AF568116

MODERN
ECONOMIC THEORY

MODERN
ECONOMIC THEORY

Micro & Macro Analysis, Money & Banking, Financial System, Money Market, Capital Market, Stock-exchange & SEBI, International Economics, Public Finance, Economic Systems, Economics of Development & Planning and Economics of Welfare

Dr. K.K. DEWETT
M.A., Ph. D.
Formerly Head of the Department of Economics
Panjab University

Revised by
M.H. NAVALUR
Department of Economics
Maharashtra College, Mumbai

Designed & Illustrated by
JANMEJOY KHUNTIA
M.Phil (Economics)
School of Correspondence Courses and
Continuing Education, University of Delhi

S Chand And Company Limited
(ISO 9001 Certified Company)

S. CHAND
PUBLISHING

S Chand And Company Limited

(ISO 9001 Certified Company)

Head Office: D-92, Sector–2, Noida – 201301, U.P. (India), Ph. 91-120-4682700

Registered Office: A-27, 2nd Floor, Mohan Co-operative Industrial Estate, New Delhi – 110 044, Phone: 011-49731800

www.**schandpublishing.com**; e-mail: **info@schandpublishing.com**

Marketing Offices:

Chennai	:	Ph: 23632120; chennai@schandpublishing.com
Guwahati	:	Ph: 2738811, 2735640; guwahati@schandpublishing.com
Hyderabad	:	Ph: 40186018; hyderabad@schandpublishing.com
Jalandhar	:	Ph: 4645630; jalandhar@schandpublishing.com
Kolkata	:	Ph: 23357458, 23353914; kolkata@schandpublishing.com
Lucknow	:	Ph: 4003633; lucknow@schandpublishing.com
Mumbai	:	Ph: 25000297; mumbai@schandpublishing.com
Patna	:	Ph: 4011400; patna@schandpublishing.com

© S Chand And Company Limited, 1946

All rights reserved. No part of this publication may be reproduced or copied in any material form (including photocopying or storing it in any medium in form of graphics, electronic or mechanical means and whether or not transient or incidental to some other use of this publication) without written permission of the copyright owner. Any breach of this will entail legal action and prosecution without further notice.

Jurisdiction: *All disputes with respect to this publication shall be subject to the jurisdiction of the Courts, Tribunals and Forums of New Delhi, India only.*

First Edition 1946
Subsequent Editions and Reprints 1948, 49, 51, 53, 55, 57, 59, 63, 64, 66, 69, 72, 75, 76, 77, 78, 79, 80, 81, 82, 83, 84 (Twice), 85, 86, 87, 88, 89, 90, 91, 92, 93, 94, 95, 96, 97, 98, 99, 2001, 2002, 2003, 2004
First Multicolour Illustrative Edition 2005 , Reprints 2006, 2008, 2009 (Twice)
Revised Edition 2010, Reprints 2012, 2013, 2014, 2015, 2017, 2018 (Twice), 2020, 2021, 2022 (Twice), 2023 (Twice)

Reprint 2025

ISBN: 978-81-219-2463-4 **Product Code:** H5ECT41ECON10ENAW10O

PRINTED IN INDIA

By Vikas Publishing House Private Limited, Plot 20/4, Site-IV, Industrial Area Sahibabad, Ghaziabad – 201 010 and Published by S Chand And Company Limited, A-27, 2nd Floor, Mohan Co-operative Industrial Estate, New Delhi – 110 044.

PREFACE TO THE 23rd REVISED EDITION (2010)

The book is now turned sixty plus. It has withstood the test of time through constant revisions, additions and upgradation. The changes which were brought in the last editions have been updated.

The monetary revolution in the world is, changing the direction of the world economies. Everybody is interested in knowing it, may it be financial system or the related markets. New chapters in some what detail have been discussed, to cater the needs of faculty members, students, community, whether from research, competitive examination, post graduate or graduate level, it is very useful and enlightening. The new chapters included are as follows:

Chapter 55: Financial system and financial reforms.

Chapter 56: Money market, capital market, stock exchange and SEBI.

+ A sub-chapter is included in international monetary fund that is WTO.
Some of the notable additions and revisions over the last edition are as follows:

- **Promotional elasticity of demand**
- **Division of labor as means of exploitation (Marx)**
- **Chamberlain's alternative approach + New strategy in monopolistic competition**
- **Rigid prices (Oligopoly market)**
- **Two sector model and the concept of measurement of national income**

Keeping in pace with the phenomenal development of information technology in the world and in an attempt to catch the imagination of our readers, the book has been presented in Multicolour containing illustrations both pictorial and graphical, which is relevant to the discussions contained in the text. This is a step forward to help the readers in understanding the subject matter in a lucid manner and make the reading smooth and interesting.

The revisor and the publisher hope that these improvements will derive maximum benefits, both at the national and at the international level concerned intellectuals. In addition, this will lead to a solution for the problems regarding economic development of mankind in the world.

Revisor

Disclaimer: While the authors of this book have made every effort to avoid any mistake or omission and have used their skill, expertise and knowledge to the best of their capacity to provide accurate and updated information. The authors and S. Chand does not give any representation or warranty with respect to the accuracy or completeness of the contents of this publication and are selling this publication on the condition and understanding that they shall not be made liable in any manner whatsoever. S. Chand and the authors expressly disclaim all and any liability/responsibility to any person, whether a purchaser or reader of this publication or not, in respect of anything and everything forming part of the contents of this publication. S. Chand and the authors shall not be responsible for any errors, omissions or damages arising out of the use of the information contained in this publication. Further, the appearance of the personal name, place and incidence, if any; in the illustrations and questions used herein is purely coincidental and work of imagination. Thus the same should in no manner be termed as defamatory to any individual.

PREFACE TO THE TWENTY FIRST EDITION (1984)

The book has been in the market for little more than sixty years now. During this period, it has undergone several revisions, additions and alterations to keep abreast of the latest developments in economic theory. In an attempt to live up to its promise, the book has also become quite comprehensive in its range and coverage embracing **Price Theory or Micro Economics, Income and Employment Theory or Macro Economics, Money and Banking, International Trade, Public Finance, Economic Systems, Economics of Development and Planning and Economics of Welfare.**

In recent revisions, special emphasis has been put on deleting out-of-date material, introducing new topics and improving the others. In the last edition added Bernoulli Hypothesis Friedman-Savage Hypothesis and Markowitz Hypothesis in the demand and theory; Baumol's Sales-maximisation principle in the theory of the firm; mark-up principle, Duopoly models, Cournot model, Edgeworth model Baumol's sales-maximisation model and Chamberlin model in price-output determination; a discussion on Impact of Technical Progress on the Relative Factor Shares, Macro Distribution Theories: Marxian Theory, Kalecki's Degree of monopoly Theory, Neo-classical Theory; Pigou Effect or Real Balance Effect; Ratchet Effect; Mathews' Model of Trade Cycle; Monetarists' Recipe to Control Inflation; Indexation; Optimising Approach, Fisal Target Approach, Harmonious Adjustment and Judicious Mix Approach in Monetary policy; in the theory of tariffs Stolper-Samuelson Theorem and the Terms of Trade Effect. In Economics of Development were added Dualism and Economic Under-development Lewis's Model of Economic Development and Relevance of Harrod-Domar Model for developing countries. In Economics of Welfare we added recent developments in, and Criticism of Compensation Principle, Market Structure and Social Welfare and Arrow's Impossibility Theorem.

These additions and improvements greatly added to the popularity of the book both in India and abroad. Several reprints and foreign editions had to be brought out accordingly. Encouraged by the big response of the students and teachers, we have now undertaken another thorough and wide-ranging revision of the book deleting old and out-of-date material and adding the following new topics which have come to be incorporated in the corpus of economic theory in recent years.

- **Retreat from Keynesianism: Supply-side Economics**
- **Inverse-J Cost Curve**
- **Maximinisation of Profit; Single-owner Entreprenuer**
- **Concept of Product Group under Monopolistic Competition**
- **Full-cost Pricing Principle**
- **Exploitation of Labour**
- **Concepts of Money and Money Stock Measures**
- **Friedman's Restatement of the Quantity Theory of Money**
- **Static and dunamic Gains from foreign trade**
- **Factor-Price Equalisation in International Trade**
- **I.M.F. Conditionality Clause**

We have no doubt that these additions, alterations and improvements will enhance the popularity of the book still further and it will be able to meet more adequately the requirements of the B.A. (Pass/Hons.), B.Com. (Pass/Hons) and M.A./M. Com. students as well as of the candidates for the various public services and other competitive examinations.

We have pleasure in thanking teachers of economics in India and abroad for the suggestions they were good enough to send us for the present edition. We shall be failing in our duty if we do not add that the sole credit of making improvements in the book not only in the present edition but also in the previous editions goes to Dr. J.D. Verma, M.A., Ph.D. (London) formerly Professor and Head of the Department of Economics, Punjab University who has been our guide, philosopher and friend. Our special thanks are due to him.

Authors

CONTENTS

PART - ONE: PRICE THEORY OR MICRO ECONOMICS

UNIT - I : NATURE AND METHODOLOGY OF ECONOMICS

UNIT - II : THEORY OF DEMAND

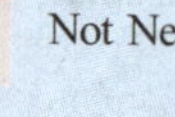

PART - TWO : THEORY OF INCOME AND EMPLOYMENT OR MACRO-ECONOMICS

UNIT - I: SOCIAL ACCOUNTING

UNIT - II: THEORY OF INCOME DETERMINATION

UNIT III: ECONOMIC FLUCTUATIONS

PART - THREE: MONEY AND BANKING

UNIT - I: MONETARY STANDARDS AND THEORY OF MONEY AND PRICES

PART - SIX: ECONOMIC SYSTEMS

PART-SEVEN: ECONOMICS OF DEVELOPMENT AND PLANNING

UNIT - I: ECONOMICS OF DEVELOPMENT

PART ONE

Price Theory or Micro Economics

UNIT I

Nature and Methodology of Economics

UNIT II

Theory of Demand

UNIT III

Theory of Production

UNIT IV

Product Pricing

UNIT V

Factor Pricing

UNIT I

Nature and Methodology of Economics

Chapters

CHAPTER 1

NATURE OF ECONOMICS : DEFINITIONS

Dr. J.M. Keynes was not far wrong when he said that "Political Economy is said to have strangled itself with definitions."[1] There are, therefore, economists like Richard Jones and Comte who would do away with the definition altogether. Economists like Pareto, Myrdal and Hutchinson think that any search for a precise definition of Economics is a barren enterprise.[2] Pareto thinks it "a waste of time to investigate what it (*i.e.,* economic phenomenon) may be." According to Mydral, "Economics is the only term regarding the precise definition of which the economist need not be concerned." In Hutchinson's opinion, "the actual assignment of a definition to the word 'Economics' does not appear to solve, or even help in the solution of any useful scientific problem whatsoever." That is why it is said that it is needless to waste words in defining Economics. It will be an exercise in futility.

Adam Smith (1723 - 1790)
In his work *"The Wealth of Nations"* he formulated the key theories of Market-driven economics.

Robbins, however, has stoutly denied that it is a waste of time to attempt a precise delimitation of the field of Economics. According to Macfie, lack of clear definition can prove harmful.

In our opinion, it is very essential for a student to have some definition in mind as a working basis. Besides, the discussion leading to a definition is very useful in giving a clear understanding of the subject. Let us, therefore, examine some of the definitions put forward from time to time.

EARLY DEFINITIONS : SCIENCE OF WEALTH

According to Adam Smith, Economics was concerned with "An Enquiry into the Nature and Causes of Wealth of Nations." The early economists called Economics, the Science of Wealth. J. E. Cairnes in his book, **'The Character and Logical Method of Political Economy'** clearly said that Economics, "deals with the phenomenon of wealth."[3]

According to the French economist **J. B. Says**, Economics is the science which treats of wealth. The American economist **F. A. Walker** says that Economics is that body of knowledge which relates to wealth.

1. Keynes. J.N.— *Scope and method of Political Economy* (1930). p. 153.
2. Kirzner, I. M. — *The Economic Point of View* (East West Edition), 1967, p. 7.
3. Ibid., p. 31

Thus, in these definitions, a key position was assigned to wealth in the study of Economics.

Comments

At a time when religious sentiment was strong and spiritual values held sway over men's minds, exclusive emphasis on wealth could only cause repulsion in the enlightened mind. This was specially due to the pampered and degenerating ways of the rich. This concept of Economics rightly called for righteous indignation from men of letters like Carlyle (describing it as a 'pig science') and Ruskin.

The early economists, the votaries of the new cult of Mammon-worship, therefore, came to be looked down upon. Economics was supposed to teach selfishness and came to be called a **"dismal science."** S. Bailey in 1835 discussed the popular view of Economics as "a man-degrading, sordid inquiry."

"The unworthiness of political economy in public opinion stemmed directly from its explicit preoccupation with so degrading a subject-matter as wealth." (Kirzner). Thus, all the vices attributed to wealth became attached to the science of wealth (i.e., Economics).

Luckily, Economics has now been extricated from this unenviable position. Exaggerated emphasis on wealth is gone. Even in the last quarter of the 19th century humanistic character of Economics has come to be well recognised. Schaffle in Germany and Droz in France placed the role of man in Economics higher that of wealth. No undue importance is now attached to wealth as such. It is now fully recognised that wealth is only a means to an end, the end being human welfare. Economists do not now regard wealth as the be-all and the end-all of human endeavour, nor can it be expected to be the sole cause contributing to human happiness.

Thus, **emphasis has now shifted from wealth to man.** Man occupies a primary place and wealth only a secondary one. As Marshall rightly puts it, Economics is **"on the one side a study of wealth; and on the other, and more important side, a part of the study of man."**[4]

Economics, thus, is not a science of wealth but a science of man primarily. It may be called the science of human welfare.

Recently, Robbins has completely freed Economics from the accusations of its detractors who called it sordid or mean. According to Robbins, Economics is not concerned with ends as such. The ends may be noble or ignoble. If their achievement involves the use of scarce resources, they have an economic aspect. Thus, Economics embraces all conduct, good or bad, provided it comes under the influence of scarcity. Hence, we can no longer blame Economics for occupying itself with bad or ignoble aims.[5]

Fraser classified the definitions of Economics into two: Type A dealing with wealth and material welfare and Type B dealing with the phenomenon arising out of scarcity of means and multiplicity of ends. Since Robbins wrote his book **'Nature and Significance of Economic Science',** in 1930, there has been a marked transition from A Type to B Type definitions.

MARSHALLIAN DEFINITION: SCIENCE OF MATERIAL WELFARE

For a long time, the accepted view was that Economics is concerned with those human activities which centre round wealth not for its own sake, but for the sake of material welfare that is promotes. The following definitions represent this traditional view:

"Economics is the study of the general methods by which men cooperate to meet their **material** needs." (Beveridge).

"The aim of Political Economy is the explanation of the general causes on which the **material welfare** of human beings depends." (Cannan).

Alfred Marshall (1842 - 1924) Famous Econimist at the Cambridge University who wrote *"Principles of Economics"* Published in 1890.

"The range of our inquiry becomes restricted to that part of **social welfare** that can be brought directly or indirectly into relation with the **measuring rod of money."** (Pigou).

"Political Economy, or Economics, is a study of mankind in the ordinary business of life; it examines that part of individual and social action which is most closely connected with the attainment and with the use of the **material requisites of well being."**[6] (Marshall).

4. Marshall, A. — *Principles of Economics, 6th edition*, p. 1.
5. Robbins, L.— *Nature and Significance of Economic Science*, 1945, p. 27.
6. Marshall, A. — *Principles of Economics* (6th Ed.) p. 1.

We can see that one thread seems to run through the definitions given above, viz., that of material welfare. Beveridge speaks of meeting "material needs", Cannan of "causes of material welfare" and Marshall of "material requisites of well-being". According to these economists, the aim of Economics is to study human activities which are conductive to human welfare in its material aspect. Wealth furnishes man with material means of satisfying his wants and a promoting his welfare. Economists, in so far as they study wealth, can be legitimately regarded as studying causes of material welfare.

We can see that Marshall's definition emphasises on four points:

(*a*) Economics does not regard wealth as the be-all and end-all of economic activities. Wealth is sought for promoting human welfare. Hence, wealth is relegated to a secondary position.

(*b*) Economics is not concerned with what is called in Economics 'economic man', *i.e.,* a man whose only motive is to acquire wealth for its own sake and who is not influenced by human considerations in the pursuit of wealth. Rather, Economics deals with ordinary men and women who are swayed by love, affection and fellow-feelings and not merely motivated by the desire to get maximum monetary advantage.

(*c*) Economics is a social science and not one which studies isolated individuals or Robinson Crusoes. We study persons living in society influencing other people and being influenced by them.

(*d*) Economics studies only 'material requisites of well-being' or causes of material welfare. It has thus a materialistic aspect and ignores non-material aspects. Actually, however, as Robbins has shown, Economics embraces both material and non-material things.

Criticism of Marshallian View

Lionel Robbins led a frontal attack on the Marshallian view. The main points of criticism are:

(*i*) Robbins does not think it right for the economists to confine their attention to the study of **material welfare,** because in the actual study of economic principles, both the "material" and "immaterial" are taken into account.

(*ii*) Robbins rejected Marshall's definition as being classificatory because it makes a distinction between material welfare and non-material welfare and says that Economics is concerned only with material welfare.

(*iii*) It unduly restricted the scope of Economics. "A theory of wages, which ignored all those sums which were paid for 'immaterial' services or spent on 'immaterial' ends would be intolerable."[7] The economists have also adopted unanimously a "non-material" definition of productivity.

In his book **"Nature and Significance of Economic Science",** Robbins has given numerous examples of goods which are highly conducive to human welfare but which have nothing material in them, e.g., services of doctors, lawyers, etc. These services have economic significance. They are scarce and have value. "It is not the **materiality** of even material means of gratification," says Robbins, "which gives them their status as economic goods; it is their relation to valuations." Economics is thus concerned with both material as well as non-material things provided they have value.

(*iv*) Robbins' objection is, however, not merely to the word "material". He would also not tie economics with welfare. The anomalous position of those who study economics in terms of welfare is evident. Intoxicants are regarded as wealth, but by no stretch of imagination can they be regarded as conducive to human welfare. Being scarce they are subject to the "pricing process". They have, in short, economic significance, though human welfare is not promoted by them. Robbins would say, "Why talk of welfare at all? Why not throw away the mask altogether?"

Apart from the anomalies into which the welfare economists have fallen, there are other reasons for discarding the welfare idea from discussions which are strictly economic. Ideas of welfare vary from age to age, from country to country, and from individual to individual. Welfare is too vague and indefinite an ideal to provide a sound foundation for building up a respectable science.

(*v*) There is further objection that, in assessing human welfare, we shall be called upon to give our verdict as to what we regard as conducive to human welfare and what is not so conducive. We shall be transported to the world of ethics, whereas Economics, according to Robbins, is neutral as regards ends. It is not supposed to be its function to pass moral judgements and say what is good and what is bad.

Thus, according to Robbins, Economics is not to be regarded as a study of the causes of material welfare. **"Whatever Economics is concerned with, it is not concerned with the causes of material welfare as such."** (Robbins).

7. Robbins, L., *op cit.,* p. 6.

(vi) According to Marshall, Economics deals with persons living in society. It ignores all others who also may have an economic problem, i.e., of using scarce means for the satisfaction of unlimited ends.

Robbins's main quarrel with the Marshallian definition is that, whereas Economics deals both with material goods and non-material services, the definition points only to the material aspect. Hence, though the contents are correct, the label is wrong.

ROBBINS' DEFINITION: SCIENCE OF SCARCITY OR SCIENCE OF CHOICE

Marshall seemed to have settled the matter of the definition of Economics long ago and a large consensus of expert opinion had been mobilised behind him. But the publication of Robbins' book, **"Nature and Significance of Economic Science"** in 1931, set the ball of controversy rolling once again.

Lionel Robbins challenged the traditional view of the nature of economic science. We have noticed some of his objections in the above section. He calls the hitherto accepted and well-known definitions of Economics classificatory and unscientific. The word "material" imposed unnecessary limitation. The welfare conception of Economics lacked universality and scientific precision. Robbins defined Economics thus:

"Economics is the science which studies human behaviour as a relationship between ends and scarce means which have alternative uses."

Robbins claimed that his definition did not suffer from any of these defects. His definition was analytical rather than classificatory. Instead of discussing a certain type of human behaviour, it focussed its attention on a particular aspect of human behaviours; *i.e.,* behaviour concerned with the utilisation of scarce resources to achieve unlimited ends.

Lionel Robins (1898 - 1984) was a famous English Econimist of the 1920s and occupied the chair of London School of Economics in 1929.

On analysis, we shall find that this definition lays down the following three fundamental propositions which constitute the basis of the structure of economic science:—

(a) "Ends" refer to wants. Human beings have wants which are unlimited in number. If one want is satisfied another crops up. Multiplicity of wants calls forth ceaseless effort for their satisfaction, and the unending cycle of economic activity moves on. If wants had been limited, they would have been adequately satisfied and there would have been no economic problem; all incentive to economic effort would have ceased. Also, since human wants are unlimited, one is compelled to choose between the more urgent and the less urgent wants. That is why Economics is also called a **science of choice.**

(b) Although wants are unlimited yet the means to satisfy them are strictly limited. No doubt, there are certain free goods which also satisfy human wants. Yet most of the things that we want are scarce. Had the means of satisfaction been unlimited, no economic problem would have arisen. But as it is, the resources at the disposal of a community are scarce, and they must, therefore, be economised. Economic resources are the various types of labour, capital, land and entrepreneurship used in producing goods and services. Since these resources are limited, the ability of the community to produce goods and services is also limited.

The term **"scarcity"** is used here in a relative sense. It is scarcity in relation to requirements. Scarcity is not to be taken in an absolute sense. A commodity may exist in a small quantity but if nobody has any use for it, we shall not call it scarce in the economic sense. Thus, rotten eggs, though much fewer than good ones, are not scarce in the economic sense. On the other hand, there may be huge stocks of a commodity like wheat or coal, yet it is called scarce because the demand is even larger than the supply. It is the demand, in relation to supply, for a commodity, and not its quantity alone, which determines whether a commodity is scarce or not. Scarcity is thus a relative term.

(c) The third proposition underlying Robbins' definition is that the scarce means are capable of alternative uses. If a commodity could be put only to one use and to none else, few economic problems would arise in its connection. After it has met that use, it will become a free good and will have no further economic significance. Actually, however, the uses to which a commodity can be put are numerous, almost unlimited. Hence, the demand in the aggregate for that commodity is almost insatiable.

Further, these alternative uses are of varying importance; some are more urgent and others less urgent. And we can select the use to which a commodity may be put. Choice comes in again.

Thus, in the Robbinsian sense, economic activity lies in man's utilisation of scarce means having alternative uses, for the satisfaction of multiple ends. ''Means'' refer to time, money or any other form of property. They are all limited. But since the ends are unlimited, choice-making is essential. That is why Economics has been called a science of choice.

From the point of view of the State, Economics may be defined as the ''study of those principles on which the resources of a community should be so regulated and administered as to secure the communal ends without waste.'' (Wicksteed). In Stigler's words, ''Economics is the study of the principles governing the allocation of scarce means among competing ends when the objective of allocation is to maximise the attainment of the ends.''[8]

In other words, **''Economics is a study of the allocation of scarce means, capable of alternative uses, among competing ends for the attainment of a maximum result in the achievement of these ends.''**

Superiority of Robbins' Definition

Robbins demolished the old structure of Economics based on material welfare and raised a new one with two foundation-stones, *viz.,* multiplicity of wants and scarcity of means.

Robbins claims that his definition is superior to the earlier definitions:

(*a*) It is more scientific, since it is not based on artificial classification of wants, as material and non-material. It is independent of such classification.

(*b*) As defined by Robbins, Economics has a much wider content. It takes into account all types of human wants, material or non-material, as well as of all types of persons whether living in society or not.

(*c*) Robbins greatly widened the scope of Economics. Marshall had restricted it to wealth and activities which related to the material welfare of man only.

(*d*) Robbins raised Economics to the level of a science whereas earlier economists regard it as both, a science and an art. As an art, it could only be an imperfect art. Thus, to Robbins belonged the credit of elevating Economics to the perfection of a science.

(*e*) Robbins made Economics a positive science whereas earlier economists regarded it also as a normative science. Economics was thus freed from the responsibility of making value judgments. It had only to enunciate general economic principles. It was no longer its function to examine the right or wrong of an economic activity. Right and wrong are relative terms.

(*f*) According to Robbins, Economics transcends the narrow boundaries within which the materialist definition confined Economics. It lays down a maxim which is true of all times and places. As Wicksteed puts it, ''Its laws are like the laws of life and are applicable to fields that have no connection whatsoever with the business or production of wealth.''

(*g*) Moreover, when Economics is defined; as Robbins does, no charge or sordidness or preaching of Mammonism can be levelled against it. It can no longer be called a ''dismal'' science, because it takes no responsibility for selecting the ends. They may be good or bad, Economics is not concerned. Wherever the ends are many and the means are scarce, Economics is directly concerned.

Thus, Robbins' definition is superior both to the early definition (science of wealth), and Marshall's definition (science of material welfare).

Criticism of Robbins' Definition

Robbins is not without his critics.

Firstly The Marshallian spirit is not altogether dead. Economists like Durbin, Fraser, Wootton and Beveridge have put a strong defence of Marshallian Economics. Wootton urges ''that it is very difficult for economists to divest their discussions completely of all normative significance.'' Robbins' idea of Economics, though admittedly more scientific, is colourless, impersonal, neutral as regards ends. He says, ''Equilibrium is just equilibrium.'' If Economics is to serve as an engine of social betterment, it cannot divest itself of normative significance. As Prof. Thomas says, **''The function of the economist is not only to explain and explore but also to advocate and condemn.''**

The ethical neutrality of Economics emphasised by Robbins has exposed it to two main criticisms: (*a*) Since search for particular ends has been abandoned, the scope of Economics has been widened to include phenomena which are not strictly economic. (*b*) Lack of concern for the nature of ends has resulted in an academic detachment from reality making economic theory a purely formal affair. Souter's essay (1933) denounced Robbins as ''a juggler with a static verbal logic'' and a ''profane sunderer of 'form' and 'substance'.''[9]

Secondly, Robbins' ends and means' formulation has been criticised as not being in conformity with human actions. It excludes the concept of purpose which is fundamental to human

8. Stigler, G. J. — *Theory of Price* (1947), p. 12.

9. Kirzner. I. M. *op. eit.,* p. 121.

action. Actually, the ends are seldom presented simultaneously with the means.

Further, there is obvious reality of the ends means scheme. Ends are generally means to further ends just as means may be ends of earlier actions.

Besides, Robbins regards ends as given, but the means may be equally given. Actually few ends are given; they are, on the other hand, deliberately chosen. Professor Knight has also criticised the attitude that Economics is only concerned with means and not ends. Economics should discuss the alternative ends and not only means for a given end.

Thirdly, Robbins, it is said, has reduced Economics merely to valuation theory. Other aspects of the study of Economics have been relegated to the background. Robbins's definition does not circumscribe an aggregate already in existence, but it leaves outside the city wall a part of the city already existing.[10] As Fraser says, **''Economics is more than a value theory or equilibrium analysis or resource allocation.''**

In Economics, we study not only how resources are allocated and how prices are determined, but we also study how total national income is generated. Keynesian Economics, which explains the determination of national income and employment, is not covered by Robbins' definition which merely assigns to Economics an **'allocative role'.** In an era in which study of economic fluctuations or of national income and employment has assumed great importance in the work of economic theorists and policymakers, this omission imposes a serious limitation on Economics as conceived by Robbins.

Fourthly, choice of individuals as such has no particular significance. As Prof. Cairncross points out, we study choices if they have social repercussions. Individual choices having no social implications cannot form the subject-matter of Economics as we know it.

Fifthly, the theory of economic growth or economic development has recently become a very important branch of Economics. But Robbins's definition does not cover it. Economics of growth explains how an economy grows and the factors which bring about increase in national income and productive capacity of the economy. Robbins takes the resources as given and discusses only their allocation.

Sixthly, Robbins's definition of Economics does not explain the problem of unemployment. For some countries this is an urgent problem. There is abundance of man-power rather than scarcity of it, whereas Economics, according to Robbins, studies the problem of scarcity.

Seventhly, in Robbins's definition, the human touch is entirely missing. It is well to emphasize with Ely that ''Economics is something more than a science, a science shot through with the infinite variety of human life, calling not only for systematic thinking but for human sympathy, imagination and in an unusual degree for the saving grace of commonsense.''[11]

Eighthly, there is no doubt that Robbins has made Economics more abstract and complex and hence difficult and unfruitful. This detracts from its utility for the common man. Utility of Economics lies, in a large measure, in its being a concrete and realistic study.

MODERN DEFINITION

During the last 40 years or so, economic thinking has moved much further from Robbins' view. According to Robbins, Economics is concerned with the best possible use of the limited resources. But it is now considered that Economics is much more than merely a theory of value or of resource allocation.

The credit for bringing about a revolution in economic thinking goes to late Lord J. M. Keynes. According to him, Economics studies how the levels of income and employment in a community are determined. Thus, in Keynesian terms, Economics is defined as the **study of the administration of scarce resources and of the determinants of income and employment.** In other words, it studies the causes of economic fluctuations to see how economic stability could be promoted.

In Benham's words, Economics is **''a study of the factors affecting the size, distribution and stability of a country's national income.''**[12]

More recently, the theory of Economic growth has come to occupy an important place in the study of Economics with reference to under-developed economies. It studies how the national income grows over years. An economy like that of India which is at the mercy of monsoons needs economic stability besides economic growth. Thus, a study of **economic growth and of economic stability** forms an integral and important part of the study of Economics. A

10. A paper read by M. H. Gopal at the Indian Economic Conference in 1940.

11. Ely and Others–*Outline of Economics*, 1930, p. 4.

12. Benham, F. — Economics, 1960.

good and adequate definition of economics must cover them.

CONCLUSION REGARDING DEFINITION OF ECONOMICS

We have seen that no short definition of a growing science like Economics would serve the purpose. To define it as a science of wealth is too narrow or uncharitable. To define it as 'a study of mankind in the ordinary business of life' is too broad and to define it as the study of material welfare is too narrow. To define it as a science of scarcity or choice or of human valuation is again too wide and to define it as ''that part of social welfare that can be brought directly or indirectly into relation with the measuring rod of money'' is too narrow.

Thus, every time we face a dilemma. One may, therefore, agree with Prof. Viner that **'Economics is what economists do'.** We know that the economists study resource allocation or resource utilisation. They also study size, distribution and stability of national income and now they study the fascinating subject of economic growth. A proper definition must cover this wide field to indicate correctly what Economics is.

In short, Economics may be defined as **''a social science concerned with the proper uses and allocation of resources for the achievement and maintenance of growth with stability.'' OR** ''Economics is a social science concerned chiefly with the way the society chooses to employ its limited resources, which have alternative uses, to produce goods and services for present and future consumption.''[13] It describes and analyses the nature and behaviour of the economy.

Definition given by Professor Henry Smith seems to be very suitable. He defines Economics as the ''study of how in a civilised society one obtains the share of what other people have produced and of how the total product of society changes and is determine''[14].

This definition covers important aspects of the study of Economics, viz., production and distribution of wealth and the determination of the level and changes in the total product of the nation which implies the theory of economic growth.

Paul Samuelson, defined economics on the basis of the modern concept of growth criteria.

''Economics is a study of how men and society 'choose' with or without the use of money, to employ scarce productive uses resource which could have alternative uses, to produce various commodities over time and distribute them for consumption, now and in the future among the various people and groups of society''.

Though Samuelson's definition takes into account, men, money, scarce resources and production aspect, but economics is not only the concern of material welfare, it has to be taken into account certain other socio-economic, politico-economic environment, which may give the human being maximum welfare. In modern day economics Physical Quality of Living Index (PQLI) and Human Development Index (HDI) has been taken as the Criteria of judging economic development of an economy. Hence, as economics is a broader concept. We should try to evolve a wider definition of economics.

Jevons referred ''Economics as the ''calculas of pain and pleasure''. or it may be the effort of earnings (disutility) and the amount of satisfaction (utility) we get from the income earned by human effort. Two things can be developed, (*i*) a more precise definition, by using mathematics, and (*ii*) extending the concept of pain and pleasure in to certain 'real' economic variables.

In contemporary society the service sector is dominating more, hence it is not only a definition of ''scarce resources and ends'' but here the resources must include the service sector also, it should not be only production of goods but also the services available to the individual. Economic problem is generally taken into account the macro-economic problem, or a very generalised micro economic problem of scarce resources, alternative uses, problem of distribution, etc. In modern days, on the basis of micro economic problems, a bigger subject, managerial economics or 'management', theories have been developed. It is essentially related to economics and the new theories have been developed to solve it, but they have been allotted different names.

MAJOR ECONOMIC PROBLEMS

What is an Economic Problem ?

In view of the scarcity of means at our disposal and the multiplicity of ends we seek to achieve, the economic problem lies in making the best possible use of our resources so as to get maximum satisfaction in the case of a consumer and maximum output or

14. Smith, Henry, *A prospect of Political Economy*, 1968, p. 20.
13. Spencer, Milton, H. — *Contemporary Economics*, 1971, p. 2.

profit for a producer. Hence economic problem consists in making decisions regarding the ends to be pursued and the goods to be produced and the means to be used for the achievement of certain ends.

Fundamental Problems Facing an Economy

From the definition of economic problem given above we can derive the following fundamental problems which as economy has to tackle:

(1) What to Produce. The first major decision relates to the quantity and the range of goods to be produced. Since resources are limited, we must choose between different alternative collection of goods and services that may be produced. It also implies the allocation of resources between the different types of goods, *e.g.,* consumer goods and capital goods.

(2) How to Produce. Having decided the quantity and the type of goods to be produced, we must next determine the techniques of production to the used, e.g., labour-intensive or capital-intensive.

(3) For Whom to Produce. This means how the national product is to be distributed, i.e., who should get how much. This is the problem of the sharing of the national product.

(4) Are the Resources Economically Used? This is the problem of economic efficiency or welfare maximisation. There is to be no waste or misuse of resources since they are limited.

(5) Problem of Full employment. Fullest possible use must be made of the available resources. In other words, an economy must endeavour to achieve full employment not only of labour but of all its resources.

(6) Problem of Growth. Another problem for an economy is to make sure that it keeps on expanding or developing so that it maintains conditions of stability. It is not to be static. Its productive capacity must continue to increase. If it is an under-developed economy, it must accelerate its process of growth.

QUESTIONS

1. "Economics was a Science of Wealth: it is now a Science of Welfare". Discuss.
2. Critically examine Marshall's definition of Economics as a link between wealth and welfare.
3. "Economics is a study of mankind in the ordinary business of life" (Marshall). Discuss.
4. Explain and comment on the following: "Economics is the science which studies human behaviour as a relationship between ends and scarce means which have alternative uses". (Robbins).
5. 'Economics is a science of choice. Discuss.
6. How far is it correct to say that Robbins definition limits the scope of Economics?
7. "Multiplicity of wants and scarcity of means are the two foundation-stones of economics". Discuss.
8. Make a comparative study of the definitions of Economics as given by Marshall and Robbins.
9. "Whatever Economics is concerned with, it is not concerned with the causes of material welfare". Discuss and examine this statement.
10. Define economics and distinguish carefully

NATURE OF ECONOMICS : SCOPE AND METHOD

Introduction

In discussing the nature and scope of Economics, we consider the nature of economic laws and limitations of Economics. We also discuss its subject - matter and consider whether it is a science, positive science or a normative science and whether it can solve practical problems.

ECONOMICS

MICRO ECONOMICS	MACRO ECONOMICS
(I) Market Economy (a) Theory of demand (consumption) (b) Theory of production (a + b = theory of product pricing). (II) Theories of distribution (i) Rent (ii) Wages (iii) Interest (iv) Profits (III) Welfare Economics	Different policy measures to solve the major economic problems. Economic problems-poverty, unemployment, inequality in income and wealth, inflation and deflation etc. Policies - Monetory, Fiscal, Industrial, Trade etc.

MANAGERIAL ECONOMICS

Managerial Economics is nothing but "the application of economics to the real business activities , so as to get the desired business results".

In a world of competition in the market, there exists thousands of rivals, due to this a businessman or an entrepreneur plans his strategies, to take control of the market. Contemporary business world has given a new threat of "diversification economics, which aims at controlling the different parts of business activities.

Managerial economics takes into account the following subject matter:

(i) Law of demand and elasticities of demand.

(ii) Demand forecasting

(iii) Production theory : Returns to scale, technology, cost, revenue etc.

(iv) Objectives of firms

(v) Determination of prices (concept of cartel's, groups, leadership) :–

(vi) Methods of pricing: Open administered national and international pricing theories and practice.

(vii) Tools to judge economic efficiency, break even points, linear programming, game theory.

(viii) Micro planning, project, capital, budgeting cost benefits analysis, public investment criteria regarding trunkey projects etc.

In the coming years of dynamic economic scenario there is a further need to study and evolve many other economic philosophies which in reality helps the mankind in achieving economic and social welfare.

(i) Engineering Economics

(ii) Health Economics

(iii) Defence Economics

A detailed study is required in this regard.

SUBJECT-MATTER: MICRO AND MACRO ECONOMICS

The study of Economics is divided by the modern economist into two parts, *viz.*, **micro-economics** and **macro-economics.**

An economic system may be looked at **as a whole** or in terms of its innumerable **decision - making units** (such as consuming units e.g., individual consumers and households), producing units, (e.g., firms, farms business and mining concerns), individual factors of production (e.g., labourers, land-owners, capitalists, entrepreneurs), and individual industries, (e.g., cotton textiles, iron and steel, toy-making): When we are analysing the problems of the economy as a whole it is macro-economic study. While an analysis of the behaviour of any particular decision- making unit, such as a firm and industry, a consumer, constitutes micro - economics.

Micro - economics is also called Price Theory and Macro-economics is called Income theory. "Price theory explains the composition, or allocation, of total production —why more of some things is produced than of others. Income theory explains the level of total production and why the level rises and falls"[1]. We explain below these terms in some detail:

MICRO-ECONOMICS

The word 'micro' means a millionth part. When we speak of micro - economics or the micro approach, what we mean is that it is some small part or component of the whole economy that we are analysing. For example, we may be studying an individual consumer's behaviour or that of an individual firm or what happens in any particular industry. If it be an analysis or price, in micro-economics what we study is the price of a particular product or of a particular factor of production and not the general price level in the country. Similarly, if it be a demand that we are analysing, in micro-economics it is the demand of an individual or that of an industry that is studied and not the aggregate demand of the entire community. Likewise, the income of an individual or of an industry, and not the national income of a country, comes within the purview of micro-economics. In respect of employment, it is the employment in a firm or in an industry that is considered in micro-economics and not the aggregate employment in the whole economy.

Thus, micro-economic theory studies the behaviour of individual decision - making units such as consumers, resource owners and business

A consumer takes dicision on consumption of goods and services for satisfaction of wants.

1. Wetson, Donald Stevensón— Price Theory and its Uses (Indian Edition), 1967, P.5.

firms. In the circular flow of economic activity in the community, micro-economics studies the flow of economic resources or factors of production from the resource owners to business firms and the flow of goods and services from the business firms to households. It studies the composition of such flows and how the prices of goods and services in the flow are determined.

A noteworthy feature of micro-approach is that, while conducting economic analysis on a micro basis, generally an assumption of full employment in the economy as a whole is made. On that assumption, the economic problem is mainly that of resource allocation or of theory of price, That is why, till recently, Economics concerned itself mainly with the theory of value and distribution, and ignored the study of the economic system as a whole.

Importance of Micro-economics

Micro-economics occupies a very important place in the study of economic theory. It has both theoretical and practical importance. From the theoretical point of view, it explains the functioning of a free enterprise economy. It tells us how millions of consumers and producers in an economy take decisions about the allocation of productive resources among millions of goods and services. It explains how through market mechanism goods and services produced in the community are distributed. It also explains the determination of the relative prices of the various products and productive services. It explains the conditions of efficiency both in consumption and production and departure from the optimum. As for practical importance, micro economics helps in the formulation of economic policies calculated to promote efficiency in production and the welfare of the masses.

Thus, the role of micro-economics is both positive and normative. It not only tells us how the economy operates but also how it should be operated to promote general welfare. In Professor Lerner's words, "Micro-economic theory facilitates the understanding of what would be a hopelessly complicated confusion of billions of facts by constructing simplified models of behaviour ....”[2]. Micro-economic analysis is also applicable to the various branches of economics such as public finance, international trade.

Limitations. Micro-economic analysis suffers from certain limitations: ***(a)*** It cannot give an idea of the functioning of the economy as a whole. An individual industry may be flourishing, whereas the economy as a whole may be languishing.

(b) As has been pointed out above, it assumes full employment which is a rare phenomenon, at any rate in the capitalist world. It is therefore, and unrealistic assumption.

A seller supplies goods and services the consumers want at some price.

MACRO-ECONOMICS OR THE THEORY OF INCOME AND EMPLOYMENT

In recent years, thanks to the late Lord Keynes, increasing attention has been given to the analysis of economic system as a whole. This is macro-economics. In macro-economics, we study, as it were, the forest, whereas in micro-economics we study the trees. Macro-economics is concerned with aggregates and averages of the entire economy, such as national income, aggregate output, total employment, total consumption, savings and investment, aggregate demand, aggregate supply, general level of prices, etc. In other words, in macro-economics, we study how these aggregates and averages of the economy as a whole are determined and what causes fluctuations in them. From theoretical reasoning and on the basis of empirical knowledge, we now know that the old assumption of full employment is not valid and, therefore, it is very vital that we should investigate how these aggregates of the economy are determined, and having known their determinants. How to ensure the maximum level of income and employment in a country.'

Macro-economics deals also with how an economy grows. In other words, it analyses the chief determinants of economic development and the various stages and processes of economic growth. This part of economic theory has been largely developed in the last two-three decades.

Economic growth is a long-run problem and as such it is a post-Keynesian development as Keynes was pre-occupied with short-run problem of economic

2. Watson, Donald Stevenson. —Price Theory and Its Uses (Indian Edition), 1967, P 5.

fluctuations. It was Harrod and Domer who extended the Keynesian analysis to the long-tun problem of growth and stability. The theory of economic growth has greatly developed these days. General growth theory applies to both developed and under - developed economies. But special growth theories have been propounded for accelerating the growth of under-developed economies. Theory of growth is in fact, long-run macro-economics.

The justification of a separate macro approach to the study of several economic problems lies in this micro approach is not only inadequate but may lead to altogether misleading conclusions. In Economics, what is true of the parts is not necessarily true of the whole. After all, the problem of the aggregate is not merely a matter of adding or of multiplying what happens in respect of the various individual parts of the whole. It may be quite different and far more complicated than a mere summation or multiplication. Take the example of saving. In times of depression, while savings by an individual may be beneficial to him, saving on the part of the entire community will deepen the depression further.

Utility of Macro-Analysis. The importance that macro-analysis has come to acquire is not without reasons. The macro-approach is useful in several ways:

(a) It is helpful in understanding the functioning of a complicated economic system. It gives a bird's eyeview of the economic world. Micro-analysis, *i.e.*, study of individual aspects of the economy will lead us nowhere. Undoubtedly, the economy is more important than the individual.

Stablising price fluctuations or containing inflation or deflation is a macro economic problem.

(b) For the formulation of useful economic policies for the nation, macro-analysis is of the utmost significance. Economic policies cannot be obviously based on the basis of the fortunes of a single firm or even a single industry or the price of an individual commodity. It is far more fruitful to regulate aggregate employment and national income and to work out a national wage policy.

(c) Macro-analysis also occupies an important place in economic theory in its pursuit of the solution of urgent economic problems. These problems relate to aggregate output, employment and national income. Economic theory seeks to explain fluctuations in the level of national income, output and employment. Thus, we are able to study the economy in its dynamic aspect.

Limitations of Macro-Analysis. Macro-analysis has limitations of its own: *(a)* individual is ignored altogether. It is individual welfare which is the main aim of Economics. Increasing national saving at the expense of individual welfare is not a wise policy.

(b) The macro-analysis overlooks individual differences. For instance, the general price level may be stable, but the prices of foodgrains may have gone spelling ruin to the poor. A steep rise in manufactured articles may conceal a calamitous fall in agricultural prices, while the average prices were steady. The agriculturists may be ruined. While speaking of the aggregates, it is also essential to remember the nature, composition and structure of the components.

Need for Integrating Macro and Micro-economics

It may be emphasised that neither of the two approaches outlined above can alone adequately help us in analysing the working of the economic system. What is true of the parts may not be true of the whole and what is true of the whole may not apply to the parts. It is very essential therefore to integrate the two approaches, if we wish to get correct solutions of our main economic problems. Take a period of unprecedented prosperity in an economy. Even in such boom conditions, it is not uncommon to come across examples of individual industries which may be languishing or may be more dead than alive. Likewise, in a period of deep depression there may yet be some individual industries which may be enjoying great prosperity. Now to apply the macro-approach to such individual industries would obviously be wrong; and it would be equally wrong to apply the micro-analysis of these industries to the economic system as a whole.

Unemployment problem is major concern for the different economies of the world.

What is needed is a proper integration of the macro and micro approaches to such problems. In fact, there are few macroproblems which have no microelements involved and few microproblems that are without macroaspects. It is, therefore, only proper to marry the two approaches both in analysing the economic problems and in prescribing policy measures for tackling them. Ignoring one and exclusively concentrating attention on the other may often lead not only to inadequate or wrong explanation but also to inappropriate or even disastrous remedial measures.

Conclusion

Thus, according to the views of the economists today, the subject-matter of Economics includes **price theory** (or micro-economics), **Income and employment theory** (macro-economics) and **growth theory**. Hence, broadly speaking, Economics may be described as a study of the economic system under which men work and live. It deals with decisions regarding the commodities to be produced and services to be rendered in the economy, how to produce them most economically, distribute them properly and to provide for the growth of the economy.

SOME MAJOR ISSUES AND PROBLEMS IN ECONOMICS

1. What to Produce that is ***(a)*** which goods are to be produced and ***(b)*** in what quantities.

2. Allocation of Resources. The economy has further to determine the ***allocation of scarce resources*** in money, men, and materials among the goods and services to be produced. The allocation of resources has also to be determined between the present and the future use *i.e.*, between consumer goods and producer or capital goods.

3. How to Produce. Another major issue relates to the ***production techniques*** to be used in production *i.e.* whether the techniques should be labour intensive or capital- intensive.

4. For whom to Produce. This problem relates to the distribution of the national product *i.e.*, who should get how much. In the matter of distribution, it is necessary to provide incentives to produce more and disincentives to curb unnecessary consumption.

5. Problems of Efficiency and Growth. This involves problems of efficiency of resource use and provision for further growth and development of the economy.

NATURE AND SCOPE OF ECONOMICS

Is Economics a Science?

While discussing the nature and scope of Economics, we may consider (*a*) the subject-matter of Economics (already discussed above), (*b*) whether Economics is a science or an art (and we think it is both, since it has both the theoretical and applied aspects; it is both light-giving and fruit-bearing), (*c*) whether it is a positive science or normative science, (*d*) whether it is a social science and (*e*) whether it can solve practical problems.

In the nature of Economics, we consider (*a*) whether it is a science and (*b*) what is the nature of economic generalisations?

We discuss below these aspects of economic science.

While considering the nature of Economics, we have to see whether Economics is entitled to be called a science. "Whenever six economists are gathered," says Wootton, "There are seven points"[3]. Bernard Shaw once remarked: "If the economists of this world were laid end to end, they wouldn't reach a conclusion". In view of the absence of unanimity among economists, the claim of Economics to be regarded as a science has been challenged. Wootton

Economic policies allow markets to function smoothly.

3. Wootton —Lament for Economics (1938), p.14.

says again, "Economists are under the suspicion of being charlatans and they cannot afford to arrogate honourable titles to themselves .... In the increasingly common application by theoretical economists or the term science to their studies, there is an element of wishfulment." Further, "The zealous student of Economic Science would do well from time to time to remind himself that of all the demand and supply schedules, cost surveys or in difference curves that give so formidable appearance to his text-books, not one (unless by accident) is founded upon fact. . . .. The reader would search far and wide through the works of analytical economists before he came upon single prediction endorsed by the weight of authoritative opinion of the course of events to be anticipated in any concrete historical situation."[4]. How can, then, Economics be called a science ?

It is further pointed out that since men are endowed with a freedom of will, economic phenomenan are highly complexed, varied and variable. It is difficult, nay impossible, to build up a science on such a slender foundation. The claim of Economics to be called a science seems therefore to have been completely demolished. The cynics often say, "where it is really scientific, it does not have much to do with economićs and what it is economics, it is not scientific."

But it is not so. Whether a particular branch of learning is entitled to be regarded a science or not, depends on what we consider a science to be. If we expect a science to formulate laws applicable everywhere and to all times, and if we expect it to predict the future course of events, then, frankly speaking, Economics is not a science. But, these requisites of a science do not accord with the modern notion as to what a science is.

By science we merely understand a systematized body of knowledge. It is not merely a collection of facts. But the facts are so arranged that they speak for themselves. That is, some laws are discovered, which explain and elucidate the facts. Only when laws have been formulated does a branch of knowledge become a science. In the words of Poincare, "Science is built up of facts as a house is built up of stones; but all accumulation of facts is no more a science than a heap of stones is a house".

Judged by this standard, Economics is certainly a science. The economist has collected his facts. The facts have been carefully analysed and put under suitable classification, and general principles governing these facts have been discovered and enunciated. What more is needed to make Economics a science? Like other sciences, Economics can claim a number of important discoveries that have improved our understanding and our economic performance. Economic theorists have taught us that a country cannot become rich merely by multiplying its currency; but later on under the leadership of Keynes, we have been taught that when resources are lying idle, money can be created with great advantages. These are no mean achievements, no less than those of other scientists, and these are just a few from among those and others.

It is now fully agreed that Economics is a full-fledged science. In fat, it is in no way less than other sciences. "Economic Laws are on all fours with the propositions of all other sciences."[5]

Both a Science and an Art. Economics is not only a science but also an art. It is a science in its methodology and an art in its application. It has a theoretical aspect and is also an applied science in its practical aspects.

True Nature of Economics

It is however, necessary to understand the true nature of Economics, The paradox of Economics is that it is a science and yet it cannot predict future course of events as the natural sciences like Physics and Chemistry can . Man is endowed with a freedom of will. Prediction in human behaviour is, therefore, difficult. To quote Durbin, "Certainty will always escape us, and prediction miss the mark ..... Just because men can learn from experience they can learn from Economics itself, and so the subject destroys its own conclusions by its own discoveries" [6]. Economics thus presents a "continually changing body of doctrine." But this does not prevent Economics from taking its due place among the well-established sciences.

Economists are handicapped in a number of ways: ***(a)*** Economic realities are complex and not easy to grasp. Just think of millions of purchasers and sellers, hundreds of thousands of commodities bought and sold. Who can advise?

(b) Further, the economist cannot hold his facts to observe them. Economic facts are constantly slipping through the fingers.

(c) Besides, in the economic sphere, experimentation is not possible as is possible in other sciences. The economists can only gather experimentation is possible in which environments can be controlled and repeated. Statistical tools are a poor substitute.

(d) Moreover, we cannot fully understand people's present actions nor appraise their future

4. Ibid, pp. 111518.

5. Robbins. op cit., p. 104
6. Economics. Man and Ilis Material Resources (New Educational Library), PP. 333-34.

intentions. Hence, sudden trends or changes in fashions and tastes upset economists' calculations.

Conclusion. In view of all this, nothing is certain. In Economics, anything is possible and everything depends on everything else. No wonder that the economists cannot agree on a certain point. But it is well to remember that the economists do agree on many things. For instance, there is substantial agreement on the policy to be pursued during recession and development policies for under developed economies or on war-time economic policies. The disagreement is only at the frontiers of knowledge. We may, however, take comfort in the thought that "absolute certainty is vouchsafed to no science and that complete conviction in this world can come only from ignorance". Hence, we may safely conclude that Economics is a Science though it has its own limitations.

Positive or Normative Science

In discussing the scope of Economics, we have also to consider whether Economics is a positive or a normative science. A positive science only explains **what is** and normative science tells us **what ought to be**, *i.e.*, right or wrong of a thing positive science describes, while the normative science evaluates. When we say, for instance, that the businessmen, while making decisions, use profit maximisation as the criterion, it is positive economics, but when we ask "ought they use this criterion", we enter the field of normative economics.

We have to consider whether Economics can pass moral judgments (normative science) or simply explain the "why" of things (positive science).

Classical view: Positive Science. The English Classical School was of the view that it was none of the functions of the economists to comment on the rightness or wrongness of an economic situation. "Almost all leading economists, from N. Senior and J.S. Mill onwards" had declared "that the science of economics should be concerned only with what is and not what ought to be."[7] Senior thought that the economist could not add even one word of advice. Cairncross said that Political Economy stood neutral as regards ends as mechanics stands neutral between rival schemes of railway construction. In the classical view, therefore, Economics was a positive Science.

Robbins' View. In recent times, Robbins has reaffirmed this neutrality and supported the above view. According to him, Economics is not concerned with the desirability or otherwise of the "ends". "The role of the economist is more and more conceived of as that of the expert who can say what consequences are likely to follow certain actions but who cannot judge as an economist the desirability of these actions." Introduction of value judgments into economic analysis is considered a transgression of the proper scope of economic theory. It is said that the **function of the economist is merely to explore and explain and not to advocate and condemn.**

Our View. This, in our opinion, is not a correct view. We agree with Hawtrey that Economics can not be dissociated from ethics. There is an "economic ought". Having analysed, for example, the causes of the maldistribution of wealth, why should the economist fight shy of saying that it ought to be better distributed? "A non-psychological Economics must, therefore, be regarded as either a superficial figment or as positively non-scientific. It is Hamlet with Hamlet left out."[8]

Economics is, therefore, **both a positive and a normative science**. We do not agree with robbins when he says that the gulf between Positive Economics and Normative Economics is so wide that no human ingenuity can bridge. It is the function of a sound economist to bridge this gulf. Even when the ends are given, Economics can pronounce on the means that ought to be adopted to achieve these ends.

The position is very well summed up by Cairncross thus: "However reluctant economists may be to introduce the brittle thread of ethics (so often snapped by disagreement) into their analysis, they cannot offer the guidance which is so urgently sought of them unless they do. They can explain how the economic system works without putting the mantle of philosophy over the rather drab working clothes of economic science. But they cannot say how the system can be made to work better. They can offer light, but not fruit; and it is fruit for which most people turn to Economics. Immediately the economist does venture to offer counsel–as is expected of him– he appears in the role of sheep in wolf's clothing, economist turned philosopher. This is a role which he must play consciously –not sheepishly, as if there were no wolf's clothing there!– if his conclusions are to command attention and respect"[9].

Macfie lucidly brings out the normative character of Economics. He says that "Economics is fundamentally a normative science, not merely a positive science like Chemistry."[10] Faced with scarce

7. Myrdal, G.– Value in Social Theory, 1958, p. 237.

8. Wolf in Tugwell's Trends of Economics (1935), p 466.
9. Cairncross, A. –Introduction to Economics (1944), p.9.
10. Macfie, A.L. — An essay on Economy and value p. 69.

resources and competing ends, the choice of a final end is to pass a value judgment. To try to achieve optimum satisfaction is to realise an objective which may be considered good and reasonable. The economic agent has to act on the principle that the scarce means should be put to the best advantage and should not be wasted. This is obviously "a universal human value" affecting all economic endeavour.

What economics should include? Economists argue on it.

Conclusion

Hence, economics act consists of not merely in allocation of scarce resources among competing ends but in maximising total satisfaction according to one's own judgement. The choice resulting from subjecting competing desires to judgement makes Economics obviously a normative Science.

Ends and Means. It has been remarked that Economics is concerned with means and ends lie outside its scope i.e., economics is neutral as regards ends. It expresses no opinion about the desirability or otherwise of the economic objectives to be pursued. It simply means that in the determination of ends or objectives, Economics has no voice. It takes the ends as given. It is for the Government, or the individuals to determine what they want to have or want to achieve. When that is settled, the economist will come in and suggest how best to achieve those ends with the minimum expenditure of resources. The economist will simply recommend the most economical use of the means for the realisation of particular ends. As stated already, Economics take ends as given in scales of relative valuation. It can only comment on the utilisation of means for the achievement of these ends. It is in this sense that ends are said to lie outside its scope.

It follows, therefore, that the economist takes no responsibility about the nature of the ends. The ends may be noble or ignoble, the economist is not concerned. Hence, there is no such thing as economic ends. "In so far as the achievement of any end is dependent on scarce means, it is germane to the preoccupation of the economist."[11]

However, as we explained in the preceding section, economists cannot altogether avoid pronouncing moral judgments, and it is good that they do. The economist today is expected to give guidance in the selection of ends or objectives considering the resources available.

Economics – A Social Science

Economics is primarily a study of man and not of wealth. **But it does not study man as an isolated individual** who has renounced the world. It studies, on the other hand, men who live in society affecting society by their actions and themselves exposed to social influences. Economics is not so much concerned with the "**economic man**" – an abstraction– but with the man of flesh and blood swayed by ordinary human motives, noble or ignoble, and having his ordinary share or human virtues and vices.

In order to understand the social aspect of economics, we should bear in mind that the workers are working in factories on materials drawn from all over the world and producing commodities to be sold all over the world in order to get in exchange goods from all other parts of the world to satisfy their wants. There is thus close inter-dependence of millions of people living in distant lands utterly unknown to one another.

In this way, the process of satisfying wants is a social process, not an individual process. Economics has thus to study social behaviour, i.e., behaviour of men in groups.

However, Economics is not a social science in the sense that it studies social acts as distinguished from the acts of the individuals.

Can Economics Solve Practical Problems?

The English economists generally hold the view that it is not the function of Economics to solve practical problems. The economic aspect of these problems may be very important and the economist's opinion is of great value. But no problem can be solved on economic grounds alone, for political and moral considerations may also be involved. **"The theory of Economics does not furnish a body of settled conclusions immediately applicable to policy. It is a method rather than a doctrine, an apparatus of the mind, a technique of thinking which helps its possessor to draw correct conclusions"** (Keynes).

We do not quite agree with this view. No economist has lived up to this ideal. Adam Smith Ricardo, Malthus and, in our times, the late Lord Keynes himself, have all actively interested

11. Robbins. L: op cit., p. 24.

Maximising profit or earning more income is a subject matter of positive economics.

themselves in the problems of their time. In the words of Fraser, **"An economist who is only an economist is a poor pretty fish."** According to Tugwell, it is only a premature flowering of Economics, which is responsible for its separation from practical life. Wooton complains that "we spend too much time forging theoretical tools and too little time in trying to make practical use of them." It is, therefore, increasingly felt that the economist must tackle practical problems. **When we study Economics, "our impulse is not the philosopher's impulse. Knowledge for the sake of knowledge but rather the physiologist's knowledge for the healing that knowledge may help to bring**". (Pigou)

Our view, therefore is that the economist must lend a helping hand in the solution of the practical problems. And he is in a much better position to do so than the statesman who may be devoid of the knowledge of economic theory. Everyday the economists are being called upon to give advice on practical problems. To quote Pigou again, "Economics is chiefly valuable neither as an intellectual gymnastic, nor as a means of winning truth for its own sake, but as a handmaid of Ethics and a servant of practice."

Limitations of Economics. It is necessary, however, to emphasise the limitations from which the science of Economics necessarily suffers. Apart from the fact that Economics cannot predict the course of future events since its laws lack definiteness, it must be recognised that economic analysis by itself cannot provide answers to questions that arise in individual or social conduct. It can furnish no magic formula by which schemes of social betterment can be tested nor a sovereign remedy to economic ills.

Boulding observes: "It is not, for instance, the business of the economist as such to decide whether large armaments are necessary, whether a marriage is successful, a religion efficacious, or oven whether a law is wise. The attention of the economist is directed principally to the area in which values can be measured in numerical terms, and consequently he cannot claim jurisdiction over the great region of valuation where such imponderable realities as friendship, patriotism, sincerity and loyalty are assessed. In all political questions such imponderable valuations are of vital importance, and economic analysis is an important witness, but is not the sole judge."[12] It is, therefore, necessary to bear in mind the limitations of Economics when an economist is called upon to tackle a practical problem.

LAWS OF ECONOMICS

Definition

Like every other science, Economics, too, has drawn its own set of generalizations, which are called the laws of Economics. These laws are supposed to govern and explain all economic activity. In the words of Marshall, economic laws may be defined thus :

"**Economic laws or statements of economic tendencies, are those social laws, which relate to branches of conduct in which the strength of the motives chiefly concerned can be measured by money price**." In terms of Robbins's definition of economic activity, we might say that economic laws are statements of uniformities which govern human behaviour concerning the utilisation of limited resources for the achievement of unlimited ends. These, in short, are the principles according to which we act when engaged in our ordinary business of life or in an economics activity.

Nature of Economic Laws

What is the nature of economic laws? What are they like? How do they compare with other laws? Are they like the government laws, or like the laws of morality or like the laws of natural sciences? The laws of the government are coercive; there is a penalty attached to their breach. The laws of morality are not so obligatory; they merely indicate how we should act in order to satisfy public opinion or our conscience. The laws of natural sciences can be stated with precision and have a universal validity. Economic laws are unlike all these, the nature of economic law is not indicated by the word "must", as in the case of statute law, or by "ought" as in the case of moral law; but their nature is indicated by the phrase, "**other things being equal**" (*ceteris paribus*).

12. Boulding, K.E.– Economic Analysis, Vol. 4, 1965, p.9.

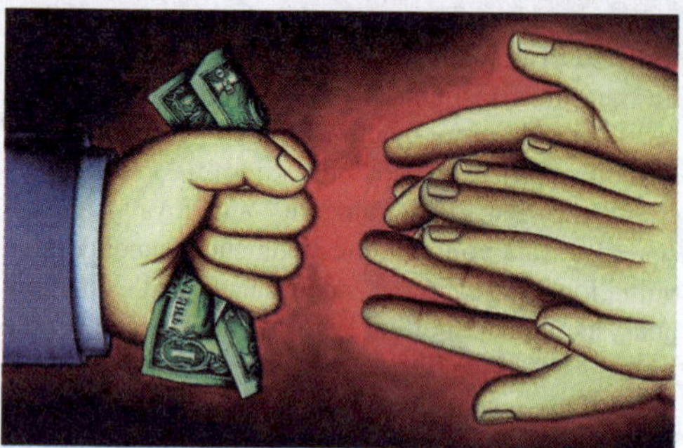

Just distribution of income is a subject matter of normative economics.

Some economic laws are axiomatic in character, e.g., greater gain is preferred to smaller gain. There are other economic laws which are of the nature of physical laws e.g., the law of diminishing returns.

Lack of Exactitude. The material of Economics is complex and ever-shifting. There is a great deal of economic friction arising out of custom and law. Social disabilities and legal restrictions thwart the operation of an economic law. There is also a preponderance of the human element. All these factors impart an element of uncertainty to economic laws. They lack the definiteness and exactitude found in laws of sciences like Physics. It is for this reason that Marshall has compared economic laws to the laws of tides rather than to the simple laws of gravitation. Economic laws are not exact; they lack definiteness.

It should, however, be remembered that the laws of Economics are more exact than those of any other social science, because the economic phenomena are capable of being measured in money price. This measuring rod of money is not available to any other Social Science like History and Political Science.

Hypothetical. Economic laws are said to be hypothetical or conditional since their validity depends upon the fulfilment of certain conditions. We say, for example, that if wages in Bombay are raised it will attract labour from other industrial centres. But some other conditions must be satisfied if other workers are actually to move to Bombay, e.g., cost of living. We also say that an increase in demand for a commodity will raise its price. But the supply of the commodity must not change in the meantime. Thus, if economic laws are to hold good other things must remain the same. Economic law simply states that given certain conditions certain results will follow.

Statement of Tendency. Economic laws are inevitable and inescapable if some necessary conditions are fulfilled. But these conditions are not always fulfilled. Hence, economic laws lack predictability. "There is no convenient yardstick by which to measure the currents in business affairs, for these are subject to gusts of fear or perhaps of fantastic optimism as unpredictable as earthquakes."[13] We cannot, therefore, say what will happen next because it depends on the fulfilment of so many conditions. We can only say what is likely to happen. Economic laws are, therefore, merely statements of tendencies of statistical probabilities. If demand increases, price tends to rise. Actually, it may rise or may not rise. It will depend also on the supply conditions.

Applicability of Economic Law

One controversial point about economic laws is about their applicability. The Classical Economists were of the opinion that economic laws were immutable, eternal, inexorable and so universally

Problems are many - we need to grow, we need more value and what not.

13. Moore and Others– Modern Economics (1940), p.3.

applicable, without any exception whatsoever. The Historical School, on the other hand, emphasized their relativity and insisted that they had only a limited application to a given environment. Bage-hot, for example, declared that the laws of Economics propounded in England were applicable to "a grown-up society of competitive commerce."

Modern economic opinion inclines to the view that in as much as economic laws are based on essentials of human nature, they hold good of almost all communities. They are simplified models of reality. They are good approximations. They are a useful guide to economic events and serve as a basis for the formulation and evaluation of economic policies. But, in the formulation of actual economic policies, allowance must be made for varying local conditions. Who can doubt that Gresham's law, the quantity theory of money, the law of diminishing utility, the law of choice and lots of other economic laws are independent of sociological and political conditions? Given the conditions under which they are true, the conclusions to which they point are inescapable. "If the data they postulate are given, then the consequences they predict necessarily follow." [14]

To say that economic laws are historico-relative and that they have no relevance outside certain historical conditions is wrong. The fact is that they are based on very wide human experience and have almost a universal applicability, though, we repeat, economic policies have to be different for different countries, and for the same country at different times.

BASIC ASSUMPTIONS IN ECONOMICS

It is seen above that economic laws are governed by the phrase "other things being equal." This means that , while reasoning out economic phenomena, we take certain things for granted. These are the various assumptions that underlie economic reasoning.

There are three broad types of these Assumptions: The first group relates to the behaviour of individuals *e.g.*, consumers, producers, workers, etc. For instance, we assume that the consumers act in a rational manner and seek maximum satisfaction. That there is mobility of labour in search of higher wages and the entrepreneurs seek maximum profit. This is known as the maximisation principle, In Mrs. Joan Robinson's words, "The fundamental assumption of economic analysis is that every individual acts in sensible manner and it is sensible for the individual to balance marginal cost and marginal gain". This sensible conduct results in maximisation of money gains. Actually the principle may not work. But, in order to simplify things, we have to assume all these things.

It is further assumed that the consumers' tastes remain unchanged for fairly long periods of time. That is, they do not suddenly change the components of their diet or their mode of dress. For instance, a vegetarian remains a vegetarian and a person continues wearing Indian dress. In other words, we assume 'economic rationality' both on the part of consumers and businessmen. We take the 'economic man' as our basis of discussion who is a sort of average of an abstraction different from 'real men' living in society. The assumption that the consumers seek maximum satisfaction out of the money they spend is fairly realistic. The assumption about the businessmen seeking maximum profits may be a little less plausible because there may be several other motives which may inspire businessmen. But it is worthwhile making this assumption because it helps us in constructing a simple theory of firm and industry. It is possible that these assumptions may not hold good in certain cases. But it seems sensible to make a simple and plausible assumption about consumers' and producers' behaviour as a basis for our study.

Then, there is the assumption of perfect competition on which the working of a competitive economy stands. It is assumed that there is a large number of buyers and sellers in the market, the commodity is homogeneous in character, that there is perfect knowledge and perfect mobility of resources and that none of the individual buyers and sellers are in a position to influence price. These assumptions are obviously unrealistic and do not hold good in the world of reality. There is no perfect knowledge, nor perfect mobility of resources, nor are the goods turned out by individual producers identical. But in discussions of economic theory, we proceed on the basis of a perfectly competitive model, because it has a fairly good predictive and explanatory value, i.e., the inferences drawn on the basis of this model fairly correspond to reality even if the assumptions only approximately hold good.

There is still another assumption which lies at the basis of economic analysis i.e., the concept of equilibrium. Equilibrium refers to a situation from which no departure is desired. It is a point of rest i.e., where a consumer is supposed to have attained maximum satisfaction and an entrepreneur maximum profit. We discuss consumers' equilibrium,

14. Robbins, L.op. cit., p. 121.

equilibrium of the firm and industry. A firm is said to be in equilibrium when it is making maximum profit and an industry is in equilibrium when it gives only normal profit. When these positions have been attained, there is no incentive to make any change.

A student of economics will also observe that most of the statements of economic laws are preceded or end with the phrase 'other things being equal' or *ceteris paribus*. This means that the law will hold good if there are no other changes taking place at the same time in the related economic phenomena. That is, economic laws are based on the assumption of 'no other change'. Actually, the world is dynamic and changes are simultaneously taking place. But this assumption isolates a particular change and thus facilitates understanding of the principles under discussion.

Conclusion

Whether the assumptions of economic analysis are true or not, it is necessary to bear them in mind so that we are all the time aware of the limitations of the conclusions at which we may have arrived. This is specially necessary when economic policies have to be formulated for the solution of certain economic problems.

The second group relates to the social, economic and political institutions. For example, we assume the existence of private property and capitalistic order of society. We assume law and order and stable political system. The existence of markets is also assumed. The market keeps the buyers and sellers of a commodity in touch with one another. That is how prices are determined and a uniform price comes to prevail in the market for a particular commodity.

Economic laws deal with those activities which can be measured in terms of money and prices.

Finally, there is a category of assumptions that relates to facts of geography and biology. We must base our conclusion on what is physically or climatically possible.

For example, the economist has to accept while discussing agricultural problems that harvest time is determined by nature. In the field of industry, it has to be assumed that the workers must have suitable rest pauses. We have also to assume that technical factors put a limit on industrial output. This leads us to the basic assumption of economic analysis, viz., that goods are scarce. Economics simply would not exist in the absence of scarcity. The basic task of economics is to distribute the available goods and services in the community in some reasonable manner.

METHODS OF ECONOMICS

One of the grounds on which Economics has been recognised to be a science is that, like other sciences, it, too, uses scientific methods. Let us now see what these methods are :

Deductive Method

The early English economists, known as the Classical School, tried to build up the science of Economics from a few simple generalizations. The method that they used is called the Deductive Analytical, Abstract or ***A priori*** method. Among these economists may be mentioned Senior, Mill Cairnes and Ricardo, the last one being its chief exponent. The advocates of this method start with a few indisputable facts about human nature and draw inferences about concrete individual cases. For example they believe that self-interest alone guides men in their daily life, and they try to explain and predict all human behaviour in terms of Self interest, which is obviously wrong.

Senior in his book **"An Outline of Political Economy"**, explains the deductive method thus. The economists' "premises consist of a few general propositions, the result of observation or consciousness and scarcely requiring proof or even formal statement which almost every man, as soon as he hears them, admits as familiar to his thoughts or at least as included in his previous knowledge and his inferences are nearly as general and, if he has reasoned correctly, as certain as his premises". J. S.

Mill too advocated the use of the deductive method in his '**Essays on some Unsettled Questions on Political Economy**'. Cairnes in his book '**Character and Logical Method of Political Economy**' Pointed out that the right method for arriving at conclusions in economic theory was the deductive method. Thus, the classical economists by and large supported the deductive method as a means of economic enquiry.

Merits of Deductive Method

(i) The deductive method is useful in analysing the complex economic phenomenon where cause and effect are inextricably mixed up. The deductive method takes a few simple general principles and applies them to draw conclusions in such complicated cases. But for this simple method it would have been perhaps impossible to establish any general relationship between two sets of facts.

(ii) This application of the deductive method yields exact and true conclusions provided the premises on which they are based are true. If we accept the general proposition that man prefers a greater gain to a lesser gain, the conclusion that Mr. A will work for a maximum profit inevitably follows. Hence, the deductive method has been Perhaps for its simplicity and exactitude, In the words of Cairnes, "The method of deduction is incomparably, when constructed under proper checks, the most powerful instrument of discovery ever wielded by human intelligence".

(iii) Deductive method is very simple and easy for application. There is no need for collecting elaborated statistical information. We just take some well known and accepted generalisation and draw inference by applying to a particular case; that is how Ricardo and his followers were able to develop pure economics on the basis of a few principles and by abstract reasoning.

(iv) In the economic field, where we have to study human behaviour, observation and experiments are simply out of the question. Also, the data are either not available at all or are inadequate. In such a situation, we have to rely on the deductive method for drawing inferences.

Limitations

(i) This deductive method has the merit of being simple, effective and certain, only if the underlying assumptions are valid, This is a very big "IF" indeed. More often than not, the assumptions turn out to be untrue of only partially true. The application of deductive method is thus misleading.

(ii) This method makes Economics dogmatic, for it refuses to admit that there can be some flaw in the premises.

(iii) The Deductive Method proves particularly dangerous when universal validity is claimed for generalisations based on imperfect or incorrect assumption, and when attempts are made to formulate practical policies of a nation in the light of these generalisations.

In view of the above shortcomings of the deductive method, the German historical school of economists bitterly attacked the classical economists for their indiscriminate use of this method for drawing hasty conclusions based on inadequate and incorrect data. It was pointed out that the use of this method led to conclusions which were unrealistic. As Professor Gide pointed out that these economists often mistook the abstraction for the reality. In a world of continuing economic changes, their conclusions had only a limited application. As Nicholson put it, "The great danger of the deductive method lies in the natural aversion to the labour of verification" No wonder that the historical school of economists came to advocate the use of inductive method in preference to the deductive method.

Different economic agents - consumers, producers etc. have different objectives to persue and they make assumptions accordingly given the time.

Inductive Method

The Historical School represents a reaction against the dogmatic attitude of the followers of deductive method. The reaction was specially marked in Germany and was represented by economists like Roscher, Hildebrand and Frederick List. The Historical School had also its supporters in England, *e.g.*, Cliff Leslie. These economists advocated a method which has come to be known as Historical, inductive or Realistic. This method insists on the examination of facts and then laying down general principles. Here we go up from "particulars" to "generals", whereas in the Deductive Method we come down from "generals" to "particulars".

Merits of the Inductive Method

The following merits are claimed for the inductive method:–

(i) The inductive method can be applied for the verification of conclusions based on deductive reasoning. In this way, deficiencies in their treatment can be brought out and their conclusions amplified or restated. Hence the inductive method proves a useful compliment to the deductive method.

(ii) The exponents of the inductive method have drawn pointed attention to the fact that economic phenomena are too complex to lend themselves to deductive reasoning. It is thus impossible to draw conclusions which may have universal validity. Rather, they are relative to time and place and have, therefore, limited applicability. Hence, inductive method is more suitable since it is based on facts rather than on abstract reasoning.

(iii) Inductive method is more suitable and useful in the formulation of economic policies for particular countries and for the same country in a particular situation. This is due to the fact that in the inductive method we proceed by examining important facts in a situation. That is how we may conclude that free trade policy may be more useful to a developed country and harmful to an under-developed economy.

Shortcomings of the Inductive Method

The main weapons in the hands of the inductive economists are observation and experiment. This method has the merit of being based on facts and having, therefore, a surer foundation But the danger is that hurried conclusions may be drawn from insufficient number of facts. Some important facts may have been ignored, and the conclusions may be unwarranted. To use Colin Clark's words, it will be "effectively putting the theoretical cart before the factual horse." Besides, observation and experimentation have very limited application in a science which deals with human activities.

But as against this it may be pointed out that although conscious experimentation is out of the question in economic science, yet history affords a number of experiments in the form of economic measures adopted from time to time. The granting of discriminating protection in India was one big experiment. In modern times, the application of the inductive method has been very much extended. There is a spate of statistical publications in every country. The "blue books" are full of facts and figures and the economist has a large and reliable supply of the material from which to draw his conclusions. That is why the modern era has been called the inductive Era.

Proper Method

The modern economist, however, does not rely on one method to the exclusion of the other. It is realised that theories without facts are barren, while facts without theories are meaningless. He uses both. **"Induction and Deduction are both needed for scientific thought as the right and left foot are both needed for walking."** [15] The economist first starts tentatively with a certain hypothesis based on deductive reasoning and then tests it on the touchstone of facts, and the hypothesis is elevated to the plane of a theory. Further checking in the light of the prevailing situation has to be done before the theory can be changed into a law. There is, thus, what Eric Rolls calls "interpenetration of deduction and induction". Thus, the two methods are complementary to one another rather than rivals. One is not to be used to the exclusion of the other.

Thus, **"true solution of the contest about method is not to be found in the selection of deduction or induction but in the acceptance of deduction and induction."** (Wagner). Which of the two methods is to be used in a particular situation depends on the nature of the inquiry, the material in hand and the stage at which the inquiry has reached.

15. Economics of Industrial Corporation, P. 241

The deductive method seems to be more suitable in the field of pure theory and the inductive method for formulating practical policies.

In short, the true scientific method consists of three different stages, *viz.*,

(*i*) Construction of Theories.

(*ii*) The deduction of conclusions from the theories.

(*iii*) The testing of Theories.

VALUE OF ECONOMIC ANALYSIS

The economists are called upon to play two distinct roles: (*a*) as educationists and (*b*) as professional economists. As teachers, they are concerned with explaining past economic experience and to instruct in the tools and techniques of economic analysis. The professional economists are involved with discovery and prediction. They are interested in developing and applying techniques that will help them in predicting future economic events. The tools are expository, analytical and illustrative devices. But they do not represent facts. They can be used to illustrate a case, but they can seldom be used to demonstrate a case (i.e., prove it).

Economics uses scientific tools for analysis for individual and institutional behavior.

It should be recognised that many assumptions made in economic analysis are really analytical tools. They may even help us purposefully to misrepresent real world conditions. Economic theory provides us with a basis for better under standing of economic behaviour. It is primarily procedural rather than substantive. We are more concerned with **how** and **why** man behaves and chooses than with **what** he actually does.

Economics is a composite discipline. It contains quantitative and very precise statements as well as statements touching on ethical and moral issues. Because of intrusion of ethical issues in so many economic problems, it is necessary to bear in mind the distinction between positive economics and normative economics. Positive economics is a scientific discipline, whereas normative economics is largely a branch of ethics. The resolution of normative problems is usually brought about through the political process and the ballot box. It is said that the economists' opinion on a normative question is of nor mere value than guessing the result of a football match.

In economics a great deal of attention is focussed on the study of the underlying axioms of the economic systems, their relevance and consistency. In the final analysis. It is the verification of the theory through observation that determines the usefulness or otherwise of the axioms employed in the theory. The axioms can turn out to be highly controversial statements and may have to be revised or rejected from time to time in keeping with the progress of ideas. "The history of science is strewn with the discarded bodies of defunct but once thriving statements that at one time or another were taken to be true by definition" [16] An economic model is like a geographical map. It does not show every aspect of the terrain, but only those features that are of interest for any task at hand. The map is not the territory nor is the model the real world. But neither can be understood without a map or a model. Economic models, like maps, increase the degree of certainty about what is likely to turn up over the hill, in the economic landscape". [17]

16. Calvo Peter and Waugh Geoffrey-Micro-Economics: An Introductory Text, 1979, P. 7
17. Ibid., Pp 10

Key terms

Micro economics, macro economics, managerial economics, positive economics, normative economics, deductive method, inductive method.

QUESTIONS

1. Discuss the nature and limitations of economic laws.

   Or

   "The laws of Economics are to be compared with the laws of tides rather than the simple and exact law of gravitation". Discuss.
2. Is economics a science? Discuss the true nature of Economics.
3. Distinguish between positive and normative economics.
4. "The true solution of the contest about method is not to be found in the selection of Deduction or Induction but in the acceptance of Deduction and Induction".

   Or

   "Induction and deduction are both needed for a scientific thought as right and left foot are needed for walking". Comment.
5. Define Micro-economics. What is its place in economic theory?
6. Define Macro-economics and discuss its importance and limitation.
7. "The economist has to study micro as well as macro economic problems. The two studies are complementary to each other than being the alternative matters of study". Discuss the statement.

PARTIAL EQUILIBRIUM AND GENERAL EQUILIBRIUM ANALYSIS

Meaning of Equilibrium

The term 'equilibrium' has often to be used in economic analysis. In fact, Modern Economics is sometimes called equilibrium analysis. Equilibrium means a state of balance. When forces acting in opposite directions are exactly equal, the object on which they are acting is said to be in a state of equilibrium. Tie a cord to a piece of stone and dangle it in the air. After oscillating from side to side, the stone will come to rest, if no further disturbance is caused. The stone is then in a state of equilibrium.

Types of Equilibria

Stable Equilibrium. There is stable equilibrium, when the object concerned, after having disturbed, tends to resume its original position. Thus, in the case of a stable equilibrium, there is a tendency for the object to revert to the old position.

Unstable Equilibrium. On the other hand, the equilibrium is unstable when a slight disturbance evokes further disturbance, so that the original position is never restored. In this case, there is a tendency for the object to assume newer and newer positions once there is departure from the original position.

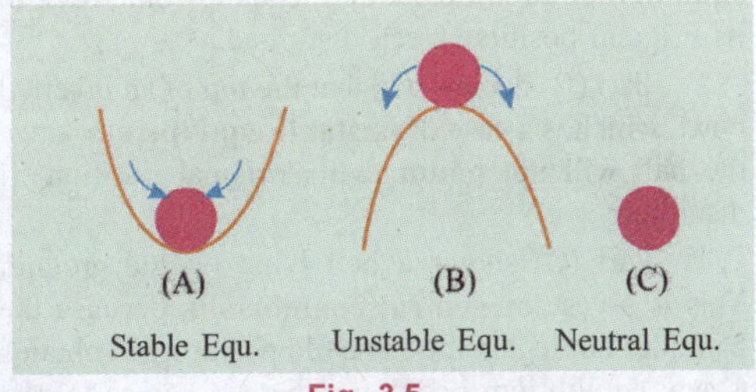

Fig. 3.5.

Neutral Equilibrium. It is neutral equilibrium when the disturbing forces neither bring it back to the original position nor do they drive it further away from it. It rests where it has been moved. Thus, in the case of a neutral equilibrium, the object assumes once-for-all a new position after the original position is disturbed.

Pigou thus describes these three equilibria: A ship with a heavy keel is in stable equilibrium; an egg lying on its side is in neutral equilibrium; an egg poised on one of its ends is in unstable equilibrium.

When the words 'equilibrium' is used to qualify the term value, then according to Prof. Schumpeter. "**A stable equilibrium** value is an equilibrium value that, if changed by a small amount, calls into action forces that will tend to reproduce the old value; a **neutral equilibrium** value is an equilibrium value, that does not know any such forces; an **unstable equilibrium** value is an equilibrium value, change in which calls forth forces which tend to move the system farther and farther away from the equilibrium value."

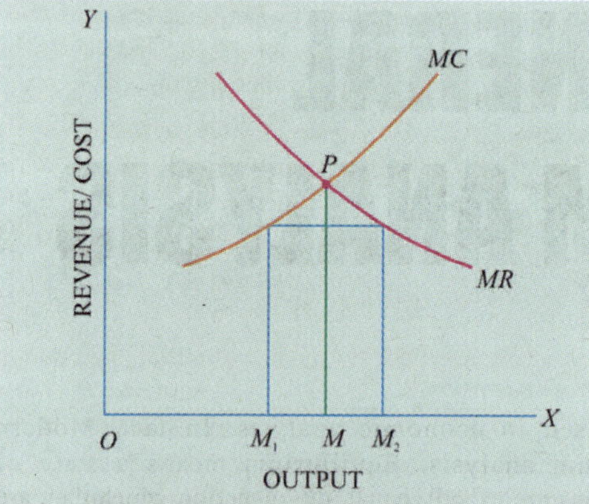

Fig. 3.2. Stable Equilibrium

Of these types, the stable equilibrium is the one most commonly used in economic analysis. Dr. Marshall made a very extensive use of it in discussion on the determination of value.

The figure below illustrates the three types of equilibria, *viz.,* stable, unstable and neutral.

Part (A) of Fig 3.1 shows a ball resting at the bottom of the bowl. This is a case of **stable equilibrium**, because the ball tends to come back to its original position when disturbed.

Part (B) depicts a ball at the top of an inverted bowl, which is a case of **unstable equilibrium**, since the ball will not return to its original position, if disturbed.

Part (C) shows a ball lying on the ground. This is a case of **neutral equilibrium**, because the ball does not regain the same old position but obtains a new equilibrium position, where it comes to rest after being disturbed initially.

Diagrammatic Representation. These three types of equilibrium can also be illustrated by making use of the marginal revenue and marginal cost curves.

The Fig. 3.2 represents **stable equilibrium** at the point P, where MR = MC. When in equilibrium at P, the producer produces an output OM and maximizes his profits. In case the producer increases his output to OM_2 or decreases it to OM_1, the size of his profits is reduced, This automatically brings in forces that tend to establish equilibrium again at P.

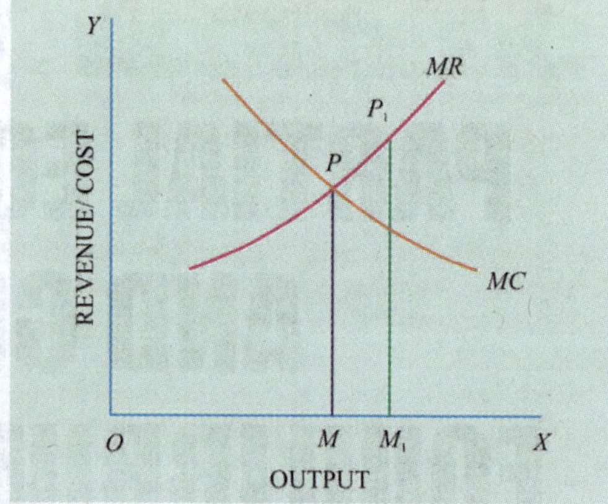

Fig. 3.2. Unstable Equilibrium

Fig. 3.3 Illustrate the case of unstable equilibrium. Initially, the producer is in equilibrium at Point P, where MR = MC and he is producing amount OM of output and maximizing his profits. If now he increases his output to OM_1, he would be in equilibrium output at P_1, where he will obtain higher profits, because, at this output, marginal revenue is greater than marginal cost. Thus, there is no tendency to return to the original position at P.

In this case, MR = MC at all levels of output so that the producer has no tendency to return to the old position and every time a new equilibrium point is obtained, which is as good as the initial one.

Short-term and Long-term Equilibria. Equilibrium may be short-term equilibrium or long-term equilibrium as in case of short-term and long-term value. In the short-term equilibrium, supply is adjusted to change in demand with the **existing** equipment or means of production, there being no time available to increase or decrease the factors of production. In the case of long-term equilibrium, however, there is an ample time to change even the equipment or the factors of production themselves. That is, a new factory can be erected or new machinery installed.

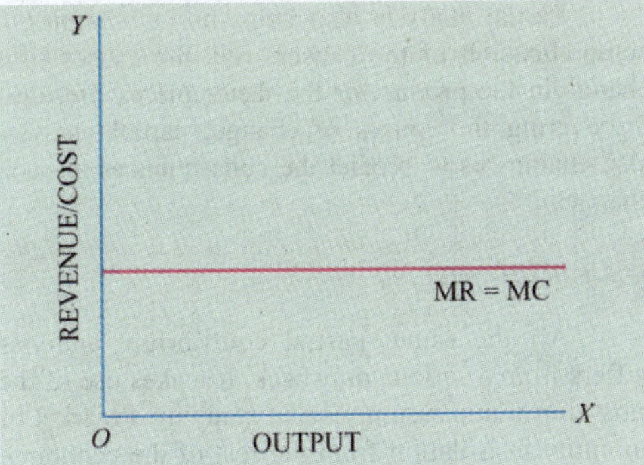

Fig. 3.4. Netural Equilibrium.

Partial or General Equilibria. There is another classification or equilibrium—partial equilibrium or general equilibrium, which we discuss at some length below:

PARTIAL EQUILIBRIUM ANALYSIS

Meaning

Partial equilibrium analysis is the analysis of an equilibrium position for a sector of the economy or for one or several partial groups of the economic units corresponding to a particular set of data. This analysis essentially entails a process of simplification, whereby, it excludes certain variable and relationship from the totality and studies only a few selected variables at a time. In other words, this method considers the changes in one or two variables keeping all others constant.

The equilibrium of a single consumer, or producer, single firm or single industry are examples of partial equilibrium analysis. Marshall's theory of value is a case of partial equilibrium analysis. Referring to this aspect of Marshallian economics, Hicks in his book **Capital and Growth** observes:

''Marshall (fixed) attention . . . . not upon the whole economy, but a sector (it had better be a rather small sector) of it: the partial equilibrium of the single ''industry'' . . . . Marshal never tired of emphasizing, the theory made no claim to be a precise theory it would be quite sufficient if (its) assumptions . . . . were very approximately true.''

It is clear from these statements that if the Marshallian method (*i.e.,* partial equilibrium analysis) is to be effective, even in its own terms, when applied to a hypothetical and idealized market, it is necessary that the market should be small enough so that its inter-dependence with the rest of the hypothetical economy could be neglected without much loss of accuracy. This procedure involves the reduction of an n-dimensional model to a two-dimensional cross-section. What it implies is that though in reality there may be n inter-dependent variables, the partial equilibrium analysis enables us to study only two of them at a time, keeping the others constant.

It is thus a case of abstraction, a process of simplification that works by choosing a few variables—we can let the others go, which do not matter for us or which are assumed not to matter. The importance of the phrase 'other things being equal' or what is also called thus *ceteris paribus* becomes obvious. For instance, in a complete demand-supply model, we know that the quantity demanded depends on a host of variables, *viz.*, the price of the product concerned, income and its distribution, prices of substitutes, selling costs, taste, *etc.* Similarly, the quantity supplied depends upon a large number of factors or variables. The partial equilibrium analysis works by picking up the most essential variables influencing the quantity demanded or supplied and assumes all other variables to be constant. It is on such assumptions that the demand and supply curves are drawn to determine the equilibrium price.

Thus, *ceteris paribus* is the crux of partial equilibrium analysis.

Applicability

There are two types of problems that the partial equilibrium analysis can deal with. In the first category fall those problems which pertain to some specific facets of economic behaviour of certain individual, firm or industry. Such a case may indeed be the market for a single product and that market alone is taken into account, while others are assumed to be constant. In the second category are included only those economic problems where the analysis is to be conducted for the first order consequences of the economic phenomena alone and it ignores the secondary effects.

With the application of partial equilibrium analysis, consumer's equilibrium is indicated when he is getting maximum aggregate satisfaction from a given expenditure and in a given set of conditions relating to price and supply of the commodity. A producer is in equilibrium when he is able to maximize his aggregate net profit in the economic conditions in which he is working. A firm is said to be in long-run equilibrium when it has attained the optimum size which is ideal from the point of view of profit and utilization of resources at its disposal. There is no tendency for it either to expand or to contract. Equilibrium of an industry shows that there is no incentive for new firms to enter it or for the existing firms to leave it. This will happen when the marginal firm in the industry is making only normal profit, neither more nor less. In all these cases, those who have incentive to change it have no opportunity and those who have the opportunity have no incentive.

Study of demand and supply of, say, apple keeping the situation of other fruits unchanged is an example of partial equilibrium analysis.

By focussing attention on a limited range of economic entities and reducing the scope of enquiry the partial equilibrium analysis renders the study of economic problems simple and understandable.

Thus, for practical problems, this method is indispensable because of its much greater simplicity in comparison with the general equilibrium analysis.

Significance

The partial equilibrium analysis is, in fact, the threshold to the general equilibrium analysis which involves the inter-dependencies of various variables. After having conducted the partial analysis, we can go on varying one more variable successively and thus by degrees explore the general working of the economic system.

Thus, the partial equilibrium analysis cannot be said to be incompatible with the general equilibrium. In Prof. Schenieder's words: "This notwithstanding, the general interdependent system may be seen as a network of particular interdependencies, a point of view which provides a complete justification for partial analysis."

The fact is that one can sometimes obtain a better notion of the properties of the general interdependencies with the help of partial analysis than one can do from Walras's highly mathematical procedure of general equilibrium.

Partial analysis also helps us in obtaining a comprehension of the causes, *viz.*: the causes of a change in the product or the factor prices. Besides, discovering the causes of change, partial analysis also enables us to predict the consequences of such changes.

Limitations

All the same, partial equilibrium analysis suffers from a serious drawback. It makes use of the most unrealistic assumption of studying a market or an entity in isolation from the rest of the economy. In the real world, the totality of all the economic dispositions and plans in an exchange economy forms one great interdependent system. The result is that economic disturbance in one market generates a chain of causation travelling from one market to another and ultimately engulfing the entire economy. Hence, the genuine course of an economic process as a whole can be visualized by means of general analysis and not by a partial one. Partial equilibrium may be regarded as a worm's eye-view, whereas the general equilibrium is a bird's eyeview.

GENERAL EQUILIBRIUM ANALYSIS

We have seen that the partial equilibrium analysis enables us to study the relationship between only a selected few variables, keeping others unchanged. For example, in the conventional price theory, the law of demand is stated thus: $(q = f\,p)$ *ceteris paribus*, meaning thereby that the quantity demanded of a commodity X is functionally related to its price and the relationship is inverse. This functional relationship considers price as the prime variable and holds all other variables such as income, tastes, prices of substitutes and complements, *etc.*, constant. Under such an abstract approach, price of every factor and commodity is a variable for the analysis of its own market and a parameter for the analysis of all other markets. This is only a piecemeal solution and there is no certainty that a consistent set of prices will result for the entire economy. However, the partial equilibrium analysis lies at the foundation of general equilibrium analysis.

Why General Equilibrium Approach

Fundamentally speaking, the price of any good or factor depends on the prices ruling in other markets. Commodities or factors must be either complementary or competitive, for there is nothing that stands unrelated (goods or factors). The complementarity arises out of the incompleteness of any single good or factor taken alone to satisfy a want. On the other hand, the goods or factors are competitive either because they are substitutable or else because with a given budget constant, a large bundle of wants is to be satisfied. Thus, the demand for, and the price of, a good depends upon the price of its substitutes or complements.

In the same way, the demand for, and the price of, a factor are influenced by the prices of other factors that can be used with or for it, Not only that; the prices of goods and of factors in turn depend upon each other because the firms enter the product market as suppliers and enter the factor market as buyers. Households, on the other hand, are buyers in the product markets and suppliers in the factor markets.

Study of interrelationship between various economic agents and markets is the subject matter of general equilibrium analysis.

However, looking from this angle, it would be committing a logical fallacy to say that the product prices are determined first and then conveyed to the consumers who thereafter make their optimum quantity adjustments. Similarly, it would be erroneous to say that the consumers first determine the quantities they wish to purchase and the market prices are decided only afterwards. This is so, because the factor prices cannot be determined till the firms have decided about the levels of output to be produced. The levels of output to be produced cannot be decided unless the product prices are known. How can the product prices be known unless the consumers have received their incomes from the sale of their factor services at certain prices? No market can adjust in isolation. It cannot adjust without disturbing the equilibrium of other markets and without having these disturbances reflect back on itself.

In fact, the economy cannot be divided into watertight compartments. The various aspects of the economic system are closely related and the whole process hangs together. It is just like an organic being that works as an integrated whole. No economic units are mutually exclusive; rather they are knit together in a mutually dependent way to form a unified whole. Every economic change will bring repercussions of a greater or less magnitude in every part of the economy. The ripples of effects of such a change pervade the entire economic system.

Repercussions of Change in Consumers' Preferences. Suppose there is a change in the tastes of the consumers which increases their relative preference for handloom cloth. The first effect that this change will produce will be to increase its price. This will impinge upon the factor prices used in its manufacture so that these will rise and that may raise their supply. Now these changes in the handloom cloth market and the handloom factor market will produce a chain of repercussions in the other markets and these in turn will react upon the handloom cloth market thus:

(i) The demand for goods complementary (if any) to handloom cloth will increase, thereby increasing their prices and the prices of factors of production used in their production.

(ii) The relative preference for handloom cloth will lead to a decrease in the demand for substitutes like mill-made cloth, thereby decreasing their prices and the prices of the factors of production used in their production (see figure .3.5).

(iii) As a consequence of the aforesaid changes, the relative prices of handloom cloth and its substitutes will be changed in favour of the former.

(*iv*) The consumers will, therefore, be confronted with new price-ratios and this will go to modify the increase in demand for, and the prices of handloom cloth and its complements. At the same time, a similar modification will occur in respect of the demand and the prices of substitutes. Similar arguments will also apply for the factors of production in each market.

(*v*) The firms engaged in the production of handloom cloth and its complements will be forced to pay higher prices to the factors of production employed by them.

(*vi*) The magnitude of increase in the price of any such factor will in turn depend upon the magnitude of increase in the production of handloom cloth and on its elasticity of supply.

(*vii*) Whether or not the prices of all factors will rise by the same percentage and their effect on the prices of handloom cloth and other commodities will depend on the relative importance of the different factors of production in different firms or industries.

(*viii*) Whatsoever the degree of the rise in the prices of factors, it will invariably stultify the fall in the price of substitutes for handloom cloth, assuming that they use the same factors. These changes in the various price-ratios will produce repercussions on the relative demands, and vice-versa.

(*ix*) Owing to a change in the relative prices of the factors of production, there will occur a substitution of dearer factors by the relatively cheaper factors.

(*x*) This process of substitution of factors shall in turn bring about a change in the demand for the factors (and in their prices), and in the costs and prices of all industries using them. The effect of all this will be to modify the changes in the relative factor prices mentioned in (*v*) and the changes in the relative prices of products mentioned in (*iii*).

(*xi*) Due to changes having occurred in the relative prices of factors of production, personal income distribution will also undergo a change.

(*xii*) The changes in the personal income distribution will further bring about changes in the pattern of demand, which will in turn impinge upon several markets.

Essence of General Equilibrium Approach

This inherent simultaneity of numerous mutual interdependencies and decisions necessitates the abandonment of partial equilibrium approach and the adoption of an approach general enough to take account of the basic mechanics of the whole economy. An analysis that treats the various individual economic units and markets as inter-related and attempts to trace the ramifications of an economic event to bring out their mutual determinations, is known as general equilibrium analysis.

Equilibrium in this general sense requires the harmony of the multitude of forces emanating from the multitude of decision-making units so as to equate the demand for, and supply of, each product and each factor at completely inter-related and consistent set of prices.

General Equilibrium and Macro-economic Equilibrium

General equilibrium is different from the aggregate or macro-economic equilibrium. In micro economic equilibrium models, the entire system is

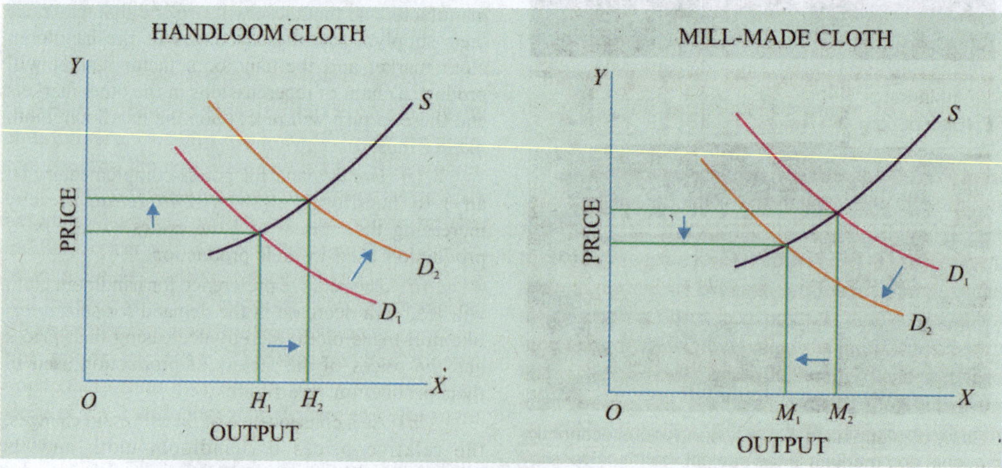

Fig. 3.5. Increase in demand for handloom cloth leads to decrease in demand for mill-made cloth.

described by relatively few, appropriately defined aggregates and functional relationship connecting aggregate variables such as total consumption expenditure, total investment, total employment, aggregate output and the like. In a macro-economic equilibrium system, such as the Keynesion type, the relations are fundamentally macro-analytical because they involve aggregate concepts and macro interpretations. In such types of analyses, many important variables and relationships tend to disappear in the process of aggregation.

Viewed from the methodological angle, the macro-economic models stand shorn of much of their appeal since their basic behavioural assumptions and relations are not derived from the individual decision-making units. However, the attraction of the aggregative analysis lies in its simplicity and the availability of date required for testing of macro-economic equilibrium models.

On the other hand, the general equilibrium models are disaggregated models which are basically atomistic and micro-analytical in nature. They intend to take cognizance of every single economic decision maker and every economic good in the economic system. The basic ingredients of a general equilibrium approach can be at once traced back to the individual decision-making units such as the consumers and the firms. The properties of the general equilibrium model relate directly to the ultimate economic units.

Further, the macro-economic equilibrium analysis, unlike the general equilibrium analysis, fails to spotlight the mutual interrelatedness and determination of the individual units and markets.

It would be pertinent to ask : Can we analyse the **putative** influences of interdependent economic forces that the general equilibrium analysis claims to cover in its ambit? While it would be difficult, in fact impossible, to analyse millions of such interdependencies that exist in any economy, the competitive markets automatically take them into account. Such types of markets are in a position to perform such a complex task because of two reasons:

(i) Firstly, in a competitive system no individual or organization has to make all the decisions. All individual decision-making units pursue their own interest and the general equilibrium solution is the outcome of all those decisions taken together.

(ii) Secondly, the competitive markets give out signals through prices which communicate to the numerous individual decision-making units the information to plan their expenditures or production.

In the process of making their decisions, the consumers and the firms affect the prices of commodities. The changes in the prices serve as signals to the various consumers and firms which adjust their decisions accordingly. In this way, the changes in prices will go on bringing forth changes in quantities supplied and demanded until equilibrium in all markets is achieved simultaneously. This solution is what we call general equilibrium.

Thus, in such a system the various individual units go on pursuing their own ends—utility in case of consumers and profit in case of entrepreneurs and the resources shall be allocated according to those ends in the state of general equilibrium. While highlighting the situation in a general equilibrium in a static state Prof. Albert L. Meyers contends that it refers to "a condition in which all prices are long-run prices, each person is spending his income in the manner which yields him the greatest satisfaction; each firm and industry is in a state of equilibrium with respect both to prices and output, and supply and demand for factors of production are equated at general equilibrium prices. In short, general equilibrium is a condition in which there are no economic motives for change".

Walras was the first person to build a model of general equilibrium of a purely competitive economy in order to express theoretically and identify practically the various markets through which the mechanism of interdependence work to bring about general equilibrium.

Uses of General Equilibrium Analysis

The general equilibrium has many theoretical and practical applications:

(i) To get an overall complete picture of the economy and study the problems involving the economy as a whole or even large segments of it, necessitates the consideration of the interrelations of production, consumption and the prices of all commodities and factors simultaneously. This requires the use of general equilibrium analysis.

(ii) The general equilibrium shows that the quantities of demanded goods are equal to the quantities supplied of them. Similarly, the quantities of factors demanded are equal to the quantities of factors supplied. Such a condition implies that the resources are being fully employed. Thus, in a state of general equilibrium, the amount of factor services which resource owners wish to supply is exactly equal to the amount which the various firms want to purchase.

In other words, all resources which seek employment are able to find it at the general equilibrium set of prices. In the absence of general equilibrium, there could be excess supply of some of the factors and, therefore, some of the resources will remain idle against the wishes of the resource owners.

Thus, we get the golden rule which states that the necessary condition for the resources to be fully employed is the existence of general equilibrium. Only in a state of full employment can the society strive to raise its standard of living.

(iii) The general equilibrium system also provides us with an ideal datum of economic efficiency. It brings out the fact that long-run competitive equilibrium is a standard of efficiency for the entire economy. Only when the competitive economy obtains general equilibrium shall its economic efficiency be at its peak and there shall be no further gains made by any reallocation of resources.

(iv) The general equilibrium system also represents the covered state from the vantage point of welfare. The consumers in this state obtain the maximum satisfaction of their wants. Maximization of satisfaction implies maximization of welfare. Not only that, the general equilibrium also represents the state of optimum production of all commodities, because there can be no over-production or under-production under such conditions. All the markets are simultaneously cleared.

(v) The theory of general equilibrium also provides an insight into the way the multitudes of individual decisions are integrated by the working of price mechanism. It, therefore, solves the fundamental problems of a free market economy, *viz.,* What to produce, how to produce, how much to produce, *etc.* This analysis shows that such decisions with regard to innumerable consumers and producers are co-ordinated by the price mechanism.

(vi) The general equilibrium analysis also gives us clues for predicting the consequences of an economic event. We have simply to peep through the complex chain of interrelationships embodied in the general equilibrium to gauge the sequence of consequences expected to be produced by the happening of an economic event.

(vii) The theory of general equilibrium also unravels the determinants of distribution of income in a community. Each individual performs certain services in the society for which he receives income. The size of the income depends on the amount of factor services which he supplies at the established prices.

As regards the functional income received by the different resources, there are two economic forces upon which it hinges: the relative productivities and the structure of demand for the output. The marginal revenue product and the equilibrium price of a factor increase or decrease in accordance with its marginal productivity. Given the state of full employment of the available resources, the income shares of the various factors will depend upon their relative marginal products. Similarly, the income shares of the various factors are also governed by the structure of demand because the income paid to a factor depends upon value attached by consumers to the product.

(viii) The general equilibrium analysis also finds application in the field of public policy. The formulation of a logically consistent public policy designed to influence business conduct requires a complete understanding of the various sector markets and aspects of individual decision-making units. General equilibrium provides the required information in this respect.

(ix) Yet another practical application of general equilibrium analysis is to be found in the input output analysis. The conceptual framework of Walrasian general equilibrium forms the basis of Leontiff static input-output system. In these days, it is being employed in the formulation of plans for economic development of underdeveloped countries.

Limitations of General Equilibrium Analysis

The general equilibrium analysis suffers from several drawbacks also:

(i) The Walrasian general equilibrium system is essentially static. It treats the coefficient of production as fixed. It considers the supply of resources to be given and constant. It also takes tastes and preferences as fixed. But, in the real world, nothing is fixed; on the other hand, everything is constantly changing.

(ii) The general equilibrium system ignores leads and lags, for it considers everything to happen instantaneously. It is supposed to work just in the same way as an electric circuit does. In the real world, all economic events have links with the past and the future.

(iii) Apart from the unrealistic assumptions on which it stands, the Walrasian general equilibrium analysis is of little practical utility. It involves astronomical volumes of calculations for estimating the various quantities and practices. This makes its application practically impossible. Even the electronic computers cannot be of much help because they can at best solve the great many equations of such a system but cannot aid in collecting and recording the

Input tranformed into output.

innumerable sets of prices and quantities that are required to formulate these equations. It is a tremendous problem.

(iv) It assumes the existence of a unique consistent real set of prices which will simultaneously equalize the demand and supplies of all goods and factors. The critics point out that the solution obtained by solving the simultaneous equations may give answers which lie in the doman of imaginary numbers. No economic meaning can be attached, for instance, if the price of any commodity comes out to be $\sqrt{-2}$ or numbers like that. Thus, the model of general equilibrium cannot be applied unless a unique real solution is obtained from the simultaneous equations. The critics further argue that even if such a solution exists, the price mechanism may not necessarily converge to it.

(v) The general equilibrium analysis is also found to flounder when the theoretical conclusions are juxtaposed with the empirical results. Large-scale unemployment has occurred under several price mechanisms. For instance, 20 per cent of the labour force was unemployed in the U.K., the U.S.A., and Germany during the 1930's. Thus, the prescription of general equilibrium analysis that in a free enterprise economy, the price mechanism shall bring about full employment is simply a myth.

(vi) Last but not least, the general equilibrium analysis falls to the ground as its star assumption of perfect competition is contrary to the actual conditions prevailing in the real world.

Need for a new concept of general equilibrium

Marshallian partial equilibrium is attached with the micro-economics, and deals with only one economic variable. Partial equilibrium gives us the picture of a smallest part of the whole economy, which may not reflect, any strong economic behaviour, whereas Leon Walras's general equilibrium is concerned with the 'macro-economics', which is very essential for governments to undertake and study and, envolve different policy measures, so as to improve the economic condition or to maximise social welfare. A number of studies are carried out in different ways, to achieve this general equilibrium. Marxian equilibrium is quite different from Keynessian 'effective demand', Harrods Ga = Gw = Gn a steady growth model equilibrium and the recent IS/LM curve determination of income and output levels etc.

In the present world of economic liberalisation and globalisation, in which to a greater extent the monetarists approach has thrown open the dynamism of economics. General equilibrium is required which should include not only the internal economics but also international economics which now-a-days has been influencing a lot. Own economic policies may not be fruitful in determining only the internal economic levels but also it must takes into account other countries policies, which influence an internal economy as well as your policies and other country's policies.

Conclusion

In spite of these drawbacks, however, the general equilibrium represents a bold attempt to view the numerous interdependencies of an economic system. As the methods of computation improve, its practical utility may considerably increase.

Summing up

In Economics, equilibrium analysis is of two kinds: Partial Equilibrium analysis and General Equilibrium analysis. In the partial equilibrium analysis, we focus our attention on individual economic units i.e. the consumer, the firm, an industry or a particular sector of an economy. It takes into account a number of variables for intensive study assuming that the economic process is not disturbed by influences external to the part of the economy we are studying. To use Schneider's words ''The surrounding world is regarded as fixed or frozen over the period for which it is being studied.'' This type of theory discusses the determination of prices and outputs of particular commodities assuming those of others remaining unchanged. In other words, in partial equilibrium analysis, we isolate a particular type of activity for special investigation in great depth even though we know that there is, in fact, much interdependence between that under investigation and that held aside.

In contrast to the partial analysis, there is the general equilibrium approach. This approach stresses the inter-relationships among the prices and outputs of the various commodities and factors. Thus the general equilibrium analysis attempts to deal with all the variables of the economic system simultaneously. Obviously it is a much more difficult proposition. In this analysis, we collect and integrate the separate individuals and markets in order to examine how they are inter-related and influence they have on one another. It is thus extremely sophisticated and requires advanced mathematical knowledge.

The partial equilibrium analysis has obvious limitations. It assumes that disturbances in a particular sector of the economy have only localised effects. In reality it is not so. Inspite of such limitations, the partial economic analysis occupies an important place in price, and resource allocation theory. According to Marshall, it is easily comprehensible and more effective. It provides simpler propositions and simpler analysis. On the other hand, general equilibrium approach is more complicated than the partial equilibrium approach. But with the advancement of mathematics this approach is becoming more popular among the economists.

Key terms

Stable equilibrium, unstable equilibrium, partial equilibrium, general equilibrium.

QUESTIONS

1. What is Equilibrium? Distinguish between stable and unstable Equilibrium.
2. Distinguish between partial and general equilibrium approach to economic analysis.
3. Explain the concept of 'Equilibrium'. Discuss its importance in economic theory.
4. Explain the uses and limitations of general equilibrium analysis.

STATICS, DYNAMICS AND COMPARATIVE STATICS

A student of modern economic analysis frequently comes across the terms 'economic statics' and 'economic dynamics'. It is, therefore, very necessary for him to understand them clearly before he embarks upon the study of economic theory proper. In fact, some economists divide economic theory into two main branches, *viz.,* economic statics and economic dynamics.

The words 'Statics and Dynamics' have been borrowed from mechanics. August Comte first introduced these words in social sciences. It was John Stuart Mill who first made use of these concepts in Economics. However, the use of these remained clouded and ambiguous till 1928, when Ragnar Frisch made a scientific distinction between them. This has been followed by a conceptual controversy between some of the leading modern economists giving rise to a great deal of confusion and fallacy. Let us, therefore, be very clear about them.

ECONOMIC STATICS

Meaning

Literally the word 'statics' implies 'causing to stand'. In common usage, the term 'statics' connotes a position of rest or absence of movement. However, economic statics does not imply absence of movement, rather it denotes a state in which there is a continuous, regular, certain and constant movement without change. It is a state wherein economic activity goes on regularly and constantly on an even keel. Thus, remarks Pigou, ''Just as the drops of water that form a stream are always changing but its form remains the same so do, in a static state, the factors change but they are not of any consequence.''

Clark maintains that a static state is characterized by the absence of five kinds of change : the size of population, the supply of capital, the methods of production, the forms of business organization and the wants of the people; but all the same the economy continuous to work at a steady pace. Marshall states that ''It is to this active but unchanging process .... that the expression static economics should be applied''.

Harrod is of the view that static analysis is concerned with a state of rest. State of rest does not signify a state of idleness but simply lack of investment with the result that the economy repeats itself over time. Harrod, of course, does not confine his concept of statics to such a rigidly defined state of affairs. He includes in it the once-for-all change whereby the economy shifts from one state of rest to another.

Prof. Hicks has a somewhat different notion of statics. According to him, we should call economic statics those parts of economic theory where we do not trouble about dating. He means to say that economic statics studies stationary situations which are devoid of any change and which do not require any relation to the past or the future. Thus, the static economy of his vision is a tameless economy in which the various phenomena and their effects are analyses without reference to time. For instance, when we say that if price is lowered by 5 percent demand rises by 3 per cent, we are in the field of static analysis.

Frisch maintains that by static analysis is meant **"A method of dealing with economic phenomena that tries to establish relations between elements of the economic system—prices and quantities of commodities—all of which have the same point of time."** In other words, in economic statics we do not study anything about the connection between conditions at various points of time, *e.g.,* sequences, lags, *etc.* The ordinary theory of demand and supply is an illustration of the static analysis. It builds up a relationship between demand and supply as they are supposed to be at any moment of time. The market situation is assumed to be immune from the influences of the decisions of past or by the future expectations of value (although actually it is not so).

Thus, static analysis being a timeless analysis assumes instantaneous adjustment of the indices. Prof. Samuelson states in this connection: "Economic statics concerns itself with the simultaneous or instantaneous determination of the economic variables by mutually interdependent relations." Since instantaneous determinations keep no link with the past or future, we can infer that economic statics contains no element of uncertainty in it. Prof. Kuznets, while commenting on this aspect, remarks that, "Static economics deals with relations and processes on the assumption of uniformity and persistence of either the absolute or relative economic quantities involved."

In simple words, economic statics presupposes that the manner in which an economic unit changes is the same as it changed in the past and will change in the future. It suffices, therefore, under economic statics, to study the economy in its present position. It gives only a "still picture" of the economy, a vision of the moment, disappearing as soon as it makes its appearance.

Stationary State

The method of economic statics is generally associated with the concept of a stationary state where everything repeats itself from year to year. The economy churns steadily like a gramophone repeating itself endlessly. However, the concept of a stationary state is a mere methodological fiction devoid of any reality, although backward economies of India and China at one time showed symptoms of

Economist making analysis by comparing graphs.

stationariness.

Further, this concept does not mean a method of analysis but an object of analysis, *viz.,* an economic process which goes on at an even rate or which merely reproduces itself. The values of all variables such as tastes, resources and technology, *etc.,* are not supposed to change over time. The factors which control production, consumption, distribution and exchange are assumed to be constant, yet there is movement, though at a uniform rate. People continue to be born and die, but births equal deaths so that there is no change in numbers, though the composition of population is changing.

Thus, it does not mean a frozen fixity. To use Pigou's words. **"Individual drops composing the waterfall are continually in movement, though the waterfall itself remains."** The economic system itself may remain static, though individual constituents may undergo change. The three fundamental sets of data *viz.,* tastes, resources and techniques remain the same.

Significance of Economic Statics

Simplicity. Though economic static is mostly unrealistic and unsuitable for most of the purposes, yet it enjoys the virtue of simplicity which has value of its own. None can deny that the study of the working of a propeller, while it is standing, is much easier than while it is in motion. In the same way, it is not only useful but necessary to possess complete understanding of the each and every part of the economic machine before it moves. Of course, economy can never stop, but it is the beauty of the static analysis that it allows the machine to move but at a constant rate so that the task of understanding is facilitated. That is why Leuthen points out that **"we**

should emphasize that static theory has an introductory pedagogical value.''

Clarity. The justification for such a value is to be found in the gain in clarity and the precision that results by studying the economic phenomena in isolation with the past and the future through higher degrees of abstraction. In Marshall's words, **''The economist segregates those disturbing causes whose wanderings happen to be inconvenient for the time being in a phrase called ''ceteris paribus''**. It is a simplifying device.

Hypothetical Model. Simplicity and clarity apart, the method of static analysis provides us with a hypothetical model of the economic phenomena in a state of unchangeability which helps us in comprehending the consequences of certain changes. This, in itself, is of no small value, for the crux of any scientific discipline lies in the discovery of the consequences. The policies can be snapped accordingly to deal squarely with the consequences.

End-View. Static theory is a study of the states of equilibria and thus it provides us an end-view of the forces in operation. In a sense, end is more important than what happens along the path to the end. Hence, utility of static theory is beyond question.

Behaviour of Variables. Static analysis also provides us with understanding regarding the behaviour of the variables in the economy. Prof. Marshall stresses that the central idea of ''equilibrium'' is statical rather than dynamical and the analysis of states of equilibria throws valuable light on the likely behaviour of the variables of an economy. For example, the study of equilibrium price tells us about the possible behaviour of the prices in the economy. Likewise, to know how demand and supply affect prices can be better understood when both demand and supply are in an equilibrium state. Economic static builds up a relationship between demand, supply and price as they are supposed to be at any given moment; nothing else is considered even though several other things may also be changing at the same time. But we shut out eyes to other changes and focus our attention only on demand, supply and price to simplify matters.

Simplifying Process. Marshall has very clearly described the simplifying process thus : ''The forces to be dealt with are so numerous, that it is best to take a few at a time; and to work out a number of partial solutions as auxiliaries to out main study. Thus we begin by isolating the primary relations of supply, demand and price in regard to a particular commodity. We reduce to inaction all other forces by the phrase 'other things being equal'. We do not suppose that they are inert, but for the time we ignore their activity . . .. In the second stage, more forces are released from the hypothetical slumber that had been imposed on them. Gradually, the area of the dynamical problem becomes larger; the area covered by provisional statical assumptions becomes smaller.''

Step to Reality. This method is known as the method of ''decreasing abstraction,'' ''successive approximation'' or the ''isolating, one-at-a-time procedure''. Recently, it has been called the ''optimistic'' approach. In the words of Joan Robinson, ''An optimist appears to be analytical economist who is prepared to work stage-by-stage towards the still far distant ideals of constructing an analysis which will be capable of solving the problems of the real world.''

Allocative Problems. Again, it is only through the method of economic statics that the various types of allocative problems of the economy are studied. We study how an individual allocates his income on the purchase of various commodities to maximize his satisfaction, how a producer combines his inputs in an optimal way to maximize his profit, and how the national product is distributed. Thus, the significance of economic static lies in penetrating the complex problems in a simple way.

Applicability. Further, as Harrod states, the central core of the doctrine and the principles related to Robbins's definition of economic fall within the purview of economic statics. **The theory of comparative costs, case for free trade and marginal analysis, etc., are all exercises in static analysis.**

Prof. Harrod also holds that **Knight's theory of profits falls within the ambit of static analysis.** He argues that ''Since change and round about production involve uncertainty—and once-over change generates more uncertainty than continuing change—I conceive the theory of profit to lie within the field of statics. I do not see anything specifically dynamic for instance in the theory of profit elaborated by Prof. F. H. Knight''.

Harrod again maintains that **Keynes's General Theory is also essentially static in character.** Except for the concept of positive saving, all other variables of the Keynesian analysis such as involuntary unemployment, liquidity preference, marginal efficiency of capital, marginal propensity to consume and the multiplier are static in character because Keynes is concerned to show once-over changes in explaining these variables.

There is also a great scope for the development of static input-output analysis with regard to **distribution of national income, internal** and **international trade** which can be of immense use in planning.

Static analysis these days is also being increasingly made of the **institutional determinants of the economic systems.**

Comparative Statics. Fundamentally speaking, the Theory of Comparative Statics has its roots in economic statics. This enables us to study the change from one equilibrium position to another.

Facilitates Dynamic Analysis. Above all, the dynamic analysis can be considered to be a sort of running commentary on static analysis. It is only the full knowledge about static analysis which enables us to apply the dynamic analysis to the problems. We cannot see what is moving and what is changing. We can study the moving picture of a functioning economy, but the picture has to be conceived as a static one. A change has thus to be broken up in bits and the bits have to be broken up into smaller bits, till each small bit is devoid of change.

Thus, the dynamic analysis has to be looked upon as if composed of innumerable small static pieces. To use Robbins' words. "We study these statical problems not merely for their own sake, but in order to apply them to the explanation of change .... their chief significance lies in their application in economic dynamics. We study the laws of rest in order to understand the laws of change."

Conclusion. Thus, economic statics occupies an important place in economic analysis today. It has a very wide application indeed. Its significance cannot be over-emphasised. It facilitates the understanding of economic theory and helps in the solution of economic problems. It can be applied to all branches of Economics.

Limitations of Economic Statics

The static analysis suffers from a few serious shortcomings: It takes us far away from the reality. It assumes variable data such as population, tastes, resources and techniques, *etc.*, to remain constant. But the actual world is a dynamic one where the data are continuously changing. Aptly Prof. Edgeworth remarks, "The treating of a constant what is variable is the source of most of our fallacies in Political Economy."

Static analysis assumes away time. We cannot, therefore, pump in much meaning into our statements regarding economic changes since they take place over time. Hence, static analysis has only a limited scope to deal with the real economic problems.

ECONOMIC DYNAMICS

Meaning.

The word 'dynamics' means causing to move. In economics, 'dynamic' refers to the study of economic change. The essence of any knowledge lies in formulating relationships between phenomena. There must be thus a sequence of events for the knowledge to be born. The main purpose is to know as to how a complex of current events will shape itself in the future. To do so, it is necessary to visualize the way it has itself arisen out of the past events. In this view, economics essentially assumes a dynamic character. The moment we talk of sequence of events, the element of time creeps into our analysis. It is this time element and its passage that imparts a dynamic flarour to our economic problems.

In economic statics, the relations between the relevant variables refer to the *same point or period of time.* In economic dynamics, however, the relations between relevant variables refer to *different points of time.* Economic Dynamics is thus a process of change through time. Since dynamic is that which changes and static which does not involve change, it is pertinent to ask what is it that changes ? An economic unit may undergo a change with respect to itself at a different place or a different time. We can therefore, say that the change may occur with respect to matter, space or time. For instance, in the process of manufacture, the matter may undergo change or in the process of transportation space undergoes a change. Similarly, in the process of hoarding, time-undergoes a change.

While the economy is in the process of change through time, the economic variables may change in two ways: One way is that, though the time element has undergone a change, the economy may not change its pattern and thus the values of the economic variable remain the same. The second way is that the economy may evolve through time and change its pattern so that the economic variables are non-stationary through time. The former way of happening of the change relates to the stationary state, while the latter type relates to economic dynamics. When the economy assumes a different pattern, the economic system will change its magnitude and direction.

We can explain this idea with the help of Fig. 4.1 given below.

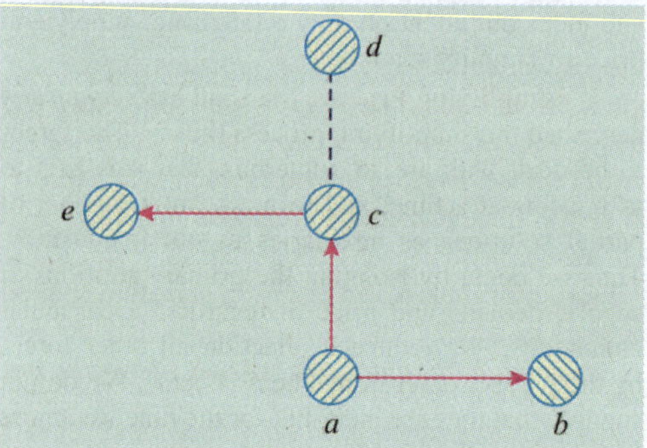

Fig. 4.1. Stationary state and change through time.

Assuming certain given values of the economic variables, the economy would have moved from the position **a** to **b**. But in case there occurs a sudden change in the pattern so that the various indices undergo some change at the initial position **a**, the economic system will change its direction and traverse towards the position **c**. Again, had there been no further change in the pattern of the economy it would have driven the economy to the position **d**. But again, if the pattern undergoes a sudden change at **c**, the economy would in that case proceed towards **e**. Economic dynamics studies the process of change from positions such as **a** to **c** and **c** to **e**. On the other hand, the analysis of the traverse from **a** to **b** and **c** to **d** would come under the subject-matter of economic statics.

However, a great deal of conceptual controversy has been raked up in recent times with regard to the notion of economic dynamics.

Hichs's View. Prof. J. R. Hicks defines Economic Dynamics ''as those parts where every quantity must be dated.'' He contends that economic statics is concerned with those situations which are perfectly devoid of change and, therefore, do not require any relation with the future or the past, and need no dating. Hence, Hick's view is that is only change which makes the analysis dynamics. Change is the force that makes the things to differ at different dates and this alone is sufficient to give a dynamic colour to the analysis. Hicks goes to the extent of including a once-over-change in the realm of dynamic analysis. However, this makes his view erroneous for it unnecessarily drags many problems in the field of dynamic analysis where static analysis would do.

Harrod's View. Criticising Hicksian definition, Prof. Harrod comments, **''Mr. Hicks appears to be analysing the effects of once-over-change in fundamental conditions. There is no recognition that a different technique may be required for analysing the effects of continuing changes.''** Thus, Harrod prefers to base his notion of economic dynamics on *continuing changes rather than once-for-all changes*, According to him, once-for-all changes simply imply the shift from one position of equilibrium to another which can be duly taken care of by economic statics.

Elaborating his point of view, Harrod emphasises that as the *economic dynamics is to be chiefly concerned with continuing change, it, therefore, necessitates the study of an economy wherein the rate of change of income (output) is itself changing*. In simple words, the continuing acceleration or deceleration is the Harrodian essence of economic dynamics.

Harrod's point can be illustrated with the help of Fig. 4.2. The horizontal axis measures time, whereas the vertical axis shows the level of income. Let us assume that OF is the full employment level of income. If, to start with, the income level is at A and for the time interval Ot the rate of growth is zero, then to Harrod, the study of the economy from A to B will be static.

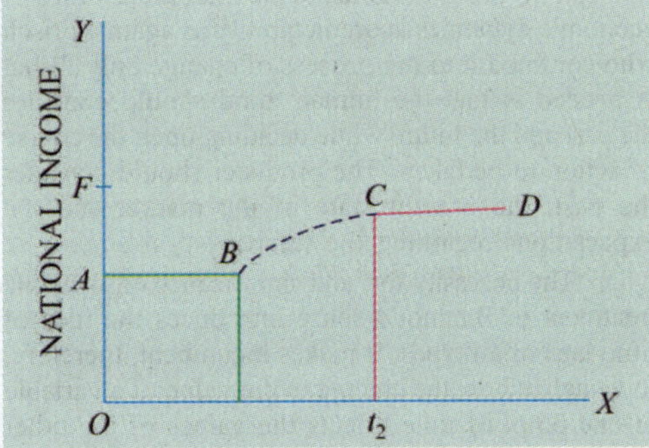

Fig. 4.2. Growth path of income over-time.

Let us suppose that the government makes an investment (say I) in some development projects so as to raise or to push the economy up to the full employment ceiling. The investment I, through the operation of the multiplier (K) will increase the income by KI amount and take the economy to the full employment level C at the point of time t. Beyond the point of time t, the rate of growth again becomes zero and the analysis of the economy from position C to D and even beyond D will be a static one. To Harrod, the dotted path between B and C is the subject-matter of economic dynamics because, during the interval t and t_2, the rate of change of income is itself undergoing a change.

Frisch's View. Ranger Frisch has broadened the vistas of economic dynamics by including in it not only continuing changes *but also the process of change*. He maintains that dynamic analysis is ***''..... one in which we consider the magnitudes of certain variables on different points of time and we introduce certain equations which embrace at the same time several of those magnitudes at different instants''***. Economic dynamics thus, according to him, should *embody functional relationships of variables with different dates appended to them.*

For instance, if we are investigating as to how many umbrellas shall be supplied by the various sellers in the market today, we should take into account the market conditions that obtained yesterday. The ramifications of the past decisions shall influence the sellers' decisions today with regard to the units of umbrellas they should supply. Proceeding in this way, we may say that Frischian definition of economic dynamics takes care of the past values of the several variables, their lags, sequences, rates of change and cumulative magnitudes, *etc.*

Baumol's Concept. Taking a cue from the Frischian approach, Baumol has further sharpened the concept of economic dynamics. He states that economic dynamics is ***"the study of economic phenomena in relation to the preceding and succeeding events."*** Thus, to Baumol the essence of economic dynamics is predictability as against Frisch who confined it to the process of change only. What is needed is that the human mind should consider the past and the future while deciding upon the course of action to be taken. The producer should consider the past, the present state of the market and the expectations regarding the future.

The necessity for, and significance of, dynamic treatment in Baumol's sense introduces the idea of time-lags of all types. It makes incumbent, therefore, to visualize how the change in the value of a variable at one point of time affects the values of the other variables at different points of time. Hence, the dynamic analysis in the Baumolian sense has to consider the inter-temporal relationship between variables and examine the course of these variables over a particular period of time.

Samuelson's Synthesis. Samuelson has however, endeavoured to clinch this controversy by offering a sort of compromise between the definitions given by Hicks Harrod. Frisch and Baumol. He states that ***"It is the essence of dynamics that economic variables at different points of time are functionally related including velocities, acceleration, or higher derivatives."*** Thus, this definition includes in its field, the phenomena of cyclical growth, cyclical fluctuations, speculation, cob-web theorems of price determinations, stagnation thesis, perspective planning, etc.

Conclusion

The upshot of this discussion is that an economy is said to be in dynamical system when the values of the variables at any point of time are dependent on their values at some other time. Moreover, if we know their values at one moment of time we can also discover their values at subsequent moments of time. The data produce the consequences and the consequences in turn give rise to data, *i.e.,* the causes of the change in data are the consequences in themselves.

Significance of Economic Dynamics

Realistic. Economic Dynamics is more realistic and light-giving than economic statics. It gives us a conspectus of the process of change and not just an analysis of the equilibrium position. Economic statics assumes constancy of resources, population, state of technique, investment, tastes, *etc.,* but all these in reality are not constant. They undergo a continuous and endless change and for a proper understanding of these changes there is no escape from the dynamic tools. Dynamics analysis takes closer to reality. Here is no assumption of *ceteris paribus*. It is a forbidden fruit as it were. In economic dynamics, we take into account all the changes, lags, sequences, cumulative magnitudes and even expectations. In statics we deal with stationary states which is a fiction. There is activity but the speed is uniform. There is movement but there is no change.

Boulding compares static equilibrium with a ball rolling at a constant speed or a forest where trees sprout, grow and die, but where the composition of the forest as a whole remains unchanged. But, in dynamics, we consider the real world which is ever-changing. It relates to a developing economy. The economic dynamics gives us a movie of the functioning economy and the process of its development by peering through the functional mechanism which propels the economy out into one period out of the preceding one.

Conditions of Stability. The fact, that dynamic analysis is concerned with the process of change and the path whereby this change leads to a new equilibrium position, enables us to analyses the way the economy traverses its path from a disequilibrium position to a new equilibrium state. By such an analysis the conditions for the stability of equilibrium can be studied.

Applicability. The dynamic analysis has assumed a place of paramount importance in the field of those **economic problems which involve time-lags, sequences and rates of growth.** With the help of dynamic analysis more general and fundamental results can be derived in the study of such problems than from static analysis.

Recent advances in the field of econometrics make extensive use of dynamic models based on the economic dynamics. Noteworthy works in this field are those of Klein, Samuelson, Goldberger and Koyack. In fact, economics is fast becoming Econometric owing to the increasing use of dynamic analysis.

Dynamic analysis has also proved to be indispensable in the **theory of trade cycles.** Some of the dynamic concepts such as accelerator and supermultiplier have been evolved to study the trade cycles. Thanks to dynamic analysis for making a clear-cut distinction between the endogenous, exogenous and mixed theories of trade cycles.

Modern economists such as Hicks, Kalecki, Domar, Harrod, Samuels on, Mrs. Robbinson, Lim dabl Frisch, Hansen, Duessenberry, Good-dahl,

Kaldor, Goodwin and others have constructed **macro-dynamic models.** These macro-dynamic models employ the dynamic analysis and have thrown a great deal of light on the inter-temporal adjustments of aggregate variables. This has placed the knowledge of economics on more scientific footing.

The short-term dynamic analysis is also being applied these days to elucidate the **dynamic stability of agricultural markets.** Such an exercise carries great importance for the underdeveloped countries which are mainly primary product producing countries.

The dynamic approach is also being used to study the **dynamics of wages, capital costs and employment in manufacturing.** Some studies are also underway to study the nature of **expectations of manufacturers** of industrial sales and of dealers about retail sales by the help of dynamic analysis. Such efforts are intended to enable an understanding of the existing complexities of the business behaviour.

Dynamic aggregate analysis has also found its application in the study of the **cumulative process of inflation or deflation**. This has proved useful in pinning down the sensitive factors in order to formulate effective policies for economic stabilization.

Conclusion. In the end, we may conclude with Prof. Samuelson's remark that "Economic dynamics is an enormously flexible mode of thought both for pinning down the implications of various hypotheses and for investigating new possibilities.''

Limitations of Economic Dynamics

Economic dynamics, though it is a more realistic method for analysing the complicated problems, yet it suffers from some weaknesses:

The method of dynamics is essentially very **complex** and only a few economists equipped with the techniques of advanced mathematics can make use of it. This in fact has reduced its popularity.

It has been held by Northrop that it is not possible to build up the theory of economic dynamics. His contention is that the theory of economic dynamics requires certain fundamental conditions, which the economic data do not possess. Economic problems being woven round the human wants are not amenable to dynamic analysis because their future structure cannot be derived from the present wants.

Conclusion

It goes without saying that dynamics is a more general and fundamental approach than statics, but at the same time it would not be proper to discount the importance of statics. Harrod has vehemently held that statics is equally applicable to various branches of economic science. The study of the working that when it is in motion. Likewise, for really useful results to be obtained, the application of dynamic analysis should be preceded by the use of static analysis.

In fact, dynamic and static are two inseparable wings. The dynamics is composed of the statics. We are in a position to study the dynamic only because it is comprised of the static. In dynamic economics, what we really study are a large number of static positions of an economy. If the economic dynamics is a movie of a functioning economy, static is a still picture depicting the stationary position of the economy. Thus, the laws of static economics must also apply to dynamics. The only thing that has got to be done is to introduce a variable that could link one static position with the other. Indeed such a link-variable are the expectations of the economic units that forge the present with the future and thus transform statics into dynamics. It is, therefore, reasonable to conclude that statics and dynamics are complementary to each other.

COMPARATIVE STATICS

The method of comparative statics is a sort of cross between statics and dynamics. It occupies a position in between the two.

We know that the dynamic analysis includes the time interval whereas the static analysis does not. Everything in the real world is subject to change with time. Notwithstanding this, static analysis remains useful, for this is a method whereby we can ignore time as a variable and still make a purposeful study of the economic system. This is possible when we are finding out the ultimate effect of a certain initial change and ignore the process through which it is brought about.

We can thus think of an analysis in which we start with a system in equilibrium, then introduce a change and study the ultimate effect of the change. This is the method of comparative statics. Here, we have in a way done away with the time element—we have ignored that time is changing. We just jump from one equilibrium position to another without taking care of as to what happens in between the two situations. We call such a method as comparative statics because in it we compare one equilibrium position with another and ignore the time element.

Thus, in comparative statics, we study the change from one equilibrium position to another as a result of changes in parameters. It helps us to know the direction and the magnitude of changes in the variable when certain data change, so as to cause a movement to a new equilibrium position. In comparative statics, there is a once-for-all change in demand conditions and supply is allowed to adjust to these changes. Fig. 4.3 illustrates this point:

The original equilibrium between the demand curve DD and the supply curve SS is at E_1. But when demand increases to D′D′ as a result of increase

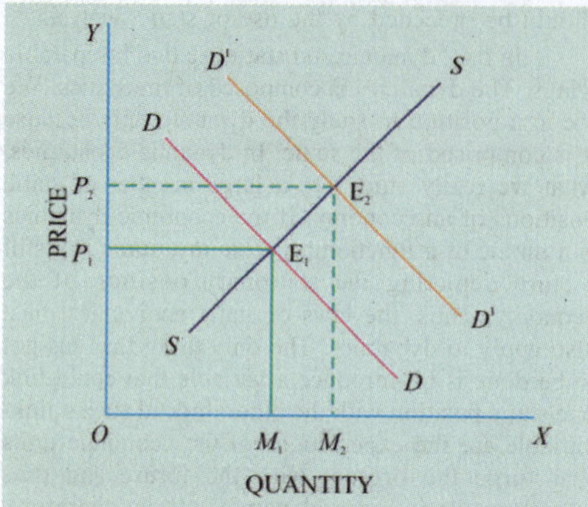

Fig. 4.3. Comparing to equilibrium position due to change in demand keeping supply constant.

in income, the new equilibrium is at E_2 at the price OP_2. In comparative static analysis, we are only concerned with explaining the new equilibrium position at E_2 and comparing it with E_1, and we are not concerned with explaining the whole path the system has travelled from E_1 to E_2. Alfred Marshall, made extensive use of comparative statics in his time—period analysis of pricing under perfect competition. Although the dynamic analysis is more comprehensive and informative of the two equilibrium positions and the different sets of data, yet comparative static treatment provides some important insights into the mechanism of the exchange economy.

Limitations of Comparative Statics

Comparative statics suffers from certain limitations. It cannot be used to tackle two types of problems: (*a*) It fails to predict the path which the market follows when moving from one equilibrium position to another, and (*b*) it cannot predict whether or not a given equilibrium position will ever be achieved. For these purposes we need dynamic analysis.

Prof. Tinbergen has pointed out that such an analysis is possible only under two circumstances: Firstly, when we are interested in the long run tendencies, when the movement produced by the changes in the data are damped and the data do not themselves undergo a change. Under such circumstances, the final position of equilibrium will be independent of time or the path traversed by the economy. Secondly, such an analysis is possible when the change in data brings about immediate adaptation of the economic magnitudes so that the new data do not take time to produce the results. Under such conditions, too, it is possible to ignore the time element.

Keynes's technique of shifting equilibrium is based upon the method of comparative statics.

The Keynesian model predicts that an upward shift in the investment function will cause a rise in the level of income, a rise in the level of saving, and a rise in the rate of interest. At the original level of income, investment exceeds saving. Equilibrium is restored by the rise in saving resulting from the rise of income, and by the fall in investment resulting from the rise in interest rates. Similarly, the Keynesian theory predicts that a fall in the transactions demand for cash will cause a rise in income, a fall in interest rate will lower the rate, raise income and raise saving and investment. Such are the shifts that Keynes studies with the aid of comparative statics.

Key terms

Statics, dynamics, Comparative Statics.

QUESTIONS

1. Distinguish between the concepts of statics and dynamics. What is their utility in economic analysis?
2. Distinguish between wealth and welfare. How far is it correct to say that the study of Economics helps in promoting welfare?
3. Define Micro-economics. What is its place in economic theory?
4. Define Micro-economics and discuss its importance and limitation.
5. "The economist has to study micro as well as macro economic problems. The two studies are complementary to each other than being the alternative matters of study". Discuss the statement.

UNIT II

Theory of Demand

Chapters

UTILITY ANALYSIS OF DEMAND

Theory of demand seeks to establish relationship between the quantity demanded of a commodity and its price. It also offers an explanation for variations in demand. There are different approaches known to the economists to the theory of demand. The oldest among them is the marginal utility approach. The marginal utility analysis explains consumer's demand for a commodity and derives a law of demand which shows an inverse relationship between the quantity demanded and the price of the commodity. That is, it states that as price falls, demand is extended, and vice-versa. Recent economists have pointed out several flaws in the utility analysis of demand and have offered new theories. For instance, we have the indifference curve technique developed by J. R Hicks and R.G.D. Allen. This has been followed by further refinements in Samuelsons' Revealed Preference Theory and Hicks' Logical Weak Ordering Theory. In this chapter, we shall take up the marginal utility analysis.

BASIC ASSUMPTIONS OF MARGINAL UTILITY ANALYSIS

We shall first mention a few basic assumptions on which the marginal utility analysis is based. We shall see later how the marginal utility analysis has been criticised on the ground that the assumptions on which it is based are unrealistic or invalid. The following are the main assumptions :

(i) Cardinal Measurement of Utility

Marginal utility analysis assumes in the first place that utility can be measured and the exact measurement can be given by assigning definite numbers such as 1, 2, 3, *etc.* That is, it is assumed that utility is a quantifiable entity. This means that a person can express the satisfaction derived from the consumption of a commodity in quantitative terms. He can say, for instance, that for him the first unit of the commodity has utility equal to 10, the second unit 8, and so on. In this way, it is possible for a consumer to compare the utilities of different goods. If, for example, fruit has for him utility 20 and sweets 10, then he can say, that for him the utility of fruits is double that of sweets. Utility is usually measured in imaginary units.

(ii) Utilities are Independent

Marginal utility analysis assumes that the utilities of different commodities are independent of one another. That is, the utility of one commodity does not in any way affect that of another. In other words, the satisfaction derived from the consumption of one good is the function of that good alone and is not

Goods have utility because they satisfy human wants. So consumers demand them.

affected by the consumption of another. It depends on the quantity consumed of one good and not of another. On this assumption, the total utility of all goods consumed by a consumer is simply the sum total of the separate utilities of all the goods consumed by a consumer. Thus, according to this assumption, the utilities of various goods are additive, *i.e.,* separate utilities of the various goods can be added to obtain the total sum of the utilities of all goods consumed.

(iii) Constant Marginal Utility of Money

Another important assumption of the marginal utility analysis is that the marginal utility of money remains constant even though the quantity of money with the consumer is diminished by the successive purchases made by him. It is assumed that while marginal utility of a commodity varies with the quantity of the commodity purchased, the marginal utility of money remains throughout the same as the quantity of the good purchased varies. This assumption becomes necessary because the marginal utility of a commodity is measured in terms of money. It is considered desirable that the measure itself should not keep changing. In the words of Professor Tapes Majumdar, **"If money is supposed to provide the measuring rod of utility, then evidently as with all measuring rods, its unit must be invariant: it must measure the same amount of utility in all circumstances"**. When a person purchases more of a good, the amount of money with him must diminish and the marginal utility of money must increase. But this variation in the marginal utility of money is ignored and it is assumed to remain constant throughout.

(iv) Introspection

The marginal utility analysis also assumes 'that from one's own experience (judging what happens in one's own mind), it is possible to draw inference about another person. This is self-observation applied to another person. It is assumed that the mind of men work identically in similar situations. This is how a system of taxation is built on the assumption that the same incomes mean the same thing to all persons irrespective of dissimilar circumstances. That is why according to the law of diminishing marginal utility, the marginal utility decreases when consumers have more of a good. The advocates of **'behaviourism'** (observing actual behaviour) do not subscribe to this view. According to them it is not possible to make a correct guess work about the working of another mind from one's own mind.

Now we shall study the two basic laws governing consumer behaviour, *viz.,* the law of diminishing marginal utility and the law of equi-marginal utility.

LAW OF DIMINISHING MARGINAL UTILITY

Statement of the Law

Satisfaction of human wants follows some very important laws and one of them is the Law of Diminishing Marginal Utility. The law refers to the common experience of every consumer. Suppose a person starts eating pieces of bread one after another. The first toast gives him great pleasure. By the time he starts taking the second, the edge of his appetite has been blunted, and the second toast, meeting with a less urgent want, yields less satisfaction; the satisfaction of the third will be less than that of the second; that of the fourth less than that of the third, and so on. The additional satisfaction will go on decreasing with every successive toast till it drops down to zero; and if the consumer is forced to take more, the satisfaction may become negative, or the utility may change into disutility.

The idea will be clear from the table 1 the given below.

(*N. B.* These figures are merely illustrative representations of the amount of utility. Any other figures may be taken, provided variations in the amount of utility are similar to those in the following table:

TABLE 1

1 Units (Toasts)	2 Total Utility (Units of Satisfaction)	3 Marginal Utility (Units of Satisfaction)
1	20	20
2	38	18
3	53	15
4	64	11
5	70	6
6	70	0
7	62	– 8
8	46	– 16

i.e., the marginal utility at every step should be diminishing.)

When our hypothetical consumer goes on taking toasts, the extra satisfaction that he gets by the consumption of each successive toast goes on decreasing till it goes down to zero at the 6th, and then it becomes negative (see column 3).

The total utility, however, goes on increasing until the consumption of the 5th; but, it is worth noting that it increases at a diminishing rate. In the words of Chapman, ''The more we have of a thing the less we want additional increments of it, or the more we want not to have additional increments of it.''

How many toasts you can consume ?

It will be seen from the table that the **total utility of a quantity of a commodity is maximum** (*i.e.,* 70) **when the marginal utility is zero** (*i.e.,* at the 6th unit).

Marshall states the law thus: **''The additional benefit which a person derives from a given increase of his stock of a thing diminishes with every increase in stock that he already has.''** We might add that with every diminution of his stock, the marginal utility will go on increasing. In other words, the marginal utility varies inversely with the stock, although not necessarily in the same proportion.

As explained below, two important reasons can be given, for diminishing marginal utility: (*a*) Each particular want is satiable, and (*b*) goods are imperfect substitutes for one another and they tend to be consumed in appropriate proportions.

Diagrammatic Representation

The following diagram illustrates the Law of Diminishing Marginal Utility as applied to the consumption of toasts, See the table given.

OX and OY are the two axes. Units of toasts are measured along OX and units of utility along OY. Utility of the first toast is represented by the rectangle standing on a portion of the axis of X (Fig. 5.1). Similarly, the utility of each successive unit consumed is represented by the rectangles as shown in the diagram. These rectangles become smaller and smaller, as consumption of units proceeds. The sixth toast has no utility. The seventh and the eighth have negative utilities, as shown by the rectangles below the axis of X.

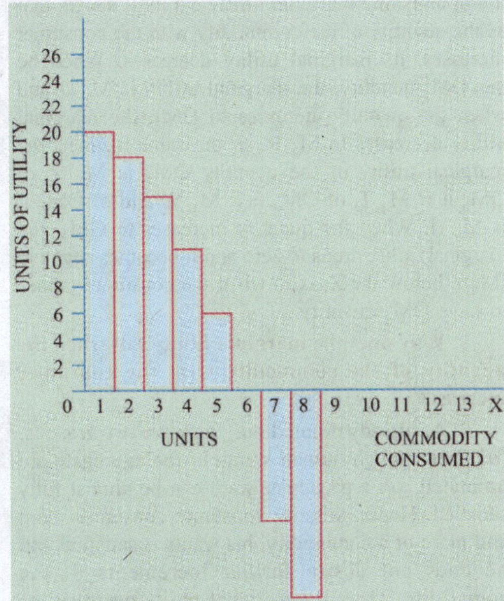

Fig. 5.1. **Diminishing Marginal Utility.**

The toasts are big units. If a commodity is

consumed in sufficiently small units, the rectangles would become thinner and thinner. We can theoretically assume that they become so thin as to be represented by a mere line. Now, if the tops of such lines, standing shoulder to shoulder, are joined together, we get a curve sloping from left to right, as shown in Fig. 5.2.

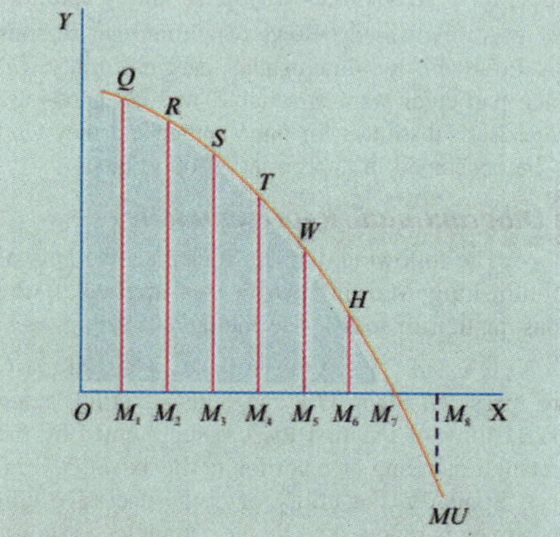

Fig. 5.2. Diminishing Marginal Utility Curve.

Diminishing Marginal Utility Curve

In this figure 5.2, a curve MU has been drawn which slopes downward from left to right. This is the diminishing marginal utility curve. It shows that as the quantity of the commodity with the consumer increases, its marginal utility decreases. When he has OM_1 quantity, the marginal utility is M_1 Q and when the quantity increases to OM_2, the marginal utility decreases to M_2 R. In the same manner, the marginal utility of the quantity OM_3 is M_3 S, of OM_4 it is M_4 T, of OM_5 it is M_5 W and of OM_6 it is M_6 H. When the quantity increases to OM_7, the marginal utility drops to zero and it becomes negative (M_8 Z below the X-axis) when the consumer comes to have OM_8 quantity.

Why does the marginal utility fall when the quantity of the commodity with the consumer increases?

As already pointed out, there are two reasons: (*a*) Even though human wants in the aggregate are unlimited, yet a particular want can be almost fully satisfied. Hence, when a consumer consumes more and more of a commodity, his wants is satisfied and he does not desire further increments of the commodity. Thus, his marginal utility decreases as his consumption of that commodity increases. A stage comes when further consumption brings the marginal utility down to zero.

(*b*) Another reason of the diminishing marginal utility is that goods are imperfect substitutes for one another. Different commodities satisfy different wants. When a consumer goes on consuming a commodity, the marginal utility falls as his want is satisfied. But if the commodity could be substituted for other commodities, it would have satisfied other wants. Hence, its marginal utility would not have decreased even though its quantity increases.

Limitations of the Law

The Law of Diminishing Marginal Utility, as enunciated above, is based on certain assumptions:

(*i*) Suitable Units. It is assumed that the commodity is taken in suitable units. If you begin taking water by spoonfuls when thirsty, or if you want to judge the utility of the morsels rather than the full chapatis, your thirst or hunger will be at first stimulated rather than assuaged, and the utility may, therefore, at first, rise instead of falling. But, sooner or later, a point will be reached when utility will begin to diminish. Unless, therefore, the units are of a suitable size, the law will not hold good. The initial quantity should be greater than the 'critical minimum.'

(*ii*) Suitable Time. It is further assumed that the commodity is taken within a certain time, otherwise the law will not apply. If you take your first meal at 10 a.m. and the next at 2 p.m., there is no reason why the utility of the second meal may be less. But in case you are compelled to take the second meal within an hour of your having taken the first, the law will apply, and the utility of the second meal will be less.

(*iii*) No Change in Consumer's Tastes. Another assumption is that the character of the consumer does not change. The consumer must not, for instance, have developed a craving. The more music one hears, the more literature one reads, the more wine a drunkard takes, the more money a miser has, the greater is the utility in each case. This is so because the character of the consumer has undergone a change. More reading lifts a person to a higher plane, and he is able to appreciate and enjoy literature better than he could before. Similarly, a drunkard is said to enjoy each successive peg more than the previous one.

(*iv*) Normal Persons. The Law of Diminishing Marginal Utility applies to normal persons and not to eccentric or abnormal persons like misers. In other words, we assume rational behaviour on the part of the consumers. In case they behave in a queer and irrational manner, the law will not hold good.

(*v*) Constant Income. It is also essential that

the income of the consumer remains the same. Any change in income will falsify the law. For instance, a rise in a man's income may raise in his eyes the value of the various plots in his big compound of which he could not make much use before.

(*vi*) Rare Collections. In the case of rare collections, the law does not hold good. If, for instance, a man is collecting ancient coins, the more he is able to collect the greater will be his satisfaction. Hence, in such cases, the law of diminishing marginal utility does not hold good.

(*vii*) Change in Other People's Stock. The law says that marginal utility decreases when there is an increase in our stock. But, in some cases, the utility changes, not because of a change in what we have but because of a change in other people's stock. For example, if I have a rival in the town collecting ancient coins, and somehow he loses his collection, the utility of my collection automatically goes up. In the same manner, utility to me of my telephone increases as the number of telephone connections increases. The value of my land goes up without any change in its dimensions when a railway station has been built nearby.

(*viii*) Other Possessions. Utility also depends on our other possessions. The law ignores the relation of complementarity. For example, a carriage may be lying useless with us, but, as soon as we are able to buy a horse, its utility at once goes up. Thus, change in our other possessions can also bring about a change in marginal utility.

(*ix*) Fashion. Further, utility depends on fashion too. The utility of my dress goes up when that dress comes in fashion. If, on the other hand, it goes out of fashion, the utility goes down.

(*x*) Not Applicable to Money. The Law does not apply to money as it is said that more money he has, the more he wants. But as explained below, it does apply to money too.

Conclusion. The law of diminishing utility, like other economic laws, is merely a statement of a tendency. It depends upon so many conditions. If the conditions are not fulfilled, the law does not apply as in the many exceptional cases mentioned above.

It is worth noting that the law of diminishing utility does not operate because the successive units of the commodity are inferior. Although it is understandable that if a unit is of inferior quality *ipso facto* its utility will be less, yet the law is far more fundamental. It is independent of quality. The toasts may all be of a uniform quality still the additional utility will decrease as consumption proceeds.

It follows from this law that more urgent wants are satisfied first. As the stock increases, it will be put to less and less urgent uses, and the reduction of the stock would mean the reversing of the process.

The law holds good in all types of satisfaction whether good or bad. We do not assume rationality on the part of the consumer. Nor do we assume that there is a rigidly fixed order in which wants are arranged by all, although the order will roughly be the same in the same class of people.

Marginal Utility

Marginal utility can be defined as the change in the total utility resulting from a one-unit change in the consumption of a commodity per unit of time. When a man is purchasing a commodity, he is consciously or unconsciously weighing in his mind the price he has to pay and the utility of each unit that he buys. He will continue purchasing till the marginal utility equals the price. Here is a fundamental proposition of the theory of consumer demand: "A consumer will exchange money for units of any commodity A, up to the point where the last (marginal) unit of A which he buys has for him a marginal significance in terms of money just equal to its money price."[1]

Refer to the table given on page 51. Where will our consumer stop? It depends upon the price. If the price is 6 paise per toast, then he will stop at the 5th, for there the marginal utility is equal to the price (marginal utility being represented in Paise units). If the price is 11 Paise per toast, he will stop at the 4th, and, if they are free, then he will go on consuming till the additional utility comes down to zero (*i.e.,* up to the 6th unit). He will not go beyond this point because disutility will be the result. The consumer stops at a point where the price and the marginal utility are just equal. This is called the marginal purchase and the **extra utility at this point is called the marginal utility. It is a point where we consider just worthwhile to purchase**, for here the pain of parting with the money and the benefit derived from the purchase of the commodity just balance.

Marginal utility has also been defined as the **addition made to the total utility by the consumption of the last unit considered just worthwhile.** In other words, it may be defined as the change in total utility resulting from a unit change in the quantity of the commodity consumed. Thus, if we buy 5 toasts, the 5th is the marginal toast. But

1. Stonier and Hague—*A Text-Book of Economi Theory*, 1953, p. 40.

marginal utility is not the utility of the 5th toast, because all the toasts are supposed to be alike. It only refers to the addition made to the previous total by the consumption of this particular toast. Marginal utility is the increase in total utility resulting from the consumption of the marginal unit. The following formula may be used to measure it.

Marginal utility (MU)

$$= \frac{\text{Change in total utility}}{\text{Change in quantity consumed}}$$

It thus measures the ratio of change in the two variables.

The margin is not something rigid or fixed. It shifts forward and backward according to changes in price. If the price falls, it will become worthwhile to purchase more of the commodity and the margin will descend and vice-versa.

Marginal Utility of Money

Does the law of diminishing marginal utility apply to money? It is said that there can be a limit to the purchase of a commodity, but there is no such limit to the acquiring of money. Money is a general purchasing power. It enables the purchaser to buy anything he likes. That is why it is said one can never reach a stage where money ceases to be desired. In other words, more money a person has more he desires to obtain it. That is, the marginal utility of money goes on increasing with its increase. This is opposed to the Law of Diminishing Marginal utility.

We may concede the strength of this argument. But it is also true that the law of diminishing marginal utility certainly applies to money too. As the quantity certainly applies to money too. As the quantity of money, that a person possesses, increases, its significance to him decreases. It can be easily seen that a rich man attaches much less importance to each unit of money than the poor. He spends it more freely and is much less worried in case he happens to lose a certain portion of it. Every increment in the amount of money that a man has brings him less and less extra pleasure. Hence, the law of diminishing marginal utility does apply to money also.

Marginal Utility and Price

It is clear from the above discussion that marginal utility and price are inter-related. The two coincide or price measures marginal utility. The consumer stops where the price and the marginal utility are equal. All units of the commodity being interchangeable, what is paid for the marginal unit is paid for every other unit. Therefore, we can say that marginal utility determines price. It is marginal utility and not total utility that determines price, otherwise the price of water should have been high, and that of gold low.

Really, marginal utility does not determine price; it simply indicates it. The determining factors are demand and supply. If the price changes, marginal utility will change too. Price and marginal utility thus move together up and down.

Marginal Utility and Supply

Marginal utility is a **function of supply**, *i.e.,* it varies with supply. In the case of a free good, where the supply is unlimited, the marginal utility is zero. Only in the case of scarce goods is the marginal utility positive. It increases as the supply contracts and decreases as it expands. It comes down to zero when the supply is super-abundant. Hence, **marginal utility varies inversely with supply**, *i.e.,* the greater the supply the less the marginal utility, and vice-versa.

Marginal Utilities of Related Goods

There are two main types of relationship between goods: (*a*) They may be substitutes; or (*b*) they may be complementary.

The **substitutes** are capable of satisfying the same want, *e.g.,* tea and coffee, air transport, rail transport and road transport. If they are perfect substitutes, they may be treated as one commodity for all practical purposes. But most goods are only imperfect substitutes. In the case of such goods, other things being equal, the marginal utility of any such goods decreases as the quantity of the substitute goods with the consumer increases.

Complementary goods are such goods which are wanted together for the satisfaction of a want, *e.g.,* paper, pen and ink for writing. In such cases, other things remaining the same, marginal utility increases as the quantities of the complementary goods with the consumer increases. If, for instance, a consumer acquires more paper, the marginal utility of the bottle of ink goes up.

Practical Importance of the Law of Diminishing Marginal Utility

Taxation. The law of diminishing marginal utility has great practical importance. We have seen that the law of diminishing marginal utility applies to money too. This law forms the basis of the theory and practice of taxation. Progressive system of taxation, imposing a heavier burden on the rich people, is a practical application of this principle in the field of public finance. Richer a person the higher is the rate of the tax he has to pay since to him the marginal utility of money is less.

Price Determination. The law explains why, with increase in its supply, the value of a commodity must fall. It thus forms a basis of the theory of value. As such its practical importance both to the general consumer and the businessman can hardly be exaggerated.

Household Expenditure. The law of diminishing marginal utility governs our daily expenditure. Since we know that a larger purchase will mean lower marginal utility, we restrict our purchase of a particular commodity, because we cannot afford to waste our limited resources. We stop further purchases at a point where marginal utility equals price.

Downward Sloping Demand Curve. It is this law which tells us why demand curves slope downwards. It is due to this law that smaller utility lines cut larger portions of the commodity line, *i.e.*, X-axis (see utility curve on page 52).

Value-in-Use and Value-in-Exchange. It also explains the divergence between value-in-use and value-in-exchange. Air has great utility (value-in-use) but little value-in-exchange, because it has no marginal utility.

Socialism. The socialists take stand on this law when they advocate the re-distribution of wealth in favour of the poor. The marginal utility to the rich of the wealth, that they might lose, is not so great as the marginal utility of the wealth which is transferred to the poor.

Basis of Some Economic Laws. Some very important laws of Economics are based on the law of diminishing marginal utility, *e.g.,* Law of Demand, the Concept of Consumer's Surplus, the Concept of Elasticity of Demand, the Law of Substitution, *etc.* These laws and concepts have ultimately been derived from the law of diminishing marginal utility.

LAW OF EQUI-MARGINAL UTILITY

Statement of the Law

Owing to multiplicity of wants and scarcity of means wants are competitive. We have, therefore, more urgent and less urgent wants. When we are weighing in our mind whether to buy a little more or a little less of a commodity, it seems we are trying to balance the marginal utility of the commodity and that of money. **But what we are really balancing is the marginal utility of that particular commodity and** the marginal utilities of a host of other commodities which we could **purchase with that amount of money.** Money thus builds a bridge for us to pass from one commodity to another. This is

When consumer purchses more than one good he/she equates the ratio of MU and P of each good in the basket which is called equi-MU.

how substitution takes place. It is not merely a substitution of one thing for another satisfying the same want, *e.g.,* substitution of tea for coffee, but substitution even of entirely different commodities.

Every prudent person wants to make the best of his or her resources. This is necessary because resources are scarce in relation to wants—a fundamental proposition with which we started the study of Economics. Every consumer aims at getting the maximum possible satisfaction. For this purpose, he will substitute the more useful for the less useful thing. When he has done so, it will be found that marginal utilities in each direction of his purchases have been equalised.

Our hypothetical consumer is acting consciously or unconsciously on the principle which has been called by various names (though different in approach), the Law of substitution, or the Law Indifference, or the Law of Economy of Expenditure, the Law of Maximum Satisfaction. It is called the Law of Substitution, because we substitute the more useful thing for the less useful one. It is known as the Law of Maximum Satisfaction, because through its application we are able to maximize our satisfaction. It is called the Law of Equi-Marginal Utility, because it is only when marginal utilities have been equalised, through the process of substitution, that we get maximum satisfaction.

It happens like this: We assume that our consumer has a given income to spend, that his tastes are also given, that he wants to maximize his satisfaction and that the marginal utility of money to the consumer also remains constant during successive purchases. Further, we assume that commodities of his purchase are subject to the law of diminishing marginal utility so that after the consumer has spent some of his money on a particular commodity, the marginal utility to him of the commodity begins to fall. Then, he feels that he would gain greater satisfaction by spending additional units of money on something else. He goes on substituting one thing for another (after a point), until the whole of the money he wanted to spend is exhausted.

Take two goods **A** and **B**. So long as the marginal utility of money spent on good **A** is not equal to the marginal utility of money spent on good **B**, the consumer will increase his satisfaction by substituting one good for the other until the marginal utility of money is the same in both the cases. The consumer will attain maximum satisfaction, hence will be in equilibrium position when he has so adjusted his expenditure that marginal utility of money to him in each direction of his purchase is the same. If marginal utility of money spent on the good **A** is greater than the marginal utility of money spent on the good **B**, the consumer will withdraw some money from the purchase of **B** and will spend it on **A** till the marginal utility of money in the two cases becomes equal. Any arrangement of expenditure, other than the one which equalised the marginal utility of money in each direction of his purchase, will yield the consumer less amount of satisfaction.

Diagrammatic Representation

The principle of equi-marginal utility can be explained with the help of the diagram (Fig. 5.3) given below. In this figure, along the axis OX, from left to right (*i.e.*, on the portion OX) is measured the quantity of the good A and from right to left, (*i.e.*, on the portion OX′) is measured the quantity of the good B. Along the axis OY is measured utility of the amounts of money spent on the goods A and B. On the right hand side of OY is drawn a curve Ua which slopes downwards from left to right. This curve shows the marginal utility of the money spent on commodity A. On the other side of OY is drawn the curve Ub which slopes downwards from right to the left. This curve shows the marginal utility of money spent on the good B.

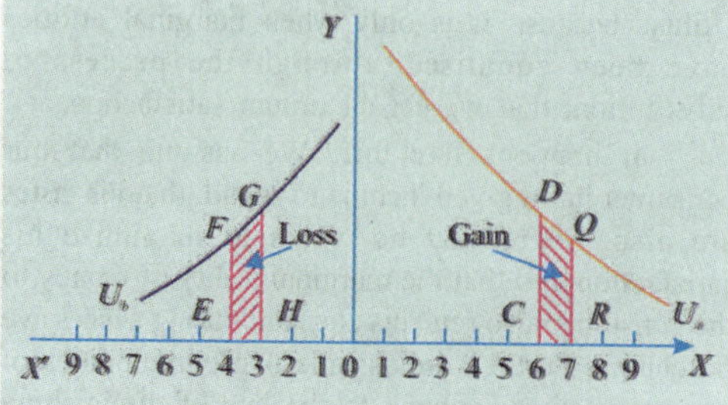

Fig. 5.3. Law of Equi-Marginal Utlity.

Suppose our hypothetical consumer has Rs. 10 to spend on the two goods A and B. It will be clear from the diagram that if he spends Rs. 6 on A good and Rs. 4 on B good, the marginal utilities of both goods are equal (CE = EF).

In this way, he will derive maximum satisfaction and any other arrangement will only reduce the aggregate satisfaction. To prove this, suppose the consumer spends Re. 1 more on the good A and consequently Re. 1 less on the good B. As a result, the marginal utilities will become unequal (GH is greater than QR). In this case, the gain in utility is less than the loss there of and his total utility will be less than before. The gain in utility and loss thereof are shown in the shaded area.

Hence, we may conclude that the consumer will get maximum satisfaction and will be in equilibrium if the marginal utilities of money spent on the various goods that he buys are equal.

Limitations of the Law

Like other economic laws, the Law of Equimarginal Utility too is a mere statement of a tendency. The actual expenditure of individuals may not conform to this law. This may be due to the following reasons:—

(i) The Law of Equi-marginal Utility involves very careful calculations of the expected satisfaction and its comparison with the amount of money spent as well as with the satisfaction which may be derived by spending the same amount of money on some other things. But how many of us are capable of making such fine calculations? How many of us have the patience and the ability to do it? Are we all so rational and calculating? The fact is that most of our expenditure is governed by habit. There is not much of conscious calculation and careful weighing of the utilities.

(ii) Only in the case of big expenditure, a prudent person goes through a certain amount of thinking. Here we may take it that this expenditure does roughly conform to the Law of Maximum Satisfaction, but not when we make small purchases.

(iii) The utmost we can say is that all rational and prudent persons are expected to act upon this law consciously or unconsciously. As Chapman puts it, "We are not, of course, compelled to distribute our incomes according to the Law of Substitution or Equi-marginal Expenditure, as a stone thrown into the air is compelled, in a sense, to fall back to the earth; but as a matter of fact, we do in a certain rough fashion, because we are reasonable."[2]

2. Chapman. *S. —Outlines of Political Economy*, p. 48.

Hence, the law will not hold good of irrational purchases.

(iv) Ignorance of consumers imposes another limitation. The consumers may not be aware of other more useful alternatives. Hence, no substitution takes place and the law of substitution does not operate. Similarly, an incompetent entrepreneur will not be able to achieve the best results from his productive resources. He may not be able to divert investment to more profitable channels.

(v) People are sometimes slaves of customs or fashion and are incapable of rational consumption. Without being rational and calculating, a consumer cannot substitute one thing for another. The is another limitation on the law.

(vi) Another limitation arises from the fact that goods are not divisible into small bits to enable consumers to equalise marginal utilities. In actual practice, therefore, the marginal utilities cannot be equalised. The law remains only on a theoretical plane.

(vii) The law of substitution has no place when the resources are unlimited as in the case of free goods. In such cases, there is no need to re-arrange expenditure because no price is to be paid whatever the quantity used.

(viii) There is no definite budget period in the case of individuals. Even if there is fixed accounting period, the application of this principle is rendered difficult by the varying degrees of durability of the goods consumed. A durable good is available for consumption in several succeeding accounting periods. It is not, therefore, easy to bring it into account of income and expenditure of a particular accounting period to see if satisfaction has been maximised during that period.

(ix) The basic criticism of the law of equimarginal utility is that it rests on some questionable assumptions. For example, we assume that utilities can be added and compared and that during successive purchases, the marginal utility of money to the consumer remains constant. The modern economists question both these assumptions. The indifference curve approach to the theory of consumer's equilibrium is based on this basic criticism of the Marshallian analysis.

Conclusion. In spite of these points of criticism, the law of equi-marginal utility occupies a very important place in economic theory. Whether it is a case of consumer's equilibrium, producer's equilibrium, allocation of resources or distribution of the national income among the productive agents, this law has a determining influence according to Marshallian analysis.

Practical Importance of the Law

The Law of Substitution, also known as the Law of Equi-Marginal Utility, has a very wide application. It is applicable to the utilisation of time, distribution of assets in various forms and the allocation of resources among various uses. It also applies to the use of money now and its use in the future, *i.e.*, in spending in the present and saving in the future. The law is applicable to all branches of economic theory.

It Applies to Consumption. Every consumer, if he is wise, wants to get maximum satisfaction out of his limited resources. In arranging his expenditure to that end, he must substitute the thing of greater utility for one possessing less utility till marginal utilities are equalized. In this way, the consumer's satisfaction is maximized.

Its Application to Production. To the businessman and the manufacturer the law is of special importance. He works towards the most economical combination of the factors of production employed by him. For this purpose, he will substitute one factor for another till their marginal productivities are made the same. In case he finds that marginal productivity of one factor, say, labour, is greater than that of capital, it will pay him to substitute the former for the latter. In this way, he will be able to maximize his profit.

Its Application to Exchange. In all our exchanges, this principle works, for exchange is nothing else but substitution of one thing for another. The substitutional character of our exchange is sufficient to bring home to us the very great importance of this basic economic principle.

Price Determination. This principle has an important bearing on the determination of value. When there is scarcity of a commodity, the Law of Substitution comes to our aid. We start substituting the less scarce goods for the more scarce ones. The scarcity of the latter is thus relieved, and its price comes down.

Its Application to Distribution. In Distribution, we are concerned with the determination of the rewards of the various agents of production, *i.e.*, determination of rent, wages, interest and profit. These shares are determined according to the principle of marginal productivity. The use of each agent of production is pushed by the entrepreneur to the margin of profitableness till the marginal product in each case is the same. In case it is not the same, the Law of Substitution will come into play to equalize their marginal productivities. This is how the Law of Substitution proves useful in the field of distribution of the national dividend among the various agents of production.

Public Finance. Public expenditure of a government conforms to this Law. Even a government is under the necessity of deriving maximum amount of benefit from its public expenditure. It must try to maximise welfare of the community. For this purpose it must cut down all wasteful expenditure.

Conclusion. Thus the Law of Substitution applies in all branches of economic theory. It has also got great practical importance.

CONSUMER'S EQUILIBRIUM

We have discussed above two important laws of consumption, *viz.,* the law of diminishing marginal utility and the law of equi-marginal utility in terms of these laws, we can indicate the position of consumer's equilibrium *i.e.,* when the consumer attains a position of maximum satisfaction and would have no further incentive to make any change in the quantity of the commodity purchased.

Equilibrium With One Commodity Purchase

The law of diminishing marginal utility tells us the position of a consumer's equilibrium in the case of a one-commodity purchase. He will go on buying successive units of the commodity till the marginal utility of the commodity becomes equal to price. If the price falls, he will buy more and the marginal utility will come down to the level of price. On the other hand, if the price goes up, naturally less will be purchased and the marginal utility goes up till it reaches the new (higher) level of price. In short, equality between marginal utility and price indicates the position of consumer's equilibrium when only one commodity is being purchased and consumed.

Equilibrium with Two Commodity Purchase

In case the consumer is buying two commodities X and Y, the position of equilibrium will be determined according to the law of equi-marginal utilities. It has already been stated that a consumer derives maximum satisfaction when the marginal utilities of the two commodities are equal. In case they are not equal, adjustment will be made in the matter of quantities purchased, (*i.e.,* buying more of the commodity with higher marginal utility and buying less of the lower marginal utility commodity) till the marginal utilities of the two commodities are equalised. This is a position of maximum satisfaction. We assume rational behaviour on the part of the consumer so that it is maximum satisfaction that he seeks and we suppose he is capable of making careful comparisons and calculations.

Let us illustrate: Suppose the consumer is buying only two commodities X and Y. For arriving at an equilibrium position, *i.e.,* a position of maximum satisfaction, the consumer will take into consideration two factors, *viz.,* the marginal utilities of the two goods and their prices, given his money income that he has to spend on the two commodities. A change in relative prices will naturally call for readjustment. Given the prices of X and Y, the consumer will be in equilibrium when the marginal utility of money expenditure on each good X and Y is the same.

Now, the marginal utility of money expenditure on a good is equal to the marginal utility of the good divided by its price. symbolically, it can be put as:

$$\text{MUE} = \frac{\text{MUx}}{\text{Px}}$$

Hence MUE is marginal utility of expenditure. MUX is marginal utility of the commodity X and Px is the price of X. This means that a consumer so spends his money income on different commodities that marginal utility of each good is proportional to its price.

From the above, we can derive a formula for a consumer's equilibrium in respect of two goods X and Y purchased by him as under:

$\frac{\text{MUx}}{\text{Px}} = \frac{\text{MUy}}{\text{Py}}$. That is, marginal utility of good X divided by the price of X must be equal to marginal utility of Y divided by the price of Y.

Suppose, however, this equation is disturbed *i.e.,* $\frac{\text{MUx}}{\text{Px}}$ is greater than $\frac{\text{MUy}}{\text{Py}}$. This would mean that the commodity X gives the consumer greater satisfaction than Y. He would, therefore, naturally substitute X for Y. The result of this substitution will be that the marginal utility of X will fall and that of Y will rise. Substitution of X for Y will continue until $\frac{\text{MUx}}{\text{Px}}$ becomes equal to $\frac{\text{MUy}}{\text{Py}}$. This would be the consumer's equilibrium position.

As we have explained already, while discussing consumer's equilibrium in the case of one-commodity purchase, a consumer goes on buying a commodity till the marginal utility of the commodity becomes equal to the price. Hence consumer's equilibrium will be indicated by the following equation:

$$\frac{\text{MUx}}{\text{Px}} = \frac{\text{MUy}}{\text{Py}} = \text{MUm},$$

Here MUm is the marginal utility of money.

This principle can also be illustrated with the help of table II and a diagram thus:

TABLE II

Marginal Utility of Goods X and Y

Units	MUx *(Utilities)*	MUy *(Utilities)*
1	33	36
2	30	32
3	27	28
4	24	24
5	21	20
6	18	16

Suppose the prices of goods X and Y are Rs. 3 and Rs. 4 respectively. The above table can be reconstructed by dividing the marginal utilities of good X (MUx) by Rs. 3 and the marginal utilities of good Y by Rs. 4. We obtain table III.

TABLE III

Marginal Utility of Expenditure

Units	$\frac{MUx}{Px}$	$\frac{MUy}{Py}$
1	11	9
2	10	8
3	9	7
4	8	6
5	7	5
6	6	4

With a given income, suppose a consumer's marginal utility of money is constant at Re. 1 = 8 utilities. From the above table, it will be seen that $\frac{MUx}{Px} = 8$ utils when our hypothetical consumer buys four units of good X and $\frac{MUy}{Py}$ is equal to 8, when he buys two units of good Y. This consumer will thus be in equilibrium when he is buying four units of good X and two units of good Y and he will be spending Rs. 20 (4 × Rs. 3 + 2 × Rs 4) on these two goods.

Consumer's equilibrium may be shown diagrammatically (see Fig. 5.4 below). We have already seen that the marginal utility curves of goods slope downward. Thus the curves portraying $\frac{MUx}{Px}$ and $\frac{MUy}{Py}$ will also slope downward (curves AB and CD respectively in Fig 5.4). Taking the income of consumer as given, suppose his marginal utility of money is constant at OE utils in Fig. 5.4. $\frac{MUx}{Px}$ is equal to OE (the marginal utility of money) when OF amount of good X is purchased, $\frac{MUy}{Py}$ is equal to OE when OG quantity of good Y is bought.

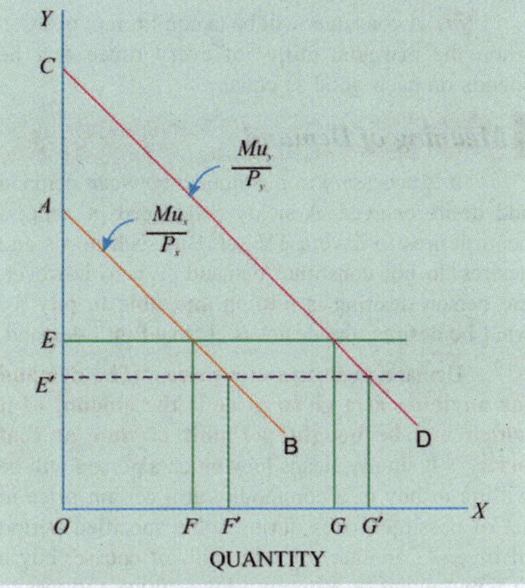

Fig. 5.4. Consumer's Equilibrium by Using Principle of Equi-margnal Utility.

Thus, when our hypothetical consumer is purchasing OF of X and OG of Y, $\frac{MUx}{Px} = \frac{MUy}{Py} = MUm$. This consumer is in equilibrium when he is purchasing OF of X and OG of Y. No other distribution of money expenditure will yield the consumer greater utility than when he is purchasing OF of X and OG of Y.

Suppose the money income of the consumer increases. As a result, his marginal utility will fall, say to OE′. The consumer will then increase his purchases of good X and Y to OF′ and OG′ respectively.

The equi- marginal position of a consumer's equilibrium can be stated in three ways as under:—

(i) In equilibrium, a consumer equalises weighted marginal utilities (*i.e.,* weighted by the price of the good) of all goods to one another and also to the marginal utility of money. Thus:

$$\frac{MUx}{Px} = \frac{MUy}{Py} = MUm.$$

(ii) Secondly, a consumer attains an equilibrium position when he equalises the ratios of marginal utilities of goods to the ratios of corresponding prices for each pair of goods consumed. Thus:

$$\frac{MUx}{MUy} = \frac{Px}{Py} \text{ and } \frac{MUy}{MUz} = \frac{Py}{Pz} \text{ and so on.}$$

(iii) A consumer will be in equilibrium position when the marginal utility of every rupee that he spends on each good is equal.

Meaning of Demand

It is necessary to distinguish between demand and desire or need. A sickly child needs a tonic; a peon desires to have a TV set. But such needs and desires do not constitute demand. When, however, the person desiring is **willing and able to pay** for what he desires, the desire is changed into demand.

Demand is always **at a price**. **"The demand for anything at a given price is the amount of it which will be bought per unit of time at that price."**[3] It simply means how much a person will be willing to buy of a commodity at a certain price in set of possible prices during some specified period of time. At another price he will, of course, buy a different quantity, more at a lower price and less at a higher price. To speak of demand without reference to price is meaningless.

Also, **the demand is always per unit of time**— per day, per week, per month or per year.

Here is a very good definition:

"By demand we mean the various quantities of a given commodity or service which consumers would buy in one market in a given period of time at various prices, or at various incomes, or at various prices of related goods." (Bober).

From the point of view of the seller, the demand price is the average revenue (revenue per unit) or income he expects to earn from the sale of a unit of a commodity. Thus, **demand price is identical with average revenue** (AR). That is why, the demand curve is also drawn as AR curve.

Types of Demand

Three kinds of demands may be distinguished:

(a) Price Demand;

(b) Income Demand; and

(c) Cross Demand.

Price Demand. Price demand refers to the various quantities of a commodity or service that a consumer would purchase at a given time in a market at various hypothetical prices. It is assumed that other things, such as consumer's income, his tastes and prices of inter-related goods, remain unchanged.

The demand of the individual consumer is called **Individual Demand** and the total demand of all the consumers combined for the commodity or service is called **Industry Demand.** The total demand for the product of an individual firm at various prices is known as firm's demand or **Individual Seller's Demand.**

Income Demand. The income demand refers to the various quantities of goods and services which would be purchased by the consumers at various levels of incomes. Here we assume that the price of the commodity or service as well as the prices of inter-related goods and the tastes and desires of consumers do not change. Just as the price demand expresses relationship between prices and quantities, the income demand shows the relationship between income and quantities demanded. For preparing demand schedule of income demand, we write incomes in one column and quantities purchased at these incomes in the second column. Superior goods or high-priced articles command brisk sales when income increases. On the other hand, inferior goods command large sales when incomes are at a lower level.

Cross Demand. The cross demand means the quantities of good or service which will be purchased with reference to change in price not of this good but of other inter-related goods. These goods are either substitutes or complementary goods. A change in the price of tea, for instance, will affect the demand for coffee. Similarly, if horses become cheap, demand for carriages may increase. In order to prepare demand schedule of this type, we write prices of one commodity in one column and the quantities purchased of the other commodity in the second column.

Of these types of demand, price demand is the most commonly spoken one. Now we study demand schedule, demand curve, etc., relating to price demand.

DEMAND CURVE

We give here a demand curve of an imaginary consumer. The demand curve simply shows how the quantity purchased varies with the variation in price. Along OX are represented the quantities of the good purchased and along OY the prices. It will be seen that at the price OP, OM quantity is purchased, a OP′ the quantity purchased is ON and at OP′ price OL. As the price falls, more is purchased, and vice-

3. Benham. F. — *Economics* (1943), p. 36.

versa. The demand curve is also known as the Average Revenue (AR) curve, because the price paid by the consumer is revenue per unit (*i.e.,* average revenue) for the seller.

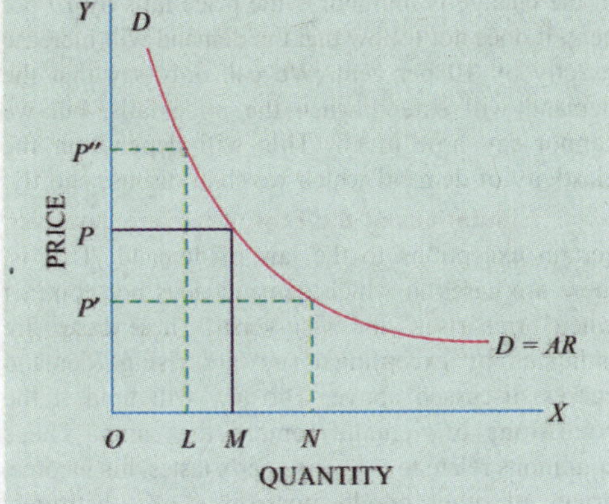

Fig. 5.5. Downward Sloping Demand Curve.

Why Demand Curve Slopes Downwards

Generally, the demand curve slopes downwards. This is in accordance with the law of diminishing marginal utility. The purchasers of most of us are governed by this law. When the price falls, new purchasers enter the market and old purchasers will probably purchase more. Since this particular commodity has become cheaper, it will be purchased by some people in preference to other commodities. Only in a curve of this slope shall we find shorter price lines cutting longer pieces on the quantity-axis. If the law of diminishing marginal utility is true—and it is generally true—the curve must slope downward, for only then the phenomenon of increasing demand with falling prices can be represented.

There are three obvious reasons why people buy more when the price falls:

(i) A unit of money goes farther and a consumer can afford to buy more. He is able and willing to buy more because the thing being cheaper, his real income increases. It is called income effect.

(ii) When the commodity becomes cheaper, it tends to be substituted wholly or partly for other commodities. This is called substitution effect.

The income effect and substitution effect combine to increase the ability and willingness of the consumer to buy more of the commodity whose price has fallen.

(iii) A commodity tends to be put to more uses or less urgent uses when it becomes cheaper. For example, if water is dear, we shall use it for drinking only; but when it becomes cheaper, we shall use it for washing and other less urgent uses.

Thus, the old buyers buy more and some new buyers enter the market. The cumulative effect is an extension of demand when price falls.

But let us go a bit deeper and try to find out **why the demand increases when the price falls**, other things being equal. Benham[4] has answered this question in this manner: Having a limited amount of money at his disposal, every consumer wants to get the maximum satisfaction therefrom. Knowing his own scale of preferences he will according to the law of substitution and equi-marginal returns, so arrange his expenditure that he gets equal marginal utility from the last paisa that he spends in different ways. He will keep to this arrangement if the prices remain the same.

But if the price of a commodity, included in his assortment of goods and services falls then he must make a corresponding alteration in his scheme of expenditure. By the fall in price, divergence has been created between the marginal utility and price and this must be rectified. This can be done by buying more of the commodity when its price falls thus bringing its marginal utility to the level of the price. That is why, people buy more when the prices fall.

Conversely, we buy less, when the price rises because: (*a*) we substitute other cheaper things for it; and (*b*) when price rises, we feel poorer (our real income falls), hence we economise and cut down our consumption.

The law of diminishing marginal utility too is the basis of the law of demand. The consumer will buy more only if the price falls because more he buys the lower is the marginal utility.

Exceptional Demand Curves

As we have said above, generally the demand curve slopes downwards to the left. But sometimes the demand curve, instead of sloping downward, will rise upwards. In other words, sometimes people will buy more when the price rises. This can be represented only by a rising demand curve. Such cases are very rare, but we can imagine some. These were first investigated by Sir Robert Giffen. The **Giffen Paradox** holds that the demand is strengthened with a rise or weakened with a fall in price.

Benham has mentioned four such cases[5] :

4. Benham, F., *Economics*, 1943, pp. 42-43.

5. Ibid, pp. 47.8.

(1) When a serious shortage is feared, people get panicky and buy more even though the price is rising. This is expectational rise in prices.

(2) In case the use of a commodity confers distinction, the wealthy people will buy more when the price rises, to be included among the few distinguished personages. Conversely, people tend to cut their purchases, if they believe the commodity to be inferior.

(3) Sometimes people buy more at a higher price in sheer ignorance.

(4) If the price of a necessity of life goes up, the consumer has to readjust his whole expenditure. He may cut down his expenses on other food articles and in order to make up, more may have to be spent on this particular good. Thus, more of this commodity will be purchased in spite of its high price.

In terms of income elasticity, the demand curves slope downward in the case of goods with positive income elasticities and upward when there is strong negative income elasticity.

Law of Demand

We are now in a position to formulate the Law of Demand. This law simply expresses the relation between quantity of a commodity demanded and its price. The law states that **demand varies inversely with price, not necessarily proportionately**. If the price falls, demand will extend, and vice-versa. The law of demand indicates this inverse relationship between price and quantity demanded.

The law can also be stated thus: **"A rise in the price of a commodity or service is followed by a reduction in demand, and a fall in price is followed by an increase in demand, if conditions of demand remain constant."**

The qualifying phrase "the conditions of demand remaining constant" is very important. Demand is subject to several influences, which will be discussed presently, and the operation of any of those influences may counteract the law.

In Marshall's words, **"The greater the amount to be sold, the smaller must be the price at which it is offered in order that it may find purchasers; or in other words, the amount demanded increases with a fall in price and diminishes with a rise in price."**[6]

Obviously, the law of demand is based on the law of diminishing marginal utility. In other words, it is the law of diminishing marginal utility which explains the law of demand.

6. Marshal, A.— *Principles of Economics*, 1949, p. 84.

Demand thus is a function of price, *i.e.,* it varies with price and can be expressed as D = F (P). Here D is demand and P is price.

It may also be added that no proportionality in the change is implied. If the price falls by 10 per cent, it does not follow that the demand will increase exactly by 10 per cent. We can only say that the demand will extend when the price falls, but we cannot say how much. This will depend on the elasticity of demand which we shall discuss shortly.

Limitations of the Law. There are, however, certain exceptions to the law of demand. That is, there are cases in which demand does not contract when price rises, and vice-versa. These cases are indicated by exceptional (upward rising) demand curves discussed above. The law will hold if the conditions of demand remain the same. These conditions relate to the consumer's tastes, his income, prices of other goods, possibility of substitutes, expected price changes, *etc.* If these conditions change, the law will not hold good. Thus, the following exceptions to the law of demand may be indicated:—

***(i)* Change in Taste or Fashion.** According to the law of demand, when price falls, demand is expected to increase. But if in the meantime consumer's tastes have undergone a change or if the commodity has gone out of fashion, more may not be demanded even if the price falls.

***(ii)* Change in Income.** A rise in price is likely to result in a diminution of demand according to the law of demand. But if the consumer's income has gone up, he may be willing to buy more in spite of the rise in price.

***(iii)* Change in Other Prices.** The law of demand says that if the price of a commodity, say tea, falls, more tea will be demanded. But if the price of coffee falls even more heavily, more tea may not be purchased; instead more coffee may be purchased. This is in contravention of the law of demand.

***(iv)* Discovery of Substitutes.** Acting on the law of demand, India may lower the price of jute by abolishing or reducing export duty to boost her sales of jute. But the discovery of cheap substitutes like synthetic bags may nullify our efforts and more jute may not be demanded even if the price of jute falls.

(v) Anticipatory changes in prices may also upset the law of demand. It is often seen that there is stockpiling of commodities and larger purchases even though the prices are rising. This may be due to the fact that either on account of the danger of war or widespread failure of rains, shortage is feared and the prices may in future go up still higher.

(vi) The law of demand does not hold good also when a commodity is such that its use confers distinction. In case of such a commodity, a fall in its price will keep off the eligible purchasers, because the use of a cheap commodity cannot be considered as a mark of distinction.

Conclusion. The above are a few exceptions to the law of demand. By and large, however, the law holds good. That is, a rise in price decreases demand and a fall in price increases it.

DERIVATION OF THE DEMAND CURVE AND LAW OF DEMAND

Having familiarised ourselves with the demand curve and the law of demand, we are now in a position to see how they are derived in the marginal utility analysis. Marshall derived the demand curve of a good from its utility function, *i.e.,* the variation of utility with the quantity purchased. As we have already mentioned the underlying assumptions are that the utility is measurable cardinally (*i.e.,* it is additive) and the utilities are independent of each other (thus ruling out substitution and complementary relations between the goods consumed). Also, the marginal utility of money MUm is supposed to remain constant.

Subject to the assumptions given above, we can derive the demand curve and the law of demand (*a*) with the help of the law of diminishing marginal utility, and (*b*) with the help of the law of equimarginal utility. We have already studied these two laws.

Demand Curve and Human Behaviour. It is very often, in simple way the relationship between the price and quantity demanded is explained. Price and quantity demanded of a product is inversely related. In this regard many questions, could be raised, why demand curve shopes downward? Why it has inverse relationship.

$$P \propto \frac{1}{d} \quad \text{, where} \quad P = \text{Price}$$

and $\quad d$ = Quantity demanded.

Let us look into the basic philosophy. According to Adam Smith, Human being is very selfish (or self love) in other words his self interest. This selfishness of human being is the main criteria of judging the relationship between "demand and price." Man "tries to weigh between what he is paying and what he is getting in return." Man "tries to give the least and wants the maximum in return." Human being weighs in terms of money and in terms of utilities of goods, when he carries out exchange in the market.

G = What he is giving (in terms of money)

R = What he is receiving (in terms of goods and their marginal utilities)

$$\left.\begin{matrix} G < R \\ R > G \end{matrix}\right\} \text{Trade or exchange goes on.}$$

G = R This is the point where trade stops or equilibrium point.

$G > R \Rightarrow$ No trade at all.

'dd' demand curve, x-axis quantity of good 'x', and y-axis price of x.

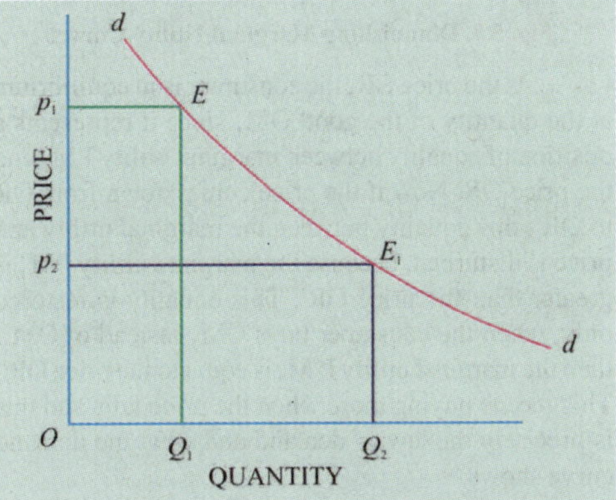

Fig. 5.6. Higher the Price Lower is Quantity and Vice versa.

At 'OP_1' price a consumer is buying less 'OQ_1,' where as at 'OP_2' price he is buying more that is 'OQ_2.'

Derivation of the Demand Curve and the Law of Demand from the Law of Diminishing Marginal Utility

The law of diminishing marginal utility states that the marginal utility of a good (expressed in terms of money) to a consumer decreases as the quantity consumed increases. This means that the marginal utility curve of a good is a downward sloping curve as shown in the figure on next page:

We have already seen that a consumer is in equilibrium when the marginal utility of a good equals its price. Now when the price of the good falls for example from OR to OR′ the consumer must buy more than before *i.e.,* OM_2 instead of OM_1 so that the marginal utility $P'M_2$ equals price OR′. From this it follows that the diminishing marginal utility curve leads us to a downward sloping demand curve which means that more of a good is purchased as its price falls. This can be seen in the given figure.

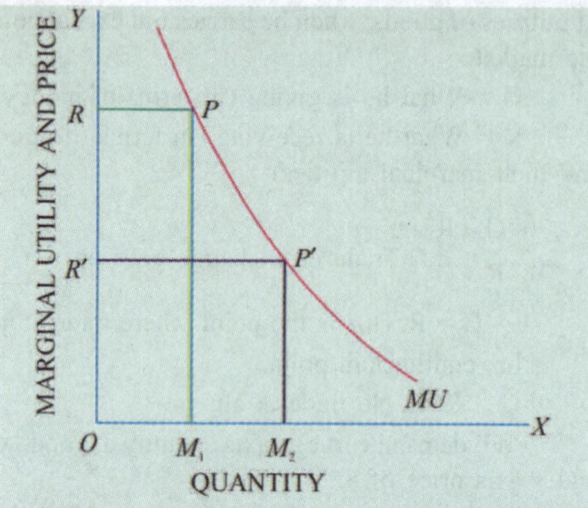

Fig. 5.7. Diminishing Marginal Utility Curve.

At the price OR, the consumer is in equilibrium at the quantity of the good OM_1 since it represents a position of equality between marginal utility PM_1 and the price OR. Now if the price comes down from OR to OR′, this equality between the marginal utility and price is disturbed, because the marginal utility PM_1 is greater than the price OR′. This equality is restored only, when the consumer buys OM_2 instead of OM_1, then the marginal utility $P'M_2$ is equal to the price OR′. This means buying more when the price falls and this is precisely the law of demand and what the demand curve shows.

Discovery of synthetic bags (above) affected demand for jute bags (below) drastically in India.

We have thus derived the law of demand which states that the quantity demanded of a good varies inversely with its price. In other words, other things remaining the same, the quantity demanded increases when the price falls, and vice-versa. This is the well known Marshallian law of demand and it is based on the law of diminishing marginal utility.

Extension of demand and Contraction of demand

Extension of demand and contraction of demand are some of the concepts which one must know, as there is an inverse relationship between demand and price.

Table IV: Demand Schedule

Price of 'x'	Quantity demanded of x
5	1000
10	850
15	650
20	500
25	400
30	200
35	100

Contraction of demand

dd' demand curve, x' axis. Quantity of 'x' y' axis. price E_1, E_2, E_3 equilibrium Q_1, Q_2, Q_3 Quantity P_1, P_2 and P_3 Price.

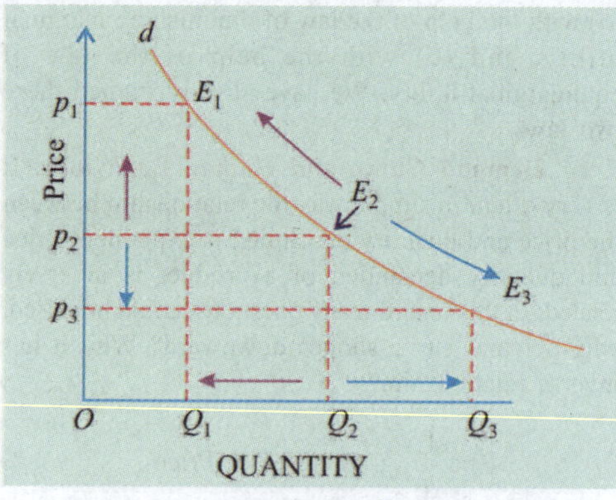

Fig. 5.8. Extension (↓→) and Contraction (←↑) of Demand.

Let us assume the economy, in equilibrium at point 'E_2' that is at 'price' OP_2 and quantity demanded is 'OQ_2.'

Case I (Contraction of demand)

Let us assume that the price increases from 'OP_2' to 'OP_1', and the quantity demanded reduces from 'OQ$_2$' to 'OQ$_1$'. This behaviour is referred as 'contraction of demand.'

Case. II (Extension of demand)

In this case the 'price' decreases from 'OP$_2$' to 'OP$_3$', due to this the quantity demanded increases from 'OQ$_2$' to 'OQ$_3$' → this is nothing but the extention of demand.

Increase in demand and Decrease in demand

In this case other factors influences the demand curve. In the extention contraction of demand we take into account "Ceteris Paribus" assumptions. Where as in case of increase in demand and decrease in demand we take into account other factors, *i.e.,* size of family, increase or decrease in income, change in fashion and styles, other government policies etc.

"dd" is original demand curve. 'd$_1$d$_1$' is decrease in demand curve. "d$_2$d$_2$" is increase in demand curve, 'OP' original price – 'OQ' original quantity

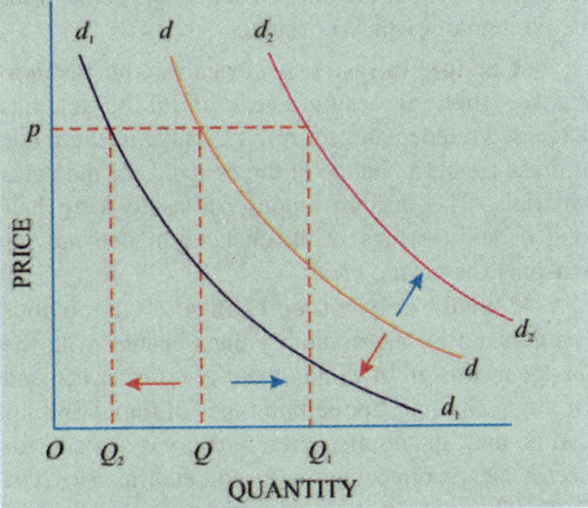

Fig. 5.9. Increase (↗) and Decrease (↙) in demand.

'OP' original price 'OQ$_1$' increase in demand

'OP' original price 'OQ$_2$' decrease in demand.

Extention of demand curve and contraction of demand curve is the movement on the same demand curve 'dd' in the diagram due to change in price, where as increase in demand is the complete shift of demand curve to the right 'd$_2$d$_2$' and decrease in demand is shift of demand curve to left that is 'd$_1$d$_1$', where as the 'price' remains same at 'OP'.

Derivation of the Demand Curve and the Law of Demand from the Law of Equi-Marginal Utility

We have already seen that in terms of the law of equi-marginal utility when a consumer is purchasing two commodities, he attains a position of equilibrium when the marginal utilities of the two goods he purchases are equal or they are proportional to their prices. The proportionality rule which the consumer must satisfy is

$$\frac{MUx}{Px} = \frac{MUy}{Py} = \frac{MUn}{Pn} = MUm$$

where Mu$_m$ is the marginal utility of money. Px is the price of X and Py is the price of Y, and so on. That is, the consumer equalises his marginal utility of money (expenditure) with the ratio of marginal utility and price of each commodity he purchases.

Now suppose that price of one good, say X, falls, the price of the other good Y and consumer's income and tastes remaining the same (*Ceteris paribus*), the proportionality rule, *i.e.,* the equality of $\frac{MUx}{Px}$ with $\frac{MUy}{Py} = MUm$ is disturbed. Since the price of X is now lower $\frac{MUx}{Px}$ will be greater than $\frac{MUy}{Py}$ or MUm. This equality can be restored only when the consumer buys more of X, whose price has come down, than before. Only then the marginal utility of X or MUx will be reduced to the level of $\frac{MUy}{Py}$ or MUm. This means that as the price of a good falls, its demand increases. This is the law of demand and it has been derived, as explained above, from the law of equi-marginal utility.

The following figure shows how the law of demand is derived, *i.e.,* how the quantity purchased increases with a fall in price.

Take the upper portion of the figure first. On the X-axis are given the quantities of the good X demanded and on the Y-axis is shown the ratio of the marginal utility and the price *i.e.,* $\frac{MUx}{Px}$. The marginal utility of money is OH. When the price of the good is Px$_1$, the consumer buys Oq$_1$, since at this quantity of the commodity, the marginal utility of money OH is equal to the ratio of the marginal utility divided by price, *i.e.,* $\frac{MUx}{Px_1}$. Now suppose the price of the good falls from PX$_1$ to PX$_2$ the demand will increase, *i.e.,* the demand curve is shifted upwards. The quantity demanded must increase to Oq$_2$ because only then the marginal utility of money OH will be equal to ratio of the marginal utility of the good and the price, *i.e.,* $\frac{MUx}{Px_2}$.

Thus, we find that when the price of a good falls, the demand curve shifts upwards and more of the good will be demanded. This is precisely the law of demand and it has been derived from the law of equi-marginal utility as explained above. On the same reasoning, if the price of the good falls further to Px_3, Oq_3 will be demanded, because only then the proportionality rule about consumer's equilibrium will be satisfied.

The lower portion of the figure shows the quantities demanded at different prices, *i.e.,* Oq_1 at Px_1, Oq_2 at Px_2 and Oq_1 at Px_3, *i.e.,* quantity demanded increases as the price falls. We can derive the demand curve DD by joining the various points.

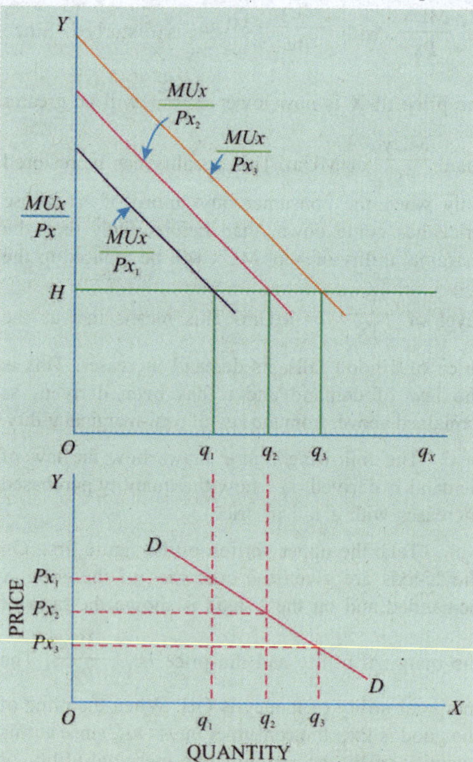

Fig. 5.10. Derivation of Demand Curve from Equi Marginal Utility.

CAUSES OF CHANGES IN DEMAND

We spell out below some of the causes which bring about changes in demand and also explain how demand will be affected by the following factors.

Change in real income. A distinction is made between money income, *i.e.,* the amount of money which a man may earn, and real income which means the quantity of goods and services which he can buy with that amount of money. In times of technical progress, there is a large output of cheap goods. The purchasing power of money increases or, as it may be said, real income increases. Less money will be needed to purchase the same quantity of goods, and the saving so made will find outlet in the purchase of some other commodities. The demand schedules will have to be recast. Some goods may be eliminated from consumption and instead entirely new goods purchased; demand for some goods will decrease and that for others increase.

Change in the level and distribution of income. Through the instrument of public finance, *e.g.,* by taxing the rich and spending the funds so obtained on the poor, wealth is redistributed. There is a transfer of spending power. This is bound to affect demand. Demands for those goods will increase which are purchased by a class whose spending power has increased, and vice versa. The larger is the average household income, greater is the demand for the commodities they consume.

Changes in tastes, preferences and fashion. We see that increasing habit of taking tea has decreased the demand for milk. Change in the mode of dress means a change in the demand for the dress materials. The fashion among ladies to keep hair long or short brings about changes in demand for hair-pins, hair-nets, *etc.*

Climate or weather changes. It is obvious that demand for a commodity must change with the change in season. In winter, there is a greater demand for warm clothing, for certain types of tonics and for coal or fuel. In summer, there is a great demand for electric fans, room coolers and cooling drinks, ice, *etc.*

Changes in the size and composition of population. If, for instance, the Commonwealth countries and America allow a free entry to Indians, we can expect emigration from India. If Indians stick to their own mode of living in food and dress in their new homes, demand for such things will be created there.

It is not merely a change in the size of the consuming population but change in the composition of the population, too, which affects demand for certain commodities and services. In a country of increasing population, like India, where lakhs of children are born every day, there will naturally be demand for toys, feeding bottles and nipples, perambulators, *etc.*

Changes in money supply. Where there is inflation, the additional money will add to the purchasing power of the community, and the prices will rise. But the rise of prices will not be uniform in the case of all goods. People will have to readjust their expenditure; demand for certain things will be reduced and for others stimulated. For example, shortage of sugar in India increased demand for **gur** and **shakker**, and restrictions on the supply of electricity have reacted a demand for kerosene lamps, and so on.

Increase in the size of population in India have led to tremendous increase in demand for goods.

Change in the price of the commodity. Obviously, demand is decisively affected by the change in the price of the commodity concerned. There is inverse relation between price and the quantity demanded. Lower the price, the greater is the demand, and vice-versa.

Change in savings. Demand for goods is affected by a change in consumer's propensity to save. Large saving means less money available for the purchase of goods. The demand will therefore decrease.

Change in asset preferences. It is quite obvious that if a consumer develops marked liquidity preference, his demand for goods will decrease, because he prefers to keep with him ready cash instead of buying things.

Conditions of trade. Demand for everything is greater in a boom even though the prices are rising. On the other hand, in times of depression, there is a general slackening of the demand.

Expectations or Anticipations. Expectations also bring about a change in demand. If prices are expected to rise in future, the demand for goods will increase now in the present. Similarly, expectations of rising incomes will restrain current purchases and postpone purchases to a future favourable situation.

Prices of Related goods. In case of substitutes, *e.g.,* tea and coffee, increase in the consumption of one will lead to a decrease in the demand for the other. When a decline in the price of one good results in a decline in the demand for another, they are substitutes. Or, two goods are substitutes if the demand for one is directly related to the price of the other.

In the case of **complements**, *e.g.,* horse and carriage, increased demand for one will augment that for the other. Two goods are complements if the price of one and the demand for the other are inversely related. For instance, if the price of the carriages falls, the demand for horses rises. Other examples of complementary goods are pipes and tobacco, tennis rackets and tennis balls, *etc.*

In the case of **joint supply**, *e.g.,* wheat and straw, the increased demand for one will lead to the late its demand too, after some time.

When there is a case of **joint demand**, the increase in the demand for the ultimate object, *e.g.,* the house, will increase the demand for everything needed in building a house.

In the case of **composite supply**, *e.g.,* light obtained from electricity, gas or kerosene, cheapening of any one of them will reduce the demand for the others.

In the case of **composite demand**, *e.g.,* water required for drinking, washing bathing, *etc.*, any extension or contraction of its uses will correspondingly change the demand.

Thus, the demand for a commodity does not depend only on its own price but the prices of other goods too.

The limited supply of money that a consumer has, is to be allocated among numerous goods that he has to purchase. Hence, the demands and prices of all goods are inter-related. A big price hike in certain commodities is bound to affect the demand for other goods that a consumer has to purchase.

These are some of the factors which bring about changes in demand.

SHORTCOMINGS OF THE UTILITY ANALYSIS

Above we have made the study of utility analysis of demand at some length. Modern economists, however, do not place much faith in the utility analysis on grounds of both theory and operational efficiency. The following are the main defects pointed out in the utility analysis or the Marshallian approach to the demand theory:

***(i)* Unsound Psychology.** It is urged that market demand is an objective phenomenon. But the utility theorists try to explain it in terms of desire, motivation, *etc*. As such, the utility theory is individualistic and hedonistic (or utilitarian). To attribute motive to the consumer is unrealistic. When the theory says that with successive increases in the quantity consumed, the marginal utility diminishes, it is too naive a description of human nature. It must, however, be said that the utility analysis given by Marshall is free from hedonistic or utilitarian interpretation. The modern economists regard the diminishing marginal utility as a familiar and fundamental tendency of human nature. It is true that the principle is based on introspection, but it has been supported by observed human behaviour.

***(ii)* Cardinal Measurement Not Possible.** The utility analysis assumes that utility is measurable cardinally, *i.e.,* it can be assigned definite numbers. But the fact is that cardinal measurement of utility is not possible. Instead, we can only have an ordinal measure, *i.e.,* we can only compare the two situations and say whether the satisfaction is more or less. As Hicks observes, it is possible to establish elementary parts of the demand theory with the help of cardinal numbers, but in advanced theory, it becomes a nuisance. He says: "**It might be, more convenient as a sort of scaffolding useful in erecting the building, but to be taken down when the building has been completed.**"[7] Thus, the utility analysis breaks down on the ground of measurability of utility and economists like J.R. Hicks want the cardinal measurability of utility to be given up as being unrealistic.

***(iii)* Wrong Assumption of Independent Utilities.** The utility analysis further assumes that utilities are independent. On this assumption, the utility of a commodity to a consumer varies with the quantity of that commodity, and of that commodity alone. This means that the satisfaction that a consumer obtains from the consumption of a particular good is not affected in any manner by the consumption of another goods. This is not correct. The utility of a pen is certainly enhanced if a good quality paper is made available. It, therefore, follows from this assumption that the total utility of all the goods consumed is merely a sum of their separate utilities. That is, the utility function is additive. Actually this is not so. All the goods consumed by a person form one system and as such the satisfaction derived from the consumption of the commodity is influenced by that from the other. The Commodities are interlinked. This makes the marginal utilities interdependent and not independent.

Hence, the marginal utility of a commodity depends not merely on its own consumption but also on the consumption of some other commodity or commodities. This is so because the commodities may be complements or substitutes of one another. Thus the assumption that utilities are independent is not a valid assumption to base the utility analysis on as, for example, Marshall did it. This is a weakness of Marshallian utility analysis.

***(iv)* Income Effect and Substitution Effect Not Brought Out.** Besides, the utility analysis does not bring out fully the income effect and substitution effect of a change in price. We know, for instance, that when the price of a commodity falls, the consumer feels as if his income has increased and he is able to purchase more. This is the income effect. Also, the consumer substitutes the cheaper commodity for some other rival commodities. This is the substitution effect in a price change. It is unable to explain how much of the increased demand is due to the income effect and how much to the substitution effect. As Hicks says, "**The distinction between direct and indirect effects of a price change is accordingly left by the cardinal theory as an empty box which is crying out to be filled.**"[8]

***(v)* Does Not Explain Giffen Paradox.** It is owing to the assumption of constant marginal utility of money and ignoring the income effect that Marshallian utility analysis failed to explain the 'Giffen Paradox'.

***(vi)* Assumption of Constant Marginal Utility of Money Wrong.** Further, the utility analysis is based on the assumption that the marginal utility of money remains constant even when a consumer is proceeding with his purchases and is parting with money at every step. Constancy of marginal utility of money is necessary in the marginal utility analysis because, according to Marshall, utility is measured in terms of money and the measure, therefore, must not change. Obviously, the reduction in the quantity of money with the purchaser must raise its marginal utility. But this facts conveniently brushed aside in the utility analysis.

***(vii)* Applies to One-Commodity World.** The Marshallian law of demand cannot be genuinely derived from the utility analysis on the assumption

7. Hicks, J.R.— *A Revision of Demand Theory*, 1959, p. 9.

8. Ibid. p. 14.

of constant marginal utility of money except in one-commodity world. The assumption of constant marginal utility is not compatible with the law of demand in a situation where a consumer has more than one commodity to spend his income on. In a multi-commodity model, the marginal utility of money does not remain the same. When a consumer has to spend his income on a number of goods, there must occur a change in the marginal utility of money with every change in the price does not remain the same, utility ceases to be measurable and the marginal utility analysis breaks down.

(*viii*) Assumes Too Much and Explains Too Little. The marginal utility analysis is based on too many assumptions like measurability of marginal utility and constancy of marginal utility of money. But it is restrictive in scope. For example, it does not split the price effect into its two components, the income effect and substitution. It does not explain the 'Giffen' paradox. On the other hand, Hicks-Allen indifference curve technique steers clear of these assumptions and is still able to deduce a more general theorem of demand which covers the Giffen Paradox too. We shall explain these fully in the next chapter.

Conclusion

We have examined above at some length the various shortcomings of the utility analysis. In conclusion, we may draw attention of the student once again to some basic weakness of this analysis also known as the cardinalist approach.

(*i*) The satisfaction derived from the various commodities cannot be measured objectively. Hence the assumption of cardinal utility is extremely doubtful. No doubt Walras has attempted to use subjective units (utils) for measuring utility but it is not a satisfactory solution.

(*ii*) The assumption of constant utility of money is also unrealistic. The marginal utility of money changes with changes in income. Hence money fails as a measuring rod because its own utility changes.

(*iii*) The law of diminishing marginal utility has been derived from introspection. It is only a psychological law which must be taken for granted. In view of its various shortcomings, the utility analysis has now been replaced, by and large, by the modern indifference curve analysis or the ordinal approach.

Modifications by Modern Economists

The modern economists have improved upon the Marshallian utility analysis in a number of ways to rid it of its restrictive assumptions:

(*i*) The modern economists have shown how demand curve can be derived from utility analysis, without assuming constant marginal utility of money.

(*ii*) The modern economists are able to explain the utility of substitutes and complementary goods with utility analysis without assuming that the marginal utilities are independent.

(*iii*) The modern economists are able to offer a satisfactory explanation of the Giffen Paradox.

The modern economists have by and large, given up the Marshallian utility analysis and have instead, adopted the indifference curve technique which we shall discuss at some length in the next two chapters. They have adopted ordinal measure of utility instead of the cardinal utility. According to them utility is a psychological phenomenon and is not therefore quantifiable. On the other hand, ordinal measure helps in comparison of utilities which is enough for practical purposes. For a proper analysis of consumer behaviour, it is sufficient if a consumer can rank his preferences. A consumer can formulate his scale of preferences independently of the market prices of goods on the basis of satisfaction he expects to derive.

All the same, the indifference curve analysis retains some of the assumptions of the marginal utility analysis: For instance it is assumed that a consumer has complete information regarding the goods he wants to purchase, i.e., the prices, satisfaction, etc. Rational behaviour on the part of a consumer is also assumed, i.e., he will seek maximum satisfaction from his purchases. Continuity is also assumed which means that the consumers are capable of ranking all conceivable combinations of goods on the basis of satisfaction that the goods are expected to yield.

In a later chapter, we shall compare in detail the Marshallian utility analysis and the indifference curve technique.

Key Terms:

Cardinal Utility, Dimnishing Marginal Utility; Introspection; Equi-marginal Utility; Consumer's Equilibrium; Extension and Contraction of Demand ; Increase and Decrease in Demand.

QUESTIONS

1. State and explain the Law of Diminishing Marginal Utility. What are the limitations and importance of the law? Bring out clearly the relationship between marginal utility and price.
2. Explain the Law of Diminishing Marginal Utility and explain its relation with the Law of Demand.
3. Estimate the importance of the Law of Diminishing Utility in shaping the theory and practice of modern taxation.
4. What are the difficulties in the measurement of utility as defined by Marshall?
5. Distinguish between marginal utility and total utility.

   Or

   Prove that the total utility of a commodity is maximum only when its marginal utility is zero. Illustrate your answer with the help of a diagram.
6. Discuss how Marshall's utility analysis is helpful in determining Consumer's Equilibrium.

   Or

   How can a consumer maximise his satisfaction in terms of utility analysis?
7. Explain the Law of Equi-marginal Utility from the particulars given below. Find out:

   (*a*) the best combination of goods that a consumer will purchase in equilibrium.

   (*b*) the total utility from the best combination.

No. of units consumed	*MUx*	*MUy*
1	30	20
2	25	18
3	20	16
4	15	14
5	10	12
6	5	10
7	1	8

Given that price of x = Rs. 5, price of y = Rs. 20 and Income Rs. 22.

8. State the 'Law of Demand' and explain 'Giffen's Paradox'.
9. How do you derive the Demand curve from (*i*) law of diminishing marginal utility and (*ii*) law of Equi-marginal Utility? What are the limitations of the Law of Demand?
10. Enumerate the factors which cause a change in the demand for a commodity. Distinguish, with illustrations, a movement along a demand curve and a shift of the demand curve.
11. Distinguish between a change in demand and a change in the quantity demanded, noting the causes of each. Illustrate your answer with examples.
12. Explain the reason why the demand curve is supposed to be downward sloping. Can you think of any exception ?
13. What are the short comings of the Utility Analysis? How the modern economists have modified the Marsrshallian Utility Theorey?

INDIFFERENCE CURVE TECHNIQUE

In view of the shortcomings of the utility analysis, modern ecnomists have adopted a new technique—called the indifference curve technique—for the analysis of demand. In the following three chapters, we shall first consider this new tool of indifference curves, then analyse consumer's behaviour with its help, and finally study the various applications of the modern technique.

Scale of Preferences

All desires of a consumer are not of equal urgency or importance. Since his resources are limited and he cannot fulfil all his desire, he must pick and choose more important and more urgent desires for satisfaction. Thus, some desires take precedence of others. This is how a consumer ranks his desires and builds up a scale of preferences. Scarcity forces him to choose. Ability to arrange preferences in order of importance or urgency is inherent in human nature.

A prudent consumer exercises a lot of discrimination in his purchases. We find him substituting one commodity, partly or wholly, for another. He purchases a certain quantity of a commodity and no more. All the time, he is striving to reach an equilibrium position, i.e., a position in which he derives maximum satisfaction from the use of money at his disposal.

Sir J.R. Hicks 1904-1989
Received nobel prize in economics in 1972.

But what is the criterion on which a consumer bases his choice? It is the relative evaluation of the utilities of the commodities included in his purchase plan. Since utility is subjective, the evaluation is obviously by himself. This means that a consumer has in his mind a definite scale of preferences which guides him in his purchases. For example, some students would like to spend their monthly allowance on the purchase of useful books, while others will squander it in the canteen. It is the consumer's scale of preferences which would determine his purchase plan. This scale of preferences is shaped by consumer's temperament and tastes. Thus, the priorities in a consumer's purchase plan are determined by his scale of preferences.

R.G.D. Allen

As we have mentioned already, a prudent consumer seeks to maximise his satisfaction from the purchases he makes, i.e., reach an equilibrium position. But in order to be able to do so, a consumer must build up a scale of preferences on which all objects of desire or pursuit find their place, and which registers the terms on which they would be accepted as equivalent, or preferred one to the other.

The consumer's scale of preference is independent of the prices rulings in the market. He builds up his scale of preferences from the commodities he consumes. On the basis of this scale of preferences, he knows that one combination of the goods yields him the same satisfaction as another.

In the discussion of consumer preference, we have to make certain assumptions to enable us to reach valid conclusions. The main assumptions are :

(*i*) Completeness. We assume that the consumer's scale of preferences is so complete that he is able to choose any one of the two combinations of commodities presented to him or is indifferent between them.

(*ii*) Non-satiation. A consumer prefers more to less.

(*iii*) Consistency or Transitivity. If a consumer regards Q better that R and R better than S, obiviously he will prefer Q to S, if this choice is open. Consumers's choices have to be consistent.

(*iv*) Continuity or Substitutability. Unless one combination can be substituted for another, the consumers' preference will not be possible.

(*v*) Convexity. The indifference curve is convex to the origin and shows the diminishing rate of marginal rate of substitution to be explained presently.

It is not to be supposed, however, that actually a consumer has a complete or consistent scale of preferences in his mind or that he is fully conscious of it all the time. Certain commodities usually figure in the weekly or monthly purchases and are thus purchased by habit. A conscious choice is made in the case of new purchases. But consumers are rational beings. We can construct a theory of demand because scales of preferences are in some degree rational and stable through time, and purchases are usually made according to them. Actually, there is sufficient degree of stability in the spending pattern of consumers so that a realistic theory of demand can be propounded.

Actual purchases made by a consumer may not, however, be in conformity with his scale of preferences. They rather depend on the amount of money in his pocket and the commodities available at the time as well as on their relative prices. Consumer's purchasing power does not depend merely on the amount of money he has. The real purchasing power depends also on the current price level. If he finds that the market has gone down, he will be able to purchase more, and vice versa. Given the scale of preferences, a consumer will arrange his purchases in the light of realised purchasing power of his resources.

INDIFFERENCE CURVES

On the basis of a consumer's scale of preferences, we can draw indifference curves. An indifference curve represents satisfaction of a consumer from two commodities. It is drawn on the assumption that for all possible points (or combinations of the two commodities) on an indifference curve, the total satisfaction (or utility) remains the same. Hence, the consumer is indifferent as to the combinations lying on an indifference curve. It is an iso-utility curve.

Let us now start by considering a consumer who wants to buy apples and mangoes. He does not make purchases of the amounts of these two commodities arbitrarily. He knows it well that one combination of apples and mangoes gives his as much satisfaction (total utility) as another combination of less apples and more mangoes or another combination of more apples and less mangoes.

The consumer cannot tell how much satisfaction he secures from an apple or from a mango but he has got a scale of preferences between these two commodities so as to be able to compare the satisfaction derived from one basketful of these two commodities. In other words, he knows what substitution of apples for mangoes or mangoes for apples will leave him with the same or equal satisfaction. Thus, our consumer has in his mind an indifference schedule.This schedule has several combinations of apples and mangoes from which he derives the same or equal total satisfaction. Or we can say that various combinations are equally preferred or desired by him.

We further clarify this point by giving an indifference schedule of the varous combinations of apples and mangoes.

To maintain a given level of satisfaction if we increase apples then we must decrease mangoes.

Table 1: Indifference Schedule

Combinations	*Apples*	*Mangoes*
1	15	1
2	11	2
3	8	3
4	6	4
5	5	5

In the above schedule, the consumer obtains as much total satisfaction (total utility) from 11 apples and 2 mangoes as from 8 apples and 3 mangoes and as well as from other combinations. In other words, our consumer feels indifferent whether he gets the 1st combination (15 A + 1 M), the 2nd combination (11A + 2 M), the 3rd combination (8A + 3M), the 4th combination (6A + 4M) or the 5th combination (5A + 5M). (Here A stands for apples and M stands for mangoes). The total satisfaction is the same in all these combinations. We shall now translate this schedule into a diagram and thus get an indifference curve IC in Fig. 6.1.

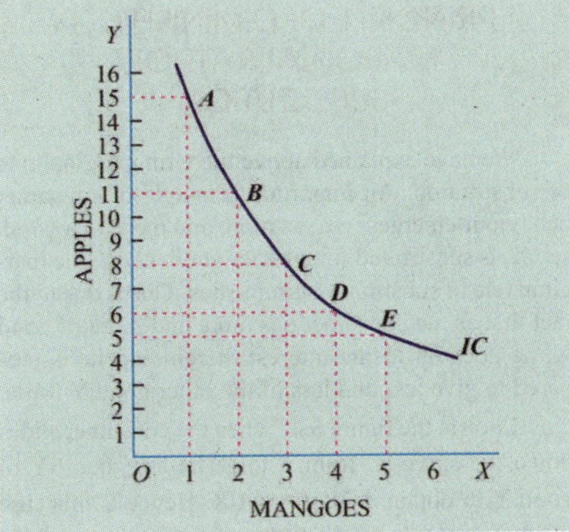

Fig. 6.1. An indifference curve.

In Fig. 6.1. mangoes are measured along the X-axis ; their number increases from left to right. Apples are meauserd along Y-axis; and their number increase upwards.

If the consumer were at point A on the curve IC with 15 apples and 1 mango, he would be just as satisfied as at point B with 11 apples and 2 mangoes or at point C with 8 apples and 3 mangoes or at point D with 6 apples and 4 mangoes, and so on. These combinations give him the same satisfaction. If we join the points A, B, C, D and E, we get a continuous curve IC, each point on it showing equal satisfaction or the indifference of the consumer towards the various com binations. This is an **indifference curve.** Each point on it shows a combination of apples and mangoes which yields the same total satisfaction to our consumer.

Indifference Map

We can draw similar indifference curves showing combinations of apples and mangoes which represent greater and lesser satisfaction than that shown on indifference curve IC (see Fig. 6.2). In this figure, all points on IC_5 and IC_4 are preferred to all the points on IC_1 or IC_2 or IC_3. All combinations of apples and mangoes on IC_2 are equally preferred and are more preferred to all the combinations at various points on the IC_1. In other words, indifference curve IC_1 represents a lower level of satisfaction as compared with indifference curves IC_2, IC_3, IC_4, IC_5. It will thus be seen that indifference curves remind us of the weather maps showing the lines of equal pressure of the contour lines on a topographical map. A set of indifference curves is called **an indifference map**.

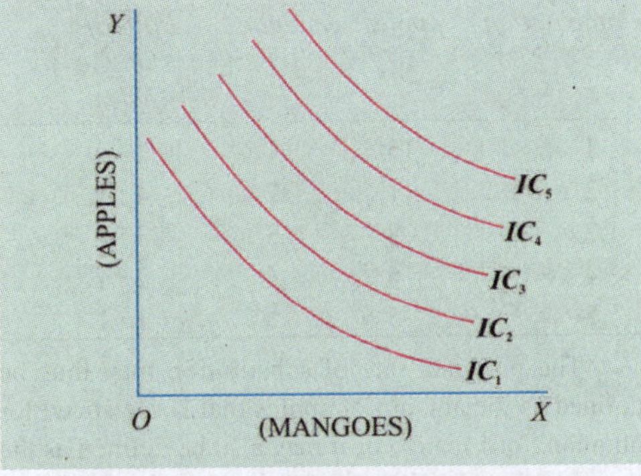

Fig. 6.2. An indifference map is a set of indifference curve. Satisfaction level is higher the farthest indifference curve from the origin.

It should be borne in mind that we cannot say how much more utility the higher indifference curve represents. That is, the aggregate utilities are rankable but not measurable ; the jumps or increase in utility cannot be ranked. We cannot say how much greater utility does IC_2 represent than IC_1 and IC_3, making cardinal measurement of utility, a Marshallian assumption that we have rejected already.

MARGINAL RATE OF SUBSTITUTION

From the schedule given above, we can see that when we move from one combination of the two commodities to another, we are in fact substituting some units of one commodity for some units of another. We can also work out the rate at which this substitution takes place.

The Marginal Rate of Substitution shows how much of one commodity is substituted for how much of another or at what rate a consumer is willing to substitute one commodity for another in his consumption pattern. The concept of marginal rate of substitution is a tool of indifference curve technique and is parallel to the concept of marginal utility in the Marshallian analysis of demand.

Taking our previous example of substitution between apples and mangoes, we notice that when our consumer has 15 apples and one mango, he will be prepared to forgo 4 apples for 1 mango and yet remain at the same level of satisfaction. Or, in other words, we can say, in case he has the second combination, then he will be prepared to accept 4 apples for the loss of one mango. Here the marginal rate of substitution of mangoes for apples is 4 : 1.

Table 4.2.

Combination	*Apples*	*Mangoes*	*MRS of Mangoes for Apples*
1	15	1	—
2	11	2	4 : 1
3	8	3	3 : 1
4	6	4	2 : 1
5	5	5	1 : 1

The marginal rate of substitution may thus be defined as the amount of apples that is sacrificed for obtaining one mango or it may also be defined as the amount of apples that may be given to the consumer for the loss of one mango so that he may remain at the same level of satisfaction.

In Hicks' words, **"we may define marginal rate of substitution of X for Y as the quantity of Y which would just compensate the consumer for the loss of the marginal unit of X."**

Let us suppose that the consumer decides upon the fourth combination, which in terms of our diagram (No. 6.1), means that he choose the combination represented by a point on IC. Now the marginal unit of mangoes is the third mango, to acquire which he has had to forego two apples; or in other words, he will agree to get the fourth mango if he is compensated by two apples. At this point, the marginal rate of substitution of mango for apples is 2 : 1.

It is common observation that, as we come to have more and more of one good, we shall be prepared to forego less and less of the other since our desire for the former becomes less and less intense with more and more of it. In technical language, it will be said that the marginal rate of substitution of good X for good Y will fall as we have more of X and less of Y. This is clearly brought out in the preceding table, where in combination 2 the marginal rate of substitution of mango for apple is 4 : 1, and it falls to 3 : 1 in combination 3 and further 2 : 1 in combination 4.

Thus, the principle is that as X is substituted for Y so as to keep the consumer at the same level of satisfaction, the marginal rate of substitution of X for Y diminishes.

This principle in indifference curve technique is termed as the Diminishing Marginal Rate of substitution, and is parallel to the Law of Diminishing Margnial Utility in Marshallian utility analysis.

The Marginal Rate of substitution is indicated by the slope of an indifference curve at a point. That is, it represents a movement along an indifference curve, but not a movement among the curves.

PRINCIPLE OF DIMINISHING MARGINAL RATE OF SUBSTITUTION

We have explained above the term marginal rate of substitution. An important principle of consumer behaviour emerges, *viz*., as more and more of a good, say X, is substituted for another good, say Y, the marginal rate of substitution diminishes. This is due to the fact that as the consumer has more and more of good X, he goes on losing interest therein and he is prepared to give less and less of the other good Y for it.

Look at the figure 6.3. When the consumer slides down the curve IC from A to B, he foregoes ΔY of good Y to obtain Δ X of good X. Hence is this case the marginal rate of substitution of X

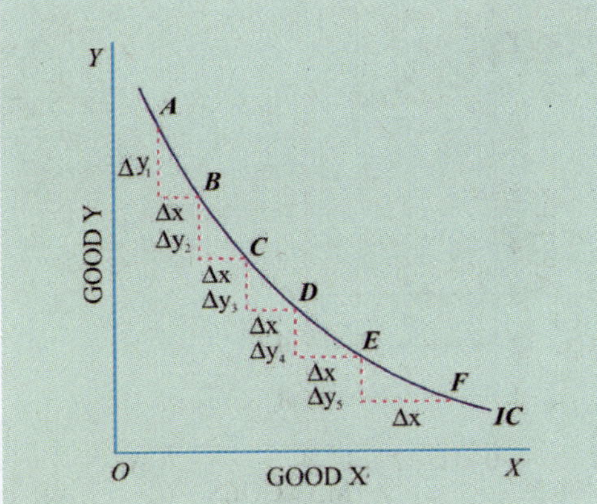

Fig. 6.3. Diminishing marginal rate of substitution implies.

for Y (MRS $_{xy}$) is equal to $\frac{\Delta y_1}{\Delta x}$ we notice that as the consumer slides down further and further on the indifference curve, ΔY becomes shorter and shorter, while ΔX remains the same. This means that as the consumer has more and more of X *i.e.*, when he moves from A to B, from B to C, from C to D and so on, he is prepared to forego less and less of Y for a unit of X. From the above figure, it can be seen that ΔY_2 is less than ΔY_1 and ΔY_3 is less than ΔY_2 and ΔY_4 is less than ΔY_3, and so on. It follows, therefore, that as the stock of X with the consumer increases and his stock of Y decreases, he is willing to give less and less of Y for a given increment of X. In other words, the marginal rate of substitution of X for Y falls as the consumer has more of X and less of Y.

That the marginal rate of substitution falls is also clearly brought out in the preceding table. As already mentioned, the marginal rate of substitution of mangoes for apples is 4.1 to start with and it falls to 3 : 1 in combination 3, 2 : 1 in combination 4 and 1 : 1 in combination 5.

Let us try to understand the reasons for the diminishing, marginal rate of substitution. Why is the consumer prepared to forego less and less of the other commodity Y for a given increment of a commodity X ? The reasons are :

(i) Since a particular want is satiable, the edge of a want for a good is blunted as the consumer has more and more of it. It is the diminishing intensity for a want that is responsible for the diminishing marginal rate of substitution (i.e. offering less for a good whose stock is increasing). That is why, as the stock of X with the consumer increase, he will offer less and less of the other good Y for a unit increase in X.

(ii) Another reason for a declining marginal rate of substitution lies in the fact that goods are imperfect substitutes for one another. If X and Y, for instance, were perfect substitutes for each other, they would be regarded as one commodity and decrease in that of the other would make no difference. Hence the marginal rate of substitution will not diminish, it will remain the same, for one commodity is good as another.

(iii) Also, the marginal rate of substitution of one good for another will not diminish if the want satisfying power of the other good has increased at the same time. For instance, if with increase in the stock of the good X, the want-satisfying power of the good Y has increased, then more and more of Y will have to be offered for a unit increase in X to keep to consumer's satisfaction at the same level.

PROPERTIES OF INDIFFERENCE CURVE

The diagram of an indefference curve given already is a typical one. From the following paragraphs, it would become clear why indifference curves normally have this shape. Besides, we shall notice the properties of typical indifference curves. There are three characteristics of indifference curves.

(i) Downward sloping to the right,
(ii) Non-interesecting, and
(iii) Convex to the origin.
(iv) Higher IC, higher is the level of satisfaction and vice, versa.

***(i)* Downward Slopping or Negatively Sloped.** To begin with, **an indifference curve slopes downwards from left to the right.** It is because when the consumer decides to have more units of one of the two goods, he will have to reduce the number of the units of the other good, if he is to remain on the same indifference curve, *i.e.*, if level of his satisfaction is to remain the same. Looking at the diagram in Fig. 6.1, we find that when the consumer moves from point A to point B, he has more mangoes than before, but the number of apples with him falls similarly from B to C and from C to D. This is the meaning or implication of an **indifference curve** sloping downwards from left to right.

To be surer of this property, let us for a moment suppose that instead of sloping downward to the right, an indifference curve is a horizontal straight line, as is indicated in the figure given above (Fig. 6.4). This shows that when the consumer is at point A, he has 7 apples and 1 mango and he is at a certain level of satisfaction, and that when he moves from the position A to the position B on the same indifference curve, he remains at the same level of satisfaction despite the fact that he has more of mangoes (*i.e.*, 2) and the same number of apples. This is obviously absurd. After all, the addition of a mango without losing any of the apples he had in the previous position, must take him on to a higher indifference curve rather than keeping him on the old indifference curve.

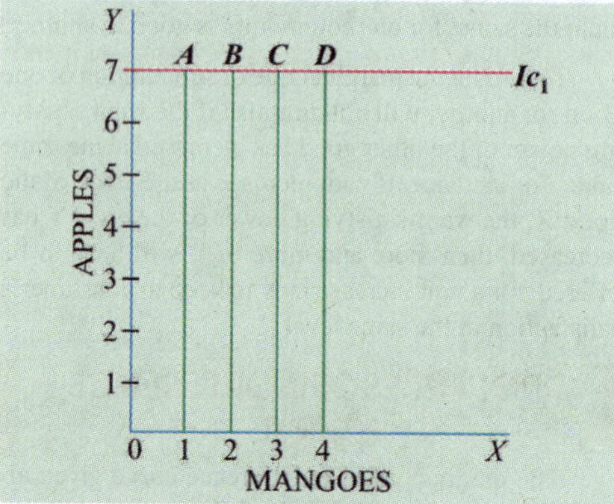

Fig. 6.4. Horizontal indifference curve.

Similarly, if the indifference curve was a vertical straight line (see Figure 6.5 below), it would mean that the consumer remains at the same level of satisfaction even though the quantity of one good increases without the decrease in the quantity of the other. Combinations A and B, for example, lie on the same indifference curve and are, therefore, assumed to yield the same number of mangoes but a greater number of apples as compared with A, give the same satisfaction as A? Hence, an indifference curve cannot be a vertical straight line.

Still another possibility, but still more absurd, is that an indifference curve may slope upwards to the right, as has been shown in diagram No. 6.6. At points A, B and C ...., our hypothetical consumer is at the same level of satisfaction, because he is on the same indifference curve, but what is indeed startling is that he derives the same level of satisfaction when he is at A with 1 mango and 6 apples, and also at B when he has 2 mangoes and 10 apples and also at C with 3 mangoes and 13 apples, *i.e.*, when the units of both goods are increasing. This is absurd. Clearly an indifference curve cannot slope upwards to the right.

Thus, we see that an indifference curve cannot be a horizontal straight line as in Fig. 6.4, nor can it be vertical straight line as in Fig. 6.5, nor sloping upwards as in Fig 6.6. Hence, by process of elimination, we come to the conclusion that an indifference curve must slope downwards to the right. This is its first property.

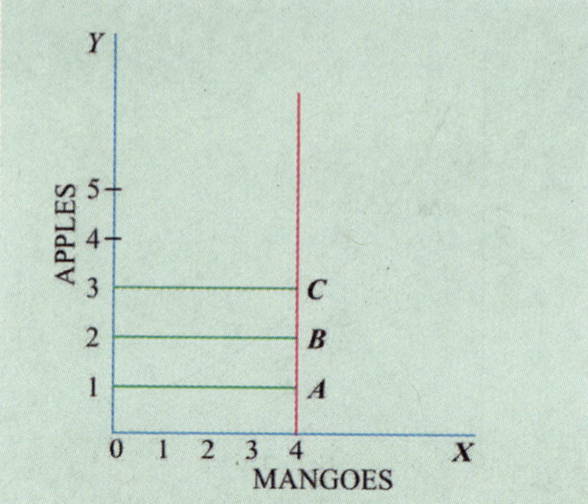

Fig. 6.5. Vertical indifference curve.

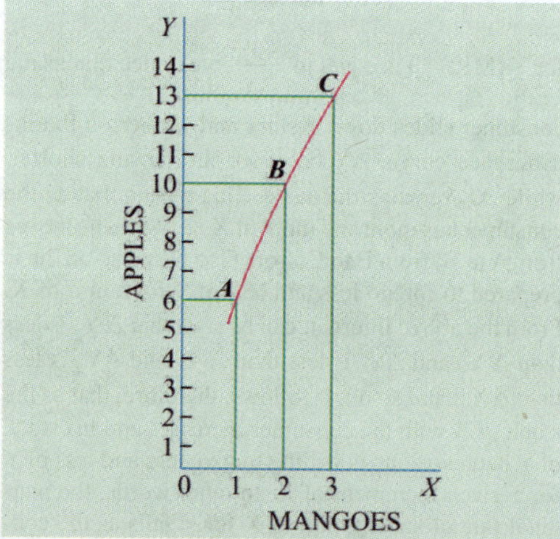

Fig. 6.6. Upward sloping indifference curve.

(*ii*) Non-intersecting. The second property or characteristic of indifference curves is that **no two such curves will ever cut each other.** What absurdity follows when two indifference curves are shown as intersecting each other may be explained with the help of diagram No. 6.7. At point B, our hypothetical consumer is on the indifference curve IC_1, while at point A, he is on the higher indifference curve IC_2, *i.e.*, the combination represented by point A gives him a level of satisfaction higher than that he enjoys when he is at point B. But since the two indifference curves have been shown to be intersecting at point C, it means that point C lies on both indifference curves, which in turn means that C is at once equal to A and B which, as seen already, represent different levels of satisfaction. How can one level be equal to two different levels ? It follows, therefore, that the indifference curves cannot cut each other.

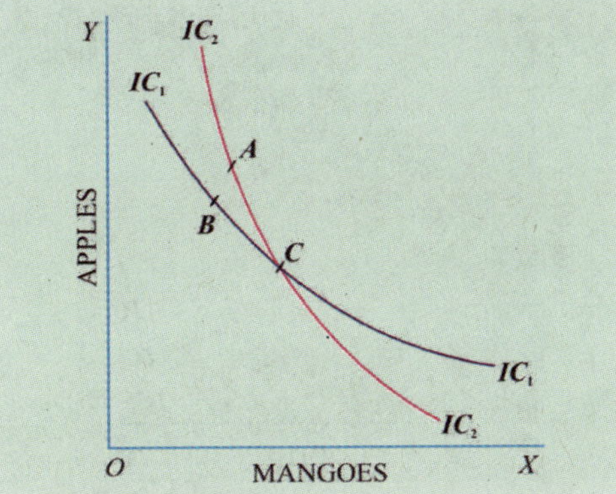

Fig. 6.7. **Indifference curves cannot intersect.**

***(iii)* Convexity.** The third property of indifference curves is that **they are normally convex to the origin.** The implication of this convexity rule is that as we have more and more of good X and less and less of Y, the marginal rate of substitution of X for Y goes on falling. This is exactly what was brought out in the table given to explain the concept of the marginal rate of substitution. (See page 74). There we said that in combination 2 our hypothetical consumer had 11 apples and 2 mangoes. Now when he acquired one mango more, he had to forego 3 apples, *i.e.*, the marginal rate of substitution of mango for apples at that stage was 3 : 1. For a further addition of one mango, the consumer was now prepared to forego a smaller of apples—two this time.

Let us prove convexity by exposing the absurdity if the curve is either convance or a straight line. Three figures of an indifference curve are given below. In Fig. 6.8 (a) the indifference curve is convex to the origin : in Fig. (*b*), it is a straight line, and in Fig. (*c*) it is concave to the origin. From Fig. (*a*) it is evident that the marginal rate of substitution (MRS) of mangoes for apples falls (*cd* is smaller than *ab*). In Fig. (*b*), the MRS of mangoes for apples remains constant (*cd* = *ab*), which is against the normal behaviour of MRS (*i.e.* diminishing). In Fig. (*c*) it actually increases (*cd* is larger than *ab*) which is quite the opposite of the normal behaviour of MRS. We have already seen that normally the marginal rate of substitution of a commodity diminishes as we have more of it. In other words, the normal shape of an indifference curve would be convex to the origin, as in given in Fig. (*a*) below. The other two shapes given in Fig. (*b*) and Fig. (*c*) are unrealistic.

Having studied the concept of indifference curve and its properties, we are now in a position to study the indifference curve analysis of demand.

Substitute Relationship and Convexity

The curvature of the indifference curves reflects the degree of substitutability between the commodities. That is, flatness or straightness of the curves shows to what extent commodities are substitutes for each other. In the case of perfect substitutes, the indifference curves are downward sloping straight lines [Fig. 6.8. (b)], whereas if they are either horizontal (Fig. 6.4), or vertical (Fig. 6.5), the consumer will not be willing to substitute one commodity for another. Goods which can be substituted somewhat (not perfect substitutes) are represented by indifference curves which are somewhat convex to the origin. But greater the degree of convexity, the poorer are the substitutes. The flatter or less convex curves represent better substitutes.

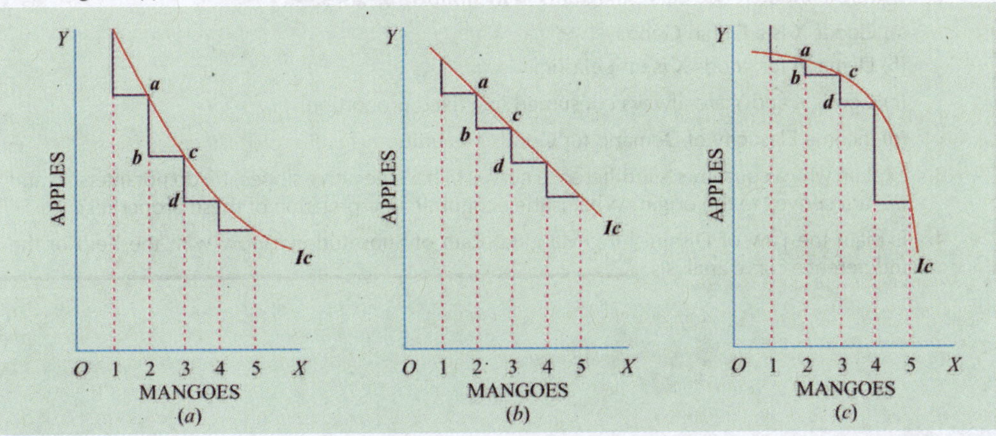

Fig. 6.8. **(*a*) Corex indifference curve implies diminishing MRS.**
(*b*) Straight line indifference curve implies constant MRS.
(*c*) Concave indifference curve implies increasing MRS.

(iv) Lower the indifference curve, lower is the level of satisfaction, and higher the indifference curve, higher is the level of satisfaction.

IC_1

x	y
1	12
2	8
3	5
4	3
5	2

IC_2

x	y
1	18
2	13
3	9
4	6
5	4

IC_3

x	y
1	25
2	19
3	14
4	10
5	7

IC_4

x	y
1	32
2	25
3	19
4	14
5	10

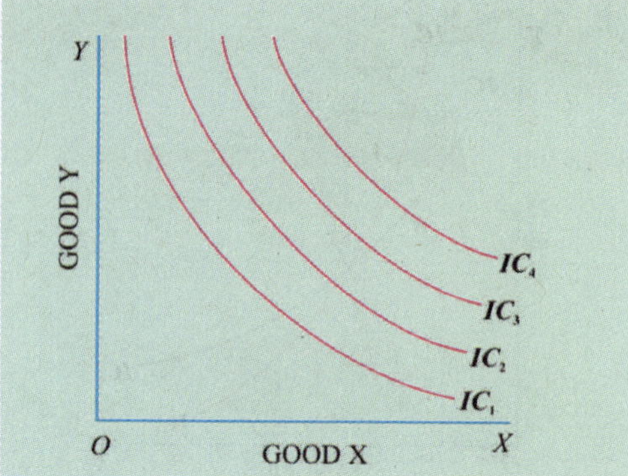

Fig. 6.9. Higher the indifference curve higher is the level of satisfaction.

In the above diagram on x-axis good 'X' and on Y axis-good y is taken. IC_1, IC_2, IC_3, and IC_4 are four different "indifference curves". IC_1 gives lower satisfaction, than IC_2, in the same way the satisfaction increases as we move on to higher level of IC curves.

$$IC_4 > IC_3 > IC_2 > IC_1.$$

Level of satisfaction

Key terms

Completeness, Non-satiation, Transitivity, Continuity, Convexity, Indifference map, Marginal rate of substitution (MRS).

QUESTIONS

1. What are indifference curves? Give their assumptions and properties.
2. Draw the indifference curve diagrams in the following cases:–
   (*a*) Goods X is a Giffan Goods.
   (*b*) Demand for goods X is unit elastic.
   (*c*) Goods X and Y are always consumed in a fixed proportion.
   (*d*) Income Elasticity of Demand for Goods Y is unity.
3. Explain why a consumer's indifference curves (*i*) have negative slopes, (*ii*) do not intersect and (*iii*) are convex to the origin. What is the economic interpretation of these properties?
4. Explain the Law of Diminishing Marginal Rate of Substitution. Show with the help of the indifference curve analysis.

INDIFFERENCE CURVE ANALYSIS OF DEMAND

We now undertake the study of the demand theory with the help of the indifference curve technique. We began with what is known as the price line.

PRICE LINE OR BUDGET LINE

It has already been explained that a higher indifference curve shows a higher level of satisfaction than a lower one. A rational consumer will, therefore, try to reach the highest possible indifference curve in order to obtain the highest possible level of satisfaction. In this pursuit, our consumer will be governed by the amount of the money or income he has to spend on goods, and the prices of the goods in the market. Suppose our consumer has Rs. 15 to spend on apples and mangoes. Further suppose that the price of mangoes in the market is Rs. 1.50 per unit and the price of apples is Re. 1 per unit. With Rs. 15, he can buy 10 (= OM) mangoes and no apples or 15 apples (= OA) and no mangoes (See Fig. 7.1).

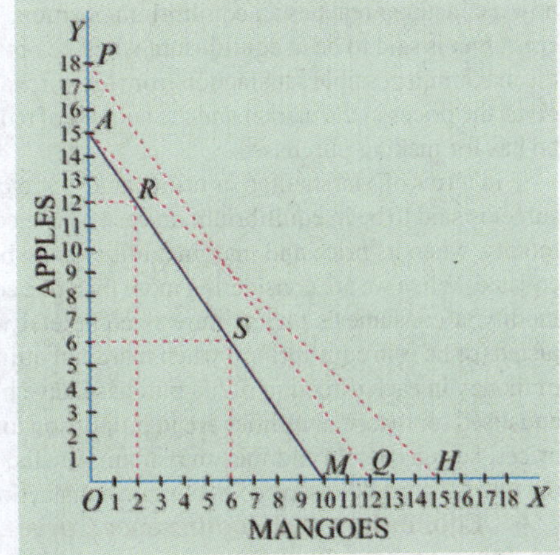

Fig. 7.1. **A budget line of the consumer.**

By joining points A and M, we get what is called **Price Line** or **Price Opportunity Line.** It is also called **Price-income Line** or **Budget Line** or **Budget Constraint Line.** This line shows all possible combinations of two goods (in our case apples and mangoes) that the consumer can buy if he spends the whole of his given sum of money on his purchases at the given prices. Thus, at point R, our consumer will be having 2 mangoes and 12 apples and will be spending all his money (Rs. 15) on the two goods—Rs. 3 on mangoes and Rs. 12 on apples. And at point S, he will be buying 6 mangoes and 6 apples with Rs. 15.

Shifting the Price Line

If money with our consumer increase to Rs. 18, the price line will shift to P.Q. For with Rs. 18, he can buy either 12 mangoes (= OQ) or 18 apples (= OP). prices of mangoes and apples remaining the same. It may be carefully noted that, since prices of mangoes and apples remain unchanged, PQ will be parallel to AM.

If the total amount of money (Rs. 15) and price of apples (Re. 1 per unit) remain the same but the price of mangoes falls from Rs. 1.50 to Re.1 per unit, the price line will shift from AM to AH. AH will not be parallel to AM because the price ratio has changed.

From the above, it follows that the shape and the position of the price line will depend on two factors : **(1)** the total amount of money a consumer has for purchasing goods ; and **(2)** price ratio of the goods in market.

The slope of the price line may be distinguished from the slope of the indifference curve. The slope of the price line is (the negative of) the price ratio, *i.e.*, the ratio of the price of X to the price of Y. But the slope of the indifference curve at any point is called the marginal rate of substitution of X for Y. The marginal rate of substitution gives the rate at which the consumer is **willing to substitute** X for Y, whereas the price ratio shows the rate at which he can substitute X for Y.

CONSUMER'S EQUILIBRIUM OR MAXIMISING SATISFACTION

Let us explain, with the help of indifference curve, how a consumer reaches an equilibrium position. The consumer is said to be in equilibrium when he obtains the maximum possible satisfaction from his purchases, given the prices in the market and the amount of money he has for making purchases.

In terms of Marshallian or utility analysis, a consumer is said to be in equilibrium, in case of one commodity, when its price and marginal utility have been equated. When we are considering more than one commodity, a consumer's expenditure is completely adjusted (or he is in equilibrium) when marginal utilities of money in each direction of his purchase have been equalised (or marginal utilities are in proportion to the prices, see chapter 5) and thus maximum satisfaction obtained according to law of maximum satisfaction.

Equilibrium with Indifference Curves. Let us now consider how a consumer reaches an equilibrium position with the help of indifference curves.

In order to explain how a consumer reaches equilibrium position, we shall make the following assumptions :

(*i*) our consumer has an indifference map showing his scale of preferences for various combinations of the two goods—apples and mangoes. This scale of preferences remains the same throughout the analysis;

(*ii*) he has a given and constant amount of money to spend on the goods and if he does not spend it on one good, he must spend it on the other ;

(*iii*) prices of the goods in the market are given and constant ;

(*iv*) each of the goods is homogenous and divisible ; and

(*v*) the consumer acts rationally, that is, he tries to maximise his satisfaction.

Suppose our consumer has an indifference map, shows in the following diagram (Fig. 7.2). Further suppose that the price line facing the consumer is AM, given a certain amount of money he has to spend on apples and mangoes and the prices of apples and mangoes in the market. Since his income and the relative prices of the two goods to be purchased are shown by the price-income line AM, his equilibrium must be on some point on this line. That is why this line is called the price-opportunity line. It is this line that contains all the possible opportunities of combining the two goods that are open to our hypothetical consumer. Any point not lying on this price line cannot be a possible equilibrium point, because his present price-income situation will not allow him to move on to that point (or purchase that combination).

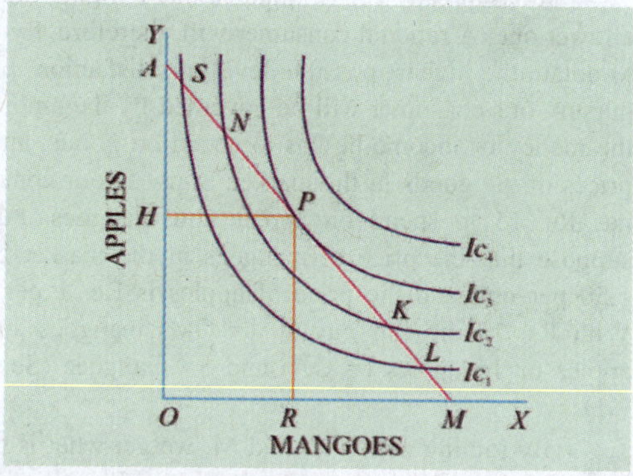

Fig. 7.2. Equilibrium of the consumer.

Actually, the consumer will be in equilibrium at the point P, i.e., he will be buying OR mangoes and OH apples. **The consumer will maximise his satisfaction and be in equilibrium at a point where the price line touches (or a tangent to) an indifference curve.** Such a point in our diagram is P which lies on indifference curve IC_3. This is the highest indifference curve to which he can go, given the money he has and the prices of the goods in the market. Given a price line, there can only be one point such as P, since no two indifference curves can cut one another and all are convex to the origin. Any combination other than P on the given price can be shown to give less satisfaction to the consumer, for all other points on the price line must lie on indifference curves of a lower order that on which P lies.

Thus, if our consumer chooses a combination of mangoes and apples represented by S, he will be on a lower indifference curve IC_1 and will thus be getting less satisfaction than when he choose the point P and is on a higher indifference curve IC_3. The combination represented by point N will also give him less satisfaction, because it lies on indifference curve IC_2, which is also lower than IC_3 at which P lies. Similarly, all other points on the price line to the left of P will be less attractive in the estimation of our consumer than P. Likewise on all points to the right of P on the price line AM, such as K and L, the consumer will not be in equilibrium because all of them lie on indifference curves lower than IC_3.

In equilibrium at point P, the marginal rate of substitution (MRS) of mangoes for apples is equal to the price ratio between these two goods, since both the indifference curve IC_3 and the price line AM have the same slope at point P (MRS of mangoes for apples is given by the slope of the indifference curve and the price ratio is given by the slope of the price line AM). Thus, at point P.

$$\text{MRS. of mangoes for apples} = \frac{\text{Price of mangoes}}{\text{Prices of apples}}$$

Conditions of Equilibrium

Thus, two conditions must be satisfied for a consumer to attain an equilibrium :

(1) The price line should be tangent to an indifference curve or MRS of one commodity for another should be equal to their relative prices. This is no doubt a necessary condition, but not a sufficient condition of equilibrium. For attaining equilibrium another condition must also be satisfied as under :

(2) At the point of equilibrium an indifference curve must be convex to the origin. We have already explained the implication of convexity to the origin, which is that MRS is falling. Thus, if the indifference curve is convex to the origin at the equilibrium point, it means that, at or near the point of equilibrium, the MRS of mangoes for apples is falling. In the preceding diagram (Fig. 7.2) showing consumer's equilibrium, this second condition is also being fulfilled at the point P.

If by some chance, the indifference curve is not convex to the origin at the point where the price line is tangent to the indifference curve, as shown in the following diagram (Fig. 7.3), equilibrium at such a point is not possible. At point R, for instance, the price

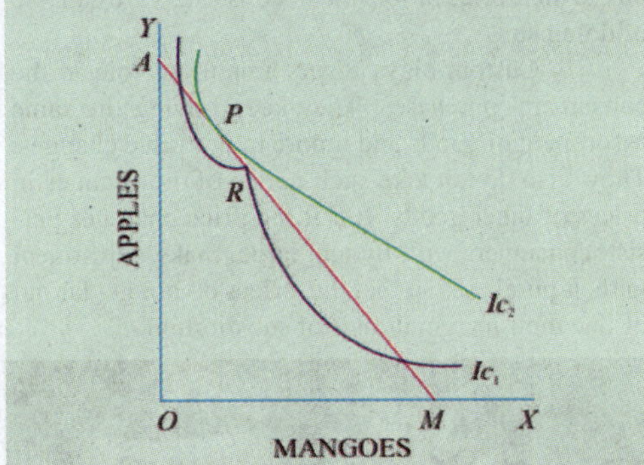

Fig,. 7.3. Strict convexity and tangency.

line is no doubt tangential to indifference curve IC_1, but in a region of the curve where it is concave to the origin rather that being convex. Here the MRS of mangoes for apples in increasing rather than decreasing. Why should he stop at point R when the MRS of mangoes for apples is still rising above the relative money prices of mangoes and apples ? On the price line AM, there can be other points at which higher indifference curves may be tangential to it. For example, IC_2, which is higher than IC_1 is tangential to the price line AM at P. Points like P will naturally be preferred to point R.

Conclusion. Thus, the point of consumer's equilibrium or of maximum satisfaction may be defined by the condition that the marginal rate of substitution between any pair of two commodities will be equal to the ratio of their prices, or (what can be deduced from it), the marginal rate of substitution of money for any commodity is equal to the price of the commodity. That is, the slope of the price line and that of the indifference curve must coincide (the former is a tangent to the latter). In other words, there must be a coincidence between the rate at which the consumer is **willing to substitute** X for Y (as depicted in the indifference curve) and the rate at which **he can substitute** (as indicated by the price line). If these two ratios are not equal, it will be possible, by changing the combination of X and Y, to reach a still higher level of satisfaction.

How far is this theory of consumer behaviour valid ?

The question is : 'How far does this theory explain the actual behaviour of real consumers in the real markets ?' Now, every rational consumer will tend to act on this principle, but the actual behaviour may not conform to it for several reasons :

(i) Few consumers actually equate consciously the marginal rates of substitution of the things they buy to their price ratio. Not all consumers are capable of doing so.

(ii) Custom plays a very important role in the consumers' purchases. They keep buying the same assortment of goods and ignore minor price changes. They also do not take such notice of the changes in prices of other goods. But if the price chan ges persist, consumers will, by and large, make adjustment in their purchases so that the prices do not get far out of line their marginal rates of substitution.

Price changes do not affect purchases to observe customs.

(iii) Many commodities are indivisible preventing precise price adjustments.

(iv) Another fact which prevents exact balancing between prices and the marginal rates of substitution is that no consumer purchases all commodities. If a commodity cannot figure in a consumer's purchase, the marginal rate of substitution of money for such a commodity is zero, and is not equal to the price.

(v) Not many consumers have the time or the energy to be devoted to the working out the precise balancing of their expenditure in the light of price changes. Only a rough balance between prices and marginal rates of substitution can be expected.

Conclusion. Considering all these limitations, the theory of consumer's equilibrium must be regarded only a rough approximation to the actual consumer behaviour.

INCOME EFFECT

Let us consider the effect on consumer's equilibrium of a change in consumer's income, relative prices of commodities remaining the same. This is called 'income effect.'

Income effect is the effect on the quantity demanded exclusively as a result of change in money income, all prices remaining constant. It has been shown above how a consumer reaches his equilibrium position with a fixed income and given and constant market prices of the two commodities. But the question arises what will happen to the consumer's equilibrium and the amounts of the two commodities bought if his income were to change while prices of the commodities remain the same. Obviously, as a result of a change in income, his satisfaction will either increase or diminish, for he has now a larger or smaller income to spend. The result ofthis type of change is described in technical language as **income effect.**

The income effect has been explained with the help of diagram No. 7.4. With price-income line $L_1 M_1$, the consumer is in equlibrium at point P_1. Now suppose the income of the consumer increases so that his new price-income line is $L_2 M_2$. As a result of this increase in income, the consumer will move to a new equilibrium position, at the point P_2, on a higher indifference curve C_2 and will be buying OH_2 of commodity X and OQ_2 of commodity Y. Thus the consumer will get on to a higher level of satisfaction as a result of an increase in his income.

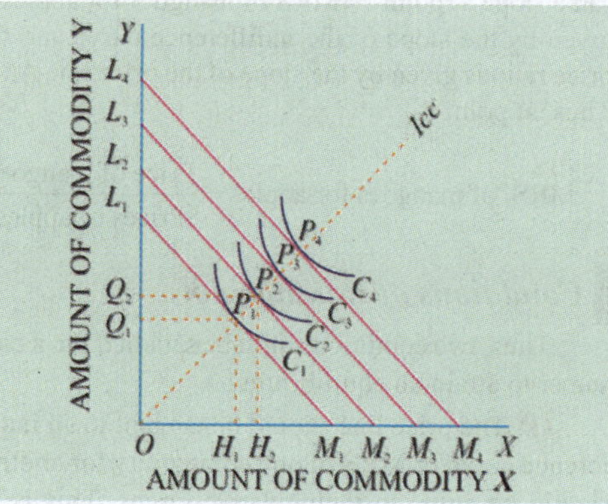

Fig. 7.4. Income Effect.

If his income increases still further, so that the new price income line becomes $L_3 M_3$, he will be in equilibrium at the Point P_3 on an indifference curve C_3, and so on for further increase in income.

Thus, we get various point of equilibrium such as P_1, P_2, P_3 for different levels of income, prices of the commodities remaining the same. If the points P_1, P_2, P_3, P_4, etc., are joined together by a line passing from the origin, we get, what is called **Income Consumption Curve. (ICC)**

The Income Consumption Curve shows how the consumption of two goods is affected by change in income when prices of both goods are given and constant. **An income consumption curve thus traces out the income as the consumer's income changes, with given relative prices of the two goods.**

Our general observation of how consumers react to an increase in their incomes suggests that most income consumption curves are of the shape presented in Fig. 7.4, *i.e.*, slopping upwards to the right. This means that, as a rule, a rise in consumer's income will make him buy more of each of any two goods he is consuming. This is the usual shape of the income consumption curve.

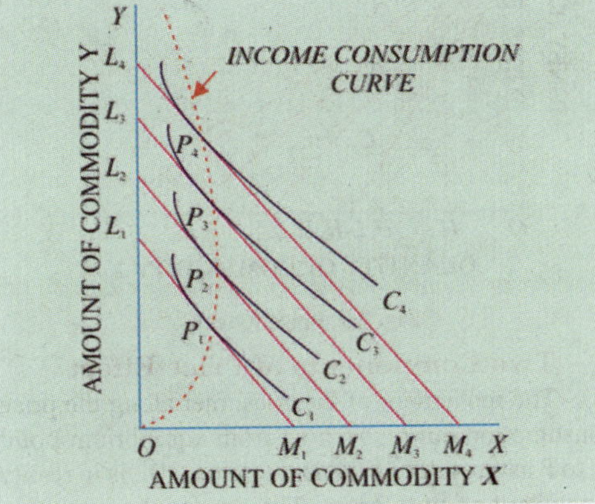

Fig. 7.5 (*a*). Income Effect: Inferior Good X.

In diagram 7.5 (*a*), however, the income consumption curve begins to move towards the OY axis on which we measure Y, showing that after a certain point, as income rises, less of X is bought. In diagram 7.5 (*b*), the curve bends towards the OX axis on which we measure X, showing that as income increases, after a point, less of Y is bought. Income consumption curves of these shapes, while rare, are not unknown. For example, it has been observed in India that when the income of a poor villager increases, he may buy less of coarser grains like millets and substitute for them superior kinds of grain like wheat or rice.

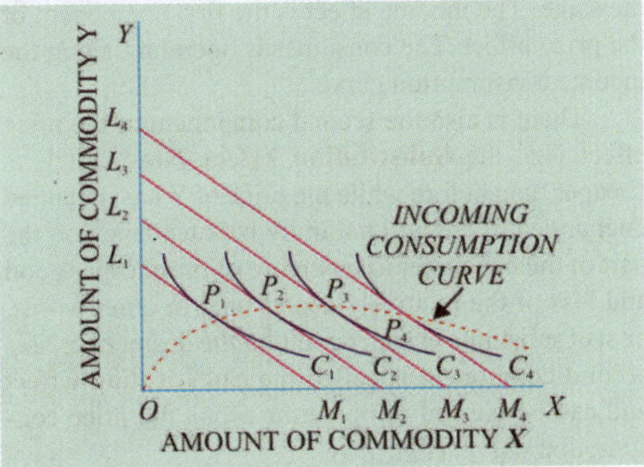

Fig. 7.5 (*b*). Income Effect: Inferior Good Y.

Inferior Goods. Those goods of which the quantity that the consumer would buy less, as his income rises, are called **inferior goods.** Thus, in diagram 7.5 (a), good X and in diagram 7.5 (b), good Y are inferior goods. Inferior goods may, therefore, be defined as goods for which income effect is negative.

SUBSTITUTION EFFECT

We have discussed above the effect on consumer's equilibrium of a change in consumer's income, relative of commodities remaining the same. Now let us see the effect of a change in relative prices, consumer's income remaining the same. This leads us to the study of what is known as the **Substitution Effect.** Substitution effect means the change in the quantity of a good purchased which is due only to the change in relative prices, money income remaining constant.

When prices of a good, say, X, falls, real income of the consumer would increase. In order to find out the change in the quantity of X purchased, which is attributable only to the change in the relative price of X, the consumer 's money must be reduced by an amount so as to cancel out the gain in real income that results from price decrease. This is necessary for us to know the effect of only a change in relative prices, consumer's income remaining the same. The amount by which the money income is reduced, so that the consumer should be neither better off nor worse off than before (*i.e* his income remains the same), is called **Compensating Variation in Income**.

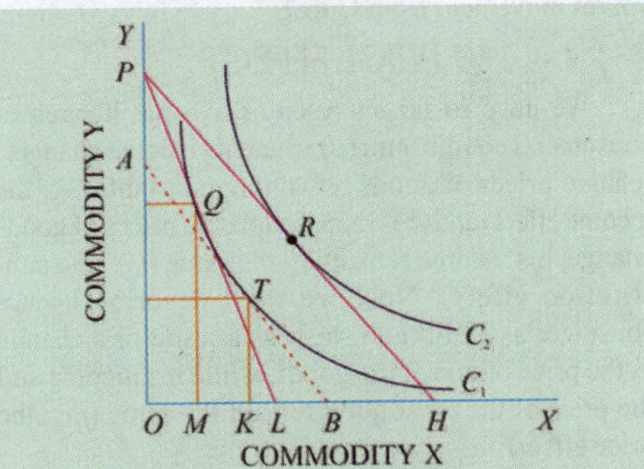

Fig. 7.6. Substitution effect is the change in quantity due to change in relative price when the utility level is held constant after compensating variation in income.

Even after compensating for the gain in real in come, the consumer would still buy more of X, because X has become relatively cheaper. **This increase in the amount purchased of X, because of the fall in its relative price, is the substitution effect.**

Thus, the substitution effect can be defined as a change in the quantity demanded as a result of a change in relative price after the consumer has beep compensated for a change in his real income. That is, there is a movement along the original indifference curve, real income remaining the same.

The substitution effect can be explained easily with the help of Fig. 7.6 given on this page. In this Fig., the consumer is in equilibrium at point Q where the given price is PL is tangent to indifference curve C_1. When the price of X falls, while the price of Y remains the same, the price line will shift to PH (because now more of X is purchased) and the consumer will be in equilibrium at R, where the new price line PH touches the indifference curve C_2. To find out the substitution effect, we draw a hypothetical price line AB parallel to the price line PH so that it (*i.e.*, AB) should touch the indifference cuve C_1. Slope of AB or PH shows the changed relative prices of X and Y. In terms of this diagram, BH or AP is the amount of money income that should be taken away from the consumer so that the gain in real income which results from the fall in the price of X is cancelled out. With price line AB, the consumer is in equlibrium at T on indifference curve C_1. At the point T, he gets the same satisfaction as at Q, because both Q and T are situated on the same indifference curve C_1. Movement from Q to T on the same indifference curve C_1 is due only to the relative fall in the price of X. At the point T, the consumer buys MK more (at Q he bought OM but at T he buys OK) of X than at Q as X is not relatively cheaper. This MK is the substitution effect which involves movement from Q to T.

PRICE EFFECT

We have so far analysed as to what happen to consumer's equilibrium (*a*) when his income changes, relative prices of goods remaining constant (*i.e.*, the income effect) and (*b*) when the relative prices of goods change, his income remaining the same (*i.e.*, the substitution effect). Now we shall describe how a consumer's equilibrium shifts as a result of a change in the price of one of the goods, while his income and the price of the other good remain the same (*i.e.*, the price effect).

Suppose, with a certain fixed income and given market prices of the two goods X and Y represented by the price-income line ML_1, the consumer is in equilibrium at point P_1 in diagram (see Fig. 7.7) Suppose the price of X falls, income and price of Y remaining unchanged, so that new price-income line becomes ML_2, the consumer will be in equilibrium at point P_2 on the higher indifference curve C_2. In this position, he will be buying OH_2 of commodity X. If the price of X falls further, so that the relevant price line is ML_3 the consumer will be in equilibrium at point P_3 and will be buying OH_3 of commodity X. In the same way, we can discover other points of equilibrium for every other price at which X might be sold. When all the points such as P_1, P_2, P_3, P_4, are joined together we have the **price consumption curve** of the consumer for good X. This shows the **price effect. It shows how the consumption of commodity X changes, as its price changes, the consumer's income and price of Y remaining the same.**

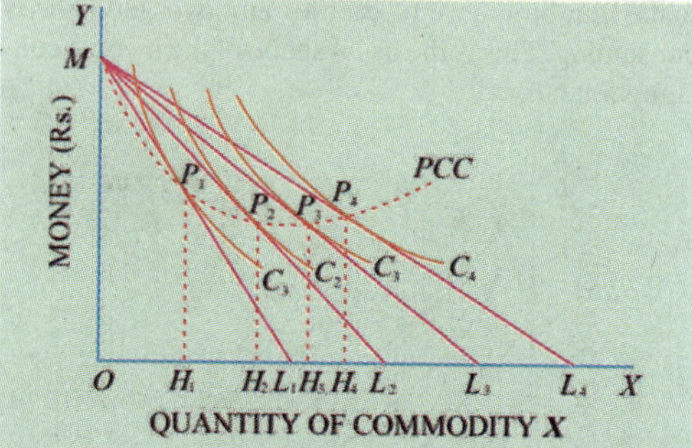

Fig. 7.7. Price Effect.

Two Components of Price Effect

The movement of the consumer along the price consumption curve, such as from equilibrium point P_1 to P as a result of a fall in the price of X, is in reality a resultant of two forces. The first of these components is the feeling of better-offness that a consumer experiences when the price of X falls. There is an increase in the potential purchasing power of the consumer's income following a relative fall in the price of X. It is **Income Effect.** It is as if his income has increased and the price of both goods has remained the same. The income effect is the first component of the price effect. The consumer is operating along the income consumption curve.

There is also the second component of the price effect viz., the **Substitution Effect.** Now that X is cheaper than before while the price of Y has remained unchanged, there will naturally be a tendency on the part of the consumer to buy more of the cheaper good and less of the relatively dearer one. In other words, he will substitute cheaper good for the dearer one. This second component is called the **Substitution Effect** and can be viewed as operating along the price consumption curve. (Fig. 7.8)

These two components of the movement from P_1 to P_2 are shown in Fig. 7.8. Initially with the price-income line ML_1, the consumer is in equilibrium at point P_1. With a fall in price of X, so that the new relevant price-income line is ML_2 he moves to a new equilibrium position P_2 on a higher indifference curve C_2. RS is a hypothetical price-income line drawn parallel to ML_1 and touching the higher indifference curve C_2 at point T. RS shows as if the price of X had

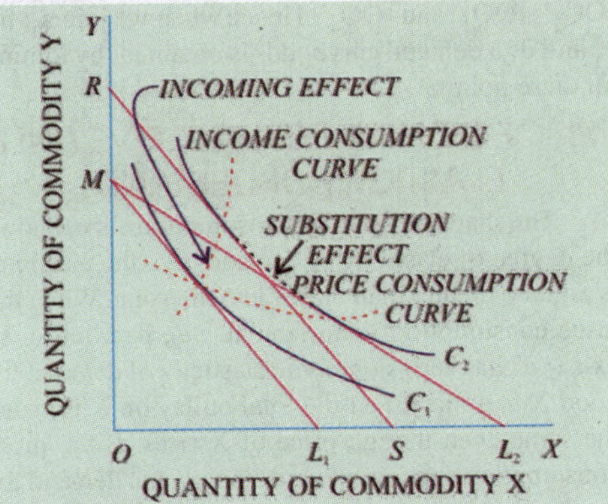

Fig. 7.8. Price Effect = Income Effect + Subsitution Effect.

remained the same (as represented by ML_1), but instead consumer's income had increased by an amount just sufficient to make the consumer as well-off as he is at point P_2, when his money income remains the same but price of X is lower than at P_1. As RS touches the higher indifference curve at T, the line passing through P_1T is the income consumption curve of the consumer.

The line PT shows both the magnitude and the direction of the income effect. The portion TP_2 of the higher indifference curve C_2 shows the direction and magnitude of the substitution effect. The substitution effect means that the cheaper good X is substituted for the dearer good Y.

The splitting up of the price effect into substitution effect and income effect is very useful in bringing out clearly the response of a consumer to a change in price of a commodity. This response will reveal itself through substitution effect and the income effect. The difference between the two may be clearly understood. The substitution effect is always positive. That is, if the price of a good falls, more of it will be purchased and substituted for other goods whose prices have not fallen. Thus, the direction of the substitution effect is very clear and certain. But we cannot be so sure of the income effect. The income effect may be positive (*i.e.*, more of the good may be purchased if the income goes up) or it may be negative (*i.e.*, increase in income may lead to less being purchased of a good). This will happen if the consumer regards it as an inferior good. Thus, the substitution effect and the income effect may move in the same direction *i.e.*, they may both be positive. In that case, the positive income effect will reinforce the positive substitution effect in increasing the demand for a good the price of which has fallen.

But in some cases, the substitution effect and the income effect pull in opposite directions. That is, the substitution effect is positive, as it generally is but the income effect may be negative. In that case, the negative income effect may dilute or negative altogether the positive substitution effect. That is, the demand for the commodity, whose price has fallen, may not much increase or it may diminish instead of increasing as in the Giffen case given below. Hence, the direction in which the quantity demanded of a good will change as a result of a fall in its price will depend upon the direction and strength of the income effect on the one hand and the strength of the substitution effect on the other.

Ordinary Inferior Goods

If the positive substitution effect over weighs the negative income effect, the net result would be an increase in the quantity of the good bought when its price falls. This will be so in case of ordinary inferior goods.

Giffen Goods

If, on the other hand, the negative income effect for a good is so powerful that it more than offsets the positive substitution effect, the net result would be a fall in the quantity of the good bought as its relative price falls. The latter case holds good in case of what are known as **"Giffen Goods."** [1]

Giffen Goods are inferior goods, because in their case, income effect is negative; but they are a special type of inferior goods in as much as in their case negative income effect is stronger than positive substitution effect. In the case of ordinary inferior goods, the negative income effect is weaker than the positive substitution effect.

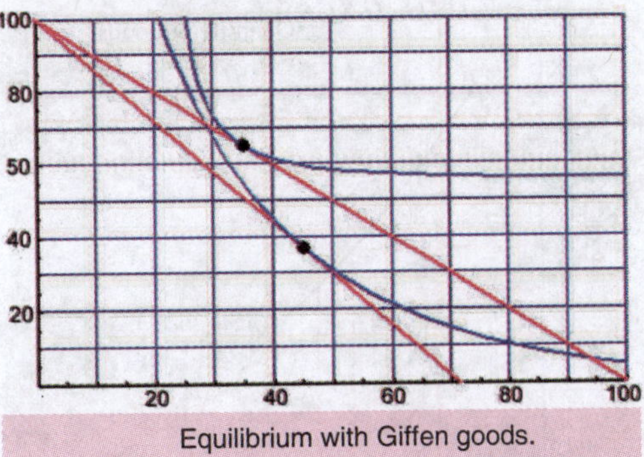

Equilibrium with Giffen goods.

The following three conditions are essential to put a good in the category of Giffen goods:

(*i*) It should be an inferior good having a large negative income effect.

1. So named after Sir Robert Giffen of Britain, who, in the mid-19th century, is said to have observed that when the price of bread rose the poor bought more bread and less meat and less of some other more expensive food stuffs.

(ii) The substitution effect of a price change must be small.

(iii) It must be an inferior good which absorbs a large proportion of the consumers' income.

Derivation of demand curve from price consumption curve

In Fig. 7.9., specially the upper part Y-axis money and X-axis quantity. A consumer has OP′ amount of income which he spends on good 'X' that means his budget line is 'OA', and it is tangent to in difference curve 'IC' at point 'a' like this as price of 'X' decreases, a consumer's budget line shifts from 'OA' to 'OB', 'OC' and 'OD', in the same way consumer moves on to higher indifference curves and they are tangent to their respective budget line. In figure IC_2, IC_3 and IC_4 are tangent to budget line, 'PB', 'PC' and 'PD' at point 'b', 'c' and 'd'. When we join all these points we get 'PCC' curve that is 'Price Consumption Curve'.

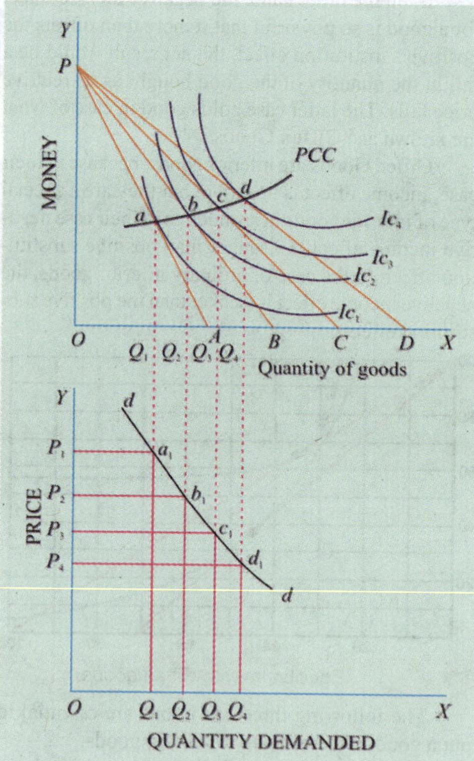

Fig. 7.9. Demand curve from PCC.

In the lower figure we take Y-axis as price, and X-axis as quantity demanded, when we draw per pendicular lines we get points 'a_1', 'b_1', 'c_1' and 'd_1', which shows relation between price OP_1, OP_2, OP_3 and OP_4 and the corresponding demand curve 'OQ_1', 'OQ_2', 'OQ_3' and 'OQ_4', Hence when we join a_1, b_1, c_1 and d_1 a demand curve 'dd' is obtained, by joining all these points.

PRICE CONSUMPTION CURVE AND ELASTICITY OF DEMAND

The shape of the price consumption curve shows the degree of elasticity of demand, *i.e.*, the elasticity is unitary, greater than one or less than one. When the price consumption is horizontal, *i.e.*, parallel to X-axis (*i.e.*, has zero slope), the elasticity of demand for good X is unitary, *i.e.*, the total outlay on X remains the same even though price of X rises. If the price consumption curve is upward sloping, the demand for the good X is inelastic; and if it is downwards sloping, the demand will be elastic.

Derivation of Individual Demand Curve

In an earlier chapter (Ch. 6), we drew a demand curve showing the various quantities of the commodity purchased at different prices. In this section, we shall describe how an ordinary demand curve of an individual consumer can be derived from his given indifference map and the size of his income.

In the earlier chapter, the demand curve was drawn on the Marshallian assumptions of utility being measurable and the marginal utility of money being constant. In the indifference curve technique, demand curve is arrived at without making these dubious assumptions.

A demand curve has been defined as the curve showing how much of a good would be bought at various prices–assuming that tastes and preferences and income of the consumer are given and constant and so are the prices of all other goods.

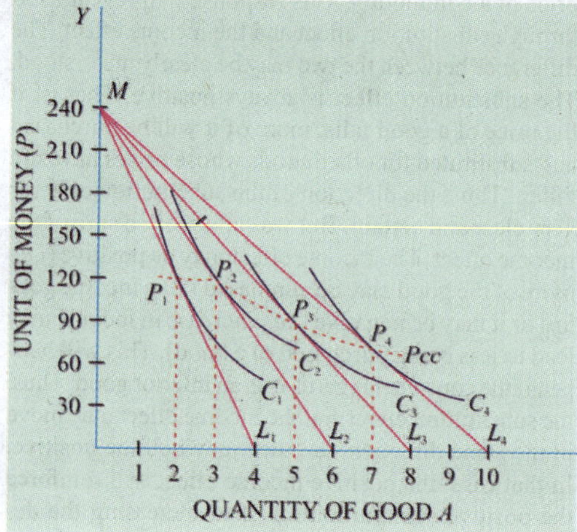

Fig. 7.10. Price consumption curve.

A little thinking will show that an individual's demand curve for a good must be related in some way to his price consumption curve for that good. In fact, both give the same information except that the former gives it directly and in a more useful form. The way in which ordinary demand curve can be drawn from price consumption curve is explained with the help of Fig. 7.10. When a demand curve is to be drawn, units of money are measured on one axis, while amounts of a good for which demand curve is to be drawn are shown on the other axis. In the above diagram, the units of money are shown on the Y-axis and the commodity A, for which the demand curve is to be drawn, is shown on the X-axis.

Suppose a consumer has a daily income of 240 P.[2] If the price of commodity A is 60 P. per unit, the relevant price-income line will be ML_1 because, at this price, 4 units can be purchased with 240 Paise. The consumer will be in equilibrium at the point P_1 of the price consumption curve PCC, because at this point the price line ML_1 is tangent to the indifference curve C_1, and will buy or demand 2 units of the commodity A. Suppose the price falls to 40 P. The relevant price line becomes ML_2 (because now 6 units can be purchased with 240 Paise). Now the consumer will be in equilibrium at point P_2 of the price consumption curve on a higher indifference curve C_2 and will buy 3 units. Similarly, the consumer will buy 5 units of the good when price is 30P., and 7 units when price is 24 P.

With the above information, we can draw up the **demand schedule** of a consumer as follows:

Table 1: Individual's Demand Schedule

Price Line	*Price*	*Quantity Demanded*
ML_1	$\frac{240}{4} = 60$ P.	2 units
ML_2	$\frac{240}{6} = 40$ P.	3
ML_3	$\frac{240}{8} = 30$ P.	5
ML_4	$\frac{240}{10} = 24$ P.	7

Now we can easily convert this demand schedule into an ordinary demand curve. By plotting the above data, we get points like Q_1, Q_2, Q_3, Q_4, (Fig. 7.11). By joining these points with a continuous curve, we get the usual demand curve of the consumer for the commodity A, We see that the demand curve drawn slopes downward from left to right as usual. This is the typical shape of the demand curve.

2. We have taken daily income, and the demand curve which we shall draw will show the demand of the consumer for the good per day. Demand is always with referemce to a certain period of time.

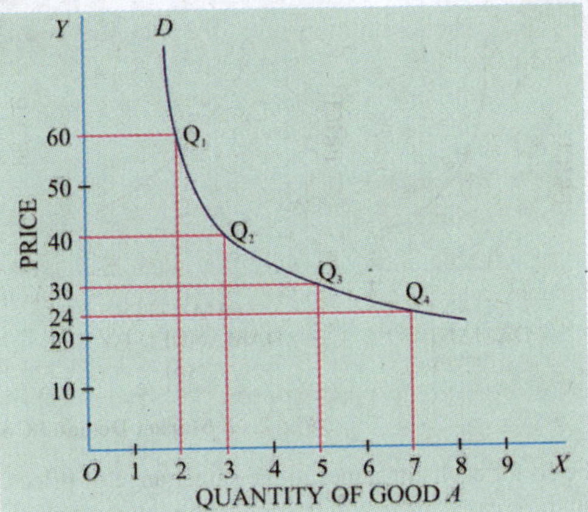

Fig. 7.11. Demand Curve.

If we had derived a demand curve for a 'Giffen Good', it would have sloped upwards from left to right because of the fact, which we have discussed earlier, that in case of Giffen Goods there is a positive relationship between price and the quantity demanded.

DERIVATION OF MARKET DEMAND CURVE

We have derived above the demand curve of a single consumer. But for price determination it is the market demand curve which is relevant. The market demand curve for a commodity is obtained by adding together the demands of all consumers who plan to buy it. The way in which this summation is effected is illustrated in Fig. 7.12. Figure (*a*), (*b*) and (*c*) show the demand of three separate and independent consumers. We get the market demand curve by adding together the quantities that each consumer wishes to buy at each price. Thus, at the price, OP_1, the consumer A's demand is a_1, B's b_1 and C's C_1. The total quantity of the commodity that all consumers demand at the price OP_1 is, therefore, **a** plus **b** plus **c** and this quantity is plotted against P_1 in Fig. (*d*) above. In the same fashion, we can discover the quantity demanded by all the three consumers at any other price. When all the points like Q are joined together, we get a market demand curve for the commodity. In our analysis, we have supposed that there are three consumers in the market. But the method will apply to any number of consumers.

The market demand curve will slope downwards to the right as individual demand curves slope downwards to the right. It is very rarely that market demand curve will slope upwards from left to right. A good may be a Giffen good for a single consumer, but it is seldom that any good will be a Giffen good for all consumers. And even if it is, it is unlikely that it will

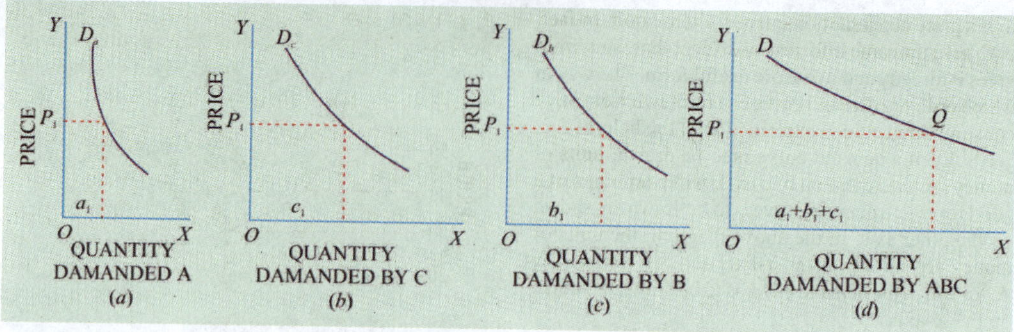

Fig. 7.12. Market Demand Curve from Individual Demand Curve.

be so for each consumer in the same range of prices. In these cases, there will generally be enough consumers who increase their quantity demanded of the good as price falls to compensate for those consumers who buy less because for them the good is a 'Giffen good' in that range of prices.

CASE OF COMPETITIVE (OR SUBSTITUTE) GOODS AND COMPLEMENTARY GOODS

The indifference curve technique has been found very useful in explaining the demand for substitutes and complementary goods. This has been facilitated by the splitting up of the price effect into its two components, *viz*., the income effect and the substitution effect. Before Hicks used the indifference curve technique for this purpose, the demand for substitutes and complementary goods was explained in terms of total price effect, or the cross elasticity of demand. According to this approach, if the price of a good, say, X, falls and consequently the demand for it increases, the demand for the other good Y decreases, then Y is said to be substitute for X. If, on the other hand, with the fall in price of X and the resultant increase in demand for it, the quantity demanded of Y also increases, Y is said to be a complement of X.

But according to Hicks, taking the income effect into account, then even with the fall in price of X, the demand for Y may also increase even though Y may be a competitive or substitute good. This is due to the fact that when the price of X falls, there may be a large income effect which may more than offset the substitution effect. Owing to income effect of the fall in price of X the demand for Y also tends to increase. This income effect may be much stronger than the substitution effect of the fall in price of X. That is why the demand for Y may increase side by side with increase in demand for X.

But we must eliminate the income effect of the price change, by making a compensating variation in income in order to arrive at a correct or accurate effect on the demand for substitute goods as a result of all in price in one of them. Using the indifference curve technique, we can now define substitute goods and complementary goods in this way. If with a fall in price of X, price of Y remaining the same, the demand for X increases due to the substitution effect and demand for Y decreases then Y is a substitute for X, income of the consumer having been reduced by compensating variation in income so that he is no better off than before. On the other hand, if with a fall in price of X and after making compensating variation in income, the demand for X increases due to the substitution effect, and along with it if the demand for Y also increases then Y is said to be a complement of X.

Thus, in the case of complementary goods, the quantity demanded of both goods increases and both of them are substituted for some other goods or goods. Professor Hicks defines the substitutes and complements thus: "I shall say Y is a substitute of X if a fall in the price of X leads to a fall in the consumption of Y: Y is a complement of X if a fall in price of X leads to a rise in the consumption of Y; a compensating variation in income being made of course in each case."[3]

There is, however, one point to be borne in mind. While the relationship of substitutes can occur only in the case of two goods, complementary relationship must involve more than two goods. In the case of two goods, the substitution effect always works in favour of the good whose price has fallen and against the other goods, *i.e.*, it tends to increase the demand for one good and reduce the demand for the other. But the case of complementarity can arise only if there are at least three goods. As Professor Hicks observes: "If consumer is dividing his income between purchases of two goods only and cannot buy any other goods than these two, then there cannot be anything else but a substitution relation between the two goods. For if he

3. Hicks, J. R. — *A Revision of Demand Theory* 1956. p 128

is to get more of one of them and still be no better off than before, he must have less of the other. But when he is dividing his income between more than two goods other kinds of relation becomes possible."

It is also worth remembering regarding the relation of substitution that all goods in a consumer's budget can be substituted for one another, but all cannot be complements. For instance, if the price of a good falls demand for it increases and the demand for other goods will decline.

Thus, we see that complementarity between a group of commodities is possible only when there is at least one commodity outside the group of complements, at whose expense the substitution in favour of the group of complement can occur. In other words out of a given number of commodities in a consumer's budget, at least one of them must be substitute for them while all other may be complements of each other. This is one extreme limit of complementrity . The other extreme limit is one where there may be no complementarity present at all, *i.e.*, all goods are substitutes for each other. In the words of Stonier and Hague. "Where there is any number of goods (n) at least one of those goods must be competitive with that in which we are interested. It could conceivably happen that all the remaining $n-2$ goods were complementary with it, but this is unlikely. It will of course be quite possible for $n-1$ of any collection of goods to be competitive with the remaining good." [4]

INDIFFERENCE CURVE TECHNIQUE VERSUS MARSHALLIAN UTILITY ANALYSIS

Whereas the indifference curve approach and the utility analysis, are similar in some respects, the former is superior to the latter in several respects:

Similarities

The two approaches are similar in the following respects:–

(i) Both approaches assume a rational behaviour on the part of the consumer in that he seeks to attain a position of equilibrium by maximising satisfaction.

(ii) Both techniques embody the same proportionality rule for the consumer to maximise satisfaction or reach an equilibrium position (see p. 67).

(iii) Both approaches assume diminishing utility –diminishing marginal utility in one case and diminishing marginal rate of substitution in another case.

(iv) Both approaches apply the psychological or introspective method. The law of diminishing utility, which is psychological in nature, lies at the bottom of law of demand. It is based on introspection. The indifference curve technique, too, is based on introspection. Thus, both approaches are introspective.

Superiority of the Indifference Curve Technique

The indifference curve technique is superior to the Marshallian utility analysis in several respects:

(*i*) More Realistic Measurement of Utility. Marshall explained consumer's behaviour assuming that utility is **measurable** and **additive** just as the weight or length of objects is measurable and additive. The consumer was, thus, assumed by Marshall to possess, what modern economists call, **'cardinal measurement of utility'.** In other words, the consumer was assumed to be capable of assigning to every commodity or combination of commodities a number representing the amount of utility associated with it. The numbers representing amounts of utility could be manipulated in the same fashion as weights.

Suppose, for example, that utility of good A is 15 units and the utility of goods B 45 units. The consumer would, therefore, like the good B three times as strongly as the good A. The differences between utility numbers could be compared and the comparison could lead to a statement such as 'A' is preferred to 'B' twice as much 'C' is preferred to 'D'.

Thus, we see that the Marshallian assumption of cardinal measurement of utility is very restrictive. It demands too much from the human mind. Utility is a mental phenomenon and the precision in the measurement of utility assumed by Marshall is unrealistic.

On the other hand, indifference curve technique assumes what is called **'ordinal measurement of utility'.** Ordinal measurement of utility means that the consumer need assign exact numbers that represent the amount of utility attributable to the various units of the commodity, but that he is capable of judging whether one level of satisfaction is equal to, lower

Cardinal Utility: It quantifies utility of a gord.

4. Stonier and Hague, *A Textbook of Economic Theory*, 1973, p. 100.

than, or higher than, the other. This is, he can compare the different levels of satisfaction. In an indifference map, one indifference curve represents a higher or lower level of satisfaction than another, but one cannot say exactly **by how much** a satisfaction is higher or lower. For this reason, indifference curves are generally given ordinal numbers to put them in the right order, I, II, III, IV *etc.*, and no attempt is made to label them in terms of units of satisfaction –since there are no such units. For an explanation of consumer's behaviour, it is sufficient to assume that he is able to **rank his preferences consistently.** The assumption of ordinal measurement of utility made by indifference curve is less restrictive and more realistic.

***(ii)* No Assumption of Constancy of Marginal Utility of Money.** Marshall in his analysis of a consumer's behaviour assumed marginal utility of money to remain constant while the consumer proceeded to make purchases. Marshall defended his assumption on the ground that since the consumer spends a small fraction of his income on a particular good, his marginal utility of money does not increase to any significant extent as he purchases more and more units of the commodity.

But this exposes Marshall to a serious criticism. With the assumption of constant marginal utility of money, the Marshallian law of demand cannot genuinely be derived from utility hypothesis except in a one-commodity world. The assumption of constant marginal utility of money is not compatible with the validity of the law of demand in a situation where the consumer has more than a single good to spend his income on. If, in Marshallian analysis, this difficulty is avoided by giving up the assumption of constant marginal utility of money, then units of money can no longer express the marginal utility of a commodity. Units of measurement must be invariant. [5]

By assuming constant marginal utility of money. Marshall ignored "the income effect" of a price change and thus failed to distinguish between the two components of the "price-effect". Indifference curve technique is superior to the Marshallian analysis in that it does not assume constancy of marginal utility of money and is therefore able to draw a **distinction between the "income effect" and "substitution effect" of a price change, as seen before.**

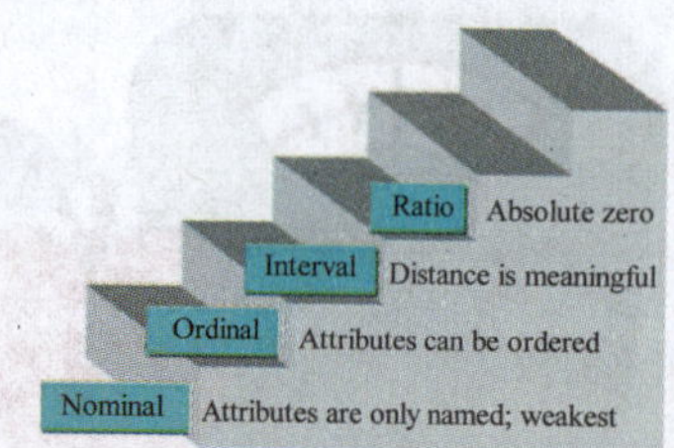

Ordinal measurement: Indifference curve ranks utility.

5. Cf. Majumdar, T. –*Measurement of Utility*, p. 56.

***(iii)* Analyses Multi-goods Model.** Marshall assumes that utility or demand for one commodity is independent of that for the other good (s) and that the marginal utility of money remains constant.

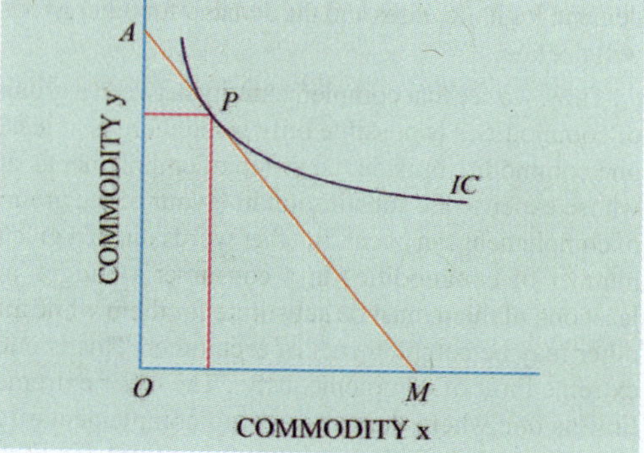

Fig. 7.13. Multigood model.

Thus, Marshall confines himself precisely to a single-good model and is unable to analyses precisely and correctly multi-good models and therefore the relationship of substitution and complementarity. The indifference curve technique, on the other hand, can successfully analyse all such cases.

By given an extra dimension, the indifference curve technique facilitates inter-commodity analysis which are of vital importance in the **price analysis.**

***(iv)* Less Restrictive.** The remarkable thing about the indifference curve technique is that it arrives at the same equilibrium condition for a consumer as the Marshallian analysis, but with less restrictive, and fewer assumptions than in Marshall's analysis. It has already been explained that a consumer is in equilibrium where a price line is tangent to an indifference curve and, therefore, the marginal rate of substitution (MRS) is equal to the ratio of prices between the goods. Thus, at P in our diagram 7.13:

$$\text{MRS of X for Y} = \frac{\text{Price of x}}{\text{Price of Y}} \qquad ...(i)$$

But MRS of X for Y is nothing else but a ratio between the marginal utility (MU) of X and the marginal utility (MU) of Y. Thus,

[6] $$\text{MRS of X for Y} = \frac{\text{M.U. of X}}{\text{M.U. of Y}} \qquad ...(ii)$$

6. This does not mean that MRS is found by measuring marginal utilities of the good and then taking out their rtio. MRS measures the **ratio** between the marginal utilities of two goods directly, without actually measuring marginal utility.

From (*i*) and (*ii*) is follows that:

$$\frac{\text{M.U. of X}}{\text{M.U. of Y}} = \frac{\text{Price of X}}{\text{Price of Y}}$$

which can be written as

$$\frac{\text{M.U. of X}}{\text{Price of X}} = \frac{\text{M.U. of Y}}{\text{Price of Y}} \quad ...(iii)$$

This, **(*iii*)** is the same "proportionality rule" of equilibrium as enunciated by Marshall, and the indifference curve technique arrives at this rule with less restrictive and fewer assumptions. This is no small achievement.

(*v*) More General Theory of Demand. The superiority of the indifference curve technique lies in the fact that even with less restrictive and fewer assumptions, it gives us a more general theory of demand. The ordinal utility theory enables us to enunciate the general theorem of demand in the following composite form of which the Marshallian law of demand constitutes a special case: [7]

(*a*) the demand for a commodity varies inversely with price when the income elasticity of demand for that commodity is nil or positive;

(*b*) the demand for a commodity varies inversely with price when the income-effect or a change in price is smaller than the substitution-effect; and

(*c*) the demand for a commodity varies directly with price when the income-elasticity of demand for that commodity is negative, and the income-effect of a change in price is larger than the substitution effect.

When either the first or the second condition is fulfilled, the Marshallian law of demand holds; and when the third condition applies, we get the Giffen case of a positively sloping demand curve. The Giffen case was an exception to the Marshallian law of demand. Marshall could not provide any satisfactory explanation of the peculiar phenomenon presented by Giffen goods; it remained a paradox to him, as to Sir Robert Giffen, after whom the problem has been named. Hicks' explanation of a Giffen case is that the negative income effect is so powerful that it outweighs the positive substitution effect and hence, when the price of a Giffen good falls, its demand also falls, instead of rising.

(vi) Chane in Welfare. By means of indifference curve technique, welfare consequences of changes in price can be translated into changes in income. A fall in the price of a good enables the consumer to shift from a lower to a higher level of welfare or satisfaction. That is, a change in price causes a change in welfare exactly as a change in consumer's income would have done. Thus, a change in price (rise or fall) brings about a change (fall or rise) in consumer's welfare exactly as if his income has changed (decreased or increased). "The equivalence of a given change in price to a suitable change in income is a major discovery of ordinal utility analysis" (T. Majumdar).

(*vii*) Closer Analysis of Price Effect. The indifference curve technique is also superior to the Marshallian utility analysis in that it furnishes a closer analysis of the effect of a change in price on consumer demand for a good by bringing out clearly the distinction between the income effect and substitution effect as already mentioned. It brings out clearly the two components of the price effect, *viz*., the income effect and the substitution effect. It thus enables us to understand more clearly the effect of a change in price on the demand for a commodity. When price falls, demand increases for two reasons: Real income increases as price falls. This is income effect. (*b*) Owing to the fall in price, the commodity becomes cheaper and this cheaper commodity is then substituted for other commodities whose prices are higher. This is substitution effect. The indifference curve technique separates the income effect from the substitution effect by the method of 'Compensating variation in income'.

(viii) Recognition of Relationship of Substitution and Complementarity. Marshall assumed independent marginal utilities. That is, he assumed that the utility of a commodity is a function of the quantity of that commodity **alone.** In other words, a change in the quantity consumed of a commodity changed its utility to the consumer and it does not affect (nor is it affected by) the utility of another commodity which can be substituted for it or which is a complementary good. Actually, this is not so. That is, the utilities are interdependent and not independent. On the other hand, the indifference curve analysis duly recognises the effect of substitutes and complementary goods on the utility of a commodity. It is able to explain the complementary and substitute goods in terms of substitution effect by splitting the price effect into substitution effect and income effects by using the technique of compensating variation in income.

Criticism of Indifference Curve Approach

(*i*) Old Wine in New Bottle. There are, however, some economists, who in spite of its merits given above, do not readily concede the superiority of the indifference curve technique. Professor D. H. Robertson is of the view that the indifference curve technique is merely "the old wine in a new bottle". The indifference curve analysis, according to him, has simply substituted new concepts and equations in place of the old ones. In place of the concept of "utility", the

7. Majumdar. T – *Measurement of Utility*, pp. 74-75.

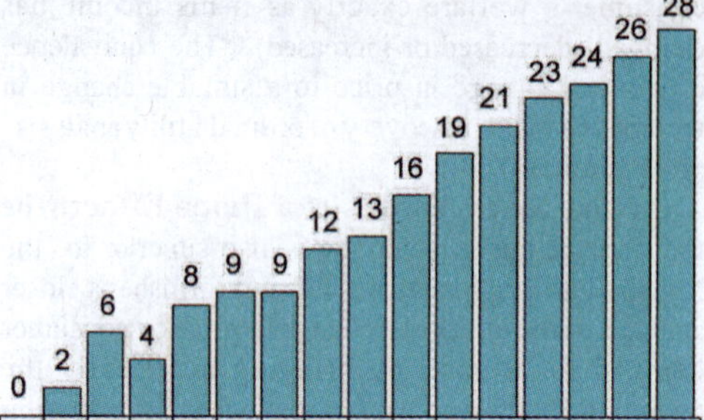

Why quantity consumed increases when price falls? Indifference technique explains better than utility through price effect.

indifference curve technique has introduced the term "preferences"; instead of the cardinal number system of one, two, three, *etc.*, which is said to measure the strength of a consumer's desire, the indifference curves have substituted ordinal number system fo first, second, third, *etc.*, to indicate the consumer's scale of preferences. The concept of marginal utility has been replaced by the marginal rate of substitution. And against the Marshallian "proportionality rule" to describe the consumer's equilibrium, indifference curve technique has advanced the equality between the marginal rate of substitution and the price ratio.

***(ii)* Marshallian Base Essential.** Professor Armstrong, too, is of the opinion that it is not possible to arrive at the Hicksian principle of diminishing MRS without making use of the "Marshallian scaffolding" of marginal utility. Why does MRS of X for Y fall as X is substituted for Y? The marginal rate of substitution diminishes and the indifference curve becomes convex to the origin, because as the consumer's stock of X increases, the marginal utility of X in term of Y falls and that of Y increases. Thus, according to Professor Armstrong, Hicks has not been able to derive the fundamental concept of diminishing marginal rate of substitution independently of the concept of utility. By a stroke of terminological manipulation, the concept of utility has been relegated to the background; but it is there all the same. Thus, it is obvious that "the principle of diminishing marginal rate of substitution is as much determinate or indeterminate as the poor law of diminishing marginal utility."

Hicks, however, claims that "the replacement of the principle of diminishing marginal utility by the principle of diminishing marginal rate of substitution is not a mere translation. It is a positive change in the theory of consumer's demand." How far his claim is justified is a matter of opinion.

***(iii)* Unrealistic.** It is argued that the new theory only jumps from **the frying pan of the difficulty of measuring utility into the fire of the unreality of assuming consumer's complete knowledge of all his scales of preferences** or indifference map. The indifference curve technique envisages a consumer who thinks of innumerable possible combinations of goods and his relative preferences for them.

***(iv)* Absurd.** Even if this feat could be performed, there is yet **another unrealistic element** in the indifference curve technique. Such curves include even the most **ridiculous combinations** which may be far removed from a consumer's habitual combinations. For example, while it may be perfectly sensible to compare whether three pairs of shoes and six shirts would give him as much satisfaction as two pairs of shoes and seven shirts, the consumer will be at a loss to compare the desirability of eight pairs of shoes and one shirt.

***(v)* Only Two-goods Model.** A further drawback of the indifference curve technique is that it can analyse consumer behaviour in respect of **two goods only;** for three goods three dimensional diagrams are needed which are difficult to understand and handle. When more than three goods may be involved, geometry altogether fails and recourse has to be taken to complicated mathematics which often tends to conceal the real point.

***(vi)* Cannot Explain Uncertaintly.** This technique cannot formalise consumer's behaviour when there exists risk or uncertainty of expectation, as regards the consequences of choice.

***(vii)* Introspective.** Samuelson has criticised this technique as being predominantly introspective and he has adopted a behaviourist method for devising the demand theory.

***(viii)* Constancy of Tastes.** This analysis assumes that consumers' tastes remain unaltered over period of time. This is not correct.

***(ix)* Continuity.** The indifference curve is supposedly smooth & continuous. This is unrealistic.

***(x)* Ignores Demonstration Effect.** An individual's consumption is often affected by level of consumption of others. Of this no notice is taken in this analysis.

***(xi)* Market Behaviour Ignored.** It considers only the prices of two goods and takes no notice of market changes in prices of other goods.

***(xii)* Relation of Transitivity Objected.** Prof. Armstrong has criticised the relation of transitivity involved in indifference curve technique. According to him, the consumer's indifference arises from his inability to perceive the difference between alternative combinations of goods. This is due to the fact that the difference is too slight to be noticed. If that is true the relation of indifference becomes non-transitive. This knocks the bottom out of the whole system of indifference curve analysis.

(*xiii*) Limited Empirical Nature. In Hicks-Allen theory, indifference curves are based on **hypothetical experimentation.** They are based on imaginary indifference curves, although attempts have been made recently to derive them experimentally.

Consumer purchases more than two goods, how indifference curve technique can explain the behaviour.

Conclusion. However, in spite of these weaknesses, the indifference curve technique is nowadays largely considered superior to the marginal utility analysis of Marshall and has of late gained considerable popularity among economists.

EXCEPTIONAL CASE OF CONSUMER'S EQUILIBRIUM

We have said that the indifference curves are usually convex to the origin. The consumers' equilibrium is at the point of tangency of the price line with an indifference curve. There are some exceptions.

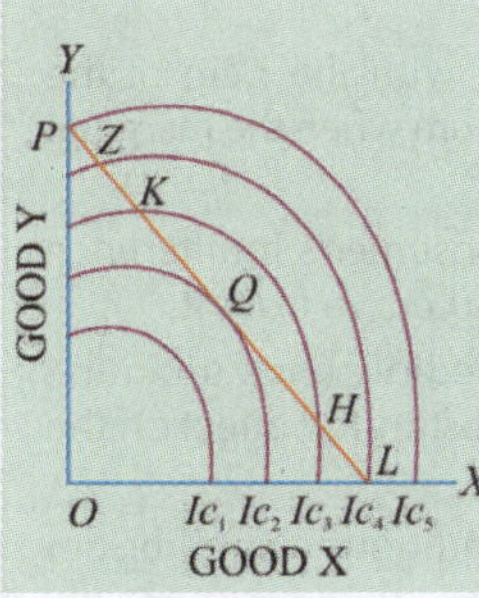

Fig. 7.14.

Fig. 7.14 gives concave indifference curves and the consumer will be in equilibrium not at Q where PL price line is a tangent to the curve but at P where consumer buys only good Y or at L where he will buy only good X, P and L being on higher indifference curves than at Q.

Fig. 7.15 and 7.16 give straight line indifference curves. It is a case of substitutes. Since these are straight lines, tangency is not possible. The equilibrium position will depend on the slope of the price line relative to the slope of indifference curves. If the slope of the price line PL is greater as in Fig. 7.15, he will be at equilibrium at P and buy only Y good. But if it is less as in Fig. 7.16, he will be in equilibrium at L and buy good X.

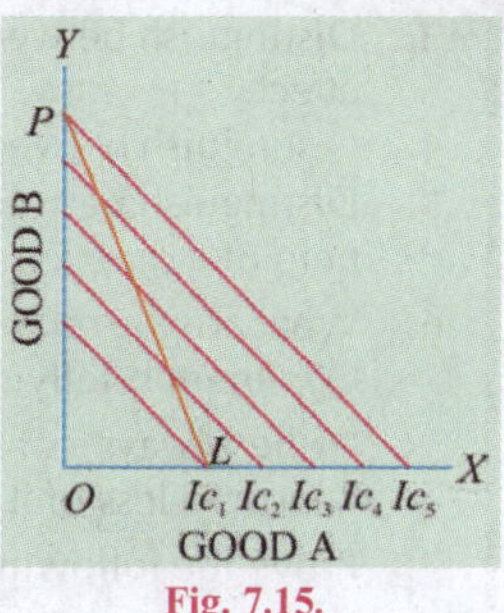

Fig. 7.15.

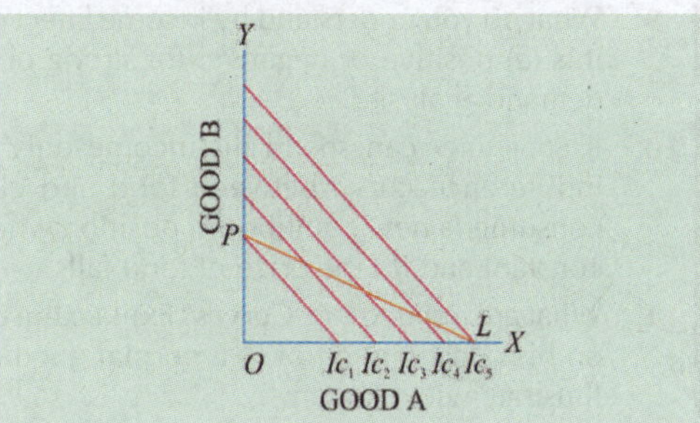

Fig. 7.16.

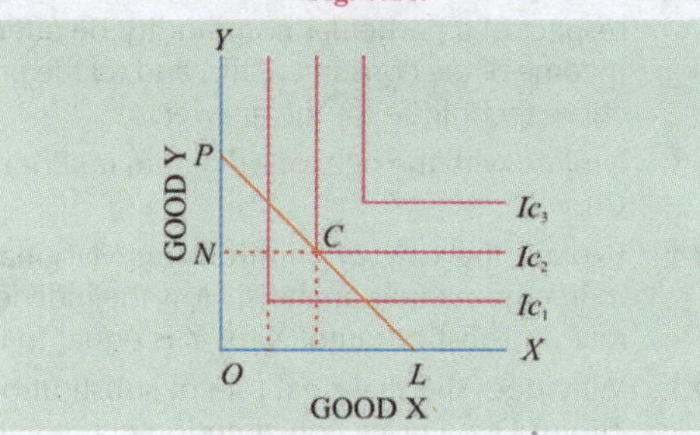

Fig. 7.17.

Fig. 7.17 represents the case of complementary goods. Here the indifference curves are right-angled. In such a case the consumer's equilibrium will be at the corner of the curve where the price line is a tangent i.e. at C.

Key terms

Budget line, Consumer's equilibrium, Income Consumption Curve (ICC), Compensating variation in income, Price consumption curve (PCC), Substitution effect, Giffen goods.

QUESTIONS

1. Explain with the help of indifference curves how a consumer allocates his income in order to attain equilibrium. How would a change in income affect his equilibrium?
2. Explain the effect of a change in the following on consumer's equilibrium: (*i*) income (*ii*) relative prices, real income remaining the same.

3. Distinguish between Income Effect and Substitution Effect Show how they are related to price effect.
4. Distinguish between Income Effect and Substitution Effect of a fall in the price of a commodity.
5. Distinguish between Income Effect and Substitution Effect of a change in price. Show with the help of a diagram how they act in case of inferior goods and 'Giffen goods.
6. What are the relationships between substitution effect, income effect and the law of demand? Comment briefly on the following statement about the rational consumer:

   "If he always consumes more of a commodity when his income alone rises, then he will consume less of it when its price alone rises."
7. Prove the following theorem for a two-commodity consumer:

   If the income effect for one of the two commodities is nil, then the consumer's demand curve for the commodity will have a negative slope.
8. 'When the price of X falls, the substitution effect cannot be negative, and a positive income elasticity of demand is sufficient to give an increase in the demand for X'. Explain.
9. What do you understand by Income Effect of a change in price; what factors determine whether it is (*a*) positive or negative, (*b*) strong or weak? How does Hicks make use of this effect in demand analysis?
10. If consumer can spend his income only on food and clothing show by using a set of his indifference curve between food and clothing and his consumption possibility line, the consumer's new equilibrium position when (*a*) his income increases, but both prices remain constant and (*b*) the price of food falls.
11. What are indifference Curves? Explain the effect of an increase in money income of a consumer on his consumption of (*i*) a normal good and (*ii*) an inferior good, other things being equal. Illustrate with diagrams.
12. What is meant by 'Consumer's Equilibrium"? How would the equilibrium of a consumer in respect of a particular commodity be affected if (*a*) the price of that commodity rises. (*b*) the income of the consumer falls, and (c) the price of a substitute commodity falls? Use indifference curve technique for the answer.
13. Explain with the help of a diagram (*a*) Price Consumption Curve, and (*b*) Income Consumption Curve'.
14. Explain the Law of Diminishing Marginal Rate of Substitution. Show with the help of the indifference curve analysis, How the individual consumer attains equilibrium when the marginal rate of substitution of X for Y is equal to the ratio of prices of X and Y.
15. Why does the marginal rate of substitution fall as we move along a consumer's indifference curve? Draw price consumption curve and derive conventional demand curve from it.
16. "As the price of any good X falls, the increase in the amount demanded depends upon the strength and direction of the income effect on the one and and of the substitution effect on the other". Discuss.
17. Show that the utility analysis and indifference analysis give the same conditions o equilibrium of the consumer. Use diagrams and/or formulae to prove your answer.
18. Explain and illustrate what is price consumption curve. Show that its shape depends on the elasticity of demand for a commodity. Compare the Price Consumption Curve with the Marshallian individual demand curve.
19. "Tangency between the price line and an indifference curve is the expression in terms of indifference curve is the expression in terms of indifference curves of the proportionality between marginal utilities and prices". Comment.
20. Describe the 'indifference curve' analysis of consumer's behaviour and discuss in what respects it is superior to the marginal utility analysis. What are its weaknesses?
21. "The indifference curve technique only jumps from the frying pan of measuring utility into the fire of the unreality of assuming consumer's complete knowledge of all his scales of preferences on indifference map". Discuss.

SOME APPLICATIONS OF INDIFFERENCE CURVE TECHNIQUE

The Indifference curve technique is not merely a tool of theoretical analysis. It can also be put to practical use in several economic spheres. As such, it occupies an important place in applied economics. It can be applied in consumption, production, index numbers, taxation and other economic matters. We shall now say a word about each.

Application in Consumption

The indifference curve technique can be used by the householder in setting his purchase plan. A consumer endeavours to reach an equilibrium position, *i.e.*, a position in which he derives maximum satisfaction from his scheme of purchases. We have already explained in the previous chapter how a consumer attains equilibrium with the help of the indifference curve technique. With any given sum of money and at any given set of prices, a consumer must decide the quantity of each commodity that he should purchase to maximise his satisfaction. He must select one of the many possible combinations of the two goods that he can purchase. These various possibilities lie on an indifference curve. Out of these, the combination that he chooses gives him the maximum satisfaction. For this purpose, he will try to reach the highest possible indifference curve touching the price line; all other points on the price line will lie on a lower indifference curve.

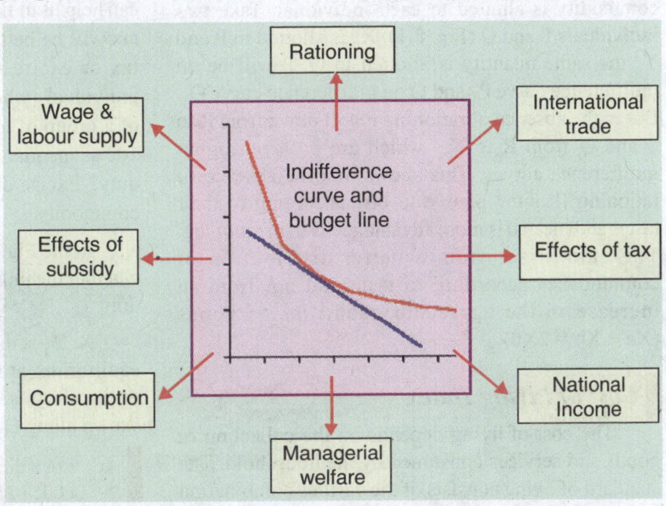

In the world of reality, a consumer has not to purchase only two goods but a number of them. But the indifference curve technique can be adapted even to represent this reality by making axis of Y represent money which is a general purchasing power, *i.e.*, all goods. With a change in the planned expenditure or in the price of a commodity, the purchase plan of the consumer will have to be revised. Such changes can be shown on the indifference curve.

Measurement of National Income

The indifference curve technique also tends itself for measuring national income. National income is the aggregate value of the net output of an economy. Each individual attaches the same relative importance to the commodities as their price ratio. National income is produced by the members of the comunity and so also it is consumed by them. An estimate of the relative valuation of the commodities composing the national income is essential for computing it. In their system of purchases, the consumers combine the commodities in such a manner as to maximise their satisfaction. The relative importance of the commodities in these combinations and the relative prices indicate the relative importance of these commodities to various members of the community. In fact, relative prices furnish the basis for combining the commodities in the purchase plans of the consumers. The indifference curves, showing the different combinations open to a consumer, can thus be used for measuring national income.

Rationing

Rationing is another field in which the indifference curve technique can be applied. Suppose in non-price rationing an equal quantity of the rationed commodity is allotted to each individual. Take two individuals P and Q (Fig. 8.1). X_0 is allotted to P and Y_0 the same quantity is allotted to Q. P will be on indifference curve P_1 and Q on indifference curve Q_1. But in the absence of rationing P will move from R to S and Q from R to N, which are both on higher indifference curves. This shows that the absence of rationing (leaving people to buy according to their tastes and means) is more advantageous than rationing. The gain arises from a better distribution of commodities according to taste and not from an increase in the aggregate quantities of goods (Xa + Xb = 2X0).

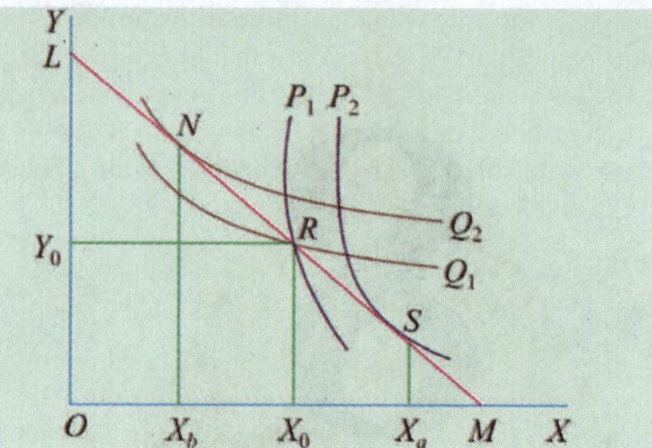

Fig. 8.1. Non-price (Quantity) Rationing.

Cost of Living Index

The cost of living depends on the collection of goods and services consumed by the household. The standard of living consists of the various combination of goods yielding equal satisfaction. Such combinations can be represented by points on the same indifference curve. If the combinations of goods purchased in two successive years are plotted on the indifference curve, it can be shown whether the standard of living has risen or fallen according as the most preferable combination is on a higher or lower indifference curve touching the respective price lines.

Price Discrimination

It can be shown with the help of indifference curves that two individuals (representing separate group of consumers) will derive greater satisfaction from the purchase of two commodities on a single price system instead of under price discrimination, (*i.e.*, when different prices are charged from each). Price discrimination prevents them from reaching the point of equilibrium at a higher indifference curve. [1]

Taxation: Direct vs. Indirect Taxes

In the field of taxation, too, the indifference curve technique can be usefully employed. For instance, it can help us to find out whether a direct tax like income-tax will be better or not than indirect taxes like sales tax or excise duty. From the point of view of an individual (who may be considered a representative of a group of tax-payers), will it be better to pay Rs. 100 as income-tax or Rs. 100 in the form of an excise duty? Excise duty is bound to raise the price of the commodity.

In the Fig. 8.2, we get the answer to the question whether the individual will prefer income tax or excise duty.

$X_1 Y_1$ is the initial price line. The individual is in equilibrium at P on indifference curve C_1. When an excise duty is imposed, the price of X commodity shown along OX rises and the new price line is $Y_1 X_2$

1. For a diagrammatic representation, see Stigler, G. J. –*The Theory of Price*, 1953, p. 92.

and now the individual is in equilibrium at Q on indifference curve C_2. It is clear that he is now buying a smaller quantity of X. To buy this quantity he has to pay SQ amount of money. If he bought no X at all, he would have spent SN amount. Thus, NQ is the amount of tax.

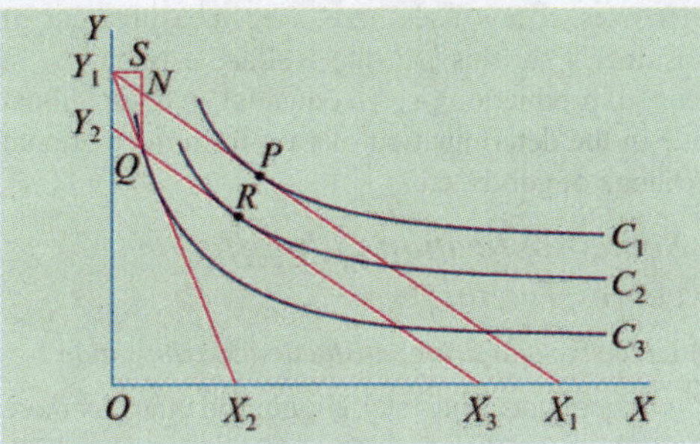

Fig. 8.2. Income tax (Direct) vs excise duty (Indirect).

In case he paid income-tax equal to NQ (= Y_1 Y_2), he is left with Y_2 O income after paying income-tax. Draw a new price Y_2 X_3 parallel to Y_1 X_1. Indifference curve C_3 touches this new price line at R. Indifference curve C_3 is at a higher level than C_2 , which shows that the tax-payer is hurt more by excise duty than by income-tax. Excise duty puts the tax-payer on a lower indifference curve. It is understandable from common sense that an excise duty upsets the budget of a consumer.

Effect of a Subsidy

Suppose the low-income groups are supplied by the Government some necessaries (say, housing accommodation) at subsidised rates, (*i.e.*, lower prices). Most welfare States like to help poor citizens in this manner. Let us suppose that the government supplies wheat at half price, the other half being a subsidy. The question is whether the benefit to the consumers is as great as the cost of the subsidy to the Government. Figure 8.3 gives the answer.

Wheat is measured along OX and income along OY. Suppose the individual's income is CO. If he spent the whole of it on unsubsidized wheat, he would buy OG quantity. Thus, CG is the price line without subsidy. The subsidy being half, the price line with subsidy is CK (OK is double of OG). The consumer is in equilibrium at P and he will, therefore, buy OF quantity of wheat and the amount of subsidy is AB. He spends AC on wheat, but in the absence of the subsidy, he would have spent BC. AB would be the cost to the Government (the vertical distance between the two price lines). The benefit to the consumer is CD. The price line without subsidy, *i.e.*, CG has moved to the right and becomes DH so as to be tangent to the indifference curve. This amounts to an increase in the money income of the consumer. It will be seen that CD is less than AB, *i.e.*, the amount of the subsidy. Hence, we may conclude that the cost of the subsidy to the government is greater than the money equivalent of the gain to the consumer.

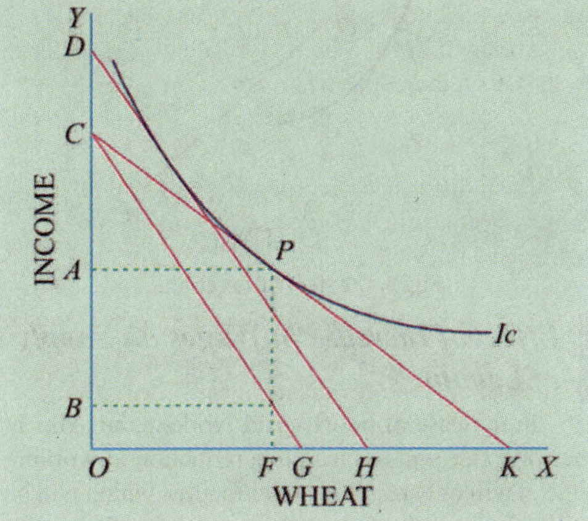

Fig. 8.3. Effects of subsidy.

Effect of Taxation on Willingness to Work

When a tax is imposed on a person, reduction in money income at his disposal will spur him on to put in more work to increase his income. But if extra work is irksome, it will have the opposite effect. Hence, a tax may induce a man to work more or work less. **A proportional tax tends to restrict output.**

In the diagram (Fig. 8.4) given above, LM′ and LM are the two price lines before and after tax respectively. P is the point of equilibrium before tax and P′ after tax. P′ Q is the amount of the tax paid. As a result of the tax, output has been reduced from OM′ to OM. Hence, this particular individual works less than before.

Suppose instead of a proportionate tax, a poll tax (*i.e.*, fixed amount irrespective of the size of the income) is levied. This is represented by the dotted price line SS′ which is parallel to LM′ but on its left. The point of tangency on this new price line will lie somewhere between P and R, which means that the tax payer will work more than when he paid income-tax. The reaction of the individual tax payers may vary. But it can be laid down as a general rule that if a fixed sum is taken away from a worker, it will restrict his output more (or increase it less) than in the cse of a progressive income tax.

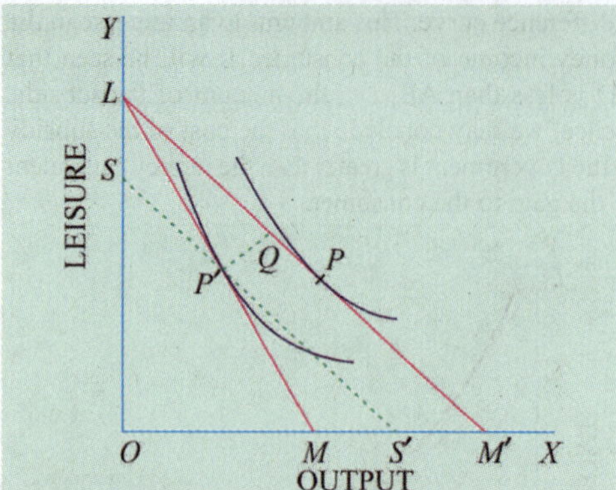

Fig. 8.4. Effect of taxation.

Effect of Increase in Wages on Supply of Labour

In the case of poorly-paid workers, any rise in the wage rate will not lead to a reduction in working time; it will only result in larger income which will be utilised in purchasing more goods. But beyond a certain stage, the worker will work less and still enjoy more goods. Study the following diagram.

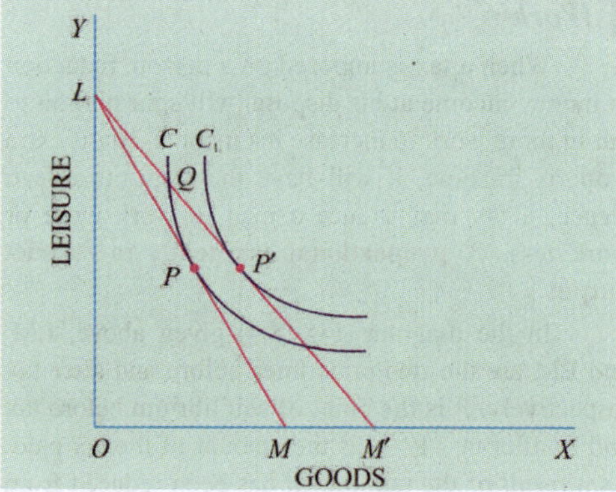

Fig. 8.5. Wage increase and labour supply.

The worker in this figure (Fig. 8.5) is in equilibrium at P on the price line LM. When the wage rate goes up, the new price line is LM′. The worker must, therefore, now move up to some point on LM′ between Q and R, which are the points on the indifference curve C. Any point between Q and R must be on a higher indifference curve like C_1 indicating that the worker will be better off. This point may be P′, a new equilibrium. Here leisure remains constant, but goods increase. The worker has moved horizontally from P outwards. If P′ is on a higher slope of C_1, it will mean more leisure and also more goods.

Other Uses of Indifference Curves

The use of indifference curve technique is not merely confined to the cases mentioned above. This technique is now being very widely used in almost the entire economic theory. We may just mention, among other uses, a few uses here, *viz.*, measurement of consumer's surplus , in the welfare economics, in theory of production (*e.g.*, Isoquants), in international trade in the determination of gain from international exchange of goods, etc.

Some Application of Indifference curves Technique

(i) *Objective of a firm: Satisfaction Maximisation*

Economists Scitovsky, Higgin and other lay more emphasis on the objective of satisfaction maximisation. With the help of indifference curves they showed how an entrepreneur is able to achieve a point which gives him satisfaction maximisation in comparison with the profit maximisation. Indifference curves are used as a relation between an entrepreneur's sale of preference between leisure and profits.

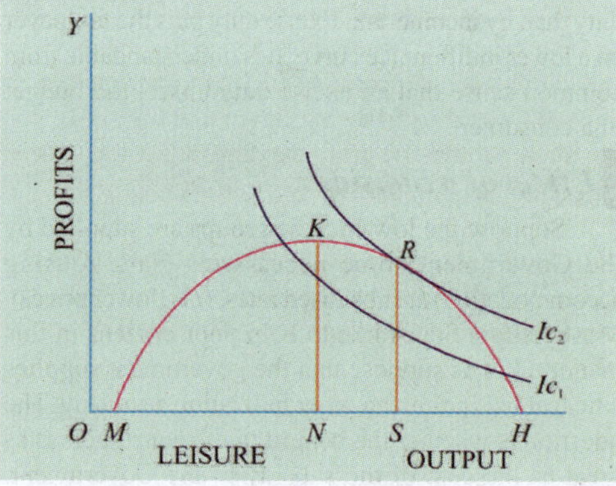

Fi.g 8.6. Maximizing satisfaction of an entrepreneur.

"Use of indifference curve to show the maximisation of satisfaction objective."

In the above diagram we measure on 'Y' axis. Profit, where as on 'x' axis from left to right that is from point 'H' towards 'N' the output, IC_1 and IC_2 are two indifference curves which shows entrepreneur's scale of preference between profit and leisure. As the entrepreneur proceed from point 'H' his, output, starts increasing. At 'HN' level of output profit is maximum that is 'KN' amount, but to achieve a balance between leisure and profit, IC_2 (Indifference curve) is tangent 'HM' curve at point 'R' , this is ideal amount of ouput which gives "satisfaction maximisation".

(ii) Objective of a firm, "Staff Maximisation".

With the help of indifference curves one can show that how managers try to keep more 'staff' then less staff even if the more staff concept gives them lesser profits. This could have been used in communists countries earlier and this may be possible in public sector enterprises where managers wants to be more safe, with more staff then, less staff and more profit.

In the diagram below we measure profit on 'Y' axis and level of staff on 'x' axis.

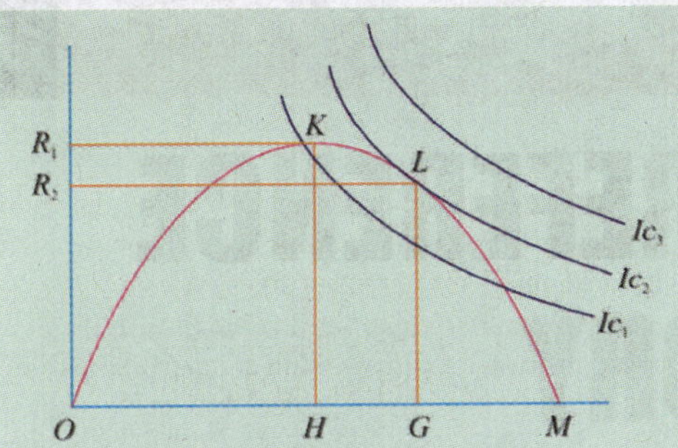

Fig. 8.7. Maximization of Staff.

'OM' is the trade-off curve and 'IC_1' 'IC_2' and 'IC_3' are managers utility function. When the size of staff is 'OH' the level of profit is 'OR', but managers try to maximise their utility by having more staff, then required, though the profit may be lower. 'IC_2', which is higher then IC_1, the managers utility functions curve which is tangent to the 'OM' trade off curve at point 'L'. At this point the manager's are satisfied, that is 'OR_2' profit and 'OG' amount of staff which is compared to 'OR_1' less profit but more staff than 'OH' amount.

(iii) Use of Indifference Curve :– To explain equilibrium between consumer prices and factor price:– (International trade theory, Hecksheir & Ohlin)

There are many uses of indifference curves, in welfare economics it has been used extensively. In recent years the reverse indifference curve is used in showing the relationship between risk & uncertaintly and the behaviour of risk-lover's.

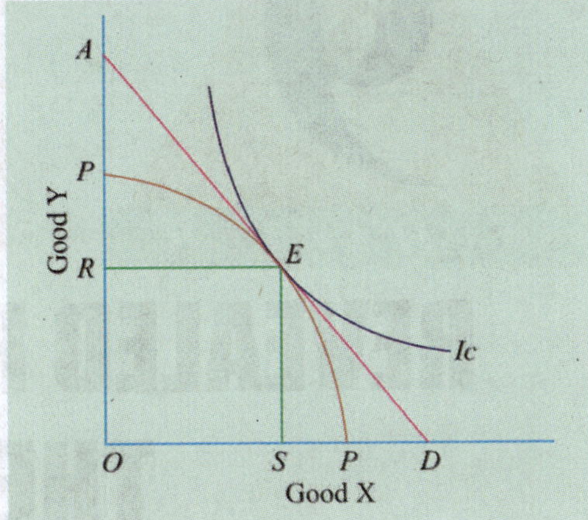

Fig. 8.8. General Equilibrium in trade.

Hecksheir-Ohlins general equilibrium theory is on the basis of concept of factor price and consumer price equilibrium which is shown with the help of a diagram below.

'AB' is the budget line, 'PP' is production posibility fronteir, and IC, is indifference curve. 'AB' is tangent to 'PP' curve as well as 'IC' at point E, which gives the equilibrium point that means.

The slope of budget line =

The slope of IC = The slope of 'PP' curves.

Point 'E' gives us the equilibrium point between consumers and producers or between demand and supply. Which is one of the starting point of Hecksheir-Ohlin's theory of general equilibrium.

Key terms

Non-price Rationing, Taxation, Subsidty, Wages, Supply of labour, Satisfaction of entre preneur

QUESTIONS

1. Explain non-price rationing by using indifference curve technique.
2. Compare the welfare implication of direct and indirect tax on an individual by using indifference curve.
3. Use indifference curve to compare the welfare implication of subsidy and monetary grant given by government.
4. Explain *(a)* effect of tax on willingness to work and *(b)* effect of increasing wages on supply of labour.
5. How you can use indifference curve technique to maximise satisfaction of entrepreneur of a firm.
6. Use indifference curve to show the following:
   (i) General equilibrium in international trade *(ii)* Cost of living index
   (iii) Staff maximisation in a firm.

REVEALED PREFERENCE THEORY

The Theory

This theory is associated with the name of Prof. Samuelson. This theory is called the behaviourist ordinal-utility theory. Instead of the unrealistic assumption that the consumers operate with a complete and consistent scales of preferences set out in the form of indifference curves, most economists now prefer to analyse situations in which their hypothesis can be tested. Both Marshallian utility analysis and Allen-Hicksian indifference curve technique apply the introspective method or the subjective method. But Samuelson's revealed preference theory makes use of hypotheses which are observable and testable. There is thus a shift from the psychological to behaviouristic explanation of consumer behaviour.

Prof. Samuelson: 1970 Nobel Laureate in Economics.

According to the revealed preference theory, the consumer is supposed to reveal the nature of his preferences. He shows the goods he would prefer to purchase in a given situation even though he may not be able to show his scale of preferences on an indifference map. Thus, in the theory of revealed preference, it is unnecessary to assume that the consumers can describe their preferences on indifference maps. This is one merit of the revealed preference theory. Also, as Sir John Hicks observes, revealed preference theory lends itself to use by econometricians.

Assumptions

Rational Consumer. When we use the revealed preference theory in order to find out the effects of a change in price of a commodity on the demand for it, we make certain assumptions. We assume that we are considering an ideal consumer or a rational consumer. That is, we assume that the consumer seeks to maximise his satisfaction from the resources he has. As such he will choose a combination of goods which he deems most satisfying, *i.e.*, which he prefers the most. It, therefore, follows that in one set of market conditions, he selects one combination and his choices will be different under different market situations.

Consistency. We also assume that the consumer's choices are consistent. The choices of actual consumers may not be consistent but those of the ideal or rational consumer may be supposed to be consistent. This consistency implies (*a*) two-term consistency and (*b*) transitivity. The two-term consistency means, for instance, that if a particular combination of goods P is better than Q combination and Q is better than R, then P must also be assumed to be better than R, and R cannot be better than P. Transitivity ensures that there should be no such circular relationship.

Positive Income-Elasticity of Demand. Another very important assumption underlying revealed preference theory is that the income-elasticity of demand of the consumer must always be positive. That is, if his income increase, his demand for the commodity must also increase; it should not remain the same (*i.e.*, zero elasticity) and it should not also decrease (*i.e.*, negative elasticity) as it happens in the case of inferior goods.

Strong Ordering. A distinguishing feature of Samuelson's theory is that of **'strong ordering'.** There are two kinds of ordering, *viz*., strong and weak. In a strong ordering, each item in a consumer's scheme of purchases is assigned a definite place or number and at each number there is only one item so that the consumer definitely reveals his preferences. For instance, a consumer reveals his preference when he is observed to choose. Say, Q combination of goods in preference to all others or he rejects the rest. In other words, choice reveals preference, by choosing one combination and rejecting others, the consumer has shown his definite preference. It is a case of strong ordering. In a weak ordering there may be some items which cannot be arranged in order or preference, so that the consumer is unable to indicate which items he prefers to which.

Strong ordering: more is preferred to less.

It may be noted that there is strong ordering so far indifference curves themselves are concerned, because each indifference represents a different level of satisfaction. As between indifference curves, you can at once say which you would prefer the most. But there is a weak ordering so far as the combination of goods on the same indifference curve are concerned because they represent the same level of satisfaction. Since they are equally satisfactory, the consumer hesitates and cannot at once reveal his preference.

A weak ordering divides the items of purchase into groups; the groups may be strongly ordered showing a definite sequence of preference but there is no such preference within the group itself, *i.e.*, there is weak ordering within the group. There may be two or more positions at the top and the choice between these cannot be easily explained. In case the ordering is strong, the consumer chooses the most preferred position and the preference explains the choice.

The conventional indifference curve is an illustration of weak ordering because all points on the same indifference curve are equally preferred to represent a non-ordered group. Samuelson's theory assumes strong ordering. The assumption underlying the indifference curve technique, *viz*., that a consumer is capable of ordering all conceivable alternatives indicated by several points on the indifference curve, appeared obviously to be unrealistic.

Weak ordering: Gulab Jamun & Rasagoolahs are preferred equally.

Samuelson, therefore, rules out the possibility of weak ordering. He does not regard indifference as an operationally significant concept. Samuelson thinks that in the choice that a consumer makes he reveals his preference. Thus, the behaviour of the individual reflects his preference. That is how the revealed preference theory derives a demand theorem from the actually observed behaviour of the consumer. The axiom of revealed preference "provides the necessary operational link between observed choice-behaviour and the behaviourist's welfare conclusions". Thus, the relation of indifference is rejected on operational grounds.

But, as already explaind, the consumer behaviour should not be self-contradictory. If, for instance, he prefers coffee to tea at one time, he cannot consistently choose tea rather than coffee at another time. Hicks has called this 'two -term consistency', which is an important assumption underlying Samuelson's theory. This consistency relates to an individual's each single act of choice.

Preference Hypothesis A strong ordering

Prof. Samuelson's revealed preference theory has laid emphasis on "Choice reveales preference" or strong ordering to explain his theory of demand. A consumer reveals his definite preference regarding the combination of two goods 'x' & 'y'consumption which he chooses. The preference hypothesis is based on the following assumptions,

(*i*) Choice of consumer reveals his preference.
(*ii*) Strong ordering concept
(*iii*) Bigger quantity of combination is preferred to smaller one.
(*iv*) It is based on "Ordinality Principle".
(*v*) It is actual behaviour of a consumer, rather than just psychological reactions.

'AB' is the budget line, If a consumer spends all his income on good 'Y', then he will buy 'OA' amount whereas if spends on good 'X' he will get 'OB' of 'X'or the consumer can buy any amount of combination within ΔOAB.

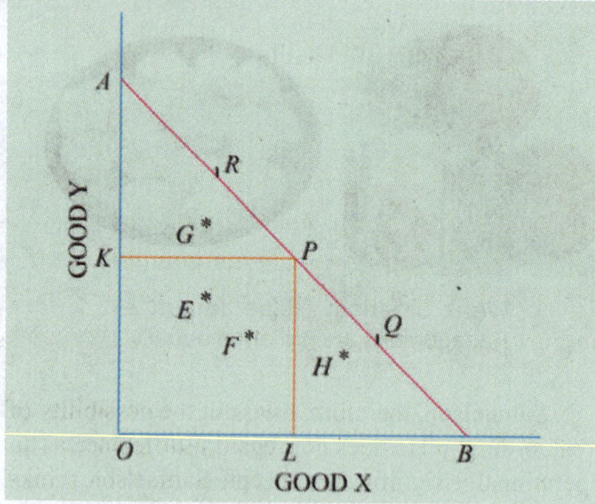

Fig. 9.1. Choice reneals preference of the consumer.

The consumer shows his strong preference at point 'P' that means, 'OK' of good 'Y' and 'OL' of good 'X'. Other combinations on line AB, *i.e.* point 'R' & 'Q' gives him less quantity of 'X' & 'Y'. Even the point below the 'AB' line *i.e.*, point 'G', 'E', 'F' & 'H' all gives less quantity of 'X' & 'Y'. Hence in the strong ordering preference hypothesis, A consumer reveals his preference which gives him the maximum amount of good 'X' & 'Y'.

Demand Theorem with Revealed Preference Hypothesis

It can be easily explained that the Marshallian law of demand can be derived with the aid of revealed preference hypothesis. According to the Marshallian law of demand, demand extends with a fall in price and contracts with a rise in price, other things remaining the same, *i.e.*, consumer's income and other relevant prices do not change. Samuelson has tried to demonstrate this inverse relationship between price and the amount demanded by **assuming income elasticity of demand to be positive.**

Samuelson states the demand theorem under the title "Fundamental Theorem of Consumption Theory" thus: **"Any good (simple or composite) that is known always to increase in demand when income alone rises must definitely shrink in demand when its price alone rises."** In this proportion, income elasticity of demand has been assumed to be positive.

This theorem can be illustrated by the following diagram (Fig. 9.2).

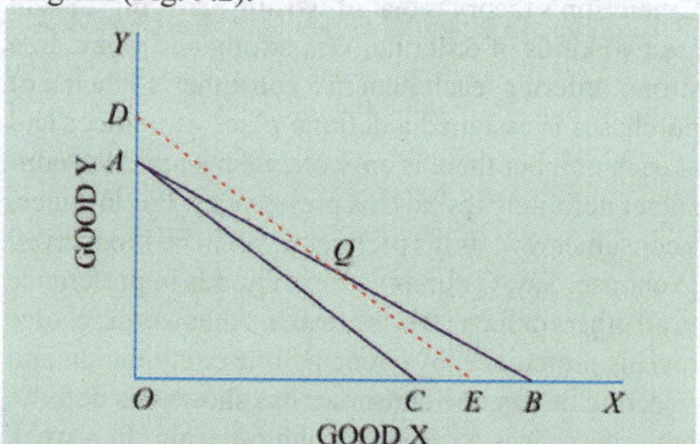

Fig. 9.2. Effect of Rise on Demand.

In this diagram (Fig. 9.2), consumer's income in terms of good X is shown by OB and in terms of good Y by OA. He is supposed to spend his entire income on these two goods X and Y. AB is the price line and as such shows all the combinations of the two goods X and Y that the consumer can buy in this price-income situation. Let us suppose the consumer is observed to choose the combination represented by Q on the price line AB as giving him the maximum satisfaction.

Price Effect. Now suppose that the price of good X rises, while the price of Y remains the same. The demand for X contracts from OB to OC. This gives the new price line AC. In this new price-income situation, Q which put the consumer in equilibrium before, becomes now beyond his reach. In order to enable him to buy the same combination Q, which had given him maximum satisfaction earlier, we give the consumer some extra money to overcome the higher price resistance. For this purpose, we draw a line DE parallel to AC but passing through Q. We give the consumer CE more money to put him on this new price line DE to enable him to buy Q combination, because Q is on this price line too. Prof. Samuelson calls the extra money as **Over-Compensation Effect** and Hicks calls it Cost- difference.

Now, since Q combination becomes available to the consumer again in the price-income situation indicated by DE price line, he will not choose any combination lower than Q (*i.e.*, lying on QE part of DE). They were available to him before since they lie within the triangle AOB made by the price line AB but were rejected by him in favour of Q. Hence, he will now choose Q or any higher combination lying on QD part of the price line DE. If he selects Q, it will mean that he is buying the same amount of goods X and Y as before. But if he chooses any combination above Q on QD portion of DE, it will mean he is buying less of X and more of Y. This shows the **substitution** effect of a price rise since some units of Y have been substituted for some units of X which has become dearer.

Thus, even when we have given some extra money to the consumer to compensate for the rise in the price of X, he either buys the orginal quantity of X or less quantity at a higher price. If extra money were not given to him, he would definitely buy smaller quantity of X when its price has risen. This establishes the inverse relationship between price and the quantity demanded when price of good has risen.

Now suppose the price of good X falls. The effect of fall in price is illustrated by the Fig. 9.3 as that of rise was illustrated by the Fig. 9.2 (The figure is given below).

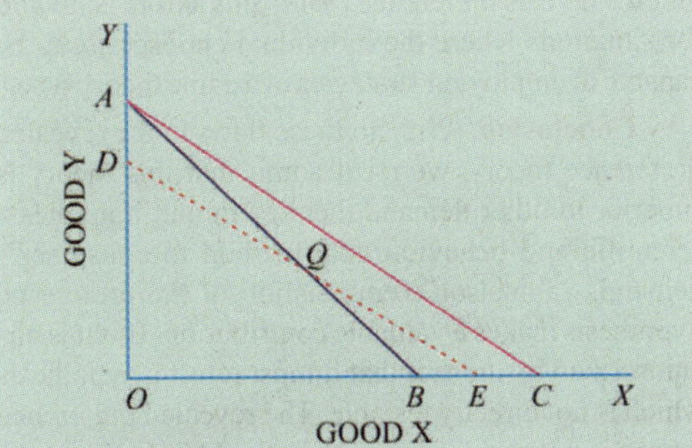

Fig. 9.3. Effect of Fall on Price on Demand.

In this diagram, take AB as the original price line and suppose our hypothetical consumer reveals his preference for Q combination of goods X and Y to all other combinations in or on the triangle OAB.

Now suppose the price of X falls and as a result the demand for X extends from OB to OC. Thus, the price line shifts from AB to AC. The consumer now feels he is better off than before. If he is to purchase the original combination of X and Y as represented by Q, we have to take away from him some money so that he is neither better off nor worse off than before. For this purpose, we draw DE price line parallel to AC. In this way, the amount of money withdrawn from the consumer is CE. Now Q being on the new price line DE also, the combination represented by Q becomes available to the consumer. But owing to reduction in his money income he cannot purchase any combination above Q, *i.e.*, lying on QD portion of DE. These combinations were available to him but had been rejected in favour of Q. Hence, he will either choose Q or any other lying below Q, *i.e.*, on the QE portion of DE. If he chooses Q, it will mean that he buys the same quantity of goods X and Y as in the orginal price-income situation represented by AB. But if he chooses any other combination below Q, it will mean that he buys more of X and less of Y than what he did originally in the price-income situation of AB.

We thus see that even when the consumer's income is reduced, he buys either the same quantity of X or more of it at a lower price. If no money is taken away, he is on the AC price line, he will definitely buy more of X at the lower price provided that his demand for X increases, as his income rises, *i.e.*, his income elasticity of demand for good X is positive.

Thus, we have proved the "Fundamental Theorem of Consumption Theory" in both cases of rise and a fall in the price of commodity. The inverse relationship between price and quantity demanded is established.

Consumer's Equilibrium. Incidentally, we have indicated how a consumer reaches an equilibrium with revealed preference hypothesis and the income effect, the substitution effect and price effect of which the former two are components.

Critical Evaluation

Merits. We have already pointed out some merits of the revealed preference theory. There is no doubt that, in several respects, it is an improvement on the Marshallian utility analysis and Hicks-Allen indifference curve technique:

(*a*) In the first place, it is behaviouristic and draws the demand theorem from the actually observed behaviour of a consumer. On the other hand, both Marshallian utility analysis and the Hicks-Allen indifference curve techniques are introspective and give psychological explanation of consumer demand. The revealed preference theory studies the actual behaviour of a consumer and not an ideal or imaginary consumer.

It is, therefore, more realistic and more scientific. As Prof. Tapas Majumdar says, "Behaviourism has certainly great advantages of treading only on observed ground; it cannot go wrong."

(b) Samuelson's revealed preference theory has another advantage over the earlier theories. It steers clear of the dubious assumptions upon which the earlier theories were based. The Marshallian and the Hicksian theories were based on the utility maximisation principle. This principle is more restrictive and difficult of realisation in actual practice. On the other hand, Samuelson's theory steers clear of the utility maximisation principle and uses instead the consistency principle to derive the demand theorem which is much less restrictive but more realistic.

(c) The indifference curve is based on the assumption of continuity, whereas revealed preference theory does not assume continuity. Indifference curve is continuous in the sense that it depicts all conceivable combinations some of which may be so unrealistic as to be ridiculous. That is why Prof. Samuelson has given up the assumption of continuity in his revealed preference theory. Although, price line is drawn continuous, yet no continuity is actually involved because the theory is based on the actually observed choice of the consumer from among such combinations as are actually available in the given price-income situation.

Demerits. Whereas the revealed perference theory has several merits as compared with the earlier theories, it is not free from defects:

(i) It is based on strong ordering and as such does not admit of indifference. But since observed choice implies a number of possible alternatives, indifference cannot be ruled out altogether. It may be that no definite preference emerges from a large number of observations. The consumer is sometimes confronted with alternatives which are equally desirable and he is hesitant to choose between them.

(ii) It is very reasonable to assume that an individual is able to compare the different alternatives open to him. Hence, there is a possibility of indifference and of remaining at the same level of satisfaction by sacrificing some units of a good in order to obtain additional units of some other good. As Mr. Tapas Majumdar points out, capacity to compare is the very basis of welfare economics.

(iii) Further, Mr. Armstrong asserts that round about evey chosen point there are points of indifference. A consumer goes through these points to reach the most desirable end. The combination actually chosen is thus a point of the series of points of indifference.

(iv) Moreover, it is pointed out that since Samuelson's revealed preference theory is based on actually observed behaviour, there is no room for making a distinction between income effect and substitution effect. And since response of demand to a change in price (*i.e.*, price effect) has two components, income effect and substitution effect, it is supposed that Samuelson's revealed preference theory gives only a partial explanation of change in demand as a result of a change in price. But Samuelson makes a clear distinction between income effect and what he calls overcompensation effect which is similar to substitution effect.

(v) Another flaw in the theory of revealed preference arises from the assumption of positive income-elasticity of demand. In view of this assumption, this theory fails to enunciate the demand theorem when income-elasticity of demand is negative. It only enunciates the demand theorem in a case in which substitution effect of a price change has been reinforced by positive income effect. It cannot, therefore, explain Giffen's paradox in which the income effect is negative and this negative effect is so powerful that it outweighs the substitution effect. Samuelson's theorem explains the inverse relationship, between price and the quantity demanded, but in Giffen paradox this relationship is direct.

Samuelson thus denies are phenomenon of Giffen paradox. But we know that this paradox is theoretically conceivable. We know that in the case of inferior goods demand changes in the same direction as price. In this respect, Hicks-Allen indifference theorem is more general than Samuelson's revealed preference theory.

(vi) Finally, objection is raised against his axiom 'choice reveals preference'. But "this axiom is invalid for situations where the individual chooser are to be capable of employing strategies of a game theory type."

Conclusion. With all these flaws in the revealed preference theory, we must admit that this theory is superior to other demand theories in that it applies a scientific and behaviouristic method to consumer's demand. Samuelson's enunciation of the preference hypothesis makes a valuable contribution. But it is circumscribed by the fact that it must reject a hypothesis which is not directly testable. The revealed preference theory is not more general than the Marshallian Law of demand and, unlike Hicks' indifference curve, it does not cover the Giffen case. It is unable to explain a case in which income-elasticity of demand is zero or is negative and the income effect larger than the substitution effect. Hence, Hicksian theory of indifference has greater operational significance than Samuelson's revealed preference theory.

A theory of consumer demand based entirely on strong ordering cannot be very satisfactory, because the consumer is actually confronted sometimes with alternatives which are equally desirable. Hence, indifference analysis cannot be altogether ruled out.

We may, therefore, conclude that neither for the purpose of formulating a general theory of demand nor on any operationally relevant consideration is it necessary to subscribe to the revealed preference theory.

Key terms

Strong ordering, Weak ordering, Fundamental theorem of consumption.

QUESTIONS

1. Outline the assumption of revealed preference theory of consumer behaviour.
2. Explain consumer's equilibrium by applying revealed preference hypothesis.
3. State and explain Samuelson's fundamental theorem of consumption.
4. Explain the effect of change in price on quantity demanded by using revealed preference theory.
5. Critically examine revealed preference hypotheses as an explanation for consumer's behaviour.

RECENT DEVELOPMENT IN DEMAND THEORY

The demand theory is primarily concerned with the elucidation of the law of demand. The law of demand states that the demand curve slopes downwards, which implies two things: (a) a fall in the price of a commodity tends to increase the quantity demanded, and (b) an increase in supply tends to lower its price. This 'price into quantity' and 'quantity into price' are the two aspects of the law of demand. The law holds good 'other things being equal.'

We can notice the following different stages of development in the theory of demand:

(*i*) The Marshallian Marginal Utility Theory.

(*ii*) Hicksian-Allen Indifference Curve Technique.

(*iii*) Samuelson's Revealed Preference Theory.

(*iv*) Hicksian Revised Theory of Demand.

(*v*) Neumann-Morgenstern Statistical Utility Theory.

(*vi*) Armstrong's Marginal Preference Theory.

We have already studied in some detail the first three, *viz*., the Marshallian utility analysis, Hicks' indifference curve technique and Samuelson's Revealed Preference Theory. The Marshallian utility analysis, we have seen, is based on the two untenable assumptions, *viz*., that utility is cardinally measurable and that the marginal utility of money remains constant. The indifference curve technique steers clear of these doubtful assumptions and arrives at the same conclusions as the Marshallian utility analysis but with fewer and less restrictive assumptions. These two theories apply the introspective method in Economics. The introspective method lays down general propositions which are not observable by themselves but which have observable consequences. Samuelson's theory of revealed preference is based on actually observed consumer's behaviour.

We shall now briefly notice the other development in the demand theory particularly Hicks' revised theory of ordinal utility, the cardinal utility theory of Morgenstern and Von Neumann, both called behaviourists who insist on observable or refutable data and the Marginal Preference Theory of W. E. Armstrong-representing a revival of the introspective cardinalism.

Hicks' Revised Theory of Demand

Hicks' first theory of demand was presented in his book **'Value and Capital.'** He revised his theory and published his book, **'A Revision of Demand Theory'** in 1956. Samuelson's revealed preference theory, the growing importance of econometrics and other allied developments led to this revision. In his revision of the demand theory. Hicks emphasised the econometric approach to the theory of demand.

Salient points in Hicks' theory may be noted: Even in his new theory. Hicks confirmed his belief in the ordinal approach to the utility theory and rejected the concept of utility hypothesis of independent utilities.

But it is curious that Hicks, who was largely responsible for popularising indifference curves in economic analysis, almost gave them up in his revision of demand theory. Among the disadvantages of indifference curves he mentions that: ***(a)*** this technique cannot include more than two commodities; and ***(b)*** it is based on the assumption of continuity which is generally not to be found in economic field. The new method that he adopted was, in his view, more effective in clarifying the nature of preference hypothesis itself.

Hicks starts by taking up an ideal consumer who is supposed to be influenced by current prices and incomes alone in his behaviour. Hicks adopts preference hypothesis for explaining the behaviour of an ideal consumer. Preference hypothesis assumes behaviour according to scale of preferences.

In his own words: "**The ideal consumer (who is not affected by anything else than current market conditions) chooses that alternative, out of the various alternatives open to him, which he most prefers or ranks most highly. In one set of market conditions he makes one choice, in others other choices, but the choices he makes always express the same ordering and must, therefore, be consistent with one another.**" [1]

According to Hicks, "**the demand theory which is based upon preference hypothesis turns out to be nothing else but an economic application of the logical theory of ordering**." After drawing a distinction between strong ordering and weak ordering, he proceeds to base his demand theory on weak ordering (as distinguished from strong ordering adopted by Samuelson in his revealed preference theory). To use his own words, "A weak ordering consists of division into groups, in which sequence of groups is strongly ordered, but in which there is no ordering within the groups." Since all combinations on an indifference curve are equally desirable or represent the same level of satisfaction, it illustrates weak ordering. It is obvious that in weak ordering, the actual choice fails to reveal definite preference. (See Figures 9.2 and 9.3 in the previous chapter). The various price-income lines drawn there represent weak ordering.

Hicks objects to strong ordering. He says that a 'two dimensional continuum point cannot be strongly ordered.' According to him, where the choice is between any good which is available in discrete units and money which is finally divisible, the possibility of equally desired combinations cannot be ruled out. The concept of strong ordering must, therefore, be given up. According to Hicks, the choice of a particular combination does not indicate preference for that particular combination over all other possible alternative combinations that have been rejected. All that is shown is that there is no rejected combination which is preferred to all one chosen. The point chosen is preferred to all points within the triangle (See figures 9.2 and 9.3 in the previous chapter) but is shows preference or indifference to all points on the price line.

Hicks is able to deduce all the major propositions of theory of consumer demand from the logic of weak ordering and the theory of direct consistency test based on it. He derives the law of demand or the downward sloping demand curve and for this purpose he adopts the same technique as was adopted in the case of indifference curve, *viz*., splitting the price effect into its two components; income effect and substitution effect. He deduces the substitution effect from the consistency theory and the income effect is based upon empirical evidence. The substitution effect is separated by means of (*a*) the method of compensating variation and by the method of cost difference.[2] (This has been explained in the previous chapter on revealed preference).

The law of demand enunciated by Hicks covers the inferior goods too, *i.e.*, where income effect is negative. This is not provided in the theory of revealed preference.

Neumann-Morgenstern Statistical Theory

There has been a neo-cardinalist revival in recent years as represented by the works of Oskar Morgenstern and John Von Neumann. The demand theory formulated by them is considered applicable to situations involving measurable risk. It is a statistical theory because it is based on a number of observations and not on a single act of choice as in Samuelson's or Hicksian theory.

1. Hicks, J. R. –*A Revision of demand Theory*, 1956, p. 18.

2. For diagrammatic illustration See *H. L. Ahuja–Advance Economic Theory*, 1975, pp. 222-223.

In statistical terms, we can have both strong and weak ordering. For example, if a person always chooses P situation rather than Q situation, P is preferred in a strong sense. Also, if he always chooses Q rather than R, then Q is strongly ordered. But between the situations like P (in which Q is never chosen) and situations like R (in which Q is never rejected), there may exist a number of intermediate situations in which Q may be accepted or rejected. We shall not, therefore, be able to predict the consumer's choice in such situations and we may say that he is in a state of indifference, which is a case of weak ordering. Samuelson's behaviour theory, therefore, cannot rationally predict individual behaviour.

When, however, an individual's choice is repeatedly observed over a set of samples of minimum size, some sort of consistency is established and the way is prepared for the statistical preference hypothesis. The Neumann-Morgenstern theory admits the concept of indifference but only by ruling out the requirement of single-events consistency. Thus, it is a hypothesis of 'weak' but consistent preference (indifference).

It is based on two possible assumptions: (*a*) the consumer is unable to distinguish clearly between two objects so that he chooses (rejects) only hesitatingly with the result that the choice sometimes turns out to be undesirable. (*b*) The consumer does not regard the two objects of his choice as 'sure prospects' and that there is an element of risk of not having one or the other. The existence of risk-explains the phenomenon of weak preference, *i.e., the* choice frequency is less than 100 per cent. The frequency of choice would vary inversely with the degree of risk. Given the degree of risk, the frequency of choice would vary with intensity of preference.This frequency serves as a measure of relative preference under conditions of risk. That is, "under conditions of measurable risk, the individual expresses his relative preference in terms of frequency of his choices."

The neo-cardinalist demand theory is simply this: A "consumer is expected to evaluate his 'prospects' in terms of statistical probability, and judged over a large number of cases, to appear to maximise the statistically expected value of his 'utility'." [3]

Armstrong's Marginal Preference Theory

W.E. Armstrong is essentially an orthodox cardinalist and stands in Marshall's tradition. He has forged his own tools to re-establish cardinalism. His theory is based on two interdependent concepts, *viz.*, uncertaintly and indifference.

3. Majumdar, T. –*The Measurement of Utility*, 1958, p. 102.

We have seen above that the two assumptions on which Neumann-Morgenstern's theory is based are: first the consumer does not regard the object of his choice as 'sure prospects'. Though the nature of the end is certain, one is not certain as to how the end is to be achieved. The second assumption is that the consumer is not able to discriminate clearly between two otherwise certainly distinct ends. It is uncertainly in discernment as distinguished from uncertainty in the prospect of achieving a given economic end which provides a basis of Armstrong's utility theory.

Like Hicks, Armstrong makes use of the concept of indifference which arises from the fact that the consumer is unable to distinguish clearly between the two situations. But, unlike Hicks, his indifference (preference) is not transitive, *i.e.*, it cannot be passed from one to the other. For instance, the consumer may not be able to distinguish between X and Y or between Y and Z, yet the difference between X and Z may be quite perceptible.

Thus, Armstrong puts forward his own concept of uncertainty and definition of indifference. Indifference may arise (*a*) from the principle of compensation, *i.e.*, loss in one direction may be compensated by gain in any other direction, or (*b*) from the idea of approximation, *i.e.*, the two situations being approximately the same, the consumer is unable to distinguish between them and is, therefore, indifferent between them. Armstrong's concept of indifference is based on approximation, whereas Hicks's idea is based on the principle of compensation. It will be seen that (*a*) is the result of weighing pros and cons and (*b*) arises from the consumer's inability to see clearly the difference between the two. Hicks's preference implies process of substitution, whereas Armstrong's indifference is the result of low state of preference.

Armstrong has introduced a concept of 'preference intensity'; the intensity may be high, low or imperceptible. According to Armstrong, preference is marginal when the consumer is just able to perceive. This will happen when the two situations are so near each other that the consumer is barely able to see that he prefers one to the other. The consumer may not be able to distinguish between these two situations. He will then be in a state of indifference. Thus, indifference in Armstrong's definition arises from the approximate identity of the two situations. His indifference is due to the triviality of difference between two situations. This relation of indifference will be intransitive, *i.e.*, there will not exist a relation of indifference between two other points.

MARGINAL UTILITY OF MONEY INCOME

Marshall assumed that the law of diminishing marginal utility applied to money too. But the recent view is that it does not. It is said that the marginal utility of money rises and falls depending on the level of income as is shown by the people taking to gambling and insurance. In this connection, the following hypotheses may be noted:

Bernoulli Hypothesis

Bernoulli offered a rational explanation of gambling and insurance. He said that the people would insist on a larger gain to compensate for the risk of a given loss. He therefore hypothesised that total utility curve of money income slopes from left upwards to right and is concave from below (or the marginal utility of money income curve falls from left to right).

Friedman-Savage Hypothesis

Friedman and Savage have suggested that the utility curve of income is first concave., then convex and finally again concave. That total utility curve is S-shaped. It shows that the poor people are willing to buy fair insurance against any kind of risk, the middle classes are induced to go in for a fair gamble and rich people are prepared to insure against small loss but not against very large losses.

The Markowitz Hypothesis

According to Markowitz, the Friedman-Savage hypothesis contradicts common behaviour. It looks strange, he says, that a poor man should go in for a fair gamble, that a rich man should insure against small losses and that both poor and rich purchase lotteries and gamble on horse races. In order to avoid these contradictions, he suggests a different form of total utility curve.

Key terms

Consistency, neo cardinalist, Statistical utility, marginal preference.

QUESTIONS

1. Explain Hick's revision of demand theory.
2. Explain in brief the satistical utility and marginal preference thories of demand.

ELASTICITY OF DEMAND

Meaning of Elasticity

We have studied the law of demand and we have seen that there is an inverse relation between demand and price. A change (rise or fall) in price leads generally to a change (contraction or extension) of demand. This attribute of demand by virtue of which it stretches or contracts under the pressure of a change in price is known as Elasticity of Demand. "The term elasticity expresses the degree of correlation between demand and price." It is the rate at which the quantity demanded varies with a change in price.

Elasticity of demand is the measure of the responsiveness of demand to changing prices. To be more exact, "The elasticity of demand is a measure of the relative change in amount purchased in response to a relative change in price on a given demand curve." [1] Another precise definition is by Mrs. Joan Robinson thus : "The elasticity of demand, at any price or at any output, is the proportional change of amount purchased in response to a small change in price, divided by the proportional change in price." [2] Other things are assumed to remain constant, *e.g.*, other prices, consumer's income. .

A Spring board is elastic.

It may be carefully noted that elasticity depends primarily on **proportional or percentage changes** and not on absolute changes in price and quantity demanded.

Elastic and Inelastic Demand

A change in demand is not always proportionate to the change in price. A small change in price may lead to a great change in demand. In that case, we shall say that the demand is **elastic** or sensitive or responsive. If, on the other hand, even a big change in price is followed only by a small change in demand, it is said to be a case of **inelastic** demand. For example, even if the price of salt varies widely, we continue to buy almost the same quantity, the demand is inelastic. But, if the price of radio sets falls, many people, who could not afford to buy before, may now be induced to buy; the demand will then stretch or expand; it is elastic.

The demand is elastic when a fall in price increases the total amount spent or the total revenue of the seller (Price × Quantity). In this case, percentage change in the quantity demanded is greater than the percentage change in price. But when a fall in price leads to a small increase in the quantity demanded so that the total outlay of the purchaser, or the total revenue of the seller (*i.e.*, Price × Quantity) decreases, we say that the demand is inelastic. In this case, the percentage change in quantity demanded is smaller than the percentage change in price.

1. Meyers, A. L. –*Elements of Modern Economics* (1951) p. 67.
2. Robbinson (Mrs.), J. – *The Economics of Imperfect Competition* (1945), p. 18).

The elastic demand is said to be greater than unity (or one) and inelastic demand less than unity (but not less than zero). It is unity (or one) when the percentage change in price results in an exactly compensating per centage change in the quantity demanded.

In the words of Marshall, **"The elasticity (or responsiveness) of demand in a market is great or small according as the amount demanded increases much or little for a given fall in price, and diminishes much or little for a given rise in price."**

There are few commodities, however, for which the demand is inelastic. Demand cannot be entirely insensitive to changes in price. Instead of saying 'inelastic', we should say 'less elastic'. Elasticity is a matter of degree only.

Demand may increase either because, with a fall in price, the existing purchasers will purchase more or some new purchasers will begin purchasing. Generally, however, it is the **potential** purchasers who lend elasticity to demand. For example, when the price of wheat falls, it is not through increased purchases by existing buyers but through increased sales to new purchasers that more wheat will now be sold.

Five Cases of Elasticity. It is usual to distinguish between five cases of elasticity: (*i*) Perfectly Elastic or Infinite Elasticity; (*ii*) Perfectly Inelastic or Zero Elasticity; (*iii*) Relatively Elastic; (*iv*) Relatively Inelastic; and (*v*) Unit Elasticity. They can be represented diagrammatically.

Diagrammatic Representation. Figure 11.1 shows an infinitely elastic demand curve DD′ which is a horizontal straight line parallel to the axis of X. It shows that even an infinitesimally small reduction in price leads to an unlimited extension of demand.

In Fig. 11.2 is shown perfectly inelastic demand or zero elasticity. The demand curve DD is a vertical straight line perpendicular to the axis of X and parallel to the axis of Y. It shows that, howsoever much the price may fall or rise, the amount demanded remains the same. In this figure, the amount demanded is OD′ both at price OP and at price OP′.

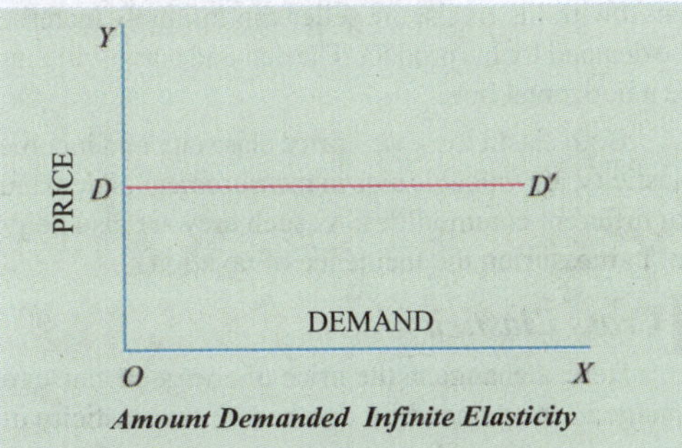

Fig. 11.1. Horizontal demand curve.

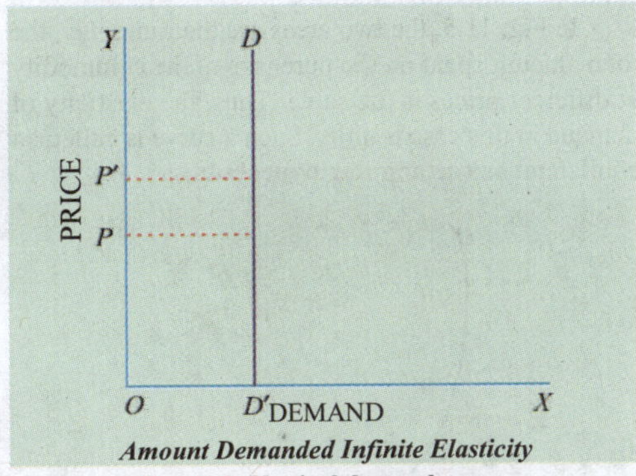

Fig. 11.2. Vertical demand curve.

It may, however, be pointed out that both perfectly inelastic demand and infinitely elastic demand are the two extreme limits which are seldom met within real life and can be conceived of only theoretically. On the other hand, in actual life we come across elasticity of demand which is somewhere between these two limits, *i.e.*, it is more than zero but less than infinity.

Fig. 11.3 shows a less elastic demand, commonly referred to as inelastic demand, while Fig. 11.4 illustrates a very elastic demand. Fig. 11.5 denotes unity elasticity of demand.

In all these diagrams, OX and OY are the two axes. Along OX are represented the quantities purchased and along OY the variations in prices.

In Fig. 11.3, as the price falls from PM (= ON) to P′ M′ (= ON′) the quantity demanded extends from OM to O′ M′ which is a small increase as compared with the fall in price. The area OM′ P′ N′, indicating total revenue received by the seller (or the total amount spent by the purchaser) after the fall in price, is smaller than the area OMPN, the total revenue received by the seller before the fall in price. Thus, the demand is inelastic. (In a subsequent section entitled Measurement of Elasticity, this method of measuring elasticity of demand has been explained at length).

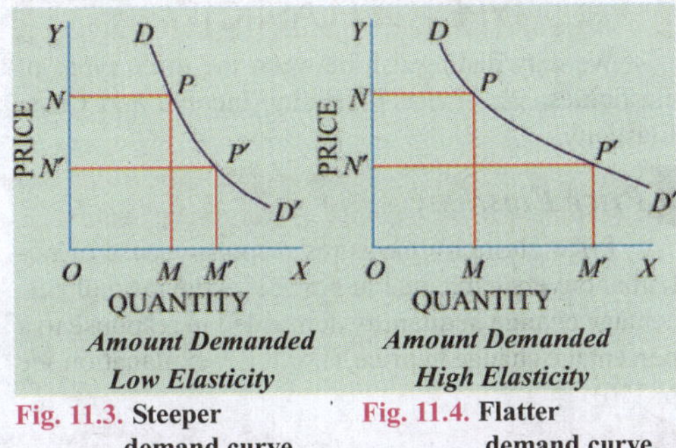

Fig. 11.3. Steeper demand curve. **Fig. 11.4. Flatter demand curve.**

In Fig. 11.4, the area OM′ P′ N′ is greater than the area OMPN and, therefore, the elasticity is more than unity in this diagram.

In Fig. 11.5, the two areas are the same, *i.e.*, the total amount spent on the purchase of the commodity at different prices is the same. Thus, the elasticity of demand in this case is unity. Such a curve is called an equilateral or **rectangular hyperbola.**

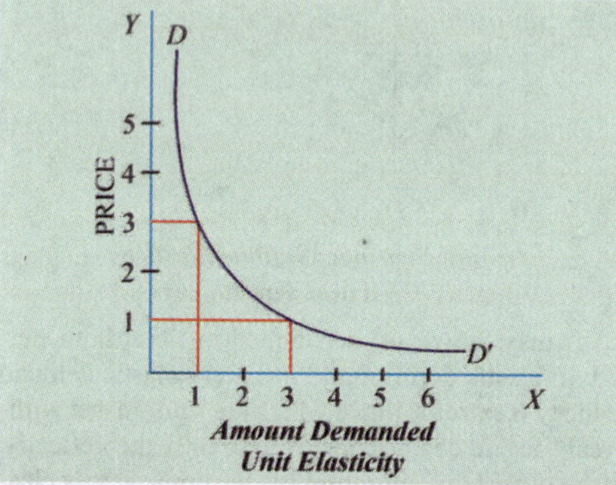

Fig. 11.5. Demand curve is rectangular hyperbola.

Relation of Elasticity with the Law of Diminishing Utility

The concept of elasticity of demand is connected with the law of diminishing utility. We know that marginal utility varies with supply. It falls when the supply is increased and rises when the supply contracts. But the fall of marginal utility does not occur at a uniform rate in all commodities. In certain cases, like salt, we soon get fed up, and the marginal utility falls very rapidly. In such cases, the demand is inelastic or less elastic and a fall in price cannot induce us to buy more. In some other cases, the marginal utility comes down very gradually, *e.g.*, luxuries. Any fall in the price of such commodities is sure to extent the demand. The demand is, therefore, elastic.

In short, **the demand is inelastic when the marginal utility falls rapidly, and elastic when it falls slowly.**

TYPES OF ELASTICITY

We may distinguish between the three types of elasticities, *viz*., Price Elasticity, Income and Cross Elasticity.

Price Elasticity

Price elasticity measures responsiveness of potential buyers to change in price. It is the ratio of percentage change in quantity demanded in response to a percentage change in price. (For fuller explanation see p. 116).

Income Elasticity

Income Elasticity is a measure of responsiveness of potential buyers to change in income. It shows how the quantity demanded will change when the income of the purchaser changes, the price of the commodity remaining the same. It may be defined thus: The Income Elasticity of demand for a good is the ratio of the percentage change in the amount spent on the commodity to a percentage change in the consumer's income, price of commodity remaining constant. Thus,

Income Elasticity

$$= \frac{\text{Proportionate change in the quantity purchased}}{\text{Proportionate change in income}}$$

while prices remain constant.

It is **equal to unity or one** when the proportion of income spent on a good remains the same even though income has increased.

It is said to be **greater than unity** when the proportion of income spent on a good increases as income increases.

It is said to be **less than unity** when the proportion of income spent on a good decreases as income increases.

Generally speaking, when our income increases, we desire to purchase more of the things than we were previously purchasing unless the commodity happens to be an "inferior" good. Normally, then, since the income effect is positive, income elasticity of demand is also positive.

It is **zero** income elasticity of demand when change in income makes no change in our purchases, and it is **negative** when with an increase in income, the consumer purchases less, *e.g.*, in the case of inferior goods.

It may be carefully noted that for any individual seller or firm, the demand for the product is highly elastic even though the demand for the product as a whole may be inelastic. By lowering the price, as compared with his rivals, the seller can infinitely increase the demand for his product. The demand curve will thus be a horizontal line.

Both elasticities, *viz*., price elasticity and income elasticity, are valuable aids in measurement of demand for different commodities. As such they are also helpful in measuring the incidence of taxation.

Cross Elasticity

Here, a change in the price of one good causes a change in the demand for another. Cross-elasticity of Demand for X and Y

$$= \frac{\text{proportionate change in purchase of commodity X}}{\text{Proportionate change in the price of commodity Y}}$$

This type of elasticity arises in the case of inter-related goods such as substitutes and complementary goods.

The two commodities will be complementary, if a fall in the price of Y increases the demand for X and conversely, if a rise in the price of one commodity decreases the demand for the other. They will be substitute or rival goods if a reduction in the price of Y decreases the demand for X, and also if a rise in price of one commodity (say tea) increases the demand for the other commodity (say coffee). The cross elasticity of complementary goods is positive and that between substitutes, it is negative.

It should, however, be remembered that 'cross elasticity' will indicate complementarity or rivalry only if the commodities in question figure in the family budget in small proportions.

Cross elasticities of demand can be used to indicate boundaries between industries. Goods with high cross elasticities constitute one industry, whereas goods with low cross elasticity constitute different industries. It is not to be supposed that cross-elasticity represents reciprocal relationship. It is not a two-way street. The cross-elasticity represents reciprocal relationship. It is not a two-way street. The cross-elasticity of tea with respect to coffee is not the same as that of coffee with respect to tea. The tastes of the consumer, his money income and all prices except of the commodity Y are assumed to remain constant.

To put in mathematical terms :

Price Elasticity of Demand is - $\frac{\Delta q^A}{q^A} \div \frac{\Delta p^A}{P^A}$

Income Elasticity of Demand is $\frac{\Delta q}{q^A} \div \frac{\Delta y^d}{y^d}$

Cross Elasticity of Demand is $\frac{\Delta q^A}{q^A} \div \frac{\Delta P^B}{P^B}$

Whereas Δ is change, Δq stands for some increase in q and $-\Delta q$ for decrease in q ; q^A is the quantity of commodity A, P^A is the price of commodity A, P_B the price of commodity B and y^d is some proportional increase in personal disposable income.

Substitution Elasticity

We may also take notice of another concept of elasticity, *viz.*, substitution elasticity. In this connection, we make use of the concept of marginal rate of substitution already discussed in the indifference curve analysis.

The elasticity of substitution shows to what extent one commodity can be substituted for another without making any change in the total satisfaction derived by the consumer, *i.e.*, he remains on the same indifference curve. In other words, the elasticity of substitution between two goods is the measure of the ease or difficulty with which one commodity can be substituted for another. Just as price effect is the measure of price elasticity of demand similarly substitution effect measures the substitution elasticity of demand.

There are two extremes, *i.e.*, two limiting cases: (*a*) The elasticity of substitution may be infinite. In this case, the goods are perfect substitutes for one another, *i.e.*, they are identical; (*b*) at the other extreme, there is a case of zero elasticity of substitution. Here, there can be no substitution at all and the goods must be used in fixed proportion or not at all. Between these two limits, there can be various degrees of substitution.

When the substitution of one good for another is difficult, then even a small change in the **ratio** of the two goods will bring about a great change in their marginal rate of substitution. If, on the other hand, the substitution of one good for another is easy, then a small change in their proportion with the consumer will not make much change in their marginal rate of substitution.

It is clear that we get an idea about substitution elasticity from the mutual relationship between the change in the proportion of the two goods with the consumer and as a result a change in their marginal rate of substitution. Elasticity of substitution is :

Proportionate increase in the amount of X with respect to Y
Proportionate decrease in the marginal rate of substitution of X for Y

Symbolically,

$$Es = \frac{\Delta\left(\frac{q_x}{q_y}\right)}{\frac{q_x}{q_y}} \div \frac{\Delta\left(\frac{\Delta Y}{\Delta X}\right)}{\frac{\Delta Y}{\Delta X}}.$$

Here Es stands for substitution elasticity : $\frac{q_x}{q_y}$ represents the original proportion between quantities of goods X and Y.

$\Delta\frac{(q_x)}{q_y}$ stands for a small change in the proportion of goods X and Y.

$\frac{\Delta Y}{\Delta X}$ is the initial marginal rate of substitution of X for Y

$\Delta\left(\frac{\Delta Y}{\Delta X}\right)$ is the change in the marginal rate of substitution of good X for Y.

Although, we may distinguish between price elasticity, income elasticity, cross elasticity and substitution elasticity, but we generally confine here to the discussion of price elasticity.

Relation Between Price Elasticity, Income Elasticity and Substitution Elasticity

We have already seen (Chapter 7) that price effect consists of two components, *viz.*, the income effect and the substitution effect. In the same manner, the price elasticity of demand, which is the measure of price effect, depends on income elasticity of demand on the one hand and substitution elasticity on the other.

This relationship can be expressed by the following formula [3] :

$e_p = K.X_i + (1 - KX)e_s$, where

e_p stands for price elasticity of demand

e_i „ „ income elasticity of demand

e_s „ „ substitution elasticity of demand

KX is the proportion of consumer's income spent on the commodity X.

In the above equation KX ei. shows the influence of income effect on the price elasticity of demand. The income effect of a change in price depends on the one hand, on the proportion of consumer's income spent on the commodity X, *i.e.*, KX and also on the income elasticity of demand for the good X, *i.e.*, ei. This explains the first part of the equation, *i.e.* KX. ei. which is the income effect.

The second component, *i.e.*, (I – KX) e_s is the substitution effect. A fall in the price of X will lead to its substitution for other goods. The magnitude of the substitution effect depends on the elasticity of substitution, E_s. *i.e.*, the extent to which X can be substituted for other goods on account of its becoming cheaper. This depends upon the extent to which other goods already figure in consumption of the particular consumer. KX being the proportion of income that is spent on the good X, 1 – KX is the proportion spent on other goods. This indicates the proportion spent on other goods. This indicates the limit to which other goods can be purchased; it shows the extent of substitutability and is thus the substitution effect.

Hence, the equation is

$e_p = KX.\ e_i + (1 - KX)e_s$.

Thus, price elasticity of demand depends upon\

(a) proportion of income spent on the particular good;

(b) Income Elasticity of demand;

(c) Elasticity of Substitution; and

(d) Proportion of income spent on the goods other than X.

3. See Ahuja, H. L. –*Advanced Economic Theory*, 1981, p. 285.

Factors Determining Price Elasticity of Demand

It is not possible to classify goods according to the nature of their demand and lay down rigid rules to determine whether demand in any particular case is elastic or inelastic. We can only formulate some general rule in this connection.

We know that elasticity is relative. For one person or at one place, the demand may be elastic and, for another person and at another place, it may be inelastic. Subjected to this important provison, we may lay down the following rules :

Necessaries and Conventional Necessaries. We must buy fixed quantities of such commodities, whatever the price. In a poor country like India, even the demand for things like salt is somewhat elastic. In Indian in 1923, the doubling of the salt duty reduced the consumption of salt. The change in the price of wheat may be immaterial for upper classes, but its consumption will certainly increase among the poor when the price falls.

It may be carefully noted that demand for wheat (a necessity of life) as a whole may be inelastic, but in a competitive market, demand for the output of any particular firm is highly elastic. If it raises the price a bit, it may lose the entire market.

Demand for Luxuries is Elastic. It stands to reason that lowering of the price of things like radio and T.V. sets, refrigerators and artistic furniture will lead to more being bought, *i.e.*, the demand is elastic. But the demand even for such luxuries on the part of the rich people is not elastic. For them these things are conventional necessaries. They must buy them and having purchased one, they will not buy another, whatever the price. Their (*i.e.*, the rich people's) demand, therefore, is not elastic; it is elastic for people of lesser means only.

Here again we cannot generalise. A luxury is a relative term. A high-priced luxury of the poor man is a low-priced necessary for the rich. A thing may be luxury in one country and a necessary in another. It is said that the luxuries of yesterday have become necessaries of today. Thus, for the same article, the demand may be elastic for some people and inelastic for others, elastic in one country and inelastic in another and elastic at one time inelastic at another.

Proportion of Total Expenditure. If a consumer good absorbs only a small proportion of total expenditure, *e.g.*, salt, the demand will not be much affected by a change in price. Hence, it will be inelastic. Conversely, if it absorbs the bulk of total expenditure, the demand will be elastic.

Substitutes. "The main cause of differences in the responsiveness of the demand for goods to change in their prices lies in the fact that there are more competing substitutes for some goods than for others." When the price of tea rises, we may curtail its purchase and take to coffee, and vice versa. In a case like this a change in price will lead to expansion or contraction in demand.

However, very few things can serve as suitable substitutes; coffee is not exactly like tea. Attempts have been made in Italy, America and Argentina to replace our jute, but without much success. It might appear that, in the matter of toilet requisites, we have several alternatives. We might use Ponds cream or Lakme cream, Colgate or Binaca tooth paste, Lux soap or Cinthol soap, Kiwi polish or Cherry Blossom and so on. But can we really use any of them ? The manufacturer does not want that his product should belong to the elastic demand category. He, therefore, gives it a special label and, by subtle and persistent propaganda, he will induce us to buy it. We become habituated to its use. We are not satisfied until we get our favourite brand. Thus, the manufacturer changes its demand from elastic into inelastic. Substitutes are, therefore, no substitutes.

Goods having Several Uses. Coal is such a commodity when cheap, it will be used for several purposes, *e.g.*, cooking, heating and industrial purposes; and its demand will increase. But, when the price goes up, its use will be restricted only to very urgent uses and consequently less will be purchased when the price rises. The demand will thus contract. When wheat becomes very cheap, it can be used even as cattle feed. Hence, demand for a commodity having several uses is elastic.

Joint Demand. If, for instance, carriages become cheap but the prices of horses continue to rule high, demand for carriages will not extend much. In other words, the demand for jointly demanded goods is less elastic.

Goods, the use of which can be postponed. Most of us during the war postponed our purchases where we Would, *e.g.*, building a house, buying furniture or having a number of warm suits. We go in for such things in a large measure when they are cheap. Demand for such goods is elastic.

Level of Prices. If a thing is either very expensive or very cheap, the demand will be inelastic. If the price is too high, a fall in it will not increase the demand much. If, on the other hand, it is too low, people will have already purchased as much as they wanted; any further fall will not increase the demand.

In Marshall's words, **"Elasticity of demand is great for high prices,** and great or at least considerable for medium prices, but it declines as **the price falls, and gradually fades away if the fall goes so far that satiety level is reached."**[4]

Level of Incomes. The demand on the part of the poor people is more sensitive to price changes. In order to derive maximum benefit from their meagre income, they must be alert to vary their purchases in response to changes in prices. The rich people, on the other hand, do not bother much and continue to buy practically the same quantities even though the price may have changed. The poor man has to run after cheaper substitutes but the rich man does not feel any such need. He can well afford to buy what he is buying. Thus, demand on the part of the poor is more elastic than on the part of the rich.

Market Imperfections. Owing to ignorance about market trends, the demand for a good may not increase when its price falls for the simple reason that consumers may not be aware of the fall in price.

Technological Factors. Low price elasticity may be due to some technical reasons. For example, lowering of electricity rates may not increase consumption because the consumers are unable to buy the necessary electric appliances.

Time Period. The elasticity of demand is greater in the long run than in the short run for the simple reason that the consumer has more time to make adjustments in his scheme of consumption. In other words, he is able to increase or decrease his demand for a commodity.

Conclusion. The above discussion confirms us in the view that it is not possible to lay down any hard and fast rule as to which commodity has an elastic demand and which inelastic. When we want to know whether the demand is elastic or inelastic, we must first know the class of people with reference to whom we wish to ascertain the fact.

MEASUREMENT OF ELASTICITY

For practical purposes, it is not enough to know whether the demand is elastic or inelastic. It is rather more useful to find out to what extent it is so. For that purpose it is essential to measure elasticity.

When people must continue to buy **exactly** the same quantity whatever the price, elasticity is zero. It means that they cannot do without this quantity, however high the price, or they cannot be induced to buy any more, however low the price. The demand is absolutely inelastic. The other extreme is when, even with a slight rise in price, further purchase will altogether stop or a minutest fall in price will extend the demand infinitely. Elasticity, here, is said to be equal to infinity, *i.e.*, it is absolutely elastic. Between

4. Marshall, A. –*Principle ofEconomics*, p. 103.

these two extremes there are varying degrees of elasticity.

Measurement of Price Elasticity of Demand

As we know that there is an indirect relationship between price and quantity demand of a good. $P \alpha \frac{1}{d}$. In other words, the increase in price brings about a decrease in demand, but this is not the same with all goods.

Let us examine the same.

(i) Perfectly inelastic demand. In the diagram vertical axis-price and horizontal axis demand is taken.

In the above diagram original price is OP′ and original quantity demanded is 'OQ'. If price is increased from 'OP' to 'OP_1', there is no corresponding change in quantity demanded. This can be expressed as :

$$Ed = \frac{\Delta Q}{\Delta P} : \frac{OQ}{PP_1}$$

Ed = Elasticity of demand.
ΔQ = Change in quantity
ΔP = Change in price

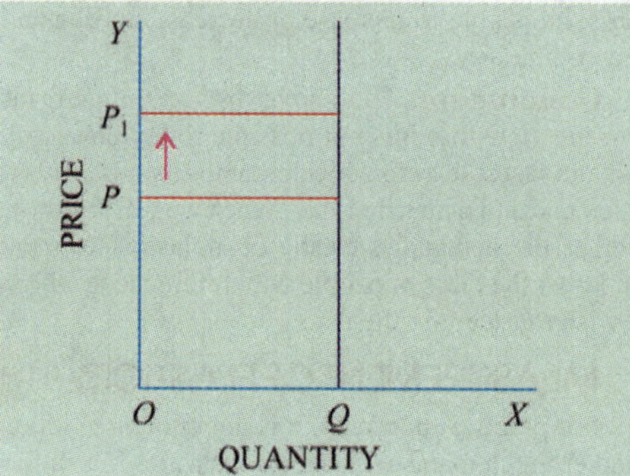

Fig. 11.6. Perfectly in elastic (vertical) demand curve.

OQ is the original quantity demanded, whereas there is change in price, that is 'OP' to 'OP_1'. In other words, numerator is zero and denominator is positive. Hence,

$$Ed = 0, \left[\frac{0}{+ve} = 0\right]$$, this means change in price has no effect on quantity demanded. This is referred as perfectly inelastic demand. The government in most of the developing countries tries to impose more tax on such type of goods, as these goods are essential or necessary goods category, and people cannot change the demand even if price increases or decreases;

(ii) Perfectly elastic demand. In this case the demand curve is perfectly elastic, or it is horizontal to x-axis.

$$Ed = \frac{\Delta Q}{\Delta P} \therefore \frac{QQ_1}{OP},$$

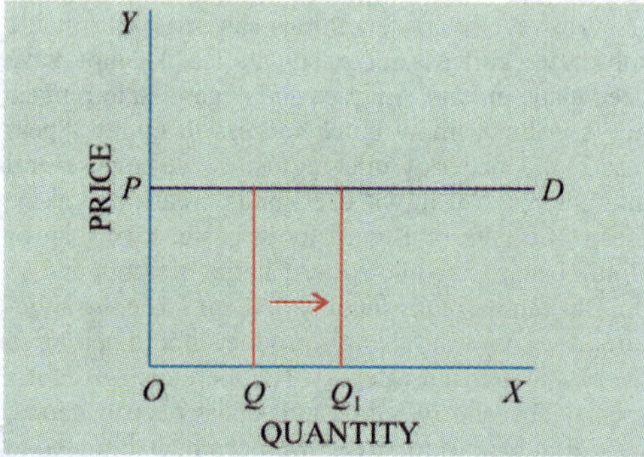

Fig. 11.7. Perfectly elastic (Horizonal demand curve).

$$Ed = \frac{\Delta Q}{OP} \therefore \frac{QQ_1}{OP}$$

In this diagram there is no change in 'price' but there is an increase in quantity demanded, this means that the elasticity of demand is perfectly elastic curve. In other words, price is not changing but quantity demanded is increasing, $Ed = \frac{+ve}{0}$ Any number divided by 'zero' will be '∝', It is referred as infinite.

Therefore Ed = ∝.

(iii) Unit elasticity of demand. In this diagram the demand curve is 45° degree line 'dd' is demand

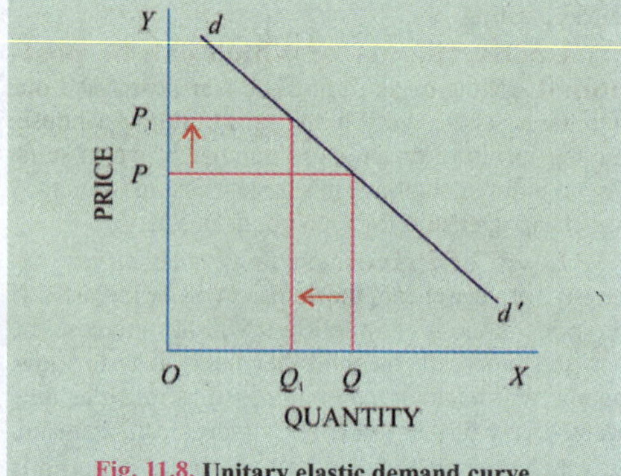

Fig. 11.8. Unitary elastic demand curve.

curve, original price is 'OP' and 'OQ' is the original quantity demanded. If there is a change in price from 'OP' to 'OP_1' then due to this there is a change in quantity demanded from 'OQ' to 'OQ_1'. In the diagram it is clear that the change in price 'PP_1' (↑) is equal to change in quantity demanded that is 'QQ_1' (↓). This is referred as unit elasticity of demand.

$$Ed = \frac{\Delta Q}{\Delta P} \therefore \frac{QQ_1}{PP_1}, Ed = 1$$

where 'PP_1' is change is price due to this there is ↓ in 'demand' that is QQ_1 but $PP_1 = QQ_1$, that means the change in price is exactly equal to change in quantity. In other words if there is a change in price of a good by 20%, then there will be a corresponding ↓decrease in quantity demanded by 20%. Such goods are known as 'comfort' goods. This is one of the essential requirement for policy framers specially the taxation policy.

(iv) Relatively Inelastic demand. In this, the change in price is more and the corresponding change in quantity demand is less. In the figure 'PP_1' is change in price due to this, there is 'QQ_1' is reduction in demand and vice-versa.

$$\text{Hence, } Ed = \frac{\Delta Q}{\Delta P} = \frac{PP_1}{QQ_1}$$

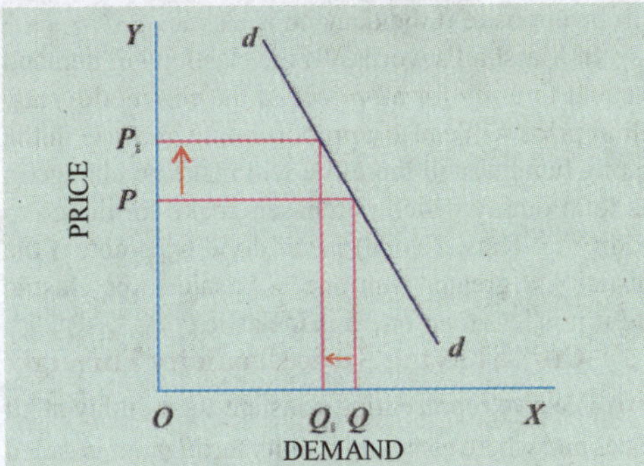

Fig. 11.9. Inelastic demand curve.

In this diagram we can see that change in price 'PP_1' is more and reduction in quantity demanded that is change in quantity is relatively less, that is 'QQ_1'

$$\therefore \quad Ed = \frac{\Delta Q}{\Delta P} = \frac{PP_1}{QQ_1}$$

$$[PP_1 > QQ_1 \text{ or } QQ_1 < PP_1]$$

This is referred as relatively inelastic demand or Ed < 1, (demand curve is steeper), in this category semi-essential goods are included, *i.e.*, clothing, shoes, watches etc.

(v) Relatively elastic demand. In this case the change in price is less, where as its corresponding effect on change on demand is more (the demand curve is flatter to 'x' axis).

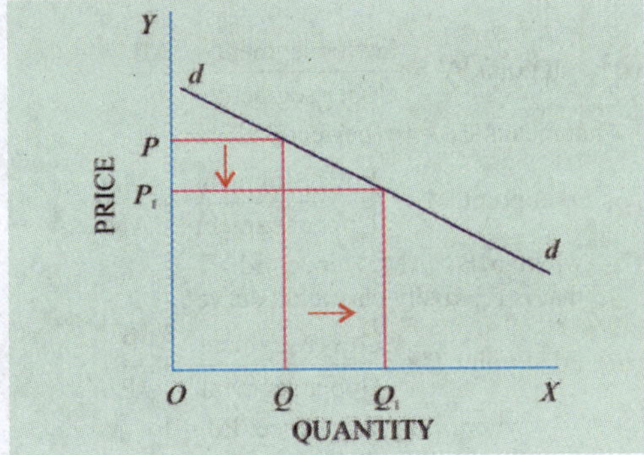

Fig. 11.10. Elastic demand curve.

In this diagram at 'OP' price 'OQ' quantity is demanded. If the price changes from 'OP' to 'OP_1' (reduced) then, quantity demanded increases from 'OQ' to OQ_1.

From the diagram we can see PP_1 is less and 'QQ_1' is more. Hence this can be referred as 'relatively elastic demand'

$$Ed = \frac{\Delta Q}{\Delta P} = \frac{QQ_1}{PP_1}$$

Where $\{QQ_1 > PP_1 \text{ or } PP_1 < QQ_1\}$

or Ed > 1, (Relatively elastic demand) Luxury goods falls under this category.

Point method of measuring Price elasticity of demand. If we take a 45° line demand curve and select different points at different places, (as shown in the diagram below) the elasticity of demand is different at different points.

There are five points on line 'AB' the demand curve. Points 'A', 'M', 'P', 'N' and 'B', Let us measure the elasticity of demand at these points.

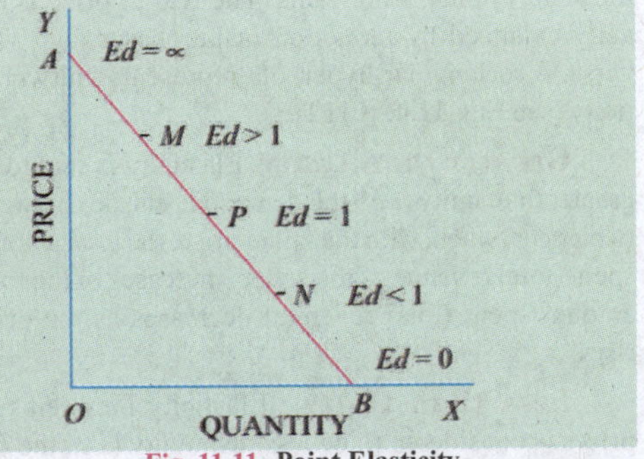

Fig. 11.11. Point Elasticity.

Elasticity varies from 0 on quantity axis to ∞ on price axis with 1 at the mid point on a straight line demand curve.

The general formula for measurement of price elasticity of demand is

$$= \frac{\text{Lower segment (of the demand curve)}}{\text{Upper segment (of the demand curve)}}$$

(*i*) Ed at point 'A' $= \frac{\text{Lower segment}}{\text{Upper segment}} = \frac{AB}{O}$

That means Ed = ∝ (perfectly elastic)

(*ii*) Ed at point 'M' $= \frac{\text{Lower segment}}{\text{Upper segment}} = \frac{MB}{AM}$

where MB > AM, Hence, Ed >1
that is relatively elastic dd curve

(*iii*) Ed at point 'P' $= \frac{\text{Lower segment}}{\text{Upper segment}} = \frac{PB}{AP}$

where PB = AP Hence, Ed = 1
that is unit elasticity of demand.

(*iv*) Ed at point 'N' $= \frac{\text{Lower segment}}{\text{Upper segment}} = \frac{NB}{AN}$

where NB < AN that is Ed <1
that means elasticity of demand is relatively inelastic demand.

(*v*) Ed at point 'B' $= \frac{\text{Lower segment}}{\text{Upper segment}} = \frac{O}{AB}$

That is Ed = 0, change in that means it is perfectly inelastic demand curve.

Total Outlay Method

According to this method, we compare the total outlay of the purchaser (or total revenue, *i.e.*, total value of sales from the point of view of the seller) before and after the variations in price. Elasticity of demand is expressed in three ways : (1) Unity (or unitary elasticity), (2) greater than unity, and (3) less than unity.

Unity. It is **unity,** when, even though the price has changed, the total amount spent (total revenue of the seller) remains the same. The rise in price is exactly balanced by reduction in purchases, and vice versa. A rectangular hyperbola represents unity elasticity (see Fig. 11.4, p.112).

Greater than Unity. Elasticity is said to be greater than unity (*i.e.*, the demand is elastic) between two prices, when, with the fall in price, the total amount spent (total revenue of the seller) increases or the total amount spent (total revenue) decreases as the price rises.

Less than Unity. Elasticity between two prices is considered to be less than unity (*i.e.*, the demand is inelastic or less elastic) when the total amount spent (total revenue of the seller) increases with a rise in price and decreases with a fall in price.

This will be clear from the following schedule:–

TABLE 1

	Price of pencils Per Dozen (1) Rs.	*Quantity Demanded* (2) Dozen	*Total Outlay (Revenue)* (3) = (1) × (2) Rs.
(1)	8.0	3	24.0
(2)	7.0	4	28.0
(3)	6.0	5	30.0
(4)	5.0	6	30.0
(5)	4.0	7	28.0
(6)	3.0	8	24.0

As between (1) and (2) and (2) and (3), the elasticity is greater than unity, because the total amount spent (total revenue of the seller) decreases when the price rises and increases when the price fall. As between (3) and (4), it is unity as the total amount spent (total revenue of the seller) remains the same even though the price has changed. Between (4) and (5) the elasticity is less than unity because the total amount spent (total revenue of the seller) increase when the price rises and decreases with a fall in price.

Thus, elasticity is a warning signal for the businessmen. It tells him that in the case of inelastic demand reduction in price will reduce his income or revenue and increase in price will increase it. The effect will be opposite if the demand is elastic.

In Marshall's words, "If the elasticity of demand is equal to unity for all prices of the commodity, any fall in price will cause a proportionate increase in the among bought, and therefore will make no change in the total outlay which purchasers make for the commodity." [5] Thus, 1 (one) is the dividing point. If the elasticity is greater than one, it is said to be elastic, and if it is less than one it is inelastic.

Curve having Same Elasticity Throughout. A curve representing constant total outlay at all prices and where elasticity is unity throughout is called **rectangular hyperbola.** Excepting such cases and cases of infinitely elastic and absolutely inelastic demand (see Fig. 11.1 and 11.2) no curve represents the same elasticity throughout its length. Usually a curve shows different elasticities at different points.

Proportional Method

In this method, we compare the percentage change in price with the percentage change in demand. The elasticity is the ratio of the percentage change in the quantity demanded to percentage change in price charged. The formula is:–

5. Marshall, A.—*Prinicples* p. 839.

Price Elasticity

$$= \frac{\text{Proportionate change in amount demanded}}{\text{Proportionate change in price}}$$

$$= \frac{\text{Change in demand}}{\text{Amount demanded}} \div \frac{\text{Change in price}}{\text{Price}}$$

Suppose, the price to a particular brand of a radio set falls from Rs. 500 to Rs. 400 each, *i.e.*, 20 per cent fall. As a result of this fall in price, suppose further that the demand for the radio sets has gone up from Rs. 400 to 600, *i.e.*, 50 per cent. Elasticity of demand will be 50/20 or 2.5 per cent.

The concept of price elasticity can be used in comparing the sensitivity of the different types of goods (*e.g.*, luxuries and necessaries) to changes in their prices. For example, by this means we may find that the price elasticity for foodgrains, in general is 0.5, whereas for fruit it may be 1.5. This means that the demand for foodgrains is less sensitive to price changes than demand for fruit. Food is a necessity of life and people must buy almost the same quantity, even if its price has risen. The consumer can, however, economise in fruit or any other commodity included in the family budget.

The elasticity of demand is always **negative,** although by convention it is taken to be positive. It is negative because change in quantity demanded is in opposite direction to the change in price. This is, a fall in price is followed by rise in demand, and vice versa. Hence, **elasticity is always less than zero,** unless of course the demand curve is abnormal, *i.e.*, sloping upward from right to left. Strictly speaking, in mathematical terms, there should be minus sign (–) before the figure indicating price elasticity. But by convention, for the sake of simplicity, the minus sign is dropped in economics.

Geometrical Method: Point Elasticity

This method tells us how to measure elasticity of demand at any point on a demand curve. The demand curve in Fig. 11.12. DD is the straight line demand curve. Elasticity is represented by the fraction: distance from D to a point on the curve divided by the distance from the other end to that point. Thus, elasticity of demand on the points P_1, P_2 and P_3 respectively is

$$\frac{D'P_1}{DP_1}, \frac{D'P_2}{DP_2} \text{ and } \frac{D'P}{DP_3}$$

Since P is the middle of the curve

$$\frac{D'P}{DP} = 1$$

i.e., elasticity is unity.

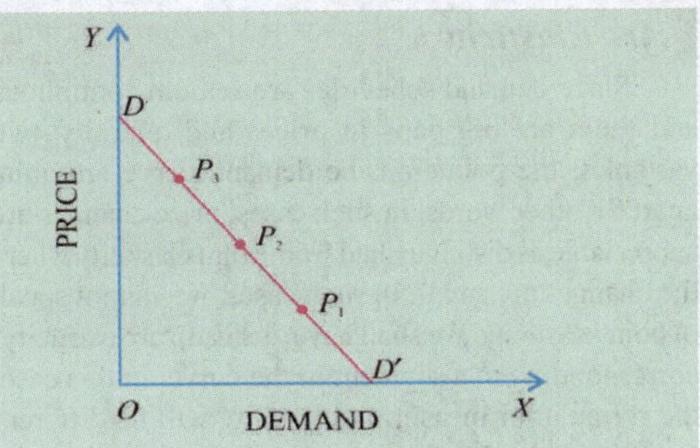

Fig. 11.12. Point Elasticity on a St. Line Demand Curve.

It can be shown that elasticity at a lower point on the curve is less than unity than at a higher point.

Even if the demand curve is not a straight line, the above formula will apply. A tangent will, however, have to be drawn at the point on the curve where elasticity is to be measured. This is illustrated in the diagram (Fig. 11.13).

DD′ is the demand curve, and two tangents PM and P′M′ are drawn respectively at the points T and T′. At the point T, elasticity will be equal to TM. This will apply only so long as the tangent and the curve coincide which means for an infinitesimally short distance. If there is any departure from the point T, a new tangent will have to be drawn and elasticity ascertained accordingly. For instance, at the point T′ elasticity = M′ T′. Clearly, elasticity at T is greater than elasticity at T′.

Two Important Conclusions. We may, therefore, note that (*a*) elasticity of demand is different at different points (or price ranges) of the same curve.

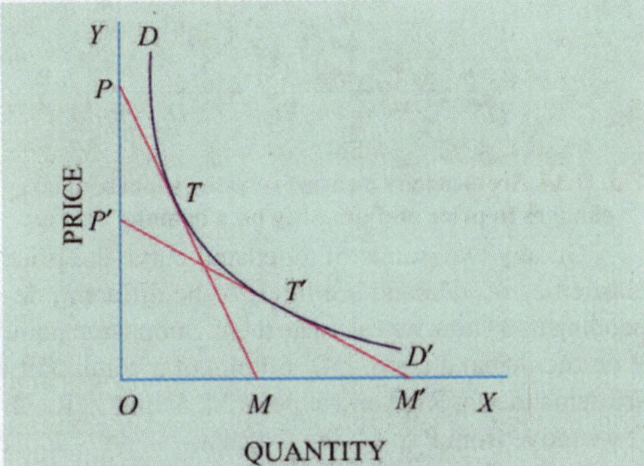

Fig. 11.13. Point Elasticity by drawing tangent.

(*b*) Elasticity is not be judged from the shape of the demand curve. That is, a steeper curve does not necessarily indicate low elasticity and a flatter curve a high elasticity. This is explained to the next page.

Arc Elasticity

Since demand schedules are seldom continuous and there are big gaps in prices and quantity–two variables, the points on the demand curve are quite apart. In other words, in such cases, price changes are appreciable as distinguished from point elasticity where the changes are small. In such cases, we cannot speak of point elasticity. We shall have, instead, 'arc elasticity' corresponding to a segment of the curve. In this case, the formula for measuring elasticity will be different from that for point elasticity. Instead of using old and new prices and quantity we take the average of both.

It will be seen that in arc elasticity, we express the price change as a proportion of the average of the initial price and change in price; and similarly, we express the change in the quantity demanded as a proportion of the average of the initial and the changed quantity. Thus, the arc elasticity is the average elasticity. Its magnitude will differ according as we make smaller or bigger move on the demand curve.

In the words of Baumol, "Arc elasticity is a measure of the **average** responsiveness to price changes exhibited by a demand curve over some finite stretch of the curve." Any two points on a demand curve make an arc. The area between P and M on the DD curve in Fig. 11.14 is an arc which measures elasticity over a certain range of prices and quantities.

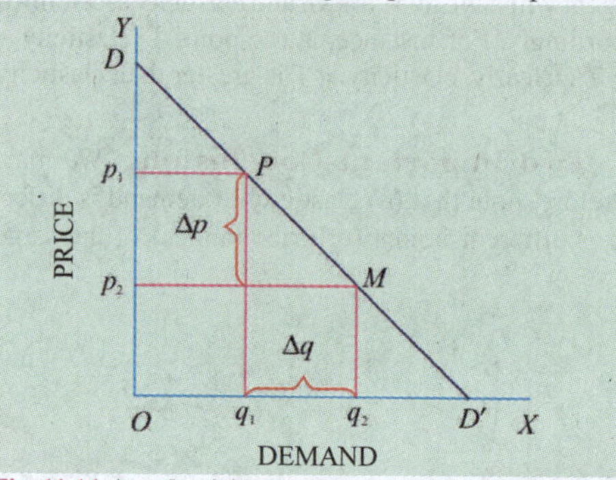

Fig. 11.14. Arc elasticity measures elasticity incase of large changes in price and quantity on a demand curve.

On any two points of a demand curve the price elasticities of demand are likely to be different, depending upon how we calculate them. Suppose at point P on the demand curve DD, 6 units of a commodity are demanded at Rs. 3 and at point M, 8 units at Rs. 2. If we move from P to M, the formula:–

$$ep = \frac{\Delta q}{q} \div \frac{\Delta P}{P}$$

gives the coefficient $\frac{2}{6} \times \frac{3}{1} = \frac{2}{2} = 1$

If, however, we move from M to P,

$$ep = \frac{2}{8} \times \frac{2}{1} = \frac{2}{4} = \frac{1}{2}$$

Thus, the point method of measuring elasticity at two points on a demand curve gives different elasticity coefficients.

To avoid this discrepancy, an average of the two values is calculated on the basis of the formula:–

$$\frac{q_1 - q_2}{q_1 + q_2} \div \frac{p_1 - p_2}{p_1 + p_2}$$

where q_1 and q_2 are the two quantities at the two prices p_1 and p_2 respectively.

Applying the above values of quantities and price, we get

$$\frac{6-8}{6+8} \div \frac{3-2}{3+2} = \frac{-2}{14} \times \frac{5}{1} = \frac{-10}{14} = \frac{-5}{7}$$

This result is more satisfactory than the two different elasticity coefficients arrived at by the point elasticity method.

The arc method may be put in simple language as under :–

$$\frac{\text{difference in q}}{\text{sum of q}} \div \frac{\text{difference in p}}{\text{sum of p}}$$

The closer the two points P and M are, the more accurate will be the measure of elasticity on the basis of the above formula. The arc elasticity is in fact the elasticity of the mid-point between P and M on the demand curve DD. If there is no difference between the two points and they merge into each other or coincide, arc elasticity becomes point elasticity.

Price Elasticity and Indifference Curve Technique

We can apply the indifference curve technique for the measurement of price elasticity. For this purpose, we take into consideration the shape of the price consumption curve. (See Figure 7.7, 7.8 and 7.9 in Ch. 7.) We can lay down the following propositions:

(1) When the price consumption curve slopes downward, the price elasticity of demand is greater than unity or one, *i.e.*, demand is elastic.

(2) When the shape of the price consumption curve is a horizontal straight line, the price elasticity of demand is unity or one, *i.e.*, it is constant.

(3) When the price consumption curve is upward sloping, then the price elasticity of demand is less than unity, *i.e.*, the demand is inelastic.

Similarly, when we want to measure income elasticity of demand, we consider the shape of the income consumption curve instead of the price consumption curve.

Slope of the Demand Curve and Price Elasticity

The slope of the curve is not to be confused with

elasticity. In other words, the slope of the curve is not a reliable indicator of the degree of elasticity.

It is, therefore, not to be supposed that a flat curve **must** mean elastic demand and a steep curve necessarily inelastic demand. The reason is that the slope of the curve depends on **absolute** changes, whereas elasticity indicates proportionate or percentage changes. The slope of the demand curve indicates the ratio of the change in the quantity demanded to the change in the price. Elasticity, on the other hand, indicates the percentage or proportionate change in the quantity demanded in response to a percentage change in price. It focusses attention on the proportionate changes as distinguished from absolute changes. If we redraw a demand curve measuring price in paise instead of rupees, it will cause a drastic decrease in the downward slope of the demand curve. But there has been no real change in the demand curve itself.

There is another drawback if we measure elasticity by the slope of the curve. Take two commodities, say wheat and radio sets. A five-rupee fall in the price of wheat may increase the demand by 5 lakh quintals but a 5 -rupee fall in the price of a radio set may increase the demand by 25 sets only. This does not mean that the demand for wheat is more responsive to the change in price than radio sets. The reason is that a 5 -rupee fall in the price of wheat is a big change whereas a 5 -rupee fall in the price of a radio set is insignificant. Also, there is no basis for comparison between a unit of wheat and a unit of radio sets.

Same Steepness but Different Elasticities. We have seen that in Fig. 11.12, the demand curve DD ' has the same steepness throughout but different elasticities at different points. If elasticity and slope were closely related, the elasticity would be constant throughout.

Same Elasticity Throughout. We have only three types of demand curve on which elasticity is the same on all points on such curves. These are demand curves showing absolutely inelastic demand (as in Fig. 11.2), infinitely elastic demand (as in Fig. 11.1) and unity elasticity of demand (as in Fig. 11.5). In all other cases, elasticity of demand is different at different points of a demand curve.

In Fig. 11.12, the demand is elastic near the price-axis (OY), say, near the point D, and unitary half way, *i.e.*, at point P_2 , and inelastic near the quantity-axis, *i.e.*, near D′.

Since elasticity depends **not on absolute changes but on percentage changes,** it really depends on the steepness of the curve relative to the price quantity ratio.[6]

6. See Samuelson, P. A. –*Economics* (1948), p. 451, especially how the formula has been worked out, in the footnote.

Different Slope but Same Elasticity. In Fig. 11.15, the curves, BP and AP have different slopes but they have the same elasticity at given price. Let OM be the price. Draw a straight line parallel to X-axis cutting BP at R and AP at S. Now elasticity of the curve BP at the point R is

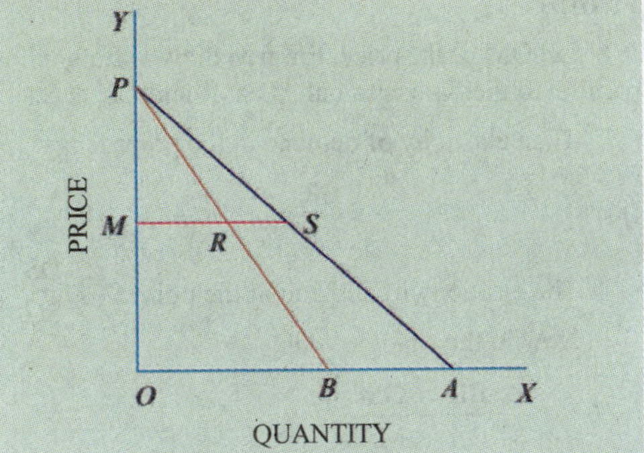

Fig. 11.15. Elasticity compared for straight demand curves originating from the same point on price axis with different slopes, the elasticity on each of them for a given price is same.

$$\frac{BR}{RP}.$$

The elasticity of the curve at the point S is $\frac{AS}{SP}$.

Now in the right-angled triangle BOP,

$$\frac{BR}{RP} = \frac{OM}{MP} \quad ...(1)$$

But in the right-angled triangle AOP,

$$\frac{OM}{MP} = \frac{AS}{SP} \quad ...(2)$$

Hence, from (1) and (2), we get

$$\frac{BR}{RP} = \frac{AS}{SP}$$

That is, elasticity at both R and S is the same even though the two curves have different slopes. Such curves are called **iso-elastic.**

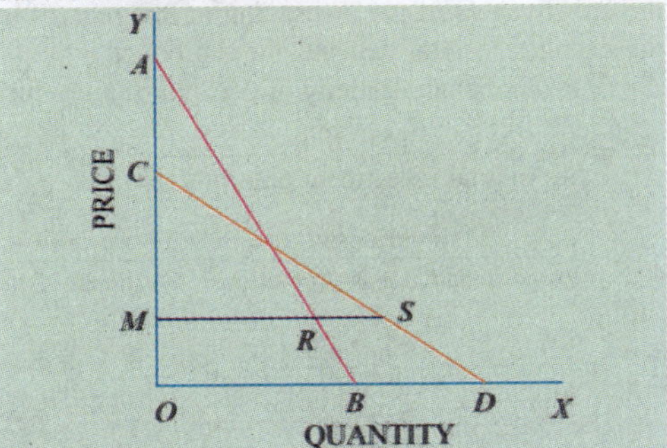

Fig. 11.16. Elasticities compared for a given price and quantity, elasticity varies inversely with slope of the demand curve.

Slope Indicating Elasticity. We can, however, conceive of one case where the relative elasticity of two curves can be known from their respective slopes. Suppose there are two curves, AB and CD, representing the demand for the same good in separate markets as shown in the following diagram (Fig. 11.16).

Let OM be the price. From M draw a straight line parallel to the X-axis to cut AB at R and CD at S.

Then elasticity of demand at the point R is

$$\frac{BR}{RA}.$$

The elasticity of demand at the point S is $\frac{DS}{SC}$.

Now in the triangle AOB

$$\frac{BR}{RA} = \frac{OM}{MA}.$$

and in the triangle COD,

$$\frac{DS}{SC} = \frac{OM}{MC}.$$

Since $\frac{OM}{MC}$ is greater than $\frac{OM}{MA}$

therefore, $\frac{DS}{SC}$ is greater than $\frac{BR}{RA}$.

That is, the curve CD, which slopes more gently represents greater elasticity than curve AB which slopes more steeply.

Promotional Elasticity of Demand

Modern markets are that of monopolistic competition and oligopoly. In these markets huge amount of investments are made in promotional measures. In other words, without the use of promotional measures to increase the sales the monopolistic & oligopolistic markets cannot survive. Hence promotional elasticity of demand measures the effectiveness of the investment in this regards to the changes in total demand for a product.

Promotional elasticity of demand of a product

$$'x' = \frac{\Delta es \text{ in sales}}{\Delta es \text{ in total investment on promotion}}$$

$$Epx = \frac{\text{Proportionate } \Delta es \text{ in sales of 'x'}}{\text{Proportionate } \Delta es \text{ in promotional investment of 'x'}}$$

$$E_{px} = \frac{\Delta S_x}{\Delta I_{px}}$$

ΔS_x = Δes in total sales of 'x'

ΔI_x = Δes in total Promotional Investment on 'x'

Epx = Promotional elasticity of demand of a product 'x'

Promotional elasticity of demand has to be taken into account in relation to the product life stage. This can be applied only in the initial stages of the product life cycle.

Practical Applications of Elasticity of Demand

The concept of elasticity of demand is of great practical importance in the sphere of government finance as well as in trade and commerce.

Taxation. The Minister of Finance can be more sure of his revenues if he taxes those commodities for which the demand is inelastic. The tax will no doubt raise the price but the demand being inelastic, people must continue to buy the same quantity of the commodity. Thus, the demand will not decrease. But, on humanitarian grounds, such taxes are generally avoided. Since such commodities are necessaries of life, their taxation is bound to affect public welfare.

Monopoly Price. In the same manner, the businessman, especially if he is a monopolist, will have to consider the nature of demand while fixing his price. In case it is inelastic, it will pay him to charge a higher price and sell a smaller quantity. If, on the other hand, the demand is elastic, he will lower the price, stimulate demand and thus maximize his monopoly net revenue. In a competitive industry, however, demand even for necessaries produced by a particular firm is elastic. No firm is in a position to dictate any price. Knowing the nature of demand of the various groups of consumers, the monopolist can practise price discrimination.

Joint Products. The concept of elasticity of demand finds application in the case of joint products also. In such cases, separate costs are not ascertained. The producer will be guided mostly by demand and its nature while fixing his price. The transport authorities fix their rates according to this principle when we say that they charge what the 'traffic will bear.'

Increasing Returns. When an industry is subject to increasing returns, the manufacturer lowers the price to develop the market so that he may be able to produce more and take full advantage of the economies of large-scale production.

Output. Elasticity of demand affects industrial output. But in this connection we have to distinguish between elasticity of demand of an individual consumer and of the market as a whole. No amount of reduction in the price will induce an individual to buy another copy of the same newspaper or magazine. The individual demand is inelastic but not the market demand, and it is the latter which matters for the producer. Reduction in price will certainly increase the sale in the market as a whole.

Wages. Elasticity of demand also exerts its influence on wages. If demand for a particular type of labour is relatively inelastic, it is easy to raise wages, but not otherwise.

Poverty in Plenty. The concept of elasticity explains the paradox of poverty in the midst of plenty. A bumper crop instead of being a cause of agricultural prosperity may spell disaster if the demand for the commodity is inelastic. This is specially so if the produce is perishable. A rich harvest may actually fetch less money than a poor one.

In the case of storable articles, however, the demand is less inelastic, or is elastic. A fall in the price may lead to increased purchases and storing. This is with reference to a particular year, but over a period of five years or so. The demand even for such commodities, *e.g.*, wheat, is relatively less elastic.

If the elasticity of demand for wheat is unity, the incomes of the growers would remain same whatever the condition of the crop (and therefore, price). In years of bad harvest, the rise in price would sufficiently compensate the grower for the reduced output. In order to ensure a stable income to the farmers, the government must, therefore, take note of the degree of elasticity of demand for a particular crop and adopt measures to counteract gluts and scarcities as the case may be.

Effect on the Economy. The working of the economy in general is affected by the nature of consumer demand. It affects the total volume of goods and services produced in the country. If also affects producers' demand for different factors of production, their allocation and remuneration.

Economic Policies. Modern governments regulate output and prices. In this, they are guided by the nature of consumer demand. They have also to control business cycles and inflationary pressures and check deflationary trends. For these purposes again, the nature of demand will have to be taken into consideration. The government can create public utilities where demand is inelastic and monopoly element is present.

International Trade. The nature of demand for the internationally traded goods is helpful in determining the quantum of gain accruing to the respective countries. This is how it determines the terms of trade.

Rate of Foreign Exchange. While fixing the rate of exchange, the government has to consider the elasticity or otherwise of its imports and exports.

Thus, it can be easily seen that the concept of elasticity of demand is of immense utility in the business world, because the degree of responsiveness of demand to changes in price affects the total revenue (*i.e.*, Price × Quantity sold) of the businessman, the seller. When the demand is elastic (*i.e.*, elasticity is greater than 1), a fall in the price of the commodity will lead to more than proportionate increase in the quantity sold. This means that the total revenue will go up, because the increase in the quantity sold will more than compensate for the fall in price. On the other hand, if the demand is relatively inelastic (*i.e.*, elasticity less than unity or 1), the increase in the quantity sold will be less than proportionate to a fall in price. As a consequence the total revenue will fall. It follows, therefore, that it pays a businessman to lower the price of his product when the elasticity of demand for his product is greater than unity (*i.e.*, the demand is relatively elastic).

However, the total revenue will not be affected, if the elasticity of demand is unity, because increase in the quantity sold will just compensate for the fall in price.

The character of demand, whether elastic or inelastic, has also an intimate bearing on the problem of price stability. It can be easily understood that if the demand is elastic, it will quickly adjust to a change in price (*i.e.*, decrease when price rises and increase when price falls.). The result will be that the original price may be somewhat restored. In case the demand is inelastic, as in the case of agricultural commodities, changes in the conditions of supply will bring about disproportionate changes in price. Hence, in such cases there is a mounting pressure on the Government to step in to stabilise price through buffer stock operations or otherwise, *e.g.*, rationing and price control in emergency scarcities.

Appraisal. The concept of elasticity of demand is, however, not without its critics. For example, Prof. Samuelson regards the concept of elasticity as of 'no consequence' and only a 'mental exercise'. He criticises it on these grounds: (*a*) Economic laws being qualitative and ordinal, the problem of dimensions is immaterial. (*b*) Elasticity co-officients are essentially arbitrary. (*c*) Its basis is partial equilibrium since while calculating the price elasticity of one commodity, we ignore other important factors like changes in prices of other commodities and in consumer's incomes.

When all is said and done the concept of elasticity of demand is not merely of theoretical interest. But it has also practical application in diverse economic fields as explained above.

THEORETICAL IMPORTANCE

Apart from the practical importance of the concept of elasticity of demand, the concept plays a crucial role in economic theory and is extensively used as a tool of economic analysis. We mention below some aspects of economic theory where use is made of this concept:

Price Determination. As will be clear from the discussion on product pricing (Part IV), the concept of elasticity of demand is used in explaining the determination of price under various market conditions. For instance, under perfect competition, the demand curve facing an individual seller is perfectly elastic which means that the producer can sell any amount by lowering the price a bit. But under monopoly or imperfect competition, the demand is less than perfectly elastic and the demand curve is downward sloping. Since the demand is less elastic, the monopolist is in a position to exercise some control over price and the buyer has to accept the price.

Relation Between Price Elasticity, Average Revenue and Marginal Revenue. There is a close relationship between price elasticity, average revenue and marginal revenue which the concept of elasticity helps to explain. This relationship enables us to understand and compare the conditions of equilibrium under different market conditions. The formula which explains this is

Price or $AR = MR\frac{e}{(e-1)}$. Also, Price or

$AR = MC\frac{e}{(e-1)}$, since in equilibrium MR = MC.

Price Discrimination. The concept of elasticity of demand is useful in explaining the conditions under which price discrimination by a monopolist becomes profitable. Price discrimination is found to be profitable if elasticity of demand in one market is different from elasticity of demand in another. The monopolist can charge a higher price in the market where elasticity of demand is less and a lower price where elasticity of demand is greater.

Measuring Degree of Monopoly Power. Elasticity of demand is also used in measuring the degree of monopoly power. Monopoly power means the power which a monopolist has to influence price. It represents the difference between marginal cost and price. This difference ultimately depends on elasticity of demand for the monopolist's product. The less is the elasticity of demand higher will be the price and wider the difference between the marginal cost and greater the monopoly power, and *vice versa*. The monopoly power is absent when there is perfect competition because the seller has no control over price. He has to accept the price as given. The demand curve facing him is perfectly elastic, i.e., a horizontal straight line parallel to the axis of X.

Classification of Goods as Substitutes and Complements. Goods are classified as substitutes on the basis of cross elasticity. Two commodities may be considered as substitutes if cross elasticity is positive and complements when elasticity is negative.

Boundary Between Industries. Cross elasticity of demand is also useful in indicating boundaries between industries. Goods with high cross elasticities constitute one industry, whereas goods with lower elasticity constitute different industries.

Market Forms. The concept of cross elasticity helps to understand different market forms. Infinite cross elasticity indicates perfect competition, whereas zero or near zero elasticity indicates pure monopoly and high elasticity indicates imperfect competition.

Incidence of Taxes. The concept of elasticity of demand is used in explaining the incidence of indirect taxes like sales tax and excise duty. Less is the elasticity of demand higher the incidence, and *vice versa.* In case of inelastic (or less elastic) demand the consumers have to buy the commodity and must bear the tax.

Theory of Distribution. Elasticity of demand is useful in the determination of relative shares of the various factors of production. If the demand for a factor of production is less elastic, its share in the national dividend is higher, and *vice versa*. If elasticity of substitution is high, the share will be low.

Conclusion. Thus, the concept of elasticity of demand is highly useful as a tool of economic analysis.

DEMAND AS SEEN BY AN INDIVIDUAL SELLER

We have been studying demand so far from the point of the consumer. It is worthwhile to shift the angle and try to look at it from the point of view of the seller. The demand price, *i.e.*, the price which a consumer is willing to pay, is the income or revenue of the seller. It is called the average revenue (AR). The income that the seller gets by selling an additional unit of the commodity is called marginal revenue or MR.

It may also be noted that the demand for a commodity, say wheat, may be inelastic from the point of view of a consumer but it can well be elastic from the point of view of the seller, because he can sell any amount at the prevailing price. That is why it is said that under perfect competition, the demand curve facing an individual seller is perfectly elastic and is represented by a horizontal straight line.

In the case of imperfectly competitive firms, whether a pure monopolist or a monopolistically competitive producer, the demand curve slopes downwards to the right. Such producers sell a significant proportion of the industry's total output. Hence, by increasing or decreasing the output, they are able to influence the market price. That is, they can sell more by reducing the price and if they decide to reduce output and sell less, the price can be raised. Such a situation can be represented by the downward sloping curve. In other words, the demand schedule is less than perfectly elastic.

Key terms

Price elasticity, Income elasticity, Cross elasticity, Substitution elasticity, Point elasticity, Arc elasticity.

QUESTIONS

1. Define 'elasticity of demand'. Distinguish between price elasticity, income elasticity and cross elasticity of demand. Discuss the factors that determine elasticity of demand.
2. Define the term Elasticity of Demand. What are the factors that affect Elasticity of Demand? Calculate the elasticity of demand in the following (the price of good X Px falls continuously).

Px (Rs)	Quantity demanded of x Units
10	20
8	30
6	35

3. What is 'elasticity of demand'? How would it be measured? Bring out its practical importance.
4. What is elasticity of demand? Illustrate how elasticity of demand varies for different incomes and different ranges of prices.
5. Define price elasticity of demand and prove that

$$e = \frac{AR}{AR - MR}$$

where e = price elasticity of demand.
AR = Average revenue. MR = Marginal revenue.

6. State the circumstances in which a demand curve throughout its length represents unit elasticity.
7. "Elasticity of Demand is different at different points on the same demand curve". Discuss. What factors affect elasticity of demand?
8. What is meant y elasticity of demand? Prove with the help of geometric method of measurement, that on a straight line demand curve, E = 1 at the central point, less than 1 at points above and more than 1 at points below it.
9. Distinguish between price elasticity and income elasticity. Prove that the higher of the two parallel straight line demand curves has lower price elasticity.
10. Define price elasticity of demand, and explain why it is usually negative.

11. When Price of a commodity increases from Rs. 10 per unit to Rs. 12 per unit, its demand falls from 96 units to 80 units. Find the price elasticity of demand for the product. Suppose you were the producer-seller of the product what would this elasticity suggest for your price policy?
12. Define income elasticity of demand. When A's income was Rs. 300, he bought 20 litres of milk per month; when his income increased to Rs. 350, he purchased 24 litres of milk per month. Assuming to change in the price of milk, what was A's income elasticity of demand for milk?
13. Define price 'elasticity of demand. Prove that (*i*) a straight downward sloping curve implies that as price falls, elasticity of demand decreases. (*ii*) Comparing two straight line demand curves of the same slope, the one further from the origin is less elastic at every price than one closer to the origin,
14. Define 'elasticity of demand' and distinguish between 'point elasticity' and 'arc elasticity'. Explain the methods of measuring point elasticity.
15. Show that the slope of the demand curve does not necessarily indicate the degree of elasticity of demand.

CONSUMER'S SURPLUS

Meaning

We owe to Marshall the introduction of the concept of consumer's surplus. His idea was to give a definite expression to something with which we, as consumers, are all familiar.

Even in our ordinary purchases there is some consumer's surplus since we may be prepared to pay more than we actually pay for a commodity. But consumer's surplus is to be found especially in the purchase of commodities which are highly useful, but which are very cheap, *e.g.*, post card, newspaper, match box, soap, salt, *etc*. For such commodities, we are prepared to pay much more than we actually pay if the alternative is to go without them. The extra satisfaction that we derive is called consumer's surplus.

In the words of Marshall, **"The excess of the price which he (*i.e.*, consumer) would be willing to pay rather than go without the thing over that which he actually does pay is the economic measure of this surplus satisfaction . . . . It may be called Consumer's Surplus."** [1] To use Hicks' words. "It (consumer's surplus) is the difference between the marginal valuation of a unit and the price which is actually paid to it." [2]

In short, **consumer's surplus** is what we are prepared to pay **minus** what we actually pay. As will be clear from the following section, the consumer's surplus is measured by the difference between total utility and the amount spent.

Consumer's Surplus and the Law of Diminishing Marginal Utility

The concept of consumer's surplus may be derived from the law of diminishing utility. The idea will be clear from the table given below.

Note: The figures in the following table are merely illustrative representations of the amount of utility. Any other figures may be taken, provided variations in the amount of utility are similar to those in the table given below, *e.g.*, the additional utility at every step should be diminishing.)

1. For later refinements in the concept of Consumer's Surplus, reference may be made to Hick's article on "The Generalized Theory of Consumer's Surplus" in the *Review of Economic Studies* (1945-46), Vol. XIII (2), No. 43.
2. Hicks, J. R. –*A Revision of Demand Theory*, 1959, p. 95.

TABLE 1

1 Units (Toasts)	2 Total Utility (Units of Satisfaction	3 Marginal Utility (Units of Satisfaction)
1	20	20
2	38	18
3	53	15
4	64	11
5	70	6
6	70	0
7	62	–8
8	46	–16

Suppose the price in the market is 6 Paise per toast. The consumer will purchase as many toasts as make his marginal utility equal to the price. Thus he will purchase 5 toasts and pay for each six Paise (one unit of utility is supposed to be one Paise worth). In this way, he will spend in all 30 Paise. But the total utility of 5 toasts is measured by 70 paise. He thus gains a consumer's surplus measured by 40 (70-30) Paise. This is so because he would have paid 70 Paise rather than go without the toasts, but he actually pays only 30 Paise. If the price rises to 11 Paise, he will purchase 4 toasts only and pay 44 Paise, whereas the total utility is worth 64 Paise. This will give a consumer's surplus measured by 20 (64-44) Paise, and so on.

Diagrammatic Representation. In Fig. 12.1, along OX are measured the units of the commodity to be purchased, and along OY is measured the utility in terms of money, which means the price that the consumer is willing to pay rather than go without a particular unit of the commodity.

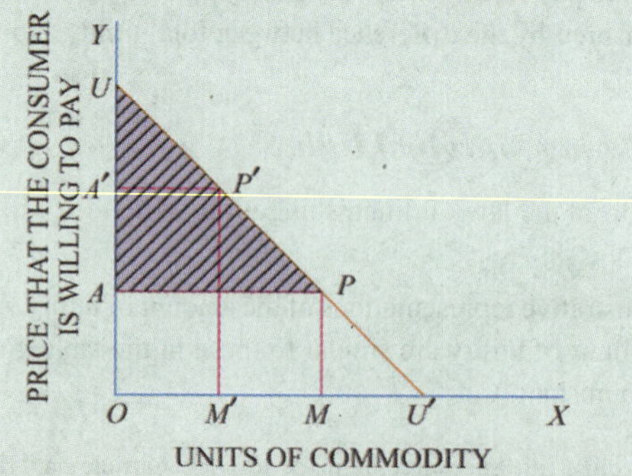

Fig. 12.1. Consumer's surplus at any point below the point on vertical axis of the demand curve is the area of the triangle above that point generated by drawing perpendicular to price axis and quantity axis from that point.

If the market price is PM, the consumer will extend his purchase up to the Mth unit, *i.e.*, he will purchase OM quantity. This is because forthis amount his marginal uitlity is equal to the price. But the marginal utility for the earlier units is more than PM. For M′ th unit, for instance, the marginal utility is P′ M′ but he only pays the market price PM (=P″ M′) for this unit as for others. He thus obtains an excess of utility for the M′ th unit equal to p′ p′′. This is consumer's surplus from this unit. Similar surplus arises from the purchase of other units. The total consumer's surplus thus derived by him, when OM units are purchased at PM price, is shown by the shaded area UAP. If the market price rises to P′M′, he will purchase only OM′ quantity, and the consumer's surplus will fall to the smaller triangle UA′ P′.

The consumer's surplus arises from the fact that some purchasers are marginal while others are not. The intra-marginal purchasers enjoy a surplus. Similarly, a consumer enjoys a surplus on intra-marginal purchases, *i.e.*, purchases which are not marginal.

Consumer's Surplus and Form of Market. In the calculation of consumer's surplus, we assume a perfect market, *i.e.*, the same price for all units. In case, however, the consumers were subjected to price discrimination, *i.e.*, higher price for earlier units and lower for the successive ones, then they would be forced to pay more for the same quantity of the commodity as compared with the perfect market. Thus, **purchases in the perfect market yield surplus over purchases in the discriminating market.**

Hicksian Refinement. As already mentioned. Hicks has defined consumer's surplus as the difference between marginal valuation of a unit and the price which is actually paid for it. The difficulty in the concept of consumer's surplus centres round the calculation of this marginal valuation. The assumption of constant marginal utility of money enabled Marshall to ignore the differences between various marginal valuations. This makes Marshall's definition inadequate.

Hicks has distinguished between various species of consumer's surplus. [3] One type of consumer's surplus is the **Increment of Consumer's Surplus.** It results when consumption of the commodity is increased consequent on a fall in price, income remaining unchanged. This increment is divided into two parts: (*a*) increment of surplus on units consumed previously and (*b*) new surplus from increase in consumption. The first is equal to the cost difference. Here there is a change in what the consumer does pay but no change

3. Hicks, J.R. –*A Revision of Demand Theory*, 1959, p. 95.

in what he is prepared to pay. The second part arises from the difference between the marginal valuation of the extra units and the price which is paid for them.

Difficulties of Measurement

We have explained above that the consumer's surplus is simply the difference between what we are prepared to pay rather than go without and what we actually pay. Or it can be ascertained by the following formula :

Consumer's Surplus = Total Utility – Price × Number of units purchased (*i.e.*, the total amount spent).

How simple it looks!

The measurement of consumer's surplus, however, is not so simple as that. There are numerous difficulties which stand in the way of the precise measurement of consumer's surplus:

A complete list of demand prices is not available. We are aware of a part only of the demand schedule. As we do not know what prices we are prepared to pay for every one of the units, the whole of the consumer's surplus cannot be ascertained. In actual life, however, we are concerned with that part of the demand schedule with which we are fairly familiar. Reactions to small changes in prices are fairly well known. In real life, we are not concerned with hypothetical scarcity prices, or unimaginably low prices.

Necessaries. Consumer's surplus, in the case of necessaries of life and conventional necessaries is indefinite and immeasurable. In case of necessaries of life as well as conventional necessaries, however, it is said that there is no positive satisfaction. In their case, there is only removal of pain rather than giving of pleasure. Patten calls it "pain economy". Only when the necessaries of life have been satisfied can there be any idea of consumer's surplus. It is to this stage which Patten calls "pleasure economy", that consumer's surplus belongs.

Consumer's Circumstances. Some consumers are rich while others are poor. A rich man is prepared to pay much more for a thing than go without it. This difference in the consumer's circumstances makes the measurement of consumer's surplus difficult and inexact. This difficulty is met by the idea of average. When there is a large number of purchasers, rich and poor, the variations in individual circumstances may be ignored.

Consumer's Sensibilities. Every consumer has his own tastes and sensibilities. Some desire a commodity more ardently than others, and are, therefore, prepared to offer more. This difficulty is also met, as in the above case, by the idea of average. When we deal with consumers in the bulk, the individual tastes and sensibilities may be supposed to cancel themselves out.

Change in Marginal Utility of Money. As we go on buying a commodity, less and less amount of money is left with us. Hence, the marginal utility of each unit of money increases. But, when we measure consumer's surplus, we do not make any allowance for this change in the marginal utility of money. In reply to this objection, we may point out that, in actual practice, only small amounts of money are spent on the purchase of individual commodities. The change in the marginal utility of money are, therefore, negligible.

Change in Earlier Units. There is the further difficulty, *viz*., that, with every increase in the purchase of a commodity, the urgency of the need for the earlier purchase is diminished and their utility decreases. This decrease in the utility of earlier units is not taken into account when calculating the consumer's surplus. To measure consumer's surplus precisely, it is suggested that the earlier parts of the list of demand prices should be continually redrawn. This objection would have valid if the utility written against each unit were the average, and not additional utility. Only the average changes at every step and not additional utility. If, for instance, the consumer buys two toasts, the average is 19, in case of three it is 53/3, and in case of four it is 16, and so on. (See the table given on p. 128). Thus, the average no doubt changes but the marginal or additional utility will not have to be altered whatever the number of units purchased.

Substitutes. Then, there is the difficulty arising out of the presence of substitutes. To meet this difficulty, the two substitutes, say, tea and coffee, can be regarded as one commodity, as suggested by Marshall.

Commodities Used for Distinction. In such cases, *e.g.*,diamonds, the fall in price will not lead to increase in demand. When such commodities become cheap, they no longer confer distinction on the user. The demand for them, therefore, may fall off. Hence, a fall in price in such cases will not increase consumer's surplus.

Conclusion. We may, therefore, conclude by saying that the exact measurement of consumer's surplus is impossible. Even so, the concept of consumer's surplus is not a useless one. In practical life, whether in business or in public finance, it is always possible to have a rough and workable idea about the measurement of consumer's surplus, and that is what matters.

Criticism of Consumer's Surplus

The concept of consumer's surplus has been subjected to scathing criticism by economists like Cannan, Nicholson, Robinson and Davenport. Its scientific character has been attacked on the ground that it is based on assumptions which are unwarranted. As pointed out above, there are several difficulties in its exact measurement so that it has little practical utility. Its measurement assumes that utilities are capable of exact measurement and can be translated in terms of money. It further assumes, that different units of the commodity have different utilities. Moreover, the utility of each commodity is regarded as something independent which it is not. It is also assumed that the marginal utility of money remains constant. While we go on spending money, the utility of each unit of the money left with us increases, while the marginal utility of the commodity falls.This makes the calculation of consumer's surplus still more difficult.

The validity of the concept has been questioned on the ground that the assumptions on which it is based do not hold good in practice. Marshall has, however, defended it by pointing out that a consumer spends only a fraction of the amount of money he has on a particular commodity. Hence, for practical purposes, the marginal utility of money may be assumed to be constant.

Hicks has, however, given a representation of consumer's surplus with the help of indifference curves which makes the concept independent of this assumption, *i.e.*, constant marginal utility of money. [4]

In the case of necessaries and conventional necessaries, it seems to have no application, for in such cases the consumer will be willing to pay any amount rather than go without. The utility is infinite.

It is, therefore, said that the whole idea of consumer's surplus is **hypothetical, imaginary and illusory.** A man cannot always say what he will be willing to pay rather than go without a thing. This inquiry seldom presents itself to him in the market. The price in the market is a fact which he must accept; what he is called upon to decide is how much he will buy. It is further pointed out that if there is a surplus, the consumer will be induced to buy more and more of that commodity till the surplus disappears. It simply cannot exist.

The criticism is indeed damaging. From the strictly scientific point of view, the validity of none of these objections can be questioned. The main point of criticism is that it is incapable of precise numerical measurement. This may at once be conceded. But it cannot be denied that something like this does exist in real life rather than go without a thing, we are prepared to pay more than what we actually pay. In this way, we do enjoy a surplus of satisfaction, though we cannot say exactly how much. It certainly tells us that a system of uniform market price does yield a surplus of satisfaction to some consumers who would have been able and willing to pay more if the alternative was to go without. In real life, the transactions are of a type which yield a surplus satisfaction to the consumers.

Thus, the concept of consumer's surplus has great practical utility and serves as a tool of modern economic welfare analysis.

Measurement of Consumer's Surplus with Indifference Curves

As has been noticed above, Marshallian measure of consumer's surplus has been severely criticised. The most important objection against the Marshallian measure of consumer's surplus with the help of demand curve (or marginal utility curve) is that it is based on the twin assumptions that utility is measurable and marginal utility of money remains constant as a person spends more of it on a particular goods.

Economists like Hicks and Allen have contended that utility is a subjective phenomenon and, hence, cannot be measured in concrete terms. Further, they contend that the assumption of the constancy of marginal utility of money is not valid. Marshall's assumption of constant marginal utility of money ignores the "income effect" of the price change, which is often important. Marshall defended his assumption by pointing out that since the consumer spends only a small fraction of his income on a particular good, the marginal utility of money does not change to any significant extent. But this need not necessarily be the case.

Prof. J. R., Hicks has rehabilitated the concept of consumer's surplus by approaching it in terms of ordinal utility function or indifference curve technique. He has given a measure of consumer's surplus without assuming utility to be measurable and the marginal utility of money to be constant.

Take the following diagram (Fig. 12.2). Money is measured on the axis of Y and commodity A is measured on the axis of X. Suppose our consumer has OY_1 of money with him to spend on goods. Indifference curve 1_0 shows that he is indifferent between OY_1 of money and any combination money and commodity A on it. For example, he is indifferent between OY_1

4. Hicks, J. R. –*Value and Capital* (1948), pp. 38.40.

of money on the one hand and OH of commodity A plus OS (= HR) of money. In other words, he is prepared to pay or forego FR (= Y_1 S) amount of money for OH of commodity A. His obtaining OH amount of commodity A as against FR amount of money depends upon his preference and is independent of any price in the market.

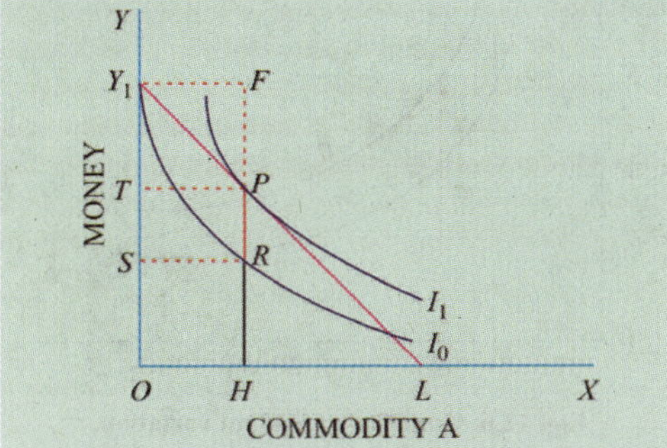

Fig. 12.2. **Measurement of Consumer's Surplus with indifference Curves.**

Suppose now that the price in the market is as represented by the price line Y_1 L, money with the consumer remaining the same. With this price in the market he will be in equilibrium at point P on a higher indifference curve 1_1 and in this equilibrium position he will actually forego FP (= Y_1 T) amount of money for OH of commodity A. But independent of the price in the market he was prepared to pay FR amount of money for OH of commodity A. Thus, he has to pay PR amount of money less than what he is prepared to pay. Hence, PR is surplus which accrues to our consumer because of the fact of this particular market price.

Prof. Hicks Concept of Consumer's Surplus

Professor Hicks has further developed the concept of consumer surplus and has propounded four kinds of consumer's surpluses which are :

(*i*) Price Compensating Variation;

(*ii*) Price Equivalent Variation;

(*iii*) Quantity Compensating Variation;

(*iv*) Quantity Equivalent Variation

The discussion of all these four consumer's surplus is beyond the scope of this book. Marshallian consumer's surplus which we have explained above with the help of indifference curve technique is called 'Quantity Compensating Variation', in the new Hicksian terminology.

(*a*) Price Compensating Variation : According to Hicks, it is the maximum amount of money the consumer will pay for the privilege of buying a commodity at a lower price :

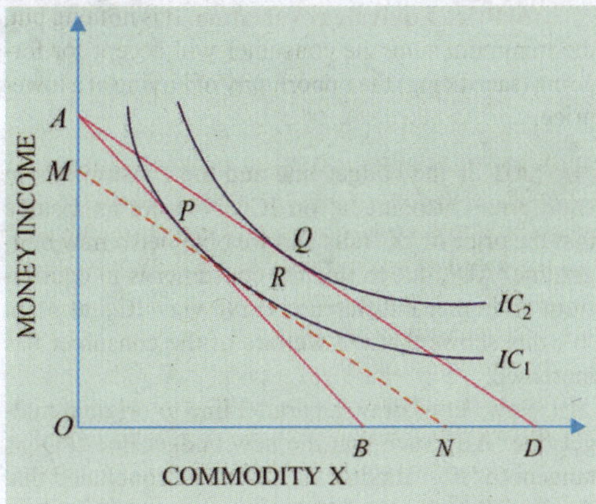

Fig. 12.3. **Compensating variation implies remaining on the original indifference curve after chnge in price of the good by adjusting the real income.**

"AB' is the budget line, 'OA' is the total amount of money with the help of this money a consumer can buy 'OB' amount of good 'X". The consumer is in equilibrium at point 'P'. Now let us assume the price of 'X' falls, due to this the budget line shifts to AD' and the consumer is in equilibrium at point 'Q' on the higher indifference curve IC_2. As the comsumer is rational one he is interested in consuming the same amount or wants to remain on IC_1, but a little better position, which was earlier not available on 'AB' budget line. Let us draw a parallel line 'MN' to budget line 'AD, MN' line is tangent to 'IC_1' at point 'R'.

In the above diagram 'AM' amount of money is taken away from the consumer. Earlier the consumer was on equilibrium on 'IC_1' at point 'P' at higher price but now he is on IC_1 only but at point 'R' which is buying with lower price. Hence, 'AM' is the price compensating variation.

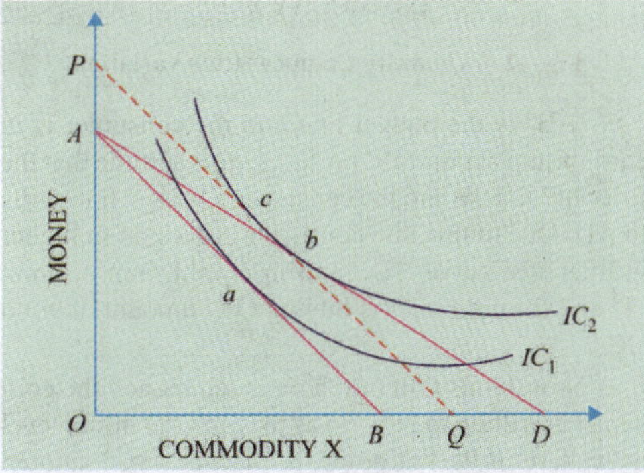

Fig. 12.4. **Equivalent variation in income implies remaining on the new indifference curve by adjusting money income reflecting change in real income due to change in price.**

(*b*) Price Equivalent Variation. It is nothing but, the minimum sum, the consumer will accept for forgoing (sacrificing) the opportunity of buying at a lower price.

'AB' is the budget line and the consumer is in equilibrium at point 'a' on IC_1. Now let us assume that the price of 'X' falls and we obtained a new budget line 'AD', due to this the consumer is in equilibrium on higher indifference curve viz, 'IC_2' at point 'b', this shows that the welfare of the consumer has increased.

Now, let us draw a parallel line to original budget line 'AB' Such that the new budget line 'PQ' is tangent to 'IC_2' at point 'C'. It can be concluded that due to fall in price of 'X' a consumer can reach to higher indifference curve 'IC_2' at point 'b', but the same welfare or satisfaction can be achieved, if the consumer income is increased from. OA to OP or by AP amount. Hence 'AP' amount is "Price equilivalent variation".

(c) Quantity Compensating Variation. It is nothing but the maximum amount of money a consumer will be willing to pay for the privilege of buying a good at a lower price.

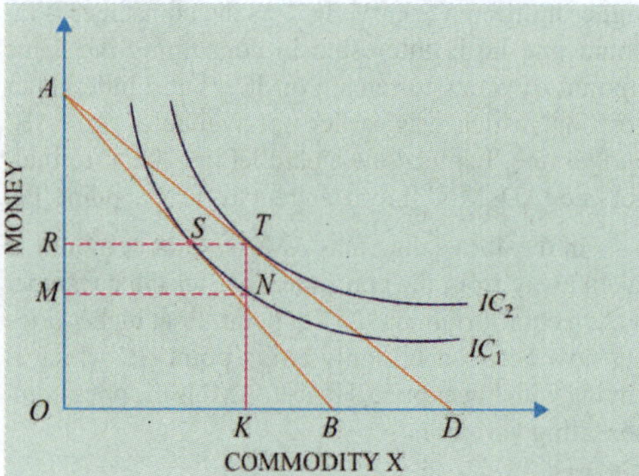

Fig. 12.5. Quantity Compensating variation.

'AB' is the budget line and the consumer is in equilibrium at point 'S' on IC_1. Let us assume that the Price of 'X' falls and the consumer's budget line shifts to AD. Due to this, the consumer moves on to higher indifference curve 'IC_2' and in equilibrium at point 'T' and the consumer is buying OK' amount of good 'X'.

Now, let us find out, how much money the consumer is willing to pay , so as to reach the initial level of welfare in IC_1' at point 'N'. Hence '$\overline{\text{IN}}$' amount which the consumer is willing to pay for 'OK' amount of good 'X'. This '$\overline{\text{IN}}$ is the 'quantity Compensating Variation.

(*d*) Quantity Equivalent Variation : It is nothing but the sum of money the consumer will accept for forgoing the opportunity of buying the commodity at a lower price.

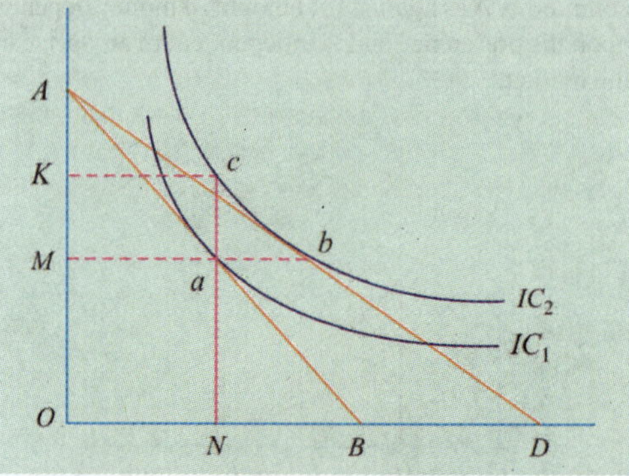

Fig. 12.6. Quantity equivalent variation.

'AB' is the initial budget line and the consumer is in equilibrium at point 'a' on 'IC_1'. Let us assume that the price of 'X' falls and the budget line shifts to 'AD' and the consumer is in equilibrium at point '*b*' on 'IC_2'. The consumer's welfare is increased, at point '*b*' the consumer will be buying more than earlier. The consumer is willing to pay 'ac' or 'KON' amount of money to remain on '*a*' or 'ON' amount of 'X'. This is because at point '*c*' he (the consumer) will be getting the same satisfaction as that of at point '*b*'. Hence '*ac*' is "quantity equivalent variation".

Practical Utility of Consumer's Surplus

Although incapable of precise measurement, the concept of consumer's surplus has a great practical utility and theoretical importance.

Conjunctural Importance. It enables us to compare the advantages of environment and opportunities, or conjunctural benefits. A person getting Rs. 500 in Delhi can enjoy better amenities of life than a person getting Rs. 1,000 in a place more remote from the centre of civilisation. It also enables us to compare the economic conditions of the people at different times. The larger the consumer's surplus the better off are the people.

Public Finance. The Finance Minister considers while proposing fresh taxation, how much the people are willing to pay for a thing and how they will be affected by a rise in price resulting from the imposition of a tax. Where the consumers are enjoying a surplus, there is scope for taxation, for the people are willing to pay more. The rise in the price will not affect the demand much.

Imposition of a tax or granting of a bounty is bound to affect consumer's surplus.[5] But the effect will differ according as the industry is subject to the law of constant return, diminishing return or increasing return.

In the case of constant return, the consumer's surplus will be diminishing by more that the gross receipts of the State. "On that part of the consumption which is maintained, the consumer looses what the State receives; and on the part which is destroyed by the rise in prices, the consumer's surplus is destroyed and there is no payment to the State." Conversely, the gain of consumer's surplus in the case of a bounty is less than the bounty itself.

Where the law of diminishing returns operates, the gross receipts from the tax may be greater than the resulting loss of consumer's surplus. A bounty will increase consumer's surplus.

How much of consumer's surplus is gained lost due to taxation.

In the case of increasing returns, the tax is more injurious and the bounty more beneficial. A tax will diminish consumer's surplus more than what it brings to the State and a bounty will increase the consumer's surplus more than the amount paid by the State.

Monopoly Value. Similarly, a businessman, especially a monopolist, will find that he can easily raise price of his product if the commodity is yielding surplus of satisfaction to the consumers. The consumers are willing to pay more, if need be. As a matter of expediency, however, the businessman will not raise the price so much as to absorb the whole of the surplus. He will not drive a hard bargain. He will like to cultivate and retain the goodwill of his customers and follow, therefore, a policy of compromise.

Value-in-Use and Value-in-Exchange. We know that the market value of a commodity is different from its utility or value-in-use. Commodities like salt and match box have great value-in-exchange. The consumer's surplus from such commodities is very large for we are prepared to pay much more for such commodities than we actually pay. Consumer's surplus depends on the total utility, *i.e.*, value-in-use, whereas the price or value-in-exchange coincides with marginal utility. The doctrine of consumer's surplus, therefore, clearly brings out the distinction between value-in-use and value-in-exchange. It is large where the value-in-use is large even though the value-in-exchange may be small.

Benefits from International Trade. By entering into trade with another country, we import certain articles which happen to be cheaper. Before we imported them, we were paying more for similar commodities. They yield a surplus of satisfaction which is measured by the excess of what we would have paid for them over what we have actually paid. The larger this surplus, the more beneficial is international trade.

Cost-Benefit Analysis. The concept of consumer's surplus is found useful in working out cost-benefit analysis of an investment. Cost-benefit analysis is considered very essential for determining the desirability or otherwise of an investment expenditure in a particular project. The extent of consumer's surplus expected from a project is a very important determining factor in decision-making in such cases. We have to weigh the costs and the benefits. The larger the consumer's surplus more beneficial is considered the investment. Thus, the concept of consumer's surplus is a useful tool for the formulation of important economic policies.

A Note on Consumer's Surplus and Producer's Surplus

Consumer's surplus was initially envolved by Marshall, which was further developed by J. R. Hicks. Along with the consumer surplus concept there is an equally important concept of producer's surplus. 'Consumers surplus' is from consumer's point of view whereas producers surplus is from producer's point of view.

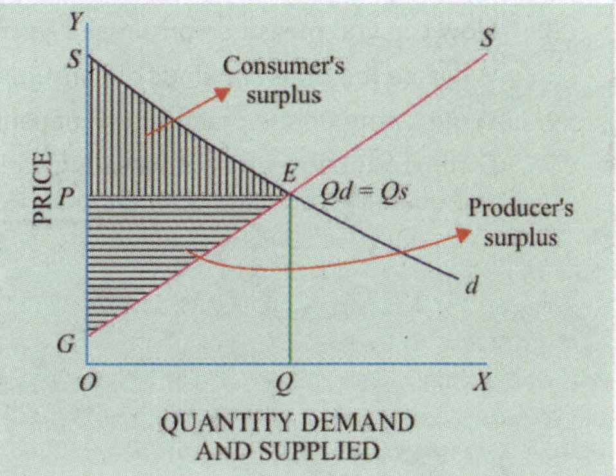

Fig. 12.7. Consumer's and producer's surplus.

5. Marshall, A. –*Principles*, *Book* V, Ch. XIII.

'SD' is the demand curve

'GS' is the supply curve

'PE' Equilibrium price

Δ SPE is consumer's surplus

ΔGPE is producer's surplus

Δ SPE = the consumer is willing to pay a total of 'OSEQ' but actually he pays only ☐OPEQ hence he gets ΔSPE, ∴ this constitute the consumer's surplus.

ΔGPE = The producer is paying 'OGEQ', but actually he gets ☐OPEQ, that means ΔGPE is more, this constitutes the producer's surplus.

Mathematically;

Consumer's Surplus,

$$C.S = \int_0^{x_0} \text{demand function} — P_0 x_0$$

Producer's Surplus

$$P.S = P_0\, x_0 - \int_0^{x_0} \text{Supply function}$$

Application of Mathematics to consumer's surplus

If the damand law for a commodity is

$$P = 20 - 2x$$

find consumer surplus at $P_0 = 6$

Solution.

Consumer's Surplus is

$$\int_0^{x_0} (20 - 2x) \cdot dx - P_0 x_0.$$

Substitute the value of P = 6 in the equation.

$$6 = 20 - 2x$$

$$\therefore \quad 2x = 20 - 6$$

$$\therefore \quad x = \frac{14}{2} = 7. \qquad \therefore \quad x_0 = 7.$$

Hence consumer's surplus =

$$\int_0^7 (20 - 2x) \,.\, dx - (6 \times 7)$$

$$\left[20x - \not{2}\frac{x^2}{\not{2}} \right]_0^7 - 42$$

Substitute the value of x = 7.

$$\{20 \times 7 - (7)^2\} - 42$$

$$\therefore \quad 140 - 49 - 42$$

$$\therefore \quad 140 - 91 = 49$$

Hence consumer's surplus = 49 Answer

Conclusion. It is thus clear that the concept of consumer's surplus is not merely of theoretical interest. It is of great practical value too.

Key terms

Consumer's surplus, Increment of consumer's surplus, Equivalent variation, Producer's surplus.

QUESTIONS

1. What do you mean by the concept of consumer's surplus? Explain the phenomena by using marginal utility analysis as given by Marshall.
2. How can you measure consumer's surplus by using indifference curve.
3. What are the different kinds of consumer's surplus given by Hicks. Explain them.
4. Write a note on the practical use of consumer's and producer's surplus.
5. Distinguish between compensating variation and equivalent variation both in terms of price and quantity respectively.

UNIT III

Theory of Production

Chapters

FACTORS OF PRODUCTION

Theory of production : Content and Importance

Having discussed the demand side of the price theory, we now proceed to discuss the supply side. Supply side relates to the production of goods and services. Production of goods depends on the cost of production which in turn depends on the prices of inputs or the factors of production. Cost of production is determined by the physical relationship between inputs and outputs. In the theory of production, we largely discuss the relation between inputs and output.

Production in economics is generally understood as the **transformation** of inputs into outputs. The inputs are what a f irm buys (*i.e.*, productive resources) and outputs (*i.e.*, goods and services produced) what it sells. Apart from physical changes of the matter, production also includes services like buying and selling , transporting and financing. But in economic analysis we restrict the use of the term 'production' to the production of goods only, because in the production of goods we can precisely specify the inputs and also identify the quantity and quality of outputs.

In the theory of production, we study the factors of production and their organization. We also study the laws of production, *i.e.*, the generalizations governing the relations between the outputs and inputs. We shall also study the theories of population which govern the supply of an important factor of production, *viz*., labour. We shall also study the 'production function, *i.e.*, the relation between the output and inputs of a firm. The analysis of production function leads us to the quantity in which the various factors of production are combined, *i.e.*, whether they are combined in fixed proportion or in variable proportions. When all the factors are varied, we have the laws of return to scale. We also see how a firm hits at the most economical or optimum combination of factors so that the unit costs are the lowest.

Production means transformation of inputs into output. –A Bakery Unit.

The theory of production occupies a very important place in economic analysis and it has a great relevance to the study of various economic problems. The theory of production plays an important role in the theory of relative prices. Specifically, (*a*) it helps in the analysis of relations between costs and volume of output; it tells us how a manufacturer combines various inputs in order to produce a given output in an economically efficient manner, *i.e.*, at the minimum unit cost. (*b*) The theory of production also provides a base for the theory of the demand of firms for productive resources. Thus, we find that the theory of production has a great relevance to the theory of firm. A firm seeks to produce that level of output at which its profits are maximum. For this purpose, it will have to consider the marginal and average cost of production besides considering the demand conditions, *i.e.*, average and marginal revenues.

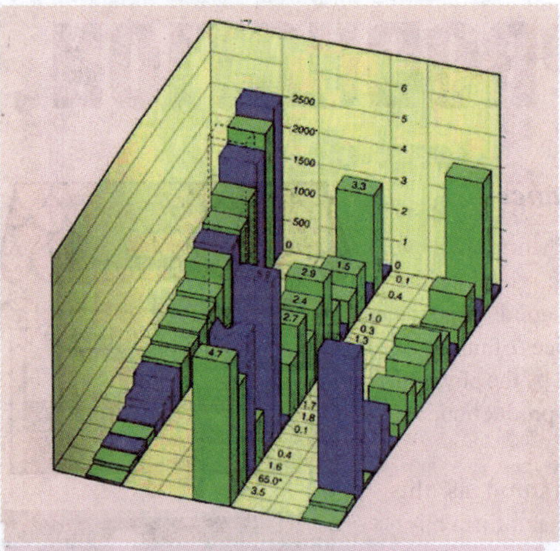

Production refers to creation of utility.

The theory of production also explains the forces which determine the marginal productivity of factors and so the prices that have to be paid for the factors of production. The relative prices of the factors form the subject - matter of the theory of distribution. In this way, the theory of production has a great relevance to the theory of distribution in its microform, *i.e.*, the relative shares of the various factors of production. It has also a great relevance to the macro theory of distribution, i.e., the aggerate distributive shares o f the various factors of production, *e.g.*, aggerative share of wages and profits in the national income. These aggregative shares are influenced by the elasticity of substitution between factors of production which is also an important concept in the theory of production.

We shall first study the various factors of production in this chapter and then in the next chapter the forms of entrepreneurial organisation. Then in the subsequent chapters, we shall study the population theories, the scale of production, the production possibility curve and production function, the laws of returns, the isoquants or equal product curves, cost and cost curves and supply. This will complete the study of the theory of production.

Meaning of Production

Production is sometimes defined as the **creation of utility** or the creation of wants - satisfying goods and services. It is said that just as man cannot destroy matter, he also cannot create matter. What he can do is to give its utility. "If consuming means extracting utility from," says Fraser, "producing means putting utility into."

But this is not a scientifically correct definition. To produce a thing which has utility but not value is not production in the economic sense. One may spread the cult of Yoga and promote the physical and spiritual well - being of one's friends—a thing of great utility—but unless one makes it one's profession, his activity will not come under production.

Production, therefore, should be defined, not as creation of utility, but creation (or addition) of value. Utilities are created in three forms: (*i*) form utility, (*ii*) time utility, and (*iii*) place utility.

Production essentially means transformation of one set of goods into another. A good may be transformed by being physically changed (from utility) or being transported to the place of use (place utility) or being kept in store till required time (time utility). Pure exchange is also an act of transformation.

Factors of Production

Productive resources required to produce a given product are called factors of production. These productive resources may be raw materials or services of the various categories of workers or of capitalists supplying capital or of entrepreneurs assembling the factors and organising the work of production. They are now generally called 'inputs'. Fraser defined "factor of production as a group or class of original productive resources."[1] The term "factor" is used for a class of productive elements, the individual members of which are known as **"units"** of the factor. Modern economists prefer to talk in terms of anonymous productive services rather than the classical factors of production.[2]

The factors of production have been traditionally classified as **Land, Labour, Capital** and **Organisation** (or Enterprise). Now we shall briefly

1. See Fraser, L.M.–*Economic Throught and Language* (1947), Ch. 12.
2. See stigler, G. J. – *Theory of Price* (1947), I, pp. 114-15.

deal with them one by one. These factors are complementary in the sense that their co-operation or combination is essential in the production process.

The typical situation in production is that a group of complementary factors is required between which there is some degree of substitutability. Between labour and capital, the relation is both of substitution and complementarity.

Specificity. A factor is said to be specific when it can be used for one purpose only and for none other, *e.g.*, spare part of a particular machine.

Versatility. A factor is said to be versatile when it can be put to every and any use.

These are, however, two extremes. No factor is completely specific or versatile. That is, a factor can be put to several uses but not all uses. A factor of low versatility is called a specialised factor. The specific or specialised nature of the factors of production plays an important role in the disposition of productive resources.

LAND

Meaning and Importance of Land

The term 'land' has been given a special meaning in Economics. It does not mean soil as in the ordinary speech, but it is used in a much wider sense. In the words of Marshall, land means "the materials and the forces which nature gives freely for man's aid, in land and water, in air and light and heat."[3] Land stands for all natural resources which yield an income or **which have exchange value. It represents those natural resources which are useful and scarce, actually or potentially.**

Peculiarities of Land

In contrast to the other factors of production, land presents certain well - marked peculiarities :

(*i*) Land is nature's gift to man.

(*ii*) Land is fixed in quantity. It is said **that land has no supply price**. That is, price of land prevailing in the market cannot affect its supply; the price may be high or low, its supply remains the same.

(*iii*) Land is permanent. There are inherent properties of the land which Ricardo called 'original and indestructible.'

(*iv*) Land lacks mobility in the geographical sense.

(*v*) Finally, land provides **infinite variation** of degrees of fertility and situation so that no two pieces of land are exactly alike. This peculiarity explains the concept of margin of cultivation.

These are a few peculiarities of land and they have a bearing on economic rent.

LABOUR

Meaning of labour

In the ordinary speech, the term 'labour' means a mass of unskilled labour. But in Economics it is used in a wider sense. Any work, whether manual or mental, which is undertaken for a monetary consideration, is called 'labour' in Economics. Any work done for the sake of pleasure or love does not fall under labour in the economic sense. In Marshall's words, **"Any exertion of mind or body undergone partly or wholly with a view to some good other than the pleasure derived directly from the work, is called labour."**[4]

The land resources.

3. Marshall, A.– *Principles of Economics* (1936), P. 138.

4. Marshall –*op.cit.*, *p.* 65.

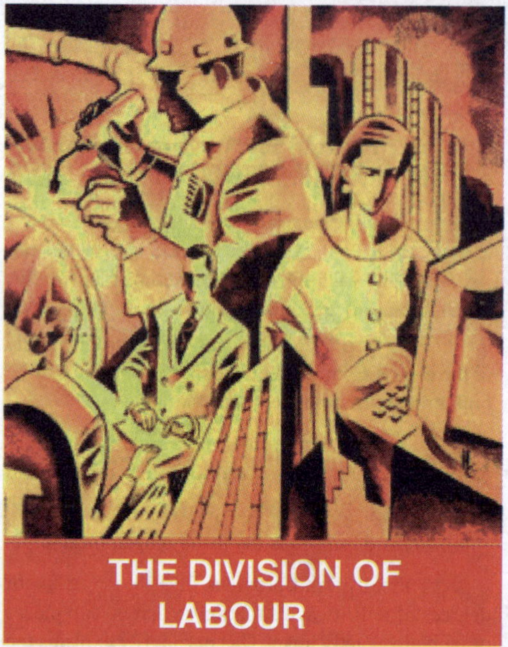

THE DIVISION OF LABOUR

Peculiarities of Labour

Labour is manifestly different from the other factors of production. It is a living thing, and that makes all the difference. Labour is not only a means of production but also an end of production. There are certain characteristics which distinguish labour from the rest of the factors of production:

(*i*) Labour is inseparable from the labourer himself.

(*ii*) Labour has to sell his labour in person.

(*iii*) Labour does not last. It is perishable. As Erich Roll remarks, "he has no reserve price." The labourer has, therefore, to accept the wage offered to him.

(*iv*) Labour has a very weak bargaining power.

(*v*) Changes in the price of labour react rather curiously on its supply. In the case of ordinary commodities, supply is directly proportionate to price, *i.e.*, the higher the price the greater the supply, and vice versa. But, in the case of labour, a fall in price (*i.e.*, wage) below a certain point may increase the supply. For instance, some members of the family, who were not working before, may start working to supplement the family income.

(*vi*) There can be no rapid adjustment of the supply of labour to demand for it, because supply cannot be increased quickly, nor can it be reduced.

These peculiarities of labour have an intimate bearing on the determination of wages.

That labour should be treated differently from a commodity is a social rather than an economic question.

Factors Determining Efficiency of Labour

The following are some of the main factors which affect labour efficiency:

(*i*) Racial Qualities. Labour efficiency largely depends on heredity and the racial stock to which a worker belongs.

(*ii*) Climatic Factors. A cool bracing climate is conducive to hard work, whereas the tropical climate is enervating.

(*iii*) Education. Efficiency also depends on education, both general and technical.

(*iv*) Personal Qualities. A worker's efficiency also depends upon his personal qualities, *e.g.*, physique, mental alertness, intelligence, resourcefulness and initiative *etc.*

(*v*) Industrial Organisation and Equipment. The level of organisation and the nature of equipment supplied to the workers, too, determine their efficiency.

(*vi*) Factory Environments. Cramped and ill-ventilated factories, situated in crowded and insanitary surroundings, are not conductive to efficiency.

(*vii*) Working Hours. Long hours impair labour efficiency.

(*viii*) Fair and Prompt Payment. A well-paid worker is generally contented and puts his heart into the job.

(*ix*) Organistion. An organised effort is always more effective.

(*x*) Social and Political Factors. Social security schemes guaranteeing freedom from want and fear, and which remove the dread of unemployment that always hangs over their head like Damocles' sword, are bound to invest labour with dignity and respect and add to their effIciency.

DIVISION OF LABOUR

Meaning and Types

Division of labour is an important characteristic of modern production. In fact, there is hardly any producing unit of a respectable size which does not organise production on the basis of division of labour. Division of labour is associated with efficiency of production. "The division of labour is not a quaint practice of eighteenth century pin factories; it is a fundamental principle of economic organisation." (Benjamin Franklin).[5]

Increasing in productivity skill.

When making of an article is split up into several processes and each process is entrusted to a separate set of workers, it is called division of labour.

The division of labour is of the following main types :-

Simple Division of Labour. This means division of society into major occupations, *e.g.*, carpenters, blacksmiths, weavers, *etc.* It may also be called functional division of labour.

Complex Division of Labour. In this case, no group of workers makes a complete article. Instead, the making of an article is split up into a number of processes and sub-processes and each process or sub-process is carried out by a separate group of people. This is division of labour proper.

Territorial Division of Labour. This form of division of labour refers to certain localities, cities or towns specialising in the production of some commodity. This is also called Localisation of Industries.

Advantages

Several advantages are claimed for the system of division of labour. Adam Smith's contribution to this part of the economic theory is still regarded as classic. Division of labour has proved beneficial in the following ways:

Increase in Productivity. Adam Smith takes the example of a pin - making industry to illustrate the immense increase in productivity. He describes pin - making as divided into 18 distinct operations. Ten men can make 48,000 pins in a day; one worker may, therefore, be considered to have made 4,800 pins in a day. In the absence of division of labour and machinery, one man could scarcely have made one pin in a day, and certainly not twenty.

Increase in Dexterity and Skill. Practice makes a man perfect. After repetitive performance of the same task, a worker becomes an expert.

Inventions are Facilitated. In division of labour, the movement becomes mechanical and the worker can freely think while at the job. New ideas often occur leading to inventions.

Introduction of Machinery Facilitated. When a man is doing the same job over and over again, he will be able to think of some mechanical contrivance to relieve himself. A machine is, therefore, bound to take over this simple movement sooner or later.

Saving in Time. Under the system of division of labour, a worker has only to do one process or a part of process. Less time is, therefore, needed to learn a specialized trade.

Saving in Tools and Implements. When a worker has to perform a part job only, *e.g.*, making the legs of a chair, he need not be supplied with a complete set of tools. One set of tools can serve many workers at the same time.

Diversity of Employment. Division of labour increases the number and variety of jobs. Employment is thus diversified.

Large-scale Production. Division of labour involves production on a large scale. The community reaps all the economies of large - scale production. Production improves not only in quantity but also in quality since goods are made by specialists.

Right Man in the Right Place. Under division of labour, workers are so distributed among the various jobs that each- worker is put in the right place. There are no round pegs in square holes.

Disadvantages

We have seen that division of labour enhances the productive capacity of the community. But as chapman puts it, "Productiveness of a method of production is not the sole test of its value –to get many commodities is not the only end in life." We have rather to see how man, for whom production is meant, has been affected by the division of labour. Considered in this light, division of labour has not proved to be an unmixed blessing.

The following may be mentioned as some of the disadvantages of division of labour :

5. Quoted by B.J. Stigler in his paper, 'The Division of labour is Limited by the Extent of the Market', in *Readings in Micro-economics*, edited by Briet and Hockman, 1967, p. 159.

Monotony. Under division of labour, a worker has to do the same job over and over again. The work becomes monotonous. It is drudgery, pure and simple. The work ceases to be interesting.

Retards Human Development. A person's development, physical and mental, is greatly affected by the job he is engaged in. Under division of labour, a worker has to repeat the same movement over and over again. His muscles and mind move in the same direction. Repetitive movement cramps a person's mind and narrows his outlook. Monotony is soul - killing.

Industry De-humanised. Under division of labour, many people combine to produce an article. "Everybody's business is nobody's business." The worker loses all sense of responsibility and pride in his work. The industry is thus de-humanised.

Loss of Skill. The master craftsman loses his skill. He knows, for instance, only either spinning or weaving, making the legs of the chair or its seat. He does not know how to make the whole chair.

Risk of Unemployment. Knowing only a part of the job, the worker is in danger of becoming unemployable. If he happens to lose his present job, he may not be able to get similar job elsewhere. He thus becomes unemployable.

Disrupts Family Life. Division of Labour facilitates employment of women and children. The influx of women into the factory disrupts domestic life and the employment of children involves the deterioration of valuable human resources of the nation. It is a great national loss.

Division of Labour and Evils of the Factory System. Division of labour is associated with the factory system which has given rise to evils like water pollution and air pollution, countryside is contaminated with foul smell; over - crowding endangers morals; and insanitary surroundings spread disease. Man becomes a slave of machine and of the factory owner.

Conclusion. Division of labour has, however, come to stay. Shortening of the working day thus increasing leisure, diffusion of education and raising of remuneration are some of the measures that can be adopted to counteract the bad effects of division of labour on a worker's life and personality.

Division of Labour is Limited by the Extent of the Market

This is so obvious. If, for instance, a shoemaker is able to dispose of one pair of shoes in six months, it will look foolish for him to employ half a dozen persons on the making of soles, half a dozen on the making of uppers, and another six persons in joining them. There must be adequate demand for his product before he can adopt such methods. Division of labour implies large - scale production, and it is meaningless to produce more in the absence of a sufficient market for goods. The limiting factor for the introduction and extension of labour is, therefore, the existence of a wide market.

But no individual entrepreneur looks at the matter like this. He no doubt considers the market while fixing the size of his plant. But when he has done that, the extent of the division of labour will depend on the nature of the machinery installed and the number and the variety of the people employed. It will depend also on entrepreneur's own organising ability. But the extent of the market is not so much in his mind.

Market also Depends on Division of Labour. Under division of labour, production is done on a large scale, which means cheaper production. When goods are cheap, more people will buy them. Thus, the boundaries of the market are extended by division of labour.

Hence, division of labour and the market are interdependent. But it is more true to say that division of labour is limited by the extent of the market than that the extent of the market depends on division of labour.

Exploitation Labour of by Division of Labour

Karl Marx considered division of labour as a means of exploitation of labour. The capitalists main aim is to increase the profits, hence they introduced different methods of exploitation, such as division of labour, increase in number of working hours, modernisation and automisation of means of production and the employment of woman and children.

S = Surplus labour

V = Variable capital the amount of labour employed

C = the amount of fixed capital

S' = the rate of exploitation of labour (assumed by Marx to be 100%)

q = organic composition of capital that is the ratio of constant capital to total capital

$$q = \frac{C}{C + V}$$

p = profit, which is nothing but $\frac{S}{C + V}$ or the ratio of surplus value to total capital.

LHS = RHS

$$P = \frac{S}{C+V} = S'(1-q)$$

$$\frac{S}{C+V} \times \frac{V}{V} = \frac{SV}{V(C+V)}$$

$\frac{SV}{V(C+V)}$ add the subtract SC

In the numerator

$$\frac{SC + SV - SC}{V(C+V)}$$

$$\frac{SC + SV}{V(C+V)} - \frac{SC}{V(C+V)}$$

$$\frac{S(C+V)}{V(C+V)} - \frac{S}{V} \times \frac{C}{C+V}$$

$$\frac{S}{V} - \frac{S}{V} \times \frac{C}{C+V}$$

where $S' = \frac{S}{V}$ and $q = \frac{C}{C+V}$

by substituting $S' - S' \times q$

$S'(1-q) = LHS$

Profits are maximized by bringing about division of labour which is one of the means of exploitation of labour. In other cases labor is substituted with machines.

TERRITORIAL DIVISION OF LABOUR

Localisation of Industries

Territorial division of labour is also called localisation of industries. By localisation we mean the establishment of an industry in a certain place or a rigion. A certain town or a territory comes to specialise in a certain place or a region. A certain town or a territory comes to specialise in a certain industry. Indian jute industry is centred in Bengal, iron and steel industry in Bihar, sugar industry in U.P. and Bihar, cotton mill industry in Bombay, and so on. For instances of localisation in State towns, we may mention hosiery industry of Ludhiana (Punjab), bangles in Ferozabad (U.P.) , silk manufactures in Hazaribagh (Bihar), *etc.*

Causes of Localisation

Among the chief factors that govern localisation may be mentioned the following:

Nearness to Raw Materials. To have raw materials near at hand is a great advantage. Transport costs will be considerably reduced. Production will be more economical. It is not surprising that most of the industries have been started in the region where abundant supplies of the necessary raw materials are available, *e,g,*, jute mills in Bengal, sugar mills in U.P. and iron and steel industry in Bihar and Orissa.

Nearness to Sources of Power. Another attraction for the industries is the availability of power resources. If coal - mines are near, several industries will soon crop up, *e.g.*, iron and steel works and several other industries in the coal regions.

Proximity to Market. It is advantageous for an industry to have a wide market at hand. There will be much saving in the cost of transport. The factories near the consuming centres have a great pull over those situated at a distance. The expansion of the Indian cotton mill industry to North India and to Bengal has been actuated by a desire to be near the markets.

Availability of Labour. If trained labour is available, it is regarded as a great facility. That is why new industrialists flock to old established industrial centres. If somebody wants to start a hosiery industry, he will find it to his advantage to start it at Ludhiana (Punjab) because there is ample trained labour available there besides several other external economies.

Availability of Capital. Finance is the very breath of industry. Where there are banks and other financiers ready to assist industry, it is a great attraction. Cities like Bombay and Calcutta are the centres of industry, because they enjoy better credit facilities.

Political Factor. Sometimes, the political factor is responsible for the establishment of an industry. Some of the old princely States in India, like Hyderabad, offered special concessions, incentives and facilities to industrialists to attract them and to induce them to set up industries in their States.

Religious Factor. In some cases, religious causes, making for larger assemblage of people, give rise to some industries. It is generally seen that places of pilgrimage specialise in the manufacture and sale of articles generally purchased by the pilgrims.

Momentum of an Early Start. In some cases, it is not possible to point to any particular cause of the localisation of industry except the momentum of an early start : the industry just happened to be started there first. The example of the pioneer industrialists is followed by others in the place. In this way, the industry becomes established in that place.

Causes of Further Concentration

After an industry has got going in a certain place, it then has a tendency to stick to and further gravitate to that place. If any new entrepreneur wants to enter this industry, he, too, will go to that place to start his business rather than start it elsewhere.

A good location has proximitry to market, rawmaterial source and power resources etc.

Several reasons account for this tendency. Trained labour is readily available there. Plant and accessories and raw materials can be conveniently had. Financing agencies are also established in that place. Several supplementary and subsidiary industries are established in course of time, and they are a valuable aid to the main industry. Technical journals are published which are found useful by the industrialists. Associations of entrepreneurs are formed to safeguard and promote common interests. Means of communication and transportation become specialised and adapted to the needs of the industry.

All these factors considerably assist the entrepreneurs. In a new place, they will find even easy and ordinary problems difficult of solution.

Above all, there is what is called industrial inertia. Once established in a place, the industry does not like to move out. It is human nature that one is prepared to put up with known difficulties rather than face unknown ones.

Consequences of Localisation

Localisation, however, is not an unmixed blessing. All the factors mentioned above as the causes of persistence of an industry, are the several advantages afforded by the place in which it has become localised, *viz.*, availability of labour, capital, raw materials, *etc.*, and the benefit of specialised transport, subsidiary industries, technical journals, associations, *etc.* Besides, there are ample opportunities for exchange of ideas: quality can be improved, costs lowered and common problems thoroughly thrashed out and successfully solved. Labour of that category is sure to find employment in that place.

Localisation, however, is not an unmixed blessing. Dependence of a place on one industry is dangerous. If the industry happens to be in a depressed state, all the people depending on the main as well as subsidiary industries will suffer. It is like placing all the eggs in one basket.

Further, there is little scope for the employment of any other type of labour.

The specialised labour loses mobility and may not find alternative openings.

Remedy

The obvious remedy is to start supplementary and subsidiary and other allied industries. The establishment of such industries goes a long way in mitigating the difficulties arising out o;f the localisation of industries and removing the evils.

Decentralisation of Industry

Several developments have taken place in modern times, which have plucked out oldindustries from their native soil and planted them in other lands.

The development in the means of transportation is one such factor. This development is really a double - edged weapon. On the one hand, it has helped the localised industries to keep to their original home. If the supply of raw materials, on the basis of which they originally developed, has been exhausted, the materials can be brought there. If the market, originally wide enough, is no longer adequate, distant markets can now be tapped through improved transport. But, on the other hand, improvement in transport hasalso helped the transfer of heavy plants to distance countries which are better markets, *e.g.*, Swedish match factories were started in India. Labour and technicians can also move out.

Further, the **rise of rents, congestion, high land prices and higher municipal taxation** in the industrial centres have driven out the old established industries, *e.g.*, cotton mills were shifted from Bombay to Ahmedabad, Sholapur and other places.

Finally, the advent of electricity, which can be carried to a long distance, has enabled the industries to start at more convenient places. They need no longer cling to the source of power, say coal mines, and suffer from other handicaps.

Conclusion. Owing to the causes stated above, several of the factors which were responsible for localisation have ceased to operate and industries have been decentralized.

CAPITAL

Meaning. Capital refers to that part of a man's wealth which is used in producing further wealth or which yields an income. But capital is not a primary or original factor of production. It is a 'produced means of production'. The term 'capital' is generally used for capital goods, *e.g.*, plant and machinery, tools and accessories, stocks of raw materials, goods in process, and fuel. The raw materials are used up in a single act of consumption. Moreover, money spent on them is fully recovered when goods made with them are sold in the market. But plant and machinery is a permanent investment.

Machines are capital good used for production.

Is Land Capital ? Land is not regarded as capital because (*a*) land is a free gift of nature but capital is man - made or is a 'produced' agent of production; (*b*) capital is perishable, whereas land is indestructible and permanent; (*c*) capital is mobile but land has no mobility; (*d*) the amount of capital can be increased but the quantity of land is fixed and limited; and (*e*) income from capital is uniform whereas rent of land varies.

Importance of Capital

Capital plays a vital role in the modern productive system. Production without capital is hard for us even to imagine. Nature cannot furnish goods and materials to man unless he has the tools and machines for mining, farming, foresting, fishing, *etc.*

Because of its strategic role in raising productivity, captial occupies a central position in the process of economic development. In fact, capital formation is the very core of economic development.

Another important economic role of capital formation is the creation of employment opportunities in the country. Capital formation creates employment at two stages. First, when the capital is produced, some workers have to be employed to make capital goods like machinery, factories, dams, irrigation works, *etc*. Secondly, more men have to be employed when capital has to be used for producing further goods.

CAPITAL FORMATION

Importance of Capital Formation

Capital accumulation is the very core of economic development. It may be a predominatly private enterprise system like the American, or a communistic economy like the Soviet, economic development cannot take place without capital accumulation. No economic development is possible without the construction of irrigation works, the production of agricultural tools and implements, land reclamation, building of dams, bridges and factories with machines installed in them, roads, railways, and airports, ships and harbours – all the "produced means of further production" associated with high levels of productivity. It seems unquestionable that the insufficiency of capital accumulation is the most serious limiting factor in underdeveloped countries. In the view of many economists, capital formation occupies the central and strategic position in the process of economic development.

Meaning of Capital Formation

Capital formation means the **increase in the stock of real capital in a country.** In other words, Capital Formation involves making of more capital goods such as machines, tools, factories, transport equipment, materials, electricity, *etc*., which are all used for further production of goods. For making additions to the stock of capital, saving and investements are essential. Professor Nurkse has, therefore, defined Capital Formation as follows:-

"The meaning of 'Capital Formation' is that society does not apply the whole of its current productive activity to the needs and desires of immediate consumption, but directs part of it to the making of Capital Goods: tools and instruments, machines, and transport facilities, plant and equipment –all the various forms of real capital that can so greatly increase the efficacy of productive efort . . . The essence of the process, then, is the diversion of a part of society's currently available resources to the purpose of increasing the stock of capital goods so as to make possible an expansion of consumable output in the future."

It is thus evident that in order to accumulate capital goods some current consumption has to be sacrificed. The greater the extent that people are willing to abstain from present consumption, the greater the extent that society will devote resources to new capital formation.

Savings depends on power and willingness to save.

From the above, it is clear that saving is essential for capital formation. But in a monetary economy, savings may not directly and automatically result in the production of capital goods. Savings must be invested in order to have capital goods. In a modern economy, where savings and investment are done mainly by two different classes of people, there must be certain means or mechanism whereby savings of the people are obtained and mobilised in order to give them to the businessmen or entrepreneurs to invest in capital goods. Therefore, in a modern free-enterprise economy the process of capital formation consists of the following three stages:

(i) Creation of Savings

Savings are done by **individuals or households.** They save by not spending all their income on consumer goods. When individuals or households save, they release resources from the production of consumer goods. Workers, natural resources, materials, *etc*., thus released are made available for the production of capital goods.

The level of savings in a country depends upon

the **power to save** and the **will to save**. The power to save or saving capacity of an economy mainly depends upon the **average level of income** and **the distribution of national income.** The higher the level of income, the greater will be the amount of savings. The countries having higher levels of income are able to save more. That is why the rate of savings in the U.S.A. and Western European countries is much higher than that in under-developed and poor countries like India. Further, the greater the inequalities of income, the greater will be the amount of savings in the economy.

Apart from the power to save, the total amount of savings also depends upon the **will to save**. Various personal, family, and national considerations induce the people to save. People save in order to provide against old age and unforeseen emergencies. Some people desire to save a large sum to start business or to expand the existing business. Moreover, people want to make provision for education, marriage, and a good start in business for their children.

Further, it may be noted that savings may be either voluntary or forced. **Voluntary savings** are those which people do of their own free will. As explained above, voluntary savings depend upon the power to save and the will to save of the people. On the other hand, taxes by the Government represent **forced savings.**

Furthermore, savings may be done not only by household but also by business enterprises and government. Business enterprises save when they do not distribute the whole of their profits but retain a part of them in the form of undistributed profits. They then use these undistributed profits for investment in real capital.

The third source of savings is **government.** The government savings constitute the money collected as **taxes** and the **profits of public undertakings.** The greater the amount of taxes collected and profits made, the greater will be the government savings. The savings so made can be used by the government for building up new capital goods like factories, machines, roads, *etc*., or it can lend them to private enterprise to invest in capital goods.

(ii) Mobilisation of Savings

The next step in the process of capital formation is that the saving of the households must be mobilised and transfered to businessmen or entrepreneurs who require them for investment. In the capital market funds are supplied by the individual investors (who may buy securities or shares issued by companies), banks, investment trusts, insurance companies, finance corporations, government, *etc*. If the rate of capital formation is to be stepped up, the development of capital market is very necessary. A well - developed capital market will ensure that the savings of the society will be mobilised and transferred to the entrepreneurs or businessmen who require them.

(iii) Investment of Savings in Real Capital

For savings to result in capital formation, they must be invested. In order that the investment of savings should take place, there must be a good number of honest and dynamic entrepreneurs in the country who are able to take risks and bear uncertainty of production.

Given that a country has got a good number of venturesome entrepreneurs, investment will be made by them only if there is sufficient **inducement to invest**. Inducement to invest depends **on the marginal efficiency of capital** (*i.e.*, the prospective rate of profit) on the one hand and the rate of interest on the other.

But of the two determinats of inducement to invest – the marginal efficiency of capital and the rate of interest – it is the former which is of greater importance. Marginal efficiency of capital depends upon the cost or supply price of capital as well as the expectations of profits. Fluctuations in investment are mainly due to the changes in expectations regarding profits. But it is the size of the market which determines the scope for profitable investment. Thus, the primary factor which determines the level of investment or capital formation in an economy is the **size of market** for goods.

Foreign Capital

Capital formation in a country can also take place with the help of foreign capital, *i.e.*, foreign savings. Foreign capital can take the form of **(*a*) direct private investment by foreigners, (*b*) loans or grants by foreign governments, (*c*) loans by international agencies like the World Bank.**

There are very few countries which have successfully marched on the road to economic development without making use of foreign capital in one form or the other. India is receiving a good amount of foreign capital from abroad for investment and capital formation under the Five- Year Plans.

In recent days foreign capital is playing a vital role in the economic development of less developed countries. After the GATT agreement as well as the establishment of WTO (World Trade Organisation) on Ist January 1995, there is an enormous increase of foreign capital from developed countries to developing countries.

Foreign capital is divided into two categories; *viz.*

(A) Foreign Direct Investments, (FDI) and,

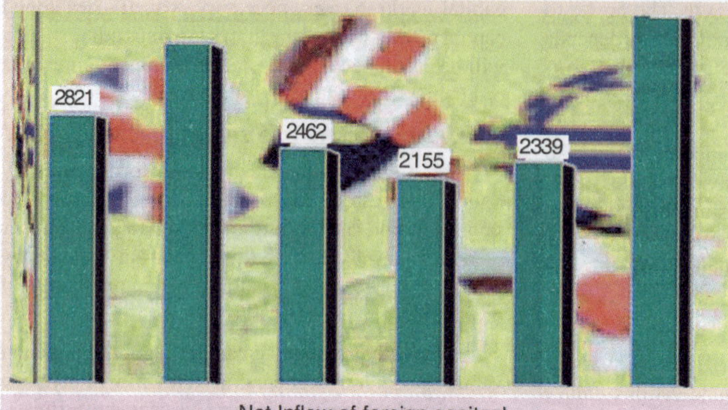

Net Inflow of foreign capitcal.

(B) Foreign Institutional Investment (FIIS).

(A) Foreign Direct Investment : (FDI) This is a very important aspect of foreign capital. The FDI means the foreigner's are allowed investment either in collaboration with corporate and government (including both state and central) or directly starting of factories, mills, departmental stores, chain stores, infrastructure and so on. The FDI plays a vital role in the economic development of a country. Due to FDI the employment and economic growth of an economy increases. This further with multiplier effect accelerate the economic growth and also commulative economic process take place. For developing countries this is a very good opportunity. There is a direct relation between FDI and economic development.

(B) Foreign Institutional Investments (FIIS) : In this category of foreign capital the foreigner's either directly or through their institutions invest in the portfolio investment of an economy. This may help the economy or may harm the economy. Generally the investment in stock–enchange is of speculative nature. Due to the liberationation and globalisation policy world-over the FII's are increasing their investment in developing countries. It has accelerated up the tempo of speculation in almost all the markets of the world.

Along with the FII's there is another kind of investment in India, that is the NRI deposits (Non-Resident Indian's) or investments. If it is in government bonds, than it may not be a non-speculative, otherwise it may be of FII's type of investment.

Deficit Financing. Deficit financing, *i.e.*, newly- created money, is another source of capital formation in a developing economy. Owing to very low standard of living of the people, the extent to which voluntary savings can be mobilised is very much limited. Also, taxation beyond limit is quite unpleasant and therefore politically inexpedient. Deficit financing is, therefore, the method on which the government can fall back to obtain funds.

However, the danger inherent in this source of development finance is that it may lead to inflationary pressure in the economy, although a certain measure of deficit financing can be had without creating much pressures.

There is specially a good case for using deficit financing to utilise the existing and under - employed labour in schemes which yield quick returns so that the inflationary potential of deficit financing may be neutralised by an increase in the supply of output in the short run.

Disguised Unemployment. Another source of capital formation is to mobilize the saving potential that exists in the form of disguised unemployment. Surplus agricultural workers can be transferred from the agricultural sector to the non - agricultural sector without diminishing agricultural output. The objective is to mobilize these unproductive workers and employ them on various capital-creating projects, such as roads, canals, building of schools, health centres and bunds for flood control in which they do not require much more capital to work with.

ENTERPRISE

The fourth factor of production is enterprise which is supplied by the entrepreneur.

Entrepreneur's Role

The role that the entrepreneur plays consists in co - ordinating and correlating the other factors of production. He starts the work, organises and supervises it. He undertakes to remunerate all the factors of production: to pay rent to the landlord, interest on the borrowed capital, and wages to labour, and pays them in advance of the sale of goods. The residue, if any, is his. Nothing may be left after he has made the necessary payments. In that case, his venture will have been miscarried. But it is also possible that he may be lucky to make a handsome profit. Whatever may be the outcome, he must be prepared to accept it. He thus takes the **final** responsibility of the business.

If he has anticipated the consumers' wishes aright and interpreted them correctly, he is amply rewarded. **Organising** and **risk-taking**, or **'uncertainty**

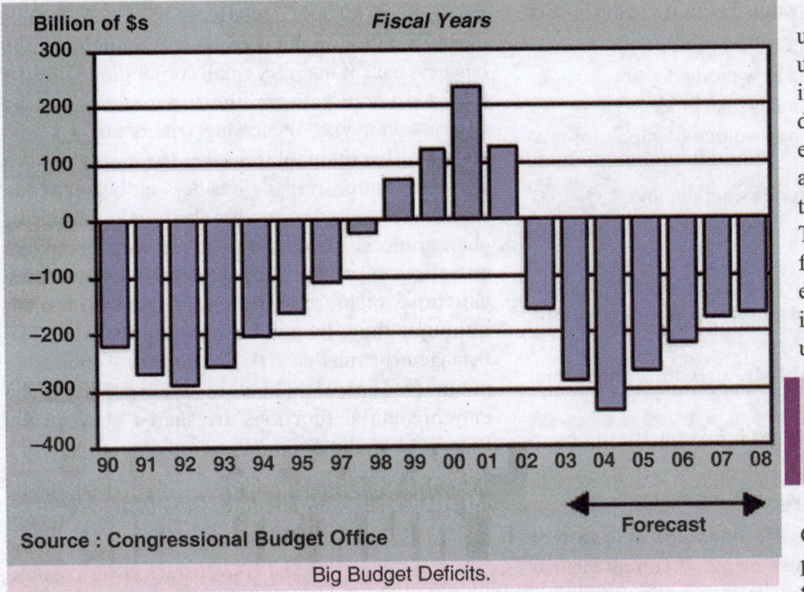

Big Budget Deficits.

It will be easily understood that uncertainty is inherent in the making of the decisions like those enumerated above and also in any innovations that may be adopted. The all - embracing function that the entrepreneur performs is, therefore, that of uncertainty - bearing.

bearing', as it is sometimes called, are the two chief functions of the modern entrepreneur.

The entrepreneur is the innovator. Innovation by the entrepreneur implies a variety of things. It may mean the introduction of a new method of production or an improvement in the old method. It may consist of the introduction of a new commodity like the transistor radio sets or a new make of an old product, *e.g* , yet another brand of toothpaste. Innovation may refer to the discovery of new materials, fresh sources of old materials, or new uses for materials or final goods. It also includes the opening up of new markets. Innovation may also take the form of new techinques in the way of administration, finance, marketing, or human relations inside the business and public relations outside, *i.e.*, with suppliers of materials and customers of products. It is involved, finally, when new forms of business organisation are instituted, such as chain stores, the merger of several establishments, or a monopolistic combination among producers.

Schumpeter's concept of Entrepreneur

J. A. Schumpeter, a German economist, has put more emphasis on the role of entrepreneur. According to him, the entrepreneur can "change the direction of an economy", in the Japanese economy during the Meiji Era after 1868 the 'Zaibtsu' (Five main Entrepreneurs) played a vital role in its economic development.

According to Schumpeter the entrepreneur is one who combines the factor of productions and carry out the production process. He is not just an investor but also one who can be a manager. An entrepreneur is dynamic and possess initiative and foresight. He is a

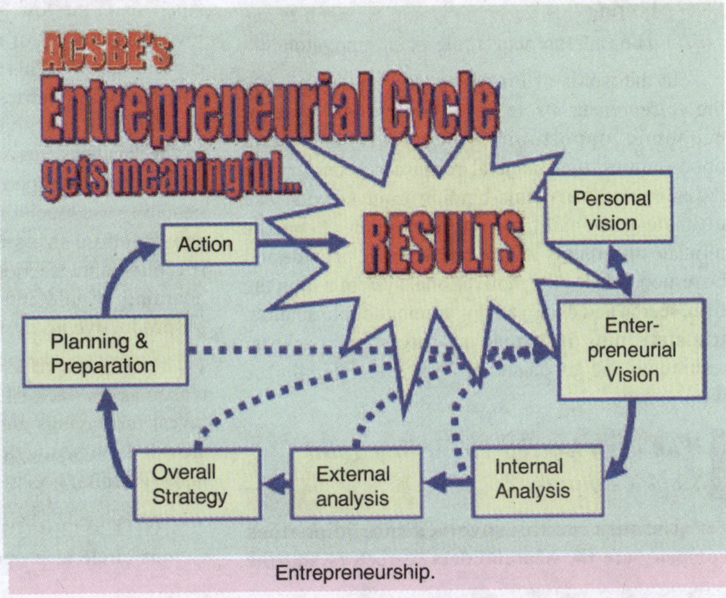

Entrepreneurship.

risk-taker and an innovator. He introduces the five types of innovations.

(*i*) Introduction of a new product
(*ii*) Introduction of a new machine
(*iii*) Discovery of a new source of supply of raw-materials
(*iv*) Opening up of a new-market, and
(*v*) Introduction of scientific methods of organisation

As a leader an entrepreneur possess the following motives, whose main aim is not only to earn profit, but also a

(*i*) Desire to establish private commercial kingdom.
(*ii*) Will to conquer and prove superiority over-others.
(*iii*) Joy of creation and getting things done.

Schumpeter said, He does not belong to a particular class, "Because being an entrepreneur is not a profession and as a rule not a lasting condition, entrepreneurs do not form a social class in the technical sense like the class of landowners or capitalists or workers."

Summing Up. The Entrepreneur's functions may be summarised thus:

(*i*) Initiating a business enterprise by mobilising and harnessing the necessary productive resources.
(*ii*) Taking the final responsibility of the business enterprise – risk-taking and uncertainty bearing.
(*iii*) The Entrepreneur's role as an innovator.

In the words of Professor Harvey Leibenstein, the entrepreneur's role is to "search and discover economic opportunities, evaluate economic opportunities, the financial resources necessary for the enterprise, make time-binding arrangements, take ultimate responsibility for management, be the ultimate uncertainty and/or risk - bearer, provide and be responsible for the motivational system within the firm, search and discover new economic information, translate new information into new markets, techniques and goods and provide leadership for the work groups."

Who is an Entrepreneur in a Joint Stock Company ?

The main parties involved in a joint stock company are the shareholders, directors and the management. The shareholders have risked their money but they do not exercise any control over the business except in a very small corporation. There is thus a divorce between the two functions of an entrepreneur, viz., ownership (risk - taking) and control. The shareholders elect the directors who exercise control over the business on behalf of the shareholders. The directors are also usually the biggest shareholders. Thus, they can be considered the entrepreneurs, for they generally initiate the enterprise, mobilise resources and risk their capital, although they do not bear the entire risk. The management runs no risk nor do they exercise the ultimate control. Thus, in a corporation the entrepreneurial functions are shared between the shareholders, the directors and top executives.

Why Low Capital Formation in Under-developed Countries

Lack of real capital is so characteristic a feature of all under - developed economies that they are often called "capital - poor economies". Low rate of capital formation in under - developed countries is due to the following reasons:

(*i*) Low Level of Domestic Savings. In under - developed countries, the level of savings is very low. The main reason is that their level of national income or per capita income is very low. Under-developed countries are, in fact, caught up in **vicious circle of poverty:** Low income - small savings - low investment - less productivity, ending in low income. Apart from the low level of absolute income, their low relative level of real income also reduces their capacity to save. This tendency of the people of under - developed countries to copy the higher levels of consumption prevailling in the advanced countries has been called "**international demonstration effect**" by Nurkse. The people, who get large incomes, generally use much of their income for conspicuous consumption, investment in land and real estate, speculative transaction, inventory accumulation and hoarding of gold and jewellery rather than using it for productive investment.

(*ii*) Lack of Entrepreneurship. Another reason is the lack of good entrepreneurs who can invest the savings and carry out innovations. They are not daring enough to bear large risks involved in making capital goods.

(*iii*) Weak Inducement to Invest. A vicious circle also operates on the demand side of capital formation. "The inducement to invest may be low because of the small buying power of the people, which is due to their small real income, which again is due to low productivity. The low level of productivity, however, is a result of the small amount of capital used in production, which in its turn may be caused at least partly by the small inducement to invest" – Nurkse.

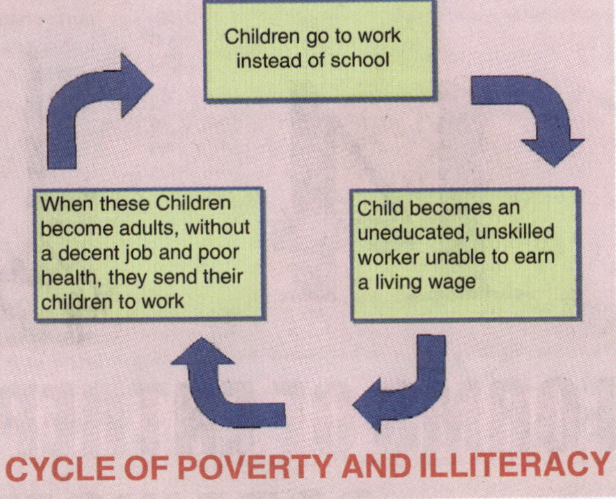

CYCLE OF POVERTY AND ILLITERACY

Conclusion

Thus, under - developed economies are caught up in the vicious circle of poverty on both the supply and the demand sides of capital formation. Once the vicious circle is broken and the country starts developing, the growth becomes cumulative and then these "vicious circles" become beneficent.

Key terms

Factors of Production, Division of Labour, Localization of Industries, Decentralisation of Industry, Capital formation Entrepreneur, innovation.

QUESTIONS

1. Indicate the criticism to which the traditional classification of the factors is subjected.
2. What are the peculiarities of traditional factors of production.
3. Distinguish between productive and unproductive labour. What are the factors which determine the efficiency of labour?
4. What is meant by Division of Labour? Briefly discuss its advantages and disadvantages.
5. "Division of labour is limited by the extent of the market." Discuss.
6. Discuss the causes of localisation of industries and its advantages and disadvantages.
7. What are the advantages of decentralisation of industries?
8. Discuss the role of the following in capital formation: (*a*) savings, (*b*) investments, (*c*) capital market and finance mechanism and (*d*) foreign capital.
9. Account for the low rate of capital formation in under developed countries. How far can disguised unemployment be regarded as a potential source of capital?

   Or

   Suggest measures to step up capital formation in under-developed countries with special reference to India.
10. Explain the role of machinery in large-scale production and state the economic and social consequences of mechanisation.
11. "The introduction of machinery may create short-run unemployment while creating general long-term employment". Discuss.
12. Examine the role and functions of an entrepreneur in a capitalist economy.
13. Explain the concept of Foreign direct investment and foreign Institutional investment.
14. Discuss the main features of Schumpeter's importance to entrepreneur and innovations.

FORMS OF ENTREPRENEURIAL OGRANISATION

Organisation of business in modern times assumes several forms, *e.g.*, sole proprietorship, individual entrepreneur or one - man business, partnership, joint - stock companies, industrial combination, co-operative enterprises and Stte enterprises.

INDIVIDUAL ENTREPRENEUR

The organiser of the 'one-man' concern invests his own capital and may also borrow some. He rents a shop and hires the service of an assistant, if necessary. He himself makes purchases and personally attends to the sales. He is his own manager. He initiates, organises, directs all economic activity and takes the entire risks. Thus, the sole proprietor combines in his person the functions of capital, enterprise and even labour in many cases.

Advantages

This form of business organisation offers several advantages:

(i) The combination of financial interest and the sole responsibility for running the business is conducive to efficiency.

(ii) All transactions and operations are, through prudent management, performed in the most economical manner; and waster of all kinds is eliminated.

(iii) It is possible to pay personal attention to all customers and give them entire satisfaction at minimum cost.

(iv) This form of business is also the easiest to start and the easiest to wind up.

Limitations

But there are limitations also which the individual entrepreneur suffers:

(i) The capital at the command of the sole proprietor is generally meagre.

(ii) Also, one man feels very much handicapped in looking after the many sides of his business.

(iii) No first - rate business can be built up in this way.

(iv) It cannot enjoy the economies of large-scale production.

PARTNERSHIP

Limitations of the one-man business give rise to another form of business organisation, *viz.*, partnership. Two, three or more people combine, contribute capital, and agree to share profits and bear losses in agreed proportions.

Advantages

This form of organisation offers several advantages over the one-man business:-

(i) It commands larger resources.

(ii) It is possible to establish wider personal contacts.

(iii) Business can be run on a larger scale enjoying the various economies of 'scale'.

(iv) The union of ownership and management is a spur to efficient and economical working.

(v) Partnership responds promptly to changes in business conditions and is very highly adaptable. There is no red-tapism.

(vi) The existence of unlimited liability curbs the speculative tendencies of the partners, and prevents the launching of rash and risky enterprises.

Disadvantages of Partnership

If the partners work in close and cordial co-operation, the business is bound to go up. But this is a very big IF.

(i) In actual practice, partners behave in a selfish manner, doing the minimum and trying to get the maximum out of the business.

(ii) According to the law, partnership must be dissolved in the event of a partner's retirement, death, bankruptcy or lunacy. There is thus no continuity of existence.

(iii) But the greatest handicap is the unlimited liability. The unlimited liability makes the policy of the firm timid and unenterprising.

(iv) Further, the partnership resources are too limited to enable the concern to do big business.

On the whole, this form of organisation cannot meet the requirements of modern trade and industry.

JOINT-STOCK COMPANY

The joint -stock company is undoubtedly the most important type of business organisation today. It seeks to remedy the disabilities and the handicaps of the partnership arising out of small financial resources and limited business talent.

Joint stock company.

Merits

There are several advantages which can be claimed for this form of organisation:

(i) The company business is generally a large-scale business. Therefore, it enjoys all the economies of large- scale production, internal and external, *e.g.*, economies arising from the use of specialised labour and machinery, economy of space, of buying and selling, publicity, research or experiments, *etc.*

(ii) Besides these, there are several advantages peculiar to the organisation itself. Shares are of small denomination, and they suit all pockets and temperaments ranging from the cautious to the speculative. Hence, large capital can be raised.

(iii) The fact that liability is limited and shares are transferable, induces many people to subscribe to the share capital. Thus, small and scattered amounts of capital are mobilised and turned into productive channels. Habit of thrift is strengthened.

(iv) The limitation of liability enables new risks to be taken and many new fields of business to be opened out. The actual loss, if any, is widely distributed. The limited liability principle encourages the prospective investor to invest freely. He need not be afraid of losing all he has. This also helps in raising large capital.

(v) From the point of view of the individual investor, too, it has great advantages. Not only is his liability limited, but he is also enabled to spread out his investment. He need not place all his eggs in one basket. Further, he is not wedded to one company for good. Whenever he wishes to leave, he can sell his shares.

(vi) Unlike the partnership, the company is a legal person apart from the shareholders or directors. It can sue and be sued upon. It thus enjoys a perpetual existence. Further, it is on account of its ever - lasting

existence that the investors can be persuaded to invest money even though for years there may be no prospect of profit.

(vii) Separation of functions has been effected between the capitalist and the entrepreneur. This specialisation has enhanced productive efficiency, because formerly the capitalist often lacked business ability, while the entrepreneur often lacked capital. This principle, therefore, is the secret of economic progress of the nations.

(viii) The management is democratic, efficient and economical. The directors are elected by the shareholders. They are supposed to be persons with wider vision, outstanding administrative ability and business acumen. Their expert advice and guidance are available to the company at a very moderate cost.

Demerits

But there is the other side too.

(i) The management is democratic only in theory: it is actually oligarchical. The directors are practically self - appointed, and they remain there as long as they choose. For practical purposes, the share - holders have little voice.

(ii) Some of the directors may be unscrupulous and exploit the unwary investor. They may use inside knowledge for their own benefit. For instance, they may falsely give out that the company is going to fail and when the value of shares goes down, they themselves purchase them.

(iii) Fraudulent publicity deceives the public. Rosy pictures given in the prospectus are sometimes misleading.

(iv) The directors are often lawyers or doctors and have no business experience or knowledge. Their only qualification is the share qualification. Such directors may not prove competent.

(v) Business is de - personalised. The owners of business, *i.e.*, the shareholders, are concerned only with profit. The welfare of the employees is utterly neglected. The paid managers express their helplessness. This loss of human touch is a great loss. The business becomes purely a mercenary affair.

(vi) The liability being limited and the shares being transferable, the shareholders take no interest in the company. Few of them attend the shareholders' meetings. Their apathy throws all the powers in the hands of a few directors. Thus, the company loses its democratic character.

(vii) Sometimes the directors launch rash enterprises, because it is easy to play ducks and drakes with other people's money.

(viii) The organisation is too ponderous and unwieldy. It cannot take quick decisions. It is only suited to a business which can be reduced to set rules, which are both fool - proof and knave - proof. This form of organisation is not fit for pioneering work, or where changing conditions require constant changes in policy of production, or where customers are won with difficulty and lost at the slightest pretext.

Conclusion

In spite of these shortcomings, it must be said that, in the absence of the joint - stock principle, industrial development and efficient exploitation of the natural resources of a country would not have been possible. It has proved to be a powerfrul and an efficient engine of economic growth.

Consumer store.

CO-OPERATIVE ENTERPRISE

Producers' Co-operation

As distinguished from the ordinary 'capitalist' enterprise, there is the co-operative enterprise. The workers are painfully awere of the fact that the entrepreneur takes away the lion's share of profits. Being convinced that they could themselves run the industry without the aid of the entrepreneur, the workers decide to take up the entrepreneurial work upon themselves. They contribute some capital themselves and borrow the rest; they elect their own foremen and managers and employ some staff. After paying all expenses, interest on capital, salaries and wages, the profits are divided among themselves. This type of co-operation is called the **Productive Co-operation or Producers' Co-operation**.

Producers' Co-operation has been generally a failure. The reasons are not far to seek. With the disappearance of the entrepreneur profits also disappear. It is his initiative, power of direction and organising ability which produce profits. The workers are not in a mood to pay well their managers.The elected foremen are not able to enforce discipline over their own people. Everybody's business is nobody's business. Little wonder that there are no profits.

Consumers' Co-operation

There is another type of co-operation which has a long record of success. It is Consumers' Co-operation. The arrangement is that the consumers of a locality contribute capital in small shares and start store of their own. The co-operative store buys goods from wholesalers like other dealers, and sells these goods to their members at the ordinary market rates. Profits are distributed among the members in proportion to their purchases or, what is more common, in proportion to the share capital. Generally, share capital is equally contributed and profits are, therefore, also equally divided among members.

These co-operative stores have been a splendid succcess and some of them count thousands among their members. In several cases, they have not contented themselves with merely retailing of consumers' goods but have added their own manufacturing organisations. They are run on ordinary capitalist lines, employing high-grade managers working under the control of able committees.

The co-operative movement has proved specially suited to agricultural and allied occupations. It was successfully applied first in Germany and Denmark, and it has now spread to almost every country. In India, Co-operative Departments are functioning in every State. Mostly these are agricultural credit societies, but non-credit and non-agricultural societies are also being established. Special attention is being paid to the establishment of co-operative farms and service co-operatives under the Five-Year Plans.

STATE ENTERPRISE

In every country, there are many public undertakings run by Central or State Governments or local bodies. Postal and telegraph arrangements are generally under the Central Government; and public utility services like water supply, gas, electric supply or tram or bus services are managed by municipal corporations.

The organisation of State enterprise is on the same lines as private enterprise with the usual paraphernalia of general manager, foremen, works manager, accountants, treasurer, departmental heads, and so on. The work is done generally in the same manner as in a joint-stock company.

Bharat Heavy Electricals Ltd. is a state enterprise.

But there is a fundamental difference. All the employees are government servants with fixity of tenure and prospect of getting a pension on retirement. The capital is provided from the State coffers, which comes ultimately from the tax-payers. The profits, if any, too, go to the State.

Merits

State enterprise has certain advantages of its own. The credit of the government stands higher than that of any private individual or company. The State has, therefore, a special facility in raising capital and on favourable terms.

In under-developed countries like India, the State has a special role to play in creating an infrastructure of overhead capital like the development of means of transport and communications. These enterprises require large amounts of capital and are generally not sufficiently productive (in the narrow sense of the term) to yield enough profits to attract private capital. Yet they are crucial for the future development of the country. Hence, government has to step in to establish these enterprises. From this point of view, public enterprise assumes a greater importance in under-developed countries than in the developed countries.

Moreover, a modern state is called upon to reduce inequalities in income and wealth. The traditional weapons of fiscal policy and progressive taxation, however, have serious limitations in being used as an instrument of bringing about greater equality. Therefore, there are many people who advocate the State operation of enterprises, the State appropriating to itself the profits of such undertakings.

Further, government is in a position to command the best talent. Government service attracts first-class brains. There is a certain glamour about government service. Thus, from the point of view of the human factor, too, the State enterprise is favourably placed.

The state enterprise is generally a monopoly. It has all the advantages of monopoly. The custom is assured. Expenditure on publicity is unnecessary. Better service at less cost is the usual rule in a government undertaking.

Demerits

But economists are generally agreed that governmental machinery, in the matter of running a business, compares very unfavourably with private management. The government manager's tenure is fixed. He gets a fixed annual increment, and will get promotion according to senjority . He canot, therefore, be expected to show the same degree of initiative or hard work as the manager of a private company. The latter may receive notice to quit any fine morning, if the management is convinced that he is not doing his best.

A government employee will not be much interested in lowering costs or improving the methods, because he himself will gain nothing thereby.

The State employee, who has no ambition to rise, can flout the senior officers. At the most, he will be transferred or his increment stopped if it comes to the worst. He does not consider himself the servant of any particular person, but the servant of the impersonal state, and that makes all the difference.

In a government-managed enterprise, routine replaces responsibility. There is the tryanny of the desk or red-tape. There are exasperating delays. A paper has to pass through very many hands, none making any material alteration or improvement.

Frequent transfers, nepotism and entry into service by the back door, merit being not necessarily the test of promotion, are some of the drawbacks in a government enterprise.

If there are losses nobody seems to bother. There is no counterpart of the shareholders whom the directors have to face every year. The tax -payers are dumb. If there is loss, nobody really feels that it is his loss. Their representatives in the legislature will no doubt raise a hue and cry, yet the government usually has a comfortable majority, and the government caravan continues to move on.

Forms of Organisation of Public Enterprises

Public enterprises may be organised as (*a*) Departmental *i.e.*, run by a Government department *e.g.* Railways and Posts and Telegraph in India (*b*) Corporation *e.g.* Life Insurance Corporation of India created by a special Act of Parliament (*c*) Limited Liability Company registered under the Companies Act.

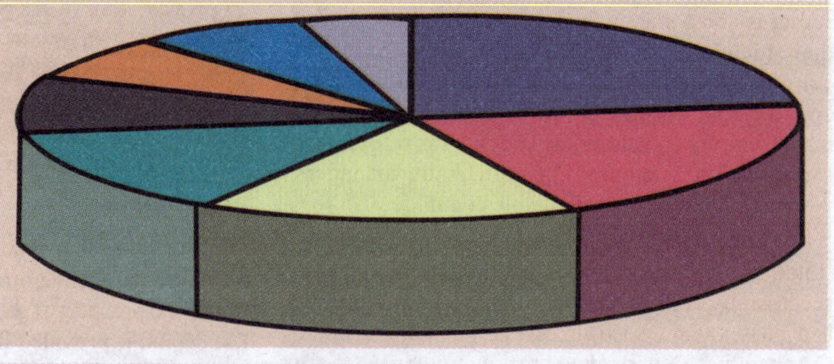

Investment in various areas.

Role of Public Enterprise in Under-developed Countries

In under-developed countries, public enterprises are badly needed to initiate and accelerate the developmental process. They can promote economic development in the following ways.

***(i)* By Creating Social and Economic Overheads.** Only State can provide educational facilities and technical training, medical aid and public health measures and develop irrigation and means of transport –all which is indispensable for economic growth.

***(ii)* By Building Basic Heavy Industries.** It is beyond private enterprise to develop basic heavy industries like iron and steel, heavy electrical and heavy engineering industries. But these are essential for providing a base for industrial development.

***(iii)* By Optimum Allocation of Resources.** Private enterprise is notorious for misallocation of the country's resources lured by profit motive. Public enterprise, which is guided by social gain rather than private profit, is needed to correct this tendency and help in bringing about an optimum allocation of resources.

***(iv)* Ensuring Balanced Regional Growth.** State, as a guardian of people's welfare, takes special pains to develop backward regions. For this purpose, industrial units are deliberately located in backward areas. In this way, regional balanced development is brought about.

***(v)* Utilising Surplus Labour for Capital Formation.** The public enterprises favourably located can drain out from the rural areas surplus labour in the form of disguised unemployment and use it more productively. This will promote economic development.

***(vi)* Creating Investible Surplus.** The profits of public enterprises are a good source of finance for economic development.

***(vii)* Planning Made Effective.** If economic planing relied on private enterprise, it would be very ineffective. Hence public enterprise is needed to make it effective.

Pricing Policy of public sector Enterprise. Public sector enterprises (PSE) were established with an economic and social obajective to be achieved within a perticuler time frame. On the basis of these objectives the following price policy was introduced.

In the diagram QP_1 is the price per unit. Hence the government is producing OQ amount such that:

$$\square ORP_1Q - \square OUVQ = \square RP_1VU.$$

$$T_R - T_C = (\pi)$$

Hence the government is able to make abnormal profit.

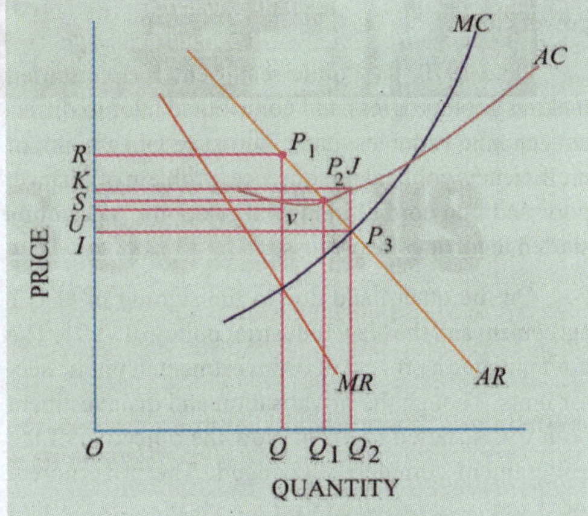

Fig. 14.1. **Pricing in PSE.**

***(i)* Monopoly price :** (MR = MC) The aim was to obtain certain amount of profit for providing other government expenditure including welfare activites. This use to include ONGC, oil, electricity etc.

***(ii)* No Profit no losses basis** (AR = AC) : In this the aim of the government was to provide the services without earning profit but to recover the cost of providing these services. In other words no loss no profit.

In this case 'P_2Q_1' price is charged. Hence $\square OSP_2Q_1 - \square OSP_2Q_1 =$ Zero

$$T_R - T_C = 0\ (\pi = 0).$$

***(iii)* Marginal cost pricing :** In this case the govt is charging only the marginal cost. In other words AR = MC. The govt. is charging only the amount of additional cost incurred to manufacture additional unit.

$$T_R - T_C = \pi$$

$$\rightarrow \quad \square OIP_3Q_2 - \square OKJQ_2 = \square IKJP_3$$

The amount of money $\square IKJP_3$ is the subsidy provided by the government.

Disinvesment Policy of Pub Sector Enterprises. Immediatly after independence the govt. Put. more emphasis on socialistic pattern of the society. Those day's the economy was picking up and require inducement. The Keynesian concept of wellfare state was applied in different countries of the world. The govt. thought of bringing more important role of pubic sector enterprise. The objective of bringing abut more public sector enterprises was to *(i)* To bring about basic & key industries. *(ii)* To accelerate the rate of economic growth, *(iii)* To achieve balance regional development *(iv)* to devlop infra structure, *(v)* to mobilise capital formation, *(vi)* to reduce the concentration of economic power etc.

Upto 1970, the Public sector enterprises started making good progress and contributed a lot to different ecnomic variables. Later, due to certain amount of inefficiency, political interference, problem of finance, poor and non cordial industrial relations, these units started incurring heavy losses.

On the other hand due to the signing of GATT agreement and the New Industrial policy of 1991. The govt initiated a process of disinvestment in public sector units. Though the privatisation and disinvestment policy was started in 1984. Now the objective of the government completely changed. The government aimed at.

(1) Concentrating on other areas of human development.

(2) The amount of money received by means of disinvestment will be invested on priority sector, which will help in economic development process.

(3) To reduce the burden on budget which was due to the losses of public sector enterprise.

(4) Modernisation of existing profit making public sector units.

(5) Other social security measures of displaced workers.

Though the policy is good in light of the competitive nature of the economy due to globalisations and liberlisation. But the disinvestment policy has raised many questions. How the government will best make use of these resources, so that the money should not be misused ? On- the other hand the government must see that the employees of these units are not put to hardship. Proper policy may give benefits, other wise private sector as well as foreign sector may take undue advantage and exploit the economy.

Key terms

Partnership, jointstock company, cooperation, State enterprise.

QUESTIONS

1. Discuss the different forms of business organisation.
2. What are the merits and demerits of joint-stock Companies ?
3. Explain. Pricing policy of public-undertakings. Discuss the role of public enterprises in UDCs.

15

CHAPTER

POPULATION THEORIES

An economy supports population, but population too, in a sense, supports the economy. It is the aim of an economy to supply people's wants for goods and services, but the people too make an important contri bution to the productive capacity of an economy. A study of population trends, therefore, is of great importance in the study of economic theory.

There are two well-known theories of population: The Malthusian Theory and Optimum Theory. We shall now briefly discuss them here. First, the Malthusian Theory.

MALTHUSIAN THEORY

The most well-known theory is the Malthusian theory of population. Thomas Robert Malthus wrote his "Essay on Principle of Population" in 1798 and modified some of his conclusions in the next edition in 1803. The rapidly increasing population of England, encouraged by a misguided poor Law, distressed him very deeply. He feared that England was heading for a disaster, and he considered it his solemn duty to warn his countrymen. He deplored "the strange contrast between over-care in breeding animals and carelessness in breeding men".

Malthus (1766 – 1834)

His theory is very simple. To use his own words: "By nature human food increases in a slow arithmetical ratio; man himself increases in a quick geometrical ratio unless want and vice stop him."

"The increase in numbers is necessarily limited by the means of subsistence. Population invariably increases when the means of subsistence increase, unless prevented by powerful and obvious checks."

Malthus based his reasoning on the biological fact that every living organism tends to multiply to an unimaginable extent. A single pair of thrushes would multiply into 19,500,000 within the life of the first pair and 20 years later to 1,200,000,000,000,000,000,000, and if they stood shoulder to shoulder about one in every 150,000 would be able to find a perching space on the whole surface of the globe. According to Huxley's estimate, the descendants of a single greenfly, if all survived and multiplied, would, at the end of one summer, weigh down the population of China! Human beings are supposed to double every 25 years and a couple can increase to the size of the present population in 1,750 years!

Such is the prolific nature of every specie including man. The power of procreation is inherent and insistent, and must find expression. Cantillon says, "Men multiply like mice in a barn." Production of food, on the other hand, is subject to the law of diminishing returns. On the basis of these two premises, Malthus concluded that population tended to outstrip the food supply. If preventive checks, like avoidance of marriage, are not exercised, then positive checks, like war, famine and disease, will operate.

The Theory propounded by Malthus can be reduced to the following four propositions:-

(1) Food is necessary to the life of man and, therefore, exercises a strong check on population. In other words, population is necessarily limited by the means of subsistence (*i.e.*, food).

(2) Human population increases faster than food production. Whereas population increases in **geometric progression**, the food production increases in **arithmatic progression**. .

(3) Population always increases when the means of subsistence increase unless prevented by some powerful and obvious checks.

(4) There are two types of checks which can keep population on a level with the means of subsistence. They are the **preventive and positive** checks.

The first proposition is that the population of a country is limited by the means of subsistence. In other words, the size of population is determined by the availability of food. The greater the food production, the greater the size of population which can besustained. The check of deaths caused by want of food and poverty would limit the maximum possible population.

The second proposition states that the growth of population will outrun the increase in food production. Malthus thought that man's sexual urge to bear offspring knows no bounds. He seemed to think that there is no limit to the fertility of man. Man multiplies at an enormous rate. But the power of land to produce food is limited. Malthus thought that the law of diminishing returns operated in the field of agriculture and that the operation of this law put a limit on increase in the supply of food.

Malthus asserted that the population of a country tends to double every twenty-five years (as it was actually happening in the American Colonies and the U.K. at that time), but the food supply could be increased much less rapidly. In fact, Malthus observed that the population tended to increase at a geometric rate (2, 4, 8, 16, 32, 64, *etc.*), but the food supply tended to increase at an arithmetic rate (2, 4, 6, 8, 10, 12). Thus at the end of two hundred years "population would be to the means of subsistence as 259 to 9; in three centuries as 4,096 to 13 and in two thousand years the difference would be incalculable." Therefore, Malthus asserted that the population would ultimately outstrip the food supply. For this reason, Malthus said that people were doomed for ever to live at a bare subsistence level. When food supply runs short, people must starve and be plunged into misery.

According to the third proposition, as the food supply in a country increases, the people will produce more children and would have larger families. This would increase the demand for food and the availability of food per person will again diminish. Therefore, according to Malthus, the standard of living of the people cannot rise permanently, unless they exercised restraints and limited the size of the family.

Malthus pointed out that there were two possible checks which limited the growth of population: (1) Preventive Checks, and (2) Positive Checks.

Preventive Checks. Preventive checks exercise their influence on the growth of population by bringing down the birth rate. They are applied by man himself. They arise from man's wisdom and foresight. He see the distress which frequently visits those who have large families. He may think that with a large number of children the standard of living of the family may be lowered. He may think that if he has to support a large family, he will have to face greater difficulties and work harder than otherwise would be the case. He may not be able to give adequate education to his children if there are many of

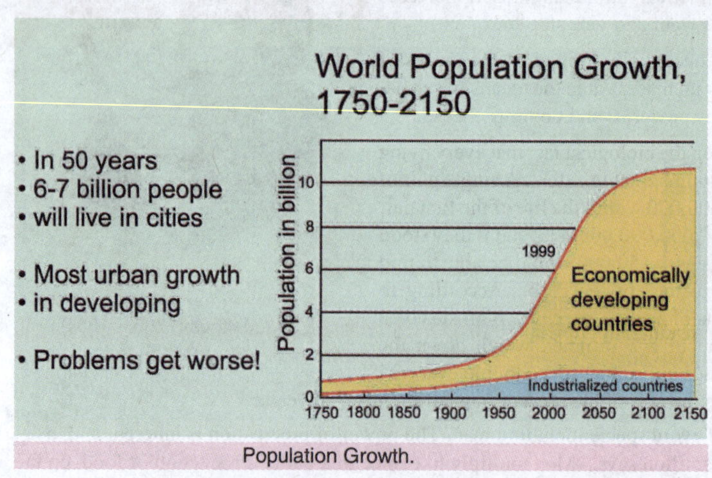

Population Growth.

"Food Supply for growing population" is a major concern.

them. Further, he may expose his children to poverty or charity by his inability to provide for them. These considerations may force man to limit his family. Late marriage and self-restraint during married life are the examples of preventive checks applied by man to limit the size of his family.

Positive Checks. Positive checks exercise their influence on the growth of population by increasing the death rate. They are applied by nature as distinguished from preventive checks which are exercised by man. The positive checks to population are many and include every cause, whether arising from vice or misery, which in any degree contributes to shorten the natural duration of human life. Unhealthy occupations, hard labour, exposure to the inclemencies of weather, extreme poverty, bad nursing of children, epidemics, wars and famines are some of the examples of positive checks. They all shorten human life and increase the death rate.

Malthus recommended the use of preventive checks if mankind was to escape from the impending misery. If preventive checks were not effectively used, positive checks like diseases, wars and famines would come into operation. As a result, the population would be reduced to the level which can be sustained by the available quantity of food supply.

In the first edition of his book, Malthus laid a great stress on the role of positive checks in keeping the population under control. The following remarks made by him in the first edition of his book show the way in which his mind was working.

"Famine seems to be the last resort, the most dreadful resource of nature. The power of population is so superior to the power of the earth to provide subsistence . . . . that the premature death must in some shape or the other visit the human race."

In later editions of his book, Malthus softened the harshness of his theory and gave preventive checks a little more importance. Thus, he held out some hope for the human race through the operation of preventive checks reducing the birth rate. But he still remained firm in his pessimistic view. He put little faith in self-restraint and late marriages, since he was of the opinion that sex urge among people was very strong. Moreover, in these later editions, Malthus also dropped the expressions of geometric and arithmetic progressions but still maintained that the increase in population would exceed the growth in food supply and if un-checked by the use of preventive checks, excessive population would lead to the operation of positive checks to take away the surplus population.

It is mainly due to this gloomy doctrine of Malthus that Economics was dubbed as a dismal science by eminent writers like Carlyle.

Criticism of Malthusian Theory

The Malthusian theory of population was the subject of a keen controversy. The following are some of the grounds on which it has been criticised:-

In the first place, it is pointed out that Malthus's pessimistic conclusions have not been borne out by history of Western European countries. The gloomy forecast made by Malthus about the miserable conditions of future generations of mankind has not proved true of the Western world. Whereas population has failed to grow as rapidly as predicted by Malthus, production has increased tremendously because of the rapid advances in technology. As a result, living standards of the people have risen insteal of falling as was predicted by Malthus.

Secondly, the Malthusian theory of population is based on the law of diminishing returns as applied to agriculture. It is on the basis of this law that Malthus asserted that food production could not keep pace with population growth. By making rapid advances in technology and larger application of capital, advanced countries have been able to increase their production greatly. In fact, in most of the advanced countries, the rate of increase of food production has been much greater than the rate of population growth.

Thus, inventions and improvements in the methods of production have belied the gloomy forecast of Malthus by holding the law of diminishing returns in check almost indefinitely.

Thirdly, Malthus considered food production alone and not the production of wealth in all its forms. He compared the population growth with the increase in food production alone. Malthus held that since land was limited in quantity, food production could not increase faster than population. But he should have taken into account all types of production in considering the question of the optimum size of the population. England did feel the shortage of land and food. If England had been forced to support its population entirely from her own soil, there can be little doubt that England would have experienced series of famines by which its growth of population would have been checked.

But England did not experience any such disaster. It is because England industrialised itself by developing its natural resources other than land like coal and iron, and by accumulating man-made capital equipment like factories, tools, machinery, mines, ships and railways. This enabled it to produce plenty of industrial and manufactured goods which it then exported in exchange for food-stuffs from foreign countries. There is thus no food problem in Great Britain.

Thus, Malthus made a mistake in taking agricultural land and food production alone into account while discussing the population question. He should have considered all types of production instead.

Fourthly, Malthus helf that the increase in the means of subsistence or of food supplies will cause population to grow so fast that ultimately means of subsistence or food supply will be in level with population and everyone would get only bare minimum subsistence. In other words, according to Malthus, living standards of the people cannot rise in the long run above the level of minimum subsistence. But, as already pointed out, living standards of the people in the Western world have risen greatly and stand much above the minimum subsistence. There is no evidence of birth-rate rising with the increases in the standard of living. Instead, there is ample evidence that birth rates fall as prosperity grows.

In the Western countries, the attitude towards children changed as they prospered. Previously, much attention was not paid to children. But now parents feel a duty to do as much as they can for each child and, therefore, they decide not to have more children than they can attend to. People now care more for higher standard of living than rearing more children. The extensive use of contraceptives in the Western world has brought down the birth rate there. This change in the attitude towards children and the wider use of contraceptives in the Western world have falsified Malthusian doctrine.

Fifthly, Malthus gave no proof of his assertion that population increased exactly in an arithmetic progression. It has been rightly pointed out that population and food supply do not change in accordance with these mathematical series. Growth of population and food supply cannot be expected to show the precision or accurancy of such series. However, Malthus, in later editions of his book, did not insist on these mathematical terms and only held that there was an inherent tendency in population to outrun the means of subsistence. We have seen above that even this is far from true.

The civilized world has kept the population in check. It is, however, to be regretted that population has been increasing at the wrong end. The poor people, who can ill-afford to bring up and educate children, are multiplying, whereas the rich, who can rear quality children, are applying breaks on the increase of the size of their families.

Is Malthusian Theory valid Today ?

We must, however, add that though the gloomy fare casts of Malthus have not turned out to be true due to several factors which have made their appearance only in recent times, yet the essentials of the theory have not been demolished. He said that unless preventive checks were exercised, positive checks would operate. This is true even today.

The Malthusian theory fully applies to countries like India. India is, at present, in that unenviable position which Malthus feared. We have the highest birh-rate and the highest death-rate in the world. Grinding poverty, ever-recurring epidemics, famine, communal quarrels are the order of the day. We are deficient in food supply. Our standard of living is incredibly low. Who can say that Malthus was not a true prophet, if not for his country, at any rate for countries like India and China ?

MODERN THEORY OF POPULATION: THE OPTIMUM THEORY

Modern economists have rejected the Malthusian theory of maximum population which, if exceeded, will spell misery in the country. Instead of the maximum population, the modern economists have substituted the idea of the optimum population.

By optimum population is meant the ideal number of the population that a country should have, considering its resources. The optimum means the best and the most desirable size of a country's population. It is the right number. When a country's population is neither too big nor small, but just that much which the country ought to have, it is called the optimum population. Given a certain amount of resources, state of technical knowledge and a certain stock of capital, there will be a definite size of the population at which the real income of goods and services per capita will be the highest. This the optimum size. **The optimum number can, therefore, be defined as the one at which per capital income is the highest**.

Under-population and its Disadvantages. If the population of a country is below the optimum, *i.e.*, below what it ought to be, then the country is said to be **under-populated**. The number of the people is insufficient to take the fullest possible advantage of the natural and capital resources of the country. This is what happens in a new country. The resources are vast. Much can be produced, but there are not men enough to carry on the work of production efficiently.

Apart from the insufficiency of working force, the second disadvantage arises from the difficulty of specialisation owing to fewness of numbers. By specialisation workers acquire job dexterity and increased efficiency in the use of specialised equipment. The community will not be able to reap the economies of large-scale production. Production would thus suffer.

Under such conditions, an increase in population will be followed by an increase in the per capital income. But this increase cannot go on indefinitely. When the shortage of man-power has been made up, the per capita income will reach the maximum, and we shall say that the optimum has been reached.

Over-population and its Dangers. If however, the population still goes on increasing and the optimum is exceeded, then we shall have a state of **over-population.** There will be too many people in the country. The country's resources will not be sufficient to provide gainful employment to all. They will be thinly spread over the teeming milions. The average productivity will diminish. Per capita income will diminish; standard of living will fall; war famine and disease will be constant companions of such a people. These are the symptoms of over-population. Capital formation will be hampered and economic development will be slowed down. The dangers of over-population, however, can be avoided by increasing the supply of capital. There is a race between productivity and population. If productivity wins the race, the danger is averted.

To be Optimum. Let us suppose that natural resources, stock of capital equipment and state of technology remain fixed in a country. Now assume that population which was initially very small relative to these other resources begins to increase. With the increase in population, labour force of the country will also increase. As more and more labour is combined with the fixed amounts of these other resources, output per capita or real income per head will rise. Why ? This is because the increase in the quantity of labour will make possible greater degree of specialisation and more efficient use of natural and capital resources of the country. With a very small population or labour force, there was a limited scope for specialisation, for each worker was required to do all sorts of jobs.

But as population and, therefore, the quantity of labour increases, specialisation becomes possible. Each man then need not do all the jobs or make all parts of a good. Everybody can concentrate on the job for which he is best suited. Division of labour among the different workers, which is made possible by the increase in population, greatly increases the efficiency and productivity of labour.

An increase in population will also permit a fuller utilization of the natural resources and capital equipment. If the quantity of labour is small relative to the natural resources, then even the actually available resources remain under-utilised. Many actually available resources, which can be utilized for producing goods, would not be utilized for lack of labour. Moreover, even the capital equipment will not be fully and effectively utilized if there is a shortage of labour. Technology requires that capital equipment be of a certain minimum size, whether output is relatively small or large. Capital equipment would not be fully utilized if only a small number of workers are available to work with it. In other words, production will be relatively inefficient if the capital equipment is grossly undermanned. If the population increases and more labourers become available to be combined with the given stock of the natural resources and capital equipment, output per capita will rise.

There is another related factor due to which production greatly increases as population expands at initial stages. When population of a country is small, market for the products of industry will also be small. With this limited market for goods, producers will be forced to produce on a small scale and thus would be unable to take advantage of the **economies of large-scale production**. As population increases, the market for goods expands and large-scale production becomes possible which adds greatly to the productivity of the economy.

At the optimum. For all these reasons, output per capita will rise for a time as population increases. As the population continuous to increase, a point will finally be reached when capital and natural resources are fully utilized and, therefore, output per capita is the highest. The level of population at which per capita output or real income is the maximum is called the optimum population. If population still goes on increasing, that is, crosses the optimum point, output per capita will start declining. The country would then become over-populated.

Beyond the Optimum. Why does the output per capita fall when the optimum point is exceeded? This is because there are now more men in the economy than needed by it. A given amount of capital and natural resources have to be shared out among a large number of workers with the result that each of them has a smaller amount of equipment, materials and natural resources to work with. For this reason the **average productivity declines.** It is very likely that many people may not get employment and, therefore, add nothing to production. Thus, there is likely to be unemployment of labour. It so happens that when people do not get employment outside agriculture, they cling to agriculture. The pressure of population on land increases. But the additional men, who get employment in agriculture, add nothing to total production. In other words, the **marginal productivity** of these extra men in agriculture is zero or nearly zero. This is what is commonly known as the phenomenon of **disguised unemployment.** Disguised unemployment exists in over-populated agriculture from where even if some workers are withdrawn total production does not fall.

When population exceeds the optimum level, it often happens that food problem crops up. An increase in population brings more mouths to eat. But the quantity of land being limited, it cannot meet the increased demand for food.

Low standard of living, open and disguised unemployment, prevalence of disease and food problem are all signs of over-population.

Thus, we see that both under-population and over-population have disadvantages. It is the optimum population, with the highest per capita output, which is the best for a country to aim at.

The concepts of optimum population, under-population and over-population are represented in Fig. 15.1 below:-

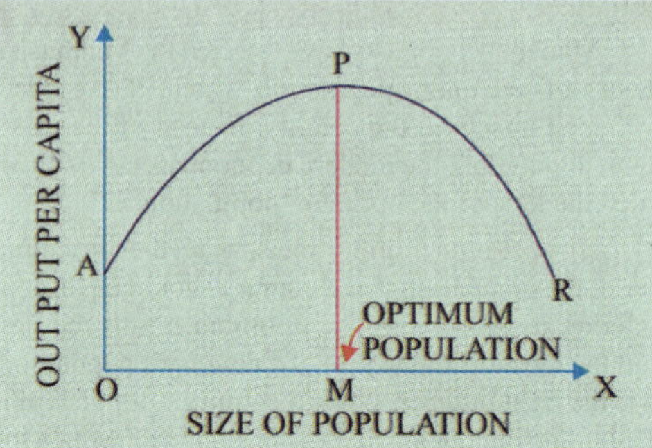

Fig. 15.1 Opitium, Over-and Under-Population.

In this figure, the size of the population is measured on X-axis and output per capita on Y-axis. It is evident from the figure that, in the beginning, as population increases, output per capita also increases. Output per capita goes on increasing with every increase in population till OM population is reached. At OM level of population, the output per capita MP is the highest. If population now increases beyond OM, output per capita falls. Therefore, OM is the optimum population. If the population of the country is less than OM, it will be under-populated and if the population is more than OM, it will be a case of over-population.

Optimum Not Fixed. But it may be noted that the optimum population is not a fixed and rigid number but is **movable**. As explained above, **optimum population is relative to resources and technology.** Given the amount of capital, natural resources and the state of technology, there is a difinite size of population at which output per capita will be maximum. But the quantity of capital and natural resources and the state of technology are subjected to change. In fact, changes in them often take place. When there is any change in them, the optimum level of population will also change. For instance, when either there is an increase in the quantity of capital equipment and available natural resources or the country makes progress in technology, per capita output curve will shift upward and to the right with the result that the optimum level of population will increase.

Shifts in Optimum. The changes in the per capita output curve, as a result of an increase in resources or progress in technology and their effect on optimum population, are shown in Fig. 15.2. With certain given resources and technology, per capita output curve is AR and the level of optimum population is OM, at which per capita income is MP, which is the highest under the given circumstances.

When the quantity of capital and natural resources increase or technology makes an advance, the output per capita curve shifts upward and to the right and is shown as A′ R′. With per capita output curve A′ R′, optimum population is OM′, which is greater than OM. Now if the resources further increase or technology makes further advance, the per capita output curve shifts to A″ R″. With the per capita output curve A″R″, optimum population is OM″, which is greater than both OM and OM′.

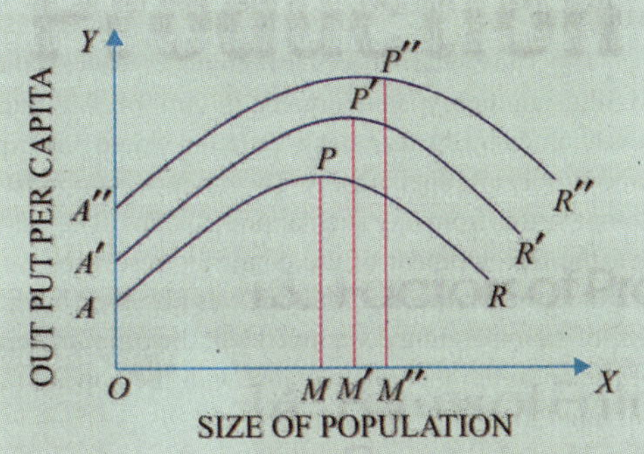

Fig. 15.2 Shifts in Optimum.

Thus, we see that with different resources or different technology, there will be a different level of optimum population.

Dalton has given a formula with which we can judge the extent to which the actual population of a country deviates from the optimum population. The extent of the deviation is called **maladjustment**. The formula seeks to measure the degree of this maladjustment. The formula is:

$$M = \frac{A - O}{O}$$

where M stands for maladjustment. A stand for actual population, and O for optimum population.

If M is negative, the country is under-populated and if M is positive, the country is over-populated. For instance, if the actual population of a country is 60 crores and its optimum population is 40 crores, then that country is over-populated to the extent of

$$\frac{60 - 40}{40} = \frac{20}{40} = \frac{1}{2}$$

Criteria of Over-population

How to know whether a country is over-populated? Several criteria have been suggested. According to Malthus, the operation of positive checks like war, famine and disease is a sure index of a country being over-populated. Besides this, economists generally suggest several other tests of over-population, *e.g.*, persistently unfavourable balance of trade, unemployment, falling living standards and average income, and high birth and death rates.

But a little reflection will show that these phenomena may not always be caused by overflowing numbers but by other factors, economic and political. For instance, adverse balance of trade may be due to increasing investments abroad, Unemployment may be caused by temporary maladjustments in the economic system. Similarly, a fall in average incomes, and hence in living standards, may be due to faulty economic policies pursued by the State. A high birth-rate may be induced by the requirements of an expanding economy or an expanding army. A high death-rate may simply be due to the inadequancy or inefficiency of health services of the country.

Conclusion. Thus, we cannot offer any infallible guide to the state of over-population. All the same, a continued state of under-employment, ill-health and poverty are fairly correct indications of the fact that ever-growing numbers are over-straining the country's slender resources.

India's Case. We, in India, find ourselves at present in this unenviable position of over-population. How can we now get back to the optimum? We must attack the problem at two ends:

(i) We must slow down the speed at which our population is growing, and *(ii)* we must accelerate the pace of our economic development. Ours is a country of unutilised or under-utilised resources. The execution of multi-purpose projects and the development of agriculture, industry, insurance and banking and of the means of transport, etc., are steps in this direction. When we try to keep down our numbers and maximize our porductive capacity, we shall be on the road to the optimum.

Thus, **"the problem of population is not of mere size but of efficient production and equitable distribution."** –(Seligman).

Limitations of the Concept of Optimum Population

The concept of optimum theory of population has been criticised on several grounds. Some economists have gone so far as to describe it as a 'fanciful concept.' The main points of criticism are:–

(i) It is said that it is almost impossible to determine the exact size of the population which may be called optimum number. It is not possible, in practice, to fix a point up to which the income per head goes on increasing and beyond which it starts declining. Population experts have suggested different and conflicting numbers as the optimum. Thus, the concept has little practical utility.

(ii) The concept is relative to natural resources, capital equipment and state of technical knowledge. It is assumed that they remain the same. Since these factors are subject to constant change, the optimum is a constantly shifting concept. As such we can seldom arrive at a stable optimum which may have significance in economic analysis and practice. Thus, the theory is based on wrong assumptions.

(iii) Also, mere size of the population is of little significance. The composition of the population, e.g., age-distribution or distribution as regards workers and non-workers matter a great deal. Even if the population of a country is of the optimum size, the existence of a large number of non-working population such as infants and the aged, is bound to affect adversly the productive capacity of the economy.

(iv) Besides, the concept of the optimum population ignores the quality of the people. It simply focuses its attention on the number. A small population consisting of efficient and hardworking people is undoubtedly more useful to the economy than a huge population consisting of lethargic and irresponsible people.

(v) The theory ignores political, social, strategic and other aspects of the population problem and considers only the economic aspect. For instance, a small population may be advocated on economic grounds but it will be dangerous from the point of view of defence. Adam Smith rightly said, "Defence is better than opulence."

(vi) The concept of the optimum population is only of theoretical interest. Actually, it is not easy to attain the optimum size by reducing population in the case of over-population and increas in it in the case of under-population. Family planning, whether aiming at reducing population or increasing it, is a long drawn affair extending over several generations. Human beings are more influenced by culture and traditions than by rigid government regulation.

Conclusion. Thus, the concept of optimum population is more of theoretical and academic interest than of practical value.

Malthusian Theory and Modern Theory Compared

From the study of these theories of population, we may notice some important differences between the two:

(i) Malthus focused his attention on food production, whereas the optimum theory takes into consideration economic development in all its aspects.

(ii) Malthus seemed to be thinking of a **maximum number** for a country which, if exceeded, would spell misery. According to the optimum theory, there is no rigidly fixed maximum.

(iii) To Malthus famine, war and disease were the indices of over-population. But the optimum theory tells us that, even in the absence of such distressing phenomena, there can be over-population, provided it can be shown that per capita income has gone down, or that with a decrease in population per capita income will go up.

(iv) The modern theory is optimistic, whereas the Malthusian theory is pessimistic in outlook. Malthus was haunted by the fear that population would outstrip food supply and spell misery. The modern economists do not suffer from any such apprehensions. They say that the development of the country's resources can brighten the prospects. "Malthus was obsessed by the fear of an impending economic Hell; the propounders of the optimum theory are elated with the hopes of a coming Paradise." –(Chatterjee).

Cost-Benefit theory of Population.

According to this theory the additional population growth is treated in two ways *(i)* as an asset and *(ii)* as a liability '*a*' '*b*' & 'c' are utility derived from additional children *(i)* 'a' is the amount of utility or satisfaction from an additional child, this remains constant whether to a 'rich' person or to a poor person.

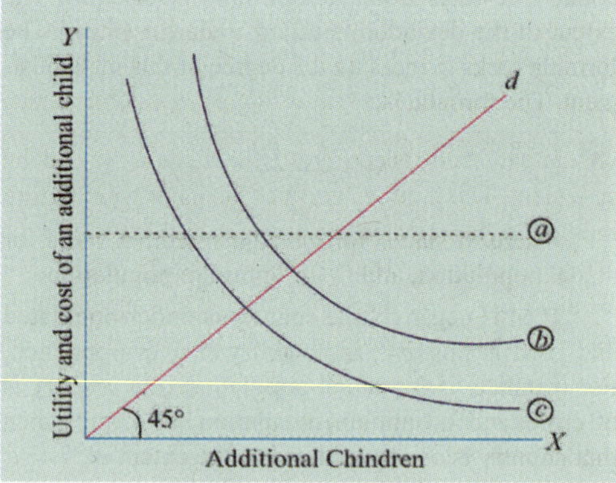

Fig. 15.3. Utility and cost of an additional child.

(ii) 'b' is the utility of additional child, because they treat this as a source of income to the family and;

(iii) 'c' is the utility, which the family feels is the source of old age security.

Generally in developing countries specially in an agrarian economies where the income of family is not secured they try to have more children. They neglect the cost aspect and gives importance to the utility aspect.

In urban areas, the people to a greater extent educated, and have a nuclear family concept in which both wife and husband is employed. If such a family wants to have an additional child, then they have to look into the concept of cost to develop the child. It is one of the basic objective of human psychology, that is, if you have a child, then he should be provided best food, best clothing and best education. The aim is to develop the child, rather than an asset or utility aspect. Due to additional child a family may undergo financial problems. It can be divided into two types of costs (*a*) Direct cost (*b*) Indirect cost.

(*a*) Direct cost is the amount of money incurred to look after the child (to develop the child-food, education etc) and when the woman is on maternity leave. She may have to lose certain amount of money (In case if maternity leave is not available, leave without pay) is to be taken. (*b*) Indirect cost is the amount of freedom or loss of entertainment due to additional child in the family. A family with more number of children may not be able to go for entertainment etc.

Though the theory neglects certain Socio, cultural aspect but to a greater extent economic aspect, play an important role in the population growth theory. This theory is found to be correct in developing countries. Specially dual economies, where a majority of the people are living in rural areas and smaller number in unban areas. Rural people donot have enough money to look after their families, they try to have additional children to bring in more income. Specially where landless labours or casual workers, even when both wife and husband is employed, the income may not be sufficient. The families may not be having any future income in the form of pension, insurance policies or other securities. Hence they feel that additional children may help them in getting additional income as well as the old age-security of the parents.

On the other hand urban people may be employed in government, semi-governments or private companies, where pensions gratuities, insurance and other benefits are available. Due to this, they concentrate more on the development of a child rather then taking child as an asset.

Population policy makers must look into this economic aspect and the so called 'governance' of public authority must concentrate on this. In many developing countries, the governments declare their social security measure only on a temporary basis, This they may announce to obtain the votes to get elected.

ECONOMIC EFFECTS OF OVER-POPULATION

We learn from the Malthusian theory of population about some adverse effects of excessive population growth. But there are some beneficial effects too. We shall spell out these effects briefly as under:–

(*i*) Food shortage. Excessive population results in food shortage, because food supply does not increase in the same proportion as the increase in the mouths to be fed. This is so because production of food is subject to the law of diminishing returns whereas population grows at a galloping speed.

(*ii*) Disease and Death. Over-population spells misery in the form of a high incidence of diseases and high mortality rates. This is so because it is difficult to arrange for wholesome food and adequate public health measures and medical aid for a large population. It is said that "it fills our roads with cars." It pollutes air and water and spoils the countryside.

(*iii*) Overstraining Resources. Excessive population overstrains the available resources of all types. We have said above that the medical facilities prove inadequate. We may also add that the transport and the educational systems are subjected to severe strain as is evident from the over-crowded schools and colleges, overcrowding in trains, long queues at the bus stops, at water taps, at the fair price shops and at the cinema houses with all attendant inconveniences of life.

(*iv*) Increase in Dependents. A rapidly increasing population means an ever growing number of children and the aged who constitute the non-working population. This lowers the per capita income and the level of living.

(*v*) Stimulating Development. A good thing about excessive numbers is an expanding market for goods and services. This stimulates economic development.

But excessive spending also generates inflationary pressures.

(*vi*) Military Advantages. A huge manpower is a great advantage from the military point of view.

Conclusion. Is growing population a curse or a blessing? No single and straight answer can be given. Such a general question cannot be answered by economics alone. "The joys and aches of family life are not to be measured in mere dollars and cents." On the whole, a rapidly growing population or excessive population is more of a liability than an asset.

ECONOMIC DEVELOPMENT AND POPULATION GROWTH

Theory of Demographic Transition

The Malthusian Theory of Populations stated in effect that if people became prosperous (especially poorer sections), population would increase. In other words, an increase in the incomes of the poor would lead to an increase in their birth rates and, through the operation of positive checks, result in high death rates so that the growth of population would slow down.

But the process of economic development, which has transformed agrarian economies into urban, industrialised and market-oriented economies, has led to the emergence of a new theory, viz., the **Theory of Demographic Transition.** The course of population growth since Malthus has been different from what he predicted. This course is more correctly described by this new theory. The theory of demographic transition brings out the relation between population growth and economic development.

Before economic development, an economy is characterised, among other things, by predominance of agriculture, small-scale industries using inefficient and old techniques of production, lack of mobility and division of labour, lack of adequate means of transport and communication, low levels of output and average income, a high degree of rural self-sufficiency and the existence of subsistence economy. But the outstanding feature, from the population point of view, is the prevalence of high birth rates, which are stable at a high level, and high mortality rates.

The birth rates are high owing to universal and early marriages, the influence of social beliefs and customs, religious attitudes and, above all, from economic necessity. This is so because children start working early and thus supplement the family income and because they are regarded as a sort of insurance against old age. The birth rates are also high because the death rates are high. A family must have more children to fill up the gaps caused by high death rates.

The death rates are high owing to poor diet, bad sanitary conditions, and absence of preventive and curative medical practices. High birth rates and high death rates prevalent in an under-developed economy are well in accord with the Malthusian Theory of Population. In fact, high death rate is essential to prevent a population explosion which may be caused by high birth rates. The result is that population growth is not rapid, but this is achieved through suffering, disease and death. In an agrarian economy, birth rates are stable at a high level but death rates fluctuate from year to year depending on availability of food and the prevalence of disease.

Let us now see how the situation is affected by the process of development and the social and economic changes which this development brings about. Economic development brings about an improvement in the economic condition of the people. The level of income, employment and productivity rises bringing about a rise in the level of living. The rural self-sufficiency is broken; the market is extended and comes to dominate production. The economy becomes industrialised and urbanized; it uses more capital and capital equipment, i.e., elaborate tools and machinery. There are rapid changes in the techniques of production. The means of transport and communication are extended and improved.

The striking trend in population in a developing economy is that death rates start declining. This follows an improvement in the standard of living, the availability of medical facilities and awareness of the benefits of smaller families. The food supply is more abundant and regular; there is greater security of life and property owing to improvement in the law and order situation. The medical innovations and the development of vaccines, antibiotics and insecticides and the improvement in sanitary conditions have eradicated many dangerous and fatal diseases. The public health measures have increasingly become more effective. The comulative effect of all these developments is to reduce substantially the incidence of disease and death. There is, thus, an increasingly pervasive pattern of rapid decline in death rates in all developing economies.

However, the birth rates prove to be more intractable. They are not so readily responsive to economic improvement. They are governed more by deeply established customs and institutions. Also, there

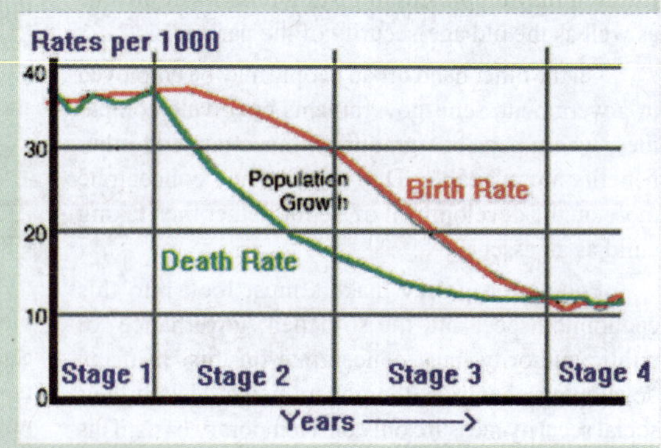

The Demographic Transition.

is a general consensus in favour of reducing death and disease but no such consensus supporting the desirability of small families. Thus, for a time, while the death rates have fallen, the birth rates continue to rule high so that during the stage of incipient economic development, population growth is accelerated rather than diminished. There is rather a population explosion. There is a time lag before the reduction of birth rates follows the reduction in death rates. This is what is happening in India at present.

But when a very high stage of economic development is reached as in the West, the birth rates fall too. There is deliberate limitation of the size of the family and this is facilitated by a widespread use of efficient contraceptive devices. The changing structure of production involves a declining importance of the family as a production unit, where women come to play an increasing role outside the home and where economic mobility can better be achieved with a small family. The children are considered more a burden than an asset. The economic advantages of a large family disappear and the fashion of having a small family first catches the higher strata of society but gradually infiltrates to the sections at the lower end of the economic scale and spreads eventually to the rural areas.

Thus, the birth rates decline too and establish a parallel with the declining death rates so that the population growth slows down. Small families and low mortality become a typical pattern.

It may, however, be borne in mind that some countries like Malaysia and Shri Lanka have reduced their death rates merely through public health measures without abandoning their agrarian structure. Also, mere urbanisation does not lead to reduction in fertility. In India and Egypt, for example, the differential fertility between the rural and urban sectors is practically non-existent.

Thus, "substantial economic improvement may be a sufficient condition for a decline in mortality, but it is not today a necessary condition." The relation between economic development and fertility is even less certain. Small economic changes may not reduce birth rates. In many under-developed countries, social and economic changes that are now going on are not likely to reduce fertility in the next two or three decades. The theory of demographic transition does not say what conditions are essential for a fertility decline and what precisely is the period during which this decline must take place.

The theory of Demographic Transition has been summarised as under:–

"The agrarian low-income economy is characterised by high birth and death rates –the birth rates relatively stable, and the death rates fluctuating in response to varying fortunes. Then as the economy changes its form to a more inter-dependent and specialised market-oriented economy, the average death rate declines. It continues to decline under the impact of better organisation and improving medical knowledge and care. Somewhat later the birth rate begins to fall. The two rates follow a more or less parallel downward course with decline in birth rate lagging behind. Finally, as further reductions in the death rate become harder to attain, the birth rate again approaches equality with death rate and a more gradual rate of growth is re-established, with, however, low risks of mortality and small family as the typical pattern. Mortality rates are now relatively stable from year to year and birth rates now responsive to voluntary decisions rather than to deeply imbedded customs may fluctuate from year to year."[1]

Over-population, An Impediment to Economic Growth

It is sometimes said that a growing population helps economic development by providing an expanding market for goods. But this is an erroneous view. Actually, over - population retards economic growth. All effort at economic development under fast growing population turns out to be "writing on sand with waves of population growth washing away all that we have written." It hampers economic development in following ways:

(*i*) Creating Food Shortage. Income elasticity of demand for food being high growing population creates serious food problem as incomes increase with economic development. Valuable foreign exchange is eaten up by food imports which would have been otherwise utilized for importing capital equipment and technical know-how.

(*ii*) Increasing Unproductive Numbers. The greater is the increase in numbers the higher is the dependency ratio. A large number of children have to be supported without making any contribution to production.

(*iii*) Problem of Unemployment. An over-populated country has to face the serious problem of unemployment and under- employment. There is disguised unemployment in rural areas and widespread unemployment in urban areas. This means that there is a large number of people who are not adding to production but have to be fed all the same.

1. Coale and Hoover: *population Growth and Economic Development in Low Income Countries*, 1958, P. 13.

In this way, productive resources have to be diverted to non-productive uses, viz., feeding the idle persons.

(*iv*) Reduction in Savings and Investment. A country having a huge population to support has little capacity to save and invest. How can the country advance economically?

(*v*) Loss of Women's Labour. Frequent maternity disables women from work and denies their contribution to production and economic development.

Conclusion. Thus, growing population aggravates the food problem, worsens the unemployment situation, adds to the number of unpoductive consumers, keeps down per capita income and the level of living and labour efficiency and militates against capital formation. In all these and many other ways, rapid rate of population growth acts as a drag on economic progress and slows down the pace of economic development.

Key terms

Positive checks, Preventive checks, optimum population, Demographic Transition

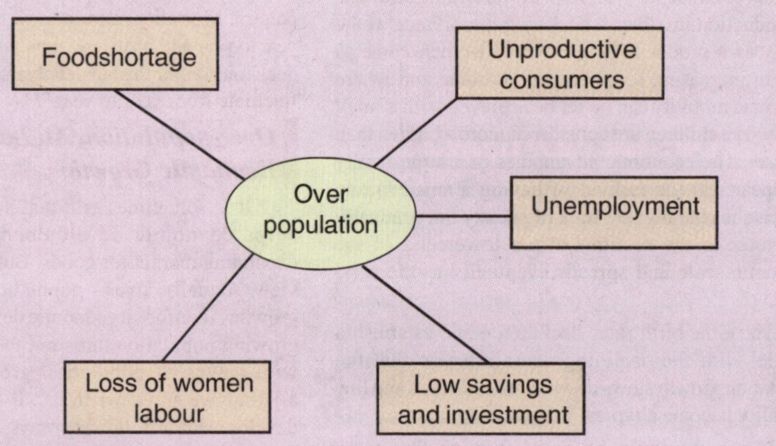

QUESTIONS

1. Explain the optimum theory population.
2. Discuss the salilent features of cost-benefit theory of population.
3. Critically examine the Malthusian Theory of Population. Is it applicable to your country?
4. Examine the Optimum Theory of Population. How far is this theory an improvement on the Malthusian Theory of Population?
5. Explain the effects of overpopulation on the economy.
6. Relate population growth with economic development.

   Or

   Explain the theory of demographic transition.

SCALE OF PRODUCTION

The scale of production has an important bearing on the cost of production. It is the manufacturers' common experience that larger the scale of production, the lower generally is the average cost of production. That is why the entrepreneur is tempted to enlarge the scale of production so that he may benefit from the resulting economies of scale. These economies are broadly speaking of two types: **Internal economies** and **external economies,** which we shall presently consider in some detail. But before we do that, we shall give in a summary way the economies and diseconomies of large-scale production.

Economies of large-Scale Production

The modern factory system, with its extensive use of machinery and division of labour, is responsible for large-scale production. The following are its chief advantages:–

Efficient Use of Capital Equipment. There is a large scope for the use of machinery which results in lower costs. A large producer can install an up-to-date and expensive machinery. He can also have his own repairing unit. Specialised machinery can be employed for each job. The result is that production is very economical. A small producer, with a small market, cannot keep the machinery continuously working. Keeping it idle is uneconomical. A large producer can work it continuously and reap the resulting economies.

Economy of Specialised Labour. In a big concern, there is ample scope for division of labour. Specialized labour produces a larger output and of better quality. It is only in a large business that every person can be put on the job that he can best perform. The large-scale producer thus gets the best out of every person he employs.

Better Utilisation and Greater Specialisation in Management. A capable manager is obviously under-utilised in a small concern. As, therefore, the scale of production is enlarged, there is fuller use of the manager's time and ability. Also, he is able to delegate some of his less important functions to his assistants and increasingly specialise in the jobs where his ability is most fruitful.

Economies of Buying and Selling. While purchasing raw material and other accessories, a big business can secure specially favourable terms on account of its large custom. While selling its goods it can attract customers by offering a greater variety and by ensuring prompt execution of the orders placed with it. A lower rate of profit results in larger sales and higher net profits in a larger-scale business.

Economies of the Overhead Charges. The expenses of administration and distribution per unit of output in a big business are much less. Interest, the pay bill, and other overhead charges are the same whether production is on a large or a small scale. Thus, the same amount of expenditure being distributed over a larger output, results in a lower cost per unit.

Economy in Rent. A large-scale producer makes a saving in rent too. If the same factory is made to produce a large quantity of goods, the same amount of rent is divided over a large output. This means a smaller addition to the cost per unit in the form of rent.

Experiments and Research. A large concern can afford to spend liberally on research and experiments. It is well-known that, in the long run, these expenses more than repay. Successful researh may lead to the discovery of a cheaper process. This may bring a large profit. Only a large-scale business can incur such expenditure.

Advertisement and Salesmanship. A big concern can afford to spend large amounts of money on advertisement and salesmanship. Ultimately they do bear fruit. Also, the amount of money spent on advertisement per unit comes to a low figure when production is on a large scale. The salesmen can make a careful study of individual markets and thus acquire a hold on new markets or strengthen it on the old ones. Thus, a large-scale producer has a greater competitive strength.

Utilization of By-products. A big busi ness will not have to throw away any of its by-products or waste products. It will be able to make an economical use of them. A small sugar factory, for instance, has to throw away the molasses, whereas a big concern can turn it into power-alcohol. By utilising by-products, it can lower the cost of production.

Meeting Adversity. A big business can show better resistance in times of adversity. It has much larger resources. Losses can be easily borne. A small concern will simply collapse under such a strain.

Cheap Credit. A large business can secure credit facilities at cheap rates. Its credit in the money market is high and the banks are only too willing to give advances. Low costs of credit reduce cost of production.

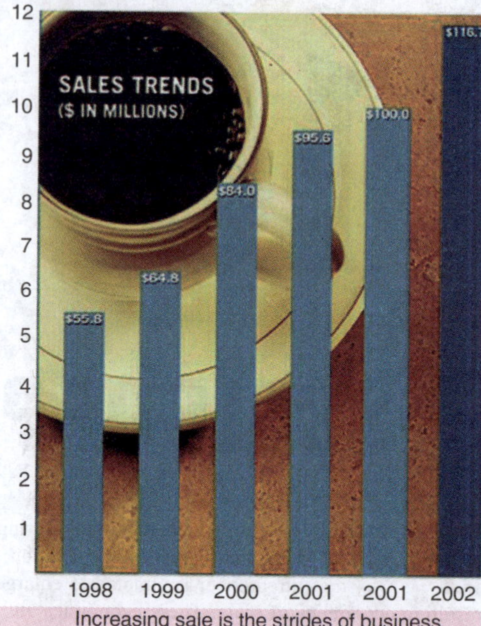

Increasing sale is the strides of business.

These are some of the advantages that a large-scale business has over a small-scale business. But let us see the other side.

Diseconomies of Scale

Large-scale production is not without its disadvantages. Some of these disadvantages are:–

Over-worked Management. A largescale producer cannot pay full attention to every detail. Costs often rise on account of the dishonesty of the employees or waste of materials by them. This is due to the lack of supervision. Owing to laxity of control costs of production go up. The management is overworked.

Individual tastes Ignored. Large-scale production is a mass production or standardised production. Goods of uniform quality are turned out irrespective of the preferences of individual customers. Individual tastes are not, therefore, satisfied. This results in a loss of custom.

No Personal Element. A large-scale business is generally managed by paid employees. The owner is usually absent. The sympathy and personal touch, which ought to exist between the master and the men, are missing. Frequent misunderstandings lead to strikes and lock-outs. This is positively harmful to the business.

Possibility of depression. Large-scale production may result in over-production. Production may exceed demand and cause depression and unemployment. It is not always easy or profitable to dispose of a large output.

Dependence on foreign markets. A large-scale producer has generally to depend on foreign markets. The foreign markets may be cut off by war or some other political upheaval. This makes the business risky.

Machinery and equipments are indivisible.

Cut-throat competition. Large-scale producers must fight for the markets. There is wasteful competition which does no good to society. Many promising business are ruined by senseless competition. There is also competition and bidding for resources and inputs.

Internatioanl complications and war. When the large-scale producers operate on an international scale, their interests clash either on the score of markets or of materials. These complications sometimes lead to armed conflicts. Many a modern war arose on account of scramble for materials and markets.

Lack of adaptability. A large-scale producing unit finds it very difficult to switch on from one business to another. In a depression, small firms are able to move away from declining trades to flourishing ones easily. In this way, they are able to avoid losses. This adaptability is lacking in a big business.

Easy Finance is a part of economies of scale.

Conclusion

In spite of these drawbacks, large-scale production offers several economies. The tendency in manufacturing and transport industries is to increase the scale. The advantages outweigh the disadvantages. The scale of production is enlarged till the firm has reached the optimum size. At this scale of production, the total profits is the maximum or the average cost per unit is the minimum. At this stage, marginal cost equals price (i.e., marginal revenue). The producer goes on producing more, so long as the price exceeds marginal cost. He will stop when marginal cost has overtaken price or marginal revenue, and the two have been equalised. "Differences in efficiency between firms will show themselves not in differences in marginal costs but in differences in output. The more efficient will have the larger output."

Concept of Indivisibility

A very important source of economy in a big concern arises from the use of an indivisible factor of production. This **concept of indivisibility** requires careful understanding. Just think of a hostel kitchen. It must have a minimum equipment of utensils and sevants, e.g., it must have at least one cook and one boy servant. This is the indivisible factor. Now if this equipment can satisfactorily serve fifteen students, it will be obviously uneconomical to have only ten students to serve. Charges per head will be unnecesarily higher and the cook and the servant will remain idle for some time. A large group of students will keep them fully employed and get the utmost out of them.

Similarly, a professor is indivisible. Suppose he can effectively impart instruction to a class of fifty students. In a small college, where the number in a class may be smaller, the authorities will not be making full use of him.

The same is the case with a factory. Take the case of a sugar factory. It must have a minimum equipment of building, plant, clerical staff and other miscellaneous establishments. Even a worker is indivisible. One operator may be required for each machine irrespective of its capacity. Similarly, a manager is indivisible whether the factory works below capacity or at full capacity. In case the factory is working below capacity, this equipment will not be fully used, a part of it will be wasted. Hence, the scale of production must be such as to use the indivisible equipment fully, otherwise it will be uneconomical.

Several of our industries, notably iron and steel and the jute industries, are generally working below capacity, which is obviously wasteful. The indivisible equipment is not being fully employed. The point, therefore, is that when production is carried on a large

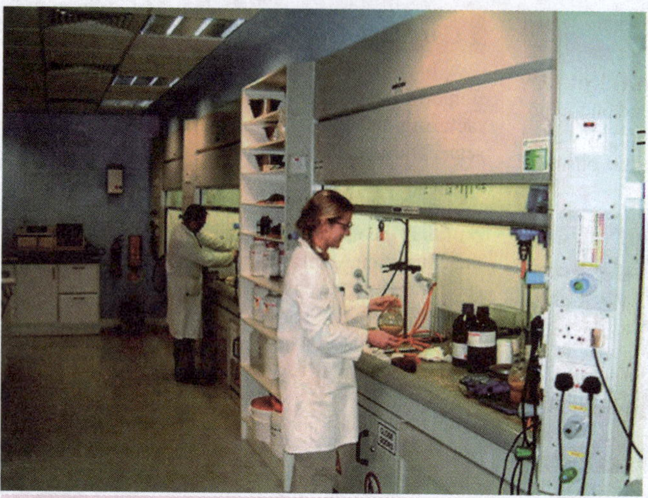
Research and Development.

scale, equipment will not remain idle, and the indivisible factors will be fully employed. It will mean more economical production.

Stigler has mentioned several types of **indivisibilities:**[1] **(1) Indivisibility of machinery. (2) Marketing indivisibilities.** These relate to the employment of salesmen, maintenance of purchasing department and advertisement. The larger the scale the smaller will be the cost per unit. **(3) Financial indivisibilities.** These relate to the managing costs of loans. Securities issued in large quantities can be listed on the stock exchange. **(4) Research indivisibilities.** Once certain costs have been incurred in investments, the larger the scale, the more economical it is.

INTERNAL AND EXTERNAL ECONOMIES

As we zhave said already, economies of large-scale production can be grouped under two headings: internal economies and external economies. We shall first take internal economies.

Internal Economies

Internal economies are those economies in production, those reductions in production costs, **which accrue to the firm itself when it expands its output or enlarges its scale of production.** The internal economies arise within a firm as a result of its own expansion independent of the size and expansion of the industry.

The internal economies are simply due to the increase in the scale of production. They arise from the use of the methods which small firms do not find it worthwhile to employ.

Internal economies may be of the following types:

(*a*) Technical Economies. They arise from the fact that it is easy to make a large machine, and there is a mechanical advantage in the use of a large machine. Technical economies pertain not to the size of the firm but to the size of a factory or establishment. A firm may own and operate several factories or establishments. The size of the establishment depends on the nature of the industry. For instance, in agriculture and dairy, large plants can be duplicated in several small establishments. In such industries, the size of the typical establishment is small. In other industries, e.g., mining, technical economies are available only in large establishments; hence the typical unit is large.

Better Management.

There are four different ways in which technical economies can arise: **(*i*) Large size.** Economies arise only when large machines are used, e.g., a bigger boiler or a bigger furnace. It has a bigger productive capacity but uses proportionately less energy. A bigger machine does not require more staff to operate it. The cost of construction is also relatively smaller. **(*ii*) Linking process.** A dairy may have its own fodder farm or a sugar factory its own cane farm: The integration of the two is more economical. Similarly, paper-making and pulp-making can be combined with great advantage. **(*iii*) Superior technique.** Some machines represent superior techniques. The bigger works can use them with greater advantage. For instance, only a big newspaper can use a rotary press. Similarly, only large establishments can use power-driven machinery

1. Stigler. G.J.–*Therory of price (1947)*, pp.135-37.

economically. **(*iv*) Increased specialisation.** Scope for specialisation is also available in a large plant. Specialisation and division of labour are highly advantageous. For instance, only in a big school, we can have specialist teachers.

(*b*) Managerial Economies. These economies arise from the creation of special departments or from functional specialisation. They also result from the delegation of routine and detailed matters to subordinates. The managerial expenses can be reduced by increasing the size of an establishment or by grouping a number of establishments under one management. In a small factory, a manager is a worker, foreman and a manager all rolled in one. Much of his time is wasted on things having little economic significance. In a big concern, such jobs can be delegated to junior employees and the manager confines himself to jobs which bring more profits. This is vertical division of labour. But there are possibilities of horizontal division too when each department is placed under an expert. The job is done more efficiently and more economically. All this is possible when production is carried on a large scale.

(*c*) Commercial Economies. They arise from the purchase of materials and scale of goods. Large businesses have bargaining advantages and are accorded a preferential treatment by the firms they deal with. They are able to secure freight concessions from railways and road transport, cheap credit from the banks, prompt delivery, careful attention, and considerate treatment from all dealers. This means more profits. A large firm can employ experts and carry on research and experiments. It can use material testing and grading machinery. It can buy and sell when the market trends are more favourable. In selling, it can cut down selling costs and in purchasing, it can have a wider choice.

(*d*) Financial Economies. These economies arise from the fact that a big firm has better credit and can borow on more favourable terms. Its shares enjoy a wider market, which encourages a prospective investor. This only shows superior bargaining strength and does not necessarily indicate greater efficiency.

(*e*) Risk-bearing Economies. A big firm can spread risks and can often eliminate them. This it does by diversifying output. Diversification imparts it strength and stability and makes it less vulnerable to changes in commercial fortunes. There is also diversification of markets, of sources of supply and of processes of manufacture.

Real and Pecuniary Economies

Internal economies can be classified as Real Economies and Pecuniary Economies. Real economies arise from reduction in the physical quantity of inputs. These may be economies in (*i*) production (*ii*) marketing or salesmanship (*iii*) managerial due to specialisation, decentralisation in decision-making and mechanisation *e.g.* computerisation and (*iv*) transport and storage economies. *Pecuniary Economies* arise from lower prices for inputs, lower interest rates, lower rates for advertising, lower transport costs paid by bigger firms.

Internal Economies (Its effect)

On y-axis cost and x-axis quantity of output. Due to the internal economies of scale the cost of production per unit will go on decreasing up to a minimum point viz M. that is 'ON' cost is the minimum possible cost. Hence the firm will be beneficial to produce 'OQ' quantity of output.

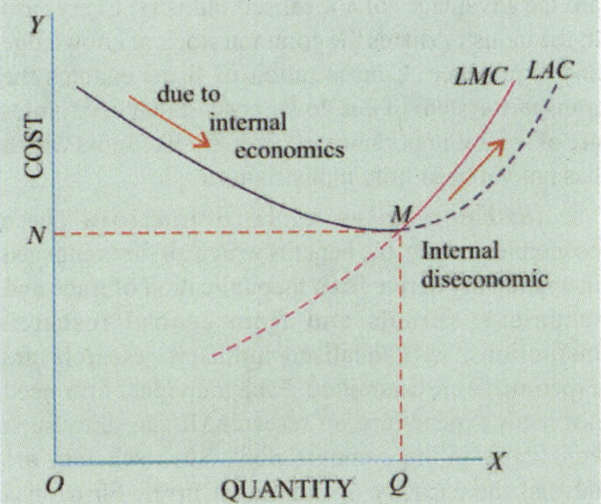

Fig. 16.1. LAC falls due to internal economies of scale.

On the other hand the 'LAC' may start increasing due to internal diseconomies of scale. that is on the right hand side of 'NM' cost.

External Economies

External economies are those economies which accrue to each member firm as a result of the expansion of the industry as a whole. Expansion of an industry may lead to the availability of new and cheaper raw materials, tools and machinery, and to the discovery and diffusion of a superior technical knowledge. Some raw materials and tools may be made available at reduced prices, because as the industry grows, subsidiary and correlated firms may spring up in the vicinity of the industry to provide it with raw materials and tools at reduced prices.

Further, as an industry expands, trade journals may appear which help in the discovery and diffusion of the technical knowledge. Moreover, with the expansion of an industry, certain specialised firms may come into existence which work up its "waste products". The industry can then sell them at a good price.

Thus, the entry of new firms enlarging the size of an industry may enable all firms to produce at lower cost. The large-scale firm reaps internal economies. The large-scale industry brings to the firms external economies. There is every possibility of external economies to be reaped when a young industry grows in a new territory. Various types of external economies are give below:

(a) Economies of Concentration. These economies relate to advantages arising from the availability of skilled workers, the provision of better transport and credit facilities, stimulation of improvements, benefits from subsidiaries, and so on. Scattered firms cannot enjoy such economies. These are the advantages of a localised industry. Every firm in the industry shares the common stock of knowledge and experience. Concentration of firms enables the transport system to cut down costs. Such economies are of special importance in a country like India which has not yet been fully industrialised.

(b) Economies of Information. These economies refer to the benefits which all firms engaged in an industry derive from thepublication of trade and technical journals and from central research institutions. In a localised industry, research and experiments are centralised. Each individual firm need not incur expenditure on research. It can draw such benefits from the common pool. Such schemes are beyond the capacity of individual firms. Firms in a scattered industry cannot have such facilities.

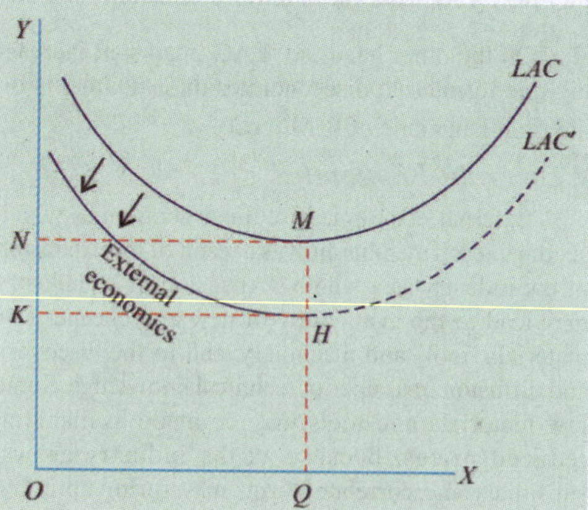

Fig. 16.2. External economies cause LAC to shift down at each level of output.

(c) Economies of Disintegration. When an industry grows, it becomes possible to split up some of the processes which are taken over by specialist firms. For example, a number of cotton mills located in a particular locality may have the benefit of a separate calendering plant.

External Economies (Its effect)

Due to external economies the cost of production per unit may be reduced. It also may help in the shift of the LAC (Long-run average cost curve) down word to LAC′. It depends on how powerful the external economies. Before the external economies the firm may be producing at 'ON' amount of cost and 'OQ' amount of quantity but now it may be producing the same quantity viz. 'OQ' at a lower cost 'OK'.

Relation between internal and external economies

No hard and fast line can be drawn between internal and external economies. When a number of firms combine into one external economies become internal economies. Whether particular economies are internal or external depends upon what operations it is profitable to combine. Internal economies are the result of expansion of individual firms, whereas external economies are the result of expansion or development of the entire industry of which the individual firms are members.

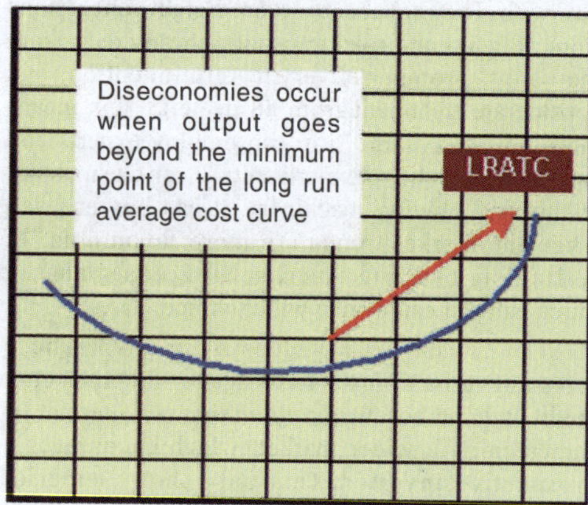

It is worth noting that as commercial and technical education spreads, and other such developments take place, the field of internal economies is being narrowed and that of external economies is being widened. This is the result of progress in different fields.

Internal and External Diseconomies

We should also take note of diseconomies, both internal and external. It is possible that the expansion of a firm's output may lead to rise in costs and thus result in diseconomies instead of economies. This may be due to the fact that inferior or less efficient factors may have been brought into use. When a firm expands beyond proper limits, it is beyond the capacity of the manager to manage it efficiently. This also is an example of an internal diseconomy.

In the same manner, the expansion of an industry may result in diseconomies which may be called external diseconomies.The result is that the individual firms in the industry are faced with diseconomies instead of economies.

It is common experience that, when an industry in an industrial centre expands, there is a keener competition among the firms for the factors of production and the raw materials. As a consequence, the prices of raw materials and of the factors of produciton go up. All firms have now to pay higher wages, higher rents and higher rates of interest besides higher prices for the raw materials. Suitable labour ceases to be available; and capital also becomes scare. The result is that, with the expansion of an industry the costs of production go up instead of falling.

The main point is that the additional factors of production, the employment of which becomes now necessary, are less efficient and they are obtained at a higher cost. It is in this manner that diseconomies result as an industry expands.

Thus, as the scale of production of an individual increases, there are internal economies as well as internal diseconomies. But, the internal economies generally outweigh internal diseconomies. That is why, as the scale of production increases, average cost of production falls. But if the scale is increased beyond a proper limit, the internal diseconomies will swallow up the internal economies and the cost of production will rise instead of falling. In the same manner, when an industry expands, the firms enjoy external economies. But too much expansion will result in greater external diseconomies than external economies. As a consequence, the cost of production goes up instead of falling.

External Diseconomies (Its effect)

Due to external diseconomies, (if they are more powerful) will shift the LAC (Long run average cost curve) upword to LAC′. In this case the firm will be producing 'OQ' amount of quantity earlier at 'ON' cost, now due to external diseconomies it will produce at 'OR' cost.

Limits to the Expansion of a Business

Although it is profitable to expand business yet it is not always possible to do so. The main obstacles in the growth of business are: ***(a)* Financial, *(b)* Managerial,** and ***(c)* Market obstacles.**

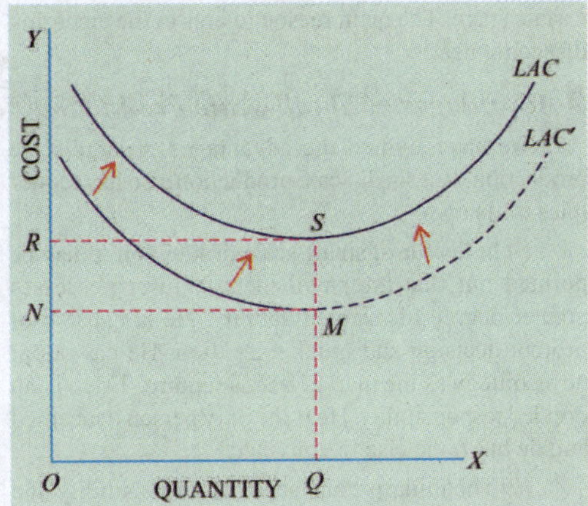

Fig. 16.3. LAC shifts up due to external diseconomies.

We take financial obstacles first. For expanding business, the entrepreneur needs fresh supplies of capital. It may not, however, be easy to arrange for more capital. Still the difficulty is not insurmountable. Successful businessmen, who have reputation for honesty and efficiency, will find ample capital forthcoming. Finance, it is said, is a mere camp follower.

A high hurdle is the managerial. An entrepreneur, however capable, cannot satisfactorily tackle problems beyond a certain range and complexity. That is why a business cannot be expanded indefinitely. A point will be reached when the entrepreneur will find that his business has become unmanageable. Supervision will then become ineffective. Safeguards against fraud will add to the cost. Internal economies will gradually disappear.

The Limit. But there are other difficulties too. As business is expanded, prices of the factors of production will rise; more may have to be paid in the form of rent, wages and interest to attract additional supplies of the inputs. The cost will, therefore, rise. On the other hand, the additional output may depress the price in the market. Hence, the cost will sooner or later overtake the revenue.

The firm will go on expanding till the marginal revenue (additional income from the additional output) exceeds the marginal costs (additional costs incurred on producing the additional output). **The limit of expansion will be reached when the marginal revenue is equal to marginal costs.** At that point, the firm will be maximising its profits and, therefore, it will have no incentive to expand its output any further.

Conclusion. These are some of the factors which govern the expansion of a business and limit its growth. No wonder that business stops growing beyond a certain stage. The main reason relates to the emerging diseconomies.

Advantages of Small-scale Production

We have studied the advantages of large-scale production. But small-scale production also has economies of its own:

(i) In favour of small-scale production it may be pointed out that the small manufacturer possesses greater degree of manoeuvrability. He is capable of prompt decision and quick execution. He can adopt new strategy as the market trends require. There is no divided responsibility. He is the only person concerned and he has none else to convince.

(ii) The initiative and sense of responsibility of a small producer have not been sapped by routine. He does not need elaborate system of book-keeping and checks to prevent fraud or eliminate waste of labour or material. As Marshall says, "the master's eye is everywhere". Close supervision makes for economic working.

(iii) Personal contact with the employees, and a kind word thrown now and then, will rule out the possibility of a strike or any other trouble. Peace generally reigns in small concern and peace means prosperity.

(iv) Personal contact with the customers, again, sends them away well satisfied and is productive of good results. Custom is stable and demand is steady. This means absence of risk.

(v) The small- scale producer's advantage is the greatest where the demand is limited and fluctuating . A large-scale business is not suited to cater for such a demand and is therefore seriously handicapped.

(vi) The small busi-nessman is usually the sole proprietor. Self-interest is a strong spur to his activity. He works long and late. Hard work is bound to make a success of a business.

Conclusion. With the wide dissemination of technical knowledge, the number of external economies is increasing while that of internal economies is decreasing. This helps the small producer. Also, where business cannot be reduced to a routine, a small producer has an advantage over a big producer. All these factors explain the advantages of small businesses.

Disadvantages

The small-scale producer cannot reap those economies which are available to a big concern. His drawbacks can be enumerated thus:

(i) There is less scope for the use of modern machinery and labour-saving devices. Hence cost per unit is high.

(ii) There is little scope for division of labour. The advantages of division of labour are, therefore, lost to him. Hence production is uneconomic.

(iii) The small-scale producer is at a disadvantage in the purchase of raw materials and other accessories. This pushes up the cost.

(iv) He cannot afford to spend large sums of money on research and experiments. Hence he cannot make innovations and thus reduce costs.

(v) Cost of rent, interest, advertisement, *etc*., per unit of output is higher. That is, he has higher overhead charges.

(vi) With his limited resources he cannot meet bad times. This means instability.

(vii) He cannot secure cheap credit. This means higher costs.

(viii) By-products have to be thrown away as so much waste.

Survival of Small Businesses

The advantages enjoyed by small-scale business enable it to compete successfully against big business. There are, besides, other circumstances which help a small business and in which large-scale production is not economical. When, for instance, the demand for a commodity is small and fitful, expansion of business is inadvisable. There are several factors which help the small producers to survive:

Small businesses.

Geographical Factors. The demand for the product may be strictly local. Small firms can meet local needs more economically.

If the raw materials are bulky and scattered, production will have to be decentralised and carried on in small units, where they can draw on the local supplies.

Similarly, in sparsely populated regions, it is more economical to carry on production in small and scattered units.

And, where markets and sources of supply overlap and the producers and consumers are in close contact with one another, e.g., in milk supply, smaller firms are found to be more economical. Thus, a small firm is sheltered by distance. Expansion of firms is checked by market resistance, especially if transport costs are high.

Psychological Factors. The small producer is also helped by psychological factors. Consumers have their own preferences based on superiority, real or imaginary, of the goods they use. Thus, it is not only the distance which breaks a market but also prejudices, tastes and habits of the consumers.This gives each a protected clientele. To overcome this resistance very expensive publicity may be necessary.

The geographical obstacles can be overcome by setting up branches and the psychological obstacles by widening the range of production. But these devices are often neither feasible nor economical, because they 'bump up' against the managerial obstacle to expansion.

Some Modern Developments. Besides, a small producer in modern times has been helped to hold his own against a big producer by developments like electricity, co-operative movement, and dissemination of scientific and technical knowledge through technical journals. Such knowledge is no longer the monopoly of the big business.

Entrepreneur's Attitude. The entre-preneur's own inclination, too, is responsible for the existence of small firms. "From a mixture of motives–from a love of independence and uncertainty, from pride or ambition, or the urge to create –men may prefer to run a small business of their own rather than act as subordinates at a higher rate of pay."

Conclusion. These are some of the reasons why a small-scale producer is able to hold his own against a big producer. That also explains why small-scale businesses exist side by side with the large-scale business.

Small Scale Industries

Small Scale industries definition has undergone many changes from time to time since 1950s. Today the definition of SSI is on the basis of investment. In February 1997 the investment limit in SSI and ancillary industries were raised to Rs. 3 crore and that of tiny units to Rs. 25 Lakh. In 1999 the ivestment limit of SSI was brought down to Rs. 1 crore

SSI play a vital role in economic devlopment of an economy specially a developing country like India. The following are the main arguments of SSI.

(1) Production arguments : SSI gives immediate production, In our country the population is more and due to this the demand for goods are more. Small scale industries helps to meet this demand.

(2) Employment argument : As the SSI are labour-intensive, it provides employment to many people. The problem of unemployment to a certain extent may be reduced.

(3) Capital-light argument : In large scale industries we require huge amount of investement, but in SSI we can start the units with smaller amount of capital.

(4) Skill-light argument : Labourers could be employed with lesser amount of training.

(5) Latent-resources arguments : SSI can help in tapping the unexploited resources into use.

(6) Decentralisation arguments : SSI helps in small town's development. They can spread to different parts of the country. In case of large scale industries concentration is in big cities only. This can stop the labour migration from small towns to big cities.

(7) Equity argument : SSI industries helps in encouraging small entrepreneurs to enter into the business. This may be vital, so as to reduced the gap between the rich and poor.

(8) Import light and Export promotion argument : As local resources are used in many SSI, less burdon on import bill. SSI are very beneficial as far as for exports are concenned. In India its share in exports is increasing. In 2000-2001. (Estimated 13.13 billiion $ worth exports were accounted from SSIs).

(9) Less-industrial disputes arguments : In SSI industries there are very less number of industrial disputes, as the number of workers in SSI are very less compare to large scale industries.

(10) Support to Large-scale industries argument : Many large scale industries output is consumed as an input in SSI;. Hence SSIs and Large scale industries are interdepending.

There are many other benefits from SSIs, that dose not mean that there are no problems. SSI; suffer; from many problems. In different countries of the world SSI have played a vital role in their economies. After the liberalisation and globalisation the role of SSI and its definition is changing in many parts of the world.

Role of Small-Scale Industry in Under-developed Countries

The small-scale industry has a special role to play in an under-developed country. Considering the resource position of the under-developed countries, the small-scale industries fit in excellently in their development plans for several reasons: (*i*) They have a vast employment potential; (*ii*) They offer limitless opportunities for self-employment; (*iii*) They are capital-light and capital is what such countries lack; (*iv*) They promote capital formation; (*v*) They are skill-light; (*vi*) They are import-light and cut the country's import bill; (*vii*) They are quick-yielding so that inflationary pressures are contained; (*viii*) They promote decentralisation of industries; (*ix*) The decentralised industries can bring about even distribution of income and wealth; (*x*) They can lend valuable support to large-scale industries; (*xi*) By diverting surplus labour from land they can reduce pressure on land.

Key terms

Positive checks, Preventive checks, optimum population, Demographic Transition

QUESTIONS

1. Carefully distinguish between internal and external economies. In what principal ways does the firm enjoy internal economies? How do they affect firm's average cost curve over different ranges of output?
2. Explain the external and internal economies in Production. Discuss the part played by them in bringing about Increasing Returns.
3. Discuss the relative merits of large and small-scale production.
4. What are the factors limiting the size of a firm? What part do "Indivisibilities: and "Economies of Scale" play in determining the size of the firm?
5. Discuss the role of small-scale industries in a developing economy.

PRODUCTION POSSIBILITY CURVE AND PRODUCTION FUNCTION

In this chapter we propose to deal with two fundamentals of the theory of production, *viz.*, Production Possibility Curve and Production Function.

PRODUCTION POSSIBILITY CURVE

We know that the resources, both human and material, at the disposal of the community are strictly limited and they are capable of alternative uses, whereas we want to produce innumerable commodities, *i.e.*, the ends are unlimited. We have, therefore, to choose the most desirable assortment of goods that we can produce with the resources that we command and with a given state of technical knowledge. Had the resources at our disposal been unlimited, there would have been no problem, and we would have produced more of everything to satisfy our wants. If some resources were lying idle, then also it would have been possible to increase the production of all goods. But, in an economy characterised by full employment, some good can be produced only by foregoing the production of some other good. This is in keeping with the opportunity cost principle.

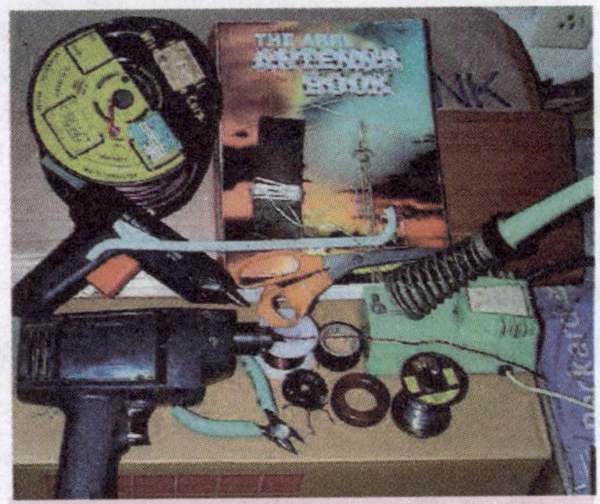

Material resources.

Natural resources. Resources are used for production of goods in the economy.

An economy has a certain population and some millions of workers of various grades; it has mastered certain techniques of production; it has certain resources in the form of land, water and other natural resources. That is, it has a certain number of factors or inputs. The society has really to decide how these resources can be utilised to produce the various possible commodities. In other words, it has to discover its **production possibility curve.**

The production possibility curve shows the maximum output of any one commodity that the economy can produce together with the prescribed quantites of other commodities produced and the resources utilised. In short, the production possibility curve tells us what assortment of goods and services the economy can produce with the resources and techniques at its disposal. The assortment on the curve is regarded as technologically efficient and below it as inefficient, for the simple reason that the economy is capable of producing a bigger assortment at least in respect of one commodity without decreasing any other. Any assortment which is beyound the frontier is really beyond the economy's power and is unattainable. The production possibility curve depicts the society's menu of choices.

We shall illustrate the concept of the production possibility curve by means of a table and a diagram. We take only two commodities, although in the real world, the commodities that can be produced are numberless. We take only two, because a larger number cannot be represented on a twodimensional diagram. But the principle will be clear and can be applied to any number of commodities.

Let us take two commodities X and Y that a firm can produce. If it decides to devote more of its resources to the production of X, it must sacrifice to that exent production of some Y. Take the following table:—

Table 1: Alternative Production Possibilities

Production Possibilities	*X (Thousands)*	*Y (Thousands)*
A	0	15
B	1	14
C	2	12
D	3	9
E	4	5
F	5	0

As in the case of indifference curves, we first suppose that all the resources at the disposal of the economy are devoted to the production of good X. In that case 5,000 X-products is the maximum that it can produce. Now let all the productive resources available be devoted to the production of Y with the result that 15,000 Y will be produced but no X. These are the two extreme limits, *viz.*, 5,000 X but no Y and 15,000 Y but no X. In between these two extreme limits, there are numerous combinations of X and Y that can be produced.

The production possibility curve can be depicted by means of diagram given below.

In this diagram (Fig. 17.1), A represents the one extreme limit at which all Y's are produced. Now if we want to produce some X, some Y will have to be sacrificed. For instance, in order to produce 1,000 X. we shall have to be content with 14,000 Y instead of 15,000. That is, we have transformed, as it were, one thousand Y into 1,000 X, and so on down the table (given above). Thus, production possibility schedule is the same thing as production transformation schedule and the curve in the diagram (Fig. 17.1) is called the Production Transformation Curve.

In the diagram, the curve marks the production possibility frontier and all points on the curve represent production possibility, the points inside the curve are attainable combinations and those outside such as s, t are unattainable combinations. Any point inside the curve represents an underutilisation of resources or under-employment. A fuller utilisation will shift the curve outwards.

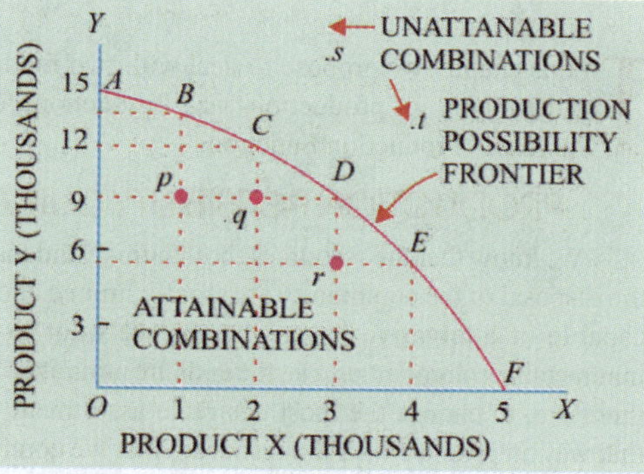

Fig. 17.1. Production possibility curve.

Increase in the resources at the disposal of the firm will take it to a higher production possibility curve.

Marginal Rate of Transformation

We have seen above that, in order to produce more X, we must sacrifice some Y, i.e., Y's can be transformed into X's. The rate at which one product is transformed into another is called **marginal rate of transformation.** For instance, marginal rate of transformation between good X and good Y is the amount of Y which has to be sacrificed for the production of X. We can also see from the table given on p. 125 that for the production of additional units of X, increasing quantities of Y have to be sacrificed.

Hence, the marginal rate of transformation increases as more of X is produced and less of Y. This makes the production possibility curve concave in the origin. The marginal rate of transformation (MRT) at any point on the production possibility curve is given by the slope of the curve at that point.

Iso-Revenue Line

We have seen that the production possibility curve shows the various combinations of the two goods which can be produced with given resources. The question remains as to which of these various combinations the firm will decide to produce. Which is considered the most desirable? Surely, the firm will have to decide which combination out of the so many available will be most profitable. In order to hit on the most desirable combination, we shall introduce the price factor or the revenue factor (Price paid by the purchaser

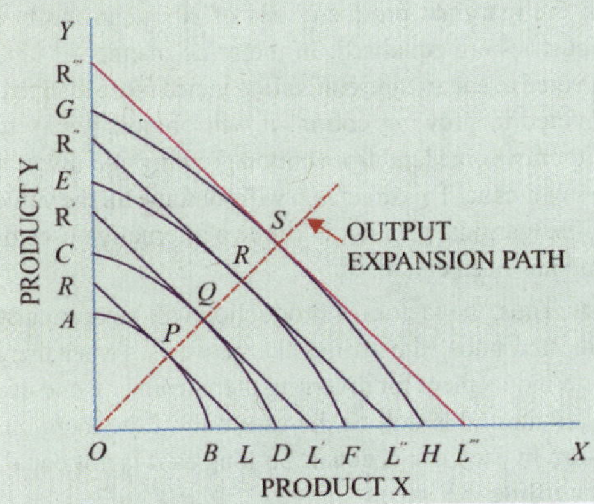

Fig. 17.2. Output Expansion path shows the revenue maximizing locus of different combinations of two products as resources of the firm change keeping prices of products constant.

is revenue for the seller). The producer must maximise his revenue. We shall, therefore, draw the Iso-Revenue line yield the same revenue. **Output Expansion Path.** In Fig. 17.2 RL, R′L′, R′′L′′and R′′′L′′′are the iso-revenue lines each showing that every point on the line represents the same revenue from the sale of the products X and Y. AB is our production possibility curve at which RL is the tangent touching it at P. Similarly, R′L′ touches CD a higher production possibility curve at Q and R′′L′′ touches EF still higher curve at R and R′′′L′′′iso-revenue line touches GH the higher curve at S. Joining P, Q, R and S, we get **Output Expansion Path.** The iso-revenue lines are parallel to one another since the prices of the products are taken as fixed. The slope of the iso-revenue line represents the ratio of the price of X to the price of Y.

If the resources at the disposal of the firm are represented by the production possibility curve AB, then it will choose for production the combination of X and Y represented by the point P. At this point, its revenue will be maximum. Here the marginal rate of transformation MRTxy on the given production possibility curve will be equal to the price ratio of the two products, *i.e.*, $\frac{Px}{Py}$. Similarly, as regards the points Q, R and S. P, Q, R, S expansion path is the locus of all the revenue maximising product combinations with the varying amount of resources that the firm commands.

Uses of Production Possibility Curve

The production possibility curve can be put to a number of practical uses. Besides helping in the solution of the basic problems of production, *viz*., what and how, *i.e.*, what is to be produced and how and with what combinations of resources is to be produced, the concept of the production possibility curve can be put to the following uses:—

(*i*) The planning authority of a developing country may decide after certain stage to divert its resources from the production of necesaries to luxuries and from producer goods to consumer goods.

(*ii*) A democratic country may decide to devote its resources less to the production of privately manufactured goods purchased by price and more by public sector enterprises supplied free but financed by taxes such as public utilities, free education, free medical services, *etc.*

(*iii*) The lproduction possibility curve can also help in guiding the diversion of resources from current consumption goods to capital goods like machines and increases productive resources to attain higher levels of production. Many more alternatives can be imagined.[1]

EFFICIENT ALLOCATION OF RESOURCES

We have been examining the problem of resource allocation from the point of view of an individual firm. Let us widen the horizon and try to see how the resources of the entire economy can be most efficiently utilised. What, in other words, is the criterion for the optimum utilisation of the country's resources? The resources will be most efficiently allocated from the consumers' point of view if highest possible level of

1. For appropriate diagram, see Samuelson, P.A. – Economics, 1970, pp. 17-22.

want-satisfaction has been attained. From the point of national income, resource allocation will be regarded as efficiently employed if they make the maximum possible contribution to the national income. There will be mis-allocation, if the net national output is less than what it can be.

In a free enterprise economy, this important function is performed by the resource prices. For attaining maximum efficiency of resource allocation, there is constant shifting and reallocation of resources between different uses in response to changes in people's tastes and preferences, changes in the category and the quantities of available resources and changes in techniques of production. Resource prices furnish the mechanism for rectifying misallocations of the resources in the economic system.

Criterion of Maximum Efficiency. Thus, the criterion for a correct or efficient utilisation of resources is that the **net national product has been maximised,** *i.e.*, at the existing technology it has attained a peak level. Conversely, the resources will not be correctly allocated if the net national product is below its potential maximum. However, in case of misallocation, automatically such forces will be set in motion as will bring about a reallocation of the resources so as to maximise the national product. Here is the traditional approach to the problem.

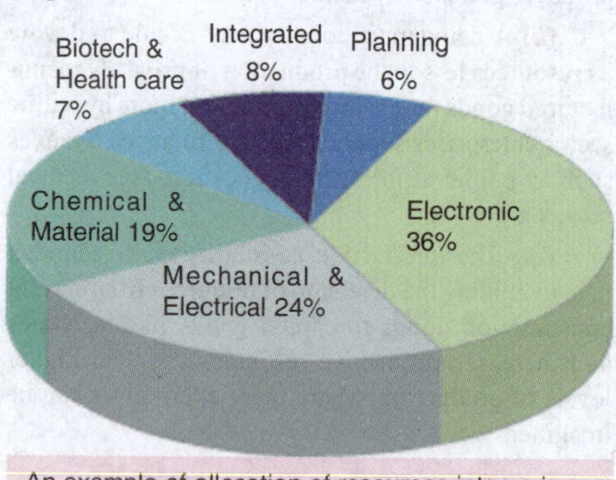

An example of allocation of resources into various areas.

The principle. The question now is as to how the optimum allocation of resources can be achieved. Or, if there is a mis-allocation of resources among the various uses, how it is to be rectified. The law of substitution or equi-marginal returns solves the problem. A community can allocate its resources in the most efficient manner by acting on this principle. This means that the resources should be so allocated among their various uses that the value of the marginal product in each use is the same. If it is not the same, then it has to be equalised by the application of the Law of Substitution, *i.e.*, by transferring resources from one use to another.

For instance, if the value of the marginal product of resources in one use is greater than it is in other uses, it is obvious that they will be more valuable to the society if they are used where the value of the marginal product is higher. Some units of the resources, therefore, must be transferred from the lower to the uses with higher value of marginal product. That would increase the total value of the economy's output.

Since some price has to be paid for a factor, no factor will be used to such an extent as to reduce its marginal productivity to zero. Each scarce factor will be allocated among the various industries or uses in such a manner as to equalise the value of its marginal product in every industry where it is employed. If the value of the marginal product of labour, say, in iron and steel industry, is greater than that in sugar industry, labour will be shifted from the latter to the former, till the marginal productivities of labour in the two industries are equalised. In the same manner, if land devoted to sugar-cane cultivation yields more than that devoted to growing cotton, it will obviously pay to withdraw some land from cotton growing and divert it to sugar-cane. This diversion will continue till the value of the marginal product in the two alternative uses of land has been equalised.

Thus, the factors of production will be optimally allocated among the various alternative uses when there is no inducement for diverting them from any one use to another. This will be the case only if the marginal return in each use is equal. So long as it is not equal, reshuffling will go on.

Thus, "**the best allocation of the factors of production is when the value of the marginal product of a factor is the same in every line in which it is employed, or the equilibrium situation with regard to allocation of factors is that in which the community places the same value upon marginal product of the factor in every industry." (Benham).**

The reshuffling of the resources as between different uses takes places through the mechanism of resource prices. When the value of the marginal product of a given resource is lower in some industries, it is clear that the firms will not be willing to pay for it more than the value of its marginal product. On the other hand, where the value of its marginal product is higher, the firms will be keen to use more of it and they will offer to pay a higher price which is above the value of its marginal product in the former case. The owner of resources keen to maximise their incomes will transfer the resources from the less remunerative to the more remunerative uses. This transfer will continue till the value of the marginal product is equalised in all uses. When equality between the values of marginal product has been attained, the resources will be making the maximum contribution to the net national product.

Input-Output.

An illustration will make it clear. Let us take firms in two industries using resource A and producing two products X and Y. In accordance with the principle enunciated above, the resources will be correctly allocated among firms of the two industries when the value of marginal product of A in firms of the industry producing X (V of MPax) is equal to the value of marginal product of A in firms of the industry producing Y = Y (v of M Pay). Thus,

V of MPax = V of MPay = Pa

or MPPax × Px = MPPay × Py = Pa

V of MP means value of marginal product.

Pa is the price per unit of resource A.

Px is the price of product X.

Py is the price of product Y.

Now if demand for the commodity X in the market increases, the price of X will rise, with the result that V of MPax increases. This means that it has become more valuable for the community to utilise resource A more in the production of X than in the production of Y. The firms producing X will feel that at price Pa, the resource A is in short suply. Hence, they will raise its price to induce the owners of A resource to transfer its units to industry producing X from that producing Y. As a consequence of larger quantities of A resource being used in X-producing industry, MPPax will decrease. As the output of X expands, its price declines. Thus V of MPax goes down. On the other hand, reduced use of A resource in Y-producing industry will result in the increase of MPPay. Since output of Y decreases, its price Py will rise. As a result of increase in MP Pay and in Py, V of MPay increase. Such transfer of resources from Y-producing industry to X-producing industry will continue till V of MPax becomes equal to V MPay. Since the value of the marginal product of A resource is now higher in both industries, the new price per unit of A will be higher. This resource will again be making its maximum contribution to the net national product.

Conclusion. The following statement clinches the issues underlying an efficient utilisation of the resources: "Efficient transformations are those in which ceteris paribus: (1) it is not possible to increase the amount of any output without increasing the amount of some input or decreasing the amount of some other output; (2) it is not possible to decrease the amount of any output without reducing the amount of some input or increasing the amount of some other output. All others are inefficient."[2]

PRODUCTION FUNCTION: INPUT-OUTPUT RELATIONSHIP

Production function may be defined as the functional relationship between physical inputs (*i.e.*, factors of production) and physical outputs, *i.e.*, the quantity of goods produced. As Stigler puts it, "the production function is name given to the relationship between the rates of input of productive services and the rate of output of product. It is the economist's summary of technological knowledge."[3]

Thus, the production function expresses the relationship between quantity of output and the quantities of various inputs used in production. The physical relationship between a firm's physical input and output depends on a given state of technological knowledge.

Like demand, production function refers to a period of time. Accordingly, it refers to a flow of inputs resulting in a flow of outputs over a period of time, leaving prices aside.

It shows the maximum amount of output that can be produced from a given set of inputs in the existing state of technology. The output will change when the quantity of any input is changed or the minimum quantities of various inputs required to produce a given quantity.

2. Benjamin Ward—*Elementary Price Theory*; 1967, p.59.
3. Stigler, G. J.—*The Theory of Price.* 1953, p.106

In real life, a manufacturer wants to know how much of the various factors or inputs, *viz.*, land (*i.e.*, natural resources), labour and capital will be required to produce a unit or given quantity of a commodity during a given period of time. It is necessary for him to know this so that he may be able not only to assess his requirements of productive services but also roughly to estimate the probable cost. It will thus indicate the varieties of the productive resources and their possible combinations used for the purposes of production.

Production function of course depends, inter alia, on (*a*) quantities of resources used, (*b*) state of technical knowledge, (*c*) possible processes, (*d*) size of the firms, (*e*) nature of firm's organisation, (*f*) relative prices of the factors of production and the manner in which the factors of production are combined. As these things change, production function will change too. For instance, output can be increased by increasing the quantity of factors of production or of some of them. It can also be increased by varying the proportion in which the factors are combined. Adoption of more efficient techniques of production, too, will add to the output. The less efficient the techniques the smaller will be the output.

Production changes with period of time. In the very long period, it changes altogether because the same inputs produce different outputs. In the long run, the production function depicts the whole set of choices open to the producer, *i.e.*, what inputs will produce what output. In the short run, the choices open to the producer are restricted because some of the factors are fixed and cannot be changed in the short period and only some can be varied. In this situation, the producer tries to find out the relation between the variable inputs and the outputs.

Since production function is concerned with physical aspects of production, it is more a concern of an engineer or a technician than of an economist. Only a technician can say what specific quantity of a good can be produced by the use of the various productive resources and their combinations.

Production function can be expressed as under:

$x = f(a, b, c, d, \ldots\ldots)$

Here X is the output of a commodity per unit of time and a, b, c, d, ... are the various productive resources which go into the making of the quantity of the commodity; f is function, *i.e.*, varying with.

Every management has to make a choice of the production function depending not only on industrial knoweldge and the prices of the various factors of production but also on its own capacity to manage. It has also to select the various factors and knit them together in economical combinations. These two choices are interlinked. The over-riding consideration is to seek a combination which gives the minimum average cost and maximum aggregate profit.

For understanding the nature of production function the following points may be emphasised:

(*i*) The production function represents a **purely technical relationship** in physical quantities between the inputs of factors and the output of the products. It has no reference to money price. The price factor is left out altogether.

(*ii*) The output is the result of a joint use of the factors of production. It is obvious that the physical productivity of one factor can be measured only in the context of this factor being used in conjunction with other factors.

(*iii*) The nature or the quantity of the various factors and the manner in which they are combined will depend on the state of technical knowledge. For instance, labour productivity will depend on the quality of labour as determined by their education and training. Similarly, the productivity of machines will be determined by the technical advances embodied in them. Again, it is on the basis of technical knowledge at the time that labour, machines and other factors will be combined in the processes of production. Thus, the state of technical knowledge is treated as given (*i.e.*, as a parameter) for specifying a production function. A change in technology will mean a shift to another production function. It will alter the cost condition. Improvement in technology will result in a larger output from a given combination of the factors of production.

(*iv*) In specifying the production function of a firm, we have to take into account the variability of the factors of production and also whether they are divisible or indivisible. These features of the factors of production will determine their physical productivities and hence the nature of the production function.

Types. Production function may take several forms: Broadly speaking (*a*) It can be a fixed-proportions production function, or (*b*) it can be a variable-proportions production function. In the case of fixed-proportions production function, the factors of production are used in definite fixed proportions. For instance, a fixed number of workers may be required to produce a unit/units of the product and this proportion cannot be varied by substituting one factor for the other factors. In the case of variable-proportions production function, the technical coefficient of production is variable. In other words, the quantity of a factor of production required to produce a given unit of product can be varied by substituting some other factor/factors in its place. This means that in this case a given quantity of a product can be turned out by several alternative combinations of factors of production as is shown in an isoquant map.

Suppose we require 40 workers to produce 200 units of a product. The technical coefficient of production in this case is 1/5. In case the technical coefficient of production is fixed then in a case like this one-fifth of labour must be employed for the production of a unit of the commodity in question and there is no scope for varying its proportion through substitution of some other factor. This is the case of **Fixed Proportions Production Function** in which the factors of production e.g. labour and capital, must be used in fixed proportions in the production of a certain level of output.

The fixed proportion production function can be illustrated by the following diagram (17.3).

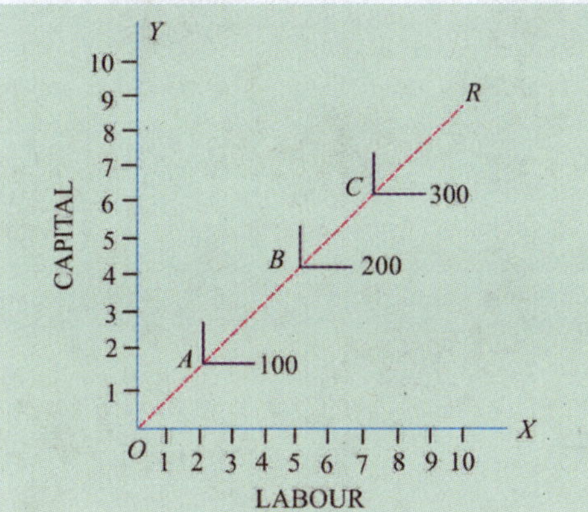

Fig. 17.3. Fixed proportion production function.

In this diagram, OR represents the fixed labour capital ratio. This ratio must be maintained whatever the level of output. Since this ratio is fixed, the isoquants relating to such a production function are shown as right-angled. Suppose the ratio is 2:3 i.e., 2 units of capital and 3 units of labour, when 100 units of the product are to be produced; then for producing 200 units 4 units of capital and 6 units of labour will be required, and so on. It may be noticed that along each isoquant, the marginal product of a factor is zero. For instance, at **B** on isoquant of 200, if the amount of capital used is fixed the use of extra labour makes no addition to the total product, i.e. the marginal product of labour is zero. However doubling both factors will result in doubling the output, and so on.

The Variable Proportions Production Function can be illustrated by the isoquant map given in Fig. 19.2, page 141. In this case, as already mentioned, the ratio in which the factors of production are used is not fixed but it is variable. That is, a given quantity of the product can be produced by several alternative combinations of factors. In the isoquant map various equal product curves are drawn to show how different combinations of factors of production can be used to produce a given level of output.

Linear Homogeneous Production Function

The Linear Homogeneous Production Function implies that if all the factors of production are increased in some proportion, the output also increases in the same proportion. That is, the doubling of all inputs will double the output and trebling them will result in the trebling of the output, and so on. This represents a case of constant returns to scale. This type of production function is called by the economists as a well-behaved production function because it can be easily handled and used in empirical studies. It can be used by computers in calculations. That is why it is widely used in linear programming and input-output analysis. It is also extensively used in model analysis of production, distribution and economic growth.

This is a production function which is homogeneous of the first degree. That is, it shows that the increase in output in the same proportion follows a given change in the factors of production. This has been put mathematically as

$$mP = f(mX, mY)$$

Here m is any number and **K** means constant. This function is homogeneous of **K**th degree. If **K** is equal to one then this homogeneous function is homogeneous of the first degree and if **K** is equal to two it is homogeneous of the second degree, and so on. If **K** is greater than one the production function gives increasing returns to scale and if it is less than one it gives decreasing returns to scale. In the case of homogeneous production function, the expansion path is always a straight line through the origin (see Fig. 19.7, P. 146). This means that in the case of homogeneous production function of the first degree, given constant relative factor prices, the proportions between the factors used will always be the same whatever the level of output. This makes the task of the entrepreneur easy. Having hit on an optimum factor proportions, he need not change the decision so long as the relative prices of the factors remain unchanged.

Cobb-Douglas Production Function

A well known empirical production function is the Cobb-Douglas Production Function. It takes two inputs labour and capital and is expressed by the following equation:

$$Q = KL^{a}C^{(1-a)}$$

Here **Q** is the quantity of output, **L** is the labour employed and **K** and **a** are positive constants (and a < 1) and **C** is the quantity of capital used.

Key terms

Production possibility Frontier, Marginate rate of trnsformation, (MRT) ISO revenue, output-Expansion path, production function, Linear - homogenous fixed and variable proprtion production function.

QUESTIONS

1. Explain a linear homogeneous production function.
2. What is 'Production Function'? How does it help in understanding producer's equilibrium?
3. Explain with the help of production possibility curve how economics is concerned with the problem of employment and allocation and growth of community's resources.
4. Explain the following problems in Economics with the help of production possibility curve: (*i*) Choice between the production of consumer goods and producer goods in an economy' (*ii*) the problem of unemployed resources; (*iii*) the problem of economic growth.

LAWS OF RETURNS

We shall first study the laws of return which are different aspects of one law, *viz.*, the law of variable proportions, then returns to scale and in the next chapter equal product curves.

There are three laws of returns known to economists, the laws of diminishing, increasing and constant return. "There is said to be increasing, decreasing or constant returns according as the marginal returns rise, fall or remain unchanged" as the quantity of a factor of production is increased. In terms of cost, an industry is subject to increasing, decreasing or constant returns according as the marginal cost of production falls, rises or remains the same, respectively, with the expansion of an industry.

As we shall explain below, **these three laws are only three aspects of one law, *viz.*, the law of Variable Proportions.** They represent three different stages of the same law. Now a word about each of these laws.

LAW OF DIMINISHING RETURNS

Statement of the Law. In the absence of the law of diminishing returns, "the science of political economy", says Cairnes, "would be as completely revolutionised as if human nature itself were altered". Such is the importance of the law of diminishing returns in economic theory.

The law of diminishing returns was supposed to have a special application to agriculture. It is the practical experience of every farmer that "successive applications of labour and capital to a given area of land must ultimately, other things remaining the same, yield a less than proportionate increase in produce." If by doubling labour and capital he could double the yield of his land and so on, it can be easily seen that one acre of land could be made to produce as much wheat as could suffice for the entire population of the world. That this cannot be done is simply due to the operation of the law of diminishing returns. If investment is increased, the total yield will no doubt increase, but at a diminishing rate.

Marshall stated the law thus: **"An increase in capital and labour applied in the cultivation of land causes in general less than proportionate increase in the amount of produce raised, unless it happens to coincide with an improvement in the arts of agriculture."** The phrase 'in **general**' in this statement is important. It means that there may be cases where the law does not hold good. It refers to limitations of the law.

Three Aspects of the Law. Consider the table below.

Table 1: Three Aspects of the Law of Diminishing Return

No. of workers	*Total Retun*	*Marginal Return*	*Average Return*
(1)	(2)	(3)	(4)
1	80	80	80
2	170	90	85
3	270	100	90
4	368	98	92
5	430	62	86
6	480	50	80
7	504	24	72
8	504	0	63
9	495	—9	55
10	440	—55	44

From the table, it appears that there are three different aspects of the Law of Diminishing Returns:

(1) Law of Total Diminishing Returns (Column 2). In this sense, the return begin to diminish from the 9th worker. Every successive worker employed does make some addition to the total output. But the 8th adds nothing and the 9th and 10th are a positive nuisance. As workers cannot be had gratis, no prudent farmer will employ more than seven workers in the conditions represented by this table.

(2) Law of Diminishing Marginal Returns (Column 3). Marginal returns go on increasing up to the 3rd worker. This is so becasue the proportion of workers to land was at first insufficient and the land was not being properly tilled. This phase of cultivation is unstable and will not be found in practice. When the farmer knows that he can get more than proportionate return by employing extra hand, he will certainly do so. The marginal, *i.e.*, the additional, return goes on falling from the 3rd man onwards till it drops down to zero at the 8th. The 9th and 10th men are merely a cause of obstruction to the others and are responsible in making the marginal return negative. The point at which the addition made to the total output by each successive unit of the variable factor starts diminishing is known as the point of diminishing marginal returns.

It can be seen that the **total output is at its maximum when marginal output is zero.**

It should be remembered that the marginal return is not what can be attributed to the last unit whose employment is considered just worthwhile, as all men are supposed to be alike. The marginal return is simply the addition that the marginal unit makes to the total return.

(3) Law of Diminishing Average Returns (Column 4). The average return reaches the maximum at the 4th worker, *i.e.*, one step later than the marginal return reaches the maximum. Then the marginal return falls more sharply. The two equalise somewhere between the 4th and 5th , *i.e.*, when the 5th worker works part-time. But we do not employ men in fractions in real life. Therefore, it is not always possible to equalise the marginal and the average returns. It is also clear that it is possible for the average output to increase while the marginal output falls.

Diagrammatic Representation. The law can be diagrammatically represented as in Fig. 18.1.[1]

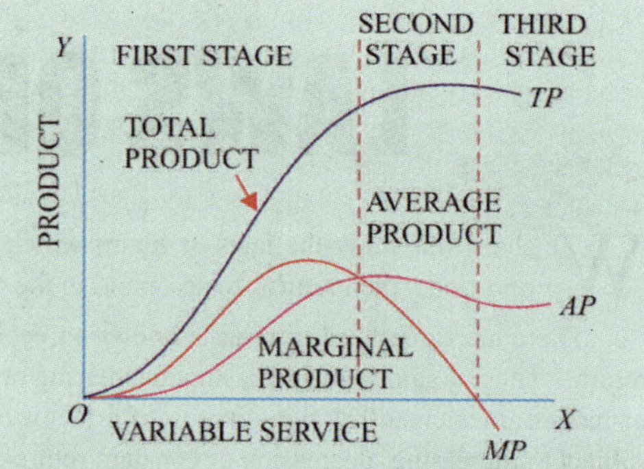

Fig. 18.1. Stages of the Law of Variable proportions.

The total production (*i.e.*, return) goes on increasing till it reaches the maximum where the third stage starts. The marginal return reaches teh maximmum the earliest and starts diminishing the first (*i.e.*, in the first stage). The average return starts diminishing next, *i.e.*, where the second stage begins.

This is in keeping with the above table. Obviously, no sensible entrepreneur will operate in the third stage where the marginal product is zero, unless, of course, the variable factor is free. Economically, the second stage is the significant region where the average product is greater than the marginal product which is still positive. It can be seen that the total output curve is the steepest where the marginal output is the largest. The law of diminishing returns is also called the Law of Diminishing Physical Productivity.

Economic Implications of the Law of Variable Proportions

The law of variable proportions (of which the law of diminishing returns is one aspect) shows the efficiency of factor combination. Incidentally, the three stages of the law of diminishing returns shown above throw light on how efficiently have the factors (land

1. Stigler—Theory of Price (1947), p. 128.

and labour) been combined in the process of production. The average return (Column 4 in the table on the page 190) shows the amount of the product obtained per unit of labour for the various land-labour ratios and the total product column (Column 2) shows the total output obtained from that unit of land for the various land-labour ratios.

In stage I, as more and more labour is used, the average product of labour increases, which reflects the increasing efficiency of labour. In this stage, the total product increases also for this unit of land which shows that the efficiency of land too is increasing. Hence, this stage shows that both land and labour are being efficiently utilised.

The second stage shows decreasing average product and marginal product of labour. But since the total output goes on increasing the marginal product is positive. This stage shows the decreasing efficiency of labour. But the efficiency of land continiues to increas because the total return continues to increase.

In the third stage, the average product (of labour) decreases still further. Also, the marginal product becomes negative and the total product is decreasing. Hence, in this stage, both labour and land have been used inefficiently.

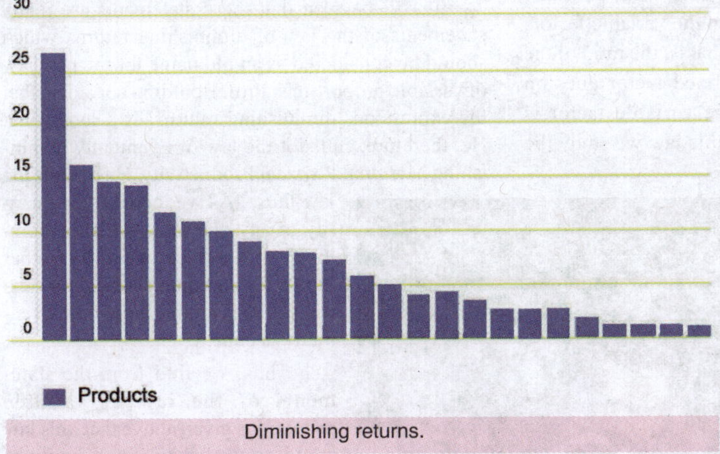

Diminishing returns.

Thus, the combination of Land and Labour attained maximum efficiency of labour at the boundary line between stage I and II and maximum efficiency ofland at the boundary line between stage II and stage III. Stage II represents higher efficiency of land-labour ratio than that of the other two stages.

The productive resources of land and labour both command a price in the market and have to be paid for. Since, in stage I, product per unit of both land and labour increases, the firm will keep expanding and move to the boundary between stage I and stage II. But when it enters the second stage, it finds that the return per unit expenditure on labour decreases while that of land increases. The proportions in which land and labour will be used will depend on their relative prices or costs per unit. If the price of land is low relative to the price of labour, the firm will operate more in the beginning of stage II, and, conversely, less the price of labour relative to the price of land, it will operate towards the end of the stage II. Stages I and III are ruled out. Stage I is ruled out because throughout this stage average product of both land and labour are still increasing and stage III is ruled out becasue the average product of both factors is decreasing.

Law of Variable Proportions

It will be seen that the name of the law "Law of Diminishing Returns" is a misnomer. It is only the third stage (as explained in Fig. No. 18.1) of one basic law, the **Law of Variable Proportions.** This law is also called the **Law of Proportionality.** This law tells us how the total output or marginal output is affected by a change in the proportion of the factors used. Since the return to the variable factor does not change at the same rate in all stages, it is also called the Law of Non-proportional Returns.

When, after a stage, the marginal return begins to diminish, it is not due to the fact that either the prices of the factors of production have gone up or the price of the output has gone down. It is rather due to the technological facts underlying the production of the product in question. Every industry has its own peculiar set of technical facts; for example, agriculture is dominated by the nature of land and manufacturing industry by capital. In agriculture, the marginal return starts diminishing early, whereas in a manufacturing industry, it starts diminishing very late, which a wise entrepreneur can altogether avoid. In some industries, the return many remain constant. This is all due to the technological peculiarities of each industry.

In agriculture, marginal return increases in the beginning but then decreases later, whereas in industry it continues increasing but may decrease if the industry is expanded too much. It is thus wrong to say that one law applies in one industry and another in another industry. The fact is that there is only one law which applies everywhere and which is property called the Law of Variable Proportions. This law operates in all industries, although its different stages are to be found in different industries or its different stages are larger or shorter in different industries. In some industries, the stage of increasing marginal return finishes earlier and diminishing marginal return starts as in agriculture and, in some other industries, the stage of increasing marginal return is so long that the marginal return starts diminishing only when the scale of production is unduly enlarged as in the case of almost all manufacturing industries.

The Law of Variable Proportion occupies a very important place in economic theory. It describes the production function with one variable factor while the quantities of other factors of production are fixed. That is, it describes the input-output relation in a situation when the output is increased by increasing the quantity of one input, keeping the other inputs constant. When the quantity of one factor is increased and the quantities of the other factors of production are kept constant, naturally the proportion between the variable factors and the fixed factor is altered. That is, the ratio of the variable factor to that of the fixed factor goes on increasing as a quantity of the variable factor is increased. It is because that in this law we study the effect on output of variations in factor proportion, this law is called the law of variable proportions. In fact, the law of variable proportions is the new name for the well known law of diminishing returns. Uptill Marshall, it was thought that there were three separate laws of production, *viz.*, the laws of diminishing, increasing and constant returns. The modern economists are of the view that these three laws are not three separate laws but are only three phases of one general law of variable proportions.

Labour and capital.

The law of variable proportions has been variously stated by the economists. In the words of Stigler, "As equal increments of one input are added, the inputs of other productive services being held constant, beyond a certain point the result in increment of product will decrease, *i.e.*, the marginal product will diminish."[2] Professor Samuelson states the law thus, "An increase in some inputs relative to other fixed inputs will, in a given state of technology, cause output to increase; but after a point the extra output resulting from the same additions of extra inputs will become less and less."[3] Professor Benham also states the law almost in similar words, "As the proportion of one factor in a combination of factors is increased, after a point, first the marginal and then the average product of that factor will diminish."[4]

It will be seen that these statements are really statements of the law of diminishing returns which should be considered as an old name for the new law of variable proportions. Prof. Boulding considers that the expression 'diminishing returns' is a loose one. He, therefore, called it the law of Eventually Diminishing Marginal Physical Productivity. He defines the law thus, "As we increase the quantity of any one input which is combined with a fixed quantity of other inputs the marginal physical productivity of the variable input must eventually decline.[5]

Thus, we find from the statements of the law of variable propotions given above that this law relates to the behaviour of output as the quantity of one factor is varied keeping the quantities of the other factors constant. It states further that the marginal product and the average product of the factor kept constant will eventually diminish.

ASSUMPTIONS OF THE LAW OF VARIABLE PROPORTIONS

The law of variable propotions, as stated above,

2. Stigler, G.J. –*Theory of price*, 1953, P, III.
3. Samuelson, P.A. –*Economics*, 8th Ed. p.25.
4. Benham, F., *Economics*, 1960, P.110.
5. Boulding, K.E. –*Principles of Economics*, p.589.

holds true under certain conditions. The following are its main assumptions:

(a) It is assumed that the state of technology remains unaltered. It is obvious that improvements in technology are bound to raise the marginal and average product and they will not diminish as the law says.

(b) It is also assumed that of the various inputs employed in production some at least must be kept constant. This is so because only in this way we can change the factor proportions and find out its effects on the output. Hence this law does not apply where all factors of production are proportionately varied. Behaviour of output when all inputs are varied comes under, 'returns to scale' which we shall discuss later.

(c) The law of variable proportions is clearly based upon the possibility of varying proportions in which the various factors are combined in production. It does not apply to cases where the factors have to be used in fixed proportions to yield fixed products. In cases where the various factors are to be used in rigidly fixed propotions, the increase in one factor would not lead to any increase in input, that is, the marginal product of the factor will be zero and not diminishing. But such cases are very uncommon and hence the law of variable propotions has almost a universal application.

Average-Marginal Relations

When we study trends in marginal and average returns (or outputs) from the table on page 190, we can discover certain unique relationship between them:

(1) So long as the marginal return exceeds the average return (see columns 3 and 4), each new average return will be larger than the previous one, *i.e.*, the average output continues to increase. Conversely, if average output is rising, it can be safely concluded that the marginal output is larger than the output.

(2) When the marginal return goes below the average return, average output begins to decline. This is so, because the new marginal return, which is lower, brings down the average. That is, when the average product is decreasing, the marginal product is les than the average product.

(3) The average output remains constant when the marginal and average returns are equal. Conversely, if the average output remains constant, it can be inferred that the margina output is also constant and the two are equal. Also, when the average product is maximum, marginal product equals average product. In such cases, the average and marginal curves coincide and they are horizontal, parallel to the X-axis.

Limitations of the Law of Diminishing Returns

The law of diminishing returns does not apply to all situations. There are several exceptions to the law as it applies in agriculture:

(i) Improved methods of cultivation. Man's ingenuity is ever striving to counteract the operation of this law by improving the technique of cultivation. Scientific rotation of crops, improved seeds, modern implements, artificial manures and better irrigation facilities, *etc.*, are bound to give increasing return. But science cannot keep pace with the increasing demand for food. The niggardliness of nature must ultimately assert itself and the law must operate sooner or later.

(ii) New soil. Again, when a virgin soil is brought under cultivation, the additional return for each successive dose of labour and capital may increase for a time. But after a point, the tendency to diminishing returns will set in. Hence, in the case of a new soil, the law of diminishing returns does not apply in the beginning.

(iii) Insufficient Capital. If capital applied hitherto has not been insufficient, increased application will, at first, yield more than proportionate return. Later, however, the marginal return will decrease. The early stage is an exception to the law of diminishing return.

How to Counteract the Law

Anything which improves the quality of the land and makes it yield more, or anything which **adds to the value of the yield,** will check the operation of the law. Use of modern implements, judicious mixing of soil and manures, careful selection of the seed and proper sowing, deeper and deeper tillage, and the provision of ample irrigation facilities, *etc.*, can enable a farmer to counteract the working of the law. **Scientific cultivation, in short, can check the operation of the law of diminishing returns.**

Application of the Law

Besides agriculture, the law also applies to extractive industries like mining, fisheries and also to building industry. The law operates when mining operations are extended to inferior, distant or deeper mines, when fishing operations are concerntrated in one place and when more and more storeys are raised on a building.

Why The Law Specially Applies to Agriculture

We have seen that the law of diminishing returns has a wide application. But it specially applies to agriculture and other extractive industries. One thing that is common to all these industries is the supremacy of nature. **It is, therefore, often remarked that the part that nature plays in production corresponds to diminishing returns and the part which man plays conforms to the law of increasing returns.** The inference is that agriculture, where nature is supreme, is subject to diminishing returns, while industry, where man is supreme, is subject to increasing returns.

There are several reasons why agriculture is subject to the law of diminishing returns:

(*i*) The agricultural operations are spread out over a wide area, and consequently supervision cannot be very effective.

(*ii*) Scope for the use of specialised machinery is also very limited. Therefore, economies of large-scale production cannot be reaped.

(*iii*) There are further limitations arising from the seasonal nature of the industry. Agricultural operations are likely to be interrupted by rain and other climatic changes. Man is not a complete master of Nature, and no wonder that the law of diminishing returns operates in agriculture.

Agriculture.

Similarly, it is understandable that manufacturing industries should be subject to the law of increasing return. Here man's ingenuity has the fullest scope to show itself. By the introduction of division of labour and the use of the most modern appliances, production can be greatly increased. Concentration of workers under one roof renders supervision easy and effective. Nature's malignant influences are thus held constantly at bay. Man is free to plan, undertake and execute. He can realise all the possible economies, internal and external.

But it is wrong to say that agriculture is always subject to diminishing returns and manufacturing always to increasing returns. The law of diminishing returns applies everywhere. To borrow Wicksteed's words, "This law is as universal as the law of life itself." Its application is not confined to agriculture only; it applies to manufacturing industries too. If the industry is expanded too much and becomes unwieldy, supervision will become lax and the costs will go up. The law of diminishing returns will, therefore, set in. The only difference is that in agriculture it sets in earlier and in industry much later. A prudent industrialist may not allow that stage to come at all. Agriculture, too, in the begining has increasing returns.

Thus, both laws apply in all types of industries, extractive as well as manufacturing. As a matter of fact, they are two aspects of the same law, which is also known as the Law of Variable Proportions.

Law of Diminishing returns in a General Form

The discussion of the law of diminishing returns in relation to land, since the times of the English Classical economiests, has obscured its real significance. There is nothing peculiar about agriculture for the law to be exclusively associated with it. As a matter of fact, in agriculture, the law has been held in check by scientific cultivation in progressive countries. This is evident from the fact that whereas consumption of food has increased on account of higher standards of living, the number of people engaged in the production of food has actually gone down.

The fact is that the law of diminishing returns does not apply to agriculture alone. It has got a general application and can, therefore, be put in a general form. The law of diminishing returns simply refers to a principle of combination of the factors. In a general way, it can be stated that if a variable factor is combined with some constant factors, the average and the marginal return for that variable factor will diminsh. Benham states the law thus: **"As the proportion of one factor in a combination of factors is increased after a point the average and marginal product of that factor will diminish."**

Why the Law of Diminishing Returns Operates

The operation of the law of diminishing returns can be attributed to several causes:

(*i*) Wrong Combination. In the initial stages, the fixed factor is not fully used since the units of variable factor are too few. Hence, increase in the variable factor in the initial stages proves productive on account of fuller utilisation of the fixed factor and of better co-operation and greater specialisation in the variable factor units. We are moving towards the optimum combination. But after a stage, increase in the variable factor brings down the marginal return. Thus, the law of diminishing returns operates because the combination of the factors of production ceases to represent a correct proportion. It ceases to be an optimum combination. There is too much of one factor in relation to the others. The fixed factor has reached its maximum capacity and there is no further possibility of specialisation of the variable factor. This explains the operation of the law of diminishing returns. When proper balance is restored the law of diminishing returns will no longer operate.

But the law of diminishing returns is a misnomer. We saw that in the beginning the marginal return increases. It is only ultimately the law operates. This is why Bounding calls it "the law of eventually diminishing marginal physical productivity."

(*ii*) Scarcity of Factors. The law of diminishing returns operates due to the scarcity of the factors of production. In the words of Chapman, **"The expansion of an industry, provided that additional supplies of some agent in production, which is essential cannot be obtained, is invariably accompanied at once or eventually by decreasing returns, other things being equal."**

(*iii*) Imperfect Substitutes. A little reflection will show that the law of diminishing returns operates because the factors of production are imperfect substitutes for one another. As Mrs. Robinson says, "What the Law of Diminishing Return really states is that there is a limit to the extent to which one factor of production can be substituted for another, or , in other words, that the elasticity of substitution between factors is not infinite. If this were not true it would be possible when one factor of production is fixed in amount and the rest are in perfectly elastic supply, to produce part of the output with the aid of the fixed factor, and then, when optimum proportion between this factor and other factors was attained, to substitute some other factor for it and to increase output at constant cost. Thus, the Law of Diminishing Returns entails that the various elements required for the production of any commodity should be divided into groups, each group being a factor of production, in such a way that the elsticity of substitution between one factor and another is less than inifinite."[6]

6. Robinson, Joan –*The economics of Imperfect Competition*(1945). p.330.

Importance of the Law of Diminishing Returns

We have already quoted Cairnes when he says that in the absence of the law of diminishing returns, "The science of political economy would be as completely revolutionized as if human nature itself were altered." Such is the great importance of the law of diminishing returns. The law of diminishing returns has a very wide, almost universal application. Uptill Marshall, it was thought that the law of diminishing returns applied to agriculture wheareas the laws of increasing or constant returns applied to manufacture. But it is now held that the law of diminishing returns applies in all fields of production, whether agriculture, mining or manufacture. Whenever we find that some factors of production are fixed and cannot be varied and other factors are varied, then techniques of production remaining the same, diminishing returns are bound to follow, sooner or later. There is no escape.

The validity of the law of diminishing returns is not merely based on theoretical reasoning but it has been supported by extensive empirical evidence. It has been remarked that if the diminishing return did not occur we could grow sufficient foodgrains in a flower pot merely by increasing the dozes of labour and capital. It is obvious that if the successive applications of dozes of labour and capital resulted in obtaining constant returns, the whole population of the world could be fed by growing crops on a tiny piece of land. As population increased, we could use more labour and capital on a piece of land to get proportionate increase in agricultural output and there would be no fear of famine and starvation. As Professor Lipsey remarks, "Indeed, where hypothesis of diminishing returns incorrect, there would be no fear that the present population explosion will bring with it a food crisis. If the marginal product of additional worker applied to a fixed quantity of land were constant, then world food production would be expanded in proportion to the increase in population merely by keeping the same proportion of the population on farms. As it is, diminishing returns means an inexorable decline in the marginal product of each additional labourer as an expanding population is applied, with static techniques, to a fixed world supply of agricultural land!".[7]

But let there be no misunderstanding. We need not arrive at the dismal conclusion that since the law of diminishing returns is universally true, the average and marginal returns must eventually decline and humanity is doomed. There is no such fear Experience

7. Lipsey, R.G. –*Introduction to positive Economics*, III edition, p.216.

of both developed technology may be able to keep the law of diminishing returns in abeyance. We see from the Indian experience that improved technology has ushered in what is known as the 'green revolution' and, in a short span of time, we have not only been able to ban hunger and starvation from the land, but we have also now a comfortable surplus. The ghost of law of diminishing returns seems to have been laid.

At the same time, we must point out that this happy experience is no contradiction of the law of diminishing returns. The law clearly states that if there is no charge in technical knowledge, capital equipment, and other aids to production, the law of diminishing returns is kept in check for the time being. But who can say that the improvement in technology and additional to capital equipment will keep pace with galloping population. We have only suspended the operation of the law of diminishing returns by improving techniques of production through the application of science and technology, but if we fail to keep up the technical progress in a sufficient measure, the law of diminishing returns may assert itself. As Lipsey observes, "Unless there is a continual and rapidly accelerating improvement in techniques of production, the population explosion must bring with it decline in living standard over much of the world and eventual wide-spread famine."[8]

The Law of Diminishing Returns has formed the basis of a number of economic doctrines propounded by the English classical economists, especially Malthus and Ricardo. It was represented as an inexorable law of nature. It accounted for a lot of pessimistic thinking in Economics and earned for it the title of a 'dismal science'.

Malthusian Theory of Population. The Malthusian theory of population, which says that population increases faster than the food supply, is obviously based on the fact that the production of food is subject to the law of diminishing returns.

Ricardian Theory of Rent. The Ricardian theory of rent explains the determination of rent on the assumption that inferior lands have to be cultivated on account of the operation of the law of diminishing returns. The margine of cultivation descends, and rent rises.

The optimum size of business is explained again by the working of this law.

Theory of Distribution. The marginal productivity theory, which determines the share of a factor of production in the national dividend, is also based on the operation of this important law.

Conclusion. The law of diminishing returns, therefore, occupies a very important place in the realm of economic thought.

LAW OF INCREASING RETURNS

Another aspect of the universal law of variable proportions is the law of increasing returns. An industry is subject to the law of increasing returns if extra investment in the industry is following by more than proportionate returns, *i.e*, if the marginal product increases. In terms of cost, the law of increasing returns means the lowering of the marginal costs as industry is expanded. As marginal cost indicates price, we can say that the law of increasing returns operates in an industry if, with every expansion of its output, the price of the product falls.

These two laws of increasing and diminishing returns can also be explained in terms of the optimum business unit. We shall have increasing returns when we are moving towards the optimum, and diminishing returns when we move beyond the optimum.

Why the Law of Increasing Returns Operates

We have already seen what economies can be reaped if the scale of production is increased. Advantages of specialisation of labour and machinery and other commercial and miscellaneous economies make it possible to lower the cost of production, and we have increasing returns.

Economies. Among the economies of mass production which contribute to greater productivity at less cost may be mentioned[9]:

(i) Use of none-human and non-animal power resources (water and wind power, steam, electricity, atomic energy);

(ii) automatic self-adjusting mechanism;

(iii) use of standardised, interchangeable parts;

(iv) breakdown of complex processes into simple repetitive operations;

(v) specialisation of functions and division of labour; and

(vi) many other technological factors.

No Scarcity of Factors. The law of diminishing returns operates when there is dearth of an essential factor. But if there is no dearth, the law of increasing returns will operate. "The expansion of an industry, provided that there is no dearth of suitable agents of production, tends to be accompanied, other things being equal, by increasing returns."[10]

8. Lipsey, R.G. *op.cit.*, p.216

9. Samuelson, P.A—Economics (1948), p.21.
10. Chapman, *op. cit.*, p.102.

Right Combination. The law of diminishing returns operates when the factors have been combined in wrong proportions.Now when we try to corresct the combination, increasing returns will follow till the balance is completely restored.

Full Use of Indivisible Factors. The concept of indivisibility, too, has a close bearing on the law of increasing returns. A manufacturer sets up a plant to cope with a peak demand, but in actual practice it may be producing below capacity. In that case, if an addition is made to some other factor or factors, the indivisible factor will be more fully employed, and increasing returns will follow.

LAW OF CONSTANT RETURNS

There can be a situation whee neither the law of diminishing returns nor the law of increasing returns operates, but there is instead constant return.

An industry is subject to the law of constant returns when, whatever the output or scale of production, **the cost per unit remains unaltered, or increased investment of labour and capital results in a proportionate increase in the output.**

Marshall pointed out that the part played by nature corresponded to diminishing returns and the part played by man to increasing returns. That is why in agriculture, where nature is said to be supreme, there is diminishing return. In manufacturing industries, where man's ingenuity has the fullest play in effecting all sorts of economies unhampered by external forces, there operates the law of increasing returns. It is conceivable that some industry may lie midway between the two, where neither there is diminishing return nor increasing return, but there is constant return.

Think of an industry where the raw materials, representing nature's part, account for the same proportion of the total cost as the manufacturing cost which is man's part. In such a case, the law of constant return will operate.

In every industy, the two opposite tendencies are at work. When it is expanded some costs rise and the others fall. It is possible that there may be an industry where these two tendencies just neutralise each other, and we have constant return. The example of an industry making blankets out of pure natural wool is sometimes given in this connection. It is said that the raw material (wool) is subject to diminishing returns, but this tendency is just counter-balanced by the economies in the manufacturing costs, and there is a constant return.

The concept of the optimum can help us to understand the operation of the laws of returns. We have said that movement towards the optimum means increasing returns, and the movement beyond it the diminishing returns. But, if we keep to the optimum, for however short a period it may be, we shall have constant returns.

RETURNS TO SCALE

Distinction between Laws of Returns and Returns to Scale

The laws of returns discussed above are often confused with 'returns to scale'. The two may be clearly distinguished. By "returns to scale" is meant the behaviour of production or returns when all the productive factors are increased or decreased **simultaneously in the same ratio.** In other words, in returns to scale, we analyse the effect of doubling, trebling, quadrupling and so on of all the inputs of productive resources on the output of the product.

The returns to scale may clearly be distinguished from the Law of Variable Proportions. In the law of variable proportions, while some co-operating factors of production may be increased (or decreased), at least one factor (*e.g.*, land in agriculture or entrepreneur in industry) remains constant or cannot be increased, so that the proportion among the factors of production changes and we see how returns or output is affected by such changes in the supply of the productive resources. In returns to scale, on the other hand, all the necessary factors of production are increased/decreased to the **same extent** so that whatever the scale of production, the proportion among the factors remains the same.

Three Phases of Returns to Scale

A layman, uninitiated into the techniques of economic analysis, would perhaps expect that, with the doubling of all productive factors, the output would also double and with trebling of all factors of production, production would also be trebled, and so on. But actually this is not so. In other words, actually the output or returns do not increase/decrease strictly according to the change in the scale.

We know that in the case of the Law of Variable Proportions, as we increase some of the co-operating factors, the marginal product or return increases at first, then stays constant and ultimately it starts diminishing. Similarly, when we increase the scale, *i.e.*, increase all the factors of production together to the same extent, the marginal product or return increases at first, *i.e.*, up to a point, then constant for some further increases in the scale of production is increased still further.

In other, words, there are three distinct phases

TABLE 1: Returns of Scale

Serial No.	Scale Product		Total or Returns (in quintals)	Marginal Product (in quintals)	
1	1 Worker	+ 3 Acres of Land	2	2	Stage I: Increasing Returns
2	2 Workers	+ 6 Acres of Land	5	3	
3	3 W*	+ 9 *	9	4	
4	4 W	+ 12 A	14	5	
5	5 W	+ 15 A	19	5	Stage II: Constant Returns
6	6 W	+ 18 A	24	5	
7	7 W	+ 21 A	28	4	Stage III: Decreasing Returns
8	8 W	+ 24 A	31	3	
9	9 W	+ 27 A	33	2	

'W' Stands for Workers and 'A' Stands for Acres of Land.

of, or stages in, the behaviour of the marginal product.

Let us take a numerical example to explain the behaviour of the returns to scale.

In the table on the page 138, we see that, at the outset, when we employ one worker on 3 acres of land, the total product is 2 quintals. Now to increase output, we double the scale, but the total product increases to more than double (to 5 instead of 4 quintals) and when the scale is trebled, the total product increases from 5 quintals to 9 quintals –the increase this time being 4 quintals as against 3 in the previous case. In other words, the returns to scale have been increasing. If the scale of production is further increased, the marginal product remains constant up to a certain point and, beyond it, it (the marginal product) starts diminishing. In the table at Serial No. 9, the marginal product or return falls to only 2 quintals. (Also see figure given below)

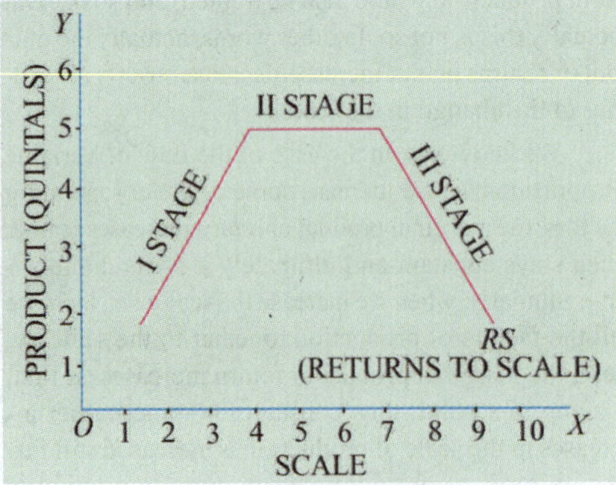

Fig. 18.2. Returns to Scale.

Explanation. Now we may try to explain why we get the above mentioned three phases or stages, *i.e.*, what makes the returns to scale behave in the manner they do.

The chief reason of this kind of behaviour is that when in the beginning, the scale of production is increased, increased division of labour becomes possible and is adopted and, as a result thereof, output increases rather rapidly. In the above table, when there is only one worker working on three acres of land, there is no scope for division of labour. When there are two workers instead and six acres of land, *i.e.*, the factors of production are doubled, there will be increased scope for division of labour and output not only doubles but increase still more and the returns to scale increase.

In this way, **up to a certain point**, the returns to scale will go on increasing until there is no further scope for division of labour. Beyond this point, the marginal product or the returns to scale will cease to increase and will remain constant for certain further increases in scale (*e.g.*, in the above table when 5 workers and 15 acres of land are used instead of 4 workers and 12 acres of land, the marginal product remains 5 quintals as before; similarly for Serial No. 5 to Serial No. 6).

But when scale is increased beyond Serial No. 6, the scope for division of labour is reduced with the result that the marginal return or product begins to decline.

In short, **the main underlying cause of the changing returns to scale is the possibility or otherwise of the division of labour or specialisation.**

However, it is very important to state here, that, in actual life, the scale of production cannot be increased beyond a certain limit. To increase the scale of production means that all factors being used in production can be increased at will and indefinitely. But it is not so in practice. While land, labour and capital can be increased at will, organisation or enterprise does not admit of being increased, since the entrepreneur or organiser remains the same. In other words, there is at least one factor of production which cannot be varied at will, and, hence when more output is desired, the proportion among the factors of production used must change.

Hence, the returns to scale are more of theoretical interest than being relevant to actual life. In practice, it is the law of variable proportions, on the other hand, which is of universal application.

Returns to scale can also be explained with the help of Isoproduct or equal product curves. This is explained in the next chapter.

Causes of Diminishing Returns to Scale

Diseconomies, both internal and external, account for the diminishing returns to scale.

(We have discussed these diseconomies in the previous chapter).

Key terms

Diminishing marginal returns, variable proportions, increasing returns, constant returns.

QUESTIONS

1. State and explain the Law of Diminishing Returns and indicate its significance in economic theory and policy.
2. "The part played by Nature conforms to Diminishing Returns while the part which man plays conforms to Increasing Returns". Critically examine this statement.
3. State the law of diminishing marginal returns and in this context explain the significance of indivisibility of factors.
4. Discuss the view that diminishing returns' arises out of defective factor proportions.
5. What do you understand by optimum factor combination? Explain fully with the aid of indifference curves.
6. State clearly the Law of Variable Proportions. Illustrate diagrammatically. How does it affect the supply curve?

   Or

   The laws of diminishing returns and increasing returns are two phases of the law of variable proportions. Discuss.
7. Explain the law of increasing returns. Do increasing returns necessarily lead to monopoly?

   Or

   How far are increasing returns compatible with competition.
8. Enunciate the Law of Constant Returns and indicate the cases where it operates.
9. Explain the reasons for the operation of (*a*) the law of diminishing returns, and (*b*) diminishing returns to scale.
10. What is the difference between Law of returns and returns to scale. Enumerate the factors that cause decreasing returns to scale.

ISOQUANTS OR EQUAL PRODUCT CURVES

Meaning of Equal Product Curves

In recent years, a new technique has been developed to study the theory of production and to show the equilibriuk of a producer regarding combination of factors. This technique is of iso-product curves which is a parallel concepts to the indifference curves in the theory of consumption.

Just as an indifference curve represent various combinations of two goods which give a consumer equal amount of satisfaction, similarly an iso-product curve also shows all possible combinations of the two inputs physically capable of producing a given level of output. Since an iso-product curve represents those combinations which will allow the production of an equal quantity of output, the producer would be indifferent between them. Iso-product curves are, therefore, called **Product-indifference Curves.** They are also known as **Isoquants or Equal-product Curves.** Any point on the isoquant is a recipe for the same output as any other point on the same curve.

The concept of equal-product curves can be easily understood from the table given below. In this table, we have assumed that two factors X and Y are being used to produce a given product.

TABLE 1. Equal Product Combinations

Combinations X	*Factor Y*	*Factor*
A	1	12
B	2	8
C	3	5
D	4	3
E	5	2

To begin with, combination A, representing 1 unit of factor X and 12 units of factor Y, produces a given quantity (say, 40 units) of a product. All other combinations in the table are assumed to yield the same amount, *i.e.*, 40 units of the product. Thus,

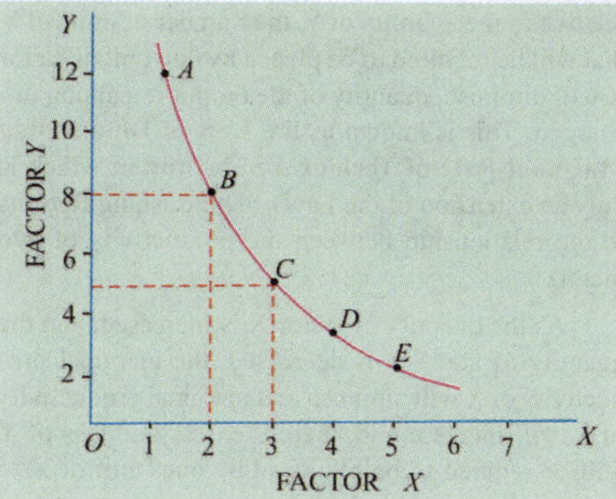

Fig. 19.1. An isoquant.

combination C representing 3X + 5Y, combination D representing 4X + 3Y and combination E haveing 5X + 2Y will all produce 40 units of the product. If we now plot all these combinations on a graph paper and join them, we shall get a continuous and smooth curve called iso-product curve on which are represented the various combinations A, B, C, D and E of the above table. IP represents all those combinations with which 40 units of the product can be produced. The shape of the isoquants shows the degree of substitutability between the two factor used in production.

Indifference Curves and Iso-product Curves Distinguished. Though iso-product curves are similar to the indifference curves of the theory of demand, one important difference between them is worth nothing. While an aindifference curve shows all those combinations of two goods which provide equal satisfaction to a consumer, it does not tell us exactly how much satisfaction is derived by the consumer from those combinations. This is because utility or satisfaction being a mental phenomenon cannot be measured in absolute terms. Thus, there are no physical units in which satisfaction can be measured. That is why we label indifference curves as I, II, III, *etc.*, showing that higher indifference curves provide greater level of satisfaction, but we cannot say how much greater. On the other hand we can label iso-product curves in the physical units of the output produced without any difficulty. Production of a good being a physical phenomenon lends itself to absolute measurement in physical units.

Moreover, if we an **iso-product map** showing various iso-product curves, it is possible to say by how much production is greater or less on one iso-product curve than on another.

We have drawn an iso-product map in Fig. 19.2 showing equal product curves IP, IP′, IP″ and IP‴, which represent 40 units, 60 units, 80 units, 100 units, of output respectively. Thus, iso-product curve IP′ represents an output 20 units greater than on iso-product curve IP and iso-product curve IP‴ yields output 60 units greater than on IP. It is, therefore, possible not only to lebel iso-product curves by physical units but also to judge how much greater or less is the size of the output on one iso-product curve than on another. This is an advantage.

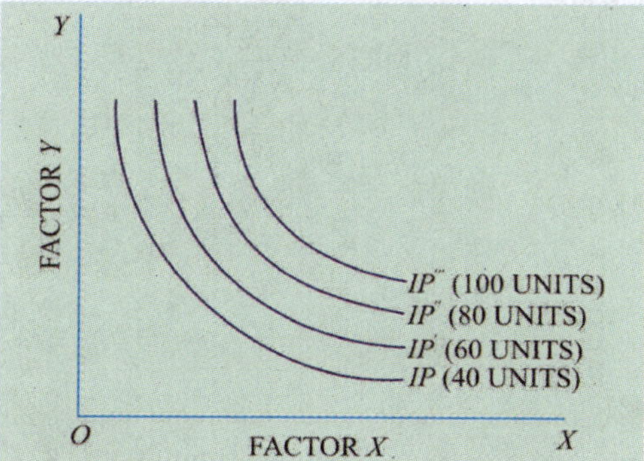

Fig. 19.2. An isoquant map is a set of isoquants. The output level increases as isoquant goes higher to the right.

Marginal Rate of Technical Substitution

Marginal rate of technical substitution is a concept similar to the marginal rate of substitution in the theory of demand. **Marginal rate of technical substitution of X for Y is the number of units of factor Y which can be replaced by one unit of factor X, quantity of the output remaining uncharged.** The concept of marginal rate of technical substitution can be easily understood from the table given above. We reproduce below the same table to find out the marginal rate of technical substitution.

As mentioned earlier, in this table various combinations of factors X and Y yield output equal to 40 units of the product. From the comparison of combinations A and B, it will become clear that here 4 units of factor Y can be replaced by 1 unit of factor X without any change in output. Therefore,

TABLE: 2

Combination	*Factor X*	*Factor Y*	*MRTS of X for Y*
A	1	12	
B	2	8	4 : 1
C	3	5	3 : 1
D	4	3	2 : 1
E	5	2	1 : 1

4 : 1 is the marginal rate of technical substitution (MRTS) at this stage.

Now by comparing combinations B and C, it will be found that there 3 units of factor Y can be replaced by 1 unit of factor X without any loss of output. Therefore, here the marginal rate of technical substitution is 3 : 1. Similarly, the marginal rate of technical substitution between C and D is 2 : 1 and between D and E is 1 : 1. Algebraically, it can be stated that

$$\text{MRTS} = \frac{\Delta X}{\Delta Y}$$

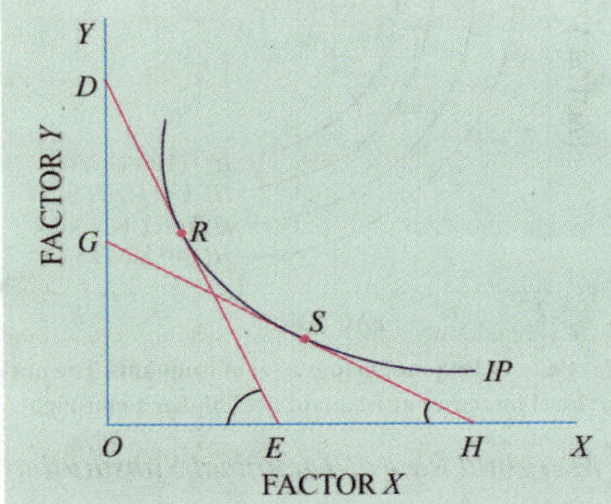

Fig. 19.3 Marginal Rate of Technical Substitution.

But $\frac{\Delta X}{\Delta Y}$ shows the slope of a curve. There fore, MRTS is the slope of the iso-product curve at a given point and can, therefore, be found out by tangent of the angle. In the Fig. 19.3 given below.

The marginal rate of technical substitution at point R will be equal to the slope of the tangent DE. Slope of the tangent DE is equal to $\frac{OD}{DE}$.

Hence, the marginal rate of technical substitution at point R will be equal to $\frac{OD}{DE}$. Likewise, marginal rate of technical substitution at point S of the iso-product curve will be $\frac{OG}{OH}$.

Law of Diminishing Marginal Rate of Technical Substitution

An important feature of the marginal rate of technical substitution is worth nothing. Marginal rate of substitution of X for Y will generally diminish as the quantity of X is increased relative to the quantity of Y. In other words, as the quantity of factor X is increased relative to the quantity of Y, the number of units of Y that will be required to be placed by one unit of factor X will diminish, quantity of the output remaining uncharged. This is known as the **Law of Diminishing Marginal Rate of Technical Substitution** which is only an extension of the Law of Diminishing Returns to the relationship between the productivity of two factors.

As the quantity of factor X is increased, and the quantity of factor Y is decreased, the marginal productivity of X will diminish and marginal productivity of Y will increase and, therefore, less and less of Y will be requied to be relplaced by one unit of X to maintain the same level of output as more and more of X and less and less of Y is used.

Elasticity of Substitution Between Factors

In the theory of demand, we explained the concept of elasticity of substitution between goods in the scheme of consumption of a consumer. That is, we explained to what extent one good could be substituted by a consumer for another good. In the theory of production, on the other hand, we are concerned with the factors of production instead of the commodities for consumption. Here we discuss to what extent a factor of production, say labour, can be substituted for another factor, say capital. That is, we are concerned with what may be called elasticity of technical substitution. Just as the marginal rate of substitution of commodity X for commodity Y falls as X is substituted for Y along an indifference curve, similarly the marginal rate of technical substitution (MRTS) of factor X for factor Y declines as factor X is substituted for factor Y along an isoquant or equal product curve. **"The relative change in the factor- proportions (or input ratios) as a consequence of relative change in the marginal rate of technical substitution is known as elasticity of substitution between factors".**[1]

The rate at which the marginal rate of technical substitution falls is a measure of the extent to which the two factor can be substituted for each other. If they are perfect substitutes, that is, if either factor can be used equally well to produce the product, the marginal rate of substitution will not fall.

The substitutability of one factor for another depends on the elasticity of substitution, *i.e.*, the degree to which it is possible to substitute one factor for another. The elasticity of substitution can be defined as the percentage change in the rates of the factors used, say X and Y, in response to a given percentage

1. Ahuja. H. L. —*Advanced Economic Theory,* 1975, p . 306.

change in the marginal rate of technical substitution. This elasticity is unity if a given percentage change in the marginal rate of technical substitution induces and equal change in the factors ratio in the opposite direction; it will be greater than unity if it induces greater percentage change and less than unity if the percentage change induced in the factors ratio is less than the percentage change in the MRTS. Thus,

$$\text{Elasticity of Substitution} = \frac{\Delta(X/Y)}{\Delta(\text{MRTS})} \times \frac{\text{MRTS}}{(X/Y)}$$

A high elasticity of substitution means that the factors can be substituted freely for one another, while in the case of low elasticity they can be used only in definite proportions.

We can refer to the shape of Isoquants or equal product curves to determine the magnitude of elasticity of substitution between factors. The measure of elasticity depends on the curvature of the isoquants. The greater the convexity of isoquant the less will be substitution elasticity, and vice versa. In case the two factors are perfect substitutes of each other and the isoquants between them are straight lines, substitution elasticity between them is infinite. On the other hand, when the two factors are perfect complements and their isoquants are right angled, the substitution elasticity between them is zero. Besides, since there is inverse relationship between the marginal rate of substitution and factor-ratio (*i.e.*, as the factor-ratio increases, the marginal rate of technical substitution falls), elasticity of substitution between factors is always negative.

The concept of elasticity of substitution also occupies an important place in the theory of distribution. It affects the distributive shares of the factors of production. For example, the relative shares of labour and capital will largely depend on the elasticity of substitution between them. If capital can be freely substituted for labour, the share of labour relative to the share of capital is bound to decline.

Application of Equal Product Curves

The isoquant technique is applicable to agriculture and to all lines of manufacture. The marginal rate of technical substitution guides in the substitution of some units of one input for some units of another input, in some cases, increased use of labour can help in making a reduction in the use of raw materials, because spoilage and wastage of material may be cut to the minimum. Similarly, by adding to the supervisory staff, labour may be economised or the introduction of machinery may cut down the use of labour. In this way, the businessman tries various permutations and combinations and the Isoquant technique helps him in reaching the most economical combination.

Properties of Equal Product Curves

Properties of iso-product curves are the same as those of indifference curves. Their properties can also be proved in the same manner as in the case of indifference curves. (See the relevant diagrams pp. 54–56). The following are the important properties of iso-product curves:

(*i*) Sloping Downwards. Iso-product curves slope downwards from left to right. This is so because if the quantity of a factor X is increased, the quantity of factor Y must be decreased so as to maintain the same level of output.

In the figure 19.4 on y-axis. K (capital) and x-axis 'L' (Labour) ISO quants are negative sloping that means as the increase in one more unit-of 'L' than we have to decrease certain amount of capital (K). Due to this the iso-quant curve slopes down word from left to right. In other words it has a negative slope.

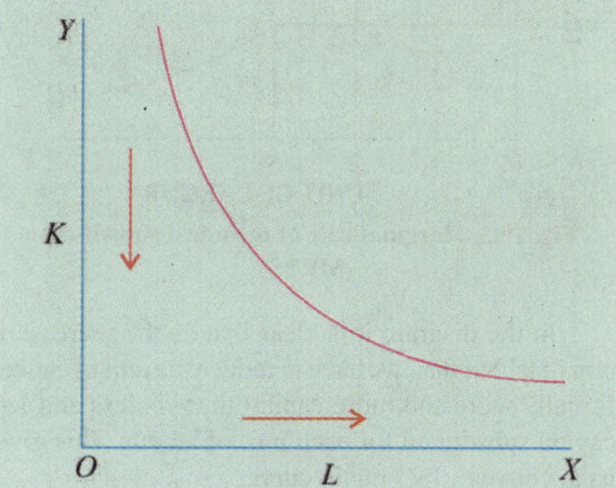

Fig. 19.4. Downward sloping isoquant.

	Labour	—	Capital	Marginmal rate of Technical sub-stitution
A	1	—	12	
B	2	—	8	1 : 4
C	3	—	5	1 : 3
D	4	—	3	1 : 2
E	5	—	2	1 : 1

(*ii*) Convexity. Iso-product curves are convex to the origin. This is due to the fact that marginal rate of technical substitution falls as more and more of X is substituted for Y. Iso-product curves being concave would mean that the marginal rate of technical substitution of X for Y increases as more and more of

X is substituted for Y. But increasing marginal rate of technical substitution is not realistic. As explained above owing to the operation of the law of diminishing returns, the marginal rate of technical substitution falls as more and more substitution takes place.

MRTS = Marginal Role of Technical Substitution

$$MRTS = \frac{\Delta K}{\Delta L}$$

ΔK = Change in Capital

ΔL = Change in Labour.

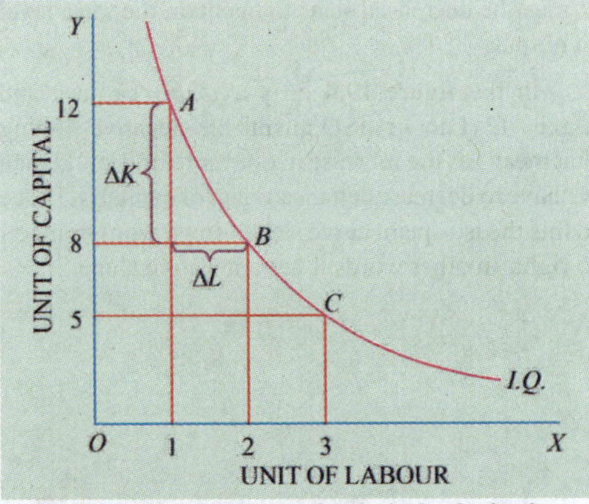

Fig. 19.5. Marginal rate of technical substitution (MRTS).

In the diagram it is clear that as the increase in unit of labour than we have to reduce the unit of capital. Initially more and more capital than is less and less capital substituted for each unit of labour. This gives us a 'convex'. ISO quant curve.

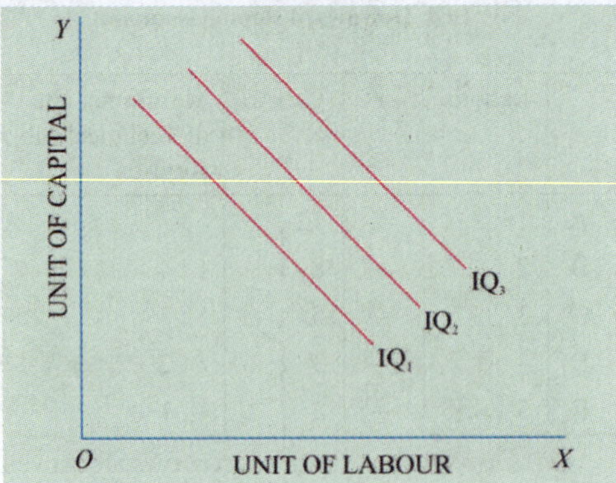

Fig. 19.6. Factors cuve perfect - substitutes.

Thus, it is the diminishing marginal rate of substitution which is a realistic phenomenon and due to which the iso-product curves are convex to the origin.

However, there are two exceptions to the rule that equal product curves are convex to the origin:

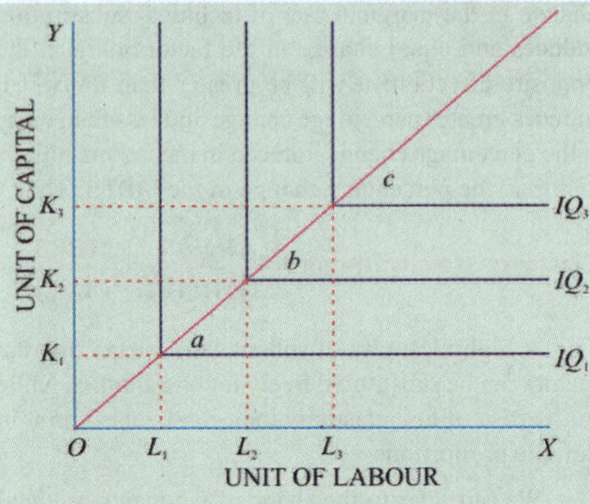

Fig. 19.7. Perfectly complementary factors.

***(a)* Perfect Substituted.** When the factors of production are perfect substitutes, then one factor can completely take the place of the other. They may, in fact, be regarded as one factor. In their case, the marginal rate of technical substitution is constant. Hence, the equal product curves will be a horizontal straight line instead of being convex to the origin.

***(b)* Complements.** The complementary factors are those which are jointly used in production in a fixed proportion. If one of these factors is increased, the other must also be increased at the same time, otherwise no additional output will be obtained. In his case, the equal product curves will be right angled (*i.e.*, one of the two arms being vertical and the other horizontal) at the combination of the two factors used in fixed proportion.

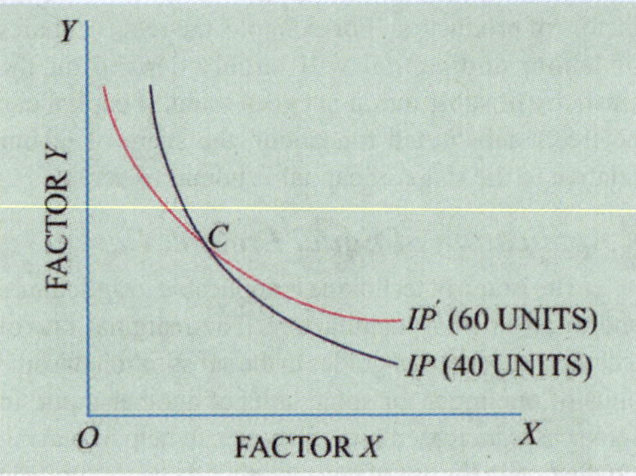

Fig. 19.8. Isoquants, like indifference curves cannot intersect.

***(iii)* Non-intersecting.** Two iso-product curves cannot cut each other. If the two iso-product curves, one of 40 units of output and the second of 60 units of output, cut each other, there would be a common combination of factors which will lie on both these curves such as combination C in Fig. 19.4. It would then mean that the same combination C which yields 40 units of output accroding to one iso-product curve, can produce 60 units according to another iso-product curve. This is absurd. How can the same combination produce two different levels of output, techniques of production being given?

***(iv)* The iso-quants is an oval-sloped curve.** As we take the combination of an abundant factor say capital (K) with relatively less factor labour 'L'. This indicates that the marginal productivity of the abundant factor say Kis zero and the vice-versa.

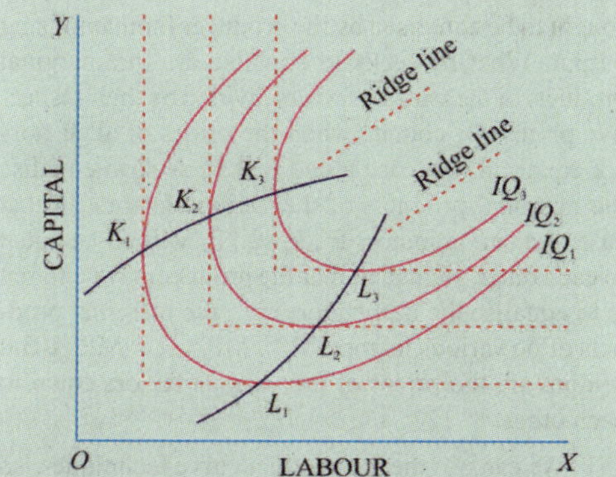

Fig. 19.9. Economic region of production falls within the two ridge lines.

K_1, K_2, K_3 are tangent to ISo-quant IQ_1, IQ_2 & IQ_3, which shows that above this point the productivity of capital is zero. In the same way L_1, L_2, and L_3 are tangent to IQ_1, IQ_2 and IQ_3 which indicate beyond this point productivity of labour is zero. When we join K_1, K_2, K_3 and L_1, L_2, L_3 we get the ridge lines.

The 'Ridge Lines' are the loans of locus of points of iso-quant where marginal productivity of the concerned factor is zero. The ridge line indicates that the region onside the ridge lines are useless or uneconomic to the producer.

Iso-Cost Line

The combination of factors with which a firm produces the product also depends on the prices of the factor and the amount of money which a firm wants to spend. Iso-cost line represents these two things–the prices of productive factors and the total amount of money which a firm wants to spend. Each iso-cost line will show various combinations of two factors which can be purchased with a given amount of total money.

Suppose a producer wants to spend Rs. 300 on factors X and Y. If the price of the factor Y is Rs.3 per unit and if he spends the whole sum of Rs. 300 on it, then he can purchase 100 units of Y. Let OH in Fig. 19.5 represent 100 units of Y.

Now if the price of X is Rs. 5 per unit and the whole sum of Rs. 300 is spent on it, 60 units of X can be purchased. Let OL in Fig. 19.5 represent 60 units of X.

If we now join together the points H and L, we shall get the iso-cost line HL on which will lie all those combinations of factors X and Y which can be purchased with Rs. 300. This line is called iso-cost line since the total cost or total money spent remains the same, whatever the combination, which lies on it, is purchased. The iso-cost line is also known as **price line** or **outlay line**.

Now if the producer decides to increase the total money to be spent on the productive factors to Rs. 400, more of both the factors can be purchased. As a result of the increase in the total outlay to Rs. 400, iso-cost line will shift to EF. Similarly, with total outlay of Rs. 500 the iso-cost line will be PT. Higher iso-cost will show greater total outlay.

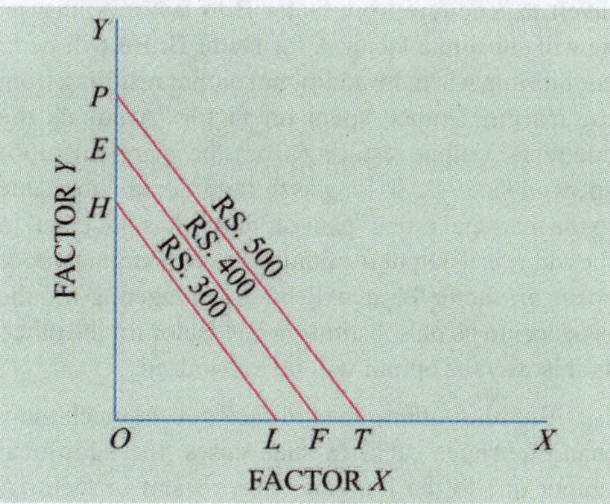

Fig. 19.10 Iso-Cost Line.

The slope of the iso-cost line represents the ratio of the price of a unit input X to the price of a unit of input Y. In case the price of any one of them changes, there would be a corresponding change in the slope of the iso-cost curve and the equilibrium would shift too.

Producer's Equilibrium: Optimum Factor Combination

Least-cost Combination. The producer will try to attam an equilibrium position by hitting at the most economical or the least cost combination of the factors of production. Just as a consumer is faced with the problem of making a choice between different combinations of two or more goods, similarly a producer is confronted with the problem of choosing between different combinations of two or more factors of production.

A rational entrepreneur would try to maximise his money profits from the production and sale of commodities, just as a consumer tries to obtain maximum satisfaction from the consumption of commodities. To produce a given output various combinations of factors of production are possible. But a rational producer or a firm would seek to produce that output with the 'optimum' or 'least-cost' combination of factors of production. (In Economics factors of production are also called 'inputs'.) The producing firm will use its productive resourcesin such proportions or such ratios that whatever the output produced, the cost outlay should be as small as possible for that output. Or, we can say that the firm should use that combination of resources which produces the maximum output for given cost outlay.

In arriving at an optimum or least- cost combination, the producer is guided by the principle of substitution or that of equil marginal returns. If a rupee spent on factor A results in a greater output than a rupee spent on factor B, it would pay the producer to divert expenditure from factor B to factor A; that is, he will substitute factor A for factor B. He will be in equilibrium when the additional output resulting from the marginal rupee spent on factor A equals the additional output resulting from the marginal rupee spent on factor B. So long as the additional output due to the marginal rupee spent on factor A is not equal to the additional output resulting from the marginal rupee spent on factor B, it will be advantageous for the producer to go on substituting one factor for the other. In this way the output will be maximised.

But most often, units of factors cost much more than one rupee each. In such cases, the additional output due to the marginal rupee spent in factor A would be equal to the marginal product of factor A divided by its price. As has been explained earlier, the marginal product of a factor is the additional product resulting from the employment of an additional unit of the factor. It, therefore, follows that the marginal product of a factor divided by the price of the factor is the additional product resulting from a rupee spent on the factor. Suppose the marginal product of a factor is 120 units of output and the price of the factor is Rs. 10. Then, 120 ÷ 10, *i.e.*, 12 is the additional output resulting from the marginal rupee spent on that factor.

The condition for the least-cost combination may, then, be put in the following form[2] :

$$\frac{MP_a}{P_a} = \frac{MP_b}{P_b} = \ldots\ldots = \frac{MP_n}{P_n}$$

Where MP_a is the marginal product of factor A and P_a is the price of A, and so on. If $\frac{MP_a}{P_a}$ is greater than $\frac{MP_b}{P_b}$ it will be to the advantage of the entrepreneur to employ more of factor A and less of factor B. He will employ more of one factor and less of the other till the above **'proportionality rule'** is satisfied.

It is in this manner, that the firm is able to discover the least-cost combination which means producing the maximum output with a given cost.

It will have been clearly understood that it is not the marginal products of the various factors that are sought to be equalised by the producer for maximising output. What he seeks to equalise are the marginal products of the various factors divided by their respective prices. Of course, when the prices of all factors are equal, in that case alone will he seek to equalise the marginal products of the various factors. In that case, the denominators P_a, P_b ..... P_n will all be equal to each other, so that all that the producer is to attempt is to equalise the numerators, *i.e.*, the marginal products ofthe various factors (MP_a, MP_b . . . . . MP_m). But seldom are the prices of the various factors equal to each other.

We can use the iso-product curve technique also for this purpose.

Producer's Equilibrium with Equal Product Curves. Iso-product curves show the various possible combinations with which a given level of output can be produced. Thus, iso-product curve shows the technical conditions of production. On the other hand, iso-cost lines represent total amount of outlay to be spent and the ratio of the prices of the two factors. Now the question arises : which combination of factors a producer will choose to produce a given level of output? In other words, at what point on the iso-product map the producer will be in equilibrium regarding the factors combination, given the level of output to be produced. This can be illustrated with Fig. 19.11.

We assume that the producer wants to produce a given level of output as cheaply as possible, becasue in doing so his profits will be maximized.In other words, the producer will try to strike a least-cost combination of factors to produce a given level of output.

2. In this case, we assume perfect competition in the factor market, which implies that our producer or the firm takes the prices of the factors as given, i.e., the price of a factor does not change as he employs more or less or it.

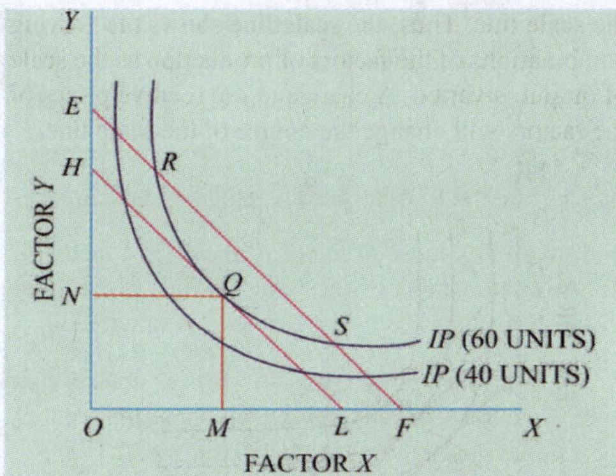

Fig. 19.11. Tangency between isoquant and lowest possible isocost line, such as the point Q, gives optimum combination of factors to minimum cost of production given the level of output.

Suppose a producer has decided to produce 60 units of a product. 60 units of the product can be produced by any of the combinations such as R, S, Q, which lie on the iso-product curve IP′ in Fig. 19.6. He will choose that combination on the iso-product curve IP′ which gives him the lowest cost of production for the production of 60 units of the product.

From Fig. 19.6, it will be clear that the produce will choose combination Q at which iso-cost line HL is tangent to the iso-product curve IP. Combination Q will cost the producer least for producing 60 units of output. The producer will not choose any other combination on iso-product curve IP\` such as R, S, because all these lie on the higher iso-cost line (EF) than iso-cost line HL and will, therefore, mean greater total outlay for producing 60 units of output. The producer will not go the left of Q, for he will not be able to produce 60 units of output by any combination which lies to the left of Q on IP′.

Hence, we conclude that the producer will be in equilibrium by choosing the factor combination Q to produce 60 units of the output. Factor combination Q is an optimum factor combination for him to produce 60 units of output.This is so because factor combination Q will give him the lowest cost of production.

Coincidence of MRTS and Price Ratio. It will be evident from Figure 19.6 that at point Q marginal rate of technical subtitution will be equal to the ratio of prices of the factors. Marginal rate of technical substitution is given by the slope of the iso-product curve and the price ratio of the factors is given by the slope of the iso-cost line. The slope of the iso-product curve IP′ and the iso-cost line HL are equal at the point of tangency Q, and the marginal rate of technical substitution (MRTS) will be equal to the price-ratio of factors X and Y at point Q.

Thus, at the point of equilibrium

$$\text{MRTS of X for Y} = \frac{\text{Price of X}}{\text{Price of Y}}$$

This means that the producer will substitute one factor for another in search of the cheapest method of production until the prices ratio and the marginal rate of technical substitution are approximately equal.

Scale Line or Expansion Path. If now the producer wishes to produce 80 units of output instead of 60 units,which combination of factors will he select? Obviously, he will choose that combination which will cost him the least for producing 80 units of output. Such a combination is Q′ at which iso-cost line is tangent to the iso-product curve IP″ which represents 80 units of output. This is shown in Fig. 19.7.

Similarly, for the production of 100 units of output, the producer will choose factor combination Q″ and for 120 units of output his equilibrium will lie at Q‴. If points like Q, Q′, Q″, Q‴ are joined together, we get what is called scale line or expansion path.

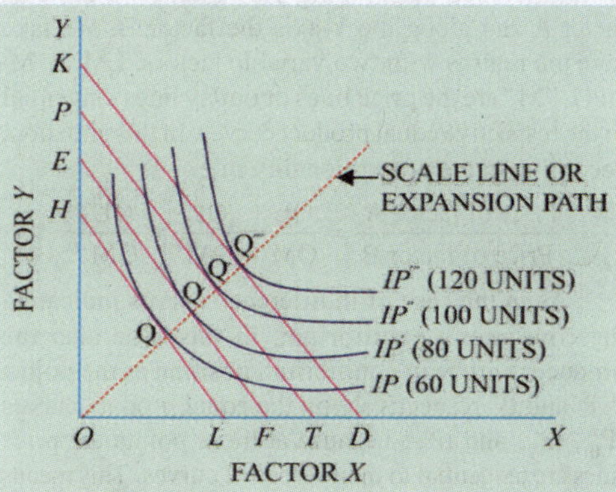

Fig. 19.12. Expansion path is the locus of various optimum combinations of factors given the factor prices.

This line is known as a scale line because it shows the way in which the producer will adjust the scale of his operations as he changes the scale of his output. This is also called expansion path as along this line he will expand his output, if relative factor prices remain the same. Given the prices of factors X and Y, a producer, who is able to vary the amounts of both these factors, will always fix his scale of output at some point along the scale line such as Q, Q′, Q″, Q‴, in Fig. 19.7. Producing onthe scale line shows the cheapest way of producing each level of output, given relative factor prices.

An iso-quant or the equal product curve represents different input combination, or input ratios which can produce a specified level of output, whereas the scale line shows different levels of output, input ratio remaining the same.

It must be noted that slope of the scale line will depend on the relative prices of the factors and the shape of the iso-product curves. One cannot know at which point on a scale line the producer will be in equilibrium until one knows that output he wishes to produce. How a producer will decide about the level of output to be produced by him will depend upon the conditions in the product market. (Determination of price and output by the producer under different market types will be subject-matter of discussion of our later chapters numbering 27–30).

Application of Equal Product Curves to Returns to Scale

The equal product curves can be used to show how returns to factors of production will vary as the scale of production is varied. In the figure 19.8, IP_0, IP_1, and IP_2 are the three equal product curves.

They constitute the firm's equal product map like an indifference map. Along the X-axis, we indicate factor A and along the Y-axis the factor B. We take here the returns with two variable factors. LM, L′M′ and L″M″ are the price lines or outlay lines tangential to the respective equal product curves. In this situation, according to the proportionality rule

$$\frac{\text{Price of factor A}}{\text{Price of factor B}} = \frac{OL}{OM} = \frac{OL'}{OM'} = \frac{OL''}{OM''}$$

As in the case of indifference curves indicating the consumer's equilibrium, in this case also the producer will be in equilibrium position at the points P, P′ and P″ respectively on the equal product curves IP_0, IP_1, and IP_2, because at these points the price lines are tangential to their resective curves. This means that only at these points will the firm be producing in the cheapest manner. At any other point (say other than P on the equal product curve IP_0), the producer will have to use either more than OM of factor A or more than OL of factor B. At the points P, P′ and P″, the marginal productivity of factor A in terms of factor B is edqual to the relative money prices of factors A and B.

By joining P, P′ and P″ we get what is known as the **Scale Line** corresponding to the income consumption curve in the case of indifference curves map. It is on some point along the scale line that the firm will fix its scale of output given the relative prices of the two factors. The scale line shows how a producer varies his scale of operations. It indicates the most economical combination of the factors of production or the cheapest way of producing each output. The shape of the equal product curves and the relative prices of the factors used will determine the shape of the scale line. Thus, the scale line shows the varying combinations of the factors of production as the scale of output is varied. A change in the relative prices of the factors will change the course of the scale line.

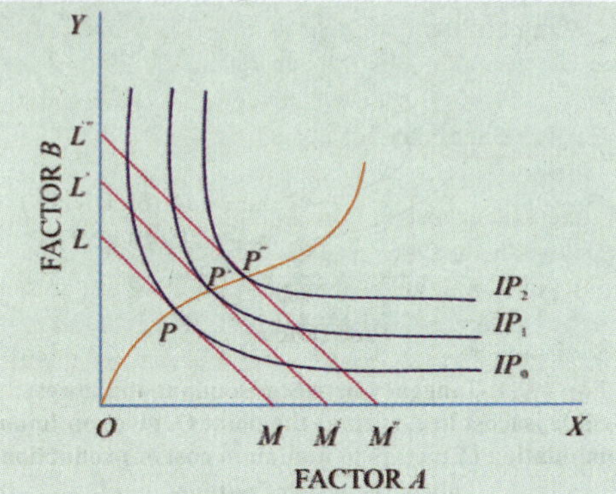

Fig. 19.13. Iso-Product Curves and Returns to Scale.

The equal product map like the one given above shows *(a)* whether the returns to scale will increase, decrease or remain constant as the scale of production is varied, and *(b)* whether the proportion between the factors of production employed will vary or remain constant as we move along the scale line.

Shape of the Scale Line

The following diagram (Fig. 19.9) shows how variations in the amounts of the factors used and in the output obtained determine the shape of the scale line. Suppose the return is constant so that doubling the amount of each factor results in doubling of the output.That is, a certain proportionate change in the amount of each factor used leads to the change in the output exactly in the same proportion.

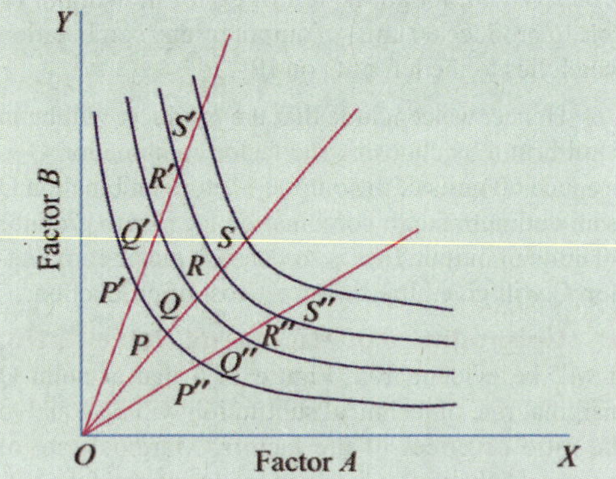

Fig. 19.14. Shape of the Scale Line.

In a situation like this, the scale lines will be straight through the origin. P′Q′R′S′, PQRS and P″Q″R″S″ are the three straight scales lines. The returns to scale along each scale line on the equal product map are constant. This is shown by the fact that the distance between the three equal product curves along each scale line is the same, *i.e.*, OP = PQ = QR = RS and OP′ = P′Q′ = R′S′, and so on.

In a diagram like this, given relative factor prices, *i.e.,* with a constant price slope, not only are the returns to scale constant but the returns to outlay are also constant. Similarly, the returns to scale and returns to outlay are interchangeable and the same.

But if there is an equal product map where the relative prices are not constant and where the returns are not constant, the returns to scale and returns to outlay will not be the same. When as the output changes, the proportion between factors also changes, it will be necessary to speak of returns to outlay instead of returns to scale. However, here for the sake of convenience and easy understanding, we assume that proportion between the factors remains constant, whatever the scale of production.

Effect of Change in Input Price on Input Use

This effect is similar to what we discussed in the case of indifference curves and it can be illustrated diagrammatically in the same manner as price effect on consumer's equilibrium by indifference curves. (See Fig. 7.8). The total effect on the use of the input of a change in its price is made up of two components: the substitution effect and the output effect. The **substitution effect** is the effect on the use of the input due exclusively to the change in the relative price of the inputs, the output remaining the same. This effect is invariably negative, because a rise in the price of an input must lead to a reduction in its use and a fall in price to its greater use. **The output effect** indicates the effect on input use due to change in the level of output, the input price remaining unchanged. This effect, too, is always negative, because increase in cost reduces both the output , and vice versa.

Substitute and Complementary Factors

Just as some goods are substitutes and complementary goods for others, similarly substitute and complementary relationship can be found to exist among factors of production. We have said above that if a factor X becomes cheaper relatively to factor Y, there will be a tendency to buy more of X and less of Y. This in effect means that factor X has been substituted for factor Y. In this case factors X and Y are substitutes of each other. **Two factors X and Y are said to be substitutes when the substitution effect on Y of a change in the price of X is greater than the output effect on it.** This is so because the negative substitution effect is greater than the positive output (or expansion) effect.

But when the marginal rate of technical substitution declines very rapidly (*i.e.*, when the equal product curves are highly convex to the origin as in Fig. 19.7), the substitution effect will be very small. In this case, the output effect of the fall in price on the purchase of Y is greater than the substitution effect. Hence the net effect of the fall in price of X will be to increase the quantity purchased of Y also. In this case, both factors X and Y will be purchased in greater quantities. This means they are complements of one another. **The two factors are said to be complementary to each other when the output effect of a fall in the price of one factor is greater than the substitution effect.**

Application to Under-developed Countries

The theory of production is not a dry and abstract theory having little relevance to practical problems. It has a special significance for the under-developed countries which are faced, like others, with factor proportions problem. These countries have excessive rural population clinging to agriculture where their marginal productivity is practically nil. That is, if a sizable proportion of them is withdrawn, it would not significantly affect output. Such countries are characterised by 'structural disequilibrium at the factor level' as Kindlebarger puts it. There is obviously a need for the adoption of more labour -intensive methods than capital-intensive methods. The factor combinations should embody high labour-capital ratios. As economic development proceeds, the composition of demanded goods will change calling forth for a change in factor proportions in the processes of production.

Key terms

Isoquant, MRTS, isocost, Expansion path, producers's equilibrium, ridge lines.

QUESTIONS

1. What are Iso-product curves? Explain their characteristics.
2. What is the significance of tangency between an Isoquant and an iso-cost line?
3. Show with the help of curves that different combinations of two factors of production give the same output (Iso-product). Explain the characteristics of the curves drawn.
4. Given the Iso-product curve of a firm and the prices of the two inputs it uses, find the condition that the firm must fulfil to produce (*i*) a given output at the least possible cost and (*ii*) the largest output at a given total cost.

COST AND COST CURVES

CONCEPT OF COST OF PRODUCTION

The cost of production of an individual firm operating in a market has an important influence on the market supply of a commodity. It is very necessary to have a clear idea about the concept of cost produc tion and then proceed to study the cost curves.

Nominal and Real Cost

Money Cost. The cost may be nominal cost or real cost. **Nominal Cost** is the **money cost** of production. It is also called **expenses of production.** These expenses are important from the point of view of the producer. He must make sure that the price of the product, in the long run, covers these expenses including normal profit, otherwise he cannot afford to carry on the business.

Real Cost. Attempts have been made to "pierce the monetary veil" and to establish cost on a real basis. The real cost of production has been variously interpreted. Adam smith regarded pains and sacrifices of labour as real cost. Marshall includes under it "real cost of efforts of various qualities" and "real cost of waiting."[1] This is called the social cost by Marshall.

Opportunity Cost. The Austrian school of economists and their followers gave a new concept of real costs. According to them, the real cost of production of a given commodity is the **next best alternative sacrificed in order to obtain that commodity.** It is also called **opportunity cost** or **displacement cost.**

From the point of view of the community, as a whole, the money costs do not tell the whole story. It is the real cost which is more important.

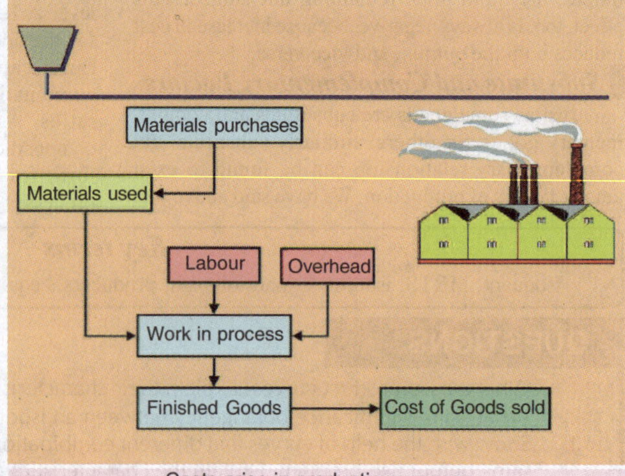

Costs arise in production process.

1. Marshall, A –*Principles of Economics* (8th ed.), p. 350.

Money Cost and the Real Cost do not coincide. It is very seldom that the real cost of a commodity may be equal to the money cost. As Marshall puts it, "If the purchasing power of money in terms of effort remained about constant, and if the rate of remuneration for waiting has remained about constant, then the money measure of costs corresponds to real costs; but such a correspondence is never to be assumed lightly."[2]

Thus, there is very little connection between money costs and real costs. The two can never be equal in a world of change, as our world is, whether we consider the long period or the short period. The value of land depends on scarcity. The question of cost in terms of effort and sacrifice in this case does not arise. The earnings of cinema stars, professors, collies, sweepers, peasants, businessmen, *etc.*, seldom correspond to the respective efforts and sacrifices undergone by each class.

Economic Costs. By economic costs is meant those payments which must be received by resource owners in order to ensure that they will continue to supply them in the process of production. This definition is based on the fact that resources are scarce and they have alternative uses. To use them in one process is to deny their use in other processes. Economic cost includes normal profit.

Implicit and Explicit Costs. Costs of production have also been classified as explicit and implicit costs. **Implicit costs** are costs of self-owned and self- employed resources such as salary of the proprietor or return on the entrepreneur's own investment. These costs are frequently ignored in calculating the expenses of production.

Explicit costs are the paid-out costs, *i.e.*, payments made for productive resources purchased or hired by the firm. They consist of the salaries and wages paid to the employees, prices of raw and semi-finished materials, overhead costs and payments into depreciation and sinking fund accounts. These are firm's accounting expenses.

If we add to the money expenses two items, *viz.*, alternative or opportunity costs and normal profits, we get the **full costs** of a firm as distinguished from **business costs** which are synonymous with firm's total money expenses as computed by ordinary accounting methods. The entrepreneur must be sure of normal profit if he is to continue in business. In this sense **normal profit too is a cost.**

2. I bid.

Alternative, Opportunity or Transfer Costs

In modern economic analysis, the term real cost is interpreted in the sense of opportunity cost or transfer cost. The American economist Davenport explains this concept as follows: "Suppose, for example, that a child has been given both a pear and a peach, that some predatory boy tries to seize them and that the only method of saving either is to drop one, say the pear, in the wayside weeds, and to run for shelter with the peach while the aggressor is picking up the pear. What has the peach cost? True, the peach was a gift. In a certain sense, therefore, it costs nothing. Nevertheless it is retained only on terms of foregoing the pear. The term cost seems not quite satisfactory to cover the case. Perhaps displacement or foregoing would be preferable. Or, if one offers you choice between a ride and an evening at the theatre, it is awkward to say that the acceptance of the one is at the cost of the other. Yet the resistance of the taking of the one is the letting go of the other. Or, if with a dollar which you have earned you are at a choice between buying a book, or a pocket knife, and finally buy the book, the resistance overcome is best expressed, not by the labour devoted to the earning of the dollar, and not by the dollar itself, but by the alternative application of the dollar. The highest cost of the book – the best test or measure of its worth to you –was in the significance of its strongest competitor, the knife."[3]

Since productive resources are limited, the production of one commodity can only be at the expense of another. The commodity that is sacrificed is the real cost of the commodity that is produced. In the words of Henderson, "Real Cost of **anything** is the curtailment of the supply of other useful things, which the production of that particular thing entails."[4] Economists define costs of production of a particular product as the value of the foregone alternative products that resources used in its production could have produced. The costs of resources to a firm are their values in their best alternative uses."[5]

Suppose with a sum of Rs. 1000' a manufacturer can produce two radio sets or a small refrigerator. Suppose further that he decides to produce the refrigerator rather than the radio sets. In this case, the real cost of the refrigerator is equal to the cost of two radio sets, *i.e.*, the alternative foregone. Conceived on

3. Devenport –*The Economics of Enterprise*, p. 61.
4. *Supply and Demand*, 1932, p. 166.
5. Leftwich, R. H. –*The Price System and Resources Allocation*, 1965, pp.126-127.

these lines, cost of production means not the effort and sacrifices undergone, but the **most attractive alternative** foregone or the next best choice sacrificed. Real costs are thus not entities, ultimate and independent of utility, but they are sacrifices of competing demands.

In a money economy, it is "the amount of money necessary to induce the factors of production to be devoted to this particular task rather than to seek employment elsewhere."

Significance of Opportunity Costs. There are competing demands (depending upon the marginal utility of the consumers) for the same resources. Since the resources are scarce, certain demands are satisfied only at the sacrifice of other demands. The resources tend to move from those uses in which their demand price (marginal utility to the consumers in the aggregate) is lower to those in which it is higher until they tend to be distributed in various uses (for the production of various commodities and services) in such a way as to equalize their marginal utilities in the various uses.

It is thus the demand price or marginal utility which determines how much of a particular factor of production will be utilized for the production of a particular commodity. The supply of a commodity, therefore, ultimately depends upon the attraction offered by the demand price (or marginal utility) to the relevant factors of production. If this demand price is not high enough, these factors will be used for the production of commodities the demand price for which is high enough to attract them.

Thus, the cost of production of a commodity is fundamentally the sum-total of retention prices that have to be paid to the productive services for retaining them in a particular industry, and this must at least be equal to what they can command elsewhere.

Application of Opportunity Cost Doctrine

The opportunity cost doctrine has a wide application in the field of economic theory. It applies to the determination of values both internally and internationally. It also applies to income distribution.

Limitations. There are, however, some limitations in its application: **(*i*) Specific.** It does not apply to productive services which are specific. A specific factor has no alternative use. Its transfer cost or opportunity cost is, therefore, zero. Hence, the payment made to this factor is of the nature of rent (preferably called non-cost outlays).

(*ii*) Inertia. Further, the doctrine of opportunity cost does not take into consideration the element of inertia. The factors may be reluctant to leave an occupation. In a case like this, where a factor's preference may have to be overcome, a payment exceeding the purely transfer cost will have to be made to induce it to an alternative occupation.

(*iii*) Non-pecuniary considerations. In view of these none-pecuniary considerations, the notion of objective costs must be given up. The theory of opportunity costs can be re-stated thus: "The cost of productive service X in making A is equal to the amount B that X could produce **plus (or minus)** the non-pecuniary returns (or cost) attached to producing B."[6] It has been suggested that non-pecuniary returns should be converted into pecuniary returns to restore objectivity to the theory. But it is not always possible to find a common monetary denominator for the purpose.

(*iv*) Factors Not Homogeneous. Besides, it should be remembered that units of productive service are rarely homogeneous.This obstructs their transfer.

(*v*) Wrong Assumption. Moreover, the theory is based on perfect competition which seldom exists.

(*vi*) Individual and Social Costs. Another discrepancy may arise on account of the difference in individual and social costs. A product may cost the factory owner Rs. 10 but to the society it will cost something in the form of ill-health due to the smoke that his factory sends out.

Conclusion. In spite of all these limitations and complications, the theory of cost, *viz.*, theory of opportunity or alternative costs, is the most acceptable one at present. Certain features of this theory are worth nothing:

(*i*) Cost of production of a commodity depends on demand prices of other commodities to thge production of which the same productive service can contribute.

(*ii*) This cost analysis is not vitiated by the fact that a commodity is produced by the combination of several factors because marginal product of each factor can be ascertained.

Social cost. It is the amount of cost the soceity bears due to industrilisation. Industrilasation has certain economic and social merits, but along with the merits, they bring about certain demerits also. They are like, development of slums, air-pollution, noise-pollution, land pollution, social inequalities, and so

6. Stigler, G.J, — *Theory of Price*, 1947, p. 108.

on. The amount of cost the scoiety bears due to industrilisation is referred as social cost. Bhopal Gas Tragedy is one of the major example of social cost. Poeple suffers from certain diseses for which the government has to incur heavy expenditure on health care and research.

Entrepreneur's Cost

In what follows, we shall use the term 'cost of production' in the sense of **money cost** or **expenses of production**. This is entrepreneur's cost.

The **entrepreneur's cost of production includes** the following elements[7] : ***(i)* Wages** of labour; ***(ii)* interest** on capital; ***(iii)* rent or royalties** paid to the owners of land or other property used; ***(iv)* cost of raw materials; *(v)* replacement and repairing charges** of machinery; ***(vi)* depreciation** of capital goods; and ***(vii)* profits** of the manufacturer sufficient to induce him to carry on the production of the commodity.

Entrepreneur's costs may be classified as –**(1)** production costs, including material costs, wage costs, interest costs, *etc.*, both direct and indirect costs **(2)** selling costs, including costs of advertising and salesmanship, **(3)** managerial costs and **(4)** other costs, including insurance charges, rates, taxes, *etc.*

SHORT-RUN AND LONG-RUN COST CURVES

After discussing the concept of cost as used in Economics, we are now in a position to study the nature of cost curves, both in the short run and the long run. The shape of the cost curve shows how a change in output affects the costs. There will be a shift in the cost curve, if factors, other than a change in output, have affected the costs.

Meaning of Short-run and Long-run

Short run is a period of time within which the firm can its output by varying only the amount of variable factors, such as labour and raw materials. In the short run, fixed factors, such as capital edquipment, top management personnel, *etc.*, cannot be varied. In other words, in the short run, the firm cannot build a new plant or abandon an old one. If the firm wants to increase production in the short run, it can do so only by overworking the existing plant, by hiring more workers and buying more raw materials. It cannot increase its output in the short run by enlarging the size of its existing plant or building a new plant of a larger size.The short run is a period of time in which only variable factors can be varied, while fixed factors remain the same.

On the other hand, **long run** is a period of time during which the quantities of all factors, variable as well as fixed, can be adjusted. Thus, in the long run output can be increased by increasing capital equipment or by increasing the size of the existing plant or by building a new plant of a greater productive capacity.

Social cost due to air pollution.

Short-run Fixed and Variable Costs

The cost of production for the entrepreneur may be analysed from another point of view. **Some costs vary more or less proportionately with the output, while others are fixed and do not vary with the output in the same way. The former are known as prime costs and the latter as supplementary costs of production or overhead costs.**

The supplementary or fixed costs must be paid even though production has been stopped temporarily. They include rent of the factory building interest on capital invested in machinery, and salaries of the permanently employed staff.

The prime costs, on the other hand, are variable costs. They vary with output.These costs include the cost of raw materials used in the making of the commodity as well as the costs of casual or daily labour employed. They are incurred only when the factory is at work.

The distinction between variable and fixed costs applies only to a short period. Nothing can remain fixed for a long time. In the long run, the staff would change, amount of capital invested would be different, the dimensions of the factory, too may change, and so on.

Hence, in the very long run, all costs are variable.

Total Fixed Cost. Total cost is the sum of Fixed cost (Factory land, building and machinery.....) plus the total variable cost (raw material charges, electricity.....)

7. For detail see Meade—*Economic Analysis and Policy,* pp. 2-5.

Cost of Production of a Firm

Units of output	*Total fixed cost*	*Total variable cost*	*Total cost* (2) + (3)	*Average fixed* cost (2) ÷ (3)	*Average variable* cost (3) ÷ (1)	*Average cost* (5) + (6)	*Morginal cost*
(1)	(2)	(3)	(4)	(5)	(6)	(7)	(8)
0	30	0	30	–	–	–	–
1	30	10	40	30	10	40	10
2	30	18	48	15	9	24	8
3	30	24	54	10	8	18	6
4	30	32	62	7.5	8	15.5	8
5	30	50	80	6	10	16	18
6	30	72	102	5	12	17	22

TC = TFC + TVC.

Total Fixed Cost = Total Fixed cost + Total variable cost

$$\therefore \quad AFC = \frac{TFC}{Q}$$

$$\text{Average Fixed Cost} = \frac{\text{Total Fixed Cost}}{\text{Quantity}}$$

$$AVC = \frac{TVC}{Q}$$

$$\text{Average Variable Cost} = \frac{\text{Total variable cost}}{\text{Quantity}}$$

$$\text{Average Cost} = \frac{\text{Total cost}}{\text{Quantity}} = \frac{TC}{Q}$$

or

Average cost = Average Fixed cost + Average variable cost

AC = AFC + AVC.

$$\text{Marginal Cost} = \frac{\text{Change in total cost}}{\text{Change in quantity}}$$

$$MC = \frac{\Delta C}{\Delta Q}$$

1. The total cost function is

$$C = 15x - 6x^2 + x^3.$$

Where as 'x' is out put and 'c' total cost.

Find out the following.

(a) Avergae cost function

$$\text{Average cost} = \frac{\text{Total cost}}{\text{Quantity}}$$

$$AC = \frac{TC}{x}$$

$$\therefore \quad AC = \frac{15x - 6x^2 + x^3}{x}$$

$$AC = 15 - 6x + x^2$$

(b) Minimum 'AC' or when is AC (Average cost) is minimum.

2. *(i)* The 'AC' to be minimum first derivation should be equal to zero, that mean

$$\frac{d}{dx}(AC) = 0$$

$$\frac{d}{dx}(15 - 6x + x^2) = 0$$

$$-6 + 2x = 0$$

$$\therefore \quad 2x = 6$$

$$x = 3$$

(ii) The second derivation of 'AC' should be greater then zero

$$\frac{d}{dx}(f) = -6 + 2x > 0$$

$$+2 > 0$$

Hence the condition is satisfied

Where x = 3 'AC' is minimum

(c) What is minimum 'AC'

Substitute in 'AC = 15 – 6x + x² the value of x = 3.

$$\therefore \quad 15 - 6 \times 3\,(3)^2$$

$$\therefore \quad 15 - 18 + 9$$

$$\therefore \quad 24 - 18 = 6.$$

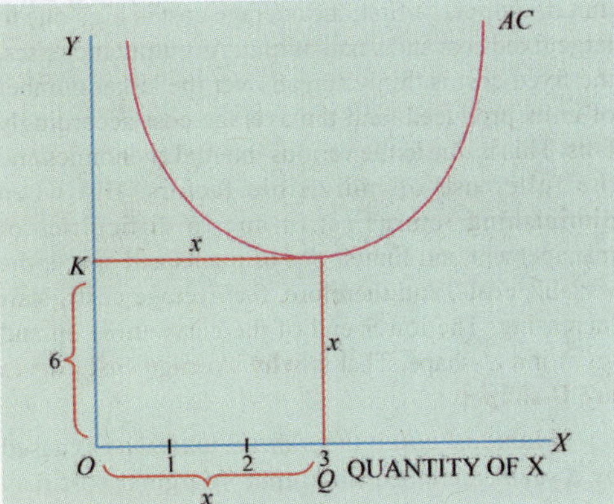

Fig. 20.1. Average cost is the cost per unit of output the AC is 'U' shaped curve.

(*d*) Marginal cost function

Marginal cost function is obtained by taking the derivation of total cost function.

$$TC = 15x - 6x^2 + x^3$$

$$\frac{d}{dx}(TC) = 15x - 6x^2 + x^3$$

$$\therefore \quad MC = 15 - 12x + 3x^2$$

(*e*) When is Marginal cost minimum

'MC' to be minimum the first derivation of 'MC' should be equal to zero.

(1) $\frac{d}{dx}(MC) = 15 - 12x + 3x^2$

$$\therefore \quad -12 + 6x = 0$$

$$\therefore \quad 6x = 12 \quad \text{or}$$

$$x = 2$$

(2) The second derivation of 'MC' should be greater then zero.

$$\therefore \quad -12 + 6x.$$

$$\frac{d}{dx}(MC)\ f'' = -12 + 6x$$

$$\therefore \quad +6 > 0.$$

Thus the condition is satisfied.

(3) How much is marginal cost.

$$15 - 12x + 3x^2$$

When x = 2 Marginal cost is minimum.

$$15 - 12x + 3x^2$$

Substitute x =2.

$$15 - 12 \times 2 + 3 \times (2)^2$$

$$15 - 24 + 12$$

$$\therefore \quad 27 - 24 = 3$$

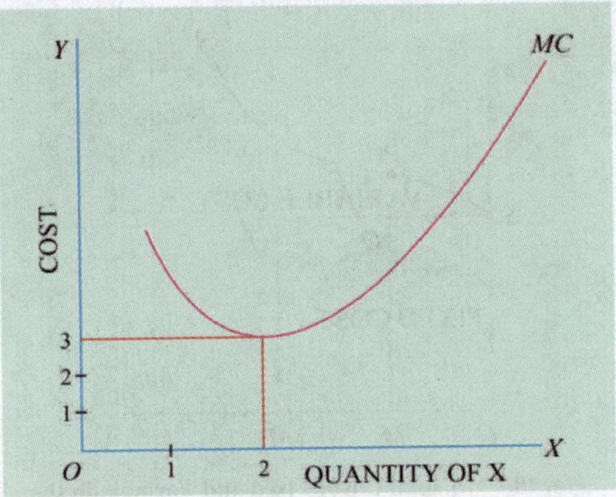

Fig. 20.2. Marginal cost curve is also U shaped. It depicts the slope (Ist derivative) of total cost curve.

Where x = 2 Marginal cost = 3 that is the 'MC' is minimum.

(*f*) When are average cost and Marginal cost equal.

At the point of minimum 'AC' 'MC' cuts AC' and that is the point when AC = MC.

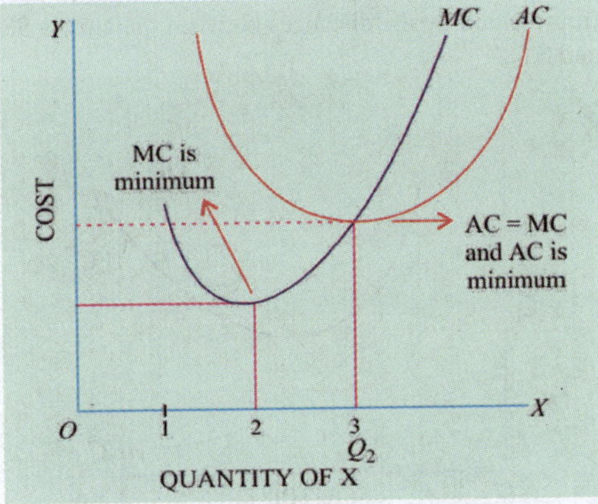

Fig. 20.3. Average and Marginal cost.

When x = 3 AC is minimum at the same point 'MC' is the cutting 'AC' thus AC = MC when x = 3.

Short Run: Total, Average and Marginal Costs

Study the above table.

Total cost of a given output is the sum of total fixed cost and total variable cost. As far as the toal fixed cost is concerned, it remains constant for all units of output, but we have to incur more variable costs, when output increases. Total variable cost is zero, when output is zero and it increases with an increase in output, though the rate of increase is not constant. At

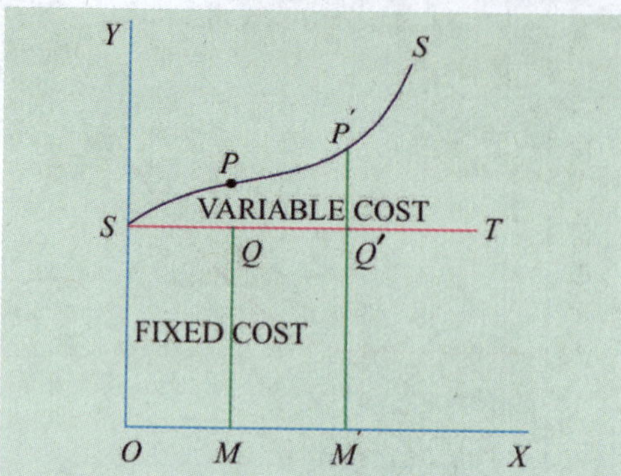

Fig. 20.4. (*a*) Total Cost : Fixed and Variable in the short run.

first it increase rapidly but, then, due to economies of larger production, it doesw not increase asfast as before, thought it jumps up rapidly at a later stage (when output increases from 4 units to 5 units) due to diseconomies that set in.

In Fig. 20.4 (*a*) SS is the total cost curve. It includesthe total fixed cost (the distance between the curve ST and X-axis) and the total variable cost (represented by the distances between the curves SS and ST).

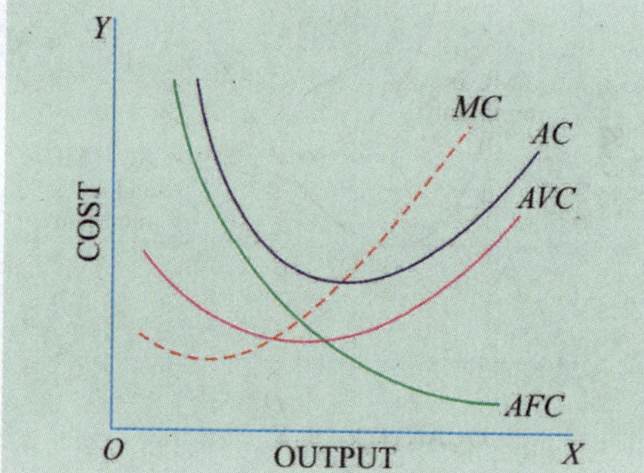

Fig. 20.4. (*b*) Average and Marginal Costs in the short run.

Average cost per unit is the total cost divided by the number of units produced. It is the sum of average fixed cost and the average variable cost. In Fig. 20.4 (*b*), we have drawn both the average fixed cost curve and the average variable cost curve.The total fixed cost being fixed for all units of output, average fixed cost is a falling curve in the shape of a rectangular hyperbola. Average variable cost curve (ACV) at first falls and then rises, as there emerge the diseconomies of the large production.

By adding the two costs, average fixed and average variable, we get the **average cost** (AC) per unit of output. At first, the average cost is high due to large fixed cost and small output. As output increases, the fixed cost is thinly spread over the larger number of units produced, and the average cost accordingly falls. This is due to the various internal economies and the fuller use of indivisible factors. But when diminishing returns set in due to difficulties of management and limitations of plants and space, the variable costs, and therefore, the average costs, start increasing. The lower end of the curve turns up and gives it a U-shape. That is **why average cost curves are U-shaped.**

Marginal cost is the addition to total cost caused by a small increment in output. Marginal cost may be defined as the change in total cost resulting from the unit change in the quantity produced. Thus, it can be expressed by the formula:

$$MC = \frac{\text{Change in Q}}{\text{Change in TC}}$$

Marginal cost curve (MC) in figurė 20.1 (b) also falls at first due to more efficient use of variable factors as output increases and then it slopes upward as further additions to the output interfere with the most efficient use of the variable factors.

Relation between Marginal and Average Costs

It can be seen that average variable cost continues to decline so long as the marginal cost is below it, but it starts rising at the point where MC crosses AVC. The marginal cost will always rise more sharply than the average variable cost. Similar relation holds between marginal cost and averagae cost.

Total-Marginal Cost Relationship

It can be seen from the table on page 214 that when total cost is increasing at increasing rate, its corresponding marginal cost is rising; when total cost is increasing at a decreasing rate, its corresponding marginal cost is falling; and when total cost has reached the maximum, *i.e.*, it is increasing at a zero rate, its corresponding marginal cost is zero.

It will be seen from the arithmetical table given on page 214 and Figure 20.1 (*b*) and Figure 20.4 that when marginal cost is less than average cost, average cost is falling, and when marginal cost is greater than average cost, average cost is rising. This marginal-average relationship is a matter of mathematical truism and can be illustrated by a simple example.

Suppose that a cricket player's batting average is 50. If in the next innings, he scores less than 50, say 44, his average will fall because his marginal (additional) score is less than his average score; if in the next innings he scores more than 50, say 58, his average will rise because marginal score is greater than his average score. If with the present average as 50, in the next innings, he scores just 50, then his average and marginal scores will be equal and his average score will neither rise nor fall.

In the same way, let us suppose that the average cost of a producer is Rs. 15. If by producing another unit, his average cost falls, the additional (marginal) unit must have cost him less than Rs. 15. If the production of the additional unit raises his average cost, the marginal unit must have cost him more than Rs. 15. And, finally, if his average cost remains unchanged, the marginal unit must have cost him exactly Rs. 15. In other words, in the third case, his marginal and average costs are equal. It is easier to remember this relationship between average and marginal costs with the help of Fig. 20.5.

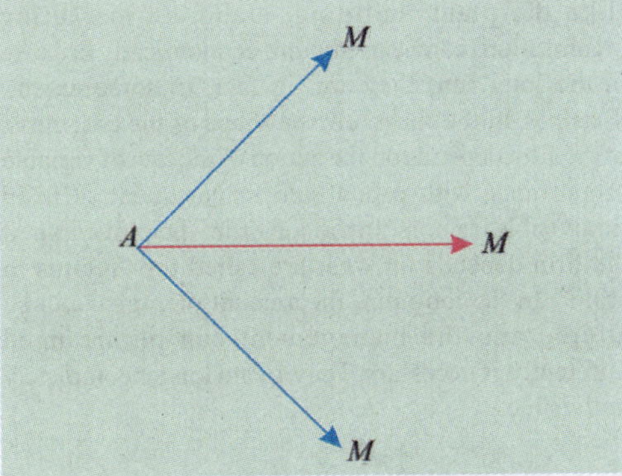

Fig. 20.5. Average and Marginal Relationship.

In Fig. 20.5, A represents average cost and M represents marginal cost. It is clear from this figure that when marginal cost is above a (greater than) average cost, average cost rises. It is as if marginal cost were pulling average cost up towards itself. Similarly, when marginal cost is below the average cost, average cost falls as if the marginal cost were pulling the average cost downwards. When marginal cost is the same as the average cost, average cost remains constant as if marginal cost were pulling average cost along horizontally.

We can see in Fig. 20.5 that so long as marginal cost curve lies below the average cost corve, the latter is falling, and where marginal cost curve lies above average cost curve, the average cost curve is rising. Therefore,at the point of inter-section, where marginal cost equals average cost, average cost curve has just ceased to fall but has not yet begun to rise. This, by definition, is the minimum point on the average cost curve.

It must be carefully understood that we cannot deduce about the direction in which marginal cost is moving from the way average cost is changing, that is, we cannot make any generalisation about whether marginal cost will be rising or falling when average cost is rising or falling. If average cost curve is falling, marginal cost must be below it but it (MC curve) may itself be rising or falling. If average cost curve is rising ,marginal cost curve must be above it, but it (MC curve) may itself be rising or falling. This can also be easily understood with the example of batting average.

Suppose that a player's batting average is 60. In his next innings he scores 54, his average score will fall to 57. But his present marginal score of 54 may well be greater than his previous marginal score. He might, for instance, have had a 'duck' in his previous innings so that his marginal score has risen considerably. But as long as average score is falling, marginal score whether rising or falling will be less than average score.

Deriving Marginal and Average Cost Curves from Total Cost Curve

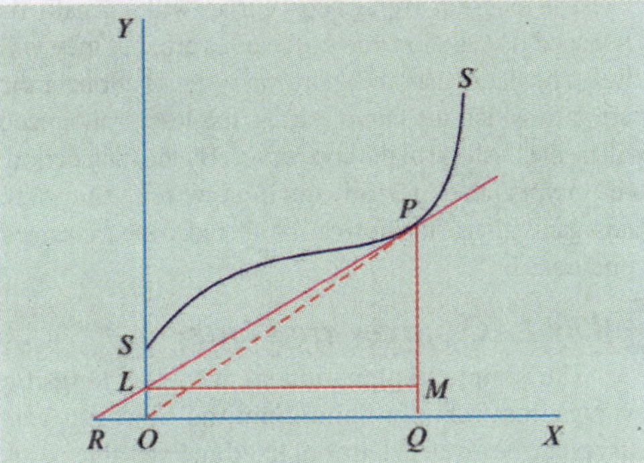

Fig. 20.6. Derivation of *AC* and *MC* Curves from Total Cost Curve.

In Fig. 20.6, SS is the total cost curve. To get the average and marginal cost for a given point P on the total cost curve, we proceed as follows:

Draw a straight line from P to the origin O. Then average cost at the point P equals the value of tangent of the angle (POX) that the st. line makes with the X-axis. In this figure, it is equal to PQ/OQ. Similarly, we can know the corresponding average costs at different points of the total cost curve. By joining all these points we get a U-Shaped average cost curve (AC in Fig. 20.6).

To know the marginal cost at the point P, we draw a tangent to the curve SS at the point P:

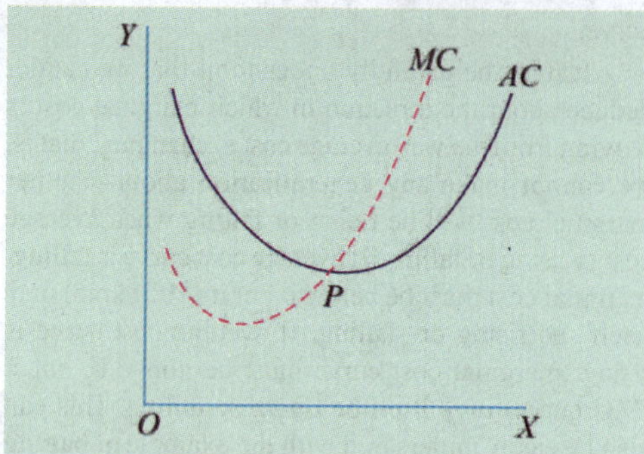

Fig. 20.7. *MC* and *AC* Curves.

Then the marginal cost corresponding to the total cost at P is given by the value of the tangent of the angle that RP makes with the X-axis. In this case, it is equal to the value of the tangent of angle PRQ and this equals PQ/RQ or which is the same thing as PM/LM.

Similarly, we can know the marginal cost at different points of the total cost curve and by joining them, we get the marginal cost curve (MC in Fig. 20.7).

LONG-RUN AVERAGE COST CURVES

The long-run average cost curves will normally be U-shaped just as short-run cost curves are, but they will always be flatter than the short-run ones. The longer the period to which the curve relates, the less pronounced will be the U-shape of the costcurves. By the long period, we means the period during which the size andorganisation of the firm can be altered to meet changed conditions.

Why LAC Curves are Flatter

The simple explanation of why the long-run average cost curve is flatter than the short-run cost curve may be given in terms of fixed and variable costs. It should be obvious that longer the period at the disposal of the producer, the fewer costs will be fixed and the more will be variable. Over a long period of time, there are very few costs which are just as great if output is small as they are if it is large. Over a long period, the size of the plant can be changed, unwanted buildings can be sold or let, administrative and marketing staff can be decreased or increased in order to deal efficiently with smaller or larger outputs and sales.

Thus, total fixed cost can be varied to a considerable extent over long periods, whereas in the short run its amount is fixed absolutely. In other words, the longer the period under consideration, the fewer costs are 'fixed' and more costs become 'variable'.

In the short run, a reduction in output will raise average costs because fixed costs will work out at a higher amount per unit of output. In the long period, however, the fixed costs can be reduced somewhat if output continues at a low level. Average fixed cost will, therefore, be lower in the long than in the short run.

Variable costs will not rise as sharply in the long run as they do in the short run. In the long run, the size of the firm can be increased to deal with an increased output more satisfactorily and the management can better tackle the various problems of larger output.

Thus, in the long run, average costs will be lower and the variable costs will not rise as sharply as in the short period. Hence, LAC cost curves are flatter than the short-run ones.

A more adequate explanation of the flatter long-run average cost curves may be given in terms of greater divisibility of the factors of production in the long run. In the long run, the indivisible factors of production (like the plant, building, elaborate marketing organisation) can be used more economically because in the long run, they are, in fact, to some extent, divisible. In the short run, the shape of the cost curve of the firm depends on the action of the law of variable proportions, with capital and management as fixed (indivisible) factors. In the long run, the cost curve of the firm depends on what are called the "returns to scale". In the long run, the amount of capital can be altered and the management can be arranged differently, if necessary. They are no longer completely indivisible.

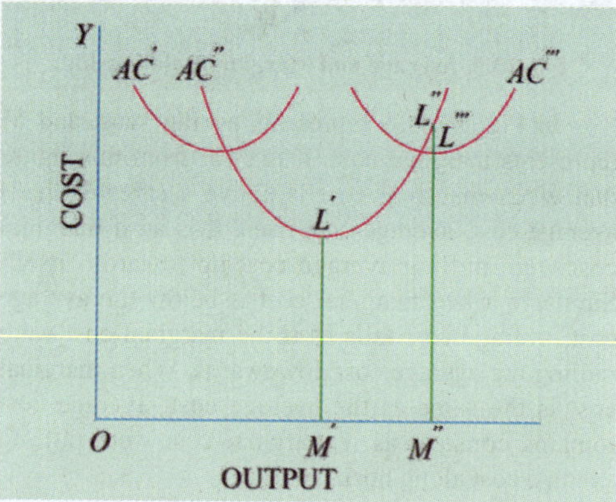

Fig. 20.7(*a*). Change the scale of operation.

If all the factors of production can be used in varying proportions, it means that the scale of operations of the firm can be changed. Each time the scale of operations is changed, a new short-run cost curve will have to be drawn for the firm. The accompanying figure (Fig. 20.7) will bring this out.

To begin with, let us suppose that the firm has the short-run cost curve
AC″. In that case, the optimum output will be OM′ at the lowest average cost M′L′. Now if output is desired to be increased to OM″, in the short run, it can be obtained at the average cost M″ L″ along the short-run cost curve AC″, because in the short run the 'scale' of operations is fixed. But, in the long run, a new and bigger plant can be built on which OM″ is the optimum output. That is, the firm now has the short-run average cost curve AC‴, and that by increasing the scale of its operations, the firm can produce the output OM″ at a cost of M″ L‴ instead of M″ L″.

Thus, it will have been seen that, at any given scale of operations, the firm will encounter regions of rising and falling costs, while in the long run the firm can produce on a completely different cost curve to the left or the right of the original one. For each different scale, there will be an output where average cost is at a minimum.

At this output, the firm is said to be producing at its **technical 'optimum',** given its scale of operations. Output is 'optimum' in the sense that average cost is at a minimum. Therefore, in the long run, the firm will be able to adjust its scale of operations so that it produces any given output at the lowest cost.

Look at the diagram (Figure 20.7). If the firm in question wishes to produce output OM′ it will find it best to produce at that scale which has the average cost curve SAC′. If OM″ quantity is desired, it will be best to produce on the curve SAC″, and for output OM‴ on the curve SAC‴. In each case, it will be producing the desired output at the lowest posible cost. It should, of course, be clearly understood that only in the long run can the scale of operations be altered; in the short run it will be fixed, and the average cost of output above or below the optimum level will necessarily rise along the short-run curve in question, whether it be SAC or SAC″ or SAC‴. A long- run average cost curve can, therefore, be drawn and it will show what the long-run cost of producing each output would be.

The shape of the long-run average cost curve will depend on the assumptions made. One assumption relates to the prices of factors. In the above examples, we have assumed constant factor prices. Various assumptions are, however, possible about the divisibility of factors of production. The simplest case is to assume that all factors are infinitely divisible and that there are no economies to be reaped from, for example, the division of labour. In other words, in the long run, all factors can be adjusted so that the proportions between them are the optimum ones and production can take place at the lowest point on the relevant short-run average cost curve. As will be seen from teh figure (Fig. 20.8), on this assumption the long-run cost curve of the firm LAC, is a horizontal straight line.

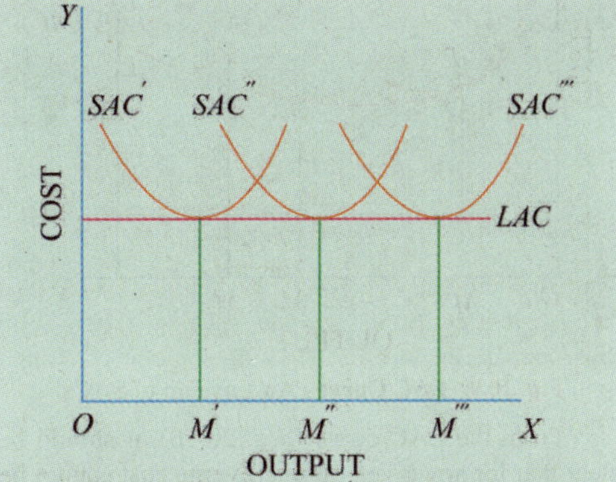

Fig. 20.8. Horizontal LAC Curve with Constant Factor Prices and Divisible Factors.

But this is not a realistic assumption. It is very unlikely that all factors are infinitely divisible even in the long run. And as output is increased, the firm may reasonably expect to reap some economies from the division of labour that will become more and more practicable as the scale of operations becomes larger.

It is common observation that some factors of production are indivisible. In particular, management is likely to be incompletely divisible. It is mere commonsense that an entrepreneur will be unlikely to produce twice a given output as efficiently as he produces a given output. It is, therefore, reasonable to expect that, even in the long run, firms will produce more cheaply at some scales of output than at others, if for no other reason, at least because, beyond a certain point, management becomes more difficult and less efficient. Certain combinations of factors will thus produce at lower costs per unit than others. This means that, in the more probable conditions, the short-run average cost curves of the firm will have different minimum points.

In the figure given below, it will be seen that the short-run average cost curve SAC_2 has a lower minimum point than either the curves SAC_3. The optimum output of the firm is obtained at point M. The long-run average cost curve, which is a tangent to all the short-run curves, will be the curve LAC. It will, therefore, be U-shaped itself. But, as will be obvious from Fig. 20.9, it will be flatter than the short-run cost curves–the U-shape will be less pronounced. Economists generally call this curve as **'envelope'**, since it envelops all the short-run curves. It is also called the "planning curve" of a firm.

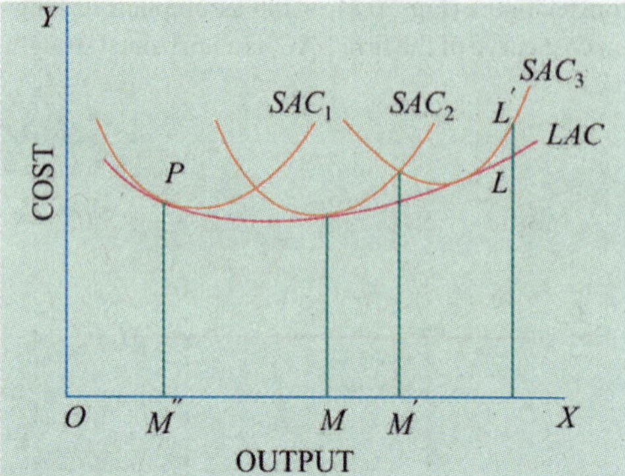

Fig. 20.9. LAC Curve : An Envelop of SACs.

From the LAC curve (Fig. 20.10), it should be clear that for any given output, averge cost cannot be higher in the long run than in the short run. After all, any adjustment in production which may be expected to cut costs, and which may be possible to make in the short-run, must also be feasible in the long run. On the other hand, in the short run, it is not always posible to produce a given output in the cheapest possible way. If a different output is to be produced, it is impossible to change the amounts used of all factors of production in the short run. While in the long run all possible adjustments can be made.

The conclusion, therefore, follows that at no point can the long-run average cost curve lie above a short-run average cost curve or the long-run average cost curve can never cut a short-run average cost curve, though they may be tangential to each other.

LONG-RUN MARGINAL COST CURVE

In diagram Fig. 20.10, we have drawn long-run marginal cost curve LMC from short-run average cost and marginal cost curves and long-run average cost curve. Just as every point of the continuous long-run average cost curve corresponds to some point of a short-run average cost curve, similarly every point of the continuous long-run marginal cost curve corresponds to some point on a short-run marginal cost curve.

If the output to be produced is OA, then in the long run it must be produced on point P on the short-run average cost curve SAC_1 and the long-run average cost curve LAC, because only point P minimizes the cost for output SAC_1. OA. Corresponding to point P on SAC_1 and LAC, there is a point R on the short-run marginal cost curve SMC_1. Then AR is the relevant short-run marginal cost for output OA in the long run. Therefore, the point R must lie on the long-run marginal cost curve corresponding to output OA.

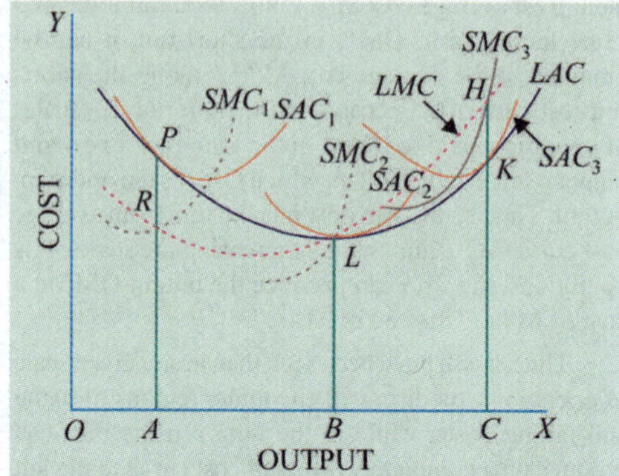

Fig. 20.10. Derivation of Long-Run Marginal Cost Curve.

If the output OB is to be produced, then in the long run it will be produced on point L on the short-run average cost curve SAC_2 and long-run average cost curve LAC, L is also the point on the short-run marginal cost curve SMC_2 corresponding to output OB. Therefore, point L must also lie on the long-run marginal cost curve corresponding to output OB.

Similarly, if output OC is to be produced, then in the long run it must be produced on point K of the short-run average cost curve SAC_3. Corresponding to K on SAC_3, the relevant point on the SMC_3 is H. Therefore, H must also lie on the long-run marginal cost curve corresponding to output OC.

By joining points such as R, L and H, we get long-run marginal cost curve LMC. The long-run marginal cost curve, like the long-run average cost curve, is U-shaped.

It is clear from Fig. 20.10 that the long-run marginal cost curve is flatter than the short-run marginal cost curves. This is what one would expect, because the U-shape of the long-run average cost curve is less pronounced than that of the short-run average cost curves. The relationship between the the long-run marginal cost curve and long-run average cost curve is the same as that between short-run marginal cost curve and short-run average cost curve. That is, when the long-run marginal cost curve lies below long-run average cost curve, the latter is falling and when the LMC curve lies above LAC curve, the latter is rising. The long-run marginal cost curve cuts the long-run average cost at the letter's lowest point. This is so because long-run marginal cost is equal to the long-run average cost when the latter is neither rising nor falling.

Why LAC curve first falls and then rises

That the LAC curve slopes downwards as the scale of production is enlarged is due to the various economies of scale, *e.g.*, (1) larger scope of specialisation of labour, (2) increasing use of specialised machinery, (3) other technological improvements.

The LAC curve rises after a point because of the various diseconomies of scale, *e,g.*, rising cost of the inputs and the difficulty of management, *etc.*

(These economies and diseconomies have already been discussed in detail in chapter 16.)

Optimum Plant. The plant is said to be of the optimum size which is operated at the point of its minimum average cost of production. It is the plant the minimum point of whose short-run average cost curve coincides with the minimum point of the long-run average cost curve. In Fig. 20.8, plant SAC_2 is opearated at its minimum cost of production for producing OB output. It is being used to its full capacity to turn over an optimum output. Any size of the plant which is either bigger or smaller than SAC_2 will be producing at higher average cost.

Optimum Output. In the Fig. 20.10, OB is the optimum output. It is optimum because it is the least cost output. If the output is smaller (e.g., OA) or larger (e.g., OC), it will be obtained at a higher cost of production as compared with OB output.

Optimum Firm. The firm which produces optimum output (i.e., the least cost output) with the optimum plant is called the Optimum Firm. In the Fig. 20.8, the firm producing OB output by operating SAC_2 plant is said to have achieved the optimum size. Since the minimum cost point of SAC_2 coincides with the minimum point of the long-run average cost curve, the optimum firm can also be defined as the firm which produces at the minimum point of the long-run average cost curve (LAC). The size of the optimum firm is different in different industries. For instance, it is smaller in agriculture and other extractive industries like mining, whereas it is bigger in manufacturing industries like automobile industry.

L-Shaped Long-run Average Cost Curve

We have said that the long-run average cost curves are U-shaped. But empirical studies have shown that the LAC curves are L-shaped, rather than U-shaped as in Fig. 20.11. We find that there is a rather rapid downward slope in the early part of the curve, *i.e.*, in the initial stages of production.

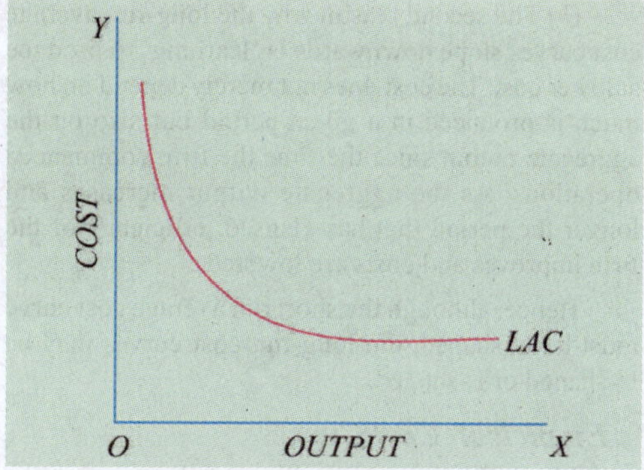

Fig. 20.11. **'L' Shaped LAC.**

The following reasons are given in support of this view:–

(a) Rapid technical progress brings about a sharp decline in unit cost. At first, the unit cost is high and remains quite high for an initial scale of production. But then the unit cost takes a downward course and remains constant so that the LAC curve is flat at the right, making the curve L-shaped. This is due to technical progress.

The figure 20.12 explains that, in absence of technical progress, the long run average cost curve is U-shaped, technical progress would convert it into an L-shaped curve. Initially, in the figure given above, the output is OM_1 and the unit cost is OC and the relevant long-run average cost curve is LAC_1, But when the output is expanded in response to increased demand to OM_2, the cost of production per unit is OC_1 on the curve LAC_1, which is quite high. But if technical progress is going apace, it may be possible to produce the same output at a unit cost of OC_2 on the curve LAC_2. This cost is much lower since a more modern plant has been installed due to technical progress. With further expansion of the output to OM_3 and technical progress gathering momentum, the unit cost drops further to OC_3 on the long run average cost curve LAC_3. It is thus that the long run average cost curve LAC takes L-shape.

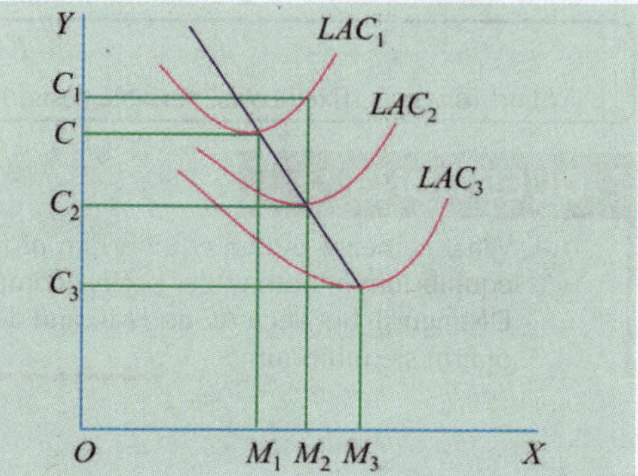

Fig. 20.12. **LAC falls with technical progress.**

(*b*) The second reason why the long-run average cost curves slope downwards is 'learning' to produce at lower cost. The cost does not merely depend on how much is produced in a given period but also on the aggregate output since the time the firm commenced operations. As the aggregate output increases and longer the period that has elapsed, efficiency of the firm improves and costs are lowered.

Hence, although the short run average cost curve must be U-shaped, the long-run cost curves may be U-shaped or L-shaped.

Empirical Cost Curves

Most of the cost curves that are discussed in the text books of economics are theoretical or conventional and they are U-shaped. But there are some cost curves of different shape which are to be found in the real world. They are called empirical cost curves.

Dish-Shaped Curve

An attempt has been made to reconcile the theoretical and empirical approaches. The U-shaped cost curves apply to cases where the plant is indivisible but can be used with changing quantities of variable factors. In such cases, change in output results though

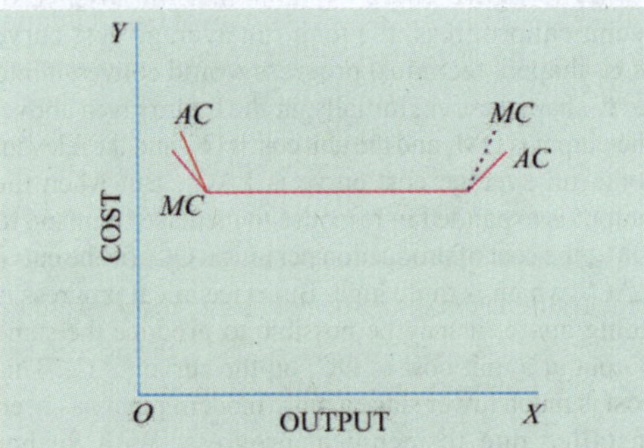

Fig. 20.13. Dish-shared *AC* and *MC*.

a change in variable factors when the returns are non-proportionate giving rise to U-shaped cost curves. But in the case of fairly divisible and fiexible plant, the cost curves may be horizontal over a range of output. When plant is divisible it is possible to maintain the factor proportion so that all the factors have to be increased in the same proportion as the increase in the output . The result is that the costs are cosntant under these circumstances the cost curves will be dish-shaped as shown in the following diagram (Fig. 20.13). You will notice that at first both Ac and Mc fall, then they remain constant for a wide range of output and then rise forming a sort of dish.

The U-shaped curve of the traditional theory was questioned by later economists both on theoretical and empirical grounds. For instance, George Stigler suggested that the short-run average variable cost curve has a flat stretch over a range of output so that the long-run cost curve is L-shaped rather than U-shaped. It has been argued that managerial diseconomics can be avoided by improved methods of modern management.

Inverse J Cost curves. More recently, the economists have questioned even the L-shaped cost curve. It has been said that there are economies of scale at all levels of output, although their magnitude becomes small beyond a certain scale of output. Hence, we get cost curves of the shape of inverse J, as is given below (Fig. 20.14).

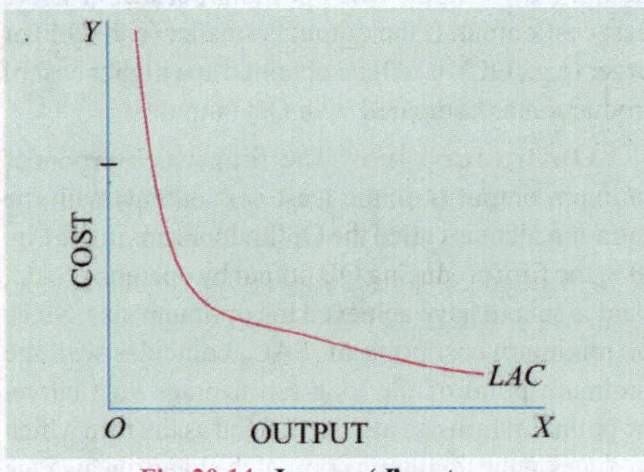

Fig. 20.14. Inverse '*J*' cost curve.

> ***Key terms***
>
> Short run costs, fixed costs, variable costs, Average costs, Marginal cost, Total costs, LAC, LMC.

QUESTIONS

1. What is meant by the equilibrium of firm and of the industry? Indicate the conditions of equilibrium of both under perfect competition.
2. Distinguish between AC and MC and discuss the significance of this distinction in the analysis of firm's equilibrium.

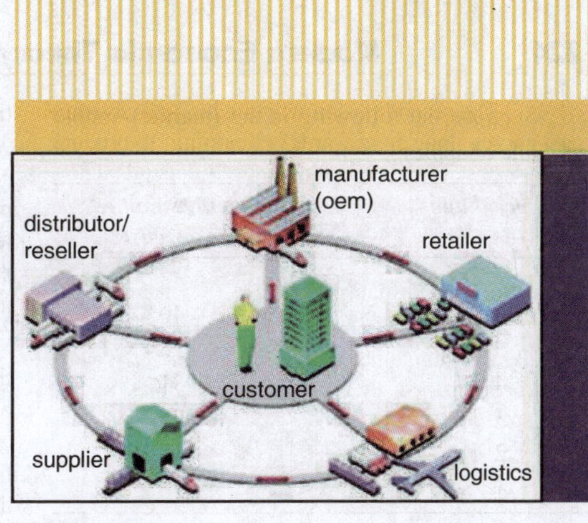

SUPPLY

Meaning

Supply means the amount offered for sale at a given price. "We may define supply as a schedule of the amount of a good that would be offered for sale at all possible prices at any one instant of time, or during any one period of time, for example, a day , a week and so on, in which the conditions of supply remain the same." (Meyers).

Supply should be carefully distinguished from stock. **Stock is the total volume of a commodity which can be brought into the market for sale at a short notice** and supply means the quantity which is **actually brought in the market.** For perishable commodities, like fish and fruits, supply and stock are the same because whatever is in stock must be disposed of. The commodities, which are not perishable, can be held back, if prices are not favourable. If the price is high, larger quantities are offered by the sellers from their stock. And if the price is low, only small quantities are brought out for sale. In short, **stock is potential supply.**

Law of Supply

Supply has functional relationship with price: **" Other things remaining the same, as the price of a commodity rises its supply is extended, and as the price falls its supply is contracted."** The quantity offered for sale varies **directly** with price, *i.e.*, the higher the price the larger is the supply, and vice versa.

Corresponding to the demand schedule already explained, we can construct an individual's supply schedule. Also, by totalling up the amount supplied at various prices by all the sellers in a market, we can obtain the supply schedule of the market. Supply shedule represents the relation between prices and the quantities that people are willing to produce and sell.

It will be seen that when price is as high as Rs. 7 per dozen as many as 43 dozen apples are offered for sale. As the price falls, the amount supplied decreases. When the price is as low as Re. 1 a dozen, only 10 dozen apples are offered for sale. This means that **as price falls supply is contracted, and as price rises supply is extended.** This is the Law of Supply.

Suppose the following is the (market) supply schedule of apples:

Price per dozen (Rs.)	*Quantity supplied (in dozens)*
7	43
6	40
5	36
4	31
3	25
2	18
1	10

The supply schedule given above can be represented in the form of a Supply Curve (Fig. 21.1 given below):

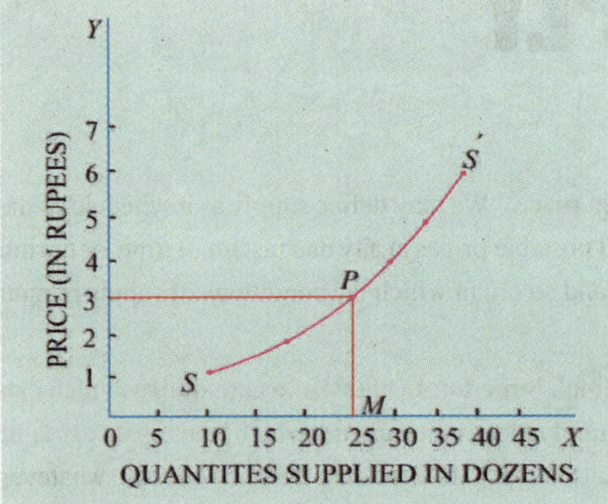

Fig. 21.1. Supply curve shows positive relationship between price of the commodity and quantity supplied.

In this diagram, quantities supplied are measured along OX, and prices along OY, SS′ is the supply curve. If from any point P on the supply curve, PM is drawn perpendicular to OX and PO′ to OY, then at PM (= O′ O) price, PO′ (= OM) quantity will be supplied.

It should be noted that the supply curve slopes downwards from right to left, as contrasted with the demand curve, which slopes from left to right. The reason is that as price falls demand is extended, but supply is contracted; and, conversely, as price rises demand is contracted, but supply is extended.

If the price falls too much, supply may dry up altogether. The price below which the seller will refuse to sell is called the **reserve price.** At this price, the seller buys his own stock, as it were.

ELASTICITY OF SUPPLY

When a small fall in price leads to great contraction in supply, the supply is comparatively elastic. But when a big fall in price leads to a very small constraction in supply, the supply is said to be comparatively inelastic. Conversely, a small rise in price leading to a big extension in supply shows elastic supply, and a big rise in price leading to a small extension in supply indicaties inelastic supply.

The elasticity of supply is really the measure of the ease with which an industry can be expanded and of the behaviour of the marginal costs. If a slight increase in price is followed by the entry of many new firms having minimum average cost equal to price and the marginal cost does not rise, the supply is said to be perfectly elastic. In case, however, the increased output can be obtained only by an infinite increase in price and no new firm is attracted to the industry, the supply will be inelastic. In between these two extremes, there will be different degrees of elasticity. The degree of elasticity will depend, in a particular case, on the slope of the marginal cost curve and the shape of the average cost curves of the successive firms.

The relation between price and the quantity supplied is rather like the relation between a whistle and a dog–the louder the whistle, the faster comes the dog; raise the price and the quantity supplied increases. If the dog is responsive–in economic terminology elastic–quite a small crescendo in the whistle will send him bounding along. If the dog is unresponsive or 'inelastic', we may have to whistle very loudly before he comes along at all."[1]

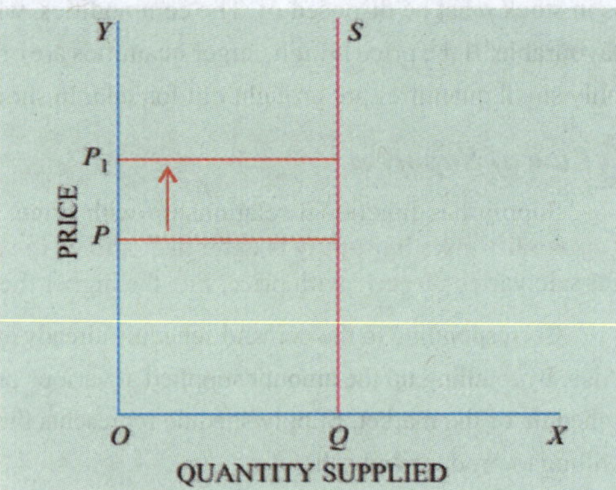

Fig. 21.2. Vertical supply curve implies zero elasticity.

Different types of elasticity of supply.

(1) Elasticity of supply when $\sum s = 0$

This means there is no change in quantity supplied due to change in price.

1. Boulding, K. —*Economic Analysis,* 1949, p. 128.

$$\therefore \quad \sum s = \frac{\Delta S}{\Delta P}$$

$$\therefore \quad \frac{O}{PP_1}$$

∴ This is when quantity supplied remains same even after price increases or decreases, then it is said to be perfactly inelasticity of supply.

In the above diagram price is increased from 'OP' to 'OP_1' but the quantity remained unchanged.

(ii) When elasticity of supply is infinite or $\sum s = \infty$.

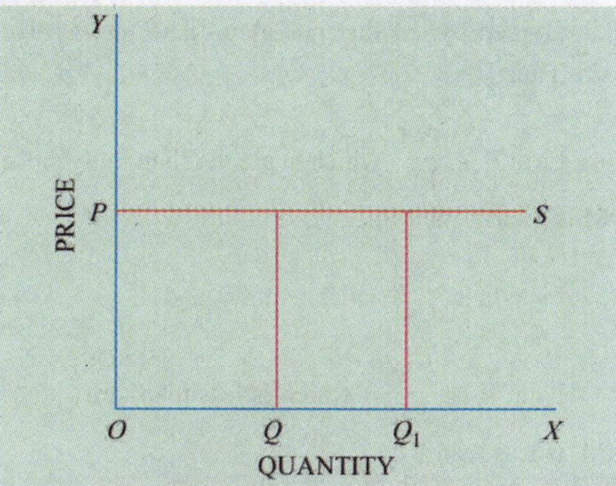

Fig. 21.3. Perfectly Elastic Supply.

$$\sum s = \frac{\Delta S}{\Delta P}$$

$$= \frac{QQ_1}{O}$$

(Numerator is changing and denominator is zero it is equal = ∝).

$$\sum s = \infty$$

In other words there is no change in price but there is change in quantity supplied this is known as '*perfectly elastic supply*'.

(iii) Elasticity of supply when $\sum s = 1$

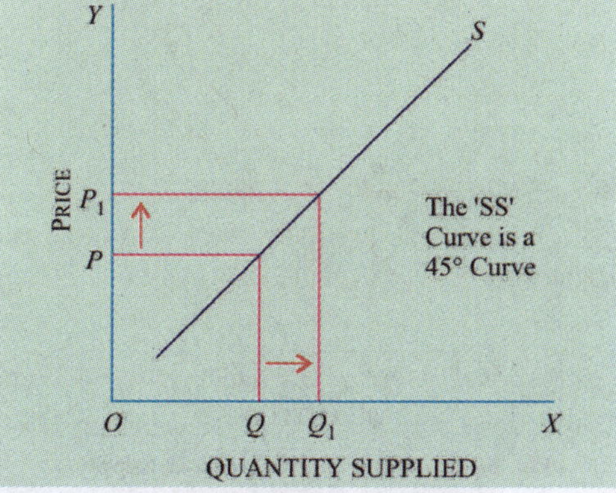

Fig. 21.4. Unitary Elastic Supply.

$$\sum s = \frac{\Delta S}{\Delta P}$$

$$\therefore \quad \frac{QQ_1}{PP_1}$$

Where $PP_1 = QQ_1$, This mean, the amount of change in price is equal to the amount of change in quantity supplied. This is known as '*Unit elastic supply*".

(iv) Relatively inelastic supply. $\sum s < 1$

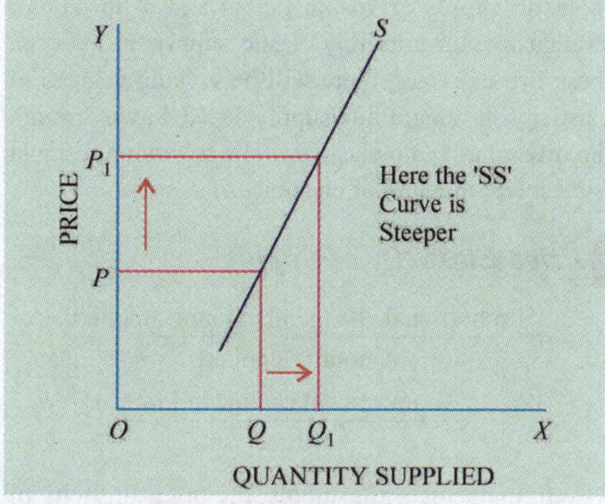

Fig. 21.5. Inelastic Supply.

$$\sum s = \frac{\Delta S}{\Delta P}$$

$$= \frac{QQ_1}{PP_1} \qquad \text{Where } PP_1 > QQ_1$$

In the above diagram the change in price is greater than the change in quantity supplied that means the price is changing more but the quantity supplied is relatively less. Hence this is referred as relatively inelastic supply.

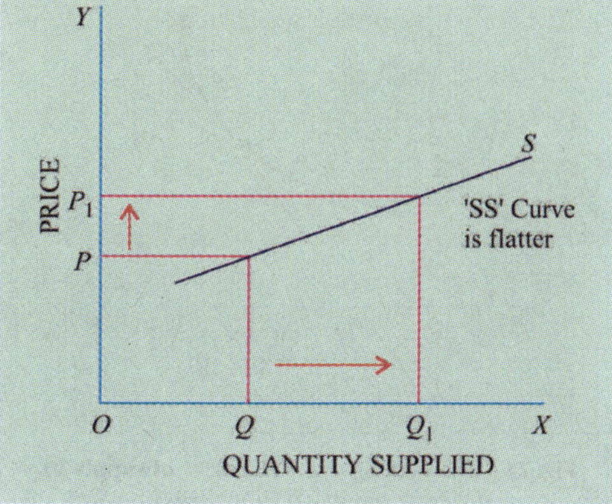

Fig. 21.6. Elastic Supply.

(*v*) Relatively elastic supply $\sum s > 1$

$$\sum s = \frac{\Delta S}{\Delta P}$$

$$= \frac{QQ_1}{PP_1} \qquad \text{Where } QQ_1 > PP_1$$

In the above diagram change in quantity supplied is more than chnage in price. Hence it is referred as relatively elastic supply.

Measurement of Elasticity of Supply

A vertical straight line will represent absolutely inelastic supply (zero-elasticity) and a horizontal straight line an infinitely elastic supply. In between these two extremes, there will be varying degrees of elasticity. A straight line supply curve drawn through the origin has a unit elasticity. The following formula is a general measure of elasticity of supply:

Price Elasticity of Supply

$$= \frac{\text{Proportional change in amount supplied}}{\text{Amount Supplied}} \div \frac{\text{Proportional change in Price}}{\text{Price}}$$

In mathematical symbols, the price elasticity of supply can be expressed as

$$Es = \frac{\Delta q}{q} \Big| \frac{\Delta p}{p}$$

Here Es is the price elasticity of supply,

q is the quantity supplied,

Δq is the proportional change in the quantity supplied.

p is the price of the good supplied,

ΔP is the proportional change in the price of the good.

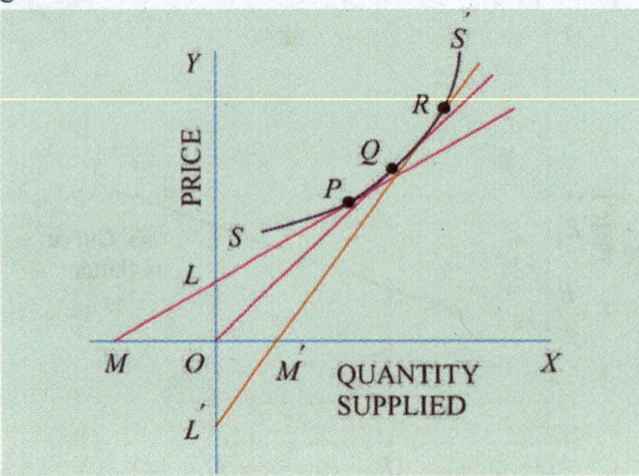

Fig. 21.7. Measuring price elasticity of supply at different points on supply curve.

The following diagrammatic method (Figure 21.7) is adopted for the measurement of the elasticity of supply:

SS′ is the supply curve and three tangents are drawn touching it at P, Q and R and are extended to intersect both axes. For instance, the tangent at P cuts the horizontal axis at M and the vertical axis at L; the tanget at Q cuts both at the origin O, whereas the tangent at R custs horizontal axis at M′ and vertical axis at L′. The price elasticity of supply at a point is measured by the distance along a tangent to the horizontal axis divided by the distance along it to the vertical axis. Thus,

Es at P is $\frac{PM}{PL}$ which is greater than unity since PM is greater than PL.

Es at Q is $\frac{QO}{QO}$ which is unity, and

Es at R is $\frac{RM'}{RL'}$ which is less than unity since RM′ is less than RL′.

Increase and Decrease in Supply

Economists usually say that, other things being equal, there is a unique demand and supply schedule at any given moment. But other things seldom remain the same. Hence, a change in supply and demand.

Supply is said to increase when, at the same price, more is offered for sale, or the same quantity is offered at a lower price. The supply is said to decrease, when, at same price, less is offered for sale or the same quantity is offered at a higher price. This is illustrated by the accompanying diagram (Fig. 21.8).

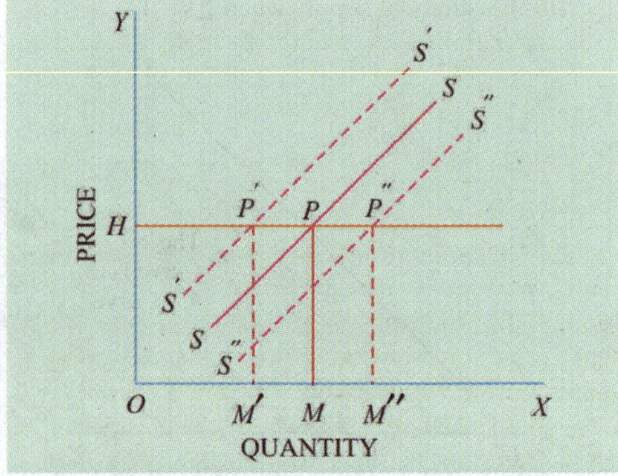

Fig. 21.8. Increase and Decrease in Supply.

Suppose SS is the supply curve before the change. S′ S′ shows a decrease in supply because at the same price PM (= P′ M′) less is offered for sale, *i.e.*, OM ′ instead of OM. S″ S″ shows an increase in supply because at the same price PM (= P″ M″) more is offered for sale, *i.e.*, OM″ instead of OM.

The student should carefully distinguish between the increase in quantity supplied (also known as extension of supply) and increase in supply. Increase in supply means that the whole supply curve has shifted to a new position to the right. It is a new curve altogether, whereas increase in the quantity supplied simply means that more is being offered at a higher price. The supply curve is the same. A movement along the same curve simply indicates changes in quantities offered as a result of a change in price It does not represnt any change in the supply schedule or conditions of supply.

Cause of Change in Supply

The increase and decrease in supply may take place on account of a number of factors:

(*i*) Cost of production a commidity may rise due to increase in the **costs of the various factors of production,** (or resource prices) like raw materials and intermediate products, used in its production. This will result in a decrease in supply. Conversely, a fall in the prices of such factors will lead to greater production and consequently an increase in supply.

(*ii*) As regards agricultural commodities, **better rainfall, improvement in irrigation, bigger doses of fertilizers, improved seeds** and **better methods of production** naturally would increase supply. On the country, **failure of rains, floods, fires, dust-strones, pests, earthquickes,** *etc*., will decrease the supply. Food supply recently increased in India owing to larger production brought about by the 'Green Revolution' and larger supply of agricultural inputs like fertilizers, water supply, pesticides, credit, *etc*.

(*iii*) Improvement in technique lowers cost of production and increases supply. On the other hand, **higher taxation** imposed on the output of a commodity or on the factors required for its production will decrease the supply.

(*iv*) Improvement in the means of communication and transport may increase the supply of a particular commodity if imports from foreign countries are encouraged. It may, however, reduce the supply if exports are facilitated.

(*v*) **Political Disturbances** or a war may disorganise or divert channels of trade and thus create scarcity of certain kinds of goods.

(*vi*) Supply may be consciously decreased by agreement among the producers, *e.g.*, agreement among the oil producing countries to cut back production. Also, a part of the supply may be destroyed in order to raise prices. During the Great Depression the production of rubber, tea and some other commodities was restricted through international agreements among the producers. Coffee was thrown into the sea in Brazil.

(*vii*) The supply of goods is also determined by the goals set by the producing firms for themselves. They can decide to produce more or less of a commodity or stop the production of one and undertake that of another.

Irrigation increases agricultural production and supply.

(*viii*) The supply of a commodity also depends on the price of that commodity and the prices of other commodities. Higher the price greater is the supply that will come forth: If the prices of other goods are more attractive, then the production of these commodities will be stimulated relatively to a particular commodity.

(*ix*) The supply also depends on the number of sellers. Entry of more sellers will increase and the exit will decrease the supply.

(*x*) **Sellers' Price Expectations.** If the sellers fear that the prices will fall in the future, they will hasten to unload the supply now and the supply will increase. On the other hand, expectation of rise in future will induce them to withhold supply and the supply will contract.

(*xi*) Taxation of output, sales, imports, *etc*., also affects the supply. By levying high import duties, a government may restrict the supply of a foreign commodity to encourage its production at home, Government may also restrict production of certain articles for reasons of health (*e.g.*, opium in India).

Conclusion. Thus, changes in prices, supply

of inputs, production techniques, monopoly control, and taxation are some of the factors which bring abount changes in supply.

SUPPLY FUNCTION

So far we have discussed the changes in supply in response to certain factors in simple, non-technical terms. We give below practically the same thing in technical terms.

The behaviour of the suppliers of goods follows a general and consistent pattern as they react to some identifiable set of functional supply determinants. Thus, the supply function identifies theimmediate determinants of supply for all goods. In other words, they explain variations in the quantity of goods supplied. This supply function can be put as under:

$$Qx = F (Px; P_Y; Pi, T, MT)$$

The supply function is merely a mathematical natation which reads as follows: The quantity supplied of any good Qx varies with the prices of that good Px, the price of ther goods Py, the price of factor inputs Pi, technology T and time periods MT. We analyse below these separate functional relationships.

Supply as a Function of Price

This functional relationship can be put in the form of an equation Qx = F (Px). This means that the quantity supplied of good X varies directly with its price. That is if the price of X goes up, its supply would increase, and vice versa. In other words the quantity supplied changes in the same direction as the price of the good concerned. That is, there is a direct functional relationship between a change in the price of a good and change in its quantity supplied. It leads to the law of upward sloping supply (See Fig. 21.1). However, direct relationship between price and quantity supplied is consistent but it is not irrefutable since there are some exception. Some factors other than mere change in price may determine the supply of a commodity e.g. change in tastes, weather, fashion, etc.

Supply as a Function of Price of other Goods

Albert O. Hirschman discusses in his book "**The Strategy of Economic Development** (Ch. 6) economic interdependence as it governs the supply of goods. According to him interdependent relationship in supply can be of two types: horizontal and vertical. There is horizontal relationship between goods when they are used at the same stage of production e.g. at the consumption or factor input level. In this case, the two goods compete with each other for the purchaser's choice. Consequently, there will be a unique, pecuniary linkage relationship between the two that is essentially a demand cross elasticity relationship.

Supply of goods.

But in the case of vertical relationship one good is an input for the production of another. A good has a forward linkage relationship when it is used as a factor input for another, but the good produced has a backward linkage relationship. Whatever the case may be there is an important functional relationship between the price of one good and the supply of another.

When the relationship is horizontal, it is almost always an inverse relationship. That is, if the price of one good rises the demand for the other good will increase. The coefficient of cross elasticity is negative. On the other hand, when the resource transferability is low as between production of say wheat and cars,coefficient of cross elasticity is low or zero.

In the case of forward vertical relationship, an increase in the price of the final product will induce a rise in the price of the factor input. The coefficient of cross elasticity will then be positive. The strength of relationship and the size of the coefficient will depend upon the extent to which one good is uniquely an input for another.

Supply as a Function of The Price of Inputs

The functional relationship between the supply of a good and the price of its factor inputs is a backward vertical relationship that is always negative. This means that as the price of factor inputs increases, the cost of production must go up which results in decrease in supply reflecting increased relative scarcity of the good. The size of the coefficient of cross elasticity for each of the several factor inputs will depend their relative importance in the production of goods.

Supply as a Function of Technology

It is obvious that technology is the most important determinant of the supply of goods. Applied technology reflects the entrepreneur's talent to make use of scientific discovery, invention and engineering advances in the production process. Technological advance results in the production of new goods, new efficiency levels in production, the development of the new industries and better resource distribution within industries.

Supply as a Function of Marshallian time periods

On the basis of time, Marshall clasified markets in time periods like the market (i.e. at a particular moment), short-run market, long run market, a very long period or secular market. Supply curves relative to time period are discussed in Ch. 27.

Key terms

Law of supply, Elasticity of Supply, Supply function, Change in supply.

QUESTIONS

1. Explain the law of Supply. What are its limitations ?
2. With the help of diagrams explain the elasticity of supply. How it can be measured at various points on a supply curve?
3. Explain increase and decrease in supply. Give the causes of change in supply.
4. What is supply function? Explain the determinants of supply.

UNIT IV

Product Pricing

Chapters

MARKET AND MARKET STRUCTURES

The father of economics Adam Smith in his book 'The Theory of Moral Sentiments' (1759), wrote about the main characteristics of human beings. According to him a human being is very selfish or posses self love as well as there exits an invisible hand. The concept of self-love in human being is one of the most important factor in "the value theory" as well as in the development of market.

"A human being weighs between what he pays and what he recieves "in return" This is one of the basic **characteristic of human being. Generally a human being carries out economic activities till a point where he** thinks that what I am paying is equal to what I am receiving. Human being willingly trade or carry out exchange till he feels that what I am giving is less and what I am receiving is more, once he realises that what I am giving is equal to what I am receiving, he stops, further trade.

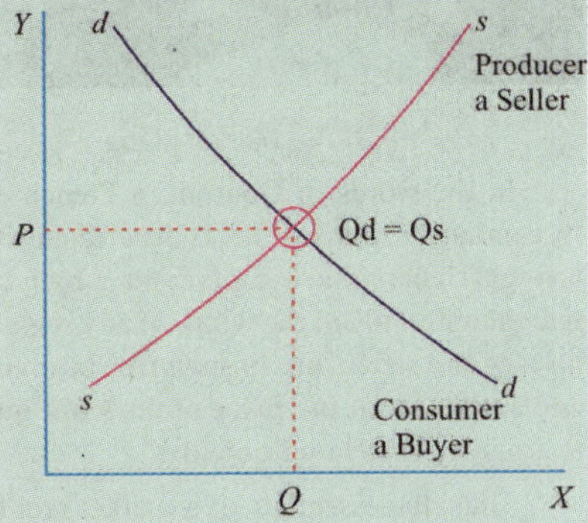

Fig. 22.1. Buyer and seller create market.

This is one of the basic philosophy of **(1)** Consumers, and the same thing in Marshallian words can be referred as consumer's surplus, on the other hand **(2)** Producer can be referred as producer surplus-Both the concept is based on human selfish motives of maximising returns in terms of their efforts (or money).

'dd' demand curve is derived from the consumers behaviour in relation to price. A consumer (demand curve) is intersted in paying least and want more in return at the point of price he feels that what he is giving is equal to what he is receiving. On the other hand a seller or producer (supply curve) is interested in getting the maximum price by giving less and less, at point 'P' he feels that what I am giving is equal to what I am receiving.

Price is determined at a place where 'dd' and 'ss' is equal. This is the concept referred as 'market'. On the basis of this 'market' the whole free enterprise or capitalistic economy is based.

Market plays an very important role in determining the shape, size and extent of the economy of a country. In value theory the,

(a) Clasical value theory is based an supply side concept (cost of production of a good).
(b) Neo-classicals, is based on demand side concept (utility of a good) and
(c) Modern-economic theorists takes into account both the supply side and demand side economics, that is nothing but the concept of market. (In other words demand and supply determines price).

MARKET

Meaning of Market

"Originally", says Jevons, " a market was a public place in a town where provisions and other objects were exposed for sale; but the word has been generalised so as to mean **any body of persons who are in intimate business relations and carry on extensive transactions in any commodity.** A great city may contain as many markets as there are important branches of trade, and these markets may or may not be localized . . . . But the **idea of locality is not neacessary.** The tradaers may be spread over a whole town, or region, or a country and yet from a market, if they are, by means of fairs, meetings, published price lists, the post-office or otherwise, in close communication with each other."[1]

Market place.

In the words of Cournot, a French economist, **"Economists understand by the term market not any particular market place in which things are bought and sold but the whole of any region in which buyers and sellers are in such free intercourse with one another that the price of the same goods tends to equality easily and quickly."**

Thus, the essentials of a market are: *(a)* a commodity which is dealt with; *(b)* the existence of buyers and sellers; *(c)* a place, be it a certain region, a country or the entire world ; and *(d)* such intercourse between buyers and sellers that only one price should prevail for the same commodity at the same time.

Classification of Markets

Markets may be classified :

(a) on the basis of **area** as **local, national** and **world markets;**

(b) on the basis of **time,** as **market price** on any particular day or moment, **short-period price, long-period price,** or **secular markets** covering a generation; and

(c) on the basis of nature of **competition** obtaining there in as **perfect markets** and **imperfect markets.**

Size of the Market

In the case of some commodities, the market is try wide covering the whole country or even the whole world, whereas in certain other cases, the size of the market is very limited covering a small village. The size of the market depends upon several factors:

Character of the Commodity. In order to have a wide market, a commodity must be *(i)* portable; *(ii)* durable; *(iii)* suitable for sampling, grading and exact description; and *(iv)* such as its supply can be increased. Such commodities are wheat, gold, government securities, *etc*. Bulky articles like bricks and perishable articles like fresh fruit and vegetables have a narrow market.

Nature of Demand. A commodity, which is in universal demand (*e.g.*, gold and silver) will have a wide market. Similarly, a commodity of general consumption has a wide market.

Means of Communication and Transport. The size of the market depends upon the extent to which means of communication and transport have been developed. A properly developed transport and communication system has enabled commodities be carried long distances and establish wide contacts. This has widened the markets.

Peace and Security. Obviously, goods cannot be marketed in distant places unless peace and ordeprevail. In war-time, due to insecurity in war zones, markets get restricted. Thus, the extent of the market depends on the peace prevailing in the region.

Currency and Credit System. If the currency and credit system of the country are well-developed, marketing can be conveniently and profitably carried on over extensive areas. The extent of the market very largely depends on the state of the currency and the confidence it inspires.

Policy of the State. Markets may be restricted by the policy of the State. Prohibitive duties and quotas restrict the market. The zoning system (*e.g.*, wheat zones) which allows free movement of goods only within a certain zone has the same effect. Thus, the Government policy can also affect the extent of the market.

1. Quoted by Marshall–Economics of Industry, pp. 134 -35.

Degree of Division of Labour. We know that division of labour is limited by the extent of the market. The converse of this is also true. That is, the extent of the market also, in its turn, depends upon the degree of division of labour. The greater the division of labour the cheaper the articles and wider the market.

Perfect and Imperfect Markets

A distinction is made between perfect market and imperfect market. **"A market is said to be perfect** when all the potential sellers and buyers are promptly aware of the prices at which transactions take place and all the offers made by other sellers and buyers, and when any buyer can purchase from any seller and conversely. Under such a condition, the price or a commodity will tend to be the same (after allowing for cost of transport including import duties) all over the market." **Thus the prevalence of the same price for the same commodity at the same time is the essential characteristic of a perfect market.**

On the other hand, a **market is said to be imperfect** when some buyers or sellers or both are not aware of the offers being made by others. Naturally, therefore, different prices come to prevail for the same commodity at the same time in an imperfect market. In a perfect market, on the other hand, the same price rules throughout the market.

Conditions of a Perfect Market

For a market to be perfect the following conditions are essential:–

(*i*) Free and Perfect Competition. In a perfect market, there are no restrictions either on the buyers or on the sellers. They should be absolutely free to buy from or sell to anybody they like. In other wor there should be no monopolies.

Transport and communications.

(*ii*) Cheap and Efficient Transport and Communication. Same price for the commodity will not rule if the information about changes in prices cannot be quickly transmitted or if the commodity cannot be cheaply and speedily transported. Hence, efficient transport and communication system is essential for a perfect market.

(*iii*) Wide Extent. A perfect market is sometimes considered synonymous with a wide market. We have already discussed above the extent on which the extent of the market depends. In order to have a wide market, a commodity should be portable, durable, gradable and should have a wide demand.

Let us now examine some cases and find out whether the markets are perfect or imperfect.

Market for invested capital (stocks and shares) is the nearest approach to a perfect market, since the stock exchange markets are highly organised.

Market for precious metals, first-class bills of exchange, foreign currencies and important raw materials are also efficiently organised and may be regarded as perfect.

Market for Consumers' goods, which are retail markets, are less perfect. Retail prices differ appreciably in different localities.

Producers' goods are, as a rule, purchased wholesale; the markets for such goods are more perfect.

Labour market is mostly imperfect. This is due to the comparative immobility of labour, their weak bargaining power and the ignorance that generally prevails in labour circles.

The market for real estate is relatively perfect. Owing to big amounts involved, the buyers take a lot of trouble before they make a purchase.

In the money market, the rate of interest vries according to the risk of default and the period of the loan. Hence, money market may be regarded as imperfect. It is especially so in India.

MARKET FORMS OR MARKET STRUCTURES

The type of market depends on the degree of competition prevailing in the market. Broadly speaking, there are two types of competition prevailing in the markets: *(i)* Perfect competition and *(ii)* Imperfect competition.

Perfect Competition and Pure Competition. Modern economists draw a distinction between perfect competition and pure competition. Perfect competition is a wider concept. In order that there should be perfect competition, the market should satisfy not only the conditions of pure competition but also a few more, as we shall show on the next page.

Imperfect competition may also take several forms, *e.g.*, monopolistic competition, oligopoly, duopoly or monopoly.

Thus, at one extreme stands perfect competition and at the other monopoly. In between these two extremes, there are all degrees of competition or lack of competition.

The following chart shows at a glance different types of market forms on the basis of the nature of competition:–

Type of the market	*No. of Firms*	*Nature of the commodity*
A. Perfect Competition		
Perfect or pure competition	Infinite	Homogeneous
B. Imperfect Competition		
(a) Monopolistic Competition	Many	Differentiated
(b) Perfect Oligopoly	A few	Homogeneous
(c) Imperfect Oligopoly	A few	Differentiated
C. Pure or Absolute Monopoly		
Pure or Absolute Monopoly	One	Homogeneous

Now we shall study these forms in some detail. We take first pure and perfect competition.

Pure Competition

Pure competition is said to exist when the following conditions are fulfilled:–

(i) Large Number of Buyers and Sellers. One condition of pure competition is that there should be operating in the market a large number of buyers and sellers. If that is so, no single seller or purchaser will be able to influence the market price, because the output of any single firm is only a small proportion of the total output and of the total demand. Hence, market price has to be taken as given and unalterable by every purchaser and seller. Thus, no individual purchaser can influence the market price by varying his own demand and no single firm is in a position to affect the market price by varying its own output. "Thus the market price is a parameter to be reacted to rather than a variable to be determined."

(ii) Homogeneous Product. The second condition is that the commodity produced by all firms should be standardised or identical. In case all farms produce Kalyan-S wheat, it is immaterial for the purchaser as to who has produced it. He can buy it as well from the other. This condition ensures that the same price rules in the market for the same commodity. The product of each firm is a perfect substitute for the products of all other firms in the industry.

It is the purchaser's opinion which will determine whether the products are identical or not. Even if the products are really identical, the purchaser may have a prejudice against the output of a particular firm and may consider it different. Hence, under pure competition, the consumers do not differentiate between the products of different firms.

When the quality is the same, the commodities are perfect substitutes for one another and their cross-elasticity is infinity. In these circumstances, if a firm raises its price, it will lose all the customers. It can sell as much as it likes at the prevailing price. Why should it then think of lowering its price? Hence, a firm cannot raise its price nor need it lower it. That is why the prevailing market price is accepted and acted upon by all the dealers.

If the above two conditions, *viz.*, homogeneous product and large number of buyers and sellers, are fund in a market, it is said to be under **pure competition.**

Shape of Demand Curve in Pure Competition

When there is pure competition, the average revenue curve (AR) or demand curve of a firm is a horizontal straight line which means that any firm can sell any quantity at the prevailing price. Since the number of firms is very large, no individual firm has the power to vary the market price. Also, since the products are identical from the consumer's point of view, the price paid by them cannot be different. This is represented by the following diagram. (Fig. 22.2.)

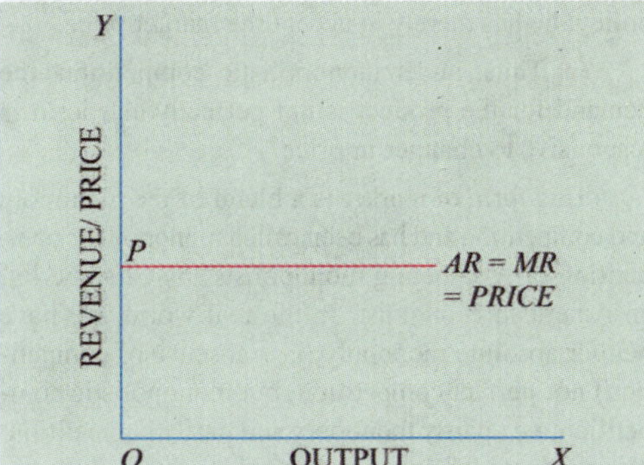

Fig. 22.2. Average Revenue Curve or Sales Curve of a Firm Under Perfect Competition

OX and OY are the two axes. Along OX is represented the output and along OY the Price/Revenue. At OP price, a seller can sell as much as he likes. He cannot charge more and he will not charge less. If he raises the price, he will lose all his customers and if he charges less, he will be unnecesarily losing.

Examples of pure competition are to be found in the case of farm products, *e.g.*, wheat, cotton, rice, *etc*. In this case, there is a large number of producers, each producing an in significant portion of the total market supply. In other fields, we seldom come across pure competition.

Perfect Competition: Conditions

There is said to be perfect competition when every purchaser and seller is so small relative to the entire market that he cannot influence the market price by increasing or decreasing his purchases or his output.

Perfect competition is a wider term than pure competition. Besides, the two conditions of pure competition mentioned above, *viz*., the homogeneity of the product and the existence of a large number of dealers, several other conditions must also be fulfilled to make it a perfect competition.

Thus, the conditions of perfect competition are:–

(i) Large number of buyers and sellers.

(ii) Homogeneous product.

(These conditions of pure competition have already been discussed above.)

***(iii)* Free Entry or Exit.** There should be no restrictions, legal or otherwise, on the firms' entry into , or exit from, the industry. In this situation all the firms will be making just normal profit. If the profit is more than normal, new firms will enter and extra profit will be competed away; and if , on the other hand, profit is less than normal, some firms will quit, raising the profits for the remaining firms. But if there are restrictions on the entry of new firms, the existing firms may continue to enjoy supernormal profit. Only when there are no restrictions on entry or exit, the firms will earn normal profit.

***(iv)* Perfect Knowledge.** Another assumption of perfect competition is that the purchasers and sellers should be fully aware of the prices that are being offered and accepted. In case there is ignorance among the dealers, the same price cannot rule in the market for the same commodity. When the producers and the customers have full knowledge of the prevailling price, nobody will offer more and none will accept less, and the same price will rule throughout the market. The producers can sell at that price as much as they like and the buyers also can buy as much as they like.

***(v)* Absence of Transport Costs.** If the same price is to rule in a market, it is necessary that no cost of transport has to be incurred. If the cost of transport is there, the prices must differ to that extent in different sectors of the market.

***(vi)* Perfect Mobility of the Factors of Production.** The mobility is essential in order to enable the firms to adjust their supply to demand. If the demand exceeds supply, additional factors will move into the industry and in the opposite case, move out. Mobility of the factors of production is essential to enable the firms and the industry to achieve an equilibrium position.

Mrs. Robinson thus defines perfect competition: "When the number of firms being large, so that a change in the output of any of them has a negligible effect upon the total output of the commodity, the commodity is perfectly homogeneous in the sense that the buyers are alike in respect of their preferences (or indifference) between one firm and its rivals, then competition is perfect, and the elasticity of demand for the individual firm is infinite."[2]

2. Robinson, J.— *The Economics of Imperfect Competition*, 1954, p. 51.

Here is a comprehensive definition: "Perfect competition is the name given to an industry or to a market characterised by a large number of buyers and sellers all engaged in the purchase and sale of a homogeneous commodity, with perfect knowledge, of market prices and quantities. no discrimination and perfect mobility of resources."[3]

Chamberlin thus brings but the distinction between pure competition and perfect competition: "Purity requires only the absence of monopoly, which is realised when there are many buyers and sellers of the **same** (perfectly standardised) product. Perfection is concerned with other matters as well: mobility of resources, perfect knowledge, *etc*. . . . .Perfection is a different thing from its purity, meaning by the latter its freedom from monopoly elements."[4]

Imperfect Competition

Imperfect competition takes three main forms:–

(a) Monopolistic Competition,

(b) Oligopoly, and

(c) Monopoly.

We shall briefly describe below these forms of imperfect competition.

Monopolistic Competition

The main features of monopolistic competition are as under:–

(i) Under monopolistic competition, the number of dealers is not large; at any rate not so large as under perfect competition.

(ii) The products are not homogeneous; they are, on the other hand, differentiated, inter alia, by means of different lebels attached to them such as different brands of toilet requisites.

(iii) Either in ignorance or on account of transport costs or lack of mobility of the factors of production, same price does not rule in the market throughout. Rather different prices are charged by different producers for products which are really similar, but are made to appear different through advertisements, high pressure salesmanship and labelling and branding. The result is that each producer comes to have a hold on a clientele from whom he can charge higher prices.

3. Spencen, Milton H.— *Contemporary Economics*, 1971, p. 380.
4. Chamberlin E.— *The Theory of Monopolistic Competion*, 1956, p. 25.

(iv) Under monopolistic competition, the demand curve or sales curve or what is also called average revenue (AR) curve, is not a horizontal straight line. It is, on the other hand, a downward sloping curve. This means that the seller can sell more by reducing price, whereas under perfect competition, he need not reduce the price for he can sell any amount at the prevailing price. Under monopolistic competition, the producer can charge higher prices, because his customers are attached to him.

The seller can thus have a price policy of his own, whereas a seller under perfect competition has no price policy; he has merely to accept the market price.

(v) Thus, under monopolistic competition, the demand for the product is not perfectly elastic; it is responsive to changes in price.

This form of market is a blend of the monopoly and competition and has been called monopolistic competition or 'competing monopolists' by Chamberlin, an American economist. In the real world, we have neither absolute monopoly (*i.e.*, absence of competition) nor perfect competition, but monopolistic competition, *i.e.*, partly monopoly and partly competition. The products are not complete substitutes for one another but they are close substitutes.

As mentioned already, monopolistic competition is only one form of imperfect competition where there is a fairly large number of sellers but products are differentiated. Other forms of imperfect competition are oligopoly andordinary monopoly.

Oligopoly

When in a market, there are only a few sellers of a product, it is called **Oligopoly.** The basic characteristic of an oligopolistic situation is the fact that every seller can exercise an important influence on the price-output policies of his rivals. This is due to the fact that the number of sellers is not very large and each seller controls a substantial portion of the supply. Every seller, therefore, is so influential that his rivals cannot ignore the likely adverse effect on them of a given change in the price-output policy of any single manufacturer. This rival consciousness, or the recognition on the part of the seller of the fact of interdependence, is the most important feature of oligopolistic situations.

Oligopoly differs from monopoly and monopolistic competition in this that, in monopoly, there is a single seller; in monopolistic competition, there is quite large number of them; but in oligopoly, there is only a small number of sellers.

Oligopoly Without Product Differentiation

Under oligopoly, the pricing theory is fundamentally the same as in other forms of competition with this difference that the larger the number of firms the greater will be differences in marginal costs and more remote will be the possibility of collusion or agreement whether tacit or explicit. When they all deal in a standardised product and each is producing a considerable portion of the total output, the price and output policy of each producer is likely to affect the others appreciably, but none can foretell precisely how. The price which will be fixed in oligopoly without product differentiation is thus indeterminate.

Oligopoly With Product Differentiation

In case there is product differentiation, monopoly agreements are even less likely. Since products are not similar, any producer in oligopoly can raise or lower his price without any fear of losing customers or immediate reactions from his rivals. Cut throat competition is unlikely. However, keen rivalry among them may create conditions of monopolistic competition. The price, in the long run, may settle at a level between the monopoly price and that in cut-throat competition.

Monopoly

When there is monopoly, a single producer or seller controls the entire market. There are no substitutes for his product. He controls the entire supply and he can fix the price. He is the firm and he also constitutes the industry. It is a one-firm industry. Thus, under monopoly, the distinction between the firm and industry disappears. The average revenue (AR) curve (or the demand curve) always slopes downwards to the right as in monopoly competition, but it is less elastic in monopoly than in monopolistic competition. In monopoly, there is no need to differentiate products because no close substitutes are available. It is one product, homogeneous and completely under the control of the monopolist.

Market Classifications and Cross Elasticity of Demand

Some economists (*e.g.*, Triffin) have used the concept of cross elasticity of demand for measuring the extent of competition among the firms. In this way, on the basis of the cross elasticity of demand an attempt has been made to classify the market structures. In other words, we can distinguish between the various types of market situations on the basis of cross elasticity of demand. Stonier and Hangue observe in this connection, "In perfect competition, the cross elasticity of demand for the product of a single firm with respect to a change in the price of the rest of industry will be infinite. That is to say, the proportionate fall in the demand for the product of a single firm will be infinitely large compared with any given proportionate fall in the price of the product of the whole industry. Similarly, in monopolistic competition, the cross elasticity of demand for the product of a single firm with respect to a change in the price of the other products made in the monopolistic 'group' will be very high. The cross elasticity of demand for the product of a monopolist with respect to a fall in the price of other products in the economy will be very low."[5] In other words, when the cross elasticity of demand is infinite, it is a case of perfect competition; when it is very high it is a case of monopolistic competition and when it is very low, it is a case of monopoly.

But cross elasticity of demand is a very unsatisfactory measure of the extent of competition pervailing in the market. It has been pointed out by some economists (*e.g.*, Chamberlin) that cross elasticityof demand of any perfectly competitive firm is zero (and not infinity). As mentioned above, under monopoly also cross elasticity of demand is zero. Hence on the basis of cross elasticity, the two market situations of pure competition and pure monopoly are lumped together whereas they are two opposite extreme cases. In a perfectly competitive situation, cross elasticity of demand is zero because a firm is producing a product that has so many identical substitutes produced by other firms. Hence if a purely competitive firm tries to raise its price, its product will be ousted by the homogeneous products of other firms.

Cross elasticity as a criterion for classification of markets is also criticised on the ground that it ignores "the two basic determinats of market structure: the degree of closeness or remoteness of substitution among products and the number of firms in the relevant group or industry."

Thus, we may conclude that cross elasticity of demand, as a criterion of market classification, is not satisfactory. The best way to classify markets is, therefore, on the basis of number of firms in the industry and the nature of the product (that is, closeness or remoteness of substitutability).

5. Stonier A. W. and Hague, D.C. –*A Text Book of Economic Theory*, IV Edition, p. 244.

CRITERIA FOR CLASSIFICATION OF MARKET

We have already given classification of markets. The following criteria for the classification of markets have been suggested:

(1) *Substitutability of Products*

This criterion refers to the existence and closeness of substitutes i.e. the extent and form of competition among the firms in the industy. This criterion may be measured by the conventional price cross-elasticity (ep) for the products of any two firms (i & j)

$$ep.\,ji = \frac{dqj}{dpi} \cdot \frac{pi}{q\,j}$$

This formula measures the degree to which the sales of the firm are affected by the price charged by the firm in the industy. If the elasticity is high, the products of the two firms will be close substitutes. In the case of perfect substitutes (*i.e.* homogeneous products), the price cross-esasticity between every pair of producers approaches infinity. On the other hand, if the products are differentiated, but can be substituted for one another, the price cross-elasticity will be finite and positive. If products are not substitutes, their price cross-elasticity will tend to zero.

(2) *Inter-Dependence*

This refers to the extent to which firms in the industry take into account the reactions of competitors. This criterion is related to the number of firms in the industry and the degree of differentiation of the products. If the number of firms is large, no firm will take into account the actions of the rivals and each firm will act atomistically. But if there are only a few firms in the industry, they will all be alert as to what the rivals may be doing and mould their own policy accordingly.

The degree of interdependence of the firms will be measured by an unconventional quantity cross-elasticity for the products of any two firms, thus

$$eqji = \frac{dpi}{dqj} \cdot \frac{qi}{pj}$$

This formula measures the proportionate change in the price of jth firm resulting from an infinitesimally small change in the quantity produced by the ith firm. The higher the value of this elasticity the stronger the interdependence of the firms. In case the number of the firms in the industry is large, each firm will tend to ignore the reactions of the competitors whether the products are close substitutes or not. In a case like this, the quantity cross-elasticity between each pair of the producers will tend to be zero. But if the number of firms in the market is small e.g. oligopoly, there will be marked interdependence even when the products are differentiated. The quantity cross-elasticity in this case will be finite.

In the case of a monopolist both elasticities will be zero, because there is only one firm in the industry and there are no close substitutes.

(3) There is the third criterion. viz the **condition of entry** i.e. whether new firms are free to entry into the industry without let or hindrance or not.

The 'condition of entry' has been defined by the expression

$$E = \frac{P\,a - P\,c}{P\,c}$$

Here E is the condition of entry, Pc price under pure competition and Pa price actually charged.

Key terms

Market, Perfect competition, Monopoly, Monopolistic Competition, Oligopoly.

QUESTIONS

1. Explain the concept of market. Give criteria for classification of market.
2. Explain the concept of equilibrium price.
3. Discuss the main features of following firm's in short.
   (i) Perfect competition *(ii)* Monopoly *(iii)* Monopolistic competition *(iv)* Oligopoly

REVENUE AND REVENUE CURVES

In an earlier chapter (No. 20), we have discussed cost and cost curves. Parallel to these we have revenue and revenue curves. We explain below marginal revenue and average revenue and their inter-relationship.

MARGINAL REVENUE AND AVERAGE REVENUE

Meaning

Average revenue is the revenue per unit of the commodity sold. It is found by dividing total revenue by the number of units sold. But since different units of a commodity are sold at the same price, in the market, average revenue equals price at which the commodity is sold. Thus, **average revenue means price.** Since the consumer's demand curve is a graphic relation between price and the amount demanded, it also represents the average revenue or price at which the various amounts of a commodity are sold, because the price offered by the buyer is the revenue from seller's point of view. Therefore, **average revenue (AR) curve of the firm is really the same thing as demand curve of the consumer.**

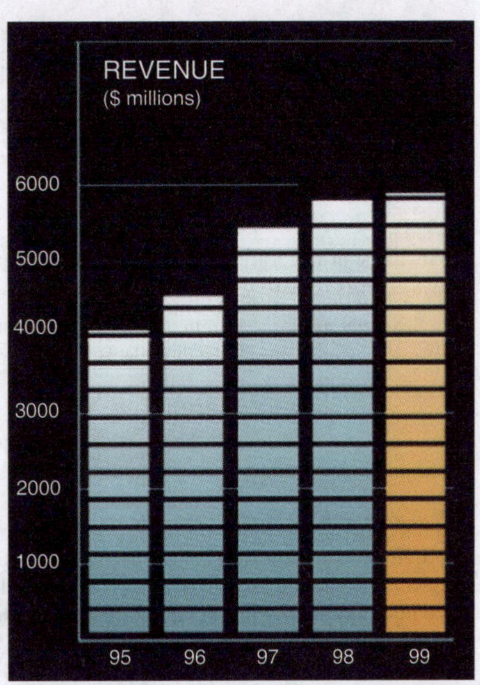

On the other hand, **marginal revenue** at any level of **firm's** output is the net revenue earned by selling **another (additional) unit** of the product. Algebraically, it is the addition to the total revenue earned by selling 'n' units of product instead of n–1, where n is any given number. The word **net** in this definition is important. If the price of a product falls when more of it is offered for sale then that would involve a loss on the previous units which were sold at a higher price before and will now be sold at the reduced price along with the additional one. This loss in the previous units must be deducted from the revenue earned by the additional unit.

Suppose a firm is selling 7 units of the output at the price of Rs. 16 per unit. Now if it wants to sell 8 units instead of 7 and thereby the price of the product falls to Rs. 15 per unit, then the marginal revenue will not be equal to Rs. 15 at which the eighth unit is sold. Seven units, which were sold at the price of Rs. 16 before, will now all have to be sold at the reduced price of Rs. 15 and that will mean the loss of one rupee on each of the previous 7 units. The total loss on the previous units would be equal to Rs. 7. Therefore, this loss of 7 rupees should be deducted from the price of Rs. 15 of the eighth unit while reckoning the marginal revenue. The marginal revenue in this case, therefore, will be Rs. 15- Rs. 7 = Rs. 8 and not Rs. 15 which is the average revenue.

The marginal revenue can also be directly found by taking out the difference between the total revenues before and after selling the additional unit as follows:

Total revenue when 7 units are sold at the price of

Rs. 16 = 7 × 16 = Rs. 112

Total revenue when 8 units are sold at the price of

Rs. 15 = 8 × 15 = Rs. 120

Therefore, Marginal Revenue or the net revenue earned by the 8th unit = 120 – 112 = Rs. 8

Thus, Marginal Revenue of the nth unit.

= difference in total revenue in increasing the sale from n – 1 to n units.

Or

= Price of nth unit minus loss in revenue on previous units resulting from price reduction.

Generally speaking, marginal revenue is less than price as indicated by the above formula. But in perfect competition, when a firm can sell any amount at the ruling market price, marginal revenue is equal to average revenue or price since there is no loss incurred on the previous units.

Relationship Between AR and MR

Let us consider the relationship between marginal, average and total revenue at previous levels of output more fully with the help of a table given below. This table represents a situation of a hypothetical firm.

Table 1. Total, average and Marginal Revenue Schedules

Number of units sold	*Price or Average revenue*	*Total Revenue AR × Quantity sold*	*Marginal Revenue (addition made to total revenue)*
(1)	(2)	(3)	(4)
1	22	22	22
2	21	42	20
3	20	60	18
4	19	76	16
5	18	90	14
6	17	102	12
7	16	112	10
8	15	120	8
9	14	126	6
10	13	130	4

In the above table, Column 2 shows the Average Revenue, while Column 4 shows the marginal revenue. Marginal revenue has been derived from the total revenue column of the table. Thus, in going from two to three units the marginal revenue is 18 and this is found out by subtracting 42 from 60, and so on. The Table further indicates that when average revenue is falling, marginal revenue is less than average revenue.

(*i*) Total Revenue = Price × Quantity

$$TR = P \times Q.$$

(*ii*) $\text{Average Revenue} = \dfrac{\text{Total Revenue}}{\text{Quantity}}$

$$\therefore \quad AR = \frac{TR}{Q}$$

(*iii*) $\text{Marginal Revenue} = \dfrac{\text{Change in Total Revenue}}{\text{Change in Quantity}}$

$$MR = \frac{\Delta TR}{\Delta Q}$$

Example 1. If the demand curve is given as $P = 10 - 4\,Q$, then find.

(*i*) the total revenue TR, and

(*ii*) the marginal revenue MR

$$TR = P \times Q.$$

$$= (10 - 4\,Q) \times Q$$

$$\therefore \quad TR = 10\,Q - 4\,Q^2 \qquad ...(i)$$

Marginal revenue = Derivation of total revenue

$$\frac{d}{dx}(TR) = MR = 10\,Q - 4\,Q^2.$$

$$MR = 10 - 8\,Q = 0$$

$$\therefore \quad 8\,Q = 10$$

$$\therefore \quad Q = \frac{10}{8} = \frac{5}{4}$$

Under Perfect Competition. When competition is perfect, as already seen, the average revenue curve of the firm is a horizontal straight line. This is so because an individual firm under perfect competition, by its own action, cannot influence the price. The seller under perfect competition can sell any amount of the commodity at the ruling market price. In this case, when average revenue curve is the horizontal line the Marginal Revenue curve coincides with the Average Revenue curve. This is so because additional units are sold at the same price as before and no loss is incurred on the previous units which would have resulted if the sale of additional units would have forced the price down.

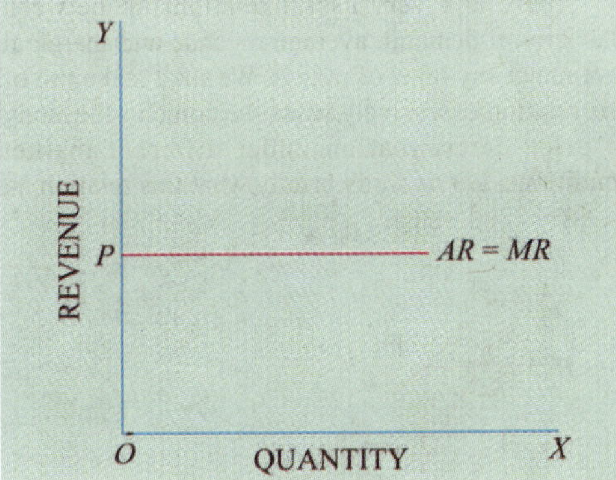

Fig. 23.1. ***AR* and *MR* Curves Under Perfect Competition.**

The average revenue and marginal revenue curves of a firm under perfect competition are shown in Fig. 23.1.

Under Imperfect Competition. By converting the schedules of Average Revenue given in table along side into curves, we get two downward sloping curves and find that marginal revenue curve is below average revenue curve. This is shown in Fig. 23.2 AR is the Average Revenue Curve and MR, the dotted curve, is the Marginal Revenue Curve. As we shall see in a later chapter, the divergence between the average revenue and marginal revenue as shown in the figure here is actually found when a firm is working under conditions of monopoly or imperfect competition. It is quite obvious that when price is falling as indicated by the declining AR curve, the marginal revenue must always be less than average revenue, because a falling price must mean some loss on the sale of additional supply. That is why MR curve lies below AR curve.

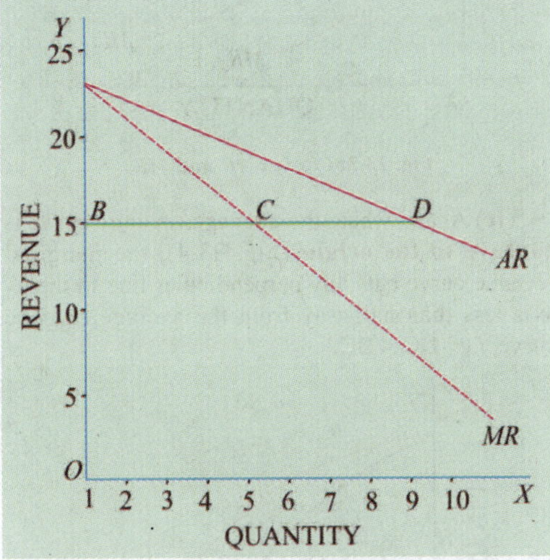

Fig. 23.2. ***AR* and *MR* Curves Under Imperfect Competition.**

How much is MR below AR? We have seen above that when average revenue curve falls downward, the marginal revenue curve lies below it (or to the left of it). Now the question arises how far to the left (or below) will it lie? This will depend on the shape of the AR and MR curves: **(*a*)** They may be straight downward sloping lines; or **(*b*)** they may be convex to the origin; or **(*c*)** they may be concave to the origin.

(*a*) When both the marginal revenue curve and average revenue curve are straight lines and sloping downwards, as shown in Fig. 23.2, the marginal revenue curve will cut in the middle of any line perpendicular to the Y-axis. That is, if from D, any point on the average revenue curve, we draw DB a perpendicular to the Y-axis, then marginal revenue curve MR must pass through the middle of this perpendicular, *i.e.*, through C where DC = BC.

(*b*) However, if the average revenue curve is **convex to the origin,** as in Fig. 23.3, the marginal revenue curve MR cuts any line perpendicular to the Y-axis **more than half-way** from the average revenue curve, *i.e.*, DC > BC.

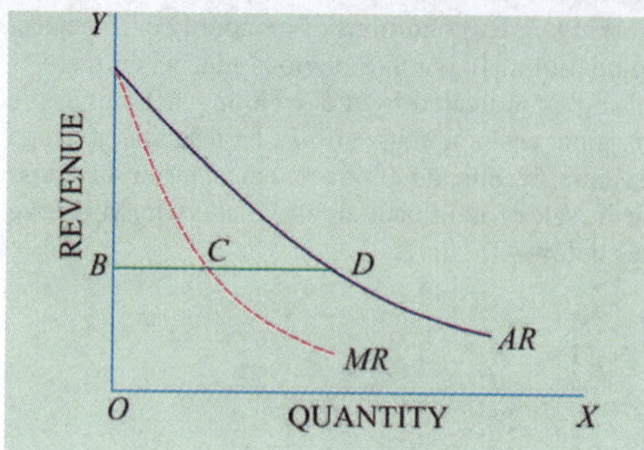

Fig. 23.3. **Convex *AR* and *MR*.**

(*c*) Again, where the **average revenue curve is concave to the origin** (Fig. 23.4), the marginal revenue curve cuts any perpendicular line to the Y-axis less than half-way from the average revenue curve, *i.e.*, DC < BC.

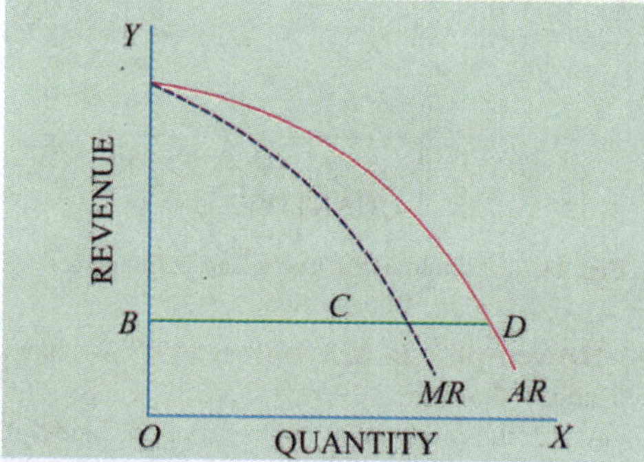

Fig. 23.4. **Concave *AR* and *MR*.**

Revenue curve in oligopoly market

In oligopoly market the demand curve is of a kinky nature. It is referred as kinky demand curve.

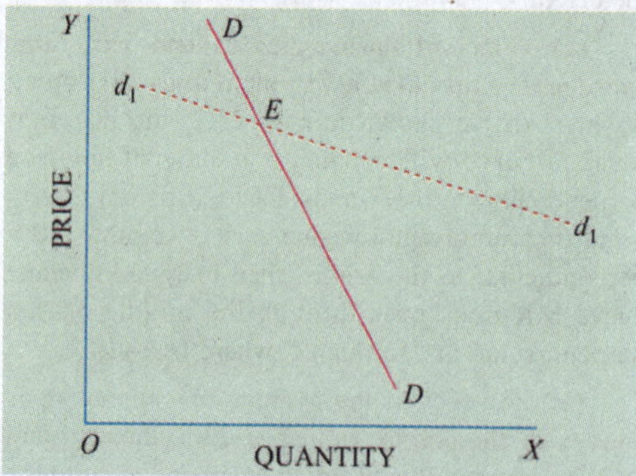

Fig. 23.5. **Demand under oligopoly.**

In the above diagram. x-axis is quantity and y-axis is price. 'DD' total market demand curve, whereas 'd_1d_1' individual firm demand curve, but this firm is a leader which is selling maximum output. Hence in the oligopoly the demand curve takes the slope of 'd_1 E D'. It is having a bend (kink) at point E.

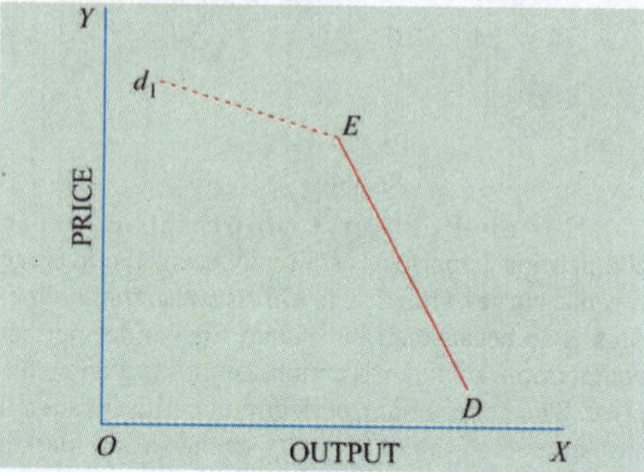

Fig. 23.6. **Kinky demand curve.**

The above diagram shows the 'kinky demand curve' concept of oligopoly market.

Elasticity of demand, Average Revenue and Marginal Revenue

There is a very useful relationship between elasticity of demand, average revenue and marginal revenue at any level of output. We shall make use of this relation extensively when we come to the study of price determination under different market conditions. Let us study briefly what this relation is.

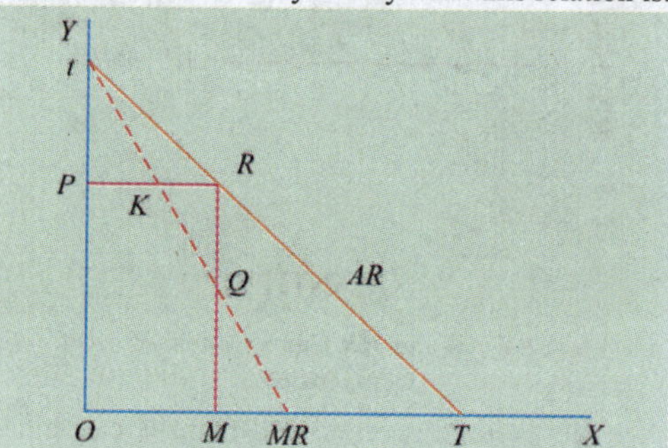

Fig. 23.7. ***AR*, *MR* and price elasticity of demand.**

We have stressed above that the average revenue curve of a firm is really the same thing as the demand curve of consumers for the firm's product. Therefore, elasticity of demand at any point on a consumer's demand curve is the same thing as the elasticity on the given point on the firm's average revenue curve. We have already seen how elasticity of demand at any point on the demand curve is measured.* With this measure of point elasticity of demand, we can study the relationship between average revenue, marginal revenue and elasticity of demand at any level of output.

In Fig. 23.7, AR and MR respectively are the average and the marginal revenue curves. Elasticity of demand at point R on the average revenue curve

$$= \frac{RT}{Rt}$$

Now, in triangles PtR and MRT

$\angle tPR = \angle RMT$ (right angles)

$\angle tRP = \angle RTM$ (corresponding angles)

$\angle PtR = \angle MRT$ (being the third angle)

Therefore, triangles PtR and MRT are equiangular,

Hence $\frac{RT}{Rt} = \frac{RM}{tP}$ ...(*i*)

In the triangle PtK and KRQ

$PK = RK$

$\angle PKt = \angle RKQ$ (vertically opposite)

$\angle tPK = \angle KRQ$ (right angles)

Therefore, triangles PtK and RQK are congruent (i.e. equal in all respects).

Hence $Pt = RQ$ ...(*ii*)

From (*i*) and (*ii*) we get

$$\text{Elasticity at R} = \frac{RT}{Rt} = \frac{RM}{tP} = \frac{RM}{RQ}$$

Now it is obvious from fig. 23.5 that

$$\frac{RM}{RQ} = \frac{RM}{RM - QM}$$

$$\text{Hence, elasticity at R} = \frac{RM}{RM - QM}$$

It will also be clear from the figure that RM is average revenue and QM is the marginal revenue at the output OM which corresponds to the point R on the average revenue curve. Therefore,

Elasticity at

$$R = \frac{\text{Average Revenue}}{\text{Average Revenue} - \text{Marginal Revenue}}$$

If, A stands for Average Revenue

M ,, ,, Marginal Revenue

e ,, ,, point elasticity on the average revenue curve

Then $e = \frac{A}{A - M}$

It follows from this that

$$eA - eM = A$$

$$\therefore \quad eA - A = eM$$

$$\therefore \quad A(e - 1) = eM$$

* See Chapter 11 on the Elasticity of Demand, p. 86.

$$\therefore \quad A = \frac{eM}{e - 1}$$

Hence $A = M\left(\frac{e}{e-1}\right)$

And also $M = A\left(\frac{e-1}{e}\right)$

The general rule therefore is : At any output,

Average Revenue = Marginal Revenue × $\frac{e}{e-1}$ and

Marginal Revenue = Average Revenue × $\frac{e-1}{e}$, where *e* stands for point elasticity of demand on the average revenue curve.

With the help of these formulae, we can find marginal revenue at any output from average revenue at the same output, provided we know the point elasticity of demand on the average revenue curve. If the demand elasticity of a firm's average revenue curve is equal to one, marginal revenue equals zero, because

$$M = A\left(\frac{e-1}{e}\right)$$

$$= A\left(\frac{1-1}{1}\right)$$

$$= A \times 0$$

$$= 0.$$

Similarly, when demand elasticity on a firm's average revenue curve is 2, the marginal revenue equals half the average revenue. This is because

$$M = A\left(\frac{e-1}{e}\right)$$

$$= A\left(\frac{2-1}{2}\right)$$

$$= A\left(\frac{1}{2}\right)$$

$$= \frac{1}{2}A.$$

By applying the formula for various elasticities of demand at different points (or at different levels of output) on the average revenue curve, it will be found that marginal revenue is always positive at any point or output where the elasticity of the average revenue curve is greater than one, and marginal revenue is always negative where the elasticity of the average revenue curve is less than one.

RELATIONSHIP BETWEEN AR, MR, TR AND ELASTICITY OF DEMAND

By making use of the formula given above MR $= AR\ \frac{e-1}{e}$, where MR is marginal revenue, AR is average revenue and **e** is elasticity of demand, we can find out the relationship between AR, MR and TR on the one hand and elasticity of demand on the other.

If the elasticity of demand **e** is equal to one then

$$MR = AR\left(\frac{e-1}{e}\right)$$

$$= AR \times \left(\frac{1-1}{1}\right)$$

$$= AR \times \frac{0}{1} = 0$$

Similarly, it can be shown that if e > 1, MR is Positive and if e > 1, MR is negative.

The relationship can be illustrated by the following diagram (Fig. 23.8)

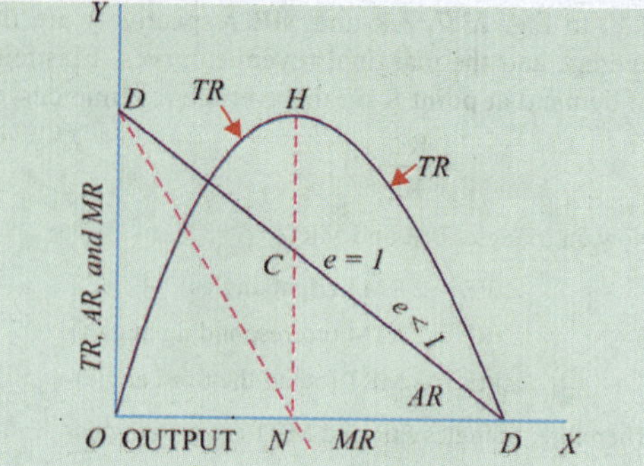

Fig. 23.8. ***AR, MR*** **and** ***TR.***

In this diagram DD is a straight line demand curve or AR curve, MR is the marginal revenue curve and OD is the total revenue curve. At the middle point C of AR curve elasticity is one (e = 1). On its lower half it is less than one-one (e > 1). Referring to the formula $MR = AR\left(\frac{e-1}{e}\right)$ given above, we can say that marginal revenue corresponding to the middle point C of the demand curve (or AR curve) is zero. This is shown by the fact that MR curve cuts the X-axis at N which corresponds to the point C on the AR curve. If the quantity is greater than ON, it will correspond to that portion of the AR curve where e < 1 marginal revenue is negative because MR goes below the X-axis. Likewise for a quantity less than ON, e >1 and the marginal revenue is positive. This means that if quantity greater than ON is sold, the total revenue (TR) will be diminishing and for a quantity less than ON the total revenue TR will be increasing. Thus the total revenue TR will be maximum at the point H where elasticity is equal to one (unit elasticity) and marginal reavenue is zero.

Key terms

Revenue, Average revenue, Marginal revenue.

QUESTIONS

1. Explain the relationship between average revenue and marginal revenue with the help of the concept of elasticity of demand.
2. Distinguish between Total Revenue, Average Revenue and Marginal Revenue. Explain their relationship.
3. Show low average and marginal revenue curve can be derived from total product curve.
4. Why do average and marginal revenue curves of a firm all under in perfect competition?
5. Explain the average revenue curve e of a firm under perfect competition. Is it identical with its marginal revenue curve? Give reasons. What is the shape of this curve?
6. What is the importance of average and marginal, revenue curves in determining Producer' Equilibrium?
7. Explain "marginal revenue curve of a firm cannot be above its average revenue curve."
8. Show that the equality between a firm's marginal revenue and marginal cost is a necessary, but not sufficient, condition for profit maximisation.
9. Explain the meaning of Average Revenue and Marginal Revenue of a firm. Explain and illustrate the nature of their respective curves in perfectly competitive and monopoly markets.
10. Establish the relationship between the marginal revenue, the average revenue and the elasticity of demand. Can the elasticity of demand be less than unity at the equilibrium price of a commodity *(a)* under perfect competition and *(b)* under monopoly?

EQUILIBRIUM OF THE FIRM AND INDUSTRY : GENERAL

EQUILIBRIUM OF THE FIRM

A firm is said to be in equilibrium when it has no incentive either to expand or to contract its output. A firm would not like to change its level of output only when its total profits are the maximum. A rational entrepreneur will expand output if he thinks he can increase his total profits by doing so, and likewise, he will contract his output if he thinks he can avoid losses and thus increase his total profits. Therefore, **a firm is in equilibrium position when it is earning maximum money profits.**

Conditions of Firm's Equilibrium

Having studied marginal revenue and average revenue in the previous chapter, we are now in a position to discuss the conditions of equilibrium of the firm. Here, we shall attempt only an analysis of the conditions of firm's equilibrium in general and not with reference to any particular market form. The firm's equilibrium conditions with particular reference to different market forms, *i.e.*, under perfect competition, monopoly and imperfect competition, will be discussed in later chapters.

Assumptions. Before explaining firm's equilibrium, we assume that the entrepreneur, *i.e.*, the owner of the firm, is rational. The rationality on the part of the entrepreneur implies that he tries to maximize his money profits. This is a fundamental assumption in the theory of production and without this, the equilibrium of the firm cannot be easily explained. A corollary from the assumption of rationality is that whatever output the firm produces, it produces as cheaply as possible given the existing production techniques. We further assume, for the sake of simplicity, that the firm produces only one product. Our analysis would, however, remain valid also in case of multiple-product firm. But when a firm produces two goods or more, certain other complications arise which we wish to avoid at this stage.

Money free giving profits.

The equilibrium of the firm can be explained in two ways:

(i) With the help of total revenue and total cost curves, and

(ii) With the aid of marginal revenue and marginal cost curves.

Equilibrium of Firm : By Curves of Total Revenue and Total Cost

A rational entrepreneur will expand output if he thinks he can increase his profits by doing so and he will likewise contract output if thereby he can avoid losses and thus increase profits. He will be in equilibrium position at the level of output where his money profits are the maximum. In other words, he will then have no inducement either to expand or contract his output when he is earning maximum money profits. Now, profits are the difference between total revenue and total cost. Hence, the point where this difference is the maximum will represent the position of maximum profits and, therefore, of equilibrium.

A cost-revenue situation of a hypothetical firm is depicted in Fig. 24.1, where TC represents total cost curve and TR represents the total revenue curve. It will be noted that total cost curve TC starts not at the origin but at the height of OF. This is so because it is assumed that even if the firm produces nothing (or shuts down), it has to bear certain costs of production due to fixed factors. These are the fixed costs.

Break-even Point. From the figure, it is clear that at any output smaller than OL, total cost exceeds total revenue and the firm is having losses. At the output OL total cost equals total revenue and the firm is having neither losses nor profits. This point L is called **'Break-even point'.** At the outputs larger than ON, the total revenue is less than total cost so that the firm is having losses. Point N is again a break-even point. Between OL and ON will lie the optimum point of maximum profits.

The maximum-profit will lie revenue-cost spread is the largest or in other words where the vertical distance between the total revenue and total cost curves is the greatest. The maximum profit point in our diagram is M where PP′ is the longest vertical distance between the two curves. Hence, at this point, the firm is in equilibrium position and is earning maximum profits PP′ by producing OM output. The maximum profit point will in fact be at that output where the slopes of the two curves are the same, that is to say, where the tangents to the total cost and total revenue curves respectively are parallel as is shown in Fig. 24.1 above.

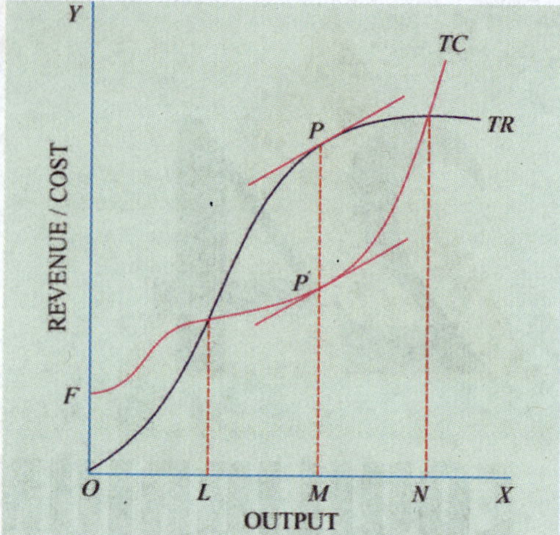

Fig. 24.1. Equilibrium of Firm: Total Revenue and Total Cost.

Limitations. This way of finding out of point of maximum profits by total revenue and total cost curves is reasonable and is also often used by businessmen but it has some limitations:

First, maximum vertical distance between the total revenue and total cost curve is difficult to see at a glance. Many tangents have to be drawn before one reaches the appropriate one corresponding to the maximum profit point. Secondly, in this method, it is not possible to discover price per unit at various outputs at first sight. Total revenue has to be divided by total number of units produced in order to get the price per unit. For example, at the equilibrium output OM the price can be found by dividing MP by OM.

Owing to these limitations, complicated problems of equilibrium analysis cannot be discussed easily and clearly in this way of representing equilibrium of the firm. Modern economists, therefore, adopt a method which shows marginal quantities, *i.e.*, marginal cost and marginal revenue at first sight.

Now we turn to this second way of representing equilibrium of the firm.

EQUILIBRIUM OF FIRM : BY CURVES OF MARGINAL REVENUE AND MARGINAL COST

We know that a firm will be in equilibrium when it is earning maximum profits. We shall see presently that for a firm, to make maximum profits, two conditions are essential:

(*i*) Marginal Revenue = Marginal Cost, and

(*ii*) MC curve cuts MR curve from below at the equilibrium point.

It is obvious that total profits can be increased by expanding output as long as the addition to the total revenue resulting from the sale of extra unit of output is greater than the addition to the total cost caused by producing an extra output. Now the addition to total revenue and total cost due to an extra unit of output are nothing else but marginal revenue and marginal cost respectively.

Thus, a firm will go on expanding output as long as marginal revenue exceeds marginal cost of production. If, at any output, marginal revenue falls short of marginal cost, *i.e.*, if an additional unit of output adds less to total revenue than to total cost, the firm will contract output to avoid losses and thus increase its profits. **The level of output where marginal revenue and marginal cost are equal is the point of maximum profit.**

Before this point of equality of marginal revenue with marginal cost is reached, the firm will be increasing its total profits by producing more as it is adding more to the total revenue than to the total cost. But if production is carried beyond this point of equality, the profits will start decreasing as the extra revenue will be smaller than the extra cost of production of a unit of output.

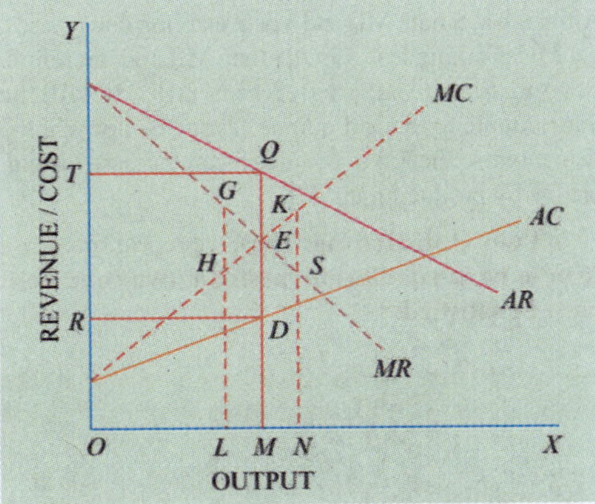

Fig. 24.2. Equilibrium of Firm : *MR* and *MC*.

The whole argument can be explained with the help of Fig. 24.2 where MC is the marginal cost curve and MR the marginal revenue curve. AC and AR are the average cost and average revenue curves respectively. At the output OM, marginal cost equals marginal revenue (MR and MC curves intersect at E above this point). This represents the point of maximum profits and hence of equilibrium.

At outputs smaller than OM, marginal revenue exceeds marginal cost and hence there is scope for increasing profits by increasing output. For example, at output OL, marginal revenue is LG and the marginal cost is LH, and LG is greater than LH. It means that by producing the Lth unit, the firm is adding more to revenue than to its cost and, therefore, it will be profitable for it to produce the Lth unit.

Similarly, for every other unit till the Mth one, the marginal revenue exceeds marginal cost, and, therefore, the firm can increase its total profits by producing up to OM output. If the firm stops producing at OL, the units of output which could have added more money to the firm's revenue than to its cost would not have been produced and profits would have been smaller by the area GHE than they could have been. Thus, a firm has an incentive to produce up to OM level of output.

But if the output is increased beyond OM, marginal cost would exceed marginal revenue and the production of each additional unit beyond OM output would add more to total cost than to total revenue. For example, at ON output, the marginal cost is KN whereas the marginal revenue is SN and KN is greater than SN. Thus, production of more units than OM would involve losses, and reduce the total profits. Therefore, the firm would not like to produce beyond OM.

Hence, we conclude that firm's profits at OM output are the maximum and **the firm is in equilibrium when**

Marginal Cost = Marginal Revenue.

This is one condition which is necessary but which is not sufficient for equilibrium.

In the Fig. 24.2, the total profits earned by the firm in the equilibrium position can be easily found. At output OM, the average cost is DM while the average revenue is QM. Therefore, the profit per unit will be equal to QD and the total profits will be equal to the rectangle QDRT.

At an equilibrium position, the **marginal cost curve must cut the marginal revenue curve from below.** The condition that for a firm to be in equilibrium marginal cost must equal marginal revenue is no doubt a necessary condition but not a sufficient condition of equilibrium. For attaining equilibrium, a second condition must also be satisfied, *viz.*, that the marginal cost (MC) curve must cut the marginal revenue (MR) curve from below at the point of equilibrium. This means that, beyond the equilibrium output, marginal cost must be greater than marginal revenue. If this condition is not met, a firm will not be earning maximum profits and hence will not be in equilibrium, as we shall see in the diagram below:

In our Fig. 24.2, the point E (*i.e.*, output OM) satisfies this second conditions also, as the MC curve cuts the MR curve from below at E and MC is greater than MR beyond E. It will be clearly not profitable, therefore, to expand output beyond OM. But there can be such a cost-revenue stituation, which satisfies the first condition of MC being equal to MR but the second condition of MC cutting MR curve from below is not met.

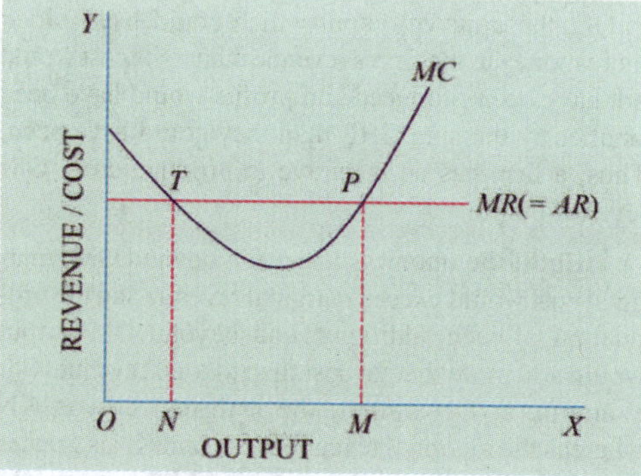

Fig. 24.3. *MC* Cutting *MR* from Below.

In Fig. 24.3, MR is the straight line marginal revenue curve (as we have already seen, a straight line marginal curve is actually faced by a firm under perfect competition). MC is the marginal cost of the firm. At point T where MC and MR intersect, the marginal cost equals marginal revenue but from the figure it is clear that at T marginal cost curve MC is cutting marginal revenue curve MR from above and, therefore, marginal cost is less than the marginal revenue beyond the point T. Obviously, T cannot be a position of equilibrium since after T, marginal cost is less than marginal revenue and it will be profitable for the firm to expand output. At T or output ON, the firm instead of making maximum profit is making maximum losses. At point P in the same figure, however, marginal cost curve is cutting marginal revenue curve from below and marginal cost beyond the point P is greater than marginal revenue. Hence, if the firm expands output beyond P (*i.e.*, OM output), it will be adding more to cost than to revenue –clearly an unprofitable move. Thus, we conclude that in this figure, the point P, and not point T is the profit maximising point. In this equilibrium position, the firm is producing equilibrium output OM.

Similarly, point E in the Fig. 24.4 (*a*) cannot be a position of equilibrium though MC equals MR at this point. This is because at E marginal cost curve is cutting the marginal revenue curve from E, both MC and MR curves are falling downwards, yet MC is falling more steeply than MR. Therefore, beyond E, MR is greater than MC. Hence, it will be profitable for the firm to expand output. Hence, E cannot be the position of firm's equilibrium. For the firm to be in equilibrium, in Fig. 24.4 (a) MC beyond E must rise upwards to cut the MR curve from below. If it does not rise upwards beyond E, then there can be no definite position of equilibrium in cost-revenue situation presented in Fig. 24.4 (*a*).

It should be carefully noted that point S in Fig. 24.4 (*b*) is really a position of equilibrium under the given cost-revenue situation. At S, MC equals MR and also MC curve is cutting MR curve from below. Although at S both MC and MR are falling downwards, yet MC is falling less Rapidly than MR and, therefore, beyond S, MC is greater than MR. It will be unprofitable to expand output beyond S; nor will the firm move to the left of S, since it can increase its total profits by producing until S.

Two Conditions. Thus, we repeat that **for a firm to be in equilibrium position, two conditions must be satisfied;**

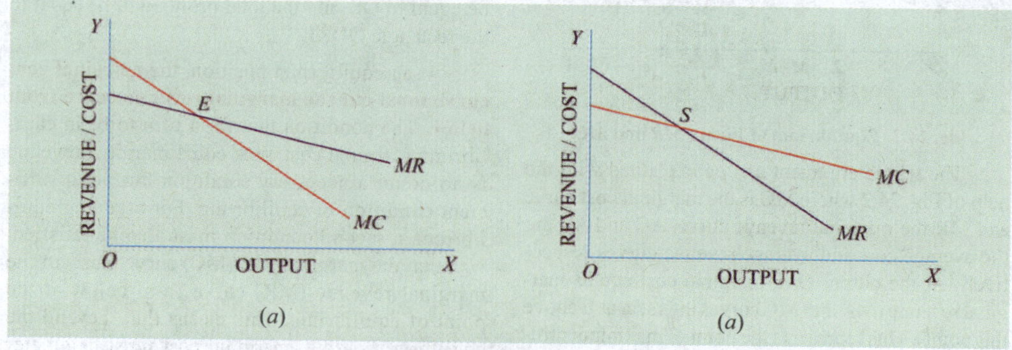

Fig. 24.4. Equilirbium when both *MC* and *MR* are falling.

(*i*) **MC = MR;** and

(*ii*) **MC curve must cut MR curve from below at the equilibrium output.**

These two conditions of equilibrium hold good both in the short run as well as in the long run. Whether the period is short or long, a firm aims at maximisation of profits and the profits are maximised only when the above two conditions are satisfied. But there is one difference. In the short run, it the short-run marginal cost curve and in the long run, it is the long-run marginal cost curve which is relevant for comparing with the marginal revenue curve.

Again, these two fundamental conditions, *viz*., marginal cost being equal to marginal revenue and MC curve cutting MR curve from below, are valid whether a firm is working under perfect competition, Monopoly or imperfect competition. The difference lies only in the shape of the marginal revenue and marginal cost curves. Under perfect competition, MR and AR curves are horizontal straight lines and they coincide,but under imperfect competition MR and AR curves are downward sloping as in Figure 23.2 and 23.3 in Chapter 23 respectively.

EQUILIBRIUM OF INDUSTRY

Meaning. An industry is said to be in equilibrium when there is no tendency for it to increase or decrease its output. Now, it will have no tendency to expand or contract its output only when the demand for and supply of its product are in equilibrium. If, for instance, the demand for its product exceeds the supply, the output is bound to increase. On the other hand, if the supply is greater than the demand for its product, the supply will have to be contracted to restore the equilibrium between demand and supply. Hence, equality between demand and supply for the product of industry is very essential if the industry is to be in equilibrium.

We know that the equilibrium of the firm does not determine the price under perfect competition. A firm operating under perfect competition has to accept the price prevailing in the market. But it is the equilibrium of the industry as a whole that determines the price under perfect competition. This means that there must be an equilibrium between demand for the product of the industry and the supply of that product by the industry. Hence we may say that industry is in equilibrium at the level of output at which the quantity demanded and the quantity supplied of its product are equal, *i.e.*, at which the demand curve for the product of industry and its supply curve intersect each other.

CONDITIONS OF EQUILIBRIUM

We have said above that an industry is said to be in equilibrium when there is no tendency for its output to increase or decrease. Now the output of the industry can vary (*a*) by the expansion or contraction of output by the individuals firms and (*b*) by the entry or exit of the firms. Thus, an industry would be in equilibrium when neither the individual firms have incentive to change their output nor is there any tendency for the new firms to enter or the existing firms to leave it.

Thus, besides equality between demand and supply of industry's products, two conditions must be satisfied if there is to be the equilibrium of the industry:

(*a*) Each and every firm should be in equilibrium. This will happen, as already explained, at the output where marginal cost is equal to marginal revenue and marginal cost curve cuts the marginal revenue curve from below at the equilibrium point.

(*b*) Industry as a whole should be in equilibrium, *i.e.*, there should be no tendency for the firms either to move into or out of the industry. This will happen when all the entrepreneurs, *i.e.*, owners of the firms in the industry, are earning only 'normal profits', that is, profits which are just sufficient to induce them to stay

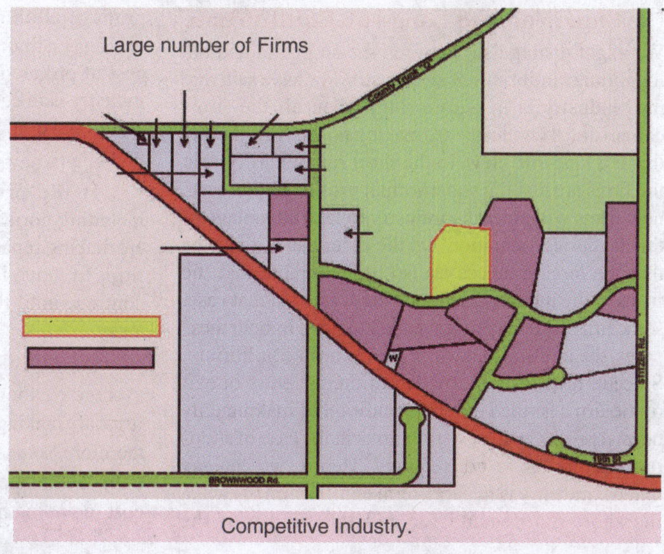

Competitive Industry.

in the industry, and when no entrepreneur outside the industry thinks that he could earn at least normal profits if he were to enter it.

Thus, the concept of normal profits is important in defining and describing equilibrium of the industry. If we assume that all the entrepreneurs in a certain industry have the same transfer earnings, there would be a fixed amount of normal profits for the whole industry. Every entrepreneur must earn at least this fixed amount of normal profits, if he is to stay in the industry.

If firms in the industry are earning profits above the normal, there will be incentive for the firms outsider the industry to enter it. This is so because there is every reason for the entrepreneurs outside there is every reason for the entrepreneurs outside the industry to expect that they would be able to earn at least normal profits if they entered this industry. Thus, there will be a tendency for the number of firms in that industry to increase.

If, on the other hand, some of the firms in the industry are earning profits below normal (or when they are having losses), they will leave the industry and search for normal profits elsewhere. Thus, the number of firms in that industry will tend to diminish.

Thus, equilibrium of the industry or **full equilibrium,** as it is sometimes called, would be attained when industry as a whole is in equilibrium (*i.e.*, there is no movement into or out of the industry) and also all the individual firms in it are in equilibrium, *i.e.*, they are equating marginal cost with marginal revenue, and their MC curves cut MR curves from below.

Short-run and Long-run Equilibrium. We might distinguish between the short-run and the long- run equilibrium of an industry. We have said that the industry is in equilibrium when all the firms comprising the industry are making normal profits. But this is a long-run view. In the short run, it may be that the firms are making supernormal profits. In that case, new firms will enter the industry to take advantage of this favourable situation. On the other hand, it may be that the circumstances are so unfavourable that the firms in the industry are incurring losses. In that case, some firms will tend to leave the industry. In both these cases, the industry cannot be said to be in equilibrium. Since in the short run, by definition, the entry or exit of the firms is ruled out, the condition of making only normal profits by the existing firms in the case of short-run equilibrium is not required. Hence, we can say that the industry is in short-term equilibrium **(*a*)** when the short-run demand for and the supply of the industry's product are equal and **(*b*)** when all the firms in it are in equilibrium, even though they may be making super-normal profits or having losses depending upon the demand conditions of the industry's product.

In the long -run, exit or entry of the new firms is possible. Hence, only normal profits will be made by the firms. Super-normal profits will be competed away by the entry of the new firms and, if there are losses, they would be eliminated by the exit of some of the existing firms. Thus, an industry will be in equilibrium in the long-run if the following two conditions are satisfied beside the equality between the long-run supply and the demand for the industry's product: **(*a*)** all the firms in the industry should be in equilibrium and **(*b*)** there should be no incentive to entry into the industry by the new firms or compulsion for the existing firms to leave it. In other words, the number of firms should be in equilibrium.

Incorporating Normal Profit into Average Cost Curve

A firm's decision to stay or leave the industry will depend not only on whether it is covering average total cost as it is generally defined but also on whether it is earning at least normal profits. It is, therefore, useful to include normal profits in average cost. This inclusion of normal profits in average cost helps us to judge easily whether firms have a tendency to stay or leave the industry. If we do not include normal profits in the average cost, we shall have to compare the current level of earnings with normal profits which is an unnecessary complication.

If price is equal to average cost including normal profit of all the firms, it means that all the firms are making just normal profits besides covering average cost of production. We can then easily conclude that industry is in equilibrium as in this situation the firms would have no tendency either to enter or leave the industry.

If the price is greater than average cost including normal profits, it means that existing firms are making super-normal profits. This will induce new firms to move into the industry. This movement will continue until the super-normal profits are competed away.

On the other hand, if the price is less than the average cost including normal profits, it follows that firms are making sub-normal profits, *i.e.*, having losses; therefore, some firms will be forced to quit the industry until the existing firms are at least covering average cost including normal profits.

In Fig. 24.6, we have drawn a curve ACP which represents average cost of production and does not include normal profits. If in ACP we add normal profits, we get AC curve which is the summation of the average cost of production and normal profits calculated per unit. The normal profits per unit will fall progressively as output increases. This is because a fixed sum of total normal profits will be spread over a progressively large number of units of output. Consequently, the vertical distance between ACP and AC = (ACP + NP) curve will steadily fall but the two curves will never meet. For instance, at the output level OM, the normal profit per unit is FG and at output ON, the normal profit per unit is RS. It should be carefully noted that rectangles showing normal profits such as EFGH and QRST would be of equal areas as we are assuming that normal profits represent a fixed sum of money.

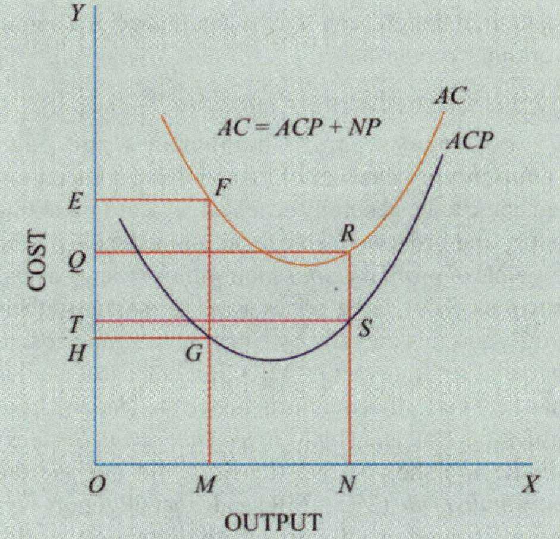

Fig. 24.5. Incorporating Normal Profits into AC.

As already pointed out, it is reasonable to assume that there will be a fixed amount of normal profits in an industry. This **normal profit, is a fixed amount, (*i.e.* independent of the level of output) which the firms must earn if they are to remain in the industry.** As the normal profits represent a fixed sum of money, it means that as output increases normal profits calculated per unit of output will fall as a fixed sum will be spread over a large number of units of output. This will be an additional reason for the average cost curve to slope downward over the low ranges of output.

VALIDITY OF PROFIT-MAXIMISING DOCTRINE

We have seen in the analysis of a firm's equilibrium, that a producer is not interested in reducing either his average cost or total cost to the minimum or in maximising his revenue. What he is interested really is in the difference between his total cost including normal profit and total revenue which is his profit. It is said that he wants to make this difference as big as possible. In other words, a firm seeks to maximise it profits. But is this assumption valid ?

But let us be clear as to what we mean by profit maximisation. The normal profits are minimum income which the entrepreneur must get if he is to stay in business. The normal profits are included in that cost and, therefore, do not come under the profit maximizing principle. Therefore, it is the super-normal profits, *i.e.*, true or pure profits, which is the residual income of the entrepreneur, which he aims at maximizing.

There has been lot of controversy over this issue. There are economists who doggedly stick to this assumption and strongly assert that a firm exists and operates for no other purpose than to maximise profits. But there are others who question the validity of maximising doctrine.

Meaning of Profit

We usually define profit in Economics as a reward for enterprise or for risk-taking or uncertainty-bearing. But this definition does not lend itself to any quantitative interpretation to enable us to settle the issue.

There are two technical difficulties in interpreting the concept of profit maximisation: First difficulty relates to the time dimension. A businessman is said to maximise his profit for each accounting period, say a year. But this is not a good assumption, when dealing with a continuing business. Because a business can certainly increase its profits in a particular year by utterly neglecting the figure, *e.g.*, clearing all the stock of finished goods at the end of the period.

The economist, therefore, as distinguished from the businessman, lays emphasis on the future in the concept of profits. According to this interpretation, profits may be defined as the maximum dividend that a company can pay without impairing its ability to pay same dividend in subsequent years.

The second difficulty about the concept of profits relates to the criterion for evaluating risk for which profit is a reward.

Leaving aside the dispute regarding the interpretation of the term 'profits', let us try to see whether the doctrine of profit maximisation is a mere theory to be found only in textbooks on Economics or whether the firms do actually try to maximise profits.

Arguments For

The following arguments are put forward to show that the assumption of profit maximisation is amply borne out by business behaviour:–

(i) The businessmen sometimes assert that it is their business to look after social welfare, rather than personal gain.

Thus, the actual behaviour of businessmen is in accord with profit maximisation doctrine.

(ii) The postulate of profit maximisation certainly applies to industries and it is the behaviour of the industry, rather than of an individual firm which determines the flow of products and the demand for inputs.

Arguments Against

Those who question the validity of the profit-maximisation postulate put forward the following arguments:–

(i) Englightened businessmen vehemently deny that their object is to maximise profits. Service of society rather than personal profit is said to be their aim.

(ii) The profit-maximisation doctrine would be the rule, if business decisions were taken by those who are to get the profits. Most business dicisions are taken by business executives or salaried managers, rather than by owners of firms.

(iii) The objective of profit maximisation is difficult of realisation. If a businessman is to maximise his profits, he must fix a price, so as to equalise marginal revenue and marginal cost. This means that he must be able to estimate demand at all prices and marginal cost at all outputs. This is a fantastically difficult task and is seldom attempted in practice.

(iv) Besides being difficult of precise calculation, profit maximisation is also regarded as immoral. "Profit maximisation requires the businessman to use every trick he can think of to keep wages and fringe benefits down, to extract the last possible dollar from the consumer, to sell as low quality merchandise as he can legally hoodwink the customer into buying, to use income solely for the benefits of the stock holder, to disclaim any responsibility to the community, to wrangle the lowest possible price from his vendors regardless of its effect on them, and so on."[1]

(v) The business policies and practices actually pursued by businessmen are not consistent with the profit maximisation doctrine. The calculus of maximisation does not fit the notions which actually sway businessmen. They are guided by a sense of fairness, adequacy, *etc*. They are satisfied with a satisfactory rate of profit instead of pursuing maximum profits with callous disregard for other interests.

Conclusion

Thus, profit maximisation maxim is unrealistic since it is difficult of calculation and not very ethical to pursue. Marginal analysis as a tool of profit maximisation is a valid technique for selecting the most efficient technique out of the various alternatives available, where the alternatives can be fairly clearly specified and where it is possible to estimate costs and revenue reasonably well. But this is not always possible.

We may conclude in the words of Robert Dorfman thus: "On balance, the maximisation hypothesis is not as firmly grounded in the facts of life as a fundamental scientific hypothesis should be. But substantial and prolonged divergences from the behaviour it implies are rare particularly in industries with many participants. It, therefore, can still be entertained as a sound working hypothesis."[2]

Full Cost Pricing Principle

For many years, Chamberlin's and Joan Robinson's price theory of monopolistic competition had come to be generally accepted. According to this theory, the firms were able to act atomistically on the principle of profit maximisation without fear of rivals' reactions. They fixed prices so as to maximise their profits and this they did by equating marginal cost to marginal revenue (MC = MR). But empirical studies made by Oxford economists under the leadership of professors Hall and Hitch (*Price Theory and Business Behaviour*) showed that the firms did not use the *marginalist rule* (MC = MR) and that oligopoly was the main market structure in the business world. According to Hall and Hitch, the firms did not act atomistically or irrespective of what their rival firms did. Rather they are continuously watching the reactions of the rival firms. The traditional theory could not adequately explain the oligopolistic interdependence.

In such a situation, the firms do not attempt to maximise short-run profits by acting on the marginalistic rule (MC = MR) but aim at maximising long-run profits by acting on the *average-cost principle*. That is, the firms do not set their price and output at the intersection of MC and MR curves but they set them at a level which covers the average variable cost, (AVC) and average fixed cost (AFC) and normal profit margin in the business in question. Thus P = AVC + AFC + Normal Profit. Firms do not seek

1. Hailstones, Thomas J. –*Readings in Economics,* 1963, pp.113-114.

2. Dorfman R. –*The Price System,* 1965, p.42.

abnormal profits for fear of losing business to rivals, actual or potential. Hall and Hitch found that the firms are ignorant not only of their demand curves but also of their marginal cost, especially in multi-product firms. Rather they follow the full cost principle which gives them a 'fair profit' and cover the full cost of production. Hall and Hitch found that the firms' main concern is with price and not output as the traditional theory implies.

Profit Maximisation and single owner-Entrepreneur

We have examined above one assumption underlying the traditional theory of the equilibrium of the firm, viz. profit maximisation through the marginalist principle (*i.e.*, equating marginal cost with marginal revenue). We have shown that, according to Hall and Hitch, it is the fall cost principle rather than the marginal principle which is found to operate in the business world.The traditional theory also assumes that the firm on which profit is sought to be maximised is owned by a single owner-entrepreneur whose sole concern is to maximise profit. In modern business world, however single entrepreneur is an exception rather than the rule. It is the professional manager who actually controls the business because the dominating form of business organisation today is a joint stock company.There is thus a divorce between ownership and management. The single owner-entrepreneur was supposed to act with 'global rationality' and there were no time information or other constraints resting upon him from pursuing the single aim of profit maximisation.

Obviously this assumption is unrealistic, because actually it is the manager who has the decision-making power. He may as well pursue goals other than profit-maximisation, *e.g.*, social welfare, employees' welfare, stability and growth. The salaried manager also lacks the motivation that a single owner-entrepreneur has for maximising profit.

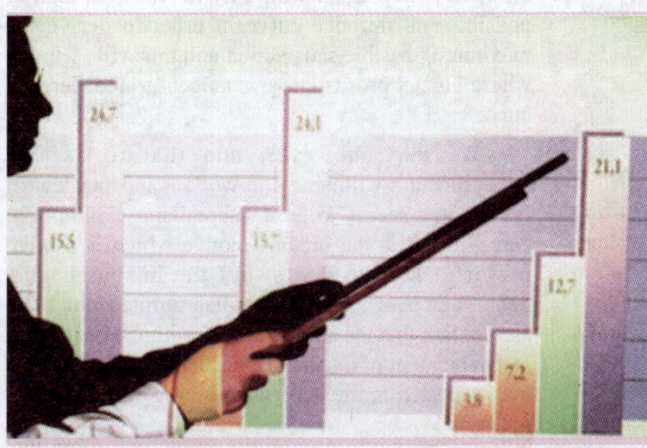

Sales maximization.

Conclusion

The fact is that given the uncertainty in and complexity of the modern business world, lack of full and accurate information, the limited time and limited activity of the manager/entrepreneur and other constraints, the firms do not seek the maximisation of profits, sales, growth or anything else. They at best try to exhibit satisfactory behaviour i.e. satisfactory profit, satisfactory sales, satisfactory growth ,*etc*. This is known as **'Behaviourism'.**

GOALS OTHER THAN PROFIT MAXIMIZATION

We have discussed above the profit maximization principle. It gives the impression that every businessman aims at maximizing his profits regardless of all other considerations. This, however, is not so. On the other hand, in the world of reality, businessmen pursue several other goals in running their business. Among these we may mention **Security Motive, Sales Maximization Motive or Utility Maximization Motive.** We shall say a word about each.

Security Motive

It is said that when an entrepreneur fixes the price for his product, his aim is not to get maximum possible profit, but to satisfy his sense of security. In other words, he aims at getting a good income for many years to come so that he does not suffer from any sense of insecurity. This means that the entrepreneur's objective is to secure a steady flow of profit for a long time. Professor K.W. Rothschild observes in this connection. "Profit maximization has uptill now serve as the wonderful master-key that opened all the doors leading to an understanding of the entrepreneur's behaviour . . . . . . But there is another motive which cannot be so lightly dismissed and which is probably of a similar order of magnitude as the desire for maximum profits; the desire for secure profits."[3]

If we take the market structure into consideration, we might say that so far as imperfect competition and monopolistic competition with a large number of firms

3. Rotheschild K.W., Price Theory and Oligopoly. The Economic Journal Vol. LVII 1974, p. 229 to 230, reprinted in *Readings in Theory* (AEA).

or absolute monopoly are concerned profit maximization seems to be a valid assumption. In the case of perfect competition, a firm has to accept the prevailing price and has no option, therefore, the question of profit maximization does not arise. In the case of monopolistic competition and absolute monopoly, the entrepreneurs are in a position to fix their price and maximize their profits. But in the case of oligopoly, profit maximization cannot be considered a valid assumption. The oligopolist has both the desire and the power to achieve a secure position. In such a market situation, therefore, the desire for security rather than the desire for maximum profit rules the entrepreneur's mind.

Sales Maximization

The sales maximization hypothesis has been put forward by Professor Baumol. In his view, maximization of sales rather than the maximization of profits the ultimate objective that the entrepreneur pursues. He says that sales have become an end of themselves and not merely as a means to further other objectives like operational efficiency and profits. Baumol, therefore, regards sales maximization as the most valid assumption governing the behaviour of a firm. By sales is meant the revenue earned by selling the product. Therefore, it is also called **Revenue Maximization Hypothesis.**

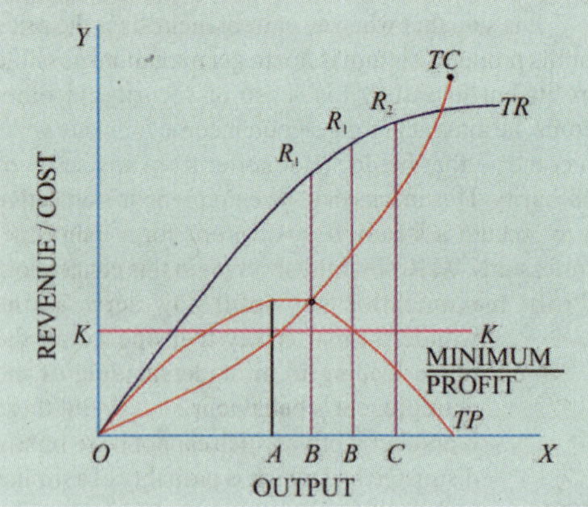

Fig. 24.6. Maximizing sales.

However, Prof. Baumol concedes that while promoting sales businessmen do not ignore altogether the goal of profits. He, therefore, modifies his position by saying that the entrepreneur promotes sales subject to the limitation that cost incurred are covered and a usual rate of return on investment is secured. Hence, according to Prof. Baumol, the objective is the sales maximization subject to minimum profit constraint. He says "So long as profits are high enough to keep stock holders satisfied and contribute adequately to the financing of company's growth, management will bend its efforts to the augmentation of sales revenue rather than to further increase in profits."[4]

The following diagram (Fig. 24.7) illustrates how, a firm aims at maximum revenue or sales consistent with earning minimum profit. This model is a compromised between total sales and profits. But it is also understood that after MR = MC, increase in sales can only be at the expense of profits. This puts a limit to sales increase because minimum profits must be made.

Here TR is total revenue, TC total cost and TP curve represents total profit. At the output OA, profits are maximum. But if the firm aims at only sales maximisation, output will be OC which corresponds to R_2 at the top of TR giving maximum total revenue. But actually this firm will produce and sell OB corresponding to R_1 total revenue because it gives minimum profit.

Utility Maximization

There are economists like Benjamin Higgins, Melvin Redder and Tibor Scitovsky who say that maximization of satisfaction or utility is the over-riding consideration which governs businessman's behaviour. This goal is also called **Preference Function Maximization.** These economists point out that profit maximization does not necessarily result in maximization of satisfaction. In their view, we should not only consider the satisfaction that an entrepreneur gets from his material possessions which he may get from his profits, but also the satisfaction which he may get from the leisure that he is able to enjoy. The entrepreneur's attitude towards work and leisure is a very important consideration if the entrepreneur is to maximize his utility or satisfaction. According to this view, an entrepreneur would try to reach the highest possible indifference curve in order to derive the maximum possible satisfaction and this will happen where his net profits curve is tangent to indifference curve.

We may, however, add that to assume entrepreneur's willingness to work as independent of his income seems to be an unrealistic assumption. Generally, it is the income motive which is a more powerful motive that sways the businessman's behaviour. But as Scitovsky has pointed out "The assumption that the entrepreneur's willingness to work is independent of his income need not imply that he is not interested in the materials rewards of his work. It

4. Baumol. W. I. –*Business Behaviour, Value and Growth*, pp. 49-50.

Utility maximization.

may also mean that he is so keen on making money that his ambition cannot be damped by a rise in income ..... This is likely to be the case partly because the desire for success is more insatiable than the demand for the material goods and partly because it is not a high but a rising income that is a sign of business success.[5] This means that it is success in business which gives greater satisfaction to the businessman **than** the money that the business brings.

According to Professor Benjamen Higgins, an entrepreneur tries to maximize his satisfaction or what he calls utility index rather than profits. He says that profit maximization is a condition of survival in perfect competition. But profit maximization motive is much weaker under the conditions of imperfect competition. There are three types of desires which in Higgins' opinion lead to non-profit maximization: **(*a*)** Desires and forces which lead the entrepreneur to produce at a point below the profit maximization motive, *e.g.*, desire for leisure; **(*b*)** forces which lead the entrepreneur to produce at a point above the profit maximization output, *e.g.*, desire to wield more power and enjoy greater prestige; and **(*c*)** forces which make the entrepreneur stay where he is irrespective of the profit maximizing output. This may be due to his reluctance to make experiments.

Key terms

Equilibrium of firm, Profit maximization, Break even point, Sales maximization.

QUESTIONS

1. Explain the necessary and sufficient condition for the equilibrium of a firm.
2. "A firm is in equilibrium where its marginal revenue is equal to its marginal cost." Explain.
3. Examine the significance of the equality between marginal revenue and marginal cost in the theory of firm under different types of market conditions.
4. "All firms do not always aim at profit maximisation". Explain.
5. Compare with the help of diagrams the equilibrium of the firm under perfect competition and under imperfect competition form the point of view of the most efficient utilisation of resources.
6. "While under perfect competition, the individual firm can attain equilibrium only under increasing cost conditions, under monopoly it can be in equilibrium, whatever the cost condition." Discuss.

5. Scitovsky, T. A. Note on Profit Maximization and Implications. *The Review of Economic Studies*. Vo. XI (1943), Reprinted in *Readings in Price Theory* (AEA).

EQUILIBRIUM OF FIRM AND INDUSTRY UNDER PERFECT COMPETITION

Conditions of Perfect Competition: Their Implications

In the previous chapter, we have discussed in detail the conditions of equilibrium of a firm and industry. As mentioned earlier, our analysis in regard to the equilibrium in the last chapter was only in general terms and not with reference to any particular market form. Now in the present chapter, we shall discuss the conditions of equilibrium of the firm and industry under conditions of perfect competition.

In chapter 22, the meaning and conditions of perfect competition have already been studied. Perfect competition, as explained there, refers to a situation when :

(i) Number of sellers and buyers is very large;

(ii) Products are homogeneous;

(iii) Both producers (or firms) and consumers possess perfect knowledge about the prevailing price and current bids in the market; and

(iv) Entry into and the exit from the industry is free for the firms.

A competitive market of many buyers and sellers of banana.

The first condition ensures that an individual firm and an individual consumer (or buyer) have no control over the price of the product. There being a large number of firms in the industry, the output of an individual firm is an insignificant part of the total output of the whole industry. An individual firm produces such a small proportion of the total output of the industry that even a large increase or decrease in its output has little or negligible effect on the total output and hence on the price of the product of that industry. Therefore, an individual firm has to take the price as given.

Similarly, the buyers or consumers of the product are also numerous and a single buyer's demand for the product is so small that changes in it cannot have any perceptible effect on the total demand and hence on the price of the product of that industry.

Thus, under perfect competition, an individual firm or individual buyer acts as if he had no influence on price and merely adjusts to a given market price.

The second condition ensures that all firms are producing goods which are accepted by consumers or buyers as homogeneous or identical. It means that product of one firm is indistinguishable from the products of other firms in the industry. Trade marks, patents, special brand labels, *etc.*, do not exist. The control over price is completely eliminated only when all firms are producing perfectly homogeneous goods, since if the product of any one firm is slightly different from that of others, it would have a degree of control over the price of his own brand. Thus, if there is to be no control over the price of the product by any one producer, the products must be homogeneous.

It should be carefully noted that whether or not products are homogeneous should be judged from the viewpoint of the consumers. If the consumers (or buyers) find some imaginary differences between the products, their prices are bound to differ, however, physically alike the products may be. Anything which makes the buyers prefer one seller to another, be it personality, reputation, convenient location, or the tone of his shop, differentiates the product purchased to that extent, since what is bought is really a bundle of utilities of which these things are a part. The utilities offered by all sellers to all buyers must be identical, otherwise individual sellers will have a degree of control over their individual prices. "Under such condition it is evident that buyers and sellers will be paired in random fashion in a large number of transactions. It will be entirely a matter of chance from which seller a particular buyer makes his purchases, and purchases over a period of time will be distributed among all sellers according to the law of probability. After all, this is only another way of saying that the product is homogeneous."[1]

The third condition guarantees that buyers and sellers are fully aware of the prevailing price in the market. Since there are no uninformed buyers, sellers cannot attempt to charge more than the prevailing price. Consumers cannot hope to buy from some producers at less than the prevailing price for similar reasons. If any seller tries to charge a higher price than the prevailing market price, the buyers will shift to some other seller and buy the commodity at the ruling price, since they are supposed to know the prevailing market price. The consumers will refuse to buy the commodity at the higher price.

The above three conditions ensure that a single price must prevail in the market under perfect competition and, further, that the demand curve or average revenue curve faced by an individual firm under perfect competition is perfectly elastic at the prevailing market price.

The fourth condition ensures that there must not be any restriction on the entry of new firms or the exit of the existing firms. As we have pointed out previously, in the short-run, the firms can neither change the size of their plants nor can the firms enter or leave the industry. But, in the long-rrn, both the size of the firm as well as the number of the firms can vary. The fourth condition of perfect competition requires that there must be absolute freedom for the entry or exit of the firms, in the long-rrn. If the prevailing price in the market is such that all the firms are making super-normal profits, new firms will enter the industry until

Banana is selling at Rs. 15 per dozen (single price).

1. Chamberlin, E.H.–*Theory of Monopolistic Competition*, 7th ed., p.8.

all firms in the industry are earning just normal profits. If the prevailing price is such that the firms are incurring losses, some of the existing firms will leave the industry so that those remaining in the industry are again making at least normal profits.

Whereas the first three conditions ensure that average revenue curve or demand curve faced by an individual firm under perfect competition is perfectly elastic at the ruling market price, the fourth condition of free entry or exit guarantees that, in the long-rrn, all firms must be earning just normal profits.

Conditions of Equilibrium

Under perfect competition, as explained earlier, price for an individual firm is given. It cannot influence the price by its own action. It works under the assumption that it can sell as much as it likes, at the prevailing price. Therefore, the demand curve or **average revenue curve facing a firm under perfect competition is perfectly elastic** at the ruling price. Since a perfectly competitive firm can sell as much as it wants without affecting the price, addition made to total revenue by an extra unit of output, *i.e.*, marginal revenue, is equal to the price (average revenue) of the commodity.

Hence, **the average revenue (or demand) curve, (AR) and marginal revenue curve (MR) must coincide with each other for a firm under perfect competition.**

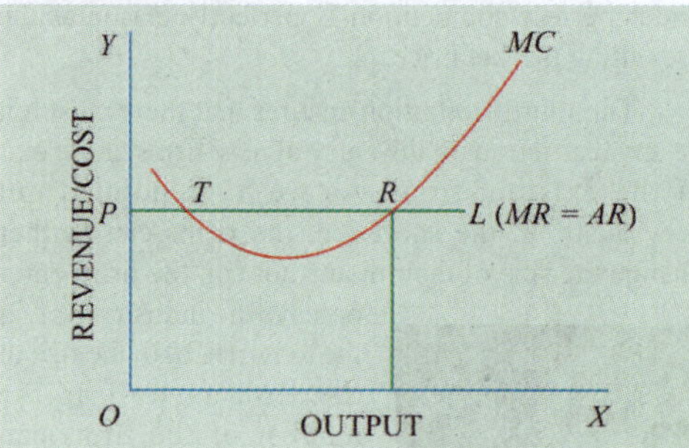

Fig. 25.1. Conditions of Equilibrium Under Perfect Competition.

In Fig. 25.1, if price prevailing in the market is OP, then PL is both the average and marginal revenue curve. MC is the marginal cost curve. It may be noted that, under perfect competition, a firm's MC curve is also its supply curve. Given the price OP, the firm will fix its output where its profits are maximum. Profits are the greatest at the level of output for which marginal cost is equal to marginal revenue and marginal cost curve cuts the marginal revenue curve from below.

As explained in the previous Chapter (Fig. 24.3), at point T though MC is equal to MR but MC is cutting MR from above rather than from below. Therefore, T cannot be a position of equilibrium. At point R or output OM, the marginal cost equals MR and marginal cost curve is also cutting MR curve from below. Hence, at the output OM or point R, the profits would be maximum and the firm would be in equilibrium position. Marginal cost, which is equal to marginal revenue in equilibrium, must also be equal to price in equilibrium under perfect competition, since price and marginal revenue are equal under perfect competition.

Hence, conditions of firm's equilibrium under perfect competition are:–

(i) MC = MR = Price.

(ii) MC curve must cut MR curve from below.

Thus, a perfectly competitive firm will adjust its output at the point where its marginal cost is equal to marginal revenue or price, and marginal cost curve cuts the marginal revenue curve from below. But producing at this point does not guarantee that the firm will always make positive profits. Whether or not there are positive profits depends on the relation between total cost and total revenue, or between average cost and average revenue (price).

Equilibrium in the Short-Run

The short-run has been defined as a period of time sufficient to allow the firm to adjust its output by increasing or decreasing the amount of variable factors of production, but during which fixed factors of production cannot be altered. Thus, in the short-run; the size and kind of plant cannot be changed, nor can new firms enter the industry.

Assumptions. In explaining the equilibrium of firm under perfect competition both in the short-run and long-rrn, we assume that all firms are working under **identical cost conditions.** Given this assumption, we shall explain the equilibrium of one firm and this explanation will apply to all other firms in the industry. Identical cost conditions for the firms mean that average cost and marginal cost curves are identical for all the firms. The entrepreneurs of all the firms are equally efficient. Further, we assume that the factors of production used by the different firms are homogeneous and are available at given and constant prices.

The above twin conditions of equilibrium ensure that profits have been maximised or losses minimised, but they do not tell about the firm's absolute profit or loss position. In this connection there are three possibilities: (*a*) When the firm makes super-normal profits; (*b*) When it makes only normal profits; and (*c*) When it incurs losses, but still does not shut down. Let us take them one by one.

(*a*) When the firm makes supernormal profits in the short-run. In Fig. 25.2, if the price is OP_1, the average-marginal revenue curve is $P_1 L_1$ and the firm is in equilibrium at point Q of output OM_1. In this case, average cost is M_1G, whereas price is OP_1(= QM_1). Hence, profit per unit is GQ. The output is OM_1 (= GH). Hence, in this equilibrium position, the firm is making supernormal profits, which are equal to the area P_1 QGH. As all the firms in the industry have identical cost curves with the firm represented in Fig. 25.2, all would be making supernormal profits. There will be a tendency for the new firms to enter the industry to complete away these supernormal profits. But the short-run is not a period sufficient for the new firms to enter; therefore, the existing firms will continue to earn supernormal profits at the price OP_1 in the short period.

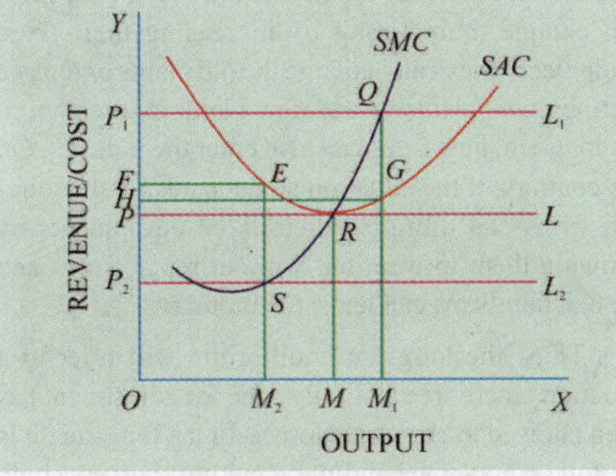

Fig. 25.2. **Firm's Equilibrium : Short-run**

Thus, with price OP_1, all the **firms** in the industry will be in equilibrium at Q but **industry,** as a whole, will not be in equilibrium as there will be a tendency for the new firms to enter the industry.

(*b*) The Firm just makes normal profit. Now suppose that the ruling price in the market is OP. PL will then be the average-marginal revenue curve and the firm will be in equilibrium at the point R. At the point R, besides marginal cost being equal to marginal revenue and MC curve cutting MR curve from below, average revenue (or price) is also equal to average cost. Hence, with OP price and at the equilibrium point R or equilibrium output OM, the firm in Fig. 25.2, and hence all the firms in the industry, will be making only normal profit (normal profits are included in average cost curve). Since all the firms in the industry are making only normal profits, there will be no tendency either for the new firms to enter or for the existing firms to quit the industry.

Thus, even in the short-run, the industry will be in equilibrium with price OP and firms Producing OM at point R. In other words, even in the short-run, full equilibrium, *i.e.*, equilibrium of all the firms as well as of the industry as a whole, will be achieved with price OP and the firm producing at point R or output OM.

But the attainment of full equilibrium in the industry in the short-run is a rare phenomenon. It is only by accident that the industry will be in equilibrium in the short-run. It is more likely that the long-run **adjustment in the number of firms takes place before the industry comes to be in equilibrium.**

(*c*) The firm incurring Losses, but does not shut down. If the short-run price in the market were OP_2 , instead of OP_1 and OP, the firm will be in equilibrium at point S, since with price OP_2 , only at S the marginal cost is equal to marginal revenue or price OP, and MC curve cuts MR curve P_1L_2 from below. But, at S or output OM_2 , the firm is incurring losses, (Average revenue SM_2 is less than average cost EM_2 at the point S or output OM_2). The total losses in this situation are equal to the area P_2 SEF. This is the smallest loss that a firm can incur under the given price-cost situation, if it is to produce at all. Given the price OP_2 in the market, the loss of the firm would be greater if it tries to produce at a point other than S.

Thus, we see that equating marginal cost with marginal revenue is optimal (when the second condition is also satisfied) even though profits are negative, because in that we losses are kept at the minimum. Since all the terms of the industry have identical cost conditions with the firm of Fig. 25.2, all would i.e. incurring losses. The firms would have a tendency to quit the industry to go in search for normal profits elsewhere. But in the short-run they cannot do so.

Thus, with price OP_2 , all the firms would be in equilibrium at point S (though all will be incurring losses), but the industry as a whole, will not be in equilibrium, since the firms will have a tendency to leave it.

The question now naturally arises: "Why at all should the firms continue operating if they are incurring losses. If they cannot leave the present industry, why do they not at least shut (which they can even in the short-run) to avoid losses ? As we have said earlier, the short-run is a period in which firms cannot alter their fixed capital equipment. They, therefore, will have to bear fixed costs in the short-run even if they shut down. Only variable cost can be avoided by stopping production. Therefore, if a firm chooses to shut down in the short-run, even then it will have to bear losses equal to the fixed cost of production.

Hence, if the firm in operation can earn revenue more than the variable cost, it will not be prudent for the firm to close merely because it is not possible to cover fixed costs fully. Instead, the firm should keep operating in the short-run, if it can cover variable costs and make anything to cover a part of the fixed costs also. The saying 'half a loaf is better than none' is suggestive of prudent action, since it is better to obtain some revenue to meet a part of the fixed costs than none at all. But if the price happens to be so low that the firm cannot cover even its variable costs, it should shut down in order to minimize the losses.

Hence, if losses are greater than total fixed costs, *i.e.*, when revenue earned is even less than the total variable costs, the firm will shut down to avoid unnecessary losses.

Shut-down Point. The whole agrument can be easily understood with the help of Fig. 25.3, where AC and MC are average cost and marginal cost curves respectively. AVC is the average variable cost curves. If price is OP_2 , the firm is in equilibrium at S and is incurring losses equal to the area P_2 SNF, but the firm is covering total variable cost and a part of the fixed costs, since price OP_2 (= M_1 S) is greater than the average variable cost M_1 K at the equilibrium output OM_1. Hence, in the short-run, it is in the interest of the firm to keep operating at price OP_2.

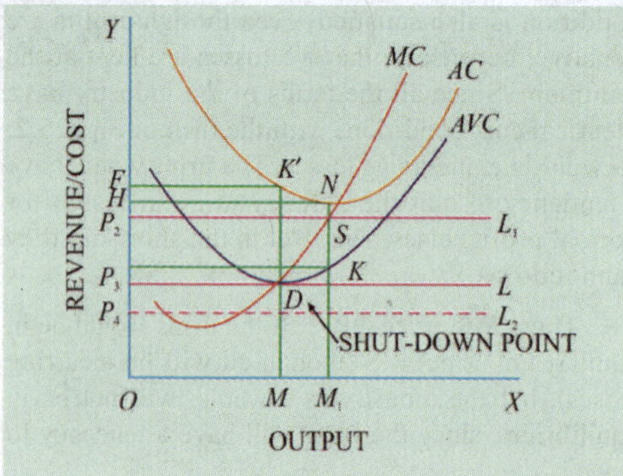

Fig. 25.3. Equilibrium of Firm—Short-Run : Shut Down Point

But if the price happens to be OP_3 , the firm will be in equilibrium at point D. At point D, the firm would be covering total variable costs but no part of the fixed costs, since price OP_3 is equal to Average Variable cost MD at the equilibrium output OM. But if the price is less than OP_3 or MD (*i.e.*, if price is less than the bottom of AVC), the firm would shut down, as in that situation it would not cover even the variable costs, since the price will be less than the average variable cost. Point D is, therefore, called the **shut down point.** For example, at price OP_4 , the firm would not cover even variable cost since OP_4 is less than the average variable cost at every level of output. With price OP_4 , the firm's losses would be equal to fixed costs plus a part of the variable cost not covered by the total revenue. Therefore, the firm will refuse to produce any output at price OP_4 and wait for some good time to re-open.

Hence, we may conclude that a firm will shut down even in the short-run, if the price falls below the bottom of Average Variable Cost curve.

Equilibrium in the Long-Run

The long-run is a period of time long enough to permit changes in the variable as well as in the fixed factors. In the long run, accordingly, all factors are variable and none fixed. Thus, in the long-run, firms can change their output by increasing their fixed equipment. They can enlarge the old plants or replace them by new plants or add new plants. Moreover, in the long-rrn, new firms can also enter the industry. On the contrary, if the situation so demands, in the long-rrn, firms can diminish their fixed equipments by allowing them to wear out without replacement and the existing firms can leave the industry.

Thus, the long-run equilibrium will refer to a situation where free and full scope for adjustment has been allowed to economic forces. In the long-run, it is the long-rrn average and marginal cost curves which are relevant for making output decisions. Further, in the long-rrn, average variable cost is of no particular relevance. It is the average total cost which is of determining importance, since in the long-rrn all costs are variable and none fixed.

We have discussed above that in the short-run a firm under perfect competition is in equilibrium at that output at which marginal cost equals price (or Marginal Revenue). This is equally valid in the long-rrn. But, in the long-run for a perfectly competitive firm to be in equilibrium, besides marginal cost being equal to price, price must also be equal to average cost. If the price is greater than the average cost, the firms will be making supernormal profits. Lured by these supernormal profits, new firms will enter the industry and these extra profits will be competed away. When the new firms enter the industry, the supply of output of the industry will increase and hence the price of the output will be forced down. The new firms will keep coming into the industry until the price is depressed down to average cost, and all firms are earning only normal profits.

On the other hand, if the price happens to be below the average cost, the firms will be incurring losses. Some of the existing firms will quit the industry. As a result, the output of the industry will decrease and the price will rise to equal the average cost so that the firms remaining in the industry are making normal profits.

Hence, in the long-rrn, firms need not be forced to produce at a loss since they can leave the industry, if they are having losses.

Thus, for a perfectly competitive firm to be in equilibrium in the long-rrn, the following two conditions must be satisfied.

Price = Marginal Cost.
Price = Average Cost.

But if price equals both the marginal and the average costs then for the long- run equilibrium of the firm under perfect competition, we have a combined condition :

Price = Marginal Cost = Average Cost.

Now when average cost curve is falling, marginal cost curve is below it, and when average cost curve is rising, marginal cost curve must be above it. Hence, marginal cost can be equal to the average cost only at the point where average cost curve is neither falling nor rising, *i.e.*, at the minimum point of average cost curve. Therefore, it is at the point of minimum average cost curve that marginal cost curve intersects the average cost curve, and the two are equal there.

Thus, the conditions for long-run equilibrium of perfectly competitive firm can be written as:

Price = Marginal Cost = Minimum Average Cost.

The conditions for the long-run equilibrium of the firm under perfect competition can be easily understood from the Fig. 25.4, where LAC is the long-run average cost curve and LMC is the long-run marginal cost curve. The firm under perfect competition cannot be in long-run equilibrium at price OP_1 because though the price OP_1 equals MC at Q (*i.e.*, at output OM_1) but it is greater than the average cost at this output and, therefore, the firm will be earning supernormal profits. Since, all the firms are assumed to be identical, all would be earning supernormal profits. Hence, there will be incentive for the new firms to enter the industry. As a result, the price will be forced down to the level OP at which price, the firm is in equilibrium at R and is producing OM output. At point R or equilibrium output OM, the price is equal to average cost, and hence the firm will be earning only normal profits (normal profits are included in average cost). Therefore, at price OP, there will be no tendency for the outside firms to enter. Hence, the firm will be in equilibrium at OP price and OM output.

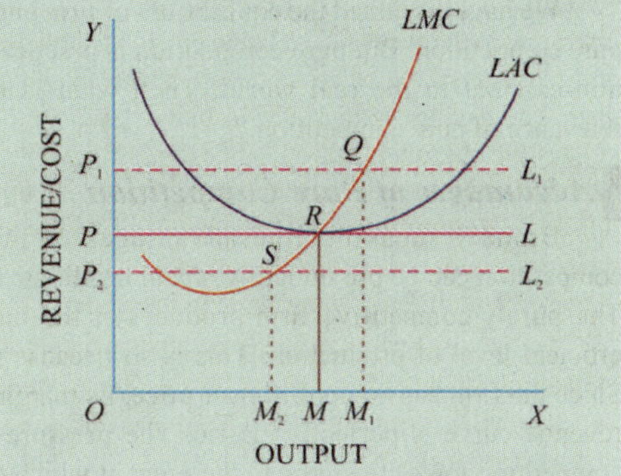

Fig. 25.4. Equilibrium of Firm : Long-Run.

On the contrary, a firm under perfect competition cannot be in the long-run equilibrium at price OP_2. Though price OP_2 is equal to marginal cost at point S, or at output OM_2 but price OP_2 is lower than the average cost at this point and thus the firm will be incurring losses. Since, all the firms in the industry are indentical in respect of cost curves, all would be incurring losses. To avoid these losses, some of the firms will leave the industry. As a result, the price will rise to OP, where again all firms are making normal profits. When the price OP is reached, the firms would have no further tendency to quit.

Thus, we conclude that at price OP, the firm under perfect competition is in equilibrium in the long-run when:

Price = MC = Minimum AC.

Now, at price OP, besides all firms being in equilibrium at output OM, the industry will also be in equilibrium, since there will be no tendency for new firms to enter or the existing firms to leave the industry, because all will be earning normal profits. Thus, at OP price, **full equilibrium,** *i.e.*, equilibrium of all the individual firms and also of the industry, as a whole, is achieved in the long-run under perfect competition.

Tendency to Optimum. An important conclusion that follows from the above discussion of firm's equilibrium in the long-rrn is that the forces of competition force all the firms to produce at the minimum point of the average cost curve. In other words, all the firms under competition tend to be of the **optimum size** in the long-rrn. This is advantageous from the viewpoint of consumers, since the product in question is being produced in the cheapest possible manner without any firm incurring a loss.

RELEVANCE OF PURE COMPETITION

We have discussed the equilibrium of firm under pure competition. But pure competition is practically non-existent in the real world, Then what is the relevance of pure competition ?

Advantages of Pure Competition

Broadly speaking, the advantages of pure competition can be put under two main headings: (1) The purely competitive firm produces at the most efficient level of production. This is so because (a) Since the firm has no control over price, its marginal revenue curve is perfectly elastic. The pressure of competition forces the price to the point at which the firm can make only normal profit. This point conforms to the level of full capacity and a level that can be achieved at the lowest per unit cost. (b) The purely competitive firm is under compulsion to use the most economical and modern methods of production so that its cost may be brought down to a competitive level. The normal-profit prices will weed out the old-fashioned and technologically backward firms by putting them to loss. (c) Pure competition is characterised by homogeneous or identical products. Hence advertisement is unnecessary. This cuts down cost and makes for economical production.

Disadvantages of Pure Competition

But pure competition is not an unmixed blessing. It has some disadvantages too: *(a)* Since the product is homogeneous, consumers' tastes for variety remain unsatisified. *(b)* In a purely competitive situation, the firms have to sacrifice economies of scale or the use of modern technology. *(c)* Purely competitive firms lack the resources to engage in extensive research and development.

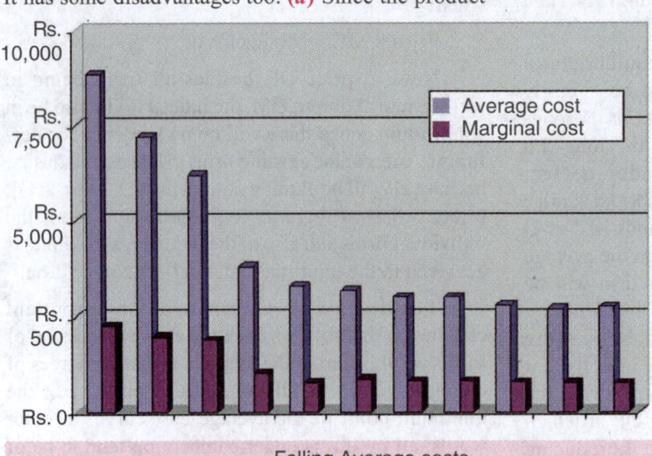

Falling Average costs.

What is then the use or relevance of the purely competitive model?

The study of the purely competitive model can be justified on the following grounds :

(a) Although pure competition is a rare phenomenon, there are at any time in existence certain industries which resemble a competitive model. The example is of a contractor's firm in a garment industry, where the number of firms is large, their size small and capital investment low.

(b) From the purely competitive model we can come to know how outside forces affect an industry. Agriculture is a purely competitive industry which is vitally affected by external factors.

(c) The study of the purely competitive market structure is helpful in understanding the imperfectly competitive model. The competitive model furnishes an ideal yard-stick for other market forms. The economists have made a good use of the purely competitive model to analyse capitalism. We can understand the monopolistic markets by reference to competitive models or as departures from pure competition.

(d) Purely competitive model is a very useful starting point for economic analysis in the real world conditions. In this competitive model, we assume a situation devoid of all interference from extraneous factors. It is a situation in a vacuum. Then one by one we introduce other factors to make the situation conform to the world of reality.

(e) An understanding of a purely competitive model can enable us to study the beneficial effects of increased production. We can understand, for instance how competition lowers prices, costs and profit margins under the impact of increased production. This is highly beneficial to the general public. When we understand the purely competitive model, we can grasp the

force of anti-trust or anti-monopoly arguments and arguments for lowering the tariff barriers, reduce import quotas and have freer international trade.

A note on equilibrium of different firms in perfect competition: Short-run equilibrium of a firm under perfect competition (Different firms)

(a) A firm making abnormal or super-normal profit.

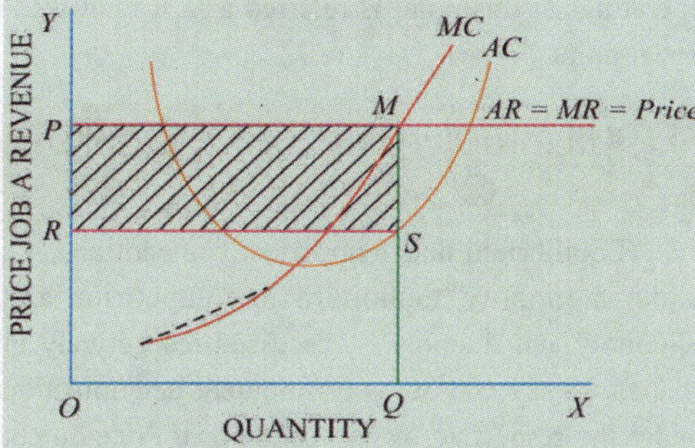

Fig. 25.5. Abnormal profit.

In the above diagram a firm is making abnormal profit. 'AC' is average cost 'MC' marginal cost, 'OP' is the price which is horizontal to 'x' axis, that means the price is fixed (MR = AR = Price). Equilibrium of a firm is achieved at point M where MR = MC. Draw a perpendicular on 'x'-axis which cuts it at point 'Q' and 'AC' at point 'S', along with this draw horizontal line which cuts at point 'P' and also a horizontal line from point 'S' on 'Y' axis we get point 'R'.

TR – TC = Π (Gross Profit)

▭ OPMQ – ▭ ORSQ = ▭ PMSR

TR = OP × OQ = Where per unit price = OP.

TC = OR × OC = Where per unit cost = OR.

Π = PR × RS (OQ) = where per unit profit = PR.

Thus a firm in short-run under perfect competetion earn's abnormal or supernormal profit. In the above diagram the shaded area ▭ PMSR is the total supernormal profit.

(b) In this case a firm is making only normal profit. Here normal profit means the firm is able to recover all the cost viz., AVC (average variable cost) and AFC (average fixed cost) that is nothing but AC (Average Cost).

AC = AFC + AVC. In this case the firm is neither making losses nor profit but as it is able to recover all the cost including the efforts put forth by the entrepreneur.

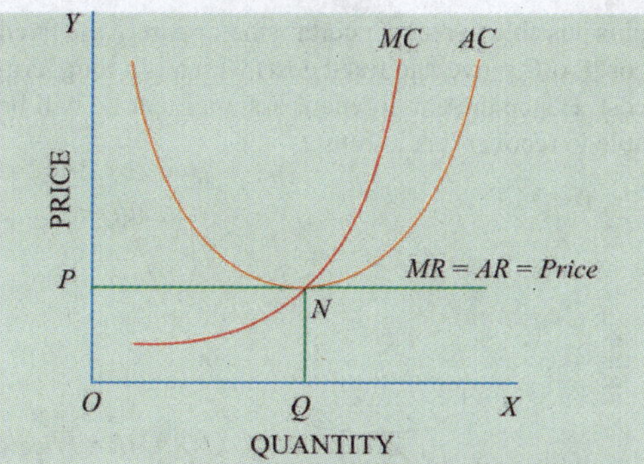

Fig. 25.6. Normal profit or break even price = Mix. AC.

In the above diagram, the equilibrium of the firm is achieved at point 'N' where MR = MC. Hence from this point, we can obtain quantity and price. 'OP' is per unit price and 'OQ' is the total quantity ∴ OQ × OP = ▭ OPNQ is the total revenue as well as total cost.

(c) In this case a firm is making sub-normal profit or incurring losses but the firm will continue to operate as it expects in the long-run to improve its demand. The demand curve (which is a horizontal curve, due to fixed prices) (AR) in perfect competition is = Marginal revenue = Price.

AR = MR = Price.

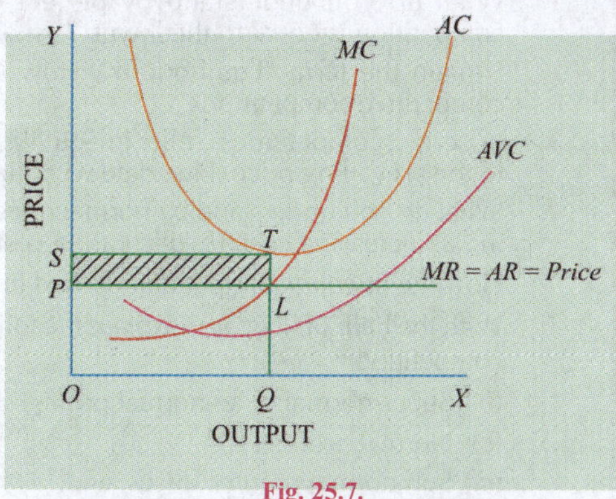

Fig. 25.7.

In the above diagram the demand curve 'PL' is between (AC) Average cost curve and (AVC) average variable cost. The equilibrium of the firm is achieved at point 'L', the total revenue is ▭ OPLQ where as the total cost is ▭ OSTQ.

▭ OPLQ – ▭ OSTQ = – ▭ STLP.

∴ ▭ STLP is referred as normal profit or losses. It is also referred as sub normal profit because the firm is able to recover, all the average variable cost plus it is able to recover certain major part of the fixed cost (AFC = average fixed cost) which is a long term cost. Hence the entrepreneur assumes that he will be able to recover this in future.

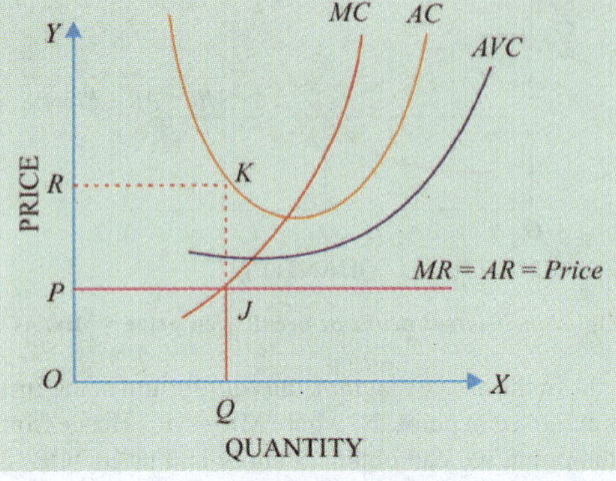

Fig. 25.8.

(*d*) A firm incurring heavy losses and it is referred as shut-down point. A firm which is not able to recover even the average variable cost, it may continue for a very short-period with the assumption it may change, but if it continues for a longer duration the firm will close-down.

In the above diagram the firms demand curve 'PJ' is well-below the average variable cost (AVC). In the diagram it is clear the firm is making huge losses that is to the amount of ▭ RKJP. Hence, the firm if operatings at this point is referred as a firm at shut-down-point.

EQUILIBRIUM UNDER IMPERFECT COMPETITION

(Equilibrium under imperfect competition, i.e., under monopoly, monopolistic competition and oligopoly and duopoly is discussed respectively in chapter 28, 29 and 30 as price-output determination under the respective market conditions. Price-output determination is nothing else except discussing conditions of equilibrium).

Key terms

Homogeneous Product, Super normal profit, Normal profit, shut-down point, loss.

QUESTIONS

1. What do you understand by perfect competition? Illustrate how price under perfect competition is equal to the lowest cost of production of a commodity.
2. Explain the term "Equilibrium". How is equilibrium price determined under perfectly competitive competition?
3. In perfect competition a seller in equilibrium does not determine price but adjust his output to the prevailing price. Elucidate with illustrations.
4. What do you understand by normal price? How is it determined under perfect competition in (*a*) increasing cost, (*b*) decreasing cost, and (*c*) constant cost.
5. How are price and output determined under perfect competition in the long-run? Explain.
6. With the help of diagrams explain the following Short-run equilibrium of a firm under perfect-competition
   (*i*) Super-normal or ab-normal profit,
   (*ii*) Normal profit,
   (*iii*) Sub-normal profitor losses, and,
   (*iv*) Shut-down point.

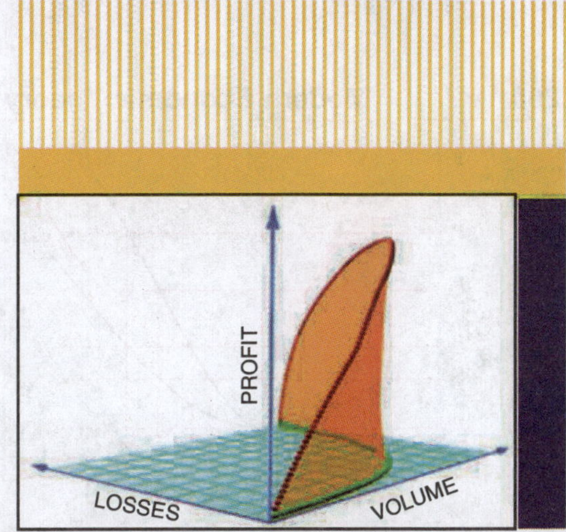

SUPPLY CURVE OF PERFECTLY COMPETITIVE INDUSTRY

Concept of Supply Curve

The supply curve of an industry depicts the various quantities of the product that it would offer to sell at various prices at a given time.

The quantities that the industry can offer to sell will depend on the price of its good in relation to the cost conditions of the firms. The cost conditions, in their turn, depend on the prices of the factors of production or inputs used by the firms and their production function. Hence, the supply of the industry will change not merely when the price of its good changes, but also as a result of a change in the production functions. This gives us the **supply function** of the industry as under :–

$S_A = f(P_A, P_X, P_Y, P_Z \ldots\ldots\ldots PF)$

Here

S_A is the quantity of the good A supplied.

f represents the functional relationship, *i.e.*, varies with.

P_A is the price of the good A.

P_x, P_y and P_z are the prices of the factors used in production.

P_F represents all the production functions of the firms.

Thus, the factor prices and the production functions are the parameters of the supply curve. That is, any change in the factor prices or the production functions will shift the supply curve to a new position, for this will mean a change in the very condition of supply (*i.e.*, the supply function). For instance, a shift in the supply curve to the right of the original supply curve will mean that owing to improvement in technology or to a fall in the factor prices, the industry is now in a position to supply a larger output at every price of its good. In other words, it is prepare to supply any output at a lower price than before. A rise in factor prices will have the opposite effect.

It is to be borne in mind that the concept of supply curve is relevant only to perfect or pure competition, and not to cases of imperfect competition, namely, monopolistic competition, monopoly and oligopoly. The reason is obvious. In the discussion of supply curve, we say how a firm adjusts (increases or decreases) its output in response to change in price. To a firm under perfect competition price is given; it cannot influence it in any manner; it has to accept it. The only thing that a firm can do is to adjust its supply to the prevailing price. Thus, under competition a firm is a quantity-adjuster. But under various forms of imperfect competition, *e.g.*, imperfect

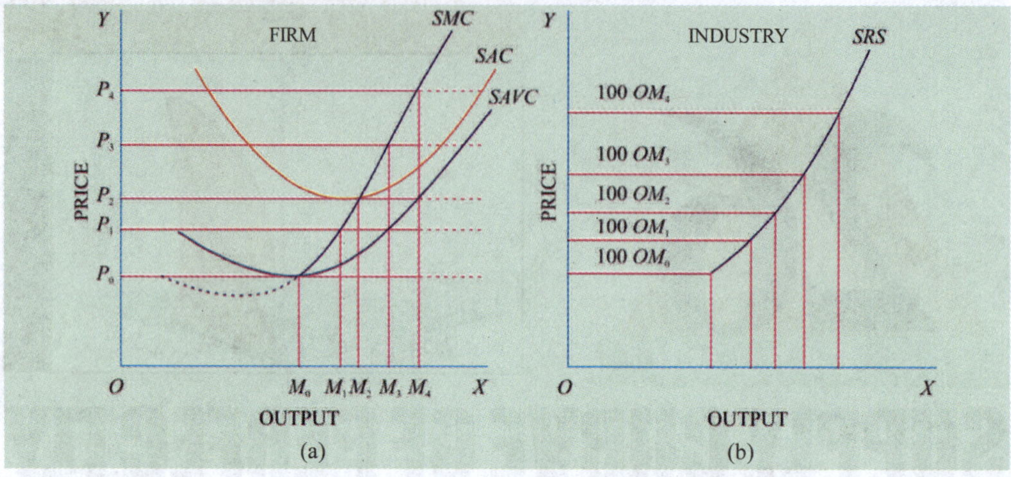

Fig. 26.1. Deriving Short-run Supply Curve under perfct competition.

competition or absolute monopoly, the firm can set its own price. Price- output determination is under its control. There is no question of adjusting output or supply to a given price as under perfect competition, but of choosing that price-output which maximizes its profit.

As professor Baumol observes, the supply curve is, strictly speaking, a concept which is usually relevant only for the case of pure (or perfect) competition .... The reason for this lies in its definition — the supply curve is designed to answer questions of the form, "How much will firm A supply if it encounters a price which is fixed at P dollars"[1]. But such a question is most relevant to the behaviour of firms that actually deal with prices over whose determination they exercise no influence". This situation is that of perfect competition and not any form of imperfect competition.

We shall now study both the short-run and long-run supply curves for a competitive industry, since its intersection with the market demand curve will determine the short-run and the long-run competitive prices respectively.

Short-run Supply Curve

As seen previously, the short-run is a period in which the capital equipment is fixed and the increased demand is met only by the intensive use of the given plant, *i.e.*, by increasing the amount of the variable factors. We have studied above that a firm under perfect competition produces an output at which marginal cost equals price. The short-run marginal cost curve of the firm, therefore, indicates the quantities which the firm will produce in the short run at all possible prices. **Thus, the short-run marginal cost curve of the firm is the supply curve of the perfectly competitive firm in the short-run.**

This is illustrated in Fig. 26.1 (a). At price OP_4, the firm will produce or supply an amount equal to OM_4, since only at this output, price OP_4 equals marginal cost. Similarly, at price OP_3, the firm will supply an amount $OM_3$and at prices OP_2 and OP_1 it will supply the amounts OM_2 and OM_1 respectively. As explained before, a firm in the short-run will not supply at prices below the minimum average variable cost, since at prices below the minimum average variable cost, it will not be covering even variable costs. Therefore, **the firm's short-run supply curve is identical with that portion of the short-run marginal cost SMC curve which lies above the minimum point of the short-run average variable cost (SAVC) curve.** The quantity supplied would be zero at all prices less than the minimum average variable cost. The firm's short-run supply curve, therefore, consists of the shaded or thick (not dotted) segment of the SMC curve in Fig. 26.1 (a).

The short-run supply curve for the whole perfectly competitive industry is derived by the lateral summation (*i.e.*, adding up sideways) of that part of all the firms' marginal cost curves which lies above the minimum points on their average variable cost curves. If a hypothetical competitive industry consists of 100 identical single-plant firms, one of which is pictured in Fig. 26.1 (a), the industry would supply an amount equal to 100 OM_1 at price OP_1, 100 M_2 at price OP_2, 100 OM_3 at price OP_3, and so on. The industry would not supply any output at prices less

1. Boumol 1. W.—*Economic Theory and Operation Analysis,* 2nd ed., p. 342.

than OP_0 . SRS is the short-run supply curve of the industry.

It may be noted that while Y-axis of both the Figs. 26.1 (a) and 26.1 (b) have been drawn on the same scale and represent price per unit, scales of the X-axes of the two Figs. 26.1 (a) and 26.1 (b) are not the same.

Thus, we see that the short-run supply curve of the perfectly competitive industry always slopes upwards, since the short-run marginal cost curve (above the minimum point of the AVC) of individual firms always slopes upwards too. How steeply will the industry's short-run supply curve rise will obviously depend on the slope of the cost curves of the individual firms in the industry. The elasticity of the short-run supply curve of the industry will depend on the elasticity of the marginal cost curves of the individual firms in the industry.

Long-run Supply Curve

As already mentioned, long run is a period sufficiently long to allow changes in both the size as well as the number of firms in the industry. If there is an increase in demand, in the short run, it will be met by over-utilisation of the existing plant. But if the increased demand persists in the long run, it will be met by both the expansion of the existing firms as well as by the entry of new firms in the industry.

Long-run supply is defined as supplies offered at various prices by the existing as well as the potential producers in the long-run. As explained before, a firm under perfect competition is in long-run equilibrium when it is equalizing price with both marginal cost and average cost. The forces of competition (*i.e.*, free entry or exit of the firms) force the firm under perfect competition to produce at the minimum point of its average cost curve in the long-run equilibrium.

On a little reflection, it will be clear that the long-run supply curve of the perfectly competitive industry cannot be the lateral summation of the long-run marginal cost curves of the firms as in short-run supply curve. This is so because, in the long-run equilibrium, owing to the free entry or exit of the firms under perfect competition, firms are forced to produce only at the minimum point of the long-run average cost curve where the long-run marginal cost curve intersects it. It is also because the expansion of the industry, *i.e.*, increase in the number of firms, brings about shifts in the cost curves of the firms due to the emergence of external economies and diseconomies of production. Moreover, the number of firms in the long-run equilibrium varies at different prices.

The concept of external economies and diseconomies is important in describing the shape of the long-run supply curve. External economies and diseconomies are those economies and diseconomies which are realised by each member firms as a consequence of the expansion of the whole industry. An expansion of the industry may lead to the availability of new and cheaper raw materials, tools and machinery, and to the discovery and diffusion of new and cheaper techniques of production.

Some raw materials and tools may be made available at reduced prices. This is so because, as the industry grows, subsidiary and correlated firms may spring up in the vicinity of the industry to provide it with raw materials and tools at the reduced prices. Further, as the industry expands trade journals may appear which help in discovering and spreading new technical knowledge. Moreover, with expansion of the industry, specialised firms may come into existence which work up its 'waste products'. The industry can then sell them at good price.

Thus, the entry of firms enlarging the size of the industry may enable all firms to produce at lower costs. The large-scale firms reap internal economies. The large-scale industry brings to the firms constituting the industry external economies. The availability of internal economies will shift the marginal and average cost curves of the firms below the previous level. There is every possibility of external economies to be reaped when a young industry grows in a new territory. But it is extremely doubtful whether external economies continue to accrue as a well-established good-sized industry experiences further growth.

On the contrary, an expanding industry may experience external diseconomies. As more firms enter into the industry, competition among them may push up the prices of scarce raw materials, skilled labour and other scarce factors or inputs. Further, the additional factors of production, other than entrepreneur, coming into the industry may be less efficient than the previous ones. The emergence of the external diseconomies will shift the marginal and average cost curves above the previous level.

Thus, whether a particular industry on expansion will experience the phenomenon of rising costs or falling costs or constant costs will depend upon the combined result of external economies and diseconomies. The long-run supply curve of a perfectly competitive industry will, therefore, have different shapes depending upon the fact:

(*i*) whether the industry in question is a constant cost industry;

(*ii*) increasing cost industry; or

(*iii*) decreasing cost industry.

We shall now examine these cases.

Supply Curve of the Constant Cost Industry

A constant cost industry will be one in which the external economies and diseconomies may cancel each other so that the constituent firms of an enlarged industry do not experience any shift in their cost curves. An industry can also be a constant cost industry if its expansion generates neither external economies nor external diseconomies.

Obviously, as the number of firms in the industry increase, there will be increased demand for productive factors like raw materials, labour, capital *etc.*, by the industry; and if the prices of these productive factors rise, as the industry expands, then the costs must rise. Hence, a constant cost industry therefore, must be one which makes little impact on the market for these productive resources. In other words, its demand for these productive factors must be a very small proportion of the total demand for these factors. It is only then that the increased demand for these factors, as a result of the expansion of the industry, will not raise the prices of these factors.

The paper-doll industry might be a case in point. This industry uses such a small proportion of the total quantity of paper produced in a year that a large increase in its demand for paper as a result of its expansion would have no perceptible influence on the price of paper. Similarly, the increased demand for labour in the paper-doll industry would have little effect of raising the wages of the labour generally.

In the case of constant cost industry, which is shown in Fig. 26.2 (*b*), the long-run supply curve will be a horizontal straight line at the level of minimum long-run average cost curve.

Every firm will be in long-run equilibrium where Price = MC = AC, *i.e.*, at the minimum point of the long-run average cost. In the long-run, new firms will enter the industry without raising or lowering the cost curves of the firms in the industry so that the industry would supply any amount of commodity at the price OP which is equal to minimum long-run average cost.

Thus, we see that in case of the constant cost industry, the new firms, which will enter the industry in the long-run, will have identical cost conditions with the already existing ones; and all firms will produce at the minimum point of the average cost curve. The additional supplies of the product will come primarily from the entry of new firms–having the same minimum average cost so that any amount can be supplied at the price equal to the minimum average cost by the increase in the number of firms.

In Fig. 26.2 (*b*), LSC is the long-run supply curve of the constant cost industry and in Fig. 26.2 (a), LAC and LMC are the long-run average and marginal cost curves respectively. The long-run marginal cost curve of the firms in its relevant Portion slopes upwards but the long-run supply curve is horizontal straight line (*i.e.*, perfectly elastic) at price OP, which is equal to the minimum average cost. Thus, it will be clear that the long-run supply curve is not the lateral summation of the long-run marginal cost curves.

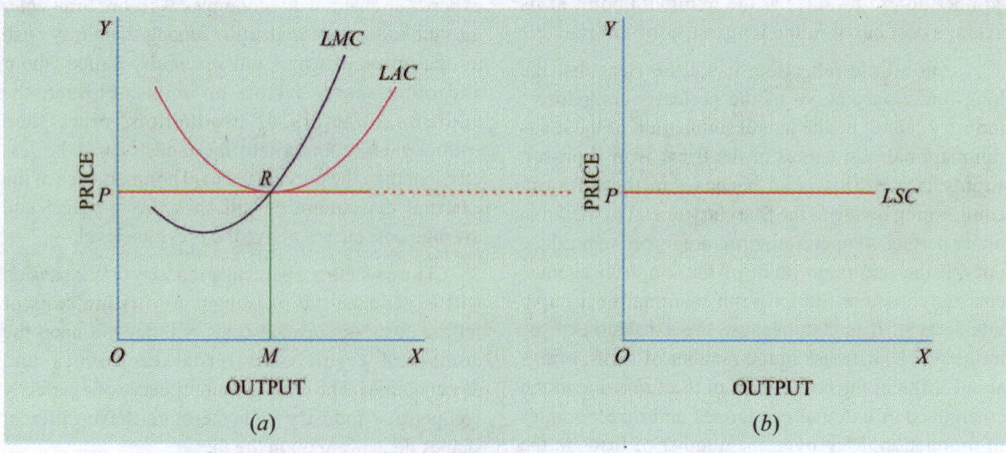

Fig. 26.2. Long-run Supply Curves of a Constant Cost Industry.

Supply Curve of the Increasing Cost Industry

If the industry is of appreciable size and its demand for productive resources constitutes a sufficiently large part of the total demand for the resources, then its expansion will cause their prices to rise. The wages of specialized labour and the prices of other scarce factors like raw materials, capital equipment are bound to rise as the demand for them increases as a result of the expansion of the industry. There may be some external economies but generally the external diseconomies will over-weigh the external economies.

Thus, these net external diseconomies will raise the costs and, therefore, shift both U-shaped average and marginal cost curves of all the firms (both existing as well as the new ones) above the previous level. As a result, the minimum average cost will rise.

Every firm will be in long-run equilibrium where Price = MC = minimum AC. But this price and minimum average cost will be higher than the one before expansion of the industry. It is, therefore, clear that the additional supplies of the product by new firm, in the case of increasing cost industry, will be forthcoming only at a higher price. The long-run supply curve (LSC) of the increasing cost industry will, therefore, slope upwards as shown in Fig. 26.3 (*b*).

In Fig. 26.3 (*a*), the new, *i.e.*, dotted long-run average cost curve (LAC) and long-run marginal cost curve (LMC) have been shifted up a little as a result of the net external diseconomies due to the increase in the number of firms in the industry. Every firm will be in equilibrium at OM_1 output, where it will be equalizing price OP_1 with new marginal cost and new minimum average cost. More will be supplied at price OP_1 than at the old price OP [see Fig. 26.3 (*b*)], because there will be **larger number of firms at price OP1 than those at OP** and, therefore, the long-run supply curve slopes upward to the right.

This case of upward sloping supply curve is probably the most typical of the actual competitive world. That is so because productive resources are used in various industries; hence higher prices have to be paid to transfer these resources from one industry to another.

Supply Curve of the Decreasing Cost Industry

It is conceivable that an industry might have decreasing costs due to net external economies. As a young industry grows in a new territory, it is likely that external economies may overweigh the external diseconomies so that, with the expansion ofthe industry, production costs would be reduced. The presence of net external economies will shift the cost curves of the firms (both existing as well as new ones) downward.

The cost curves of a young industry with its expansion may be lowered (*a*) because cheaper and better trained labour becomes available, (*b*) because better information centres and markets created, (*c*) because productivity of the factors in one firm is enhanced by expanded production in others or (*d*) because raw materials produced at decreasing costs by other specialised industries are obtained cheaply.

Owing to the external economies, the additional supplies of the product will be forthcoming at reduced prices. Every firm after expansion will be in equilibrium where it is equating price with marginal cost and minimum average cost. But this new price and minimum average cost will be lower than the original ones.

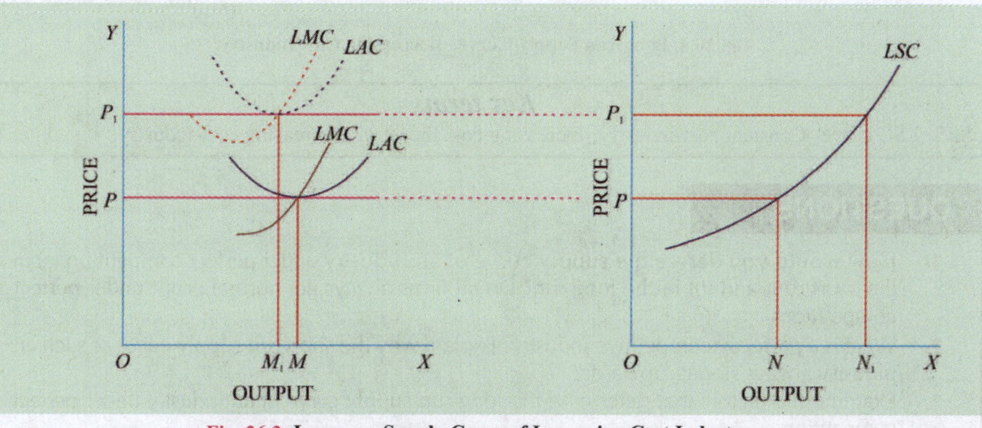

Fig. 26.3. Long-run Supply Curve of Increasing Cost Industry.

Fig. 24.4 (a) depicts the position of one firm but all firms are supposed to have identical conditions. At the initial price OP, before expansion of the industry, even firm will be in equilibrium at E and will be producing OM. The total supply of the product by the industry at price OP would be ON [Fig. 26.4 (b)]. As the new firms enter, in the long run under the stimulus of increased demand, additional supplies of the product will be coming at the lower price OP_1, since costs would be reduced with the expansion of the industry. The new dotted LAC and LMC curves are long-run average and marginal cost curves respectively after the industry has expanded due to the entry of new firms. In this new position, every firm will be in long-run equilibrium equating price OP_1 with new marginal and minimum average cost at E_1 and producing upwards or sloping downwards depending upon the fact whether the industry is a constant cost, an increasing cost or a decreasing cost industry. But as mentioned above, the long-run upward sloping supplý curve is more in conformity with the actual world, since external economies are very much limited in scope in the real world. The productive resources are required in all lines of production and increased demand for them by any industry is bound to push their prices up. OM_1. The total supply of the product by the industry will be ON_1[Fig. 26.4 (b)]. The total supply will be greater at the new price OP_1 than at the old price OP partly because of the larger production by the existing firms but mainly because there will be a greater number of firms at OP_1.

Summing up

From the above discussion, it follows that while the short-run supply curve of the industry alwasys slopes upwards, the long-run supply curve may be a horizontal straight line, sloping upwards or sloping downwards depending upon the fact whether the industry is a constant cost, an increasing cost or a decreasing cost industry. But as mentioned above, the long-run upward sloping supply curve is more in conformity with the actual world, since external economies are very much limited in scope in the real world. The productive resources are required in all lines of production and increased demand for them by any industry is bound to push their prices up.

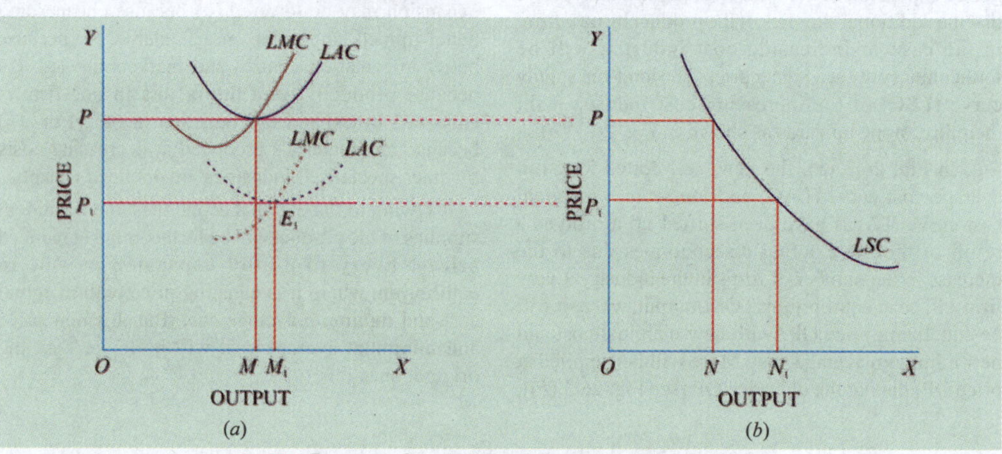

Fig. 26.4. Long-run Supply Curve, Decreasing Cost Industry.

Key terms

SRS, LSC curve, Constant cost-industry, Increasing cost Industry, Decreasing cost-industry.

QUESTIONS

1. How would you derive the supply curve of an industry under perfect competition (*a*) in the short run, and (*b*) in the long run? Do all firms always get normal profit under perfect competition?
2. What is a perfectly competitive industry? Explain why the short run supply curve of such an industry always slopes upwards?
3. Examine the factors that determine the long-run supply curve of an industry under perfect competition.

PRICE-OUTPUT DETERMINATION- PERFECT COMPETITION

Our main purpose in the preceding chapters was to bring us to a position where we can explain how price is determined under conditions of perfect competition. In the discussion of consumer's behaviour, we assumed that, under perfect competition, a single buyer or consumer is unable to influence the price and, therefore, takes the market price as given and allocates his money expenditure so as to obtain maximum satisfaction. On this assumption, we derived demand curve for product of a single consumer as well as of the market as a whole (*i.e.*, of all the consumers or buyers of the product) both according to the old Marshallian utility analysis and the new indifference curve technique.

Similarly, we studied the behaviour of the entrepreneur or firm under perfect competition assuming that a single firm or producer cannot affect the price of his product by his own individual action. A single firm under perfect competition then takes the market price as given and adjust its output so as to obtain maximum profits. On this assumption, we discussed in details the conditions for the firm's equilibrium in perfect competition and derived both short-run and long-run supply curves of the firm as well as of the whole industry.

Now the interaction between these two forces of demand and supply determines price in the market. It is not the demand and supply of a single buyer and a firm respectively that determines price but it is the demand of all the buyers taken together and the supply of all the buyers taken together that determine the price by their interaction. We see, therefore, that the price of a commodity which is given for each individual consumer or firm is determined by all the consumers and firms that buy and sell.

Two Approaches

There are two well known approaches to pricing under perfect competition, *viz*., partial equilibrium approach and the general equilibrium approach. The first is set by Alfred Marshall and the second by Walras. We have already discussed partial Equilibrium and General Equilibrium in Chapter 3 of this book.

Partial Equilibrium Approach

In the partial equilibrium approach to pricing, we explain price determination of a single commodity, keeping the prices of other commodities unchanged. We assume that the prices of various commodities are independent of one another and do not mutually affect one another. Marshall explains this approach thus, "The forces to be dealt with are however, so numerous that it is best to analyse a few at a time and work out a number of partial solutions as auxiliaries to our main study. Thus, we begin by isolating the primary relations of supply, demand and price in regard to a particular commodity. We reduce to inaction all other forces by the phrase 'other things being equal.' We do not suppose that they are inert, but for the time we ignore their activity."

Thus, in the Marshallian or partial equilibrium approach to pricing under perfect competition, demand for a commodity is determined on the assumption that prices of other commodities, tastes and incomes of the consumer remain constant. Similarly, supply is determined on the assumption that the prices of other commodities, price of resources or factors and production functions remain the same. The partial equilibrium analysis discusses only the price determination of a commodity in isolation and does not explain how the prices of the various commodities are inter-dependent and inter-related.

Thus, the partial equilibrium analysis is based on the assumption that the changes in any single sector of the economy do not significantly affect the other sectors. As Prof. Lipsey observes, "All partial equilibrium analyses are based on the assumption of *ceteris paribus*. Strictly interpreted, the assumption is that all other things in the economy are unaffected by any changes in the sector under consideration (say sector *A*). This assumption is always violated to some extent, for anything that happens in one sector must cause changes in some other sectors. What matters is that the changes induced throughout the rest of the economy are sufficiently small and diffused so that the effect they in turn have on the sector *A* can be safely ignored."[1]

General Equilibrium Approach

The general equilibrium analysis does not assume that the price of a good is determined independently of the prices of other goods. It supposes rather that a change in the price of a particular good affects prices and quantities demanded of other goods and the charges in prices of the other goods affect the price and quantity demanded of this particular good. Thus, the general equilibrium analysis explains the mutual and simultaneous determination of the prices of all goods and factors. It thus "looks at **multi-market equilibrium.** It considers the way in which the prices of all goods in an economic system are set simultaneously each in its own Flex-price market."[1]

We have said above that the partial equilibrium approach assumes that the effect of a change in price of a particular good will be so diffused in the rest of the economy that it will have a negligible effect on the prices of other goods. But when the effect is significant as in the case of inter-related goods, the partial equilibrium analysis ceases to be applicable. In such cases, we have to resort to the general equilibrium approach. As stonier and Hague observe, "If X and Y are either strongly complementary or strongly competitive, a fall in the price of X can have a substantial effect on the demand for Y. General equilibrium analysis attempts to take account of such relationship."[2]

Hence "to explain the inter-relationship and inter-dependence among the prices and quantities of goods and factors ultimately to explain the determination of the relative prices of all goods and factors, the proportion in which different goods are being produced and different factors are being used for the production of different goods is the essence of general equilibrium analysis."[3]

Professor Ryan explains the general equilibrium thus, "Let us suppose that the whole economy is initially in 'general' equilibrium; that is, that at the going prices the planned sales of each commodity and productive services are equal to the planned purchases . . . . . . When a 'general' equilibrium is disturbed by some economic event there will ensue a process of adjustment and re-adjustment during which each price affects, and is in turn affected by, each other price. The change in pattern of prices is in part the cause, and in part the consequence, of revision in the purchases and sales plans of individuals, households and firms . . . . . Ultimately, a new equilibrium will emerge in which the planned sales of each commodity and productive services will again be equal to the planned purchases. In the new 'general equilibrium', full adjustment will have been made to the new conditions."[4] In this chapter, we shall confine ourselves to partial equilibrium approach. The general equilibrium approach is beyond this level of this study.

1. Lipsey, R. G. –*An Introduction to Positive Economics*, III Ed. 1971, p. 404.
2. Stonier and Hague, *Text Book of Economic Theory*, IV Ed. 1972, p. 383.
3. Ahuja H. L. *Advance Economic Theory* 1975, p. 489.
4. Ryan. W. J. L., *Price Theory* 1958, p. 244, 246-47.

Price Determination: General Statement

Before Marshall, there was a dispute among economists on whether the force of demand (*i.e.*, marginal utility) or the force of supply (*i.e.*, cost of production) is more important in determining price. Marshall gave equal importance to both the demand (or marginal utility) and supply (or cost of production) in the determination of the value or price.

Marshall's famous analogy of a pair of scissors is worth quoting. "We might as reasonably dispute whether it is the upper or the under blade of a pair of scissors that cuts a piece of paper, as whether value is governed by utility or cost of production. It is true that when one blade is held still and the cutting is effected by moving the other, we may say with careless brevity that the cutting is done by the second, but the statement is not strictly accurate and is to be excused only so long as it claims to be merely a popular and not a strictly scientific account of what happens". Thus, neither the upper blade nor the lower one taken separately can do the work of cutting, both have their importance in the process of cutting. The lower blade may be kept stationary and only the upper one may be moved, yet both are indispensable for the process of cutting.

"The only really accurate answer to the question whether it is supply or demand which determines price is that it is both. At times it will seem that one is more important than the other, for one will be active and the other passive. For example, if demand remains constant but supply conditions vary, it is demand which is passive and supply active. **But neither is more or less important than the other in determining price.**"[5]

Thus, the demand of all consumers and the supply of all firms together determine the prices which are then taken as given by each one of them.

Equilibrium Price

In the chapters on demand analysis–both in Marshallian utility analysis and indifference curve technique, we concluded that a demand curve normally slopes downwards. In other words, it means that, other things remaining the same, more quantity of a commodity will be demanded at a lower price than that at a higher price. Similarly, we saw in an earlier chapter that the supply curve of the commodity normally slopes upwards. In other words, the producers will offer to sell larger quantity of the product at a higher price than at a lower one. Supply depends on the number and size of firms, production techniques and the prices of the productive resources.

Thus, quantity demanded and quantity supplied vary with price. The price which will tend to settle down or come to stay in the market is one at which the quantity demanded is equal to the quantity supplied. Only at the price at which quantity demanded is equal to the quantity supplied, will all the buyers' and sellers' wishes be satisfied. This price at which demand and supply are equal is known as an **equilibrium price,** since, at this price, the forces of demand and supply are balanced, or are in equilibrium. The quantity bought and sold (or the amount demanded or supplied) at this equilibrium price is known as **equilibrium amount.**

If the equality between quantity demanded and supplied does not hold for some price, buyers' and sellers' desires are inconsistent: either the amount demanded by the buyers is more than that offered by the sellers is greater than the amount demanded by the buyers. In either case, this price will change so as to bring about equality between quantity demanded and quantity supplied.

An example both in terms of schedules and curves will make the whole thing clear. The table given below gives the demand and supply schedules relating to a variety of common cloth and in Figure 27.1, DD is the demand curve and SS is the supply curve. A glance at the table and the figure will show how the price is determined between the demand and supply.

TABLE 1.

Price per metre	*Quantity demanded (million metres) per month*	*Quantity supplied (million metres) per month*	*Pressure on price*
Rs.			
5	9	18	↓ Falling
4	10	16	↓ Falling
3	12	12	Neutral
2	15	7	↑ Rising
1	20	0	↑ Rising

It will be seen that when price is Rs. 3 per metre, 12 million metres are supplied and 12 million of metres are demanded, *i.e.*, the quantity demanded is equal to the quantity supplied. Rs. 3 per metre, therefore, is the equilibrium price. Price is at equilibrium at Rs. 3. In other words, price of Rs. 3 will persist in the market,

5. Stonier and Hangue–*A Text-book of Economic Theory*, p. 155.

because at this level there is no tendency for it to rise or to fall. Of course, this equilibrium price may not be reached at once. There may have to be an initial period of trial and error and of oscillations around this equilibrium level before the price finally settles down and supply balances demand.

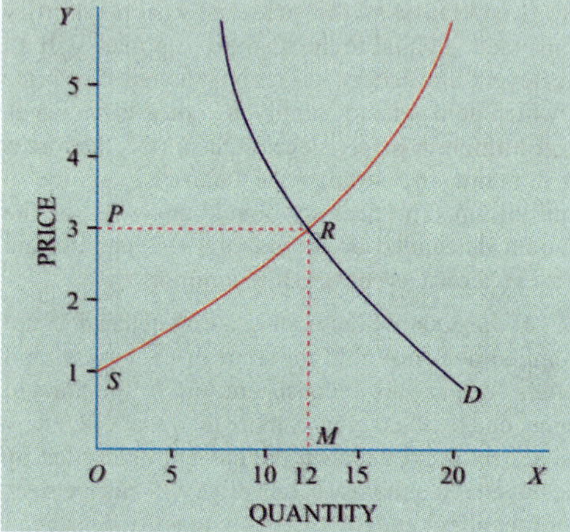

Fig. 27.1. Interaction of Demand and Supply.

If the price is Rs. 5 (*i.e.*, above the equilibrium level), the quantity offered (18 million metres) by the sellers will be greater than the quantity demanded (9 million metres) and there will be a tendency for the price to fall. At the price of Rs. 5 some of the sellers will be unable to sell all the quantity they want to sell and will, therefore, cut down the price in order to attract customers.

On the other hand, as the price falls, the quantity demanded will increase and the quantity supplied will decline in the way shown in the table until at the price of Rs. 3 per metre at which supply balances demand. At this price, the whole quantity of the product, which all sellers are willing to sell, will be purchased by the buyers.

Similarly, if the price is Rs. 2 per metre, *i.e.*, below the equilibrium price, the amount of the cotton cloth demanded (15 million metres) by the buyers will exceed the amount offered to supply (7 million metres), therefore, the price of cotton cloth will tend to rise. Since at Rs. 2 the quantity demanded exceeds the quantity supplied, the buyers who are willing to buy at this price will find that the quantity offered is not sufficient to satisfy their wants, *i.e.*, sellers are not willing to supply as large a quantity as buyers demand. Hence, some of the consumers, who have not been able to satisfy their demand, will be induced to bid the price up in the hope of getting more supplies. This action of unsatisfied buyers will push up the price in the market up to the equilibrium level.

Thus, Rs. 3 is the equilibrium price and 12 million metres is the equilibrium amount, because only at this price of Rs. 3 per metre will there be no tendency for the price to rise or to fall; only at this price the same quantity is demanded and supplied. Only at this price will there be no unsatisfied buyers or sellers who are prepared to let prices alter to satisfy their desires.

From the above discussion, it follows that the equilibrium between demand and supply, or what is often called market equilibrium, determines the price in the market. Price comes to stay in the market at the level where demand and supply curves intersect each other.

The equilibrium price will change if either the demand or the supply curve change due to a change in demand or supply conditions. Given the supply curve, an increase in demand (*i.e.*, shift of the demand curve to the right) will raise the price and a decrease in demand (*i.e.*, shift of the demand curve to the left) will lower the price. On the contrary, an increase in supply (*i.e.*, shift of the supply curve to the right) demand curve remaining the same, will lower the price and a decrease in supply (*i.e.*, shift in the supply curve to the left) will raise the price.

The change in equilibrium price as a result of change in demand or supply curve is shown in Fig. 27.2 given below. In Fig. 27.2 (a) SS is the supply cure and DD is the demand curve. If now there is an increase in demand from DD to D′D′, the supply curve remaining the same, equilibrium price will rise to OP′ (= M′ R′) at which the new demand curve D′ D′ intersects the supply curve SS at the point R′. As a result of the increase in demand, equilibrium amount demanded and supplied will also rise to OM′. On the contrary, if the demand decreases from DD to D″D″, the equilibrium price will fall to Op″ (= M″ R″) and the equilibrium amount will decrease from OM to OM″.

On the other hand, in Fig. 27.2 (b), demand curve DD remains the same and it is the supply curve which shifts. To begin with, SS is the supply curve which instersects the demand curve DD at the price OP. If now the supply curve increases from SS to S′S′, the equilibirum price will fall to OP′ (= R′ M′) and the equilibrium amount will increase to OM′. If supply decreases from SS to S″S″, the equilibrium price will rise to OP″ (= R″ M″) and the equilibrium amount will decrease to OM″.

Thus, we see that changes either in demand or supply will change the equilibrium price.

Demand and Supply only Superficially Affect Price

From the above analysis, it seems that price is determined by the interaction of demand and supply. But it should be remembered that demand and supply are themselves governed by a host of other factors. 'Supply and Demand' is only a superficial formula. Professor Samuelson rightly remarks: "Supply and demand are not ultimate explanations of price. They are simply useful catch-all categories for analysing and describing the multitude of forces, causes and factors impinging on price. Rather than being final answers supply and demand simply represent initial questions. Our work is not over but just begun."[6]

For example, the cost of production is the main determinant of supply curve. A change in cost of production will change the supply curve and will thus change the equilibrium price. Similarly, the market demand for a commodity may change because the incomes of the consumers have changed or the total number of consumers have changed because of the change in the number of population.

Thus, we see that factors like cost of production, incomes of the consumers, and the size of the population, *etc.*, take part in determining price but all of them work through either supply or demand.

In the last analysis, the firms seek to minimise costs and maximise profits. This will govern the amount of resources they will use. The resources are supplied by the households. The price of a resource will depend on the amount which the firms want in relation to the household's ability and willingness to provide the resource. The price of a good will depend on the amount which the households want in relation to the firms' willingness to produce it.

Thus, prices depend on the willingness and ability of the households to sell resources and buy goods and the firms' ability and willingness to sell goods and buy resources. The price will be established at a point where (*a*) the quantity of goods produced must be the same as the households want to buy and (*b*) the quantity of resources used must be the same as those which the households want to sell.

IMPORTANCE OF TIME ELEMENT

We have seen that the price is determined by the equilibrium between demand and supply. But Marshall, who propounded the theory that the price is determined by the interaction of demand and supply, also laid emphasis on the role of time element in the determination of price. This is so because supply conditions vary with the length of period under consideration.

Three Time-Periods

On the basis of response of supply over time to a given and permanent change in demand, Marshall distinguished three periods in which equilibrium between demand and supply was brought about:

(*i*) Very short period or market period equilibrium when supply is fixed or is limited to the existing stock in hand;

(*ii*) Short-run equilibrium when firms can expand output with the existing plants by changing the amounts of variable factors employed; and

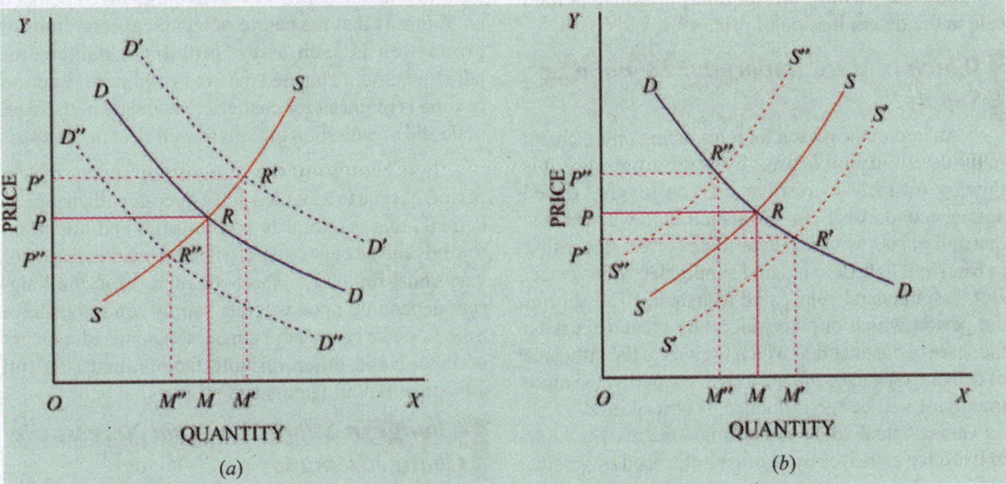

Fig. 27.2. (*a*) Effect of Change in Demand on Equilibrium Price.
(*b*) Effect of Change in Supply on Equilibrium Price.

6. Samuelson, P. A.–*Economics*, 1970 Edition, p. 369.

***(iii)* Long-run equilibrium** when firms can abandon old plants or build new ones and when the new firms can enter the industry or old ones can leave it.

It is on the basis of time allowed to the forces of demand and supply for mutual adjustment that Marshall talked of **market price, short-run price or long-run normal price.** Let us see how price changes in these time periods.

Market Period. If a sudden and once-for-all increase in demand takes place, there will be a sharp rise in market price but, there can be no change in the amount supplied, because, in the market period, firms can sell only what they have already produced, *i.e.*, what is in stock.

Short-run Period. This period is sufficient only to make limited output adjustment with the existing equipment by expanding output along the short-run marginal cost curves. The new short-run equilibrium price will be higher than the price before the increase in demand, but not as high as the market price or very short-run price just after the increase in demand. The output will be greater in short-run equilibrium than it was before the increase in demand.

Long-run Period. In the long-run, the time is long enough for the firms to change in size of their plants or build new plants. Also, new firms can enter the industry. In the long-run equilibrium, therefore, the price will be established at a lower level and output at a higher level than in the short-run position.

Thus, we see that the price that will tend to prevail in the market depends on the period under consideration. In other words, time plays an important role in the determination of price.

Which is More Important: Demand or Supply?

An important reason for introducing time element in the determination of price by Marshall was that it is thereby possible to resolve the controversy raised among economists before Marshall as to whether it is demand or supply which determines price. According to Marshall both demand and supply determine price. But, "as a general rule", said Marshall, "The shorter the period which one considers the greater must be the share of our attention which is given to the influence of demand on value; and the longer the period the more important will be the influence of cost of production on value. Actual value at any time –the market value as it is often called –is more often influenced by passing events and causes whose action is fitful and short-lived than by those which work persistently. But in the long-run these fitful and irregular causes in a large measure affects one another's influence, so that in the long-run persistent causes dominate values completely."[7]

Roughly speaking it can be said that in the very short-run it is demand which determines price and in the long-run it is supply which determines price. Thus, the economists who contended that price is determined by demand were right and so were those who held that price is determined by supply. Only the former were emphasising the price determination has no influence on price, and the latter were stressing the price determination in the long-run in which cost of production, which affects supply, has an important bearing.

But, as already pointed out, a correct scientific answer to the question whether it is demand or supply which determines price is that it is both. The above statement of either demand determining price in the market period or supply determining price in the long-run is only a rough one. As it is clear from the analogy of scissors provided by Marshall from the viewpoint of scientific accuracy, fixity of supply in the market period is as much a determinant of price as the variability of demand.

Conclusion. Thus, we see that, as factors determining price, both supply and demand are important. Only their influence varies over different time periods.

Time Affects Supply

From the above analysis, one important conclusion follows that it always takes time for the supply to adjust fully to the changed conditions of demand. The reason why changes in supply conditions take time to adjust themselves to the changed demand condition is that the nature of technical conditions of production is such as to prohibit instantaneous adjustment to a changed demand condition. A period of time is required for changes to be made in the size, scale and organisation of firms as well as of the industry.

It is because of the response of supply over a period of time to a sudden and a once-for all change in demand that economists find it useful and important to study the pricing process (*a*) in the market period or very short-run, (*b*) in short-run, and (*c*) in the long-run, depending upon whether supply conditions have time to make (*i*) no adjustment, (*ii*) some adjustment of labour and other variable factors, and (*iii*) full adjustment of all factors and all costs.

Change in Supply Does not Necessarily Change Demand

On the other hand, the economists do not study the adjustment in demand as a consequence of the

7. Marshall –*Principles of Economics*, pp. 349-50.

changes in supply conditions. This is because, "There is no reason why, if supply conditions change, demand conditions should change as well, or, if they do, why should they change differently in the short-run and the long-run. Changes in consumers' tastes are not dependent on technology in the way that supply conditon are. Admittedly consumers' tastes may, and probably will, change as time goes on. But this will be a change of data and not a change induced by the changed supply conditions. Thus, there is no necessary reason why the long-run demand curve should differ from the short-run demand curve, however odd the behaviour of supply has been . . . . We must expect that the longer is the period during which demand and supply are coming into equilibrium, the more changes will have time to take place. If we were to study the changes in demand and supply which would take place, in response to any change of data, during many successive very short periods of time, we should find that we had introduced unnecessary and intolerable detail into the analysis."[8]

We shall now study how the equilibrium between demand and supply is brought about in three periods of time. In other words, we shall study the determination of :

(*i*) market price,

(*ii*) short -period price, and

(*iii*) long -period price.

In this discussion, we shall describe the way in which the supply of a commodity adopts itself to a sudden and once-for all change in demand for it in various periods and thus influences price.

DETERMINATION OF MARKET PRICE

Market price is determined by the equilibrium between demand and supply in a market period or very short-run. The market period is a period in which the maximum that can be supplied is limited by the existing stock. The market period is so short that more cannot be produced in response to increased demand. This market period may be an hour, a day or a few days or even a few weeks depending upon the nature of the product, *i.e.*, in case of perishable commodities like fish, this market period may be a day and for a common textile industry it may be a few weeks.

What will be the nature of supply curve in a market period? Two cases are prominent –one is that of **perishable goods** and the other that of **non-perishable durable goods,** or reproducible goods.

Perishable Goods

In the case of a perishable commodity like fish, the supply is limited by the quantity available or stock in a day and which cannot be kept back for the next period. Hence, the whole of it must be sold away on the same day, whatever may be the price.

In Fig. 27.3, therefore, the supply curve of the fish has been shown as a vertical straight line like MS in the figure, where OM is the quantity of the fish available on that day. DD is the market demand curve. With perfect competition between buyers and sellers, an equilibrium price OP (= EM) will be established at which the quantity demanded is equal to the available supply, that is, equilibrium price will be established at the point E where downward sloping demand DD intersects the vertical supply curve MS.

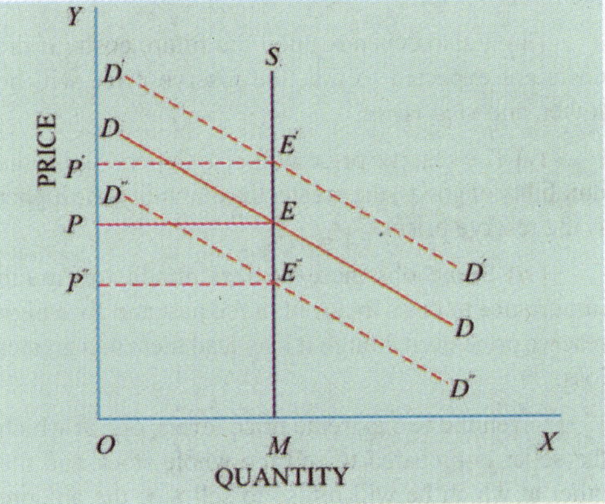

Fig. 27.3. Market Price of Perishable Goods.

Now suppose that there is a sudden increase in demand from DD to D′ D′. With the supply of fish remaining unchanged, the increased demand will raise the market price sharply from OP to OP′(= E′M). On the contrary if there is a decrease in demand DD to D″ D″, the price will fall to OP″ (= E″ M). The quantity sold remains the same in all cases.

Reproducible Goods

In case of non-perishable but reproducible goods, the supply curve cannot be a vertical straight line throughout its length, because some of the goods can be preserved or kept back from the market, and carried over to the next market period. There will then be two critical price levels. The first, if price is very high, the seller will be prepared to sell the whole stock. The second level is set by a very low price at which the seller would not sell any amount in the present market period, but will hold back the whole stock for some better time.

8. Stonier and Hague –*A Text-book of Economic Theory*, Ist ed. pp. 152-53.

Reserve Price

The price at which a seller will refuse to sell is called the reserve price. There are several factors which govern the reserve price of a seller:

(i) The reserve price will depend upon the seller's expectations regarding the figure price. If he expects a high future price, the reserve price will be higher, and *vice-versa*.

(ii) The seller's liquidity preference is another determining factor. The more urgent is his need for cash, the lower will be the reserve price.

(iii) The reserve price also depends on the changes which have to be incurred for carrying stocks. The period for which the stocks have to be held is, therefore, important. The longer is the period the lower will be the reserve price.

(iv) It also depends upon the future costs. If the costs are expected to fall, the reserve price will be lower, and *vice-versa*.

(v) The reserve price will also depend upon the durability of goods; the greater the durability, the higher is the reserve price..

(vi) Some obstinate dealers attach too much importance to costs incurred in the past and fix a high reserve price even though it may lead them to a greater loss.

Given the two extreme price levels, one at which the seller is prepared to sell the whole stock and the other at which he will refuse to sell any, the amount which he will offer for sale will vary with price. Given his anticipations of future price and intensity of his need for cash, *etc.*, he will be prepared to supply more at a higher price than at a lower one. The supply curve of a seller will, therefore, slope upwards to the right. Beyond a price at which he is prepared to sell the whole stock, the supply curve will be a vertical straight line whatever the price. Similarly, analysis will apply to each of the sellers.

There is an additional reason for the total market supply curve to slope upwards in some of its portion. This is that the reserve price will be different for different sellers. At a given price, some of the sellers will be prepared to sell while others will hold back, and, at a higher price, some more sellers will offer the output for sale. At a very high price, all sellers may be prepared to supply the whole stock of the product, and, at a very low price, all may refuse to sell.

In Figure 27.4 SRFS is the supply curve of the durable goods while OQ is the total amount of the stock of the goods. Up to the price OP′ (= QF), the quantity supplied varies with price so that at a higher price more is supplied than at a lower one. At the price OS, nothing is sold, the whole stock being held back. Therefore, SF portion of the supply curve slopes upwards from left to right. At the price OP′ (= QF), the whole of stock is offered for sale, and beyond OP′, the quantity supplied remains the same whatever the price. Therefore, beyond price OP′, the market supply curve has been shown as a vertical straight line. DD is the demand curve which slopes downwards from left to right.

Market price determined is OP (= RM) as at this price quantity demanded is equal to the quantity supplied since the demand curve DD and the supply curve SF intersect at the point R.

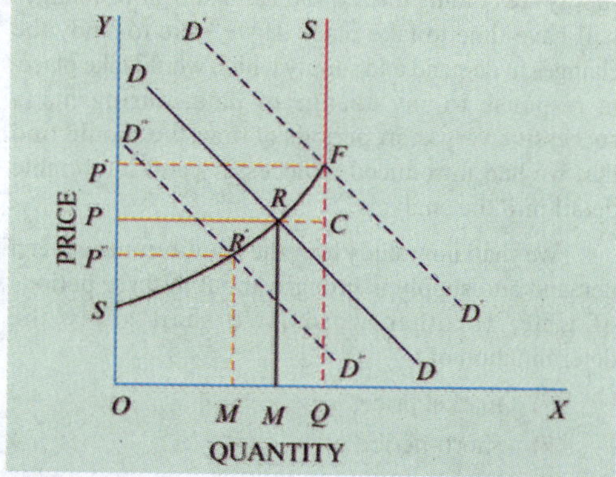

Fig. 27.4. Market Price of Durable Commodity.

At this equilibrium price OP (= RM), OM amount from the stock is sold, while the rest of the stock, *i.e.*, MQ (= RC) is held back from the market.

If now the demand increases from DD to D′D′, the price will rise to OP′ (= QF) and the whole stock OQ will be sold. In case, the demand further increases from D′D′ to some higher level, the quantity supplied or sold will remain the same, *i.e.*, equal to OQ, which is the entire stock, only the price will rise so that at the new equilibrium level quantity demanded is equal to the available supply.

If, however, the demand decreases from DD to D″D″ the price will fall to OP″ (R′M′) and the amount sold will fall to OM′.

Since in a perfectly competitive market, the product is homogeneous and no buyer has any preference for a particular seller, therefore, a single uniform market price will be established in the market. Once the market price is determined, an individual seller in the market will take the price as given and constant, and sell any quantity he likes. Hence, the demand curve, which is downward sloping for all sellers, is a horizontal straight line, *i.e.*, perfectly elastic at the level of ruling market price for a single seller.

Thus, a single seller, under perfect competition, can dispose of his entire output at the ruling market price, there is no reason why he should lower his price even though his reserve price may be less than the ruling market price.If his reserve price is above the market price, he will not be able to sell anything, because demand for him is perfectly elastic.

Costs Do Not Affect Market Price

One important conclusion that follows from the above analysis of price determination in the market period is that costs of production do not enter into the calculation of the seller and, therefore, costs have no influence on the market price. For example, if the market price 'today' is below the cost of production but the seller expects further fall 'tomorrow', he will try to dispose of the stock today. On the other hand, he would not be inclined to sell his stock even at a price above cost 'today', if he expects the price to rise still higher 'tomorrow'.

The costs of production have influence only when the amount supplied can be varied. The costs, therefore, enter into calculations in the short-run as well as in the long-run. In the market period, only the output which has already been produced can be offered for sell and, therefore, the question of increasing or decreasing output does not arise. Hence, costs of production are no consideration in deciding the amount to be offered for sale.

Price as a Rationing Device

We shall discuss more fully later the role of prices in a modern economy. We may only say here that price is a signal to the producers to expand or contract production and a warning to the consumers as to the possible shortage of the commodity or signal to the possible glut. Also, price reflects marginal social value of the commodity. But the function that we see price performing here is of a rationing device. In a market period (*i.e.*, a very short period), the supply is fixed. Price, therefore, rations or distributes the available supply among the consumers who are willing and able to pay the price equal to, or more than, the equilibrium price.

DETERMINATION OF SHORT-RUN PRICE

In a preceding chapter, we explained that in the short-run a firm is in equilibrium at the output at which price equals marginal cost. It was also pointed out that, during the short-run, fixed costs are disregarded in making a decision whether to produce or not. It is the average variable cost rather than average total cost which is of determining importance to decide whether to produce or not. If the price falls below the minimum average variable cost, then even in the short-run firms will shut down to minimise losses.

Thus, the minimum average variable cost sets a minimum limit to the price in the short-run since at a price below it no amount of output will be produced. We also pointed out that short-run supply curve of the industry is the lateral summation of the short-run marginal cost curves of the firms. The supply curve of the industry lies above the minimum average variable costs. The short-run supply curve of the industry slopes upward from left to right since the short-run marginal cost curve of the firms slopes upwards too.

The determination of the short-run price can be explained with the help of the Fig. 27.5. DD in the Fig. 27.5 (b) is the demand curve facing the industry. This demand curve as usual slopes downwards from left to right. MPS is the market period supply curve (its vertical shape shows that it is fixed) and SRS is the short-run supply curve of the industry. If there is an increase in demand from DD to D′ D′, the market price will rise sharply from OP to OK at which level the new demand curve D′ D′ intersects the market period supply curve MPS, supply of output remaining unchanged.

But, under the stimulus of this increased demand, the firms will increase their production in the short period, by making intensive use of the fixed capital equipment and increasing the amount of variable factors. It should be borne in mind that, in the short period, no change in the fixed capital equipment can be made, nor can new firms enter the industry. The supply of the commodity will increase as a result of the expansion of output by the firms, using more variable factors, in response to increase in demand. Hence, in the short-run price will fall to OR at which new demand curve D′ D′ intersects the short-run supply curve SRS.

Thus, OR is the short-run normal price which is higher than the original market price OP but not as high as the second market price of OK. The quantity supplied has also increased from OM to OM′. Hence, in the short-run, a larger amount of the quantity is sold and the price is not quite as high as in the market period.

Given the demand curve D′ D′, the short-run normal price OR is established in the market. Individual firms will take this price as given and constant and will adjust their output level so that the price equals marginal cost. From Fig. 27.5 (a), it is clear that, at price OR, the firm is making super-normal profits, since price OR is greater than the average cost at equilibrium output ON′.

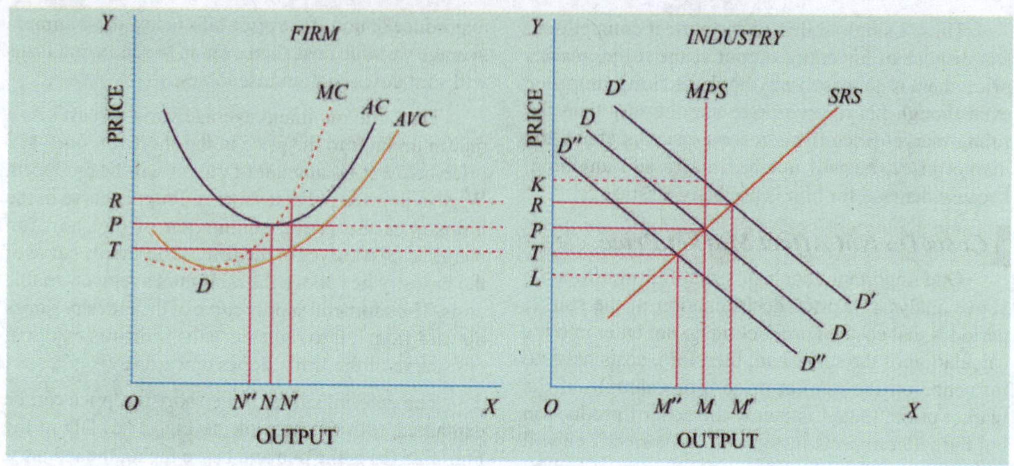

Fig. 27.5. Determination of Short-run Price

Now, if there is a decrease in demand from DD to D″ D″, the market price will fall sharply from OP to OL at which level demand curve D″ D″ intersects the MPS curve, the supply of the output remaining the same. But, in the short-run, firms will contract output by diminishing the variable factors and,as a result, the quantity supplied will decrease. The short-run normal price will be OT at which short-run supply curve SRS intersects the new demand curve D″ D″.

Thus, short-run price OT will be higher than the new market price OL but will be lower than the original market price OP. Again, OT, the new short-run price, will be taken as given and constant by the firms and they will adjust their output at which OT equals marginal cost. It will be seen from Fig. 27.5 (a) that at price OT firms would be incurring losses. Price cannot fall below the point D since at prices below D firms would not produce any amount of the commodity and the quantity supplied will be zero.

DETERMINATION OF LONG-RUN NORMAL PRICE

Market price may fluctuate owing to a sudden change either on the side of supply or on that of demand. A big arrival of fish, for instance, may depress its price in a particular market. A sudden heat wave may raise the price of ice. These are, however, temporary influences and cause temporary disturbances in the market price. In the absence of such disturbing causes, the price tends to come back to a certain level. This level itself may not be a fixed point for all times. But if the techniques and scale of production remain on the whole constant, this level may be taken as a fixed anchor around which, in its day-to-day movements, market price oscillates.

Adam Smith called this level "natural" price and Marshall called it "normal" price. In the words of Marshall, " 'Normal or natural value of a commodity is that which economic forces would tend to bring about in the long-run. It is probably worth purifing out that "Normal Prices are not the same thing as 'average' prices unless prices are constant. Normal prics are those prices to which are may expect the actual prices to tend. They will not only be influenced by fluctuations and oscillations, but will also take account of the general trend towards the 'normal' price."[9]

In order to describe how long-run equilibrium is brought about and thus normal price is determined, it is useful to refer to the market period and short-run period also. As we have stated above, the market period is so short that no adjustment in the output can be made. There is a given amount of the stock of the goods on hand, and, in case of perishable goods, the whole of it must be sold at whatever price the market will fetch. In the market period or very short-run, costs of production have no influence on price.

The short-run period, however, is sufficient to allow the firms to make limited output adjustment. If there is an increase in demand, the firms will expand output, by more intensive use of the fixed capital equipment and by greater use of the variable factors, to the point where new price equals marginal cost. As shown above, the new short-run price will be higher than the price before the increase in demand but not as high as the market price, and the output will be greater.

In the long period, the supply conditions are fully adapted to meet the new demand conditions. If there

9. Stonier and Hague—*A Text-book of Economic Theory*, Ist ed., pp. 160.

is a sudden and once-for-all increase in demand, the firms in the long-run will expand output by increasing the use of variable as well as of the fixed factors of production. They may enlarge their old plants or build new plants. Moreover, in the long-run, new firms can also enter the industry and thus, add to the supplies of the product.

In the long period, average variable cost is of no particular relevance, since, in the long-run, all factors are variable and none fixed. In this period, all costs ever incurred by the firm must be covered, and hence all are price-determining. Price, in the long-run, or normal price, under perfect competition, therefore, must be equal to the minimum long-run average cost.

In a previous chapter (No. 25), we explained that a firm under perfect competition is in long-run equi-

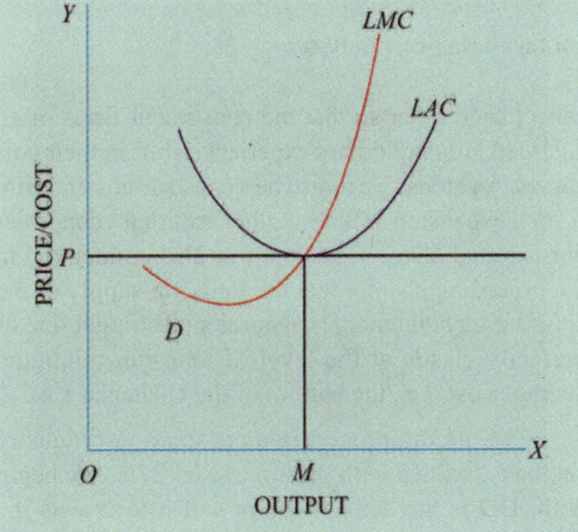

Fig. 27.6. Long-run Normal Price = Long-run Minimum Average Cost.

librium at the output where Price = MC = minimum LAC. Fig. 27.6 shows that price OP = LMC = LAC. If the price is above the minimum long-run average cost, the firms will be making supernormal profits. Therefore, in the long-run, new firms will enter the industry to compete away these extra profits and the price will fall to the level where it is equal to the minimum long-run average cost. Neither can the price fall below the minimum average cost since in that case the firms will be incurring losses. In long-run, if these losses persist, some of the firms will leave the industry. As a result, the price will rise to the level of minimum average cost, so that in the long-run firms are earning only normal profits.

Thus, we see that if the price is above or below the minimum long-run average cost, adjustment takes place in he output primarily by the entry of new firms or exit of some existing firms so that new price once more equals the minimum average cost.

But whether this long-run minimum average cost is equal to or is higher or lower than the previous one will depend on whether the industry in question is subject to the law of constant cost, increasing cost or decreasing cost. How the normal price is determined under conditions of increasing cost, constant cost or decreasing cost is explained below.

Long-run Normal Price in Increasing-Cost Industry

As we explained in the previous chapter, supply curve of an increasing-cost industry slopes upwards from left to right. This is so because when a full-sized industry expands as a result of the increased demand for its product, it expriences certain external economies and diseconomies. But external diseconomies in the case of an increasing-cost industry outweigh the external economies and this brings about an upward shift in the cost curves of all firms. When the industry expands, the costs rise primarily due to the intensive bidding of the prices of specialised labour and raw materials by new firms. As already expained, the increasing -cost industry is the most typical of the actual competitive world.

The whole pricing process in the increasing-cost industry can be explained with reference to Fig. 27.7. In Fig. 27.7 (*b*), LRS is the long-run supply curve of the increasing-cost industry. MPS is the market period supply curve and SRS the short-run supply curve. To begin with, DD is the market demand curve and OP is the market price. Now suppose that there is a sudden and once-for-all increase in demand from DD to D′ D′. In the market period or very short-run, the firms can sell only what they have already produced. The total amount supplied will remain unchanged at output OM. Thus, as a result of increase in demand from DD to D′ D′, the market price will rise sharply from OP to OP′, because the new demand curve D′D′ intersects the market period supply curve MPS at OP level.

In the short-run, however, the firms will increase output OM to OM′ along the short-run marginal cost curve. Therefore, the price in the short-run will fall to the level OP″ at which the new demand curve D′ D′ intersects the short-run supply curve SRS, which is the lateral summation of the short-run marginal cost curves of the firms. In this short-run equilibrium, every firm will be producing output for which the price OP″ is equal to short-run marginal cost. In this short-run equilibrium position, firms would be earning supernormal profits, because the price OP″ is above the LAC (long-run average cost). [see Fig. 27.7 (*a*)].

Lured by these supernormal profits, new firms will enter into the industry in the long-run. But since

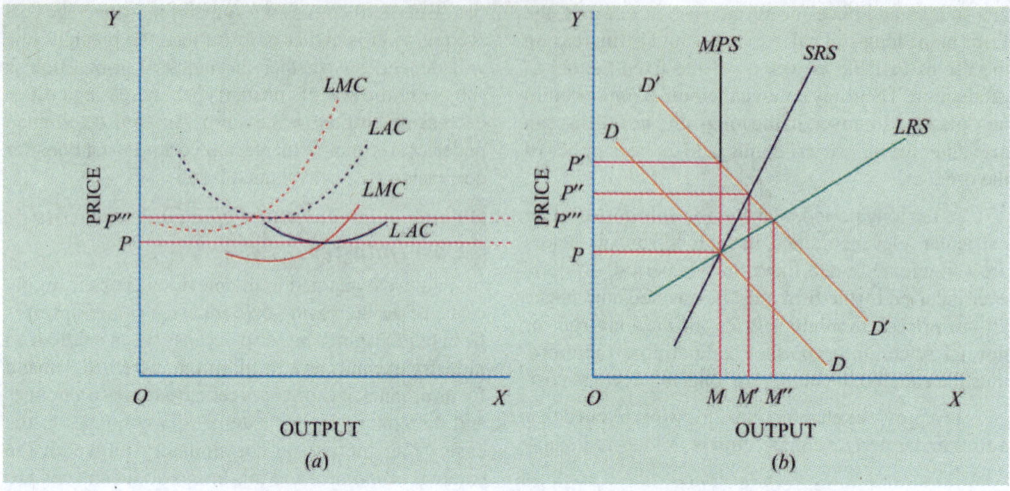

Fig. 27.7. Long-run Normal price in Increasing-cost Industry.

we are dealing with the increasing-cost industry, as the new firms enter, the cost curves of all the firms will shift upwards due to the **net external** diseconomies. As the output of the industry increases OM to OM″ as a result of the entry of new firms, price in the long-run will fall to OP‴ at which the demand curve D′D′ intersects the long-run supply curve LRS. Thus, OP‴ is the long-run normal price.

This long-run normal price OP‴ must be equal to the minimum long-run average cost since new firms will continue entering the industry until all firms are earning only normal profits. But this new minimum average cost [shown by the dotted curve in Fig. 27.7 (*a*)] in the case of increasing-cost industry will be higher than the initial minimum average cost, because costs have risen due to the entry of new firms in the industry. Therefore, the price OP‴ will be higher than the initial price OP. All this is clear from the Fig. 27.7.

From the above, it is clear that, in the long-run, in the case of increasing-cost industry, more quantity of the output can be got only at a rather higher price. The extent to which the long-run price differs from the original price depends on the extent of increase in costs following the expansion of the industry. It must be carefully noted that each point on the long-run supply curve of the industry LRS represents a long-run equilibrium as the demand shifts to the right inducing ultimately the expansion of the industry, with more firms each with higher cost curves.

Long-Run Normal Price in Constant-Cost Industry

We explained in the preceding chapter that industry will be a constant-cost industry if, on its expansion, external economies and diseconomies cancel each other so that the constituent firms of an enlarged industry do not experience shift in their cost curves. An industry can also be a constant-cost industry if its expansion breeds neither external economies nor external diseconomies. It was also pointed out in the preceding chapter that the long-run supply of the constant- cost industry is a horizontal straight line or prefectly elastic at the level of long-run minimum average cost, *i.e.*, the bottom of the U-shaped LAC.

The pricing process in a constant-cost industry can be explained with the aid of Fig. 27.8. To begin with, DD is the demand curve and it intersects the market period supply curve MPS at price level OP. Thus, OP is the market price.

Now if the demand increases to D′D′, there will be a sharp rise in the market price from OP to OP′ where the new demand curve cuts the Market Supply Curve (MPS), the supply remaining unchanged. In response to the increased demand, the firms in the short-run will increase production. Therefore, in the short-run equilibrium, price will fall to OP″ at which the short-run supply curve SRS intersects the new demand curve D′D′.

In the long-run, the output will increase further and the price will fall to the original level. In the case of of a constant-cost industry, the new long-run normal price will be the same as the original equilibrium price OP. The output of the industry, in this new long-run equilibrium, will be OM″. Every firm in the long-run will be producing at the long-run minimum average cost as in the original equilibrium position and will be earning only normal profits.

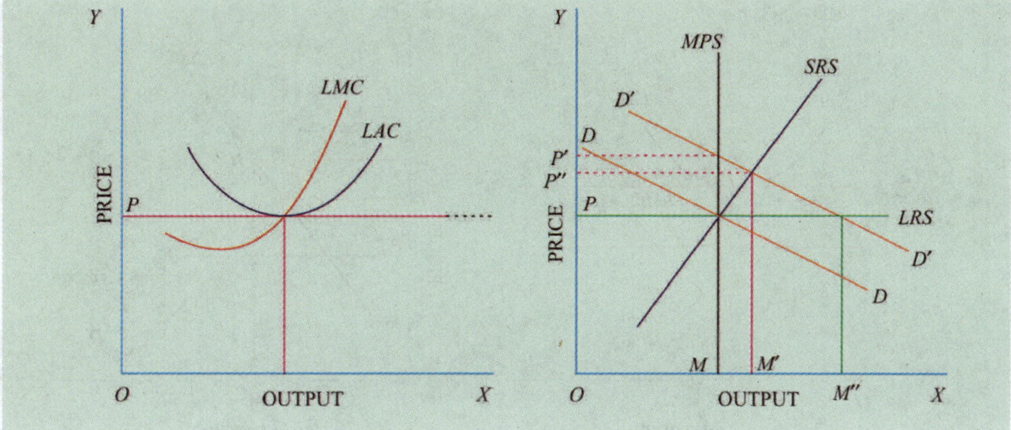

Fig. 27.8. Long-run Normal Price in Constant-Cost Industry

Thus, we see that, in this constant-cost case, an increase or decrease in demand will, in the long-run, simply change output by changing the number of firms. It will have no effect on price in the long-run or on the scale and costs of each firm under perfect competition is always forced to the bottom of U-shaped LAC curve and no shift takes place in cost curves in the constant-cost industry.

Long-run Normal Price in Decreasing-Cost Industry

As already pointed out in the preceding chapter, in the case of a young industry in its early stages of growth, the external economies may overweigh the external diseconomies. This phenomenon of net external economies lowers the cost curves of all firms.

The external economies, which may be available when the industry grows in size, arise because : (*a*) cheaper and better trained labour becomes available; (*b*) better information centres and markets are created; (*c*) productivity of factors in one firm is enhanced by expanded production in others; (*d*) raw material produced at decreasing costs by other specialized industries are made available at reduced prices; (*e*) cheap credit becomes available; and (*f*) there is the benefit of specialized transport.

The presence of the net external economies will lower the cost curve of all firms and, therefore, the industry will experience the phenomenon of decreasing costs as it expands by the entry of new firms.

Thus, in the case of a decreasing-cost industry, the additional supplies of the product will be forthcoming at reduced costs and, therefore, the long-run supply curve of the industry will slope downwards from left to right.

The determination of normal price in the case of a decreasing cost industry can be explained with the help of Fig. 27.9 where LRS is the long-run supply curve of the decreasing-cost industry.

To begin with, DD is the demand curve which intersects the market period supply curve MPS at price OP. Therefore, OP is the market price. Now suppose that there is a sudden and permanent change in demand from DD to D′D′. As a result of this increased demand, the market price will rise sharply to OP′, output remaining the same.

In the short-run, the firms will increase output and, therefore, amount supplied will increase. As a result, the price in the short-run will fall to OP″, at which the new demand curve D′D′ intersects the short-run supply curve SRS.

In the long-run, however, new firms will enter the industry and cause a downward shift in the cost curves of all the firms. The new long-run price will be determined at the level OP‴ at which new demand curve D′D′ cuts the downward sloping long-run supply curve LRS. In this new long-run equilibrium, more will be produced and supplied at a lower price than in the original equilibrium position. Whereas in the original equilibrium position, OM amount of the product is produced and supplied at price OP, in the new long-run equilibrium position, a larger amount OM″ is produced and supplied at a lower price OP‴. Thus, in the long-run, larger supplies of the product will be forthcoming at reduced prices.

Therefore, we conclude that, in the case of a decreasing-cost industry, an increased demand for its products will, in the long-run, lower the price and increase the quantity supplied.

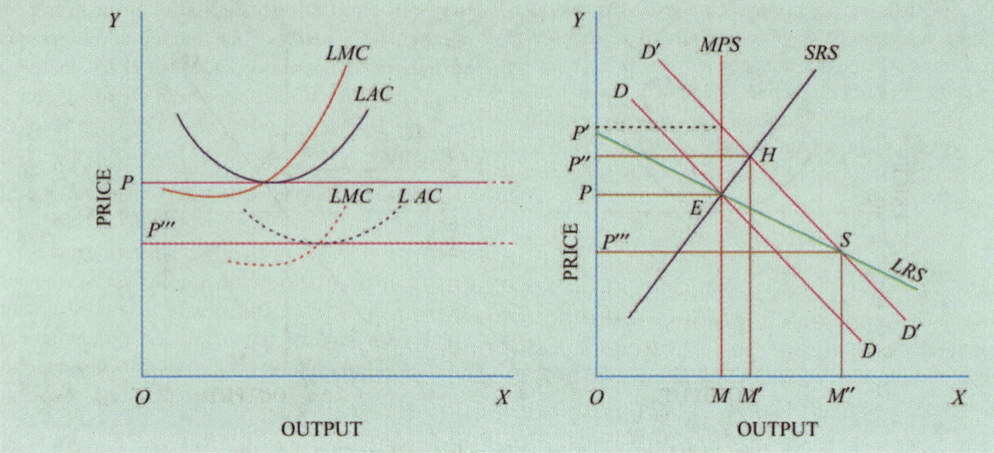

Fig. 27.9. Long-run Normal Price in Decreasing-Cost Industry.

Conclusion. From the above discussion, it is clear that, as demand increases, the long-run normal price increases, remains the same, or decreases depending on whether the industry in question is an increasing-cost, constant-cost or decreasing-cost industry.

Decreasing-Cost Industry is Incompatible with Perfect Competition

In case of a decreasing-cost industry, even if there is competition to start with, competition will gradually disappear resulting in a monopoly or oligopoly (a few monopolists). Suppose initially there is a large number of firms in the industry. There will be a tendency for them to expand to take advantage of economies of scale, resulting in lower and lower average costs as the scale of output is enlarged. But all firms are not equally efficient and quick enough to realise the economies of scale. Those who are left behind in the race have ultimately to drop out. Bigger firms keep driving down the prices, till only a few survive, resulting in an oligopoly, or only one firm survives, and a monopoly is established.

Figure 27.10 illustrates this. We see here that average cost curve AC declines very sharply up to its point of intersection with the demand curve DD. The marginal cost curve MC lines below AC over this range of output. MC cuts DD at E where price EM′ is lower than average cost E′M′. At this point, total cost (OM′ × E′M′) exceeds total revenue (OM′ × EM′), therefore, losses are incurred. But few firms will have the endurance to reach this point. Long before, most of them would have dropped out. The survivor, the monopolist, would restrict output to OM and charge OP_2 (= MQ_2) price, and make a handsome profit of $P_1Q_1Q_2P_2$, which is measured by the excess of total revenue (OM × OP_2) over (OM × OP_1).

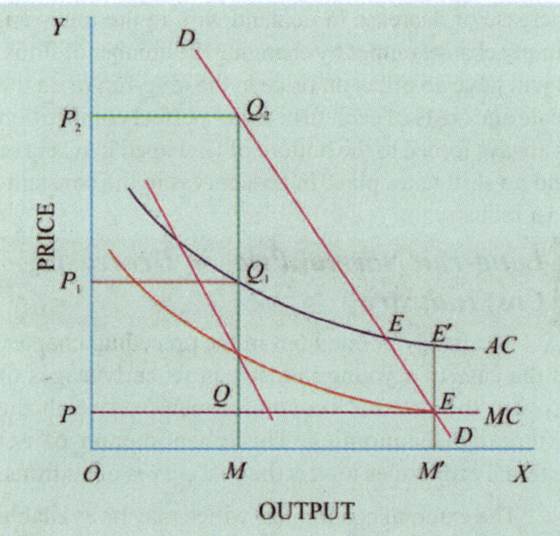

Fig. 27.10. Decreasing-Cost Industry and Competition.

If the shape of AC were such that after declining, it remained constant over a large part of the output, it will permit a fair number of firms to continue and an oligopoly will be the result.

Normal Price and Market Price Compared

We have already discussed what is meant by the market price and the normal and how they are determined under conditions of perfect competition. We are now in a position to make comparison between them in some detail:

(i) While market price is determined by the temporary equilibrium between the force of demand and supply at a particular time, normal price is the result of the long-run equilibrium between demand and supply, when the supply conditions have fully adjusted themselves to the given demand conditions.

(ii) Market price may actually be reached at a given moment or day as a result of a temporary equilibrium. But the long-run normal price may, in practice, never be reached. There will usually be a change in either the demand or supply conditions underlying the long-run equilibrium before it has had time to come into being. The long-run–like tomorrow–never comes.

(iii) Market price is governed by temporary causes and passing events, whereas normal price is influenced by permanent and persistent causes. For, in the long-run, temporary causes disappear or neutralize one another. Market price, therefore, fluctuates from day to day due to a temporary change either on the side of demand or that of supply. Normal price is the centre round which the market price oscillates or it is the level to which it tends to return after having departed from it temporarily.

But it should be remembered that this normal price is not a fixed level. For example, if there is a permanent change in the demand conditions, the normal price will change. In the determination of normal price, under increasing-cost industry in Fig. 27.7 (*b*) (which we reproduce here also as Fig. 27.11), we saw that, when there was a permanent change in demand from DD to D′D′, the normal price increased from OP to OP‴.

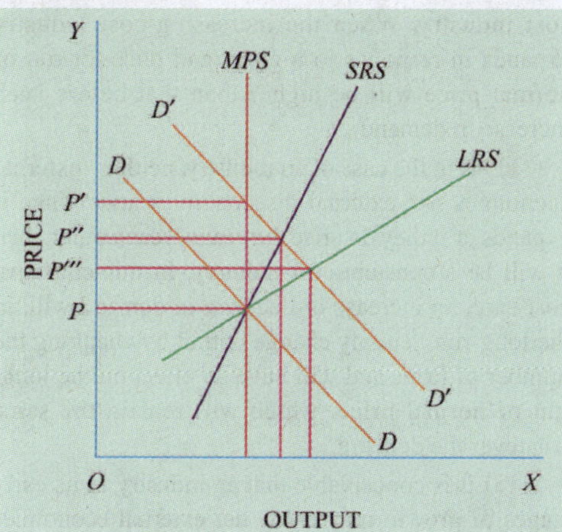

Fig. 27.11. Market Price Fluctuating A Round Normal Price.

But it must be understood that given the D′D′ and LRS as permanent conditions of demand and supply respectively, the market price will fluctuate around the new normal prcie OP‴, owing to temporary changes in demand and supply. Before the permanent increase in demand from DD to D′D′, the market price fluctuated around the original equilibrium price OP. In fact, what we studied was the movement from one long-run equilibrium position or normal price to another. As a result of the sudden and permanent change in the demand from DD to D′D′, there is a sharp rise in the market price from OP to OP′, but in the long-run, the price will fall to OP‴, the new long -run normal price.

As already mentioned, every point on the long-run supply curve LRS with the corresponding demand curve represents a long-run equilibrium position and hence normal price. We saw that when there is a permanent increase in demand, in the case of increasing-cost industry, the normal price increases; and, in the case of constant-cost industry, the normal price remains the same; and in the case of decreasing-cost industry, the normal price decreases.

It should be further noted that even long-run supply curve LRS can alter if there is a fundamental change in technical conditions of production. If there is a fundamental improvement in the technical know-how, the long-run supply curve LRS will shift downwards and there will be a new normal price corresponding to given demand curves.

(iv) Since in the market period, the quantity of the output cannot be varied, the cost of production has no influence on market price, the market price may be above or below the marginal and average cost of production, depending upon the demand conditions. If, in the market period, the demand is relatively greater than supply, the market price may be established at the level well above both the marginal and average cost of production. But the long-run normal price must be equal to both the marginal cost and the minimum long-run average cost.

(v) All commodities have a market price but only reproducible commodities can have a normal price. If commodities cannot be produced at all, their supply is fixed for all time. If the output of a commodity cannot be varied in response to changes in demand, there is no sense in speaking of their normal price. Such commodities may be pictures of old masters, unique manuscripts, *etc.* These commodities have a market price, but no normal price.

PRICE DETERMINATION UNDER PERFECT COMPETITION SUMMED UP

We may now sum up the theory of price determination under perfect competition in the following propositions:

We repeat that perfect competition assumes that (*a*) the firms in the industry are of a small size but large in number, (*b*) their products are homogeneous or identical, (*c*) that all productive resources are perfectly mobile as between uses and places, and (d) consumers, producers and resource owners possess perfect knowledge.

(1) Price is determined by the interaction of the forces of demand and supply. **Equilibrium price** is established at the level at which demand curve intersects the supply curve, or at which the quantity demanded is equal to the quantity supplied. At any price higher than the equilibrium price, the quantity supplied will exceed the quantity demand; competition between sellers will force the price down to the equilibrium level. Similarly, at any price lower than the equilibrium one, the quantity demanded will be greater than the quantity supplied; competition between buyers will push the price up to the equilibrium level.

(2) The element of time plays an important role in the determination of price. On the basis of the response of supply over time to a given and once-for-all change in demand. Marshall distinguished equilibrium between demand and supply in three periods: (*a*) Very short-run or momentary equilibrium when supply is fixed or limited by the total stock on hand; (*b*) short-run equilibrium when output can be varied within given fixed plants and firms; (*c*) long-run equilibrium when both the size of the plants and number of the firms can adjust themselves to the new level of demand.

(3) Market price is the result of momentary equilibrium between demand and supply. This period is so short that the output cannot be varied in response to changes in demand. The firms can sell only what they have already produced. In case of perishable commodities like fish, the whole stock must be sold whatever the price, and, therefore, the supply curve is a vertical straight line throughout its length. However, in the case of durable goods, some part of the stock may be held back from the market in the hope of getting higher price in future. Therefore, in the case of durable goods, supply curve in part of its length slopes upwards to the right but runs vertical beyond a price at which the whole stock of the goods is offered for sale. An important point to note about market price is that demand plays a predominant part in its determination and cost of production has no influence on price whatsoever.

(4) Short-run price is the result of the equilibrium between a given demand curve and the short-run supply curve, firms having been given enough time to expand output only along short-run marginal cost curves. In the short-run, price must equal marginal cost of production. But at this point, profit may be supernormal, normal or subnormal depending upon the demand conditions. The short-run price, however, cannot fall below the minimum average variable cost, and, therefore, losses cannot be greater than the fixed cost (why?).

(5) Long-run or normal price is the result of equilibrium between a given demand curve and the long-run supply curve, supply conditions having been fully adjusted to the given demand condition. Long-run or normal price must be equal to minimum long-run cost (why?). But whether this long-run minimum average cost increases, remains constant or decreases as the industry expands by the entry of new firms, depends upon whether the industry in question is an increasing-cost, constant cost or decreasing -cost industry respectively.

(6) If there are net external diseconomies as the industry grows in size, it will be a case of increasing-cost industry. When the increasing-cost industry expands in response to a given and once-for-run or normal price will be higher than that before such increase in demand.

(7) If in the case of an industry, neither external economies nor external diseconomies arise when it expands or if they do arise they cancel each other, then it will be a constant-cost industry. In this constant-cost case, an increase or decrease in demand will, in the long-run, simply change output by changing the number of firms and will have no effect on the long-run or normal price, which will remain the same whatever the demand.

(8) It is conceivable that an industry in its early stages of growth may enjoy net external economies when it grows in size. Such a case will be one of a decreasing-cost industry. In this case, as the industry expands in response to a given and once-for-all increase in demand, new long-run or normal price will be lower than that before the increase in demand.

Key terms

Short run price, Long run normal price, Equilirbium price.

QUESTIONS

1. Comment on the role of price mechanism in a competitive economy.
2. Show how in perfectly competitive equilibrium the price of a commodity is equal to its marginal and average cost of production. Illustrate your answer diagrammatically.
3. "Value is determined by marginal utility." "Value is determined by the equilibrium of demand and supply". Are these statements consistent?
4. "We might as reasonably dispute whether it is the upper or the under blade of a pair of scissors that cuts a price of paper as whether value is determined by utility or cost of production'. Discuss.
5. "Through demand and supply, production becomes profitable to producers and price acceptable to consumers". Discuss.
6. What do you understand by perfect competition? Illustrate how price under perfect competition is equal to the lowest cost of production of a commodity.
7. Explain the term "Equilibrium". How is equilibrium price determined under perfectly competitive competition?
8. In perfect competition a seller in equilibrium does not determine price but adjust his output to the prevailing price. Elucidate with illustrations.
9. What do you understand by normal price? How is it determined under perfect competition in (*a*) increasing cost, (*b*) decreasing cost, and (*c*) constant cost.
10. How are price and output determined under perfect competition in the long-run? Explain fully.
11. Distinguish between market price and normal price. In what respects is the determination of these two prices different?
12. What do you mean by "Normal Equilibrium Value"? How is it determined? Can you account for the paradox that sometimes a rise in normal demand for a commodity may lead to a fall in price?
13. Bring out the importance of time element in the theory of value and eluceate the following statement:

    "The shorter the period the greater will be the influence of demand on price and longer the period the more important will be the influence of supply on price".
14. What would be the effect of changes in demand for a commodity on its price (*a*) in the short period, and (*b*) in the long period. Use diagrams to illustrate your answer.
15. Distinguish between the "Short" period and the "long" period. How is long period average cost curve of a producer drawn?
16. Analyse the relationship between price and cost of production for a firm under perfect competition in (*a*) short-run equilibrium, and (*b*) long-run equilibrium.

PRICE OUTPUT UNDER MONOPOLY

In the preceding chapters, we studied the conditions of equilibrium under perfect competition. We have also seen how price and output are determined in a perfectly competitive industry. We shall now study price-output determination under imperfect competition which may take the form of a monopoly, monopolistic competition or oligopoly. The present chapter will deal with monopoly.

Meaning of Monopoly

As already mentioned in Chapter 22, **the monopoly is that market form in which a single producer controls the whole supply of a single commodity which has no close substitutes.**

Two points should be noted in regard to this definition: First, there must be single producer or seller, if there is to be a monopoly. The single producer may be an individual owner or a group of partners or a joint-stock company or any other combination of producers or the state. If there are many producers, there will be competition, perfect or monopolistic, and, if there are a few producers, we face oligopoly. Hence, there must be a sole producer or seller in the market, if it is to be called a monopoly. Since there is only one firm under monopoly, that single firm constitutes the whole industry. Therefore, **the distinction between the firm and industry disappears under conditions of monopoly.**

Secondly, the commodity produced by the producer must have no closely competing substitutes, if he is to be called a monopolist. This ensures that there must not be any rival of the monopolist. By the absence of close substitutes we mean that there are no other firms producing similar product or products varying only slightly from that of the monopolist. The producer of the 'Lux', for instance, cannot be called a monopolist as there are other varieties of soap like Rexona, Breeze, Hamam, Sunlight, *etc.*, which closely compete with

Single seller.

Lux in the market. But there are no close substitutes for electricity and water supplied by the local public utilities. These local public utilities thus provide economists with the examples of a monopoly.

We can also express this second condition of monopoly in terms of cost-elasticity of demand. As we have seen in an earlier chapter (No. 11), cross-elasticity of demand shows a change in the demand for a commodity as a result of change in the price of another commodity. If there is to be monopoly, **the cross elasticity of demand between the product of the monopolist and the product of any other producer must be very low.**

The above two conditions ensure that the monopolist can set the price of his product and can pursue an independent price policy. **Power to influence price is the very essence of monopoly.** From this it must not be gathered that the monopolist is so powerful that he can dictate the price as well as the amount sold. Monopolist can do one of these things only; either he can fix the price leaving the amount sold to the consumers, or he can fix the quantity he wants to produce and sell and leave the price to be determined by the demand of the consumers.

Bases of Monopoly: Barriers to the Entry of Rivals

It is noteworthy that monopoly can exist only when there are strong barriers to the entry of rivals. In general, the persistence of profits above the normal shows the lack of freedom of entry of other firms. The monopolist can maintain his position as the sole producer or seller of a product only when certain circumstances keep the rivals away from his line of production. These barriers also explain the existence of oligopoly. But in the case of a monopoly, the barriers to entry are so great and strong that they block all other producers form entering in the field of production of the monopolist.

Barriers are of two types: (*a*) First type of barriers are **economic in nature.** In a given industry or in a great area, the consumers can best be served by a single firm and it is not profitable for other firms to enter the field of the monopolist. The total market is not big enough to permit even one firm to operate at the optimal scale of output. Until a firm reaches this optimal scale, it is operating in its range of **"decreasing costs."** That is, by increasing output it can cut its cost per unit produced. Such reductions in costs are described as the **"economies of large-scale production".**

If the market in an industry is not big enough to support even one big optimum-sized firm, it is reasonable to assume that there will be established a monopoly of the existing firm, which is still enjoying economies of scale and, therefore, working in the range of 'decreasing costs'. This is so because new firms, if they were to enter the market as small scale producers will have little or no chance to survive and expand. These small-scale entrants will be unable to realise the cost economies enjoyed by the existing big firm and will not be able to compete with it. The other option for the new entrants is to start big, that is, to enter the industry as a large-scale producer. In practice, this is virtually impossible. Apart from other handicaps for a new and untried enterprise, the financial obstacles in the way of starting big are so great in many cases as to be prohibitive. The automobile, aluminium and steel industries reflect such conditions of the economies of scale, and, in these industries, monopolies or at least oligopolies are generally to be found.

In some industries, economies of scale are so particularly pronounced that competition is impractical, inconvenient or simply unworkable. Such industries are called **natural monopolies,** and most of the so called public utilities –the electric and gas companies, bus and railway companies, water and communication facilities –can be so classified. These industries are generally given exclusive rights by the governments. But in return for this sole right to supply electricity, water or bus service in a given geographic area, Government reserves the right to regulate the operations of such monopolies to prevent abuses of the monopoly power it has granted.

(*b*) The second type of barrier to entry is institutional or else artificial in nature. Thus

(i) A firm may enjoy the **exclusive ownership or control of the raw materials** which are absolutely essential in making the product, and prohibiting the creation of rival firms.

(ii) By granting an inventor the exclusive right to control a product for some years, patent laws protect an inventor from the competition of rivals.

(iii) The entry of new competitors may be blocked or the rivals may be eliminated by aggressive cut-throat tactics of the monopolist. Familiaring techniques are: aggressive price- cutting designed to make the competitors bankrupt, disparagement of the product, pressure on the banks not to grant credit and pressure on resource suppliers to withhold materials, spurious and exhausting law suits, the luring away of strategic personnel and spying and sabotage.

The above-listed barriers to entry are seldom effective cent per cent and, therefore, monopoly is a rare phenomenon. With these points in mind, let us analyse how price-output equilibrium is established in case of a monopoly.

PRICE-OUTPUT DETERMINATION UNDER MONOPOLY

Price-output analysis in the case of a monopoly is also an analysis of the equilibrium of the firm and industry under monopoly.

Since in a monopoly, a single firm constitutes the whole industry, there is no need for a separate analysis of the equilibrium of the firm and of the industry, as is done in case of perfect competition. Also, the price-output equilibrium of the firm will mean the price output determination under monopoly.

In the discussion of perfect competition (Chapter 22), we saw that the demand curve or the average revenue curve faced by a perfectly competitive firm is perfectly elastic and is represented by a horizontal straight line parallel to the X-axis. This is so because a producer under perfect competition cannot affect price by his own individual action. He has to accept the ruling market price as given and constant, and at this price, he can sell any quantity of the commodity.

But this is not true in the case of a monopoly. A firm under monopoly faces a downward sloping demand curve or average revenue (AR) curve. Therefore, if the monopolist lowers the price of his product, the quantity demanded increases, and, if he raises the price, the quantity demanded decreases. In other words, if the monopolist wants to sell a larger output, he has to reduce the price of his product. In that way, it is not only the price of the additional units that falls but the price of his total output goes down. Since his output affects the price at which he can sell, price is not a given factor for him as it is for the man producing under perfect competition.

Further, in perfect competition, since the average revenue curve is perfectly elastic and a horizontal straight line to X-axis, the marginal revenue is always equal to the average revenue, *i.e.*, the marginal revenue curve coincides with the average revenue curve. But unlike this, in a monopoly, since average revenue falls as more units of output are produced and sold, the marginal revenue is always less than the average revenue. In other words, under monopoly the marginal revenue curve lies below the average revenue curve.

From the above analysis, it follows that even the monopolist is not free of the market forces in establishing his price. The monopolist cannot set his price high without losing sales, nor can he gain sales without charging a lower price. The question now arises: which particular price-output combination on his demand curve will the monopolist choose? This depends not only on the demand conditions but also on the cost situation faced by the monopolist.

On the cost side of the picture, as in perfect competition, the average cost curve is generally U-shaped. Marginal cost curve, as elsewhere, cuts the average cost curve at its minimum point.

Equating Marginal Revenue and Marginal Cost

The aim of the monopolist, like every other producer, is to maximize his total money profits. Therefore, he will produce up to a point and charge a price which gives him the maximum money profits. In other words, he will be in equilibrium at that price-output level at which his profits are the maximum. He will go on producing so long as additional units add more to the revenue than to the cost. He will stop at that point beyond which additional units of production add more to cost than to revenue. In other words, he will be in equilibrium position at that level of output at which marginal revenue equals marginal cost. That is, he will continue producing so long as marginal revenue exceeds marginal cost. He does so because profits will go on increasing as long as the marginal revenue exceeds the marginal cost. At the point where marginal revenue is equal to marginal cost, the profit will be maximised, and here he stops. If the production is carried beyond this point profits will start decreasing.

The price-output equilibrium of the monopolist can be easily understood from diagram No. 28.1. AR is the demand curve or average revenue curve facing the monopolist. MR is the marginal revenue curve which lies below the average revenue curve AR. AC is the average cost curve and MC is the marginal cost curve. It can be seen from the diagram that uptill OM output, marginal revenue is greater than marginal cost but beyond OM the marginal revenue is less than marginal cost. Therefore, the monopolist will be in equilibrium at the output OM, where marginal revenue is equal to marginal cost and profits are the greatest. The price at which output OM is sold in the market can be known from looking at demand or average revenue curve AR. It can be seen from the diagram that corresponding to equilibrium output OM, the price on the demand or average revenue curve is MP ' (= OP). Thus, it is clear that, given the cost-revenue situation as presented in Fig. 28.1, the monopolist firm will be in equilibrium at the output OM and will be charging price equal to MP′ (= OP).

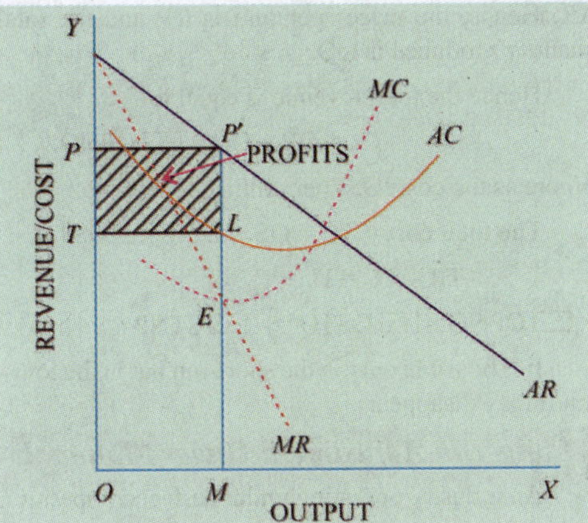

Fig. 28.1. Price-Output Equilibrium Under Monopoly.

Now the question is : what amount of actual total profits—although maximum they would be in the given cost-revenue situation—will be earned by the monopolist in this equilibrium position? This can be known in the following way:

At output OM, while MP′ is the average revenue, ML is the average cost (being on the AC curve). Then, P′L is the profit per unit.

Now the total profits = Profits per unit × total output sold

$$= P'L \times OM$$
$$= P'L \times TL$$
$$= P'LTP$$

Thus, the total profits earned by the monopolist in the equilibrium position are equal to the rectangle P′LTP, *i.e.*, the shaded area.

Monopoly Price and Elasticity of Demand

A very important point about the equilibrium position of the monopolist is worth mentioning. It is that the equilibrium of the monopolist will always lie at that level of output where the elasticity of demand for his product is greater than one, provided that his costs are positive. In other words, monopolist will never fix the output of his product at any level where the elasticity of his average revenue curve is less than one. If he were to do so, it would be possible for him to increase his total profits by decreasing output.

As already seen, when elasticity on the demand or average revenue curve is less than one, total revenue decreases when output is increased. In other words, marginal revenue is negative at those levels of output where elasticity of demand is less than one. Since marginal cost can never be negative, therefore monopolist cannot be in equilibrium at those output-levels where elasticity of demand is less than one.

There are some cases where the cost of production is zero or is not relevant to the pricing decision. For example, in case of mineral spring, costs of production are zero. Further, in the very short-run, if a good is already on hand in excessive amount, cost of production is not relevant for fixing price. In these cases, monopolist has only to decide at which output his total revenue will be maximum.

This can be easily seen in Fig. 28.2. In this figure, the equilibrium position of the monopolist will be at output OM and price OP (= MP′). At OM output, MR is equal to zero. The equilibrium condition is satisfied at OM as in this case we are assuming that MC is zero. Therefore marginal revenue is equal to marginal cost. It will be seen that P′ is the midpoint of the line TT′ where the elasticity of demand is unity. Therefore, when marginal cost is zero, the equilibrium of the monopolist is established at that output where elasticity of demand is unity.

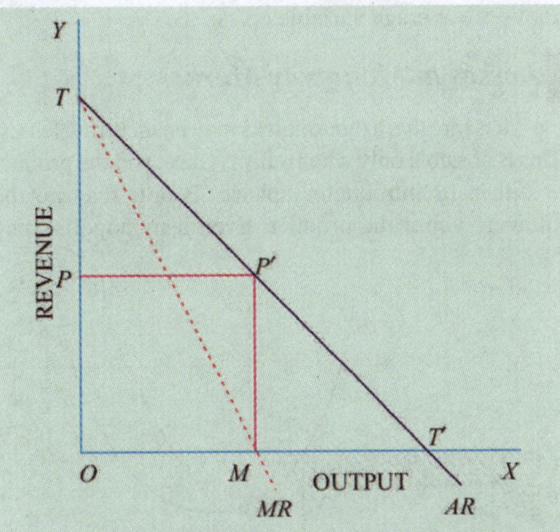

Fig. 28.2. Monopoly Equilibrium when MC is Zero.

Short-run and Long-run View

We have discussed above the equilibrium of the monopolist without making distinction between his behaviour in the short-run and the long-run. The analysis made above is general which applies both to the short-run as well as to the long-run situations. In the short-run, it should be carefully noted that the monopolist has to keep an eye on the variable costs. His price must not go below his average variable cost, otherwise he will stop producing. In the long-run, the monopolist can change the size of plant in response to a change in demand. In the long-run, he will make adjustment in the amount of the factors, fixed and variable, so that marginal revenue equals not only short-run but also long-run marginal cost. In the short-run, he equates the marginal revenue with marginal cost but in the long-run he seeks to bring about equality between the marginal revenue with the long-run marginal cost which reflects the fact that the scale of the whole firm has been adjusted for maximisation of profits.

Does the Monopolist necessarily Make Profit?

The general impression is that since the monopolist is in a position to influence both price and output, he must always make a profit. But, it is not so. There can be situations, when his costs are so high and the market for his output so small that at no output will the average costs be covered. He may thus incur losses in the short-run and continue in business if the price more than covers average variable costs. He can, however, minimise the losses by keeping the price above the average variable costs.

Losses in Monopoly Market

It is rare that a monopolists may be incurring losses. This is possible only when a firm is new, and the product is still in its introductory phase. People may not be knowing about the product. Even a monopolist may

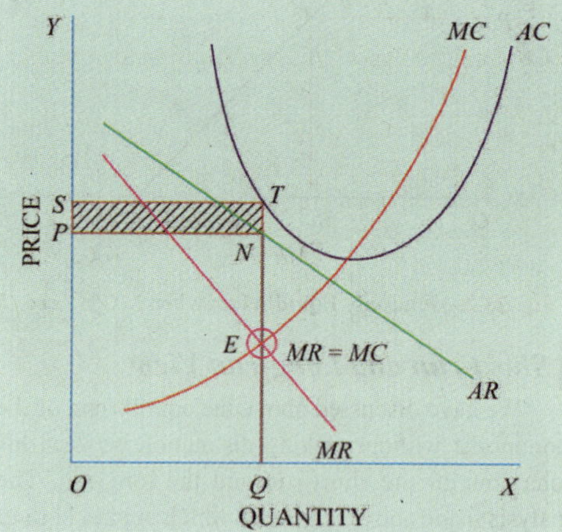

Fig. 28.3. Loss under monopoly.

incur losses when the costs are more and the demand is lower.

In the above diagram 'AC' and 'MC' is average cost and marginal cost. Average revenue and marginal revenue is below the 'AC'. The equilibrium point is at 'E' and price is fixed at point 'N' on demand curve AR. Hence, the price per unit is OP and the total quantity produced is OQ.

Hence the total revenue is equal to

$$TR = OP \times OQ = \square\, OPNQ.$$

Where as the cost 'OS' per unit.

$$\therefore \quad \text{The total cost} = TC = OS \times OQ = \square\, OSTQ.$$

$$TR - TC = \Pi$$

$$\square\, OPNQ - \square\, OSTQ = -\square\, STNP$$

It is possible only in the short-run but in the long-run it may disappear.

Long-run Adjustment Under Monopoly

An industry operating under perfect competition makes adjustment in the long-run by the entry of new firms or exit of old firms and attains an equilibrium position. But under monopoly, the entry of new firms is blocked in several ways: The monopolist may be in control of some essential raw materials or he may hold some patents or the market may be too limited to give scope for profit to more firms. Entry may be blocked in other ways too. Thus, entry into the industry blocked, the monopolist seeks to secure a position of vantage through adjustments in the scale of plant in the long-run. Considering the size of the market for his product and his long-run average costs, the monopolist may maximise his profits by building (*a*) a less than optimum scale of plant, or (*b*) an optimum scale of plant or (*c*) greater than optimum scale of plant.

If the monopolist is incurring a loss in the short-run and there is no plant size that can earn profit, then in the long-run the monopolist will go out of business. If he is already making a profit, then in the long-run, he will try to see if he can increase his profit by varying the size of the plant. A multi-plant monopolist will, in the long-run, adjust the number of plants to attain a long-run equilibrium. The monopolist can, in the long-run, construct each plant of such a size that short-run average cost coincides with long-run average cost at the minimum point on the latter curve. In other words, he can increase output by constructing more plants of suitable size instead of producing more units per plant at a higher unit cost.

Monopoly Equilibrium and Competitive Equilibrium Compared

We have now seen the conditions of firm's equilibrium both under conditions of perfect competition and monopoly and have also studied how price is determined under them. We are now in a position to compare the two.

Similarly. The only really general feature which is common to both is that both under perfect competition and monopoly, the firm is in equilibrium at that level of output where marginal revenue is equal to marginal cost.

Differences. But there are many important differences which we give below:

(i) Under perfect competition, demand curve or the average revenue curve faced by an individual firm is perfectly elastic and is a horizontal straight line parallel to the horizontal axis. Therefore, under perfect competition, marginal revenue is equal to average revenue at all levels of output and marginal revenue curve coincides with the average revenue curve. But unlike this, under monopoly, demand curve or average revenue curve faced by the firm is falling downwards from left to right. Therefore, marginal revenue is less than average revenue at all levels of output and marginal revenue curve lies below the average revenue curve. Hence, in the equilibrium position, the marginal revenue will be smaller than the average revenue or price.

(ii) Both under perfect competition and monopoly, the firm is in equilibrium at that level of output where MC is equal to MR. But in perfect competition since MR is equal to average revenue or price, therefore, MC, when equal to MR in equilibrium condition, is also equal to price or AR. This is not true in case of a monopoly. Since under monopoly, MR is always less than AR or Price, in equilibrium MC will, therefore, be equal to MR but it will be less than price.

Hence, under perfect competition, MC = MR = AR (Price). But under monopoly, MC = MR < AR (Price).

Therefore, we conclude that whereas in perfectly competitive equilibrium the price charged by the firm equals its marginal cost, under monopoly, the price set is above the marginal cost. In fact, the difference between marginal cost and price is said to measure the degree of monopoly power.

(iii) Another main difference is that, whereas in perfect competition a firm is in the long-run equilibrium at the minimum point of long-run average cost curve, in monopoly the firm is in equilibrium at the point where AC is still declining and has not reached the minimum. It often happens in monopoly that the marginal cost curve cuts the marginal revenue curve to the left of the point of minimum average cost. The chief reason for this limitation of output is that, as output is increased MR drops below this thus lowering AR, whereas marginal cost is likely to increase. Under perfect competition, it pays the firm to expand production so long as the average cost is falling , because under perfect competition average revenue and marginal revenue both stay high for a large output as for small output.

(iv) While discussing the conditions for the equilibrium of the firms under perfect competition, we saw there that a firm is in equilibrium at that level of output at which marginal cost is rising. Only in this way the second condition of equilibrium, *viz.*, marginal cost curve must cut the marginal revenue curve from below at the equilibrium output, is satisfied. Since in perfect competition the marginal revenue curve is a horizontal straight line, then if the marginal cost curve is to cut it from below, the marginal cost curve must be rising at and near the equilibrium output. But under conditions of monopoly marginal revenue curve is sloping downwards, and therefore, it is possible for

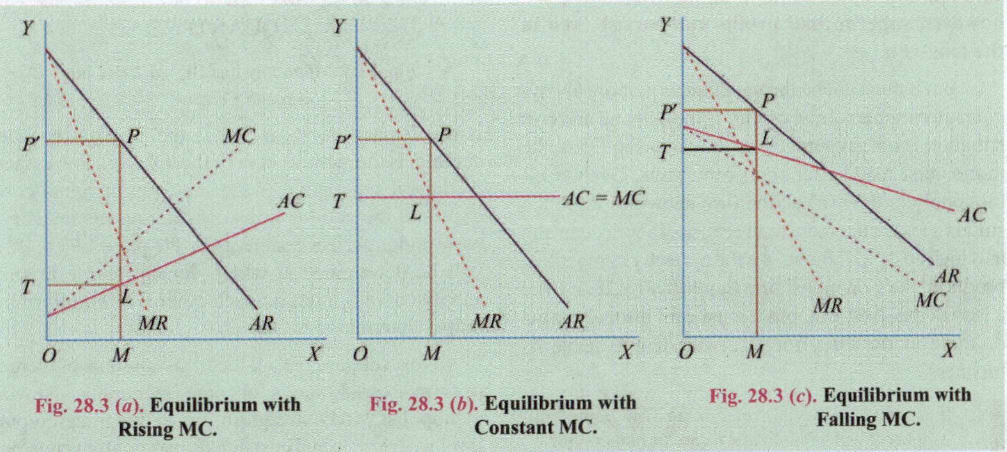

Fig. 28.3 *(a)*. **Equilibrium with Rising MC.**

Fig. 28.3 *(b)*. **Equilibrium with Constant MC.**

Fig. 28.3 *(c)*. **Equilibrium with Falling MC.**

the marginal cost curve to cut it from below whether it (MC) is rising, falling or running parallel to horizontal axis.

These three cases of rising, constant and falling marginal cost at the equilibrium output are illustrated by diagrams (*a*), (*b*) and (*c*) respectively in the Fig. 28.3. In the Fig. 28.3 (*a*), the equilibrium of the monopolist is shown when marginal cost is rising at the equilibrium output. In Fig. 28.3 (*b*), the monopolist is in equilibrium when marginal cost remains constant at and near the equilibrium output. In Fig. 28.3 (*c*), the equilibrium of the monopolist is established at the output at which marginal cost is falling. In all these cases, the price set is OP′ (= MP), the equilibrium output is equal to OM and total profits PLTP′.

Thus, while in the case of equilibrium under perfect competition, the marginal cost curve must be rising at or near the equilibrium output, under monopoly, a firm can be in equilibrium with rising, falling or constant marginal cost.

(*v*) Still another difference between the monopoly equilibrium and perfectly competitive equilibrium is that while under perfect competition in the long-run, a firm can earn only normal profits, but a monopolistic firm may be earning supernormal profits even in the long-run. If a perfectly competitive firm is earning supernormal profits in the short-run, they are competed away in the long-run by the entry of new firms in the industry. But in the case of a monopoly, there are sufficient barriers to the entry of new firms in the monopolised industry. Therefore, new firms cannot enter the industry in the long-run to compete away the monopoly profits.[1]

Thus, under perfect competition, there may be supernormal profits in the short-run, but they will be competed away in the long-run. In monopoly, however, supernormal profits can persist even in the long-run.

But it must not be through that monopoly always guarantees supernormal profits. If the demand and cost situation is not favourable, as shown in Fig. 28.4, the monopolist may suffer short-run losses. Despite his monopoly in the market, the firm shown in Fig. 28.4 suffers a loss in the short-run because of a weak demand and high costs. Of course like the perfectly competitive producer, the monopolist firm shown in Fig. 28.4 suffer a loss in the short-run, but it must earn normal profits or more in the long-run otherwise it will leave its business.

1. If in spite of the barriers, some firms enter the industry it will be no longer a case of monopoly.

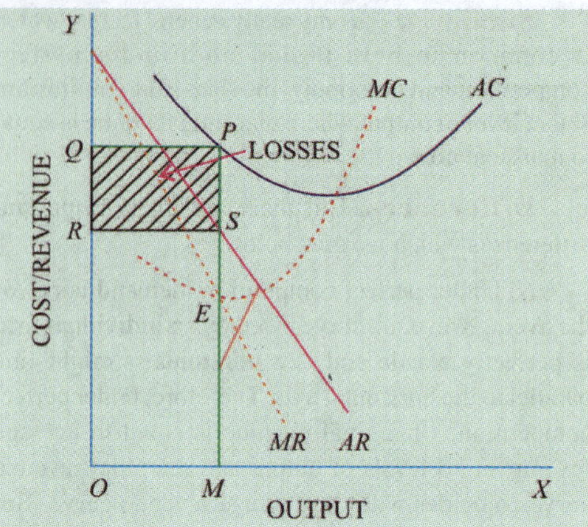

Fig. 28.4. **Monopolist Suffering Short-run Losses.**

(*vi*) Another difference between competition and monopoly is that under monopoly price set is higher and output smaller than under perfect competition, given the same cost-revenue situation. This is so because the monopolist restricts output to raise price. This can be explained with Fig. 28.5. In this figure, D

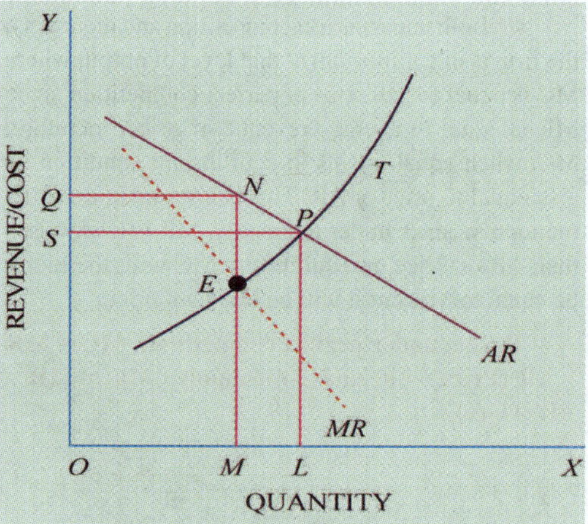

Fig. 28.5. **Monopoly has Higher Price but Smaller Output.**

is the demand curve. It is also the average revenue curve. S is the supply curve of the industry. It is in fact the lateral summation of the short-run marginal cost curves of the various firms constituting the industry. Now under perfect competition, the price LP (= OS) will be determined at which demand curve D and supply curve S intersect each other. The equilibrium output determined is OL.

Now suppose that all the firms combine or merge to form a cartel, that is, become monopoly.[2] Now a monopolist will be in equilibrium at that price-output level where marginal cost equals marginal revenue. In this figure, marginal cost equals marginal revenue at output OM and price fixed is MN (N being on the demand or AR curve). It is quite evident from the figure that when all the firms have merged together and become a monopoly, they have reduced the total output from OL to OM and raised the price from LP to MN.

Thus, in monopoly the price is higher and the output less than in perfect competition, conditions of cost and demand remaining unchanged.

(vii) Another difference between monopoly and perfect competition may be noted: A monopolist can charge discriminatory prices or his goods but a firm operating under perfect competition cannot. Under perfect competition, the price is fixed by the market and the producer cannot exercise any control over it. The question of charging different prices from different set of customers does not arise. On the other hand, a monopolist finds price discrimination both possible and profitable. For this purpose, he splits the market for his goods into sub-markets on the basis of elasticity of demand for his goods. Under perfect competition, the seller confronts a perfectly elastic demand curve at the prevailing price. If he charges a little higher price than the market price from some buyers, he will lose the customers. On the other hand, the monopolist has sole control over the supply of a product which has no close substitutes. Hence, the demand curve for the monopolist's product is relatively inelastic. He can, therefore, charge different prices in different parts of the market, but the condition is that the elasticity of demand for the product should be different in different parts of the market.

(viii) Competitive industry implies more efficient allocation of national resources. The competitive industries operate, in the long-run, at the minimum point of the average cost curves where average cost equals price. In case they tried to make higher profits, the entry of new firms will drive down prices and the extra profits will be competed away. In a competitive industry, a rupee worth of additional resources will produce a rupee worth of additional output, because average cost equals price. But since monopoly price is generally higher, the consumers are willing to pay more than a rupee for this additional output. This means that if these resources were used in the monopoly, the consumers would get greater satisfaction. But the monopolist does not permit this. It does not suit him. On the contrary, he restricts the output and thus reduces the consumers' satisfaction. Hence, from the point of consumers' welfare, the resources used in a monopoly represent a less efficient utilisation.

2. We assume that no extra economies of scale arise when the different firms combine.

REGULATION OF MONOPOLY

A monopolist is a suspect in the public eye. He generally exploits the consumers. All governments, therefore, consider it necessary to curb his profit-making propensity in the interest of the consumers and the community at large.

The two common methods are: (a) Price regulation and (b) Taxation. Now a word about these.

Price Regulation

It is usual for the Government to regulate prices charged by public utilities like gas and electric companies. The underlying object is to call forth the maximum output consistent with the monopolists' cost and consumer demand. This is shown in diagram Fig. 28.6. In the absence of price fixation by the Government, the monopolist would produce OM output and charge OP(= MQ) price, because here MR = MC and Q is a point on the demand curve and shows the consumers are prepared to Pay. Now let us suppose the Government fixes a lower price OP′ (= M′L). At this price, the monopolist produces a larger output OM′, since this price cuts the demand curve DD at L. Although the monopolist has been compelled to charge a lower price, yet the consuming public has taken a larger quantity. This compensates the monopolist. OM′ is the new profit-maximising output and his profit will be

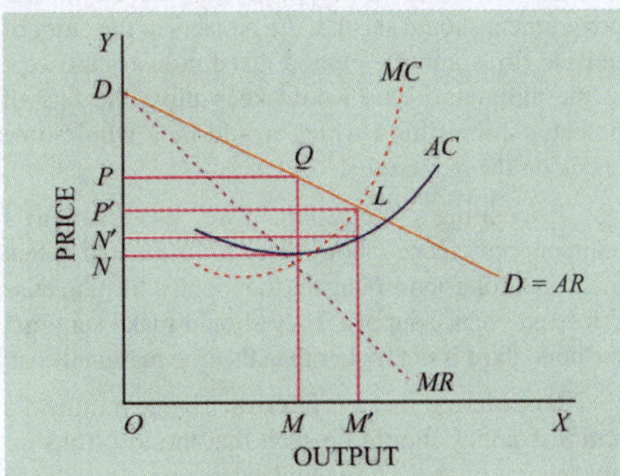

Fig. 28.6. Price Regulation.

OM′ output × P′N′. The consumers are benefited by a larger amount being made available to them at a lower price.

Taxation

Taxation is regarded as a very suitable device for regulating monopolies so that they are not able to exploit the consuming public by misusing their monopolistic power. Such taxes may be of two types: (*i*) Lumpsum tax irrespective of the quantity of the output and (*ii*) a fixed tax per unit of the output.

The lumpsum tax has to be borne entirely by the monopolist since it cannot be shifted to the consumers by way of the price rise. Already, the monopolist is supposed to have fixed a price which maximises his profit. If he could decrease the output to increase his profit, he would have done so. Since he has already fixed price and output which brings him maximum profit, he cannot now touch them. Hence, by imposing a lumpsum tax, the government can take away all or any proportion of his profit without adversely affecting the general welfare. This is, therefore, a very effective way of controlling the monopolist's behaviour.

As for the tax per unit of output the monopolist will be induced to reduce output and raise the price in order to maximise his profit after paying the per unit tax. The price rise affects the consumer. The profits after the tax too are smaller than profits before the tax; since the tax is a variable cost. The total costs of the monopolist at the various levels of output are increased, but the total revenue remains the same. Hence, prices being higher and the output smaller, the general welfare is adversely affected. Such a tax is a wholesome check on the misuse of monopolist's power.

Other Methods of Control

There are several other regulatory devices for curbing the exploitative propensity of the monopolist.

Reducing Barriers to Entry. The government should see that the barriers to the entry of outside firms into the monopolised industry are kept at the minimum. This would keep alive the fear of potential competition which would be a wholesome check on the monopolist.

Preventing Collusion. The government's antimonopoly agency should keep a close watch so that there is so collusion among the monopolist firms to raise price and control supply. They should make sure that the price fixed is not higher than the true marginal cost.

Breaking Large Firms. The government's antitrust policy should be such that the big firms do not become bigger. The capital issue cannot may be so exercised that they are not permitted to issue more capital. Further, they may not be given the supply of scarce materials. In these and other ways, large firms should be prevented from expanding.

Monopolies Commission. Periodical report on the working of monopolies by a Commission may focus public opinion on the evil doings of the monopolists. This itself may keep them straight, failing which legislation may be adopted to weed out the known evils. Greater attention should be paid to preventing a bad market behaviour than to punishment after the misbehaviour.

Conclusion

There is no complete remedy to monopolist misbehaviour. But sustained efforts have to be made to keep a close watch on the working of the monopolies and take necessary measures for their regulation and control. We have to console ourselves with the fact that things would have been worse and the consumer hit harder in the absence of such measures.

DISCRIMINATING MONOPOLY

Meaning of Price Discrimination

So far we have assumed that the monopolist charges only one price from all the purchasers of his commodity. This is generally not the case. The monopolist can, and some monopolists do, charge different prices for the same commodity from different people provided these people from "different markets" or belong to what are called non-competing groups. This is known as price discrimination or discriminating monopoly. Mrs. Robinson defines it as "charging different price for the same product, or same price for the differentiated product." The product may be differentiated by time, appearance or place so that the purchasers are not able to shift to the low-price commodity. Stigler defines price discrimination "as the sale of various products at prices which are not proportional to their marginal costs."[3]

Types of Price Discrimination

Price discrimination may be (*a*) personal, (*b*) local, or (*c*) according to trade or use. It is personal when different prices are charged from different persons. It is local when the price varies according to locality (*e.g.*, dumping). Discrimination is according to use when different prices are charged according to the uses to which the commodity is put, *e.g., electric* current is usually sold cheaper for industrial uses than for domestic purposes. Sometimes the monopolist introduces product differentiation by means of special labels and charges different prices for the differentiated products.

Degrees of Price Discrimination

According to Prof. A. C. Pigou, there are three degrees of discrimination as under:–

(*i*) Price discrimination of the first degree in which the monopolist charges a different price for each unit of the commodity sold. He charges the maximum that

3. Stigler, G. J. –*The Theory of Price*, 1953, p. 214.

each buyer is able and willing to pay, leaving him to consumer's surplus. Obviously, this involves maximum exploitation of the buyers. This is known as perfect price discrimination.

(ii) Instead of setting price for each buyer as in the first degree discrimination, in the second degree, the buyers are divided into groups and from each group a different price is charged, which is the lowest demand price for that group. Thus, all units with a demand price greater than, say X, are sold at X price, all units with demand price greater than Y but less than X are sold at Y, and so on. Such a price discrimination is possible. The demand of each individual buyer is perfectly inelastic.

(iii) In the third degree discrimination, the monopolist splits the entire market into a few sub-markets and charges a different price in each sub-market.

Conditions of Price Discrimination

The essence of price discrimination is that the monopolist can charge different customers different prices although there is no fundamental difference between the goods offered to the different customers. Let us study the conditions (*a*) under which price discrimination is possible and (*b*) when price discrimination is profitable.

When Price Discrimination is Possible

As already mentioned, a monopolist can practise price discrimination by dividing his market into sub-market and charging different prices in the monopolist can keep these sub-markets absolutely separate. According to Pigou, there are two main conditions for this purpose:–

First, it should not be possible to transfer any unit of the commodity from one sub-market to another. That is, the goods sold in the cheaper market cannot be resold in the dearer market, otherwise monopolist's purpose will be defeated.

Secondly, it should not be possible for the buyers in the dearer market to sneak into the cheaper market to take advantage of the low price. For example, a patient, who is really rich, should not be able to pass as a poor person to avail himself of the lower fee charged by a doctor from the poor patients.

For the monopolist to keep his sub markets separate to successfully practice price discrimination is possible under the following conditions:–

***(i)* When consumers have certain preferences or prejudices.** Certain consumers, especially belonging to the upper class, usually have the irrational feeling that they are paying higher prices for a good because it is of a better quality, although actually it may be of the same quality. As Mrs. Joan Robinson observes, "various brands of a certain article which in fact are almost alike may be sold as different qualities under names and labels which induce rich and snobbish buyers to divide themselves from the poor buyers, and in this way the market is split up and the monopolist can sell what is substantially the same thing at different prices."[4]

Similarly upper class snobbish people prefer to shop in fashionable quarters, (*e.g.*, Connaught Place in New Delhi) to going to a cheaper locality (*i.e.*, Chandni Chowk, Delhi). This enables the monopolist to charge discriminating prices.

(ii) When the **nature of the good** is such as makes it possible for the monopolist to charge different prices. This happens particularly when the good in question is a **direct service.** While goods like combs and hairpins can be resold by those who are charged lower prices to those required to pay prices, it is not possible to resell haircuts or beauty treatment effected in a beauty parlour, so that different prices can be charged from different persons. There may be some difference in the standard of service rendered, but the difference in prices charged is usually far greater than the difference in the standard of service rendered. We often find that surgeons charge different fees from rich and poor patients for performing similar surgical operations.

***(iii)* When consumers are separated by distance or tariff barriers,** the monopolist can charge different prices. A good may be sold in one town for Rs. 1 and in another for Rs. 2 and so long as the cost of transport exceeds the difference in prices, resale will not be profitable. Similarly, the monopolist can charge higher prices in a country levying import duty on his commodity and lower prices elsewhere where no such duties are levied. Because of import duty it is obviously not profitable to import the commodity from countries where it is sold cheaper.

***(iv)* Government Regulations.** Sometimes, the price discrimination occurs when the government rules and regulations permit. For instance, according to rules, electricity rates are fixed at lower level for industrial purposes and higher for domestic uses. Similarly, railways charge by law higher fare from first class passengers than from the second or third class passengers.

***(v)* Ignorance and Lethargy.** Monopolists also take advantage of the ignorance of the customers

4. *Economics of Imp fect Competition*, pp. 180-81.

or of their disinclination to take the trouble of comparing prices. In this way, they can charge higher prices from some customers than from others. They also sometimes cash on the impatience of the buyers, *e.g.*, charging higher price for the Ist edition of a book.

(*vi*) Same Service for Different Purposes. When a monopolist, while rendering the same service, is able to cater for different needs of his customers, it is possible for him to charge discriminating prices. For example, railways charge different rates for carrying coal, silk and fruit even though the same train carries them all.

(*vii*) Special Orders. A monopolist can easily charge discriminating prices when goods are being supplied to special orders. In such a case, there is no question for the buyers to compare prices.

Possible only in Imperfect Competition. It is obvious that price discrimination can be practised only under imperfect competition. It is not at all possible when perfect competition prevails in a market. Under perfect competition, price prevailing in the market has to be accepted both by the buyers and sellers. The buyers can only adjust their purchases and the seller the supply to the prevailing price. It is not in the power of the buyers or of the sellers (for the obvious reason that they are so many of them) to influence or modify the price in any manner. The seller faces a perfectly elastic demand curve. But when there is imperfect competition, taking the form of a monopoly or monopolistic competition, the seller is in a position to fix the price. The degree of price discrimination will depend on the degree of imperfection of the market.

When Price Discrimination is Profitable

We have studied above the conditions which make discrimination by a monopolist possible. Now let us see when such discrimination becomes profitable. Price discrimination is profitable only if elasticity of demand in one market is different from elasticity of demand in the other. Then the monopolist can go on dividing and sub-dividing his market till no two buyers with different elasticities are put in the same group, or till in each market the elasticity of demand is the same. The monopolist will find it profitable to charge more in the market where elasticity is low and low price where it is high. To quote Mrs. Robinson, "The sub-markets will be arranged in ascending order of their elasticities, the highest price being charged in the least elastic market, and the lowest price in the most elastic market."[5]

5. Economic of Imperfect Competition, pp. 180-81.

Discrimination Not Profitable When the Demand Curves Are Iso-elastic

In order to prove that unless the elasticity of demand in the sub-markets is different discrimination will not be profitable, we shall take the two markets where the demand curves are iso-elastic, *i.e.*, where, at every price, elasticity of demand curve is the same.

When in the two markets elasticity of demand is the same, then the marginal revenue will also be the same.[6] Marginal revenue in the two markets being the same, it will not be profitable to transfer any unit of the commodity from one market to another in order to charge a different price. This will be clear from the above diagram (Fig. 28.7).

In this diagram, the demand curves ARa (in market A) and ARb (in market B) have the same elasticity at the price OP as at any other price ($OP = M_1 H_1 = M_2 H_2$). At this price (OP), marginal revenue in the two markets is the same ($M_1S_1 = M_2 S_2$). Now if the monopolist transfers some units of the commodity from the market A by reducing $M_1 N_1$ to the market B by adding $M_2 N_2$, then the loss in market A shown in the shaded area $M_1 S_1 T_1 N_1$ is greater than the gain $M_2 S_2 T_2 N_2$ in the market B. This shows that when the demand curves have the same elasticity in the sub-markets price discrimination will not be profitable.

Price Discrimination Profitable when Elasticities Differ

The monopolist will find it profitable to charge discriminating prices, on the other hand, when the elasticities of demand in the two markets are different. Rather, this is the only way for him to maximise profits. In case he charged a single price in the two markets, his profits will not be maximum. But if elasticity of demand is different in the two markets, he would charge higher price in the market where elasticity is low and low price where it is high. When elasticity of demand at the single monopoly price are different in the two markets, the marginal revenue will also be different. The marginal revenue in the market with higher elasticity of demand is greater than the marginal revenue in the market where elasticity is lower. It will be obviously worthwhile for the monopolist to transfer some units of the commodity from the market where elasticity is high. By such a transfer he will be increasing his profit. The market from which the units are transferred will experience a rise and the market to

6. This follows from the formula

$$MR = AR\left(\frac{e-1}{e}\right)$$ (See page 171).

e stands for elasticity of demand.

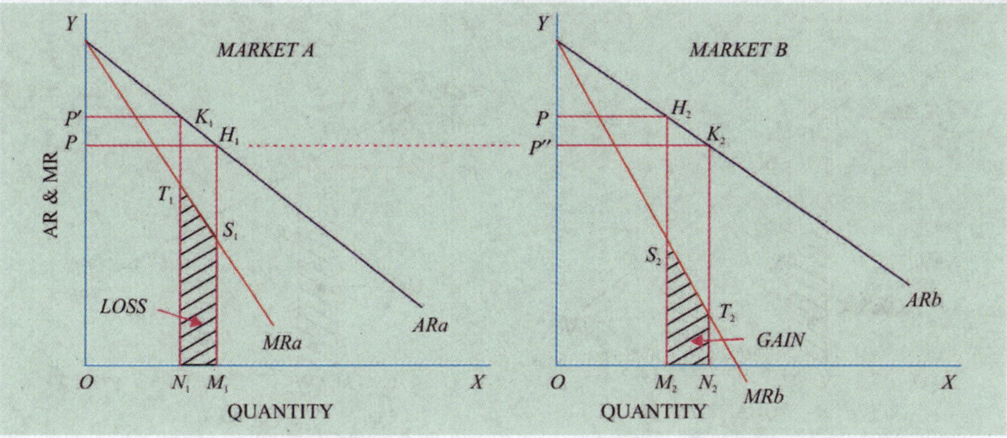

Fig. 28.7. With Same Elasticity Discrimination is Not Profitable.

which the units are transferred will experience a fall in price.

How this is more profitable is illustrated in the Fig. 28.8 given on next page.

In this diagram, elasticity of demand is greater in market B than it is in market A. This is indicated by the slope of the AR curves (ARb has a greater slope). In market B, marginal revenue M_2 S_2 is greater than marginal revenue M_1 S_1 in Market A. Now if sale in the market A is reduced by N_1 M_1 the loss in revenue (M_1 S_1 T_1 N_1) is much less than the gain (M_2 S_2 T_2 N_2) in market B by increasing sales thereby M_2 N_2. It can be seen that, when M_1N_1 units are withdrawn from market A, the price rises from OP to OP′. On the other hand, when M_2 N_2 units are added in the market B, the price falls from OP to OP″. That is, now the monopolist is charging different prices in the two markets as against one single price OP before and we see that his profit has increased thereby. Shifting of units of the commodity from market A to market B will continue till marginal revenues in the two markets are equalised, the profit will have been maximised and there will be no further shifting. This is so because, so long as MR is higher in market B, the monopolist will be adding more to his revenue than his loss in market A by transferring some amount of goods from A market to B market.

Price-output Equilibrium in Discriminating Monopoly

We have studied already how price and output are determined under conditions of simple monopoly. In the simple monopoly, a single price is charged for the whole output. But as explained above in discriminating monopoly, different prices are charged for a commodity. We shall now see how a monopolist decides the output to be produced under price discrimination and how he sets different prices for a commodity.

First of all, the monopolist divides his total market into sub-markets. The monopolist can divide his total market into several sub-markets but we shall explain the case of two sub-markets only. There is no difference in analysis even if the sub-markets are many rather than two. Our analysis can, therefore, easily be extended to cover several sub-markets.

Price discrimination by the monopolist has been illustrated in Figs. 28.9 (*a*), (*b*) and (*c*). In these figures, we see that the monopolist has divided his total market into sub-markets A and B on the basis of elasticity of demand for the product in these two markets. Elasticity of demand is greater in market B than in market A. In market A, AR′ is the average revenue curve and MR′ is the corresponding marginal revenue curve. Similarly AR″ and MR″ are the average revenue and marginal revenue curves respectively in market B. CMR is the combined marginal revenue curve. CMR has been obtained by the lateral summation of MR′ and MR″, MC is the marginal cost curve of the total output of the product.

The discriminating monopolist has now to decide what level of output he should produce. Like every other producer, he aims at maximizing his profits. As elsewhere, his profits will be maximum, and, hence he will be in equilibrium position, at the output at which MR = MC, and MC curve cuts the MR curve from below. It is evident from Fig. 28.9 (c) that equilibrium of the discriminating monopolist is established at the output OM at which MC cuts CMR.

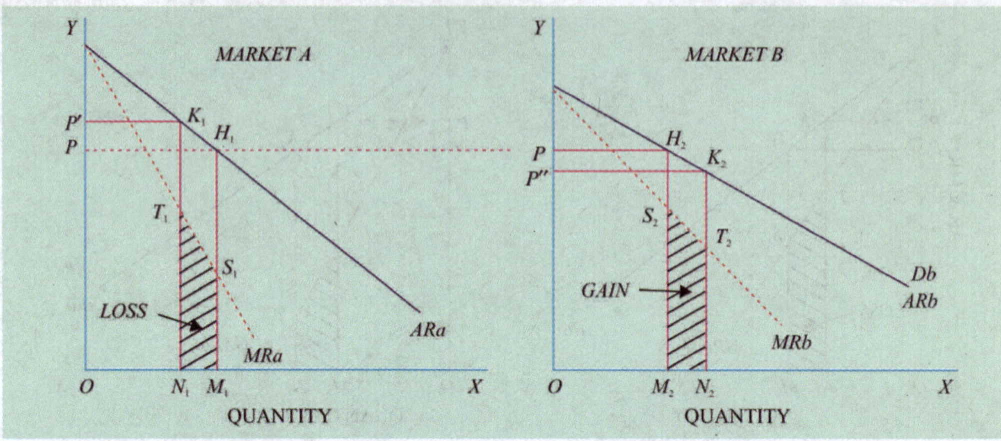

Fig. 28.8. Price Discrimination is Profitable when Elasticties Differ.

Now the output OM has therefore to be distributed between the two markets in such a way that marginal revenue in each is equal to ME which is the marginal cost, being on the MC curve. Therefore, he will sell output OM_1 in market A, because only at this output marginal revenue MR′ in market A is equal to ME (M_1E' = ME). The price charged in the market for output OM_1 is equal to M_1 P_1 P_1 being on the average revenue (AR′) or demand curve. The output OM_2 will be sold in market B as only at this output, marginal revenue in market B, that is MR″ is equal to ME (M_2E'' = ME). Price charged in market B for output OM_2 is M_2 P_2 which is lower than the M_1 P_1 which is charged in market A. Thus, in market B in which elasticity of demand is greater, the price charged is lower than that in market A, where the elasticity of demand is less.

Hence, for the discriminating monopolist to be in equilibrium the following two conditions must be satisfied:

(i) Marginal Cost of Total Output = Combined Marginal Revenue.

(ii) Marginal Revenue in Market A = Marginal Revenue in Market B = Marginal Cost.

Price Discrimination and Output

Will the output in a Discriminating Monopoly be more or less than in a simple monopoly? When the elasticities of demand in the two markets are different, it will be found that marginal revenue from the sale of a unit of output will be more where the elasticity is higher than where it is low. It will be, therefore, profitable to reduce the output and raise the price where the elasticity is low and increase the output and lower the price where the elasticity of demand is high. In this way, the marginal revenue in the two markets will be equalised.

But will the output on the whole increase, or decrease, or remain the same? Mrs. Robinson gives the answer: "It is possible to establish the fact that total output under discrimination will be greater or less than under simple monopoly according as the more elastic of the demand curves in the separate markets is more or less concave than the less elastic demand curve; and the total output will be the same if the demand curves are straight lines, or in any other case in which the concavities are equal."[7] This holds good, however, if marginal cost under simple monopoly and discriminating monopoly is the same. But if marginal cost is falling, the increase in output in a discriminating monopoly will be accentuated and if the marginal cost is rising , then the decrease in the output will be accentuated.

On the whole, it is more likely that discrimination will increase rather than decrease output.

A few illustrations will make this point clear. In this case of certain books, the first edition is issued at a high price. The readers, whose marginal utility (intensity of demand) for the book is very high, purchase it at this price. After this edition is exhausted, a second edition is issued which is priced lower than the first. People of lower marginal utility also can now purchase the book. This process may be repeated several times and a very wide sale obtained. People with greater intensity of demand will not wait for cheaper editions. In this way, the monopolist appropriates the major portion of the consumer's surplus and increases his monopoly revenue to a point otherwise not possible.

7. See Robinson, J. –*OP. cit.*, Chapter 10.

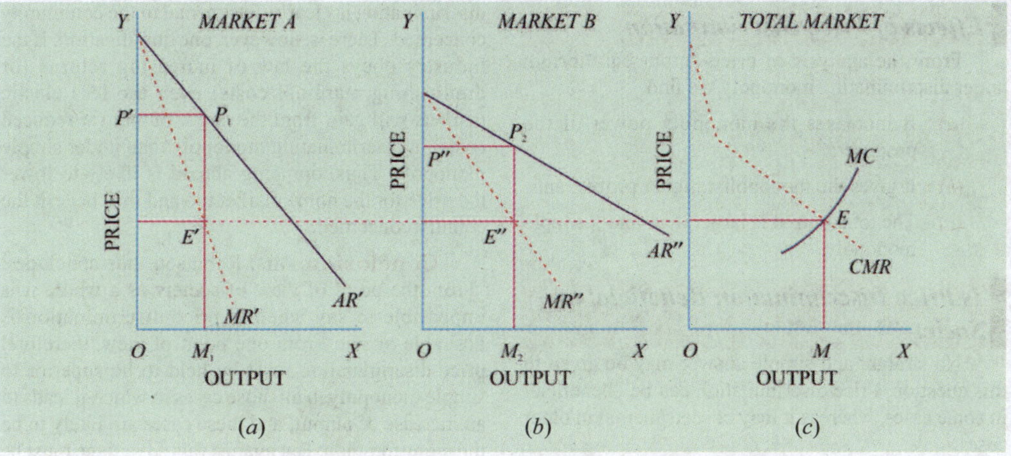

Fig. 28.9. Price-Output Equilibrium under Discriminating Monopoly.

Price Discrimination by Dumping

When discrimination takes the form of dumping, it is regarded as an obnoxious practice. Dumping occurs when producers (usually monopolists) of one country sell their goods in another country at prices below those charged from the consumers in the country of origin. In some cases, it may pay a monopolist to sell his commodity in the foreign market below even his cost of production.

The monopolist may have several motives for dumping: (*a*) to dispose of an over-stock casually produced due to wrong judgment of demand. (*b*) to develop new trade connections by charging low prices, (*c*) to drive competitors out of the foreign market whether foreigners or native producers, and (*d*) to reap economies of large-scale production.

An extreme case of dumping may be illustrated by the following table:

TABLE 1: HOME MARKET

Sale Price	*Cost Price*	*No. of Units*	*Net Revenue*
Rs. Ps.	Rs. Ps.		Rs. Ps.
10.00	5.00	100	500.00
9.75	4.75	150	750.00
9.25	4.50	200	950.00
8.50	4.25	250	1062.50
7.75	4.00	300	1125.00
7.00	3.75	350	1137.50
----	----	----	--------
5.75	3.25	400	1000.00
4.75	2.75	450	900.00

It will be seen from the above table that, if the monopolist only produced for the home market, he would produce 350 units and sell them at Rs. 7 a unit. This will give him the largest net revenue, *i.e.*, Rs. 1,137.50.

Suppose he produced 450 units instead of 350. His total cost will be Rs. $450 \times 2\frac{3}{4}$ = Rs. 1,237.50. For 350 units his total cost would have been Rs. $350 \times 3\frac{3}{4}$ = Rs. 1,312.50.

Thus the monopolist can lower his total cost by Rs. 75 (Rs. 1,312.50 – Rs. 1,237.50) by producing 100 units more.

It will be to his advantage to produce these extra 100 units even if he has to destroy them. He can thus sell these additional units in a foreign market with profit if he can charge a price just above the cost of transporting them. No foreign producer can compete with him at such a price.

Such a big advantage, however, is rare. We took an extreme case to illustrate the principle involved. Moreover, if the difference between the home price and the foreign price is greater than the cost of transporting the commodity back to the country of its origin, the commodity may be re-exported, unless high tariff walls stand in the way. Foreign countries usually raise high tariff walls against dumping, especially if it affects their own industries. It is a temporary phenomenon and does not confer any permanent benefit on the country into which goods are dumped. "The possibility of dumping in a foreign market will raise the home price if marginal costs are raising, lower if they are falling and leave it unaltered if they are constant." (Benham).

Effects of Price Discrimination

From the analysis of price-output equilibrium under discriminating monopoly we find –

(*a*) It increases the monopoly power of the producer;

(*b*) It gives the monopolist higher profits; and

(*c*) The total output is larger than under simple monopoly.

Is Price Discrimination Beneficial to Society?[8]

No straight and simple answer may be given to this question. Price discrimination can be beneficial in some cases, whereas it may be detrimental in other cases.

In certain cases, price discrimination may be to the advantage of the community, for instance, when a particular service may be very useful to the community. If the price is fixed low enough for the poorer classes, production costs may not be met due to absence of normal profit per unit. If the price is fixed too high, the total receipts again may be low due to meagre sales. The commodity may, therefore, not be produced at all. At any rate, some output may be held up, because average revenue in a discriminating monopoly is greater than under simple monopoly. "It may happen, for instance, that a railway would not be built, or a country doctor would not set up in practice, if discrimination were forbidden. It is clearly desirable that price discrimination should be permitted in such cases." If discriminatory prices are charged, the total receipts may be adequate to meet the total cost with profit. Thus, every one may gain from the production of such a commodity when discriminatory prices are charged.

Since discrimination involves raising the price for some people and lowering for some others, it is obvious that price discrimination is beneficial to some and harmful to others. But the net effect on social welfare will depend on which group the society likes to favour. If the price is lowered for the masses and raised for the 'classes' the society has nothing to regret, for such an arrangement is obviously intended to promote economic welfare.

But, in the case of geographical discrimination, it is also possible that the less elastic market (for whom the price is raised) may be the home market, whereas the market abroad may happen to be more elastic and for them the price will, therefore, be lowered. In a case like this, the foreigners gain at the expense of the nationals of the country. Such a price discrimination is clearly detrimental to the community concerned. There is, however, one qualification. If the industry obeys the law of increasing returns (or diminishing marginal costs) even the less elastic markets will gain from the larger output (at reduced costs) in discriminating monopoly than under simple monopoly. Thus, dumping abroad is likely to lower the price for the home market too and thus benefit the country concerned.

Conclusion. Mrs. Robinson thus concludes: "From the point of view of society as a whole it is impossible to say whether price discrimination is desirable or not. From one point of view, therefore, price discrimination must be held to be superior to simple monopoly in all those cases in which it leads to an increase of output, and these cases are likely to be the more common. But against this advantage must be set the fact that price discrimination leads to a maldistribution of resources as between different uses .... Before it is possible to say whether discrimination is desirable or not, it is necessary to weigh up the benefit from the increase in output against this disadvantage. In those cases in which discrimination will decrease output, it is undersirable on both counts."[9]

Dumping. In modern market, a number of countries resort to dumping. It is a situation in which a monopolist sells his product in home market at higher price (that is monopolists price) and foreign market at low price (that is competitive price).

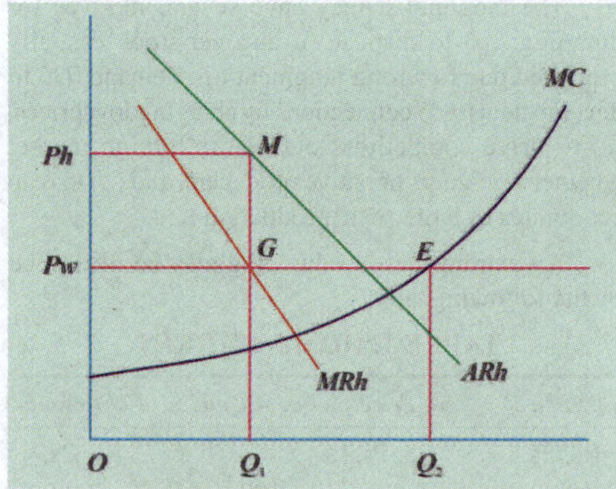

Fig. 28.10. Dumping by monopolist.

Dumping is very common in modern days global economy. Due to automization and modern technology advanced countries are able to produce huge quantity. Their home market demand is less than the production, they release only that much of quantity and maintain a high price. The remaining quantity they sell or dump it in developing countries at a competitive price. In general we assume a monopolists faces monopoly

8. See Robinson, J. –*op. cit.*, Chapter 10.

9. *ibid.*, p. 206.

market in home market and a perfectly competitive market in world market.

$OQ_1 < Q_1Q_2$ — OQ_1 Quantity in Home Market
Q_1Q_2 in Foreign Market

OP_h price (Monopoly and OQ_1 Quantity in Home Market

OP_w Price (competitive) and OQ_2 Quantity in Foreign Market

MC—Marginal Cost

AR_H—Average Revenue Home Market.

MR_H—Marginal revenue Home Market.

ARW = MRW—Foreign market (world) demand curve.

P_h—Price in home market (monopoly price).

P_w—Price in world market (competitive price).

In the above diagram the concept of dumping is shown. AR_H is the demand curve. That is relatively elastic or unit elasticity of demand, whereas AR_W and MR_W is perfectly elastic demand curve of world market. The equilibrium point of total quantity is achieved at point 'E' that mean 'OQ_2' quantity. Out of which 'OQ_1' quantity of goods is sold in home market at P_h price (higher price and less quantity) and the other part 'Q_1Q_2' is sold in world market or foreign market at P_w price (higher quantity at lower price).

The aim of monopolists is to maximize his profit by sales maximisation. He intends to sell his maximum output by maintaining a high price at home and a competitive price in world market. In modern days management a monopolist tries to maintain high price in home market, so as to maintain or attract demand from foreign markets.

MONOPOLY POWER

All monopolies are not equally powerful. Some monopolists are able to exercise greater control on price-output than others. We should not, therefore, think that all monopolists have the same capacity for influencing price and output in an industry. The degree of monopoly power is indicated by the extent of influence that a monopolist can exercise on price and output. **By monopoly power we mean the amount of discretion which the monopolist possesses or the intensity of competition which affects him in shaping his policy with regard to the ouput and the price of his product and to the differentiation of his production by quality and service.**

In short, monopoly power indicates the extent of the departure from the competitive behaviour.

Measurement of Monopoly power

Now let us see how this monopoly power can be measured. Have we got any measure by which we can say that this particular monopolist has so much monopoly power or so much more or less than another monopolist?

There are different ways of measuring monopoly power:–

(*i*) Excess of Price Over Marginal Cost. We have said above that the monopoly power indicates a departure from the competitive behaviour. It is the extent of this departure which indicates the extent of monopoly power. We have already seen that in a perfectly competitive equilibrium, marginal cost equals price or AR. But this is not so under monopoly. Under conditions of monopoly, AR (Average Revenue) curve slopes downwards to the right, whereas under competition, the two curves AR and MR (Marginal Revenue) coincide, and both are horizontal straight lines. In a monopoly, MR curve is always below the AR curve. Since the firm is in equilibrium where marginal revenue is equal to marginal cost, the MC (Marginal Cost) is less than AR (Average Revenue), and AR, *i.e.*, average revenue is price. This can be put as under :

In equilibrium (whether monopoly or competition), MR = MC.

But in monopoly MR is less than AR (*i.e.*, Price).

∴ MC is less than AR (*i.e.*, Price).

On the other hand, in perfect competition MC = Price.

This is the major difference between monopoly and competition, *viz.*, (to repeat) in competition MC (marginal cost) is equal to price whereas under monopoly MC (marginal cost) is less than the price. We can, therefore, say, that **monopoly power is indicated by the extent to which marginal cost departs from price.** In other words, the size of the difference between marginal cost and price is sometimes used to measure the extent of a firm's monopoly power.

A. P. Lerner has given the following formula for the measurement of this monopoly power:–

$$\text{Measure of Monopoly Power} = \frac{P - MC}{P} \quad ..(1)$$

Here, P is price and MC is Marginal Cost.

Under competition P = MC. ...(2)

From 1 and 2, we get

$$\frac{MC - MC}{P} = \frac{O}{P} = O$$

In this case (*i.e.*, under competition), therefore, monopoly power is nil. To the extent price exceeds marginal cost, the monopoly power is greater than what is under competition.

Elasticity of Demand and Monopoly Power. We have explained above that the difference between marginal cost and price measures the degree of monopoly power. The larger is the difference the greater is the firm's monopoly power, and *vice versa*. This difference ultimately depends upon the elasticity of demand for the firm's product. Differing elasticities of demand measure the degree of monopoly power. The less is the elasticity of demand the greater is the power or degree of monopoly.

(*ii*) Amount of Supernormal Profits. There is another way to measure monopoly power, *viz*., by the amount of supernormal profits. Under perfect or free competition, firms can earn only normal profits in the long-run. If there are supernormal profits they are competed away. This is due to the fact that the new firms will enter the industry and the existing firms will also expand. The result will be that price will come down and costs will go up so that extra profits disappear. But this cannot happen under a monopoly. Since competition is absent, supernormal profits will persist in a monopoly; they are not competed away.

Hence, the size of the supernormal profits will measure the degree of monopoly power. The stronger the monopolist's position the larger will be the size of the supernormal profits.

Thus, there are two measures of monopoly power:

(*i*) The difference between the marginal cost and the price; and

(*ii*) the size of the supernormal profits.

Is Monopoly Price a High Price?

Not necessarily. We have seen that monopoly power enables a monopolist to restrict his output and charge a price higher than the marginal cost. Competitive price, however, tends to equal the marginal cost. This, however, does not mean that monopoly price is necessarily and invariably higher than competitive price. Several influences may keep the monopoly price down and in some cases may bring it to a level lower than what is would be under competition.

The monopolist may be able to produce an article at a lower cost per unit on account of the exceptional advantages that he may enjoy as regard the scale of production, in advertising, marketing expenses and other overhead charges. Thus, even though he may charge a price higher than his own marginal cost, it may be lower than what would be the marginal cost under competition. This is the case especially with industries using large and expensive indivisible equipment, and the demand for the products of which is elastic. Expansion of output in such industries reduces cost per unit, and larger output can be sold at remunerative, though low, prices.

Normally, however, monopoly price is rarely lower than the price under competition. But this does not mean that monopoly price is inordinately a high price. As we shall see below, there are serious limitations on the power of a monopolist. He is not always able to charge price which would theoretically maximize his profit. Apart from the fact that the monopolist may be ignorant of the level of the price, which gives him maximum returns due to difficulties of assessing the factors involved, there are certain considerations which few monopolist can ignore. (There are discussed on page 295).

Conclusion. But in spite of these restraining influences, monopoly prices are generally higher than the competitive prices. Our conclusion is that the monopolist is in a position to charge less, but he does not. Monopoly price thus need not be higher, but it actually is.

CRITICISM OF MONOPOLY

People look at monopolies with suspicious eyes because it is thought that monopoly involves exploitation of the consumers. Because of their anti-social consequences, governments have taken steps to control and regulate monopolies so as to compel them to work in public interest. The various objections raised against monopoly are stated below:

Firstly, it has below pointed out, as explained earlier in the chapter, that monopolist finds it possible and profitable to restrict output and charge higher prices than would the competitive producers. The profit maximising price of the monopolist is very likely to set a scale of production below the optimum size possible for the monopolist. This means that monopoly does not seek to use fully the internal economies of production and thereby lower the cost per unit, and the price. The result is that the consumers pay more for the product than the cost of production. That is, they pay more than what is necessary to put the resources in the industry.

Owing to the reduction in output, the complementary factors have to seek employment elsewhere, there their marginal productivity will be lower. Consequently, the price that these complementary factors will fetch will be correspondingly lower. On the other hand, the volume of output in other industries, to which these productive resources have been transferred will expand. Thus, the owner of the monopolised resource has a higher income, whereas the owners of the other resources are worse off. Such will be the consequences brought about by the revisions in consumer income allocations induced by these income and price changes. They will also be the result of ripples of changes affecting the organisation of production.

Futher, monopoly involves misallocation of resources. The monopolist will not use resources at their peak potential efficiency. His profit maximisation does not necessarily indicate either the optimum rate of output or the optimum scale of the plant. In other words, under monopoly the allocation of resources is not conducive to maximum welfare or satisfaction. Maximum welfare of the society requires that the level of output should be fixed at the point where marginal cost equals price. But price set under monopoly stands above marginal cost and does not therefore maximize welfare.

Price is indicative of the marginal utility or satisfaction derived by the society from the good. Therefore, society will gain in welfare if more resources are employed to produce more of that good so that price (*i.e.*, marginal utility) becomes equal to marginal cost. But the monopolist finds it profitable to restrict output to a level at which price is higher than marginal cost, and, therefore, he employs fewer resources than are justified from the point of view of social welfare. The monopolist forbids the entry of resources in the desired quantities. They must, therefore, remain in use elsewhere, where their contribution to consumer's satisfaction is smaller.

Another criticism of monopoly is that the supernormal profits, which monopolists make, contribute to greater inequality in the distribution of income. Under competitive conditions, firms will earn only normal profits in the long-run. But surplus profits are persistently realised by monopolist evening the long-run. But surplus profits are persistently realised by monopolists even in the long-run. By virtue of their monopoly power, monopolists obtain a large share of the national income. Thus, monopolies increase income inequalities in the country.

Further, it has been alleged that monopoly retards technological progress. Incentives to develop new products and new techniques on the part of monopolist are very weak. This is because there are no rivals of the monopolist. It is only competition which induces one to introduce improved techniques so as to improve efficiency and productivity. Because of the absence of competition, monopoly can afford to be inefficient and lethargic.

Moreover, it has been argued that a monopolist is likely to resist or withhold technological improvement in both product and productive techniques in order to use the present capital equipment fully. Introduction of new and improved products and techniques may be resisted by the monopolist to avoid any losses caused by the sudden obsolescence of existing machinery and equipment.

The monopolist may, through advertisement and sale promotion measures, enlarge the demand for his products and even may make the demand less elastic by convincing the people of the desirability, nay the indispensability, of his product.

Finally, it is argued that monopoly creates unemployment. As explained before, monopoly restricts output to raise the price. When output is smaller, fewer men will be employed, hence, retrenchment and unemployment. In other words, monopoly equilibrium is an equilibrium with **'excess capacity',** which means that there is under-utilisation of resources.

RESTRAINTS ON MONOPOLIES

It will perhaps seem that the monopolist would be able to charge whatever price he liked, his sole consideration being to maximise his profit regardless of social welfare. But the monopolist cannot, in actual practice, behave like an autocrat. There are several checks on the abuse of monopoly power:

In the first place, a monopolist is always afraid of **potential rivals.** If he charges too high a price, some other entrepreneurs will surely enter the field to take advantage of the high price and wrest from him a share of the high profits that he is making.

Secondly, the consumers may not take it lying down. There is a limit to their exploitation. An increase of one Paisa in the price may prove to be the last straw on the camel's back. **The consumers may actively organise a boycott.** No monopolist can afford to alienate the sympathies of his customers.

Thirdly, there is hardly any commodity for which substitutes, more or less satisfactory, cannot be found. The monopolist's greed can be effectively checked by resort to substitutes. The consumers are willing only to allow a certain margin between the price of the monopolised product and the substitute. As soon as that margin is exceeded, the substitute comes in.

Fourthly, the monopolist cannot ignore the **conditions of demand** and take independent unilateral action. He is bound to consider at every step the state of demand. If the demand is elastic, the monopolist's position is correspondingly weak.

Fifthly, we have seen that a combination (*i.e.*, monopoly) is constantly threatened by forces from within. It is not so easy to maintain a combination. It is usually a house divided against itself and they cannot, therefore, do as they please.

Finally, there is the fear of State intervention. The State, as the custodian of the interests of the general public, cannot allow a monopolist to exploit the community. If need be, it is prepared to intervene. This acts as a wholesome check on the autocratic tendency of the monopolist.

Summing up. Thus, the price-output policies of the monopolist are constrained by the threat of potential competition, competition from close substitutes and by indirect competition from all commodities that can be purchased with consumer's income and fear of state intervention.

PRICE UNDER MONOPSONY

The difference between competitive buying and monopsony buying is that, in the former case, there is a large number of buyers, and the purchases of none of them can affect the market price. To each the supply is perfectly elastic. A slight variation in his price offer will vitally affect the amount of his purchases; for instance, if he offered even a little less than the market price he will be able to buy nothing. The market price, so far as such individual purchaser is concerned, is given. He will buy an amount which equates his marginal utility to the price. But under monopsony there is one buying agency or the buyers are supposed to act in a concerted manner.

A monopsonist will so regulate his purchases as to equate marginal cost to marginal utility, since he must pay the supply price of the commodity. Under competition, it is the price or average cost which is equal to marginal utility. The difference between marginal cost and price will arise only when the industry is working under increasing or decreasing cost.

When the industry is operating under the constant supply price, the average cost (*i.e.*, price) and marginal cost are equal and the amount purchased under competition and monopsony will be the same.

When, however, the industry is working under increasing supply price, the larger the amount the monopolist purchases, the higher will be the price that he has to pay. The marginal cost to him will be greater than the supply price of the commodity.

But, under conditions of decreasing supply price, the larger the amount purchased, the lower will be the supply price, and the marginal cost to him will be less than the supply price. In this case, he will buy more than under competition.

Just as the monopolist aims at maximising his profit, in the same manner the monopsonist aims at maximising his consumer's surplus, and consumer's surplus is maximum when the marginal cost is equal to marginal utility. This may be called the optimum purchase. If the amount purchased exceeds this, the marginal utility will be less than the marginal cost and the consumer's surplus will be reduced. Purchasing short would mean that the utility is reduced more the saving in cost.

A monopsonist can also resort to price discrimination like monopolist by tackling the sellers separately. "The monopsonist will buy from each source of supply in such a way that the marginal costs to him of the outputs bought from each source are equal to each other and to the marginal utility of the whole amount purchased, in just the same way as the monopolist will sell in each separate market such an amount that the marginal revenues are equal in each market and equal to the marginal cost of the whole output. The possibility of discriminating with advantage will depend upon a difference in the elasticities of supply from various sources, that is the elasticities of the average cost curves of each group of sellers."[10] To what extent the monopsonist can discriminate will depend on the number of the sellers and the supply conditions of each.

In a way, a monopolist is a monopsonist of the factors that he uses and if the factors are not homogeneous, he will be able to discriminate between them, especially in the case of an imperfectly elastic supply.

BILATERAL MONOPOLY

The term 'bilateral monopoly' is applied to a situation when a monopoly of purchase is matched with the monopoly of sale *i.e.*, single monopolist is facing a single monopsonist. In the real world, it is not common to come across such a situation.

The monopolist wishes to operate on a scale where the marginal cost is equal to marginal revenue, because that will bring him the maximum monopoly

10. *Ibid*, p. 224.

profit. On the other hand, the monopsonist wishes to purchase an amount at which marginal cost is equal to marginal utility. This indicates one optimum price for the buyer and another for the seller.

Which price between these two sides will be actually established, there is no economic principle to determine. Full knowledge about the demand and cost curves is lacking and it is not possible to indicate definitely the output and the price which will rule. The price will depend on the circumstances of each case. In most of cases, it will be a compromise price which may be influenced by the respective bargaining skill of the parties. Besides economic motive, the administrative factors may also enter into the decision.

We may, therefore, conclude that, in case of bilateral monopoly, the price and output are **indeterminate.**

The following diagram (Fig. 28.11) illustrates the price-output determination in the case of bilateral monopoly.

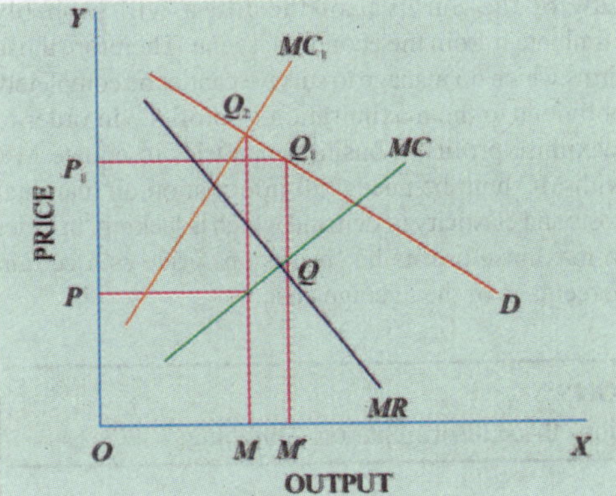

Fig. 28.11. Price-output in Bilateral monopoly.

In this diagram DD is the demand curve, MC the marginal cost curve and MC_1 represents the marginal cost of buying an additional unit.

In bilateral monopoly, each side wants to get the better of the other through bargaining skill. The monopolist will like the monopsonist to behave –as if he were one of the many buyers as in perfect competition, so that he (*i.e.*, buyer) may accept the price fixed by him (the monopolist producer). Similarly, the monopsonist will like the monopolist to behave as if he were a perfect-competition producer (*i.e.*, one of so many) unable to influence price, so that he (the monopsonist buyer) can purchase at his own price. Now nothing can be said as to who will succeed and how far. Most probably, there will be a compromise between the two extremes.

According to the analysis presented by this diagram, the monopolist will be maximising his profit (MR = MC) if he sold OM′ output and charged OP_1 (= M′Q) price, since Q_1 is a point on the demand curve D showing what the purchaser will be willing to pay under perfect competition. On the other hand, the monopsonist will like to buy OM at OP price, since Q_2 , where D and MC_1, intersect is a point where buyer's marginal valuation equals marginal cost of purchase. As we have said before, none can hope to achieve his objective completely and there will be a compromise between the positions that each would like to take. Hence, price will be somewhere between OP and OP_1 and the output between OM and OM′ depending on the relative bargaining skill of the parties.

APPENDIX
REGULATING MONOPOLY THROUGH TAXATION

Diagrammatic Representation

In order to prevent exploitation of consumers by the monopolist, the government may use the tax weapon. The tax may be: (1) Specific tax or (2) a lumpsum tax.

Specific Tax

A specific tax is a variable cost and as such pushes up both MC and AC by an amount equal to the tax. Since the monopolist is supposed to have already pitched high his price, he may not altogether succeed in transferring the tax burden on to the consumer. The following diagram represents this situation:

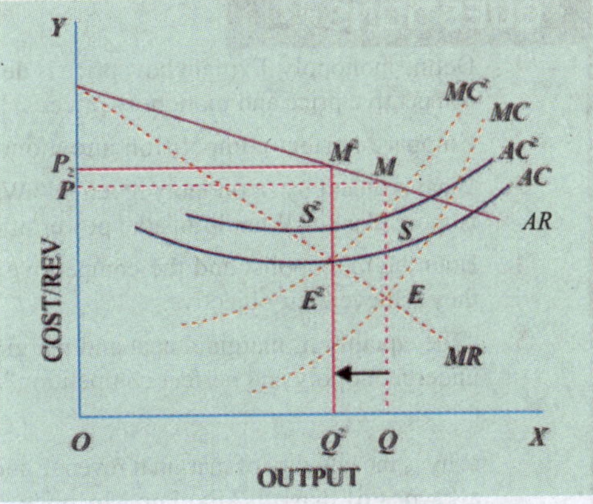

Fig. 28.12. Specific shifts in *MC* and *AC* lead to change.

Before the tax:

MR and MC interest at E; hence = OP = MQ and output is OQ.

After the Tax:

MR and MC^2 intersect at E^2; Price = $OP^2 = M^2 - Q^2$ and output is OQ^2 Since $M^2 S^2$ X output – MS × output, the monopoly profit will be smaller than before. It results in higher prices and smaller output.

Lumpsum Tax

A lumpsum tax is an excess profit tax and is levied primarily to reduce inequalities of income distribution. It may also aim at regulating profits at a socially desirable level. The following diagram illustrates this situation:

Before Tax:

MR = MC at E; Price is OP, output OQ and monopoly profit = PKEM

After Tax:

Lumpsum tax is like a fixed cost. When such a tax is levied AC is pushed up to AC^2. It does not affect MC. Hence equilibrium output remains the same. Thus monopoly output is OQ and price is OP. Since the average cost is now higher, the monopolist's profit is reduced after the tax as we can see PSFM< PKEM. Thus the incidence of a lumpsum tax is entirely on the monopolist. But it confers no benefit on the consumer since price remains the same.

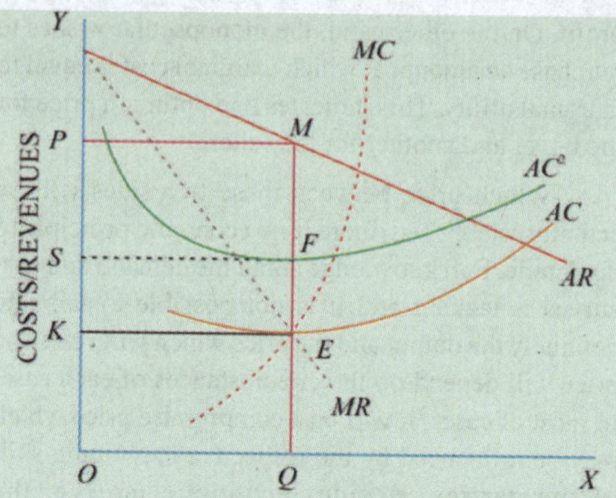

Fig. 28.13. Lumpsum tax shifts AC up. Price is unchanged. Profit is reduced.

(2) MAKE-UP PRINCIPLE

The businessmen can ignore the principle of maximisation of profits only at their peril. As Prof. Samuelson observes, "If a firm is absolutely reckless in calculating costs and revenues, then the Darwinian Law of the Survival of the fittest will probably eliminate it from the economic scene. Therefore those firms which do manage to survive cannot be completely oblivious to the maximisation of profits." In order to maximise profits, a businessman tries to equate MR with MC buth he needs full information on marginal costs and elasticity of demand which is lacking. In order to maximise profits he 'marks up' price as a certain percentage of the average cost.

Key terms

Monopoly price, Bilateral monopoly, Price regulation, Price discrimination, Dumping.

QUESTIONS

1. Define monopoly. Explain how price is determined under monopoly. Indicate the difference between competitive price and monopoly price.
2. Compare perfect competition and monopoly in respect of price, output and profits.
3. What is meant by 'monopoly revenue'? Will it be higher if the demand curve facing a monopolist is more elastic? What limits the power of the monopolist to raise price?
4. Both the monopolist and the competitive producer aim at maximising their net gain. Show how they achieve their objective.
5. "The equality of marginal cost and marginal revenue is the basis for determination of price both under monopoly and perfect competition". Explain.

   Or

   Why is the equality of marginal revenue and marginal cost essential for profit maximisation in all types of markets? Explain why price can be substituted for marginal revenue in the MR = MC rule when an industry is purely competitive.
6. "Monopoly equilibrium is not possible if elasticity of demand is less than one". Explain.
7. Explain : (*a*) the demand curve is horizontal under perfect competition.

8. Compare price and output policies under monopoly and perfect competition.
9. "A monopolist is a price maker, a seller under competition is price taker". Elucidate.
10. (*a*) Explain how the pricing policy of a monopolist is influenced by elasticity of demand for his product.

    (*b*) At the point of equilibrium, elasticity of demand for the monopolist's product is 1.5 and marginal revenue earned by him is Rs. 20. Find out the equilibrium price.

    (*c*) At equilibrium price, if the elasticity of demand for the monopolist's product is 1.5, the MC for equilibrium output is $\frac{1}{3}$rd of the equilibrium price". Explain and illustrate.
11. What are the foundations of monopoly power? How do the monopolists exercise it to 'maximise profits in markets' where consumers can be given discriminating treatment?
12. What is a discriminating monopoly? Under what conditions is discrimination possible, profitable and socially desirable.
13. "Different demand elasticities is a condition necessary but not sufficient for price discrimination". Explain.
14. Discuss the principles governing the price-output policy of a discriminating monopolist.
15. How doe a discriminating monopolist determine his total output and the price, profit and output to be sold in the market?

    Or

    How does a discriminating monopolist fix : (*a*) his total output, (*b*) division of the total output in different markets, and (*c*) prices to be charged in different markets. Explain diagrammatically.
16. Explain the concept of dumping.
17. Draw diagram and show how a monopolists divides his output in two different market.
18. Explain the behaviour of a monopolists, regarding prices and output in the policy of dumping.

PRICE-OUTPUT UNDER MONOPOLISTIC COMPETITION

Meaning of Imperfect Competition. We have now seen how prices and output are deter mined in a perfectly competitive industry and also in monopoly. In fact, the case of ordinary mo nopoly described in the last chapter is an extreme form of imperfect competition. Imperfect competition covers all situations where there is neither pure competition nor pure monopoly. [1] Both perfect competition and pure monopoly are very unlikely to be found in the real world. In the actual world, it is the region of imperfect competition lying between these two extreme limits which prevails.

The fundamental distinguishing characteristic of imperfect competition is that the average revenue (AR) curve slopes downwards throughout its length, but it slopes downwards at different rates in different categories of imperfect competition.In some cases, firm's average revenue curve slopes downwards only gently where competition is nearly perfect and in some other cases, it slopes very steeply where competition is extremely imperfect. "There is no single case of imperfect competition but a whole range or series of cases representing progressively more and more imperfect competition." [2]

We discussed in the last chaper one case of imperfect competition, namely, that of ordinary monopoly. In the present chapter, we shall discuss the another form of imperfect competition, *viz.*, monopolistic competition.

MONOPOLISTIC COMPETITION

Meaning and Nature

Monopolistic competition refers to a market situation in which there are many producers producing goods which are close substitutes of one another or where output is differentiated.

The important distinguishing characteristics of monopolistic competition are, (a) Product Differentiation, (b) existence of many firms supplying the market, and (c) the goods made by them are close substitutes. *i.e.*, their products are similar but not identical.

1. We have defined pure monopoly in the way defined by Prof. Sraffa, that is, pure monopoly is that situation when a producer is so powerful that he is always be able to take the whole of all consumers' incomes whatever the level of his output.
2. Stonier and Hague –*A Text-book of Economic Theory*, 1953, p. 164.

Product Differentiation. In sharp contrast to perfect competition, where there is only one homogeneous commodity, in monopolistic competition there is **differentiation of products.** "Products are not homogeneous, as in perfect competition, but neither are they only remote substitutes as in monopoly. What this really means is that in monopolistic competition there are various 'monopolists' competing with one another. These competing monopolists do not produce identical goods. Neither do they produce goods which are completely different. Product differentiation means that products are different in some ways, but not altogether so." [3]

Many examples of monopolistic competition and product differentiation can be cited. Many firms in India produce toothpaste, but the product of each differs from its rivals in one or more respects. Different toothpastes like Colgate, Binaca, 'Forhans, Kolynos, McClean, and soaps Lux, Sunlight, *etc.*, provide examples of monopolistic competition. Other examples of monopolistic competition are those of the producers of soap (Lux, Rexona, Breeze, Hamam, Sunlight, *etc.*). toothbrush (Colgate, Dr. West's, Wisdom, *etc.*), retailers shops, barber shops, *etc.*

'Real' or physical differences, like those of materials used, design and workmanship, are no doubt important means of product differentiation. But "imaginary" differences created through advertising, packing and the use of trade marks and brand names are the more important methods by which products are differentiated, even if physically they are identical or almost so. Finally, the conditions of sale also help in the differentiation of the products. For example, the location of a shop, the courteousness of those who serve at the counters, *etc.*, makes for the differentiation of products.

Many Firms. Under monopolistic competition, there are many firms, but it must not be assumed that it requires hundreds or thousands of firms. It requires only a fairly large number –say 25, 30, 60 or 70. Many important conclusions follow from the existence of a fairly large number of firms: First, an individual firm has relatively small part of the total market so that each has a very limited control over the price of the product. Again, the presence of relatively large number of firms ensures that collusion by them to restrict output to raise price is most unlikely. Finally, with a large number of firms in the industry, there is no feeling of mutual inter-dependence that each firm determines its price-output policies without considering the possible reactions of rival firms.

In other words, a monopolistically competitive firm follows an **independent price policy.** And this is a very reasonable way to act in a market where one's rivals are numerous. If a firm lowers its price, its gain in sales will be spread thinly over many of its rivals so that the extent to which each of the rival firms suffers will be negligible. Hence, these rivals will have no reason to retaliate.

As in perfect competition, in the monopolistic competition too, in the long-run, there is freedom of entry and exit. That is, in this case, there are no barriers to entry as found under monopoly.

As explained above, where there is monopolistic competition, the commodity bought and sold is not a standardised commodity but a differentiated product. Hence, competition is no longer exclusively on the price basis. Buyers are now buying a combination of physical product and the services which go with it (location of store, packing, trade mark, personality of sales people, and so on). The buyers are willing to pay for their favourite product something more than the market price of a standardised product. This will depend on the estimate **in their own minds** as to the superiority of their favourite product, regardless of its intrinsic worth, or what the seller claims it to be.

Because of consumer's attachment to a particular brand, the seller acquires a monopolistic influence on his market. If he raises his price a little, he may lose many of his customers, but not all of them. Similarly,

3. Stonier and Hague –*A Text-book of Economic Theory*, 1953, p. 183.

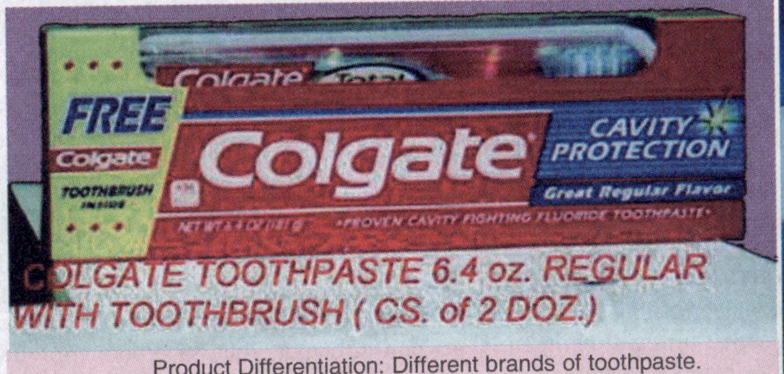

Product Differentiation: Different brands of toothpaste.

a reduction in price may bring him some additional customers but not many. Thus, the demand curve facing a firm under monopolistic competition is a downward sloping curve, *i.e.*, if he wants to sell more, the seller has to lower his price. This is unlike the demand curve in perfect competition, where for any individual seller, the curve is absolutely elastic at the ruling price (*i.e.*, it is a horizontal straight line parallel to the X-axis). He cannot influence the market price but he can sell any amount at the prevailing price, without having any fear of depressing it. But, under monopolistic competition this is not so. The seller has some amount of monopolistic control over his brand but his control is tempered by the realisation that there are close substitutes (similar though not exactly identical products) available in the market. Hence, too high a price will mean his customers shifting to the rival brand.

Thus, unlike as in perfect competition but as in monopoly, the demand curve (or the average revenue curve) for a firm under monopolistic competition is a downward sloping curve. But unlike monopoly, where there are no close substitutes available for the monopolised commodity, the demand or average revenue curve under imperfect competition is fairly elastic, because of the presence of close substitutes.

Price-output Determination Under Monopolistic Competition

It may be borne in mind that price-output determination is the same thing, as an analysis of equilibrium of a firm.

Since, under monopolistic competition, different firms produce different varieties of the product, therefore, different prices for them will be determined in the market depending upon their respective demand and cost conditions. Each firm under monopolistic competition seeks to achieve equilibrium or profit-maximising position as regards (1) price and output, (2) product adjustment and (3) adjustment of selling costs. In other words, the producer, under monopolistic competition, must make optimal adjustments not only in the price charged and as regards the quantity of output sold but also in the design of the product and the way in which he promotes the sales.

Further, we have to study not only individual equilibrium of a firm but also group equilibrium of the firms in the market.

We shall now analyse these aspects. We first take up **Individual Equilibrium.**

Price-output Equilibrium

The question arises at which price-output level the monopolistically competitive firm will be in an equilibrium position? Here we have to remember that every seller, whether a monopolist or one working under perfectly or imperfectly competitive situation, wants to maximise his profit. As we saw in the previous chapter, the seller will go on producing till the extra receipts to be had from additional production exceed the extra costs to be incurred in the production process, and he will stop where the extra receipts and extra costs have been equalised. This will be the point of maximum profit. In other words, profits will be maximised when marginal revenue is equal to marginal cost. So long as the marginal revenue is greater than the marginal cost, the seller will find it profitable to expand his output; and, if the marginal revenue is less than the marginal cost, obviously it is to his advantage to reduce his output to the point where marginal revenue is equal to marginal cost.

Short-run Equilibrium

In the short-run, therefore, the firm will be in equilibrium when it is maximising its profits, *i.e.*, when Marginal Revenue = Marginal Cost.

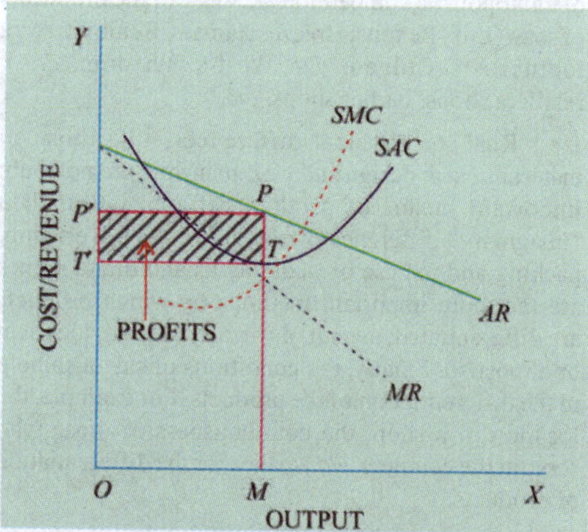

Fig. 29.1. Equilibrium under Monopolistic Competition : Short-run.

In the figure (29.1 and 29.2), AR is average revenue curve, MR is marginal revenue curve, SAC is the short-run average cost curve, and SMC is the short-run marginal cost curve. In these figures, marginal revenue curve (MR) and marginal cost curve (SMC) intersect each other at the output OM at which price is OP′ (= MP), because P is point on AR (average revenue), *i.e.*, price.

In Fig. 29.1, the firm is earning supernormal profits. Supernormal profit per unit of output is the difference between average revenue and average cost at the equilibrium point. In this case, in equilibrium, the average revenue is MP and average cost is MT (T is on SAC). Therefore, PT is the supernormal profit per unit of output. Total supernormal profit will be measured by the area of the rectangle PTT′ P′, *i.e.*, output multiplied by supernormal profit per unit of output.

But if the demand and cost situations are less favourable, then the monopolistically competitive firm will be realising losses in the short-run as illustrated in Fig. 29.2. Here, the price is OP′ (= MP) which is less than the average cost MT. TP is the loss per unit of the output OM (= PP′). Hence, the total loss is represented by the shaded area TPP′T′.

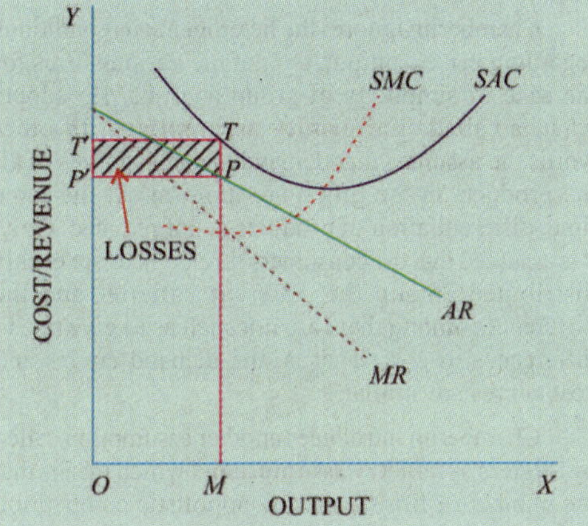

Fig. 29.2. Equilibrium Under Monopolistic, Competition : Short-run (with Losses).

Thus, in the short-run, the monopolisti cally competitive firm may either realise profits or suffer losses.

Long-run Equilibrium of Firm and Group Equilibrium

We have seen above that the firms under monopolistic competition can earn supernormal profit in the short-run. But, in the long-run, such profits disappear. This is because we assume that entry is free and new firms will enter the industry, if the existing firms are making supernormal profits. As new firms enter and start production, supply will increase and the price will fall, *i.e.*, average revenue curve faced by the firm will shift to the left, and, therefore, the supernormal profits will be competed away and the firms will be earning only normal profits. If, in the short-run, firms are realising losses, then, in the long-run, some firms will leave the industry so that the remaining firms will be earning normal profits.

Another point which is to be noted in regard to the long-run equilibrium is that **average revenue curve in the long-run will be more elastic (*i.e.*, flatter), since large number of substitutes will be available in the long-run.** Therefore, in the long-run, equilibrium is established when firms are earning only **normal profits.** Now profits are normal only when Average Revenue = Average Cost.

Therfore, **there is equilibrium in the long-run under monopolistic competition when**

Average Revenue = Average Cost.

In Fig. 29.3, average revenue curve (AR) is a tangent to the average cost curve (LAC) at P. Therefore, the equilibrium output in the long-run is OM and the corresponding price is MP (= OP′). At this point, average cost is also MP and so is averagae revenue. Therefore, there are no supernormal profits; there are only the normal profits which form part of the cost of production.

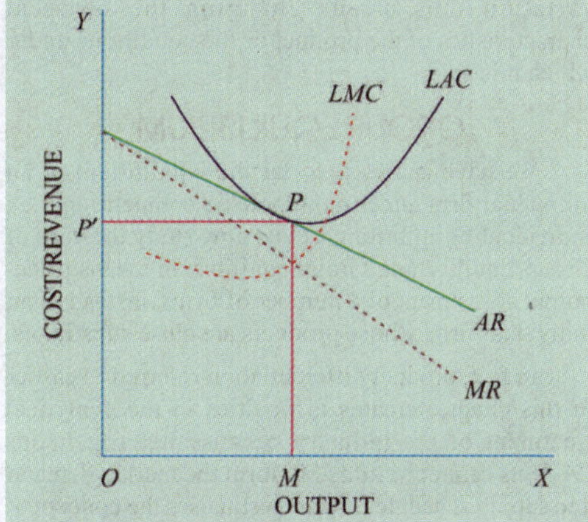

Fig. 29.3. Equilibrium Under Monopolistic Competition : Long-run.

In the long-run, therefore, the firm is in equilibrium when output is OM, and the price is MP (= OP′).

In the short-run there is only one condition of equilibrium, *i.e.*,

Marginal Revenue = Marginal Cost.

In the long-run, however, both the conditions must hold, *i.e.*,

Marginal Revenue = Marginal Cost.
Average Revenue = Average Cost.

Product Variation Equilibrium

An important problem that a firm under monopolistic competition has to tackle is concerned with product adjustment. This problem does not arise under perfect competition. Since the product is homogeneous. But under imperfect competition, there is product differentiation. The product has to be adjusted to consumer's preferences so that the profit is maximised. The product adjustment may take place through an "alteration in the quality of the product itself, technical changes, a new design, better materials; it may mean new package or container, it may mean more prompt or courteous service, or different way of doing business, or perhaps a different location. In some cases, an alteration is specific and definite –the adoption of new design, for instance. In others, a change in the quality of service, it may be gradual, perhaps unconscious."[4] The choice of the differentiated product will be made on the principle of profit maximisation. In case variety A gives more profit than variety B, the producer will produce more of A and less of B so that he maximises his profit. Thus, a firm operating under monopolistic competition must work out a product equilibrium in addition to the price-output equilibrium. It should also adjust selling cost for maximising profit which we discuss below. Product variation thus means changing the physical characteristics of the product or the conditions under which it is sold.

GROUP EQUILIBRIUM

We have analysed so far the equilibrium of an individual firm under monopolistic competition, *i.e.*, Individual Equilibrium. Let us now study the case of Group Equilibrium. Group equilibrium means price-output adjustment of a number of firms, instead of an individual firm, whose products are close substitutes.

In fact, product differentiation referred to earlier in this chapter creates difficulties in the analytical treatment of the industry because heterogeneous products cannot be added to form the market demand and supply schedules. Chamberlin uses the concept of '**product group**' for industry. The product group includes products which are closely related, *i.e.* are technological and economic substitutes. *Technological substitutes* are products which can technically cover the same want and *economic substitutes* refer to products which cover the same want and have similar prices. An operational definition of the product group is *that the demand for each single product be highly elastic and that it shifts appreciably when the price of the other products in the group changes. That is, products forming the 'group' or industry should have high cross and price elasticities*. Product differentiation enables each firm to charge a different prices.

In each industry, one can imagine different groups of firms forming an industry of their own. For example, in the automobile industry, a group of firms may be manufacturing light cars and another group making heavy trucks. The firms in the car group may be making various types of cars, *e.g.*, Fiat, Ambassador, Standard cars which are close substitutes for one another but net perfect substitutes or completely homogeneous products because it is a case of monopolistic competition.

Each firm within a group has a monopoly of its own product, yet there is competition among those firms which are producing closely related products. The price-output decision of one firm will affect the decisions of rival firms. The qualitative difference among the products of the monopolistically competitive firms results in large variation in cost and demand (AR) curves of the various firms. The demand curves also differ in elasticity. Similarly, the shape and position of cost curves too differ. As a result, there are differences in prices, output and profits of the various firms in the group.

Chamberlin ignores the heterogeneous conditions regarding prices, output, *etc.*, of the various firms for the sake of simplicity of group analysis. He adopts what is called **'uniformity assumption.'** In other words, he assumes that demand and cost curves of all the products in the group are uniform. At the same time, differentiation of products is not reduced. Only, it is assumed that the consumers' preferences are evenly distributed among the different varieties and the differences among them are not such as to give rise to differences in cost. That is, the demand curves and cost curves are similar.

Chamberlin introduces another assumption called by Stigler **"symmetry assumption,"** which means that the number of firms under monopolistic competition is large enough to ensure that individual decision regarding price and output adjustment has negligible influence on the rivals. There is thus no possibility of retaliation.

We now proceed to the analysis of group equilibrium subject to the assumptions made above. Within the group, if a firm has successfully designed a popular brand, it will be making supernormal profits but, in the long-run, other firms will imitate the design so that extra profits will tend to disappear. This is what happens within the monopolistically competitive groups. But if the group as a whole is making supernormal profits in the short-run, outside firms will enter into the group, unless the entry is legally or economically barred. In this way extra profits will be competed away.

This is illustrated by the following diagram (Fig. 29.4).

Fig. 29.4 (*a*) represents short-run equilibrium and Fig. 29.4 (*b*) the long-run equilibrium. In the short-run the price is OP (= RM), whereas average cost is MN at the output OM where marginal revenue is equal to marginal cost. Hence there is supernormal profit represented by the shaded area $PRNP_1$. But in the long-run, shown in Fig. 29.4 (*b*), the surplus profit will be competed away. In this diagram, the marginal revenue equals marginal cost at the output level OM_1 and the average revenue curve (LAR) is a tangent to the average cost (LAC) which means that the average (*i.e.*, price) is equal to average cost and there is not extra profit,

4. Chamberlin, E. H., *The Theory of Monopolistic Competition*, p. 71.

i.e., only normal profit is being made.

This situation is similar to the one prevailing under perfect competition. But the differences may also be carefully noted. The main difference is that under perfect competition, the average revenue curve is a horizontal straight line, whereas under monopolistic competition it is a downward sloping curve. The result is that with a U-shaped average cost curve, the equilibrium under monopolistic competition must occur at a smaller output than under perfect competition.

SELLING COSTS

Meaning of Selling Costs

The costs incurred on advertising, publicity and salesmanship are known as selling costs. Selling costs have been defined "as the costs necessary to persuade a buyer to buy one product rather than another or to buy from one seller rather than another."

Obviously, if the markets were perfect, *i.e.*, if the buyers were well informed about the prices and quantity, advertising will be a waste. It will not win over any buyer. Advertising will also be unnecessary in a purely competitive market dealing in standardised products. Monopolist also need not spend on advertisement, for there are no rivals. Actually, however, perfect competition and perfect monopoly are rare. Few buyers can be considered connoiseurs of quality or fully acquainted with market conditions. There is a very large number of brands contesting for a buyer's choice. This creates a large scope for advertisement either to herald a new product or to remind the customers that an old product is still going strong. Advertisement may be **promotional** which gives general information about the industry and promotes its sales. This advertisement is on behalf of the entire industry say, cement industry or life insurance. The advertisement may be competitive when it seeks to push the products of one firm against another.

Selling costs are thus, specially associated with imperfect markets or monopolistic competition, Product differentiation necessitates selling effort.

How Far Are Selling Costs Efficacious?

Advertisement is a very delicate weapon and it is impossible to assess its value. First, it is difficult to generalise. The same expense on advertising may yield a handsome dividend when incurred in a certain manner or under certain circumstances and may prove utterly barren otherwise. This is due to the fact that its success depends almost entirely on its appeal to uniqueness or novelty. When this element is missing, advertisement is a waste.

Secondly, there is no relation between the selling costs and the volume of business secured by a firm.

Thirdly, since advertisement evokes counter-advertisement, selling costs are influenced very much by what the rival businessmen are doing. This competitive advertisement may eat up the profits so that none may benefit except the advertising agencies and the salesmen.

Fourthly, the benefit from selling costs may accrue not only to the firm incurring them but also to its rivals. An advertisement by New India Insurance Company may prepare a person for insurance but he may go in for a policy in the Oriental Insurance Company instead.

Fifthly, advertisement is based on the assumption that a large number of customers are prepared to change their preferences. This may not be the case. Resistence comes from the force of habit. It is not possible to

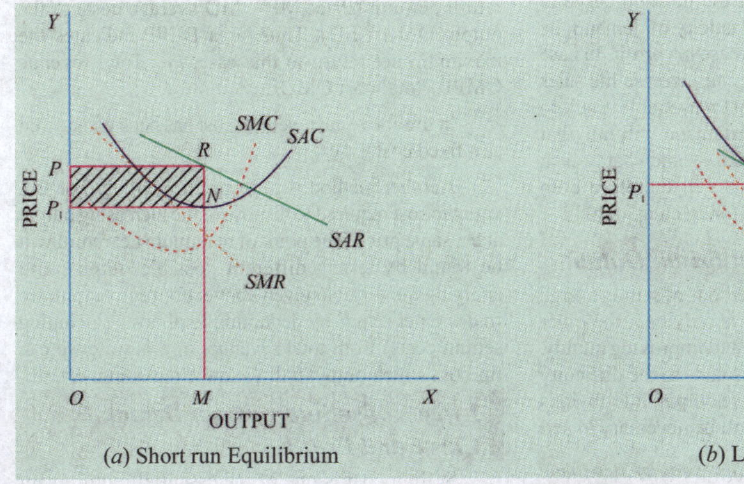

Fig. 29.4. Group Equilibrium.

find out how much of the business is due to repeat customers and how much to new customers won by advertisement. In the former case, selling costs should be treated as fixed costs and in the latter, variable costs. Full costs of advertisement should be charged to new business.

Effect of Selling Costs on the Demand Curve

Selling costs (*i.e.*, advertisement and salesmanship) are likely to induce old buyers to buy more and also to attract new buyers.This means an increase in demand. The new demand curve representing an increase in demand will be above the old curve or to the right of it. But it is not sure whether the new curve will have the same elasticity as the old one. It will depend on the buying habits of the new customers. In case they are sensitive to price changes, it will be more elastic, otherwise less elastic than the old curve. If the new customers are fully and permanently convinced of the superiority of the product, the new curve will be less elastic in the upper segments because price can be safely raised. If, on the other hand, the customers feel they can afford to purchase it only at lower prices, the new curve will be more elastic than the old one in the lower regions.

The main point is that the producers by spending money and effort on advertisement can alter or shift the demand curve. Persuasive advertisement usually result in increasing sales by attracting the attention of a large number of prospective buyers. The aim is to increase the sales of one firm at the expense of the other firms.

The effect of advertisement may be (a) to increase the sales and (b) to make the demand for the commodity less elastic. But the producer is more interested in increasing the sales by shifting the demand curve to the right. If he can lower the elasticity of demand, he can raise the price and thus increase his profit. In case he cannot reduce elasticity, he can increase his sales by lowering the price. "The most reasonable result to expect will be that elasticity of demand will fall, that the volume of demand will increase somewhat at each price and that price and output will therefore both increase as a result of the advertising campaign." [5]

Selling Costs and Equilibrium Output

There are three possible methods of selling a large output of which advertisement is only one; the other two methods are lowering price and improving quality. The intervention of selling costs adds to the difficulty of determining the most profitable output. It is obvious that higher total selling costs will be necessary to sell a larger output at the same price or the same output a higher prices.

In order to ascertain the equilibrium output the following formula may be used:–

Net returns = (Price × Output) – (Production Cost + Selling Cost).

The problem is to find out that output at which the net returns will be the highest. We have already seen that selling costs create a new demand curve. One method of finding out the most profitable output is to regard the selling costs as a fixed cost in connection with that particular demand curve. A diagram may be drawn for such possible selling cost and the demand curve that it creates.

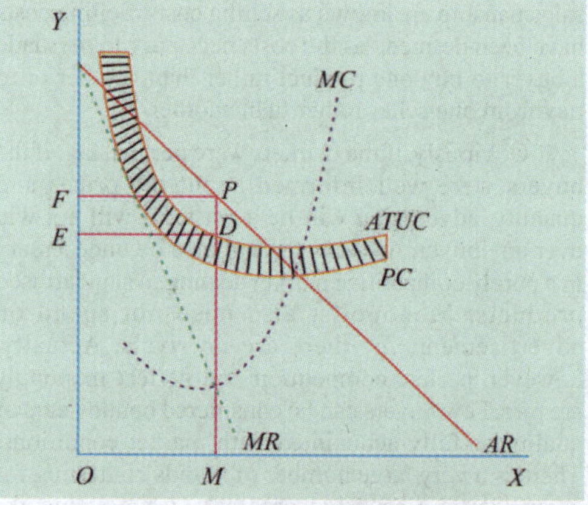

Fig. 29.5. Equilibrium with Selling Costs.

In Fig. 29.5, AR is the average revenue (demand) curve; MR is the marginal revenue curve; PC the average production cost, the shaded area above it represents the selling costs. By adding this to PC, we get ATUC, *i.e.*, average total unit cost. DP is the net return per unit (Price MP – MD average cost) of the output OM (= ED). Thus, area DEFP indicates the maximum net return in this case, *i.e.*, Total revenue OMPF –total cost OMDE.

In the above case, selling cost has been considered as a fixed cost.

Another method is to regard the selling cost as a variable cost required to dispose of the increasing output at the same price. The point of maximum net return will be found by taking different possible outputs and applying the formula given above. For each output, we find the net return by deducting total costs (including selling costs) from total revenue. In this way, we can find out which output will yield the maximum return.

Effects of selling Cost on Demand Curve and Profits

Selling cost is one of the essential requirement of monopolistic competition. Monopolistic and

5. Stonier and Hague –*A Text-book of Economic Theory*, 1953 p. 196.

Oligopoly market cannot survive without the use it. Selling cost has more use in monopolistic competition, as there are many sellers and many buyers with heterogeneous goods, the level of competition directly varies with the amount of advertising as well as other means of selling cost and promotional measures. From time to time producer or sellers are involved in evolving new ways and means of inducing buyers to buy the product. This has resulted in very often the increase in the sale of the product. The question is how long and upto what level of output the use of selling cost is profitable.

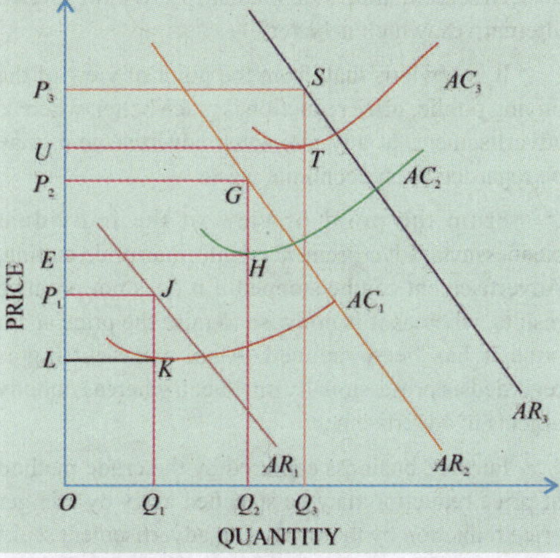

Fig. 29.6. Effect of selling cost on demand. (Economics)

In the above diagram a firm with its initial expenditure on advertising is able to make profit to the tune of □ 'P_1JKL' 'AR' is the 'demand' curve, the firm is producing 'OQ_1' quantity and making profit of □ P_1JKL. As the advertisement (Selling cost) increases due to this 'AC_1' shifts to 'AC_2' and due to this the demand curve increases more, that is upto 'AR_2', and the said firm is producing 'OQ_2' and it is making enormous amount of profit viz, □P_2GHE. In the third case if you further increase your advertisement or selling cost this increases the cost to AC_3 the demand curve shifts to AR_3. The firm is selling 'OQ_3' output and making profit to the amount of □ P_3STV. The following table gives you the compelete picture of the relationship between selling cost, increase in demand curve and the total profit.

S.N.	Total Average Cost	Demand Curve	Output	Profit
(1)	AC_1	AR_1	OQ_1	□ P_1JKL
(2)	AC_2	AR_2	OQ_2	□ P_2GHE
(3)	AC_3	AR_3	OQ_3	□ P_3STV

From the above table and the diagram one can make out that due to increase in selling cost there is an increase in sales and profit but the profit and quantity is more in case two. This birngs out the two important conclusions.

(1) It is not always true that increase in selling cost brings about increase in profit.

(2) There exists a direct relationship between increase in selling cost and increase in profit.

(3) In the diagram it is clear that in second case increase in selling cost has essentially brought about an enormous increase in profit, but further increase in selling cost has resulted in less profit.

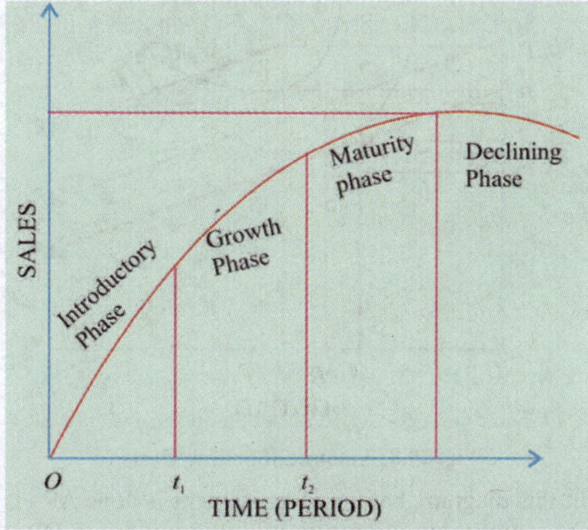

Fig. 29.7. Growth path of sales. (The product life cycle) (Marketing Management)

The above conclusion is correct because the relationship between increase in advertisement cost may bring more and more sales and profit upto a point only specially when the product is in the growth and maturity phase of a product life cycle.

If the product has reached the declining phase, then increase in selling cost not necessarily brings about increase in profit and sales, rather it may decrease the sales and profit. There can be some exceptions to this problem, in recent year radio's and jute has re-emerged and significantly its revival of demand is giving more profit.

Optimum Selling Costs?

The question arises: how much advertising expenditure will the firm find it worthwhile to incur? Obviously, by spending a certain amount on advertisement a producer gets a certain revenue. A firm will incur extra expenditure on advertising when it finds it worthwhile, *i.e.*, when it brings additional revenue. So long as the marginal revenue exceeds the marginal cost on advertising, the firm will go on increasing the advertising expenditure and it will stop when the additional (marginal) revenue generated equals extra (marginal) cost incurred. Profit will be the maximum in that position. In order to find the most profitable sales promotion programme, the monopolistic competitor identifies the cost and revenue curves associated with the various sales promotion programmes and on this basis he finds out that particular level of selling costs which would maximise his profit and he adopts this for his purpose.

Following diagram (Fig. 29.8) illustrates this.

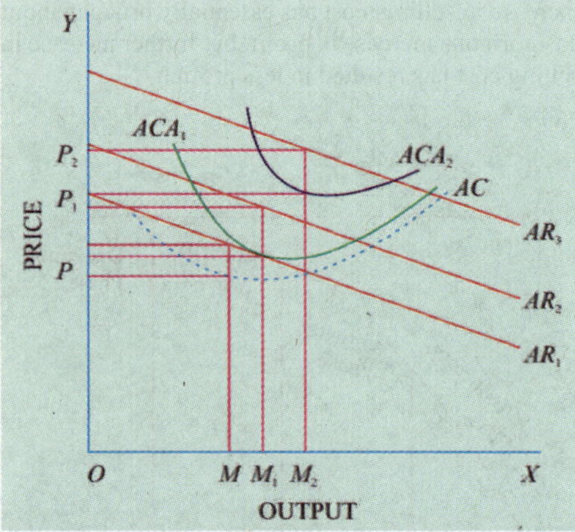

Fig. 29.8. Amount of Selling Costs.

In this diagram, before advertisement is done AR_1 is the average revenue curve, AC is the cost curve, OP is the price and OM the equilibrium amount. Suppose, Rs. 1,000 are spent on advertisement. This increases the demand from AR_1 to AR_2. The average cost curve ACA_1 includes now Rs. 1,000, the cost of advertisement. Now the equilibrium will be at the price OP_1 and the amount OM_1. This again is the profit-maximising position. Here the output is larger and the price higher than in the original equilibrium. But the important point to note is that the firm does not bother about the price or the size of the output; it is only concerned with maximising of profit. That is, the total revenue minus total cost must rise by more than Rs. 1,000 when the selling costs amount to Rs. 1,000. Since profits have increased, the firm will be tempted to increase the advertisement expenditure. The profits will be the maximum when, as mentioned before, the marginal revenue equals marginal cost. This situation is represented in the diagram where AR_3 is the average revenue curve, ACA_2 is the average cost curve, OP_2 is the price and OM_2 is the output. Beyond this, further expenditure on advertisement will reduce profit since it will add more to the cost than to the revenue. Thus, for a firm under monopolistic competition, corresponding to different levels of selling costs, there are series of average revenue of selling costs, there are series of average revenue curves and average cost curves. The producer has to select that set of cost and revenue curves where the profits are the maximum.

Increased Selling Costs vs. *Price-Cutting*

We have mentioned before that apart from improving quality, there are two methods of increasing the sale or output, *viz.*, reducing the price or increasing selling costs (*i.e.*, spending more money on advertisement and salesmanship). Of these two alternatives, which is better?

It is obvious that, from the point of view of the buying public, price reduction is much better, whereas advertisement, at any rate some advertisement, may be regarded as an economic waste.

From the point of view of the individual businessman, advertisement is better than price-cutting. Advertisement can be stopped if it does not produce results, whereas it is not wise to raise the price again once it has been reduced. Also, price-cutting is regarded as professionally unethical, whereas nobody objects to advertisement.

Further, business captured by the crude method of price reduction may be snatched away by a larger price reduction by the rivals. But advertisement seeks to create a delusion in the minds of the customers in favour of the advertised product. To the extent it succeeds, the gain is permanent.

EXCESS CAPACITY UNDER IMPERFECT COMPETITION

Discussion of monopolistic competition by Chamberlin and Joan Robinson have shown that firms under imperfect competition operate with excess capacity. According to these economists, a firm under monopolistic competition or imperfect competition produces on output in thelong-run equilibrium, which is less than socially optimum or ideal output. In other words, they do not produce that level of output at which long-run average cost is minimum. This will happen when the firms operate at a point on the falling portion of the long-run average cost curve. A firm under monopolistic competition attains long-run equilibrium when the demand curve (or average revenue curve) facing it is tangential to the long-run average cost curve so that it may earn only normal profits. Since they are operating on the falling portion of the long-run average cost curve, the firms can reduce their average cost, (and hence price) by expanding their output to the minimum point of the long-run average cost curve. But they do not increase their output, because their profits have already been maximized at the level of output smaller than at which their long-run average cost would be minimum. This happens at a point where equality between marginal revenue and marginal cost has been attained.

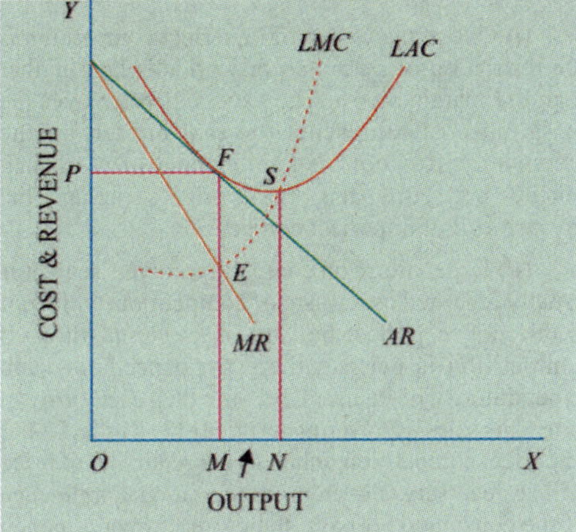

Fig. 29.9. Excess capacity.

It is clear that productive resources of the community are fully utilized only when they are used to produce that level of output which brings down the long-run average cost to the lowest point. But the monopolistic firms produce less than that level of output which is socially optimum or ideal output. This is quite different from what happens under perfect competition when the firms operate at the minimum point of long-run average cost curve. Thus, the actual long-run output of the firm under monopolistic competition falls short of what is produced under perfect competition which can be considered the socially ideal output. This gives the measure of excess capacity which lies unutilized under imperfect competition.

The two figures (Fig. 29.9 and Fig. 29.10) show the existence of excess capacity. Fig. 29.9 represents the long-run position of a perfectly competitive firm. The firm is in long-run equilibrium at the level of ON output where the long-run average cost is minimum. At this point, Price = MC = AC, which means that the double condition of long -run equilibrium is satisfied. This represents the socially ideal output.

The operation of the firm under monopolistic competition is shown in the figure 29.9. In this case, the long -run equilibrium is achieved at OM output at which the marginal revenue is equal to marginal cost and price is equal to average cost. Here average revenue curve AR is tangential to average cost curve AC at point F corresponding to output OM. It can be seen that at output OM average cost is still falling and it continues to fall upto ON and thus reduce its long-run average cost to the minimum. Hence, the ideal output is ON where the long-run average cost is minimum. This means that this firm is producing MN quantity less than the ideal output. Hence MN output represents excess capacity which emerges under monopolistic competition.

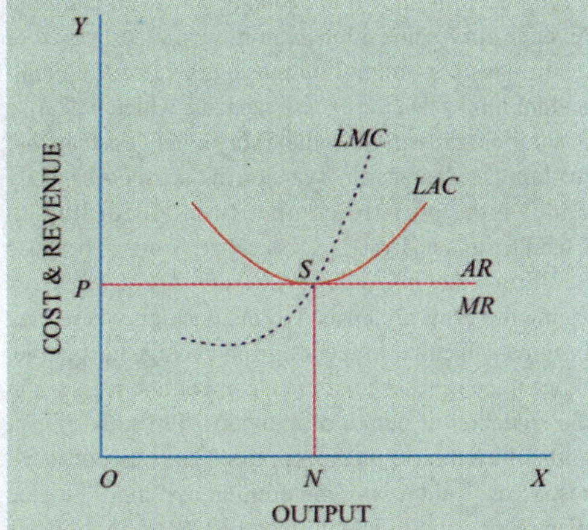

Fig. 29.10. Competitive output in the long-run.

It may be noted that this concept of excess capacity refers only to the long-run, because in the short-run under any type of market structure (including perfect competition), there can be all types departures from the ideal output showing incomplete adjustment to existing market conditions. It may also be noted that excess capacity arises because under monopolistic competition, the average revenue curve or the demand curve can be a tangent to a U-shaped average cost curve only at the latter's falling portions. This happens under monopolistic competition because under it the demand curve slopes downwards. On the other hand, under perfect competition, it is only the horizontal demand curve or average revenue curve which can be tangent to a U-shaped average cost curve at the latter's minimum point. It follows, therefore, that the greater the elasticity of average revenue (or demand) curve confronting a firm under monopolistic competition, the less will be the excess capacity, and vice versa. On the other hand, under perfect competition when a firm faces a perfectly elastic demand curve, there can be no excess capacity.

Chamberlin, however, considers that this 'competitive ideal' cannot be considered as 'ideal under monopolistic competition. He thinks, on the other hand, that under monopolistic competition, where there is product differentiation and free entry and active price competition, there is a different 'ideal' output.

The concept of excess capacity under monopolistic or imperfect competition has been criticised by some economists, especially Harrod and Kaldor. According to Harrod, there is inconsistency in the description of excess capacity by Chamberlin and Mrs. Robinson arising from the fact that the entrepreneur is shown to be using short-run marginal revenue curves and a long-run marginal cost curve to determines his optimal output and size of the plant. Kaldor thinks that the excess capacity, which will arise in some circumstances, will be very much less than that made out in Chamberlin's version of the excess capacity under monopolistic competition. According to Chamberlin's analysis, excess capacity arises because new firms enter into industry so that the demand curves facing the firms are pushed to the position where they become tangential to the long-run average cost curve. Since there is absence of price competition it results in the reduction of output of individual firms and rise in costs which represents excess capacity or waste of social resources. Kaldor is of the opinion that high degree of excess capactiy under monopolistic competition has been shown to arise on account of the unrealistic assumptions made explicity or implicity by Chamberlin.

CRITIQUE OF MONOPOLISTIC COMPETITION

Effects of Monopolistic Competition

Based on the above analysis, we may sum up the effects of monopolistic competition as under:

(*i*) Unlike pure competition, under monopolistic competition, output is slightly less and the prices slightly higher.

(*ii*) Under monopolistic competition, the consumers have the pleasure of enjoying the use of wider range of goods in types, design and quality.

(*iii*) The firms engage in high pressure salesmanship, the expenditure on which does not confer on the community proportional benefit.

(*iv*) Under monopolistic competition, inefficient firms are helped to carry on.

The brings us to the wastes of imperfect competition.

Wastes of Monopolistic Competition

Some other evils, besides those noted under monopoly, are associated with imperfect competition. Superficially, these are sometimes considered "wastes of competition" but they can more fitly be described as "wastes of monopolistic conditions"[6] or of imperfect competition. They are mostly due to what are technically called irrational buyers' preferences, *i.e.*, buyer's preference for a commodity or a shop due not to any real differences in quality but to irrational factors like habit, prejudices or ignorance. Some of these wastes are given below:

(*i*) One of the wastes of imperfect competition is the restriction of output so that price is kept higher than the marginal cost. The excess of price over the marginal cost represents the real burden on the community. It is not the total amount of profit that pinches but setting too high a price is perhaps the greatest evil of imperfect competition.

(*ii*) Expenditure on competitive advertisement is usually regarded as a waste of competition. In fact, it is due not to perfect but imperfect competition. If competition is perfect, there is no need for such expenditure to be incurred, because then each firm can extend its sales by lowering its price only a little. Under imperfect competition, much larger reduction of price will be necessary to overcome the irrational preference of the consumers. It pays, therefore, to spend money on advertising and thus persuading the consumers that the product of the advertising firm is better than that of its rivals. Such expenditure is a waste from the point of view of the community.

(*iii*) Another similar waste is "expenditure" on cross-transport. A firm in the north of India may be selling a commodity to the consumers in the south. At the same time, the same (or substantially the same) commodity is perhaps being sold by a firm located in the south to consumers living in the north. This state of affairs is also due to the absence of perfect competition, which in its turn is due to irrational buyer's preferences. If competition were perfect, the firms in the north would have attracted all the buyers in the north and the firms in the south all the buyers there, by slightly lowering the price. This would have saved the cost of transport. As it is, the firm deem it worthwhile spending considerable sums on advertisement and transport cost, rather than reduce the price sufficiently to attract the neighbouring consumers with irrational preferences.

(*iv*) A third waste of imperfect competition is the failure of each firm in an industry to specialise in the production of those things for which it is best suited. Under perfect competition, such a specialisation would naturally take place, provided it led to any real economies. Under conditions of imperfect competition, since each firm has to spend money on advertisement or to sell at considerably lower prices in order to attract customers from its rivals, "each firm may find that it pays it better to produce varied assortment of types and qualities to sell to its own particular customers, rather than face the cost of attracting a large number of customers for one type of product alone."

6. Meade—*Economic Analysis and Policy*, pp. 165-68.

(v) Still another waste of imperfect competition has already been noted. This is that, under such conditions the efficient firm which can produce at lower cost may fail to drive out the inefficient ones as would happen if competition were perfect. If competition is perfect, the efficient firm (or firms) will increase output until the price comes down to the marginal cost of production at which the inefficient firms will not be able to supply. But, if competition is imperfect and the efficient firm has to spend considerable sums to attract consumers from inefficient rivals, or it has to lower its price considerably to achieve the same end, it might prefer not to drive out the inefficient firms, even though the latter were charging a price higher than the marginal cost of the efficient firm. Thus, valuable resources are wasted because of excess capacity resulting in idle plant and manpower in each firm.

(vi) Finally, imperfect competition may prevent that standardization of commodities which is essential if the most efficient methods of production are to be adopted. Different types of cars may be produced by a large number of firms each at a high cost of production. If only a few designs were produced cost per unit could be lowered considerably due to the economies of large-scale production. Under imperfect competition, such large producing units would emerge. Under imperfect competition, no producer would take the risk of producing, any particular design on a large scale, since the cost of attracting buyers from his rivals would outweigh the economies of scale obtained by producing the large output.

(vii) Monopolistic competition has also been criticised on the ground that the firms under this type of market operate with excess capacity.

Conclusion

Thus, under imperfect competition, producers incur losses, valuable resources of the community are wasted and the consumers suffer from too high prices.

MONOPOLISTIC COMPETITION: AN APPRAISAL

The important of Chamberlin's contribution to the theory of pricing cannot be denied. He has introduced product differentiation and selling strategy as the two additional variables in firms decision-making process. Also, his model has provided some sort of solution to the dilemma of falling costs.

But we may also notice the criticisms levelled against Chamberlin's theory of monopolistic competition: (*i*) The assumptions of product differentiation and of independent action by the rivals are inconsistent. Actions of competitors, whose products are close substitutes, are well known to the firms. (*ii*) The assumption of product differentiation is also inconsistent with the assumption of free entry. Product differentiation and brand loyalty of the buyers is a barrier to the entry of new firms. (*iii*) Product differentiation destroys the very concept of industry. This makes each firm an industry because heterogeneous products cannot be added to get the industry demand supply curves. (*iv*) Chamberlin's 'heroic model' cannot be accepted as an approximation to the real world in which demand and costs are different among the firms giving rise to cluster of prices rather than a unique price. (*v*) Finally, the model assumes that the products should be close substitutes with high price and high cross elasticities but it is not clear what should be the exact value of elasticities to put the products in the same group.

(*vi*) Chamberlin's Alternative Approach: Alternative Approach of Chamberline is to explain, how the firm naively behave with the assumption that, if they decrease the price then, they will be able to induce more buyer and will be able to make more profits. In other words Chamberline tried to explain how the short-sightedness (myopic) attitude of a firm's behavior with regards to price-cut and increase in sale will not result in much to gain in a real monopolistic competition.

The following are the assumptions underlying to explain such behavior

1. There are two types of demand curves 'perceived demand' curve and 'proportional demand' curve. Perceived demand curve' is the individual firms behavior, that if it reduces the prices from P_0 to P* it will be able to sell more output, with the assumption other firms will not react (d_0d_0).

'Proportional demand curve' is that if firms decrease the price from p_0 to p^*, the other firms will also behave in the same proportion immediately.

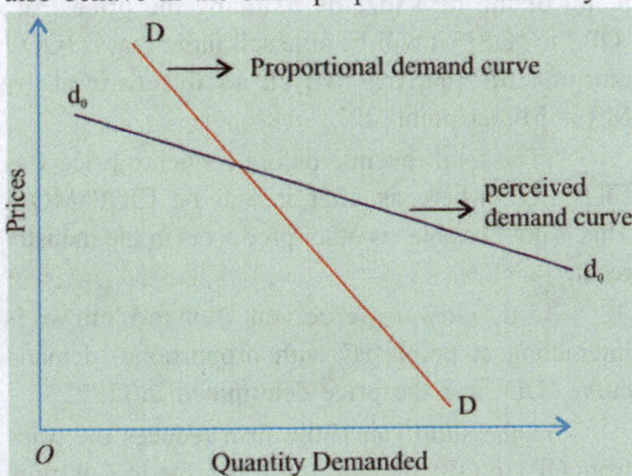

2. 'DD' proportional demand curve may be the same, as that of the total demand curve of the

industry.

3. The intersection point between MR (perceived demand curve) and that of MC firm determines price output.

4. MR = MC will be the price-out determination-point curve (d_1d_1) intersect proportional demand 'DD', corresponds to it, C at price P*.

'do' original perceived demand curve

'DD' proportional demand curve (which is generally equal to market demand curve of the product) The firm assumes that it will increase the sales from 'QQ_0 to QO_2' by decreasing price from 'OP_0 to OP*'. Due to the interaction point between the perceived demand 'd_1d_1' and proportional demand 'DD' this bebavior will 'backfire' and his naive decision will result in only 'Q_0Q_1' increase in quantity sale, instead of 'Q_0Q_2', with the 'myopic' belief.

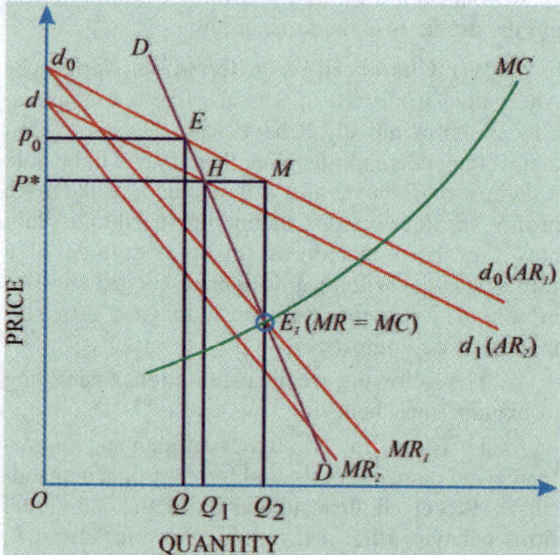

Original equilibrium is at point 'E' where 'DD' proportional demand curve and 'd_0d_0', the initial perceived demand curve intersects each other, which determines price 'OP_0'. The naive or short-sighted belief of the firm that by reducing the price from 'OP_0' to 'OP*' it will be able sell more that is 'OQ_2' amount of quantity which is determined by MR = MC at point 'E_1'.

[The total revenue before reducing price was □OP_0EQ_0, where as after it will be □OP^*MQ_2]. This is not possible, as other producers in the industry react.

'd_1d_1' lower perceived demand curve is interacting at point 'H' with proportional demand curve 'DD' and the price determined in OP*.

In the short run if the firm reduces the price from OP_0 to OP* though it will be able to sell more quantity 'OQ_2'. This may not be possible as this may reduce the monopoly element in terms of quality difference of the product. Unless and until the firm maintains a good quality without changing the price or maintaining competitive prices, it will not influence the market. It will be able to sell only 'Q_0Q_1' amount of quantity.

Modern Day Behaviour of Firms under Monopolistic Competitions

A firm instead or reducing the price with the concept of proportional demand curve and perceived demand curve, a different perspective is followed. A firm without changing the price' of the product, instead involves into improving the quality of the product. For quality improvement the cost of production may increase but this may bring about an increase in total sales. (Sales maximization one of the prime objective of firm according to William. J. Baumol).

Initially a firm is selling 'OQ_1' quantity of good 'x' at price 'OP'. AC_1 is the average cost, and the minimum 'AC' and 'Q_1S' therefore per unit profit is 'MS'. By selling 'OQ_1' quantity the firm is able to make □PMSR amount of profits TR – TC = π

□$OPMQ_1$ – □$ORSQ_1$ = □PMSR (profits)

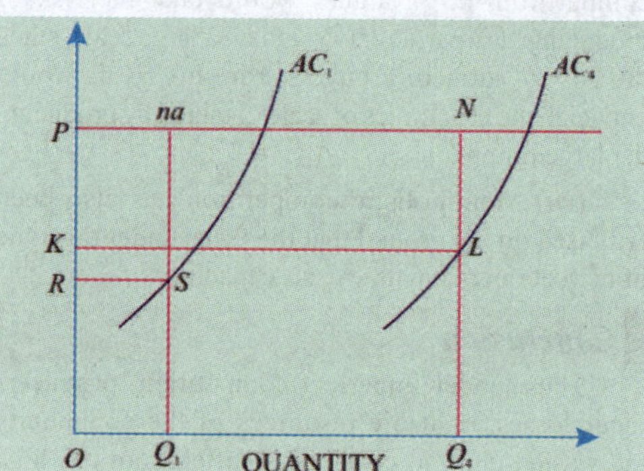

Now the firm will undertake a strategy of improving the quality, this will push up the costs. The firm will keep the prices same but through different promotional strategy, increases the sales. This will result in enormous increase in the total profits.

AC_1 shifts to 'AC_4' due to the quality improving techniques as well as other promotional strategies, the total quality sold will increase from 'OQ_1' to 'OQ_4' The profits will increase from □PMSR to □PNLK. □$OPNQ_4$ – □$OKLQ_4$ = ^ PNLK.

A per unit cost of production will increase from 'Q_1S' to 'Q_4L' ($Q_1S < Q_4L$) and also open per unit profit will decrease from 'MS' to 'NL' (where MS >

NL); But the gross profits increases from □PMSR to □PNLK which further builds up the confidence of the producer for diversification and other objectives. This is possible only when the said product is in the growth and maturity stage of the 'product life cycle', otherwise even if you increase the quality and other promotional measure the sales may not increase.

Key terms

Monopolistic Competition, Imperfect Competition, Product differentiation, Selling cost, Excess capacity.

QUESTIONS

1. What do you mean by monopolistic competition? How are price and output determined under monopolistic competition?
2. State the characteristics of monopolistic competition and explain why the demand curve under monopolistic competition is more elastic than that under monopoly.
3. What are the main characteristics of the traditional theory of value? How does Chamberlain's theory of monopolistic competition constitute an advance over it?
4. Discuss the relation between marginal cost and price (*a*) under competition, (*b*) under monopolistic competition, and (*c*) under ordinary monopoly.
5. What are 'selling costs'? Under what market conditions would a producer incur selling costs? How does a producer incurring selling costs reach equilibrium?
6. What are selling costs? How do they differ from production costs? Why are selling costs incompatible with perfect competition?
7. How do selling costs differ from production costs? Discuss how the group attains equilibrium when selling costs alone vary.
8. What is the shape of selling costs curve of a firm under monopolistic competition? How is the blending of monopoly and competition reflected in the price output results of long-run equilibrium under monopolistic competition?
9. Discuss the effects of selling cost on Profit and output.
10. How far selling costs is beneficials ? Explain with the help of diagram.
11. "There is a direct relationship between increase in selling cost and profits". How far it is true? Comment.

OLIGOPOLY AND DUOPOLY

We have so far discussed where there is a very large number of producers supplying a market as under perfect competition, or a single monopolist an individual or a single group of individuals, dominates the entire market, or there are many producers as in imperfect competition but not as many as in perfect competition.

But other situation may also arise in the real world. One is that there may be two monopolists instead of one who share the monopoly power. This is called **Duopoly.** The other is when more than two or a few sellers are found in a monopolistic position. This is called **Oligopoly.**

Important characteristics of an oligopolistic situation are : (*a*) Every seller can exercise an important influence on the price-output policies of his rivals. (*b*) Every seller, therefore, is so influential that his rivals cannot ignore the likely adverse effect on them of a given change in the price-output policy of any single manufacturer. (*c*) This rival consciousness, or the recognition on the part of the seller of the fact of interdependence is the most important feature of oligopolistic situation. (*d*) The demand curve under oligopoly is indeterminate as we shall see, because any step taken by his rivals may change the demand curve. It is more elastic than under simply monopoly and not perfectly elastic as under perfect competition.

As compared with perfect competition, the number of firms in an oligopoly is much smaller. Oligopoly differs from monopoly and monopolistic competition in this that, in monopoly, there is a single seller; in monopolistic competition, there is quite a large number of them; and in oligopoly, there is only a small number of sellers.

We discuss these two market situations at some length below :

DUOPOLY

Duopoly may be of two types : (*a*) Duopoly without product differentiation and (*b*) Duopoly with product differentiation.

Duopoly means two sellers.

Duopoly Without Product Differentiation

Under duopoly the simplest cases will be those where the two monopolists are supposed to be selling an identical commodity and there is no product differentiation. Very likely there will be a collusion between the two. They may agree on a price, or assign quotas or divide the territory in which each is to market his goods. This will specially be the case if their respective cost curves are identical or nearly so, and if the demand is stable and less elastic. Obviously, this collusion creates conditions almost analogous to a monopoly and the price determination will be similar to that under monopoly.

In case, however, there is no agreement between the two, a constant price war will be the most probable consequence. The important factors to be considered then would be the costs and gains in driving out the rival, the relative sizes of the two firms, the demand elasticity and mobility of the purchasers, the promptitude with which the rival reacts to change in the other's policy and the extent to which price concession can be kept secret, and so on.

If there is no product differentiation and goods are identical, the consumers are indifferent between the two producers and the same price must be charged by both in the long-run, otherwise the one charging more will not be able to sell any. They must fix a price as if they were a single monopolist rolled in one. Only in that way they will be maximising profits.

In case there is a price is a price-war between them, they will be able to earn only normal profits as under perfect competition. If their costs are different, the one with lower costs will squeeze out the other and a simple monopoly would be established. The best course for the duopolists will be to fix the monopoly price and share the market and profits.

It is possible that, in the short-run, duopoly price may be lower than the competitive price, none of the producers earning normal profit. In the long-run this price may be somewhere between the monopoly price and the competitive price.

DUOPOLY MODELS

Cournot Model

The following diagram illustrates the Cournot model. It shows how A and B producers share the total market and adjust output (not prices) and how they maximise their profit.

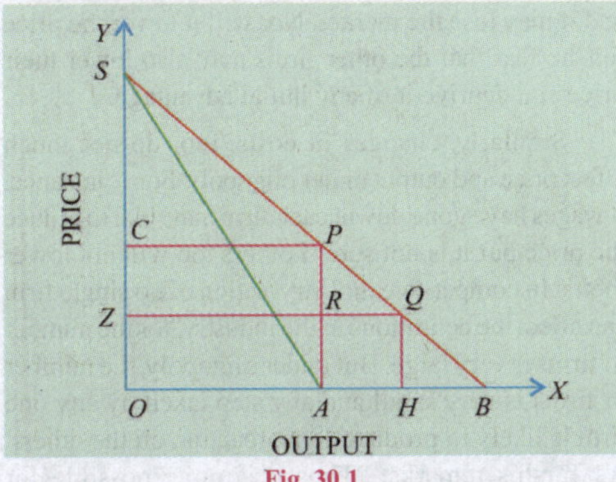

Fig. 30.1.

In this diagram (30.1) SB is the total demand. Let the unit cost be zero i.e. MC = O. Therefore, MR is also zero. MR is zero at A.

Before B enters the market, A produces OA = $\frac{1}{2}$ AB. The price is OC giving maximum profit OAPC. Then B enters the market and produce AH s.c. $\frac{1}{2}$ AB the remaining market, or $\frac{1}{4}$ OB. The price falls from OC to OZ. B gets total profit AHQP. A's profit falls from OAPC to OARZ, the total profit being OHQZ. When B produces AH which is $\frac{1}{4}$ of the whole, the total output left for A is $\frac{1}{2}(1-\frac{1}{4})=\frac{3}{8}$. What is left over by A and which now B produces is $\frac{1}{2}(1-\frac{3}{8})=5/16$. A may now react by producing $\frac{1}{2}(1-5/16)$ i.e. $11/32$. This process will continue till equilibrium output and price are achieved. As more and more firms enter, they will produce output approaching the competitive output. If the number of firms goes up to N they will produce $\frac{(N)}{N+1}$ OB.

Edgeworth Model

The basic difference between this model and the cournot model is that in Cournot model, the output (and not the price) of the rival firm is assumed to remain unchanged. Here, the rival firm is supposed to keep the price unchanged.

The following diagram (Fig. 30.2) illustrates the situation. It is assumed that each producer's capacity is limited to 3/4th of his entire market and each is confronted with his own demand curve made up of one half of the consumers. The maximum output that A can produce is OB and B can produce OB′.

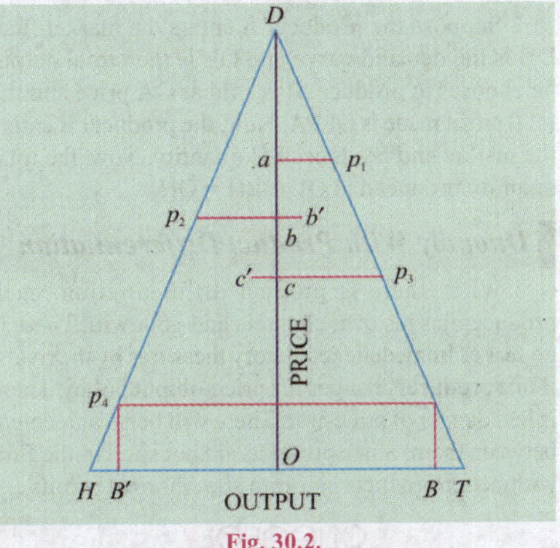

Fig. 30.2.

The demand curves of A and B respectively are DT and DH. A first enters the market and sets his price P_1 he sells the total output ap_1. Then B enters the market and sells at price slightly lower than A and thus captures his market. B then sells the whole output at P_2 and snatches from A bb′ of sales. Now A reacts and captures B's market to the extent of CC′. This process of price-cutting, continues until one of them say B fixes his price at P_4. At this point none can snatch the market from the other by lowering the price. Then A raises the price back to p_1 to maximise his profit from his share of the market knowing that B has already thrown his entire supply. B then follows suit. There is thus continual oscillation of price between P_1 and P_4 i.e. the upper and lower limits.

Chamberlin Model

Unlike Cournot and Edgeworth models, Chamberlin model is based on the assumption that both the producers recognise their mutual interdependence. The following diagram (Fig. 30.3) explains this model :

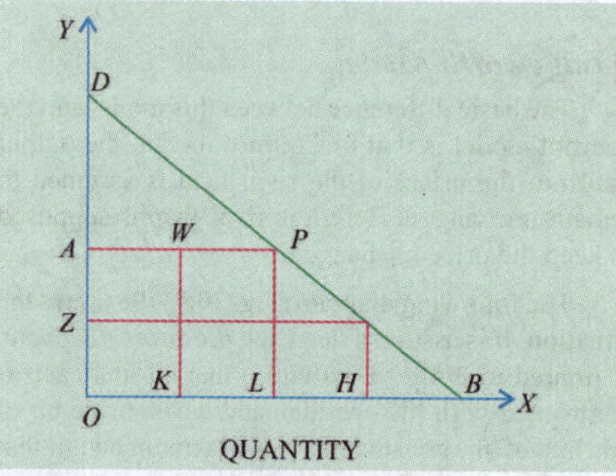

Fig. 30.3.

Suppose the producer A enters the market first. DB is the demand curve and OL is the total output he chooses to produce. It is sold at OA price and the total profit made is OLPA. Now, the producer B enters the market and produces LH quantity. Now, the total quantity produced is OL + LH = OH.

Duopoly With Product Differentiation

When there is product differentiation, each producer has his own clientele and goodwill. There is no fear of immediate retaliatory measures by the rivals, if one producer changes his price-output policy. There is less danger of price-war. There will be no agreement between them. Since products are not similar, the firm with better products can earn supernormal profits.

OLIGOPOLY

Oligopoly Without Product Differentiation

Under **oligopoly**, the pricing theory is fundamentally the same as in duopoly with this difference that the larger the number of firms the greater will be the differences in marginal costs and more remote will be the possibility of collusion or agreement, whether tacit or explicit. The element of predictability as regards the proper scale of advertisement research investment and returns is almost missing. The temperaments of entrepreneurs, whether pessimistic or optimistic, make the situation still more complicated and obscure. Since they all deal in a standardised product and each is producing a considerable portion of the total output, the price and output policy of each is likely to affect the price and output policy of each is likely to affect the others appreciably, but none can foretell precisely how. "The price which will be fixed in oligopoly without product differentiation is thus indetermination but is likely, in general, to be lower, the larger the number of producers, until in the end there are enough for a perfectly competitive equilibrium to be reached."

Oligopoly With Product Differentiation

In case there is product differentiation, monopoly agreements are even less likely. Since products are not similar, any producer in oligopoly can raise or lower his price without any fear of losing customers or immediate reactions from his rivals. Cut-throat competition is unlikely. However, keen rivalry among them may create condition of monopolostic competition. The price, in the long-run, may settle at a level between the monopoly price and that in cut-throat competition.

Stability of Price under Oligopoly

It is often noticed that price under oligopoly is stable. It is neither much responsive to changes in demand nor to changes in supply. For instance, if demand increases, no firm will venture to raise the price for fear that other firms may not raise the price and it may lose the market. Nor will it lower the price for the fear that the other firms may also lower their price and deprive it of any initial advantage.

Similarly, changes in costs, too, do not much affect price and output under oligopoly. For instance, if wages have gone down, each firm may like to reduce the price but it is not sure if others too will not lower theirs. In competitive industry, action of no single firm can affect the conditions in the industry, for the number of firms is very large. But under oligopoly, the number of firms is very small and any step taken by any one firm is likely to produce some reaction on the others. As Tarshis remarks. "Thus it is quite possible for demand and cost to change frequently and yet to produce no change, or at any rate very few changes, in price. Thus, the existence of oligopoly accounts for some of the price inflexibility that characterises our economy."

The oligopolist avoids experimenting with price changes. He knows that if he raises the price, he will lose his customers and if he lowers it he will offend his rivals. He has a clientele of his own when there is product differentiation. Why should he experiment? He is, therefore content to leave the price and output as they are.

Price Rigidity

Very often the question arises why the prices in oligopoly market are fixed for a longer period of time or they do not fluctuate more as in the case of monopolistic competition. Here it is not the question of the number of competitors, One of the distinct features of oligopoly market is that if the leader increased the price, the other follower's do not do so, where as if the leader decreases the price, other producers also reduce the price.

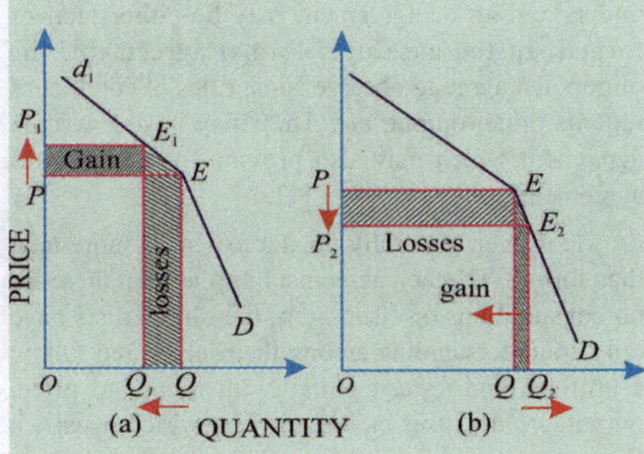

'd_1E' is the 'demand' segment of the leaders individual demand curve where as ED is the 'market demand' curve segment. Let us assume the price is 'OP' and the quantity offered as 'OQ'. Price 'OP' is fixed on the basis of the leadership concept.

1. If the leader increases the price from 'OP' to 'OP_1', than the gain to the seller will □P_1EKP, where as the losses will be □E_1Q_1QE. (Fig. a).

2. If the oligopolist firm decreases the price from 'OP to OP_2', the quantity sold will increase from "OQ to 'OQ_2', but the gain is □E_2Q_2QH where as the losses will be □PEE_2P_2. This shows that the losses are more than the gain.

Total Revenue	Original price OP □OPEQ	Increase in Price OP_1 (Case I) □O$P_1E_1Q_1$	Decrease in Price OP_2 (Case II) □O$P_2E_2Q_2$
Gain	–	□P_1E_1KP	□E_2Q_2QH
Losses	–	□E_1Q_1QE	□PEE_2P_2
Result	–	□E_1Q_1QE >	□PEE_2P_2 >
		□P_1E_1KP	□E_2Q_2QH

This clearly indicates that in both cases viz. increase and decrease in prices the oligopoly firm is about to bear more losses and gain less. Hence the prices are generally rigid or sticky.

One of the important differences between the oligopoly and monopolistic competition is that of huge amount of infrastructural investment. Where the number of firms are less, it is due to the requirement of heavy capital investment and that too for a longer period of time.

KINKY DEMAND CURVE

It is impossible to find a single generalised solution to the problem of oligopoly pricing. This is because of the difficulty of knowing the exact position of the demand curve facing a firm under oligopoly. This in turn is due to the fact that the effect of a given price change by a seller on the demand for his product depends very much on the reaction of his rivals and, as we explained earlier rival consciousness is a basic characteristic of oligopolistic situations.

As for the possible reactions of the rivals, there can be any number of hypothesis. Under some circumstances, a price cut by a seller may pass unnoticed by his rivals; at other times, it may invite

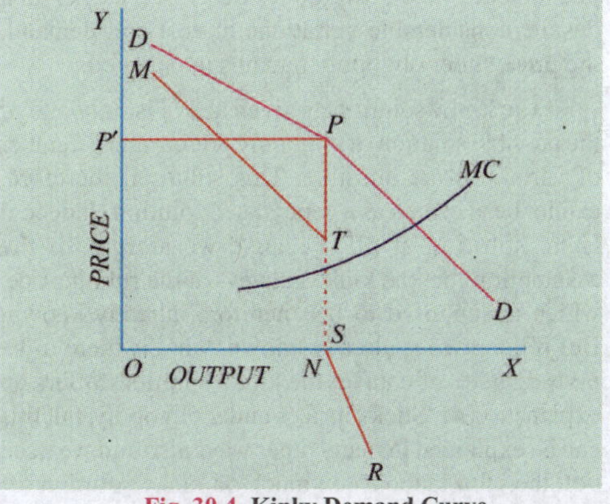

Fig. 30.4. Kinky Demand Curve.

immediate retaliation, so that the position and the shape of the demand curve of a firm under oligopoly will vary with the hypothesis that we adopt about the reaction to its moves on the part of the rival firms.

There is, however, one particular shape of demand curve under oligopoly which has become very popular, *i.e.*, the kinky demand curve. This curve is drawn on the assumption that the kink in the curve is always at the ruling price. Taking the ruling price as given, it assumes that a rise in price (beyond the ruling price) on the part of a given firm under oligopoly, will not invite retaliation from the rivals, *i.e.*, they will not come forward with a price increase of their own to neutralise the effects of price increase by the first seller. Rather, they will allow him to raise his price and lose customers to his rivals, so that the upper part of the curve is more elastic than the part of the curve lying below the kink. This is because a price cut (below the ruling price) will invite immediate retaliation from the rivals who wish to protect their own sales. The result will be that if a firm under oligopoly lowers its price, it cannot push up its sales very much because the rival firms also follow suit with a price cut, so that there are no customers to be drawn from the rivals. Hence, the lower part of the demand curve is less elastic than the upper one.

Having drawn the demand curve, we can draw the corresponding marginal revenue curve (MR) (Fig. 30.1). We shall notice that there is a discontinuity in the marginal revenue curve just below the point corresponding to the kink. Next we can draw the marginal cost curve (MC). The equilibrium of the firm will be at the point where marginal revenue equals marginal cost. We shall further notice that, because of discontinuity in the marginal revenue curve, shifts in the marginal cost curve between the points T and S will not alter the equilibrium position as regards output and prices. The firm helps to explain an often observed phenomenon under oligopoly described earlier that despite considerable variations in cost and demand, the price under oligopoly remains unchanged.

The kinky solution as given above is only one of the possible solution of oligopoly pricing and a number of variations are possible. This solution, therefore, cannot be accepted as a generalised solution. Indeed it is no solution at all, because we start with the assumption that the kink is always at the ruling price, which is supposed to be, therefore, already known. But if the price is already known, what is there to be investigated? of course, the kinky solution offers an explanation of 'Sticky' prices under oligopoly, but this can be explained in many other ways also and we need not, therefore, labour too much on kinky solution for this purpose alone.

PRICE LEADERSHIP UNDER OLIGOPOLY

In an oligopolistic situation, there are more than two or a few sellers who are able to exercise monopolistic influence. In such a market situation, we generally find that there exists what is called the 'price leadership'. Under price leadership, one firm assumes the role of a price leader and fixes the price of the product for the entire industry. The other firms in the industry simply follow the price leader and accept the price fixed by him and adjust their output to this price. The price leader is generally a very large or a dominant firm or a firm with the lowest cost of production. It often happens that price leadership is established as a result of price war in which one firm emerges as the winner.

Thus, we find that in an oligopolistic market situation, it is very rare that prices are set independently and there is usually some understanding among the oligopolist is operating in the industry. This understanding or agreement may be either tacit or formal. In the case of a formal agreement, the oligopolist agree to observe some rules of conduct as regards price, output, *etc.* They may have a written agreement which may also provide for violation of agreement.

However, generally the agreement is more tacit than formal. The tacit agreement implies that there are no consultations or discussion; the oligopolists have only an understanding among themselves and follow a uniform and agreed policy with regard to price, output, *etc.* It is this tacit agreement which usually a feature of price leadership. That is, under price leadership there is no formal agreement or setting up of an agency to control and regulate the activities of the firms in the industry. Some times, however, price leadership may emerge from a formal agreement among the rival firms in which a leader is chosen whom the other firms in the industry agree to follow in setting the price.

Dominant Firm. A dominant firm is one which has a large capacity to produce and sell in the market. In oligopoly such a practice is possible. It is a very efficient and effective firm as such can dominate the market, it can produce the goods at possible lowest cost then the other small firms exists in the market. We assume that the dominant leader has the knowledge of the supply of small firms as well as the total demand for the product in the market.

P_1L_1 is small firm's supply 'L,K' is leaders supply. The total 'DD' (for the product) and 'SS' is small firm's supply curve. The point of interaction

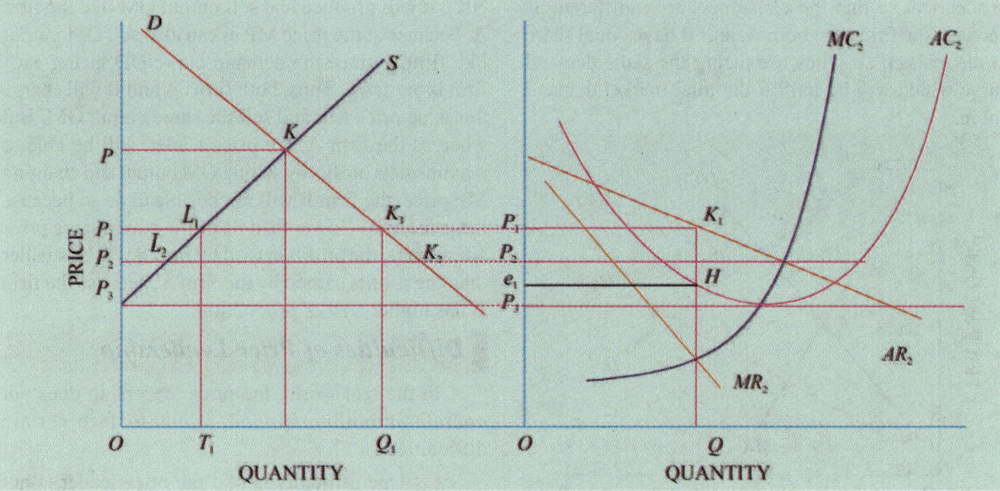

Fig. 30.5. Price leadership by dominant firm.

between DD and 'SS' at 'K' and the price determined will be 'OP'. At this point the dominant firm is not able to sell any amount. At 'OP_3' price at which the supply curve of small firm cuts the y-axis, but this price is not profitable to the leader, as its amount of profit may be less (which is explained in other diagram). If the dominant firm operates at OP_2 price then the leader may sell 'LK_2' amount of out put and 'P_2L' may be left over to the small firms. This also may not maximise the profits of the dominant firm. At price 'OP_1' the dominant firm leaves 'P_1L_1' = OT_1 amount of output for small firms and the remaining $L_1K_1 = T_1Q_1$ amount of output is sold by the dominant firm. This output level is the level at which the dominant firm maximises the profit. It is the point at which MR = MC point of equilibrium of dominant firm which is explained in the right hand side diagram, which is equal to 'OQ' or 'P_1K' and (in the main diagram it is [($L_1K_1 = T_1Q_1$)].

There are several types of price leadership. The following are the principal types:

(*a*) Price Leadership of a dominant Firm. Under this type of price leadership, it is found that there is generally one firm, among the firms operating in the industry, which produces the bulk of the product of the industry. By virtue of this position, it is able to dominate the entire market. It sets the price and the other firms simply accept this price. The other firms are not in a position to exercise any influence on the market price. Naturally the dominant firm, considering its own interest, fixes a price so as to maximize its profits. The other firms have to adjust their output to the price so fixed by the dominant firm.

(*b*) Barometric Price Leadership. Under this type of price leadership, an old, experienced and the largest firm assumes the role of a leader, but undertakes also to protect the interests of all firms instead of merely promoting its own interest. In a way it acts as the custodian of firms operating in the industry. It fixes a price which is found to be suitable for all the firms in the industry. This price is fixed by taking into consideration the market conditions with regard to the demand for the product, cost of production, competition from the rival producers, *etc.* Since the interest of all firms are protected by this dominant firm, all the firms in the industry are only too willing to follow the price leader.

(*c*) Exploitative or Aggressive Price Leadership. In this case, one big firm comes to establish its supremacy in the market by following aggressive price policies. This firm compels other firms to follow it and accept the price fixed by it. In case the other firms show any independence, this firm threatens them and coerces them to follow its leadership with the result that the price set by this firm comes to be accepted willingly or unwillingly.

Price-output Determination Under Price Leadership

Economists have developed various models concerning price-output determination under price leadership on the basis of certain assumptions regarding the behaviour of the price leader and his followers. We take a simple case here to show price-output determination under price leadership on the following assumptions:— (*a*) There are only two firms **A** and **B** and the firm **A** has a lower cost of production than **B**; (*b*) the product of the firms is homogeneous or identical so that the consumers are indifferent as between the firms; (*c*) both **A**. and **B** have equal share in the market, *i.e.*, they are facing the same demand curve which will be half of the total market demand curve.

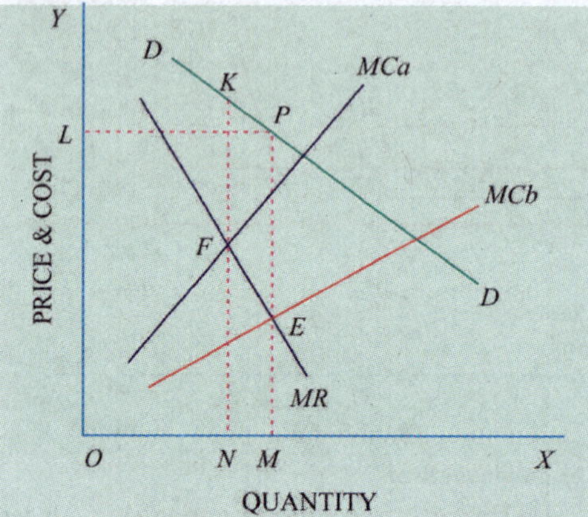

Fig. 30.6. Equilibrium Price-output Under Price Leadership.

The preceding diagram illustrates price-output determination in this case subject to the assumptions given above.

In this figure DD is the demand curve facing each firm which is half of the total demand curve for the product, MR is the marginal revenue curve of each firm. MC_a is the marginal cost curve of firm **A** and MC_b is the marginal cost curve of the firm **B**. Since we have assumed that the firm **A** has a lower cost of production than the firm **B**, MC_a is drawn below MC_b.

Let us take the firm **A** first. **A** will be maximizing its profits by selling output OM and setting price MP, because at the output OM its marginal cost is equal to its marginal revenue. As regards the firm **B**, the profits will be maximum when it sells ON output and fixes NK price, because at this output its marginal cost is equal to its marginal revenue. It can be seen that the profit-maximizing price MP of the firm **A** is lower than the profit-maximizing price NK of the firm **B**. The two firms will have to charge the same price since the products of the two firms have been assumed to be homogeneous. This means that the firm **A**, whose price **MP** is lower, will dictate the price to the firm **B** whose profit-maximizing price NK is higher. In case the firm **B** refuses to fall in line, it can be ousted by the firm **A** which will be charging the lower price. This shows that in this situation, the firm **A** is the price leader and the firm **B** has to follow it.

It can also be seen that although the firm **B** is compelled to follow **A** and has to charge the price MP (which is lower than its own profit-maximizing price NK), it will produce and sell output OM like the firm **A**, because at the price MP, it can also sell OM output like firm **A** since the demand curve DD facing each firm is the same. Thus, both firms **A** and **B** will charge the same price MP and sell the same output OM. But whereas the firm **A**, the price leader, will be able to maximize its profits by selling OM output and charging MP price, the firm **B** will not be able to do so because the price MP is lower than its profit-maximizing price NK. Hence, the profits earned by firm **B** will be smaller than the profits earned by the firm **A**, because the firm **B** has higher cost of production.

Difficulties of Price Leadership

In the real world, the price leadership does not operate smoothly. Instead, it has to face certain difficulties :

(*a*) One difficulty is that the price leader is not able to assess correctly the reactions of his followers. The rival firms may not follow its lead.

(*b*) The rival firms may secretly charge lower prices when they find that the price leader has fixed unduly higher price. In this way, they may seek to increase their share of the market without challenging the price leader openly. The price-cutting devices generally are : offer of rebates, favourable credit terms, 'money back' guarantees, after-delivery free services, easy instalment sales with low rates of interest and liberal entertainment given to the buyers. In this way, the price leadership is rendered infructuous.

(*c*) The price leader has to face another difficulty, when it finds that the rival firms are indulging in 'non-price competition' to increase their sales even though they charge the price set by the price leader. These 'non-price competition' devices include advertising and other methods of sales promotion like improvement of the product besides the secret price-product concessions mentioned above.

(*d*) When the price leader fixes a high price, there is an inherent tendency on the part of the rival producers to make secret price-cuts and thus adversely affect the sales of the price leader. The high price set by the price leader may also attract new entrants into the industry and these new entrants may not accept his leadership.

(*e*) Finally, the differences in cost of production also pose a problem. If the cost of production of the price leader is higher on account of which he fixes a high price and the rival producers have lower cost of production, they will have no difficulty in undercutting the price. On the other hand, if the price leader has a lower cost, he will set a low price which may not suit his rivals. This will antogonize them and induce them to break his leadership.

COLLUSIVE OLIGOPOLY

There can be a collusion among the oligopolists operating in an industry. Under this situation, the oligopolists arrive at a tacit or a formal agreement on a uniform policy as regards price to be charged. When the agreement is formal, the oligopolists form what is known as a cartel.

The collusive oligopoly may take various forms. An extreme form of collusion is when the firms entering into an agreement surrender completely their rights of price-output determination to a central agency. In this way, they secure collectively maximum profits for themselves. The total profits are distributed among the member firms in agreed proportions which may not be necessarily in proportion to the output quota assigned to each firm. The total cost is sought to be minimized by asking the firms of the cartel to produce such separate outputs as to make their output costs equal.

In the real world, formation of perfect cartels is not very common even when their formation is not legally prohibited. In actual collusion, the agreement is only on the price which is generally the joint-profit maximizing price and the member firms are free to produce and sell the output which will maximize their individual profits subject to the fixed agreed price. Each firm will be able to earn profits on the basis of the output produced and sold by it and the costs incurred.

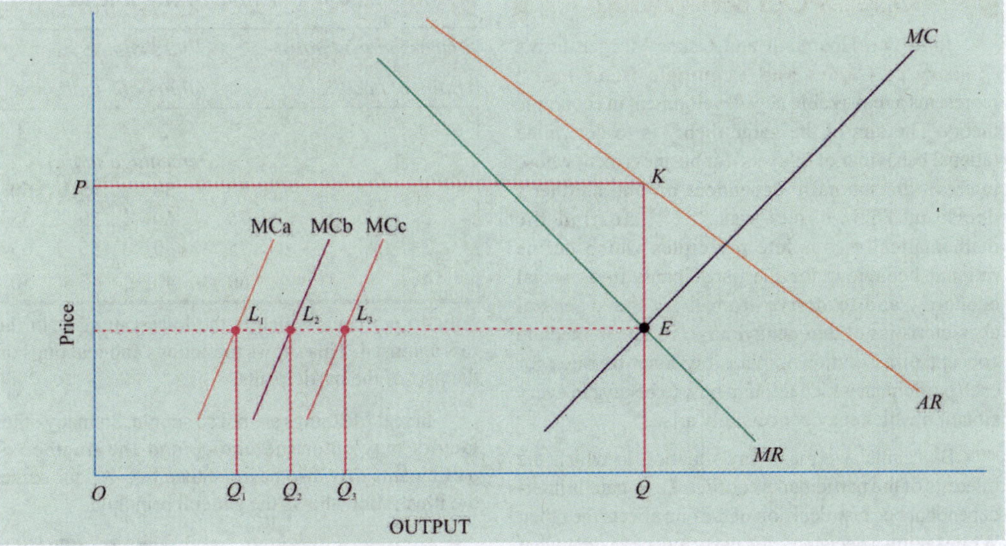

Fig. 30.7. Equilibrium of cartel-collusive oligopoly.

Collusive Oligopoly

'Cartel's are a kind of 'collusive' oligopoly. OPEC' Organisation of Petroleum Export countries is one of the example of collusive oligopoly. In this type of oligopoly, a group is formed under an agreement, where they decide regarding price of the product output and area of distribution and marketing. Collusive oligopoly is a kind of market in which the whole market is controlled and divided by the group, and they changed the output as well as price whenever they decide.

In the present world of globalisation and liberalisation many companies are either merging with other big concerns or forms a 'pool' or it is completely 'taken-over' by the big firms. Cartels are taking new shapes. Some companies they come together and form a group and decide the pricing and output policy which is explained below.

'AR' is the total demand for the product in the market (including both national and international market). 'MR' is the marginal revenue and 'MC' is the marginal cost. Equilibrium is achieved at point 'E' which determines the output 'OQ'. If we raise the line 'QE' it will cut at point 'K' on average revenue AR curve. Draw 'PK' horizontal curve. Hence 'OP' is the price and the total quantity produced in an economy or group is 'OQ'.

From point 'E' when we draw a horizontal curve to 'y' axis it cuts MC_a, MC_b & MC_c at point 'L_1' 'L_2' AND L_3. MC_a, MC_b and MC_c are marginal cost of firm's 'a', 'b' and 'c'. Draw perpendicular's L_1Q_1, L_2Q_2 & L_3Q_3 which is nothing but the three firms 'a', 'b' and 'c' are producing 'OQ_1', 'OQ_2' and 'OQ_3' output.

The total output OQ

OQ_1 firm 'a''s output

OQ_2 firm 'b''s output

OQ_3 firm 'c''s output

$\therefore OQ_{1a} + OQ_{2b} + OQ_{3c} = OQ$

In this way the oligopolists form a group called collusive – oligopoly and determines the price 'OP' and they share their output in the total market demand.

GAME THEORY AND OLIGOPOLY BEHAVIOUR

John von Neumann and Oskar Morgenstern's **'Theory of Games and Economic Behaviour'**[1] represents a remarkable new development in economic theory. The aim of the game theory is to determine rational behaviour of 'players' (or business men) whose interests are mutually dependent on one another's decision. Their object was ". . . . to find the mathematically complete principles which define rational behaviour for the participants in a social economy, and to derive from them the general characteristics of that behaviour . . . . The immediate concept of a solution is plausibly a set of rules for each participant which tell him how to behave in every situation which may conceivably arise."

By 'game' we mean any situation in which the interests of the participants conflict. Their gain is inter-dependent because decision of the one affects the other. While taking a decision each party must consider what probably will be the decision of the other so that he may make a choice most profitable to himself. This is what usually happens in a game of chess or cards. This is applicable to situations arising in an oligopoly.

The two common games are the "constant-sum" game in which the participants take share or the 'zero-sum' game in which the winnings of one are matched exactly by the losses of the other.

We give here an illustration of the 'constant-sum' game. Suppose the total Indian demand for cars is shared by the two manufacturers, of the Ambassador and the Fiat. Suppose, they want to choose for their next model the number of headlights. The table on the next page gives the choices and Ambassador's share of the market :

Ambassador's four choices are given vertically and Fiat's four choices horizontally.

If Ambassador chooses one pair of headlights and Fiat 3, the Ambassador will capture 45 per cent of the market. While deciding, Fiat will focus attention on the lowest in the row. Corresponding to choice of one, 45 is the lowest number in the row. Corresponding to choice of one, 45 is the lowest number in the row and it comes under 3. That is why Fiat chooses 3, so that it gives Ambassador the lowest share in the market. The lowest numbers in each row are called "row minima". If Ambassador selects 4, Fiat will decide on 2, so as to give Ambassador only 40 per cent, which is the lowest number in the row against 4. This shows the actions and reactions on the part of the participants.

Ambassador's Share of the market

Ambassador's choice (Pairs of headlights)	*Fiat's choice (Pairs of headlights)*			
	1	2	3	4
	(Percentage share)			
1	60	50	45	60
2	76	60	50	55
3	75	60	55	65
4	60	40	45	50

In real life things are not so simple. So many other factors may enter the choice and the number of participants may also be more than two. All the same, the illustration shows the general principle.

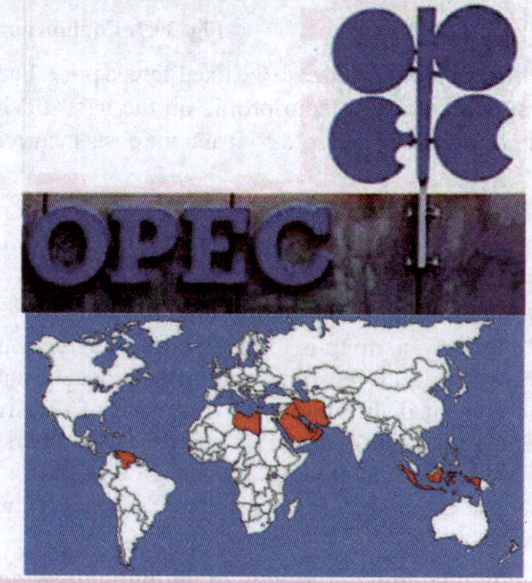

OPEC – World Oil Cartel.

1. John von Neumann and Oskar Morgenstern — Theory of Games and Economic Behaviour, 1953, p. 31.

EFFECTS OF OLIGOPOLY

We may mention, in a summary way, the following economic effects of the oligopolistic markets which we can derive from the above analysis :

***(i)* Small Output and Higher Price.** As compared with perfect competition, oligopoly results in the restriction of output and charging of higher prices.

***(ii)* Price Exceed Average Costs.** Owing to restrictions, partial or complete, on the entry of new firms, the prices fixed, under oligopoly, are higher than the average cost. The consumers have to pay more than is necessary to retain the resources in the industry. The resources of the economy cannot move into the making of products desired more by the consumers from those where they are desired less. In other words, the economy's productive capacity is not utilised in conformity with the consumer's preferences.

***(iii)* Lower Efficiency.** There is no tendency, under oligopoly, for the firms in the industry to build optimum scales of plant and operate them at the optimum rates of output. They do not, therefore, attain maximum potential economic efficiency. This is so because the firm's output depends on the quota or the share of the market allotted to it or on its judgment as to the future behaviour of marginal revenue and marginal costs.

***(iv)* Selling Costs.** In order to snatch markets from their rivals, the oligopolistic firms engage in aggressive and extensive sales promotion effort by means of advertisement and by changing the design and improving the quality of their products. The resources employed in sales promotion must be regarded as wasted since they do not add to the consumers' satisfaction.

***(v)* Wider Range of Products.** As compared with pure competition or pure monopoly, differentiated oligopoly places at the consumer's disposal a wider range of commodities. To this extent, it promotes consumer's welfare.

***(vi)* Welfare Effect.** Under oligopoly, since output does not generally correspond to the minimum long-run unit cost, more units of resources per unit of output are utilised than it is necessary. Also, price is higher than both AC and MC. Vast sums of money are poured into sales promotion to create quality and design differentials. Hence, from the point of view of economic welfare, oligopoly fares fairly badly. The oligopolists push non-price competition beyond socially desirable limits.

Conclusion. Oligopoly shows poor performance from all angles. For the participants it is an awkward organisation, because they can neither avail of individual opportunities as in perfect competition nor building up an efficient money-making organisations as in a monopoly. It is also unresponsive to market changes because (*a*) they are not interested in short-run condition and (*b*) they are anxious not to spoil their mutual relations for a temporary advantage. In the absence of prompt transmission of market information through price change, the consumer's response is also weakened. They do not know whether to buy more when the products are plentiful or less when they are scarce. The oligopolists also have the unpleasant experience of wasteful fluctuations in their sales and output. Besides, there is huge wasteful expenditure on advertisements. In the U.S.A. the total bill on advertising by industries is $ 12 billion a year, which is 5 per cent of the value of their products and 1/30th of the entire national income. It has all the drawbacks of a monopoly in addition to rigidity and wasteful competition peculiar to itself.

EVILS OF OLIGOPOLY

There is generally a continuous price war which finally results in disastrously low level of prices. When some of the producers find themselves at an advantage, they will push up the prices creating an anomalous and discriminatory pattern of prices charged from the consumers. Such cut-throat competition in industries characterised by heavy overheads and increasing costs proves ruinous to all producers.

Realising this, they may tacitly or explicitly enter into price agreements; which may result in the exploitation of the consumers. A tendency to earn a fair return on past investments, resulting in the excessive plant capacity, is detrimental to consumer's welfare, because they face scarce output and high prices. Hence, cut-throat competition may be, essential to liquidate excess capacity through losses or sub-normal profits.

Unlike perfect competition, under which price falls when demand decreases, output remaining the same, in oligopoly, prices stay firm, and only output varies resulting in idle plants. This is bad for the society and bad for the consumers.

Remedies. Government regulation is necessary (*a*) to pull down barriers to the entry to new firms, (*b*) to frown on collusions to maintain prices and restrict supply, and (*c*) to break big firms or to prevent them from becoming bigger.

Key terms

Oligopoly, Duopoly, Kinky demand, Price Leadership, Collusive Oligopoly, Cartel.

QUESTIONS

1. Examine the significance of a firm's kinked demand curve in the theory of price under oligopoly.
2. "The size of the gap in the two portions of the MR curve of an oligopoly firm depends upon the difference between the elasticities of the two segments of its kindly demand curve". Illustrate and explain.
3. Discuss the main features of oligopoly market.
4. Explain the Duopoly model of
   (*a*) Chamberlin
   (*b*) Edgenorth and
   (*c*) Cournot
5. What do you mean by 'leadership' concept in oligopoly market ?
6. Discuss the different types of price leadership in oligopoly market.
7. Draw diagram and explain the Collusive-oligopoly behaviour.
8. Define the concept of 'Cartel'. Explain equilibrium under cartel.

UNIT V

Factor Pricing

Chapters

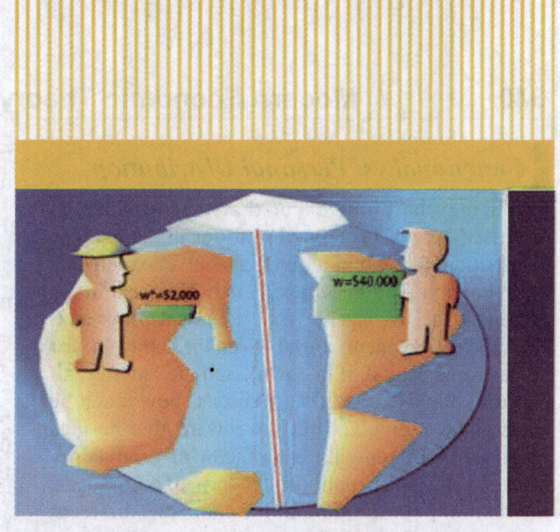

THE GENERAL THEORY OF FACTOR PRICING

Significance of Factor Pricing

The prices paid by businessmen to the various factors of production in the form of rent, wages, interest, *etc*., are a major determinant of money incomes. Thus, the resource prices play a crucial role in determining the distribution of income in the community. The households supply the human and property resources and get money incomes in return.

Further, factor prices serve as a rationing device for the utilisation of the productive resources. These resources are allocated among various industries and firms through the mechanism of factor prices. These prices facilitate the shifting of resources from the less remunerative uses to the more profitable ones. Dynamic societies cannot function without this shifting.

From the point of view of the firms, the resource prices enable the application to production of the most economical or least cost combination of factors. To the firms factor prices are costs and these costs must be minimised in order to maximise profits.

Finally, since resource prices constitute incomes for the various sections of the society, a very important consideration is the attainment of equality of incomes. This trend in modern societies highlights the ethical and political significance of factor prices.

Theory of factor pricing is also called theory of distribution.

Meaning of Distribution

By "distribution" in the present context, we do not mean the distributive activities of traders and middle men. "The economics of distribution," says Chapman, "accounts for the sharing of the wealth produced by a community among the agents, or the owners of the agents, which have been active in its production."[1]

The theory of distribution is concerned with the evaluation of the services of the factors of production, a study of the conditions of demand for the influences that bring about changes in their market price.

For instance, in the factor market, it is not acres of land which are being bought or sold but the services of land. Similarly, neither labour nor capital goods are being bought and sold but the services of labour and of capital. Thus, rent is not the price of land but the price of service or the use of land; wages, the price of service of labour; interest, the price of the use of capital; and profit, the reward for entrepreneur's services.

1. *Outlines of Political Economy*, p.278.

Functional vs. Personal Distribution

It may be pointed out that the distribution discussed here is **functional and not personal**. It is distribution not among individuals but among agents of production. The same person may represent in his person all the four agents, *e.g.,* a peasant-proprietor. He is the entrepreneur, the labourer, the capitalist (for he has some capital of his own), antl the landlord all rolled in one. Here we do not discuss how much he earns as an individual but the reward that he gets separately for supplying each factor of production. Thus, we study distribution in the form of rent, wages, interest and profits and not among the different individuals in the community.

It may also be understood that the prices of the factors of production are really the prices paid for them by the firms using them in producing a commodity. From the point of view of the firms they are the cost of production. In other words, what is cost to a firm is income to the factors of production. Wages, rent, interest, profit are the functional incomes respectively of the labourer, the landlord, the capitalist and the entrepreneur. The reward that each factor gets is the price paid for his service by the entrepreneur. Thus, from one angle it is income and from the other it is cost.

Role of Factor Prices

Price theory covers both product-pricing and factor-pricing. So far we have studied product-pricing and now we turn to factor-pricing. The factor prices play a key role in the free- enterprise economy. Briefly :

(a) It is through factor prices that employment levels of the various productive resources are determined. That is, how much of a factor of production should be utilised in the process of production. A fall in the price of a factor will lead to increase in its demand and more of it being employed, and vice-versa.

(b) The second important function of the factor prices is to allocate the productive resources among the various alternative uses. They signal the resources from the less important to the more important uses. This sort of discrimination will be simply out of the question in the absence of guide lines furnished by the factor prices.

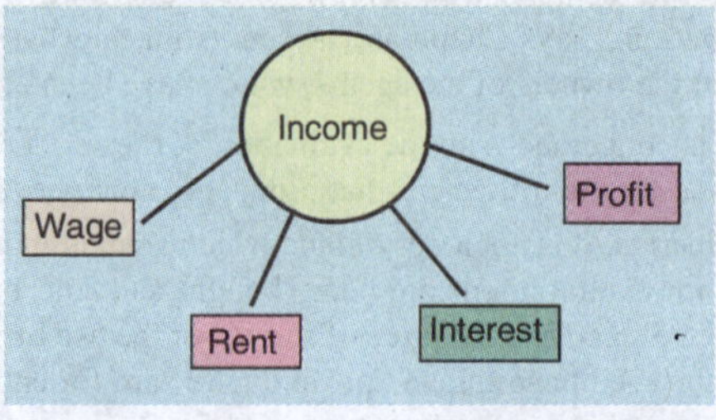

(c) As a corollary from the second function, the factor prices not only guide the individual firms regarding the use of resources, they also bring about the most efficient allocation of the resources of the community. Without pricing of factors, optimum utilisation of factors will not be possible.

(d) Finally, since we all are suppliers of one resource or another, factor-pricing determines the incomes of all of us, *i.e.*, our respective shares in the national output.

MARGINAL PRODUCTIVITY THEORY

Now let us see how the services of factors of production are evaluated. One theory put forward in this connection is the marginal productivity theory. We find references to marginal productivity theory in von Thunen's **Der Isolierte Staat** 91826), Long-field's Lectures on **Political Economy,** and in Henry George's **Progress and Poverty** (1879). But John Bates Clerk's name is most widely associated with its development. In 1880's and 1890's Jevons, Wicksteed, Marshall, Wood, Walras and others made important contribution to its development.

The entrepreneur buys the services of the various factors of production. Since he works for profit, he can only pay a price for a factor which he finds just worthwhile. Obviously, he cannot afford to pay more than its marginal productivity. Since there is open competition, nobody will accept less than marginal productivity. That is how marginal productivity (not total productivity) determines the remuneration or the price of a factor of production.

The entrepreneur, in employing the various factors of production, acts on the principle of substitution. He substitutes one factor for another till the marginal productivities of all the factors he uses are equalised. In this way, he maximises his profit, What is marginal productivity?

Marginal product may be **physical marginal product,** *i.e.*, the increase in output secured by an increase in the use of a factor. If we multiply increase in output by the prevailing price, we get the value of the marginal product or the revenue from the marginal product. This is called **Marginal revenue product,** *i.e.*, the addition to the total revenue resulting from the use of one more unit of a factor of production. We use briefly marginal productivity in place of marginal revenue productivity.

We repeat that by the marginal productivity of a factor of production we mean the addition made to total production by the employment of the marginal unit, *i.e.*, the unit which the employer thinks just worthwhile employing. It may be distinguished from average productivity which is obtained by dividing the total product by the number of factor units employed.

At the margin of employment, the payment made to the factor concerned is just equal to the value of the addition made to the total production on account of the employment of the additional unit of a factor. If, for instance, the prevailing wage is less than the marginal productivity, then more labour will be employed. Competition among employers will raise the wage to the level of marginal productivity. If, on the other hand, the marginal productivity is less than the wage, the employers are losing and they will reduce their demand for labour. As a result, the wage will come down to the level of marginal productivity. In this way, by competition wage tends to equal the marginal productivity. This applies also to the marginal production and their reward.

This is illustrated in the Fig. 31.1 given below.

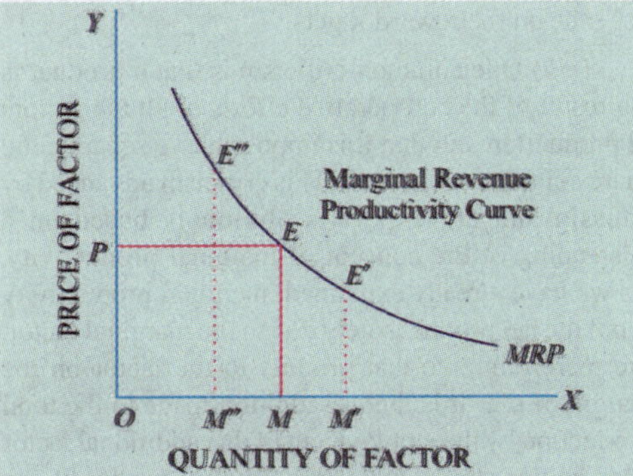

Fig. 31.1. Marginal Revenue Product.

Here, MRP is the marginal productivity curve. It is the demand curve for a factor of production. At the price OP, the quantity of the factor employed is OM, because at this level of employment, marginal productivity equals price. If he employed more, *i.e.* OM′, the marginal productivity E′ M′ will be less than the price he has to pay. He will thus be a loser. And if he employed less, *i.e.*, OM″ the marginal product E′ M″ is more than the price and he will add to his profit by employing more, till at OM when marginal revenue productivity equals price.

Thus, the marginal productivity theory lays great emphasis on the close connection between the price of a factor and the price of the product that it produces. It seems that the factors of production earn that they get. Under perfect competition, a firm will be maximising its profit by equating marginal revenue product of each factor with its price. This indicates the extent to which the use of a factor of production will be pushed in production.

Also, factors of production tend to move from those uses in which their marginal productivity is low to those in which it is high. In this way, a given supply of a factor of production is distributed in such a way that its marginal productivity is equal in all the uses. Thus, we can say that the price of a factor of production is determined by its marginal productivity and this marginal productivity is the same in all its uses.

It also follows that in a competitive market assuming full knowledge of the various alternatives and of the right technology, paying factors of production according to their marginal productivity implies an efficient allocation of the community's productive resources. It gives a least-cost combination of the factors of production in a productive process.

Thus, in a position of competitive equilibrium:

(*i*) the marginal productivity of a factor of production is the same in all its employments, (*ii*) the marginal productivity of a factor of production is measured by the price of the factor of production, and (*iii*) marginal productivities of various factors are proportional to their respective prices.

Hence, over the whole field of employment, therefore, each factor of production tends to be paid in proportion to its marginal productivity.

Thus, the distribution of National Dividend is not a scramble as the strikes or lock-outs make it appear to be. It is governed by a definite economic principle, *viz*., marginal productivity theory.

It should be noted that for any individual employer working under competition, the prices that he has to pay for the factors of production are already determined. Since his demand for the factors of production is only an insignificant proportion of the total demand, his employing more or less of the factors does not appreciably affect their prices. What he does is to push the use of each of the factors to such a point as to make its marginal productivity equal to its price as already determined by the market forces.

Hence, the price of a factor of production is determined by the marginal productivity not of any particular employer but of employers in the aggregate.

Criticism of Marginal Productivity Theory

The theory, explained above, is true only under certain assumptions which make the theory unrealistic and render it inapplicable to actual conditions. It thus fails to explain the actual rewards earned by the factors of production. We give below the various ground on which the marginal productivity theory is criticised :

(*i*) It assumes that all the units of a factor are homogeneous, so that any one unit is as good as any other. This is not actually the case. All labourers are not alike; they are of varying efficiency : nor are all the units of land similar. The capital equipment is also of different types. Thus, we cannot talk of marginal productivity of a factor in general.

(ii) It is assumed that different factors are capable of being substituted for one another, so that, at the margin, it is possible to use a little more land, or a little more labour or capital, *etc.* If this substitution is not possible, marginal productivity of the various factors may remain unequal. Actually, it is not always possible to substitute labour for capital, and **vice versa.** Different factors of production are not close substitutes for one another.

(iii) It is also assumed that the amount of a factor used can be continuously varied, so that it is possible to apply a little more or a little less of the same factor. If this cannot be done, as is sometimes the case, the use of the factor cannot be pushed to the point at which its marginal productivity becomes equal to its price.

(iv) It is assumed that the factors of production are mobile as between various uses. We know that land lacks mobility; nor are labour and capital perfectly mobile. Human package is said to be the least portable. If a factor cannot be moved from one use or employment to another, its marginal productivity in the various employments may remain unequal.

(v) The theory is based on the law of diminishing returns as applied to the organisation of a business. This means that, other things being equal, a disproportionate increase in the supply of one factor increases total production at a diminishing rate. We know, however, that in manufacturing industries, the operation of the law of diminishing returns is held in check.

It is under these assumptions that the reward of each of the four factors of production, *viz*., rent of land, interest on capital, wages of labour and profits of enterprise, tends to equal the value of its marginal net product. These assumptions do not always hold good. The theory has been criticised on other grounds too.

(vi) The marginal productivity theory has been criticised by Keynes thus : One implication of this theory is that if employment is to be increased, wages should be lowered, so that more labour will be employed to make marginal productivity equal to the wage. This argument is fallacious. This may be true in the case of an individual industry or a firm. But it cannot apply to the economy as a whole. The total employment in a country depends on effective or aggregate demand, and not on the level of wages.

(vii) According to marginal productivity theory, marginal productivity determines the reward of a factor of production. In other words, the two are independent. This is not really the case. One affects the other. The marginal productivity or efficiency of a factor also depends on the reward it gets.

(viii) One common criticism is that a product is the result of the co-operative efforts of all the factors of production and that it is impossible to separate the share contributed by each. This criticism advanced by Taussig and Davenport is obviously based on a misreading of the concept of marginal productivity. As we have already explained, marginal productivity is not the net product solely due to the marginal factor. We merely impute that product to the factor on the margin of use. It is the net addition made to the total production by the employment of this additional factor or deduction caused in it if this factor were withdrawn.

(ix) Another attack is made by Hobson. It is held that if any particular factor unit is withdrawn, the whole business will be so disorganized that the loss to production will be much more than the productivity of the unit withdrawn. The criticism is also due to the wrong application of the theory. In this criticism, we are thinking of a small business organisation and large

Skilled labour

Unskilled labour

Labour is not homogeneous.

units of factors. If we conceive of a large business and small units of factors, it will be clear that withdrawing a unit at the margin will not appreciably affect the productivity of other factors.

(*x*) Then there is the view, according to which the sum of the marginal net products of all the factors will be less than the total product, the surplus being due not to any particular factor but to their co-operation. Wicksteed has answered this criticism. He assumes that the increase of all the factors will increase the quantity of the factors will increase the quantity of the product in the same proportion. But this assumption, which implies that the industry obeys the law of constant returns, is not always valid and introduces certain difficulties.

(*xi*) Another serious difficulty, which relates to the measurement of the marginal net product, has been pointed out by Joan Robinson,[2] Pigou and J. R. Hicks. It is argued that when there are economies of large-scale production, the marginal productivity of a unit of a factor to a particular firm will be considerably less than that to the industry as a whole. This is so because, when an additional unit is made available to an industry, it brings about a greater division of labour. But, when the industry has adjusted itself to the new supply, it is quite possible that the marginal productivity of a factor to an individual firm is less than that to the industry as a whole. This is so because its withdrawal will mean a much greater loss to the industry than to an individual firm. In such industries, therefore, marginal productivity of a factor is indeterminate.

(*xii*) Finally, to call marginal productivity theory, a theory of distribution is a misleading statement. At the most it analyses the factors affecting the demand for a factor of production. The supply is taken as fixed. It is objected, however, that in actual practice, the reward enjoyed by a factor does affect its supply. The theory only approaches the problem from the side of demand. It is thus a one-sided explanation.

Conclusion. It should be remembered that the theory is valid only under the assumption of perfect competition. In real life, since competition is not perfect, actual rewards paid to the factors of production do not conform to their relative marginal productivities.

Moreover, this explanation of the determination of the shares of the various factors of production, in a capitalistic economy, should not be regarded as a justification from the ethical point of view, of the system of distribution under such a system. The theory is essentially positive and not normative. It does not say that the reward of a factor according to marginal productivity is a just reward.

2. The Economics of Impetition, p. 327.
3. Economics of Welfare.

As Samuelson remarks, "It (marginal productivity theory) is not a theory that explains wages, rents or interests; on the contrary, it simply explains how factors of production are hired by the firm, once their prices are known."

Commenting on the theory of distribution, Fraser remarks, "No economist would claim that the theory is as yet complete, even as a purely academic structure or framework. It has the defects of its qualities. Being simple and self-consistent it is abstract and impersonal. It is guilty of sins both of omission and commission, its postulates are unduly rigid and narrow."[6]

FIRM'S EQUILIBRIUM IN FACTOR EMPLOYMENT

We have already seen in chapter 19 how a firm achieves equilibrium in regard to a factor combination. A firm will be in equilibrium in this respect when it is combining the various factors of production in such a way that the marginal rate of technical substitution between any two factors is equal to their price ratio. In this way, the producer will be using the most economical combination or the least-cost factor combination. Thus, the firm will be in equilibrium in regard to the employment of factors of production when

$$\frac{MP_a}{P_a} = \frac{MP_b}{P_b} \ldots\ldots = \frac{MP_n}{P_n},$$

This is as regards using the most economical combination of the factors of production.

But here the problem is different. Instead of finding the optimum factor proportion, the firm now wants to find out the **absolute amounts** of the factors of production which it should use or employ in order to be in equilibrium. In this connection, we may say that the various market situations are possible, *viz.*, (*i*) perfect competition in both the factor market and the product market; (*ii*) perfect competition in the factor market but imperfect competition in the product market; (*iii*) monopsony in the factor market but perfect competition in the product market, and (*iv*) monoposony in the factor market and monopoly in the product market.

Since the entrepreneur is supposed to be rational, he will compare revenue and cost of utilizing an extra unit of a factor. If he finds that the marginal revenue (*i.e.* the additional income from the use of an additional unit of a factor) is greater than the cost of hiring it, he will use more of that factor. He will stop employing

4. The Theory of Wages.
5. Economics, p. 198, 526, 528.
6. *Economic Thought and Language*, 1941 p. 354.

extra factor units when the marginal revenue product of the factor is equal to its marginal factor cost (*i.e.* MRP = MFC).

We shall now discuss the employment of a factor of production (*a*) under perfect competition, and (*b*) under imperfect competition.

Equilibrium Under Perfect Competition In The Factor Market

When there is perfect competition, an individual firm cannot influence the price of a factor, by buying more or less of it, because its own demand for the factor constitutes a small fraction of the total demand. Consequently, a firm has to accept the price of a factor, say, labour, prevailing in the market (*i.e.*, wage) as given. Similarly, no individual supplier of a factor supplies an appreciable quantity thereof so as to be able to affect its price in the market. In this case, therefore, marginal factor cost (MFC) and average factor cost (AFC) will tend to be equal and their curves will be the same or they will coincide, and will be a horizontal straight line as in the case of product prices. In the commodity market also, under perfect competition, marginal revenue (MR) and average revenue (AR) are equal and they are represented by horizontal straight line.

The following diagram (Fig. 31.2) represents this state.

MRP is the marginal revenue productivity curve and the same curve represents the value of marginal productivity (VMP), because we assume perfect competition in the product market. PW horizontal straight line represents both marginal factor cost MFC and average factor cost AFC. This firm will obtain maximum profit where marginal revenue productivity (MRP = VMP) is equal to the marginal factor cost (MFC). They are equal at the point E where the two curves intersect. At the point of equilibrium, the firm will employ ON quantity of the factor and pay OP (= EN) as the price or wage. This is the position of maximum profit.

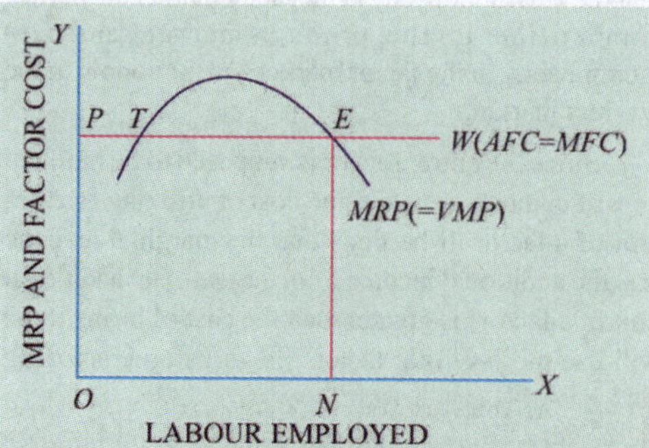

Fig. 31.2. Equilibrium Under Perfect Competition.

In the diagram, it will be seen that these curves intersect also at an earlier point, T. But this cannot be the position of maximum profit, since at this point marginal revenue productivity (MRP) is still rising, whereas the factor cost is the same. Hence the producer will not stop at T; he will continue to employ more labour till he reaches E where MRP is falling. It is thus clear that E is the real point of equilibrium. We can, therefore, lay down a principle that a purely competitive producer maximises short run profits (or minimises losses) only when he employs each productive resource or a factor of production up to the point where the value of its marginal product equals the market price of the factor.

Thus, under perfect competition, since marginal factor cost (MFC) is equal to average factor cost (AFC), at equilibrium marginal revenue productivity (MRP) is equal to marginal factor cost, it is also equal to average factor cost. This means that for a firm to be in equilibrium in a competitive factor market, two conditions must be satisfied, *viz.*

(1) MRP = MFC

(2) MRP curve must cut the MFC curve from above.

From the above diagram (Fig. 31.2), we cannot say whether the firm makes a profit or incurs a loss and if there is profit how much? This we shall be able to know from the following diagram (Fig. 31.3)

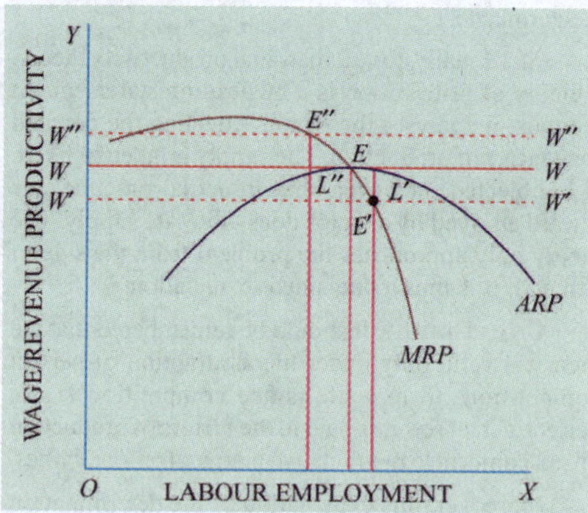

Fig. 31.3. Profit or Loss.

In this diagram ARP is the average revenue productivity curve and MRP is the marginal revenue productivity curve. MRP curve cuts the ARP curve at its highest point E. At the OW′ wage level, the equilibrium will be at E′. Here there is extra profit per unit E′ L′. This is however, a short-run situation.

In the long-run new firms will enter the industry because super-normal profit is being made. When the new firms enter, the demand for labour will increase : hence the wage level will go up to OW, where E is the point of equilibrium. Here supernormal profit has disappeared, because wage is equal to average revenue productivity. If on the other hand, the wage level is OW″, the equilibrium will be at E″. In this case, the wage is higher than the average revenue productivity. Hence, there is loss instead of profit. In the long-run, therefore, some firms will leave the industry; the demand for labour will decrease till the wage-level comes down to OW and the loss will disappear. The equilibrium at E will be restored and the wage will be OW. Here, the wage is equal both to ARP and MRP.

Thus, we conclude that, **under competitive conditions, wages tend in the long run to equal marginal revenue productivity as well as average revenue productivity.**

Equilibrium Under Imperfect Competition in the Factor Market

We have analysed above conditions of equilibrium in a factor market under perfect competition. But we know that in the real world, perfect competition does not prevail. The real world is of imperfect competition. We shall now see how a firm reaches a state of equilibrium under imperfect competition in respect of the quantity of the factor employed and the price paid for it.

We shall take here an extreme case of imperfect competition, *i.e.*, monopsony, in which there is only a sole purchaser of a factor, *i.e.*, a sole employer and no one to compete with him, *i.e.*, there is none else who needs that factor. Unlike under perfect competition, here the employer has control over the price he pays for the factor, say, wage, *i.e.*, he can raise it or lower it as it suits him, for there is no fear of competition from any other employer. If he needs more labour, he will have to pay a higher wage. Hence, the average wage curve AW will rise upward from left to right and the marginal wage curve MW will be above it.

In the diagram (Fig. 31.4). ARP is the average revenue productivity curve and MRP the marginal revenue productivity curve. In this case, the firm will be in equilibrium position where marginal wage (MW) is equal to the marginal revenue productivity (MRP). This is at the point E, because it is here that MW and MRP curves intersect. In this equilibrium position, we see that the average wage OW (= NP) is less than marginal revenue productivity MRP which is EN in this diagram. This Means that the labour gives to the employer more than the wage the employer pays him. In other words, he is exploiting labour. This is known as monopsonistic exploitation. It is natural that, when there is no competition and the employer enjoys a monopoly of purchasing a factor, he must pay as little as possible. Hence, under imperfect competition, labour will usually be exploited at the equilibrium position.

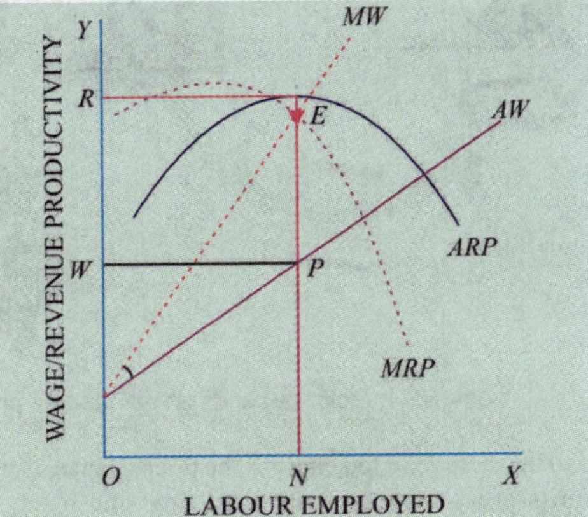

Fig. 31.4. Equilibrium Under Imperfect Competition in the Factor Market.

Conditions of Monopsony

A monopsonistic situation, inter alia, may arise in the following ways :

(i) Units of a factory may become specialised to a particular use. Having become thus specific, they have no use for other purposes. For example, a labour of specialised skill may be developed to meet the requirements of a particular firm and no other firm has any use for it; or a big automobile manufacturer may be the sole purchaser of certain parts. In the film line, certain artists may be bound by agreement to work for a certain produce only and cannot work for any other during the currency of the agreement.

(ii) Monopsony may also arise owing to the immobility of a productive resource. For instance, a certain body of workers may be attached to a certain firm on account of emotional ties or caste considerations. Ignorance or dread of the unknown may keep them tied to a particular place or employer. They may be too poor to seek jobs elsewhere. Seniority, provident fund or pension rights earned already do not permit the employees to leave. There is also geographical immobility.

Under perfect competition, each firm maximises its profits by employing larger and larger quantities of the factor till the marginal revenue product of the factor is equal to the price paid for it. But a monopsonist maximises his profit by employing smaller quantity that would equalise marginal revenue to its price per unit. That is, the marginal product exceeds the price

Demand for factor depends on demand for product.

and the factor cost too exceeds the price. Hence, factor units are paid less than what any one of them contributes to the total receipts of the firm. In other words, the monopsonist restricts the quantity of the factor employed and keeps down the price that he pays. This is how the factor supplies are exploited by a monopsonist.

The Remedies. Is there any remedy to prevent this exploitation? Broadly speaking, two remedies are possible :

(i) The factor suppliers may organise themselves and they or the government may fix minimum prices for the supply of the factor exploited. The firms using these resources must be made to pay these minimum price. The minimum price will not only eliminate exploitation but, if fixed at a reasonable level, may also increase the quantity of the factor used. If it is fixed too high, it will create unemployment of the resource. Fixing a correct price may not be so easy. Hence, collective bargaining on a firm to-firm basis may be more appropriate.

(ii) Measures may be adopted to increase the mobility of the factor. In case of labour, where exploitation is general, steps can be taken to reduce geographical mobility by spreading information, improving transport or by subsidising migration; horizontal mobility may be increased by facilitating transfer from one industry to another and vertical mobility by imparting technical and general education.

MODERN THEORY OF DISTRIBUTION

The marginal productivity theory, which we have discussed above only tells us how many workers will an employer engage at a given wage-level in order to maximise his profit. It does not tell us how that wage-level is determined. We also saw that the marginal productivity theory approaches the problem of the determination of the reward of a factor of production from the side of demand only. It ignores the supply side. Hence, the marginal productivity theory is not an adequate explanation of the determination of the factor prices.

The modern theory of factor price which provides a satisfactory explanation of factor prices is the **Demand and Supply Theory**. Just as the price of a commodity is determined by the demand for, and supply of, a commodity, similarly the price of a productive service also is determined by demand for, and supply of, that particular factor. We shall now analyse these two aspects, *viz.*, demand and supply.

Demand Side

About the factor demand, we should remember two things :

(a) Demand for a factor is not a direct demand but a derived demand and

(b) the demand for it is a jointly interdependent demand.

The demand for a factor of production is not a direct demand; it is an indirect or derived demand. It is derived from the demand for the product that the factor produces. For instance, labour does not satisfy our wants directly. We want labour for the sake of the goods that it produces. The demand for a factor of production is, therefore, ultimately determined by the desires and preferences of the consumers for the final product. It follows, therefore, that if the demand for such goods increases, the demand for the factor, which help to produce these goods will also increase. Also, if the demand for goods is elastic or inelastic, the demand for factor, too will be elastic or inelastic. The higher the price of the commodity produced the higher the price of the productive service used.

No factor of production works alone. It is generally required to work in combination with others. The demand for a factor of production, therefore depends on the quantity and the prices of the other factors required in the process. Generally speaking, the demand price for a given quantity of a factor of production will be higher, the greater the quantities of co-operating productive services. The factors of production are not only complementary to one another, they also some times compete with one another and are, therefore, substitutes for one another. Hence, the price of one factor effect the price of another. Hence, their cross elasticities are as important as their own elasticities.

If more of a factor of production is currently employed, the marginal productivity of the factor will fall and the lower will be the demand price for the unit of the productive service. This is another rule connected with the demand for a factor of production.

The demand price of a factor also depends on the value of the finished product in the production of which the factor is used. The demand price will generally be greater, the more valuable is the finished product in which the factor is used.

Also, the more productive the factor, the higher will be demand price of a given quantity of the factor.

The demand for a productive service also depends upon technological changes. Improvement in technology makes a factor more productive and thus increases its demand.

On the demand side, we have also to consider the elasticity of a factor demand. In this connection, we may note that the elasticity of demand for a factor varies directly with the elasticity of demand for the final product. Also, the demand for a factor will be more inelastic, the smaller the cost of a given factor in the total cost of the final product. But the demand for a factor will be more elastic, the easier it is to substitute some other factor for it.

To Sum Up. The demand for a factor of production depends on (*a*) the demand for the commodity produced, (*b*) the price of the factor concerned, (*c*) the quantity and the prices of the co-operating factors, (*d*) the quantity and the quality of the factor currently employed and (*e*) changes in technology.

These are a few points connected with the demand for a productive service. We know that the demand curve of the industry is the sum-total of the demand curves of the various firms in the industry. By a similar summing up, we can have the demand curve of all the industries using a particular productive service.

The demand of the employer for a factor depends on its marginal revenue productivity (in short marginal productivity) and the quantity of the factor that a firm will employ will depend on the prevailing wage-level. That is, more labour will be employed if wages are low and less if the wages are higher.

Fig. 31.5 (*a*) is the diagram representing the position of a firm regarding the employment of a factor say, labour. When the wage is OW, the firm is in equilibrium at the point E and the demand for the factor is ON; similarly, at OW′ wages the demand is ON′ and at OW″ the demand is ON″. MRP (marginal revenue productive curve) is the demand curve for a factor of production by individual firm.

But for the determination of price it is not the demand of the individual firm that matters. What matters is the total demand, *i.e.*, the sum-total of the demands of all firms in the industry. The total demand curve is derived by the industry. The total demand curve is derived by the lateral summation of the marginal revenue productivity curves of all the firms in the industry. This curve DD is shown in Fig. 31.5 (b). It may be carefully noted that Y-axes in both curves are drawn to the same scale, but X-axes are drawn on different scales.

We have supposed that there are 100 firms in the industry. At OW wage, the demand of the individual firm is ON, but the demand of the whole industry at the same wages is OM which is equal to 100 ON (because the number of firms in the industry is 100). In the same manner, at OW′ the demand of the firm is ON′ but the demand of the entire industry is OM′, which is equal to 100 ON′ and similarly at OW″, the

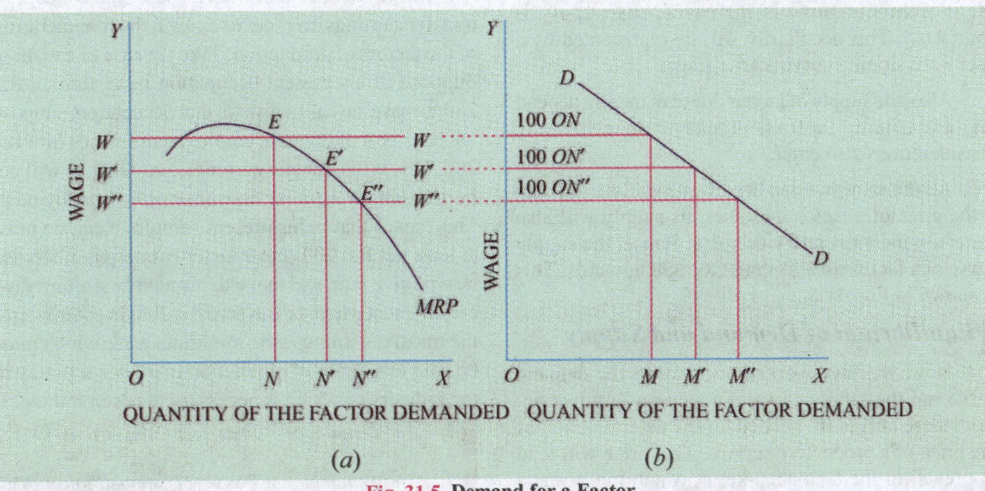

Fig. 31.5. Demand for a Factor.

demand of the firm is ON″ and that of industry OM″, which is equal to 100 ON″.

It can be seen that the demand curve DD also slopes downward to the right. The reason is that MRP curve whose summation is represented by DD also slopes down similarly to the right in the relevant portion. This means that according to the law of diminishing marginal productivity, the more a factor is employed, the lower is the marginal productivity.

Now we turn to the supply side.

Supply Side

The supply curve of a factor of production depends on the various conditions governing its supply. Take the case of labour–a very important productive service. The supply of labour depends on the size and composition and geographical distribution, labour efficiency, cost of education and training, costs of movement, the expected income, relative preference for work and leisure, and so on. In this manner, by for work and leisure, and so on. In this manner, by considering all the relevant factors, it is possible to construct the supply curve of a productive service.

We may, however, add that the supply is a bit complicated affair. We generally say that the supply of land is limited. But the fact is that although for the community as a whole, land is limited, but for a particular firm or an industry, its supply is not limited. The supply can be increased, if higher rent is offered.

In the case of commodities, we see that generally an increase in price brings forth larger supplies. This, however, does not necessarily hold good in the case of the factors of production. It may happen in some cases that if wages go up, labour may be able to satisfy their needs by working for a short time. They may prefer leisure to work. In this case, when the price of a factor (or its remuneration) is increased, the supply is contracted. This peculiarity will be represented by a backward sloping curve after a stage.

Also, the supply of labour does not merely depend on economic factors; many non-economic considerations also enter.

All the same, we can lay down a general rule that if the price of a factor increases, its supply will also generally increase, and vice versa. Hence, the supply curve of a factor rises from left to right upwards. This is shown in Fig. 31.6.

Equilibrium of Demand and Supply

Now, we have worked our way to the demand curve and the supply curve of a factor of production. Both these curves are needed for the determination of the price of a productive service. That price will tend to prevail in the factor market at which the demand and supply are in equilibrium. This equilibrium is at the point of intersection of the demand and supply curves.

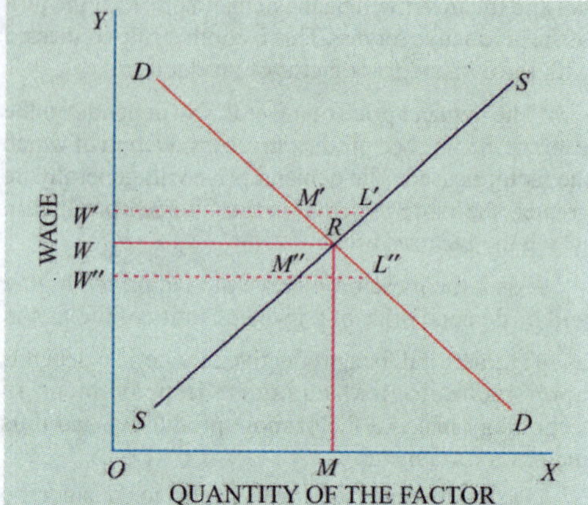

Fig. 31.6. Determination of a Factor Price.

In the diagram 31.6, they intersect at the point R and the price of the factor will be OW (= MR). At OW′ wage demand W′ M′ is less than the supply W′ L′. Hence, the competition among the sellers of the service will tend to bring down the price to OW. On the other hand, at OW″ price, the demand W″ L″ is greater than the supply W″ M″; hence price will tend to go up to OW at which the demand and supply will be equal.

This is how price of a factor of production in the factor market is determined by the interaction of the forces of demand and supply relating to that factor of production. The modern economists consider this theory as a satisfactory theory of distribution.

TRANSFER EARNINGS

Modern economists make use of the concept of transfer earnings, in order to explain the remuneration of the factors of production. Take the case of a worker. Suppose in his present occupation he is earning Rs. 250. In case, he has to give up that occupation, suppose the next best alternative employment fetches him Rs. 200. This is his transfer earnings, *i.e.*, what he will get on transfer to the next best alternative employment. This means that in his present employment, he must at least get Rs. 200 (his transfer earnings), otherwise he will give it up and move to his next best alternative employment where he can earn Rs. 200. In other words, the transfer earning is the minimum price which must be paid to a factor of production to induce it to stay in the industry or which is necessary to retain it there. If

7. *The Economics of Imperfect Competition*, 1945, p 104.
8. *The Economics of Imperfect Competition*, 1945, p. 107.

this price is not forthcoming, the factor unit will transfer itself to its next best alternative use.

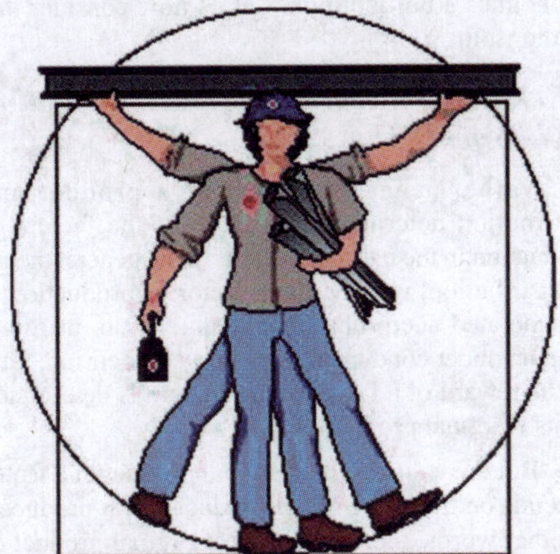

Transfer Earning–Earning in alternative use.

In Benham's words, **"The amount of money which any particular unit could earn in its best paid alternative use is sometimes called its transfer earnings."** To quote Mrs. Robinson, "The price which is necessary to retain a given unit of a factor in a certain industry may be called **its transfer earnings** or **transfer price,** since a reduction of the payment made for it below this price would cause it to be transferred elsewhere; and any particular unit of a factor may be said to be at the margin of transference, or to be a marginal unit, if the earnings, which it receives in the industry, where it is employed, are only just sufficient to prevent it from transferring itself to some other use."

Take the case of land. Suppose, a land used for the cultivation of cotton earns a little more than when it is used for the growing of sugar-cane. If the profit in cotton cultivation falls a little or that in cane cultivation rises a little, the cotton land will be converted into cane land. Thus, fluctuations in prices of different crops may make the cultivation of one crop more profitable than that of another. There will then be a tendency for the land to be transferred from one use to another in search for higher earnings. If an agent is earning more than what it would earn when transferred to the best-paid alternative, the surplus is rent.

As Mrs. Robinson says, "Each individual unit of each factor will be fitted into the place where its earnings will be greatest; when its earnings in that use fall it will retreat to its next most profitable use and, if there is an appreciable difference between its actual earnings and its earnings in the next most profitable use to which it could be put, it will be receiving rent. If each productive unit is like its neighbour, both in respect to their efficiencies in the industry employing them and in respect to their efficiencies in alternative uses, there will be no rent."

The concept of transfer earnings has a great significance in the theory of value. The supply of a factor for a particular industry depends on its transfer earnings. The industry must pay a price for the use of a factor which is at least equal to its transfer earnings. This is how transfer earning affects the supply of a factor which is one of the two factors affecting the price of a factor. In this way, the concept of transfer earnings has an intimate bearing on factor pricing.

EQUITY IN INCOME DISTRIBUTION

We have studied above the general theory of income distribution. Two questions arise : (*a*) Is the distribution equitable, fair and just? (*b*) Why is there inequality of incomes? The first question is ethical and involves value judgment and does not admit of any objective measurement. Also, no two opinions agree on the criterion of fairness or justice. It is futile, therefore, for economic theory to attempt to answer this question.

As for inequalities of income, they arise from two basic sources : (*a*) Differences in quality and quantity of resources owned by individuals and (*b*) differences in prices paid for the use of the productive resources.

The various causes responsible for the inequalities of income may be spelt out below :

(i) So far as differences in labour earnings are concerned, horizontal differences are due to differences in demand and supply conditions for a particular type of labour. Quantitative differences in the amount of work done and qualitative differences in the abilities and skills of the workers account for differences in earnings; vertical immobility also gives rise to differences in earnings of certain professions. Vertical mobility depends on the opportunities for training and for going up and it is also accounted for differences in social inheritance.

(ii) Differences in earnings also arise from differences in ownership of capital, *e.g.*, business assets, land factories and property of all kinds. This may, in turn, be due to inequalities of inheritance or gifts received, qualities of thrift and saving propensity and opportunities for investment or windfalls, chance or luck.

(iii) Differences in income may also arise from interference with the price mechanism. The owners of resources may manipulate the prices of the resources they own and the producers, the price of their products, *e.g.*, farmers getting high procurement prices fixed up, cane-growers getting minimum price of sugar-cane. In an aera of price control, all manufacturers endeavour

Training accounts for higher earning.

to get minimum prices fixed for their products. How far the owners of resources are able to raise their distributive share will depend upon the elasticity of demand for the factor concerned. By restricting the resource supplies, the resource prices, and hence their income, can be raised. The existence of a monopoly or monopsony result in the manipulation of factor incomes.

Remedies

There are two broad remedies :

(*a*) Via Administered Prices. Prices may be fixed or manipulated in favour of the proper sections of society.

(*b*) Via resources Redistribution. Labour resources can be redistributed by increasing vertical mobility, by providing greater equality in educational and training opportunities, greater economic opportunities by reducing inequalities of capital ownership and breaking down barriers to entry into higher jobs and professions. Appropriate fiscal and taxation measures can be adopted not only to reduce economic inequalities directly by heavy taxation of the top classes but also to provide greater equality in capital accumulation and holdings of capital resources. Provision of more comprehensive social security and social welfare programmes will have the same effect.

Relation between Production, Value and Distribution Theories

According to the traditional division of Economics into different parts, value, production and distribution are considered its principal parts, but there exists an intimate relation between them so as to give Economics a unified look. Let us now consider this relationship.

Relation Between Value and Distribution Theories

Value means the price of a product and distribution determines the share of the factors of production in the national output. In the general theory of distribution, we say that a factor of production is remunerated according to the value of its marginal product under conditions of perfect competition. That is, the reward of a factor of production is determined by its marginal productivity.

But the value of the marginal product of a factor depends on the value of the product that it produces. In other words, the value of the marginal product of the factor is equal to the marginal physical product of the factor multiplied by the price of the product that it helps to produce. Obviously, higher the price of the product, the higher will be the value of the marginal product of the factor that produces it, and hence, greater will be its reward or the income. In case the value of the product goes up, the demand for the factor required to produce that product will rise and as a result the price or the income of the factor will go up. In this way, the demand for the factor is derived from the demand for the product.

Thus, the value of the products and the distribution of the income of the factors of production are very closely related to each other.

Relation Between Production and Distribution Theories

We have seen above how value and distribution (that is the share of the factors of production in national income) are intimately related to each other. Let us now see how production is related to distribution. Theory of distribution, as we have said above, determines the share that goes to a factor of production out of the national output. It can be easily seen that the greater the share of a factor of production, the better will be his standard of living and greater his efficiency in production. The more efficient the factors of production, the higher will be the national income. In this way, the character of distribution in a country

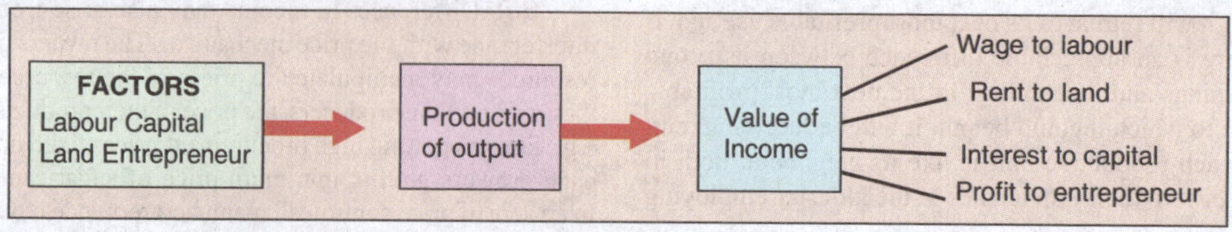

determines its productive efficiency, which in turn determines the level of output in the country.

Thus, we find that the theories of production and distribution are very closely related to each other.

We have already explained in Chapter 17 how a production function can be expressed. The formula is X = F (a, b, c, d, *etc*. . . .). Here X is the output of a commodity and a, b, c, d, *etc*. are the various productive resources whic go into the making of the commodity and F means the function of *i.e.* it varies with. From this equation, it is clear that production varies with the quantities of the various factors of production used. We do not merely consider their number but also when we employ the factors of production on their efficiency which depends on whether distribution of the national dividends is fair or uneven.

Marginal product of factors of production, say labour and capital, plays a vital role in the theory of distribution (*i.e.* marginal productivity theory). According to this theory, wages are equal to the marginal product of labour and interest equal to the marginal product of capital. The equality of factor rewards with their marginal productivities is based upon the assumption that the entrepreneurs aim at maximizing their profits. They combine labour and capital in a proportion which is most advantageous to them. The most advantageous combination will be where the marginal productivities of each factor are equalized. It is said that the forces are constantly at work which bring about an equality between the remuneration of the factors of production and their marginal productivities. This clearly brings out a synthesis between production theory and distribution theory.

Diminishing marginal return, which is a special feature of production function, has great relevance for the theory of distribution. We know that the entrepreneur continues to employ labour or capital till its marginal product comes down to the level of wage or interest. Had the marginal product increased or remained constant instead of diminishing the equality between the factor rewards and the marginal product could not have been achieved and the theory of distribution would have been nowhere.

The possibility of substitution between the factors, of production is another feature of production function which has a bearing on the theory of distribution. If it were not possible to substitute one factor for another and if the factors were to be used in rigidly fixed proportions, their marginal productivities would have been zero, and zero marginal productivity does not furnish any basis for the.theory of distribution. It is only the possibility of substitution between factors which makes it possible to build a theory of distribution based on the concept of marginal productivity.

It was Prof. Hicks who introduced the concept of elasticity of substitution between factors and pointed out its importance for determining the distributive shares of the various factors of production. If there were a change in the ratio of the prices of factors of production, the cheaper factor would be substituted for the factor whose price is relatively higher. If for instance, wages rise relatively to interest, the entrepreneur will substitute capital for labour. This would naturally reduce the distributive share of labour and raise that of capital.

It may also be pointed out that the possibility of substitution between the factors discourages unions from unduly pressing for higher wages. Any unreasonable behaviour on the part of unions will simply compel the enterpreneur to substitute capital for labour. The result would be that volume of employment will diminish and the labour itself would suffer.

Thus, we find that there is a very intimate relation not only between the theories of distribution and production but also of between value and distribution.

Product Exhaustion Problem or Adding-Up Problem

The marginal productivity theory of distribution states that each factor of production is paid remuneration equal to its marginal product. It has been urged out that if that were so, the total product would be just exhausted without leaving any surplus or deficit. This problem is called the adding-up problem.

The following figures numbering 31.7 and 31.8 illustrate the product exhaustion problem.

We assume that there are only two factors, labour and capital, used in production. Let A stand for Labour and B for Capital. The marginal product of a factor can be found by varying its quantity and keeping the other factor constant. The reward of a variable factor is equal to its marginal product when a certain quantity of it is used. Then the reward for the fixed factor can be shown as surplus (or residual income) of the total product over the marginally determined reward of the variable factor. In figure 31.7, labour (*i.e.* A has been treated as a variable factor and is shown on the X–axis whereas capital has been taken as a fixed factor. When OL is the equilibrium amount of the labour employed, its marginal product is LM and the wage rate determined is OW. The total wage bill is OLMW. The total product is the whole area under the marginal productivity curve *i.e.* OSML. After paying the total wage bill *i.e.* OLMW, the residual income SWM will go to capital as interest. In this way, when we have

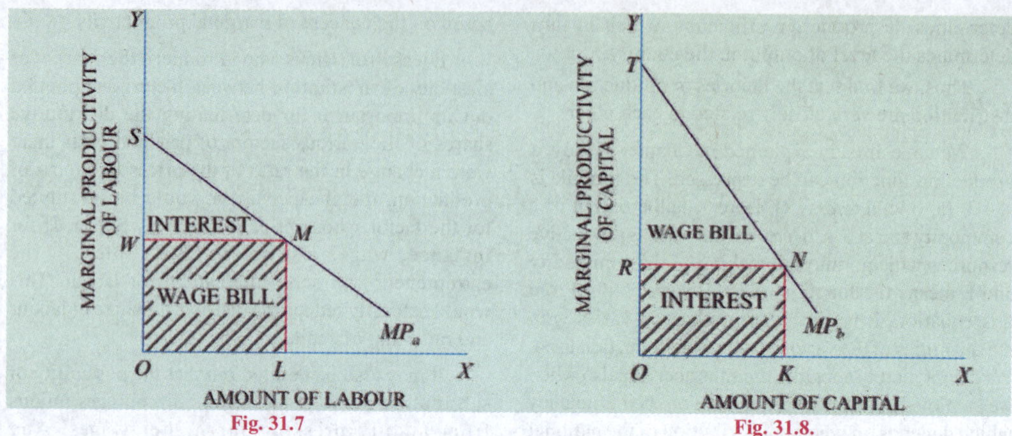

Fig. 31.7

Fig. 31.8.

paid the total wage bill OLMW and interest SWM, nothing is left, *i.e.* the total product is exhausted.

In order to show that the total product is exhausted, we may now take capital as the fixed factor and labour as the variable factor. This has been shown in figure 31.8. In this figure, capital gets ORNK as the marginally determined interest out of the total product OTNK. Labour receives the residue in the form of the wage bill *i.e.* RTN. Here, again the total product is just exhausted by the rewards paid to labour and capital, leaving no surplus or deficit.

We have now to prove that the area OKNR in Figure 31.8 is equal to the area WMS in figure 31.7 and area RNT in figure 31.8 is equal to OLMW in figure 31.7. Only in this way we can show that the payments made in accordance with marginal productivity to both labour and capital exactly exhaust the total product. We can thus show that the marginally determined reward of a factor is equal to the income of the factor determined as residual. In this way, we can illustrate the problem of product exhaustion. But illustration is not a proof.

Professor Wicksteed was one of the first economists who posed this problem of product exhaustion and also furnished a solution. This he did by applying a mathematical proposition known as the Eular's Theoren. He proved that the total product will be just exhausted if all the factors of production are paid according to their marginal product. Wicksteed's solution was criticised by economists like Walras, Edgeworth and Pareto. These writers say that production function is not homogeneous of the first degree, *i.e.*, returns to scales are not constant the actual world.

The critics have pointed out that production function is such that it yields a U-shaped long-run average cost curve. This implies that increasing returns to scale occur upto a point and then there are diminishing returns to scale. If a firm is operating under increasing returns to scale, then payment to factors of production according to their marginal product would make the total factor rewards greater than the total product. If, on the other hand, the firm is working under diminishing returns to scale and all factors are paid equal to their marginal product, the total factor rewards would not fully exhaust the total product and there will be a surplus. It is pointed out, therefore, that Eular's Theorem does not apply and the adding-up problem does not hold good either when there are increasing returns to scale or decreasing returns to scale.

It is also pointed out as a defect in Wicksteed's solution that when there is a constant return to scale, the long-run average cost curve of the firm is a horizontal straight line which is incompatible with the perfect competition. But competition is essential to the marginal productivity theory and so to Wicksteed's solution.

Economists like Wicksell and Walras advanced more satisfactory solution after Wicksteed to the problem that marginally determined rewards would just exhaust the total product. They pointed out that in the long-run, under perfect competition, the firm is in equilibrium and the minimum point of the long-run average cost curve is where the returns to scale are momentarily constant *i.e.*, constant within the range of a small variation of output. Thus, it was pointed out that the condition required for the marginally determined rewards to exhaust the total product (*i.e.*, the operation of constant return to scale) was fulfilled at the minimum point of the long-run average cost curve, where a firm operating under perfect competition is in long-run equilibrium. Hence, in the case of perfectly long-run equilibrium, the marginally determined rewards of the factors would exactly exhaust the total product.

From the above discussion, two solutions of the problems of product exhaustion, emerge : (*a*) Wicksteed's solution which assumes the operation of the constant return to scale and (*b*) the solution by Wicksell and Walras which assumes that the firms operated at the lowest point of the long-run average cost curve.

IMPACT OF TECHNOLOGICAL PROGRESS ON RELATIVE FACTOR SHARES

Recent technical advance in agriculture, industry, trade and transport has raised the question of its effect on the relative remuneration of the factors of production, in particular of labour and capital. Technological progress implies the introduction of innovations *i.e.* new processes, new products or more economical methods of production.

The analysis of relative factor shares requires a detailed examination of the nature of technical progress as well as the underlying production function. In this analysis two basic concepts are involved *viz.*, the elasticity of substitution and the linear homogeneous production function.

Elasticity of substitution (a concept developed by J. R. Hicks in his book 'Theory of Wages') is measured by the ratio of the proportional change in a factor combination to a proportional change in the marginal rate of substitution between factors represented by the ratio of the marginal products of the two factors. If the production functions are of Cobb-Douglas type (*i.e.* the unitary substitution elasticity) the relative shares of the factors will remain constant. If elasticity of substitution between labour and capital is less than one, the share of labour will go up relatively to the share of capital, and if it is greater than one opposite will be the result.

Now, take the linear homogeneous production function called the Cobb-Douglas production function. This production function represents constant returns to scale.

Key terms

Marginal Revenue Product, Average Revenue Product, Marginal Factor Cost, Average Factor Cost, Marginal Value Product, Transfer Earning, Product Exhaustion.

QUESTIONS

1. Explain the term 'National Divident'. Briefly discuss the principle which governs its distribution among various agents of production.
2. How does pricing of factors of production differ from pricing of commodities? What is the significance of marginal productivity approach in the theory of factor pricing?

   Or

   "The theory of factor pricing is only an extension of he general price theory". Discuss.
3. Discuss fully the meaning of marginal productivity of a factor of production. How is price of a factor related to its productivity under conditions of perfect competition and imperfect competition.
4. "When each factor is paid according to its marginal product, the total product i s exhausted". Critically examine.
5. Why is productivity important in determining the factor prices? Why is the marginal productivity and not the average productivity that concerns the economists?
6. Distinguish between marginal revenue product and marginal value product of a factor of production. Under what conditions will the price of a factor be equal to its marginal value product?
7. Explain the concept of 'marginal revenue product'. What role does it ply in the determination of the price of a factor?
8. What do you understand by the equilibrium of the firm in the factor market? What are the conditions of this equilibrium (*a*) under perfect competition and (*b*) under imperfect competition?
9. Discuss the Marginal Productivity Theory of Distribution. Does it provide a satisfactory explanation of the determination of the reward of a factor of production?
10. Explain the marginal productivity theory of distribution and compare it with the modern theory of distribution.
11. Explain what do you understand by 'transfer Earnings'. Indicate its significance in the theory of factor pricing.

WAGES

Having studied the general theory of distribution, we are now in a position to take up the study of the determination of the share of the factors of production separately. We shall first take up wages followed by rent, interest and profit.

Meaning of Wages

The term 'wages' means payments made for the services of labour. "A wage may be defined," says Benham, "As a sum of money paid under contract by an employer to a worker for services rendered." A wage payment is essentially a price paid for a particular commodity, *viz.*, labour services.

Is Labour a Commodity?

We have said that wage is the price of labour as if labour is a commodity. There is no doubt that labour has peculiarities of its own which differentiate it from other commodities (see next page) and labour protests against its being described as a commodity, yet it is true that from the aspect with which the economist is concerned, labour is regarded as a commodity. Like a commodity it is bought and sold. Labour participates in an exchange relationship, *i.e.*, the worker gives his time or labour and, in exchange, gets money including some fringe benefits, if any.

Nominal Wages vs. Real Wages

According to the classical wage theory, labour supply was considered a function of real wages, But according to Keynes, the workers acted irrationally and generally bargained for money wages and they sharply reacted against any cut in money wages. That is, a rise in prices does not offend labour so much as a cut in the money wage. The money wage has also been called nominal wage.

Money Wage.

The distinction between nominal wages and real wages may be clearly understood. Nominal wages are wages paid or received in terms of money. But money wages alone may not give us a correct idea of what a worker **really** earns from his work. In order to ascertain real wages, which determine the standard of living of a person, the following factors have to be taken into consideration :

(*a*) Purchasing Power of Money. When comparing wages at different places and at different times the changes in the purchasing power of money must be taken into account. The purchasing power of money varies inversely with price level, *i.e.*, higher the price, the lower the purchasing power of money, and vice versa. A part of the high wages in England and America may be due to higher prices prevailing in those countries. Three hundred rupees in a village in India may provide a much more comfortable life than a similar amount in a town or vice-versa, according to circumstances and tastes of the person concerned. One hundred rupees in 1950 had much greater purchasing power than in 1976. Even an increase of money wages thus leaves real wages at a lower level in 1976 as compared with 1950.

It is generally supposed that the prices rise faster than money wages during the times of rising prices and fall faster than money wages during the periods of falling prices. The result is that money wages decline in the former and rise in the latter case.

(*b*) Subsidiary Earnings. In addition to the regular money wage, an employee has extra earnings in the form of money or goods. For example, free board and lodging are provided to the domestic servants and may in some cases be given to peons. Professors earn additional income by marking examination papers or from tuition fees, and so on. Subsidiary earnings may also arise from opportunities of employment available to other members of the worker's family.

(*c*) Extra Work Without Extra Payment. If an employee is required to do extra work without any compensation, his real wages are less by that extent. Peons are paid for doing their duty during working hours, but quite often they are required to work late. For such extra work they are paid nothing. This means that their real earnings are reduced to that extent.

(*d*) Regularity or Irregularity of Employment. Regular or more secure employments may give lower money wages, but the real wages may be higher than irregular and insecure employments which give high money wages. For instance, a person with Rs. 10 daily wage but whose employment is intermittent, may not be so well off as another, who earns regularly Rs. 5 a day. Hence, it is good to distinguish between wage rates and earnings.

(*e*) Conditions of Work. Some occupations are healthier than others, and in some, the hours of work are shorter than in others; the work may be more pleasant or less pleasant; the employer may be more sympathetic or less, and so on. All these things should be taken into account in estimating a person's real earnings.

(*f*) Future Prospects. A low money income will be considered a high real wage if there are good prospects of a rise in the future. On the other hand, a high initial salary may not be considered as good in the absence of prospects for a further rise.

Why a Separate Theory of Wages?

It is demand and supply relationship or scarcity in relation to demand, which explains all values whether values of commodities or values of services of the factors of production. Why should we then have a separate theory of wages?

The ordinary theory of prices, *i.e.*, demand and supply theory, is not fully applicable to the determination of wages for the following reasons :

(*i*) The demand for goods depends on their utility to the purchaser, whereas the demand for labour services depends on their productivity (and not utility) to the employer. Hence, demand for the labour needs a special treatment.

(*ii*) The human element in the labour market deserves special consideration. The labourer and the labour services are inseparably tied up; hence the importance of the human element.

(*iii*) The peculiar institutional and behavioural factors affect bargains in the labour market. For instance, in the rural areas of backward economies, wages are fixed by custom instead of competition.

(*iv*) Certain peculiarities of labour, which distinguish it from a commodity, also necessitate a separate theory of wages. These peculiarities are :

(*a*) Labour has weak bargaining power as against the powerful employer. Hence, the actual wage is less than what a worker may be entitled to by his productivity.

(*b*) Labour is most perishable. Hence, the worker has to accept a lower wage than to what he may be entitled. He has no staying power and must accept what is offered.

(*c*) The changes in the price of labour react rather curiously on its supply. It amy be that when wages have gone up, the supply of labour may decrease instead of increasing, unlike what happens in the case of a commodity. The worker may prefer leisure to work. That is why supply of labour may be a backward bending curve.

(*d*) Another peculiarity is that the supply of labour cannot rapidly adjust itself to the changes in demand. It takes a generation to increase the supply of labour. When, therefore, demand increases, wages must go up. Nor can the supply of labour be decreased when there is unemployment.

Conclusion. In view of the above peculiarities of labour, it becomes necessary to formulate a separate theory of wages. All the same, it is well to remember that wages being a price (of labour services), the fundamental principle of pricing, *i.e.*, the interaction of the forces of demand and supply, applies to the wage determination also. The various theories of wages only differ in the assumptions regarding the basic conditions of demand and supply.

OLD THEORIES OF WAGES

Subsistence Theory[1]

Several theories have been put forward to explain the general level of wages prevalent in a country. Take first the Subsistence Theory. This theory originated with the Physiocratic School of the French economists and was developed by Adam Smith and the later economists of the classical school. The German economist Lassalle called it the Iron Law of Wages or the Brazen Law of Wages. Karl Marx made it the basis of his theory of exploitation.

According to this theory, wages tend to settle at the level just sufficient to maintain the worker and his family at the minimum subsistence level. If wages rise above the subsistence level, the workers are encouraged to marry and to have large families. The large supply of labour brings wages down to the subsistence level. If wages fall below this level, marriages and births are discouraged and undernourishment increases the death-rate. Ultimately, labour supply is decreased, until wages rise again to the subsistence level. It is supposed that the supply of labour is infinitely elastic. That is, its supply would increase if the price (*i.e.*, wage) offered rises.

Criticism. In backward countries, wages no doubt are to be found at or near the subsistence level. But the theory does not apply to advanced countries like England and America. The theory evidently is based on the Malthusian Theory of Population. But it is wrong to say that every increase in wages must inevitably be followed by an increase in birth rate. An increase in wages may be followed by a higher standard of living which in turn influences the wage level.

Ricardo, one of the exponents of the theory, stressed the influence of custom and habit in determining what was 'necessary' for the workers. But habits and customs change over time. Hence, the theory can hold good for only a limited period of time and cannot be true of all times, especially of a world characterised by fast changing habits. Ricardo, therefore, admitted that wages might rise above the subsistence level 'for an indefinite period in an improving society.'

Another criticism of the theory is that the subsistence level is more or less uniform for all working classes with certain exceptions. The theory, thus, does not explain differences of wages in different employments.

Further, it may be said that the theory explains wages only with reference to supply; the demand side is entirely ignored. On the demand side, the employer has to consider the amount of work which the employee give him and not the subsistence of the employee.

Moreover, the fundamental weakness of the subsistence theory lies in its long-term character. It explains the adjustment of wages over the lifetime of a generation and does not explain wage fluctuations from year to year. As such it has little practical value.

Finally, the 'subsistence minimum' is a very vague term. Does it refer to the minimum requirements of a modern man or of a tribal savage? There is no rigidly fixed minimum and it is not independent of the wages ruling over a period of time.

Wages Fund Theory[2].

This theory is associated with the name of J.S. Mill. "Wages." wrote Mill, 'depend upon the demand and supply of about, or, as it is often expressed, on the proportion between population and capital. By population is here meant the number only of the labouring classes or rather of those who work for hire, and by capital, only circulating capital and not even the whole of that but the part which is expanded on the direct purchase of labour." Mill asserted : "Wages not only depend upon the relative amount of capital and population, but cannot, under the rule of competition, be affected by anything else."

According to this theory, therefore, wages depended upon two quantities, *viz*., (*i*) the wage fund or the circulating capital set aside for the purchase of labour and (*ii*) the number of labourers seeking employment. Hence, the level of wages can be ascertained by means of a simple arithmetical operation : by dividing the wages fund by the number of workers. In other words, wages vary directly as the quantity of capital and inversely as the number of workers.

Wages, thus, cannot rise unless either the wage fund increases or the number of workers decreases.

1. See Dobb, M. — *Wages*, 1932, Ch. IV, Sec. 3, p. 100.

2. *Ibid*. Ch. IV. Sec. 6. See also *Marshall's Principles*. Appendix (a).

But since the theory takes the wage fund as fixed wages could rise only by a reduction in the number of workers.

It would appear, therefore, that according to this theory, the efforts of trade unions to raise wages are futile. If they succeeded in raising wages in one trade, it can only be at the expense of another, since the wage fund is fixed and the trade unions have no control over population. According to this theory therefore, trade unions cannot raise wages for the labour class as a whole.

Criticism. In contrast to the subsistence theory, which represented a rigid view and attempted to provide deterministic long-term or static theory, the wages fund theory tried to explain movement of wages in a changing world.' Instead of a single equilibrium to which wages must inevitably return, determined by 'cost of production of labour,' the wages fund theory provided a varying 'natural rate,' determined by varying ratio of capital to population.

The theory has been widely criticized and stands rejected now. Mill himself recanted it in the second edition of his **"Principles of Political Economy."**

Mill thought that wages were paid out of circulating capital alone. Whether the source of wages is capital or the present products, has been the subject of a keen controversy in the past. The fact is that in some cases, where the process of production is short (*e.g.*, final stages of the productive process, wages are paid out of the present production. On the other hand, when a process of production is long, the labourer obviously does not obtain wages from the product of his labour either directly or through exchange. In such cases, wages mainly come out of capital.

Mill argued that wages were paid out of a certain fixed proportion of capital set aside for this purpose. This also is not true. There is no fixed wages fund in this sense. The fund, if we can at all call it so, is elastic. Its volume changes according to the prospects of profits. The productivity of labour at a given time is an important factor in determining these prospects.

Further, the theory is a mere truism. It does not tell us about the sources of the wages fund and the method by which it is estimated. It simply tells us what is self-evident, namely, that the wage can be ascertained by dividing the wages fund by the number of workers.

Again, the theory assumes a degree of antagonism between labour and capital that does not actually exist. According to this theory, wages can increase only at the expense of profits. But this is not necessarily so. In times of business prosperity, both wages and profits can go up.

It is also wrong to assume that the forcing up of the wages will drive capital abroad. Capital is not so sensitive, not are the profits so inelastic. The theory fails to show why wages cannot be increased at the expense of rent and profit.

We cannot accept its corollary that the trade unions are powerless to increase wages and that any measures which hindered the accumulation of capital, *e.g.*, heavy taxation, were bound to lower wages by reducing the wages fund. The theory is too unsympathetic to labour when it says that "the only hope of improvement for the workers lay in limiting the size of their own families and helping to increase the prosperity of their masters" (Dobb).

It is difficult to subscribe to the implication of the theory, *viz.*, that if any section of labour wrested a higher wage, it will be at the expense of other workers who must receive less or face unemployment. It also looks absurd that low wages paid to a certain section of workers would benefit others for it left larger wages fund available for them.

The theory ignores the principle of Economy of High-Wages. We know that a rise in wages would improve labour efficiency and increase the demand for labour to satisfy which the employers would set aside a larger fund for the purchase of labour. That is why the economists regard capital not as a fund but a flow.

Moreover, the wages fund theory does not explain why wages differ in different occupations. Besides, the wage rates prevalent in different countries donot correspond to the total amount of capital available there. In new countries capital is scarce but the wages are high; the opposite is the case in the old countries.

Conclusion. In spite of the above criticism, it may be stated that the theory contains an element of truth. It may not apply to a highly industrialised country, but, in an under-developed country suffering from capital deficiency, wages cannot be increased unless national income is increased and capital accumulated through industrialisation.

Residual Claimant Theory

The Residual Claimant Theory has been advanced by the American economist, Walker. According to him, wage are the residue left over, after the other factors of production have been paid. Walker says that rent and interest are governed by contracts but profit is determined by definite principles. There are no similar principles, says the theory, operating as regards wages. According to this theory, after rent, interest and profit have been paid, the remainder of the total output goes to the workers as wages.

The theory admits the possibility of increase in wages through greater efficiency of labour. In this sense, it is an optimistic theory, whereas the subsistence theory and the wages fund theory are pessimistic.

Criticism. This theory also has been rejected by most economists. It has several defects. In the first place, it does not explain how trade unions are able to raise wages. Secondly, it ignores the influence of supply of labour on wages. Thirdly, one fails to understand why the same laws of supply and demand, that explain the remuneration of other factors of production cannot be applied to wages as well. Finally, it is not the worker who is the residual claimant but the entrepreneur, who undertakes to pay the other factors of production before he can expect to get anything.

Marginal Productivity Theory of Wages

Towards the end of the nineteenth century, the economists abandoned the Wage-Fund doctrine. Economists like Marshall treated demand for labour as derived from the demand for the products of labour and not from a pre-determined decision of the employers regarding the amount of capital they proposed to utilise in the purchase of labour. This view is represented by the marginal productivity theory.

While discussing the general theory of distribution (Chapter 31), we have given a detailed account of the marginal productivity theory and its criticism. There we explained the theory states that, under conditions of perfect competition, every worker of same skill and efficiency in a given category will receive a wage equal to the value of the marginal product of that type of labour.

We may repeat that the marginal product of labour in any industry is the amount by which the output would be increased if a unit of labour was increased, while the quantities of other factors of production employed in the industry remained constant. In short, it is the output attributable to a single unit of labour unaccompanied by any change in other factors of production. The value of the marginal product of labour is the price at which the marginal product can be sold in the market.

Under conditions of perfect competition, an employer will go on employing workers until the value of the product of the last worker he employs is equal to the marginal or additional cost of employing the last worker. Further, the condition of perfect competition implies that the marginal cost of labour is always equal to the wage rate, irrespective of the number of workers the employer may engage. Every industry being ultimately subject to the law of diminishing returns, this marginal product must start declining sooner or later. Wages remaining constant, the employer stops employing workers at that point where value of the marginal product of a worker is equal to the wage rate.

So far we have assumed that the quantities of other factors remain constant while that of labour alone increases. This, however, is not true because quantities of factors increase all round though this may not be true in the short-run. To allow for this fact, the economists make use of the term "marginal net product of labour" instead of "marginal product of labour." The value of a marginal net product of labour may be defined as being the value of the amount by which output would be increased by employing one more worker with the appropriate addition of other factors of production, less the addition to the cost of the other factors caused by increasing the quantities of other factors.

The theory may thus finally be re-stated as follows : Under conditions of perfect competition in the labour market and in the market for the products of the industry, and irrespective of the number employed, every worker will receive a wage equal to the value of marginal net product of his labour.

Limitations of the Marginal Productivity Theory. We have already studied in detail the various limitations and criticisms of the Marginal Productivity Theory as a general principle of distribution.[3] With reference to its application to wages, we may repeat that the theory is true only under certain assumptions such as perfect competition perfect mobility of labour from employment to employment, homogeneous character of all labour, constant rates of interest and rent and given prices of the product.

It is a static theory. The actual world is dynamic. All the factors assumed to be constant are in fact constantly changing. Competition is never perfect; mobility of labour is restricted for various reasons; all labour is not of the same grade; remuneration to other factors of production doesn't remain constant; and the prices of the products of labour vary. All these changes modify the theory when applied to actual conditions. The theory, however, as an assertion of a tendency, is true and is valuable in understanding the basic forces that determine wage rates.

In the real world, owing to the absence of the above assumptions, there is no single rate of wages that may be applicable to all labour of a particular type. Wages differ from place to place, from person to person and from employment to employment.

The following further points of criticism may now be noted :

Firstly, the theory has little applicability to reality. Labour is not perfectly mobile. Workers of the same skill and efficiency may not receive the same wages at two different places.

3. See Chapter 31.

Secondly, though the condition of a large number of independent buyers of labour is fulfilled for a few industries of all countries and for most industries of some countries, the employers usually combine to the disadvantage of the worker. It is a case of monopsony, *i.e.*, one buyer and many sellers. The employers succeed in pulling down the wages below the value of the marginal net product of labour. If employees are also collectively organised, the wage rates may or may not be equal to the values of marginal net product of labour in the occupations or industries concerned. The wages are determined by the relative bargaining strength of the two parties, but cannot exceed the value of the marginal net product of labour.

Thirdly, the market for goods is in general characterised by imperfect competition, this also unsettles the theory.

Fourthly, the productivity of workers is also dependent on factors such as the quality of capital and efficient management. These factors are outside the control of workers.

Fifthly, it should be borne in mind that the marginal net product of labour depends not merely on the supply of labour but also on the supply of all other factors of production. If other factors are plentiful and labour relatively scarce, the marginal net product of labour will be high, and vice-versa.

Finally, productivity is also a function of wages. Low productivity may be the cause of low wages, which may tell on the efficiency of the worker, lower his standard of living and ultimately check the supply of labour. The theory takes the supply of labour for granted.

Conclusion. In short, the marginal productivity theory ignores the effect of wage changes on the supply of labour, bargaining strength and monopoly conditions, *etc.*

Rejecting the marginal productivity theory, Marshall said: "This doctrine has been put forward as a theory of wages. But there is no valid ground for any such pretension . . . Demand and supply exert equally important influences on wages; neither has a claim to predominance; any more than has either blade of a scissors, or either pier of an arch . . . . (but) the doctrine throws into clear light one of the causes that governs wages."[4]

Taussig's Theory of Wages[5]

The American economist Taussig gives a modified version of the Marginal Productivity Theory of Wages. According to him, wages represent the **marginal discounted product** of labour.

Taussig thinks that the labourer cannot get the full amount of the marginal output. This is because production takes time and the final product of labour cannot be obtained immediately. But the labourers have to be supported in the meantime. This is done by the capitalist employer. The employer does not pay the full amount of the expected marginal product of labour. He deducts a certain percentage from the final output in order to compensate himself for the risk he takes in making an advance payment. This deduction, according to Taussig, is made at the current rate of interest.

Thus, wages equal the total product of labour on the marginal land or in the marginal firm minus the amount discounted explained above. The present value of the product is ascertained by discounting its anticipated future returns.

Two weaknesses of the theory have been recognised by Taussig himself. First, that it is "a dim and abstract one, remote from the problem of real life". To this he replies that this weakness is common to all economic generalisations. Second, and a more serious, objection is that the joint product is discounted at the current rate of interest. But according to his own analysis, the rate of interest is a result of the process of advance to the labourers, because it depends on the excess of what the labourers produce in the future over what is advanced to them in the present. This would mean arguing in a circle. To meet this difficulty Taussig suggests that we determine the rate of interest independently of marginal productivity by the rate of time preference, and with the interest thus determined discount the marginal product of labour. This, however hardly solves the difficulty; it merely evades it.

Taussig's theory ultimately analysed is another version of the Residual Claimant Theory of Wages. He says, in fact, that wages are what is left after rent, interest and profits are deducted from the total output. As such, the theory is open to all the objections put forward against the Residual Claimant Theory.

MODERN THEORY OF WAGES

Although labour has certain peculiarities and cannot be regarded as an ordinary commodity, still wages are very largely determined by the interaction of the forces of demand and supply as in the case of an ordinary commodity. Thus, the Modern theory of wages is the demand and supply theory.

Demand for Labour

"The demand for labour by the individual firm is a function of both the productivity of labour and the money demand for the firm's product."[6] In other words,

4. Marshall A., *Principles*, pp. 518, 538.
5. For a detailed study consult *Readings in the Theory of Income Distribution*, pp. 278-293.
6. Allen M. Carter. *The Theory of Wages and Employment.* 1959. p. 45.

the demand for labour reflects partly labour's productivity and partly the market value of the product at different levels of production.

The demand for labour is a **derived demand. It** is derived from the demand for the commodities it helps to produce. Greater the consumer demand for the product, the greater the producer demand for the labour required in making it. It may be observed that it is expected demand and not existing demand for the product that determines demand for labour. Hence, an **expected** increase in the demand for a commodity will increase the demand for the type of labour that productes this commodity.

Apart from the magnitude of demand (*i.e.,* big or small), we have also to consider its elasticity or responsiveness to change in wages. The elasticity of demand for labour depends on the elasticity of demand for its output. Also, demand for labour will generally be inelastic if their wages form only a small proportion of the total wages. The demand, on the other hand, will be elastic if the demand for the commodity it produces, is elastic or if cheaper substitutes are available.

The demand for labour also depends on the prices and the quantities of the co-operating factors. Suppose, the machines are costly, as is the case in India, obviously more labour will be employed. The demand for labour will be more. Also, the greater the demand for the co-operating factors the greater will be the demand for labour.

Another factor that influences the demand for labour is the technical progress. In some cases, labour and machinery are used in definite proportions. For instance, the introduction of automatic looms reduces the demand for labour.

Thus, demand for labour is determined by (*a*) the nature of demand for the product of labour, (*b*) the proportion of the cost of labour to the total cost of the product, (*c*) its substitutability by other factors, and (*d*) supply of capital as determined by the ability and willingness of investors to save and invest.

After considering all relevant factors, *e.g*., demand for the products, technical conditions, the prices of the co-operating factors, *etc*., the employer is governed by one fundamental factor, *viz*., marginal productivity. The demand for labour, under typical circumstances of a modern community comes from the employer, who employees labour and other factors of production for making profits out of his business. The demand price of labour, therefore is the wage that an employer is willing to pay for that particular kind of labour.

Suppose, the employer employs labourers one by one. After a point, the law of diminishing marginal returns will come into operation. Every additional labour employed will add to the total net production at diminishing rate. The employer will naturally stop employing additional labourers at the point at which the cost of employing a labourer just equals (in fact it is little less than) the addition made by him to the value of the total net product.

Thus, the wages that he will pay to such a labour (the marginal unit of labour) will be equal to the value of this additional product or marginal productivity. But since all the labour units are supposed to be homogeneous, what is paid to the marginal worker will be paid to all the labourers.

The demand schedule of the employer for labour is like the demand schedule of the consumer for a commodity, *i.e.*, lower the wage, the larger the number of workers demanded. With the larger labour force, output will expand and each unit of output will have to be sold at a lower price. This is an additional reason why marginal productivity of industry as a whole declines, the other reason being a decline in the marginal output.

The change in wage rate determines the **direction** of change in the demand for labour but the **degree** of this change depends on the elasticity of demand for labour. In case of elastic demand, a small change in the wage rate will lead to a considerable change in demand for labour, and vice-versa. Whether the demand for labour is elastic or not will depend on (*a*) the technical conditions of production and (*b*) elasticity of demand for the commodity which that labour produces. Generally, the short-term demand for labour is less elastic that the long-term demand. That is why the employers and the trade unions adopt a stiff attitude in wage negotiations.

In fact, for any particular employer, working under perfect competition, wages are already settled by the market forces. Each firm constitutes so small a portion of the entire industry that it cannot influence wages appreciably by employing more or less of labour. The supply curve of labour confronting each producer is perfectly elastic, *i.e.*, horizontal line at the level of the market wage rate. The individual demand curve is determined by marginal productivity. The individual employer hires as many labourers as will equate the marginal productivity of labour with the rate of wages in the market.

In Chapter 31, we have given two diagrams. Have a look at them again. Fig. 31.5 (*a*) shows the demand for labour of an individual firm and Fig. 31.5 (*b*) the demand of the industry. It is necessary to remember that it is the demand of the entire industry, not of an individual firm, which determines wages in the market. The individual firm has to accept the market rate of wages and adjust its own demand for labour accordingly. The demand curve of the industry is derived from the lateral summation of the demand curve of individual firms.

Supply of Labour

The supply of labour depends on (*a*) the number of workers of a given type of labour which would offer themselves for employment at various wage rates and (*b*) the number of hours per day or the number of days per week they are prepared to work. The Supply of labour may mean three things : (*a*) Supply of labour to firm, (*b*) Supply of labour to the industry and (*c*) Supply of labour to the entire economy.

To a given firm, the supply of labour is perfectly elastic because at the current wage rate, it can engage as many workers as it wants. Its own demand constitutes only a negligible fraction of the total supply of labour.

But for the industry as a whole, the supply of labour is not infinitely elastic. Hence, if it wants more labour it has to attract it from other industries by offering a higher wage. it can also work the existing labour force overtime. This in effect will mean an increase in supply. The supply of labour for the industry is subject to the law of supply, *viz*., supply varies directly with price, which means low wage small supply and high wage large supply. Hence, the supply curve of labour for an industry rises upwards from left to the right.

The long-run supply curve of labour in any occupation is a horizontal straight line, if earnings in other occupations are constant. This is due to the mobility of labour among occupations. Even in the short-run, it will be approximately horizontal if the occupation is an old one and does not require much training. In case an occupation requires extensive training, the short-run supply curve will be inelastic.

The supply of labour for the entire economy depends on economic, social and political factors or institutional factors, *e.g.*, attitude of women towards work, working age, school and college age and possibilities of part-time employment for students, size and composition of the population and sex distribution, attitude to marriage, the size of the family, birth control, standard of medical aid and sanitation, *etc.*

A given supply of labour, under conditions of perfect competition, gets distributed in various employments in such a way as to make the marginal productivity of labour in all the employments the same. but if labour cannot move freely from one employment to another, the marginal productivity will be different in different employments, and consequently, wages will also be different even for the same kind of labour.

The supply of labour may be decreased by labourers refusing to work for a time. This happens when labour is organised into trade unions. The labourers may not accept wages offered by the employer, if such wages do not ensure the maintenance of a standard of living to which they are accustomed. But, as we shall see, it is only when higher wages are justified by higher marginal productivity that high wages will have a chance to stay. Thus, labourers with low marginal productivity cannot demand high wages merely on the basis of their standard of living. In the long-run, however, marginal productivity, wages and the standard of living tend to adjust to one another.

On the whole, we might say that, the number of potential workers being given, the supply of labour may be defined as the schedule of units of labour at the prevailing rates of wages. This depends on two factors : (*a*) the number of workers who are willing and able to work at different wages and (*b*) the number of working hours that workers are willing and able to put in at different rates of wages.

In case, the workers have no staying power and the only alternative to work is starvation, the supply of labour in general will be perfectly inelastic. This means that wages can be driven down. Over a short period, reduction in wages may not cause any reduction in the supply of labour. But if wages are driven too low, competition among employers themselves will push them up. Even over a long period, the supply of labour is not very elastic.

There is a certain minimum wage below which labour will not work at all. Once this minimum is exceeded, supply of labour will increase as the wage rate goes up. But this will happen only up to a point beyond which wage increase will lead to a reduction in the supply of labour. Again, after a point, this tendency will be reversed when the worker thinks that he can move to a higher level of living. Hence, a rise in wages may lead to rise or fall in the supply of labour. It will depend on the worker's relative valuation of goods and leisure.

Thus, the supply of labour will depend on the elasticity of demand for income which will vary according to the worker's temperament and social environment. (We have already explained in Chapter 8 how indifference curves can be used to depict worker's preference for income and leisure). When the worker's standard of living is low, they may be able to satisfy their wants with a small income and when they have made that much, they may prefer leisure to work.

That is why it happens that sometimes increase in wages leads to a contraction of the supply of labour. This is represented by a backward bending supply curve as in Fig. 32.1. For some time this particular individual is prepared to work longer hours as the wages go up (wage is represented on OY-axis). But beyond OW wage, he will reduce rather than increase his working hours.

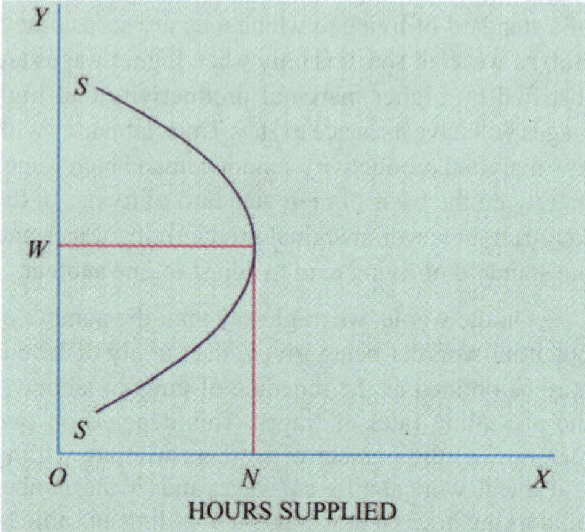

Fig. 32.1. Backward Bending Supply Curve of Labour.

Under perfect competition, the supply of labour, as already mentioned, is perfectly elastic, since no single firm can influence the price of labour in the market as a whole. But actually competition in the world is not perfect. Under imperfect competition, we have an upward sloping supply curve. The particular slope of the supply curve will depend on a number of inter-related factors such as the existence or absence of unemployment in the neighbouring labour market, the reaction of the other firms to a change in the wage rate made by the firm in question, differences in the efficiency of the workers, and so on.

The supply of labour becomes less elastic as the margin of full employment is reached or if the particular firm accounts for a large share of total employment.

Interaction of Demand and Supply

Having analysed the demand side and supply side of labour, we shall now see how their interaction determines the wage level. This is shown by the diagrams given on next page.

In Fig. 32.2 (*a*) we take the case of an industry. The curve SS represents supply to the industry. DD is the demand curve. They intersect at E. The wage level, therefore, is OW (= EN).

Fig. 32.3 (*b*) represents the case of a firm. Under perfect competition, the firm has to accept the market wage OW settled by the industry above. From the OW level in Fig. 32.2 (*a*) draw a straight line towards Fig. 32.2 (*b*) representing the condition of the firm. We see that this extended line W-AW cuts the MRP (marginal revenue productivity) curve of the firm at F′ in Fig. 32.2 (*b*). But at this level, the average revenue productivity (ARP) is MR which is greater than the wage OW. Hence, all the firms (this particular firm is representative of all firms in the industry) are making supernormal profits at this wage level. This will lead to entry of new firms in the industry; the demand for labour will increase and the wage level will go up. Thus, the supernormal profits will be competed away in the long-run by the entry of new firms.

The new demand curve D′ D′ cuts the supply curve SS in Fig. 32.2 (*a*) at F. The wage level in this situation will be OW′ which is higher than the original

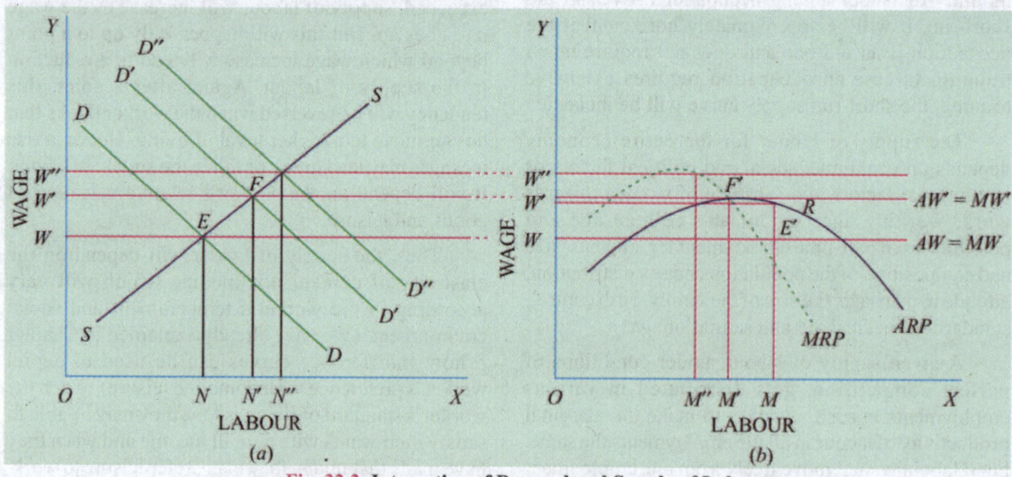

Fig. 32.2. Interaction of Demand and Supply of Labour.

wage level OW. This is how the interaction of demand and supply determines the wage. We can see that when the wage rises to OW′, the equilibrium is at F′. At this point, average revenue productivity (ARP) and marginal revenue productivity (MRP) are equal, and the average wage OW′ is equal to both of them.

It can also happen that the occurrence of supernormal profits attracts some firms from outside, which may further increase the demand for labour to D″ D″. The wage level will then be OW″. Here, the average revenue productivity (ARP) is less than the wage OW″, *i.e.*, the firms are suffering losses. The result will be that some firms will leave the industry and the wage will come down to the level of OW″. Here, the wage, the marginal revenue productivity and the average revenue productivity are all equal.

Thus, **under competitive conditions, wages are, in the long run equal to the marginal as well as average productivity of labour.** If marginal productivity is greater than average productivity, it will be worthwhile to employ more labour till marginal productivity falls to the level of average productivity. On the other hand, if marginal productivity is less than average productivity, less labour will be employed and the marginal productivity will rise to the level of average productivity. Marginal productivity and average productivity thus tend to be equalised. Since wages are equal to marginal productivity, they are also equal to average productivity.

This can be shown in a simpler diagram as in Fig. 32.3. Here, OR represents the wage level, AP is the average productivity curve and MP the marginal productivity curve. They intersect at P which shows that wages are equal both to the marginal productivity and average productivity. When AP is rising MP > AP, and when AP is falling, MP < AP. But when AP is neither rising nor falling, MP = AP. Hence,

Wage = MP = AP.

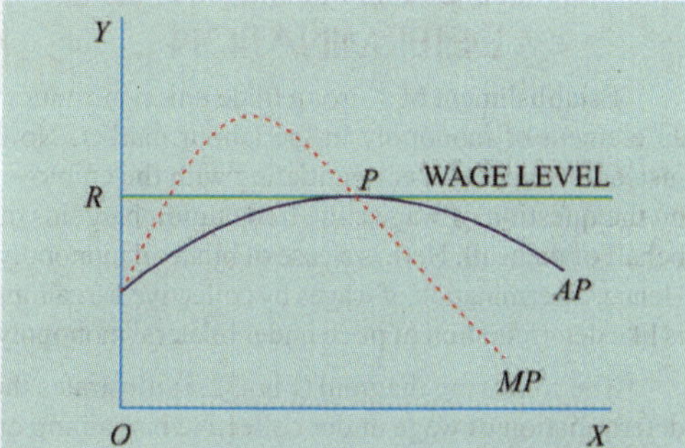

Fig. 32.3. Wages Equal Marginal and Average Productivity.

WAGES UNDER IMPERFECT COMPETITION

We have discussed above wage determination under perfect competition. But in the world of reality there is imperfect competition rather than perfect competition. Imperfect competition may result (*a*) when strong employer's associations are confronted with strong labour organisations. It is a case of Bilateral Monopoly, (*b*) when an industrial employer or a group of employers occupy a very strong monopolistic position as compared with labour to constitute what is called monopsony.

In bilateral monopoly, wage will be determined as price is determined under bilateral monopoly.

Monopsony. The usual case of imperfect competition so far as labour is concerned is that of monopsony where the employer embodies in his person concentrated monopoly power of being the sole purchaser of labour, whereas labour occupies a very weak position in comparison. Monopsony also occurs when a big employer employs proportionately a very large number of a given type of labour so that he is in a position to influence the wage rate. It may also occur when a group of big employers come to an understanding not to compete for labour and thus act as a single hirer of labour.

In the Fig. 32.4, the marginal revenue productivity curve (MRP) is the demand for labour. The supply curve of labour is Aw (Average wage curve) which is rising to the right which shows that higher wages have to be paid to engage more labour. MW is the marginal wage curve corresponding to the average wage curve AW.

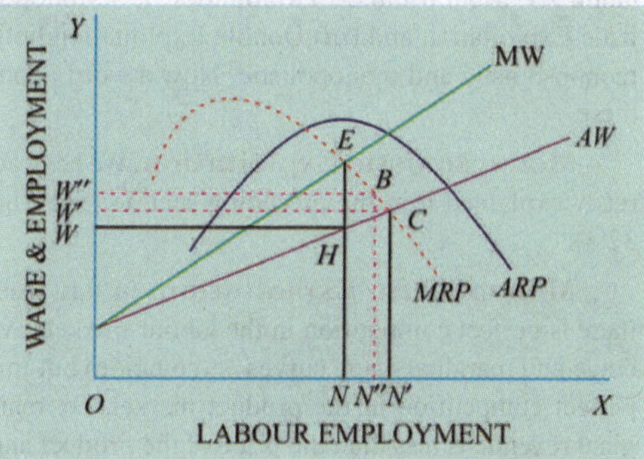

Fig. 32.4. Wages Determination Under Monoposny.

The two curves, *viz.*, marginal wage curve MW and the marginal revenue productivity curve (MRP) intersect at E. It is at this point that the monopsonist will be in equilibrium. Here the marginal wage is equal to the marginal revenue product at the level of labour employment ON. In this situation, the wage is NH (= OW).

It can be seen that this wage NH (= OW) is less than marginal revenue productivity which is NE. Thus, each worker gets EH less than his marginal revenue product. This is the measure of labour exploitation under monopsony. This is called by Mrs. Robinson as '**monopsonistic exploitation.**'

Thus, under monopsony, wage is lower and employment is less than under perfect competition in the labour market. Under perfect competition, the equilibrium would have been at C where the supply curve AW cuts the demand curve MRP. At this point, the wage would have been higher at OW (= N C) and the labour employed would have been larger at ON.

EXPLOITATION OF LABOUR

It is well-known that labour has weak bargaining power in relation to the employer; hence exploitation of labour. But what precisely do we mean by exploitation? As defined by Joan Robinson, labour is said to be exploited when the wage is less than the value of the marginal product (VMP), which is equal to the physical product multiplied by the sale price of the product. Obviously, there can be no exploitation of labour under perfect competition both in the labour market and in the product market. In this case, price and marginal revenue are equal (VMP = MRP) and labour is paid the wage rate equal to the value of its marginal product (see Fig. 32.3 where there is no exploitation of labour).

But in other market situations, labour exploitation occurs. We may distinguish three types of exploitation : (*i*) Monopsonistic Exploitation, (*ii*) Monopolistic Exploitation and (*iii*) Double Exploitation both monopsonistic and monopolistic. Now a word about these.

Monopsonistic Exploitation. We have already explained it in the preceding section (See Fig. 32.4).

Monopolistic Exploitation. In this case, there is perfect competition in the labour market (average and marginal wage curves coincide) but imperfect competition in the product market, i.e. marginal revenue is less than the price of the product and therfore the marginal revenue product (MRP) is less than the value of the marginal product (VMP). In equilibrium, the firm will equate wage with marginal revenue product. This means that labour is paid less than the value of the marginal product which shows exploitation. This is shown in Fig. 32.4A given on next page.

Double Exploitation. It occurs when there is imperfect competition both in the labour market (monopsony) and in the product market (monopoly). Thus, there is double exploitation of labour both monopsonistic and monopolistic and labour is exploited the most.

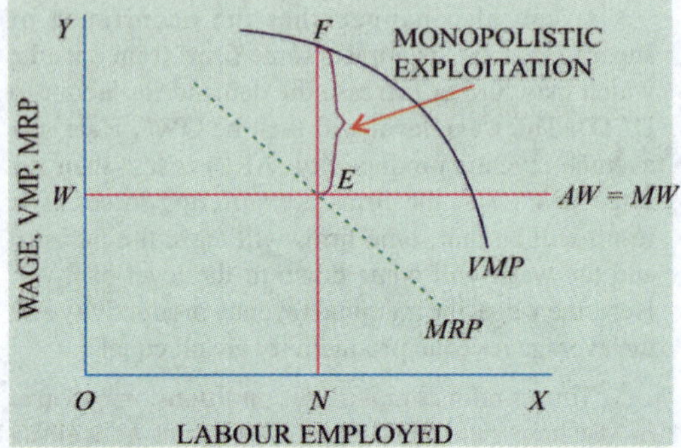

Fig. 32.4A.

How to Stop Exploitation. The two weapons to stop exploitation are (*a*) Government action and (*b*) Trade Union action. Since monopolistic exploitation arises from the monopoly power of the employer, it cannot be stopped either by the trade union or the government calling upon the employer to raise wages. If the trade unions compel the employers to pay high wages, they can reply by employing smaller number of workers so as to equate the new higher wage with the marginal revenue product of labour. Since the value of marginal product (VMP) will be greater than the marginal revenue product (MRP), labour will still be exploited. The only way to remove exploitation is to create conditions of perfect competition in the product market. The government can take some measures to remove monopolistic conditions. In the case of monopsonistic competition, the trade union or the government can remove exploitation by raising wages.

TRADE UNION AND WAGE DETERMINATION

Establishment of a strong trade union introduces an element of monopoly in the labour market. Now, instead of each worker negotiating with the employer on the question of wages, the trade union bargains on behalf of them all. Here is a case of bilateral monopoly. Hence, determination of wages by collective bargaining is like determination of price under bilateral monopoly.

The following diagram (Fig. 32.5) illustrates the determination of wage under collective bargaining on the assumption that the trade union seeks to achieve maximum wage regardless of its effect on employment.

In this figure ARP is the average net revenue productivity curve and MRP is the marginal net revenue productivity curve and IC_1, IC_2, IC_3, IC_4 and IC_5 are indifference curves showing different wage levels corresponding to the satisfaction of the trade union with the respective wage rate. The indifference curves show a constant rise in satisfaction between successive indifference curves. We can see that as the wages go up the gap between the wage levels widens. This is due to the fact that as wages increase only a larger increase will yield constant satisfaction.

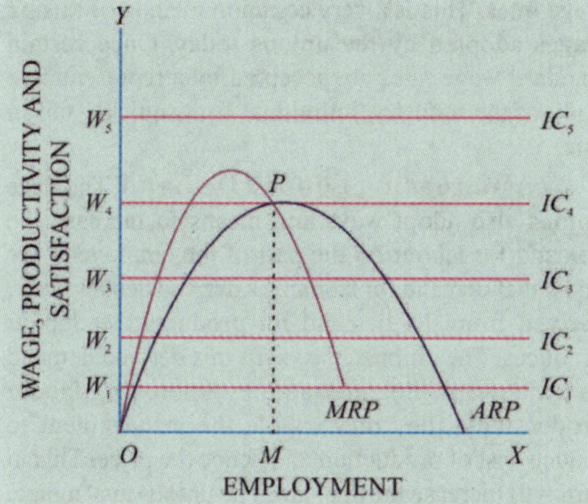

Fig. 32.5. The Two Limits in Collective Bargaining.

If the union had its way and could choose the wage rate unilaterally, it would choose that wage rate at which the corresponding indifference curve is a tangent to the average net revenue productivity curve (ARP). This happens at the point P in the figure given above and the wage rate will be set at OW_4 (= PM), where the indifference curve IC_4 is tangent to ARP curve. The number of workers employed will be OM. A wage rate above OW being above the average net revenue productivity will put the employer to loss and hence will not be at all acceptable to him. He would rather stop production which would be detrimental to the workers who would lose their jobs. Thus, OW_4 is the upper limit.

But the employer would like to fix wages at as low a level as he could considering industrial conditions, elasticity of demand for the product, elasticity of substitution between labour and capital, prevailing wage rates, labour efficiency, their cost of living, etc.

Can Trade Union Raise Wages?

For a long time, the economists held the view that the trade union action in increasing wages was futile and ineffective.

The classical economists argued that wages could be raised only at the expense of profits and a fall in profits, by reducing industrial activity, would reduce demand for labour and cause unemployment.

It is said that the wage level is determined ultimately by economic forces to which the strength of the contracting parties is irrelevant and which the bargaining power of the trade unions is powerless to bend.

Hubert Henderson hald a similar opinion : "It is . . . . . an illusion to suppose that the general level of wages can be appreciably and permanently raised by trade union action, except in so far as it increases the efficiency of workers or incidentally stimulates the efficiency of the employers."[7]

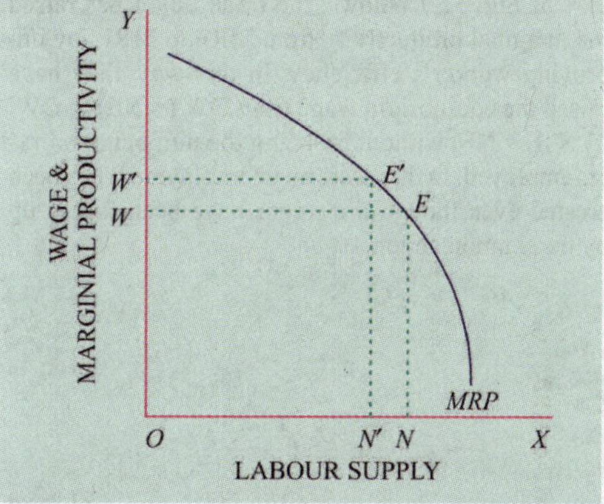

Fig. 32.6.

Futility of trade unions in raising wages is illustrated by the diagram 32.6. Here MRP is the Marginal Revenue Productivity curve which is the employer's demand curve. When ON is the supply of labour, equilibrium of demand and supply is at E and at OW (= NE) wage, ON is the number of workers employed. But if the wages are forced up through trade union action to OW′ (= N′ E′), the number of workers employed is reduced to ON′ *i.e.*, NN′ remains unemployed or through competition they will bring down the wages to OW, the previous level.

But, the modern economists do not subscribe to the above view. On the other hand, they strongly hold that trade unions can raise wages in a number of ways:

(*i*) Stopping Exploitation. The trade unions can ensure that labour is paid the full value of its marginal productivity. Under perfect competition, no doubt, wages tend to equal the marginal productivity of labour. But competition, in the real world, is not perfect. Hence, wages do not come up to the marginal productivity level due to the weak bargaining power of labour. By improving their bargaining power, the trade unions can raise wages up to the marginal

7. Supply and Demand, p. 145.

productivity level and put an end to the exploitation of labour by powerful employers.

(*ii*) **Raising Marginal Productivity.** Trade unions can improve the marginal productivity of labour itself : (*a*) They can force the employer to use more up-to-date appliances and organisation (*b*) They improve the efficiency of labour itself. Thus they do by fostering habits of sobriety, thrift and honesty and by helping the younger generation to acquire better education and training and (*c*) Trade unions may also increase the marginal productivity of a particular group of labourers by restricting its supply.

In Fig. 32.7 below : the trade union has raised the marginal productivity from MRP to MRP′ by improving worker's efficiency. In this way, they have raised the equilibrium wage from OW (= NE) to OW′ (= N′ E = NF) without reducing the number of workers employed. In this case, no unemployment has been created even though the wages have been forced up by trade union action.

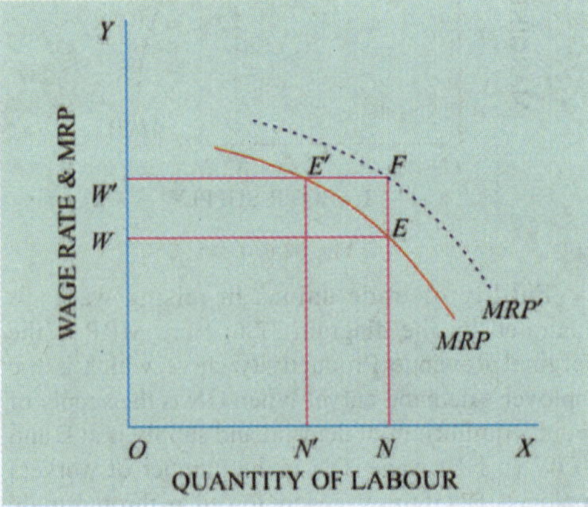

Fig. 32.7.

(*iii*) **Restricting Labour Supply.** The trade unions usually adopt a number of restrictive devices, *e.g.*, forcing the government to pass immigration laws, pressing for the reduction of working hours, long apprenticeships, restricting entry to the union and not permitting non-union labour to work, and so on. The aim clearly is to raise wages by reducing supply of labour when demand for it remains the same. When men workers get higher wages and are able to support the family, women workers may withdraw or the workers may work short-time preferring leisure to wages. In these ways, reduction in the supply of labour may raise the equilibrium wage rate.

There are special circumstances in which a particular set of workers can raise their wages by withdrawing their supply : (*a*) when the demand for that group of labour is inelastic, (*b*) when the wages of the said group form a small proportion of the total cost of production of the commodity concerned, and (*c*) when the other factors of production are "squeezable." In the long run, however, if the employers are forced to pay too high wages, there is a danger that they may adopt labour-saving devices and the demand for labour may fall, thus bringing down wages.

(*iv*) **Raising Standard Wage Rates.** Instead of putting restrictions on the supply of labour, modern trade unions fight for the raising of standard wage rates. This is a very common method of raising wages adopted by the unions today. Once certain standard wage rates are accepted by a representative body of the industry, individual firms quickly fall in line.

(*v*) **Increasing Labour Demand.** The trade unions also adopt ways and means to increase the demand for labour on the part of the employers. We know that demand for labour is a derived demand, *i.e.*, derived from the demand for products that labour produces. The unions try to shift this derived demand curve upward. For instance, by improving labour productivity, they may enable the management to reduce cost of production and hence the price. This in turn will increase the demand. The unions may agitate for the protection of the industry so that domestic industry expands and employs more labour. They may influence the government to pay higher rates on public contracts for the goods made by the industry. They may help the employers to charge a high monopoly price and wrest a share for labour out of monopoly price and wrest a share for labour out of monopoly profits. Some unions have agitated for higher tariff in order to increase the domestic demand for goods they produce and consequently for labour used in their production.

By collective bargaining they can raise wages and increased wages mean higher marginal productivity. Higher marginal productivity means shifting of the demand curve upwards.

(*vi*) The trade unions, can raise wages, because a large part of this rise can come about by squeezing the rent-element in the other factors of production and monopoly gains in other incomes.

(*vii*) It may also be argued that the raising of wages by the unions will not necessarily discourage investment. Today the bulk of investment comes not from individuals but from big corporations which usually maintain the level of investment but reduce dividend to shareholders when their income falls.

However, trade unions can raise wages if they are all-inclusive and it is difficult to import 'blacklegs'.

Adverse Effect of Trade Union Action

We may note certain implications of wage determination by trade unions. By imposing a high wage, a trade union may prevent undue expansion of an industry when the only attraction to the new firms was the prevalence of a low wage. But it may also cause unemployment by insisting on a wage which is beyond the capacity of the industry to bear. Some employers will be forced out and others will contract output. In both cases, some labour will be discharged. The movement of the discharged labour into other industries will depress wages there too.

Conclusion

If a trade union can wrest monopoly profits from a monopolist, it is all right. The proper function of a trade union is to stop or prevent exploitation and when it goes beyond, it is bad. "The whole question of labour's bargaining power in a free enterprise economy boils down, therefore, to the question how far it can make inroads into capitalist consumption without endangering the capital substance on which its own long-run productivity and income depend."[8]

WAGE DIFFERENTIALS

Relative Wages

So far we were concerned with general wages. The problem of relative wages is different. Here we have to explain the causes of differences in wages in different employments or occupations or grades of employments and also between different persons in the same employment or grade. Wages everywhere tend to approximate to the marginal productivity of labour. But, the marginal productivity of labour is different in different employments and grades. It varies with the degree of scarcity of each kind of labour in relation to the demand for it, or ultimately in relation to the demand for the products of each kind of labour.

If there were free mobility of labour over the whole field of employment, real wage would tend to be in proportion to the relative efficiency of labour engaged in each kind of work. Real wages (not nominal wages) of workers of the same level of efficiency would tend to be the same. If workers in one employment were getting real wages more than in proportion to their efficiency, labour would tend to move to that employment until increased supply would bring down its marginal productivity and wages. An opposite movement would take place if in an employment lower wages were paid than those justified by the relative efficiency of labour. Actually, however, labour cannot move freely from employment to employment especially in different grades. Different grades thus tend to become "non competing groups."

We may summarise here the causes which create differences in wages in different employments professions, and localities :

(*i*) Differences in Efficiency. These may be due to different inborn qualities, education, training and conditions under which work is performed. When efficiencies are different, wages must be different.

(*ii*) Existence of Non-competing Groups. As explained above, these groups arise because of the difficulties in the way of mobility of labour from low-paid to high-paid employments. These difficulties may be due to geographical, social or economic reasons. They may arise from lack of transport facilities, existence of family ties or caste barriers, and lack of means for better training, *etc.*

(*iii*) Difficulty of Learning a Trade. The number of those who can master difficult trades is small. Their supply is less than demand for them, and their wages are higher.

(*iv*) Differences in Agreeableness or Social Esteem. Disagreeable employments must pay higher wages in order to attract labourers. If, however, disagreeable work can be performed by unskilled workers, who cannot do anything better (due to caste or other disabilities), wages may be quite low, *e.g.*, sweepers in India.

(*v*) Future Prospects. If an occupation provides opportunities for future promotion, people will accept a lower start in it, as against another occupation offering higher initial rewards but no chances of rise in the future. The number of top prizes available in a profession also accounts for differences in wages.

(*vi*) Hazardous and dangerous occupations generally offer higher emoluments.

(*vii*) Regularity or irregularity of employment also exerts a strong influence on the level of wages. Regular employment generally carries a low salary.

(*viii*) Collective Bargaining. The differences in the strength and militancy of trade unions also account for differences in wages in different industries.

To Sum Up. We may sum up broadly the causes of differences in wages as worker's preferences, transfer costs, ranges of abilities and effects of collective bargaining.

It should be borne in mind that all these factors create differences in wages by affecting the adjustment of supply of labour to demand for it in various employments and grades. Wages are, in every case,

8. Rothschild, K. W., *The Theory of Wages*, 1965, p.

determined by the degree of scarcity in relation to demand for labour, or by the marginal productivity of labour with respect to each kind of work.

Low Wages of Women

In most cases, women are paid lower wages for doing the same kind of work. There are several reasons for this : In the first place, it is due to long habit and custom. Until comparatively recently, a woman was regarded as a household drudge even in advanced countries. Even today women tend to crowd into occupations involving drudgery and depress wages there.

Secondly, since women do not make their work a life career, they do not equip themselves with proper education and training. Their aim normally is to get married, and after marriage most of them cease to earn independently.

Thirdly, for the same reasons, women do not organize themselves into trade unions to enforce higher wages for themselves. Their employment being only a stop gap between school/college and marriage, they do not try to improve their economic position.

Fourthly, women workers are prepared to accept lower wages because they have very limited obligations and responsibilities. In most cases, they do not depend merely on their own earnings, even when they are in employment. Husband, brother or father, may and does, give them financial support.

Finally, male workers are supposed to be more capable of continuous and efficient work than female workers due to various reasons. Men are physically stronger and can undertake more strenuous work and can bear much greater nervous strain. Moreover, a woman, on account of biological reasons, is partly or wholly incapacitated for full work during certain periods of her life.

WAGES UNDER FULL EMPLOYMENT

When there is no full employment, pressure for increase in wage rates may lead to some reshuffling of demand for labour and hence of employment without upsetting the price system. For example, if as a result of increase in wages, there is increase in propensity to consume, level of investment remaining the same, output will increase to meet the increased demand and prices will not rise. If on the other hand, investment declines, the national income will decline and prices, too, will fall in line. Thus, the wage increase will not affect prices if the productive resources of the community are not fully employed so far.

But under full employment, the conditions are not likely to remain stable. Since the resources are already fully employed, increase in wages will not be followed by increase in output; hence prices are bound to rise. The Government will make good by public investment any falling off of private investment which might have depressed prices.

Also, the existence of full employment strengthens the bargaining power of labour. There can be no fear of unemployment as a result of rise in wages. This will only provoke labour to clamour for higher wages. The employers can maintain or increase production by offering higher wages, since there is no unemployed labour to draw upon. The employers, therefore, are likely to combine to resist an all-round increase in wages without their being able to get better supply of labour. But the labour will be in a stronger position and will succeed in securing wage increases. However, since as explained above prices are likely to rise, their real wages are not likely to go up.

Hence, under full employment, there will develop an inflationary spiral consequent on a rise in wages. This can be neutralized only by increase in the level of labour productivity. Further, insistent demand for higher wages may lead to the adoption of labour saving and other technical improvements. Persistent rise in prices, wages and profits will lead to transfer of purchasing power from the fixed incomists to workers and entrepreneurs which is quite desirable socially.

Besides, inflationary situation and consequent instability, another consequence of permanent full employment is to rob the labour market of its flexibility. Changes in the industrial structure can no longer be met by redistribution of unemployed labour but by transfer of labour from one sector to another. In the absence of unemployment, helping in the process of adjustment, some new and more positive methods will have to be devised and adopted to ensure flexibility of the economic system. A national wage policy will have to be adopted which can be easily done in a planned system.

SHARE OF WAGES IN THE NATIONAL INCOME

Factors Affecting Share of Wages

Among the factors affecting the share of wages in the national income we may mention the following :

(*i*) Labour Productivity. Other things being equal, the wages per worker would be higher where the labour productivity is higher and would increase with increases in labour productivity.

(*ii*) Introduction of Labour-Saving Machinery. With the progressive introduction of labour-saving machinery the share of wages in the aggregate national output would decline. It will be high where the work is mainly manual and low where it is highly mechanised.

(*iii*) Condition of the Labour Market. Labour's share in the total market is subject to various influences in the labour market. For instance, if labour is plentiful, their share will be low and it will be high if it is scarce. Similarly, collective bargaining, where there are strong labour unions, will increase labour's share.

(*iv*) Mobility of Labour. If there are no barriers to the entry of labour into the ranks of self-employed persons as small farmers, artisans, *etc.*, labour will get a large share in the national income.

(*v*) Growth of Monopolies. The monopolists are in a position to exploit labour; hence labour's share in the national product would be reduced under monopoly.

(*vi*) Export of Capital. If capital migrates to other countries, where cheap labour and raw materials are available, there is a corresponding reduction in employment, and so in labour's share, in the exporting country.

(*vii*) Cheaper Imports. The real wages, and hence labour earnings, go up when cheap food and other consumable commodities can be imported from abroad.

From a continuous rise in wages, one is likely to get the impression that labour's share in the national income must have gone up. This, however, is not borne out by facts. The fact is that the share of wages in the national income has remained remarkably stable. This is so even in advanced countries where trade unionism is well established and very strong. In Great Britain, in the whole period 1880 to 1944, it fluctuated between 39 and 41 per cent.[9]

According to an estimate by Sir Dennis Robertson, the share of wages in the net national income at factor cost varies from 40.3 per cent in 1938 to 43.6 per cent in 1953.[10] As regards the U.S.A, Dr. King's estimate showed that this share was just under 38 per cent in 1909 and just over 40 per cent in 1925.[11] Thus, the share of wages in the national income has been remarkably steady.

There are two forces which seem to be responsible for keeping stable the labour's share in the national income : (*a*) The level of raw material prices, and (*b*) the degree of monopoly. These are the forces which in a capitalist economy determine the share of wages in the national income under conditions of imperfect competition.

In an economy, where productive capacity is not fully used, additional units of output can be obtained by combining more manual workers and raw materials with the given capital equipment without raising the wage and material costs of these additional units. Constant average wage and raw material costs are typical of the major part of the economy. Other items of costs being negligible, the marginal costs of production approximate to the average cost of labour and raw materials.

The difference between the price and the marginal cost goes to the capitalists in the form of surplus profits or in the form of profit, interest, rent, depreciation, *etc*. The share of gross capitalist income and salaries in the total national income is determined by the average degree of monopoly; it increases or decreases if the degree of monopoly rises or falls. The rest of the national income is accounted for by wages and cost of raw materials.

Hence, the share of wages in the national income will depend on the cost of raw materials and degree of monopoly power. Therefore, a rise in the degree of monopoly power or in the cost of raw materials will reduce the share of wages and increase the gain of capital.

It should be clearly understood that the above analysis is applicable to an economy characterised by imperfect competition with some degree of monopoly power and not to an economy operating under perfect competition where the degree of monopoly power is zero. The world of imperfect competition is the world of reality.

Under perfect competition, the relative share of labour in the total output depends on the extent to which labour can be substitute for capital, and vice-versa. The greater the substitution (technical or commodity substitution) of labour for capital, when the total output expands, the greater will be labour's share in the new output, and vice versa. This substitution will depend on elasticity of substitution. The relative share of labour will be greater or smaller according as the elasticity of substitution is greater or smaller than one. As Hicks observes, "An increase in the supply of any factor will increase its relative share, (*i.e.*, its proportion of the National Dividend) if its elasticity of substitution is greater than unity."[12]

That the labour's share in the national income has remained stable is due to the fact that, on the one hand labour's attempts to raise wages have been baffled by their inability to reduce the degree of monopoly power; on the other hand, increase in the degree of monopoly power has been neutralised by a fall in the price of raw materials. During depression, the firms try to recover as much of their fixed expenses as possible and labour's share falls. But there is a greater fall in the prices of raw materials which checks the tendency of the wages to fall. In this manner, forces operating from opposite direction keep the share of wages in the national income more or less constant. This has been called a **law of capitalist economy.**

9. See Rothschild, K. W. — The Theory of Wages, 1965, p. 164.
10. Stamp Memorial Lecture for 1954, quoted in Maurice Dobb's Wages, 1956, p. 20.
11. Maurice Dobb — *Wages*, 1956, p. 20.
12. Hicks J.R. - *Theory of Wages*, 1932, p-117.

Key terms

Derived demand, Backward bending supply of labour, Monopolistic Exploitation, monopsonistic exploitation. Trade Union collective Bargaining.

QUESTIONS

1. How fare is the determination of wages affected by the peculiarities of labour? Can labour be treated as a commodity?
2. Distinguish between real and money wages. What factors would you take into consideration in determining real wages? Under what conditions is it possible for the two to move in the opposite directions?
3. 'Fairly acceptable wages of 1969 became too low in 1975'. What are the economic principles in solved in this statement?
4. Discuss how wages are determined
   (a) Under perfect competition.
   (*b*) Under imperfect competition.
5. "Wages under pure competition are equal both to the marginal and average product of labour". Explain.
6. Critically discuss the marginal productivity theory of wages. Does this theory satisfactorily explain changes in the wage rate?
7. State the modern theory of wages. How fare is it true to say that the theory of wages is an application of the general theory of value?
8. Show how the concept of a uniform wage rate implicit in the old theories of wages is incompatible with the existence of non-competing groups.
9. How do you account for difference in wages among (*a*) individual workers; (*b*) different occupations and industries and (*c*) within the same occupation?
10. Will an increase in the wage rate necessarily increase the quantity of labour supplies? Give reasons for your answer.
11. Analyse the effect of a wage increase on the supply of labour. When can the supply curve of labour be backward sloping? Illustrate diagrammatically.
12. How do the following factors influence the wage rates in labour market:
    (*a*) Non-competing groups, (*b*) bargaining power, (*c*) mobility of labour, (*d*) nature of work, and (e) Government policy.
13. Discuss the functions and utility of Trade Unions.
14. How far can the Trade Unions raise wage without adversely affecting the volume of employment in an industry?
15. Can collective bargaining raise (*a*) the general wage level, (*b*) wages in an individual industry? Explain fully.
16. What is meant by collective bargaining? What are the consequences of collective bargaining in the labour market?
17. Analyse the effect of collective bargaining on wages and employment in the following conditions:–
    (*a*) Perfect competition in both markets.
    (*b*) Monopsony in the factor market and imperfect competition in the product market.
18. "Trade Unions can raise wages in a particular industry but the result will be less employment". Comment.
19. Discuss the economic consequences of minimum wage fixation and collective bargaining.
20. Discuss the desirability and feasibility of (*a*) national minimum wage and (*b*) minimum wage for selected occupations.
21. Explain monopolistic exploitation of Labour.
22. Outline the factors affective share of wages in National Income. Explain the forces responsible for maintaining stability in labour's share.
23. Discuss the implications of a policy of Full Employment with special reference to under-developed economies.

RENT

MEANING OF RENT

In ordinary speech, the term 'rent' is used in a wide sense to mean a hiring charge, *e.g.*, rent of a house, a tonga or a machine. But, in Economics, rent, or **economic rent** as it is called, is used in a special sense. **It refers to that part of the payment by a tenant which is made only for the use of land, i.e., free gift of nature.**

Economic Rent and Contract Rent

The payment that an agriculturist tenant actually makes to the landlord is not necessarily equal to this economic rent. A part of this payment may consist of interest on capital invested in the land by the owner in the form of buildings, fences, drainage, wells, *etc*. That part of the payment which is made for the use of land **only is economic rent** and the total payment made by a tenant to the landlord is called **contract rent.**

Rent as Surplus

In Economics, the term 'rent' is being increasingly used in the sense of a **surplus,** *i.e.*, what a factor of production earns over and above what is essential to maintain its supplies in its present occupation. It can be easily understood that rent in this sense can arise only when the supply of a factor of production is less than perfectly elastic, and this is the case with most of the factors. In case the supply of a factor is perfectly elastic, it cannot earn any surplus over and above its supply price. Because whenever such a factor is found to be earning

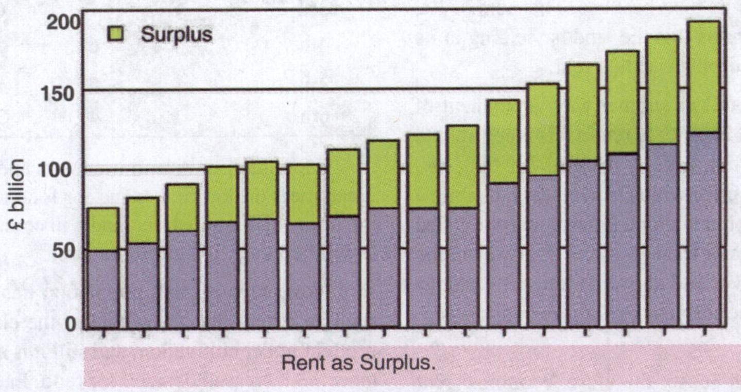

Rent as Surplus.

more than its supply price, more units of this factor will rush in and the surplus earning will disappear. This is so because, under perfect competition, the market price of a factor must equal to its supply price.

But when the supply of a factor is not perfectly responsive to changes in the reward of the factor, it can continue to earn more than what is necessary to call forth its supplies without any fear of new units of factors coming in to deprive it of extra reward. The supply of land in general, though not for a particular use, is absolutely inelastic, and as such, its supply is independent of what it earns. That is a higher rent cannot attract more of it and a lower rent cannot drive it out. That is why it is said that land has no supply price. That is, no payment is necessary to call forth its supply; it is there already. Its supply price being zero, the whole of its earnings is rent in the economic sense.

Economic rent is the surplus which remains to the supplier of a factor after he has paid all the expenses of production and has remunerated himself for his own productive effort.

We have said above that, **from the social point of view,** the whole of the earnings of land (and of other free gifts of nature) can be termed as rent because land has no supply price, or its cost of production is zero. Why then is any payment made for the use of such factors of production? This is simply due to the fact that they are scarce in relation to demand for them.

Rent and Transfer Earnings

Modern economists make use of the concept of transfer earnings in explaining economic rent. As was explained in a previous chapter (no. 31), the transfer earnings represent the amount which a factor can earn in its next best paid alternative use. Suppose, a piece of land yields in its present use Rs. 500 a year and suppose further that if it is transferred to its next best use, it will yield Rs. 400. In its present use, it yields Rs. 100 more than its next best use. This sum of Rs. 100 is a sort of surplus that the land is yielding in its present use. This surplus is called rent.

We can look at it in another way. A payment of Rs. 400 is essential in order to retain this piece of land in its present use, but actually it yields Rs. 500, *i.e.*, Rs. 100 extra. The price which is necessary to retain a given unit of a factor in a certain industry may be called its transfer earnings or transfer price. If, however, the factor is earning over and above its transfer earnings or transfer price, the surplus or excess earnings is economic rent.

In the modern sense, therefore, economic rent means surplus or excess over transfer earnings. This sort of surplus or economic rent is not peculiar to land, it can be found in other factors of production too.

RICARDIAN THEORY OF RENT

How Does Rent Arise?

More than a century ago, David Ricardo supplied the answer in the Theory of Rent associated with his name.

Ricardo defined rent as follows : "Rent is that portion of the produce of the earth which is paid to the landlord for the use of the **original and indestructible powers** of the soil." Economic rent, according to Ricardo, is the true surplus left after the expenses of cultivation as represented by payments to labour, capital and enterprise have been met.

Differential Rent

How this surplus arises may be illustrated by an example. Suppose, in a country, there are four kinds of land — A, B, C and D. Some pieces of land are more fertile than other and some areas are more advantageously situated as regards centres of population and means of transport, *etc.* But taking all the factors into consideration, let us suppose that we have four grades of land as mentioned above, so that land A is the most superior and B, C and D are 2nd, 3rd and 4th grade lands, respectively. Further, suppose that standard units of labour and capital called "doses" of labour and capital, when applied to these categories of land, produce wheat as given in the following table :

Doses of labour and capital	*Return in quintals of wheat per acre*			
	A	B	C	D
1st	10	9	8	7
2nd	9	8	7	6
3rd	8	7	6	5
4th	7	6	5	4
5th	6	5	4	3
6th	5	4	3	2

Suppose class A land is enough and to spare and it can meet the entire demand for food at the prevailing price. In this situation, land will command no rent. It will be like a free gift of nature.

Now, suppose that population has increased to such an extent that the whole of the class A land is brought under cultivation, and still it is not enough to meet the increased demand for food. In order to meet

Original and indestructible powers of the soil.

the growing demand for food, more labour and capital will be put into lands of class A, and lands of class B will also be brought under cultivation. This will happen only when the price of wheat rises so much as to make it worthwhile putting one more dose (*i.e.*, two doses in all) of labour and capital into land A and putting first dose of labour and capital into land B.

In other words, according to our table above, 9 quintals of wheat must sell for as much as is the cost of second dose of labour and capital. The price of 9 quintals of wheat produced on land B is equal to the cost of labour and capital put in this land for producing this quantity. Since the price of wheat produced on land B just covers the cost of production on this land, there is no surplus and hence no rent. In other words, B is the no-rent land. But on lands of class A, two doses of labour and capital give a return of 10 + 9 = 19 quintals of wheat are enough to pay for the two doses. Hence, one quintal of wheat is the surplus on land A. Thus, cultivators of land can either cultivate B class lands free of rent and get 9 quintals of wheat per dose of labour and capital per acre, or they can pay one quintal of wheat (or its equivalent in money at the prevailing price) per acre to the owners of land A as rent. By applying one more dose of labour and capital per acre of land, they can obtain 19 quintals of wheat (*i.e.*, by applying two doses in all). The application of second dose on A class land yields 9 quintals of wheat per dose of labour and capital. If there is perfect competition, at this stage, this rent (*i.e.*, one quintal per acre) for A class lands is bound to be established, but B is no-rent land.

As the demand for food still grows and the price of wheat rises, this process will continue. More and more units of labour and capital will be applied to the superior lands on the one hand, and still inferior lands will be brought under cultivation, on the other. The available doses of labour and capital will be applied in such a way as to get equal returns at the margin of cultivation. For instance, if there are 10 doses available, 4 will be applied to land A, 3 to land B, 2 to land C and 1 to land D. In this way, the marginal or the last dose applied to each class of land will give the same return, *i.e.*, 7 quintals of wheat. The total production under these conditions will be 34 + 24 + 15 + 7 = 80 quintals of wheat. No other arrangement will give more than this total. These doses will be applied only if the price of wheat is such as to make only of quintals of wheat enough to meet the cost of application of doses of labour and capital.

Since the number of doses applied to each class of land is different, the output of these lands will also be different. On A class land, 4 doses of labour and capital will yield 34 quintals (10 + 9 + 8 + 7 = 34), B land with 3 doses will yield 15 (*i.e.*, 8 + 7 = 15) quintals and one dose applied to D class land will yield only 7 quintals which will just cover the cost of production there, yielding no rent.

It is clear that rent of each class of land is equal to the surplus output over and above the cost of production, which is equal to 7 quintals of wheat.

Under such circumstances, rent per acre of the various kinds of land will be :

Rent of A grade

= (total produce) — (total cost)

= 34 – 28 = 6 Qtls

Rent of B grade = 24 – 21 = 3 Qtls

Rent of C grade = 15 – 14 = 1 Qtls

Rent of D grade = 7 – 7 = 0 (zero) Qtls.

We have calculated the rent in terms of the produce. It can be easily converted into money value at the prevailing price of the produce.

Thus, rent arises on account of natural differential advantages enjoyed by a piece of land over the marginal land. The natural differential advantage may be due either to superior quality of land or its better situation.

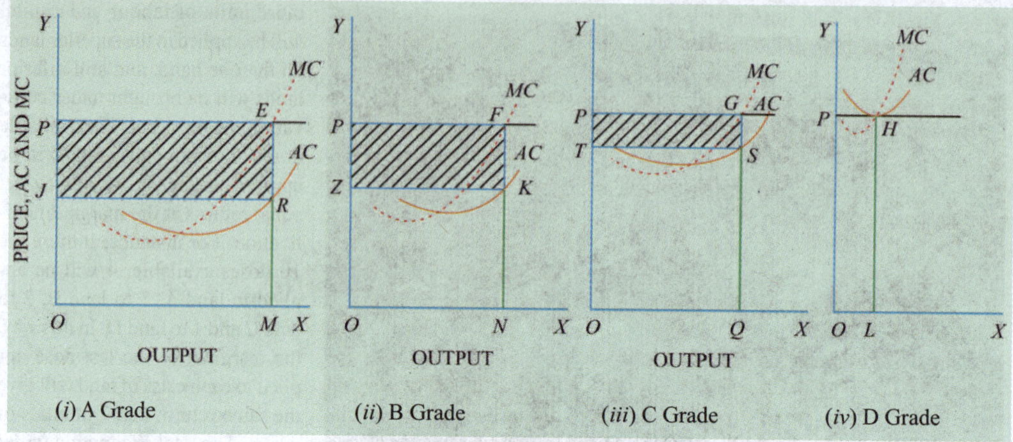

Fig. 33.1.

Marginal or No-Rent Land

When marginal produce is 7 quintals, there will be no rent of D grade land. It is then the marginal land or land on the margin of cultivation. This is also called the "no-rent land". It produces no surplus over cost of production. Its produce is just enough to cover the expenses of production on it. The rent of all superior lands is measured upwards from, and with reference to the marginal land.

Now, the marginal land may not be the poorest or the worst land. We have to look not to the quality of land but to its best alternative use. The marginal land, *i.e.*, the land on the margin of transfer, may be the best land. The land which is best for the cultivation of cotton may also be the best for the cultivation of wheat. If the price of cotton falls, it is this land which will be first diverted to wheat, and will, therefore, be marginal from the point of view of cotton. This may be considered the modern version of marginal land.

Diagrammatic Illustration of the Ricardian Theory of Rent

The following diagram (Fig. 33.1) illustrates the Ricardian theory of rent. These four figures show how much rent each grade of land yields. The Fig. (*i*) indicates A-grade land which is the most superior land, Fig. (*ii*) shows the B-grade land which is next best. Fig. (*iii*) shows the C-grade land and Fig. (*iv*) shows D-grade land which is the least productive land or which is most inferior. In all these figures, the curve AC is the average cost curve and MC is the marginal cost curve.

The D-grade land will be cultivated only when the price of agricultural output is equal to the average cost of production. It will be seen that the minimum average cost of production on D-grade land is LH. If this D-grade land is to be cultivated then the price of the produce (wheat) must be equal to OP. In other words, when the demand for wheat increases so much that price OP is determined, only then will this land be cultivated. Now, suppose that the demand for wheat has increased so much that OP price is determined. In this situation OL quantity of D-grade land will be cultivated. In the figure (*iv*), the total cost of production is equal to the total value of the produce obtained (because price OP = Average cost of production LH). Thus, in this case of D-grade land, there is no surplus above the cost of production. In other words, there will be no rent on D-grade land. This is the no-rent land or marginal land.

Now take C-grade land (Fig. *iii*). In this case also, price is OP (because under perfect competition price in the market must be the same whatever land may be producing that commodity), but the average cost is QS. Hence, there is GS per unit surplus or total surplus above total cost, is shaded area GPTS. This is the rent on the C-grade land. Similarly, the rent on B class land is represented by the shaded area FPZK and on A-grade land it is EPJR.

Does Marginal or No-rent Land Really Exist?

One would think that such a land cannot exist. Everybody will be keen on having such a land so that the owner may be in a position to demand some rent for it. But this is a superficial view. No rent land does really exist. The whole of the payment as rent for the use of land may be due to investment of capital, *i.e.*, interest. The land itself may be such as not to yield any surplus at all. For example, there may be some waste land lying useless and nobody may be willing to pay anything for its use. But a prospective-tenant may agree to pay something. If the owner sinks a well there. Obviously, the well and not for the land which is really a no-rent land.

Sometimes, the existence of no-rent land is concealed in a big farm, where the rent takes the form of so much money per acre. But in a farm there are mixed up good acres as well as bad ones. The latter, if let out alone, may fetch nothing.

Also, the rent paid may not be economic rent, but scarcity rent. This happens in an old country with a growing population. Then even the marginal land pays some rent which is scarcity rent, economic rent due to the natural differential advantages enjoyed by them.

Finally the marginal land, with regard to an old country, like England may exist in Australia or Canada supplying the same market.

Scarcity Rent

Besides economic rent, we have seen above, there is also scarcity rent. As the price of wheat rises, the worst land is also subjected to intensive cultivation and it yields a surplus over cost. This surplus is not a differential one compared to no-rent land, which does not exist. It is due to the scarcity of land as such. Hence, it is called scarcity rent.

The rent yielded by superior lands thus contains two elements : (*a*) differential surplus over the marginal land, and (*b*) payment due to scarcity of land as such. For instance, in our illustration, if cultivation is carried to a point where the worst land pays 2 quintals of wheat as rent, the superior land will pay a scarcity rent of 2 quintals in addition to the differential rent. The superior land will pay scarcity rent at the same rate as the worst land, but they will also pay a differential rent. As Marshall says, "in a sense all rents are scarcity rents, and all rents are differential rents."[1] Differential rents arise because of scarcity of each particular grade of land.

Criticism of the Ricardian Theory

The Ricardian theory of rent has been widely criticized. **First**, it has been pointed out that there are no "original and indestructible powers of the soil." Good lands, after being constantly cultivated, lose their fertility to a large extent and get exhausted. To this may be replied that, if after exhaustion, good lands are manured equally with the bad ones, the former regain their productive power much more readily than the latter. It is also pointed out that, in an old country, where land has been constantly manured, the upper layer, which grows crops, is all man-made. There is nothing 'original' about it. But this is not correct. The climate sunshine, air, situation, *etc*., of a particular piece of land are all fixed by nature. They are all 'original and indestructible'.

Secondly, it is objected that Ricardo uses the term fertility of land in a vague manner. Apart from the factor of situation, fertility depends upon the ability of the farmers and the methods of cultivation used. Moreover, fertility is relative to the crops grown.

Thirdly, Ricardo's theory assumes that there exists a no-rent land which only repays the cost of cultivation. In most cases, it is true; there are lands which pay only a nominal rent. Such lands yield no true economic rent. The concept of scarcity rent can also explain this situation. For the substance of the theory, it is not necessary that there should exist a no-rent land. The concept of no-rent land is merely imaginary and theoretical and is not realistic.

Fourthly, according to the Ricardian theory, rent arises on account of natural differential advantages of superior lands over the marginal one. But even if all the land is of A-grade, rent will still arise. It will arise owing to the operation of the law of diminishing returns when land is intensively cultivated. The marginal unit of labour and capital applied must be compensated by the yield obtained. The earlier units will give surpluses over their costs (because their costs are less than the cost at the margin), which will constitute the rent.

The fact is that rent arises not on account of superiority or inferiority of land, but because land is scarce. If land, good or bad were in a state of abundance, there would have been no question of paying or receiving rent. Even if the lands were homogeneous, rent will still arise owing to its scarcity. Ricardian Theory explains that superior things have superior prices, but it does not explain why prices emerge.

Fifthly, as Carey and Roscher point out, it is historically wrong to assume that, in a new country, the best lands are cultivated first. In fact, lands that are first cultivated are not usually the best; they are only the most easily accessible. To this Walker replied that by the best land Ricardo meant not the most fertile land but that which was the best both from the point of view of fertility and situation.

Sixthly, criticism is levelled against Ricardo's corollary that since the marginal land pays no rent and price is determined by cost of the marginal land, rent does not form a part of the price of the produce. The modern economists think that it is only from the point

1. Principles of Economics p. 422.

of view of economy as a whole that land has perfectly inelastic supply and earns a surplus or rent. This surplus is not included in cost and hence it does not enter into price. But, from the point of view of an individual farmer or industry, a payment has to be made to prevent land from being transferred to some other use. The payment called transfer earnings, is an element of cost and hence enters into price. For the individual farmer the whole of rent is cost.

"This concept of transfer earnings helps to bring the simple Ricardian theory—where transfer earnings are zero because it is the whole economy which is being studied—into a close relation with reality." (Stonier and Hague).

Finally, the most important criticism of Ricardo, however, comes from those who deny the necessity of explaining rent by a special theory not applicable to the rewards of other factors of production. They explain rent in the same way as wages, interest and profits. They deny its peculiar nature as contended by Ricardo. No specific and separate theory of rent is called for. The demand and supply theory which determines all values, also determines the rent of land. This point of view is explained below.

Further Appraisal of the Ricardian Theory

In the Ricardian theory, two facts stand out prominently : (*a*) That rent arises because some lands are superior and other inferior; and (*b*) that rent is measured from the no-rent margin.

Modern writers question both these contentions. In the first place, they assert that it is a matter of indifference to the general principle of rent whether the land is uniformly good, uniformly bad or gradable. The essential factor of rent is the relative scarcity of the products that land can yield. The scarcity of land is in fact derived from the scarcity of its products. If the problem is approached from this point of view, the necessity of assuming different grades of land disappears. The "differential principle" only explains why one particular acre of land **commands a higher rent** than the less fertile one; it does not explain **why rent arises.**

Fundamentally speaking, rent is paid because the produce of the land is scarce in relation to its demand. In the face of this scarcity, rent will arise even if all the lands in the country are exactly alike. The same is the case with wages, interest and profit. These payments arise because the products of the factors concerned are scarce in relation to the demand for them. Just as a superior labourer gets higher wages and a superior entrepreneur earns higher profits than the inferior ones, superior land also commands a higher rent. "Fundamentally, all that the Ricardian theory of rent amounts to is the truism that the better article will always command the higher price. A more fertile acre will be worth more than a less fertile one simply because they are different things. The same truism applies to wages."[2] Wicksell has pointed out that rent and wages are almost parallel cases.

Thus, there is no justification for placing rent in a special category. Land commands rent according to its marginal productivity just as labour commands wages or capital commands interest.

The second point of attack is the idea of the no-rent margin. This is the starting point of measuring rent according to the Ricardian theory. It is contended by modern writers that the no-rent margin may exist in some cases, but it is not fundamental to the emergence of rent. For instance, some lands may be fit only for a specific use, *e.g.*, growing corn. If it is not profitable to grow corn on them due to fall in the price of corn, such lands may go out of cultivation, or they may just pay for the cost of the crop grown on them. Such lands may have significance from the point of view of rent but in a different sense than held by Ricardo. If such lands are cultivated, they tend to increase the supply of corn and thus lower rents, and if they go out of cultivation, rent rises due to a decrease in the supply of corn. The existence of such marginal land does not give any ultimate explanation of rent.

But when we do not refer to any particular crop, especially in a fully developed country, there is probably no land that cannot be put to some profitable use. Thus, the margin of cultivation may vary according to the use to which a particular land is put.

Conclusion

It is concluded, therefore, that the theory of no-rent margin and a series of differential rents created upon it, while true in particular cases, is a partial, not an ultimate, explanation of the phenomenon of rent. It does not reach the bottom of the problem. The real approach to rent, as to other phenomena of value, is through the principle of scarcity. The Ricardian Theory has, therefore, been rejected.

Although the Ricardian theory has been rejected, but we should not ignore the elements of truth contained in it. Who can deny that with the increasing

2. Briggs and Jordan, *op cit.*, p. 355.

pressure of population, inferior land would be brought under the plough? It is true even today and not only historically true. The scientific improvements and new technology going under the label of 'green revolution' can only put off the process. Further, the theory exerted powerful influence on the contemporary economic and political thought, It highlighted the conflicting interests of the landlords and the rest of society. That is why abolition or socialisation of rent was advocated.

MODERN VIEW OF RENT OF LAND

Modern economists have furnished a better explanation of the rent of land. According to the modern view, rent is a payment for the use of land. Rent, in this sense, is obviously determined by the demand for and the supply of land. Take first the demand side.

Demand for the Use of Land. The demand for land is a derived demand. It is derived from the demand for the products of land. If the demand for these products rises or falls, the demand for the use of land will correspondingly rise or fall leading to increase or decrease of rents. For instance, if population of a country increases, the demand for food will increase, resulting in increased demand for land and rise in its rent, and vice-versa.

We have seen in a previous chapter (no. 31) that the demand for a factor of production depends on its marginal revenue productivity (or in short marginal productivity). The productivity is subject to the law of diminishing marginal productivity. That is why, as in the case of other factors, the demand curves shown in the Fig. 32.2 slope down from the left to the right.

Thus, on the side of demand, rent of land is determined by its productivity, not total productivity, but marginal productivity.

Supply Side. On the supply side, the supply of land is fixed so far as the community is concerned, although individuals can increase their own supply by acquiring more land from others or decrease its supply by parting with land. In spite of reclamation projects, the effect of which on the total supply is negligible, the supply of land remains practically fixed. It is a case of perfectly inelastic supply which means that whatever the rent (the rent may rise or fall), the supply remains the same. That is why it is said that **land has no supply price**. In other words, the supply of land in general is absolutely inelastic and as such its supply is independent of what it earns.

Interaction of Demand and Supply. We have analysed the demand and the supply side of land. The interaction of these forces is shown in the diagram (see Fig. 33.2). We assume that land is homogeneous and it is sued for raising only one crop.

Only then there can be one demand curve and one supply curve. We also assume perfect competition. SS supply curve, a vertical straight line, represents fixed supply. We start with DD as the total demand curve for land. These two curves intersect at E. In this OR (= SE) is the rent. If the rent is less than OR, say OR″ (= SE″), the demand for land will increase; but the supply is fixed, hence rent will again rise to OR. If, on the other hand, rent rises above OR to OR′ (= SE′), the demand for land will decrease and bring the rent back to OR.

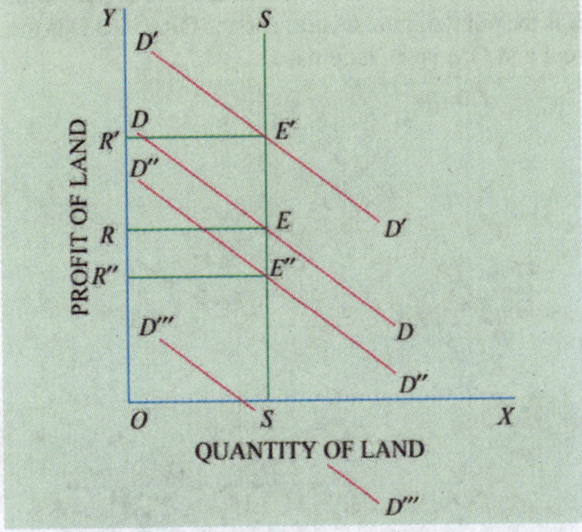

Fig. 33.2. Interaction of Demand and Supply of Land.

Suppose now that on account of increase in population or otherwise, demand for land has increased from DD to D′ D′. Supply curve is still the same SS. The new point of intersection will be E′, and, therefore, the rent will be OR′ (= SE′). If demand falls to D″ D″ then the demand and the supply curves intersect at E″, and the rent will be OR″ (= SE″). In case, the country is entirely new and land of good quality is surplus, then there will be no rent. This condition is shown by D‴ D‴.

If the land is of different qualities, then each quality will have a separate demand curve and each quality of land will command different rent. Hence, the theory explains differential rent too.

Conclusion. Thus, the rent of land, like the remuneration of other factors of production, is determined by the equilibrium between demand for, and supply of land. In other words, it is scarcity in relation to demand that determines rent. Fundamentally speaking, rent is paid for land, because the produce of land is scarce in relation to its demand. The scarcity of land is in fact derived from the scarcity of its products.

It is this scarcity which explains all values and rent is no exception.

Land for a Particular Use

We have analysed above the total demand and the total supply of land for the community as a whole. Let us now consider it from the point of a particular industry or use. For a particular use or industry, the supply of land cannot be regarded as fixed. By offering more rent, the supply can be increased; the supply will decrease if the rent in this particular case goes down. The supply is thus elastic and the supply curve will rise upward from the left to the right as is shown in the Fig. 33.3. DD is the demand curve to start with E is the point of intersection : hence OR (= EM) is the rent and OM is the land used.

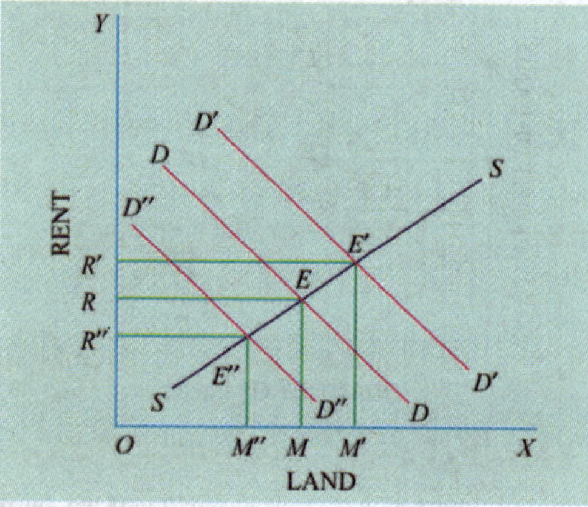

Fig. 33.3. Land Rent for a Particular Use.

Suppose the demand increases to D′ D′. Now the two curves intersect at E′ and the rent will be OR′ (= E′ M′) and the land used OM′. This means that, since for this particular use the rent of land has gone up. MM′ land has been withdrawn from other uses and put to this use. If the demand for land decreases to D″ D″, the rent will come down to OR″ (= E″ M″) and the quantity of land will come down to OM″. This will mean that MM″ land has gone out of this particular use. Since the rent has fallen.

MODERN THEORY OF RENT

Modern theory of rent does not confine itself to the determination of the reward of only land as a factor of production. Rent according to the modern sense can arise in respect of any factor of production. It is a surplus payment in excess of transfer earnings of that factor. We have already explained that transfer earnings means the amount of money which any particular unit of a factor could earn in its next best alternative use.

Economic rent of a factor of production is the excess over its transfer earnings, *i.e.*, what a factor may be earning in its present employment over what it could earn in its next best employment. In other words, transfer earnings of a factor mean what a unit of factor can earn in its next best alternative use, occupation or industry. We can also define transfer earnings as the minimum earnings which a unit of factor of production must be paid in order to induce it to stay in its present use or industry or occupation. If a factor is getting less than this minimum, it will give up its present employment and shift to its next best alternative employment. But if a factor in its present employment is earning more than the minimum necessary to keep it in that employment, the excess is called economic rent.

This concept of rent is applicable not merely to land but to all factors of production. That is, labour, capital and entrepreneurs too can earn economic rent in this sense.

Let us give some examples to explain this concept. Suppose, a lecturer in economics is getting Rs. 600 per month as salary. Suppose, further that his next best employment can be in a bank where he can get Rs. 500. If he cannot get Rs. 500 in a college, he will take up a job in a bank and earn that much. But since he is actually getting Rs. 600 as a lecturer in a college, he is earning Rs. 100 more than his next best alternative employment. That is, he is earning Rs. 100 as economic rent. Take another example. Suppose, a piece of land is devoted to the cultivation of cane in which the owner of land is earning Rs. 1,500. If in the next alternative use, say cultivation of cotton, it can fetch Rs. 1,200, then in its present use it is earning Rs. 300 more than its transfer earnings. This excess of Rs. 300 is surplus or economic rent. In the same manner, we can take the example of capital. Suppose, one is getting 10 per cent on a certain investment of capital. Suppose further the next best investment is fixed deposit in a commercial bank where one can get 7 per cent. This means that the present investment gives an excess of 3 per cent over its transfer earnings. This is economic rent.

From the above analysis it is clear that a unit of factor of production can earn more in its present use than its next best alternative use or the transfer earnings. Economic rent in such a case is the difference between the present earnings and transfer earnings. In Joan Robinson's words, "The essence of the conception of rent is the conception of a surplus earned by a particular part of a factor of production over and above the minimum earnings necessary to induce it to its work"[3].

3. *Economics of Inperfect Competition.* p. 102.

How Economic Rent Arises?

Now the question is how economic rent arises. Economic rent in the sense of surplus over transfer earnings will arise when the supply of the factor units is **less than perfectly elastic or not perfectly elastic.** From the point of view of elasticity of supply, there are three possibilities: (*a*) when the supply is perfectly elastic, (*b*) when it is less than perfectly elastic, and (*c*) when it is inelastic. Let us examine these possibilities from the point of view of rent.

(*a*) When the supply of factor units is perfectly elastic. In this case, there will be no surplus or economic rent and the actual earnings and transfer earnings will be equal. If there is any difference it will be competed away. When the supply of a factor is perfectly elastic, it means that at a given price, or remuneration, the entrepreneur can engage or employ any number of the factor units. It is obvious that, when the factor units are available at a minimum price or transfer earnings, their equilibrium price will be equal to that minimum price at when the present earnings are equal to the transfer earnings. Thus, no factor unit in such a situation will be able to earn more than its transfer earnings. That is, there will be no rent or surplus earnings.

This is shown in diagram 33.4 given below. Along OX is shown the quantity of the factor and along OY its price.

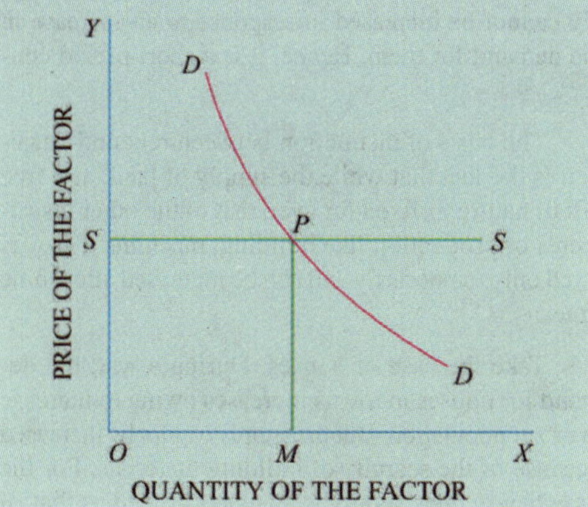

Fig. 33.4. Perfectly Elastic Supply.

In this figure, the supply curve of the factor of production SS is perfectly elastic and is, therefore, shown as a horizontal straight line. This means that all factor units are available at the given price OS or in other words, the transfer earnings of each factor unit are also equal to OS. DD is the demand curve. The two curves intersect at P. OM is the quantity of the factor used. The price determined is OS (= PM). The total earnings are OSPM. But since transfer earnings are equal to the actual earnings, they are also equal to OSPM. There is no surplus and hence no rent. If this firm does not pay the price OS, the factor units will be shifted to some other use and earn there as much, because present earnings are equal to transfer earnings.

Thus, it is clear that if the supply of factor units is perfectly elastic for a particular use or industry, then no factor unit can earn surplus or economic rent.

Now, let us have a situation when the supply of a factor is less than perfectly elastic.

(*b*) Less than Perfectly Elastic Supply. We have seen above that if the supply of a factor is perfectly elastic, there can be no rent. Now let us take a case when the supply is less than perfectly elastic, *i.e.*, it is somewhat elastic. This means that the transfer earnings of all the factor units are not equal. As, in some industry or use, the price of the factor increases, more and more of the factor units will offer their services to this industry in use, a factor unit can earn Rs. 200 p.m. It is obvious that only such units of the factor will offer their services to this industry whose price in other alternative occupations is less than Rs. 200 or in other words the transfer earnings are less than the present earnings. In this manner, as the price paid for a factor in a particular industry or occupation increases, the supply of the factor will increase if the transfer earnings are less. It is clear that the supply of a factor of production depends on its transfer earnings.

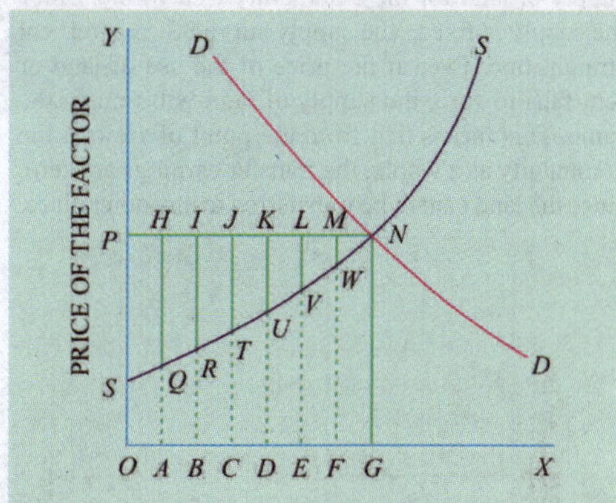

Fig. 33.5. Elastic But Not Perfectly Elastic Supply.

This is shown in the diagram 33.5 given below.Along the X-axis the quantity of the factor is shown and along OY its price. SS is the supply curve sloping upwards to the right. It is somewhat elastic but not perfectly elastic as in the case (*a*). The supply curve SS indicates what quantity of the factor will be available at various prices. In other words, it shows the transferearnings of different factor units. Thus, the transfer earning of A unit of the factor, is AQ whereas the price is OP. Therefore, surplus or rent is HQ. In the same manner, the other units earn surplus or rent. It is assumed that all factor units are equally useful for this industry. Hence, the price of all factor units in the industry will be the same. The supply curve cuts DD demand curve at N. In this case, OG is the quantity of the factor used. The rent or price per unit is OP (= GN). But the transfer earnings of each factor unit are less than the price OP. All units except the last G unit are earning more than their transfer earnings. That is they are earning economic rent. Economic rent or surplus will be different for different units because the transfer earnings are different, although the price is the same.

The total earnings are OGNP. But the transfer earnings are OGNS. If we take away the transfer earnings, we get PNS, the thick-lined area as surplus or rent.

(c) Absolutely Inelastic Supply. Now we come to a case when the supply of a factor is absolutely inelastic. The obvious example of this case is the supply of land for the community as a whole. We know that land for the community is fixed and it cannot be increased or decreased whatever the price offered. High price will not increase it or low price will not decrease it. That is why it is said **that land has no supply price.**

In the diagram 33.6, the supply curve SS shows an absolutely inelastic supply which represents the supply of land for the community as a whole. Since the supply is fixed, the supply curve SS′ is a vertical straight line. Even if the price of the use of land or rent falls to zero, the supply of land will remain the same. This means that from the point of view of the community as a whole, the transfer earnings are zero, since the land cannot be transferred to any other place.

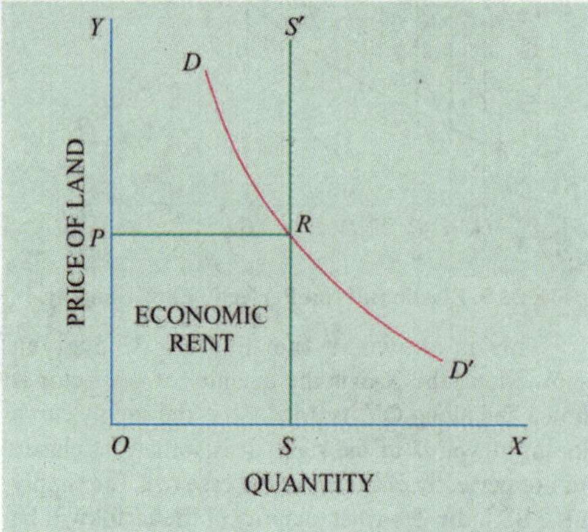

Fig. 33.6. Absolutely Inelastic Supply.

Look at the Fig. 33.6 again D′D′ is the demand curve for the whole land. The supply curve SS′ and the demand curve DD′ intersect at R. In equilibrium, the price of land or rent is determined at OP and the total earnings of land are equal to OPRS area. Since in this situation the transfer earnings of land are zero, the entire earning of land, *i.e.*, OPRS is rent. From the point of the community as a whole, there are two alternatives, *viz.*, either the land should be cultivated or it should be kept idle. Hence, for the community, the transfer earnings of land are zero and whatever earnings are made in any use thereof constitute its rent or surplus.

Thus, it is clear that in case the supply of a factor is absolutely inelastic, its earnings are rent.

Conclusion. We may conclude that rent arises when the supply of a factor is less than perfectly elastic.

QUASI-RENT

The concept of Quasi-Rent was first introduced in Economics by Marshall. Quasi-rent, according to him, is the surplus earned by the instruments of production other than land. The term 'rent' is applied to income from land and other free gifts of nature, and quasi-rent to the income derived from appliances and machines which are the product of human effort. Quasi-rent stands for the whole of the income which some agents of production yield when demand for them has suddenly increased. It is earned during the period when their supply cannot be increased in response to an increase in the demand for them. Hence, it is a short-period concept.

The basis of distinction between rent and quasi-rent is the fact that while the supply of land, as a free gift of nature, is fixed for ever, that of the other instruments of production like building, machinery, *etc.*, is fixed only temporarily and can be increased after some time.

Take the case of houses. During a war, the demand for houses in towns increases owing to increase in urban population. But the supply cannot be increased because of the scarcity of building materials. For the time being, their supply is as much limited as that of land. This abnormal increase in the return on capital invested in buildings is quasi-rent. It is not pure rent, because the supply of houses can be increased in the long-run.

We may repeat that Quasi-rent is only a temporary surplus. With the increase in the supply of houses, as building materials become available, this surplus will tend to disappear. A similar surplus may arise in the case of other durable goods like machines, ships, *etc.* Similarly, quasi-rent may arise due to a temporary scarcity of a particular kind of skill which can be increased only if enough time is given.

The earnings from such durable goods like machines must, in the long run, equal the prevailing rate of interest. Temporarily, however, due to shortage, they may yield surplus earnings which are called quasi-rent.

We can apply the concept of transfer earnings also to explain quasi-rent. In the short run, a specialised machinery must remain in its present use. It cannot be transferred to any other use. This means that its transfer earnings are zero. Hence, in the short run, the whole of the earnings of machinery and capital equipment is a surplus over transfer earnings and is rent. But it is called quasi-rent because it is temporary. Their supply during the short period is fixed, and cannot be increased howsoever keen the demand may be. The surplus will, therefore, continue to be earned and cannot be competed away. But, in the long run, the supply can be increased and the surplus earnings will disappear. This cannot happen in the case of land whose supply is perfectly inelastic and is permanently fixed. Hence, rent of land will persist in the long run.

Quasi-rent has also been defined as the excess of total revenue earned in the short run over and above the total variable costs.

Thus,

Quasi-rent = Total Revenue—Total Variable Cost.

In the long run, all costs are variable and in the long run competitive equilibrium, total receipts are equal to total costs (including normal profit). There are no excess earnings over and above costs and hence no quasi-rent.

Quasi-rent can be illustrated by the following diagram (Fig. 33.7).

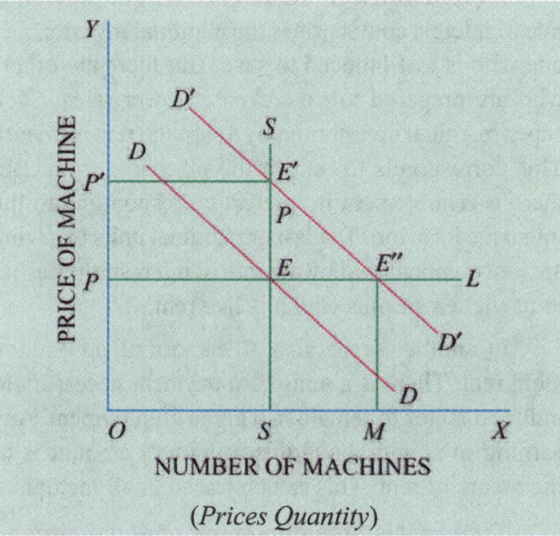

(*Prices Quantity*)

Fig. 33.7

In this diagram (Fig. 33.7), SS is the absolutely inelastic supply curve of machines. It cuts the demand curve DD at E. That is, at OP (= SE) price, OS machines are supplied. If in the short run, demand increases to D′D′, the price will go up to OP′ (= SE′) but the supply of machines remains OS. Since the number of machines is fixed in the short run, the transfer earnings are zero, the whole price is quasi-rent. It was OP before and it has become OP′ now. But, in the long run, the supply is perfectly elastic and is represented by PL so that any number of machines will be supplied at OP. Supply having now increased to OM, the price comes down to E′ ′M (= OP). Now the quasi-rent has vanished, because the price E′ ′M just covers the supply price (or transfer earnings) which is OP.

It is thus clear that capital goods earn quasi-rent in the short run, because the supply is fixed, but it disappears in the long run, when supply becomes perfectly elastic.

Quasi–Rent

Quasi-rent can be shown with other diagram (33.8) as follows:

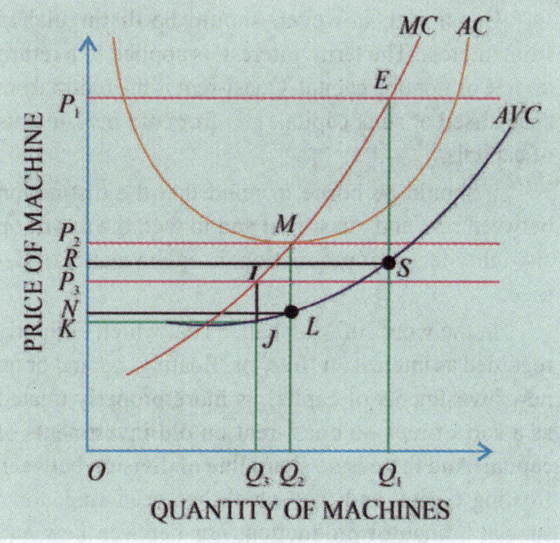

Fig. 33.8

In the above diagram AC = Average cost, AVC = Average variable cost and MC = Marginal cost. Let us find out the amount of quasi-rent at different prices.

(1) At OP_1, Price, equilibrium is at point 'E' and 'OQ_1', is the total quantity produced earlier explained as, quasi-rent is the earnings over and above the AVC.

Hence $\square\, OP_1EQ_1 - \square ORSQ_1 = \square P_1ESR$

(2) At OP_2 Price equilibrium is at point 'M' and 'OQ_2' quantity is produced.

Hence □ OP_2MQ_2 — □ $ONLQ_2$ = □ P_2MLN

(3) At OP_3 Price, equilibrium is at point 'I', 'OQ_3' quantity of output is produced.

□ OP_3IQ_3 — □ $OKJQ_3$ = □ P_3IJK.

Price	Total revenue	—Total variable Cost	= Quasi -rent
At OP_1	□ OP_1EQ_1	□ $ORSQ_1$	= □ P_1ESR
At OP_2	□ OP_2MQ_2	□ $ONLQ_2$	= □ P_2MLN
At OP_3	□ OP_3IQ_3	□ $OKJQ_3$	= □ P_3IJK

It is clear that

□ P_1ESR > □P_2MLN > □ P_3IJK.

From the diagram and the table it is clear that higher the price, higher is the quasi-rent and lower the price lower is the quasi-rent. Marshall made it clear that quasi-rent is a temporary phenomenon, it will disappear in the long-run [due to the use of more and more fixed capital].

Quasi-Rent and Interest

Quasi-rent, however, should be distinguished from interest. The term 'interest' is applied to a return on free or floating capital. Quasi-rent is the return from specialised or sunk capital, *i.e.*, from old investments of capital.

It should be borne in mind that the distinction between rent and quasi-rent and in fact, the return on any other factor of production, is only a matter of degree.

In the words of Marshall, "That which is rightly regarded as interest on 'free' or 'floating' capital or on new investments of capital, is more properly treated as a sort of rent—a quasi-rent on old investments of capital. And there is no sharp line of division between floating capital and that which has been sunk for a special branch of production, nor between new and old investments of capital; each group shades into the other gradually."[4] Rent is thus **"a leading species of a large genus."**

Land, old investments and new investments they are all scarce in relation to demand. Differential surpluses arise in all of them. But since the supply of land in the absolute sense is limited in a larger degree than that of other factors, land is put in a separate category by economists. Fundamentally speaking, there is no justification for this distinction.

It is necessary to clear one misconception. Quasi-rent has been called "unnecessary profit," that is, it does not form part of costs. This misconception arises from not making a clear distinction between the long-run and short-run view. For the short period, quasi-rent may be regarded as unnecessary profit. It does not form part of price, because the appliances are already there in existence and no special costs have to be incurred. But, in the long run, several supplementary costs may have to be incurred and the businessman must be duly compensated for them. These will certainly form part of costs and must be regarded as 'necessary profit.'

Rent Element in Other Factors

The rent element is not peculiar to land. But it can be traced in other agents of production as well.

Rent Element in Profits. All entrepreneurs are not of the same ability. At one extreme are those who are just able to keep their heads above water earning low profits. But at the other extreme are those who, on account of their superior organising ability, are able to produce at a lower cost. They enjoy higher profits which are similar to the surplus enjoyed by superior lands. Corresponding to situational advantages possessed by land, certain entrepreneurs make large profits on account of birth or business influence. There is thus the rent element in profits. Profits have been called **'rent of ability'.**

Rent Element in Wages. There are varying degrees of efficiency to be found among the workers. Roughly speaking wages correspond to personal efficiency. The more efficient workers enjoy a surplus or extra-wages as compared with the marginal worker. This is analogous to the rent of more accessible lands.

Rent Element in Interest. The prevailing rate of interest compensates the marginal investor, *i.e.*, one who is just induced to save. But there are others who are prepared to save even at lower rates. Such super-marginal investors enjoy a surplus (rent element). This corresponds to rent in the extensive form. But there is rent element in interest corresponding to the intensive form too. The last or marginal units of saving are just compensated by the rate of interest; the earlier units yield a surplus which is like rent.

In another sense also all factors of production yield rent. There is a minimum payment necessary to induce a factor to remain in a given employment. Any earning over and above this minimum amount is of the nature of rent. This can be traced in all factors.

Thus, **rent is "a leading specie of a large genus."**

4. *Principles of Economics*. 1936, p. 412.

RELATION BETWEEN RENT AND PRICE

According to Ricardo, rent does not enter into price. But the modern theory of rent deviates from the Ricardian theory in this respect. Ricardo held that rent did not enter into the cost of production of the produce and hence did not affect its price. Rent rises because of the rise in price and not the other way round. We have seen that, according to this theory, rent is surplus over cost. Price is determined by the cost of production at the margin where there is no rent. Hence, rent does not enter into price. The marginal dode of labour and capital just pays for itself and leaves no surplus.

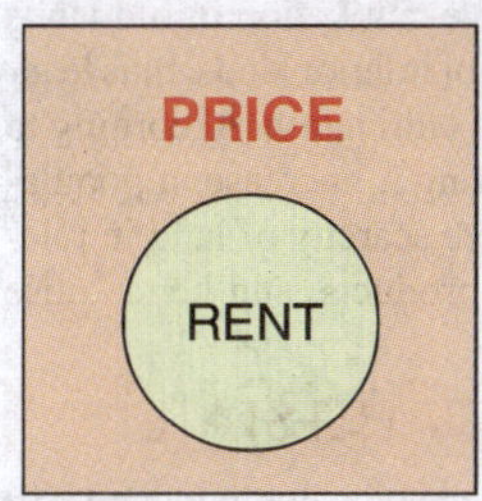

In fact the position of the margin, according to the Ricardian theory, is determined by price and not price by the position of the margin. Rent is thus not a part of price. Rent is price-determined and not price-determining.

It is true that the differential aspect of land is not a cause of price. If land A gives more valuable service than land B, the extra payment yielded by land A would not affect the price of the produce. In fact, here we are considering two different things, each being paid according to its efficiency or marginal productivity. There can be a similar differential aspect of wages, and we can argue that such differential payments do not affect the price of the product of labour. But wages do enter into price.

In another sense also, it may be argued that rent does not form a part of price. Land is free gift of nature. No payment is necessary to maintain the total supply of land. In this sense, rent is not a part of the supply price of land and consequently of the products of land. Since the supply of land is inelastic, it will always work for whatever it fetches under competition. Thus, the value of land completely depends on the value (*i.e.*, price) of the product, and not vice versa.

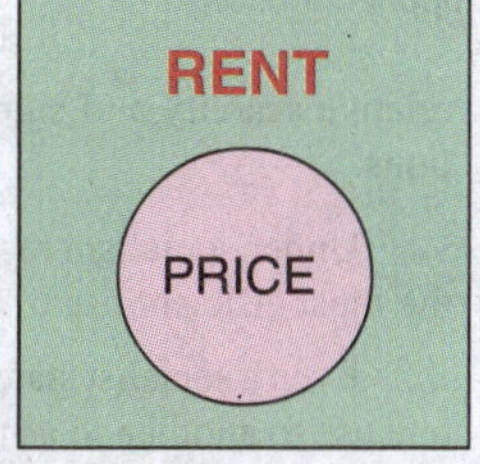

Suppose land is specific and it can be put to only one use and to none else, *e.g.*, when land can be used for production in one dominant industry only. It is again a case of inelastic supply to a particular industry, since land has no other use. Here also it will work for whatever it can get. In this case also rent will be price-determined and not price determining.

When Rent Enters Price

When we are thinking, not of all the lands of the country, but of the land available for particular uses, rent does form an element of cost and hence affects price. This is clear from the conception of the opportunity cost. Most of the land is capable of being put to alternative uses. If it is put to one use, it is not available for another use. The minimum price that has to be paid for the use of land is the amount which this land could earn in its most profitable **alternative** use. This payment for the use of land enters into price.

From the point of view of an individual farmer, prices paid for all factors (including the price for the use of land) must of course be included in the cost of production, and must, therefore, enter into price. If a farmer is using land belonging to someone else, the rent that he pays is obviously a cost for him. In the case of an owner-cultivator, too, the rent as a cost is there, only its presence is obscured. The payment that he could have received, if he did not cultivate himself, is the opportunity cost of this land.

The problem may be approached in another way. Prices are determined by the scarcity of the products in relation to demand. The rent that an entrepreneur pays is part of his cost of production. If the rent is high, the entrepreneur will tend to hire less land; and, conversely, he will use more land, if rent is low. If he uses more land the supply of land for other purposes is reduced; if he uses less land, the supply available for other purposes is increased. Thus, rent, by influencing relative scarcity of land for different uses; affects the prices of different products.

Thus, to use Samuelson's words, "What is a price-determined rent return to a factor which is inelastic in supply to the whole community or a dominant industry may to each firm and to any small industry that is only one of many potential users, appear as a price-determining cost."[5]

Conclusion

In the last analysis, however, as Davenport points out, **rent neither determines price nor is determined by price. Both price and rent are governed by the relative scarcities of the products of land.** They both vary with the changes in this relative scarcity. The same principle applies to wages, interest and profits.

Rent and Economic Progress

How is rent affected by economic progress? Broadly speaking economic progress may be indicated

5. Samuelson, P.A. — *Economics*, 1970, p. 540.

by (*a*) technical advances in methods of production, (*b*) improvements in transport, and (*c*) growth of population.

(*a*) Improved methods of agricultural production may affect all agricultural lands equally, or they may affect only the better or only the marginal lands.

If all lands are affected equally, the supply of the produce will increase, demand remaining the same, its price will, therefore, fall; marginal lands will go out of cultivation and, according to the Ricardian theory, rents of superior lands will fall.

If the improvements only affect the marginal land, according to the Ricardian theory, rents will again fall because the surplus of the superior land over the marginal land will be reduced.

If, on the other hand, the improvements affect only the best lands, their rents will rise, since their productivity, compared with that of the marginal land, will be higher. But if, in this latter case, the higher productivity of superior lands depresses the prices of the product, rents may fall again.

Thus, ultimately rents will depends upon the relation between supply and demand of the product of the land. **Agricultural improvements will affect rent not so much by affecting the margin of cultivation as the degree of scarcity of land or its products.**

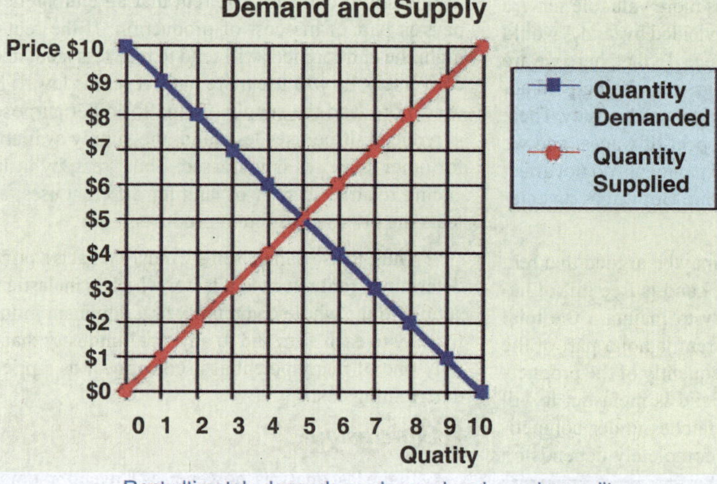

Rent ultimately depends on demand and supply conditons.

(*b*) As regards transport improvements, according to the Ricardian theory, better transport will affect rent by affecting the factor of situation. Distant lands will become nearer the market as it were. Their rents will rise. The rents of more favourably situated lands will fall. This can also be explained in terms of scarcity. If improved transport increases scarcity (by leading to exports from the given region), rents will rise; in the contrary circumstances, the rents will fall.

(*c*) As for the growth of population, its result is to raise rents. According to the Ricardian theory, this will be due to more intensive cultivation of old lands and extension of cultivation of inferior lands, thus leading to a fall of the margin of cultivation. According to the more recent way of putting it, increase in population will increase the relative scarcity of land in relation to the demand for its products, and hence raise rents.

RENT IN A SOCIALIST STATE

In a socialist state, private ownership in land will end, but a socialist state cannot do away with the concept of rent. Change of economic order from capitalism to socialism will not turn scarce land into an unlimited quantity. Rent as an index of productivity will help in the best allocation of the available land among its various uses. An accounting price tag will have to be put on the various types of land, the good land being put a higher tag. As Samuelson puts it, "Only by putting a price upon inert sweatless land are we using it, and sweating breathing labour, most productively! The price or rent of land rises so as to ration its limited supply among the best uses." Thus, rent makes for the most efficient use of the land resources of the community. In this way, it solves the problems of FOR WHOM and HOW of the society. In countries, like India, where land is scarce and rents are high, farmers will take to cheaper labour-intensive production. On the other hand, as in the U.S.A., where labour is relatively more expensive, the farmers will use land-intensive methods. It is rent which indicates the relative scarcity and signals the best factor substitutions.

Under socialism too, the community must make the most efficient use of its resources.

Even a socialist state will have to direct land from one use to another so as to make its marginal productivity in all uses the same. The marginal productivity will be indicated by rent.

Thus, the existence of rent ensures a correct allocation of valuable human or non-human resources.

ECONOMIC RENT AS A BASIS FOR A SINGLE LAND TAX

Henry George, an American economist in his well-known book '**Progress and Poverty**' (1879) advocated a single tax on land rent to replace the numerous other taxes which were then being levied. From the social point of view, land is a free gift of nature and as such land rent is not necessary to ensure its supply. Hence Henry George argued that taking away rents in their entirely would not affect the supply of land or impair the working of the economy. He justified such a tax on the ground that land rents went on rising as a result of social progress and not in no way due to the personal efforts of the land owners. The incidence of tax or rent is entirely on the land owners for whom this represents unearned income. A tax levied on a completely in elastically supplied good is absorbed entirely by the suppliers of that good. Hence Henry George argued that a single tax on land rent could take the place of numerous other taxes without producing any ill effects on the economy. Besides, it would not distort the allocation of land usage, because it will leave the supply and demand for land unaffected.

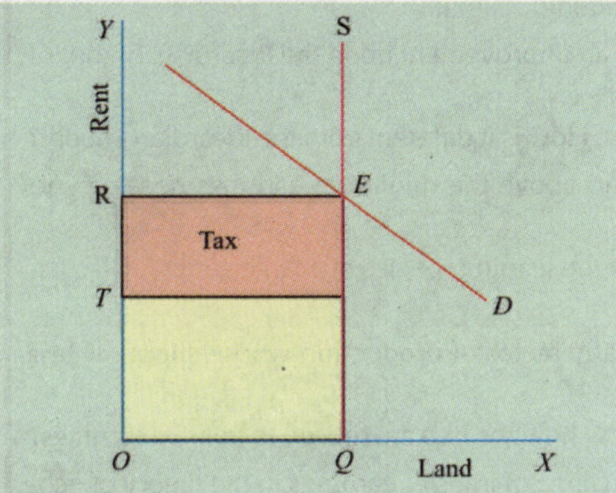

Fig. 33.9. Taking the rent from land. (inelastic supply).

However, the proposal had little practical value.

Key terms

Economic rent, Differential Rent, Scarcity Rent, Quasi Rent, Contact Rent, marginal Land.

QUESTIONS

1. Distinguish between Economic Rent and Contract Rent. How is Economic Rent determined? Explain.
2. Distinguish between Economic Rent and Scarcity Rent. In what sense is rent peculiar to land?
3. Explain the Ricardian Theory of Rent and discuss the amplifications and modifications made in the theory by modern economists.
4. "Rent is paid for the origin and indestructible power of the soil." Explain.
5. "The among of rent earned depends both on quality and quantity of the factor in relation to the demand for it". Examine this view.
6. What is "No-rent Land"? Under what circumstances will such land start yielding positive rent?
7. "Rent can arise only when the supply of any factor of production is less than perfectly elastic." In the context of this statement describe the modern theory of rent.
8. Do you agree with the view that no rent will arise, if all land is equally fertile and equally well situated?
9. Would here be rent (*a*) if all lands were equally fertile; (*b*) if the land owner himself is the cultivator of land; (*c*) if there were no tendency to diminishing returns; (*d*) if the Government owned all lands; (*e*) if the supply of better lands were practically unlimited; and (*f*) if land revenue were abolished? Give reasons in each case.
10. Explain the occurrence of rent—

    (*a*) When land is homogeneous and has a single use.

    (*b*) When land is not homogeneous.

    (*c*) When it has alternative uses.

11. State and explain the modern theory of rent. Does rent, according to this theory, enter into price?
12. Discuss the modern theory of rent what is the role of opportunity cost in it?
13. 'Rent is not a payment for the factor land but for the land-element in factors'. In the light of this statement discuss the modern theory of rent.
14. "Rent is price determined and not price determining". Explain.
15. What is Modern Theory of Rent? How far is in an improvement upon the Ricardian Theory of Rent?
16. Explain the modern concept of rent as a surplus. How is it different from the Ricardian Theory?
17. "Rent is a surplus earned by a factor over and above the minimum earnings necessary to induce to do its work". Discuss.
18. "The rent of the land is not a thing by itself but the leading species of a large genus". Discuss.

    Or

    "Rent is not peculier to land; it can arise to any factor of production whose supply is less than perfectly elastic'. Discuss.
19. Distinguish between Rent and Quasi-Rent Show how the two are related to transfer earnings?
20. What are transfer earnings? What is the significance of transfer earnings in the theory of economic rent ?
21. Distinguish between Transfer Earnings and Economic Rent. Mention cases where the entire earnings of a factor may be regarded as (*a*) Transfer Earnings and (*b*) Economic Rent.
22. Discuss the probable effects of the following on agricultural rents: (a) growth of population; (*b*) growth of international trade; (*c*) industrialisation; (*d*) agricultural improvements; and (e) improvements in the means of transport.
23. Analyse the nature of rent and indicate the position it is likely to hold under a socialistic regime.

INTEREST

What is Interest?

Perhaps interest has been the most controversial topic in the whole theory of distribution. Economists have differed regarding the nature of interest as well as how it is determined. In fact, the subject of interest is still an unsettled question of Economics. The very definition of interest depends on the interest theory which one accepts. Those, who believe in the classical or real theory, regard interest as payment for the use of capital goods. They also believe that interest is necessary to induce people to save. The followers of liquidity preference theory believe that interest is a price for surrendering liquidity preference. Still others who accept the loanable funds theory hold that interest is the price paid for the use of loanable funds.

Just as rent is a payment for the use of land, similarly interest is a payment for the use of capital. In Marshall's words, interest is "the price paid for the use of capital in any market."[1] Just as wage is the price of the service of labour, similarly, interest is the price of capital. It is expressed as a percentage return on capital invested after allowing for risks of investment.

Interest is percentage return on capital inverted.

Samuelson defines interest thus: "The market rate of interest is that percentage return per year which has to be paid on any safe loan of money, which has to be yielded by any safe bond or other type of security, and which has to be earned on the value of any capital asset (such as a machine, a hotel building, a patent right) in any competitive market where there are no risks or where all risk factors have already been taken care of by special premium payments to protect against risk."[2]

In this chapter, we shall discuss all these divergent views about the nature of interest

1. *Principles*, (8th Edition), p. 534.
2. Samuelson. P. A. –*Economics*, 1970. P. 595.

and determination of its rate, and shall attempt a synthesis among them.

Gross and Net Interest

Much of what is called interest is not the price of the service of capital as such. What people generally call interest is really gross interest. Pure interest is only a small proportion of gross interest as explained by this fact. Pure interest tends to equality in different employments, provided competition is free and perfect.

Gross Interest. The total amount which the debtor pays to the creditor is known as gross interest as already indicated. All that the borrower pays to the lender is not pure or net interest, *i.e.*, the price paid for the services of capital only. It is mixed up with so many other elements, of which Pure or Net Interest is only one. Gross interest consists of the following elements:–

(*a*) Pure Interest. This is a payment only for the services of capital as such or for the money borrowed.

(*b*) Insurance against Risk. The lender is exposed to risk when he lends money. A certain amount must be paid to him to cover these risks. These risks are of two kinds: (*i*) personal risks due to the unreliable character of the borrower himself, and (*ii*) trade risks. Trade risks are due to the varying fortunes of the business in which the money is invested. Thus, the lender may fear that either the borrower may refuse to pay back the loan and the interest on it or he may lose the money in his business. The greater the risk of this kind, the higher will have to be the insurance money that the lender will expect before he is willing to lend.

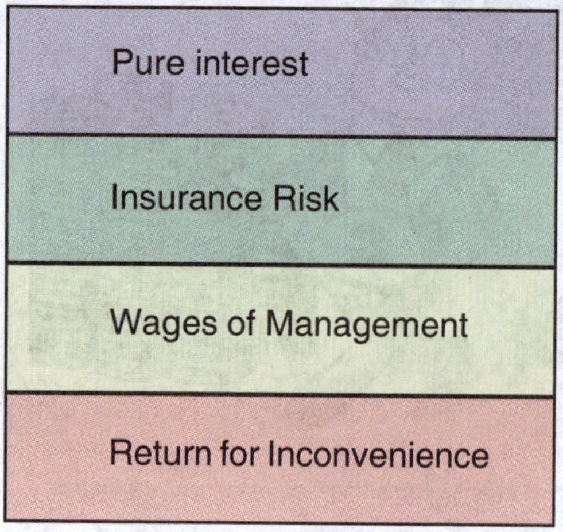

Pure interest
Insurance Risk
Wages of Management
Return for Inconvenience

Gross interest.

(*c*) Wages of Management. A part of the payment may be due to the wages of management. The lender has to keep accounts and to arrange for new loans for short period. Money-lending is his whole time job.

(*d*) Return for Inconvenience. A lender has to suffer certain inconveniences for which he seeks compensation in the form of interest. When a man lends money, he loses command over it for a period. He is unable to make use of it for himself, if he wants to. Favourable opportunities for its investment may also slip by. Inconvenience is of two types: The lender may not get back the money when he needs it and he may have to borrow from others on interest. Or, he may get the money when he cannot find for it some safe and remunerative investment so that the money lies idle and he loses interest. He must, therefore, compensate himself for such losses. Hence, he charges something extra over and above pure or net interest.

Keeping, these facts in mind, it will become clear why the village money-lender's rates of interest are high in spite of competition among the lender. This is due to the fact that he faces greater risk and inconvenience. Similarly, the pawn-brokers seemingly charge very high rates when calculated on an annual basis. But they have to undergo a lot of trouble in their business in keeping small individual accounts, *etc.* This also explains why governments, especially those with sound financial traditions, can borrow at extremely low rates of interest. Here the risk and inconvenience to the lender are negligible and the interest paid is mainly "pure interest". The return on government securities is an example of pure rate of interest.

Differences in Interest Rates

There is an element of monopolistic competition in the money market in as much as different borrowers are charged different rates of interest. It may be noted, however, that pure interest tends to be the same, if calculated over the same period of time in the same money market. The actual differences that prevail are differences in gross interest. In other words, they are due to difference in the degree of risk involved and inconveniences suffered by the lenders.

Differences in Pure Interest

Pure interest may be different in different investments, when the market is not the same owing to the following reasons:–

(*a*) Differences Due to Distances. People are usually more willing to invest their capital nearer home than at a long distance. This may create differences in supply and demand due to the comparative immobility of capital.

(*b*) Differences Due to Time. If people have to part with their money for a longer period, they expect higher rate of interest even though risks and other factors are the same. Of course, if money is lent for very short periods and has to be re-lent again and again, the inconvenience of management will increase gross interest. But that will not be net interest.

(*c*) Differences Due to the Amount of the Loan. It is generally seen that the rate of interest varies inversely with the amount of the loan. The rate decreases as the amount of the loan increases, and vice versa.

(*d*) Differences in Liquidity. By 'liquidity' we mean the ease with which the loan given can be called back or the ease with which an asset like securities can be sold without monetary loss when its owner requires cash. The sale of some securities may involve delay, cost or capital loss, while others may be readily disposed of without such cost or monetary loss. The more liquid securities will carry a lower rate of interest and **vice-versa.**

(*e*) Maturity Period. Another reason for differences in interest rates is the maturity of the loan, *i.e.*, the length of the loan. Other things being equal, long-term loans will carry higher rates of interest than do short-term loans, since the long-term lenders suffer greater inconvenience and possible financial sacrifice of foregoing alternative uses for their money for a longer period of time. On a long-term loan, there is a risk of drop in the value of the securities or a possible rise in the price level. The lender must, therefore, charge more to cover the possible loss. Hence, a long-term bond will have to offer a higher rate of interest than a short-term bond, other thing being equal.

(*f*) Market Imperfections. Another factor which explains some of the differences in interest rates is the market imperfections or monopoly element. A bank in a small town, which has a monopoly in local money market, may charge a higher rate of interest from the local people, because there the people find it very inconvenient to "shop around" at banks in distant cities. On the other hand a large corporation (*i.e.*, joint-stock company) being not confined to a local market enjoys a more competitive position and can survey or shop around all possible lending houses. Therefore, a large nationally known corporation can sell its bonds on favourable terms.

Differences in Gross Interest

Differences in gross interest may, in addition to the causes already considered, be due to:–

(*i*) Differences in Social Esteem. A person with better reputation or integrity can borrow at lower rates. This is partly due to the element of lower personal risk already considered.

(*ii*) Differences in Productivity. Where capital can earn greater reward for the producer, he will be willing to pay higher interest. Such trades are usually more speculative and higher interest can be attributed to higher risks. Moreover, **under perfect competition, as we shall see, marginal productivity of capital, and hence the pure rate of interest, tends to equality.** Higher rewards in particular employment, if not justified by greater risks or inconvenience, tend to disappear through force of competition. But if competition is imperfect, such differences may persist.

Productivity of capital may differ in different countries. In new States, for instance, the demand for capital is great, while the supply is very limited. Capital thus has a high marginal productivity, and interest is high. This is due to the immobility of capital over distance as already noted. Partly it is due to greater risk. In the latter case, it is **gross** interest which will be higher, and not **net** interest.

Thus, ultimately differences in interest rates can be reduced to differences in inconvenience or risks of lending except in cases where we are not dealing with the same market. **Pure interest tends to be the same in the same market.**

To sum up: "The interest rate charged on individual business is usually determined in personal negotiation between bank and borrower. It reflects such attributes as the borrower's size and general credit standing, his access to alternative credit sources, the size and maturity of the loan, the character of the borrower's business, the value to the bank of his deposit account and of other business relationships, and the nature of the security, if any, to be pledged. Certain other factors not related directly to the borrower of the loan but rather to the lending bank or perhaps the banking structure can also be shown to have some effect on interest rates charged for bank business loans. There are the size of the lending bank, the size of the centre in which the bank is located, and the area of the country where the loan was made." [3]

3. Richard Youngdahl on "Structure of Interest Rates", *Federal Reserve Bulletin*, July 1947.

THEORIES OF INTEREST

A theory of interest should explain two things: (*a*) How interest arises and (*b*) how the rate of interest is determined. Some theories of interest explain only one of these aspects whereas others explain both. For instance, Productivity Theory, Abstinence or Waiting Theory, Agio Theory and Fisher's Time Preference Theory are all classical theories which explain only why interest arises or why interest is paid. On the other hand, the Classical Theory, the Loanable Funds Theory and Liquidity Preference Theory explain both how interest arises as well as how the rate of interest is determined.

We now start the discussion of the theories of interest with the first set of theories which explain how interest arises or why interest is paid.

HOW INTEREST ARISES

Productivity Theory

The Theory. To take the Productivity Theory first, some older economists thought that capital was productive of goods in the same sense as land was productive of crops. They held that interest was paid because production with the aid of capital was greater than without it. Capital is productive in the sense that labour, assisted by capital, produces more than labour without capital. A fisherman with a net catches more fish than without it. A farm labourer with a tractor can produce more than without a tractor.

Criticism. Physical productivity of capital goods, however, does not explain interest. If people were willing to lend unlimited amounts of money without interest, business would expand up to a point where the falling price of the product would simply cover other changes (without any interest) in making thereof. **Interest would not be a cost.** But interest is a cost which every entrepreneur must reckon with. Hence, price, in the long run, must cover **all costs including interest.** Since demand for capital, when it is free of interest, must exceed the supply of it, interest is bound to emerge. Even if some lenders were willing to lend without interest, prevalence of competition would ensure that loans would be advanced only to those who would pay interest rather than to those who would not.

Hence, it is scarcity rather than productivity which explains interest.

Further, if interest depended merely on productivity (not marginal productivity), interest rates should vary in proportion to the productiveness of capital. In actual fact, pure rate of interest tends to be the same in the same market.

Saving today implies waiting for consumption tomorrow.

Moreover, if capital helps labour to produce more, it has to be seen how much of this extra production is due to capital and how much to labour, since capital without labour produces nothing.

Then, what about loans for consumption purposes? They are not productive, but interest has to be paid on them all the same.

Again, it may be pointed out that the productivity theory attempts to explain interest from the side of demand only. It ignores the supply side altogether. It is thus a one-sided explanation.

As we shall see later, the above objections can be overcome, if we talk in terms of marginal productivity and not mere productivity of capital.

Conclusion. Thus, it is clear that it is not productivity, as such which explains why interest is paid.

Abstinence or Waiting Theory

The Theory. Another theory of interest is the Abstinence Theory. Whereas the Productivity Theory tries to explain interest from the side of demand; the Abstinence Theory approaches the problem from the side of supply. It was Senior who first pointed out that saving involved a sacrifice or "abstinence" as he put it. Saving was an act of abstaining from consumption. Since to abstain was painful, it was necessary to reward people for this act. This reward was in the form of the interest paid to those who saved, rather than consumed their incomes, or a part of their income.

Criticism. The idea of abstinence was widely criticised on the ground that it suggested positive discomfort, while the rich people, who are the main source of capital, save without the least inconvenience. That is why Marshall substituted the term "waiting" for "abstinence". Saving implies waiting. When a person saves, he does not refrain from consumption for all time; he merely postpones present consumption to a future data. Meanwhile, he has to wait. But since most people do not like to wait, an inducement is necessary to encourage this postponement of consumption. Interest is this inducement.

Some "waiting", however, may be forthcoming without any inducement in the way of interest payment. Other people will "wait" even with a negative rate of interest. But aggregate of savings thus made will not be adequate to meet the total demand for capital. Interest must be paid to induce many more people to save in the case of whom "waiting" does involve inconvenience. The rate of interest must be high enough to bring forth the marginal increment of saving or "waiting" in order to meet the aggregate demand for capital. The rate of interest will be fixed at a level at which the supply of "waiting" will be equal to the demand for it.

This theory has a considerable element of truth in it, but it does not clearly analyse forces acting on the side of demand for capital.

Austrian or Agio Theory

This theory is also called Psychological Theory of interest. First advanced by John Rae in 1834, this theory was given its final shape by Bohm Bawerk of the Austrian school of economists. It became popular later among some American economists, like Fisher, with slight modifications.

The Theory. The gist of the theory of Bohm Bawerk, is that interest arises because people prefer present goods to future goods, and that, therefore, there is an 'agio' or premium on present goods. One bird in hand is said to be worth two in the bush. The present gratification is attached greater importance than the future satisfaction.

In other words, future satisfactions when viewed from the present angle undergoes a discount. Interest is this discount which must be paid in order to induce people to lend money or postpone present satisfactions to a future data. That is, interest is intended to equate future satisfaction with present satisfaction. To induce a person to part with Rs. 100 now, it is not enough to give him a promise of the return of only Rs.100 after a year. The borrower must pay more, otherwise the lender will feel that he is a loser. The human mind is so constituted that there is commonly an under-valuation of the future purchasing power as compared with the present purchasing power.

Why do people prefer present satisfaction to future satisfaction? Bohm Bawerk gave three reasons for this fact. One is the "prospective under-estimate for the future". The future is less clearly perceived than the present. It is uncertain. In the second place, present wants are felt more keenly than the future wants. The result is that the demand for present goods is greater than that for future goods. Thirdly, present goods possess "a technical superiority over future goods." This is so because the passage of time allows the use of more round about methods of production, which are more productive.

Another reason is that one may hope to improve his economic position in future as a result of which the marginal utility of his income will decline. He will, therefore, prefer to use his income at the present when the marginal utility of his income is high.

There is still another reason for a consumer to prefer present satisfaction to future satisfaction. He may expect growth of the economy making more and better goods and services available when the general standard of living will be higher indicating declining marginal utility of money.

These reasons, however, do not apply to all, at any rate, to the same extent.

Fisher's Time Preference Theory

Fisher emphasizes the fact of "time preference" as the central point in the Theory. Individuals prefer present satisfactions to equally certain future satisfactions. They are thus impatient to spend their incomes now. The degree of impatience depends upon the size of the income, the distribution of income over time, the degree of certainly regarding enjoyment in the future and the temperament and the character of the individual. Thus, people with larger incomes are likely to have their present wants more fully satisfied and will thus discount the future at a lower rate than poorer people.

As regards distribution of income over time, three kinds of situations may be imagined. The income may be uniform throughout one's life, or increase with age, or decrease with age. If it is uniform, the degree of impatience to spend (*i.e.*, the rate of discounting the future) will be determined by the size of the income and the temperament of the individual. If the income increases with age, it means the future is well provided for, and the tendency will be to discount the future at a higher rate. If the income decreases with age, the converse will be true, *i.e.*, the future will be discounted at a lower rate.

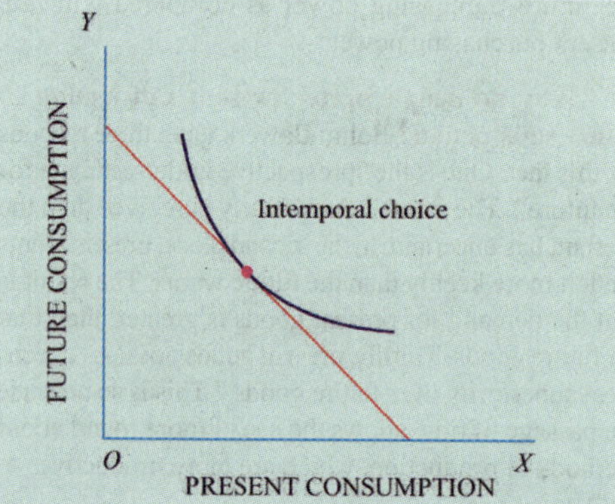

As for the degree of certainty, it is clear that the greater the certainty of future enjoyment of income the smaller the degree of time preference or the rate of discounting the future, and vice-versa.

Finally, the character of the individual will also influence this time preference. A man of forethought will discount the future at a lower rate compared with a spendthrift. The rate of time preference is also influenced by expectation of life. If a man expects to live long, his preference for purchasing power in the present will be comparatively low. Similar will be the case of a man who desires to leave behind a handsome patrimony.

The rate of time preference of an individual also depends on the proportion of his income that he is asked to lend. The larger the amount of loan, the higher must be the rate of interest, because it entails a greater sacrifice of liquidity on the part of the lender.

Thus, the rates of individual time preference, after having been determined in this way, tend to become equal to the rate of interest. An individual with a higher rate of time preference compared with the market rate of interests tends to borrow money in order to satisfy his more pressing wants. If his rate of time preference is lower than the market rate of interest, he will lend to the market and make a gain thereby. Thus, the individual will vary his income-stream by borrowing or lending. This process will tend to equalise the rate of interest with the rate of time preference.

Liquidity Preference Theory

According to Keynes, interest is not a reward for waiting, nor is it a payment for time preference. The rate of interest is a reward for parting with liquidity. This theory not only explains why interest arises, but it also explains how the rate of interest is determined. We shall discuss this theory in a later section of this chapter.

HOW RATE OF INTEREST IS DETERMINED

Among the theories which seek to explain the determination of the rate of interest we might mention:

(i) Classical or Real Theory.

(ii) Loanable Funds or Neo-Classical Theory, and

(iii) Keynesian or Liquidity Preference Theory.

All these theories of interest seek to explain the determination of the rate of interest though the equilibrium between the forces of demand and supply. In other words, all these three theories of interest are 'demand and supply theories' with rate of interest as the mechanism which brings about equilibrium between demand and supply. The difference among the theories of interest lies in the answer to the question: demand for what and supply of what?

According to the Classical Theory of interest, rate of interest is determined by demand for **saving to invest** and supply of **savings.** Loanable Funds theory seeks to explain the determination of the rate of interest through the equilibrium between demand for **loanable funds** and **supply of loanable funds.** Apart from current savings, loanable funds **include** other things also. Keynesian Theory of interest asserts that the **rate of interest** is determined by the demand for **money** to hold (*i.e.*, liquidity preference) and the supply of **money.**

We will now discuss these theories one by one.

CLASSICAL OR REAL THEORY OF INTEREST

There was no unanimity among the classical economists on the point as to how interest arises or why interest is paid. They had different views on this point. But they all agreed that the rate of interest is determined by the equilibrium of savings and investment.

The classical theory of interest also goes by the name of real theory as it seeks to explain the determination of the rate of interest by real factors like productivity and thrift, *i.e.*, productivity of capital goods and saving of goods. According to this theory the rate of interest is a payment for saving. The rate of interest is, thus, determined by the demand for saving to invest in capital goods and the supply of savings. Let us explain these demand and supply sides.

Demand for Savings

The demand for capital goods comes from firms which desire to invest, that is, to purchase or to make new capital goods. Capital goods are demanded because they can be used to produce consumer goods –because they have a revenue productivity like all other factors. For any given type of capital asset, *e.g.*, a machine, it is possible to draw a marginal revenue-productivity curve showing the addition made to the total revenue by an additional unit of a machine at various levels of the stock of that machine.

We have said that capital, like other factors of production, has marginal revenue productivity. But the marginal revenue productivity of capital is a more complex concept than that of other factors, because capital has a life of many years. A capital asset continues to yield returns for many years. Therefore, the entrepreneurs have to take into consideration the uncertainties of the future and estimate the percentage yield or returns from capital after making allowance for maintenance and operating costs. In other words, they have to find out the **net expected return** of a marginal unit of capital expressed as percentage of the cost of the capital asset. The more capital assets of a given kind an entrepreneur has, the less revenue or income he will expect to earn by purchasing one more machine of the same kind. Therefore, the marginal revenue productivity curve of capital slopes downwards towards the right. (See Fig. 34.1 below).

Now, under perfect competition, it is profitable for a firm to purchase any factor up to the point at which the price of that factor equals its marginal revenue productivity. The price of the savings required to purchase the capital goods is obviously the rate of interest. Hence, the entrepreneur will demand capital goods or (which is the same thing) 'will demand savings to purchase capital goods' up to the point at which the expected net rate of return on the capital goods equals the rate of interest. Since the marginal revenue productivity curve of capital slopes downwards, it follows that, as the rate of interest falls, more capital goods will be demanded and also more money will be required to purchase these capital goods.

The way in which the demand for capital goods rises as the rate of interest falls is shown in Fig. 34.1, where MRP, is the marginal revenue productivity

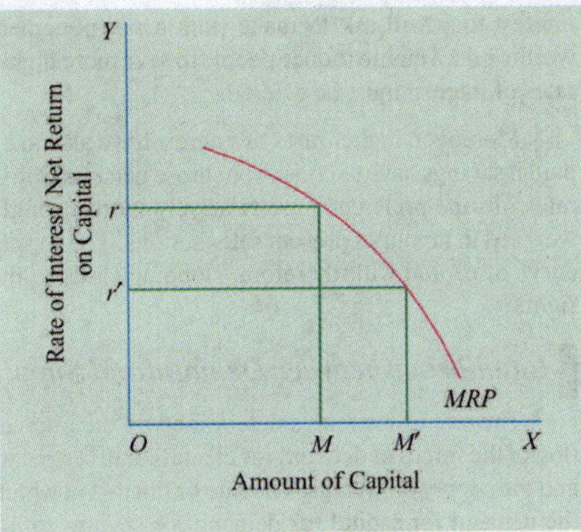

Fig. 34.1. Demand for Capital.

curve. On the Y-axis net rate of return on capital and the rate of interest are shown, while X-axis represents the amount of capital.

At Or rate of interest, OM amount of capital is demanded. This is so because only at OM amount of capital the falling net rate of return on capital becomes equal to the prevailing rate of interest Or. Now, if the rate of interest falls from Or to Or′, the amount of capital demanded will increase from OM to OM′, since at OM′ the falling net rate of return equals the new interest rate Or′.

Thus, it is clear that the marginal revenue productivity curve of capital shows the demand for capital and further that the demand curve for capital (or demand for savings to buy the capital) slopes downwards towards the right. This is true of individual firms, of individual industries and of the community as a whole.

Thus, we conclude that demand for individual capital goods and for capital goods in general will increase as the rate of interest falls.

Supply of Savings

According to this theory, the money which is to be used for purchasing capital goods is made available by those who save from their current income. By postponing consumption of a part of their current income, they release resources for productive purposes. Saving involve the element of waiting for the future enjoyment of savings. But people prefer the present enjoyment of goods and services to the future enjoyment of them. Therefore, if people are to be persuaded to save money and to lend it to entrepreneurs, they must be offered some interest as reward. More savings the people will do, the more consumption they will have to postpone, the higher must be the rate of interest they will ask to make such a postponement worthwhile. Thus, to induce people to save more higher rates of interest must be offered.

Moreover, higher rates of interest have also to be paid if savings have to come from those persons whose rates of time-preference are relatively more strongly weighed in favour of present satisfactions. The supply curve of capital will, therefore, slope upwards to the right.

Equilibrium between Demand and Supply

The rate of interest is determined by the interaction of the forces of demand for capital (or investment) and the supply of savings. The rate of interest at which the demand for capital (or demand for savings to invest in capital goods) and the supply of savings are in equilibrium will be the rate determined in the market.

How the rate of interest is determined by the interaction of demand for investment and supply of savings is shown in Fig. 34.2, where SS is the supply curve of saving and II is the demand curve of savings to invest in capital goods (II is also called demand curve for investment or simply investment demand curve). The demand for investment and supply of savings are in equilibrium at Or rate of interest, where the curves intersect each other. Hence, Or is the equilibrium rate of interest, which will come to stay in the market. In this equilibrium position, OM amount of money is lent, borrowed and invested. If any change in the demand for investment and supply of saving comes about, the curves will shift accordingly, and, therefore, the equilibrium rate of interest will also change.

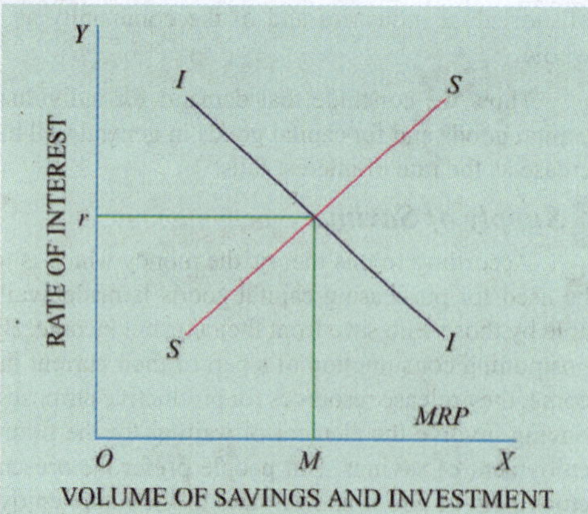

Fig. 34.2. Demand and Supply Equilibrium.

Criticism

The Classical Theory of Interest came in for serious criticism at the hands of Keynes. Firstly, it is pointed out that Classical Theory of interest is based upon the assumption of full employment of resources. In other words, it assumes that an increase in the production of one thing must mean the withdrawal of some resources from the production of other things. "Within the framework of a system of theory, built on the assumption of full employment, the notion of interest as a reward for waiting or abstinence is highly plausible. It is the premise that resources are typically fully employed that lacks plausibility in the contemporary world."[4] If at any time in the country, unemployed resources are found on a large scale, there is no need for paying people to abstain from consumption, *i.e.*, to wait in order that more resources should be devoted to the production of capital goods.

Secondly, according to the Classical Theory of interest, more investment (production of capital goods) can take place only by curtailing consumption. Greater the reduction of consumption more are the saving and, therefore, more investment. But a decrease in the demand for consumer goods is likely to lessen the incentive to produce capital goods and therefore, will affect investment adversely.

Thirdly, by assumpting full employment, the classical theory has neglected the changes in the income level. By neglecting the changes in the income level, the classical theory is led into error of viewing the rate of interest as the factor which brings equality of saving and investment. As keynes asserts, equality between savings and investment is brought about not by changes in the rate of interest but by changes in the level of income.

Fourthly, according to the Classical Theory, the investment demand schedule can change or shift without causing a change or shift in the saving curve schedule. For example, according to classical theory, if investment demand schedule or curve II shifts downwards, then the new equilibrium rate of interest will be determined where this new investment demand curve cuts the old saving curve which has remained unchanged. But this is wrong. As we know from Keynesian Economics, fall in investment leads to decrease in income and out of the reduced income, less is saved and therefore savings curve also changes. Thus, we see that classical theory ignores the effect of changes in investment on savings.

Lastly, the Classical Theory, as pointed out by Keynes, is indeterminate. Position of the savings schedule or curve depends upon the income level, that is, the position of the savings curve or schedule will vary with the level of incomes. There will be different savings schedules for different levels of incomes. As

4. Dillard –*Economics of J. M. Keynes*, p. 162.

income rises, for example, the savings schedule or curve will shift to the right. Thus, we cannot know what the rate of interest will be unless we already know what that the income level is. And we cannot know the income level without already knowing the rate of interest, since a lower interest rate will mean a large volume of investment and so via the multiplier, a higher level of real income. The classical theory, therefore, offers no solution and is indeterminate.

LOANABLE FUNDS THEORY OF INTEREST

The loanable funds theorists believed in the Time Preference explanation of how interest arises. According to Loanable Funds Theory, also called the Neo-classical Theory, interest is the price paid for the use of loanable funds. Like the Classical and Keynesian theories of interest, it is also a demand and supply theory. It asserts that rate of interest is determined by the equilibrium between demand and supply of loanable funds in the credit market. There are several sources of both supply and demand of loanable funds which we discuss below.

Supply of Loanable Funds

The supply of loanable funds is derived from four basic sources, namely, (*a*) savings, (*b*) dishoarding, (*c*) bank credit, and (*d*) disinvestment.

(*a*) Savings. Savings by individuals or households constitute the most important source of loanable funds. In the lonable funds theory, savings are looked at in either of these two ways, firstly, as ex-ante savings, *i.e.*, savings planned by individuals at the beginning of a period in the hope of expected incomes and anticipated expenditures on consumption; or secondly in the Robertsonian sense savings of the difference between the income of the preceding period and the consumption of the present period. In either case, the amount saved varies at various rates of interest. Savings by individuals and households primarily depend upon the size of their incomes. But, given the level of income, savings vary at various rates of interest. More savings will be forthcoming at higher rates of interest, and vice versa.

Savings.

Like individuals, businesses also save. A part of the earnings of a business concern is consumed as declared dividends; the undistributed part constitutes business or corporate savings. Such savings depend partly upon the current rate of interest. A high rate of interest is likely to encourage business savings as a substitute for borrowings from the loan market. But these business savings are often demanded for investment purposes by the firms themselves and, therefore, they do not enter the market for loanable funds.

(*b*) Dishoarding. This is another sources of loanable funds. Individuals may dishoard money from the hoarded stock of the previous period. Thus, cash balances, lying idle in a previous period, become active balances in the present period and are available as loanable funds. At higher rate of interest, more will be dishoarded. At very low rates of interest, there is a greater tendency to hold on to money.

(*c*) Bank Credit. The banking system provides a third source of loanable funds. Banks, by creating credit money, can advance loans to the businessmen. Banks can also reduce the amount of money by contracting their lending. The new money created by the banks in a period adds greatly to the supply of loan funds. The supply curve of funds provided by banks is to some degree interest-elastic, *i.e.*, it varies with various rates of interest. Generally speaking, the banks will lend more money at higher rates of interest than at lower ones, other things remaining the same.

(*d*) Disinvestment. Disinvestment is the opposite of investment and takes place when, due to the structural changes or bad venture, the existing stock of machines and other equipment is allowed to wear out without being replaced or when the inventories are drawn below the level of the previous period. When this happens, a part of the revenue from the sale of the products, instead of going into capital replacement, flows into the market for loanable funds.

"Disinvestment is encouraged somewhat by a high rate of interest on loanable funds. When the rate is high, some of the current capital may not produce a marginal revenue product to match this rate of interest. The firm may decide to let this capital run down and to put the depreciation funds in the loan market." [5] Thus, disinvestment adds to the supply of loanable funds. In Fig. 34.3, DI is the disinvestment curve and slopes upwards to the right.

By the lateral summation of the four curves, saving (S), dishoarding (DH), disinvestment (DI), and bank credit (BM), we get the total supply curve of loanable funds which slopes upwards to the right showing that a greater amount of loanable funds will available at higher rates of interest, and vice versa.

Demand for Loanable Funds

The demand for loanable funds comes mainly from three fields: (i) investment, (ii) consumption and (iii) hoarding.

The bulk of demand for loanable funds comes from business firms which borrow money for purchasing or making new capital goods, including the building up of inventories. Demand for loanable funds for investment purposes by business firms is the most important constituent of total demand for loanable funds. The price of the loanable funds required to purchase the capital goods is obviously the rate of interest. It will pay businessmen to demand loanable funds up to the point at which the expected net rate of return on the capital goods equal the rate of interest. Businessmen will find it profitable to purchase larger amounts of capital goods, when the rate of interest (*i.e.*, the price of the loanable funds) declines.

Thus, the demand for loanable funds for investment purposes is interest-elastic and slopes downwards to the right. The demand for loanable funds for investment purposes is represented by curve I in Fig. 34.3 given on the next page.

The second big demand for loanable funds comes from individuals or households who want to borrow for consumption purposes. Individuals or households demand loanable funds when they wish to make purchases in excess of their current incomes and cash resources. Generally, the loans for consumption are demanded for buying durable goods like automobiles, refrigerators, radios, television sets, *etc*. Lower rates of interest will encourage some increase in consumer borrowing. Demand for loanable funds for consumption purposes is shown by the curve 'C' in Fig. 34.3, which is interest-elastic and slopes downward to the right.

5. Bober, M. M. –Intermediate Price and Income Theory, ed. 1955, p. 371.

Lastly, the demand for loanable funds may come from those who wants to hoard money, *i.e.*, to satisfy the liquidity preference. Hoarding signifies the people's desires to hold their savings as **idle cash balance.** An important point to be noted here is that the one who supplies the loanable funds is the same person who demands the loanable funds for hoarding. A saver who hoards his savings can be said to be supplying loanable funds and also demanding them to satisfy his liquidity preference.

Demand for hoarding is shown by curve H in Fig. 34.3. The demand for hoarding money is interest-elastic and slopes downwards to the right. At higher rate of interest, people will hoard or hold less money, because much of the money will be lent to take advantage of the higher interest rates. Similarly, at lower rates of interest, people will hoard more money, because the loss incurred by hoarding in this case is not very much.

Equilibrium Between Demand for and Supply of Loanable Funds

The rate of interest will be determined by the equilibrium between the total demand for loanable funds and the total supply of loanable funds as shown in Fig. 34.3 below.

In this figure LS is the total supply curve of loanable funds, which has been derived by the lateral

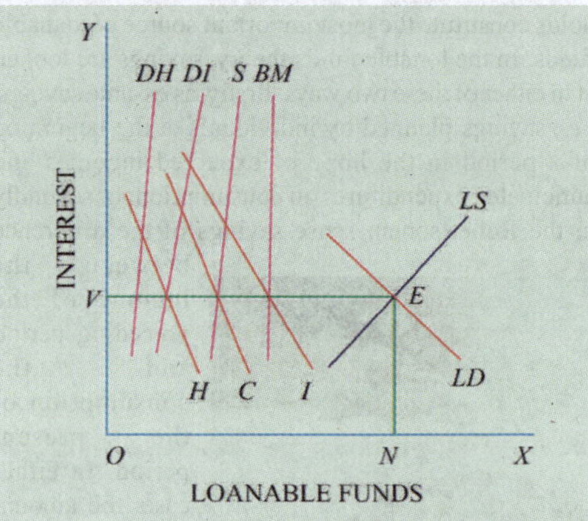

Fig. 34.3. Demand and Supply of Loanable Funds.

summation of the saving curve S, dishoarding curve DH, Bank credit curve BM and disinvestment curve DI. Total demand curve for loanable funds is LD which has been found out by the lateral addition of curves I, C and H, which show respectively the demand for loanable funds for investment purposes, consumption purposes and for hoarding. The curve LD of total demand for loanable funds and curve LS of the total supply of loanable funds intersect each other at the rate of interest Or (= NE). At this rate, the loanable funds lent or supplied are equal to the loanable funds borrowed or demanded. Hence, Or is the equilibrium rate of interest which will tend to settle in the loan market.

Criticism

Most of the criticisms made against the classical theory are valid also in the case of the loanable funds theory. In fact, there is not much difference in the classical and loanable funds theories. The difference lies only in the meaning of saving. In the classical theory, 'savings' is in fact the same thing as the "loanable funds" of the loanable funds theory. In classical theory, savings mean savings out of the income of the previous period. In the loanable funds theory, loanable funds consist of saving out of the income of the previous period plus borrowed bank deposits plus activated idle balances. In classical language, savings out of current income may well exceed the savings of loanable funds theory, because current income is increased by bank loans or the injection of idle balances. Thus, the supply schedule of savings of classical theory amounts to the same thing as the supply schedule of loanable funds of the loanable funds theory.

Further, the Loanable Funds Theory like the Classical Theory is indeterminate. According to this theory, the rate of interest is determined by the intersection of the demand curve for loanable fund with the supply curve. Now, the supply of loanable funds is composed of savings plus Bank credit and dishoarding. But since the 'savings' part of the supply curve varies with the level of income, it follows that the total supply of loanable funds will also vary with income. Thus, the theory is also indeterminate.

LIQUIDITY PREFERENCE THEORY

In this epoch-making book, "The General Theory of Employment, Interest and Money", the late Loard Keynes gave a new view of interest. According to him, "Interest is the reward for parting with liquidity for a specified period." [6]

A man with a given income has to decide first how much of this income he is going to consume and how much to save. The former will depend on what Keynes calls, the **propensity to consume.** Given this propensity to consume, the individual will save a certain proportion of his given income. He now has to make another decision. How should he hold his savings? How much of his resources will he hold in saving? How much of his resources will be hold in the form of ready money (cash or non part with or lend). This latter decision will depend upon what Keynes calls his **"liquidity preference."**

Meaning. Liquidity preference means the demand for money to **hold** or the desire of the public to hold cash. In the words of Prof. Meyer, "Liquidity preference is the preference to have an equal amount or cash rather than of claims against others."

Factors Governing Liquidity Preference

Liquidity preference of a particular individual depends upon several considerations: The question is: Why should the people hold their resources liquid or in the form of ready money, when they can get interest by lending such resources? The desire for liquidity arises because of three motives: (*i*) the transactions motive, (*ii*) the precautionary motive, and (*iii*) the speculative motive.

Transactions Motive. The transactions motive relates to the demand for money or the need for cash for the current transactions of individual and business exchanges. Individuals hold cash in order "to bridge the interval between the receipt of income and its expenditure." This is called the **'Income Motive.'** Most of the people receive their income by the week or the month, while the expenditure goes on day by day. A certain amount of ready money, therefore, is kept in hand to make current payments. This amount will depend upon the size of the individual's income, the interval at which the income is received and the methods of payments current in the locality.

The businessmen and the entrepreneurs also have to keep a proportion of their resources in ready cash in order to meet their current needs of various kinds. They need money all the time in order to pay for rqw materials and transport, to pay wages and salaries and to meet all other current expenses incurred by any business. This Keynes calls the **'Business Motive'** for keeping money. It is clear that the amount of money held, under the business motive, will depend to a very large extent on the turn-over (*i.e.*, the volume of trade of the firm in question). The larger the turn-over the larger, in general, will be the amount of money needed to cover current expenses.

Precautionary Motive. Precautionary motive for holding money refers to the desire of the people to hold cash balances for unforeseen contingencies. People hold a certain amount of money to provide for the danger of unemployment, sickness, accidents and other more uncertain perils. The amount of money held under this motive will depend on the nature of the individual and on the conditions in which he lives.

6. *Ibid.*, p. 167.

The combined sum of balances held for transactions and precautionary motives, Keynes termed 'active balances' and labelled M. The demand for active balances can be referred to as L_1 and thus $L_1 = f(Y)$. This relationship is shown diagrammatically in Fig. 34.4. According to keynes, L_1 is directly proportionate to the level of national income. OL_1 is the demand for active balances at OY_1 of national income. When the national income increases from OY_1 to OY_2 the demand for active balances goes up from OL_1 to OL_2. It should be noted here that the demand for active balances, according to Keynes, is independent of the rate of interest or the demand for active balances with respect to the rate of interest is absolutely inelastic. OM is the demand for active balances which does not change, whether the rate of interest is 8% or 6% as given in Fig. 34.5.

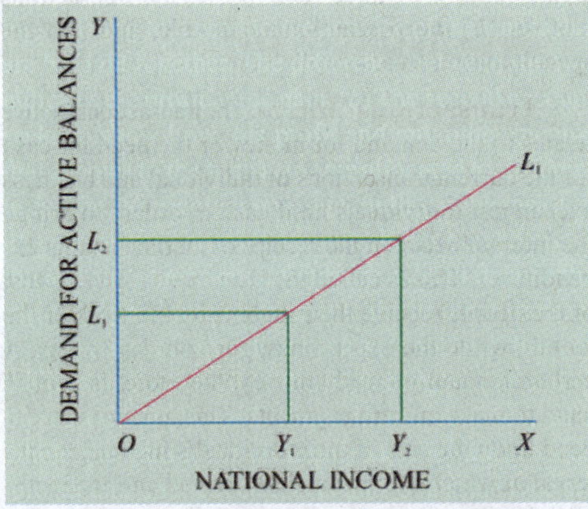

Fig. 34.4. **Transactions and Precautionary demand.**

Speculative Motive. The speculative motive relates to the desire to hold one's resources in liquid form in order to take advantage of market movements regarding the future changes in the rate of interest (or bond prices).

The notion of holding money for speculative motive is a new typically Keynesian idea. Money held under the speculative motive serves as a store of value as money held under the precautionary motive does. But it is a store of money meant for a different purpose. The cash held under this motive is used to make speculative gains by dealing in bonds [7] whose prices fluctuate. If bond prices are expected to rise, which in other words means that the rate of interest is expected to fall, businessmen will buy bonds to sell when the price later rises. If, however, bond prices are expected to fall, *i.e.*, the rate of interest is expected to rise, businessmen will sell bonds to avoid capital losses. Nothing being certain in this dynamic world, where guesses about the future course of events are made on precarious bases, businessmen keep cash to speculate on the probable future changes in bond prices (or the rate of interest) with a view to making profits.

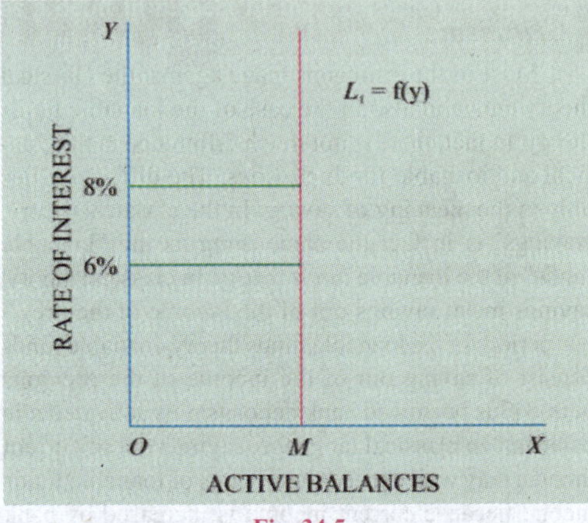

Fig. 34.5.

Given the expectations about the changes in the rate of interest in future, less money will be held under the speculative motive at a higher current or prevailing rate of interest and more money will be held under this motive at a lower current rate of interest. The reason for this inverse correlation between money held for speculative motive and the prevailing rate of interest is that at a lower rate of interest less is lost by not lending money or investing it, that is by holding on to money; while at a higher rate the holders of cash balances would lose more by not lending or investing.

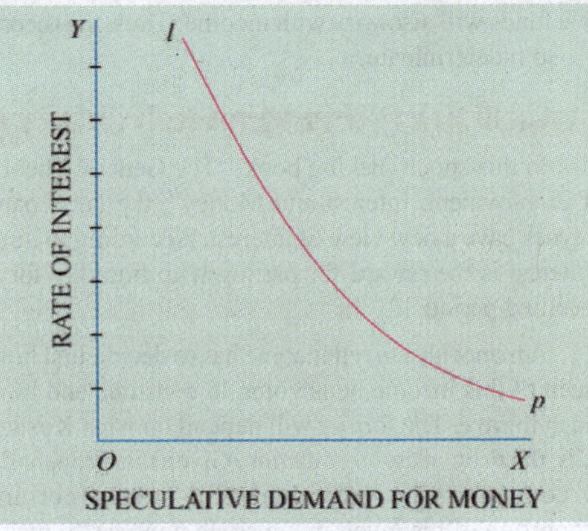

Fig. 34.6. **Liquidity Preference Schedule.**

Thus, the demand for money under the speculative motive is a function of the current rate of interest, increasing as the interest rate falls and decreas-

7. All securities and other such papers as yield a fixed and known amount of interest over a period of time are known as bonds.

ing as the interest rate rises. In other words, demand for money under this motive is decreasing function of the rate of interest. This will be clear from the following diagram (Fig. 34.6).

Along OX-axis is represented the speculative demand for money (called inactive balances, by Keynes) and along OY the rate of interest. The liquidity preference schedule lp is a downward sloping curve towards the right signifying that the higher the rate of interest, the lower the demand for speculative motive, and vice-versa. The schedule becomes more elastic towards the right end at very low rates of interest.

But the demand for money to satisfy the speculative motive does not depend so much upon what the current rate of interest is as on expectation of changes in the rate of interest. If there is a change in the expectations regarding the future rate of interest, the whole curve or schedule of liquidity preference for speculative motive will change accordingly. Thus, if the public on balance expect the rate of interest to be higher (*i.e.*, bond prices to be lower) in the future than they had previously supposed, the speculative demand for money will increase and whole liquidity preference curve for speculative motive will shift upwards.

If the total supply of money is represented by M, we may refer to that part of M held for transactions and precautionary motives as M_1, and to that part held for the speculative motive as M_2. Thus, $M = M_1 + M_2$. The money held under the transactions and precautionary motives, *i.e.*, M_1, is completely interest-inelastic unless the interest rate is very high. Also, the amount of money held as M_1, that is for transactions and precautionary motive, is mainly a function of the size of income and business transactions together with the contingencies growing out of the conduct of personal and business affairs. On the other hand, money demanded for speculative motive, *i.e.*, M_2, as explained above, is primarily a function of the rate of interest.

Determination of the Rate of Interest

According to Keynes, the demand for money, *i.e.*, the liquidity preference and supply of money, determine the rate of interest. It is, in fact, the liquidity preference for speculative motive which, along with the quantity of money, determines the rate of interest. We have explained above the speculative demand for money in detail. As for the supply of money, it is determined by the policies of the Government and of the Central Bank of the country. The total supply of money of coins plus notes plus bank deposits.

How the rate of interest is determined by the equilibrium between the liquidity preference for speculative motive and the supply of money is shown in Fig. 34.7.

In Fig. 34.5 (*a*) , IPS is the curve liquidity preference for speculative motive. In other words, LPS curve shows the demand for money for speculative motive. To begin with, OM_2 is the quantity of money available for satisfying liquidity preference for speculative motive. Rate of interest will be determined where the speculative demand for money is in balance or equal to the (fixed) supply of money OM_2. It is clear from the figure that speculative demand for money is equal to OM_2 quantity of money at Or rate of interest. Hence, Or is the equilibrium rate of interest. Assuming no change in expectations, an increase in the quantity of money (via open market operations) for the speculative motive, will lower the rate of interest.

In Fig. 34.7 (*a*) when the quantity of money increases from OM_2 to OM'_2 , the rate of interest falls from Or to Or ' because the new quantity of money OM'_2 is in balance with the speculative demand for money at OR' rate of interest. In this case we move down the curve. Thus, given the schedule or curve of liquidity preference for speculative motive, an increase in the quantity of money brings down the rate of interest.

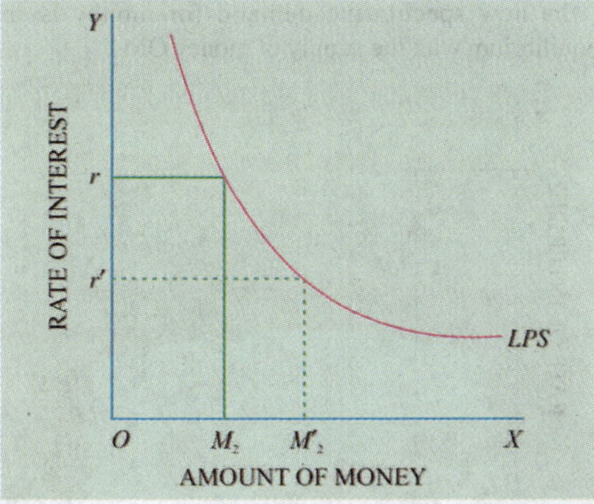

Fig. 34.7 (*a*)

But the increase in the quantity of money may cause a change in the expectations of the public and thereby cause an upward shift in liquidity schedule or curve for speculative motive pushing the rate of interest up. But this is not certain. "New developments may only cause wide differences of opinion leading to increased activity in the bond market without necessarily causing any shift in the aggressive speculative demand for money schedule. If the balance of market expectations is changed, there will be a shift in the schedule. Central Bank policy designed to increase the money supply may, therefore, be met by an upward shift of speculative demand function leaving the rate of interest virtually unaffected."[8]

Thus, a large increase in the quantity of money may exert only a small influence on the rate of interest in certain circumstances.

It is worth mentioning that shifts in liquidity preference schedule or curve can be caused by many other factors which affect expectations and might take place independently of change in the quantity of money by the Central Bank. Shifts in the liquidity function may be either downward or upward depending on the way in which the public interprets a change in events.

If some change in events leads the people on balance to expect a higher rate of interest in the future than they had previously supposed, the liquidity preference for speculative motive will increase, which will bring about an upward shift in the curve of liquidity preference for speculative motive, and will raise the rate of interest.

In Fig. 34.7 (*b*), assuming that the quantity of money remains unchanged at OM_2 , with the rise in the liquidity preference curve from LPS to L′ P′ S′, the rate of interest rises from Or to Or″ because at Or″ , the new speculative demand for money is in equilibrium with the supply of money OM_2.

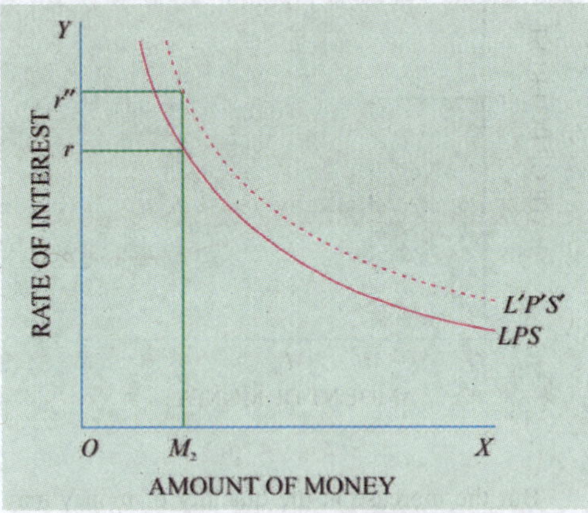

Fig. 34.7 (*b*)

It is worth noting that when the liquidity preference for speculative motives rises from LPS to L′ P′ S′, the amount of money held does not rise: it remains as OM_2 as before. Only the rate of interest rises from Or to Or″ to equilibrate the new liquidity preference for speculative motive with the available quantity of money OM_2.

8. Hansen –*Guide to Keynes*, p. 133.

Thus, we see that Keynes explained interest in terms of purely monetary forces and not in terms of real forces like productivity of capital and thrift which formed the foundation-stones of both classical and loanable fund theories. According to him, demand for money for speculative motive together with the supply of money determines the rate of interest. He agreed that the marginal revenue product of capital tends to become equal to the rate of interest, but the rate of interest is not determined by marginal revenue productivity of capital. Moreover, according to him, interest is not a reward for saving or thriftiness or waiting but for parting with liquidity. Keynes asserted that it is not the rate of interest which equalises saving and investment. But this equality is brought about through changes in the level of incomes.

Criticism of Liquidity Preference Theory

Keynes theory, too, has met with criticism: Firstly, it has been pointed out that the rate of interest is not purely a monetary phenomenon. Real forces like productivity of capital and thriftiness or saving by the people also play an important role in the determination of the rate of interest.

Secondly, Keynes makes the rate of interest independent of the demand for investment funds. Actually, it is not so independent. The cash-balances of the businessmen are largely influenced by their demand for savings for capital investment. This demand for capital investment depends upon the marginal revenue productivity of capital. Therefore, the rate of interest is not determined independently of the marginal productivity of capital or marginal efficiency of capital, as Keynes calls it.

Thirdly, liquidity preference is not the only factor governing the rate of interest. There are several other factors which influence the rate of interest by affecting the demand for and supply of investible funds.

Fourthly, the liquidity preference theory does not explain the existence of different rate of interest prevailing in the market at the same time. Owing to the perfect homogeneity of cash balance, the rates of interest have to be uniform. Actually it is not so.

Fifthly, Keynes ignores saving or waiting as a means or source of investible fund. To part with liquidity without there being any saving is meaningless.

Sixthly, the Keynesian theory only explains interest in the short run. It gives no clue to the rates of interest in the long run.

Seventhly, the borrower's intention is not so much to reward parting with liquidity as to get a return on investment.

Finally, exactly the same criticism applies to Keynesian theory itself on the basis of which Keynes rejected the classical and loanable funds theories. Keynes's theory of interest, like the classical and loanable funds theories, is indeterminate. According to Keynes, rate of interest is determined by the speculative demand for money and the supply of money available for satisfying speculative demand. Given the total money supply, we cannot know how much money will be available so satisfy the speculative demand for money, unless we know how much the transactions demand for money is. And we cannot know the transactions demand for money, unless we first know the level of income. Thus, the Keynesian theory, like the classical theory, is indeterminate.

"In the Keynesian case the supply and demand for money schedules cannot give the rate of interest unless we already know the income level; in the classical case the demand and supply schedules for saving offer no solution until the income is known. Precisely the same is true of loanable-funds theory. Keynes's criticism of the classical and loanable-fund theories applies equally to his own theory. " [9]

Income forms the basis of Keynenan, Clamical and Loanable fund theories.

KEYNESIAN AND OTHER THEORIES OF INTEREST COMPARED

Keynesian vs. Classical Theory

The Keynesian Theory differs from the Classical Theory in the following respects:–

(*i*) The classical theory applies to a situation of full employment and constant national income, whereas the Keynesian Theory assumes an equilibrium with less than full employment, where both employment and income are fluctuating.

(*ii*) The second difference derived from the first is that since in the classical theory income is assumed to be constant, saving is also regarded as fixed and the rate of interest is determined by investment demand curve. It is the rate of interest which brings about equality between saving and investment. On the other hand, according to the Keynesian theory, there is a separate savings curve corresponding to each level of income and employment and the rate of interest is determined by the intersection of the liquidity preference and money supply schedule.

(*iii*) The classical theory regards the available funds as the supply factor, whereas Keynes treats them as a demand factor since they are determined by people's liquidity preference.

(*iv*) Keynesian saving is out of income. Therefore, according to Keynes, higher rate of interest will not increase savings as is the belief of the classical economists, because it will discourage investment and so decrease income out of which saving has to come. According to the view of the classical economists, saving automatically leads to investment. But Keynes held quite the opposite view, *viz.*, investment result in saving out of current income. In the classical view, investment could be increased by saving more, but according to keynes it is investment which determines the volume of saving through the multiplier process. The classicals confused the amount saved with propensity to save (*i.e.*, thrift).

Keynesian vs. Loanable Funds Theory

We may note below a few points of difference between the Keynesian Theory and the Loanable Funds Theory:–

(*i*) Keynesian theory regards money as stock, whereas the loanable funds theory treats money as a flow. That is why Keynesian Theory explains the rate of interest at any given moment when the money stock is assumed to be fixed. On the other hand, the Loanable Funds Theory explains interest over a period of time when the supply of money is supposed to be fluctuating.

(*ii*) In the Keynesian theory, the quantity of money is regarded as an independent variable and is not

9. Hansen –*Guide to Keynes*, p. 141.

affected by changes in the rate of interest. On the other hand, according to the loanable funds theory, the stock of money itself depends on the rate of interest.

Keynes treats money as stock.

(*iii*) Keynesian theory explains interest in a situation of less than full employment, while the loanable funds theory is valid in the long-run period when full employment of human and material resources has been realised. In this sense, the two theories may be regarded as complementary.

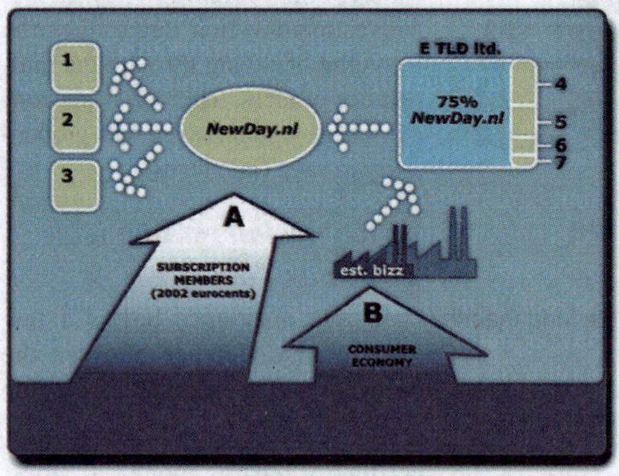

Loanable funds theory treats money as flow.

(*iv*) According to the Keynesian theory, it is the demand for and supply of money which determine the rate of interest, whereas according to the loanable funds theory, the rate of interest is simply the price of credit and, as such, is determined by the demand for, and supply of, credit. Hence, the banking system can influence the rate of interest by expanding or contracting credit. In the Keynesian theory, supply of money is regarded as given.

(*v*) The loanable funds theory emphasises the crucial interdependence between the loan market and the commodity market, since money can be used for different alternatives like purchasing of consumption goods, investment in industries and for purchasing bonds. Keynes, on the other hand, ignores this interrelationship.

(*vi*) Unlike Keynes, the loanable funds theory does not accept the notion that shifts in liquidity preference can affect the long-run equilibrium rate of interest.

MODERN THEORY OF INTEREST: HICKS-HANSEN SYNTHESIS[10]

We have discussed above the various theories of the rate of interest put forward from time to time. But we have seen that all these theories suffer from various drawbacks and are indeterminate. The Keynesian theory considered only the monetary factors and the classical theory only the real factors as determining rate of interest. Modern economists have considered both types of factors, monetary and real. The economists like Prof. Hicks and Hansen have made a synthesis between these various theories and have given an adequate and determinate theory of interest. They are of the opinion that the classical and loanable funds theories amount to the same thing. The difference between these two theories, *i.e.*, classical and loanable funds theories, lies only in the meaning of saving. "The Pigovian supply schedule of savings amounts to the same thing as the Robertsonian or Swedish supply of loanable funds."[11]

How the modern economists make synthesis between the classical or loanable funds theory on the one hand and the Keynesian theory on the other to give an adequate and the determinate interest theory, we state in Prof. Hansen's own words:

"The classical or loanable fund formulation and the Keynesian formulation, taken together, do supply us with an adequate theory of the rate of interest. From the loanable-funds formulation we get a family of loanable-fund schedules (or saving schedules in the Pigovian sense) at various income levels. These together with the investment demand schedule give us the Hicksian IS curve. In other words, the neo-classical formulation can tell us what the various levels of income will be (given the investment demand schedule and a family of loanable-funds schedules) at

10. See H. L. Ahuja. *Advanced Economic Theory*, 1975, pp. 944-95.
11. *Ibid*, p. 143.

different rates of interest. But it does not tell us what the rate of interest will be.

From the Keynesian formulation, we get a family of liquidity preference schedules at various income levels. These together with the supply of money fixed by the monetary authority give us the LM curve (Fig. 34.7). The LM curve tells us what the various rates of interest will be (given the quantity of money and the family of liquidity preference curves) at different levels of income. But the liquidity schedule alone cannot tell us what the rate of interest will be. It is the intersection between the IS curve and LM curve which will determine the rate of interest.

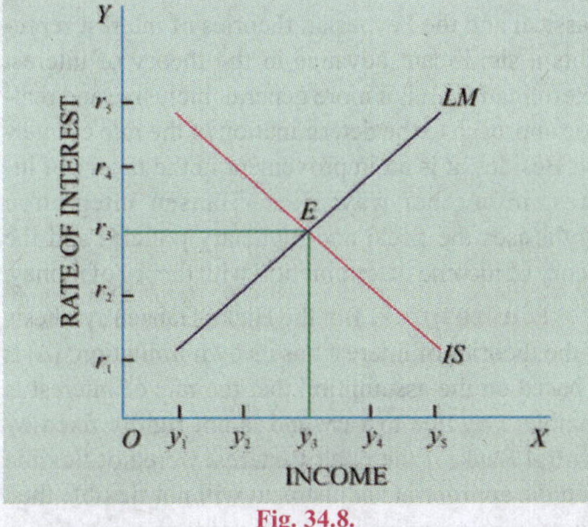

Fig. 34.8.

In the above Fig. 34.7, the IS curve and the LM curve are curves relating to the two variables: (a) income and (b) rate of interest. Income and the rate of interest are, therefore, determined together at the point of intersection of these two curves, *i.e.*, the point E. Equilibrium rate of interest thus determined is Or_3 and the level of income determined is OY. At this point, the income and the rate of interest stand in relation to each other such that investment and saving are in equilibrium, and that the demand for money is in equilibrium with the supply of money. It should be noted that LM curve has been drawn by taking the supply of money as fixed.

Effect of Changes in the Variables

With the aid of Hicks-Hansen analysis, we can explain more satisfactorily the effect of changes in certain important economic variables such as desire to save, the supply of money, investment, liquidity preferences on the rate of interest. This is illustrated in Fig. 34.8.

Changes in the Supply of Money. Now suppose that the supply of money has been increased by the action of the Central Bank. Given the liquidity preference schedule, with the increase in the supply of money, more money will be held for speculative motive at each level of income and the rate of interest will come down.

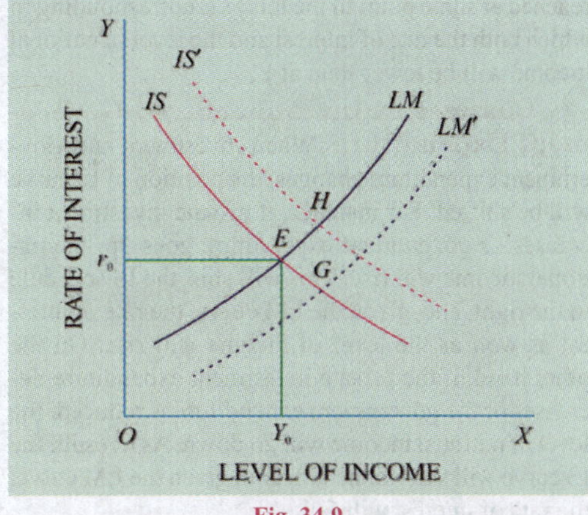

Fig. 34.9.

We see in the above Fig. that the LM curve has shifted to the right. When the LM curve has so shifted rightward, in the new equilibrium position, the rate of interest will be lower and the level of income higher than before. Point E is the intersection of LM and IS curves. When the supply of money has increased LM shifts to the dotted position LM ' and with IS schedule remaining the same, the new equilibrium will be at point G corresponding to which the rate of interest is lower and the level of income greater than at E. On the other hand, if the Central Bank has reduced the money supply, less money will be available for speculative motive at each level of income. As a result, the LM curve will shift to the left of E; and the IS curve remaining unchanged, in the new equilibrium position, the rate of interest will be higher and the level of income lower than before.

Changes in the Desire to Save or Propensity to Consume. Let us now consider the effect of changes in the desire to save or propensity to consume. Suppose people's desire to save decreases, *i.e.*, the propensity to consume goes up. As a result, the level of national income will go up at each rate of interest. The result will be that the IS curve will shift to the right. This is shown by IS curve shifting rightward to the doted position IS '. With LM curve remaining unchanged, the new equilibrium position will be established at H corresponding to which the rate of interest as well as the level of income will be greater than at E. We find that decrease in the desire to save has led to the increase in both rate of interest and the level of income. If, on the other hand, the desire to save increases *i.e.*, the propensity to consume decreases, the level of national income will fall for each rate of interest. As a result, the IS curve will shift to the left. With this shift and the LM curve remaining unchanged, the new equilibrium position will be reached at some point to the left of E corresponding to which both the rate of interest and the level of national income will be lower than at E.

Changes in Investment and Government Expenditure. When investment and Government expenditure changes, the position of IS curve will be shifted. For instance, if private investment increases or government expenditure goes up, the national income will rise. This will shift the IS schedule to the right, and, given the LM curve, the rate of interest as well as the level of income will rise. On the other hand, if the private investment expenditure decreases or the government expenditure is reduced, the level of national income will go down. As a result, the IS curve will shift to the left, and, given the LM curve, the rate of interest will fall.

Changes in Liquidity Preference. The position of LM curve will also shift as a result of changes in the liquidity preference. If, for instance, the liquidity preference of the people rises, the LM curve will shift to the left, because the higher liquidity preference, supply of money remaining the same, will raise the rate of interest corresponding to each level of national income. When the LM curve has shifted leftward, given the IS curve, the new equilibrium rate of interest will be higher and the level of national income lower. On the other hand, if the people's liquidity preference decreases, the LM curve will shift to the right because, given the supply of money a downward shift in the liquidity preference curve means that, corresponding to each level of income, there will be a lower rate of interest. When the LM curve has shifted right wards, given the IS curve, the new equilibrium level of the rate of interest will be lower and the equilibrium level of the national income higher.

Thus, we see that changes in factors like propensity to consume (or desire to save) investment or government expenditure, the supply of money and the liquidity preference will bring about shifts in IS or LM curves. As a result, the rate of interest as well as the level of national income will change.

Hicks-Hansen integration of the classical and the Keynesian theories of interest shows clearly that the government is in a position to influence the level of economic activities or the level of national income by monetary and fiscal measures. We find, therefore, that Hicks-Hansen Theory of interest explained above has integrated the theory of money with the theory of income determination. In this way, the modern theory of interest has succeeded in synthesising the monetary and fiscal policies. Hence, both monetary and fiscal policies can play a useful role in regulating the rate of economic activity in the country.

Thus, a determinate theory of interest is based on: (1) the investment demand function, (2) the saving function (or conversely the consumption function), (3) the liquidity preference function and (4) the quantity of money. Hence, according to modern economists both monetary and real factors, *viz.*, productivity, thrift, liquidity preference and the money supply play their part in the determination of rate of interest.

Critical Appraisal of Hicks-Hansen Synthesis Merits. Hicks-Hansen synthesis of the classical and the keynesian theories of interest represents a significant advance in the theory of interest determination. It is a more general, inclusive and realistic approach to the determination of the rate of interest. Besides, it is an improvement in the theory of interest in another way. Hicks-Hansen integration synthesises the fiscal and monetary policies and the theory of income determination with theory of money.

Limitations. But the Hicks-Hansen synthesis of the theories of interest has its own limitation: (*a*) It is based on the assumption that the rate of interest is flexible, *i.e.*, free to vary and is not rigidly fixed by Central Bank. If the rate of interest were not flexible then the appropriate adjustment will not flexible then the appropriate adjustment will not take place.

(*b*) This synthesis of interest theories is also based upon the assumption that investment is interest-elastic, *i.e.*, investment varies with the rate of interest. If investment were not interest-elastic, then also the Hicks-Hansen synthesis breaks down because, the necessary adjustment will not take place. (*c*) Don Patinkin and Milton Freidman have criticised the Hicks-Hansen synthesis as being too artificial and oversimplified. They think that the division of the economy into two sectors, *viz.*, monetary and real, is artificial and unrealistic. On the other hand, they are of the opinion that the monetary and real factors are interwoven and act and react on each other. (*d*) Patinkin also has pointed out that Hicks-Hansen synthesis ignores the possibilities of changes in the price level of commodities. He thinks that the various economic variables such as money supply, propensity to consume or save, investment, and liquidity preference not only influence the rate of interest and the level of income but also the prices of commodities and services. He, therefore, suggests a more integrated and general equilibrium approach which involves the simultaneous determination of not only the rate of interest and the level of income but also prices of commodities and services.

CAN THE RATE OF INTEREST FALL TO ZERO?

Theoretically, a zero rate of interest can be conceived. As pointed out above as time goes on, people's power to save and will to save tend to increase. The former because of the rising productive capacity and the latter because of the greater foresight and the latter because of the greater foresight and the tendency to discount the future at a low rate among the more advanced people. A stage can be imagined in which capital accumulation may outstrip the demand for capital, thus lowering the marginal productivity of capital to zero, even making it negative; that is, people may even pay something for the care of their savings.

It is, however, extremely improbable that such a stage will be ever reached. In the first place, the demand for capital will increase with the increase in population and the increase in the variety of people's wants. Moreover, technical progress, including new inventions and discoveries, is constantly taking place which raises the net productivity of capital and so interest rates. It is true, of course, that new inventions may substitute methods, which economise capital; this may lead to a fall in the rate of interest. But the marginal productivity of capital will still be positive, and, hence there will always be a positive rate of interest. Moreover, the difference between the present gratification and future gratification cannot altogether be removed. The rate of interest is a measure of this difference.

Looking from the side of supply also, we come to the same conclusion. Some people may save even if the rate of interest is zero or negative. But the volume of savings would be seriously reduced if there were no compensation for postponing consumption, thus creating relative scarcity of capital.

Thus, there is no possibility of the rate of interest falling to zero. We can expect a zero rate of interest only if capital loses its character of scarcity. As it is, capital is scarce relatively to demand for its services. There are so many alternative uses to which capital can be put. It is the rate of interest which determines to what uses may be put.

That the zero rate of interest is improbable is also brought out by the Keynesian Theory of Interest , *viz*., Liquidity Preference Theory. Look at the shape of the lp curve in Fig. 34.6. It has three distinct parts: the upper reach which is steep, the middle one with a medium slope and the tail which is a horizontal straight line. The upper portion which is steeply falling indicates that, at a high rate of interest, the demand for money has low interest-elasticity. That is, even if the rate of interest falls, the demand for money to hold does not increase much. But when the rate of interest is neither very high nor very low (which is shown by the middle part of the curve), then the demand for money is interest-elastic, which means that even with a small fall in the rate of interest, the demand for money is interest-elastic, which means that even with a small fall in the rate of interest, the demand for money will increase considerably. But when you come to the flat portion, *i.e.*, the tail of the curve, the demand for money is infinitely elastic. In other words, the demand for money is perfectly elastic in respect of interest rate and as the liquidity preference reaches its maximum, *i.e.*, at the very low rate of interest, there is no limit to the amount of money which the people would like to hold. This is a position of Absolute liquidity Preference. It is also called **Liquidity Trap** by some economists.

Now, suppose that the position of liquidity trap or absolute liquidity preference is reached at 2 per cent rate of interest shown by that portion of the 1p curve which is a horizontal straight line. All increase of money now will be absorbed by the people and it will not lower the rate of interest. They will not now like to invest any portion of their money in bonds. The reason is that they do not expect the rate of interest to fall further to the price of bonds to rise. Since the price of bonds is not expected to rise, why should they take the risk of investing money in them? That is, they will like to keep the entire stock of money with themselves. In other words, at this stage no amount of increase in the money supply will lead to a reduction in the rate of interest.

Thus, from this characteristic of liquidity preference (being perfectly elastic in respect of low rate of interest) an important conclusion can be drawn, *viz.*, that the rate of interest is not likely to fall below a certain low figure. There is no way of depressing the rate of interest further even though such a fall may be in public interest. In other words, an important implication of perfect elasticity of liquidity preference at a certain low rate of interest is that the rate of interest cannot fall to zero.

Conclusion

We may conclude in Samuelson's words, "As long as any increase in time-consuming process could be counted on to produce any extra product and dollars of revenue, the yield of capital could not be zero. Also, as long as any land or other asset exists with a sure perpetual net income –and as long as people are willing to give only a finite amount of money today in exchange for a perpetual flow of income spread over the whole future–then we can hardly conceive of the rate of interest as falling to zero." [12]

12. Samuelson P.A.- *Economics*, 1970 p. 579.

SOCIAL IMPORTANCE OF INTEREST

Every society, socialist or capitalist, is faced with the problem of using its scarce resources in an optimum manner. Capital resources are scarce everywhere even in a socialist society.

Its Allocative Function. In all types of societies, therefore, all projects have to go through a screening process to find their place in the order of priorities.

Even in a socialist society interest cannot be abolished, though it may not be paid to private individuals. Even there, through its instrumentality, priorities regarding the use of scarce capital resources for various possible employments will be determined. The order of priorities in a socialist society will probably be different from the one in a capitalist society, but the rate of interest will perform its function all the same. It has the same function as the function of price, *viz.*, it adjusts demand to the supply available. It enables capital to be apportioned between competing demands of alternative uses. It is through the rate of interest that those uses which promise the highest future returns receive the first consideration. Of course, the criterion of the highest future returns will differ in a capitalist society from that in a socialist society. In the former, expectations of profits for private entrepreneurs and in the latter the conception of welfare of the planning authority, will determine the priorities in investment.

Interest cannot be abolished; it can be socialised, if capital is socialised. Even if capital is socialised, the rate of interest will still be needed as an accounting device to give expression to the prevailing scarcity or abundance of capital for the guidance of the managers of public enterprises in a socialist economy.

Whatever the type of economic system, interest acts as a rationing device or performs an allocative function. Since capital is a scarce commodity, only those projects can be undertaken where the return on capital invested is greater than, or equal to, the rate of interest. Those projects whose prospective yield is lower than the rate of interest have to be dropped. Thus, the rate of interest directs the use of capital and the growth of productive capacity.

The interest rate is socially important because it determines both the level and composition of investment. According to Keynes' theory of investment, the level of investment is determined by marginal efficiency of capital and the rate of interest. The lower the rate of interest, the greater is the investment, and vice versa. However, the influence of the rate of interest depends on the interest-elasticity of investment. It may, therefore, be understood that raising interest rates as an anti-inflationary device will curb the rate of growth by reducing investment.

As pointed out above interest rate affects the composition of investment through its price-rationing function. Whether investment goes into consumer goods industries or the producing goods industries or into long-term or short-term investment depends on the rate of return in these investments.

There are, however, some limitations in its performance as an allocative mechanism, because government allocates a substantial portion of available capital to projects which it considers in public interest and oligopolistic firms can obtain capital on more favourable terms.

Key terms

Gross interest, Net interest, Time preference, Liquidity preference, Loanable Fund, Transaction motive, Precautionary motive, Speculative motive.

QUESTIONS

1. How is the rate of interest determined? Account for the varying rates of interest in the same market.
2. Discuss: "The rate of interest is the price of money and is determined by the supply of money and demand for it".
3. What is liquidity preference? How do changes in liquidity preference influence the rate of interest?
4. State and explain the liquidity preference theory of interest. Is interest a monetary phenomenon?
5. Explain Keynes' Liquidity Preference Theory of Interest and explain how it differs from the classical theory.

6. Explain the keynesian Theory of Interest. Do you consider it a fully satisfactory explanation? Give reasons. What according to keynes is the role of rate of interest in determining equilibrium level of investment?
7. What is meant by the speculative demand for money? What role does it play in the determination of the rate of interest?
8. "Interest is the reward for parting with liquidity for a specified period". Discuss.
9. Critically examine the Loanable Funds Theory of rate of interest.
10. Explain how supply of and demand for loanable funds differ from the supply of and demand for savings. Bring out the significance of this difference in the theory of interest.
11. "Keynes' criticism of the classical and Loanable Fund Theories of indetermenancy applies equally to his own theory". (Hansen). Discuss.
12. Examine the Loanable Funds Theory of Interest. What is the main difference between this theory and the Keynesian Theory of interest.
13. Discuss the view that (*a*) interest is reward for waiting.

    (*b*) The rate of interest depends upon the marginal productivity of capital.
14. "Both the Classical and the Keynesian theories of interest are inderterminate and therefore incomplete". Elucidate.
15. Distinguish between time-preference and liquidity preference. What part do they play in the theory of interest?
16. "The rate of interest is determined by the demand for and the supply of savings"

    Or

    "The rate of interest is determined by the demand for and the supply of money". Comment.
17. Discuss and explain clearly the part played by rate of interest in maintaining equilibrium between savings and investment.
18. Explain carefully the grounds for the existence of a positive rate of interest.
19. Explain the relation between Interest, Rent and Quasi-rent.
20. What is the role of interest in a socialist economy? Is the concept of interest necessary under socialism?

PROFIT

Nature of Profits

Profit is the reward of the entrepreneur, rather of the entrepreneurial functions. Profit differs from the return on other factors in three important respects: (*a*) Profit is a residual income and not contractual or certain income and not contractual or certain income as in the case of other factors. (*b*) There are much greater fluctuations in profits than in the rewards of the other factors. (*c*) Profits may be negative, whereas rent, wages and interest must always be positive.

In the ordinary speech, people understand by the term 'profit' all excess of income over costs and this includes the earninorsesgs of self-used factors, *i.e.*, entrepreneur's own land, capital and his own labour work called respectively implicit rent, implicit interest and implicit wage. But in economics, profit is regarded as a reward for the entrepreneurial functions of final decision-making and ultimate uncertainty-bearing.

Analysis of Gross Profits

The best way to understand the true nature of profits is to analyse the gross income of the entrepreneur into its various component parts. Gross profits stand for the total earnings of the entrepreneur, not necessarily for the entrepreneurial functions only. It is a mixture composed of several elements.

Prof. Walker was the first economist to draw the distinction between interest and profit in this mixture. According to him, the entrepreneur's income consists of two elements only, *viz*., interest and profit.

There have been further refinements, in modern times, of the several items of which pure profit, however, is the return for the entrepreneurial functions only. From the total receipts of the business must be taken out what has to be paid out to the various factors of production engaged on a contract basis. Thus, the rent of land, the wages of labour, and interest on capital have to be a deducted out of the total income of the entrepreneur.

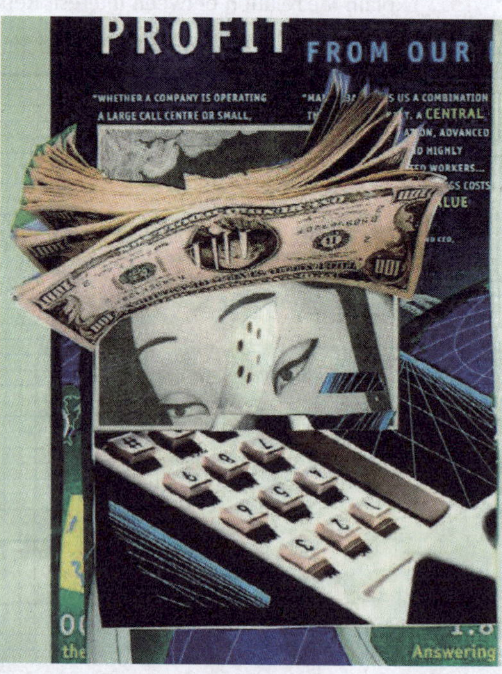

Apart from pure profit, the following are the main constituents of gross profit:–

(*i*) Interest on Entrepreneur's Own Capital. The entrepreneur could earn this interest by lending his capital . We must, therefore, make a deduction out of gross profit, for interest on the entrepreneur's own capital, at the current rate of interest in order to ascertain net profit.

(*ii*) Rent of Land Owned by the Entrepreneur. This rent cannot be counted as profits. The entrepreneur could earn this rent by giving his land to a tenant. A deduction must, therefore, be made, out of gross profit, for this rent at the current rate of the rent of land similarly situated and possessing similar other advantages for calculating net profit.

(*iii*) Entrepreneur's Wages of Management or Superintendence. This is the return for the work done by the entrepreneur as manager, and could have been done by him on a salary basis for another firm. This is also included in gross profit. The entrepreneur must be allowed a salary, which should be considered his wages rather than profits.

The above three elements, strictly speaking, are not the reward of the entrepreneur as such but he gets them as capitalist, landlord and manager. These he could earn without setting himself up as an entrepreneur. These are included in gross profit and must be deducted for finding out the net profit.

(*iv*) Reward of The Entrepreneur as Risk-taker. The function as a risk-taker must be performed by the entrepreneur himself. Certain risks, however, are insurable, *e.g.*, risks of accident, fire and marine, *etc.* But, as we shall see, many risks cannot be insured, and these must fall on the entrepreneur.

(*v*) Gains as Superior Bargainer. Certain gains accrue to the entrepreneur when he bargains with labourers, capitalists, landlords, suppliers of raw materials and consumers–all those with whom he has dealings. These gains he makes owing to his superior skill in bargaining. They are also mixed up with gross profit.

(*vi*) Monopoly Gains. These gains are due to imperfect competition, which enables the entrepreneur to charge higher prices or to pay lower rewards to the factors hired by him and thus increase his profits. They, too, form part of gross profits.

(*vii*) Conjunctural Gains. Another element contained in gross profit are the conjunctural gains. They are also called "windfall profits." These are due to favourable circumstances or pure luck, *e.g.*, outbreak of a war giving high profits to producers of essentials of war and even to other producers. During the second world war, many entrepreneurs made enormous profits due to war demands and high prices in India and elsewhere.

Sudden rise in price is not the only source of windfall profits. They may also arise on account of sudden increase in demand due to non-monetary causes like changes in tastes or discovery of new uses of a product. Windfall profits will also emerge from a shift in population.

Pure or Net Profit

The tendency among modern economists is to accept the American view of profits as being the reward for purely entrepreneurial functions, *i.e.*, functions which cannot be performed by paid employees. The income from **risk-taking and gain from bargaining are regarded by some economists as "pure profits"** of the entrepreneur as against the "gross profits" which include all the items enumerated above.

Pure or net profit is "the amount that accrues to the entrepreneur for assuming the risk inseparable from all business under the system of production in anticipation of demand." "It **(pure profit)** is a payment made exclusively for bearing risk. The essential function of the entrepreneur is considered to be something which only he can perform. This something cannot be the task of management, for managers can be hired, nor can it be any other function which the entrepreneur can delegate. Hence, it is contended that the entrepreneur receives a profit as a reward for assuming **final responsibility,** a responsibility that cannot be shifted on the shoulders of any one else." [1]

THEORIES OF PROFITS[2]

Profit as Rent of Ability

One view of profits makes them analogous to rent. The Rent Theory of Profit, as it may be called, was propounded by the American economist, F. A. Walker. He was the first to introduce a distinction between a capitalist and an entrepreneur. An entrepreneur need not be a capitalist. He is a person who may undertake a business without using any of his own capital.

1. Thomas, S. E. : *Elements of Economics*, 1939, pp. 293-94.
2. For the history of the theories of profit see F. H. Knight–*Risk, Uncertainly and Profit*, 1940, Ch. II.

The Theory. Walker regards profits as rent of ability. Just as there are different grades of land, there are different grades of entrepreneurs. The least efficient entrepreneur, who must remain in the field of production to meet the current demand, just recovers his cost of production. Above him are entrepreneurs of superior ability. Just as rent arises because of the differential advantages enjoyed by a superior land over the marginal land, profit also is the reward for differential ability of the entrepreneur over the marginal entrepreneur or the no-profit entrepreneur. **Profits are thus like rent and, like rent, they do not enter into price.**

Wages of management are not profit and the marginal employer only earns the wages of management, and no more. With a slight unfavourable turn of prices or costs, he may have to work as an employee rather than as an employer. Wages of management, thus, must be paid to maintain the given supply of entrepreneurs. Such wages thus enter into price.

Criticism. This theory has the same weakness as Ricardo's theory of rent. The employer, who will leave the business with a slight unfavourable turn of events, is not necessarily the least efficient. He may be higher up in the scale and may be attracted by more profitable alternative ventures.

The theory, moreover, does not explain the real nature of profits; it merely provides at best a measure of profits.

It is wrong to say, again, that profits do not enter into price. They may not enter in the short period, but they must be covered by price in the long-run. The entrepreneur performs the essential function of risk-bearing and unless the price of the commodity is high enough to compensate the entrepreneur for this, the supply of entrepreneurs will decrease until the price rises high enough to pay for the risk-bearing service.

Some entrepreneurs may earn high profits and others may suffer heavy losses. When the average is taken over a long period, the so-called surplus tends to disappear.

Finally, the theory even fails to explain the size of the profit. The differential gain is due to scarcity of superior entrepreneurs; but why does this scarcity arise? In the case of land, scarcity is due to natural limitations. In the case of entrepreneurs, there are no such limitations. The theory of profit must explain the cause of such scarcity.

Profit is rent of ability.

Thus, there is no doubt a differential element in profits as in rent, superior entrepreneurs earning higher profits. But the analogy ends here. There may exist no-rent land, but there cannot exist no-profit entrepreneur. Rent may not enter into price but normal profits do. This is due to the fact that the supply of land is, there, rent or no rent. But the supply of entrepreneurs cannot be maintained unless profits are earned. Expected profits or prospective profits do enter into price, though the realised profits may not. But even realised profits enter indirectly into price in the long-run by influencing expectations of profits.

Wages Theory of Profits

The connection between profits and wages can be looked at from two points of view: (*i*) The socialists regard profits as simply deductions from the produce of the worker's labour. According to this view, profits are not justified; because they are earned at the expense of the wage-earners. (*ii*) The second view is represented by Prof. Taussig. He regards profits as simply a particular kind of wages.

As for the socialist view, it may be pointed out that, under perfect competition, rates of wages for the same type of labour tend to equality in the same industry. The same wages are paid by the employer who earns no profits as by the one who earns high profits. The superior employer earns profits, not because he pays lower wage (this he cannot do under competition) but because, on account of his superior organising ability and uncertainty-bearing powers, he can produce at a cost lower than that of his inferior rival.

Now consider Taussig's view that profits are merely wages for a special kind of labour. "Profits," say Taussig, "are best regarded as simply a form of wages."

Criticism. The position taken up by Taussig cannot be accepted. There are fundamental differences between wages and profits:

(*i*) Profits are essentially a reward for assuming risks of business. But the labourer takes no risk. His reward or wage is primarily for the work done by him. His risk is insignificant as compared with the risk taken by the employer.

(*ii*) There is much greater element of chance gains in profits than in wages. Wages thus are "earned incomes" in a much more real sense than profits.

(*iii*) Part of profits, and in some cases a major part, is due to imperfections of competition. Under imperfect competition, while profits tend to swell, wages tend to be depressed, for reasons already noted.

Marginal Productivity and Profits

Does the marginal productivity theory apply to profit? The answer is "in a way, yes." Marginal productivity, as we have already explained, is the expression of relationship between scarcity and demand. The supply of entrepreneurs is short and it is not easy to increase it. The demand for the entrepreneur's services, especially entrepreneurs of exceptional ability, on the other hand, is great in the modern conditions of production. Since the marginal productivity of entrepreneurs is high, therefore, profits are high. The greater the factor of uncertainty and the greater the scarcity of entrepreneurs of ability high enough to make a success of business, the higher the profits.

The only difference in the application of the theory of marginal productivity to entrepreneurs, as compared with other factors, is that here the forces of competition work directly, while in the case of the other factors they work through the employer. The ultimate substance is the same. It is the community's competing demands that have to be satisfied, and thus entrepreneurial ability has alternative uses. Forces of competition tend to equalise the profits of entrepreneurs of equal ability.

The theory of marginal productivity, however, cannot be applied in such a clear-cut way to profits as it applies to other phenomenon of value. This is due to the fact that the entrepreneur performs a complex set of functions and the element of uncertainty refuses to be standardised. Moreover, the entrepreneurial factor cannot be increased or decreased in minute doses, since it constitutes one large unit. Withdrawal of one unit may disorganise the whole business. It is thus difficult to measure the marginal net product of the services of the entrepreneur.

Marginal revenue productivity of the entrepreneur to an industrial firm cannot be measured as the marginal revenue productivity of other factors–land, labour, and capital-can be measured. You cannot compare the marginal revenue productivity of one entrepreneur with that of two or three or of two with three or four and so on. Contribution of an entrepreneur to a firm cannot be measured in any physical units. No set rules are available to measure entrepreneurial ability. That is why to try to calculate the marginal revenue productivity of the entrepreneur to an individual firm is unrealistic.

But the marginal revenue productivity of an entrepreneur to an industry can be measured in principle. This is so because, the number of entrepreneurs in an industry can vary and results of such variations or alterations can be studied. However, it will be necessary to assume that all entrepreneurs in the industry are homogeneous.

In Fig. 35.1, MRP is the marginal revenue productivity curve or the demand curve of the industry for entrepreneurs. SS is the supply curve of entrepreneurs. The equilibrium is at E, the point of intersection of the curves, where all entrepreneurs make normal profit OS (= EM) in the long-run. In the short-run, the number of entrepreneurs being OM ' instead of OM, they may make-super-normal profit E ' M ' (=

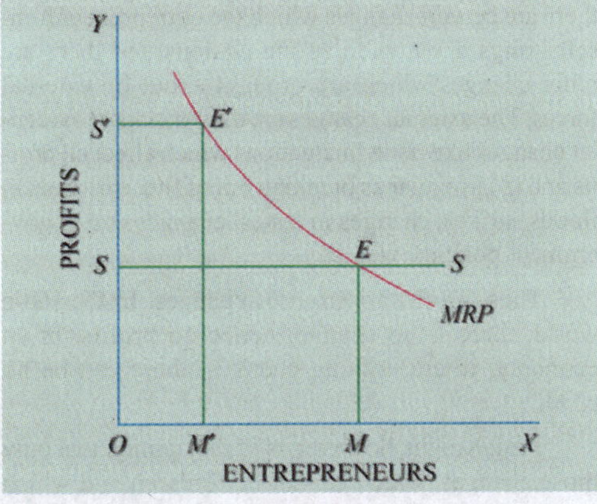

Fig. 35.1.

OS '). But, in the long run, the number of entrepreneurs will increase to OM and the extra profits will be competed away so that the profits fall to the normal level EM (= OS).

Dynamic Theory of Profit

No Profit in Stationary State. This theory is associated with the name of the American economist, J. B. Clark. He says that in a static world, where the size of the population, the amount of capital, the quantity and quality of human wants, the methods of production, technical knowledge, the organisation of business, *etc.*, remain the same, profits tend to disappear under the force of competition. Profits represent the difference between selling price and cost. It is surplus above costs. But if competition works in a frictionless manner, the surplus will vanish. Wherever there is a surplus, production will increase, bringing down the price. That is how the surplus will disappear. "In the static state each factor secures what it produces, and since cost and selling prices are always equal, there can be no profits beyond wages for the routine work of supervision." [3] In a stationary state everything is known and knowable. There is no risk and no uncertainty; hence no profits.

Profits Arise in Dynamic World. But we are not living in a stationary state. Ours is a dynamic world and some changes are constantly taking place. The clever entrepreneur foresees these changes. He is a pioneer. Somehow by invention or otherwise he lowers the cost and makes profits. The changing world offers limitless opportunities to the farsighted, daring and clever entrepreneurs to make profits by turning the facts of the situation in their favour. It is only because the world is dynamic that it is possible for them to keep the lead and reap the profits.

That the world is dynamic is due to two sets of factors: (*a*) internal and (*b*) external. In other words, there are certain changes which the entrepreneur himself brings about such as innovations and there are other changes which are brought about by external forces. The external changes are of two kinds; (*a*) regular changes like trade fluctuations which affect all profits and (*b*) irregular as breaking out of fire, earthquake, floods, strikes, changes in tastes, changes due to government policies, war, *etc.*

Thus, profits arise out of changes. In the static world, there is no change; hence no profits. In an economy, where nothing changes, there can be no profit.

Prof. Knight, however, is of the opinion that only those changes, which cannot be foreseen and which cannot be provided for in advance, will yield profits and not others. He says, "It cannot, then, be change, which is the cause of profit, since **if the law of change is known,** as in fact is largely the case, no profits can arise. Change may cause a situation out of which profit will be made, if it brings about ignorance of the future." [4]

Thus, it is ignorance of the future or uncertainty, and not necessarily change, which, according to Knight, is the cause of profit.

Innovations Theory of Profits

In the dynamic changes, which give rise to profits according to the dynamic theory of profits, Joseph Schumpeter has singled out for special treatment the part played by innovations. The daring and the dynamic entrepreneurs continue to hit at one innovation or another, keeping their business ahead of others and thus make a handsome profits. According to schumpeter, the principal function of the entrepreneur is to make innovations and profits are a reward for performing this important function.

Schumpeter 1883-1950

Schumpeter has given the term innovation very wide meaning. Discovery of a new material or a new technique of production resulting in the lowering of the cost of production or improving the quality of the product is an innovation. Any new measure or new policy initiated by the entrepreneur comes under innovation as Schumpeter uses the term. Innovations may be of two types: (*a*) Those which change the production function and reduce the cost of production, and (*b*) those innovations which stimulate the demand for the product, i.e. which change the demand or utility function. In the first type are included the introduction of new machinery, improved production techniques or processes, exploitation of a new source of raw material or a new and better organisational pattern for the firm. The second type of innovations are those which are calculated to increase the demand for the product by introducing a new product or a new variety of an old product, new and more effective mode of advertisement, discovery of new markets, *etc.* Success of any of these innovations brings a handsome increase in profits. Profits increase because either the cost of production is lowered or the product fetches a higher price.

It may be pointed out, however, that profits owing to innovations are only temporary and tend to be competed away. Soon the innovation come to be imitated by the rivals and they cease to be innovations or lose their novelty. Only when the innovation is got patented can the originating entrepreneur continue to enjoy it. But in a dynamic world and progressive economy, the superior entrepreneurs continue to make innovations and enjoy the profits thereof. As Stigler observes, "These profits may exist for a considerable time because of the ignorance of other firms of their (innovations) existence or because of the time required for the entry of new firms. More important, the successful innovator can continuously seek new disequilibrium profits since the horizon of conceivable innovations is unlimited." [5]

3. Knight, F.H. –*Risk, Uncertainty and profits*, 1940, p. 33.
4. *Ibid*., p. 3.
5. Stigler, G. J. –*The Theory of Price*, 1952, p. 182.

We may also remember that profits are both the cause and effect of innovations. Profits serve as a necessary incentive for making innovations; hence profits are a cause of innovations. But since innovations result in profits, profits are the effect of innovations.

Criticism. Schumpeter's innovation theory can be criticised on the same ground as Clark's dynamic theory:

(a) Schumpeter also like Clark ignores uncertainty as a source of profit.

(b) He also denies that risk-bearing plays any role in the determination of profit.

Risk-bearing Theory of Profits

Most people do mind the risk which makes them hesitate to take a plunge in business. The greater the risk the higher must be the expected profit in order to induce them to start the business. All businesses are more or less speculative, and unless the risk-taker is going to be amply rewarded, business will not be started. As risk acts as a great deterrent, the supply of entrepreneurs is kept down, and those who do take the risk earn much more than the normal return on capital. Hence, profits are regarded as a reward for risk-taking or risk-bearing.

This theory of profit is associated with F. B. Hawley's name. [6] He says profits is the reward for risks and responsibilities that the undertaker . . . . .subjects himself to. Drucker mentions four kinds of risks: replacement, risk proper, uncertainty and obsolescence. Replacement generally known as depreciation, is calculable and is counted as cost. Obsolescence is the least calculable but is also an item in the cost Risk proper (*i.e.*, risk of marketability of the product) and uncertainty are not costs in the conventional sense, but are charges against profits. They may be called costs of staying in business. Physical risks like fire, accident, *etc*., can be provided against by insurance, and are, therefore, included in costs. There are, however, risks that cannot be foreseen, and hence cannot be provided against. It is for undertaking these risks that the entrepreneur is rewarded.

Criticism. As against this, there is the view that though profits do contain some remuneration for risk-taking, yet the high profits made by entrepreneurs cannot in their entirely be attributed to the element of risk. They are not, at any rate, in proportion to the risk undertaken. On the contrary, it is pointed out by Carver that profits arise not because risks are borne, but because the superior entrepreneurs are able to reduce them. [7] We might say–though it may seem paradoxical–that profits are made not because risks are borne but because they are avoided. Still, it cannot be denied that a great deal of pure profit is the reward for risk-bearing.

Uncertainty-bearing Theory of Profits

The Theory. According to Prof. knight, it is uncertainty-bearing **rather than risk-taking** which is the special function of the entrepreneur and leads to profit. We have seen that there are certain risks which are foreseen and provided against. Risks of death and of accident like fire and ship sinkings are statistically determinable. Their incidence is measurable. The insurance companies undertake these risks in return of premia paid to them. The payments of these premia are included in the cost of production. The entrepreneur gets no profit on account of these risks. Hence, risk-taking is not the function of the entrepreneur, but of the insurance companies.

But the genuine economic risks of the marketability of the product due to shifts in demand, are unforeseen and unpredictable. Knight will not call them risks but uncertainty. The term 'risk' is applied to those dangers which can be known and foreseen. The entrepreneur gets a remuneration for bearing uncertainties (unforeseeable risks) and nothing for the risks which have been foreseen, the incidence of which is on the insurance companies.

Just as waiting (capital) is a factor of production, uncertainty-bearing has also been given the status of a factor of production. Like other factors of production, uncertaintly-bearing has a supply price, *i.e.*, unless a certain return is expected, no entrepreneur will be induced to face uncertainty. The supply of this factor, uncertainty-bearing, depends on the temperament of the entrepreneur, the total resources at his command and the proportion of these resources he is inclined to expose to uncertainty. A rich entrepreneur of a bold and venturesome spirit, who has made up his mind to invest a big proportion of his wealth, can bear greater uncertainty. A greater gain is necessary to induce an entrepreneur to expose a large proportion of his capital than when only a small proportion is exposed.

Criticism. The theory of uncertainty-bearing, as a cause of profit, has been criticised on the following grounds:

(i) Uncertainty is not the only factor that limits the supply of entrepreneurs. Lack of funds, lack of knowledge, lack of opportunities and the presence of ecomomic friction are some of the factors that restrict the supply of entrepreneurs.

6. *Enterprise and the Productive Process*. 1907.

7. *Distribution of Wealth*, p. 273.

(*ii*) Uncertainty-bearing is not the only function of the entrepreneur. The profit that he gets is also the reward for other services that he renders, *e.g.*, initiating, co-ordinating, *etc.*

(*iii*) Uncertainty-bearing cannot be elevated to the status of a factor of production. It is an element of real costs which means exertion, absitence, sacrifice, *etc.*, as distinguished from money cost. Cost is not generally measured in terms of real cost. We know that capital is a factor of production but not abstinence that is needed to have capital.

Prof. Knight.

(*iv*) Knight's theory does not seem to have much relevance to the real world Businessmen continue to estimate profits **ex-ante** in defiance of this theory. This theory has been criticised as heavily insulated from empirical testing and empirical relevance.

Conclusion Regarding Theories of Profit

We have discussed above the various thoeries of profits. The question arises: which theory shall we accept? How do profits arise? Here we are thinking of not gross profit but net profit. The fact is that in the real world there are several causes which give rise to profit, but the principle cause is uncertainty. This uncertainty is due to the dynamic nature of the world. In this real world of ours, some or the other change is always taking place. But such changes only are causes of profits as cannot be foreseen as we have read in K6. *Enterprise and the Productive Process.* 1907 Nnight's theory.

However, in a static world, profits can arise in one way, *viz.*, owing to monopoly. The monopoly profits arise in the dynamic world also. Besides monopoly profits can arise also from any other position of advantage.

In short, we can say there are two sources of profits: (*a*) uncertainty and (*b*) position of special advantage, monopoly or otherwise.

Normal Profit

Some writers introduce the concept of normal profits. As Prof. Knight points out, normal profits, belong to the equilibrium state, or to the state in which changes are taking place which can be anticipated and calculated. Of course, it is difficult to imagine a world entirely devoid of change. But we can have societies, specially old established societies, in which conditions are relatively static and business methods have become more or less of a routine nature.

Absence of Uncertainty. In a static society (or state of equilibrium), resources are more or less fixed and have attained such a distribution among various industries that there is no motive for transferring them from one employment to another. There is no tendency for any firm to enter or leave the industry. Uncertainty, therefore, would be at a minimum and competition perfect. Under such conditions, pure profits will tend to disappear and the entrepreneurs will earn only wages of superintendence. Normal profits, therefore, practically amount to earnings of management. They are just sufficient to induce an entrepreneur to stay in the industry.

In a progressive state also, similar results can follow, provided competition is unrestricted and changes can be anticipated. But since changes are not uniform, entrepreneurs in some industries may be able to make higher profits than in others.

Surplus profits can arise, in the short-run, in a dynamic world even though the factor of uncertainty is absent . But this will only be a temporary condition. In the long run, industries yielding profits higher than the normal will attract entrepreneurial ability and other factors of production. The rate of profits in such industries will tend to fall. In industries, which are being depleted of such factors, profits will rise, until the normal level of profits is established.

But normal profits in a dynamic world need not necessarily be equal to the wages of a hired manager, even though the factor of uncertainty is absent. The very fact that change exists, even though it can be anticipated, means heavier responsibility on the entrepreneur than in a purely static state. To keep up the supply of entrepreneurs, therefore, inducement must be given to them to take up such responsibility. But this additional payment will be kept within narrow limits by the forces of competition.

Existence of Uncertainty. In a dynamic world, with element of uncertainty in existence, even under competition profits can be kept permanently above the normal level. Super-normal profits also can permanently arise, where the supply is in the hands of

Uncertainty gives rise to profit.

a monopolist and demand is inelastic. This will be so whether uncertainty exists or not.

It should be noted that uncertainty in its turn is not something constant. There are degrees of uncertainty. The greater the degree of uncertainty, the higher must be the profits to compensate the entrepreneurs for bearing its risks.

Monopoly and Profits

So far we assumed that the employer is working under conditions of competition. Under perfect competition, there are no profits in the long-run. Profits must, therefore, be either temporary or monopoly profits. The monopolist is able to control output so that the price is not allowed to fall to the level of cost, as is the case under competition. By restricting entry of new firms into business by means of agreements and through the use of patent rights and similar devices, monopolists are able to reap monopoly profits. But the most common source of monopoly profits lies in monopolistic competition or product differentiation.

An element of monopoly profits can also be traced in what have been called **innovation profits** or pioneering profits. A firm which produces a new product, or is able to discover a new material or a cheap process or a new market, will always be able to make extra gains, till its rivals make an inroad into its business. Since competition is absent, partially or totally, gains arising out of innovation or pioneering may be termed as monopoly gains.

In the actual world, the typical cases are of imperfect competition, since absolute monopoly is rate. And, therefore, the element of monopoly gains is not as rare as one would think. In fact, monopoly element will be found almost in all profits.

A monopolist is able to make profits both in static and dynamic conditions. He is able to so fix the price of the product that he may make substantial profits by exercising his monopoly power. In order to make profits he raises the price by restricting the level of his ouput.

Monopoly is a matter of degree only. Monopoly power is exercised by a pure monopolist who produces a product which has no close substitute. Monopoly is also exercised, though to a somewhat lesser extent, by firms under monopolistic competition and oligopoly as mentioned above. Under various categories of imperfect competition, we know that the demand curve slopes downwards. Hence monopoly is associated with a downward sloping demand curve. Since the demand curve under conditions of pure monopoly, monopolistic competition and oligopoly slopes downwards, firm's equilibrium (*i.e.* equality between marginal revenue and marginal cost) is achieved at a price which is higher than the marginal cost of production. Also, the price so determined is often higher than the average cost of production which, therefore, yields positive profits to the firm enjoying monopoly power. Since there is strong resistance to the entry of new firms into the industry, the firms working under the monopoly or monopolistic competition continue to make supernormal profits even in the long-run.

Even under monopolistic competition, owing to product differentiation, entry into the industry by new firms is not wholly free since product differentiation gives a firm a certain degree of monopoly power so that it can set own price. No new firm can produce exactly the same product as that of the existing firms. Since the entry of new firms is restricted, demand does not fall, even in the long run, to the tangency position with average cost curve. The result is that entrepreneurs working under monopolistic competition continue to enjoy positive profits by virtue of their monopoly power.

The monopolist enjoys profits owing to his monopoly power. In a previous chapter (No. 28), we have given Prof. A. P. Lerner's quantitative measure of the degree of monopoly power. This measure of the degree of monopoly power is based on the fact that the price set by the monopolist is higher than the marginal cost due to the demand curve sloping downwards. This measure of the degree of monopoly power is based upon the ideal market, *i.e.*, that is a market under perfect competition in which monopoly power is completely absent and, in equilibrium, price is equal to the marginal cost.

Some economists, especially Prof. M. Kalecki, have asserted that the greater the degree of monopoly, the greater the size of profits made by the firm. Kalecki thinks that the degree of monopoly power is the most important determinant of the value of profits; in fact,

Monopoly profit

he thinks that it is the only determinant of the level of profits. It may be borne in mind that the degree of monopoly power a firm (*i.e.*, its power to set the price above the marginal cost of production) depends upon the elasticity of the demand curve facing the monopolist. That is, smaller the elasticity of demand for the product, the greater is the power of the monopolist to set the price and hence to make profits. But elasticity of demand for a firm's product depends upon the extent to which the product can be differentiated. The greater the product differentiation, the less elastic is the demand for the product. The degree of monopoly power also depends upon the firm's share in the market for its product. The greater is its share, the greater is the monopoly power.

Thus, an entrepreneur is able to set the price for its product owing to monopoly power that it has gained by the extent of distinctiveness of its product and its share in the total output or market. The entrepreneur earns profits based on its ability to set the price as high above the marginal cost as he can.

But it may be noted that the enjoyment of monopoly power is no guarantee that positive profits will be made. Much depends upon the demand-cost situation. If the demand-cost situation is unfavourable, which means that costs are higher and the demand or revenue is less, even under pure monopoly, monopolistic competition and oligopoly, under which the firms enjoy varying degrees of monopoly power, will be incurring losses. As Professor Bober observes, "He skates on thin ice who identify profits with monopoly and monopoly with profits."[8]

But generally through the devices of advertisement, product differentiation and other sales promotion activities, the firms enjoying monopoly power make sure that the demand for the product remains above the marginal cost of production yielding a good deal of profits. They can not only exploit the consumers by setting a higher price and making profits but also by virtue of their monopsonistic power are able to exploit the various factors of production and underpay them.

It may be emphasised that in order to make their monopoly power lasting, the firms already in the market must be able to raise strong barriers to the entry of new firms into the industry. Hence, the ability of the monopolist to enjoy monopoly power and make profit depends ultimately on the restrictions they are able to impose on the entry of the new firms. By control over the supply of an essential raw material or legal restrictions such as patent rights, the existence of goodwill enjoyed by the existing firms, reputation of their brands, and trade marks of their products, economies of large-scale production *etc.*, the entry of new firms into the industry will be effectively barred and the existing firms will continue to earn monopoly profits.

Critical Evaluation of Monopoly Theory of Profits

It cannot be denied that monopoly is a very important source of profit. The firms operating under monopoly or monopolistic competition, with a downward sloping demand curve and so enjoying price-setting power, are able to make positive profits. But the assertion, as of Prof. Kalecki, that monopoly is the sole source or determinant of profit cannot be accepted. Dynamic changes, innovations by the bold entrepreneurs and uncertainty also contribute to profits. In any theory of profits, the influence of these factors cannot be ignored. It may also be mentioned that there is no contradiction between uncertainty and monopoly theories of profits as kelecki thinks. In fact, market imperfections in monopolistic competition increase uncertainty, which also makes the entry of new firms into industry difficult. Hence, the monopoly theory of profit only supplements the uncertainty theory of profits.

Kalecki's concept of the degree of monopoly power has also been criticized. For instance, under perfect competition, the degree of monopoly power is zero. Hence the rate of profits should also be zero and the share of labour and other factors should be 100 per cent which is really ridiculous. We must add that a great deal of criticism against monopoly theory of profits is really against Kalecki's measure of degree of monopoly power as a source of profits. There is no doubt that monopoly is an important cause and source of profit.

8. Bober, M. M. *Intermediate Price and Income Thoery*.

DO PROFITS TEND TO EQUALITY?

Here again, we cannot give a straight answer. It will depend upon the conditions that prevail. In a state of equilibrium, profit in the sense of wages of superintendence will be equalised. Pure profit will disappear.

Absence of Uncertainty. In a state of society, in which change is present but the factor of uncertainty is absent, profits will tend to equality about the normal level as already explained. Difference however, will not be entirely absent because of the differences of ability. But these differences will be kept narrow by the force of competition.

On the whole, one may say that the greater the routine character of an industry, the greater the tendency of profits to equality, provided the period is fairly long and competition unrestricted. In the short period, however, inequalities can exist.

Existence of Uncertainty. But when we are dealing with a changing society, in which the factor of uncertainty is prominent, there is no tendency towards equality of profits even in the long run. Here profits may show considerable variations.

SOCIAL FUNCTION OF PROFIT[9]

It is commonly thought that the profit is for the entrepreneur; it is his concern, and it is at the expense of the consumer or the general public. It is supposed that there is an inherent conflict between the interests of the individual entrepreneur and social welfare or between private net product and social net product, as Pigou would put it.

But this view is a mere delusion. Far from there being a conflict, there is an underlying harmony between what the entrepreneur gets and the society gives. The conflict is more apparent than real. Whatever the form of society–capitalist, socialist, communist or fascist–profit performs a very, essential and useful function.

Philanthropically inclined entrepreneurs sometimes speak of their duty to promote the welfare of the society and of those who are associated with them as workers in the enterprise. They say their duty is not to make profits but to make the people happy. But the foremost duty of an economic enterprise is economic performance, which means the preservation of the resources entrusted to it. "The preservation of these resources is the corporate enterprise's first obligation to itself and to society. If it fails in this it not only weakens its own power to survive, but

9. See P. F. Drucker on "The Function of Profit" in Fortune, March, 1949.

Profit is not only for entrepreneurs but also for workers.

impoverishes the whole society." In order to keep its resources intact, the enterprise must avoid losses and work for the maintenance of normal rate of profit.

In its battle for survival, it is the duty of each individual enterprise to try to cover (*a*) current costs of business: and (*b*) the future costs of **staying in business** arising out of four kinds of risks already mentioned, (*viz*., replacement, obsolescence, risk proper and uncertainty).

In addition to these, there are two more functions which a profit-making industrial enterprise must perform: (*a*) One is to fill what Drucker calls "dry holes," *i.e.*, a successful enterprise must from the social point of view, cover the losses of the unsuccessful ones. "Just as a productive oil well must pay for the pipe and labour that went into a dry hole, so the surviving company must pay for the economic loss of its competitor's failure." This is the insurance principle. Any individual enterprise may try to avoid these dry holes, but the society as a whole cannot.

(*b*) There is still another function which profit must discharge, *viz.*, to bear the **social burden.** The successful industrial ventures must bear the cost of social service or social security measures like education, health services, poor relief, old-age pensions, maternity relief, defence, civil administration, *etc.*

These four functions profit has to perform for the sheer maintenance and preservation of modern industrial economy. But no modern community could be satisfied with mere maintenance or survival. It must provide for **a progressive growth and development.** The economy must expand and increase productivity not only by the exploitation of **virgin** resources, but also by making a fuller and better use of existing resources through technological advances, so that they are made more productive than what they have been. All this has also to be achieved out of profits.

Finally, we may add that the rate of profit is an indicator of the directions in which the community's resources should move. It is a **guide for the optimum allocation of the available resources.** Whatever the economic system, no community can ignore the imperative necessity of deriving maximum benefit out of its resources. It can ignore it only at its peril. The punishment will be economic degeneration. Even a communist society is faced with scarce resources and multiplicity of wants. The rate of profit, regardless of the pockets it goes into, will guide the investment. Broadly speaking, profits stimulate innovations by inducing businessmen to undertake new ventures. Further, desire for profits leads to efficient allocation of the country's productive resources. In a free enterprise or capitalistic economy, profit is prime mover or energiser of all economic activity.

Thus, even under a socialist or communist organisation of society, profit will have an essential function to perform. Hence, whatever the form of our economy, the rate of profit guides the economy.

Here is an excellent summing up of the role of profit by Samuelson: "Profits and high factor returns are the bait, the carrots dangled before us enterprising donkeys. Losses are our penalty kicks. Profits go to those who have been efficient in the past–efficient in making things, in selling things, in foreseeing things. Through profits, society is giving the command over new ventures to those who have piled up a record of success." Again, "profits are the report card of the past, the incentive gold star for the future, and also the grubstake for new ventures." [10]

Thus, the most important function of profit is resource allocation. Occurrence of profit gives the signal for reallocation of resources. It is, therefore, an important part of the signal–incentive mechanism which facilitates the functioning of the price-mechanism in a free enterprise economy. The rate of profit influences both the level of resource utilisation as well as the allocation of productive resources among alternative uses.

Profit is also meant for social development.

MACRO-THEORIES OF DISTRIBUTION

We have discussed so far micro-theories of distribution i.e. how wage is determined in an individual firm/industry, rent of a particular piece of land and profit of an individual firm or an entrepreneur. But we should also understand how national income is shared among the **aggregative** shares of rent, wages, interest and profits. This is macro theory. We shall now briefly notice some macro-distribution theories.

THE RICARDIAN OR CLASSICAL THEORY

The Ricardian theory makes use of two principles in income distribution viz., the 'marginal principle' and 'surplus principle'. With the marginal principle, the theory explains the determination of the share of rent in the aggregate national output and with the surplus principle the shares of wages and profits in the remaining national income. As Kaldor observes, rent is the difference between the product of labour on the marginal land and the product of average land.

In the Ricardian Theory, the marginal product is assumed to be equal to the sum of wages and profits. The wage rate is said to be determined by the minimum subsistence level. The balance of the marginal product (i.e. after deducting the subsistence level wage) is the share of profit. Thus profits are a residual income (i.e. what is left over after paying rent and wages).

With economic growth the share of wages increases at the expense of profits. Thus in the Ricardian Macro economic model, there is a

10. Samuelson, P. A. –*Economics*, 1970, P. 602.

continuous tendency towards a declining rate of profit, with growth in output and employment.

THE MARXIAN THEORY

As Prof. Kaldor observes, the Marxian theory is an adaptation of Ricardo's surplus theory. According to Marx, the value of a commodity is determined by the labour-time necessary for its production. But labour produces more than the value of its labour power i.e. more than what is necessary for maintaining the minimum subsistence standard. Hence a surplus emerges which is exploited by the capitalists in the form of profits. This is Marx's Theory of **Surplus Value.** Thus, according to Marx profits represent exploitation of labour by the capitalists. The capitalists are able to exploit labour through the ownership of the non-human means of production (i.e. machines).

Karl Marx referred his surplus value as nothing but the profits earned by the capitalists. According to him,

Use Value – Exchange Value = Surplus Value or Profit

$$U - E = S.$$

Use Value is nothing but the total value (utility created or produced).

Exchange Value is the amount of money paid to workers as wages or (subsistence) and the surplus value is the profits pocketed by the capitalists. Marx said the capitalists exploits the labour by 100%, in other words, if the total value created is Rs. 100 than Rs. 50 is paid as exchange value and Rs. 50 is the capitalists profit.

$$100 - 50 = 50.$$

Marx took the surplus value (Profit) as the indicator of the capitalists progress and decline. One of the main factor responsible for the collapse of capitalism is due to the falling rate of profit and this happens as the capitalists increases the fixed capital to replace the labour force.

The falling rate of profit as one of the indicator of the collapse of capitalism.

The notion of surplus value is crucial to the Marxian theory; It is the amount of this surplus that determines the relative share of profits in the national income. Wages remaining constant at the subsistence level, the difference between total output and the subsistence output (i.e. the rate of exploitation) increases with technical progress. Hence under the capitalistic system the relative share of wages in the national income declines and the share of profits increases (quite the opposite of what Ricardo thought), though the *rate* of profit will go down as a result of capital accumulation. $q = \frac{c}{c+v}$ is organic composition of capital. This gives the ratio of constant capital to total capital. The table shows as 'q' increase profit 'p' goes on decreasing. This is what Marx calls 'immiseration of the proletariat.'

Total 'C' Fixed capital	Variable capital V = wages	Surplus value profit = S	Organic composition of capital $Q = \frac{C}{C+V}$	Profit $= \frac{S}{C+V}$
50	50	50	$\frac{50}{100} = 50\%$	$\frac{50}{100} = 50\%$
100	50	50	$\frac{100}{150} = 66\%$	$\frac{50}{150} = 33.33\%$
150	50	50	$\frac{150}{200} = 75\%$	$\frac{50}{200} = 25\%$
200	50	50	$\frac{200}{250} = 80\%$	$\frac{50}{250} = 20\%$

(Here the assumption of constant V and 'S' is taken into account).

But Marx has proved to be a bad prophet of future events. Worker's living conditions have continued to improve and the rate of profit has not fallen. Labour theory of value on which he bases his theory has been rejected.

KALECKI'S 'DEGREE OF MONOPOLY' THEORY

According to Kalecki, the distribution of national income into profits and wages depends upon the degree of monopoly in the economy. The degree of monopoly of a firm is measured by (p-a) which is the difference between the price of the product and the average cost on manual labour and raw materials per unit of output. This difference is made up of entrepreneurial profits, interest, depreciation and salaries and thus represents gross capitalist income (inclusive of salaries) per unit of output. We can get his total income by multiplying it by the total number of units produced. Also, in order to get the gross capitalist income of the economy as a whole, we have to sum up the gross capitalist incomes of all firms which may be represented by the formula Ex (p-a). If we divide it by T (aggregate turn over), we get

$$\text{macro - degree of monopoly} = \frac{\text{Groos capitalist income}}{\text{Aggregate turn over}}$$

Kelecki shows the dependence of labour's share in national income on the macro-degree of monopoly power. The relative share of wages in national income is given by the formula Wages National Income. This

Profit results by paying labour less than its share.

share is inversely related to the degree of monopoly power. In other words, increase in the degree of monopoly power will reduce the relative share of wages (i.e. manual labour's share).

Labour's share in national income has remained constant by and large. This, according to Kalecki is due to the fact that increasing degree of monopoly power has been counter-balanced by a fall in the price of basic raw materials.

NEO-CLASSICAL THEORY

According to Neo-classical theory, the marginal principle can be applied to all factors of production by taking them as variable factors, and their rewards are equal to their marginal products. It is just like the micro theory of distribution. The total absolute share of a factor is determined by marginal products multiplied by the amount of the factor used. The absolute share of labour in the national income is determined by the amount of labour multiplied by its marginal products. The relative share of labour in the national income is the absolute share divided by the total national income.

KALDOR'S OR KEYNESIAN THEORY OF INCOME DISTRIBUTION

Kaldor has called his income distribution theory as Keynesian Theory since he employs Keynesian theoretical framework in its elucidation; Kaldor also divides the national income into two parts, viz., wages and profits. Since profits are defined as the incomes of property owners, it includes rents and interest besides ordinary profits.

In Kaldor's model, the share of profits in the national income is a function of investment-income ratio (I/Y); the greater this ratio, the greater the share of profits, and vice versa. According to Kaldor's theory, a shift in the distribution of income in favour of capitalist class is essential if full employment equilibrium is to be maintained.

Modern Concept of Profit

I. Economists Concept : An Economists takes into account the gross profit as the surplus obtained over and above the average cost. In other words he takes into account.

TR = OP Price Per unit × OQ quantity sold.

TC = OR Cost per unit × OQ quantity sold;

Where TR = Total revenue and

TC = Total cost

$\therefore$ TR – TC = π (Gross Profit)

▭ OPMQ – ▭ ORSQ = ▭ PMSR

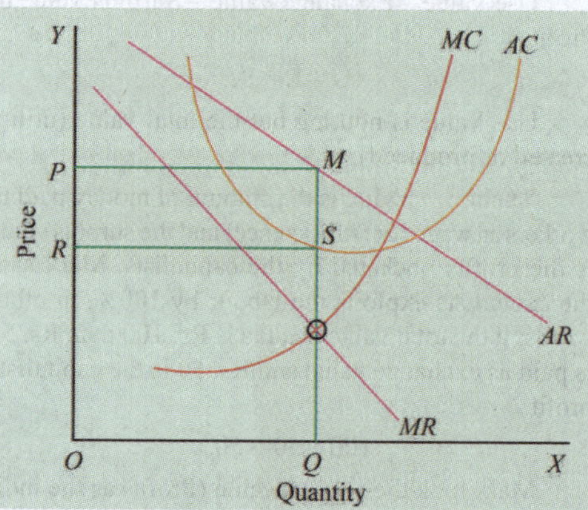

Fig. 35.2.

(An example of a monopolistic firm or monopolist)

AR = Average revenue

MR = Marginal revenue

AC = Average cost

MC = Marginal cost.

II. A corporate sector concept.

Total revenue – Total Cost = Gross Profit

Total revenue is nothing but Price × quantity, whereas total cost is nothing but the expenses incurred for raw material wages, manufacturing cost, advertisement, wages, salaries and so on.

$$\text{Gross profit} - \left\{ \begin{array}{l} (a)\ \textit{Reserved fund} \ + \\ (b)\ \textit{Depreciation} \ + \\ (c)\ \textit{Corporate taxes} \end{array} \right\} = \text{Net Profit}$$

Key terms

Gross Profit, Net Profit, Risk, Uncertainty, Normal Profit, Monopoly Profit.

QUESTIONS

1. Distinguish between Gross Profits and Net Profits. Account for the variations of profits of different units in the same industry.
2. Critically examine Knight's Theory of Profit.
3. Critically examine the view that profit is the reward for the entrepreneur for bearing non-insurable risks and uncertainty.
4. "Uncertainty and not risk forms the basis of a valid theory of profits". Discuss.
5. Discuss the role played by the following in the determination of profits:–
   (*i*) Risk and uncertainty.
   (*ii*) Dynamic Changes.
   (*iii*) Innovation.
   (*iv*) Monopoly.
6. Critically examine the Dynamic Theory of Profits.
7. "Profits are said to be both causes and effects of economic dynamics."

   Or

   "A true theory of profits must reconcile the risk theory and dynamic theory of profits". Comment.
8. "Rent and profit are alike because both are surplus, but they differ because there might be rent in all incomes but not profit". Discuss.
9. Indicate the nature of profits and indicate the position they are likely to hold under a socialistic regime.
10. Explain the Marxian theory of Profit.
11. Explain the Marxian concept of
    (*a*) Use value,
    (*b*) Exchange value and
    (*c*) Surplus value.
12. Do you think falling role of Profit is one of the main cause of collopse of Capitalism? Comment, and is it prevailing now, in the post liberalisation era ? Comment.

CHAPTER 36

ROLE OF PRICE MECHANISM

Having studied the pricing process under different market conditions, we should discuss briefly the role of the price system in a Modern Economy.

In order to appreciate the role of price in a modern economy, we should have some idea of what a modern economy is. A modern free enterprise economy is based on economic freedom, where every individual is free to take up any job he likes and give up the one he does not like. He is free to work or not to work. Further, every individual is free to own any property and use it as he likes. Also, every individual is free to enter into any contract or agreement, that he thinks most profitable for himself. Thus, freedom of occupation, freedom of owing and using property and freedom of contract are three main pillars of a modern capitalistic economy.

As a result, we find minute division of labour and specialisation creating millions of businesses, enterprises, millions of farmers, professional men, governmental and non-profit and philanthropic institutions all working in the economic system giving a fair degree of satisfaction to all concerned. In this system, every individual, including legal individuals like firms and corporations, decides for himself what contribution, in the form of goods and services, he will make to the economy and be sure that he will get the price acceptable to himself and the buyers thereof. Also, he is confident that he can get goods and services contributed by others at prices acceptable to them.

What is the instrument of this remarkable achievement? It is the 'invisible hand' –the price system–about which Adam Smith spoke so eloquently thus: . . . . "Every individual necessarily labours to render the annual revenue of the society as great as he can. He generally, indeed, neither intends to promote the public interest, nor knows how much he is promoting it . . . . by directing that industry in such a manner as its produce may be of the greatest value, he intends only his own gain, and he is, in this, as in many other cases, led by an invisible hand to promote an end which was no part of his intention."

PROBLEMS TO BE TACKLED BY PRICE SYSTEM

The given system seeks to tackle the following problems:

(1) The consumers constituting the household have a variety of unlimited wants; but the resources at their disposal for the satisfaction of these wants are limited. They seek to select such combination of goods and services which will give them maximum satisfaction. The consumer's demand schedule or curve indicates how much they would be willing to purchase at various prices.

Free enterprise economy.

(2) The businessmen or producers supply the goods and services to the households. Their supply schedule or curve communicates to the consumers the amounts they would be able to supply at various prices. But they have to select for production those goods and services and the quantities to be produced which will maximise their profits. For this purpose, they must choose the most economical or least-cost combination of productive resources.

(3) The producers will maximise profits and minimise costs by substituting low-priced resources for high-priced resources. The resource's demand curves will indicate to the resource suppliers how much of the resources the firms would be willing to employ at the various prices of the productive resources.

(4) The households, as resource suppliers, offer to the firms productive resources in the form of land, labour, capital and entrepreneurial talents. The decisions of the competing resource suppliers are communicated to the producers by means of resource supply curves. The resource suppliers tend to shift their resources from the less remunerative to more remunerative employments. In this way, they seek to obtain the maximum return from the resources they supply.

Through the price mechanism, the product demand intentions of the consumers or the households and the product supply decisions of the firms result in series of product prices. In the same manner, the resource demand decisions of the firms and the resource supply decisions of the households will establish a series of resources prices. In short, "The competitive price system is a mechanism both for communicating the decisions of the consumers, producers and resource suppliers to one another and for synchronizing those decisions toward consistent production objectives." [1] This is series of inter-related decisions on the part of consumers, the resource suppliers and producers or resource users. These decisions or choices are based on the fact of scarcity of resources at the disposal both of consumers and producers and are influenced by considerations of substitutability of both products and resources, because both products and resources are capable of being put to alternative uses. The prices of products and resources reflect the relative scarcities and when the products and resources become scarce, their prices rise and it is a signal for substitution. Through substitutability, the society uses less of scarce resources and products and more of those which are comparatively less scarce.

Thus, the price system enables the community to tackle the fundamental problems of the economy, *viz.*, (*a*) what to produce, (*b*) how much to produce, (*c*) how to produce, *i.e.*, organising production and (*d*) for whom to produce, *i.e.*, the distribution of the total output and (e) to adapt itself to change or flexibility.

Let us now study in some detail the operation of the price system.

FUNCTIONS OF THE PRICE SYSTEM

The price system performs the following useful functions:

Coordination. The price system functions in such a manner that the adjustments in the economic system take place almost automatically without any direction or dictation from a central authority. Price is the co-ordinator both of production and consumption. The consumers are able to convey their preferences through the prices they are willing to offer. Similarly, the producers are able to indicate the scarcity or abundance of a commodity by means of the price they are willing to accept. If price rises, it checks demand and stimulates supply, and vice versa. If there is a greater demand for a commodity than the supply thereof, then the adjustment between the two will be brought about through a rise in price. Conversely, if the supply is greater than the demand, the price will fall and bring about an equilibrium between the two.

The same type of dovetailing is effected in the sphere of distribution where we are concerned with the remuneration of services of the agents of production. Rent, wages, interest and profits are the prices paid for the factors of production. If, for instance, there is a large supply of labour, wages will fall and induce the employers to employ more and absorb the extra supply. If, on the other hand, the supply of labour has been curtailed by war or epidemics, the wages will rise and give a warning signal to the employers of this shortage. The price system collates and transmits to millions of consumers and producers the required information, as it were, regarding the availability of, and desires for in conceivably large number and

1. Mc Connel, Campbell, R. –*Economics, Fourth Edition*, p. 75.

bewildering variety of goods and services and the industries are motivated to react appropriately.

Guides Economic Activity. The price obtained either for a commodity or a service constitutes an income which, through its purchasing power, determines the extent and the direction of economic activity. There seems to be every justification, therefore, for the present economic system to be designated as "government by price."

Harmonizes Conflicting Interests. The price - mechanism is supposed to harmonize the interests of both the consumers and the producers. In Benham's words, "It tends to harmonize the desire of entrepreneurs for profits and the desire of consumers to satisfy their wants as fully as possible from the factors of production available."

This harmony, however, is not always realized in actual practice. We may find that either the consumers are being exploited or the entrepreneurs are suffering a loss. While the consumers enjoy the benefits of cheap production, they are sometimes deliberately defrauded, or they are at the mercy of the monopolist who does not hesitate to exploit them. On the other hand, the joint-stock company may suffer because of the inefficiency of the directors or because the directors are enriching themselves at the expense of the company. Thus, we generally find divergence rather than harmony between the interests of the producers and the consumers, for the price-mechanism does not often work smoothly and freely.

Allocation of Working Force. Everybody has his own preference for jobs. He may like to be a top business executive, a barrister, a top physician or a chief engineer, but he cannot. He must be put in his proper place. This is the unpleasant task of the price system to assign each individual a task which befits him. Not only that, the price system allocates the available labour force of a country numbering millions among thousands of trades, professions and occupations some of which are monotonous, irksome and hazardous. A change in wages and terms of employment matches the demand for, and supply of, each type of the workers. By adjusting the patterns of economic activity, the price system balances the relevant supply and demand. There is no favouritism and no injustice. No other alternative, *e.g.*, job assignment by a central authority can do the trick except allocating jobs and workers by a free labour market.

Curbing Consumption. There may be times, for instance, when saving is essential for the growth of the economy or when shortage is feared and consumption has to be curtailed. In a free enterprise economy, a rise in the price will achieve the objective. Rationing cannot be tolerated for long and is out of place in normal times. An economy exists to provide the people with goods and services they want, unless they voluntarily withdraw their demand in the face of a forbidding price. The price system compels the consumers to express their preferences in a manner to match these preferences to the producer's costs. The price system thus makes an economy responsive to the desires of the consumers and the potentialities of the producers.

Allocation of Resources. The productive resources of the community, human and material, are automatically as it were, allocated among the various uses in such a manner that each makes a maximum contribution to the total output. Any misallocation will be rectified by transfer of resources from one use to another through the price indicator. For instance, if land can make more valuable contribution, when devoted to the cultivation of food crops, the object will be accomplished by higher food prices.

Making for Adaptability. Unless an economy is flexible and can quickly adapt to changed situations, efficient administration of its resources over time will not be possible. It is the price system which provides this flexibility. As consumers' tastes and preferences change, new techniques of production are discovered and resource supplies undergo change, the particular allocation of resources will cease to be appropriate and efficient. Adjustment to change takes place through price-mechanism. For instance, if consumer's tastes change, this will be communicated to the producers through changes in price of the goods concerned. If certain goods are in greater demand, the prices will rise giving supernormal profits to the existing firms and new firms will enter the industry. In this way, industry expands to meet increased demand. On the other

Conflict between private interest has social consideration

hand, the industry, for whose goods the demand is decreased, contracts. Thus, the price system elicits appropriate responses from the firms as well as resource suppliers to a given change in consumer's preferences. This is its **guiding and directing function.** By and large, the competitive price system is conducive to technological improvements and capital formation and other inter-related changes which result in greater productivity and higher level of materials well-being.

CRITICAL APPRAISAL OF THE PRICE SYSTEM

Let us assess the functioning of price-mechanism in order to see whether the price system is an unfailing guide as to what is to be produced, how much to be produced, how production is to be organised and how total output is to be distributed. Opinions naturally differ on this point. There are people who are all praise for the competitive price system which is a characteristic feature of capitalism and there are those with whom it does not find favour. We shall briefly notice the case for and the case against the price system.

Case For

(i) In support of the price system, it is urged that it results in the most efficient allocation of the community's resources. All errors of judgment on the part of the producers are heavily penalised by losses. At the risk of being squeezed out, the producers have to employ the most economical techniques of production. Self-interest of the producers induces them to produce goods which consumers want the most. In short, the price system makes for maximum economic efficiency. The consumers get maximum satisfaction, the producers maximum profit and the community maximum welfare.

(ii) On the non-economic considerations, the proponents of the price system point out that it makes for economic freedom, *i.e.*, freedom of enterprise for the businessmen and freedom of choice for the consumers. They are free to pursue their self-interest subject to rewards and punishments imposed by the price system itself.

Shortcomings

The price system is criticised on the following grounds:

(i) The economic freedom permitted by the price system kills wholesome competition which is beneficial to the consumers and the workers. Instead, the self-seeking and profit-greedy entrepreneurs combine to extract highest prices from the consumers and pay the lowest wages to the workers. This is sheer exploitation. "Combination, conspiracy, cut-throat competition, sheer productive efficiency are all means to the end of reducing competition and escaping its regulatory powers." (McConnel)[2] Attainment of maximum economic efficiency requires that the number of producing firms should be small rather than large. Hence, rivals are ruthlessly squeezed out. The sovereignty of the producers kills the sovereignty of the consumers.

(ii) There is a clash between private interest and social welfare. The entrepreneurs are out to enrich themselves unabashed at the expense of the society. Social considerations are thrown overboard. Private individual interest runs amuck.

(iii) It is wrong to say that the price system leads to the production of goods which the consumers the consumer's prefers the Rather are hypnotised through high pressure salesmanship, to buy goods which the producers think most profitable to produce. The consumer's sovereignty is a myth. Besides, the competitive price system may not provide the consumers sufficient range of choice or for the development of new products. Pure competition entails product standardisation nor is it sufficiently progressive to develop new products.

(iv) The price system accentuates economic inequalities. It enables the big landlords and industrial magnates to acquire vast property which they can bequeath to their heirs and successors. Further, owing to differences in the quality and amount of human resources supplied by the households, there are galling differences in incomes.

(v) The critics also point out that the price system fails to register all costs and benefits. It shows only the cost of the producers, but not the social costs (*i.e.*, harm which a system of production may do to the society, *e.g.* air and water pollution). Similarly, it only registers utility of purchase to the individual consumers but takes no notice of the benefits to the society, *e.g.*, purchase of an X-ray plant for a hospital.

(vi) The price system is an indicator of individual wants but not the collective wants of the community. For example, public parks, libraries, education and public health system cannot be purchased individually.

(vii) The price system does not help the economy of the country to adjust quickly to drastic changes in community's production targets. The actual pattern of resource allocation always legs behind the country's production targets. This is due to geographical and occupational immobility of the productive resources.

(viii) The price system has proved to be an imperfect mechanism for achieving full employment.

2. *Economics*, p. 86.

Unemployment persists even in highly developed and prosperous societies.

(*ix*) The price system does not necessarily entail the use of most efficient productive techniques or the development of improved techniques. This is due to the fact that profit from innovations may be competed away; hence it is discouraged. A typical competitive firm is too small to be able to finance research programmes.

Conclusion

While we cannot ignore the various criticisms levelled against the price system and some of them are reasonably valid, we have to concede that the functioning of the price system is conducive to economic efficiency, *i.e.*, efficient allocation of community's productive resources.

On the whole, it may be said that working of the capitalistic system is out of the question without price-mechanism. It is price-mechanism which brings about the necessary adjustments between the various parts of the economic system. It is really difficult to think how the economic system could functions justly or smoothly. But price-mechanism certainly enables it to work normally without any serious jolts and jerks.

PRICE SYSTEM IN A DEVELOPING ECONOMY

In a mixed economy like ours, where a substantial part of economic activity is in the private sector, the price-mechanism has an important role to play. Decisions regarding what to produce, how much to produce and how to produce are based on prices of products. This has been recognised in our plan documents.

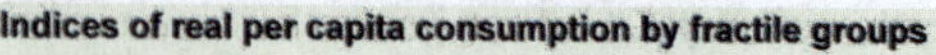

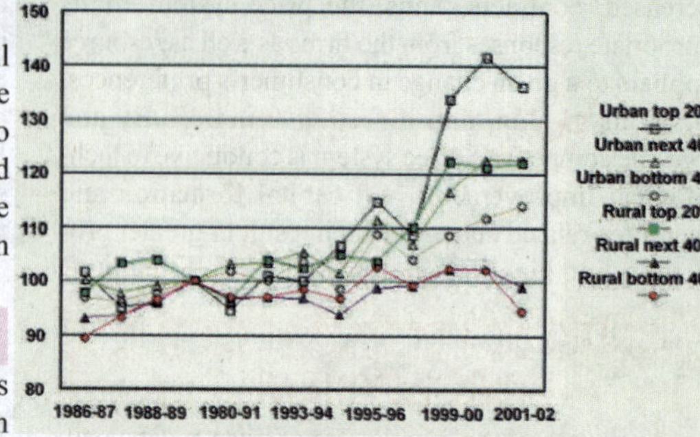

Chart showing distribution of consumer expenditure in India.

One cannot, however, rely entirely on the free play of market forces. The prevailing price-relations in an under-developed economy are often the result of market imperfections and rigidities. Nor can the changes in relative prices by themselves always bring about the necessary re-allocation of resources quickly or adequately. In a developing economy, the basic trend of government operations in the fiscal and monetary fields is inevitably expansionary. Hence economic policy in a planned economy must influence the allocation of resources through direct controls, allocations, taxation and subsidies, so that it conforms more closely to the objectives of planning. Thus, the government has to play a positive role in using the price-mechanism for purposes of planning.

There is no aspect of economic policy which does not, in some way or another, have a bearing on prices. Therefore, we should not view price policy in isolation. It must be viewed as an integral part of general economic policy. We may conclude that within a broad framework of a properly conceived plan, the evolution and implementation of an appropriate price policy can be of assistance in securing the plan objectives.

Key terms

Price mechanism, Allocation of resources.

QUESTIONS

1. Explain the concept of Price Mechanism.
2. Discuss the main functions of the price system.
3. Give a critical appraisal of price system.
4. Discuss price system in a developing economy.

PART TWO

Theory of Income and Employment or Macro-Economics

UNIT I

Social Accounting

UNIT II

Theory of Income Determination

UNIT III

Economic Fluctuations

UNIT I

Social Accounting

Chapters

SOCIAL ACCOUNTING

Introduction: Importance

Social accounting or preparation of social accounts has assumed great importance in modern times. This is so because economic theory is being increasingly applied for the solution of practical problems. If study of economics is to be fruitful, knowledge of social accounts is absolutely essential. In the absence of a clear picture of the working of the economy, an economist is seriously handicapped in giving practical advice to the government or to businessmen. It is only with the help of social accounting that one can clearly trace the effects of changes in one section of the economy on its other sections. Nature of economic relationship is very complex in the present-day world, and therefore, no student can clearly grasp the principles of economics without having in his mind a clear picture of the economy which only social accounting can give.

What is Social Accounting?

As we have said above, the nature of economic relationship has become very complicated in modern times. We have also said that it is the business of social accounting to make the understanding of this relationship easy and simple. But what precisely is social accounting? 'Social accounting' is a term which is applied to the description of the various types of economic activities that are taking place in the community in a certain institutional frame-work. In social accounting, we are concerned with statistical classification of the economic activity so that we are able to understand easily and clearly the operation of the economy as a whole. In the words or Stone and Murray, "The term social accounts is used in a general sense to denote an organized arrangement of all transactions, actual or imputed, in an economic system. In such a system distinctions are drawn between: (*i*) Forms of economic activity, namely, production, consumption and accumulation of wealth:

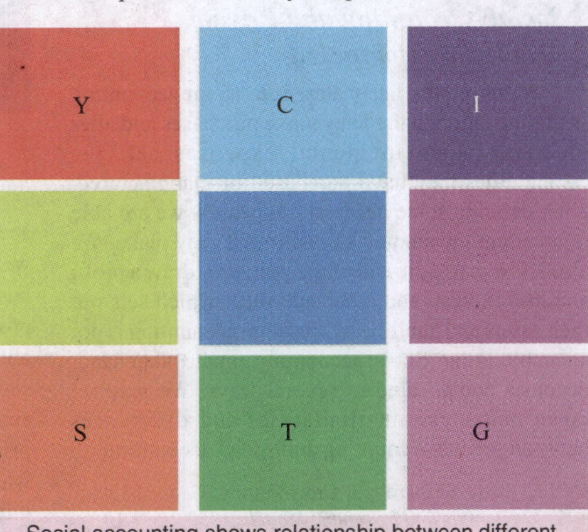

Social accounting shows relationship between different economic activities.

(*ii*) sectors or institutional division of the economy; and (*iii*) types of transactions, such as sales and purchase of goods and services, gifts, taxes and other current transfers, *etc.*" [1]

Here is another description of the field of social accounting, "The field of studies-summed up by the words 'social accounting' embraces, however, not only the **classification** of economic activity, but also the **application** of the information thus assembled to the investigation of the operation of the economic system."[2] Social accounting is thus concerned with the analytical as well as the statistical elements of the study of national accounts.

In social accounting, a transactor is supposed to keep a set of three accounts in which transactions are entered: (*a*) In the first account, incomes and outgoings relating to a productive activity of the transactor are brought together. The difference between the two indicates the profit or the gain. (*b*) The second account seeks to show how this profit and any other income that accrues to the transactor are allocated to different uses. The excess of income over outlay is the measure of savings. (*c*) The third account shows how this saving and any other capital funds are used to finance the capital expenditure or to give loans to other transactors. These accounts show the assets and liabilities of the person concerned at the beginning and at end of the accounting period. Since in the economy as a whole, the transactors are numerous, they are grouped into sectors. In the sector, accounts of a same type are consolidated. The sector accounts form the units in a system of social accounts.

Social Accounting and Private Accounting Compared

We have all a fairly clear idea about accounting of private individuals. They make purchases and after incurring some incidental expenses sell the commodities they have purchased or manufactured. After debiting some necessary expenses, we are able to ascertain the amount of profit that they make. We also know that at the end of the year, they draw a profit and loss account and a balance sheet which sets out their assets and liabilities. But social accounting is not as simple as that. Social accounting, on the other hand, becomes complicated in several ways. We may set down below certain similarities and differences between private accounting and social accounting :

1. Stone, Richard and Croft-Murray, G. *Social Accounting and Economic Models*, 1959, pp. 9-10.
2. Eday, H. C. and Peacock, A. T., *National Income and Social Accounting*, 1959, p. 11.

(*a*) It is common knowledge with those dealing with accounts that private accounting is done on the method of double entry book-keeping. That is, each transaction is recorded twice in the books of the businessman. For instance, a cash sale will be entered once in the appropriate ledger account as a credit to the good sold, and it is again entered in the cash account as a debit in respect of the cash received. In social accounting, however, cash transactions are not separately presented. On the other hand, cash balances are recorded in the capital transaction account. This shows that social accounting also adopts the double entry method but the second entries are not recorded in detail.

(*b*) Another difference between private accounting and social accounting is that private accounts relate to the individual businessmen. Each transaction is thus recorded from one point of view only. On the contrary, social accounts relate to a connected and closed network of all businessmen. There are no loose ends. Each transaction is recorded from the point of view of the two transactors connected with it.

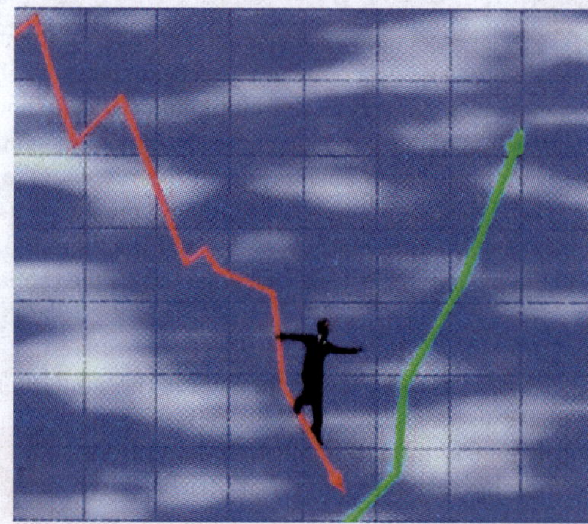

Private accounting relates to accounts of individual business.

(*c*) Still another difference between private accounting and social accounting may be noted. As we have mentioned above, the accounts of private businessmen are usually presented in the form of a profit and a loss account which shows income and its allocation. There is also set out a balance sheet which shows the stock of assets and liabilities at the end of accounting period. The profit and loss account of a private individual resembles in social accounting to what is called as the appropriation account. The only difference is that in private accounting, the profit often includes some elements of costs such as depreciation on plant and machinery and fees paid to the directors of the company. On the other hand, in social accounting, these incomes are shown net. There is no counterpart at all of a balance sheet in social accounting since there are insuperable difficulties in collecting the necessary information completely and on a uniform basis regarding assets and liabilities of all transactors in the economy.

Uses of Social Accounting

One might as well ask what after all is the object and purpose of preparing social accounts. To what uses are the social accounts put? We may give below in a summary fashion the purposes for which the social accounts are prepared or the uses to which they are put:

(i) One purpose of the preparation of social accounts is to give the reader a clear picture of the economy as a whole. As we have mentioned above, in social accounting we find a classified account of the various transactions entered into in the various sectors of the economy. From these transactions, we can have a fairly clear view of the working of the entire economic system. These days we are not so much interested in the accounts of private businessmen, however big and prominent they may be. On the other hand, we are interested in the health of the economy and the way in which it functions. It is understood that a healthy economy is able to impart strength and health even to the economic affairs of private individuals. Intelligent citizens are keen on knowing how an economy is faring at a particular moment or in a particular period of time. This is clearly reflected in social accounting.

(ii) We are all interested in the health, efficiency and stability of the economy since, as it has been mentioned above, a healthy and efficient economy results in the health and efficiency of individual businesses. We are all fairly familiar with the objectives placed before our Five-Year Plans. They all relate to the economy as a whole. We want economic growth with stability or we want to build up a self-reliant and self-generating economy. How far we are able to achieve these objectives can be very well found out from the description of various transactions and activities given in social accounting. Thus, if we want to promote efficiency and stability of our economy, preparation of social accounts is a 'must'.

(iii) Measurement of economic welfare is another purpose of the preparation of social accounts. We have mentioned above our Five-Year Plans. At the end of each plan, we naturally like to know how far the masses have benefitted from the plan. In other words, we want to know to what extent economic welfare of the masses has been promoted. From social accounting and its study we can know at a glance to what extent the masses are better off than at the time when planning started.

(iv) There is another important use which social accounting serves. From a study of social accounts, we are in a position to find out how the different sectors of the economy are inter-related to each other. We can, for instance, find out to what extent the industrial sector depends on the agricultural sector, and vice versa. We can also know to what extent the growth of our export sector is conditioned by our industrial and agricultural growth. To the economist and to the person engaged in economic planning these inter-relationships are of very great use. In fact, the information that social accounting furnishes about the mutual relationship of the various sectors of the economy is indispensable, if planning is not going to be a leap in the dark.

(v) Social accounting serves a very practical purpose for the statesman, the government administrator and the politician. It is on the basis of social accounts that intelligent and effective government policies in fiscal, monetary and other economic spheres can be formulated and executed. In the absence of social accounts, such policies can well be mis-leading and may result in economic disasters. The national resources are limited and it will be criminal to fritter them away. It is, therefore, very necessary that every care is taken in the formulation of national policies. Only social accounts can give us proper guidance in this connection.

PREPARATION OF SOCIAL ACCOUNTS

We shall now see how social accounts are prepared *(a)* in a closed economy and *(b)* in an open economy.

Social accounting concerns estimation of income, consumption etc. of whole society.

3. See Richard Stone and Giovauna Croft Murray, *A Social Accounting and Economic Models*, 1959, p. 12.

Social Accounts in a Closed Economy

A closed economy is one which is self-contained and self-sufficient so that it has no economic dealings with the outside world. In a closed economy, the accounts may be prepared on a uniforms basis and classified as (*i*) transactions relating to productive activity, (*ii*) transactions relating to the use of gain from productive activity, and (*iii*) transactions relating to capital. By consolidating these accounts, prepared for each firm, household, government agencies and every other transactor, we get three consolidated national accounts: (*a*) Production (or operating) Account (*b*) Consumption (or appropriation) Account and (*c*) Accumulation (or capital transactions) Account. These accounts can be illustrated for purpose of easy understanding, by a diagram given below. These transactions are represented as flows of money by arrows.

Let us now say a word about these accounts one by one.

Production (or operating) Account. In this account, we include all productive activities being carried on in the entire economy. It is a consolidated production statement relating to all firms operating in the economy. These firms manufacture commodities meant for consumption and capital goods and equipment for generating and accumulating wealth. The income obtained by these firms, therefore, comes through two channels, *viz*., partly by selling consumption goods and partly by selling capital equipment. The flow of this revenue is indicated by the direction of the arrows. In these accounts, purchases and sales by the firms from one another have obviously to be left out. They may be important for individual accounts but in the national or social accounts they cancel out.

In the above diagram, all proceeds of the sales of production are shown as being paid out as income to the factors of production, *i.e.*, to those who have taken part in the process of production. These payments take the form of wages to labour, salaries to the other employees, interest on capital, rent to the landlord, *i.e.*, the owners of land and business premises and profit going to the entrepreneur. The incomes are shown in the diagram as flowing from production to consumption by an arrow.

The incomes received by the factors of production may be either spent on consumption, *i.e.*, for the satisfaction of their immediate wants or they may be partly saved. The income spent on commodities is shown by an arrow going towards production from consumption and the part which is saved is shown by the arrow going from consumption to accumulation. Transactions of the consumers among themselves paying cash to one another are ignored just as we ignored the buying and selling activities of the producers among themselves.

We have seen that the whole of the sale proceeds of production go to consumption and consumption income is divided into spending and saving. It follows, therefore, that saving is equal to capital expenditure on real assets (or investments). We thus get the following two independent equations:

$$Y = C + S \quad ...(1)$$

$$S = 1 \quad ...(2)$$

In these equations Y stands for income paid to the factors of production, C stands for consumers' expenditure on commodities and services and S is savings (or income not consumed) and I is investment (or capital expenditures on real assets). If we substitute for S from equation (2) into equation (1), we get the

Diagram 1

Simplified Flow Diagram for Closed Economy

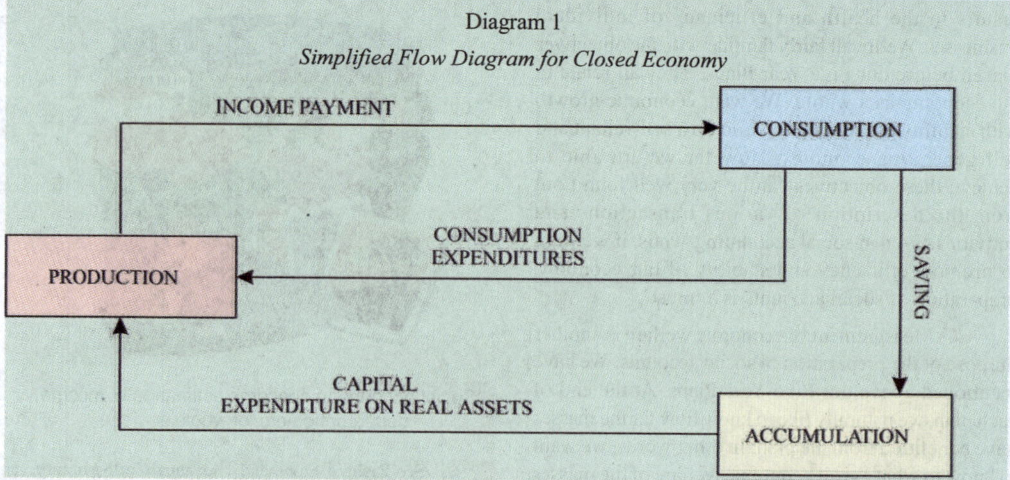

Fig. 37.1.

following equations:–

$$Y = C + 1 \qquad ...(3)$$

As we shall see in the Keynesian theory discussed in the chapters that follow, these equations are the fundamental identities around which the Keynesian theory is built up. These relationships pertain to a simple closed economy which has no trading or financial relations with the rest of the world.

Social Accounts in an Open Economy

An open economy is an economy having economic dealings with other countries of the world. Simple representation of an economy given above seems to be unrealistic when we think of what happens in the economic systems actually. We find that in practice economic systems are seldom self-contained. On the other hand, they enter into extensive economic relationship with other economic systems. To put it into simple language we can say that no country in the world is self-sufficient. There may have been a time when various territorial units were ignorant of the existence of one another and led a self-contained economic life. It is often said that the Indian villages were at one time economically self-sufficient, *i.e.*, they consumed what they produced and produced only for domestic consumption. Such a situation no longer exists. On the other hand, we find that there are extensive trading and capital transactions taking place between one country and another. Even China, a big communist country, is not self-sufficient. Thus, we find that economic systems of the world represented by individual countries are very closely inter-related. If social accounts are to be realistic, we have to introduce this new element in social accounts which may be represented by 'rest of the world'. Hence, for an open economy, we can classify the social accounts into (*a*) Production, (*b*) Consumption, (*c*) 'Rest of the world' and (d) Accumulation. The 'rest of the world' stands for the totality of other economies with which the economy in question is connected by virtue of economic relationship, *i.e.*, buying and selling, borrowing and lending, *etc.*

Open economies.

The diagram 2 given on next page represents the social accounting picture of an open economy.

It will be seen that this diagram is partly a reproduction of the earlier diagram. But we can also notice the additional items namely imports and exports of the country in question from and to the rest of the world. These are shown by flows connecting production with the rest of the world. In view of the fact that the value of the exports and imports is seldom equal to each other, we show in the diagram an arrow towards the rest of the world from accumulation. This flow is called 'net lending abroad'. This is a situation in respect of a country which has a favourable balance on current account which it lends abroad.

Like diagram No. 1, the flows into any given box in diagram 2 sum up to the same total as the flows which go out of that box. The total has to be same, it cannot be otherwise. We, therefore, get the following equations:

$$Y = C + S \qquad .....(4)$$

$$S = I + L \qquad .....(5)$$

$$X = M + L \qquad .....(6)$$

In the above equations, as before, Y stands for income (paid or payable to the factors of production), C is consumers' expenditure on commodities, S the saving (or the income not consumed) and I the investment (or capital expenditure on real assets). The new letters X, M and L stand respectively for exports, imports and the net amount lent by a country in question to the countries in the rest of world.

Coming to the equations we can see that equation (4) is the same as equation (1). It is with equation (5) that we come to difference made by introducing the 'rest of the world'. This equation shows that saving is no longer equal only to domestic investment as in diagram (1); but it is equal to domestic investment plus foreign investment. That is, saving of a country finances investment (or capital expenditure on real assets) both in the country itself and also includes the

Diagram 2

Simplified Flow Diagram for an Open Economy

Expenditure on Imports

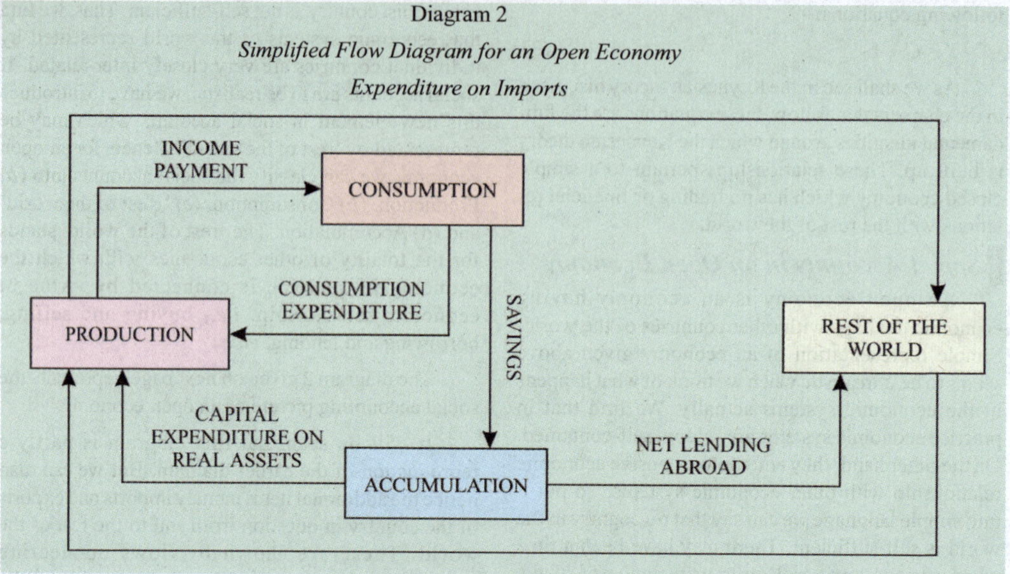

Fig. 37.2. **Revenue from Exports.**

amount which it lends abroad. In the new equation (6), showing relationship between transactions with the rest of the world, value of exports of the country in question is equal to the value of its imports plus the amount which it lends to the foreign countries. By substituting for L from equation (6) into (5) and then for S from (5) into (4), we get the equation

$$Y = C + I + X - M \qquad .....(7)$$

This equation shows that income payments are equal to consumption expenditures plus capital expenditures on real assets (*i.e.*, investment) plus the excess of the value of exports over the value of imports.

There is no doubt that the second diagram is more realistic than the first one, but even this diagram is not sufficiently detailed as to give a complete picture of an economic system actually in operation. It does not contain provision for depreciation which is very necessary since buildings and machinery do not last for ever. Provision for depreciation is taken directly to 'accumulation' to serve as a source for funds meant for the replacement of real assets. It has, therefore, to be represented by an arrow pointing from production to accumulation.

Secondly, we have to take into account taxes, both direct and indirect, levied by the government and also subsidies given by it. Indirect taxes are paid from 'production' into 'consumption' which includes 'consumption' by government also. Actually, all subsidies paid by the government are set off against the indirect taxes received by them and the resulting flow is labelled 'indirect taxes (net)'.

We have also to take note of the fact that the number of transactions between the economy in question and 'the rest of the world' is much greater than described here. For instance, a firm belonging to the country may have set up branches abroad from which profits flow in. Also, the citizens of the countries may earn dividends from investments abroad. These flows of income payments, from and to the rest of the world, have also to be taken into account. These are shown as received by and paid out by 'consumption'. Then there are gifts to and from abroad and also inter-governmental grants.

Thus, the actual situation to be represented by social accounts becomes very much complicated. If the social accounts are to be realistic, the flow called 'consumption expenditures' going from 'consumption' to 'production' should include not only the consumption expenditures of individuals and of non-profit institutions but also public consumption, *i.e.*, of public agencies. It may be more convenient to route these expenditures abroad through the domestic productive system which will, therefore, appear both as imports and as purchases from production. Similarly, the flow of savings going from consumption to accumulation should include not only the savings of individuals, non-profit institutions and business firms but also savings by government agencies. In case the government has a deficit on current account showing negative saving, the flow of saving will represent the excess of positive saving by the private sector over the

Diagram 3

Basic Economic Activities

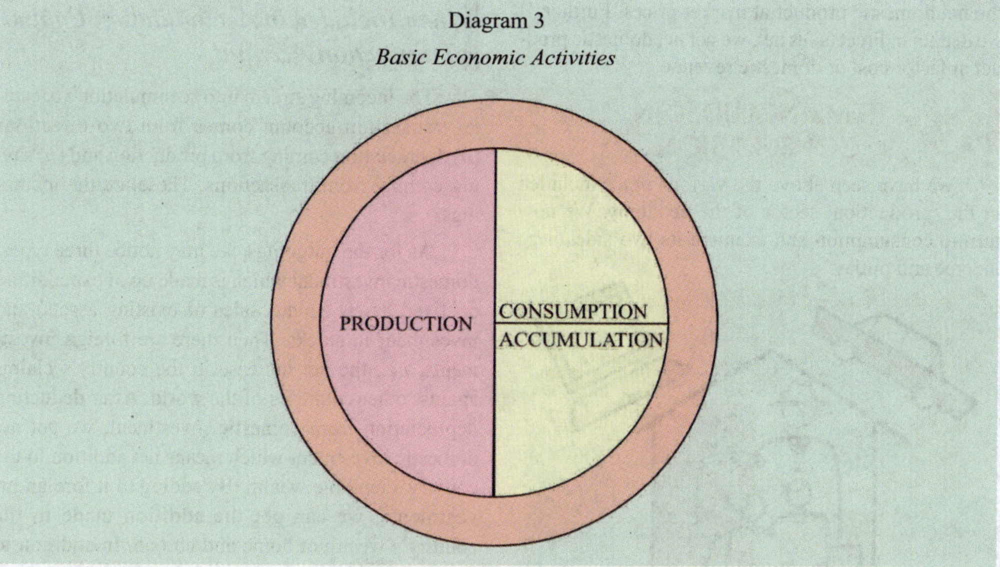

Fig. 37.3.

negative saving of the public sector.

Look at the above diagram. The outer circle represents the world economy and the inner circle domestic economy. The domestic economy is divided into two equal parts of which one is production and the second includes consumption and accumulation. This diagram can give some idea of the economic activities in a domestic economy and its relation with the world outside.

ITEMS INCLUDED IN THE VARIOUS SECTORS OF THE ECONOMY

We have classified the various-sectors of the economy as production, consumption and capital transactions account. We shall now say a word about the various items included in the social accounts relating to each sector.

Items included in the Production Sector

The production sector has two sides: (*a*) the incomings (or revenues) and (*b*) outgoings (or costs). The sale proceeds of commodities is the principal source of revenue or income of the firms. The goods are sold to other producers to enable them to carry on current production, to consumers consisting of households, private non-profit institutions or departments of central and local government. Then there are sales to other producers for the purposes of maintaining or adding to their capital equipment ; and finally, there are sales to the rest of the world. The second source of revenue consists of the value of increase in stocks. The stocks increase when production exceeds sales. Still another source of revenue is subsidies given to industries, agriculture, *etc.*

As far the costs, they are incurred on the intermediate products used in production which are bought from domestic producers or from abroad. Depreciation is another item of costs. It represents that value of a fixed asset which is deemed to have been used up in current production. The third item on the cost side is the indirect taxes or taxes on sales.

When we balance the costs mentioned above against the revenue of sale proceeds of the goods, we shall get what the business has gained and which is represented by excess of revenue over costs. Out of this profit only that part will accrue to the entrepreneur which is left after paying wages and salaries to the employees and interest to the bond-holders.

An account is prepared on above lines for every producer in the country and all accounts are added together. Sales and purchases of intermediate products will be equal and are, therefore, to be cancelled out. Subsidies may be treated simply as reduction in costs instead of revenue and hence subtracted from indirect taxes. Conversely, imports instead of being considered as costs may be treated as reduction in revenues from exports. In this way, we can get a total revenue consisting of the proceeds of final sales to the domestic product. From this if we deduct depreciation, we get

4. Stone, R. and G, *National Income and Expenditure*, 1961, p. 29.

the net domestic product at market prices. Further, if we deduct indirect taxes net, we get net domestic product at factor cost or domestic revenue.

ITEMS INCLUDED IN CONSUMPTION

We have seen above the various items included in the 'production' sector of the economy. We now turn to consumption and examine its two sides, *viz.*, income and outlay.

Balance of payment records transactions between two countries.

The consumers' income consists of the income which accrues to a country from its productive activity at home and abroad. In other words, it is the national income. Besides, there is some income from indirect taxes, which is counted as usual net of subsidies. As far as consumers' expenditure, we may say that most of the income that a country derives from its productive activity is spent on the purchase of goods and services. The second item of outgoings of the consumer is what are called current transfers abroad. They take the form of private remittances and government grants given to foreign countries. After taking into account similar remittances and grants received from foreign countries, we can show these transfers as net. These two items, however, namely consumers' expenditure on purchase of goods and services and current transfers abroad, do not exhaust the consumer, income. There is another item in consumers' outlay that is savings. Saving represents the excess of consumers' income over expenditure and their transfers abroad. Saving then flows from consumption into accumulation and thus finances capital expenditure.

Item Included in Accumulation Capital Transaction Account

The incoming stream into accumulation *i.e.* capital transaction account comes from two directions (*a*) depreciation coming from production and (*b*) saving coming from transactions. These are the incomings.

As for the outgoings, we may notice three types: domestic investment which is made up of expenditure on fixed assets (minus sales of existing assets) and investment in stocks. Then there are foreign investments, *i.e.*, the net increase in the country's claims against other countries of the world. After deducting depreciation from domestic investment, we get net domestic investment which means net addition to the country's tangible wealth. By adding to it foreign investments, we can get the addition made to the country's wealth at home and abroad. In addition to the two outgoings mentioned above, there is the third, *viz.*, capital transfers abroad. After deducting similar transfers received from abroad they are shown net.

Rest of the World: Balance of Payment Account

Let us now bring in 'rest of the world' and see the balance of payment account of a country with respect to the totality of the other countries of the world. We have to take notice of the mixture of income flows and transfer flows and current and capital transactions. The total income of country consists of the income derived from production, from transfers abroad both current (net) and capital (net) and borrowings from abroad. Against these, we set off the total outgoings consisting of imports and incomes from productive activity.

Conclusion

This briefly is the description of the process of the preparation of national or social accounts of a country. Social accounts show the structure of an economic system in the simplest form possible. The accounts are classified as production, consumption and accumulation. It may, however, be noted that it relates only to flows. This means that it only shows the additions to the country's wealth during a given period, but it leaves out the accumulated wealth already existing at the commencement of a period. That is, it does not give a balance sheet.

PROBLEMS OF CLASSIFICATION AND DEFINITION[5]

The description and classification of social accounting given in the previous sections seems to be a very simple affair. But it is not so. Actually when we come to define the various concepts and make an attempt to classify the accounts of an economy, we encounter several difficulties some of which appear to be formidable and insurmountable. We discuss below the main problems which arise from classification and definitions adopted in social accounting.

(i) Classification into Sectors and Accounts

One problem that has to be faced in the preparation of social accounts relates to classification into sectors and accounts. The relationships between production, consumption, investment and saving are easy to identify in hypothetical examples. But when we consider the actual accounting behaviour, we may not find it possible to ignore the various types of transactors operating in the economy. For instance, the directors of the company will not act as the owners of private businesses will do. The decisions of both are different from those of the government administrators running trading and manufacturing corporations. Hence it may be necessary to divide and sub-divide further the firms or production accounts corresponding to different types of business organizations. For example, it may be proper to sub-divide the government accounts into accounts for central and local government. Similarly, the accounts of the firms can be split into parts like 'production' or 'operating account' and the 'operating account' and the 'appropriation account'. It may be found necessary to have separate operating account and a separate appropriation account for each sub-division.

(ii) Transactions Recorded

Social accounts which are usually prepared do not give a complete picture of an economy. There are several items which are not included in the accounts. These items relate to the flow of value resulting from the production of new goods and services during the accounting period, the incomes accruing to the factors of production in respect of a particular product, current transfers of wealth between the various factors and to and from abroad in the forms of gifts, grants, taxes, interest payments, *etc.*, and capital transfers. The social accounts also exclude domestic transactions in second-hand goods. A common difficulty relates to the inclusion of the value of paid services of wives and

Social accounting faces problems of definition of concepts and clarification of accounts.

other members of the family.

The payments of interest and dividends also raise a conceptual problem. We have to see to what extent should such payments be deemed to have been made in respect of current services and therefore, treated as part of the aggregate gross national product and to what extent should they be treated as mere transfers of income between sectors. Business payments of interest and dividends to share-holders also raise some difficulties. We have to decide whether such payments are to be considered as part of factor income or as transfers for the purpose of social accounting.

There is still another problem which arises in dealing with financial intermediaries such as banks, investment trusts, *etc. The* payments that these organizations receive for services rendered in the form of commissions, *etc.*, the payments that they make to the factors of production (*e.g.*, salaries and rents and payments for goods and services purchased) are similar to what the other firms do. The difficulty is that these institutions make profit from the excess of interest and dividend received over interest paid. If interest received and payments are treated as transfers, it may give a negative figure for their gross product which does not reflect the true state of affairs.

(iii) Principles of Measurement

The items included in social accounts are measured in terms of exchanges at market values. When payments are made in terms of money, the valuation problem does not arise. But difficulty arises when we come to measure transactions which are not to be settled in money terms. These problems arise in the case of, for instance, valuation of farm products

5. Edey, H. C. and Peacock, A.T. *National Income and Social Accounting*, 1959, p. 63-78.

consumed by the farm household or the imputation of rental values to owner-occupied property. Difficulty particularly arises in the case of the valuation of investment in the form of both fixed capital formation and stock changes including the problem of depreciation. The difficulty also relates to the valuation of semi-manufactured and unsold finished stock held by the firms. No market transactions may be available as guidance for setting value on them. Deductions may also have to be made for obsolescence, *etc*., in the case of stocks. To make allowance for depreciation is not easy because capital equipment undergoes changes both in quality and quantity. The wornout capital equipment may not be replaced by identical equipment.

(iv) Collection of Data

Difficulties arise in connection with collection of data also. The difficulties relate to method of collection as well as the reliability of the data collected. Theoretically, if we independently calculate the sum of the net output of individual industries, sum of factor incomes and the sum of purchases of final output, it would furnish a check on each other in respect of different estimates of national income. But actually independent estimates can be made only to a limited extent, partly because some components of each aggregate are available from one source only and partly because of the practical difficulties in finding adequate reliable statistics.

As for the reliability of the data, it can be ensured if all economic units are required to keep accurate accounts and classify them according to official definition and reveal the information required correctly and completely. But the accounts actually kept are defective in all these respects. Even if the business

Collection of data and measurement of value create lots of problems.

units cooperate with the authorities, errors of computations may still arise and errors of classification may also be committed. Hence statistical discrepancies may arise when we aim to achieve consistency in the estimation of the national income from different sources.

Conclusion

There is no doubt that the task of preparing social accounts is beset with difficulties, but as the data improve both qualitatively and quantitatively, we may succeed in preparing national accounts in which errors are reduced to the minimum and the accounts become more reliable and dependable.

Key terms

Social Accounting, Private Accounting, Production Account, Balance of Payment, National Income Accounting.

QUESTIONS

1. Explain how national income accounts are organized.
2. With the help of diagram explain the concept of social accounting in
   (*a*) Closed economy
   (*b*) Open economy.
3. Distinguish between social and private accounting. What are the uses of social accounting?
4. What are the items included in production and consumption sectors of the economy.
5. Explain the problems of social accounting.

NATIONAL INCOME : MEANING AND CONCEPTS

Introduction

In the foregoing chapters, we were mainly concerned with the principles determining the pricing of products and of productive resources. The theory of value and distribution is mainly concerned with these principles. Although prices are very important yet of much greater importance is the volume of activity and employment in the economy as a whole. This subject, however, did not receive sufficient attention till recently. The Great Depression of the 'thirties of this century led economists to think much more seriously about this question and Keynes' "General Theory of Employment, Interest and Money" was the pioneering attempt in that direction.

The subject has further gained in interest and importance as a result of the quest for rapid economic development in the under-developed areas of the world. The factors on which the state of employment in a country depends deserve serious consideration. We, therefore, now enter a new and much more extensive territory. Our interest now shifts from the constituent parts of an economy (micro-economics) to the economy as a whole. We referred to the term macro-economics in the second chapter of the book while discussing the scope of economics. We repeat that macro-economics is concerned with aggregates such as national income, total output and employment, total consumption, saving and investment, aggregate demand, aggregate supply and the general level of prices.

Various products in the economy.

The problem which we have now to investigate is: What determines the level of total output and employment in the economy and fluctuations in this level from one time period to another? Thus, the problem has two aspects: (*a*) the determination of aggregate output and employment **at a moment** of

Economic Activities.

time; and (*b*) the analysis of causes of fluctuations in this level over a **period of time.** The second aspect opens out into the theory of industrial fluctuations more commonly known as the theory of trade cycle. Output and employment in a country depend on the size of national income (in fact they depend on each other) to the study of which we now turn.

Dr. Alfred Marshall defines National Income (or National Dividend) thus: "Labour and capital of a country acting on its natural resources, produce annually a certain 'net' aggregate of commodities, material and immaterial, including services of all kinds. The word 'net' means that from the gross value of the output depreciation of capital must be deducted. In Pigou's words, national income "is that part of the objective income of the community including, of course, income derived from abroad, which can be measured in money." Prof. Fisher bases his idea of national income on consumption instead of production. According to him national income refers "solely to services received by ultimate consumers, whether from their material or human environment."

The concept of national income has three interpretations. It represents a receipts total, it represents an expenditure total and it arises out of the fact every expenditure is at the same time a receipt (expenditure by one is received by another); and if goods or services bought are valued at their sales prices, we have three-fold identity that the value received equals the value paid, equals the value of goods and services given in exchange.

Definition of National Income

Keyne's concept of national income is somewhere between G.N.P. and N.N.P. (discussed below). From G.N.P. he subtracts only the 'User Cost', *i.e.*, reduction in the value of capital equipment actually used and not full depreciation.

According to present ideas, National Income may be defined as the aggregate factor income (*i.e.*, earning of labour and property) which arises from the current production of goods and services by the nation's economy. The nation's economy refers to the factors of production (*i.e.*, labour and property) supplied by the normal residents of the national territory.

There is a circular flow which can be shown in the above diagram:

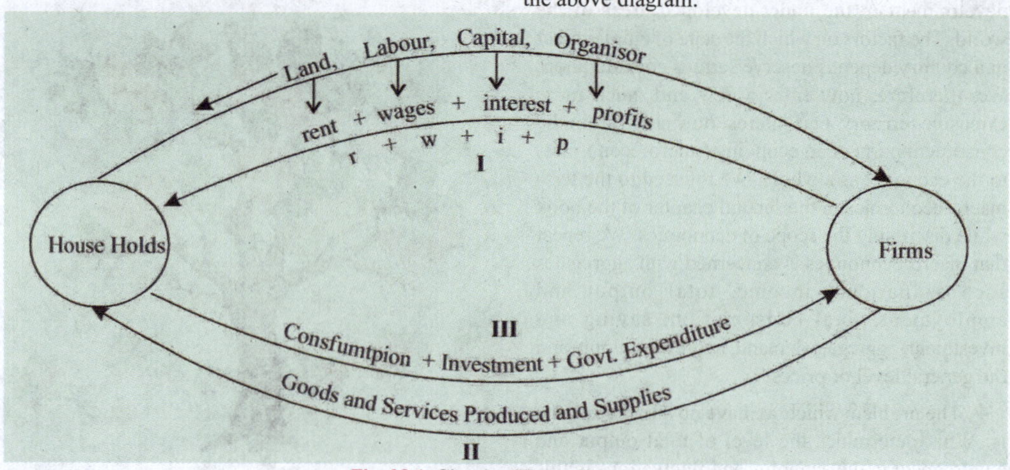

Fig. 38.1. Circular Flow of Income.

National Income by.

(I) Income Method = Aggregate of all income such as $NY = \Sigma(\Sigma_w + \Sigma_r + \Sigma_i + \Sigma p)$

(II) Production Method = Money value of all final goods and services produced in an economy

(III) Expenditure method = Aggregate of Expenditures of consumption + Investment + Government

To explain the above idea let us take an economy, where there are only two sectors: households and firms. Firms are required to produce goods. To produce them, they require services of the factors of production. Thus, incomes of these factors arise in the course of production. The sales value of net production must equal the sum total of payments made by the firms to the factors of production in the form of wages, rents, interest and profits. These incomes in turn become the sources of expenditure.

Thus, income flows from firms to households in exchange for productive services while products flow in return when expenditure by the households takes place.

Thus, there are three measures of national income of a country:–

(a) as the sum of all incomes, in cash and kind, accruing to factors of production in a given time period, *i.e.*, the total of income flows;

(b) as the sum of net outputs arising in several sectors of the nation's production;

(c) as the sum of consumers' expenditure, government expenditure on goods and services and net expenditure on capital goods.

The total of income flows, net outputs and final expenditures will be the same but the significance of each arises from the fact that they reflect the total operations of the nation's economy at the level of three basic economic functions—production, distribution and expenditure.

The discussion of the various concepts of national income will make the meaning of national income clear.

CONCEPTS OF NATIONAL INCOME

We study below the five important concepts of national income, *viz.*, the Gross National Product, Net National Product, National Income, Personal Income, Disposable Income.

Gross National Product (G.N.P.)

This is the basic social accounting measure of the total output or aggregate supply of goods and services, **Gross National Product is defined as the total market value of all final goods and services produced in a year.** It is a measure of the current output of economic activity in the country.

Two things must be noted in regard to gross national product:

(i) It measures the market value of the annual output. In other words, G. N. P. is a **monetary measure.**

Measurable output.

There is no other way of adding up the different sorts of goods and services produced in a year except with their money prices. But in order to know accurately the changes in physical output, the figure for gross national product is adjusted for price changes by comparing to a base year as we do when we prepare index numbers.

(ii) For calculating gross national product accurately, all goods and services produced in any given year must be counted once, but not more than once. Most of the goods go through a series of production stages before reaching a market. As a result, parts or components of many goods are bought and sold many times. Hence, to avoid counting several times the parts of goods that are sold and resold, gross national product only includes the market value of **final** goods and ignores transactions involving intermediate goods.

What do we mean by final goods? Final goods are those goods which are being purchased for final use and not for resale or further processing. Intermediate goods, on the other hand, are those goods which are purchased for further processing or for resale. The sale of final goods is included in gross national product, while the sale of intermediate goods is excluded from gross national product. Why? Because the value of final goods includes the value of all intermediate goods used in their production. For instance, the value of cloth includes the value of cotton used in the making of cloth. The inclusion of intermediate goods would involve double counting and will, therefore, give an exaggerated estimate of gross national product.

Another important thing to be borne in mind while calculating the G. N. P. is that non-productive transactions should be excluded. These are purely financial transactions or transfer payments like old-age pensions or unemployment doles which are merely grants or gifts or transactions relating to existing shares or second-hand shares.

Net National Product (N.N.P.)

The second important concept of national income is that of net national product. In the production of gross national product of a year, we consume or use up some capital, *i.e.*, equipment, machinery, *etc.* The capital goods, like machinery, wear out or depreciate in value as a result of its consumption or use in the production process. This consumption of fixed capital or fall in value of capital due to wear and tear is called **depreciation.** When charges for depreciation are deducted from the gross national product, we get net national product. It means the **market value of all final goods and services** after providing for depreciation. Therefore, it is called **'national income at market prices.'** Thus,

Net National Product
or
National Income at
Market Prices

= Gross National Product—Depreciation.

National Income or National Income at Factor Cost (N. I.)

The difference between 'national income at market prices' and national income at factor cost may be clearly understood. National Income at **factor cost** means the sum of all incomes earned by resource suppliers for their contribution of land, labour, capital and entrepreneurial ability which go into the year's net production. In other words, national income (or national income at factor cost) shows how much it costs society, in terms of economic resources, to produce net output. It is really the national income at factor cost for which we use the term 'National Income.' The difference between national income (or national income at factor cost) and net national product (national income at market prices) arises from the fact that indirect taxes and subsidies cause market prices of output to be different from the factor incomes resulting from it.

Suppose a meter of mill cloth sold for Rs. 5 includes 25 P. on account of the excise and the sales tax. In this case, while the market price of the cloth is Rs. 5 per metre, the factors engaged in its production and distribution would receive only Rs. 4.75 P. a metre. The value of cloth at factor cost would thus be equal to its value at market price less than indirect taxes on it. On the other hand, a subsidy causes the market price to be less than the factor cost. Suppose handloom cloth is subsidized at the rate of 20 P. a metre and it sells at Rs. 2.80 P. Then, while the consumer pays Rs. 2.80 per metre, the factors engaged in the production and distribution of such cloth receive Rs. 3 per metre. The value of the handloom cloth at factor cost would thus be equal to its market price plus the subsidies paid on it.

Thus, national income (or national income at factor cost) is equal to net national product **minus** indirect taxes plus subsidies.

National Income
or
National Income
at Factor Cost

= Net National Product (National Income at Market price)—Indirect Taxes + Subsidies.

Personal Income (P.I.)

Personal Income is the sum of all incomes actually received by all individuals or households during a given year. National income, that is, income received, must be different for the simple reason that some income which is earned—social security contributions, corporate income taxes and undistributed corporate profits—is not actually received by households and, conversely, some income which is received—transfer payments—is not currently earned. (Transfer payments are old-age pensions, unemployment doles, relief payments, interest payment on the public debt, *etc.*).

Obviously, in moving from national income as an indicator of income earned, to personal income, as an indicator of income actually received, we must subtract from national income these three types of incomes which are earned but not received and add incomes received but not currently earned. Therefore,

Personal Income = National Inocme – Social Security Contributions – Corporate Income Taxes – Undistributed Corporate Profits + Transfer Payments.

Disposable Income (D.I.)

After a good part of personal income is paid to government in the form of **personal taxes** like income tax, personal property taxes, *etc.*, what remains of personal income is called **disposable income.**

Disposable income is personal income minuses taxes.

Concepts Summarised. The following chart summarises the various concepts of National Income.

Disposable Income = Personal Income – Personal Taxes.

Disposable Income can either be consumed or saved. Therefore,

Disposable Income = Consumption + Saving.

MEASUREMENT OF NATIONAL INCOME

We have already pointed out that there are three possible measures of national income: (*a*) total income flows, (*b*) Net outputs, and (*c*) final expenditures. We have also said that all these methods arrive at the same result. Which of these methods is adopted in actual practice in calculating the national income of a country depends on the nature and condition of its economy as well as the purpose of undertaking this exercise. We discuss below briefly these methods.

Production or Output Method

This method approaches national income from the output side. According to this method, the economy is divided into different sectors such as agriculture, mining, manufacturing, small enterprises, commerce, transport, communication and other services. Then, the gross product is found out by **adding up net values of all the production** that has taken place in these sectors during a given year.

In order to arrive at the net value of production of a given industry, the purchases of the producers of this industry from producers of other industries or sectors are deducted from the gross value of production of that industry. The aggregate or net values of production of all the industries and sectors of the economy plus the net income from abroad will give us the **Gross National Product.** By subtracting the total amount of depreciation from the figure of gross national product, we get the net national product, or national income.

This method of estimating national income enables us to trace the origin of the national income aggregate to the different sectors of the economy. Therefore, this is called **national income by industrial origin.**

This method can be used where there exists a census of production for the year. In many countries, figures of production of only important industries are known. Hence, this method is employed along with other methods to arrive at the national income. The one great advantage of this method is that it reveals the relative importance of the different sectors of the economy by showing their respective contribution to the national income.

National Income Concepts Summarised

GNP	GNP	NNP	NI	PI	DI
Expenditure Approach	*Income Approach*	*National Product*	*National Income*	*Personal Income*	*Disposable Income*
Personal Consumption Expenditure	Wages	Wages	Wages	Wages	Consumption
	Rent	Rent	Rent	Rent	
	Interest	Interest	Interest	Interest	
	Dividends	Dividends	Dividends	Dividends	
Government Purchases	Income of the unincorporated business	Income of the unincorporated business	Income of the incorporated business	Income of the unincorporated business	Savings
	Corporate Income Taxes	Corporate Income Taxes	Corporate Income Taxes	Subsidies Transfer Payments	Personal Taxes
	Social Security contributions	Social Security contributions	Social Security contributions		
Gross Private Domestic Investment	Undistributed Corporate Profits	Undistributed Corporate Profits	Undistributed Corporate Profits		
	Indirect Business Taxes	Indirect Business Taxes	Subsidies		
Net foreign Investment	Depreciation				

Income Method

This method approaches national income from the distribution side. In other words, this method measures the national income after it has been distributed and appears as income earned or received by individuals of the country. Thus, according to this method, **national income is obtained by summing up of the incomes of all individuals in the country.** Individuals earn income by contributing their own services and the services of their property such as land and capital to the national production. Therefore, national income is calculated by adding up the rent of land, wages and salaries of employees, interest on capital, profits of entrepreneurs (including undistributed profits of joint-stock companies) and income of self-employed people.

This method of estimating national income has the great advantage of indicating the distribution of national income among different income groups such as landlords, capitalists, workers, *etc*. Therefore this is called **national income by distributive shares.**

Expenditure Method

This method arrives at national income by adding up all the expenditure made on goods and services during a year. Income can be spent either on consumer goods or investment goods. Thus, we can get national income by summing up all consumption expenditure and investment expenditure made by all individuals as well as the government of a country during a year. Hence, the gross national product is found by adding up—

(*a*) what private individuals spend on consumer

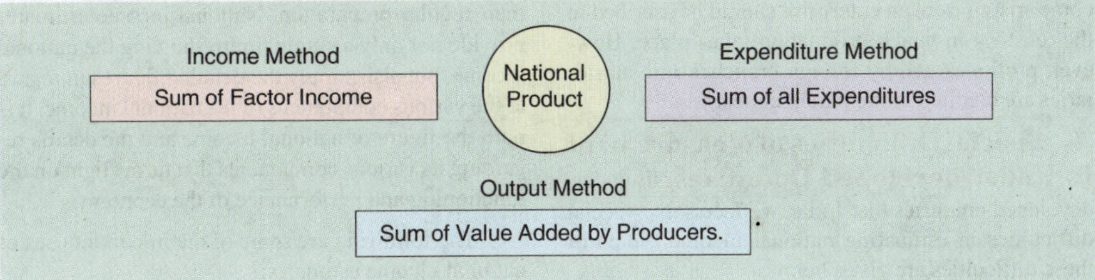

goods and services. This is called **personal consumption expenditure;**

(b) what private businesses spend on replacement, renewals, and new investment. This is called **gross domestic private investment;**

(c) what the foreign countries spend on the goods and services of the national economy over and above what this economy spends on the output of the foreign countries, *i.e.*, exports minus imports.

(d) what the government spends on the purchase of goods and services, *i.e.*, **government purchases.**

We have explained above the three alternative methods of estimating national income. The best way to arrive at national income will be to employ all these three methods so as to permit their cross-checking ensuring greater accuracy and throwing more light on details.

Identity of the Methods

It can be shown that the results obtained by any of these methods are similar to those obtained by any other method. But allowance will have to be made for all errors of omission and commission and all discrepancies removed before they can be found to be exactly the same. Hence in actual practice more than one method is used in combination with one another so as to provide a cross check.

By way of a hypothetical illustration we may take total GNP as 18,564 (figures in crores of rupees) by the income method composed of Rental Incomes 692 wages, salaries and supplements 9,564. Net interest earnings 844, Dividends of Companies 760, undistributed profits 240. Profit Tax Liability 292, Inventory Valuation adjustment 144, Indirect Taxes 1,872, Business Transfer Payments 92, Subsidies 96, Depreciation (Capital consumption) 1,620, Income of Unincorporate enterprises 2,256, Statistical Discrepancy 92.

By the Expenditure Method, we can get the same result, *i.e.*, total GNP 18,564 consisting of Personal Consumption Expenditure 13,488, Gross Private Domestic Investment 1,800, Government Purchases of Goods and Services 3,096, Net Foreign Investment 176.

Difficulties of Measurement

There are some conceptual problems that crop up when we start measuring the national income of a country. Some of these problems are enumerated below:–

(i) The first problem relates to the treatment of non-monetised transactions such as the services of housewives to the members of their families and farm output consumed at home. On this point, the general agreement seems to be to exclude the services of housewives while including the value of farm output consumed at home in the estimates of national income. This, however, gives rise to certain anomalies. For example, if a man employs a maid-servant for household work, payment to her will appear as a positive item in national income. If next day, the man were to marry the maid-servant, she would be performing the same services as before but without payments. In this event, the value of national income would go down though the real amount of goods and services performed remains the same as before.

(ii) The second difficulty arises with regard to the treatment of the government in national income accounts. On this point, the general viewpoint is that, so far as the administrative functions of the government like justice, administration and defence are concerned, they should be treated as giving rise to final consumption of such services by the community as a whole, so that the contribution of general government activities will be equal to the amount of wages and salaries paid by the government. As regards capital formation by the government, this is treated at par with capital formation by any other enterprise.

(iii) The third major problem arises with regard to the treatment of income arising out of activities of the foreign firms in a country. Should their income form a part of the national income of the country in which they are located or should it belong to the national income of the country owing the firms? On this point, the IMF viewpoint is that production and in-

come arising from an enterprise should be ascribed to the territory in which production takes place. However, profits earned by foreign branches and subsidiaries are credited to the parent concern.

Special Difficulties of Measurement in Under-developed Countries. In under-developed countries like India, we face some special difficulties in estimating national income. Some of these difficulties are given below:–

(*i*) The first difficulty arises because of the prevalence of non-monetised transactions in under-developed countries like India, so that a considerable part of output does not come into the market at all. Agriculture, still being in the nature of subsistence farming in these countries, a major part of output is consumed at the farm itself. The national income statistician, therefore, has to face the problem of finding a suitable measure for this part of output.

(*ii*) Because of illiteracy, most producers have no idea of the quantity and value of their output and do not keep regular accounts. This makes the task of getting reliable information from a large number of petty producers all the more difficult.

Barter system and overall underdevelopment in rural India create difficulties in measurement of national income.

(*iii*) Because of under-development, occupational specialisation is still incomplete so that there is a lack of differentiation in economic functioning. For instance, an individual may receive income partly from farm ownership, partly from manual work in industry in the slack season, *etc.*

(*iv*) There is a general lack of adequate statistical data and this adds to the difficulties of estimating national income.

SIGNIFICANCE OF NATIONAL INCOME STATISTICS

There are several important uses of national income statistics and, therefore, there is great need for their regular preparation. National income estimates provide not only a single figure showing the national income, but also supply the detailed figures in regard to the various components of the national income. It is both the figure of national income and the details regarding its various components that throw light on the functioning and performance of the economy.

The following are some of the important uses of national income estimates:

First, national income estimate reveals the overall production performance of the economy, as it seeks to measure the level of production in a year. Per capita income, which is found by dividing the total national income by the population, gives us an idea about the average standard of living of the people. Economic welfare depends to a considerable degree on the level of national income and the average standard of living of the people. Thus, the figures of national income and per capital income indicate the level of economic welfare of the people of a country.

Secondly, by comparing national income estimates over a period of time, we can know whether the economy is growing, stagnant or declining. If the national income increases over years, it means that the economy is growing. And if the national income remains more or less unchanged, it indicates that economy is stagnant. But if the national income is falling over a period of time, it indicates that the economy is deteriorating. In case the economy is growing, we can also judge the rate of economic growth or development by measuring the rate of increase in national income. Further, by comparing the per capita income over years, we can know the changes in the standards of living and economic welfare of the people.

Thirdly, the national income estimates show the contribution made by the various sectors of the economy, such as agriculture, manufacturing industry, trade, *etc*., to the national income. Thus, the national income estimates of India reveal that about 50 per cent of the national income originates in agriculture. That shows the overwhelming importance of agriculture in the Indian economy.

Fourthly, national income estimates throw light on the distribution of national income among different categories of income such as wages, profits, rents and interest. The distribution of national income between wages on the one hand and profits, interest, rent on the other, is of special significance, since inequality in personal incomes depends to a large extent on the share of the working classes (*i.e.*, wages) and the share of property owners (*i.e.*, rents, profits and interest).

Fifthly, the national income estimates also contain the figures of consumption, saving and investment in the economy. Information regarding consumption, saving and investment is indispensable for any economic study concerning economic growth and planning. It is the rate of saving and investment in the economy that determines the rate of economic growth. Further, consumption plus investment constitutes the level of aggregate demand on which depends the level of income or employment in a country.

Sixthly, with the help of national income estimates of various countries of the world, we can compare the standards of living and the levels of economic welfare of the people living in those countries. For this purpose, we have to adjust the national income figures for differences in production and in price levels. In other words, by the figures of the 'real' national income per capita, we can compare the standards of living or levels of welfare in different countries of the world. Moreover, developed and under-developed countries are usually classified on the basis of per capita income.

Finally, national income estimates are a valuable guide to economic policy, especially in these days of development planning and active government intervention in the economy. By looking at the national income statistics, the government can decide if the economy or its various sectors need any stimulus or regulation. From the national income estimates we can see the part played by the government in the national economy.

Only GNP cannot measure welfare. Better Quality of life is necessary for welfare.

In fact, no development planning is possible without national income estimates. National income estimates prove very useful for formulating plans and fixing targets of production. Preparation of plans depends very much on the availability of data regarding national income, consumption, saving and investment which are all provided by national income estimates. Further, we can assess and evaluate the achievements or otherwise of the development targets laid down in the plans from the changes in national income and its various components.

Conclusion. We may conclude in Samuelson's words thus: "By means of statistics of national income, we can chart the movements of a country from depression to prosperity, its steady long-term rate of economic growth and development, and finally, its material standard of living in comparison with other nations."

LIMITATIONS OF THE GNP APPROACH

Is Growth of GNP an Unfailing Index of a Country's Economic Welfare?

We are accustomed to judging a country's economic welfare from the rate of growth in GNP (Gross National Product). The GNP represents the total value of goods and services produced in the country in that year. It also includes the amounts set aside as saving or investment, expenditure incurred by Government and by the people.

But this concept of national income is not altogether valid in a country like India, where everything is not commercialised. For instance, the value of the services rendered by a son in the firm or a wife on the farm are not generally evaluated and paid for on the basis of the ruling wage rates. Besides, much of the work done in institutions like panchayats, village co-operatives, *etc*., is honorary. Hence tremendous amount of national economic effort is not recorded in GNP. Nor is a good deal of production in villages like food grains, milk, vegetables by self-employed small and marginal farmers reckoned in GNP.

It has, therefore, been suggested that it would be more appropriate or sensible for the developing countries to measure economic welfare in terms of improvement in the conditions of the people, *i.e.*, in terms of increase or decrease in human suffering. That is, we can measure it by the size and magnitude of poverty and unemployment. Recently, a few economists in America, having recognised the unreliability of GNP as an instrument to measure a backward country's progress, have come up with a new index which they call the 'quality of life' to measure a developing country's progress.

The quality of life criterion consists of three factors, *viz.*, literacy, life expectancy and infant mortality. Since this index does not say anything about the distribution of income or relative level of poverty (things which are vital for judging a people's economic conditions), it may not be considered very sound. Hence it is necessary to take into account the indices of consumption by people belonging to economically weaker sections of the people.

Production of 'use values' is, suggested as another criterion. 'Use values' is defined as basic goods and services necessary for a person's survival. Thus, the total output of a country can be classified as 'basic goods or use values' and non-basic goods or 'exchange values.' In India 'use values' could include foodgrains like rice, wheat, pulses, oils, vegetables, milk, sugar, salt, clothing, bricks, timber, *etc*.

Thus, the inadequacy of GNP as a yard-stick to measure the welfare of developing countries is sought to be replaced by 'quality of life' and the 'production of use values.'

Key terms

National Income, Factor cost, Market price, Depreciation, Net indirect taxes, GNP, GDP, NNP, NDP, Personal income, Disposable income, Economic welfare, Income method, Expenditure method, Output method.

QUESTIONS

1. What is national income? Is it a reliable index of economic welfare?
2. Distinguish between :—
   (*i*) Gross National Product and Net National Product.
   (*ii*) National Income at market prices and National Income at Factor Cost.
   (*iii*) National Income and Domestic Income.
   (*iv*) National Income at current prices and National Income at constant prices.
3. Explain the following terms:—
   (*i*) National Income.
   (*ii*) Personal Income.
   (*iii*) Disposable Income.
   (*iv*) Real Income.
4. Given N.N.P. at market prices, what adjustments will you make and why to get N.I. at factor cost ?
5. Define National Income. What are the various methods of estimating national income ? Point out its imperfections.
6. Explain how national income is a flow and not a stock; it is realised flow and not any expected flow. What are the problems and difficulties in calculating its size?
7. Explain the 'flow of product' approach and the 'income' aproach to the problem of calculation of a country's National Income. How are the following problems dealt with, while calculation of country's National Income. How are the following problems dealt with, while calculating National Income: (a) Double counting ; (b) Government transactions, taxes and transfer payments?
8. Discuss the importance and significance of national income estimates in modern economic analysis.
9. Explain how the changes in the size and distribution of national income affect economic welfare.

UNIT II

Theory of Income Determination

Chapters

THEORY OF EMPLOYMENT

Having familiarised ourselves with the national income and its various concepts, we are now in a position to study the theory of Income and Employment. It is also called simply 'income theory' or 'employment theory.' In macro-economics, 'income' and 'employment' are interchangeable terms, since in the short run national income depends on the total volume of employment or economic activity in the country.

The problem of employment has exercised the minds of the economists from time to time. We shall first study the theory of employment as propounded by the classical economists and then the modern theory of employment, the Keynesian theory. In his book **"General Theory of Employment, Interest and Money",** the Late Lord Keynes is said to have ushered in a revolution in economic thinking and "opened up new vistas and new pathways to a whole generation of economists." It has also been called 'New Economics' or "Keynesian Revolution." There have been also subsequent modifications and refinements in the theory of employment introduced by later economists. The classical economists assumed the prevalence of full employment. They thought that there might occasionally be unemployment, but there was a tendency in the economic system towards full employment all the same. But the Great Depression of 1929-1934, engulfing the entire world in widespread unemployment, low output and low national income for about five years, upset the classical theory. Keynes showed convincingly that the classical doctrine was untenable on theoretical grounds while it had been proved untrue in the practical world.

Crowds clog wallspect during stock market crash of 1929.

CLASSICAL THEORY OF EMPLOYMENT:

The term 'classical economists' was first used by Marx to describe economic thought of Ricardo and his predecessors including Adam Smith. But by classical economists' Keynes meant the followers of David Ricardo including John Stuart Mill, Alfred Marshall and A.C. Pigou. The term 'classical economics', as used by Keynes, refers to the traditional or orthodox principles of economics which had come to be accepted, by and large, by the well-known English economists since the time of David Ricardo. They were so widely accepted and well established for over more than a century that they were labelled as 'classical'. Being a student and disciple of Marshall, Keynes had himself accepted and taught these classical principles. But he repudiated the doctrine of laissez-faire which the classical economists strongly advocated.

The classical economists did not formulate any specific theory of employment as such. They only laid down certain postulates. The two broad features of the classical theory of employment were: (*a*) the assumption of full employment of labour and other productive resources and (*b*) the flexibility of prices and wages to bring about full employment.

Assumption of Full Employment. The classical economists assumed that labour and other resources were always fully employed. According to them, the general over-production, and hence general unemployment, is impossible. There may be lapses from full employment at times but these were regarded as temporary and abnormal. The normal situation is stable equilibrium at full employment. If at any time unemployment persists for a long time, according to classical economists, it is because of the interference by government or private monopoly with the free play of market forces or wrong calculations of businessmen or artificial resistances in the economic system. In the view of classical economists, thus, in a free competitive capitalist economy, the persistence of general unemployment is unlikely and that there always exists full employment or a tendency towards full employment.

The classical economists believed that the policy of laissez-faire guaranteed normal full employment. According to them, the laissez-faire capitalism was self-adjusting. They had great faith in free and perfect competition, efficacy of the profit motive and price mechanism to remedy the temporary ills of the economic system and ensure full employment.

The classical theory does not explain what determines the level of employment. Instead, it assumes full employment and tries to explain the allocation of given resources in production and the distribution of income among the participating resources. The market forces of demand and supply allocate the resources as well as determine their rewards. It is the general relations of demand and supply which determine the relative values of commodities and services. The pricing system serves as the planning mechanism.

Flexibility of Price and Wages. Apart from full employment of resources, the classical economists believed that it is the flexibility of prices and wages which automatically brings about full employment. For instance, if there is general overproduction resulting in depression and unemployment, prices would fall as a result of which demand would increase, prices would rise and productive activity will be stimulated and unemployment would tend to disappear. Similarly, unemployment would be cured by cutting down wages which would increase the demand for labour and would stimulate activity. As Prof. Pigou says, "With perfectly free competition, there will always be at work a strong tendency for wage rates to be so related to demand that everybody is employed."

Thus, if the prices and wages are allowed to move freely without any let or hindrance from the Government or monopoly interests, unemployment would disappear and full employment level restored in course of time.

Further, the classical economists treated money as a mere medium of exchange. They ignored its role in affecting income, output and employment. In other words, they took note only of the transactions motive for holding money and overlooked the precautionary and speculative motives.

Say's Law

Say's Law is the foundation of Classical Economics. Assumption of full employment as a normal condition of a free market economy is justified by classical economists by a law known as **'Say's Law of Markets.'** It was this law on the basis of which classical economists thought that general over-production and hence general unemployment were impossible.

J.B. Say
1767 - 1832

Statement of the Law. According to J.B. Say, an early nineteenth century French economist, **'supply creates its own demand.'** In Say's words: "It is production which creates market for goods; for selling is at the same time buying and more of production, more of creating demand for other goods. Every producer finds a buyer." In other words, every supply of output creates an equivalent demand for output, so that there can never be a problem of general over-production. Say's law, thus, denies the possibility of the deficiency of aggregate demand.

Say's law so conceived describes an important fact about the working of the free exchange economy that the main source of demand is the sum of incomes earned by the various productive factors from the process of production itself. The employment of hitherto unutilised labour and other resources pays its own way, because it enlarges the market demand for goods by an amount equivalent to the income created and the value of output produced. A new productive process, by paying out income to its employed factors, generates demand at the same time that it adds to supply. It is thus production which creates market for goods. It is the cause and sole cause of demand. David Ricardo, the chief among the classical economists, said : "No man produces but with a view to consume or sell, and he never sells but with an intention to purchase some other commodity which may be useful to him or which contributes to future production. In the words of James Mill; "Consumption is co-extensive with production." Say's law was faithfully followed by the neo-classical economists like Marshall and Pigou.

Thus, supply creates its own demand not only at the same time but also to an equal extent. Demand is generated simultaneously through the act of supply because supply creates income in the form of wages, interest and profit.

Suppose 1,000 metres of cloth are produced. The value of cloth has been distributed in the form of wages, rent, interest and profit as reward to the participating factors of production. The purchasing power so generated will be spent either on purchasing the cloth or some other commodity. The factors of production

Supply creates its own demand.

producing the other commodity will receive purchasing power as reward which may be spent on the purchase of cloth or again some other commodity. Thus, the circle of production as well as of purchase goes on widening till the supply of no commodity remains unsold in the market. Hence, the total or aggregate supply of commodities in the economy would be exactly equal to aggregate demand. There being no deficiency of demand, general overproduction is out of the question. It may be that at any given time, the supply of commodity may exceed the demand for it, but it will be only a temporary disequilibrium; ultimately demand will equal supply and the entire production will be taken off the market, provided, of course, there is no interference in the working of the free market forces.

"In brief, Say's law of markets is a denial of the possibility of general overproduction, that is, a denial of the possibility of a deficiency of aggregate demand. Therefore, the employment of more resources will always be profitable and will take place to the point of full employment, subject to the limitation that the contributors of resources are willing to accept rewards no greater than their physical productivity justifies. There can be no general unemployment, according to this view, if workers will accept what they are 'worth.'[1]

Equality of Savings and Investment.

According to Say's law, there will always be a sufficient rate of total spending so as to keep all resources fully employed. Most of the income, which is earned by resources or factors participating in the productive processes, is spent on consumer goods and a part of it is saved. But according to classical economists, savings are spent automatically on investment goods. Savings and investment are interchangeable terms and are equal to each other. "Since saving is just another form of spending, according to the classical theory, all income is spent, partly for consumption and partly for investment. There is no reason to expect a break in the flow of income stream and, therefore, supply creates its own demand."

(*i*) Postulate of classical theory of Employment.

(*ii*) Interest Rate Flexibility : The classical economists believed that through the free market interaction, I I (demand for investment) and 'SS' (Supply of savings) will be equal. I I (Investment) demand is an inverse function of rate of interest 'i' whereas savings 'SS' is a direct function of rate of interest 'i' this is the belief of the classical economists that, there is always fluctuation and through these, the economy achieves equilibrium automatically. The classical economists believe that all savings are invested and they agree that there may exists some 'leakages'.

I I is the investment demand as the rate of interest is high investment is low, and as ROI (rate of interest) is low investment is high $i \propto \frac{1}{I\,I}$ and where as the savings is directly related to interest rate. In other words $i \propto SS$. In the diagram 'I I' and 'SS' interacts at point

1. Dillard, D. – *Economics of J.M. Keynes*, p. 19.

'E' which determines the 'ROI' 'i'. If there is a shift on the right hand side of I I (↑ in the investment) then the interest will increase to 'Oi_1', and savings and investment will be shifted to a new equilibrium 'E_1' and there will be an increase in 'SS' and I_1I_1, to 'OQ_2'.

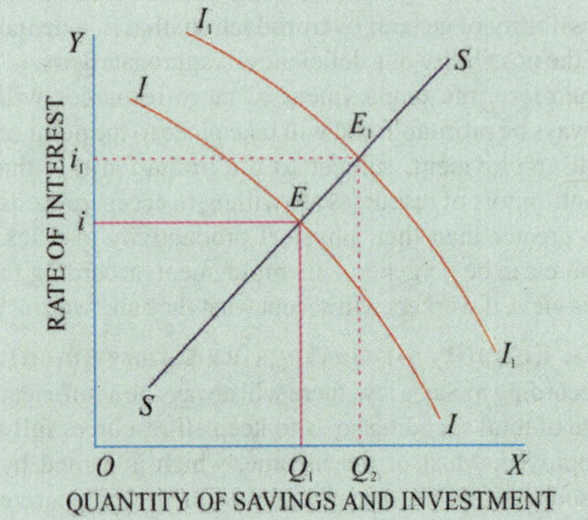

This shows that as the economy fluctuates the problems of 'business cycle' and 'unemployment' is settled. As the classical economists believed in the 'Laissez Faire' economy concept.

(iii) Wage Rate Flexibility : The classical economists were of the opinion that "unemployment is of a temporary nature and this could be corrected by wage cut policy. Voluntary unemployment may exist but involuntary unemployment could be corrected by wage cut policy, which through self adjusting process in which economy will lead to full employment. Dillard says: "Monopolistic behaviour on the part of labour and labourer's friend is responsible for unemployment". In free enterprise economy : if wages are allowed to find their own level, then through perfect competition involuntary unemployment will disappear.

Prof. Pigou was of the opinion that money wage-cut policy will solve the problem of involuntary unemployment.

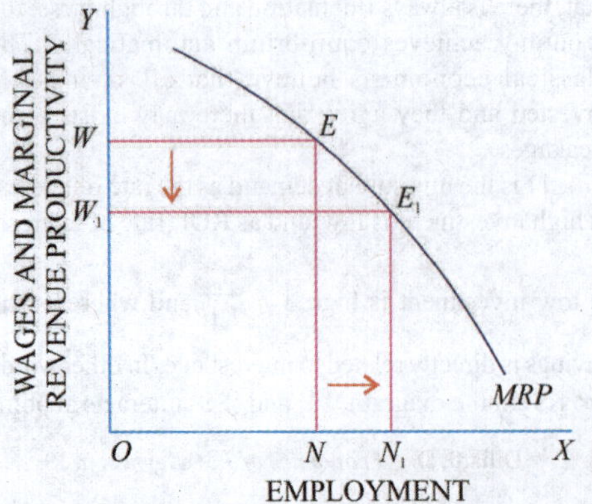

In the above diagram 'MRP' Marginal revenue productivity is given. At 'OW' wages the total employment is 'ON', if the wages were reduced to 'OW_1' then the employment will increase upto 'ON_1'. This was the basis of Pigou's, wage cut policy so as to solve the problem of involuntary unemployment.

(iv) Balanced Budget :– The classical economists believed in Laissez-faire economy, and they said that government is, "the best government which in-terferes the least in economic activities and taxes the least". They believed that government must maintain its revenue and expenditures in equilibrium.

Equilibrating Rate of Interest. If there is any gap between saving and investment, the rate of interest brings about equality between the two. In McConnell's words, "As classical economists saw it, the economy was analogous to a gigantic bath-tub wherein the water-mark measured the level of output and employment. Any leakage down the drain of saving would be returned to the tub through the tap of investment. This had to be so because the interest rate connected the drain pipe and the tap." [2]

Pigou's Modification

According to Prof. Pigou, the unemployment which exists at any time is because of the fact that changes in demand conditions are continually taking place and that frictional resistances prevent the appropriate wage adjustment from being made instantaneously. Thus, according to classical theory, there could be small amounts of **frictional unemployment** attendant on changing from one job to another, but there could not be **involuntary unemployment** for a long period of time. All people who sought employment would fairly quickly find it, if the wage rate is perfectly elastic. If all people seeking jobs at the current wage rate could not obtain them, then the wage rate would be bid down. A decrease in the wage rate would reduce the cost, shifting individual product supply curves to the right, thereby lowering the price of the products. With given demand curves, a larger quantity would be purchased at lower prices; then more people would be employed to produce the larger output. In short, Pigou applied to the labour market what Say said about the commodity market.

Thus, according to the classical analysis, if people were unemployed, wages would fall until all seeking employment were in fact employed. Involuntary unemployment which was found at times of depression was because of the fact that wages were kept too high

2. Mc Connell, C.R. — *Economics* 1969, p. 208.

by the actions of labour unions and government. Therefore, Prof. Pigou advocated that a general cut in money wages at a time of depression would increase employment. Hence, according to Prof. Pigou perfectly elastic wage policy would abolish fluctuations of employment and would ensure full employment of labour.

Basic Assumptions of Say's Law

It is clear from the statement of the law given above that it is based on certain assumptions. The main assumptions are:

(i) The law can operate only in a free-exchange economy where there is perfect freedom for the buyers to buy and sellers to sell. There prevails perfect competition and there are no restrictions imposed either on the producers or on the consumers and there is no price control.

(ii) There is free flow of money incomes. As these incomes are received they are immediately spent. Even savings must be invested and spent on acquiring producer's goods.

(iii) Savings are equal to investment and this equality is brought about by flexible interest rate.

(iv) The government follows the policy of laissez-faire and does not interfere in any manner with the operation of the market forces.

(v) The size of the market is limited by the volume of production; only then will demand equal supply or supply create its own demand.

Implications of Say's Law

From the above study of Say's Law some conclusions logically follows. The following are its main implications:

(i) One of the implications of Say's Law is that the economic system is self-adjusting and functions automatically without being directed by any controlling authority. If there is any disequilibrium, it will be only temporary and there is a persistent tendency for the equilibrium to be restored. For instance, if there is over-production, prices will fall, demand will increase and the extra supply will be cleared. Similarly, if there is unemployment, wages would fall and it would become worth while to employ more labour so that unemployment disappears. That is how there is automatic adjustment in the economic system. There is built-in flexibility.

(ii) An important policy conclusion that follows from Say's Law is that the governments should act on the policy of laissez-faire (let alone) or of non-interference in economic activities. Any interference by the government in the automatic working of the economic system will simply create imbalances and disequilibria. In the absence of government interference, the disequilibrium will be temporary and will tend to be rectified by the free operation of market forces. Hence, government should not raise barriers in the way of smooth working of the economy and economic forces. Owing to built-in flexibility in the economic system, prices, wages and interest rates and the volume of production keep changing as the economic situation may require and there is no need for the government to interfere.

(iii) Another important conclusion that follows from Say's Law is that general over-production is not possible. This is so because as soon as phenomenon of over-production appears, prices will fall and increased demand under the impact of fall in prices will clear the surplus stock. At times, there may be over-production in a particular industry as distinguished from general over-production. But this would also be temporary because automatically adjustments would come about. But, in a free and fully competitive system, general over-production is simply out of the question. Whatever the amount of the annual products, it can never exceed the amount of annual demand.

(iv) Similarly, under free and perfectly competitive economic system, general unemployment is impossible. It follows from Pigovian formulation of Say's Law that a general reduction in wages would create enough demand for labour to remove unemployment. Only there should be no wage regulation by government and no trade union pressure to resist reduction in wages. There will thus be persistent tendency to full employment. There may be sometimes unemployment in a particular industry but no general unemployment is possible. Whatever the state of demand, there will always be, via wage adjustment, tendency towards full employment.

Say's argument can be explained by taking into account the money flows in an economy, based on the following simplifying assumptions:

1. All income received by households is immediately spent on consumption.

2. There is no government activity of any nature, *i.e.*, no government expenditure, taxation, subsidies, price control, *etc.*

3. It is a closed economy.

The following figure shows the money flows between the firms and the households in the economy. Firms pay for factor services in money-wages, rent, interest and profit which in turn is the income of households.

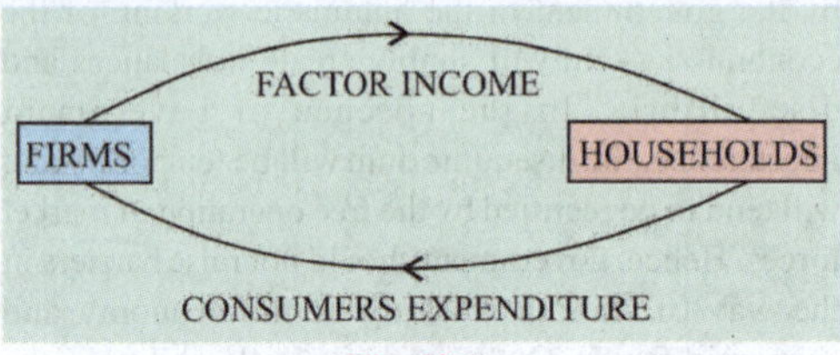

Fig. 39.1.

Households spend their income on goods and services. There is thus a circular flow of money from firms to households and from households to firms.

The assumption that all income is spent is of course unrealistic. However, it does not make any difference with the working of this law even if we assume that some income is not spent, *i.e.*, part of income is saved.

The real question then is what happens to the unspent income or saving. Suppose we have an economy which has been in equilibrium with income = Rs. 1,000 and consumers expenditure Rs. 1,000. Households now decide to save 1% of their income. The result will be firms' receipts fall to Rs. 900. Profits will fall and firms will tend to react by reducing output and hence reducing employment and income. But it should be pointed out here that in the above discussion we have assumed that firms only produce consumption goods and services, which is not true because they also invest in factories, machinery and stocks of raw materials and unsold goods. Provided that the firms wish to borrow and spend exactly the same amount that households wish to save, the circular flow of income can be maintained and so can employment. This is shown in the following figure, when savings are channelled to firms through banks.

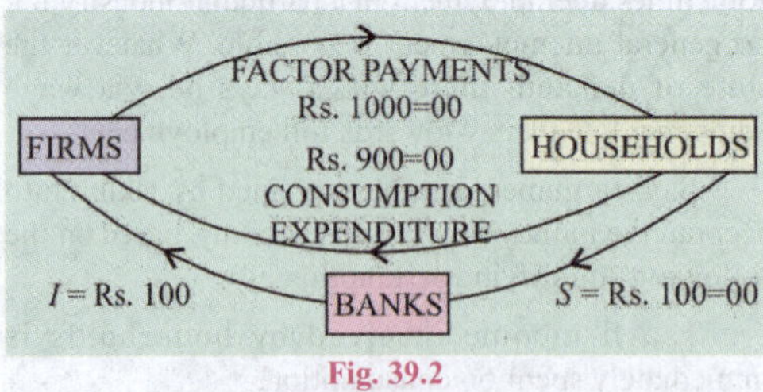

Fig. 39.2

(*v*) It also follows from Say's Law that it always pays to employ the unemployed or under-employed productive resources in the economy. The incomes earned by them will be sufficient to purchase their output and provide profit to the entrepreneurs. Thus, according to Say's Law, it would be unwise to let the resources remain idle. They can be made to pay their way.

(*vi*) Since supply is supposed to create its own demand, there is no limit to productive activity in the economy. In other words, economic development can be carried out to any extent; for there can be no deficiency of aggregate demand. This opens out unlimited possibilities of economic development in under-developed countries.

Criticism of Classical Theory and Say's Law

Keynes in his General Theory made a vigorous attack on the classical theory of employment; mainly, it was two-pronged attack: (*a*) He bitterly criticised Say's law, "supply creates its own demand" and (*b*) in particular the Pigovian assertion that money wage-cuts would help to promote employment at a time of depression and unemployment.

As explained above, according to Say's law every supply of output creates an equivalent demand for output, so that there can never be a problem of general over-production and hence of general unemployment. Now, it is true that supply does create demand for goods and services, because various factors of production earn their incomes in the process of production by helping to create additional supply of output. When factors of production are employed, for instance, to produce cloth, they get their reward in the form of wages, rents, interest and profits.

But, from this, it does not follow that the entire supply of national output will always be demanded by them. The incomes of the factors of production are necessarily equal to the value added in the productive process, but it does not mean that the entire income will be automatically spent on goods and services created in a given time period. A part of income will be saved so that this part of income is not available to create demand for goods and services. Saving thus causes a break or leakage in the income stream and obstructs the income expenditure flow. Unless investors are willing to invest to an equivalent extent of intended savings, the total effective demand which consists of demand for consumers' goods and producers goods will not be sufficient to absorb the entire available supply of output. And, if it happens like this, there will be over-production and the producers will not be able to sell their entire output, their profits will fall and they will reduce their production and this will create unemployment. Thus, supply does not necessarily create its own demand.

In a given time period, consumers are planning to spend a given part of their income and save the rest. Similarly, entrepreneurs are planning to invest in factories, machines, *etc.*, to a given extent. The total

John Manynard Keynes
1883-1946
Author of "The General Theory of Employment, Interest and Money". Founder of Modern Macro Economics and Keynesian Economics.

effective demand is the sum of consumption and investment demand. Savers are saving for reasons different from the investors and, in a free enterprise economy, there is no mechanism to ensure that what savers are planning to save is just equal to what investors are planning to invest. If the planned investment expenditure is not enough to fill up the gap of savings, then the present level of income and employment will not be maintained and, therefore, there will be a fall in income and employment.

Hence, the basic weakness of Say's law arises because of lack of any agency to ensure that intended savings are just equal to intended investment; and since savings and investment are undertaken by different persons and for different reasons, a discrepancy between the two is bound to arise, and, when it arises, the necessary mechanism to correct it is through changes in the volume of employment and income.

Thus, according to Keynes, there is no inherent reason to believe that investment expenditure plus consumption expenditure would always be equal to the cost of any given output; there is thus no assurance that demand would equal any given supply. Savings are determined primarily by income. But investment demand depends mainly, in the short run, on marginal efficiency of capital and rate of interest, and , in the long run, on factors like changes in technology and population growth. Therefore, investment demand, so determined, will not necessarily fill the savings gap between the income and consumption at the level of full employment and thus unemployment will be the result.

In sharp contrast to the classical view that full-employment equilibrium in the normal situation, Keynes in his General Theory firmly held the view that in a free private enterprise economy, there are more chances for the equilibrium to be established at less than full employment level.

Further, Keynes strongly opposed the Pigovian view that unemployment would disappear, if a general cut in money wages was applied. A general cut in wages, according to Keynes, will fail to bring about increase in employment, because it will mainly cause a reduction in aggregate demand. No doubt, the costs in all industries would be reduced as a result of a general wage-cut, but that in itself would not increase demand for the products, because the purchasing power in the hands of workers would have been reduced by cutting down their wages. A general wage-cut, by bringing about decline in aggregate demand, may actually decrease the volume of employment, and thus deepen the depression. As Hansen observes, "Demand determines employment and employment determines marginal productivity or real wage, not the other way round". Employment cannot be increased by manipulating wages.

Besides, worker's organisations are too strong to permit general wage cuts. Thus, Pigou's theory has no relevance as a guide to policy. Hence, the classical theory of employment must be rejected both on theoretical and practical grounds.

The fundamental fallacy in Say's Law is that partial equilibrium analysis which could apply to a particular industry, has been extended to the economy as a whole. Lowering of wage rate in a particular industry may increase employment there without decreasing demand. But if wages are reduced all round, it will reduce income and so effective demand and the volume of employment.

Besides, capitalism is not a self-regulating system as it is supposed to be. It cannot be depended to run itself.

The difference between the Pigovian and Keynesian views is fundamental. While Pigou is of the view that employment depends upon the level of money wages, and can be increased by lowering wages, Keynes contends that the volume of employment is determined by the level of aggregate effective demand, which may be adversely affected by the cuts in money-wages. In Keynes' view, even if wages rates were perfectly flexible, unemployment could still exist, if the aggregate demand was deficient. Hence, it is wrong to assert, as the classical economists did, that wage adjustment ensures full employment and interest rate adjustment tends to solve the saving-investment problem.

Summing Up. We can give the main points of criticism in a summary fashion as under:

(i) Supply may not create its own demand when a part of the income is saved. Aggregate demand is not always equal to aggregate supply.

(ii) Employment in the economy as a whole cannot be increased by means of a general wage cut though it may be possible in a particular industry. It is

Full employment is a myth as unemployment has become a major problem every where.

wrong to apply micro-economic principles to macro-economic activities or situations.

(iii) The classical economists looked at wages only from the employers' point of view, *i.e.*, the cost aspect and ignored the income aspect of wages. There is no direct relationship between wages and employment, nor is unemployment due to wage rigidities or artificial resistances.

(iv) **Interest-rate** adjustment cannot solve savings-investment problem. Savings and investment are not interest-elastic.

(v) The economic system is not so self-adjusting as it is supposed; hence government intervention in the economic sphere becomes necessary. Wages and prices are not so flexible as was supposed.

(vi) Assumption of free and perfect competition is not realistic.

(vii) **It is wrong** to suppose that money is a mere medium of exchange and has no role in affecting output and employment.

(viii) Say's Law cannot explain the occurrence of trade cycles.

(ix) The classical theory does not explain how the level of employment is determined. It evades the problem by assuming full employment.

KEYNESIAN THEORY OF EMPLOYMENT

We have discussed above the classical theory of employment. We have also subjected it to detailed criticism .This criticism is mainly based on Keynes. In his epoch-making book, **"General Theory of Employment, Interest and Money",** Keynes has not only pointed out the shortcomings of the classical theory but he has also propounded his own theory of employment which is widely accepted by modern economists. In fact, as already pointed out, Keynesian Economics has been called 'New Economics' and 'Economic Revolution.' While propounding his theory of employment Keynes has invented and used new tools of economic analysis such as 'consumption function' or 'propensity of consumer', 'multiplier', 'marginal efficiency of capital', 'liquidity preference', 'effective demand', *etc.* We shall discuss these concepts in their proper place. Here we shall give in brief the Keynesian theory of employment.

At the outset, it may be pointed out that Keynesian theory is based on a short-run view. In the short run, it is assumed that capital equipment, population or manpower, technical knowledge, labour efficiency remain constant. That is why, according to Keynesian theory, volume of employment depends on the level of national income and output. Because if capital, working force and technology, labour efficiency remain fixed, the national income can be increased only by employing more labour (which was lying idle before). Hence, in Keynesian short-run, the increase in national income would mean increase in employment. The larger the volume of employment, the larger the national income and smaller the volume of employment the smaller the national income, and vice versa. That is why the Keynesian theory is called the theory of employment determination and also theory of income determination.

However, to simplify the analysis in this chapter, we shall explain Keynesian theory in terms of employment determination and the diagrams given in this chapter are intended to clarify the determination of the level of employment. In the next chapter, we shall explain the Keynesian theory regarding national income determination. But the factors that determine level of employment and national income are the same; only the diagrammatic representations are different.

PRINCIPLE OF EFFECTIVE DEMAND

The basic idea underlying or starting point of Keynesian theory of employment is the Principle of Effective Demand. According to Keynes, the level of employment in the short run will depend on aggregate effective demand for goods in the country. Greater the aggregate effective demand, the greater will be the volume of employment, and vice versa. Total employment depends on total demand and unemployment is the result of a deficiency of total demand.

Effective demand represents the total money spent on consumption and investment. The total national expenditure is equal to total national income which is equal to national output. Effective demand being equal to total output as well as total expenditure, is also equal to national income.

Thus:

Effective Demand = National Income (*Y*).

= National Output (*O*).

Hence, effective demand holds the key at the same time to the volume of employment in the economy, to the level of national income and to the total national expenditure. Since, effective demand determines the volume of employment in the economy at a particular time, the deficiency of effective demand results in unemployment. The deficiency of effective demand is due to the gap between income and consumption. As income increases, consumption also increases but in a smaller proportion than the increase in national income. Since consumption is less, the demand is less. The gap must be filled up by increasing investment and hence effective demand, in order to maintain employment at a high level. Thus, it is increase in effective demand which results in increase in employment or total output or national income.

In terms of expenditure, effective demand means the total expenditure of the community at a particular level of employment. This expenditure is just equal to the economy's aggregate supply price, *i.e.*, the total cost of production of goods and services at that level of employment. In short, effective demand is the aggregate or total demand of the community both for consumption and investment.

Determination of Effective Demand

Keynes used two terms: Aggregate Demand Function or Price and Aggregate Supply Function or Price to explain the determination of effective demand. These are the two Keynesian 'blades of scissors' like Marshall's blades of scissors of demand and supply. Aggregate Demand Price and Aggregate Supply Price together determine effective demand which in turn determines the level of employment in the economy at a particular time.

An entrepreneur will employ that number of workers in his firm which gives him maximum profit. In the economy as a whole, the level of employment depends on the decisions of all individual employers, added together, as to how many workers should be employed so that it is most profitable. The volume of employment in an economy will be determined by aggregate supply price and aggregate demand price. Let us understand these two concepts.

Aggregate Supply Price

At any given level of employment of labour, aggregate supply price is the total amount of money which all the entrepreneurs in the economy, taken together, **must receive** from the sale of the output turned out by that number of workers which it is just worthwhile employing them. In other words, the aggregate supply price, when any given number of workers is employed, is the total cost of production of the output at a certain level of employment. It is the sum total of all payments made by entrepreneurs to all

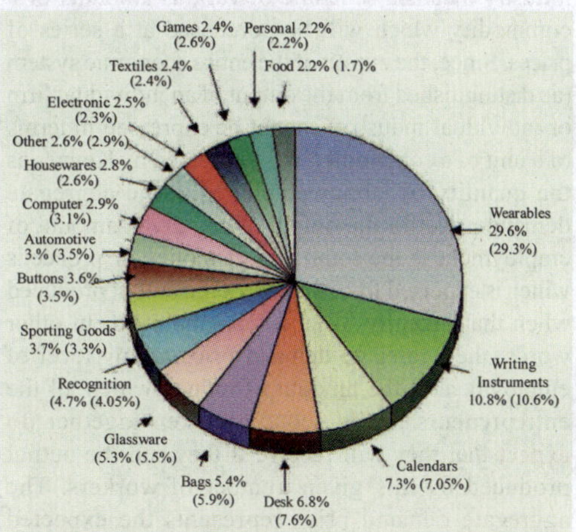

Sales proceeds from various sources: aggregate supply is the sum of all such revenue to producer.

the factors of production producing that output. Obviously, the entrepreneurs will not employ that number unless they can recover the total cost of employing them. A certain minimum amount of proceeds is necessary to induce employers as a whole to offer any given aggregate amount of employment. "This minimum price or proceeds, which will just induce employment on a given scale, is called the aggregate supply price of that amount of employment." (Dillard).

If the output of these workers does not fetch sufficient price so as to cover the cost, the entrepreneurs will employ less number of workers. In this way, aggregate supply price will be different for different number of workers employed. That is, we can prepare aggregate supply price schedule according to the total number of workers employed in the economy and we can have a corresponding aggregate supply price curve or **Aggregate Supply Function.** Thus, aggregate supply price is a schedule of the minimum amounts of proceeds required to induce varying quantities of employment. The greater the amount of proceeds, the greater the amount of employment offered by the employers, taken together, to the workers in the economy. Since more workers will be employed only if the employers in the aggregate expect to be paid more money for the larger output produced by these workers, the aggregate supply price curve will slope upwards to the right.

Aggregate Demand Price

Aggregate demand must be distinguished from the demand for the products of an individual firm and individual industries. The demand for a firm or industry means a schedule of various amounts of a commodity which will be purchased at a series of prices. Since, the output of the entire economic system (as distinguished from the output of an individual firm or individual industry) cannot be expressed in terms of a unit of a commodity, it is expressed by Keynes as the quantity of labour employed. "The aggregate demand price for the output of any given amount of employment is the total sum of money or proceeds which is expected from the sale of the output produced when that quantity of labour is employed. In other words, the aggregate demand price at any level of employment is the amount of money which all the entrepreneurs in the economy taken together **do expect** that they will receive if they sell the output produced by this given number of workers. The aggregate demand price represents the expected receipts when a given volume of employment is offered to workers. The aggregate demand curve or **Aggregate Demand Function** represents a schedule of the proceeds expected from the sale of the output produced by different amounts of employment. The greater the number of workers employed, the larger the output. That is, the aggregate demand price increases as the amount of employment increases, and vice versa. The aggregate demand curve rises upwards to the right showing that demand increases with an increase of employment. This is quite the opposite of demand curve for the product of a firm or an industry which slopes downwards to the right showing that the quantity sold will increase as the price falls.

The student should carefully see the difference in the wording in the definitions of aggregate supply price and aggregate demand price since the wording seems to be similar. In the case of aggregate supply price, it is the amount of money which all employers taken together **must expect to receive** to induce them to offer certain amount of employment and in the case of aggregate demand price, it is the amount of money which they **do expect to receive** by the sale of the output produced by varying number of men. One is necessary payment, the other is **an expectation.**

Determination of Equilibrium Level of Employment

After having understood the concepts of Aggregate Supply Price and Aggregate Demand Price, we are now in a position to explain the determination of the level of employment with the help of the Aggregate Supply (AS) and Aggregate Demand (AD) curves.

In Fig. 39.3, AS (Aggregate Supply) and AD (Aggregate Demand) curves relate to an imaginary economy. Both AS and AD curves slope upwards to the right, but they do not follow the same course. For each level of employment there will be both an aggregate demand price and an aggregate supply price. There will be some levels of employment for which the receipts expected exceed the receipts necessary to induce given volumes of employment and at certain other levels of employment for which the receipts expected will not be sufficient to induce that amount of employment. In between these two limits there will be some level of employment for which the expected receipts are just equal to what is necessary to make the employment worth while to the employers. This will be a point of intersection of the Aggregate Supply Curve and the Aggregate Demand Curve. This point of intersection determines the actual level of employment at any time. This is the point E in the Fig. 39.3.

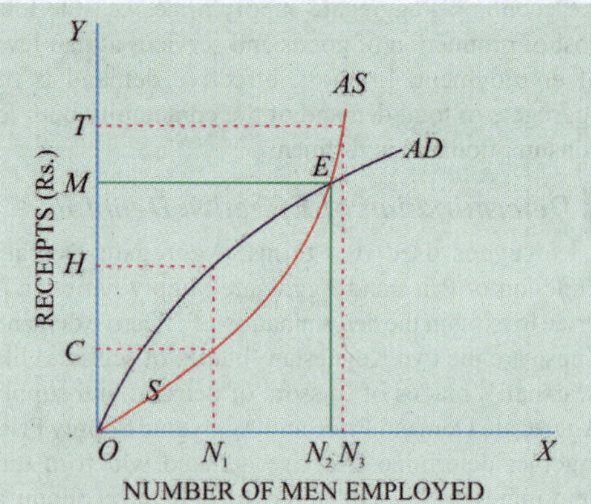

Fig. 39.3. Determination of Level of Employment.

In Fig. 39.3, the number of men employed are shown along the X-axis and receipts or proceeds of the goods and services produced by all the entrepreneurs are shown up the Y-axis, *i.e.*, the total amount spent by the community on the output made by the entrepreneurs.

Take first AS curve. It shows the different total amounts which all the entrepreneurs taken together **must receive** to induce them to employ a certain number of men. For instance, if the entrepreneurs are convinced that they must receive OC amount of money, then they will employ ON_1 men. Now take AD curve. It shows the different total amounts which all the entrepreneurs, taken together, expect to receive at different levels of employment. For instance, if they employ ON_1 men, then they expect to receive OH amount from the sale of the total output. This means that at ON_1 level of employment, the total amount expected is greater than the amount necessary to be paid; hence there is no equilibrium at this point.

Look at the shape of AS curve. At first it rises slowly and then after a point it rises sharply. It means that in the beginning as more and more men are employed, the cost of output rises slowly. But as the amount received by the entrepreneurs increases they employ more and more men. So much so that all men who offer for work are given employment. In Fig. 39.3 ON_3 men altogether seek employment and as soon as the entrepreneurs start getting OT amount, they will be prepared to employ all of them.

Now look at the shape of AD. In the beginning, it rises sharply, but flattens towards the end. This shows that in the beginning as more men are employed, the entrepreneurs expect to get sharply increasing amounts of money from the sale of the output. But after employment has sufficiently increased, the expected receipts do not rise sharply.

The aggregate demand and aggregate supply for any community together determine the volume of employment which is actually offered by the entrepreneur. If the situation is such that the total amount of money which all the entrepreneurs, taken together, expect to receive from the sale of output exceeds what they consider necessary to receive, there will be competition among the entrepreneurs to offer more employment to the workers and employment will increase. For instance, on the left of N_2 (*i.e.*, till the employment level reaches ON_2). Aggregate Demand (AD) is greater than Aggregate Supply (AS), *i.e.*, the amount expected to be received is greater than the amount considered necessary. It is natural that there will be competition among entrepreneurs to employ more men.

On the other hand, if the number of men employed is greater than ON_2, AD curve lies below the AS curve, that is, the amount expected by the entrepreneurs in the aggregate from the sale of the total output is less than what is considered necessary by them, and consequently they are losers. They will, therefore, reduce the number of persons employed. The retrenchment will continue till ON_2 level of employment is reached. At ON_2 level, AS and AD intersect. This is the point of equilibrium of the level.

Thus, employment in the economy as a whole will be in equilibrium only when the amount of proceeds which entrepreneurs **expect to receive** from providing any given number of jobs is just equal to the amount which they **must receive** if the employment of that number of workers is to be worthwhile for the entrepreneurs.

Further Discussion on Effective Demand

At the outset of the Keynesian theory of employment, we said that the Principle of Effective Demand is the starting point of the theory and greater the effective demand, the larger the volume of employment, and vice versa. After familiarising ourselves with the concepts of Aggregate Demand Price and Aggregate Supply Price, we are in a position to understand more clearly what 'effective demand' means and how it determines the level of employment.

We have seen in the above discussion that when in an economy, the Aggregate Demand and Aggregate Supply are equal to each other then employment in the economy is in equilibrium. When both aggregate demand and aggregate supply change but again are equal to each other, the equilibrium level of employment also changes. But in the short run, when aggregate demand remains the same, then it is a short-run equilibrium of aggregate demand and aggregate supply. There is, in the economy, a schedule of aggregate demand (or aggregate demand price) which shows the aggregate demands at varying levels of employment. But of these varying levels of employment that aggregate demand is called effective demand which, at that level of employment, is also equal to the aggregate supply and which shows the short-run equilibrium of aggregate demand and aggregate supply. In other words, **effective demand is that aggregate demand price which becomes 'effective' because it is equal to aggregate supply price and thus represents a position of 'short-run' equilibrium.** There are several other points on the aggregate demand schedule but what distinguishes effective demand from all these points is that at this point aggregate demand price is equal to aggregate supply price. On all other points, aggregate demand price is either more or less than aggregate supply price.

It is clear that employment in the economy in the short run is determined by effective demand. The higher the level of effective demand, the greater is the volume of employment, and vice versa. Unemployment is due to the deficiency of effective demand and the basic remedy to remove this unemployment is to raise the level of effective demand. The classical economists believed that effective demand was always large enough to ensure full employment. But Keynes proved that it was not so and that is why the phenomenon of unemployment was common in all economies.

Effective demand means the total amount of money, actually spent on goods and services produced in the economy. Since money can be spent both on consumption goods and investment goods, effective demand will equal national expenditure both on consumption goods and investment goods. Thus, the main determinants of effective demand are total expenditure on consumption goods and on investment goods.

In the **Post-Keynesian sense,** government expenditure is also added to the total expenditure on consumption and investment on private account. Also, since all the money which all the entrepreneurs, taken together, receive from the sale of goods and services must be paid out in the form of wages, rent, interest and profit, effective demand will equal national income—the receipts of all the people in the country. Effective demand also represents the value of national output because the value of national output is nothing else but the total amount of money received by the entrepreneurs from the sale of goods and services. And money received by the entrepreneurs from the sale of goods is equal to the money spent by the people on these goods. Hence, effective demand equals national income or value of national output or national expenditure.

Thus,

Effective Demand = National Income.
= Value of National Output.
= National Expenditure.
= Expenditure on consumption goods + expenditure on investment goods.

Importance of Effective Demand

The concept of effective demand occupies a very important place in Keynesian theory of employment. We have seen that the total volume of employment in the community depends on the state of effective demand. It is the deficiency of effective demand that results in unemployment in the country.

The concept of effective demand explains under-employment equilibrium as we shall show presently. We learn from the principle of effective demand that whatever is produced in the economy is not automatically consumed. That is, supply does not create its own demand as Say's Law said. It also shows that a general wage-cut is no remedy for unemployment.

Thus, the principle of effective demand demolishes the main notions of the classical theory. It brings out the crucial importance of investment in filling the gap between total income and total consumption.

Equilibrium Not Necessarily at Full Employment

It is not necessary that the equilibrium level of employment is always at full employment. Equality between aggregate demand price and aggregate supply price does not necessarily indicate the full employment level. It can be in equilibrium at less than full employment or an under-employment equilibrium. The classical economists assumed full employment. Actually, however, there is always some unemployment even in the most developed countries. Keynes demolished the classical thesis of full employment both on theoretical grounds and by illustrations from real life. Full employment is important only as a limiting case. It is the level of employment beyond which further increases in effective demand do not increase output and employment.

At the point of intersection of AS and AD, the entrepreneurs are maximising their profits. The profits will be reduced if volume of employment is more or less than at this point. But there is no reason to assume that this point represents full employment. Aggregate demand and aggregate supply will be equal at full employment only if investment demand is sufficient to cover the gap between the aggregate supply price corresponding to full employment and the consumption expenditure out of income at full employment. The view of Keynes is that the typical investment demand falls short of this gap. Hence, the aggregate demand schedule and aggregate supply schedule will intersect at a point less than full employment. Unless there is some external change there will be no tendency to depart from this under-employment equilibrium. Although with given aggregate demand and supply curves, there will normally be one position of equilibrium (where the two curves intersect), this need not be at the level of full employment. It is possible that the aggregate demand curve and the aggregate supply curve intersect each other at such a point at which the number of workers actually employed is less than those seeking employment. All the seekers of employment have not been able to secure employment and thus remain unemployed.

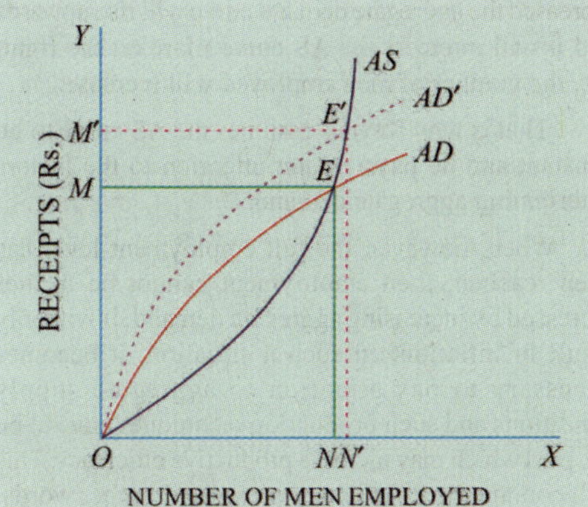

Fig. 39.4. Employment Equilibrium at Full and Less than Fall Employment Levels.

Look at the diagram (Fig. 39.4). Employment is measured along OX-axis and income or money receipts along OY-axis. AD curve shows expected incomes at various levels of employment. It shows that expected income increases as volume of employment increases. It has a diminishing slope and it becomes horizontal to X-axis after a certain level of employment showing that further employment will not increase the expected income. AS curve representing total cost of production rises steeply. This means that due to rising costs the entrepreneur will increase employment only if the maximum income that they must receive rises faster. It represents two situations, one of full employment and another of less than full employment. AS, the aggregate supply curve and AD, the aggregate demand curve, intersect at E. This means that ON men are employed and the entrepreneurs expect to get from this level of employment OM amount of money. In this situation of aggregate demand and aggregate supply in the economy, ON represents equilibrium level of employment. But as is shown in this diagram, in this situation of aggregate supply (AS), ON′ number of men were seeking employment, whereas only ON number could secure employment. In this situation there is equilibrium level of employment but it has not yet reached the full employment level, because NN′ men are still unemployed. This unemployment will be removed only if on account of some favourable circumstances, aggregate demand increases so much (*i.e.*, it should increase from OM to OM′ and there is shift from AD to AD′) that the entrepreneurs now find it worthwhile to employ ON′ men so that none who seeks work remains unemployed. In this diagram only at point E′ there is full employment.

The situation in which an economy is in equilibrium at the level of full employment is called the optimum situation. In any other situation, it is in a state of less than full employment or there is unemployment. The classical economists denied that there could be an equilibrium at less than full employment. But we have seen in the above diagram that when AD and AS intersect at the point E, there is equilibrium level of employment but at less than full employment or there is under-employment equilibrium. There is unemployment indicated by NN', i.e., NN' men are seeking employment but are not actually employed.

Why Under-employment Equilibrium

According to Keynes, the root cause of the under-employment equilibrium is the deficiency of Aggregate Demand. This deficiency is due to the fact that there is a gap between income and consumption. As income increases, consumption increases but not proportionately, *i.e.*, marginal propensity to consume (to be discussed later) is less than unity. Coupled with this is the cause of insufficiency of investment. If investment increases sufficiently to cover this gap, there can be full employment, otherwise not. Investment is low owing to low marginal efficiency of capital (to be discussed later), *i.e.*, profit expectations are low.

Hence, the gap between income and consumption and insufficiency of investment to fill this gap are responsible for under-employment equilibrium. According to Keynes, under-employment (or unemployment) equilibrium is a normal feature of private free enterprise economy. To increase employment, government must step up its own investment and not leave things to the private investor.

Factors Determining Aggregate Supply and Aggregate Demand

We have seen above that we have to use Aggregate Supply Price curve and Aggregate Demand Price curve to determine the equilibrium level of employment. Let us know a little more about them. This will enable us to understand more clearly the principle of effective demand.

First take the Aggregate Supply Price curve. The Aggregate Supply Price Schedule or curve of the economy depends in the last analysis on physical and technical conditions. The physical and technical conditions of production remain constant in the short period. Hence, given these technical conditions, production can be increased only by increasing employment. But production and employment can be increased only if the expenditure on production is increased. Production may be subject to the law of increasing, diminishing or constant returns, additional expenditure must be increased to increase production

Aggregate supply depends on present amount of usable resources which are constant in the shortrun.

or employment. Hence, more men will be employed only if the entrepreneurs expect to increase their income from the sale of output produced by these men. That is why the aggregate supply curve slopes upwards to the right. The slope of the aggregate supply curve will depend on the physical and technical conditions of produced in the economy. But when all the men seeking employment have been provided employment, then the AS curve will rise vertically, because even though the entrepreneurs may expect to receive larger income, employment cannot be increased since there are no unemployed men left. This has been shown in the diagram 39.4. As soon as ON′ men are employed, the AS curve rises vertically.

We have said that the Aggregate Supply Schedule is determined by the physical and technical conditions prevailing in the economy, that is, the nature and quantity of labour, capital and raw materials available in the economy. As these change, or as productive resources are improved, *AS* curve will also change. But in the analysis of the problem of unemployment, it is unnecessary to pay more attention to aggregate supply schedule or curve. This is for the simple reason that at that time the main problem is how to employ idle resources to increase production and not that the techniques of production be improved. That is, AS curve need not be changed. The need of the moment is to increase employment and to increase aggregate demand for the purpose. When aggregate demand is increased the aggregate demand curve will rise upwards and it will intersect the AS curve more on the right, *i.e.*, the number of men employed will increase.

That is why Keynes assumes the AS curve to be constant and he pays greater attention to the factors determining aggregate demand.

When, however, the full employment level has been reached, then employment cannot be further increased by increasing aggregate demand. It will only result in inflation. In such a situation, it becomes necessary to pay attention to aggregate supply conditions and such production techniques have to be adopted which may increase productive efficiency. This will contain the inflationary pressure. In other words, we have to pay attention to aggregate supply only when full employment level has already been achieved and the economy is involved in inflation.

Since normally there is less than full employment (*i.e.*, there is some unemployment), aggregate demand has greater importance in the theory of employment than aggregate supply. Whereas aggregate supply depends on technical factors, aggregate demand schedule depends more on psychology of the people than on technology. The aggregate demand schedule shows the varying amounts of money that the entrepreneurs expect to receive at different levels of production or employment. In other words, it shows the varying amounts of total expenditure –which all the purchasers of goods and services are prepared to incur at different levels of employment. The purchasers of goods spend money on the purchase of two types of goods: (*a*) consumption goods and (*b*) investment goods. Thus, the shape and position of aggregate demand curve at each level of employment depends on the expenditure of the members of the community on consumption on the one hand and on investment on the other.

Summary of Keynesian Theory of Employment and Income

From the theory of employment explained above, we learn that in the short run, employment is determined by effective demand and the effective demand is equal to the total expenditure on consumption goods and investment goods. Hence, it is clear that employment depends on the total expenditure incurred on consumption and investment. In other words, if at any time owing to some reasons either consumption increases or investment increases, it would mean that effective demand has increased which in turn would increase employment in the country, and vice versa. This means that the key to employment and income determination lies in consumption and investment.

Keynes has introduced several new concepts in the discussion of consumption and investment. In the succeeding chapters, we shall discuss these concepts and principles such as propensity to consume and marginal efficiency of capital. We shall see how consumption expenditure is determined by propensity to consume and investment by marginal efficiency of capital and the rate of interest. Marginal efficiency of capital depends on (*a*) future expectations of profit from investment and (*b*) present cost of replacing capital equipment. Obviously, higher the expected rate of profit, the greater the inducement to invest. Also, lower the replacement cost, the greater is the inducement to invest. If the expectations of profit remain the same and the rate of interest falls, then investment would increase. Keynes introduced the concept of liquidity preference to explain the determination of the rate of interest.

Thus, the two determinants of investment are the marginal efficiency of capital and the rate of interest.

After we have learnt fully the tools and principles used by Keynes in the theory of employment, we shall be able to understand clearly Keynesian theory of employment and income. We give below this theory in summary fashion:

(1) Total income depends on the volume of total employment.

(2) Total employment depends on total effective demand and in equilibrium aggregate demand is equal to aggregate supply.

(3) Aggregate supply depends on physical and technical conditions of production, and, in the short run, these do not often change; hence, it is the changes in the aggregate demand that bring about changes in income and employment.

(4) Effective demand is made up of (*a*) consumption demand and (*b*) investment demand.

(5) Consumption demand depends on consumption function or propensity to consume, and, in the short run, consumption function is relatively stable.

(6) Investment demand depends on (*a*) the marginal efficiency of capital, and (*b*) the rate of interest.

(7) The marginal efficiency of capital depends on (*a*) the expectations of profit yields, and (*b*) replacement cost of capital assets.

(8) The rate of interest depends on (*a*) the quantity of money, and (*b*) the state of liquidity preference.

Key terms

Say's law of market, Wage, Price Flexibility, Unemployment-equilibrium.

QUESTIONS

1. Explain clearly the classical theory of employment and point out its main shortcomings.
2. Explain Keyesian Theory of Employment. Show how Keynes proves that equilibrium can be achieved at a point much below the level of full employment.
3. "Although with a given Aggregete Demand and Aggregate Supply, there will normally be only one position of equilibrium, this need not be at the level of full employment". Explain.
4. Explain under what conditions an economy happens to be in a state of 'under-employment equilibrium'.
5. What factors govern the level of employment in a free enterprise system according to Lord Keynes?
6. What are the fundamental differences between Keynes' Theory of Employment and the Classical Thoery of Employment? Which is more relevant for India ?
7. State and criticise Say's Law of Markets and bring out its main implications. On what grounds has it been criticised by Keynes?

   Or

   "Supply creates its own demand". Critically examine this statement.

DETERMINATION OF NATIONAL INCOME

In the previous chapter, we have given Keynes' theory from the point of view of the determination of the volume of employment. As we explained there, Keynes gives a short-run view in which the amount of capital, labour efficiency, techniques of production, the system of business organisation, *etc*., are assumed to be constant. In such a situation, the volume of employment and the level of national income increase and decrease together. This is, the determinants of income and employment are the same. They are both determined by aggregate demand and aggregate supply.

In this chapter, we shall explain the Keynesian theory in terms of the determination of national income. Since the determining factors of income and employment are the same, some repetition of what we have given in the previous chapter is unavoidable. The diagrammatic representation, as we shall see, will be different.

How the Level of National Income is Determined

As we have mentioned above, the level of national income, in the short period, is determined by aggregate demand and aggregate supply. The supply of goods and services in a country depends on the productive capacity of the community. But during the short period this productive capacity does not change. But it is not necessary that the actual production or aggregate supply should be always equal to productive capacity. The total output or aggregate supply will correspond to aggregate demand. If aggregate demand increases, output will also increase and the level of national output (*i.e.*, national income) will rise. On the other hand, if aggregate demand decreases, the national output or national income will also decrease. It follows that the equilibrium level of national income is determined by aggregate demand since aggregate capacity remains more or less the same during the short period. We assume here that the national output (or income) will be as much as the effective demand.

GDP of Ration	=	House hold demand + Producers demand + Governments demand + Rest of world's Demand

There are two components of effective demand: (*a*) consumption demand, *i.e.*, demand for consumption goods and (*b*) investment demand, *i.e.*, demand for investment goods or producer's or capital goods. Hence, by effective demand, we mean how much total expenditure the government and the people are willing to incur on consumption goods and investment goods.

Thus,

Aggregate Demand = Consumption Demand + Investment Demand, *i.e.*, AD = C + I.

(Here *C* is consumption demand and I is investment demand).

So far as consumption demand is concerned, it depends on propensity to consume (consumption function) and income. Given propensity to consume, as income increases, the consumption demand will also increase.

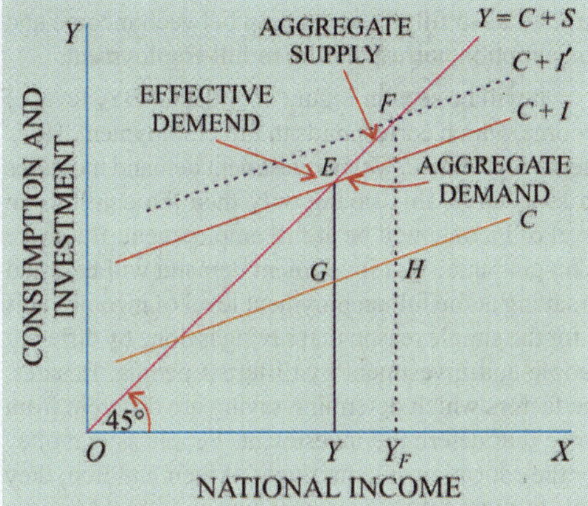

Fig. 40.1. Determination of National Income.

Look at the diagram (Fig. 40.1) below. In this figure, national income and national output (G. N. P.) are shown along the X-axis and along the Y-axis are shown the consumption demand (C) and investment (I). A straight line making an angle of 45° is drawn along the X-axis. This 45° line represents aggregate supply curve and it is also called Income Line. This 45° line shows two things: (*a*) total output or aggregate supply (consumption goods + investment goods) and (*b*) national income in terms of money. Actually, national output (G. N. P.) and national income are two different names of the same thing.

In this diagram, C curve represents propensity to consume. It will be seen that this curve C rises upwards to the right which means that as income increases consumption (or consumption demand) also increases. Since 45° line also represents national income, the distance between the curve C showing propensity to consume and 45° line represents saving because a part of income is consumed and the rest is saved. Thus, national income = consumption + saving or Y = C + S.

(Here Y is national income, C is consumption and S is saving).

It will be seen in the diagram that the distance between the national income line Y (*i.e.*, 45° angle line) and C (propensity to consume) goes on increasing which means that as income increases, the amount of saving increases.

One noteworthy thing about propensity to consume is that it remains stable or constant during the short period. This is because propensity to consume (or shape of *C* curve) depends on the tastes and needs of the people and these do not change in the short period. When we say that propensity to consume remains stable, it does not mean that there is no change in the consumption demand. As we have said above, consumption demand increases with increase in income. What we mean by the constancy or stability of propensity to consume is that the total consumption schedule or the shape of propensity to consume curve C does not change in the short period. Since consumption is more or less stable, variation in national income depends on variation in investment.

The second component of aggregate demand, *viz.*, investment is a very important determinant of national income. Investment depends on two things: (*a*) marginal efficiency of capital and (*b*) the rate of interest. Of these two, interest rate is comparatively stable. Hence, change in investment is largely determined by change in marginal efficiency of capital. The marginal efficiency of capital means expectation of profit from investment. That is, expected rate of profit is called marginal efficiency of capital. The marginal efficiency of capital, too, depends on two things: one is the replacement cost of the capital goods and the other, profit expectations of the investors. Of these two, again, profit expectations are a more important determinant of investment. This means that when a country wants to increase its national income or employment then it should create conditions in which profit expectations of investors and businessmen go high.

At any time in a country, keeping in view, the rate of interest and marginal efficiency of capital, the entrepreneurs wish to invest a certain amount of capital or there is a certain demand for investment goods. We assume that investment demand does not increase with increase in income. Actually, as people's income goes up, then their demand for goods will increase and as a result the entrepreneur's profit expectations go up. When profit expectations go up, the marginal efficiency of capital goes up which will result in increase in investment. But it is obvious that the amount of investment does not directly depend on income. That is why in our diagram, we do not show investment demand rising with increase in income.

As we have said above, at any given time, in a country, the entrepreneurs are desirous of investing a certain amount of capital. If we join this investment demand with the curve C of propensity to consume, we get aggregate demand curve C + I in which C represents consumption and I investment. The distance between prospensity to consume curve C and aggregate demand curve C + I is equal to investment (I). If propensity to consume curve is given, then higher the investment, the higher will be the aggregate demand curve (C + I).

What level of national income will be determined in any country at any time? The level of income will be determined at a point at which the aggregate demand curve (C + I) of the country and the aggregate supply curve, *i.e.*, 45° angle line intersect each other, *i.e.*, where the aggregate demand and aggregate supply are in equilibrium. This has been shown in the Fig. 40.1 on the previous page.

We see in this figure that aggregate demand curve C + I intersects the aggregate supply curve (*i.e.*, 45° angle line) at *E*. Hence, the equilibrium level of income is OY. It will be seen in this figure that when income is either more or less than OY, then the aggregate demand and aggregate supply are not in equilibrium. You will see that if income is more than OY, then total output or aggregate supply is greater than aggregate demand C + I so that the entire output cannot be sold out. The result will be that output will be decreased and income will decrease. On the contrary, if income is less than OY, then the total output or aggregate supply will fall short of aggregate demand. As a result, output will be increased and national income will increase. It is only when income is OY that aggregate demand and aggregate output (supply) are equal so that there will be no tendency for output or income to decrease or increase. Hence, OY income will be determined. We have seen how the equilibrium level of income is determined by the interaction of aggregate demand and aggregate supply. The equilibrium level of employment (discussed in the previous chapter) is also determined by the interaction of aggregate demand and aggregate supply. This is as it should be because national income, output and employment are interchangeable terms.

Equilibrium Not Necessarily at Full Employment

We may repeat here that it is not necessary that equilibrium level of national income may be achieved at the point of full employment. This view of Keynes is altogether opposed to the classical view. According to the classical economists, the economy is always in a state of full employment. The lapses from full employment are strictly temporary, since there is persistent tendency in the economic system to restore the state of full employment. Keynes completely demolished this view and established both on theoretical grounds and with reference to reality the possibility of under-employment equilibrium.

Look at the figure 40.1 again. Suppose OY_F is the full employment level of national income. But in this diagram, OY is the equilibrium level of income and OY is less than OY_F which represents full employment level. It is obvious that the equilibrium level of income is at less than full employment. That is, it is an under-employment equilibrium. The equilibrium will be established at full employment income only when investment demand is sufficiently large so as to fill the saving gap between income and consumption corresponding to full employment.

It will be seen in Figure 40.1 that at OY_F level of income, which corresponds to full employment, HF is the saving. Hence, when investment demand increases so as to cover this saving only then the equilibrium level of income will be at full employment. But there is no guarantee that investment demand will be equal to saving at the full employment level of income. This is for the simple reason that saving is done by different people and investment by different people. Besides, the factors which determine saving are different from those that determine investment. People save money for the education and marriages of their children; they save to meet future contingencies or to build houses or for their old age. But investment at any time depends on the marginal efficiency of capital and the rate of interest. And it is not necessary that investment should be equal to saving at the full employment level of national income. When investment is less than saving at the full employment level of income, as it usually is, the equilibrium will be established at less than full employment.

EQUILIBRIUM LEVEL OF INCOME: EQUALITY OF SAVING AND INVESTMENT

We have seen how equilibrium level of national income is determined by the interaction of aggregate demand and aggregate supply. The equilibrium level of national income is established at the point where aggregate demand equals aggregate supply. But there is also another method for the explanation of the determination of national income. This alternative method explains the determination of national income directly by saving and investment.

Look at the Figure 40.1 again. In this figure, at the equilibrium level of national income OY, saving and investment are equal; they are both equal to GE. Given the aggregate demand curve C + I, the amount of saving at income more than OY is more than investment and for income less than OY, investment is more than saving. It is obvious that saving and investment are equal only at the equilibrium level of national income and when saving and investment are not equal, then the national income will not be in equilibrium. Let us see why it is so and how national income is determined by saving and investment.

When at a certain level of national income, intended investment by the entrepreneurs is more than intended savings by the people, this would mean that aggregate demand is greater than the total output or aggregate supply. This would induce the firms to increase production raising the level of income and employment. The result will be that national output will be increased on account of which national income will increase. Hence, when at any level of income, investment is greater than saving, there will be a tendency for the national income to increase. On the contrary, when at any level of national income, the investment demand is less than saving, it means that aggregate demand is less than aggregate supply. That is, the entrepreneurs will not be able to sell their entire output at given prices. The result will be that output will be reduced which will result in the reduction of national income.

Hence, when, at any level of national income, investment demand of the entrepreneurs is less than the intended savings of the people, the national income will decrease. It will come down to the level at which investment spending is just equal to the planned savings by the community. But, when at any level of national income, intended investment demand on the part of the entrepreneurs is equal to intended saving of the people, it means that aggregate demand is equal to the total output or aggregate supply as a result of which the national income will be in equilibrium.

Hence, equilibrium level of national income will be established at the level at which the amount of intended investment by the entrepreneurs is equal to the amount of intended saving by the people.

We can explain the determination of national income by saving and investment in another way. Saving is withdrawal of some money from the income stream. On the other hand, investment is injection of money into the income stream. Now if intended investment is more than intended saving, it means that more money has been put into the income stream than has been taken out of it. This would mean that the income stream, *i.e.*, national income would increase. On the contrary, if investment is less than intended saving, it means that less amount of money has been put into the income stream and more has been taken out of it. The result would be that national income would decrease. But when investment is just equal to saving, it would mean that as much money has been put into the income stream as has been taken out of it. The result will be that the national income will neither increase nor decrease, *i.e.*, it will be in equilibrium. It is thus clear that the equilibrium of national income will be established at the level at which the intended investment is equal to intended saving.

The determination of national income by investment and saving is illustrated by Fig. 40.2.

In this figure (40.2), income is shown on the X-axis and saving and investment on the Y-axis. SS is the saving curve which shows intended saving at different levels of income. II curve shows investment demand, *i.e.*, intended investment. The II investment curve has been drawn parallel to the X-axis. This is done on the assumption that in any year the entrepreneurs intend to invest a certain amount of money. That is, we assume that investment does not change with income.

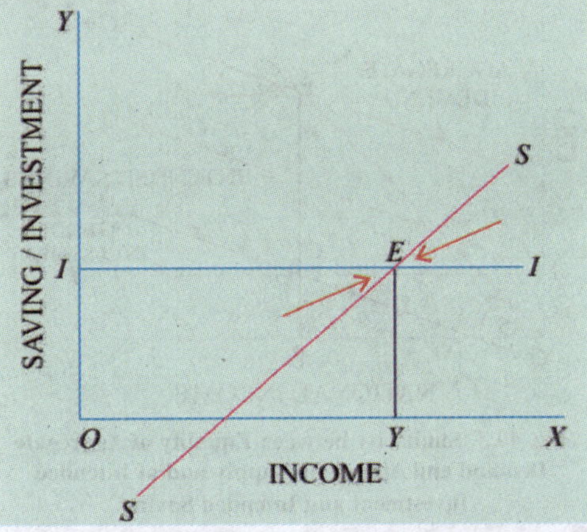

Fig. 40.2. Determination of National Income by Saving and Investment.

The saving curve SS and the investment curve *II* intersect each other at E. That is, the intended investment and intended saving are equal at the OY level of income. Hence, OY is the equilibrium level of income.

It will be seen in the Fig. 40.2, that at the level of income less than OY, the amount of intended investment is more than intended saving. As a result income will increase. On the contrary, at the level of income greater than OY, the amount of intended investment is less than the intended saving with the result that income will decrease. The decrease in income will continue till it becomes equal to OY. At the level of OY income, intended investment and intended saving are equal so that there is neither the tendency for income to increase nor to decrease. Hence, OY national income is determined. It is thus that national income is determined by investment and saving.

Conclusion

The determination of national income has been explained above by two methods: The equilibrium level of national income will be determined where two conditions are fulfilled:

(*i*) **Aggregate Demand = Aggregate Supply, and**

(*ii*) **Intended Investment = Intended Saving.**

In reality, the equality between Aggregate Demand and Aggregate Supply and between Intended Investment and Intended Saving mean the same thing.

This is illustrated in diagram 40.3 below.

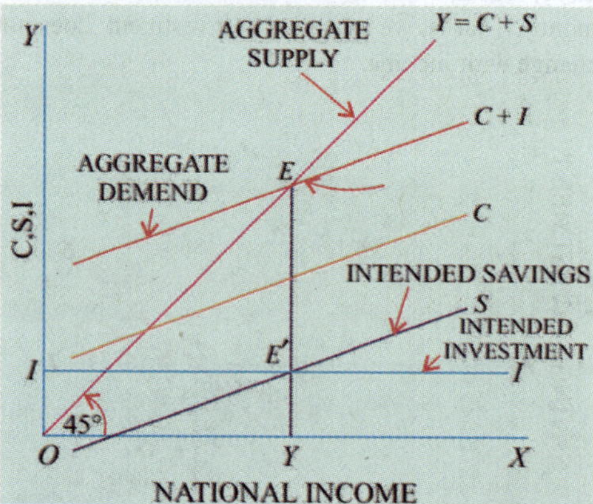

Fig. 40.3. Similarity between Equality of Aggregate Demand and Aggregate Supply and of Intended Investment and Intended Saving.

Keynesian Theory of Employment The Principle of Effective Demand

The classical economic theories completely collapsed during the late 20's. In 1919, the "Great Depression" showed that, the classical theories, completely failed to correct the disequilibrium in the economic activities, though the classical economists were of the view that business cycles are of temporary nature and unemployment is a short term phenomenon, which can be corrected easily by varying the rate of interest or by reducing the wage rate. All these suggestions failed. President However, took many steps to correct the economic situation, but the measures were "too little and too late". Hence, he was supposed to resign and on 04-03-1933 President Roosevelt took over as President of America. In 1936 the Keynesian 'General Theory" of Employment 'Interest and Money' changed completely the classical economic thought. This resulted in the emergence of the Keynesian revolution, which completely transformed the old economic thinking based on monetarist's approach to a new approach based more on fiscal economics, better known as 'welfare oriented economic policy'.

Principles of Effective Demand

The Keynesian approach was to rescue the capitalists economy from the great depression situation. Hence it is better known as a solution to the "depression economics". In general term the Keynesian injection of "General Theory" rescued the dying bed ridden 'laissez-faire' economy, and later the same has emerged as the most strong economies of the world in the 21st century.

In Keynes opinion the depression has occurred due to lack of 'effective demand', and there is a need to strengthen or raise the level of 'effective demand'. If we raise the level of effective demand the other economic variables will move in upward direction.

$$\Delta O = \Delta N = \Delta Y$$

$$\Downarrow$$

⇐ Effective Demand

ΔO = Aggregate output in an economy

Δ(N) = Aggregate employment in an economy

ΔY = Aggregate income in an economy.

There are two important elements of "Effective demand", "Aggregate Supply Function" and Aggregate Demand Function.

$$\Delta O = \Delta N = \Delta Y$$

$$\downarrow$$

Effective Demand

Aggregate Supply Function	Aggregate Demand Function
"Aggregate Supply Function" is the expectation of entrepreneurs or total amount of money expected from the sale of output in the economy.	"Aggregate Demand Function" the total (aggregate) demand from consumers and producers, in the economy as a whole.

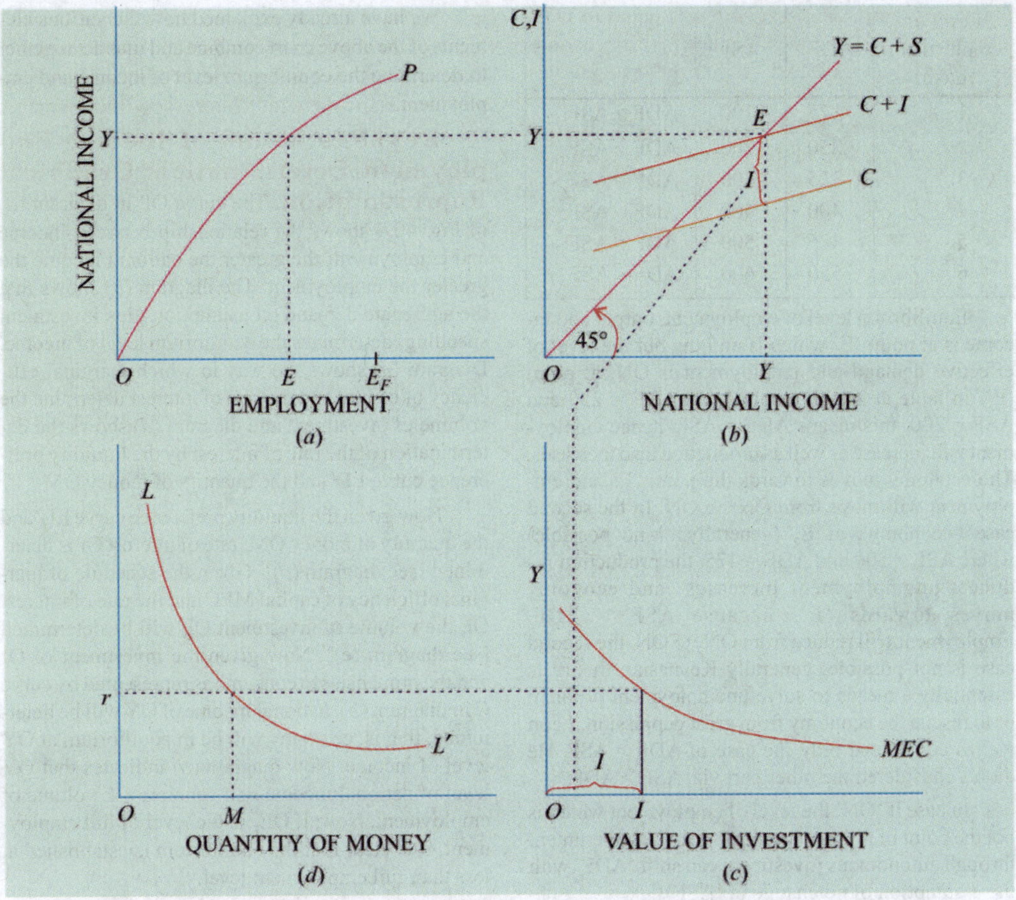

Fig. 40.4. Income-Employment Determination Model.

Adam Smith, 'the father of economics' has laid down more emphasis on human behaviour, specially his 'self-love' concept. As human being is very selfish whether from consumers point of view or from producer's point of view. Consumers tries to maximise his returns in the form of utility or value of his money "Quid Pro Quo" concept, whereas seller wants to maximise his sales. A seller will undertake more economic activities in the form of production process. A producer (being a human being) first estimates the market demand, then he adjusts his production process. Keynesian economic principle is also based on this philosophy. As long as ADF > ASF, economic activities will increase and this leads to increase in employment etc, further Keynesian multiplier effect as well as acceleration principle adds to the acceleration of the economic activities.

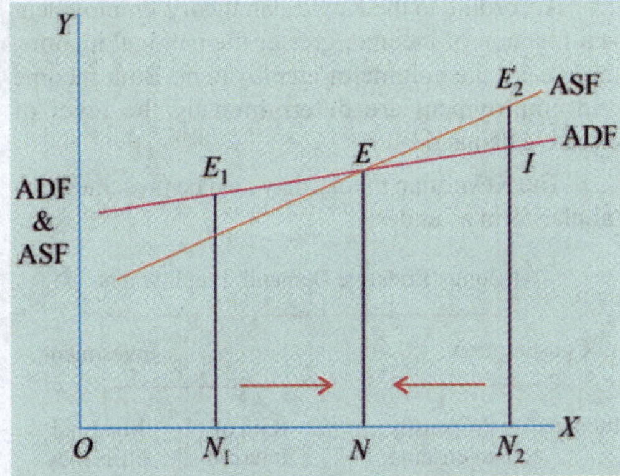

Fig. 40.5. Level of Employment.

In the above diagram the interaction between ADF and ASF at point 'E' determines the level of employment 'ON'.

Level of employment (Lakh)	ADF	ASF	
1	175	100	ADF > ASF
2	250	200	ADF > ASF
3	325	300	ADF > ASF
4	400	400	ADF = ASF
5	475	500	ADF < ASF
6	550	600	ADF < ASF

Equilibrium level of employment, output and income is at point 'E' which is nothing but the level of effective demand and employment is ON, at point 'E'. In table at 2 lakh employment ADF = 250 and ASF = 200, this means ADF > ASF, hence employment will increase as well as production also increases. The economy moves towards the point 'E' and employment will move from ON_1 to ON. In the second case if economy is at 'E_2' (generally it is not possible) where ASF = 500 and ADF = 475, the production reduces, unemployment increases and economy moves towards 'E', because ASF > ADF. Employment will reduce from ON_2 to ON, the second case is not possible, generally Keynesian theory is essentially a means to solve unemployment problem or to rescue the economy from great depression. Leon walras considered only the case of ADF > ASF. He didn't considered the other part viz. ASF > ADF.

In case if 'ON' the level of employment which is not the point of full employment, then the government through autonomous investment can shift 'ADF' with the assumption of no change in 'ASF'.

Keynes' Theory in Outline

According to the Keynesian theory, employment is a function of income; greater the national income, the greater the volume of employment. Both income and employment are determined by the level of effective demand.

The Keynesian theory may also be presented in a tabular form as under:

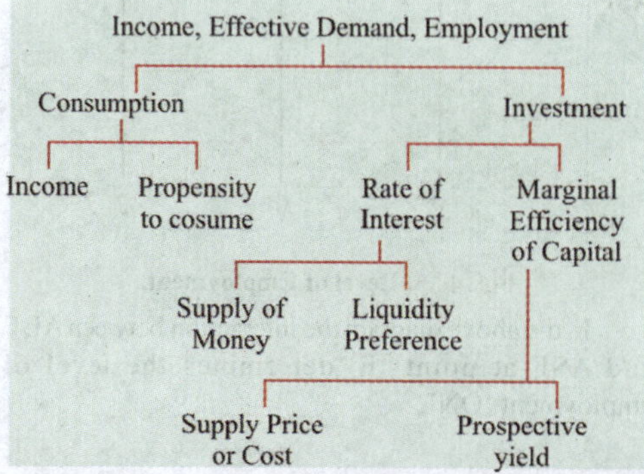

We have already explained how the various elements of the above chart combine and interact together to determine the equilibrium level of income and employment.

Keynes's Model of Income-Employment Determination: Graphical Representation. The curve OP in diagram (*a*) of Fig. 40.4 shows the relationship between income and employment; the greater the national income the greater the employment. The diagram (*b*) shows that the aggregate demand (consumption plus investment spending) determines the equilibrium level of income. Diagram (*c*) shows the way in which marginal efficiency of capital and the rate of interest determine the volume of investment and diagram (*d*) shows the determination of the rate of interest by the liquidity preference curve LL′ and the quantity of money OM.

Now given the liquidity preference curve LL′ and the quantity of money OM, rate of interest Or is determined [see diagram (*d*)]. Given the schedule of marginal efficiency of capital MEC and the rate of interest Or, the volume of investment OI, will be determined [see diagram (c)]. Now given the investment of OI and the propensity to consume as represented by curve C in diagram (*b*), national income of OY will be determined, that is, economy will be in equilibrium at OY level of income. Now diagram (*a*) indicates that OY level of national income will generate OE volume of employment. Now, if OE_F is the level of full employment, it is clear that the equilibrium is established at less than full employment level.

If the quantity of money in the economy is increased, it can be shown by the above diagram that the equilibrium income and employment will rise.

INFLATIONARY AND DEFLATIONARY GAPS

We know that equilibrium is not always at the full employment level. Rather it can be at a level when there is less than full employment. Thus no particular virtue need be attached to what we call the equilibrium level of national income or employment. On the other hand, equilibrium level may involve much unemployment and waste of national resources, if the investment is not sufficiently high to ensure full employment. Hence, the only level of equilibrium that may be considered desirable is that which provides full employment or near full employment. This level can be reached if investment opportunities happen to match full employment saving. In actual practice, therefore, we may have inflationary gap or deflationary gap.

Inflationary Gap

Inflationary gap arises when consumption and investment spending together are greater than the full employment GNP level. This means that people are demanding more goods and services than can be produced. In other words, the implication of inflationary gap is that national income, output and employment cannot rise further. The only consequence of increased demand for goods and services on the part of people will be to raise the price level. Or, we may say that there will be an inflationary gap if scheduled investment tends to be greater than full employment saving. In a situation like this, more goods will be demanded than the economic system can produce. The result will be that the prices will begin to rise and an inflationary situation will emerge. Thus, if full employment saving falls short of scheduled investment at full employment (which means that peoples' propensity to spend is higher than the propensity to save), there will be an inflationary gap.

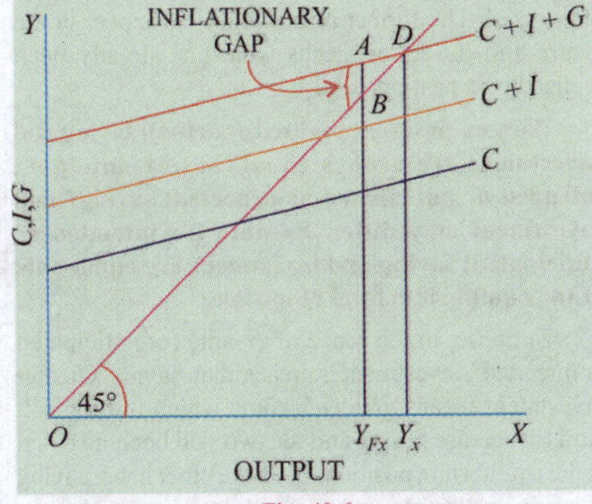

Fig. 40.6.

The inflationary gap can be explained with the help of the above diagram. C, I, G stand for the consumption, investment and Government expenditure respectively. (C + I + G) line shows the total expenditure on demand in the economy. At this level, Yx is the total real output, as shown by the intersection, point D, with the 45º line. Y_{FX} represents a full employment limit on real output Y_{FX}. Real income of the economy, obviously cannot reach Yx. At Y_{FX}, total demand (C + I + G) exceeds total output, leaving a gap AB, which is the inflationary gap in the Keynesian sense.

Deflationary Gap

Similarly, we can show with the help of a diagram "deflationary gap". This would come into existence, if total aggregate demand is insufficient to create full employment. Y_X is the total output at full employment. Let us assume that the total demand is (C + I + G)′ which cuts the 45º line at B, with real output Y'_X. AB then is the deflationary gap.

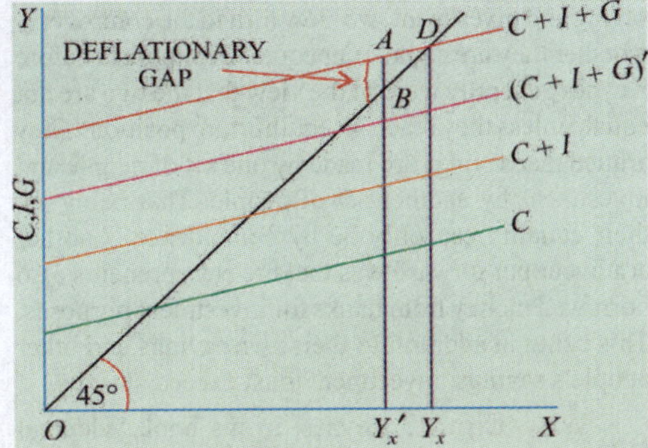

Fig. 40.7. Real Output or National Income.

SAVING-INVESTMENT CONTROVERSY

To a beginner in the Keynesian Theory; this controversy is one of the perplexing ones. Are savings equal to investment or are they unequal? A layman may say that a man may not invest all his savings; how can then saving be equal to investment? Let us clear this matter.

The first thing is to understand the meanings of these two terms, saving and investment. Investment in Keynesian Theory means the net addition to the stock of capital goods like machinery, equipment, factories, *etc*. It also includes inventories. Investment in this sense does not mean the total stock of capital goods in existence but the net addition thereto in a certain period. Thus, the term investment is different from the term capital. Capital means the total stock of capital goods in existence, whereas investment means what has been added to this stock say in a year.

Saving means that amount which a man saves out of income after he has incurred his consumption expenditure. Saving thus means the income which is not consumed. It has been defined as the excess of income over consumption expenditure. This even a leyman can understand. Suppose a man is earning Rs. 5,000 per annum. Out of it he spends Rs. 4,000 on food, clothes, housing accommodation and on other household needs. His saving amounts to Rs. 1,000. Suppose he is a farmer and spends Rs. 500 on irrigation, agricultural implements or in repairing the farm house. We should not then think that his saving is Rs. 500. The saving will still be Rs. 1,000, for Rs. 500 spent on irrigation, agricultural implements, *etc*., is called investment and cannot be included in consumption expenditure. For finding out saving, we should deduct from income only domestic or consumption expenditure and not investment expenditure. This point needs to be remembered.

Why Unequal? Having defined the terms saving and investment, we now turn to the controversy whether they are equal or unequal. Economists before Keynes generally were of the view that the two are not equal, unless they reach an equilibrium position. They argued that savings are made by one set of people and investment by another set of people. That being so, their equality can only be by coincidence. Another argument put forward was that the entrepreneurs also borrowed money from banks for investment purposes. This being in addition to their own savings and other people's savings, investment must exceed savings.

Why Equal? Keynes, in his book "General Theory", has established that savings and investment are equal. The national income, he says, is derived from the production and sale of (*a*) consumer's goods and (*b*) investment goods. We therefore get the equation;

Income = Consumption + Investment

or $Y = C + 1$ ...(1)

Y stands for income, C for consumption expenditure and I for investment expenditure.

This is the production and sales side of income. But income has also another side, *i.e.*, spending side. From this point of view, income is exhausted in consumption and saving and we get the equation

Income = Consumption + Saving

or $Y = C + S$ ...(2)

Y stands for income, C for consumption expenditure and S for saving out of the income.

Bringing equations (1) and (2) together we get

$\therefore$ $C + S = C + 1$

$\therefore$ S (Saving) = I (Investment).

We find that saving and investment are equal by the very definition we have given. In Keynesian Economics, the terms 'income', 'consumption', 'saving' and 'investment' have been so defined as excess of income over consumption expenditure; such is also the definition of investment. The two must therefore be equal. Hence, both saving and investment are equal, because they have been equated to each other by the definition of both as excess of income over consumption expenditure.

We may remind the reader that we are now studying Macro-Economics and not Micro-Economics. The words 'savings' and 'investment' are used in the aggregate sense and not individual sense. For instance, saving does not mean here savings of an individual but that of the community. Similarly, income means aggregate income and consumption aggregate consumption. In the case of an individual, saving may not be equal to investment, but for the community or the economic system as a whole, saving must be equal to investment as defined by Keynes.

It may happen sometimes that the nation cuts down consumption expenditure in response to appeals by leaders in a national emergency. Savings will then increase. It may be asked how can saving be equal to investment in this case. The answer is that, if consumption has been decreased, the inventories or finished goods are lying idle; they have not been sold to the consumers. And those inventories are included in investment. Hence, investment is as large as savings.

In What Sense Unequal? Is there any sense in which saving and investment may not be equal to each other? The answer is that as the words have been defined in Keynesian Economics, they must be always equal. In this controversy, it is essential for the student to understand two words: ex-ante and ex-post. Ex-ante means anticipated or intended and ex-post means actual or realised. The former means what we expect in the future and the latter means what has already been realised by a past process.

Now ex-post (*i.e.*, realised or actual) saving and investment are always equal, but ex-ante (*i.e.*, intended or anticipated or expected) savings and investment may differ. Ex-ante (or intended or anticipated) saving and investment are equal only at the equilibrium level of income.

Suppose, in the sense of ex-ante (or anticipated or intended), investment is greater than saving. Greater investment means greater income which in turn will tend to increase saving and the two will become equal at the equilibrium position. If, on the other hand, saving exceeds investment, income will decrease, leading in turn to a decrease in saving so that saving and investment will tend to be equal.

This can be shown by the diagram (Fig. 40.7). SS is the saving curve and II is the investment curve. The point of intersection of the two curves E represents the equilibrium level of income. Here both saving and investment are equal. At the OY_1 level, $Y_1 P_1$ is the ex-ante or intended investment and $Y_1 L_1$ is the ex-ante or intended saving, which is less than intended investment. Hence, income must increase and reach the OY level where the intended saving and investment are equal. At the OY_2 level, intended saving $Y_2 P_2$ is more than intended investment Y_2L_2. Hence income must decrease and tend to reach OY level where again the two are equal.

It is clear that ex-ante (or intended or anticipated) saving and investment are equal at the equilibrium level of income, and not at any other level of income (*i.e.*, more or less). It is just like demand and supply, which are equal at the equilibrium price, and not at any other price. Just as price goes up and down and equates demand and supply at the equilibrium level, similarly, income increases or decreases to reach the equilibrium level and thus equates saving and investment.

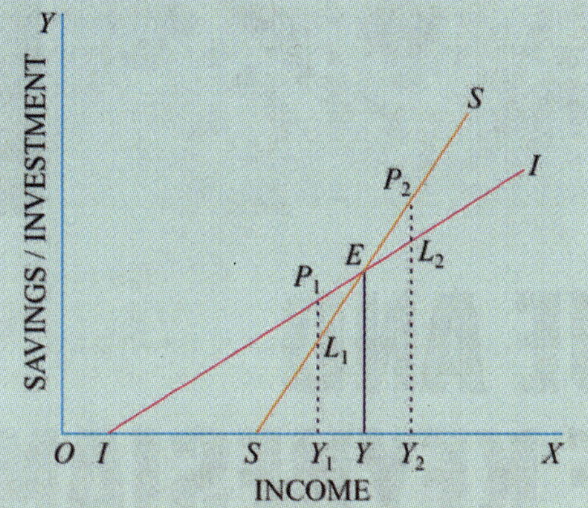

Fig. 40.8. Equality of Saving and Investment.

SOME MACRO-ECONOMIC TERMS

Stocks and Flows

The variables in macro-economics may be called 'Stocks' or 'Flows'. There is no time dimension in stocks but flows have a time dimension. That is, a stock must be specified at a point of time, but the magnitude of stock has no time dimension. On the other hand, a flow can be expressed only in terms of time units. It is clear that money is a stock but expenditure is a flow. Similarly, wealth is a stock but income is a flow.

We can trace stock-flow relationship in certain economic problems. Stocks' change only through flows. It is the fast or slow changes in stock due to current rates of flow that certain macro-economic problems arise.

Macro-Statics

In macro-static, attention is given to the state of the economy at a given moment of time. That is, we confine our attention to equilibrium positions. We explain certain aggregative relationships in an equilibrium but we do not show how this equilibrium position was reached. In other words, we do not show the process of adjustment implied in reaching the equilibrium position.

For example, when we say Y = C + 1, we only show that to maintain a certain level of income, the expenditure of the consumers and businessmen must be C + 1, but we do not show how the total income reaches that particular level of Y. That is, there is no room for time analysis in macro-statics. It is looking at a still picture and not a movie.

Macro-Comparative Statics

As against static analysis, the comparative statics involves a comparison between two equilibrium positions. That is, we compare the state of economy at one particular time with that of another. In other words, we compare two levels of income or employment achieved by an economy at two different times.

Macro-Dynamics

In macro-dynamics, we investigate the process by which the economy moves from one equilibrium position to another. For instance, the national income of India at constant prices rose from nearly Rs. 9,000 crores in 1950-51 to Rs. 22,000 crores nearly in 1975-76. The macro-dynamics will investigate the changes in the economy which raised the income to that level in 25 years. It describes the time paths of macro variables and aggregate relationships. Thus it shows us a movie picture of the progressive changes that occurred in the economy during this period. For instance, it shows present savings depending on past rates of interest, level of consumption and cumulative total of past savings and dissavings.

Obviously, it is a more realistic description of complex phenomenon of cyclical fluctuations and secular growth.

The dynamic analysis is of particular importance in macro-economics since it is widely used in the study of national income, principle of acceleration, trade-cycle theories and growth economics.

Key terms

Effective demand, Ex-ante, ex-post, Inflationary gap, Deflationary gap.

QUESTIONS

1. Define Aggregate Demand and Aggregate Supply Schedules and show how they help determine the equilibrium level of income. What according to Keynes are the factors that determine the equilibrium level of employment in the economy?
2. Explain Inflationary and Deflationary gap ?
3. State and explain Keynes' principle of Effective Demand. What is its importance ?
4. Give a brief outline of the Keynesian Theory of Employment, bringing out clearly the role of 'effective demand', in determining the level of employment in an economy.

CRITIQUE AND RELEVANCE OF KEYNESIAN SYSTEM

KEYNES vs. CLASSICAL ECONOMISTS

While discussing Keynes's theory of income and employment, we have had often to refer in this con nection to the classical economists. We may at this stage sum up the main differences between Keynes and the classical economists:

(i) The most important difference is that the classical economists said, according to Say's Law, that the economy was in a state of stable equilibrium at full employment. It might for a short time depart from full employment, but the equilibrium would be restored through wage adjustments. Keynes, on the other hand, said that, barring periods like wars, there was seldom full employment and the equilibrium was mostly at less than full employment.

(ii) Keynes's theory relates to Macro-Economics, which studies the economy as a whole but the classical economic theory dealt with individual aspects of the economy and was Micro-Economics. Keynes dealt with aggregates, whereas the classical economists studied the economic system in terms of its innumerable decision-making units, *e.g.*, consumer's equilibrium, producer's equilibrium, equilibrium of the firm, and so on. Keynes dealt with the general price level, instead of the price of an individual commodity. His concern was with the level of employment in the community, instead of the employment of any particular class of labour.

(iii) The classical economists believed that a state of full employment could be brought about through cuts in money wages, and whatever the state of demand, there will always be, via wage adjustment, a tendency towards full employment.

But Keynes held that this theory was not only unrealistic but theoretically unsound. According to Keynes, lowering of wages in any particular industry might increase employment there. But, if wages were reduced all round, it will reduce income and so effective demand and the volume of employment. In these days of democracy and trade unionism, only a foolish government would allow wage reductions.

(iv) According to classical economists, interest is the reward for 'waiting' or for time preference. But according to Keynes, it is a reward for parting with liquidity. The classical theory of interest states that the rate of interest is determined by the intersection of the saving and investment schedule. The Keynesian Theory gives us a set of liquidity preference schedules at various levels of income. These, together with the supply of money fixed by the monetary authority, give us a curve that tells us what the various rates of interest will be at different levels of income.

(v) The classical theory is based on the conception of static economy, whereas Keynes's theory is dynamic. The classical economists concentrated on equilibrium at a certain time, but Keynes introduced future expectations into economic analysis and thus analysed a dynamic economy. Keynes is thus realistic, whereas the classical economists all the time dealt with an unrealistic picture.

(vi) Keynes's theory is a general theory and as such has a very wide application to all situations – unemployment, partial employment and near full employment. The classical analysis relates only to full employment. They thought a general and permanent unemployment was impossible. They believed that wage flexibility provided a self-adjusting mechanism which made for full employment. Hence, all their theories are based on the assumption of full employment –a thoroughly unrealistic proposition.

(vii) Keynes integrated the theory of money with the theory of value and output. The classical economists segregated these theories from one another and dealt with them as if they were unrelated to one another, which is actually not the case. Here again, Keynesian is more realistic, whereas the classical economists were all theoretical and dealt with abstract situations. Money supply affects output and employment. Hence, the theory of money and prices cannot be isolated from the analysis of income and employment in the country.

Keyne's approch is more integrated for whole economy.

(viii) The classical economists believed in orthodox finance and balanced budgets. But, according to Keynes, a country's budget should reflect the financial situation and should vary as the situation demands. There is no special virtue in a balanced budget. There are times when a deficit budget is dictated by the economic situation prevailing at the time. That is why deficit financing is the common feature in all developing economies.

(ix) According to the classical economists, increase in money supply brings about inflation and must, therefore, be avoided. This arose from their contention that there always existed full employment. But Keynes pointed out that full employment was a rare phenomenon; actually there was generally less-than-full employment so that some productive resources of the community lay idle and unemployed, totally or partially. That being so, an increase in money supply would increase employment and output and may not thus necessarily result in inflation.

Thus Keynes's theory has greater relevance to the world of reality and has great practical value; whereas the views of the classical economists are more or less theoretical and devoid of any practical importance.

These are a few points of departure of the Keynesian theory from the classical theory. In fact, Keynes's theory is entirely new and marks a revolution in economic thinking. It has been aptly called a **"Keynesian revolution".**

CRITICISM OF THE KEYNESIAN THEORY

Keynesian theory does not represent the last word in economic thinking as it is sometimes supposed. On the other hand, the Keynesian theory can be criticised on the following grounds:

(i) Some economists, *e.g.*, Schumpiter, say that the Keynesian theory is really 'depression theory' and as such has limited application and has little relevance to general economic situation. But "his (Keynes's) models clarify both deflationary and inflationary episodes and prosperous and depressed economies".

(ii) It is said that Keynesian theory is a theory of capitalist economies. It is said that "if Communism comes, Keynes will be a dead as Ricardo". However, even the Socialist countries strive to raise their national income and have to use the Keynesian tools like savings, investment, consumption function, marginal efficiency of capital, and so on.

(iii) It is further pointed out that the Keynesian theory is not sufficiently dynamic and it may more properly be called comparative statics. Thus, it is not much different from the classical theory. Keynes does not use the concept of time-lag.

(iv) The Keynesian model is too static in character. It assumes the amount of capital to be fixed and the output as a function of employment only. The model fails to explain short-run fluctuations.

(v) It is also held that Keynes altogether ignores Micro-analysis and as such is not helpful in the solution of the problems of individual firms and industries. The Keynesian theory is altogether a Macro-theory concurring itself with national income and employment. The Keynesian theory is too aggregative.

(vi) The Keynesian theory has not given any place to the accelerator principle. But we know an integration between the multiplier and the accelerator is essential to explain adequately the economic problems.

(vii) It is also said that the Keynesian theory is largely a monetary theory since it pays excessive attention to money in economic analysis.

(viii) Shortcomings can also be pointed out in the various aspects of the Keynesian theory: For example, his interest theory is indeterminate and the theory of consumption function is inadequate.

(ix) The economists also question the various assumptions underlying the Keynesian model *e.g.*, the assumption of a stable consumption function, the assumption that the aggregate production function is based on the law of diminishing returns, the assumption of fixed money wages and fixed speculative demand, schedule for money. Also, as Shapiro has observed, the Keynesian model is wrong in assuming that the supply of capital is available in unlimited quantity at the given rate of interest.

Retreat from Keynesianism: Supply side Economies

Keynesian theory has dominated economic thinking for nearly 50 years. But in view of the criticism of the theory in recent years, a major revaluation in economic thinking is now under way representing retreat from the Keynesian theory. Even in his time there were serious doubters but Keynes's brilliant and highly intellectual and persuasive exposition made them lie low. Economists like Milton Friedman and Friedrich Hayek rejected Keynesian conclusions. In the thirties, the British and American economies had been experiencing an unusually high rate of unemployment and depression and Keynes's theory seemed to have a great relevance as a corrective prescription for prolonged unemployment. But his ideas were not found appropriate for the U. S. economy of 1960's and 1970's. Hence, retreat from Keynesian economics began in American universities. Some of this thinking is reflected in what has come to be called 'Supply side' economics.

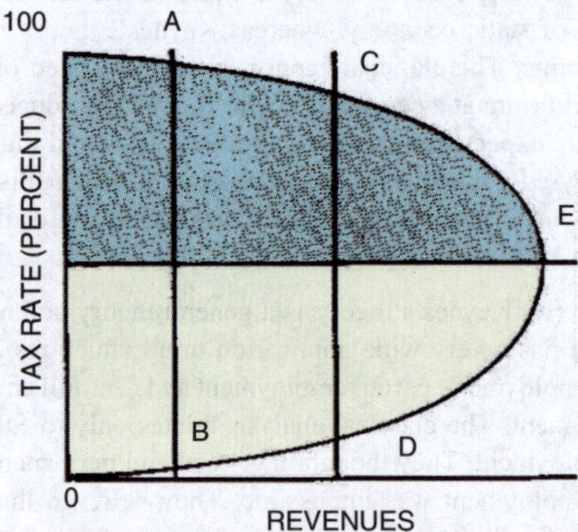

The Laffer Curve.

Slow economic growth, persistent inflation, diminishing increase in productivity have focussed increasing attention to supply-side economics. This new economic thinking emphasises measures to increase production as opposed to consumption. Keynesian economics was demand-oriented economics, whereas supply-side economics is supply or production-oriented economics. Supply-side theory puts emphasis on stimulating production side of the economic equation by means of *substantial tax cuts and reducing government spending as key incentives for individuals and businesses to produce, invest, work*

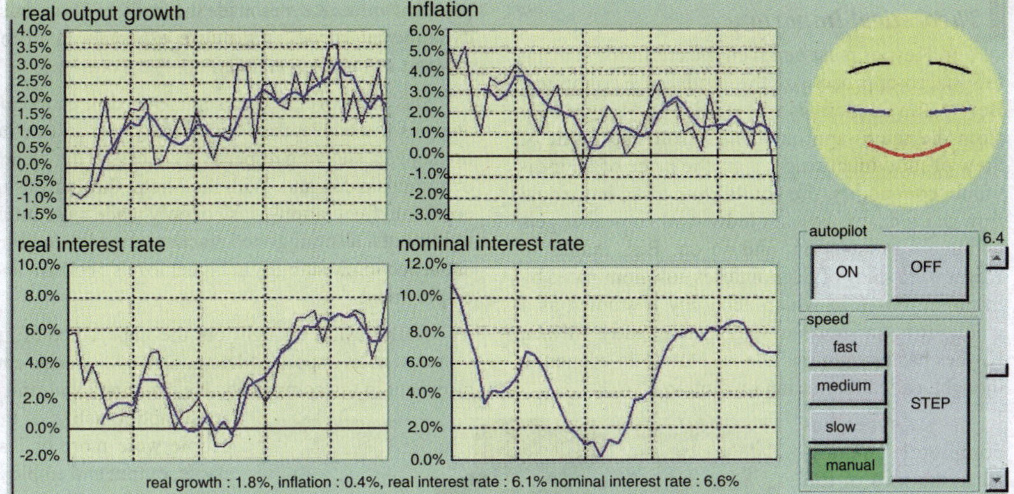

and save more, and imposition of non-inflationary monetary policy. Professor Arthur Laffer of Southern California, a leading proponent of supply-side economics has in effect introduced what is known after his name as the **Laffer Curve** with the help of which he shows how to determine the optimum rate at which taxes can be set to maximise government revenue via increase in productive supply. He maintains that "Supply-side economics is nothing more than classical economics in modern dress." J. B. Say, a 19th century French economist laid down a law "Supply creates its own demand". This law is the essential enactment of supply-side theory.[1] To use Dr. Laffer's words again, 'Basically, supply-side economics is that branch of economics that focusses on very personal and very private incentives" with a view to increasing production and productivity and promote private savings.

It has been pointed out that supply-side economics has historical roots dating back to Adam Smith, who was known as father of political economy and who advocated a policy of Laissez-faire or government non-intervention in economic sphere to create a free market and give other incentives that will spur greater economic growth. This is in contrast to the prevailing Keynesian approach which emphasises the need for government to manage and manipulate through fiscal and monetary policies-aggregate demand so as to maintain full employment. Supply-side economists say that the government cannot really do this. This is too much for the government. But if private enterprise is permitted to function freely with minimum of government interference, it will innovate, produce more, save move and invest more so as to create requisite demand for the goods it produces. This will undoubtedly stimulate economic growth and increase national income and employment. Supply-side economics looks at the economy from the ground level, as it were, from the point of view of the entrepreneurs who are the prime movers. In contrast to this, Keynesian economists look at the economy from the above-from the stand-point of a government which is supposed to intervene, in its omniscience, intervene discretely to *preserve* a harmonious economic universe.

Conclusion

It is well to remember, however, that we cannot think of demand and supply to the exclusion of one or the other. They are really two sides of the same coin co-existing of necessity and there is no question of emphasis depending on the prevailing economic climate.

SIGNIFICANCE OF THE KEYNESIAN THEORY

In spite of the criticism levelled against the Keynesian theory by some economists, the fact cannot be denied that it has great significance even today. It has continued to exercise considerable influence on economic thinking almost all over the world. The Keynesian theory has both theoretical and practical importance. Since the various points relating to them have been already discussed in the previous chapters, we shall dwell on these two aspects of this theory in a summary fashion.

1. See *Impact*, Number 35, Supply-side Economics Innovative Ideas.

Theoretical Importance

(*i*) Keynes must be given the credit for starting the macro-approach to the study of Economics. Before him Economics was studied and taught only from the micro-approach, *i.e.*, from the point of view of individual study, *e.g.*, the price of an individual commodity, the equilibrium of an individual firm and industry, how an individual consumer gets maximum satisfaction, and so on. But, thanks to Keynes, the study of Economics is now dominated by macro-approach in which economy is studied as a whole. It is, in short, an aggregative study. In fact, Keynes has brought about a revolution in economic thought, called Keynesian revolution.

(*ii*) Keynes has completely demolished the idea of full employment equilibrium so elaborately built up by the classical economists. Instead, he put forward the idea of under-employment equilibrium. He proved that the economy of a country is generally in equilibrium even though there is under-employment. He showed how employment could be increased by increasing investment.

Keynesian Economics calls for policy frame work for curing economic Problems.

(*iii*) The economists of today have got from Keynes several new tools of economic analysis which enable them to draw correct conclusions. Some of these tools are consumption function, the multiplier, the investment function, liquidity preference, and so on. These are now the current coins of the science of Economics. They are valuable allies of economists in the study of an economic system.

(*iv*) Keynes integrated the theory of money with the theories of value and output which when studied in an isolated fashion, led to one-sided and incorrect conclusions. The monetary theory now is studied from a realistic and practical point of view. Thus, this study has been made more fruitful.

(*v*) Another service that Keynes has rendered to Economics is the introduction of the dynamic element in its study. Before him, the classical economists made it a study of economic statistics in which the economy was supposed to remain standstill. The assumption of motionlessness was made to facilitate the study of the effects of a single change. The result obviously was to make the whole study unrealistic and devoid of any practical value. Keynes made the study of Economics dynamic by introducing future expectations in the analysis of business activity.

(*vi*) Moreover, Keynes introduced in economic analysis the concepts of inflationary gap and deflationary gap, showing respectively excess or deficiency of aggregate demand. With their help, the analysis of economic fluctuations was not only made more intelligible but it also suggested practical remedies to bring about economic stability at higher levels of output and employment.

(*vii*) Keynes brought out the importance of investment as an important determinant of aggregate employment in the community. He explained that, since consumption habits of the people were more or less stable, output and employment could readily be increased by increasing investment. The marginal propensity to consume being less than unity, (*i.e.*, as income increases, consumption does not increase by as much as the increase in income), it brings out the crucial importance of investment.

(*viii*) Keynes' is a general theory and not a particular one applying to a particular type of economic system. His theory applies to all economic situations, whether full employment or under-employment.

Practical Importance

(*i*) The classical economists believed in the policy of laissez-faire but Keynes showed how this policy was utterly unsuitable to modern economic conditions and how inadequate this policy was to cure the economic ills from which a community might be suffering. The influence of Keynes on government policy can be seen from the increasing intervention of the State in the interest of promoting general welfare. Keynes showed that full employment could only be achieved through State help, because effective demand could only be increased by enlarging State activity. Thanks to Keynes, the policy of laissez-faire is dead and gone.

(*ii*) Another way in which Keynes influenced practical policies was by criticising the policy of surplus budgets. He advocated deficit budgeting, if that suited the economic situation in the country. Thus, surplus budgeting is no longer regarded as sacrosanct.

(iii) Keynes put great emphasis on suitable fiscal policy as an instrument for checking inflation and for increasing output and employment in a community. Thus, extensive public works programme now forms an integral part of government programme in all countries for expanding employment opportunities.

(iv) Monetary policy, as an instrument of controlling cyclical fluctuations, received due attention from Keynes. He also pointed out the limitations of monetary policy. Central banking control over credit now occupies a very important place in the economic policies of a nation. These are the weapons taken from Keynesian armoury of economic instruments.

(v) Again, it was due to Keynes that deficit financing has come to pay an important part in the economic development of under-developed economies. Keynes showed how deficit financing (*i.e.*, creating new money) could be used for a time to further economic development, if it is kept within proper limits.

(vi) Keynes completely demolished the classical doctrine which said that employment could be increased through wage cuts. Keynes refuted the theoretical validity as well as practical feasibility of wage-cut as a means of promoting full employment. He cautioned the governments against the dangers of such a policy.

(vii) We owe it to Keynes that the economists and governments today give a lot of attention to social accounting. We now see that, in every country, statistics of national income are being collected. This enables a suitable economic policy to be evolved and adopted.

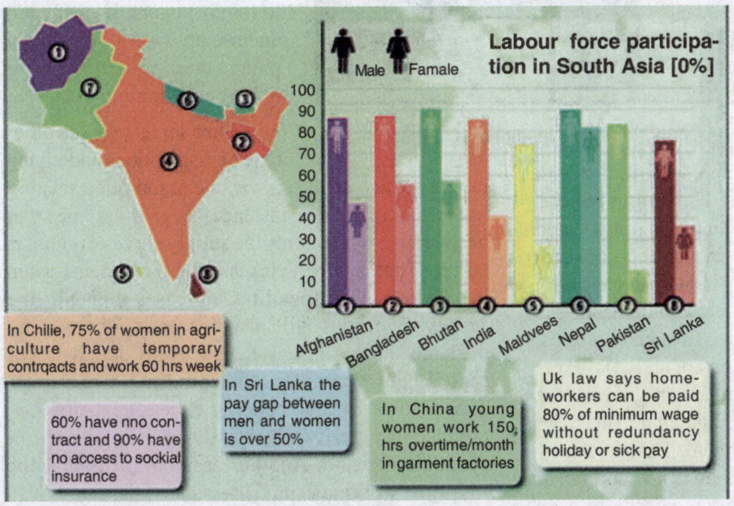

Conclusion. We, thus, see that Keynesian theory has exercised tremendous influence not only on economic theory but also on economic policy. We find today that, on the one hand, economists conduct economic analysis on the basis of Keynesian theory (in fact Keynes has given birth to what is called Keynesian Economics) and, on the other, the governments are increasingly relying on Keynesian Economics for tackling their economic problems.

RELEVANCE OF KEYNESIAN ECONOMICS TO UNDER-DEVELOPED ECONOMIES

In order to see how far Keynesian income and employment analysis is relevant to under-developed economies, we have to bear in mind the assumptions on which this analysis is based. We have, therefore, simply to see how far the assumptions underlying Keynesian analysis are valid in the case of under-developed countries. To the extent that they do not hold good in the case of under-developed countries, the Keynesian analysis will not have relevance to such countries.

The assumptions on which the Keynesian theory of income and employment is based are of two types: (*a*) the assumptions which are associated with the multiplier and (*b*) those which are required for a short-term analysis and do not apply to the long-term analysis. We first take the latter type, *viz.*, those which are needed for a short-term analysis. Keynes assumes that capital equipment, technology, organization, the working force and its efficiency in a country are constant and do not vary. He considers that the problem relating to income and employment in developed countries arises only on account of the deficiency of demand.

But the problem in the case of under-developed countries is to increase capital equipment, to improve technology and labour efficiency because only in this way can the level of income and employment in such countries be raised. The problem of unemployment or under-employment in the developed countries is a short-term problem since it arises from a deficiency of effective demand at a

UDCs suffer from economic backwardness.

particular period of time. As soon as this deficiency is removed by monetary or fiscal measures or through a public works programme, the problem is solved. But, in the case of under-developed countries, the problem is chronic because capital formation, improvement of technology or of labour efficiency is a long process. Keynes regards these things as given. That is, what an under-developed economy requires, Keynes just assumes away.

Let us take the case of India. The basic cause of under-employment and unemployment in an under-developed country like India is to be found in the dearth of capital equipment, which, in turn, is due to low rate of saving and investment. The various policies like public works, deficit spending, *etc*., advocated by Keynes as a cure for unemployment do not seem to have any relevance here. They have relevance only if unemployment is due to deficiency of demand as is the case in developed economies. In such countries, there is no dearth of capital equipment and of workers willing to work, so that an increase in government expenditure financed by deficit financing leads to an increase in output and employment. But, in under-developed economies, though there is no shortage of man-power, capital equipment is scarce and an increase in government spending is more liable to create inflation rather than lead to an increase in output. This happens because, for want of complementary resources in capital, the supply curve of output tends to be inelastic. Thus Keynesian analysis is not much helpful to an under-developed economy.

Poverty is a cause of nonfunctioning of multiplier in UDCs.

Let us illustrate it by referring to major sectors of the economy of an under-developed country. Agriculture is the predominant occupation in backward countries contributing to national income to the extent of fifty per cent or even more. Suppose the government tries to bring about an increase in national income by deficit spending. This will lead to increase in demand for food, as at low income level, income elasticity of demand for food tends to be high. But the supply curve of agricultural output in under-developed countries is notoriously inelastic. There are several bottle-necks in increasing agricultural output which arise because of extremely uneconomic size of holding, lack of efficient tools and implements. Thus an increase in the demand for food arising out of deficit financing is more likely to raise the prices of foodgrains rather than the supply of output. Similarly, in the industrial sector also, there is no idle capacity to be utilized, and, for these reasons, reliance of Keynesian remedies to remove unemployment and under-employment will simply plunge these countries into an inflationary spiral.

Now let us take the other type of assumptions underlying the Keynesian analysis, *viz*., the assumption relating to the multiplier. For instance, Keynes assumes that in an industrial economy the supply curve of output is elastic. That is why he takes it for granted that when the Government spending increases demand, the supply of output will also increase. There is no difficulty in this because there is no deficiency of capital equipment and other productive resources. There exists in the economy excess capacity, *i.e.*, productive capacity which is lying idle for want of adequate demand. Another assumption is that the supply of working capital, raw materials, *etc*., is also elastic and can also be increased without difficulty. This, however, is not the case in under-developed countries which suffer from all types of shortages.

Still another assumption underlying Keynesian analysis is of involuntary unemployment which means that people are willing to work but they do not get work. The working of the multiplier is based on such assumptions. Only on these assumptions can a multiplier increase income and employment. That is, the principle of the multiplier states that when a new investment is made, the incomes of productive factors will increase and the demand will increase. Keynes assumes that the supply of goods is elastic, since there is excess capacity in the economy and working capital and raw-materials can be increased. It is only on these assumptions that output can be increased and workers willing to work will be able to get jobs, and income and employment will increase manifold in accordance with the multiplier.

Due to overall backwardness including disguised unemployment multiplier does not work in UDCs like India.

But these assumptions do not hold good in the case of under-developed countries like India. These countries are not predominantly industrial. On the other hand, they are predominantly agricultural, hence the supply of goods is not elastic; nor is there any excess capacity in the economy, because there is great scarcity of capital equipment. Nor can the working capital, raw material, *etc.*, be increased. Also, most of the people are self-employed and the number of workers engaged on wage is comparatively small. The national output mostly is meant for domestic consumption and not for the market; there is also lot of disguised unemployment. In all these respects, the under-developed countries are different from developed countries. The Keynesian theory, on the other hand, is applicable to developed countries because all these assumptions hold good in their case. The case of under-developed countries is entirely different. They cannot, therefore, derive any help from the application of the Keynesian theory.

The multiplier does not work under the conditions found in under-developed countries. Suppose new investment is made in such countries, there is no doubt that increased investment will lead to establishment of new factories; workers will also get jobs; their incomes will increase; thus demand will increase. But the chain stops here. Although demand has increased, the supply of goods cannot increase because there is no excess capacity and the supply of productive factors, especially capital, is not elastic. Hence, increased income will only be absorbed in enhanced prices without creating any additional output and employment. The primary increased income following a given increment of investment does get spent to a large extent on the output of agriculture and leads to a corresponding increase in the incomes of the agricultural producers. But it is not followed up by these producers increasing their output and thus adding to both employment and real income.

There is another thing to be found in the under-developed countries, *viz.*, that increased income in such countries is spent on consumer's goods because propensity to consume in such countries is very high. The bulk of increased income is absorbed in increase in demand for food, because their income elasticity for demand for food is generally very high. As a result, the marketable surplus is reduced. This also raises prices in such countries. If there is any surplus income, it is spent on consumer's goods but their supply cannot be increased. Hence their prices also rise. In this way, inflationary spiral starts both in the agricultural and the industrial sector. This has happened in India. Mounting investment undertaken under the five year plans financed by deficit financing has raised prices all round. The multiplier has not worked; neither the agricultural output nor the industrial output has increased; but the prices have continued to soar higher and higher. We, therefore, find that the Keynesian remedies to remove unemployment and under-employment in backward countries will only plunge them into an inflationary spiral.

As we have already mentioned, in underdeveloped countries there is no involuntary unemployment in the Keynesian sense; yet millions of people are unemployed in the clearly economic sense as in the case of disguised unemployment. As Dr. V. K. R. V. Rao observes, "The particular form which unemployment takes in the under-developed countries, *viz.*, that of disguised unemployment makes the economies for Keynesian purposes practically analogous with one of full employment and to that extent prevents the multiplier from working in the direction of an increase in either output".

We should not, however, conclude from the above discussion that Keynesian remedies have no place at all in under-developed countries. Deficit financing for instance, has a definite role to play in such countries for mobilizing resources for the public sector. Only, in resorting to Keynesian policies, we must bear in mind the inflationary effects and use it with all possible caution, keeping it within proper limits. If inflation occurs, strong measures should be taken in time to cure it as India has done recently with great success.

The basic solution for the problem of unemployment or under-employment in the under-developed countries is economic development. Economic development, however, is a long-term process. In a way, it depends on capital formation, which, in turn, depends on the surplus of income over consumption of the community. The greater the surplus, the faster will be the rate of growth, if there are entrepreneurs to utilize the resources for capital formation. To save more and to consume less, therefore, is a good remedy for under-developed economies, whereas for an advanced economy the opposite is the case during a depression. The Keynesian remedy is primarily for fighting depression.

While Keynesian policies may not have much relevance to the problems of under-developed countries, the tools of analysis developed by Keynes are indispensable even for under-developed countries. The discussion of monetary flows, the concepts of national income accounting, the problems of inflationary gap, *etc*., are as useful to an economist in an under-developed country as to one in a developed country.

Conclusion

We may, thus, conclude that Keynesian economics, though originally developed to fight depression, has a good deal relevance to an under-developed country. Hence, these countries have lot to benefit from the study and application of policies advocated by the late Lord Keynes.

Key terms

Keynesian Economics, Supply side Economics.

QUESTIONS

1. Critically evaluate the Keynesian theory of employment.
2. Discuss the factors responsible for retreat from supply side economics.
3. Discuss the relevance of Keynesian economics to developing countries.

42

CHAPTER

DETERMINANTS OF INCOME AND EMPLOYMENT : PROPENSITY TO CONSUME

It must have been clear from the previous two chapters how equilibrium level of income and employment is determined. We have seen that in the position of equilibrium aggregate demand and aggregate supply in the economy are equal to each other. Also, aggregate demand is the sum-total of two types of demand: (*a*) consumption demand and (*b*) investment demand. In this chapter, we shall explain consumption demand. We shall study the factors which determine consumption demand, and we shall see what law can be enunciated in this connection. Consumption demand plays a very important role in the determination of the level of employment and income. Normally, if in a country consumption (or propensity to consume) is high, employment and income will increase, and vice versa. Hence, it follows that an effective way of increasing employment and income in a country is to adopt such measures as to increase consumption or strengthen propensity to consume.

Let us study the propensity to consume in some detail.

CONSUMPTION FUNCTION

Propensity to consume is also called 'consumption function'. In the Keynesian theory, we are concerned not with the consumption of an individual consumer but with the sum total of consumption spending by all the individuals. However, in generalising about the consumption behaviour of the economy, as a whole, we can draw some useful conclusions from the study of the behaviour of a normal consumer which may well be valid for the consumption behaviour of the economy also. Our observations about the consumption behaviour will help us immediately to generalise about the saving behaviour of the economy also,

Consumption.

for saving equals income not consumed. Aggregate consumption depends on Consumption Function or propensity to consume, as it is called.

Meaning

The distinction between consumption and consumption function will make the meaning of consumption function clear. Consumption means the amount spent on consumption at a given level of income, but consumption function or propensity to consume means the whole of the schedule showing consumption expenditure at various levels of income. It tells us, in short, how consumption expenditure increases as income increases. The consumption function or propensity to consume, therefore, indicates a functional relationship between two aggregates, *viz*., total consumption expenditure and the gross national income. It is a schedule that expresses relationship between consumption and disposable income.

Normally, when income increases consumption also increases but by less than the increase in income as we shall explain in Keynesian Psychological Law given below.

Factors influencing Consumption

Consumption spending of the people is influenced, among others, by the following factors:–

(*a*) the real income of the individual,

(*b*) his past savings,

(*c*) rate of interest.

Of these, the influence of real income seems to be the strongest of all. For a great majority of people, past savings are very small and they too are for specific purposes like contributions to social security schemes, pension and provident funds and life insurance. These savings are not readily available for spending by the individuals. Therefore, their influence on current consumption seems to be negligible. The rich, who have sufficient savings, can satisfy their current needs adequately out of their current incomes; hence their consumption spending is not greatly affected by their past savings.

As regards an increase in the rate of interest, it may encourage some people to save more because the saved money now earns a higher rate of interest. But if a person is saving for some specific purpose a given sum at a future date, an increase in the rate of interest enables him to accumulate the given sum with lower current savings. Suppose I need 105 rupees at the end of one year. Now if the rate of interest is 5 per cent, I have to save 100 rupees to get Rs. 105 at the end of the year but if is more than 5 per cent 1 need to save less than 100 rupees. Hence, the net influence of the rate of interest seems to be in determinate. This leaves income as the major determinant of consumption spending.

Average and Marginal Propensities to Consume

The relationship between income and consumption is measured by the average and the marginal propensities to consume. The average propensity to consume is a relationship between total consumption and total income in a given time period, while the marginal propensity to consume measures the incremental change in consumption as a result of a given increment in income. In other words, average propensity to consume is the ratio of consumption to income. But the marginal propensity to consume is the ratio of change in consumption to the change in income.

Thus

$$\text{apc} = \frac{C}{Y}$$

where C stands for consumption and Y for income;

$$\text{mpc} = \frac{\Delta C}{\Delta Y}$$

ΔC is incremental change in consumption.

ΔY is incremental change in income.

The normal relationship between income and consumption is such that when income increases consumption also increases, but by less than the increase in income. In other words, in normal times, the marginal propensity to consume is less than one. It is drawn as a straight line with a slope of less than one. This slope indicates the percentage of additional disposable income that will be spent. It is less than one or unity, because it is assumed that the whole additional income is not spent, *i.e.*, a certain percentage of it is spent and the remainder is saved.

Take the following table:–

(*Rupees*)		
Income	*Consumption*	*Saving*
100	75	25
120	90	30
140	105	35
180	135	45
220	165	55

The figures of the above table have been plotted in the diagram Fig. 42.1 where income is represented on the X-axis and consumption on the Y-axis. OL is the line which makes an angle of 45° with both the axes and any point on this straight line will be equidistant from both the axes. Should the income-consumption curve coincide with this line, it will mean that the marginal propensity to consume is equal to one which is not normally true. Hence, the income-consumption curve OP lies below the 45° line through its entire length. The marginal propensity to consume will be measured by the tangent of the angle that the income-consumption curve makes with X-axis, *etc.*,

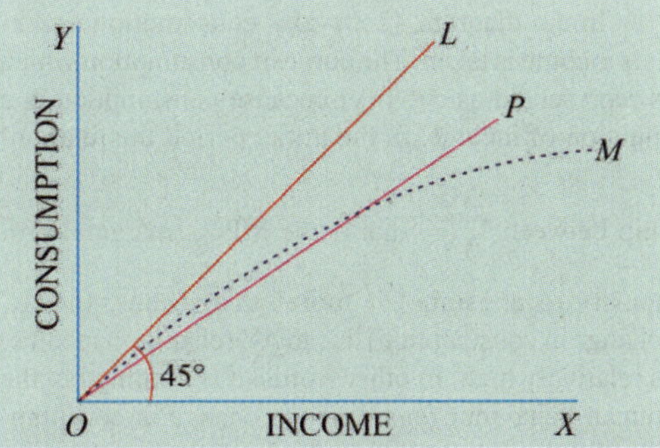

Fig. 42.1. Income-Consumption Relationship.

$mpc = \tan \angle \text{POX}$

The curve as we have drawn turns out to be a straight line rising from the origin, which means that the marginal propensity to consume is constant throughout. This, however, need not be so and the curve may well become flatter as income rises, for as more and more consumption needs have been satisfied, a greater share of an increase in income than before may be saved. The dotted curve OM represents such a relationship showing that as income rises, marginal propensity to consume becomes smaller and smaller.

There is some level of disposable income at which the entire income is spent. This is often called a "point of zero savings". Below this level of disposable income, the consumption expenditure will exceed the disposable income. There may be cases in which the consumer has no income at all. In such cases, the income-consumption curve may not rise from the origin but from further left showing that when income is zero, consumption is not zero and that the individual is living on his past savings. These complicated cases, however, we are not going to consider. From individual consumption-income relation, we can construct a consumption-income curve for the economy as a whole.

Income	Consumption	Savings	$APC = \frac{C}{Y}$	$APS = \frac{S}{Y}$	$MPC = \frac{\Delta C}{\Delta Y}$	$MPS = \frac{\Delta S}{\Delta Y}$
1000	950	50	$\frac{950}{1000} = 0.95$	$\frac{50}{1000} = 0.05$	—	—
1100	1040	60	$\frac{1040}{1100} = 0.94$	$\frac{60}{1100} = 0.06$	$\frac{90}{100} = 0.9$	$\frac{10}{100} = 0.1$
1200	1125	75	$\frac{1125}{1200} = 0.9375$	$\frac{75}{1200} = 0.062$	$\frac{85}{100} = 0.85$	$\frac{15}{100} = 0.15$
1300	1205	95	$\frac{1205}{1300} = 0.926$	$\frac{95}{1300} = 0.073$	$\frac{80}{100} = 0.80$	$\frac{20}{100} = 0.2$
1400	1280	120	$\frac{1280}{1400} = 0.914$	$\frac{120}{1280} = 0.093$	$\frac{75}{100} = 0.75$	$\frac{25}{100} = 0.25$

Keynesian "Consumption Function" Concepts

APC = Average Propensity to consume
MPC = Marginal Propensity to consume
APS = Average Propensity to save
MPS = Marginal Propensity to save.

$$APC = \frac{C}{Y}$$

C = Total Consumption and
Y = Total Income

$MPC = \dfrac{\Delta C}{\Delta Y}$ It is nothing but the ratio of change in consumption due to the ratio of change in income. Mathematically if we take the derivative of total consumption function, we get the 'MPC'.

$$APS = \frac{S}{Y}$$

S = Savings = Y = Income

It is generally referred as average savings.

$$MPS = \frac{\Delta S}{\Delta Y}$$

It is nothing but percentage or ratio of change in savings due to percentage or ratio of change in income. If we take the derivative of total savings function, we obtain the 'MPS'.

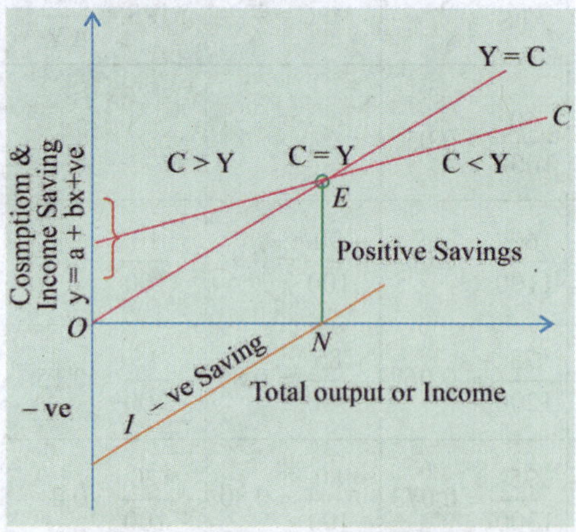

Fig. 42.2. Propensity to consume and save.

In the above diagram 'C' is consumption line, the 45° line is Y = C, (income = consumption) on y-axis consumption, savings and on x-axis, total output and income is measured. At point E, consumption = income. [C =Y], before 'E' (C > Y) consumption is greater than income, at this point savings is negative or the individual is either using his past savings or borrowing money to fulfill his consumption needs. After point 'E' on the right hand side Y > C or C < Y, that means the consumption is less than income.

The Keynesian Psychological law of consumption states that as the income increases than the consumption also increases but less than proportionate. In general we can say that in a number of developing countries, a large section of their population may be experiencing, the first case *viz*. C > Y, where as in most of the developed countries a majority of the people may be in the state of Y > C.

The Keynesian psychological law of consumption is expressed in the diagram below.

In the diagram 42.3 y-axis consumption and x-axis income is taken. The curve of consumption which is represented as c = f (y) because consumption is a function of income. In the initial period the relationship between $\dfrac{\Delta C}{\Delta Y}$ that is the MPC, (marginal propensity to consume) is more that means, the ΔC (change in consumption) due to ΔY (change in income) is relatively high. In other words, it is nothing but the human behaviour regarding the change in consumption due to change in income, is relatively more. As we move towards right it is clear that ΔY is changing by the same amount but ΔC is decreasing. In the second curve $\dfrac{\Delta C}{\Delta Y}$ is comparatively very less than the first case.

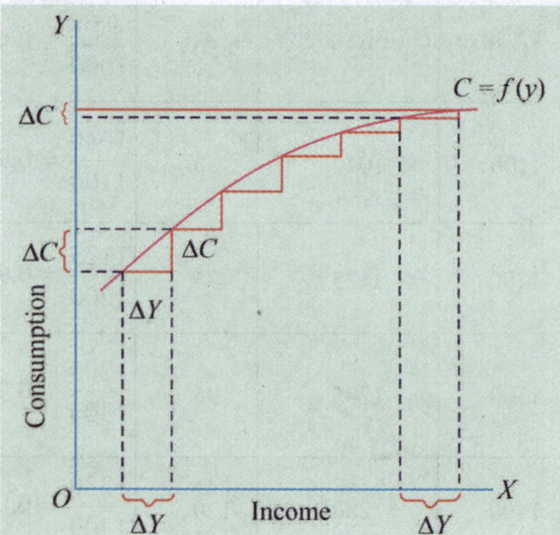

Fig. 42.3. Consumption function.

This is what Keynes wanted to show that as income increases, consumption also increases but relatively with lower and lower rate. This is referred as Keynesian psychological law of consumption.

Propensity to Save

The income-consumption relation can be used to derive also the savings-income relation, for income not consumed is income saved (see the table in first column). Now plotting savings on Y-axis and income on X-axis, we get the saving-income curve ON in diagram 42.4. Savings corresponding to a given level of income can also be read off from the distance between a point on income-consumption curve and corresponding point on the 45° line (Fig. 42.1). Just as the marginal propensity to consume is measured by the slope of the income-consumption curve, similarly the marginal propensity to save is given by the slope of the income-saving curve. Marginal propensity to save is the increment in savings caused by a given increment in income. The marginal propensity to save is always one **minus** marginal propensity to consume.

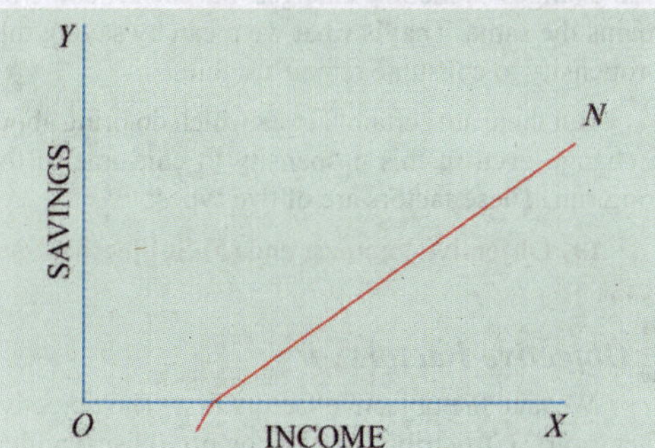

Fig. 42.4. Savings-Income Curve.

$$\text{Marginal propensity to save } mps = \frac{\Delta s}{\Delta y}$$

$$= 1 - \frac{\Delta c}{\Delta y}$$

Average propensity to save or *aps*

$$= \frac{S}{Y} = \frac{\text{total saving}}{\text{total income}}.$$

KEYNES' LAW OF CONSUMPTION

Keynes propounded a Law based on the analysis of consumption function. This law is called Fundamental Law of Consumption or Psychological Law of Consumption. It states that aggregate consumption is a function of aggregate disposable income.

Propositions of the Law

This law consists of three related propositions: (*a*) When aggregate income increases, consumption expenditure will also increase but by a somewhat smaller amount. The reason is that as income increases, more and more of our wants get satisfied, hence not as much is again spent on consumption as the increase in income. Consumption expenditure will no doubt increase but not to the same extent as increase in income.

(*b*) The second proposition is that when income increases, the increment of income will be divided in same proportion between saving and consumption. This really follows from the first proposition. Since consumption spending does not increase at the same rate as the increase in income, a part of the increase is saved and only a part is consumed. That is why consumption and savings go side by side. What is not consumed is saved. Saving is, thus, the complement of consumption.

(*c*) The third proposition included in Keynes' Psychological Law is that as income increases both consumption spending and savings will go up. An increment of income is unlikely to lead either to less spending or less savings than before. It will seldom happen that a person may decrease his consumption or his savings when he has got more income. He will spend a little more than before and also save more than before.

These three propositions form Keynes' Psychological Law of Consumption.

Assumptions

This law is based on three assumptions:

(*i*) It is assumed that habits of the people regarding spending do not change or that the propensity to consume remains the same. Normally, the propensity to consume does remain the same; it is more or less stable. This means that we assume that only income changes, whereas the other variables like income distribution, price movements, growth of population, *etc.*, remain more or less constant.

(*ii*) The second assumption is that the conditions remain normal; for instance there is no hyperinflation or there is no war or other abnormal conditions.

(*iii*) The third assumption is that of a capitalistic laissez-faire economy. In an economy, where the State interferes with consumption or productive enterprise, the law will not hold good. In that case, the government may check consumption even when income increases. If a country is very poor, the question of choosing between consumption and saving does not really rise. This law can, therefore, apply to a free economy and in peace time and over a short period.

These assumptions are more or less valid in a short time and in normal conditions. We can, therefore, say that Keynes' Law is a rough approximation to the actual macro-behaviour of free consumers in the normal short period. It is true that, as a rule and on an average, as income increases, consumption will increase, but not by as much as the increase in income.

There is one and only essential characteristic of the slope of the consumption function, *viz*., the marginal propensity to consume. $\frac{\Delta C}{\Delta Y}$ will be less than unity. It ultimately results in low-consumption and high-saving economy. This law boils down to this that the position and the shape of the consumption function curve depends entirely on income That is consumption can be increased only by increasing income.

Implications

Some implications of Keynes' Law may be noted. One implication is that since consumption largely depends on income and consumption function is more or less stable, it is necessary to increase investment to fill up the gap of declining consumption as income increases. If this is not done, increased output will not be profitable. This law, therefore, underlines the crucial importance of investment.

This law states that even when income increases, consumption lags behind. Hence general over-production is possible. The government will have to step in to remedy the situation. The policy of laissez-faire will not do. If somehow consumption is not increased, marginal efficiency of capital will go down. The demand for capital will diminish and all economic progress will come to a standstill.

Keynes' Law explains the turning points in the business cycle. When the trade cycle has reached the highest point of prosperity, income has gone up. But since consumption does not correspondingly go up, the downward cycle starts, for demand has lagged behind. In the same manner, when the business cycle has touched the lowest point, the cycle starts upwards, because consumption cannot be diminished beyond a certain point. This is due to the stability of marginal propensity to consume.

Also, since marginal propensity to consume is less than unity, this law explains the over-saving gap. As income goes on increasing, consumption does not increase as much. Hence saving process proceeds cumulatively and there arises a danger of over-saving.

Keynes' law also explains the unique nature of income generation. If money is injected into the economic system, it will increase consumption but to a smaller extent than increase in income. This again is due to the fact that consumption does not increase along with increase in income.

To sum up, we can say that since marginal propensity to consume is less than unity, it brings out (*a*) the crucial importance of investment, (*b*) possibility of general over-production, (*c*) declining tendency of the marginal efficiency of capital, (*d*) turning points of business cycles, (*e*) danger of over-saving and (*f*) unique nature of income generation.

FACTORS INFLUENCING CONSUMPTION FUNCTION

When we say that the propensity to consume is stable, it does not mean the consumption expenditure remains constant. Consumption expenditure does no doubt vary as income varies. But consumption changes according to a set pattern. The amount of consumption changes as income changes, but the schedule remains the same. That is what we mean by saying that propensity to consume remains stable.

But there are certain factors which do bring about a change even in this propensity to consume in the long run. These factors are of two types:

(*a*) Objective Factors; and **(*b*) Subjective Factors.**

Objective Factors

We take the objective factors first. The objective factors are: (*i*) distribution of income, (*ii*) fiscal policy, (*iii*) substantial changes in rate of interest, (*iv*) changes in business expectations, (*v*) windfall gains and losses, (*vi*) liquidity preference.

Apart from the size of national income, consumption behaviour of the economy will also be influenced by the **pattern of income distribution.** It will be generally observed that the average and marginal propensities to consume of the poor people are greater than those of the rich. If, for example, you give an additional 10-rupee note to a poor man, the assumption is that of this additional income, he will spend a greater proportion than will be the case if the same amount were given to a rich man. This is because the poor man has a lot of unsatisfied wants and he is likely to seize every opportunity that comes his way to satisfy them. On the other hand, the rich have already a high standard of living and relatively less urgent wants remain to be satisfied, so that in their case, an addition to their incomes is more likely to be saved than spent on consumption.

Consumption is typically the function of the poor

and saving typically the function of the rich. Therefore, given the national income, a more equal distribution of incomes will make for a higher marginal propensity to consume and, therefore, will raise the value of the multiplier.

Similarly, **fiscal policy** of the government will also influence the consumption behaviour of an economy. A reduction in taxation will leave more post-tax incomes with the people and this will stimulate higher expenditure on consumption; an increase in taxes will depress consumption. Of the two types of taxes, *i.e.*, direct and indirect, the latter will have more immediate effect on consumption than the former, particularly when direct taxes are progressive in their incidence. Commodity taxes penalise consumer expenditure directly by raising the prices of the commodities while taxes on income reduce commonly indirectly by reducing the post-tax income of the individual.

Hence, the structure of fiscal system has an important influence on the consumption behaviour of the economy. Changes in fiscal policy are liable to bring about shift in the consumption-income curve. Modern trend towards welfare state financed by progressive taxation tends to shift upwards the consumption function.

Business expectations by affecting the incomes of certain classes of people affect consumption function, The **windfall losses and gains** arising out of changes in capital values affect the 'saving brackets' mostly and not the spending sections. Hence, their influence on consumption function is not so well marked.

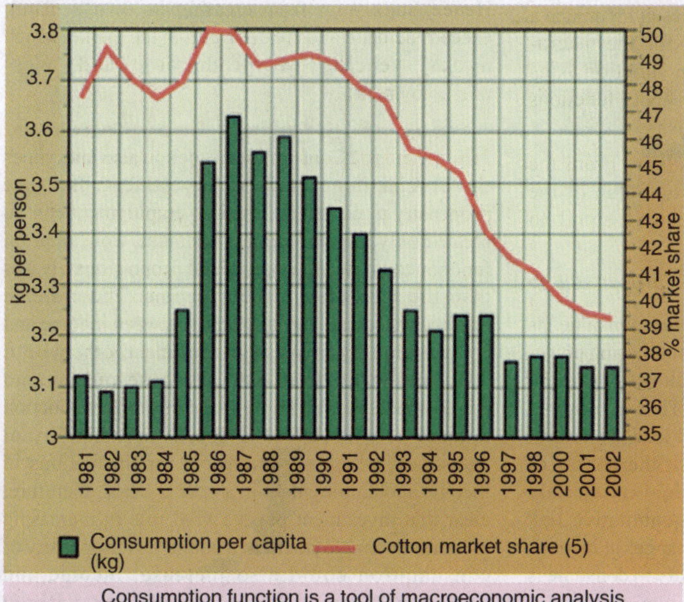

Consumption function is a tool of macroeconomic analysis.

Also, if people prefer to keep their **income in liquid form,** consumption is reduced correspondingly.

Subjective Factors

It is the **subjective factors** which, according to Keynes, basically underlie and determine the propensity to consume. Keynes laid stress on the role of the psychology of human nature in determining the consumption function. Subjective factors relate both to the behaviour pattern of individuals and of business corporations.

As regards motives which lead individuals to save, Keynes mentioned factors such as building of reserves for unforeseen contingencies as illness or unemployment; the desire to provide for anticipated future needs such as daughter's marriage and son's education; the desire to enjoy an enlarged future income by investing funds out of current income, the desire to bequeath a fortune to one's heirs; the enjoyment of a sense of independence, power to do things and to hold one's head high in the society, and for some people the satisfaction of pure miserliness.

In regard to the behaviour patterns of business corporations, among the factors which induce them to save, Keynes mentioned: the desire to expand one's business; the desire to face emergencies successfully; the desire to demonstrate successful management; and the desire to ensure sufficient financial provision against depreciation and obsolescence.

We may repeat that the factors mentioned above can only produce effect in the long run. Over a short period, the propensity to consume remains stable more or less.

Since consumption function is a major factor determining the level of income and employment in the country, it is worthwhile considering what measures can be adopted to stimulate consumption. This, in turn, would stimulate investment and add to the national income and create more employment.

Measures for Raising Consumption

(*i*) Redistribution of Income. If income is redistributed in favour of the poor, whose propensity to consume is higher, from the rich whose propensity to save is greater, it will go a long way in raising the consumption function.

***(ii)* Comprehensive Social Security.** The weaker sections of the society can be helped to increase their consumption through social security measures like unemployment doles, old-age pension, sickness insurance, *etc*. It will solve the paradox of thrift, which usually characterises the affluent sections of society.

***(iii)* Liberal Wage Policy.** This will help the workers, who constitute the masses, in raising their living standards and increasing their consumption.

***(iv)* Credit Facilities.** Poor and middle class people can be enabled to buy more consumer goods through liberal consumer credit. The nationalised banks in India are trying to do something in this direction.

IMPORTANCE OF CONSUMPTION FUNCTION

Consumption function is not to be considered merely a subject of study and analysis. It has a great theoretical and practical importance. All countries want to remove unemployment from their midst, raise their national income and enjoy prosperity. For this purpose a policy of planned economic development is essential. In the formulation of this policy, consumption function plays a very useful role.

We briefly discuss below the importance of consumption from various points of view:

Important Tool of Macro-economic Analysis. Consumption function is an important tool of macro-economic analysis given to us by Keynes. Without the consumption function, we would not have been able to find a determinate link between changes in investment and the resultant changes in income of a country. From this point of view, for the macro-economic theory, the consumption function is as important a tool as the demand and supply functions are in the theory of firm and the industry.

The value of the Multiplier. From the consumption function, we derive the value of the multiplier, which as we have seen is equal to $\frac{1}{1 - \text{mpc}}$. Here mpc is marginal propensity to consume. Since marginal propensity to consume is less than unity, an initial injection of purchasing power into the income stream leads to a multiple expansion of total income in a peculiar way. That is, original injection of money into the economy leads to several successive increments of income in the course of **responding to the increase in original purchasing power.** The multiplier gives us a quantitative link between changes in investment and changes in income. If, for example, the marginal propensity to consume is $\frac{3}{4}$, we know that the multiplier will be 4 so that if investment increases by say, Rs. 1,000, national income will rise by Rs. 4,000. Even before Keynes, the economists knew that changes in investment bring about changes in income but by how much and through what process was not clear, till Keynes gave us tools of consumption function and the multiplier.

Invalidates Say's Law. Consumption function helps to invalidate Say's Law which said that supply creates its own demand. Since marginal propensity to consume is less than unity, the whole of the income is not spent on the output produced. According to Say's Law, general over-production in the country is not possible since supply is supposed to create its own demand. This law may hold good in the long run, but not in the short run. In the long run, the market forces establish equilibrium automatically so that demand may be equated to supply. But no such automatic adjustment is possible in the short run. Hence, for some time, there may occur general overproduction. According to Say's Law, an act of producing is simultaneously an act of creating proportional effective demand. There is no doubt production creates value equal to itself but that value is not **wholly** spent then and there. Since marginal propensity to consume is less than unity, the classical law of markets does not hold good, because the entire output cannot be taken off the market or the entire income is not spent. We know that marginal propensity to consume is less than unity, *i.e.*, as income increases, consumption increases less than increase in income. Hence, supply far from creating its own demand, exceeds demand and creates a glut in the market which means general overproduction and mass unemployment.

Shows Crucial Importance of Investment. Consumption function also underlines the crucial importance of investment. Because propensity to consume is stable, employment can be created only by increasing investment. Consumption function tells us that people spend proportionately less than the increases in their income. Therefore, it becomes necessary to fill the gap between income and consumption by increasing investment, otherwise it will not be profitable to increase output and employment. We also know that consumption function is more or less stable. Hence, it is instability of investment which is responsible for fluctuations in income and employment in a country. It is, therefore, clear that investment plays a vital role in increasing income and employment in a country. If propensity of consumption could also increase, income and employment could be increased even without

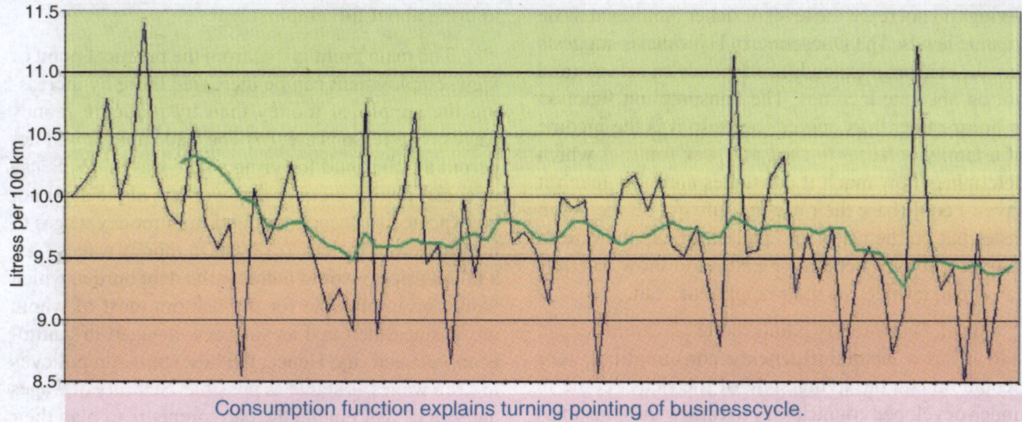

Consumption function explains turning pointing of businesscycle.

increasing investment. But, since consumption function is stable, investment is the crucial and initiating determinant of the levels of income and employment.

Explains the Declining Marginal Efficiency of Capital. Consumption function explains the declining marginal efficiency of capital. Since consumption function does not increase which could raise the level of consumption expenditure, the prospective yield of capital assets falls. Once the demand for capital goods decreases, the marginal productivity of capital cannot rise unless the marginal propensity to consume rises. Thus, the fall in the marginal productivity could be checked, if the marginal propensity to consume could be increased. Hence, the marginal efficiency tends to decline because the demand for goods is discouraged on account of the marginal propensity to consume not rising or the marginal propensity to save not falling. It is the stability of the marginal propensity to consume which explains the declining marginal efficiency of capital.

Explains the Turning Points of the Business Cycle. Consumption function explains the turning points of the business cycle. The trade cycle takes the downward course because the marginal propensity to consume is less than unity, *i.e.*, the people do not spend proportionately more as their income increases. Similarly, the consumption function explains the upturn of the business cycle. This is due to the fact that since consumption is stable, people are unable to cut down their consumption expenditure to the full extent of a decrease in their income. It shows the danger of permanent over-saving gap and thus explains the secular decline in the marginal efficiency of capital.

Thus, consumption function occupies a very important place in the theory of employment.

POST-KEYNESIAN DEVELOPMENTS REGARDING CONSUMPTION FUNCTION

There have been several developments and refinements in regard to consumption function since Keynes. These have been briefly noticed below:

Duesenberry Doctrine

The Ratchet Effect. Among the factors affecting consumption function, we may take a note of the observations made by Prof. Duesenberry known as the **"Duesenberry Hypothesis."** He says that in matter of consumption, an individual is not merely influenced by current income, but also by the standard of living he has enjoyed in the past. There is no doubt that consumption expenditure will decrease as income decreases, but not to the same extent since it is difficult to depart from the standard of living to which a person has got accustomed. The consumers are not easily reconciled to fall in their income. They do not find it easy to scale down their consumption as their income falls. On the other hand, they try hard to maintain their position and status among their neighbours. They do not want their neighbours to know that they cannot now afford to keep to their former mode of life. Whatever the reason, a study of family budgets has revealed that a fall in income leads to a smaller reduction in consumer expenditure. Consumption, as a proportion of income, goes up as income increases but does not fall in the same proportion as income falls. In other words, the consumption function is not reversible. This is known as the **'Ratchet effect'.**

Demonstration Effect. Statistical evidence suggests that after the families have adjusted to the change in their incomes, they save roughly the same proportion of their income as before. As income increases, the poor families no doubt save more but their savings do not reach the level of richer families at those income levels. The Duesenberry Hypothesis suggests that the consumer expenditure depends on **relative** and not on absolute incomes. The consumption function is linear rather than curved, because it is the income of a family **relative to that of other families** which determines how much it consumes and how much it saves. People base their expenditure not on their own tastes but on the tastes and pattern of expenditure of their neighbours. People are anxious to show that they can spend as much as their neighbours can.

Prof. Duesenberry points to the **"Demonstration Effect"** as a factor influencing consumption. Poor people imitate the living style of the rich. People in under-developed countries try to follow the consumption pattern of the affluent nations. This is dangerous because money which should be saved and invested is spent on consumption goods. This retards economic growth (For fuller discussion see Ch. 70).

We may also take note of two other factors which affect a person's consumption, *viz*., (*a*) 'Pigou Effect' or Real Balances Effect and (*b*) Government expenditure.

Pigou Effect. When prices fall as a result of a cut in money wages, the purchasing power of money with a consumer increases or there is increase in the real value of money balances. People feel that they are now 'better off' and they increase their consumption expenditure. This leads to economic expansion or increase in G.N.P. The way in which an increase in the real value of money balances results in the expansion of economic activity has been described as the "Pigou effect" after the late Prof. A.C. Pigou. It is also called the real balances effect.

Arthur C Pigou (1877-1959).

Many modern economists are sceptical about the real balances effect being so strong as to bring about full employment. But it seems to be theoretically possible. Keynes seems to be agreed that theoretically it is possible to bring about full employment by sufficiently lowering the money wages. But according to him the process was so slow that it could be ignored as a practical possibility. It would be more realistic to assume that wages are not so flexible as to permit the working of the Pigou effect to bring about full employment.

The main point is that from the practical point of view, employment can be increased more by increasing the supply of money than by reducing money wages. The reasons are: (*a*) The trade unions will not permit an all round lowering of the wages. (*b*) Sense of social justice dictates that workers alone shall not be expected to accept a reduction in money wages to increase employment, (*c*) A cut in money wages (*i.e.*, a fall in prices) would increase the debt burden which would be intolerable for the debtors most of whom are businessmen and as such are engaged in gainful economic activity. Hence, the best short-run policy is to keep wages as stable as possible. Stability of wages and prices will enable the entrepreneurs to plan their business properly so as to minimise the possibility of economic fluctuations. It will ensure a steady employment level.

Government Consumption. Another factor which affects consumption and therefore the level of economic activity is the government expenditure or government consumption. The size of government expenditure is determined by political attitudes and decisions. It differs from country to country and in the same country it differs over time. It depends on the decision of the community about the extent to which it would meet its needs collectively rather on an individual basis. It should, however, be borne in mind that it is the total expenditure on public and private account which determines the level of economic activity and not how much is spent by the government and how much by private individuals. Thus, the division of expenditure into public and private has little bearing on the level of income and employment in the country.

THREE THEORIES OF CONSUMPTION FUNCTION

In the short run consumption increases less than increase in income, but it increases equal to increase in income in the long run. Hence consumption-income relationship is one of non-proportionality in the short run but that of proportionality in the long run.

There are three different theories explaining consumption-income relationship: (*a*) Absolute Income Theory; (*b*) The Relative Income Hypothesis and (*c*) The Permanent Income Hypothesis.

Absolute Income Theory

According to Keynes, on average "men increase their consumption as their income increases, but not by as much as the increase in income." In other words, the average propensity to consume goes down as the absolute level of income goes up. Hence, according to this theory, the level of consumption expenditure depends upon the absolute level of income and the relationship between the two variables is non-proportionate. However, it is pointed out that although this relationship is one of non-proportionality, yet there is illusion of proportionality caused by factors other than income, *viz*., accumulated wealth, migration to urban areas, new consumer goods, etc. Owing to such factors as these, the consumers spend more and the relationship appears to be proportional.

Absolute Income Hypothesis

Keynes was of the opinion that the level of income determines the level of consumption. Accordingly, lower the income, lower is the level of consumption and vice-versa. [Consumption function, $c = f(y)$]. Further the absolute income hypothesis is that, the income determines the consumption, as the income increases, consumption also increases but less than the proportionate.

$Y = a + bx$

Where Y = income, a = autonomous consumption, b = the change in consumption due to change in x = change in income (a = autonomous consumption even if $y = 0$ $c = +ve$).

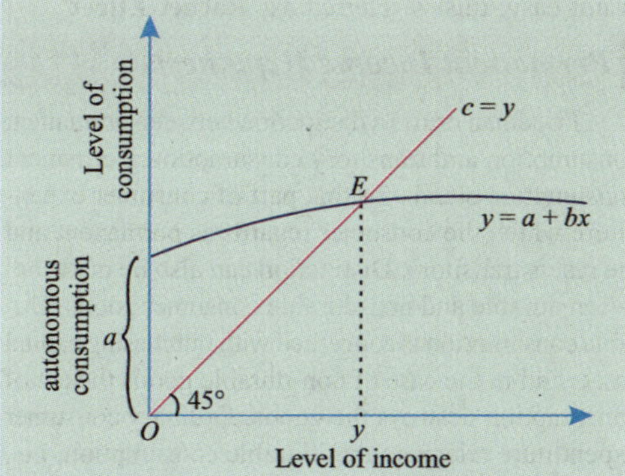

It clearly indicates that beyond the point 'E' as income increases, consumption increase, less than the proportionate, that means APC goes on falling and APS increasing, (APC = c/y, & APS = s/y). Simon Kuznets (1946) studies revealed that the short run consumption functions (Y = a + bx) in the long run becomes constant. It is not proportionate but becomes constant that is 0.9. (APC = MPC). Simon Kuznets (1946), James Tobin (1951), Arthur Smithie (1945), and also Edward Shapiro (1989) showed that in the long run the consumption and incomes relation are more or less proportional (APC = MPC). Kuznet did not take into account the absolute consumption that is when income = 0 the consumption is positive. He considers only the relationship between income and consumption from the origin.

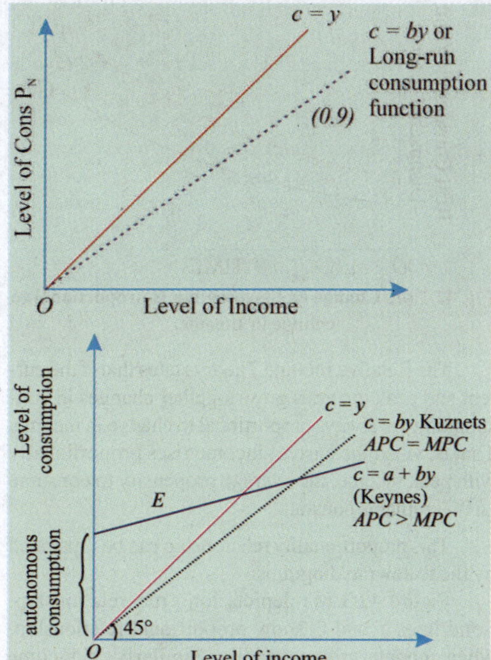

Keynes considered the increase in accumulated wealth, migration to urban areas, new consumer goods (modern day FMCG's) consumption pattern of the old people and to add the modern day technique of marketing strategies and promotional measures such as discount, guarantees, warranties, services after sales etc. influences the consumption pattern.

Relative Income Hypothesis

The Relative Income Hypothesis was first introduced by Dorothy Brady and Rose Friedman. It states that the consumption expenditure does not depend on the absolute level of income but instead on the relative level of income. Dussenberry lent it empirical and psychological support.

According to Dussenberry, there is a strong tendency for the people to emulate and initiate the consumption pattern of their neighbours. This is the 'demonstration effect' already explained above i.e., relative income affecting consumption.

Also, the relative income theory tells us that the level of consumption spending is determined by the households' level of current income relative to the highest level of income earned previously. People are then reluctant to revert to the previous low level of consumption. This is the 'Rachet Effect' discussed above.

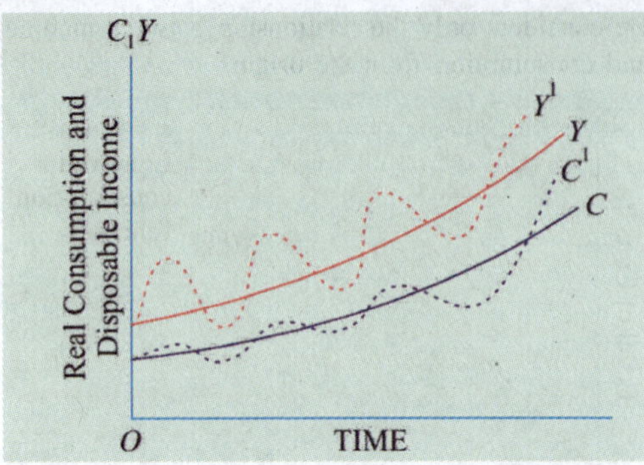

Fig. 42.5 (*a*). **Change in consumption is proportional to change in Income.**

The Relative Income Theory states that if the current and peak incomes grow together changes in consumption are always proportional to change in income. That is, when the current income rises proportionally with peak income, the average propensity to consume (APC) remains constant.

This proportionality relationship can be illustrated by the following diagrams:

Figure 42.3 (*a*) depicts long run relationship. Solid lines Y and C show proportional relationship, when income grows steadily. Similarly, if income grows in spurts and dips, the response of consumption is the same. Thus C′ Y′ show proportional relationship. Fig. 42.5 (*b*), however, shows non-proportional relationship. Here we have only one Cycle as compared with many shown in Fig. (42.5(*a*).

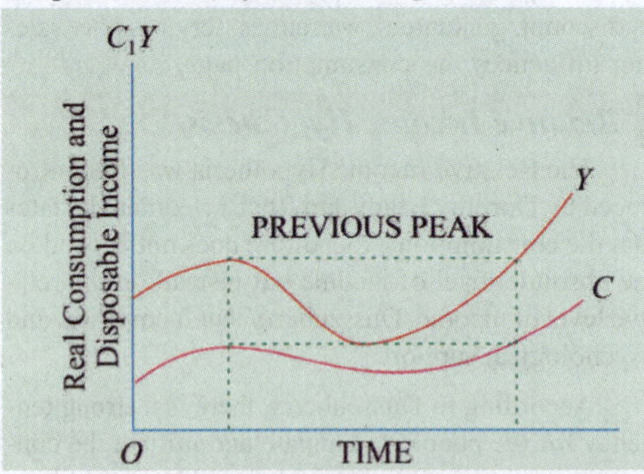

Fig. 42.5 (*b*). **Change in consumption is not proportional to change in Income.**

Relative Income Hypothesis

Dussenberry took into account the relative income hypothesis, as the income increase, the consumption increases not due to 'absolute' concept, but due to relative concept.

(a) As income increases people copy the living and consumption behavior pattern of higher income level therefore the consumption increases (Demonstration Effect), on the other;

(b) As the income decreases, the consumption does not decrease with the same rate (Rachet Effect)

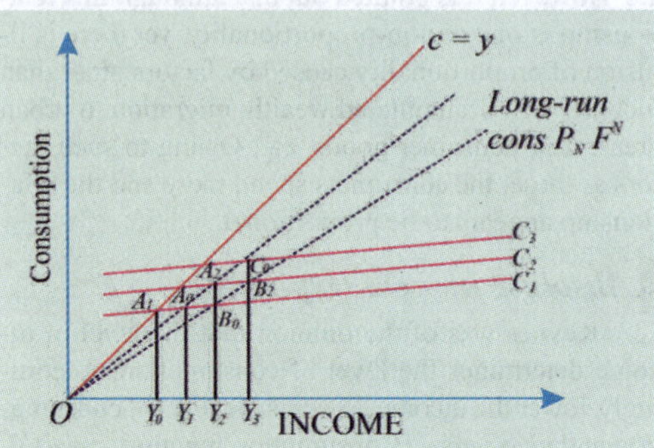

C_1, C_2, C_3, short run consumption A, B, C, are consumers.

(1) Let consumer 'A' is at 'A_0' on 'C_1' consumption curve at income level 'OY_1' As his income 'increases to 'OY_2' the consumption shifts on 'C_2' this is the movement from 'A_0' to A_2 is '**Demonstration Effect**'. On the other hand if the income decreases from 'OY' to 'OY_0' the consumption does not shift to point 'A_1', movement from 'A_0' to 'A_1' is difficult and it is not easy, this is referred as '**Rachet Effect**'

Permanent Income Hypothesis

Friedman draws a distinction between permanent consumption and transitory consumption. Permanent consumption stands for that part of consumer expenditure which the consumer regards as permanent and the rest is transitory. Distinction can also be made between durable and non-durable consumer goods. Durable consumption is concerned with purchasing capital assets and in the case of non-durable goods the act of consumption destroys the goods. Ordinary consumer expenditure relates to non-durable consumption, *i.e.*, consumption of goods which are quickly used in consumption. These are the 'flow' items since a flow of them is being continuously consumed. On the other hand, durable consumption, which relates to the purchase of capital assets, is an act of investment. They are the stock items.

The permanent income hypothesis takes into account this distinction. This hypothesis gives the relationship between permanent income and permanent consumption and states that the ratio between the two does not merely depends on the size of the permanent income, it also depends on some other variables.

Friedman gives his permanent hypothesis in the form of three equations:

(1) $Y = Yp + Yt$

(2) $C = Cp + Ct$

(3) $Cp = k(i,w,u)\ Yp$

Here Y stands for income, Yp is permanent income, Yt is transitory income. Similarly, C stands for consumption; therefore, Cp is permanent consumption and Ct is transitory consumption.

Equation No. (1) means that total income Y is made up of permanent income Yp and transitory income Yt, and equation No. (2) means that total consumption C is equal to permanent consumption Cp and transitory consumption Ct. In other words, the first two equations state that both income and consumption are made up of permanent and transitory elements.

Equation 3 gives the permanent income hypothesis. Look at equation 3 again. As mentioned already, it gives the relationship between permanent income and permanent consumption. It gives the variables on which the ratio between the two depends. These variables are interest (i); the relationship between the income from his property and that from his own abilities and efforts (w); and the preference of the consumer for immediate or transitory consumption as distinguished from addition to his wealth, *i.e.*, permanent consumption (u).

Thus equation (3) means that permanent consumption Cp is a function of (*a*) the rate of interest, (*b*) rates of consumer's income from property and his personal effort, *i.e.*, human and non-human wealth (w) and (*c*) his preference for immediate consumption (u) multiplied by permanent income Yp.

Milton Friedman 1912— 2006

Actually, it is the size of income rather than the rate of interest which determines consumption. As for the second element, *viz.*, human and non-human wealth, statistical evidence suggests that the size of consumption expenditure depends a great deal on the value of consumer's assets. A consumer, who has considerable income from his assets, is likely to spend more on consumption and save a smaller proportion of his income than one who has no assets at all but desires to have them. This shows the importance of (u) in equation (3).

Permanent income is derived both from human and non-human capital of the consumer. The permanent income hypothesis really emphasises the important role of capital assets or wealth in determining the size of consumption. It shows how both income and consumption are closely linked with the consumer's wealth. It is capital and wealth (both human and non-human) which affects the level of consumption rather consumer's income.

Life Cycle Hypothesis [1]

There is another approach to consumer expenditure. It is said that consumption function is affected more by consumer's whole life income rather than his current income. This view has been put forward by Modigliani, Brumberg and Ando.[2] The permanent income hypothesis focusses attention on the income of the consumer earned in recent past as well as expected future earnings (and wealth). But the 'Life cycle' hypothesis makes the consumption function depend upon consumer's whole life income. In childhood, the consumer earns nothing but spends all the same (his parents spend on him); in the middle age, when he comes to have a family, he earns and spends. But he will be earning more than he spends. He tries to save enough to maintain himself in his old age when he will not be able to earn or earn much. Over his life span, the consumer tries to maintain a certain uniform standard and with that end in view he organises whole life's uneven income flows of cash receipts. In other words, he will arrange his income and expenditure in such a manner as to maintain a certain standard of living which he desires.

Assuming a rational age of a community or citizens that, say up to 30 years, the consumption is greater than the income, $(c > y)$ since $y = c$. $Y - c = -s$) (negative saving $-S_1$), after 30 years the income starts increasing and consumption tends to fall in other words, $Y > C$ and savings are positive, up to 60 years,

1. See Stonier and Hauge, *A Text Book of Economic Theory*, p. 476.
2. Modigliani F. and Brumberg R., "*Utility Analysis and Consumption Function*" in Kurihara (ed.), *Post Keynesian Economies*, pp.383-436; and Ando, A and Modigliani, F., The Life Cycle Hypothesis of Saving, *etc.*, American Economic Review, 1963, pp. 55-84.

it continues in such tendency. After 60 years as due to retirement etc, forces the income to decline and consumption continues with the earlier rate, it changes to C > Y, and that is negative savings.

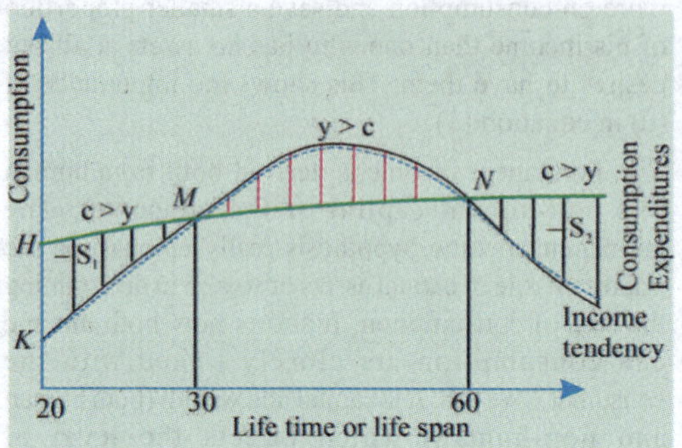

Negative saving $S_1 + S_2 = S$

Positive savings S_3

Modigliani was of the opinion that

$S_3 > S$ [where S_3 = the positive, saving S = negative saving].

On 'X' axis age of the community (lifetime) and on 'Y' axis consumption. Initially the income is lower and consumption is higher generally because education, training, etc. 'OH' is consumption &' OK' is income this shows that there is a negative savings (dis-saving 'S_1') up to point 'M' which is break-even point, where C = Y and savings = 0, as the age increases the income of the community may increase due to more opportunities, abilities ....etc. Y > C, up to break-even point 'N' the consumption is lower and the income is greater, 'S_3' (the + ve saving). Beyond point 'N' further due to 'old age', retirement or so, the income falls and consumption tends to be more or less same or more, this gives negative saving 'S_2' that is C > Y. If we add both negative saving, $S_1 + S_2 = S$ total negative savings and the 'S_3' as positive savings (Area between point 'M' & 'N'), than according to Modigliani $S_3 > S$, that means a community leaves some money for their heir.

If all individuals forming the community earn just enough to maintain their standard of living till the end of their life, such a community will have no net savings. But since nobody can say precisely when he would die it will not be possible for people just to balance their income and expenditure. Hence it is very likely that people will leave some saving at their death. Most people consciously want to leave some money for their heirs. Hence, over life time, people will earn more than they spend and saving is inevitable. The amount of net saving of the community will depend on the growth of population, their age-structure, on income and the amount they desire to leave to their heirs.

Franco Modigliani 1918-2003.

Thus, the life cycle theory links the net saving of the community to the growth rate of population and to the rate of increase in incomes. When in a country population is increasing and people are earning to spend, at any moment of time there will be net saving. Net savings will go on increasing as time passes; there will be more saving in each year than in the previous year. If people are better off than their parents, as is usually the case, more saving will be effected.

The 'Life Cycle' hypothesis seems to be quite realistic and plausible. It may be noted, however, that this hypothesis emphasises income as derived from wealth more than cash receipts. It also draws our attention to the fact that consumers have to make a choice between immediate consumption and accumulating of assets for future use. Thus, **economic theory is progressively moving from theory of consumption to the theory of capital.** In other words, the life cycle hypothesis brings out the fact that consumers build up capital stock which they might hold in cash or invest in various ways and a part of the consumer's stock invested is in durables. It is clear that the theory of consumption function in future is likely to be firmly linked to capital theory. The consumer are keen to build up a stock of capital assets of a certain size which they consider appropriate to their level of income.

Key terms

MPC, APC, MPS, APS, Permanent Income, Life cycle consumption and Savings multiplier, Demonstration effect, Pigou effect, Psychological law of consumption.

QUESTIONS

1. Define the term "Propensity to Consume." Discuss the factors which govern propensity to consume. How is it relevant to employment multiplier?
2. What do you understand by consumption function? Discuss its significance in Keynesian theory of employment.

   Or

   Define marginal propensity to consume, what is its importance in determining the level of income and employment in a country? What measures can be adopted to raise the propensity to consume?
3. Clearly distinguish between Average Propensity to Consume and Marginal Propensity to Consume and Show:—
   (*a*) MPC 1 ;
   (*b*) MPC dectives as income rises, and
   (*c*) Propensity to consume is generally stable.
4. Explain permanent Income hypothesis of consumption.
5. Explain life cycle hypothesis of consumption.
6. Write short notes on (*a*) Absolute Incoune Hypothesis, (*b*) Relative Income Hypothesis.
7. Explain the factors influencing propensity to consume.

DETERMINATIONS OF INCOME AND EMPLOYMENT : INDUCEMENT TO INVEST

Meaning of Investment

It may be stated at the outset that the meaning of investment here is different from the common use of the word. One often hears of a person investing money in buying shares of a company or buying an existing security or bond or property or title to property. These are purely financial transactions and are merely transfers of assets from one person to another. It is an investment by one and disinvestment by another and as such, transactions cancel out. They do not constitute real investment since they do not **add** to the nation's physical stock of capital.

Investment, in the theory of income and employment, means an addition to the nation's physical stock of capital like the building of new factories, new machines as well as any addition to the stock of finished goods or the goods in the pipelines of production. Investment includes additions to inventories as well as to fixed capital. Investment in this sense does not refer to the total stock of capital **in existence,** but **net addition** to this capital over a period of time, say a year.

Thus, investment in the present context does not mean the purchase of **existing** securities or titles—bonds, debentures' shares, *etc.* Such

Investment means creation of capital goods.

transactions do not add to the existing capital but merely mean a change in ownership of the assets already in existence. They do not create income and employment. Real investment, on the other hand, means the purchase of **new** factories, plants and machines, because only newly constructed or created assets create employment or generate income.

Types of Investment

Investment may be counted on the **gross** or the **net** basis. Net investment is gross investment minus depreciation. In the theory of income and employment, investment means net investment and not gross investment.

Investment may be **ex-ante** or planned or anticipated or intended investment; or it may be **ex-post,** *i.e.*, actually realised investment or when investment is not merely planned or intended but which has actually been invested or implemented.

Another classification of investment may be **Private Investment** or **Public Investment. Private Investment** is on private account, *i.e.*, by private individuals and public investment is by the government. Private investment, *i.e.*, by private investors or entrepreneurs is influenced by marginal efficiency of capital (*i.e.*, profit expectations) and the rate of interest. It is profit-elastic. **Public Investment** is by the State or local authorities, such as building of roads, irrigation projects, school buildings, public parks, electricity works, *etc*. In the public investment profit motive does not enter into consideration. It is undertaken for social good and not for private gain.

From the point of view of the theory of income and employment, the more important classification of investment is into autonomous investment and induced investment.

Autonomous Investment. Investment which is independent of the level of income is called autonomous investment. Such investment does not vary with the level of income. In other words, it is **income-inelastic.** Autonomous investment depends more on population growth and technical progress than on anything else. The influence of change in income is not altogether ruled out, because higher income would probably result in more investment. But the influence of income is negligible as compared with the influence of population growth and progress of technical knowledge.

Examples of autonomous investment are 'long range' investments in houses, roads, public buildings and other forms of public investment. Such investment is generally done by the State as necessitated by the growth of population and facilitated by technical progress and not as a result of change in national income. Most of the investment undertaken to promote planned economic development or defence, investment comes under autonomous investment. It also includes long-range investment to bring about technical progress or innovations. In Hicks' words, "Public investment means investment which occurs in direct response to invention and much of the long-range investment (as Harrod calls it) which is only expected to pay for itself over a long period, all of these can be regarded as autonomous investments." These investments are independent of changes in income and are not governed by profit motive. They are generally made by governments and local authorities more for promoting general welfare than for making profit.

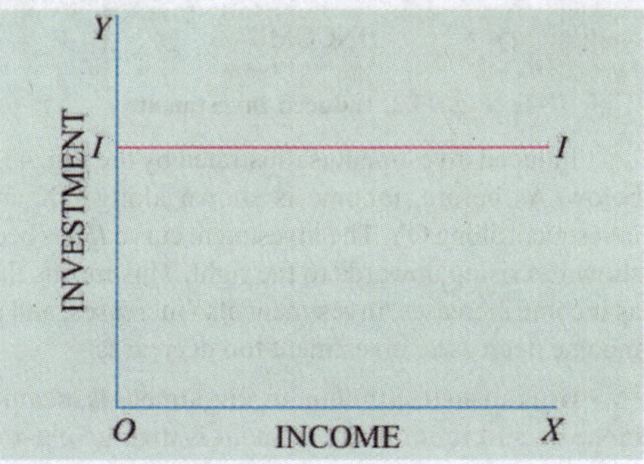

Fig. 43.1. Savings-Income Curve.

Autonomous investment can be represented diagrammatically as in the figure given below. Income is shown along the X-axis OX and investment along the Y-axis OY. II is the investment curve drawn parallel to the X-axis. This means that whatever the level of income (changes in income are shown on OX), investment remains the same.

Induced Investment. Investment which varies with the changes in national income is called induced investment. Changes in national income bring about changes in aggregate demand which in turn affects the volume of investment. When, for instance, national income increases, aggregate demand too increases. Investment has to be undertaken to meet this increased demand. This induced investment is income-elastic, *i.e.*, it increases as income increases, and vice versa.

Induced investment is investment not only in fixed capital but also in inventories which is undertaken to enable the economy to produce a larger output in order to meet the increased demand.

Induced investment is made by the people as a result of changes in income level or consumption. It is also influenced by price changes, interest changes, *etc.* which affect profit possibilities. It is undertaken for the sake of profit or income and it changes with a change in income. Thus induced investment is governed by profit motive. It is sensitive to changes in income, *i.e.*, it is income-elastic.

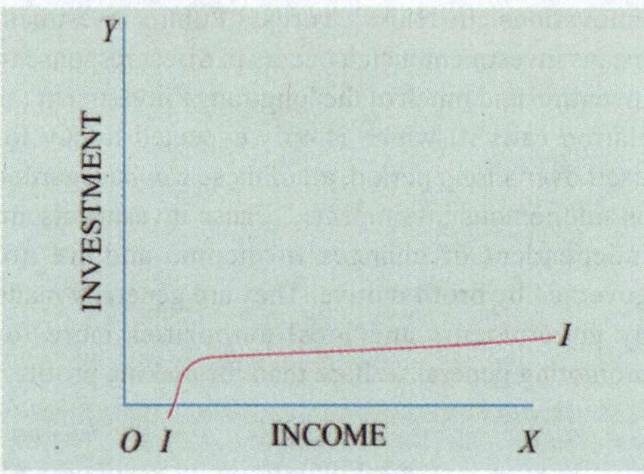

Fig. 43.2. Induced Investment.

Induced investment is illustrated by the Fig. 43.2 below. As before, income is shown along OX and investment along OY. The investment curve *II* has been shown as rising upwards to the right. This means that as income increases, investment also increases, and as income decreases, investment too decreases.

In a nutshell autonomous investment is income-inelastic and induced investment is income-elastic.

Investment is an important economic activity.

Importance of Investment

We have seen that, in the Keynesian system, employment depends upon effective demand. There are two major constituents of effective demand – investment and consumption. Of the two, investment is more volatile and unpredictable as well as a more strategic variable. "A fundamental principle is that as the income of a community increases, consumption will also increase but by less than the increase in income. Hence, in order to have sufficient demand to sustain an increase in employment, there must be increase in real investment equal to the gap between income and consumption out of income. In other words, employment cannot increase, unless investment increases".[1]

In the previous chapter, we have already emphasised the crucial importance of investment. The real solution of the problem of unemployment is to step up the level of investment in the economy. Being a more volatile variable, investment determines effective demand more than its other constituent, *viz.*, consumption spending.

Factors Affecting Investment

We have said above that there are two determinants of income and employment in a country which constitute effective demand, *viz.*, consumption and investment and we have also said that the more important of the two constituents of effective demand is investment. What induces businessmen to undertake investment? Obviously, profit expectations seem to exercise a major influence on investment decisions of businessmen and these profit expectations in turn are influenced by the current and the expected level of economic activity, changes in technique, *etc.*

Broadly speaking, inducement to invest depends on two factors, *viz.*,

(*a*) the marginal efficiency of capital (which according to Keynes is another name for the expected rate of profit); and

(*b*) the rate of interest.

Suppose a man borrows money to invest. He will have to pay interest on the loan. But he expects profit from this investment. He must compare the rate of interest which he has to pay and the rate of profit that he expects to obtain. Obviously, the rate of return or profit must at least be equal to the rate of interest, otherwise no investment will continue to be made. So long as the expected rate of profit exceeds the rate of interest, investment will continue to be made. The yield expected from a new unit of capital is called by Keynes **marginal efficiency of capital.** This marginal efficiency of capital must never fall below the current rate of interest, if investment is to be worthwhile.

Hence, the inducement to invest depends on the marginal efficiency of capital on the one hand and the rate of interest on the other.

1. Dillard, Dudley – *The Economics of J.M. Keynes,* 1958, p. 29.

Of these two determinants of inducement to invest, *viz*., the marginal efficiency of capital and the rate of interest, which is of greater importance? The rate of interest does not quickly change, it is more or less sticky or constant. Hence, the inducement to invest, by and large, **depends on the marginal efficiency of capital.** If the business expectations are good or if the marginal efficiency of capital is high, more investment will be made in spite of high rate of interest. On the contrary, depression or bleak prospects of profits will discourage investment, even if the prevailing rate of interest is low. Thus, fluctuations in investment are mainly due to the fluctuations in the marginal efficiency of capital.

Other Factors. There are some other factors that affect investment. For instance, if a firm has already **excess capacity** and can easily handle increased future demand, it will not go in for further investment to increase its capital equipment.

Technological progress also affects current level of investment. For example, a new invention may render the present capital stock of a firm obsolete and adversely affect its ability to compete. In this case, further investment will be called for.

We may sum up the Keynesian argument at this stage: The level of income and employment depends on (*a*) consumption and (*b*) investment. Consumption being more or less stable, we are left with the more important factor, *viz*., investment. Investment depends on (*a*) the rate of interest and (*b*) marginal efficiency of capital or the expected rate of profit. Now the rate of interest being more or less constant, we are left with the marginal efficiency of capital as the sole determinant of the level of income and employment in a country.

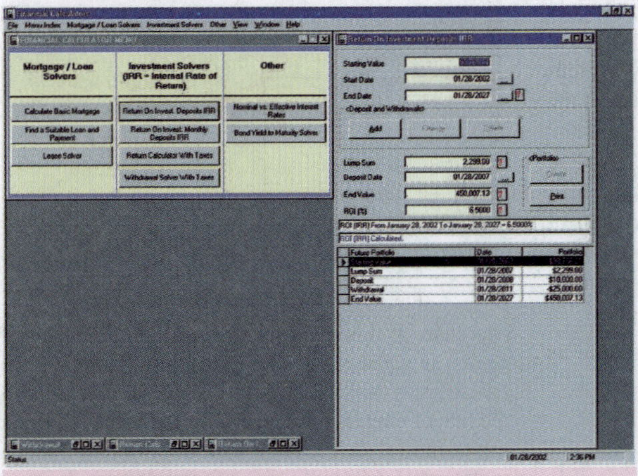

Calculating Returns on investment.

We discuss these two determinants of investment, *viz*., marginal efficiency of capital and the rate of interest, in the following sections.

MARGINAL EFFICIENCY OF CAPITAL

Meaning

In the modern world, an act of investment involves a great amount of risk. It means locking up of funds for a long time to come in the hope of getting profits as a reward over the expected economic life of the capital asset. When an entrepreneur instals a new machine, he is undertaking an act of investment, expecting to reap profits in future from the sale of the output of the machine. But the future by its very nature is uncertain. It is quite possible that when the machine is ready for production, the demand for its product may no longer be there, so that instead of profits there may be losses.

The great uncertainty about the future gives rise to the extreme instability and fluctuations in the rate of investment in modern capitalist economies. To compensate them for bearing these risks, the entrepreneurs want a higher enough rate of profit so as to induce them to take such risks on behalf of the community. If this rate of profit is not adequate, the inducement to invest will be very weak.

The businessmen try to reduce the unpredictably of the future by trying to base their decision in the light of past and present trends. **Marginal efficiency of investment is the highest expected rate of profit which is likely to be had by a marginal increase in the rate of investment.** Since it refers to the expected rate, rather than the current rate of profit, marginal efficiency of investment is liable to a great deal of fluctuations in the short run. **It is the prospective yield which gives the marginal efficiency of capital its most important characteristic, *i.e.*, instability.**

While making investment, the businessmen compare the supply price or replacement cost of the machine and its prospective yield. The marginal efficiency of a capital asset can be calculated by relating the prospective yield of the asset to its supply price. Keynes himself defines marginal efficiency of capital thus: "I define the marginal efficiency of capital as being equal to that rate of discount which would make the present value of the series of annuities given by the returns expected from the capital asset during the life just equal to its supply price". In other words, marginal efficiency of capital is the rate at which prospective yield of an asset is discounted so as to make it just equal to the supply price or replacement cost of the asset. The formula is

Supply Price = Discounted Prospective Yields

$$\text{Or } Cr = \frac{R_1}{1+r} + \frac{R_2}{(1+r)^2} + \frac{R_3}{(1+r)^3} \ldots + \frac{R_n}{(1+r)^n}$$

Here Cr is the replacement cost or supply price. $R_1, R_2 \ldots\ldots R_n$ are the series of the prospective annual returns or yields; r stands for the rate of discount which would make the present value of the series of annual return just equal to the replacement cost or supply price of the capital asset. This is really the marginal efficiency of capital.

The above is the marginal efficiency of a particular asset. But in macro-economics we are concerned with the marginal efficiency of capital in general. The marginal efficiency of capital in general is the highest of all individual marginal efficiencies. We can prepare a schedule of the marginal efficiencies at various levels of investment.

Investment Demand Curve

The marginal efficiency of capital falls as investment increases. There are two reasons for this: One, the installation of a larger number of similar machines leads to a reduction in their prospective yields just as consumption of more units leads to a decrease in marginal utility. Secondly, the prices of such machines will go up as their demand increases. This will add to the costs. Thus costs go up on the one hand and the market price of their products goes down as production increases. Hence, the marginal efficiency of capital goes down as investment increases. This is because with more investment the productive capacity of the economy will increase and this will depress the expected rate of profit. It is clear that marginal efficiency of capital will be different at different levels of capital investment. As investment increases, marginal efficiency of capital goes down. Thus, the curve of marginal efficiency of investment is likely to be a curve falling from left to right.

We can construct an imaginary schedule as under:

Diminishing Marginal Efficiency of Capital

Investment Rs.	*Marginal Efficiency of Capital*
10,000	12%
12,000	10%
14,000	8%
16,000	6%
18,000	4%
20,000	2%

We see from the above schedule that when investment is Rs. 10,000, the marginal efficiency of capital is 12 per cent. But as investment increases, say to Rs. 20,000, the marginal efficiency goes down to 2 per cent.

This schedule can be easily converted into MEC curve as shown in Fig. 43.3 below. On the OX-axis are shown the different amounts of investment and on OY the marginal efficiency of capital and the rate of interest. The MEC curve represents the marginal efficiency of capital. It slopes down from left to the right which means that as investment is increased its marginal efficiency goes down.

Investment at any time depends on the rate of interest prevailing at that time. If the rate of interest is 6 per cent, then it will be seen in Fig. 43.3 that the entrepreneurs will invest Rs. 16,000 in capital goods,

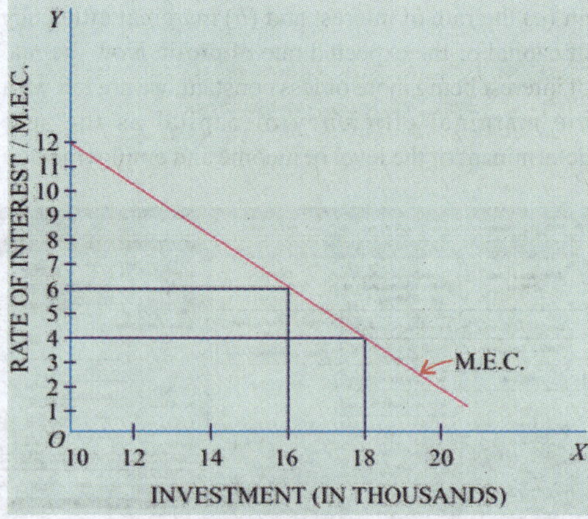

Fig. 43.3. Marginal Efficiency Curve.

because, at this investment, marginal efficiency of capital is equal to the rate of interest. The marginal efficiency of capital represents the investor's return and the rate of interest is his cost. Obviously, the return on capital must at least be equal to the rate of interest, which is its cost. Suppose the rate of interest goes down to

4 per cent, then it will become worthwhile to invest Rs. 18,000. Thus, the marginal efficiency of capital and the rate of interest move together. We may thus conclude that **given a marginal efficiency schedule or curve, the investment will depend on the prevailing rate of interest.**

The Position and Shape of the MEC Curve

The elasticity of the MEC determines the extent to which the volume of investment would change consequent upon changes in the rate of interest. If the MEC is relatively interest-elastic, a little fall in the rate of interest will result in a considerable expansion in the volume of investment. On the other hand, if MEC is relatively interest inelastic, then a considerable fall in the rate of interest may not lead to any increase in the volume of investment. This is shown in the Fig. 43.4 and Fig. 43.5.

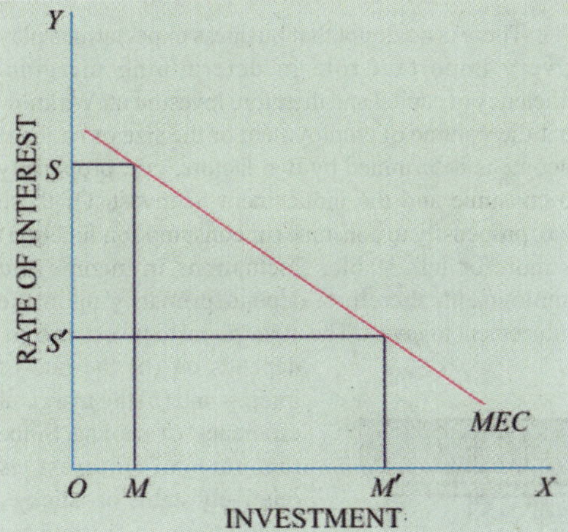

Fig. 43.4. Interest-elastic MEC Curve.

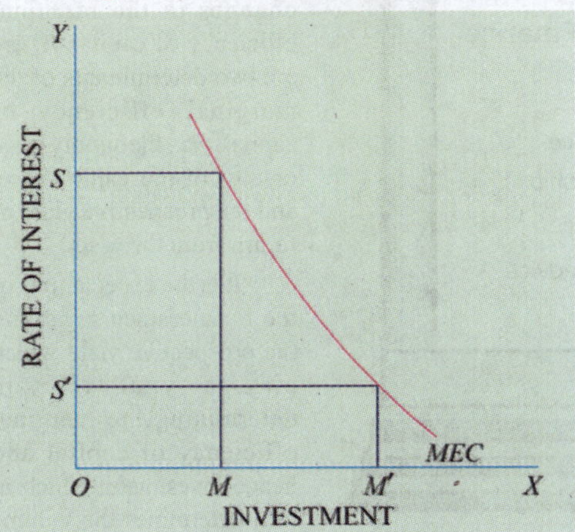

Fig. 43.5. Interest-inelastic MEC Curve.

Shifts in MEC

It can be easily understood that as the expectations regarding the prospective yields change,the marginal efficiency of capital will change too and the MEC curve will shift upwards or downwards.

This is shown in Fig. 43.6 below. Suppose a war breaks out or demand goods increases on account of some other reason. As a result, entrepreneurs' expectations of profit will rise high and the investment demand curve or the MEC curve will shift upwards to MEC′. This means that a given rate of interest, investment will be greater than before. From the Fig. 43.6, it will be seen that whereas the rate of interest *i*, investment was OM before, it now becomes OM′. Similarly, if for some reason demand for goods has decreased bringing down the marginal efficiency of capital to MEC″, at the same rate of interest *i*, investment will only be OM″ as compared with OM before.

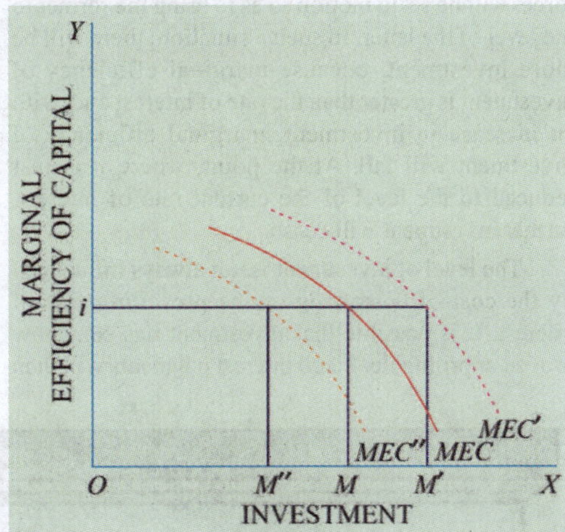

Fig. 43.6. Shifts in Marginal Efficiency of Capital.

Influence of the Rate of Interest. Thus, the rate of interest, along with the marginal efficiency of investment, determines the volme of investment. If the rate of interest is higher than the marginal efficiency of investment, it will not be profitable to create a new physical asset. This is because we assume that the aim of the individual investor is to maximise his money profits. Two courses of action are open to an investor; either he can use his money to create additional physical assets, *i.e.*, he can invest in the Keynesian sense of the term, or else he can lend his money to others at a certain rate of interest. Now, if marginal efficiency of investment is lower than the current rate of interest, it is more profitable to lend one's money rather than use it for creating new assets. On the other hand, if marginal efficiency of investment is higher than the rate of interest, it is better to invest more. At the point, where marginal efficiency of investment equals the current rate of interest, we have the equilibrium level of the rate of investment.

It follows, therefore, that the rate of investment also depends on the rate of interest. It is interest-elastic. A low rate of interest tends to stimulate investment. But it may fail to do so, if marginal efficiency of investment is already lower than the rate of interest (as may well happen during a depression). Of the two determinants of the rate of investment, marginal efficiency of investment is more volatile than the rate of interest.

The rate of interest is usually 'sticky' in the short run, while marginal efficiency of investment fluctuate from one extreme to another. If there is a divergence between the two, usually the marginal efficiency of investment will adjust to the rate of interest. If, for example the marginal efficiency of investment is 6 per cent, while the current rate of interest is 4 per cent, forces will be set in motion so as to bring the former to the level of the latter. In such a situation, there will be more investment, because marginal efficiency of investment is greater than the rate of interest and, with an increase in investment, marginal efficiency of investment will fall. At the point, where it is just reduced to the level of the current rate of interest, further investment will cease.

The level of investment is not always influenced by the cost of borrowing or the prevailing rate of interest. It is possible that investment has somehow proved unprofitable. Fixed interest payments will then reduce the future earnings on the equity issue of the firm and thus discourage investment.

Also, instead of borrowing, the firm has the option of increasing the ordinary stock issue.

Besides, if profits increase proportionately to increase in share capital, the proposition cannot be attractive to the investing firm. Moreover, the firm can plough back its accumulated profits and may not resort to borrowing.

Thus, although, for the economy as a whole, the supply of funds may be interest-elastic, yet an individual firm may not find borrowing from the market worthwhile. In actual practice, we find that investment demand is not much influenced by rate of interest (*i.e.*, it is interest-inelastic). Investment demand is largely determined by marginal efficiency of capital.

ROLE OF BUSINESS EXPECTATIONS IN DETERMINING MEC

There is no doubt that business expectations play a very important role in determining marginal efficiency of capital and therefore investment. We know that the volume of employment or the size of national income is determined by two factors, *viz.*, propensity to consume and the inducement to invest. Of these two, propensity to consume (or consumption function) is more or less stable, fluctuations in income and employment, therefore, depend primarily upon the inducement to invest. The inducement to invest, in turn, depends on (*a*) the rate of interest and (*b*) the marginal efficiency of capital. Since the rate of interest is relatively stable or 'sticky', fluctuations in investment depend primarily upon the changes in the marginal efficiency of capital. There are two determinants of the marginal efficiency of capital, *viz.*, the supply price or cost of the capital asset and the prospective yield or return from the asset.

It is the expectations of the businessmen regarding the prospective yield which play a vital role in determining the marginal efficiency of capital and hence investment, which in turn determines the volume of employment or size of the

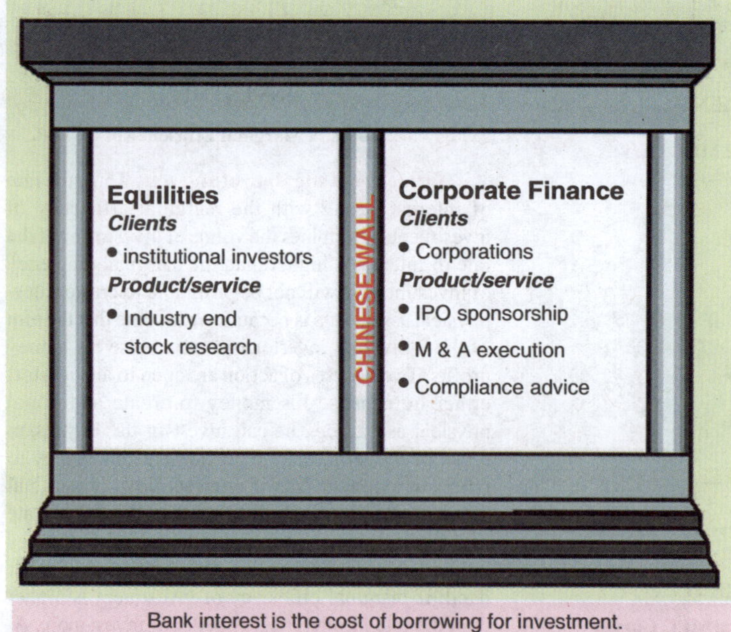

Bank interest is the cost of borrowing for investment.

national income. The most important characteristic of the marginal efficiency of capital is its instability and this is caused by the uncertainty in prospective yield or business expectations.

In a capitalist economy, the instability of economic life (or economic fluctuations) is mainly attributable to the unstable character of prospective yields from capital assets. Whether the demand for capital goods is stable or unstable will be determined by the stability or instability of prospective yields, *i.e.*, by business expectations. As business expectations change, the volume of investment changes and so does the volume of business activity or the volume of employment.

It may be emphasised that the marginal efficiency of capital refers to the yield that is expected in future from investment in a brand-new asset and not the return actually obtained from an existing plant, till it becomes useless. Further, it may also be borne in mind that the prospective yield is made up of the total returns expected from the asset during the **whole** of its life, and these returns may vary from year to year.

Following are the two types of expectations regarding the prospective yields of capital assets:

(*a*) Short-term expectation; and

(*b*) Long-term expectations.

The short-term expectations are based on existing facts which are more or less known to be certain such as the size of existing stock of capital assets and the intensity of consumer demand for the goods which can be produced with these assets. Short-term expectations relate to the sale proceeds of the goods made with the existing plant.

On the other hand, **long-term expectations** relate to the sale proceeds of output resulting from the alterations in the size of the plant or from entirely a new plant. In other words, they are expectations about future changes in the size of the stock of capital assets and about changes in the level of aggregate demand during the future life of these assets. Obviously, the factors on which long-run expectations are based are uncertain.

Thus, short-term expectations are more stable because what has happened in the recent past is a safe guide for the near future. But no past experience will tell us as to what will happen in the long run. The long-run expectations are highly unstable. The horizon becomes more clouded as we look ahead. But long-term expectations are more important in explaining fluctuations in investment and employment.

Factors Influencing Expectations

In view of the important role that the business expectations play in determining marginal efficiency of capital, let us analyse the forces which influence the prospective yields of an asset.

The long-term expectations are influenced by the following factors:

(*a*) The State of Confidence. Much depends on how confident the businessmen are about the future changes, *i.e.*, not only what they expect to happen but how certain and confident they are that it **will** happen.

(*b*) Stock Exchange Valuation. The value of the assets also depends a great deal on the value attached to it by the dealers in stock exchanges. Given the rate of interest, changes in the capital values of investments will depend on the prospective yields as shown by dealings in stock exchange.

(c) Irrevocable Decisions. Investment decisions depend not so much on cold calculations or precise calculations of expected profits but decisions are irrevocably made and risks taken by bold and dynamic entrepreneurs. In other words, investments are not

Stock market influences peoples expections about investment.

based on accurate knowledge of prospective yields but on mere adhoc decisions of entrepreneurs who ventured to take the risk.

(*d*) Elements of Instability. In modern times, elements of instability have been imported into the economic system by divorce between ownership and control and by the working of stock exchanges. Prospects of the various investments are assessed and reassessed almost daily, even several times in a day. It has now become possible to invest one day and disinvest the next day.

(*e*) Link with Investments. The stock exchange dealings regarding the revaluation of the existing investments inevitably influence similar new investments. Thus, the present investments are linked with new investments which is the real investment.

(*f*) Behaviour of Investors. Dealings in the stock exchange by ignorant and unintelligent investors may give a perverted view of the entrepreneur's long-term expectations. They rather think that the present state of affairs will continue. But actually conditions often change. Since there is mass valuation of assets on the stock exchange, there are alternating waves of pessimism and optimism. Even a professional dealer is more concerned with making money than with giving a correct valuation of the assets. He also takes a short-run view.

(*g*) Non-economic Factors. Then there are several non-*economic* factors. Some political events such as threat of a war, success of a particular party in elections or a diplomatic triumph also affect the value of assets or their prospective yields.

THEORY OF SECULAR STAGNATION

It has been observed that the marginal efficiency of capital shows a declining tendency in the long run. The economists used to call it a falling rate of profit, but now they call it a diminishing marginal efficiency of capital. It is the view of most economists that in a capitalist society, the rate of profit goes on falling in the long-run. It is called **"Stagnation Thesis."**

Although most economists agree that the rate of profit continues to fall in the long run. There is, however, difference of opinion on why is it so? According to Adam Smith, the rate of profit falls because the amount of capital in a country goes on increasing. Ricardo and Mill were of the opinion that this was due to the niggardlines of nature. Owing to increase in population even inferior lands have to be brought under cultivation and naturally the output decreases. Keynes's view is somewhat similar to the view of Adam Smith and that of Karl Marx. He thinks that as the stock of capital goods increases, its return goes on decreasing. He says that marginal efficiency of capital decreases in the long run because with a growing stock of capital assets, prospective yield decreases.

The marginal efficiency of capital depends on two factors: (*a*) Supply price or cost of production and (*b*) prospective yields. The marginal efficiency of capital decreases because either the cost of production increases or the prospective yield decreases. In the short run, marginal efficiency of capital decreases because the cost of production of capital increases, but the longer the period the greater is the influence of the prospective yields. Thus, the secular decline in the marginal efficiency of capital is almost entirely the result of a fall in the prospective yields. The prospective yield decreases because there is increase in the supply of capital goods. As investment increases, production increases. The increase in capital and other factors leads to an increase in output which results in fall in prices. The result is that future expectations from investment goes down.

But so long as the marginal efficiency of capital is more than the current rate of interest, further investment will continue since the rate of interest is less than the rate of profit. If the rate of interest falls to zero, the production of capital goods will increase up to the point where the rate of profit also falls to zero. The capital goods will be no longer scarce and the marginal efficiency of capital will drop to zero. Keynes is of the view that if the output of capital goods continues to increase without any limit, the situation as above will be created in a generation or two. But because some difficulties do appear in the way of production of more capital goods, the marginal efficiency of capital has not fallen to zero.

What checks the decline in marginal efficiency of capital? Some of the factors which prevent the marginal efficiency of capital from falling to zero are increase in population, territorial expansion and technical progress. These are growth factors. Also, the wars break out off and on and they check the fall in the rate of profits. In case these growth factors cease to operate, there will be secular stagnation. In rich countries, where there is abundance of capital goods and investment ceases to be profitable, there is unemployment. Hence such countries cannot maintain full employment without social control on investment.

The above analysis of the marginal efficiency of capital leads Keynes to the conclusion that control on investment cannot be left in the hands of private individuals. The long-term expectations are so uncertain that they cause fluctuations in the marginal efficiency of capital, which cannot be set right by changes in the rate of interest. There is a great fear of fall in the long run return resulting from the continuing uncontrolled increase in capital goods. This may irreparably damage the future productive capacity of the community. Hence government control is essential. State can understand much better the long-term needs of the community and it has the power to keep it in a state of comfort.

Thus, the theoretical concept of marginal efficiency of capital has its practical counterpart in socialisation of investment. This necessitates overall economic planning.

Determination of Rate of Interest. As regards the determination of the rate of interest, we have already discussed the Keynesian theory of the rate of interest in the Chapter on Interest.[2] To repeat, the rate of interest is determined by the demand for and supply of money. The demand for money is the demand for money to hold. It is determined by three motives, *viz.*, transactions motive, precautionary motive and speculative motive. The supply of money is fixed by monetary authorities in a country, while demand for money arises because of liquidity preference of the people, arising out of transactions, precautionary and speculative motives. The demand for money, however, is not absolute. People can be induced to part with liquidity if the reward, *i.e.*, the rate of interest, being offered in return is attractive. Generally, the higher the rate of interest the lower will be the demand for liquidity, and as the rate of interest falls the demand for liquidity increases, and, at very low rates of interest, it may become absolute, *i.e.*, people may refuse to part with any amount of money with them.

Given the demand for money, an increase in supply of money will lower the rate of interest. However, when the rate of interest is very low, say, 2 per cent, it may be difficult to lower the rate of interest any further by increasing the supply of money. This is so, because at the very low rates of interest, the demand for money becomes nearly absolute. When the rate of interest is already low, the reward for parting with money is only nominal. At very low rates of interest, people expect that sooner or later the rate will rise, and they prefer to wait till then for lending rather than lending money just now.

Summing up. Broadly speaking, investment depends on:

(*a*) Marginal efficiency of investment;

(*b*) rate of interest.

Marginal efficiency of investment is subject to violent fluctuations in the short run, while the rate of interest is somewhat 'sticky'. Fluctuations in investment, therefore, are largely determined by fluctuations in the marginal efficiency of investment.

INVESTMENT AND THE LEVEL OF INCOME

Recently, a view has been put forward that investment is more responsive to the level of income than to interest rate. In its support, empirical evidence is cited which indicates that a major determining factor in respect of the level of investment is the level of demand for goods rather than the prevailing interest rate. Two arguments are given to support this view: (*a*) The higher the level of demand and income, the more **willing** will the businessmen be to invest in the risky enterprises because they expect higher return. (*b*) the higher the level of demand, output and hence profits, the more will the businessmen be **able** to invest. It will be seen that the first argument refers to the **willingness to invest** and the second to the **ability to invest.** It is assumed that the businessmen are unable to borrow from the market all the funds they require for investment at the prevailing rate of interest. Hence he is compelled to fall back on their own resources or funds to finance the investment projects they consider worth while. These funds may be obtained by not distributing the entire profits to the shareholders but hold back a portion for investment. And the profits will tend to be high when demand and income are high. Hence we arrive at the conclusion that investment will depend upon the level of income (or demand) rather than on the rate of interest.

The theory that investment is influenced by level of profits (or income) has raised lot of controversy. There are statistical difficulties in determining whether empirical evidence conforms to the theory. There is no conclusive evidence supporting the theory that investment is high when profits are high. Rather, the causal connection points in the opposite direction. It is seen that high investment causes high level of income by the multiplier process which causes high profits.

Thus, the controversy is not settled one way or the other. All that we can say is that the available empirical evidence is not adequate to reject the theory that investment depends on demand or income or is influenced by the level of profits.

2. Chapter 34.

Key terms

MEC, Investment demand, Business Expecations Secular stagnation.

QUESTIONS

1. What are the determinants of invesment? How do business expecations affect the inducement to invest?
2. Discuss the role played by "Business Expectations" in the Keynesian theory of the Marginal Efficiency of Capital.
3. What do you understand by "Inducement to Invest"? Discuss the factors which govern inducement to invest in a capitalist economy.
4. What do you understand by marginal efficiency of capital? Explain how it affects inducement to invest.
5. Explain Keynes' definition of marginal efficiency of capital and account for the short-run fluctuations in the position of MEC curve.
6. Explain the concept of marginal efficiency of capital what part does it play in the Keynesian Theory of Employment and Fluctuations?
7. What do you understand by 'Marginal Efficiency of Capital'? What factors influence marginal efficiency of capital in a community ?
8. Critically examine the relationship between investment and income.
9. Distinguish between autonomous investment and induced investment. Explain the various measures that can stimulate 'private' and 'public' investments.
10. Explain the following statements:—
    (*a*) Marginal Propensity to consume is less than one.
    (*b*) Saving is a function of income and not rate of interest.
    (*c*) Investment is a function of marginal efficiency of capital.
11. Examine the view that capital investment depends of changes in the demand for goods and services rather than on the absolute level of demand.
12. Discuss the extent to which the volume of investment can be controlled by purely monetary methods.

44 CHAPTER MULTIPLIER AND ACCELERATOR

Concept of Multiplier

We have studied the determinants of income and employment in a country. There we saw that the volume of employment depends on aggregate demand. The aggregate demand is composed of (*a*) consumption demand and (*b*) investment demand. Consumption depends on the consumer's income and his propensity to consume and investment depends on (*a*) the marginal efficiency of capital and (*b*) the rate of interest.

We have discussed the propensity to consume in a previous chapter. [1]Higher the propensity to consume the higher will be the level of income and employment in the country. Hence, if there is unemployment in a country, steps should be taken to raise the propensity to consume. When investment is increased then also the level of income and employment rises. As income increases, consumption expenditure too increases, but proportionately less than the increase in income. This is due to the fact that the marginal propensity to consume is less than unity. We have discussed this in a previous chapter (42).

In this chapter, we propose to study how much or how many times income increases as investment is done. This can be known from the concept of the multiplier. We shall see that as investment is increased the national income increases proportionately much more. How many times it increases depends on the marginal propensity to consume. As we have said already, the higher the marginal propensity to consume, the greater will be the increase in income as a result of investment. The higher the marginal propensity to consume the bigger will be the multiplier. We shall explain this fully presently.

Since the national income increases many times more as a result of a given investment, Keynes

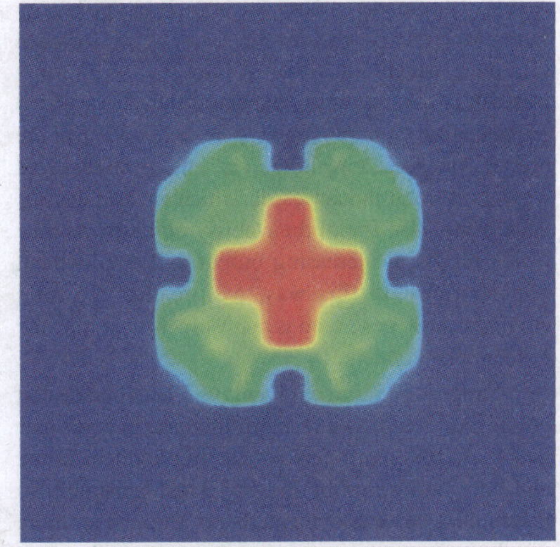

Lagrange multiplier.

1. Chapter 42.

multiplier theory attaches great importance to increase in public investment and Government expenditure for raising the level of income and employment. The multiplier theory emphasises that public investment is highly useful, nay necessary, for increasing income and employment in the country.

It may be borne in mind that both consumption and investment create employment. If there is unemployment or less than full employment, increase both in consumption and investment will increase employment. In this respect they stand in complementary relationship with one another. When investment increases, consumption increases too and helps in creating employment. It is only when the level of full employment has been reached that investment and consumption become competitive instead of being complementary; then increase in one will reduce the other; one will be at the expense of the other.

Kahnes's Employment Multiplier

Before understanding Keynes's multiplier, it seems to be essential to have an idea about Kahn's employment multiplier. Keynes's multiplier is known as 'Keynes's Investment Multiplier' or 'Keynes's Income Multiplier', whereas Kahn's multiplier is known as 'Kahn's Employment Multiplier'.

When government undertakes public works like roads, railways, irrigation works then people get employment. This is initial or primary employment. These people then spend their income on consumption goods. As a result, demand for consumption goods increases, which leads to increase in the output of concerned industries which provides further employment to more people. But the process does not end here. The entrepreneurs and workers in such industries, in which investment has been made, also spend their newly obtained income which results in increasing output and employment opportunities. In this way, we see that the total employment so generated is many times more than the primary employment.

1 + 1 = 11

Multiplier increases income manyfolds due to increase in investment.

Suppose government employs 3 lakh persons on public works and, as a result of increase in consumer goods, 6 lakhs more persons get employment in the concerned industries. In this way, 9 lakh persons have been able to get employment, that is, three times more people are now employed, whereas initial employment generated was only for 3 lakhs people. In other words, Kahn's employment multiplier means that by the government undertaking public works many more times total employment is provided as compared with initial employment.

Keynes' Income or Investment Multiplier

On the other hand, Keynes' income multiplier tells us that a given increase in investment ultimately creates total income which is many times the initial increase in income resulting from that investment. That is why it is called income multiplier or investment multiplier. Income multiplier indicates how many times the total income increases by a given initial investment.

Suppose Rs. 10 crores are invested in public works and as a result there is an increase of Rs. 30 crores in income. In this case, income has increased 3 times, *i.e.*, the multiplier is 3. If Δ1 represents increase in investment, ΔY indicates increase in income and K is the multiplier, then

$$k = \frac{\Delta Y}{\Delta 1}$$

The multiplier is the numerical co-efficient showing how large an increase in income will result from each increase in investment. The multiplier is the number by which the changes in investment must be multiplied in order to get the resulting changes in income. It is the ratio of change in income to the change in investment. If an investment of Rs. 5 crores increases income by Rs. 15, the income multiplier is 3 and if Rs. 20 crores, the multiplier is 4, and so on.

With the help of marginal propensity to consume, we can express in a systematic manner the relationship between a given increment in investment and the resulting change in income. Suppose on a given day an investment of 1,000 rupees takes place. Now, the first impact of this change will be that incomes of persons engaged in investment activity will go up by 1,000 rupees. The process, however, does not end there. The recipients of incomes will spend a part of their additional income and save the rest–the magnitude of their additional spending will depend on their marginal propensity to consume.

Suppose marginal propensity to consume is 3/4. Then they will spend 750 ($1000 \times \frac{3}{4}$) rupees and save 250 rupees. When they spend these 750 rupees in buying goods and services, the incomes of the sellers of these goods and services go up by Rs. 750. They in turn will spend a part of it, depending on their marginal propensity to consume. If their marginal propensity to consume is also $\frac{3}{4}$, they will spend 562.5 ($750 \times \frac{3}{4}$) rupees and save the rest increasing income by Rs. 562.5. Thus, one primary round of expenditure creates income much higher than the original amount. If the marginal propensity to consume is stable, the series of successive expenditure become a geometric progression.

$$1000 + 1000 \times \frac{3}{4} + (1000)\left(\frac{3}{4}\right)^2 + 1000 \times \left(\frac{3}{4}\right)^3 + 1000 \times \left(\frac{3}{4}\right)^4$$

$$\Delta Y = 1000\left[1 + \left(\frac{3}{4}\right) + \left(\frac{3}{4}\right)^2 + \left(\frac{3}{4}\right)^3 + \left(\frac{3}{4}\right)^4 + ...\right]$$

$$= 1000\left(\frac{1}{1-\frac{3}{4}}\right) = 1000\left(\frac{1}{\frac{1}{4}}\right)$$

$$= 10000 \times 4$$

$\Delta Y = 4000$ rupees.

Δ stands for the increase.

Thus, we see that an initial, primary investment of 1,000 rupees gives rise to an increase of 4,000 rupees in the national income. **The investment multiplier measures the relationship between an increase in income caused by a primary increase in investment.** If ΔY is increase in income and $\Delta 1$ is increase in investment,

$$\text{Investment Multiplier} = \frac{\Delta Y}{\Delta I}$$

In the above case, multiplier $= \frac{4000}{1000} = 4$

We observe from the above that the multiplier is given by the following formula:

$$\text{Multiplier} = \frac{1}{1 - mpc}$$

Since $1 - mpc = mps$(marginal propensity to save),

$$\therefore \text{ The Multiplier} = \frac{1}{mps}$$

(Here *mpc* is marginal propensity to consume and *mps* is the marginal propensity to save).

If the marginal propensity to consume is $\frac{2}{3}$, the multiplier can be found as under :–

$$\text{Multiplier} = \frac{1}{1 - mpc} = \frac{1}{1 - \frac{2}{3}} = \frac{1}{\frac{1}{3}} = 3$$

If marginal propensity to consume is $\frac{1}{2}$,

$$\text{multiplier} = \frac{1}{1 - \frac{1}{2}} = \frac{1}{\frac{1}{2}} = 2$$

The formula for the calculation of the value of the Multiplier is derived as follows:

We know $Y = C + I$, (*i.e.*, total national income = total Consumption

Or $\Delta Y = \Delta C + \Delta I$ and Investment expenditure.)

Divide both sides by ΔY

$$1 = \frac{\Delta C}{\Delta Y} + \frac{\Delta I}{\Delta Y}$$

$$\text{or } 1 - \frac{\Delta C}{\Delta Y} = \frac{\Delta I}{\Delta Y} = \frac{1}{\frac{\Delta Y}{\Delta I}}$$

By definition we know that $k = \frac{\Delta Y}{\Delta I}$

$$\therefore 1 - \frac{\Delta C}{\Delta Y} = \frac{1}{k}$$

$$k = \frac{1}{1 - \frac{\Delta C}{\Delta Y}} = \frac{1}{1 - mpc} = \frac{1}{mps}$$

$$\therefore k = \frac{1}{mps}$$

In other words, the simple method is that from marginal propensity to consume we find marginal propensity to save which can be found by deducting marginal propensity to consume from 1 (*i.e.*, $1 - mpc$) and then find its reciprocal. Thus, the multiplier is the reciprocal of marginal propensity to save (*mps*). If the marginal propensity to consume is 4/5, the multiplier will be 5; if it is 9/10, the multiplier will be 10; if marginal propensity to consume is 1, the multiplier will be infinity and a given dose of primary investment will lead automatically to full employment; if marginal propensity to consume is zero, the multiplier will be I so that total increase in income will just equal the increase in primary investment.

Thus, the size of the multiplier varies directly with the size of the marginal propensity to consume. When the marginal propensity to consume is high, the multiplier is high and when the marginal propensity to consume is low, it is low.

It may be emphasised that the multiplier works not only in money terms but also in real terms. In other words, the increase in income takes place not only in form of money but in the form of goods and services. When the incomes increase as a result of investment and these incomes are spent on consumer goods, then the output of these goods has to be increased to meet the increasing demand for them. Hence, increase in money incomes is matched by increase in output or increase in real income. We assume that excess productive capacity exists in consumer goods industries.

Diagrammatic Representation of Multiplier

We know that national income is determined at the level where aggregate demand (= consumption demand + investment demand) curve C + 1 cuts the aggregate supply curve (line forming an angle of 45° with the X-axis). This point of intersection is at *E* in the Fig. 44.1. We can show the multiplier effect also with the help of this diagram. Here income is shown along OX and consumption + investment along OY. The curve C, represents the marginal propensity to consume which is assumed to $\frac{1}{2}$. This is why the slope of C curve is 0.5. Since the aggregate demand curve C + I cuts the 45° angle line at E, OY_1 is the level of

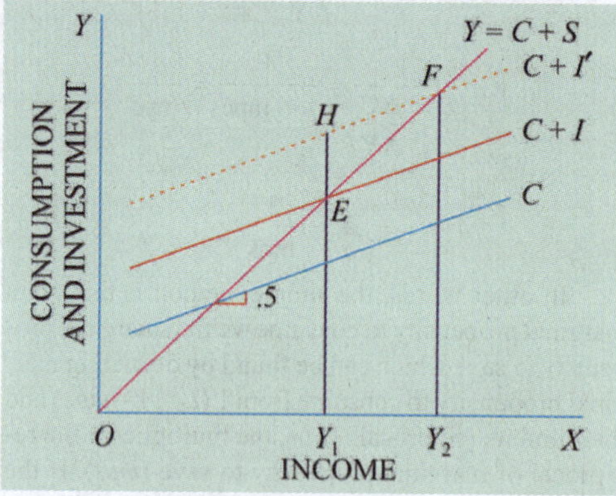

Fig. 44.1. Multiplier Effect.

income determined. If now investment is increased to EH (Δ1) we can find out the increase in income (ΔY). As a result of investment EH, the aggregate demand curve shifts upwards to C + 1. This new aggregate demand curve cuts the 45° angle line at F, so that OY_2 income is determined. Thus, income increases by Y_1Y_2 as a result of investment increase of EH, which (Y_1Y_2) is double of EH (This can be measured).

It is clear, therefore, that the multiplier is 2. We also derive this from our formula $\frac{1}{1 - \text{mpc}}$. When marginal propensity to consume

(*mpc*) is $\frac{1}{2}$, the multiplier

$$= \frac{1}{1 - \text{mpc}} = \frac{1}{1 - \frac{1}{2}} = \frac{1}{\frac{1}{2}} = 2$$

We can also show, with the help of a saving and investment diagram, Fig. 44.2, the multiplier effect of an increase in investment on the equilibrium level of income. In diagram 44.2, SS is the saving curve and I – I is the investment curve showing the total level of investment of Rs. 20 crores. These two curves intersect at point E and the equilibrium level of income of Rs. 330 crores is determined. If now there is a change in investment from Rs. 20 crores to 30 crores, *i.e.*, an increase of 10 crores, then the I – I curve will shift to

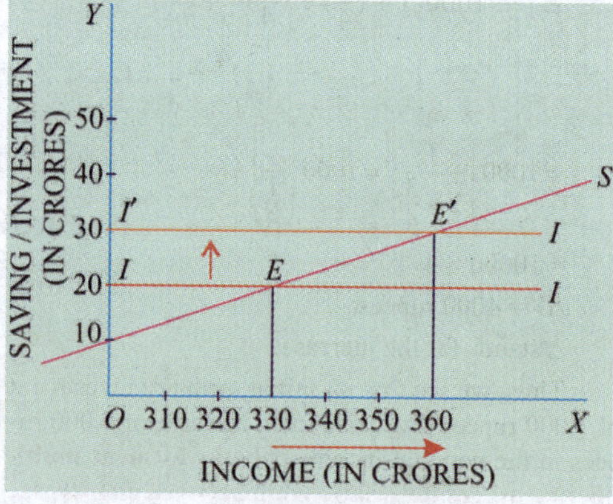

Fig. 44.2. Multiplier Effect.

the position of I′ I′ and the two curves I′ I′ and SS intersect at point E′ and the new equilibrium level of income of Rs. 360 crores is determined. Now it is clear that when propensity to save is $\frac{1}{3}$, an increase in investment by Rs. 10 crores has led to the increase in income by Rs. 30 crores (*i.e.*, from Rs. 330 crores to Rs. 360 crores). Obviously, the value of the multiplier is equal to 3.

Limitations of Multiplier

On a theoretical plane, the multiplier principle seems to be very attractive, but in actual practice, things may not materialise as desired. Its working is subject to several limitations:

***(i)* Efficiency of Production.** If the production system of the country cannot cope with increased demand for consumption goods and make them readily available, the incomes generated will not be spend as visualised. As a result, the marginal propensity to consume may decline.

***(ii)* Regular Investment.** The value of the multiplier will also depend on regularly repeated investments. A steadily increasing investment is essential to maintain the tempo of economic activity.

***(iii)* Multiplier Period.** Successive doses of investment must be injected at suitable intervals if the multiplier effect is not to be lost.

***(iv)* Full Employmeant Ceiling.** As soon as full employment of the idle resources is achieved, further beneficial effect of the multiplier will practically cease.

Uses of Multiplier

In spite of the above limitations, the multiplier principle occupies a very important place not only in economic theory but also in shaping economic policy. It plays a vital role as an instrument of income building. It tells us how a small increase in investment can result in large increase in income. It is of special importance in the study and control of business cycles. It furnishes guidelines for appropriate income and employment policies. It also explains the expansion of public sector in modern times.

Paying off debts reduces effect of multiplier.

Leakages in Income Stream and Their Effect on the Multiplier

In the discussion of the propensity to consume, we saw that as income increases, consumption does not increase to the same extent or proportionately, because a part of the income is saved. The part of the income that is saved (*i.e.*, not spent) is as if a leakage from the flow of income stream. These leakages obstruct the growth of national income. In the absence of these leakages, marginal propensity to consume would have been unity. The consumption expenditure would have increased 100 per cent of the increase in income and there would have been full employment. Why does not an investment of Rs. one crore increase income equal to Rs. one crore? In other words, why does the increase in income decrease at every step of investment? The answer is that the whole of the newly obtained income is not spent, but a part leaks out. Leakages break the chain reaction. An initial investment brings about infinite number of constant additions to income, but the successive additions diminish at each stage. This is due to leakages.

The following are the principal leakages:

***(i)* Paying Off Debts.** It generally happens that a person has to pay a debt to a bank or to another person. A part of his income goes out in repaying such debts and is not utilised either in consumption or in productive activity. Income used to pay off debts disappears from the income stream. If, however, the creditor uses this amount in buying consumer goods or in some productive activity, then this sum will generate some income, otherwise not.

***(ii)* Idle Cash Balances.** It is well known that people keep with them ready cash which is neither used productively nor in purchasing consumer goods. Keynes has mentioned three motives for holding ready cash for liquidity preference, *viz.*, transactions motive, precautionary motive and speculative motive. This means that the respent part of income goes on decreasing. In this way, a part of the initial expenditure leaks out of the income stream. The cash may be kept in current account or saving account. But it is kept away from the expenditure all right; it would have otherwise added to the future income.

***(iii)* Imports.** This part of the money spent by country for importing goods also leaks out of the country's income stream. It does not encourage or support any business or industry in the country. It only helps trade and industry of the exporting country. This money must be supposed to have leaked out of the country's income stream. This is specially so if the imports do not help the trade and industry of the country or if they are not used for export promotion. The net import is a leakage.

***(iv)* Purchase of Existing Securities.** Some monied people buy securities from others and the sellers of securities hoard this money. This money also leaks out of the income stream. The result will be the same if a person buys shares or debentures of an existing company or gets an insurance policy or undertakes some such financial investment. Money so spent is not used in consumption expenditure and thus does not help in increasing income. This is a leakage.

***(v)* Price Inflation.** Inflationary situation is also responsible for leakage. In such a situation, investment does not help in generating employment or increasing income. If there is already full employment in the country, increase in investment, far from increasing demand for consumer goods, it decreases it as a result of which employment in the consumer goods industries contracts and demand for capital goods decreases. Whatever increase in income there is, it is spent in high prices and it does not help in creating income and employment.

Conclusion. As a result of leakages of income from the main income stream of the country, the multiplier effect of the primary or initial investment in increasing income is reduced. If somehow these leakages are plugged, the multiplier effect of investment in generating income and employment would increase. If they cannot be plugged altogether, they should be reduced or the propensity to consume should be increased or propensity to save should be reduced, otherwise the new investment will not have full effect in increasing income and employment. Suppose one-third of the new income leaks out in one form or another at each expenditure sequence. This means that marginal propensity to consume is $\frac{2}{3}$. With $\frac{2}{3}$ marginal propensity to consume, an initial investment expenditure of Re. 1 crore, *i.e.*, primary employment and the resulting sequence of consumption expenditure, *i.e.*, secondary employment, would add up to Rs. 3 crores which in the absence of leakages, would have been much more.

Reverse Operation of the Multiplier

It may be pointed out that the multiplier operates both backward and forward depending on the direction of the initial change in investment, *i.e.*, whether investment is increased or decreased. An initial reduction in investment precipitates the reverse operation of the multiplier.

In this case, higher the marginal propensity to consume, the greater will be the cumulative decline in income. A community with a high propensity to consume is hurt more by the reverse operation of the multiplier than one with a low propensity to consume. Conversely, a community with a high propensity to save is hurt less than one with a low propensity to save.

The marginal propensity to consume being less than one serves as a check to a downward cumulative decline of income when investment declines, otherwise, the reverse operation of the multiplier would bring about a collapse of economic activity. This never happens. This shows that propensity to consume being less than one saves the situation.

Reserve Operation of the Multiplier can be explained with the help of the following diagram:–

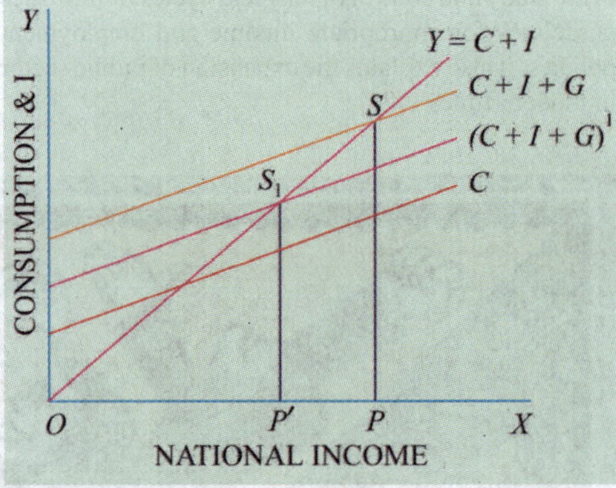

Fig. 44.3.

The initial equilibrium is at point *S*, with *OP* as the level of national income. Let the government expenditure fall, shifting the total demand curve from $(C+I+G)$ to $(C+I+G)$.[1] The $(C+I+G)^1$ line intersects the 45° line at the point S_1 and the level of income falls to *OP′*.

Importance of the Multiplier

So far we have discusssed the multiplier from the theoretical point of view. Now let us see its practical importance. These days governments actively interfere in the economic activity of the community. Therefore, it is essential to realise the importance of the multiplier in connection with investment. If there is depression and unemployment in the country, the people would like the government to undertake public works so that some employment should be provided to the unemployed. But if it is realised that an investment of Rs. one crore will create employment worth many times, the importance of government investment will become clear. That is, the multiplier principle has added to the importance of public investment.

When a country is engulfed in depression, the entrepreneurs are discouraged from investment, because in such a situation profit expectations are very low. Therefore, if depression is to be lifted and the level of national income and employment is to be raised, it becomes necessary to increase public investment. If during such times, the government undertakes investment, the demand for consumer goods and hence the level of income and employment will increase manifold on account of the working of the multiplier. The operation of the multiplier rapidly removes depression through government investment and the economy moves towards full employment.

It is worth noting that when, owing to government investment to remove depression and unemployment, the demand for goods and the level of income and employment rises, the private entrepreneurs too are encouraged to invest. This happens because as the demand for goods increases and incomes rise owing to government investment, the profit expectations of the entrepreneurs go up and as a result the marginal efficiency of capital rises. Hence when government makes investment in public works to fight depression and unemployment, private investment is also encouraged on account of the operation of the multiplier. Depression is quickly lifted on account of investment both by the government and private entrepreneurs. If the multiplier did not operate, the increase in income and employment would not have been so much as when it operates. Influenced by the Keynesian principle of the multiplier, the Government of the United States of America undertook large-scale investment in public works to remove the Great Depression of 1929-34. This met with great success and the Depression was lifted.

MULTIPLIER AND UNDER-DEVELOPED COUNTRIES

It may be understood that Keynes's principle of the multiplier does not apply to the under-developed countries like India. The reason is that there are certain essential conditions for the operation of the multiplier. One important condition is that the supply curve of output should be elastic. In other words, when demand for certain goods or services increases, its supply can be increased without much difficulty. This condition is fulfilled in industrialised countries but not in under-developed countries.

Allied with this is another assumption that there is excess productive capacity in consumer goods industries. This being so, the supply of goods can be easily increased when demand increases. If, somehow, demand decreases, this productive capacity lies idle and there is unemployment. In under-developed countries, there is little excess productive capacity in the economy.

The third condition is that the supply of raw materials, working capital, *etc.*, should also be elastic

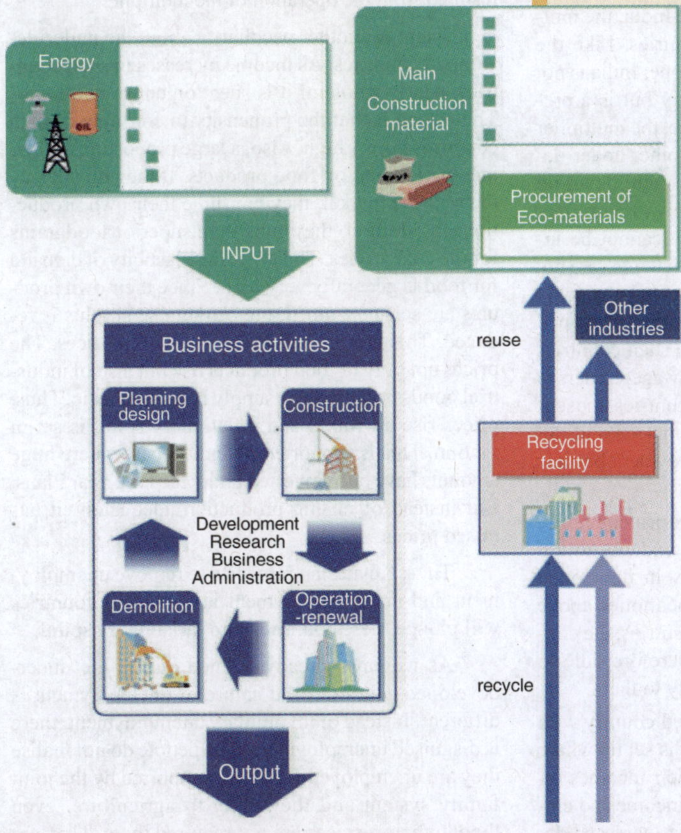

Smooth supply of inputs is a condition for working of multiplier.

and it should be easily increased when need arises. Such is not the case in under-developed countries.

The fourth condition is that there should be involuntary unemployment. That is, there are people who want work at the prevailing wage rate, but are not getting it. In under-developed countries, most of the people being self-employed, this condition is not fulfilled.

These are some of the assumptions on the validity of which alone Keynes's multiplier will operate. Only in these conditions the multiplier increase income manifold from a given investment. Thus Keynes assumes that (*a*) the supply of goods and services is elastic; (*b*) there is sufficient excess capacity in industries; (*c*) the working capital, *etc*., can be increased; and (*d*) the workers seeking employment will be able to find employment and as a result income and employment will increase from a given investment according to the multiplier. For example, if the multiplier is 4, an initial investment of Rs. 1000 will increase income equal to Rs. 4,000.

But since the above conditions are not fulfilled by the under-developed countries like India, the multiplier does not operate in such countries. Like the U.S.A. and the U.K. and Western Europe, India is not a predominantly industrialised country but is a predominantly agricultural country. Hence, the multiplier principle does not apply to India and other under-developed countries. In such countries, there being no excess capacity in industries, the supply of consumer goods is not elastic, *i.e.*, their supply cannot be increased much. Machines, working capital, *etc*., are not easily available and their supply cannot be quickly increased. Another peculiarity of the under-developed countries is that most of the people in such countries are self-employed and the number of wage-earners is comparatively small. Thus, in these countries, most of the output of goods is for self-consumption and not for the market. There is lot of unemployment but it is disguised unemployment.

It is clear that Keynes's multiplier principle fully applies to the developed economies and not to the under-developed ones, because only in developed economies the various assumptions mentioned above hold good. In the under-developed countries, the conditions are entirely different. It is, therefore, idle to expect the multiplier principle to apply to them.

Suppose in some under-developed country with an investment of Rs. 1 crore a factory is set up where some workers get employment and their incomes increase. But the process of increase in income and employment ends here. The reason is that increased demand for consumer goods resulting from increased incomes cannot be met because the supply of goods is not sufficiently elastic. The only result of increased demand is to raise their prices because their supply cannot be increased. Thus, the increased income is absorbed in enhanced prices without creating any additional output and employment.

In under-developed countries, the principal occupation of the people is agriculture and the greater proportion of their national income is spent in the production of agricultural products like foodgrains. But we know that the supply of agricultural products is inelastic because their production is subject to uncertain natural factors like climate and rainfall. Agriculture is said to be a 'gamble in the rains'. The farmers also lack machinery and other inputs like fertilizers, *etc*. There are also insufficient credit facilities. Hence, it is difficult to increase production. Since the people are generally underfed, the increased incomes resulting from new investment are spent on foodgrains. But since their supply cannot be increased to meet the increased demand, the only consequence is to raise their prices and not increase income and employment which would have resulted from the operation of the multiplier.

There is another peculiarity about the under-developed countries. As income increases in such countries, nearly whole of it is spent on consumer goods. The reason is that the propensity to consume in such countries is very high. Also, a large proportion of their income is spent on food products. If they do not buy them in the market, they consume their own production. In addition, they substitute superior foodgrains for the coarse ones. Their income-elasticity of demand for food is generally very high. Since their own products are self-consumed, the marketable surplus is reduced. This is another reason of a rise in prices. The prices not only of food products rise but also of industrial goods because their supply is also inelastic. Thus, prices rise all round and inflationary spiral is set in motion. This is supported by India's case where huge amounts have been invested under the Five Year Plans. But instead of raising production adequately, it has raised prices.

Thus, Keynesian remedies to remove unemployment and under-employment in backward countries will plunge these countries into inflationary spiral.

As we have already pointed out, in the under-developed countries, the nature of unemployment is different. Instead of involuntary unemployment, there is disguised unemployment. The people do not realise they are unemployed. They are supported by the joint family system and they cling to agriculture, even though their services are not required there. They are not really involuntarily unemployed in the Keynesian sense and yet they are unemployed or under-employed in the clearly economic sense. The particular form which unemployment takes in the under-developed countries, *viz*., that of disguised unemployment makes the economy for Keynesian purposes practically analogous with one of full employment and to that extent prevents the multiplier from working in the direction of an increase in either output or employment.

Thus, Keynes's multiplier principle is not applicable to the under-developed countries.

ACCELERATOR

Concept of Accelerator

In the study of the multiplier, we have seen how a small change in investment exerts a magnified effect on consumption and hence on income and employment. In other words, the multiplier describes the relationship between investment and income, *i.e.*, the effect of investment on income. The multiplier concept is concerned with original investment as a stimulus to consumption and thereby to income and employment. But there is another type of relationship between investment and income which is the other way about. In this relationship, we are not concerned with the effect of investment on income (*i.e.*, the multiplier effect), but we are concerned with the effect of increase in income on the resultant investment. This effect involves what has been called the 'principle of acceleration'. This traces the effect of added consumption upon the demand for investment . It is a case of derived demand, *i.e.*, demand for investment goods, derived from increase in consumption or income.

The principle of acceleration dates back to 1914 and beyond. It is associated with the name of J. M. Clark who was mainly responsible for popularising it. It has proved to be a useful tool of economic analysis since 1914, although Keynes entirely ignored it. In fact, it is not considered a part of Keynesian Economics. Keynes emphasised psychological concepts like marginal propensity to consume, marginal efficiency of capital and the multiplier rather than the accelerator which is regarded as a technical concept.

Let us be clear about the concept of the Accelerator. When income increases, people's spending power increases; their consumption increases and consequently demand for consumer goods increases. In order to meet this enhanced demand, investment must increase to raise the productive capacity of the community. Initially, however, the increased demand will be met by over-working the existing plants and machinery. All this leads to increase in profits which will induce entrepreneurs to expand their plants by increasing their investments. Thus, a rise in income leads to a further induced investment. The accelerator is the numerical value of the relation between an increase in income and the resulting increase in investment.

In other words, the acceleration principle simply tells us that if owing to increase in people's incomes, the demand for consumption goods increases, the derived demand for the factors of production, producers's goods in particular, say, machines to make the consumption goods, will increase. But the point to be noted is that invesment in the making of machines will even increase faster than the demand for the product.

But the accelerator in Economics is not to be confused with the accelerator in a motor car. In the case of a car, the accelerator makes it run faster and ever faster. That is not the case with investment in business. It does not increase faster and ever faster, the downtrend also appears after some time. The accelerator in Economics expresses only a functional

	Demand for cloth in rupees 1	*Needed stock of Capital* 2	*Replacement expenditure* 3	*Net investment* 4	*Gross investment* 5
Period 1	500	5 machines = 1500 rupees	1 machine = 300 rupees	0 machine	300 rupees
Period 2	500	5 machines = 1500 rupees	1 machine = 300 rupees	0 machine	300 rupees
Period 3	800	8 machines = 2400 rupees	1 machine = 300 rupees	3 machines = 900 rupees	1200 rupees
Period 4	1000	10 machines = 3000 rupees	1 machine = 300 rupees	2 machines = 600 rupees	900 rupees
Period 5	1000	10 machines = 3000 rupees	1 machine = 300 rupees	0 machine	300 rupees
Period 6	800	8 machines = 2400 rupees	1 machine = 300 rupees	– 2 machines = 600 rupees	– 300 rupees

relationship between consumption demand and investment demand, *i.e.*, demand for machines which make the final product or the consumers's goods. "It makes the final product or the consumers goods. It make the level of investment a function not of the level of consumption but of the **rate of change** of consumption."[2] The level of investment is a function of the rate of change in the level of income. "This expression of the acceleration maintains the hypothesis that a fluctuation in the independent variable will give rise to a greater fluctuation in the dependent variable."[3]

Working of the Accelerator

An illustration will make the working of the acceleration clear. Suppose we are living in a world, where the only commodity produced is cloth. Further suppose that to produce cloth worth 100 rupees, we require one machine worth 300 rupees, which means that the value of the accelerator is 3 (*i.e.*, capital-output ratio 1:3). That is, if demand rises by 100 rupees, additional investment worth 300 rupees takes place. If the existing level of demand for cloth remains constant, let us say, at 500 rupees, then to produce this much of cloth we need five machines worth Rs. 1,500. At the end of one year, let us suppose, that one machine becomes useless as a result of wear and tear, so that at the end of one year, a gross investment of 300 rupees must take place to replace the old machine in order that the stock of capital is capable of producing output worth 500 rupees.

In the third period, demand rises to 800 rupees. To produce output worth 800 rupees, we need 8 machines. But our previous stock consisted of only 5 machines. Thus if we are to produce output worth 800 rupees, we must instal 3 new machines, worth 900 rupees. In addition, since at the end of one period one old machine has become useless, even to maintain previous stock of 5 machines, we need to instal one new machine in place of the old one. Thus, net investment will be 900 rupees and replacement investment 300 rupees so that our gross investment rises from 300 rupees in period 2 to 1,200 rupees in period 3. A 60 per cent rise in demand gives rise to 400 per cent increase in gross investment. Here we have a glimpse of the powerful destabilising role of accelerator.

In the fourth period, demand rises from 800 rupees to 1,000 rupees (25%), but total gross investment is only 900 rupees which is 25% less than the period third. In the fifth period, even though demand remains constant at 1,000 rupees, gross investment falls to 300 rupees which is 33.3% of the fourth period while net investment falls to zero. Thus, in order to keep the economy prosperous, mere standing still or running at a slow pace is no good. We must run and run faster and faster in order to ward off the danger of a depression. This is because of the extremely destabilising role of the accelerator.

We assume (*a*) a constant sum of replacement expenditure which falls due each period; (*b*) relationship between capital stock and the total output, *e.g.*, 1:3 ratio, is determined by technological factors. This ratio is to be considered an average of the various industry ratios, and (*c*) we assume the real profits move with aggregate output. We are not, therefore, concerned with the problem of capacity and its effect on the accelerator nor with the problem of profits. The anticipated output with planned expenditure is assumed to be equal to the realised output.

In the above table, we see that when output or income becomes stabilised round the peak (*e.g.*, period 4 and 5), the pressure for the decline becomes more intense, because a halt in the increase in output means an accelerated constraction in investment spending. There is no gross investment at all in period 6, which means that relative to the lower level of output the system is still in excess capacity. The wear and tear of equipment is a technical process and is divorced from the rate of economic contraction. The decline in investment expenditure cannot go beyond zero replacement.

It may be noted that the acceleration principle does not act as well as in the down-turn as it does during the up-turn; regardless of the rate of change in output, the limit to the decline in investment is zero replacement.

We may note that investment goods fluctuate more intensely than do aggregate output. The acceleration principle explains, the large cyclical fluctuations of investment spending.

Criticism of the Acceleration Principle

In the acceleration principle, we find a powerful explanation of the destabilishing forces working in the economy during a trade cycle. If the accelerator is the only force at work, then we shall have too much of instability in the economy–more than is actually found. In real life, we find that there are limits to instability, both in the upward as well as the downward direction, so that the trade cycle must have a peak as well as a bottom.

The principle of acceleration has come in for a good deal of criticism in recent years. For example, it has been pointed out by Kaldor that we cannot as-

2. Stonier and Hague – *A Text Book of Economic Theory*, 1973, p. 501.
3. Bober, Stanley –*The Economics of Cycles and Growth*, 1971, p. 142.

sume a constant value of the accelerator throughout the trade cycle, that it is not true that an increase in demand for 100 rupees must always give rise to an increase in investment of 300 rupees (as in our example). This is because, if already some machines are lying idle, we shall try to use them before rushing in for new equipment. Also, if our expectation is that the rise in demand is a temporary one, we shall try to meet by overworking the existing machinery rather than installing a new plant.

Accelerator does not remain constant. It may change as new plants are installed.

Further, it may be easier for a firm to take advantage of a small increase in demand than big ones–for the financial resources of a firm may not be sufficient to take immediate advantage of big increases, while small additional equipment is not likely to strain its financial resources to any great extent. Hence, its response to the latter may be quicker than to the former.

Conclusion. Thus, the simple type of acceleration principle turns out to be a crude instrument, for the value of the accelerator will vary at different stages of the trade cycle. But this does not mean that the basic principle, underlying the acceleration principle, is wrong. It is based on a sound principle that a change in national income will tend to induce corresponding additional changes in the rate of investment.

Limitations of the Accelerator

It seems that the explanation of fluctuations in the capital goods industries provided by the principle of acceleration is too good to be realistic. The assumptions on which it is based are too rigid and do not hold good in real life. If increase in demand for consumption goods led to much more than proportionate increase in the capital goods, fluctuations in the capital goods industries would be much larger than they actually are: We have assumed great inflexibility of output in the consumer goods industries and great flexibility in capital goods industries.

The following assumptions made in the discussion of the accelerator make it unrealistic:

(i) We have assumed that there is no excess capacity existing in consumer goods industries. In other words, we have assumed that no machines are lying idle and shift working is not possible. If there had been excess capacity and shift working was possible, the supply of goods could be increased with the existing equipment and the accelerator would not come into play.

In the capital goods industries, we have assumed the existence of surplus capacity. If there was no excess capacity in the machine-making industry, increased demand for machines could not lead to increase in the supply of machines. Actually, the things are not so rigid as supposed.

(ii) The second assumption is the flexibility of output. It is assumed that the machine-making industry is capable of increasing its output for the time being at least. The supply can be increased by reducing stocks of finished machines, by working extra shifts, and so on. But stocks cannot be reduced below zero and working double shifts or adoption of other experiments is found to be expensive. Only when the demand has increased permanently, will the entrepreneur find it worthwhile to increase investment for installing additional machines.

(iii) The size of the accelerator does not remain constant over time. Its value will be affected by the businessman's calculations regarding the profitability of installing new plants to make more machines on the basis of their probable working life. It also assumes that the demand for machines will remain stable in future, although the increase in demand has suddenly cropped up. The entrepreneur will have to make so many complicated calculations like the future demand for the final product made by the machines, about the future demand for machines themselves, about the cost and availability of machines, about interest rates, and so on. This indeed is too much for an average entrepreneur.

Utility of the Accelerator

In spite of these limitations and difficulties, the concept of the accelerator has proved a very useful tool of economic analysis. There is no doubt that it has restricted application but it does not mean that it has no place in any realistic discussion of the factors affecting income and employment. Some economists have made use of the acceleration principle in formal, mathematical models to bring out how an economy would react if there was a sudden increase in demand for goods.

Comparison Between the Accelerator and the Multiplier

Now that we have studied both the multiplier and the accelerator, we can pause and compare the two. There seems to be some resemblance between the two but the difference should be quite clear by this time. We have to repeat what we have said already. The multiplier shows the effect of a change in investment on income (and consumption) whereas the accelerator shows the effect of increase in income (and consumption) on investment.

Another remarkable difference is that the multiplier ultimately depends on psychology; it depends on the propensity to consume which is determined by consumers' tastes and habits and the marginal efficiency of capital, which depends on entrepreneurs's expectations of profit or their confidence in the success of the investment. This is all psychological. But the accelerator depends on technical factors. It depends on the fact that a given amount of capital (*i.e.*, a machine) is required to produce a given amount of final product, *i.e.*, a consumption good. Hence, the accelerator is based on technology, whereas the multiplier depends on psychology.

APPENDIX THREE CONCEPTS OF THE MULTIPLIER

Three concepts of the multiplier are: Static Multiplier; Comparative-Static Multiplier and Dynamic Multiplier.

Static Multiplier

The multiplier discussed earlier in this chapter (pages 374-75) is an example of a static multiplier. It shows a still picture analysing the forces bringing about an equilibrium at a given time.

Comparative-Static Multiplier

The comparative static multiplier is the third type of multiplier. It is 'timeless' in the sense that it leaps over the time interval between two successive static equilibrium positions. It does not show the path actually travelled between the two positions of equilibrium. In other words, the process and the time it takes from one equilibrium level to another is ignored. It is assumed that there are no changes in the MPC of the various income recipients as the economy moves from one equilibrium level to the next. The comparative static analysis simply leaps over the transition period. It skips from one equilibrium position to another. It leaves out of account the time path in between.

Dynamic Multiplier

The dynamic multiplier shows a movie picture. It is a moving equilibrium or logical theory of the multiplier which holds good continuously without time lag. The dynamic analysis of the multiplier attempts to trace the steps by which income changes from one equilibrium level to another. Obviously, such changes can occur only over time and not instantaneously. In dynamic multiplier, we assume that production adjusts to changes in demand instantaneously, that expenditures are instantaneously translated into income receipts; but consumption responds to change in income with a lag of one period.

Multiplier is increase in income due to increase in investment auelerator is increase in capital stock due to increase in income.

We begin with an initial equilibrium income level Y. Now suppose that autonomous investment rises by $\Delta 1$ in the first period and that subsequent investment remains above the initial level by the amount $\Delta 1$. That is, increase in investment is supposed to be permanent. In the first period, income will rise by the amount of increase in investment. Hence $Y = Y + \Delta 1$. In the second period, income will be in excess of the initial level Y not only because investment remains in excess of the initial level but also because a fraction say b of the first periods' income increase is re-spent on consumption. Hence

$$Y_2 = Y + \Delta 1 + b\,(Y_1 - Y)$$

$$= Y + \Delta 1 + b\,\Delta 1 \text{ or}$$

$$Y_2 - Y = \Delta 1 + b\,\Delta 1.$$

Similarly in the third period, income will exceed the initial level by $\Delta 1$ increase in investment spending plus b times the excess of income in the second period over the initial level. Hence

$Y_3 = Y + \Delta 1 + b\,\Delta 1 + b_2\,\Delta 1$, and so on for any period n –

$$Y_n = Y + \Delta 1 + b\,\Delta 1 + b_2\,\Delta 1 + b_3\,\Delta 1 + b^{n-1}\,\Delta 1.$$

It is thus that the dynamic equilibrium traces the path of income as it adjusts from the old equilibrium level to the new equilibrium level.

THE BALANCED BUDGET MULTIPLIER

The multiplier effect may be associated with changes in both taxes and transfers. This multiplier effect is normally smaller than the multiplier effect associated with a change in government expenditures. Any increase in government expenditures may have an expansionary effect even though these expenditures are matched by an equal increase in taxes. This possibility has been called **balanced budget thesis.**

How will the combined impact of the increase in both government expenditures and taxes affect the income level? This effect depends upon the combined impact of the increase in government expenditures and the taxes upon the aggregate demand function.

Key terms

Multiplier, Accelerator, Static multiplier, Dynamic multiplier, Leakages of multiplier, Reverse operation of multiplier. Balanced budget multiplier.

QUESTIONS

1. Explain the concept of the multiplier and its role in the theory of employment.

Or

Explain the importance of Multiplier in economic analysis and economic policy.

2. "The multiplier depends ulitmately on a psychological factor whereas the accelerator is based on technogical factors". Explain.
3. Explain the limitations and leakages of multiplier.
4. What is the investment multiplier? How is its value measured?

Or

Explain the working of the 'investment multiplier' along with its limitations.

5. What is meant by investment multiplier and on what factors does it depend? Explain its role in determination of the level of national income.
6. Explain the meaning of accelerator. Explain its working. Give its utility and Limitations.

WAGES AND EMPLOYMENT

The relationship between wage rate and the volume of employment has been a subject on which acute controversy has raged. We shall here examine in this connection the views of the classical economists, the Keynesian view and the view of the modern economists.

CLASSICAL VIEW

The classical economists held the view that the economic system automatically adjusted itself at the level of full employment through wage-price flexibility. According to this view, there was a strong tendency towards full employment via-wage adjustment. For example, if during depression, money wages were reduced all round, it would be possible not only to reduce unemployment but eventually to create a situation of full employment. A cut in money wages will lower marginal production costs and as a result, lead to increase in output and employment.

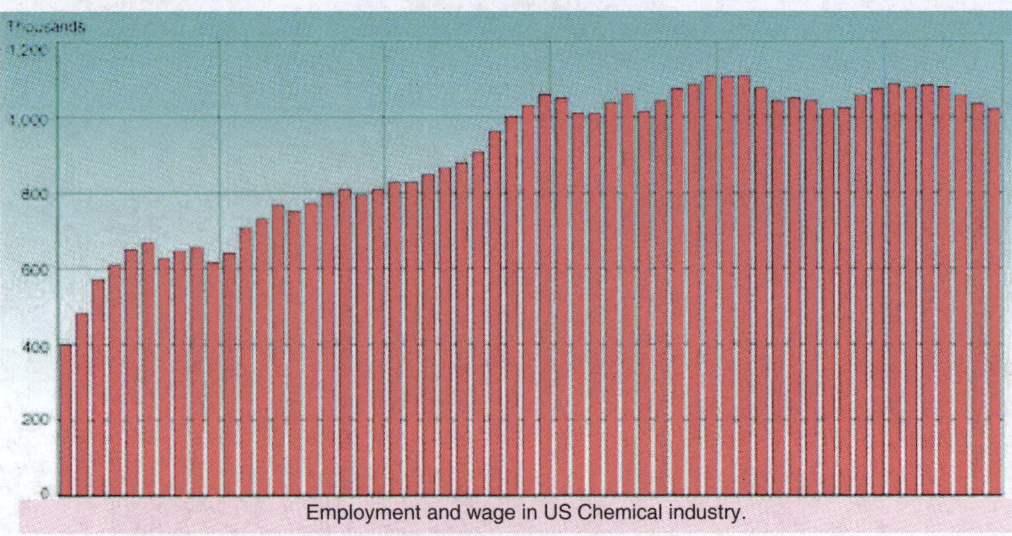

Employment and wage in US Chemical industry.

The output (and hence employment) will increase, because reduction in production costs will enable the producers to lower prices and stimulate demand. Unemployment, if any, will be a temporary phase.

It will appear that the classical remedy for unemployment is to cut down the money wages all round. The process of bidding down the wages should continue till the employers find it worthwhile to employ all people seeking jobs. According to this view, unemployment exists because wages are kept at a higher level than what some employers consider worthwhile. So long as there is some involuntary unemployment, wages and prices must continue to fall. This will lead to increase in investment, output and income, until unemployment is eliminated.

Assumption

The classical theory is based on one big assumption, *viz.*, that a cut in money wage results in reduction in the real wage. It is reduction in real wage which will stimulate investment and increase output and employment. With cut in money wages, costs and prices fall. But, since prices do not fall to the same extent as the cut in wages, real wages are reduced. Reduction in real wages, without a corresponding fall in prices, widens profit margins, and hence provides incentive to the producers to increase investment. In this way, output will continue to increase till full employment equilibrium is established.

Criticism

Keynes severely criticised the classical view. He made a comprehensive analysis of the problem and pointed out serious flaws in the classical argument. The main flaw is that the classical economists have ignored the demand aspect. They hold that reduction in wages will leave the aggregate effective demand unaffected. There is no doubt that reduction in wages will, as explained already, lead to increase in output. But, unless the increased output is purchased and consumed, investment will be discouraged and output and employment reduced.

The classical economists simply saw that when wages in a particular industry were reduced, profits there increased, resulting in larger output and employment. Cut in wages in a particular industry or by a particular firm does not reduce the demand for the products of that industry. This is so, because their particular labour is a small fraction of the total labour force. Their purchasing power may be reduced by a cut in their wages, but the purchasing power of the rest of labour is not reduced. Hence, the demand for goods will not be reduced. On the contrary, the cheapening of the goods produced by them will increase demand for them. Their output will increase and so employment in that particular industry will increase.

But what is true of a particular industry cannot be true of the economic system as a whole. If there is a general wage cut, *i.e.*, cutting of wages in all industries, then the incomes, and so the purchasing power, of all workers will decrease. Reduction in aggregate effective demand will result in reduction of output and curtail the volume of employment. It is to be remembered that so far as the economy is concerned, wages are not only cost but also source of demand.

It is not necessary that a cut in money wage may lead to a reduction in real wage. If prices fall to the same extent as wages fall, real wages remain the same. Real wages will be reduced only when prices do not fall to the same extent as fall in wages. It is reduction in real wages which is going to provide incentive to the producers to invest and increase output and employment.

Thus, the fatal flaw in the classical analysis is that it suffers from the lack of a theory of effective demand and it arises from the classical economists' attempt to apply, to the economy as a whole, the logic of a theory designed to apply to a particular industry. They ignored the fact that an all-round reduction in wages or a general or overall cut in wages would reduce effective demand or aggregate demand which will reduce employment rather than increase it.

The classical and Keynesian ideas can be explained with the help of the following diagram (45.1):

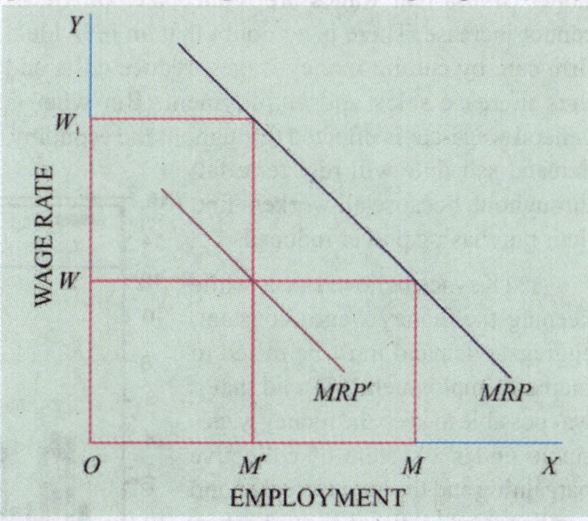

Fig. 45.1

OM is the level of full employment. MRP is the marginal revenue productivity curve. With OW_1 wage rate, OM′ people are employed, leaving M′M as unemployed. Unemployment leads to competition for jobs in the market, forcing wage rate down to OW. At this wage rate, OM persons are employed, which is a situation of full employment. Hence reduction in wages has helped in achieving full employment, through wage reduction. According to Keynes, however, if there is an all round wage cut, then people will have less purchasing power. Reducing money wages means less spending. This would result in a fall in price and hence the total receipts of the firm fall. A fall in the prices pushes the MRP curve leftwards, *i.e.*, to MRP′. With MRP′ as the marginal revenue productivity curve, employment will not increase as a result of a wage cut from OW_1 to OW.

KEYNESIAN ANALYSIS

We shall now briefly summarise the Keynesian analysis regarding the relationship between wages and employment as under :

(1) In the first place, Keynes agreed with the classical economists that other things being equal, employment varied inversely with the level of real wages. That is, when real wages rose, the volume of employment was curtailed, and *vice versa*. In other words, the demand for labour depends on the real wage rates: It increases when the real wage rate falls and decreases when the real wages go up.

(2) Keynes did not agree that a cut in money wages for the economy as a whole will necessarily cut the real wages. On the other hand, a reduction in the money wages reduced *proportionately* the total outlay, demand and prices so that the real wages remained the same. Unless real wages are reduced, employment cannot increase. There is no doubt that an individual firm can, by cutting money wages, reduce costs and thus increase sales and employment. But when a general wage-cut is effected throughout the economy, demand schedule will register a fall throughout, because all workers find their purchasing power reduced.

(3) Keynes believed that, while keeping the money wages constant, aggregate demand must be raised to increase employment. He said that it was possible to keep the money wages stable under a system of collective bargaining and the aggregate demand can be raised by fiscal and monetary measures.

(4) Keynes further believed that a rise in aggregate demand, while the money wages are kept constant, would normally lead to a reduction in real wages. And a reduction in real wages would stimulate investment and increase employment. He agreed that since organisation, equipment and technique do not change in the short run, an increase in aggregate demand would result in increased output and a rise in marginal cost and prices. Rise in prices would mean a cut in real wages. **It is increase in employment which reduces real wages, and not the other way round.**

(5) According to Keynes, the wage-earners do not mind a small rise in prices and do not agitate for a corresponding rise in money wages. But they vigorously resists a cut in money wages. Hence, a better and more practical method of increasing employment is to raise aggregate demand and not cut money wages. For instance, the wage earners are offended at a cut in money wages, but they cannot blame the employer for a reduction in real wages. A cut in money wages also increase the burden of their debt. The wage earners are not satisfied even if the prices fall in proportion to the cut in money wages, because they fear that the prices may again rise to their old level. Thus, according to Keynes, it is neither wise nor feasible to cut money wages. The wage earners oppose cut in money wages even when the prices are falling. Thus, in modern times of strong trade unionism, it is impossible to cut money wages.

(6) In order to explain why a general cut in money wages would not increase employment, Keynes analyses the effect of cut in money wages on the main determinants of income and employment, *viz.*, marginal efficiency of capital, consumption function and the rate of interest (discussed on the next page). He shows that all these factors are adversely affected by a cut in money wages. Hence, we cannot hope to increase employment by cutting money wages, unless other factors are favourable.

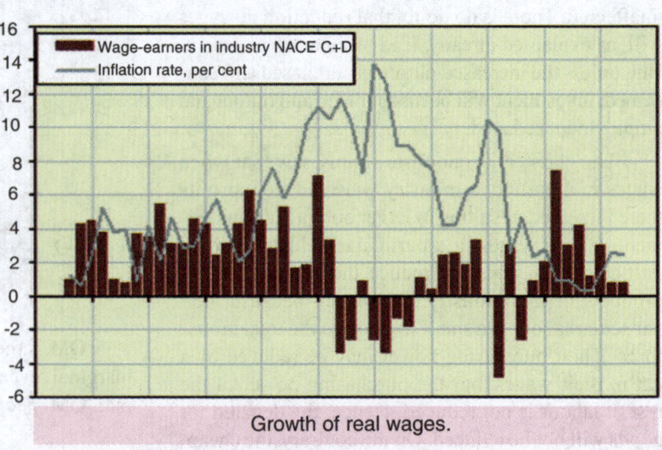

Growth of real wages.

Conclusion. Keynes comes to the conclusion that a cut in money wages is no remedy for unemployment nor a suitable prescription for increasing employment.

Money Illusion

In this connection we would like to refer to a concept called 'money illusion'.

Professor Irving Fisher introduced in economic theory the term 'Money Illusion' in his book of the same name based on a series of lectures that he delivered at Geneva School of International Studies in 1927. By 'money illusion' he meant that the people thought that a rupee was a rupee for ever. That is, its value or purchasing power in terms of goods and services never changes. People generally fail to perceive that a unit of money does not always buy the same quantity of goods and services, *i.e.*, its purchasing power varies from time to time. Thus, the constancy of the purchasing power of money is a myth, but somehow people cling to the illusion that it is not so.

It is the existence of money illusion which explains that there is a great discontent among the workers whenever their employers cut money wages and they do not hesitate to go on a strike. But, when their standard of living suffers owing to rising prices, the discontent is not so great. Rise of prices hits them underhand, as it were, while the cut in money wages is deemed a direct attack. As the late Lord Keynes observed, "Whilst workers will usually resist a reduction in money wages, it is not their practice to withdraw their labour whenever there is a rise in the price of wage goods".

What explains the existence of the money illusion in the minds of the people? There are two possible explanations: (*a*) when prices rise, the workers in a particular industry feel that the workers in other industries are also hit to the same extent and their relative position does not suffer in any manner. The workers seem to be more keen on maintaining their relative position than to raise their absolute wages. (*b*) The workers strongly resent a cut in their money wages, because they feel that it has been imposed by their own employers and they must retaliate by going on a strike. On the other hand, the rise in prices (*i.e.*, reduction in real wages) is not considered in any way due to any action on the part of their own employers.

Thus, the existence of money illusion has a practical implication. It is this that workers will resent any reduction in their money wages, but will not take much notice of a reduction in real wages. Hence, if there is unemployment in the country due to high wages, the proper solution will be to reduce real wages and not touch the money wages. In other words, it would be preferable to increase employment by reduction in real wages than by cuts in money wages.

EFFECT OF WAGE-CUT ON DETERMINANTS OF EMPLOYMENT

We have said above that employment cannot be increased by cutting money wages. Why not? For this purpose, we shall have to consider the effect of the wage-cut on the main determinants of employment, *viz*., marginal efficiency of capital, propensity to consume and the rate of interest.

Effect on Marginal Efficiency of Capital

It is obvious that if money wages are reduced, the profit expectations improve or the marginal efficiency of capital increases. This will stimulate investment and increase employment.

But a cut in money wages will promote investment only if the entrepreneurs believe that there will be no further fall in money wages. If a further fall in wages is expected, then the entrepreneurs will wait and put off their projects. Under a system of perfect competition, there is no guarantee that if wages have once fallen, they will not fall further.

Also, wage-cuts may provoke agitation on the part of the workers resulting in industrial disputes. Such a state of affairs is not conducive to profitable investments. In this case, marginal efficiency of capital is likely to go down.

There is another reason why marginal efficiency of capital may be adversely affected by a cut in money wages. When wages fall, prices are likely to fall too. A fall in prices will increase the burden of debt, both private and public. Increase in public debt will necessitate increase in taxation. All this will have a depression effect on investment and employment.

However, profit expectations or marginal efficiency of capital will rise in export industries, because wage-cut will cheapen export goods. But it will have to be considered what retaliatory measures the importing countries may adopt to meet our competition.

Effect on Consumption Function

It is quite clear that a general cut in wages will reduce the purchasing power of the masses of workers. Their consumption will diminish. Hence, effect of a wage cut on propensity to consume is more likely to be unfavourable than favourable. Income distribution in the community will become more unequal. This redistribution of income favouring the saving class and unfavourable to the consumption class is likely to lower the consumption function.

Money illusion.

Cut in money wages may, however, raise consumption function in some cases. This effect was ignored by Keynes but pointed out by Pigou who was the chief supporter of the classical view. That is why it is called "Pigou effect". It is clear that a cut in money wages leads to reduction in prices and income, which means the value of money goes up. As a result, the real value of various forms of money assets, *e.g.*, bank deposits, government securities goes up. This creates a **'money illusion'** and makes the owners of these assets feel richer than before, whose propensity to consume, therefore, increases.

Now we have to see whether Keynesian effect is stronger or the Pigou effect is stronger. That is, whether the redistribution of income resulting from a fall in money wages affects the propensity to consume more than the rise in the real value of money assets. The majority of the economists hold that the adverse effect as pointed out by Keynes is far stronger than the favourable effect pointed out by Pigou. We may, therefore, conclude that a reduction in money wages would lower the consumption function rather than raise it.

Effect on Rate of Interest

According to Keynes, cut in money wages will lower the general price level. Therefore much less amount of money is needed for transactions. That is, transactions motive demand for money is reduced. This means that the remaining quantity of money exceeds the existing speculative demand for money. This will result in lowering of the interest rate which will tend to stimulate investment and increase employment. The greater the fall in wages and prices, the greater the quantity of money released from active balances to inactive balances, and, therefore, greater the fall in the interest rate.

It is well to remember three things in the analysis of Keynes's effect of cut in wages on interest rate:

(*a*) The fall in the interest rate will depend on amount of money released from transactions motive. It also depends on whether the speculative demand for money is interest-elastic or interest-inelastic. It may be that the liquidity preference of the people at the time may be so strong that in spite of a large amount of money having been released from the transactions and being available for speculative motive, the rate of interest does not fall. However, if speculative demand for money is interest-inelastic then the rate of interest will fall, when money for speculative motive has been increased.

(*b*) Investment and employment are not likely to increase if, in spite of a fall in wages, the profit expectations of the entrepreneurs have been adversely affected somehow.

(*c*) It should also be borne in mind that Keynes' effect of cut in money wages on interest takes place through the monetary route. That is, it is the same as increasing the total amount of money in order to increase the amount available for speculative motive. But, from a practical point of view, flexible money policy is preferable to flexible wage policy. This is so because policy of cutting wages has to face many difficulties. Keynes has shown that the favourable effect of wage reduction can be achieved far more effectively by deliberate expansion through deficit financing. In this case, harmful effects of falling prices on profits can be avoided, while the favourable effect will be more pronounced.

Summing up

The effect of money wage cuts on the level of employment may be summed up as under:–

"The effect of money wage cuts on the level of employment will depend to some extent on the importance of Pigou effect, on the significance of foreign trade, on the effect of 'money illusion' (thinking increase in money wages as increase in real wages), on consumption, on money illusion in the tax structure, on the effect of redistribution of income on consumption, and finally on the nature of expectations induced by wage cuts".[1]

MODERN THEORY OF WAGES AND EMPLOYMENT

The modern economists by and large agree with Keynesian analysis. But there are some differences which we shall try to bring out here.

According to Keynes, a decline in the real wage is a condition for increase in employment. We have already referred to his argument that since organisation, equipment and technique do not change in the short run, an increase in aggregate demand would lead to increased output and a rise in marginal cost and prices. Rise in prices means a fall in real wages even when money wages remain constant.

Protest in South Korea over fear of wage cut.

But the modern economists do not agree that an increase in employment resulting from increase in effective demand would necessarily lower real wage. They put forward the following arguments in support of this view:

(i) It is pointed out that in fixing prices of their products, the producers usually follow "full cost" pricing policy rather than fixing them on the basis of marginal cost. When prices are fixed on a full cost basis, costs will fall as output expands up to a point at which rising marginal cost rises above total unit cost. Till this point is reached, it is possible to expand output at prices lower than those obtaining before the expansion of output started.

(ii) Keynes has assumed that, in the short run, there is no change in organisation, equipment and technique so that marginal costs must rise. But we know that improvements in these respects are continually being made, which check the tendency of the marginal costs to rise.

(iii) The modern economists believe that the marginal cost curve remains flat over considerable range of output, whereas Keynes believes that the marginal cost curve rises upwards even with a small increase in output. It follows, therefore, that in the view of the modern economists, it is not necessary for the costs and prices to rise as output expands and the real wages need not fall. Improvements in techniques may even result in the fall of the marginal cost. Hence, real wages may even rise instead of falling. The modern economists do not, therefore, subscribe to the view that there is an inverse relationship between wage rates and employment. They are more optimistic in thinking that there are possibilities of expanding employment through raising aggregate demand. This is because, according to modern theory, prices need to rise less as employment and output expand than what Keynes had believed.

Conclusion. Barring the points mentioned above, the modern economists subscribe to Keynesian analysis of relationship between wages and employment.

Application to Wage Policy

Analysis of wage-employment relationship given here is not a mere theory but it has great practical importance. It helps governments in formulating and following a suitable wage policy. It needs hardly be emphasised that co-operation of labour is a key to the progress and stability of industrial economies. Hence, the importance of a suitable labour policy.

It is clear from the analysis given above that employment cannot be increased by a general cut in money wages. If a policy of cutting money wages all round is adopted, it will have adverse repercussions in the economy on account of decrease in aggregate effective demand. Economic conditions will become worse than before.

Reduction in money incomes of the people or deflation will adversely affect the main determinants of output and employment. These determinants can be favourably influenced only through appropriate monetary and fiscal policies. Fiscal and monetary measures can , therefore, be far more effective in increasing employment than a policy of a general cut in money wages. It will avoid deflation which is detrimental to the growth of output and employment

1. Dernburg and McDougall—*Macro-Economics, International Student Edition*, p. 148.

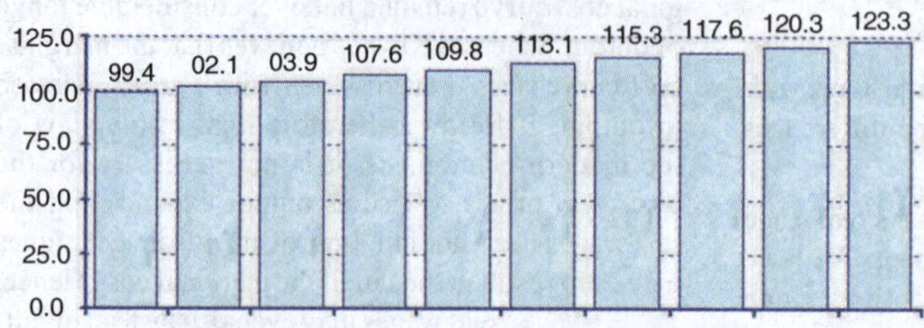

Wage policy aims at stable wages and employment.

but which is bound to result when money wages are cut over the entire economy.

Hence, an appropriate wage policy will be one which keeps the money wages stable. Modern wages-employment theory indicates efficiency wages as the appropriate goal of wage policy. If somehow, even by mistake, efficiency wages (*i.e.*, labour cost) have been raised, it is now the generally accepted view to recognise the situation as an accomplished fact and not to attempt a wage cut and get involved in a deflationary situation.

It does not, however, follow that wages should be allowed to go on increasing without any increase in productivity. If through pressure or wrong policies, wages are raised heedlessly, it will usher in an inflationary situation which is equally dangerous for economic stabiltiy. Hence, it is more appropriate to maintain wage stability as far as possible.

PIGOU EFFECT OR REAL BALANCE EFFECT

We have already referred to Pigou Effect. But we would like to elucidate it further in view of its theoretical and practical importance. Keynes held that shift in the consumption function came from changes in income distribution incident to wage reduction. But Pigou was of the opinion that shifting of consumption function upward was due to increase in the **real** value of money assets resulting from a fall in money wages and prices. This is the **'real balance effect'.**

When wages and prices fall, the total **real** value of the public's holding of wealth which has fixed money value, (in the form of money assets like bank balances, bonds, government securities etc.) will increase though wealth in the form of goods, land or equities will depreciate. Thus a fall in prices will increase in **real** terms the wealth of consumers to the extent that its money value is fixed. Now consumption is an increasing function of the level of wealth and income. Hence a rising real value of wealth stimulates consumption outlays at all levels of income.

Thus we see that Pigou concentrates exclusively on the 'real-value-of-money-assets' effect, called the real balances effect.

Key terms

Real Wage, Money illusion, Real Balance Effect.

QUESTIONS

1. Discuss the classical and Keynesian view on wages and employment.
2. Write a note on 'Money illusion".
3. What do you mean by Pigou effect or 'real balance effect'?

46 CHAPTER

UNEMPLOYMENT AND FULL EMPLOYMENT

TYPES OF UNEMPLOYMENT

Structural Unemployment

In the modern world, man by himself hardly produces anything. Even the primitive man needed some elementary tools like the bow and the arrow to engage in hunting for the earning of his livelihood. With the growth of technology and specialisation, he needs much more capital with which to engage in the productive activity. All these instruments of production constitute community's stock of capital. Now, if the working force grows faster than the stock of capital of a country, the entire addition of the labour force cannot be absorbed in productive employment–because not enough of instruments of production are there to employ them. The resulting unemployment is known as the **structural, long-term or Marxian unemployment.**

Seasonal Unemployment

Seasonal unemployment arises because of the seasonal character of a particular productive activity so that people become unemployed during the slack season. Indian agriculture is a seasonal occupation so that the farmers have not sufficient work to do during the slack season. Other examples of seasonal industry are the ice factories, the rice mills, the sugar factories, *etc.* The solution has to be found in re-arranging the process of production, and, where this is not possible, complementary and subsidiary jobs have to be created for the people suffering from seasonal unemployment.

Indian agriculture is a seasonal occupation.

Frictional Unemployment

Frictional unemployment exists when men are temporarily out of work because of the lack of perfect mobility on the part of the labour. In a growing and dynamic economy, in which some industries are declining and others are rising and in which people are free to work wherever they wish, some volume of frictional unemployment is bound to exist. This is so because it takes some time for the unemployed labour to learn new trades or to shift to new places, where there is a demand for labour. Thus, frictional unemployment exists when there is unsatisfied demand for labour, but the unemployed workers are either not fit for the jobs in question or are not in the right place to meet this demand.

In frictional unemployment, workers are only temporarily unemployed, the reasons being immobility of labour, the seasonal work, shortages of materials, breakdowns in machinery and equipment, ignorance of the job seekers, *etc*.

We cannot conceive of frictional unemployment, unless there is unsatisfied demand for labour somewhere in the economy. If, in a country, the total demand for labour falls short of the total supply of labour, then the cause is not frictional but some other. Some action can be taken to minimize the harmful consequences of frictional unemployment by offering quick retraining facilities to the unemployed, providing labour exchanges, and by arranging adequate social security measures to help the unemployed during the transition and by regulating, in an orderly manner, the pace of technological change.

In spite of some frictional unemployment, we can say there is employment if those who wish to work are able to get work.

Keynesian Unemployment or Cyclical Unemployment

We have explained above that the equilibrium level of income and employment may well be established at less than full employment level. Consequently, there is some unemployment. This is Known as Keynesian unemployment. It is due to deficiency of aggregate effective demand. This is also called **cyclical unemployment.** It is so called because business depression occurs at more or less regular intervals. During times of depression, business activity is at a low ebb and unemployment increases. Some people are thrown out of employment altogether and others are only partially employed. Advanced capitalist countries have been suffering from time to time from this type of unemployment. This type of unemployment arises not because of 'too little' capital as in the case of structural unemployment, but because of 'too much' capital for a short while in relation to demand for goods and services.

In others words, this type of unemployment is due to the fact that the total effective demand of the community is not sufficient to absorb the entire production of goods that can be produced with the available stock of capital. In a free private enterprise economy, production takes place in response to the profit motive. When businessmen cannot sell their entire output, their profit expectations are not fulfilled so that their reaction in the next period is to reduce their output. Now, factors of production earn their incomes because of their participation in the process of production and, when entrepreneurs decide to reduce their production, some factors of production become unemployed. Since employment is the major source of incomes for a great majority of people, a fall in employment signifies a fall in their incomes also.

Measures to Remove Cyclical or Keynesian Unemployment. We know that the Keynesian unemployment is due to the deficiency of effective demand. We can, therefore, remove this type of unemployment by boosting up the level of effective demand. This can be done by raising the rate of investment or shifting the consumption function to the left. To increase the rate of investment, the government can adopt the following measures:

(i) The government may decide to induce the private investors to invest more. For this reason, the government may pursue a cheap money policy of lowering the rate of interest. We know that ordinarily, the lower the rate of interest, the higher will be the level of private investment.

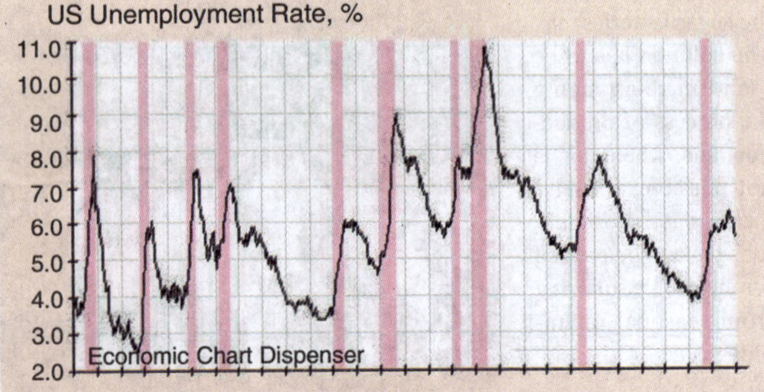

Cyclical unemployment is a phenomenon in capalist countries such as USA.

(ii) Alternatively, the government may encourage private investment by reducing the taxes on profits so that the post-tax rate of profit will now be higher than before.

(iii) If in spite of all these measures, adequate private investment is not forthcoming, the government may try to boost up private consumption by reducing the tax rates on incomes and commodities. The government may also offer direct subsidies to increase private consumption.

(iv) If all these measures do not lead to full employment, the government may itself decide to increase its investment by resorting to a public works programme. This will offer additional employment to the factors of production which, in turn, will experience the familiar multiplier effects.

Nature of Unemployment in Under-developed Countries

Bulk of the unemployment in under-developed countries is of a different nature from that in advanced and developed countries. A major part of the unemployment in developed countries is of cyclical nature which is due to deficiency of aggregate effective demand. But most of the unemployment in under-developed countries is not cyclical. Instead, it is a long-term problem. The major cause of unemployment and under-employment in under-developed countries like India is the deficiency of the stock of capital in relation to the needs of the growing labour force.

The classical economists were mainly concerned with structural or Marxian unemployment. A nation's stock of capital can be enlarged by increased investment which, in the absence of any unutilised resources, requires additional savings on the part of the community. The concern of the classical economists was to ensure that the rate of capital formation was kept sufficiently high so that employment opportunities were successively enlarged to absorb the additions to working force of the country as a result of population growth.

Agriculture in UDCs suffer from disguise unemployment.

This is the problem that underdeveloped countries like India are facing today. Since our stock of capital has not been growing at a rate fast enough to keep pace with the growth of population, the country's capacity to offer productive employment to the new entrants to the labour market has been severely limited. This manifests itself in two ways–firstly, the prevalence of large-scale unemployment in the urban areas as evidenced by the statistics of employment exchanges; secondly, it manifests itself in the form of growing numbers engaged in agriculture, resulting in disguised unemployment.

It is common knowledge that with minor changes in organisation and with existing techniques, our agriculture can be looked after by a much smaller number of persons than are actually engaged in it. If alternative employment opportunities were available, these people could be removed from agriculture, where their marginal productivity is very low (if not zero or negative), to occupations with higher marginal productivity, and the national income of the country would rise. Since employment opportunities in the non-agricultural sector are not growing rapidly, the new entrants to the working force are compelled to remain in agriculture and perpetuate the phenomenon of **disguised unemployment.** This means that people are engaged in occupations, where their marginal productivity is very low (if not zero or negative). Consequently, a shift to alternative occupations will improve their marginal productivity and add to the national income of the country.

The Solution. The basic solution to the problem of this sort is the faster rate of capital formation so as to enlarge employment opportunities. For this purpose, every possible encouragement should be given to savings and their productive utilisation in increasing the rate of investment. In under-developed countries, investment incentives are very low and the State can assist in the process of capital formation directly as well as indirectly. Through a fiscal policy, which encourages savings and investment, and through a sound monetary policy, the State can do much to encourage investors.

The State itself can participate in the process of capital formation by undertaking such development activities as the private entrepreneurs do not find it profitable to undertake. Under-developed countries suffer from a notorious shyness on the part of private investors; therefore, the State has got to assume a special role in speeding up the rate of economic development. The other line of attack has got to be on the rate of population growth. Malthusian theory may not be valid so far as advanced countries are concerned, but it is true of under-developed countries. If population grows at a rapid rate, then, to maintain the people even at their existing levels, large amounts of capital are needed. This capital could otherwise have been used to raise the amount of capital available per man and hence raise the living standards at a faster rate. Hence, it becomes absolutely necessary to check rapid population growth.

FULL EMPLOYMENT

Meaning of Full Employment

To attain and maintain the level of full employment is one of the chief objectives of the present-day economies. But what does full employment precisely mean?

The classical economists believed that there was always full employment and lapses, if any, were strictly temporary. According to them, full employment is a situation when there is no involuntary unemployment, though there may be voluntary, casual, seasonal, structural, technological and frictional unemployment. In their opinion, in a free competitive economy, serious unemployment was a passing phase. All job seekers are able to find jobs sooner or later at the prevailing wage rate. This view, however, is not accepted by economists these days. Actually, there is always some unemployment.

Employment would be full literally, when every able-bodied adult worked the number of hours considered normal for a fully employed person at the current wage level. This level of employment, however, normally appears to be unattainable in private enterprise economies. For, under such economies, quite a few have enough unearned incomes to be able to afford a life of well-paid idleness. Pigou, accordingly, defined full employment as one when "everybody who at the ruling rate of wages wishes to be employed is in fact employed."

But even Pigovian full employment appears to be unattainable for, at any given time, there is bound to be some seasonal and frictional unemployment. This led Keynes[1] and many after him to define full employment as the level of employment which falls short of Pigovian full employment. The Economic and Social Council of the U.N. has accepted the same definition, for it required countries to fix the full employment standard in this sense. The purpose of such a standard is to provide **full employment which is consistent with the smallest amount of unemployment that a country can reasonably be expected to have, after a minimum allowance is made for seasonal and frictional unemployment.**[2]

Full employment refers to such a state of economy that all productive resources of a community–land, labour, capital and enterprise–are fully employed. In other words, when none of the productive resources are lying idle or are under-employed. Full employment may also be defined as an amount of employment beyond which further increase in effective demand does not increase output and employment but results in inflation. In this sense, even the under-employed countries may be supposed to be in a state of full employment because increase in demand creates an inflationary pressure owing to the fact that, on account of deficiency of capital equipment, the supply of output is inelastic.

Keynesian full employment is, by definition, the maximum level of employment that private enterprise countries can attain without experiencing strong inflationary pressures. According to Keynes, "full employment is a situation in which aggregate employment is inelastic in response to an increase in effective demand for its output." But, for purposes of practical policy, it is necessary to reduce the concept to quantitative terms. It should be possible to say precisely when employment is less than full so that remedial measures can be adopted to achieve the full employment level.

Measurement of Full Employment Level

The concept, as defined above, raises two quantitative problems, namely, how to determine (1) the amount of employment sought by those who at the ruling wage-rates wish to be employed, and (2) the inevitable minimum of frictional and seasonal unemployment. The first, in turn, depends upon (*a*) the number of people able and willing to work for wages, and (*b*) the average number of hours of work which each of them wants to be employed. The number of wage-employment seekers depends upon the size of the population of working age, the number who, having sufficient unearned incomes, choose to remain idle, the number who, being in command of the requisite means of production, are self-employed; and the prevailing wage-rates and other incentives provided.

1. *The General Theory*, pp. 15-16.

2. U.N., *Problems of Unemployment and Inflation*, 1950 and 1951, p. 5.

Normally, apart from the size of the population of working age, these factors are likely to be more or less stable over short periods. For instance, the span of life regarded as falling within the working age, while subject to variation as a result of changes in the period of schooling or in the normal age for retirement consequent on changes in health standards and longevity, is likely to remain unchanged in the short period. Again, since most workers have no large unearned income or accumulated savings, they are obliged to remain continuously in employment. They cannot, therefore, throw their labour-power on the market or withhold it therefrom in some unpredictable manner. Accordingly, the number who choose to remain idle is unlikely to vary much in any short period.

Moreover, even when some of these factors change somewhat, the net quantitative effect may not be important. **Higher wages, for instance, may induce some of the older workers to postpone their retirement, while these may impel some of the married women workers, now that their husbands are better off, to relinquish their jobs. The net effect of a rise in wages will not, therefore, be quantitatively important.** [3] **The same applies to other of these factors.** The size of the population of working age, too, though not invariant is measurable as changes according to definite trends. It follows that the number of wage-seeking population can be determined with a great measure of accuracy. And since the average number of hours of work which each wage-employment seeker wants to put in is likely to be more or less stable, in any short period, the total amount of wage-employment sought is quite precisely measurable.

Similar observations may be made regarding the permissible allowance for seasonal and frictional unemployment. It will have to vary from season to season, and from year to year, in accordance with the inevitable seasonal variations in employment and in the magnitude of the structural shifts in demand and production that together with immobility of labour cause frictional unemployment. It may, therefore, be better defined as a range rather than as a precise figure. Since normally **structural** shifts in demand and production are unlikely to be violent or spasmodic and since in industrialized countries the incidence of seasonal unemployment is bound to be quite low, the allowance for frictional and seasonal unemployment needs to be very small. A U.N. study has suggested that this allowance need not be beyond a range of 2.4 or 3.5 per cent of the available labour force.

Thus, the possibility of measuring the size of the available labour force and the inevitable minimum of frictional and seasonal unemployment makes full employment a determinate quantity. As suggested by a U. N. study, [4] as a necessary step in the effective implementation of full employment policies, each country should fix a full employment target expressed in terms of the permissible range of frictional and seasonal unemployment. Unemployment in excess of the fixed target would indicate a lapse from full employment calling for remedial action. The fixation of such a target would help to reduce the chances of government inaction or vacillation in the face of growing unemployment. It may also help to maintain confidence among businessmen, whose pessimism ordinarily plays a notable part in magnifying the downswing. There is, of course, the danger of the government acting on a false scent. For at times, unemployment may exceed the target due to causes other than insufficient demand. This danger may be minimized by allowing the government the discretion to disregard the signal if it has clear evidence that rise in unemployment is not due to demand deficiency.

POLICY FOR FULL EMPLOYMENT

To create a state of full employment is not an easy job. No simple and straight remedy can be prescribed for the purpose. There is no panacea which can cure a country of unemployment and create conditions of full employment. The problem has to be fought on all fronts and a comprehensive policy covering the various aspects of the economy has to be formulated. It will cover:–

(1) Fiscal Policy

(2) Monetary Policy

(3) Income Policy

(4) Price Policy

(5) International measures.

Now a word about each of the above policies.

Fiscal Policy for Full Employment

The principal instrument of fiscal policy is the public finance or the budget. It involves purposeful manipulation of public expenditure, taxation and public debt. This is known as functional finance. Public expenditure, taxation and public borrowing have to be geared to fight inflationary and deflationary tendencies so that the national economy moves on an even keel.

The level of full employment—the classical economists were more concerned with the fuller

3. *Pigou, Lapses from Full Employment*, 1945, p. 5.

4. U.N., *Measures for Full Employment*, 1949, p. 14.

utilisation of resources in relation to the manpower resources. Though prior to the classical economists, the early thinkers put this concept indirectly in the form of wealth (*i*) The physiocrats were of the opinion that, that country is the wealthiest country which possesses huge amount of cultivable land, be (this is prior to modus prosperity more cultivable land, more employment more output and operate of the economy. (*ii*) The merchants on the other hand concentrated more on the material aspect, in their opinion, a country is rich because of its material wealth in the form of gold, silver and other precious metal, *etc.* (*iii*) Adam Smith was the first to elaborate this concept in a more refined way, that a country's wealth is nothing but the aggregate productive capacity of its citizens. As Adam Smith laid more emphasis on Laissaz-Fair economy as well as on the invisible hand concept. If the masses of a country is hardworking and productive than that country can be referred as the wealthiest country. In modern concept the Japanese economy can be Adam Smith's ideal, full employment developed wealthiest economy concept.

J. B. say a french economist evolved a theory of employment on the basis of supply creates its own demand. According to the classical economists that there always exists full employment, where as unemployment may occur due to business cycles and that may be a temporary phenomenon. On the basis of this ideology many economists specially balanced growth approach, big, push and unbalanced approach theories emerged.

Employment Concepts
Classical
Marxian
Keynesian
(IS-LM) Frame work (Modern)

Marxist concept of full employment is rather a more radical and extreme ideology. Everything in his ideology rests and the exploitation of labour and justification for a complete change in the economic ideology that of Socialism. Marxs in materialistic interpretation of economic history, exploitation of labour, the theory of surplus value the alienation theory, in almost all he laid more emphasis on the exploitation of labour and the short comings of capitalists economy. In his opinion equilibrium can be achieved only when, there exists full employment and fulfilment of human wants. Here quality is not given importance, it is only the basic needs of people and an eqalitarian society is, taken into account. It is a very difficult problem which Marx failed to bring about a solution as he was confused between cultural, political, social and economic equilibrium. Marx's main idealogy was that of socialists, but in general human beings have been bestoved with different types of intelligence and abilities, Hence we cannot more achieve an economic equilibrium with the assumption of labour equality or "work according to your ability and take according to your needs." Human being is very intelligent and if utilised with proper means, than economic technical prosperity is not impossible.

The keynesian revolution which emphasised more on role of government without interfering in the economic activities of the people. The so called welfare state concept" with the help of important weapon of fiscal policy in the form of the theory of pump-priming was responsible for new economic revolution. Keynes attack on classical theory, and the functional finance approach, gave a new lease of life to political economic philosophy. Politicians with their hidden agenda moved with the weapon of discriminatory fiscal policy essentially in the form of deficit finance, to control and achieve their political objectives along with to same extent the objective of full employment. Keynes concentrated more on the "Principle of Effective Demand" to raise the level of economic development. He took into account only certain rational assumptions of consumption function and investment function. Keynes main set back was that of technological development. The role of government as an investor, the regional intelligence, the cultural attachment and the zeal of the people to acquire richness or development is neglected. In Japan after the than Thnkgura regime, is 1869 the Meiji era encouraged foreign colla- baration, where as the top five Zaibatsh, played pivotal role in economic development a that country. Keynesian ideas regarding the rate of interest and the role of money is also vague. In modern economic system, financial institutions are unfusing huge amount of purchasing power (effective demand), which may collapse at any time.

The next state of full-employment equilibrium in the second half of Nineteenth century was that of the marriage of *IS*/*LM* curves. The so called goods market and money market which brings about an equilibrium on the basis of fiscal policy and monetary policy. The fiscal policy is responsible for goods market and the monetary policy for money market. The equilibrium can be altered as and when the policy maker's feel to increase or decrease the policy weapons. One of the most important aspect of the modern economic scenario is that of fast moving 'service sector'. Service sector has been dominating in the economies of the so called liberalised economics along with never ending acceleration of money supply. If the service sector outpaces the primary and secondary sector than it may **lead to more conflict in the form of inequalities** of income and wealth". The history may repeat in the form of depression and economic chaos, in future, if not controlled properly. New revolution may emerge unless and untill "full employment' concept is properly developed. The *IS*/*LM* curve theory has neglected the importance of service sector.

Among the broad aims of fiscal policy are :

(*a*) To improve the efficiency of productive capacity of the economic system by an optimum allocation of the productive resources in men, money and materials. These productive resources are so allocated and utilised that they make a maximum contribution to national output, income and employment.

(*b*) The fiscal policy aims not only at maximising national income and output but to bring about an equitable distribution thereof. It seeks to reduce inequalities of income and wealth in order to promote general welfare of the community.

(*c*) The overriding objective of fiscal policy is to increase employment opportunities in the country and to make the economy march towards full employment. Public expenditure, taxation and borrowing policies are aimed at increasing consumption, saving and investment. Unnecessary or conspicuous consumption is to be ruthlessly curtailed and mass consumption which creates employment should be stimulated by means of suitable taxation and by giving suitable direction to public expenditure. But side by side, all possible incentives should be provided for saving and even compulsion may be resorted to so that the incomes are not recklessly squandered. On the other hand, sizable proportion of incomes should be saved towards capital formation. The savings must be channelised into productive investments. For this purpose, necessary mechanism must be provided like a sound capital market and healthy stock exchanges. Thus both taxation and public expenditure should be geared to economic growth and development.

(*d*) To maintain economic stability and price stability is another important objective of fiscal policy. It must be so designed as to maintain a reasonably stable price level and to eliminate cyclical fluctuations. A suitable fiscal policy has to be formulated for an inflationary situation and for depression.

During depression there is wide-spread unemployment and fiscal policy must not only remove this unemployment but generate additional employment. The government should adopt a taxation policy which encourages private consumption and investment. Taxes are reduced to provide incentives for investment; public expenditure is increased through budget deficits which are financed by borrowing from the public, commercial banks and the central bank of the country. During depression government spending assumes a great importance. It seeks to lift the economy out of the morass of stagnation. Public expenditure (pump priming) revives economic activity and compensatory spending by government is intended to make up the deficiency of private investment. Government increases its expenditure on public works and there are transfer payments like subsidies and relief payments. "Massive deficit-financed spending can almost surely put millions back to work and push the economy back to reasonably high level of employment."[5]

During inflation, however, the fiscal policy has to be different. Through taxation and borrowing, the government must withdraw money from the income stream so that the purchasing power is taken away from the public. This will exercise deflationary pressure and tend to bring down prices. But the crucial thing is that the withdrawal of money from the income-stream should not be replaced by Government spending.

Thus, fiscal policy should remove both inflationary and deflationary pressures and make the working of the economy smooth and steady.

To sum up, fiscal policy can serve as a powerful instrument in taking the economy to the goal of full employment, by mobilising productive resources and their optimum utilisation, increasing government expenditure and investment to cover the gap between income and consumption by raising consumption function, by encouraging private investment, by maintaining economic stability, by promoting capital formation and by suitably altering distribution of income.

Monetary policy for Full Employment

Monetary policy refers to the measures which the central bank of a country adopts to expand and contract credit as the economic situation may demand. It is aimed at influencing the availability and cost of funds with which the community may have to finance economic activity.

For this purpose, the central bank uses the well-known instruments of credit control, *viz*., manipulation of the bank rate, open market operations and other measures of general and selective credit controls. The central bank regulates the rates of interest and other terms of lending in the money market and it also regulates the money supply with the public.

Among the objectives of monetary policy we may mention maintaining neutrality of money, exchange stability, price stability, steady economic growth and

5. Bach. G. L. –*Economics*, p. 280.

above all full employment. The attainment and maintenance of full employment is now regarded as the most important aim of monetary policy. According to Crowther, the main object of monetary policy is to bring about equilibrium between saving and investment in the country and to create conditions for full employment. Keynes strongly favoured the use of monetary policy for maintaining economic activity at the highest possible level.

Monetary policy can generate employment through increased investment. Through cheap money policy (*i.e.*, low rates of interest) it can induce the entrepreneurs to borrow and invest. Judicious investment encouraged by a suitable monetary policy can, through multiplier and acceleration effects, raise the level of employment in the country. It can not only take the country to the goal of full employment but also maintain the level of full employment by maintaining in the economy stable cost-price structure.

Monetary Policy for achieving full employment.

In order to ensure economic growth (which means more employment) with stability the monetary policy must protect the economy from the baneful influences of both depression and inflation.

During depression, a suitable monetary policy should be pursued to offset the decline in the velocity of money, to stimulate lending for investment by bringing down interest rates and try to inject cash into the economy and raise prospects of profit. On the other hand, when there exists an inflationary situation, the monetary policy can slow down the rate of expansion of money supply, to offset the increase in its velocity, to reduce liquid assets with the people, to reduce consumption spending and investment by raising the interest rates. In this way, it can restore health and stability to the economy and create conditions for the growth of income and employment.

But monetary policy alone cannot play the trick. A suitable combination of monetary policy and fiscal policy including prudent management of public debt is required to increase the level of employment in a country.

It may, however, be emphasised that in the under-developed economies, the role of monetary policy is extremely limited, since the central bank control does not extend to the entire money market. A major portion of the money market is unorganised over which the writ of the central bank does not run. Stock exchanges are also not properly developed. The nature of unemployment in under-developed economies is not cyclical; hence it cannot be set right by the manipulation of credit policy. But even here, the monetary policy can be used to influence the pattern of investment and output through control of bank credit. It can be made effective through selective credit control. In various ways, monetary policy can influence economic growth and the growth of employment. It can help in the solution of balance of payments problems. In all these ways, the weapons of monetary policy can be used to raise the level of employment.

Incomes Policy for Full Employment

There is no doubt that income policy can have a far-reaching effect on the level of economic activity, and hence the level of employment in a country. For instance, if the government does not properly control incomes, *i.e*, salaries, wages, dividend incomes, *etc*., it may end in inflation or damage the industrial structure. A suitable income policy is essential to achieve and maintain a high level of employment. Instrument of income policy can be used to reconcile economic growth and price stability. Increase in wages and other incomes must be in tune with the rate of growth in the national output. It can curb private consumption expenditure and thus create savings which can be invested to increase employment.

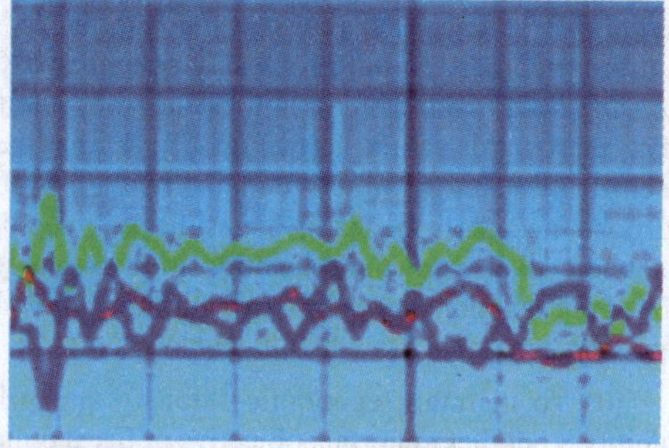

It is essential that wage and non-wage incomes should be properly regulated in the interest of economic growth and economic stability and full employment.

Price Policy for Full Employment

We have already seen that in the interest of a high level of employment, a suitable price policy is essential. Price fluctuations are inimical to steady economic growth. Both inflation and deflation are detrimental to economic activity. Booms and slumps have a disturbing effect on the volume of employment. Price policy must seek to protect the economy from these business fluctuations. Lowering prices of goods and services may result in expansion of their markets and the resultant increase in supply will increase employment. A fall in factor prices will raise marginal efficiency of capital and hence promote investment and create employment. Price control and price support policy can be used to maintain economic activity at a high level, which means increased employment.

International Measures for Full Employment

Co-operation and contacts with the other nations and international political and economic organisations can go a long way to increase economic activity and level of employment. Obviously, loans from the I.M.F., the World Bank, and other international bodies have helped in maintaining economic stability of economically advanced nations and promoted economic development of under-developed economies. This has no doubt resulted in increasing the volume of employment. Domestic fiscal, trade and monetary policies must be properly co-ordinated with international measures.

Conclusions

Thus, policy for full employment must embrace suitable fiscal policy, monetary policy, income policy, price policy and international measures to achieve and maintain a high level of income and employment. A sound policy for full employment must control economic fluctuations and for this tax rates should be properly adjusted and public expenditure properly channelised. Interest rates should be suitably adjusted by a wise monetary policy. In the matter of income policy, wage rates should be so controlled as to promote an equilibrium ratio of wages to profits; there should be a balanced wage structure. Consumption should be controlled, propensity to consume raised and private investment stimulated and public investment increased.

IS/LM FRAME WORK

To determine an equilibrium with the help of fiscal policy and monetary policy :

Fiscal policy came to the forefront after the keynesian revolution of 1936. It was Keynes functional finance approach, which helped in rescuing the economies, which was shaken by the great depression. Even today it is the fiscal policy which has dominated the policy making of the governments all over the world irrespective of whether they are developed or under developed. On the other hand monetorists still are of the opinion that "economy is essentially to a greater extent based on monetary phenomenonn. Though today it is the monetary revolution which has resulted in a greater degree of flexibility in the economies. For the time being it may be the monetary economics which is dominating in the form of the role of international financial institutions, the developed as well as under developed countries financial institutions, flow of easy capital (portfolio as well as direct foreign investments), the governments deficit finance policies, the innovation in banking systems in the form of *ATM*, credit cards, easy availability of loans for whether productive purpose or unproductive purpose, and the change in the habits and motives, of demand for money has resulted in the dynamism of the economies of the world. "It is very difficult to predict the collapse of international monetary economic system, as well as the domination of service sector in the economy in the days to follow".

"There is no time bound for such a collapse".

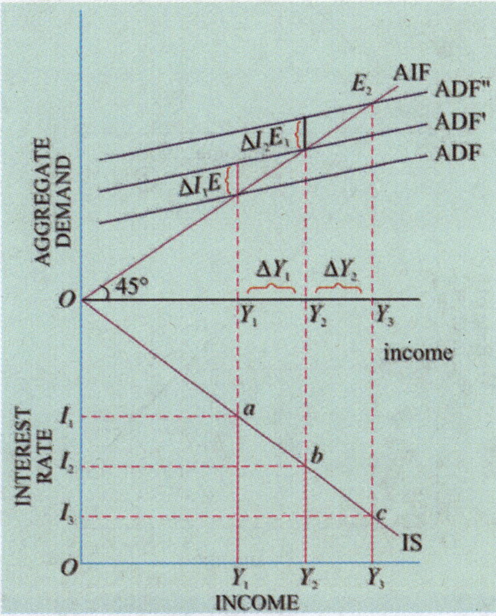

Fig. 46.1. Goods markets equilibrium and IS curve.

The economies of the world today is not fully dependent on only monetary or fiscal policy but a blend of both along with some adjustments.

IS curve is obtained with the help of fiscal policy or the so called goods market.

In the above diagram

ASF = Aggregate Supply function,

ADF = Aggregate demand function,

ADF′ and *ADF*′′ is increase in aggregate demand due to governments spending (Fiscal Policy) that is ΔI_1 and ΔI_2 which is nothing but autonomous investment by the government.

In the diagram, 46.1 the upper part is aggregate demand on *y*-axis and real income on *x*-axis, in the lower part it is interest-rate on *y*-axis and real income on *x*-axis. '*ASF*' aggregate supply function is given, the initial equilibrium is at point '*E*' where '*ADF*' intersects '*ASF*'. If we draw a perpendicular on *x*-axis we get 'OY_1' as the income. Now the government, through its fiscal economies increases the public expenditure to the tune of ΔI_1, which shifts the ADF^1 and this through the multiplier effect increases the income from 'OY_1' to 'OY_2'. In the same way as government spending increases by 'ΔI_2', (*ADF*) bring equilibrium at 'E_2' which results through multiplier effect to increase income up to 'OY_3'.

In the lower diagram it is the relationship between the rate of interest and real income. To a certain extent this is based on the real return of investment.

In the lower part at OI_1 rate of interest OY_1, is income which is obtained from the perpendicular drawn from the upper diagram. In the same way when we draw perpendicular on '*x*'-axis of lower diagram through upper diagram, we get the points, *i.e.*, OI_2 interest rate to OY_2 income, and OI_3 interest rate to OY_3 income.

When we join all these equilibrium points of '*a*', '*b*', '*c*' we get a line which is nothing but *IS*′ curve.

Let us explain this concept of '*IS*' curve which is nothing but the classical concept of *I I* = *SS* or investment demand = savings.

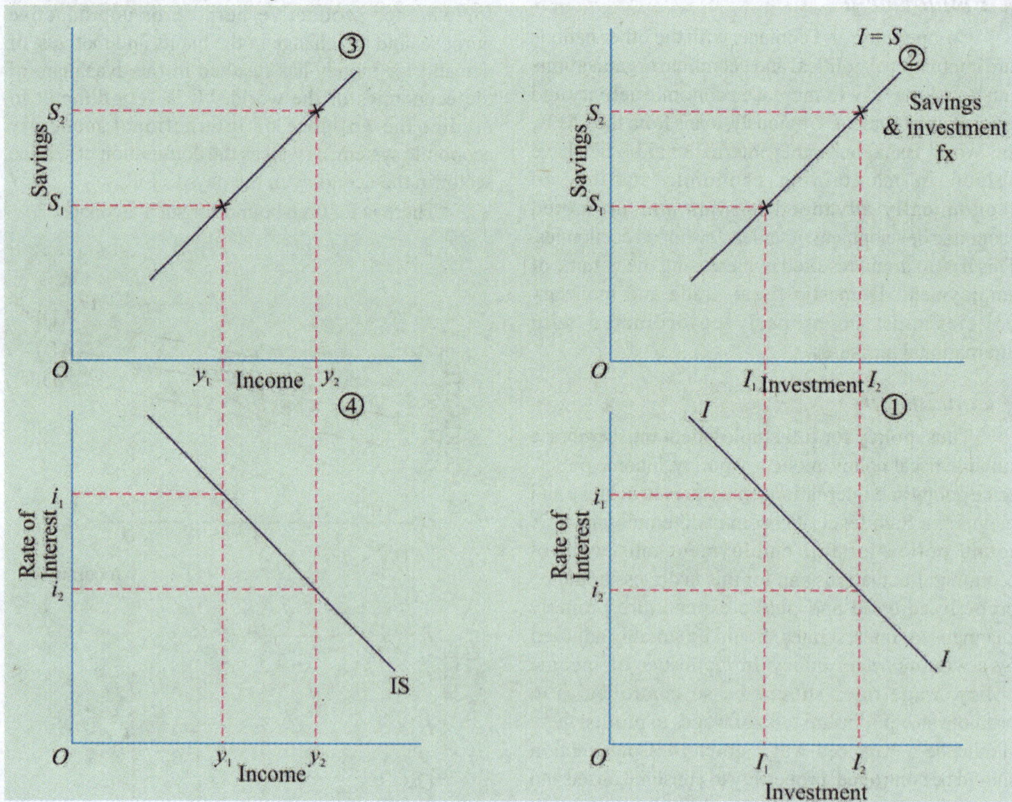

Fig. 46.2. Derivation of IS curve from Saving Investment equality.

	Quadrant I	II	III	IV
x-axis	Investment I_1 & I_2	Investment I_1 & I_2	Income Y_1, Y_2	Income Y_1, Y_2
y-axis	Interest i_1 & i_2	Savings S_1 & S_2	Savings S_1 & S_2	Interest i_1 & i_2

$Y = C + S.$

Income = Consumption + Savings.

According to classical economists $S = I$

Savings = Investment

$C = f(y)$ Consumption is a C function of income

$I = f(i)$ Investment is a function at rate of interest.

Savings is a function of income.

$S = f(y)$

$\therefore \quad Y = f(y) + f(i) \quad \rightarrow \quad Y = C + I$

$Y = f(y) + f(y) \quad \rightarrow \quad Y = C + S$

$\therefore \quad f(y) = f(i).$

$\therefore$ '*IS*' curve is derived on the basis of relationship between '*income*' (y) and rate of interest (i).

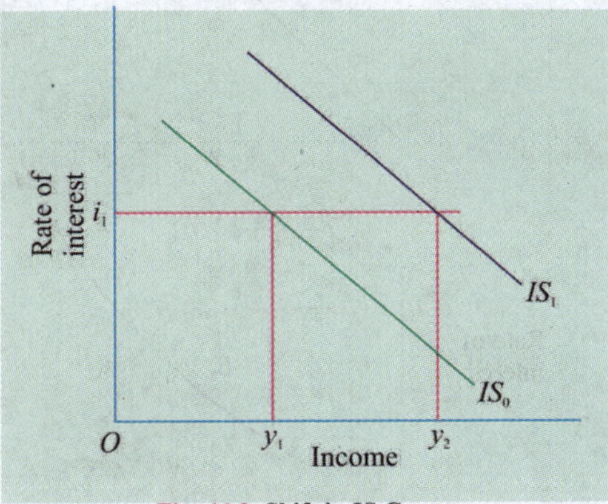

Fig. 46.3. **Shift in IS Curve.**

Shift in the IS curve :–

"The derivation of *IS*' curve shows that the goods (product) market equilibrium between the planned investments equals to planned savings". If at all the government plans to shift the complete '*IS*' curve than this needs the fiscal policy frame up in which the government has to increase the total planned investment. That can be shown by the diagram below.

Money Market

The equilibrium of money market is essentially the work of the central bank which must be framed or evolved under the monetary policy. The money market concept is developed on the basis of Keynesian liquidity preference theory. Keynesian liquidity preference theory which takes into account that the "interest is the outcome of demand for money and supply of money."

In the below diagram 46.4 on '*x*'-axis in figure '*a*' is

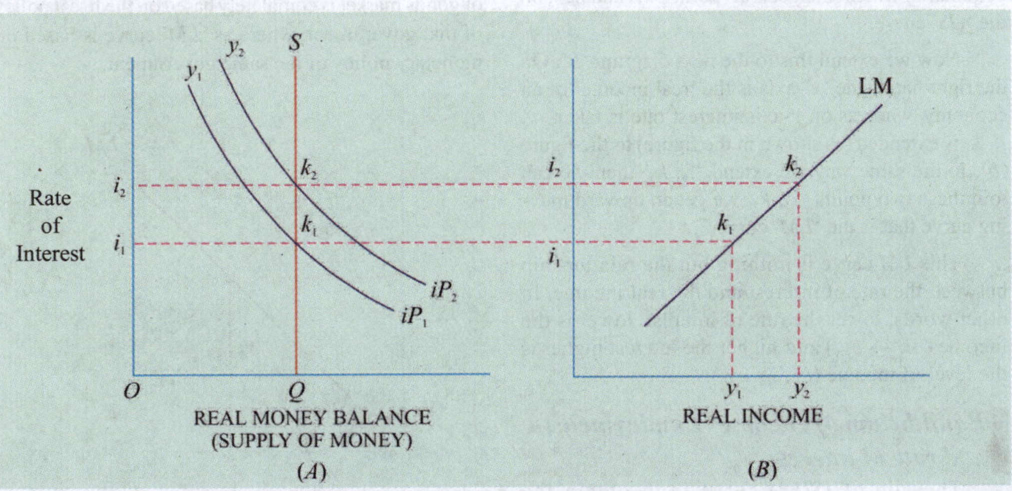

Fig. 46.4 **Money market equilibrium and LM curve.**

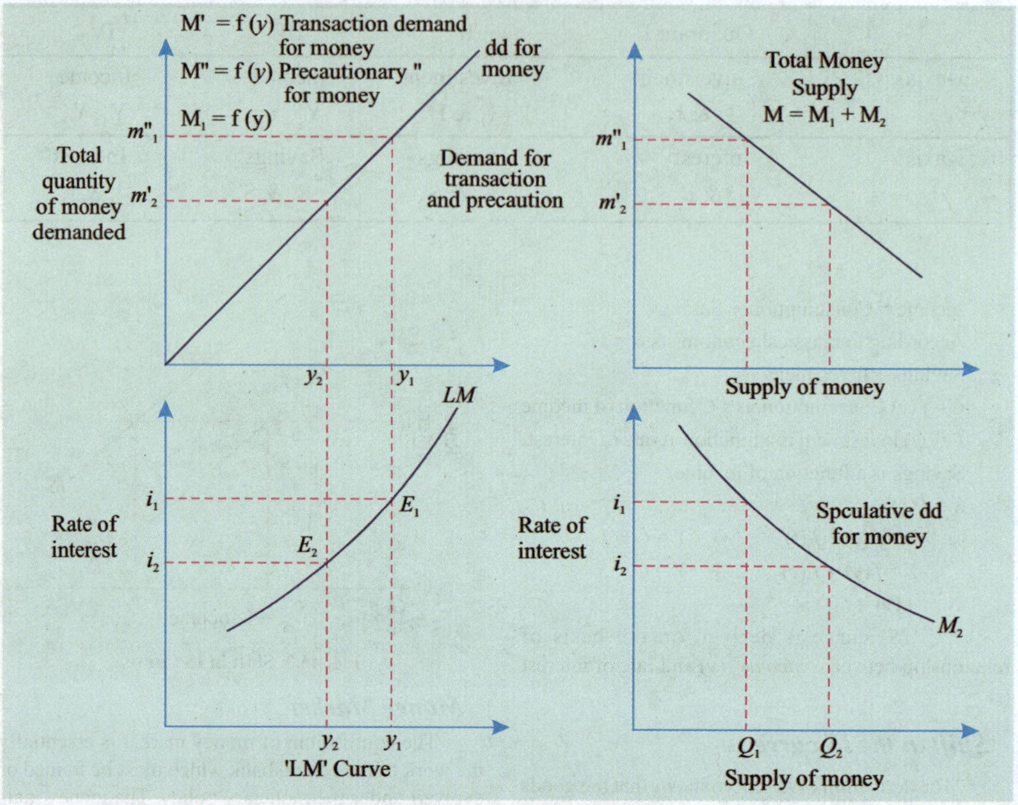

Fig. 46.5. Derivation of LM curve from equilibrium of demand and supply of money.

the total supply of money (Real money balances) which is a perfectly inelastic supply curve '*QS*'. (In other words the supply of money is fixed in an economy by the government). On *y*-axis the rate of interest is taken 'LP_1' and 'LP_2' are two liquidity preference of a community which intersects at 'point' 'k_1' and 'k_2', on the '*QS*' curve.

Now we extend this to the next diagram '*B*'. On the right hand side '*x*'-axis is the 'real income' of an economy, whereas on *y*-axis interest rate is taken. . . i_1, k_1 is extended (as shown in the figure) to the figure '*b*', in the same way we extend 'i_2, k_2' then we can join these two points 'k_1, k_2' we get an upward moving curve that is the '*LM*' curve.

This *LM* curve is nothing but the relationship between the rate of interest and the real income. In other words, lower the rate of interest, lower is the income ($oi_1 \rightarrow oy_1$) and higher the interest higher is the level of income ($oi_2 \rightarrow oy_2$).

Equilibrium of Income (Employment) and rate of interest

The aim of *IS*/*LM* curve is to obtain the equilibrium level of income and employment in the Keynesian sense. It is a blend of classical economists (*IS* curve-goods market) and Keynesian economists (*LM*-curve-money market), so as to determines the desirable level of income and employment in the economy. In modern contemporary economics *IS* curve or goods market is completely based on the fiscal policy of that government, where as '*LM*' curve is based on monetary policy of the same government.

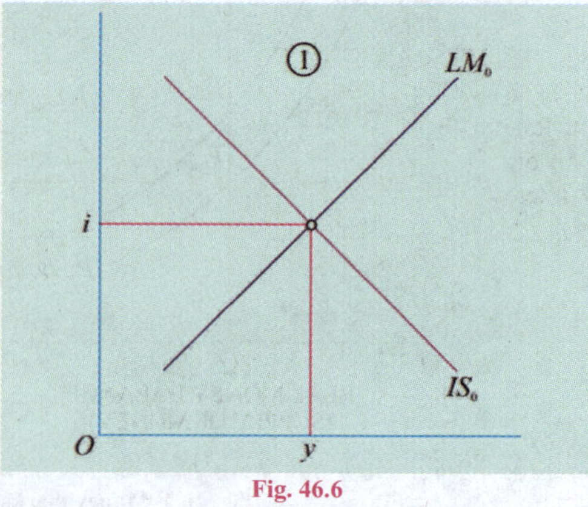

Fig. 46.6

Crowding Out Effect

Crowding out effect is nothing but the exit of some private entrepreneur from the investment in the economy due to the fiscal policy measures (goods market). The aim of the monetary policy is to bring about a reduction in crowding out effect so as to increase the level of income and output in the economy, without disturbing the rate of interest.

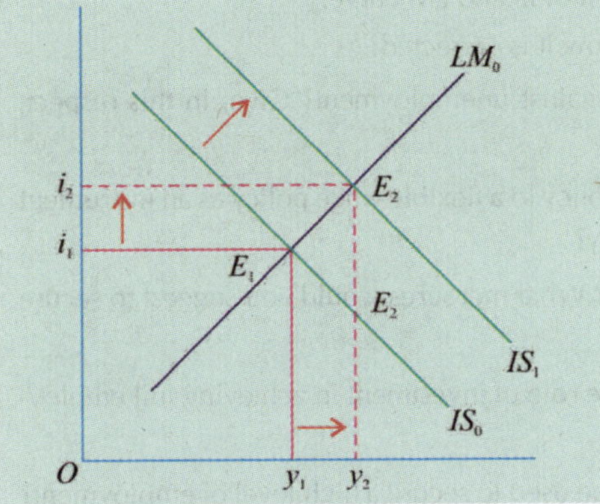

Fig. 46.7. **Crowding Out**

(i) In the above diagram initial economic equilibrium of income and interest rate is at point '*E*' which determines 'OI_1' → 'OY_1' that is OI_1 rate of interest and 'OY_1' level of income and employment. That is given by IS_0 and LM_0 curves.

(ii) Now the government increase ↑ public expenditure through its fiscal policy. This brings a shift in the *IS* curve from IS_0 to IS_1.

This leads to certain changes in the overall economic set-up. That is the rate of interest shifts from 'oi_1' to 'oi_2' and the level of income and employment changes from 'oy_1' to 'oy_2'. Due to this there are certain repercussions on the economy that is the concept of "crowding out effect".

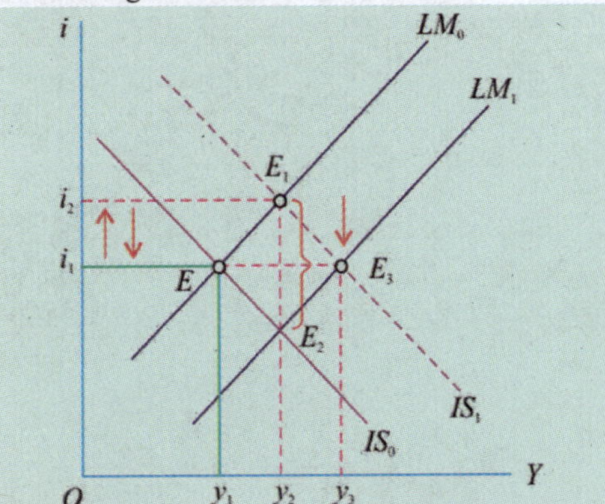

Fig. 46.8. **Monetary Policy to eliminate crowding out.**

"Crowding out effect" is nothing but, the exit of the private entrepreneurs from the economy due to increase in rate of interest from oi_1 to oi_2. In the diagram 'E_1E_2' is the crowding out effect.

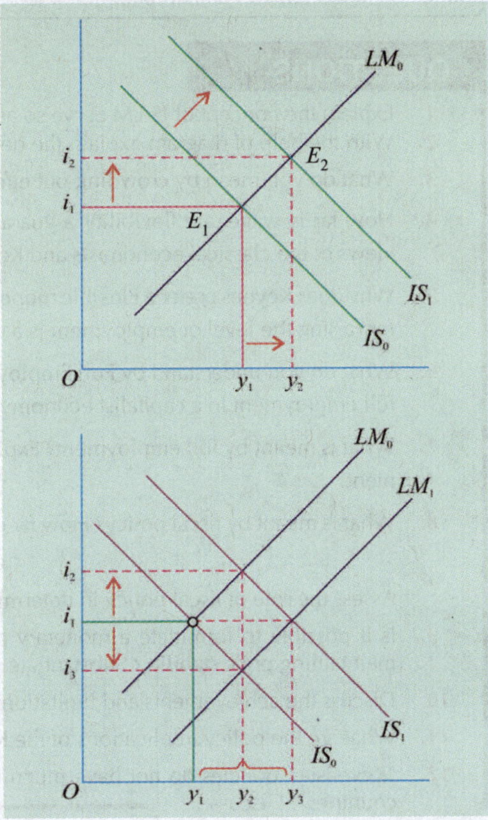

Fig. 46.9.

(iii) Now the government wants to minimise this crowding out effect. Hence the government resorts to the monetary policy (money market). In the diagram there is a shift of *LM* curve from 'LM_0' to 'LM_1' due to this monetary policy measure which intersects the IS_1 curve at point 'E_3'.

'E_3' is the new level of economy income and employment, which shows that the 'rate of interest' is reversed back to 'OI_1' from 'OI_2', but the economy's income and employment level is increased from 'OY_1' to 'OY_3'. This is the net result of both monetary and fiscal policy, which has resulted in an increase in income with a minimum level of crowding out, by bringing about the pre-policy rate of interest *viz.* oi_1.

In modern contemporary economic policy measures, the blend of fiscal policy and monetary policy is used so as to correct the economic disequilibrium.

Key terms

Seasonal unemployment, Keynesian unemployment or Cyclical unemployment, Nature of unemployment in underdeveloped countries, Full employment, Policy for full employment, International measures for full employment, IS/LM Framework.

QUESTIONS

1. Explain the concept of IS-LM curve so as to obtain economic equilibrium.
2. With the help of diagram explain the derivation of IS and LM curve.
3. What do you mean by crowding-out effect? How it is corrected?
4. How far is wage-rate flexibility a guarantee against unemployment? Give, in this respect, views of the classical economists and Keynes.
5. Why does Keynes prefer a Flexible monetary policy to a flexible wage policy as an instrument for raising the level of employment is a country?
6. What do you understand by Full Employment? What measures would you suggest to secure full employment in a capitalist economy?
7. What is meant by full employment? Explain the role of investment in achieving full employment.
8. What is meant by fiscal policy? How far can it be used to secure a high level of employment?

   Or

   Assess the role of fiscal policy in determining income and employment.
9. Is it possible to formulate a monetary policy designed to achieve full employment while maintaining price stability? Substantiate your answer.
10. Discuss the achievements and limitations of Keynesian economics.
11. What are the policy implications of the Keynesian Economics?
12. "Keyensian policies do not have much relevance to the problems of the under-developed countries". Discuss.

UNIT III

Economic Fluctuations

Chapters

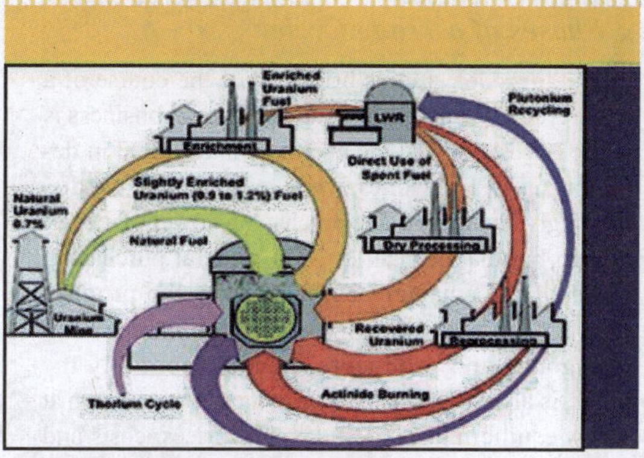

TRADE CYCLES

Meaning of a Trade Cycle

The world has registered remarkable economic progress especially during the last 150 years. But it would be wrong to think that this economic progress has been a steady upward swing and a continuous movement forward. On the other hand, every businessman knows that, after ten or twelve years, the production machinery receives a rude shock, which throws it out of gear for a number of years. There are upward swings and then downward swings in business. The periods of business prosperity alternate with periods of adversity. Every boom is followed by a slump, and vice versa. This is a trade cycle. The trade cycle simply means the whole course of trade or business activity which passes through all phases of prosperity and adversity.

Economic Crisis

An economic crisis, on the other hand, means a period of stress and strain when businessmen find it difficult to meet their commitments. In the words of Adolph Wagner, "Crises imply the overwhelming and simultaneous occurrence of inability on the part of independent entrepreneurs to pay their debts." Or in J. S. Mill's words, "There is said to be a commercial crisis when a great number of merchants have or apprehend they have a difficulty in meeting their engagement. It is a commercial crisis when only merchants are involved in a difficulty. But when it is accentuated and leads to bank failures it is called financial crisis."

Trading in Stock Exchange.

Phases of a Trade Cycle

Depression. Let us briefly trace the course of a trade cycle. We might start at a point when business is at the lowest ebb and the economy is engulfed in depression. The lucky ones, who are employed, get distressingly low wages. The purchasing power of money is high but that of man low. The general purchasing power of the community being very low, the productive activity, both in the production of consumers' goods and producers' goods, especially the latter, is at a very low level. Business settles down at a new equilibrium at a low level of prices, costs and profits. This new adjustment or equilibrium may last for a number of years.

Recovery. But the things are not going to continue to be in a depressed state, for ever. After the depression has lasted for some time, rays of hope appear on the business horizon. Pessimism gives place to optimism. The depression contains within itself the germs of recovery. After the depression has lasted for some time, the situation is found favourable for a business venture. Wages are low even for efficient workers, sufficient number of whom is now available. Money is cheap and so are the other materials and the factors of production. Prices may be low but the costs too are low. This induces an entrepreneur, who may have sufficient financial backing, to take the risk. He orders repairs, renewals and replacements and, perhaps, a new plant. Constructional and allied industries receive orders and re-employ workers who spend their newly-acquired purchasing power on consumers' goods. This stimulates further investment and production in several other industries. Lo! the business has turned the corner.

Boom. Recovery once started gathers momentum. The slender stream of recovery, when it has started flowing, is strengthened by numerous tributaries on its way. The revival of investment in one industry leads to a revival in another. With the general revival of demand, prices show an upward trend. The businessman's income takes a forward jump while wages, interest, and other costs lag behind. Profit margins are thus widened. Optimism grows and spreads far and wide. Exceptional business prosperity turns businessman's head, and they indulge in over-trading. This phase of the trade cycle is known as boom.

End of the Boom. But just as depression created the conditions for recovery, similarly the boom conditions generate their own checks. All idle factors have been employed and further demand for them must raise their prices, but the quality available now is inferior. Less efficient workers have to be taken on higher wages. Rate of interest rises and so, also the prices of the essential materials. As a consequence, costs take an upward swing. They overtake prices and the profit margins are first narrowed and then begin to disappear. The boom conditions are thus almost at an end.

Crisis. Then starts the downward course. Fearing that the era of profits has come to a close, businessmen stop ordering further equipment and materials. The Government applies the axe mercilessly. The bankers insist on repayment. The bottlenecks appear and stocks accumulate. Desire for liquidity increases all round. This accentuates the depression. Just as the recovery is self-reinforcing, the forces of depression are also self-accumulating. There is general distress. This phase of the trade cycle is known as the crisis –a point of critical convulsions.

Slump. The crisis is the period of utmost suffering for businessmen. But they recover in course of time from the stunning blow. Their commitments are liquidated somehow and business enters into the stage of what has already been described as depression or slump or a state of stagnation.

Loard Overstone describes the course of a trade cycle: "state of quiescence – next improvement – growing – confidence – prosperity – excitement –

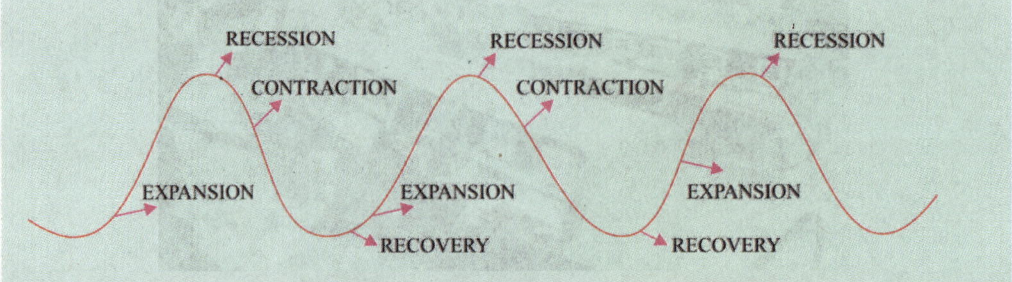

Fig. 47.1

over-trading –convulsion – pressure – distress – ending again in quiescence."[1] To use Mitchell's terminology, we can mark four distinct phases of a business cycle, *viz.*, Expansion (upward movement). Recession. Contraction (downward course) and Recovery. The above figure 47.1 represents these four phases.

Characteristics of a Trade Cycle

A study of trade cycles has revealed two important characteristics: (1) Its cyclical nature, *i.e.*, **periodicity,** (2) its general nature or **synchronism.**

In the first place, it has been found that trade cycles occur periodically at fairly regular intervals. The interval is not a precise one but the degree of regularity is sufficient to demonstrate the periodicity of a trade cycle. There is a general consensus of opinion that the cycle takes seven to ten years nearly to complete itself.

The second characteristic is synchronism or its all-embracing character. The business world is one economic unit, like a living organism. An attack on one part of the business organism is bound to send a shock to the other parts. If one firm is in grief, those who deal with it cannot remain unaffected, and they, in turn, will affect others with whom they may be in commercial intercourse. Thus, depression passes from one industry to another. A time comes when all industries in all districts and all firms in the country are engulfed. Few can escape the deluge.

The Cobweb Theory of Trade Cycle

The cobweb cycles are generally of three types (*i*) Continuous (*ii*) Diverging and (*iii*) Converging. The Cobweb theory of cycles are generally a short term phenomenon. In these cycles the equilibrium and disequilibrium concepts are partial in nature, it may not be of a macro-economic nature : the theory is based on demand and supply aspect and neglectes the time lag. Generally the theories application is to a greater extent limited to agriculture productivity, some economists extended this theory to durable goods.

(1) Continuous type. In this case the demand forces and supply forces adjust themselves automatically.

In 47.2 diagram the forces of 'demand' and 'supply' moves into disequilibrium. If price is high say 'P_1' quantity supplied may be more but at 'P_1' price quantity demanded may be less. Hence more quantity of goods produced in the economy may bring down the 'price' to 'P_0' and this may result in the decrease in the quantity supplied, In this case the action and reaction of 'price' factor and quantity supplied or production factor may move upward and down- word. This type of cycle may be of a theoretical importance, in reality it may happen for a very short-period.

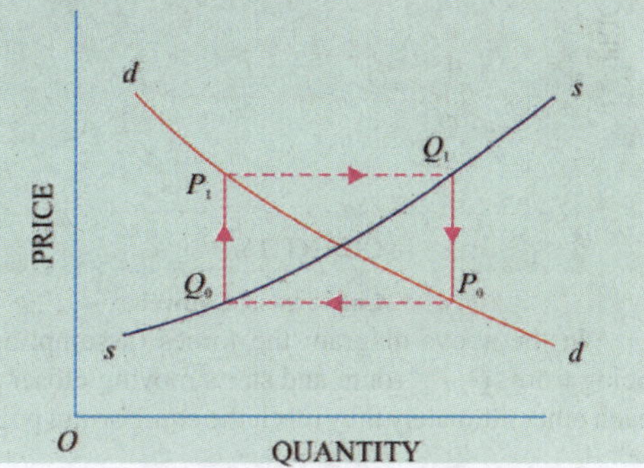

Fig. 47.2. **Continuous Cobweb.**

(2) Divergent type. In this case the forces of demand and supply may move away from the equilibrium due to the upward downword trend of action and reaction.

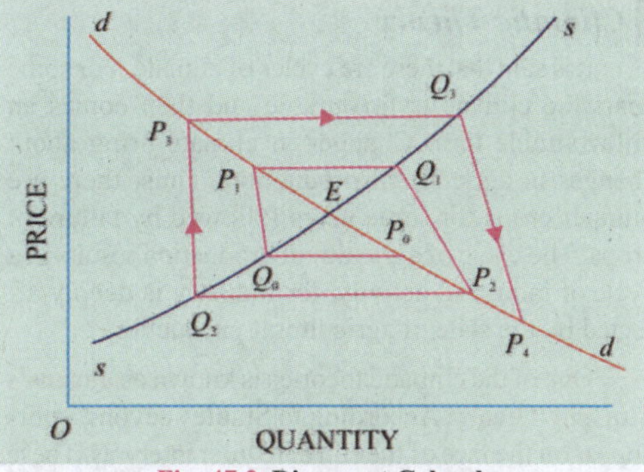

Fig. 47.3. **Divergent Cobweb.**

In diagram, 47.3 '*dd*' demand (consumers) curve which gives the price factor and '*SS*' is supply curve (from producers) the quantity supplied. The forces are moving away from the equilibrium point '*E*'. Initially it may move from the path, 'P_0' 'prices' and 'Q_0' quantity leads to increase in prices, as price increase it induces more production of goods, *viz.* 'P_1' leads to 'Q_1'→ this may bring down the price to 'P_2' and so on.

$$P_0 Q_0 \rightarrow P_1 Q_1 \rightarrow Q_1 P_2 \ldots$$

(3) Convergent type. In this the demand forces and supply forces narrows down towards the equilibrium. The gap between the demand and supply forces reduces, and ultimately they reach an equilibrium point.

1. Quoted by Marshall in *Money, Credit and Commerce*, p. 246.

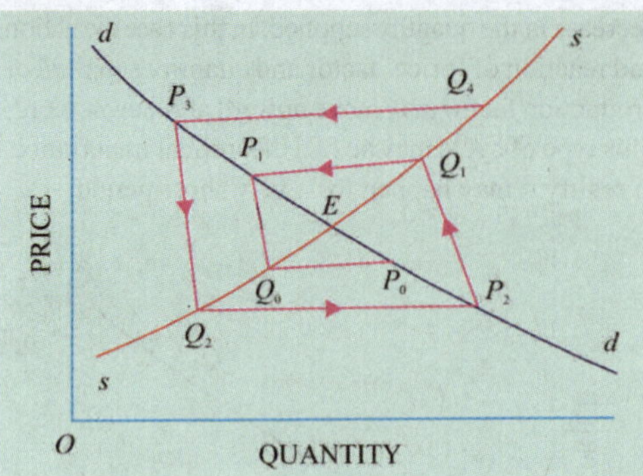

Fig. 47.4. Convergent Cobweb.

In the above diagram the forces (assumption) being from 'Q_4 P_3' route and starts moving closer to each other ultimately they reach the equilibrium point 'E'.

THEORIES OF TRADE CYCLE

Several theories of trade cycles have been put forward from time to time. We shall say here a word about some well-known theories.

Climatic Theory

It is said that there are cycles of climate. For some years the climate is favourable and then comes an unfavourable turn. Changes in climate bring about changes in agricultural production. Thus, there are bumper crops for some years followed by failure of crops. The cycle of agricultural production results in a cycle of industrial activity, for industry is deeply affected by the state of agricultural production.

One of the climatic theories is known as **Jevons's Sunspot Theory.** According to Stanley Jevons, spots appear on the face of the sun at regular intervals. These spots affect the emission of heat from the sun, which, in turn, conditions the degree of rainfall. The rain affects agriculture, which, in turn, affects trade and industry. That is how trade cycles are caused.

Comments. Modern economists do not place much reliance on climatic theories. Nobody can say with certainty about the nature of the sunspots and the degree to which they affect rain. There is no doubt that climate affects agricultural production. But the climatic theory does not adequately explain periodicity of the trade cycle.

Psychological Theory

Attempts are made by some economists to explain trade cycles in terms of psychology. There are moods of optimism alternating with moods of pessimism without there being any tangible basis for the same. At some stage, people just think that trade is good and that it is going to remain good. Business activity is intensified and becomes feverish. Then, all of a sudden, people start thinking that the period of prosperity has lasted long enough and adversity is round the corner. Thus, although there was no valid reason for depression to come about, but it is brought about by the people themselves. It is all psychological.

Comments. The psychological theory lacks any sound basis. There is conjectural element in it. There is no doubt that industrial fluctuations are affected by the waves of optimism and pessimism and are intensified by them. But they do not explain the course of the trade cycles or their periodicity aspect.

Under-consumption Theory

According to under-consumption theory, there is too much of saving during a boom and further additions to saving reduce the level of consumption. A reduction in the level of consumption, in the face of increasing productive capacity, must sooner or later lead to the collapse of the boom. This theory is associated with the names of J. A. Hobson and Major Douglas.

But why does over-saving or under-consumption take place? This is because during the boom, though prices rise wages lag behind, so that profit margins are progressively increased. There takes place a shift in the distribution of incomes in favour of profits and against the wage-earners. The saving propensity of the rich is greater than that of the poor, so that a shift in income distribution in favour of the rich leads to an increase in the volume of saving. This process goes on till prices keep on rising and wages lag behind. However, one result of such a state of affairs is that the demand for consumption goods gets steadily reduced. This leads to contraction in their output which precipitates the crisis.

Comments. The under-consumption or over saving theory contains an element of truth. But it cannot be the sole or adequate explanation. For example, if the under-consumption theory were to be exclusively relied on, we should expect the consumption goods industries to fluctuate more than investment goods industries. But exactly reverse is the case in real life during a trade cycle.

Monetary Theory

R. G. Hawtrey was a firm believer in the monetary theory. According to him, variations in flows of money are the sole and sufficient determinants of business activity and account for alternating phases of prosperity and depression. Non-monetary causes like drought, floods, earthquakes, wars, strikes, unbalanced development of certain industries, *etc.*, can at best cause a **partial** as distinguished from **general depression.**

The argument is something like this: Most of the business is done with borrowed money. When business prospects are good, the banks freely extend credit facilities. Assured of cheap and easy credit facilities, the businessmen go on expanding their business, entering into further and further commitments. A huge superstructure of credit is built up. This superstructure can be maintained by the continuance of cheap money conditions, if not their further extension. But a point is reached. When banks think that they have gone a bit too far in the matter of advances. Probably their reserve ratio has fallen dangerously low. In self-defence, they apply the brake, curb further expansion of credit, and begin to recall advances. This sudden suspension of credit facilities proves a bomb-shell to the business community.

Businessmen have been counting on the renewal of overdrafts and cash credit facilities. But contrary to their expectation, moneys are being called in. They have to sell off their stocks in order to repay. This general desire for liquidity depresses the market, for the stocks are being unloaded all round. Some firms, weaker links of the chain, fail to meet their obligations and bring to grief those whom they could not pay. Very solvent firms may fail, simply because they do not receive timely financial assistance from the banks.

Thus, the monetary phenomena of hoarding and dishoarding, credit expansion and credit contraction have a lot to do with business cycles, since they represent a succession of inflationary and deflationary processes.

Comments. No doubt banking institutions play an important part in building up trade activity. But it is a bit unkind to say that they cause a crisis. The most that we can say is that they aggravate matters. They prop up a boom by an over-issue of credit and they accentuate a depression by its suspension. But neither the boom nor the depression originates with them. Secondly, a world phenomenon like a modern slump cannot be attributed to the isolated action of banks in one country. A trade cycle cannot, therefore, be exclusively attributed to the misbehaviour of money.

Over-investment Theory

Some writers attribute the boom to excessive investment and regard the slump as the necessary corrective for the imbalances created during the boom. That investment becomes excessive during the boom is borne out by the fact that investment goods industries expand faster than consumption goods industries during the upward phase of the cycle. During the depression, investment goods industries suffer more than consumption goods industries.

But why do investment goods industries expand faster than consumption goods industries in the boom phase of the cycle? On this point, there is a difference of opinion among the various theorists, who believe in the over-investment theory. Some economists like Hayek, Machlup, Ropke and Robbins trace this to the banking system. Though they do not regard the trade cycle to be a purely monetary phenomenon, yet they believe that the disparity in the growth rates of consumption goods industries and investment goods industries could not occur, if the banking system were not elastic. According to this version, an increase in investment opportunities is fed by a low rate of interest. In this way, there is encouragement to adopt more and more roundabout methods of production. Resources are increasingly withdrawn from consumption goods industries through a process of "forced saving".

Comments. The over-investment theory correctly states that fluctuations in the rate of investment are the main cause of trade cycles. However, the theory fails to offer a convincing explanation as to why investment fluctuates in so regular a manner. Many authors trace back fluctuations in investment to the behaviour of the banking system and that we have seen already is not a very satisfactory answer.

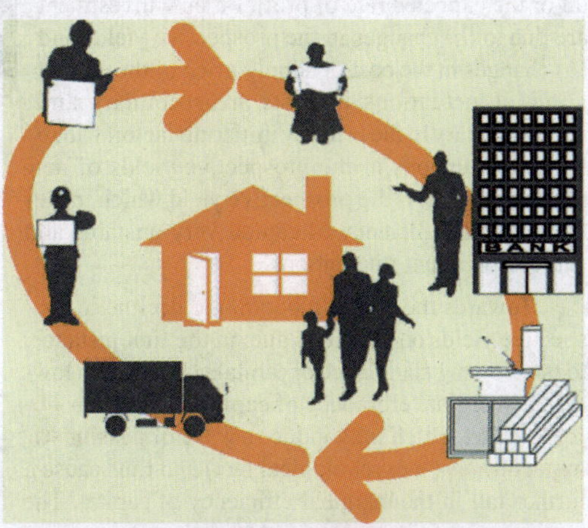

Money flow influences business cycle.

Keynes' s Theory

In explaining what determines at any time the prevailing level of income, output and employment, Keynes's 'General Theory' also provides an explanation of business cycle, because the business cycle is nothing more than a rhythmic fluctuation in the overall level of income, output and employment.

However, Keynes' 'General Theory' "is not a theory of business cycle as such. It is much more and also much less than that. It is more than a theory of the business cycle in the sense that it offers a general explanation for the level of employment quite independently of the cyclical nature of changes in employment. It is less than a complete theory of the business cycle because it makes no attempt to give a detailed account of the various phases of the cycle, and does not examine closely the empirical data of cyclical fluctuations, something which any complete study of the business cycle would presumably do."[2]

According to Keynes's, fluctuations in economic activity are caused by fluctuations in the rate of investment. And fluctuations in the rate of investment are caused mainly by fluctuations in the marginal efficiency of capital. The rate of interest, which is the other determinant of investment, is more or less stable and does not play a significant role in cyclical fluctuations in investment, but at times it reinforces and supplements the primary motivating factor (*i.e.*, changes in marginal efficiency of capital). Now, the marginal efficiency of capital is a new Keynesian name for the **expected rate of profit** on new investment. Therefore, the economic fluctuations result from the changes in expectations about the rate of profit on new investment.

Fluctuations in the marginal efficiency of capital or the expected rate of profit on new investment are due to (*a*) changes in the prospective yields and (*b*) changes in the cost or supply price of the capital goods. Fluctuations in costs are secondary and supplementary to the primary initiating factor, which is the fluctuations in the prospective yields of new capital goods. It is the prospective yield which makes the marginal efficiency of capital very unstable and subject to violent fluctuations.

Towards the end of a boom, the decline in prospective yields on capital is due, in the first instance, to the growing abundance of capital goods which lowers the marginal efficiency of capital. This is an **objective** fact which may induce a wave of **pessimistic expectations** (a psychological fact) and thus cause a further fall in the marginal efficiency of capital. The turning point from expansion to contraction is, thus, explained by a collapse in the marginal efficiency of capital. As investment falls, because of the decline in marginal efficiency of capital, the income also falls. The multiplier works in the reverse direction. A given fall in investment leads to a multiple fall in income. As income is falling rapidly, under the multiplier effect, the employment also goes tumbling down.

Just as the collapse of marginal efficiency of capital is the main cause of the upper turning point in the trade cycle, similarly the lower turning point *i.e.*, change from recession to recovery, is due to the **revival** of the marginal efficiency of capital. The interval, between the upper turning point and the start of recovery, is conditioned by two factors: (*i*) the time necessary for wearing out of durable capital assets, and (*ii*) the time required to absorb the excess stocks of goods left over from the boom. Just as the marginal efficiency of capital was pushed down by the growing abundance of capital goods during the period of boom, similarly as the stocks of capital goods are depleted and there grows a scarcity of capital goods, the marginal efficiency of capital rises, thereby inducing the businessmen to invest more. Income increases due to the multiplier effect. So the cumulative process starts upward.

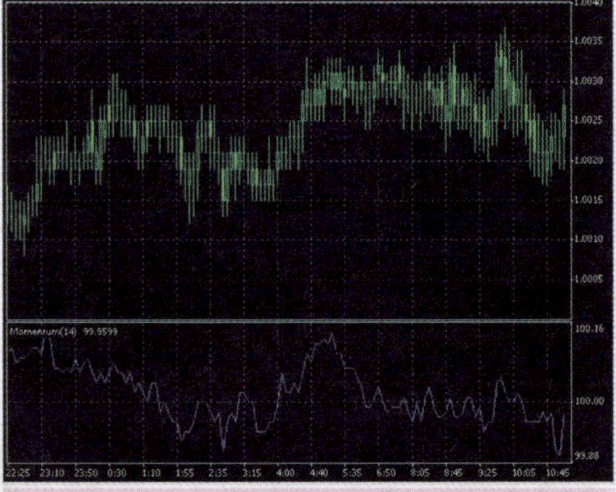

Fluctuations in rate of investment affect clonomic activity according to Keynes.

Comments. Since Keynes's 'General Theory', the theories of trade cycle have shown a great degree of convergence. Of course, even before Keynes, it was agreed that fluctuations in the rate of investment have something to do with the fluctuations in the level of activity, yet a systematic exposition was lacking. In a previous chapter (46), we investigated the relation between a change in investment and the resulting change in the level of national income. This is the familiar theory of multiplier. The theory of multiplier tells us that changes in investment will bring about magnified changes in the level of income and employment. This theory helps us in understanding the relation between investment and income.

But the theory of multiplier alone does not offer a full and satisfactory explanation of the trade cycle.

2. Dillard—Economics of J.M.Keynes, p. 276.

As has been observed above, a basic feature of the trade cycle is its cumulative character both on the upswing as well as the downswing, *i.e.*, once economic activity starts rising or falling, it gathers momentum and for a time feeds on itself. Thus, what we have to explain is the cumulative character of economic fluctuations. The theory of multiplier alone does not prove adequate for this task.

Suppose that investment rises by 100 rupees and that the magnitude of multiplier is 4. Then, from the theory of multiplier, we know that national income will rise by 400 and, if multiplier is the only force at work, that will be the end of the matter, with the economy reaching a new stable equilibrium at a higher level of national income. But, in real life, this is not likely to be so, for a rise in income produced by a given rise in investment, will have further repercussions on the economy. We have already studied this reaction in the theory of the accelerator.

Modern Theory: Interaction of Multiplier and Accelerator

Having studied the various theories of trade cycle, we turn to the modern theory. None of the theories explained above is fully satisfactory. The chief drawback of Keynes's theory of trade cycle is that he ignored the acceleration effect in his explanation of the trade cycle. As pointed out above, the multiplier alone cannot provide an explanation of the cyclical fluctuations. It is the interaction between multiplier and accelerator that gives rise to cyclical fluctuations in economic activity. An autonomous increase in the level of fixed investment raises income by a marginal amount according to the value of the multiplier. This increase in total income will induce further increase in investment through acceleration effect. When this happens, the chain of causation is linked round in a 'loop': investment affects income, which in turn affects investment plans.

How interaction between the multiplier and accelerator causes fluctuations in income can be easily understood from the following table:

In the table, we have assumed that the marginal propensity to consume is 2/3, the accelerator is 2, and that there is one-period lag. One-period lag means that an increase in income in one period induces an increase in consumption in the succeeding period. We have further assumed that an autonomous investment of Rs. 10 crores is added in each period which is continuously maintained in the succeeding periods. It will be noticed from the table that, when autonomous increase in investment of Rs. 10 crores is added in period 1, it gives rise to an increase in income of only Rs. 10 crores. It does not induce increase in consumption in period 1, as we have assumed a lag of one period.

Now with marginal propensity to consume of 2/3, the increase in income of Rs. 10 crores in period 1 induces an increase in consumption of Rs. 6.7 crores in period 2. With the value of accelerator as 2, there will be induced investment of Rs. 13.4 crores in period 2. Now the total increase in income in period 2 over the base period will be equal to the autonomous investment of Rs. 10 crores which is maintained in the second period plus the induced consumption of Rs. 6.7 crores plus the induced investment of Rs. 13.4 crores (total increase in income in period 2 = 30.1). Now, in the third period, the consumption would be equal to 30.1 × 2/3 = Rs. 20 crores.

The increase in consumption in period 3 over period 2 is Rs. 13.3 crores (*i.e.*, Rs. 20 crores–Rs. 6.7 crores). This increase in consumption of Rs. 13.3 crores will induce investment of the value of Rs. 26.6 crores in period 3. Thus, the total increase in the income in period 3 over the base period is equal to Rs. 56.6 crores. In the same manner, the changes in income for the succeeding periods will be determined. A glance at column 5 will show that there are great fluctuations in total income. Under the combined effect of the multiplier and accelerator, the income increases up to the 6th period, but, beyond the 6th period, it begins to decrease. 1st to 6th is the stage of expansion or upswing. The 6th one is a turning point and from 6th onward is the phase of contraction or down-swing.

In the above table, it has been assumed that there is no limitation of productive resources. In other words, there is no full employment ceiling. In the table, we have only tried to convey the idea that interaction between the multiplier and accelerator gives rise to fluctuations in total national income. We have taken certain values of the marginal propensity to consume (and hence of the multiplier) and the accelerator. The different values of the marginal propensity to consume and the accelerator will produce fluctuations of different magnitudes.

Now introducing the fact that there is a limit to the increase in national income set by the full employment ceilings, we may explain the different phases of the trade cycle with the aid of diagram used by Prof. Hicks. In Fig. 47.2, *AA* is the line representing autonomous investment. Prof. Hicks assumes that autonomous investment grows annually at a rate given by the slope of *AA*. Given the marginal propensity to consume, the simple multiplier is determined. Then, the multiplier and autonomous investment together determine the equilibrium level of income shown by the line *LL*. Hicks calls this the floor line. But induced investment has not yet been taken into account. If national income grows from one year to the next, as it would along the line *LL*, there is some amount of in-

(1)	Autonomous Investment (deviation from base period) (2)	Induced Consumption (3)	Induced Investment (4)	Total Deviation of Income from base period (5)
	Rs.	Rs.	Rs.	Rs.
Base Period	0	0	0	0
Period 1	10	0	0	10
,, 2	10	6.7	13.4	30.1
,, 3	10	20.0	26.6	56.6
,, 4	10	37.8	35.6	83.4
,, 5	10	55.6	35.6	101.2
,, 6	10	67.5	23.8	101.3
,, 7	10	67.6	0.2	77.8
,, 8	10	51.8	– 10.0	51.8
,, 9	10	34.6	– 10.0	34.6
,, 10	10	23.0	– 10.0	23.0
,, 11	10	15.4	– 10.0	15.4
,, 12	10	10.2	– 10.0	10.2
,, 13	10	6.8	– 6.8	10.0
,, 14	10	6.6	+ 0.2	16.8

duced investment via accelerator. The line *EE* shows the equilibrium time path of national income determined by autonomous investment and the combined effect of multiplier and accelerator. *FF* is the full employment ceiling. It is a line that shows the maximum national output at any period of time.

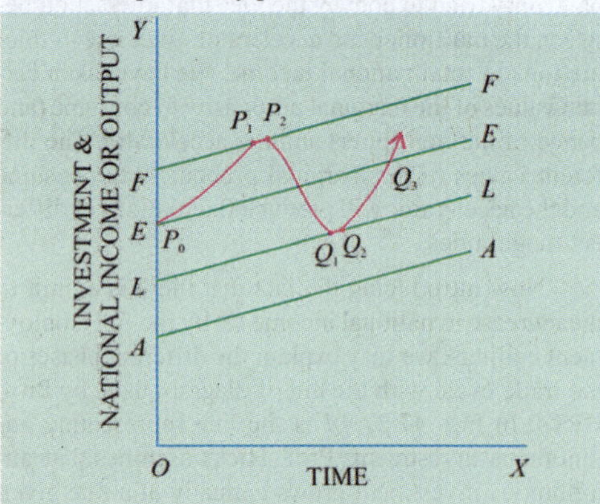

Fig. 47.5. **Phases of Trade Cycle.**

Starting from point *E*, the economy will be in equilibrium moving along the path *EE* determined by the combined effect of multiplier and accelerator and the growing level of autonomous investment. When the economy reaches point P_0 along the path *EE*, suppose there is an external shock, say an outburst of investment due to certain innovations or jump in government investment. When the economy experiences such an outburst of autonomous investment, it pushes the economy above the equilibrium path *EE* after point P_0. The rise in autonomous investment due to external shock causes national income to increase at a greater rate than shown by the slope of *EE*. This increase in national income will cause further increase in **induced investment** through acceleration effect. The increase in induced investment causes national income to increase by a magnified amount through multiplier.

Thus, under the combined effect of multiplier and accelerator, national income or output will rapidly expand along the path from P_0 to P_1. But this expansion must stop at P_1 because this is the full employment ceiling. The limited human and material resources of the economy do not permit a greater expansion of national income. Therefore, when point P_1 is reached, the rapid growth of national income must come to an end. Prof. Hicks assumes that the full employment ceiling grows at the same rate as autonomous investment. Therefore, *FF* slopes gently unlike the greater slope of the line from P_0 to P_1. When point P_1 is reached, the economy must grow at the same rate as the usual growth in the autonomous investment.

For a short time, the economy may crawl along

the full employment ceiling *FF*. But because national income has ceased to increase at the rapid rate, the induced investment via accelerator falls off to the level consistent with the modest rate of growth. But the economy cannot crawl along its full employment ceiling for a long time. The sharp decline in induced investment, when national income, and hence consumption, ceases to increase rapidly, initiates a contraction in the level of income and business activity. Thus, there is a slackening off at P_2 and the level of national income moves towards *EE*. Investment falls off rapidly and multiplier works in the reverse direction.

The fall in national income and output resulting from the sharp fall in induced investment will not stop on touching the level *EE* but will go further down. The economy must consequently move all the way down from point P_2 to point Q_1. But at point Q_1, the floor has been reached. National income will not fall further, because this is the equilibrium level given by the working of ordinary multiplier and autonomous investment free from the simultaneous operation of the accelerator. The economy may crawl along the floor through the path Q_1 to Q_2. In doing so, there is a growth in the level of national income. This rate of growth as before induces investment and both the multiplier and accelerator come into operation, and the economy will move towards Q_3 and the full employment ceiling *FF*. This is how the interaction between multiplier and accelerator causes economic fluctuations.

Kaldor's Contribution to Modern Trade Cycle Theory

We have explained above how Hicks explains the occurrence of trade cycles through the interaction of multiplier and accelerator. Kaldor also subscribes to the view that fluctuations in the level of economic activity (*i.e.*, trade cycles) take place due to the interaction of multiplier and accelerator but he uses a modified and more realistic form of accelerator and investment function. According to the conventional concept of accelerator, the investment or demand for capital depends upon the **rate of change** of the level of economic activity (*i.e.*, the level of income and employment). Kaldor has put forward the view, and most of the modern economists agree with him, that a more realistic concept of accelerator of investment function is that which considers that the demand for investment (or capital goods) depends upon the **level of activity** rather than the rate of change of that level. It should be remembered that in Kaldor's analysis the level of activity means the level of national output, income and employment. Further, the Hicksian analysis of accelerator and investment demand does not consider the effect of capital accumulation on the productive capacity and, therefore, on the new investment decisions by the entrepreneurs. In Kaldor's model of trade cycle, the capital accumulation by raising the productive capacity affects the investment decisions of the entrepreneurs. The effect of the capital accumulation on the investment decision of the entrepreneurs makes the investment function non-linear in the real world (that is, investment-incomes or investment-employment curve is not a straight line). Through this non-linear investment function Kaldor has been able to explain the conditions of stability and instability of the economic system.

Kaldor explains the occurrence of trade cycles through saving and investment which by their interaction determine the level of activity, that is, the levels of national output, employment and income. It is worth noting that Kaldor uses the ex-ante concepts of saving and investment, since it is the **ex-ante** saving and **ex-ante** investment that determine the level of economic activity and not the **ex-post** or realised saving and investment. **Ex-ante** investment means planned net addition to the stock of fixed capital and inventories of goods. This **ex-ante** investment differs from the realised, actual or **ex-post** investment by the amount of unintended accumulation or disaccumulations of inventories of goods which arise due to the difference between the planned and realised sales of goods. **Ex-ante** saving means the savings planned by the people for a period if they had accurately forecast their incomes. Therefore, unexpected changes in the level of income will make the realised or **ex-post** saving different from the planned or **ex-ante** saving.

As has been explained in an earlier chapter, when **ex-ante** investment exceeds **ex-ante** savings, the level of activity or income and employment will rise and, on the other hand, when **ex-ante** saving exceeds **ex-ante** investment, the level of activity or income and employment will fall. The equilibrium level of activity (income and employment) is determined at which **ex-ante** saving is equal to **ex-ante** investment.

Let us now see how Kaldor explains the stability or instability of the level of economic activity and the course of the trade cycle. Kaldor takes first the cases of linear (straight line) saving and investment functions. Consider Figure 47.6 where linear saving and investment functions (*i.e.*, curves) are shown and where the investment curve *II* is more steeply inclined than the saving curve *SS*. The two functions intersect at point *C* and seem to determine the level of income Y_0. But this equilibrium between **ex-ante** saving and **ex-ante** investment is quite unstable. This is because in Figure 47.6, if once the equilibrium between saving and investment is disturbed, the economy will move either towards hyper-inflation or towards collapse. Thus, if, as a result of some change, **ex-ante** investment exceeds **ex-ante** savings (Figure 47.6), then the level of activity (*i.e.*, income) will go on rising unchecked and will ultimately result in hyper-inflation. On the other hand, if some disturbance sends the system towards the right of the cross between saving and investment in Fig. 47.6 so that **ex-ante** saving exceeds **ex-ante** investment, then the level of income or activity will go on falling unchecked and will ultimately collapse. Thus the situation depicted in Figure 47.6 with linear investment curve more steeply inclined than the saving curve is quite unstable; any disturbance in the equilibrium situation either sends the system towards hyper-inflation or towards collapse. Since such an instability is not actually found in the real world, Kaldor rules out this case.

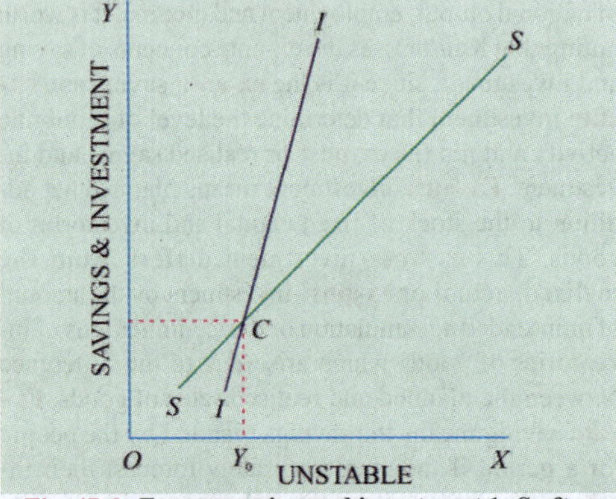

Fig. 47.6. Ex-ante saving and investment 1>S after equilibrium income.

Now, take Figure 47.7 where also saving and investment curves are intersecting at point *C* and determine the level of income Y_0. But in Figure 47.7, investment curve *II* is less steeply inclined than the saving curve *SS* so that the equilibrium between them at point *C* or at the level of income Y_0 is quite stable. In this case any disturbance, which sends the system on either side of the equilibrium level, will not reinforce itself and the system will tend to come back to its equilibrium level Y_0. For example, if as a result of some disturbance, the level of income rises beyond equilibrium income Y_0, **ex-ante** saving exceeds **ex-ante** investment which will tend to reduce the income to the equilibrium level Y_0. On the other hand, if in Figure 47.7. the income falls below Y_0, **ex-ante** investment will exceed **ex-ante** savings and as a result the level of income will rise to Y_0. Thus, the equilibrium is quite stable in Figure 47.7 where investment curve is less steeply inclined than the savings curve. But such a stability is also not realistic because economic system in the real world shows great instability. We thus see both the cases depicted in Figures 47.6 and 47.7 having linear **ex-ante saving and investment functions** are quite unrealistic and therefore Kaldor rules them out. Kaldor points out that in the real world both the saving and investment functions are **non-linear** (that is, they are not the straight lines) and explain trade cycles or fluctuations in the economic activity with non-linear saving and investment functions.

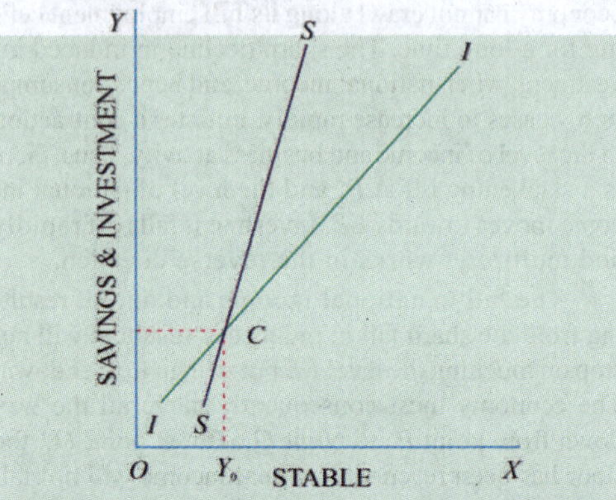

Fig. 47.7. Ex-ante saving and investment S>1 after equilibrium income.

The interaction between the non-linear saving function *SS* and the non-linear investment function II is shown in Figure 47.8. Given the shapes of these two functions, they intersect at three points, *A*, *B* and *C*. Equilibrium at point *B* is quite unstable both upward and downward. Above point *B*, investment exceeds saving and, therefore, once as a result of some disturbance investment exceeds saving, the income (*i.e.*, the level of activity) will go on moving upwards till point *C* is reached, and below point *B* saving exceeds investment and any disturbance which moves the system below point *B*, the level of activity will go on moving downward till point *A* is reached. Above point *C*, saving exceeds investment and, therefore, if the system goes above point *C*, it will come back to it. Therefore, the system is stable upward. On the other hand, below point *C*, investment exceeds saving and, therefore, any disturbance which sends the system below point *C*, it will be corrected by the return to the point *C*. Thus, the level of activity at point *C* is also stable downward. It, therefore, follows that the level of activity is in stable equilibrium at point *C*.

A glance at point *A* in Figure 47.5, will reveal that it also represents a stableS equilibrium; above point A saving exceeds investment and below point A investment exceeds saving which means that the level of activity will tend to return to point *A* if any disturbance, causing movement either upward or downward, occurs. It, therefore, follows that both the extreme points, C representing boom period and *A* representing depression, are stable equilibrium points. This means that economy should tend to be in **stable equilibrium** at either a very high or a very low level of

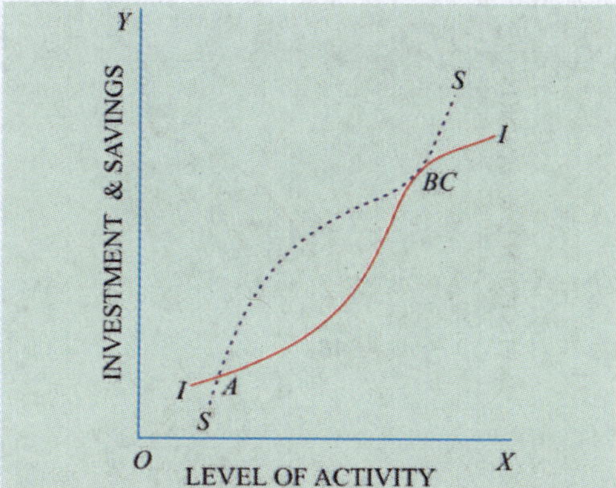

Fig. 47.8. Non linear saving and investment functions.

activity. This is, however, a quite unlikely and improbable result since in the real world the economy is not found to be stable at these extreme levels of activity. In the capitalist system of the real world there occurs, if Government does not take any steps, self-generating trade cycles. That is, a good deal of instability is found in the capitalist system in the real world. But the stability at these two extreme levels of activity seems to be necessary if the saving and investment functions remain fixed and also if the non-linear saving and investment functions are actually of the shape as shown in Figure 47.8. Kaldor shows that these shapes of the two functions approximate to the real world situation.

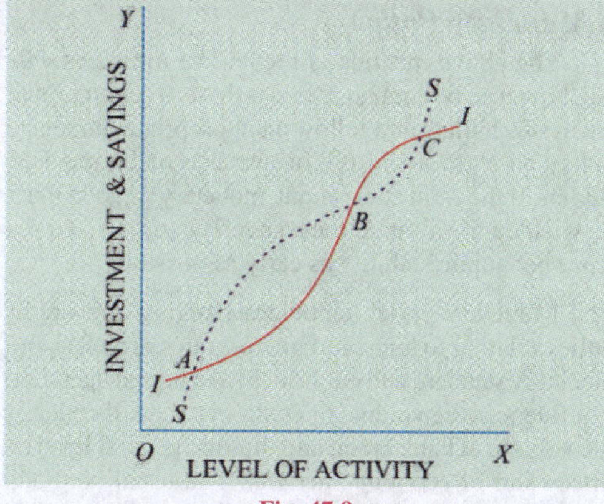

Fig. 47.9.

It is through the **changes or shifts** in the investment function and saving function curve that Kaldor explains the self-generating trade cycles found in the free-market capitalist economies. According to Kaldor, when the level of investment is very high, production of consumer goods increases and as a result both consumption and saving increase. This means that saving function curve *SS* will shift upward when the high level of activity is reached. Besides, with a high level of investment the opportunities for further investment may become temporarily restricted and as a result of this investment function curve *II* tends to shift downward. Thus, when the economy is at a high level of activity, *i.e.*, at point *C*, the saving function curve *SS* tends to move upward and the investment function curve *II* tends to move downward and consequently the point *C* tends to move down and point *B* tends to move up as in Figure 47.9, until they meet each other at the combined point *BC* as in Figure 47.10. It will be seen from Figure 47.10, that saving exceeds investment on both sides of the combined point *BC*, which means that the level of activity at the combined point *BC* is unstable downward. Thus, because saving exceeds investment at the combined point *BC*, the contraction in the level of activity will not stop at point *BC* but will continue further until point *A* is reached.

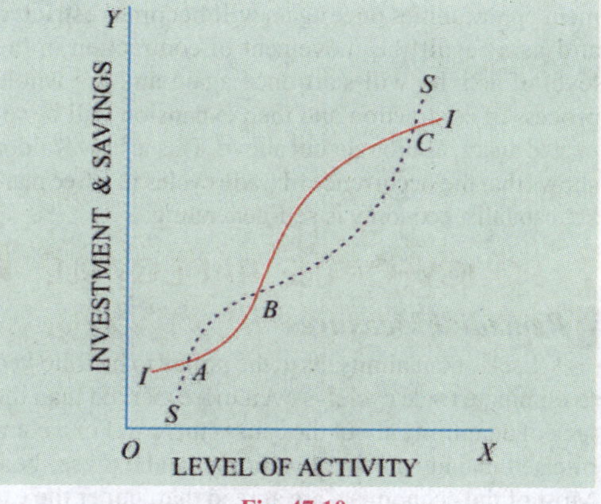

Fig. 47.10

The economy will not go below point *A* in Figure 47.10, because, as explained above, saving and investment are in stable equilibrium at point *A*. But, according to Kaldor, reversal movement of the cycle will start because the investment function curve will shift downward. Given the level of activity at *A*, investment in machines or equipment may not be sufficient to cover the depreciation. This creates opportunities for more investment, which causes the investment function curve to move upward. With the level of activity at *A*, as the investment. Function curve *II* moves upward relative to the saving function curve *SS*, the point *B* will separate from point *C* and tend to move towards *A* as in Figure 47.11 (*a*). The investment function curve *II* will go on shifting upward till combined point *AB* is reached as in Figure 47.11 (*b*). But the combined point *AB* is unstable upward, for above combined point *AB*, investment exceeds saving. As a result, the expansion in the level of activity will not stop at point *AB* but will continue until once again point C is reached. Now, with the point *C* representing again

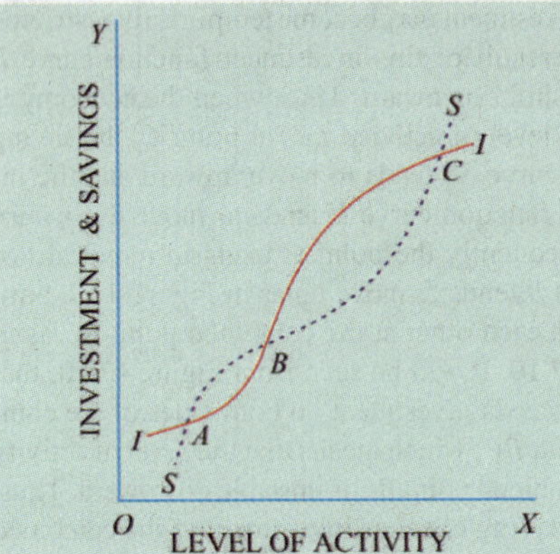

Fig. 47.11(*a*)

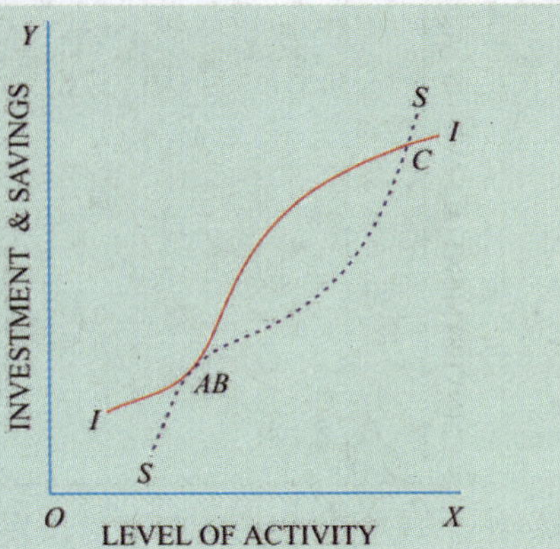

Fig. 47.11(*b*)

the situation of boom having been reached, the investment opportunities once again will become restricted and as a result the movement of contraction in the level of activity will start once again and the whole process of contraction and then expansion will be repeated again, as brought out above. This is how Kaldor shows that the occurrence of trade cycles in a free market capitalist economy is self-generating.

POLICY FOR THE TRADE CYCLE

Remedial Measures

Lack of unanimity, as to the policy to be followed to eliminate trade cycle, is even more marked than the lack of unanimity about the causes thereof. For a complicated malady no simple remedy can be prescribed. Most of the economists are agreed that, under the existing economic order, crisis are unavoidable; you can only delay them or mitigate their severity when they come. We need, therefore, two sets of measures: the **preventive** and the **curative,** for the stabilisation of the economy.

For preventing or avoiding crisis, the remedy will depend on the diagnosis. Influences of climatic factors on the supply of raw materials cannot be ruled out altogether. In a country like India, where nearly two-thirds of the people depend on agriculture, it is necessary that dependence on rains should be reduced as far as possible so that agriculture no longer remains a gamble in the monsoons. A network of canals, wells and reservoirs may be provided to ensure an adequate and regular supply of water. Other external factors like wars, earth-quakes, and epidemics cannot be provided against. They do not, however, play an important part in a trade cycle. At any rate, they do not occur with any degree of regularity.

Imperfect adjustment of demand and supply can be rectified by collecting and disseminating correct and up-to-date statistical information about the condition of crops, quantities of goods produced by the main industries, state of employment, imports and exports, per capita income, prices and cost of living index numbers and of company floatations, profits, *etc*. This will help the businessman to form an intelligent forecast of the probable changes in the demand for, and supply of, certain types of goods. The intelligence bureau may issue directives and warnings from time to time so that undue pessimism or optimism is nipped in the bud. In the boom period, the companies may be asked to follow a cautious policy in the distribution of dividends and to build up reserves.

Monetary Policy

The above-mentioned preventive measures will not, however, be enough. Besides these, a country must always formulate and follow an appropriate monetary policy so as to avoid the occurrence of booms and slumps. If they still come about, monetary weapon must be wielded to mitigate their severity and also to restore economic stability as early as possible.

Monetary policy embraces banking and credit policy relating to loans and interest rates as well as the monetary standard and public debt and its management. It influences the volume of credit base and, through it the volume of bank credit and thus the general level of prices and of economic activity. The usual methods through which it works are fully discussed in another chapter [3]. We may mention here that the important ones among such methods are: manipulation of bank rate and open market operations. When boom conditions are developing, bank rate is raised and thus credit is contracted with the consequent brake upon the undue expansion of business activity. In a depression, a policy of **cheap money** may be adopted to stimulate business investment and thus assist recovery.

3. Chapter 53.

The bank credit policy involves two types of controls: the quantitative and the qualitative. The quantitative control is aimed at general tightening or easing of the credit system as the situation may demand. It is exercised by influencing the reserves of the banks. The qualitative or selective control seeks to regulate particular type of credit. Its object is to stimulate, restrict or stabilise bank advances for specific business schemes. In recent years, the Reserve Bank of India has been following a policy of selective credit controls.

Obviously, monetary policy has much to commend itself and was, therefore, rightly regarded, in the early thirties, as the best anti-cyclical instrument. But there are limitations of the policy relating to the bank rate and open market operations. Its success will depend on how far certain assumptions are true. For example, how far the various members of the banking system are prepared to accept the lead given by the central bank; how far the banks can make their borrowers use their credits for purposes for which such credits have actually been created; Further, how far monetary causes are responsible for the economic fluctuations; and still further, and most important, whether the business community will adjust their investment exactly in accordance with the altered rates of interest.

Limitations. Thus, since these assumptions are only partially true, it is understandable that monetary management can claim only limited efficacy. The most serious limitation, in periods of depression, when the business community is so completely in the grip of pessimism, is that even a substantial reduction in the interest rates does not make them embark upon expansion of production and new investments. The horse may be taken to water, but it may refuse to drink. The monetary authority can only encourage business enterprises. The only result of lower interest rates may be to create a state of liquidity.

The existence of a huge public debt has also blunted the edge of monetary control. For the sake of their own solvency, the banks must keep the prices of bonds stable.

Hence, modern expert opinion is not inclined to place much reliance on monetary policy, as a tool for keeping economic activity in proper trim.

Fiscal Policy

The inadequacy of monetary policy led, therefore, to the search for suitable supplementary methods. Fiscal policy was the most important new find. But, for reasons to be explained presently, this new method, though it was "designed to supplement and strengthen monetary policy, has ended up by threatening to supplant monetary policy altogether." (Williams). Since public expenditure in all modern States constitutes a fairly respectable proportion of the total national income, fiscal policy is bound to affect the level of prices, production and employment, irrespective of the fact whether this policy is deliberately aimed at this or not.

Fiscal Policy, broadly speaking, consists of : (*a*) **Public spending or a policy of public works** and (*b*) **appropriate taxation.**

We have already seen that, according to Keynes explanation, trade cycle is primarily caused by a disequilibrium between saving and actual investment. If, therefore, the capital outlays of the State and public bodies could be adjusted to the varying private (business) investments, disequilibrium can be prevented from arising, and, thus, economic stability ensured. And if disequilibrium has somehow come about, it can be rectified by adjusting public spending. Public spending has, thus, to be varied according to the exigencies of the business situation.

In a year of depression, that is, when private investment is at a low ebb, the deficiency in investment will have to be made up by large capital outlay by the State, and, conversely, during the upward swing of the cycle, the State will have considerably to cut down its spending programme. Thus, during the depression years, the State must be ready to spend beyond its current revenues.

In other words, the State should be prepared to have deficit budgets during depression. Conversely, there should be surplus budgets during the years of prosperity. To put it in another way, instead of having balanced budgets every year, the State should aim at budget-balancing over a series of years.

On the revenue side, rates and taxes should be lowered during depression, while they should be raised during boom years. To stimulate business investment during depression, not only the rates of taxes should be lowered but also more liberal allowances for depreciation and obsolescence, *etc*., should be granted.

Thus, fiscal policy, which is also called the contra-cyclical management of public finance, may be operated both through public revenues and public expenditure. Between these two, the expenditure method is far more effective in stimulating business activity. Moreover, the revenue method leaves the entire initiative to the business community and is also not capable of directing expenditure into channels which may be particularly desired. However, best result will be achieved if both of them are combined.

Public Spending or public works policy, in view of its greater efficacy, deserves rather a detailed treatment. We shall begin with its theory. When during depression, economic activity is at a low ebb, and consequently there is considerable unemployment, the propensity to consume is naturally low. One important thing (apart from lowering the rate of interest) is to increase this propensity to consume. If somehow additional employment could be created by starting public works and thus purchasing power increased through the wages paid to the newly employed, propensity to consume will rise and, in turn, stimulate private business investment, on the principles of multiplier and acceleration. The government expenditure on its public works will, thus, have brought about many times greater investment and, thus, contributed greatly towards all-round economic recovery. The public works expenditure of the State will have, thus, performed the function of **'priming the pump'** of economic activity in the country.

This is to fight a depression, when it has already occurred or is developing. But there is another function that public spending programme may be made to perform, namely, that of stabilizing economic activity over a long time, and making it free from booms and depressions. This long-term aim can be achieved, as has been mentioned already, by constantly and appropriately adjusting public investment to the changes in private investment. The function is called the **'compensatory action'** of fiscal policy.

In the words of the American Economic Association, "In a system where the great majority of workers are in private employment, government stabilisation policy consists primarily in altering the general economic climate so as to mitigate or offset developing fluctuations in private business." Among the measures that a government may adopt to even out cyclical fluctuations, their report mentions the following :

(i) Alternative in tax rates and in the design of tax structure to bring about changes in incentives to individuals.

(ii) Changes in government contributions to the income stream through transfer payments, *i.e.*, employment benefits, *etc*.

(iii) Change in public expenditure on public works and other government purchases.

(iv) Monetary control to bring about a change in the cost and availability of bank credit.

(v) Public debt or monetary policy to bring about changes in the financial assets and liabilities of the public.

(vi) Timely announcement of a clearly defined government policy with a view to influencing investment decisions as well as those relating to current scheduling of output and employment,

(vii) An appropriate international economy policy.

Two strategic principles have been recommended for the achievement of economic stability.

(1) Government tax revenue should be higher relative to government expenditure in periods of high employment than in periods of substantial unemployment.

(2) Money and credit should be relatively tight in periods of high employment and relatively easy in periods of substantial unemployment.

Complete unanimity is, however, still lacking amongst economists regarding the merits of public spending policy as a means of securing continuous equilibrium between saving and investment. As against this, all are agreed about the great utility of fiscal policy in regard to its narrower, but surer, application for combating cyclical fluctuations, when these have already occurred.

Apart from the infinite gain in assisting investment during depression, public spending or public works policy, during such a period, will enable the State to complete such works at much lower cost. Wages, prices and interest rate during depression are low. Moreover, the net expense by the State is lower still. After all, if such schemes are not undertaken, unemployment 'doles' would have to be paid. The net cost of public works is, therefore, their total cost minus the unemployment 'doles', which would have otherwise been paid.

Limitations. The limitations of fiscal policy must not, however, be lost sight of. To begin with, many of the public works may be non-shiftable in time. Some of them cannot wait for depression to set in. Most of them are directly connected with the general business movement, rather than being used as corrective.

Then, owing to immobility of labour, the policy may fail in creating additional employment. Road making, for example, cannot absorb the unemployed textile workers.

Besides, in a democratic State, the public may bitterly oppose heavily surplus budgets during period of prosperity and may demand tax reductions.

Further, sufficient care will also have to be taken to ensure that the spending by the State is in such spheres only which would not have been taken up by private investors, otherwise public investment does nothing more than merely replace private investment. Moreover, public spending should not increase the difficulties of private investors by raising the cost of construction materials, building labour, *etc*.

Notwithstanding these limitations, fiscal policy is a powerful anticyclical weapon. Its efficacy will be further heightened, if suitable monetary management is also combined with it. The two could be so devised as to be "mutually reinforcing". "In recovery from depression the deficit budgeting may play the larger role, both by creating new income directly, and by

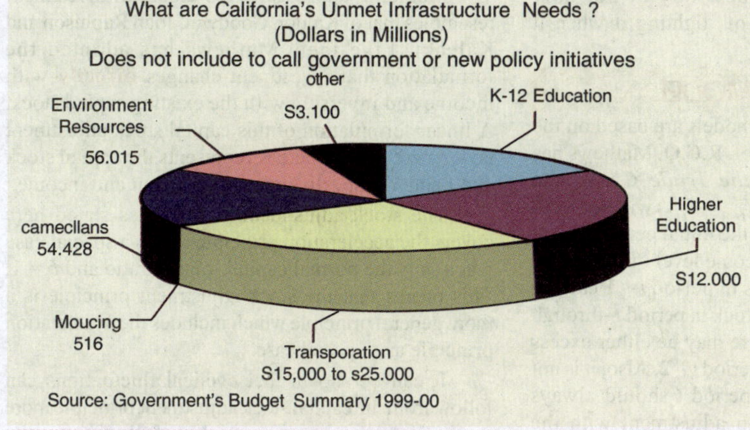

Investment on various social activities by state.

helping to implement an easy money policy, while in a boom, monetary policy would play an important and perhaps even the predominant role."

State Control of Investment. In recent years, economists have been advocating something farther than direct public investments for the purpose of counteracting business fluctuations. They urge that private investment should also be effectively controlled by the State for the same purpose. Control of private investment in certain countries dates from the thirties, when it was adopted as an emergency measure. It was further extended and tightened during the War of 1939-45 by the belligerent countries and by some neutral countries as well. But then the object was the diversion of resources for war purposes. After the war, though such control of investment was relaxed, yet its role is being greatly emphasised by the economists as a permanent measure of economic stabilization. In developing economies, as in the Indian economy which have adopted a course of planned economic development, control on new capital issues is generally instituted.

The danger of such a policy lies in this that too much State direction and intervention will hamper private enterprise. But leaving private investment entirely free is also not very safe. A happy mean will have to be struck. Keynes was of the opinion that such a golden mean could be struck. When that is done, economic stabilization will become more practicable.

International Measures

So far we have been discussing individual national efforts at stabilisation. But trade cycle is an international phenomenon and no country is hermetically sealed from the rest of the world. In fact, this international aspect creates complications and makes crisis control all the more difficult.

The measures which are suggested to be adopted on an international scale are: International Production Control, International Buffer Stocks and International Investment Control. International Production Control envisages control of production and prices of the important primary products. The difficulties of such control are indeed formidable, notably because agriculture in countries like India is usually carried on a small scale and more as a mode of living than as business, so that even though it ceases to be profitable, it will be continued. But production control, as far as possible, combined with buffer stocks to counteract sudden changes in supply and demand, will go a long way in preventing rise or fall in their prices, which give rise further to serious fluctuations in the entire economy.

An international investment control for developing backward regions would help in raising the standards of living of their people and thus reduce the inequalities in the standard of living of different peoples. Such reduction in those inequalities is bound to strengthen the forces of stabilization. The I.B.R.D. and President Truman's Point-Four Programme and the Colombo Plan are attempts in this direction.

Conclusion. These are some of the measures that can be adopted to alleviate suffering. But the world has not been able to discover any panacea or sovereign remedy for a commercial crisis. Nothing short of reorganisation of the economic system can provide against the recurrence of crisis. These are by-products of capitalism and so long as capitalistic system of production continues such disturbances must continue to take place. A planned economy or some form of socialism may remove such a contingency.

Even a Socialist State will commit mistakes about organisation of production. It will also have to anticipate demand. No human organisation can be infallible, yet planning of the entire economic field will so co-ordinate the various economic activities that maladjustments will be a rare phenomenon. Even when dislocations do occur, the vast resources of the State can easily meet such a situation. No failure of individual firms or displacement of labour will take place; losses can be easily borne. When the whole world was suffering from acute depression and unemployment during the early' thirties, no such dark clouds threatened the economic horizon of Russia. Planned economy seems to be the best way of not only preventing a crisis, but also of fighting it when it comes.

MATHEWS' MODEL

Samuelson and Hicks's models are based on the acceleration principle. But Prof. R.C.O. Mathews has pointed out in his book, *the Trade Cycle*, the acceleration principle It = $Y(Y_{t-1} - Y_{t-2})$ will not work because the stock of capital at the initial period **t** is not necessarily adjusted to the income level of the period t – 2, after which income rises in period t – 1 calling for re-adjustment of capital stock in period *t*–through fresh investment. Instead, there may be either excess capacity or short capacity in period t – 2. Also, it is not necessary that investment in period t should always bring the stock of capital in adjustment with the income level of period t – 1. Hence level of investment in period t cannot be expressed satisfactorily as a function of ($Y_{t-1} - Y_{t-2}$) as it is postulated in the acceleration principle, Mathews has therefore discarded the acceleration principle in his model and has instead adopted another principle known as the **capital stock adjustment principle.**

Mathews' approach to the theory of investment resembles that of Kaldor, Goodwin, Joan Rabinson and Kalecki. Like them Mathews has adopted the formulation that investment changes **directly** with income and inversely with the existing capital stock. A linear formulation of this capital stock adjustment is: It $t = aY_t - bK_t$ where K represents the capital stock and I and Y respectively are investment and income.

The stock-adjustment principle as stated here covers the acceleration principle too as a special case when a is the normal capital -output ratio and $b = 1$. This means that the stock adjustment principle is a more general principle which includes the acceleration principle as a special case.

It can be shown that cyclical fluctuations can follow from the capital stock adjustment principle more or less in the same way as they follow from the acceleration model, either 'lags' or 'buffers' or both are a necessary condition for the interaction between the stock adjustment principle and the multiplier to generate endogenous cyclical fluctuations.

Key terms

Meaning of trade cycles, Economic crisis, Characteristics of trade cycle, The Cobweb theory of trade cycles, Theories of trade cycles, Over investment theory, Keynes' theory, Policy for the trade cycles, Mathews' Model.

QUESTIONS

1. What is a trade cycle? Explain its main characteristics.
2. Write a short note on the parts played by the (*a*) real and (*b*) monetary factors in a trade cycle.
3. Bring out the part played by the following in the trade cycle : (a) Variations in bank credit, (*b*) Fluctuations in the marginal efficiency of capital, (*c*) Waves of optimism and pessimism.
4. Discuss the role of the acceleration principle in the explanation of the trade cycle.
5. Comment on the view that a trade cycle is a purely monetary phenomenon.
6. Give an outline of the Hicksian Theory of Trade Cycle.
7. Discuss what you consider to be the most satisfactory explanation of the Trade Cycle.
8. Discuss the various measures which should be adopted to fight business fluctuations.
9. Discuss the policies that can be followed to control cyclical fluctuations.
10. Discuss the objectives of monetary policy. How far can a suitable monetary policy bring business revival?
11. What monetary measures would you advocate to cope with recession? How far effective would each of them prove to be?
12. "Monetary policy can back a boom, but it cannot deal with recession". Discuss the statement.
13. What are the different monetary explanations for the 'recession' phase of the trade cycle? How far are they adequate?
14. Explain the need for and limitations of fiscal policy as a means of reducing economic stability.
15. Briefly analyse the nature and working of compensatory fiscal policy. To what extent can it control cyclical fluctuations?
16. Discuss the various phases of the business cycle. How do variations in savings and investment influctuence the course of a cycle?
17. Explain the principle of acceleration and indicate the conditions under which it works.
18. Distinguish Acceleration principlefrom Investment multiplier. Explain and illustrate Acceleration principle.

PART THREE

Money and Banking

UNIT I

Monetary Standards and Theory of Money and Prices

Chapters

NATURE AND FUNCTIONS OF MONEY

Meaning of Money

Money has been defined in various ways. Some say, **'Money is what money does.'** (Walzker). In other words, anything that performs the functions of money is money. In the widest sense, the term 'money' includes all media of exchange—gold, silver, copper, paper, cheques, commercial bills of exchange, etc. But this definition is too wide. Cheques, bills, *etc.*, have been called representative money as they are only convenient representatives of the standard of value. Some writers narrow down the definition to include only the commodity (*e.g.*, gold) that may serve the purpose of money. This excludes bank notes or government currency notes from the category of money. These instruments cannot, logically speaking, be excluded, because they possess all the attributes of money, as we shall see presently.

The most commonly agreed view is that, **"anything which is widely accepted in payment for goods, or in discharge of other kinds of obligations"** is money (Robertson).

In Crowther's words. "The only essential requirement is general acceptability. Money .... need not itself be valuable. It must, indeed, be relatively scarce, since it would hardly do if money could be plucked off every tree. But, provided precautions are taken to keep it relatively scarce and, it may be added, comparatively invariable in amount–money can consist of things as worthless as a scrap of paper or the scratch of a clerk's pen in the books of a bank."

Money.

CONCEPTS OF MONEY

Theoretical Debate on the Definition of Money

In recent years, there has been a keen controversy on what is and what is not money. This controversy hinges on what functions money is expected to perform *i.e.* whether money is to be regarded as a mere medium of exchange or a store of value. The functions are discussed in detail in a subsequent system. As pointed out by Prof. Harry G. Johnson, in his recent survey of developments in *monetary theory and policy*, there are four main schools of thought on the definition of money and money supply. We refer to them briefly as under:—

Conventional Approach. There are economists who define money on the basis only of its function being a medium of exchange. They include in the term 'money' currency and demand deposits in banks. Since they think that to serve as a medium of exchange is still the primary function of money, only currency and demand deposits in banks should be included in the definition of money because they are perfectly liquid and are generally and immediately acceptable as medium of exchange.

Thus, according to this school, Money Stock =– Cash + Demand Deposits. This is called *M*. This definition of money includes only currency and demand deposits, but excludes, all other assets (not so liquid) like time deposits, post office savings bank deposits and liabilities of non-banking financial institutions which are known as *near money*. They cannot be used as medium of exchange. It costs something to convert these assets into currency or cash or demand deposits. They are also called 'frozen assets' which can be sold at a substantially lower price.

Chicago Approach. Prof. Milton Friedman is the leader of this school. The basic idea underlying their approach is that they do not regard money as a mere medium of exchange but also as a *store of value*. Keynes also used the term 'money to hold'. Obviously, when money is to serve as a store of value, other assets besides currency and demand deposits must also be included in the term money. These economists regard money as a temporary abode of purchasing power separating the act of purchase from the act of sale. Thus money is supposed to include, besides currency and demand deposits in banks as in the conventional approach given above, other assets like time deposits in banks as well as savings bank deposits. The time deposits are very closely linked with demand deposits and may appropriately be called *near money.* They are also liquid assets though not so liquid as currency and demand deposits because one cannot spend them as money. They have to be converted into case or currency before they can be spent. Money in this sense is ML_2.

Thus M_2 + Time Deposits = Currency + Demand Deposits + Time Deposits

1. *An Outline of Money*, 1950, p. 21.

Money includes Bank Deposits.

Emperical studies have brought out the close relation between money income and money supply. It has been found that correlation between changes in money supply and changes in money income is more clearly brought out if time deposits are also included in the definition of money supply.

Gurley and Shaw Approach. The other school of quantity theorist is one led by Gurley and Shaw. They emphasise the implications of velocity of circulation of money and the existence of substantial volume of liquid assets closely substituable for money like short-term Government securities, liabilities of non-banking financial institutions, time deposits in banks, post office saving bank deposits, etc. Thus the definition of money as currency and demand deposits in banks is to be broadened to include time deposits in banks and other assets mentioned above.

Gurley and Shaw are also of the opinion that money supply should be defined as a *weighted* sum of currency, demand deposits, time deposits and liabilities of non-banking financial institutions, weights being assigned on the basis of degree of their substitutability for currency. For instance weight of unity be assigned to currency and demand deposits in banks and weights between zero and unity to other assets depending on the degree of substitutability between a particular asset and currency.

Credit Approach. There are two broad groups representing this approach. One group, consisting of the financial experts of the Federal Reserve System of the U.S.A., emphasise the close substitutability between currency and bank credit. They would rather substitute credit for currency, since credit instruments are very close substitutes for money.

The second group adopts the views of the Radcliffe Committee whose theoretical basis was provided by R.S. Sayers. This group wants to replace the concept of money by the general liquidity situation of the economy. They are of the view that money supply and its velocity have little significance for an economy can substitute credit for money without any limit. A credit card can enable the holder to buy anything. This means a decrease in the velocity of circulation. In other words, Radcliffe-Sayers Thesis is that money supply is not the main lever of monetary action, because spending decisions do not depend only on money supply but the fate of liquidity of the economy. Liquidity means the case with which funds can be raised for financing purchases which in turn depends on the borrowing power of the community as a whole. Hence these economists reject money as an operationally useful concept and substitute for it general liquidity position of the economy.

Conclusion. Thus we see that there is no consensus among economists as to what is money and what is not money.

Money Stock Measures in India

In recent years, there has been a great deal of debate as to what constitutes money supply with the public. While all are agreed on money supply with the public in the sense in which it has been explained above (*i.e.*, currency plus demand deposits with banks), many monetary theorists have expressed the opinion that in a country like India where the branches of banks are confined to cities, towns and only to a proportion of villages and where the people maintain substantial deposits with post office saving banks, it would be a true measure of total money supply with the public, if the peoples's deposits with postal savings banks are also included. Accordingly, **money supply with the public in the sense of currency and demand deposits with banks and other deposits with *RBI* may be designated as M_1. Another measure of money stock in the country, called M_2, would be if post office saving bank deposits are also added to M_1.** In this case, apart from currency which is most liquid form of money, demand deposits with banks and savings deposits with post office saving banks are also taken into account.

Some economists would like to go further and include time deposits with banks also in the country's money stock. When that is done, the aggregate of money supply is designated M_3 in India. **This is equal to the sum of M_1 and time deposits with banks.** The justification advanced for this is that the holders of time deposits regard their such deposits as *near money assets* and in time of need can use their time deposits by obtaining bank loans against them or by getting them converted into cash by receiving payment of such amounts before their maturity by foregoing interest which would have accrued had those deposits been retained till their maturity.

The process of extending the concept of money supply or money stock measures does not stop here. Logically speaking, apart from demand deposits and time deposits with banks, quite substantial amounts are kept by people in India with post offices not only in the postal saving banks, but also in the form of term deposits (medium-term and long-term) in the form of post bonds/cash certificates. **The money stock in this comprehensive sense-currency with** the public plus demand deposits with banks plus time deposits with banks plus total post office deposits (both saving deposits and term deposits) has, in India, been designated M_4.

Difficulties of Barter

When exchange is done without the intervention of money, we call it barter. Barter, however, is possible only under extremely simple conditions of exchange. As social organization became more complex through a more minute division of labour and multiplicity of human wants, it was realised that exchange by barter was not a satisfactory method.

The following are the main difficulties of the barter system:

(*i*) Double coincidence of wants. Barter requires a double coincidence of wants. If '*A*' possesses a cow, for instance, and wants to exchange it for a horse, he has to find a person, who not only can spare a horse but also wants a cow. Suppose he meets '*B*' who wants a cow but can only offer sheep. '*A*' may then have to find a man who wants sheep, and so on until he can get the commodity he wants by a series of barter transactions. It is obvious that this method involves much inconvenience and risk.

(*ii*) Lack of a common measure of value. The difficulties of barter do not end here. Even if two persons, who want each other's goods happen to meet, a second difficulty arises: In what proportion the two goods are to be exchanged? There is no common measure of value.The ratio will be arbitrarily fixed according to the necessities of the two parties or the intensities of their reciprocal demand. One party is bound to suffer under conditions, where each exchange is an isolated transaction.

(*iii*) Indivisibility of certain articles. Even if an agreement is reached regarding the proportion in which things should be exchanged, a third difficulty may arise when the commodities concerned are indivisible. For instance, take the case of a man who wants to purchase wheat equal to half the value of his cow. With the other half, he wants to purchase cloth which is in the possession of a third person. How is the cow to be divided? Many similar situations can be imagined.

The difficulties of barter can be illustrated by taking the example of a French singer who gave performances in an island where money was not in use. She was paid in the form of pigs, goats, fowls, apples, bananas, *etc.* She had to give the fruits and other things to her pigs and goats to keep them alive. What did she gain? Nothing. Had she been paid in money for these performances, she would have become rich.

Difficulties of barter led to the introduction of money which passed through several stages, *viz*., commodity money, metallic money, paper money and then credit money.

ROLE AND IMPORTANCE OF MONEY IN MODERN ECONOMY

There is no doubt that money facilitates and motivates all economic activity relating to consumption, production, exchange and distribution. Money enables a consumer to maximise his satisfaction. Money measures the intensity of desire and the utility of a commodity to a consumer. Money facilitates production by stimulating saving and investment. It gives mobility to capital and helps in capital formation. It enables the harnessing of various factors of production so that the entrepreneur is able to maximise his profit. Introduction of money facilitates exchange and helps in the development of trade and commerce, both national and international. Money functions as a common denominator for the distribution of social product. It is in terms of money that, wages, rent, interest and profits are determined. Money helps the price mechanism to operate and serve as an instrument for the allocation of resources among competing uses. Money is an extremely valuable social instrument which has largely contributed to the growth of national wealth and social welfare. It has ensured the smooth functioning of the economic system. It has accelerated the process of industrialisation. In money economy, there is a continuous flow of money payments. This circular flow is essential for promoting economic welfare.

Whatever the type of economic system money is found to be of great service. In a capitalist economy, money plays an important role because capitalism basically depends, on price mechanism which operates through the medium of money. As Prof. Robertson observes, "the existence of monetary economy helps society to discover what people want and how much they want....... and to decide what shall be produced and in what quantities, and to make the best use of its limited productive power. And it helps each member of society to ensure that the means of enjoyment to which he has access, yield him the greatest amount of actual enjoyment which is within his reach."* Even in a socialist economy, price tags are essential for its smooth, efficient and economical working. It is said while money is a master in a capitalist economy, it is a servant in a socialist economy. Money also plays a significant role in a mixed economy. It plays a crucial role in determining employment, output and income in the private sector. In the public sector, it is helpful in the allocation of resources and for changing the pattern of income distribution. It is a powerful instrument for capital formation and economic development in a developing economy.

Dangers of Money

Money is not, however, an unmixed blessing. Money is a good servant but a bad master.

Money in Modern Economy.

Money has proved dangerous in several ways:

(i) Economic Instability. Some economists are of the view that money is responsible for economic instability that is to be found in capitalist economies.

When there was no money, saving was not divorced from investment. Those who saved also invested. But in a monetised economy, saving is done by certain people and investment by some other people. Hence, it does not follow that savings and investment should be equal. When saving in a community exceeds investment, then national income, output and employment decrease and the economy is engulfed in depression. On the contrary, when investment exceeds savings (*i.e.*, investment financed not by genuine savings but through deficit financing), then national income, output and employment increase and there is a spell of prosperity. But if the process of money creation and investment continues beyond the point of full employment, inflationary situation will be created. Hence, disparity between savings and investment resulting form the creation of money, is said to be the main cause of economic fluctuations.

The main danger of money lies in its liability of being over-issued in the case of inconvertible paper money. The over-issue of money may result in hyper-inflation as in India in 1973-74. Excessive rise in prices hits hard the consuming public and the fixed-incomests. It engenders speculation and inhibits productive enterprises. It also upsets debtor-creditor relationship. It adversely affects distribution of income and wealth in the community so that the gulf between the rich and poor widens.

(ii) Economic Inequalities. Money has proved to be a very convenient tool for amassing wealth and of the exploitation of the poor by the rich. It has created a yawning gulf between the 'haves' and the 'have-nots' The misery and degradation of the poor is, thus, to no small measure due to the existence of money.

(iii) Moral Depravity. Money has weakened the moral fibre of man. The evils to be found in the affluent society are only too obvious. The wealthy monopolise all the social evils like corruption, the 'wine and the woman'. In their case, money has proved to be a soul-killing weapon. In the words of an eminent German economist Von Mises, "money is regarded as the cause of theft and murder, of deception and betrayal. Money is balmed when the prostitute sells her body and when the bribed judge perverts the law. It is money against which the moralist declaims when he wishes to oppose excessive materialism. Significantly enough, avarice is called the love of money and all evil is attributed to it."[2] Money in itself may not be bad, but its possession no doubt facilitates corruption and crime.

Thus, "money which is a source of so many blessings to mankind becomes, unless we control it, a source of peril and confusion."[3]

Money in a Socialist State

In view of the evils mentioned above, especially the exploitation of the poor by the rich, prominent socialists like Marx and Lenin condemned money. No wonder that when the Communists came to power in Russia, they took steps to abolish money. But it was soon realised that to run a modern economy without money was impossible. All economic activity has to be based on monetary calculations. As Leon Trotsky observed, "The blueprints produced by the offices must demonstrate their economic expediency through commercial calculation. Without a firm monetary unit, commercial accounting can only increase the chaos."[4]

Accordingly, money is fully and firmly established in all Socialist States. Even there it performs the essential functions, *viz.*:

(*a*) It facilitates optimum allocation of the country's resources.

(*b*) It functions as medium of exchange and a measure of value.

(*c*) Money guides economic activity.

(*d*) Money is essential for facilitating distribution of national income.

FUNCTIONS OF MONEY

Money performs five important functions:—

(*i*) It serves as a medium of exchange.

(*ii*) It is used as a store of value. In more modern terminology, it helps to keep resources liquid.

(*iii*) It is a standard for measuring values.

(*iv*) Money serves as a standard for deferred payments.

(*v*) It transfers value.

Money as Medium of Exchange

The most important function of money is to serve as a medium of exchange. As a medium of exchange, moeny removes all the difficulties of barter. There is no necessity for a double coincidence of wants in a

2. Von Mises—*Theory of Money and Credit*, p. 93, quoted by K.P.M. Sundharam in his money, *Banking and International Trade*, P. 27.
3. Robertson, D.H.—*Money*, p. 15.
4. Trotsky, L.D.—*Soviet Economy in Danger*, p. 30.

money economy. The man with the cow, who wants to purchase a horse, need not hunt for a horse-seller, who wants a cow. He can sell his cow in the market for money and then purchase a horse with the money thus obtained. The convenience is very great when the person has to sell his services or goods in an unfinished state which no consumer in the narrow sense wants. They can be easily turned into money, the general purchasing power. The difficulty of indivisibility of certain articles is also eliminated. Money units are of all denominations and it is easy to make fractional purchases, which is not possible under most cases of barter.

Money is Medium of Exchange.

Money as a Standard Measure of Value

When money serves as a medium of exchange, it incidentally measures the values of things for which it is exchanged. One inconvenience of barter, as noted, was the lack of common measure or a common denominator of value in terms of which other values could be expressed and added and accounts kept. Money removes this difficulty too. Money serves as a **unit of account.** In a money economy, it is easy to compare the relative values of commodities and services which are dissimilar and entirely different from one another. The values are in proportion to their respective prices. Expression of values in prices enables us to add them up and have a definite idea of a person's or a community's wealth. In matters of exchange, a common standard of value makes the transaction easy and also fair.

Money as a Standard of Deferred Payments

Money also serves as a standard of payments made after a lapse of time. Lending and borrowing, therefore, must take place in terms of a commodity which will, reasonably speaking, keep its value stable over time. Most commodities deteriorate with the passage of time. But if the money material is properly selected and managed, its value can be kept more stable than that of other articles. By serving as a standard measure of payments over time, money makes borrowing and lending much less risky. Thus, it helps in stimulating all kinds of economic activity which depends on borrowed money or credit.

Money as a Store of Value

Money serves as a store of value or, more correctly, it enables a person to keep a portion of his assets liquid. Liquid assets are those which can be used for any purpose at any time one likes. Most persons in the modern world have to keep currency notes in their pockets or at home, or they may keep current accounts with the banks withdrawable by cheque. The necessity arises from the fact that the two streams of income and expenditure do not keep time with each other. An employer has to pay wages, *etc.*, periodically, even daily, while his income does not come to him in the same periodical intervals. Money is best kept as a store of value to be used as and when need arises.

Functions of money have been summed up in a couplet thus:

"Money is a matter of functions four,
A medium, a measure, a standard, a store."

It should be noted that all these functions of money are not independent of each other. They are inter-related. Money is kept as liquid assets, for instance, because it serves as a medium of exchange. It is accepted as a medium of exchange, because it has comparatively stable value. For the same reason, it serves as a standard for deferred payments and measure of value.

Money as a Means of Transferring Value

There is also another function which money performs. One can sell one's immovable and movable belongings at one place and with the money so acquired he can buy them elsewhere. Value will thus be transferred. Such things have happened on a very large scale in India after the partition of the country.

Primary, Secondary and Contingency Functions

According to Kinley, functions of money can be classified as under:

(*a*) Primary functions, *e.g.*, as medium of exchange and measure of value, (*b*) Secondary Functions, *e.g.*, as standard of deferred payments, as store of value and as a means of transferring value, and (*c*) Contingent Functions such as distribution of national income, as basis of bank credit, imparting liquidity and uniformity to wealth and equalising marginal utility.

Static and Dynamic Functions

Paul Einzig classifies the functions of money as (*a*) Static and (*b*) Dynamic.

Static Functions are those mentioned above, *viz.*, servings as a medium of exchange, measure of value, a standard of deferred payments, store of value and transfer of value.

The **Dynamic Functions** of money are those by which money influences the working of the economy by influencing price level, level of consumption, volume of production and distribution of wealth in the economy. The dynamic functions thus determine the economic trends. It is well-known that there is a close connection between money supply with the public and the general price level in the country. It is also admitted that a high price level (inflation) and low price level (depression) have a profound effect on the level of production, one stimulating and the other depressing it. Deficit financing (*i.e.*, created money) can be resorted to for bringing about a fuller utilisation of the human and natural resources of the country which may otherwise be lying idle or underutilised. The monetary system also facilitates public debt.

Time is money.

Dynamic functions have assumed great importance in modern times as is evident from the monetary policy pursued by modern governments.

When Does Money Cease to Perform its Functions?

The basic function of money is to serve as a stable medium of exchange so that it can serve as a standard of deferred payments on the basis of which debts can be contracted and repaid. But money ceases to perform its functions properly and satisfactorily in a highly inflationary situation when money is fast losing its value. Such a situation arose in Germany in and after the two great wars. Hyper-inflation causes a serious breakdown of the monetary system. In such a situation, the first consequence is that money ceases to act as a standard of deferred payments. The debts are then contracted in terms of some other universally acceptable currency as the American dollar or the English £.

Since all the functions of money are interdependent or inter-connected, it ceases to perform other functions too. When money ceases to function as a standard of deferred payment, it also ceases to act as a store of value. It is not considered worthwhile to hold or hoard money when its value is being fast eroded. In India, for instance, in 1974, instead of keeping bank balances, people were eager to invest in real estate or keep jewellery or gold instead of cash owing to rapidly depreciating value of money. Since, owing to instability in value, money ceases to be a bridge between the present and the future, people prefer to keep their assets in other forms of wealth.

When money can no longer function satisfactorily as a store of value, it can no longer function satisfactorily as a medium of exchange and a unit of account or a measure of value. All calculations become difficult when money is fast losing its value. Money is thus no longer a satisfactory unit of account. As for medium of exchange, when there is hyper-inflation, no one is inclined to receive money because it loses value in their hands. Hence, no one likes to keep or hold money at all.

In such a situation of a complete monetary breakdown, old money must be demonetised and some new money created to take its place.

Essentials of Good Money

From the above discussion, one can easily infer what the essentials of good money can be: (*a*) The basic ingredient of good money is that, it must be **stable** and not rapidly change in value. (*b*) It must then be a generally acceptable medium of exchange. (*c*) It must be a dependable measure of value. (*d*) It must be a suitable store of value. (*e*) Being generally acceptable, it should be capable of transferring value.

DEMAND FOR AND SUPPLY OF MONEY

Before we discuss the value of money in the next chapter, it will be useful to have an idea of the demand for and the supply of money. The modern notion about these aspects of money is different from the traditional one. Let us analyse demand for and supply of money separately.

Demand for Money

The old idea about the demand for money was that money was demanded for completing the business transactions. In other words, the demand for money depended on the volume of trade or transactions. As such, the demand for money increased during boom period or when the trade was brisk and it decreased during depression or slackening of trade.

The modern idea about the demand for money was put forward by the late Lord Keynes, the famous English economist, who gave birth to what has been called the Keynesian Economics. According to Keynes, the demand for money, or liquidity preference as he called it, means the demand for money to hold. Broadly speaking, there are three main motives on account of which money is wanted by the people, *viz*.:

(*i*) transactions motive.
(*ii*) Precautionary motive.
(*iii*) Speculative motive.

Now a word about each one of them.

(*i*) Transactions Motive. This motive can be looked at (*a*) from the point of consumers who want income to meet the household expenditure which may be termed the **income motive** and (*b*) from the point of view of the businessmen, who require money and want to hold it in order to carry on their business, *i.e.*, the business motive.

(*a*) Income Motive. The transactions motive relates to the demand for money or the need for cash for the current transactions of individual and business exchanges. Individuals hold cash in order "to bridge the interval between the receipt of income and its expenditure." This is called the **'Income Motive.'** Most of the people receive their incomes by the week or the month, while the expenditure goes on day by day. A certain amount of ready money, therefore, is kept in hand to make current payments. This amount will depend upon the size of the individual's income, the interval at which the income is received and the methods of payments current in the locality.

(*b*) Business Motive. The businessmen and the entrepreneurs also have to keep a proportion of their resources in ready cash in order to meet current needs of various kinds. They need money all the time in order to pay for raw materials and transport, to pay wages and salaries and to meet all other current expenses incurred by any business of exchange. Keynes calls it the **'Business Motive'** for keeping money. It is clear that the amount of money held, under this business motive, will depend to a very large extent on the turn-over (*i.e.*, the volume of trade of the firm in question). The larger the turn-over the larger, in general, will be the amount of money needed to cover current expenses.

(*ii*) Precautionary Motive. Precautionary motive for holding money refers to the desire of the people to hold cash balances for unforeseen contigencies. People hold a certain amount of money to provide for the risk of unemployment, sickness, accidents and other more uncertain perils. The amount of money held under this motive will depend on the nature of the individual and on the conditions in which he lives.

(*iii*) Speculative Motive. The speculative motive relates to the desire to hold one's resources in liquid form in order to take advantage of market movements regarding the future changes in the rate of interest (or bond prices).

The notion of holding money for speculative motive is a new typically Keynesian idea. Money held under the speculative motive serves as a store of value as money held under the precautionary motive does. But it is a store of money meant for a different purpose. The cash held under this motive is used to make speculative gains by dealing in bonds whose prices fluctuate. If bond prices are expected to rise, which in other words means that the rate of interest is expected to fall, businessmen will buy bonds to sell when the price actually rises. If, however, bond prices are expected to fall, *i.e.*, the rate of interest is expected to rise, businessmen will sell bonds to avoid capital losses. Nothing being certain in this dynamic world, where guesses about the future course of events are made on precarious bases, businessmen keep cash to speculate on the probable further changes in bond prices (or the rate of interest) with a view to making profits.

Money is Needed for Transaction.

Given the expectations about the changes in the rate of interest in future, less money will be held under the speculative motive at a higher current or prevailing rate of interest and more money will be held under this motive at a lower current rate of interest. The reason for this inverse correlation between money held for speculative motive and the prevailing rate of interest is that at a lower rate of interest less is lost by not lending money or investing it thus at higher rate.

Friedman in his restatement of the Quantity Theory of Money draws a distinction between *demand for money and the demand function for money*. Friedman takes note only of the asset demand for money, not so much of the transactions demand. Among the other post-Keynesian economists, Baumol and Tobm are of the view that transactions demand for money is influenced not only by the level of income but also by is influenced not only by the level of income but also the rate of interest (for fuller discussion see chaper 50)

Supply of Money

We have described the demand for money as the demand for the stock (not flow) of money to be held. The flow is over a period of time and not at a given moment. In the case of a commodity, it is a flow. Goods are being continually produced and disposed of. This is the essential difference between the demand for money and the demand for a commodity. Similarly, the supply of money conforms to the 'stock' concept and not the 'flow' concept. Just as the demand for money is the demand for money to hold, similarly, the supply of money means the supply of money to hold. Money must always be **held** by some one, otherwise it cannot exist. Hence, the supply of money means the sum total of all the forms of money which are held by a community at any given moment.

The stock of money, which constitutes the supply of it, consists of (*a*) metallic money or coins, (*b*) currency notes issued by the currency authority of the country whether the Central bank or the government, and (*c*) chequable bank deposits. In old times, the coins formed the bulk of money supply of the country. Later, the currency notes eclipsed the metallic currency and now the bank deposits in current account withdrawable by cheques have overwhelmed all other forms of money. In modern times, the supply of money really means the chequable bank deposits.

The modern economists include in money stock not only currency or cash balances and demand deposits in banks together called M_1. They also include time deposits in the banks called near money and call it M_2 (= M_1 + time deposits and deposits in post offices.) The total money stock in this sense is called M_3. Further, term deposits in the form of postal bonds/cash certificates are also included. Thus money stock in this comprehensive sense includes currency, demand deposits in banks, time deposits with banks plus total post office deposits, savings bank and term deposits. It has been designated as M_4.

The total supply of money in a country, by and large, depends on the credit control policies pursued by the banking system of the country.

Key terms

Conventional definition of Money, Chicago approach to money, Barter, Medium of exchange, Store of value, Transaction and Precautionary demand, Speculative demand, Concepts of money, Role and importance of money in modern economy, Function of money, Demand for and supply of money.

QUESTIONS

1. Explain the inconveniences attendant upon barter system and show how the introduction of money removes them.
2. Define Money and its functions. Does bank money perform these functions satisfactorily?
3. "Thus money which is a source of many blessings to mankind becomes also, unless we control it, a source of peril and confusion" (Robertson). Discuss the statement carefully.
4. "Money is what money does". Discuss.
5. Explain the role of money in a capitalist economy. How would it be different in a socialist economy?

MONETARY STANDARDS

Various monetary systems or monetary standards have been adopted in practice from time to time. These are (*a*) **Bimetallism,** (*b*) **Monometallism,** silver standard or gold standard, and (*c*) **Paper Standard.**

Bimetallism has now only a historical interest. We shall discuss here gold standard.

GOLD STANDARD

Although gold standard of the orthodox type ceased to function a long time back but gold standard still retains some of its old halo. Gold standard still figures in the discussions of the monetary system. There are several distinct phases through which gold standard has passed. We are familiar with gold currency standard, gold exchange standard, gold bullion standard and now, its latest variety, gold parity standard. We shall now say a word about each of these types of gold standard.

Gold Currency Standard

This is also called Full Gold Standard. A country is on a full gold standard when gold serves not only as standsrd of value but also circulates as coins. Before 1914, Britain had this kind of gold standard and so had the U.S.A., France, Germany and other European countries. Gold provides for the currency a solid and tangible base. It is called the traditional or the orthodox gold standard.

We may illustrate its working from the example of pre-1914 Britain. Gold circulated in the form of sovereigns of a given weight (113 – 1/623 grs.) of pure gold, plus a little alloy. The actual weight of the sovereign was 123.27447 grammes 11/12 fine. In other words, one ounce of gold 11/12 fine could be coined into £3 17s. $10\frac{1}{2}$d. in English money. Actually the Bank of England only gave £3 17s. 9d. for every ounce of such gold. To purchase an ounce of standard gold from the Bank, one had to pay £3 17s. $10\frac{1}{2}$d. per oz. Under this system, therefore, the purchasing power of a British sovereign could not rise appreciably above or fall appreciably below 123.27447 grammes of gold 11/12 fine or 113.1/623 grammes of pure gold.

Gold Bullions.

This system could not be maintained during the World War of 1914–18, and had to be given up. The reason was that, for the prosecution of war, paper money had to be issued on a very large scale and there was not enough gold with the Central bank to maintain convertibility of note-issue. In April 1925, however, Great Britain restored the Gold Standard but of a different variety, *viz*., the Gold Bullion Standard.

Gold Bullion Standard

Under the gold bullion standard, the value of the currency is fixed in terms of gold by making such currency convertible into gold (bullion not coin), and vice versa. But gold does not circulate as coins.

In the United Kingdom, under the Gold Bullion Standard, the Bank of England was willing to buy any amount of gold at £3 17s. 9d. per ounce 11/12 fine and to sell it in minimum amount of 400 ounces, at £3 17s. $10\frac{1}{2}$d. This was the same rate as before 1914. Gold was allowed freely to move into or outside the country. As a measure of economy, no gold coins circulated in the country. But gold was made available for foreign payments.

The Gold Bullion Standard was adopted in India in 1927 on the recommendation of the Hilton Young Commission. The currency authority was placed under an obligation to buy or sell gold at rates announced beforehand subject to a minimum of 400 ozs. of gold.

Merits. The Hilton Young Commission claimed that it had all the advantages of a full gold standard minus its disadvantages:

(i) It is economical as no gold coins have to be minted and put into circulation. In their daily dealings, the public use a cheap medium of exchange, either paper money or rupees.

(ii) It makes for national prestige, because gold is made freely available both for use inside the country and for exporting it abroad and not merely for exchange purposes as under the gold exchange standard.

(iii) The paper currency, under gold bullion standard, has a more tangible and solid backing. It is convertible into gold. But, under the gold exchange standard, one token money (currency note) is convertible into another token money (rupee).

(iv) It is also claimed that, under this system, an automatic mechanism for expansion and contraction of currency is maintained. The currency will be expanded when gold is sold to the currency authority, and it will be contracted when gold is purchased by the public.

(v) It is considered that gold kept as a reserve in the central bank is much more useful and gives more valuable support to the national currency than gold put into circulation. This is provided under the gold bullion standard.

Gold.

(vi) The gold bullion standard provided for the public the facility to obtain gold and liberty to melt or export it.

But these merits of the gold bullion standard are more or less theoretical; at any rate, they turned out to be so in the case of India. For the average man, the convertibility of notes into gold was a farce, for who could bring sufficient paper money to purchase 400 oz. of gold (400 oz. = 1,065 tolas)? Thus, under gold bullion standard, automatic expansion and contraction of currency was not brought about.

In 1931, England went off the gold standard and so did India. The gold bullion standard made an exit 'unhonoured and unsung.'

Gold Exchange Standard [1]

The first country to adopt gold exchange standard seems to have been Holland, which it did in 1877. Russia followed Holland in adopting it in 1894. Austria-Hungary too adopted it at the same time. The credit, however, of perfecting it and working it effectively belongs to India where it started functioning in 1907. The philippine Islands had established it a few years earlier. The Genoa International Conference held in 1922 passed a resolution recommending the adoption of the gold exchange standard. India was on this system when the war of 1914–18 broke out.

As this system worked in India, the internal currency consisted of silver rupees which were token

1. See "International Currency Experience," League of Nations, 1944, Ch. II.

coins and paper currency. But for foreign payments sterling (convertible into gold in London) was sold by the Government in return for rupees at a fixed rate. In London, the Secretary of State sold rupees (called Council Bills since they were sold by the authority of the Secretary of State-in-Council) to those who wanted to make payments to India. When the Government of India sold drafts on the Secretary of State, they were called Reverse Councils. The rates[2] for buying and selling of rupees were fixed in such a way as to maintain the sterling-rupee ratio at 1 s. 4d., or nearabout.

Thus, the gold exchange standard necessitates the keeping of two reserves, one in the country, which has adopted it, in the form of home currency, and the other at a foreign centre, the former to make payment for the Council Bills and the latter to pay the Reverse Councils. The successful functioning of the system depends on the adequacy of these reserves. The Government of India maintained a reserve for the purpose called the Gold Standard Reserve.

The system broke down during the war of 1914 – 18 due to great demand for rupees accompanied by an excessive rise in the price of silver. High price of silver made the rupee a full-valued coin (instead of being a token coin that it was) leading to its melting and hoarding. The Government was unable to supply rupees at the old rates. First, the rate was raised, but later the attempt to maintain the rupee in terms of the sterling was given up altogether.

After the war (in 1920), the gold exchange standard was again tried at the rate of 2s. (gold) per rupee, but had to be given up. This time for opposite reasons, *viz*., a fall in the price of silver accompanied by a great demand for sterling due to excess of imports over exports. The Government was unable to sell sterling (by rupees) at 2s. gold or even at 2s. sterling.

Essential Features. Thus, the essential features of gold exchange standard are:

(*i*) The monetary standard is fixed either directly or indirectly in terms of a certain number of grammes of gold. For instance, the Indian rupee was made equal to 7.53 grammes.

(*ii*) The local currency is pegged to a foreign currency and the local mints are closed to free coinage so that there may be no difficulty in maintaining its value.

Gold Cube.

(*iii*) It is essential to maintain in the 'planet' country a reserve in gold and in the 'satelite' country a reserve in the local currency to provide resources for the maintenance of the exchange value of the currency.

(*iv*) To ensure that the actual rates of exchange do not vary widely from the fixed rate, drafts are sold freely in both countries.

Advantages. Among the advantages claimed for the gold exchange standard one was that it give all the advantages of the full gold standard without involving the use of gold. It is thus economical. Moreover, linking the rupee with the sterling was said to benefit India, because of her considerable trade relations with Great Britain and financial status of London in the international field. International payments, when made through sterling, were considerably facilitated, while the sterling link gave the rupee a high status.

The general advantages of such a system are:

(*i*) It is economical.

(*ii*) It facilitates foreign trade.

(*iii*) It keeps the external value of the currency stable.

(*iv*) Possibly it may also make for comparatively stable price levels.

Defects of the Gold Exchange Standard. Gold Exchange Standard, as it worked during the inter-war period, was criticised on several grounds:

In the first place, it was charged with breeding inflation. But it was really anti-deflationary rather than inflationary.

Secondly, the central banks did not follow any concerted or uniform policy in their reliance on exchange reserves as against gold, so that their isolated actions tended to produce a financial chaos.

2. Before the war of 1914–18 the selling and buying rates of the rupee were 1 s. 4d. and 1st. 3–29/32d, respectively, the former in London (Council Bills) and the latter in India (Reverse Councils).

Thirdly, keeping of reserves in the form of a foreign currency was deemed to be a blow to national prestige.

Fourthly, it was considered to be a British fad and disliked by many countries on that account.

Fifthly, there was an inherent danger of depreciation of the foreign currency in which the reserve was kept.

Finally, it was said that, unlike gold movements, the movements in foreign exchange reserves did not bring into play the reciprocal tendency towards contraction or expansion of currency.

So far as the working of this standard in India is concerned, the gold exchange standard was criticized by the Hilton Young Commission in scathing terms. The following points may be mentioned in this connection:

(i) It was too abstract, far from simple and 'unintelligible to the uninstructed public.' Not even educated Indians could easily understand its working. Such a system could not inspire popular confidence or enthusiasm. It made the currency authority a suspect in the eyes of the public.

(ii) As the system operated in India, there was unnecessary duplication of the reserves. There were three reserves in India—the Gold Standard Reserve, the Paper Currency Reserve and the Government of India's balances, Those reserves had their counterparts in England.

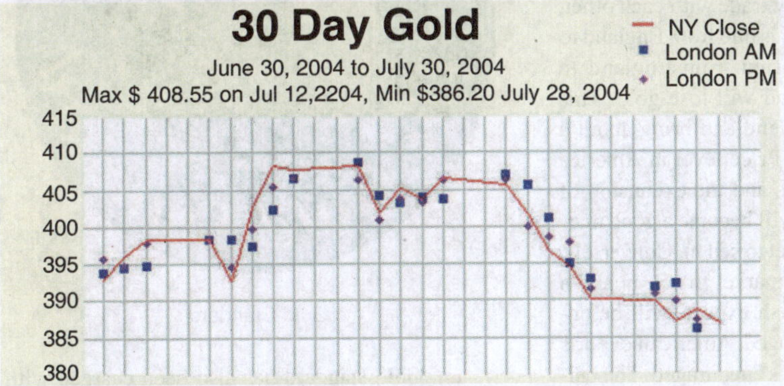

(iii) The system was not automatic. In its operation, it depended too much on the will of the currency authority.

(iv) It lacked elasticity. Expansion of currency did take place in India when rupees were issued to meet Council Bills, but once issued, the rupees remained in circulation. There were no means by which contraction of currency could be effected.

(v) A very serious defect is that currency policy of one country becomes subservient to that of another country. The Indian rupee was subject to all the misfortunes to which the English currency may have been subject to.

The Hilton Young Commission was of the opinion that the gold exchange standard had inherent defects and it was not possible to correct them. They came to the conclusion that it could not be mended, it must be ended. Accordingly, they recommended its replacement by the gold bullion standard (already studied above).

Gold Parity Standard

The latest to enter the list of gold standards is the **gold parity standard.** This is the type which is supposed to prevail under the aegis of the International Monetary Fund. Under this system, no gold coins are put into circulation. Gold does not serve as a medium of exchange. The internal currency consists largely of notes and some form of metallic money but certainly not of gold, nor are these notes convertible into coins as under the full gold standard, nor into gold bullion as under the bullion standard, nor into particular foreign currency based on gold as under the gold exchange standard. But the only respect in which gold comes into play, under this system, is that the currency authority takes upon itself the obligation of maintaining the exchange rate of the domestic currency stable in terms of a certain quantity of gold. This is the type of gold standard which the member countries of the I.M.F. were supposed to have till 1975 when gold was replaced by SDR's for that purpose.

30 Day Gold
June 30, 2004 to July 30, 2004
Max $ 408.55 on Jul 12,2204, Min $386.20 July 28, 2004
NY Close
London AM
London PM

Advantages of Gold Standard

Several advantages are claimed for the gold standard, especially when it is adopted simultaneously by a number of countries, *i.e.*, international gold standard.

(i) It is an objective system and is not subject to the changing policies of the government or the whims of the currency authority.

(*ii*) Gold standard enables the country to maintain the purchasing power of its currency over long periods. This is so because the currency and credit structure is ultimately based on gold in possession of the currency authority.[3]

(*iii*) Another important advantage claimed for gold standard is that it preserves and maintains the exteranl value of the currency (rate of exchage) within narrow limits.[4] As a matter of fact, within the gold standard system, it provides fixed exchanges, which is a great boon to traders and investors. International division of labour is greatly facilitated.

(*iv*) It gives, in fact, all the advantages of a common international currency. It establishes an international measure of value. As Marshall pointed out before the Fowler Committee (Report on Indian Currency) in 1898, the change to a gold basis is like a movement towards bringing the railway gauge on the side branches of the world's railway into unison with the main lines.[5] This greatly facilitates foreign trade, because fluctuations in rates of exchange hamper international trade.

(*v*) It is further claimed that gold standard helps to adjust the balance of payments between countries automatically. How this happens may be illustrated by a simple example. Suppose England and America are both on gold standard and only trade with each other, and that a balance of payments is due from England to America. Gold will be exported from England to America. The Bank of England will lose gold. This will contract currency in England and bring about a fall in the British price level. Price level in America will rise due to larger reserves and the expansion of currency and credit. England will become a good market to buy from and a bad market to sell in. Conversely, America will become a good market to sell in and a bad market to buy from. British exports will be encouraged and imports discouraged. American exports will be discouraged and imports encouraged. The balance of payments will tend to move in favour of Britain until equilibrium is reached. It is in this way, that movement of gold, by affecting prices and trade, keeps equilibrium among gold standard countries. More of this later.

(*vi*) Gold standard inspires confidence and contributes to national prestige, for "so long as nine people out of ten in every country think the gold standard the best, it is the best."

3. See Chapter on Central Banks.
4. See Chapter on Foreign Exchange.
5. Report, Fowler Committee, para 34.

Disadvantages of Gold Standard

(*i*) Gold standard is costly and the cost is unnecessary. We only want a medium of exchange; why should it be made of gold? It is a luxury. 'The yellow metal could tickle the fancy of savages only.'

(*ii*) Even the value of gold has not been found to be absolutely stable over long periods.

(*iii*) Under the gold standard, currency cannot be expanded in response to the requirements of trade. The supply of currency depends on the supply of gold. But the supply of gold depends on the success of the mining operations, which may have nothing to do with the factors affecting the growth of trade and industry in the country.

Recently even the gold standard has been a managed standard. The central banking technique has been applied deliberately to control the working of the gold standard. It is thus no longer as automatic as it was claimed to be.

Gold Standard.

(*iv*) Gold standard has also been charged with sacrificing internal stability to external (exchange) stability. It is the international aspect of the gold standard which has been paid more attention to.

(*v*) Another disadvantage is that, under gold standard "gold movements lead to changes in interest rates, so that investment is stimulated or checked solely in order to expand or reduce money income" (Benham).

(*vi*) A country on a gold standard cannot follow an independent policy. In order to maintain the gold standard or to restore it (as in England after World War I), it may have to deflate its currency against its will. Deflation spells ruin to the economy of a country. It brings, in its wake, large-scale unemployment, closing of works and untold suffering attendant on depression.

Conditions for Successful Functioning of Gold Standard

There are certain pre-conditions for the successful functioning of the gold standard:

(*i*) Observance of the Rules of the Gold Standard.

Gold standard cannot function successfully unless certain rules are observed by the countries on the gold standard. These have come to be known as the **"Rules of the Gold Standard Game."** The principal rules are:

(*a*) There should be no restrictions on the movement of gold from one country to another.

(*b*) There should be a high degree of freedom of trade so that dis-equilibrium arising out of balance of payments may be adjusted through the movement of goods. Gold should move only to cover small gaps.

(*c*) The economic structure of gold standard countries should be kept fairly elastic so that prices and wages respond readily to gold movements.

(*d*) The most important of all—the government and central banks should not offset the effects of gold movements. A country losing gold must contract its currency and allow its price-level to fall, and the one that gets it must expand its currency and allow the price level to rise. As Crowther says, "The golden rule

Goldbars.

of the gold standard is: expand credit when gold comes in; contract credit, when gold is going out."[6] In other words, there should be automatic expansion and contraction of currency and credit as gold inflows and outflows respectively.

Violation of these rules on the part of the gold standard countries will inevitably lead to the break-down of the standard.

6. Crowther, G.—*An Outline of Money,* 1950, p. 304.

(*ii*) Exchange Stability. Besides the above, it is essential for the successful functioning of the gold standard that the countries concerned should maintain stable exchange rates. Exchange instability is bound to create chaos in international economic relations and render it impossible for a country to keep on the gold standard if there is a danger of its losing gold by doing so.

(*iii*) No Large Capital Movements. Another danger to the functioning of gold standard arises from international capital movements on a big scale. Short-term capital movements may be essential to remove temporary disequilibrium in the balance of payments. But large scale capital movements may result in economic, social and political disturbances. Panicky outflow of capital or gold is inimical to the smooth working of the gold standard.

Absence of the above conditions in the inter-war period (1919–1939) led to the breakdown of the gold standard.

Causes of the Break-down of the Gold Standard

The gold standard broke down in country after country soon after its rehabilitation during the post-1914–18 war decade. There were several reasons for this development:

(*i*) Gold was very unevenly distributed among the countries in the inter-war period. While the U.S.A. and France came to possess the bulk of it, other countries did not have enough to maintain a monetary system based in gold.

(*ii*) Owing to **general political unsettlement,** a habit arose on the part of certain Continental countries to keep their funds for short periods in foreign central banks, especially in Great Britain. These funds were liable to be withdrawn at the earliest danger signal. Withdrawal of such funds from Britain on the part of France led to gold standard being suspended in 1931 in the former country. The Bank of England could not afford to lose its gold resources in large quantities at such a short notice.

(*iii*) International trade was not free. Some countries often imposed stringent restrictions on imports which created serious balance of payments problems for other countries. Not having enough gold to cover the gap, they threw the gold standard overboard. This specially happened during the Great Depression of early thirties.

(*iv*) International obligation in the form of reparations and war debts arose out of World War I. Since the creditor countries refused to accept payments in the form of goods and also refused to continue lending to the debtors countries, the **debts had to be cleared through gold movements.** This led to concentration of 34 per cent of the world's gold in the U.S.A., and France, the two chief creditor countries. The gold left with the other countries was not enough to enable them to maintain gold standard successfully.

(v) The **gold-receiving countries did not "play the game of the gold standard".** They (especially the U.S.A.) did not allow this gold to have any effect on their price levels. **The gold was "sterilised" or made ineffective.** Had prices risen in these countries, imports would have been encouraged and exports discouraged and an unfavourable balance of trade would have led to movement of gold in the reverse direction. Since this was not allowed to happen, the gold standard failed to work automatically.

(vi) Gold standard failed also because the **economic structure of the countries concerned had become less and less elastic** after the World War of 1914–18. This was due to several reasons: The enormous growth in the indebtedness of governments and local authorities resulted in a mass of interest payments fixed by contract over a long period of years. The huge expenditure in the form of payment to social services could not be easily reduced. The trade unions were now able to offer a much stronger resistance to wage cuts than before 1914. The prices of raw materials and finished goods were becoming more and more fixed by partial monopolies, cartel agreements, *etc*. The result was that prices no longer moved in the directions warranted by gold movements and equilibrium failed to be restored as of old.

(vii) Another weakness that was discovered in the gold standard in practice was that **it was always liable to collapse in a crisis.** It has often been called **a 'fair weather standard' only.**

(viii) Another objection that was frequently urged against the system was that **gold movements caused inconvenient changes in interest rates.** Deflation, for instance, may be made necessary at a time of crisis to prevent suspension of the standard. But deflation, which involves falling wages and prices, may prove a cause of serious trouble. Wage cuts are resisted by trade unions, and falling prices increase the burden of fixed payments which the government or the people may have to make. Moreover, falling prices discourage enterprise and create unemployment.

(ix) A large volume of short-term capital was moving for safety from one financial centre to another. Big flows of this hot money necessitated large gold movements which the slender gold reserves of the countries could not maintain. Hence, gold standard was given up.

Thus, it was that country after country abandoned the Gold Standard in the inter-war period.

Future of Gold Standard

It is unlikely that, after the experiences of the inter-war period, gold standard would be established in the conventional sense by any country of the world. Gold standard worked more or less automatically under the pre-1914 conditions of trade and finance. The experience of inter-war period, however, showed that the gold standard required quite a fair degree of management and still greater degree of co-operation of the gold standard countries for its smooth working. "The gold standard will work if every nation is content to march in step with every other." Unless the rules of the gold standard are observed, it cannot function successfully. Also, the rigidities of the economic system stand in the way of proper adjustment of price levels and costs necessary for its successful working.

The International Monetary Fund, which was set up, after the Second World War, is supposed to achieve all the advantages of a gold standard without its disadvantages by international co-operation. Gold still plays a role but not such a dominant role as it did under the gold standard. We shall discuss the I.M.F. (International Monetary Fund) in a later chapter,[7] where the position of gold in the present international monetary system will be indicated. Thus we can confidently assert that the gold standard of the old type has no future.

PAPER CURRENCY STANDARD

In modern times, metallic money is supplemented or replaced by paper money altogether. Paper money has been very useful. It economises the use of precious metals. It is convenient to carry and easy to store. Its value can be kept stable by properly controlling its issue. It is of great fiscal advantage to the government. A government can tide over a period of difficulty by the issue of paper money. Hence, it has largely replaced coins.

In early times, when notes were introduced, they were backed by an exactly equal amount in gold or silver kept in reserve by the issuing authority. Such notes could be exchanged for coins whenever needed and did nothing more than represent coins. They were called **representative paper money.** American gold certificates (Greenbacks) were of this type. This practice was very expensive and is no more current now.

7. Chapter 59.

Paper money is not wholly backed by specie (*i.e.*, precious metal) now. Only proportional reserves are maintained and a good deal of the paper money rests on people's confidence in the word of the issuing authority, be it the Government or the Central Bank of the country. Such a currency is called **fiduciary issue** (*i.e.*, depending on trust or confidence). The total notes in circulation in India at the end of March 1982 amounted to Rs. 14,752 crores nearly. This amount was backed by nearly Rs. 226 crores worth of gold, supplemented by foreign securities and securities of the Government of India. Thus, currency is of a fiduciary issue.

Paper money can be convertible or inconvertible. If the issuing authority promises to convert notes into standard money on demand it is called **'convertible paper money.'** But sometimes after an overissue of paper money in an emergency like war, the authority feels unable to convert its notes into coins. Then it breaks its promise of converting notes into standard money and thereby makes the money **'inconvertible'** or **fiat money** (money by order). When the link with metal is broken, there is a tendency to over-issue paper money. Its value then depreciates. Prices shoot up, which results in suffering for the people with fixed incomes.

Indian notes are convertible into the standard money of the country—rupees—as and when desired by holders. But it should be clearly noted that the rupee coins in India were themselves only token coins. The Indian rupee was called a note printed on silver and later nickel. Even these rupee coins of nickel are also no longer in circulation. One-rupee notes are not legally convertible into rupee coins—they are treated as rupees. They are issued by the Government of India while all other notes are issued by the Reserve Bank of India.

Advantages of Paper Money

Paper money has got several advantages and disadvantages. The following advantages can be mentioned:

***(i)* Economical.** Paper money practically costs nothing to the Government. Currency notes, therefore, are the cheapest media of exchange. If a country uses paper money, it need not spend anything on the purchase of gold or silver for minting coins. The loss which a country suffers from the wear and tear of metallic money is also avoided.

***(ii)* Convenient.** Paper money is the most convenient form of money. A large amount can be carried conveniently in the pocket without anybody knowing it. It is very risky to carry on one's person Rs. 5,000 in coins, but not in notes. It possesses, in a very large measure, the quality of portability which a money material should have. In a very small bulk it can contain a very large value. Think of a currency note of Rs. 10,000.

***(iii)* Homogeneous.** One essential quality in money is that it must be exactly of the same type. Even among the coins there are good and bad coins. But currency notes are all exactly similar. It is, therefor, a very suitable medium of exchange.

***(iv)* Stability.** The value of paper money can be kept stable by properly regulating its issue. That is why there are many advocates of **'managed' paper currency.**

***(v)* Elasticity.** Paper money is absolutely elastic. Its quantity can be increased or decreased at the will of the currency authority. Thus, paper money can better meet the requirements of trade and industry.

***(vi)* Cheap Remittance.** Money in the form of currncy notes can be cheaply remitted from one place to another in an insured cover.

***(vii)* Advantageous to Banks.** Paper money is of

WORLD PAPER MONEY

very **great advantage to the banks.** They can keep their cash reserves against liabilities in this form, for currency notes are full legal tender.

***(viii)* Fiscal advantages to the Government** of the paper currency are undoubtedly very great, especially in times of national emergencies like a war. A modern war cannot be prosecuted by taxes or loans alone. All governments have to resort to the printing press. In recent years in India there has been a high degree of inflation. We must remember, however, that by this means our Government has been able to spend hundreds of crores of rupees on various ambitious programmes of economic development. Hence, within limits the issue of paper money comes very handy to the government at the time of dire need.

Disadvantages of Paper Money

(i) Paper money is of **no value outside the country of issue.** Gold and silver coins are accepted even by foreigners, as they have got some intrinsic value.

(ii) Paper currency may result in instability of foreign exchange rates when the domestic prices and external prices do not move in harmony.

***(iii)* There is a possibility of damage to paper.** Fire may burn it; if the place is flooded, it is gone; it may also be eaten up by white ants.

Currency Principle.

(iv) A serious drawback in paper currency is the ease with which it can be issued. There is always a **danger of its over-issue** when the Government is in financial difficulties. The temptation is too great to be resisted. Once this course is adopted, however, it gathers momentum and leads to further noteprinting, and this goes on till the paper currency loses all value. This happened in various countries in recent times: in Russia (1917), in Germany (1919), in China (1944), and so on.

An over-issue of notes, in other words 'inflation'. brings many evils in its train. Some of them are:

(a) Prices rise steeply. As a result, labourers and people with fixed incomes suffer greatly. In fact, the whole public feels the pinch.

(b) The indirect result of the excessive rise in prices is a fall in exports and a rise in imports. This leads to the export of gold from the country, which is not a desirable thing. Its balance of payments becomes unfavourable.

(c) The rise in prices also leads to a fall in the external value of the home currency. The rate of exchange falls. More home currency will have to be paid to buy units of foreign currencies.

Conclusion. Really, paper money, if it is issued and regulated carefully, is without any disadvantage. All countries issue paper currency, and, in normal times, they do not suffer from it in any manner. Only when it is over-issued, it becomes a great danger and a curse. It may cause grave discontent among the masses. When paper money is over-issued, there is inflation and prices rise. It hits hard several important sections of the people like workers and fixed-incomeists. The people might lose confidence in the currency and it might become useless. Such a situation arose in many European countries during and after World War I, and later more recently in China.

Principles of Note-Issue

In the issue of notes, two conflicting aims have to be reconciled. On the one hand, the note issue must be elastic. The circulation should expand and contract in accordance with the requirements of trade. On the other hand, the confidence in the notes must be preserved by maintaining its convertibility. The first is the principle of elasticity, and the second is that of security. This requires a proper regulation of note-issue.

Banking Principle.

Currency Principle vs. **Banking Principle.** On the eve of the passing of the Bank Charter Act in England in 1844, there was a keen controversy as to what should be the right principle of note-issue. There were two opposing schools of thought, one advocating what is known as the Currency Principle and the other the Banking Principle.

The advocates of the **Currency Principle** insisted on full metallic backing (*i.e*, 100% reserve). For every note issued, there must be kept in the currency chest coins of the same value. In their opinion, the currency note was merely a convenient economical substitute for metallic money. Naturally, the paper currency under this system was absolutely safe, but it lacked elasticity.

Those who advocated the **Banking Principle** were in favour of leaving the business of note-issue entirely to the discretion of the banks. This would enable them to vary the amount of currency in response to the legitimate needs of trade and industry. Any excess of note-issue would automatically come back to the banks by being presented for cash payments. They held that the banks in their own interest would maintain adequate reserves to honour these notes. No reserve requirements need be laid down by law. In their opinion, the banks could be safely relied up to the regulate the note-issue properly. The Banking Principle undoubtedly made the note-issue elastic, but it lacked security.

We thus find that the Currency Principle provides security but lacks elasticity, whereas the Banking Principle ensures elasticity but is wanting in security. A sound system of note-issue, however, must provide both elasticity and security. Hence, all countries have evolved systems each of which represents a compromise between these two principles.

Systems of Note-Issue

As mentioned above, there was at one time a controversy whether notes should be issued on the **currency principle** (*i.e.,* 100 per cent reserve) or the **banking principle,** leaving the question of paper currency reserve entirely to the discretion of the banks of issue. We may repeat that the Currency Principle provides safety but lacks elasticity, whereas the Banking Principle ensures elasticity but is wanting in security. A sound system of note-issue, however, must have both **elasticity** and **safety.** Hence, all countries have evolved systems each of which represents a compromise between these two principles. Among these we may mention:

(*a*) **Maximum Fiduciary Issue**

(*b*) **Fixed Fiduciary Principle** or **Partial Deposit System.**

(*c*) **Proportional Reserve System.**

(*d*) **Minimum Reserve System.**

Maximum Fiduciary Issue. Under this system, the government fixes a maximum amount of paper currency that the central bank can issue without backing of metallic money. This maximum is subject to revision from time to time. This may, however, result in inflation when a needy government may raise the maximum to finance an excess of expenditure. Such a system was introduced by many countries including England since 1939.

Fixed Fiduciary System. In Great Britain, the Fixed Fiduciary System was embodied in the Bank Charter Act of 1844 as amended subsequently. Under this system, a given quantity of notes can be issued by the central bank without keeping any metallic reserves. This portion could be covered only by Government securities. This is called the **fiduciary limit.** Notes issued in excess of fiduciary limit must be covered pound for pound by gold.

This method was attacked from time to time as lacking in elasticity. It, however, acted as a brake on the over-expansion of currency. In abnormal circumstances, the fiduciary limit could be raised by amending the Act. In 1928 the Treasury was given power to increase the fiduciary limit beyond the legal ceiling. This gave some elasticity to the system. It was, however, objected that the raising of the fiduciary limit was always interpreted as a sign of weakness. Thus, it was held that elasticity was imparted but there was loss of confidence. In spite of criticism, the system has survived owing, mainly perhaps, to the force of tradition. Japan and Norway, in fact, have introduced this system.

Proportional Reserve System. This system has been adopted on the European continent. France keeping 35 per cent and Germany 40 per cent reserve. With some modifications it has also been followed by the Federal Reserve System of the U.S.A. "The essential feature of this method, which has now spread over a large part of the world," says De Kock, "is the provision of a proportional metallic reserve against the note circulation (25, 30, 33–1/3, 40 per cent), the remainder of the notes to be covered by trade bills and Government securities, with the further provision that, subject to certain conditions and penalties, the reserve ratio may be allowed to drop below the legal minimum." The banks generally keep a 'cushion' above the legal minimum for fear of breaking the law.

However, it should be borne in mind that the central bank reserve is not merely intended as a cover for notes issued. "The amount of international currency a country needs does not depend at all closely on the amount of its domestic currency and credit; it depends on its liability to suffer fluctuations in the balance of external payments." And what is kept as 'cover' is not available for external settlements.

This system is more elastic than the Fixed Fiduciary Principle. If the bank obtains, say, Rs. 40 worth of gold, it can issue Rs. 100 worth of notes under the Proportional Reserve System, but only Rs. 40 worth of notes under the Fixed Fiduciary Principle, once it has exhausted the fiduciary limit. The element of safety, however, is less under this method of issuing notes.

Gold and Foreign exchange reserves.

Some people think that if the State issues notes, as was done in India until the Reserve Bank of India took over this function, the note-issue can be better controlled. But, in times of emergencies, the notes will be over-issued, whether the State does it directly or indirectly through its influence over the central bank. In fact, note-issue by a central bank is slightly better from this point of view, since there may be some resistance by the central bank to the proposals of the government to use the method of printing additional notes for its finance.

So far as India is concerned, the Reserve Bank of India has the monopoly of note-issue. For this purpose, the Reserve Bank, like some other central banks (*e.g.*, the Bank of England), maintains a separate department called the **Issue Department.** The assets of this department are kept distinct from those of the other department of the Bank, the Banking Department.

Till 1956, the Reserve Bank of India issued notes on the basis of the proportional reserve system. The assets of the Issue Department consisted of silver, rupee coins, Government of India (rupee) securities, gold coins, gold bullion, or **foreign sterling** securities, provided that the amount of gold coin, gold bullion and foreign securities must be at least 40 per cent of the total reserve. With the sanction of the Central Government, this 40 per cent limit could be reduced for limited periods on payment of a specified tax on the deficiency. Thus, the system adopted in India was a compromise between the two systems discussed above.

Fixed Minimum Reserve System. However, in 1956, the proportional reserve system was replaced by the **Fixed Minimum Reserve System** in India. A minimum holding of foreign securities worth Rs. 400 crores including gold worth Rs. 115 crores was prescribed. In 1957, it was cut down to Rs. 200 crores including gold worth Rs. 115 crores. This drastic reduction was necessitated by the rapid depletion of foreign exchange reserves due to adverse balance of payments. Under this system of note issue, paper currency in India has now become practically inconvertible.

ESSENTIALS OF A SOUND CURRENCY SYSTEM

Broadly speaking, a sound currency system must fulfil the following conditions:

(i) It must maintain a reasonable stability of prices in the country. This means that its internal value (or purchasing power in terms of goods and services in the country concerned) must not fluctuate too violently. As we shall see later, this involves regulation of the amount of money in circulation to suit the requirements of trade and industry in the country.

(ii) A sound currency system must maintain stability of the external value of the currency. This means that its purchasing power over goods and services in foreign countries, through its command over a definite amount of foreign currency, should remain constant. This is the problem of foreign exchange, which we shall tackle in a later chapter.[8]

(iii) The system must be economical. A costly medium of exchange is a national waste. It is unnecessary. That is why all countries use mostly paper money.

8. Chapter 58.

(iv) The currency must be elastic and automatic so that it expands or contracts in response to the requirements of trade and industry.

(v) The currency system must be simple so that an average man can understand it. A complicated system cannot inspire public confidence.

PAPER GOLD STANDARD OR THE SDR STANDARD

The IMF was an improvement on the gold standard. The IMF had all the merits of the gold standard minus its demerits. It ensured exchange stability without the country having to undergo the expense of maintaining a costly currency system. Under the IMF system, exchange parities were fixed in gold but it was unnecessary to keep large gold reserves for currency purposes. Besides gold stocks and current output were utterly inadequate to meet the requirements of ever-expanding volume of international trade, thus giving rise to the serious problem of international liquidity (This problem has been considered at length in Chapter 59). The IMF sought to provide multilaterism. The IMF quota facilitated foreign exchange transactions and there was no need to export gold to meet a trade deficit. It also facilitated convertibility of currencies and provided adequate and convenient currency reserve for the use of member countries.

However, fast changing circumstances is necessitated changes in the I.M.F. system. In September 1967, the Board of Governors approved a plan for a new type of international asset known as the S.D. Rs. (Special Drawing Rights). They have been called "Paper Gold Standard". Under the Scheme, the I.M.F. is empowered to allocate to various member countries Special Drawing Rights (SDR's) on a specified basis, which in effect amounts to raising the limit to which a member country can draw from the IMF in time of need. Besides, the SDR's supplement gold dollars and pounds sterling most countries now use as monetary reserves. They can be used unconditionally by the participating countries to meet their liabilities and they are not backed by gold. They are meant to be used by the Central banks of the Fund's member countries. With the SDR's, the Central banks can buy whatever currencies they need for settling their balance of payments deficits. The resources of the new scheme are not a pool of currencies but simply the obligation of participating members to accept the SDR's for settlement of payments between them. Thus, SDR's serve as an international money as good as other reserve currencies.

But a nicely and diligently built up system of exchange stability by the *I.M.F.* collapsed like a house of cards. This was caused by the dollar crisis created by the adverse American balance of payments.

Among the measures taken by the American administration, there was one which delinked dollar from gold. The delinking of dollar from gold knocked out the very foundation of the IMF.

In January 1975, the IMF abolished the official price of gold and SDR's have instead become the basis of the present international monetary standard. The *SDR*'s are not convertible into gold; that is why alternatively the present standard may also be referred to as Paper Gold Standard.

Money Supply In India

Money supply does not mean only the supply of money in the form of coins and currency. In modern economic activities any financial paper which represents money or near money also a part of money supply. Thus in modern day business sense money supply includes coins, currency, demand deposits and time deposits with bank and other financial assets such as deposits with non-bank financial intermediaries, post office savings deposits, money market instruments like, treasury and exchange bills as well as bonds and equities *etc*. The money supply concept in India is divided into four components such as.

***(i)* Narrow Money Concept [M_1].** it can be considered as reserved money or high powered money, which includes.

C = Currency and coins.

DD = Demand deposits with banks

OD = It is the deposits with *RBI* with reference to employees pension, provident and guarantee funds + deposits of some non-bank financial institutions and + other compulsory deposits.

$$M_1 = C + OD + DD$$

***(ii)* "Money Stock" Concept [M_2].** It is nothing but an extention of M_1 along with the addition of Post office Savings Bank Deposits (*POSBD*). As people love money and material wealth. They keep their money in the safest institutions. Post offices are government organisation where common people feel safe to keep their money. Hence *POSBD* is added to M_1.

$$\therefore \quad M_2 = M_1 + POSBD$$

***(iii)* Broad Money Concept [M_3].** Milton Friedman included time deposits also as part of money supply. Even Chakravarty committee (1985) took M_3 for monetory planning.

$$M_3 = M_1 + TD.$$

(iv) **Aggregate Monetary Resources. (M_4).** In M_4 total post office deposits are added as post offices are all over the country. Hence their deposits are also included in the money supply.

$$M_4 = M_3 + TPOD.$$

Key terms

Gold standard, Paper money, Minimum revenue system, Proportional measure system, Fiduciary systems, SDR, M_1, M_2, M_3, and M_4 in India.

QUESTIONS

1. What is gold standard? Why is it called an 'automatic standard'? Compare gold standard with the present I.M.F. standard.
2. Discuss the main features of Gold Standard. What are the rules to be observed for its successful functioning?

   Or

   The case for the Gold Standard is the case for a strict dejure gold standard, with each country following 'the rules" so that no gold standardd currency becomes distrusted Explain and illustrate.
3. Gold Standard failed due to the failure of countries to observe its golden rules. Examine the truth of this statement.
4. 'The Gold Standard mechanism secures stability of exchange rates at the cost of domestic price stability." Elucidate.
5. Discuss how balance of payments disequilibrium is corrected under an intenational gold standard.
6. Define the term 'monetary standard'. Describe the main features of the Gold Exchange Standard.
7. What is meant by managed currency? Give its merits and demerits.
8. What are the essentials of a good monetary system? How far are they found in a paper currency standard?
9. Discuss the elements or constituents of 'money supply' in India.
10. Explain paper currency standard. What are its advantages and disadvantages.
11. What are the principles of note issue? Explain different systems of note issue.

THEORY OF MONEY AND PRICES

In the theory of money, we are concerned with the determination of the value of money which has an inverse relationship with the general price level. There are two main questions concerning the value of money, *viz.*, (*a*) how changes in the value of money (or prices) are measured and (*b*) how the value of money is determined, *i.e.*, the factors governing price fluctuations.

We first take up the measurement of the changes in the value of money which is done by means of index numbers.

INDEX NUMBER

Meaning

In the world, as we see there are numerous commodities being offered for sale. Prices of all these commodities do not always move together. It is quite possible that while prices of some commodities are rising, those of other commodities may be falling. Even if all the prices are moving together, the rate of change of some prices may be faster than that of others, *i.e.*, some prices may be rising or falling faster than others. In order to introduce an element of uniformity, the concept of general price level is used, which, in a sense, is the average of price changes of diverse commodities. This is done by means of index numbers.

Index numbers are devices for measuring the differences in the magnitude of a group of related variables. An index number of prices is then a number which indicates the price level at any given date as compared with the level of prices at some standard date called the base.

Stock Indices.

Preparation of Index Numbers

The following are the various steps in the construction of such an index number:—

***(i)* Choice of the base year.** The first step is to choose a year to serve as the base year, *i.e.*, the year with reference to which the price changes in other years are expressed as percentages. Care must be exercised in its selection. It should be an average year, neither a year of boom nor of depression. Sometimes an average (of prices) of a number of years is taken to serve as the base.

***(ii)* Selection of commodities.** The second step is to select commodities the prices of which have to be taken to represent the general price-level. The commodities should be really representative and should be sufficiently large in number. The selection of commodities also depends on the object with which the index is prepared. For instance, if the object is to study how the cost of living of working class has been affected by price changes, we select those commodities which figure in the consumption of the working class.

***(iii)* Price lists are then taken for each commodity.** It is better to have an average of wholesale prices of the same commodity from a number of representative markets. These prices are taken for the base year (or years) and also for the subsequent years, the index number for which we want to construct. Retail prices are bette;r because it is the retail prices which consumers actually pay. But retail prices are not taken because they differ widely from locality to locality.

(iv) The next step is to **represent the price of each commodity for the base year as 100 and the price of the same commodity for the subsequent year as a percentage of the price for the base year.** For instance, if the price of wheat in the base year is Rs. 70 per quintal and is called 100, a price of Rs. 154 in the subsequent year should be called 220 and so on in the case of all the commodities taken and all the years.

(v) The final step is to strike the average of the numbers thus obtained with reference to each year. The average for the base year will of course come to 100. The other average will be higher or lower than 100 according as the general price-level has risen or fallen.

The above table illustrates how index numbers are constructed. (Figures are imaginary).

According to this table, there was a rise of 194 per cent in general prices in 1983, as compared with 1970. This means that in 1983, as compared with 1970, the value of money in India (on the basis of the above figures) had fallen by about 66 per cent.

Weighted Index Numbers. The type of index number constructed above is called an unweighted index number. Here every commodity is given the same importance. But actually to a consumer a small rise in the price of a particular commodity may mean a greater disadvantage than a big rise in another commodity which is not so important in his household expenditure. This fact is specially to be taken into account when we are constructing what is called the 'cost of living index number,' *i.e.*, the one for measuring changes in the cost of living of a particular class of people.

Suppose the above articles represent goods consumed by a particular class of people, and we want to know how the war affected their cost of living. All these articles are not of the same importance to these consumers. To show their relative importance, we can assign a **"weight"** to each commodity by multiplying its index number by a certain figure indicating the degree of its importance. Such a figure is usually based on the proportion of money spent on particular commodities in a typical family budget.

The following table illustrates how a weighted index number is constructed. The same figures are taken as in the previous illustration:

Thus, we have given 3 times importance to wheat as compared with sugar, kerosene and milk and four times to cloth.

Commodities	*Base year (1970) Price*	*Base year Index*	*Current year (1983) Price*	*Current year Index*
1. Wheat	Rs. 70 (per quintal)	100	Rs. 154	220
2. Sugar	Rs. 2.40 (per kg.)	100	Rs. 4.80	200
3. Milk	Rs. 1.50 (per litre)	100	Rs. 3.75	250
4. Cloth	Rs. 2.00 (per metre)	100	Rs. 8.00	400
5. Kerosene Oil	50 paise (per litre)	100	Rs. 2.00	400
Average	$\frac{500}{5} = 100$			$\frac{1470}{5} = \mathbf{294}$

Commodities		Base year (1970) Price	Base year Index	Current year (1983) Price	Current year Index
1.	Wheat	Rs. 70 (per quintal)	100 × 4	Rs. 154	220 × 3 = 660
2.	Sugar	Rs. 2.40 (per kg.)	100 × 1	Rs. 4.80	200 × 1 = 200
3.	Milk	Rs. 1.50 (per litre)	100 × 1	Rs. 3.75	250 × 1 = 250
4.	Cloth	Rs. 2.00 (per metre)	100 × 3	Rs. 8.00	400 × 4 = 1600
5.	Kerosene Oil	50 paise (per litre)	100 × 1	Rs. 2.00	400 × 1 = 400
Average			$\frac{1000}{10} = 100$		$\frac{3110}{10} = 311$

The cost of living on this basis has not risen as much as indicated by the unweighted index number, if that was regarded as a cost of living index number. These figures, however, are only by way of illustration. Actually the same index could not be employed to measure changes in the general level of prices and changes in the cost of living. Moreover, the commodities taken to measure changes in the cost of living of different classes will not all be the same. It will depend upon what commodities figure in their scheme of consumption.

We have only chosen a few commodities. Actually a large number of commodities is chosen. For instance, the oldest series of index numbers in India was the one constructed by the Commercial Intelligence Department of the Government of India. It included 28 exported and imported articles. The series was unweighted and took 1873 as the base year. At present the most important index number of wholesale prices is compiled and issued by the office of Economic Adviser to Government of India.

Weighting can be indirectly introduced by taking prices of more than one variety of a commodity, *e.g.*, 3 varieties of wheat, 2 of cloth.

About 20 different cost of living index numbers are now published in India from various important urban centres.

Weighted Index Numbers

(1) Laspeyers Index Number :– In case of Laspeyer, the ratio of current year price and base year price are multiplied by the base year quantity :–

$$Po_1 = \frac{\Sigma p_1 q_0}{\Sigma p_0 q_0} \times 100$$

Po_1 = Prices (or index number) change from base year to current year.

Σ = Summation or aggregate.

P_1 = Current year prices.

P_0 = Base year prices.

q_0 = Base year quantity

(2) Paasche's Index Number :– In Paasche's index number the ratio of current prices to base year prices are multiplied by current year quantity.

$$Po_1 = \frac{\Sigma p_1 q_1}{\Sigma p_0 q_1} \times 100$$

where q_1 = current year quantity

(3) Fisher's Index Number :–

$$Po_1 = \sqrt{\frac{\Sigma p_1 q_0}{\Sigma p_0 q_0} \times \frac{\Sigma p_1 q_1}{\Sigma p_0 q_1}} \times 100$$

or $$Po_1 = \sqrt{\text{Laspeyer} \times \text{Paasche}}$$

or $$Po_1 = \sqrt{\text{L} \times \text{P}}$$

(4) Dorbisch and Bowley's Index Number :– Dorbisch and Bowley's took the average (arithmetic mean) of Laspeyer and Paasche index number.

$$Po_1 = \frac{L + P}{2}$$

$$= \frac{\left\{\left(\frac{\Sigma p_1 q_0}{\Sigma p_0 q_0}\right) + \left(\frac{\Sigma p_1 q_1}{\Sigma p_0 q_1}\right)\right\}}{2} \times 100$$

(5) Marshall and Edgeworth's Index Number :–

$$Po_1 = \frac{\Sigma p_1 \left\{\frac{q_0 + q_1}{2}\right\}}{\Sigma p_0 \left\{\frac{q_0 + q_1}{2}\right\}} \times 100$$

$$= \frac{\Sigma p_1 (q_0 + q_1)}{\Sigma p_0 (q_0 + q_1)} \times 100$$

$$= \frac{\Sigma p_1 q_0 + \Sigma p_1 q_1}{\Sigma p_0 q_0 + \Sigma p_0 q_1} \times 100$$

Example: From the following data calculate Laspeyer, Paasche, Fisher, Dorbisch-Bowley and Marshall-Edgeworth's index-numbers.

Commodity	Base year		Current year	
	Price (p_0)	Quantity (q_0)	Prices p_1	Quantity q_1
A	8	12	10	15
B	5	10	8	12
C	10	25	12	25
D	15	15	20	20

Commodity	Base year		Current year		$p_1 q_0$	$p_0 q_0$	$p_1 q_1$	$p_0 q_1$
	p_0	q_0	p_1	q_1				
A	8	12	10	15	120	96	150	120
B	5	10	8	12	80	50	96	60
C	10	25	12	25	300	250	300	250
D	15	15	20	20	300	225	400	300
					800	621	946	730
					$\Sigma p_1 q_0$	$\Sigma p_0 q_0$	$\Sigma p_1 q_1$	$\Sigma p_0 q_1$

(1) Laspeyer $= \frac{\Sigma p_1 q_0}{\Sigma p_0 q_0} \times 100$

$$= \frac{800}{621} \times 100 = 128.82$$

(2) Paasche $= \frac{\Sigma p_1 q_1}{\Sigma p_0 q_1} \times 100$

$$= \frac{946}{730} \times 100 = 129.58$$

(3) Fisher $= \sqrt{\frac{\Sigma p_1 q_0}{\Sigma p_0 q_0} \times \frac{\Sigma p_1 q_1}{\Sigma p_0 q_1}} \times 100$

$$= \sqrt{\frac{800}{621} \times \frac{946}{730}} \times 100 \quad \text{or}$$

$$= \sqrt{L \times P}$$

$$= \sqrt{1.28 \times 1.29} \times 100 = 128.29$$

(4) Dorbisch and Bowley's $= \frac{L + P}{2}$ or

$$= \frac{\left[\frac{\Sigma p_1 q_0}{\Sigma p_0 q_0} + \frac{\Sigma p_1 q_1}{\Sigma p_0 q_1}\right]}{2} \times 100$$

$$= \frac{\frac{800}{621} + \frac{946}{730}}{2} \times 100$$

$$= \frac{1.28 + 1.29}{2} = \frac{2.575}{2}$$

$$= 1.2879 \times 100 = 128.79$$

(5) Marshall and Edge worth.

$$= \frac{\Sigma p_1 (q_0 + q_1)}{\Sigma p_0 (q_0 + q_1)} \times 100$$

$$= \frac{\Sigma p_1 q_0 + \Sigma p_1 q_1}{\Sigma p_0 q_0 + \Sigma p_0 q_1} \times 100$$

$$= \frac{800 + 946}{621 + 730} \times 100 = \frac{1746}{1351} \times 100$$

$$= 1.2923 \times 100$$
$$= 129.23$$

Uses of Index Number

Measuring Changes in Price Level. The method of index numbers is used for measuring changes in the price-level. This is essential for maintaining price stability. Price stability is conducive to the maintenance of economic activity at the desired level.

Measuring Other Economic Changes. We can measure any quantitative change in addition to changes in the value of money and the cost of living. There may be index numbers of wages, imports, exports, industrial activity, employment, change in areas under cultivation, change in population, *etc*. These measurements indicate social and economic trends and help in framing policies with respect to them.

Adjusting Wages and Prices. An index number of cost of living can guide us in the adjustment of wages to changing prices.

Exchange Stability. Index number of wholesale prices can guide the currency authority not only in stabilizing price-levels but also in stabilizing foreign exchange.

Comparing Economic Conditions. We can compare, with the help of index numbers, economic conditions of a class of people at two different periods.

Comparing Purchasing Power of Two Currencies. Index numbers can also be used to compare the purchasing power of two currencies and to fix the purchasing power parity.

Equitable Discharge of Debts. Index numbers can be used as a basis for an equitable discharge of contracts, *i.e.*, borrowing and lending. When prices rise, the creditor is a loser, for the same amount returned to him has less purchasing power. It should be more just to ensure that the creditor gets back the same purchasing power. If that is so, then the amount of the principal should be increased in proportion to the increase in prices. Similarly, when the prices fall, the debtor should be asked to pay correspondingly less, otherwise the burden of the debt in terms of commodities and services will be increased in proportion to the fall in prices.

Limitations

Index numbers are thus very useful, nay their preparation is essential for modern governments otherwise all the economic policies will be a leap in the dark. But it is necessary to recognise that the index numbers suffer from certain limitations:

(i) Index numbers are just approximations. They cannot be taken as infallible guides. Their data are open to question and they lead to different interpretations.

(ii) International comparisons are difficult, if not impossible, on account of the different bases, different sets of commodities or difference in their quality or quantity.

(iii) Comparisons between different times are also not easy. Over long periods, some popular commodities are replaced by others. Entirely new commodities come to figure in consumption, or the commodity may be vastly different from what it used to be. Think of a modern railway engine and one of the early ones. Ford car 1983 is a different commodity from the 1940 Ford.

(iv) Index numbers only measure changes in the **sectional price-levels.** An index, therefore, prepared for one particular purpose, may not be useful for another. An index number that helps us to study the economic conditions of mill-hands or railway coolies will be useless for a study of the conditions of college professors. An entirely different set of commodities will have to be selected. Different people use different things and hold different assets. Therefore, different classes of people are affected differently by a given change in the price-level. Hence, the same index number cannot throw light on the effects of a price change on all sections of society.

Giving different weight to different types of commodities.

(v) One set of weights may yield quite a different result from another, and weighting is all arbitrary.

As Coulborn observes, "No general price-level is, in fact, compiled in this way because the practical difficulties of collecting the various prices and assessing weights strictly appropriate to the base year, and approximately relevant to the subsequent ones, prove to be difficulties which are insuperable in practice."

THEORIES OF MONEY AND PRICES

Value of Money: Its Meaning

The term 'value of money' has been variously

used. Thus, it may mean (*i*) its command over a definite weight and fineness of gold or silver, as is the case under gold and silver standards respectively, or (*ii*) the units of foreign currency that it will purchase (e.g., £1 = Rs. 15.55 as on January 17,1983. or (*iii*) its command over goods and services with a country, *i.e.*, the internal purchasing power of money. When we use the term "the value of money" without qualification, we mean it in the third sense.

The value of money, then, is the quantity of goods and services in general that will be exchanged for a unit of money. In other words, the value of money is its purchasing power, *i.e.*, **the quantity of goods and services that a unit of money can purchase.**

It should be noted that the value of money, or its purchasing power, has a definite, though inverse, relation with the general level of prices in a country. When general price-level rises, the value of money falls and conversely, when general price-level falls, the value of money rises.

There are three principal approaches to monetary analysis:

1. The Quantity-Velocity Approach or Cash Transaction Approach/Friedman's Restatement.
2. The Cash Balances Approach.
3. The Income-Expenditure Approach.

The first two, *viz.*, quantity-velocity approach and the cash balances approach are grouped together as the quantity theories of money. The income-expenditure theory is generally considered the modern theory. We shall now discuss these theories one by one.

QUANTITY THEORIES OF MONEY

The Quantity-Velocity or Cash Transactions Approach

Till recently, the economists believed that the major cause of fluctuations in the general level of prices was to be found in the changes in the quantity of money. Some economists still hold this view to be correct, though with many qualifications. However, most economists today regard the quantity theory of money as theoretically unsound and practically misleading. Quantity of money includes cash (*M*) and its velocity (*V*). The velocity of circulation depends upon the frequency of transactions, the volume of trade, the nature of business conditions (whether boom or slump), the level of prices (inflation or deflation), facilities for borrowing and lending, *etc.*

Statement of the Theory. Basically, the quantity theory of money states that **other things remaining constant,** changes in general price level are to be explained with reference to changes in the quantity of money in circulation so that an increase in the quantity of money leads to a rise in the price level, while a contraction in the quantity of money will lead to a fall in general price level. In an extreme version of the theory, it is asserted that, other things remaining the same, the value of money falls **proportionately** with a given increase in the quantity of money. Conversely, the value of money rises **proportionately** with a given decrease in the quantity of money. In other words, the changes in the general price level, other things remaining the same, are **directly proportional** to changes in money supply. Double the quantity of money and the price level will be doubled.

Qualifications. In the milder as well as the stronger version of the theory, we use the phrase "other things remaining the same." Now what is meant by this phrase. It means that there should be no change in the following factors while the quantity of money changes:—

1. Velocity of circulation of money. Velocity or rapidity of circulation of money means the number of times a money unit changes hands. If, for instance, during a given period, a five-rupee note changes hands five times, then the quantity of money in this case will be Rs. 25 and not Rs. 5.

2. The use of **credit instruments** as money. If there is an increase (or decrease) in the use of credit instruments, such as cheques, book credit, *etc.*, it should be regarded as an increase (or decrease) in the quantity of money in circulation. Similar is the case as regards the velocity of circulation of credit instruments.

3. Barter transactions. If some exchanges are done without the use of money, they should either be excluded altogether or be regarded as an increase in the quantity of money (supply) or decrease in the quantity of transactions (or demand for money).

4. Finally, the **volume of transactions** must remain constant. This means that the work to be done by money, or the transactions to be performed, must remain the same. Not only the amount of goods exchanged, but also the number of times goods change hands (rapidity of circulation of goods) must remain constant.

In a word, other things being equal, the value of money varies inversely with its quantity and directly with the volume of goods and services in existence.

Equation of Exchange. Professor Irving Fisher has expressed the relationship between he quantity of money and its value in the form of a formula, which he calls the equation of exchange. This is :—

$$P = \frac{MV + M'V'}{T}$$

Here P = Price level, or P = the value of money; T = Transactions to be performed by money; M = Metallic money; M' = credit money; V = Velocity of metallic money; and V' = velocity of credit money.

This formula equates the supply of money to the demand for it. Price-level multiplied by the transactions gives the total value of transactions which means demand for money (PT). This is equal to the supply of money which consists of cash and credit instruments with their velocities of circulation ($MV + M'V'$).

Thus $\quad PT = MV + M'V'$

$$P = \frac{MV + M'V'}{T}$$

Professor Fisher contends that, in the short period, T. V, V' remain constant. The proportion of M' to M also remains constant. Therefore, P varies directly with M. In other words, I/P (value of money) varies inversely with M or quantity of money in circulation.

Why do "other things" (T, V, V' and proportion of M' to M) remain constant? Professor Fisher holds that:

Transactions or amount of work to be done by money remains constant in the short period, because in the short period, population does not change, production per head of population does not change, percentage of consumption by producers does not change, percentage of exchange by barter does not change and the rapidity of circulation of goods does not change, Methods of production and habits of the people in this connection are practically fixed. Thus, the demand for money remains constant.

As regards the supply side, rapidity of circulating of money and credit depends upon custom and business habits of the people. The proportion of M' to M depends upon the policy of the banks. These things also do not change appreciably in the short period. Hence, we can say that the value of money varies inversely with its quantity.

Critical Evaluation of the Quantity Theory

The Quantity Theory has been widely criticised. It is a static theory, whereas the real world is dynamic where changes are constantly taking place. With the qualification "other things remaining the same" it is a useless truism. It is an over-simplified version. The real trouble is that 'other things' seldom remain the same. They change not only in the long period but also in a comparatively short period. Population, amount of business transacted per head of the population, velocity of circulation, policy as regards the proportion of credit to cash all are subject to change and changes in them are constantly taking place.

Thus, many factors, other than the quantity of money, may bring about a change in the price level, and hence the value of money, *e.g.*, change in the volume of trade, improvement in transport facilities, gold movements, extension of banking and credit facilities, *etc.*. All such factors can bring about changes in the price level, Hence, exclusive emphasis on the quantity of money is not proper.

Process Not Spelt Out. The quantity theory is said to be only a short-hand expression and does not fully explain the whole process by which a change in the quantity of money brings about a change in the price level or the value of money.

Money Not Merely a Medium of Exchange. Fisher's theory regards money as merely a medium of exchange which must be exchanged for goods. But money may be wanted for its own sake to be held as idle cash balances. It is also a store of value and may be wanted for speculative purposes.

Not Independent Variables. Moreover, these factors are not independent variables as Fisher assumes. For instance, a change in M in itself may cause a change in V, and thus cause a change in P more than in proportion to a change in M. After the First Great War, the German mark was depreciating fast and no one was willing to hold it. The rapidity of circulation money (V) increased progressively and out of all proportion to the increase in the note-issue (M). Similarly, a change in M may cause, and does cause, frequently a change in T, and a change in P may lead to a change in M. An increase in the supply of money may raise prices, increase profits and stimulate production beyond the profitable level thus again depressing prices. Moreover, higher price-level may necessitate the issue of more money to carry on transactions. Thus, high price-level

Money and its velocity of circulation.

may be the cause rather than the effect of the increase in the quantity of money.

M and V Differ. *M* refers to a point of time and *V* to a period of time, and it is wrong to multiply two different things, *e.g.*, *MV*.

Wrong Assumptions. Basically, for the quantity theory to be true, the following two assumptions must hold:—

(i) An increase in money supply leads to an increase in spending, *i.e.*, no part of additional money created should be kept in idle hoards.

(ii) The resulting increase in spending must face a totally inelastic supply of output.

Both the assumptions lack generality and, therefore, if either of them does not hold, the quantity theory cannot be accepted as a valid explanation of the changes in price level. Let us take the first assumption. Under this assumption, the entire increase in the quantity of money must express itself in the form of increased spending. If spending does not increase, there is no question of a change in prices or output. But is it valid to make such an assumption? Obviously, there is no such direct link between the increase in the quantity of money and the increase in the volume of total spending. No one is going to increase his expenditure simply because the government is printing more notes or the banks are more liberal in their lending policies.

This is not to say, however, that changes in the quantity of money have no influence whatsoever on the volume of aggregate spending. As we shall show below, changes in the quantity of money are sometimes capable of inducing changes in the volume of aggregate spending. What we are denying is the assertion that there exists a direct, simple, and more or less a proportional relation between variation in money supply and variations in the level of total spending.

Coming to the second assumption, this will be valid only under conditions of full employment. It is only then that we can assume a totally inelastic supply of output, for all the available resources are being already fully utilised. In conditions of less than full employment, the supply curve of output will be elastic. Now, if we assume that aggregate spending increases with an increase in the quantity of money, it does not follow that prices must necessarily rise. If the supply curve of output is fairly elastic, it is more likely that the effect of an increase in spending will be more to raise production rather than raise prices. Of course, at full employment, every further increase in spending must lead to an increase in prices as output is inelastic in supply. Since full employment cannot be assumed to be a normal feature, we cannot accept the quantity theory of money as a valid, general explanation of changes in the price level in the short run.

Not useful. Apart from challenging the basic assumptions underlying the theory, it is criticised on the score of its utility. It is not regarded as particularly helpful either as an analytical tool or as a guide to policy. It is pointed out that neither the volume of transactions nor the velocity of money is stable.

Merits of the Theory. Although the quantity theory of money is widely criticised by modern economists and is rejected as an adequate explanation of the value of money, it has some merits too:

(i) It is historically true for whenever there has been over-issue of currency, prices have invariably risen. The currency history of every country has demonstrated it.

(ii) The practical utility of the theory is evident from the fact that whenever the monetary authorities seek to control prices they do so by regulating and controlling the issue of currency. The manipulation of the bank rate and open market operations of the central bank are based on this assumption.

(iii) Although every change in the quantity of money may not produce a proportionate change in the price level, yet the theory seems to be broadly true.

Cash Balances Approach; Cambridge Equation

As already mentioned, there are two main lines of approach to the problem of relationship between the quantity of money and its value (or the price-level). This has given rise to two types of quantity theories. One is the Quantity Theory of Money proper, called the Transactions Approach theory which we have discussed above and which is represented by Fisher's Equation. This approach has been more popular in the U.S.A. The other approach, known as the cash-balances type, which has been more popular in Europe, especially in England, is represented by the Cambridge Equation.

The latter is an improvement on the former Quantity Equation in the sense that it is based on the National Income approach and takes into account the concept of liquidity, both of which form part of Keynesian Economics.

As mentioned above, the Cambridge Equation represents what has been called the cash-balances approach to the value of money.[1] It simply says that the value of money depends on demand for cash-balances and the supply thereof **at any given time.** We have discussed in the preceding sections the

1. Robertson, D.H.—*Money*, 1932, Ch. II and Appendix A.

determinants of both demand and supply of money. Here we want to draw the attention of the student to one point on the demand side. The demand for money does not merely depend on the physical quantity of resources or of the goods and services which are sought to be exchanged, but it largely depends on the **period of time** which the transactions are intended to cover. Take the case of a consumer of wheat. Is it necessary for him to purchase his whole year's requirement of wheat at once or, what comes to the same thing, keep sufficient liquid cash to buy the whole year's requirement? No, it is unnecessary. Few consumers will do that unless they happen to be foolish. A consumer may decide to buy wheat from month to month. It will then be necessary for him to keep cash equal to 1/12 of his total requirement of wheat for the year. Similarly, he will keep liquid funds just enough to enable him to purchase his requirements of other goods and services for a certain **period only** and not for the **whole year**.

If the members of a community are in the habit of keeping cash to cover their purchases over a long period, obviously their demand for cash will be greater. Only a fraction of the whole income is kept in cash, the rest is invested. The amount of cash held should not be too much, because to keep cash locked up idly means a loss, besides being a danger, although a large cash balance makes business smooth and easy. Nor should the amount of cash held be too small, because it may be risky from the business point of view. As

Cash Balance.

Marshall observes, "A man fixes the appropriate fraction (of his income) after balancing one against another the advantages of a further ready command and the disadvantages of putting more of his resources into a form in which they yield him no direct income or other benefit."[2] An individual has thus to keep only a fraction of his income in titles to legal tender (*i.e.*, liquid cash) to carry on his business smoothly and to guard against emergencies. Let this fraction be denoted by k.

The equation is usually put in the form:

$M = kpR$

where M is the quantity of money and is the same as M of Fisher's Equation of Exchange. R is the real national income, *i.e.*, it is the sum total of goods and services **finally** brought to the market and sold for money, *e.g.*, cotton is not part of R but a suit of clothes made by a tailor is a part of R . Similarly, wheat is not included in R, but bread is.

p is the average price-level of the real national income. That is, it is the average of price of clothes, food, shelter and other goods, and services consumed by the public.

Thus, pR is the monetary national income,

Now, a proportion of the monetary national income is held by the community in cash. This proportion is k and represents the desire of the public to have liquid resources, This is called the liquidity factor for buying it. If all money circulated only once, then the amount of money required would be the same as the monetary national income. If money circulated twice in a year, then obviously half pR will be required to purchase the national product, *i.e.*, to create the monetary national income which is shown as pR above. The number of times money circulates for buying the national production in a year is V_1 , *i.e.*, income-velocity of circulation of money, k is the proportion of the monetary national income which the community desires to hold in cash. pR then is the demand for money for purchasing the national product, This must be equal to the money supply.

$M \times$ velocity of circulation of money = $M \times V$.

$$M = kp\,R \text{ where } k = \frac{I}{V_1}$$

We have seen that in the Fisher's Equation of Exchange in its simplest form

$$M = \frac{PT}{VT} = \frac{I}{V_1} \times PT$$

By Cambridge Equation

$$M = kpR$$

Now as $$k = \frac{I}{V_1}$$

$$\therefore \quad M = \frac{I}{V_1}\,PR$$

Differences between Fisher Equation and Cambridge Equation. The differences between the

2. Marshall, A.—*Money, Credit and Commerce*, 1, iv. 3.

two equations are as follows:

(*i*) T in the Fisher Equation is the sum total of all transactions, whereas R is only the final product which comes to the market. For example, Fisher will include in T the transactions of production and sale of cotton, sale of yarn, sale of cloth and finally brought to the market, *e.g.*, tailored clothes.

(*ii*) Similarly, *P* in the Fisher equation is the average of the price-level of each good and service at each stage of production and includes the average price-level of all transactions. *p* in the Cambridge Equation is the price-level of only the goods finally brought to the market. They may tend to move up and down in the same direction, but are not the same.

(*iii*) The meaning of *V* and V_1, *i.e.*, velocity of circulation, also differs between them. In the Fisher Equation, it takes the form *VT*, *i.e.*, Transactions Velocity of Circulation. It represents the number of times a unit of money circulates for performing all the transactions taking place in the economy in a year. V_1, on the other hand, is only Income Velocity of circulation and represents the number of times a unit of money circulates for buying the final product.

Superiority of Cambridge Equation. The Cambridge equation, which in fact was a later form of the Quantity Theory, sought to remove some of the shortcomings of the latter and took several steps on the way to the modern theory of money and prices. The old theory did not provide any explanation of the velocity or circulation of money. Instead of explaining the frequency with which money changed hands, the Cambridge equation tried to explain why money rested (instead of moving) in people's hands. This was an important shift in the emphasis. An attempt was now made to analyse the motives on account of which people wished to hold money.

Cambridge version ignores speculative demand for money.

Similarly, there was a switch away from the analysis of causes of changes in the supply of money to an analysis of the causes of changes in the demand for it.

Another important new element in the Cambridge version was that instead of being concerned with the total number of transactions, it was concerned only with the transactions relating to final goods only, *i.e.*, the level of income. It thus concentrated attention on a concept which occupies an important place in the whole of modern economic theory.

The Cambridge equation went some way towards explaining both short and long-run changes in the level of income. But the theory did not satisfactorily separate price changes and changes in the level of output both of which are included in the changes in the level of money income.

Criticism. However, the Cambridge version is an over-simplified explanation of the theory of money and prices. It ignores the speculative demand to hold money. Thus, it loses sight of an important fact that the quantity of money may change without corresponding changes in the level of money income or that money income may change without corresponding changes in the quantity of money.

Also, ignoring the speculative demand meant that the theories of interest were not linked with the theories of level of income through demand for money. This is an important omission.

Thus, the Cambridge version is an inadequate guide to the understanding of the mechanics of price changes. Its misleading simplicity obscures more than it reveals.

In the words of A.C.L. Day, "Although the Cambridge version of the Quantity Theory represented a big advance on the Fisher version, it is not in itself an adequate monetary theory. Its weakness is that it is too simple to deal adequately with the complexities of the economic system."[3] Its weakness lies in this that it does not pay attention to the fact that effective demand for goods and services does not necessarily vary at all closely with the quantity of money. In order to understand variations in effective demand, we must analyse the causes of changes in expenditure.

3. Day, A.C.L.—*Outline of Monetary Economics*, 1960, p. 257.

The second weakness is that it pays inadequate attention to the fact that the price level does not necessarily change in proportion to the changes in effective demand.

Thus, we can say that the Cambridge Equation lays stress on the national income, its price-level and the liquidity of the public. Keynes uses the concept of national income in the modern Keynesian analysis and it is with the fluctuations of the price-level of final goods and output with which the modern trade cycle economists and governments are concerned. The concept of liquidity, slightly modified, is used by Keynes for his theory of rate of interest and investment, as a determinant of total production.

But, for Keynes, there are other factors more important on which total national income depends. These are the profitability of investment and thriftiness. The Cambridge Equation does not take note of these and is, therefore, not used for analysis these days.

Friedman's Restatement of the Quantity Theory of Money

Milton Friedman, a leading luminary of what has come to be known as the **Chicago School** of economists has put forward his own quantity theory of money. In his restatement of the theory, he restored the quantity theory of money almost to its original position. That is, he resuscitated and rehabilitated the Fisher formula of the quantity theory of money, but in a more sophisticated manner. In view of the importance of his restatement of the theory and the influence his theory exercised on economic thinking and policies it deserves a fuller treatment which has been attempted in a subsequent section.

FRIEDMAN'S RESTATEMENT OF THE QUANTITY THEORY OF MONEY

Special Features

Milton Friedman's restatement of the quantity theory of money has already become a modern classic. He says that his quantity theory of money is essentially a theory of *demand for money*. Hence his analysis in this connection is primarily concerned with exploring and explaining the nature of the demand function for money! Its objective is to discover the relatively more significant variables which determine the demand for money and to find out whether this function is stable or not. The traditional quantity theory of money was based on the assumption of a constant velocity of money.

Friedman draws a distinction between velocity and velocity function. He says that while velocity of money may and does fluctuate, the velocity functions is stable. Thus the modern quantity theorists like Friedman draw a distinction between *demand* for money and the *demand function* for money or between velocity of money and velocity-of-money function. The velocity-of-money function is highly stable, much more stable than the Keynesian consumption function. Friedman therefore prefers economic analysis in terms of changes in the money supply and a money multiplier derived from velocity relationship rather than use autonomous expenditures and the multiplier which emerges from the consumption function as emphasised in the Keynesian theory.

The modern quantity of money theorists regard the money demand function not only stable but also of vital importance in determining the variables which are very important for the economy as a whole *e.g.* the level of national income, employment and price level.

Friedman is of the opinion that the demand function and the money supply function are independent of each other. That is, there are some important variables which determine the supply of money but which do not affect the demand for money. The notion of stable demand function is useful in order to trace out the effect of changes in supply, but it is useful only if supply is influenced by at least some factors other than those regarded as affecting demand. Thus the modern quantity theorists would reject the notion that the supply of money expands or contracts according to the needs of trade.

Wealth is an important factor in Friedman's Quantiz theory..

We can also say that the modern quantity theorists reject the concept of the Keynesian liquidity trap or infinite elasticity of demand for money. Friedman makes out a strong case for the quantity theory if the elasticity of demand for money is approximately zero.

Without going into how Friedman derives or expound his version of the Quantity Theory, it may suffice to give his restatement of the Quantity Theory of Money; this is set out below:

$$Y = M, V\left(e_b, r_e, \frac{1}{P}, \frac{dp}{dt}, W \frac{p}{y}, u\right)$$

Friedman's above equation is equivalent to the Equation of Exchange of the traditional Quantity Theory, *i.e.* $M = PY$, however, with the difference that Y is the real income in the traditional equation instead of the money income that Y represents in Friedman's equation given above.

It is very necessary to bear in mind that the traditional quantity theory is only superficially equivalent to Friedman's restatement of it. The fundamental difference betweent the two approaches is that Friedman has substituted the velocity function, $V\left(r_b\, r_e \frac{1}{P}, \frac{dp}{dt}, W, \frac{y}{p} V\right)$· in place of the velocity constant V, or its reciprocal, k, in the traditional statement of the Quantity Theory. This is by no means a mere formal difference; it is instead a very significant *difference of substance.*

Criticism

Friedman's Restatement of the Quantity Theory of Money gives a highly formalised model of the determination of the demand for money. But one can pick a number of holes or gaps and inadequacies which are mentioned below:

(*i*) Friedman's derivation of money demand takes explicit note of the *asset* demand for money only, but the transactions demand for money has not been adequately analysed. This means that he has practically ignored the function of money as a means of payment. It provides no analysis of the cost of transactions and how these costs could be relevant in the determination of the demand for money and for alternative forms of assets.

Also, as Miles Fleming puts it, "The nature of the services provided by money balances is not enquired into closely" and this makes Friedman's analysis rather too abstract.

(*ii*) In Friedman's analysis it is implied that the different forms of assets mentioned by him are close substitutes of one another. How this substitutability will influence the demand for money and alternative assets is not clearly spelt out.

(*iii*) Friedman's model has been given in a static term. It takes no notice of the time lags involved and implications for the demand of money. The nature of the time lags will determine the values of the variables from period to period. Time lags in the adjustment of the values and structure of assets in the wealth-holders portfolios to the desired levels and structure are also important in the determination of demand for money. But Friedman's model does not take note of these factors.

(*iv*) Empirical investigations have not borne out Friedman's assertion that his money demand function and the monetary multiplier based on it are much more stable than the Keynesian consumption function and the Keynesian multiplier based thereon.

(*v*) An important implication of Friedman's model is that there is a very regular relationship between the supply of money, the money income and prices. This proposition is however challenged by certain studies.

(*vi*) Friedman's definition of money is too broad. It includes even time deposits which cannot be regarded as ready money.

Conclusion

In sum, the Friedmanites think that the economy is like a 'black box' and it is difficult to know or show precisely what processes are taking place in this 'black box', which connects changes in *M* to changes in *GNP*. They would like to hold that whatever the processes are, the interest elasticity of demand for money is very low or zero. A study covering the period 1897-1958 showed that the quantity of money was a better predicator of consumption than was investment. In other words, it was found that the quantity of money furnished a better explanation of the *GNP* than the multiplier did except during the Great Depression of the 30's (thirties).

Thus, we come to the conclusion that the quantity theorists of today seem to have established a broad relationship between the *GNP*, consumption and money supply. It may be that this relationship does not hold uniformly satisfactorily throughout the various periods of economic history. They hold that money supply is the principal factor leading to fluctuations in income, though causal influences work slowly and variably. One implication of the contemporary quantity theory of money is that the monetary authorities should not use monetary policy for the "fine-tuning' of the economy when one is trying to deal with short-term fluctuations in economic activity"[4].

4. Stonier, A.W., and Hague, D.C., *A Textbook of Economic Theory,* 4th Edition, p. 567.

KEYNESIAN THEORY OF MONEY AND PRICES: THE INCOME APPROACH

The modern theorists, especially the Keynesians, do not deny that changes in money supply can bring about changes in the price-level. However, what they do deny is that there is a simple, direct and easily predictable relation between the quantity of money and the level of prices.

The modern theory emphasises that **the value of money or the price level is in fact a consequence of the total incomes rather than of the quantity of money.** The real cause of fluctuations in prices is to be found in fluctuations in the level of aggregate income or expenditure. Therefore, changes in the quantity of money can bring about changes in the level of prices only if they change aggregate spending in relation to the supply of output. Unless spending increases, there can be no increase in demand for goods. And if demand for goods does not increase, the question of price rise does not arise. However, even if aggregate spending does increase, prices may still not rise if the supply curve of output is fairly elastic. Therefore, the effects of a change in quantity of money on the price-level depends on the following factors :—

Increase in Quanlity of Money ⇒ Increase in Aggregate spending/ output ⇒ Increase in Prices

(*i*) effect of changes in money supply on the level of aggregate demand or spending;

(*ii*) relation between aggregate spending and the volume of production.

As regards the volume of spending, it depends on the following:—

(*i*) The consumption function.

(*ii*) The investment demand schedule.

(*iii*) Liquidity preference schedule.

(*iv*) Supply of money.

An increase in the quantity of money in the Keynesian system will lower the rate of interest. But if the rate of interest is already very low, further increases in the quantity of money will not be able to reduce it still further. And we know that a fall in the rate of interest encourages new investment. Thus, if the rate of interest is reduced as a result of an increase in money supply, the rate of investment will rise and the increase in investment will lead to increase in income via the multiplier. If this happens, there will be an increase in aggregate spending. But if the rate of interest cannot be reduced any further by increases in the quantity of money, *i.e.* we are operating along the perfectly elastic part of the liquidity preference curve, the rate of investment will not increase; and if investment does not increase, income and spending cannot increase.

Thus, there are circumstances when an increase in the quantity of money may fail to increase the level of aggregate spending. If this is the case, prices will not rise at all, even though the quantity of money has increased.

Even if aggregate spending does increase because of an increase in the rate of investment, it is not necessary that prices must rise at all, much less proportionately to the increase in money supply. If we have less than full employment and there are idle capital and labour resources, the supply curve of output will be fairly elastic, and increases in aggregate spending will lead to an increase in production without much increase in prices. On the other hand, if there is full employment, an increase in aggregate spending will largely result in an increase in the level of prices rather than output.

To sum up. In the modern theory, money has an important place. But the relationship between changes in money supply and changes in prices is much more indirect and uncertain than was assumed by the quantity theory of money. It all depends on its effects on aggregate spending and the elasticity of supply of output.

Determination of the General Price Level; Keynesian View

We are now in a position to give the modern view regarding the determination of general price level. In the classical and neo-classical monetary theory, the general price level was supposed to vary directly with changes in the quantity of money, so that an increase in the quantity of money, was supposed to be the cause of a rise in the price level. That view, it is now generally agreed, is a gross over-simplification of what happens in real life.

In modern theory, the general price-level is thought to be determined by the same forces which determine the level of national income and employment, *i.e.*, aggregate effective demand and aggregate supply. As we have discussed elsewhere, aggregate effective demand in a given period is the sum of the demand of the consumers for current goods and services, the demand of the government for current goods and services and net capital formation in the economy as determined by the decision of entrepreneurs. Similarly, aggregate supply of output of all sorts of goods is determined by the profit expectation of entrepreneurs.

It is quite likely that the total of effective demand (at constant prices) in a given period may not equal the aggregate supply of output (at constant prices) forthcoming. The result will be that in the process of adjustment, the real value of a given monetary effective demand will have to be cut down to be just equal to available supply of output. The mechanism of this adjustment is provided by the change in prices. If aggregate demand tends to be greater than aggregate supply, the general price level will move up, and vice versa.

Policy Significance

In conclusions, let us clearly understand the policy significance of the theories of money and prices. The quantity theory of money suggests that if prices are too high, the monetary authority should contract credit and reduce the money supply. On the other hand, when there is depression, money should be pumped into the economic system so that economic activity or investment is stimulated through the lowering of the rate of interest. The income theory, on the other hand, seeks to control prices through changes in the level of national income and expenditure. It follows that during depression, government must increase its expenditure which will raise the level of incomes and effective demand. Similarly, a business boom can be checked by reducing effective demand through taxation and reduction of government expenditure.

Post-Keynesian Developments in Theory of Money and Prices

The economists coming after Keynes have tried to fill up the gaps in the Keynesian theory and refined it. The post-Keynesian monetary economists have tried to discover and emphasise additional variables which have influence on the demand for money. As a refinement of the monetary theory, these economists have given a more elaborate and rigorous application of the capital theory to the analysis of demand for money.

In the application of capital theory to money, they have denied the Keynesian proposition that the demand for speculative money is interest elastic and the transaction-cum-precautionary demand for money is interest inelastic. For instance, Baumol's "*Transactions Demand for Cash*' : *An Inventory Theoretic Approach*" and Tobin's "*Interest Elasticity of Transactions Demand for Cash*" have put forward the view that transactions demand for money is influenced not only by the level of income but also by the rate of interest. Tobin is of the view that there is an inverse relationship betweent the rate of interest and the transactions demand for money. This adjustment is based on inventory-capital theory. In a well developed modern economy, with a well, organised bond market, the transactions demand for money is determined both by the level of income and the rate of interest. The number of transactions will increase if income and the rate of interest rise. The larger is the number of these transactions, the greater is the proportion of income and the rate of interest rise. The larger is the number of these transactions, the greater is the proportion of income held in the form of bonds and smaller the proportion of income kept in the form of cash balances. Thus the transactions demand for money is not a constant proportion of income held in bonds but varies with the rate of interest and is inversely related to it. Hence it is meaningless to distinguish between transactions-cum-precautionary demand for money and put the money demand function in the Keynesian form $M = M_1 + M_2 = L_1(Y) + L_2(r)$; It should be written as $M = L(y.r)$.

Portfolio balance approach.

Tobins Portfolio Balance Approach

An important post-Kevnesian development is what is known as Tobin's **Portfolio Balance Approach** to the analysis of the asset demand for money. In his paper *Liquidity Preference as "Behaviour Toward Risk"* Tobin has liberated the concept of the speculative or asset demand for money from reliance on expectations regarcing future changes in the rate of interest. He has done away with unrealistic Keynesian assumption that the only alternative to holding assets in the form of cash balances is to hold single-maturity bonds. These economists hold that money as well as various forms of non-money assets can be liquid as distinguished from the Keynesian view that money is the only liquid asset, although money is perfectly liquid whereas non-money assets possess less perfect liquidity. The various assets can be arranged in a descending order of liquidity thus-money, time deposits, bills, bonds, equities and goods. The normal individuals or the risk averters tend to arrange their portfolio in such a way as to balance, at the margin, the utility of additional return against the disutility of additional uncertainty. An important implication of Tobin's theory is that the demand for money, as an asset is determined by the total size of wealth and not merely by change for the rate of interest.

Patinkin's View. Anothere post-Keynesian development has been brought out in **Patinkin's** "*Money, Interest and Prices*". Patinkin suggest that *wealth Effect* is like the *Income Effect.* Thus an increase in the wealth of an asset holder induces him to distribute the increment over all the form of assets except in the exceptional case, when a particular assets is looked upon as 'inferior'. Hence demand for money will increase if wealth increases.

Conclusion. Thus the post-Keynesian version of the demand function for money may be mentioned as

$$M = \frac{M}{P} = L\,(y, r, w)$$

Where m denotes demand for money, M for quantity of money, P for price level, L for functional relationship, Y for real national income r for rate of interest and w for wealth.

Neutrality and Non-Neutrality of Money

The issue of neutrality or non-neutrality of money has an important bearing on the question of effectiveness or otherwise of monetary policy. The supporters of neutrality of money say that a change in the quantity of money may generate economic fluctuations. It is held that creation of money may generate prosperity. The classical economists regarded money as netural and a veil. It is regarded as simply a medium of exchange and not affecting output and employment in any manner. But to Keynes, it was no longer a veil. Money affects rate of interest and through it rate of investment and hence general economic activity in the country.

Money is regarded as neutral if a change in the quantity of money does not alter the real equilibrium of the economic system. That is, the relative prices, and interest rates are not affected by a change in the quantity of money.

Conditions for Neutrality

Money will be neutral under the following conditions:

1. Existence of only one kind of money *i.e.*, either inside money (created against private debt and constituted by claims against financial institutions) or outside money (backed by foreign and government securities).
2. Absence of money illusion (see p. 385)
3. Absence of distribution effects.
4. Price-Wage flexibility
5. Absence of open market operations.
6. Unitary Elasticity of Expectations.

Key terms

Index number Quantity theory, Velocity of Circulation, Cash-balance approach, Friedman's Quantity theory, Portfolio balance, Neutrality of money.

QUESTIONS

1. Explain the effects of the following facotrs on the value of money:— (*a*) Increase in the volume of bank credit; (*b*) Decrease in the liquidity preference; (*c*) Excess of investment over savings.
2. Critically examine the quantity thoery of money. Does the quantity theory offer an adequate explanation of rise and fall of prices?
3. "The value of money, other things being the same, varies inversely with its quantity." Discuss.
4. Outline the processes by which a change in money supply would affect the general price level.
5. "The modern tendency in economic thiking is to discard the old notion of the quantity of money as the sole determinant of rhe value of money". Elucidate.

6. "The Quantity Theory of Money comes into its own during periods of full employment". Discuss this statement.
7. Do you agree with the view that Say's Law and the Quantity Theory of Money are consistent and complementary? Give reasons for your answer.
8. Give a critical appraisal of the Quantity Theory of Money. To what extent does Keynes' Income-Expenditure approach constitute an improvement on the Quantity Theory?
9. Explain the "Cash' Balance" approach to the value of money. How far is this an improvement over the "Transactions" approach?
10. Compare and contrast the cash-balance and cash-transactions approaches to the value of money. How far is it correct to say that the value of money is a consequence of the total incomes rather than of the quantity of money?

    Or

    Compare the relative merits of Fisherian and Cambirdge approach to the explanation of changes in the value of money.
11. "Changes in money incomes rather than changes in the quantity of money account for movements of the general price level." Discuss.
12. Discuss the view that price change are better explained by Saving-Investment Theory than by the traditional Quantity Theory.
13. "The value of money, like value of anything else, is mainly a question of demand and supply". Elucidate.
14. "The demand for money fluctuates mainly due to the speculative motive". Discuss.
15. "The demand for money is the demand for money to hold". Discuss.
16. "Men speculate prices fluctuate; prices do not fluctuate because men speculate". Comment.
17. What do you understand by an 'Index Number'? Construct a table of a simple index number. What principles should be borne in mind in constructing such a number? What are the difficulties involved?
18. Distinguish clearly between Simple and Weighted Index Number. Prepare a Simple Index Number of the cost of living of a labourer for 1977 taking 1960 as the base.
19. What are Index Numbers? Discuss the utility of index numbers in formulating public policies.
20. Explain the phrase 'value of money'. How would you measure changes in the value of money?
21. Explain Quantity theory of money given by M. Friedman.

INFLATION

Definition of Inflation

By inflation, in ordinary language, we mean a process of rising prices. A situation is described as inflationary when either the prices or the supply of money are rising, because in practice both will rise together. In the Keynesian sense, true inflation begins when the elasticity of supply of output in response to increase in money supply has fallen to zero or when output is unresponsive to changes in money supply. When there exists a state of full employment, the conditions will be clearly inflationary, if there is increase in the supply of money. But since we do not subscribe to the classical view that there is full employment, we can say that when money supply increase it results partly in the increase of output (GNP) and it partly feeds the rise in prices. And when the supply of output lags far behind, the rise in prices is described as inflationary. In Coulborn's words, it is a case of "too much money chasing too few goods." Thus, inflation is generally associated with an abnormal increase in the quantity of money resulting in abnormal rise in prices.

Rising Prices.

Inflationary Gap. Keynes invented the term 'inflationary gap' to describe a situation when there is "excess of anticipated expenditures over the available output at base prices." In simple words, it is a gap between money incomes of the community and the available supply of output of goods and services. This has already been explained and illustrated earlier in chapter 40.

However, when discussing inflation, we are thinking of a persistent rise in prices rather than a once-for-all rise in prices (which may, for example, be brought about by a bad weather leading to destruction of crops). A rise in prices is one of the indicators of inflation rather than being its cause.

There are three main features of inflation: (*a*) It is a process of rising prices; (*b*) it is initiated by some change which makes it impossible to satisfy the whole of the demand which is forthcoming at existing prices, so that initial price rises occur; and (*c*) it is propagated by the reactions of buyers or group of buyers to the initial price rise so that further rise in prices is induced.

Then, there is a type of inflation which is called **suppressed inflation.** Sometimes deliberate policies are pursued to prevent price rises in the present, but it is only a temporary muzzling of the inflationary forces. These forces are in the meantime accumulating and are bound to burst in future. Ultimately, the inflationary pressures exert themselves in full strength. This is the case with war-time price controls. When the controls are abolished the pent-up demand leads to inflationary spiral.

The various causes of inflation and methods of combating inflation are discussed in the later sections of this chapter.

Deflation is the opposite of inflation. It usually means an excessive fall in prices and money incomes of factors of production.

Reflation refers to a moderate degree of controlled inflation.

Disinflation refers to a process of a bringing down prices moderately from their high level.

"Stagflation" is used when there is stagnation as well as inflation, both side by side as prevailed in India in 1974 -75 and again in 1979-80.

Inflationary Process

Basically, inflation represents a situation whereby the pressure of aggregate demand for goods and services exceeds the available supply of output (both being counted at the prices ruling at the beginning of a period). In such a situation, the rise in price level is a natural consequence. Now, this disparity between aggregate demand and aggregate supply may be the result of more than one force at work. As we know, aggregate demand is the sum total of consumers' spending on current goods and services, government spending on current goods and services and net investment being contemplated by the entrepreneurs.

The ordinary functioning of an economy should result in distributing and using income in such a manner that aggregate demand for output is equivalent to the cost of producing the total output including profits and taxes. At times, however, the government, the entrepreneurs or the households may attempt to secure a larger part of output than would thus accrue to them. If other sectors are not prepared to acquiesce in this increase in the share of output used by any one sector, all the sectors together will be trying to get more of the national output than production has provided. **This is the basic framework for the inflationary process, when aggregate demand for all purposes– consumption, investment and government expenditure–exceeds the supply of goods at current prices.**

To illustrate the above point, let us assume that the government wants to use more of national output than the ordinary functioning of the system provides through taxes and loans from the public. If the government is insistent on securing additional resources, it will get them in one way or another –by issuing currency or by borrowing from the central bank or from commercial banks. If other sectors, particularly the active sectors–entrepreneurs and wage earners, are unwilling to reduce their investment or consumption by the amount of these additional resources used by the government, an inflationary process will be initiated. Similarly, an inflationary process will be initiated if entrepreneurs wish to use more of national output than the ordinary functioning of the economy provides (through savings out of profits and savings lent or invested by the public) and other sectors do not willingly reduce their demands for resources to the extent that entrepreneurs want to use them more.

Wage--price Spiral. If the total claims on output exceed the available supply of output, prices will rise. The rise in prices provides the necessary mechanism whereby the real resources being used by the inactive sectors are reduced for being used by the more active sectors. If, for example, the initiative for the inflationary pressure comes from the government demand for more resources, the only way that the government can have more resources is by the consumers and private entrepreneurs having less of them (assuming that all the resources were fully employed already). If they are not willing to reduce their claims on resources voluntarily, the prices will rise and the result will be that real value of spending

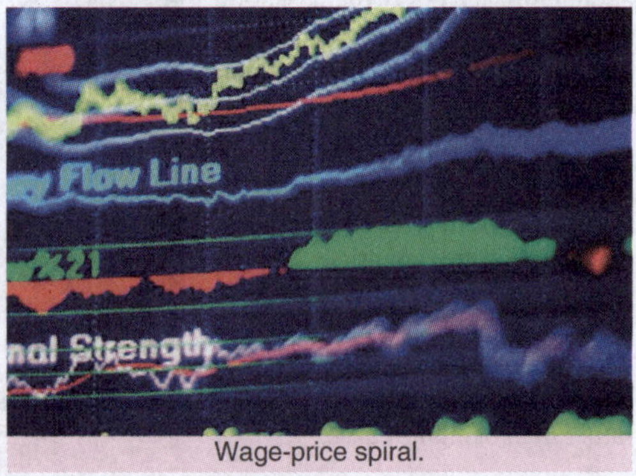

Wage-price spiral.

by these sectors will be reduced and to that extent resources will be made available for use by the government.

But that will not be the end of the story. A rise in prices reduces the real consumption of the wage earners. They will, therefore, press for higher money wages to compensate them for the higher cost of living. Now, an increase in wages, if granted, will raise the prime cost of production and, therefore, entrepreneurs will be tempted to raise the prices. This adds fuel to the inflationary fire. A further rise in prices raises the cost of living still further and the workers ask for still higher wages .In this way, wages and prices chase each other and the process of inflationary rise in prices gathers momentum. If unchecked, this may lead to **hyper-inflation** which signifies a state of affairs where wages and prices chase each other at a very quick speed. This is a state of galloping inflation. This state of affairs seemed to prevail in India in 1974–75 and again in 1979-80.

Distinction is sometimes made between Demand-pull Inflation and Cost-push Inflation.

(*i*) Demand-pull Inflation. This represents a situation where the basic factor at work is the increase in demand for resources either from the government or the entrepreneurs or the households. The result is that the pressure of demand is such that it cannot be met by the currently available supply of output. If, for example, in a situation of full employment, the government expenditure or private investment goes up this is bound to generate an inflationary pressure in the economy.

Demand pull inflation could be of two types (*a*) Perishable goods and (*b*) non-perishable goods.

(a) Perishable goods

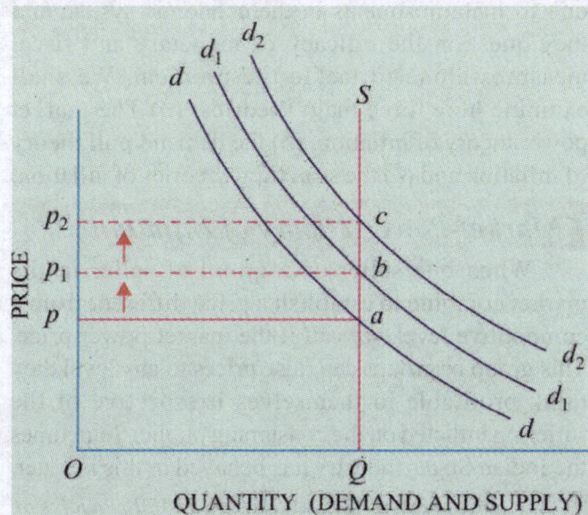

Fig. 51.1. **Perishable goods.**

'*QS*' is 'supply of goods' which is perfectly inelastic curve. This is because the supply of goods is fixed in market period. It is the demand factor which plays an important role in determining the price level. Initially '*dd*' is the demand curve and equilibrium is at point '*a*' and the price is at '*OP*'. As the demand increases from '*dd*' to 'd_1d_1' and further to 'd_2d_2', the equilibrium is at point '*b*' and '*c*'. This birngs about an increase in price from '*OP*' to 'OP_1' and 'OP_2'.

This is due to the demand forces pulling the prices upwards.

(b) Non-perishable goods

The '*SS*' curve is supply curve which is initially 'price elastic' till the stocks are more and later it becomes perfectly inelastic due to non-availability of more stocks. Initially '*dd*' is demand curve and the equilibrium is at point '*a*', which determines the price '*OP*' and quantity '*OQ*'. As the demand increases from '*dd*' to 'd_1d_1' the equilibrium is achieved at point '*b*' which gives 'OP_1' price and 'OQ_1' quantity.

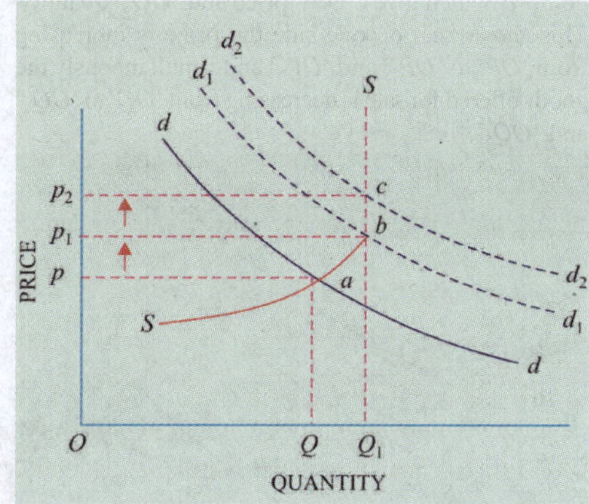

Fig. 51.2. **Non Perishable goods.**

Further increase in demand to 'd_2d_2' the price will increase to 'OP_2' but the quantity supplied will be 'OQ_1' only. The increase in price is due to 'demand' pull.

(*ii*) Cost-push Inflation. We can visualise a situation where even though there is no increase in aggregate demand, prices may still rise. This may happen if the costs, particularly the wage costs, go on rising. Now, as the level of employment increases, the demand for workers rises progressively so that the bargaining position of the workers is enhanced. To exploit this situation, they may ask for an increase in wage rates, which are not justifiable either on grounds of a prior rise in productivity or of cost of living. The employers in a situation of high demand and employment are more agreeable to concede to these wage claims, because they hope to pass on these rises in costs to the consumers in the shape of higher prices. If this happens we have another inflationary factor at work.

The cost-push inflation may also be explained with the help of the figure given on next page.

Cost Push Inflation

On *y*-axis 'price' and *x*-axis quantity demanded and supplied are taken in fig. 51.3. Initially '*dd*' is the demand curve and '*SS*' is the supply curve,equilibrium is at point '*a*'; '*OP*' is the price and '*OQ*' is the quantity determined. As the cost of productions, *i.e.* transportation cost raw material cost, electricity charges, wages and other expenses increase, due to this the '*SS*' curve decreases and it shifts on the left hand side, new equilibrium is reached at point '*b*', which gives 'OP_1' price and 'OQ_1' quantity. In the same way further increase in cost of production, the new equilibrium will be achieved at point '*c*' which gives 'OP_2' price and 'OQ_2' quantity. This shows that on one side the price is increasing from '*OP*' to 'OP_1' and 'OP_2' and simultaneously the goods offered for sale is decreasing from '*OQ*' to 'OQ_1' and 'OQ_2'.

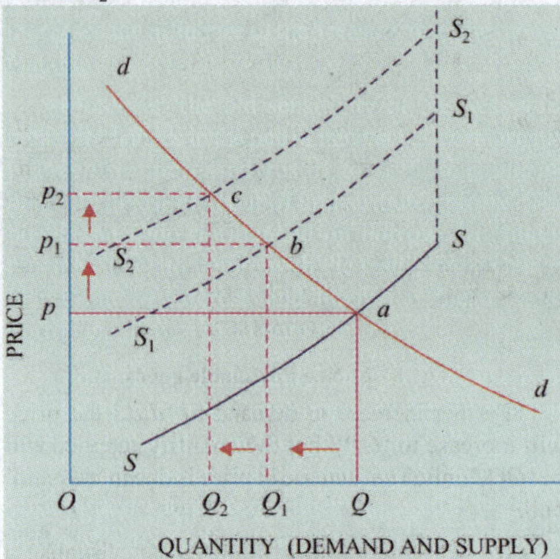

Fig. 51.3. Cost-Push Inflation.

Thus the 'price' increase is due to 'cost-push' and also it reduces the quantity supplied in the market. It is nothing but the 'cost-push' inflation.

The same can be explained with reference to 'aggregate demand' and 'aggregate supply' forces in Fig 51.4.

In this figure *AZ* and *AD* are the usual aggregate demand and supply curves. A rise in the wage rates in the economy shifts *AZ* curve upward, *i.e.*, to *AZ'*. This would in turn induce a rise in aggregate demand curve from *AD* to *AD'*. Let us assume that *ON* is the output at full employment. This would push up prices. At *ON* output with *AD* as the total demand, the average

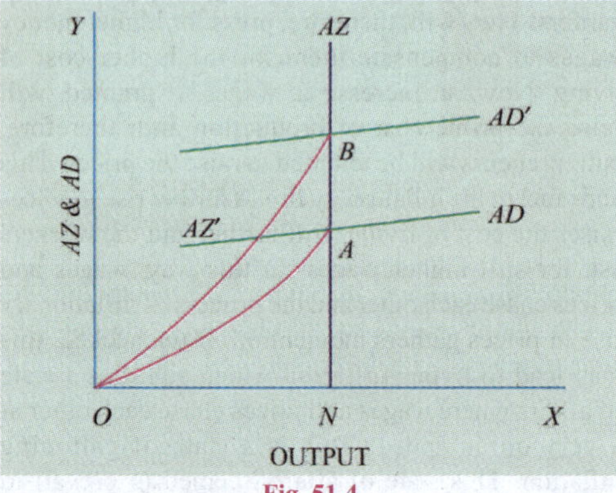

Fig. 51.4.

price level is $\frac{AN}{ON}$. At *ON* output with *AD'* as the aggregate demand, the average price level is $\frac{BN}{ON}$ which is clearly higher than $\frac{AN}{ON}$. This higher price level would further lead to increase in the general wage rate and hence there will be another rise in the aggregate demand curve.

THEORIES OF INFLATION

Several theories have been put forward by economists from time to time. Broadly, the inflation theorists can be grouped under two labels, *viz.*, the monetarists and the structuralists. The monetarists attribute inflation to monetary causes and they rely on monetary measures to control it. On the other hand, the structuralists are of the opinion that inflation is due to maladjustments in the economic system and they question the efficacy of monetary and fiscal measures alone to tackle the problem. We shall examine here three main theories: (*a*) The market power theory of inflation, (*b*) the demand pull theory of inflation and (*c*) the structural theories of inflation.

Market-Power Theory of Inflation

When one seller or a group of seller in the market combine to establish a price different from a competitive level, we call it the market-power price. This group or groups can raise prices to any level they think profitable to themselves irrespective of the suffering inflicted on the consuming public. Sometimes the Indian Sugar Industry has behaved in this manner.

1. See Ferguson, C.E., and Kreps, J.M., *Principles of Economics*, 1962. pp. 686-709.

The unduly high prices of sugar prevailing in the market may be attributed to the group action of the industrialists.

Many economists have advanced the market-power theory of inflation. That is, it is their view that oligopolists are normally in a position to increase their profit by raising the price of their products even when there is no increase in demand. The trade unions keep pressing for increase in wages and fringe benefits. They succeed in securing such increases since increase in wage in the entire industry can be passed on in higher prices. Hence, oligopoly price has a constant tendency to rise corresponding to increase in wage rate. Thus an inflationary situation is created.

Policy Implications. This has led some economists to contend that monetary and fiscal policies are practically useless in preventing a rise in prices. These policies try to curb inflation by restricting demand. But, in a case of oligopolist rise in prices, it is not increase in demand that is responsible for inflation; it is the cost which is responsible. Obviously, monetary and fiscal policies cannot affect costs. Monetary authorities can raise the rate of interest by imposing curbs on credits, but this is of no avail, because increase in cost can be passed on in higher prices. Besides, the oligopolists raise prices step by step. They are also more credit-worthy. Hence credit curbs can affect only competitive firms and not oligopolists. Moreover, big oligopolists have open to them credit facilities provided by organized financial markets. Monetary and fiscal policies are, therefore, generally ineffective against the oligopolists. They can only control the firms operating under competition.

Market Power inflation.

In this connection, we may refer to the view expressed by Professor A.P. Lerner who says that there are two basic kinds of inflation: One of the conventional sort which is caused by excess demand and the other quite different which occurs even in the absence of excess demand. This second type of inflation may be called sellers' inflation or what has been called the market-power inflation.

A peculiar feature of this type of inflation is that it is accompanied by depression, *i.e.*, inflation and depression are to be found side by side. Prof. Lerner aptly calls it inflationary depression. Depression is inevitable because the government seeks to check inflation by reducing effective aggregate demand. Hence, Lerner also says that under these circumstances monetary and fiscal policies are worse than useless; they are positively harmful. Lerner suggests that market-power inflation can be controlled by regulating administered prices, *i.e.*, prices administered by powerful trading groups. He recommends the establishment of a governmental regulating agency which would permit the raising of the administered prices only under certain circumstances. Rather, it may enforce decreases in such prices.

There are, however, economists like Professor Ruggles of America who regard market-power with administered pricing as relatively insignificant in the inflationary process. This view is not accepted because oligopolistic organisations do have a substantial effect upon inflationary price movements.

Conventional Demand-Pull Inflation

The market-power theorists stand at one extreme and say that inflation occurs even when there is no excess in demand. At the other extreme stand the conventional demand-pull theorists. They are of the opinion that excess in aggregate demand over aggregate supply is the only cause of inflation. They refuse to admit that there can be any other cause.

When an economy is operating at full employment equilibrium, and there is increase in demand, inflation is inevitable. This is so because the economy has already reached its maximum productive capacity as it is operating at full employment level. Since the quantity of goods and services cannot be increased, inflation inevitably results from increase in demand. We have witnessed in our own country how during war and post-war years demand for goods increased manifold, and inflationary pressures were built up to raise prices to great heights.

Structural Theories of Inflation

In between the two extremes mentioned above stands a middle group of economists. According to this group, market-power can be only one force causing inflation, but not the exclusive force. They try to explain inflation in terms of structural maladjustments in the country itself or of certain institutional features of the business world. Several explanations of inflation are put forward by these economists such as the Mark-up Theory, the Bottleneck Theory, and the Demand-composition Theory.

Mark-up Theory. Prof. Gardner Ackley puts forward the mark-up theory of inflation. He says that it is wrong to attribute inflation exclusively either to demand or cost. Actually, inflation is caused both by demand-pull and cost-push factors. The demand-pull inflation is caused by excessive demand for goods so that it is natural that their prices go up. But the increase in prices stimulates production and causes excess demand for factors of production and, as a result, costs rise and prices rise.

Increase in cost of basic materials leads to inflationary situation.

Sometimes wages may rise (as a result of trade union pressure) without excess demand for the product. This would mean that at the prevailing level of prices (which have gone up as a result of increase in wages), there is an actual or potential shortage in the supply of goods. When there is a shortage in the supply of goods, prices tend to rise.

Thus Professor Ackley suggests a model of mark-up inflation in which both elements of demand and cost inflation are to be found. An increase in demand makes the prices rise because customers spend more on goods. When goods are sold to firms, and not to consumers, the price rise becomes also a cost rise resulting in further price increases. Similarly, when wages increase costs increase resulting in higher prices. We, therefore, find that an inflationary situation may be built up or initiated either by excess commodity demand or by an autonomous increase in wage rates. To strengthen the mark-up inflation analysis, Professor Ackley suggests that average level of mark-up used by the firms tends to rise as total demand for goods increases, and conversely it tends to fall as demand decreases. Similarly, the mark-up that unions supply to the cost of living in setting their wage rate demand also tends to rise and fall as the volume of employment respectively rises and falls.

Since, according to Ackley, total demand contributes to inflation, the tools of monetary and fiscal policies will be found somewhat useful in checking inflation, though in themselves they will not be sufficient to curb inflation.

Bottle-Neck Inflation

According to Professor Otto Eckstein, the wage-price spiral is an important cause of inflation. All the same, it does not mean that either a simple wage push-theory or the market-power theory is an adequate explanation of inflation. After examining empirical evidence regarding inflationary periods, Eckstein came to the conclusion that the recent inflation was associated with capital goods boom and with a wage-price spiral. He found that although prices of manufactures rose generally but one or two particular industries had a very sharp increase in prices. He calls these 'bottle-neck industries' and it was his opinion that general price rise was substantially due to such industries. Of these steel was a chief bottle-neck industry. Inflation, he found was not entirely due to excess demand because there was wide-spread prevalence of excess productive capacity. It was the concentration of demand on the products of the bottle-neck industries that accounted for a considerable share of inflation.

Demand-Composition Inflation

The last of the structural theories of inflation is what is known as 'demand-composition theory' recently propounded by Professor Charles L. Schultze. According to Schultze, neither cost-push nor demand-pull theories can offer an adequate explanation of inflation. He points out that prices and wages are comparatively insensitive to decrease in demand, but they respond rather quickly to increase in demand. In other words, if demand decreases prices and wages do not go down quickly, but if demand increases the increase in price and wages is almost simultaneous.

Schultze thinks that it is a rapid shift in the composition of demand which will lead to a general price rise, even though there may have been no increase in the overall aggregate demand or a general increase in the level of wages. A change in the composition of demand means, for instance, that there is an increase in the demand for the product of one particular industry, whereas there is a similar decrease in demand for the product of another industry; hence total demand remains the same; only its composition has changed. The prices of the products of that industry will not change much whose demand has decreased because prices are relatively insensitive to decrease in demand. On the other hand, prices of the products of that industry will go up whose demand has increased because prices are relatively sensitive to increase in demand.

Increase in demand causes inflation.

Thus, according to the demand-composition theory, it is a change in the composition of the demand, as explained above, which is responsible for inflation and not either increase in aggregate demand or a cost-push in wages. The inflationary situation of 1955-57 period seems to conform reasonably well to the demand-composition theory.

The policy implication of this theory is that because inflation does not arise from aggregate excess demand but largely from excess demand in particular sectors of economy, prices cannot be controlled by general monetary and fiscal measures. Hence what is required is the adoption of selective controls or selective monetary and fiscal policies. In India, in recent years, the Reserve Bank of India has made an extensive use of selective credit controls to combat inflationary trends.

Schultze's theory gets support from many economists now. Of course, there can be pure-demand pull inflation when goods are in short supply and demand is excessive as in the post-war II period. But demand-pull inflation does not explain why prices rise faster than increase in demand or increase in wages. Schultze's theory precisely explains this. He has explained why there can be inflation in the absence of demand-pull or cost-push forces.

Summing-up

We have examined above the three important types of inflation theories. At the one extreme, there is the market-power theory which says that inflation is largely attributable to the market power of oligopolists and to their ability to pass on the cost increases to increases in prices, even though demand for their product has not increased. At the other extreme, is the view that if aggregate demand exceeds aggregate supply at the full employment level, inflation is inevitable. This is the demand-pull theory. Between these two extremes of demand-pull and cost-push theories lie a number of structural theories which attribute inflation to structural maladjustment in an economy. Among the structural theories, we have mentioned the demand-composition theory of Schultze which says that a shift in the composition of demand will create an inflationary situation even the absence of either excess of aggregate demand or autonomous cost increases.

CAUSES OF INFLATION

In the detailed analysis of inflation given above, we have referred to the basic cause of inflation, that is when aggregate demand for output tends to be excessive in relation to the supply of output. Thus, the causes of inflation may be grouped under two headings:

(1) Increase in Demand which may be due to:

(*a*) increase in money supply;

(*b*) increase in disposable incomes;

(*c*) increase in community's aggregate spending on consumption and investment goods;

(*d*) excessive speculation and tendency to hoarding and profiteering on the part of producers and traders;

(*e*) increase in foreign demand and hence exports;

(*f*) increase in salaries, wages or dearness allowance; and

(*g*) increase in population.

These causes may operate singly or in combination with one another. Generally, the most important cause of inflation is excessive public expenditure financed by deficit financing during war or on the implementation of plans for economic development. The newly created money increases government demand for goods and services and also the purchasing power of the people through increase in disposable income.

(2) No corresponding increase in the output of goods and services which may be due to:

(*a*) deficiency of capital equipment;

(*b*) Scarcity of other complementary factors of production, *e.g.*, skilled labour or technicians essential raw materials or lack of dynamic entrepreneurs;

(*c*) increase in exports for earning the required foreign exchange;

(*d*) decrease in imports owing to war or restrictions on imports necessitated by an adverse balance of payments and efforts to rectify it;

(*e*) speculative hoarding by the producers, traders and middlemen in anticipation of a further rise in prices;

(*f*) drought, famine or any other natural calamity adversely affecting agricultural production; and

(*g*) prolonged industrial unrest resulting in reduction of industrial production.

The demand-pull inflation is caused primarily by factors operating on the demand side resulting in excess of aggregate demand over the available supply of goods and services. The cost-push inflation, on the other hand, is caused by increase in salaries, wages, the rising cost of machinery and capital equipment and of essential raw materials. Actually, all the above factors operate simultaneously to exert inflationary pressure and, if continued sufficiently long, to create hyper-inflation.

FULL EMPLOYMENT AND INFLATION

Broadly speaking, we might distinguish in any economy two phases in its development:

(*i*) a zone below full employment; and

(*ii*) a full employment zone.

In the 'below full-employment zone,' it is assumed that large amount of productive resources are lying idle and are waiting for employment. In these conditions, if there is an increase in effective demand, it will lead to fuller employment of the productive resources of the community and to a higher level of business activity and output, but it will not result in higher prices.

But as the process of expansion and development proceeds apace, the volume of idle resources will shrink, since most of them will now be gainfully employed. The margin of unemployment falls and the economy is heading towards the full employment zone.

"As full employment is approached, the pressure for costs and prices increases progressively because the bargaining strength of labour is greatly enhanced and the remaining unemployed resources become less and less efficient as the bottom of the barrel is scraped. The number of the bottlenecks multiplies rapidly. Shortages are more and more difficult to overcome as substitutes are difficult to find, because the most satisfactory substitutes have already been fully employed, or nearly so. But as long as there is unemployment, increase in effective demand will increase employment. When full employment is at last attained, further increases in effective demand no longer increase employment. They spend themselves entirely on increase in prices. **A condition of true inflation sets in as full employment is reached.**"

We may, however, point out that it is not correct to assume that there is one precise point of full employment below which increase in effective demand is reflected by increase in output and employment, and above which the increase in effective demand results in higher prices. The fact is that the changes in effective demand can simultaneously affect the level of prices and the level of output in a country. Even where there is a considerable amount of unemployment, say, in a manufacturing industry, the general prices may show a tendency to rise with an increase in effective demand owing to rise in prices of primary products, especially agricultural products. The rise in prices may lead to rise in wage rates. The rise in prices and wage rates push the economy to the verge of inflation.

Keynes showed why **semi-inflation is likely to develop with increasing money supplies before the point of full employment is reached** and prices rise gradually as output and employment increase. This happened in India in 1974–75.

There are five important causes which contribute to this semi-inflation: (*i*) Effective demand (the flow of monetary expenditure) is shared among the rise of prices, the rise of costs and the rise of output and employment. (*ii*) Since the productive resources are not homogeneous, the use of less and less efficient ones will lead to a diminishing return. This means higher costs and the rising supply price of output. (*iii*) Some resources have a perfectly inelastic supply and

2. Dillard, D. –*The Economics of J.M.Keynes*, p. 234.

a series of bottlenecks are bound to raise factor prices and, therefore, commodity prices in some sectors. (*iv*) Increase in wage rates cannot be avoided for long. Hence, costs, and, therefore, prices, must rise. (*v*) Some variable factors have different degrees of price elasticity of supply. Hence, the marginal costs curve will move upwards via diminishing returns in cases where the supply of factors is perfectly inelastic.

In a structurally balanced economy, the point of full[3] employment and full capacity output will be reached simultaneously in all sectors, where as in the case of an unbalanced economy, there may be reached full employment condition in some sectors with extensive unemployment in others. Once conditions of full capacity output and very low unemployment are reached in some sectors of the economy, price rises become more marked and show increasingly strong tendencies to lead to other price rises. Thus, the inflationary price rises become cumulative in the full employment zone.

Hence, there is a bias to secular inflation in modern industrial economy unless a very high level of employment is maintained. We may, therefore, conclude "that below a certain level of unemployment all changes in effective demand showed themselves solely as price changes and above a certain level of unemployment, the changes in effective demand showed themselves solely as changes in the level of activity." In terms of quantity theory, **"So long as there is unemployment, employment will change in the same proportion as the quantity of money, and when there is full employment prices will change in the same proportion as the quantity of money."**

Short-term Problem. There is no doubt that full employment economy is highly susceptible to inflation. But the problem is a short-run problem, because it is only in short run that output cannot be expanded except by slow degrees. "That is why inflation is typically a short-run phenomenon peculiar to a stationary, full-employment economy." In the long run, for a dynamic and expanding economy, inflation is no problem. It is capable of increasing output to match with the increasing demand. Thus, full employment can be maintained continuously without price inflation provided the economy continues to grow at the desired rate.

The Phillips' Curve

Professor Phillips, formerly of London School of Economics, urged that there was a close link between the level of unemployment and the rate of wage increase. We know that Keynes was of the opinion that trade unions would tend to raise wages more rapidly when unemployment rates were higher. Phillips studied the relationship between unemployment and the rate of changes in money wages in the U.K. over the period 1862-1957. As a result of this study he seems to have discovered a stable relationship over the whole period between the rate of wage increase and the percentage of unemployment. Phillips Curve shows this relationship. It may also be considered a relationship between inflation and unemployment, because when there is inflation money wages invariably go up under trade union pressure.

Phillips' Curve is shown in the follow ing diagram.

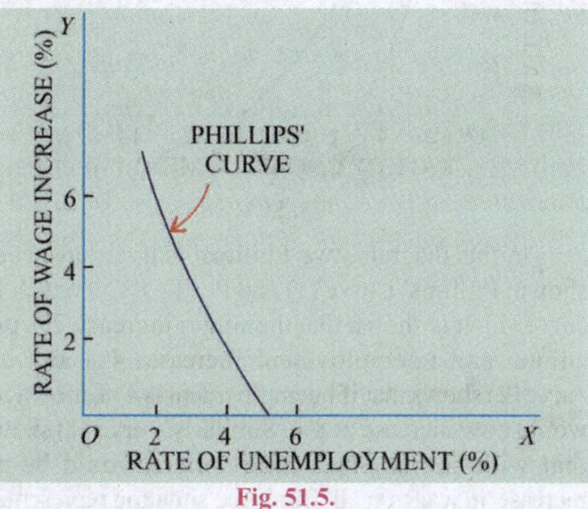

Fig. 51.5.

In the figure, rate of unemployment is shown along the *x*-axis and the rate of wage increase along the *y*-axis, both in percentages. From this figure, which represents a hypothetical economy, we find that when wages rise by 2% per annum, unemployment goes up by 4%. Thus we may say that as wages rise unemployment rises more than proportionately. But the curve also shows that when unemployment has reached a very high level, say 5%, wages do not rise at all, which means that, in the case of wide-spread unemployment, the workers are more keen to get employment than to fight for higher wages.

The concept of Phillips Curve has been widely accepted as a useful concept, though there are economists who question its realism, *i.e.*, they do not regard it as representing a realistic situation. There is no doubt that, as we have said above, in the case on widespread unemployment, there is a keen competition for securing jobs and consequently pressure for securing higher wages is correspondingly reduced.

However, Phillips' Curve may be used for establishing actual relationship between unemployment and the increase in money wages. This means that Phillips' Curve does not establish a

3. Day, A.C.L. –*Outline of Money Economics*, 1960, pp. 295-96.

permanent or universally applicable relationship between an increase in unemployment and increase in the rate of wages. On the other hand, a new Phillips' Curve may have to be drawn to represent a new relationship between these two variables at a particular period of time. This shift in the position of the Phillips' Curve may be represented by the following diagram.

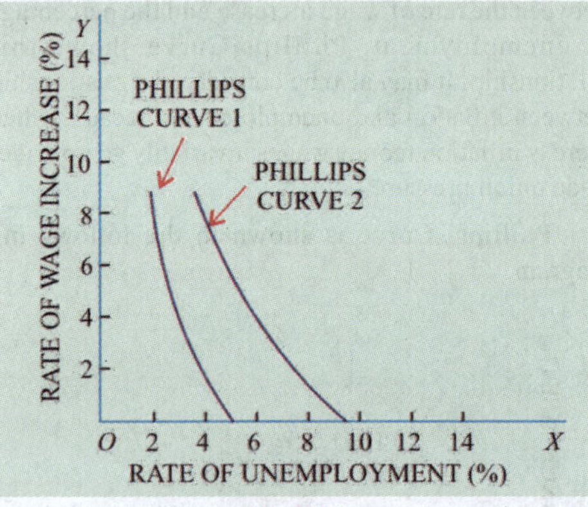

Fig. 51.6.

In this diagram, two Phillips' Curves have been shown: Phillips' Curve (1) and Phillips' Curve (2). In curve (1), it is shown that the wages increase 2% per annum and unemployment increases 4%. But the curve (2) shows that if unemployment is 4%, the wages would now increase at 8%. Similarly, curve (1) shows that with 5% unemployment, there would be no increase in wages at all. But in the situation represented by curve (2), the wages would not increase further only when unemployment has reached 9%.

Thus, Phillips introduced an empirically measurable relationship between the rate of wage increase and the rate of increase in unemployment into economic analysis. But it has to be admitted that it is not easy to discover exactly where the Phillips' Curve is in any economy at a particular moment. This means that no stable relationship has been discovered by Phillips between the rate of increase in wages and the rate of increase in unemployment. In view of this, it is not possible to make use of the Phillips' Curve in the formulation of economic policy.

Trade-off Between Degree of Unemployment And Wage-Price Rise

So far we have described Phillips' curve as a relationship between unemployment and money wage rates. But, as has been mentioned earlier, Phillips' curve also depicts a relationship between the level of unemployment and price rise. The diagram[6] given below illustrates this double relationship (or 'trade-off' as it has been called), between the level of unemployment on the one hand and the rates of wage rise and price rise on the other.

In this diagram (Fig. 51.7), the level of unemployment (per cent) has shown on the *x*-axis. The annual price rise (per cent) on the *y*-axis and the annual wage rise (per cent) on the right hand on the line perpendicular to the *x*-axis.

It will be seen that the right hand vertical line shows a wage rise higher (9%) than the price rise on the *y*-axis (6%). This difference is explained by the 3% rate of average annual productivity growth which has been assumed. This means that if money wages rise by 9%, the real wages will rise only by 6%. In other words, the price rise of 6% would correspond to wage rise of 9%. We see in this figure that greater is the unemployment, as shown on the *x*-axis, the lower is the rate of price inflation. The United States' experience, in the recent decades, shows that the Phillips' curve has shifted higher to the right as in Fig. 51.6. This means that now the degree of inflation would be kept down only by greater unemployment. If we move leftward, we shall see that unemployment is reduced as the rates of price and wage rise become higher. It also follows that if the rate of annual average productivity growth goes up, there will be a corresponding decline in both prices and wages. For instance, if productivity rate rises to 6% a year, 8% wage increase would correspond to only a 2% annual price rise.

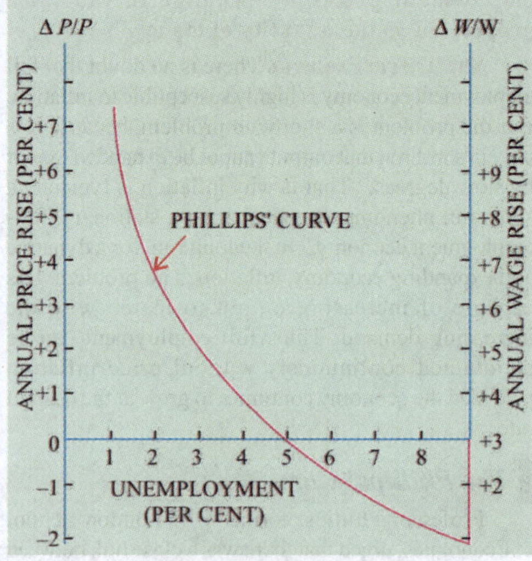

Fig. 51.7. Trade off Between Inflation and Full Employment.

4. Stonier, A.W., and Hague, D.C., *A Taxtbook of Economic Theory*, 4th Edition, p. 569.
5. *Ibid*., p. 570.

6. Samuelson, P.A., *Economics*, 9th Edition, p. 832.

NATURE OF INFLATION IN A DEVELOPING ECONOMY

Developing countries in their bid to raise the standards of living of their people through development plans have often found themselves in the grip of inflation. But the nature of inflation in under-developed but developing economies is quite different from that found in advanced or developed countries. As discussed above, in advanced countries true inflation starts after the level of full-employment is attained. But in under-developed countries like India huge unemployment and inflation exist side by side. In other words, in under-developed countries, serious inflation is in evidence long before the level of full-employment is reached. This is so because the nature of unemployment in under-developed countries differs from that which prevails in developed countries during times of depression.

In order to get the economy out of depression, governments in advanced countries take various steps to increase the level of investment. The additional investment expenditure leads to an increase in effective demand depending upon the magnitude of the multiplier. But this increase in investment and effective demand does not generate serious inflationary pressures because of the elastic nature of the supply curve of output. Instead, increase in investment and effective demand helps a great deal in removing depression and unemployment which are caused by the lack of effective demand. This is the case of developed economies.

In advanced countries, during depression, there is a lot of excess capacity in the system so that an increase in output presents no difficult problems. Thus, when the supply of output can be increased easily so as to match increase in effective demand, there need be no inflationary pressures.

The situation in under-developed countries is, however, different. Here an increase in investment does create additional demand but a corresponding increase in the supply of output cannot be taken for granted .Unemployment in under-developed economies is not due to the lack of effective demand but due to the dearth of real capital.

In these countries, level of national income can be increased and the unemployment can be removed by accumulating more real capital. But increase in the rate of capital formation requires stepping up the level of investment. Now, under-developed countries, under their development plans, are making huge investment expenditure to increase the rate of capital formation and thus to obtain rapid economic growth. This huge investment expenditure leads to a sharp increase in aggregate demand for consumer goods, especially the agricultural products. Since, in under-developed countries, there is no excess capacity in the system, the supply of consumer goods cannot be increased sufficiently and rapidly to match the increase in demand for them. This leads to inflationary rise in prices.

It is worth nothing that it is the food prices which first start rising rapidly in a developing economy. Rise in food prices is then followed by the rise in the prices of other consumer goods. This is so because a greater part of the increase in demand generated by the investment expenditure is spent on the food products such as wheat and rice. But the supply of these food products cannot be sufficiently increased in the short run due to the tiny size of the farms, lack of irrigation facilities, of superior seeds, fertilizers and owing and owing to inefficient techniques of cultivation. **Income elasticity of demand for food is very high,** because the vast majority of the people are undernourished. Thus, as a result of huge investment expenditure, there is a sharp rise in demand for foodgrains, leading to increase in food prices.

In under-developed countries like India, which are predominantly agricultural, the prices of agricultural commodities, especially of food crops, hold the key position in the price structure of the country. Any distortion in agricultural prices leads to a distortion in the whole price structure.

A steep rise in food prices increases the cost of living of the people. Consumers are hit hard, as their incomes do not increase so easily to offset the increase in prices. Workers, whose cost of living rise, press for higher wages. When wage increases are conceded, the cost of production of manufactured articles rises and this, in turn, increases their prices, and so on.

Moreover, some agricultural products are raw materials for industries and increase in their prices will directly increase the cost of production of industrial goods. Hoarding of, and speculation in, both agricultural and industrial products add fuel to the inflationary fire. Thus, **once the prices of agricultural goods rise, they are likely to cause an inflationary spiral in the economy.**

A factor which deserves special mention in this connection is the mode of financing development plans. The developing countries are not in a position to finance their plans fully from voluntary savings of the people and taxes by the government. They have often to resort to deficit financing (*i.e.*, the creation of new money) as a method of financing their development plans. Deficit financing to some extent is good and can be absorbed by the economy without experiencing inflation. This is so because, as the economy grows, its monetary sector expands and also there is an increase in production for which extra money is needed.

But, owing to acute shortage of finance, the underdeveloped countries have often indulged in deficit financing to an excessive degree. Sharp increase in the money supply with the public as a result of excessive deficit financing adds greatly to the level of aggregate demand for consumers' goods. On the other hand, the supply of consumers' goods, especially of food products, cannot be increased rapidly and sufficiently. The pressure of demand, therefore, leads to an inflationary rise in prices.

UDCs face the problem fo shortage of finance.

It may, however, be pointed out that investment expenditure made by the government under the development plans not only generates the additional demand for goods, it also increases the productive capacity. **Investment has a dual effect. On the one hand, it generates demand or income, on the other it increases the productive capacity.** As a result of increase in productive capacity, more output of goods can be obtained which will counteract inflationary tendencies. But, in the earlier stages of development, investment expenditure is largely made on huge dams, steel plants and other heavy and basic industries which have long-gestation periods. In other words, the long-term projects can help in increasing the supply of consumers' goods only in the long run. In the short run, prices generally shoot up under the pressure of excessive demand for goods. And once inflationary spiral starts operating, it is difficult to control it.

CONTROL OF INFLATION

Inflation is a very complex phenomenon. There is no one sovereign remedy to combat it . On the other hand, measures have to be taken on several fronts, monetary and non-monetary, to fight it. All these measures have one common aim. They aim at reducing aggregate monetary expenditure taking the available output as given. Broadly speaking, the anti-inflationary measures can be classified as under:–

(i) Monetary measures.

(ii) Fiscal measures.

(iii) Physical or non-monetary measures.

We shall now say a word about each.

Monetary Measures

The best remedy for fighting inflation is to reduce the aggregate spending. Monetary policy can help in reducing the pressure of demand. Briefly speaking, monetary policy works by controlling the cost and availability of credit. During inflation, the central bank can raise the cost of borrowing and reduce the credit creating capacity of the commercial banks This will make borrowing more costly than before and thereby the demand for funds will be reduced. Similarly, with a reduction in their credit creating capacity, the banks will be more cautious in their lending policies. The result will be a fall in the volume of spending. The mechanics of dear money policy is as follows:–

***(i)* Raising Bank Rate.** The bank rate is the rate at which the central bank is willing to rediscount eligible paper offered by the commercial banks. The rise in the bank rate will be followed by the rise in other market rates of interest. There will be an all-round hardening of the rates of interest. A rise in the rate of interest will tend to reduce the amount of aggregate spending for the following reasons:

(a) Borrowing becomes more costly than before. The potential borrowers will, therefore, postpone their investment plans. They would like to wait till interest rates fall to their more normal level. A cut in investment will usually mean a reduction in the volume of spending and thereby help moderate the inflationary pressures.

(b) Further, an increase in the rate of interest has some adverse psychological effects on business confidence. In a way, it is a red signal to the businessmen that bad times are ahead. This by itself will help to dampen their enthusiasm for additional spending on investment.

(c) An increase in the rate of interest may make saving more attractive than before so that some people will be tempted to consume less of their income than before. This will reduce consumers' spending.

***(ii)* Directly Controlling Credit Creation.** The other method is to cut directly the credit creating capacity of banks. We know that in their own interest, banks want to keep a minimum reserve of cash which bears more or less a definite relationship to the volume of their deposits. If the central bank of the country can reduce the cash available to the banking system, the capacity of the banks to lend money to the borrowers will be reduced. The banks, therefore, in their own interest will be induced to contract the supply of credit. The borrowers, now not being able to get help from the banks as easily as previously, will be forced to postpone their investment plans. The various methods of controlling the credit creating capacity of banks are:

(*a*) Open market operations. If the central bank wants to reduce the credit-creating capacity of commercial banks, it will sell government securities to the public or to the banks themselves. Either way, the result will be that the amount of cash with the banks will diminish and this will force them to reduce the supply of credit.

(*b*) Varying Reserve Ratios. The same effect may be brought about by varying reserve ratios in countries where the banks are required to keep certain minimum cash in relation to the volume of their deposits and the central bank has the power to change these ratios from time to time. When it desired to reduce the credit created by commercial banks, the cash ratios can be raised, so that, for a given amount of deposits, the banks now need to keep higher cash reserves than before. This will exercise a contractional effect on bank credit.

Thus, monetary measures consist in fixing (*a*) higher discount rates, (*b*) higher reserve requirements, (*c*) open market operations, (*d*) and selective credit controls or regulation of consumer credit and varying margin requirements.

Limitations of Monetary Policy. Monetary policy, however, is not without its limitations. These limitations are discussed in the chapter on central banking (Ch. 53). Some of these difficulties are as follows:–

(*i*) An increase in bank rate may be ineffective if commercial banks do not follow the rise in the bank rate by raising their own interest rates. Where there is no tradition of close cooperation between the central bank and commercial banks, or where the central bank has no legal powers to force the commercial banks to fall in line, this difficulty will prove a great limitation on the effectiveness of monetary policy.

(*ii*) Even if the rates of interest do rise, they may not be able to curb spending significantly. For example, if the prospects of profits are very good, businessmen do not mind paying a slightly higher rate of interest on their borrowings. Further, investment is increasingly being financed out of undistributed profits so that the dependence of firms on banks for funds has been greatly reduced. Therefore, a change in interest rate may not disturb very much the plans for investment.

(*iii*) As regards the efficiency of open market operations as a curb on the lending activity of the banks, their success depends on the existence of available, broad-based market in government securities; otherwise open market operations even on a minor scale will exercise a greatly destabilising influence on the prices of government securities and will hamper the efficient conduct of government's borrowing operations.

(*iv*) A major difficulty, particularly in underdeveloped countries, arises from the fact that the central bank has often not enough control over all the banks. In our own country, the organised banking sector, which is easily amenable to control by the central bank, is very small. The indigenous bankers and the village money-lenders, who do the bulk of the business of lending in the rural areas, are outside the control of the Reserve Bank.

Fiscal Measures

The two wins of fiscal policy are government revenues and government expenditure. The government's fiscal policy can contribute to the control of inflation either by reducing private spending by increasing the taxes on private sector or by decreasing government expenditure, or combining both the elements. If private spending tends to be excessive, the government can moderate the inflationary pressure by reducing its own expenditure. But reduction or postponement of government expenditure in modern times is not an easy task. There may be projects already under construction and these obviously cannot be postponed. Similarly, other types of expenditure may be necessary to meet the normal

Private spending is reduced when state takes away money from household through taxation.

requirements of the 'collective consumption' of the community–defence, police, justice, *etc.* Then, there may be social expenditures on education, health, *etc.*, which are very difficult to cut because of undesirable political effects. Therefore, the major emphasis of fiscal policy in inflation has been on reducing private spending through increased taxation.

An increase in taxes tends to reduce private spending. If the rates of direct taxes on incomes and profits are raised, the private disposable income is reduced and this will tend to reduce private consumption spending. If the rates of commodity taxes are increased or fresh levies are made, the effect on consumption will be more immediate. An increase in the tax rates on a commodity will penalise spending directly by raising the cost of purchases.

Thus, in periods of inflation, the government should curb its own spending and increase the tax rates to reduce private spending. It is a good thing to plan for a budget surplus during inflationary periods.

Summing Up. Thus, the fiscal measures consist in (*a*) reduction of government spending, (*b*) imposition of new taxes or increasing the old ones to curtail the size of disposable income in the hands of the people and to reduce the magnitude of the inflationary gaps, (*c*) the encouragement of savings or introduction of compulsory saving schemes, (*d*) public debt management so as to reduce the money supply, (*e*) gold sterilisation as done in the United States, and (*f*) over-valuing domestic currency in terms of foreign currencies.

Physical or Non-Monetary Measures

Apart from the monetary and fiscal measures, it becomes necessary also to resort to some measures of non-monetary nature. But it should be clearly understood that such measures are much less practicable than the monetary-fiscal ones. Several causes–psychological, institutional, technological and other non-economic causes–hinder the success of the non-monetary measures. Hence, full reliance cannot be placed on such measures. They can only be considered as supplementary to more effective measures.

The non-monetary measures, among others, include: (*a*) increasing output or increasing imports and decreasing exports so as to increase the available supply of goods in short supply, (*b*) controlling money wages to keep down costs and (*c*) price control and rationing.

Rationing-Queue for food during worldwar I in Europe at controlled price.

In a symposium held in Bombay in February, 1975 on "Inflation, India and world economy," the problem of inflation was discussed at some depth. Mr. L.K. Jha, a former Governor of Reserve Bank of India, and Prof. J.K. Galbraith, a distinguished American economist and a former U.S. Ambassador in India, participated. Prof. Galbraith advocated a greatly reduced reliance on Central banks and monetary policies in meeting the current economic situation in which inflation and recession went hand in hand. It is necessary to recognise, he said, the impossibility of reducing consumption among people of average income or less, for restraints on income and consumption at the lower levels of the income period were possible only if the higher levels were restrained as well. He emphasised that wage increases which could not keep trade unions and white collar incomes within the capacity of the economy were self-defeating because they were taken away by price increases. As a balancing mechanism, he suggested that the aggregate demand be kept roughly equal to the supply of goods and services available at full-resource employment in the interest of price stability. For short-term adjustments, reliance should be on taxation-prompt, horizontal increases when aggregate demand exceeded supply and the reverse when it was deficient.

Mr. L.K. Jha said that there was need to increase investment in basic essential goods which were carce and costly. He pleaded for a judicious use of regulatory instruments to achieve a shift in production from luxury goods to essential goods. Fiscal measures could be devised to curb the profitability of non essentials and make investment in essential goods more attractive. Excise duties, corporate taxation and industrial licensing for new capacity were instruments which could be used to achieve this objective. Curb on monetary expansion must be within the framework of continuous investment in agriculture and in those industrial products which were major elements in fixing the cost of living. Curbs on credit and on budgetary outlays must, therefore, be selective and not quantitative. In India, a steady increase in the supply of basic necessaries was a pre-requisite for price stability.

We discuss below the economics of price control because this is a widely used weapon to fight inflation.

PRICE CONTROL

One method of preventing prices from rising is to impose price control on important commodities. This is an attempt to suppress inflation rather than to control it effectively. The basic pressure will not be allowed to express themselves in the form of a rise in prices which are now deliberately sought to be controlled. Such a state of affairs is called **suppressed inflation.** The logic of economic analysis as well as historical facts amply proves that price controls by themselves are no solution of the inflationary pressures. During the war, all governments imposed price controls to check a rise in prices yet in all countries prices kept up their upward march.

Failure of Price Control. The reasons for relative ineffectiveness of price controls as an anti-inflationary measure are discussed below :

(i) By merely controlling the prices, the government is tackling the symptoms rather than the basic causes of inflation. If the underlying pressure of demand is not allowed to express itself in the form of a rise in prices, it will express itself in the form of much longer queues of the potential purchasers. There will be a tendency for black-markets to flourish.

(ii) Further, to deal with now longer queues, the government will soon be forced to controls will have to be extended to production also so that producers do not sell their output in the black-market. This ever-widening system of controls is liable to prove administratively costly as well as economically inefficient.

(iii) It is impossible to control prices of each and every commodity. Usually, the government will restrict itself to controlling the prices of only the important commodities: By so doing, the government is interfering with the normal working of price-mechanism. As we saw earlier, a rise in price of a commodity is a green signal to producers to produce more. By artificially controlling the prices of the basic commodities, the government will be discouraging the movement of more resources into these urgent lines of production. On the other hand, if people cannot spend all their incomes on basic necessities, they will shift their spending towards luxuries which are uncontrolled. Price of luxury goods will also rise and existing resources will be diverted from necessities to the production of luxuries. Thus, price controls lead to an inefficient and wasteful allocation of resources.

(iv) Lastly, there are technical difficulties of price fixation—what margin of profit should be allowed to the producers; should prices vary between the different parts of the country or should they be uniform; what should be the proper structure of relative prices, *etc.*? These are important questions to which it is difficult to find satisfactory answers.

Conclusion. For all these reasons, price control cannot by itself help to fight inflation effectively. This, however, does not mean that price controls have no place in the armoury of anti-inflation policies. They can provide the much-needed breathing space and hold the price line till more effective weapons go into action.

FURTHER MEASURES TO CONTROL INFLATION

The following further measures for containing inflation may be mentioned.

Price Income Policy. Successive rounds of high wages resulting from trade union pressure is regarded as an importatn cause of inflation. This arises from the monopoly power of the unions. Since the trade unions would not agree only to wage freeze, a comprehensive approach is called for. That is, prices and profits will also have to be controlled to ensure workers' cooperation. Since wages are downwardly rigid and profits are already reduced by an all round increase in costs, the price-income policy cannot be effective in containing inflation.

Monetarists' Recipe. The monetarists hold that inflation can be controlled by regulating money supply combined with appropriate credit policy. They believe that wage-price spiralling can be checked by reducing the rate of monetary expansion below the money income level. In course of time, it is said people will try to restore their initial real balances by cutting consumption expenditure and raise the level of saving.This decline in aggregate expenditure will affect businessmen who may decide to keep the product prices steady. But output will be reduced and unemployment would increase. Or the product prices may be lowered to avoid accumulation of inventory of finished products. The level of profits would fall and there may be liquidity crisis. This would also cause increased unemployment which may undermine the power of the unions to demand higher wages. This is the main lever to reduce the rate of inflation. The wage-price spiral is set in the reverse gear. The rate of inflation becomes in tune with the rate of monetary expansion. This is how the economic system steers through the danger of excessive inflation or unemployment. It is reduction in money supply which initiated the process.

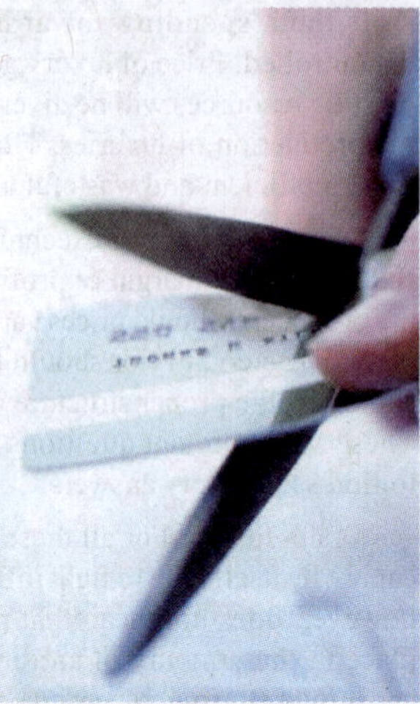

Inflation can be checked by controlling credit.

We see that the monetarist prescription rests on controlling the rate of monetary expansion and the resultant effect on expanditure. But the impact operates with a time lag. Hence direct management of demand through monetary and fiscal policy is recommended because it involves shorter time lags. Lowering of tax rates should be combined with tight control over money supply. It should also be associated with a reduction in public expenditure otherwise budgetary deficits would emerge and fan the inflationary fire. A reduction in the level of taxation would stimulate investment and reduce unemployment. In this way, aggregate demand can be kept in check, investment expenditure increased and the level of unemployment lowered.

Indexation. An effective supplementary device for controlling inflation is what has been called indexation. Economic variables are indexed to maintain the real value of variables which are measured in money units. The technique is to link a variable with a selected index e.g. wages may be linked to retail price index. The object is to prevent the erosion of real wages irrespective of changes in the price level. Similarly, the rate of interest can be indexed so that positive rate of return on money can be protected in real terms. Tax system constitutes an important area of indexation so that the proportion of deducted earnings can be kept relatively constant over time.

Conclusion. One school of economists (monetarists and non-monetarists) holds that the root cause of inflation are the economic factors, viz., continued existence of excess demand. The other school (Sociological-institutional) lays emphasis on the non-economic factors as the basic cause of inflation. To the monetarists excess demand originates in the excess money supply which arises from fiscal deficits, behaviour of the banking system and balance of payments surpluses. Non-monetarists ascribe the continued excess demand to fiscal overspending and money supply is assigned a passive role. But monetarists and non-monetarists both agree on the techniques of containing inflation vis., the regulation of money supply, credit curbs, avoidance of fiscal deficits, funding of deficits by savings rather than by monetary expansion. The non-monetarists rely heavily on taxation and reduction of public expenditure. Both monetarists and non-monetarists recommend indexation of economic variables like wages, interest rates, profits and dividends. Price-and-income policy is also recommended to contain inflationary pressures.

Key terms

Inflationary process, wage-price spiral, Demand full inflation, Cost-push inflation, Market-Power inflation, Phillips curve, Anti-inflationary measures, Indexation.

QUESTIONS

1. What are the causes of inflation? Discuss the monetary and different classes of people.
2. "Monetary Policy is far more effective in controlling inflation than fiscal policy. Discuss.
3. Distinguish between Demand-Pull and Cost-Push types of inflation.
4. (a) What is meant by inflationary gap? (b) What are the methods of controlling price rise?
5. "Inflation is unjust and inequitable and deflation is indexpedient" (Keynes). Discuss.
6. Discuss the economic consequences of inflation. How far can monetary measures control inflation? Account for inflation in any economy and discuss its consequences.
7. "Inflation and unemployment cannot co-exist in an economy" Comment.
8. "True inflation begins only after the level of full employment". Explain.
9. What do you understand by 'price control'? What are its objectives? Explain the difficulties of controlling prices effectively.
10. Discuss the effect of rising or falling prices on production, consumption and employment.

UNIT II

Banking

Chapters

BANKING

What is a Bank?

A bank is an institution which deals in money. Broadly speaking, bank draw surplus money from the people who are not using it at the time, and lend to those who are in a position to use it for productive purposes. Modern banks have developed from very small beginnings. The earlier bankers were goldsmiths.

Crowther observes that "the present-day banker has three ancestors: merchant money-lender and goldsmith. A modern bank is something of each of these. It is said money has two properties. It is flat so that it can be piled up, and it is round so that it is can circulate. The progeny of the money-lender are concerned with flat money, piled up money, savings. The progeny of the goldsmith are concerned with round money, circulating money, cash."[1]

FUNCTIONS OF COMMERCIAL BANKS

Broadly speaking, there are three principal functions that banks (other than central banks) perform: (*a*) receiving deposits; (*b*) advancing loans; and (*c*) discounting bills.

(*a*) Receiving Deposits. This function is important, because banks mainly depend on the funds deposited with them by the public. Deposits are of three kinds: (*i*) current or demand deposits, (*ii*) fixed or time deposits, and (*iii*) savings deposits. On current or demand deposits, the bank pays practically no interest. They can be withdrawn in part or in full at any time by issuing a cheque. Field deposits are so called because they are left with the bank for a certain fixed period before the expiry of which they cannot be withdrawn except after giving due notice. On such deposits, the bank pays higher interest. Savings deposits can be withdrawn subject to certain limitations regarding the amount with drawn or the frequency of withdrawals. There is, for instance, a limit to total weekly withdrawals. Modern banks are now more liberal in this respect and have relaxed most of these restrictions.

Banking.

In actual fact, only a small percentage of saving is withdrawn at any particular time. But since withdrawals can and do take place, the bank has to keep a certain proportion of its assets in

1. *An Outline of Money*, 1950, pp. 24-25.

liquid form. The rest can be lent for varying periods. This brings us to the second function of banks.

(*b*) Advancing Loans. In this respect, the banker has to shoulder a heavily responsibility. The bank makes profit by advancing loans. But the bank deals in other people's money. It has, therefore, to keep ready cash to meet the depositors' demands. Hence, great care has to be exercised in the matter of lending and keeping reserves. The bank must strike a fine balance between liquidity and profitability. If it keeps its assets in too liquid a form, it loses profit, and, if it tries to make too much profit, it may not be able to meet the depositors' demands. It must aim at both liquidity and profitability.

It should be noted that the bank does not merely lend funds actually deposited with it by its clients. The bank can itself create deposits and thus make advances considerably in excess of the sums deposited with it. After satisfying itself that the purpose for which the loan is required is economically sound and after taking precautions as regards security, the bank gives its client the right to draw cheques. The loan thus becomes a deposit to the credit of the customer concerned. If the customer, by a cheque or a series of cheques, withdraws this amount, the payment is made to somebody. These cheques, in their turn, come back either to the same bank or to other banks of the country or locality. They appear as deposits in the credit of the various people to whom the payments were made. Thus, it is that **"loans create deposits."** That is why it is said that in modern times, **deposits of cash have changed into deposits of credit.**

(*c*) Discounting Bills. Discounting of bills is, practically speaking, lending for short periods. A trader, for instance, who does not wish to lock up large funds in trade credits, may draw a bill of exchange on his debtor, and , after it has been accepted by ,or on behalf of, the debtor, he may get it discounted by his banker. This gives the trader immediate possession of the money due to him less a deduction for the loss of interest and for the commission to the bank. These bills are usually for three months, and when they mature, the bank realises the face value of the bills. Thus, the bank earns a profit in addition to facilitating trade. These bills mature after short periods, and if the worst happens, they can be rediscounted at the central bank.

This is a common way of keeping a part of the assets of the bank in a liquid form. The bankers regard discounting of bills as a very good investment. That is why it is remarked that a good bank manager knows the difference between a bill and a mortgage. In modern times, trade bills occupy a very small position in the discount market as compared with Treasury Bills.

Summing Up. The main functions of the banks can be summed up in one sentence: **The banks borrow to lend.** They borrow in the form of deposits, *viz*., (*a*) Fixed Deposits, (*b*) Savings Bank Deposits, and (*c*) Current Deposits in Accounts. The banks lend in three ways: (*a*) on open account for overdraft; (*b*) loans on the cash credit basis; and (*c*) discounting of bills.

The banks borrow short and lend long. Their liabilities mature earlier than their loans. Their liabilities are money and their assets partly money and partly near-money. The interest they have to pay on their liabilities is, therefore, less than what they earn on their assets. "The nearer to money that near-money is, the lower is the income it will yield. The further away from money the higher is the yield."[2]

Other Services. Apart from the above main functions, the banks perform a number of other services for the clients: They help in the transfer of funds from one place to another and from one person to another through the use of cheques. Some banks **accept** bills on behalf of their clients and thus make them more easily negotiable. They also supply information and advice to their clients on matters relating to investment. In addition, they perform miscellaneous services like taking charge of valuables and securities, acting as agents, trustees and bailees of their customers, purchasing and selling stocks and shares on their behalf, and making sundry payments on behalf of their customers, *e.g*., paying rent, insurance premium, subscriptions to clubs and charitable institutions at regular intervals. *etc*.

CREATION OF CREDIT

Creation of credit is one of the most important functions of a modern bank. A bank has sometimes been called a factory for the manufacture of credit. Let us see what we mean by credit creation, how it is created by the banks and, finally, whether the power of the banks to create credit is absolute and unlimited or whether it is subject to certain limitations.

How Banks Create Credit

Banks create credit in two ways:

(*i*) By advancing loans.

(*ii*) By purchasing securities.

A bank deposit is created entirely by the banking system. Every advance made by the bank creates a corresponding deposit. In fact, the two things happen simultaneously. The granting of a loan results in creation of deposit.

2. Crowther. G. –*An Outline of Money*, 1950. p. 66.

It is an open secret that the banks do no keep cent per cent reserve against deposits in order to meet the demands of depositors. **The bank is not a cloak room** where you can keep your currency notes or coins and claim those very notes or coin back when you desire. It is generally understood that deposits received by the bank are meant to be advanced to others. A depositor has to be content simply with the bank's promise or undertaking to pay him whenever he makes a demand. Thus the banks are able to do with a very small reserve, because all the depositors do not come to withdraw money simultaneously; some withdraw, while others deposit at the same time.

Thus, the bank is enabled to erect a vast superstructure of credit on the basis of a small cash reserve. The bank is able to lend money and charge interest without parting with cash. The bank loan creates a deposit, as we have seen above, or it creates a credit for the borrower.

Similarly, the bank buys securities and pays the seller with its own cheque which again is no cash; it is just a promise to pay cash. The cheque is deposited in some bank and a deposit is created or credit is created for the seller of the securities. This is credit creation. Also, when a bank discounts a bill of exchange, it is seldom that the amount is paid in cash; instead the customer's account is credited with the amount. This is creating credit.

Thus, every time that a bank acquires an earning asset whether by advances or investments, it creates a deposit (or credit) in the name of the person or institution from whom. the asset has been acquired.

The term 'credit creation' implies a situation, to use Benham's words, when "a bank may receive interest simply by permitting customers to overdraw their accounts or by purchasing securities and paying for them with its own cheques, thus increasing the total bank deposits."[3]

Process of Credit Creation

Let us see the actual process. Suppose a customer deposits Rs. 1,000 in a bank. The bank has to pay him interest; therefore, the bank must seek a safe and profitable investment for this amount. It must lend it to somebody. But this amount is not actually paid out to the borrower; on the other hand, it is retained by the bank to meet its obligations, *i.e.*, to pay to those of its depositors who need cash and draw cheques for the purpose. The banker's experience tells him that for this purpose only a certain percentage of cash reserve to total liabilities need be kept In countries like England, they keep nearly 10 per cent. The ratio of cash to liabilities is much higher in countries like India, where banking habit has not yet fully developed.

Suppose the bank, in which a depositor has deposited Rs. 1,000, keeps 20 per cent cash reserve to meet the demands of depositors. This means that as soon as the bank has received Rs. 1,000, it will make up its mind to advance loans up to the amount of Rs. 5,000 (only one-fifth reserve is kept). When, therefore, a businessman comes to the bank with a request for a loan of Rs. 5,000, he may be sure of being granted accommodation to this extent, provided, of course, his credit is good. The bank would have liabilities of Rs. 5,000, although it has only Rs. 1,000 in cash. It is here that credit comes in.

Credit Creation.

This transaction is rendered possible, because the borrower is not given the loan in cash; only an account is opened in his name and/or the amount is credited to that account. He is simply given a cheque book, *i.e.*, the right to draw cheques as and when he needs money. Even when he withdraws cash, it may be deposited in another bank, for businessmen do not raise funds to keep them locked up in a cash box but to run their business and to make payments to their creditors. When this particular businessman draws cheques on this bank to pay his creditors, these cheques are passed on by them to their own banks, where the amount is deposited in their accounts. Cash is seldom withdrawn. The banks settle their mutual obligations through a system of bank clearing. Thus, the bank has succeeded in creating a credit of Rs. 5,000 against a cash reserve of Rs. 1,000.

But the process of credit creation does not stop here. The banks generally keep their spare cash into the central bank. A portion of Rs. 1,000, therefore, is deposited in the central bank which in its turn uses it as a basis for similarly creating further credit. Just as the banks go on creating credit (*i.e.*, advancing loans on cash credit) all the time relying on their cash balances with the central bank, in the same manner the branch banks go on accommodating their local customers relying on the resources of the head office. The movement of credit creation thus goes apace. This is one way of creating credit.

3. *Economics*, 1940, p. 354.

The second way of creating credit is very simple. The bank can purchase securities without paying any cash. It issues its own cheque to pay the purchase price. The cheque is deposited in this bank or some other bank and the small cash reserve which the bank keeps is sufficient to meet the obligation arising from this transaction too.

It is thus that, on a small cash foundation, a vast superstructure of credit is built up.

Process of Credit Creation

New Deposits /Primary „	Demand Deposits	Derivative or secondary deposits (Loans)
1000	200	800
800	160	640
640	128	512
512	102.4	409.6
—	—	—
—	—	—
—	—	—
5000	1000	4000

$\bar{k}$ = money multiplier

$\bar{k} = \frac{1}{r}$ where r = the rate of demand deposit which the banks keep to meet the cash needs of deposits. In the above case, $r = 20\%$.

$$\bar{k} = \frac{1}{r} = \frac{1}{\frac{20}{100}} = \frac{1}{\frac{1}{5}} = 5$$

$$\therefore \quad \bar{k} = 5$$

If the government changes the money supply (ΔM) = 1000 crores. Then, through banking system.

$\therefore \quad \Delta D = \Delta m \,.\, \bar{k}$

$\therefore \quad \Delta D$ = aggregate money supply or total demand

$\therefore \quad \Delta D$ = 1000 crore's × 5

ΔD = 5000 crore's.

Limitations

From the account of credit creation given above, it would seem that **"the banks reap where they have not sown.'** They advance loans or buy securities without actually paying cash. But they earn interest on the loans they give or earn dividends on the securities they purchase all the same. This is very tempting. They make profits without investing cash. They would, of course, like to make as much profits like this as they can. But they cannot go on expanding credit indefinitely. In their own interest, they have to apply the brake, and they do actually apply it, for it is well known that the profits made by the banks are not very high. **The overriding limitation arises from the obligation of the banks to meet the demands of their depositors.**

Benham has mentioned three limitations on the powers of the banks to create credit:

(*i*) The total amount of cash in the country;

(*ii*) The amount of cash which the public wishes to hold, *i.e.*, the ratio in which the public wishes to hold bank notes and bank deposits; and

(*iii*) The minimum percentage of cash to deposits which the banks consider safe, *i.e.*, the reserve ratio.

As for (*i*) it may be said that credit can be created only on the basis of cash. The larger the cash (*i.e.*, legal tender money) the larger the amount of credit that can be created assuming no change in (*ii*). But the amount of cash that a bank may have is subject to the control of the central bank or it depends on the monetary policy of the Central bank. We shall study this influences in full in the next chapter. Here it may suffice to say that the central bank has the monopoly of issue of cash. It may increase it or decrease it, and credit will expand or contract accordingly. The Central bank can also influence the amount of cash in the country through open market operations (to be discussed later). It can increase cash with the commercial banks by purchasing securities and reduce it by selling securities. Thus, the power of the central bank to control currency is the controlling influence on the extent of credit that the banks can create.

The second limitation arises from the habit of the people regarding the use of cash. If people are in the habit of using cash and not cheques, as in India, then as soon as credit is sanctioned by the bank to a borrower, he will draw a cheque and get cash. When the bank's cash reserve is thus reduced, its power to create credit is correspondingly reduced. On the other hand, if people use cash only for very small and odd transactions, then the cash reserve of the banks is not much drawn upon, and their power of creating credit remains unimpaired. This is the case in advanced countries like the U.S.A., the U.K. and other European countries. There the banks hardly keep 10 per cent cash reserve.

The third limitation is the most important. It arises from the traditional reserve ratio of cash to liabilities, which the banks must maintain to ensure their safety and to retain the degree of liquidity that is considered desirable. It is clear that when a bank creates a credit or sanctions a loan, it undertakes a liability. There is an increase in its liabilities and there is correspondingly a fall in the reserve ratio. The bank will not let the ratio fall below a certain minimum. When that minimum is reached, the power of the bank to create further credit comes to an end. To grant any further credit will be risky unless the bank's experience is reassuring enough to permit the adoption of a lower cash ratio. Then that would be the limit.

To these may be added the fourth limitation. The bank cannot create credit without acquiring assets (in this case the borrower's promise to pay on some security). An asset is a form of wealth. Thus, the bank only turns immobile wealth into mobile wealth. Hence, as Crowther observes, **"the bank does not create money out of thin air, it transmutes other forms of wealth into money."**[4]

To Sum Up: The essential conditions for the creation of credit are that the banks obtain fresh cash reserves, they should be willing to lend and the businessmen should be willing to borrow, and the borrowers should not withdraw the amount of the loan but be content to leave it in the form of deposit with the bank. The initiative is in the hands of the borrowers .The deposit is, in fact, created not by the amount borrowed but by the amount not withdrawn.

Significance of Credit Creation

Credit creation vitally affects the level of economic activity (and hence national income, output and employment) in the country. It is no wonder that the policy pursued by the monetary authority in the country is directed to the control of credit expansion or contraction. Left to itself, credit expansion or contraction may 'boom the booms' and 'depress the depressions.' Thus, credit creation has a lot to do with the cyclical fluctuations in the economy.

In the case of under-developed economies, credit creation has to be controlled to ensure economic growth with stability. It can be easily understood that when credit is unduly created, prices rise and wages rise along with. Inflationary situation is inimical to economic growth. Similarly, credit contraction is injurious, as it slows down economic growth because entrepreneurs are deprived of the necessary funds. Hence, the monetary authority pursues a policy of controlled expansion of credit to ensure growth with stability.

Thus, since money supply in the country depends on the volume of credit created, credit creation plays a vital role in determining the level of national income and volume of employment in the country.

4. *Op cit.*, p. 30.

Money tree.

Investment Policy: Liquidity vs. Profitability

A bank exists to make profit. Its investment policy is, therefore, mainly governed by the profit motive. But a bank is a very sensitive institution and must always keep in view its own security. 'Safety first' is the rule and subject to this, the bank must try to make maximum profit. Thus, profitability and safety (*i.e.*, liquidity) are the two considerations governing a bank's investment, although it is not easy to reconcile them.

If the bank management is more keen on making profits, it may invest its funds in lines which are highly remunerative but which may not be converted into cash quickly when the need arises. On the other hand, if the bank is swayed only by safety considerations, it may not earn much profit because safe investments are generally not very remunerative.

The secret of sound banking consists in the maintenance of adequate reserves, while at the same time making profits. A bank, we have seen, deals with other people's money (*i.e.*, deposits) and the money can be withdrawn with or without notice. They must, therefore, maintain adequate reserves to meet this demand and make profit by lending the rest. A wise banker must maintain a proper balance between liquidity and profitability. Too much caution will mean too little profit, while reckless lending may endanger the safety of the bank itself.

The liquidity and profitability are opposing considerations. There has to be a compromise, but it is an uneasy compromise. Because whatever the form and quantity in which the banks keep their reserve, they are found to be unnecessary in normal times and insufficient when the depositors' confidence is shaken.

In order to ensure liquidity for their own safety, a bank must keep adequate reserve. The amount of reserve kept by a bank is governed, among others, by three factors [5] : (*a*) day-to-day fluctuation in the amount of bank's deposits; (*b*) the variability of the customer's borrowing needs; and (*c*) the nature of secondary reserves, and the character of reserve organisation in the banking system.

Importance of Liquidity. The proportion in which the various forms of assets are kept vary from country to country, from bank to bank, and vary also with the state of trade .The larger the 'liquidity' of the assets, the more confidence will a bank inspire, but the lower will be its profits.

The whole banking business rests on the confidence of the people in the ability of the bank to pay their money back on demand. If such confidence is shaken for any reason, there is a 'run' on the bank. No bank can face a run because all the assets of the bank are not in liquid form.

Banking business is said to be a 'fair weather' business. So long as the skies are sunny, *i.e.*, so long as the depositors are happy with the bank and nobody wants to withdraw his money, the bank says, "Anybody can have his money back." But as soon as the skies are overcast and the depositors get nervous and all depositors wish to take out their money, then none can have it. If there is only a single patch of colour on the sky, *i.e.*, if only one bank is involved in a run, it may perhaps be able to meet its liabilities by converting its assets into cash. But if the whole atmosphere is gloomy, and there is a general panic, depositors of all banks will have to go disappointed.

Thus, it is necessary for a bank not only to keep a certain proportion of its assets liquid, but also to see that people's confidence in its soundness is not shaken. Bankers must take into account a certain degree of proclivity on the part of the depositors. When they know they can have their money back, they do not have it, and as soon as they suspect they cannot have it, they insist on having it. The best way to inspire confidence is freely to give credits in times of panic. Central banks also come to the help of other banks on such occasions.

Bank Balance Sheet

To keep the people informed of their financial position, the banks are required by law to publish their accounts in the form of what is called a "Balance Sheet". A bank's balance sheet is a statement of its financial position. Usually such a statement is issued at the end of the financial year. The central bank, however, issues it weekly. The balance sheet is a mirror that reflects the financial position of the bank.

The balance sheet consists of two columns. The column on the left hand side gives the liabilities of the bank. The liabilities include capital and Reserve Fund which the bank owes to the shareholders .Then there are deposits which belong to the depositors and the bank is liable to meet their demands. On the right side of the bank balance sheet are given the assets , *e.g.*, cash in hand, cash at the central bank, money lent at call, bills discounted for which the persons whose bills have been discounted are liable, and finally furniture and other property that the bank owns.

The Bank Balance Sheet is usually given in the following form:–

Liabilities	*Assets*
Capital	Cash
Reserve Fund	Cash at Central Bank
Deposits	Money at Call
Acceptance for Customers	Bill discounted
(*as per contra*)	Investment
	Liabilities of Customers for Acceptance (*as per contra*)
	Furniture and Fittings
	Premises and other Property

Usually a bank keeps its assets in descending order of liquidity or realisability into cash. Its first line of defence, as the term goes, is to maintain a certain amount in ready cash. This cash is kept either in the form of coins or in the form of currency notes or as a balance with the central bank.

The balance with the central bank can always be withdrawn in the form of legal tender currency. The banks thus treat such balance as cash. All major banks, either by law or by convention, keep a certain proportion of their liabilities in the form of balances with the central bank of the country. It may be incidentally mentioned that the existence of such balances gives the central bank a power over other banks of the country in the matter of controlling the credit expansion by the latter.

The second line of defence in maintaining reserves is the money lent for very short periods, technically

5. Kilborne and Woodworth–*Principle of Money and Banking*, 1937, p. 291.

called in England money 'at call and at short notice.' This is mainly lent to discount houses, bill brokers and petty stock brokers. Such loans can be recalled either on demand or within a few days.

After this come the bills discounted. These become liquid as they mature. These may be Treasury Bills issued by the Government or commercial bills.

Then come investments. These are mainly government securities. The fixed interest-yielding securities also called "gilt-edged" securities in England, are most popular with the banks, since there is practically no risk in such investments.

Then come advances to customers. They may take the form of loans or overdrafts. They bring the highest profits, though the risk is the greatest in their case, since they are the least liquid.

In the balance-sheet, the banks are anxious to show that their position is very sound. This they can do by keeping a big cash reserve or higher ratio of reserve to liabilities. For this purpose, they call back, on the eve of the preparation of the balance sheet, the amounts lent on call or at short notice on the understanding, that they may be re-lent the next day. These efforts at putting up a good show are called "window dressing".

Utility of Banks

It should be clear by this time the banks are extremely useful, nay indispensable, for a modern community. "Bankers are the custodians and distributors of the liquid capital, which is the life-blood of our commercial and industrial activities; and upon the prudence of their administration depends the economic well-being of the nation."[6] More concretely we may summarise the uses of banks as follows:

(*i*) The banks create purchasing power in the form of bank notes (*e.g.*, central bank currency notes) cheques, bills and drafts and thus economise the use of metallic money which is very expensive.

Banks promote capital formation.

(*ii*) They make money more mobile, by bringing lenders and borrowers together and by helping funds to move from place to place and from person to person in a convenient and inexpensive manner, through the use of cheques, bills and drafts. In this way, they help trade and industry.

(*iii*) The banks encourage the habit of saving among the people and enable small savings, which otherwise would have been scattered ineffectively, to be accumulated into large funds and thus made available for investments of various kinds. In this way, they promote economic development through capital formation.

(*iv*) By encouraging savings and investment, the banks increase the productivity of the resources of the country and thus contribute to general prosperity and welfare by promoting economic development.

(*v*) The bank's agency functions are very useful to the customers of the bank. They undertake to make petty payments of various kinds on behalf of their customers and also make several types of collections on their behalf.

Thus, the banks are useful not only to the community in general but also to the individual customers.

There are special functions of very great importance that are performed by the central bank of a country to the study of which we shall direct our attention in the next chapter.

Role of Banks in Economic Development

Banks play a vital role in economic development of under-developed economies in several ways:

(*i*) Banks Promote Capital Formation. In any plan of economic development, capital occupies a position of crucial and strategic importance. No economic development of sizable magnitude is possible unless there is an adequate degree of capital formation in the country. A very important trait of an under developed economy is deficiency of capital which is due to small saving made by the community. Backward economies hardly save 5 per cent of the

6. Stephenson and Branton –*Economics of Banking Trade and Finance*. p. 180.

national income, whereas they should save and invest at least 12 per cent in order to secure a reasonable level of development. In 1950, Colin Clark estimating the capital needs of China, India and Pakistan pointed out that they must save 12.5 per cent of the national income to absorb the increasing labour force and maintain the past rate of increase in productivity.

In the under-developed countries, not only is the capital stock extremely small but, as pointed out above, the current rate of capital formation is also very low. For example, in India and Pakistan, gross investment is only 6-7 per cent of gross national product and in Indonesia only 5 per cent, whereas in the United States, Canada and Western Europe it is 15-18 per cent. A small rate of saving (5-6 per cent) does not permit large investment in new industries. In fact, in economically backward countries, the amount of net capital formation is hardly sufficient to provide the growing population with a constant per capita equipment. Thus, the serious capital deficiency in under-developed countries is reflected in the small amount of capital equipment per worker and in limited knowledge, training and scientific advance. These are serious handicaps in economic development and they all arise from capital deficiency and the banks can play a useful role in making up the deficiency.

The role of the banks in economic development is to remove the deficiency of capital by stimulating savings and investment. A sound banking system mobilises the small and scattered savings of the people and makes them available for investment in productive enterprises. In this connection, the banks perform two important functions: (*a*) they attract deposits by offering attractive rates of interest, thus converting savings which otherwise would have remained inert into active capital, and (*b*) they distribute these savings through loans among enterprises which are connected with economic development.

(*ii*) Optimum Utilisation of Resources. It is difficult to see how, in the absence of banks, could small savings of the people be mobilised or even made possible. It is also difficult to see who would distribute these savings among entrepreneurs. It is through the agency of the banks that the community's savings automatically flow into channels which are productive. The banks exercise a degree of discrimination which not only ensures their own safety but which makes for optimum utilisation of the financial resources of the community. We see in India that the period of economic development has coincided with a phenomenal increase in bank deposits and increasing advances for agricultural and industrial development.

(*iii*) Banks Finance Priority Sectors. In order to meet additional demands arising out of economic development, the banking system has to undergo certain changes in its structure and organisation. The banks and other financial institutions must operate in such a manner as to conform to the priorities of development and not in terms of return on their capital. The banks have now to play a more positive role. Thus, the central bank is not merely to content itself with its regulatory role, *i.e.*, regulation of bank credit. It must play a developmental role. It must create or help to create a machinery or agencies for financing development plans. It must ensure that the available finance is diverted to the right channels. For successful implementation of the development programmes it becomes necessary to make credit facilities available to high priority sectors and to see that the available funds are not squandered a way in non-essential or non-plan expenditure.

(*iv*) Banks Promote Balanced Regional Development. By opening branches in backward areas, the banks make credit facilities available there. Also, the funds collected in developed regions through deposits may be channelised for investment in the under-developed regions of the country. In this way, they bring about more balanced regional development.

(*v*) Expansion of Credit. It is recognised that to maintain a high level of economic activity, credit must expand. In an era of economic development, banks create credit more liberally and thus make funds available for the development projects. In this way, the banks make a valuable contribution to the speed and the level of economic development in the country.

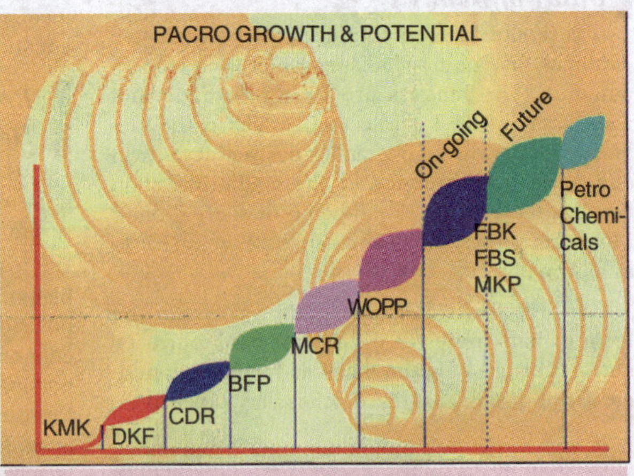

Banks promote growth with stability.

***(vi)* Banks Promote Growth with Stability.** Through their influence on the rate of interest, the banks can regulate the rate of investment. If cheap money is helping development at too great a speed , they will raise interest rates under the direction of the central bank. On the other hand, they can encourage investment when the speed of development has slowed down. In this way, the banks promote growth with stability.

In India, the primary function of the Reserve Bank of India was to regulate the issue of bank notes and keep adequate reserves to ensure monetary stability. But now it has assumed wider responsibility to help in the task of economic development. In addition to the traditional responsibility of regulating currency and controlling credit, the Reserve Bank of India has been playing a vital role in financing and supervision of the development programmes for agriculture, trade, transport and industry. It has created special funds for promoting agricultural credit and it has created special institutions for widening facilities for industrial finance. The other banks too readily fall in line. They open new branches to tap the savings of the people and lend them to entrepreneurs. An increasing degree of control is exercised in respect of management, financing and development of banks so that they do not sabotage the development programmes but are made to further these programmes.

Conclusion. Thus, the banks come to play a dominant and useful role in promoting economic development by mobilising the financial resources of the community and by making them flow into desired channels.

A NOTE ON NON-BANKING FINANCIAL INTERMEDIARIES (NBFIS)

We have studied banks and their functions. Besides the banks there are other financial institutions too which practically perform the same functions (*e.g.* deposit mobilisation and advancing loans as the banks but in a different way. These are the non-banking financial institutions.

Meaning. The NBFIs are just intermediaries or middlemen transferring funds from ultimate lenders to ultimate borrowers .The financial intermediaries obtain funds by issuing to the public their own liabilities (*e.g.*, saving deposits and loan shares) and then use this money to buy financial assets (stocks, bonds and mortgages) for themselves. In this way, the financial intermediaries 'intermediate' between original savers and final borrowers.

Functions of the NBFIs

The following are the main functions performed by the NBFIs –

(i) They produce and provide near money and not money.

(ii) They provide liquid assets to the community, because their liabilities are close substitutes for money.

(iii) They pass on savings to ultimate investors and issue indirect securities to the ultimate savers in return for savings.

(iv) They create loanable funds or add to their net supply by mobilising existing money balances in exchange for their own newly, issued financial claims or liabilities.

A note on innovation in banking sector

Commercial banks are financial intermediaries, with the sole objective of making profits. In 1969 Mrs. Indira Gandhi all of a sudden on 19-07-1969 announced the take-over (nationalisation) of commercial banks. Then the objectives were of two fold, *(i)* Profit making and *(ii)* development oriented. In a socialistic pattern of society the government aims at maximisation of total welfare of people including both economic as well as non-economic. The nationalisation of banks were essentially to over-come certain demerits as well as direct towards social commitment of commercial banks. In the late ninetees due to Narasimhan Committee Report as well as the so called liberalisation and globalisation policy the government initiated the process of privatisation as well as allowing foreign and Indian participation in the government owned banks and non-bank financial institutions. Capitalistic economies main base is profit

ATM–Innovation in Banking.

and business, whether they create social benefits or brings about huge inequalities. This brings about conflicting question in the academic circles. (*i*) Whether the government is moving away from social responsibilities ? [In terms of providing employment, priority lending, reduction in inequalities *etc*]. (*ii*) Is 'profit' the main criteria of judging the efficiency of a banking institution in a country like India ? and (*iii*) The future of monetary economics ?

In modern day banking sector, new methods of financial activities have been introduced. Commercial banks are concentrating more on secondary function, Commercial banks investment in stock-exchange (de-mat banking) *etc.*, ATM (Automated Teller Machine), drafts, credit cards, lockers, safe deposits vaults, e-banking etc., are the new ways and means to enlarge banking business. This is essentially increasing indirectly or directly the employment opportunities, but this may be of a temporary nature and is based on the success and future of monetary economics. The commercial banks have neglected the importance of providing direct employment with the excuse of bringing about modernisation as well as profit as the main criteria of judging the efficiency of the banks. The government can increase employment opportunities in this sector by bringing about certain reforms which may induce the staff to increase their efficiency.

'Profit' should not be the basis of judging the efficiency of a bank. If banks are creating more deposits or enlarging the banking habits among the masses and helping a larger section of the people in their economic activities, which may bring either directly or indirectly the economic activities. Further more studies are required to justify this point.

No economic policy is of a permanent nature. In the past, in 1930's monetary economies collapsed. Then emerged the fiscal economic policy of pump-priming. Many countries governments are following deficit finance or functional finance approach to redress their economic problems. This has led to increase in fiscal imbalances and specially the developing countries are at the mercy of international monetary institutions. In recent years after the GATT proposals and the emergence of WTO, the monetary economics has taken the front seat, which at present taking the economies into that direction which does not know its destination. There is a need for consenses among the economic policy makers to assess the real picture of economic course in future and envolve a policy which may help, rather than create problem for the economies.

Key terms

Deposits, Bills of exchange, Credit creation, Liquidity, Profitabiliy, Balance sheet of commercial Bank, NBFI.

QUESTIONS

1. What are the main functins of banks? Explain the role played by commercial banks in the economic development of a country.
2. What are the functions of nationalised commercial banks in a mixed Economy?
3. What is meant by 'liquidity' of commercial banks? How does a commercial bank achieve it?
4. Describe the principles underlying the distribution of assests of a commercial bank.
5. How do commercial banks reconcile the conflicting aimes of Liquidity and Profitability in their operations?
6. How does a bank create credit? Examine the limitations on the power of a bank to create credit.
7. Do you agree with the view that every loan creates a deposit? Give reasons for your answer.
8. what is meant by the net liquidity ratio of commercial banks? Discuss its role in the process of expansion of money supply and the mechanism of credit control by the central bank.
9. "Banks are not merely traders in money but also in an important sence manufacturers of money". (Sayers.) Comment.
10. Write an explainatory note on innovation in banking.
11. "Loans are children of deposits and deposits are children of loans". Explain.

CENTRAL BANKING

Importance of Central Bank

Now every country has a central bank. It is a symbol of financial sovereignty and stability of the country. A central bank is an institution which is responsible for safeguarding the financial stability of the country. It holds the ultimate reserves of the nation, controls the flow of purchasing power –whether currency or credit–and acts as a banker to the State.

In recent years, the importance of central banks has enormously increased. This has been due to various causes: the growing interdependence of economic life within and between countries; the greater necessity of management and control of currency system; he post-war (1914-18) confusion in currency and exchange matters; the Great Depression and realisation that control over supply of money through central banks could avoid to a large degree cyclical fluctuations; and the element of planning and regulation that has been introduced in the economic systems of various countries in recent years. All these have increased the importance of an institution which could co-ordinate, control and manage the various complicated and conflicting factors, economic and financial, which affect the economic stability in the national and international field.

Reserve Bank of India

Reserve Bank of India, Mumbai.

CENTRAL BANKING PRINCIPLES

The principles on which a central bank is run are quite different from the ordinary banking principles:

(i) An ordinary bank is run for profit. A central bank, on the other hand, is primarily meant to shoulder the responsibility of safe guarding the financial and economic stability of the country. "The guiding principle of a central bank," says De Kock, "is that it should act only in the public interest and for the welfare of the country as a whole and without regard to profit as primary consideration."[1] Earning of profit for a central bank is thus a secondary consideration.

1. *Central Banking*.

(ii) Since the central bank is not a profit or dividend-hunting institution, it does not act as a rival of other banking institutions. That is why it seldom allows interest on deposits nor can it advance money against the security of immovable property or grant unsecured overdrafts. It is primarily concerned with the maintenance of the solvency of the entire banking system of the country. It must, therefore, keep its own assets as liquid as possible.

(iii) The central bank is a reservoir of credit and a lender of last resort. All other banks and financial houses can look to it for accommodation, of course, at a price. But the central bank cannot rely on any other institution to come to its aid and give it cash or take bills and securities off its hands.

(iv) The central bank must follow an active policy. It should not be merely an idle spectator when something goes wrong with the credit machinery of the nation. It must take active steps to remedy the situation. For this purpose, it may resort to two weapons: (*a*) the manipulation of the bank rate policy; (*b*) the open market operations. Their working is explained the sections below. It may also adopt other measures of credit control, general or selective credit controls.

(v) For the efficient discharge of its functions, the central bank is provided with special equipment: (*a*) It is given the monopoly of the note issue. (*b*) It is made a banker to the government. (*c*) It is a bankers' bank. With the position so acquired, it can effectively control currency and credit, and this control is the raison d'tere of a central bank.

(vi) Finally, a central bank should not be subservient to any political party. It must be independent of all political influence, so that it can act freely, without fear or favour, in the best interests of the nation as a whole. However, there is usually very close co-operation between the government and the bank.

FUNCTIONS OF CENTRAL BANKS

What functions are more characteristically the central banking functions has been widely discussed question among economists. Hawtrey thinks that it should primarily be the "lender of last resort." Vera Smith stresses the monopoly of note issue and Shaw regards control of credit as "the one true, but at the same time all sufficing, function of a central bank." Kisch and Elkins[2] regard "the maintenance of the stability of the monetary standard" as the essential function of central bank. It is, however, difficult to single out any particular function as characteristic of a central bank.

Broadly put, a central bank acts in the following capacities:–

(i) As the note-issuing agency;

(ii) as the banker to the State;

(iii) as the bankers' bank;

(iv) as the guardian of the money market, through control of credit;

(v) as the lender of last resort;

(vi) it undertakes to maintain the external value of the domestic currency;

(vii) it ensures the stability of the internal value of the currency, *i.e.*, the price level;

(viii) it undertakes exchange control operations, &

(ix) it fights economic crises and fluctuations and ensures economic stability of the country.

Above are given what are known as the traditional functions of a Central Bank. In the advanced countries of the West, it is these functions which their central banks have been performing. Largely these functions are regulatory in nature. In the under-developed countries, however, whose main concern is to accelerate development of their economic potentialities, the Central Banks have a special role to play, which is not merely regulatory to maintain stability, but developmental and promotional. This latter role is discussed at length in the last section of the present chapter.

We shall now proceed to consider some of these functions in some detail.

Note-Issuing Agency

In the early periods of banking development, almost every bank enjoyed the right of issuing notes. This led to frequent troubles. Notes were over-issued and the resulting inflation disorganized the currency system and brought other serious economic and financial consequences. The government, therefore, had to exercise strict control over the issuing of notes. Grdually, the practice of entrusting this important function to the chief bank of the country, the central bank, became established. Now, in almost every country ,the central bank enjoys a monopoly of note issue. Such a monopoly is of great importance. It gives uniformity to the system of note-issue. Moreover, the notes of a central bank have greater prestige and even

2. *Central Banks*, p. 74.

in times of shaken confidence, are seldom presented for encashment into coins or metal. Above all, this monopoly gives the central bank control over other banks in the matter of expansion of credit, since it is the cash reserve which constitutes the ultimate limit of such expansion.

(The various systems of note-issue have already been given in Chapter 49).

Banker of the State

The second important function of a central bank is to act as a banker to the government. **All the balances of the government of the country are kept with the central bank.** On these balances, usually the central bank pays no interest. On the other hand, the bank performs a number of services to the government. Generally speaking, it is the fiscal agent of the government, and advises the latter in matters relating to currency and exchange as well as finance. It carries out their exchange, remittance and other bank operations including the management of public debt. "Central banks everywhere operate as bankers to the State not only because it may be more convenient and economical to the State, but also because of the intimate connection between public finance and monetary affairs."

Currency notes of India.

An important function of the central bank with respect to the State is the **provision of short-term loans.** This is usually done through the central bank discounting the government treasury bills either directly or when presented by other banks. This is to enable the government to meet its current financial obligations in anticipation of its revenues.

During times of crisis like a war, such lending to the government can lend to serious inflation as happened in the case of France, Germany and elsewhere in Europe during and after the war of 114-18. "History is full of examples," says De Kock, "of inflation and currency depreciation resulting from credit creation on behalf of the State. In fact, experience has shown that heavy government borrowing either directly from the central bank or indirectly through rediscount, is the easiest means, and sometimes the only means, of bringing about substantial inflation."[3]

When a central Bank gives advances to the government against treasury bills or other government securities, the money spent by government is again deposited with commercial banks by those who receive payments. This, in fact, means an increase in the commercial banks' balances with the central bank which, as we have seen, are as good as cash. On the basis of this cash, the commercial banks are able to increase their loans and advances. Thus, inflation starts.

Bankers' Bank

Broadly speaking, the central bank acts as a banker's bank in three capacities: (*i*) As the custodian of the cash reserves of the commercial banks; (*ii*) as the lender of last resort; and (*iii*) as a bank of central clearance, settlement and transfers.

(*i*) Custodian of the Cash Reserves of Commercial Banks. The practice of the commercial banks of keeping their cash reserves with the central bank developed slowly and it has been closely associated with the functions of the central banks as the bank of issue and as banker to the government. It was convenient to keep cash reserves with the central bank, because its notes commanded the greatest confidence, and also because government's banking transactions took place through this institution. Originally, keeping of cash with the central bank was optional; later on, in most countries, it was made a statutory obligation.

The practice has many advantages: First, it economists cash. The nation's cash can be more

3. De Kock–*Op. cit.*, p. 64

Lender of Last resort.

effectively used when centralised than when scattered in the vaults of numerous banks. Secondly, it enables commercial banks to increase their reserves merely by discounting bills with the central bank in times of need instead of having to rely upon their own resources. Thirdly, it gives the central bank control over the credit policies of the member-banks as we shall presently see.

***(ii)* Lender of Last Resort.** The central bank is the lender of last resort to the commercial banks. When the commercial banks have exhausted their own resources and have failed to supplement their funds from the usual outside resources, the central bank is called upon to function as the lender of last resort. It acts in this capacity mainly through its rediscount operations.

In the narrow sense, rediscounting is applied only to first class trade and agricultural bills brought to the central bank by commercial banks and bill dealers or brokers, who are temporarily in need of funds and want to convert some of their short-term assets into cash. In the wider sense, as now current in most countries, rediscounting is defined as "the conversion directly or indirectly of commercial bank credit into additional central bank credit."[4] Redis counting is thus applied also to treasury bills and to short-term collateral loans to banks and other financial institutions made by the central bank against bills or promissory notes and government securities.

4. De Kock –*Op. cit*., p. 106.

Rediscounting facility enables commercial banks to carry on their day-to-day business on smaller cash reserves, since they can always rely upon the central bank in times of crisis. It gives increased elasticity and liquidity to the assets of the commercial banks.

Rediscounting, however, should not be abused. It should be resorted to only in times of emergencies and not in times of normal business activity. The central bank, in its turn, should be ready to help in times of distress, but should be less liberal in ordinary times. This is necessary to encourage self-reliance among commercial banks and to conserve the strength of the central bank for emergencies.

***(iii)* Clearing and Settlement.** The central clearing function is performed by all central banks. In some countries, it is merely a matter of tradition or convenience, in others it is a duty imposed upon the central bank by law. This is a logical step from the position of the bank as custodian of cash reserves of the commercial banks. Since banks keep cash reserves with the central bank, settlements between them can be easily effected by means of debits and credits in the books of the central bank. In some countries, separate clearing houses are set up to settle mutual obligations between the banks, including the central bank. In such countries, the balances ultimately to be paid can be paid without cash transfers through mere book entries in the accounts of commercial banks with the central bank.

This method of settling accounts, apart from being convenient, is economical as regards the use of cash. It also strengthens the banking system by reducing withdrawals of cash in times of crisis. Moreover, it enables the central bank to be well informed about the state of liquidity being maintained by the commercial banks with regard to their assets. This information helps the central bank in its function of controlling the credit expansion in the country.

Credit Control

The most important function of the central bank is the control credit. The control of credit means the regulation and control of bank advances. It goes without saying that the nature and volume of bank advances have a vital bearing on the state of the economy. There is a time when trade and industry need finance, whereas the banks may feel shy. The central bank must step in to stimulate bank advances. At other times, the banks' lending may assume undesirable proportions or they may be flowing into undesirable proportions or they may be flowing into underisable channels. It is the duty of the central bank to curb these undesirable tendencies by regulating and controlling credit creation by banks.

Cash management and Credit control.

In view of the great importance of the control of credit, we discuss it below at some length.

CONTROL OF CREDIT

Objectives of Credit Control

A central bank controls credit with the following objects in view:

(a) to safeguard its gold reserves against internal and external drains;

(b) to maintain stability of internal prices;

(c) to achieve stability of foreign exchanges;

(d) to eliminate fluctuations in output and employment; and

(e) to assist in economic growth.

This assistance is required not only in under-developed countries desirous of accelerating economic development but also in developed countries desirous of maintaining and improving their living standards.

Now a word about each.

Safeguarding Gold Reserves. The necessity of safeguarding gold reserves arises under a gold standard. In a gold standard country, gold can be freely imported and exported as the currency of the country is convertible by law into gold coin or gold bullion. In such a country, an over-expansion of credit causes inflation. High prices at home first lead to withdrawal of more cash from the banks and then gold from the central bank to carry on transactions at a higher level. This is called the "internal drain."

Secondly, the home price-level being higher than the international price-level, imports are encouraged and exports discouraged. An unfavourable balance of trade is created which has to be met by export of gold .This is called the "external drain."

Gold may also move out because the foreign investors have lost confidence in the future of the currency under question and they begin to withdraw their funds.

In these circumstances, the central bank must take steps to contract credit, bring prices down and stop the internal and external drain of gold.

Now no country is on a gold standard and movement of gold is generally banned. It is now the duty of the central bank to safeguard the foreign exchange reserves of the country.

Price Stability. Another object of credit control is to maintain stability of internal prices. We have already referred to the various disadvantages of fluctuating prices. Price instability causes disturbances in economic relations, maladjustments and serious social consequences. The central bank by regulating the supply of purchasing power, according to the needs of the people, can reduce economic fluctuations to a large extent.

External Stability. In the interest of smooth flow of international trade and for settlement of international obligations, stability of foreign exchange rates is essential. Instability of foreign exchange rate (value of foreign money in terms of home money) disturbs international trade and makes the settlement of international obligations difficult.

There has been considerable controversy as to which of the two objects, *viz*., internal price stability or exchange stability, should the central trade (*e.g.*, India) would concentrate more on internal stability.

Economic Stability. A more recent view rejects the aims both of exchange stability and of internal price stability. It is held that the central **bank** should aim at smoothening out the business cycle, which may not result merely from price movements. The aim should be to maintain a normal steady growth of business activity and prevent booms and slumps.

Regarding the adequacy of the banking policy in this regard, Crowther remarks, "Banking policy will never be sufficient by itself to bring economic utopia into being. Its first task should be to prevent the natural instability of a complex credit system from increasing the amplitude of economic fluctuations. Its second task should be to attempt deliberately to offset some of the causes of disturbance that are beyond its control. But for those causes themselves we must look outside the realm of money."[5] (For detailed discussion see Chapter 58 on Foreign Exchanges).

5. Crowther–*Op. cit*., p. 201.

Difficulties of Credit Control

There are several difficulties in the way of the central bank being able to control credit:

First, bank credit is not the only form of credit. There is commercial credit like book credit, bills of exchange and promissory notes (not discounted by banks). Over these, the central bank has little control. They are as much purchasing power as any other form of credit.

Secondly, even as regards bank credit, all banks of the country do not have direct relations with the central bank. In the U.S.A. for instance, one-half of the commercial banks with one-fifth of resources are outside the Federal Reserve System. In India, the indigenous bankers, accounting for nearly 90 per cent of the banking business in the country, are still beyond the influence of the Reserve Bank.

Thirdly, even if all banks were member-banks, commercial banks may not always co-operate with the central banks and may not follow its lead. Such co-operation, as we shall see, in indispensable for a successful control of credit.

Fourthly, there are non-banking elements in the financial structure of a country. Among these are the various circumstances that affect the temper of the business community. These are beyond the scope of central banking action.

Finally, the central bank cannot control the ultimate use to which credit may be put. Strictly commercial loans, for instance, may be used for speculative purposes.

Conclusion. This, however, does not mean that any attempt to control credit on the part of the central bank is bound to fail. These are the limitations to which the action of the central bank is subject.

METHODS OF CREDIT CONTROL OR INSTRUMENTS OF MONETARY MANAGEMENT

Now we proceed to discuss the methods of credit control, also called the central banking techniques.

There are broadly speaking, two types of controls used by the central banks in modern times for regulating bank advances: (*a*) Quantitative or General Credit Controls and (*b*) Qualitative Controls or the Selective Credit Controls. The aim of the quantitative controls is to regulate the amount of bank advances, *i.e.*, to make the banks lend more or lend less. The object of the selective credit controls is to divert bank advances into certain channels or to discourage them from lending for certain purposes. These selective controls have of late assumed great importance.

The following are the principal methods of credit control used by the central banks in modern times:–

Quantitative or General Controls

(*i*) Manipulation of the Bank Rate;

(*ii*) Open market operations;

(*iii*) Varying reserve requirements;

(*iv*) Credit rationing;

Qualitative or Selective Controls

(*v*) Regulation of consumer credit or regulating volume of instalment credit buying (*a*) by regulating the minimum down payments for specified goods. (*b*) by fixing the coverage of selective consumers' durable goods, (*c*) by regulating the maximum maturities (payment period) on all instalment credit, and (*d*) by fixing the maximum exemption costs of instalment purchases of specified goods;

(*vi*) Varying margin requirements for certain bank advances; and

(*vi*) Issuing directives to restrict certain bank advances.

Let us take these in turn.

General Credit Controls: Manipulation of Bank Rate

The **bank rate** is the rate at which the central bank of a country is willing to discount first class. bills. It is, thus the rate of discount of the central banks, while the market rate is the rate of discount prevailing in the money market among the other lending institutions. Since the central bank is only the lender of the last resort, the bank rate is normally higher than the market rate. The term **'rate of interest'** is the rate which the commercial banks pay to those who keep deposits with them. The banks' **call rate** is the rate at which money is advanced by banks for very short periods to bill brokers, *etc*.

In a perfectly developed money market, all these rates bear a more or less constant relationship with each other. Before World War I, for instance, in England the banks usually fixed their deposit rate. $1\frac{1}{2}$ per cent below the bank rate. The call rate was fixed usually $\frac{1}{2}$ per cent above the deposit rate to enable the banks to have a margin of profit between what they charged and what they paid. The banks charged about 1 per cent above the bank rate on advances to their customers, subject to a minimum of 5 per cent. The relationship between the bank rate and the market rate of discount was determined by the conditions of the money market.

Under such conditions, therefore, if the bank rate was changed all the other rates normally moved in the same direction, though this did not always happen as we shall see.

In countries, where the money market is not so well organised, the relationship between the bank rate and the other rates is not so close. To that extent, therefore, the central bank is unable to influence these other rates by changing its own rate of discount.

Theory of Bank Rate Policy. According to the theory, changes in the bank rate of the central bank are followed by corresponding changes in all the local money rates. If the bank is raised, the market rates and other lending rates of the money market also go up, Conversely, the market rate of discount and the other rates go down when the central bank lowers its bank rate. These changes affect the supply and demand for money. Borrowing is discouraged when the rates go up and encouraged when they go down. In the former case a contraction of credit and in the latter its expansion, is the result.

The flow of foreign short-term capital is also affected. There is an inflow of foreign funds when the rates are raised and an outflow when they are lowered.

Internal price-level tends to fall with the contraction of credit and it tends to rise with its expansion.

Business activity, both commercial and industrial, is stimulated when the rates of interest are low, and discouraged when they are high. An adverse balance of international trade can be corrected through lowering of domestic costs and prices by contraction of credit, since this stimulates exports and discourages import.

Bank Rate Policy under Gold Standard. The theory of this policy is specially adapted to gold standard. It operated most successfully, therefore, in Great Britain before 1914. Under gold standard, an adverse balance of trade is indicated by movement of the exchange rate to the gold export point and outflow of gold. This may be due to excessive export of capital or excessive import of merchandise. Conversely, when the balance of payments[6] is favourable, there is an inflow of gold.

Under such conditions, raising of the bank rate led to contraction of credit. This was followed by greater sale of commodities and securities since their holding became more costly due to higher rates of interest, fall in domestic demand due to fall in the incomes of various groups, decline in new investment and speculation and fall in prices and wages.

The ultimate result was encouragement of exports, inflow of foreign capital, discouragement in the withdrawal of foreign capital, *etc*. In due course, equilibrium was restored and the outflow of gold stopped. If the policy was continued long enough, there would be inflow of gold, thus relieving credit stringency, lowering money rates and reviving business activity.

Thus, the raising of the bank rate has two effects: (*i*) **immediate,** and (*ii*) **ultimate,. Immediately,** borrowing is discouraged as the discounting of bills becomes a costly affair. Money, therefore, does not leave the banks. Instead, funds flow in even from abroad as the raising of the bank rate is followed by the raising of the bankers' deposit rate. **Ultimately,** prices fall through contraction of credit and currency. Exports are stimulated and imports are checked. The objective of raising the bank rate is thus achieved, *viz*., drain of gold out of the country is checked and, instead, gold comes in.

Conversely, if there was a continued inflow of gold, the central bank would lower the bank rate. This would cheapen money and encourage expansion of credit, trade, production, investment and speculation. It would raise domestic prices and costs, encourage imports and discourage exports. Investment in foreign countries would be encouraged. If the policy is continued long enough, an adverse balance of payment would arise and gold inflow would be changed into outflow.

Limiting Conditions of Bank Rate Policy. For a successful working of such a policy, a little reflection will show that a number of conditions have to be satisfied:

(*i*) All the other rates should follow the bank rate in its movement so that credit should expand and contract as the case may be.

(*ii*) The economic structure of the country should be elastic so that changes in credit conditions should lead to corresponding changes in wages, rents, production, trade, *etc.*

In a well-organised money market like that of Great Britain, the first condition is satisfied. In Great Britain, as we have seen, all other rates have a more or less constant relationship with the bank rate as a matter of convention.

As regards the second condition, again, conditions in Great Britain were most favourable,

6. For Balance of Payments, see Chapter 67.

especially before 1924. The economic structure was fairly elastic. Wages, rents and production responded within limits to changes in money rates and credit conditions. In subsequent years the British economic structure considerably lost its old elasticity. This was due to various reasons among which were the breakdown of the gold standard and coming in of the managed currency and regulation of wages and prices.

As regards other countries, the bank rate policy was always much less successful due to the absence of the above two conditions. The decline in its relative importance is due to changes in money market conditions and the greater rigidity of the economic system as already noted.

Several recent developments in the money markets have made the bank rate policy less efficacious. For instance, domestic trade is financed now more through bank overdrafts and less through bills of exchange which play an important part in discounting operations. Foreign bills have also lost a good deal of their importance due to the fact that London no longer enjoys the same financial status as it used to before the war of 1914-18. Moreover. short-term Treasury Bills have taken the place of bills of exchange for short-term investments. This has increased the influence of the Treasury over the money market.

Moreover, the old sensitivity of business with regard to changes in the rate of interest has been greatly reduced by increased resort to self-financing of business investment out of undistributed profits. The businessmen do not depend on borrowed funds as much as they did before with the result that a change in the rate of interest, and interest is the price of borrowing, leaves them unmoved.

Further, with the quickening of the pace of technical progress, riskiness of business has increased so that even though the normal economic life of capital assets may extend over a long period, businessmen want to recover their capital costs in a short period of three to four years. In such a situation, the rate of interest does not exercise an important influence on investment decisions.

Another contributory factor has been the growth of progressive system of income and profit taxation. An increase in the rate of interest increases the cost of production and, given the sales receipts, reduces the pre-tax profit. But with the lowering of pre-tax profits, the tax rate also is reduced so that profits **post-tax** do not fall as much as profits pre-tax. From the businessmen's point of view, profits post-tax are more

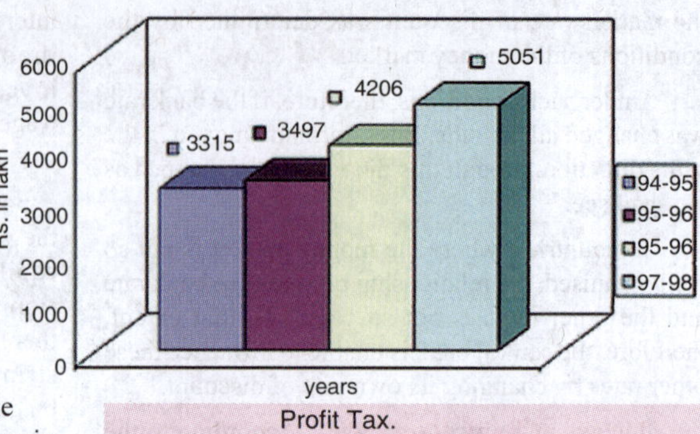

Profit Tax.

important than pre-tax profits and the progressive system of taxation neutralises somewhat the adverse effects of high interest rates on the profitability of investment.

Keynes's View of the Bank Rate Policy. According to the late Lord Keynes, the traditional theories of bank rate concentrated largely on the influence of bank rate as a means of regulating the quantity of bank money and of protecting a country's gold reserves. It had not taken account of the influence of bank rate on the rate of investment relatively to saving, and the influence of changes in the relation between investment and saving on prices, production, employment and wages.

Keynes criticised Hawtrey who had emphasized investment but only one particular kind of investment, namely, "investment by dealers and middle-men in liquid goods, to which," said Keynes, 'a degree of sensitiveness to changes in bank rate is attributed which certainly does not exist in fact."[7]

According to Keynes, economic situation is affected not through the changes in short-term rate of interest and in the stocks of working capital goods, but through the long-term rates of interest and the volume of fixed capital goods. Changes in the bank rate lead to changes not only in short-term rates of interest, but also in long-term rates, since the last two are inter-connected.

In his 'General Theory, *etc*.,' Keynes emphasised the importance of equilibrium between saving and investment for general economic stability. He was, however, of the view that apart from regulation of quantity of money through open market operations (to be studied presently) such equilibrium should be attained, not by the bank rate policy but by the State directly organizing investment and starting public works in periods of depressions. Keynes regarded bank rate policy as an out-of-date method of controlling credit.

7. *A Treatise on Money*, Vol. 1, p. 193.

Conclusion. The bank rate policy, however, has not yet gone completely out of use, though its relative importance has been much reduced .It is still used as an instrument for correcting wrong trends and restoring equilibrium through its influence on the supply of, and demand for, money. Whether it acts through affecting short-term interest rate and investment in liquid goods, as Hawtrey holds, or through long-term interest rates affecting investment in capital goods as contended by Keynes, is a matter which is difficult of verification. Interest, moreover, is only one of the elements of cost, whether the investment is in liquid goods or in capital goods. The state of trade and prices is affected by several other factors. It should also be remembered that the explanations of the process given by Hawtrey and Keynes are not mutually exclusive. A change in bank rate may lead to changes in holding of stocks as well as investments in fixed capital goods. The difference is only of emphasis.

Open Market Operations

The Theory. The term **'One Market Operations'** in the wider sense means purchase or sale by a central bank of any kind of paper in which it deals, like government securities or any other public securities or trade bills, *etc*. In practice, however, the term is applied to purchase or sale of government securities, short-term as well as long-term, at the initiative of the central bank, as a deliberate credit policy. This method of credit control has attained great importance during the last two or three decades.

The theory of open market operations is like this: The sale of securities by the central bank leads to contraction of credit and the purchase thereof to credit expansion. When the central bank sells securities in the open market, it receives payment in the form of a cheque on one of the commercial banks. If the purchaser is a bank, the cheque is drawn against the purchasing bank. In both cases the result is the same. The cash balance of the bank in question, which it keeps with the central bank, is to that extent reduced. With the reduction of its cash, the commercial bank has to reduce its lending. Thus, credit contracts. When the central bank purchases securities, it pays through cheques drawn on itself. This increases the cash balance of the commercial banks and enables them to expand credit. **"Take care of the legal tender money and credit will take care of itself"** is the maxim.

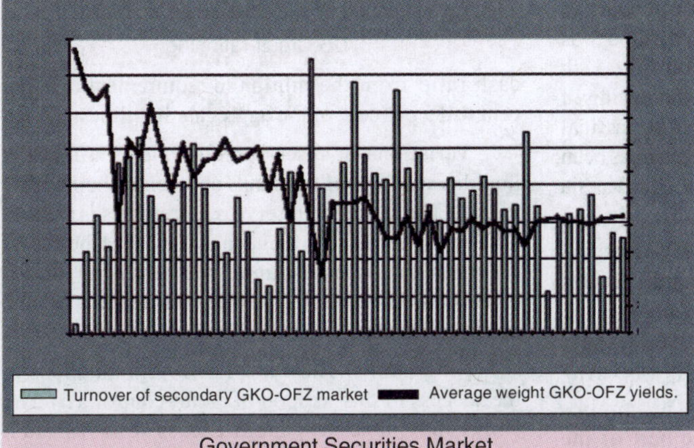

Government Securities Market.

This method is sometimes adopted to make the bank rate policy effective. If the member-banks do not raise their rates following the rise in the bank rate, due to surplus funds available with them, the central bank can withdraw such surplus funds by the sale of securities and thus compel the member-banks to raise their rates. Scarcity of funds in the market compels the banks directly or indirectly to borrow from the central bank through rediscounting bills. If the bank rate is high, the market rate cannot remain low.

Limitations of the Theory. It is obvious that the above will be valid only if certain conditions are satisfied. The limitations are discussed below:

(i) The theory is that when the central bank purchases securities, the cash reserves of the member-banks will be increased and conversely, the cash reserves will be decreased when the central bank sells securities. This, however, may not happen. The sale of securities may be offset by inflow of gold into the bank or by return of notes from circulation and hoards. The purchase of securities, on the other hand, may be accompanied by an outflow of gold or withdrawal of notes for increased currency requirements or for hoarding. In both the cases, therefore, the cash reserves of the member-banks may remain unaffected.

(ii) But even if the cash reserves of the member-banks are increased or decreased, the banks may not expand or contract credit accordingly. The percentage of cash to credit is not rigidly fixed and can vary within quite wide limits. The banks will expand and contract credit according to the prevailing economic and political circumstances and not merely with reference to their cash resources.

(iii) The third condition is that when the commercial banks's cash resources increase the demand for

loans and advances should increase too, and vice versa. This may not happen. Owing to economic or political uncertainty, even cheap money rates may not attract borrowers. Conversely, when trade is good and prospects of profits bright, entrepreneurs would borrow even at high rates of interest.

(iv) Finally, the circulation of bank credit should have a constant velocity. But the velocity of bank deposits is rarely constant. It increases in periods of rising business activity and decreases in periods of depression. Thus, a policy of contracting credit may be neutralised by increased velocity of circulation, and vice versa.

Conclusion. In spite of these limitations, however, there is a fairly close relationship between the sale and purchase of securities by the central bank and contraction and expansion, respectively, of bank credit.

Since for the success of market operations it is necessary that there should be broad and active market in short and long-term government securities, and such markets exist only in the U.S.A. and Great Britain, this method of credit control has been most effectively used in these two countries.

In Great Britain especially, this method has been widely used with the objects of making bank rate effective, or counteracting the effect of seasonal movements of funds, or offsetting the inflow and outflow of gold and for creating and maintaining conditions of cheap money in the interest of business.

Credit Rationing

Credit rationing means restrictions placed by the central bank on demands for accommodation made upon it during times of monetary stringency and declining gold reserves. The credit is rationed by limiting the amount available to each applicant. Further, the central bank restricts its discounts to bills maturing after short periods. This method was used by the Bank of England till the end of the 18th century when the usury laws prohibited the raising of discount rate beyond 5 per cent. After the critical period following World War I, credit rationing has been adopted as a policy by a number of countries like Russia and Germany.

This method of controlling credit can be justified only as a measure to meet exceptional emergencies because it is open to serious abuse.

Direct Action and Moral Suasion: The other methods of credit control may be noted only briefly. There is what is called 'direct action.' This implies coercive measures like refusal on the part of the central bank to rediscount for banks whose credit policy is not in accordance with the wishes of the central bank or whose borrowings from the central banks are excessive in relation ot their capital and reserve. The central bank may, on the other hand, request and persuade member-banks to refrain from increasing their loans for speculation or non-essential activity. The method of publicity is also used. The means issuing of weekly statistics, periodical review of the money market conditions, public finances, trade and industry, the issue of weekly statement of assets and liabilities in the form of balance sheets, *etc.*

Varying Reserve Requirements

When it is sought to restrict credit, the central bank may raise the reserve ratio. In 1960, for instance, the Reserve Bank of India required the scheduled banks to maintain with it additional reserve equivalent to 25 per cent of the increase in their bank deposits (later raised to 50 per cent). The Reserve Bank Act was amended in 1962 which requires all banks to maintain at the close of business on any day a minimum amount of liquid assets equal to not less than 25 per cent of their total demand and time liabilities exclusive of the balances already maintained with the Reserve Bank. Also, the Reserve Bank was empowered to vary the

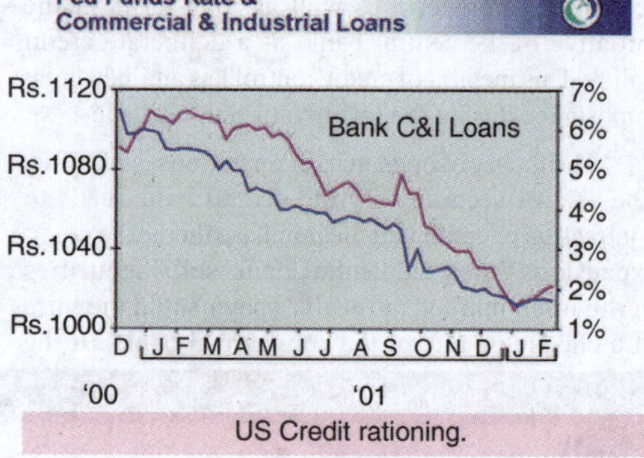

US Credit rationing.

cash ratio from the minimum requirement of 3 per cent to 15 per cent of the aggregate liabilities.

Variations of reserve requirements affect the liquidity position of the banks and hence their ability to lend. The raising of reserve requirements is an anti-inflationary measure in as much as it reduces the excess reserves of member-banks for potential credit expansion. The lowering of the reserve ratios has the opposite effect.

Limitations. There are, however, limitations to the success of this weapon of credit control: (*a*) The banks may have very large excess reserves and it may not be easy to alter legal reserve requirements;

(*b*) the banks have ready access to reserve funds which may nullify the rise in reserve requirements; (*c*) a large net inflow of gold in payment of persistent export surplus may increase the banks' power to lend; and (*d*) the government policy of keeping interest rates low and stable would keep large reserves in the banks and may discourage too drastic increases in reserve requirements.

Selective Credit Controls: Varying Margin Requirements

Another weapon in the hands of the central bank for controlling credit is to vary the margin requirements. While lending money against securities, the banks keep a certain margin. They do not advance money to the full value of the security pledged for the loan. In case it is desired to curtail bank advances, the central bank may issue directives that higher margin be kept .In 1960, for instance, the Reserve Bank of India raised to 50 per cent the minimum margin requirement for bank advances against equity shares. The raising of margin requirements is designed to check speculation in the stock markets and to prevent the typical 'boom-bust' pattern in the stock markets. In this way, the demand for speculative credit is controlled. The higher the margin required, the less credit one would obtain for the purchase of stocks.

Some of the beneficial effects of raising margin requirements are:

(*a*) High margin requirements divert investible funds from speculative to productive channels.

(*b*) They also check undue monetary expansion because the commercial banks are to this extent prevented from manufacturing speculative 'bank money' and thus increasing the total money supply.

(*c*) High margin requirements reduce the inflationary effect of speculative profits upon the income-expenditure structure of the company, and thus contribute to the prevention of a 'boom bust' development.

(*d*) Finally, the high margin requirements contribute to the stability in the economy by eliminating or curbing speculative activity in the country. It is useful in minimising cyclical disturbances. The margin requirements can also be lowered to foster 'bullish' sentiment in a period of low activity.

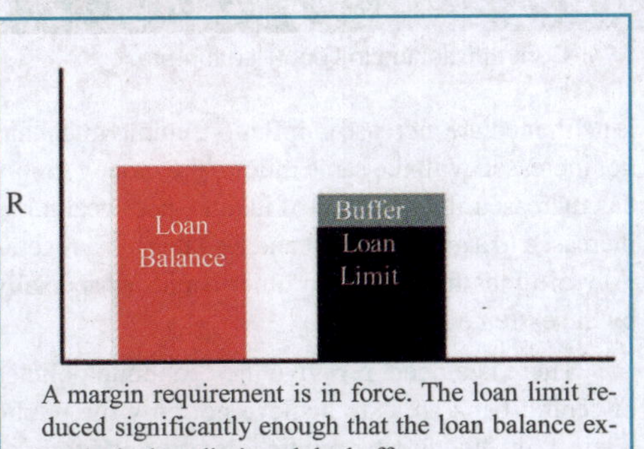

A margin requirement is in force. The loan limit reduced significantly enough that the loan balance exceeds the loan limit and the buffer.

You have 3 business days to reduce the loan balance to below the loan limit.

Margin requirement.

The Reserve Bank of India made use of selective credit controls for the first time in 1956. It issued directives to banks to refrain from excessive lending against foodgrains, sugar, groundnuts and shares. As already mentioned, in 1960, margin requirements for advances against equity shares were raised to 50 per cent. The selective credit controls have been operated by the Reserve Bank with suitable modifications from time to time in the light of demand and supply position of the commodities. The credit restraint measures were intensified in May, 1960, but it later relaxed these measures with a view tó easing pressure of seasonal stringency. Similarly, in 1962, the improvement in the supply and price situation led to the relaxation of some of the controls. In this way, the Reserve Bank of India has been adjusting the control machinery to changing situations.

Limitations of Selective Credit Controls. It is not to be supposed that selective controls can be freely operated so as to fully achieve their objectives. They are subject to some serious limitations:

(*i*) The selective credit controls are concerned with bank advances only. But there are other sources of finance which are beyond these controls, *e.g.*, borrowing from non-banking institutions like insurance companies. Moreover, the companies have reserve funds and undistributed profits to fall back upon or they can issue capital or debentures.

(*ii*) It is also possible that the loans taken for other purposes may be diverted to the lines which are forbidden under the selective credit controls. It is not easy to keep track of the purposes for which the bank advances may be utilised.

(*iii*) Further, the banks themselves lend money under different labels on the understanding with their customers that they can invest them in forbidden uses. Such a collusion between the banks and their customers may reduce the selective credit controls to naught.

Conclusion

On the central bank's power to control credit, Crowther concludes thus: "There are thus limits on the central bank's ability to control the volume of money in existence in the country. But they are broad and elastic limits . . . Over the quantitative aspects of money in a modern State the control of the central bank is very great. To the question: 'What determines the quantity of money in existence?' the answer is: 'The policy of the central bank, using its free discretion within limits that are normally vary broad' . . . In its own field the central bank is clearly a dictator."[8]

Central Bank (In an era of globalisation)

"A 'central bank' is a bank of the government which regulates, controls, directs and manages the complete financial system in an economy with the sole objective of public interest by varying the total supply of money in an economy."

The majority of central banks in the world are not able to follow their own independent policies. They used to depend on their functioning of their central banks on the basis of developed countries or western central banks policies. There used to arise many problems as their financial system was not as much developed as the developed countries. Some developing countries either with democratic government or dictator government used to influence the functioning of central bank, so as to achieve their personal or political objectives. Due to this the economic development was very slow or not upto the expectations.

The main objective of a 'central bank' to work for the benefit and welfare of the whole society is further pushed back due to the liberalisation and globalisation policies. The emergence of WTO and the dictates of IMF in the policy framing of developing countries. There can be a resemblence in the so called Russian dictatorial policy after the second world war on the Warsaw pact countries for economic and other plannings. Only Marshall Tito, stood against such policy.

Liberalisation and globalisation policy has opened the doors of the developing countries economies (*i*) For the flow of either direct foreign investment or institutional foreign investment in their economies, (*ii*) Financial assistance from different international financial institutions *i.e.*, I.M.F., World Bank, Asian Development Bank *etc*., has increased, and (*iii*) The innovations in commercial banks and allowing the easy loan policies for any purpose (productive and unproductive) as well as the ATM Services. All these factors has increased the total money supply in the economy.

In India the total inflow of foreign funds in the economy is increasing day by day, which is clear from the amount of foreign reserve accumulation to nearly 102 billion $s this is a record for the Indian economy. This may induce the public authorities to bring about those projects which may benefit them politically and economically without taking into account the public interest. To day the economic policies as well as the real economic situation are quite conflicting. Though money supply in the economy has increased, but there

Central Banking in Globalisation era.

is no immediate increase in inflation, employment has not increased with the same ratio as the money supply has increased. Inequalities of income and wealth has increased to a greater extent and also there is a reverse flow of funds from India to other countries specially by the extreme rich people.

There is a need to revive the economic policies of central bank so as to achieve not only the public interest but "the greater public interest in the form of uplifling the lower income groups without disturbing the higher income groups and the over-all economy."

8. *An Outline of Money*, 1950, p. 58.

Key terms

Note issuing agency, Bankers' Bank, Banker to state, Lender of last resort, Bank rate, Open market operation, Credit control, Selective credit control, Quantitative credit control.

QUESTIONS

1. Critically evaluate the role of Central Bank (RBI) in the era of Post-liberalisation and globalisation.
2. Describe the main functions of Central Banks and point out the peculiarities of the Reverse Bank of India.
3. Briefly explain the methods by which the Central Bank controls the volume and creation of credit.
4. Distinguish between general credit control and selective credit control and examine their relative merits.
5. Assess the efficacy of open market operations and bank rate policy as instruments of credit control.
6. Compare teh relative merits of open market operations and variable reserve ratio as methods of credit control.
7. Discuss the working and efficiency of selective credit controls.
8. Examine the case for and against the use of the methods of variable reserve ratios for the control of bank credit.
9. Discuss the objectives and limitations fo monetary policy especially in an under-developed country.
10. Enumerate the general objectives of economic policy. To what extent can monetary or fiscal instruments by themselves achieve these objectives?
11. 'The role of Central Bank in a developing economy is not so much to regulate the quantum of credit as to direct the flow of credit? Elucidate.
12. What role can the Central Bank play in promoting economic growth with stabiility? Illustrate your answer with reference to India.
13. Describe the functions of a Central Bank with reference to economic development of a country.
14. How far can (1) price stability and (2) full employment be attained through monetary policy? Are the two objectives compatible?

MONETARY POLICY

Objectives

The principal objectives of monetary policy are:

(*a*) The safeguarding of the country's gold reserves,

(*b*) Price stability,

(*c*) Exchange stability,

(*d*) Elimination of cyclical fluctuations

(*e*) Achievement of full employment, and

(*f*) In the case of under-developed economies, accelerating economic growth.

Which particular objective is to be pursued at any given time will depend on the economic situation to be tackled.

We may consider whether a country should follow a dear money policy or a cheap money policy or a neutral money policy. We shall also consider a suitable monetary policy for a developing economy. We have already discussed monetary policy for full employment.

Dear Money vs. Cheap Money

Meaning. In a discussion on money, we think it necessary to take notice of controversy centring round the policy to be pursued regarding money.

When the economy has been shattered by war or disrupted by depression, one controversy looms large on the economic horizon, *viz.*, should the country follow a dear money policy or a cheap money policy?

But what do we mean by dear money or cheap money? Some students are prone to think that dear money means that its value in terms of commodities and services is high, *i.e.*, prices are low, and that cheap money, on the other hand, implies that the value (or purchasing power) of money is low and prices have gone up. Now dear money may be associated with low prices, and cheap money, with high prices, but the terms 'dear money' and 'cheap money' are not defind in this sense. The price of money, which the terms 'dear' or

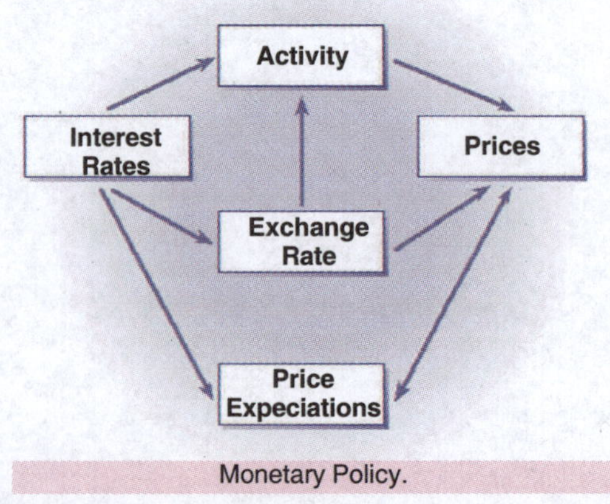

Monetary Policy.

'cheap' are supposed to indicate, is not in term of its exchange value of purchasing power.

The 'price' of money more appropriately refers to the rate at which money can be had or borrowed. Thus, **'dear money'** means that the borrowing rates or interest rates are high and **'cheap money'** means that interest **rates are low.** The price of money, in short, is the rate of interest.

Which is Better? Some economists advocate dear money policy, while others are in favour of cheap money policy. Which is better? It all depends on the economic situation with which we are faced. The rate of interest has been recognised to be an important tool for the execution of an economic policy. There are times when the appropriate economic policy demands that the rate of interest in the money market should be kept low, and there are times when interest rates have to be kept high in view of the economic objective before the community.

When Dear Money? When there is a state of galloping or hyper-inflation, when there is hectic speculative activity, when there is reckless investment by industrialists, when credit creation by the banks has crossed all prudent bounds, when balance of payments is heavily against the country or threatens to continue unfavourable, a dear money policy is indicated. It is a deflationary move. It will apply a brake on senseless capital investment; it will check reckless credit creation by the banks; it will stem the rising tide of prices; it will muzzle and mad career of the speculator; and it will ultimately put the balance of payments position of the country on a stable footing.

When Cheap Money? Cheap money policy, on the other hand, is indicated in opposite set of circumstances. For instance, when the business enterprise is groaning under the benumbing and baneful effects of depression, when the banks are shy of lending, when the low price-level is killing economic incentive, when there is widespread unemployment, and when a comprehensive building programme has to be put through, and so on, a cheap money policy, or a policy of low interest rates is the best. It will stimulate investment, create employment or reduce the incidence of unemployment; it will oil the wheel of the industrial machine; it will, in short, tend to lift the blanket of depression and remove its deadening influences.

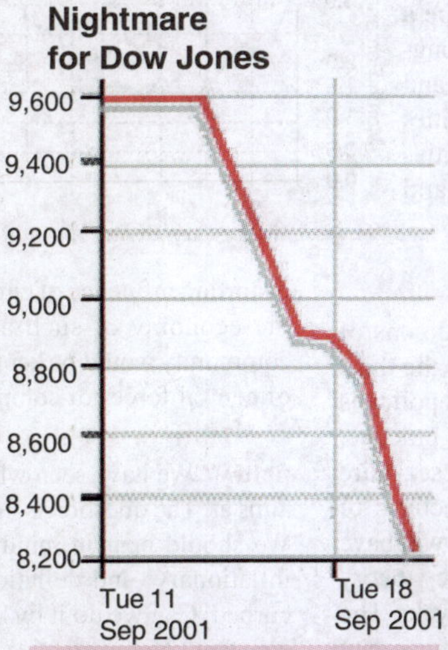

Nightmare for Dow Jones

During depression cheap money policy is helpful.

Thus, Cheap money policy (*i.e.*, cheapening of credit services) is a tool for (*a*) combating slump, (*b*) fighting unemployment, and (*c*) financing development programmes. When a cheap money policy is adopted, the government has to borrow in the open market. In case there is dearth of credit, the prices of securities will rise and the demand for them will fall. The government will have to rely on institutional investors. Cheap money policy means the monetisation of public debt, *i.e.*, the public debt is turned into liquid cash. If a stage of full employment has already been reached, it will mean an inflationary finance.

How Far Feasible? Now the question arises: It is in the power of the State through the central bank or otherwise to fix and control interest rates to keep the money cheap or dear? Is not the rate of interest determined by the operation of natural forces relating to demand and supply of loanable funds? As has already been explained, the theory that the rate of interest brings about an equilibrium between demand for saving and supply thereof has now been exploded. As Sir William Beveridge points out, "The rate of interest cannot ulfil the function (of equilibrating demand and supply), because capital expenditure brings into existence the very savings necessary to finance it. There is no question of 'equilibrating' the one to the other because they are kept in equality by changes in the level of income."[1] If there is a low rate of interest, investment is encouraged. Any expenditure incurred by the community out of loans and reserves will bring additional income and create new sources of saving. Thus, low rate of interest does not discourage saving, but it encourages expenditure and investment and makes more savings possible.

It is now accepted by modern economists that it is in the power of the State to fix and maintain low rates of interest, and the rate is not determined by any natural factors. This is shown by the fact that the ever-mounting demands for loans during war and post-war years have been satisfied at low rates of interest. This clear ly indicates the possibility of controlling interest rates.

Let us see how it is done. The interest rate can be controlled through a control over savings. For this, it is essential to know the

1. *Full Employment in a Free Society*, 1945, p. 307.

different forms that savings take. There are four ways in which people hold their savings, *viz*., cash balances, bank deposits, bills *i.e.*, short-term investments) and bonds (*i.e.*, long-term investments). The government may decide to fix a particular rate of interest considering the overall economic picture of the country and then leave the saving public to adjust their savings and the forms in which they would wish to hold their savings at that rate. As Beveridge puts it, "That is to say, that government must offer long-term bonds and short-term paper 'on tap' so that savings can flow into them according to the wishes of the savers."

In case, however, it is found that the government is unable to raise the desire amounts at the rates announced and the public subscription to long-term and short-term issues falls short, the government can obtain the balance from the central bank through "Ways and Means" advances. As the government expenditure proceeds, new savings will be created and the cash balances of the banks will go up. The savings that the public can hold in cash and bank deposits are governed by the business turnover; they will also invest their surplus savings in short or long-term paper.

The feasibility of fixing stable rate of interest is thus beyond question. The government has simply to decide the rate and then offer to the public what they would wish to hold given this rate. The only safeguard is that the change in the rate must be gradual. There should be no sudden break. That is why it will not be feasible to fix a zero rate and then try to maintain it as described above. In case of sudden reduction of the rate, there will be a sudden appreciation of capital assets and long-term money claims; it will create a chaos and social tension. The stream of gilt-edged securities will dry up and the very foundation of activities of financial institutions like the banks and insurance companies will crumble.

Neutral Money Policy

We have discussed above the pros and cons of dear a money *vs*. cheap money. But there is the third course open *viz*., neutral money policy. This policy is based on the philosophy of laissez-faire. In practice, however, it is a depar ture from the laissez-faire doctrine, inasmuch as, to achieve the objectives of neutral money policy, the monetary authority will have to pursue an active policy. The neutral money theory is associated with the name of Prof. F.A. Hayek.[2] The Advocates of this theory believe that the most important causes of economic instability lie in the monetary changes. Eliminate them and you ensure a smooth and steady economy.

It is a policy which seeks to neutralise or eliminate the dislocating and disturbing influences caused by the creation or expansion of money on the one hand, and its destruction or contraction on the other. The creation or injection of new money is supposed to cause inflation whereas withdrawal or contraction of money produces a deflationary effect. Inflation is associated with cheap money and deflation with dear money. From the point of view of economic stability or stability of price, output and employment, both inflation and deflation are considered bad. We should have neither the one nor the other. Money should be neither dear nor cheap.

The neutral money policy is thus identified with zero-mark of inflation and deflation. It seeks to create a state of affairs as if money did not exist, lest it should be inflationary or deflationary; and, as if exchanges (trade) were all by barter. But since money does not disappear altogether, inconveniences of barter do not exist. In the pursuit of the neutral money policy, the monetary authority has to so regulate the supply of money that the production levels, price-level and the volume of transactions are such as if the community did not use any money. It is supposed that if the distorting influence of circulating media were kept out, the economy of such as imaginary non-monetary community would be kept stable through the operation of neutral forces of competition.

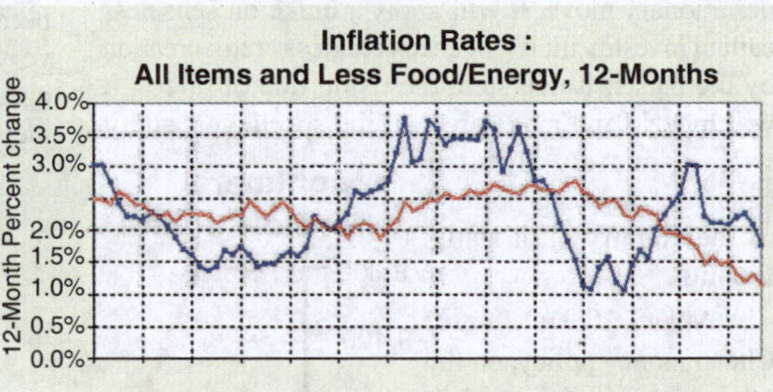

Monetary Policy aims at controlling inflation.

How to achieve the aim of neutral money policy? We have seen what the neutral money policy aims at. The question is, how is this aim to be realised? We should bear in mind that under this policy both inflationary and deflationary tendencies have to be curbed. Can we do it by keeping the supply of money constant? Not at all.

We know that price changes are not merely caused by change in the supply of money but also by such factors as changes in output, in population, improvement in technique and transport, changes in

2. Hayem, F. A. –*Prices and Production*—Monetary Theory, and Trade and Trade Cycles.

velocity of circulation of money, *etc*. These changes must also be neutralised. If the supply of money were kept rigidly fixed, economic progress and improvement in productive efficiency would bring about a disastrous fall in prices in a generation, and this is precisely what a neutral money policy does not want. Thus, merely avoidance of money creation and money contraction will not achieve the objective of neutral money policy.

What then should the monetary authority do? If population increases, demand for money will increase and this demand must be satisfied, otherwise shortage of money will cause deflation and this is what the neutral money policy must avoid. If velocity of circulation of money increases, it will be inflationary, and to check that, the speed at which money is being created must be slowed done. If due to inventions and other technical improvements or improvements in the productive efficiency of the factors, the volume of production goes up, then the quantity of money is not to be increased because in this case the fall in prices is not dangerous or disturbing. If due to improvement in transport, business turnover increases, more money must be created to cope with the increased traffic. If the movement towards verical integration of business becomes strong, demand for money will be correspondingly reduced. The monetary authority should take this factor, too, into consideration and adopt compensatory measures. It must also keep a close watch on the policies of the monopolists to keep their prices at reasonable levels.

In short, it has to keep its eye on the price-level rather than keep the supply of money constant so that dangerous turns in prices are avoided.

How far could this policy be efficacious? On paper, the theory looks simple and the neutral money policy seems straight. Actually, there are so many complications. The theory wrongly assumes that the sole or the important determinants of business cycles are the monetary changes. So diverse are the factors affecting price-level, volume of output and employment that no amount of moentary regulation can ensure stability. The modern economists are not prepared to subscribe to the view that the business cycle is a purely monetary phenomenon. The neutral money policy thus suffers from serious limitations.

How does neutral money policy differ from the policy of price stabilisation? In order to distinguish between the neutral money policy and the policy of price stabilisation as such, we should bear in mind that there are two types of price-levels; one is the general price-level, a sort of average of all price-levels; and the other is the relative price-level. In one sense, the aim of both these policies is the same. Both seek to neutralise money and to make it play a passive role so that if there are any economic fluctuations, money should not be held to blame. The aim of both is to remove a major cause of economic fluctuations.

But there is this difference between the two: the aim of the policy of price stabilisation is to prevent changes in the general price-level so that money as a unit of account remains neutral or behaves in a stable manner. The aim of the neutral money policy is to keep the structure of **relative** prices stable. For this purpose, it seeks to regulate the total effective quantity of money so that money as a medium of exchange is not allowed to cause any disturbance in the economy.

MONETARY POLICY FOR A DEVELOPING ECONOMY

In a developing economy, monetary policy has a special role to play. A developing economy has to make a very large-scale mobilisation of productive resources of all types and has to organise their most efficient allocation. The task of implementing the development plans of sizable dimensions is a big task and an all-out effort is required on the part of all authorities to ensure their successful implementation. The monetary authorities have to play their full part.

One important requirement for steady economic growth is the environment or atmosphere of comparative price stability and absence of inflation. For a steady and sound economic advance and for efficient utilisation of resources, for avoidance of distortion and dislocation of investment programmes and for the promotion of the objective of greater economic equalities or of lessening inequalities of income and wealth, it is essential that there should prevail in the economy an atmosphere of general financial stability including price and exchange stability. "A non-inflationary environment is conducive to sustained, continuous and efficient development rather than fitfil, uneven and unstable growth."

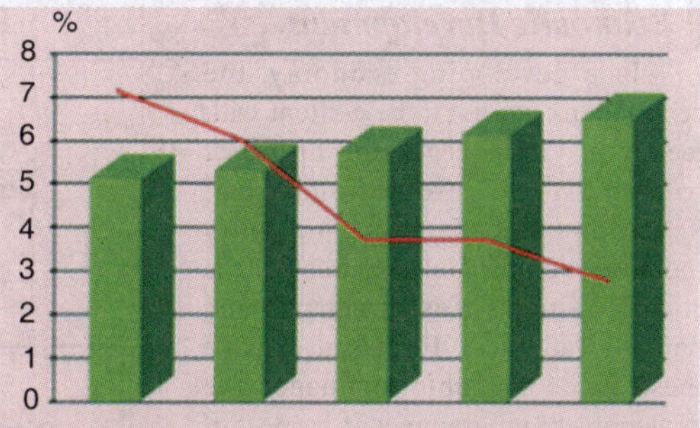

Increasing GDP and containing inflation are major challeges for Developing countries.

Now let us see what weapons can be used to ensure financial and price stability. There are the physical or direct controls like price control and rationing of essential commodities in short supply. But owing to vast numbers of producers and consumers, physical controls are difficult to administer. In an under-developed economy, the administrative organisation cannot successfully cope with the complicated and difficult task of operating physical controls. Beyond a point, these controls become too vexatious and hamper initiative and enterprise. On the other hand, monetary controls are more efficacious and less vexatious and do not raise many administrative problems.

Then, there is the fiscal instrument or budgetary action on the part of the government involving income and commodity taxes. Fiscal policy involves a direct draft on the financial resources and purchasing power is the hands of the public and with the particular classes of producers and consumers. Taxes can also differentiate between various classes of consumers and producers through reliefs and rebates and are, therefore, more fair.

But, in under-developed countries, fiscal policy has serious limitations inasmuch as the proportion of taxation to national income is very low: 9 per cent in case of India as against 28 per cent in the U.K., 33 per cent in the U.S.A., 27 per cent in Germany, 25 per cent in France, 22 per cent in Itlay and 21 per cent in Japan. Hence, monetary action is also called for.

The fact is that all types of weapons–physical, fiscal and monetary–have to be used in combination with one another to ensure the requisite atmosphere for the successful implementation of the development plans and to promote steady and healthy growth of the economy. We are here concerned with the monetary policy.

Role of Central Bank in Economic Development

In a developing economy, the central bank has not to be content with merely playing a **regulatory role.** Its role must be promotional and developmental. It must not only mobilise the financial resources of the country by means of expansion of sound banking facilities, it must also make these funds available to finance the development programmes in respect of agriculture, trade, transport and industry and create specialized financial institutions for the purpose.

In the words of Indian Planning Commission, "Central Banking in a planned economy can hardly be confined ot the regulation of the overall supply of credit or to a somewhat negative regulation of the flow of bank credit. It would have to take a direct and active role, **first,** in creating or helping to create the machinery needed for financing development activities all over the country, and **secondly,** in ensuring that the finance available flows in the directions intended."[3]

The central bank can promote economic development in a number of ways. In particular, it can make a satisfactory provision for the following:–

***(i)* Sound Currency System.** Economic development leads to the expansion of market and increasing specialisation. To cope with this growth it is essential that the soundness and efficiency of the payment mechanism or the currency system must be maintained. It is obvious that if the currency loses value as in hyper-inflation, economic activity may be seriously hampered.

***(ii)* Regulated and Adequate Money Supply.** Not only should the money supply be adequate for the expanded economic activity, but it should be properly regulated so that too much of it may not create an inflationary situation and too little result in recession or depression. By means of controlled expansion of credit, the monetary authority ensures growth with stability.

***(iii)* Creation of New Financial Institutions.** The central bank creates special financial institution for promoting economic development in different sectors such as Agriculture Finance Corporation, Industrial

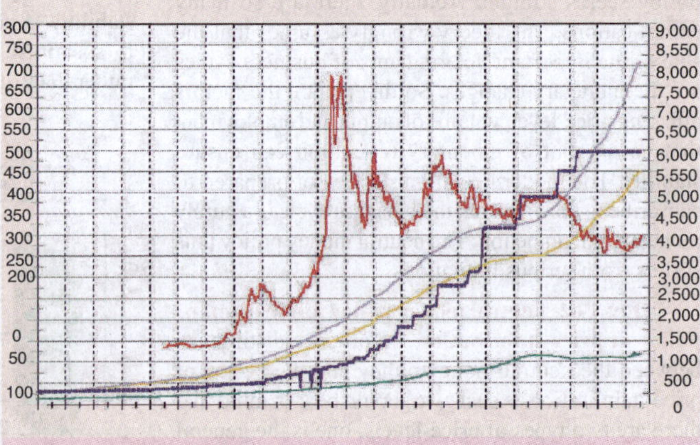

Central Bank must ensure adequate money supply.

3. *First Five Year Plan*, p. 38.

Finance Corporation, Export Finance Corporation, Small Industries Development Corporation, *etc*. These institutions provide much needed finance to accelerate development in their respective spheres.

(*iv*) Tackling Balance of Payments Problem. In a developing economy, owing to mounting imports of foodgrains, machinery and capital equipment, essential raw materials and technical know-how, the balance of payments turns adverse. The monetary authority tackles this problem by export promotion, import substitution, raising foreign loans so that economic development proceeds on an even keel.

(*v*) Restraining Inflationary Pressure. In a developing economy, the Government budgetary operations owing to increasing size of Government expenditure, generate strong inflationary pressure. It is the responsibility of the monetary authority to restrain these pressures by freezing part of the liquidity thus generated. This the monetary authority is able to do through its pivotal tool–the rate of interest, The prevailing rate of interest enters into assessment of profitability or remunerative character of projects. The productive enterprises even in the public sector cannot be immune from the pervasive influence of the rate of interest. The targets cannot be fixed only by administrative decisions independently of consideration of the rate of interest. The interest rates are governed by monetary policy. Hence, its vital role in a developing economy.

For the implementation of development programmes borrowing from banks is essential. The money is borrowed for investment for expanding the capacity of the existing plant or build a new plant or for holding additional stock or for consumption. Naturally, there is expansion of bank credit. The fresh money supplies generated by the bank credit add to the active demand for goods and services. This tends to start the inflationary spiral. Then it becomes necessary for the monetary authority ot step in and restrain the extension of bank credit, for increase in the bank credit has price raising effects. Even though restraints on bank credit may adversely affect productive enterprises, they are essential all the same in the interest of sound and steady economic growth in the country.

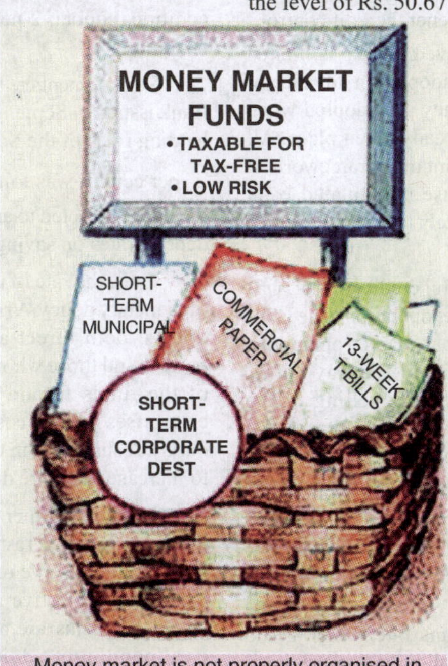

Money market is not properly organised in UDCs.

Thus, the monetary policy consists in central bank's action in the sphere of bank credit. The central bank seeks to regulate bank advances leaving the operation of the price mechanism intact and leaving productive enterprises freedom of initiative and autonomus functioning.

Limitations of Monetary Policy

The monetary policy has to face several difficulties in under-developed countries: the existence of a large non-monetised sector, perhaps one-third of the economy, in under-developed countries seriously limits the scope of the use of the monetary weapons. However, two-thirds of the economy offer large enough scope for monetary action.

Another limiting factor is the existence of a large non-organised money market, *e.g.*, indigenous banking in India (it was 90 per cent in 1930 and is roughly 50 per cent now).

Moreover, in under-developed countries like India currency occupies a relatively more important position than bank deposits. In recent years, however, there has been a phenomenal growth of bank deposits. The bank deposits in India grew from Rs.881 crores in 1950-51 to Rs. 14.155 crores at the end of 1975-76 and reached the level of Rs. 50.671 crores at the end of December 1982. The total bank deposits have out-stripped the currency money. This has increased the significance of Central Bank policies in the developing economies.

Also, in India, high expansion of banking credit during the busy season takes place through borrowing from the Reserve Bank. Co-operative inance completely relies on the Reserve Bank. Thus, the Central Bank has an increasing role to play. This is specially so because, in under-developed countries like India, there is lack of other financial institutions like building societies, finance houses, hire-purchase companies, *etc.*

The inadequate development of the capital market adds to the importance of commercial lending and correspondingly the importance of Central Bank policies. Greater dependence of commercial banks on central bank borrowing enchances the ability of the central bank to influence the credit policies of banks.

Role of Monetary Policy in Indian Economic Development

Let us briefly notice the role that the monetary policy has played in India in recent years. That would illustrate the role of monetary policy in a developing economy. During the last twenty five years of planning, the Reserve Bank of India has tried to regulate (*a*) the cost of credit, (*b*) the quantity of credit, and (*c*) the purpose or use of credit. For regulating the cost and the quantity of credit, the Reserve Bank has used the weapons of general or quantitative controls, *e.g.*, regulating the bank rate and the open market operations and for regulating the purpose or the use of bank credit, the Reserve Bank has had resort to what are called the 'selective credit controls.'

The selective credit controls have been used primarily for regulating bank advances against foodgrains and other selected articles or raw materials like sugar or groundnut, temporarily cotton textiles and recently raw jute and jute goods. These measures have been useful in restraining excessive speculative stockpiling of the commodities concerned, though their success is largely due to the fact of their bring used in conjunction with measures of general credit control.

The efficacy of the selective controls is limited by the fact that they cannot be adopted in advance of future pattern of production; they are adopted when 'excessive bank lending has already taken place. All the same, it is necessary to maintain a framework of selective credit controls because unregulated bank credit for building of stocks is likely to accentuate price fluctuations.

As for instruments of general credit control, *viz.*, the bank rate and the open market operations, the latter is more continuous and informal market operations have tended to become increasingly one-way traffic, *i.e.*, there has been more and more selling of the Government securities to reduce the gap in the budgetary operations. The scope of the open market operations is also limited by the capacity of the market to absorb the stream of Government securities flowing from the Reserve Bank pool. In effect, the open market operations have become more and more ancillary to Government debt management.

In India, the use of the Bank rate, which is the prime instrument of monetary policy, had neither been frequent nor considerable. The bank rate remained constant since the inception of the Reserve Bank in 1935 to 1951 when it was raised from 3 per cent to $3\frac{1}{2}$ per cent and to 4 per cent in 1957. But in recent years, the weapon of the bank rate was used quite frequently. The bank rate was raised to $4\frac{1}{2}$ per cent in 1963 to 5 per cent in 1964 and further to 6 per cent in 1965. In 1968, however, there was a reversal of dear money policy when in March, 1968, the bank rate was cut 1 per cent to 5 per cent. Considering again that bank credit was showing a tendency of expanding too much, the bank rate was raised to 6 per cent in January, 1971 and further to 7 per cent on May 30, 1973. In July 1974, the bank was raised to 9 per cent and the minimum lending rate to be charged by commercial banks was stepped up from 11 per cent to 12.5 per cent. Simultaneously, interest rates on various categories of commercial bank deposits were enhanced. All these measures had the effect of restraining the growth in money expenditures.

In 1960, the Reserve Bank introduction a system of graded lending rates with the bank rate remaining unaltered. Under this system, borrowing quotas for scheduled banks were fixed at 50 per cent of their statutory deposits with the Reserve Bank and 1 per cent above the bank rate was charged for any borrowing in excess of the quota up to an amount equal to the basic quota and for further borrowing, above this additional quota, 2 per cent above the bank rate was charged.

Complementary to these measures, the Reserve Bank issued in September 1960 a directive raising the lending rates of the Scheduled banks by minimum of $\frac{1}{2}$ per cent. It was followed by a move on the part of the banks directed to an upwards shift in the pattern of deposit rates on savings and fixed deposit.

Thus, the rate of interest continues to be the core of monetary policy. A rise in interest rates has important effects, both direct and indirect, upon those who borrow and those who lend and also on the movement of the funds to and from the country. For some enterprises interest costs are a crucial part of the total outlay. A sharp rise in the interest rate is also expected to increase the more desirable kinds of savings.

There is another instrument which the Reserve Bank has used of restrain expansion of bank credit, *viz.*, varying reserve requirements. This instrument is particularly effective in freezing additional liquidity when the banks are acquiring large new resources, corespondingly adding to their lending capacity. Twenty-five per cent (later 50 per cent) of the increase in deposits was frozen in 1960. This method is more appropriate as a temporary expedient to meet exceptional liquidity situations, while changes in general interest rates are more appropriate for a long-term structural adjustment to a situation of steadily improving liquidity.

The Reserve Bank of India was called upon to use the above weapons of credit control, for a serious inflationary situation had developed in the country during the last few years. There has been great increase in money supply and liquidity has outrun the pace of growth of real national income. Consequently, prices and cost of living have been rising.

A 20 per cent rise in prices from Feb. -end 1939 to Sep. -end 1979 i.e. since the presentation of the 1979-80 budget made the situation alarming. Among the factors responsible were a big increase to money supply of Rs. 1,182 crores during end-April to end-Aug. 1979 as against that of only Rs. 158 crores during the corresponding period of 1978. In order to curb the runaway expansion in bank credit and money supply, the RBI in August-Sept. 1979 reduced banks' resources under participation certificates, kept down cash credit and bill discounts, curtailed refinance, offered incentive to saying by raising rates of interest on fixed deposits, fixed ceiling rates on short-term advances, and so on. Such strong action on the monetary front was definitely called for to reduce the pressure of growing money supply and liquid funds generated by bank credit. It is good that the Reserve Bank adopted various credit-freeze measures.

It must be said to the credit of the Reserve Bank of India that it has fully risen to the occasion to meet the requirements of the developing economy. Besides, taking monetary measures mentioned above to maintain the general financial stability in the country and restraining inflationary pressures, it has helped in the creation of specialized institutions so that financial facilities are made available to agriculture and industry. Its developmental effort is indeed commendable.

We might enumerate a few things that the Reserve Bank of India has done in the field of developmental finance. It has made available shorterm, medium-term, and long-term finance to agriculture through are hierarchical network of co-creation of two funds, *viz.*, the National Agricultural Credit (Long-term Operations) Fund and the National Agricultural Credit (Stabilisation) Fund deserves mention. It has also been instrumental in setting up Agricultural Refinance and Development Corporation and lately NABARI. It has organised industrial finance so that industries, big and small , can secure all types of loans, short-term, medium-term and long-term. It has helped in the creation of Industrial Finance Corporation of India, State Financial Corporations, Refinance Corporation, National Small Industries Corporation, National Industrial Development Corporation, Industrial Credit and Investment Corportation and the Industrial Development Bank and the Unit Trust.It has introduced a scheme of guarantee of bank loans to small industry.

"Monetary Policy In Post Liberalisation Era"

A 'monetary policy' is defined as the policy of a central bank, so as to achieve certain pre-determined socio-economic objectives with the help of techniques of monetary instrumetns. or,

"A monetary policy is nothing but the concious policy of a central bank with the sole objective of achieving certain desirable effects on the economy and to avoid undersirable effects on the economy by the use of quantitative or selective

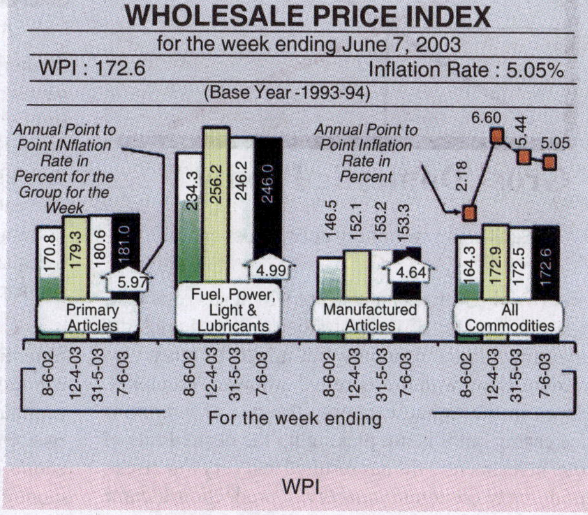

WPI

credit control techniques or both."

In recent years it is becoming more difficult to bring about a precise and very effective monetary policy. This is due to the following reasons:–

(i) Liberalisation and globalisation has opened the gates of foreign direct investment or foreign institutional investment.

(ii) The resurgence of monetary economies, which is increasing with a rapid pace,

(iii) More freedom to commercial banks plus the entry of foreign and private commercial banks, which

has increased the innovation in banking system, and the increasing , use of credit cards, ATM etc has increased the money supply,

***(iv)* More liberal policy of "cheap money policy", has initiated the concept of "aaj udhar kal nakkad" (Today credit tomorrow cash), which is offering the financial product (personal loans, home loans, car loans . . . . .), etc., without taking into account, the use of money for productive and unproductive uses.**

Overall the capitalists economy of laissez-fair has recentered in the developing countries. This may harm the economy in near future, if it is not controlled with wise policy. The economies of developing countries (with reference to India), is facing many problems, *i.e.*

(i) Stagflation, or a lower rate of inflation which is not picking up more investment and generating the desired economic results.

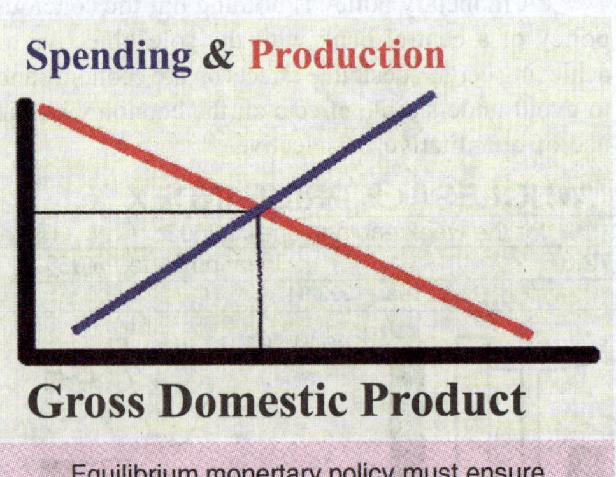

Equilibrium monertary policy must ensure.

(ii) The Keynesian concept which suggests that, it is not the rate of interest alone which guides the investment in the economy, but it is to be taken into account along with the marginal efficiency of capital. Hence in the Indian economy the rate of interest is decreasing but it is not picking up the desired rate of total investment. This has resulted in a very low rise in the different economic variable *i.e.*, production, income generation and so on.

(iii) Though there is huge increase in economic activities of service sector, which may put the economies in a more difficult situation, as service sector being a supportive sector in the over-all economy.

(iv) The changes in the government's vision of monetary system; Earlier it use to concentrate on socialism, today it is based on a pro-capitalists approach. (This was one of the reason why Mrs. Gandhi nationalised commercial banks on 19-07-1969).

(v) The Indian economy still is of a seasonal nature, the ups & downs in the economy is to a greater extent based on the performance of agriculture sector.

Conclusion. The Reserve Bank of India has thus helped to broaden and deepen the structure of institutional finance for accelerating economic development of the country with itself as the central arch of the banking and monetary framework of the country. It has sought to preserve a proper climate for economic development and has tendered to the Government and the planning authority its expert and invaluable advice. In short, it has acted as a guide, philosopher and friend to the Government in the sphere of finance.

CONFLICTING OBJECTIVES OF MONETARY POLICY

Before we take up the conflict between the various objectives of monetary policy, we might enumerate once more the various objectives: (1) Price Stability (2) Exchange Stability. (3) Full Employment. (4) Economic Growth. (5) Balance of Payments Equilibrium.

Other Objectives. In addition to the above the other objectives are:

(i) Creation, working and expansion of different financial institutions. *(ii)* Provision of an efficient payment mechanism. *(iii)* Proper debt management. *(iv)* Evaluation of a rational interest rate structure. *(v)* Operation of credit control measures. *(vi)* Income Stabilisation by preventing or mitigating cyclical fluctuations. *(vii)* To ensure neutrality of money. *(viii)* To bring about monetary equilibrium in the economy by equalising savings and investment and demand for and supply of money.

Compatibility of the Objectives. Some of the objectives seem to be conflicting and mututally contradictory. For instance, take price stability and economic growth. In the period of growth, some price rise or inflation is inevitable. This is borne out by the economic history of various countries. Additional money has to be injected into circulation to finance development projects. This results in price rise. But inflation which is mild at first becomes hyper-inflation after some time and becomes an obstacle to economic growth. Thus price stability and economic growth are not compatible objectives.

Let us next consider price stability and full employment. The classical economists and Prof. Patinkin point out that full employment can only be achieved under conditions of price-wage stability. Phillips, Samuelson and Solow also hold the same view. But various studies undertaken in this connection show that ther is a positive correlation between price flexibility and full employment. Some trade-off between unemployment and inflation is to be found. Thus price stability and full employment are conflicting objectives.

Similarly, there is a conflict between full employment and balance of payments equilibrium. If monetary policy is designed to maximise domestic employment and economic growth, balance of payments deficit is bound to emerge. With the rise of domestic income, imports increase fast. Expansionary monetary policy will create inflation and exports will decrease. In this way balance of payments equilibrium will be disturbed.

The objectives of full employment employment and economic growth too will be found to be conflicting. Full employment is a static concept whereas economic growth is a dynamic concept. Full employment is concerned with raising output to the level of production possibility, whereas economic growth concerns itself with the raising of production possibility itself. If full employment increases income and imports and results in balance of payments dis-equilibrium, the measures adopted to correct it may militate against economic growth.

There is also some conflict between exchange stability, price stability and economic growth. In the initial stages of economic development, imports increase whereas exports are static. This results in exchange insability. Artificially raising the exchange rate will worsen the balance of payments position and slow down the rate of economic growth.

COORDINATION OF OBJECTIVES

There is no doubt that some objectives of monetary policy are in conflict with others. But they can be also reconciled to some extent. There are two approaches to this reconciliation: (*a*) The optimising approach and (*b*) fixed targets approach. The authorities may lay down preference pattern regarding the objectives they would like to achieve. They may also select some rate of **trade off** or substitution between the conflicting objectives. In other words, it may be laid down to what extent one objective can be sacrificed for the achievement of another. It is thus possible to indicate the trade-off and lay down priorities among the objectives.

Optimising Approach. We can make use of Phillips curve (See P. 441) for illustrating the optimising approach and the fixed-target approach. Phillips curve shows an inverse statistical relationship between the rate of change of money wage-rate (inflation) and unemployment. We can express the relationship between the rate of change of prices and the rate of unemployment. The trade-off between the rate of change of prices and unemployment rate can be illustrated by the following diagram.

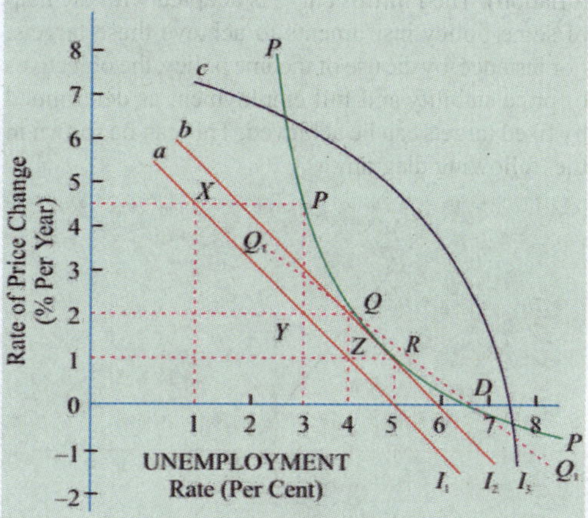

Fig. 54.1.

In this figure (54.1) the rate of price change is represented on the vertical axis and unemployment percentage on the horizontal axis. *PP* is the Phillips curve. Point *D* shows a situation of price stability at an employment rate of 7 per cent (*OD*) **'a', 'b', 'c'** are the indifference curves representing the policy preferences of the authorities regarding unemployment and inflation. Each of these curves shows equallly acceptable combination of unemployment and inflation *e.g.* points *x.y.z.* on the indifference curve **'a'**. But the indifference curve nearer the origin (*i.e.* **a**) is preferred to those which are further off from the origin, because on this curve a certain level of unemployment is associated with smaller rate of inflation as compared with other curves. The authorities will choose a combination which will maximise social welfare. Obviously, they would like to choose point *O* where there is not only full employment but also price stability. But at this point there is a conflict between price stability and full employment. The authorities must therefore choose from the economically possible combinations which lie on the Phillips curve PP. The optimum combination will be where the indifference curve is a tangent to the Phillips curve. This is point *Q* where 2 per cent inflation and 4 per cent unemployment would maximise social welfare. In case the authorities prefer lower rate of inflation with inflation with higher rate of unemployment, they may choose '*R*' which is a point of tangency between the Phillips curve and the indifference curve '*a*'. This means that the authorities regard 5 per cent unemployment and 1 per cent inflation as maximising social welfare. Thus, the actual trade-off between unemployment and inflation will be determined by the preference pattern of the authorities.

Fixed Target Approach. In the fixed target approach, the authorities fix certain desirable targets (say 95 per cent employment and 5 per cent rate of inflation). The Phillips curve is adapted with the help of some policy instruments to achieve these targets. For instance, by the use of income policy, the objectives of price stability and full employment as determined by fixed targets can be achieved. This can be shown in the following diagram:

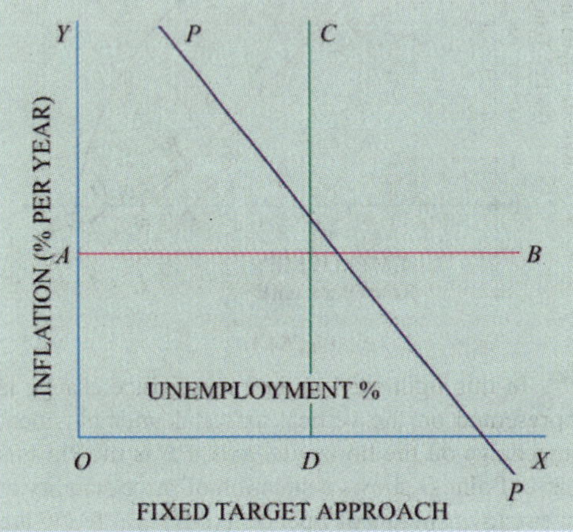

Fig. 54.2.

The Phillips curve *PP* will have to be lowered in order to enable the authorities to keep below the area of *AB* and to the left of *CD*.

Harmonious Adjustment and Judicious Mix.

Some conflicting objectives can be reconciled by making a harmonious adjustment and a judicious mix. For example, the conflict between the objectives of exchange stability and price stability can be resolved if the authorities adopt an action which while maintaining exchange rate coincides with the policy of stabilisation.

In the case of conflicting objectives, the authorities should assign priorities, make a choice and try to have optimal combination depending upon the economic and social conditions of the country. For instance, an optional combination between some rate of wild inflation and economic growth may be found out.

The best way to coordinate the conflicting objectives is to give priority to the solution of short-term problems, but the short-term objectives must be subordinated to the long-term objectives.

MONETARY POLICY VS FISCAL POLICY

Monetary policy affects income and expenditure through cost and availability of money, whereas fiscal policy affects income and spending through government revenues (*i.e.* taxes) and government expenditure. Monetarists assign more important role to monetary policy than to fiscal policy.

Key terms

Monetary policy, Dear money, cheap money neutral money, objectives of monetary policy, regulation of money supply.

QUESTIONS

1. Discuss the main features of post-liberalisation objectives of monetary policy.
2. Under what conditions and to what extent is it possible to improve the terms of trade by deprecaiting the rate of exhange?
3. (*a*) Distinguish between Balance of Trade and Balance of Payments.

   (*b*) Explain the concept of 'balance of payments equilibrium'. What are the methods usually adopted for correcting an adverse balance of payments? How is the disequilibrium in the Balance of Payments corrected?

FINANCIAL SYSTEM

A financial system is essential for an economy, It is better known as, the blood of an economy. It is needed at every function of the economic system whether it is consumption, production distribution or ex change. It has to play a vital role in bringing and developing the economy so as to achieve the required economic and non-economic welfare of a country. A financial system consists of four important units:

1. Financial Institutions
2. Financial Markets
3. Financial Instruments &
4. Financial Managements

Government of any country, through an independent institution called as a 'Central Bank', with a Governor as head, work for the countries financial requirements along with the different objectives needed to be achieved from time to time, with the directions and the measures, support by the respective governments.

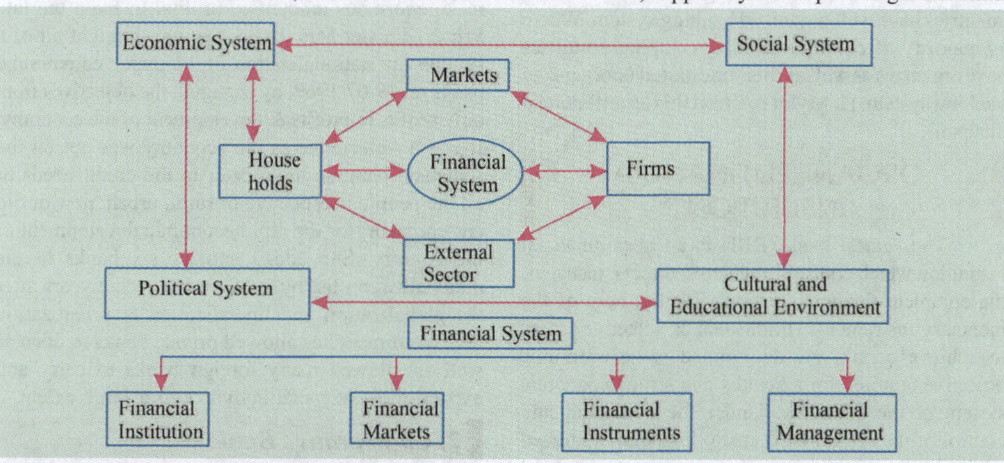

(I) Financial Institutions.

These are the main pillars of any economic system, which determines the complete structure of the total economic activities and responsible for carrying out the main objectives of any financial system viz., the process of capital formations. In the opinion of Ragnar Nurkse, capital formation is that, the society does not apply all of its current productive activity to the needs and desires of immediate consumption, but directs a part of it to the making of capital goods, tools, plants, equipments .... which further increases the efficacy of production. In other words to carry out the capital accumulation needed for the economy to function,

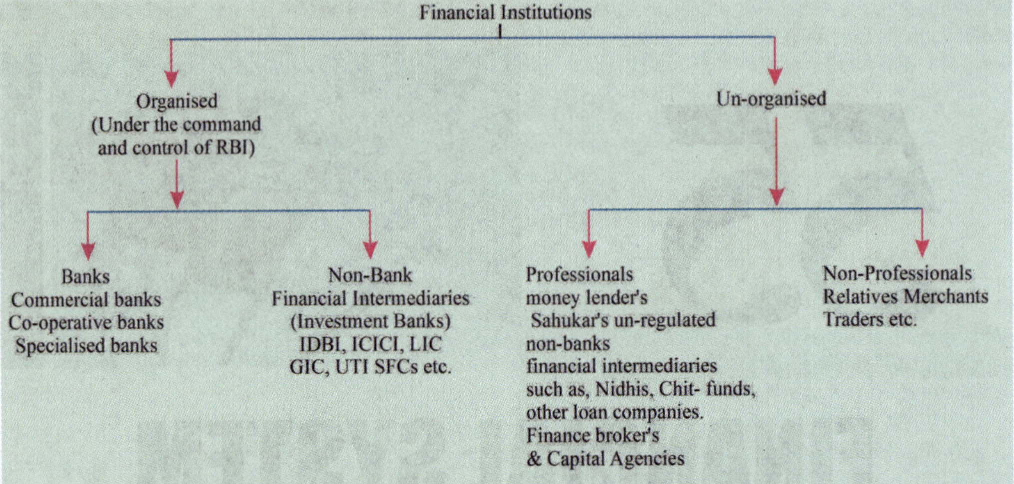

the process of capital formation is needed. This process is nothing, but, the creation, mobilization and channelisation of savings into productive activity. A well established and organized financial institutions or banking is a pre-condition for rapid economic development of any economy. Encouraging or inducing people to save, by different incentives of interest etc., mobilization of these savings and then directing the same for productive activities is the basic function of any financial system and institution.

The financial institutions are further divided into two viz, organized and unorganized. Advanced countries have well organized banking system. Where as majority of colonial ruled developing countries have organizes as well as their traditional unorganized banking system. H. Myint referred this as a 'financial dualism'.

ORGANIZED FINANCIAL INSTITUTION

The central bank (RBI) is an apex financial institution which controls, regulates, directs, manages, the complete financial system with the help of the monetary instruments (traditional & selective) so as to achieve certain pre-determined socio-economic objective required for a healthy and strong economic system of the economy. Under the command and control of the central bank many financial organized institution works, which really help in bringing about the effective measures for the required objectives. Where as some institution do not come directly under the command & control of the central bank, but they are regulated through different other directives. Majority of non-bank financial intermediaries are not directly under the central bank but they have to satisfy certain requirements of it. Most of the unorganized financial institutions do not come under the direct control as well as they avoid the rules and regulations of the central bank. This makes very difficult for the monetary authorities to bring the effectiveness in the regulatory system.

1. *Commercial Banks*

A commercial bank could be defined as "a financial intermediary who lures the depositor to save their money at a lower rate of interest and the same money is offered at higher rate of interest to the business community (barrowers) in the process they make enormous amount of profits. In India the late Prime Minister Mrs. Indira Gandhi, brought all of a sudden the nationalization of 14 major commercial banks on 19/07/1969, by changing the objectives from only profits to profits & development of the economy. It was a right move as the economy was put on the socialism path, so as to cater to the credit needs of all the people irrespective of rural, urban, new or old entrepreneur, for the rapid economic development of the country. She added another six banks to the nationalization list by 1982. In the recent years after the globalization and liberalization & privatization the government has allowed private banks to open as well as allowed many foreign banks to carry and expand their financial activities to a large extent.

2. *Co-operative Banks*

A Co-operative bank may be defined as "an institution of economically weaker sections coming together to mobilize funds by means of membership and non-membership and to provide it to members and non-member to achieve their economic ends earning a nominal profit". It is said that co-operative societies have not much developed as expected but they must develop if you want to achieve higher economic and social welfare. A country like India where most of the commercial banks and co-operative banks are operating to a large proportion of banking system but their performance in terms of economic upliftment has not been very encouraging. Some of the urban cooperative banks have suffered a lot; this is essentially due to the deviation of the objective by the managing committee members, which has led to the increase in non-performing assets. One of the main reasons is, due to either lack of religious faith or moral, ethical values and degrading attitude of becoming rich, a diversion of co-operative spirit from all members & society's welfare to the member's gain, specially those who control the business of the co-operatives.

3. *Specialized Financial Institution*

This is with reference to India, but a number of developing countries can take this experience and derive the benefits of this, as those institutions has contributed to a real prosperity of India from different perspectives of economic, social, equity and balance development concepts etc.

(i) Housing Banks : These banks were created to cater to the housing needs of especially ever increasing urban population. Both private and public banks have been in operation one of the leading private banks is the HDFC (Housing Development Financial Corporation) and the other ICICI, etc. Beside this there are government housing banks such as HUDCO (The Housing and Urban Development Cooperation of India Ltd) & NHB (National Housing Bank).

(ii) EXIM BANK : This was set up on 1st January 1982, so as to cater the financial needs of import & export. The main aim was to improve and develop the external sector of the economy. After globalization and the new industrial policy of July 1991, the role of the EXIM Bank has further increase to higher responsibility.

Other financial institution such as film finance, SIDBI (Small Industries Development Bank of India, April 1990), Risk capital formation [now it is known as IFCI venture capital funds Ltd (IVCF) 1998] & Tourism finance corporation of India etc., has been set up to cater to the different sector needs. This can be included in specialised financial institution. They have been helping the respective sectors on the way for a rapid economic growth.

NON-BANK FINANCIAL INTERMEDIARIES (NBFI)

These institutions are long term financial institution, the main business is to deal in time deposits from depositors point of view and advance loan in thousands of crores of rupees. In America & other developed countries they are known as Investment banks. In the recent October 2008, collapse of stock market specially in America was due to the increase in the non-performing assets (NPA) of these banks. NBFI's offer higher rate of interest and they do not come under the direct control of the RBI (Central Bank). These institutions are the major players in the country's stock market. IDBI (Industrial Development Bank of India) was established in 1964, as an apex refinancing & industrial development oriented financial institutions. ICICI (Industrial Credit and Investment Corporation of India) established in 1955, and now is merged

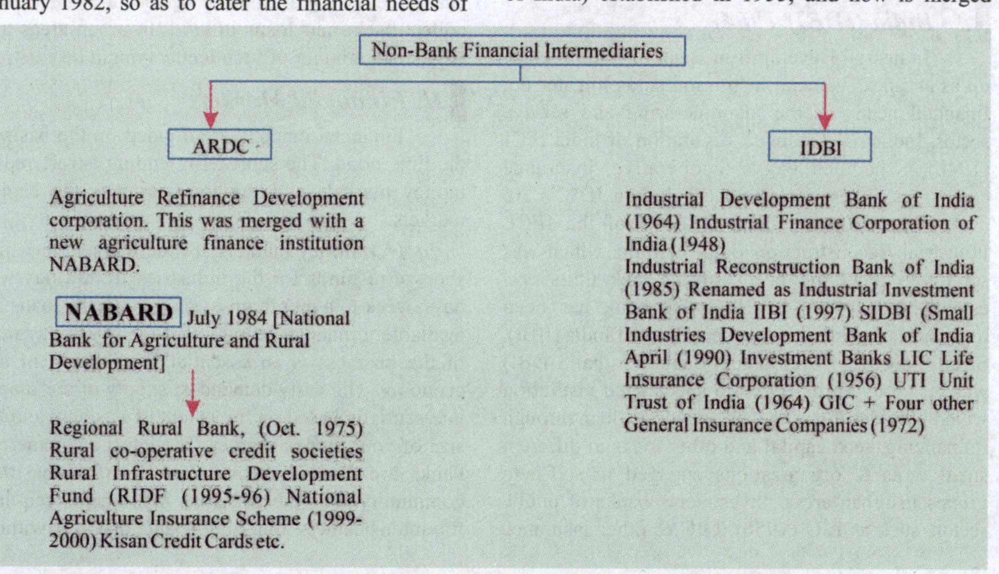

with ICICI bank and it is no more a non-banking financial institution (private bank).

1. *Agriculture Refinance Development Corporation*

Agriculture Refinance Development Corporation was looking after all the agricultural finance including the refinance activities. Mrs. Indira Gandhi the late Prime Minister in 1984 introduced a separate apex rural financial institution to cater to the financial requirements of the rural sector. Reserve Bank of India, was over burdened with different financial activities, hence there was a need for a separate financial institution to look into independently the rural finance and achieve the desired rural development along with the active role of organized institutional finance in agriculture sector. NABARD was established in 1984 which caters to the different needs of finance. Direct, supervisory technological development along with the main role of refinancing the RRB's rural co-operative credits societies, and other activities. Regional Rural Banks were set up on October 2nd 1975, so as to encourage the rural savings mobilization as well as to advance loans to the farmers. This was not brought into complete with the rural co-operative credit societies but to strengthen the institutional finance and get rid of the influence of money lenders. Further the cooperative societies were provided all type of refinance and other facilities by NABARD. NABARD has been playing a vital role in rural development such as Rural Infrastructure Development Fund (RIDF) and contributions to insurance schemes etc.

2. *Industrial Development Bank of India (IDBI) 1964)*

Industrial Development Bank of India was set up as an apex financial institution so as to cater the financial needs of the manufacturing and service sector. Industrial Finance Corporation of India IFCI (1948), Scheduled banks, cooperative, insurance companies, investments trusts including IDBI's are among the different share holder's of the IFCI. Industrial Reconstruction Bank of India which was set up to meet the needs of the sick units was established in1985. In 1997 this bank has been renamed as industrial Investment Bank of India (IIBI). Small Industries Development Bank of India (SIDBI) was set up in April 1990 as a specialized institution which provides direct as well as indirect loan through refinancing, seed capital and other loans to different small units & organizations engaged in self-help groups in urban areas. Investments banks of public sector, such as LIC (1956), GIC & other insurance companies (1972) and UTI (1964), etc were established to mobilize savings, long term capital formation for economic development. Besides this, these institutions play a direct role in industrial activities and also they are the major players in the stock-exchange.

UNORGANIZED FINANCIAL INSTITUTION

Professional unorganized institutions refer to those financial intermediaries who carry out their financial business individually in cities & rural areas, independently. They are not organized one and they do not come under the direct control of the central bank (RBI). Though they take the permission (license) from the central bank to carry out their operation where some Nidhis & chit funds especially in south India are very popular . Nidhis, group collecting money from members and advancing loans to members at lower rate where as to non-members at higher rate of interest. Chit funds, on the other are very common in which members collect certain fixed amount of money as one chit and on the basis of draws; they take the money in lump-sum. Loan companies, Finance brokers, Capital agencies, forms groups and borrow funds from rich individuals specially those who have surplus funds with them, may not be necessarily belongs to industries, and the same money is offered to small businessmen or units, at higher rate of interest. Before independence the Capital Agency system used to exists and finance huge amount to industries.

In rural areas some non-professionals & merchants advances loans to farmers and others & charge heavy rate of interest besides they very often collect back their loans in kind. In urban areas too, very small amount of such lenders might be existing.

II. Financial Markets

Financial markets are divided on the basis of the time bond. The short term lending is referred as money markets and the long term as the capital markets.

(A) Money markets are the markets in which short term funds for the industries from a day to 7 days, week to a month up to six months the loans are available. Financial requirement for day to day need of the business is an essential requirement of any economy. The daily demand & supply of the money is essentially based on the extent of business and the size of your money market. Though the commercial banks are there to provide loans to the business community, but the different instruments required for inter-business transaction and that too without any hurdles, is the role of money markets. Inter-bank lending where a surplus banks gives/offers loans to a deficit bank and the rate of interest is general known as call money market rate. Bill's of exchange or bill market is essentially another types of instruments, besides these certificate of deposits, commercial papers also exists.

(B) Capital market is one of the main indicators of economic activities. Generally the capital market is a market, where loans are available for long term. No. economy can develop without huge amount of investments, in infrastructures, basic and heavy industries and other industries which requires huge amount of investments. The concepts of block, seeds, promoter's capital etc, is essential for inducing either the private investors or the public (government) sector. The experience of Russia during its early planning period gave rich dividends to its defence industries, during Second World War was the result of such investments. Late Prime Minister Jawaharlal Nehru gave its recommendation to the heavy based industries, second five year plan by Mahalnobis. During the early liberalization period the government of India permitted many multinational corporations, to invest huge amount of capital in infrastructure industries. Never the less the capital market is an over all important indicator of an economy's growth rate as well as development.

3. *Financial Instruments*

Financial instruments are the means with which the business transactions are carried out. The general financial instruments are all the near money concepts such as cheques, drafts, credit cards, etc., where as the main instruments which include the money markets call money market bill of exchange Treasury bill, repo's & reverse repose (Liquidity Adjustment Facility), certificate of deposits, commercial paper & money market mutual funds (MMMF). On the hand the capital markets instruments include Government securities (gilt edge securities), industrial securities markets, [New issues (equities etc), old issues (stock exchange)]. etc.

4. *Financial Management*

Financial management are of two types (1) Main the macro management carried out by the central bank through its different methods of credit control measures, such as quantitative (traditional) and selective (qualitative). This aims at controlling and regulating the over all financial system by increasing or decreasing the total money (liquidity) supply (elasticity of supply of currency notes) in the economy. (2) Micro financial management refers to individual organization or government, (central & state, local self) through budgets or financial management departments etc., carried out within the micro management. There are private individual or firms carry out financial management services for which they charge their fees.

In financial system we concentrate on the central banks managements of the total economic system, so as to achieve the desire socio-economic objectives. The government of any country through its central bank regulates, manages, control, directs, the complete financial system, with the aim of achieving certain desirable effects. The measure goes on changing from time to time, depending on the course or phases of the economy as well as the objectives and the goals laid down by the respective governments.

FINANCIAL MARKET REFORMS

To bring about an active financial system in case of developing countries to achieve their desired socio-economic objective, there is a need to have a very optimistic and strong financial management. The central banks of different countries frame the management policies, by bringing about different reforms in their financial system. Some of them are very effective and help the country to achieve the desired results, in favor of the system as well as the economy, for the welfare of the people to increase. There are certain cases where the central banks have failed in their approach and had resulted in a monetary chaos, which had forced them to change their currency units. In South American industrialized countries, specially Argentina and Brazil and some other countries in that region along with some African, Russian block countries faced financial crisis with regards to currencies, due to higher inflation rate, declining unemployment & lower growth rate etc. There was a complete failure of a financial management. The rate of interest being less and the rate of inflation being higher, induced the barrower to barrow huge money and the same pumped in the economy which resulted in higher rate of inflation, in fact 'stagflation'. The economy was not moving in terms of different positive economic variables where as the price continues to rise which increases the inequalities of income and wealth and the concentration of economic power in the hands of few.

1. If the rate of interest is lower and the inflation rate is higher, that means you rare barrowing 'good' money and paying 'bad' money.

GM < BM [GM = Good money, BM = Bad money]

$f > i$

This is beneficial for barrowers and harmful for the lenders (the banking system).

2. If the rate of interest in higher and the rate for inflation is lower than the lenders benefits and borrower suffers. This is depending upon the difference between the rate of interest (i) and the inflation rate (f). $i > f$.

BM > GM. This is the case with the Indian economy where the rate of interest on lending varies from 10% onwards. $(i > f)$

There is a need for the central banks to carry out their policies with regards to their financial management. This needs a review of their management policies from time to time, besides this the influence and the policy of the political parties controlling the system & their agenda also has an effect on the management.

After independence Jawaharlal Nehru did not bring any radical changes in the financial system as the currency was very strong and the rate of inflation was also very less. Indian currency had a smooth sailing as there were no sever effects either from inside and outside the economy. The role of the government towards the economy was very passive with some strong forces in the form of economic planning and deficit finance. In the late sixties, certain external factors combined with internal such as droughts, political changes and also the Hazari committee report (1969) and the strong will-power of the late Prime Minister Mrs. Indira Gandhi for socialism and her bold decision to nationalize the 14 major commercial banks and abolishment of privy purses, initiated the first big financial reforms in the economy. In 1975, further the regional rural bank concept was introduced. Meier and Baldwin were of the opinion that "the currency and credit system must be responsive to stimulate of development, but monetary and financial institutions in themselves cannot be expected to be the primary and active movers of development in direct sense". In 1984, the ARDC (Agriculture Refinance Development Corporation) was merged with a new apex agriculture finance institution was established named NABARD (National Bank of Agriculture and Rural Development) NABARD was to relieve the RBI from its heavy burden of financial activities. It was created to bring out an active dynamic role in agricultural finance, not only the refinance, but technological, infrastructure, direct assistance to all agriculture activities. In the mid eighties the Chakravarty committee was established. Review of working of stock-exchanges, establishment of SEBI and other reforms helped the financial system. It was in July 1991, on the eve of the liberalization, privatization; globalization policy adopted by the government under the GATT agreement the M. Narasimhan (former RBI governor) submitted its report to the government in November 1991. This was essentially in the line with the future (signed the GATT, Dunkel Draft Text DDT) of the Uruguay Round Final Act of 15th December 1993 along with 117 nations on April 15th 1994.

NARSIMHAN COMMITTEE REPORT (1991)

This was the basic input required to strengthen and develop the overall financial system. A financial systems health indicated the functioning of an economy, without which whether the main components of the economy, the household and firms cannot carry out the required activities. So the committee's main core was that "The solvency, health and efficiency of the institutions should be central to effective financial reforms". The committee emphasized more recommendation on the following:

1. With reference to banking system
2. Financial institution including new one
3. Liberalization of control technique of RBI
4. On interest rates
5. On directed credit programs
6. Liberalization of capital markets & other recommendation.

The main thrust of the committee was to strengthen the over all banking and financial institutions. Specially with regards to commercial banks to increases the branch & deposits mobilization which must help in pushing both savings mobilization as well as barrowers, to increase the rural banking, overall banking for strengthening the economy, so that the priority sector and other neglected sectors of the economy is taken care off. It was a kind of synchronized and over all financial development with deeper penetration in agriculture sector as well as unbanked states.

1. *Banking system*

The committee was of the opinion that to improve the profitability and productivity of the banking sector, the following suggestions were made.

i. Three to four large banks (including the state banks of India) which must develop into international standard.

ii. Eight to ten banks with branches all over the country that could be national or universal in nature.

iii. Specific region, local banks to deal with all the financial needs.

iv. Rural areas banks along with regional rural banks (RRB) to meet to the needs of agriculture and allied activities.

The committee suggested that there should be no need for nationalization of banks, further private banks be permitted and the licensing system must be withdrawn.

Foreign banks and Indian banks can develop joint venture, especially in investment & merchant banks as well as other financial activities. Foreign banks should also be allowed to open their branches or subsidiaries, keeping in mind the social obligation of the banks in the line with the national banks.

2. *Financial Institutions (including new one)*

Newly started financial institutions as well as investments banks dealing in merchants banks, mutual funds, leasing companies, venture capital companies, could be given permission and a new agency under RBI should look after their functioning & supervising. The required laws, rules, should be framed as to meet the Indian social obligation. The aim was to bring about a healthy and strong financial system so as to achieve the desire socio-economic objectives. On other hand, banking should be in line with the international standard and character in the light of the globalization aspect. The banking system restructure along with the new financial institution should become a link between the national and international standards to meet the global requirements of the financial system. This may also emerge as one unit and foreign direct investment can flow easily and also there is possibility of reverse flow.

3. *Liberalization of control techniques of RBI*

To increase the efficiency and productivity of the commercial banks, the committee recommended certain liberalization process, which will enhance the profitability of the banks, and bring further development of trade, industry and financial sector. Earlier the banks were suppose to invest 38.5% (SLR) + 15% (CRR) = 53.5%. It means the banks will have only 100 – 53.5% = 46.5% available funds to carry out their day to day business. It was very difficult for the banks to make the necessary profits and maintain efficiency, and compete at the international level with the foreign banks. Under the banking regulation act, 1949 section 24, the commercial banks are to maintain liquidity assets in the form of gold and cash in government securities of their deposits (time + demand). It was raised to 38.5%. In the opinion of the committe, SLR was a fraud perpetrated by the Finance Ministry. The rate of interest offered of SLR and CRR was 10.5%, which was below the market rate. The repercussion of this on the banking system was two fold (a) less funds for banking business and (b) the funds taken by the government offering lower rate of interest than the market rate.

The aim of the government was two fold, one was to have a stronger control over the banking system and the other to invest huge amount of money on social welfare projects, so as to generate a better healthy economic prosperity from the socialism aspects. Through the aim's were good, but to carry out this, there was a need for a "will power" and "good leadership".

The committee recommended that SLR should be reduced in phased manner to 25% and the CRR from 15% to 3 to 5%. By June 2002 the SLR was reduced to 25% and CRR to 5%.

4. *On Directed Credit Programs*

The governments had laid certain major objectives at the time of nationalization of commercial banks in the 1969. One of the main objectives was the importance of loans to priority sector. Over the period the quality of loans to the priority sector was under many problems. The loan melas or loan waiver policy etc. though the banks was instructed that the loans should be 'purpose oriented' than earlier concept of security oriented'. There were many problems. In the priority sector the non-performing assets were increasing, the funds were used for the purpose other than ear-marked; therefore the committee recommended gradually phasing out of the 'directed-credit-program'. The committee redefined the priority sector including small-marginal farms, rural, artisan, tiny industry & cottage industry etc. The total direct credit should be fixed at 10%, and every three years there must be a review, whether to continue the direct program to priority sector'.

In the recent years there are many other problems in this regard, that of the farmer's suicide in Maharashtra etc.

5. *On Interest rates*

The committee was more for an open economy. In its recommendation the committee emphasized on a market based interest rate, rather than completely determined by the monetary authorities. The interest rates controls over the deposits and lending rates of all the financial institutions including banks, as well as with regard to debentures fixed deposits of companies etc must be removed. There is need to phase out the priority sector lending rates to small scales and also the subsidy offered on IRDP etc should be stopped. The committee was of the opinion that the structuring of the interest rate is essential to induce competition and operational efficiency among the banks and financial authorities. Besides the RBI must be the sole authority to restructure, bank rate, deposit rates, prime lending rates, government barrowing rates, etc, so that the real rate of interest must be positive (If the rate of interest is greater than the inflation rate than it is positive, on the other if the rate of interest is lower than the rate of inflation, it is negative, $i > f = i + ve$ & $i < f = i - ve$) (i = the existing rate of interest, f = the prevailing inflation rate for the year).

6. *Liberalization of Capital Market & Other Recommendation*

The committee recommended more openness and liberalization of capital market. This will enhance more investment in the capital market on the other hand SEBI must function as a market regulatory institution, so that it can protect the interest of the investors. With regards to the instruments of debt, their nature, pricing, terms and condition etc should be left to the issuer and more freedom must be given to the concern companies / institutions. The capital market must be given enough freedom so that it can gradually open up for foreign investors and induced the total quantity of trading in it. There was need for the nationalized banks to have access to capital market to raise funds through capital issue.

With the recommendation of Narsimhan Committee Report, the SLR was reduced from 38.5% to 25% as well as the CRR was gradually decreased to 5.5% by December 2001. Many reforms accepted and the interest rates were also reduced on deposits etc. Many loan interest were decontrolled. Under the reforms prudential norms were introduced by RBI, so as to bring about a strong and healthy financial system. So as to strengthen the over-all economy, trade, industry, service sector etc. On 23rd April 1998, second Narsimhan Committee Report was submitted. The committee was of the opinion that there is a need to bring about high efficiency in the banking system, stronger & healthy banking is the need of the hour, to face the challenges of the open liberalized economy. The capital account convertibility (CAC) reforms, with regard to international trade as the total volume of inflow and outflow of capital and its emerging complication can destabilize the domestic economy as well as exchange rate management. In the recent October 2008, economic crisis this was evident that the Rupees value in terms of American dollar ($) started depreciating very fast. This was due to international factors of recession, under which many foreign investors started unloading shares and took away their investments in terms of $. The committee was concerned with the public sector weak banks. This is because their NPA (Non-performing Assets) were increasing therefore the concepts of narrow banking is to be followed. These banks should put their funds only in short term risk free assets. There is also need for the setting up of Assets Reconstruction Funds (ARF). The committee advocated that 8 to 10 large banks with all India level branches and must cater to the needs of large & medium corporate sectors and entrepreneurs. 2 to 3 large banks like SBI with an international level functioning and standard, while local needs should be taken up by small banks with branches over all the interior of the country. The committee stressed the needs for technological upgradation and professional competence at the top management level to take effective & positive decision making. Therefore the requirement of a high degree of professionalism in management is a must. Overall the aim of financial environment, which must induce and motivate the free and smooth functioning of the economy so that the desired socio-economic objectives are achieved within a short-period of time.

MONEY MARKET, CAPITAL MARKET, STOCK-EXCHANGE AND SEBI

Any economy to run efficiently needs money. Money is the required energy to put the economy on the road. The different policies are introduced by respective governments to achieve certain pre-determined socio-economic objective or to increase the economic & social welfare of the society through the total supply of money in the economy. The monetary authorities goes on changing the elasticity of supply of currency notes in the economy, as to the need of the economy concerned. No economy can carry out its total economic activities with the use of only liquidity or money (cash). Though the total amount of money determines the extent of market. In the modern economies the total purchasing power determines the size of an economy. Since the world is experiencing the liberalization era, hence the total purchasing power must be in line with not only the internal economic requirement but also the external economy has to be taken into account. The concept of near money which has been playing an important role in easing the business transaction. In our country the so called 'Hundis' (the commercial exchange bills) in the form of Muddati (time bond) and Darshani (Bearer) were existing since the early 19th century onwards. Due to industrial revolution & further the World War I, II, after the era of free countries from 50's onwards and the domination of market oriented goods, energized by the Japanese miracle growth which was referred as the 'FMCG' (Fast Moving consumer Goods Industries). Initiated the need for more 'near money' concept. The development of further service sector, specially the communication process, innovation in banking due to the computer and mobiles has increased enormously the role of near money in the economy. Majority of the banking and non-bank financial intermediaries have been engaged in the economic activities, more with near money than the actual liquidity or cash. The commercial banks have been using the investments such as cheques, demand drafts, emergency vouchers etc, to facilitate and speed up their business transaction, besides this we have 'money market' and 'capital market', in which some specialized instruments have been used so as to ease the business transaction, so that the economy can move faster and achieve its desired economic and other objectives. Money market refers to a place where the short-term funds up to 1 year is available in the economy, with the different forms of instruments accepted in the business and floated by either the monetary authorities or the banking sector including the non-banking institutions. On the other hand capital market is a place where long-term' funds are available for industries and other sector in the form of government bonds 'company equities and so on. Over-all the aim is to strengthen and stimulate the economy, to achieve the desired economic effects.

Main functions of a money market

1. A link between the supplier of funds and the need (demand) for short-term funds. Thus achieving a balance between them, which is reflected through the call money rates, etc?
2. 'Near Money' market which helps the over-all economy's purchasing power needs, along with the supply of currency notes'.
3. Helps in bringing about an effective & efficient monetary policy, so, as to achieve the desire economic & non-economic objectives.
4. It is a dual returns oriented, place, where the supplier of funds get their fair return and also to the needs of working capital of the business concerns for their return and their investment.
5. It helps the government to obtain the non-inflationary funds to cater to its developmental requirements. (The indirect taxes of the government are inflationary in nature).
6. The different instruments help the functioning & speed up of the economy, which in turn results in many economic gains.

Diagram – I

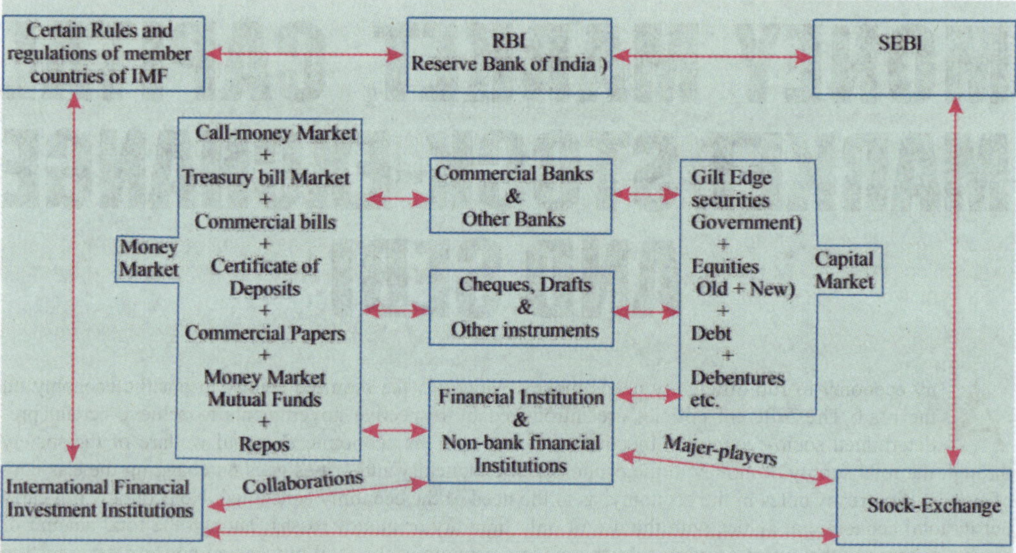

MONEY MARKET

Market is a place where buyers and sellers bargain each other to buy & sell a product. Here product is with reference to near money which is essential component of any economy's requirement; hence a money market is defined as "a market dealing in near money for short term up to one year, by the banking, non banking and business concern under stipulated directives, rules of the RBI". A money market provides the required motive power or an economy for day to day business especially for working capital. Its dealings depend upon the size of an economy and market money (cash) alone cannot solve the immediate required funds for any economy in the world, hence the role of money market enters into it.

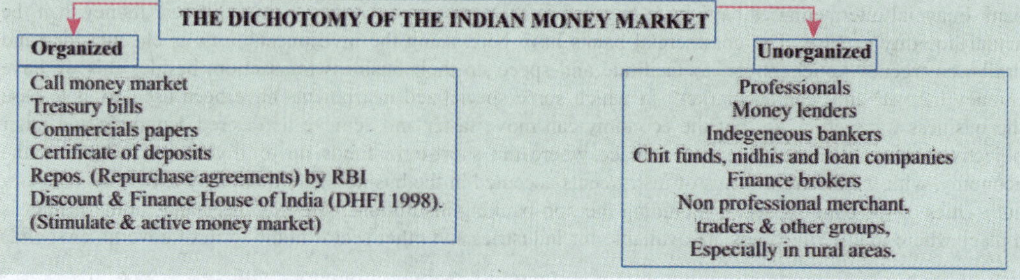

ORGANIZED SECTOR

1. Call money market: It is one of the most basic components of money market where generally the immediate needs of the different economic agents are available. It meets the day to day, weekly .... requirements of the different banks for their further business transactions. Call money market is a place where a bank with surplus funds, supplies it to a bank in need with deficit funds. The rate at which the bargaining point is reached is referred as "Call Money Rate". The call money in terms indicates two important aspects (i) The economic activity (ii) The total availability of funds such as a cheap or dear money policy of the financial authorities.

Diagram – I

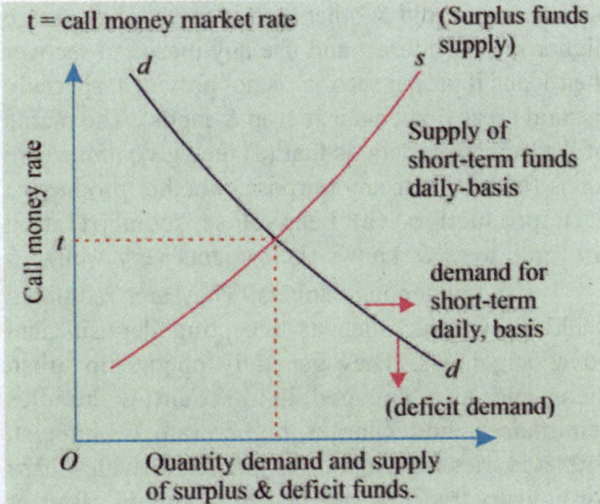

The shape of demand for short term funds that is steeper & flatter is based on the total economic requirements of short term funds where as the 'ss' supply for short term funds is depending upon the efficiency of commercial banks to attract & mobilize the savings (funds) in the economy, further on their policies as well as the RBI rate of interest and other fiscal policies etc. Higher the call money rate, the dear money policy is an operation, where as lower the call money market rate, the cheap money policy. Since, the call money market is very sensitive and temporary in nature, and the over all economic activities cannot be judged by it, the call money markets are generally centered in the cities which are commercially very active.

2. Treasury bill market: The RBI issues the treasury bills on behalf of the government to meet its deficits etc. The treasury bills are considered to be highly liquid as well as easily available with assured yields. Thus bills are fortnightly auction and between (14 days, 91 days, 182 days, 364 days) the commercial banks can invest their SLR's (statutory liquid ratios) with the government in the form of these treasury bills. The banking sector claims that they are getting lesser rate of returns of these investments then the market rate of return.

3. Commercial bill market : The commercial bill is known as bills of exchange or trade bill it is bill drawn by the seller to the buyer. The bill period is 90 days, and interest charged is the rate of discount which is based on the market demand and supply. During the usance period that is fixed period, the bill can be discounted and rediscounted by the commercial bank, this makes the bill as self liquidating short term fund. The government introduced two bills in 1952 and 1970, so as to strengthen the bill market system. In 1971 to encourage and motivate the business activities the RBI under the bill culture advised the bank, that the 25% of the inland credit purchases of borrowers should be carried out with the help of commercial bills & also withdraw the 12.5% interest rate ceilings on the bills rediscounting. There are many limitations with regard to bill market scheme and still it is referred as under developed. The government has appointed a committee under chairmanship of U.R. Ramamoorthy.

4. Certificate of deposits: The certificate of deposits was introduced by the RBI in 1989. The commercial bank issues CDs to the depositor, the certificate is used at a rate of discount on to its maturity period (face value). It is to be issued in multiples of Rs. 25 lakh and the minimum size should be Rs: 1 crore in recent years it has been reduced to Rs. : 5 lakh and this can be increased in the multiples of Rs 1 lakh. Earlier the CDS were transferred freely after 45 days from the date of issue, now it is reduced to 15 days (lock-in-period). Scheduled banks and financial institutions are allowed to issue, with the maturity period of 15 days to 1 year, where as non-bank financial institutions form a maturity period of 1 year to 3 years. It is not doing well and continuously on the decreasing trend.

5. Commercial paper market: The commercial paper concept was introduced by the RBI in January 1990. High reputed leading nationally & internationally credit worthy Indian manufacturing, finance companies are allowed to issue certificate of deposit to the investors. This is essentially to raise the required funds as well as an opportunity to investors to earn through investments in reputed companies. A company with not less than Rs. 4 crore of investment of working capital and Rs. 4 crore in tangible asset can issue up to 75% of its working capital. The period is between 15 days to 1 year, the rate of interest on commercial paper by the companies offered are lower than the prime lending rate of the commercial banks, thus helping them to get their required funds at lower costs. Reputed corporate bodies, standard commercial banks, mutual funds. LIC, GIC & UTI are the major participants in this market.

6. Repos (repurchase agreements): It is dealing between a buyer and a seller. A seller sells the security to a buyer under a mutually agreed agreement in which the seller buys the same security at a particular future date & price. Selling with an agreement to repurchased at future price & date is referred as 'repos' (from seller's point) and reverse repo (from buyer's point), it was introduced in December 1992. It is a regular feature of RBI's operation, dealing central government securities. There are two repos (i) Inter Bank & (ii) the RBI's. (i) Inter-banks public sector under taking (PSU) bonds and private corporate debt securities and (ii) the RBI's government securities. Earlier the rate of interest was very less and due to inflationary trend in the economy the reverse-repo at 6%, but due to the October 2008, depression trend all-over the world, the RBI brought many monetary measures as liquidity adjustment facilities to lower the repo and reverse-repo rates, and the total liquidity in the economy must increase, and the level of effective demand must be pushed up. Even with such measures in December 2008, the economy did not pick-up, rather the rate of inflation reached less than 8%.

7. Money Market Mutual Funds. (MMMF): In the late 90's mutual funds entered with a bang, in the Indian financial system. In line with the same the RBI introduced in April 1992, a new fund to encourage and motivate individual investors, the MMMF was set up. This was an attractive scheme and very helpful in mobilizing additional funds for the economy. The banks, public financial institutions, non-banking financial institutions, & private sector institutions were allowed to set up MMMF. The individuals and also the corporate sectors can participate in it. The money thus obtain must be invested only in the money market instruments. The lock in period is 15 days, earlier it was '46' days, MMMF's including the private sectors are required to obtain RBI's permission and they are under the regulation of SEBI since March 2000.

8. Discount and Finance House of India (DFHI): It was set up jointly by RBI & private sector banks in April 1988. The aim was to accelerate the money market. The bills and short-term papers of commercial banks to be bought by DFHI's, so that, these institution can put their idle cash balance in short-term investments. Besides this the DFHI is involved in government securities, call money market (inter-banks lending) and term deposit market, as both lender and borrower. Due to these activities of stimulating money market, it has been accredited as 'primary Dealer', In February 1996. RBI has been providing enough funds to deal in government securities. It has branches in major cities in Chennai, Kolkata, Delhi, Bangalore, Ahemadabad, etc.

The Unorganized Sector

It consists of three important components.

(*i*) Indigenous bankers,

(*ii*) Money lenders

(*iii*) Unregulated financial intermediaries

(*i*) Money lenders are the common forms of indigenous bankers specially in agriculture sector, but they exists in urban areas too. They give 'loan against crops, gold & other securities etc. They charge higher rate of interest and use any means to recover their loans if proper security is not provided, specially in rural areas (loan against crop & lands). The merits of the money lenders, is that (a) they give immediate loans (b) loans for any purpose, whether productive & unproductive, (c) keep close social relation (in rural areas & knows their clients very well).

(*ii*) Indigenous bankers: They are traditional banking systems, such as accepting deposits and advancing loans. They generally operate in urban areas and also engaged in discounting hundies remittances, and charges higher rate of interest. Interest varies from market to market. Provides loans for industry trade, & they belong to certain castes or groups such as, Multanis, Shroff, Marwari, Kayas, Chettiars etc. They generally combined their activities of banking along with trade, brokers, general merchant, proprietors of sugar, flour mills, etc.

(*iii*) Unregulated non-banking financial intermediaries: Generally this includes the chit funds, nidhis and loan companies. Chit funds are very common means of group activities, where members, contribute a fixed amount of money and the beneficiary will be on the basis of previously agreed criteria or by drawing lots, bids etc. They are very popular in South India especially in Kerala & Tamilnadu. Every member is assured the lump-sum amount. On the other hand Nidhi are mutual benefit funds, member collect huge amount of money and the same money is advanced as loans to members and non-members. For members they charge reason able rate of interest, where as for non members higher rate of interest. They are very popular in south India. Loan companies consists of group of people coming together contributing their own funds, and also accepts deposits from others by offering lucrative incentives and the money is partly deposited in fixed deposits of commercial banks (depending on business conditions) and remaining advances loans to other. They give loans to self-employed, artisan, retailer, wholesalers, traders, small scale industries, etc & charges very high rate of interest. There are some middle-man who helps in the business especially in cloth, grains and other markets in major cities and are referred as finance brokers.

FEATURES & DEFECTS OF THE INDIAN MONEY MARKET

1. It is of a dual nature: It consists of organized sector and unorganized sector. Both are involved in providing short-term funds for economic activities, both have merits and demerits. The main difference is, that the organized one is under the direct control & supervision of the RBI and whatever changes the monetary authorities brings, so as to correct the economy, it is very effective. They follow a set of rules and regulation charges lower rate of interest. On the other hand the unorganized do not come under direct control, beside this they do not separate short-term & long term loans as well as the purpose of loans, hence very difficult to correct their activities, so that the financial system could be strengthen.

2. Lack of integration: There is no balance between the activities of the different organized sector as well as between the organized and unorganized sector. The main objective of the different organized money market viz., the SBI, the commercial, foreign, cooperative, development & investments banks are not completely in line with the socially necessary objective of the economy. There is lack of economic & social development concept, individual profits making objective is at the top, and this is in conflict with the purpose of their advancement. There is no check on the amount of black-money or unaccounted money put into the economy by the banks & companies in the form of the different instruments. Thus with the on slaught of liberalization, privatization and globalization, the amount of liberty provided to private sector & to foreign investments, it is very difficult to keep the social obligation of the banks into the mind set. There is difference of rate of interest and returns as well as, no-coordination between the organized and unorganized sector.

3. Multiplicity in rate of interest: The rate of interest differs from one organized unit to another. The barrowing rate of government deposits, lending rate, the commercial banks, foreign banks, co-operative banks non-banks financial institutions are different. There is lot of variation. The rate of interest offered is less than the market rate of return, therefore the Narsimhan Committee suggested, the reduction in SLR. Different banks offer different rates under different schemes, under the time deposits. Easy liquidity concept is also helping the banks to increase their rate of interest on the borrowers in money market. There is lot of difference between rural and urban cooperatives, this has resulted in the executive committee members of rural cooperatives in diverting the rural saving to urban markets especially in unproductive activities, etc.

4. Absence of organized bill market: In land bills and foreign bills needs to be enlarged. The use of commercial bill is less, though the banks find it very, lucrative as well as easily transferable into liquidity. Due to the preference of cash and instead of discounting the bills, they prefer to barrow from banks. To enlarge the business activities, there is a strong need to bring about an effective strong bill market system. If the business expands than due to the multiplier effect the economy can gain many benefits. The banks have surplus funds and they want to finance, because it may be giving them more returns than the other investments. The RBI can use these bills effectively for its open market operation, especially when the economy is in depression or there is need for more money supply, than it can bring it in the open market, which will enhance the liquidity in the economy, and bring the required effect.

5. Seasonal stringency of money: Though the Indian economy is not an agrarian economy and the contribution of agriculture sector to the total national income is continuously declining, on the other hand the service and manufacturing sectors is increasing, even than, the agricultural seasonal activities has a direct effect on the total money supply and the activities of money market. The busy season is from November to June and July to October is the slack season. The demand for money increase to a greater extent and the supply does not keep pace with it, this results in the problems of shortages and the rates of interest in the unorganized sector to increase. July to October is off season as well as many festivals etc. fall in the busy season and very less in slack season. Due to this the banks are having a surplus funds in slack season and shortage of funds in the busy season. Though there were some measures by the RBI, but this is to be corrected not only with the increase or decrease in money supply, but along with the government economic activities is to be introduced so that even in the slack seasons the demand for money exists. The macro-economic policies, specially external sector, must be encouraged and incentives provided, so that, the external economic activities can keep the demand for money in the line of supply, as well as other economic gain could be achieved.

6. Highly Volatile Call Money Market: Call market rates goes on changing very fast, as it is based on market behaviour. Money at call or short-notice is the inter-bank lending rate in which a surplus bank provides loans to a deficit bank in need of money. Though the RBI interfere with the help of open market operation to correct the demand and supply of money in the economy. If we take the highest call rate and lowest call rate of some years, for e.g. 1990-91, highest 70, lowest 4, 2000-2001, highest 14, lowest 4, 2004-2005, highest 6.25, lowest -0.60. If there is a dear money policy by the government it can cross even 100 mark, on a particular day or if cheap money policy, than it can decrease below 1. There is need to do more to narrow down the volatility in call rate by the RBI.

7. Inadequacy of credit instruments: Earlier the instruments were very limited, such as call money market, bill market & treasury bills. In the 90's the government introduced the concepts of certificate of deposits, commercial papers, MMMF etc. Besides the DFHI's setting up and its role to boost the money market activity has helped in this regard. There is still more proper decision making and introduction of new instruments, along with the encouragement and incentives to the trading community to use these instruments, so as to increase the total financial activities. In comparison with the London & New York money market Indian market needs more instruments to be introduced for an effective and efficient money market to achieve its desired result.

8. Absence of well-organized banking system: The banking system still needs more supervisory functions, rather than the development functions. Through the nationalization the urban oriented banks have been diversified to rural and unbanked areas. The branch expansion, saving mobilization, advances has increased but there are many other defects. The banks loyalty with the RBI is still not 100%. The functioning of the commercial banks may be is in line with the socio-economic development. The case of Japan, in which the Zaibatsu and other corporate sector takes active role in social development equally with their economic objectives. The Harshad Mehta, banking scam (1992) Ketan Parekh (2001), C.M. Agarwal (March 2002), are some of the examples where the different banks funds were used and diverted for speculative gain, putting the whole society into financial chaos or crisis. The insolvency of many banks had put the faith of many depositors and dealers in money market into dilemma. Further due to more freedom under financial reforms, especially to establish the Indian banks on line with foreign banks, there is a need to see, how much faithful the commercial banks and other financial institutions.

Reforms in Indian Money Market

The appointment of different committees and their recommendations, such as S. Chakarvarthy (1985), N. Vaghul (1987), M. Narsimhan (1992, 1998) has further helped and strengthened the functioning of Indian money market.

1. Relaxation of interest rate regulation: The RBI had earlier introduced controlled rate of interest to control inflation. On the basis of different recommendation the RBI has initiated more on a competitive, market oriented rate of interest. Ceiling rate reduced on bank advances, call money rates (inter-bank lending) and short notice money. The minimum lending rate of commercial banks and public sector development financial institution gradually declined from 18.5% to 10.5% (2004-05) to increase the liquidity in the economy, The RBI continued to reduce the bank rate from 10% (1990-91) to 6% (2003-04).

2. Introduction of new instruments in the money market: On the basis of the recommendation of the Vaghul working group, RBI introduced new money market instruments, such as changes in treasury bills, dated government securities, certificate of deposits, commercial papers etc. Repo, and reverse repo's that is repurchase auctioned dated government securities were introduced, this has helped the authority to enhance liquidity in the economy and one of the effective measures of the liquidity adjustment facility (LAF). Repo's is a deliberate policy of the RBI to increase the liquidity in the money market. In the recent crisis on October 2008, the Repo & reverse repo's have been effectively used by the RBI to a greater extent, in temporary managing the on-slaught of the sudden collapse of the economy.

3. Stamp duty reforms: Due to the imposition of stamp-duties on the different money market securities and lending, had a number a repercussions on their functioning. Hence there was need to get away with the stamp-duties instead a flat-rate fee could be imposed, so as to enhance &

improve the smooth trading instruments in the money market there was further suggestion to exempt the stamp-duties on the transaction of securities in dematerialized (demat) from.

4. Electronic dealing system: To have a better transparency and efficiency in the money market operations there is a need for this system. Banks, financial institutions, and RBI can use this system to observe and act in the money market activities. The rate of different instruments such as call money rates, repo's, treasury bills etc. can provide immediate information and hence it can activate and speed up the money market transactions.

5. Money market mutual funds (MMMF): This new instrument has been encouraged to mobilized and channelized the funds. This was introduced in April 1992, on one hand the individuals and corporate bodies can invest and on the other commercial banks; financial institutions and private sectors can set up the funds. The money can be invested in money market instruments such as debentures, well rated corporate bonds etc. The minimum lock in period is 15 days.

6. Discount and finance house of India (DFHI): It was set up jointly by RBI with public sector commercial banks and financial institutions in 1988. The aim was to bring about all the organized financial institutions such as commercial banks, financial institutions, cooperative banks & foreign banks to play an active role in money market with regards to the demand for and supply of funds.

7. Development of inter-bank call / notice / term money market: Generally there are inter-bank lending there were certain restriction with regard to borrowing & lending the banks & primary dealer (PD), were given both, the barrowing & lending facilities where as the financial institutions and mutual funds were only lenders, this has been removed, so as to enlarge and bring about competition and stabilize the rates in the call money market.

8. Regulation of (non-banking financial companies NBFC's): To incorporate and regulate the unorganized sector, through an amendment in the RBI act 1997, all the NBFC's can carry out there, acceptance of deposits and financial activities only after obtaining a certificate of registration from RBI. There is regulation on their rate of interest offered as well as they have to submit periodical report to the RBI. This has been done so as to have greater transparency, organizational stability to avoid the excessive rate of interest and commissions to agents etc.

9. The clearing corporation of India (CCIL): The state bank of India as chief promoter, the CCIL was registered on April 30, 2001 under the company's act 1956. The CCIL clears all transaction of government securities & repos reported under the negotiated dealing system (NDS) of RBI and also rupee / US $ foreign exchange spot & forward deals. It is Mandatory to settle less than Rs. 20 crores dealing through CCIL and above Rs. 20 crores through the RBI or the CCIL.

CAPITAL MARKET

Capital market is a market in which the long term financial dealings are carried out. Generally the funds are used for fixed or block capital or seed capital by big corporate sector, including public (government) and foreign. The governments through RBI, the corporate sectors, financial institutions,

Diagram – III

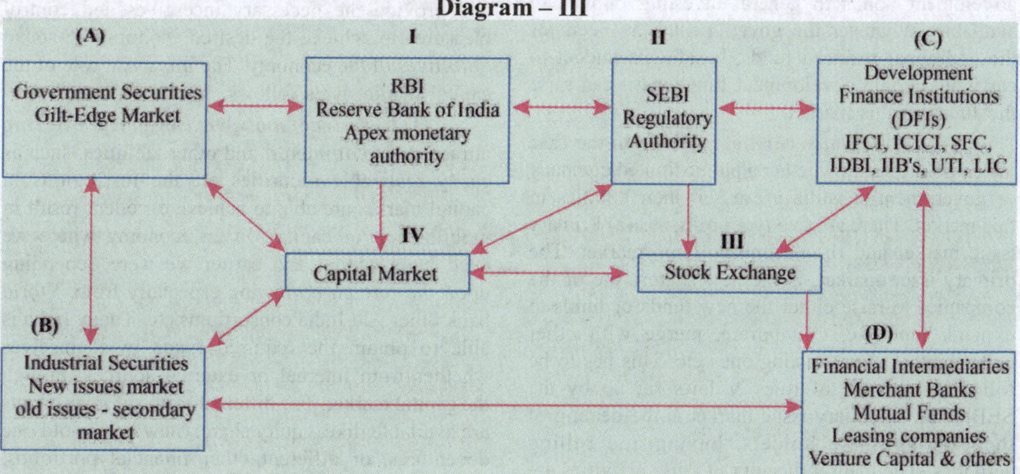

development banks, mutual funds, foreign direct investors or institutions are the major players along with the small investors etc.

1. RBI is the monetary and financial authority which has to look after the complete functioning of the financial system along with the needs & requirements of the government, the corporate sector, the investors (local & foreign), the economy, common man's interest specially in the total economic activities so that whatever economic & social agenda, the government has purposed to achieve within a time frame work and achieve the desired standard of living.

2. SEBI: The security & exchange board of India has been established as non-statutory board (1988) and accorded statutory status (January 1992). It is a regulatory authority to look into the functioning of stock exchange, new issues of the companies, operation of mutual funds and the activities of the merchant banks on their issue activities etc.

3. Stock exchange: It is the centre of all long term financial activities. It measures the economic activities of the country; generally it has been referred as the pulse indictor of an economy's strength & weaknesses. Major Players operate in the stock exchange, the over all economic activities and the players keep watch on it, especially from investment & other financial activities, point of view.

4. Capital market is the name assigned to the place where the long term financial dealings are carried out, there are four main components of it.

***(i)* Gilt Edge Securities market:** This deals in the government and semi-government securities. The commercial banks, other banks & financial institution can invest in this. Some of the investment is mandatory and some are open. Even the government bonds to general investing public are available. Whatever the government is in need for the additional required funds, besides its budget to carry out certain development functions it can raise the funds in this market.

***(ii)* Industrial securities market:** In the case the corporate sector whether a public limited company or government subsidiary can sell their equities in this market. There are two types of issues (a) Primary issue market and (b) Secondary issue market. The primary issue market, is the new share issue of the companies to raise either the new funds or funds to expand, innovate, collaborate, merge with other companies of their existing ones etc. This has to be followed by a set of rules & laws set up by the SEBI. The secondary issue market is the dealing of the existing share holders, buying and selling activities. The main indicators of these activities are reflected through the stock exchange index, in which the share price of the company is based on, the total demand for and the total supply of it. The index may motivate or discourage the buyers & seller depending on the situation.

***(iii)* Development Financial Institutions:** Special institutions were set up to develop the economy from time to time after independence. This was an essential ingredient and to push the economic activities under the mixed system, now it is a kind of welfare capitalism concept. IDBI, ICICI, IFCI, SFC, UTI & LIC & other general insurance companies are referred as the development financial institutions. These are the main institutions which mobilize capital for long term period and invest money in industrial, infra-structural and service sector development. Overall economic activities are accelerated with the inputs from these institutions.

***(iv)* Financial intermediaries:** These are the institutions which are providing different types of long term financial activities to the corporate sector and other government and semi-government sector. They have been playing a vital role and in India a new form of investment activities and facilities are provided which in real terms will accelerate the aggregate economic activities. Merchant banks, mutual funds, leasing companies, venture capital & other facilities are the different components of these financial intermediaries.

Role of capital market in India

The capital market in India plays a very active and dynamic role in mobilization and channelizing of long term funds into the economy. Though the capital market was not so active in the pre-independence as it is today. The government, through the Finance Ministery & the RBI has to keep a vigil and provide the necessary incentives and control measures to achieve the desired economic & social objectives of the economy. The important role of the capital market is as follows.

(1) Resource mobilization: By offering attractive rate of interest and other facilities, such as easily realizable securities etc the institutions in capital market are able to achieve excellent result in mobilization of capital. In an economy where we need huge capital and earlier we were depending upon the foreign borrowing especially from, World bank other Aid India consortiums etc. Today India is able to obtain the required funds by themselves whether from internal or external sources through the capital market. The different forms of investments are available, like, equity share, (new one or old one debentures, or different other financial portfolios, including gold, ornament land etc, with easy accessibility and in cashability. They offer higher rate of return than the common banking system.

(2) Channelization of funds (investments): A capital market is a place where funds are mobilized and the same is offered to industrialists for further investments activities, this is a very important function of an economy. Without this the economy can not achieve long term economic development. Long term investments are essential for further cumulative economic activities, Arthur Lewis & W.W. Rostow and others have given important place for capital investment. In the contemporary world both industrial sector (metal & chemical based) and service sector (infra-structure including communication, dams, transportation, hospitality industries etc.) are fast developing which needs huge investments for long term. The development of capital market thus indicates the development of an economy.

(3) Industrial & service sector development: The domination of industrial sector and service sector needs a quick availability of funds, to carry out their long term requirements. Since finance is an essential component and ingredient of these sectors. The development of capital markets helps into a sustained economic activities. New entrepreneurs may emerge, more technological development (especially in investments carried out in R & D), diversification, collaboration, amalgamations, merger's etc can go on and which brings along with it many economic gains.

(4) Economic Development: Economic development is the prime concerns of many developing countries. One of the essential requirements is that of capital '(money)'. After 1950's many international agencies in collaboration with the developed industrialized countries offered their funds for the investments in these countries. When economies start opening up due to the GATT / WTO, institutions, financial revolution started picking up. The modern day, financial activities are a world-wide phenomenon. It is easily moving in those directions where it is required in terms of the investors gain. In India due to this the FDI & the foreign institutional investments increased enormously, which helped the economy to achieve certain positive economic benefits. From October 2001 onwards India was able to provide finance to IMF as a creditor country. Huge amount of foreign exchange has not been properly and gainfully used in India.

(5) Indicator and guide to corporate sector: The movement in the capital market with regard to companies shares (buying and selling) indicates its performance and deficiencies. The total turn over of a corporate sector can show the importance of it in the market. If the companies shares are appreciating than, it can get further boost to its diversification, expansion and other related objectives. Even if a company is able to raise additional funds by means of other forms of securities or barrowing at lower rate of interest than it reveals the strength of the company. Modern corporate sector needs dynamism, and must have flexible organization structures to cope-up with the changing needs of consumers (internal and external) of an economy. Therefore they constantly need the funds as and when required and this they can easily obtain, if their financial health in the capital market is strong.

(6) Source of modernization & technical assistance to industries: In India there are some specialized financial developmental institutions in operation which caters to this need. IFCI, ICICI, IDBI, IIBs and others have been helping the industries, beside major players in the stock exchange and also the source of funds to the corporate sector. In case of venture capital, the financial institutions are providing new technological adaptation, to technocrat entrepreneurs. There are separate financing agencies for software and IT industry (NVFSIT National Venture Funds for Software and IT Industry)

Growth of Indian Capital Market

There are a number of factors which are responsible for the growth of capital market in India. It is not only responsible for the expansion, enlargement, but also the activities in the capital market have increased enormously as well as attracted huge amount of transaction internationally. It has provided quick information of the activities & the so called appreciation and depreciation of the shares, the governments policy through the liberalization, decontrol, and to a more open competitive market and the different form of development & financial institution have helped in the growth of capital market.

1. Growth of stock exchanges: The first stock exchange was established in Bombay in India in 1987. Over the years the stock exchanges have become stronger. The number of stock-exchange in India has increased from 8 (1970-71) to 23 (2003-04). The number of listed companies increased from 5,969 (1990) to 89, 871 in March (2000). The total resources mobilization, including debt and equity securities from 6970 crores (2002) to Rs. 30,391 crores (2005).

2. Progress of development banks: There has been a continuous increase in the number of development banks and industrial financing institutions, IFCI (1948), ICICI (1955), IDBI (1964), IRCI (1971). 18 state finance corporations (SFCI) 26, state industrial corporations (SICs) the LIC (1956), UTI (1964) and General Insurance Corporation & its subsidiaries (1972) etc. These institutions are the major players in the stock-exchanges. They are engaged in subscribing to the shares & debentures of new and old companies, offers loans & underwriting new issues, where as the UTI, LIC, GIC etc are the institutions which mobilize huge amount of long term funds and put them in the stock-market as well as in the government securities. The total assistance sanctioned by the term lending institution, increased from Rs 230 crores (1970-71) to over Rs. 57,000 crores in (1996-97) and further at Rs. 66,420 crores (2001). Due to these emerging institutions and their active participation, the capital market has further strengthened.

3. Progress of commercial banks: Commercial banks have been playing a vital role in the economic development. In the recent years they have been progressively involved in the capital market adopting new role in the form of mutual funds, merchant banking, core banking solutions, on line banking, venture capital funds. Some of the banks have been allowed to raise capital to limited amount from the capital market. New issues and portfolio management is another form of activities. Some of the commercial banks, have brought their own subsidiaries such as SBI capital market Ltd, Can bank financial services Ltd etc to deal in capital market.

4. Merchant banking: A few financial services companies in association with foreign banks and money market institutions have set up merchant banks. The merchant banks, underwrite new issues, they undertake syndication of credit as well as advising on how to raise funds for corporate and other clients. The merchants banks direct involvement in the capital market has enhanced the activities further, besides the Narsimhan Committee (1991), considered that there is more potential role for greater operation in future.

5. Mutual fund: In the late 80's the government encouraged some of the commercial banks and financial institutions to set up their mutual funds. The common savings (investors) is mobilized in small amounts (units) by these institutions and the same is invested in the capital market. They started on a high note, but due to the Harshad Mehta scam, they suffered heavy losses. Today it is increasing in different forms. Mutual funds are purely financial intermediary activities. The money (savings) from small investors (indifferent units) is to be mobilized, initially when they started it was for a lock in period of 3 years, and the same funds is to be invested in the securities & equities and after the period the profit earned due to appreciation of the instruments, distributed according to their investments. It induced many salaried people to invest, thus even the small investors became a part of the capital market. There are open end MF's in which the day to day trading is carried out and from to time the funds announced their repurchase value (NAV). In the case of close ended funds, the lock in the period is for three or five years, once you purchased the units, additional units are not sold. These funds are listed on the stock-exchanges; there are other funds which are floated to raise funds from abroad etc.

6. Venture capital funds: This is a new type of financial assistance provided, especially to technocrat entrepreneurs who have excellent expertise but lack of funds, hence to develop and support in new ideas and introduction and adaptation of emerging new advance technology, funds are provided by the concerned banks & institutions. There is high risk as well as high profitability in the venture capital business. The venture capital funds, vary from company to company and demands a share in the capital appreciation as well as in decision making at the top management level. The investments are for 3 to 5 years. Though it is a very recent one, there are 43 domestic & six foreign venture capital funds. Due to high risk involved in the business the Narsimhan committee recommended the reduction in capital gain tax. The government in 2000-01 budgets liberalized the tax on venture capital funds, so as to provide a strong boost to the NRIs from Silicon Valley and other places to invest their capital in knowledge & other enterprise ventures in India.

7. Securities and Exchange board of India (SEBI): The SEBI was set up in 1988 it is a regulatory authority. It has issued many regulations for the functioning of primary & secondary, markets, market intermediaries mutual funds etc. to safe guard the interest of the investors and avoid any kind of manipulation in the capital market.

8. Credit rating agencies: The three credit rating agencies,

(*i*) CRISIL (credit rating and investment corporation of India Ltd), this was set up by ICICI & UTI as a public limited company with its headquarters at Mumbai in 1987.

(*ii*) ICRA (formerly, it was known as investments information and credit rating agency of India) was set up by industrial finance corporation of India, the promoter, as its headquarters in Delhi (1991).

(*iii*) Credit analysis and research Ltd (CARE) was promoted by IDBI, some banks, investment institutions & finance companies in October 1993.

These agencies provide up to date information & guidance to the investors, with regard to the equities and debt instruments. Beside this they provide knowledge about the new equities, business & financial risk involved, the management plans, credit review committee etc.

9. Establishment of national stock exchange (NSE): This was set up in 1993 and started its operations in November 1994. It is a system based on modernization and competition, it provides electronic screen based system to all over the cities and thus provide access and opportunity to all the investors with regard to the different equities & debt market instruments. In 1996 it had branches in 21 cities of which six cities have no stock exchange & planned to extend the services to other major cities. Approximately 1200 companies' listed / permitted against 5999 listed companies in BSE in 1996.

10. Depository system: Script less trading mechanism was introduced in 1996. To eradicate the forged certificates, counterfeit scrips, bad deliveries delays and other exploitation of investors, this system was initiated. This is an organization which holds the shares and other securities in electronic form. All the further process of dealing is carried out through this facility.

11. The emergence of the middle-income investment-oriented class: further due to the fiscal and other tax concessions provided by the government, large number (at least 60%) of the middle income group has emerged as new short-term investors in one or the other form. They have been playing active role. The electronic media, the immediate information, the reviews in the newspaper & magazines and commercial banks, brokers and other initiatives from financial institutions has accelerated the development of capital market.

Reforms in Capital Market

The government from time to time introduced many reforms in capital market along with the establishment of NSE, SEBI, depository system, and credit rating agencies, screen based trading, the different institution such as venture capital, merchant bank, leasing companies, more reforms were brought in to strengthen and speed up the capital market. Along with this, further additional measures were as follows.

1. Abolition of controller of capital issues: Earlier the capital issues were administered by the controller of capital issues (CCI). The government abolished this; instead SEBI looks after the different rules, regulation to be followed by the companies. Many new measures have been taken with regard to primary and secondary issues separately. The different 'IPO' (initial public offer) has to follow a set up SEBI rules.

2. Over the counter exchange of India (OTCEI): It was set up in 1992 and first screen based trading system and also to companies and investor a source of multi-tired market of securities and liquidity. To avoid all kinds of problem in security dealings, help investors in providing the different avenues of investment, cheap form of capital availability to companies etc, are the benefits derived from the OTCEI.

3. Screen based trading: With the help of computers screen based trading system (SBTS,) to reduce and cut down the cost-time and delays, the modernization process of stock-exchange initiated in 1990's, this has encouraged more participants as well as accelerated the functioning of capital market.

4. Rolling settlements: To enhance the efficiency and integrity of securities market and shifts from the traditional account period settlement, the rolling settlement was introduced which marks an important change from the age old practices. SEBI introduced under this system, any transactions made on a particular day, necessarily result in delivery after a fixed period of time (days). The Finance Minister in March 2001 introduced rolling settlement 200 scrip's, which were further eligible for trading under, modified carry forward scheme (MCFS) automated lending and borrowing mechanisms (ALBM) and borrowing & lending securities scheme (BLESS) gave boost and strength to the rolling settlements.

5. Derivative trading: To manage the risk through hedging, speculation, and arbitrage, the derivative trading was introduced in India in June 2000. At present there are four equity derivatives, such as index options, stock future, stock option and index future. Contract between counterparties, whose value is derived from that of underlying assets, is referred as derivatives. There is high degree of volatility in the asset prices (equity / forex / any other asset) the derivative products comes to rescue.

6. Investors-protection: Besides to protect the interest of investors, guide and enlighten them with regard to the securities claims and disclaims of dividends through issues, advertisement and also the government establishment the investors education protection fund (IEPF) with effect from 1st October 2001. The unpaid dividend accounts of companies, the money due for refund of application money received for allotment of securities, the interest and capital amount of matured deposits and debentures with companies which has been unclaimed for seven years shall be credited to IEPE, the government further appointed a committee under the chairmanship of N.L. Mitra in 2001 to study this issue.

7. The clearing corporation of India limited (CCIL): The CCIL was promoted by SBI and registered under the companies, Act 1956, on April 30, 2001 and commenced its operation from February 15, 2002. It clears all government securities and repo's, which are reported on negotiated dealings system (NDS) of RBI and also deals in spot and forward rupee/US$ forex.

8. Demutualisation: Earlier the stock exchanges were owned, controlled and managed by the brokers. They use to frame their own rules and laws, with regard to disputes etc, which very often leads to inevitable conflict of interest of companies and investors. Because of these the regulators insisted on 50% membership to non-brokers. Due to extreme volatility in securities market the government insisted to corporatise stock-exchange to segregate the ownership, management and trading membership from one another. Some of the exchanges have already initiated demutualisation process and NSE adopted a pure demutualisation governance process under which ownership, management and trading are with three different group people. This is a process in favor of decentralization against the centralized and domination of one groups viz the brokers.

9. The setting up of national securities clearing corporation Ltd (NSCCL): It was set up in July 1996 and responsible for post trade activities especially with regard to all clearing, settlement of trades as well as the risk management. It clears all the trades executed on NSE. The clearing corporations clearing members, custodians, clearing banks and institution depositories are all involved in the clearing process. A strong risk management system is an integral and to a efficient clearing and settlement system which is regulated and directed under the supervision of NSCCL to avoid any pre-scrip market failures.

10. Accessing global funds market: Indian companies have been allowed to raise capital (resources) through issues of American depository receipts (ADR'S) global depository receipts (GDR's), foreign currency convertible bands (FCCB's) and external commercial borrowing (EBC's). In the line with the liberalization, globalization, privatization process the Indian financial system encouraged, invited and opened up for foreign investment fund through non-resident Indian (NRI'S), foreign institutional investors (FII's), overseas corporate bodies (OBC'S) and others.

Stock-Exchanges

Industrial revolution introduced the concept of joint-stock companies on a large scale. Earlier it was concentrated only in the European countries. Due to colonial rules and its imposition of their influence on the different economic cultures, the stock-exchanges came to the forefront of the economies. The World War I and II initiated the development of basic and heavy industries on a large scale. After the Second World War the freedom aspect of colonial ruled countries, were of the opinion that, industrialization is a pre-conditioned for their economic development. Huge investment either by the government or by the private sector initiated the pace of industrialization. The 1970's miracle growth of Japan and emergence of developed countries dictates, in terms of GATT / WTO, and the financial revolution of 1990's energized the stock-exchange culture to a greater extent. A stock exchange is a market 'where long term funds are traded between the financial investors and the financial barrowers under the rules and regulation of the concerned country'. Further a stock exchange (market) is a place where the government, private companies, equities, debt securities etc are sold and bought for a long term basis, which reveals the internal economic pulse of a country".

The securities contracts (regulation) act of 1956 defines stock exchange as "an association or organization or body of individual, whether incorporation or not, established for the purpose of assisting, regulating and controlling business in buying, selling and dealing in securities".

Features of stock exchanges

1. It is an organized long term financial market. It deals in buying and selling of equities and other debt securities.
2. It measures the pulse of an economy; the behavior of the market could indicate the strength of an economy.
3. It is a place where the people (investors) with surplus funds, interested in putting their money for profit on the other hand, the industrialists, businessman, entrepreneur, corporate sector wants to borrow the funds for their onward business so as to make profits.
4. A market purely based on the interest of profits or gain in terms of rate of returns on their investments whether the investors or borrowers.
5. Modern day commercial banks, financial

institutions, development banks are the major players, those who can change the directions of the stock exchanges trend.

6. It is a market in which the corporate sectors or the government could raise the required fund (capital) for their onward activities or put the funds into it.
7. It is a place, which directs the monetary authority to take the necessary steps, with regard to the correction of the economy, in terms of cheap or dear money policy.
8. It operates under the rules, regulation and direction put forth by the RBI and other statutory organizations & regulations of SEBI etc.
9. The aim of the direction of the monetary authority is to see that the economy benefits from the social and economic points of view.
10. Facilitates orderly marketing of equities & other securities, under a particular authority keeping check on their activities.
11. It has its own system of tracking any scams, manipulations and frauds.
12. It is an strong indicator of the internal and external economy, which may be a political, economic & social agenda with the government.
13. It may have its own ups and downs depending upon the economic variables & other political, social environment.
14. It is an essential ingredient of a free enterprise economy, without which the long term financial market will not be active.

Functions of stock-exchange

1. It provides a market for raising long term funds which are very essential for rapid economic development.
2. It is a place in which the investors, such as private individual, government, banks, financial institutions (inland or foreign) put their money for higher earnings.
3. It shows the economy's strength and weakness, which help the monetary authorities to take the necessary steps of actions.
4. It induces, encourages, and stimulates the investments in the economy.
5. It is one of the major source of both mobilization and channelization of the capital formation, which further increases the efficacy of production.
6. It encourages the general investors to put their money into those companies in which the shares are appreciating and vice versa.
7. It guides the management to take the necessary steps to improve the standing with regard to their appreciation and depreciation of shares.
8. It builds up the confidence required for the corporate sector to go for their diversification, expansion, rennovation, collaboration, merger and amalgamation plans if their shares are appreciating.
9. It is one of the main centers, from where the government is able to raise its required funds by selling or auctioning the debt instruments.
10. It helps the government in regulating, monitoring, controlling and accelerating the financial activities of the financial system.
11. It acts as a middle-man / agent between government private sector and other institutions with regard to funds required for respective activities.
12. It helps the government in carrying out the macro-economic policies, generally about monetary & fiscal, policy measures which, gets the input from the stock-exchange.
13. It is a place where speculation is an essential ingredient.
14. According to Marshall "Stock exchanges are no merely chief theaters of business transaction, they are also barometers which indicate the general conditions of the business atmosphere".

The first stock exchange was established in 1887 in Bombay. Today there are 23 (2003-04) stock exchanges, with 9871, listed companies as on March 31, 2000. BSE, the Bombay (Mumbai) stock exchange is the oldest and the main along with the others which are inter linked with the electronic means.

National stock exchange of India Ltd (NSEIL), over the counter exchange of India Limited (OTCEI), the BSE (Mumbai), and the other Indian stock exchanges ware adopted the screen based trading system (SBTS). Internet trading has been permitted by SEBI. We need the means of education to the common man, so that he can join the stock exchange by whatever his meager saving in different ravenues rather than with the assumption and mind set, that it is a place of gambling and speculation'.

Main terms of stock exchange

1. Shares (Equity): A company issues equity shares, each equity with a price, accordingly the share holder, has right to vote in general body meeting and annual rate of return (dividends) if any.
2. Scrip: Provisional certificate of money, subscribed to a bank or company, entitling the holder to dividends.

3. Stock: The capital of a company raised through the selling of shares
4. Bonds: A long term certificate, which assures fixed returns irrespective of the ups & downs in the market after a fixed period of time.
5. Debentures: A loan raised by company promising a fixed rate of interest for a particular period of time and with fixed returns.
6. Brokers: He is the middle man between the buyer and seller of a scrip or share.
7. Bull: He is a speculator in the stock exchange Bullish behaviour means an upwards movement in the stock. If the companies are interested in selling more shares, it creates a bullish behaviour. (Tejiwala as it is referred)
8. Bear: He is a speculator in stock exchange interested in purchasing the stock when we say the bearish behaviour it is the downward trend in the stock-exchange. (Mandiwala)
9. Scrip less trading: Is generally referred as shares traded electronically.
10. Dematerialization: It is a process in which a physical share certificate is transferred into as electronic share maintain in the participants depository system.
11. BSE SENSEX Bombay (Mumbai) Stock-Exchange: It is the main stock exchange index. Index number (base year 1978-79 = 100) comprising 30 scripts from the specified & non-specified list.
    'Sensitive Index' all major market leaders in this. The Mumbai stock exchange is compiled as BSE National Index (1983 – 84) base year 30 + 70 scrip added to it.
12. S & P CNX NIFTY: Is a well diversified 50 stocks accounting for 25 sectors of the economy. Dow Jones + NASDAQ (American) , FUTSE (U.K.) CNC (French), DAX (German), NIKKI (Japan), KOSPI (Korean) are some of the other stock exchanges.

Security and Exchange Board of India (SEBI)

There were many problems with the functioning of stock exchange in India such as price rigging, long delays, insider trading, lack or transparency in procedures, leading to exploitation of investors, frauds etc, to cope with it and remove all these defects and to regulate, it in the interest of all the members, the security & exchange board of India (SEBI) has been set up in 1988. It was initially a non-statutory body but from January 1992, as a statutory body. SEBI was authorized to regulate and create a more cordial and conducive environment to mobilize resources and put them into proper channels keeping in mind the interest of not only the concerned members but also the overall economy's objectives. It has been assigned wide range of regulatory and other control measures such as, merchant bank issues, operation of mutual funds, functioning of stock exchanges, & the new issue activities of the concerned companies.

Main objectives

SEBI was concerned with the protection of investors and regulation and growth of an orderly functioning of the stock exchanges.

1. To bring about such environment in which there is orderly, smooth growth of capital market (securities market)
2. To protect the interest of the investors by regulating the market with proper rules & regulation.
3. To initiate such atmosphere in which there is smooth & proper functioning of banks, financial institutions, brokers, underwriters, portfolio managers & mutual funds.
4. To create an environment so that the government, the companies and other can raise the capital required through equities, debentures & other debt securities etc.
5. To guide the investors with regard to their interest, grievances and claims etc

Besides this it aims at

(*i*) Regulation of stock markets
(*ii*) Registration of all brokers & other intermediaries.
(*iii*) Issuing regulatory norms, laws etc.
(*iv*) To avoid fraudulent practice of middleman
(*v*) Proper regulation of functioning of mutual funds.
(*vi*) To help develop self regulating organizations.
(*vii*) To avoid & prohibit inside trending with regard to acquisition of shares and take over of the companies. In the light of the liberalization era there are many cases of take over.
(*viii*) It has been bestowed with the powers to exercise the capital issue control act 1956, as directed by the central government. The M.N. Shoes East Ltd was literally aborted by SEBI in February-March 1995.

Measures and important Achievements of SEBI

1. SEBI issued guide lines to different issuing companies so as to follow an orderly manner and ovoid the earlier defects of the functioning of stock market, even than there were some problems such as M.S. Shoes East Ltd. episode. Companies before the issue must take the permission of SEBI, thus it has control over new issue market. Beside this the companies must follow as code of conduct with regard to the advertisement of public issue.
2. Keeping in mind the different securities scams the SEBI brought out a systematic regulating and policing method of portfolio investments. The portfolio management services were brought under the control of SEBI in January 1993.
3. With regard to non payment of refunds and delay in transfer of share companies the SEBI took action against such companies. This is in line, with the protection of investors' interest.
4. The different issuing companies must provide complete & correct financial and other information of the companies so as to provide a clear guide lines to the investors.
5. To educate the investors the SEBI initiated the different publication so as to highlight investor's grievances, rights & remedies, market behaviour news, different problems emerging in the market, new rules and regulation coming into force from time to time etc.
6. A proper guide line to the financial intermediaries and their role in the functioning of the capital market and the rules and regulation taken in this regard.
7. Efficient and effective functioning of the stock exchange was one of the main motives. In this process the SEBI instructed about the transparency of transactions of membership, settlement periods and also education of brokers & other intermediaries involved in the activities, to bring more professionalism along with the use of computers etc.
8. From January 20, 1993, all the mutual funds were brought under the direct supervision of the SEBI. The MF's were barred from option trading, short selling or other forward transaction, which may harm the functioning of capital market & create problem for the investors.
9. SEBI issued firm guide line with regard to take over, mergers, collaboration and amalgamations etc. The concerned companies must announce their respective intentions, in relation to their acquisitions of shares and other assets.
10. All the new forms of development and investment banks, activities such as merchant banks etc were brought under the regulatory frame work of SEBI. The merchant banks have to follow different norms with regard to capital adequacy, different code of conduct, so that investors' interest is not harmed. Now the merchant banks have a greater amount of accountability in the matters of their dealings as well as they have to inform in their prospectus, all the required financial & other details.
11. After the liberalization and the opening up of Indian capital market for different types of foreign investments, the SEBI issued the different guidelines to them.

Other important measures besides this is that to stop the fraudulent, trade practices SEBI imposed prohibition and penalties on the concerned parties, entry norms, penal margins and other forms of actions including prudential norms for introducing of securities, debts instruments & other depositories. Further the stock exchanges introduced the screen based transaction to provide immediate information to encourage the small investors to take active part in it. Many measures such as investors' education, prevention of insider trading, ban on badla and strict norms for share transfer etc. The SEBI also initiated certain rules with regard to corporate governance as well as risk management concept etc., where different guidelines in relation to disclosures etc., through electronic media is to be provided by the companies concerned.

PART FOUR

International Economics

UNIT I

International Trade Theory

UNIT II

Balance of Payments and International Monetary System

UNIT I

International Trade Theory

Chapters

THEORY OF INTERNATIONAL TRADE

Inter-regional vs. International Trade

Inter-regional trade is trade between different regions within the same country, whereas international trade is between different countries. It should be noted that the difference between inter-regional trade and the international trade is only one of degree, not of kind. The fundamental principles in both cases are the same. International trade, like inter-regional trade, is the result of division of labour. In internal or inter-regional trade, people specialise in producing goods in which they have a greater comparative advantage; the same thing happens in international trade.

Why a Separate Theory of International Trade

Differences between Internal Trade and Foreign Trade. There are, however, several differences between domestic trade and foreign trade which necessitate the formulation of a separate theory of international trade:

Mobility of Factors of Production. Ricardo advocated a separate theory of international trade on the ground that within the same country, labour and capital are more mobile than they are between different countries. As regards labour, as Adam Smith puts it, "Of all sorts of luggage man is the most difficult to be transported." Several causes are responsible for this: differences of language, tradition, religion, customs, social and political life, *etc*., or mere inertia may keep labour at home. Capital is more mobile than labour. But even here people prefer to invest their savings in their own country for various reasons. An investor feels a greater sense of security if his capital is invested in his own country.

Trade involves the whole world.

The result of this **comparatively greater immobility of labour and capital** between different countries is that competition fails to make costs of production of similar goods equal, as it does in the same country. This gives unequal advantages to different countries in the production of different commodities. The different countries thus constitute non-competing groups.

There is another consequence of comparative immobility of labour and capital as between one country and another: "Within a country, the price of a commodity, in the long run, tends to approximate to its cost of production. This is so because labour and capital can easily move into or move out of an industry, if the price is respectively more or less than the cost of production. This cannot happen in the case of international trade. Labour and capital being immobile, price and cost of production can seldom approximate.

Also, the consequence of this immobility of factors internationally is that returns to factors tend to equality within, but not between countries.

Trade brings Nations together.

Natural Endowments. Differences in advantages of trade to different countries may arise because of natural causes like geographical and climatic conditions. These lead to territorial division of labour and localization of industries. For instance, some countries may have particular mineral resources like coal, iron ore, copper, *etc*. Others may have land or climate peculiarly suitable for certain crops, *e.g.*, jute in Bengal. Either these advantages cannot be transferred to other countries at all or the cost of moving them is prohibitive.

Human Capabilities. Countries differ in human capabilities too. People in some countries are physically more sturdy, whereas in others they are intellectually superior. Some have greater skill and dexterity and others excel in spirit of enterprise and organisational ability.

Stock of Capital. Some countries possess large stock of capital goods like the U.K., and the U.S.A. and others like India suffer from capital deficiency. This makes a great difference in the type of goods produced in different countries.

Political Sovereignty. In international trade, certain problems arise out of the fact that countries are independent sovereign States and can pursue independent policies with respect to the movement of goods, wages and prices, fiscal matters, banking law, foreign loans, *etc*. Several kinds of restrictions may be placed on the movement of goods beyond their frontiers by the States.

Currency Systems. Different countries have different currency systems. This hampers smooth flow of trade as between one country and another. A number of foreign exchange problems arise in foreign trade which are non-existent in internal trade. To the man in the street this is the main difference between international and domestic trade. Really, it is not the different currencies so much as the possibility of change in their relative values which differentiates between international trade from inter-regional trade.

Separate Markets. There are cultural distinctions between markets. The national markets are frequently separate from one another. For instance, the British use right hand drive cars, whereas the French use the left hand drive. Thus, the markets for automobiles are effectively separated. But markets are also separated by language, customs, usage, habits, tastes and host of other causes of difference. Standards differ, some goods are designed in inches, feet and short tons and others in metric measurements. "Export and import trade must get outside of the culture of the domestic market to become acquainted with different goods, described in different words, using differing measurements, bought and sold on different terms, for different currency units."[1]

Economic Nationalism. Different countries have their separate national economic life. "Along with political independence has grown a demand for economic self-reliance, self-esteem expressed largely in plans and hopes for economic development." The national units have been striving for increasing consumption, production, capital formation, *etc*. Thus, political and economic nationalism is rising especially in newly independent countries widening the difference between international and inter-regional trade.

1. Kindleberger, C.P.—International Economics, 1963, p. 10

Trade and Exchange Controls. We find that trade and exchange controls are instituted by almost all modern States which obstruct the movement of goods and services from one country to another. This also necessitates a separate theory of international trade.

All these difference give rise to a separate theory of international trade.

THE BASIS OF INTERNATIONAL TRADE

The fundamental basis of international trade lies in the fact that countries are endowed by nature with different elements of productive power. In other words, factor endowments are unevenly distributed among the countries of the world. This is due to geographic facts, physical features and climatic differences. Some countries have the monopoly of certain minerals, *e.g.*, Bengal and Bangla Desh for jute.

Thus, international trade is inevitable when there are marked differences in the countries regarding materials, natural vegetation, climate, soils and other physical and geographical conditions.

International trade is also affected by several other factors besides the natural or geographical factors, *e.g.*, stage of economic development, accumulation of capital by a nation and its foreign investments, technological progress, trade and financial regulations, political affiliations, and so on.

CLASSICAL THEORY OF INTERNATIONAL TRADE

Let us briefly review the historical background of the theory of international trade propounded mainly by Adam Smith and Ricardo, the principal exponents of the classical school of economics.

The economic philosophy that prevailed during the 17th and 18th centuries was that of Mercantilism. The main feature of the mercantilist doctrine was that a country could grow rich and prosperous by acquiring more and still more precious metals especially gold, and, therefore, all the efforts of the State should be directed to such economic activities as help a country to acquire more and more precious metals. According to the mercantilist school of economists, if international trade is not properly regulated then people might exchange gold for commodities of daily use or required for a luxurious living to the depletion of the stock of precious metals with the nation. Thus, exports were viewed favourably so long as they brought in gold but imports were looked at with apprehension as depriving the country of its true source of riches, *i.e.*, precious metals.

Adam Smith and Ricardo strongly repudiated the mercantile nations of international trade.

THE THEORY OF ABSOLUTE ADVANTAGE

Adam Smith argued that a country could certainly gain by trading with other nations. Just as a tailor does not make his own shoes but exchange a suit for shoes, and hence both the tailor and the shoe-maker gain by trading, in the same manner, Smith argued that a country as a whole would gain by having trade relations with other countries. According to Smith, if one country has absolute advantage over another in one line of production, and the other country has an absolute advantage over the first country in another line of production, then both countries would gain by trading.

For example, if it takes 10 units of labour to produce one unit of good *X* in country *A*, but 20 units of labour to produce the same good in country *B*, and if it takes 20 units of labour to produce one unit of good *Y* in country *B* and 10 units of labour to produce the same good in country *A*, then both the countries will gain by trading. After the opening of trade, country *A* will specialise in the production of good *X*, while country *B* will specialise in the production of *Y*.

Comparative Cost Trade Theory of International Trade, By David Ricardo

David Ricardo, the British classical economist, known for his original theories in economics, came out with the theory of comparative cost, which was a unique theory at that time. Adam Smith's absolute cost theory had its own limitations. Ricardo developed absolute cost into a new comparative cost trade theory.

Adam Smith : Absolute Cost Theory : Adam Smith gave the following example to explain his theory, which is based on traditional labour theory of value.

Country	Cotton in bales	Wheat in bushels
A	10	25
B	15	10

In the above example it is clear that in country '*A*' certain amount of labour is able to produce '10' bales of cotton, where as country '*B*' is producing '15' bales of cotton. On the other hand country '*A*' is producing '25' bushels of wheat and country '*B*' '10' bushels of wheat. It is clear from the above example that country '*A*' is superior or efficient in the production of wheat (25 > 10 bushels), where as country '*B*' is efficient in the production of cotton (15 bales > 10 bales). Hence country '*A*' will specialise in the production of wheat and export it to '*B*', on the other hand '*B*' will specialise in cotton production and export to '*A*', Both the countries gain. Adam Smith's theory was very simple and it can be criticised at length.

David Ricardo came out with a unique theory on the basis of labour theory of value.

Assumptions :

(1) There are two countries *viz*., England and Portugal, producing two goods, wine and cloth,
(2) Labour is the only factor of production.
(3) All labours are homogeneous.
(4) Factors of production are perfectly mobile within a country and imperfectly mobile between the countries.
(5) Constant returns to scale as well as no change in technology.
(6) Perfect competition as well as no intervention of the government in economic activities.
(7) Full employment exists.
(8) No transportation cost.

The Crux of Comparative Cost Trade Theory

"A country having greater absolute advantage in the production of the good, will export to the other country, and the other country will specialise in the production of that good in which it has absolute least disadvantage".

Let us explain it with the following information :

Absolute cost advantage

$$\frac{a_1}{b_1} < 1 < \frac{a_2}{b_2} \qquad \frac{80}{90} < 1 < \frac{120}{100}$$

Comparative cost advantage

$$\frac{a_1}{a_2} < \frac{b_1}{b_2} < 1 \qquad \frac{80}{120} < \frac{90}{100} < 1$$

In the above example Portugal is efficient in the production of both the goods viz wine and cloth as it require less amount of time 80 hrs and 90 hrs Where as England is in efficient compare to Portugal as it requires 120 hrs for wine and 100 hrs for cloth which is more than Portugal's time : On the basis of absolute cost theory there will be no trade, where as Ricardo evolved the comparative cost trade theory and came to the conclusion, that trade does take place and both the countries will gain from international trade.

According to Ricardo "Portugal is efficient in the production of both the goods viz wine and cloth but it has absolute greater advantage in the production of wine. Hence it will specialise in the production of wine and export it to England. On the other England is having disadvantage in the production of both the goods, but it has least disadvantage in the production of cloth hence it will specialise in the production of cloth and export it to Portugal".

Comparative cost trade theory is beneficial, to both the countries. Let us explain the gains from international trade.

Country	Wine 1 unit	Cloth 1 unit	Internal Terms of trade
Portugal	80 hrs. a_1	90 hrs. b_1	80/90 $1W = 0.89\ C.$ or $1\ C = 1.13\ W.$
England	120 hrs. a_2	100 hrs b_2	120/100 $1\ C = 0.83\ W.$ or $1\ W = 1.2\ C.$
Comparative Cost	80/100 1 : 0.67 – 0.33	90/100 1 : 0.9 – 0.1	International terms of trade $1\ W = 1\ C$

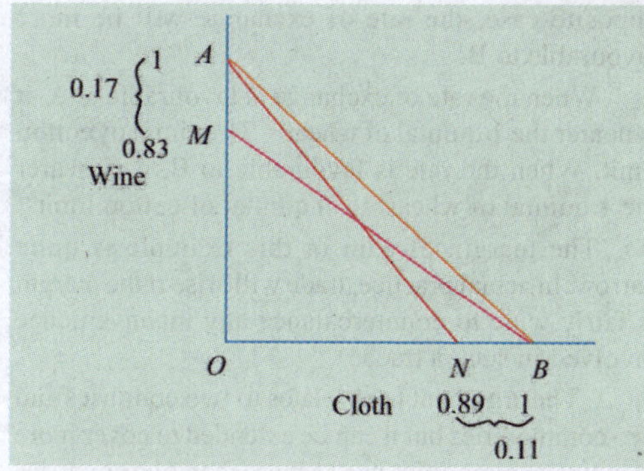

In the above diagram on y-axis wine is taken and on 'x' axis cloth is taken.

AB = International terms of trade where 1 W = 1 C.

AN = Portugal's internal terms of trade where 1 W = 0.89 C.

MB = England's internal terms of trade where 1 C = 0.83 W

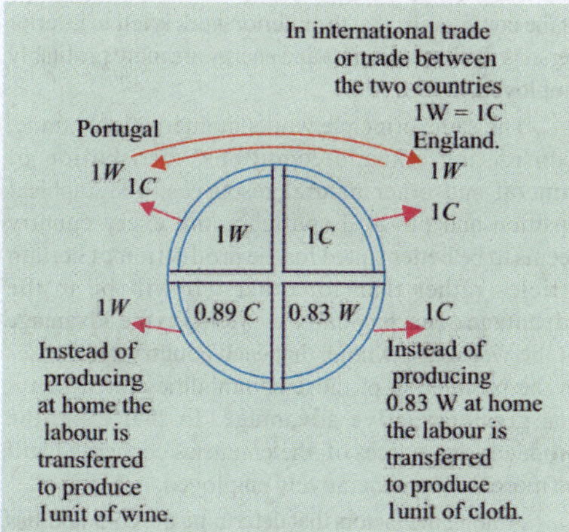

According to comparative cost trade theory. Portugal will specialise in wine production and export it to England in return for 1 unit of cloth (1 W = 1 C), whereas England will specialise in cloth production and export it to Portugal in return for 1 unit of wine. Thus both the countries gain (NB) amount of Portagal gains 0.11 units more of cloth, (as international trade gives it 1 unit of cloth, against 0.89 units of cloth production at home). England gains 0.17 (MA) amount of wine because of international trade 1 unit of wine is received, against 0.83 units produced at home).

There is no transport cost if Portugal is producing cloth at home it is producing 0.89 C but by international trade (that is 1 W = 1 C) it gets 1 C by giving 1 W, on the other hand England gets 1 W where as it used to produce only 0.83 W.

Both the countries gain by international trade.

0.11 'C' units of gain to Portugal.

0.17 unit of 'W' gain to England.

THE THEORY OF COMPARATIVE COST

Ricardo agreed with the analysis of Smith that international trade would be of mutual advantage if one country has absolute advantage over another in one line of production and the other country has an absolute advantage over the first country in another line of production. But Ricardo went further and argued that any two countries can very well gain by trading even if one of the countries is having an absolute advantage in both the goods over another, **provided the extent of absolute advantage is different in the two commodities in question**, *i.e.*, comparative advantage is greater in respect of one good than in that of the other. In other words, when there are comparative differences in costs.

Let us take a numerical example.

Comparative Differences in Costs. When the comparative advantage is different, trade will arise and it will continue. Suppose that

In Country A { Marginal cost of producing wheat is Rs. 70 a qtl. Marginal cost of producing cotton is Rs. 140 a qtl. }

In Country B { Marginal cost of producing cotton is Rs. 70 a qtl. Marginal cost of producing wheat is Rs. 50 a qtl. }

In this case, country B can produce both, wheat and cotton cheaper than country A. But the comparative advantage is higher in the production of cotton than in that of wheat. On the other hand, A has a comparative disadvantage in the production of both the commodities but the disadvantage is lower for wheat than for cotton.

Thus :

	Cost Ratio
Country A:	
1 qtl. of wheat = ½ qtl. of cotton	1 : 2
Country B :	
1 qtl. of wheat = 5/7 or .71 qtl. of cotton	1 : 1 - 2/5

It will, therefore, pay country B to specialise in the production of cotton and A in wheat.

Gain with Comparative Differences in costs. In this case, a surplus arises with specialization.

Without specialization:

A = 1 quintal of wheat + .50 quintal of cotton

B = 1 quintal of wheat + .71 quintal of cotton.

A + B = 2 quintals of wheat + 1.21 quintals of cotton.

With specialization, A producing wheat and B producing cotton only :

A = 2 quintals of wheat.

B = 1.42 quintals of cotton.

A + B = 2 quintals of wheat + 1.42 quintals of cotton.

Surplus = .21 quintal of cotton.

This is the gain from trade.

Size of the Gain. The total gain from international trade depends upon the differences in the cost ratios in the two countries. The larger the range between the comparative costs the greater the total gain. In the words of Harrod:-

"A country gains by foreign trade if and when the traders find that there exists abroad a ratio of prices very different from that to which they are accustomed at home. They buy what to them seems cheap and sell what to them seems dear. The bigger the gap between what to them seems low points and high points, and the more important the articles affected, the greater will the gain from trade be."[2]

Sharing the Gain. As regards the share of this gain accruing to the parties, this will depend also upon the terms of trade, *i.e.*, the ratio in which wheat exchanges for cotton in our example for instance. This ratio, as we have explained, depends upon the elasticities of the demand of one country for the goods of the other, or the intensity of reciprocal demands. Whoever is more keen to purchase or sell will be the loser in the bargain.

What will be the terms of trade? B will gain as long as she can get a quintal of wheat by parting with less than .71 quintals of cotton. A will gain as long as she get more than .50 quintal of cotton by parting with a quintal of wheat. The rate of exchange will lie between.

1 quintal of wheat = .05 quintal of cotton.

1 quintal of wheat = .71 quintal of cotton.

The actual rate will depend upon the relative elasticities of demand of each party for the goods of the other.

If the demand of A for cotton is more elastic than the demand of B for wheat, the rate of exchange will be more favourable to A. This is so because A will be less anxious for cotton than B is for wheat. In the opposite case, the rate of exchange will be more favourable to B.

When the rate of exchange is favourable to A, it is nearer the 1 quintal of wheat = 71 quintal of cotton limit. When the rate is favourable to B, it is nearer the 1 quintal of wheat = .50 quintal of cotton limit.

The margin of gain in this example is quite narrow. In actual practice, trade will arise if the margin is fairly wide to counterbalance any inconvenience involved in such a trade.

The argument here relates to two countries and two commodities but it can be extended to cover more than two commodities and to more than two countries without invalidating the essential principle.

We may sum up the theory of comparative cost in general terms. An individual is able to perform many tasks but he does not perform them all. He selects this work which pays him the most. A doctor can also do the dispensing but he not do it; a lawyer can perhaps type, but he does not do it; a professor can teach his son reading in a school but he does not do it. All these people find it to their advantage, and it is also to the advantage of the community, that the inferior work is left to inferior persons. In that case, time and energy are more profitably employed.

The same principle works in international trade. Considering climatic conditions, distribution of mineral and other natural resources, geographical position and physical configuration, every country seems to be better suited for the production of certain articles rather than for others. It will be to the advantage of each country, as well as to the advantage of the world as a whole, that each country specialises in the production of those commodities for which it has greater relative advantage. In that case, the productive resources of the countries concerned will be more that remuneratively employed.

Among the factors that determine the commodities in which a country should specialise, we may mention the rate of exchange, the monopoly element, transfer costs, prices of the factors and their relative efficiency. A country would lend to specialise in the production of those commodities in which transfer costs and factor prices are low but productive efficiency is high.

A Paradox. The application of the theory of comparative cost may give rise to a paradoxical situation. A country may specialise in the production of certain commodities and import certain other articles, even though it can produce them at a lower cost than the country from which it imports them. For instance, England imports dairy products from Denmark although their cost of production in England is less. The reason is that England is able to get much better return from labour and capital employed in other

2. *International Economics*, p. 34.

directions, say, machinery, and the loss from the puchase of cheese and butter is more than made up.

"The theory of comparative costs as applied to international trade is, therefore, that each country tends to produce not necessarily what it can produce more cheaply than another country, but those articles which it can produce at thegreatest relative advantage, *i.e.*, at the **lowest comparative costs.**"

Limitations

Like other economic laws the principle of comparative cost is also a statement of a tendency. In actual practice, the operation of the theory is hindered by frictional influences such as differences in language, custom, religion and above all the unwillingness of labour and capital to be guided by purely economic considerations. They are also influenced by political motives, commercial practices and general security. The cost of transport and the behaviour of the cost of production are the other limiting factors. Specialisation tends to increase the scale of production, but if the industry is subject to the law of increasing cost, the principle of comparative cost will cease to function.

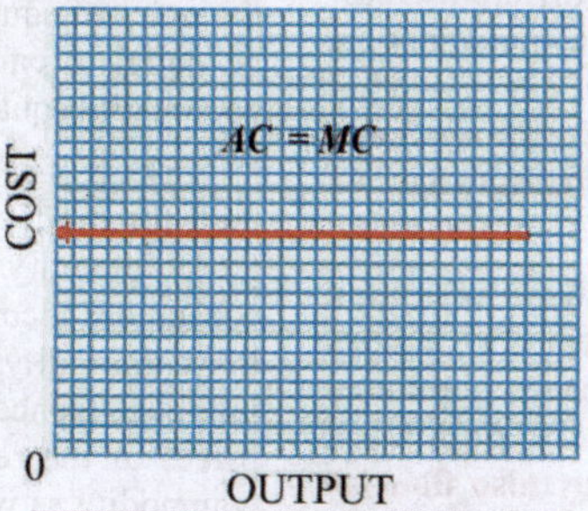

Assumptions

The comparative cost theory is based on the following assumptions:

(*i*) Cost of production consists of labour costs only since labour is regarded as the sole factor of production.

(*ii*) The cost ratio between the two goods is assumed to be constant since production is considered to be subject to the law of constant returns.

(*iii*) It is assumed that within a country the factors of production have perfect mobility, whereas between different countries they are perfectly immobile.

(*iv*) There are no restrictions whatsoever on the movement of goods from one country to another. That is, it is assumed that there exist free and unfettered trade between the countries concerned.

(*v*) The theory is based on the quantity theory of money since it is assumed that if a country receives more money for its goods than it pays, the price level there will go up.

These were some of the assumptions on which the classical theory (or the comparative cost theory) of international trade was based and propounded.

Criticism of the Comparative Cost Theory

The comparative cost theory is unrealistic since it is based on assumptions the validity of which can be questioned.

The comparative cost theory has been criticised on the following grounds:

(*i*) Assumption of Constant Cost. The theory is based on the assumption of constant costs. The classical economists were of the opinion that in accordance with the law of constant unit costs, additional quantities of a commodity could be obtained with the same expenditure of labour per unit as previously. But this is not a valid assumption, sicne beyond a point the law of increasing or decreasing costs operates. The cost ratios are bound to change when specialisation between the two countries has gone apace.

(*ii*) Some Static Assumptions. The comparative cost theory is based on static assumptions of fixed tastes, identical production functions between trading countries and fixed supplies of land, labour, capital, *etc*. It cannot apply to the real world which is dynamic. The static world no longer exists. Tastes change owing to demonstration effect; technology is altered by innovation; factors also change. With changing technology and factors, it is impossible to calculate comparative costs.

COST | AC = MC | 0 | OUTPUT

Constant costs.

(*iii*) No Transport Cost Assumption. The comparative cost theory also ignores transport costs. When transport costs are introduced, it no longer follows that the price ratios between export and import goods are the same in the exporting and importing countries. Export goods must be lower in price to overcome transport costs costs; import goods higher. If transport are wider than price differentials in the absence of trade, trade cannot take place. That is why many goods and services do not enter into international trade.

(*iv*) Labour Costs Assumption. The great weakness of the theory springs from the fact that it assumes that there are no other costs except labour costs. It ignores altogether other costs like cost of raw materials, cost of capital, *i.e.*, interest and other fixed costs like rent. This makes the theory utterly unrealistic. Money, rather than labour alone, could well form the basis of comparative cost theory. The problem of international trade can be easily and satisfactorily explained in terms of prices.

(*v*) Assumption of Perfect Mobility Inside and Immobility Outside. The comparative cost theory makes a very big assumption, *viz*., the factors of production are perfectly mobile inside a country but perfectly immobile between one country and another. However, the development of cheap, quick and safe means of transport and communication has broken down this immobility. As Bertil Ohlin points out, this assumption does not accord with reality. Even within the same country, there is no freedom of movement of the factors of production as is supposed, especially in the case of a big country, and as between countries the factors are not altogether immobile.

Besides being based on the unrealistic assumptions mentioned above the comparative cost theory can be criticised on several other grounds as explained below.

(*vi*) Complete Specialisation Not always Possible. It may be possible for a small country to specialise in the production of one commodity or a few commodities. But it is simply out of the question for a big country like India, the U.S.A. and the U.S.S.R. to specialise. Even industrially advanced small countries like the U.K., Germany and Japan do not specialise. Thus, again the theory, though looks plausible, is not realistic.

(*vii*) Difference in comparative costs arise because of the fact that different countries have different factor endowments and because different commodities are best produced with a predominance of one or another factor. **Trade is said to arise out of differences in relative factor prices, but trade also tends to narrow these differences.**

(*viii*) Differences in factor endowments explain the movement of goods between tropical regions and temperate zones, between densely populated industrial countries and sparsely populated agricultural countries. But **trade may also flourish between countries with similar factor endowments,** *e.g.*, indus-trialised countries, owing to differences in comparative costs produced by historically increasing returns.

(*ix*) The comparative cost **theory concerns itself with one side of the question only, *i.e.*, the supply side.** It only tells us what goods a country will buy and sell. It does not tell us at what prices will these goods be traded. For that purpose, a study of the demand side is essential. Ricardo said that the law of comparative cost determines what commodities would be bought and sold in foreign trade. Mill explained that the law of reciprocal demand set the prices at which they would be traded. But it is not correct to separate demand and supply sides of international trade like this. **In general equilibrium theory, both demand and supply together determine the quantities of goods bought and sold as well as their prices.** We are reminded here of Marshall's analogy of the pair of scissors where demand and supply are compared to upper and lower blades.

(*x*) Actually, the trade between two countries may be dictated by strategic or military considerations and not by comparative costs. For these reasons, country may deliberately attempt to encourage production of a commodity, even though it may have no special advantage in its production.

(*xi*) According to Bertil Ohlin, the comparative cost theory is dangerous. It takes only two countries and two commodities and applies uncritically the generalisations so obtained to world at large. It is thus unrealistic.

MODERN THEORY : GENERAL EQUILIBRIUM THEORY

The modern theory of international trade is an extension of the general equilibrium theory of value. This analysis known as the 'factor-proportions-analysis' has been given by Bertil Ohlin and it has replaced the traditional comparative cost theory.

We know that the price of a commodity is determined by the demand for and supply of it, *i.e.*, the preferences and incomes of consumers, on the one hand, and production possibilities, on the other. At the point of equilibrium the demand and supply will be equal to each other and also the price of the commodity equals its cost of production per unit.

The cost of production is composed of the prices paid for the factors required for the production of the commodity. These factor prices determine the consumers' incomes from which arises the demand for the commodity. Ohlin thus points out the mutual interdependence of prices of the commodities, the prices of the required factors, the demand for the commodity as well as the demand for and supply of the factors.

Just as individuals specialise in some economic activity or activities in which they have comparative advantage on the basis of their talents and aptitudes, similarly countries specialise in the production of certain commodities in which they have comparative advantage on the basis of factor endowments. Just as differences in individual capabilities is the cause of exchange between individuals, similarly difference in factor prices is the cause of inter-regional or international trade. The analysis which is applicable to a single market in a region or a country, Bertil Ohlin extends to the determination of values internationally or to exchange between different regions or countries.

Thus, Ohlin observes: "International trade is but a special case of inter-local or inter-regional trade." Hence, according to Ohlin, there is no need to have a separate theory of international trade. He says that the same fundamental principle holds good of all trade, whether it is trade between individuals of the same country or between different nations. The classical theory of comparative cost is based on the assumption of comparative immobility of the factors of production between different countries. But Ohlin points out that this immobility is to be found even between two regions of the same country.

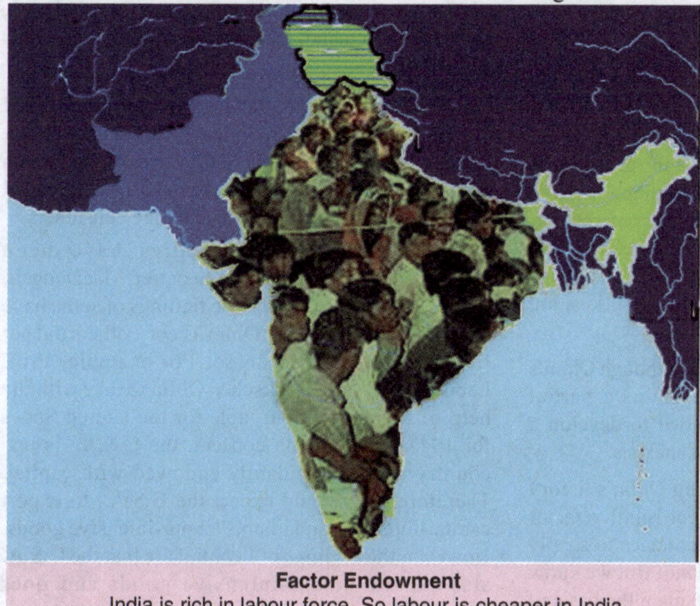

Factor Endowment
India is rich in labour force. So labour is cheaper in India.

According to Ohlin, the immediate cause of international trade is the difference in commodity prices which in turn is due to the differences in factor prices. Goods are purchased from outside because it is cheaper to buy them from outside. The establishment of a rate of exchange between the two countries facilitates the comparison between the commodity prices prevailing in the two countries.

Thus, in Ohlin's opinion, there are no fundamental differences but only quatitative difference between inter-regional and international trade.

We may summaries the main point of Ohlin's theory as follows:[3]

1. International trade is a special case of inter-regional trade. Thus the terms 'inter-regional' and 'international' trade can be substituted for each other. (For, in a country there may be many regions, and sometimes two or more countries may form only one region geographically).

2. Heckscher-Ohlin approach is based on two suppositions:

(i) Products differ in factors requirements.

(ii) Countries differ in factor endowments.

3. The immediate cause of international trade is the difference in relative commodity prices in the two regions.

4. Differences in relative commodity pricesarise due to differences in factors prices and the different proportions of various factors required for producing different goods.

5. Differences in factor prices are caused by differences in factor endowments and their relative scarcities in the two regions.

6. When rate of exchange is established, relative price differences are translated into absolute price differences. This will indicate which of the factors are cheap and which dear in each region and, therfore, in what commodities each region should specialise. Evidently, a capital-abundant country will tend to specialise in capital-intensive products and shall export some of them to import labour-intensive goods. Likewise, a labour-abundant country will specialise in labour-intensive products and shall export some of them in order to import capital-intensive goods.

7. Since factors of production are immobile between two countries, free mobility of commodities in international trade, according to Ohline, can serve as a partial substitute for factor mobility.

8. Further, free trade will also lead to a partial equalization of relative (and absolute) factor prices. Due to transport costs and other impediments in practice, a complete factor price equalization is improbable.

This theory is applicable to any number of regions without affecting its conclusions. Even if the regions are identical as regards factor endowments it will still be profitable for them to enter into international exchange because extension of the market would offer them economies of scale. The qualitative differences in the factors of production facilitate their classification for the purpose of international comparison. Ohlin takes into full account transport costs and relative scarcities of the factors of production to determine international price relationship. He points out barriers to inter-regional mobility of productive factors. He also explains how

3. Mithani, D.M., *Introduction to International Economics*, 1972, pp. 124-25.

factor movements can take the place of movement of goods.

Most economists accept the classical theory of international trade as stated by Haberler, a German economist, in terms of opportunity cost.

Criticism of Heckscher-Ohlin's Theory

The following points of criticism has been offered against Ohlin's 'factor-proportions' theory:

(i) Ohlin's theory is criticised on the ground that since it is based on over-simplified assumptions, it is unrealistic. But, as against this, it may be pointed out, the simplified assumptions have been taken to make it easily understandable, otherwise the theory holds good even in situations where these assumptions are absent.

(ii) Haberler has pointed out that although Ohlin's theory is more realistic, yet it remains a partial equilibrium analysis. Ohlin has failed to develop a comprehensive general equilibrium analysis.

(iii) One assumption underlying Ohlin's theory is that relative factor prices reflect relative factor endowments. This gives undue importance to supply and attaches less importance to demand. But we know that the demand conditions also explain the basis of international trade.

(iv) Also, it may be pointed out that if demand conditions are given due weight, the commodity price-ratio may not correspond to cost ratios.

(v) The critics have also urged that differences of relative factor endowments (which is the very basis of Ohlin's theory) are only of the several explanations for the commodity price differences of the internationally traded goods. Differences in production techniques or in factor qualities, consumers' demand, *etc.*, are also important in this connection.

(vi) It is also said that the prices of commodities are not determined by factor costs, but it is the other way about. That is, the prices of the factors of production (*e.g.*, the raw materials) are determined by the prices of final goods paid by the consumers.

Various empirical studies have been conducted by economists like Leontief, MacDougall, Karvis and Balassa. While the findings of some have supported the Heckscher Ohlin Theory, others did not find enough basis to do so. For example, Prof. Leontief tested the Heckscher-Ohlin theory with the help of an input-output table for the United States for 1947. By common consent, the U.S.A., is one country that is abundantly endowed with capital. Therefore, one would expect the U.S.A., to export capital-intensive and import labour-intensive goods. However, the findings of Leontief are that the U.S.A. also exports labour-intensive goods and does import capital-intensive goods.

The findings of Leontief have also been supported by Prof. B.S. Minhas, on the assumption that factor reversal exists. The meaning of factor reversal is that at a certain set of factor prices, one good is labour-intensive, whereas at another set of factor prices, the same good is capital-intensive. With factor reversals, it is understandtable that a capital-rich country may export labour-intensive goods and a labour-abundant country may export capital-intensive goods.

The differences in comparative cost ratios may also be caused by other factors, when there are differences in factor qualities or production technique in the trading countries. The Heckscher-Ohlin theory assumes that the factors of production are of the same quality, which is rarely so.

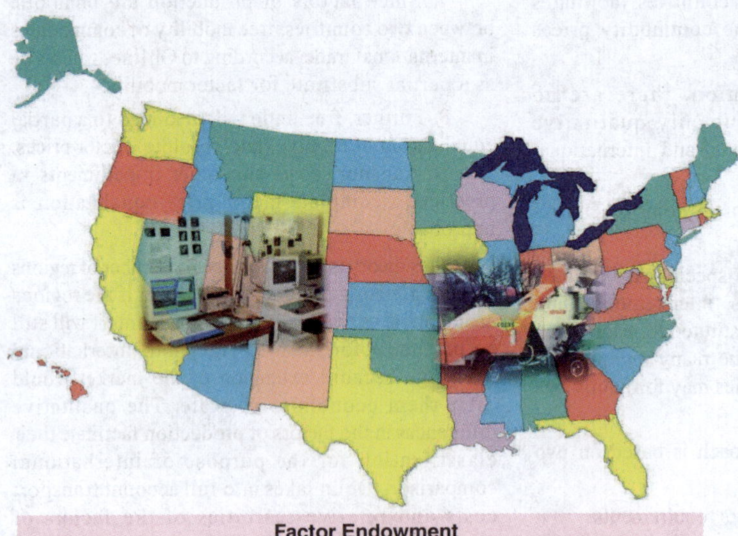

Factor Endowment

USA is rich in capital. So capital is cheaper there.

Conclusion. In spite of all the short comings pointed out above, Ohlin's theory offers a crucial explanation, nay the best of all possible explanations, of the basis of international trade.

Comparison between the Classical Theory and Ohlin's Theory

Ohlin's theory departs from the classical (Comparative Cost Theory) in the following respects:

(i) It seeks to explain the phenomenon of international trade in terms of general theory of value rather than the Labour theory of value.

(ii) Unlike the classical theory, Ohlin's theory asserts that there is no need for a separate theory of international trade.

(iii) Ohlin's theory is a type of location theory and stresses the space element. It is simply the multiple market theory of pricing. Hence it is more realistic than the highly abstract classical theory of comparative costs.

(iv) Since Ohlin's theory takes two or more factors of production into account, factor supplies become crucial determinant of comparative advantage. In the classical theory, only one factor–labour–is considered, hence factor supply aspect is rendered irrlevant.

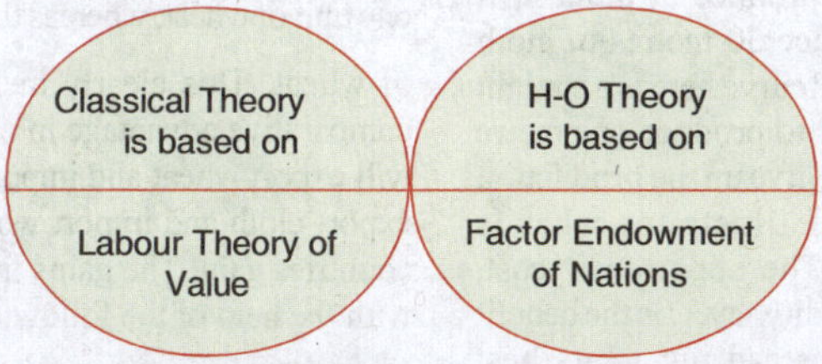

Classical Theory is based on | H-O Theory is based on
Labour Theory of Value | Factor Endowment of Nations

Thus Ohlin's theory integrates factor markets into international trade theory.

(v) The classical theory seeks to establish the welfare propositions of the international trade theory. On the other hand, Ohlin's theory represents a contribution to positive economics. It attempts a scientific explanation of the structure of international trade.

(vi) The classical theory laid emphasis on the quality of a single factor–labour. On the other hand, in Ohlin's theory it is the quantity of all factors and not their quality in different regions which account for the emergence of international trade.

(vii) In the classical theory, comparative advantage arises from superior skills or techniques. But theis superiority may vanish when others have learnt the technique. Hence, international trade will come to an end. But Ohlin's theory asserts that international trade will always continue, because international trade arises from differences in relative commodity costs which are due to relative differences in factor prices and relative differences in factor requirements.

(viii) The classical theory does not explain why there are differences in comparative costs, but Ohlin's factor-proportions analysis is able to do so.

Conclusion. Thus, Ohlin's theory represents a real departure from the classical doctrine and is a great improvement thereon.

THE THEORY OF OPPORTUNITY COST

The theory of absolute advantage and the theory of comparative cost has been based on the labour theory of value which has been widely criticized. Goods are not produced by labour alone, but by the various combinations of all the factors of production, *viz*., land, labour and capital. Prof. Haberler restates the theory of comparative cost by taking two factors of production, *viz*., labour and capital and in terms of opportunity cost. According to Haberler, each country exports goods which it produces at lower opportunity cost and imports those with higher opportunity cost.

The concept of the opportunity cost will be clear from the following example. Let us assume that the U.S.A. can produce either 100 bushels of wheat or 100 metres of cloth when all its factors of production are fully employed in the production of either wheat or cloth. It is a common knowledge, however, that a country interested not only in the production of one good but a range of goods. Let us assume that the U.S.A. is interested in producing both wheat and cloth. The various combinations of both of these goods then can be shown with the help of a production possibility (*PP*) curve, also called transformation curve. The PP curve shows the combination of two goods that a country can produce with the help of all the resources at its disposal. The PP curve of the U.S.A., has been drawn in the following diagram (Fig. 55.1) on the assumption of constant returns to scale.

On the *x*-axis, the quantity of cloth while on the *y*-axis the quantity of wheat has been measured. All the points on this *PP* curve show the various combinations of cloth and wheat that the U.S.A. can produce with its resources. It should be noted here that it cannot reach a point in the commodity space outside this curve. The reason for this is that with the amounts of factors of production the country has, it can only produce some combination of goods indicated by the *PP* curve. The country can, on the other hand, produce any combination of goods represented by a point inside the curve, such as k_1. This is clearly an inefficient position because by moving further to point, which is on the curve the country can produce the same amount of wheat (50 bushels of wheat) as at k_1 and a larger amount of cloth.

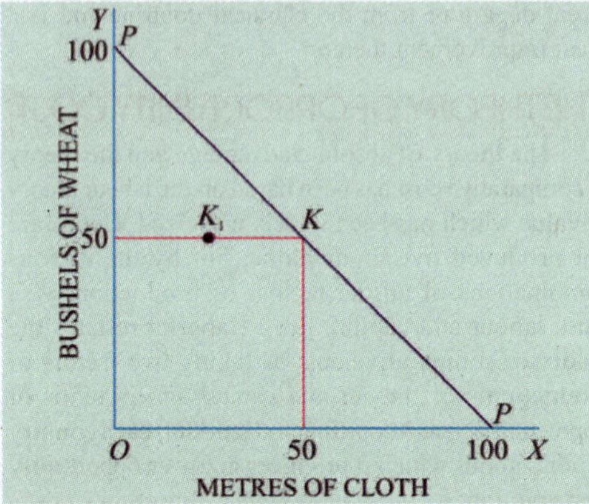

Fig. 55.1. Production Possibility Curve of the U.S.A.

If the U.S.A. decides to produce at point *k*, it means that it chooses to produce 50 metres of cloth and 50 bushels of wheat. The *PP* curve here is a straight line, which shows that in order to produce one metre of cloth, the U.S.A. will have to give up the production of one bushel of wheat. This illustrates what is meant by opportunity cost. The opportunity cost, therefore, of a particular commodity say *X*, is the benefit of opportunity lost if *X* is instead put to its best alternative use. In the above example, the U.S.A. can produce either 100 bushels of wheat or 100 metres of cloth, so that opportunity cost of cloth in terms of wheat is 1:1. In other words, this means that in order to have one additional unit of cloth, the U.S.A. will have to forego one unit of wheat.

Similarly, the *PP* curve of another country, say the U.K., can also be drawn. Let us say the U.K. can produce either 100 metres of cloth or 50 bushels of wheat with given resources. The opportunity cost of

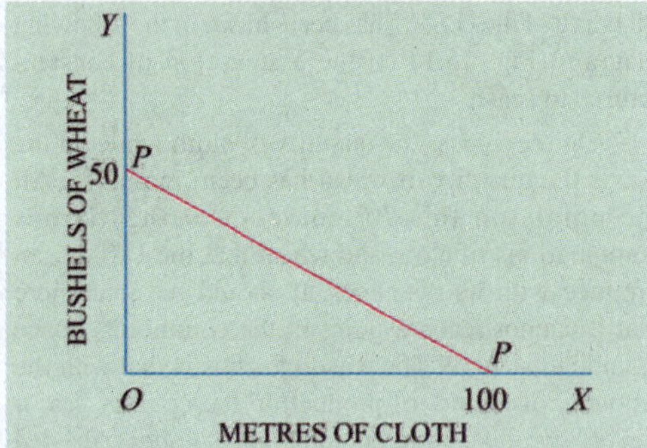

Fig. 55.2. Production Possibility Curve of the U.K.

cloth in terms of wheat in the case of the U.K., in that case, will be 100:50. In other words, it means that in order to have one additional unit of cloth it will have to forego $\frac{1}{2}$ unit of wheat. The *PP* of the U.K. has been drawn in the following diagram (Fig. 55.2).

For the U.S.A. the opportunity cost of wheat in terms of cloth is 1:1. For the U.K., the opportunity cost of wheat in terms of cloth is $1:\frac{1}{2}$. Trade will benefit both the nations so long as the rate of exchange between wheat and cloth lies between

1 unit of cloth: from $= \frac{1}{2}$ unit of wheat to 1 unit of wheat.

From the above data, it can easily be concluded that between the two countries, wheat will be relatively cheaper in the U.S.A. and cloth will be relatively cheaper in the U.K. This is because of the fact that in order to have one additional unit of wheat, the U.S.A. has to forego one unit of cloth, whereas the U.K. has to give up 2 units of cloth. On the other hand, in order to have one additional unit of cloth, the U.S.A. has to give up one unit of wheat, whereas the U.K. has to give up $\frac{1}{2}$ unit of wheat. This clearly means that the U.S.A. has a comparative advantage in cloth. Therefore, the U.S.A. will export wheat and import cloth, while the U.K will export cloth and import wheat. By doing so, both the countries gain. The gains from trade can be illustrated with the help of the following Fig. (Fig. 55.3).

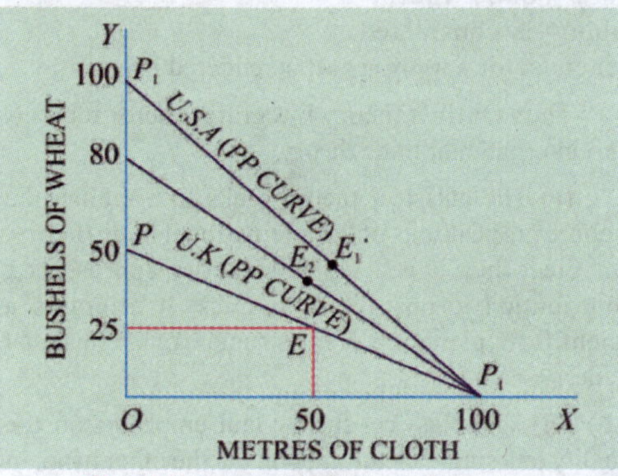

Fig. 55.3. International Trade Situation.

This Fig. (Fig. 55.3) shows the *PP* curve, of both the U.K. and the U.S.A. On the *X*-axis, the quantity of cloth and, on the *Y*-axis, the quantity of wheat have been meansured. P_1P and P_1P_1 are the production possibility curves of the U.K. and the U.S.A. respectively.

Let us assume that the U.K. chooses to produce at *E*, before the opening of trade. At *E*, it will produce and consume 50 metres of cloth and obviously, 25 bushels of wheat. After the opening of trade, it will produce and specialise in cloth only and import wheat from the U.S.A. Within the U.K., 50 metres of cloth were equal to 25 bushels of wheat, but from the U.S.A., it can have 50 bushels of wheat by parting with 50 metres of cloth (because the opportunity cost of colth in terms of wheat is 1:1 in the U.S.A.). This means that after the opening of trade, the U.K. will move from E to E_1, which is clearly a better position than E.

Here, of course, we are assuming that the U.S.A. is exchanging wheat for cloth at 1:1 price. If this is so, then there seems to be no gain for the U.S.A. by trading with the U.K. But in the real world, it will not be so. The actual terms of trade will be determined by the demand and supply conditions of both the countries. The terms of trade will fall as explained earlier between 1 unit of cloth = $\frac{1}{2}$ unit of wheat or 1 unit of wheat. Let the new terms of trade to be 1 unit of cloth = .8 unit of wheat, which means 100 units of cloth = 80 units of wheat. At this rate, the U.K. will get from the U.S.A. 40 bushels of wheat in return for its 50 metres of cloth. In the above diagram, the U.K. will reach E_2 instead of E_1. This reduced share of the U.K. in the gain is the gain of the U.S.A.

Comparative Cost Theory and the Opportunity Cost Theory Compared

Firstly, in the case of the opportunity cost theory, the differences in labour cost between the trading partners are not measured by the absolute amount of labour but by the alternatives foregone.

Secondly, the opportunity cost approach recognises the existence of many different kinds of productive factors as compared with comparative cost theory which takes into account only one factor of production, *viz.*, labour and hence clearly is a major step forward from Ricardo's simple theory.

Thirdly, the opportunity cost theory shows that even if we discard the labour theory of value on which the Ricardian theory of comparative cost is based, and rely on opportunity cost theory, the conclusions of comparative cost theory are still valid: Countries will specialize in the production of those goods in which they have a comparative advantage and will import those goods in respect of which they are in a position of comparative disadvantage.

Fourthly, while the Ricardian theory of comparative cost is based on the unrealistic assumption of constant returns to scale, the opportunity cost theory is equally valid in the case of increasing/decreasing cost too. The production and trade taking place under conditions of increasing cost help in explaining the fact that a country may depend upon its own production for part of its own supplies and on foreign markets for the remainder of its output.

The Ricardian theory of comparative cost explains that international trade arises because of differences in comparative cost of the commodities produced. The theory of opportunity cost explains that international trade arises because the *PP* curves of the various countries differ. But these theories do not fully explain why comparative cost ratios or *PP* curves between the trading countries are different. The answer to this question was supplied by Heckscher, a Swedish economist, in 1919 and elaborated by his pupil Bertil Ohlin. The reason for this, according to them, is twofold: Firstly, different goods require different factor inputs. Secondly, different countries possess different factor endowments. By factor endowments is meant the nature, quality and quantity of different factors of production with which a country is endowed. In Ricardian theory, how much of a good a country could produce depends on how much labour a country has. Hence, total working labour force was regarded as the total factor endowment. But in the Heckscher-Ohlin model factor endowments comprise of two factors of production, *viz*., labour and capital. Some countries have ample capital and others have ample labour. According to them , the countries that are 'rich in capital' will export capital-intensive goods and the labour-abundant economies will export labour-intensive goods.

The terms 'rich in capital' and 'rich in labour' are not very precise so far. Two alternative definitions have been given for them. One of these definitions runs in terms of factor prices: country *A* rich in capital as compared with country *B*, if capital is relatively cheaper in country A than in country *B*. The second definition compares over-all physical amounts of labour and capital: country *A* is rich in capital if the ratio of capital to labour is higher in country *A* than in country *B*. Ohlin, however, takes the first definition. According to this theory, country *A* is rich in capital if $\frac{PCA}{PLA}$ is less than $\frac{PCB}{PLB}$, where *PcA* and *PLA* stand for the prices of capital and labour in country *A* and *PcB* and *PLB* for the prices of capital and labour in country *B*.

Hence, if $\frac{PLA}{PCA}$ $\frac{PLB}{PCB}$ country *A* will export labour-intensive goods and country *B* will export capital-intensive goods.

The following example will make the theory very clear. If country *A* is having abundance of labour but very little capital, then the price of labour will be lower as compared with the price of capital. This will result in lowering the prices of those goods which require more labour and less capital. Therefore, country *A* should produce and export those goods which require more labour and less capital. On the other hand, if country *B* possesses plenty of capital but very little of labour, the price of capital will be lower as compared with the price of labour. This will result in lowering the prices of those goods which require more capital and less labor. Therefore, country *B* should produce and export capital-intensive goods.

Assumptions

This theory is based on the following assumptions:

(i) There are no transport costs.

(ii) There is perfect competition in both commodity and factor markets.

(iii) Factors of production are immobile between countries but freely mobile within them.

(iv) There are constant returns to scale in the production of each commodity.

(v) All production functions are homogeneous of the first degree.

(vi) Production functions for different commodities are such as can be distinguished by factor intensity.

(vii) There exist no barriers to international trade.

(viii) Factors are of identical quality in the two countries.

TERMS OF TRADE

Three Main Concepts

There are several measures of terms of trade, each representing a different concept. The important measures among them are: (*i*) **Net barter terms of trade;** (*ii*) **Gross barter terms of trade;** and (*iii*) **Income terms of trade.** There are other measures too like single factoral and double factoral terms of trade, which, however, are not used frequently. The most widely used measure is the net barter or the **commodity** terms of trade. Now a word about these three important measures.

Net Barter Terms of Trade

It is obtained by dividing the index of export prics by the index of import prices both indices expressed in percentages and the quotient thus obtained also expressed in percentage. In symbols it is $\frac{Px}{Pm} \times 100$: *where Px* stands for the index number of export prices and *Pm* stands for the index number of import prices.

Let us take an example. If the index number of export prices of country *A* is 200 and index number of import prices is 100, then the net barter terms of trade will be equal to $\frac{200}{100} \times 100 = 200$. This means that the Net barber terms of trade of a country *A* have shown an increase of 100 per cent over the base period. If the value of the Net barter terms of trade comes to lower than 100, that means that the terms of trade have fallen to that extent. From the point of view of a country, a rise in the net barter terms of trade is favourable because as a result of the rise, the country has now to pay a smaller quantum of exports in return for the same volume of imports or alternatively the same volume of exports for a larger quantum of imports.

Gross Barter Terms of Trade

It is obtained by dividing the index of the physical quantity of exports by the index of the physical quantity of imports, all epressed in terms of percentages. In symbold, $\frac{Qx}{QM} \times 100$ where Qx stands for the index number of quantity of exports, and Q_M stands for the index number of quantity of imports. If $Qx = 100$ and $Q_M = 80$ then the gross barter terms of trade will be equal to $\frac{100}{80} \times 100 = 125$ which means that the gross barter terms of trade have shown an improvement of 25 per cent.

Income Terms of Trade

This is obtained by dividing the value of exports (Value index = Quantity index × Price index), divided by the index of import prices. In symbols, $\frac{Q_x \times P_x}{P_M} \times 100$

A rise in this index means that a country can obtain a larger volume of imports from its sale of exports in a given year relative to the base year.

Factors on which Terms of Trade Depend

The following are the main factors on which the terms of trade of a country may depend:

(i) Elasticity of demand and supply;
(ii) Availability of substitutes;
(iii) Size of demand;
(iv) Rate of Exchange;
(v) Production pattern of a country.

Elasticity of Demand. If the demand of a country for her exports is relatively less elastic as compared with her demand for imports, then the prices of her exports may be higher as compared with the prices of her imports. This will make the terms of trade favourable to that country. On the other hand, if the demand of a country for her exports is relatively more elastic as compared with her demand for imports, then the prices of her exports may be lower as compared to the prices of her imports. This would make terms of trade unfavourable to the country concerned.

Elasticity of Supply. If the supply of exports from a country is relatively elastic as compared with the elasticity of supply of its imports, then it is possible that she may be able to enjoy favourable terms of trade. This is so because of the fact that she will be able to adjust her supply according to demand. She will not then allow the prices of her exportables to fall in case the demand of her products fall in the foreign markets.

Availability of Substitutes. A country may be able to enjoy favourable terms of trade, given the demand conditions, if the products exported by her do not have close substitutes. This is so because in case of the non-availability of the substitutes, the country may be able to sell her products at a higher price.

Size of Demand. The terms of trade of a country are also considerably influenced by the size of the effective demand. A highly populated country like India may be relatively in a stronger position to bargain over price for her imports. However, this factor is such as can cut both ways.

Rate of Exchange. A country may be able to have favourable terms of trade by appreciating the exchange value of her currency. This is because of the fact that the prices of her exports will become relatively higher as compared with the prices of her imports by currency appreciation. However, if the other country also appreciates her currency, then there would be no impact on the terms of trade of either country.

Production Structure. Production structure of a country also influences its terms of trade. If the country produces primary goods (*e.g.*, food and raw materials), there is every possibility that the country may experience unfavourable terms of trade, for the reason that the demand for these products is normally

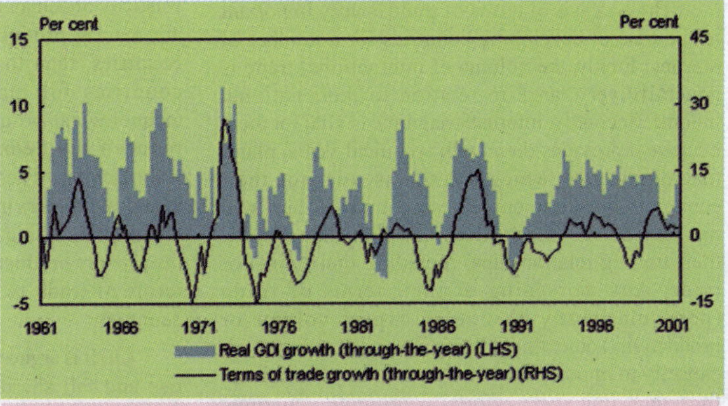

Australia's terms of trade and gross domestic income.

declining with economic development. It is partly because of the operation of the the Engel's Law, which states that as the income of a country rises, less is spent on food products, *etc.*, and partly because of technological advances which usually are of the raw materials displacing or economising nature. In other words, the primary producing countries have usually to sell their products at falling prices. On the other hand, their main demand consists of industrial goods the demand for which is of a rising rather than falling nature and they have no option but to accept the prices dictated by their more advanced industrialised suppliers.

Raul Prebisch has shown that prices of primary products (of under-developed countries) deteriorated in relative terms (*i.e.*, relatively to manufactured products) which means a reduction in the export earnings of the countries producing such goods. That is, the under-developed countries have not benefited from international trade relatively to the exports of industrial goods (*i.e.*, the developed countries). In other words, the gains from international trade have not been equitably distributed between the developed and under-developed countries.

Terms of Trade and Economic Growth

Terms of trade play an important role in the economy of a country. Improved terms of trade enable a country to import a larger quantity of goods from her trading partners in return for the same quantity of her exports or the same quantity of imports in exchange for a smaller quantity of exports. This greatly influences the income of the countries engaged in trade. Secondly, the terms of trade play a significant role in explaining changes in income differentials among countries. Changes in terms of trade may affect the international distribution of income and unfavourable terms of trade may provide some explanation for the low levels of income in developing countries.

The analysis of terms of trade is very important in the case of developing countries for a number of reasons: Firstly, the volume of international trade is generally very large in relation to their national income. Secondly, international trade is vital for them because it provides them with technical skills, plant, machinery, *etc.*, which are so essential for their economic development. These countries then will naturally be very much concerned with all aspects of their trading relationships, including their terms of trade. Any worsening of their terms of trade (particularly any change in export volume or productivity) other things being equal will reduce their capacity to import and shift income away from them, thus retarding their efforts to promote economic growth.

There are two views. The classical economists believed that the terms of trade would shift in the long run in favour of countries producing primary goods and against those producing manufactured goods. This is so because of the fact that primary products are subject to diminishing returns whereas manufactured goods obey the law of increasing returns. The net effect of this tendency would be an increase in the prices of primary products and a reduction in the prices of manufactured goods. This would in turn make the terms of trade of developing countries favourable.

Recently, however, a group of economists, *viz.*, Raul Prebisch, Singer and Myrdal are of the view that the terms of trade of developing countries tend to move against them. Their view, termed secular deterioration hypothesis, was based on the trend in the terms of trade of the U.K, from the latter part of the 19th century to the late 1930's. At the end of this period, a given quantity of primary products exported to the U.K., purchased 40 per cent less of manufactured goods than at the beginning. The main reasons for it given by them are as follows:

(i) The developed countries keep most of the gains of the increased productivity in manufactures by increasing wages and profits and not reducing prices. Strong trade union organisations make sure that the gains in productivity are followed by wage-increases. On the other hand, growth in the productivity in primary products results in lower product prices. The result of this is unfavourable terms for the primary product producing countries, where there is practically perfect competition in the factor markets.

(ii) There has been a relative increase in the demand for manufactured goods produced by developed economies and decrease in their demand for primary products. This is partly explained by Engel's Law, which states that as income increases a small proportion is spent on food items. Their income elasticity of demand is thus lower for such items which are mainly produced and exported by developing countries, than that of the demand of developing countries for manufactured goods. Secondly, technological progress in manufactures has greatly reduced the demand for raw materials used in manufactures. Therefore, Engel's Law coupled with technical progress in manufactured goods have worked together in causing a reduction in the total demand for the primary products, which in turn have shifted the terms of trade to the detriment of the developing countries.

(iii) It is argued that the prices of primary products rise and fall sharply in periods of both boom and depression thus losing all the gains of the boom periods.

But the prices of manufactured goods do not fall in depression as much as they rise in boom periods, because of the presence of strong trade unions. As a result, there arises a wide gap between the prices of primary products and manufactured goods over successive cycles which in turn make the terms of trade of developing countries unfavourable in the long run.

Raul Prebisch has shown, as pointed out above, that the developing countries are handicapped in their attemps at economic development, since terms of trade are unfavourable to them relative to the developed countries. That is why they have to seek loans and grants from the developed countries. The terms of trade are unfavourable to the developing countries since their export earnings are derived from a few commodities only known as the traditional exports, *e.g.*, jute, tea and oilseeds in the case of India. The prices of such commodities do not rise as much as the prices of capital goods and other manufactured goods that they have to purchase. Prices of imported manufactures being relatively high and prices of primary goods exported being relatively low, the terms of trade are unfavourable to the developing countries. There is a secular decline in their terms of trade. Prof. Haberler has questioned this thesis of a secular decline. But Prof. Kindlebeger supports Raul Prebisch and asserts that the terms of trade have been generally favourable to well-developed countries and unfavourable to developing countries.

For economic development, the developing countries have to purchase from abroad machinery and capital equipment, essential industrial raw materials and technical know-how. But owing to the terms of trade being unfavourable to them they do not have adequate export earnings to be able to purchase their requirements of economic development. This is a great handicap.

In view of the above, we might say that economic development has not benefited the developing countries as much as the well-developed countries.

Thus, fair terms of trade are very important for the economic development of the under-developed countries. Favourable terms of trade enable a country to import a large quantity of goods for the same quantity of exports or the same quantity of imports for a smaller quantity of exports. This is a potential source of capital formation. In Nurkse's words, "The great advantage of this potential source of capital formation is that it gives rise neither to foreign debt burden nor to the various frictions that may arise from inter-governmental loans and grants." Unfavourable terms of trade accentuate balance of payments and budgetary difficulties. It may, however, be emphasised that unless the additional resources made available by the favourable terms are turned into saving and investment, economic development will not be promoted. Favourable terms by themselves do not accelerate development automatically.

GAINS FROM FOREIGN TRADE: STATIC AND DYNAMIC

Benefits from foreign trade arise from specialisation on the basis of comparative cost theory. It brings about improvement in production and promotes economies development. It prevents monopolies. It is beneficial to consumers by providing them new and cheap commodities. It also facilitates international payments. There is no doubt that the participating countries enjoy numerous benefits from international trade.

The gains from international trade can be broadly classified into **static gains and dynamic gains.** Static gains arise from optimum use of the country's factor endowments or resources in men, money and material, so that the national output is maximised resulting in increase in social welfare. Dynamic gains, on the other hand, refer to those benefits which promote economic growth of the participating countries. Now a word about these two types of gains.

Static Gains

As pointed out above, static gains result from the operation of the theory of comparative cost in the field of foreign trade. Acting on this principle, the participating countries are able to make optimum use of their resources or factor endowments so that the national output is greater than it otherwise would be. This raises the level of social welfare in the country. Utility or welfare can be measured by indifference

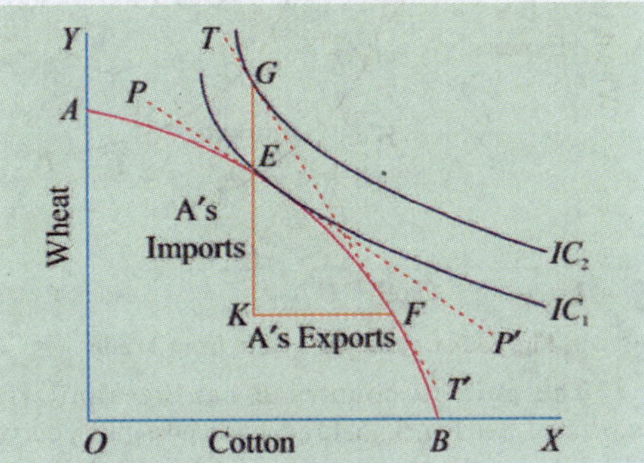

Fig. 55.4. Country A's Gain from Trade.

curves. We find that as a result of introduction or extension of foreign trade, the people can move to a higher indifference curve. This has been shown in Figs.

55.4 and 55.5. Take two countries A and B both producing wheat and cotton. Production possibility and indifference curves are shown in Figs. 55.4 and 55.5.

It can be seen that, before the commencement of foreign trade, country *A* would be in equilibrium at the point E where the price line *PP'* is tangent to both production possibility curve AB and indifference curve *IC*., The slop of the price line shows the price ratio or cost ratio of the two commodities in the country A; *TT'* is the terms of trade line showing the price ratio at which goods can be exchanged between these two countries, *TT' i.e.* terms of trade line is tangent to *A's* production possibility curve *AB*. Fig. 55.4 shows that at F, *A* will produce more of cotton in which it has comparative advantage and less of wheat at *F* than at *E*. Taking the pattern of demand in the country *A*, we have the indifference curves IC_1 and IC_2 representing the demand for the two commodities. Now *TT'*, the terms of trade line is tangent to IC_2 at G which shows the quantities of wheat and cotton consumed by the country *A*. It can be seen that as a result of introduction of foreign trade, the country *A* has moved from *E* on the indifference IC_1 to *G* on the indifference curve IC_2, which represents a higher level of social welfare in terms of larger consumption of the two trade goods. This is called *Static Gain* resulting from specialisation brought about by the introduction of foreign trade. It can also be seen that the quantities of the two goods consumed and different from the quantities produced. The quantities produced are shown at *F* and quantities consumed at *G*. The difference is accounted for by exports and imports. The country *A* will be exporting *KF* quantity of cotton importing *KG* quantity of cotton.

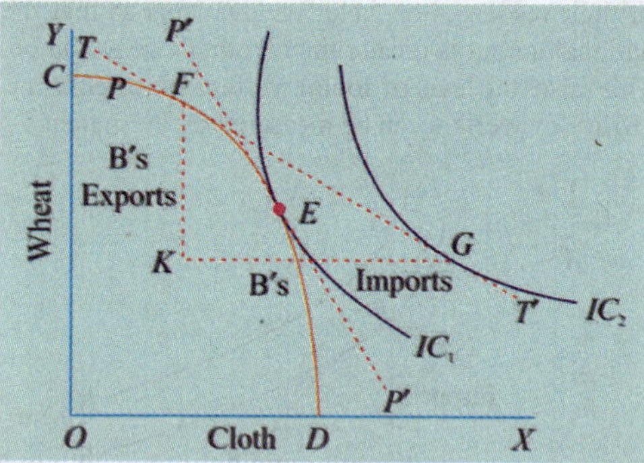

Fig. 55.5. Country B's Gain from Trade.

The gain to country *B* can be similarly explained. See Fig. 55.5. Production possibility curve of *B* between wheat and cotton is shown by the curve *CD*. It is clear that given the factor endowments, it is more profitable for *B* to produce wheat. The country *B* fixes her production and consumption at point *E* before the introduction of foreign trade. At this point, price ratio line *PP'* and indifference curve IC_1, are tangent to production possibility curve *CD*. The country *B* would gain, from trade if it can sell at a price ratio different from *PP'*. Given the terms of trade lin *TT'*, the country *B* will produce at *F* on its production possibility curve *CD*.

It can be seen from Fig. 55.5 that it will produce more of wheat in which it has comparative advantage and less of cotton in which it has comparative disadvantage. But given the price ratio as represented by terms of trade line *TT'*, B will consume the quantities of two goods as shown by the point *G* where the terms of trade line *TT'* is tangent to the indifference curve IC_2. It is clear that specialisation resulting from the introduction of foreign trade has enabled the country *B* to move to the higher indifference curve IC_2 and thus consume more of the two goods. This is her gain from international trade. The country will now export *KF* quantity of wheat and import *KG* amount of cotton. It may be borne in mind that in the case of constant opportunity cost, each country resorts to complete specialisation i.e. producing only one of the two goods. On the other hand, in case of increasing opportunity cost, specialisation is not complete so that a country produces relatively larger quantity of the commodity in which it has comparative advantage.

Dynamic Gains: Foreign Trade and Economic Development

Apart from the fuller utilisation of the factor endowments resulting in increase in output (i.e. more of all goods) and improvement in social welfare which foreign trade brings to a country explained in the static gains above, international trade also brings to the participating countries what are known as *dynamic gains*. They relate to economic growth and development which results from the introduction of international trade. Specialisation by different countries in producing commodities for which they are best fitted, according to the theory of comparative cost, results in a larger, volume of production and improves productivity. This obviously promotes economic development, there is no doubt that extension of international trade has accelerated economic growth in the participating countries. As Professor Haberler observes, "International division of labour and international trade, which enable every country to specialise and to export those things which it can produce cheaper in exchange for what others can provide at a lower cost, have been and still are one of the basic factors promoting economic well-being and increasing national income of every participating country." As distinguished from static gains, which accrue to a country from mere re-allocation of a given amount of resources, dynamic gains accrue to a country in terms of promotion of its economic growth. Foreign trade has been described as "an egine of economic growth" (Robertson). Besides the static gains flowing out of the operation of the theory of comparative costs, some indirect benefits and gains also accrue to the particapating countries which promote economic growth. These are known as *dynamic gains*.

Let us see how international trade promotes economic growth. International trade increases national income and facilitates saving and opens out new channels of investment. Increase in saving and investment is found to promote economic growth. Exports earn foreign exchange which can be utilised in buying capital and equipment and know-how from abroad which can serve as instruments of economic growth. The larger the national income and output, the higher will be rate of growth. The higher level of output enables a country to avoid the vicious circle of poverty and put the country in 'take-off, or self-sustaining , growth. Production possibilities and cost of production in different countries differ so widely that foreign trade brings to the participating countries tremendous gains in terms of national output and income.

Foreign trade promotes economic development in the following different ways.

(i) The under-developed countries are enabled by foreign trade to obtain in exchange for their goods capital equipment, machinery and raw materials which are highly useful in accelerating the rate of economic growth. Take the case of India, there was a time when she used to import manufactured goods but the pattern of her foreign trade has undergone a perceptible change so that instead of importing manufactured goods she is now importing large quantities of raw materials, capital goods, machinery and equipment.

(ii) Besides raw materials, machinery and capital equipment, international trade enables, a country to import technical know-how, technical skills, managerial talents and entrepreneurship through foreign collaborations. As Professor Haberler observes "Today the under-developed countries have a tremendous, constantly growing store of technical know-how to draw from" which is essential for economic growth.........Trade is the most important vehicle for the transmission of technical know-how.

(iii) International trade has brought about a tremendous movement of capital from the developed to the under-developed and developing countries. This the foreign trade does by facilitating the payment of interest or repatriation of capital which, in the absence of foreign trade, would have presented tremendous difficulties. The existence of a large volume of foreign trade serves as a guarantee for the payment of interest and the principal.

Thus, dynamic gains represent the contribution that foreign trade makes to the economic growth or development of an under-developed country.

FACTOR-PRICE EQUALISATION THEOREM

Factor-price equalisation Theorem is an important corollary from Heckscher-Ohlin theory of international trade. This theory assumes immobility of the factors of production as between different countries. Hence their prices in different countries must be different. But if we assume full mobility of these factors, then factor prices, like prices of goods, must be equal.

Obviously, when there is no trade between countries, prices of commodities in different countries must rule at different levels. But when trade channels are opened and international trade starts, there will be a tendency for the prices of internationally traded goods to equalise. Take two countries *A* and *B* producing wheat and cotton, respectively. Suppose wheat is cheapter in *A* and cotton is cheaper in *B*. Now suppose trade starts between these two countries. *B* will buy wheat from *A* which is cheaper there and *A* will buy cotton from *B* where it is cheaper. When *A*'s market is flood with cotton from *B* and *B*'s market with wheat from *A*, the price of cotton will start falling in *A* and price of wheat in *B*. This will go on till the prices of the two goods are equalised in both countries. Thus in the absence of transport costs and tariffs, the effect of trade would be to equalise the prices of commodities in the countries participating in trade.

But what about the equalising of factor prices? The factors of production are not so mobile as between different countries as the goods. Their comparative immobility stands in the say of the equalisation of their prices. In modern times, however, even factors of production have acquired a degree of mobility. Also, the factors of production are after all embodied in the production of goods and we might say movement of goods is a substitute for the movement of the factors of production needed in the production of those goods. In this way, there is a tendency to equality of factor prices. Trade tends to equalise not only commodity prices but factor prices too. Besides, labour and capital have become fairly mobile. For instance, Indians are emigrating in large numbers to foreign countries where wayes are high so that wages are going up in India on account of labour shortage.

Take two countries Great Britain and India. In Great Britain, capital is relatively adundant and cheap, whereas labour is relatively scarce and wages are relatively higher. In India, on the other hand, labour is abundant and relatively cheaper whereas capital is scarce and relatively expensive. With these factor endowmeant, it will pay India to export labour-intensive goods to Great Britain and import therfrom capital-intensive goods like machinery. The result will be that the demand for labour in India will increase and push up wages. Great Britain will concentrate on the production of capital-intensive goods and hence demand for labour there will decrease and wages will go down. In this way, the cost of labour in the two countries would approximate to each other. Similarly, demand for capital would go up in Great Britain because the demand for capital goods would increase. On the other hand, in India the demand for capital goods would decrease since they would be imported from Great Britain. Thus demand for capital would decrease in India, but increase in Great Britain. In this way, the rate of interest would tend to fall in India but tend to rise in Great Britain. Hence the rate of interest would tend to equalise.

Thus, according to Heckscher-Ohlin theory establishment of free trade between the two countries will result in the equalisation of factor costs. But how far this equality will be established will depend on the degree of mobility. However the movement of goods makes up for this immobility. Hence what would have been accomplished by the free movement of the factors of production is indirectly accomplished by the free movement of goods. In this way, according to Ohlin, *international trade in commodities serves as a substitute for international mobility of factors and equalises the factor costs*.

There are, however, certain assumptions on the basis of which equality between factor costs would be realised. It is assumed for instance, that (*a*) demand pattern or tastes are the same in the two countries, (*b*) supply conditions of the factors or technological progress should be almost the same, (*c*) production function of the commodities should be the same, (*d*) there are no restrictions in the free movement of goods (*e*) there are no transport costs and (*f*) perfect competition prevails both in the commodity market and factor market.

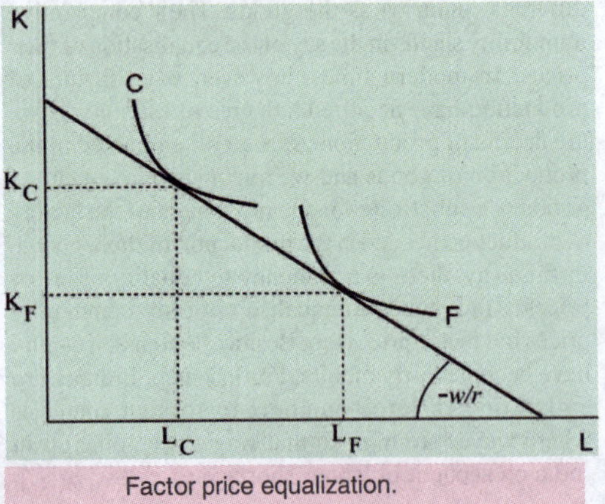

Factor price equalization.

Conclusion

These assumptions are quite restrictive and unrealistic. Hence in the real world perfect equality in the factor costs in different countries participating in international trade is unattainable.

Consequences of International Trade

We have discussed above the various advantages and disadvantages of international trade. These constitute the good and bad effects of international trade. We shall mention here in a summary way some other effects:

(*i*) Equalisation of commodity Prices. Obviously, one direct effect of international exchange of goods is to equalise the prices of similar goods in the trading countries. Absolute equality is, however, out of the question, because the transfer of goods must invole transport costs and other incidental expenses. There must, therefore, remain some difference in the prices of the internationally traded goods to compensate for these costs.

(*ii*) Equalisation of Factor Prices. Commodity prices in the ultimate analysis depend on the factor prices. Hence, equalisation of commodity prices msut tend to equalise factor prices. The prices of relatively scarce factors will fall since the good in which they are used will be imported and demand for such factors will diminish. On the other hand, there will begreater demand for the relatively cheap and abundant factors, for the goods in which they enter will be exported. Their price will, therefore, tend to rise. But complete equalisation cannot be expected.

(*iii*) Equitable distribution of Scarce Materials. Nature has blessed some countries with some raw materials, *e.g.*, oil in Arab countries, jute in Bangla Desh, gold in African countries. These scarce materials are equitably distributed among the countries of the world through international trade.

(*iv*) Effect on Factor Supplies. It is also possible that the fall in the prices of scarce factors may lead to contraction in their supply and rise in the prices of abundant factors may result in the extension of their supply. This may accentuate differences in factor supply of the two countries.

(v) Specialisation and international division of labour will be of mutual advantage to the trading countries. Not only will their standard of living rise but they will also progress economically and industrially. Their productive resources will be put to optimum use. Disadvantages arising from uneven distribution of factor endowments will disappear, although, it must be admitted that the gain accruing from international trade will not be distributed equally. Advanced countries will gain relatively more than the under-developed countries.

(vi) International trade affects people's tastes and desires. This means that demand for certain goods will increase and demand for some new goods will arise. In this manner, international trade will affect both the volume and the nature of demand.

These are a few important effects of international trade.

Key terms

Interregional trade, International trade, Absolute advantage, Comparative costs, Complete specialization, Factor endowment, Factor requirement, Factor-price equalization, Static and Dynamic gains from trade, Terms of trade, Barter terms of trade, Income terms of trade.

QUESTIONS

1. Distinguish between domestic and international trade and point out the advantages aristing from the participation international trade.
2. "International trade is only a special form of interregional trade. Explain the statement.
3. Why is a separate theory of international trade considered necessary? Explain the conditions under which international trade is possible.
4. Distinguish between equal absolute and comoparative differences in costs. Show how comparative cost difference make international division of labour and exchange gainful.
5. Explain the theory' of comparative costs. What are its limitations as the theory of international trade?
6. Examine the validity of comparative costs Theory of inter-national trade in relation to under-developed countries.
7. Critically examine the classical theory of International trade and state the modern theory.
8. Explain the doctrine of comparative advantage as developed by modern economists.
9. Compare and evaluate the views expressed in the following two statement:—
   (*a*) "Two countries trade with each other those commodities in which they have a comparative cost advantage" (*b*) "Differences in factor endowments of the countries determine the course of their commodity trade".
10. Discuss the General Equilibrium Theory of international trade.
11. State and explain Ohlin's theory of international trade. In what ways is it superior to the classical theory?
12. What is the economic justification of international trade? How is the gain from internatioanl trade determined? In what way is this gain distributed between the trading countries?
13. Explain carefully the basis of trade between developed industrial countries taking similar factor endowments.

FREE TRADE vs. PROTECTION

THEORY OF FREE TRADE

A policy of no restrictions on the movement of goods between countries is known as the policy of Free Trade. Restrictions placed with a view to safeguarding home industries constitute the policy of protec tion. In the words of Adam Smith, the term 'free trade' has been used to denote "that system of commercial policy which draws no distinction between domestic and foreign commodities and, therefore, neither imposes additional burdens on the latter, nor grants any special favours to the former."[1] Free trade, however, does not require the removal of all duties on commodities. It only insists that they shall be imposed exclusively for revenue and not at all for protection.

Adam Smith wrote: "If a foreign country can supply us with a commodity cheaper than we ourselves can produce, better buy it from them with some part of the produce of our own industry, employed in a way in which we have some advantage." He continued further: "Whether the advantage which one country has over another be natural or acquired is in this respect of no consequence. As long as one country has those advantages and

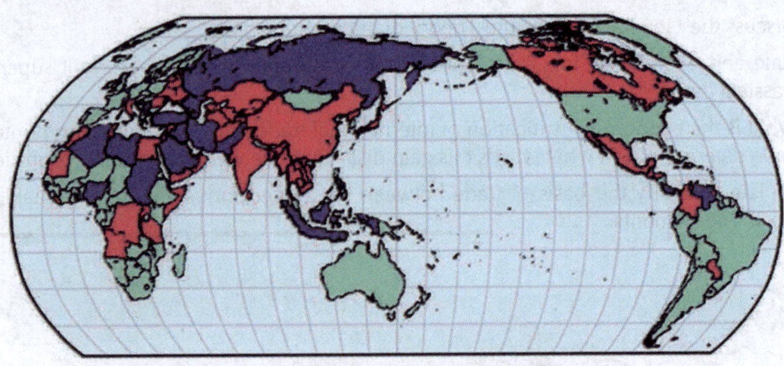

Trade between nations be free of restrictions.

1. Quoted by Palgrave in *Dictionary of Political Economy*, Vol. II, p. 143.

the other wants them, it will always be more advantageous for the latter rather to buy of the former than to make."[2] The only exception that Adam Smith would make was industries necessary for defence. These might be protected since defence is more important than opulence, he said.

The doctrine of free trade is the extension of the doctrine of division of labour to the international field. In the words of Adam Smith again, "Individuals find it for their interest to employ their industry in a way in which they have some advantage over their neighbours." And he adds, "What is prudence in the conduct of every private family can scarce be folly in that of great kingdom." In short, the free trade theory is that such a policy enables every country to devote itself to those forms of production for which it is best suited on the basis of comparative advantages.

Case for Free Trade

(For arguments in favour of Free Trade see advantages of foreign trade given in the previous chapter.)

PROTECTIONISM

The term 'protection' is used to denote a policy of encouraging the home industries by the use of bounties or by the imposition of high customs duties on foreign products. The objects is to build up great national industries even by sacrificing utilities on the part of existing consumers.

Arguments for Protection

The main arguments that are usually advanced in favour of protection are discussed below:

(*i*) 'Infant Industry' Argument. This argument was put forward by Friedrich List, a German economist, in 1840. In those days, Germany was making all-out efforts to industrialise its economy. On the other hand, the U.K. had already built, by that time, a sound industrial base. Germany was then facing lot of difficulties in competing with the more established British industry. List was of the firm view that the development of industries is a pre-requisite of economic progress. Free trade was good for Britain whose economic position was already well established. For young emerging German industry, however, protection of a tariff wall was essential. In the words of J.S. Mill, "The superiority of one country over another in a branch of production often arises only from having begun it sooner. There may be no inherent advantage on one part or disadvantage on the other, but only a present superiority of acquired skill and experience."[3]

Thus, J. S. Mill, one of the advocates of free trade, accepted only one argument in favour of protection, *viz.*, the infant industry argument. In Mill's words it ran thus: "A protective duty, continued for a reasonable time, might sometimes be the least inconvenient mode in which a nation can tax itself for the support of such an experiment (introducing new industries). But it is essential that protection should be confined to cases in which there is good ground of assurance that the industry which it fosters will after a time be able to dispense with it."[4] Alfred Marshall, the eminent English economist, too, conceded the force of the infant industry argument, although the English economists by and large advocated free trade. However, for protection to produce social benefits, an infant industry must first grow up. It must eventually be able to compete at world market prices. Not only has it to grow up, for a protectionist policy to be profitable, according to Sodersten, it will have to be able to pay back the losses due to protection during the infant industry period. Only then is there a clear-cut case for infant industry protection.

J.S. Mill (1806-1823)
Mill was an advocated of free trade.

This argument specially applies to countries that enter the industrial field at a later stage. Such countries possess potential advantages which may not become effective unless foreign competition is excluded for a period of time. Unless an industry in its infancy is protected till it acquires strength and maturity, it will die in the face of foreign competition.

The infant industry argument rests on the following grounds: (*a*) Every country has its own potentialities for developing some industries in the form of labour skill, raw materials and entrepreneurial talent. No country is completely devoid of productive elements which may yet be latent.

(*b*) Every nation has the right to develop its potentialities or discover its latent productive powers. No nation would like its efforts for economic development to be smothered before it has had a full chance for trial and error.

2. *Wealth of Nations*, Book IV, Ch. 2.
3. *Principles of Political Economy*, Vol. II. pp. 537-38.
4. *Ibid.*, Book V, Ch. 10, Sec. 1.

(*c*) It takes time for the productive elements to be developed. Labour can be trained; raw materials can be improved; and entrepreneurs can become competent by experience. But they should have enough time to develop and discover themselves.

(*d*) Infant industries cannot be expected to withstand competition from old and well-entrenched industries. It will be unfair to expose new industries to face cut-throat competition from fully developed industries.

(*e*) If infant industries are not duly protected against competition from strong and well-established industries, they are bound to die. This will mean waste of valuable national assets invested in the industry and a serious setback to entrepreneurial venture in future.

The 'infant industry' argument, however, has been refuted on two grounds: (*a*) that once an infant always an infant. Once protection is given, vested interests are created and it becomes almost impossible to withdraw it. (*b*) that all sorts of industries begin to claim protection once this basis is admitted. The result is political corruption.

Tariff may save employment in domestic economy.

In spite of these weaknesses, the argument has been widely accepted and many countries have industrialised themselves through protection given on the basis of this argument, *e.g.*, the U.S.A. and several members of the British Commonwealth, including India. But it is recognised that protection should not be given on a permanent basis. It should be given for a definite period considered sufficient for the industry to grow. Moreover, it should not be given indiscriminately to all industries. The industries to be given protection should be selected with proper care and discrimination so that scarce productive resources of the community are properly allocated.

(*ii*) 'Diversification of Industry' Argument. This argument was advanced, among other writers, by Frederich List in Germany. According to it, a nation should have a variety of sources of production and employment. Depending on one industry or on a few industries is dangerous both politically and economically. Politically it means too much dependence on foreign trade which may be cut off during a war. Economically, a country depending on a few industries is exposed to the danger of serious economic dislocation in case some adverse circumstances affect such an industry.

But it must be understood that this argument cuts at the root of the principle of comparative cost according to which each country must specialise in the production of certain articles. According to this argument a country must produce even those articles in which it may not have comparative advantage.

(*iii*) 'Employment' Argument. It is argued that industrial development through protection increases employment in a country. Conversely, if protection is not given to old established industries, foreign competition may ruin them and create unemployment in the country. The decay of the Indian handicrafts, during the 19th century, as a result of foreign competition, and the resultant unemployment and distress among the artisans, is a case in point.

Free traders meet this argument by saying that protection does not increase total employment; it merely transfers employment to the protected industries at the expense of other industries. Conversely, if due to foreign competition, old industries have to disappear, the people so set free can move to export industries for which the country concerned possesses greater comparative advantage, or migrate to other lands.

This reasoning assumes that labour and capital can easily move from industry to industry or from one country to another. In actual practice, due to economic friction, this happens very slowly or may not happen at all. It also assumes that productive resources of the country are already fully employed, whereas, in a country like India, there is a chronic under-employment of such resources.

At any rate, the employment created in the protected industries is bound to offset any contraction of employment in the export industries so that there is net increase in employment in the country. It is very likely that some previously unemployed workers are able to find jobs in the protected industry.

Some economists are, however, of the view that protective tariffs are only short-term palliatives to cure temporary unemployment. For instance, frictional unemployment, which arises from the inability of the workers to adjust to the new industrial changes owing to lack of mobility on their part, may be absorbed in the protected industries temporarily. Similarly, tariffs can lessen temporarily cyclical unemployment arising out of depression. That explains that during the Great Depression of the early thirties, nearly all countries raised tariff walls. Also, chronic unemployment resulting from high real wages can to some extent be cured by means of tariffs. The late Lord Keynes advocated protection as a means of combating permanent mass unemployment for an economy which is 'neither in equilibrium nor in sight of equilibrium.'

But tariff is no panacea for unemployment of any type. Sectional unemployment can be cured by technical training of workers to equip them for other jobs. General permanent unemployment can be cured by technical progress to raise marginal productivity of workers and by lowering real wages and by economic development of under-developed countries. The cyclical unemployment may be expected to vanish at the full recovery of the economy from depression.

Hence, protection by itself cannot create employment. It is like medicine which cannot be made a daily food.

(*iv*) 'Conservation of National Resources' Argument. Carey and Patten had argued that free trade resulted in the export of agricultural commodities from America and thus led to the exhaustion of the soil. Jevons in England applied the same argument against the export of coal which exhausted coal-fields. The same argument has also been applied in the Union of South Africa regarding gold mining and in India regarding the export of manganese and mica.

The argument has some force. If a country exports its exhaustible materials in a raw state, it losses the manufacturer's profits. It may also be seriously handicapped when such materials have been altogether exhausted.

(*v*) 'Defence' Argument. Adam Smith, remarked, "Defence is better than opulence." It is said that it is essential to make a country militarily strong even though it may not be economically prosperous. Hitler preached to the German nation, "Guns are better than butter." According to this argument, a country must actively encourage the development of those industries which are essential from the point of view of defence, even though it may result in uneconomic distribution of the national resources.

The advocates of free trade point out that this is politics and not economics. On purely economic grounds, they say, free trade is the best.

(*vi*) 'Revenue' Argument. Protection is also advocated for revenue purposes. When protective import duties are imposed, they certainly bring in revenue. Customs duties in India have been fairly productive.

But it may be pointed out that there is a certain degree of incompatibility between the revenue and protection. If full protection is given, the government will not get any revenue, because full protection will mean that our goods have driven out foreign goods altogether. When foreign goods do not come in, there will be no revenue from import duty. On the other hand, if we want revenue then foreign goods must come in and compete with our goods. Then our industries do not get any protection. This incompatibility, however, arises between **maximum** protection and **maximum** revenue. But if the duties are moderate, they will yield revenue besides affording protection. It is, however, much better to advocate protection for the sake of protecting industries rather than for raising revenues.

(*vii*) 'Key Industry' Argument. If the industrial structure of a country is to be stable and sound, it must develop 'key' or basic industries; otherwise the foundation of industries will have been laid on sand. The country may not have any comparative advantage in such industries. But since they are of crucial importance and have to be developed, protection must be granted to them.

(*viii*) 'Balance of Payment' Argument. It may become necessary to check imports by means of tariff in order to rectify an adverse balance of payments. The I.M.F. regulations permit the member countries to impose temporary restrictions on trade to cure a balance of payments deficit. Import restrictions on non-essential imports also become necessary in the interest of accelerated economic growth.

(*ix*) 'Patriotism' Argument. Protection is advocated on patriotic grounds also. It is the duty of every citizen to use home-made goods as far as possible. We must, therefore, develop our industries, through protection, if necessary, so that home-made goods in the right quantity and of good quality are made available for use. There was a widespread Swadeshi sentiment in India in the first decade of the present century which gave Indian industry great stimulus.

(*x*) 'Self-sufficiency' Argument. Another argument in favour of protection is that we should become self-sufficient and not depend on other countries for our necessaries. Such a dependence proves very dangerous during war when foreign trade is cut off. This argument has a particular force in present times when war clouds are constantly threatening overhead.

(xi) Protection also becomes necessary **against unfair competition** from abroad arising from dumping, depreciated exchanges, bounties, *etc*.

(xii) **For Economic Stability.** Protection is also advocated to shut out the baneful influences of trade cycles from abroad. It is expected to make the domestic economy immune from the destabilising effects of external disturbing factors. In the Macmillan Committee (1931), the late Lord Keynes put forward the opinion that protection and not free trade was needed to restore the much-needed economic stability for an economy which is out of gear.

Tariff creates rifts between nations.

Arguments Against Protection

Let us now look at the other side of the shield and see if there are any drawbacks in the policy of protection. The usual arguments are:–

(i) Vested interests are created. Once certain industries are given protection, they claim it as a matter of right. It then becomes very difficult to take away protection. The 'infants' begin kicking if you touch them in any manner. Such infants refuse to admit that they have grown into adults.

(ii) Protection produces lethargy and acts like an opiate. When foreign competition has been removed, it sends the home manufacturers to sleep, as it were. They do not try to make any improvement, and technical progress comes to a standstill.

(iii) Then there is the danger of corruption. The industrialists bribe legislators so that protection is not taken away. This evil was rampant in the U.S.A. at one time.

(iv) Protection creates monopolies. Tariff is said to be the mother of trusts. When foreign competition has been removed, the home manufacturers are tempted to combine to reap monopoly profits. That explains, for instance, the birth of the Indian Sugar Syndicate.

(v) Consumers and unprotected industries suffer. This is so because imposition of import duties invariably leads to the rising of prices.

(vi) The distribution of wealth becomes more unequal. Protection favours the rich capitalists who grow still richer. The gulf between the 'haves' and 'have-nots' is thus widened still further.

(vii) Protection leads to conflict, friction and retaliation in international dealings. It thus creates Mifts between nations and breeds the germs of future wars.

(viii) The most important argument against protection on economic grounds is that it militates against optimum utilisation of resources. It hampers international division of labour so that labour, capital and other factors of production do not find their most remunerative employment. Their distribution is not governed by natural economic forces but they are artificially forced into certain channels. The result is that they do not make their maximum possible contribution in the production of commodities. The world output is lower is than it could be, so that the standard of living is necessarily lowered. A natural movement towards world prosperity is hindered.

To this argument it may be replied that so long as world citizenship does not come into existence, the economically backward countries must safeguard their interests against cut-throat competition from the economically powerful countries.

Conclusion

On the whole, therefore, we come to conclusion that in theory free trade may be the best, but in practice protection is, in some cases, essential, especially in the case of economically under-developed countries like India.

ROLE OF PROTECTION IN UNDER-DEVELOPED COUNTRIES

There is no doubt that historically speaking protection was an instrument used by industrially backward countries to catch up with the advanced countries. The U.S.A. as well as the countries of the European continent adopted the policy of protection against the United Kingdom which was industrially ahead of them. Their industries could not face the British competition since they had entered the race of industrialisation later. The force of 'infant-industry argument' was admitted even by the eminent English economist like Alfred Marshall, although the English economists have, as a rule, favoured free trade as against protection.

Now protection is being given extended application in developing economies. They are not backward generally in economic development. Protection may be needed even by farm products. The developing economies are desirous of registering economic advance in all sectors of the economy, of course, in accordance with a scheme of priorities. Fresh economic development cannot obviously last if exposed to the withering competition from abroad. There is a period during which newly gained economic gains must be protected and consolidated. 'Nurse the baby, protect the child and free the adult' is a maxim which still holds good.

In all plans of economic development, protection occupies an important place. What is generally done is that when a certain industrial project is taken up as a part of the economic development plan, the imports of competing manufactured goods are substantially curtailed or totally banned for some years so that the field is left free for domestic manuf actures. The home market is thus preserved by protection for the home manufactures. If this is not done, all investment in the new lines of manufacture may go to waste, because foreign competition will not allow the home manufacturers to acquire a foothold in the home market. Unless there is prospect of protection for the new products, no investor will come forward and make investment in that particular field. As a consequence, the development plans will fall through.

Protection is known to be of two varieties: the safeguarding variety and the developmental variety. In India, we first introduced what came to be known as discriminating protection. This was more or less protection of the safeguarding variety. In spite of its being in operation for more than a quarter of a century, the goal of industrial development remained as far as ever. After the country became independent, a new look had to be given to the fiscal policy and a Fiscal Commission was appointed in 1950. It recommended a new fiscal policy which may be described as 'developmental'. It fitted in with the requirements of a developing economy.

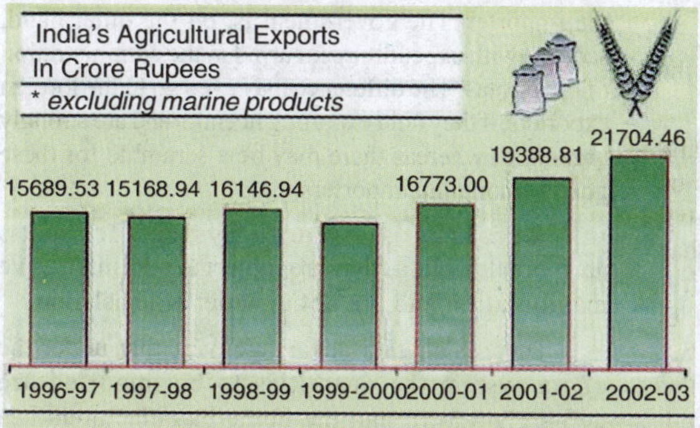

Agricultural Exports of India.

Fiscal policy is now being used as an instrument of planning. It plays a vital role in economic development. It must be such as to encourage saving and investment in the country. Fiscal policy can be used as a device to bring about greater investment and increase in income and employment in the country. It can also be used for reducing inequalities of income and wealth in the country which is a desirable objective of economic development.

A developing country has very carefully to work out import policy to be pursued from year to year. Imports are strictly controlled and quotas fixed. While fixing quotas, the main consideration is the availability of foreign exchange. As a rule, where the country has the capacity to meet entire domestic demand, tariffs are increased even up to 100 per cent. When the home industry can meet home demand partically, the imports are regulated by quotas. As for exports, export promotion drive is launched. Export incentives are provided by removal or reduction of export duties and by giving several concessions to exporters.

Thus, protection is of special value, say an urgent necessity, for the under-developed and developing countries. We indicate below in a summary way why so:

(i) The 'infant industry argument' specially indicates the need for protection for the developing countries. But it should be selective or of a discriminating type.

(ii) As Pigou observes, "The case for protection with a view to building up productive power is strong in any agricultural country which seems to possess natural advantages for manufactures". It is especially the case for under-developed, predominantly agricultural countries like India.

(iii) Protection preserves the available foreign exchange for the import of capital equipment, essential raw materials and the technical know-how so urgently needed to give a push to the development process.

(iv) Protection strengthens the economy of under-developed countries and increases the GNP and eventually results in the expansion of international trade.

(v) Protection will strengthen defence and promote self-sufficiency and full employment in such countries. This is all the more necessary in a world of political uncer tainty.

(vi) Protection is an essential ingredient of planned economic development for which control and regulation of all economic activity are so very necessary.

Thus, protection has come to play a vital role in developing economies to bring about rapid economic development.

BARRIERS TO FOREIGN TRADE

In view of the protectionist sentiment prevailing in economically backward countries, obstacles have been raised in the way of free foreign trade. Obstruction to foreign trade may take various forms. Among these are: (1) Prohibition of imports or exports, (2) exchange control, (3) customs duties, (4) preferential treatment, (5) quotas, (6) import licences, and (7) import monopolies. A few words may be said about each of these.

Import Prohibition. Sometimes import of certain commodities is prohibited by law or allowed only under defined conditions. For instance there are "sanitary regulations". The United States once excluded beef from a certain region in Argentina where foot and mouth disease had attacked cattle. Later, the embargo was extended to the whole of Argentina. Sometimes countries indirectly curtail imports by refusing to export certain materials until they have been processed at home. "Rumania did not let her oils out except on the condition that it be first refined at home, while Hungary will not admit Rumanian oil except on the condition that it be refined after it is received."[5]

Exchange Control. Exchange control implies government interference with the buying and selling of foreign exchange. In this way, foreign trade is curtailed and driven into fixed channels. Government may "allot" exchange or ration it out so that importers can buy only a limited amount of goods in foreign countries. Or they may "block" exchange. For instance, an American exporting goods to Germany may be required to use the marks exchange thus obtained in purchasing goods in Germany. Another way is known as exchange "clearing ." Thus, a German buying goods worth $ 1,000 from America may be required to deposit this amount in a German bank, while a German selling goods worth $1,000 to an American may draw on the bank for payment. In this way, an attempt is made to carry on foreign trade without the use of foreign exchange.

Customs Duties. This is an old method and consists in imposing import or export duties on goods coming into or going out of the country, respectively. Import duties are more common than export duties. A duty is said to be **specific** when it is imposed according to a standard of weight or measurement, *e.g.*, 6 Paisa per yard of cloth or two rupees per 40 kg. of wheat, *etc*. The duty is called **advolerem** when it is imposed according to value, *e.g.*, 10 per cent on motor cars or radio sets.

Customs duties or tariffs may have either revenue or protection as their aim. To protect cotton industry, an export duty on raw cotton may be imposed to cheapen it for the home manufacturer or an import duty on cotton manufactures may be levied. The latter is the usual method. The revenue duty is for revenue primarily and is levied for the financial year. It may be revised or discontinued in the next budget. The protective duty has greater continuity. Since the intention is to attract labour and capital to a particular industry, it must be levied for a number of years.

Preferential Treatment. Sometimes discrimination is made in the rate of duties with regard to different countries. For instance, India gave preferential treatment to certain British goods under the Ottawa Agreement of 1932. India also received preferential treatment in the British markets against non-Empire goods. This is known as **Imperial Preference.** Such arrangements curtail international trade and lead to the development of trade blocs. Moreover, countries whose goods pay higher duties may retaliate and impose high duties on the discriminating country in return.

Quota Restrictions. There are two kinds of quotas: "Customs quotas" and "import quotas". The first type allows a certain amount of a commodity at a favourable duty; beyond this the normal duty is charged. The limits are settled by agreements, *e.g.*, the U.S.A. does this with the Canadian cream and some other commodities coming under the reciprocal trade agreements. The "import quota" has more serious effect on trade. Here an arbitrary limit is set beyond which imports during a given period are not allowed.

Quota System vs. **Import Duties.** The import duties bring revenue to the State Treasury but under the quota system the differences between the foreign price and the home price, which arises on account of the restricted supply, is pocketed by the importer. The government is, on the other hand, saddled with expenditure incurred in the administration of the quotas. The difference may even go to the foreign exporters, if they hold exporting licences and are strongly organised, whereas there may be a scramble for these goods among the importers.

Advantages of Quota System. The quotas are more flexible, as they are subject to administrative manipulation and are not a matter of legislation.

There is another advantage, *viz.*, that under the quota system the quantities to be imported are definitely known and the home manufacturers can regulate their output accordingly. The quotas are not

5. B.W., Knight –*Economic Principle in Practice*, p. 344.

so much resented as the import duties are. The quotas are useful as bargaining counters in trade negotiations with other countries. The quotas can be reduced to grant further protection when a trade agreement may preclude the raising of import duties. Further, under the quota system the 'Most-Favoured Nation' clause can be evaded.

Disadvantages. The quota system has also several disadvantages: The home market is altogether isolated from the world market. Prices may be falling outside, but they will have no effect on the home market, because the quota is fixed and no goods can be imported beyond the quota. In the case of import duties, changes in the world prices bring about corresponding changes in the home prices. Similarly, if the foreign exporters are able to reduce costs, the home consumer cannot benefit under the quota system, as he would have benefited under a stable import duty. Under the quota system, government suffers a loss of revenue which it could get if it had imposed import duties. Finally, the quota system puts too much power in the hands of administrative officials as against the legislators.

Import Licences. Under this system, the government does not allow import of certain goods without a licence being obtained by the importer. In this way, imports can be cut down and certain goods discriminated against.

Import Monopolies. The Government may take the import of goods a State monopoly, as Russia does, and thus reduce imports or discriminate against certain countries.

Conclusion. We may conclude in Samuelson's words, "A system of prohibitive tariffs puts a society inefficiently inside the consumption-possibility frontier that would be available if the efficiencies of international exchange and division of labour were utilised. This is absolutely true of the world as a whole, and particularly true for a country that cuts off all imports and becomes self-sufficient."[6] The citizens are forced to curb their consumption of goods they desire the most and to channel their resources from uses of true comparative advantage to economically inefficient uses.

A Note on The Theory of Tariffs

Tariff is an important tool of commercial policy. Although it is primarily a potectionist device yet it proves to be a double-edged weapon. On the one hand, it limits consumer's choice by forcing him to cut consumption of the goods he likes and, on the other, it shifts the use of resources from one use to another. The effect of tariffs is to change relative prices of goods and services and to change the relative prices of the factors of production. The following diagram illustrates the effects.

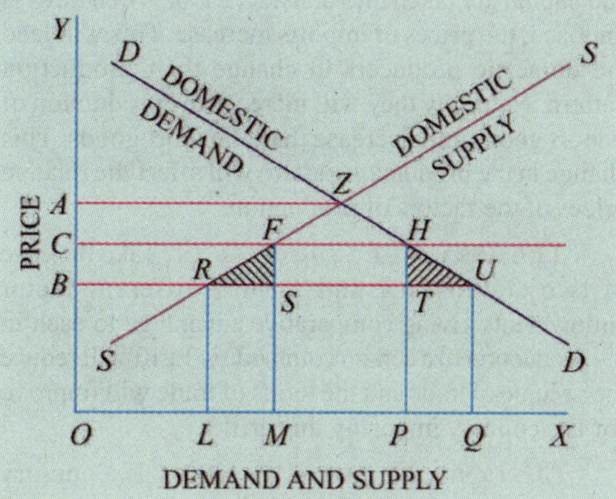

Effects of tariff.

In this diagram, demand and supply are represented along the *X*-axis and price along the *Y*-axis, *DD* and *SS* respectively are demand and supply curves. Before the imposition of the tariff, domestic supply is *OL* and domestic demand is *OQ*. *OB* is the price. At this price, demand exceeds the supply and the excess is met by imports equal to *LQ*. Now suppose tariff equal to *BC* is imposed. Since at *OB* price the imports have infinite elasticity, they will not be affected by the tariff. But it will raise the price in the domestic market from *OB* to *OC*. At *OC* price, foreign supply line shifts to *CWW* and imports are cut down from *LQ* to *MP*(= *FH*). As a result, the domestic production increases from *OL* to *OM* (*i.e.* by *LM*).

Protective Effect. Tariff reduces the imports of competing goods thus affording protection to the domestic producer. Domestic production is increased as shown above as a result of the imposition of tariff. This is known as **Protective effect.**

Consumption Effect. When tariff is imposed, price of the commodity rises and domestic consumption is reduced from *OQ* to OP. This is called the **Consumption effects.**

Revenue Effect. The government derives revenue from the tariff which is measured by the quantity of the imports multiplied by the rate of the tariff. This is represented by the area FSTH. This is the **Revenue effect.**

Redistribution Effect. The imposition of the tariff increases the price of the commodity and thus reduces the consumers' surplus. In this way, some income is transferred from the consumers to the producers. This affects distribution of income. It is called the **Redistributive effect.** In the diagram it is represented by the quadrilateral *BRFC*.

6. Samuelson, P.A.–*Economics*, 9th Edition, p. 678.

Stolper-Samuelson Theorem. The redistributive effect can be studied with the help of the Stolper-Samuelson theorem. Two factors labour and capital are taken into consideration. When tariff is imposed, the prices of imports increase. This will lead the domestic producers to change their production pattern. Naturally they will increase the production of import goods and decrease that of export goods. This change in the production pattern will affect the relative prices of the factors of production.

The Terms of Trade Effect. Take the case of two countries *A* and *B* with different factor endowments giving comparative advantage to each in the production of a certain commodity. Tariff will reduce the volume of trade and the terms of trade will improve for the country imposing the tariff.

Effect on National Income. If a country is facing unemployment problem, imposition of tariff will increase employment and thus increase national income. This happens because with the imposition of tariff consumers' demands are diverted to the domestically produced goods. To meet this increased demand new production units will be set up. As a result lot of employment will be created and national income increased.

Optimum Tariff. A tariff is said to be optimum when its rate maximises the welfare of the country *i.e.* when the rate is considered best from all points of view; it is neither high nor low. It is the ideal rate.

Globalisation and The Theory of Protection

The theory of protection was based on the prove verb "that a baby is to be nursed, a child is to be protected and an adult is to be left free". The developing countries economies were like an infant and they were not so much developed as that of the western European countries. Hence they use to follow the theory of protection for certain arguments which were essential for the growth of their economies, along with their social, political and cultural environment. The period between 1985 and 1995, saw some violent economic revolutions in the world, not in favour of common man, but in favour of those who have enough economic power. The collapse of Socialism, the emergence of Capitalism, as the undisputed economic policy in the world and to support this the Dunket Draft Text in the form of GATT agreement. This forced most of the countries in the world to opt for liberatisation and globalisation policy. The TRIPS (Trade Related Intellectual Property Rights) and TRIMS (Trade Related Investment Measures, Multinational Trade negotiations and the MFN (Most Favoured Nation) Concept helped the developing countries to withdraw their theory of protection.

The present economic scenario in the world is that your economy or any country's economy is a part of the world economy and it is opened to other countries of the world. The developed countries have succeeded in super-imposing their economic, political and cultural environment on the developing countries with the help of the above mentioned measures as well as with the establishment of WTO on 01-01-95. Thus the developing countries are at the mercy of developed countries; whatever benefits, they used to get by way of the policy of protection, now they cannot get the same. Though there are many arguments in favour and against liberalisation, but it has increased the prices of certain essential products *i.e.* drugs pharama ceuticals *etc.* . . . . In the absence of the theory of protection the developing countries governments, very often are at the mercy of developed countries and it has also increased more cases to be filed for patents, dumping, ... In case of India, the patent of Haldi, Neem, Basmati Rice, Tulsi *etc.* are some of the examples, Though the Indian exports during the post-liberalisation period is increased to certain extent.

Key terms

Free trade, Protectionism, Tariff, Consumption effect of tariff, Redistibution effect of tariff, Optimum tariff, Import quota, Customs quota, Stolper-Samuelson theorem.

QUESTIONS

1. Discuss the present scenario of the theory of protection.
2. Examine critically the case for and against free trade. How far does it increase the volume and value of trade?
3. Explain the term 'protection' and give arguments for and against the poolicy of protection.
4. Discuss the rationale of a protectionist policy in a developing economy.
5. Under what conditions would it be preferable for a country (*i*) to resort to tariffs rather than quotas and (*ii*) to impose quotas rather than tariffs?

UNIT II

Balance of Payments and International Monetary System

Chapters

BALANCE OF PAYMENTS

Definition of Balance of Payments

In the modern world, there is hardly any country which is self-sufficient in the sense that it produces all the goods and services that it needs. Every country imports from other countries the goods that cannot be produced at all in the country or can be produced only at higher cost than foreign supplies. Similarly, a country exports to other countries the commodities which those countries prefer to buy from abroad rather than produce at home.

The balance of payments is a comprehensive record of economic transactions of the residents of a country with the rest of the world during a given period of time. The record is so prepared as to provide meaning and measure to the various components of a country's external economic transactions. Thus, the aim is to present an account of all receipts and payments on account of goods exported, services rendered and capital received by residents of a country, and goods imported, services received and capital transferred by residents of the country. The main purpose of keeping these records is to inform government of the international economic position of the country and to help it in reaching decisions on monetary and fiscal policy on the one hand, and trade and payments questions on the other.

Balance of Payments: Current and Capital Accounts

The balance of payments on current account includes items like imports and exports, expenses on travel, transportation, insurance, investment income, *etc.* These relate to current transactions.

The Capital Account, on the other hand, is made up of capital transactions, *e.g.*, borrowing and lending of capital, repayment of capital, sale and purchase of securities and other assets to and from foreigners–individuals and governments. When both current and capital accounts are taken, it is called over-all balance of payments. It is the over-all balance of payments which must balance.

By way of illustration, we give on the next page India's Balance of payments on Current Account and on Capital Account for the year 1979–80.

Balance of Payment records transaction between domestic residents and rest of the world.

India's Overall Balance of Payments-Current Account, 1979-80

	Items	*Credits (in crores)*	*Debits (in crores)*	*Net (in crores)*
1.	Merchandise			
	(i) Private	6181.0	4837.6	+ 1343.4
	(ii) Government	20.4	4738.1	– 4717.7
2.	Non-monetary gold movement	5.2	–	+ 5.2
3.	Travel	920.0	88.2	+ 831.8
4.	Transportation	318.5	252.7	+ 65.8
5.	Insurance	42.8	28.1	+ 14.7
6.	Investment income	643.0	378.8	+ 264.2
7.	Government, not included elsewhere	86.4	87.8	– 1.4
8.	Miscellaneous	558.6	562.1	– 3.5
9.	Transfer payments			1624.2
	(i) Official	347.5	8.7	+ 338.8
	(ii) Private	1631.9	7.7	
10.	**Total Current Transactions**	**10,755.3**	**10989.8**	**+ 1,734.7**
11.	*Errors and omissions*			**– 234.5**
				+ 10.6

Source: *RBI Bulletin, April*, 1982

Items Included in the Balance of Payments

The various items in the balance of payments (current account) are given below:

(i) The chief item is the international trade in commodities. Export of commodities to foreign countries adds to our foreign receipts, while imports add to the payments that we have to make to the foreigners. **The difference between the value of commodity exports and imports is known as the Balance of Trade.** If exports exceed imports, the balance of trade is said to be favourable, and if imports exceed exports the balance of trade will be unfavourable. As we see from the following table, in 1979–80. India had an unfavourable balance of trade because our imports exceeded exports. The commodity exports and imports entering the balance of trade are also called **visible** items because they are recorded at the customs barriers of the country.

(ii) In additional to the import and export of goods, we also import and export certain services. Such services may be of various kinds for which payments have to be made or received, *e.g.*, transport charges, shipping freight, passenger fares, harbour and canal dues, commercial services (fees and commissions), financial services (broker's fees, *etc.*) and services connected with the tourist traffic and payment of interest on external debt. As against commodity or merchandise transactions, which are **visible,** these services are called **invisible** items of the balance of payments as they are not recorded at the customs barriers. If we render more invisible services to the foreigners than they render to us, we shall have a surplus on invisible account.

Previously, India used to have a deficit on invisible account as our payment on this account exceeded our receipts. India had to pay for the services of British officers working in India, their salaries, pensions and gratuities, shipping charges for use of foreign ships, bank charges for use of the foreign banking services, *etc*. However, in recent years, India is having a surplus on invisible account as the above table shows. This is because now she renders more services to the foreigners than they render to her and also because of official donations and private remittances from the foreign countries sent to India.

(iii) If we group together both the visible and invisible transactions, we get balance of payment on current account. If the value of our visible and invisible receipts is greater than the value of visible and invisible payments by us, then we shall have a favourable balance or a surplus balance of payments on current account, and *vice versa*. In recent years,- India has been suffering from huge deficits in our balance of payments on current account depite sizable remittances from abroad by Indians residing there.

(iv) In addition to current transactions, there are also capital movements between the countries. For example, capital may move from one country to another. The country which receives capital will add to its foreign receipts at the time when such capital is received, but at the time of repayment of debt it will

increase our payment to the foreigners. Capital between the two countries may move at the inter-governmental plane–*i.e.*, loan from one government to another. It may also move on private account–when, for example, Amercian investors invest their capital in Indian industry. Capital movements may be short-term or long-term. Short-term capital inflow carries with it the risk of early outflow and is liable to add an element of uncertainty to the country's international transactions.

In recent years, to finance a heavy deficit on current account, India has been getting lot of foreign loans both from the friendly foreign governments as well as from private investors.

(*v*) By summing up the balance on the current account and the balance of capital account, we get a country's overall balance of payments. If there is a deficit on overall account, and a country is not able to find sufficient capital inflow to neutralise the effect of a deficit on the current account, it will have to draw upon its reserves of foreign exchange. If on the other hand, the current account surplus is greater than the capital outflow from a country, its foreign exchange reserves will increase. In recent years, the inflow of foreign capital–official as well as private–being insufficient to finance fully India's deficit on current account, she was forced to draw down her foreign exchange reserves which have been drastically cut down.

Balance of Payments and Balance of Trade

As we have already said, balance of trade refers only to the merchandise balance or balance of visible transactions alone. On the other hand, the balance of payments refers to the sum of both the balance on visible as well as invisible items. It also includes capital and financial accounts. We have already explained the meaning of the terms visible and invisible. To repeat, visible items are those which are duly recorded at the customs barriers, while invisible transactions are incapable of being so recorded.

For the country's overall international economic position, what really matters is its balance of payments and not the balance of trade alone. A country may have a deficit on trade balance, while it may have a surplus in balance of payments on current account. England for a long time used to have a deficit on trade account and this deficit was more than made up by surplus on invisible account so that her balance of payments position remained favourable. As against this, India under the British rule used to have a favourable trade balance, but her surplus on balance of payments was considerably reduced because of a host of invisible payments like the 'home charges' that she had to make to England.

How Does the Balance of Payments Balance?

The balance of payments (on current account) is said to balance when the total of the credit items is exactly equal to the total of the debit items. But, it is seldom so. Hence, there is either a deficit or a surplus in the current account of the balance of payments. This deficit or surplus is met by transfers in the capital account. In other words, the balance of payments is made to balance through the capital account.

Suppose there is a deficit in the current account of the balance of payments. This deficit will be covered

India's Overall Balance of Payments-Capital Account 79-80

Items	*Credits (in crores)*	*Debits (in crores)*	*Net (in crores)*
1. Private			
(*i*) Long-term	93.9	133.9	– 40.0
(*ii*) Short-term	—	0.3	– 0.3
2. Banking	205.7	287.4	– 81.7
3. Official			
(*i*) Loans	982.3	87.0	+ 895.3
(*ii*) Amortisation	3.4	479.4	– 476.0
(*iii*) Miscellaneous	632.4	336.5	+ 295.9
(*iv*) Reserves	863.2	1,232.5	– 369.3
Total Capital and Monetary Gold	**2,780.9**	**2,557.0**	**+ 223.9**

SOURCE: *Reserve Bank Bulletin*, April 1982, 5212.

by (*a*) drawing upon the country's foreign exchange reserve, (*b*) by borrowing from abroad, and (*c*) by exporting gold. Now the I.M.F. grants temporary accommodation to bridge the gap.

EQUILIBRIUM, DISEQUILIBRIUM AND ADJUSTMENT

Balance of Payments Equilibrium

Before we analyse the conditions of disequilibrium, we would like to explain what is meant by equilibrium balance of payments. "Equilibrium is that state of the balance of payments over the relevant time period which makes it possible to sustain an open economy without severe unemployment on a continuing basis."[1] The essentials in this definition are: (*a*) relevant time period, (*b*) openness of economy (*i.e.*, no undue restrictions on imports). (*c*) absence of unemployment, and (*d*) continuing basis of the equilibrium (*i.e.*, it is capable of being sustained). The period is generally one year. Thus, seasonal inequality between exports and imports is not a sign of disequilibrium.

Balance of payment Equilibrium.

Static Equilibrium. A distinction is also made between static equilibrium and dynamic equilibrium. The distinction between static and dynamic equilibrium depends upon the time period. In static equilibrium, exports equal imports including exports and imports of services as well as goods and the other items on the balance of payments–short-term capital, long-term capital and monetary gold, are on balance, zero. Not only should the balance of payments be in equilibrium, but also national money incomes should be in a equilibrium vis-a-vis money incomes abraod. The foreign exchange rate must also be in equilibrium.

Dynamic Equilibrium. The condition of dynamic equilibrium for short periods of time is that exports and imports differ by the amount of short-term capital movements and gold (net) and there are no large de-stabilising short-term capital movements.

The condition for dynamic equilibrium in the long run is that exports and imports differ by the amount of long-term autonomous capital movements made in a normal direction, *i.e.*, "from the low-interest-rate country to those with high rates."[2]

When the balance of payments of a country is in equilibrium, the demand for domestic currency is equal to its supply. The demand and supply situation is thus neither favourable nor unfavourable. If the balance of payment moves against a country, adjustments must be made by encouraging exports of goods, services or other forms of exports, or by discouraging imports of all kinds. No country can have a permanently unfavourable balance of payments, though it is possible–and is quite common for some countries–to have a permanently unfavourable balance of trade. Total liabilities and total assets of nations, as of individuals, must balance in the long run.

This does not mean that the balance of payment of a country should be in equilibrium individually with every other country with which she has trade relations. This is not necessary nor is it the case in the real world. Trade relations are multilateral. India, for instance, may have an active balance of payments with the United States and passive balance with the United Kingdom and/or other countries. But each country, in the long run, cannot receive more value than she has exported to other countries taken together.

Equilibrium in the balance of payments, therefore, is a sign of the soundness of a country's economy. But disequilibrium may arise either for short or long periods. A continued disequilibrium indicates that the

1. Kindleberger. C.P.–*International Economics*, 963. p. 501.

2. *Ibid.*, p. 506.

country is heading towards economic and financial bankruptcy. Every country, therefore must try to maintain balance of payments in equilibrium. To know how this can be done involves the study of the theories and causes of disequilibrium in the balance of payments of a country.

Types and Causes of Disequilibrium

There are several variables which join together to constitute equilibrium in the international economic position of a country, *viz*., national incomes at home and abroad, the prices of goods and factors, the supply of money, the rate of interest, *etc*. At the back of these variables lie the supply of factors, production functions, the state of technology, tastes, the distribution of income, the state of anticipations, *etc*. If there is a change in any of these variables and there are no appropriate changes in other variables, disequilibrium will be the result.

The bulk of balance-of-payments difficulties is the result of **domestic inflation;** and disinflation is the obvious remedy. The decline in income will reduce domestic demand for goods and release them for sale abroad. The reduction in prices will make the country a better country to buy from than to sell to thus increasing exports and reducing imports. Halting of inflation and correction of exchange rate tend to reverse speculation which had depleted foreign exchange reserves and will lead to a return flow of domestic capital and build up again foreign working balances.

There are three main types of disequilibria: (*a*) Cyclical Disequilibrium, (*b*) Secular Disequilibrium, and (*c*) Structural Disequilibrium.

Cyclical Disequilibrium. Cyclical disequilibrium is caused by countries having different cyclical patterns of income, or the same income pattern with different income elasticities, or identical income patterns and income elasticities by different price elasticities. "If prices rise in prosperity and decline in depression, a country with a price elasticity for imports greater than unity will experience a tendency for a decline in the value of imports in prosperity, while those for which import price elasticity is less than one will experience a tendency for increase. These tendencies may be overshadowed by the effects of income changes, of course. Conversely, as prices decline in depression, the elastic demand will bring about an increase in imports, the inelastic demand a decrease."[3]

It is said that the under-developed countries suffer in terms of the balance of payments both from low prices in depression which hurt exports and from high incomes in prosperity which give rise to heavy imports. The developed countries are hurt consistently by high import prices during periods of world prosperity, and by low incomes abroad during periods of depression.

But these are too sweeping statements and are also contradictory. There is no doubt that the balance of payments of under-developed countries is adversely affected by the income effect in prosperity and the terms-of-trade (price) effect in depression. But before any conclusion can be drawn about the net impact on such countries of trade cycles, one must study the income effect in depression and the terms-of-trade (price) effect in prosperity; and the converse for developed countries.

Secular Disequilibrium. As for secular (long run) disequilibrium in balance of payments, they occur bacause of long-run and deep-seated changes in an economy as it advances from one stage of growth to another. The current account follows a varying pattern from one state to another. In the initial stages of development, domestic investment exceeds domestic savings and imports exceed exports. Disequilibrium arises owing to lack of sufficient funds available to finance the import surplus, or the import surplus is not covered by available capital from abroad. Then comes a stage when domestic savings tend to exceed domestic investment and exports outrun imports. Disequilibrium may result, because the long-term capital outflow falls short of the surplus savings or because

Capital outflow from the economy.

3. Kindleberger, C.P.–*International Economics*, 1963, p. 525,

surplus savings exceed the amount of investment opportunities abroad. At a still later stage, domestic savings tend to equal domestic investment and long-term capital movements are, on balance, zero.

Now if there is any change, it will cause a disequilibrium. This is a balanced stage and a secular disequilibrium will occur when either the long-term capital movement gets out of adjustment with deep-seated factors affecting savings and investment, or scheduled savings and investment change without an offsetting change in the movement of long-term capital. If investment adjusted itself readily to the amount of domestic savings plus foreign capital, there could be no tendency for secular disequilibrium.

The balance-of-payments position will also be in order, if the international capital flow fell into line with the requirements of domestic investment minus domestic savings. There is a tendency to secular disequilibrium, because domestic savings and domestic investment are independent of the foreign capital flow and are of different magnitudes. There is a strong tendency for under-developed countries to over-invest and/or undersave. These countries are anxious to narrow the gap between their economic level and that of the advanced countries.The tendency to overspend follows fairly automatically from the character of the economic effort. This must cause a disequilibrium in balance of payments.

Technological changes are another major cause of disequilibrium in the balance of payments. Each technological change implies a new comparative advantage, which the other country adjusts to, but the adjustment process itself produces a balance of payments deficit. The innovation leads to increased exports if it is a new good or an export biased innovation; or it may lead to a decline in imports if the innovation is import-biased. This will create a disequilibrium. A new equilibrium will require either increased imports or reduced exports.

To the extent, the secular disequilibrium is due to the incongruence of foreign lending or borrowing, with excess domestic savings over investment or of investment over savings, the obvious remedy lies in changing foreign lending or borrowing, on the one hand, or domestic savings and investment, on the other, or both.

Structural Disequilibrium. There is another type of disequilibrium, *viz*., structural disequilibrium. Let us see how this type of disequilibrium is caused. "Structural disequilibrium at the goods level occurs, when a change in demand or supply of exports or imports alters a previously existing equilibrium, or when a change occurs in the basic circumstances under which income is earned or spent abroad, in both cases without the requisite parallel changes elsewhere in the economy."

Suppose demand for Indian handicrafts falls off. The resources engaged in the production of these handicrafts must shift to some other line or the country must restrict imports, otherwise the country will experience a structural disequilibrium. Suppose Indian jute crop fails, export will fall and disequilibrium will be created .Apart from goods, a loss of service income may also upset the balance-of-payments position on current account. The loss of income may arise, because foreign investment has proved a failure or it has been confiscated or nationalised, *e.g.*, nationalisation of Anglo-Iranian Company in Iran. A war also produces structural changes which may affect not only goods but also factors of production.

A deficit arising from a structural change can be filled by increased production or decreased expenditure, which in turn affect international transactions in increased exports or decreased imports. Actually, it is

War affects flow of both goods and factors of production adversely.

Income must increase to correct BOP disequilirbium.

not so easy, because the resources are relatively immobile and expenditure not readily compressible. Disinflation or depreciation may be called for to correct a serious disequilibrium.

"Structural disequilibrium **at the factor level** result from factor prices which fail to reflect accurately factor endowments. . . . *i.e.*, when factor prices, out of line with factor endowments, distort the structure of production from the allocation of resources which appropriate factor prices would have indicated". If, for instance, the price of labour is too high, it will be used more sparingly and the country will import goods with a higher labour content. This will lead to unemployment, upsetting the balance in the economy.

We have explained above four types of disequilibria–cyclical, secular and two kinds of structural disequilibria and how they are caused. In each case, the causes manifest themselves through changes in export and import of goods and services making one exceed the other.

We have already detailed the various items that enter into the balance of payments. Any cause that leads to a persistently one-sided movement in those items may cause a disequilibrium. For instance, certain causes may lead to a falling off in the export or merchandise, imports remaining unaffected or moving in the opposite direction. Falling off in exports may be due to all sorts of causes.

Take the case of merchandise for illustration. Our exports may fall because of decreased production due to seasonal factors or other causes. The demand for our goods in the international market may fall off because of a fall in the purchasing power of the consumers of such goods or because of a comparatively high cost of production in India which reduces our competitive strength in the international market. Our exports may become dear to foreigners because of an appreciation of our exchange, a rise in the value of the rupee, say from Is. 6d. to 1s. 8d. If we persist in artifically keeping the value of the rupee at a higher level than justified by economic forces (which we shall study in the next chapter), unfavourable balance of trade and of payments will tend to persist.

In the same way, disequilibrium may arise due to excessive imports or services neither balanced by exports nor by import of capital, *etc*. Compulsory exports in the form of reparations or indemnities also cause international disequilibrium and obstruct the harmonious trade relations between the countries concerned.

Theories Concerning Disequilibrium in Balance of Payments

There are broadly the following three main theories which explain how a disequilibrium in balance of payments is caused:

(*i*) Classical Theory of Price Theory.

(*ii*) Keynesian Theory or Income Theory.

(*iii*) Demonstration Effect Theory.

Now a word about each of these.

Classical Theory. This theory explains disequilibrium in the balance of payments of a country in terms of relative costs and price structures. A country is likely to have an adverse balance of payments if her cost and price structure is relatively higher as compared with that of her trading partners. This theory assumes that there exists a significant element of substitutability between the home-made goods and foreign goods. If this is so, then the consumers in the country whose cost and price structure is relatively higher will substitute home-made goods by foreign goods. This will increase the imports of the country significantly and thus create balance of payments problem for the country.

Income Theory. Joan Robinson, Harrod and Haberler were mainly responsible for developing this theory. By using Keynesian tools, these economists came to the conclusion that the disequilibrium in the balance of payments of a country can be explained in terms of relative incomes. According to this theory, a country would face a disequilibrium in the balance of payments if her income is rising faster than that of her trading partners. This theory assumes that imports are a function of income, *i.e.*, with an increase in income, imports of a country would rise. Therefore, if the income of a country is rising faster than that of her trading partner countries, her imports are bound to increase faster, which in turn will give rise to a disequilibrium in her balance of payments.

Demonstration Effect Theoy. This theory was propounded, chiefly by Ranger Nurkse. It was suggested by Nurkse and also by MacDougal, that the high standards of living of the advanced countries had the effect of inducing the developing countries also to raise theirs. The aspirations of these countries to imitate the living standards of the advanced countries, resulted in their undertaking heavy investment programmes and in huge imports of luxury items. In other words, the standards of living of advanced countries serve as a 'demonstration model' for the less developed countries. The result of this is a fantastic increase in their imports, which in turn creates balance of payments problems for them.

Conclusion. No single theory can explain the disequilibrium in the balance of payments of a developing economy. There are a number of factors operating simultaneously which cause this disequilibrium. The main causes are:

(i) Ambitious development programme necessitating large-scale imports of machinery, plant and equipment, raw materials and technical know-how;.

(ii) Exports lagging behind owing to low level of productivity in agro-based industries and competition and stagnant or declining demand for traditional exports, and increased domestic consumption;

(iii) Food imports owing to high elasticity of demand for food and increase in population.

Methods of Correcting Disequilibrium in Balance of Payments

When serious disequilibrium arises in a country's balance of payments, steps must be taken to correct it, if the country's economy is to be kept in a sound condition. Obviously, the causes which are responsible for such a state of affairs must be removed. The 'classical' view of the adjustment mechanism is: "An active or passive balance, accompanied by an inflow or outflow of gold, was normally supposed ot result in an expansion or contraction of the domestic money supply; and this expansion or contraction was expected to bring about a rise or fall in the level of domestic costs and prices tending, in the former case, to stimulate imports and discourage exports or, in the latter, to discourage imports and stimulate exports. Gold flows, changes in relative price levels thus appeared as the principal factors in the mechanism of adjustments."[4]

Recent currency experience has, however, led to certain modifications in the classical theory. It is now thought that changes in the flow of income induced by balance of payments serve as an equilibrating factor. "The main point is that any active or passive balance of current transactions . . . . tends directly to expand or contract the total flow of money income within a given country . . . . The change induced by the balance of payments in the flow of income and outlay affect, in turn, the demand for imported as well as home-produced goods and so react on the balance in an equilibrium manner".[5]

There are five well-known methods of correcting an adverse balance of payments:

***(i)* Stimulating exports** and/or **checking imports.** If the exports have fallen off, step should be taken to encourage them. To encourage exports the level of costs in the country may have to be brought down. This may involve cutting down of wages and interest rates and other incomes and also contraction of currency to bring the prices down.

Exports are also encouraged by granting bounties to manufacturers and exporters. Imports may be discouraged either by total prohibition or by imposition of import duties or by adopting the quota system.

(ii) Another method is to **depreciate the external (exchange) value** of the home currency, thus cheapening domestic goods for the foreigner. This latter course, however, has serious limitations, because other countries may start doing likewise and 'competitive' depreciation of exchange rates may start, as it happened during the depression years in the thirties.

It may be noted that the rate of exchange serves as an equilibrating factor between the balance of payments. If, for instance, the demand for American goods increases, the demand for the dollars will increase, and, in the absence of exchange control the price of dollar in terms of foreign currencies will go up. This by itself will discourage the foreign buyers from buying in America and encourage Americans to buy from abroad. In this way the balance may be restored. Normally, it will be so. But if a further rise in the price of the dollar is feared, the foreigners will increase their purchases of American goods now lest they should become dearer still; it will also hold back

4. League of Nations—*International Currency Experience*, 1944, p. 9.
5. *Ibid.*, p. 600.

Stimulating Exports and Checking Imports will correct BOP disequilibrium.

the Amercians from buying more from abroad. In this way, the disequilibrium may be accentuated, instead of being cured.

(iii) The third method is to **deflate the currency.** As currency contracts, prices will fall, which will stimulate exports and check imports. But the method of deflation is also full of dangers. If prices are forced down while costs, which are proverbially rigid (especially as regards wages in countries where trade unions are well organised), do not follow suit, the country may face a serious depression and unemployment. Correcting the balance of payments, therefore, once a disequilibrium has arisen is not an easy matter.

(iv) The fourth method is **devaluation.** Its effect is the same as that of depreciation. When a currency is devalued (*i.e.*, its metallic content is reduced), its value in terms of foreign currency decreases. The result is that foreigners are able to buy in our country more goods than before with the same amount of their currency. This would stimulate exports. But when we want to buy foreign goods, our currency, having become cheaper, we have to pay more for them. Imports are thus discouraged, and, in course of time, the balance of trade turns in our favour and corrects the balance of payments.

The success of devaluation in improving the balance of trade, and through it the balance of payments, depends upon the demand elasticities of imports and exports of the devaluing country. In other words, an improvement in the balance of trade will depend upon whether the demand for imports and exports is elastic or inelastic. Devaluation makes the imports of the devaluing country costlier than before and in case her demand for imports is inelastic, a higher amount will be spent for the same imports, thereby worsening her balance of trade. Similarly, if her export demand is inelastic, then, after devaluation, lesser amount will be spent by the foreigners thereby affecting adversely the balance of payments of the devaluing country. However, if her demand for exports is elastic then with a fall in the prices of the exports as a result of devaluation, more will be purchased by the foreigners, which, in turn, will help in restroing the equilibrium in her balance of payments. Likewise, if her demand for imports is elastic, then the imports of the country will be significantly reduced by devaluation, which in turn would improve the balance of payments of the devaluing country.

However, some rule is needed to relate the required degrees of elasticities for the success of devaluation in improving the balance of trade. In this connection we have what are called the **Marshall-Learner Conditions.** According to it, devaluation will improve the balance of trade of a country if the sum of the elasticities of demand for imports and exports is greater than one. When the sum of these elasticities is equal to one, devaluation will leave the size of the deficit unchanged; and when this is less than one, it will make the balance of payments worse than before.

It should be noted here that the Marshall-Learner conditions relate only to the demand for commodity exports and imports. The response of capital, both official and private, to devaluation must also be taken into consideration before it can be determined whether devaluation will improve the balance of payments. (This is because of the fact that both the current account and the capital account constitute the balance of payments of a country). Then, if sufficient amounts of autonomous capital flow into the devaluing country, it would be possible to have the sum of elasticities of demand less than one and yet devaluation may lead to an improvement in the balance of payments of the devaluing country. If the country has investment opportunities and the devaluation is sufficient to allay fears of further devaluation, then capital will feel induced to flow into the country in search of profits.

Devaluation of currency improves BOP situation.

into domestic savings and not used for imports. Thus, change in prices or exchange rate will be essential for full equilibrium.

After the Second World War was evolved a new international machinery for maintaining equilibrium in the balance of international payments and for correcting disequilibrium when it does arise. This new machinery is the International Monetary Fund (I.M.F.), which we shall discuss in Chapter 59. It may, however, be mentioned here that no country now need be forced into deflation (and so depression) to root out the causes underlying disequilibrium as had to be done under the gold standard. On the contrary, the I.M.F. provides a mechanism by which changes in the rate of foreign exchange can be made in an orderly fashion.

On the other hand, if the flow of capital is reduced, as a result of devaluation, then the devaluation even with the sum of the elasticities greater than one, will agravate the deficit. This would occur, if capital were discouragred by devaluation and investors fear further devaluation.

The success of devaluation in improving the balance of trade also depends on the reactions of her trading partners. If the trading partners retaliate, then devaluation will not make any impact on the imports or exports of the devaluing country, even though her demand of imports and exports may be elastic.

(*v*) Finally, there is the method of exchange control. We know that deflation is dangerous depreciation has a temporary effect and may provoke others also to depreciate; and devaluation hits the prestige of a country. These methods are, therefore, avoided and, instead, foreign exchange is controlled by the government. All the exporters are ordered to surrender their foreign exchage to the central bank, and it is then rationed out among the licensed importers. None else is allowed to import goods without a licence. The balance of payments is thus rectified by keeping the imports within limits. (Exchange control is discussed in detail in the next chapter.)

When gold standard was effectively at work in most countries, disequilibria in international payments were automatically corrected to a fair degree. Some economists have recently expressed the opinion that changes in level of national incomes can restore the equilibrium. Increase in export, for instance, increases national income which, in its turn, adds to our capacity to purchase from abroad. This means that the imports will also increase and an equilibrium between exports and imports maintained. But modern economic analysis has shown that increase in imports will only partially cover up exports, because some portion of national income is bound to leak

Conclusion. In short, correction of disequilibrium calls for a judicious combination of the following methods:

(*i*) Monetary and fiscal changes affecting income and prices in the country;

(*ii*) exchange rate adjustment, *i.e.*, depreciation or appreciation of the home currency;

(*iii*) trade restrictions, *i.e.*, tariffs, quotas, *etc*.; and

(*iv*) capital movement, *i.e.*, borrowing or lending abroad.

No reliance can be placed on any single tool. There is room for more than one approach and for more than one device. But the application of the tool depends on the nature of disequilibrium. There are, we have said, four types of disequilibrium, two in income (cyclical and secular) and two in price or structural (at the goods and the factor level). It is more appropriate that the cyclical and secular disequilibria be tackled by monetary and fiscal measures. In structural disequilibria, exchage rate adjustment plays a greater role. Generally, trade restrictions should be avoided. Capital movements by time in short-run disturbances and are needed to offset deep-seated forces in secular disequilibrium.

The main methods of desirable adjustment are, therefore, monetary and fiscal policies which directly affects income, and exchange depreciation which affects prices in the first instance. It can also have income effect through price effects. Monetary and fiscal policies affect relative prices also.

ECONOMIC DEVELOPMENT AND BALANCE OF PAYMENTS

It is the usual experience of all developing economies to have serious difficulties in their balance of payments. This will be clear if we analyse the requirements of development and some of its consequences.

The balance of payments has two aspects, *viz.*, the import aspect and the export aspect. On the imports side, we can easily see that in the initial stages of development; the import bill must rapidly mount up from year to year. The country which has chosen the road to rapid economic development must be prepared to face heavy imports. What is being attempted is the conversion of a predominantly agrarian economy into a highly industrialised economy within a reasonable span of time. For this purpose, the country needs machinery, equipment and industrial raw materials. It must also import technical know-how. All these things an under-developed country lacks and for them it must rely on foreign countries. An under-developed country also lacks capital. It has, therefore, to borrow capital from abroad. The loans have to be repaid and it has to meet yearly liabilities arising out of interest payments. All these developments tilt the balance of payments against the developing economy.

Now let us see the export side. A developing country must build up, of course, an export surplus to pay for constantly pouring imports. But in the early stages of development, it is unable to export much. It has yet to build up export industries. Most of the domestically produced materials are absorbed in the home manufactures. Nor can it spare capital for investment abroad, because under-developed countries suffer from serious capital deficiency. The country is also not advanced enough to export services of any type. Most of the goods and services produced at home are absorbed at home in a rising tempo of economic development.

The rising tempo of development expenditure fed by deficit financing unleases the inflationary forces so that the country is good for selling to and not a good country to buy from. Inflation, therefore, adversely affects the balance of payments position.

Rising imports and lagging behind or stagnant exports lead to the widening of the deficit on current account and there is a widening gap on the capital account too. The balance of payments becomes increasingly unfavourable from year to year as development programme proceeds apace.

How is this situation met? It is the generosity of foreign friendly countries which comes to the rescue. Foreign aid in the form of loans is sought and obtained. In additon, foreign exchange reserves are drawn upon. International organisations like the I.M.F. also come forward to help the country out of the balance of payments difficulties.

But no country can go on borrowing from abroad indefinitely, if it is to retain its credit-worthiness in international financial circles. Foreign reserves are not a bottomless pool. Ultimately, the country must stand on its own legs and move to a stage called self-sustained growth. At this stage, it must find out of its own resources all the means for economic development. It should be able to do without foreign aid. It must meet its import bill out of its own export earnings. The export earnings should be sufficient to cover not only development imports but also maintenance imports. It is neither desirable nor feasible to cut down imports (except the non-essential ones) without hampering economic development. The development targets must be achieved and essential imports must continue to flow. Hence, vigorous and determined drive in the direction of export promotion is essential. It is the only sane course to adopt.

"Balance of Payment" The Present Case

The overall exports and imports of the Indian economy has increased over a period of 10 years in the post liberalisation period. Indian economy had severe balance of payment crisis during Prime-Minister Chandrasekhar's government. Due to certain measure and the policies adopted and introduced by the then Finance Minister Manmohan Singh. The economy was put on the road of recovery. The late ninetees and the early 21st century saw the rise in both the exports and imports. Earlier our exports were 0.54% but now it has increased to 0.82%. The government has introduced from time to time the Export and Import Policies, along with this, export promotion, the trade is increasing. This has helped in not only an increase in export but also imports. At present India is one of the most developed country among the developing nations as far as its items of exports and the quality of products. India's service sector exports is also increasing.

The over-all balance of payment situation is good, but there are certain other factors which is emerging in between. Due to the flow of *NRI* deposits as well as direct investments along with the *FDI* (Foreign Direct Investment) and *FII*'s (Foreign Institutional

Investment) there is enormous rise in the foreign exchange reserves. It is all time high at 104 billion $S. On the other hand recently the rupee has started appreciating against the U.S $. This may bring about certain repercurssion's which may harm the exports and imports.

There is a need for proper Exim Policy. India should not base its policy on the slogan of the seventies, that of, export or perish.

Key terms

Balance of payment, Current Account, Capital account, Balance of trade, Invisibles, Disequilibrium in BOP, Devaluation.

QUESTIONS

1. (*a*) Distinguish between Balance of Trade and Balance of Payments.
   (*b*) Explain the concept of 'balance of payments equilibrium'. What are the methods usually adopted for correcting an adverse balance of Payments? How is the disequilibrium in the Balance of Payments corrected?
2. What do you mean by equilibrium in the balance of payments? Explain fully the conditions necessary for such equilibrium.
3. Analyse the causes of adverse balanace of payments. Assess the efficacy of tariff and subsidy as corrective measures.
4. Discuss the role of devaluation as a method of correcting disequilibrium in the balance of payments.
5. What is meant by fundamental disequilibrium in a country's balance of payments" Discuss the relative usefulness of the measures suggested in the International Monetary Fund Agreement for correcting it?
6. Analyse the dictum that 'Exports pay for Imports'. How should this notion affect tariff policy?
7. Explain the relationship between a change in the foreign trade of a country and change in its national income.

EXCHANGE RATE DETERMINATION

Obviously, it is the supply of, and the demand for, foreign currency that would determine at any time the rate of exchange of a country's currency just as the market price of commodities is determined by the forces of demand and supply. We also know how the demand for, and supply of, foreign currency (or conversely supply of, and demand for, home currency) arise. When the supply is equal to demand, the rate of exchange is said to be at par. If supply of foreign currency is greater than demand, the value of the foreign currency falls below (or of the home currency rises above) the par. And conversely, if the demand for foreign currency is greater than supply thereof, the value of foreign currency rises above (or of the home currency falls below) the par.

1 $ = ? Rs.

Up to what limits can the exchange rate rise above, or fall below the part? These limits are determined differently under different conditions. The par of exchange also has different meanings under different conditions.

We shall see how rate of exchange is determined under different monetary systems.

Rate of Exchange under Gold Standard

When the two countries concerned are on gold standard (none now) as already explained, their currency units are either gold coins or are convertible into gold at fixed rates. Moreover, gold freely moves between the countries. The par of exchange between such countries is called the **"mint par of exchange".** This is arrived at by equating the amount of gold contained in the currency units (or given in exchange for them by currency authorities respectively) of the two countries.* There can be no mint par between a gold standard and a silver standard country.

For instance, before 1914, England and France were both on gold standard. Their mint par of exchange could be calculated as above.

The mint par between London and Paris was 25.2215 francs to £ 1. If the exchange is at par, under these conditions a French importer would get £ 1 in London by paying 25.2215 francs in Paris to meet his liability. An

English importer would get 25.2215 francs in Paris by paying £ 1 in London.

Specie Points. Now suppose the French people have to make more payments to the English people than the latter have to make to the former. The demand for the English currency in France will be greater than its supply. The value of the £ will rise in terms of the francs. The French importer will have to pay more than 25.2215 francs in order to get £ 1 in London.

But how much more will he be willing to pay? We have already said that an importer will send gold if he can get it and thinks it cheaper to send it. Gold standard countries always provide gold in exchange for their currency and allow it to leave the country. But gold involves cost of transport (shipping, insurance, interest charges, *etc.*) when it has to be sent out. The importer in France will, therefore, only send gold if the rate of exchange is higher than the par to the extent of more than the cost of transporting gold from Paris to London.

Suppose the cost of transporting 25.2215 francs worth of gold from Paris to London is .3 franc. Then it will be worthwhile sending gold if the exchange rises above 25.2215 francs to the £ by more than .3 franc. If the exchange actually rises above this point, gold will begin to move out from France to England. This point is thus called gold export point from the point of view of France and gold import point from that of England. This point is obtained by adding the cost of transport to the mint par of exchange. It is also called the **gold export point or the upper specie point.**

In the same way, there is a **lower specie point,** or **gold import point** for France and gold export point for England. This is obtained by deducting the cost of transport from the mint par. In the above example, it will be 24.9215 francs to the £. If the exchange falls below this point, the English importers will send gold rather than purchase title to francs.

Two Limits. Thus, if gold is available and is allowed to move freely between two countries (on gold standard), the rate of exchange will move between the two limits set by the upper and the lower gold points, also called the "specie points". If, however, gold is not available, the rate of exchange will pass beyond the specie points. These are the two limits within which the fluctuations will be caused by the changes in supply of, and the demand for, foreign currency, *i.e.*, bills, drafts, *T.T.s.*, *etc.*

Exchange between Gold and Silver Standard

The above is a case where both the countries concerned are on gold standard (none now). If, however, one is on gold standard and the other on silver standard, the par of exchange will be determined by the price of gold in terms of silver in the country on silver, and price of silver in terms of gold in the gold standard country. This discussion is now of purely academic interest.

The Purchasing Power Parity (PPP) Theory

The purchasing power parity theory which was developed by Gustav Cassel, a swedish economists, has its own beauty, but not without criticism. Earlier the exchange rate was determined on the basis of the gold standard or the gold mint-parity theory. This, theory had its own weakness as it is to help those countries who have huge gold reserves. It was Gustav Cassel, who introduced this unique theory of exchange rate. The main theme of Cassel was to compare the internal purchasing power of one country's currency with that of the internal purchasing power of another country's currency and then to bring or evolve the exchange rate on the basis of both currencies purchasing power comparison. Cassel's purchasing power parity theory was based on simple assumptions, that the two countries trading are free countries and there are no restriction whatsoever in their internal economies as well as their trade with the said country.

Let us explain the theory on the following assumptions.

(i) Two countries India and America.

(ii) Both countries are independent and free countries.

(iii) There is no pressure of any kind on them either on their internal trade or external trade.

(iv) In India we measure in terms of Rupees and in U.S.A. (America) in term of U.S $.

(v) The trade is in a given period of time, which can be fixed as a year or half a year *etc.*

* One English Sovereign = 7.98815 grammes of gold 11/12 fine
= 7.32238 grammes of pure gold.

One French Napoleon (20 francs) = 6.45161 grammes of gold 9/10 fine
= 5.80645 grammes of pure gold.

Therefore, one Sovereign $= \frac{7.32238 \times 20}{5.80645}$ francs = 25.2215 francs.

(*vi*) The year selected must be normal one, that means it must be free from either natural calamities as well as man-made crisis, in both the countries.

In second version that is Relative Version the commodities which we select in both the countries must be of same quality and quantity.

Cassel explained his theory with two versions.

(*i*) Absolute Version and

(*ii*) Relative Version

(i) Absolute Version

10 gram of gold of the same quality in India is Rs. 300 and that of in America is 10 $.

$$\therefore \quad 300 \text{ Rs.} = 10 \,\$$$

$$\therefore \quad 1 \,\$ = \frac{300}{10} = 30 \text{ Rupees.}$$

or

Let us take a bale of cotton. In USA it is available at 10 $ where as in India it is available at Rs. 400.

$$\therefore \quad 10 \,\$ = 400 \text{ Rs.}$$

$$\therefore \quad 1 \,\$ = \frac{400}{10} = 40 \text{ Rupees.}$$

(ii) Relative Version

In this case Cassel selected two baskets of same commodities of same quality in both the countries. Here we assume that the quality of commodities in both the countries are same.The quantity is measured in the same weights in both the countries. Let us explain the same.

Basket I In India Rs. 250			Basket II In USA. 10 $	
Milk	= 50 Rs.		Milk	= 2 $
Sugar	= 50 "		Sugar	= 2 "
Bread	= 40 "	=	Bread	= 1.50 "
Butter	= 50 "		Butter	= 2 "
Rice	= 30 "		Rice	= 1.50 "
Oil	= 30 "		Oil	= 1.00 "

Taking two baskets and selecting the day to day need of common commodities in both the countries and selecting their weights, and putting the prices existing at the same time in both the countries. In the above example '6' commodities are selected and the same amount of commodities are available in India at Rs. 250 (aggregate of all six commodities) and on the other hand in America it is available at $ 10.

According to Cassel if we bring out the parity between the two currencies then we will be able to get the exchange rate.

$$E_R = \frac{P_I}{P_A}$$

Rs. = 250 equal to $ 10.

ER in terms of Rupees per $ can be.

$$1 \,\$ = \frac{250}{10} = 25 \text{ Rs.}$$

ER → 1 $ = 25 Rs. The same can be compared to two different period of time (1990, 91).

$$ER = \frac{\dfrac{P_{I_1}}{P_{I_0}}}{\dfrac{P_{A_1}}{P_{A_0}}}$$

$$ER = \frac{P_{I_1}}{P_{I_0}} \times \frac{P_{A_0}}{P_{A_1}}$$

$$= \frac{P_{I_1}}{P_{A_1}} \times \frac{P_{A_0}}{P_{I_0}}$$

P = Prices

I = India

A = America

1 = Current Period

0 = Base Period

P_{I_1} = Prices in India in Current Period.

P_{A_1} = ,, ,, America ,, ,,

P_{I_0} = ,, ,, India in base ,,

P_{A_0} = ,, ,, America ,, ,,

Cassel's unique theory has its own beauty, and with certain amount of modification it can be of immense help, in the determination of exchange rate. Certain amount of work is already been done by the author in this regard that is the application of Cassel's theory for the determination of one currency for the SAARC countries.

Critical Evaluation of the Purchasing Power Parity Theory

This theory was popularised after World War I by Gustav Cassel, a Swedish economist. "The rate of exchange between two currencies," wrote Cassel, "must stand essentially on the question of the internal purchasing power of these currencies." This is easily seen if we reflect on the fact that the price paid in a foreign currency is ultimately a price which must stand in a certain relation to the prices of commodities on the home market." But the theory is criticised on several grounds:

(i) The strongest point of criticism is that the purchasing power parity theory compares the general price-levels in the two countries and not merely the price-levels of goods actually entering international trade. The prices of the latter kind of goods, of course, are the same in all countries allowing for the cost of transportation, tariff, *etc*. It is quite easy to verify the theory if we only compare prices of internationally traded goods. In fact, when its application is confined to such goods, it becomes an empty truism, because, as Halm says, "it is obvious that the national prices of internationally traded goods tend to equality as between different markets when translated into each other at the current exchange rates."[1]

But, when we try to compare the index numbers of the prices of the whole mass of goods marketed in the countries concer ned, the rate of exchange will not always conform to the points thus determined. This is so because price of domestic goods may not move in the same direction, at least not in the short period, as of those entering into international trade.

(ii) The theory is true only in the long run. In the long run, the rate of exchange and price-levels will tend to move in the same direction, especially if international trade is a major factor in a country's economic life. The theory, therefore, only holds good in the long period. Even in the long period the theory will be valid only if the essential conditions of international trade remain unchanged. But such conditions seldom remain unchanged. For instance, the barter terms of trade are constantly in a process of change between countries due to change in the demand for foreign goods or changes in the condition of supply of domestic goods.

(iii) Further, there is no permanence about the goods which do or do not enter into international trade. This depends on the rate of exchange itself. If the price of foreign currency goes up, it will make profitable the export of some hitherto domestic goods, and vice versa.

(iv) Moreover, changes may occur in the volume of foreign loans, cost of transport or in any other items of invisible balance of trade. Changes in barter terms thus brought about may disturb the relationship between the price-levels, and the parities based on such price-levels may not correspond to the rate of exchange. As Cassel observes, "Differences in the two countries' economic situation, particularly in regard to transport and customs, may cause the normal exchange rate to deviate to a certain extent from the quotient of the currencies' intrinsic purchasing powers"[2] If a country puts up tariffs, the exchange value of the currency will rise but its price-level will remain the same.

(v) Besides, many items of balance of payments like insurance and banking transactions and capital movements are very little affected by changes in general price-levels. But these items do influence exchange rates by acting upon the supply of, and the demand for, foreign currencies. The Purchasing Power Parity Theory ignores these influences altogether.

(vi) The theory, as propounded by Cassel, says that changes in price level bring about changes in exchange rates but changes in exchange rates do not cause any change in prices. This latter part is not true, for exchange movements do exercise some influence on international prices.

***(vii)* Keynes' Criticism.** According to Keynes there are two basic defects in the purchasing power parity theory, *viz*., *(i)* it does not take into consideration the elasticities of reciprocal demand, and *(ii)* it ignores the influence of capital movements. In Keynes' view, foreign exchange rates are determined not only by the price movements but also by capital

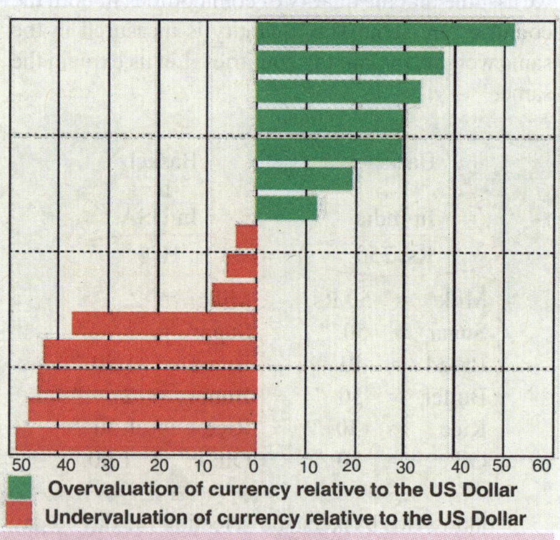

Purchasing Power Parity (PPP).

1. *Monetary Theory*, 1964, p. 224.

2. Cassel, G.–*Money and Foreign Exchange After* 1914, P. 139.

movements, the elasticities of reciprocal demand and many other forces affecting the demand for, and supply of, foreign exchange.

"By elasticity of reciprocal demand is meant the responsiveness of one country's demand for another country's exports with respect to price or income." As for price elasticity, generally speaking, greater the proportion of luxuries and semi-luxuries in the exports demanded, the more elastic will be the country's demand for another country's exports. It will also be more elastic, the greater the number of alternative markets in which to buy and greater the capacity to produce the effective substitutes for goods imported. As for the income elasticity of demand for imports, changes in demand for goods and services and in the derived demand for foreign exchange is functionally related to the changes in national income. How far is one country's demand for another's exports responsive to a change in its national income? That will influence the rate of exchange. In other words, it is the character of the propensity to import out of a given income that is supposed to affect the exchange rates independently of international price movements.

(viii) Technological improvements adding to the productivity of the country and making its goods cheaper and better, tariff changes and export subsidies affect exchange rates via their influence upon reciprocal demand quite independently of international price movements.

(ix) Capital movements, both short-term and long-term, are the other important influences. There is 'hot money' flying from a country trying to make profit or avoid loss on exchange fluctuations and there is a 'refugee capital' seeking safety and security abroad. An actual or expected change in the domestic price of a foreign currency may lead to inflow or outflow of 'hot money' causing a further change in the exchange rate without there being price changes in either country. The inflow tends to raise the exchange value of the country of the capital receiving country and outflow will lower it. Long-term movement of capital also has a similar effect.

Thus, there is no direct link between the purchasing power parity of the currency and its rate of exchange, because there are several other factors too which affect the rate of foreign exchange, *e.g.*, tariffs, speculation, capital movements, *etc*.

In conclusion, we may say that the Purchasing Power Parity Theory attempts to explain the ultimate rather plan the immediate forces determining the rate of exchange.

Its Superiority. The theory is applicable to all currencies. It is superior to the old theory according to which the rate of exchange was determined by balance of indebtedness. This theory goes even to the root of the balance of indebtedness. It explains how balance of trade, of indebtedness itself, is determined. This theory lays proper emphasis on the influence of price-level on the determination of rates of exchange.

The actual rate at any particular moment may diverge from the equilibrium rate as indicated by the purchasing power parity due to the various factors affecting the terms of trade or the balance of payments for the time being.

MODERN THEORY OF EXCHANGE RATE DETERMINATION

In view of the defects pointed out above, the purchasing power parity theory does not offer an adequate and satisfactory explanation of the fluctuations in the rates of exchange. The determination of the exchange rate depends not only on international price relations but also on many other factors as mentioned above. This leads us to a more adequate explanation of the determination of foreign exchange rates, *viz.*, balance of payments theory or demand and supply theory.

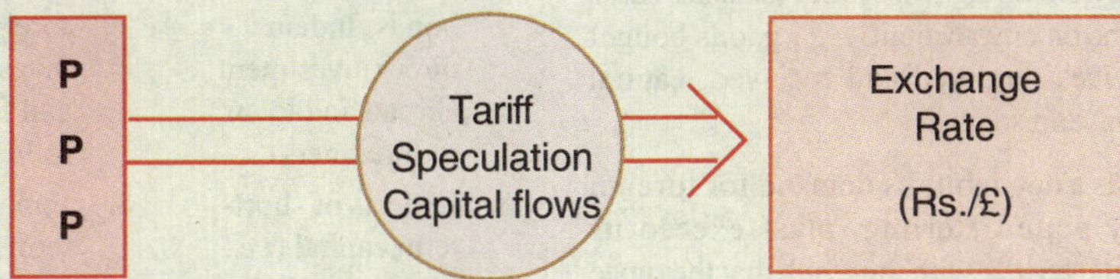

Demand and Supply Theory or Balance of Payments Theory

The most satisfactory explanation of the determination of the rate of exchange is that a **free exchange rate tends to be such as to equate the demand and supply of foreign exchange.** For example, the external value of the rupee in Bombay depends on the demand for, and supply of, rupees on the foreign exchange market in Bombay. The demand for rupee comes from those who offer foreign exchange in order to obtain rupees, while the supply of rupees comes from those people who are offering rupees to obtain foreign exchange. The Indian exporters to England, for instance, constitute the demand for rupees, for they have a claim on pound sterling which they want to convert into rupees; and the Indian importers, who have to make payments to England, offer rupees in order to get pound sterling.

The intersection of the sterling-supply curve and the sterling-demand curve gives the equilibrium price of sterling that equates the amount of pound sterling offered and the amount of pound sterling demanded. If the equilibrium pound sterling price in Bombay is Rs. 18 per pound sterling, the equilibrium price of the rupee on the London market is the reciprocal of Rs. 18, *i.e.*, 1/18 of a £.

Now, what lies at the back of demand for, and supply of, foreign currency? These are the various items in the country's balance of payments. The demand for foreign exchange arises from the debit items in the balance of payments, whereas the supply of foreign exchange arises from credit items. The debit items relate to all payments made during a given period by resident of the country to foreigners, and credits include all payments received during the given period from foreigners by the residents. These payments may be on any account, *e.g.*, goods bought and sold, services rendered and received, capital borrowed or lent, and so on.

If India has a net debit, its demand for foreign exchange, say pound sterling, must exceed its supply of pounds sterling with the result that the rupee price of pound sterling will go up, or, what comes to the same thing, the external value of the rupee must go down relative to pound sterling. The rupee becomes cheap in terms of £. Conversely, a net credit in India's balance of payment will lead to a fall in the rupee price of £, which means a higher value of the rupee or expensive rupee relative to the £.

It is well to remember that the demand for, and supply of, foreign exchange in the final analysis is nothing else than the demand for, and supply of, foreign goods and services. As already mentioned, the supply of foreign exchange arises from the credit items in the balance of payments, while the demand for foreign exchange results from the debits. In other words, the debit and credit items in the balance of payments constitute respectively the demand for, and supply of, foreign exchange.

These items can be put in the form of a balance sheet as under:–

Debits (demand)	**Credits** (supply)
1. Commodity imports.	1. Commodity exports.
2. Services rendered by foreigners.	2. Services rendered to foreigners.
3. Travel expenditure by Indian nationals abroad.	3. Travel expenditure by foreigners in India.
4. Interest and dividends on Indian securities owned by foreigners.	4. Interest and dividends on foreign securities owned by Indians.
5. Remittances and charitable contribution by Indian nationals.	5. Remittances and charitable contribution by foreigners to Indians.
6. Government expenditure by Indian Government abroad.	6. Government expenditure in India by foreign nations.
7. Exports of long-term capital (*i.e.*, import of foreign stocks and bonds, Indian direct investment abroad and loans to foreigners),	7. Imports of long-term capital (*i.e.*, export of stocks and bonds to India by foreigners, foreign direct investment in India and foreign loans to India).
8. Exports of short-term capital (*i.e.*, increase of Indian bank balances abroad).	8. Imports of short-term capital (*i.e.*, increase of foreign owned bank balances in India).
9. Gold imports.	9. Gold exports.
10. Miscellaneous import items.	10. Miscellaneous export items.

The balance sheet contains items both on current account (items 1 to 6) and capital account (items No. 7 and 8). Among these items, the largest single source of demand for, and supply of, foreign exchange is represented by commodity exports and imports, though the quantitative significance of the various items differs from country to country.

The balance of payments is said to be adverse if the total of visible and invisible imports exceeds those of exports. The country is then said to have been deficit on current account which must be paid off by drawings on foreign exchange reserves or by exporting gold or by borrowings for short terms from the I.M.F. or from the creditor countries. Conversely, a favourable balance of payments means that the invisible and visible exports together exceed the invisible and visible imports. Then the country has a surplus on current account and is accumulating claims on foreign currencies.

When the balance of payments is unfavourable, the country is said to have a weak exchange rate position. There will be increase in the demand for foreign exchange relative to the supply thereof because more payments have to be made than receiving payments from abroad. In this case, there will be decline in the external value of the domestic currency. But the depreciated external value of its currency will stimulate exports and help it to wipe out the deficit.

If a country has a surplus on current account, it is said to have a favourable balance of payment. There are more people abroad who have to make payments to this country. The demand for this country's currency will increase on the part of the holders of foreign currency. The result will be that the external value of the domestic currency will appreciate.

This is how the balance of payments affecting demand for foreign exchange and supply of foreign exchange determines the rate of exchange.

Evaluation of The Balance of Payments Theory

Superiority. The balance of payments theory of exchange rates is superior because (*a*) it facilitates equilibrium analysis; (*b*) it is more realistic because the price of foreign currency is seen here as a function of many significant variables and not merely purchasing power expressed in general price level, and above all (*c*) it clearly shows the possibility of adjusting balance of payments disequilibria through exchange rate adjustment rather than through domestic price deflation as implied by the purchasing parity theory.

Criticism. The balance of payments theory is criticised on the following grounds:

(*i*) It is unrealistic because it assumes perfect competition and absence of all interference with the movement of money from country to country.

(*ii*) It follows from this theory that there is no causal connection between the rate of exchange and the internal price level. Actually, there is a close connection between the two, because price-cost structure affects the balance of payments position.

(*iii*) The theory assumes that the balance of payments is a fixed quantity. Actually it is not so. It varies with the changes in the internal and external price levels.

(*iv*) The balance of payments theory is a mere truism, *i.e.*, it is self-evident.

EQUILIBRIUM RATE OF EXCHANGE

After fluctuations, the rate of exchange may reach a certain comparatively stable level which may be called an **equilibrium rate.** In the history of Indian currency, we read about the battle of ratios; 18d. *vs*. 16d. Which was the correct ratio? The advocates of each ratio said that, at the rate they recommended, there was proper adjustment between the rate and other economic factors like prices, wages, interest rates, *etc*. In short, it was the equilibrium rate. **When all relevant factors have been taken into consideration, the rate which is the most suitable may be called the equilibrium rate.** It is correct rate; at this rate there are no disharmonies in the economic system, *e.g.*, there is no cost-price disparity, and no sector of the economy shows any sign of maladjustment or disequilibrium.

The equilibrium rate of exchange has been defined as "the rate which, over a certain period, maintains the balance of payments in

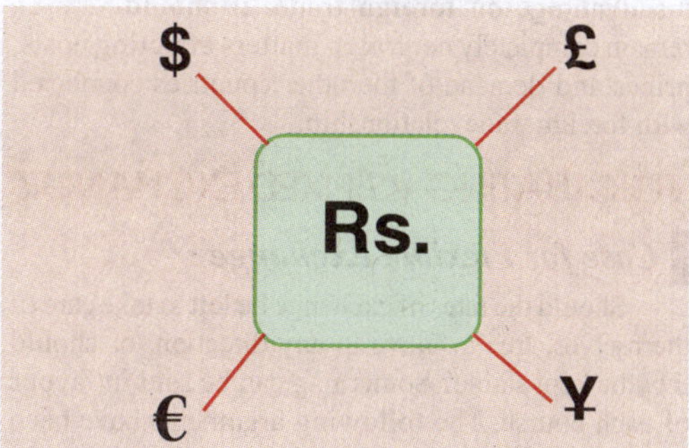

equilibrium without any net change in the international currency reserves". It has also been defined "as one that maintains the balance of payments equilibrium without a degree of unemployment greater than in the rest of the world."[3] We may also say that the equilibrium rate is one at which the demand for currency would be equal to the supply of it and no account is taken of speculative and abnormal capital movements. It expresses a balanced relationship between different economies. At the equilibrium rate, the domestic currency is neither undervalued nor overvalued in terms of foreign currency, so that neither it gives an artificial stimulus to exports nor to imports. It remains neutral.

3. *International Currency Experience*, pp. 124 and 126 respectively.

Scammel has defined equilibrium rate of exchange thus:[4]

"An equilibrium rate is that rate which, over a standard period, during which full employment is maintained and there is no change in the amount of restriction on trade or on currency transfer, causes no net change in the holding of gold and currency reserves of the country concerned".

Halm mentions the following criteria of an equilibrium rate[5] :–

(i) It should be inconformity with an average degree of domestic stability. For instance, as has already been said, unemployment inside should not be greater than unemployment outside.

(ii) It should not be necessary to overstrain the national gold reserves nor should it lead to depletion of foreign balances to maintain this rate. If domestic currency has to be contracted for the maintenance of the exchange rate which causes depression or impedes recovery, it is obviously not an equilibrium rate.

(iii) It should not offer any artificial advantage or inflict any out-of-the-way disadvantage on foreign trade. It should remain completely neutral in matters affecting costs, prices and demand of the other countries connected with foreign trade relationship.

FLUCTUATING *VS.* FIXED EXCHANGE

Case for Flexible Exchange

Should the rates of exchange be left to take care of themselves, free to move in any direction, or should they be kept stable? Something can be said in favour of each course. The following arguments have been put forward in favour of flexible rates of exchange:

(i) The advocates of flexible rates of exchange say that a system of free rates enables a country to pursue an independent economic policy. Its monetary policy is not tied down rigidly to a certain rate of exchange to maintain which it may have to deflate its currency and plunge the country into depression and unemployment.

(ii) Internal stability is a better aim to pursue. Hence, a country should look to internal stability, *i.e.*, stability of prices, output and employment and leave the exchange rates to vary as they would. Such a policy would eliminate outside interference with internal economy.

(iii) The rate of exchange has an equilibrating influence on the balance of payments and it is better, it is said, to let this equilibrating factor work freely and automatically.

(iv) The rate of exchange acts as a shock absorber. If the rates of exchange are kept rigidly fixed, the shocks of inflation and deflation from abroad are transmitted to the internal economic system. But variations in the rates of exchange can ward off the invasion of the inflationary and deflationary forces.

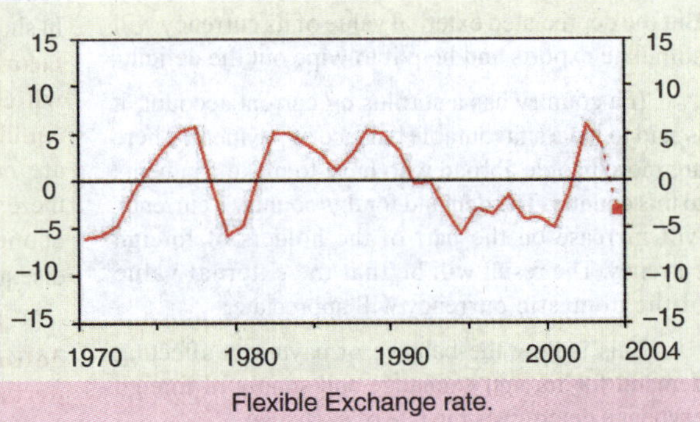

Flexible Exchange rate.

(v) It is also asked: "If demand and supply formula works so excellently in all economic spheres, why not in the foreign exchanges?" Hence, it is better to leave the rate of exchange be freely determined by the forces of demand and supply.

(vi) Flexible exchange is in no way detrimental to the smooth flow of international trade. The importers and exporters are able intelligently to anticipate the trends in exchange rate and protect themselves by means of forward exchange rate transactions. Fixed rate are of no particular advantage to international trade.

(vii) Fluctuating rates of exchange do not discourage long-term investments as it is supposed. The investors can never be sure of any fixed rate of exchange for decades to come. Hence, fluctuating rates cannot be rejected on the ground of long-term investment.

Case for Fixed Exchange

There seems to be a great deal of force in the above arguments, but the policy of free fluctuating rates of exchange has been almost universally abandoned on the following grounds[7]:

4. Scammel, W.M., International Monetary Policy, p. 56.
5. *Monetary Theory*, 1946, p. 219.
6. See League of Nations–*International Currency Experience*, 1944, pp. 47-52 and also Ch. 11.
7. See Halm; G.N. –*Monetary Theory, 1949*, pp. 211-216.

(i) Since variations in rates of exchange affect imports and exports, a policy of fluctuating exchanges is inimical to domestic stability. It will necessitate constant reshuffling of the national resources as between the import industries and export industries, which may involve waste besides making the internal economy precarious.

(ii) A fluctuating rate of exchange adds to the hazards of international trade, and, by making it risky and uncertain, proves prejudicial to its healthy growth. A fixed rate of exchange, on the other hand, ensures a smooth flow of international trade. The importers and exporters go on confidently in their business believing that the existing rate of exchange will be maintained.

(iii) Under a system of fluctuating exchange, there are always anticipatory dealings in foreign currencies which lead to self-aggravating and cumulative movements in the rate of exchange making it highly unstable. If, therefore, there is merely an anticipation of exchange depreciation, it proves dangerous and leads to fight of capital. Thus, fluctuating exchanges cannot always be relied upon to promote adjustment. A fixed rate of exchange eliminates speculative tendencies.

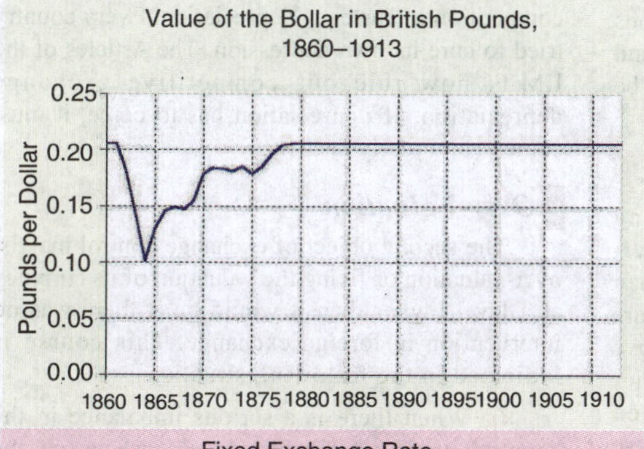

Fixed Exchange Rate.

(iv) Fluctuating rates of exchange cause windfall profits and losses. In order to be able to take advantage of a sudden turn in the rate of exchange, businessmen have to maintain a high state of liquidity which means contraction of credit, higher rates of interest and diminution in the volume of employment.

(v) The fluctuating rates are also calculated to discourage long-term international investments, since anything which dislocates internal economy must have a deterrent effect on the prospective investor. A fixed rate of exchange, on the other hand, is said to promote long-term investment.

Conclusion. From the above discussion, it is clear that neither fluctuating exchange rates nor rigidly fixed rates would serve the purpose. No exchange rate can be maintained for ever. "While exchange variations are certainly an unsuitable and undersirable means of dealing with short-term discrepancies in the balance of payments, an absolute rigidity of exchange rates in the face of drastic changes in other factors at home or abroad may thus be equally harmful. The general interest may call for an occasional revision of currency values so as to eliminate as far as possible any chronic and structural disparity between price-levels and exchange rates in different countries." That is why there is provision for revision of the rates of exchange in the Articles of the International Monetary Fund. But a start has to be made with a fixed par of exchange. According to Mr. Pierre-Paul Schweitzer,

> the stability of exchange rates has made a key contribution to the balance expansion of the world economy. The rate of exchange has a major impact on employment, output, price stability, and other major economic variables.

Since the fixed rates are not feasible and fluctuating rates are not acceptable to most countries, the world is heading towards a hybrid or compromise system of 'crawling pegs' or' gliding bands'. Under this new system, the exchange parities, with bands round them within which they can move, can float up or down to a maximum of, say, 1 or 2% in a year, which would mean 10 to 20% change in a decade.

EXCHANGE CONTROL[8]

This dangers and disadvantages of the fluctuating exchanges have led to the introduction of the system of exchange control.

Since World War I, the State has exercised a growing control over the movement of exchange for various reasons.

Objectives of Exchange Control

The object of controlling exchange is to fix it at a level different from what it would be if the economic forces were permitted free interplay. The objectives of exchange control may be:–

(*a*) To correct a serious imbalance in the economy of the country relatively to the outside world; or

(*b*) To conserve the country's gold reserves which are being depleted; or

8. See *International Currency Experience*, Ch.7 and also Halm, G.N.—*Monetary Theory*, 1946, Ch. XIV, and LEgue of Nations' *Report on Exchange Control*, 1938.
Crowther, G.—*An Outline of Money*, 1950, Ch. VIII.

(*c*) to correct a persistently adverse balance of payments; or

(*d*) to prevent a flight of capital from the country; or

(*e*) to conserve foreign exchange reserves for large payments abroad; or

(*f*) **to maintain stable exchange rate,** or

(*g*) to ensure growth with stability, and so on.

In all these circumstances, a free exchange would be either embarrassing or prejudicial to the object in view, and exchange control becomes an imperative necessity.

There are three possible courses that a country adopting exchange control may like to pursue, considering the economic situation in which it may find itself.[9] (1) It may like to under-value or depreciate currency; or (2) it may decide on over-valuation; or (3) it may decide to avoid fluctuations and maintain a stable rate. Let us consider when and with what consequences each of these courses may be adopted.

Under-valuation

Under valuation is advocated for curing depression. When a country decides on under-valuation or depreciation, *i.e.*, fixing a rate lower than it would be in a free exchange market, exports are stimulated and imports are discouraged. It will give stimulus to export industries and domestic industries will also benefit because imports have been discouraged. Thus, under-valuation will increase economic activity in the country, add to the total output (GNP) and will create more employment.

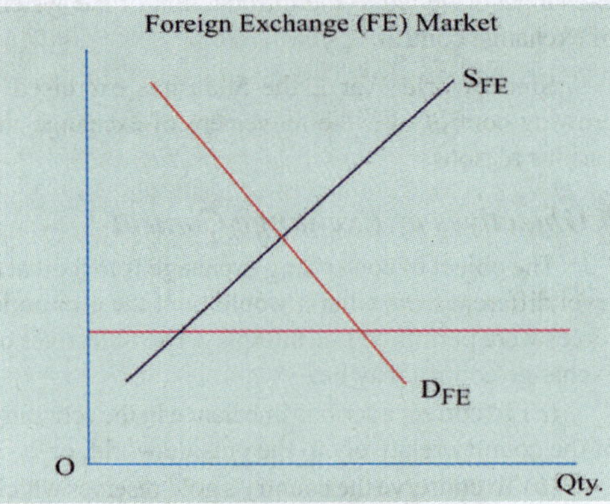

Under valuation of Exchange rate.

But this object may not be fulfilled. Instead of internal prices rising, the external prices may fall. This would happen in the case of a big country like India and the U.S.A. Also, since prices are affected through exports and imports, the desired objective of modifying the price level is more likely to be achieved when foreign trade is extensive than when it forms only a small proportion of the aggregate trade of the country.

The policy of under-valuation is more suitable for a country whose exports consist of foodstuffs and raw materials, for during depression, prices of these goods are depressed to a greater extent. Since, however, under-valuation will make the imports dear, the purchasing power of the producers of raw materials and foodstuffs will be reduced. But it is considered more advantageous to prevent a fall in the prices of goods it has to sell than to prevent a rise in those which it has to buy.

During the Great Depression (1929-34), many countries adopted a policy of under-valuation and depreciated their currencies. In fact, there was regular competition in currency depreciation. Every country tried to cure its own depression. The Articles of the I.M.F. now rule out competitive exchange depreciation. If depreciation has to come, it must come in an orderly fashion.

Over-Valuation

The second object of exchange control may be over-valuation or fixing the valuation of its currency at a level higher than it would be if there was no intervention in foreign exchange. This course is indicated in the following situations:

(*i*) When there is a serious imbalance in the country's trade relationship. As a consequence, the supply of national currency may far exceed the demand for it.

(*ii*) The country may be in great need of foreign goods either for prosecution of a war or for reconstruction after the war or for economic development. If exchange rate were permitted to fall in these circumstances, it would make these much needed imports very costly, or almost prohibitive. When a country finds itself under the sudden necessity of making large purchases from abroad, over-valuation is found to be most suitable.

(*iii*) If a country is suffering from inflation, the exchange value of the national currency will go down when exchanges are left free to move. If foreign trade plays a very important part in the economy of the country, this downward trend must be arrested by over-valuing the domestic currency, otherwise imports will become very dear and the exporters will have windfall profits.

(*iv*) A policy of over-valuation is also in the interest of a country which has to meet a large debt

9. This discussion leans heavily on Crowther's *Outline of Money*, Ch. VIII.

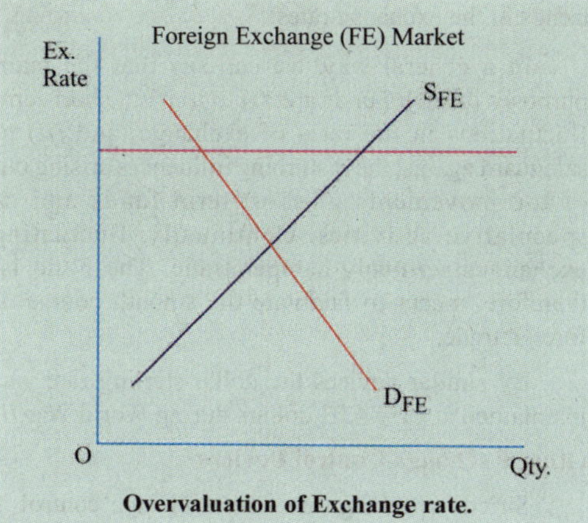

Overvaluation of Exchange rate.

payments expressed in foreign currency. This was the case with our "Home Charges". If the rate of exchange fell, the burden of foreign debt would correspondingly increase.

We cannot lay down dogmatically whether a country should under-value or over value. It all depends on circumstances. Over-valuation may suit certain countries and under-valuation certain others. The same country may find over-valuation more suitable at one stage and under-valuation at another. In Crowther's words, "The rough rule-of-thumb, therefore, is in times of slump and surfeit, under-value your currency".[10]

The third course is neither to under-value nor to over-value but to avoid fluctuations. Even here the object is not to keep exchanges rigidly fixed but simply to avoid sudden and big changes. It is intended only to iron out temporary ups and downs and to keep off the adventitious influences. This was done by Exchange Equalization Account. The I.M.F. is also intended to achieve the same objective.

Methods of Exchange Control

Influencing Exchange Rate. Exchange control is exercised either by regulating international movements of goods through various devices or by the purchase and sale of foreign currency at specified rates in order to maintain a particular range of exchange fluctuations. Exchange control can be exercised by influencing demand for, and supply of, currencies in the exchange market. This can be done indirectly by devices like tariffs, quotas, bounties, changes in interest rates, *etc.* Imposition of import duties and of import quotas will reduce imports, cut down the demand for foreign currency, lower its value or raise the value of the domestic currency. Export duties, which are not so common, will have the opposite effect. Bounties affect the other way about. Export bounty will raise and import bounty (which exists nowhere) will lower the value of the home currency. A rise in the interest rates attracts funds from abroad, increases demand for domestic currency and raises its value, and vice versa.

But these are the ways in which exchange is influenced and not controlled. The effect of such devices can be offset by similar devices adopted by rival nations. These measures are not necessarily adopted for controlling exchange and are not sufficiently strong to bring rates of exchange under effective control. Hence, more direct methods have to be adopted.

Controlling Exchange Rate. There are two methods generally adopted for controlling exchange:

(*a*) **Intervention.** In this case, the government enters the exchange market either to purchase or to sell foreign exchange in order to bring the rate up or down to the desired level. This method has been called intervention and leads to 'exchange pegging' described below. Or, (*b*) **Restriction.** In this case, the government can prevent the existing demand for, or supply of, the country, in which they are interested, from reaching the exchange market. This method has been called restriction. The second method has been more popular because intervention proved a weak weapon and was also expensive.

Exchange Control Proper. Exchange restriction is exchange control proper. For this three things are done: (*a*) All foreign dealings are centralised, usually in the central bank; (*b*) the national currency cannot be offered for exchange without previous permission, and (*c*) it is made a criminal offence to enter into an unauthorised foreign exchange transaction.

The usual procedure is to order all exporters to surrender claims on foreign currency to the central bank and ratio the foreign exchange made so available among the licensed importers. Exchange, control thus involves import control. Up to 1939, Germany was a pioneer in the method of exchange control although exchange control was adopted in several other European countries also during the Great Depression (1929-33).

Forms of Exchange Control

The various forms that exchange control has taken are briefly discussed below:

Exchange "Pegging". This device is usually adopted during war in order to minimize exchange fluctuations. The internal value of a currency may depreciate due to inflation but the government may

10. *An Outline of Money*, 1950, p. 240.

seek to keep its external value at a higher level than warranted by the purchasing power parity in order to facilitate international transactions. The method was adopted by England during First World War and again the Second War. Between 1916 and 1919, the sterling was kept artificially pegged at 4,765 dollars—a value which was higher than the real value of the sterling. This was done by raising loans in America and through these funds, purchasing exchange in London at the above rate. Success in exchange pegging evidently depends on the resources at the command of the nation. Exchange pegging can iron out more or less sporadic and adventitious fluctuations and cannot avoid fundamental changes in the equilibrium rates of exchange.

Exchange Equalisation Account. Exchange funds were the out-growth of the transformation of the international gold standard convention into an international gold settlement system[11] under which gold came to be used as a balancing item in international trade. After the suspension of the gold standard in 1931 by England, there again arose the necessity of preventing violent exchange fluctuations. For this purpose, the device of the Exchange Equalisation Account (or Exchange Stabilisation Fund) was utilised. "An Exchange Stabilisation Fund is a collection of assets segregated under a central control for the purpose of intervention in the exchange market to prevent undesirable fluctuations in exchange rate."[12] Foreign currency was purchased or sold, as the necessity arose, with the help of this fund, and thus exchange was kept within a narrow range in the face of uncertain movements of short-term funds into and out of England. The Fund is not used to prevent long-term adjustments in the value of the currency concerned.

The purposes for which Exchange Stabilisation Funds have been used have differed in different countries and in the same country at different stages. "The aim of the British Exchange Equalisation Account was that the Account was designed, without resisting general trends, to iron out undue fluctuations in the exchanges caused by erratic movements of capital and the disturbing activities of the speculators."[13] Gradually, the object of the fund was extended, and it was used to combat seasonal exchange fluctuations. The major purpose of other Exchange Funds was to establish and define appropriate exchange levels, *i.e.*, to resist general trends in the exchange rates.

In a general way, we can say that the main purposes of such Funds are: (*i*) to iron out short-term fluctuations in the rates of exchange, and (*ii*) to safeguard against the disturbing influences arising out of the movements of short-term funds and of speculative activities. Continually, fluctuating exchanges seriously hamper trade. The Fund is, therefore, meant to facilitate the smooth course of foreign trade.

By similar devices the dollar-sterling rate was maintained at £1 = 4.03 dollars during World War *II*.

Other Exchange Control Devices

Strictly speaking, the term exchange control is applied to several devices most of which were first introduced in Germany during the Nazi regime. Later, other countries also adopted some of them.

Some of these devices we have already considered while discussing restrictions on international trade. Here we shall look at them again from the point of view of foreign exchange rather than of foreign trade. Such devices are: (*a*) Clearing Agreements. (*b*) Standstill Agreements, (*c*) Transfer Moratoria, and (*d*) Blocked Accounts.

Under a **clearing agreement** between two countries, importers in both countries pay into an account at their respective central banks the purchase price of the goods imported. This money is then used to pay off exporters .The rate between the currencies is usually fixed by the terms of agreement. The object is to regulate imports according to the wishes of the government, to ensure equilibrium in the balance of payments and to prevent uncertainties of fluctuating exchanges. The system tends to encourage bilateral trade at the expense of multilateral trade and thus has a restrictive effect on international trade. On the other hand, it discourages dumping and currency depreciation. On the whole, the system stands condemned except under special circumstances of a war or as a temporary measure to tide over a period of disequilibrium in a country's balance of payments until the basic causes of such a disequilibrium have been removed.

A standstill agreement is a device to prevent the movement of capital through a moratorium on outstanding short-term foreign debts of a country and to give her time to put her house in order. Either the short-term debt is converted into long-term debt or provision is made for its gradual repayment. This device was used in Germany after the crisis of 1931.

Transfer moratoria is another device of the same kind. Under this system, importers or others pay their

11. For characteristics of the Gold Settlement system, see *International Currency Experience*, p. 155.
12. League of Nations—*International Currency Experience*, 1944, p. 143.
13. *Ibid.*

foreign debts in their domestic currency to a specified authority. When the moratorium is concluded these funds are remitted abroad. A foreign creditor is sometimes allowed to use his funds in the country imposing the moratorium in a way specified by the government.

Blocked accounts spring from the previously considered two devices of standstill agreement and transfer moratoria. When foreign debts paid in domestic currency to the central bank cannot be remitted abroad without the permission of, the government, blocked accounts are said to arise. Since idle funds in the country lead to contraction of credit, the foreign creditors are not altogether prevented from using them. But they have to be used in manner prescribed by the government. Usually, they are allowed to be sold in the open market. In most cases, they are sold at a heavy discount.

Key terms

Gold export point, Purchasing Power Parity (PPP) Fixed exchange rate, Fluctuating exchange rate, Exchange control, Intervention, Exchange pegging.

QUESTIONS

1. Differentiate between the internal value and the foreign exchange value of a country's currency. Show how the foreign exchange value of a currency is determined.
2. How is the rate of exchange determined when both the countries are on the gold standard? Also explain the limits within which the rate of exchange flutuates.
3. What are specie points? Explain their significance in the determination of mint par rate of exchange.
4. Explain how the rate of foreign exchange is determined under a system of inconvertible paper currencies.
5. Examine critically the Purchasing Power Parity Theory and compare it with the Balance of Payments Theory of foreign exchanges.
6. Explain with illustrations the balance of payments theory of foreign exchange. What are its limitatins?
7. What is foreign exchange? Explain the causes of 'fluctuatios in the rates of foreign exchange. Are they any limits to these fluctuations?
8. Discuss the relative advantages and disadvantages of fiexible exchange rate over a rigidly fixed exchange rate. Can you suggest a method by which the advantages of both system can be combined? State the case for flexible rates of exchange.
9. It is said that the balance of payments always balances. How, then, do you explain the disequilibrium in the balance of payments? How can this disequilibrium be corrected?
10. What do you understand by exchange control? Discuss its objectives and technique.

INTERNATIONAL MONETARY FUNDS

The establishment of an International Monetary Fund was the outcome of a conference held at Bretton Woods, New Hampshire, in the summer of 1944. The main purposes for which the I.M.F. was set up were to provide exchange stability, temporary assistance to countries falling short of foreign exchange and international sponsoring of measures for curing fundamental causes of disequilibrium in balance of payments. The I.M.F. is a pool of central bank reserves and national currencies which are available to its members under certain conditions. It can be regarded as an extension of the central bank reserves of the member-countries.

PURPOSES AND OBJECTIVES

According to Article[1] of the Fund, the main purposes of the Fund are:

(1) To promote international monetary co-operation through a permanent institution.

(2) To facilitate the expansion and balanced growth of international trade, and to contribute thereby to the promotion and maintenance of high levels of employment of the member-countries.

(3) To promote exchange stability, to maintain orderly exchange arrangements among members, and to avoid competitive exchange depreciation.

Headquarter Buildings of International Monetary Fund (IMF), Washington D.C.

(4) To assist in the establishment of a multilateral system of payments in respect of current transaction between members and in the elimination of foreign exchange restrictions.

(5) To give confidence to members by making the Fund's resources available to them under adequate safeguards, thus providing them with opportunity to correct maladjustments in their balance of payments without resorting to measures destructive of national or international prosperity (*e.g.*, deflationary policies).

(6) In accordance with the above, to shorten the duration and lessen the degree of disequilibrium in the international balance of payments of members.

1. See the excellent article on "The International Monetary Fund" by Alvin Hansen in America's Role in World Economy reprinted by Hess and other in *Outside Readings in Economics*, pp. 752-64. See also Halm, G.N.—*Monetary Theory*, Ch. XV.

ORGANISATION AND FUNCTIONS

Organisation of the Fund

The International Monetary Fund (I.M.F.) was constituted by subscriptions from members agreeing to participate in the Fund amounting to 8.5 billion dollars out of which India's contribution was 400 million dollars. The subscription was to be partly in the form of gold and partly in domestic currency. A member-country is required to pay 25 cent of its quota or 10 per cent of its holdings of gold, whichever is smaller, in the form of gold. The resources of the I.M.F. are thus partly gold and partly currencies of the member-countries, the latter being kept in the central banks of the countries concerned. Members' liability to pay a part of its quota in gold has been now (1976) abrogated under the New Articles.

In 1958, there was made a general increase of 50 per cent in members' quotas and a specially higher increase for Canada, Germany and Japan. In 1965 and in 1970, quotas were again raised by 25 per cent each time. India's quota, which was originally equal to $ 400 million, was raised to $ 600 million in 1958 and $ 750 million in 1965 and subsequently to $ 940 million.

A substantial increase in Fund quotas was made in 1979 from *SDR* 40 billion to *SDR* 60 billion and subsequently in February 1983 making a 47 per cent increase in member quotas raising the Funds' resources from about $ 66,000 million to $ 98,000 million.

It may, however, be added that the above increase in the Fund quotas has not meant a corresponding in their borrowing facility. For instance, in 1979 when Fund quotas were raised, the ceiling, on borrowing was reduced from 6 times a member's quota to 4.5 times. Thus India's ceiling rose only from *SDR* 7.2 billion to *SDR* 7.6 billion, though its quota had been increased by 50 per cent. Now when quotas were increased in 1983, the controlling group demanded that the ceiling on borrowing should be reduced from 4.5 times to 3 times the quota. The maximum that India could borrow would, in that case instead of rising, come down from *SDR* 7.6 billion to *SDR* 6.6 billion, but it might be allowed to retain its old ceiling of *SDR* 7.6 billion.

The Fund can purchase and sell currencies of member-countries for one another subject to the condition that the holding of no member-country's currency should exceed 200 per cent of its quota, raised later to 600 per cent but reduced in 1979 to 450 per cent. Thus, a debtor-country is saved from gold exports and consequent deflation (as happened under gold standard) through the help of the Fund.

The creditor-countries, whose export surplus exceeds 75 per cent of their quota, will have their currencies declared scarce. Such currencies are rationed among countries needing them. The I.M.F., however, can increase the supply of scarce currencies by borrowing them or by purchasing them against gold. If even then these currencies are not enough, debtor-countries must restrict their imports from credit-countries and thus achieve equilibrium in their balance of payments.

Thus, a member's quota has four-fold significance: It determines (*a*) a member's subscription to the Fund. (*b*) its access to Fund's resources through drawings from the Fund, (*c*) its relative voting power in the Fund management, and (*d*) its share of any allocation of *SDRs* among participants in the Special Drawing Account.

As regards the rates of exchange, member-countries are required to fix parities of their currencies with gold. But these parities need not be fixed for all time. An all-round uniform change in them can be brought about by the consent of the member-countries contributing individually more than 10 per cent of the aggregate quota. Apart from this, the member-countries can alter exchange value of their currencies by 10 per cent. Another 10 per cent can be brought about with the consent of the Fund. Changes beyond this can be brought about with the consent of the Fund, only to correct fundamental disequilibria.

Executive Board of the IMF (April 4, 1999)

"Thus, exchange depreciation, which may be necessary for a country, whose money is over-valued, can be accomplished without inviting retaliation. In this way, the Fund not only provides temporary assistance in tiding a country over a period when it cannot acquire an adequate supply of foreign exchange; it also sponsors measures to remedy more fundamental difficulties. An by holding member-countries to their agreement not to engage in competitive exchange depreciation, it introduces a measure of disarmament into the field of international economic relations."[2]

The Fund does not interfere in the internal economy of member-countries in order to restore equilibrium in their balance of payments. The members can withdraw from the fund by a simple notice in writing.

The *IMF* is managed by an Executive Board of 20 directors—5 assigned to the largest quota holders (U.S.A., U.K., West Germany, France and Japan), 3 elected by the South African countries, 3 by Latin American countries, 5 by Far East Pacific countries and 4 by Continental Europe.

IMF provides Machinery for international consultations.

This is a system analogous to exchange stabilization account evolved by individual countries during the depression years of the thirties. The same principles have been carried to the international plane. It seeks to achieve the purpose of international gold standard without its shortcomings.

Functions of the Fund

From the brief account of the International Monetary Fund given above, it can be seen that the Find performs five major functions:

***(i)* It serves as a short-term credit institution.** If any country is in a temporary difficulty in liquidating an adverse balance of payments, the Fund will come to its aid. It does not, however, undertake to supply all the foreign exchange that a country may need. All countries are supposed to have their separate monetary and foreign exchange reserves to meet their normal requirements. The Fund is not intended to supplant them but to provide only a second line of defence in case of emergency. The borrowing country has to pay interest and maintain its quota intact. Should a counrty borrow unnecessarily, the rate of interest rises as the amount of loan increases. Lower rates are charged if a loan is taken for a short period. If the amount of the loan and its duration are such as to raise the rate of interest to 5 per cent, the Fund can then raise the rate to any level by way of penalty, for this is regarded as an abuse of the privilege of membership.

Thus, it is clear that the credit operations of the Fund are not only conducted on sound business principles but they also ensure that the object of the Fund, *viz.*, to provide short-term loan only, is not defeated.

***(ii)* The Fund provides a mechanism for improving short-term balance of payments position.** For this purpose, its rules provide for orderly adjustment of exchange. No member-country can indulge in irresponsible and competitive exchange depreciation thus introducing the law of the jungle in international monetary relations. Whenever a country feels that its rate of exchange is out of line with its economy, the rate can be altered but only after due deliberation between the country and the authorities of the Fund. There is thus provision of the careful determination of the initial rate and its orderly adjustment subsequently. This procedure at once reconciles the claims to internal stability and full employment on the one hand and to international stability and high level of world trade on the other. Every country must now rely on its own productive efficiency rather than on artificial stimulus of exchange depreciation to hold its own in the world markets.

***(iii)* The Fund provides machinery for international consultations.** It brings together representatives of the principal countries of the world and affords an excellent opportunity for reconciling their conflicting claims. This constructive approach and the measure of international co-operation have had not only a stabilising influence on world economy but they have also led to the expansion and balanced development of world trade and world production. The Fund has thus contributed to the promotion and maintenance of high levels of employment and real

2. Tarshis, L.—*The Elements of Economics*, 1946, p. 619.

income and to the development of the productive resources of the member-countries. For this purpose, the Fund is engaged in constant study and research relating to the important and urgent economic problems of the world.

(iv) It provides a reservoir of the currencies of the member countries and enables members to borrow one another's currency.

(v) It promotes orderly adjustment of exchange-rate to promote exchange stability.

I.M.F.: AN IMPROVEMENT ON GOLD STANDARD

There is no doubt that the I.M.F. is a vast improvement on the gold standard. To maintain a gold standard was a very costly affair and it was also unnecessary. What matters is that a currency system retained the confidence of the people and should provide stability of its internal and external value.

There should be no crisis of confidence. Under gold standard, the currency system depended on the volume of gold output or the acquisition of gold. A scramble for the yellow metal led to its maldistribution and the breakdown of the gold standard. Under intense economic nationalism, it became almost impossible to make the countries to observe the Rules of the Gold Standard.

The I.M.F. has all the merits of gold standard minus its demerits. It ensures exchange stability without a country having to undergo the expense of maintaining a costly currency system. The exchange parities are fixed in terms of gold but it is unnecessary to keep large gold reserves for currency purposes. The I.M.F. provides multilateralism because it encourages multilateral transactions. Under the gold standard, a country having a net deficit in the balance of payments had to export gold to meet this deficit. But under the I.M.F., this function of gold is performed by the I.M.F. quota. Under the gold standard, there were no trade restrictions. The I.M.F. also seeks to restore multilateral trade on the basis of freely convertible currencies and reasonably stable exchanges.

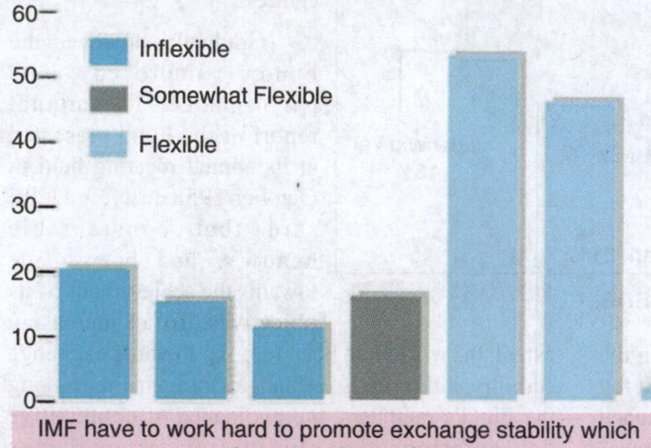

IMF have to work hard to promote exchange stability which has not come so far.

Under the gold standard, excess of imports were met by the export of gold which resulted in contraction of credit. This was a serious defect of the gold standard. Under the I.M.F., a country is enabled to meet an adverse balance by the help of the Fund without unfavourable effects on its credit structure which a deflationary policy must produce.

Another serious defect of the gold standard (which is avoided by the I.M.F.) was that exchange stability was made the first objective of the monetary policy and it was maintained by deflation of credit in the country losing gold. The country receiving gold was expected to expand credit. This method of maintaining equilibrium in balance of payments worked successfully only so long as wages and other costs were flexible. But now these cost have become more and more rigid due to trade union pressures. In these circumstances, deflation paralyses economic activity. The I.M.F. avoids there rigidities. There is provision for change of rates of exchange, if circumstances warrant.

Conclusion. In short, the I.M.F. combines the advantages of gold standard with those of free exchange and avoids its disadvantage by preventing competitive exchange depreciation, prohibiting exchange restrictions in a normal situation, by facilitating convertibility of currencies and by providing a convenient and adequate currency reserve for the use of the member countries.

WORKING AND EVALUATION OF THE FUND

It is clear that the Fund can play a vital role in achieving international economic stability and in promoting healthy international monetary relations. However, the I.M.F. failed to achieve its objectives in the early years of its operations.

(i) For many years, the Fund was not able to achieve its fundamental objective of pulling down trade barriers. Agricultural protection dominates fiscal policies in Europe and the U.S.A. It is a pity that the U.S.A. still clings to the protectionist policy in spite of her tremendous competitive strength. These policies are repugnant to the underlying objectives of the Fund. Lack of

international co-ordination of monetary, import and stockpiling polices has aggravated the difficulties.

(ii) The Fund is helpless in restraining inflationary pressures in a country and in maintaining monetary stability. The seventh report of the Fund emphasized internal monetary stability as the primary need and it issued a warning to the member-countries to end inflation or the world will move further towards restrictions on trade and currency convertibility. But the warning went unheeded.

(iii) The I.M.F. was unable to promote exchange stability in the member-countries. Perhaps the post war dislocation proved a little too much for the I.M.F. In 1948, France carried 44.4 per cent devaluation and established a free market in gold and U.S. dollars in Paris which was incompatible with the principles of the Fund. But still the Fund treated France in distress with sympathy and enhanced its reputation for its principles, and for its management. Up to September, 1949, there was no general devaluation; but Great Britain devalued her pound at that time by 30.5 per cent and the British example was followed not only by the Common wealth nations (except Pakistan) but also by 13 other countries. India devalued her currency by 36.5 per cent in June, 1966 and England again devalued the £ in November, 1967 by 14.3 per cent. The Fund could object to this big change in the par value of the currencies involved, but did not. It felt that the action was necessary to correct a fundamental disequilibrium. The change, though not agreeable, was inescapable.

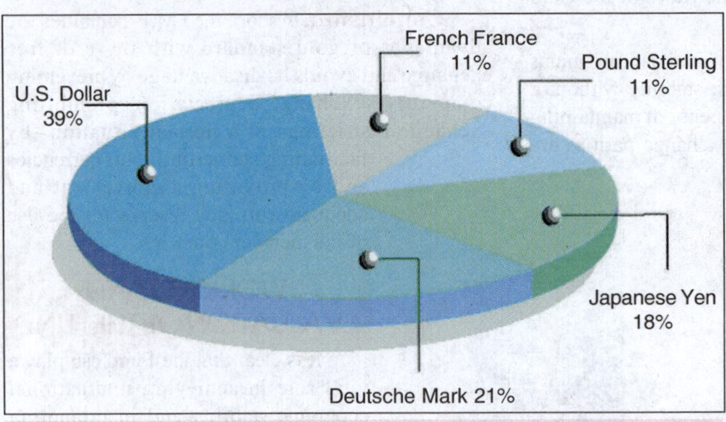

Valuation of the SDR.

(iv) The Fund was unable to prevent dollar shortage in the late forties. It should have declared dollar as a scarce currency and adopted measures to make the dollar freely available. But it did nothing of the kind.

(v) The Fund has suffered all along from inadequacy of funds. Funds of the I.M.F. may not be sufficient to cope with the sudden movements of hot money when there are no exchange controls to stop them. Then there are national sovereignties to be reckoned with. "The I.M.F. agreement is a transparent piece of paper stretched across the cracks which exist in the world polity of every national character."

An apt picture of the working of the Fund is given by Coulborn: "There are fifty (1952) countries trying to play the semi-gold standard game, whereas there used to be six principal players and few lesser ones. Yet it is the same game (because I.M.F. is essentially an amalgamation of the Exchange Equalisation Accounts of gold standard days put under international control), and the chief players are the same, as the voting strengths show. It remains to be seen whether it is a better game played somewhat publicly in Washington, with fairly precise rules codified for it and a large number of amateur players taking a small part, or whether it was better when six stars played with skill and without distraction, making the rules as they went along. It may be a reasonable guess that the best game of all will prove to be a combination of the present from with the earlier one. There might be added both strength and flexibility to the I.M.F. system if the Exchange Equalisation Accounts, provided a new with resources in some cases, came into the exchange market again in the more important financial centres."

Gradually, however, the Fund improved its performance. The annual report of the Fund presented at its annual meeting held in October 1958 in New Delhi said that considerable headway had been made towards the achievement of its objectives. To an increasing extent, the world had been moving towards exchange stability with orderly exchange arrangements, among the Fund's members, the avoidance of competitive depreciation, the elimination of exchange restrictions and establishment of a multilateral system of payments. The Managing Director the Fund declared at the opening of the annual conference in September 1962 that there were indictions that the world was approaching a state of economic equilibrium solid enough to withstand monetary tension. The improvement has continued since then.

A plan for a new international asset, known as the **'special drawing rights'**, was approved by the I.M.F.'s Board of Governors in September, 1967. It is like a normal account in a bank except that no deposits are required to build up the account. Once the allocation is made, a participating country automatically receives a share corresponding to its quota in the I.M.F.'s general account. They are treated as part of the monetary reserves to finance their international trade. The special drawing rights supplement the gold, the dollars and pounds sterling most countries now use as money reserves.

In order to mitigate the hardship of the developing countries arising from the unprecedented oil price hike, the I.M.F. set up a three-billion **"Oil facility"** Fund in 1974 in the form of special drawing rights. The developing countries get a credit out of this fund at a low rate of interest (2.5 per cent) to enable them to pay their enhanced oil bills and meet balance of payments difficulties caused thereby. It was decided to keep the "oil window" open for another year and to raise the oil facility funds from $3 billion to $6 billion. Interest is subsidized from a fund contributed by oil exporting and industrial countries. The Oil Facility was wound up in 1976.

Another facility provided by the Fund to its members is the **Compensatory Financing Facility.** Established in February 1963, it is designed to extent the Fund's balance of payments short-term support to such member countries—particularly primary producting countries as suffer from fluctuations in their export receipts due to circumstances beyond their control. Expect in the case of natural disasters or other major emergencies, the drawings under this facility cannot exceed in any one year, more than 50% (previously 25%) of the member's quota and the total drawings more than 75% (previously 50%) of the quota. Drawings under the compensatory financing facility are additional to those under the Fund's regular tranche policies.

Mention may also be made of the **Extend Facility** which was established by the Fund in October, 1974. The object of this facility is to provide medium-term assistance for member countries that need to make structural adjustments to correct balance of payments difficulties. This facility represents an important development in Fund practice. While the usual duration of **stand-by-agreement** is not more than one year, the extended arrangement provides an assurance of Fund support for a period up to three years, as well as providing larger amount and on longer re-purchases terms than are available under the Fund's other facilities. This facility is designed to benefit largely the developing countries.

The following table gives a summary of the transactions of the *IMF* for 1978-1982

TABLE: SUMMARY OF TRANSACTIONS. 1978-82

(In millions of SDRs)

	Calendar YEAR				January-March	
	1978	1979	1980	1981	1981	1982
Total purchases	**3,744.3**	**1,842.8**	**3,752.7**	**7,081.7**	**1,505.7**	**1,826.2**
Reserve tranche	2,535.5	147.1	359.2	310.4	202.9	592.4
Credit tranche	421.0	853.1	1,798.6	3,436.6	1,117.3	419.8
(Of which,supplementary. financing facility)		205.4	(943.1)	(1,468.9)	(342.6)	(300.7)
(Of which, enlarged access	(–)	(–)	(–)	(305.5)	(–)	(10.0)
Compensatory financing	577.7	572.0	980.4	1,242.5	19.4	309.9
Extended facility	174.0	233.0	614.5	2,092.2	166.1	504.1
(Of which, supplementary financing facility)	(–)	(101.5)	(275.2)	(570.7)	(51.0)	(108.8)
(Of which, enlarged access)	(–)	(–)	(–)	(480.6)	(–)	(150.0)
Buffer stock	36.1	37.7	—	—	—	—
Total repurchases	**4,845**	**4,215.3**	**3,344.8**	**2,109.8**	**592.4**	**528.2**
Trust Fund loans	688.1	526.6	1,256.0	367.7	367.7	—

Source : *Finance and Development*, June 1982, p. 3.

It was also agreed on August 31, 1975 to establish a **Trust Fund** out of the profits derived from the sale of the Fund's gold. This fund is used to provide balance of payments assistance on concessionary terms to members with low per capita income, initially those with 1973 per capita income not exceeding *SDR* 300. It was estimated that the trust fund could provide assistance between $ 400 million and $ 500 million a year.

We may summaries the achievements and shortcomings of the *IMF* thus:

Achievements

(*i*) The *IMF* has provided an excellent forum for the discussion and solution of the economic, fiscal and financial problems having an international aspect.

(*ii*) It has promoted the expansion of international trade in a variety of ways to the mutual benefit of the member countries.

(*iii*) It has promoted exchange stability while at the same providing for an orderly adjustment of exchange rates.

(*iv*) It has simplified to some extent the multiple exchange system.

(*v*) The Fund has been instrumental in promoting steady progress towards the establishment of a multilateral system of payments in respect of current transaction.

(*vi*) It has liberalised the use of its resources by members in a number of ways.

(*vii*) By promoting economic stability of the member countries, it has accelerated the pace of economic development of the under-developed countries.

(*viii*) The Fund has shown great interest in the economic growth of less-developed countries.

Shortcoming

(*i*) The Fund was unable to tackle the immediate post-war economic problems affecting its members.

(*ii*) The insistence on devaluation in some cases as a cure of disequilibrium in balance of payments was not well-advised.

(*iii*) The Fund followed a passive and weakened policy in the fixation of exchange rates both initially and subsequently.

(*iv*) In spite of persistent shortage of dollars, it did not declare it as a 'scarce currency' and take steps to ensure its ready availability.

(*v*) It is said to have granted undue credit to certain countries without making sure of their credit-worthiness.

(*vi*) The Fund has been charged as being partial to the developed countries and not helping adequately the developing countries.

(*vii*) The domination of American administration over the Funds' operations has laid it open to severe criticism by other member countries.

Conclusion. In spite of the shortcomings pointed out above, it must be conceded that the Fund has been a striking success. Considering the growth of the Fund in size, composition and resources and the important role it has played in solving international monetary problems and in formulating international monetary policies, the Fund must be pronounced a great success. There is no doubt that the Fund has remarkably succeeded in the achievement of its main objectives, *viz.*, expansion of international trade, elimination of restrictive practices, stabilising exchange rates and ensuring easy convertibility of currencies. In its operations, it has shown imagination and dynamism.

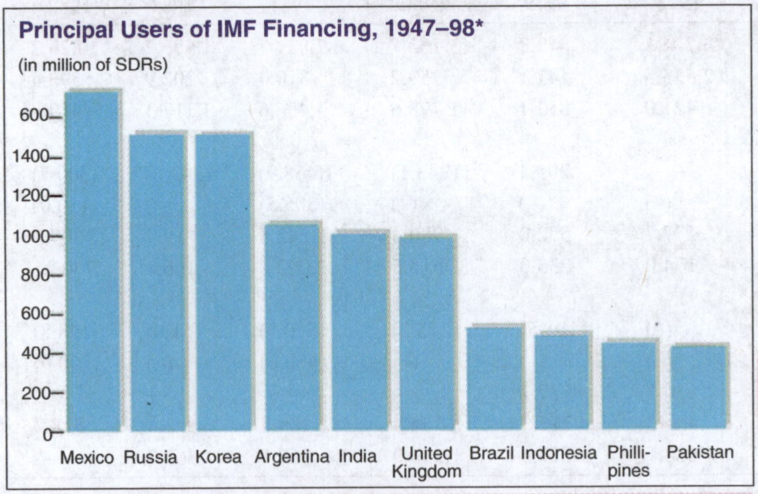

Principal Users of IMF Financing, 1947–98*

(in million of SDRs)

Users of IMF Financing.

I.M.F. and Less Developed Countries

From the point of view of the L.D.C.'s (less developed countries), the working of the I.M.F. has not been satisfactory. It did not pay sufficient attention to the problems of the L.D.C's. It was supposed that the domestic economic considerations of the L.D.C.'s and the world objectives of international co-operation were not really incompatible, but even mutually reinforcing. That is, the expansion of world trade depended virtually on the monetary stability of the developed countries and that economic development and full employment in the L.D.C.'s would automatically follow. It was not realised that, in economic theory as well as in practice, considerations of full employment and economic development in L.D.C.'s require policies which would usually run counter to the principles of international economic co-operation, free trade and exchange stability.

IMF must give more attention to less Developed countries.

Thus, a major drawback of the Fund's rules, in principle as well as in practice, has been the asymmetry of its adjustment mechanism as between the high reserve countries and low reserve countries, that is, the well-developed and the developing countries. The Fund expects normal adjustment of the balance of payments through changes in domestic expenditure and change in the exchange rate is to be made as a last resort, when the Fund is convinced that there is a fundamental disequilibrium. This adjustment is very easy for the rich countries because, they have huge stocks of international reserve and abundant provision of international liquidity. They were able, therefore, to avoid going through painful process of adjustment by domestic measures. The L.D.C.'s, on the other hand, had to curtail their domestic investments and slow down their development programmes to adjust their exchange rates. Mr. Pierre-Paul Schweitzer, the Managing Director of the Fund, in his address in April, 1973 observed, "a system in which the burden of adjustment is not equitably shared between surplus and deficit countries, produces strains and frictions which may be political as well as economic."

The funds of the I.M.F. have been largely flowing to the rich countries. The use of the Fund resources by L.D.C.'s during 1966-72 fell to 25% of the total world use. In the sixties, however, the attitude of the Fund improved under the leadership of Mr. Schweitzer. The Fund set up its compensatory finance in order to give assistance to primary producing countries experiencing temporary short-falls in their export earnings. In 1964, the Fund introduced a facility to finance buffer stocks. The annual reports of the Fund are now more sympathetic to the requirements of the L.D.C.'s.

It may be mentioned that an over-whelming majority of the memebrs of the Fund are developing countries and should be able to take care of their special needs. The compensatory financing facility for example, is specially designed to benefit them. Mr. Witteveen, the Managing Director of the Fund, estimated that the value to the developing countries of the trust fund, increased access to Fund's resources and the recent liberalisation of the Fund's compensatory financing facility could be of the order of 3 billion a year, in addition to the normal use of the Fund's credit facilities.

It may also be pointed out that it is not the function of the IMF to transfer real resources for development (that is the function of the World Bank). The proper function of the Fund is to supervise the international monetary system and to give members **temporary** assistance to overcome their balance of payments problems. That is why the Fund has always emphasised three aspects of its policies regarding the use of its resources: (*a*) non-discrimination among its members, (*b*) the temporary nature of use of its resources, and (*c*) its conditionality.

PROBLEM OF INTERNATIONAL LIQUIDITY AND S.D.R.'S

International liquidity means the resources or the reserves at the disposal of the various countries of the world for setting trade and other imbalances in the international sphere. It is common knowledge that a country's international transactions on current account are rarely in balance, *i.e.*, the total value of exports of goods and services and the total value of imports of goods and services are seldom equal.

Components of International Liquidity

Under the present international monetary system, which underwent a severe crisis in recent years, the total liquidity or reserves at the disposal of a country consists of (*a*) the gold reserves of the national monetary authorities with the central bank, (*b*) holdings of the key currencies acceptable internationally, *i.e.*, the U.S. dollar and the U.K. pound sterling, and (*c*) I.M.F. reserve position which represents the drawing potential of the I.M.F. countries. Out of these three components of international liquidity, the holdings of gold and dollar are more important in determining the extent of liquidity. It means that the supply of international liquidity is linked with the supply of gold, and the dollar which in turn is a function of the external balance, *i.e.*, the balance of payments position of the U.S.A. vis-a-vis the rest of the world.

It has been argued by many economists that in the present times, the amount of international liquidity at the disposal of the countries of the world especially of developing countries is quite inadequate.

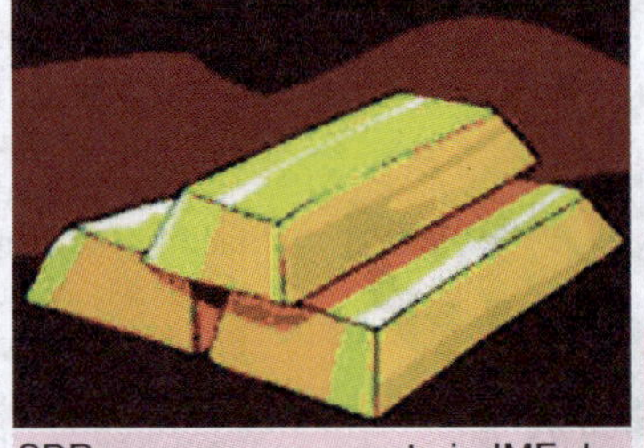

SDRs are reserve assets in IMF designed to supplement reserves of gold and convertible currencies to maintain exchange rate stability.

Causes of Inadequacy

The main reasons advanced for the inadequacy of liquidity are as follows:

(*i*) While, on the one hand, total gold reserves have grown since 1950 at 1.4 per cent per year, and total international liquidity at 2.7 per cent per year, on the other hand, the world trade has since 1950 grown at the annual rate of 7.5 per cent per year. In other words, the supply of liquidity has not been keeping pace with the demand for liquidity. The world trade is expected to grow in the future at 6 per cent to 7 per cent annually; therefore, the total reserves should also grow at least by this rate.

(*ii*) Distribution of liquidity among the various countries of the world is also very uneven. Some countries have too much liquidity, whereas others have too little. For example in 1968, the E.E.C. countries and Switzerland held over 40 per cent of the total gold stock in the world. The U.S.A. and these countries between them still had more than 75 per cent of the gold stock.

(*iii*) The supply of gold-one of the major components of liquidity–is very much limited and also cannot be increased according to the needs. For example, during the period 1958-68, gold has not practically contributed to the growth of international liquidity. The total stock of world gold, which was 38.0 billion of U.S. dollars in 1958, increased to 38.9 billion U.S. dollars in 1968. Therefore, the growing need of international reserves could be met by increasing the supply of the key currency, *i.e.*, dollars. But the supply of the U.S. dollar is ultimately linked with her gold stock and her external position. In the present times, however, the chances of increasing the supply of dollars are very limited.

As long as there is confidence in the key currency, it will be acceptable internationally and will, therefore, serve as an international medium of exchange. But this confidence in dollar was shaken. The ability of the U.S.A. freely to convert these dollars into gold was called into question. On August 15, 1971, the U.S.A. announced that it was no longer prepared to buy and sell gold freely which undermined the present system considerably. Now under the present system, supply of dollar, hence liquidity, can be increased only if the U.S.A. is willing to have more and more deficits in her balance of payments which seems to be next to impossible under the present circumstances.

Special Drawing Rights or 'Paper Gold'

In order to solve the problem of liquidity, in July 1969, the Group of Ten agreed to establish Special Drawing Rights (S.D.R.'s). Under the scheme, the I.M.F. is empowered to grant special drawing rights (S.D.R.'s) on a specified basis. When a member country has been sanctioned S.D.R.'s, it is entitled to obtain defined equivalent of currency from other participating members to meet its liabilities. The essence of this plan is that they create a new international reserve asset. They can be used unconditionally by the participating countries and they are not backed by gold. The new reserves are designed to supplement the gold and the reserve currencies, *i.e.*, the pound sterling and the dollar. They are meant for use by the central banks of the Fund's member countries; they are not to be made available for commercial use for payments in the ordinary course of business. With the help of the S.D.R.'s the central banks can buy whatever currencies they need for setting balance of payments. The creation of S.D.R.'s is essentially similar to credit creation by central banks to supplement the resources of the banking system.

Three features of the S.D.R.'s deserve notice: Firstly, they constitute a permanent part of the reserves of each country. Secondly, a country is free to decide as to how and when to use its S.D.R.'s. Thirdly, the scheme implies that each country will be prepared to take S.D.R.'s and supply its own currency. Since the value of S.D.R.'s is fixed in gold it is called 'paper gold' (= 0.88671 grams of the fine gold).

The S.D.R. facility departs from ordinary I.M.F. procedures in a couple of ways: First, The attractiveness of the S.D.R. as a reserve asset derives from the obligation of all members to accept them. If a deficit country, say France, finds itself in need of convertible foreign currencies, it can acquire say German marks or any other currency in exchange for the S.D.R.'s. The purchase is directly made from Germany and does not affect any of the I.M.F.'s holdings of the currencies involved. S.D.R. transactions are outside the regular Fund operations, and the role of I.M.F. is only that of an intermediary and a guarantor. The transaction will deplete France's holdings of S.D.R. and will increase that of Germany. The French are not required to meet any fixed repayments schedule as under normal I.M.F. quota operations. Secondly, the scheme recognises the fact that international reserves can be created without the need for assets to back the new international liabilities. The use of any money depends ultimately on its acceptability in settlements. This fact has been used in connection with the special drawing rights. The resources of the new scheme are not a pool of currencies. It is simply the obligation of the participating members to accept the special drawing rights for settlement of payments between the member countries. Thirdly, countries now have immediate access to 25 per cent of their basic quota in the Fund but that increasingly stringent conditions of approval are needed if a country wishes to use more than 25 per cent. But S.D.R.'s have an automaticity that will lead to international liquidity being automatically increased when needed.

On January 2, 1970, the I.M.F. announced the first allocations of $3,414 million worth of S.D.R.'s to 104 countries. Each country's allocation was made at 16.8 per cent of its quota as in December last and India was allocated $126 million (Rs. 94.5 crores). On January 1, 1971 and January 1, 1972, the next two allocations of nearly $3,000 million each were made.

On January 1981, the Fund allocated a total of SDRs 4.05 billion to the member countries on the basis of 6.8 per cent of their quota. The total of *SDRs* allocated till then amounted to nearly *SDRs* 21 billion. The *SDR* basket then was composed of the currencies of five countries with largest export of goods and services *viz*. The U.S.A., West Germany, France, Japan and the U.K.

The IMF announced on August 30, 1979 that it had distributed $ 396 million to 104 countries from profits made out of the sale of gold. India was the biggest beneficiary receiving nearly 46 million ($ 119.38 million in January 1979). The distribution was made in proportion to each country's quota. Two previous distributions had totalled $ 363 million.

Benefit of the scheme to India as also to other developing countries is indirect. By increasing international liquidity, the scheme provides a more assured flow of multilateral foreign aid and more liberal trade and aid policies by the richer countries. Increase in world trade facilitated by the S.D.R.'s may be regarded as a factor in boosting India's exports. A highly comfortable foreign exchange reserve position enabled India to pay off 260 million S.D.R.'s to the Fund in September, 1976.

Comments. Although S.D.R.s represent an important advance, they may also create a problem. S.D.R.s will now serve as reserves alongside the two existing reserve assets, *i.e.*, gold and dollar. Presumably the stock of S.D.R.'s will grow much faster than that of the other assets. There is no doubt that the stock of gold is more or less fixed. But an international multiple-reserve assets system cannot work well unless the different reserve assets are equally attractive. Otherwise central bankers may hoard a preferred asset and use a less attractive one in international settlements, the operation of a sort of Gresham's law. In contrast to the traditional value attached to gold and the linkage of the dollar to the strongest economy in the world, the attractiveness of S.D.R.s depends solely on an agreement by all participating countries to accept them. At least at the outset they may be considered less attractive than the other two assets.

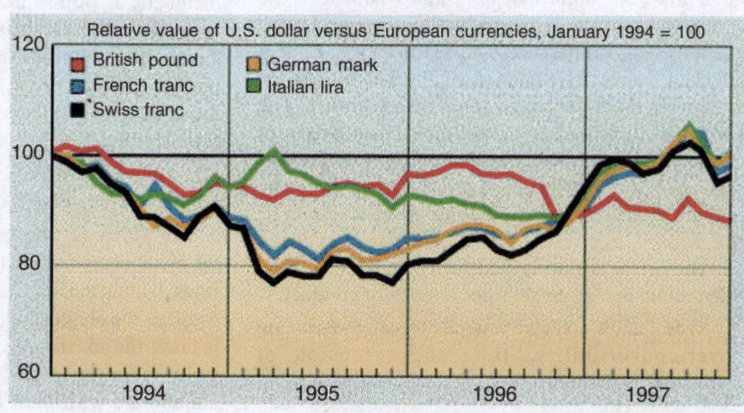

Besides, as Dr. Brahmanand has observed, "the S.D.R. instead of being a panacea may aggravate the financial disequilibrium in the world." This is because of the fact that the distribution of S.D.R.s on the basis of the I.M.F. quota, does not satisfy the canon of equality and justice. The developed countries which are already having enough of liquidity, have been allotted a major share of the total S.D.R.s. The problem, therefore, of creating more liquidity for the developing countries remains partially unsolved.

Further, the rate of interest on S.D.R.s is very low, *i.e.*, 1.5 per cent per annum. It is possible that the deficit countries may start using S.D.R.s intensively for covering up their deficits as compared to the other assets, because of low rate of interest. On the other hand, the developed countries may not much like to accumulate more and more S.D.R.s. This might create a situation involving lack of adjustment as among the developed and developing countries of the world in implementing this scheme successfully in the long run.

Conclusion. It will, however, be admitted that the system of S.D.R.s represents, a bold attempt to tackle the serious problem of international liquidity. It is to be hoped that as the scheme is worked, its inadequacies and shortcomings will be sought to be removed so as to make it a success.

REFORM OF THE INTERNATIONAL MONETARY SYSTEM

Breakdown of the Brettonwoods System

A nicely and diligently built up system of exchange stability by the I.M.F. seemed to have collapsed like a house of cards. This was brought about by the dollar crisis created by the adverse American balance of payments which reached a record-breaking and back-breaking figure of 11,300 billion in the first half of 1971. A package of measures announced by President Nixon delinked dollar from gold and the exchange rates started floating all round. A firm dollar-gold link and stable exchange rates had been the cornerstones of the monetary system created by the Brettonwoods Conference. The Nixon announcement knocked the very foundation of the I.M.F. and the system of fixed exchange rates disintegrated. The I.M.F. pathetically accepted the Smithsonian agreement on the realigned exchange rates. But the Fund report for 1973 did not give any indication that the realigned rates were expected to stablise. In fact, the report explicitly stated that the prevailing currency relationship lacked firm foundations of an internationally agreed set rules or code of conduct.

The Fund's collapse was due to its emphasis on "over-convertibility," *i.e.*, the extension of convertibility to short-term capital movements beyond Fund's normal expectations. The removal of restrictions on **"hot money flows"** and maintaining at the same time the Fund system of stable exchange rates really spelt the doom of the Fund. The American dollar could not bear the strain of these hot flows. The seasaw movements of exchange were caused by the uncertain movements of speculative capital. The speculators shifted large volume of funds with great rapidity making mockery of attempts to manage balance of payments.

Abolition of Gold Basis of I.M.F. on January 16, 1975. On January 16, 1975, the International Monetary Fund (I.M.F.) agreed to abolish the official price of gold. This put an end to the privileged role that gold had played in the international monetary system for the past 30 years. This decision opened the way to the elimination of any reference to gold in the I.M.F. statutes and it amounted to a new step towards the release of gold stocks held by central banks. The I.M.F. members agreed to lift the obligation to pay one-fourth of their I.M.F. quotas in gold.

Reforms. The first stage of the reform of the international monetary system began when the Governors of the International Monetary Fund took a decision to this effect in their Annual Meeting held in 1971 in Washington. It reached a final stage when the Interim Committee of the Board of Governors in their meeting held in Kingston, Jamaica on 7-8 January 1976 reached an agreement on an important package of reforms relating to *IMF*. This most comprehensive package of monetary reforms, since the establishment of the Fund, was approved by Board of Governors at the end of April 1976. These reforms are in the form of a proposed amendment to the Articles of Agreement of the Fund. They are subject to the approval of the three-fifths of member countries representing four-fifths of the total voting power. This formality may take a year or so. Besides amendment to the Fund's Articles of Agreement, the reforms include a substantial quota increase for almost all members, as well as increase in access to the Fund's resources, the establishment of a trust fund for developing countries financed through the sale of a portion of Fund's gold, the sale of another portion of the gold to all members in proportion to quotas at the official price.

Below we give a short summary of the main features of the reforms of the IMF.

Exchange Rates. The amended Articles give the member countries a freedom of choice of exchange rates which means that, in effect, the amendment legalises the present system of floating exchange rates; it ends the existing system of par values based on gold; it imposes on members an obligation to collaborate with the Fund and with each other to

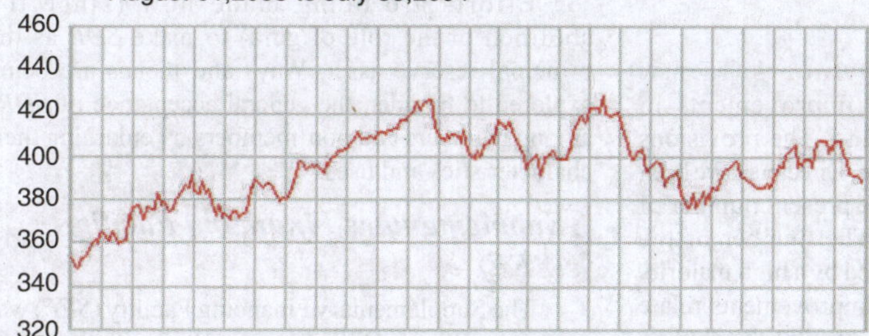

promote better surveillance of international liquidity. By decisions taken by 85% majority of the total voting power, the Fund will be able to recommend exchange arrangements that accord with the development of the international monetary system, or to determine what conditions permit the introduction of a system based on stable but adjustable par values. But any such arrangements will respect the right of members to maintain exchange arrangements of their choice. Thus, the new arrangements give the members "freedom of choice of exchange arrangements but not freedom of behaviour".

Role of Gold. The amended articles provide a gradual reduction in the role of gold in the international monetary system thus:

(a) elimination of the function of gold as the common denominator of par values and as the unit of the special drawing rights;

(b) the abolition of the official price of gold;

(c) the abrogation of obligatory payments in gold by member to the Fund and by the Fund to the members, and elimination of the authority for the Fund to accept gold except under decisions taken with a high majority of the total voting power;

(d) The Fund is to complete the disposition of 50 million ounces of gold;

(e) the authorisation of the Fund to dispose of the remainder of its gold holdings in various ways by sale at market prices or official price;

(f) "profits" on the sale of gold to be placed in a special account for use in the ordinary operations or for other uses, including those for the special benefit of members with low per capita income;

(g) the Fund is to avoid the management of the price, or the establishment of a fixed price, in the gold market; and

(h) the members to collaborate with the Fund and with other memebrs in order to promote better surveillance of international liquidity and making SDR's the principal reserve asset in the international monetary system.

S.D.R.'s. There are changes in the characteristics and expansion of the possible uses of the S.D.R.'s so as to assist it to become the principal reserve asset of the international monetary system. Some of these changes are given below:

(i) Permission to enter into transactions without the necessity of the decisions by the Fund;

(ii) the Fund may authorise operations where otherwise not provided by the Articles subject to appropriate safeguards,

(iii) the Fund may review the rules for the reconstitution of participants, holdings at any time and adopt, modify, or abrogate the rules by a lower majority of the total voting power than is necessary at present, (70% instead of 85%);

(iv) expansion of the possible uses of the S.D.R.'s in operations and transaction conducted through the General Department of the Fund; and

(v) the Fund may broaden the categories of other holders of S.D.R.'s although not beyond official entities, and the operations and transactions in which they may engage.

Financial Operations. There is in the new Articles simplification and expansion of the types of the Fund's operations and transactions, particularly those conducted through the General Department. Certain policies and practices, which have been found useful, have been incorporated. For instance, Fund's policy on repurchase, which is designed to ensure that the use of the general resources will not extend beyond three to five years. Provisions have also been adopted to ensure that the Fund's holdings of the currencies of the members will be usable by the Fund in its operations and transactions. Similarly, the members will be able to obtain the currencies of other members. Members will be permitted to engage in transactions under special policies without at the same time foregoing their reserve tranche positions.

Council. The amended Articles give the Fund's Governors the authority to decide, by 85% majority of the total voting power, to call into being a new organ, the Council, composed of Governors, Finance Ministers, or persons of comparable rank. The Council will have decision-making powers. Its authority would extend to matters concerning adjustment process and global liquidity and the review, in this connection, of developments in the transfer of real resources to developing countries.

Organisational Improvements. The new Articles seek to make certain improvements in Organisational aspects of the Fund. The provisions. governing the election of Executive. Directors have been updated by the incorporation of the present number of elective Executive Directors. The number of the Executive Directors can be modified by a high majority of the total voting power. Other improvements relate to the classification and simplification of the distribution and delegability of powers among the organs of the Fund and reduction of special majorities to 70% and 85%. Some changes have also been made in the nomenclature in use in the Fund. These changes, however, do not involve changes of substance in the legal or operational organisation of the Fund.

Second Amendment

Under the Second Amendment of the Fund's Articles adopted in March 1978, wide powers were given to the Fund over exchange rate practices, to abolish the official price of gold and to increase use of the I.M.F.'s Special Drawing Rights. The members can now buy and sell gold among themselves at market prices.

The amendment also provides for the setting up of a new council which will have decision-making power unlike the existing committee which could act only as advisory body.

The Second Amendment to the Articles of Agreement of the *IMF* came into force on April 1, 1978. The amended Articles have abolished the System of fixed par values determined in terms of gold and the new exchange rate provisions give the members wide latitude in the choice of exchange rate practices best suited to their needs. Each member, however, undertakes a general obligation to direct its policies towards orderly growth with reasonable price stability and a specific obligation to avoid manipulation of exchange rates to prevent balance of payments adjustment or gain unfair competitive advantage.

The new system assigns to the IMF the responsibility for conducting a continuing surveilling over the operation of the international monetary system and the members' compliance with their obligations regarding exchange rate policies and in the operations of the balance of payments adjustment process. The amended articles also authorise the Board of Governors to establish a permanent machinery for exercising general supervision over the international monetary system, including the continuing operation of the adjustment process and development in global liquidity.

Efforts are being made now (since the abolition of the role of gold) to make *SDR* as the principal reserve asset. Ways and means are being explored to broaden the general acceptance of *SDRs* among members and non-members by enlarging their characteristics and uses.

Supplementary Financing Facility (SFF)

The Supplementary Financing Facility (*SFF*) was established by the *IMF* in August 1977 with the object of extending financial assistance to those member countries which were expected to face large payments imbalances in relation to their economies and their quotas in the Fund.

Compensatory Financing Facility

Under the Compensatory Financing Facility introduced since February 1963, the *IMF* provides financial assistance to members particularly primary exporting countries experiencing balance of payments pressures arising from fluctuations in their export earnings.

Trust Fund

The Trust was established by the IMF in May 1976. The object was to provide additional balance of payments assistance on concessional terms to eligible developing countries during two periods; first ending with June 30, 1978, and the second period on June 30, 1980. The resources of the Trust Fund comprise mainly the profit from the sale of a portion of the Fund's own gold and income from investments of funds held by the Trust.

Subsidy Account

A Subsidy Account was established by the *IMF* in August 1975 to assist member countries most seriously affected by oil price hike. It is designed to provide subsidy to such members in meeting the cost of using the resources made available to them through the 1975 Oil Facility. Contributions to the Subsidy Account were expected from 24 members including oil exporting and industrial countries.

Substitution Account

A Substitution Account administered by the *IMF* would accept deposits of US dollars in exchange for equivalent amounts of special drawing rights (*SDRs*). This Account is a device to change the asset composition of official reserves by converting surplus money into assets priced in special drawing rights (*SDRs*). This would allow the member countries to exchange some of their unwanted dollar balances for funds denominated in *SDRs*. The countries holding these dollar reserves are put to great loss when dollar depreciates which is a very common phenomenon. This loss can be avoided if the excess dollars are transferred to another account in *SDR* denominations. This is the Substitution Account.

Buffer Stock Financing Facility

This is a recent facility provided to the members in order to help them overcome serious balance of payments difficulties. Financial aid is given for creating and maintaining buffer stocks of essential commodities in danger of falling short.

Common Fund

In June 1980, it was decided to establish a Common Fund to promote the stabilisation of commodity prices under international agreements. The Fund assured to extend its fullest cooperation in the working of the common Fund.

In February 1983, the Interim Committee of the *IMF* decided to raise the quota resources by 47 per cent (40 per cent equiproportional and 60 per cent on other considerations, raising the Fund's own resources from about $ 66,000 million to $ 98,000 million. India's quota was expected to go up from *SDRs* 1,717 million to *SDRs* 2,207 million, but its relative position down from 2.8 to 2.45 per cent.

SDRs Allocation

As on January 1, 1981, the *IMF* allocated 4,052.5 million *SDRs* to its 141 member countries. This was the third and final allocation of 4000 *SDRs* each was made in 1979 and 1980. The total allocations stood at 21,433.35 *SDRs*. As a result of this allocation India got 116,790,000 *SDRs* which lent much-needed strength to India's dwindling foreign exchange reserves.

A Serious Problem

The problem of all problems that has dominated the working of the Fund during recent years is the mounting deficits of non-oil developing countries arising out of four-fold oil price hike and inflationary prices they have to pay for the manufactures of the developed countries. On the one hand, the current account surpluses of the oil exporting countries, which had receded to $5 billion in 1978, rose to $68 billion in 1979 and was projected to reach $115 billion in 1980. On the other hand, the deficit of the non-oil developing countries on current account rose from $36 billion in 1978 to $68 billion in 1979 and $78 billion in 1980.

Liberalised Lending by the Fund

The *IMF*'s policy setting Interim Committee approved new lending programmes under which the members would be allowed to borrow currencies worth up to 200 per cent of the *IMF* quotas a year and to make these drawings for three consecutive years which would mean that their maximum drawings, outstanding at any one time could be as high as 600 per cent of quotas as against 125 per cent of quota under the previous rules. This is in addition to the balance of payments assistance available under the existing facilities mentioned above.

In 1980, *IMF*'s lending to poor countries more than tripled to $9,144 billion as against $2,838 billion in 1979. India would for the first time borrow from the *IMF* Trust Fund about Rs. 550 crores.

Thus the Fund is prepared to play an expanded role both by lending larger amounts in relation to quotas and through stretching adjustment and financial assistance over larger periods.

Fund Conditionality

In recent years, the *IMF* started attaching conditions to the use of the Fund's resources by the members to support circumstances. These conditionality practices naturally varied with the changing nature of the condition of the borrowing member and the nature and the dimension of the problems faced by it. The object is to safeguard the revolving character of the Fund's resources and to meet the genuine needs of the country concerned. Owing to the severe and widespread payments imbalances of 1970's, the Fund's conditionality practices assumed an elaborate character. For instances, under the 1975 oil facility, the borrowing members were required, in addition to qualitative commitments, to provide a quantitative description of the policies that they intended to pursue to solve their balance of payments problem. These quantitative targets of the programme constituted what has come to be known as *performance criteria,*

A typical example of the conditionality clause is furnished by the loan of Rs. 5000 crores granted to India in 1981. In memorandum submitted to the Fund, the Government of India agreed on two sets of criteria (*a*) *adjustment criteria* and (*b*) *performance criteria*. The *adjustment criteria* included such policies as curbing the inflationary spiral, correcting the adverse balance of payments, reduction in the quantum of deficit financing, reduction in credit to the economy particularly of net bank credit to the government sector. The *performance criteria* related to the performance of the economy in terms of growth rate or in other concrete and quantitative terms such as money supply, the budgetary deficits, the quantum of bank finance, etc. These conditions in effect require that the economy should function efficiently, the resources utilisation should be no under-utilisation of capacities.

Critical Evaluation

The International Monetary Fund has been criticised by Third World governments intent on growth with social justice for its ideological bias to an unfettered market economy and free enterprise. It is also accused of frustrating efforts to protect the "weaker sections of the population" by insisting on cutting down spending on welfare measures as a condition for its loans. By insisting on short-term "performance" tests for "adjustment policies" it prevents moves towards an equitable restructuring of society.

The net effect of the Fund's prescribed stabilisation programmes, even in the rare cases when these are successful in restoring external balance, has been to worsen the income distribution, reduce growth rates during the period of the programme, and increase the long-term dependence of the economy on imports and foreign investment. Many experts are, therefore, questioning the economic foundations and the relevance of the policies being prescribed by the Fund in the context of developing societies.

The direction of economic policies, they argue, should be a country's own concern, the Fund must not be allowed to take advantage of a crisis in balance of payments to force a change in a country's development strategy.

These issues are of course known to the *IMF*. In the face of mounting criticism, the Executive Board of the *IMF* adopted in 1979, a new set of guidelines on conditions attached to *IMF* assistance. The new guidelines reflect an awareness of the problems, but leave substantial scope for the exercise of discretion by the Fund's management in the interpretation and application of these guidelines. Among other provisions in the new guidelines, there is the requirement that "the Fund will pay due regard to the domestic, social and political objectives, the economic priorities, and the circumstances of members including the causes of their balance of payments problems".

Conclusion

Thus the *IMF* has stepped up its lending to countries that are making serious efforts to adjust their economic policies to current realities.

Fund's lending commitments had amounted to 4,300 million *SDRs* during 1979 while in the first nine months of 1980 they had risen to 5,900 million *SDRs*.

In the words of the President of the Fund, "The Fund stands ready to assume an increasing role in recycling and to make flexible and sensible use of its resources".

GATT, WTO, & CURRENCY CRISIS

It is a general tradition in the world history that the victorious countries start either initiating or super imposing their authorities in different fields, so as to strengthen their control over others. The same happened after the World War II, a new international counselling authority in the name of United Nations Organization emerged. New ways and means were initiated, so as to see new era of economic and political activities. IMF is one of the outcomes At Britten Woods in July 1944, it took birth. Along with this the World Bank and international trade organization also entered. In 1947 at the Geneva tariff conference, 23 countries signed and in 1948, the general agreement on tariff trade was established. Different rounds of conference were held, in September 1986 & April 1994 the 8th round of GATT held at Punta Del Este in Uruguay, emerged as an important international trade cooperation outcome. When GATT was established, it had 23 members and at the end of GATTs life in December 1984 it had increased to 118 members. The aim of GATT was to bring about smooth increase in world trade cooperation and the benefits of it must reach to all its member countries. If there is any problem it should be solved by the different agencies. The main objective of GATT was to increase the multilateral world trade with reduction in tariff, to improve trade relation, putforth a framework to accelerate and promote the international trade, to initiate laws, to eliminate the trade barriers if any & set rules for taking any actions, if there are any problems. The important aspects of GATT were the clause of most favored nation (MFN) multilateral trade instead of bilateral trade, reduction in tariff, free trade, promoting fair competition among trading nations and encouraging development in the member countries. The eight round at Uruguay was signed on April 1994 by 118 countries, the Uruguay round contained the mandate to have negotiation in 15 areas of which part I, 14 & part II, part I, trade-in goods included tariff, non tariff measures, tropical products, natural resources based products, textile and clothing, agriculture, GATT articles, safeguards multilateral trade negotiation (MTN) agreements and arrangements, subsidies & countervailing measures, disputes settlements trade related aspects of intellectual property rights trade related investments measures, functioning of GATT system (FOGS) and part II services. The detailed document was known as Dunkel Draft Text (DDT) signed by its Director General Mr. Arthur Dunkel on April 15,1994 by 117 countries. The DDT text included the reduction in duties and export subsidies, patents regime. Patent or patent like protection in agriculture, TRIPS & TRIMS textile & clothing. Beside it contain a social clause in which the low labour cost prevailing in the exporting countries must impose duty so that the labour should be paid more, the social clause was not accepted and in fifth conference held at Delhi on 19 January 1995 the labour ministers of non aligned countries referred it as "totally unacceptable".

WORLD TRADE ORGANIZATION (WTO)

WTO came into existence on 01-01-1995, under the Marrakesh agreement with 85 member countries, now it has 144 countries. It is a legal entity to provide an organizational set up to look after the objectives, laid down with different institutional setups, having equal voting powers of the members. It is a permanent legal body of members to look after multilateral trade in goods & services, foreign direct investments, anti dumping laws & intellectual property rights etc. The IMF was setup in 1944 to function as central bank of the world so as to look after the functioning of the monetary systems of the member countries and solve their short term balance of payments problems as well as exchange rate and international liquidity aspect. The world bank was setup to look into the economic development of the countries to only governments, but loans to semi governments etc were provided, where as the establishment of WTO is an organized institution with the sole objective of enlarging the multilateral international trade & service & cooperate and provide the legal framework and safeguard the interest of the member countries with equal voting rights.

Beside this there are subsidiary bodies such as agriculture, textile, intellectual property rights, investment measures, antidumping measures, subsidies and countervailing measure & safeguard, dispute settlement and appeals etc.

The Director General is appointed by the Ministerial Council for a tenure of four years and he is assisted by four deputy directors from different member countries.

Main Objectives of WTO

1. To bring about the increase in world trade which was increasing due to the GATT agreement and also opening up the economics and there by bringing about reduction in tariff and reduce or solve any barrier imposed by member countries.

2. To bring about a non discriminatory policy & eliminate discriminatory treatment for a smooth international trade relation. This is an essential requirement as many countries in the world are in continuous strained relationship.

3. To bring about the positive economic gains, specially the increase in economic variables in the member countries such as production, income generation, level of effective demand, employment etc so as to achieve standard of living condition in member countries.

4. To help in the achievement of different economic requirements of the developing countries, so that they can get a positive share of international trade and improve their economic conditions.

5. Competition due to enlargement of trade and services can lead to an optimal uses of international resources.

6. Whatever positive aspects of the Uruguary round declaration of DDT's is to be, incorporated and its benefits must reach to all member countries.

Code of conduct for eradicating hurdles in

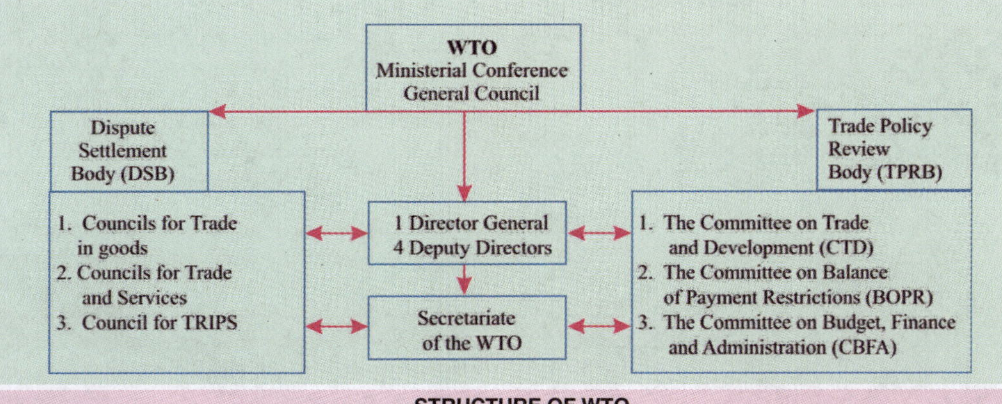

STRUCTURE OF WTO

international trade, institutional frame work with set of norms, for smooth global trade, institutional and administrative implementation for achieving and fulfilling the objectives, as a stage for further liberalization of trade, and to cooperative with other international agencies. So as to disperse the economic gains to different member countries there are major trade agreements which includes (1) TRIPS, (2) TRIMS and (3) GATS.

Key terms

IMF, SDR, Compensatory financing facility, Supplementary financing facility, Subsidy amount, Trust fund, International Liquidity.

QUESTIONS

1. State the objectives of the International Monetary Fund. How far has it achieved them?
2. Describe the organisation and working of the International Monetary Fund.
3. Discuss the role of International Monetary Fund in promoting the stabillity of the exchange rate. Why has it failed in recent years in maintaining stabiility of foreign exchange rates?
4. Examine the role played by the I.M.F. in the settlement of the balance of payments problems of the member countries.
5. How far is the International Monetary Fund an improvement over the international gold standard?
6. To what extent does the International Monetary Fund meet the requirements of an international currency system?
7. What steps have been taken by the International Monetary Fund in order to strengthen the international monetaryt system in the past two decades? How far have they been effective?
8. Explain the concept of international liquidity. What is the role of Special Drawing Rights in solving the problem of international liquidity?

PART FIVE

Public Finance

Chapters

CHAPTER 62

NATURE AND SCOPE OF PUBLIC FINANCE

Distinction Between Public Finance and Private Finance

Before we launch on the study of Public Finance, it may not be without interest to note some similarities and differences between government finance and individual finance. It will help us to understand the difference in the method of approach as well as the aim of a government and of an individual.

There are some similarities between the finance of private individuals and that of public authorities: (*a*) Both have to balance their incomes and expenditure; (*b*) both try to maximise the benefit with the minimum use of resources; (*c*) both have to borrow to bridge the gap between their current revenue and current expenditure; and (*d*) both can increase their income by increasing their investment expenditure. But there are marked differences between the two:

Ministry of Finance Government of India.

(*i*) Adjustment of income and expenditure. To an individual we preach: "Cut your coat according to your cloth." But a government first settles the dimensions of the coat and then proceeds to arrange for the cloth required. In other words, the individual must live within his income, *i.e.*, he must adjust his expenditure to his income. On the other hand, a government first prepares an estimate of expenditure and then devises ways and means to raise that sum. The government, unlike the individual, adjusts its income to its expenditure.

This, however, is not always true. The individual, too, sometimes first take a note of his obligations and commitments and then tries to work up his income to the requisite figure. The governments also, sometimes, act like the individuals in adjusting their expenditure to income. When the government realises a surplus, it may decide to increase expenditure in certain desirable directions. And when the public revenues shrink, the government tries to bring about a corresponding reduction in its expenditure through a policy of retrenchment.

1. For a fuller discussion see Findlay Shirras—*Principles of Public Finance*, 1936, Vol. I, Ch. IV.

But, on the whole, we can say that there is a real difference in approach towards the finance of an individual and that of a government. The individual ordinarily knows his income and he must arrange his scheme of expenditure accordingly. A government, on the other hand, first calls for an estimate of expenditure from the various departments, settles the total expenditure, and then levies the taxes accordingly.

(*ii*) Budgeting. For the public authorities, the unit of time for the budget is one year. But the individual attaches no special sanctity to the period in which the earth revolves round the sun (*i.e.*, one year). He need not balance his budget by a particular date or during a given period.

(*iii*) No internal borrowing for an individual. In their resources, too, a government and an individual differ. When hard-pressed, a government can borrow both at home and abroad, *i.e.*, it can raise either an internal loan or an external loan or both. But the only way open to an individual is external loan. There can be no internal loan for an individual.

(*iv*) Deficit Financing a peculiar privilege of a government. There is another source of income open to a government. It can have resort to the printing press. All belligerent governments, more or less, printed currency notes to meet the huge war expenditure. During the war of 1914-18, Germany almost ruined herself by the reckless issue of currency. When a government feels that the taxable capacity of the nation is overstrained and public confidence has been shaken, it can use this 'hidden hand', wave the magic wand and create money. Can the individual do it? No, unless he is prepared to go behind the bars.

(*v*) Different objectives. Whereas an individual tries to maximise his satisfaction or profit from a given amount of resources, the objective of government expenditure is to maximise social benefit. We have seen that according to the law of equimarginal utility, every individual tends to so arrange his expenditure that he gets the same marginal utility from every unit of money that he spends. For this purpose, he can weigh the utilities of buying different commodities. But when a government, an impersonal entity, spends money such conscious weighing is not possible, for utility is subjective. This does not, however, mean that public expenditure is indiscriminate.

Further, the governments seek to achieve full exployment, an equitable distribution of income and rapid economic growth or economic stability through their fiscal operations. But these objectives have no counter-parts in individual finance.

(*vi*) Deliberate and big changes in public finance are easier. For an individual, big and deliberate changes either in income or in expenditure are not so easy. Everybody likes to supplement or double his income. But how many can do it? In the same manner, a man gets used to a certain standard of living which does not admit of easy alterations and adjustments. But governments are in a much better position to make big and fundamental changes in the scheme of public income and public expenditure. If a socialist party comes into power, it will surely make revolutionary changes both in the State income and State expenditure. The individual finance lacks this elasticity.

(*vii*) Provision for the future. In the matter of providing for the future, a government is much more liberal and far-sighted. The stateman is a trustee for the future generations. Governments spend large amounts of money on schemes of afforestation, public works or social security schemes from which either there may be no monetary return or the return may be delayed for generations. The individual, on the other hand, is anxious to reap quick returns. Human life is so uncertain that some individuals discount the future at a very heavy rate. But the community outlasts the individual. It exists in perpetuity. Hence, the States are bound to make a suitable provision for the future.

(*viii*) Surplus budgeting is a virtue for an individual but need not be for the State. A prudent individual must spend less than he earns. He must have a surplus budget. For an individual this is considered a virtue. But for a State it need not be so. Deficit budgeting during times of a depression to stimulate effective demand has become increasingly acceptable. On the other hand, during periods of inflation, the emphasis is on surplus budgeting so as to reduce the level of effective demand. But surplus budgeting, however, is not necessarily a virtue. It may mean that the level of taxation is kept unnecessarily high and public expenditure is kept unduly low. Certain services, *e.g.*, social services may be starved. To make surplus budgeting a normal feature is not good finance. We should not make a fetish of a surplus. If big surpluses recur from year to year, it is better either to give relief to the tax-payer or to increase the scale of social expenditure.

(*ix*) Individual finance is shrouded in mystery. Secrecy surrounds individal finance. Every man of money must aviod the unwelcome gaze of others. Individual credit depends not on what a man has but on what he is supposed to have. He must keep, the people guessing and try to given them some vague and exaggerated idea about his financial position. But publicity, on the other hand, is the essence of public finance. Budgets are published and the widest publicity is given to them. Publicity strengthens, rather than weakens, public credit.

(*x*) The private individual lacks the coercive authority which a government has. A government has simply to pass a law and compel the citizens to pay a tax or subscribe to a compulsory loan (*e.g.*, compulsory deposit), but an individual cannot do anything of the kind.

These are some of the features which distinguished public finance from private finance.

Importance of Public Finance

'Money makes the mare go' is a very common saying. Everybody realises the necessity of money in all he does. If the importance of money is great to an individual it is greater still to a government. Earlier in this chapter, we saw the many functions which we expect a modern government to perform. The importance of public finance thus arises from the increasing functions of the state. It is obvious that, for the performance of these functions, money is needed. The strength of a nation is reflected in its budget. The extent of State activity and its efficiency are primarily dependent upon the length of its purse.

We often complain that educationally India is very backward, that the system of medical relief is utterly inadequate and that agriculture and industry in India are still backward. Why is it so? There is only one answer: lack of funds. The amounts spent on social and developmental services in India are ridiculously small. With the meagre resources placed at the disposal of these services, no spectacular progress can be expected. "The revenue of the State," it has been said, "is the State." Everything depends upon it. Kautilya, the earliest of Indian economists, writing more than 2,000 years ago, said : "The beginning of every undertaking is finance."[2]

Public Finance is a very important function of any state.

The importance of public finance not only lies in the increasing functions of the state as mentioned above but also in the effect of fiscal operations on the economic life of the nation. Public finance can be used as a powerful instrument to bring about desired social and economic changes. For instance, the system of public finance in a country affects the entire economic field. Public finance is no longer considered as a mere means of raising the State revenues. To use Colbert's words, it is no longer considered simply "the art of so plucking the goose as to cause the least amount of squealing." On the other hand, public finance is now regarded as a powerful instrument of social justice. It is employed by modern governments to bridge, as far as possible, the gulf between the rich and the poor. An equitable system of public finance would tax the rich and spend the proceeds in the supply of such services as are calculated to benefit the poor primarily.

The power to tax is really the power to regulate economic activity; it can retard it or stimulate it. The effect of taxation is felt not merely when revenues are raised but also when they are spent. Taxation and public expenditure can be so arranged as to encourage production or guide production along the desired lines. Certain industries can be exempted from taxation or given protection through import duties. Social and development expenditure can stimulate economic growth. As Buchler observes, "And the burdens or benefits resulting from a particular tax policy are not simply monetary, they are also psychological, affecting emotions, the reasoning and the economic behaviour of the tax payers and the community."[3]

In modern times, thus, taxation has a dual purpose: (*a*) to raise funds for the State, and (*b*) to achieve its social and economic objectives. Such purposes of Public Finance have today assumed a very great importance.

According to Dalton, the most fundamental principle of public finance is what he calls the principle of Maximum Social Advantage.[4] Public finance operations affect a series of transfers of purchasing power. The tax transfers the purchasing power to the government which is then transferred to the individuals to whom the government makes the payment, such

2. Shirras Findlay—*Science of Public Finance*, 1939, Vol. I, p.2.

3. Alfred G. Buchler—Article on "*Taxation and Economy*" *in National Journal*, July, 1950.

4. *Principles of Public Finance,* 1948, pp. 10-11.

as government contractors and government servants. The one aim underlying all these transfers is the attainment of maximum social advantage. The tests of social advantage, according to Dalton, lie in the preservation of the community and the improvement of both consumption and production.

To an economist, who is primarily concerned with the promotion of human welfare, the importance of the study of public finance is indeed very great.

The importance of public finance lies in the following:

(i) It is one of the most effective instruments of state control over the economy. It is not merely a means of collecting state revenues and making disbursements.

(ii) The state activities, which have to be financed by public revenues, are ever expanding. This has added to the importance of public finance manifold.

(iii) Growing significance of fiscal policy in tackling economic problems has also increased the importance of public finance.

(iv) The study of public finance is specially important for the under-developed countries. Only a prudent management of state finances is essential to break the vicious circle of poverty in which the under-developed countries are involved. Fiscal policy is a powerful tool for increasing capital formation, accelerating economic growth, increasing national income and raising the level of employment.

The importance of public finance can be easily understood from the functions of public finance which we give below.

Functions of Public Finance

According to Musgraves, the major functions of the Public Finance are the following.[5] These functions underline the importance of public finance:

(i) Allocative Function. It refers to the process by which total resource use is divided between private and social goods and by which the mix of social goods is chosen. This is done by the budgetary policy.

(ii) Distributive Function. The budgetary policy also affects the distribution of income in the community. The tax and expenditure measures are adopted to modify the existing distribution with a view to reducing economic inequalities. In this way, optimal income distribution is brought about.

(iii) Stabilisation Function. The budgetary policy can also be used to maintain a high level of employment, a reasonable degree of price level stability, an appropriate rate of economic growth and stability in the balance of payments.

The above functions are sufficient to bring into focus the vital role that public finance plays in modern economic life. In fact, there is no aspect of economic activity which can escape being affected by the budgetary policy.

CLASSICAL VIEWS ON PUBLIC FINANCE

In the classical economic theory, it was assumed that in a private enterprise, competitive economy authomatically ensures full employment of resources. If the resources are already optimally employed, there is no need for the government to interfere in the economic life of the country. On this basic assumption, the classical economist laid down certain principles of public finance which are given below:

(i) Keep the budget as small as possible. If it is assumed that private enterprise ensures ideal use of economic resources, then any withdrawl of resources from the private sector to the government must involve less efficient use of resources. Of course, the government needs some resources to carry on its normal activities, but in the interest of efficiency, it is desirable that the size of the government draft on private resources should remain as small as possible, otherwise there will be an unduly wasteful use of resources.

(ii) Keep the budget balanced. In a situation of full employment, if the government increases its expenditure without increasing its revenues, this will lead to inflationary rise in prices. This follows from the assumption of full employment, so that there are no idle resources willing to be employed. The budget deficit signifies an increase in the demand for resources on the part of the government without the private sector being willing to release the resources. Thus, in the classical theory every budget deficit is inflationary.

(iii) Borrow only for productive purposes. If it is necessary for the State to borrow, then this borrowing must be confined to the financing of productive enterprises. Otherwise, borrowing will mean withdrawl of resources from their more productive uses in the private sector to less productive use by the government.

(iv) Pay off the debt at the earliest. A debt of the government generally represents an opportunity that has been wasted. Hence, the government should try to repay its debt as early as possible.

(v) Tax consumption rather than saving. If we want to pay off the public debt, it is necessary to increase taxation. For this purpose, the government

5. Musgrave, R.A. and Musgrave, P.B.—*Public Finance in Theory and Practice,* 1973, p. 6

should tax the consumption of the people but not saving, for a tax on saving will reduce the rate of capital formation in the economy.

Modern View

Modern economists do not subscribe to any of the principles laid down by the classical economists. Owing to increase in state functions, both qualitatively and quantitatively, the budgets of modern governments have become swollen in size and, what is more, they are continually going up. As for balancing the budget, the modern trend is towards deficit budgeting especially during depression or recession. Thus, to keep the budgets small and to have a **balanced budget is neither feasible nor desirable.** Just as a deficit budget is more desirable to combat unemployment, surplus budget is more suitable during inflation. Through taxation, government seeks to withdraw purchasing power from the public to keep down prices. In the same manner, it is better to tax saving during depression so that consumption is stimulated, and increase in propensity to consume would promote investment. Increase in effective demand will increase income and employment in the country. On the other hand, consumption should be taxed during inflation so that demand is reduced and price rise is checked.

Classicals talked about balanced budget system.

Thus, we see that it all depends on the prevailing economic conditions or the social objectives of the State whether budget should be small or whether it should be balanced or deficit or surplus or what should be the income and expenditure of the State. In other words, public finance should be functional. The eminent economist, the late Lord J.M. Keynes, who brought about a revolution in economic science by propounding his income and employment theory, rejected the above-mentioned principles of public finance of the classical economists. We shall now give Keynes' view of public finance and shall explain the concept of functional finance arising from his views.

KEYNESIAN VIEWS ON PUBLIC FINANCE

As discussed in an earlier chapter, Keynes challenged the classical view that private enterprise economy automatically ensures full employment. On the other hand, he said that employment depended on effective demand and there is no guarantee that there will always be adequate effective demand to generate full employment. Unemployment arises because of the deficiency of demand. And, when there is unemployment, the classical prescription of public finance is no longer valid.

If there are unemployed resources, there is no special virtue in keeping the budget small and balanced. When resources are unemployed, it is the duty of the State to increase effective demand by increasing its expenditure. Far from being an evil, a budget deficit during a depression helps to raise the level of employment and output. Similarly, when resources are unemployed, it is no longer true that the use of resources by the government is unproductive and inflationary and, therefore, there is no special virtue in not resorting to borrowing to finance an increase in government expenditure. Similarly, during periods of demand deficiency, it is no good taxing consumption; it is better to tax saving rather than consumption, as we want to raise the level of demand, and not reduce it.

With the Keynesian revolution, therefore, the scope of public finance has been greatly enlarged. It is emphasised that it is the duty of the fiscal authorities to avoid the extremes of both depression as well as inflation.

During a depression, fiscal policy should help in increasing demand. For this purpose the government can increase its expenditure and spend more on public works. This will provide employment to more people. Or else, the government can increase its expenditure on subsidies to producers of mass consumption commodities so as to increase consumers' spending. Similarly, the government can lower its tax rates so as to stimulate consumption and investment. Thus, a budget deficit during a depression is a positive help in fighting unemployment.

On the other hand, during periods of inflation, there is too much of demand; hence the government should reduce its own expenditure and also curb private spending by increasing taxes. Thus, in periods of inflation, we should have surplus budgets. Therefore, there is no inherent superiority in a balanced or a surplus budget. It all depends on the prevailing economic situation.

This view of public finance is called by the name of **functional finance,** because revenues and expenditures are not to be considered as being occasioned solely by the requirement of government finances but with regard to the requirements of attaining and maintaining full employments.

THE PRINCIPLE OF MAXIMUM SOCIAL ADVANTAGE

Just as an individual seeks to maximise his satisfaction or welfare by the use of his resources, similarly the State ought to maximise social advantage or benefit from the resources at its command.

This is one principle for judging the desirability or otherwise of public finance operations. The public finance operations include both taxes and expenditures. Each such operation, whether it be the imposition of a tax or incurring of public expenditure, affects economic life of individuals or the community as a whole and we want to see that it promotes maximum social welfare. In order to determine whether the tax or the expenditure has proved to be of the optimum benefit we apply the **Principle of Maximum Social Advantage.** This has been called The Principle of Public Finance. As Dalton observes, "This (principle) lies at the very root of public finance." According to him "the best system of public finance is that which secures the maximum social advantage from the operations which it conducts."[6] It may also be called the Principle of Maximum Social Benefit. Pigou has called it the Principle of Maximum Aggregate Welfare[7] and we may repeat, it applies to all public finance operations, *viz.*, taxes, public expenditure and public borrowing.

Attainment of maximum social advantage requires that:

(a) both public expenditure and taxation should be carried out up to certain limits and no more;

(b) public expenditure should be utilised among the various uses in an optimal manner; and

(c) the different sources of taxation should be so tapped that the aggregate sacrifice entailed is the minimum.

Let us take these one by one.

Limits of Public Expenditure and Taxation

Dalton has enunciated this principle thus: "Public expenditure in every direction must be carried just so far that advantage to the community of a further small increase in any direction is just counter-balanced by the disadvantage of a corresponding small increase in taxation and in receipts from any other source of public income. This gives the ideal of public expenditure and of public income."[8] It is clear that the principle covers both expenditure and revenue.

Pigou has stated the same law in the following words which are more or less similar: Expenditure should be pushed in all directions up to the point at which satisfaction obtained from the last shilling expended is equal to the satisfaction lost in respect of the shilling called up on government service."[9] Here again, as in Dalton's statement, there is balancing of utility of expenditure with the disutility of a tax.

Public finance aims at maximum social advantage.

This principle indicates the limits up to which both public expenditure and taxation should be carried out.

This is the same principle by acting on which a consumer maximises his satisfaction and a producer maximises his profit. A consumer's satisfaction is maximised when the marginal utility of the last unit of a commodity purchased is equal to its price. This

6. Dalton—*Public Finance*, pp. 6 and 7.
7. Pigou, A.C.—*A Study in Public Finance*, p.43.
8. Dalton—*Public Finance,* p. 7.
9. Pigou, A.C.—*Public Finance*, p. 31.

is how he balances the benefit from the purchase of the commodity with the sacrifice he has made in the form of a price. In the same manner, a producer maximises his profit when he has equalised the output of the marginal unit of a factor of production with the payment he has made for it, *i.e.*, when marginal productivity is equal to price.

Public Finance aims at maximizing social benefits.

In the case of public finance, the government should try to maximise the benefit to the community as a whole from its public finance operations. The community's welfare is maximised when marginal social utility of an item of expenditure has been equated to the marginal social disutility of the tax imposed for the purpose. Obviously, expenditure confers a benefit and the tax entails a sacrifice and the two must be balanced against one another. If, for instance, the benefit is greater than the sacrifice entailed, it is an indication that the expenditure should be increased further in this direction: and, if, on the other hand, the sacrifice is greater than the benefit, the tax must be reduced. Only at the point of equilibrium of the two (tax and expenditure) will there be the optimum or maximum welfare of the community as a whole.

Public finance operations involve series of transfers of purchasing power from some people to the government by means of taxation and from the government to the people by way of public expenditure. The tax payers make a sacrifice and public expenditure confers a benefit. The ideal system of public finance is one where the net benefit (*i.e.*, the aggregate benefit minus sacrifice) is the maximum. This is what the principle of maximum social advantage means.

Public Expenditure: Maximum Social Welfare

Achieving maximum social advantage also involves the use of the principle of equi-marginal utility. We know that a consumer maximises his satisfaction by arranging his expenditure in such a manner that the utility of every rupee that he spends on different commodities is equal. The government also should act on the principle of equi-marginal utility in order to maximise social advantage from the alternative modes of expenditure.

Public expenditure has to be incurred on numerous items, *e.g.*, defence, law and order, social and development expenditure. No government can just heedlessly go on spending its revenues. It knows of the various demands on public revenue. A wise government should exercise all possible discrimination between the various uses to which public revenue can be put. It should arrange a list of priorities, just as a prudent consumer does. A consumer has also to spend his income on a number of items like food, clothing, housing, *etc.* Only by striking a proper balance between the various items of expenditure can he derive maximum satisfaction out of his resources.

How does he do it? By equalising marginal utilities of the purchases he makes. The government should also do the same. Suppose it has to develop both agriculture and industry. It should spend its resources on each in such a manner that the marginal utility from the two is equal. If it finds that it has overspent in the development of industries and under-spent on agriculture, it should increase its expenditure on agriculture and decrease on industry so that the benefit from the two types of expenditure is equal. In this way, the public revenues will have been spent in the best possible manner from the social point of view, *i.e.*, the social advantage will be maximised. In other words, the principle of maximum social advantage states that social marginal utility from each direction of public expenditure is equal. Obviously, if expenditure is pushed too far in any particular direction and the government has been miserly in some other desirable direction, the social advantage will be less than maximum. By acting on the law of substitution or equi-marginal returns, the social advantage from public expenditure can be maximised.

Distribution of Tax Burden: Minimum Social Sacrifice

We have seen above the proper limits of expenditure and taxation and the allocation of public expenditure among the various items which would be in keeping with the principle of maximum social advantage. Let us now see how the tax burden should be distributed in the community so that the sacrifice entailed is the minimum (or the advantage is maximised). Each tax calls forth for a sacrifice from the tax payer. A wise government should see that this suffering or sacrifice is not increased unnecessarily.

The sacrifice entailed by the various taxes should be compared and optimum combination of the taxes should be found out.

For instance, if it is felt that raising of the income tax and corporation taxes further will result either in increasing the sacrifice entailed or in the discouragement of productive enterprise, it will be better not to put extra burden on the income-tax payers, and instead, commodity taxation (especially taxing luxuries) may be resorted to. In this way, the tax burden will be more equitably distributed.

We can lay down broadly that the tax system as a whole should conform to the various canons of taxation. Above all, it should be equitable and convenient. The broadest shoulders should be made to bear the heaviest burden. In that way, the burden on the community as a whole will be the minimum and the tax system as a whole will confer the maximum social advantage.

Diagrammatic Representation

The Principle of Maximum Social Advantage has two main aspects, *viz.*, one relating to public expenditure and the other taxation. The principle of maximum social welfare applies to the expenditure side and the principle of minimum sacrifice applies to taxation. In other words, public expenditure has to be so distributed among the various items so that the total benefit to the society is maximised. As for taxation, its burden is to be so distributed in the community that it entails the minimum social sacrifice.

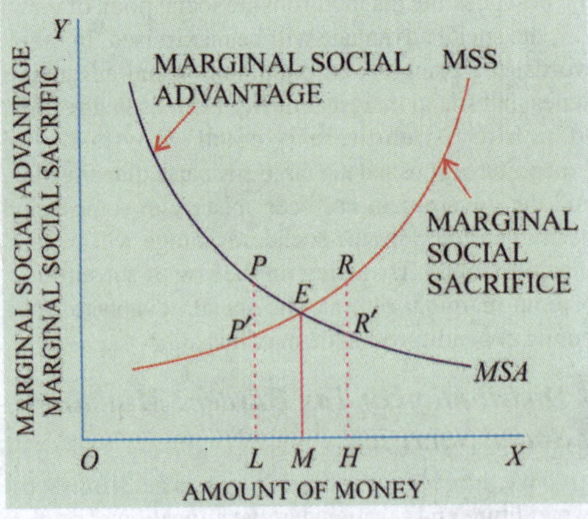

Fig. 60.1.

As more and more funds are collected from the people by way of taxation, marginal social sacrifice increases. Hence, the marginal social sacrifice curve rises upwards from left to the right. On the contrary, since with every increase in expenditure marginal social advantage decreases, its curve slopes downwards from left to right. This is shown in the following diagram (Fig. 60.1) where amount of money is shown along the *X*-axis and marginal social advantage and marginal social sacrifice on the *Y*-axis.

Government should increase taxation if the marginal social benefit derived from its expenditure is greater than the marginal social sacrifice entailed thereby, because in this way there will be derived net social advantage. The net social welfare or advantage will be maximum where the marginal social sacrifice from taxation is equal to the marginal social advantage from expenditure. This is at the point *E* or at the amount of money *OM* in the diagram where the curve *MSS* (Marginal Social Sacrifice) and the curve *MSA* (Marginal Social Advantage) intersect. That is, if the amount of money *OM* is raised by taxation and the same is spent in public expenditure, the net social advantage is the maximum. Hence, the amount *OM* represents Optimum Public Finance. In other words, if amount of taxation and that of public expenditure is more or less than *OM*, then the social advantage or welfare will not be the maximum.

For example, if the amount is less than *OM*, *i.e.*, *OL*, the maximum social advantage is *PL* but the marginal social sacrifice is *P′L* which is much less; hence it is advantageous to increase the amount; this increase will go on till it reaches *OM* where again the marginal social advantage and the marginal social sacrifice are equal. If, on the other hand, the amount is greater than *OM*, *i.e.*, *OH*, then the marginal social sacrifice *HR* is much greater than the marginal social advantage *H′ R*. Taxation is too much and it must be cut down to *OM* where the marginal social advantage and marginal social sacrifice are equal to each other. This is the optimum point or point of maximum social advantage; here the net aggregate welfare is maximised. This is what the Principle of Net Aggregate Social Welfare or Maximum Social Advantage says.

Conclusion

Thus, we may conclude that the Principle of Maximum Social Advantage will be satisfied if (*a*) the marginal utility from each direction of public expenditure and marginal disutility of taxation, borrowing, *etc.*, are the same, (*b*) marginal utility from each item of public expenditure is the same and (*c*) marginal sacrifice from each type of taxes is the same.

Criticism of the Principle of Maximum Social Advantage

It must be pointed out, however, that these are only theoretical principles. As a general principle perhaps no exception can be taken to it. But when we come to the actual application several difficulties crop up:

How to measure benefits?

(i) **Difficulty of Measuring Sacrifice and Benefits.** We know that public expenditure confers benefits and taxation entails a sacrifice. The Principle of Maximum Social Advantage assumes that the benefits and sacrifices are calculable. This is not a valid assumption since exact measurement in such cases is out of the question. For example, how can we estimate in quantitative terms benefit resulting from a certain expenditure on education, public health or police? There is no objective measure available for this purpose.

Similarly, in the case of a tax, we can at best assess its money burden but not the real burden. Whereas a tax entails a sacrifice it has also several good and bad side-effects. A tax may reduce consumption, but it can also promote saving and investment so as to raise the level of income and employment in the country. It is difficult to measure and balance sacrifices and benefits of taxation. Taxation affects consumption, prices and factor allocation. If all these good and bad effects are borne in mind, it is really impossible to say what have been the benefits and sacrifices to society. Correct measurement of benefits and sacrifices is still more difficult.

Besides, in the principle of maximum social advantage, the sacrifices entailed in taxation and benefits conferred by expenditure are sought to be measured in terms of utility, and utility to different individuals is compared. That is, it involves interpersonal comparison of utility. But the well-known economist Robbins has declared that the interpersonal comparison of utility is unscientific. Utility is subjective; it cannot be measured and it cannot be compared. Prof. J.R. Hicks has pointed out the shortcomings of cardinal measurement of utility. There is no doubt that it is difficult, nay impossible, to measure the social sacrifice of taxation and public benefit of expenditure. Hence, it is difficult to put into practice the principle of maximum social advantage which is based on measurement of social sacrifice of taxation and public benefits of expenditure in terms of utility.

(ii) **Impropriety of the use of Equi-marginal Utility in Public Expenditure.** We know that an individual consumer maximises his utility from a certain expenditure by acting on the law of equi-marginal utility. But this law cannot be extended to public expenditure, since public expenditure is not supposed to benefit particular individuals. Most of the public expenditure confers a collective or social benefit as distinguished from individual benefits, *e.g.*, public expenditure on defence, on general administration, maintenance of law and order, economic development, *etc.* How much benefit accrues to individuals, cannot be ascertained. Hence, if individual benefits cannot be ascertained, it is impossible to equi-marginalise their utility.

(iii) **Difficulty Arising from the Huge Amounts of Taxation and Expenditure.** In the principle of maximum social advantage, it is said that the marginal benefit of public expenditure to various individuals should be equalised and similarly, the marginal sacrifice of taxation of the various individuals should be equalised. But actually it is not possible to equalise marginal units. The State has to spend crores of rupees on education, on public health, on defence, and so on. It is simply out of the question to equalise their benefits and sacrifices in terms of marginal units.

(iv) **Replacement of the Principle of Maximum Social Advantage by Functional Finance.** Most of the modern economists have adopted the concept of functional finance instead of the Principle of Maximum Social Advantage. This is due to the fact that in the principle of maximum social advantage the revenue raised by the government through taxation and public expenditure must be equal. That is, the budget must be a balanced one. But a balanced budget is not necessarily useful for the economy. The great economist, late Lord J.M.Keynes, showed that during depression, when there is widespread unemployment, it is more beneficial to have a deficit budget. Similarly, in an inflationary situation, surplus budget is called for. Whether the budget should be

balanced or surplus or deficit, it depends on the economic conditions prevailing at the time. This means that budget is an instrument for the achievement of certain objectives or it has to fulfil certain functions, *e.g.*, to remove unemployment and achieve full exmployment or to check inflation or to accelerate economic development, and so on. The budget has to be deficits or surplus according to the objectives to be achieved and the taxation and public expenditure policy has to be shaped accordingly. This is the concept of functional finance which we shall explain more fully presently.

Conclusion. In spite of the difficulties and limitations mentioned above, the principle of maximum social advantage is of fundamental importance in public finance. The public finance operations of modern governments are no doubt governed by considerations of maximum social benefit whether exactly measurable or not. This principle serves as a good guide for conduct of public finance operations.

Functions of Government

Defence

Maintaining Peace

Economic Stability

Ensuring Equitable distribution of Income

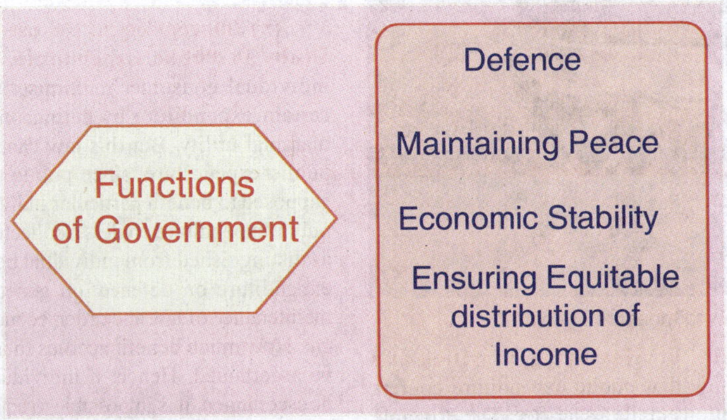

As a practical interpretation of the principle of maximum social advantage, Dalton has laid down the following guidelines for modern governments.

(*i*) They should make adequate provision for defence against external aggression and for maintenance of peace and stability in the country.

(*ii*) Production should be improved. For improving production, productive efficiency of the workers should be improved, organisation of production should be improved and productive resources should not be wasted. Further, the composition of national output should be improved so that the goods and services produced conform to the consumers' preferences.

(*iii*) The distribution of national income should be improved, *i.e.*, it should be more evenly distributed. This can be done by progressive taxation and by increasing transfer expenditure like old-age pensions, social insurance, provident fund schemes, *etc*. That is, the rich should be taxed more heavily and a larger share of public expenditure should go to benefit the poor.

(*iv*) Business fluctuations should be reduced and economic stability ensured. This can be done by the government increasing its spending during depression and reducing it during the periods of boom.

According to Dalton, a government will be conferring maximum social advantage by conducting its public finance operations in such a manner as to achieve the above objectives.

CONCEPT OF FUNCTIONAL FINANCE

We have referred above to the concept of functional finance, especially in the Keynesian views on public finance. The main point in Keynesian view of public finance is that Keynes has given it the form of functional finance. The essence of functional finance is that public finance should be used as an instrument for the achievement of certain economic and social objectives. Before Keynes, the sole concern of public finance was to raise sufficient revenues for meeting public expenditure. In other words, before Keynes, public finance was concerned with the raising of financial resources for the State. But Keynes made a fundamental change in the nature and scope of public finance. Keynes and his followers emphasised that public finance is to help in the achievement of certain social and economic objectives and finance some essential economic activities.

Keynes underlines the fact that the taxation and public expenditure policy of the State vitally affects the level of income and employment in the country. Keynes showed that during depression, the government can remove depression by increasing its expenditure on public works and raise the level of income and employment in the country. When the government increases its investment expenditure on public works, then the level of income and the volume of employment in the country increases many times more than the initial investment. This is in accordance with the Keynes' Income Multiplier.

It is clear that the function of public finance is not merely to raise financial resources for the State but to help in the performance of certain important tasks facing the economy, *e.g.*, raising the level of income and employment in the economy. This is entirely a new concept altogether different from the classical view of public finance. It may be mentioned here that the term 'functional finance' was first used by an American Professor Lerner. But it is more explicit in the Keynesian theory of Income and Employment and Keynes put it more emphatically. It was Keynes who strongly advocated that public expenditure on public works should be increased to remove depression and unemployment and to increase national income and employment in the country.

Appropriate Expenditure and taxation policy are necessary to check inflation and depression.

When there is inflation in the economy and the prices are soaring higher and higher, the government should levy heavy taxes and in this way withdraw purchasing power from the people and should also reduce its own expenditure. The demand having been reduced in this way, prices would tend to come down. It is clear that to fight inflation, the government should frame a surplus budget. A surplus budget means that the government should collect more money from the public by imposing more taxes but keep its expenditure less than the revenue raised. The result will be that less purchasing power will be left with the people and the aggregate demand for goods will be reduced. Consequently, the prices will have a tendency to fall. On the contrary, as we have seen above, the government should increase its expenditure during depression more than its revenue. The deficit can be covered by deficit financing, *i.e.*, by creating new money. The result of deficit financing is that the purchasing power with the people increases and aggregate demand for goods and services increases. Owing to increase in aggregate demand and the operation of the multiplier, the depression will tend to disappear and the economy will move towards full employment.

It is clear from the above analysis that the essence of functional finance is that the government should solve both the problems of depression and inflation by making appropriate changes in its taxation and expenditure policies. By removing both depression and inflation, it should establish an equilibrium in the economy at the level of full employment. Public finance has this important function to perform in developed or advanced countries.

But in under-developed countries like India, the problem is not so much of cyclical instability as of promoting economic development and accelerating economic growth. The under-developed countries are caught up in the vicious circle of poverty and their main problem is to break this circle and move towards economic development so that poverty is removed and the living standard of the people is raised. Thus, the objectives of public finance in under-developed countries are different from those in the developed countries. Whereas in the developed countries, the objective is to ensure economic stability at the level of full employment, in the under-developed countries, its function is to accelerate economic development so that the widespread unemployment and poverty prevailing in the country are removed. Hence, in the under-developed countries, public finance is to play a developmental role.

Besides the main function of accelerating economic growth, public finance has, in the developing countries, also to check price hike and reduce inequalities of income and wealth. Reduction of inequalities in income and wealth can bring about social justice in the country. Hence, in the developing countries, the objective of public finance is to ensure growth with social justice.

We may repeat that the essence of functional finance is that public finance is not merely an instrument of raising financial resources for the State, but it has also to perform several other important functions for the economy. The functions of public finance are, however, different in the developed and under-developed or developing economies. Whereas in the developed countries, its objective is to eliminate cyclical fluctuations and maintain economic stability, in the under-developed countries, its function is to give a fillip to capital formation and economic development.

The concept of functional finance was made very clear in his budget speech on February 8, 1975 by Mr. C. Subramaniam, the Union Finance Minister. He says, "what, one might ask, has been the underlying approach, the basic philosophy, in framing these (*i.e.*, the budget) proposals? Is it merely an ostrich like exercise to balance receipts and expenditure of the exchequer? Or does the budget seem more positively and purposively to subserve larger national objectives? The answer is, of course clear and unequivocal. We do look upon the budget as an important tool for reaching our cherished socio-economic goals. Development, the security of our country and growth along with social justice continue to govern our priorities. These objectives determine the decisions on how much to spend, on what programmes to spend and in what manner the resources are to be raised."[10]

ROLE OF PUBLIC FINANCE IN A DEVELOPING ECONOMY

In a developing economy, the State must play a very active role in promoting economic development and public finance is the instrument that the State must use. This instrument has to be used to break the vicious circle of poverty and to accelerate economic growth. Hence, the great importance of public finance in under-developed countries desirous of rapid economic development.

There are several reasons why the State must play an important role in a developing economy. The vast and varied natural resources have yet to be exploited and this is obviously beyond the capacity of individual citizens or group of them forming corporations. The technical know-how is lacking; means of transport and communications are under-developed; and irrigation and power need rapid development. Who can do these things except the State? Low ratio of savings to national income in under-developed countries is another compelling reason for the State to step in to promote capital formation.

As an Instrument of Capital Formation

Capital formation is of strategic importance in the matter of rapid economic development and the under-developed economies suffer from capital deficiency. It is, therefore, necessary to achieve a higher ratio of savings to national income. This can be best done through fiscal measures.

People of developing countries are extremely poor and they can hardly make two ends meet, not to speak of making a saving. The government has to see how savings can be generated and capital formation promoted. There are some rich people too who are in a position to save but do not save since they indulge in conspicuous consumption. The increased incomes arising from whatever little economic development is made are spent under the demonstration effect in imitating the higher standards prevailing in the developed countries. The result is that not much money is available for productive investment. The government can raise financial resources for development by levying taxes on the rich. Thus, when voluntary savings are not forthcoming, the government generates forced savings through taxation. In this way, savings in the country can be increased. It may be pointed out that a tax is a collective saving which is available for capital formation through the government.

Public finance helps generating capital in developing countries.

It does not follow from the above analysis that people should reduce their consumption. Rather, it indicates that they should save relatively more from their increased incomes. That is **their marginal rate of savings should be greater than their average rate of savings.** When the marginal rate of savings increases, the average rate of savings also goes up with the result that capital formation and economic development in the country are accelerated.

In early days of capitalism, payment of low wages and the existence of inequality of incomes helped capital formation. But no democratic country can adopt this method in modern times; the effort rather is to raise wages and reduce inequalities of income and wealth.

Under a regime of socialistic dictatorship, capital formation is brought about by ruthlessly curtailing consumption and keeping down the standard of living. But in modern democracies, to raise the standard of living is the first concern of the State. Hence, the State must rely on other methods to raise capital resources for economic development. This increases the importance of public investment side by side with private investment. Taxation can be used to generate collective savings and also to promote private investment.

10. *Times of India*, March 1, 1975, p. 4.

A well-conceived scheme of taxation is a surer way of raising the ratio of savings which is one of the crucial determinants of the rate of economic growth. As Nurkse says, "public finance assumes a new significance in the face of the problem of capital formation in under-developed countries."

As an Instrument for Regulating Consumption and Production

There are other methods also, besides public finance or fiscal policy, by which capital formation can be promoted, *e.g.*, taking the various means of production under government control.

But in a democratic society like that of India there is an inherent dislike for direct (physical) control and regulation by the state. The entrepreneurs would not like to be ordered about to produce this or that, how much to produce or where to produce. Incentives in the form of tax concessions, rebates or subsidies are, therefore, preferable. Through appropriate fiscal measures it can discourage unproductive investment, and encourage productive investment. Similarly, the consumers would not like to be told directly to curtail their consumption or to consume this and not to consume that. Taxation of articles whose consumption is to be discouraged is, therefore, preferable.

Hence, a democratic State must rely on indirect methods of control and regulation and this is done through fiscal and monetary policies.

Also, under a democratic constitution, a State cannot command resources. It must, therefore, operate through price-mechanism which is susceptible to the influence of public finance. Thus, in democratic countries, public finance is the most powerful and least undesirable weapon on which the States can rely for promoting economic development. In this way, they can raise resources not only for the public sector but also encourage savings and investment in the private sector.

Matching Physical Development

In any plan of economic development, a physical plan must be matched by a financial plan. The Indian Planning Commission says, "It must be emphasised that the balance to be achieved in the plan has to be both in real and financial terms. Money incomes are generated in the process of production and supplies are utilised in response to money demands. It is important, therefore, to operate upon and modify money income flows so as to maintain a balance between the supply of consumer goods and the purchasing power available for being spent on them, between savings and investment and between receipts and payments abroad."[11]

It is quite clear that only through fiscal and monetary measures—the chief instruments of public finance—the financial plan can be implemented and targets in money terms achieved. Hence, public finance has a vital role to play in the development programmes of a developing economy.

Influencing Rates of Saving and Investment

Public finance can exercise an important influence in increasing the rate of saving and investment. For example, the tax system can be so devised as to discourage the consumption of less essential goods and thereby release resources for being employed in more productive channels. Further, the tax system can be used to increase public saving which in turn can be used to finance an increase in public investment. On the expenditure side, there is positive need for public investment, especially in those branches of economic activity where the private investors are not easily tempted—for example, the development of means of transport and communications, basic heavy industries, education and research. Such investments are very often the very foundations of rapid economic advance. Since the government takes active part in economic development by launching public sector enterprises, it has to raise resources for the expansion of the public sector. Not only more taxes have to be levied but resources have to be raised through public borrowing too and also deficit financing (newly created money).

Conclusion

Thus, public finance is of crucial importance in accelerating the pace of development in under-developed countries by promoting capital formation. It can help reduce inequalities of wealth and income in the country, thus ensuring growth with social justice. For this purpose, progressive taxes like wealth tax, death duties, *etc.*, are levied on the rich and social security provided for the poor with the proceeds. Fiscal and monetary measures can also be used for checking price rise and thus ensuring growth with stability. Thus, public fiance in developing economies has to be functional and help in the achievement of economic and social objectives.

ROLE OF PUBLIC FINANCE UNDER DIFFERENT ECONOMIC SYSTEMS

It is well-known that public finance is not regarded merely as an instrument for collecting revenue for the states but is now increasingly used as an

11. Second Five Year Plan, pp. 15-16.

instrument for the achievement of certain economic and social objectives, whatever the economic system. The basic role of public finance is to mobilise resources through taxes, loans, etc. and utilise these resources for accelerating economic growth and for bringing about the desired redistribution of income and wealth in the community.

Public finance influences rates of saving.

In capitalist countries, there is private property and private ownership of means of production and the profit-motive provides the incentive for economic activity. Most of the wants of the people are satisfied through price mechanism in the market economy. However certain services are supplied collectively by the State on payment of a reasonable price, while others are supplied free and are financed by taxation or compulsory levies. Health services, law and order and defence are financed by taxation. Some revenue is raised through public enterprises also. The non-tax revenue are becoming quite important, although the tax revenue still continues to dominate.

In several under-developed countries, where some basic raw materials like crude oil occupy an important place in export trade, state trading provides significant amounts of revenue. Where some industries have been nationalised, significant amount of revenue is provided by the corporations managing such services. The allocation of resources is done on the principle of Maximum Social Advantage. Public utilities, public health, sanitation and education are subsidised by the State. Public fianance policy is used in capitalist countries for promoting economic growth and providing employment opportunities. The State also utilises its taxation and expenditure policies to reduce economic disparities.

In Socialist States, means of production are collectively owned by the State and wages and salaries are the main forms of distribution. Taxation accounts for a small part of state revenue, services and goods are collectively produced.

Key terms

Public finance, Maximum social advantage, Functional finance.

QUESTIONS

1. What is a Balanced Budget? Under what conditions can a budget be allowed to remain unbalanced?
2. Examine the significance of budget as an instrument of economic policy.
3. Assuming a balanced budget to start with, explain the effects on the national income of (*a*) an increase in government expenditure resulting in a budget deficit and (*b*) an increase in government expenditure with a balanced budget again.
4. Explain the different ways in which a 'managed budget policy' may be used to reduce economic instability. Which, if any, of these ways would you advocate and why?
5. Distinguish between Private and Public Finance. Account for the growing importance of public finance in recent times.
6. Examine critically the priniciple of maximum social advantages as the cardinal doctrine of public finance. What are its limitations? Distinguish between progressive and proportional taxes. How are direct taxes made progressive?
7. What is meant by 'Functional Finance'? Discuss its usefulness in the formation of fiscal policy in a developing economy.

63 CHAPTER

PUBLIC EXPENDITURE

Of the two important aspects of Public Finance, *viz*., Public Revenue and Public Expenditure, let us first study Public Expenditure. This department of public finance received scant attention at the hands of writers on public finance throughout the 19th century. Attention was almost exclusively focussed on public revenues. It is only in the present century that it came to be realised that public expenditure is far more important in its implications and bearing on public welfare than public revenue. The main reason for the early neglect of the subject of public expenditure seems to be that the amount of public expenditure was very small as the field of governmental activity was restricted. Now public expenditure has reached astronomical figures.

Adam Smith had concentrated only on passive role of government under which a government can support the smooth flow of economies with least interference in economic activities. The government must look after,

(*i*) Expenditure on defence, to protect the citizens's from external aggression,

(*ii*) expenditure on internal law and order so as to bring about peaceful functioning of economic activities,

(*iii*) expenditure of government on administrative activities, for bringing about co-ordination of different economic activities to achieve economic and social welfare, and

(*iv*) expenditure on certain amount of infrastructure development, to help the economy grow.

Distribution of public expenditure among various state activities.

The role of government started increasing with increase in urbanisation and industralisation. Even in today's economies the economic activities of the government is increasing many folds. (*i*) Adolph Wagner a German economists stated that the government activities whether economic or non-economic starts increasing, this results in an increase in the government expenditure. This may be due to two aspects (*i*) increase in more intensive activities of the existing one and (*ii*) increase in additional extensive activities. This can be termed as "deepening and widening" of governments' activities so as to achieve certain pre-determined socio-economic objectives.

Public expenditure policy of the government came to the forefront due to the application of Keynesian "functional finance approach", which was an intense success in pushing the Amercian economy upwards from the great depression. The success of Keynesian theory of pump-priming and the application of multiplier effect in accelerating the pace of economic activities, boosted the confidence of many governments to increase the public expenditure and achieve its desired results. This concept has increased the active role of government in a "welfare state" policy which has resulted in an enormous increase in public expenditure. Peacock and Wisenam came to the conclusion after a thorough study that the increase in public expenditure is not smooth but it is of a sudden nature, it increases in jerks and stabilises and so on . . . . Peacock and Wiseman explained the growth of public expenditure and its resulting effect, (*i*) Displacement effect, (*ii*) Inspection effect and (*iii*) Concentration effect.

Peacoack and Wiseman From 1891 to 1955 carried out the study of public expenditure of the United-kingdom. They were of the opinion that due to certain social disturbances, there can be a sudden jump or jerk in the increase of public expenditure, This is referred as displacement effect, Generally during war-time the governments are in immediate need of more expendituire on defence requirements, hence this is a kind of jerks. As the economy stabilises after the increase in public expenditure and the simultaneouse increase in taxation by the government, a new fiscal plateau is reached. Here the government is neither interested in reducing public expenditure nor reducing taxes. Hence a new equilibrium is reached. This is referred as "inspection effect" as the government will review the situation. Once this situation prevails and economy is settled for some period, this concept may be referred as "concentration effect".

Again after certain period of time a new social disturbance may occur and a new "displacement, inspection and concentration effect may take place."

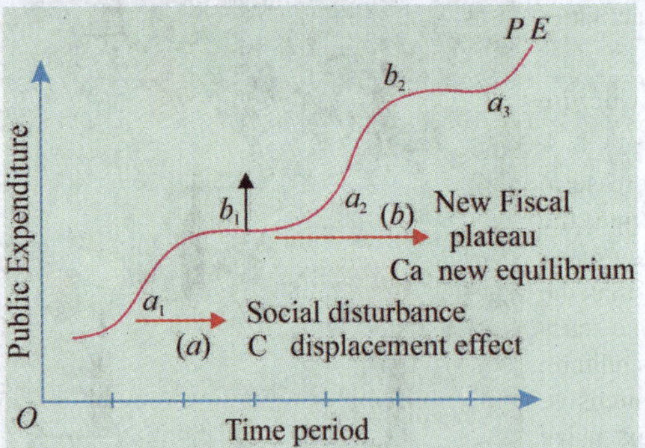

On *y*-axis the increase in public expenditure (as percentage of Gross national product '*GNP*') and on *x*-axis the time period. '*PE*' the public expenditure increase path, '*a*', is the first social disturbance, which causes an enormous increase in public expenditure (displacement effect) and after reaching certain point the economy is about to settle, at this point the government reviews the situation and 'b_1' is 'inspection effect' and once every thing becomes normal the 'concentration effect' takes place.

Though the peacock Wiseman hypothesis is based on their study and to a greater extent the natural process of a strong economy is taken into account, In developing countries there are many continuous jerks in the form of un-intentional and intentional, the un-intentional jerks are (that of Peacock-Wiseman's hypothesis) due to natural calamities, wars and civil disturbances *etc*., on the other hand the intentional public expenditure is that of for political reasons or may be depending on social and cultural expenditure. In developing countries it has become a regular feature of increase in public expenditure with jerks which may or may not be for economic purpose or for the human resource development.

CAUSES OF INCREASE IN PUBLIC EXPENDITURE

In recent times, public expenditure has increased enormously. The main reason is that the functions of the state have increased manifold. In the past, the state was regarded only as a police state concerned with defence from foreign aggression and maintenance of law and order within the State. Now the State is regarded as a Welfare State which is concerned with promoting the welfare of its citizens. As such, it has to provide not only social security but it has also to look to economic stability and economic growth which calls for ever increasing investment expenditure.

The following are the principal causes of growing public expenditure:

(*i*) Increase in Area and Population. In the first place, the increase in public expenditure is due to the fact that the physical boundaries of the States have been widened. 'No-man's lands' have been brought under organised government. Also, in certain cases, even if the area has not increased, the population figures have considerably gone up. Governments have, therefore, to cater to the needs of millions of more people scattered perhaps over a much wider area.

(*ii*) Growth of State Functions. As already pointed out, the modern States are no longer police states concerned mainly with the maintenance of law and order. They are now regarded as welfare states. This has resulted in a tremendous increase in their functions. While old functions are being performed more intensively such as administrative functions and functions relating to internal security and protection against aggression but numerous new functions are being undertaken, *e.g.*, optimum utilisation of national resources, economic growth, reduction of economic inequalities.

(iii) Higher Price-Level and Rising Cost of Public Services. Another reason which accounts for the mounting public expenditure is the higher price-level. Persons who have seen 'good old days' in India, or have heard about them, tell us that there was a time when ghee was selling at 4 annas a seer, whereas now it sells at twenty rupees per kg. There has been a similar rise in prices of other commodities. Governments, like individuals, therefore, have to find larger amounts of money to pay for the commodities and the services they have to purchase.

(iv) Increase in National Wealth. There has been almost a continuous improvement in agriculture, trade and industry in every country, though in some countries like India it has been painfully slow. There has been a steady increase in the per capita income and consequently an improvement in the standard of living. There has also been a corresponding improvement in public revenues and public expenditure.

(v) Ability to Tax. In a low-income economy, it is difficult to impose and collect taxes. But as economy develops, a much wider range of taxes becomes available to the State and as State revenue swells, public expenditure increases. Ability to tax raises the ability to spend.

(vi) War and Prevention of War. We know it to our cost now how costly a modern war is. England was spending £ 15 million daily during the last war. Even when the war is not on, large amounts are spent on preparing for it or on adopting means for its prevention. War has been one of the main factors responsible for increasing public expenditure.

(vii) Provision of Public Utility Services. Another important cause of increase in public expenditure is the provision of more and more public utility services, *e.g.*, water, electricity, transport services. It is now realised that some of the important wants of man can be satisfied more efficiently and economically if these are supplied collectively rather than each individual making his own arrangements. It is not considered desirable or economical that in a town there should be different companies supplying these services on a competitive basis. However, these public utility services are best provided by the State Government or local authority. Naturally, public expenditure goes up.

(viii) Expansion in Social Services. In modern times, there has been a remarkable expansion in social services like education, public health measures and medical aid. Expansion in educational facilities has led to the establishment of schools, colleges and technical institutions in very large numbers. The number of hospitals and medical colleges has multiplied manifold. Public health and sanitary measures are taken on a vast scale. There are also undertaken slum clearance programmes. Expenditure on these social services is also regarded as productive investment since it leads to increase in income and employment. Such expenditure builds up what is called human capital.

(ix) As Musgraves observes, "Efficient product mix between private and social good changes as per capita income rises, and this change involves a rising share of social goods."[1] In other words, when G. N. P. or per capita income rises it indicates the transformation of an economy from an agricultural or low income state to an industrial or high-income state. When this happens the output of social goods, *i.e.*, goods for the society as a whole, increases and public expenditure must inevitably go up.

(x) Technological Changes. Technological inventions call for larger or new production in the public sector, because it happens that improvements in techniques can be best exploited by the state. For instance, invention of internal combustion gave rise to a massive automobile industry necessitating the construction and improvement of highways. State expenditure naturally goes with the expansion of the public sector.

(xi) Expansion of Public Sector. Socialistic tendencies have in modern times resulted in the expansion of the public sector. As a consequence, public expenditure has gone very high.

(xii) Defective Financial and Civil Administration. Not a small increase in public expenditure is due to defective financial and civil administration. Duplication and unnecessary multiplication of governmental agencies is not uncommon. Wrong allocation of resources and functions also leads to extravagance. A lax control over public expenditure swells it to an unnecessarily high figure.

(xiii) Political and Social Factors. Political Development and changing social views have led to a great expansion of the public sector and increase in public expenditure. In a democratic State, there are several political parties and each party is anxious to enlist the support of the people. The supporters constantly clamour for concessions and benefits at the expense of public fund. From every corner of the country and from every section comes the call for more and more amenities. Ministers are asked by the people

1. Musgrave, R. A., and Musgrave, P. G.— *Public Finance in Theory and Practice,* 1973, p. 126.

to open colleges in their home districts. Governments have thus been pressed by the democratic forces to take upon themselves more and more functions. According to Wagner's Law of Increasing State Activity, governments' functions have increased both intensively and extensively. The old functions are being performed more thoroughly and many new functions are being undertaken.

(*xiv*) Welfare Activities and growth of Transfer Expenditure. All modern States wish to make liberal provision for social security schemes, or social insurance, *e.g.*, free medical aid, free education, old-age pensions, provident fund schemes, *etc.* These are known as transfers or transfer expenditure. These transfers were unimportant up to the thirties but they have phenomenally grown since then. All such transfers have substantially pushed up the State budgets.

(*xv*) Requirements of Full Employment. A modern State is anxious to underwrite full employment. To provide employment for all, the State must launch ambitious schemes of public works and public undertakings. Naturally, the public expenditure must shoot up.

(*xvi*) Economic Development. In all countries, whether developed or under-developed, the States have given top priority to economic development. The developed countries are desirous to raise their standard of living still higher, whereas the under-developed countries are anxious to attain a certain minimum standard. Economic development is a very costly affair. Lot of money has to be spent on economic and social overheads and many costly projects have to be undertaken. Measures have to be taken for the development of agriculture and industry, and so on. There is no wonder, therefore, that the size of the State budgets has become swollen everywhere.

Conclusion. Alfred Buehler says in his **Public Finance:** "To some persons a relative increase in public expenditure seems a calamity, to others it is a cause of rejoicing and to still others it is a matter of indifference. No definite percentage of national income can be named as the proper limit for the cost of government since such a limit must depend upon relative circumstances. The proper size of the expenditure depends on the desires and needs of a community, the effects of government spending and the revenues supporting the spending, the willingness of the population to be taxed, existing burdens of taxation, the resources and population of a community, the distribution of wealth and incomes, the stage of economic development and other variables. The real issue is the advisability of a particular expenditure of a particular government at a particular time."

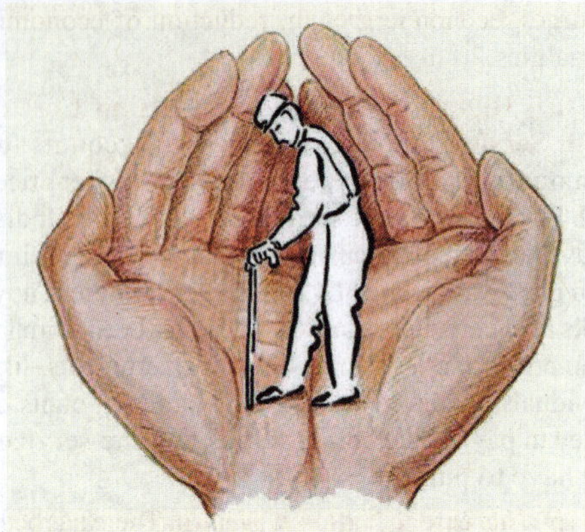

Transfer expenditure such as old age pension has increased recently by the governments.

Revenue And Capital Expenditure

Public expenditure has been classified into revenue and capital expenditure. Revenue Expenditure is current expenditure, *e.g.*, administrative and maintenance expenditure. This expenditure is of a recurring type while Capital Expenditure is of capital nature and is incurred once for all. It is nonrecurring expenditure, *e.g.*, expenditure in building multipurpose projects or on setting up big factories like steel plants, money spent on land, machinery and equipment.

Developmental and Non-developmental Expenditure

Money spent on the maintenance of internal security, law and order, *i.e.*, on police, jails and judiciary and money spent on the army to provide defence against aggression is generaly regarded as non-developmental, whereas the developmental expenditure includes expenditure on irrigation projects, rail and road transport, expenditure on agricultural and industrial development, and so on. Even expenditure on education and research is also regarded as developmental.

PRINCIPLES OF PUBLIC EXPENDITURE

Just as there are well-known canons of taxation, similarly it is possible to formulate some canons or principles to which prudent public expenditure should conform. These principles are:—

Principle of Maximum Social Benefit

It is necessary that all public expenditure should satisfy one fundamental test, *viz.*, that of Maximum Social Advantage. That is, the government should discover and maintain an optimum level of public expenditure by balancing social benefits and social costs. Every rupee spent by a government must have as its aim the promotion of the maximum welfare of the society as a whole. Care has to be taken that public funds are not utilised for the benefit of a particular group or a section of society. The aim is the **general** welfare. Government exists for the benefit of the governed and the justification of the government expenditure is, therefore, to be sought in the benefit of the community as a whole. (The principle of maximum social advantage has already been discussed in the previous chapter.)

Canon of Economy

Although the aim of public expenditure is to maximise the social benefit, yet it does not exonerate government from exercising utmost economy in its expenditure. Economy does not mean niggardliness. It only means that extra vagance and waste of all types should be avoided. Public expenditure has great potentiality for public good but it may also prove injurious and wasteful. In the words of Coleridge, "The sun may draw up the moisture from the river, the morass, and the ocean to be given back in general showers to the garden, the pasture and the cornfield; but it may likewise force away the moisture from the fields of tillage, to drop it on the stagnant pool, the saturated swamp, or the unprofitable sand waste."[2] Thus, if revenue collected from the tax-payer is heedlessly spent, it would be obviously uneconomical.

To satisfy the canon of economy, it will be necessary to avoid all duplication of expenditure and overlapping of authorities. Further, public expenditure should not adversely affect saving. In case government activity damaged the individual's will or power to save, it would be repugnant to the canon of economy.

Canon of Sanction

Another important principle of public expenditure is that before it is actually incurred, it should be sanctioned by a competent authority. Unauthorised spending is bound to lead to extravagance and over-spending. It also means that the amount must be spent on the purpose for which it was sanctioned. Allied to the canon of sanction, there is another, *viz.*, auditing. Not only is previous sanction of public expenditure essential but a post-mortem examination is equally imperative. That is, all the public accounts at the end of the year should be properly audited to see that the amounts have not been mis-spent or misappropriated.

2. Macgregor—*Public Aspects of Finance*, 1939, p. 67.

Parliament in session: public expenditure must be sanctioned by the state authority.

Canon of Elasticity

Another sane principle of public expenditure is that it should be fairly elastic. It should be possible for public authorities to vary the expenditure according to need or circumstances. A rigid level of expenditure may prove a source of trouble and embarrassment in bad times. Alteration in the upward direction is not difficult. It is easy, rather tempting, to increase the scale of expenditure. But elasticity is needed most in the downward direction. When the economy axe is applied, it is a very painful process. Retrenchment of a widespread character creates serious social discontent.

It is very necessary, therefore, that when the scale of public expendtiure has to be increased, it should be increased gradually. A short spell of prosperity should not lead to long-term commitments. A fair degree of elasticity is essential if financial breakdown is to be avoided at a time of shrinking revenue.

No Adverse Influence on Production or Distribution

It is also necessary to ensure that public expenditure should exercise a healthy influence both on production and distribution of wealth in the community. It should stimulate productive activity so that income and employment in the country increase, and it may be possible to raise the standard of living. But this object of raising of living standards of the masses will be served only if wealth is evenly distributed. If newly created wealth goes to enrich the already rich, the purpose is not served. Public expenditure should aim at reducing the inequalities of wealth distribution.

Principle of Surplus

It is considered a sound or orthodox principle of public expenditure that as far as possible public expenditure should be kept well within the revenue of the State so that a surplus is left at the end of the year. In other words, the government should avoid deficit budget. But the modern economists, especially Keynes, do not regard surplus budgeting as a virtue, rather deficit budgeting is more useful in raising the levels of income and employment in the under-developed countries. All the same, budget deficits running over a series of years are considered bad for the financial stability of the country.

Promotion of Economic Growth and Stability

In modern times, a very important principle of public expenditure is that it should promote economic development and economic stability, directly or indirectly. No public expenditure should impair the economy's potentialities for economic growth. In all public expenditure requirements of economic growth and economic stability (avoiding economic fluctuations) are kept in the forefront.

Conclusion

Public expenditure to be beneficial must conform, as far as possible, to the principles enumerated above. But the all pervading principle is that of **functional finance.** That is public expenditure should be directed to the achievement of economic and social objectives in which the country may have set its heart.

Public expenditure creates infrastructure for the economy.

EFFECTS OF PUBLIC EXPENDITURE

Effects on Production

There is a type of public expenditure which is regarded as unproductive. This refers to expenditure on the prosecution of, or the preparation for, a war. This belief, however, is not entirely correct. Military expenditure, if not overdone, does indirectly assist production by ensuring to the community an ordered economic life. Actually, it is overdone and a great deal of military expenditure may be regarded as unproductive. Also, we have to admit that a short and successful war may bring to the nation much economic gain by securing some economic privileges. In the same manner, by preventing an invasion of the country, the armed forces may enable the community to avoid an economic loss. Thus, military expenditure may be considered indirectly or broadly productive.

Most of the public expenditure is productive directly or indirectly. Governments, in every country, are running commercial enterprises which are directly productive. The Indian Government has created solid and lucrative assets in the form of canals and railways. The State enterprises make a direct contribution to production in the community. In the same manner, schemes of reclamation and afforestation are also directly productive. In all these ways, the level of employment in the country goes up.

A great deal of public expenditure is, however, only indirectly productive. In this connection we may consider the effects of public expenditure on —

(*a*) Power to work and save;

(*b*) will to work and save;

(*c*) diversion of resources as between employments and localities; and

(*d*) the total volume of employment and income.

As for **power to work and save,** it may be pointed out that much of the socially desirable public expenditure incurred by modern governments undoubtedly increases the community's productive power and, consequently, also the power to save. Such expenditure includes the provision of means of communication and transport, education, public health, scientific research and industrial research, controlling of human, animal and plant diseases, and expenditure on social insurance, like health insurance, unemployment insurance and old-age pensions.

As for **the will to work and save,** much depends on the character of public expenditure and the policy governing it. By giving the people expectation of future benefits from public expenditure, it may blunt the edge of the desire to work and save. The granting of old-age pension, insurance against sickness and unemployment and provision of education at State expense may make the people indifferent towards the future and make them neglect saving. This is bound to affect adversely exertions in the present. People will work less. But if such expenditure is kept

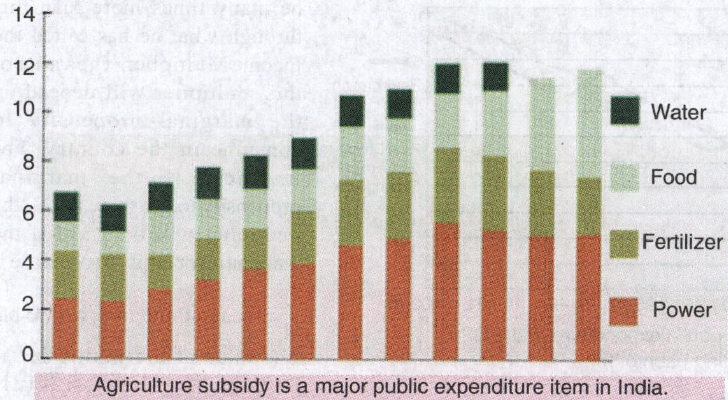

Agriculture subsidy is a major public expenditure item in India.

within proper limits and if it helps the really helpless, the check to work and saving may be negligible.

Regarding the **diversion of resources as between employments and localities,** the public expenditure may have distinctly a beneficial effect on production. Through the system of bounties and subsidies a government may succeed in diverting resources to hitherto neglected channels and thus create new industries. In the same manner, by spending money on the development of backward areas, the government may add to the total production in the country. A wisely conducted policy of public borrowing stimulates saving and the habit of investment in the community, which are certainly beneficial to production. It also diverts resources into channels which may add considerably to the wealth of the community.

We may thus safely conclude that wise public expenditure exerts a very wholesome influence on production. It assists production indirectly by adding to the power to work and save, and by a profitable diversion of resources. This is besides taking up directly the work of production through State enterprises.

Till recently, the discussion of the effects of public expenditure was mostly confined to the indirect effects discussed above. However, with the Keynesian revolution, it has come to be realised that public expenditure can exercise directly **an important influence on the level of economic activity, accelerate economic growth and help maintain economic stability.** We have seen previously that unemployment in the Keynesian system is due to deficiency of effective demand. Public expenditure has a direct influence on the level of effective demand. An increase in public expenditure during a depression helps to create more demand and thereby increases the level of output and employment. Indeed, at times, this direct effect may outweigh the indirect effects of public expenditure discussed above. (See also "Role of Public Finance in a Developing Economy" in the previous chapter.)

Conclusion. Thus, public expenditure increases production (*a*) by improving the productive efficiency of workers, (*b*) by providing economic and social overheads, (*c*) by giving direct assistance in the form of loans, grants and subsidies and technical advice, and (*d*) by investment in public enterprises. Besides raising the level of production, public expenditure can influence the pattern of production or composition of output.

Effects on Distribution

Public expenditure can have a very wholesome influence on the distribution of wealth in the community. It can reduce inequalities of incomes. It is an admitted fact that the benefit to the poor from State activities is far greater than to the rich. A rich man can protect himself. He can make arrangements for the education and medical relief of himself and his family. But a poor man is helpless. It is, therefore, the poor man who benefits the most from the State activity. To this extent, the State expenditure seeks to bridge the gulf between the rich and the poor.

There is a certain expenditure which benefits the poor exclusively and primarily, *e.g.*, poor relief, old-age pensions and unemployment and sickness benefits. The benefits derived from such social services by the poor may be regarded as a net addition to their incomes. And when we remember that the revenue is obtained by taxing the rich, the conclusion is inescapable that inequalities of wealth distribution have been reduced to some extent.

But much depends, here again, on the character of public expenditure and the policy underlying it. Just as there are proportional, progressive and regressive taxes, in the same manner the government grants may also be proportional, progressive, and regressive. If public expenditure is really to make the distribution of wealth more even and fair, it must be progressive. It must be according to 'ability to receive' (corresponding to 'ability to pay' in taxation).

Corresponding to the principle of minimum sacrifice in taxation, there is the principle of maximum

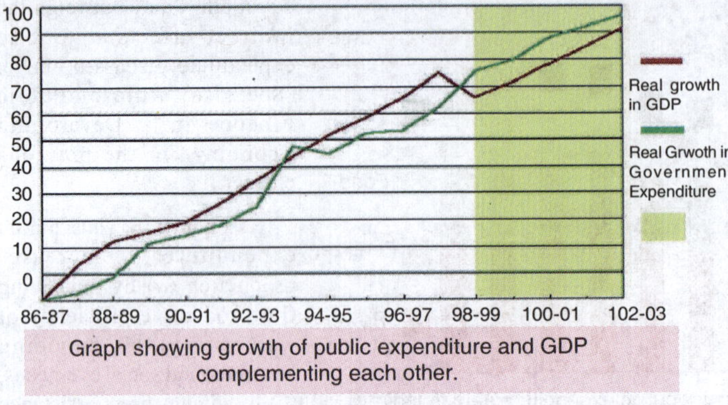

Graph showing growth of public expenditure and GDP complementing each other.

benefit in public expenditure. Public expenditure must be so arranged as to confer a maximum benefit on the community as a whole. This is the guiding principle. Judged in this light, we can see that expenditure on debt services is regressive, because it gives more income to the already rich. Granting of old-age pensions and benefits of social insurance are progressive. If a government subsidizes the production of commodities largely consumed by the poor, it is progressive otherwise regressive.

We have also to consider the reaction of public expenditure on individual income. If a government grant reduces the individual's desire to work and save, it may lead to reduction of incomes of the beneficiaries. In this case, the inequalities of wealth distribution are not reduced.

On the whole, public expenditure in modern times tends to make the distribution of wealth in the community more equitable.

Effects on Level of Income and Employment

We have discussed above the effects of public expenditure on production and distribution. We have also noticed that in modern times the sphere of state activity has very much widened. As a result public expenditure on several new items has increased manifold. This public expenditure affects the level of income and employment in the country. Keynes has shown that the government can remove widespread unemployment during periods of depression through liberal public expenditure on public works. It can thus raise the level of income and employment in the country.

Keynes showed that when government increases its investment expenditure on public works, then the increase in level of income and employment in the country will not be merely equal to increase in income and employment in those activities, but it will be many times more than this through what he has called the Income Multiplier. The value of this multiplier will depend on the marginal propensity to consume in the country. For instance, if the marginal propensity to consume is 2/3, the multiplier will be 3 and if the marginal propensity to consume is $\frac{3}{4}$, the multiplier is 4, and so on. The value of the multiplier is found by the principle propounded by

Keynes thus: $\text{Multiplier} = \dfrac{1}{1 - \text{mpc}}$

If the value of the multiplier is 3, it would mean that if the government makes an additional investment of Rs. 100 crores on public works, then the national income and output in the country will not increase only by Rs. 100 crores but equal to Rs. 300 crores. In the same way, the volume of employment will not increase only as much as is provided by the public works launched by the government, but many times more. This happens because when government increases its investment expenditure, then at first employment increases in those works and the incomes of people employed in those works increase. Further, when these people spend their additional income on the purchase of consumers' goods, the demand for these goods increases and to meet this increased demand, their production will have to be increased. To increase production, some more people will be offered employment.

The effect of increase in public expenditure on the national income and employment is shown in the diagram (Fig. 61.1). In this diagram, national income is shown on the *X*-axis and consumption and investment demand on the *Y*-axis. *OZ* making a 45° angle with *X*-axis is the income line. As we have already read in the theory of income and employment, this 45° line is also called aggregate supply curve (Ch. 39). The equilibrium level of income is determined at a point where this line (*e.g.*, aggregate supply curve) cuts the aggregate demand (consumption and investment demand) curve and employment level will be determined corresponding to this income level.

In the diagram below, the aggregate demand curve $C + I$ cuts the aggregate supply curve OZ at E according to which OY_1 national income is determined. Now if consumption and investment demand remains constant and government does not increase its expenditure, then *OY* will remain the national income and correspondingly the level of employment. Rather, it is possible, and it happens during depression, that this level may go down owing to decrease in aggregate demand and there may be widespread unemployment in the country.

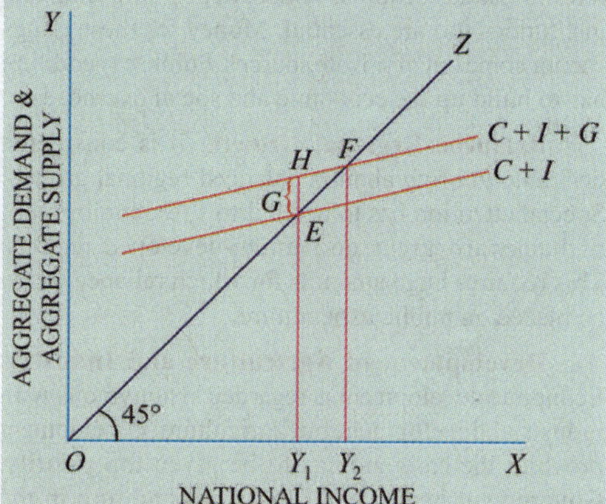

Fig. 61.1. Multiplier effect of increase in government expenditure on national income.

Now, according to Keynes, the government should increase its expenditure in such a situation so that the level of national income and employment in the country may increase. In the above diagram, if the government increases investment expenditure by *EH*, the aggregate demand curve moves upwards as shown by the curve $C + I + G$. Now this new aggregate demand curve $C + I + G$ cuts the aggregate supply curve at F and accordingly the national income increases to OY_2. It will be seen that even though the government has increased its investment expenditure by *EH*, the national income has increased by $Y_1 Y_2$ which is many times more than the increase in investment.

In this way, Keynes has shown that during depression the government can remove unemployment by increasing its public expenditure. Thus, public expenditure can vitally influence the level of national income and employment in the country and maintain economic stability by eliminating economic fluctuations.

Effect on Income and Employment in a Developing Economy

Above we have explained the effect of public expenditure on income and employment in developed countries, *viz.*, it is to ensure economic stability by eliminating economic fluctuations. The problem of developing economies is different. Here the low level of income and employment is due not so much to deficiency of demand, as in developed countries during depression, but to deficiency of capital stock. It is for the state to make up this deficiency through a wise policy relating to public expenditure. Public expenditure in developing economies is to be mainly directed to the acceleration of economic development.

The government in a developing economy can with adequate and properly directed public expenditure, build up the requisites of economic growth, *viz.*, social and economic overheads or the required infrastructure, *e.g.*, sound educational base, adequate public health measures and medical aid to improve human capital in the form of physically strong and healthy and skilled labour. The government can also launch public enterprises and build up heavy and core industries of strategic importance. It can also promote agricultural development by making adequate provision for the supply of critical inputs in the form of irrigation facilities, fertilizers, improved seeds and pesticides. In these and many other ways, public expenditure can be used as an instrument for raising the level of income and employment in the country. Through public expenditure, government can raise the rate of capital formation in the country and thus promote economic development. It would provide employment and build up productive capacity of the economy.

In India, we see that the government is spending lot of money under the five-year plans on schemes of capital formation. It has spent crores of rupees on irrigation and power by undertaking multipurpose projects, on roads, railways, on huge steel plants, machine-making industry, heavy engineering and heavy electrical industry, fertilizer industry, and so on. This has substantially added to the volume of employment and productive capacity in the country. These are important steps towards removing unemployment and poverty in the country.

For creating employment directly, the government in India has started special employment schemes. Rural Public Works Programmes have been launched to provide employment for the people in the rural areas. These public works included irrigation schemes, road construction, flood control, soil conservation schemes, *etc.* It is proposed to increase substantially expenditure on these schemes during the Fifth Plan period. In this way, the government has created additional employment opportunities and added to people's incomes.

To create opportunities for self-employment in the rural areas, the government has started special schemes. Small Farmers Development Agencies (*S.F.D.A.*) have been set up which help the small

Indian government spends a lot on development of farmers.

farmers in getting improved seeds, fertilizers, pesticides, irrigation facilities, *etc.* They thus make their employment more productive and increase their incomes. Then there are Agencies for Marginal Farmers and Landless Labourers (*MFAL*) which impart them training in, and provide finance for, poultry, dairy, animal husbandry, *etc.* Thus, gainful employment is provided for such people and their earnings are increased.

Similarly, to remove unemployment among the educated people and to provide them opportunities for self-employment they are assisted through technical training and financial assistance, to start small-scale industries. Financial aid is given directly by the State and also through the nationalised banks and other financial institutions set up for the purpose.

Thus, the governments of under-developed countries like India, by increasing their expenditure on economic development and capital formation, can make valuable contribution towards increasing income and opportunities of employment in the country. Public expenditure in developing countries, therefore, plays a very vital role in raising the level of income and employment in the country.

ROLE OF PUBLIC EXPENDITURE IN A DEVELOPING ECONOMY

Under-developed nations are keen on rapid economic development which requires huge expenditure to be incurred in the various sectors of the economy. The private sector is either unable to find and invest these huge amounts or it is unwilling because the return from such investments may be uncertain or long delayed. Hence, economic development has to depend almost entirely on public expenditure. Public expenditure, therefore, plays a vital role in economic development of an under-developed economy.

Public expenditure promotes economic development in the following ways:

Social and Economic Overheads. Economic development is handicapped in under-developed countries on account of the lack of the necessary infrastructure. Economic overheads like the roads and railways, irrigation and power projects are essential for speeding-up economic development. Social overheads like hospitals, schools, and colleges and technical institutions too are essential. Money for these things cannot come out of private sources. Public expenditure has to build up the economic and social overheads.

Balanced Regional Growth. It is considered desirable to bring about a balanced regional growth. Special attention has to be paid to the development of backward areas and under-developed regions. This requires huge amounts for which reliance has to be placed on public expenditure.

Development of Agriculture and Industry. Economic development is regarded synonymous with industrial development but agricultural development provides the base and has to be given top priority. Government has to incur lot of expenditure in the agricultural sector, *e.g.*, on irrigation and power, seed farms, fertilizer factories, warehouses, *etc.*, and in the industrial sector by setting up public enterprises like the steel plants, heavy electricals, heavy engineering, machine-making factories, *etc.* All these enterprises are calculated to promote economic development.

Exploitation and Development of Mineral Resources. Minerals provide a base for further economic development. The government has to undertake schemes of exploration and development of essential minerals, *e.g.*, coal and oil. Public expenditure has to play its role here too.

Subsidies and Grants. The Central government gives grants to State governments and the State governments to local authorities to induce them to incur some desirable expenditure. Subsidies have also to be given to encourage the production of certain goods especially for export to earn much-needed foreign exchange.

Conclusion

Thus, public expenditure has to play a vital role in economic development. It is required to create and maintain conditions essential for economic growth. It must improve climate for investment and provide incentives for savings. The private entrepreneurs have to be assisted and inspired in every possible manner to venture forth and launch industrial and commercial undertakings. Public expenditure creates the necessary environment for the expansion of private enterprise and initiative.

THE PURE THEORY OF PUBLIC EXPENDITURE

The pure theory of public expenditure seeks to determine the optimum amount of public expenditure. Erik Lindahl sought to build a model for a simultaneous determination of the optimum amount of public expenditure and the optimum distribution of tax shares both on benefit principles. The difficulty in this model was that the optimum tax structure could not be determined without knowing the optimum amount of public expenditure, nor could the optimum expenditure be determined independent of tax structure.

The English economists developed an entirely different approach. These economists viewed the determination of public expenditure as a planning problem. They held the view that expenditure could be determined independent of revenue determination. Once the amount of expenditure has been determined, the revenue required to finance this expenditure could be determined without difficulty.

Pigou and Dalton attempted the formulation of a theory of optimum budget incorporating both expenditure and taxation. The Pigou-Dalton approach is based on the assumption that the marginal social benefit of government expenditure, optimally distributed amongst different sectors, diminishes as the amount of expenditure increases whereas the marginal social cost of taxation increases as the amount of taxation increases. Hence with the expansion of public expenditure we shall reach a break-even point where the social benefit derived from an additional amount of government expenditure is equal to the social costs of additional amount of taxation needed to finance this expenditure. Hence it is inferred that a theory of determination of the public expenditure must be based on the benefit approach particularly so in a normative theory of public finance where the supply of public goods is so planned that the community derives the greatest attainable satisfaction within its budget restraints.

Public expenditure for exploitation of mineral resources.

Prof. Musgrave has, in fact, given us a theory of the public household where the optimum amount of public expenditure is sought to be so determined that the community is able to reach its highest possible indifference curve. This theory is based on two important assumptions: (1) The preference patterns of individuals comprising the community for goods and services as also leisure have been known and determined and (2) There is a given distribution of income in the community in the post-revenue expenditure situation which is considered ideal *i.e.*, the distribution branch of the budget is optimally determined.

These assumptions are 'heroic' in the sense that it is very difficult, rather impossible to get the preferences of individuals revealed. But for planning of public expenditure these revelations are a 'must'. All the same, this theory of determination of public expenditure can be utilised as a guide to the determination and allocation of the two branches of the budget.

Key terms

Public expenditure, Causes of increase in public expenditure, Wagner's law, principles of public expenditure, Public expenditure and Production and distribution.

QUESTIONS

1. Explain the "Peacock-Wiseman" hypothesis. How far it is applicable in developing countries?
2. What are the basic objectives of public expenditure in a developing economy?
3. Explain the main principles which should guide public expenditure in a growing economy.
4. Explain the causes of growth of public expenditure in modern times. Is this growth always justifiable?
5. Discuss how public expenditure influence production and distribution in various ways.

64
CHAPTER

PUBLIC REVENUE

A modern State taps a number of source to collect its revenue. Broadly speaking, the government revenues can be classified as (1) **Tax Revenue** and (2) **Non-Tax Revenue.**

Tax revenue derived from the various taxes: (*a*) Direct Taxes, *e.g.*, income-tax, wealth tax, gift tax, expenditure tax, *etc.*

(*b*) Indirect taxes, *e.g.*, customs duties, excise duties, sales tax, *etc.*

Non-tax revenue is derived from public undertakings called **Prices** and other miscellaneous receipts. It also raises loans, short-term and long-term, to augment its revenues.

The major sources of revenue are **Taxes and Prices.** The minor sources are **Fees, Special Assessment, Fines, forfeitures and Escheats, Tributes and Indemnities, Gifts and Grants.**

Taxes

As we have mentioned above, that the most important source of public revenue is taxation. But taxation revenue takes several forms. It consists of taxes, fees, prices, special assessments, rates, *etc.* Let us distinguish between all these forms.

Tax. Plehn defines taxes thus: "Taxes are general compulsory contributions of wealth levied upon persons, natural or corporate, to defray the expenses incurred in conferring **common benefit** upon the residents of the State."[1] This definition brings out the true nature of a tax. The essence of a tax is (*a*) that it is a compulsory levy under certain conditions, and (*b*) it is meant for the general purposes of the State. The individual cannot expect that the State should render him a specific service in return for the tax paid by him. If I pay income-tax, I cannot claim in return that the State should post a policeman at my gate during night to protect my property which is a source of income to me.

This, however, does not mean that State undertakes to do nothing in return for the taxes that it receives from the people. The State carries on the general administration and confers lot of benefit on the community. But these are **common** benefits meant for all and not any special benefit meant for a particular tax-payer. There is no direct quid pro quo. The taxes are intended to meet the **general expenses of the government** which confer a common benefit. In the words of Taussig, "The essence of a tax, as distinguished **from other charges by government,** is the absence of any direct quid pro quo between the tax-payer and the public authority."[2]

Price. In modern times, public sector occupies a very important place in the economy. We find public enterprises being run side by side with private enterprises. The government has to launch public enterprises when private sector is either unwilling or unable to enter certain fields because the return is either uncertain or it takes a long time to mature, such as multipurpose projects, railways, hydroelectric works, water works, huge

1. *Introduction to Public Finance*, 1921, p. 59.
2. *Principles/ of Economics*, Ch. LXVI, I.

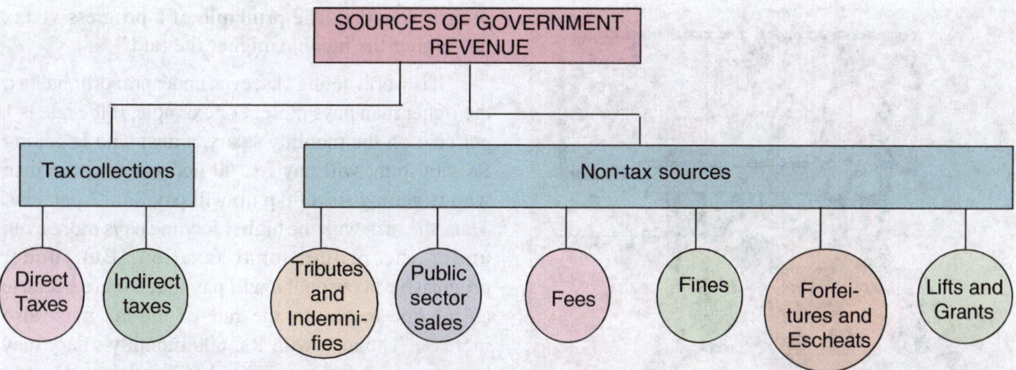

iron and steel works. The government does not supply these services or goods manufactured in government undertakings free but charges a price. When public authority sells a commodity or renders a service, the charge made on the consumer, who avails of the service or buys a commodity, is called a price. Income from public enterprises now constitutes a substantial source of revenue.

Fee. It is also a compulsory payment made by those who obtain a definite service in return. The fee is intended to cover a part of the cost of the service rendered. It is never more than the cost of service. Also, some public purpose is kept in view in the service rendered. The obvious example is of the educational fees. In the words of Plehn, "A fee may be defined as a compulsory contribution of wealth made by a person, natural or corporate, under the authority of public power to defray a part or all of the expenses involved in some action of the government which while creating a common benefit, also confers a special benefit, or one that is arbitrarily so regarded." In short, a fee is charged for a specific service which is rendered primarily in public interest. A licence fee, however, is much more than the cost of service, and there is not much of a positive service in return.

The difference between a fee and a price is that in a fee public interest is prominent, whereas a price is a payment for a service of business character, *e.g.*, charges for travelling on State railways. You can escape the price by not purchasing a service. Price also differs from a tax. A tax is paid for a common benefit, whereas both fees and prices are paid for specific benefits.

Special Assessment is defined by Prof. Seligman as "a compulsory contribution levied in proportion to the special benefit derived to defray the cost of the specific improvement to property undertaken in the public interest." Suppose government builds a road or makes suitable drainage arrangements, all the property in the neighbourhood will appreciate in value. The State has a right to appropriate a part of this unearned increment. Special assessment is compulsory like a tax. But the tax imposed for a special purpose is called special assessment. These assessments are intended to cover a part of the extraordinary expenditure incurred by the public authority in this connection. They are levied on property proportionately to the benefit conferred.

Seligman analyses the essence of a special assessment thus: (*a*) there is the element of special purpose; (*b*) the special benefit is measurable; (*c*) these assessments are not progressive but proportional to the benefit received; (*d*) they are for specific local improvements; and (*e*) they are intended to extend and improve, as it were, the permanent plant of the community. Unlike a fee, there is an element of coercion in special assessment.

Rates. Rates are levied by local bodies, *i.e.*, municipalities and district boards, for local purposes. They are generally levied on immovable property of the residents but not necessarily for any special improvements effected or special benefits conferred. The rates generally vary from locality to locality.

Fines. Fines are imposed as a penalty for breaking the law. A fine is compulsory like a tax but it is imposed more as a deterrent than as a source of revenue.

Forfeitures. If an undertrial jumps a bail or a party to contract fails to carry his part of the contract, the money deposited is forfeited. The money so forfeited goes to the State. It is, however, a minor source.

Escheat. When a person dies heirless or without a successor or leaves no will behind, his property or assets will go to the State. This claim of the State to a deceased's assets is called escheat.

Tributes and Indemnities. These are paid by foreign countries. Tributes are paid by conquered countries and indemnities for any damage done to the country either by war of aggression or otherwise.

Government schools charge nominal fee for providing education.

Grants and Gifts. Grants are given by a government at a higher level to that at the lower level, *e.g.*, from the Central government to the State government or from the State government to a District Board, Municipality or a Corporation. These are given for a specific purpose, *e.g.*, for economic development or some public works or for public health or education.

Gifts are received either from governments of some private bodies or individuals. Gifts are sometimes received from foreign governments for relief in natural calamities like earthquake, floods, droughts, cyclones, *etc*. Donations are given by individuals for specific purposes such as building a hospital or relief fund.

CLASSIFICATION OF TAXES

Taxes have been variously classified. Some classifications are given below:

Taxes may be proportional, progressive, regressive and degressive.

Proportional Tax

A proportional tax is one in which, whatever the size of income, same rate or same percentage is charged. If all the tax payers have to pay, say one per cent of their income as tax, it is a case of proportional taxation. The same percentage is charged from all tax-payers.

Progressive Tax

If, on the other hand, the rate of the tax rises as the taxable income increases, the tax is called a progressive tax. The principle of a progressive tax is: "higher the income, higher the rate."

It is worth noting that, even under proportional tax, the richer man pays more. For example, if the rate is 1 per cent on the monthly salary, a man who is getting Rs. 500 p.m. will pay Rs. 60 per year and the man who is getting Rs. 600 p.m. will pay Rs. 72 per year. Thus, the man with the higher income pays more even under the proportional taxation. But, under progressive taxation, he will pay much more because as income increases, the rate of the tax must also increase. The man with Rs. 600 monthly salary may have to pay 2 per cent instead of 1 per cent. He will pay, therefore, Rs. 120 instead of Rs. 60 per year. All countries have adopted the progressive system of taxation, as it is considered more equitable. This is due to the fact that the sacrifice entailed in proportional taxation is less than it ought to be. We shall consider the pros and cons of progressive taxation in a subsequent section.

Regressive Tax

A tax is said to be regressive when its burden falls more heavily on the poor than the rich. It is the opposite of a progressive tax. No civilised government imposes a tax in which, as income increases, the rate of tax is lowered. That would be palpably unjust. But there are several taxes on commodities whose burden rests mainly on the poor. The Indian salt tax was regarded as a regressive tax, as it pressed more heavily on the poor than on the rich. As a matter of fact, the rich man did not feel it at all.

Degressive Tax

A tax is called degressive when the higher incomes do not make a due sacrifice, or when the burden imposed on them is relatively less. This will happen when a tax is only mildly progressive, *i.e.*, when the rate of progression is not sufficiently steep. A tax may be progressive up to a certain limit beyond which a uniform rate is charged. In that case, there will be a lower relative sacrifice on the larger incomes than on the smaller incomes.

Types of taxes	Income >1,00,000	Income >2,00,000	Income >3,00,000
	Rate of tax	....	....
Progressive	10%	18%	30%
Regressive	+ 20%	12%	5%
Proportional	10%	10%	10%

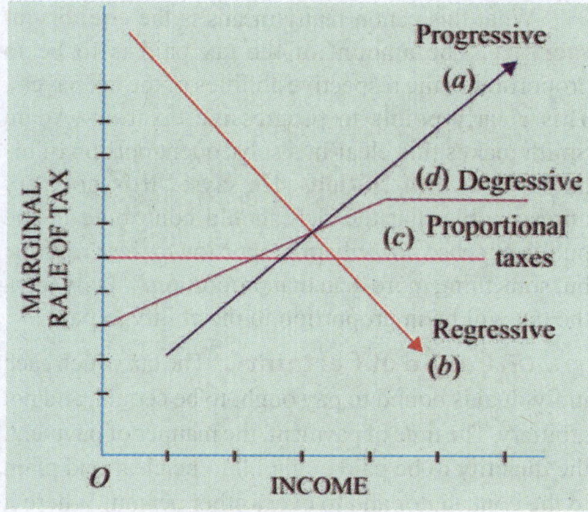

Different types of taxes.

In the above diagram on vertical axis marginal rate of tax is measured and in the horizontal axis, the size of income is measured.

(a) is progressive taxes, which shows an upword rising line.

(b) is regressive taxes, which gives a downward moving line.

(c) is proportional taxes line which is horizontal to *x*-axis.

(d) is degressive taxes which rises showly but after reaching a point it becomes horizontal to *x*-axis.

Comparison of direct and indirect taxes. [From imposition of burden point of view.]

It is said that direct taxes imposes lesser burden compared to the indirect taxes. This is due to the reason that direct taxes are paid directly by the tax payer to the government, where as indirect taxes are paid through the middleman. Hence the middleman exploit the tax-payers.

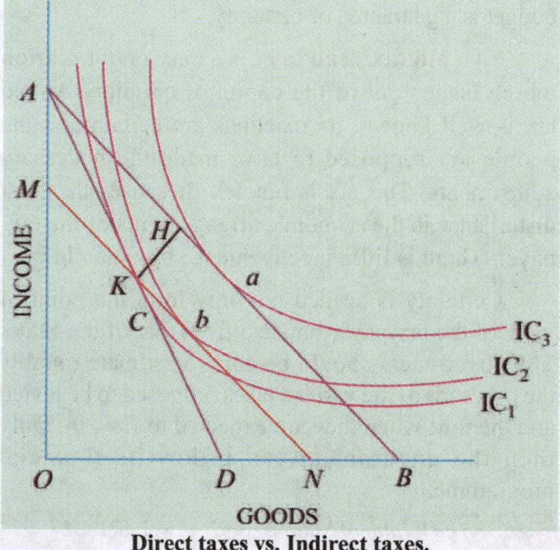

Direct taxes vs. Indirect taxes.

In the above diagram *y*-axis income is measured where as on *x*-axis the quantity of goods is measured.

(1) *AB* is the budget line and IC_3 is tangent to it at point 'a'. In '*OA*' amount of income the consumer is able to get '*OB*' amount of goods. As the consumer is on higher indifference curve, he is getting more satisfaction, compared to, when he pays taxes.

(2) '*MN*' is new budget line, as '*AM*' amount of money is taken away from the consumer by the government by means of direct taxes, due to this he is on 'IC_2'. By means of this he is getting '*ON*' amount of goods.

(3) '*AD*' budget line is due to the imposition of indirect taxes, the consumer is on IC_3, and getting '*OD*' amount of goods. Though the government is imposing or getting the same amount of revenue whether by direct taxes or indirect taxes, *viz.*, '*AM*' amount which is equal to '*KH*'.

Before taxes consumer is on 'IC_3' and getting '*OB*' amount of goods.

After direct taxes consumer is on IC_2 and getting '*ON*' amount of goods.

After indirect taxes consumer is on 'IC_1' and getting OD amount of goods.

$OB > ON > OD$

It is clear that indirect taxes gives lesser amount of goods, than direct taxes.

'*DN*' amount of less goods are obtained by the consumer due to indirect 'taxes', though the government receives the same amount of taxes *viz.*, ($AM = KH$). This is referred as the exploitation of consumer by the middleman or indirect taxes puts more burden on consumer's than direct taxes.

Direct and Indirect Taxes

Another classification of taxes is as **Direct Taxes** and **Indirect Taxes.** In the case of a direct tax, the man who pays it is also intended to bear it. But an indirect tax is expected to be shifted to other persons. If I pay income-tax, I have to bear it. I cannot pass it on to somebody else. It is a **direct tax.** But if a tax is imposed on sugar, the dealer who first pays it, charges it from the next buyer till ultimately it is borne by the consumers of sugar. The tax has been shifted. It is called an **indirect tax.**

In the case of direct taxes, as Mrs. Hicks explains, the liability varies with the circumstances of the tax-payer and the relation between the tax-payer and the revenue authorities is direct and personal. But, in the case of indirect taxes, the liability depends on the amount or value of a particular product or service bought. Here there is an indirect relation between the tax-payer and the revenue authorities, for the taxes are collected unofficially through the agency of merchants. Direct taxes are taxes on income and indirect taxes are taxes on outlay.

We shall discuss the merits and demerits of direct and indirect taxes in a later chapter (No. 64).

Specific and Ad Valorem Taxes

Taxes may also be classified as **specific** and **ad valorem taxes.** A specific tax is according to the weight of the commodity. An **ad valorem** tax is according to its value. If imposed on coarser or cheaper articles, the specific duties mean a heavier burden and are considered regressive in character. But they are simpler to administer. For the administration of ad valorem duties an elaborate administrative machinery is needed. The invoice has to be checked and a host of appraisers needed for evaluating the goods.

CANONS OF TAXATION

Adam Smith's Canons

Adam Smith's contribution to taxation part of economic theory is still regarded as classic. His statement of the canons of taxation has hardly been surpassed in clarity and simplicity. Adam Smith's canons still constitute the foundation of all discussions on the principles of taxation. We give below his four celebrated canons:

(*i*) Canon of Equality. "The subjects of every State ought to contribute towards the support of the government, as nearly as possible, in proportion to their respective abilities, that is, in proportion to the revenue which they respectively enjoy under the protection of the State."

This canon embodies the principle of equity or justice. This is the most important canon of taxation. It lays the moral foundation of the tax system. The canon of equality does not mean that every tax-payer should pay the same sum. That would be manifestly unjust. Nor does it mean that they should pay at the same rate which means proportional taxation, and a proportional tax is also not a just tax.

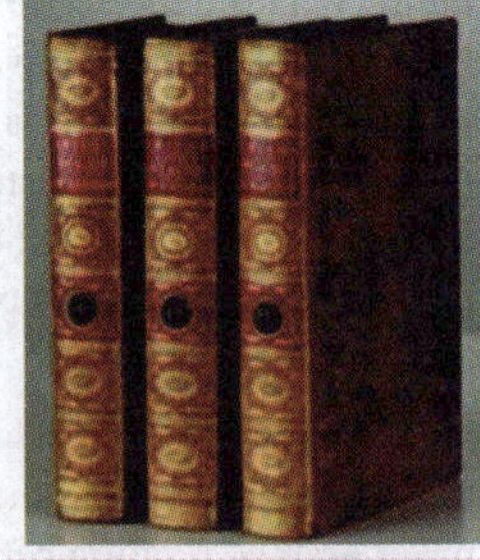

Adam Smith's "The Wealth of Nations", 1786.

What this canon really means is the **equality of sacrifice.** The amount of the tax paid is to be in proportion to the respective abilities of the tax payers. This clearly points to progressive taxation. Adam Smith makes this clear in a subsequent portion of his book **Wealth of Nations.** He says: "It is not very unreasonable that the rich should contribute to the public expense not only in proportion to their revenue but something more than that proportion."[3] Only then, the tax will be in proportion to the ability to pay.

(*ii*) Canon of Certainty. "The tax which each individual is bound to pay ought to be certain, and not arbitrary. The time of payment, the manner of payment, the quantity to be paid ought all to be clear and plain to the contributor and to every other person. Where it is otherwise, every person subject to the tax is put more or less in the power of the tax-gatherer, who can either aggravate the tax upon any obnoxious contributor, or extort, by the terror of such aggravation, some present or perquisite to himself."

Uncertainty in taxation, according to Adam Smith, encourages insolence or corruption. He regards this canon as very important, for in his view "very considerable degree of inequality . . . . is not near so great an evil as a very small degree of uncertainty." Hadley also regards it as the most fundamental canon, for, according to him, all attempts at equality will prove illusory without the taxes being certain.

The canon of certainty demands that there should be no element of arbitrariness in a tax. It is not to be left to the caprice or the sweet will of the income-tax department. The tax-payer should be able to see for himself why he is called upon pay a particular sum. That is why wide publicity is given to the budget proposals and discussions thereon. The passing of the budget is a guarantee of certainty.

"An old tax is no tax" is a maxim of taxation which issues out of the canon of certainty. An old tax is well known, its reactions are certain and the people are supposed to have made the necessary adjustments. The tax is not felt. It causes the least disturbance in the economic arrangements of the tax-payer. There is little inconvenience from an old tax.

Certainty is needed not only from the point of view of the tax-payer but also from that of the State. The government should be able to estimate roughly the proceeds of the various taxes proposed to be levied and the time when they are expected to flow in. Only then the government can follow its financial programme.

3. *The Wealth of Nations*, Book V, Vol. II, P. 327.

Income tax does not follow cannon of convenience.

***(iii)* Canon of Convenience.** "Every tax ought to be levied at the time or in the manner in which it is most likely to be convenient for the contributor to pay it."

The canon of certainty says that the time and the manner of payment should be certain. But the canon of convenience says that the time of payment and the manner of payment should be convenient. If a tax on land or house is collected at a time when rent is expected to be paid and acceptable by cheque, the manner is convenient, but not so if it is to be paid personally to the taxing authority. In the latter case, there will be a lot of inconvenience and harassment.

Taxes on consumers are very convenient. The consumer pays them when he makes purchases and at a time when he can afford to pay because the purchaser chooses his own time for purchasing. The manner is also very convenient for he has to make no special arrangement for paying a tax. He pays it when he buys the commodity. The tax is wrapped up in the price of the commodity.

The Indian land revenue conforms to the canon of convenience, because it is paid in instalments and after the harvest time. Income-tax, on the other hand, infringes the canon of convenience. The assessee has to take his account books to the income-tax officer in order to satisfy him about the accounts. This necessitates a series of personal interviews with consequent loss of time. It also involves a lot of trouble and oppression.

But land revenue conforms to cannon of convenience.

***(iv)* Canon of Economy.** "Every tax ought to be so contributed as both to take out and to keep out of pockets of the people as little as possible, over and above what it brings into the public treasury of the State."

One implication of the canon of economy is very obvious. The tax is economical if the cost of collecting it is very small. If, on the other hand, the salaries of the officers engaged in collecting the tax take away a big portion of the tax revenue, the tax is certainly uneconomical. As far as possible, as much should come into the State treasury as is taken out of the people's pockets. Nothing should evaporate in the way. If there is corruption or oppression involved in the frequent visits to the income-tax office and the odious examination by the taxing officer, the canon of economy is not satisfied.

But the tax should also be economical in another, perhaps broader sense. It would infringe the canon of economy, if it retarded the development of trade and industry in any manner. If incomes are subjected to a very heavy tax, saving may be discouraged, capital will not accumulate and the productive capacity of the community will be seriously impaired. This would obviously be uneconomical. A tax is economical if it does not hamper in any manner the economic progress of the country.

Taxes on harmful drugs and intoxicants are regarded as economical, because they not only bring income to the State, but also discourage unproductive expenditure. But taxes on raw materials are uneconomical because they raise the price of the manufactured goods and weaken the competitive power of the industry. Also, every middleman goes on adding something to the tax that he has paid.

The first canon of Adam Smith is ethical and the other three are administrative in character.

Other Canons

Since Adam Smith wrote, the science of Public Finance has continued to grow. Subsequent writers have added canons of their own to his four canons. The following are some of those which have been subsequently added:

***(v)* Fiscal Adequacy or Productivity.** The State should be able to function with the revenue raised from the people by means of taxes. The government should be free from financial embarrassments. It will be necessary, therefore, that the tax proceeds should adequately cover the government expenditure and the government does not run into a deficit. But the government should also not err on the side of excess. In their zeal to raise more revenue, they should not cripple, in any manner, the productive capacity of the community or impair the economic resources of the country.

The canon of productivity would indicate that a few taxes bringing a large revenue are better than many taxes each bringing a very small revenue. Too great a multiplicity of taxes is to be avoided, because each tax is likely to cause some vexation to the citizens. But here again, we must warn that the principle of concentration should not be carried to excess, otherwise it may become either uneconomical or inequitable.

***(vi)* Elasticity.** The canon of elasticity is closely connected with that of fiscal adequacy. As the needs of the State increase, the revenue should also increase otherwise they will cease to be adequate. To meet an emergency or a period of stress and strain, the government should be in a position to augment its financial resources. Some of the taxes should be capable of yielding more if need be. Income-tax is a very good example of an elastic tax. By raising the rate a bit or by levying a surcharge, the yield from income-tax can be considerably increased.

***(vii)* Flexibility.** The canon of flexibility looks like that of elasticity but the difference between the two is quite clear. Flexibility means that there should be no rigidity in the tax system so that it can be quickly adjusted to new conditions, and elasticity means that the revenues can be increased. Unless the system is flexible, the revenue cannot be increased, for alterations will not be possible. Thus, presence of flexibility is a condition of elasticity. If a tax system cannot be altered without bringing about a revolution, it lacks flexibility.

The Permanents Settlement of Bengal (1793) is an example of rigidity or lack of flexibility in a tax. Under this arrangement, the Government bound itself to collect the same sum from the land-owners in perpetuity. The lack of flexibility was, in no small measure, the cause of the financial troubles of Bengal.

***(viii)* Simplicity.** In the words of Armitage Smith, "A system of taxation should be simple, plain and intelligible to the common understanding." This canon is essential if corruption or oppression is to be avoided. If a tax is complicated so that the tax-payer cannot understand how much he is to pay and why he is to pay it, a great power will pass into the hands of the tax-gatherers. The door will be widely opened to corruption and oppression.

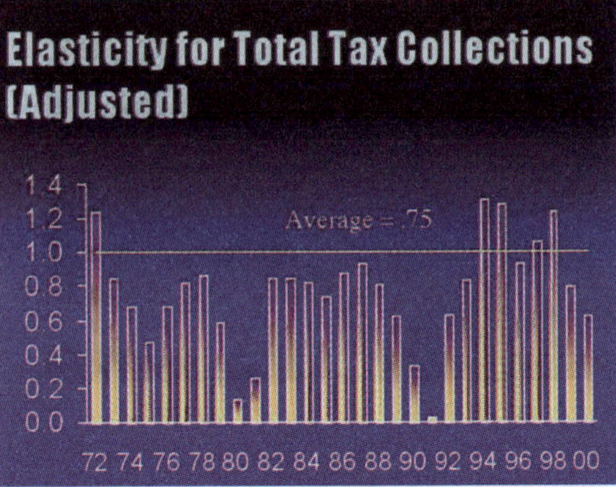

Tax Elasticity of the state of Tennessele USA (1972-2000).

***(ix)* Diversity.** Another important principle is that of diversity. A single tax or only a few taxes will not do. There should be a large variety of taxes so that all the citizens, who can afford to contribute to the State revenue, should be made to do so. They should be approached in a variety of ways. There should be a wise admixture of direct and indirect taxes. In this manner, the canons of fiscal adequacy and equity may be better satisfied. But too great a multiplicity will be bad and uneconomical.

***(x)* Achievement of Social and Economic Objectives.** Considering the role that taxation is called upon to play in modern times, another principle is being emphasized, *viz.*, that the effects of taxation should be compatible with the economic and social objectives that the community has placed before itself and with the institutions and processes considered essential for the attainment of these objectives.

The neutrality principle or 'leave-them-as-you-find-them' principle no longer holds the field. The taxation policy today has to be more positive. It is intended to bring about economic stability and development besides the attainment of other political and social goals. In conjunction with economic controls and monetary measures, taxation has to be freely used to combat threats of economic instability and stagnation by means of a "managed compensatory fiscal programme."

It was Adolph Wagner, a German economist, who in his book **Finanzwissenschaft,** published in 1880, developed a "social compensatory or social political theory of taxation" for the purpose of reducing economic inequalities. The application of this theory can be seen during the depression dilemma of the 'thirties and during and after the Second World War when taxation was used as a tool for fighting inflation.

Several other considerations have been put forward. It is recommended, for instance, that a tax should fall on revenue and not on capital. It should not cut down the minimum subsistence of the tax-payer, and so on.

SOCIAL AND ECONOMIC OBJECTIVES OF TAXATION

Among the social and economic objectives of taxation, the following principal ones may be mentioned:

(*a*) Reduction of Inequalities in Income and Wealth. One of the main objectives of taxation is to reduce, if not to remove, inequalities of income and wealth. For this purpose, steeply progressive taxes must be levied on the affluent sections of society. This is the trend in all democratic countries.

(*b*) Accelerating Economic Growth. Another important objective is to accelerate economic growth. For this purpose, the tax system must be so designed as to raise the rates of saving and investment. This is a very important objective for developing economies like India. But in the developed economies, during periods of depression, the aim is to increase consumption and reduce saving so that aggregate demand may increase and remove depression, and the prevailing unemployment may diminish. On the contrary, when there is inflation, the objective of taxation policy is to reduce consumption (*i.e.*, to increase saving) so that aggregate demand may diminish and price rise is checked.

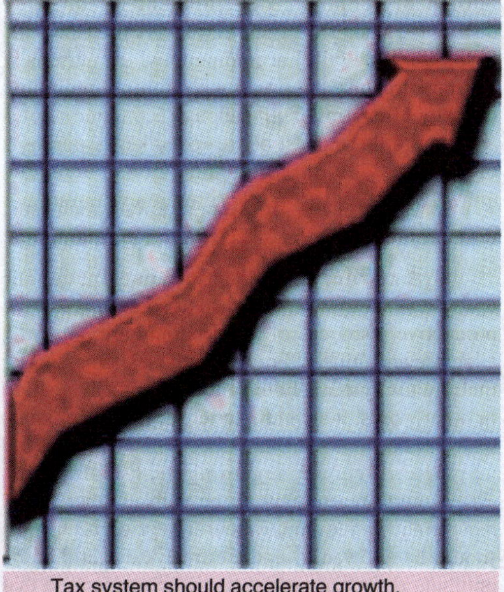

Tax system should accelerate growth.

(*c*) Price Stability. In under-developed countries, there is another objective that the tax system has to achieve, *viz.*, price stability to ensure growth with stability. When these countries launch economic development programme they have to face the problem of inflation or soaring prices. They should follow an integrated tax policy to solve this problem.

Objectives in a Developing Economy

A dominant aim of under-developed countries is to accelerate economic development. This calls for a rational reorganisation of their tax system on the basis of the concept of functional finance. The tax policy of such countries is to be attuned to the raising of resources required for development. In the developed countries the aim is to ensure economic stability and to avoid economic fluctuations. But the aim in the under-developed countries is to ensure rapid economic growth, and taxation is to be used as an instrument of economic progress. Accordingly, the under-developed economies must ensure collective savings (raising the ratio of savings to national income) through taxation, because in such countries saving is not practised voluntarily. But mere saving is not enough; the savings must be invested.

Thus the tax policy must strengthen incentives to savings and investment. The traditional canons of taxation developed in the West will not serve the purpose. The under-developed countries have to act on different canons.

Take the case of the canon of 'ability to pay'. In the realm of theory of taxation, this canon still enjoys pride of place among the canons of taxation. This is favoured because it leads to progressive taxation and results in reduction of inequalities. But the question of reduction of inequalities must be taken up separately keeping in view the requirements of a developing economy. From the point of view of development, taxation is not to be viewed as solely a contribution to meet the costs of common services rendered by the State. It is to be viewed rather as a powerful tool to raise the rate of investment in the economy.

The following few canons of taxation may be suggested as more appropriate to a developing economy:

(*i*) Ability to Contribute to Economic Development. Each person should be made to contribute to economic development, according to his ability to do so. All his unused capacity must be utilised, through appropriate tax measures, for

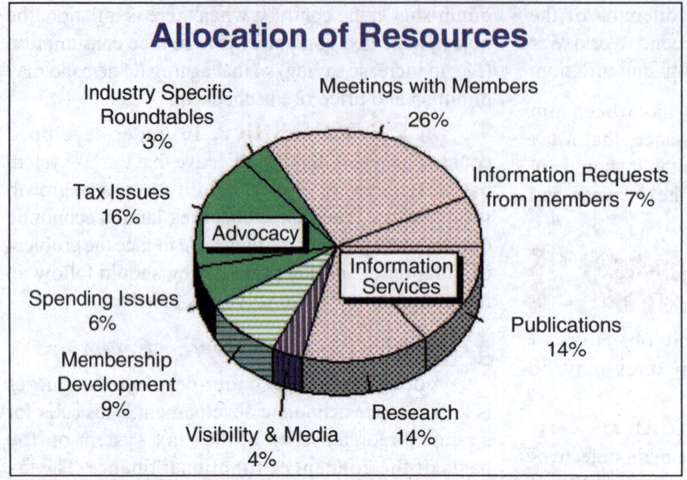

Chart showing allocation of resources of california, USA.

incomes. Thus, taxation must also mobilise **any** increase in economic surplus accruing to individuals. For achieving this purpose commodity taxes are quite effective.

(*iv*) Income Elasticity of Taxation. In backward economies, the share of taxation out of the national income is less than 10 per cent. This share must be progressively raised as national income increases as a result of economic development. This needs built-in flexibility in the tax system. Progressive taxation of incomes provides this flexibility. Taxation of goods having a high income-elasticity of demand also imparts to the tax system much needed flexibility.

purposes of economic development. Suppose a person is making a large saving but he lets it lie idle. Such saving must be mobilised and channelised into investment. The Compulsory Deposit Scheme (later replaced by Annuity Deposit Scheme) in India and Cumulative Time Deposit in post offices promote this purpose. If a person's income exceeds what is required to maintain his efficiency and incentive (*i.e.*, willingness and ability to work and save), this excess must be taken away and used for economic development, of course on reasonable compensation.

(*ii*) Mobilization of Economic Surplus. In all backward economies, a significant proportion of national output goes to the big landlords and the other idle rich or propertied people. A large portion of their income is spent on conspicuous consumption, *e.g.*, building of palaces, *etc*. This is unproductive expenditure and a waste from the point of national development. Economic growth can be accelerated if an appreciable portion of this 'surplus' income is mobilised and made available for productive investment.

Hence, an important canon of taxation in a developing economy is the mobilisation of economic surplus generated in the various sectors of the economy.

(*iii*) Increasing the Incremental Saving Ratio. As economic development proceeds apace, incomes rise. But there is a danger that propensity to consume may also increase so that extra incomes generated in the economy are utilised in consumption rather than invested in production. This has to be prevented. In other words, consumption is not to be allowed to increase in proportion to increase in

(*v*) Equity. The canon of equity demands that the burden of economic development must be distributed among the different sections of the community equitably. That is why the richer classes are prevented from increasing their consumption in proportion to the rise in their incomes. This is how they make a sacrifice for the economic development of their country. The poor people also make a sacrifice because rising prices curtail their consumption. In this manner, sacrifices in consumption are shared by all sections of the people. Thus, the burden of economic development is equitably distributed among all. There is what is called the **'rule of horizontal equity'** according to which persons in similar circumstances and with similar economic behaviour (in terms of utilisation of economic surplus accruing to them) must be treated alike for purposes of taxation.

These are a few of the principles which must underlie the tax system of a developing economy.

Optimum Allocation of resources. The tax system should be so framed as to ensure that the productive resources of the economy are optimally allocated and utilised. For this purpose, it is essential that the tax system should be economically neutral. In other words, it should interfere as little as possible with the consumers' choices for consumption goods and the producers' choices regarding the use of factors. The owners of factors should be enabled to seek their most remunerative employment. The price mechanism should be allowed to operate freely so that there is optimum output of goods. It can be understood that the imposition of a tax leads to diversion of resources from the taxed to the non-taxed sector. This reallocation of resources may be a departure from the optimum utilisation of resources. Hence, the nature of the taxes and the rate of taxes should be such as to ensure optimum utilisation of resources.

Above all, the tax system should conform to the principle of maximum social advantage so that the society as a whole is benefited to the maximum extent possible.

Conclusion

It may, however, be emphasised in conclusion that no tax system in the world can satisfy all the criteria of a good tax system mentioned above. Some of the objectives conflict with one another, whereas others are complementary. For instance, too high progressiveness in the tax system may reduce inequalities but they may also reduce national output and employment by damaging productive efficiency. Similarly, protective import duties may promote industrial development but they may reallocate productive resources in such a manner as to depart from the optimum. The best thing to do is to adapt the tax system to the prevalent economic situation and to make it conform to aims and objectives considered most desirable under the circumstances.

Evaluation of the Indian Tax System

According to Kaldor, who was invited to report on the Indian tax system, there are three main considerations that should be taken into account in framing an effective tax system, *viz.*, **equity, economic effects, administrative efficiency.**

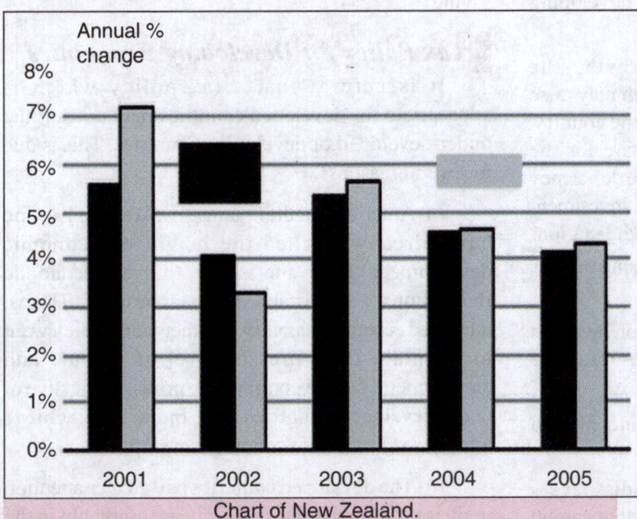

Chart of New Zealand.

From the point of view of equity, the most important consideration is that the tax system should not contain a systematic bias in favour of particular groups of tax-payers and against others. From the point of view of economic effects of taxation, the major consideration is to prevent the tax system from becoming too much of a disincentive on effort, initiative or enterprise. From the point of view of administrative efficiency, all loopholes for evasion should be plugged and the main requirements are: simplicity and comprehensiveness embracing all forms of beneficial receipts, a single comprehensive return, self-checking system of taxation and an automatic reporting system.

According to Kaldor, the present system of direct taxation in India is, however, both inefficient and inequitable. It is inequitable because the present base of taxation, *i.e.*, income, as defined in law, is defective and is capable of being manipulated by certain classes of tax-payers. It is inefficient because of the possibility of large-scale evasion on account of the limited information furnished by tax-payers and on account of the absence of any comprehensive reporting system on property transactions and property income.

Kaldor made proposals which aimed at broadening the tax base through the introduction of an annual tax on wealth, a tax on capital gains, a general gift tax, and a personal expenditure tax. All these five taxes were to be assessed simultaneously on the basis of a single comprehensive return and they are self-checking in character so that concealment or understatement of income from certain items will involve an added liability with regard to others. He says that it is far better to have a foolproof system of taxation with a moderate rate schedule than a system which has the appearance of high progressivity, but which cannot be effectively or impartially administered.

Judged from the point of view of economic development, however, the tax effort in India has been quite satisfactory. The ratio of savings to national income has been going up. It has been estimated that 25 per cent of the increase in incomes (*i.e.*, marginal savings rate) has been saved which is quite commendable. The investment has been going up by leaps and bounds as from one five-year plan to another. The second plan outlay was more than double of the first and the third more than double of the second and the fourth plan more than the three earlier plans combined.

ROLE OF TAXATION IN DEVELOPING ECONOMIES

For under-developed or developing countries, it is very essential to have an appropriate taxation policy, if economic growth is to be accelerated. In the absence of a suitable tax policy, the rate of economic growth is bound to be tardy. In modern times, the aim of public finance is not merely to raise sufficient financial resources for meeting administrative expenses, for maintenance of law and order and to protect the country from foreign aggression. On the other hand, the sphere of public finance has been very much extended. It is now considered a powerful instrument in the hands of the State for the achievement of important economic and social objectives. The most important objective before these countries is to accelerate their economic growth.

The under-developed countries, like India, are caught up in the vicious circle of poverty. Consequently, such countries are not able to save much, whether we consider individual savings or collective savings by corporations and firms. Their annual savings are only a small fraction of their national income. In India, the rate of domestic savings has been projected to grow from 12.2% of G.N.P. in 1973-74 to 15.7 per cent in 1978-79. In the same period, the rate of investment is expected to rise from 13.7 per cent of G.N.P. in 1973-74 to 16.3 per cent of G.N.P. in 1978-79. But our annual rate of growth has been round about 3 per cent. This means that a much greater tax effort is called for to raise our growth rate to a reasonable level. Since private savings and capital formation are meagre in India, the responsibility of resource mobilisation for economic growth falls on the State. That is why the role of public finance in developing countries is very important.

For accelerating economic growth, the government has to adopt a tax policy which may raise the rates of saving and capital formation in the country. Since private investment is not adequate for the purpose, the government has to make up the deficiency of private investment by increasing public investment and for that purpose raise resources through taxation.

There are several advantages of increasing savings and investment through taxes:

(a) Taxation is the only effective weapon by which private consumption can be curbed and thus resources transferred to the State.

(b) Through taxation inequalities in income and wealth can be reduced.

Since developing countries like India have a mixed economy, care has also to be taken that capital formation and investment in the private sector is not discouraged. The primary objective of tax policy is, therefore, to promote investment both in the private and public sectors. Taxation policy is to be directed to raising the ratio of savings to national income. Hence, such taxes should be levied as encourage savings and investment. If the people do not make savings out of their increasing incomes, then the government should take away from them a part of their income through taxes and invest it in development programmes. In other words, taxes result in forced saving.

TABLE : Gross Doemstic Saving and Gross Domestic Capital Formation in the Indian Economy

(Rs. crores at current prices)

	Gross Domestic Saving (1)	*Net Capital Inflow (2)*	*Gross Domestic Capital Formation (3 = 1 + 2)*
1950-51	887 (8.9)	-21 (–0.2)	866 (8.7)
1960-61	1,989 (11.6)	481 (2.8)	2,470 (14.4)
1970-71	6,649 (14.6)	394 (0.8)	7,043 (15.4)
1980-81	27,136 (18.9)	2,094 (1.4)	29,230 (20.3)
1990-91	1,31,340 (23.1)	16,196 (3.2)	1,49,536 (26.3)
1995-96	2,98,747 (25.1)	20,780 (1.8)	3,19,527 (26.9)
1999-00	4,66,640 (24.1)	21,988 (1.1)	4,88,628 (25.2)
2000-01	4,91,761 (23.4)	12,977 (0.6)	5,04,738 (24.6)
2001-02	5,49,963 (24.0)	4,872 (–0.3)	5,45,091 (23.7)

Note: Figures in brackets are percentages of GDP at market prices.

SOURCE: Central Statistical Organisation and ***Economic Survey (2002-03)***.

Tax Policy for Developing Economies

It is natural that a tax policy which is appropriate for developed countries may not suit the under-developed or developing countries. This is due to several reasons:

(a) America and the countries of Western Europe have already reached the height of economic development. Their aim is now to avoid economic fluctuations, *i.e.*, ups and downs in business. That is, they need economic stability. In other words, they want to maintain their present level of income and employment. On the contrary, the primary objective of under-developed countries, like India, is to achieve a higher standard of economic development.

(b) The developed countries pay greater attention in their tax policy to ability to pay or equity; but in the

under-developed countries more attention is given to the amount of revenue raised and practicability.

(*c*) The governments in developed countries generally pursue the policy of laissez-faire in economic matters. On the other hand, the governments in developing countries have to intervene to make sure that the productive resources, are utilised in strategic or key industries and in other essential economic activities.

(*d*) Whereas, the objective of developed countries is to reduce inequalities in income and wealth distribution, the primary objective of the developing countries is to accelerate economic growth.

Hence, under-developed countries should not borrow or imitate the tax policies adopted in the developed countries.

It does not follow from the low per capita income of the under-developed countries that the rate of savings must also necessarily be low. Even in under-developed countries, there are many rich people like big industrialists, big landlords and owners of vast urban property. They enjoy large incomes out of which sizable savings can be made. But since these savings generally seek investment in jewellery and real estate, they are not utilised for economic development. If these economic surpluses are mobilised through taxation and used in productive investment, economic development can be accelerated beyond doubt.

If an economy enjoys an economic surplus after satisfying consumption needs, it can be expected to develop economically. Economic surplus is the difference between current output and essential consumption. Some countries waste this surplus in unproductive consumption, *e.g.*, maharajas building palaces. In agriculturally predominant countries such surpluses go into the hands of big zamindars, sahukars and big businessmen, who have no experience of utilising them for productive investment. The bulk of their wealth is squandered in marriages and house building. It is the task of the tax policy of a developing country to mobilise the economic surplus, direct it into productive investment and enlarge it.

So far we have referred to direct taxes. Now let us take indirect taxes. In under-developed countries, indirect taxes occupy a relatively more important position than direct taxes. We have to see how these taxes should be levied so that they not only yield revenue to the State but also ecourage investment in economic development programme. The question is whether commodities of mass consumption should be taxed or not. It is argued that the incomes of poor people are already very low; hence these commodities should not be taxed. But this argument is not valid. Such taxes have great importance for economic development, because only by means of these taxes, increase in consumption can be checked as incomes increase and thus saving can be increased which can be used in economic development.

Indirect taxes promote economic development in three ways:

(*i*) They check consumption of luxuries and use the saving so made for economic development;

(*ii*) they mobilise resources for public sector investment; and

(*iii*) they increase the savings ratio.

For the achievement of these objectives taxation is used for (*a*) diversion of resources from private the to public sector, (*b*) diversion from consumption goods industries to investment goods industries, and (*c*) diversion of demand for import goods to export goods.

The Theory of Tax Structure Development

It is common knowledge that tax structure has undergone changes from time to time. The theory of tax structure seeks to explain changes in tax structure of an economy over time under the impact of economic development and of political and social factors.

To take economic development first. Tax structure is affected by economic development in three ways: (*a*) Tax base undergoes a change as the developmental process proceeds; (*b*) change in tax base brings about changes in the revenue system: and (*c*) Economic development leads to changes in the objectives of tax policy.

Changes in Tax Structure Under The Impact of Economic Development

Earlier Stages of Development. In the beginning we find that these countries are predominantly agricultural and have a slender industrial base. But since agriculturists have low taxable income, it is difficult to reach this sector through income taxation. As regards the industrial sector, since the manufacturing base is thin, the effective tax has to be confined to large-scale establishments.

At this stage following guidelines are indicated: (1) There should be inter-locking of taxes to ensure better tax compliance. That is, a tax on income should be accompanied by expenditure tax and wealth tax. And there should be simultaneously an estate duty and gift tax. (2) There should be a system of fines and penalties for tax evasion and under-reporting. There should be adequate administrative devices to minimise opportunities of tax evasion. Greater emphasis should be put on commodity taxes because they cannot be evaded. New tax bases like foreign trade sector should be tapped.

Calculating tax collections.

Changes in the Later Stages of Development. As a result of economic development, there are three distinct changes in the tax structure: (*a*) Since the economy becomes monetised, a broader tax base becomes available as a large volume of output and income pass through the market.

(*b*) There is a wider scope for indirect taxation as consumption and exchange of commodities increases.

(*c*) As economic development takes place, there is improvement in the accounting practices of businessmen making for better assessment of business incomes and taxation. Taxation of incomes becomes more efficient and effective.

Inspite of these improvements, the tax-structure suffers from two serious drawbacks: In the first place, the tax system suffers from the weakness of administrative machinery. As the scope for taxation becomes wider tax collection becomes more complicated. Multiplicity of taxes creates legal and institutional problems from the variety of ways in which incomes are received and outlays made. For instance, estate duty and gift tax give rise to many technical problems. In the early stages of economic development, the problem was how to assess an "elusive herd of cows," but in the later stages the problem is how to assess an "elusive flow of capital". Devices like holding company, trust arrangements, etc. add to the difficulties of the tax administration.

As for social and political factors affecting the development of tax structure, we might say that under feudalism property was an ideal base for taxation. As feudalism gave place to modern capitalism, property as a base for taxation was relegated to the background and its place was taken by income as a base for taxation. Under a predominantly agricultural economy, land taxes were supreme. But as trade and industry developed, sales and excise duties occupied a pride of place. Under the impact of social philosophy, equity started bothering the taxation authorities.

Key terms

Tax Revenue, Non-tax revenue, Direct tax, Indirect tax, Progressive tax, Regressive tax, Proportional tax, Cannons of taxation, Tax Structure, Indian tax system.

QUESTIONS

1. Distinguish between progressive and proportional taxation. Examine the limitations of progressive income taxation in an under-developed economy.
2. Examine the basic principles of progressive taxation and their impact on saving and investment.
3. What do you mean by Progressive Taxation? How can it help in ensuring the equitable distribution of national income?
4. Discuss the effects of taxation and public expenditure on the production and distribution with special reference to a developing country.
5. Outline a tax policy designed to promote the economic development of an under-developed country.
6. Do you agree that indirect rather than direct taxation will provide large public revenue needed in a developing economy.
7. Discuss the various cannons of taxation and explain their importance in a tax-system.

PROBLEM OF EQUITY

"It is equitable that people in the same economic position should be treated in the same way for purpose of taxation." But how to measure economic position? In order to achieve the ideal of justice in taxation several principles have been suggested. We examine some of these principles below:

Cost of Service Principle

It is said that it would be just if people are charged the cost of the service rendered to them. However equitable it may appear to be, 'the cost of service principle' cannot be applied in actual practice. The cost of service of the armed forces, police, *etc.*,—the services which are rendered out of tax proceeds—cannot be exactly determined. We have to calculate how much it costs to render a service to the particular tax-payer.

We know that in case of taxes there is no direct quid pro quo to the tax-payer. Hence, the question of ascertaining the cost of service to an individual tax-payer does not arise. Only in those cases, where the services are rendered out of prices, *e.g.*, supply of electricity, railway or postal service, a near approach can be made to charging according to the cost of service. Even here the exact cost cannot be ascertained, and for fixing the charges, we have to fall back on the principle of "charging what the service will bear."

The cost of service principle, therefore, must be rejected as being impracticable.

Benefit or 'Quid Pro Quo' Theory

It is suggested that the taxes should be levied according to the benefit conferred on the tax-payers. But on grounds similar to those mentioned above, the benefit theory also breaks down when an attempt is made to give it a practical shape. Most of the public expenditure is incurred for common or indivisible benefits. It is impossible to calculate how much benefit accrues to a particular individual. There are a few cases only where the benefit to the individual is ascertainable, *e.g.*, old-age pensions. Applied to this case, the theory would demand a refund of the pension itself, for that precisely is the measure of the benefit. Nobody would seriously put forward such a proposal. It is, therefore, impossible to ask the people to contribute according to the benefits received by them.

Quid-Pro-Quo.

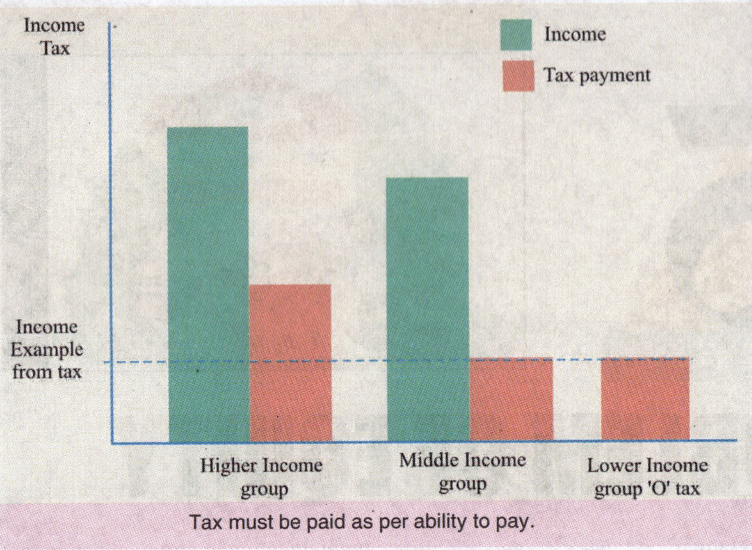

Tax must be paid as per ability to pay.

'Ability to pay' or Faculty Theory

The most popular and the plausible theory of justice in taxation is that every tax-payer should be made to contribute according to his ability or faculty to pay. The tax is to be based on his taxable capacity. Nothing would appear to be more just. But the acceptance of the principle does not mean the end of our difficulties; rather the difficulties begin. The question which we then face is: 'What is the measure of a man's ability to pay?'

Several other objections can be raised against the Benefit Theory. It is against the basic principles of the tax. A tax is paid for the general purposes of the State and not in return for a specific service. The Benefit Theory can have meaning only if we think of the benefit to the community as a whole. But this is obviously useless for the purpose of taxing the individual. If you want to make some exceptions you will be in a difficulty. On what basis will you make the exceptions?

Moreover, it is commonly believed that the poor benefit more from the State activities than the rich. If that is so, then to apply the 'Benefit Theory' would mean making those people pay who cannot afford to pay and letting off those who can and who should. This would be absurd.

In the words to Plehn, "Common benefits are the peaceful enjoyment of life, liberty and property." So far as life and liberty are concerned, the benefit of State protection is the same for all. This would indicate a uniform tax, say a poll tax. But poll tax has been long discarded on account of its relatively small yield and greater cost and botheration of collection. If we take protection of property as the basis, then it should be proportional tax, proportionate to the capital value or the income yielding capacity of the property. But proportional taxation has also been rejected in modern times as being less than just. We cannot, therefore, take benefit as a criterion of justice.

The Benefit Theory has, however, a place in all modern tax systems. The idea of benefit stands out prominently in the case of fees, licences, special assessment and local rating.

In the search for a proper criterion of a person's ability to contribute to the State exchequer, we can proceed on two lines, subjective and objective:

Subjective Approach. If we examine the position of the tax-payer in its subjective aspect, we shall consider the inconvenience, the pinch or the sacrifice involved. On this point, three distinct views have been advanced: (*a*) The Principle of Equal Sacrifice; (*b*) The Principle of Proportional Sacrifice; and (*c*) The Principle of Minimum Sacrifice.

In the words of J. S. Mill, "Equality of taxation, as a maxim of politics, means equality of sacrifice. It means apportioning the contribution of each person towards the expenses of government, so that he shall feel neither more nor less inconvenience from his share of the payment than every other person experiences from his.[1] According to this principle, the money burden of taxation is to be so distributed as to impose equal real bur den on the individual tax-payers. This would mean proportional taxation.

According to the principle of **proportional sacrifice,** the real burden on the individual tax-payer is to be not equal but proportional either to their income or the economic welfare they derive. This would be more just than if the sacrifice involved were equal. Those who can make a greater sacrifice should be asked to do so. This would mean progressive taxation.

The **minimum sacrifice principle** considers the body of tax-payers in the aggregate and not individually. According to this principle, the total

1. '*Principles of Political Economy*', Book V, II, p. 2.

real burden on the community should be as small as possible.

In the words of Edgeworth, the chief exponent of the theory of minimum aggregate sacrifice, "The minimum sacrifice is the sovereign principle of taxation. If one is a utilitarian and believes not only in the measurability of utility but also in the view that the law of diminishing marginal utility is applicable to money also, then this principle would involve a high level of minimum exemption and a very steep progression as income increases. This is because if we assume that marginal utility of money falls as income increases, then money has less marginal utility to the rich than to the poor. And assuming that a given tax revenue is to be collected, it would involve least aggregate sacrifice if the tax revenue were to be collected from the people in the higher income brackets. The less the aggregate sacrifice the better the distribution of the tax burden in the community. The State exists to maximize human welfare. This it will be able to do by minimizing the sacrifices involved."

Cohen-Stuard and Edgeworth developed the following three distinct features of equal sacrifice.

(1) Equal Absolute Sacrifice:– The Principle of equity is based on "ability to pay approach". The burden of tax on the tax payer's must be the same, in other words.

$U(Y) - U(Y - T)$ must be same for all

Here Y = Income

T = Tax

U = Utility

$U(Y)$ = Pre-tax utility of income

$U(Y - T)$ = Post-tax utility of income

(2) Equal Proportional Sacrifice:– Under this the burden is same for all but it is taken in proportion to their income.

$\therefore \quad \dfrac{U(Y) - U(Y - T)}{U(Y)}$. Only difference between equal absolute sacrifice and equal proportional is that we take only the difference between the pre-tax income satisfaction, but in the case of equal proportional we divide it by the pre-tax income satisfaction.

$$\therefore \quad \frac{\text{Equal absolute sacrifice}}{\text{Pre-tax income satisfaction}}$$

(3) Equal Marginal Sacrifice:– In this concept, the marginal utility or satisfaction derived after the payment of tax must be same for all.

In this we take the first order derivative of $U(Y - T)$.

$\therefore \quad \dfrac{dU(Y-T)}{d(Y-T)}$ is equal for all the individuals.

Let us explain all these three concepts with the help of the following diagram.

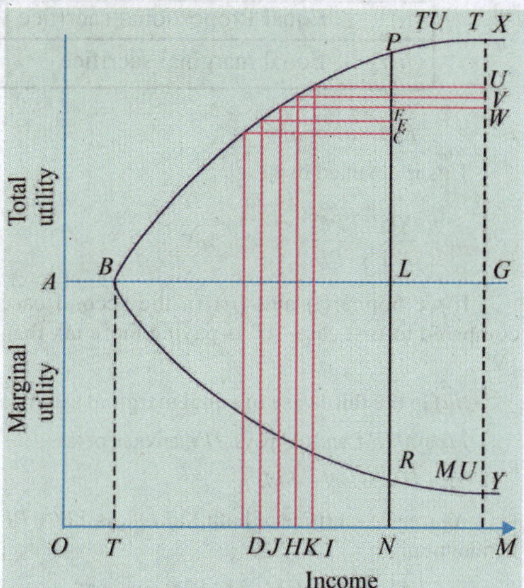

Equal-Absolute, Proportional and Marginal Sacrifice.

In the above figure on *x*-axis income is measured and on y-axis upto '*OA*' is marginal utility and from above '*A*' total utility is measured. '*AB*' amount of income is exempted from tax or it is subsistence income, beyond this income tax will be imposed. '*BX*' is total utility curve and '*BY*' is marginal utility curve. Let us assume that tax payer '*M*' has '*TM*' amount of income and tax payer '*N*' has '*TN*' amount of income.

'*M*' is getting '*GX*' amount of total utility

'*N*' is getting '*LP*' amount of total utility

M is getting '*MY*' amount of Marginal utility

N is getting *NR* amount of Marginal utility.

Now let us assume that the government imposes income tax which yields '*SM*' amount of tax revenue. In case of (*i*) equal absolute sacrifice, '*M*' will pay '*IM*' amount of tax and '*N*' will pay '*DN*' amount of tax.

$$\therefore \quad IM + DN = SM$$

The amount of *IM* and *DN* we get and the loss of total utility of M is '*XU*' and that of '*N*' is '*PC*'.

$$(\therefore \quad XU = PC).$$

(*ii*) In the second case that is equal proportional tax.

M pays '*KM*' and '*N*' pays '*JN*'.

		Amount of tax payed		Total
		By	By	Tax yield
	Tax Payers →	M	N	SM
(*i*)	Equal absolute sacrifice	IM	DN	SM
(*ii*)	Equal Proportional sacrifice	KM	JN	SM
(*iii*)	Equal marginal sacrifice	HM	HN	SM

$\therefore \quad KM + JN = SM$

This is obtained by

$$\frac{XV}{XG} = \frac{PE}{PL}$$

If we notice (*i*) and (*ii*) In the second case compared to first case '*M*' is paying more tax than '*N*'.

(*iii*) In the third case of equal marginal sacrifice *M* pays '*HM*' and '*N*' pays '*HN*' amount of tax.

$\therefore \quad HM + HN = SM.$

Aggregate sacrifice of both '*M*' '*N*', is $XW + PF$ is minimum.

$\therefore \quad IM > KM > HM.$ for '*M*' tax payer.

$\therefore \quad DN > JN > HN$ for '*N*' tax payer

Objective Approach. We must, therefore, take our second line of approach to measure a man's ability to pay, that is, proceed objectively. Here we are on surer grounds. But here again, we find that several criteria have been suggested. A man's ability to pay may be measured according to (*a*) consumption, (*b*) property, or (*c*) income.

Consumption, as a criterion of ability to pay, is not a sound criterion, because consumption or utilisation of the services of the State by the poor is considered to be out of all proportion to their means, and, as such, it cannot be taken as a practical principle of taxation.

Property also cannot be a fair basis of taxation, for properties of the same size and description may not yield the same amount of income; and some persons having no property to show may have large incomes, whereas men of large property may be getting small incomes. Thus, to tax according to property will not be taxation according to ability.

Income, however, remains the single best test of a man's ability to pay. But even in the case of income, the tax will be in proportion ability, if there is a minimum exemption to allow for a reasonable subsistence, if there is an allowance made for the number of dependants, and, finally, if the principle of progression is applied by taxing the rich at a higher rate.

Besides, we have to consider 'the ability to pay' not merely of the individual tax-payer but of the community as a whole. In this light, it is necessary that the tax system as a whole is not oppressive. It should not discourage saving or retard accumulation of capital. Also, it should not, in any manner, impair the productive capacity of the community by hampering the development of trade and industry in the country.

Summing up. This is the solution of the problem of justice in taxation. The ends of justice are not served by applying the cost of service principle or by taxing according to benefit, but according to faculty or ability to pay. The ability to pay cannot be judged subjectively by the amount of sacrifice involved, but objectively according to the man's income and not according to his consumption or property. What is intended is that the tax system as a whole should be equitable. Each individual tax may not be absolutely just or equitable. The inequity of one tax may be neutralised by the equity of another. "There may be inequity in the parts but equity in the whole."

It is said that equity is a matter of opinion. There is no generally accepted definition of equity. It is, in the words of Dalton, "an elusive mistress whom perhaps it is only worth the while of philosophers to pursue ardently and of politicians to watch warily."

PROPORTIONAL VS. PROGRESSIVE TAXATION

In our discussion of the various theories of a fair distribution of the tax burden, we have almost invariably been led to the conclusion that there must be some degree of progression, wherever possible, in a tax.

Case for Proportional Taxation

There have been advocates of proportional taxation. McCulloch's well-known remark is typical of the attitude of the nineteenth century. He said: "When you abandon the plain principle (of proportion) you are at sea without rudder and compass and there is no amount of injustice you may not commit." J. S. Mill was even more emphatic. He said: "A graduated income-tax was an entirely unjust mode of taxation and, in fact, a graduated robbery." According to him, progressive taxation was a step towards confiscation.

Case Against

According to the principle of equality of sacrifice, proportional taxation could be justified only on the assumption that the marginal utility of income decreases slowly as income increases. But this assumption is not correct. If we keep in view the principle of proportional sacrifice, then the proportional tax can be justified only on the assumption that as income increases, the marginal utility of income does not at all decrease. This assumption is absurd, because when income increases, its marginal utility must decrease. Hence, proportional taxation can be justified neither on the principle of equality of sacrifice nor on the principle of proportional sacrifice.

Proportional taxation will entail equal sacrifice, whereas sacrifice itself should be proportional to the tax-payer's capacity. Proportional taxation is, therefore, not equitable. Furter, it is also not sufficiently productive. Moreover, the element of arbitrariness even in proportional taxation is not altogether absent.

Hence, the theory of proportional taxation has been abandoned generally so far as direct taxation is concerned and, wherever possible, the principle of progressive taxation has been adopted instead.

Case for Progressive Taxation

The principle of progressive taxation is justified on the following grounds:–

(i) It is argued that as income increases, the utility of each addition to the income decreases. Hence, the payment of the tax by the rich entails much less sacrifice than by the poor. The rich people should, therefore, pay tax at high rates.

(ii) It is further argued that as income increases the expenditure on luxuries tends to increase, whereas necessaries are more important than luxuries from the point of view of economic welfare. It follows, therefore, that by taxing the rich more, we only compel them to cut down luxuries. The sacrifice so entailed is not as great as the benefit to the poor on whom the tax proceeds may be spent.

(iii) Progressive taxation yields much greater revenue and hence it is more productive. It is very difficult to see how modern governments can balance their budgets today in the absence of the principle of

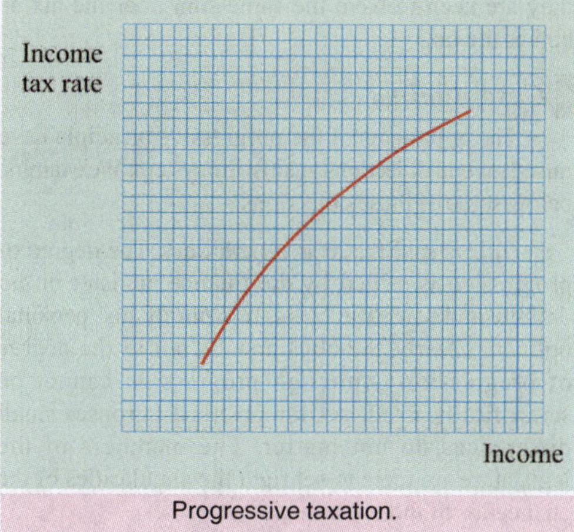

Progressive taxation.

progression.

(iv) Progressive taxation is more economical and equitable. The cost of collection of the taxes does not increase when the rate of the tax increases. About the equity of progressive taxation there can be no question. It calls forth a proportional sacrifice from the tax-payers. It places the heaviest burden on the broadest shoulders.

(v) The principle of progression gives to the tax system much-needed elasticity or flexibility. When there is an emergency, only a little raising of the rates may be sufficient to meet the situation.

(vi) The maintenance of law and order by the government benefits the rich much more than the poor. It enables the rich to make much more money. It is only proper, therefore, that they pay taxes at progressively higher rates.

(vii) Progressive taxation promotes economic stability and checks cyclical fluctuations. Progressive taxes mop up the purchasing power in the hands of the people. In this way, they ease inflationary pressures. In a deflationary situation, on the other hand, the amount of tax paid would fall as income falls and a much larger proportion of income may be left in the hands of the tax-payer to be spent. This would arrest the deflationary tendency. Hence, progressive taxes are contra-cyclical.

(viii) Progressive taxes are badly needed for reducing economic inequalities and for bringing about more equitable distribution of wealth in the community. It would curb the luxurious living of the rich which is resented by the poor, who cannot have even basic necessities of life.

(ix) Progressive taxes may increase the desire to work, save and invest on the part of the rich because

they are keen to have the same sum after the tax as before the tax.

Case Against

The opponents of the progressive principle have raised several objections against the system. We examine below some of these objections:–

(i) It is said that it is all arbitrary. The degree of progression is settled by the finance minister on no definite and scientific basis. It is purely his personal opinion. Clearly, the objecti0on is not to the degree of progression. Although progression cannot be scientifically fixed, yet for practical purposes small differences do not matter. The members of the legislature are there to set right the angularities of the chancellor of the exchequer.

(ii) It is pointed out that the principle of progression cannot be advocated on the ground of promoting welfare, because welfare is subjective and cannot be measured. There is no scientific apparatus to test whether welfare has increased consequent on reduction of inequalities of income. The rich are perhaps vexed more than the poor are comforted.

(iii) Again, it is said that progression will discourage saving, drive out capital and thus hamper trade and industry. It will, in short be uneconomical. But such dire consequences will follow only if the rate of progression exceeds the limits of reason and expediency. This has seldom been the case. Capital is not so sensitive as it is supposed to be.

(iv) The principle of progression is said to break down on scientific grounds. Its fundamental assumption that the same income measures the same satisfaction is not at all valid. Further, the law of diminishing marginal utility may not hold good in the case of money. "Money," they say, "does not represent one good, but goods in general; and since human wants in general are unlimited, it may be questioned whether the wealthy person does require the additional pounds less and less. It may even be that his desire for additional income increases as his income increases. Such may be the case when an increase in income causes the possessor to move into a higher social circle, and so bring about an extension in his necessary wants."[2]

But Robbins regards the use of the principle of diminishing marginal utility in this field as entirely illigitimate and unscientific.[3] Marginal utility being subjective cannot be ascertained by observation. As Robbins says, "There is no means of testing the magnitude of *A*'s satisfaction as compared with *B*'s .... Introspection does not enable *A* to measure what is going on in *B*'s mind, nor *B* to measure what is going on in *A*'s." In progressive taxation, we assume that persons with same income derive equal satisfaction therefrom. But we cannot prove that this assumption rests on ascertainable fact because satisfaction cannot be measured. "It would be rather silly," says Robbins, "if we continued to pretend that the justification of scheme of things was in any way scientific." Although on scientific grounds, the argument is unanswerable, but progression can be advocated equally strongly on ethical and political grounds.

Taxable capacity.

(v) Investments which are risky but which yield rich harvest are discouraged because the proportion of tax increases as income increases. Reduction of investment will reduce the level of income and employment in the country.

(vi) Progressive taxes put premium on idleness and leisure since they penalise those who work hard and make more money. It amounts almost to graduated confiscation of rich man's income.

(vii) It is said that progression will lead to taxevasion. But the possibility of evasion in proportional taxation is not less. It all depends on the social conscience.

Conclusion

Progressive taxation, whether it can be scientifically justified or not, is ethically sound, socially desirable and it conforms to the canons of equity, economy, productivity and elasticity. This principle has been universally adopted in all tax systems.

TAXABLE CAPACITY

The concept of taxable capacity had racked the brains of not a few economists and publicists. Dalton calls it "a dim and confused conception," He says,

2. Thomas, S.E.—*Elements of Economics*, 1936, p. 332.
3. Robbins, L.—*The Nature and Significance of Economic Science*, 1931, Ch. VI.

"Absolute taxable capacity is a myth and should be banished from all serious discussions on Public Finance." To the question whether taxable capacity can be measured, he thinks Cannan's 'No-how' is the best answer. Findlay Shirras, on the other hand, thinks that it is of great practical importance. "It is always wise and useful," he says, "for a government to know even roughly the limit that the country can contribute by way of taxation both in the ordinary and extraordinary circumstances." He goes on: "The necessity in post-war finance especially of balancing budgets heavily laden with public debt of short maturity, has made the question of absolute taxable capacity a real and an abiding problem of taxation."[4]

Meaning

The term taxable capacity can be used in two senses:

(i) in the absolute sense, and

(ii) in the relative sense.

The absolute taxable capacity has been variously defined. It means how much a particular community can pay in the form of taxes without producing unpleasant effects. Relative taxable capacity, on the other hand, means the respective contribution which the two communities should make towards a common expenditure, *e.g.*, provincial contribution to Central expenditure. Dalton says the former is a myth and the latter a reality. The relative limit may be reached without reaching the absolute limit, *i.e.*, we may have reached the limit of how much a particular community should contribute without reaching the limit beyond which it possibly cannot contribute.

Absolute Taxable Capacity

There are two extreme views about absolute taxable capacity: (*a*) the capacity to pay without suffering, and (*b*) the capacity to pay regardless of suffering. In the former sense, taxable capacity is practically nil, for every tax must entail some suffering. In the latter case, there is practically no limit to taxable capacity except the one imposed by the extent of the resources of the community.

Sir-Josiah Stamp defines taxable capacity as "the margin of total production over total consumption, or the amount required to maintain the population at subsistence level." This means the utmost that a community can pay "without having a really unhappy down-trodden existence and without dislocating the organisation too much."

Findlay Shirras defines absolute taxable capacity

as "the maximum amount which the citizens of a country can contribute towards the expense of the public authorities, without having to undergo an unbearable strain. Briefly, taxable capacity is the limit of squeezability . . . . It is the taxation of a nation, the minimum amount of taxation of a nation, the maximum amount of taxation that can be raised and spent to produce the maximum economic welfare in that community."

These definitions lack scientific precision and have an element of vagueness. Sir Stamp's "level of subsistence" and "unhappy downtroden existence" and Shirras's "unbearable strain" and "maximum economic welfare" cannot be scientifically defined and laid down in exact terms. This, however, does not detract from the practical importance and the utility of the concept of taxable capacity. The meaning conveyed by the definitions given above is fairly clear, although we must admit that any attempt to measure the taxable capacity is foredoomed to failure. Cannan's 'No-how' is really the correct answer.

Limit of Taxable Capacity

Views also differ as to what are the symptoms to show that taxable capacity has been exceeded. Sir Stamp mentions two limits: (*a*) the check to total production, and (*b*) the check to total revenue yield. But the check may be due to causes other than excessive taxation. Taxation is not the only factor that affects production. Ellinger thinks that "the limits would be reached when so much is taken out of the tax-payers' pockets that the incentive to produce is reduced, and when insufficient remains to provide the necessary capital to make up for wastage and to set to work new workers in an increasing population." He obviously ignores the beneficent effect of public expenditure on production.

Factors Governing Taxable Capacity

The fact is that the taxable capacity is not rigidly fixed. It is a moving point. It is relative to so many factors that any change in any of them is bound to change our estimate about the taxable capacity of a nation. Findlay Shirras gives the following factors which determine the taxable capacity of a nation:

4. *Science of Public Finance*, 1936, p.227.

(i) **Number of Inhabitants.** It is quite obvious that the larger the population the greater is the taxable capacity of the community to contribute towards the expenses of the government. From this point of view, India is well placed. Its taxable capacity will infinitely increase when the country is economically developed.

(ii) **Distribution of Wealth.** If wealth is more equally distributed, the table capacity will be correspondingly reduced. But if there are large accumulations of wealth in a few hands, the government can raise more money by taxing the rich.

(iii) **Method of Taxation.** A scientifically constructed tax system with a wise admixture of the various types of taxes, direct and indirect, is sure to bring a larger yield. The Indian tax system is not much diversified; there are no taxes on large agricultural incomes. This certainly reduces the taxable capacity.

(iv) **Purpose of Taxation.** If the purpose of taxation is to promote welfare of the people, they will be more willing to tax themselves. For a popular cause, the people will be willing to stretch their capacity to the utmost. If the government proceeds to raise money for fighting famine, disease or for spread of education, there will be a surprising expansion in the yield of taxes. But if the bulk of the public funds is to be spend on the maintenance of foreign armed forces and for the upkeep of a costly civil service, the case in India, the taxable capacity must correspondingly shrink.

(v) **Psychology of Tax-payers.** Much depends on the people's attitude towards a government. A popular government can galvanise the spirit of the people and prepare them for a greater sacrifice. An appeal to patriotism is often the cause of the success of a financial measure. This is what makes war loans successful. Psychology of the people is an important factor, and unless they are properly approached, they may be unwilling to tax themselves.

(vi) **Stability of Income.** If the income of the citizens is precarious, there will be not much scope for further taxation. The vagaries of the monsoons in India account for a lower taxable capacity. It is only on stable incomes that long-term financial arrangements can be based.

(vii) **Inflation.** It lowers the purchasing power of the people and it cripples many; it has an adverse effect on taxable capicity.

(viii) **Level of Economic Development.** The level of economic development attained by a country is an important determinant of its taxable capacity. Undoubtedly, all highly developed countries of the world have greater taxable capacity than the under-developed countries.

(ix) Taxable capacity in a country also depends on political conditions prevailing at the time. Political stability relieves businessmen of all worries and uncertainty. It provides a congenial climate for the blossoming of variegated economic activity. On the other hand, political upheavals sap all business activity and hence adversely affect taxable capacity.

Conclusion

All these factors must be taken into account before we can have an idea about the taxable capacity of a nation. It may be that on account of the multiplicity of the factors influencing taxable capacity, we cannot measure this capacity. But this does not mean that the attempt is useless. The interest lies in the journey itself rather than in the destination. As Findlay Shirras puts it, "A road leading to an important centre has often many crossings, signposts, danger signals, but this does not lessen its value to the cautious sojourner."[5]

A Further Note on Case for Progressive Taxation

We have already discussed the case for and against progressive taxation. We should like to add a further note on the case for progressive taxation.

The terms 'proportional', 'progressive' and regressive refer to the relation between the tax rate and the tax base. But a sales tax is typically a proportional tax because the rate is the same whatever the tax base. It is, however, regressive when it is related to the buyer's income because rich and poor shall be paying at the same rate. Thus a tax may be proportional with regard to the tax base but regressive with respect to income.

The case for progressive taxation rests on the grounds of (*a*) revenue productivity, (*b*) optimum allocation of the tax burden, (*c*) promotion of stability and growth and (*d*) optimum allocation of resources.

For Revenue Productivity. The rising requirements of the State for providing social goods need a large revenue to meet them. The government cannot increase the rates of proportional taxation because that would press heavily on the poor. Obviously, the new rate increase must be concentrated on the rich people. Hence the only way to raise more revenue with less out-cry is to resort to progressive taxation.

For Optimum Allocation of Tax Burden. Marginal utility principle is helpful in this connection. It is as applicable to income as to goods. It is obvious that paying one additional rupee as tax from a large income is less burdensome than giving up a marginal rupee of a small income. In other words, if we want to equalise tax burdens, we should take a larger number of rupees from a large income than from a small income.

5. *Op. cit.*, 1936, p. 31.

For Promoting Growth and Stability. A progressive tax has an automatic counter-cyclical effect. As income rises, marginal income pushes into higher brackets, raising both the marginal and average tax rates on these incomes. It is obvious that with progressive rates, taxes rise and fall more rapidly than income, whereas the proportional rates change the tax in proportion to income. Progression thus has the maximum counter-cyclical effect. It may also be noted that this effect is automatic and immediate and does not require any legislation. It may be clearly understood that this automatic reaction is not the result of progression in tax rates but because income is the tax base. Since individual income tax is progressive, it is regarded as an effective instrument reacting favourably, quickly and strongly in the interest of economic stability.

For Optimum Allocation of Resources. Progressive taxation can also be justified on the ground that it brings about optimum allocation of community's resources. Certain goods are considered preferable to others. It is therefore necessary that the community's resources should be allocated to the production of certain goods which are considered worth while rather than to others, while may be trivial or unimportant. Social judgement is substituted for individual preference in order to select goods which are preferable. It can be assumed that large incomes are preferable. It can be assumed that large incomes are more likely to be utilised in the satisfaction of trivial wants than small incomes. There is thus a case for heavier taxation of large incomes. In this way, progressive taxation can be used as an instrument for redistribution of income and resources in the community for achieving social objectives.

Conclusion. The diminishing marginal utility argument may not be very scientific but it is broadly correct. And the case for progressive taxation on the ground of revenue productivity, compensatory use and redistribution of community's resources is clear and strong. Nobody now seriously questions the validity and necessity of progressive taxation. If there is any difference of opinion, it is only about the degree of progression.

Key terms

Ability-to-pay, Equal absolute sacrifice, Equal marginal sacrifice, Equal proportional sacrifice, Taxable capacity.

QUESTIONS

1. What are the principles of taxation? Explain the difficulties involved in following these principles in practice.
2. Define tax. What are the characteristics of a good tax system?
3. What is the significance of "equity" in the principles of taxation? How is equilty introduced in a tax system?
4. "Expenditure is a better index of ability of pay than income". Elucidate.
5. "The principle of equity necessarily implies least aggregate sacrifice for scociety". Discuss.
6. What do you understand by the Principle of Minimum Sacrifice? What is its usefulness and application in the thoery of taxation?

66 CHAPTER

INCIDENCE OF TAXATION

Meaning of Incidence

The problem of the incidence of a tax is the problem of who pays it. Taxes are not always borne by the people who pay them in the first instance. They are sometimes shifted on to other people. Incidence means the final resting place of a tax. Thus, incidence is on the man who ultimately bears the money burden of the tax.

New Concept of Incidence. To determine as to who bears the money burden of the tax is the conventional meaning of incidence. Some modern economists like Ursula Hicks and Musgrave have introduced a new concept of incidence. According to this new concept, incidence means the changes brought about in income distribution by changes in the budgetary policy, *i.e.*, changes both in taxes and public expenditure. The difference between the traditional concept and new concept may be carefully noted. In the conventional sense, incidence refers simply to the money burden of a tax but the new concept refers to distributional changes resulting both from taxation and public expenditure.

Impact and Incidence. We may distinguish between impact and incidence. The impact of a tax is on the person who pays it in the first instance and the incidence is on the one who finally bears it. If an excise duty is imposed on sugar, it is paid in the first instance by the sugar manufacturer; the impact is, therefore, on him. But the duty will be added to the price of the sugar sold, which, through a series of transfers, will ultimately fall on the consumer of sugar. The incidence is, therefore, on the final consumer.

Incidence and Effects. The term 'incidence' should be distinguished from the effects of taxation. The effect of a tax refers to incidental results of the tax. There are several consequences of the imposition of tax which are quite distinct from the problem of incidence. The imposition of an excise duty on sugar, we have seen, is shifted ultimately to consumer of sugar. The incidence is on the consumer.

But the effects of this duty may be far-reaching; a heavy excise duty may cripple the industry. The manufacturer's profits will be reduced. Wages may be reduced. Labour and capital may have to leave the industry. Thousands of middlemen engaged in the distribution of sugar may find their earnings reduced. Reshuffling of their family budgets may affect the demand for certain other goods. The consumption of sugar may decrease and that of its substitutes may increase. All these are the effects of the tax. It is a much wider problem as distinguished from the incidence which is a narrow and a special problem of finding who bears the money burden of the tax.

Incidence of tax—Who ultimately pays the tax.

Money Burden and Real Burden. We may also distinguish between the money burden of a tax and its real burden. The money burden of a tax is represented by the total amount of money received by the treasury. If a consumer has to spend Rs. 5 more per month on the sugar consumed by him on account of the levy of a duty on sugar, it is the money burden that he has to bear. But he may have reduced the consumption of sugar which may mean a reduction of his economic welfare. He may have to pinch in the consumption of some other commodities too. **This pinching, inconvenience, sacrifice, or, in short, loss of economic welfare is the real burden of the tax.** In incidence, we are concerned with the money burden and not the real burden.

Importance of Incidence

The study of incidence is very important. A tax system is not merely aimed at raising a certain amount of revenue, but the aim is to raise it from those sections of the people who can best bear the tax. The aim, in short, is to secure a just distribution of the tax burden. This obviously cannot be done unless an effort is made to trace the incidence of each tax. We must know who pays it ultimately in order to find out whether it is just to ask him to pay it, or whether the burden imposed on him is according to the ability of the tax-payer or not. If the tax system is to conform to Adam Smith's first canon of taxation, *viz.*, the canon of equality, it becomes imperative to make a careful study of the reactions and repercussions of each tax and find out its final resting place.

There are certain taxes, called direct taxes, which are borne by the people who pay them first. The incidence in such cases is apparent. But the tax system of a country is not merely composed of direct taxes. There are indirect taxes also, whose reactions are a complicated affair. These taxes are intended to be shifted. But in actual practice, on account of economic friction, the shifting may not take place at all or it may be partial, or the tax may be shifted on to a class of people quite different from those intended to bear it.

If Public Finance is to serve as an instrument of social justice, the question of incidence at once assumes great importance. The rich have to be taxed and the proceeds have to be spent for the benefit of the poor. If we have to tax the rich, the incidence must be on the rich, otherwise the object is not served. We must, therefore, follow each tax and make sure that it finds a rich home to rest in.

Direct tax is paid by the person on whom it is imposed.

Factors Determining Incidence

It would appear that the incidence of a tax or where its ultimate burden rest, depends on a number of factors. We give below some of them in a summary way:

(*i*) Elasticity. While considering incidence we consider both elasticity of demand and elasticity of supply. If the demand for the commodity taxed is elastic, the tax will tend to be shifted to the producer but, in case of inelastic demand, it will be largely borne by the consumer. In case of elastic supply, the burden will tend to be on the purchaser and in the case of inelastic supply on the producer.

(*ii*) Price. Since shifting of the tax burden can only take place through a change in price, is a very important factor. If the tax leaves the price unchanged, the tax does not shift.

(*iii*) Time. In the short-run the producer cannot make any adjustment in plant and equipment. If, therefore, demand falls on account of price rise resulting from the tax, he may not be able to reduce supply and may have to bear the tax to some extent through loss of profit resulting from a fall in demand. In the long period, however, full adjustment can be made and tax shifted to the consumer.

(*iv*) Cost. Tax raises the price; rise in price reduces demand and reduced demand results in the reduction of output. But a change in the scale of production affects cost and the effect will vary according as the industry is decreasing, increasing or constant costs industry. For instance, if the industry is subject to decreasing cost, a reduction in the scale of production will raise the cost and hence price shifting the burden of the tax to the consumer.

(*v*) Nature of the Tax. A tax, for instance, on surplus of windfall will tend to remain where it is levied.

(*vi*) Market Form. Under perfect competition, no single producer or single purchaser can affect the price; hence shifting of the tax in either direction is out of the question. But under monopoly, a producer is in a position to influence price and hence shift the tax. Incidence of a tax on monopoly will be discussed in detail shortly.

DIRECT AND INDIRECT TAXES

Distinction between the Direct Taxes and Indirect Taxes

We have said before that the question of incidence is very simple in the case of a direct tax, because the impact and the incidence are on the same person. But, in the case of an indirect tax, the impact is on one person and the incidence on another. A direct tax is not intended to be shifted, whereas an indirect tax is so intended .The question of incidence, therefore, really arises in the case of indirect taxes.

Taxes on commodities are generally called indirect taxes, for they are ultimately shifted completely or partially into the consumers, whereas they are first collected from the dealers or producers. But we should remember that the mere fact that a tax is a commodity tax does not make it an indirect tax. A tax can be called an indirect tax, if its burden can be shifted and this happens when its price is affected by the tax. It is just possible that the commodity may be taxed, yet its price may remain unaffected. In this case, the consumer is not touched, and the tax will be called direct and not indirect, even though it is a tax on a commodity.

A lump-sum tax imposed on a monopolist or a as a percentage of monopoly net revenue is not shifted, while a monopoly tax in proportion to the output tends to be shifted. In the former case, it will be a direct tax, and in the latter it will be indirect. The inheritance tax is commonly considered a direct tax. It falls on the successor and it tends to stay there. But the predecessor, while he was alive, may have taken an insurance policy to cover the amount of the tax. In this case, it imposes an indirect money burden on him. Income-tax, again, is a direct tax but in exceptional cases a part of it may be shifted. To that extent it will become an indirect tax.

We may thus conclude by saying that we cannot draw hard and fast lines between taxes which are direct and those which are indirect. The distinction between the two types is settled by the question whether the tax has been shifted or not. If it is shifted, it is indirect, otherwise direct.

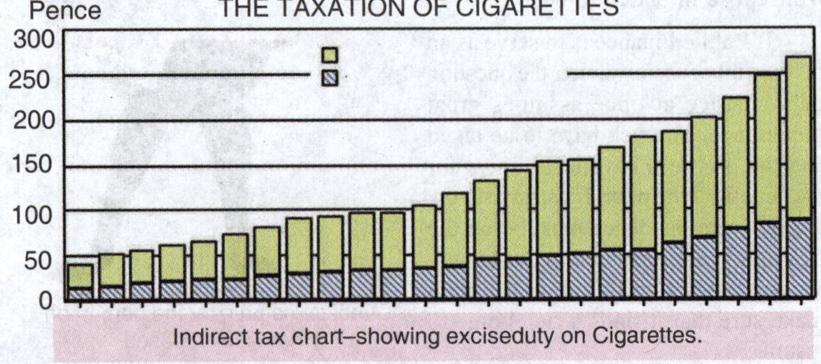

Indirect tax chart–showing exciseduty on Cigarettes.

Relative Merits and Demerits of Direct and Indirect Taxes

We compare these two forms of taxes not with the object of choosing whether we should have the one or the other. No country relies exclusively on one type . . Both direct and indirect taxes are needed to make up an equitable and adequate tax system. "I can never think," said the great Scotsman, "of direct and indirect taxation except as I should think of two attractive sisters who have been introduced into the gay world of London, each with an ample fortune, both having the same parentage—for the parents of both I believe to be Necessity and Invention—differing only as sister may differ . . . ." However, direct taxes are better in some respects and indirect taxes in some other respects.

Merits of Direct Taxes

The following merits are claimed for direct taxes:–

***(i)* Equitable.** Direct taxes are more equitable as progression can be applied to them. The rate of the tax is varied to make the tax conform to the ability to pay.

***(ii)* Economical.** They are economical as the cost of collection is small. There being no intermediary between the tax-payer and the State, no part of the tax evaporates in transit.

***(iii)* Certain.** The yield of direct taxes can be calculated with a fair degree of precision. The tax-payer is also certain of the amount that he has to pay.

***(iv)* Elastic.** Direct taxes have a high degree of elasticity. Income-tax has remarkably responded to the enormously enhanced needs of the State of defence and development.

***(v)* Civic Consciousness.** They create a civic consciousness among the tax-payers. A man who pays a direct tax feels that he is contributing towards the State expenditure. He is expected to take keener, interest in civic affairs.

(vi) Reduction of Inequalities. Progressive taxes are used as an instrument for the reduction of economic inequalities. The rich persons are called upon to pay taxes at a higher rate so that the gulf between the rich and the poor is narrowed down. However, economic inequalities cannot be reduced by taxes alone. Public expenditure should also be so directed as to benefit the poor more than the rich.

Demerits

The following are the chief demerits of direct taxes:

(i) Inconvenient. Direct taxes are very inconvenient to pay. Every tax-payer feels the pinch. The tax has to be paid in a lump sum; the filling of returns is a complicated affair; and there is a lot of harassment.

(ii) Unpopular. Direct taxes are very unpopular. Nobody likes to pay them. To part with money is not an easy thing especially when there is no direct quid pro quo.

(iii) Evasion. They can be easily evaded and the State defrauded of its due. That is why, it is said that a direct tax is a tax on honesty.

(iv) Arbitrary. The direct taxes are arbitrary in the sense that the rates of taxes are fixed arbitrarily by the government. The rate could as well be different. The rates are not determined on any scientific principle. A leftist government will fix higher rates and a rightist government lower rates. It is all arbitrary.

Merits of Indirect Taxation

Some advantages of indirect taxes are given below:

(i) Convenient. An indirect tax is convenient. We pay the tax when we buy a commodity, and at a time when we can afford it. It is paid in small trickles rather than in a lump sum. 'Many people prefer to be taxed in the dark.' The tax-payer does not feel than he is paying it. The tax is wrapped in the price of the commodity he buys.

(ii) No Evasion. It is very difficult to evade an indirect tax, because it is mixed up with the price of the commodity one purchases.

(iii) Equitable. Indirect taxes can also be made more equitable by being imposed on articles generally consumed by the rich. That is why luxuries are generally taxed at a higher rate.

(iv) Elastic. When imposed on necessaries of life or articles for which the demand is inelastic, indirect taxes are also fairly elastic. They can, therefore, be varied according to the State needs.

(v) Beneficial Social Effects. Indirect taxes have a beneficial social effect in that the consumption of harmful drugs and intoxicants can be discouraged by means of such taxes.

(vi) Capital Formation. Indirect taxes are levied on the consumption of commodities. In this way, consumption is reduced. The savings so made can be invested in some productive employment.

(vii) Re-allocation of Resources. Taxation of some commodities will discourage their production. The resources used in their production may be utilised in the production of more desirable commodities. In this way, resources devoted to the production of luxuries can be diverted to the production of goods required by the masses.

(viii) Wide Coverage. Indirect taxes can be levied on a large number of commodities. In this way, larger sections of consuming public can be made to contribute to the public exchequer. In India, the tax net of central excise duties is being spread wider and wider.

(ix) Productive. Since they can be given a wide coverage, indirect taxes can be very productive. It is the Indian experience that Union excise duties and sales tax have yielded a very substantial revenue and have become the mainstay of the respective governments.

(x) Reduce Disincentiveness of Direct Taxation. Since indirect taxes have proved very productive of revenue, it has obviated the necessity of steeply progressive direct taxation which would have been very disincentive of saving and investment.

Demerits

The following are some of the disadvantages of indirect taxes:

(i) Uncertain. Indirect taxes are uncertain. It is not always possible to anticipate the various repercussions of a tax imposed on a commodity. A finance minister cannot precisely calculate the estimated yield of a tax.

(ii) Regressive. They are regressive. Every consumer of the taxed commodity, rich or poor, pays the tax at the same rate. Therefore, the real burden of the tax on the poor is greater than on the rich. If the tax is imposed on the necessaries of life, its regressive character is accentuated. According to Engel's Law of Consumption, the bulk of a poor man's income is spent on necessaries of life. The poor man pays the tax, therefore, on almost all his income, while the rich man pays it on a relatively smaller portion of the income spent on necessaries of life.

(iii) No Civic Consciousness. Indirect taxes do not develop any civic consciousness in the tax-payer, because nobody feels that he is paying a tax as it is concealed in price.

(iv) Uneconomical. Although the shopkeeper is considered an unpaid tax collector, yet it is though that the cost of collection of certain indirect taxes is very heavy. In the case of customs duties, a highly-paid staff of customs officials, appraisers, raiding parties to prevent smuggling have to be engaged. These taxes are uneconomical in another way as well. The taxed commodity passes through a number of middlemen and each middleman ads something to the tax, so that the final consumer pays much more than what the State receives.

(v) Inflationary. The indirect taxes have one serious danger especially in developing countries, *viz.,* they contribute to the inflationary pressures in the economy. Every tax levied on a commodity must inevitably raise its price and if prices are already rising, it feeds inflation.

(vi) Evasion. Certain of the indirect taxes are easily evaded. For example, excise duty on manufactured goods are collected at the factory gate when the goods roll out. But one cannot be sure that all goods going out actually pay the duty for there may be leakages. Similarly, if a tax is levied on the farm products, the portion consumed by the grower escapes taxation.

(vii) Loss of Economic Welfare. Taxation on commodities raises their price. But in case of goods produced under the conditions of the law of increasing returns (or decreasing cost), the price rises more than the cost. In this case, the consumers suffer and the community suffers a loss of economic welfare.

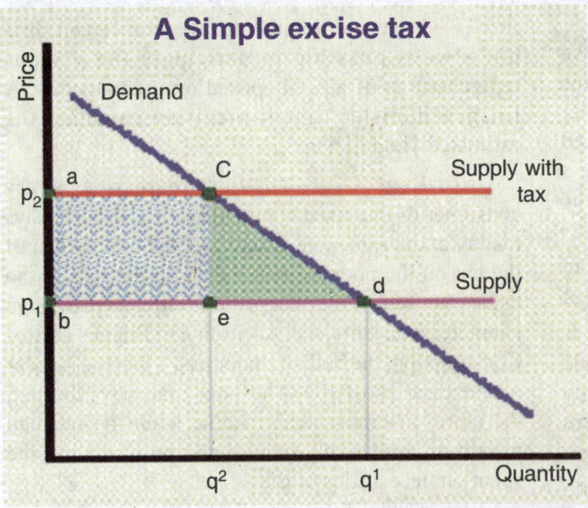

Social loss of taxation is measured by area ced.

Conclusion. The distinction between direct taxes and indirect taxes is not of much practical importance. We cannot assume that the entire burden of direct taxation falls on the rich and that of indirect taxation on the poor. Indirect taxes, like taxes on luxuries, fall on the rich and not on the poor. It is, however, generally true that direct taxes like inheritance tax and income-tax and super-tax fall exclusively on the rich. In a good tax system, we must have a proper balance between direct and indirect taxation. One corrects the other. Indirect taxation relieves exclusive pressure on the rich and makes the system of taxation broad-based. Thus, the two taxes are complementary, A good tax system has a goodly proportion of both types.

ROLE OF INDIRECT TAXATION IN A DEVELOPING ECONOMY

Indirect taxes have to play a very important role in a developing economy. This is due to the fact that owing to general poverty and low level of G.N.P. or low individual incomes, the scope for direct taxes is limited or their yield is comparatively very low. For instance, in India wealth tax, death duties, gift tax, *etc*., do not yield much. Hence, greater and greater reliance has to be placed on indirect taxes. No wonder that range of Union excise duties in India is becoming wider and wider every year. Indirect taxation has proved to be a very potent weapon of resource mobilistion. They raise the rate of investment by curtailing consumption and raising the incremental ratio of saving.

The developing countries have to rely more on indirect taxes for the following main reasons: In the first place, low levels of income in the under-developed countries provide only a limited scope for direct taxation, *e.g.*, income tax and wealth tax. The tax net can be spread much wider through commodity taxation. Even commodities of universal consumption can be taxed to raise adequate revenues.

Secondly, Indirect taxation is specially important from the point of view of economic growth on which such countries have set their heart. To accelerate economic growth, the rates of saving and investment must be raised sufficiently. This cannot be done without curtailing consumption and in these countries propensity to consume is notoriously high. Duesenberry's Demonstration Effect' operates very sharply. To tax commodities is the only effective way of putting curbs on consumption and release funds for productive investment.

Thirdly, Indirect taxation also transfers the growing agricultural surplus from the rural to the urban areas by taxing the farm sector and by checking consumption on the part of the newly prosperous farmers.

In the words of Taxation Enquiry Commission, "For any substantial receipts from commodity taxation and appreciable restraints on consumption in the economy as a whole, it will be necessary to extend excise and sales taxation to the consumption of lower income groups and of goods which are commonly classed as necessaries."[1]

The basic objective is to raise resource for public investment and indirect taxes play a significant role in bringing about diversion of resources from consumption to production and from private sector to the public sector. By means of taxation, the government acquires purchasing power from the people and then uses the funds so raised in productive investment which is essential for rapid economic growth.

INCIDENCE OF SOME TAXES

Incidence of Taxes on Personal Income

Income-tax, super-tax, excess profits tax are all direct taxes and are as such borne by the people who pay them in the first instance. They cannot ordinarily be shifted. But a businessman, who is in an exceptionally strong position relative to the persons he deals with, may be able to shift a part of the tax to is customers. May be that he is the seller of a very popular brand; may be that he is the seller of a very popular doctor in whom his patients have implicit faith. In such cases, the patients may be willing to pay a bit more. But these conditions are rarely present, and the income-tax payers must ordinarily bear the burden of the tax. A tax on the businessman's income has no influence on price which is determined by demand and supply.

Taxes on personal income.

1. *Report*, Vol. I, p. 149.

Businessman's income depends on his profits. Profit depends on price, and not vice versa. A tax on profit, therefore, cannot be passed on to the consumer by raising the price. In the long run, however, a heavy tax may check enterprise by reducing the anticipated profits. But it will depend on elasticity of supply and alternative channels of investment available. It is very difficult to say what will happen in the long run. The probability is that a moderate tax will not have any undersirable repercussions.

If, however, the income-tax is extremely heavy, it may discourage saving, check accumulation of capital or drive it abroad. The productive capacity of the community will thus be impaired and there will be widespread repercussions of such a heavy tax. But the tax is seldom so heavy. Ordinarily, therefore, it rests on those on whom it is imposed.

A heavy income-tax may discourage incentive and enterprise. This, however, will depend on whether the tax falls on average income or marginal income. In the former case, the tax-payer is transferred to a lower income group and he must work harder to maintain his customary standard of living. If the increase in tax falls mainly on the marginal income, it will mean a positive discouragement to the earning of that income. How far actually the enterprise will be affected will depend on the tax-payer's ability to vary his income and hence, his liability to be taxed, by varying his effort. Ordinarily, few workers have the ability to vary their income by varying their effort; only, when there is a great demand for overtime, they may be able to do so.

Incidence of Corporation Tax

It is a tax on companies. It is imposed on the net profit of the corporations or joint stock companies. By reducing the fund available for re-investment, the corporation tax militates against expansion and development.

Also, the amount available to be distributed as dividends is reduced. This also serves as a disincentive to the investing public. Capital formation is checked thereby. Thus, flow of equity capital is checked. The prices of goods manufactured by such corporations rise which may give place to cheaper substitutes resulting in a shift of resources in their favour.

Further, since corporation taxes discourage investment, the level of national income and employment is reduced. If, however, the corporation which is taxed, maintains the dividend rate by paying dividend out of the undistributed profits, then neither is consumption reduced nor the flow of equity capital checked.

A corporation tax, by reducing the earnings of the existing firms, discourages the entry of new firms into the industry which may result in a monopoly or a semi-monopoly for the existing firms with all the attendant evils.

Further, its disincentive effect may lower efficiency. A part of the corporation tax may be shifted to the buyers through a price rise.

Incidence of Tax on Profits

The problem of incidence of tax on profits is complicated by the fact that there is difference of opinion among the economists about the definition of profits and the elements that compose it. Some economist, like Prof. Walker, regard profits as analogous to rent. In this sense, profit is a surplus earned by the entrepreneur superior to the marginal entrepreneur. The price in the market is determined by the marginal producer. Hence, profits, like rent, do not enter into price. It cannot, therefore, be shifted to the consumer. It will be borne by the businessman who pays it. This is Walker's view.

But we do not subscribe to this view. Even the marginal entrepreneur must have profit in the long run. Normal profit is, therefore, not a surplus but a part of the necessary cost. This, however, does not lead us to the conclusion that a tax on profit will be shifted to the consumer, unless the entrepreneur is able to influence the price which he rarely can. For an individual entrepreneur, price in the market is fixed. The being so, a tax on his profit must come out of his own pocket. A general tax on profits, as a rule, is not shifted unless the price are rising rapidly and the consumers are anxious to buy. This, however, is very rare.

But if the tax is a speçial one on profits from a particular trade and industry, there will be a tendency on the part of the entrepreneurs to withdraw themselves from such lines. If this happens, the incidence will ultimately be shifted to the consumers of the commodity or the users of the service supplied by the entrepreneurs. A great deal depends upon the elasticity of demand and the mobility of capital.

A tax on profits may take the form of a licence duty. Even this will be borne by the producer. In order to reimburse himself, the producer may increase his output. The consumer benefits but the incidence of licence duty will remain on the producer. It is generally too small to make the producer try to shift it.

Although complete exemption of profits from taxation is not desirable, yet a high tax is highly undesirable. It will put a brake on invention and enterprise and it will cut down revenues and thus hinder modernisation of plant. In the words of Mrs. Hicks, "The effect of an additional tax on profits on a curve of expected returns is to shift the curve bodily to the left, but without altering its shape or the chance of loss. The chance of very high gains which formerly balanced the big chance of loss in the risky investment curve is thus cut off, and the scales are consequently tipped against it; while the safe investment, being relatively unaffected, will become the more attractive.

"The discrimination of high profits tax against 'venture capital' is serious for any country that means to keep abreast of modern development; it is perhaps especially serious in an established industrial equipment, and where, consequently, new enterprise needs to be especially on the alert. This tax has also important cyclical relevance; in depression, curves of expected returns flatten out; many normally safe investments pass into the risky class".

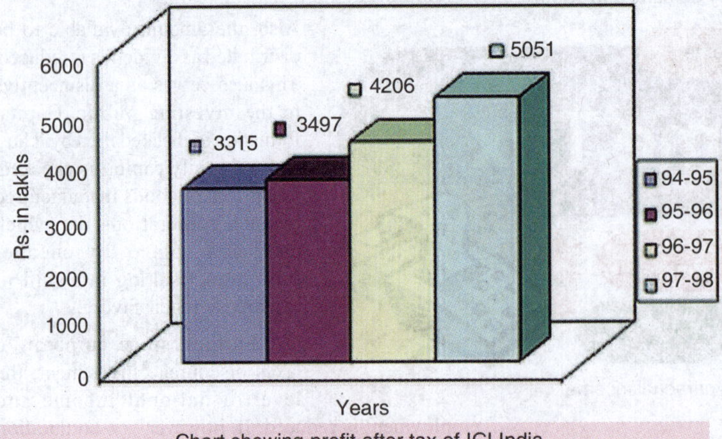

Chart showing profit after tax of ICI India.

Effect of Wealth Tax

Wealth tax is imposed on value of a person's stock of wealth at a point of time, say at the end of financial year. The wealth tax does not discriminate against risky investment. In this way, it promotes economic development. By enabling the government not to raise the income tax rates too high, the wealth tax encourages investment in modern industries. Another obvious effect of wealth tax is the reduction of economic inequalities by reducing the size of the inherited wealth. The tax is borne by the persons on whom it is levied. It reduces the size of unearned income. The wealth tax discourages productive investment. It influences the supply of money capital. It encourages consumption and discourages saving or capital formation. The tendency to purchase non-durable goods will increase.

Incidence of Property Tax

The distinction between wealth tax and property tax may be clearly understood. The wealth tax is imposed on the net wealth of the individual. In calculating the net wealth outstanding claims of others are deducted fro the gross value of the assets. But the property tax is levied on the gross value of the property irrespective of the ownership and no deduction is allowed for the outstanding claims of others against the property.

Property includes real estate like lands and buildings, machinery, inventories, household effects, jewellery, bank balances, bonds, *etc*. In actual practice, only the real estate like land and buildings are taxed.

In case of property used for consumption, (*e.g.*, jewellery, house and household effects), there is no shifting of the tax and the incidence is on the person on whom the tax is levied. But when the property is used for production, the producers will attempt to shift it to the consumers. But much depends on the elasticity of demand and supply.

Property tax.

We shall, therefore, consider now incidence of land taxation and tax on buildings.

Incidence of Land Taxation

The value of land depends on two sets of factors: (*a*) Natural factors like the fertility of the soil, the situation of the land, some other natural conditions; and (*b*) investment of capital in drainage schemes, anti-erosion measure, irrigation facilities and other measures necessary to increase and sustain productivity.

The tax depending on the first set of factors is a tax on economic rent and has a tendency to fall on the owners. The landlord cannot shift it to the tenant, for economic rent is determined by factors independent of land tax. The owner is supposed already to be charging rent fully measuring the superiority of his land over the marginal land. But in case, through ignorance, indifference or indulgence, he has not been charging full economic rent, he will, when the tax is imposed, sharply look round and take in the 'slack'. To this extent, the tax is shifted to the tenant.

Tax of this nature, *i.e.*, the tax on economic rent, cannot be passed on to the consumer, for the consumer can only be reached through the price. We know that economic rent does not enter into price. The rising or lowering of the rent does not affect price. The fact that the tax is paid by the occupier makes no difference. If he pays it in the first instance, he can deduct it when he pays the rent to the owner.

Thus, tax on economic rent is borne by the owner of the land and not by the tenant or the consumer of the product.

But, where the owner can vary his investment in land, we will reduce this investment when the tax is imposed. This will affect the yield and hence the price of the commodity. In this case, *i.e.*, in the case of improvements, it is shifted to the consumer.

Tax on building sites also tends to be thrown on those owners of sites who enjoy surplus income on account of more favourable situation of their sites.

Can the land tax be shifted to a prospective purchaser of the land? No, the tendency is that it will be borne by the present owner. The purchaser, while purchasing land, will be in mind that he will have to pay the tax. He will, consequently, offer less price. The tax is thus capitalised or absorbed in the lower price that the land will command. This will happen to the extent that future tax payments can be accurately forecast. But there is also neutralising tendency. Future increases in land values may also be anticipated and more price offered.

Incidence of Tax on Buildings

There are two parties in immediate contact with

each other so far as housing is concerned, *viz.*, the owner and occupier. If the tax is imposed on the owner, he will try to raise the house rent and thus shift the tax to the occupier or the tenant. But he cannot do this during the currency of the lease. Further, there may be a rent law controlling rent and forbidding the landlord from raising the rent. Even if he can raise the rent, the tenant may shift to some other house preferring smaller accommodation to paying a higher rent. In such cases, therefore, the incidence will be on the landlord, at any rate, for some time.

But the effect will be that building houses for letting out may not remain a paying proposition. A heavy tax will check building activity and the muneration of the builder and of other people engaged in the trade may fall. The demand for building sites may decrease. If they try to sell off, the new purchaser will bear in mind the tax, and offer correspondingly less. But, in course of time, the supply of houses will fall off and the rents must rise thus shifting the burden, to some extent, to the tenants. Thus, the tax may fall partly on the owner partly on the builder and partly on the occupier.

If, on the other hand, the tax is imposed on the occupier, it will tend to stick to him. It is not easy to find a new house nor so convenient to shift. One likes to stay on, where one is. The demand for a house is inelastic. The landlord, therefore, is in a much stronger position. The tax will, thus, stay where its first impact is. But if the occupier is a shopkeeper, he may be able to shift the tax to his customers in the neighbourhood by raising a bit the prices of the commodities he sells. We must remember, however, that the development of the means of communication and transport brings the travelling salesman to our very door and weakens the grip of the neighbouring store.

We shall, thus, conclude that the tax on buildings will fall generally on the occupier but under certains circumstances may be shifted to the owner, the building or the consumer.

Incidence of Death Duty

In almost all advanced countries, death duties form an important part of the tax system. Death duties take two forms: Estate Duty and Succession Duty. The estate duty is levied on the total value of the estate (*i.e.*, movable and immovable property) left by the deceased irrespective of the relationship of the successor. It is graduated with reference to the total value of the property. The succession duty varies with the relationship of the beneficiary to the decreased. It is graduated on the basis of the windfall element which increases with the distance of relationship. Further, it takes into consideration individual share of the successor and not the total value as in estate duty.

Death duties are justified on the ground that the government is said to be a silent partner in the creation of wealth. It is aimed at reducing inequalities of wealth and concentration of economic power in the hands of a few persons. By reducing unearned income from wealth, this tax makes for equality of opportunity. But the death duties may reduce savings by discouraging savings to avoid a heavy death duty. This tax also reduces the ability to save on the part of the heirs. Thus, capital formation is adversely affected.

Government collects Estate duty on property left by the deceased for successor.

The death duty tends to disrupt small enterprises because they are forced to sell themselves to larger firms in order to pay the tax. This promotes the growth of monopolies. By encouraging the formation of trusts in order to avoid substantial tax liabilities, the death duties favour conservative investment policies.

The willingness to work may be affected by death duties. If a person wants to leave to his hires assets of certain size after the payment of tax he may have to work harder. On the other hand, if the marginal rate of tax rises with every increase in his estate he will tend to work less. It is possible that the rich people may dissipate their wealth during their lives. But if they have greater concern for their heirs, they may consume less and save more. If, however, the marginal tax rate is very high, it may encourage consumption and discourage saving.

The transfer of property at death may disrupt small business which may not be in the interest of the community. By reducing the successors' amount of wealth, death duty will decrease their consumption and investment and adversely affect the level of income and employment.

Where is the incidence of death duties? Is the incidence on the deceased or the beneficiary, *i.e.*, the successor? The owner is dead and it is said that death pays all debts. He can be taxed no more. No further burden can be placed on him. If, however, he had got insured to pay such a tax, he certainly bore it when he paid the insurance premium. In the absence of any such anticipation by the owner of the property, when he was alive, the tax will obviously fall on the beneficiary.

Incidence of Tax on Monopoly

The question of incidence is a part of the larger question of the theory of value. As value determination differs in the case of monopoly from the value determination under competitive conditions, the incidence of a tax on monopoly works our differently.

The monopoly tax may be (*a*) independent of the output of the monopolised product; or (*b*) it may vary with the output, *i.e.*, increase or decrease with the output.

(*a*) When the tax is independent of the quantity produced, it may either be lump-sum tax on the monopolist or a percentage of the monopoly net revenue (profit). In both these cases, it will fall on the monopolist. He cannot shift it to the consumer. This could be done by raising the price. But he is already supposed to have fixed a price which yielded him the maximum monopoly net revenue. If it had been possible for him to raise the price consistent with the policy of maximising his profit, he would have done it already. Any alteration in the price, thus, would be at the expense of his profit. That being the case, he must now pay the tax out of his own profit. He will get maximum profit now after paying the tax by leaving the selling price unchanged and the consumer unaffected.

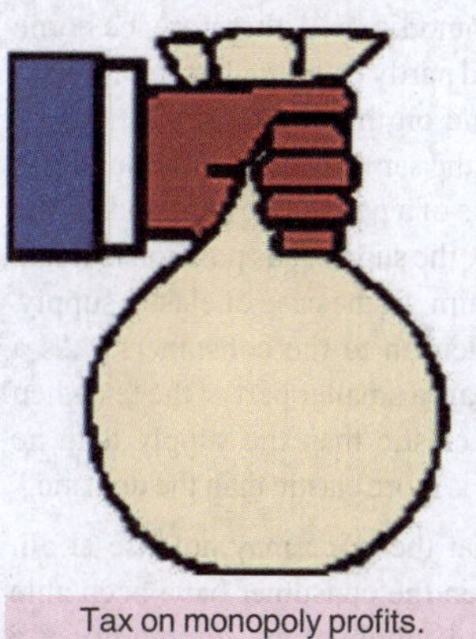

Tax on monopoly profits.

It is possible that, instead of re-calculating how he would maximise his profit after paying the tax, he may simply put up the price shifting the tax to the consumer. But by so doing he may have reduced his monopoly profit. "He may prefer this to a rather greater profit at the expense of a greater effort."

In case, however, he has been charging less out of consideration for consumers' welfare than what he could charge for maximising his profit, he will, when the tax is imposed, take in the 'slack'. To this extent, the burden of the tax will be shifted to the consumers.

(*b*) Now let us see what happens when the tax varies directly or inversely with the quantity of the commodity produced. In this case, as discussed in the previous section, elasticities of demand and supply and the influenced. In this case, as discussed in the previous section, elasticities of demand and supply and the influence of the laws of returns will have to be taken into account. The tax will enter into the cost of production. It will mean an addition to the cost of production. Taxing of the commodity, therefore, raises the price which will tend to reduce the demand.

If, however, the demand is inelastic, it cannot be appreciably reduced and the tax will be borne by the consumer. If the demand is elastic, the consumers may buy less when the tax has raised the price. In this case, the tax will partly be borne by the monopolist. Instead of facing a decline in demand, the monopolist may reduce the price and decide to bear the tax himself. If the supply is more elastic, then the producer is a stronger position. Thus, if the demand is more elastic than the supply, the consumer will bear less burden of the tax, and if the supply is more elastic than the demand, then the producer will bear less.

If the production of the commodity obeys the law of increasing returns, the reduction in output, consequent upon the imposition of a tax, will raise the price more than if it were subject to the law of diminishing returns. The burden on the consumer in the former case will be greater than in the latter case. When the marginal costs are constant and the demand curve facing the monopolist is a straight line, then, according to the theory of monopoly price, the price of the taxed commodity will be raised by half the amount of the tax; under competition it would have risen by the full amount of the tax.

In case the demand curve is concave, the rise in price will be greater than this. Where the demand curve is so concave as to make the marginal revenue curve parallel to the demand curve over the relevant range, the price will be raised by the full amount of the tax. In cases, however, the demand curve is not only concave but indicant elasticity, the ratio between price and marginal cost will be constant. The marginal revenue being necessarily less than price, the slope of the marginal revenue curve will be less than that of the demand curve so that the price will rise by more than the tax.

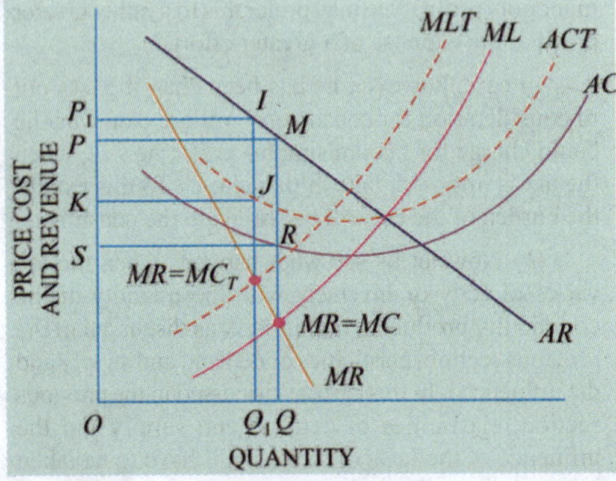

Tax under monopoly.

If in order to stimulate production, the rate of the tax varies inversely with the output, then the monopolist will be tempted to produce more and keep the price low. The burden of the tax will thus be entirely on the monopolist who will, in fact, be transferring a part of his monopoly profit to the consumers.

The fact is that, owing to the exceptional ability of the monopolist to manipulate the price and control the market, the incidence of a monopoly tax is uncertain.

AC = average cost

MC = marginal cost

AR = average revenue

MR = marginal revenue

ACT = average cost after tax

MCT = marginal cost after tax

(*i*) Before tax the equilibrium is reached at a point where *MR* = *MC*. Which determines price and '*OQ*' amount of quantity, '*OP*' price before tax.

$TR - TC = \Pi_1$

TR = Total revenue

TC = Total cost

Π = Profit

$\square\, OPMQ - \square\, OSRQ = \square\, PMRS$

(*ii*) After imposition of tax on monopoly the equilibrium changes. The equilibrium is achieved at point where *MR* = *MCT*. Which determines 'OP_1' price and 'OQ_1' quantity.

$TR - TC_T = \Pi_2$.

$\square\, OP_1IQ_1 - \square\, OKJQ_1 = \square\, P_1IJK$

Π_1 (Profit before tax)

Π_2 (Profit after tax),

$\therefore \quad \square\, PMRS > P_1IJK$.

A monopolists bears some amount of tax and some amount he shifts on the consumer's (buyers), therefore the rise in prices is only 'PP_1' or marginal.

Incidence of a Commodity Tax

Taxes on commodities may take different forms: (*a*) a tax on manufacture or production of a commodity called excise duties, (*b*) a tax on sale of a particular commodity or general sales tax, and (*c*) import or export of commodity known as customs duty.

A tax on a commodity tends to be shifted from the producer forward to the consumer and from the consumer backward to the producer. A tax on production of a commodity tends to raise its price and will, therefore, be normally borne by the consumer. But a tax on consumption is likely to check consumption and tends to be shifted backward to the producer.

The extent to which a commodity tax will actually be shifted will depend upon the nature of demand and supply curves. If demand is inelastic, as is the case with the necessaries of life, the people must buy the commodity. The producer will be in a stronger position and almost the entire burden of the tax will be shifted on to the consumer. But in the case of elastic demand, the people will buy less. In that case, the price will not rise by the full amount of the tax, and the tax will be partly borne by the producer.

The tax on a commodity will, therefore, be borne partly by the buyer and partly by the sellers. How much exactly? It will depend on the degree of elasticity of demand or supply. In the same manner, if the supply is inelastic, as in the case of a perishable commodity, the seller cannot withdraw the supply. His position is weak. The tax will stick to him. In the case of elastic supply, he can shift the burden on to the consumers. "As a rule, the consumer bears a smaller part of the tax when the demand is more elastic than the supply than he does when the supply is more elastic than the demand."

It is possible that the price may not rise at all. This will happen when the consumer have been able to discover an untaxed supply of the commodity or a satisfactory untaxed substitute. In this case, the entire burden of the tax will fall on the producer or the seller.

On the supply side, the laws of returns will also exert their influence. The taxing of a commodity tends to check its demand which, in its turn, will check production. Now if the industry is subject to the law of increasing returns, the reduced production will be obtained at a higher cost and, in the case of the law of diminishing returns, at a lower cost. In the former case, the price will be higher than in the latter with a corresponding burden on the consumer.

Much also depends on the amount and the method of taxation. Nobody bothers about a small tax. No producer would like to annoy his customers for a paltry sum. He would cheerfully bear it himself. Only when the tax is heavy will the shifting take place. A tax on marginal output will raise the price and not the one on the surplus output.

The nature of the commodity also will make a difference. A tax on a commodity like sugar gets rapidly adjusted and shifted. But a tax on a house cannot be so readily shifted for rent is fixed for a period and during the currency of the lease no change can be made.

Other factors which govern the course of shifting of a commodity tax are whether competition is perfect, and whether labour and capital are freely mobile. Only in case of free and unfettered competition can the tax be passed on to the consumer otherwise it will stick to the producer. If labour and capital are freely mobile, it will add to the ability of the producer to shift the burden on to the consumer. If, on the other hand, large fixed capital is locked up in the industry, the position of the producer is correspondingly weakened, and the probability is that the tax burden will be borne by him. He cannot withdraw his capital. He must continue in the field even though he may be losing for a time.

Since the demand for a taxed commodity is reduced, productive resources may be shifted from the taxed to the non-taxed industries. Thus, the investment pattern will change to the disadvantage of the consumer. Hence, economic welfare is reduced. Also, economic inequalities are accentuated because commodity taxes are regressive, unless they are imposed on undesirable or injurious products.

Diagrammatic Representation. How the burden of a commodity tax is distributed between the buyers and sellers or producers according to ratio of elasticities of demand and supply is shown in the following diagram (Fig. 64.1):

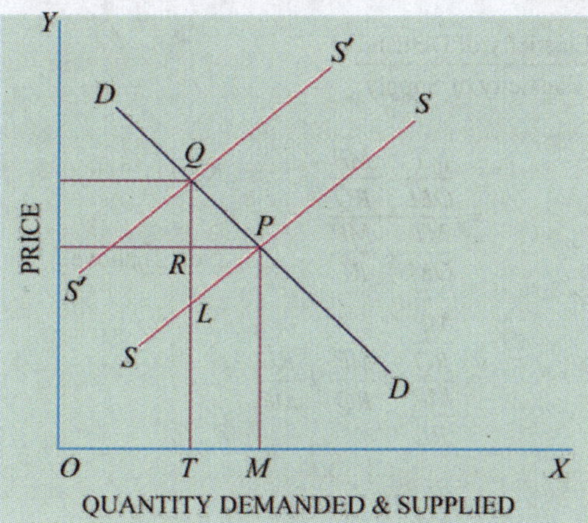

Fig. 64.1. Incidence of Commodity Taxes.

In this diagram, *DD* is the demand curve and *SS* is the supply curve. They intersect at *P* and *MP* is the price determined. Now suppose a sales tax per unit of the commodity has been levied. As a result, its supply curve will shift upward equal to the tax per unit, because the tax will be added to the supply price. The new supply curve will be *S′ S′* cuts the demand curve at *Q* and, therefore, now *TQ* is the price determined which is higher than the old price *PM* by *RQ*. Hence, *RQ* is the burden of the tax borne by the consumer even though the tax per unit is *LQ*. Therefore, *RL* (*LQ* – *QR*) is the burden of the tax borne by the seller or he has *RL* price less than before (*PM* being the first price).

We can show that the splitting of the burden of the tax *LQ* into *RL* on the seller and *RQ* on the buyer is equal to the ratio of elasticities of demand and supply thus:

$$\frac{RL}{RQ} = \frac{\text{Burden of the Tax on the seller (producer)}}{\text{Burden of the Tax on the buyer (consumer)}}$$

Elasticity of Demand

$$= \frac{\text{Proportionate decrease in the quantity demanded}}{\text{Proportionate increase in price}}$$

$$= \frac{MT}{OM} \div \frac{RQ}{MP}$$

$$= \frac{MT}{OM} \times \frac{MP}{RQ} \quad ...(1)$$

Elasticity of Supply

$$= \frac{\text{Proportionate decrease in the quantity supplied}}{\text{Proportionate decrease in price}}$$

$$= \frac{MT}{OM} \div \frac{RQ}{MP}$$

$$= \frac{MT}{OM} \times \frac{MP}{RL} \quad ...(2)$$

$$\frac{\text{Elasticity of Demand}}{\text{Elasticity of Supply}}$$

$$= \frac{\dfrac{MT}{OM} \times \dfrac{MP}{RQ}}{\dfrac{MT}{OM} \times \dfrac{MP}{RL}} \quad \begin{array}{l} \text{.........No. (1) above} \\ \text{.........No. (2) above} \end{array}$$

$$= \frac{\dfrac{MP}{RQ}}{\dfrac{MP}{RL}} = \frac{MP}{RQ} \times \frac{RL}{MP}$$

$$= \frac{RL}{RQ}$$

We have seen above that *RL* is the burden of the tax on the seller and *RQ* is the burden of the tax on the buyer on consumer.

$$\text{Hence } \frac{RL}{RQ} = \frac{\text{Burden of the tax on the seller}}{\text{Burden of the tax on the consumer}}$$

$$= \frac{\text{Elasticity of Demand}}{\text{Elasticity of supply}}$$

It clear that the limits within which a commodity tax is shared between the buyers and sellers depends on the elasticities of demand and supply. If the demand is inelastic, as is the case with the necessaries of life, the people must buy, them whatever the increase in the price as a result of imposition of a tax. In such a situation, the seller's position is stronger and the entire burden of the tax will be shifted to the consumer. But if the demand is elastic, it will contract when the price rises. Hence, price will not rise to the full amount of the tax. Therefore, a part of the tax will be borne by the sellers or producers and a part by the buyers or consumers. But exactly how much? This will depend on the ratio of elasticity of demand and elasticity of supply. In the same manner, if the supply is inelastic as is the case with perishable commodities, the sellers cannot reduce the supply as price rises and their position is weaker. In such a situation, the burden of the tax will be on the sellers or producers—and it cannot be shifted to the purchasers or consumers. On the contrary, if the supply is elastic then the sellers can withdraw the supply if the price does not suit them. In such a situation, the burden of the tax will be on the buyers or consumers.

Conclusion. Thus, incidence of a commodity tax is a very complicated affair. It is a part of a large problem of price determination. There are various conflicting influences on price. We say that generally a tax on a commodity tends to be borne by the consumer. But this tendency may or may not be actually realised. Unless the price is affected, the consumer is not touched and he is touched only to the extent that the price is raised by the imposition of the tax.

Elasticity of demand	Total tax	Burden on buyer, increase	Burden on seller in price	Remarks
Ed = 0 on	PP_1	PP_1	Nil	complete burden buyer
Ed < 1	MN	MT	TN	MT > TN More on buyer less on seller
Ed = 1	RS	RX	XS	RX = XS Equal burden on both
Ed > 1	GH	GI	IH	GI < IH More on seller & less on buyer
Ed = α	KJ	Nil	KJ	Complete burden on seller

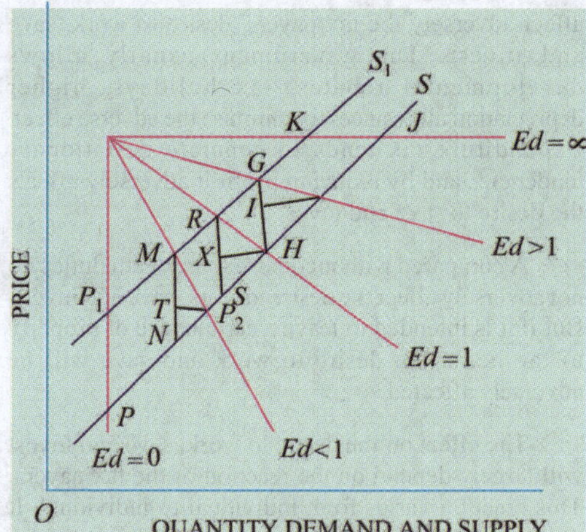

Elasticity of demand and incidence of tax on commodity.

On *y*-axis price and on *x*-axis quantity demanded and supplied.

$\Sigma d = 0$ Elasticity of demand is perfectly inelastic.

$\Sigma d < 1$ „ „ „ is relatively inelastic

$\Sigma d = 1$ „ „ „ equal to 1 or unit elastic demand.

$\Sigma d > 1$ „ „ „ relatively elastic.

$\Sigma d = \alpha$ „ „ „ perfectly elastic.

'*SS*' is original supply curve and 'S_1S_1' is supply curve after imposition of tax.

Incidence of Sales Tax

The sales tax is levied on the turnover, profits or no profits. Its incidence is a complicated affair, because it covers commodities of widely divergent nature. If the demand for a commodity is inelastic, its price can be raised and the tax will be then shifted to the consumer to that extent. But if the demand is elastic, it may be shifted partly to the consumer and may remain partly on the seller. If the supply is perfectly elastic, the entire burden of the tax will fall upon the buyer and if the supply is perfectly inelastic, the entire burden will be on the seller. If the supply is only relatively elastic or inelastic then the tax burden will be shared between the buyer and the seller.

There are possibilities of incidence shifting forward (to the buyers) and backward (to the seller of factors of production) in the long run. For instance, if the demand falls, the output will be reduced and demand for factors may go down reducing their reward.

The sales tax may make heavy inroads into profits which may lead to retrenchment in staff and management, restrict enterprise and employment leaving some business premises unoccupied. Thus, its incidence may fall upon the employees, management and landlords. Sales tax indeed hits a large number of people of direct types.

Incidence of Import and Export Duties

Import duties are generally, and almost exclusively, borne by the home consumer. The duty paid by the importer is added to the price that he charges from the next buyer, and so on. The duty is ultimately shifted to the consumer. Only, in very rare case, the burden of such duties may be shifted to the foreign producer. If, for instance, our demand for the imported product is elastic so that we may or may not buy it, and the supply is inelastic and the foreign producer has no alternative market, then in such a case the burden can be shifted to the foreign producer. But these conditions are rarely present the import duty must be borne by the home consumer.

Export duty is similarly borne by the exporter. The price in the world markets is fixed so far as he is concerned. No individual exporter is in a position to influence the world price. But, here again,; we can imagine a situation in which the exporter is in an exceptionally strong position so that the export duty can be shifted to the foreign purchaser. For example, we may have a monopoly of the supply of a commodity and the demand of the foreigners for our product may be inelastic, whereas so many other alternative markets may be open to us. In such circumstances, we can certainly make the foreigners pay the export duty by raising the price of the commodity by the full amount of the duty. But such conditions are very rare and, unless they are present, the export duty must be borne by the exporter.

Dalton lays down the rule in this connection thus: "Taxes on imports and exports may be regarded as obstacle to exchange and, in accordance with the preceding theory, the direct money burden of any such

Exporter pays export duty.

obstacle is divided between the two parties of the exchange in inverse proportion to the elasticities of their respective demand. In other words, it is divided in direct proportion to the urgencies of their respective needs which are satisfied by the exchange."

EFFECT OF TAXATION ON PRODUCTION, CONSUMPTION AND DISTRIBUTION

an earlier chapter (61), we discussed the effect of public expenditure on production and distribution. Let us now study the effects of taxes on production and distribution.

Effect on Production

Production is affected by taxes in two ways: (*a*) by affecting ability to work, save and invest and (*b*) by affecting the desire to work, save and invest.

Effect on the Ability to Work, Save and Invest. This effect will depend on so many factors including the nature of the tax and the reaction of the tax payers to the tax. We can take a few instances: A tax on the necessaries of life, will obviously affect the worker's productive efficiency and hence reduce production. This adverse effect on production can be avoided by exempting the goods of mass consumption or tax them at very low rates. A heavy tax on income tends to reduce the ability to save and invest on the part of individuals. A tax on the net profits of business firms will reduce their ability to save and invest. A decrease in investment is bound to affect adversely the level of output in the country. But increase in government expenditure may offset the decrease in investment in the private sector.

In an inflationary situation, taxes will tend to contain inflationary pressures and in a normal situation, high taxation will result in the fall of the price level and decline in output.

Effect on the Desire to Work, Save and Invest. Normally, taxation induces the people to work harder, earn more, save more and invest more to increase their income or enjoy the same income after tax. Some taxes have no adverse effect, *e.g.*, a tax on windfalls, inherited wealth, tax on monopolies irrespective of the output. Import duties too increase the domestic producers' desire to work save and invest. Low export duty may also encourage production. Every duties or sales tax may not affect the people's desire to work, save and invest if they are spending only a small portion of their income on the taxed commodities. But if they are spending a large proportion of their income on such commodities, savings will fall and a fall in demand may also reduce output.

High marginals rates of income tax are likely to affect adversely the tax payers' desire to work, save and invest. The government usually allows developmental rebates, tax holidays, higher depreciation allowances to minimise the adverse effect. Expenditure tax tends to generate deflationary tendencies and by reducing profit it adversely affects the desire to save and invest.

A compared with income tax, the death duties do not adversely affect the desire to work, save and invest. But if it is intended to leave a certain size of property to the heirs, the desire to work and save will be adversely affected.

The effect on the desire to work, save and invest will largely depend on the reaction of the tax payers. This reaction varies from individual to individual. It depends on the individual's elasticity of demand for income, *i.e.*, individual's keenness to earn an income. When an individual's demand for income is relatively elastic, the tax will lessen his desire to work and save. The effect will be the opposite if this demand is relatively inelastic. This is actually the case in the real world. Hence, a tax will induce the tax-payers to work more, save more and invest more, especially those who want to maintain a certain standard of living or earn certain amount on their savings, or who want to improve their social status or acquire power or those who wish to provide comfort and security in old age, and so on.

Production Pattern. Taxes may modify the pattern of production. Entrepreneurs may avoid the production of goods which are taxed. There is likely to be a diversion of resources from some sectors of the economy to others. For instance, if luxuries are heavily taxed production ofnecessaries may be stimulated. There will be diversion from the present to the future if consumption is taxed and savings are encouraged.

Effect on Income Distribution

Modern governments levy taxes not merely to raise revenue but also to levy such taxes as would reduce economic inequalities. It is recognised that if economic welfare of the masses is to be promoted, incomes and wealth in the country must be more evenly distributed.

The effect of taxes on income distribution depends on the type of taxes and the rates of taxes. Taxation of goods of mass consumption are regressive and redistribute incomes in favour of the rich. But if such commodities are exempted and luxuries are taxed, and taxation is made progressive, then incomes will be redistributed in favour of the poor.

The direct taxes like income tax, wealth tax, death duties and property tax levied at progressive rates tend to reduce inequalities of income and wealth.

The direct taxes like income tax, wealth tax, death duties and property tax levied at progressive rates tend to reduce inequalities of income and wealth.

It may, however, be emphasised that taxation alone cannot reduce economic inequalities. But levy of progressive direct taxes combined with public expenditure, mainly for the benefit of the poor, may go a long way in lessening economic inequalities. However, extremely high progressive rates may adversely affect production.

Effect on Consumption

Taxes can affect consumption in a number of ways. By imposing a heavy tax on a consumable good which is injurious to health, its consumption can be checked. It raises its price and reduces the demand for it. Similarly, by taxing luxuries, their consumption can be decreased and resources diverted to the production of goods of mass consumption. Taxes on necessaries are not considered desirable since their prices for the poor people will rise and their standard of living will fall.

Conclusion

Thus, taxation plays a regulatory role. It regulates consumption, production and income distribution. Taxation alone, however, may not be able completely to regulate them. It may have to be supplemented by other measures of control to make its regulatry role effective.

MODERN THEORY OF SHIFTING AND INCIDENCE

Various theories have been put forward to explain the shifting and incidence of taxation.

Earlier Theories. The earlier theories may be classified into (*a*) Concentration Theory or Surplus Theory and (*b*) Diversion or Diffusion Theory. According to the concentration theory or the surplus theory, each tax tends to concentrate on a particular class of people who happen to enjoy surplus from their products. The diffusion theory held on the other hand, that the tax eventually got diffused in the entire society. That is, the final resting place of the tax is not one but multiple. The process of diffusion took place through shifting or through the process of exchange.

Modern Theory. The concentration theory and the diffusion theory are only partially true. Actually, there is both concentration and diffusion of taxes according to the conditions present. The modern theory seeks to analyses the conditions which bring about concentration or diffusion.

Take a tax an a commodity payable by a producer. A producer has a dual price-relationship. He has price-relationship with he customers through selling price as well as with the suppliers of factors of production through purchase price. The producer will try to shift the tax to the customers by raising the price or to the factors by reducing the price he has to pay. The former is called forward shifting and the latter backward shifting. It is possible that the producer is able to shift it partly to the customers and partly to the factors of production and in this way shake off the entire tax burden.

Backward shifting is by and large, difficult because factor remuneration is determined by market forces of demand and supply. As regards forward shifting, we notice that the producer enjoys surplus in the form of profit s and the consumers enjoy consumer's surplus. The producer wants to retain his entire surplus, whereas the consumer resists a reduction in his surplus. The producer will threaten to cut production and the consumer to cut consumption. In this way, the shifting will depend on the conditions of demand and supply.

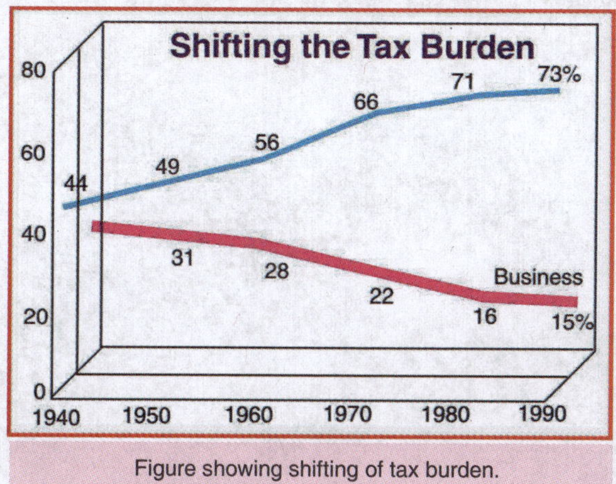

Figure showing shifting of tax burden.

Key terms

Impact and Incidence of tax, Effects of tax on production and distribution, Shifting of tax.

QUESTIONS

1. What are the factors on which incidence of tax depends? Trace the incidence of estate duty and inheritance tax.
2. Distinguish between (*a*) Impact, (*b*) Incidence, (*c*) Effects of a tax. Briefly discuss the general principles determining the incidence of indirect taxes.
3. Distinguish between incidence and effects of taxation. Discuss the effects of the following taxes on distribution and production: (*a*) Excise duty on sugar, (*b*) Corporation Tax, and (*c*) Estate Duty.
4. Explain with the help of a diagram how a tax payer is better off with an income tax of an equal amount rather than a commodity tax.
5. Explain the principles governing the incidenc of commodity taxation. Examine the conditions under which the price of a taxed commodity rises (*i*) by more than; and (*ii*) by less than the amount of the tax.
6. Discuss incidence of the following taxes:
   (1) Expenditure Tax, (2) Export Duty on Tea, (3) Entertainment Tax.
7. Discuss carefully the nature and direction of the incidence of sales taxes, indicating the factors on which these depend.
8. What is 'incidence' of taxation? Examine the incidence of income tax and excise duties.
9. Examine the effects of (*a*) 10% tax on all rents paid for the use of land, (*b*) a 5% tax on the value of all land and (*c*) a 5% on all urban land.

PUBLIC DEBT

Public debt refers to borrowing by a government from within the country or from abroad, from private individuals or association of individuals or from banking and non-banking financial institutions.

CLASSIFICATION OF PUBLIC DEBT

Public debt may be classified as under:

1. Internal and External. Internal debt is raised from within the country and external debt is owed to foreigners or foreign governments or institutions.

2. Productive and Unproductive. The productive debt is expected to create assets which will yield income sufficient to pay the principal and interest on the loan. In other words, they are expected to pay their way; they are self-liquidating. On the other hand, loans raised for war do not create any asset; they are a dead weight and are regarded as unproductive.

3. Short-term and Long-term. Short-term loans are repayable after short interval of time, *e.g.*, Treasury Bills payable after three months, ways and means advances from the Central bank. They are intended to bridge the gap temporarily between current revenue and current expenditure. It is called floating debt.

Long-term loans are payable after a long time covering several years. They are also called funded debt.

GROWTH OF PUBLIC DEBT

Borrowing by public authority is a modern practice. In the past, whenever there was an emergency, usually a war, the monarch relied on the hoarded wealth or borrowed on his own personal credit. Books on history abound in instances of fabulous hoards and accounts of loots and sacks of hoarded wealth either from king's treasuries or from temples and churches. But this method of finance is not suited to modern conditions. It will be inadequate and uneconomical.

Map of the world and Debt.

The system of public credit, making it easy for the States to borrow, has led to tremendous increase in the indebtedness of modern States. The public debt of 27 countries in 1900 was £6,079,000,000, in 1913 it increased to £8,566,000,000; and in 1933 to £22,000,000,000. Almost the sole responsibility for this phenomenal increase lies on war. The net cost of the war of 1914-18 was estimated at £42,000,000,000. The war of 1939-45 was innately more costly.

Causes of Increase in Public Debt

Besides war, there are several other causes which have brought about great increase in the size of public debt:

(i) The most important cause of increase in public debt is war or war-preparedness. Nations attach a great importance to their territorial integrity and they consider no sacrifice too much to defend their country. Every war, therefore, leaves the country under greater debt.

(ii) The increase is also due to fairly frequent budget deficits on current account. The deficits arise from the necessity of maintaining full economic activity in the economies which may have ceased to expand.

(iii) Increase in public debt is also due to the undertaking of welfare schemes by governments in modern times.

(iv) In public utilities, where there is no convenient profit check, no tight control over costs can be maintained and there are more losses than gains. They also add to the weight of public debt.

(v) In recent years, urge for economic growth has induced the under-developed countries to contract debts both internally and externally. The volume of public debt has consequently swollen.

The following are the principal purposes for raising public loans:

(*i*) Bridging Gap Between Revenues and Expenditure. It often happens that towards the end of the financial year, government experiences shortage of funds. To cover this gap between revenue and expenditure, the government raises temporary loans or gets 'ways and means' advance from the Central Bank. In India, the government issues what are called 'Treasury Bills' which are repayable after three months.

(*ii*) Financing Public Works Programme. During depression, the government has to launch public works programme to provide employment. In this way, money is injected into the economy to lift the depression. For this purpose, it becomes necessary to raise public loans to ensure economic stability.

(*iii*) Curbing Inflation. When inflation is rampant and it is desired to bring down the prices, the government issues public loans. In this way, money or purchasing power is drawn from the public. Reduction in money supply will bring down prices.

(*iv*) Financing Economic Development. The underdeveloped countries are now very keen on speedy economic development, which involves huge investment. They are unable to raise adequate finances through taxation. Hence resort to public borrowing becomes necessary.

(*v*) Financing the Public Sector. An economic system, which is becoming increasingly popular, is that of mixed economy. For several reasons, economic, political and social, there has to be a rapidly expanding public sector. The financing of this sector is not possible without resort to public borrowing.

(*vi*) War Finance. A modern war is a very costly affair. To prosecute a modern war by taxation is simply out of the question. Public borrowing becomes essential.

Thus, public borrowing is necessitated by the requirements of filling the gap between revenue and expenditure, public programme, economic development and war finance.

METHODS OF DEBT REDEMPTION

Modern governments make it a point of honour to repay their debts. Debt repayment maintains and strengthens the national credit. If a national emergency arises later, it will be easy to raise funds. Repayment of loans also releases funds for trade and industry.

The following are some of the methods adopted:

(*i*) Utilization of Surplus Revenue. This is an old method and badly out of tune with the modern conditions. Budget surplus is not a common phenomenon. Even when there is a surplus, it is insignificant that it cannot be used for making any substantial reduction in the public debt.

(*ii*) Purchase of Government Bonds. The government may buy its own stock in the market, thus wiping off its obligation to that extent. This may be done by the application of surplus revenues or by borrowing at low rates, if the conditions are favourable.

(*iii*) Terminable Annuities. When it is intended completely to wipe off a permanent debt, it may be arranged to pay the creditors a certain fixed amount for a number of years. These annual payments are called annuities. It will appear that, during the time these annuities are being paid, there will be much greater strain on the government finances than when only interest has to be paid.

(*iv*) Conversion. This is a method for reducing the burden of the debt. A government may have borrowed when the rate of interest was high. Now, if the rate of interest falls, it can convert a high-rated loan into a low-rated one. The government gives notice to the creditors that they should either agree to reduce the interest rate for future payments or it will exercise the option of repaying the loan. In case the bond-holders do not accept the lower rate, then the government will raise a new loan at lower rate of interest and, with the proceeds, pay off the old debt. The effect is to convert a high-rated loan into a low-rated one. The financial burden is consequently reduced.

(*v*) Sinking Fund. This is the most important method. A fund is created for the repayment of every loan by setting aside a certain amount every year out of the current revenue. The sum to be set aside is so calculated that over a certain period, the total sum accumulated, together with the interest thereon, is enough to pay off the loan.

Some Revolutionary Proposals

Apart from the above methods of repayment of debts normally adopted by modern governments, sometimes unorthodox and revolutionary proposals are also made from time to time for wiping off or reducing public debt, *e.g.*, Debt repudiation, compulsory scaling down of capital and/or interest and capital levy.

These methods are not considered honourable and no responsible government entertains such proposals. Hence, they need not detain us.

BURDEN OF PUBLIC DEBT

In order to assess the burden of public debt, we shall have to consider the nature and the purpose of the public debt. If the debt is taken for productive purposes, *e.g.*, for irrigation and railways, it will not mean any burden. On the other hand, it will confer a benefit, provided the scheme has been successfully executed. But if the debt is unproductive, it will impose both money burden and real burden on the community. The measure of the burden will depend on whether the debt is internal or external.

Burden of Internal Debt

Internal debt involves a series of transfers of wealth within the community. For example, when the loan is raised, money is transferred from the lenders to the government. The government then makes payments to contractors, government servants or to those people from whom it buys goods and services .Money is, thus, transferred from some sections of the community to the other sections. In this case, there is obviously no direct **money burden** of the debt on the community as a whole.

Real Burden of Debt.

But there will be a direct **real burden** (*i.e.*, sacrifice, hardship or loss of economic welfare) on the community depending on the nature of these transfers of wealth. If by these transfers, wealth comes to be more evenly distributed, *i.e.*, wealth is transferred from the rich to the poor, then public debt will be considered beneficial instead of being burdensome. If, on the other hand, the public debt enriches the rich at the expense of the poor, it imposes a real burden.

Let us analyses carefully the nature of the transfer. In order to repay the interest and the principal of the debt, the Government must levy taxes. What the tax-payers pay, the bond-holders receive. The bond-holders are generally rich people. But the tax burden does not exclusively fall on the rich, unless it is very sharply progressive which is seldom the case. The tax burden falls on the rich and the poor both, and, in the case of indirect taxes, it may be more on the poor than on the rich. The net result may be that the wealth is transferred from the poor to the rich. This means a net loss of economic welfare.

This burden is accentuated by the fact that the transfer is from the young to the old (the bond-holders, the creditors of the goverment, are generally advanced in age) and from the active to the passive members of the community. "Here", says Dr. Dalton, "if nowhere else in the sphere of public finance, the voice of equity rings loud and clear. There is also a general presumption, on grounds of production (besides those on grounds of distribution) against the enrichment of the passive at the expense of the active, whereby work and productive risk-taking are penalised for the benefit of accumulated wealth."

Thus, internal debt has adverse repercussion both on production and distribution of wealth. This is its direct real burden.

Its **indirect real burden** will lie in the **check it imposes** on Production. The production is likely to be

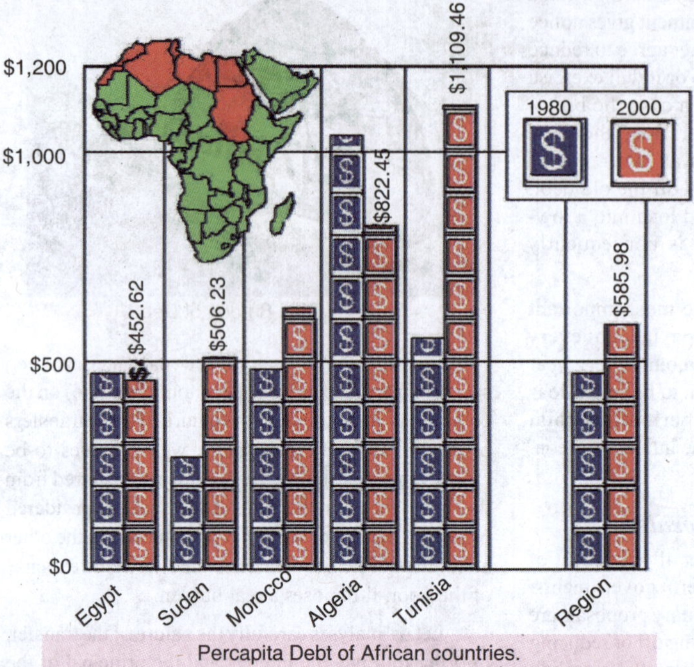

Percapita Debt of African countries.

checked, if the desire and ability to work and save are reduced. If the repayment of debt involves very heavy taxation, it is likely to reduce the ability and the willingness to work and save.

Burden of External Debt

The external debt also involves a series of transfers of wealth but not within the same country like the internal debt. This makes all the difference. When the loan is raised, wealth is transferred from the lending to the borrowing country, and when it is repad the transfer is in the opposite direction. The account of money paid by the debtor-country towards interest and the principal is the measures of the **direct money burden** on the community.

But if we want to know the direct real burden (*i.e.*, loss of economic welfare), we shall have to consider the proportions in which the rich and the poor contribute to these payments. The government will raise the required money by taxes. If the taxes fall largely on the rich, the direct real burden will be less than it would be if the incidence is largely on the poor. The payment that we make to the foreign creditor gives him a control over our goods and services. He does not take away our money; it is of no use to him. He buys with that money goods in our country. An external loan thus sets up a drain of goods from our country. In the absence of debt payments, these goods would have been enjoyed by ourselves. This means a diminution of economic welfare; hence a **direct real burden.**

The indirect burden of the foreign debt lies in the check to production of wealth in the economy. Taxes imposed, in order to raise funds for debt payment, may reduce willingness and ability to work and to save. The debt payment made by the government may reduce public expenditure in the directions which would have stimulated production. Hence, production may be checked.

International payments can be made only by exporting goods. For this purpose, a country must produce more. Hence, it is said that production is stimulated. But production is stimulated only in certain directions. There is no general increase in production and employment. Factors of production are limited. If they are needed in the export industries, they will have to be drawn from the other industries which must consequently shrink. Thus, there is only a diversion of resources and no net increase in production and employment.

ROLE OF PUBLIC BORROWING IN A DEVELOPING ECONOMY

A developing economy has to tap all possible sources to mobilise sufficient financial resources for the implementation of its economic development plans. It has to utilise revenue surplus for the purpose, seek external aid, pitch up its level of taxation and resort to public borrowing in addition. But taxation and public borrowing are the two major instruments of resources mobilisation.

Public borrowing has one advantage over taxation. Taxation, beyond a certain limit, tends to affect economic activity adversely owing to its disincentive effect. There is no such danger in public borrowing. It does not have any unfavourable repercussions on economic activity by being disincentive, partly because of its voluntary nature and partly because of expectation of return and repayment.

According to expert opinion, taxation should cover at least current expenditure on normal government services, and borrowing should be resorted to finance government expenditure which results in creation of capital assets. In that case, growing public debt will not be a burden on the

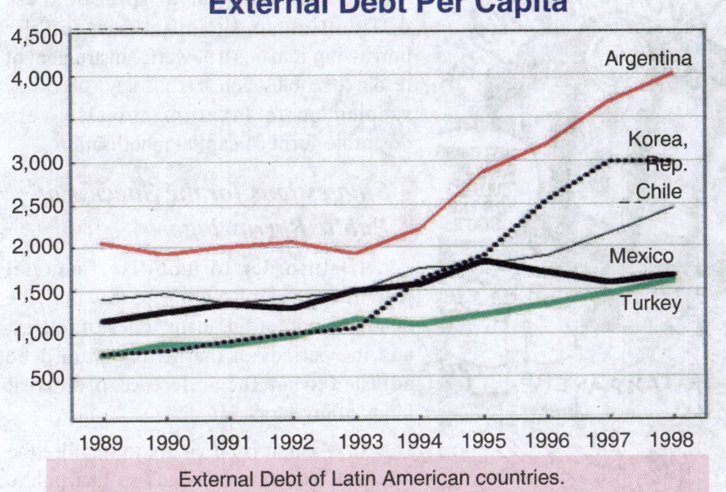

External Debt of Latin American countries.

economy, because such a debt is self-liquidating. But there is a limit to public borrowing, which is considered safe. Additional taxation is also necessary to implement the development plans.

The classical theory frowned upon public borrowing. It was thought that the use of resources by the government was less productive than their use in private hands. But the classical reasoning was based on the assumptions of full employment, inelasticity of money supplies and unproductiveness of public expenditure. These assumptions, we know, are not valid today. Public borrowing for financing productive investment generates additional productive capacity in the economy, which otherwise would not have been possible. It is used as an instrument to mobilise resources which, in an under-developed economy, would otherwise have gone into hoards or invested in real estate or jewellery. Public debt would thus divert the flow of resources into the right channels.

Thus, in an under-developed economy, public borrowing, if prudently managed and skilfully operated, can become a powerful instrument of economic development.

Besides, growing public debt provides the people opportunities to hold their wealth in the form of safe and stable income-yielding assets, *i.e.*, government bonds.

Growth and composition of public debt provides the monetary authorities with assets which they can manipulate to give effect to a monetary policy considered desirable in the context of economic development. Thus, monetary policy, which is considered essential for achieving the objectives of economic policy, becomes vitally related to public debt management. The management of public debt is used as a method to influence the structure of interest rates.

Thus, a growing public debt, in an under-developed economy, has become a powerful tool of developmental monetary policy.

There are two important ways in which the governments of under-developed economies raise resources through public loans: (*a*) **market borrowing,** *i.e.*, sales to the public of government bonds (long-term loans) and treasury bills (short-term loans) in the capital market, (*b*) **non-market borrowing,** *i.e.*, issue to the public of debt which is not negotiable and is not bought and sold in the capital market, *e.g.*, issue of national savings certificate; and national plan bonds and accepting deposits in the government post offices.

Voluntary or Forced Loans

Most of the types of public loans are voluntary. But, if the voluntary loans do not prove sufficient for the purpose, forced loans become necessary and are resorted to. An important example of forced loans familiar in India is that of Compulsory Deposit Scheme. Compulsory borrowing is a compromise between taxation and borrowing. Like a tax it is a compulsory contribution to the government but like a loan, it is to be repaid with interest.

Compulsory loans have a special advantage in the context of an inflationary situation and are superior to voluntary public borrowing. They sterilise funds, whereas voluntary public loans result in the creation of readily cashable bonds. They are monetised to increase liquid assets in the community which produce an inflationary effect. Also, lower rate of interest can be paid on compulsory loans thus reducing the most of public debt. But a continuous policy of compulsory borrowing may arouse public resentment. Normally, it is the voluntary public borrowing programmes which should be chiefly relied upon.

Difficulties of Public Borrowing in Under-developed Countries

Public borrowing, however, has to face special difficulties in under-developed economies: (*i*) There are no organised capital and money markets and, where

they exist, they constitute a very small portion of the total capital and money markets in the country. Also, there may be no organic relationship between the organised and unorganised markets. Besides, the resources of the organised capital market are too inadequate to fulfil the capital needs of the economy.

(ii) Special difficulties of public borrowing in the under-developed countries arise from the fact that the people have a predilection in favour of investment in real estate, that gives them social prestige and for jewellery because it can be easily concealed and can be easily converted into cash in case of need.

(iii) A substantial volume of savings in these countries originates in the rural sector but these people have no tradition of investment in trade and industry. The rural saving cannot be mobilised effectively because rural incomes do not move through monetary channels. That is why most of the financial institutions are concentrated in the urban areas. Also, agricultural interests are entenched strongly, politically and resist all proposals to tax them.

(iv) The prevalence of very high rates of interest militates against the flow of funds towards agricultural improvement, savings accounts, government bonds, small-scale industry or other channels of investment where the yield cannot be so high.

(v) The response to government securities is also poor because of rising prices which reduce the value of the yield from government securities.

Conclusion. But in spite of these difficulties and limitations, public borrowing remains a powerful instrument of resource mobilisation. It is not only a necessary supplement to taxation but also very desirable form of capital mobilisation.

Suggestions for the Success of Public Borrowing

(i) In order to mobilise financial resources through public borrowing, the denomination of the loans, rates of interest and the periods of maturities should be adjusted to suit the preferences of different kinds of investors.

(ii) Also, it is necessary to stabilise the prices of government bonds so that public confidence in the government bonds is retained and response to future issues is encouraging.

(iii) Financial institutions should be set up to attract voluntary savings.

(iv) The facilities for deposit of savings should be varied and widespread and easily accessible.

(v) A reasonable stability in the value of money (*i.e.*, price level) must be assured, otherwise confidence of the savers will be shaken and saving will be discouraged.

(vi) Some under-developed countries have found the lottery system very useful because, according to this system, savings are attracted at lower rates of interest. Thus, prize bonds have been issued to attract savings into the public sector.

(vii) A suitable monetary policy constitutes an important factor in the success of the borrowing programmes of governments in under-developed countries. The aim of the monetary policy is to maintain sufficient liquidity in the economy as a pre-requisite of the success of the borrowing programme. A growth-oriented monetary policy has to be both regulatory and developmental.

Effects of Public Debt on Production, Consumption, Distribution and Level of Income and Employment

In modern times, public borrowing is both extensive and intensive. Almost all countries resort to public borrowing and they get deeper and deeper into it. Financial operations, which public borrowing of modern dimensions involve, are bound to affect production, consumption, distribution and the level of income and employment in the country.

Effect on Production

Vast sums are raised through public loans by modern governments both in the domestic capital market and abroad. They are raised to finance productive enterprises of various kinds, *e.g.*, steel works, multipurpose projects, construction of ships, railway lines and national highways, heavy electrical and engineering works, and so on. Obviously, such enterprises build up the economy's production base and, in course of time, make an enormous increase in the country's output. Public borrowing transforms inactive bank balances of the people into active capital. Repayment of loans also transfers money from expenditure to savings. Thus public borrowing stimulates the process of capital formation which increases the productive capacity of the country.

Effect on Consumption

When people subscribe to government loans, they generally have to curtail consumption. In this way, the propensity to consume is curbed. Since investment of funds raised by borrowing raises the level of employment, and so increases people's incomes, their consumption is increased. Much, however, depends on the manner in which funds raised by public borrowing are spent by the government.

Effect on Distribution

Public loans transfer money from the rich to the government. But the fiscal operations in modern times are meant to benefit the poor primarily. Either the incomes of the poor increase directly through increased employment or it benefits them indirectly through the enlargement of social services. In this way, national wealth comes to be redistributed in favour of the poor. In India, the Prime Minister's 20-Point Programme is aimed at reducing poverty. To the extent it is financed by public borrowing, public loans will have been used to change the distribution of wealth in the country. The rich will become less rich and the poor less poor. In this way, the gulf between the rich and the poor will be narrowed.

Effect on the Level of Income and Employment

In modern times, public borrowing is resorted to in order to raise funds for financing agriculture, industry, extension of the means of transport and communications or for construction of major irrigation works. Sometimes local development projects are launched to increase employment opportunities in rural areas. In this way, not only are the economic activities in the country multiplied but the volume of employment is also increased and the level of incomes goes up.

Key terms

Internal and External Debt, Short-term and Long-term Debt, Burden of Debt.

QUESTIONS

1. Public debt has a secular tndency to go up in every country. Discuss.
2. In what cases and in what manner is it proper for the government to raise loans?
3. State the objects for which public debt may be contracted. Describe the economic effect of public debt.
4. What are the principle methods of redeeming public debt? Explain their relative merits.
5. Distinguish between the burden of internal and external public debt. How would you deal with the problem of their repayment?
6. What do you understand by the burden of public debt? Can any generation shift the burden of public debt to future generations?
7. Discuss the effects of public debt on (*a*) money supply, (*b*) price level and (*c*) rate of interest.
8. Examine the relative merits of taxation and borrowing as methods of mobilising resources for development.
9. Discuss the comparative significance of taxation and borrowing as instruments for financing public expenditure in a developing economy.
10. Compare the effects of taxation and borrowing on production and distribution of wealth in a country.

DEFICIT FINANCING AND FISCAL POLICY

In the face of a fall in private spending, the use of deficit financing to maintain total spending or effective demand in the economy at the level required to buy the full employment output at the current level of price, was an important discovery of the Depression Economics of nineteen-thirties. To-day, it is a major instrument in the hands of government in the advanced countries to ensure continued high levels of economic activity. Lately, the under-developed countries have increasingly realised its potentialities for adding to the resources available for development. India has made quite a liberal use of deficit financing to carry her economic development plans through.

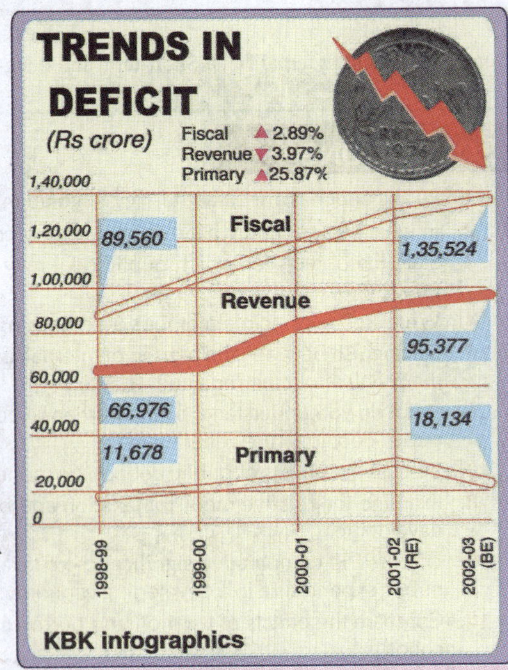

Deficit financing in India.

Definition

It is not possible to give precise definition of deficit financing applicable to all countries at all times. The definition of deficit financing adopted by the Planning Commission in India is that it is equal to the net increase in the purchasing power of the economy arising out of the budgetary operation of the government. Deficit financing is said to have been practised whenever government expenditure exceeds the receipts from the public like taxes, fees and borrowings from the public. Such an excess of government expenditure can be financed either by drawing down the cash balances of the government (held in the Reserve Bank of India or in the State Treasuries) or by borrowing from the Reserve Bank of India. Both these methods of financing the deficit would have the effect of expanding money supply held by the public.

"The term deficit financing is used to denote the direct addition to gross national expenditure through budget deficits whether the deficits are on revenue account or on capital account. The essence of such a policy, therefore, lies in government spending in excess of revenue it receives in the shape of taxes, earnings of State enterprises, loans from the public, deposits and funds and other miscellaneous sources. The government may cover the deficit either by running down its accumulated balances or by borrowing from the banking system mainly from the Central Bank of the country and thus creating money."

The pre-budget Economic Survey for 1974-75 defines deficit financing as "the net credit given to the government sector by the Reserve Bank."

Thus, deficit financing is that part of government expenditure which is met either by drawing down the cash balances of the government or by resorting to borrowing from the Reserve Bank of India. This definition of deficit financing, therefore, identifies it with that part of government expenditure the finance of which leads to a net increase in money supply with the public.

There is a difference in the method of deficit financing practised by the developed countries and the under-developed countries. In advanced countries, deficit financing takes place by the Government borrowing from the banking system when the Government sells government securities either to individual bank depositors or directly to the banks. In both cases additional credit is created by the banking system. In the case of under-developed countries, where the banking habit is not fully developed, deficit financing takes the form of the government borrowing from the central bank instead of the banking system in general. The central bank issues paper currency in lieu of the government securities deposited with it. Thus, deficit financing in the ultimate analysis means issuing of more notes.

Deficit Financing and Deficit Budgeting. Deficit financing may be distinguished from deficit budgeting. When current expenditure exceeds current revenue it is said to be deficit budgeting. In this case, no item on capital account is taken into consideration.

On the other hand, when we take into consideration not only current receipts but also receipts on capital account, *e.g.*, public borrowing, and we still find a gap between receipts and expenditure, the method of financing used to cover this gap is called deficit financing. In other words, in the case of deficit financing, the volume of deficit budgeting is measured in terms of the overall budget deficit, *i.e.*, the aggregate of the deficit on both the revenue and capital accounts.

Uses of Deficit Financing

There are three types of situations in which resort to deficit financing becomes necessary :

(*a*) For prosecuting a war,

(*b*) for fighting depression, and

(*c*) for financing economic development. We shall leave out war and discuss the other two uses.

Deficit Financing during the Depression

We have discussed, in the chapter on Trade Cycle (Ch. 47), the causes of unemployment in advanced and developed countries. There we observed that a deficiency of effective demand is the major cause of cyclical unemployment. In a situation like this, the obvious remedy is to boost effective demand. The government can assist in this process in a number of ways. It can stimulate private consumption and investment. It can do so by lowering the tax rates while maintaining its own expenditure. In this case since the government is spending more than it raises in taxes, it is practising deficit financing, the deficit being covered by borrowing.

If, however, this method of stimulating economic activity does not produce sufficiently effective results, the government can increase its own expenditure on public works programme. The government's tax revenue remains constant but its expenditure has gone up, the deficit once again being met by borrowing. In this case, as government investment rises, the level of national income and employment also increases by multiplier times the increase in primary government investment.

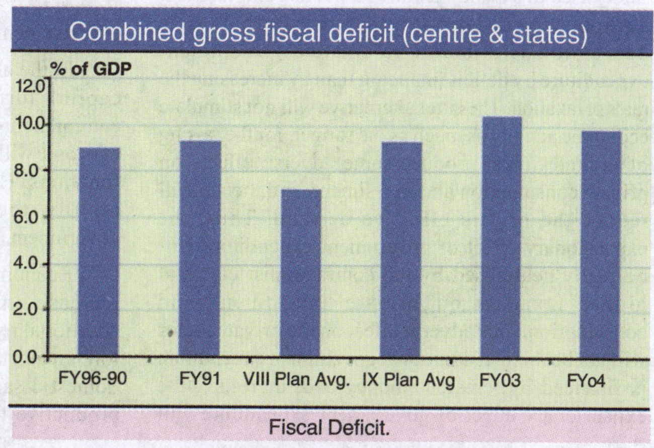

Fiscal Deficit.

Thus, deficit financing can be used to create additional employment, when the economy is suffering from a deficiency of effective demand. It is an instrument of recovery after depression. It is used to mitigate the severity of cyclical fluctuations. In this context, it takes three forms, *viz.*, pump priming, cyclical deficit spending and secular deficit spending to fill the inflationary gap.

This line of approach was made fashionable by the late Lord Keynes. Before him, there was a great deal of prejudice against a government, practising deficit financing. The classical economists were against deficit financing, except for financing productive enterprises. This opposition to deficit financing, on their part, was based on the assumption that in a private enterprise economy the level of activity had the tendency to be always full—an assumption we discussed in an earlier chapter under Say's Law of Markets (Ch. 39). Obviously, if there is already full employment in the economy, government expenditure, financed by the created money, is bound to create inflationary rise in prices. This fear of inflation constantly haunted the classical economists, and this was their main argument against deficit financing.

Lord Keynes, however, established it conclusively that in a situation, where there was large-scale unemployment of labour and excess capacity in the stock of capital, the fear that deficit financing would create inflation was baseless. For, when more employment was created by deficit spending on the part of the government, there would simultaneously take place an increase in the supply of output. When there is depression, an increase in supply can be had without any rise in average and marginal costs of production, so that additional demand creates additional supply of output without any rise in prices.

Thus, during depression, deficit financing can be safely used to expand income, output and employment without any inflationary danger. Rather, in a depression it is better to finance government expenditure by deficit financing than by increasing the rates of taxation. The latter alternative will not stimulate economic activity as much as the former, for the raising of tax rates must produce some adverse effects on private consumption and investment, and, hence will reduce the private effective demand. Thus, the expansionary effect of government expenditure will be partly neutralised by the contractionist effect of higher taxation on private investment and consumption. This adverse effect on the private sector will not be there, if additional government expenditure is financed by 'created' money and, therefore, the expansionary effect of government expenditure will correspondingly be greater. Increased spending offsets the deficiency of effective demand and puts into motion the stagnant wheels of the productive machinery. In this way, deficit financing makes for economic stability.

ROLE OF DEFICIT FINANCING IN A DEVELOPING ECONOMY

What scope is there for deficit financing to be used as an instrument of economic development in the under-developed countries like India? In the chapter on 'Determination of National Income' (Ch. 40), we observed that the basic problem confronting these countries is that of a population growing much faster than the rate of capital formation. If these countries are to provide full employment to their labour force, they need huge amounts of capital. Unlike the advanced economies, the problem facing under-developed countries is not one of deficiency of effective demand but of deficiency of capital.

Deficit financing results in the creation of new money.

In the advanced capitalist countries, the task of capital formation is in the hands of private entrepreneurs; but, in poor countries there is a dearth of people willing and able to undertake entrepreneurial functions. Hence, if these countries are to develop rapidly, the responsibility must rest with the government.

Economic growth can be accelerated only by increasing the rate of investment. This requires additional resources and, in the absence of sufficient foreign aid, they can come out only through increased domestic savings, these being channelised along productive lines. One way of increasing domestic savings is through additional voluntary effort on the part of the public through small savings schemes. These savings add to the resources available to the government.

But, in a country, where a majority of people are living at the subsistence level, the marginal between income and consumption is very low so that voluntary savings, howsoever welcome, cannot by themselves provide sufficient resources for development. The government may also attempt to increase the volume of resources by additional taxes. Yet, because of extreme poverty of the great mass of the people, additional taxation beyond a point raises difficult problems, both economic as well as political.

"Due to the low levels of income and high propensity to consume, aggregate savings in the economy are low. Investment being inadequate as compared to national requirements, the level of production, incomes, savings and thus of investment again, cannot increase sufficiently. It is, therefore, necessary to break such a vicious circle of poverty in these economies."[1] Since investment expenditure required for speedy economic development is too large to be financed through normal sources of revenue, deficit financing becomes inevitable.

As pointed out already, deficit financing results in the creation of new money. The increase in the money supply tends to raise prices because the supply of goods cannot be increased in the short run in proportion to increase in the people's purchasing power. As a result of rise in prices, entrepreneurs' profits go up and there is an increase in the inducement to invest on their part. Thus, there is increase in investment in the private sector.

Investment increases in the public sector too. Deficit financing puts in the hands of the government huge amounts of money with which they launch public enterprises, carry out multipurpose projects and build up the essential infrastructure. All this accelerates economic development. Thus, deficit financing gives the government command over productive resources which are utilised more fully and more fruitfully.

In this way, deficit financing stimulates economic development both in the public and private sector. It also promotes economic development by reducing consumption through a price rise.

In short, deficit financing accelerates economic development,

(a) by building up social and economic overheads,

(b) by using unemployed or under-employed resources and surplus labour more fully,

(*c*) by helping to create additional productive capital, and

(d) by mobilising additional resources for development.

Precautions

There is inherent danger of inflation in deficit financing which must be guarded against to ensure economic growth with stability. To avoid this danger, it will be necessary to take the following precautions in the use of deficit financing:

(i) Deficit financing should be used in moderate doses only and for this purpose constant watch should be kept over the price index.

(ii) The prices of consumer's goods and of essential raw materials should be effectively controlled.

(iii) To ensure a corresponding increase in the availability of goods, it will be necessary to concentrate on the quick-yielding projects.

(iv) In order to keep down the prices of food-grains, food imports should be arranged well in time and in adequate quantities.

(v) The rise in wages and salaries should be checked lest the country should be caught in a vicious circle.

(vi) To withdraw from the public excess purchasing power, the excess money supply should

DEFICIT FINANCING IN INDIA'S FIVE-YEAR PLANS

Deficit financing was given a very important place in India's five-year plans, rather too much reliance on it. The following table gives the amount of deficit financing in the five-year plans in India.

Deficit Financing in India's Five-Year Plans

Plan of Year	*Deficit Financing (Rs. Crores)*
First Five-Year Plan (1951-56)	333
Second Five-Year Plan (1956-61)	950
Third Five-Year Plan	1,150
Fourth Five-Year Plan (1969-74)	2,060
Fifth Five-Year Plan (1974-75-1977-78)	5,830
Sixth Plan (1980-85)	15,680
Seventh Plan(1985-90)	28,260
Eighth Plan (1992-97)	33,040

1. Kulkarni, R.G. —*Deficit Financing and Economic Development*, 1966, p. 32.

be mopped up through taxation and borrowing and through attractive small savings scheme.

(vii) Above all, it will be essential to provide clean and efficient administration to ensure whole-hearted co-operation from the people in tackling the difficult economic situation resulting from a liberal use of deficit financing.

CONSEQUENCES OF DEFICIT FINANCING

The possible effects of deficit financing are:

(a) Increase in money supply with the public;

(b) the rise in the level of incomes; and

(c) the rise in the general price level.

Whether deficit financing is utilised for war purposes or for bringing about recovery after depression or for initiating the process of economic growth, the direct and immediate result is to increase the volume of total money supply with the public. However, the actual expansion of currency will depend on the credit policy of the central bank and the commercial banks and the balance of payments position.

Deficit financing also results in the increase in the level of incomes. Increase in government expenditure facilitated by deficit financing adds to the incomes of the people in the form of wages, salaries, rent, interest payments, profits, *etc.* Large amount of public spending promotes business investment and hence increases national income.

But the most striking effect of deficit financing is on the price level. Since, as mentioned above, deficit financing results in the expansion of money supply with the public, it tends to be inflationary. We discuss this effect in the section below.

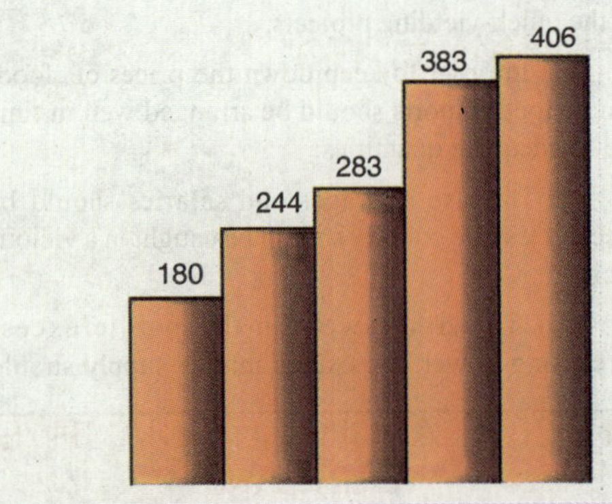

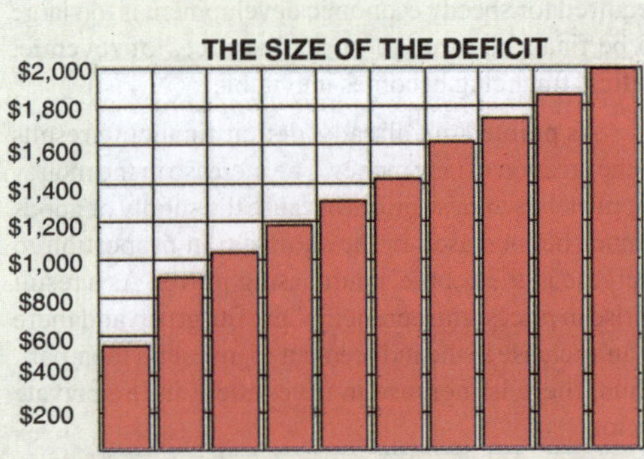

Deficit financing increases level of income.

Deficit Financing and Inflation

Deficit financing practised during the depression in advanced countries does not generate inflationary pressures, because of the elastic nature of the supply curves of output. Additional government expenditure leads to an increase in effective demand, depending on the magnitude of the multiplier. Similarly, when supply of output can be increased easily to match additional demand, there need be no inflationary pressures. In advanced countries, during the depression, there is lot of excess capacity in the economic system, so that an increase in output presents no difficult problems.

The situation in under-developed countries, however, is different. Here, an increase in investment does create additional demand, but a corresponding increase in the supply of output cannot be taken for granted. Firstly, an under-developed country suffers from the dearth of capital, and there is no excess capacity to be utilised for creating additional supply of consumer's goods.

Besides, the basic wage-goods industry, *i.e.*, agriculture, suffers from an inelastic supply curve, in the short run. In a subsistence agriculture, when the demand for agricultural products goes up, the farmer often lacks the willingness as well as the ability to increase his output.

The farmer's demand for non-agricultural consumer's goods is limited so that when agricultural prices rise relatively to the prices of industrial products, the farmer can satisfy his needs with less effort than before, and his reaction may well be to work less in the next period. Moreover, even if he wants to increase his output, his ability to do so is very limited. His holding is a small one and often lies scattered all over the village. He lacks resources to buy more and better seeds and manures; irrigation facilities are also lacking so that even with the best of wills in the world, unaided by any outside agency, the farmer's efforts to increase his output may not bear fruit.

Thus, in the absence of an elastic supply of consumers' goods, a development plan carries with it a great inflationary bias.

In the earlier stages of development, the inflationary danger is very real indeed. This is because of the urgent need to invest large sums in the creation of an adequate system of transport and communications. Such investments generate demand like any other investment outlays, yet they do not directly add to the supply of consumption goods. For all these reasons, deficit financing in under-developed countries is full of inflationary potentialities and these have to be watched carefully so as to keep them under control.

Not Necessarily Inflationary

As already mentioned, deficit financing results in a net increase in the money supply with the public. Of course, there is no direct relation between an increase in money supply and the inflationary rise in prices. If, for example, the newly created money is merely hoarded or saved, no inflationary pressure is generated. But to the extent that new money is used to offer additional employment to the hitherto unemployed or the new recruits to the working force, a large part of it will be spent and hence add to the volume of effective demand.

Similarly, if sufficient additional supply of consumers' goods can be made available with the help of additional investment, once again there need be no inflationary pressures and supply and demand may be in equilibrium at a higher level.

The inflationary impact of deficit financing also depends on the extent of monetisation of an economy. In case of a 100 per cent monetisation, the impact of a given amount of deficit financing will be less inflationary than when it is only partly monetised. In the case of non-monetised sector, the increase in money supply is to be viewed against that output which enters into monetary transactions.

Deficit financing creates inflationary revenue.

The propensity to consume also affects the inflationary impact of deficit financing. In case propensity to consume is low, the inflationary impact is reduced ,whereas a high propensity to consume intensifies the inflationary pressure. Since propensity to consume is constant in the short run, the inflationary impact cannot be managed through the marginal propensity to consume. Conversely, the inflationary impact of deficit financing will be less when the marginal propensity to save is high, and **vice versa.**

Also, the inflationary pressure generated by deficit financing depends upon the proportion which the amount of deficit financing bears to the total national income. The lower this proportion, irrespective of the amount, the lower will be inflationary impact. In other words, when the amount of national output rises proportionately to deficit financing, the prices too will behave proportionally and the inflationary impact will be lower. If deficit financing leads to utilization of unused resources of the economy and results in increase in output, it will neutralise the inflationary impact.

The inflationary impact of deficit financing also depends upon the nature of public expenditure. If public expenditure only adds to money incomes without an increase in output, the inflationary impact will be higher. It will be lower if public expenditure goes into production of goods and services. On the whole, deficit financing generates inflationary pressures unless supply of goods is increased rapidly and sufficiently.

The management of inflation depends on the effectiveness of government controls, public cooperation and future outlook.

Minimising Inflationary Potential of Deficit Financing

The following measures will minimise the inflationary potential of deficit financing:

(*i*) Fiscal Policy. Through a proper disinflationary fiscal policy, the inflationary pressures generated by deficit financing can be controlled to some extent. This involves raising taxes on income and consumption and reduction of non-essential government expenditure. Through various tax measures, the government can mop up a part of the increase in incomes generated by the development expenditure. All these measures will reduce the pressure of demand on the available goods and services.

***(ii)* Monetary Policy.** By adopting a restrictive monetary policy, non-essential private investment can be kept under control, thereby releasing resources for the expansion of essential investment.

***(iii)* Economic Controls.** Through selective credit controls, physical and fiscal controls, the government can influence the behaviour of private investment and channelise it into desirable lines. For example, scarce materials can be rationed, building activity can be controlled and controls imposed on new capital issues by the companies.

***(iv)* Proper Allocation of Resources.** All the above measures have for their aim the reduction of pressure of demand. But attempts should be simultaneously made to increase the supply of output of consumption goods. In this connection a proper balance must be kept between agriculture and industry and heavy and light industries. Agriculture is the supplier of basic wage-good, *i.e.*, food. Therefore, a programme of economic development which fails to lay proper emphasis on the increase in agricultural production must run into inflationary difficulties. Similarly, industries requiring small investment and maturing quickly should also receive due emphasis.

***(v)* Developing Import Surplus.** The supply of goods can also be increased by having an import surplus. In the Indian First Five-Year Plan, for instance, there was a provision, for drawing down our sterling balances by Rs. 290 crores to finance imports in order to dampen the inflationary effects of deficit financing. (Actually, however, deficit financing was much higher than anticipated and withdrawal of sterling balances was smaller than expected). However, there is a limit to which a country can have an import surplus. This is limited by the availability of resources of foreign exchange by the previously accumulated or by receiving fresh foreign loans.

Thus, suitable fiscal and monetary policy can go a long way in counter-acting the inflationary effect of deficit financing. But beyond a limit, it is bound to prove inflationary.

Conclusion

The above discussion indicates alike the scope and limitations of deficit financing. Deficit financing has a definite place in development finance but it is desirable to keep it within "safe limits". The extent of deficit financing depends on our ability to control inflationary pressures by keeping demand in check as well as by simultaneous increase in production. It is indeed gratifying that through discipline and hard work and realising the dangers of inflation, our country has a unique distinction of having successfully controlled inflation and actually achieving a negative rate of inflation. This has paved the way for economic growth with stability.

Concept and Principles of Federal Finance

Federal Finance seeks to maximise total welfare. The economic welfare of an under-developed region in a federation can be increased by the diversion of resources from the developed regions.

The general principle to maximise economic welfare is that each regional or State government should try to equate marginal social benefit (*MSB*) with marginal social cost (*MSC*). The federal government will try to do so for the whole county. Thus the principle of federal finance would be

$MSBa = MSBb = MSBc$ and also

$MSCa = MSCb = MSCc$

Here, ***a***, ***b*** and ***c*** are three regions or States.

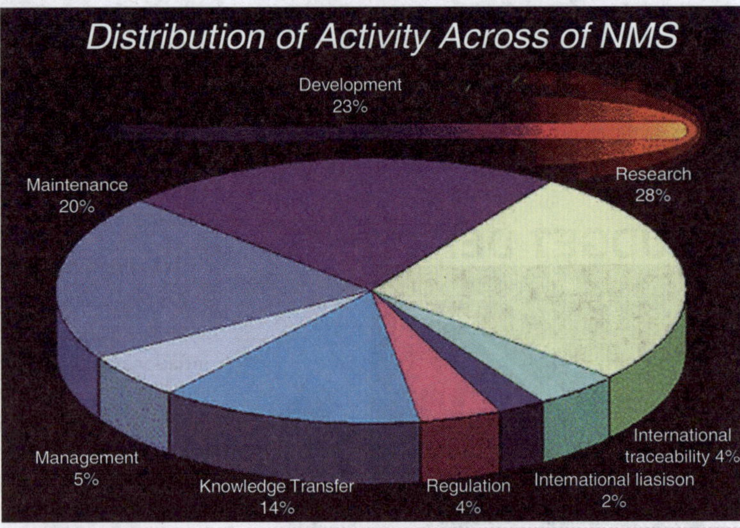

Deficit financing is an important source of financing development activities.

Inter-Personal Equity: Equalising of marginal

social benefits and marginal social cost in the union as well as the units would require a substantial inter-area transfer of resources in a federation for achieving what Prof. Buchanan calls **inter-personal equity.** Inter-personal equity means equal treatment to equals. Suppose the per capita in one federating unit is higher than in another. If the same amount of a tax is collected in both the federal units, (States) and the same amount of expenditure is incurred in both the states, the total tax collection and the total expenditure made in the rich state will be higher than in the poor state. The same amount of expenditure in both states would mean that a resident of the rich state will be subject to less tax than his equal income counter-part in the poor state. A transfer of resources will thus be necessary to achieve **horizontal equity.** Also, the total benefits derived by the individuals in the two units from public goods may not be equal; being more in the richer units than in the poor ones. This inequality too must be removed or minimised.

The two practical problems to be tackled in federal finance are (*a*) the allocation of resources between the different regional governments and (*b*) the balancing of resources with the needs of the regions. For the solution of these two problems, the following principles have been suggested. These may be called the principles of federal finance:

1. Uniformity. The principle of uniformity implies that there should be no discrimination in levying taxes between one unit and another. That is why, for instance, in India, income tax, central excise duties, etc. are levied by the Central government and sales tax, land revenue, *etc.* by the state governments.

2. Independence of Freedom. The federal constitution earmarks certain resources to the unit in which they are free to levy taxes and also free to spend. There is no dependence on each other and the central government does not interfere. In this way, each unit will try to develop resources assigned to it.

3. Adequacy. It is also necessary that both the Central government and the federal units have at their disposal sufficient resources to carry on their normal functions, so that there is no dependence of one on the other.

4. Elasticity. The resources assigned both to the Centre and the states should be capable of expansion as the requirements increase. In India, this is made possible by the appointment of a Finance Commission every five years to recommend further devolution of resources.

5. Efficiency. Federal finance should also provide for efficiency or administrative economy. The taxes should be so levied and collected that there is minimum evasion and minimum cost of collection. Also, adverse effects on trade and industry should be minimised. To ensure the observance of this principle, taxes of inter-state importance are collected by the union government and taxes of state importance by the States.

6. Grants-In Aid to Deficit States. Since usually the State resources are comparatively inelastic and inadequate to meet their requirements it is necessary that there should be a provision for grants-in-aid to meet these deficits. For instance, the Indian Seventh Finance Commission recommended a total transfer of Rs. 20,842 crores from the Centre to the states for the five-year period 1979-84.

Conclusion. The basic fiscal problems in a federation relate to allocation, distribution and stabilisation and it is the duty of federal finance to offer suitable solutions to these problems.

FISCAL POLICY

Fiscal policy is one of the important macro-economic policy. After the publication of Keynesian General Theory, the fiscal policy took the driver's seat in the policy formulation of the governments so as to achieve their objectives. In modern day economics fiscal policy is quite ahead of monetary policy and other policies as an instrument in the hands of the governments to achieve their desired economic and non-economic results.

Fiscal policy can be defined as "the conscious policy of a government so as achieve certain pre-determined socio-economic objectives with the help of public revenue, public expenditure and public debt". It can also be defined as the policy of the state, so as to achieve certain desired economic and non-

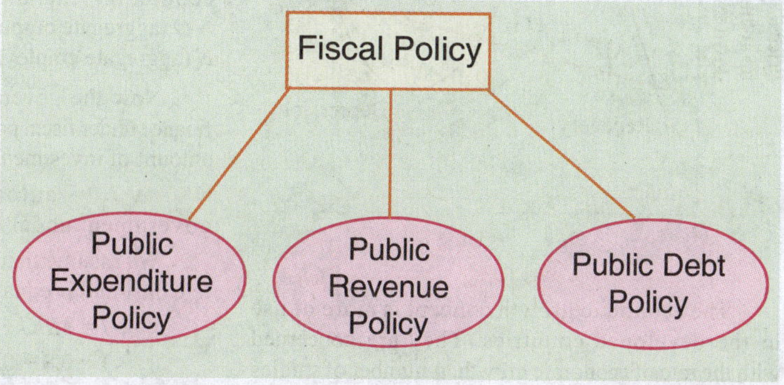

economic objectives, and avoid undesired effects, with the help of public revenue, public expenditure and public debt. Mrs. Ursula Hicks, says, "Fiscal Policy is concerned with the manner in which the different elements of public finance, while still primarily concerned with carrying out their own duties (as the first duty of a tax is to raise revenue), may collectively be geared to forward the aim of economic policy".

According to Otto Eckstein Fiscal policy is nothing but "changes in taxes and expenditures which aim at short-run goals of full employment and price-level stability".

Objectives of Fiscal Policy

The following are the main objectives of fiscal policy :–

(i) Economic growth

(ii) Full employment

(iii) Price stability and

(iv) Social justice.

***(i)* Economic Growth.** "Economic growth is nothing but an increase in the economic activities or economic variables over a period of time." In simple means, by reducing, *(a)* direct taxes, a state can induce the investors or entrepreneurs to increase the rate of investment, which will automatically increase production, employment and income generation *etc.*, and *(b)* indirect taxes, which will motivate the buyers (consumer's) to demand more goods which will automatically increase the economic activities.

On the other hand by bringing about an increase in public expenditure on infra structure *etc.*, the government can accelerate the rate of economic growth.

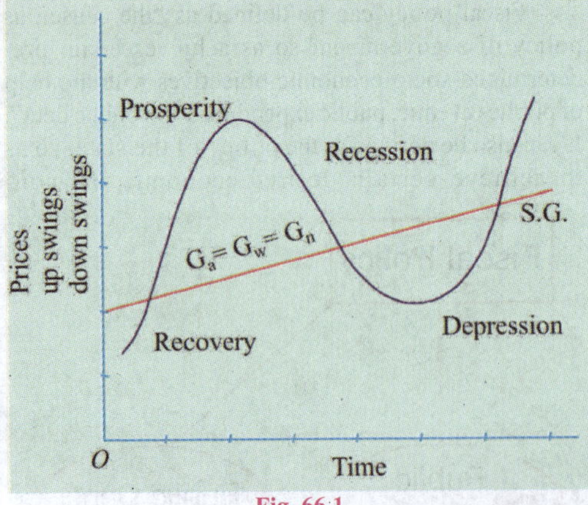

Fig. 66.1

The economic growth concept is more of use in the developed countries. They are concerned with the rate of economic growth. A number of studies were carried out, Harrod and Domar, initiated a new growth rate model independently.

Let us explain the concept of gradual growth putforth by Harrod, who said, could be achieved by equating $Ga = Gw = Gn$. The simple schmpeterian phases of business cycles diagram is taken into account. The four phases are recovery, prosperity, recession and recovery. According to Harrod economic growth must increase with a gradual or steady rate. Economic growth must increase without the sudden up -swings (prosperity) and downswings (depression). For this he advocated $Ga = Gw = Gn$.

	growth	rate
Ga = Actual		
Gw = Warranted	,,	,,
Gn = Natural	,,	,,

'*SG*' is the steady growth rate, which is increasing slowly over a period of time without the upswings and downswings. Hence the aim of fiscal policy is to help achieve "$Ga = Gw = Gn$".

***(ii)* The Full Employment.** The Keynesian functional finance approach, came to the help of President Roosevelt to rescue the American economy from "the great depression". President Hoover failed to stabilise the economy though many different measures were taken. It was the 'deficit finance' or 'autonomous investment' measures which helped the economy to revive. The theory of pump-priming' was of intense success.

The Theory of "Pump Priming"

In the below diagram, '*x*' axis income in both upper part as well as lower part and on '*y*' axis upper part *ASF* (Aggregate supply function) and ADF (Aggregate demand function) and lower part y-axis upswings and downswings of a business cycle is taken.

Δ Output = Δ Income = Δ Employment

(I) Let the economy is at point 'E_1' which in lower part is at a very low-level of economic activity at 'I_1'. The income-level is at y_1, (According to Keynesian economics the effective demand determines, ΔO (aggregate output) = ΔY (aggregate income) = ΔN (aggregate employment)]

Now the government with the help of deficit finance under fiscal policy brings about of an additional amount of investment ($ = 1000) million.

ΔI_1 = autonomous investment by the government under fiscal policy = 1000 $ million.

We assume that the *MPC* (Marginal Propensity to Consume) is equal to 0.8, and that mean $Y = C + S$

$$I = MPC + MPS.$$

$$I = 0.8 + 0.2.$$

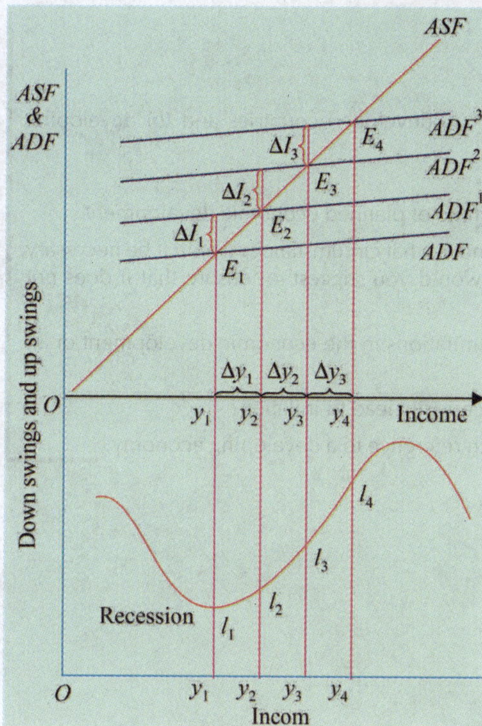

Fig. 66.2.

Multiplier $K = \frac{1}{1 - MPC}$ or $\frac{1}{MPS}$

$$K \frac{1}{1.08} = \frac{1}{0.2} = \frac{1}{\frac{1}{5}} = 5$$

Hence $\Delta Y_1 = \Delta I_1 \times k.$

$= 1000 \$ \times 5 = 5000 \$$ Million.

Thus under the fiscal policy the government brings out $\Delta I_1 = 1000$ \$ (million) in the public infra structure or other activities, which through, the multiplier effect increases. The income, output and employment that is $\Delta Y_1 = 5000$ \$ million due to multiplier effect.

This helps the economy to move up (in the lower diagram) from 'l_1' to 'l_2'. The economy moves from point 'y_1' to 'y_2'.

ΔI_1 leads to ΔY_1 which increases the economy from Y_1 to Y_2.

(*II*) Now again the government brings about another \$ 1000 million in the economy, which will increase the economy through multiplier effect.

$\Delta Y_2 = \Delta I_2 \times K$

$= 1000$ million $\times 5$

$= 5000$ million \$

This will lift the economy upward from 'l_2' to 'l_3' point and thus increases the economy from OY_1 to OY_2 to OY_3.

(*III*) Again the same process, that means $\Delta I_3 =$ Additional \$ 1000 million is put in the economy through public expenditure (Fiscal policy). This through the multiplier effect increases the economy from OY_2 to OY_3, due to this $\Delta I_3 = 1000$ million \$ investment the economy increases from 'OY_3' to 'OY_4'.

This is due to $\Delta Y_3 = \Delta I_3 \times k$.

The same process shifts the economy from 'l_3' to 'l_4' which puts the economy on prosperity phase.

"The out-come of the theory of pump-priming is that the government increases under fiscal policy the investment from ΔI_1 1000 \$ million \$, to $\Delta I_2 = 1000$ million \$, $\Delta I_3 = 1000$ million \$, after a certain amount of time interval, which leads the economy to increase from OY_1 to OY_2 to OY_3 and the lower diagram the economy moves from 'l_1' → 'l_2' → 'l_3' and 'l_4 which is in the prosperity phase."

This was one of the essential outcome of Keynesian theory of pump-priming, which helped in rescuing the American economy from 'great depression'. Keynesian economy has been referred as the "economy of depression" is true to the point in this sense.

(*III*) Economic Stability or Demand Stabilisation. Through the fiscal policy we can follow the below mentioned policy measures to bring about demand stabilisation.

(*IV*) **Social Justice.** The government can achieve social justice by imposing higher rate progressive taxes on rich and giving subsidies and concession to lower income and middle income groups.

Fiscal policy in Developing Countries. The following will be the main objectives in developing countries.

(*i*) To accelerate the rate of economic growth.

(*ii*) To help build-up-basic and heavy industries.

(*iii*) To achieve regional balance development.

(*iv*) To help mobilise capital formation

(*v*) To help develop infarastructure.

(*vi*) To bring about decentralisation of the economy.

(*vii*) To reduce the concentration of economics power in the hands of few.

QUESTIONS

1. Define "fiscal policy".
2. Discuss the main objectives of fiscal policy in (*a*) developed countries and (*b*) developing countries.
3. Critically evaluate the theory of "Pump-priming".
4. Analyse the role of deficit financing in a programme of planned economic development.
5. Evaluate benefits and dangers of Public Debt. Under what circumstances would it be necessary to resort to deficit financing? What safeguards would you suggest to ensure that it does not produce adverse effects?
6. What is deficit financing? Discuss its role and limitations in the economic development of an under-developed country.
7. What is meant by Deficit Financing? Does it necessarily lead to inflation?
8. What is fiscal policy? Examine its objectives with reference to a developing economy.

PART SIX

ECONOMIC SYSTEMS

Chapters

69

CHAPTER

CAPITALISM

There is hardly any country today which can be called a pure free enterprise or capitalistic economy. Even the economies of the U.S.A. and the U.K., which are called capitalistic economies, are examples of mixed economies. But basically, they are still free market or capitalistic economies, because even now major role in their economies is played by private enterprise and capital.

Definition

Under capitalism, all farms, factories and other means of production are the property of private individuals and firms. They are free to use them with a view to making profit, or not to use them, if it so suits them. The desire for profit is the sole consideration with the property-owners in the use of their property. Besides free and unfettered use of their property, everybody is free to take up any line of production he likes and is free to enter into any contract with other fellow-citizens for his profit.

Although all modern States do impose certain restrictions on economic freedom in the interest of general welfare, yet even these restrictions leave much latitude to the propertied class to use their property in any manner they like, to start any business they think profitable to themselves, and to enter into contracts they think necessary in their own interest.

What to produce, how to produce and for whom to produce—all these central problems of economics are settled by the free working of the forces of demand and supply. The economic development of the U.S.A., the U.K. and the Western European countries took place under capitalism or under the system of free enterprise. In the words of Prof. Loucks, "Capitalism is a system of economic organisation featured by the private ownership and the use for private profit of man-made and nature-made capital."[1]

The definition of capitalism, given by the Webs, brings out the necessary implications of the system. They define it thus: "By the term 'capitalism' or the capitalistic system' or as we prefer the 'capitalist civilization', we mean the particular stage in the development of industry and legal institutions in which the bulk of the workers find themselves divorced from the ownership of the instruments of production in such a way as to pass into the position of wage-earners whose subsistence,

Capitalism refers to private ownership of property.

1. Loucks—*Comparative Ecconomic Systems.*

security and personal freedom seem dependent on the will of a relatively small proportion of the nation, namely, those who own and, through their legal ownership, control the organisation of the land, the machinery and the labour forces of the community and do so with the object of making for themselves individual and private gains".

Outstanding Features of Capitalism

A study of capitalism reveals several outstanding features of this system:

(*i*) Right of Private Property. The most important feature of capitalism is the existence of private property and the system of inheritance. Everybody has a right to acquire private property, to keep it, and, after his death, to pass it on to his heirs. The result of this system is that inequalities of wealth distribution are perpetuated. The rich people become richer and the poor become poorer.

Allied with this feature is another, *viz*., that instruments for production are owned by private individuals and they are managed by the owners of farms and factories. They carry on the business of agriculture, trade and industry for their own personal profit and not for the benefit of the society. The result is that the lion's share of the national dividend goes to the powerful capitalist and the rich landlord. The masses are exploited and do not get a fair return on their labour.

(*ii*) Freedom of Enterprise. A very outstanding feature of the capitalistic order of the society is economic freedom. This freedom implies three things: (*a*) freedom of enterprise, (*b*) freedom of contract, and (*c*) freedom to use one's property. Everybody is free to take up any occupation that he likes or start any business he likes and to enter into contracts or agreements with his fellow-citizens in a manner most profitable to him. Every citizen has the freedom to form any firm or company and set up a factory anywhere he likes provided he has the requisite capital and ability.

Actually, however, there is no absolute freedom in these respects: In the interest of general welfare, certain restrictions are imposed by all States on individual rights. Freedom to choose one's occupation is only in name. Family influence, the resources of an individual, prejudices, and other social restrictions stand in the way of a person choosing the occupation that he likes. The result is that only poorly-paid occupations are open to the poor.

(*iii*) Freedom of Choice by the Consumers. Another important feature of capitalism is that every consumer enjoys a freedom of choice of the commodities and services that he wishes to consume. He cannot be forced to consume any particular commodity or service nor can he be forced to give up the use of any commodity or service. Under capitalism the consumer is sovereign. Of course, the consumer's sovereignty is limited by the consumer's income and the availability of goods. It is the consumer's likes and dislikes which determine the magnitude and pattern of production. (We discuss it more fully below).

(*iv*) Profit Motive. Still another characteristic of capitalism is that the profit motive of individuals governs business enterprise. It is the profit motive which induces people to undertake any productive activity. To make profit is the primary motive of entrepreneurial activity and not love of society or social service. Those commodities and services are produced under capitalism which are expected to yield maximum profit. Hence, what to produce and how much to produce is determined by individual profit rather than by social benefit. It is the profit motive which induces businessmen to make the optimum use of the factors of production. Thus, profit motive is the mainspring of all economic activity under capitalism.

(*v*) Class-Conflict. From this arises another feature of this economic order, *viz*., that there is class-conflict. The society has been divided into two classes, the "haves" and the "have-nots" which are constantly at war with each other. Conflict between

Capitalism creates two classes "Haves" and "Have-nots".

agent of the community in the matter of production. It is difficult to see how the present system can work at all in the absence of the entrepreneur. Every thing hinges on him.

Capitalism encourages enterpreneurship.

labour and capital is going on in all capitalistic countries, and there seems to be no near solution of this problem. One regards the other as its natural enemy. It seems that this class conflict is inherent in capitalism.

***(vi)* Un-co-ordinated Nature.** A very remarkable feature of this economic order is its unco-ordinated nature. There is no conscious regulation or central direction of economic activity. Everything seems to go on automatically. Production is conducted as a result of the decisions of numerous isolated entrepreneurs. It is also at the same time influenced by the vast army of individual consumers who make their decisions without consulting one another. The consumer is the king. It is consumer's preferences (or aversions) which finally decide what should be produced and what should not be produced. They furnish the demand side and the unco-ordinated activities of the producers the supply side. Somehow the demand and supply adjust themselves to each other. Price serves as the sign-post or the signal. Price influences the consumers as well as the producers. That is why the present system has been described as a "government by price."

***(vii)* Entrepreneur's Role.** A prominent feature of this economic order is the vital role which the entrepreneur plays under this system. The entire productive machinery of the country is under his direction. It is he who hires the other factors of production and undertakes to pay them. He is the sole

***(viii)* Control with Risks.** We also notice another feature of the present economic system, *viz.*, the control of business goes with risk. This has been called the Golden Rule of Capitalism. He who risks his money must also control the business. He who pays the piper must call the tune. If capital belongs to some other people and the control is vested in the hands of those who have no stake in business, we can imagine that the decisions will be made in a very irresponsible manner.

***(ix)* Competition.** This is another characteristic of capitalism. The producers compete with one another to get the consumer's choice or in selling the commodity as much as they can through advertisement. They may cut the price or improve the quality of the product or offer other concessions to the purchasers. On the other hand, there is also competition among the buyers to obtain the commodity who bid against one another and offer higher prices for the purpose. Similarly, there is competition among workers for jobs.

It may also be pointed out that pure or perfect competition is rare in capitalism. In the real world, there is imperfect or monopolistic competition. Pure competition is only an exception. Also, the producers generally combine to form monopolies or oligopolies to maximise their profits by charging the maximum prices they can.

We may also notice that this economic order is not only based on competition, but also on combination or co-operation among the various interests. The buyers compete with buyers and the sellers with sellers; the labourers compete with one another in order to get jobs but they also combine in trade unions to fight the capitalists. Similarly, the employers not only compete among themselves but they also combine to form associations to safeguard their interests. Thus, under capitalism, combination and competition go side by side.

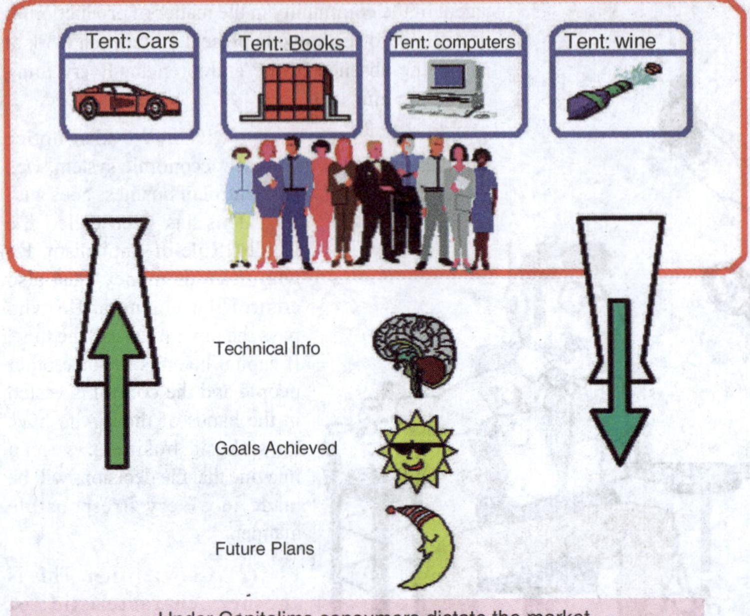

Under Capitalims consumers dictate the market.

(x) Importance of Price System. Capitalism is said to be governed by price. It is the price-mechanism which facilitates the functioning of capitalism. It is the price which equates the demand and supply of commodities and factors of production. For instance, if supply is short, price rises and demand is cut to the size of supply. If supply is large, the price comes down so that the extra supply is taken off the market. Price is a signal which guides the producers as to what to produce and what not to produce. A higher price is also a warning to the consumers to cut down their consumption.

(xi) Economic Inequalities. A feature of capitalistic countries is the glaring inequalities of wealth and income. A few are very rich indulging in all sorts of conceivable luxuries, whereas the masses are not able to get even two square meals a day. What is more painful is that the gulf between the rich and poor is ever widening. The inequalities arise from unearned incomes which are due to uneven distribution of wealth. Larger wealth yields higher income.

SOVEREIGNTY OF THE CONSUMER

Under capitalism or the system of free enterprise, the consumer has been compared to a king. The entire productive machinery is supposed to work under his sovereign sway. His whims, prejudices and desires seem to rule the world of production. The entrepreneurs of modern industry are his bond slaves and so many servants to carry out his commands. If the consumer is pleased, the entrepreneurs are happy and prosperous and if the consumer is dissatisfied, the entrepreneurs' fate is sealed. Thus, the consumer is said to be the monarch of all he surveys.

In the past, the consumer's rule was manifest. The consumer placed the order, say, for shoes, clothes, *etc.*, and the market simply carried out the order faithfully. The consumer got what he wanted. He was undoubtedly the sovereign.

But the modern producer does not work to order. He anticipates demand. It is the business of the entrepreneur to make a shrewd guess as to what would satisfy the consumer the most. Here again, the consumer's preference exert their full weight. If the entrepreneur is not sufficiently intelligent to gauge rightly the requirements of the consumers, or if the prices fixed by him do not suit the pockets of the consumers, his goods will not sell.

In a capitalist eco-nomy, such ventures will succeed as satisfy the consumers the most. Universal consumption is something like universal suffrage; it is a democratic means of control. The only qualification required for consumption is the possession of income with which to acquire the desired goods. "In economic elections, a consumer casts as many votes as he has dollars to spend. If the economic electorate decides to spend its money for baubles instead of essentials, for shoddy goods instead of genuine articles, for things that are ugly instead of things that are beautiful, such things will be produced. Consumer's choice, whether it is wise or foolish, guides the operations of our industrial system. It is like closing an electric circuit and thereby turning on a current that sets the wheel of the productive mechanism into motion."[2]

Thus, the rationale of all economic activity is the satisfaction of the consumer's wants.

2. Kleckhofer. W.H., *Economic Principles, Problems and Policies*, 1936, p. 652.

Limitations

But the consumer is not so despotic a monarch as he is supposed to be. At best his case may be one of constitutional or limited monarchy. A constitutional morarch reigns but does not rule. There are some serious limitations on the authority of our sovereign, the consumer.

The most important check on his authority arises from the **size of his income.** The things do not move according to his command unless he uses the money-whip. The consumer wants pure ghee but he has to be content with Dalda for lack of means to pay. Thus, the real wants of the consumers go unsatisfied under capitalism and only those wants can be satisfied which are expressed in money.

Consumers, sovereignty is a myth. Infact instruments such as advertising has targeted the consumers, the way producers want.

Further, the individual consumer does not count. It is only the combined demand which rules.

The satisfaction of the consumer depends on the **goods actually available** in the market. There are physical limitations too. Actual production depends upon technical knowledge at the moment, and the development of technique may lag behind consumer's desires. We want noiseless trains but we must wait till the technique develops. Consumer's preferences are generally ahead of what is available at the moment.

High pressure salesmanship and persistent advertisement modify the real desires of the consumers. The propaganda machinery is directed to mould and to control consumer's tastes. They are thus induced to buy something different from what they would have purchased otherwise. Our sovereign, the consumer, is impotent and helpless. That businessman succeeds who does not merely satisfy the felt wants of the consumers, but who is able to direct the consumers' tastes towards his particular brand. Huge amounts of money are being spent on advertisement in every country. At every strategic corner on the roadsides, on the railway platform, on the trunks of tree and telegraph poles, or the houses and buses and trams, a consumer is faced with attractive advertisements.

According to Ely, "Expenses in the United States for national advertising alone are estimated to average nearly 10 dollars for every man, woman and child. The cost of advertising in each issue of the *Saturday Evening Post* is nearly a million dollars."[3] Here is another estimate: "In the United States alone about half a million persons are normally employed in advertising and that nation's annual advertising bill runs from $1\frac{1}{2}$ to 2 billion dollars."[4]

These amounts are not being spent to please the consumer but to enrich the producer. Every rupee spent on advertisement and salesmanship is a nail in the coffin of the consumer's sovereignty. We do not agree with Benham when he says that a monarch may be advised and cajoled as to some of his activities even by his slaves, but he remains a monarch nonetheless. This is a case of nominal sovereignty, a very poor specimen of monarchy indeed.

Here is an evidence of the consumer's helplessness. "No doubt the public is spending a tremendous amount yearly—and it comes from those who can least afford it—for lamps that are both a fire and health hazard, for toasters that we dare not touch once they are heated up, for automatic irons that burn and destroy fine rayon goods when set for the lowest temperature, for curling irons, vibrators, massagers which are so poorly insulated that only a person totally ignorant to the potential shock of 110-120 volt supply would dare use such an appliance."[5] This is true of most lines of production.

The monopolists too exercise control over the consumers. In modern times, there is a tendency towards combination or cartelisation, and a few firms or companies come to control the entire output. They can easily dictate their terms to the consumers, who have no say in the matter of price or the range of production.

Then, there is the **Government control** with which we have now become well acquainted. Even in normal times the government either prohibits or restricts the consumption of certain articles, *e.g.*, intoxicants. The Government can exert influence on the trends of production. Besides, the Government itself is the biggest consumer and is in a position to

3. Ely. R.T.—*Outlines of Economics*, 1930, p. 145.
4. Kiekhofer, *op. cit.*, p. 154.
5. Moore and Others—*Modern Economics*.

set the pace in the matter of price as well as the quality of goods produced.

Consumer's own habits bind him and he is reluctant to make any departure from his set scales of preferences. The freedom to choose, therefore, is not exercised.

Environments and **conventions of society** also exercises a restraining influence on the consumer's choice. Therefore, the unrestricted freedom of the consumer is a mere myth.

Capitalism rewards hardwork by giving incentives.

The **consumer are generally ignorant** and do not know what is best for them. Their blind choice does not always accord with their self-interest. Lack of knowledge, therefore, is another hindrance in the way of exercise of the consumer's sovereignty. If the consumer is a giant, he is surely a blind giant.

Production of standardised goods, irrespective of the individual tastes, is a conclusive proof that the modern economic system pays scant attention to the consumers' wishes. The consumers are bulked together and treated en masse, not like a king but a herd of sheep.

Conclusion

It is really very difficult to convince a poor villager or a factory hand that he is the sovereign of all he surveys and that factories are working, trains and ships are moving and the businessmen sitting at their shops or running to and fro in the market—are all trying to serve him and satisfy him rather than line their own purses.

The fact is that neither consumers nor producers alone are sovereign. Economic prosperity of a country lies in a proper balance between consumption and production. In the words of Ely, "Progress is dependent on alert and responsive consumers as well as on prudent and efficient producers. Sluggish consumers, sluggish producers."

MERITS OF CAPITALISM

That capitalism has survived for centuries and is still going strong shows that the system must have certain inherent merits. We may note below the main merits:

(*i*) Automatic working. One merit of capitalism is that it does not require any central directing authority for its functioning. It functions automatically through the price-mechanism as we have explained above. If at any time, there is some disturbance in the economy, it is rectified through price change. On the contrary, socialism can function only through active state intervention. Thousands of people are employed in preparing a plan for working of the system and crores of rupees are spent in the formulation and implementation of the plan. But capitalism functions automatically through the price system without there being any need for incurring such expenditure simply to make the system work.

(*ii*) Higher Efficiency and Incentive to Hard Work. Another merit of capitalism is that under capitalism workers and entrepreneurs are encouraged to imporve their efficiency and put in hard work. The entrepreneurs are induced to work hard and work more efficiently to earn higher profits. Since the more efficient and hard working labour can earn higher wages, they have the incentive to improve their efficiency. Hence, under capitalism, the entire manpower resources of the country (labour and entrepreneur) work the hardest and most efficiently. In this way, the national output increases and economic development is accelerated.

(*iii*) Higher Rate of Capital Formation. As we have already mentioned, people under capitalism have the right to hold property and pass it on in inheritance to their heirs and successors. Owing to this right, people save a part of their income so that it can be invested to earn more income and leave larger property for their heirs. The rate of capital formation increases when savings are invested. This accelerates economic growth.

(*iv*) Economic Development and Prosperity. The supporters of capitalism point to the rich variety and abundant supply of goods and services. The lure of profit compels the entrepreneurs to take risk, and to conquer new fields in production. Standard of living has risen all round, comforts of life have increased, and life has become richer and fuller. This is the service rendered by capitalism to society. As we have already said, capitalism offers great incentive for saving and large opportunities for investment. It encourages innovation and technological progress and the optimum use of

Wasteful competion: Too many varieties of same product.

resources. It is thus conducive to economic growth and prosperity.

(v) Optimum Uti-lisation of Resources. The limited resources of the community are put to the most economical uses with as little waste as possible. There is keen competition among producers and entrepreneurs to produce and sell goods. Every producer and entrepreneur tries to use the productive resources at his disposal in the most economical manner in order to make maximum profit. The person responsible for the waste receives prompt punishment for his miscalculation in the form of losses or bankruptcy. In this way, capitalism encourages the most efficient use of the resources of the country.

(vi) Just System. The richest reward under capitalism goes to the ablest, the most daring as well as the most prudent entrepreneur. A man who takes the initiative and shows extraordinary resourcefulness and pluck makes the highest profits. Nothing seems to be more just than that the rewards should be apportioned according to merit.

(vii) Democratic. The consumer's control gives the system a democratic tinge. Nobody likes that his consumption should be dictated by some superior authority. In the capitalist economy, an attempt is made to adjust production to the consumer's wishes. They consume what they like and not what is supplied to them. That is, the consumers control production. The consumers constitute the general public, Hence, the system is democratic.

(viii) Encouragement to Enterprise and Risk-taking. Another important merit of capitalism lies in this that it encourages the entrepreneurs to take risks and adopt bold policies, because in this way they can make higher profits. Higher the risk, greater is the profit. They also make innovations in order to cut their costs and maximise their profits. These innovations result in the improvement of production techniques and lowering of the costs of production. Hence, capitalism brings about a great technological progress in the country.

(ix) Adaptability. Finally, if the survival of the fittest is any criterion of the soundness of a system, capitalism is indeed sound and strong. So many crises have overtaken the system, but it somehow emerges, a bit crippled no doubt, but victorious. Its adaptability to the changing economic conditions is indeed surprising. What greater proof do we need of its toughness and resiliency than the wonderful manner in which it has stood the straing of costly wars?

DEMERITS OR CRITICISM OF CAPITALISM

But capitalism is now being assailed from all directions. The following are the main grounds on which its is attacked:

(i) Wasteful Competition. Competition, which is the cardinal feature of capitalist economy, is a sheer waste. Colossal expenditure is incurred on advertisement and salesmanship simply to defeat a rival. Resources employed by those who are defeated in the race, go to waste. Cut-throat competition does not confer any corresponding social benefit, though it may be advantageous to the firms concerned.

Competition results in the production of too many varieties. A reasonable variety is all right, because it offers alternatives to consumers. But too much variety is wasteful, because a small variety, but each large in quantity, can be more economically produced.

There is no doubt that the efficiency of the capitalistic system depends on the existence of free

Capitalism breeds income equality in the society.

competition and the mobility of the factors of production. But the existence of friction, legal, social and economic, hampers free competition with the result that the factors of production often lie idle.

***(ii)* Human Welfare Ignored.** The supposed harmony between the interests of the consumers, *i.e.*, the society, and those of the producers, does not actually exist. Lack of free competition, deliberate deceit practised by unscrupulous producers and the ignorance and the impotence of the individual consumer turn the consumer-king into an abject slave, a victim of exploitation. The economic decisions made by individual entrepreneurs and producers under capitalism are based on their self-interest and not from the point of view of good of society. The producers produce those commodities and in such quantities that the difference between price and cost is the maximum so that their profit is maximised. However necessary and useful the commodity may be the producers will not produce it if price does not exceed the cost, because it is only the profit motive which drives them. Social welfare is ignored altogether.

***(iii)* Economic Instability and Unemployment.** The recurrence of the trade cycles, due to over-competition and over-saving resulting in over-production, must be considered one of the bitterest fruits of capitalism. Production is unplanned and is being augmented by ever increasing accumulation of capital, while the bulk of the consumers are being impoverished more and more. In these circumstances, it will be a miracle if there is a proper balance between production and consumption. The result is economic instability. Booms are followed by slumps and when there is depression there is large-scale unemployment. The workers, who constitute the bulk of the nation, have to live under a perpetual dread of losing their job. They have no sense of security. There was mass unemployment during the Great Depression of 1929-34 and even political stability of certain States was threatened. When there is boom, there is the danger of inflation which also entails large-scale suffering especially of the poor and fixed incomists.

***(iv)* Property Rights Take Precedence Over Human Rights.** Capitalism lays undue emphasis on property rights as against human rights. Man, the first of God's creation, is treated like an ordinary chattel. Money, not man, rules the world and debases humanity.

***(v)* Class-Conflict.** Capitalism has sown the seeds of eternal social unrest by dividing the society into two hostile camps of capital and labour, the 'leaves' and 'have-nots'. They look sullently at each other, and are ever on the look out for an opportunity to fight. This is due to the fact that their interests mutinually clash. The labour wants higher wages and short working hours which is against the interests of capitalists. Strikes and lock-outs are inevitable.

***(vi)* Social Injustice and Economic Inequity.** The extreme inequality of wealth distribution, which is being accentuated as time goes on, is the most galling outcome of capitalism. As G.D.H. Cole remarks, "There is a world of difference in terms of happiness between the high priest and the slaves in the temple of industry."[6] On the one hand, there are a few rich people and, on the other, the vast masses fabulously steeped in abject poverty. The formers are enjoying a luxurious life even without working, whereas the latter cannot get two square meals a day even after putting in hard labour. They are clothed in rags and live in hovels and their children often die from lack of milk and medicine, whereas even the rich man's dogs are better fed. A system which results in such social injustice and economic inequalities deserves to be condemned.

Thus, capitalism is full of frustrating anomalies, the few indulging in all conceivable luxuries and the majority living under-semi-starved conditions. The crops are rotting while human beings are starving, and machines are lying idle inside the factories, while unemployment is raging in all its fury outside.

***(vii)* Misallocation of Resources.** Capitalism is also criticised on the ground of the misallocation of the productive resources of the country. Production under capitalism is not undertaken merely to satisfy

6. *Principles of Economic Planning*, 1935, p. 3.

Capitalims has evolved towards a welfare state.

the basic needs of the masses of people. The productive resources are utilised for the production of luxuries for the rich without producing sufficient quantity of goods for mass consumption. It is true that under capitalism production is carried on according to the wishes of the consumers. But since there are great inequalities in income and wealth, and demand depends on the purchasing power of the people, the rich people are able to exert greater pull in the product market.

The producers take decisions about production on the basis of market price, hence it is more profitable for them to produce luxuries because the rich people can buy them at higher prices. On the other hand, sufficient quantity of consumer goods cannot be produced for the poor because they cannot afford today sufficient prices for such goods. The aggregate satisfaction can be increased by using productive resources in the production of goods for the poor instead of for the rich. But this is not possible under capitalism where production is governed not by the wishes and needs of the poor but by market prices. The market prices are not a correct index of the wishes and needs of the general public, because the rich people are able to influence the market prices by their higher incomes.

(*viii*) Emergence of Monopolies and Concentration of Economic Power. It also happens under capitalism that perfect and free competition ceases to prevail and instead big combinations of powerful producers and monopolies emerge against whom it becomes difficult for an ordinary entrepreneur to compete. These big monopolies come to control the market on account of the huge resources that they command, and small producers are squeezed out. Thus, under capitalism free enterprise is merely nominal; it is not free enterprise for all. Actually, only those entrepreneurs are able to undertake business who command large resources. The monopolists produce small quantity but charge higher prices and thus exploit the consumers. Also, the big businesses control many types of business and industrial concerns at the same time. Hence, there is lot of concentration of economic power in a few hands. The concentration of economic power is considered to be one of the major defects of capitalism.

(*ix*) Malpractices. In recent years, the image of capitalism has been tarnished by sharp practices (or malpractices) indulged in by big industrialists and businessmen. Such practices include payment of handsome salaries to influential directors, the large-scale evasion of fiscal laws, luxurious living at nation's cost and persistent generation of black money through clandestine deals and surreptitious transactions. The seamy side of capitalism has been thoroughly exposed by the scandals circulating about the big business personalities. For example, the recent Lonrho affair rudely shook the U.K. by the misdeeds of the British mining and trading tycoons. In a debate in the House of Lords, even Prime Minister Edward Health conceded that the malpractices "constitute the unpleasant and unacceptable face of capitalism." The labour peers warned that the system was "so uncivilized that it gravely imperilled the future."

Conclusion. These few points constitute a sufficient indictment on the present system. Ruthless exploitation of women and children, callous disregard of the aged, the sick and the unemployed, and the mercenary motives mainly governing human relations have all pricked the social conscience, and people are furiously looking round for an alternative. Already, the death-knell of capitalism has been tolled over a large part of the globe. People now proudly put forward their progressive views in capitalist countries. As an escape from the intolerable conditions prevalent under capitalism, the chief alternatives suggested are: Planning Capitalism, Socialism and Communism. In the meantime, the governments of capitalistic countries are taking active steps to remove the glaring defect of capitalism like economic instability, unemployment, economic inequalities by adopting appropriate fiscal and monetary policies and by converting themselves into welfare states.

CHANGING FACE OF CAPITALISM: TOWARDS THE WELFARE STATE

Capitalism has shown wonderful vitality, resilience and adaptability to changing circumstances and situations. No wonder that it has not merely survived but has been flourishing and it has belied the hopes and fears of those who predicted its disintegration and doom. What is remarkable is the swift transformation which has come about in the structure of capitalism, and the welfare state has emerged as an aspect of capitalism. This is a self-corrective step. The liberal constitutional tradition which built capitalism is now moulding it into a concept of welfare state.

What is a Welfare State?

"The welfare state is a form of society characterised by a system of democratic, government sponsored welfare placed on a new footing and offering a guarantee of collective social care to its citizens, concurrently with the maintenance of a capitalist system of production". (Piet Thoenes). It is a system which guarantees of the citizens freedom from want and fear. It looks after him from the cradle to the grave, meeting all his vital and reasonable requirements in the matter of education, health, housing, employment, old-age pensions, etc. It takes off all his wordly worries as it were. Welfare State may also be defined as under:

"A civil community in which the instrumentalities and the authority of government are employed to establish, maintain and guarantee to its citizens certain specific conditions of physical and sociological protection, beneficial services, and institutionalised opportunities that are considered to be essential to general public welfare of the State and to the corresponding personal well-being of each citizen."[7]

Worlds leading MNCs.

This is the direction in which modern capitalism is moving. It was due to Keynes' strong advocacy of State intervention and expansion of State activities that this social revolution was brought about.

In England, the National Insurance Act of 1946 provides to every one in the country sickness benefit, guardians' allowance, death grant, maternity benefits, widows' benefits, un-employment benefit, *etc*. Now children attending school run by local authorities do not pay any fees and they get books and equipment free. They are also provided milk during school hours free. Meals and milk on a modest scale are provided in India too. A number of social security measures are on the statute book *e.g*. Employees' Provident Fund, Maternity Benefit Act, Employees State Insurance Scheme, Social Security for Old and Disabled, Family Pension Scheme, Pension for windows. It is, however a far cry from the comprehensive social security provided in the west.

7. Perspectives on the Welfare State edited by S. P. Aiyar, 1966, p. 133.

Thus the transformation of capitalism to a sort of welfare capitalism is the most remarkable development of modern times. It is due not only to the working of democratic forces in the State, but what is important to note is, that several capitalist enterprises have introduced welfare schemes for their workers.

The Capitalism of 21st Century

Capitalism is nothing but an economic system based on laissez-faire economic policy, which opens up all economic activities to individual in a natural way and the government plays just a supporting passive role to achieve economic welfare by the individuals. In 1936, the concept of capitalism changed into a welfare state concept, because of (*i*) the great depression and consequently (*ii*) the publication of Keynesian functional finance approach. A number of governments (due to the changing economic and political environment in the world) started opting more of the characterisations of capitalism along with more active indirect role in the form of monetary and fiscal policies. The Japanese and the other eastern countries started emphasising more on foreign trade and the slogan of "export or perish" gave another jerk to free market economy concept. President Mikhail Gorbachov; Prestrioka and Glasnots' along with the collapse of Warswa Pact countries, socialism further strengthen the capitalists economy. The Berlin wall was demolished in 1989. These historical back ground helped indirectly the capitalists economy. The GATT agreements and its collapse as well as the emergence of WTO on 01-01-95 added further strength to the capitalists economy.

Following are the main features of capitalists economy in the world.

(*i*) Modern capitalism is not the system of a country but of many countries. The world is treated as one economy. It is a global economy concept.

(ii) Industrial giants in the form of "Multi National Corporations" (MNC) and "Trans National Corporations (TNC) are its main capitalists Agents.

(iii) Big industries concept, that is the merger, pools, amalgmations are the distinct feature of market agents.

(iv) Monetory economics and cheap money flow and easy credit policy in the form of foreign money has increased temporarily the purchasing power of the people in the world.

(v) Easy transportation and new soft-ware technology development has boosted the service sector based economy in the world.

(vi) Economies are threatened and controlled by western technology, and culture. Different countries are invaded by cheap-technology, superficial increase in economic growth, and independent economies have been transferred into dependent economies.

(vii) Widening inequalities of income and the concentration of economic power in the hands of few, may lead the different countries, to the same condition of Southern American countries or Latin American countries.

Key terms

Private property, Freedom of enterprise, Consumer's sovereignty, Haves and Have-nots, Class conflict, Wasteful competition, Welfare state.

QUESTIONS

1. State the essential characteristics of capitalism and show in which respects capitalism is superior to socialism.
2. What are the essential characteristics of capitalists economy? How far can its evils be removed by planned economy?
3. What are the basic problems of every economy? How does a capitalism system of economy try to solve them?
4. Critically examine the concept of consumer's sover eignty. Is it desirable under present conditions?
5. Describe the evils of capitalism and explain in what way socialism seeks to overcome them.
6. How far is market mechanism effective in efficiently allocating the resources in a capitalist economy?
7. What are the main features of capitalism? Discuss its merits and demerits.

70 CHAPTER

SOCIALISM

Definition

Socialism, as an alternative to capitalism, has the widest appeal. A Swedish king once remarked to his minister, "If one is not a socialist up to the age of twenty-five, it shows that he has no heart; but if he continues to be a socialist after the age of 25, he has no head". Socialism seems to have caught the imagination of youth all over the world.

For a long time, the definition of socialism as given by the Webbs was accepted by a majority of the socialists. Their definition runs thus: "A socialised industry is one in which the national instruments of production are owned by public authority or voluntary association and operated not with a view to profiting by sale to other people, but for the direct service of those whom the authority or voluntary association represents". This definition does not correspond to the present notion of socialism, because it does not imply any idea of planning.

Socialism.

The definition given by Dickenson seems to be better. According to him, socialism is an economic organisation of society in which the material means of production are owned by the whole community and operated by the organs representative of, and responsible to, the community according to general plan, all members of the community being entitled to benefits from the results of such socialised planned production on the basis of equal rights.[1]

According to another definition which brings out the implications of socialism more clearly. "Socialism refers to that movement which aims at vesting in society as a whole, rather than in individuals, ownership and management of all nature-made and man-made producers' goods used in large-scale production to the end that an increased national income may be more equally distributed without materially destroying the individual's economic motivation or his freedom of occupational and consumption choices."[2] In Morrison's words, "the important essentials of socialism are that all the great industries and the land should be publicly or collectively owned, and that they should be conducted (in conformity with a national economic plan) for the common good instead of private profit.[3]

1. Dickenson, H.D.—*Economics of Socialism*, 1939, p.
2. Loucks and Weldon Hoot—*Comparative Economic Systems*, 1948.
3. *Readings in Economics*, edited by P.A. Samuelson, Second Edition, p. 430.

There is no complete agreement as to what socialism exactly is. It seems there are as many types of socialism as there are socialists. Socialism has been compared to a hat which has lost its shape because everybody wears it. It has been aptly remarked that "Socialism has been called many things and many things have been called socialism."

The kaleidoscopic nature of socialism has been described by Shadwell thus:[4] It is both abstract and concrete, theoretical and practical, idealist and materialist, very old and entirely modern; it ranges from a mere sentiment to a precise programme of acting; different advocates present it as a philosophy of life, a sort of religion, an ethical code, an economic system, a historical category, a judicial principle, it is a popular movement and scientific analysis, an interpretation of the past and a vision of the future, a war cry and the negation of war, a violent revolution and a gentle revolution, a gospel of love and altruism, and a campaign of hate and greed, the hope of mankind and the end of civilisation, the dawn of the millennium and a frightful catastrophe." How paradoxical !

From the definitions given above, we are in a position to understand the basic idea/ideas underlying socialism. In simple words, socialism implies social ownership of means of production. But besides social ownership of instruments of production, socialism implies several other things. It implies equality of incomes and equality of opportunity for all. Socialism does not mean that all productive resources should be owned by the State, only the major instruments of production should be under the State control so that economy is run for social benefit rather than private profit. Socialism wants to change the old capitalistic structure of society and replace it by a new economic order based on equality and social justice. Instead of special prerogatives and vested interests, socialism lays emphasis on work and ability and equal opportunities for all regardless of caste, class and inherited privileges.

Authoritarian Socialism versus Liberal Socialism

It may be instructive to distinguish between two types of socialism: (*a*) Authoritarian Socialism, and (*b*) Liberal Socialism. In authoritarian socialism, State ownership covers all the means of production and allocates them by planning for the production of various goods. In this system, there is no sovereignty of the consumer nor any freedom for the labour to organise themselves. What to produce, how to produce and how is output to be distributed, how much is to be invested for economic development—all these decisions are made by the government. This authoritarian socialism is generally called communism which is prevalent in countries like Russia and China.

On the other hand, under **Liberal** Socialism, the government takes up the ownership of the means of production, but the price system or market mechanism is retained. The consumers are given the choice of consumption. The managers of factories appointed by the government produce commodities considering the consumers' demands and the prices of the factors supplied by the government. The concept of Liberal Socialism has been propounded by the economists like Dickinson, Lange and Taylor.

4. *The Quarterly Review*, July 1924, p. 2.

MARXIAN SOCIALISM

Karl Marx, who wrote in 1867 his famous book **Das Kapital,** the Bible of socialism, is considered to be the father of scientific socialism. He tried to put the theory of socialism on a scientific basis. His theory led him to the conclusion that capitalism was doomed to decay.

Karl Marx (1818-1883).

Main Elements in Marxian Theory

The chief points of the Marxian theory are discussed below:

(*i*) Materialistic Conception of History. Karl Marx seeks to explain every events of history on economic ground. He gives an economic interpretation of history. All wars, riots and political movements have their origin in economic factors. There is an appropriate political organisation, corresponding to every economic stage. A capitalist economy, for example, will evolve a system of government which perpetuates and supports property rights.

He goes on to explain how capitalism will generate conditions which will replace it by socialism. The capitalists will grow in wealth as time passes, but will become fewer and fewer, the bigger whales swallowing the smaller ones. Monopolies will be created, production will expand necessitating scramble for markets abroad. This will lead to an imperialist war, and one war will be followed by another more terrible than the preceding one till capitalism perishes in the conflict, and the dictatorship of the proletariat is established.

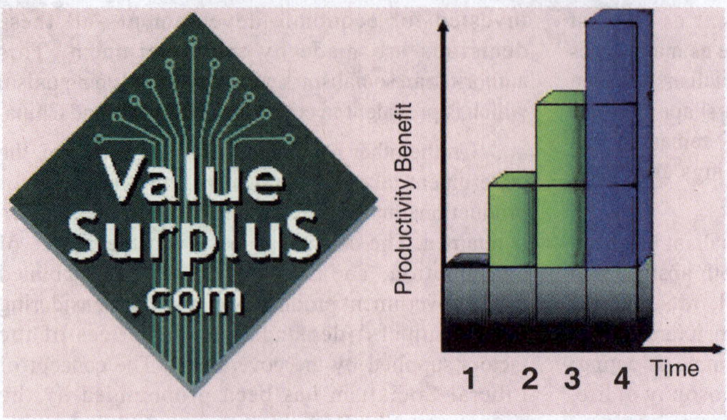

Surplus value is the excess of market value over losts of production and is a creation of labour.

(ii) Labour Theory of Value : According to Karl Marx, value represents the human labour used in production. In other words, the value of a commodity depends on the labour used in the production of that commodity. It is equal to the socially necessary labour time. Marx defined value of a commodity "as the labour time required to produce an article under the normal conditions of production and with the average degree of skill and intensity prevalent at the time."[5]

Karl Marx has given the same definition of capital as Ricardo has defined it on the basis of past labour. As for differences in quality of labour, he considered efficient labour as a form of intense labour. According to him, a given quantity of skilled labour is equal to a bigger amount of ordinary labour. He said this deficiency is continuously being made good. Whatever may be the amount of skilled labour used in the production of a commodity but if it is equated to a commodity produced by ordinary labour, its price will represent only a given quantity of ordinary labour. According to Marx, the ratio of skilled labour and unskilled labour is fixed by convention. In his view, skilled labour is more valuable because, as compared with unskilled labour, it requires more time and labour.

(iii) Theory of Surplus Value and Exploitation. Marx propounded his theory of surplus value on the basis of his theory of value. He said that in order to enable labour to carry on the work of production, he should have some instruments of production and other facilities but he lacks these facilities. Hence, he has to sell his labour to the capitalist. It is, however, not necessary for the capitalist to pay labour the full value of the product produced by him. **Here Karl** Marx supported his theory on the basis of a classical theory, *viz.*, the subsistence theory of value according to which the level of wages is determined by the subsistence of the worker. What happens is that a worker continues working even after he has earned sufficient amount of money for his subsistence. That is, he continues working even beyond the time when he has put in labour worth its price. Sometimes he works for 12 hours, whereas six hours' labour was enough to compensate the capitalist. Thus, work of labour force is not merely to produce value equal to its price but much more. This surplus value is the difference between the market value of the commodity and the cost of the factors used in the production of the commodity. Karl Marx says that the manufacturer gets for his commodity more than what he has spent on labour and other costs. The excess of market value over the costs is the surplus value. By using this surplus value, the capitalist can get still more surplus.

This surplus is the creation of labour. It is created because labour is paid much less than is due to it. He characterised the appropriation of the surplus value by the capitalist as robbery and exploitation. A commodity, according to him, is simply 'crystallised labour' or 'congealed labour'. In this way, the capitalist class goes on becoming richer and richer through exploitation of the working class. Thus, Karl Marx propounded his theory of exploitation on the basis of the theory of surplus value.

(iv) Capitalist Development and its End. According to Karl Marx, the forces that operate in the capitalistic system lead to greater and greater exploitation of labour. The capitalists compete against one another to increase their profits. Like Ricardo, Karl Marx asserted that in the long run wages have a tendency to fall to the minimum subsistence level. In other words, according to Marx, excepting in the short run, wages do not exceed the subsistence level. But the reason put forward by Marx for the wage being equal to subsistence level are different from those given by Ricardo. According to Ricardo, wages keep to the subsistence level owing to increase in population. But according to Marx, it is the excess of current supply of labour over demand that prevents the wages from rising above the subsistence level.

Since the supply of labour continues to be in excess of the demand for it, there is always in existence a large supply of labour which Marx calls the reserve army of labour. Hence, it is this large reserve army of labour (*i.e.*, mass of unemployed labour) which prevents wages from rising above the subsistence level. The supply of labour exceeds the demand for it because

5. *Capital*, Vol. I Chapter I, Sec. I.

the capitalist entrepreneurs are unable to absorb all the labour rendered jobless by the destruction of handicrafts or when the precapitalist entrepreneurs are displaced by the capitalist entrepreneurs owing to lower per capita productivity in the pre-capitalist period. So long as the capitalist entrepreneur flourishes at the expense of the pre-capitalist entrepreneur, the supply of wage earners exceeds the demand for them.

Owing to wages continuing at the subsistence level, the techniques of production which increase productivity also increase the rate of exploitation. In this way, the profits of the capitalists go up. According to Marx, the capitalists, who are owners of the physical means of production, compete against one another so that they may be able to raise the rate of exploitation and thus maximise their profits. That is why Prof. Patterson has said that in the Marxian theory, competition among the owners of physical means of production for increasing the rate of exploitation or the non-wage share takes the form of a conflict or struggle.

There are three ways of increasing the rate of exploitation or the surplus value : (*a*) to increase the rate of exploitation by increasing the length of the working day. When the working hours are increased, total output increases, but wages being fixed, the rate of exploitation increases or the profits extracted by the capitalists increase, (*b*) surplus value or the rate of exploitation is increased by the more intensive use of labour. The working hours are not increased but the workers are made to produce more. But the surplus value cannot be substantially increased by these two methods; (*c*) according to Marx, there is a third and more important method of increasing surplus value, *viz*., to increase the physical productivity of labour by technological progress. Technical progress implies improvements in techniques of production by which labour is able to produce more, working the same number of hours as before or working with the same intensity as before. The result is that the total-output of labour increases. Since wages continue at the subsistence level, the margin between the subsistence output and the improved technique output widens. In this way, there is increase in surplus value or the rate of exploitation.

But technical progress can be achieved only through the accumulation of capital. The result is that there is keen competition among the capitalists to accumulate capital. But in the Marxian system, as Kaldor says, the accumulation of capital is done not for the lure of profit but it is thrust on the capitalists by the competitive struggle among them.

Thus, discussing the hidden motives of capital formation, Kaldor observed that Ricardo explained it as arising from the desire for higher rate of profit. The capitalists of their own desire accumulate capital so long as the rate of profit from the productive use of capital is more than the minimum required for risk-taking. For Marx, capital accumulation by capitalist entrepreneurs is not a matter of their own choosing but a matter of necessity. This is due to a keen competition among the capitalists themselves. This has been explained with the help of economies of scale. There is an implicit assumption that capital used by a particular capitalist is governed by his own accumulation. Considering the fact that larger the scale of operation, the more efficient will be his production, every producer automatically led to an increase in his scale of output by the reinvestment of his profits. He does so because he does not want to lag behind in the competitive race.

Technological progress increases labour producting. But with wages remaining same the result is surplus value.

Thus, we see that owing to technical progress and stepping up of capital accumulation as capitalism develops, the rate of exploitation or surplus value of labour increases on account of competitive struggle among the capitalists. Consequently, as capitalism develops, the national income will rise but the relative share of wages (*i.e.*, share of labour) will fall and the relative share of profit (or the share of the capitalist) will go up.

Thus, the working of capitalistic system results in the worsening condition of the working class. Marx has called it the law of increasing misery of the working class. According to this law, owing to technical progress, increase in capital accumulation and the consequent increase in national income under

Marx said that capitalism is doomed to fail. Socialism is the answer to capitalistic exploitation.

capitalism, the relative share of wages in national income is bound to fall and that of capital is bound to go up.

It is thus clear that the conclusion at which Marx arrives regarding the changes in the relative shares in the national income owing to the development of capitalism, is contrary to that of Ricardo. Ricardo thought that with the development of capitalistic economy, the relative share of wages in the national income would rise whereas the share of profits would decline.

Prof. Patterson has rightly remarked that in the Marxian model of income distribution, the fundamental reason of the decline in the relative share of wages is technical progress, the full benefits of which go to the owners of physical means of production. The increasing hardship of the working class is not due to the declining level of real wages because, in absolute terms, their hardship is not aggravated. The reason is that there may not be any increase in real wages along with increase in productivity, yet there is no decline either. This is the essence of Marxian theory of distribution. Although Marx came to the conclusion that, on the development of capitalism, the relative share of profits will increase owing to technical progress and the accumulation of capital, but following Ricardo, he too accepted the view that owing to the accumulation of capital the **rate of profit** would decline. It may be specially noted that according to Marx on the development of capitalistic economy when the **relative share** of profits goes up there is a fall in the rate of profit. It looks paradoxical but Marx fully explained the co-existence of these two trends, *viz.*, the share of profit and the rate of profit. But Marx did not explain the declining rate of profit with the help of the law of diminishing returns which Ricardo had emphasised. Instead, Marx explained the declining rate of profit on the basis of an increase in the organic composition of capital.

Surplus value is basic for profits and accumulation. The aim of the capitalist is to increase surplus value to the maximum. At first, when the supply of labour is large, wage rate remains constant at the subsistence level, but sooner or later, the demand for labour exceeds the available supply and wages rise, reducing thereby surplus value. With the loss of surplus value, there is a 'crisis', as the capitalist has no incentive to invest. He also tries to create again a surplus of labour by using labour-saving machinery but this also is temporary solution as a too frequent resort to this device will lower the rate of profit and thereby reduce the capitalists' incentive to accumulate.

Thus, capitalism is doomed to fail and give place to socialism. This is the picture which Marx himself gives of the end of capitalism; "Along with the constantly diminishing number of the magnates of capital who usurp and monopolies all advantages of this process of transformation, grows the mass of misery, oppression, slavery, degradation, exploitation; but with this too grows the revolt of the working class, a class always increasing in numbers, and disciplined, united, organised by the very mechanism of the process of capitalist production itself . . . . centralisation of the means of production and socialisation of labour at last reach a point where they become incompatible with their capitalist integument. This integument bursts asunder. The knell of capitalist private property sounds. The expropriators are expropriated".[6]

Criticism of Marxian Theory

Marx has proved to be a poor prophet of future events. Some of the predictions of Marx have proved to be true while others have proved wrong. His prediction regarding the increasing hold of monopoly has been proved to be true by later events. But his other prediction regarding continuous misery for the working class under capitalism has proved to be wrong in countries where capitalism has been successful. In countries of Western Europe and the U.S.A. the standard of living of the worker has been steadily rising and not falling.

He had predicted that the relative share of wages in the national income would decline and the economic condition of the workers would deteriorate. But this has not happened. Empirical research has shown that in the countries in the pre-capitalist stage, labour's

6. *Readings in Economics* edited by P.A. Samuelson and others, Second Edition, p. 420.

share in the national income has remained constant and, as Marx had said, there has been no decline in this share either. In the capitalist countries, labour has got sufficient share in the increase in physical productivity which has taken place on account of technical progress and capital accumulation. As a result, there has been marked improvement in the living conditions of workers. That is why they are now less revolutionary than before.

Capitalism has survived Marx's prediction as indicated by strong and growing dollar.

Besides, there is no evidence of decline in the rate of profit. It is in view of the declining rate of profit and concentration of purchasing power in the hands of a few people that Marx had predicted that capitalism would face crises off and on, and capitalism would ultimately come to an end. The actual events have falsified the gloomy predictions of Marx. It is true that trade cycles keep recurring in the capitalistic economies. But in spite of short-term ups and downs, the capitalistic economies made a very rapid economic progress in the first 100 years and it is on account of this that these countries became affluent. Prof. Patterson has rightly remarked that Marx had thought that capitalism would rapidly disintegrate on account of ever recurring serious crises and it would finally and completely end on account of revolution by labour, and communism would be ushered in this way. Marx had not only wrongly predicted about the behaviour of labour's share in national income but also about the long-term development of capitalism.

Moreover, there are several theoretical flaws in the Marxian theory of declining rate of profit as a result of a change in organic composition of capital. Some writers have said that the law of declining rate of profit cannot be derived from the law of increasing organic composition of capital. Since Marx assumed that the real wages of labour remained stable at the subsistence level, there will be great increase in per capita productivity as a result of increase in the organic composition of capital owing to capital accumulation and technical progress. The rate of profit will also increase on account of real wages remaining constant at the subsistence level and rapid increase in the surplus value earned by the capitalists. It is worth noting Prof. Kaldor's views in this connection. He says: "Since, Marx assumed that the supply price of labour remains unchanged in terms of commodities, when the organic composition of capital and hence output per head rises, there is no more reason to assume that an increase in organic composition will yield a lower rate of profit than a higher rate. For even if output per man were assumed to increase more slowly than ("constant" plus "variable") capital per man, the "surplus value" per man (the excess of output per man over the costs of reproduction of labour) will necessarily increase faster than output per man, and may thus secure a rising rate of profit even if there is diminishing productivity to successive additions to fixed capital per unit of labour."[7]

Finally, Marx's theory of income distribution is based on the labour theory of value which is not accepted by modern economists. Marxian analysis of surplus value or the exploitation of labour is obviously based on the concept that aggregate value is produced by labour, and capital only transfers its value to the value of the commodity. Capital makes a significant contribution to productivity and substantially adds value. To deny this is only to show one's bias. Besides, the labour theory of value is only a form of the cost of production theory. As Marshall had said long time back, only costs of production (cost of labour together with cost of capital) do not determine value. Price of a commodity also depends on its marginal utility or demand for it. The price of a commodity is determined by the interaction of the forces of demand and supply. Hence, Marx's view that the value of commodity is determined by that labour time which has been used in making it is wrong and the modern economists do not accept it. Thus, if the labour theory of value is wrong, the theory of surplus value or theory of exploitation based on it is also proved to be wrong.

SOME OTHER FORMS OF SOCIALISM

Collectivism or State Socialism

The collectivists or the State socialists believe in parliamentary democracy and nationalisation of the means of production. They want to capture the political machinery, strengthen it and use it for the realisation of the socialists' aims and ideals. The powerful State engine is to be utilised for the production of wealth and its equitable distribution. State is to be all in all, and as soon as the socialists have captured it, they have reached the goal. The State will do for them all that they want. Private enterprise will be put an end to.

7. Robinson, Joan—*An Essay on Marxian Economics*, pp. 75–80 and N. Kaldor—*Alternative Theories of Distribution*.

Guild socialism calls for handing over business management to labour organisations.

All production will be carried on by salaried State officials and profits will go to the State coffers and utilised for the uplift of the masses.

The only difference between capitalism and State socialism is that under the latter, means of production are owned and managed by the State instead of the private entrepreneur, otherwise the exchange mechanism of capitalism, *e.g.*, pricing, marketing, *etc.*, is retained.

Among the chief tenets of the socialist creed may be mentioned (*a*) State ownership of productive resources, (*b*) redistribution of national income, (*c*) economic planning, and (*d*) peaceful and democratic evolution of the economic system.

Guild Socialism

The guild socialists have no faith in the State running economic activity. Unlike the collectivists, the guild socialists do not believe that the State can successfully use the productive resources of the community. According to the guild socialists, it is necessary to do away with the private capitalists. But they want the business organisations, factories and productive resources, *etc.*, to be handed over to labour organisations for management and operation. In their view, guilds of the workers can best run them. They want to put industries under the administration and control of these guilds. They want the State merely to supervise, fix prices and look after the quality of the products and thus safeguard the interests of the consumers.

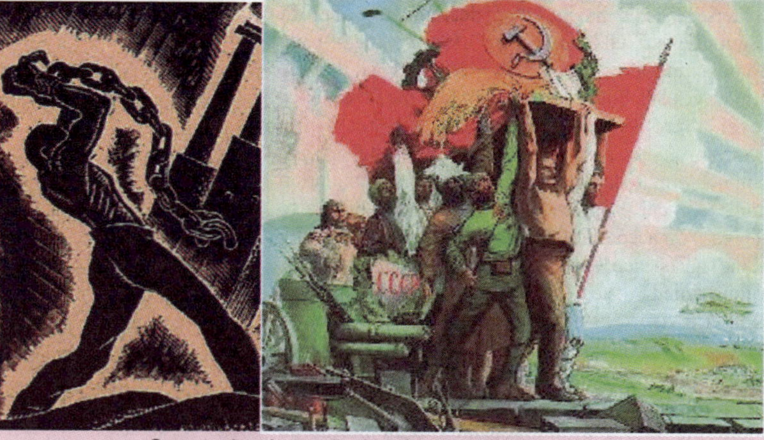
Communism is a radical social movement.

The basic principle is that the means of production should be under the ownership of the State but the actual implementation of this ownership should be in the hands of the workers. The State should only see that the consumers are not exploited or cheated. The aim of the guild socialists is to avoid the evils of excessive concentration of power and inefficiency of bureaucracy in running the economic activities. They claim that according to their system decentralisation will usher in real democracy in the world and improve the working capacity of industries.

Syndicalism

The syndicalists too, like guild socialists, do not consider political power as an appropriate weapon for the achievement of socialist aims. Whatever the type of political authority, it invariably has special type of bureaucratic tendency. It can never understand the aspirations of the workers. It has a bad habit of dominating over others. Hence, according to the views of the syndicalists, if the State is made all powerful, it will produce many petty tyrants. That is why the syndicalists want to build up social, political and economic structure on the foundation of trade unions.

They have no faith that they can achieve their aims through constitutional means. They know that political authorities are very powerful. Hence, they (*i.e.*, the syndicalists) believe in direct and violent action. Strike is their main weapon. They believe that even if the strike is unsuccessful it gives the workers an experience in economic warfare. Through strikes, the workers become more strongly organised and their hatred for the capitalists becomes more bitter and this hatred should not be allowed to diminish. Their strategy is that there should be strike after strike and a long strike in the end to paralyse the administration and capture power. The syndicalists lay great stress on the destruction of existing economic and political structure. They deliberately do not throw any light on the structure of society which they propose to create after the revolution. Their policy is that of destruction rather than construction.

Communism

The Communist Manifesto of 1845 lays down the strategy that the communists want to adopt for the achievement of their aims. The communists lay stress on the formation of a network of communist organisations all over the country and the world, capturing key posts in other organisations and carrying on their work silently adding to the number of adherents. When the party has become sufficiently strong, it attempts to capture government machinery and lay the foundation of the proletariat State. The State machinery is utilised to crush all opposition and to expropriate the capitalists. The aim is to create a classless society where there is no distinction of high or low, rich or poor. When the objective is achieved, the State is considered unnecessary. It will 'wither away'.

As for the type of society which the Communists envisage, some idea can be gathered from Plato's *Republic* or Well's *New Worlds for Old.* The Communists propose to abolish all forms of private property, not merely in the instruments of production but also in the consumers' goods. Those consumers' goods which are intimately connected with the person of the consumer, *e.g.*, food and clothing, are transferred to individuals and families and those which are not so connected, *e.g.*, houses, are owned by society, only their services are transferred to the consumers.

People are supposed to work according to capacity and get according to need. Everybody is to be assigned a definite job. He cannot choose his own occupation. Nobody will have a house of his own or a bank account. Everyone will be a government employee; he will not be paid cash but he will get his meals in the State kitchens and live in Government quarters. He will be provided commodities and services for consumption not of his choice but what the State chooses to give according to production at the time. The bringing up of the children, their education and employment, will be the State concern. The pricing system will disappear. The State will control production, assign jobs, fix remuneration and prices of goods and services without profit motive. A very alluring dream indeed! It is utopian.

In the communist society, there will be no trade cycles or unemployment nor can there be differences of the rich and the poor. The conflict between labour and capital will disappear. This view is undoubtedly imaginary and impractical. In the beginning, the Russians tried to implement these ideas. They abolished money and exchange. But it did not work. The money economy had to be re-established. In order to provide incentives for efficiency and goods work, different wages had to be offered.

Anarchism

The ultimate aim of the communists is to build a social structure in which there will be no need for the State. As we said above "the State will wither away." This is technically known as anarchy. In ordinary language, anarchy means absence of government rule and disorder. But in the socialist phraseology it simply means 'statelessness' when the administration has become superfluous and the society regulates itself out there is no disorder. The communists believe that when capitalism has come to an end, all greed, selfishness, cheating, tyranny, *etc.*, generally associated with capitalism will disappear from the world and in their place will be established virtues of self-sacrifice, social service, goodwill, *etc*. Instead of grabbing, the people will adopt an attitude of sacrificing for others. Man will have been so much uplifted then, that there will be no need for the police. The courts will be closed. Is it not surprising? Fahien tells about the ancient Indian society that there were no thefts and no robberies and people did not lock their houses. It is possible that sometime the anarchists' dream may come true.

The economic and social life will be organised into self-regulating or self-governing institutions. All the functions of the State will be automatically carried out. Every individual will respect the rights of others and there will be no difficulty of any type. The State will be like an automatic traffic signal. When the policeman is off the traffic duty, the traffic regulates itself. This is how the society will itself regulate its affairs in the absence of a government. This is another sweet dream. We get an outline of this plan from Prince Kropotkin. The anarchists say that government is needed only to protect the unjustly obtained wealth, undue profits and loot of the capitalists. When capitalism goes, the government will follow suit.

Fabian Socialists

Fabian socialists are men of literature. Bernard Shaw was one of them. They sincerely believe that socialism is a question of conviction. If the people can only be convinced of the virtues of socialism, no power on earth can prevent its coming about. Through literary propaganda—novels, dramas, short stories—they expose the evils of capitalism and bring out the merits and necessity of socialism. It is hoped that, in course of time, the world will come to believe in socialism, and socialism will then come to prevail. They may not be wrong.

GENERAL FEATURES OF SOCIALISM

Although there is a great diversity of views among the socialists and there are as many types of socialism as there are socialists, yet it is possible to pick up a few general features of socialism.

(*i*) Social Ownership of Means of Production. The socialists believe in the abolition of private ownership in the instruments of production. Land, factories, railways, mines and every other means of production must be nationalised. Their ownership and control are to be vested in the State so that the State may provide work for everybody.

Socialisation of the means of production is so important a characteristic feature of socialism that some writers define socialism as social ownership of the means of production. The means of production are the property of the State and not of private individuals. The profits of all enterprises go to the State exchequer to be utilised for the benefit of society rather than for the benefit of a few private individuals.

But it may be mentioned that it is not necessary to nationalise all means of production to bring about socialism. Generally, it is considered sufficient and useful to nationalise only the principal means of production like heavy and basic industries, mines, banks, means of transport like railways, motor transport, *etc*. However, State control-extends over

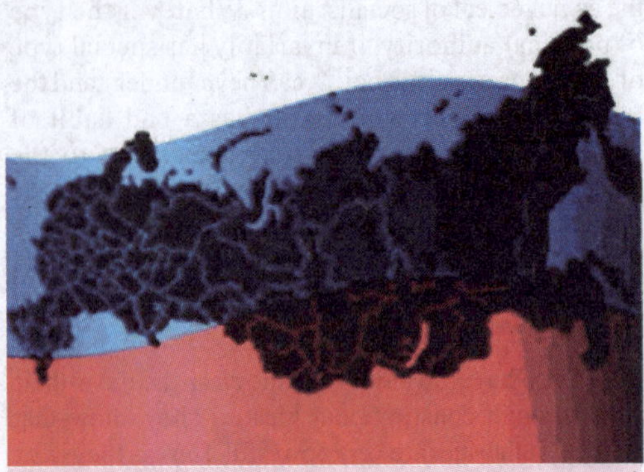

Russia follows socialism where resources are owned by state.

all means of production and the entire economy to make sure that the economy functions to promote the interests of the society as a whole. So far as land is concerned, the actual tiller or a co-operative society can be given the ownership. In fact, 'land to the tiller' is the principal objective of socialism. Several other land reforms are introduced so that the tiller is actually made the owner of land and he gets a proper reward for his labour. Besides, the farmers are encouraged to form co-operative farming societies so that large-scale farming can be undertaken.

(*ii*) No Private Enterprise. Generally, there is to be no private enterprise. Production is to be initiated and conducted by the State which will pay wages and other costs and keep profits to itself. Interest and rent as payments respectively to the capitalists and the landlords will disappear, for the State will be the capitalist, landlord and entrepreneur. However, in agriculture, as mentioned above, co-operatives may be permitted.

(*iii*) Economic Equality. Living on unearned income is to be discouraged. Remuneration for work is to be according to the nature of work and is not to be equal. Earnings will vary according to ability. A limited operation of the law of demand and supply in this connection is envisaged.

There is, thus, no basis for the belief that under socialism all would be equal economically. No economic equality is guaranteed. But there are to be no glaring inequalities. All possible steps are taken to reduce economic inequalities of income and wealth. Since industrial and business enterprises belong to the State, there is little possibility of amassing wealth by private individuals. In other words, perfect economic equality is not the aim of socialism. However, it aims at social justice in the distribution of national income. It therefore, aims at giving a fair share to all in the national income. Some inequality in incomes is considered essential to provide incentive for harder and better work. Unless efficient workers are paid better no one will try to be efficient in his work. Hence, workers will not fully use their skill, ability and experience unless they are better rewarded. Thus, in case of perfect equality of incomes national output will go down and the nation is bound to suffer. The national economy will suffer in performance if income equality is insisted upon. Thus, instead of perfect equality of incomes, the socialists aim at minimum practicable inequality. As Douglas Jay observes, "Basic aim of socialism is not literal or absolute equality but the minimum equality that is workable if human beings are actively to use their talents, not equal share but fair shares, not perfect equality but social justice." System of inheritance which leads to unearned incomes is not permitted. Those factors of production, *e.g.*, land, capital which can yield unearned incomes are nationalised. But interest on savings given to the government is permissible.

(*iv*) Equality of Opportunity. Although, as we have said above, socialism does not guarantee perfect equality of income, it aims at providing equality of opportunity. In fact, to provide equality of opportunity is a basic objective of socialism. Every individual, whether he belongs to a rich family or a poor family has an equal opportunity to rise in life under socialism. Every young person is given equal opportunity to receive education or training according to his aptitude so that he can enter a profession of his choice. Children of poor parents have to face lot of difficulties in life. The poor parents are not in a position to provide their children basic minimum means to equip themselves mentally or physically for life. They have no resources at their disposal to give the necessary education and training. Either they cannot afford to send their children to school or they have to withdraw them from the school early to supplement their income by putting them to a job. The inequality of opportunity starts from the birth itself. The atmosphere in which these children are brought up is suffocating and causes them intense worry. The socialist society does not tolerate it.

Under socialism such steps are taken that every child, whatever his family background, gets full opportunity to develop his inborn and latent faculties. To ensure equal opportunities for all, it is essential to provide free education and health services up to the secondary standard. At the university level also, it is essential to provide talented students a scheme of stipends and free ships. All these things are provided under a socialist regime.

(*v*) Economic Planning. The State is in charge of both production and distribution. The allocation of the productive resources of the community will be determined according to the direction of a central authority. In fact, economic planning is an essential feature of socialism.

Planning.

Economic planning is most closely associated with the Russian system. Although now for some years, economic planning has been adopted by capitalist countries too, yet it cannot be comprehensive and effective as under socialism, because under capitalism the means of production are under the control of private individuals and the direction of production and of productive resources is done through price-mechanism. There can be only indicative planning or planning by inducement under capitalism which does not prove so effective. Since under socialism, the principal means of production are owned and controlled by the State, it is possible to direct the production of commodities and the utilisation of resources in the desired channels. If it is desired to use the productive resources effectively and to product a certain set of commodities, economic planning is essential for socialism.

Under socialism, the place of price-mechanism is taken by planning commission which is entrusted with the work of laying down the objectives of planning and to settle the targets and priorities of planning. The planning commission formulates five-year plans for economic development which are implemented through the various governmental agencies.

Economic planning ensures speedy economic development. It ensures efficient and optimum allocation of resources. In the underdeveloped countries, where without raising the level of national income and wealth, socialism cannot be brought about, economic planning is absolutely essential for socialism, because without it the level of production cannot be raised.

But under socialism, only increase in production is not considered sufficient. The objectives of socialism is also to ensure a fair distribution of gains in production and income. Hence, economic planning is required for socialism not merely to accelerate economic development but also to ensure a fair distribution of fruits of economic growth. In

Socialism answers social justice.

pursuance of the socialist objectives, economic planning in India is not only to raise the level of national income but also to reduce economic inequalities and to prevent concentration of economic power.

***(vi)* Social Welfare and Social Security.** Another important feature of socialism is that it is social welfare consideration which guides productive activity in the economy rather than private profit. Under capitalism, only production of such commodities and services is undertaken which are expected to yield maximum profit. It follows, therefore, that under capitalism, luxury goods are produced for the rich rather than goods of mass consumption required by the poor. The poor are thus deprived of the necessaries of life while the rich are enabled to lead a luxurious and wasteful life. This is so because production of luxuries is more profitable than the production of necessaries of life. In this way, profit motive is the determining factor of economic activity under capitalism. But situation is entirely different under socialism. Commodities and services of such type and in such quantities are produced which are essential for promoting social welfare. The motive power of economic activity under socialism is social welfare and not private profit. The work which is performed by market mechanism under capitalism is performed by central economic authority under socialism, which determines and guides all economic activity. Planning Commission keeps social welfare uppermost in consideration.

Under socialism, the State devotes its attention to ameliorating the lot of the common man by providing him and his family with adequate medical aid, full and free education and ample means of recreation and entertainment. Freedom from want is guaranteed and fear, born of insecurity, is to be banned.

***(vii)* Classless Society.** The socialists believe in a class less society where the distinction between the rich and the poor and the 'haves' and the 'have-nots' has completely disappeared. Thus, the caste system that prevails in India is repugnant to socialists. In a socialist State, every individual enjoys equality of opportunity regardless of caste, creed, family and religion. A socialist state is really a secular State.

The prime objective of a socialist State is that the society is not divided into two classes of labour and capitalists as under capitalism. That is why big zamindars and capitalists have no place under socialism. Severe restrictions are imposed on the control and ownership of private wealth. Every individual gets a reward according to his work and ability. It is in this way that class-conflict, which prevails under capitalism, is put an end to under socialism and a classless society is created.

CASE FOR SOCIALISM

The evils of capitalism have given birth to socialism. Socialism has started as a reaction to industrial revolution that took place in the Western European countries. The industrial revolution of the Western European countries made some people very rich in the midst of poverty elsewhere. It resulted in the exploitation of labour, women and children by the capitalists. Above all, capitalism failed to maintain economic stability. Periodically, the capitalist economy is engulfed in depression which is responsible for large-scale unemployment of, and hardship to, millions of people. Also, capitalism has given rise to extreme inequalities of income and wealth. The poor were deprived of social justice. Owing to the domination of the individual profit motive, the capitalistic economy witnessed a serious misallocation of resources. Socialism seeks to rectify all these evils and create a just social order. Socialists claim the following merits for their system :

***(i)* Social Justice.** The chief merit of socialism is that it assures of social justice. Under socialism, the inequalities of income are reduced to the minimum and the national income is more equitably and evenly distributed. The socialist principle provides for a fair share for all. No one is permitted to have unearned income. Exploitation of man by man is put an end to. Every individual is assured of equal opportunity to develop his latent faculties through proper education and training.

***(ii)* Better Allocation of Resources.** As compared with capitalism, the productive resources of the national are more economically and optimally allocated among the various productive uses. Owing to extreme inequalities of income and the existence of monopolies in the industrial sector, capitalism is incapable of a rational and economical allocation of

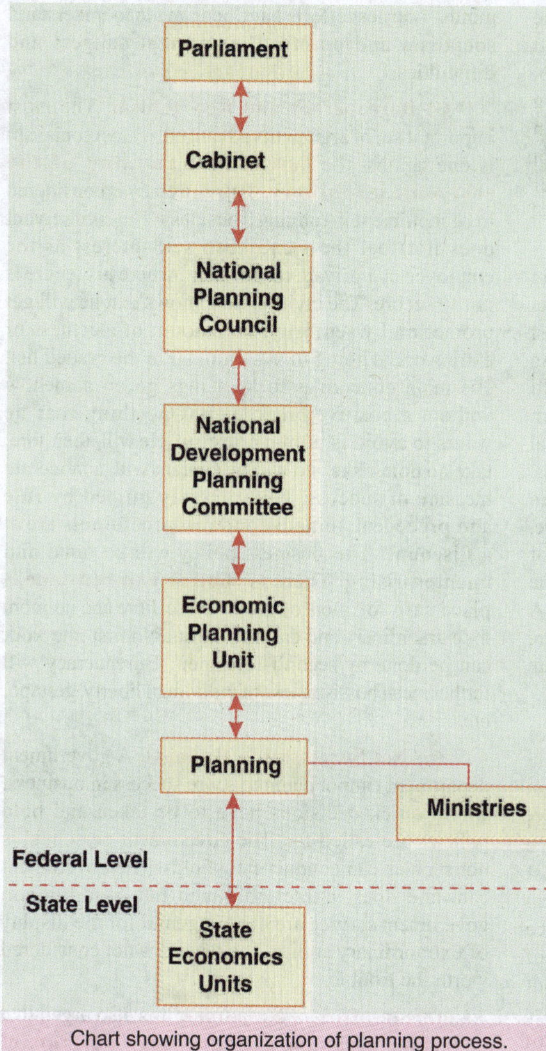

Chart showing organization of planning process.

the productive resources of the community. Besides, private entrepreneurs do not take into consideration social costs while deciding about the allocation of resources. As a result, the productive resources of the community are misallocated.

On the contrary, under socialism a central planning authority determines the allocation of resources among the various uses whose sole aim is to promote social welfare and social security. A planning authority is in a better position to assess the basic needs of the people and the intensity of their desires and to devote the resources to satisfy these desires and meet these needs in the best possible manner. It is wrong to say that socialism completely ignores consumers' preferences and demand for the various commodities and services. In a socialist economy, State can fix the prices of finished goods and give to the consumers a free choice of the goods available in the market at fixed prices. The consumers' demand and preferences can be estimated from the purchases made by them in the market and resources can be devoted to the production of commodities accordingly. But there is no harm also in ignoring certain desires of the consumers if they conflict with social welfare. Often a consumer is unable to understand what is best for him.

Hence, the planning commission under socialism has to strike a desirable balance between social welfare considerations and the individual consumers' preferences. Thus, the allocation of resources under socialism proves to be much better and more rational. In the allocation of resources, due consideration is given to human wants, consumers' preferences and social costs.

(*iii*) Improving Productive Efficiency. Another important merit of socialism is that under it national output can be significantly increased. This is due to the fact that under socialism, the production is undertaken to increase social welfare and not for the benefit of any particular individual. Under socialism, improved techniques of production and scientific research are made freely available to all organisations that may need them. On the other hand, under capitalism, improved production techniques and results of scientific research, which are known to certain firms, are generally kept absolutely secret so that the competing firms, cannot avail themselves of them. And what is more, the monopoly concerns under capitalism limit their output so that they may raise the prices of their products in order to increase their monopoly profits. This means that their output is below the welfare level. But this cannot happen under socialism because none can benefit from the policy of reducing output. All major industries are under complete social control and they are run for social benefit. It is quite clear that the society cannot benefit by reducing output, for the reduction of output means reduction of national income and so of social welfare.

Under socialism, production techniques are also improved because it avoids all wastes of competition. In a capitalist economy, large quantity of financial resources are wasted in competitive advertisement. Different entrepreneurs compete against one another to attract consumers or purchasers of goods. Besides, resources are wasted in the production of unnecessarily large variety of goods. Since, under socialism, the State controls production, there is no need to waste resources on competitive advertisement. However, under socialism, some expenditure is incurred on information and educative programme which is not wasteful. Also, under socialism, concentrating production in big firms results in improvement of production techniques. Moreover, there is no idle capacity kept under socialism as is usually the case under capitalism. A socialist State, makes the fullest use of productive activity.

(*iv*) Social Security and Welfare. Socialism provides social security for all citizens. The socialists believe that people should be given protection against uncertainties relating to income, work and living conditions and the burden of this provision should be borne by the entire society. That is why modern socialists include in their programme schemes of social insurance covering unemployment, accidents, sickness, old-age pensions, death grants, *etc*. In fact, an individual is provided security from cradle to the grave. Most of the things which are considered essential for individual's health and training are provided by the socialist State either free or at cost of production. A socialist State can provide free of cost milk for children, nursing, education and medical aid. A socialist State is truly welfare State.

(*v*) Economic Stability. There is another advantage of socialism, *viz*., it ensures economic stability. Socialism eliminates trade cycles which cause a great hardship to the people. We do not come across depression, unemployment and idle productive capacity in socialist economies. In the capitalist countries, absence of effective demand causes cyclical unemployment and business depression. This absence of monetary effective demand is due to the excess of people's savings over investment expenditure. But since under socialism, the means of production are owned and controlled by the State the level of investment and the level of aggregate demand can also be effectively determined. This ensures economic stability. Sometimes in socialist economies too there can be an imbalance between aggregate demand and aggregate supply but it can be effectively tackled. A socialist State can prevent the imbalance between aggregate demand and aggregate supply from creating trade cycles in the economy and thus makes for economic stability.

DEMERITS OF SOCIALISM

The critics of socialism claim to have picked numerous holes in the socialist fabric. Apart from some silly objections, which have been exploded since long—*e.g.*, socialism would ban religion, abolish marriage and family life, and the dangling of Malthusian bogey to frighten the simple and ignorant minds—earnest efforts have been made to understand socialism and point out some real dangers and difficulties.

(*i*) Bureaucracy and Red Tapism. The most important set of arguments advanced against socialism is one against the **bureaucratic running of the economic machinery.** Bureaucracy is considered to be inefficient in running a business. The civil servant does not feel the same keen self-interest as the employee of a private corporation, where his tenure is not so secure. The civil servant knows that he will get promotion by seniority; no amount of alertness or extra work is going to push him up in the graded list. His main concern is to let things go on somehow without a positive breakdown. One thing that he wants to avoid is public criticism. He will, therefore, take no bold risks and will be content with a moderate measure of success, being merely guided by rule and precedent. Initiative and resourcefulness are at a discount. The business policy will be timid and unenterprising. There is **routine and red-tape,** a place safe for men of mediocre calibre and no room for extraordinary and dashing spirits. No first-rate work can be done by second-rate men. Bureaucracy will further mean bossism, loss of individual liberty, gestapo, *etc*.

(*ii*) Not Successful in Business. A government department cannot claim to score success in business, where quick decisions have to be taken and bold policies are called for. The government personnel is not such as can conquer new fields. The government can, and does, attract able men but conditions in government service are not congenial for the display of extraordinary ability. The reward is not considered worth the trouble.

(*iii*) Insufficient Resources. It is also urged that **government cannot raise the huge amounts of capital** which are necessary for the efficient running and expanding of all industries and trades.

(*iv*) Misallocation of Resources. Under socialism, there will be no automatic indicator for the most economical allocation of the resources of the community among different industries. Under capitalism, there are consumers' preferences which, through price-mechanism, bring about an optimum allocation of these resources. But, under socialism, it will be all groping in the dark. Some commodities will be produced in excess and wasted, whereas there may be a shortage of others resulting in unsatisfied demand. **A chronic mal-adjustment in demand and supply** is feared. The task of organising production, of allocating every acre of land to its proper use, of setting every worker on the right job and of investing every rupee in the direction of maximum benefit is too big to be performed by any single authority.

(*v*) Loss of Consumer's Sovereignty. Under capitalism, the consumer enjoys sovereignty. Of course, this sovereignty is limited by his income, existence of monopoly, *etc*., yet the domain is wide enough for him to pick and choose. But, under socialism, he will loss this sovereignty altogether. Consumption will have to adjust itself to production. This loss to the consumer is a real loss. He will not be able to maximise his satisfaction.

The State will no doubt fix the prices, but it will be all arbitrary. The price fixation will be rigid and will lack the resiliency of market mechanism, which is sensitive to even the slightest change in the consumers' preferences.

(*vi*) Lack of Incentives. It is also feared that incentive to hard work and stimulus to self-improvement will disappear altogether when personal gain or self-interest is eliminated. People will not give their best. Inventive ability, enterprising spirit and the go-ahead attitude will languish, and creative work will become impossible. It is remarked that "a government could print a good edition of Shakespeare's works, but it could not get them written."[8]

(*vii*) Loss of Economic Freedom. There will be loss of economic freedom under socialism. A serious charge against socialism is that, when freedom of enterprise disappears, even the free choice of occupation will go. Workers will be assigned certain jobs and they cannot change them without the consent of the planning authority. Every worker is dovetailed in the scheme, and he must remain there. This loss of freedom may be really galling.

(*viii*) No Economic Equality. Some people have been disappointed in socialism, because in Russia, where it has been in operation, it has **failed to bring about economic equality.** The difference between the rich and the poor is still there. The dream of a classless society is far from being realised. The workers under capitalism, *e.g.*, in the U.S.A. and the U.K., are not so worse off. They enjoy a high standard of living. They are not convinced that under capitalism the poor go on becoming poorer. The rich are no doubt getting richer but the lot of the poor is also undoubtedly improving. It is thus that some degree of scepticism in the efficacy of socialism as a panacea for all social ills has grown and damped the ardour of some enthusiastic socialists.

(*ix*) Concentration of Power in the State. The greatest danger of socialism is that too much power is concentrated in the State. Under socialism, the State is not merely a political authority but it also exercises unlimited authority in the economic sphere. To the extent all power is concentrated in the State; the danger is that the State is everything and individual nothing. He may not count at all. He is reduced to a cypher. After all, the human institutions are for man and not man for these institutions.

(*x*) Loss of Personal Liberty. That under socialism there is no unemployment is conceded, but the critics retort by saying that there is also no unemployment in a jail. They regard a socialist State as **one big prisonhouse** and they do not think that employment is any compensation for the loss of liberty.

(*xi*) Not Scientific. It may also be pointed out in the end that Marxian **socialism is not so scientific after all.** Labour is not the only source of value and has not the sole right to its appropriation. Few are convinced of the accuracy of Marx's materialistic interpretation of history. Economic motives are no doubt the strongest but they are not the only ones to sway human actions.

Criticism Answered

This looks a formidable array of arguments against socialism, but it is not so formidable as it may seem. The strength of socialism lies in the proved evils of capitalism. The world is periodically plunged into depression causing much dislocation, unemployment and suffering. Capitalism has not been able to ensure stable economic conditions. National resources have been exploited for personal profit. Human beings, especially women and children, have been used as so many machines simply to enrich the capitalists. Who can help hearing the "Cry of the Children"?

> How long, O cruel nation,
>
> Will you stand, to move the world, on a child's heart, —
>
> Stifle down with a mailed heel its palpitation.
>
> And tread onward to your throne amid the mart;
>
> Our blood splashes upward, O gold heaper,
>
> And your purpole shows your path!
>
> **(Elizabeth Barret Browning)**

The social conscience feels outraged at the sight of a poor family **working the hardest,** yet not getting two square meals a day, dressed in rags, living in dirty cells, and children dying because they cannot get medical aid or milk. On the other hand, the rich are rolling in luxuries, their horses and dogs are better fed and housed than their fellow-human beings. They perhaps think that the poor man is not after all a human

8. Pigou—*Capitalism and Socialism*, p. 80.

being; he is some other specie! A system which produces such iniquities and callousness stands self-condemned.

Look at the alternative. **Socialism bans trade depression and removes unemployment** which, under capitalism, always hangs over the worker's head like a Damocle's sword. A great worry is off. Free choice of occupation under capitalism is a farce. Who can really choose his occupation? The choice is limited by his parents' means and influence. Sometimes a man would like to get any work that he can. But there is no work. Capitalism throws him on the scrapheap. Who would not like to be put on to a job compulsorily rather than face enforced unemployment and starvation? A socialist State provides permanent and pensionable job for everybody according to his aptitude and capacity.

A socialist State can allocate the resources of the community among the various uses with the sole consideration of **social security and welfare.** Consumer's wishes have to be replaced by higher social valuations. It is possible that at one stage there may be a shortage of some type of consumers' goods, but this is deliberately done in the higher interests of the society. Surely, there is no harm in making a temporary sacrifice so that we or our children may be able to enjoy better standards later. Only a socialist State can build up a solid foundation for the country's strength and prosperity. The policy of a capitalist economy is a short-sighted one guided by the immediate gains of the entrepreneur.

Under socialism, vast funds can be devoted to the expansion of education of all types, for provision of adequate medical facilities and for relationalisation of industry and reorganisation of agriculture. The result is that **human and material resources of the nation are immensely improved and fully utilised.** A socialist State can easily find resources to help the poor, because the profits of industry, which, under capitalism, go to enrich the already rich and surfeited, are pooled in the State treasury.

Many things, the consumption of which is considered essential for health and efficiency, may be **supplied free or below cost.** Not doubt, consumption is regimented and it is curtailed in certain directions, yet there need be no hardship, for it may be expanded in some other and more desirable directions. A socialist State can provide free milk for children, free nursing, free education and free medical aid. It can give free cinema shows to the workers and provide for them swimming pools, recreational clubs, railway passes to week-end resorts , and light refreshment in the factory gratis. Such things are

Socialism ensures social welfare.

impossible in a capitalist economy where lure of the lure rules. A capitalist only looks to his dividend.

Production of all types can be immediately increased by a socialist State. The achievements of the Russian Five-Year Plans are a standing monument to what can be achieved under socialism by people who not long ago were illiterate, ignorant, backward, conservative and poor peasants. Russia, too, like India, was a country of small farmers, almost all illiterate. Now there is nearly cent per cent literacy; and in production Russia has beaten every other European country which started in the race of industrialisation nearly one century ago. This shows that it is only in a socialist State that planning can really be effective. This is all due to the fact that all phases of economic life are under the central State direction.

Dangers of bureaucratic management have been exaggerated. There is a lot of red-tapism in company management even under capitalism. A socialist State can also regulate credit and banking operations, so that financial maladjustments are eliminated.

As for incentive to hard work, a socialist State can, by persistent propaganda and through instruction in the educational institutions, change the very psychology of the people and create **new scales of values.** It can offer production bonuses so that every worker does his best.

Who will do the dirty work? The socialists' answer is that most of it will be done by machinery. Machinery is not being put to such tasks at present simply because man is cheaper than machinery. Thousands of semi-starving people are available under capitalism to do such jobs on a small wages, because capitalism has impoverished the masses. But a socialist

State, not working for profit, will be in a position to relieve man from all dangerous dirty and degrading jobs.

Socialism may not be able to make everybody economically equal. This is due not to lack of organising ability in a socialist State. The cause lies in the innate inequalities among human beings. Nature does not make everyone alike. Everyone is endowed with varying degrees of intelligence and working capacity. No state can help it. It is not a matter for legislation. But a socialist State can discover the aptitude and ability of each citizen and develop them further by training and education so that every citizen is enabled to make his best contribution to the welfare of the State. Real worth will not be allowed to be suppressed or depressed by poverty. **The socialist State can pick up genius even from the lowliest of families and provide it with the fullest facilities and opportunities.** If, therefore, the attainment of economic equality is not considered feasible, at least equality of opportunity can be assured, to each, and this will be no mean achievement. There can also be a considerable levelling up of the masses.

Recently socialistic countries have undergone transformations such as allowing private property, price mechanism in some degree.

The balance seems to be heavily tilted in favour of socialism.

Some Problems of Socialism

It will be of interest to know how Soviet Russia has tackled the various economic problems :

Private property. Private property in the form of a house, a car, a few animals and other consumers' goods is allowed. A man is free to buy government bonds or securities. He can keep to a deposit in the bank. Property up to the amount of 50,000 roubles can be transmitted by inheritance. But living on unearned income is discouraged and all unearned income is subject to very heavy taxation. Only bourgeois property which is the result of exploitation, is sought to be abolished.

Pricing System. Under the free-enterprise, competitive and individualistic system, the pricing system automatically solves the major economic problems. Some economists, however, notably Mrs. Hayek and Robbins, are of the opinion that rational accounting is impossible under a socialist regime and that it is all groping in the dark. But there are other economists like Pigou who do not see any difficulty in this. Dickinson and some other economists are of the opinion that the capitalist apparatus of marketing and pricing can be retained in socialism.

Russians have been able to fix prices of the goods. Costs of raw materials and wages, transport and all other costs are added and then a small percentage for a little profit. This gives a selling price. It is a little arbitrary. The prices do not reflect the intensities of consumers' demands, although some note is taken of the relative scarcities. But, in a socialist society, prices of goods will be low enough to clear the available supplies and also high enough to cover the socially necessary marginal costs of production. The price under socialist planning need not be market price as under capitalism. It is purely a book-keeping or accounting price set by the planning authority.

In recent years, however, the crude quantitative goods in the physical units are being replaced by profitability criteria of performance. By this process of economic valuation socialism seems to be moving in the direction of capitalism.

Supply of Labour and Wages. There is no freedom of choice of occupation. There are also ample facilities for technical training. The Government is prepared to bear the cost of training on the condition that the trainees, after completing training, work in government factories for a term of years on conditions settled beforehand. Money wages are paid and there are variations according to ability efficiency and the nature of work.

Standard wages are fixed after a thorough motion-study and time-study in order to ascertain the standard time required for a job. Efficiency premia are paid to better workers who take less time. Wages are also supplemented by the payment to the workers of a lump-sum social dividend payment. This payment varies with the size composition and health status of the family. By means of such payments, inequalities of income and mitigated. If there is a comparative shortage of some type of labour, higher wages are of course offered to attract the right type and sufficient supply of labour.

Workers are assigned definite jobs. The workers could also be transferred from one place to another just like government servants. The government tries to adjust supply to demand.

Wages. The system of setting accounting prices on labour, as in the case of other productive resources will not do, for the amount of labour is not a fixed quantity. People can choose their occupation and they can also choose whether to work more or work less, *i.e.*, whether to prefer income or leisure. Hence, it is essential to have a system of **actual market wages rather than accounting wages.** These rates will vary according to the agreeableness or disagreeableness of the job, possibility of supplementary earning, training or skill required to do a job, productivity of individual workers, *etc*. Marginal productivity will determine the wage.

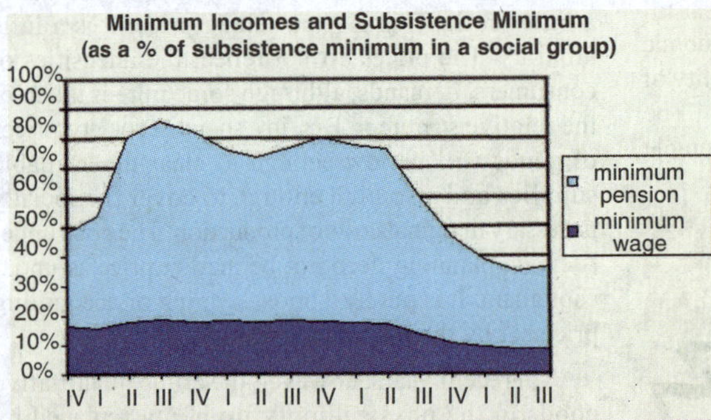

Chart showing minimum pension on minimum wage in Russia.

Thus, there will be no dead level of wages in a socialist State. The wages will depend on the valuation that society places on the needs and worth of individual workers and the necessity for compensation to those who have to do dirty, irksome and arduous jobs. Inequality of incomes will no longer be accounted for by inequalities of property but by such factors as mentioned above.

Finance. The Russians had repudiated foreign debts and could not hope to secure foreign loans. They relied, therefore, mostly on created money. Paper money was issued by the State in enormous amounts. There was inflation with all the usual consequences—exorbitant prices and a very high cost of living, *etc*. They also raised loans from the people. Later on, income from socialised industry flowed in and helped to finance the later stages of planning.

Rent. Even a socialist State cannot do away with the concept of rent. Change of economic order from capitalism to socialism will not turn scarce land into an unlimited quantity. Rent as an index of productivity will help in the best allocation of the available land among its various types of land, the good hand being put a higher tag.

As Samuelson puts it, "Only by putting a price upon inert sweatless land are we using it, and sweating breathing labour, most productively! The price or rent of land rises so as to ration its limited supply among the best uses."[9] Even a socialist State will have to direct land from one use to another so as to make its marginal productivity in all uses the same. This marginal productivity will be indicated by rent. This is the only way to ensure a correct allocation of valuable human or material resources.

Interest. The Russians have not abolished interest altogether. The Government itself pays interest on State loans. Interest shows an attempt to bring the demand for, and supply of, capital into equilibrium. The banks also pay interest on personal accounts. Interest as remuneration to the capitalist, *i.e.*, payment to private owners of idle money, does not occupy an important place in Russian economy, since private capital has practically disappeared. The State borrows and pays interest and appropriates the profit of industry.

What role does interest play in a socialist State? In a capitalistic State, we know that interest performs three important functions (*a*) It determines people's income from bonds and other assets; (*b*) it is a necessary payment to induce people to part with liquidity; and (*c*) it relates future and present economic values, *i.e.*, it helps society to decide how much of the national income should be invested in capital formation and where should the capital be used.

Now the first two functions have no bearing in a socialist State. Since capital is no longer the property of private individuals, interest as an income-determining factor or as an inducement for dishoarding does not exist. But whatever the form of economy, interest must continue to perform the third function, *viz.*, to determine the allocation of the economic resources of the community as between present and future and the allocation of capital among different uses in the present.

The rate of interest acts like a sieve or a rationing device. Capital is scarce and the uses for which it is wanted are unlimited. The rate of interest is the indicator of the directions in which capital should move. Obviously, enterprises with a prospective yield at 12 per cent are to be undertaken in preference to those yielding 10 per cent. "The rate of interest must

9. *Economics*, 1948, p. 598.

be used to allocate scarce capital supplies optimally and to determine the order of priority of alternative projects."

Allocation of factors of production. The State planning authority tries to estimate the amounts of factors required for the targeted production in an industry and arranges for the supply. It is first decided which industries have to be developed and to what extent. The factors of production are diverted in channels set by the State and according to consumers' preferences. For example, the Russians concentrated first on heavy industries. Naturally, there was a shortage of consumers' goods whose prices shot up. In a capitalistic system, factors of production would rush towards consumers' goods industries to make up for the deficiency. But a socialist State does not allow this diversion. Shortage would continue and rationing and price control introduced. In Russia, the normal functioning of the price-mechanism, which brings about an optimum distribution of resources, as judged by the consumers' valuations, is nullified by State action.

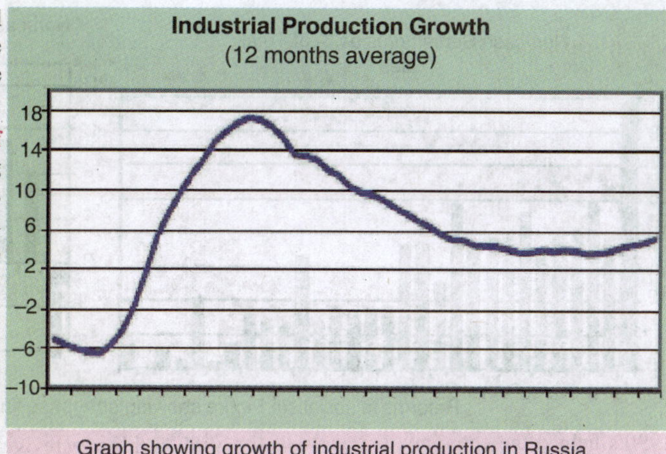

Graph showing growth of industrial production in Russia.

Thus, the resources are allocated, not according to the valuation of the consumers but, according to the valuation of the State. The State decides what is best for the nation at a particular period of its life and arranges the distribution of resources accordingly. The consumers must adjust their demands according to production and the exigencies of the State.

Future of Socialism After 1989

A number of countries opted for free enterprise economy after the 1989 demolition of Berlin wall. Today socialism in its traditional form of authoritarian or market socialism is rarely exists in the world. Only Vietnam or North Korea, Cuba and certain small pockets in different parts of the World it exists, that too not a powerful one. It is only in a simplest form. Socialism once a powerful economic system was ruling the world during the second half of the twentieth century. Socialism in real sense was a good economic system, though it had not given many economic freedom to people. The causes of collapse of socialism is not the system, but its application by the leaders. Socialism became one of the powerful weapon among the Russian Leaders and other Warswa pact countries to exploit people for their own benefits. Socialism means welfare of society or mankind but it was used for exploiting the mankind. Giving the people the bare necessities and the rest for the personal use of the leaders. There was no difference between the Czars and Joseph Stalin. The Czars build up huge war machines at the cost of people the same thing did by Stalin in a different or some what refined way. Marshall Tito, former Yugolsalvian President was the only leader who declined to accept the hagemony of the Russians. This was regarding the Planning and expansion of market programme, which the Russian's under Stalin were interested in carrying out over the Warsaw Pact countries. Tito, said, we are competent enough to carry out our internal economic planning for our country and denounced the interference of the Russian in their internal-affairs.

Pandit Jawaharlal Nehru the first Prime Minister of India, appreciated the way Russians achieved economic development in a short-period and based the economic idealogy of India on socialistic pattern of society. Mrs. Gandhi in real term brought about certain bold decisions in the form of nationalisation of commercial banks, abolishment of privy purses and nationalisation of some foreign corporate sectors as the government undertakings. The environment of capitalists economy all over the world engulfed the basic principles of socialism. Today in India, the government which at once used to take care of the common masses by providing jobs, social security measures, educational facilities, health and other measures is backing out and handing over it to the private-sector. Dis-investment policy, privatisation of education health care and other essential services are being reduced by the government from its functions.

Generally for any economy to get its fruits, it requires certain amount of time. The education, health, poverty alleviation programmes which the government initiated some time between 1970's and

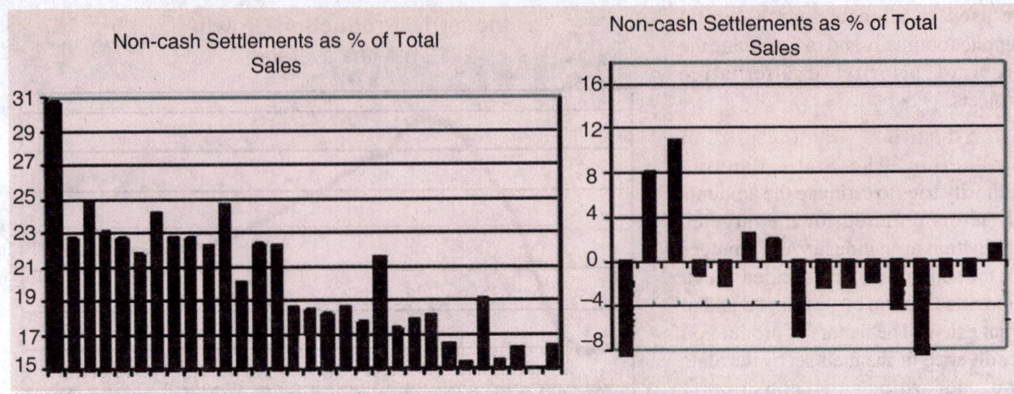

Reforms in socialism Figure showing enterprise finance in Russia.

1990's helped the economy to review in the 21st century. Now the market socialism is no more in India and we are following completely the capitalists economy. There is a possibility of wider inequalities of income and wealth and other problems may come, as that of the case of Latin American countries, and this may revive the beginning of socialism in its new form. History repeats, if exploitation of common man increases than it may sow the seeds of revolution and which may initiate the beginning of yet another form of socialism.

Key terms

Socialism, Marxian socialism, Authoritarian socialism, Liberal socialism, Guild socialism, Communism, Syndialism, Surplus value, Anarchism, Fabian Socialism, Economic planning.

QUESTIONS

1. Critically evaluate the future of socialism.
2. What are the main features of capitalism? Discuss its merits and demerits.
3. Compare the economic role of the state in a socialist economy with its role in a capitalist economy.
4. Distinguish between capitalism and socialism. In what respects is socialism superior to capitalism?
5. How does a capitalist society differ from a socialist one? To what extent are the defects of both eliminated in a mixed economy?
6. Examine critically the case for 'socialism' as a system more conducive to the progress of society than capitalism.
7. What can be the incentives to production under a socialist economy? Can they be more effective than those under capitalism?

MIXED ECONOMY

Meaning

We have discussed in the preceding chapters the two economic system, *viz*., capitalism and socialism. But there is also a third one, *viz*., the mixed economy. It is neither pure capitalism nor pure socialism but a mixture of the two. In the system we find the characteristics both of capitalism and socialism. As Samuelson observes, "Within the advanced countries themselves, the scene was drastically changed from the Victorian days of laissez-faire capitalism. Almost unconsciously, undiluted capitalism had been evolving into a mixed economy with both private and public initiative and control. The clock of history sometimes evolves so slowly that its moving hands are never seen to move."[1]

In the modern world, what we find mostly are mixed economies. Mixed economy means that it is operated both by private enterprise and public enterprise. That is, private enterprise is not permitted to function freely and uncontrolled through price-mechanism. On the other hand, the government intervenes to control and regulate private enterprise in several ways. It has been realised that a free functioning of private enterprise results in several types of evils. For instance, free functioning of private enterprise produces trade cycles, *i.e.*, sometimes depression and unemployment and at other times booms and inflationary situation. Besides, free functioning of private enterprise results in extreme inequalities of income and wealth. Under the laissez-faire policy pursued by the State in the free enterprise economy, the weaker and vulnerable sections of society as well as the indigenous industries do not get protection.

It is also realised that in the under-developed countries, like India, economic development cannot be achieved at the desired rate of growth without any active government help and guidance. Hence the government in such countries actively participates in economic activities in order to minimise the evils of unadulterated capitalism and to accelerate economic growth. That is why most of the capitalistic economies of the world have become mixed economies, because in all economies the economic functions of the State have increased.

The laissez-faire policy propounded by Adam Smith and other classical economists has been almost altogether abandoned and the economies even of the U.S.A. and the U.K. have become mixed economies. Eminent American

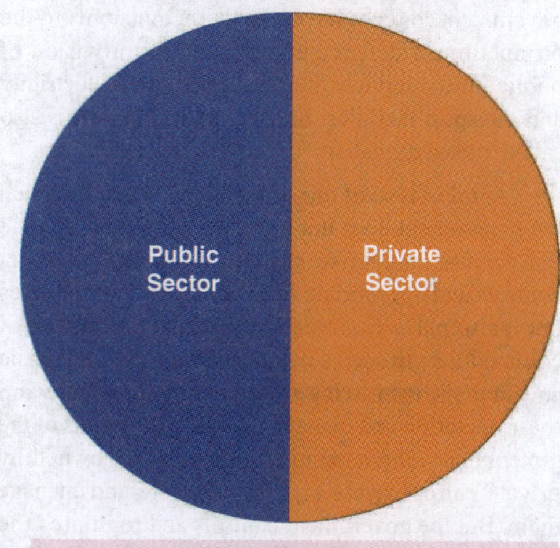

Mixed Economy.

1. Samuelson, P.A., *Economics*, Ninth Edition, p. 867.

economists like Prof. Samuelson and Hansen call the American, English and the French economies as "Mixed Capitalist System" on "Mixed Enterprise System" because their governments interfere in the working of the economy by controlling and regulating it and they actively participate in economic activities.

Mixed economy contains positive aspects of both capitalims and socialism.

Two Types. In one type, the means of production are owned by private entrepreneurs. But the government directly controls and regulates the working of the economy through its monetary and fiscal policies. For, example, it institutes price control, licensing system, import control, exchange control, control over capital issues, *etc*. The government does not take over the ownership of the means of production to undertake production itself. Even if it undertakes production directly, it is comparatively very little as compared with the volume of production under the control of private entrepreneurs. That is why such a mixed economy is called **'mixed capitalist system'.** It is predominantly capitalistic and the government only influences its working and growth through appropriate fiscal and monetary policies. It controls and regulates private enterprise so that the evils of free private enterprise and of the price system are avoided and some pre-determined objectives are achieved.

In such mixed enterprise systems the government confines its productive activity only to the production of defence equipment and provision of public utility services like water, gas and electricity and transport facilities. Such a mixed economy is also called 'mixed capitalism' or 'controlled capitalism."

Another type of mixed economy is one in which the government does not merely control and regulate the private enterprise system by means of direct controls and appropriate fiscal and monetary policies but it also plays vital role in the actual production of commodities. In such a mixed economy, several basic and strategic industries are owned by the State and their operation and management is in the hands of the government. The remaining industries are owned by private entrepreneurs and they operate and manage them. But the government controls and regulates the private sector through direct controls and appropriate monetary and fiscal policies.

The main difference between the mixed economy of this type and of the former type is that in this type of mixed economy, the government controls the means of production in a much larger measure and itself undertakes production. Whereas, the first type of mixed economy is biased more towards capitalism, the latter type is biased more towards socialism, the Indian economy is an example of this second type of mixed economy.

In the Indian economy, both the public sector and private sector are in operation. The foundations of mixed economy in India were laid by the Industrial Policy Resolution of 1948 which was modified by the Industrial Policy Resolution of 1956. According to these resolutions, the various industries were divided between the two sectors, *viz*., the private sector and the public sector. The responsibility for the development of several basic, heavy and strategic industries was assigned to the State and the development of the rest of the industries was left to the private sector. Even the private sector is controlled and influenced by the Government of India by means of direct controls or through appropriate fiscal and monetary policies.

It is clear from the above that the mixed economy is a mixture of capitalism and socialism. The mixed economy tries to avoid the two extremes of pure capitalism and pure socialism and the evils associated with each. In other words, it strikes a middle path between capitalism and socialism. We have mentioned above that in pure capitalism only private sector establishes and runs industries and the government does not interfere in any manner. As against this, under pure socialism all the means of production, *i.e.*, industries, agriculture, land, mines, *etc*., are owned and controlled by the State and the State operates them. In the mixed economy, on the other hand both private and public sectors operate. Some industries are owned and managed by the State and other industries are owned and managed by the private sector. It is thus clear that, in a mixed economy, all industries are not nationalised. Only those industries are nationalised and put under the operation of the public sector which are very essential for the speedy economic development of the country but in which the private entrepreneurs are reluctant to invest because either the return is insufficient or long delayed. In a mixed economy, the sphere of two sectors, *i.e.*, the private sector and the public sector, are clearly demarcated, and they combine and co-operate in the work of economic development of the country.

Steel Industry in India has both public and private participation.

As we have said already, the economies of the U.S.A. and the U.K. have also today become mixed economies. But the Indian mixed economy is different from them, because in the Indian economy, the public sector has been assigned a much more extensive, more active, and more strategic role to play.

Main Features of Mixed Economy

Having understood the meaning of mixed economy, we are now in a position to bring out the main features or characteristics of such an economy. It will also be clear from these characteristics how a mixed economy functions. The following are the main characteristics of a mixed economy:

(*i*) Co-existence of the Public and Private Sectors. The chief characteristic of a mixed economy is that in this economy both public sector and the private sector function together. They co-exist. The industries of the country are divided into two parts. In one part are the industries the responsibility for the development of which is entrepreneurs to the State and they are owned and managed by the State. Other industries are left under the authority and control of the private entrepreneurs. The private sector is free to develop them and start new enterprises in this sector. Generally, the basic and heavy industries;, the industries concerned with the production of defence equipment, atomic energy heavy engineering industries, *etc*., are put in the public sector. On the other hand, the consumer goods industries, small and cottage industries, agriculture, *etc*., are generally assigned to the private sector. It may be borne in mind that the government does not work against the private sector. On the contrary, the government helps and encourages the private sector by providing them several incentives and facilities so that the industries in the private sector are able to develop properly and make the country's economy efficient and strong.

(*ii*) Role of Price System and Government Directives. Another characteristic of mixed economy is that it is operated both by the price system and the government directives. So far as the public sector is concerned economic decisions relating to production, prices and investment are made by the government or authorities appointed by the government. But the private sector in the missed economy is operated by price-mechanism. In other words, in the industries in the private sector, the decisions regarding investment, production, prices, *etc*., are made by private entrepreneurs—capitalists and industrialists—with the object of making maximum profits on the basis of the price system. It is clear that in the mixed economy the allocation of productive resources is partly determined by the price system and partly by the government directives.

(*iii*) Government Regulation and Control and Private Sector. In a mixed economy, the government adopts necessary measures to regulate and influence the private sector, so that it may function in the interest of the nation rather than exclusively in the interest of the private entrepreneurs. For this purpose, it introduces the licensing system according to which government approval or licence is essential for setting up a factory. If the government considers that in a certain industry already there is excessive investment or excess capacity, no new licences are issued for setting up factories in that industry. Licensing system is the instrument by which the government controls and regulates industrial investment and output. The government also controls and regulates the private sector through appropriate monetary and fiscal policies. For this purpose, the government gives rebates and tax concessions and credit facilities at low and reasonable rates so that the private entrepreneurs are induced to invest in those industrial lines.

(*iv*) Consumers' Sovereignty Protected. In mixed economy, the sovereignty of the consumers is protected. Like socialism, the mixed economy does not put an end to consumer's sovereignty. The consumers are free to buy commodities of their choice and the private entrepreneurs produce commodities according to consumers' demands or preferences, although the government can control their prices in public interest so that they can be prevented from rising unduly high. In fact, the aim of price control is to protect the consumers from exploitation by private producers and capitalists. Besides, the government can also ration the commodities in short supply so that the limited available quantities can be fairly distributed. It is clear that, in spite of some

JRD Tata – 1904-1993.
India's Leading Industrialist.

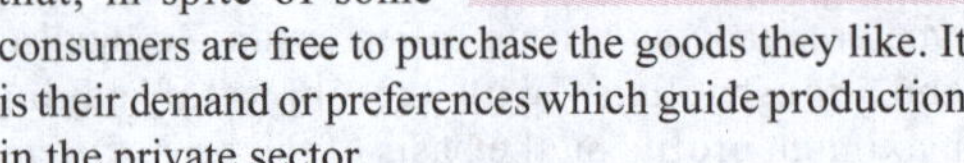

consumers are free to purchase the goods they like. It is their demand or preferences which guide production in the private sector.

(*v*) Government Protection of Labour. In a mixed economy, government protects the weaker sections of society especially labour. That is, it saves labour from exploitation by the capitalists. In the developed countries, in the beginning of Industrial Revolution, the greed and selfishness of the factory owners inflicted untold hardships on male labour, women and children. Social conscience was roused on seeing the pitiful and miserable working and living conditions of such labour. The government realised its responsibility or protecting labour from exploitation by industrialists and factory owners. Now several factory Acts have been passed to regulate the working conditions of labour. Minimum wages and the working hours have been fixed. Restrictions have been imposed on the employment of small children in factories. Labour is paid compensation for accidents while at work. The government also tales necessary steps to prevent industrial disputes. These things are done even in mixed economies of 'controlled capitalism' type.

(*vi*) Reduction of Economic Inequalities. The government in mixed economies take necessary steps for the reduction of inequalities of income and wealth. Extreme inequalities of income and wealth are socially unjust, politically undesirable and economically harmful. Extreme inequalities of income reduce social welfare. Income inequality creates inequalities of opportunities for education and training in favour of high-income groups. The extreme inequalities of income create class distinctions and generate class-conflict which splits the whole society into two warring camps—the rich and the poor or the 'haves' and the 'have-nots'. The rich exploit the poor. Modern governments try to reduce economic inequalities for promoting social justice, and social stability and social welfare, increasing production and for providing equal opportunities for all. For this purpose, government levies progressive taxation, wealth tax, death duties, gift tax, *etc*. On the other hand, free education, free medical aid and old-age pensions, for the poor, stipends for poor students are some of the remedies adopted for distributing the extra income of the rich among the poor.

As a result of the above-mentioned measures, which have been adopted by the governments of different countries like the U.S.A. the U.K., Norway and Sweden, inequalities of income and wealth have been somewhat reduced. The Government of India also has decided to introduce a socialistic pattern of society and for that purpose reduce inequalities of income and wealth. This is a major objective of our Five-Year Plans. But so fare the Government has not succeeded in achieving this desirable objective. In fact, it is said that in India economic inequalities have increased instead of decreasing the planning era. The fruits of economic development are concentrating in the hands of a few rich people. Our Government is now fully seized of the problem of growing economic inequalities and it may be hoped that in future strong measures will be adopted for reducing economic inequalities. In this way, it will be fulfilling one of the main purposes of a mixed economy.

(*vii*) Control of Monopoly. In a mixed economy. The government tries to control and regulate monopolies. A charge against monopolies is that they reduce output and raise prices in order to get maximum profit. The monopolist thus uses his monopoly power to exploit the consumers. He fixes a price which is above the marginal cost of production and in this way reduces consumers' welfare. Such a price-output policy results in misallocation of productive resources of the community. Besides, the excessive profits made by monopolists result in accentuating economic inequalities in the country. Moreover, monopoly creates unemployment by reducing output and thus hampers industrial development.

The government tries to control and regulate monopolies in order to remove the above evils and make them function in public interest. It appoints an ad hoc or permanent commission to fix a fair price of the monopolised products. Only a reasonable return is permitted on investments made by monopolists. In other words, a monopolist can earn only a fixed rate of dividend. Also, when the government considers it necessary in public interest, it takes over monopolies and operates them in public interest. Moreover, some governments have passed legislation to prevent the establishment of business combinations which lead to the creation of monopolies.

Conclusion. We have studied above that in a mixed economy public sector and private sector operate side by side. In the pubic sector, the development of industries is directly under the government: hence it is possible to make sure of their operation according to plan and with proper organisation. In the private sector, however, there is need for some controls and incentives so that they are also developed according to plan, *e.g.*, price controls, influencing them by means of proper investment, licensing of new industries control over capital issues, control over imports, prevention of concentration of economic power and creation of monopolies, *etc*.

Critical Evaluation of Mixed Economy

Let us assess briefly the working of the mixed economy system. Although, as we have said above, all capitalistic economies have become more or less mixed economies, yet we do not propose to make a survey of the working of the system elsewhere. We confine ourselves to the assessment of the working of mixed economy in India, for, as India is the biggest democracy, it is also the biggest experiment in mixed economy.

We may notice two opposite views on the working of mixed economy: one represented by the business community or 'big business' properly speaking and the other by the political leaders in the Government. These views are usually given expression to in the annual conferences of the Chambers of Commerce which are addressed usually by the Prime Minister and other high government spokesmen. There is usually a wordy warfare between the two. The business leaders are frankly critical of the government and the government spokesman of the business community. The government charges the business of the community with black marketing, profiteering and not being patriotic enough to play a proper role in the economy whereas the business leaders hold the government responsible for inflation, economic stagnation and for the ills of the economy and of trying to squeeze out the private sector in a variety of ways.

For instance, in the annual meeting of the Associated Chamber of Commerce and Industry held in April, 1975, J.R.D. Tata said that mixed economy was dead or dying. He said, "our economy will continue to stagnate while our population grows and we shall end up before the turn of the century under dictatorship or in a state of chaos and violence." The Prime Minister, on the other hand, extolled the virtues of the public sector and harped on its achievements. Mr. P. N. Haksar, Deputy Chairman of the Planning Commission, addressing the annual session of the Federation of Indian Chamber of Commerce and Industry termed Mr. Tata's speech as a 'funeral oration' and said that this oration would be justified if mixed economy was really dead. He said that the problems of the country could not be solved by "composing lyrical passages on the death of mixed economy, raising 'macabre' vision of the hold of communists". He further said that it would be doing an injustice to argue that the concept of mixed economy obtained only abroad and what obtained in India was "mixed-up economy."

These charges and counter-charges only blur the true vision of mixed economy. The reality is that despite the present ills of the Indian economy, the marriage of the public and private sectors in Indian economy is merrily going on and doing well. Both sectors are making a valuable contribution to the successful functioning of the Indian economy. As pointed out by Mr. Haksar, the country produced in terms of output 90% of the goods and services through private economy. This bears ample testimony to the vitality and virility of he private sector. Far from being dead, it is alive and kicking. There is little danger of its becoming extinct or being swallowed up by the public sector. While private sector was a part of the national economy, State control is essential in the interest of integrated growth of the economy. Mixed economy in India is a byproduct of the government involvement in the task of economic development of the country. There is no doubt that government has played a remarkable role in developing infrastructural facilities and setting up big industrial units which have helped the private sector a great deal in its functioning.

The fact is that the public sector and the private sector are the two necessary limbs of the economy and both must be in good health and functioning properly. There should be cordial co-operation between the two. Mixed economy cannot function in a State of cold war. Besides, government regulation is essential to bring about a proper co-ordination between the two wings of the economy. It may also be borne in mind that mixed economy cannot function in a static framework. It is a dynamic concept and the proper relationship between the two sectors must go through a continuous evolutionary process to ensure that they do not work at cross purposes. Both sectors must work in the interest of the economy as a whole rather than promote their own selfish interests. "That mixed economy which reflects the callous indifference of the omnipotent bureaucratic machine of the public sector on the one hand and massive profiteering with unutilised capacities and high prices of he private sector on the other, stands totally condemned in the eyes of the people. . . . The amorphous opportunism of the political elite and the greed of the private big business stare us in the face every day."[2] This situation must change so that the economy is restored to full health and soundness.

MIXED ECONOMY IN THE CONTEXT OF INDIAN ECONOMY

The Industrial Policy Resolutions passed in 1948 and 1956 gave a concrete shape to the concept of mixed economy. According to the Industrial Policy Resolution of 1948, industries in India were broadly divided into four categories: (*i*) Exclusive government monopoly; (*ii*) Government-controlled sphere; (*iii*) Industries subject to State regulation and control: and (*iv*) the rest of the industrial field which was to be the sphere of private enterprise under general control of the State. In other words, the whole industrial field was split up into two broad sectors *viz*., public sector which was exclusively reserved for the government and the private sector in which private enterprise could operate freely. The Industrial (Development and Regulation) Act, 1951 was the main instrument by which the Government controlled and regulated private industrial enterprise *i.e.*, controlled the location, setting up and expansion of private industrial undertakings.

Mixed Economy in Dilemma

Many countries after the IInd world war either embraced socialism (some of them forced) or opted for mixed economy. Some economists are of the opinion that there is no pure capitalism and pure socialism, but nearly all of them to a certain extent is mixed form. The Indian economy after independence opted for a mixed economy concept, it became a very strong economy during the late seventies and early eighties. The "Dumkel Draft Text" opened the gates of all developing countries for the entry of MNC and TNC which announced the slow death of mixed economy. The collapse of GATT and a more refined WTO came into existence in 1995, which further wiped out the concept of mixed economy in the world. The mixed economy came into existence with the positive aspects of capitalism and socialism, with the rejection of negative aspects of both the system. Today mixed economy concept has remained only in the book as that of an academic interest, the rest is controlled by the capitalists economy. Mixed economy concept was very much responsible for the rapid development of the economies of the west. The British, The French, the Swedish economies to certain extent was dominated by the mixed economy. The infra structure, including transportation and other activities were controlled by the government. These facilities were owned and managed successfully by the respective governments. Even today in some countries including India, transportation, education, banking and some other facilities are still owned by the governments, but it is in the process of privatisation.

Key terms

Mixed Economy, Public Sector, Private Sector, Government regulation and control.

QUESTIONS

1. What do you understand by 'Mixed Economy'? Discuss its merits and demerits with reference to Indian conditions.
2. What are the basic features of a mixed economy? Illustrate with reference to India.
3. How does a mixed economy differ from both capitalism and socialism?
4. Discuss the merits and limitations of mixed economy.

PART SEVEN

ECONOMICS OF DEVELOPMENT AND PLANNING

UNIT I

Economics of Development

UNIT II

Development Planning

UNIT I

ECONOMICS OF DEVELOPMENT

Chapters

ECONOMIC UNDER-DEVELOPMENT

We now pass from statics of comparative statics to dynamic analysis. In static analysis, for example, we discuss how equilibrium price is determined when the demand and supply curves are known and remain unchanged. Static analysis helps us to an analyse a situation where consumers, producing firms, industries *etc*., are in stable or static equilibrium at certain levels of prices, output, income and employment. In comparative statics, we analyse a situation, which has come about after a once-for-all change. In other words, we compare the two stable equilibria—one before and the other after the change. For example, suppose demand has permanently gone up. Now there will be new equilibrium price or an equilibrium different from the first.

But these methods of analysis have their limitations and cannot analyse many important and pressing problems, for example, the problems of economic fluctuations—booms and slumps and the problems of economic growth. In the study of economic growth. In the study of economic growth, instead of looking at the rates of output per period of time, we look at the rates of change in the rate of output between periods of time. In static analysis, certain basic elements in the economy (*e.g.*, size and composition of the population, natural resources, consumers' tastes, production techniques, *etc.*) are taken as given and fixed. These basic factors determine the levels of income, output and employment. In analysis of economic growth, some or all these basic elements are supposed to change and we have to determine the rates at which output is changing. We study the conditions of steady growth rate or determinants of economic growth.

Let us first study how the theory of economic growth has emerged and has come to occupy the attention of economists today.

Emergence of Theory of Growth

In the course of the last twenty five years or so, a separate branch of economic theory has emerged which studies the factors which contribute to increase the level of national income and output of a country and raise the standard of living of its people. This new branch of economic theory is variously levelled as **'Economics of Growth,' 'Economics of Under-development,'** or **'Economics of Development.'** For our purpose here, we shall use the term "Economics of Development."

The factors determining economic growth were discussed by Adam Smith, the father of political economy, and other classical economists. But, after the classical economists, owing to ascendency of marginalism, the economists mainly concentrated on the study of allocation of resources and determination of relative prices. In the beginning of the present century, and especially in the early 1930's, when the Great Depression engulfed the capitalist countries, the economists were largely engaged in finding out suitable explanation of depression and trade cycles. In 1936, Keynes's **General Theory of Employment, Interest and Money,** various aspects of which have already been discussed, brought about a revolution in economic thinking. Keynes explained clearly the true nature of depression and economic fluctuations.

But Keynesian theory only deals with the determination of income and employment in the short run, on the contrary economic development is a long-run process. It is, therefore, widely recognised that the Keynesian theory of income and employment has serious limitations when applied to under-developed countries. The problem which Keynes was out to solve in the nineteen thirties was one of economic instability and of low national output brought about not by the dearth of capital but in spite of the availability of capital. In under-developed countries, the main problem has been one of insufficiency of capital. In these countries, the problem essentially is one of narrowness of the margin over and above the consumption demand based on the extremely low standards of living.

Since the end of World War II, the economists started taking lot of interest in economic development. The reason was that the capitalist countries like the U.S.A., the U.K. and European countries were keen on stabilising the conditions of full employment. In this connection, economists like Sir Roy Harrod in England and Evsey D. Domar in the U.S.A., put forward models of steady economic growth. According to them, in order to maintain full employment it is necessary to have steady and continuous growth and increase in net investment. Besides, the governments in under-developed countries—in Asia, Africa, Latin America, and East European countries—have increasingly become development-minded. A good many of these countries have embarked on development planning to cross the curdle of stationary equilibrium of under-development. Their aim is to catch up with the advanced and highly developed nations of the world in the shortest possible time.

Poverty, hunger, disease, illiteracy, and lack of opportunity for self development have been the lot of a large majority of people in under-developed countries. Poverty there is old but the awareness of poverty and the hope that something can be done about it are new. In fact, **a "revolution of rising expectations"** is currently sweeping the under-developed countries. In these countries, many theories were propounded about initiating and accelerating the process of economic growth.

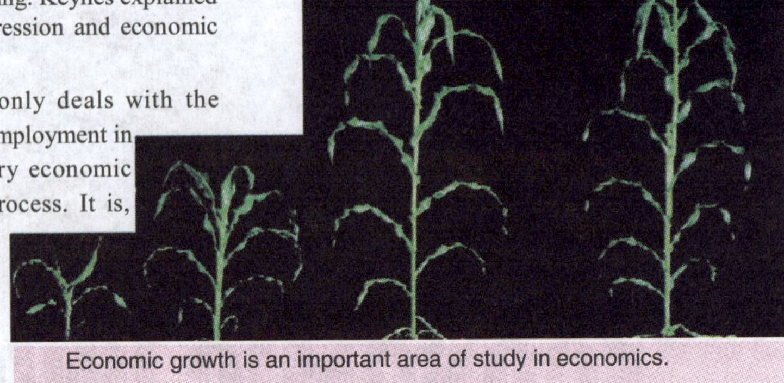

Economic growth is an important area of study in economics.

Definition of an Under-Developed Economy

It is not easy to define an under-developed economy. According to the United Nations experts, an under-developed country is one "in which per capita real income is low when compared with the per capita real incomes of the U.S.A., Canada, Australia and Western Europe."[1] This definition, though it focusses attention on a very important characteristic of under-development, *viz.*, poverty, can by no means be considered adequate. A country may be poor and yet not under-developed in relation to its resources if the resources happen to be scanty or inadequate. It may have fully developed its resources and yet be among the poorest countries in the world.

According to Prof. Ranger Nurkse, 'under-developed' countries are those which "compared with the advanced countries, **are under-equipped with capital in relation to their population and natural resources.**"[2] But this too is not a wholly satisfactory definition. As Nurkse himself points out, "Economic development has much to do with human endowments, social attitudes, political conditions and historical accidents. Capital is necessary but not a sufficient condition of progress."[3]

The Indian Planning Commission defines an under-developed country as one "which is characterised by the co-existence, in greater or less degree, of uniutilized or under-utilized manpower, on the one hand and of unexploited natural resources

1. U.N.O. *Measures for Economic Development of Under-developed Countries*, 1951, p. 3.
2 Nurkse, Ragnar: *Problems of Capital Formation in Under-developed Countries*, p. 1.
3. *Ibid.*, p. 2.

on the other." The existence of idle resources as stressed by this definition, is undoubtedly an important characteristic of an under-developed economy. But there is a snag in it: It does not clearly indicate the causes of the existence of idle resources. Resources may be, and are very often, idle even in the highly developed capitalist countries, particularly in times of depression. But such countries cannot be classed as 'under-developed' on that ground. As such, an acceptable definition of an under-developed country must pinpoint the main factors which lead to the existence of idle or under-utilized resources in such an economy. If the resources are idle because they have not been properly exploited or developed, it indicates a state of economic under-development.

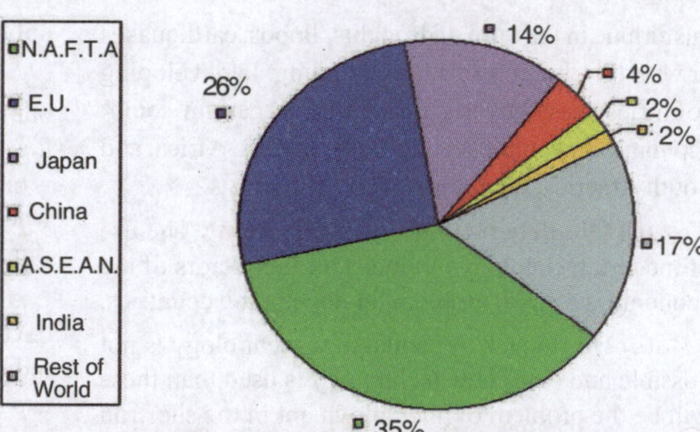

Chart shows share of different economics and economic regions in the world income. UDCs are poorly placed.
Source — World Bank.

Hence, an economy will considered under-developed:

(a) if its per capita income is how.

(b) if the natural resources and manpower in the country remain unutilised or under-utilised on account of lack of economic development; and

(c) if it is possible to raise its level of national income and per capita income by properly utilising its natural resources and manpower.

Prof. Viner observes: **"A more useful definition of an under-developed country is that it is a country with good potential prospects for using more capital or more labour or more available natural resources or all of these to support its present population on a higher level of living."**[4]

To Colin Clark, one of the pioneers in the studies of under-developed economies, economic development consists in the progressive enlargement of the proportion of tertiary occupations in the economy. But under-developed economies are those in which primary occupations predominate. While it is broadly true that, with rising standards of living there occurs a proliferation of the various kinds of personal services (*i.e.*, tertiary occupations), it has been often observed that in 'under-developed' countries the proportion of domestic servants is usually quite large. And since domestic service also fall in the category of tertiary occupations, this test of tertiary occupations cannot, therefore, be regarded as an unmistakable one.

Eugene Stanley gave a very precise and simple definition of under-developed countries, "these countries are characterised by (*i*) mass poverty of long standing, which is not due to a misfortune and (*ii*) old and obsolete methods of production along with socio-economic conditions which are not conducive to economic development.

The definition concentrates on (*i*) mass poverty (*ii*) obsolete methods of production and (*iii*) socio-economic conditions.

(*i*) Mass Poverty : Under-developed countries are suffering from mass poverty, that means a certain percentage of population is not able to get the basic needs of life. This phenomenon is not due to the

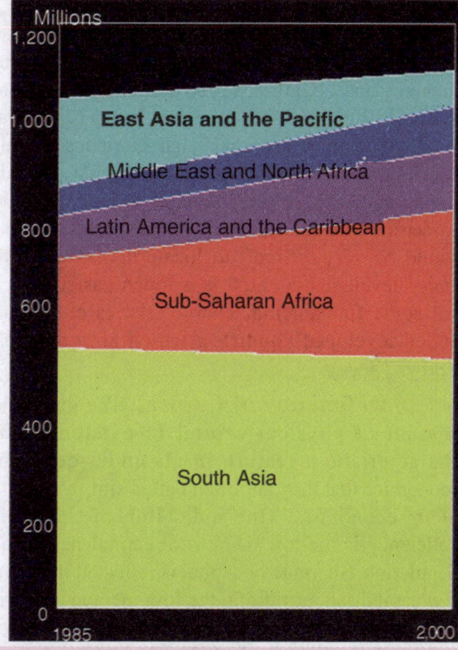

Poverty in the developing world is a major concern of development economics.

4. Viner. J.— "The Economics of Development" in *The Economics of Under-development*, edited by A.N. Agarwal and S.P. Singh. p.12.

misfortune in the form of droughts, floods, earthquakes or wars etc., but it is of a long standing. In developing countries mass-poverty exists due to certain socio-economic and political conditions. In Asia, Africa, and South America, the mass poverty still exists.

***(ii)* Obsolete methods of production :** The use of modern technology in almost all the sectors of the economy is a major problem for developing countries.

(*a*) Due to lack of capital new technology is not possible and (*b*) If new technology is used than these will be the problem of unemployment in the shortrun and other problems may arise.

(iii) Socio-economic conditions are one of the major hurdle in economic development. People are still backward and under developed.

From the above discussion, it is obvious that defining an under-developed country is by no means a simple task. In current discussion, all low-income countries are generally classified as under-developed. In general, all those countries with per capita income less than 25 per cent of the United States level or roughly less than $500 per year are included among under-developed countries. There is also a broad agreement among economists that low-income levels are largely associated with deficiency of capital.

CHARACTERISTICS OF UNDER-DEVELOPED ECONOMIES COUNTRIES (UDCs)

The general nature of an under-developed economy may be gathered from the common economic characteristics of such an economy. It may be too much to talk of common economic characteristics of under-developed countries in view of the wide diversity; among under-developed countries, as revealed by the numerous case-studies that have been made. While it would be very difficult to locate a **representative** under-developed country, it is much easier to bring out some fundamental characteristics common to under-developed countries, which are considered below:

***(i)* Deficiency of Capital.** The insufficient amount of physical capital in existence is so characteristic a feature in all under-developed economies that they are often called simply **'capital-poor'** economies. One indication of the capital deficiency is the low amount of capital per head of population. Shortage of capital is reflected in the very low capital-labour ratio in the low-income countries. According to a survey by the United Nations Department of Economic Affairs in 1949 real capital per worker in Asia and Far East excluding Japan was only 10 per cent of the U.S.A.[5]

Not only **is the capital stock extremely small**, but the current **rate of capital formation** is also very low. In most under-developed countries, investment is only 5 per cent to 8 per cent of the national income, whereas in the United States, Canada, and Western Europe, it is generally from 15 per cent to 18 per cent.

The low level of capital formation in an under-developed country is due both to the weakness of the inducement to invest and to the low propensity and capacity to save. In such an economy, the low level of per capita income limits **the size of the market demand for manufactured output,** which weakens the inducement to invest. The low level of investment also arises as a result of the lack of **dynamic entrepreneurship,** which was regarded by Schumpeter as the focal point in the process of economic development.

At the root of capital deficiency is the shortage of savings. The level of per capita income being quite low, most of it is spent in satisfying the bare necessities of life, leaving a very low margin of income for capital accumulation. Even with an increase in the level of individual incomes in an under-developed economy, there does not usually follow a higher rate of accumulation, because of the tendency to emulate the higher levels of consumption prevailing in the advanced countries. Nurkse has called this tendency **"demonstration effect."** It is usually caused through media like films, or through foreign visits.

Generally, there exists a marked inequality in the distribution of incomes in under-developed countries. This should have resulted in a greater volume of savings available for capital formation. But most often the sector in which the greatest concentration of income lies is the one which derives its income primarily from non-entrepreneurial sources, such as unearned rent and interest. The attitudes and social values of this sector are often such that it is prone to use its income for **'conspicuous consumption,'** investment in land and real estate, speculative transactions, inventory accumulation and hoarding of gold and jewellery. If these surpluses were channelled into productive investment, they would tend to increase substantially the level of capital formation.

As the capitalist sector, either private or State, constitutes a very small part of the economy of an under-developed country, industrial profits constitute a much smaller proportion of its national income as

5. U.N. Development of Economic Affairs— *Economic Survey of Asia and the Far East*, 1949, (1950), p. 296.

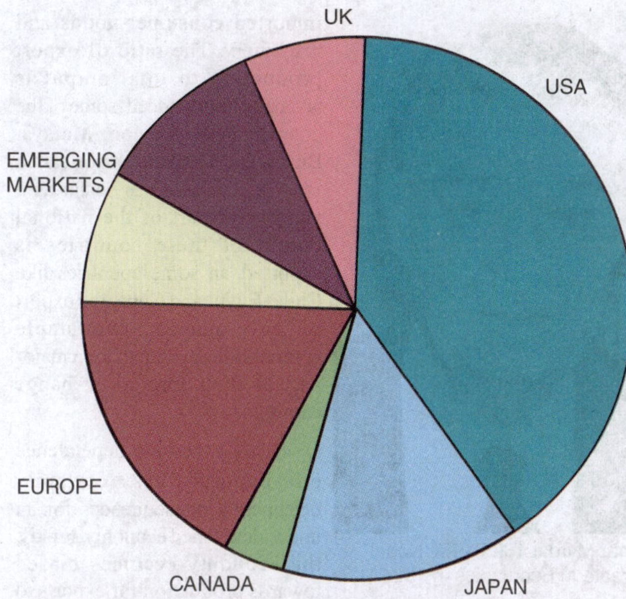

UDCs share in global capital distribution is meagre on the chart shows.

compared with that in advanced countries, where they constitute a considerable proportion of the national income. It was the increasing volume of profits arising in the private capitalist sector in England in the 19th century and in recent times in the State capitalist sector in the USSR that played an important part in the accumulation of capital in these countries.

***(ii)* Excessive Dependence on Agriculture.** Most under-developed countries are predominantly agricultural. A great majority of population, usually between 70 and 80 per cent, are engaged in agriculture and allied occupations, whereas in the developed countries 15 per cent or even less draw their sustenance from agriculture. This excessive dependence on agriculture is due to the fact that non-agricultural occupations have not grown at a rate commensurate with the increase in population owing to lack of sufficient investment outside agriculture. Hence, a growing labour force has had to be absorbed in agriculture. With the accelerated growth of population in the last few decades, the pressure of papulation on the available land has become very great and has produced serious consequences. The labour-land ratio being high, agricultural holdings have become subdivided into small plots, which do not permit the use of modern mechanical methods of production.

Under-developed countries produce relatively large proportion of their national income, in the agricultural sector. However, the share of agriculture in the national income is considerably smaller than its share in the total employment in the economy, reflecting low productivity per man in the agricultural sector. For instance, in India, while agriculture accounts for about 50 per cent of the total national income, it employees no less than 70 per cent of the country's total population.

Thus, though under-developed countries are predominantly agricultural, they are nevertheless much less efficient in agriculture than are the industrial countries. As Prof. J.K. Galbraith has put it, "a purely agricultural country is likely to be unprogressive even in its agriculture." Prof. Gunnar Myrdal explains this paradox thus: "Industrialization creates technology which can then be applied to agriculture, but not vice versa." Too much concentration on land and too low a ratio of capital per worker explains the low productivity per worker in the agrarian sector. Harvey Leibenstein observes: "As long as industrial capital remains relatively scarce and as long as the vast majority of the labour force is engaged in agriculture, it would appear to be reasonably safe to postulate that, under these circumstances and at least for the early stages of development, the system is operating under diminishing returns with respect to labour."[6]

***(iii)* Inequalities of Income and Wealth.** Another distinguishing characteristic of the under-developed economies is the disparities in income and wealth enjoyed by the rich and poor sections of society. The lower national income of the economically backward countries is more inequitably distributed than in the advanced countries. According to Colin Clark's estimates, labour's share of net income in the rich countries, like the U.S.A., the U.K. Canada, Australia, New Zealand and Switzerland was more than 70 per cent in 1950, while in Chile and Mexico it was below 60 per cent.[7] According to a recent estimate, the share of wages and income of self-employed persons in India is 24 per cent of the total national income.[8] In the under-

6. Leibenstein, Harvey—*Economic Backwardness and Economic Growth*, 1950, p. 56.
7. Clark, Colin, *Conditions of Economic Progress*, 1957, pp. 618–619.
8. Mukherjee, M., *Papers on National Income and Allied Topics*, ed. Dr. V.K.R.V. Rao, 1962.

developed countries, unearned income of land-owners in the form of rent forms a very higher proportion as compared with the developed countries. But owing to a decline in the share of property income, there is tendency for the share of the incomes of the richest group in advanced countries to go down. On the other hand, the share of wages is gone up.

Gunnar Myrdal 1898-1987 Nobel Laureate in Economics in 1974.

Although, in the under-developed countries, there is concentration of incomes in a few hands, yet in absolute terms such incomes are too small to meet the requirements of the economy. Besides, such incomes are usually diverted to non-economic investment such as jewellery and real estate or they are dissipated in unproductive social expenditure, *e.g.*, on marriages and are, therefore, not available to finance economic development.

***(iv)* Dualistic Economy.** The under-developed countries present sharp contrast in all walks of life. There is the old and new, developed and under-developed, the educated and the illiterate, the rich and poor existing side by side. It is both a bullock cart and motor car economy. There are pockets of extra rich and ultra modern people and vast masses steeped in abject poverty. There are efficient modern industries and the languishing indigenous handicrafts, and so on.

***(v)* Lack of Entrepreneurial Ability and Skilled Technicians.** In the under-developed countries generally, there are very few people, who can be described as daring and dynamic entrepreneurs. There is also woeful lack of technical know-how.

***(vi)* Inadequate Infrastructure.** The under-developed countries are also characterised by the lack of sufficient economic and social overheads. The means of transport and communication, irrigation and power, the banking system, the educational and medical facilities are all imperfectly developed and they are utterly inadequate to serve the existing population.

***(vii)* Foreign Trade Orientation.** An under-developed economy is generally foreign trade-oriented. Traditionally under-developed countries have exported raw materials and imported consumer goods and machinery. The ratio of export production to total output is normally high. Indeed, some of the countries like Ceylon, Malaya, Burma and Thailand can be called **export economies** in so far as a significant part of the national output of these countries is exported. In some countries like Chile, Egypt and Cuba, the export of only one or two staple commodities accounts for a major part of their foreign exchange earnings.

This excessive dependence on exports has certainly detrimental consequences for an under-developed economy. Firstly, the economy becomes biased towards production for exports to the comparative neglect of the other sectors of the economy. Secondly, the economy becomes unstable owing to frequent changes in foreign exchange earnings caused by fluctuations in the international prices of the export commodities. That is, the national income of these countries is highly susceptible to fluctuations resulting from varying trends in the foreign markets for their products. Thirdly, it is pointed out that of late there has been going on a secular deterioration in the terms of trade of primary producing countries, so that the richer developed countries are benefiting at the expense of the poor under-developed countries. Fourthly, the export-orientation of such economies has stepped up their marginal prospensity to import.

***(viii)* Rapid Population Growth and Disguised Unemployment.** The diversity

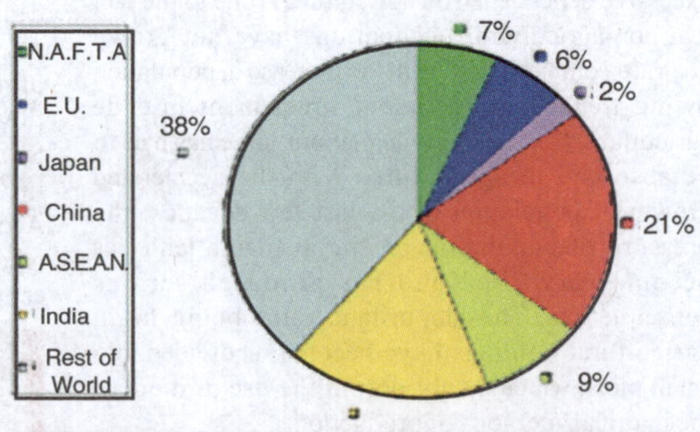

World Population distribution—UDCs have a larger share in world population as well as unemployment.

among under-developed economies is perhaps nowhere so much in evidence as in respect of the facts of their population as regards its size, density and growth. While we have examples of India and China with their teeming millions and galloping rates of growth, there are the Latin American countries which are very sparsely populated and whose total population in some cases numbers less than the single metropolitan cities in India and China. In several newly emerging countries of Africa too, and in some of the Middle Eastern countries, the size of their population cannot be regarded as excessive considering their large expanse. The South-east and Eastern Asia, on the other hand, have swarming populations.

However, there appears to be a common feature, namely, a rapid rate **of population increase.** This rate has been rising still more in recent years, thanks to the advances in medical sciences which have greatly reduced the mortality due to epidemics and diseases. While the death-rate has thus fallen phenomenally, birth-rate does not yet show any significant decline, so that the natural survival rates has become much larger. In countries like India, Pakistan and Burma, a veritable population-explosion is feared.

The great relevance of this important trend consists in this that it sets at ought all attempts at development in as much as the increased output is swallowed up by the increased population.

One important consequence of this rapid of population growth is that it throws more and more people on land to eke out their living from agriculture, since alternative occupations do not simultaneously develop and thus are not there to absorb the increasing numbers seeking gainful employment. The resultant pressure of population on land thus gives rise to what has been called **"disguised unemployment."** Low land-labour and capital-labour ratios must result in under-employment and disguised unemployment in agriculture. It means that there are more persons engaged in agriculture than are actually needed, so that the addition of such persons does not add to land's productivity; or putting it alternatively, given the technique and organisation, even if some of the persons are withdrawn from land, no fall in production will follow from such withdrawal.

(*ix*) Under-utilisation of Natural Resources. The natural resources in an under-developed economy are either unutilised or under-utilised. Generally speaking, under-developed countries are not deficient in land, water, minerals, forest or power resources though they be untapped. In other words, these constitute only potential resources. The main problem in their case is that such resources have not been fully and properly utilised due to various difficulties, such as their inaccessibility, shortage of capital, primitive techniques, and the small size of the market. This means that they have the potentialities for development but the level and character of their economic performance is too poor to take them forward.

(*x*) Economic Backwardness of the People. The people in under-developed countries are economically backward, that is, the quality of the people as productive agents is low. Instead of acquiring the greatest possible control over their physical environment, the people have struck a balance with nature at an elementary level. They have been relatively unsuccessful in solving the economic problem of man's conquest of his material environment. Particular manifestations of this are low labour efficiency, factor immobility, limited specialization in occupations and in trades, and a lack of entrepreneurship, economic ignorance, and a value structure and social structure that minimize the incentives of economic change.

(*xi*) Poor Consumption Pattern. The low level of earnings in the under-developed countries is reflected in their low level of living. The bulk (nearly 60 per cent) of their income is spent on necessaries of life, particularly food consisting mostly of cereals and devoid of nourishing items like fruits, meat, eggs, milk, *etc*. They are too poor to afford comforts and luxuries. The proportion of expenditure on housing and clothing is also very small. General poverty is also reflected in the very low standard of consumption of industrial goods and services.

(*xii*) Peculiar Demographic and Social Characteristics. There are certain demographic and social characteristics typical of the under-developed countries. Leaving a few under-populated and under-developed countries, the density of population is very high considering the resources and employment opportunities available. There is a very high proportion of the population in the age-group 0–15, and a lower proportion in the working group 20–60 years. Average expectation of life is low and infant mortality is very high.

Summing up. The socio-economic characteristics of under-developed countries have been comprehensively summarised thus: "Low aggregate and per capita incomes, limited availability of land, natural and capital resources per head; hence low productivity of labour which explains the low earnings of workers the meagreness of savings and capital formation; the dependence of the major part of the population on agriculture and the extractive industries for earning a living, poor yield of agriculture per capita as well as per unit of land; great disparity in the

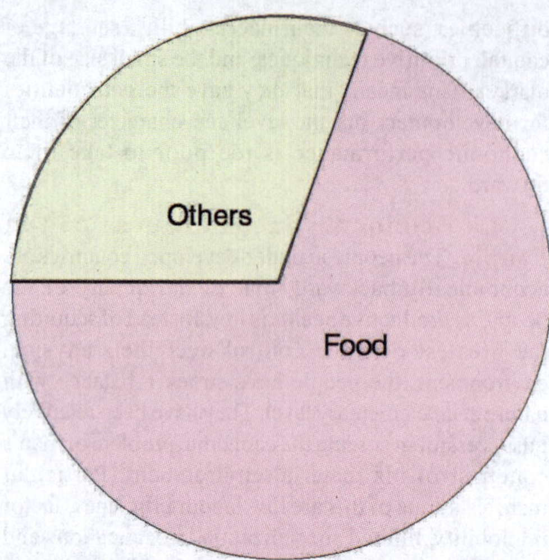

Necessities such as food accounts for more than 60% of total consumption of people in UDCs.

distribution of income and wealth, concentration of large rental incomes in the hands of a few property owners; low levels of consumption expenditure and predominance of the outlay on food items; very unsatisfactory housing conditions and negligible spending on the ordinary comforts of life; great density of population and high rates of growth; high infant mortality rate, uneconomic distribution of population in the different age groups, heavy dependency load, concentration of population in urban centres; low standards of literacy, inadequate medical facilities, poor health standards and short expectation of life—all these are the common economic and social characteristics of the poor and backward countries of the world today."[9]

A very apt and easily understandable description of an under-developed country is given by Paul Hoffman thus: "Every one knows an under-developed country when he sees one. It is a country characterised by poverty, with beggars in the cities and villages eking out a bare subsistence in the rural areas. It is a country lacking in factories of its own usually with inadequate power and light. It usually has insufficient roads and rail-roads, insufficient government services, poor communications. It has few hospitals and few institutions of higher learning. Most of its people cannot read and write. In spite of the generally prevailing poverty of the people, it may have isolated islands of wealth with a few persons living in luxury. Its banking system is poor, small loans have to be obtained from money-lenders who are little better than extortionists. Among the striking characteristics of an under-developed country is that its exports to other countries usually consist almost entirely of raw materials, ores or fruits or some staple product with possibly a small admixture of luxury handicrafts."[10]

DUALISM AND ECONOMIC UNDER-DEVELOPMENT

Dualism is a major characteristic of an under developed economy. Daulism refers to that condition of a country when two sectors (*i.e.*, advanced or modern sector and the backward or traditional sector) exist side by side. For instance, we have modern industries and the old cottage industries working side by side as well as modern farming and medieval farming being practised at the same time. In other words, in an under-developed country, there is the bullock-cart economy and modern transport operating at the same time. Usually, modernisation is confined to the trade sector mainly organised managed and financed by the foreign capitalist. Along with this advanced sector, there is a very large indigenous sector following traditional modes of production and distribution.

Types. In technical language, it may be called **Technological Dualism** as Benjamin Higgins mentions in his book **Economic Development.** Advanced sector is capital-intensive and the backward sector is labour-intensive.

There is also **Social Dualism** mentioned by J. H. Bocke in his book *Economies and Economic Policy of Dual Society*. The Society in under-developed countries is split into two parts, the upper and lower. The upper strata of society are influenced by modern ways of living and thinking, not tied by customs, enterprising and pursuing profits and having unlimited wants, whereas the lower strata are conservative, custom-ridden and follow the traditional modes of business and having limited wants, high preference for leisure and lacking in enterprise. In the under-developed sector, increase in wages lead to leisure and absenteeism in industry, and prices do not affect farming which is customary. Agriculture, in short is not commercialised.

There are people, however, who would not accept such sweeping generalisations. To some extent they apply to certain sections of western society too. Rather, it has been amply demonstrated that in under-developed countries too, there are progressive elements in which workers, by and large, respond to increase in wages and farmers to increased prices. For instance, it has been shown that producers of rubber in Malaya and rice farmers in Burma responded to the

9. Bright Singh, D.—*Economics of Development*, 1966, p. 26.

10. Quoted by Stephen Erke in *Economic for Development*, p. 16.

continuously growing world demand for, and rising prices of, their products. It is the opportunity and the existence of infra structural facilities which matter. The fact is that in the under-developed economies, people would respond in the same way to opportunities available for increasing income as in the advanced countries.

Skyscrapers and slum coexist in India and many UDCs.

There is another type of dualism, *viz*., **financial dualism-** modern banking institutions existing side by side with indigenous banking. This type has been discussed by H. Myint in his book, *The Economics of Developing Countries*. There exist a large unorganised financial market and a small organised financial market working in isolation with one another.

Key terms

Economics of Development, UDCs, Dualism, Demonstration effect, Conspicuous consumption.

QUESTIONS

1. Discuss the characteristics of under-developed economies.
2. Define economic growth. What are the main factors on which economic growth depends?
3. What do you understand by 'economic growth'? How could a steady rate of economic growth be maintained in a developing economy?
4. Explain the vicious circle of poverty. How does it check the growth of capital in a poor country?

   Or

   What do you understand by 'vicious circle of poverty'? How can it be converted into a beneficient circle?
5. "A country is poor because a country is poor". (Nurkse) Discuss.

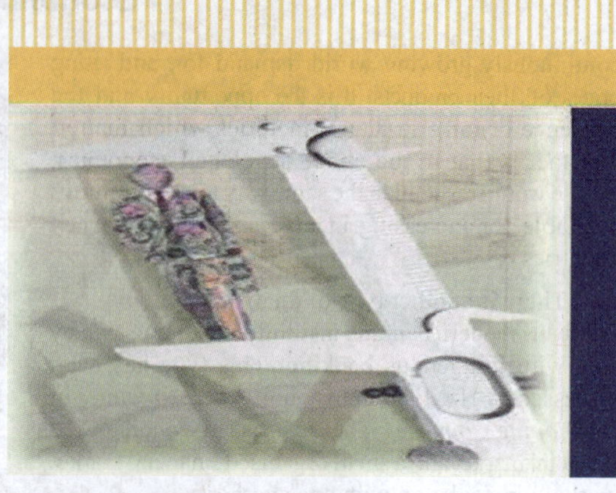

OBSTACLES TO ECONOMIC GROWTH

We have already studied the main characteristics of under-developed countries. The question is: What has stood in the way of their economic development? There are several causes, economic, social and political which have hindered the growth of under-developed countries. We briefly examine these obstacles below:

ECONOMIC FACTORS IMPEDING GROWTH

First we discuss the main economic factors impeding growth.

Foreign Domination

Most of the countries of Asia and Africa, which are under-developed, have been at one time or another under an alien rule. The most important cause of poverty in India and its under-development is its subjection to the British rule. The foreign rulers, naturally, exploited the dependent countries and used their resources to promote their own interests. These countries were made to supply raw materials at low prices. The foreign industrialists also made investments in primary industries such as mining, drilling of oil wells, tea, coffee, rubber plantations, *etc*., the products of which were exported. The domestic workers were exploited and were paid very low wages. High profits thus made were taken out of the country. They sold their manufactures in the under-developed countries in exchange for raw materials.

Thus, the foreign masters used these countries as suppliers of raw materials to their industries and markets for their manufactured goods. They did not take any interest in their economic development. Rather, there is ample evidence to show that they raised all sorts of obstacles in the way of their industrial development as in India, where competing small and cottage industries were destroyed by the unfair use of the political weapon. This resulted in increasing pressure on agriculture, disguised unemployment and poverty. That is how foreign domination has been a great impediment in the economic growth of under-developed countries. Now that these countries are free they can plan their own development.

Misuse of Resources due to market Imperfections

Another important reason for the economic backwardness of the under-developed countries is the misuse of resources owing to market imperfections. By the market imperfections we mean the immobility of the factors of production, price rigidities, ignorance regarding market trends, static social structure, lack of specialisation, *etc*., These market imperfections are great obstacles in the way of economic growth. It is due to market

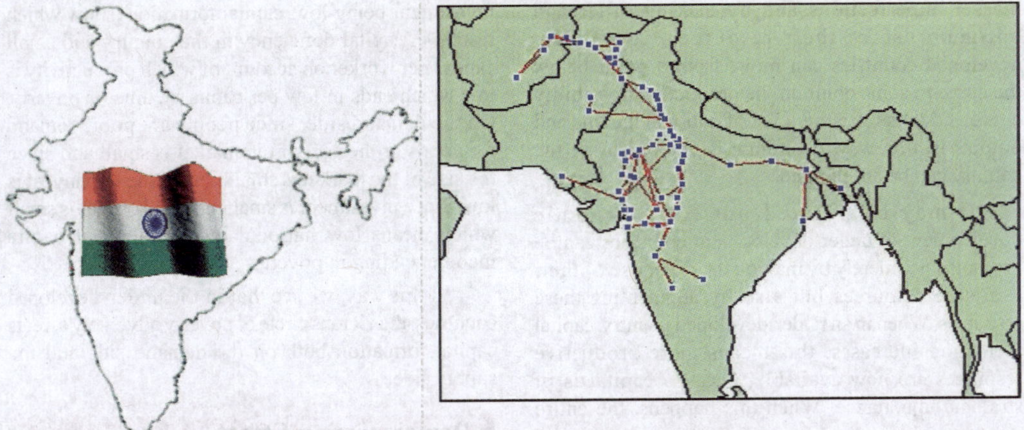

Till its independence in 1947 India was constantly under foreign aggresion. Mughals ruled for nearly 400 years and then Britishers ruled for nearly 200 years.

imperfections that productive efficiency in these countries is low, the resources are either unutilised or under-utilised and the resources are misallocated.

When the resources are perfectly mobile and there is perfect competition among them, they can easily move from one sector to another in search of a better return and in this way they make an optimum contribution to the national output. But in the under-developed countries, it is found that the workers are engaged in occupations where their marginal productivity is zero (*e.g.*, in disguised unemployment in agriculture). Even then they do not move out into industries where they can earn higher waves. Similarly, there is misallocation of capital in the under-developed countries, various customs, habits and social inhibitions stand in the way of free mobility of labour and capital. Poverty also impedes mobility of labour from one place to another or from one industry to another. Lack of employment opportunities and ignorance about the market trends are also responsible for market imperfections. The manufacturers and entrepreneurs too are ignorant of the market trends in domestic and world markets. Then there are monopolistic practices which aggravate the market imperfections and are responsible for the misuse or misallocation of the resources of under-developed countries.

To the extent of these imperfections, the resources of their countries are misused or under-utilised. There is no doubt that the output in these countries can be increased by fuller and better use of the productive resources by removing these market imperfections. This can be made clear by the production possibility curve given below:

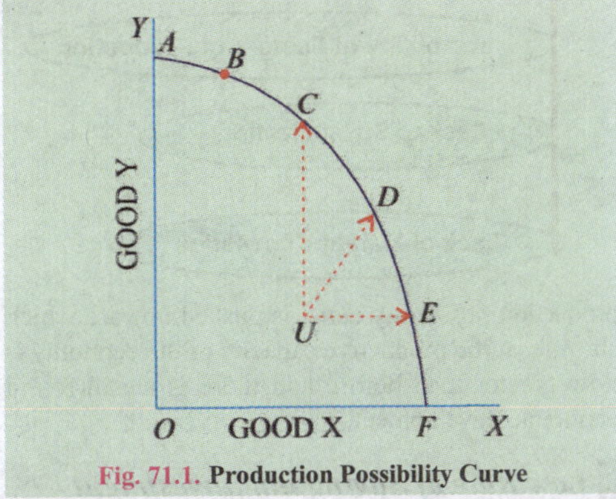

Fig. 71.1. Production Possibility Curve

In the Fig. 71.1, a production possibility curve AF is drawn on the assumption of a given amount of productive resources available and given technology. The good X is shown on X-axis and the good Y on the Y-axis. The production possibility curve shows that if a full and optimum use is made of the productive resources of the country, how much of good X and how of Y will be produced with a given amount of the resources and with a given technology. When a country is making the fullest and optimum use of its available resources and technology, then it is operating at a point on the production possibility curve.

We have said above that owing to market imperfections, the under-developed countries are not making the fullest and most efficient use of their productive resources with the result that these resources remain unutilised or under-utilised in large quantities. In such a situation, their economy does not operate on the production possibility curve but at a point below it, *e.g.*, at the point U in the diagram. By removing the market imperfections and by making fuller and optimum use of their resources, the under-developed countries can move from a point below the curve to some point on the production possibility curve and thus raise the level of national income and output. In this way, economic development of the country can be accelerated.

It may be pointed out that economic development of under-development countries can be promoted not merely by making the fuller use of their available resources but also by augmenting these resources. When in an under-developed country, capital formation increases, this means more productive resources are now available, because capital is of strategic importance. When this happens, the entire

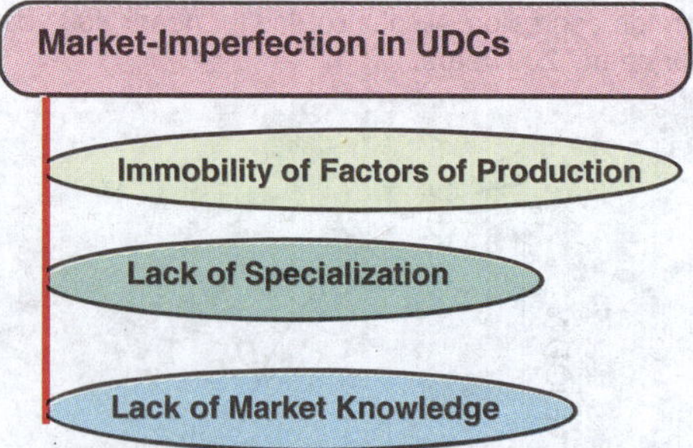

production possibility curve is pushed upward which shows that the productive capacity of the economy is now greater than before and there is an all-round economic development.

Low Rate of Saving and investment

Another main reason of the poverty and under-development of the under-developed countries is that the rate of saving and investment in these countries is very low. In these countries, only 5–8 per cent of the national income goes into savings, whereas the rate is 15–20 per cent and even more in the developed countries. When the rate of saving in a country is low, the rate of investment is bound to be low and the rate of capital formation is low too. Since capital per man is low, the productivity is also low. Productivity being low, the per capita income and the national income too are low. It is truly said that the under-developed countries are caught up in a vicious circle of poverty which we shall discuss presently. This vicious circle of poverty is the greatest obstacle in the way of their economic development.

The vicious circle of poverty affects both demand side and supply side of capital formation. On the supply side, the saving capacity is low on account of poverty and low per capita income. Since the rate of saving is low, investment is low and the rate of investment being low, capital formation is low which results in capital deficiency in the country and small capital per worker on account of which productivity is low which ends in low per capita income or poverty. On the demand side, since people are poor, demand for goods or the size of the market is small and since the size of the market is small, inducement to invest is low. Since investment is small, national output is small which means low national income and per capita income, ending in poverty.

In this way, we see that in the under-developed countries, the vicious circle of poverty adversely affects capital formation both on the demand side and the supply side.

Demonstration Effect

The under-development of the economically backward countries is also due to what has been called the 'demonstration effect.' The demonstration effect increases propensity to consume which reduces the rate of savings and investment. A very important principle has been propounded regarding consumption, *viz*., that an individual's consumption does not merely depend on individual's own income but it is very much influenced by the standard of living or consumption of his friends and relations. When a man sees that some of his friends and relatives have refrigerator, scooter, radio or TV set, good furniture, good clothes, *etc*., he likes to imitate them and is desirous of possessing and using these things. As soon as he can afford or when his income increases he buys such things. This means that instead of increasing his savings, when his income increases, he increasehis consumption.

Thus, consumption does not depend upon absolute real income but on relative level of real income. That is, consumption expenditure does not depend on our own purchasing power but on what is being spent by other on the purchase of luxury articles. An eminent American economist Duesenberry has called it 'Demonstration Effect.' The demonstration effect has adversely affected people's capacity to save. It has been estimated that 75 per cent Americans are unable to make any saving. It does not mean that they are too poor to save. But they cannot save because they imitate the superior standard of living of the people richer than they.

Ragnar Narkse–1907-1959 A Leading development economist.

Nurkse has applied the Duesenberry doctrine to international levels of living. According to him, the economic development of the under-developed countries has been greatly influenced by the disparities in real income of different countries. Whereas on the one hand, the rich developed countries are trying to help the under-developed countries in breaking the vicious circle of poverty, they also export to them their higher standard of living. Their superior standard of living increases their propensity to consume, because they try to imitate their standard of living. Nurkse calls it **'International Demonstration Effect.'** He says, " When people come into contact with superior goods or superior patterns of consumption, with new articles or new ways of meeting old wants, they are apt to feel after a while certain restlessness and dissatisfaction. Their knowledge is extended, their imagination is stimulated new desires are aroused the propensity to consume is shifted upward."[1]

Thus, we see that international demonstration effect reduces the savings of under-developed countries and in this way hinders their economic growth. Television, movies, radios, foreign travel, expansion of education and travelling facilities are such powerful media which extensively advertise, new articles or propagate new higher standards of living and thus increase propensity to consume.

Propensity to consume directly affects propensity to save: Higher the consumption less is the saving. When poor countries imitate the higher standards of living of the rich countries, they have to pay the price for it. The price is that their capacity to save is reduced. As Nurkse observes: "The great and growing gaps between the income levels and, therefore, living standards of different countries, combined with increasing awareness of these gaps, may tend to push up the general propensity to consume of the poor nations, reduce their propensity to save." The decrease in their propensity to save is bound to prove a big obstacle in the path of their economic development.

Moreover, increase in propensity to consume also adversely affects the potential savings of surplus labour in disguised unemployment. This potential saving can be utilised for capital formation only if original consumption or standard of living is maintained when incomes rise in the process of economic growth. In the developing economies, there is a sharp conflict between the necessity to save and the desire to raise propensity to consume. Generally, the consumption expenditure goes up and saving goes down. No wonder that economic growth suffers.

1. Nurkse, R. — *Problems of Capital Formation in Under-developed Countries*, pp. 58–59.

Rapidly Growing Population

In the under-developed countries, especially in the over-populated countries of Asia, population increases very rapidly. This has very adversely affected their rate of economic growth. In fact, rapid population growth is the greatest obstacle to economic growth. Whatever increase takes place in the national output and income in such countries as a result of development is devoured by the everpouring torrent of babies. It is like writing on the sand. That is why their standard of living and income per capita cannot rise. For example, the major part of increase in national income that has accrued in India during the five-year plans has been nullified by the rapid population growth. As a result, though there has been substantial increase in national income, but the per capita income has not increased much. Obviously, a rapidly growing population is a great obstacle in the way of raising the level of living in such countries.

A rapid population growth is an impediment to economic growth in as much as it slows down the rate of capital formation. But to accelerate economic growth, it is imperative to step up the rate of capital formation. How can capital formation be stepped up when the per capita income increases slowly on account of a rapid rise in population? A rapidly growing population increases the number of consumers in the country and hence consumption expenditure. Owing to increase in consumption expenditure, it becomes difficult to increase the rate of saving and investment which is so essential for economic growth. It is clear that a rapidly growing population retards economic growth by retarding the growth of capital formation.

Whereas rapid increase in population slows down the increase in the rate of investment on the one hand, it necessitates a higher rate of investment required for rapid economic growth, on the other. For instance, in India owing to 2.5 per cent annual rate of population growth, it has become necessary to increase the rate of investment and capital formation so that the per capita income remains constant (*i.e.*, it should not decrease). According to the eminent development economist Colin Clark, if there is 1 per cent increase in population, it becomes necessary to increase national income by 4 per cent just to keep the per capita income constant. In other words, with a 2.5 per cent increase in population in India, the national income must rise by 10 per cent just to maintain the per capita income at the old level and to prevent it from sliding down. But if the per capita income, and hence the standard of living, is to be raised, the national income must rise by much more than 10 per cent. This shows what a great obstacle the rapidly growing population is in the way of rapid increase in the per capita income.

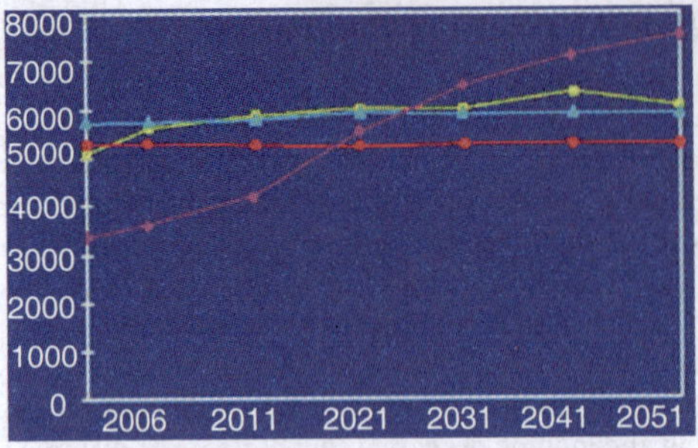

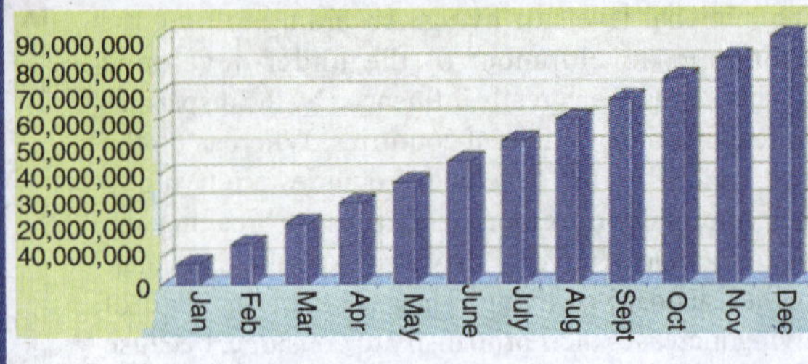

Besides, a rapidly growing population creates several other problems on account of which it becomes difficult to accelerate economic growth. In the first place, a rapidly growing population requires larger quantity of food- grains. In India, the explosive rate of population growth has increased the demand for foodgrains manifold. This is due to higher income elasticity of demand for food. It has created a serious food problem in the country. India has been importing now for many years large quantities of foodgrains and losing valuable foreign exchange on this account. If there had been no food problem, we would have been able to import plant and machinery and other equipment and necessary industrial raw materials all of which would have promoted rapid economic growth in the country.

Unemployment is another very serious problem created by rapid increase in population. We know that in India backlog of the unemployed has been increasing at the end of each five-year plan. This is due to the fact owing to low rate of capital formation, industrialisation has been going on at a slow rate and it has not been possible to increase employment opportunities commensurate with the rate of population increase. Unemployment means waste of potential manpower resources. Instead of being used in the work of economic development, the unemployed act as a drag on economic progress, since they have to be fed all right even though they are not making any contribution to the growth of national output.

SOCIAL AND POLITICAL OBSTACLES TO GROWTH

There are several other factors which have retarded the economic growth of under-developed countries. Among these we may mention the following:

Inefficient Agrarian System. In the under-developed countries like India, agriculture has been carried on in a very inefficient manner. Lack of adequate irrigation facilities and fertilizers, primitive agricultural practices, proverty of the peasant, out-moded systems of tenure, uneconomic holdings are some of the reasons for the backwardness of Indian agriculture. Excessive dependence on agriculture itself is a major cause of the economic backwardness of these countries.

Shortage of Entrepreneurial Ability and Spirit of Experimentation and Innovation. The under-developed countries are generally wanting in dynamic entrepreneurship. No wonder trade and industry have been conducted at a very low level and few new grounds have been broken.

Scarcity of Skills. Economic development requires an army of trained and skilled personnel who serve as instruments of economic progress. These the under-developed countries lack and consequently remain backward.

Lack of Technical Know-how. The use of modern techniques in the field of agriculture, trade and industry is indispensable for economic progress. But industrialists and businessmen in under-developed countries are blissfully ignorant of such techniques and thus feel terribly handicapped in the economic race.

Inadequacy of the Transport and Credit Systems has also contributed to our economic backwardness. It is obvious that if a country is to develop, it must have sound infrastructure in the form of means of transport and communication to facilitate trade and industry and an efficient banking system to assist it financially.

Social Structure. Not only have the economic factors handicapped economic progress of the under-developed countries but social factors, too, have played their part to keep them economically backward. Social structure has proved inimical to economic progress. Among the social forces impeding, for instance, India's economic progress we may mention the following:

Caste System has divided the Indian society into water-tight compartments and has rendered cooperation in the economic sphere impossible. It has created divergence between aptitude and the

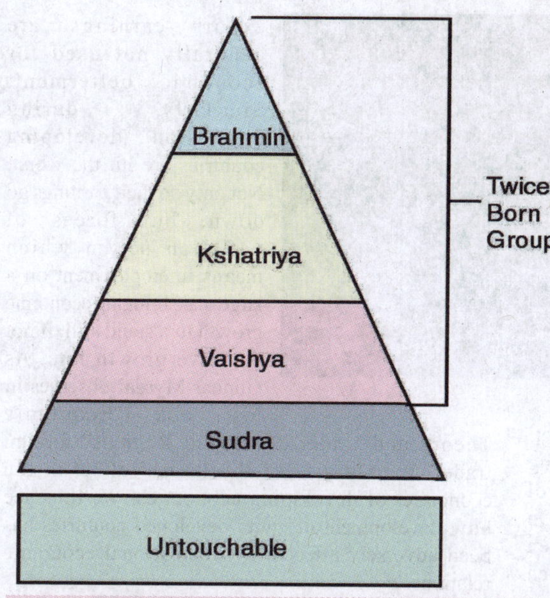

The Caste System.

occupation actually pursued. By making functions hereditary, it killed initiative and enterprise. Untouchability has demoralised millions of our people striking at the very root of dignity of labour. Mobility of labour so essential for economic progress, has been rendered difficult, if not impossible. Healthy trade union movement cannot grow in a society split by caste considerations. In this and other ways, the Indian caste system has stood in the way of her economic progress.

Joint Family System acts as another serious obstacle to economic progress. The system breeds drones, seriously imperils the will and the power to save, since it leads to extravagance on the part of some members. It kills initiative and enterprise in the younger members of the family, for they expect to be comfortably looked after by the head of the family. In short, the joint family system results in shortage of capital and low rate of capital formation which is a major cause of the tardy economic growth in India.

Laws of Inheritance guaranteeing equal share in father's property to all his children, sons and daughters, is an important cause of successive impoverishment of the people in India. It has resulted in sub-division and fragmentation of land holdings which have barred all agricultural improvements. This is another important cause which has impeded economic development in India.

Out-moded Religious Beliefs and lack of secular and rational out look generate other-wordly attitude to the neglect of economic endeavour in the present life. They encourage austere living. As such they are in no small measure responsible for India's economic backwardness. Positive attitude towards work and wealth is wanting. Superstitious and costly rituals eat up the savings of many years, creating shortage of capital and resulting in much national waste of resources. The philosophy of Karma makes the people fatalists and dampens their enthusiasm for work.

Unprogressive Social Attitudes, *e.g.*, irrational attitude to having children, are also obstructing economic progress in India.

Political Factors. In addition to the economic and social factors enumerated above, there are the political factors which have retarded economic growth in India. During the British regime, the Government promoted British interests at the expense of Indian interests. For example, the development of Indian industry was deliberately discouraged. Vested British interests in India also stood in the way. The masses were kept in a state of illiteracy and abject poverty without any economic uplift. They were dumb-driven cattle viewing life in a callous and fatalistic manner. After Independence, too things did not improve. Some dishonest and corrupt leaders came to the fore. There was absence of clean and efficient administration. Favouritism, nepotism and corruption were rampant all over the country. The people too lacked sense of duty and devotion to the country and were trying to enrich themselves at the expense of the country. Such conditions were hardly conducive to economic growth.

But in 1975–76, owing to certain government measures and cooperation of the people putting in greater effort, there was a welcome change on the economic front. Consequently, the process of development picked up with amazing speed.

Adverse International Factors. Economic relations with the advanced countries have also kept the under-developed countries in a state of under-development. In other words, international trade has worked to the disadvantage of the under-developed countries and perpetuated their poverty. As Prof. Raul Prebisch has observed, there has been a secular stagnation in the terms of trade of the under-developed countries. He says that "over the last seventy years, the peripheral under-developed countries have suffered with fatal effects of a continuous weakening in their capacity to impact. It has led to the weakening of the capacity of their existing primary producing industries to support their growing population, it has resulted in a failure to transmit to them the benefit of technical progress; ... it has finally lowered their rates of capital formation and thus of their economic growth."

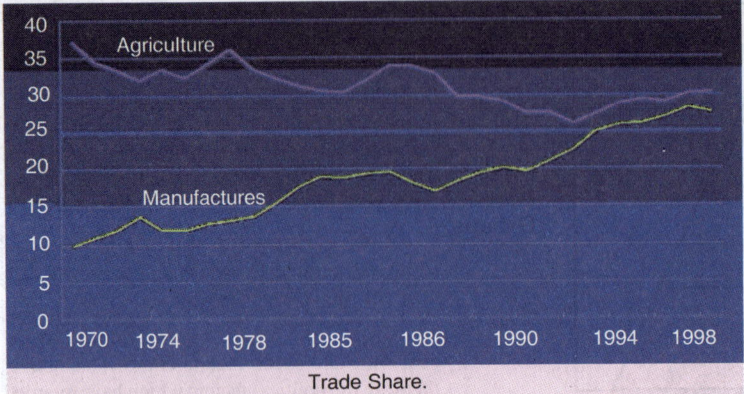

Trade Share.

Foreign trade has a very limited 'spread-effect' on developing economies. That is, developing economies are not exposed to the beneficial effect of foreign trade in terms of economic development. On the other hand, developing economies are often exposed to the cyclical effects of foreign trade which inevitably results in economic instability and thus impedes economic growth. During prosperity, most of the earnings of these countries are frittered away on consumption goods which are mainly imported. The excess spending creates inflationary situation which also is inimical to economic growth. Thus export earnings are generally not used for economic betterment. Similarly, during depression developing countries are hit the worst. Not only do their earnings go down, but forces of deflation set in which means unemployment on a large scale bringing economic growth to a stand still, if not negative growth rate. As Gunnar Myrdal observes in his book "Economic Theory and Under-developed Regions" foreign trade has only yielded 'backwash' effect in the economies of developing economies. We thus see how development of under-developed countries has been adversely affected by international economic relations.

Conclusion

Thus, various factors, economic and noneconomic, *i.e.*, social, political and international, have conspired to retard economic growth of the under-developed countries.

Key terms

Foreign domination, International demonstration effect, Caste system.

QUESTIONS

1. "Population growth is not always an obstacle to the growth of per capita income". Discuss.
2. Discuss the factors that impede economic development.
3. In what way does the small size of a market inhibit economic development? Suggest measures for the enlargement of the size of the market.
4. What are the basic determinants of economic growth? How far are they present in India?

74 CHAPTER VICIOUS CIRCLES OF POVERTY

Among the obstacles to economic growth, we referred briefly to the vicious circle of poverty. In view of its importance, we now devote a separate chapter to it. Looking at things from individual point of view, we find that a poor man is caught in a vicious circle. Being poor, he lacks the means to prosper and since he lacks the means to prosper, he must remain poor. The vicious circle is complete. Poverty leads to inefficiency and incapacity to do well, and inefficiency and incapacity must end in poverty. That is why we generally find that poverty is perpetuated from generation to generation. It is cumulative. In the capitalist world, it is indeed a miracle for a poor man to become rich; and who does not know that the rich people go on becoming richer and richer. That is the curse of poverty and its vicious circle.

What is true of an individual is true of the community as a whole. For an under-developed economy to develop economically is indeed an uphill task. In fact, the main cause of the under-developed countries remaining poor and under-developed is that they are caught up in the vicious circle of poverty. Poverty means that their per capita income is low and per capita income is low because the level of productivity per man is generally low in such countries. Since productivity per man in low, naturally income per capita is low, which means poverty. Thus, the vicious circle is complete.

Now the question is: why is productivity per man low? On what factors does productivity per man depend? Productivity per man depends on the quantity of capital equipment or machinery at the disposal of a worker. The higher level of productivity in the developed countries is due to the fact that each worker is provided with superior capital equipment. In the under-developed countries, however, a worker is supplied with primitive tools both in industry and agriculture. Naturally, the level of productivity is low. Hence, the amount of capital is of crucial importance in determining the level of output and income in a country. In the under-developed countries, capital equipment per worker is poor in quality and meagre in quantity because the rate of capital formation in such countries is low.

Poverty.

The crux of the problem is capital formation. The rate of capital formation is affected both by demand for and supply of capital. Favourable factors operating on demand and supply will increase capital and adverse factors will result in diminution of capital and slacken its rate of growth. On the demand side, capital accumulation depends on the inducements or incentives to invest and on the supply side on the willingness and the ability of the people to save. Both on the side of demand and on the side of supply we are face to face with a vicious circle.

In the under-developed countries, the rate of capital formation is low because on the one hand, the rate of savings (*i.e.*, the supply of capital) is low and on the other the inducement to invest (*i.e.*, demand for capital) is less owing to small size of the market. The rate of savings and investment in an under-developed economy is too low to make for rapid development and since the rate of savings and investment are too small, it must remain under-developed. Here is the vicious circle of poverty embracing the entire economy. "It implies a circular constellation of forces tending to act and react upon one another in such a way as to keep a poor country in a state of poverty. A country is poor because a country is poor." (Nurkse).

Let us now analyse the demand and supply sides of the vicious circle.

Vicious Circle on the Demand Side of Capital Formation

In a poor county, the level of productivity and so of incomes is very low which means a low purchasing power. Since the purchasing power of the people is low, the scope for business and industry is correspondingly limited. The inducement to invest is practically absent. The rate of investment being low, productivity is low and the incomes are small completing the vicious circle. (See Fig. 72.1 below.)

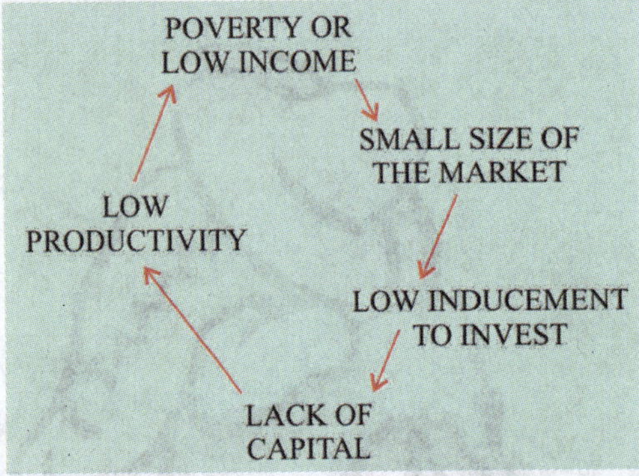

Fig. 72.1. Vicious Circle on Demand Side.

Thus, the under-developed countries face the vicious circle of poverty on the demand side of capital formation because the size of market is too small. The result is there is not much inducement for the businessmen and industrialist to make investments. Just as division of labour is limited by the size of the market ,similarly , the inducement to invest is also limited by the size of market. Since in the under-developed countries, the size of the market *i.e.,* the demand for goods is limited ,the inducement to invest is small.

Let us clearly see how the vicious circle is created on the demand side of capital formation. Since the people of the under-developed countries are poor *i.e.*, their income per capita is low, their purchasing power is low and demand for goods is less (*i.e.*, the size of the market is small). The market for goods being limited, their output is low and the industrialists cannot afford to use more productive capital equipment. Hence, investment is discouraged. Since, there is less inducement to invest, the rate of capital formation is low and the capital equipment available to each worker is small, and since capital available per worker is less, productivity per worker is low. Productivity per worker being low, income per capita is low and there is proverty. In this way, the vicious circle of poverty is complete on the demand side.

As Nurkse observes, "The inducement to invest may be low because of the small buying power of the people, which is due to their small real income, which again is due to low productivity. The low level of productivity, however, is a result of the small amount of capital used in production which in turn may be caused at least partly by the small inducement to invest,"[1] This completes the vicious circle.

Vicious Circle of Poverty on the Supply Side of Capital Formation

The vicious circle of poverty on the supply side of capital operates in this manner: Poverty in the under-developed countries means that the per capita income in such countries is low. Since per capita income is low, their capacity to save is low. When people cannot make even the two ends meet with their low income, the question of saving does not arise. That is why the rate of savings in the under-developed countries is extremely low. The rate of savings being low, the rate of investment in turn is bound to be low. Since the rate of investment is low, the rate of capital formation is low and hence there is great shortage of capital in the under-developed countries. Since the amount of capital per man is of vital importance in determining productivity, the level of productivity per worker is extremely low in the under-developed countries. The productivity

1. Nurkse, R., *Problems of Capital Formation in Under-developed Counries*, p. 5.

per worker being low, the real income per capita is low and there is poverty. This is how the vicious circle is complete on the supply side.

Owing to poverty or low per capita income saving is less and when saving is less, the rate of investment is low. The rate of investment being low, the amount of capital per worker is small and when capital per worker is small, productivity per worker is low. Since productivity is low, the income per capita is low which means that the country is poor. In this way, we see that the cause of a country's poverty is poverty itself and as Nurkse says, "Under-developed countries are poor because they are poor."

We thus see that the vicious circle of poverty operates on the supply side of capital formation and the main problem is how to break this vicious circle. We can show the vicious circle of poverty on the supply side by the Fig. 72.2.

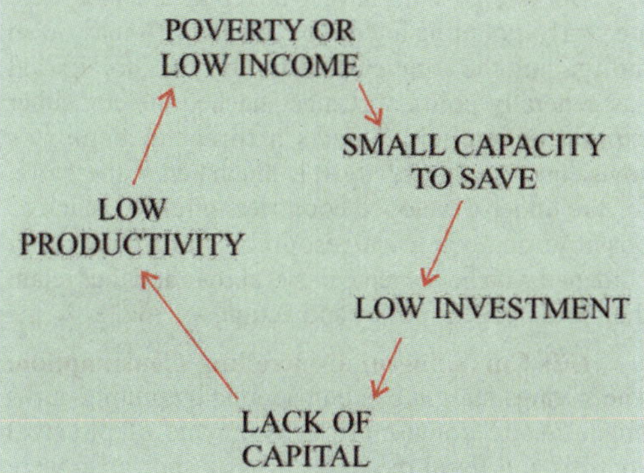

Fig. 72.2. Vicious Circle on Supply Side.

In addition to the vicious circle of poverty explained by Nurkse, Prof. Meir and Baldwin have given another vicious circle.[2] According to them the natural resources of the under-developed countries have not been fully tapped or developed and remain unutilised, or under-utilised in large quantities. The exploitation of these natural resources depends on the quality of human resources of these countries. But these human resources or population of such countries is economically backward. That is, they have not the ability and capacity of developing the natural resources or of making productive use thereof. Since these countries are poor they are unable to improve the efficiency, ability and capacity of their people and owing to this inefficiency, incapacity or inability to make a fuller use of their natural resources, these resources remain unexploited or under-utilised. Owing to the natural resources remaining unused or under-utilised, the level of output in such countries is low and the levels of national income and per capita income are low, *i.e.*, these countries remain steeped in poverty. That is how from this point of view also, these countries are caught up in a vicious circle of poverty.

But it is now the ambition of under-developed countries to tread the road leading to full economic development and they are anxious to break the vicious circle of poverty to accelerate the process of economic growth. The vicious circle must be attacked at both ends, but it will be more effective to try to break it at the supply end. That is, the rate of savings must be raised so that the rate of investment may be increased and investment should be encouraged in all possible ways. Foreign aid can also be helpful. We discuss below how the vicious circle of poverty can be broken.

Measures to Break the Vicious Circle: Measures to Promote Capital Formation

We have seen above how the under-developed countries are caught up in the cicious circle of poverty and how this vicious circle is a great obstacle in the way of their economic development. Now we have to see whether the vicious circle of poverty can be broken and if so how. Modern economists are of the view that the vicious circle can be broken if an economic effort is made in such countries. The developed and rich countries of today were also poor at one time and reached their present stage of development and prospensity by somehow breaking the vicious circle of poverty. From the study of their economic history, we learn that the poor countries of today can also remove their poverty and reach the goal of a developed state through economic endeavour. The people of under-developed countries believed in the past that to be rich or poor depended on their destiny. But education and enlightenment have exploded these false notions. Now it is fully realised that if a serious and determined effort is made poverty can be removed. It is truly said that poverty is an old thing but the belief that poverty can be removed by human effort is new.

We have said above that capital formation is the crux of the whole problem. We can, therefore, break the vicious circle by stepping up capital formation. The following measures may be suggested:—

(*i*) Raising the Rate of Savings. The Government can raise the rate of savings in the country by taxation, deficit financing and by borrowing from the banks and the public. In this way, the low level of voluntary savings, which is due to low per capita income, can be raised by forced savings. The increased savings can be used for capital formation.

It is wrong to say, as is implied in the supply side of vicious circle, that since the under-developed

2. Meir and Baldwin — *Economic Development, Theory, History and Policy.*

Saving must increase to increase investment.

countries are poor, it is not at all possible to increase their savings. In spite of low level of per capita incomes in such countries, there is still a great scope for increasing the rate of savings. There are extreme inequalities in the distribution of income and wealth. Per capita income is only an average income of the country. Actually, there are many people whose incomes are far higher. For instance, the per capita income in India at current prices was Rs. 850 in 1973-74. It is true that a person earning Rs. 850 per year cannot make any saving. But in India there are numerous people like Birla, Dalmia, Tata whose incomes are far higher. They earn crores of rupees a year. This means that there are numerous people in the under-developed countries who can save a lot.

But it is seen that in the under-developed countries, the rich people, who can make lot of savings, actually do not do so. They indulge in unproductive investments like jewellery, house building, *etc*., or dissipate their resources in costly social ceremonies like marriages or other forms of conspicuous consumption. That is why the rate of productive investment in such countries is low. Arthur Lewis, a specialist in economic development, is of the opinion that the under-developed countries are not so poor that they cannot save even 10 to 12 per cent of their income. Financial resources can be mobilised by taxing the high-income groups and the rate of investment can be raised thereby.

***(ii)* Use of Foreign Capital.** The vicious circle of poverty can be broken and economic development accelerated by raising foreign capital also to supplement domestic resources. The developed countries of today were once poor and they developed themselves with the help of foreign capital in one form or another, at one time or another. The under-developed countries, too, can make up the deficiency of domestic savings by getting capital from abroad.

It is gratifying that the rich countries of the world like the U.S.A., Canada, the U.K., Western Germany, France and Japan are generously helping the under-developed countries to promote their economic development. There is a regular Aid-India Club (consisting of the rich countries) helping India financially with loans and grants to accelerate her economic growth. There is also Colombo Plan under which the under-developed countries of the Commonwealth are receiving aid for development. Besides, there are international organisations like the World Bank, I.M.F. and International Development Association by which financial aid for development is being given on reasonable terms.

But foreign loans have to be repaid and then there are yearly mounting interest payments. This may mean mortgaging the country's future. Besides, foreign aid has generally political strings attached thereto, either explicit or implicit. This is a threat to country's sovereignty and integrity. It is much better, therefore, for the under-developed countries to rely as much as possible on their own resources and avoid being burdened with heavy repayments abroad and thus retain their independent policy and action.

***(iii)* Curtailing or Controlling Consumption.** The savings margin can be widened by putting curbs on domestic consumption by means of physical controls and fiscal measures. Russia and Japan were able to raise the level of their investment to 30 per cent of their national income to achieve a high level of economic development by adopting austerity measures and cutting consumption to the minimum. But in the under-developed countries, the standard of living is already very low and their governments are committed to the raising of living standards and improving economic welfare. This coupled with democratic form of government rules out the large-scale adoption of such restrictive measures. However, the consumption of luxury or semi-luxury goods can be controlled.

But there is a way out. Without cutting down the level of consumption, it is possible to raise the rate of savings and investment, if there is a relatively higher rate of savings from the increase in incomes. For example, if the rate of savings in a country is 5 per cent as a result of which 5 per cent of the national income is being invested, then there must be some increase in the national income. Suppose the national income goes up by Rs. 100 lakhs and if the major part of this additional income of Rs. 100 lakhs is saved, then the rate of aggregate savings in the country will increase. If, for instance. Rs. 25 lakhs are saved or Rs. 75 lakhs are spent on consumption, then the rate of savings in the country will rise higher from 5 per cent.

It may be borne in mind that even when the rate of savings has risen, consumption has not been cut down. Actually, consumption has increased by Rs.75 lakhs and the rate of savings too has increased. If the entire additional income of Rs. 100 lakhs had been spent on consumption, obviously, the rate of savings would have gone down — savings Rs. 25 lakshs out of the additional income of Rs. 100 lakhs means that the marginal rate of savings is 25 per cent which is much higher than the previous average savings rate. When the marginal rate of savings exceeds the average rate, there is a tendency for the average savings rate to go up.

The upshot of the whole argument is that in the under-developed countries the rate of capital formation (savings and investment) can be raised even without lowering the level of consumption and in this way the standard of living of the people can be improved.

(*iv*) Raising the Level of Production. It is possible to widen the saving margin and step up the rate of capital formation by raising the level of production. This can be done in a number of ways:

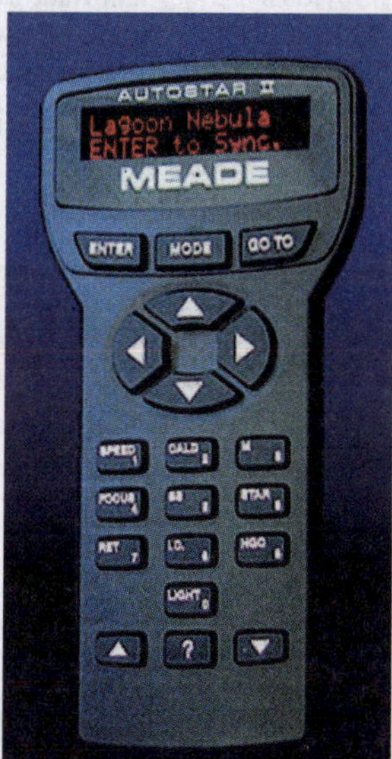

Technology must be improved.

(*a*) Better Utilisation of Existing Capital Equipment. It is generally seen that in the under-development countries factories are working below their installed capacity either for the lack of raw materials or of shortage of power or on account of inadequacy of complementary resources such as skilled and trained personnel, or due to defective management. By removing these handicaps, fuller use can be made of the existing capital equipment. By raising the level of productivity in the country, the level of per capita income, and hence the capacity to save, can be increased. Since the under-developed countries suffer from scarcity of capital, it is only prudent that maximum possible use should be made of the existing capacity.

In this way, the aggregate output in the country can be increased without increasing the stock of capital. Japan provides a classical example of how a country can accelerate its economic growth and lift itself by its bootstraps. Owing to maximum utilisation of its installed capital capacity in the secondary and tertiary sectors by means of multiple shifts and better utilisation of labour, the capital-output ratio in Japan declined from 2.50 in 1883-92 to 1.29 in 1893-1902. This enabled Japan to escape a low level equilibrium trap and enter the Harrodian world of developed economies.[3]

(*b*) Improvement of Technology. The low level of production prevailing in the under-developed countries and hence the level of national income, can be raised by improving techniques of production or by adopting modern techniques. Modern technology is capital saving (which amounts to increasing capital) and helps in achieving larger output with relatively smaller use of real resources. Productivity in the U.S.A. and Western European countries was substantially increased by automation and rationalisation. There is undoubtedly great scope for the underdeveloped countries like India to adopt the advanced technology of the West to suit their own requirements and factor endowments. "Without any exaggeration it may be said that economic growth is a function of technological expansion of the right type."[4]

(*c*) Optimum Use of Labour Resources. There is no doubt that labour in the advanced countries works harder and works more willingly than is the case in the under-developed countries, where labour is generally a shirker and indisciplined. Germany and Japan have built up their war-devastated economies rapidly mainly with the help of efficient labour force. Generally, in the under-developed countries, labour is abundant and cheap and there is vast scope for increasing the national output by a fuller and better utilisation of their manpower. It is a sad commentary on the state of affairs prevailing in the low-income countries where labour insists on the rights and privileges and conveniently ignores their duties and responsibilities.

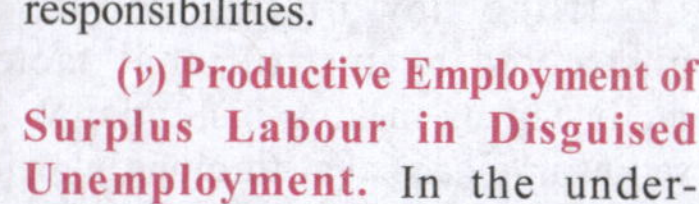

(*v*) Productive Employment of Surplus Labour in Disguised Unemployment. In the under-developed countries, there is lot of surplus labour to be found in the form of disguised unemployment. In view of its importance as a potential source of capital formation we discuss it more fully in the next chapter. Here it may suffice to say that in the agricultural sector, in the under-developed but over-populated countries, more people are apparently employed than there is need for them. This surplus

3. See D. Bright Singh, *Economics of Development*, 1966. p., 175.
4. *Ibid*., p. 176.

labour can be withdrawn from agriculture without in any way diminishing the agricultural output (since in agriculture their marginal productivity is zero) and they can be employed elsewhere more productively, *e.g.*, in road making, irrigation works which are labour-intensive. But the full effect of capital contribution from the transfer of surplus labour from agriculture would follow only if their consumption level does not rise. That is, the labour left behind does not consume more than before nor does the labour transferred to more remunerative employment, start consuming more, otherwise the saving and investment potential will be reduced. The level of consumption can be prevented from rising by means of direct or indirect taxation.

(*vi*) Encouraging Investment. So far we have tried to tackle the problem of capital formation from the supply side, *i.e.*, side of savings. Now let us see what can be done to break the vicious circle of poverty on the side of demand, *i.e.*, investment side. We said that the under-developed countries are poor because there is not much inducement to invest. Obviously, if active steps are taken to encourage investment, the level of output and income will rise. Through wise monetary and fiscal policies, the Government can encourage investment. The Government may follow cheap money policy and give tax concessions and rebates on new investment. For instance, there are provided in India tax holiday for new enterprises, liberal depreciation allowance in corporation tax, *etc.* Protection is granted to domestic industries from foreign competition. Infrastructure (*i.e.*, economic and social overheads) are built up to promote trade and industry. Industrial estates are set up and so on.

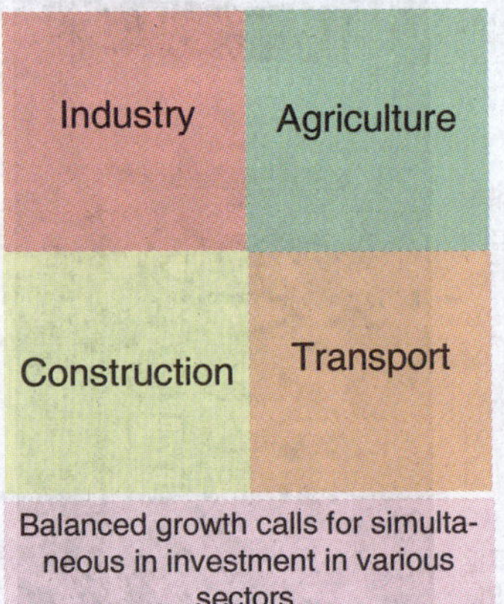

Balanced growth calls for simultaneous in investment in various sectors.

If the flow of finance into investment is obstructed by institutional factors, it can be facilitated by making institutional changes and by setting up financial institutions, *e.g.*, in India were set up Industrial Finance Corporation of India, State Financial Corporations, Industrial Credit and Investment Corporation, Industrial Development Bank of India, *etc.*

(*vii*) Strategy of Balanced Growth. Again, to break the vicious circle of poverty on the demand side of capital formation, Nurkse recommends the strategy of balanced growth. According to him, if investment is made in one particular industry, it is likely to fail owing to low income and low purchasing power of the people. That is why private investors are discouraged from investment in a particular industry. But Nurkse says if investment is made in several industries simultaneously, then the persons employed in different industries become consumers of the goods produced by one another since they have all acquired more purchasing power. That is, the industries in which investment has been made create demand for one another. In this way, balanced growth, in which investment is made simultaneously in a number of industries, creates its own demand. This is how, in Nurkes's opinion, the vicious circle of poverty can be broken on the demand side by means of balanced growth.

It may be pointed out that Nurkse seems to have exaggerated the difficulties on the demand side of the vicious circle. Actually, the demand in the under-developed countries for certain products is quite substantial and if investment is made in these directions, it can prove quite fruitful. The reason is that even though per capita income is low in such countries, yet there are many people whose incomes are high enough to be able to purchase the newly manufactured goods. Who does not know that in India—a low income country, the demand for scooters, cars, and many other commodities is almost insatiable? Who can say, therefore, that investment in these industries is less because the demand is less?

Another noteworthy thing in this connection is that many commodities are imported in large quantities in the under-developed countries which shows that there is a great demand for them. Hence, through a policy of import substitution investment can profitably be made in the manufacture of such commodities or their substitutes. For them there is no dearth of demand or small size of the market.

Conclusion

The vicious circle must be broken at both ends. The supply of savings, both from domestic and foreign sources, must be increased and the State must provide incentives for investment by means of a suitable monetary and fiscal policy. The low level of real income reflecting low productivity is the crucial point both in the demand circle and the supply circle. Of these, the supply end is more difficult to break than the demand end. It is obviously easy to create or increase demand for capital but it is not so easy to make up the deficiency of capital. The country may also suffer from lack of natural resources like water and mineral resources or the poverty of the soil. But in the matter of economic development, the things of crucial importance are the small capacity to save and small inducement to invest. Other deficiencies can be made up and the handicap of the natural factor removed, if the problem of capital formation is successfully tackled.

FOREIGN AID AND ITS ROLE IN ECONOMIC DEVELOPMENT

We have already referred to a low rate of capital formation as one of the primary causes of the vicious circle of poverty in the under-developed countries. The domestic saving rate being very low in such countries, foreign aid assumes great significance if a poor country wants to come out of the vicious circle. Let us therefore consider at some length first the concept of foreign aid and then its role in economic development.

The Concept of Foreign Aid

The term foreign aid is generally used in the sense of flow of resources from the rich countries to the poor under-developed countries. But it has been variously defined. According to the United Nations, economic aid means outright grants and long-term loans for non-military purposes by Governments and various international organisations. An appropriate definition of foreign aid is given by R. F. Mikesall according to whom, foreign aid is a transfer of real resources or immediate claim on resources from one country to another, which would not have taken place as a consequence of the operation of market forces or in the absence of specific official action designed to promote the transfer by the donor country. Thus foreign aid so defined includes both direct government transfers and those promoted by special official action such as government guarantees. It avoids some other motivation on the part of a donor country on the ground that motivations do not in themselves determine the nature and extent of the benefits of the recipients. The transfer of resources should have as their main objective the promotion of economic development and welfare of the developing countries.

Role in Economic Development

The objective of foreign aid is the achievement of sustained economic growth by the recipient country *i.e.* achieving a given target rate of growth which can be sustained without further external assistance.

We may notice three basic approaches to foreign aid requirements for a developing country: (*i*) The Savings-investment gap approach, (*ii*) Foreign exchange earnings and expenditure gap; and (*iii*) the capital absorption approach. The first two approaches viz., the Savings-investment gap and foreign exchange earnings and expenditure gap yield identical results. Foreign aid is equal to both the gap between imports and exports and the gap between domestic investment expenditure and domestic savings.

The third approach *viz*., the capital absorption approach assesses the capital requirements of a developing country on the basis of the ability of an economy to utilise both domestic and foreign capital efficiently *i.e.* it should yield a minimum rate of return. In other words, it has to be seen that foreign aid is not just frittered away in senseless and useless plans. Foreign aid is regarded as a means of overcoming internal obstacles to growth and as a catalyst for mobilising domestic resources for economic development. According to H.M. Chenery and H.M. Strout, foreign aid should make a contribution to the transformation of a poor stagnant economy by raising the levels of skills and improving economic organisation through removing resource bottle-necks and encouraging self-help measures in the administration of foreign aid. This is a more comprehensive view than merely focussing attention on investment-saving gap or import requirements and foreign exchange earnings gap.

Thus, foreign aid makes a significant contribution to the acceleration of the pace of economic growth (*a*) by overcoming shortages and (*b*) by supplementing domestic resources.

Key terms

Vicious circle of poverty, Balanced growth, Foreign Capital, Foreign investment.

QUESTIONS

1. Explain the vicious circle of poverty. How does it check the growth of capital in a poor country?

   Or

   What do you understand by 'vicious circle of poverty'? How can it be converted into a beneficient circle?
2. "A country is poor because a country is poor". (Nurkse) Discuss.
3. "Population growth is not always an obstacle to the growth of per capita income". Discuss.

75 CHAPTER

DISGUISED UNEMPLOYMENT AND ECONOMIC GROWTH

In the previous chapter, we briefly referred to disguised unemployment as a potential source of capital formation. In view of its importance in the theory of economic growth, we examine it more fully here.

In the under-developed countries, we find large-scale open unemployment and disguised unemployment, especially in the agricultural sector, owing to rapidly increasing population. Specialists in the theory of economic development like Ragnar Nurkse, Maurice Dobb and Arthur Lewis, have suggested the use of surplus labour found in disguised unemployment in the under-developed countries for capital formation and for promoting economic development. According to them, disguised unemployment, which indicates surplus labour and which at present is a great liability, can be converted into a great asset. Hidden in the surplus labour in agriculture is substantial saving available for capital formation. Nurkse and other development economists are of the view that there is great scope for increasing the rate of capital formation and for accelerating economic growth if the surplus labour is withdrawn from agriculture and is used in more productive employments elsewhere.

We shall discuss below what disguised unemployment means and how it can be used for capital formation and for promoting economic development.

Meaning of Disguised Unemployment

Joan Robinson was perhaps the first economist who used the term 'disguised unemployment'. But she used this term for the people taking to occupation with comparatively low productivity and income instead of occupations of high productivity and large income during periods of depression in the developed and advanced countries. But the term 'disguised unemployment' is used in a different sense in the under-developed countries.

In the under-developed countries, 'disguised unemployment' refers to a situation where too many people are engaged in agriculture. A common characteristic of the over-populated under-developed countries is that a large majority of population draw their livelihood from agriculture. In a situation of rapidly increasing population and owing to slow rate of industrialisation, naturally a large number of people gravitate to land, because sufficient employment opportunities are not available in the non-agricultural sector to absorb the growing population. The result is that more people are apparently engaged in agriculture than are warranted by the size of the land holdings and capital available and the techniques of cultivation. If some of them are withdrawn, it will not reduce agricultural output and may perhaps increase it, because as it is said too many cooks spoil the broth. This disguised unemployment is found in the self employed agricultural population. The term 'disguised unemployment' is used to refer to such a situation because such people are only apparently employed. In fact they are unemployed or only partly employed and their unemployment is concealed. Since more people seem to be working in agriculture than it is necessary, some of them can be withdrawn without reducing the total output. In other words, their marginal productivity is zero.

In Nurkse's[1] words, "There is disguised unemployment in the sense that even with unchanged techniques of agriculture, a large part of the population engaged in agriculture could be removed without reducing agricultural output .... The same farm output could be got with a smaller labour force."

Some economists are of the view that the term 'disguised unemployment' refers to seasonal unemployment, because all workers are able to get full employment during the harvesting season. This is true to some extent, but even in the harvesting season, work can be so arranged as to be able to manage it with a smaller number of people. Even when employment is seasonal, there is still the question of making a productive use of this labour. The seasonal unemployment too has an important role to play in capital formation in under-developed countries. Economists like Nurkse think that disguised unemployment is not merely seasonal in the under-developed countries but is to be found throughout the year.

Difference between Disguised Unemployment and Open Industrial Unemployment. The disguised unemployment of under-developed countries in agriculture is different from the open industrial unemployment to be found in the developed countries. The cause of open unemployment in the industrial countries is the deficiency of effective demand during depression. Owing to a reduction in aggregate demand, output is reduced in some factories and other factories are altogether closed on account of lack of demand for their goods. As a result, labour employed in such countries is retrenched. Thus, there is open unemployment of industrial labour, in spite of the availability of capital. The cause of this unemployment, as we have said just now, is the reduction in aggregate demand. This type of unemployment can be removed by increasing aggregate demand by creating new money or by deficit financing, *i.e.*, by putting new purchasing power in the hands of the people.

On the contrary, the disguised unemployment to be found in the agricultural sector in the under-developed countries is due not to the deficiency of demand, as in the case of open unemployment in the industrial sector of the developed countries, but to the deficiency of capital equipment, *i.e.*, a low rate of capital formation as compared with a high rate of population growth.

In other words, the disguised unemployment in the under-developed countries is caused by a lack of capital formation, industrialisation and economic development commensurate with the rapid increase in their population. That is why it cannot be cured by deficit financing and by creating new money. Deficit financing would merely raise prices in such countries and there would be inflation because owing to deficiency of capital, output of goods cannot be increased in these countries as fast. Hence, deficit financing will have no effect in removing this unemployment.

Another important difference between agricultural disguised unemployment in the under-developed countries and the open industrial unemployment in the developed countries is that, in the developed countries unemployed industrial labour can take up minor jobs for a temporary period during depression. But in the under-developed countries, disguised unemployment is more or less a permanent feature arising out of excess of labour and the scarcity of capital, and not because of any deficiency of demand.

Characteristics of Disguised Unemployment. Nurkse mentions the following characteristics of disguised unemployment:-

(*a*) The marginal productivity of labour in disguised unemployment is zero.

(*b*) It is usually associated with family employment or self-employed labour and not wage labour.

1. Nurkse, R. — *Problems of Capital Formation in Under—developed Countries*, p. 33.

(*c*) It is not possible to identify personally disguisedly unemployed labour.

(*d*) It is to be distinguished from seasonal unemployment caused by climatic factors.

(*e*) The disguised unemployment in under-developed countries is to be distinguished from industrial under-employment in the developed countries.

Extent of Disguised Unemployment

The magnitude of disguised unemployment in the under-developed countries has been roughly estimated at about 25%[2]. A study by the Royal Institute of International Affairs in 1943 estimated disguised unemployment for the Eastern European regions as the lowest at 20 to 25%. Doreen Warriner placed the surplus labour in Egypt in 1937 at about one-half of the farm population. According to a body of U.N. experts, for many regions of India and Pakistan, and for parts of Philippines and Indonesia, the surplus cannot be less than the pre-war average for the East European region. Nurkse himself is of the view that in many countries ranging from South East Europe to South Eastern Asia, the magnitude of disguised unemployment may be 15 per cent, 20 per cent, or as much as 30 per cent. A study of nine selected villages in the Bombay Karnataka region revealed that 71 per cent of the farmers had less than normal employment and 52 per cent less than half the normal employment.

Disguised Unemployment as a Potential Source of Capital Formation

Nurkse recognised disguised unemployment as a saving potential. That is, in Nurkse's view there is a hidden saving in disguised unemployment which can be used for capital formation in the under-developed countries. According to Nurkse, surplus labour can be withdrawn from agriculture and utilised for capital formation activities like road building, irrigation projects, railway construction, building of houses, factories, *etc.*

The question is : Where form should the finance be obtained for such projects? How are the workers transferred from agriculture to these projects of capital formation to be fed? In Nurkse's view, the best solution to this problem is that the surplus labour transferred from agriculture to capital formation projects should be given their own food that they left behind in the farm families. It is assumed that when surplus labour is withdrawn from agriculture there is no

Disguised unemployment as a potential source of capital formation.

diminution in agricultural output. This means that with the families left behind in agriculture there is surplus food which was being consumed by the people who have not been with drawn from agriculture. In a nutshell, the work of capital formation should be carried on by the people transferred from agriculture supported by the very food that they were consuming before when they were attached to agriculture. That is, capital formation effected by the surplus labour transferred from agriculture is the result of saving not from any other sector or of foreign aid but their own saving concealed in disguised unemployment in agriculture. That is why Nurkse has put forward the view that there is a saving potential in the disguised unemployment in agriculture in the under-developed countries. That is how additional capital can be generated in the under-developed countries by productive employment of surplus labour without extra cost.

How this source of capital formation can be exploited by the under-developed countries can be explained in this manner : The people who are engaged in agriculture have the capacity to save. The productive workers (*i.e.*, those who are fully employed) support those unproductive workers who are only partly employed or those who are only apparently employed but are actually making no contribution (*i.e.*, their marginal productivity is zero). These unproductive workers can be transferred elsewhere from agriculture to productive employments, *i.e.*, to capital formation projects. The productive workers in agriculture are really making a saving. They are producing more than their own consumption and with this extra production

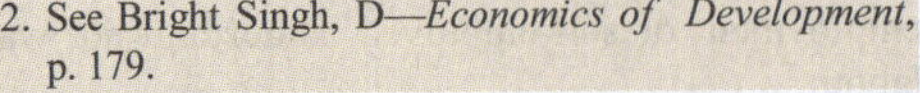

2. See Bright Singh, D—*Economics of Development*, p. 179.

Shift of surplus labour from rural to urban areas.

they are supporting the unproductive workers who are their own kith and kin. But this saving of the productive workers is going to waste because it is consumed by those who can be taken away from agriculture without reducing agricultural output. In Nurkse's words, "If the productive peasants were to send their useless dependants—their cousins, brothers and nephews who live with them, to work on capital projects and if continued to feed them there, then their virtual saving would become effective saving. The unproductive consumption of surplus farm population would become productive consumption".[3] and we add it would become a source of capital formation.

Suppose there are 1,000 persons engaged in agriculture in a village and 25 per cent of them, *i.e.*, 250 are surplus. These are being supported by the remaining 750 persons. Now suppose these 250 workers are transferred to some capital projects elsewhere. If consumption is maintained at the old level, then the 750 persons remaining back in agriculture can transfer the food consumed by 250 before to feed them in their new occupation. What they produce in their new occupation becomes a net contribution to capital without lowering the per capita consumption of the farming population (though aggregate consumption in the village will be reduced).

Thus, we see that the disguised unemployment in agriculture (*i.e.*, surplus labour) can be used for capital formation in under-developed countries and the resources for this purpose can be obtained from the disguised unemployment itself. The farming population need not lower its level of consumption. But it is necessary that they should not raise the level of their consumption. Nor is it necessary for these agricultural workers to lower their consumption who have been transferred from agriculture to some other productive employment. But they have also to see that their level of consumption does not rise. Hence, capital formation out of disguised unemployment is possible without lowering the level of consumption. In this way, the rate of capital formation in the under-developed countries can be raised without lowering the level of consumption.

Here, the relationship between consumption and investment (*i.e.*, capital formation) is midway between the classical and the Keynesian views of this relationship. According to classical theory, as we have already pointed out, it is necessary to reduce the level of consumption in order to raise the rate of capital formation. As against this, according to the Keynesian view, both consumption and investment can be increased at the same time. In fact, Keynes advocates raising of consumption to increase investment. But the relationship between consumption and investment (*i.e.*, capital formation) set out above (*i.e.*, Nurkse's view) is different from Keynesian view in this that here consumption and capital formation do not rise at the same time; only capital formation rises and consumption level remains the same. This is a new theory that the rate of capital formation can be raised without sacrificing consumption.

"Hence, Nurkse argues that while the classical economists stressed the need of restricting consumption so that the level of savings could be raised to support a higher level of investment and Keynes pointed out that by raising the level of consumption and spendings, income level and thereby the level of investment can be raised, the method which he has suggested would raise investment without lowering consumption."[4]

Critical Evaluation of Disguised Unemployment as a Source of Capital Formation

The view put forward by Nurkse of the possibility of using disguised unemployment seems to be plausible and theoretically possible. But let us see how far it is practically feasible. As we have already said, the transfer of surplus labour can result in capital formation only if the level of consumption is prevented from rising and if the transfer does not cost much and transferred labour can be put on suitable jobs and are provided with suitable equipment without increasing much cost. This indeed is a very big 'IF'. Hence, the proposal to make use of surplus labour for capital formation suffers from serious limitations and there can be several leakages. That is why many economists do not subscribe to Nurkse's thesis. They

3. *Ibid.*, pp. 37-38.

4. Bright Singh, D. — *Economics of Development*, p. 179.

admit that there is surplus labour in agriculture in the form of disguised unemployment. But owing to several difficulties they do not agree that its saving potential can be actually realised :

(i) It is very likely that the consumption level of the labour left behind as well as of the labour transferred rises to nullify the saving potential. Since the consumption level is already very low, the agricultural output may fall, when some labour is withdrawn, unless consumption level is raised. Also, when surplus labour moves from the rural to urban areas where the level of consumption is higher and the wages are higher too, the propensity to consume of the transferred labour is bound to go up. They will tend to consume more because they have now to put in more work. The workers who have been left behind in agriculture and whose dependents are now gone, will feel a little better off and will have more to eat. They will, therefore, be tempted to raise their level of consumption, when they have now more to eat. They must also consume more, because they have now to work more to maintain the old level of output, since the number of workers has been reduced on account of transfer of some of their co-workers.

Thus, we see that, some labour is transferred from agriculture to other productive employment, the level of consumption of those who have been left behind and of those who are transferred, has a strong tendency to go up. The rise in consumption of the workers concerned will eat up the saving potential of disguised unemployment. In fact, the leakage in the savings potential will the substantial.

(ii) Another leakage will arise on account of cost of transport. Costs will have to be incurred in transporting labour from villages to urban areas or to the sites of construction works started for the purpose of absorbing surplus agricultural labour. There will be costs involved too in transporting food to feed the surplus labour that has been transferred to new areas. These costs of transport must be set off against the saving expected from the transfer of surplus labour from agriculture.

(iii) There are some other costs too which the scheme will involve. Obviously, labour cannot be dislodged from their native places and taken to other areas unless higher wages are offered. This will increase the cost of the investment works undertaken in this connection. Capital equipment will have to be supplied to the labour transferred to new projects. There will be additional administrative burden. Competent personnel will have to be engaged to supervise and organise the work. These costs may add up to a much higher figure than it is assumed and may

Transportation of labour from one area to another area involves high cost.

substantially cut down the saving potential of disguised unemployment.

(iv) Besides, there is the difficulty of choosing a suitable job for the transferred labour and to plant them in a convenient location. It may not be possible to start development projects in the vicinity of the village from which the workers are sought to be transferred. Further, these people have no training and can do only unskilled labour. They are tied to the native place by a sentimental attachment. Unless they expect to get the jobs which are congenial and unless the place of work is congenial and the working conditions are congenial, the transfer of labour may provoke adverse reaction. They may, in fact, return to their native place.

(v) Further, it is most likely that the type of people who are transferred from the village are backward and poor. Hence, the wage goods released may be of the lowest consumption level. Consequently, the savings so made may not be substantial and worthwhile.

(vi) Another difficulty relates to the procurement of foodgrains from the farming population left behind in agriculture and making it available to the transferred labour in their new place of work. Will the Government collect it by means of a tax or through procurement at fixed price or will it require the transferred labour to purchase it in the free market with the cash wages paid to them? Thus, it is very difficult to procure foodgrains and to arrange its distribution among the transferred labour. The Government will be powerless to collect such large quantities of foodgrains by means of a tax. If it is compulsorily procured at fixed prices, payment in cash will have to be made to the farmers and they will spend it on the purchase of other commodities. This means that the output of industrial consumer goods will increase.

In this way, consumption will increase which Nurkse's doctrine assumes to be kept at the previous level. If the distribution of foodgrains is left to the free market forces the prices of foodgrains will be pushed up in the country and an inflationary situation will be created. The reason is that the consumption level of the transferred labour will have gone up and so also of the farmers left behind. On the one hand, the marketable surplus will be reduced and on the other the consumption of transferred labour will go up and the prices will rise. Thus, we see that the saving potential for capital formation in disguised unemployment is reduced and the possibility of price rise is increased which will impede economic growth in the country.

This doctrine may well work socialist countries like the U.S.S.R. and China where the governments can compulsorily procure foodgrains from the farming population without paying any price and use it for feeding the transferred labour. The Government, can also compel the people to keep their consumption at the old level. But such things are simply out of the question in a democratic country like India. Hence. Saving potential in disguised unemployment cannot be used for capital formation without increasing consumption. It is true that some people in India were persuaded to give their free labour for the community under the leadership of Acharya Vinoba Bhave but its impact is negligible. Also, under the community development programme in India people have been asked to give their free labour for the construction of roads, school buildings, construction of hospitals, minor irrigation works, *etc.* But this also made only a limited contribution to capital formation.

Thus, there are several difficulties in individualistic and democratic countries like India in using saving potential in disguised unemployment for capital formation. Although it is admitted that there is a large-scale disguised unemployment in agriculture but its saving potential for capital formation is denied.

(vii) There is another formidable difficulty of identifying the disguisedly unemployed labour in agriculture. Who is going to pick and choose to transfer this labour elsewhere, the state or the farming families or such workers will themselves opt out? In actual practice, it will be found that the task is not only difficult but impossible. Agricultural operations provide work for all young and old and even children. Some persons are fully occupied some time and some others at other times. It is very difficult to lay finger on those workers whose marginal productivity is zero. Because calculation of marginal productivity itself is too difficult a task to be lightly undertaken.

Conclusion. The difficulties mentioned above are quite real and the doctrine of surplus labour as a potential source for capital formation as propounded by Nurkse suffers from serious limitations. But the phenomenon of disguised unemployment in the under-developed countries cannot be denied. It does constitute a potential source of capital formation without putting undue strain on the economy if the Government concerned can devise an effective way of putting it into practice. The under-developed countries, which suffer from capital deficiency but which are keen on economic development, have to make a start in capital formation and Nurkse has suggested how it can be done. The central idea of the scheme is to avoid wastage of resources, natural or human and to make optimum utilisation of them by transferring them from less productive uses to more productive uses and to increase the G.N.P. Looked at from this angle, the doctrine is based on sound economic logic.

Solution of the Problem of Disguised Unemployment

In the under-developed countries, there is disguised unemployment not only in the agricultural sector, but there is also large-scale unemployment in the urban areas. In agriculture, unemployment is hidden and disguised but in the urban area it is open, full and visible. Now the question is whether employment should be provided to those who are totally unemployed or to the partially employed or disguisedly unemployed people.

When there is not much scope of saving potential in agriculture for capital formation, the best thing would be to create employment opportunities in the urban areas for people who have no jobs. The wise course seems to be first to put the altogether unemployed persons on the job and then solve the problem of disguised unemployment. Our view is that the best method of removing disguised unemployment is to raise agricultural productivity through agricultural improvements. Agricultural productivity can be raised by the use of modern agricultural inputs like high-yielding varieties of seeds, fertilizers in heavy doses, pesticides and ample irrigation facilities. Then there will be new employment opportunities available in agriculture. For instance, more labour is required in a system of multiple-cropping. If this system is extensively adopted, employment will certainly increase or disguised unemployment will decrease.

In this way, the problem of disguised unemployment or under-employment can be solved by raising agricultural productivity or by agricultural development. Since in disguised unemployment some workers do not get enough work to do and their removal will not reduce output, their marginal productivity is zero. But when there is a green revolution, as a result of which agricultural productivity will go up and more and new employment opportunities will be available, the problem of disguised unemployment will be automatically solved.

Thus, we see that to remove disguised unemployment it is not necessary to withdraw those workers from agriculture whose marginal productivity is zero. But we should raise their marginal productivity in that very sector by improving agricultural practices. This would solve their problem and there will be no difficulties that have to be faced in withdrawing the disguisedly unemployed labour and putting them to productive work elsewhere.

LEWIS MODEL OF ECONOMIC DEVELOPMENT WITH UNLIMITED LABOUR SUPPLY

W. Arthur Lewis has presented a theory of economic development with the use of unlimited supply of labour. The supply of labour in under-developed countries generally is perfectly elastic at the current wage rate. That is, an unlimited supply of labour is available at the subsistence wage. This unlimited supply of labour is drawn from surplus agricultural labour, domestic servants, women in households, *etc*. In all these sectors, the marginal productivity of labour is negligible or zero.

Sir W. Arther Lewis got nobel Prize in economics in 1979.

Some economists contend that there is not much surplus labour actually available for capital formation so as to be useful for economic development. Lewis model is more in accord with this reality. His model is not based on disguised unemployment but on some other conditions, *viz*., (*a*) The wage rate in the industrial sector is above its marginal productivity in the subsistence sector by a small but fixed margin. (*b*) The investment in the industrial sector is not large relative to population growth. (*c*) The cost of training of the skilled workers is constant.

In his model, Lewis analyses the process of economic development in terms of inter-sectorial relationships in a dual economy composed of a 'capitalist' (manufacturing, mining, *etc*.) Sector and a 'subsistence sector or the self-employment sector. In an overpopulated country, the capitalist sector draws labour from the subsistence sector of which there is an almost unlimited supply. The wage in the capitalist sector depends on what labour gets/earns in the subsistence sector and is a bit higher so as to attract labour. Hence at this wage, the supply of labour is perfectly elastic which means the capitalist sector can have as much labour as it requires. Subsistence wage, in turn, is governed by the conventional view of the minimum required for subsistence or by average product per worker in subsistence agriculture.

Since marginal productivity in the capitalist sector is higher than the current wage rate, it yields a surplus or profits to the capitalist. The surplus is reinvested and creates new capital which in turn raises the marginal productivity and increases employment in the capitalist sector. This process does not raise wages but increases the surplus or share of profits in the national income. This process goes on. Profits grow relatively as the capitalist sector expands and capital formation increases.

In this diagram, quantity of labour is represented along OX and wages and marginal productivity along OY. OS represents subsistence earnings and OW capitalist wage. WS is the perfectly elastic supply of labour at OW the capitalist wage. Initially the demand for labour is represented by the marginal productivity curve of labour $N_1 D_1$. Labour is employed up to the point where the marginal productivity equals the current wage rate OW. Thus the amount of labour employed initially is OL_1. Labour share (*i.e.* wages) in the total product $ON_1 M_1 L_1$ is $OWM_1 L_1$ and share of profits or surplus going to the capitalist is $WN_1 M_1$

On reinvestment of the profits, the marginal productivity of labour rises to $N_2 D_2$, and employment of labour will increase to OL_2. In the same way, further investment will raise the marginal productivity of labour to $N_3 D_3$ and employment increases further to OL_3 and capitalists surplus on profits to $WN_3 M_3$. This process repeats itself. Capital formation resulting from credit creation and deficit financing adds to the capital formed out of real savings and leads to accelerated rate of investment and quicker utilisation of surplus labour. This results in inflationary price rise. But according to Lewis such inflation will be self-destroying rather than cumulative, because increase in the production of goods and services will, in course of time bring down prices. Larger profits will facilitate more saving so that capital formation out of real savings overtakes capital formation out of credit creation and deficit financing. This means that in course of time, credit creation deficit financing will become unnecessary.

The following diagram illustrates this process:

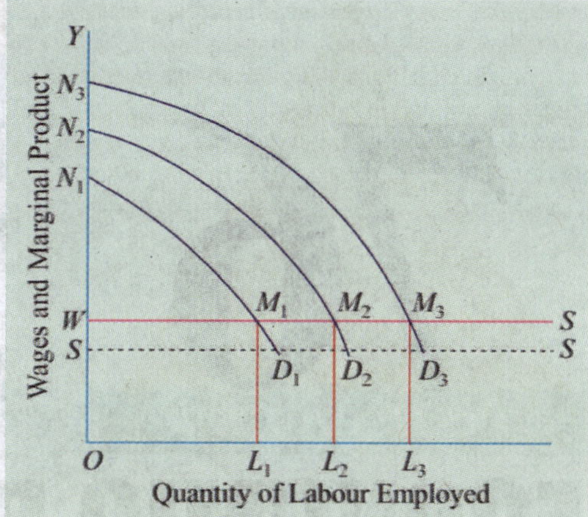

Development with unlimited supplies of Labour.

Arthur Lewis, however, points out that the process of economic growth must come to an end (*a*) when no surplus labour is left (*b*) when population declines (*c*) when food prices rise pushing up wages and (*d*) when workers press for higher wages.

Key terms

Disguised unemployment , Surplus labour as saving potential.

QUESTIONS

1. Distinguish between disguised and under unemployment.
2. Explain the concept of disguised unemployment as source of capital formation.
3. Critically evaluate the Arthur Lewis theory of economic development with unlimited supply of labour.

CHAPTER 76

ECONOMIC DEVELOPMENT

Meaning

Economic development or economic progress has been defined in two ways: According to one definition, economic growth means growth of national income of the country. In other words, it implies an increase in the net national product in a given period, say, a year. Some economists consider this definition as inadequate and unsatisfactory. They argue that even if the national income goes up, the general standard of living may go down. This can happen if population of the country is rising more rapidly than the growth of the national income. If the national income is rising at the rate of 2 per cent and population is increasing at the rate of 3 per cent, the level of living of the people is bound to go down. This is because on account of population increasing at a higher rate than the growth of the national income, per capita income falls and when per capita income goes down, we cannot call it economic growth. The country will have registered economic growth only if per capita income has gone up and this will happen only if the national income grows at a higher rate than the growth rate of the population.

Thus, a better definition of economic development will be to base it on per capita income. According to this definition, economic growth means the increase in per capita income of the country at constant prices. A higher per capita income would mean that people are better off and enjoy a higher standard of living, and to raise the level of living of the people is the main objective of economic development. But the increase in national income or per capita income must be maintained for a long time. A temporary or short-lived increase will not connote real economic growth.

In an earlier chapter (70), we mentioned the characteristics of under-developed countries. The best definition of economic development would be to say what a developed country would be like. "Viewed in this manner, economic progress is the advancement of a community along the line of evolving new and better methods of production, and raising of the levels of output through development of human skill and energy, better organisation and the acquisition of capital resources" ... Economic development also brings in its wake important social, institutional and organisational changes. A rise in national and per capita income is implicit in economic growth. This improvement in income helps and in turn is facilitated by larger savings, increased capital formation and technological development. Rise in the per capita availability of capital resources, improvement in the skill, efficiency and earning power of labour, better organisation of production, development of means of transport and communications, growth of financial institutions, urbanisation, rise in standards of health and education and expectation of life, greater leisure and increased recreation facilities and widening of the mental horizon of the people, all these characterise economic growth."[1] This is, in a nutshell, what economic development means.

The essence of economic development consists in the growth of output or real income per head of the population. Economic growth means the transformation of an economy from the state of underdevelopment to a state of development, from an agrarian to a highly industrialised society, from a low saver to high saver and from a predominantly rural to a predominantly urbanised society. This transformation is mainly reflected in a sustained and steady rise in national income and per capita income.

Schumpeter said "economic development constitutes a spontaneouse and discontinuous change in the channels of flow, a disturbance of equilibrium which for ever alters and displaces the equilibrium state previously existing."

According to Buchanan and Ellis, "Development means developing the real income potentials by using investment to effect those changes and to augment those productive resources which promise to raise real income per person."

Economic growth and economic development is used by different economists in different ways :

(*i*) In general economic growth refer's to a quantitative change in economic variables, where as economic development is an over-all increase in the quantitative as well as qualitative aspects. Therefore Michael Todaro writes "Development must therefore be conceived as a multi-dimensional process involving major changes in social structures, popular attitudes and national institutions as well as acceleration of economic growth, reduction in income inequalities and the eradication of absolute poverty." (*ii*) Economic growth is just an increase in an economic variable and it is a simple phonemenon, where as economic development is a multi-dimensional changes involving economic social, institutional aspects, hence it is a more complex phenomenon. (*iii*) Economic growth is a continuous concept, whereas economic development is a discontinuous and spontaneous concept. (*iv*) Many developed countries are concerned with their economic growth rate. Hence a number of economists developed growth theories, on the other hand economic development is concerned with developing countries as they have many problems including economic, social, political *etc.* (*v*) Economic growth may be a micro concept where as economic development is a macro-concept, which can be referred as a "Walrasian concept".

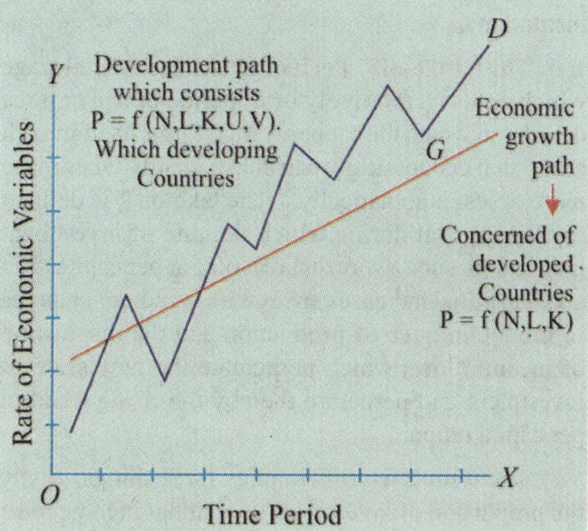

G = Growth path

P = Production function

N = Land (resource utilised)

L = Labour (labour employed)

K = Capital (capital used in production process.)

$P = f(N, L, K,)$ These are growth components, which are common in many countries.

D = Economic development path. which is concerned of developing countries. It consists of

$P = f(N, L, K, u, v,)$

u = Socio-economic conditions +

v = Technological know-how

Growth + Development components = Economic Development path.

$N, L, K + u, v, = p = f(N, L, K, U, V)$

Stages of Economic Development

Prof. Rostow, an eminent economic historian and a specialist in economic development, has divided the historical process of economic growth into three states: (1) the preparatory stage, (2) the 'take-off' period and (3) the period of self-sustained growth. Now a word about each of these.

Preparatory Stage covers a long period of a century or more during which the preconditions for take-off are established. These conditions mainly comprise fundamental changes in the social, political and economic fields; for example (*a*) a change in

1. Bright Singh, D. — *Economic Development,* p. 1.

society's attitudes towards science, risk-taking and profit-earning; (*b*) the adaptability of the labour force; (*c*) political sovereignty; (*d*) development of a centralised tax system and financial institutions; and (*e*) the construction of certain economic and social overheads like rail-roads and educational institutions.

The "Take-off" Period. This is the crucial stage which covers a relatively brief period of two or three decades in which the economy transforms itself in such a why that economic growth subsequently takes place more or less automatically. " The take-off " is defined as "the interval during which the rate of investment increases in such a way that real output per capita rises and this initial increase carries with it radical changes in the techniques of production and the disposition of income flows which perpetuate the new scale of investment and perpeture thereby the rising trend in per capita output."

The term 'take-off' implies three things; firstly the proportion of investment to national income must rise from 12 to 15 per cent definitely outstripping the likely population increase; secondly, the period must be relatively short so that it should show the characteristics of an economic revolution; and thirdly, it must culminate in self-sustaining and self-generating economic growth.

Period of Self-sustained Growth. This is, of course, a long period of self-generating and self-propelling economic growth. The rates of savings and investment are of such magnitude that economic development becomes automatic. Overall capital per head increases as the economy matures. The structure of the economy changes increasingly. The initial key industries which sparked the take-off decelerate as diminishing returns set in. But the average rate of growth is maintained by a succession of new rapidly-growing sectors with a new set of pioneering leaders; the proportion of the population engaged in rural pursuits declines, and the structure of the country's foreign trade undergoes a radical change.

It is both with the problems and the cyclical movements of national income in such growing economies in the third stage that the bulk of modern theoretical economics is concerned. The students of contemporary under-developed countries and also of economic history are more likely to be concerned with the economics of the first two stages, that is, the economics of the preparatory and the 'take-off' stages. If we are to have a useful and adequate theory of economic growth, it must, obviously, be comprehensive enough to embrace these two stages as well, especially the economics of the "take-off".

On *y*-axis capital, investment and savings are measured on x-axis income is measured. The 45 degree line measured $I = S$ (investment = savings) and S_0, S_1, S_2 .... is higher rate of economic growth.

(*i*) Initially the economy is at 'Y_0' which brings about 'S_0' savings which leads to increase in I_0' investment, this increases the rate of income in the economy from 'Y_0' to 'Y_1'. (Due to K_1Y_1 Capital-output ratio)

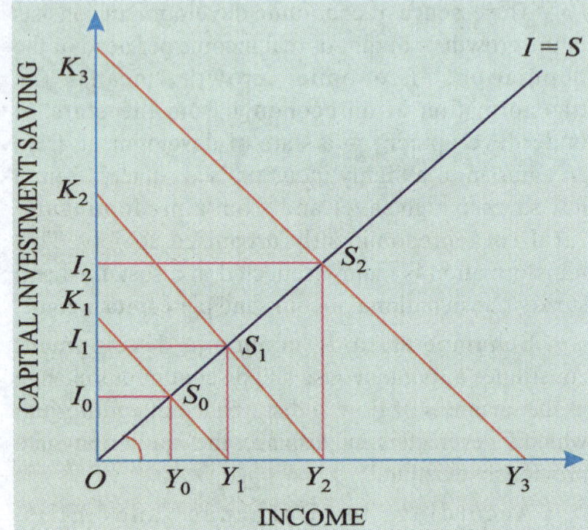

Self sustained emmulative process.

(*ii*) When economy settles at Y_1' income, which brings 'S_1' savings and 'I_1' investment. This shifts the economy from Y_1 to Y_2 (Due to K_2Y_2 capital output ratio) through "$I_1S_1Y_2$ route.

(*iii*) As economy settles at 'Y_2' this brings about "S_2" savings to and 'I_2' investment. Hence through the '$I_2S_2Y_3$' route, that means on due to I_2 investment the income increases to 'OY_3' and further the capital output ratio increases to 'K_3Y_3.

In this way the economy reaches into a self-sustained commulative process, which automatically increases the growth rate from S_1, S_2, S_3 ...... and so on.

DETERMINANTS OF ECONOMIC GROWTH

We have said that economic development means the transformation from low income to high income society. Let us see now the conditions which facilitate this transformation and maintain a sustained and steady rate of growth. The process of economic development is a highly complex phenomenon and is influenced by numerous and varied factors, such as political, social and cultural factors. As such, economic analysis can provide only a partial explanation of this process. To repeat here the remark of Prof. Ragnar Nurkse in this connection, "Economic development has much to do with human endowments, social attitudes, political condition and historical accidents. Capital is a necessary but not a sufficient condition of progress." The supply of natural resources, the growth of scientific and technological knowledge—all these too have a strong bearing on the process of economic growth. We shall briefly notice some of these factors one by one. Form the standpoint of economic analysis, the most important factors determining the rate of economic development are :

(*i*) Availability of natural resources;

(*ii*) The rate of capital formation;

(*iii*) Capital-output ratio;

(*iv*) Technological progress;

(*v*) Dynamic Entrepreneurship;

(*vi*) Rate of growth of population;

(*vii*) Social overheads like education and health.

(*viii*) Non-economic factors.

Availability of Natural Resources

The quantity and quality of natural resources vitally affect the economic growth of a country. Among the natural resources, we generally include the land area and the quality of the soil, forest wealth, good river system, minerals and oil-resources, good and bracing climate, *etc*. A country's productive capacity largely depends on the natural resources available. Without a minimum availability of natural resources it is idle to expect any sizable economic growth. But it may be noted that the existence of natural resources is not a sufficient condition of economic growth. For instance, India is blessed by natural with good and sufficient resources, yet it is poor and under-developed. This is due to the fact that the natural resources have not been properly harnessed and fully exploited. Hence, availability of natural resources by itself cannot bring about economic development. Ability to utilisation is also required.

The supply of natural resources can be increased by research and technological progress. Technological progress helps in the discovery of new resources, *e.g.*, oil resources in India and putting to economical use resources which have been lying useless hitherto. Also, the shortage of some natural resources can be made good by synthetic materials. For instance, in the advanced countries, synthetic rubber is being used more and more in place of natural rubber and nylon is being largely used for natural silk.

The use of natural resources and their contribution to economic development depends on the type of technology. The resource use has a close connection with the type and level of technology. To know this one need not go far in to history. For instance, petroleum which is considered so valuable today was not considered so important a short while ago. Now on account of scientific discoveries and technological development petroleum is regarded very useful. Besides, just now radioactive substances are considered very valuable. There is no doubt that there exists in the under-developed countries abundant mineral resources which are not being used owing to the lack of technological progress.

Capital Formation

According to classical economists, the main factor, which helped capital formation, was the accumulation of capital. Profits made by the business community constituted the major part of the savings of the community and what was saved was assumed to be invested. Adam Smith too emphasised the virtues of savings. He said: "Capitals are increased by parsimony and diminished by prodigality and misconduct." Keynes also ascribed the economic development of Europe to the accumulation of capital. He said: "Europe was so organised socially and economically as to secure the maximum accumulation of capital." Later, Schumpeter showed that increased investment made possible a rise in gross output in money terms.

Thus, the crux of the problem of economic development in an under-developed economy lies in a 'rapid expansion of the rate of its capital investment so that it attains a rate of growth of output which exceeds the rate of growth of population by a significant margin. Only with such a rate of capital investment will the living standards begin to improve in a developing country.

Need for Capital Formation. We have already discussed capital formation in a previous chapter and also the measures for promoting it to break the vicious circle of poverty.[2] Here we discuss it from the point of view of economic growth. Capital formation is the very core of economic development. It may be a predominantly private enterprise system like the American, or a communist economy like the Soviet, economic development cannot take place without capital accumulation. No economic development is possible without the construction of irrigation works, the production of agricultural tools and implements, land reclamation, building of dams, bridges and factories with machines installed in them, roads, railways, and

2. Chapter 72.

Capital formation and economic Development go together.

airports, ships and harbours—all the "produced means of further production" associated with high levels of productivity. It seems unquestionable that the insufficiency of capital accumulation is the most serious limiting factor in under-developed countries. In the view of many economists, capital occupies the central and strategic position in the process of economic development.

Capital formation indeed plays a decisive role in determining the level and growth of national income, hence economic development. This is due to the fact that of all factors of production capital has unlimited expansibility. It is man-made and is capable of increasing in quantity and improving in quality. There is no doubt that productive capacity of an economy can be increased only by increasing the quantity and improving the quality of its capital equipment.

Thus, in any programme of planned economic development capital formation must be assigned a significant role on account of a very close connection between economic growth and capital growth. It enables the adoption of more productive methods of production. Capital widening makes the economy diversified and broad-based. It exerts an interacting and cumulative effect on the whole economy. It facilitates technical progress. In all these and several other ways, capital formation promotes economic growth.

It could of course be argued that without the presence of other factors favourable to development, the supply or creation of capital alone would not be of much avail. indeed, as pointed out above, it has often been argued that economic development is a matter of changing social attitudes and economic institutions rather than a simple process of increasing capital per head. Yet the history of economic development shows that widespread changes in attitudes, values and institutions came about in the very process of economic development and not prior to development.

Process of Capital Formation. The process of building up the necessary stock of capital equipment requires huge resources for financing it. Either a part of national income must be saved for the production of capital goods or the necessary funds for the purpose must be borrowed from abroad. The various methods of financing economic development, will be discussed in detail in a separate section. Here we may only emphasize that domestic saving is a sine qua non of capital formation. In fact, Professor Arthur Lewis has defined the process of economic growth as one of transforming a country from a 5 per cent to a 15 per cent saver. But savings though necessary are not sufficient for the purpose of capital formation, which involves the following three independent activities :

(*a*) an increase in the volume of real savings so that resources that would have been used for consumption purposes may be released for the purpose of capital formation.

(*b*) a finance and credit mechanism, so that the available resources may be availed of by private investors or government for capital formation; and

(*c*) the act of investment itself, so that resources are used for the production of capital goods.

Although Schumpeter showed that investment can and does exceed voluntary savings through credit creation by the banking system, yet the requirements of capital accumulation cannot be simply met by monetary expansion. **Without additional real savings, monetary expansion may merely generate inflation.** The basic point is that the cost of development must be measured in real terms and not in monetary terms. The real costs are those of the resources that must be mobilized to carry out the development programme: the foreign and domestic services, materials, and equipment directly required for its execution; and the additional goods and services for which more demand will indirectly be created through development expenditures.

Can capital accumulation take place without technological progress? A community could just go on building more transport facilities, more sources of power, more factories of the **existing type.** This process of duplicating the existing technique is sometimes called **"widening of capital,"** in contrast with **"deepening of capital"**, which implies use of more capital-intensive techniques. In fact, capital accumulation and technological progress go hand in hand. Technological improvement is virtually impossible without prior capital accumulation. This is because the most efficient techniques require heavy investment for their introduction, even if they reduce capital costs per unit of output, once they are installed and are operating. Thus, no nation, that is not willing either to save and pay taxes or to borrow abroad, will enjoy the fruits of the advanced techniques.

Capital-output Ratio

Meaning. Apart from the ratio of capital formation to the aggregate national income, the growth of output depends upon the capital-output ratio. "The capital-output ratio may be defined as the relationship of investment in a given economy or industry for a given time period to the output of that economy or industry for a similar time period."[3] The capital-output ratio thus determines the rate at which output grows as a result of a given volume of capital investment than a higher capital-output ratio. For example, a capital-output ratio of 3 : 1 would mean, in Indian rupees, that a capital investment of Rs. 3 results in the addition of output worth Re. 1. Hence, given the output, smaller capital investment would be needed if the capital-output ratio is lower than when it is higher.

Factors Determining Capital-output Ratio. It is difficult to estimate the capital-output ratio for an economy. The productivity of capital depends upon many factors such as the degree of technological development associated with capital investment, the efficiency of handling new types of equipment, the quality of managerial and organizational skill, the existence and the extent of the utilization of economic overheads and the pattern and rate of investment. For instance, the higher the proportion of investment devoted to the production of direct commodities, the lower the capital-output ratio; and higher the proportion of investment devoted to public utilities, *i.e.*, economic and social overheads, the higher shall be the capital-output ratio, and vice versa. Higher the investment devoted to heavy industry, the higher will be the capital-output ratio, and vice versa. Higher the rate of investment and greater the technological progress, the lower will be the capital-output ratio. The capital-output ratio also varies with the prices of inputs.

Why High in Under-developed Countries. It is agreed that capital-output ratio in under-developed countries is generally higher, *i.e.*, the capital is less productive in them than in developed countries. This is so because there is a relative inefficiency of the industries which produce capital goods. There is the greater wastage of capital in the process of production due to low level of technical knowledge and there is the scarcity of economic overheads. Besides, owing to indivisibilities, certain kinds of investment are bound to be initially under-utilized. As development proceeds, naturally the pattern of demand will shift towards the more capital intensive industries.

Various estimates have been made of capital output ratios in poor countries. A group of experts appointed by the United Nations used a ratio ranging from 2 : 1 to 5 : 1. The Second Five-Year Plan of India assumed an average capital-output ratio of 23 : 1. It was 2 : 1 in the First Five-Year Plan. Kurihara has assumed that in most under developed countries the ratio is of the order of 5 : 1. Singer in his model of economic development assumed a ratio of 6 : 1 in the non-agricultural sector and 4 : 1 in the agricultural sector and Rosentein-Rodan estimates that the ratio is at least 3 : 1.

Importance. Thus, the objective of capital accumulation, howsoever important, should not be over stressed. For to gain the most from capital formation, a country must also undergo technological and organizational progress, so that the capital may be used more productively. The growth of the rate of output depends not only on the amount of capital accumulated but also on how much capital is required per unit increase in output (*i.e.*, capital-output ratio). A low capital-output ratio is, thus, as significant as capital accumulation. But it must also be pointed out that a low ratio requires technological and organizational progress, so that capital becomes more productive.

Thus, capital-output ratio plays a vital role in accelerating economic growth. The lower the capital-output ratio, more accelerated is the economic growth. The capital-output ratio can be reduced by means of technological progress and administrative improvements.

Limitations. It may, however, be pointed out that the concept of capital-output ratio suffers from certain limitations. Its precise calculation presents some formidable difficulties. Hence, the quantitative relationship between capital investment and output, which the capital-output ratio suggests, may prove to be misleading. It would, therefore, be hazardous to base the estimates of capital requirements of an industry or economy on such ratios. Neigher can the capital stock be assessed with any exactitude; nor is the other side of the ratio, *i.e.*, output capable of any precise measurement. Besides the index number problems, a

3. Rosen, George—*Industrial Changes in India*, 1959, p. 37.

clear distinction cannot be often made between capital goods and non-capital goods. Returns to social overheads, in particular, cannot be calculated accurately. Further, capital-output ratio is influenced by several variables, *e.g.*, technological improvements, better utilisation of equipment organisational improvements, labour efficiency, and such factors elude quantitative assessment.

Hence, the concept of capital-output ratio has only a limited practical significance, because it cannot indicate the actual contribution of capital alone in a given scheme of investment. Great caution is, therefore, necessary in making use of a particular capital-output ratio in the formulation of actual investment policy.

Technological Progress

Adam Smith, the father of political economy, pointed out the great importance of technological progress in economic development. Ricardo visualised the development of capitalist economies as a race between technological progress and growth of population. The great importance of technological progress in capitalist development was recognised by Karl Marx too.

There is no doubt that technological progress is a very important factor in determining the rate of economic growth. In fact, even capital accumulation is not possible without technical progress. A country may be added to its means of transportation and communications, its power resources and its factories. According to modern technique, it is called **widening of capital.** The use of improved techniques in production and technological progress bring about a significant increase in per capita income. Technological progress has something to do with the research into the use of new and better methods of production or the improvement of the old methods. Sometimes technical progress results in the availability of natural resources. But generally technological progress results in increase in productivity, *e.g.*, green revolution. In other words, technological progress increases the ability to make a more effective and fruitful use of natural and other resources for increasing production. By the use of improved technology it is possible to have greater output from the use of given resources or a given output can be obtained by the use of a smaller quantity of resources.

It is a matter of common knowledge that technological progress adds greatly to our ability to make a fuller use of the natural resources, *e.g.*, generation of hydro-electricity. With the aid of power-driven farm equipment a marked increase has been brought about in agricultural yields per acre and per worker. Technical progress also increases the ability to make a more effective use of capital equipment. Technological progress has very close connection with capital formation. In fact, both go hand in hand. Without capital formation technical progress is out of the question because heavy investment is required for making use of better and more efficient methods of production, although after they are well established, capital cost per unit of output may fall.

Thus, technological progress has a very important role to play in the economic development of a country. No backward country can hope to march ahead on the road of economic development without adopting newer and newer techniques of production and unless it is assisted in its march by technological progress. We have already brought out the importance of capital accumulation in economic growth. But capital accumulation promotes economic growth because it facilitates technological improvements, which raise labour productivity and thus add to the national and per capita income.

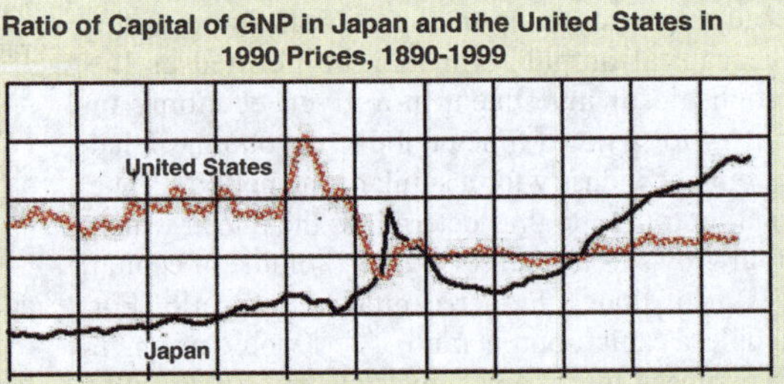

Developed countries such as US and Japan home low.

Dynamic Entrepreneurship

According to the classical economists, an entrepreneur or an organiser acts merely as an agency for bringing together the various agents of production and undertaking to remunerate them for the work done. But the modern economists recognise the dynamic role that an entrepreneur plays in promoting the economic growth of the country. This was specially underlined by Schumpeter who thought that the entrepreneur played a key role in economic development. Even Karl Marx had emphasised the fact that in trying to widen the profit margin by adopting new technology and improved methods of production, the entrepreneur in fact makes an important contribution to economic growth.

The entrepreneur earns profit by ensuring that the value of the final product exceeds the sum of the remuneration of the factors of production, *i.e.*, the value of the means of production. This surplus constitutes his profit. It is the entrepreneur's main aim to enlarge this surplus or profit. Obviously, the greater the surplus, the greater is the entrepreneurial activity and greater the entrepreneurial activity, the faster is the rate at which the economy grows. The entrepreneur tries to maximise his profit by making innovations, *i.e.*, by bringing out a new product, tapping a new market, tapping new sources of raw materials and by adopting an optimum or most economical combination of the factors of production. In all these ways, while he succeeds in making higher profits for himself, he is making a significant contribution to an increase in the national income. We can imagine that cumulative effect of the individual activities of the daring and dynamic entrepreneurs is to accelerate the process of economic growth.

Entrepreneurship is an important factor in growth and development.

Population Growth

The size and the rate of population growth has an important bearing on the economic development of a country. If the population is too small, it does not afford full scope for specialisation or division of labour nor a sufficient market for the goods produced in the country. If, on the other hand, population is too large, then also it is a great impediment to economic growth. It is a serious hindrance to capital formation. The feeding of a huge population leaves little scope for saving, and saving is very essential for economic growth, because capital formation is the very crux of the process of economic growth. Hence population should be of a proper or optimum size.

Apart from the proper size of the population, it is also essential that the rate of population growth should not be too rapid, otherwise it will swallow up whatever little economic progress may have been made and the country may only mark time. In such a situation, efforts at development will be simply a writing on the sand.

Thus, a rapidly growing population aggravates the food problem, worsens the unemployment situation, adds to the number of unproductive consumers, keeps down per capita income and labour efficiency and militates against capital formation. In all these and many other ways, a rapid rate of population growth acts like a drag on economic development and slows down the pace of economic growth.

In view of the great importance of the population factor in determining the rate of economic growth, we discuss it at some length at the end of this chapter.

Social Overheads

Another important determinant of economic growth is the provision of social overheads like schools, colleges, technical institutions, medical colleges, hospitals and public health facilities. Such facilities make the working population healthy, efficient and responsible. Such people can well take their country economically forward.

Non-economic or Institutional Factors

Thus far we have dwelt on the economic factors. But perhaps equally powerful are the various non-economic forces like the social and political factors. In Kaldor's words, "A study of the dynamics of economic growth leads beyond the analysis of economic factors to a study of the Psychsiological and sociological determinants of these factors."[4] Karl Marx also emphasised the inter-relationship between institutional factors and economic change. Let us first take the **political factors,** which include political sovereignty of the country, the complexion of its government—whether it is development-conscious or is completely laissez-faire in its outlook or is dominated by vested interests who would oppose bitterly any departure from the status quo, the quality of administration, and the political ideology of the government, particularly in relation to the problems of development. Compare in this connection the faith of the Indian Government in democratic planning with the authoritarian planning pursued in China.

Social and Cultural Factors are no less important and are very extensive in scope. In a work like this, we can at best just mention a few of them. Each society has certain social institutions which have a strong bearing on economic development. In India, for example, the institutions of caste, joint families, non-materialistic attitude of the people, and their fatalism based on the philosophy of **karma** have been some of the serious impediments to economic

4. Kaldor, N.—*An Expenditure Tax*, 1955, p. 180.

development. Any attempt at accelerating development must aim at changing these age-long institutions and a fundamental change in the outlook and attitudes of the people must be brought about. Similarly, the prevalence of custom as against contract and the religious taboo among large sections of the population against usury are still other examples of social factors that inhibit the growth of the economy. Likewise, the rampant illiteracy among the people in under-developed countries and their apathy towards the multiplication of their numbers, are the other social factors which hinder economic development.

Naturally, the various relevant social and cultural factors will have to be suitably adapted before the tempo of economic development can be expected to quicken. "Planned development in the economically backward countries, mostly sponsored and engineered by governments, has meant the superimposition of an advanced form of economic structure on a social foundation which is ill-fitted to bear the burden."[5] Naturally, the economic growth is slow.

Conclusion

The factors that go into the process of economic growth are numerous, since this process involves the transformation of the entire economy. All facets of the economy have to be affected. We have mentioned a few of the important factors and in conclusion we may again sum up the basic determinats of economic growth which are: The natural resources like the mineral, forest, water and power resources, geographical factors like climate and rainfall, the size, composition and the quality, *i.e.*, the efficiency of population in the matter of education, skill, health, sense of discipline and patriotism, spirit of co-operation, ability and willingness to work and above all their character, entrepreneurial and organising ability, social and institutional factors conducive to economic effort, stable and helpful government keen on economic development and welfare of the people, clean and efficient administration, favourable external factors facilitating foreign aid and stimulating foreign contacts, and so on.

HARROD-DOMAR GROWTH MODELS

The classical economists laid stress on savings and accumulation of capital and the role of investment and technology in economic growth. They thus concentrated on the supply side of the problem of economic growth. The demand for capital was taken for granted. But this is true of the mature economies in which investment, *i.e.*, the demand for capital tends to lose its momentum. The problem of demand for capital or investment received Keynes' attention. In his 'General Theory,' Keynes analysed the aggregate problem like the levels of output, income and employment, savings, investment, *etc*. But Keynes' was a short-run analysis and excepting his emphasis on savings and role of expectations, it was mainly static, whereas analysis of economic growth has to be dynamic since it involves changes of some fundamental variables in the economy. But Keynesian analysis opened the way for dynamic analysis, *i.e.*, analysis of the problems of growth. The tools of economic analysis forged by him, *viz*., multiplier and the accelerator (introduced by J.M. Clark) have been used by modern economists in growth analysis. They have used his analysis of saving as a demand reducing factor and investment as demand generating factor to examine the role of these factors in economic growth.

Sir Roy F. Harrod, 1900-1978.

Thus, Keynesian analysis and concepts have furnished the basis for modern models of economic growth. The foundations of modern growth analysis lie in the ideas and concepts contained in Keynes's book, 'General Theory of Employment, Interest and Money.'

How Keynesian Economics has been used in the analysis of economic growth will be clear from the growth models given by Harrod, Domar and others. Harrod[6] and Domar[7] analysised the dynamic nature of investment and demand and showed how variations in capital and in demand were responsible for instability in economic growth.

We have studied above the main determinants of economic growth, *viz*., natural resources, rate of savings and capital, formation, technological progress, population growth, *etc.* These determinants of economic growth influence the rate of growth by influencing two important factors: (*a*) The Rate of Investment and (*b*) Capital-output Ratio. Hence, the rate of economic growth in a country, *i.e.*, growth of G.N.P. depends on the rate of investment and capital-output ratio.

5. Bright Singh, D.—*Economic Development*, p. 100.

6. Harrod, R.F. — *Towards Dynamic Economics.*
7. Domar, E.D., *Essays in the Theory of Economic Growth.*

We give below Harrod-Domar growth equations:—[8]

If G_y is taken to represent proportionate increase in income, I is investment and $\frac{\Delta Y}{\Delta K}$ extra capital stock and the resultant output, *i.e.*, capital-output ratio, then the following equation will give the growth rate:

$$G_y = \frac{1}{Y} \times \frac{\Delta Y}{\Delta K} \quad \ldots \quad \ldots \quad \ldots \quad (1)$$

In a balanced growth economy, saving (S) is equal to I (investment), we can, therefore, write $\frac{I}{Y}$ as $\frac{S}{Y}$ and $\frac{S}{Y}$ is written merely as 's' representing savings ratio—the fraction of income saved. Then equation (1) can be written as

$$G_y = s \times \frac{\Delta Y}{\Delta K} \quad \ldots \quad \ldots \quad \ldots \quad (2)$$

While discussing the determinants of economic growth, we mentioned the important role of the concept of capital-output ratio. If each unit of a given capital stock yields larger output, the rate of economic growth will be higher. For instance, if a machine worth Rs. 5,000, produces output worth Rs. 1,000 the capital-output ratio is $\frac{\text{Rs.}5{,}000}{\text{Rs.}1{,}000}$ *i.e.*, 5 and if capital worth Rs. 10,000 produces goods worth Rs. 2,500, the capital output ratio is $\frac{\text{Rs.}10{,}000}{\text{Rs.}2{,}500}$ or 4, and so on. Thus capital-output ratio is simply the inverse of the annual return on (productivity of) capital. If the capital-output ratio is 5, the return is 20 per cent and if it is 4, the return is 25 per cent. The capital-output ratio is represented by the symbol *v*. '*v*' represents the actual marginal capital-output ratio. That is, it shows the extra amount of capital invested divided by the extra output, obtained. Hence, $\frac{\Delta Y}{\Delta K}$ in equation (1) above is the inverse of the marginal capital-output ratio. It shows the marginal increment of output (income) produced by a marginal increment of nation's capital stock. Hence, $\frac{\Delta y}{\Delta k}$ in equation (1) can be written as $\frac{1}{v}$ and equation (2) can be written as

$$G_y = s \times \frac{1}{v} \quad \text{or}$$

$$G_y = \frac{s}{v} \quad \ldots \quad \ldots \quad \ldots \quad (3)$$

This equation (3) means that increase in output during any period is equal to extra units of capital invested multiplied by the output obtained from each unit of capital invested.

Warranted Growth Rate. Equation (3) only tells us what has happened (*i.e.*, output actually obtained from a certain amount of capital invested). But it does not say whether this growth is satisfactory or not from the point of view of a steady growth of the economy or from the point of view of the entrepreneur. The fundamental equation for growth rate which the entrepreneurs would find just satisfactory from the point of profitability can be put down in the following form.:

$$G_w = \frac{s}{v_r} \quad \ldots \quad \ldots \quad \ldots \quad (4)$$

Prof. Harrod has called G_w as the warranted rate of growth. The entrepreneurs would regard this rate of growth as just satisfactory and would like it to be repeated. That is why 'r' is written on the right side of the equation at the foot of 'v'. This is the overall rate of growth and not the rate of growth relating to certain sectors of the economy which may be rising in some and declining in others.

We may repeat that equation (3) shows what has actually, *i.e.*, the growth rate actually realised but not the rate which the entrepreneurs as a whole would consider just satisfactory and worthwhile repeating. This latter rate is shown in equation (4). It is the warranted rate of growth (G_w) which is considered just satisfactory and the entrepreneurs would like it to be repeated. The growth rate shown in equation (3) depends on circumstances varying with economic fluctuations—booms and slumps. But the growth rate of equation (4) is deliberate and is based on technological progress. This shows the rate of increase in output arising from the extra amount of capital invested on the basis of existing state of technical knowledge and the existing production techniques. This increase in output is regarded as optimally profitable. Thus, V_r is determined by capital-output ratio which is governed by the currently accepted production techniques and the acceptable rate of profit.

Hence, at the warranted rate of growth (G_w), the growth of the economy as a whole would be regarded as satisfactory. It may be regarded as an equilibrium

8. Stonier and Hauge. *A Textbook of Economic Theory*, 1971, pp. 593-599.

rate of growth in the sense that it would perpetuate itself.

Natural Growth Rate. It is not necessary that the warranted growth rate should be in keeping with the available natural and human resources. That rate would be called 'the natural rate of growth.' We may show it by Gn. It is the rate of growth which can be achieved by the optimum utilisation of all the resources of the economy. The rate of population growth and the rate of technical progress are the two most important factors that determine the natural rate of growth. It is assumed that there is no unemployed labour that can be drawn upon and there is no further scope of technical improvement so that the number of workers is fixed and their efficiency (*i.e.*, productivity per worker) has reached the peak as a once-for-all process.

If 'l' represents population growth and 't' technical progress, the natural growth rate (G_n) will be shown by the following equation:—

$$G_n = 1 + t \quad \ldots \quad \ldots \quad \ldots \quad (5)$$

Harrod-Domar Model. The fundamental equation (3) given above, *i.e.*, $G_y = \frac{s}{v}$ has been called the "Harrod-Domar Equation." In view of its basic character and of being widely known and accepted model of growth, we explain it by a numerical illustration to make it easily understandable as under:

$$G_y = \frac{s}{v} = s \times \frac{1}{v}$$

['s' is investment and 'v' is the capital-output ratio.]

$$\therefore \quad \text{Growth Rate} = \text{Investment} \times \frac{1}{\text{Capital-Output ratio}}.$$

Suppose investment rate is 10 per cent of the national income and capital-output ratio is 4, then

$$\text{Growth rate} = \frac{10}{4} = 2.5.$$

This hypothetical country has achieved a growth rate of 2.5 per cent in its national income or output.

Harrod and Domar Compared. Profs. Harrod and Domar, though working independently, reached similar conclusions and constructed similar growth equations but they were not exactly the same. Domar's equation aimed at showing that growth in the output which would fully utilise the additional productive capacity created by a given amount of capital accumulation. He arrived at the conclusion that investment must rise quickly and sufficiently to absorb all the savings arising out of the rising incomes in a growing economy. He represented this by the equation:

$$\frac{\Delta I}{I} = sa \quad \ldots \quad \ldots \quad \ldots \quad (8)$$

Here I is investment, ΔI is increase in investment. s the proportion of income saved and a is the capital-output ratio.

This equation, therefore, means that the investment growth rate $\left(\frac{\Delta I}{I}\right)$ must be equal to the proportion of income saved (s) multiplied by the capital-output ratio (a) assuming full employment.

If you compare equation (3) and equation (6) you will find that the result given by the right-hand sides of the two equations is the same. Domar multiplies s by the capital-output ratio and Harrod divides s by the capital-output ratio. The difference is due to the fact that Domar is concerned with finding the rate of investment (growth of the rate of income with constant capital-output ratio) which would provide full employment. On the other hand, Harrod concerned himself with three types of growth rates. His equation (4) dealing with warranted growth rate $\left(G_y = \frac{S}{V_r}\right)$ approximates to Domar's equation. But there is no guarantee that warranted growth would ensure full employment. That is why Harrod brings in the natural growth rate (Gn) to hit on the growth rate which would provide full employment. Again, full employment of labour does not necessarily mean the full employment of capital assets. Domar's equation provides for full employment simultaneously of both labour and capital assets. Harrod gives a series of equations to a complete growth theory whereas Domar does it by one equation.

RELATION BETWEEN POPULATION GROWTH AND ECONOMIC GROWTH

For effecting a significant improvement in living standards, the rate of capital formation and the consequent rate of growth of output must be viewed in relation to the rate of population growth. It may be that the population may be increasing so fast as to offset even a quick rate of capital formation and the resultant increase in output. It is, therefore, necessary to ensure that the rates of population growth and of capital formation must be such as to yield a high per capita output.

Conflicting opinions have been expressed by economists as to whether population growth is a stimulant to economic growth or an obstacle in the way. Owing to inadequate response to agricultural production to meet the requirements of a growing population, Malthus and Richardo dreaded a rapid increase in population and thought it would spell misery and starvation. But with the remarkable growth of industry, world trade and revolution in agricultural techniques the bogey of over-population was laid at rest and the western economists veered round to the view that growth of population stimulated economic growth.

Prof. Hansen regards a high rate of population growth as one of the conditions for economic expansion. Prof. Arthur Lewis shows how a capitalist economy expands by drawing on cheap labour from the subsistence sector of the economy. Prof. Colin Clark feels that the neo-Malthusian fear is very much exaggerated. Prof. Hirschman holds the view that the pressure of population will be a stimulant to economic growth. At the World Population Conference at Rome in 1954, Prof. Alfred Bonne expressed the view that the bogey of overpopulation should not be exaggerated. At the same Conference, the Russian economist Ryabushkin stressed the need for considering the dynamics of population along with the dynamics of production or the possibilities of increasing production when population grows.[9]

Let us see how population growth can stimulate economic growth. Population growth means an increase in the supply of labour. Now the economic significance of labour lies in the fact that labour is both a producer and a consumer. The contribution of population to economic growth is determined by its impact on consumption and production. Increase in population increases consumption and strengthens the inducements to invest which results in increase in output. The increase in the supply of labour, of course, directly increases production when all workers can be put on productive employment. Thus increase in population means an increase in demand for goods or expansion in the size of the market which promotes economic development. When the market for goods is enlarged, scale of production is increased with the resultant economies of large-scale production. The economic history of America and Europe and of other developed countries shows that an increase in their population accelerated their economic growth.

But what is true of the developed countries cannot be true of the under-developed countries. The economists who say that growth of population helps in economic growth do not seem to understand the realities of the situation prevailing in the under-developed countries. The extent to which population growth stimulates economic growth does not depend much on the increase of number but also on its organisation, the availability of complementary resources, the techniques of production, and so on. So long as size of the population is small in relation to land and capital resources, growth in its size will undoubtedly promote economic development. But if a country is overpopulated and there is deficiency of capital, growth of population will be inimical to economic growth.

Hence, whether growth in population is beneficial to economic growth or not depends on the present size of the population and the availability of natural and capital resources and existing technology. In America and Europe, where the supply of capital and other resources is relatively abundant and where technology is in an advanced state, the increase in population increases output. But in under-developed countries like India, where population is already excessive and, on the top of it, it increases at an explosive rate, and where natural resources and capital equipment in relation to population are scarce, the growth of population instead of helping economic growth hinders it.

Thus, population growth can be beneficial to economic growth and it can bring about an increase in national income only if along with increase in population the supply of capital and other resources also increases. But, as pointed out already, if natural and other resources are in short supply in relation to the existing population, growth of population will increase unemployment instead of increasing the national output.

As we have already said, economic development requires an increase in the supply of capital equipment. The supply of capital goods can be increased by raising the level of investment. But the rate of investment can be increased only if the rate of savings is increased. Now increase in population increases the number of consumers and hence the level of consumption which in turn reduces the capacity to save and the rate of investment. Thus, in the under-developed countries, increase in populations reduces the rates of saving and investment on account of which economic growth is impeded. Hence, in a situation like that of India, growth of population is an impediment to economic growth.

Whereas, on the one hand, rapid growth of population in the under-developed countries reduces the rate of investment, it increases the necessity for increasing investment, on the other. In a situation of rapidly growing population, a higher rate of investment is required to bring about a significant increase in per capita output. Suppose the country *A*'s population is increasing at the rate of 1 per cent per annum and country *B*'s at the rate of 3 per cent per annum. If the

9. For these references see Bright Singh, D.— *Eco nomic Development*, pp. 115- 117.

capital-output ratio is 3 : 1, the country *A* will have to invest 3 per cent of its national income to maintain its per capita income at the existing level, whereas the country *B* will have to invest 9 per cent of its national income to keep its per capital income at the existing level. Hence, if population is increasing at a rapid rate, relatively greater effort and higher investment will be required to achieve a given rate of economic growth.

Population growth prevents the per capita income from rising substantially. The under-developed countries have to make a supreme effort to increase their national income so that the per capita income of the people may rise and their standard of living may be raised. But the rapid increase in their population nullifies all their efforts in this direction. Owing to greater increase in population along with increase in national income, the per capita income does not rise significantly. Asoka Mehta has very aptly remarked that population growth is like a thief who robs us of the benefit of economic development. Hence, increase in population swallows up the major part of increase in national income on account of which there can be no significant rise in the per capita income and in the level of living. This is what has happend in India in the era of planned economic development.

In India, national income increased by 18 per cent in the First Plan and 20 per cent in the Second Plan, whereas increase in the per capita income respectively was only 8 per cent and 9 per cent nearly. Similarly, whereas in the Third Plan, national income increased by 13.5 per cent, the per capita income increased by only 1 per cent. This highlights the adverse effect of a rapid population growth which is responsible for a far lower increase in the per capita income as compared with the increase in the national income.

Thus, it is clear that a rapid increase in population is a great obstacle in the economic growth of under-developed but over-populated countries. It can be beneficial to economic growth only if there are present some pre-conditions which are altogether lacking in the under-developed countries, *e.g.*, if social attitudes and values of the people are conducive to economic progress. They should have the will and preparedness to face and surmount economic difficulties and turn seeming obstacles into opportunities for economic advance.

Critical Minimum Effort Thesis

The economic, political and social conditions in under-developed countries are such as to make their growing population inimical to economic growth. Most of the economists are of the view that many under-developed countries, especially of the South East Asian countries, are over-populated and the population pressure is a great barrier in the way of their economic development and unless this barrier is broken all efforts at accelerating economic growth will prove futile.

However, a way out of this population barrier has been suggested in the form of a 'critical minimum effort.' The 'Critical Minimum Efforts' thesis has been put forward by Prof. Harvey Leibenstein[10]. According to him, the under-developed over-populated countries are in a Malthusian **Under-employment Equilibrium** position based on a subsistence structure. He quotes Dupont's capillarity thesis according to which when a community realises that there are greater chances to rise socially with a fewer children than with a larger family, there is a change in social attitudes and strong motivation for restricting the family as per capita income rises.

Leibenstein bases his thesis on the assumption that population is an increasing function of income up to a certain level of income, but beyond that point it is a decreasing function of income. In a low income group, the cost of rearing children is low but their utility in the form of early employment is high. Hence, population has a tendency to increase rapidly. But to a high income group, whose social attitudes are assumed to have changed, the significance of children as contributors to family income is reduced, but the cost of bringing them is high. Hence, there is a strong motive to restrict the size of the family.

Thus, it follows that if a country is to break the population barrier and to come out of the under-employment equilibrium trap, the per capita income must be raised sufficiently high. For this purpose, a certain minimum amount of investment has to be made which has been called the **'critical minimum effort.'**

The initial increase in the per capita income, necessary to displace the under-employment equilibrium, can be secured by (*a*) procuring foreign capital in a sufficiently large amount, (*b*) technological innovations and improvements and (*c*) emigration. The initial rise in the per capita income will set in motion forces which will ultimately take the income level to a sufficiently high level so as to act as a brake on population growth. The point to be emphasised is that per capita income must rise sufficiently high if it is to be effective in brining down the rate of population growth so that further increase in per capita income and investment becomes easier. We may then say that the economy has reached the self-sustained stage.

How long will it take to reach this stage? No dogmatic or straight answer can be given to this question. It will all depend on (*a*) the magnitude of the initial increase in the per capita income; (*b*) the capital-labour ratio; (*c*) the rate of population growth; and (*d*) how rapidly the social attitudes changes. Thus, if incomes rise more rapidly and population rises

10. Leibenstein, Harvey—*A Theory of Economic Demographic Development.* 1954, and *Economic Backwardness and Economic Growth*, 1957, pp. 164-167.

slowly, it will take less time to reach the point of time beyond which further growth of income and investment becomes easier. Hence, in over-populated and under-developed economies, economic development can be secured if a sufficiently large investment is made in the income generating projects. When a sufficiently high level of incomes is reached, the rate of population growth will slow down and the rate of economic growth will be accelerated. Since there is a biologically determined maximum population growth rate, it is possible to have sufficiently high level of investment to break the population barrier.

Leibenstein conceives of a critical minimum effort in terms of this initial investment and the resultant increase in income. Any effort below this minimum will be futile. The investment will be a waste from the point of view of growth. Growing population will simply eat up whatever has been achieved so that the country either stands still or goes backward instead of marching forward. That is why Leibenstein argues that the backward economies remain backward because the "efforts to escape backwardness be they spontaneous or forced, are below the critical minimum required for persistent growth."[11]

Limitations. 'The critical minimum effort thesis' seems to be plausible but suffers from serious limitations from the point of view of its practical significance :

(i) Dependence on foreign capital is precarious: emigration may be ruled out in view of stringent immigration laws of the countries where it would be worthwhile migrating to; and technological innovations cannot be made to order. In the absence of these, the initial rise in income can be secured by lowering consumption and thus increasing the rate of savings and investment. The sacrifice will be much greater, probably beyond the capacity of the country to bear, because the investment required out of current domestic resources will be much larger.

(ii) The under-developed countries lack reliable statistics on the basis of which it is possible to know the exact population, its rate of growth, the size of the capital stock, the level of income, the rates of saving and investment and the extent to which investment should increase to produce a much higher increase in income, and so on. Accurate knowledge of production functions of the various factors of production is required. It is rather too much for an under-developed country to have this information.

(iii) The level of investment which can have perceptible influence on population growth and produce the required increase in income is beyond the capacity of most of the under-developed countries. For instance, if we assume a population growth of 1.7 per cent per year and per capita income at $65 (which were the average rates in the ECAFE region excluding Japan in 1956) and capital-output ratio of 3 : 1, the investment required to increase per capita income by 3 per cent a year would be 14.1 per cent of national income.[12] But it would take 24 years for the per capital. income to double at 3 per cent increase per year. To double income in a shorter period, say 10 years, it would require an investment of 26.1 per cent of the national income (under the same assumptions). This is obviously beyond the capacity of the under-developed countries. This would mean cutting of consumption to an extent as would adversely affect labour productivity.

(iv) The 'critical minimum effort' thesis assumes that a sufficiently high increase in per capita income will reduce the rate of population growth. This implies that there is a direct relation between increase in income and downward trend in population growth. It also assumes that if increase in income is only moderate, the rate of population growth will increase. Actually, however, the population problem in the backward countries is too complex a problem to lend itself to such simple mathematical formulae. It is a social problem and as such it is profoundly influenced by customs, religious beliefs, social attitudes, cultural patterns, *etc*., and not merely by changes in income. Hence, it is necessary to attack the problem on the social front and not merely on the economic front to break the population barrier.

Conclusion. In spite of these limitations, it has to be conceded that there is a great deal of substance in the 'critical minimum effort' thesis. The population barrier can be broken by making an efficient and optimum use of labour so as to increase its productivity. If there is lack of complementary factors, say capital, they must be imported. The capital-output ratio should be lowered by devising capital-saving technological improvements, by making more economical use of the existing capital resources, avoiding all waste in the use of plants and equipment. It would be possible to increase the level of incomes by such measures without any back-breaking investment. The resources made available by enlarged incomes should be carefully mobilised and efficiently utilised by appropriate fiscal, monetary and trade policies so that further rise in incomes can be secured without much difficulty.

RELEVANCE OF HARROD-DOMAR MODEL FOR DEVELOPING COUNTRIES

Harrod-Domar models were formulated primarily to protect the developed countries from

11. Leibenstein, Harvey—*Economic Backwardness and Economic Growth*, 1960, pp. 45.

12. U.N.—*Economic Bulletin for Asia and Far East*, June 1959, p. 39.

chronic unemployment and they were not meant to provide guidelines to the developing economies in their economic development. Since they were formulated primarily for the developed countries they were based on high propensity to save and a correct estimate of the capital-output ratio, which should remain fixed over time. On the other hand, the main problem of the under-developed countries is to raise their propensity to save because it is generally low there. Nor is it possible to assume a fixed value of the capital-output ratio. This ratio happens to be very high in such countries. Thus the two important bases of the Harrod-Domar models are non-existent in the case of developing economies. Further, the nature of unemployment problem in developing countries is different from that in the developed countries. It is cyclical unemployment due to deficiency of demand in the developed economies and it is disguised unemployment in the developing economies. In developed economies, unemployment can be removed by raising the level of investment so that aggregate demand increases which was not keeping pace with the growth of productive capacity. In the developing economies there is unemployment because available productive capacity is inadequate to employ fully the existing labour force. Thus in such countries, the rate of investment is to raise productive capacity rather than aggregate demand and fully utilise the existing idle capacity.

Evsly Domar, 1914-1997.

Thus we see that the peculiar conditions prevalent in the developing countries *e.g.* disguised unemployment, low propensity to save and low productive capacity make the Harrod-Domar model in applicable to them. Also, these models assume no government intervention, fixed prices and no institutional changes. All these assumptions too make these models inappropriate for the developing economies.

But we should not reject these models wholesale and emphasise their inapplicability to developing economies. With slight modifications and reinterpretation they can be made to furnish suitable guide-lines even for the developing economies. In some cases, it is only a question of changing the emphasis. For instance, Domar's model recognizes the capacity creating role of investment. But it is intended to increase effective demand in developed countries, while in developing countries, the capacity creating role of investment is to be seen as a means of overcoming the problem of unemployment. Hence to make the model applicable to the developing countries Domar's model has to be suitably reinterpreted.

Key terms

Economic development, Determinants of growth, Stages of economic development, Harrod-Domar growth model, Critical minimum effort, warranted growth rate, National growth rate.

QUESTIONS

1. What are the basic determinants of economic growth ? How far are they present in India?
2. Comment on the Harrod-Domar model regarding economic grwoth. How far is it relevant to developing economy in India?
3. Distinguish between economic growth and economic development.
4. Explain Rustun's Stages of economic development.
5. Discuss the applications of Harrod-Domar model to under-development countries what are its merits and demerits?
6. What are the basic determinants of economic growth? How far are they present in India?
7. Comment on the Harrod-Domar model regarding economic growth. How far is it relevant to developing economy like India?

STRATEGY OF ECONOMIC DEVELOPMENT : BALANCED AND UNBALANCED GROWTH

Just as a war cannot be won without a suitable strategy, similarly the objective of rapid economic development cannot be achieved without adopting an appropriate strategy. It implies the most effective way of utilising the available resources of the country. Strategy, however, does not mean a set of magic rules which will at once take us to the goal of economic development. It is only comprised of the major decisions that go into the making of a development plan. Thus, the major elements in the plan strategy are the size of the plan, the pattern of investment envisaged in the plan, the allocation of investment among the various sectors of the economy, the techniques of resource mobilisation, the policy, mix, *etc.*, appropriate fiscal policy, monetary policy, policy regarding controls, extent of reliance on foreign, *etc.*

Types of Strategies

The strategies known to the planners commonly are :

(1) Balanced *vs*. Unbalanced Growth.

(2) Big Push Strategy.

(3) Balanced, Unbalanced, Big Push (B.U.B.) Strategy.

We reserve balanced *vs*. unbalanced growth strategy for detailed discussion.

Big Push Strategy

The 'Big Push' strategy is associated with the name of Rosenstein-Rodan and Harevy Leibenstein. It is contended that a big push is needed to overcome the initial inertia of a stagnant economy. Rosenstein-Rodan observes: "There is a minimum level of resources that must be devoted to a development programme if it is to have any chance of success. Launching a country into self-sustaining growth is like getting an airplane off the ground. There is a critical ground speed which must be passed before the craft can become airborne."[1] According to Leibenstein, it is not advisable for an economy to inch along the path of development, the economy must cover a certain distance in one leap or it does not move at all.

1. Notes on *Theory of Big Push*, 1957, p. 47.

Balanced, Unbalanced, Big Push

The advocates of this strategy suggest that no single strategy will take us to the goal of economic development. Not only has the strategy to be changed from time to time as the situation may require, but it may be necessary sometimes to strike a balanced between the alternative strategies.

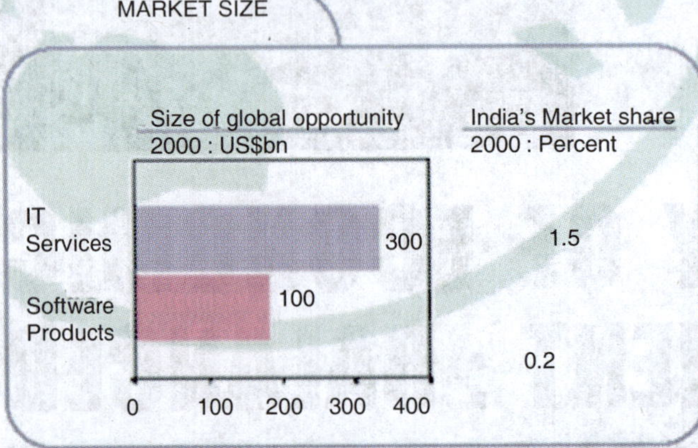

Market size.

In the initial stages characterised by imbalance, counter-imbalances will be a more effective remedy. But once an appropriate balance is attained by a fair dose of big push, the strategy of balanced growth may be applied to further planning.

The strategy adopted in Indian planning may be described as balanced B.U.B., *i.e.*, a happy compromise of Balanced, Unbalanced and Big Push strategies. More prominent, however, is the strategy of balanced growth. This is indicated by varying emphasis on a single aspect in successive plans, *e.g.*, self-sufficiency in food in the First Plan, rapid industrialisation in the Second Plan, self-sustaining growth in the Third Plan and growth with stability in the Fourth Plan.

Let us now turn to the study of Balanced *vs.* Unbalanced Growth.

BALANCED VS. UNBALANCED GROWTH

Currently, there are among the development specialists two major schools of thought regarding the pattern and process of growth according to which development should take place. On the one side, there are economists, like Ragnar Nurkse and Rosentsein-Rodan who are of the view that the pattern of investment should be so designed as to ensure a balanced development of the various sectors of the economy. They, therefore, advocate simultaneous investment in a number of industries so that there is a balanced growth of different industries. Economists, like H.W. Singer and A.O. Hirschman, on the other side, believe that rapid economic growth follows **concentration** of investment in certain strategic industries rather than an even distribution of investment among the various industries. In other words, in the view of these latter economists, unbalanced growth is more conducive to economic development than a balanced one. We may now pause to consider both these views at some length.

In an earlier chapter,[2] we explained how the under-developed countries are caught up in a vicious circle of poverty. We also pointed out how difficult it is to break this vicious circle. We explained how the vicious circle of poverty operates both on the demand side of capital formation as well as on the supply side of capital formation. Nurkse has put forward the doctrine of balanced growth (which we shall discuss presently) in order to break the vicious circle of poverty on the demand side of capital formation. It will be useful to have again a cursory look on the vicious circle.

In an under-developed country, the level of per capita income is low which means that the people's purchasing power is low. Owing to small incomes and low purchasing power their demand for consumer goods is low. As a result of low demand for goods, the inducement for investment is less and capital equipment per capita (*i.e.*, per worker) is small. Since the amount of capital per capita is small productivity per worker is low. Low per capita productivity means low per capita income, *i.e.*, poverty. This completes the vicious circle of poverty. In a poor country, the size of the market for goods is small so that sufficient opportunities for profitable investment in trade and industry are lacking. This is the main reason for lack of inducement to invest which we discuss presently.

Size of Market and Inducement to Invest

Investment means the expenditure on the making and installation of capital goods, *e.g.*, construction of factories and the making of machines and their installation, execution of irrigation and power projects, the construction of roads, railway, *etc.* Obviously, an entrepreneur will be induced to invest in factories, machinery, *etc.*, if he expects sufficient return on his investment. Businessmen will have incentive to invest only from a motive of earning a profit. It is the expectation of profit which is a fundamental factor

2. Chapter 72.

influencing the amount of investment in a country at a given time. In a poor country, the low level of investment is due to low expectations of profit because of less demand for goods or a small size of the market.

Let us understand clearly why there is less inducement to invest in a poor country. It is easily understandable that, in under-developed countries, there is a great need for capital for economic development. People are too poor even to have two square meals a day or a reasonable housing accommodation or clothing to cover their bodies. Hence, there is an urgent need for large-scale production of consumer' goods, but it cannot be done without the production and use of capital goods in large quantities. Agricultural improvements, the establishment and expansion of industries, the optimum use of the natural resources and harnessing the natural resources into the service of the people, all require capital. The need for capital can be great but the inducement to invest can be weak. The level of investment depends not on the need for capital but on the inducement to invest in the form of attraction to earn profit from the capital invested. Without reasonable expectations of profit, much capital will not flow into investment.

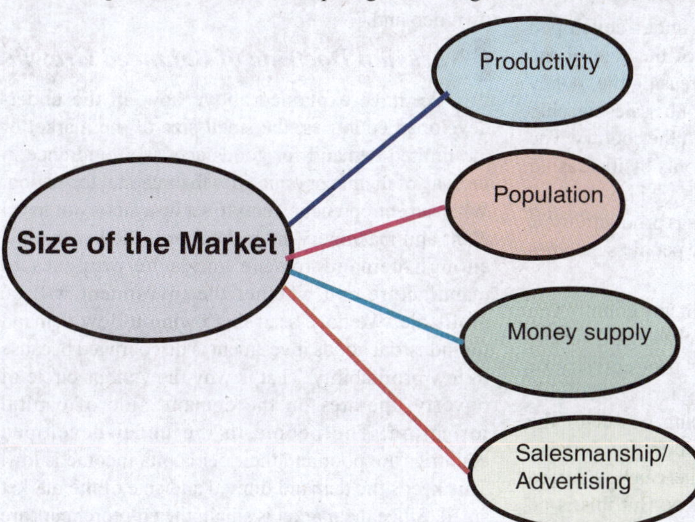

The quantity of profitable investment in a country depends on the size of the market. Adam Smith said, "Division of labour is limited by the size of the market." We can say in the same manner that inducement to invest depends on the size of the market. Inducement to invest, in the last analysis, depends on the size of the demand or market. The small size of the market or the low level of demand for the products concerned discourages the entrepreneurs from investing.

This will be clear from an illustration. In a modern dairy, milking, filling up bottles and their loading all these operations are done with the aid of automatic machinery. Will the installation of such a machinery in every Indian town be profitable for individual entrepreneurs? Obviously, it will not be profitable. Per capita income being low in India, the demand for milk in each town will be too small to make a full use of such automatic machinery. Such costly plant and machinery will remain mostly idle and there will be work for such a machinery only for a few hours during a week. This means a great waste of valuable capital asset. Which entrepreneur dare start such a business? As an inducement to invest, the entrepreneurs should be sure that the capital equipment will be profitably employed. This will be possible only if the machinery can be kept in continuous use, and this cannot be done unless there is sufficient demand for the products made by this machinery.

Take another example Suppose the handmade cloth is very attractive and it can fetch a very high price. But it will not be economical to instal a big machine to make a cloth of a special design because owing to its high price and low incomes of the people, there will not be sufficient demand for this type of cloth *i.e.,* the market will be too small. In America, the cars are cheap but they are very expensive in India. What is the reason? The sole reason is that the demand for cars in India as compared with that in America is so small that the manufacturers of cars cannot be induced to make them in large quantities which would have made them cheap on account of the economies of scale. Examples can be multiplied. The conclusion is clear than inducement to invest depends on the size of the market or the purchasing power of the people.

It may be clearly understood that in the under-developed countries, demand for consumer goods cannot be increased merely by the expansion of the money supply in the country. The real demand will increase only if there is increase in the productivity per worker and as a result thereof there is increase in the real per capita income. By mere expansion of money supply and thus putting more money into people's pockets demand can increase only in the form of money which result in inflation or higher prices, but not increase in the real aggregate demand.

Similarly, the demand for goods or the size of the market cannot be large merely because a country is big or its population is large. If the purchasing power of the people is low because of their extreme poverty, the demand for goods in that country will be small or the size of the market will be small even though the country is big in size or its population is large.

Similarly, in poor countries, where the people's purchasing power is low on account of low per capita income, the demand for goods, and hence the size of the market, cannot be increased by high pressure salesmanship and vigorous advertising campaign. There should be enough people to buy them.

Thus, it is clear that, in the under-developed countries, the demand for goods, or the size of the market, cannot be increased by increasing the money supply, or by increase in population or by salesmanship and advertisement or the large size of the country. The size of the market can be increased only by increasing productivity. As Nurkse puts it, "The crucial determinant of the size of the market is productivity."[3] Increase in productivity will increase people's incomes and hence their purchasing power.

The level of people's income in any country can be raised and consequently their purchasing power can be increased only by increasing productivity or aggregate output. A situation of higher productivity, higher incomes and high purchasing power of the people will provide a profitable field for investment. It may be said that the size of the market can be enlarged by lowering the price of the products. But this is no solution of the problem. The real solution of the problem is only an increase in productivity. Only as a result of increase in productivity, there is increase in income and increase in purchasing power which will increase demand and enlarge the size of the market.

Say's law propounded by classical economists which we have studied earlier, [4] tells us that production or supply creates its own demand. But this law cannot be accepted in the sense that the production of cloth creates its own demand because the workers engaged in the making of cloth will not spend their entire earnings on the purchase of cloth. In the same way, production of shoes cannot create its own demand. The reason lies the variety of man's demands.

However, Say's law can be applied to some extent to the under-developed countries. If, in the under-developed countries, investment is made simultaneously in a large number of industries, incomes of a large number of workers engaged in these industries, will increase. This will create demand for goods produced by one another. In other words, if investment is made simultaneously in a large number of industries and production is increased, then supply will create its own demand. The Say's law will hold good in such a situation.

Thus, we see that investment in a particular industry and the resultant production or supply cannot create its own demand but simultaneous investment in a number of industries can. As Nurkse says, "An increase in production over a wide range of consumables, so proportioned as to correspond with the pattern of consumer's preferences, does create its own demand."[5]

Nurksian Doctrine of Balanced Growth

We have explained above how, in the under-developed countries, the small size of the market or the limited demand for goods acts as a hindrance in the way of their economic growth or capital formation. When an entrepreneur wants to set up a factory or instal plant and machinery, he makes sure whether there is enough demand for the goods he proposes to manufacture and whether the investment will be profitable. We have seen that owing to low demand for industrial goods investment is discouraged because of low profitability. That is why the vicious circle of poverty operates on the demand side of capital formation. The people in the under-developed countries are poor and their per capita income is low. This keeps the demand limited and size of the market small. Since the market is small, the entrepreneurs are discouraged from investment in plant and machinery on which only large-scale production is possible and economical.

The result is that capital formation in the country is discouraged. Owing to lack of capital, productivity is low and since productivity per worker is low, the per capita income is low which means there is poverty. This is how the vicious circle of poverty operates in the under-developed countries.

According to Nurkse, it is the vicious circle operating in the under-developed countries, which stands in the way of their economic development, and accordingly, if this vicious circle can be broken, economic development will follow. The operation of the vicious circle can also be described thus: Inducement to invest depends ultimately upon demand, *i.e.*, the size of the market, and the size of the market in turn depends upon productivity, because the capacity to buy is ultimately based on the capacity to

3. Nurkse. R.— *Problems of Capital Formation in Under-developed Countries*, p. 8.
4. Chapter 39.

5. *Ibid.*, p. 12.

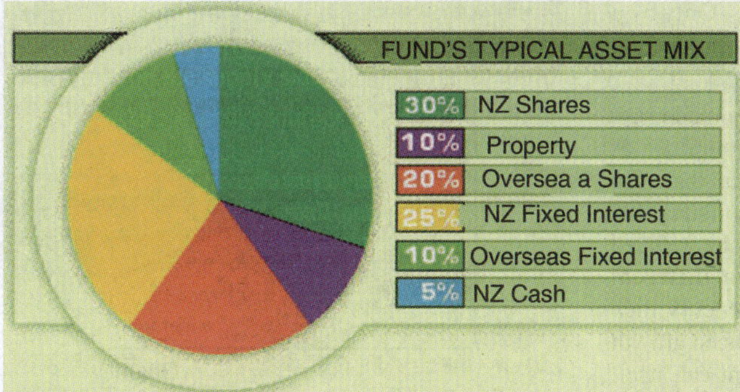

produce. Productivity, in its turn, largely depends on the use of capital. But, for an entrepreneur, the small size of the market will limit the use of capital so that productivity will remain low, thus keeping the size of the market small. The vicious circle will then repeat itself. This vicious circle of poverty, according to Nurkse, can be broken by a simultaneous investment in a large number of industries, *i.e.*, by a balanced economic growth.

We have explained how Say's law cannot be helpful in under-developed countries, if investment is made only in one industry. The output of any single industry newly set up with capital equipment cannot create its own demand. Human wants being diverse, the people engaged in the new industry will not wish to spend all their income on their own products. Suppose a shoe manufacturing industry is set up. If, in the rest of the economy, nothing happens to increase productivity, and hence the buying power of the people, the market for the additional output of shoes is likely to be deficient. People, outside the shoe industry, will not give up the consumption of essential food, clothing, *etc.*, to create a sufficient demand for shoes every year. The supply of shoes is likely to outrun demand, and, thus, the industry is likely to be failure. Hence, if investment is confined only to one particular industry, it cannot prove fruitful.

But if investment is made simultaneously in a large number of industries, it will provide work for a large number of industries, it will provide work for a large number of people producing diverse commodities. It will increase their income and they will be in a position to buy for consumption the goods made by one another. This is how supply can create its own demand (as Say's Law asserts) through the process of balanced growth. The producers become customers of one another's goods and demand is increased or the size of the market is enlarged. The expansion of one industry helps in the expansion of others and there is all round growth. This is how the difficulty arising from small size of the market is overcome and the obstacle in the way of economic growth cleared.

In Nurkse's words, "The difficulty caused by the small size of the market relates to individual investment incentives in any single line of production taken by itself. At least in principle, the difficulty vanishes in the case of more or less synchronised application of capital to a wide range of different industries. Here is an escape from the deadlock; here the result is an overall enlargement of the market. People, working with more and better tools in a number of complementary projects become each other's customers. Most industries catering for mass consumption are complementary in the sense that they provide a market for, and thus support, each other. This basic complementarily stems in the last analysis from the diversity of human wants. The case for balanced growth rests on the need for a balanced diet."[6]

Taken separately, a number of industries may be unprofitable so that the private profit motive would not suffice to induce investment in these industries. However, undertaken together in a synchronized manner, a balanced increase in production would enlarge the size of the market for each firm or industry so that the "synchronized undertaking" would become profitable. This wave of capital investment in a number of different industries is called by Nurkse **"balanced growth."**

In this way, as we have already said, the hindrance to economic growth owing to the small size of the market is removed. The aggregate demand is increased owing to simultaneous investment in a large number of industries, because the incomes and productivity levels of persons employed in different industries go up. Hence, the under-development equilibrium trap and the vicious circle of poverty can be broken by balanced growth. If once this circle is broken then, since it is a circular connection, this circle will turn from poverty to balanced growth and to all-round development of the economy. In this way, the circle can be given a beneficial form.

Now the question arises: Which industries should be selected for investment? The answer is to be found in the above solution offered by Nurkse. Investment should be made simultaneously in such industries the manufactured products of which are in accordance with the demand or the preferences of the consumers or on which the persons engaged in different industries spend their incomes. These should be complementary projects

6. Nurkse, *op. cit.*, p. 11.

so that they become each other customers. Only by a simultaneous investment in such industries, production or supply will create its own demand.

Then the question is: How is it to be made sure that simultaneous investment in large number of industries is actually made? Nurkse answers that, if in the country there are dynamic and constructive entrepreneurs and industrialists, they can be induced to make investment simultaneously in different industries. If there is lack of such entrepreneurs, then the government can take the work of balanced growth in its own hands. That is the government can itself make simultaneous investment in several industries and can thus increase people's incomes and productivity. As a result of investment in several industries, it will be possible to increase the use of capital goods in large quantities which will raise the level of productivity and there will be a large increase in the aggregate output of consumers goods and service. As a result of this, the level of national income will rise which will help to raise the standard of living of the people. In this way, the poverty of the people will go. What is needed to remove the poverty of the people is to launch an attack on the various sectors of the economy **simultaneously.** This will remove the obstacle arising from limited demand or narrowness of the market and the inducement to investment will increase.

It seems to be proper to refer in this connection to external economies. When one industry creates demand for another, it will be profitable to the other industry. When one industry benefits from the growth of another industry, then we say that external economies are available from one industry to another. We have seen above that it proves profitable to make investment in complementary industries, because people engaged in such industries become one another's customers or create demand for one another. It is clear, therefore, that the doctrine of balanced growth is based on the concept of external economies.

It is to be noted that here we do not use the term 'external economies' in the sense in which Marshall used it. By 'external economies Marshall meant those economies which arise from the localisation of a certain industry in a particular place and these economies are enjoyed by each firm in the industry by the establishment of numerous firms there. But in economic development, by external economies are meant those benefit which accrue to other industries by the establishment of new industries or the extension of the existing industries. We have seen above how, according to Nurkse's doctrine of balanced growth, these benefits accrue to the other industries by the establishment of new industries of the expansion of old industries through simultaneous investment in such

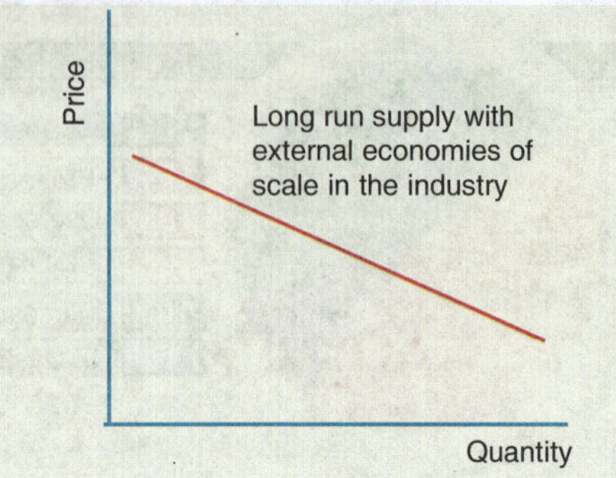

industries in the form or increased demand or extension of the market. In fact, the increasing returns which arise from the process of economic growth, are mainly due to the creation of external economies in the form of extension of the market or increase in demand and not due to the economies mentioned by Marshall such as technical information from the journals, improvement in the technical skill of labour, development in the means of communication and transport, *etc.*, which arise from the location of an industry in a particular place.

It is worthwhile knowing whether, in balanced growth, investment will be made in agriculture or not. Nurkse has not discussed this point in his book **'Problems of Capital Formation in Under-developed Countries.'** But later on he made it clear that in his balanced growth, appropriate investment will be made in agriculture. Thus, he has not ignored agricultural development in his doctrine of balanced growth. In fact, investment in agriculture is implied in his book referred to above, because he has said that investment would be made in such industries simultaneously as produce goods conforming to consumers' demand or preferences. Since when, in the under-developed countries people will get employment in the various industries, they mostly spend their incomes on the foodgrains, investment in agriculture will be necessary to meet their demand and to promote balanced growth.

Nurkse has not made clear in his doctrine of balanced growth whether investment should be made in capital goods industries and social overhead capital like transport and communications, to promote balanced growth. Actually, Nurkse has suggested investment in consumer goods industries. But how will the machinery and capital equipment required in these industries be obtained: If they are not to be imported from abroad, they will have to be produced in the country and for that purpose investment will have to be made in their production.

Thus, we see if the doctrine of balanced growth is to be fully implemented, then investment will have to be made in consumer goods industries,agriculture, capital goods industries and social overhead capital. But when investment is to be made in all such sectors and industries, then, in order to bring about balanced economic growth, large quantities of resources will be required. It is doubtful if the under-developed countries have the moanr to mobilise resources in such large quantities.

Singer's Critique of Balanced Growth Doctrine

Prof. Hans Singer and Albert Hirschman, erninent American economists, have criticized Nurkse's doctrine of balanced growth. They contend that what is needed is not balanced growth, but a strategy of judiciously-planned unbalanced growth.

According to Singer, balanced growth cannot solve the problem of the under-developed countries, nor do they have sufficient resources to achieve balanced growth. Singer maintains that balanced growth doctrine might be better expressed as follows: "As hundred flowers may grow whereas a single flower would wither away for lack of nourishment." But where are the resources to grow hundred flowers? Singer agrees that the slogan "stop thinking piecemeal and start thinking big" is a sound advice for under-developed countries, but he also feels that there are "several areas of doubt" about the balanced growth theory in its Nurksian form.

First, if the balanced growth doctrine is interpreted to advise the under-developed countries to embark on large and varied packages of industrial investment with no attention to agricultural productivity, it can lead to trouble. At the initial stages of development,as the income grows with new industrial investment and employment, the relatively greater demand would be created for food and other agricultural goods. In order to sustain industrial investment, the agricultural productivity would have to be greatly raised. Thus, the big push in industry must be accompanied by a big push in agriculture as well, if the country is not to run short of foodstuffs and agricultural raw materials during the transition to an industrialized society.

But when we start talking about varied investment packages for industry and "major additional blocks of investment in agriculture" at the same time, we run into serious doubts about the capacity of under-developed countries to follow the balanced growth path. Singer quotes Marcus Fleming, "Whereas the balanced growth doctrine assumes that the relationship between industries is for the most part complementary, the limitation of factor supply assures that the relationship is for the most part competitive." Singer adds: "The resources required for carrying out the policy of balanced growth . . . . are of such an order of magnitude that a country disposing of such resources would in fact not be underdeveloped."

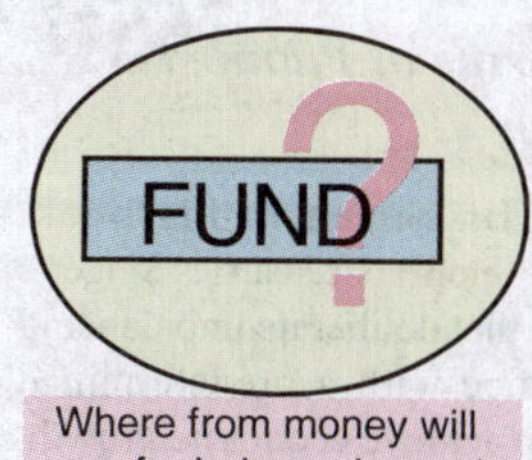

Where from money will come for balanced growth.

Investment may be of whatever type, it necessarily induces some additional investment and some other productive activities. According to Singer, the expansion of social capital overheads and the improvement of production techniques cannot take place simultaneously, because the under-developed countries, have only limited capabilities of making use of their resources. In the under developed countries, not only are the resources and the capabilities to bring about balanced growth lacking but, according to Hirschman, balanced growth lacking but, according to Hirschman, balanced growth is not even desirable. His view is that if economic growth is to be accelerated, it will have to be brought about by unbalanced growth. If we promote growth by creating imbalances in the economy, the growth will be accelerated, because it will produce such incentives and pressures which will encourage development in the private sector.

"The doctrine is premature rather than wrong," Singer concludes. It is applicable to a subsequent stage of self-sustained growth rather than to the breaking of a deadlock. For launching growth "it may well be a better development strategy to concentrate available resources on types of investment which help to make the economic system more elastic, more capable of expansion under the stimulus of expanded markets and expanding demand." He instances investment in social overhead capital and removal of special bottlenecks as examples of such "strategic" investment.

The fundamental trouble with the balanced growth doctrine, Singer further concludes, is its failure to come to grips with the true problem of under-developed countries, the shortage of resources. **"Think Big"** is a sound advice to under-developed countries, but **"Act Big"** is unwise counsel, if it spurs them to bite more than they can possibly chew.

Moreover, the balanced growth doctrine assumes that an under-developed country starts from a scratch. In reality, every under-developed country starts from a position that reflects previous investment and previous development. Thus, at any point of time, there are highly desirable investment programmes which are not in themselves balanced investment packages but which represent unbalanced investment to complement existing imbalance.

Hirschman's Doctrine of Planned Unbalanced Growth

Professor Albert Hirschman in his book, **'Strategy of Economic Development,'** carries Singer's idea further and contends that deliberate unbalancing of economy, in accordance with a predetermined strategy, is the best way to achieve economic growth. Like Singer, he argues that balanced growth theory requires huge amounts of precisely those **abilities** which have been identified as likely to be very limited in supply in the under-developed countries. He characterises the balanced growth doctrine as "the application to under-development of a therapy originally devised for an under-employment situation." In an advanced country, during depression, "industries, machines, managers, and workers as well as the consumption habits" are all present, while in under-developed countries this is obviously not so.

As an under-developed country is incapable of financing and managing simultaneously a balanced "investment package" in industry and the needed investment in agriculture, in order to give a big push to lift an under-developed country from a position of stagnation, Hirschman prescribes big push in strategiclly selected industries or sectors of the economy. After all, he points out, the industrialized countries did not get to where they are now through "balanced growth." True, if you compare the economy of the United States in 1950 with the situation in 1850, you will find that many things have grown, but not everything grew at the same rate throughout the whole century. Development has proceeded "with growth being communicated from the leading sectors of the economy to the followers, from one industry to another; from one firm to another."[7]

According to Professor Hirschman, the real scarcity in under-developed countries is not the resources themselves **"but the ability to bring them into play."** He divides the initial investment into two related activities: (*a*) **directly productive activities,** and (*b*) **social overhead capital.** An under-developed country may follow the method of unbalanced growth by undertaking initial investment either in social overhead capital or the directly productive activities. Whichever the type of investments, it will yield an 'extra dividend' of induced decisions resulting in additional investment and output. He contends that social overhead capital, and directly productive activities cannot be expanded simultaneously, because of the limited ability to utilize resources. Thus, the planning problem is to determine the **sequence** of expansion that will maximize induced decision-making.

Albert O. Hirschman.

Balanced growth (of social overhead capital and directly productive activities) is not only unattainable in most under-developed countries, it may also not be desirable. The rate of growth is likely to be faster with chronic imbalance, precisely because of **"the incentives and pressures"** it sets up.

Having demonstrated the virtues of strategic imbalance, we are left with the problem of discovering what kind of imbalance is likely to be most effective. Any particular investment project may have both **"forward linkage"** (that is, it may encourage investment in subsequent stages of production) and "backward linkage" (that is it may encourage investment in earlier stages of production). The task is to find the projects with greatest **"total linkage."** The projects, with the greatest total linkage, will vary from country to country and from time to time and can be discovered only by empirical studies of the "input-output tables."

In determining the sequence of projects, planning authorities should also give attention to the alternation of **"pressure-creating"** and **"pressure-relieving"** investments. In countries with vigorously expanding private enterprise sectors, the government's function can be largely limited to **"pressure-relieving."** As private investment takes place, shortages and bottlenecks will appear in transport, public utilities, education, and other activities traditionally assigned (in whole or in part) to public enterprise in such societies. Government ought not to feel "restless and slighted" when confined to this "induced role."

Where expansion through private investment is not assured, the government's role must be more active. For example, it might build an iron and steel plant. "It is interesting to note," says Hirschman, "that the industry with the highest combined linkage score is iron and steel. Perhaps the under-developed countries are not foolish and exclusively prestige motivated in attributing prime importance to this industry, because of the high total linkage effects of iron and steel industry." The building of it by the government will lead to a spurt of investment and production in a variety of fields both in the stages before and after this industry. In this way, it accelerates economic growth. The investment in iron and steel industry in turn will reveal

7. Hirschman, A., *Strategy of Economic Development*, pp. 62-63.

deficiencies in the preceding and succeeding sectors of industry that the government must fill up. To remove these deficiencies and obstacles, further investment will be stimulated. When these deficiencies are filled up, further private investment will take place, and so the process of growth goes on.

Conclusion

The foregoing discussion leads us to the conclusion that the balanced growth doctrine is neither attainable nor desirable. On the other hand, for rapid economic development the under-developed countries should rely largely on judiciously-planned unbalanced growth. In fact, Soviet Russia and India have been following this course.

Mahalnobis Strategy of Economic Growth

There has been lot of controversy in our country on the appropriate strategy to be adopted for planned economic development. There was no clear strategy in the First Five-Year Plan. In this plan, emphasis was laid on increasing agricultural production to achieve self-sufficiency in foodgrains and to stabilise prices. That is why agriculture was given top priority in its development outlay.

But when the Second Five-Year Plan was being formulated the question arose as to what strategy should be adopted for the planned development in India. At this time, Prof. P. C. Mahalnobis prepared a growth model in which he showed that to achieve a self-sustained growth quickly in the country, it would be essential to devote major part of the development outlay to building basic heavy industry, *e.g.*, of capital goods industry like steel and the engineering industry for making different types of machines, the multipurpose river valley projects for irrigation and power.

According to Prof. Mahalnobis, the rate of real capital formation in a country like India did not depend merely on savings in the form of money but it depends on the capacity for making capital goods. He said that even if the rate of savings was substantially raised and it was desired to accelerate economic growth and capital formation by investing it in the consumer goods industries, it would be futile. The reason is that the capital goods required for the consumer goods industries are not produced in the country in sufficient quantities.

Thus, Prof. Mahalnobis was of the view that if large investment is not made in the heavy basic industry and capital goods industry, the country will for ever remain dependent on foreign countries for the imports of steel and capital goods like machinery for economic development and real capital formation. Since it is not possible for India to earn sufficient foreign exchange for the purpose by increasing exports, the capital goods cannot be imported in sufficient quantities owing to foreign exchange constraints. The result will be that the rate of economic growth and the rate of real capital formation in the country will be slow indeed.

Prof. Mahalnobis was of the opinion that without adequate investment in heavy basic industry, it was not possible to achieve self-reliant and self-sustained economic growth and the economic development of the country will be dependent on the imports of capital goods from foreign countries. Thus, we see that according to Prof. Mahalnobis, to achieve rapid economic growth and self-reliance, it would be necessary to give a high priority to basic and capital goods industries in the development strategy of a plan.

It is necessary in this connection to mention Prof. Mahalnobis's views on increasing employment opportunities and to achieve a state of full employment. According to him, productive employment can be increased only by increasing the production of capital goods like steel, electricity, machinery, fertilizers, *etc.* Whether it is increase in employment in the agricultural sector or in the industrial sector, it cannot be achieved without increasing the output of capital goods. Thus in Prof. Mahalnobis's opinion, even to achieve full employment, it will be necessary to accord high priority to capital goods industries in the development strategy.

The above development strategy as laid down by Prof. Mahalnobis was adopted in India in the Second and Third Five-Year Plans.

Appraisal. However, Mahalnobis's strategy was subjected to severe criticism, especially by Profs. C. N. Vakil and Brahmanand of Bombay University. They criticised Mahalnobis's strategy suggested for the Second Five-Year Plans. These two economists jointly wrote a book **"Planning for an Expanding Economy"** in which they raised objections against the strategy. According to Profs. Vakil and Brahmanand, the increase in employment in a country depends on increasing the supply of essential consumer's goods and wage goods. When in a country employment is provided to a large number of people, the demand for the essential consumers' goods and wage goods will increase. If these goods cannot be supplied to them, they cannot be given employment. Hence, Profs. Vakil and Brahmanand laid emphasis in the development strategy on large investment in the production of essential consumers goods like foodgrains, cotton textiles, sugar, *etc.* They recommended a growth model in which important place was assigned to agriculture and the essential consumers, goods industries.

Another criticism of Prof. Mahalnobis's strategy is that owing to large investment in the heavy basic industries, there is a great and rapid increase in money incomes on account of which there is great increase in demand for consumers' goods. But their supply cannot be increased quickly or in a short time. The necessary consequence of this state of affairs is a great rise in prices or the creation of an inflationary situation.

Mahalonobis advocated for heavy industry strategy India's development.

Another serious flaw of Mahalnobis's model lies in its assumption of the mutual independence of the productivity coefficient and the technology parameters. How can the two coefficients be independent of each other because the investment per unit of employment directly depends on the productivity of investment?

Further Prof. Mahalnobis assumes investment as a single homogeneous fund which is not correct. This assumption holds only if there is a single type of investment good.

Again his choice with regard to key variables-proportion of investment allocation to the investment goods sector is arbitrary.

Moreover, Prof. Mahalnobis's model suffers from a serious handicap in that it is framed in the capital-output ratios and the capital-labour ratios which have been assumed to be strictly invariant. Production techniques are regarded as rigidly fixed. There is also a rigid and unrealistic assumption about the complete absence of mobility of capital from the consumer goods sector tothe investment - goods sector and even within the investment - goods sector itself.

Prof. Shigeto Tsuru calls the Mahalnobis's model as one-eyed model becuase it pays attention only to the supply side and ignores the demand altogether. Thus it fails to relate the sectoral outputs with sectoral demands.

Inspite of the drawbacks mentioned above, Mahalnobis's model is an operational model of growth amenable to practical use. It provides an actual approach to investment planning which can be adopted for the execution of a plan. It correctly emphasises the fact that a very high proportion of investment needs to be allocated to the investment goods sector to ensure a high level of marginal rate of savings. It also underlines the need to create maximum growth potential for the future.

Key terms

Balanced growth, Size of the market, Unbalanced growth, Directly productive activities, Social overhead capital, Forward Linkage, Capital goods industries.

QUESTIONS

1. State and criticise the Theory of Balance Growth.

   Or

   What do you mean by the concept of 'balanced growth'? Examine the desirability and capacity of the under-developed countries to follow the balance growth path.
2. Analyse the case for and against balanced growth strategy for initiating economic development in developing countries.
3. Distinguish between 'Balance Growth' and the 'Unabalanced Growth' as system of economic development. Which one is more suitable for India?
4. Explain doctrine of unabalanced growth. Do you think it is a sound strategy for the growth of undeveloped countries?
4. What is self-sustained growth? Under what circumstances does it become possible?

78
CHAPTER

INVESTMENT CRITERIA AND CHOICE OF TECHNIQUES

Since the investible resources in the low-income countries are very much limited in face of growing and urgent needs for them, the problem of choosing between alternative employment of these resources assumes great importance. Given the total investment and its distribution over different sectors and given the alternative technical and locational possibilities, the question is how to rank alternative projects so that some of them are preferred to others. For the same level of output, it may be possible to use several alternative techniques or different factor combinations and we have to discover the most economical technique in a given situation. Obviously, for a planned unbalanced growth we must explore suitable criteria for investment, *i.e.*, to discover the main bases on which to determine the distribution of limited investible funds and skills among the numolous claimant fields of investment. We have discussed above the investment criteria of total linkage effects as recommended by Hirschman, which form a part and parcel of his theory of planned unbalanced growth. Now we shall discuss other investment criteria which have been put forward.

There are lots of investment projects to choose from

Cost-Benefit Analysis[1]

While selecting projects for investments out of a number of technically feasible alternatives, the most important consideration seems to be to weigh their costs and benefits and to select those which maximise the difference between costs and benefits. The costs include the cost of capital, *i.e.*, interest, cost of raw materials, rent, salaries, wages and other expenses and benefits refer to the return on the capital invested based on the size of the output resulting from the investment. "The aim is to maximise the present value of all benefits less that of all costs." The purpose of the cost-benefit analysis is to indicate whether a particular project is worthwhile or which is economically the best of the several alternative projects that can be undertaken subject to specified constraints.

The alternative projects which present themselves for our choice differ in the type and the number of workers required, the nature and the quantity of raw materials and equipment required, the period involved in

1. Prest. A. R. and Turvey, R. —The '*Main Questions*' in *Cost-Benefit Analysis,* 1972, ed. Richard Layard, pp. 73–99.

their completion and the life of the project and in the resultant output from that particular investment. These differences affect the costs and benefits of these projects and we have to attempt a social valuation of these costs and benefits so as to determine the choice of a particular alternative in preference to others.

The weighing of costs and benefits seems to be a simple affair but in its application several ticklish questions crop up:

(*a*) Which costs and which benefits are to be considered? (*b*) How are the costs and benefits to be evaluated? (*c*) Since we have to find the present values of costs still to be incurred and benefits still to accrue, at what rate of interest are they to be discounted? and , (*d*) What are the relevant constraints?

It may be noted that we have to consider social costs and social returns as distinguished from individual or private costs and returns. Social cost means the opportunity cost from the social point of view incurred by the use of scarce resources, and social returns mean the additions to the total output of the

Project-Planning Accounting and Auditing.

community as a whole resulting from that particular investment. Social costs and benefits are different from the purely accounting costs and returns. "The costs and benefits of a project are the time streams of consumption foregone and provided by that project." This follows from the social opportunity cost of funds transferred from the private sectors to the public sector.

It has also to be noted that returns or benefits of a project are reinvested and create new investment opportunities. Some of the funds used for the project would otherwise have been invested or it has been rendered impossible to invest these funds in some other and mutually exclusive investment project, because the cost has been used here in the sense of opportunity cost.

What Costs and Benefits? Now let us see what costs and benefits are to be included in the cost benefit analysis. As mentioned earlier, in the cost-benefit analysis of a project, we should not merely confine ourselves to the consideration of direct costs and benefits but we should also consider the external or side effects and secondary benefits. That is, the costs and benefits have to be taken in a wider sense which means that we must take into account costs and benefits which accrue to the bodies other than the one sponsoring the project. This is necessary because investment in a particular project alters the physical production possibilities of the other producers or the consumption possibilities of other consumers thus affecting their satisfaction from given resources.

For instance, construction of a reservoir upstream will necessitate more dredging by the downstream authority, or improvement of a certain road increases the incomes of garages and restaurants on that road. But it has to be offset by the losses incurred by those on the other roads owing to diversion of traffic.

In order to avoid double counting, we have to ignore purely transfer or distributional items from cost-benefit evaluation. That is we have to take into account the value of the increment of output resulting from a given investment and not the increment in the value of existing assets.

It follows from the above discussion that investing authority should take into account technological spillovers, *e.g.*, the effect of the construction of a dam on the productivity of land elsewhere in the neighbourhood. The decrease in production will be considered an item of cost.

Then there are the secondary effects. An irrigation project will not only increase output in the area it commands but also confer other benefits. The primary benefit is the increase in the value of agricultural output less the costs incurred by the farmers concerned. But increased output will result in increased business activity, and hence profits, of the grain merchants, millers, transporters, banks, bakers, *etc.* These are the secondary benefits. In case the output has a market value, then this value plus the consumer's surplus, if any, will constitute the benefit. In case the output is not sold in the market in a normal way but it is supplied to the consumers at a price based on welfare considerations, value will have to be imputed.

Valuation of Costs and Benefits. As for the valuation of costs and benefits, if they are expressed in terms of money, we have to make adjustments to the expected prices of future inputs and outputs in order to make allowance for the anticipated changes in the relative prices of the conerned items, but not for expected changes in the general price level. The expected changes in the output levels must also be taken into account. Notice has to be taken of monopolistic elements or other market imperfections. In such cases, investment decisions based on market prices will not be correct. Some correction will be needed for the distortions resulting from market imperfections. Account must also be taken of taxes and controls because they also create divergence between market price and social cost or benefit. Taxed inputs should be measured at their factor cost instead of their market value.

Benefit.

There is still another cause of divergence between social cost and private cost, *viz.*, unemployment. When at the prevailing price there is excess supply of any input or factor of production (*e.g.*, labour in the case of unemployment), the price exaggerates the social cost of a project using that input. The utilisation of unemployed labour in investment projects involves no social cost since it does not reduce output anywhere, because the unemployed labour is not supposed to make any contribution to output. In this case, the society as a whole does not forego anything. Hence, in such cases, the use of market values to ascertain direct costs and benefits of a project overstates its social cost and understates its total benefit.

Social costs of materials, machinery and equipment should be calculated like that of labour. In case a material is available free, *e.g.,* sand and stones, the only social cost is that involved in the use of labour for collecting, digging, *etc*. As for scarce materials, their social cost is the cost to the investing agency. Machinery and equipment have usually to be imported and they involve a draft on foreign exchange. In view of this, the social cost is higher than the private accounting costs.

In the case of collective goods, *e.g.*, defence, public health measures, educational facilities, it is not obviously possible to use market price to evaluate their benefits. The quantity of such goods and services supplied to any person in the community cannot be independently varied. Although individuals may differ in their marginal valuation of such goods and services, they are all supposed to use the same amounts. In such cases, there is no basis for making an investment decision by computing their present values.

Then, there are intangible costs and benefits (*e.g.*, scenic effect of building a dam). These costs and benefits are not quantifiable and cannot be valued in any market sense.

Rate of Discount. Now we come to the question of ascertaining the present value of the future costs and benefits, *i.e.*, discounting process. Which rate of interest is to be used for the purpose? There is a large number of interest rates prevailing in the private sector and there seems to be no ground for selecting any of them. It is not clear whether any market-determined rate would be sufficient for community investment decisions. It is said that social time preference rate attaches greater importance to the future than private time preference. It seems best to use the government borrowing rate since it is easily applicable and is also a risk-free rate of interest. Usually, the interest rate is selected on the basis of observed rates ruling at the time for calculating present values.

Social cost of time has also to be determined. Projects differ in their gestation period and in the durability of construction. On what basis are we to impute social value of time? Take first the gestation period. The social cost in gestation is the value of the output that could alternatively be obtained in the meanwhile with the same resources, the maximum that could be obtained within the shortest possible time. Projects with shorter gestation period but with higher output have, of course, to be preferred. But if the rate of output in a shorter gestation period is lower, as is generally the case, then we have to balance the advantage of having a higher rate of output in the longer period against the disadvantage of having to forego the output which could be had in the shorter period even if it be at the lower rate, in the intervening period.

Appropriate rate of discount must be applied on account of time preference. The individuals value the volume of output in future less than in the present. But in the case of the society, which is a continuing entity, there is no justification for applying this rate of discount. It is, therefore, necessary to confine calculations about future streams of output and balance of discount on account of time preference to be zero, the social cost of time would be the maximum rate of output realisable per annum through the alternative with the shortest gestation period. In case, the assets created by the alternative investments are less durable, the annuities to be taken into account will be fewer.

As for the durability of the assets created by an investment, it affects curent costs via the rates of depreciation. Less durable project is subjected to a higher rate of depreciation, and vice-versa and hence a larger deduction must be made from its gross output to arrive at the net addition per annum of the project. But the society calculates the rates of depreciation in a different manner from private accounting. The community values capital equipment on the basis of what it can produce relatively to the use of labour involved. Hence, if the same equipment can be produced at less cost owing to improvement in labour productivity, the value of the equipment installed earlier will depreciate in terms of its output.

Estimation of the Social Product. Here we repeat that, in the under-developed countries, there is likely to be considerable divergence between the private and social product, especially in the case of building up the necessary infrastructure or the social and economic overheads. This divergence is due ultimately to external economies which in practical life are not easy to define and calculate. An investment creates external economies by increasing the demand for certain factors of production and products and thus making it possible for the existing units of production to turn out larger output.

When completed, an investment helps to increase productivity in existing units by either increasing the supply of inputs or making possible new and more economical combinations of factors. Thus, there is expansion of output, as a result of an investment. Sometimes this expansion needs further investment. The divergence between the private and social product of the initial investment will appear only to the extent that these induced investments are actually undertaken.

In this, we face some difficulties: In estimating the social product of an investment, account must be taken of the increase in output accruing from investments whose profitability it has increased. The output of the supplementary investments can be treated as the social product of initial investment if it creates by itself the additional capital required for the supplementary investments. Since one investment leads to another how far can we go on pursuing the effects of an investment? It is better, therefore, to avoid this pursuit and confine ourselves to a definite time period and region and lump together the initial and the likely induced investments and relate this total to the total of expected increases in output resulting therefrom. If increases in output save foreign exchange either by increasing exports or by replacing imports, greater value should be put on them, since foreign exchange presents a great problem to the under-developed countries.

Relevant Constraints. These constraints are physical, legal, distributional constraints and budgetary constraints. The most common physical constraint is the production function which relates the physical inputs and outputs of a project. This directly enters into the calculation of costs and benefits. One of the inputs or some inputs may be in totally inelastic supply. Then , the investment must conform to the legal framework. The legal constraintstarise, for instance, from regulated pricing. Administrative constraints arise from what can be administratively handled. The distributional constraints arise from the fact that no section should be unfavourably affected in the matter of income distribution. It is not always possible to make the gainers compensate the losers. There are budgetary constraints, since projects have to be executed within the budget allotment.

Conclusion. The whole purpose of the cost-benefit analysis is to select the projects for investment or lay down the investment criteria. Where no projects are inter-dependent or mutually exclusive, and where there are no constraints, the projects which maximise the present value of total benefits less total costs can be indicated as under.[2]

1. Select all projects where the present value of benefits exceeds the present value of costs:
2. Select all projects where the ratio of the present value of benefits to the present value of costs exceeds unity;
3. Select all projects where the constant annuity with the same present value of benefits exceeds the constant annuity (of the same duration) with the same present value as costs;
4. Select all projects where the rate of return exceeds the chosen rate of discount.

Capital-output Ratio Criterion

An investment criterion that has often been advocated by various economists is that of capital-output ratio. That is, in choosing among investment projects and in determining priorities, capital output ratios of different investment projects be compared. Those investment projects (or their technical forms) should be selected that minimize the capital-output ratio. If capital-output ratio of investment A (3 : 1) is less than the capital-output ratio of investment B (5 : 1), then, in developmental planning, investment. A must get priority over investment B.

The underlying assumption of this criterion is that products in which capital investment is to be made are substitutes of each other. If every project is a substitute of every other, there is no reason why we should not prefer a low marginal ratio of capital to net output. The classic case of substitutability is provided by the problem of choosing between alternative techniques to produce the same commondity. Various examples

2. Prest, E.R. and Turvey, R., '*The Main Questions*' *in Cost-Benefit Analysis,* edited Richard Layard, 1972, p. 96.

can be given of it. Additional foodgrains production can be had either from constructing major irrigation works or by building small irrigation works or by producing and using more fertilizers. Electricity can be produced either by thermal projects or by hydel projects. Further, more cloth can be produced either in the handloom (khadi-cloth) sector or in the mill sector (mill-cloth). We select a project with a lower capital-output ratio.

But the criterion of capital-output ratio has been subjected to severe criticism. It is maintained that the economic world is not an abode of perfect or very high substitutability. For example, the allocation of investment between agriculture and industry or between consumption goods and investment goods cannot be adjudged on the basis of capital-output ratio, since the degree of substitutability between these products is very limited. Agricultural products and industrial products are complementary rather than substitutes.

Again, what should be compared in choosing among investment projects is not their capitaloutput ratios, but their contribution to income during a crucial period. The goal of development policy is not the maximum output at a **point of time** but a maximum rate of growth over time.

Moreover, capital-output ratio may be one of the criteria when substitutes are involved, but it is not the sole criterion. There are many other considerations too, such as the labour-investment ratio and the effect of investment on income distribution. In a developing country like India, where fuller employment and better distribution of income and wealth are also the cherished aims of the Five-Year Plans, these other considerations of any investment projects are of paramount importance.

Marginal Social Productivity Criterion

A more general criterion of investment proposed is that of social marginal productivity. According to this criterion, those investments should be made in which social marginal productivity is the highest. Those who advocate social marginal productivity as the main investment criterion have also deduced several corollaries as practical guides to policy. Some of these are: (1) A given volume of investment should be allocated in a manner that maximizes the ratio of current output to investment, *i.e.*, capital-output ratio be minimized; (2) Those investment projects should be selected that will maximize the ratio of labour to investment; and (3) To reduce pressures on the balance of payments, investment should be allocated in a manner that will maximize the ratio of export goods to investment.

The use of these specific principles in specific

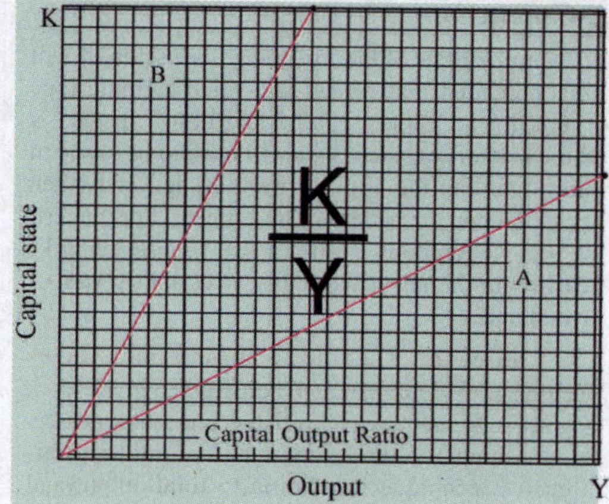

Less the value of $\frac{K}{Y}$ for any project better the prospects are.

situations is, however, likely to be difficult. For development is a dynamic process which involves changes in the size and quality of population, tastes and pattern of demand, technological knowledge and social and institutional factors. The criterion of social marginal productivity must, therefore, be interpreted within the total dynamic complex. To do this, one must make value judgments regarding the various social objectives some of which can be conflicting. Suppose different projects are likely to result in different distributions of income. If a project maximizes total output or income but at the same time involves a more unequal distribution of income than would another project, should it be preferred? Answers to questions like this involve value judgments and different individuals may reach different conclusions.

Like the capital-output criterion, the marginal social productivity criterion is also ambiguous as a guide to investment decisions, when the shape of income stream over time is considered. To determine the most productive investment projects, future yields of capital assets must be discounted to their present values, and these discounted values compared with their present costs. Investment decisions will differ according to the future shape of the income stream which is desired. For instance, from the standpoint of having a maximum increase in national output during the next five years, one type of investment, say, cotton textile production, might be the best. From the standpoint of having the highest national output 15 years hence, however, investment in some other direction, say, steel production, might be better.

These and other similar questions which come readily to mind mean that specific decisions regarding the direction of investment cannot be made without first deciding on a set of social objectives.

Conclusion

On the basis of the foregoing discussion, it will be appreciated that no cut-and-dried formula type criteria for investment can be laid down. Instead, a whole host of considerations will have to be borne in mind. Nor can the above criteria be ignored when deciding upon the pattern of investment. For the rest, the best we can do is to offer a few general remarks bearing on the allocation of resources among various investments.

Choice of Technique and Time Series Technique — Amartya Sen. Amrtya Sen in his work "Choice of techniques has given the time series criterion. He has compared the labour intensive and capital-intensive technique in relation to total output and employment generation with relation to a time-bound concept. In Amartya Sen's opinion if the society is prepared to wait for certain period of time (say about thirty years) regarding its social welfare function more capital intensive techniques are better otherwise they can opt for labour intensive technique.

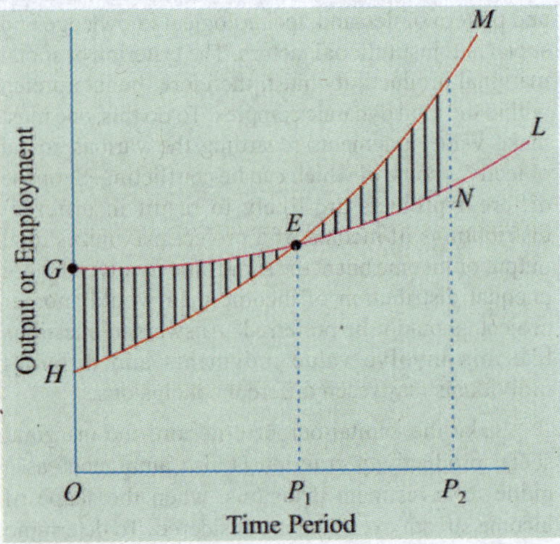

On *x*-axis time period is taken, on *y*-axis total ouput or employment generation is taken. '*GL*' curve shows the growth of output and employment by means of labour-intensive techniques where as '*HM*' curve is by capital-intensive technique. At 'OP_1' period of time both the techniques give the same rate of output and employment, before 'OP_1' period it is labour - intensive technique that is giving greater output where as after "OP", period of time it is the capital-intensive technique which giving more output and employment than labour-intensive technique. After OP_1, period of time it is the capital-intensive technique which is giving more output and employment than labour-intesive technique. At 'OP_1' period of time whatever initial losses of output and employment generation due to capital-intensive technique can be covered between the time period 'P_1P_2'.

That means

$\Delta\, HGE = \Delta\, EMN$

Initially $OH < OG$

This is terms of $\Delta_O = \Delta_Y = \text{M}$

OG continues to be greater till point 'E' where $(ON)_L = (ON)_K$

This is terms of $\Delta_O = \Delta_Y = \text{N}$

Where ON = output employment generation, 'L' Labour-intensive technique, 'K' is capital-intensive technique.

After 'OP_1' time period

$EM > EN$

That is

$(ON)_K > (ON)_L$

At point 'P_2' "$HG = MN$"

Beyond 'OP_2' period of time capital intensive techniques is more fruitful (It will give more output and employment generation).

Prof. Amartya Sen has taken into account output and employment generation as two variables, this can be equated with the inome as well. Keynes took that $\Delta\, O = \Delta\, Y = \Delta\, N$ is determined by effective demand.

$\Delta\, O$ = aggregate output

$\Delta\, Y$ = aggregate income

$\Delta\, N$ = aggregate employment

The time concept of 'OP_1' or 'P_1P_2' or say 'P_1P_2' as thirty years is an assumption. This is to be taken into account not only the economic variables but also all those depending on the culture, social, political and the desire to opt for better technology, *etc*.

Some General Guidelines

External Economies. It has generally come to be accepted that the basic consideration in selecting industries for development in an under-developed economy is the prospect of external economies. Allyn Young drew attention to this important consideration in 1928, and Rosenstein-Rodan made out in 1943 a strong case of developing those industries which would create conditions favourable to the growth of other industries. For example, the development of transport or of sources of fuel and power influences both the costs and the market possibilities of diverse manufacturing industries. Similarly, iron and steel and engineering industries increase the growth and potentiality of industry in general. From the standpoint of supply, it thus emerges that one of the requirements of investments should be that it creates additional external economies.

Market. On the demand side, when considering particular industries, one cannot assume that supply will create its own demand. There must be markets for the commodities produced. Where are the potential markets in the poor countries? Investment should be made in those industries which produce commodities having a readily-available demand. The deamand for building and construction is likely to be high, since poor countries are deficient in roads, railways, houses and public utilities. Investment in export industries, for which there is foreign demand, is another attractive area, and import competing industries provide still another potential choice of investment.

Growing Points. These considerations of external economies and of available market demand may be summarised by saying that investment should be directed to "growing points" in the economy. In the initial stages of economic development, it is highly useful to concentrate on certain focal points which seem to have the promise of more rapid growth. From these local areas, a chain reaction usually starts that gradually spreads chain to the remaining areas of the economy. Thus, even an unbalanced process of initial economic growth has every possibility of ultimately merging into the broader requirement of balanced growth.

Balance of Payments Criterion

Investment should also satisfy what we may call the **"balance of payments"** criterion. Alternative types of investment expenditures will have different effects on the country's export capacity and import requirements. One investment project may be more export-creating than another and one project may be more import-requiring than another. Knowing that under-developed countries are particularly prone to balance of payments difficulties, investments should be directed, as far as practicable, to those projects that will reduce imports or increase exports, other things being equal.

Quick-Yielding Investments

Some industries have a long gestation period, while for some others there is a short time-lag between incurring the investment expenditure and the reaping of fruits. While comparing the benefits of the extra output with the costs, the cost of time-lag must never be forgotten. Unless eventual benefits are outstandingly great. priority should be given to those industries or production techniques which have a relatively short time-lag. Mr. Hicks has called such industries **"quick investment type".** In a developing economy, with a high inflationary potential and a need for a rapid rise in the living standards, industries which have a high **"fruition co-efficient"** (*i.e.*, a high ratio between output and investment) and also a short **'fruition-lag'** should generally be preferred. This point is particularly important when one is comparing the two ways of producing the same result. Thus, extra agricultural output may be secured by major irrigation schemes or minor irrigation schemes. By and large, the major irrigation schemes should be regarded as less desirable than the minor irrigation schemes, because of the time-lags and high capital costs of the former unless the eventual benefits are outstandingly great.

Labour-Intensive vs Capital-Intensive Techniques

Further, there is a problem of choosing between labour-intensive industries or labour-intensive methods and capital-intensive industries or capital-intensive techniques. Since in poor under-developed countries, there is a chronic unemployment and the price of labour is low compared with the price of capital, a relatively high ratio of labour to capital should, as a rule be favoured. In general, where market opportunities exist, and technological restrains are not a problem, the most efficient use of resources in the less developed countries will tend to favour labour-intensive methods. With respect to innovations, it would also follow that capital-saving and labour-using innovations should be favoured as against labour-saving and capital-using innovations.

But it is possible that, as between a technique involving less capital but large labour-employment and another involving a large capital and relatively small labour-employment, there may be such a large differential in productivity in relation to costs that it will be profitable to adopt the capital-intensive technique, despite the high cost of borrowing and amortisation. Again, to strengthen its balance of payments, the country may have to direct some of the new investments into export production. If the export industries are capital-intensive, such as mining and mineral refining, then, even though there is a surplus of labour, investment may have to be directed to these capital-intensive industries for the sake of earning the necessary foreign exchange.

Local Community Assets

In a country like India, where the problem of disguised unemployment in the agricultural sector is very acute and of wide proportions, there is another important consideration affecting the choice of investment. The building of local community assets should be a particularly suitable type of investment, since such local assets will absorb the otherwise unemployed and under-employed labour force in the rural areas and add to productive capacity. Minor irrigation works, contour-bunding, land reclamation, village approach roads, bunds against floods, buildings for schools and health centres are some of the instances of local community works the nature of which amply speaks of their fitness for being undertaken in planned development.

Among the other criteria for choosing between techniques of production in an under-developed economy, we may discuss (*a*) The Rate-of-Turnover Criterion, (*b*) The Surplus Rate Criterion, (*c*) Employment Absorption Criterion and (*d*) The Time Series Criterion.[3]

The Rate of Turnover Criterion

According to Prof. J.J. Polak, the investment should be chosen on the basis of the rate of turnover, *i.e.*, the ratio of output to capital. We have already discussed above the capital-output ratio. As explained by Prof. Norman S. Buchanan, "If investment funds are limited, the wise policy, in the absence of special considerations, would be to undertake first those investments having a high value of annual product relative to the investment."[4] That is, investment projects with a high rate of capital turnover should be given preference. In other words, capital coefficient is to be minimised in order to maximise output.

Amartya K Sen (1933 –) Nobel Laureate in Economics in 1998.

But, as a general guide to policy, this criterion suffers from some serious limitations: (*a*) The high rate of turn-over may entail a high rate of depreciation so that the net output is not necessarily high.

(*b*) 'Short-fruition-lag projects' may have a lower capital-output ratio in the short period but not necessarily so in the long period.

(*c*) This criterion ignores the cost of complementary factors like labour used in operating the capital.

(*d*) This criterion also ignores the 'project-complementarity', particularly the vertical and horizontal transmissionof external economies. In order to avail of the external economies, it may become necessary to choose an investemnt with a higher capital-output ratio.

(*c*) In a sector like agriculture, the amount of fixed capital investment is small in proportion to total inputs. Hence, factors other than capital investement may substantially change the fixed capital-output ratio.

3. (1) Sen. A.K. — 'Some Notes on the Choice of Techniques of Capital Intensity in Development' Planning' in "*Accelerating Investment in Developing Economics,*"ed. A.N. Agarwal and S.P. Singh, 1969 pp. 213–238 and (2) Chaudhuri, A.K., Investment Criteria and Choice of Technique, *Lok Udyog,* January 1973, pp. 29–33.
4. *International Investment and Domestic Welfare,* p.24.

The Surplus Rate Criterion

This criterion seeks to maximise the per capita income at some future point of time rather than maximise the national income now. For this purpose, the rate of savings should be maximised so that the rate of reinvestment can be maximised. Hence, for each unit should be chosen "that alternative that will give each worker greater productive power than any other alternative".

This criterion assumes that profits are largely saved and re-invested and that wages are largely spent on consumption. Hence, it is recommended that the capital resources should be so allocated among the alternative uses that the marginal per capita reinvestement quotient is the same in different alternatives. The application of the law of equimarginal return will bring about an optimal utilisation of scarce capital resources.

According to this criterion, capital-intensive projects should be undertaken in under-developed countries even though capital is scarce because in this way output per capita will be maximised. The capital-intensive projects are advocated also on the ground that they will provide training and experience to management and the working force and these are the things that the developing countries lack the most.

But the application of this criterion is likely to produce some undesirable social effects: It will accentuate inequalities in income and wealth in the community, because the capitalists will gain at the expense of the wage earners.

Employment Absorption Criterion

It is well-known that in the under-developed but over-populated countries, labour supply is abundant and cheap. There is large-scale unemployment or under-employment especially in the agricultural sector in the form of disguised unemployment. Hence, it is suggested such techniques should be adopted as are labour-intensive. We have already discussed above the pros and cons of labour-intensive *vs*. capital-intensive techniques. We discuss it here from the point of view of employment. Techniques with greater employment content should be preferred to others which may absorb less labour.

Besides providing more employment, such techniques will raise the level of consumption because the newly employed labour will spend their incomes on consumption. Higher propensity to consume will stimulate further investment which will accelerate economic growth. Also, such techniques will be conducive to a high degree of economic equality by raising the level of income of the working class people.

But the defect of such techniques is that they do not necessarily maximise the national output. Labour-intensive techniques are not as productive as the capital-intensive techniques. Low labour productivity may be perpetuated. Besides, the quality of the end-products suffers.

Employment absorption criterion prescribes labour intensive tehnology.

The Time Series Criterion

When several techniques are available to choose from, we may estimate real income flows resulting from each technique. For this purpose, we apply the rate of investment with corrections due to the variability of the volume of investment arising from different spending habits and varying import-content of investments. When we have taken two time series of real income flows, we have to apply the relevant rates of time discount. The time discount is necessary because of (*a*) the diminishing marginal social utility of income with the rising income level and (*b*) the uncertainty of the future. In the case of quickly falling marginal social utility, the higher rate of income growth may not mean higher level of social satisfaction. Since future is uncertain, it is necessary to have a valuation of uncertainty discount.

This criterion suffers from some serious limitations when we consider it as a policy prescription. It is not easy to arrive at utility and uncertainty functions. A more practical method seems to be to fix the period of time we want to consider and weigh the loss of immediate output arising form the adoption of more capital-intensive techniques against a gain in increased output later.

Socially Desirable Income Distribution Criterion

Another important investment criterion is the socially desirable income distribution. It means that investment should be so planned as to achieve equitable distribution of benefits. This criterion may be regarded very important because economic development in under-developed countries tends to accentuate disparities of income and wealth distribution in the country. Such disparities cause grave discontent and pose a great threat to political stability. Such desirable investment may be in the form of public utilities, education, public health, improving means of transport and communications, *etc*. In this type of investment benefits are evenly distributed, may be more in favour of the poor than the rich.

Conclusion

From the above analysis of the various investment criteria and the choice of techniques, it is clear that we cannot lay down dogmatically the criterion or criteria which should guide us in investment. Nor can we make a categorical choice of any particular technique.

Thus, there is no single, simple, precise and objective criterion for planning investments. The best that the planners can do is to strike a balance among the various considerations we have discussed above.

It is clear that investment criteria should not be linked with any one of the objectives. For, promoting economic growth, output, profits, savings and employment all must be increased. To use Prof. Rostows' terminology, the leading sectors of the economy should be developed or investment should create increase infrastructural facilities.

Key terms

Cost, benefit, Social cost, Social Product, Rate of discount, Present value, Labour intensive technique, Capital intensive technique.

QUESTIONS

1. State and explain the different concepts of investment criteria.
2. Critically evaluate the labour-internsive and capital intensive techniques used in developing countries.

FINANCING OF ECONOMIC DEVELOPMENT

For accelerating capital formation and promoting other developmental activities huge resouces are needed. Wherefrom are the underdeveloped countries to find such resources? Owing to the narrowness of the margin of aggregate output over consumption demand, the resources needed for the financing of development plans pose a very difficult problem. There are several methods of financing economic development. The principal methods are discussed below:

Savings

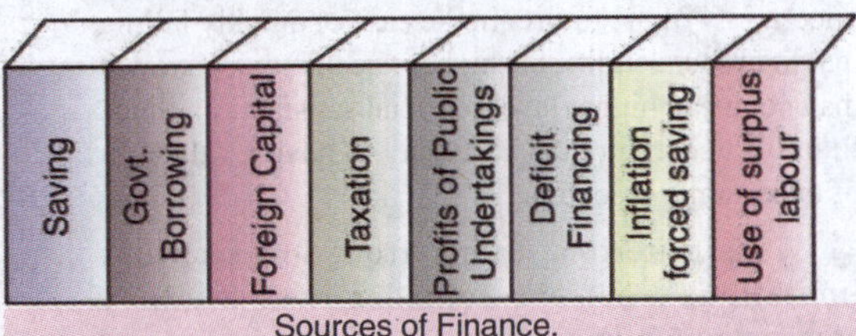

Sources of Finance.

The total investible resources available at any time in a country are made up of domestic savings and external resources which are obtained from abroad in the form of foreign capital. To take savings first. The aggregate savings of an economy consist of government savings, saving by the business sector and savings by the households. Government savings are the tax revenues minus public expenditure; the business savings are the gross income of trade and industry minus the dividends and the taxes paid and the savings of the households are the disposable income minus consumption expenditure. In India, in 1958-59, government savings accounted for 10.6 per cent, corporate savings 3.5 per cent and the savings of the household sector 85.9 percent.[1]

Broadly speaking, savings are determined by the rate and pattern of growth and the institutional and social factors. In order to promote economic development, savings have not only to be generated but they have also to be mobilised to the maximum extent possible and then canalise them into productive investment. The conditions in the under-developed countries are not very conducive to economic growth from the point of view of capital formation: The rate of savings is very low (about 5 per cent of the national income), the financial institutions to mobilise these savings are not adequate; nor is the climate for investment favourable.

Finance is needed both for private and public sectors. So far as the **private sector** is concerned, it primarily depends on the **voluntary savings** of the people. Profits of private undertakings can also be ploughed back into investment. Institutions like Finance Corporations set up by the Government can also provide the needed development finance to the private sector.

1. *Reserve Bank of India Bulletin,* August 1961, p. 1204

To finance capital formation and other development activities in the public sector is the responsibility of the Government. There are various methods of financing development in the public sector. Owing to the shortage of voluntary savings, the govern-ments are often compelled to resort to the device of forced saving. Below we shall discuss each method of development finance, for the public sector, one by one.

Taxation

There is considerable unanimity among economists about the usefulness, nay necessity, of taxation and fiscal policy for mobilising resources for economic development in the under-developed countries. When development has proceeded to achieve a certain rate of growth, the level of savings by households and businesses rises sufficiently to meet the requirements of development. But in the early stages, some measure of compulsion is necessary to compel the people to save by means of suitable taxation measures, because the rate of domestic savings is low and propensity to consume is very high.

Thus, taxation is an important method of increasing the volume of savings by restricting domestic consumption. Both direct and indirect taxes can play a part in augmenting the resources of the governments to be spent on developmental activities. For achieving best results, taxes should be imposed on non-entrepreneurial incomes and luxury consumption. But the taxation of non-functional surplus may not yield a substantial volume of development finance, because most of the income of the vast majority of the people in an under-developed country is devoted to the consumption of necessaries. Thus, the need to raise an adequate volume of development finance makes it inevitable for the government to extend the coverage of indirect taxes to include the staple commodities of mass consumption. Moreover, the taxation of agriculture has to play an important part in the mobilization of resources for the public sector in a developing economy.

Thus, taxation is the most important means available to the State for mobilising nation's resources for economic development. Its yield can be more accurately estimated and its economic effects can be better foreseen. It can be used to finance development with minimum adverse effects on economic stability. Hence, it is necessary to intensify the tax effort, especially because the savings are meagre and the rate of capital formation low, whereas the development requirements are very large.

But taxation as a method of development finance has some difficulties. While involuntary savings are increased, voluntary savings may be diminished, since individuals may reduce their voluntary savings in order to maintain their former consumption levels. This may reduce the resources going to the private sector. Another major drawback of taxation is its negative effects which it may have on incentives. If taxes on wage-earners diminish their incentive to work harder, if taxes on profits of the higher income group reduce their incentive to save and to make investments in new enterprises, and if taxes on the output or income of the farmers diminish the incentive to improve agricultural techniques, then, the forced savings extracted through these taxes will not be an unmixed gain.

Taxes in India (Central and State)

(Rs. crores)

Year	*Direct taxes*	*Indirect taxes*	*Total taxes*	*Total taxes as percentage of GDP*
1950-51	230	430	660	6
1960-61	420	1,040	1,460	10
1970-71	1,100	3,590	4,690	14
1980-81	3,690	16,100	19,790	17
2002-03	100,970	2,89,660	3,90,630	17

SOURCE: Calculated from Economic Survey (various issues)

Note : Figures for 2002-03 represent revised budget receipts for the Centre and budget figures for the States.

Thus, it is necessary to devise a tax system that will not weaken the incentives to work, save and invest nor will it violate the accepted notion of equity.

Tax policy of the government can exert a powerful influence both on savings and investment—the two crucial factors determining economic growth. The primary objective of the tax policy in the under-developed countries is to transfer from the community to the State as large a volume of resources as possible with minimum of adverse effects on incentives for production and investment. It is generally agreed that there is a considerable scope for broadening and deepening the tax system by improving the tax structure and by toning up the tax machinery. A sound tax policy can provide incentives for private enterprise. Taxation can be used as means for controlling economic fluctuations, for containing inflationary pressures and to achieve social justice by reducing inequalities in income and wealth. These are principal objectives of tax policy in under-developed countries.

Government Borrowing

Borrowing by the government is another method by which the saving of the community may be mobilized. But there exist a number of obstacles which hinder the success of borrowing policy in an under-developed economy. In many such countries, there are no organized money and capital markets and in those where such markets exist, they constitute a very small segment of the total money market of the country. There may not, besides, exist any organic relationship between the organized and the unorganized parts of the money market. Moreover, the resources of the organized capital market may be too inadequate to fulfil the needs both of the private and of the public sector. Further, in the capital market the competition for funds between the government and the private sector will raise the rate of interest and this will have a highly disincentive effect on the increase of investment in the private sector.

For the success of government's borrowing policy, it is necessary that financial institutions be developed and extended into the rural sector of the economy. This will inculcate the habit of thrift in the population and mobilize for productive purpose the amount of savings, originating in this sector. Besides, for the mobilization of savings, it will be necessary to check and regulate the diversion of savings into unproductive investment such as real estate and inventory accumulation. Suitable techniques of borrowing must also be devised. For example, bonds issued by the Government should be adjusted to the preferences of the general public. Bonds of large denomination and long maturity may be offered to the institutional investors, whereas those of small denomination and short maturity may be reserved for the non-institutional investors. If properly devised and conducted, small savings campaign can mobilize a sizable amount of resources.

Further, the mobilization of the hoarded gold and jewellery through government programmes constitutes a highly desirable source of development finance. Of course, suitable techniques of public borrowing for the mobilization of these resources have to be evolved.

Foreign Capital

The importance of foreign capital in accelerating economic development is undoubted. But which are the main sources of foreign capital? In the 19th and the early 20th centuries, most of the foreign capital which went to develop the resources of the developing countries was private capital investment either of the equity type or the portfolio variety. In more recent times, though private foreign capital continues to be invested largely in primary production for the purpose of export to the investing countries, yet, in its size, it has been far eclipsed by the flow of capital either on government-to-government level or through borrowing from international financial institutions like the International Bank for Reconstruction and Development (known as the World Bank) and its affiliate the International Development Association. In India's five-year plans, for example, a great deal of reliance has been placed on government-to-government long-term borrowing (through the Aid-India Club comprising several capital-rich countries) and on loans from the World Bank.

We discuss below some important aspects of foreign capital at some length.

Forms of Foreign Capital. From the point of view of the country receiving foreign capital, it can take three forms: (*a*) Loans, (*b*) Direct Investments and (*c*) Grants and Aid. These three forms of foreign capital differ in respect of impact, the benefits they confer on the receiving country and the strains they produce in its economy. For instance, loans involve regular servicing costs in the form of interest payments and amortization and grants and aid constitute a net gain if no political strings are attached thereto. Direct investment involves the transfer of resources in the form of dividends and profits. Direct investment takes the form of equity capital, *i.e.*, share capital. This means buying of shares by the enterpreneurs or firms of one country in firms of another country. It involves foreign control of the firm in which investment is made. Reinvestment of profits in the firms or companies of the receiving country by the foreign capitalists is also called direct investment. Private foreign capital also takes the form of loans which is called portfolio investment as distinguished from direct investment. In portfolio investment, capital is transferred from one country to another through the purchase of bonds and debentures of a firm or company in the borrowing country.

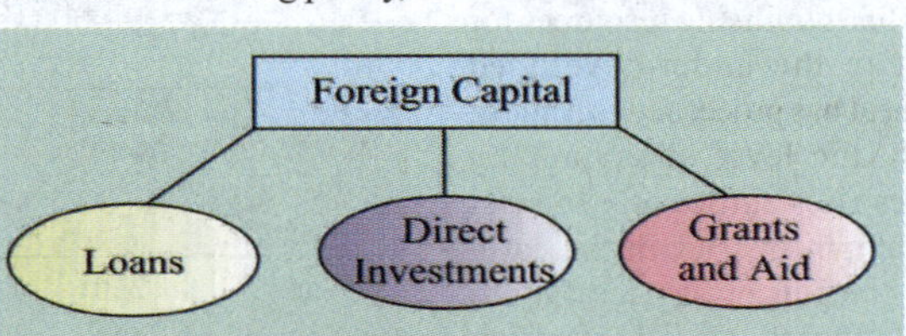

Trends in the Flow of Foreign Capital. Before the First World War, there was tremendous flow of foreign capital to the needy countries form the rich countries like the U.K., Germany and France owing to the need for securing key raw materials from abroad, the lure of fabulous profits and owing to the legal and economic advantages enjoyed by the owners of capital. However, during the inter-war period, the outflow declined considerably on account of the unsettled political and economic conditions and the Great Depression of the early 1930's which created balance of payments problems resulting in exchange control and exchange restrictions. But since the Second World War, there has been significant revival in the flow of foreign capital. In seven years 1946-52, the net outflow of private long-term capital from the industrial countries amounted to $ 11 billion and in four years from 1955-58, it exceeded $ 17 billion.[2] The

2. Bright Singh, D.—*Economic Development*, p. 421.

emergence of the West European countries and of the U.S.A. as lenders and the establishment of theWorld Bank largely contributed to this revival. In recent years, the flow of foreign capital from governments and international agencies has increased very rapidly (from an annual average of $2 billion in 1954-56 to $3.3 billion in 1958-59).[3]

The basic reason of the outflow of private capital is the prospect of profits in the receiving countries as compared with the level of profits at home. So far as the under-developed countries are concerned, the marginal productivity of capital (hence the rate of profit) is expected to be higher than the lending countries owing to the existence of rich natural resources lying untapped and the cheapness of labour. Against these, however, have to be set off the low productivity of labour, inadequate economic overheads or infrastructure and the lack of other sources of external economies. Also, the economic and political conditions prevalent in the under-developed countries are not very conducive to any large inflow of foreign capital. Impediments arise out of procedural dilatoriness, red tape, bureaucratic delays and corruption. The spirit of nationalism manifesting itself in unfriendliness and sometimes hostility to the foreign investor also stands in the way. No wonder the respone of the foreign investor to efforts made by the under-developed countries to woo foreign capital is poor.

For instance, in India, between 1948-53, the inflow of foreign private capital amounted to meagre Rs. 130 crores. During the Second Plan out of a total investment of Rs. 7,000 crores, the foreign investment was about Rs. 150 crores as against a target of Rs. 200 crores. In the Third Plan, an inflow of Rs. 300 crores was anticipated, which was less than 3 per cent of the total outlay, but the actual receipt was much less. Again in the Fourth Plan Rs. 300 crores was the targeted amount, the actual inflow did not exceed Rs. 100 crores.

However, an important recent trend is that the decline in the inflow of private foreign capital is being made up by contributions from foreign friendly governments and international agencies like the World Bank, International Development Association and the I.M.F. At the government level, the transfer of capital is effected in the form of loans and grants, technical assistance and food supplies.

Economic Significance. Beyond doubt, the inflow of foreign capital has accelerated the economic growth of the under-developed countries in a number of ways.

(i) Foreign capital supplements domestic savings and harnesses them to secure a rapid rate of growth. It serves as a stimulant to additional domestic investment in the recipient country. By increasing the rate of capital formation in the country, it goes a long way in removing the capital deficiency which is the main hurdle in economic growth.

(ii) Foreign capital generally brings along with it technical know-how. By providing technological expertise it helps in building modern industrial structure in the receiving countries. In this way, it adds to their aggregate national product and per capita income which not only works towards removing their proverty but increases the rate of savings which in turn accelerates the process of their growth. In course of time, the vicious circle of poverty is broken and the beneficial circle of prosperity is set in motion.

(iii) Foreign capital provides valuable foreign exchange which is the desperate need of the developing economies. It is generally observed that, in the early years of development, the import bill of such countries goes on mounting because they have to import foodgrains, machinery and capital and essential industrial raw materials but their exports lag woefully behind. This creates balance of payments difficulties in the solution of which foreign capital proves a god-send.

(iv) Benefits also accrue from foreign capital to domestic labour in the form of higher real wages, to consumers in the form of greater supply of consumer goods, larger in quantity, better in quality and greater in variety and to the government in the form of higher tax revenues. The economy benefits through the realisation of external economies. Since foreign capital helps in building up economic infrastructure in the form of means of transport and communications, railways, roads, hydro-electric projects supplying irrigation and power, it undoubtedly results in acceleration of the rate of growth.

World-Bank—HQ.

But there is the other side too. Foreign capital is not an unmixed blessing. Usually, there are political strings attached to foreign capital, either implicitly or explicitly. The receiving countries suffer a loss in independence in action or policy and even their sovereignty is threatened. Besides, the loans have to be repaid and the interest payments and amortisation put a very severe strain on the economy. According to the Union Finance Minister's statement made in Rajya

3. *Ibid*., p. 440.

Sabha on November 16, 1971, foreign private investment in India at the end of month 1970 stood at Rs. 1,298 crores. The remittance of profits on foreign private investment amounted to Rs. 12 crores in 1969-70. All such payments add to the balance of payments difficulties.

Conclusion. Proper utilisation of foreign capital is the crux of the problem. It should be so utilised as to transform the economy into a self-reliant and self-sustained economy. Its ability to meet the service and repayment obligations will depend on the extent to which the economy is so transformed.

Profits of Public Undertakings

In a developing economy, where the scope of the public sector has been progressively expanding in the industrial, financial and commercial spheres, it is desirable that a large amount of resources should be generated and mobilized in this sector also. **"No-profit-no-loss"** basis of the price policy of the public undertaking should give place to a policty of reasonable profits on the output produced and sold. Similarly, state trading organizations conducting any domestic and /or foreign trade should suitably adjust their price policy to mobilize the resources in the form of trading profits.

In advanced countries, public undertakings contribute a sizable proportion of resources for economic development. In Soviet Russia, of course, 90 per cent of the public revenue is derived from the public undertakings (private undertakings there are practically non-existent). Even in the U.K., nationalisation of some industries has expanded this source of development. But in some countries of South Eastern Asia, this source of revenue has become very important because of state ownership of certain industries and state trading in some important commodities, *e.g.*, rice trading in Mayanmar (Burma).

In India, there is a very large number of public undertakings operating at present. After the initial period of pioneering losses some of them are now yielding handsome dividends. This is an expanding source of revenue available for economic development. The Fifth Five-Year Plan estimated that the Central and State undertakings would contribute Rs. 6,000 crores to its total outlay.

Deficit Financing

We have devoted a full chapter to deficit financing.[4] Deficit financing, *i.e.*, newly created money, is another source of capital formation in a developing economy. The danger, inherent in this source of development finance, is that it may lead to inflationary pressures in the economy. But a certain measure of deficit financing can be had without creating such pressures. As the aggregate real output increases under stimulus of development plans, new money has to be created to match this increased output. Further, in a developing economy, Other demand for money increases as the monetized sector of the economy expands at the expense of the non-monetary and subsistence sectors. New money has to be created to satisfy this increased demand for money. Besides, there exists some possibility of using deficit financing to utilise the existing unemployed and under-employed labour in schemes which yield quick results, so that the inflationary potential of deficit financing may be neutralized by an increase in the supply of output in the short time.

4. Chapter 66

Disguised Unemployment

Another source of development finance and capital formation is to mobilize the saving potential that exists in the form of disguised unemployment. Surplus agricultural workers can be transferred from the agricultural sector to the non-agricultural sectors without diminishing agricultural output. The objective is to mobilize these unproductive workers and employ them on various capital-creating projects such as roads, canals, buildings of schools and health centres, bunds for controlling floods in which they do not require much capital to work with.

But how will these workers be fed? previously they were subsidized by the productive workers. This must continue. For this, the Government will have to mobilize resources from the remaining productive workers. The consumption of these remaining productive workers must be kept at their former level.

Government Enterprises

As on March 31	*No. of Units*	*Total Investment (Rs. crores)*
1951	5	29
1961	47	950
1980	179	18,150
1990	244	99,330
2001	242	2,74,198
2002	240	3,24,632

SOURCE : Government of India, ***Public Enterprise Survey***, (2001-2002).

We have already discussed disguised unemployment in a separate chapter.[5]

Inflation and Forced Saving

Taxation, surpluses of public enterprises and borrowings are non-inflationary methods of resource mobilisation and are ideal methods for achieving economic growth with stability. But the under-developed countries are under strong political pressure to hasten economic development and for that purpose adopt ambitious plans of economic development. For the implementation of such big plans only non-inflationary resources are not enough. The gap may be too wide to be bridged by foreign aid

5. Chapter 73

Contribution of public enterprises to Central exchequer

(*Rs. crores*)

Year/period	*Amount Contributed* *Total*	*Average**
Sixth Plan (1980-85)	27,570	5,510
Seventh Plan (1985-90)	69,410	13,880
Eighth Plan (1992-97)	1,33,780	26,760
1997-98 and 2001-02	2,69,110	53,822

* Figures rounded

Source: ***Public Enterprises Survey***, 2001-02, p. 28.

or private investment. Hence resort to inflationary resource mobilisation become necessary. We have already mentioned deficit financing but deficit financing may not necessarily be inflationary when it results in increase in production of goods and services sufficient to neutralise its inflationary effect.

Inflation may provide resources for development in the following ways:–

(i) There is the forced saving mechanism of inflation. Rising prices due to inflation lower real wages and tend to increase profits when wages lag behind. Similarly, the real income of the farmer falls. In this way, income is transferred from those who have lower propensity to save to those whose propensity to save is higher. Inflation thus acts as a disguised taxation. 'Inflationary tax' on consumers and savers works to the advantage of investors and the government, where the government acquires in this way real resources for development, people are forced to save. It is a hidden tax and evokes no opposition and the government is able to raise resources for development easily. This is its chief merit.

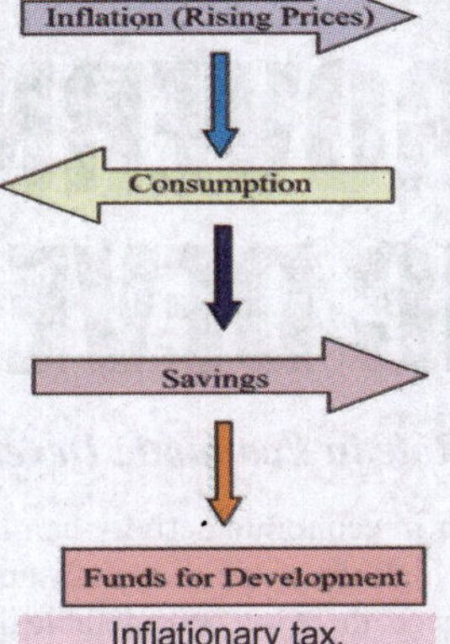

Inflationary tax.

(ii) In the under-developed countries, the growth process is hampered by the existence of several rigidities and immobilities. Rise in prices and wages compel the workers to move from the traditional subsistence sector to the expanding industrial sector. In this way, labour and other resources tend to be optimally allocated and more fully utilised so that economic growth is promoted. There is no fear of agricultural production falling as a result of the movement of these workers because their marginal productivity there was zero or nearly zero.

The advocates of inflationary finance contend that a moderate degree of inflation is the logical concomitant of efficient economic mobilisation. But care has to be taken that it remains moderate and does not become hyper-inflation. Such inflation can be 'self-liquidating' as Prof. A. Lewis puts it. It will lead to increase in the output of consumer goods and bring down the prices. In this way, inflation will disappear. On the other hand, spiralling inflation has a tendency to go out of control. Organised labour will protect itself by adopting militant measures and succeed in getting wages and dearness allowances linked to the price index. The farmers clamour for higher prices of their produce and succeed in getting them. As inflation proceeds, commodities are preferred to money in an effort to evade the inflation tax. All such developments introduce serious distortions in resource allocation which more than offset the earlier gains. This is hyper-inflation.

The method of inflationary finance is considered wasteful as a method of raising the rate of saving. The net increase in saving is generally less than the decline in consumption. Those who are hit by inflation are forced to lower their consumption. This forced decline in consumption constitutes the potential for saving. The gainers from inflation *i.e.* those whose real income has gone up owing to rising prices find themselves with more income than before. They will divide this increase in income between consumption and saving according to their propensity to consume and save. The forced saving hypothesis assumes that the propensity to consume of the gainers from inflation is less than that of the losers. This means that the decline in consumption of the losers is greater than the increases in consumption of the gainers. Net result is an increase in saving.

Key terms

Voluntary savings, Forms of foreign capital, Profits of Public undertakings, Inflationary tax.

QUESTIONS

1. Discuss in detail the various methods of internal resource mobilisation for economic development.
2. Examine the relative roles of taxation, borrowing and deficit financing in promoting economic development.
3. Discuss the role of capital formation in economic development.
4. Distinguish between Foreign Institutional investments and foreign direct investments.
5. What are the merits and demerits of Foreign direct investments ?

80 CHAPTER

ROLE OF GOVERNMENT IN ECONOMIC DEVELOPMENT

Importance of Government's Role in Economic Development

In modern times, State participation in economic activity can hardly be a matter of disagreement. The free play of economic forces, even in highly developed capitalist countries, has often meant large unemployment and instability of the system. Hence, there is a considerable dilution of the laissez-faire principle and the governments are now called upon to intervene in economic fields which were considered sacrosanct. In these advanced countries, State intervention has been invoked to ensure economic stability and full employment of productive resource of the community.

But state action is all the more inevitable in under-developed economies. Here the state has to play a vital and ever-expanding role to accelerate process of economic growth. These countries are struggling hard to get rid of poverty and to attain higher living standards. In an under-developed economy, there is a circular constellation of forces tending to act and react upon one another in such a way as to keep a poor country in a stationary state of under-development equilibrium. The vicious circle of under-developed equilibrium can be broken only by a comprehensive government planning of the process of economic development.

Rashtrapati Bhavan.

It is obvious that a high rate of investment and growth of output cannot be attained in an under-developed country simply as a result of the functioning of the market forces. Even the operation of these forces is hindered by the existence of economic rigidities and structural disequilibria. Economic development is not a spontaneous or automatic process. On the contrary, it is evident that there are automatic forces within the system tending to keep it moored to a low level. Thus, if an under-developed country does not wish to remain caught up in a vicious circle of poverty, government must interfere with the market forces to break that circle.

In the initial phase, the process of development is an under-developed country is held up primarily by the lack of the basic **social and economic** overheads such as schools, technical colleges and research institutes, hospitals and railways, roads, ports, harbours and bridges. Provision of these overheads requires very large investments. Such investments will lead to the creation of external economies, which, in their turn, will provide incentives for the expansion of private enterprise in the field of industry as well as of agriculture.

Private enterprise will not undertake investments in social overheads, because the returns from them in the form of an increase in the supply of technical skills and higher standards of education and health can be realised only over a long period. Also, it will accrue to the whole society rather than to those entrepreneurs who incur the necessary large expenditure on the creation of such costly social overheads. Therefore, investment in them is not profitable from the standpoint of the private entrepreneurs, howsoever productive it may be from the broader interest of the society. This indicates the need for direct participating of the government by way of investment in social overheads, so that the rate of development be quickened.

Investments in economic overheads require huge outlays of capital which are usually beyond the capacity of private enterprise. Besides, the returns from such investments are quite uncertain and take very long to accrue. Private enterprise is generally interested in quick returns and will seldom be prepared to wait so long.

Nor can private enterprise easily mobilise resources for building up all these overheads. The State is in a far better position to find the necessary resources through taxation, borrowing and deficit-financing– sources not open to private enterprise. Thus, private enterprise lacks the capacity to undertake large-scale and comprehensive development programme. Not only that; it also lacks the necessary approach to development.

The role of government in development is further highlighted by the fact that under-developed countries suffer from a serious deficiency of all types of resources and skills, while the need for them is so great. In these circumstances, what is needed is a wise and efficient allocation of limited resources. This only the State is best fitted to do through central planning, according to a scheme of priorities well suited to the country's conditions and needs. Until the country has attained the stage of self-sustained growth, the Government must make determined and conscious efforts to push the economy through the 'take-off' period of development.

Besides, the conditions in the under-developed countries are not conducive to rapid economic growth. "The tendency towards the formation of monopolistic organisations under the free enterprise system, he unpreparedness and reluctance on the part of entrepreneurs to make investments in schemes of collective value, the lack of attention to the long-run problems of the economy and too much concentration on the immediate prospects of profits, the absence of integration among the various sectors of the economy

Indian Parliament makes law for Indian and its development.

and the possibility of adverse economic results arising from uncoordinated economic decisions, constitute the major defects of the private enterprise system."[1] A decisive role by the government is called for to rectify these defects and to overcome obstacles to economic growth.

GOVERNMENT MEASURES TO PROMOTE ECONOMIC DEVELOPMENT

In view of the peculiar circumstances in which politically, socially and economically the under-developed countries are placed, there is not only a great urgency about economic development but also an infinitely much greater effort is required to generate the forces of economic growth. This effort is obviously beyond private enterprise in such countries. Owing to adverse political, economic and social factors, these countries have been for long in a state of economic stagnation. They are now becoming painfully aware of the widening disparity between their economic condition and that of the advanced countries, which are getting richer everyday whereas they are caught up in the vicious circle of poverty. This necessitates a comprehensive set of measures to be adopted by the government not only to rouse them up from the state of economic slumber but to see them march quickly on the road of development.

The following are the principal measures, which are necessary for the government of an under-developed country to take in order to accelerate the process of economic growth.

Provision of Economic and Social Overheads

If economic growth is to be accelerated, it is necessary for the government to provide in adequate measure economic and social overhead facilities also called the overhead capital and services or infrastructure. Economic infrastructure includes transport facilities,

1. Finer Herman, "The Role of Government,". *Economic Development, Principles and Patterns*, Williamson, H.F. and J.A. Buttrick, 1954, p. 369.

e.g., railways, roads, harbours, airfields, *etc.*, means of communications, *e.g.*, postal, telegraph and telephone facilities, electric and even atomic energy, irrigation facilities, *etc.* The social overheads or infrastructure consists of educational institutions (schools, colleges and universities) both for general educational and technical training, public health, and medical aid facilities, housing, water supply and other welfare schemes. "The availability of adequate overhead facilities brings about external economies to other industries, lowers their capital coefficient and by thus improving the efficiency of general investment, makes possible a more rapid rate of economic growth."[2]

The under-developed countries are woefully suffering form the lack of such facilities on account of which their rate of growth has been slow and tardy. Only the government can have the ability and willingness to make investments in these directions, where the private investor cannot hope to get any tangible return, and remove a big hurdle in the way of economic growth. Actually, the governments in under-developed countries are making large investments in the provision of overhead facilities. Of total public investment (1950-59), they have ranged from 54 per cent in Ceylon (now Sri Lanka) , 56 per cent in India, 66 per cent in Burma and 72 per cent in Thailand.[3]

Provision of Financial Facilities

Finance is the crux of the problem of development. We know that the under-developed countries suffer from scarcity of capital which is the greatest handicap in their economic growth. No doubt that their savings are meagre but even the meagre savings are not available for economic development. To mobilise these savings, a sound banking system is essential and other financial institutions are required to canalise these savings into investments and supply the credit needs of trade and industry. The government is to see that appropriate financial institutions are set up to meet the requirements of the entrepreneurs.

In India, for instance, the government took steps to reform the banking system and put it on a sound footing. Fourteen major commercial banks were nationalised in 1969. In the agricultural sector to meet the short-term credit needs of the farmers, co-operative societies were set up and, for long-term credit, land mortgage banks or land development banks have been organised. Two funds were set up–National Agricultural Credit (Long-term) Operations Fund and National Agricultural Credit (Stabilisation) Fund. The former is meant to give long-term loans to State Governments to enable them to buy shares of co-operatives and to grant medium-term loans to co-operatives and long-term loans to land development banks and the latter fund to give medium-term loans to State Co-operative Banks to enable them to convert short-term loans into medium-term loans. Agricultural Refinance Corporation was set up to serve as a refinancing agency for agricultural credit and to give assistance for reclamation of land, development of special crops, mechanical farming and development of animal husbandry dairy farming, poultry, *etc.* Small Farmers Developments Agencies (S.F.D.A.'s) were established and Marginal Farmers and Agricultural Labour (M.F.A.L.) schemes were taken up. Agro-Industries Corporations have also been set up to give loans for the purchase of tractors and agricultural machinery. In 1984 the government set up an open agriculture finance institution that is "the National Bank of Agriculture and Rural Development" (NABARD). The agriculture refinance corporation was merged with NABARD.

In the industrial sector too, financial and other institutions were established to promote industrial development. To assist the small scale and cottage industries several boards were set up such as the Cottage Industries Board, All India Handicrafts Board, Central Marketing Organisation, Inventions Promotion Board, State Financial Corporations, National Small Industries Corporation, *etc.* For the large-scale industries were set up the Industrial Finance Corporation of India and the Industrial Development Bank Of India. Unit Trust of India was created to promote investment. National Industrial Development Corporation was established to grant special loans for the rehabilitation and modernisation of cotton textile mills and jute mills. Industrial Credit and Investment Corporation was set up to assist the creation, expansion and modernisation of industrial enterprises in the private sector. For re-lending facilities Refinance Corporation for Industry was set up. Export Credit and Guarantee Corporation was created to insure against export risks, financial and political, and to furnish guarantees to banks to assist exporters

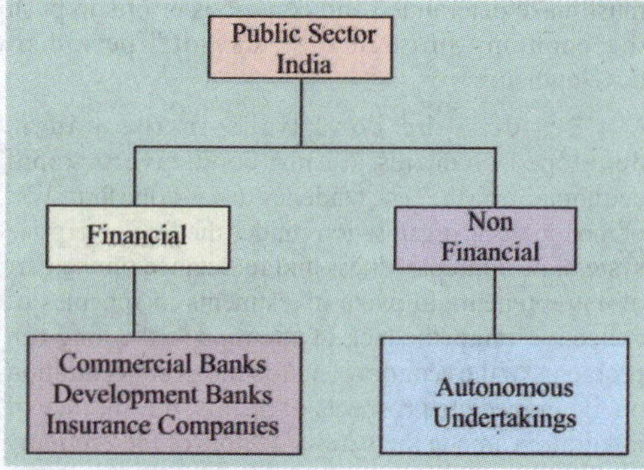

2. Bright Singh, D.—*Economic Development*, p. 544.
3. United Nations, *Economic Survey of Asia and Far East*, 1960, p. 75.

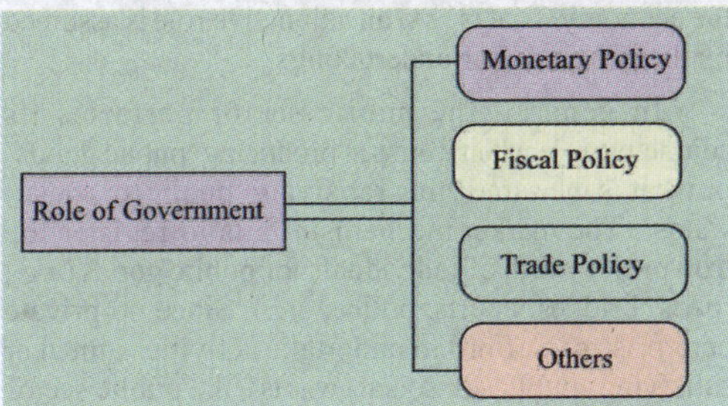

to secure liberal credit facilities. This gives some idea as to what a government in an under-developed country can do in the matter of provision of financial facilities.

Institutional Changes

Out-model institutions and legal and social structure too stand in the way of economic development of the under-developed countries. Lot of reform and reorganisation is essential to initiate and accelerate the process of growth. These institutional changes include land reforms like the abolition of the feudal system, tenancy reform to give security to the tenants and fix fair rent payable by them, ceilings on land holdings community development projects in the rural areas to promote self-reliance and local leadership, *etc*. In the sphere of trade and industry, government encourages small industries and regulates and controls the big corporations to prevent the creation of monopolies. To improve labour efficiency, technical institutions are set up, social security schemes are introduced and housing schemes and welfare activities are undertaken. Producer's co-operatives are set up.

The state also regulates relations between labour and capital to maintain industrial peace by means of labour legislation to increase output and minimise losses. The government also promotes marketing to enable the producers to get a fair price for the products.

These measures accelerate economic growth by improving the organisation of production and building up non-material or intangible capital which assist productive effort as much as material capital.

Direct Participation

In addition to the measures mentioned above, the governments in underdeveloped countries directly participate in economic enterprises to assist private enterprise or to set for them a model to follow. In pursuance of the Industrial Policy Resolutions of 1948 and 1956, the Government of India has set up huge public undertakings in diverse fields like the steel plants, heavy electricals, heavy engineering machine tools, fertilizers, oil refineries, antibiotics, *etc*. The profits of these undertakings are available for use in economic development plans. The government mainly confines itself to basic, heavy and key industries which help other industries, whereas the private sector operates in manufacturing and consumption goods industries.

Indirect Measures

Besides promoting economic development directly as explained above, the governments of under-developed countries promote economic growth of their countries indirectly too. The indirect measures relate to the adoption of economic policies which may be conducive to economic growth. These policies mainly are: monetary policy, fiscal policy and commercial policy. The objective of monetary policy is to control and regulate credit to ensure growth with stability. Credit is liberalised to help industrial and business enterprise, but when it is felt that too easy monetary conditions are hampering growth, credit curbs are applied to check speculation and inflation. As for fiscal policy, taxation is used as an instrument for checking consumption, increasing savings and for preventing investment in undesirable channels and canalising them into desired directions so that economic growth is accelerated and not slowed down. Commercial policy is so designed as to check undesirable imports and promote exports. Foreign exchange dealings are regulated and exchange control instituted to prevent balance of payments position getting out of hand.

Conclusion

Thus, the government in an under-developed country has a vital role to play in stepping up its rate of growth directly by participation in economic activity, by providing economic and social overhead capital or building the necessary infrastructure, by creating financial institutions and by moulding the social structure and adapting the legal framework to the tasks of development and indirectly by pursuing suitable monetary, fiscal and trade policies.

Rationale of Public Sector in Economic Development

We have referred above to the direct participation of the government in industrial enterprises with a view to promoting economic growth in the country. This means the launching of public sector enterprises. The rationale of the public sector lies in a large number of imperatives of development which may now be dealt with at some length.

The raison d'etre or a rationale for the public sector undertakings is to be found in the inadequacies or weakness of the price system. The price system, as it actually functions, is far from being an ideal mechanism for the efficient running of an economy-especially, in terms of the three vital considerations of resource allocation, income distribution and employment.

(i) **The Compensatory Role.** The participation of the public sector undertakings in the economic activities is called for when it has a compensatory role to perform. The compensatory role, in turn, would be necessitated when there is a need to compensate for the deficiencies or shortfalls of the price system.

When the public sector assumes a compensatory role it serves to provide a substitute for the private sector of the economy. In fact, the public sector enterprises, then, perform the functions of a corrective activity or device. This in itself provides a rationale for the participation of public enterprises in economic activity.

In the same way, where the price mechanism hinders the full utilisation of resources due to the existence of monopolistic tendencies or externalities, the public sector has to step in to remedy the situation. The public sector, in such cases, makes for the deficiency by its direct participation in productive and distributive activities of the economy.

Again, the compensatory role of the public sector becomes necessary where the price system left to itself, fails to achieve some socially desirable objectives. For instance, if education, health and other welfare activities were in the purview of the private sector, it will lead to both inadequate quantity and inequitable distribution of the service. The public sector can compensate for these deficiencies by undertaking these activities under its own aegis.

(ii) **The Adjunctive Role.** The price system may not only fail to function satisfactorily, but also in a number of situations it may fail altogether. And when the market mechanism fails to operate, certain goods and services would not be produced in the economy. Under such a situation, it is necessary for the public sector to undertake to produce these goods and services. These public activities would, in effect, be an addition to the overall level of economic activity of the economy. That is how an adjunctive role is assumed by the public sector undertakings.

In general, the public sector performs its adjunctive role when it aims at producing 'public goods' or what is the same thing satisfying 'public (or social) wants'. The market mechanism fails to register the true preferences of individuals for public goods (*e.g.*, roads, bridges, courts, police, *etc.*). Since no private enterprise can afford to undertake activities aimed at satisfying 'public (or social) wants', the public sector has necessarily to step-in in this direction.

Role of Public Enterprises in Economic Development

It is now recognised that in the underdeveloped countries, the vicious circle of under-development can be broken only by a bold intervention by the government in the form of public sector enterprises.

The role of public enterprises both in accelerating development and realising the avowed social objectives of under-developed countries can be brought as under:

(*a*) Achieving Socialistic Pattern, (*b*) Building Industrial Base, (*c*) Capital Formation, (*d*) Optimum allocation of resources strategies, (*e*) Balanced and Unbalanced Growth, (*f*) Balanced Regional Development, (*g*) Achieving Social Objectives.

Some other ways in which public sector can promote economic development are as under:–

(i) Diversification of economic structure,

(ii) Enlargement of employment,

(iii) Bridging the entrepreneurial gap,

(iv) Generating foreign exchange earnings,

(v) Supporting private enterprise,

(vi) Bulwark against maleficent tendencies.

Key terms

Economic and Social overheads, Reforms, Land reforms, Role of Public sector.

QUESTIONS

1. Discuss the role of government in promoting economic development.
2. Critically evaluate the role of government in India since 1950.

UNIT II

Development Planning

Chapters

ECONOMIC PLANNING : MEANING AND TYPES

Popularity of Planning

In the previous part, we discussed the theory of economic development. But economic development has been closely linked with planning. Economic planning has become a craze in modern times especially in under-developed or developing countries. The idea of planning acquired a tremendous support after the end of World War II when advanced but disrupted economies had to be rehabilitated and the under-developed economies were fired with the ambition of rapid economic development. This idea was not taken up kindly in some countries by some people. It was perhaps due to the fact that planning came to be most actively associated with socialist economies. Hatred of socialism was transferred to planning too. But such unreasoned opposition to planning has now almost vanished. On the other, hand remarkable achievements of Nazi Germany and Soviet Russia popularised the idea of economic planning.

Even in capitalist countries, where the economy is governed and directed by market incentives, planning is being practised more or less in one or the other sector of the economy. Planning has become popular owing to the basic defects of capitalism and free enterprise and owing to the realisation that, unless a free enterprise economy is regulated and controlled, it would not ensure stable growth or maximise social welfare. That is why about 20 per cent of American economy is planned, because to this extent current resources are controlled and disposed of by the State. Although the distinction between planned and the unplanned economy is there, yet planning has been universally accepted and the planned sector almost everywhere is expanding.

For, the under-developed countries, desirous of accelerating development after achieving political freedom, planning is a *sine qua non* of progress. As Robbins says, "Planning is the grand panacea of our age". It is no longer a forbidden fruit. To quote Lewis: "There are no longer any believers in laissez-faire except on lunatic fringe." The popularity of planning may be summed up in these words: "The change in ideology of the people, their growing social consciousness and the realisation of the social and economic evils of maldistribution of income and wealth have drawn attention to the need for directing economic growth in a manner that would bring about not only increased production but would ensure more equitable distribution of the larger output; egalitarian measures have, therefore, been called for, and regulation of economic mechanism has become necessary to ensure social justice and equility."[1]

1. Bright Singh, D.—*Economic Development*, p. 557.

Although both advanced capitalistic countries and the under-developed countries have adopted planning but there is this difference between the two: in the former it is corrective planning to ensure economic stability, in the latter it is developmental planning to secure rapid growth.

Meaning of Planning

There is lack of unanimity among economists and political thinkers as to what planning means. No precise and universally acceptable definition can be offered. The idea underlying planning is a conscious and deliberate use of the resources of the community with a view to achieving certain targets of production. The State, through a planning authority, takes the responsibility of planning. It represents a complete break from the policy of laissez-faire.

Thus, Prof. H. D. Dickinson defines economic planning as "the making of major economic decisions—what and how much is to be produced and to whom it is to be allocated by the conscious decision of a determinate authority, on the basis of a comprehensive survey of the economic system as a whole."[2] In the words of the Second Five-Year Plan of India, economic planning is "essentially a way of organising and utilising resources to maximum advantage in terms of defined social ends. The two main constituents of the concept of planning are: (*i*) A system of ends to be pursued, and (*ii*) knowledge as to the available resources and their optimum allocations."[3] Thus, planning is a technique for achieving certain self-defined and pre-determined goals laid down by a central planning authority.

The idea of planning will be clear by drawing distinction between a planned economy and an unplanned economy.

Distinction between Planned and Unplanned Economy. The unplanned economy relies on market mechanism for the utilization of the community's resource of productive purpose. The market mechanism interprets consumer's preferences to the producer through the medium of higher prices and promise of higher profits. A planned economy, on the other hand, represents a much more determinate organisation of resources and specifying goals to be achieved and the commodities to be produced. The State is vested with the necessary powers to pursue these goals and exploit the resources along the pre-determined channels in conformity with the goals already fixed.

Thus the main implications of planning are:–

(*a*) Formulation of objectives or goals;

(*b*) Fixing targets to be achieved and priorities of production for each sector of the economy;

(*c*) Mobilisation of the financial and other resources required for the execution of the plan;

(*d*) Creation of the necessary organisation or agency for the execution of the plan; and

(*e*) Creating assessment machinery for assessing the progress made.

It is immaterial whether there is public ownership and/or control of resources or not, although public ownership and control would be more conducive to effective planning. State initiative and State regulation and control are, however, essential for successful execution of a plan. Robbins says: "Planning in the modern jargon involves government control of production in some form or other." A central economic authority regulates output, prices and costs.

In the words of Mrs. Barbara Wootton, "Planning may be defined as the conscious and deliberate choice of economic priorities by some public authority." But the public authority must also carry out these priorities through the agency of the State organs.

Thus, planning, in short, may be defined as conceiving, initiating, regulating and controlling economic activity by the State according to set priorities with a view to achieving well-defined objective within a given time.

FORMS OF PLANNING

Authoritarian and Democratic Planning

The type of planning that has been done in Soviet Russia, China and other socialist countries is authoritarian planning and that in India and other democratic countries is democratic planning. In authoritarian planning, the government is the sole centralised agency which draws the plan and implements it. It is move comprehensive, systematic and rigid—and is more efficient. In democratic planning, the plan is prepared by an expert body called the planning commission, which is outside the government or the executive and it is finally approved by legislature which represents the people. It is based on the system of free enterprise, but economic activity outside the public sector is sought to be regulated and guided indirectly by providing incentives for investment through fiscal or monetary policies.

General and Partial Planning

Several other varieties of planning are now known to the students of Economics. There is general planning in which a comprehensive and integrated plan is conceived, initiated and executed by a central authority. The plan covers all aspects of the economy and the central authority completely controls the investment

State plays its active role in indicative planning.

2. Dickinson, H.D., *Economics of Socialism*, 1939, p. 41.
3. Government of India, *First Five-Year Plan,* 1951, p. 7.

and utilisation of resources.

As against general planning, there is partial planning, a sort of piece-meal planning in which the plan covers only some important sectors of the economy. Strictly speaking partial planning is no planning.

Functional and Structural Planning

Then again, planning may be attempted within the existing socio-economic framework or it may seem to change the existing order radically. The former is known as **functional planning** and the latter **structural planning.** Functional planning assumes that planning is possible even in a capitalistic economy, whereas advocates of structural planning think that planning and capitalism are incompatible. Quite respectable opinions have taken sides on this question. For instance, Dr. Ludwig Von Mises is of the view that "planning and capitalism are utterly incompatible." On the other hand Professor Landauer holds the opinion that planning and capitalism could be reconciled. We are inclined to agree with the latter view and hold that even capitalist countries can have a measure of planning and benefit from its technique in order to carry the economy forward on the road of economic progress or eliminate serious imbalances in the economy.

Planning by Inducement and Planning by Direction

Sometimes the State try to achieve objectives of planning in an indirect manner. There is private enterprise throughout the economy and market mechanisms in full operation. The State just offers certain inducements and incentives. That is what a predominantly capitalistic economy like the American economy would do. As against **induced planning** or indicative planning, there is compulsory planning or planning by direction under a central directing authority.

Indicative Planning. Planning by inducement is often referred to as indicative planning. In this type of planning, the planner either subsidies production or controls prices, if it is intended to increase the consumption of a commodity. The first acts on the supply side and the latter on the demand side. Cheaper price is an inducement for the consumer and subsidy an inducement for the producer. This is planning through the market mechanism. The citizen wants freedom of choice in consumption. This freedom exerts pressure for free adjustment of production to consumption. Similarly, the worker demands freedom to choose his own job. This means that besides consumers market there must also be a labour market. This leaves a narrow sphere for State control.

The basic idea is that the market controls the entrepreneurs and State can control the entrepreneur by controlling the market. The State tries to manipulate the market by means of incentives and inducements through price fixation, taxation and subsidies. The government seeks to influence economic and investment decisions by offering incentives to entrepreneurs via fiscal and monetary policies but does not control or regulate the functioning of the economy directly. Planning by inducements avoids swollen bureaucracy. Thus, it is planning by persuasion rather than compulsion. There is freedom of enterprise, freedom of production and consumption subject to some regulation or control by the state.

However, immobility of resources imposes serious limitations on planning by inducement. This immobility creates shortages which cannot be eliminated merely by price control and rationing. Measures have to be taken not only to distribute supplies equitably but also to augment supplies. There are writers who are not prepared to consider indicative planning as planning in the real sense of the word. According to them, there can be no planning without direct orders or directions so as to compel economic activities to conform to the plan programmes and objectives.

The **merit** of indicative planning are: (*a*) Consumer's sovereignty remains intact; (*b*) There is freedom of enterprise; (*c*) It is flexible; (*d*) It is democratic.

As against these merits, there are some **demerits** too: (*a*) It fails to achieve the objectives of planning or targets of production; (*b*) The private entrepreneurs care more for profit than for the growth of the economy; (*c*) The fiscal and monetary policies of the government are not so successful in the under-developed countries; controls lead to black markets. (*d*) The producers may not find the incentives offered by the state attractive enough to follow the state guide-lines. The disincentives for the consumers may not be deterrent enough to curb wasteful consumption; (*e*) The working of the market forces fail to bring about proper adjustment between demand and supply and thus create inbalances in the economy.

As Prof. Dobb observes: "Without large public sector and large government investment the plan targets may remain pious hopes that are unrealised in practice."

Planning by direction implies minute and detailed instructions being given both to producers and consumers. A list of all commodities to be produced with the quantity of each has to be prepared as well as a separate list for each of the complements and substitutes. Planning by direction is very comprehensive. It covers the entire economy. There is complete concentration of economic authority in the state. There is one authority which is in sole charge of planning, directing and execution of the plan in accordance with pre-determined targets and priorities. Only planning by direction can guarantee the success of the plan, otherwise the targets would turn out to be mere pious wishes. This means that the economic plan should have at its back the full authority of the state not merely in planning but also in its implementation or execution. As Dr. Oskar Lange observes, "With regard to the socialist sector the national plan represents a binding directive. The targets of the national plan and its financial provisions represent orders to be carried out of the various ministries and the enterprises subject to them. They are duty bound to carry out the directives of the plan."

Planning by direction suffers from certain shortcomings: (*i*) It is undemocratic since the people are ignored all along. It is bureaucratic and totalitarian and, as such, involves the treatment of human being as mere pegs in a big bureaucratic machine. There is no economic freedom. Rationing and control result in black marketing and corruption. (*ii*) Owing to the complexity an many-sidedness of modern economic system, planning by direction does not yield satisfactory results. It is too formidable a task. No person or body of persons can perform this task satisfactorily. (*iii*) There is bound to be shortage of some and surplus of other commodities. (*iv*) Besides, this sort of planning is bound to be inflexible. The plan once prepared must be adhered to, on part of the plan can be altered affecting the whole plan. (*v*) The fulfilment of the plan cannot be anticipated, because conditions keep changing. Black markets emerge to overcome the imperfections of the plan. (*vi*) Planning by direction also leads to excessive standardisation which impinges on consumers sovereignty. (*vii*) It also involves huge administrative costs—elaborate censuses, numerous forms and army of clerks.

Planning by direction is too bureacratic and totalitarian.

As Lewis remarks, "When government is doing only a few things we can keep an eye on it, but when it is doing everything it cannot even keep an eye on itself." These are a few difficulties or shortcomings of Planning by direction. But the choice between these two types of planning is determined by the system of government prevailing in the country. A democratic government adopts indicative planning whereas a socialist state will adopt planning by direction.

Centralised Planning vs. *Decentralised Planning*

Some other forms of planning may be (*a*) centralised planning and (*b*) decentralised planning. In the case of the former, planning is done by a central authority. It is done from the top. Each citizen, producer or consumer, has simply to carry out the instructions or the job or duty assigned to him. In the case of decentralised planning, however, we plan from the bottom. For instance, each village panchayat may be asked to prepare a plan for the economic development of the village and each industry may be asked to prepare its own plan. Out of these plans, an integrated plan may then be evolved for the country as a whole.

Physical and Financial Planning. Here we come to the question whether we fix the size of investment in terms of real resources which is known as physical planning or in terms of money which is known as financial planning. Ultimately, however, financial resources will have to be translated into real resources for money as such serves no purpose. If adequate finance is not available, it can be created through deficit financing. In under-developed countries, there always exist unutilised or under-utilised resources, for instance, uncultivated land, unemployed labour, hoarded wealth, *etc*. These resources can be mobilised by "creating" money.

In the case of financial planning, the planners determine how much money will have to be invested in order to achieve the pre-determined objectives or targets. Total outlay is fixed in terms of money on the basis of growth rate to be achieved, the various targets of production, estimates of the required quantity of consumer goods and the various social services, expenditure on the necessary infrastructure, *etc*., as well as revenue from taxation borrowings and savings (The financing of economic development has been discussed in an earlier chapter No. 77). This money is then used to mobilise the required resources. There has thus to be an integration between physical planning and financial planning. Indian planning has been mostly financial planning although some targets have been set in concrete and real terms, *e.g.*, the output of food-grains.

A merit of financial planning is that it facilitates adjustment between demand and supply. As India's Second Five Year Plan States, "The essence of financial planning is to ensure that the demands and supplies are matched in a manner which exploits physical potentialities as fully as possible without major and unplanned changes in the price structure".[4]

Finance holds the key to the success of a plan. If

4. p. 16.

the country is able to raise adequate financial resources the success of the plan is assured. But failure to raise the required resources will spell its failure. It will not be able to achieve the targets set out for it.

Limitations of Financial Planning. Financial planning has its own limitations: (*a*) An attempt to raise taxes to too high a level will adversely affect the capacity of the people to save which may hamper the development process. (*b*) Owing to smallness of organised money sector and the existence of a larger non-monetised sector, the estimates of financial resources may go wrong. Even the physical targets may be upset. Imbalances between the monetised and non-monetised sectors may result in shortages and in inflationary pressures. Hence financial planning is more suitable for sector planning than for over all planning. (*c*) Financial planning may not provide for the expansion of employment opportunities at a scale so as to absorb the new entrants to the labour market. Hence people's needs both for work and employment may remain unsatisfied.

Physical Planning. In physical planning, the planning authority has to work out how much land, labour, materials and capital equipment will be required to implement, the plan and achieve the targets set out for it. Physical planning makes for concreteness in planning. As is stated in India's Second Five Year Plan, physical planning "is an attempt to work out the implication of the development effort in terms of factor allocations and product yields so as to maximise incomes and employment".[5] It is an input-output analysis. It implies proper evaluation of the relationship between investment and output. In physical planning, the planners have to determine not only the account of investment but also work out its composition in terms of the various goods and services required to obtain a certain increase of output of product. For instance, it has to be worked out as to how much of cotton, coal or electric power and other ingredients will go into an output of 1,000 metres of cloth. That is how calculations have to be made for each type of goods to achieve the targeted quantity. In this way, planned increase in the output of various goods is matched with the amounts and various types of investments. Financial planning is only a means to achieve the various targets laid down in the plan.

Thus, in physical, we make an overall assessment of the available real resources like raw materials, manpower and capital equipment and devise ways and means to mobilise them in amounts sufficient to enable us to achieve the various targets of production. These targets are laid in physical terms, *e.g.*, so many tons of steel, foodgrains, coal, sugar and so many million metres of cloth, *etc*., in agricultural and industrial sectors and also for economic overheads like roads and rail kilometrage, *etc*., or so many million jobs to be created, so many doctors and engineers to be trained and the number and type of educational institutions, and so on. But the various targets have to be properly matched and balanced. The test of the soundness of planning lies in the avoidances of imbalances, stresses and strains of any type in the economy.

Financial Planning.

Limitations of Physical Planning. It is not to be understood that physical planning is a straight and simple affair and presents no difficulties. Rather, there are formidable difficulties in the way: (*a*) In the under-developed countries there is statistical blackout so that adequate and reliable statistics regarding the various types of real resources are lacking. It, therefore, becomes really difficult to lay down with any degree of certainty the targets. (*b*) To build up a sound sectoral balance is also a tight-rope dance. That is why when the plan is being implemented all sort of stresses and strains, bottle-necks, shortages and gluts and inflationary pressures appear to thwart the planner's effort. (*c*) Physical planning is not enough to prepare a sound plan for economic development. It has to be supplemented with financial planning. If this is not done, the economic plan will go down against financial rocks. Lack of adequate financial resources has been a major cause of the failure of planning in India.

Thus, both physical and financial planning are necessary to assure the success of the plan. They are complementary to each other just as the right and left legs are needed for walking. There has to be a proper balance between the two. Both techniques must be integrated in the development process.

Conclusion

We have in the world today the above main types of planning or their permutations and combinations. In Soviet Union and China there is general, structural and directional planning. In Nazi Germany and Fascist Italy, planning was general and directional. In the U.S.A. and the U.K. whatever planning is there it is

5. p. 14.

partial, functional and by inducement. In India it is general and partly structural and a combination of planning by inducement and planning by direction. Also, physical and financial planning go side by side.

Case for Planning

An unplanned economy is like a ship moving rudderless on uncharted seas with no fixed destinational and unlikely to reach it if there be any. Such an economy works blindly and haphazardly. It caters for the rich and makes them still richer. It ignores the real wants of the people and fails to promote general well-being. It is the profit motive rather than service of the masses which is the mainspring of economic activity in such an economy. How it operates is no guarantee of economic progress for the less developed economies. The economically advanced countries may not feel enamoured of the idea of planning but for the under-developed economies it is a stark necessity as economic development is now regarded as imperative. Majority of the under-developed countries realise very clearly that they must develop economically and that too very soon.

As Galbraith says, "There is much that market can usefully encourage and accomplish. But the market cannot reach forward and take great strides wen these are called for. As it cannot put a man in space so it cannot bring quickly into existence a steel industry when there was little or no steel making capacity before . . . To trust the market is to take an unacceptable risk that nothing or too little will happen."[6] It is planning alone which can guarantee quick economic growth in the under-developed countries. This explains why there is a clear and pronounced swing of opinion in favour of planning.

We shall now put forward a few arguments for economic planning. Some of these arguments are in favour of planning in general for all countries and some of them apply with a special force to under-developed economies:

(i) Planning is advocated on the ground that the **judgement of the State is superior** to that of the citizen, however wise and able he may be. As Arthur Lewis remarks, "The state now claims to know better than its citizens for how many years they should send their children to school, between what hours they should drink, what proportion of income should be saved, whether cheap houses are better than cigarettes, and so on." Economic development is a more serious matter and should not be left to the individual entrepreneurs. The State represents the accumulated wisdom of centuries and provides talent and

Physical Planning refers to amount of physical resources required for certain objective.

experience beyond the capacity of individual and isolated businessmen. Planning by collective action is indispensable if a country is to develop economically on the right lines and develop at the desired speed.

(ii) Planning also becomes necessary for **equitable distribution of economic power.** The price-mechanism rewards people according to the resources they possess but contains in itself no mechanism for equalisation of the distribution of those resources. There is no wonder, therefore, that there are wide gaps between the 'haves' and 'havenots' which seriously offend against sense of social justice. Shocking economic inequalities are a marked feature of an unplanned economy. Inequalities result in heart burning and social tensions. They also paralyse some of the ablest members of the society. Reduction of inequalities in income, wealth and economic opportunities is, therefore, now the avowed aim of modern welfare States and it is impossible of achievement without the instrument of planning. In the absence of planning, inequalities will not only be perpetuated but accentuated from generation to generation.

(iii) It has been seen that labour legislation alone cannot **protect** labour and harmonise wage relations when market mechanism is permitted to operate freely. A planning authority must step in to so regulate the economic growth of the country as to ensure to the actual workers the fruits of their labour. If there was perfect competition and full employment, the price mechanism, shorn of its imperfections, would have afforded due protection of labour rights. But this is a big 'IF'. The State is a more effective guardian of labour rights than self-adjusting and automatic economic forces. By proper planning, it will be possible to provide perfect social security to all workers.

(iv) Planning has also proved to be a powerful instrument for eliminating instability which is necessary concomitant of free market economy. Private enterprise left to itself would produce trade cycles,

6. Galbraith, John Kenneth—*Economic Development in Perspective*, p. 29.

unemployment and misery. As Barbara Wootton remarks, "The progress of an unplanned capitalist economy has always been liable to interruptions from the tendency of the system to fall over its own toes, from a certain continued instability in its gait." It is now generally agreed that planning of economic activity goes a long way in smoothening the violent oscillations and swings in business, thus preventing undeserved gains and undue hardships. It is on this ground that planning is advocated even for developed and advanced economies. These countries may not need any further economic development; but they certainly need a mechanism which prevent violent ups and downs in the movements of business activity and smoothen the course of business. In the last thirties, every country suffered from Depression except Russia, which was a planned economy.

(v) Again, it is planning alone which can ensure that the terms of **trade remain favourable** to a country. The volume and direction of foreign trade in a country admittedly plays a very important part not only in economic development but also in determining the level of general well-being in a community. But handling of foreign trade by the market has proved utterly inadequate. Foreign trade must be thoroughly planned, if fruits of economic development are not to be thrown away. This aspect of economic development has been paid special attention by planners everywhere.

John Kenneth Galbraith
American Economist.

(vi) Without the aid of planning no country can **cope with major economic changes.** Such changes, *e.g.*, industrial revolution or rationalisation movement, are bound to turn the economy topsy-turvy. The economic system may be thrown out of gear altogether. Private enterprise will feel helpless and stand simply aghast. The planning authority with its resources of men and money can meet all such situations and control the disturbing factors. Major changes can even be anticipated and provided against in good time. The market mechanism cannot move the resources in the desired directions in quantity and with speed which a major change may necessitate. Only a planning authority can eliminate bottle-necks. Under a free market economy, a few persons receive abnormally large income at public expense and the scarce commodities are unjustly distributed. Overproduction is a common phenomenon bringing suffering to the poor. A planned action to speed up the movement of resources at times of major changes is absolutely essential.

***(vii)* Planning eliminates wasteful competition.** The merit of the free market lies in competition being perfect; but in actual life perfect competition is a rare phenomenon. At any rate, there is nothing in the market mechanism that establishes or maintains competition. Only State action can ensure fair competition. Hence, market economy can also be helped to function adequately with the positive support of the planning authority. Huge man-power need not be dissipated in distributional trades nor huge funds frittered away in advertisement and salesmanship. Planning can be combined with a market economy in various degrees. Only by means of planning by direction rather than by means of persuasion or inducement can an economy achieve a desired objective. That is the only way to direct economic life economically, wisely and safely.

(viii) Only a planned economy provides for **proper co-ordination and avoids unnecessary duplication** of staff and equipment. In an unplanned economy, millions of producers work in an independent and isolated fashion without bothering as to what the other businessmen are doing. The cumulative consequence may be confusion and chaos. We might well question with Professor Dobb: "How could order emerge from the conflict of a myriad of independent and autonomous wills?" An unplanned economy, according to Learner, is like "an automobile without a driver but in which many passengers keep reaching over to the steering wheel to give it a twist." It will be a miracle indeed if the automobile reaches its destination safely.

On the whole, therefore, economic decisions in an unplanned economy are likely to be irrational, shortsighted, self-frustrating and socially disastrous. A planning authority, on the other hand, can take farsighted decisions and produce a balanced economy. It can take an overall view, whereas in an unplanned economy each entrepreneur looks to his own interest and nobody bothers about the economy as a whole as a central planning authority can do. As Prof. Durbin remarks, "The general officers on the hill must be able to see more than the ensign in the line of battle."

(ix) Planning makes for **optimum utilisation of a country's resources.** A planning authority is able to lay down what is essential and what is non-essential activity, encouraging the former and sharply cutting down the latter. On the other hand, private enterprise

is guided solely by the profit motive regardless of social benefits or evils. Only a planning authority can ban lipstick and face powder, otherwise valuable national resources will be directed towards the production of useless luxuries for the rich and starve the masses of the necessaries of life. It is to the obvious advantage of a country to concentrate on the production of essentials and avoid wasting its resources on the non-essentials. As Professor Harris says, "Surely no well functioning planned society would allow expenditure of 3 billion on education, and 2 billion on social security, as in the U.S.A. and seven billion on alcoholic beverages."

(*x*) A planned economy will **prevent artificial shortages** being created by profit-greedy businessmen. By means of trusts, cartels, price agreements and market sharing they increase their profits at the expense of the society. The planning authority can smash such designs by positive action in favour of the community. It possesses enough power to ensure the working of the economy in a healthy manner in the best interest of all rather than for the benefit of the few.

(*xi*) By planning it is possible to **keep down or eliminate social costs** which usually take the form of industrial diseases, industrial accidents, overcrowding and insanitary conditions and cyclical unemployment. These social costs are the by-products of capitalism. Since planning extends the sphere of public ownership and control, the evils of capitalism are mitigated. Full co-operation of labour can be secured and anti-social 'go slow' tactics rendered unnecessary resulting in increase in national output.

(*xii*) Planning also results in **higher rate of capital formation.** Private enterprise is more intent on immediate gain rather than future good. It takes a short-sighted view of thing. On the contrary, the planning authority, as the custodian of the national interests, takes a farsighted view. It can look more to the distant future than to the immediate present. It is in a position to sacrifice petty present gains for the future substantial benefits. The surpluses of the public undertakings add to the capital assets of the national instead of going into the pockets of private persons and spent on consumption goods. That is why under planning capital formation receives a great fillip.

The Industrial Revolution.

Planning brings economic change.

Special Case of Under-developed Countries

The arguments given above apply to all countries at all stages of economic development. They largely take their stand on the failure of laissez-faire policy and its general abandonment. It is now realised that lack of co-ordination, recurrence of business cycles, economic inequalities, social parasitism, economic insecurity, wastes of competition, absence of industrial peace and huge social costs which characterise an unplanned economy, can be done away with by resorting to planning. An unplanned economy must act in an erratic and irrational manner.

But planning has a specially strong case of the under-developed economies. In their case, it is not merely necessary to maintain the country's economy in sound health and to ensure a rational and optimum use of the community's resources but also to speed up economic development. They are lagging behind in the race and they are keen to catch up with the advanced economies or at any rate reduce dependence on them as fast as possible. This impatience for accelerating economic development leads inevitably to economic planning. The achievements of the Russian and Chinese economies under planning serve as an example.

The private enterprise in India has not taken India any far on the road of economic progress. It has left untouched and undeveloped some of the vital sectors of the Indian economy. The entrepreneurial ability is lacking in India or exists only in an insignificant measure. The Indian entrepreneurs take up hackneyed lines and give no evidence of innovation. They are more intent on rich quick methods and pursue speculative profits rather than long-term industrial development. They have been attracted more by commerce than by industry. In such countries, it becomes necessary for the State to intervene and provide the right type of entrepreneurship to bring about economic development.

Even in advanced countries the edge of price-mechanism has been blunted. It has failed to function efficiently on account of economic rigidities and structural disequilibria. But in the under-developed countries, intent upon accelerated economic development, little reliance can be placed on price-mechanism for the optimum utilisation of resources and for giving a right direction to the productive machine of the community. It will only function erratically, fitfully and irrationally. There will be no guarantee that the equality and quantity of production is what the nation needs. Much more positive action is needed to give right direction to productive activity. In order to speed up the rate of economic development, price-mechanism, as governing economic development, must go or its functioning confined to unimportant sectors of the economy like the purchase and sale of consumer goods. Only then, the under-developed countries will come out of the morass of poverty and economic stagnation. Only by planning can specific objectives be attained and targets of production achieved. At every five-year period, progressively higher targets can be fixed and effective means to achieve them adopted.

Capital formation and skill formation are of crucial importance for any stage of economic development. These two determinants of economic growth have a very tardy and unsatisfactory development in backward and under-developed economies. Planning is essential to build up these necessary elements of productive power. Planning authority can launch a vigorous savings drive and control and guide investment of the mobilised resources in the desired channels. Normally in backward countries, rich people prefer investment in land, housing property and jewellery. This sort of investment is no good for speedy economic development of the country. That is why Indian government has come hard upon the gold hoardings. Drastic measures have to be taken to take over hoarded wealth lying unproductively in lockers and private hoards in order to help capital formation. This can only be done under planning.

Voluntary savings can be supplemented by revenue surplus 'Disguised unemployment', which is a special feature of an under-developed economy, is another source that can be tapped. We have surplus labour in agriculture which represents disguised unemployment. Such labour can be withdrawn from agriculture and put to more productive employment. The State, in an under-developed country, can also resort to deficit financing and thus increase the financial resources available for economic development.

Even then foreign aid may become necessary. For planned economic development, foreign aid is readily made available. A country which has no plan and which may rightly be considered as going nowhere, cannot hope to secure foreign financial assistance, but planned economies can. Colombo Plan and foreign aid given to Pakistan and India are the examples which can be cited. These are a few measures by means of which financial resources of a country can be built up under planning.

Glaring inequalities of wealth and income and of economic opportunities is another painful feature of under-developed countries. These inequalities can also be reduced through planning. Slogan of equality whips up the enthusiasm of the people and induces them to put in their best effort.

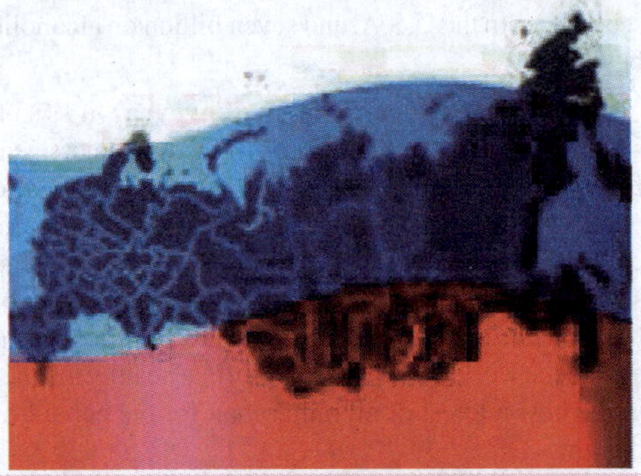

Planning in Russia has been a story of success.

The demographic factor is another hindrance in backward countries which can also be overcome by planning. A country with increasing population must run fast in order to keep up its present position. Increase in national wealth is swallowed up by still many more mouths. There is no escape from planning in such countries.

The socio-religious attitudes of the people also call for an effective State action to make them act in a more rational manner. It is well known that social and religious institutions of India have hindered economic growth in the past. A planned programme is essential to neutralise the adverse effect of such obsolete notions and institutions.

The paucity of trained, competent and honest administrators in backward countries has also to be made up and calls for a planned endeavour.

Conclusion. These are some of the special problems which an under-developed country has to tackle. It is now already realised and universally admitted that these problems can be effectively tackled by planning and by planning alone. Planning in such countries is needed, above all, for accelerating economic development. There is need in such countries, as Galbraith says, not only for development "but an urgent demand that it should occur promptly."

Planning in UDCs such on India is a gateway to development.

Prof. D.R. Gadgil indicates the need for, and justification of, planning in these words, "Planning for economic development is undertaken presumably because the pace or direction of development taking place in the absence of external intervention is not considered to be satisfactory and because it is further held that appropriate external intervention will result in increasing considerably the pace of development and directing it properly. Planning seeks to bring about a rationalisation and, if possible and necessary, some reduction of consumption to evolve and adopt a long-term plan of appropriate investment of capital resources with progressively improved techniques, a programme of training and education through which the competence of labour to make use of capital resources is increased, and a better distribution of the national product so as to attain social security and peace. Planning, therefore, means, in a sense, no more than better organisation, consistent and far-seeing organisation and comprehensive all-sided organisation. Direction, regulation, controls on private activity, and increasing the sphere of public activity, are all parts of organisational effort."[7]

Pre-requisites of Successful Planning

Although planning has been almost universally adopted but the development plans have not invariably been successful. The successful implementation of the plan requires the existence of certain pre-conditions:

(i) It needs a **strong and efficient government** and a clean administration to ensure the success of the plan. It is the government which has to get the plan prepared and it is the government machinery through which the plan is to be implemented. Weak and inefficient government and corrupt administration will distort everything and the plan will end in a smoke. Planning will be a farce and not a reality.

(ii) Besides a sound and strong political frame, the **economic organisation of the country should also be sound** and susceptible to rapid growth. That is why stress is laid on reorganisation of the agrarian system or restructuring of the industrial system of the country to ensure success of planning. In India, zamindari system had to be abolished and tenants given proper protection to make agriculture efficient. There was reform also of the banking system and of company organisation.

(iii) The **objectives of planning** should be well-defined and co-ordinated. Confused and conflicting objectives will lead the economy nowhere. For instance, it should be clear whether the plan aims at increasing output or at more even distribution of wealth and income or whether food self-sufficiency is the aim or rapid industrialisation is the objective.

(iv) For the successful implementation of a plan a **whole-hearted co-operation of the people** is essential. People are no dumb-driven cattle. Unless they co-operate nothing can be achieved. Coercion will merely lead to the adoption of subterfuges. It is necessary that the people at large should feel the urge for development and should welcome planning for development. They should have the necessary will to carry out the plan and behave in a disciplined and patriotic manner. They should be convinced that their self-interest coincides with the broad objectives of the plan.

(v) It is also very necessary for the formulation of the plan that the necessary **statistical data** should be available. The data should be adequate, up-to-date and correct. In the absence of correct statistical information, planning will merely be a leap in the dark.

(vi) Successful planning requires that reasonable and **appropriate targets** should be fixed. If the targets are too ambitious, their non-achievement may cause frustration, and, if they are too low, the pace of development may be less than it can be. Similarly, it is necessary that since the resources at the disposal of the country are limited, a proper order of priorities should be laid down so that first things are tackled first. Only in this way, the limited available productive resources will be made the best use of.

(vii) To ensure success of planning, it is also very necessary that there should be proper balance in the various parts of the plan or sectorial planning. If the plan does not provide for proper balances, bottlenecks or shortages and gluts are bound to appear and upset the plan.

7. Gadgil, D.R., *Planning and Economic Policy in India*, p. 88.

Coperation is essential for planning.

(viii) Proper development policy is another desideratum of successful planning. Proper development policy should embrace careful survey of national resources, scientific research, market research, building up of adequate infrastructure (transport and communications, irrigation and power, *etc.*), provision of specialised training and educational facilities, suitable legal framework, assistance for the entrepreneurs, promoting saving and investment, and so on.

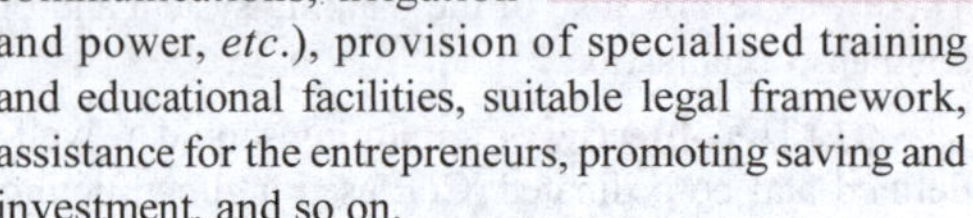

Conclusion. Very few under-developed countries fulfill the above conditions. That is why there is generally a wide gap between promise and performance. It is seldom that the targets are fully achieved. People get despaired and disgusted and planning loses credibility. If planning is to succeed earnest effort should be made to create the conditions which will be conductive to the success of planning.

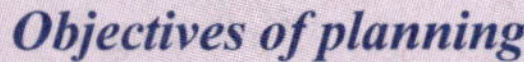

Objectives of planning

Planning is regarded as a panacea for all economic ills. It is, therefore, advocated for the achievement of a variety of objectives. It may be introduced for increasing national income or raising living standards or to fill up gaps in economic structure or to achieve self-sufficiency in food and raw materials or for bringing about rapid and adequate industrialisation or to correct serious imbalance or lopsidedness in economic development or to reduce inequalities and establish a socialistic pattern of society and so on.

The objectives are not the same for all countries or the same for a country at all times. What precisely are the objectives placed by the planners before them depends on the stage of economic development, the nature of economic development, socio-economic conditions prevalent at the time and the requirements of a particular situation. It may be pointed out at the same time that all these objectives are inter-related and complementary rather than exclusive.

We may now say a word about some major objectives of planing:

Achieving Full Employment. In economically advanced countries the aim of the State is to provide full employment. All modern States have, in fact, underwritten employment. If they cannot provide work, they have to give doles which are demoralising and inadequate. Unemployment is the byproduct of capitalism and is considered to be the biggest headache of a modern capitalistic society. If capitalism cannot be ended, at any rate, unemployment must be ended. In such cases, efforts of planned development and directed to those directions and those sectors where unemployment is found to exist. The State can redistribute labour and create work opportunities.

We in Indian may not be able to create conditions of full employment at any foreseeable future but we can certainly reduce the incidence of unemployment. For instance, India's Five-Year Plans have aimed at providing additional employment opportunities for millions of additional hands. The objective of British planning during 1945-57 was one of achieving full employment. Thus, creating employment or reducing unemployment may well be a major objective of planning.

Maximisation of National Income and Raising Living Standards. This is another laudable objective that the planners seek to pursue especially in poor countries like India. Over the First Plan period, our national income increased by 18 per cent, over the Second Plan by 21.4 per cent and over the Third Plan it was estimated to have risen by 20 per cent. The Fourth Plan aimed to raise it by 25-27 per cent. Only a concentrated and planned effort can raise national income .The unplanned development does not register any substantial progress in this direction, because the productive effort is diffused. Maximisation of national income has been the objective before planning authorities in the U.S.A.

Rapid Industrialisation. This is another important objective which the planners try to pursue. This objective assumes importance in countries which have been left behind in the race of industrialisation. South America had this objective before it while framing its development plans. India also aimed at rapid industrialisation in the Second Plan. It is realised that industrialisation makes more significant contribution to the raising of national income and to the solution of the problem of unemployment. Few countries can become prosperous by merely confining themselves to agriculture as India has been doing in the past. Economies predominantly agricultural are bound to remain backward. Rapid industrialisation is, therefore, a very desirable aim of planning.

Self-sufficiency in Food and Raw Materials. As a preparation for more systematic and intensive planning, it may be considered necessary first to make the country self-sufficient in food and essential raw materials. That would provide a solid and sound base for the economy and prepare it for further building up. India, in the First plan, concentrated mainly on agriculture. Dependence on foreign food is dangerous. The first duty of a nation is to feed its people. Political freedom may prove a farce without freedom from foreign fòod, especially when war clouds may be hovering overhead. It is understandable, therefore, that this objective may take precedence over other objectives when a Plan is being conceived.

Reduction of Inequalities. It is now realised that political equality is illusory unless it is accompanied by economic equality. Glaring inequalities of wealth, income and opportunities are shocking to the democratic conscience. Socialism is in the air; it has a very wide appeal in modern times. In poor countries, it is a painful sight that the masses of people should be on the border line of starvation, whereas a few rich people should be rolling in all conceivable luxuries. It is natural, therefore, that the planners, who are custodians of general welfare, should so shape their plans as to make the poor people less poor and the rich a little less rich, so that the gulf between the two is narrowed down as much as is humanly possible. The Indian planners have before them the establishment of socialistic pattern of society as one of the objectives.

Redressing Imbalances in the Economy. It is sometimes found that the economic development in a country is lopsided, for instance, an economy may be predominantly agricultural. In India, nearly three-fourths of the people are engaged in agriculture, whereas nearly one-tenth pursue industry. This is an example of unbalanced economy. To lend stability to the economy, it becomes essential first to reduce this imbalance. The planning authority cannot ignore this aspect of development.

It is not necessary that the planning authority should adopt only one objective. That perhaps may be possibly for countries like the U.S.A. and European countries which are economically well advanced and they have not much to seek now. But the under-developed countries suffer from several shortcomings and the planners must pay attention to various important objectives simultaneously. Their plans are generally multi-objective. However, lest the effort should get diffused, it is necessary to confine to a few principal objectives at one time, choosing those which may be felt to be most essential in the context of the economic situation prevailing at the time.

Self sufficiency in food ensures success in planning for developemnt.

Formulation and implementation of a plan

Let us now have some idea about planning techniques or methodology. The first step that the planners take is to lay down the broad objectives of the plan. As we have said before, the choice of objectives depends on the economic situation that the country may be facing.

The next step is to fix the size of the plan or to determine investment. Growth models are now available with the help of which it is possible to arrive at the investment figure. The planners make use of the concept of the capital-output ratio or capital co-efficient as the necessary tool. This tool is used to ascertain how much capital would be needed to secure a given unit of increase in income. For instance, if in a country capital-output ratio is 3 : 1 it will mean that an investment of Rs. 3 will add to national income or Rs. 1. The capital-output ratio is ascertained by means of a careful study of the industrial situation. In India, the capital-output ratio for the First Plan worked out at 1.8 : 1 though the Planning Commission had assumed it as 3 : 1, for the Second Plan it was estimated at 2.3 : 1 and for the Third Plan at 2.6 : 1.

The Harrod-Dommar model is the most popular growth model. This enables us to determine the rate of investment (or saving-income ratio) necessary for achieving a certain rate of economic growth. In Indian planning, investment as a percentage of the national income rose from 6.6 per cent in the First Plan to 9.5 per cent in the Third Plan. The Fourth plan aimed at raising it from 11.3 per cent in 1968-69 to 14.5 per cent in 1973-74. In the Western countries, the rate of capital formation ranged from 10 to 15 per cent, in Japan 16 to 20 per cent between 1913 and 1939. The U.S.S.R. has maintained a high investment rate of 15 to 20 per cent.

It is generally considered desirable that under-developed countries, intent on rapid economic development, must be prepared to invest 15 per cent of the national income. According to Prof. Rostow, a rise of investment from 5 to 10 per cent of national income is essential to enable a country to reach the 'take-off' stage. Since, however, these countries are poor and having low living standards, the investment ratio cannot be very high if hardship is to be avoided. Thus, low saving-income ratio acts as a limiting factor on economic growth. On the basis of the capital-output ratio and considering the percentage increase in national income aimed at, it is possible to work out the aggregate investment required.

Fixing a target for an economic effort is important in Planning.

Having fixed the size of the Plan, the next stage is to work out the details and fix targets for each individual economic effort on the basis of certain priorities. In order to evolve a sound and workable plan, it will be essential to ensure a **proper balance between the several major portions of the plan** to avoid either gluts or shortages.

A crosswise balance will establish an equilibrium between the aggregate output targets and the aggregate resources available. For the soundness and efficiency of the plan, it is essential that there should be close correspondence between the available resources and the aggregate production schedules. Power, labour and transport are the most important resources which require balancing with the targets of production. In order to ensure that the targets fixed are mutually consistent, balances will have to be established between production targets and the productive resources. Physical targets must be balanced against financial resources that can be mobilised. A 'backward balance' is also required between the final products and the numerous components which enter into their production. Inter-industry balances are a *sine qua non* of sound and efficient planning. The Indian plans did not establish cross-wise balances or backward balances so that bottlenecks held up the execution of the plans.

No plans need considered as absolutely final. In the course of implementation of a plan, new situation appear and have to be provided for. Hence, there should be provision for supplementary planning or for a revised plan. For the under-developed countries it is wise to split the plan into two parts: (*a*) **'core' plan** which must be carried out at all costs and (*b*) **'contingent' plan** which may be implemented if the funds are available. That is what India did in the case of re-appraisal of the Second Plan in 1958.

It is necessary that there should be a certain degree of flexibility in planning. The plan can then be modified in the light of new requirements or new situations or new experiences. However, the main structure or character of the Plan should stand firm. Too much flexibility may nullify planning altogether. The basic structure or the core of the plan should not be tampered with.

We have now reached the final stage in the process of planning. The broad objectives have been laid down, the size of the plan has been fixed, financial resources mobilised, priorities determined and targets fixed. Now administrative machinery must be created to carry out the plan with faith and vigour. Even a good plan may come to nought unless competent and efficient administration is there to implement it. There should also be provision for supervision and regular assessment or evaluation of the work done. In the Soviet Union, the Gosplan acts as the watcher. The Planning Commission in India has set up the programme evaluation organisation for community projects. But what is needed is that the work of the entire plan should be evaluated.

Features of a Planned Economy

If we have a look at the planned economies, say, Russian, Chinese or even Indian economy, we shall discover some common characteristics. Formulation of the plan and its implementation call for a certain type of economic and administrative organisation and a certain type of endeavour and set up. It is only natural, therefore, that the planned economies reveal some common features. The distinction between planned and unplanned economies rests largely on the dominant role played by the State in the planned economy and the laissez-faire doctrine swaying the State in the unplanned economy. State initiative, State regulation, State control of foreign trade, investment, price, *etc*., largely shape the economy under planning. The desire for accelerated economic development colours the social, political and economic outlook. The attitude of the people is to look at the economy as a whole rather than looking exclusively at their own individual affairs.

The following are some of the main features of a planned economy:

Existence of a Central Planning Authority. All countries, launching economic planning, have at the top of economic affairs a Planning Commission or a Central Planning Authority, *e.g.*, Gosplan in the U.S.S.R. and a Planning Commission in India. Planning has no meaning unless it is centrally planned. Planning by individual industries or organisations will simply constitute plans and not planning. For successful and efficient planning, a central planning body is essential and all planned economies have established such bodies. This body conceives the plan, prepares the plan, suggests measures for its implementation, supervises the working of the plan and assesses the achievements. Only a central body can perform these functions so that it may look at the economy as a whole.

Communist Party → Gosplan → Ministries → Directors

Structure of top down soviet decision making process.

Laying down Objectives. Planning to be fruitful must keep steadily in view certain broad objectives which have to be realised. In the absence of such objectives planning will merely be a leap in the dark. Planning is not a policy of drift and the economic endeavour under planning has not to be haphazard. Certain very desirable objectives are laid down beforehand after careful consideration and due deliberation. However, it is essential that objectives are not to be mere dreams or distant ideals but they should be realistic and should look feasible and within reach. As we have discussed in an earlier section, the usual objectives are maximisation of national income and rapid industrialisation, providing full employment, achieving a socialistic pattern, achieving self-sufficiency, *etc*. Of course, the objectives will be laid down in the context of economic situation.

Fixing Targets. Allied with the laying down of objectives is the fixing of targets. The objectives indicate the directions in which the economy is to move and targets are fixed for the realisation of those objectives. Targets are fixed for each industry and for each sector of major industries, transport and communication, for imports and exports, and also in the field of education and public health. The target indicates the job assigned to each sector of the economy. When we take the aim carefully the chances are that we may hit the target. Thus, fixing to targets is essential to give a concrete shape to our aims and make each sector of the economy move on the road to progress with determination. Fixing of targets enables the Planning Commission to determine the success or failure of each component part of the economy. In the case of failure, weak spots can be discovered and remedial measures adopted.

Controls. A planned economy has of necessity to be subjected to a variety of controls. The working of free market economy has to be modified and controlled in the interest of overall planned development. Price mechanism ordinarily guides the capitalistic economy, but, when planning is adopted, free functioning of price mechanism has to be restrained. A limit has to be put on consumer's sovereignty. All types of markets, *e.g.*, consumer's markets, producer's markets, labour market, capital market, *etc*., must either be suspended or their activities seriously curtailed so as to make them conform to the requirements of planning. Thus, in a planned economy, we have price controls on the distribution of essential goods and scarce raw materials through fair price shops and co-operative stores, import control, export control, exchange control, control of capital issues, licensing of factories, *etc*. Laissez-fair is dead and gone in all planned economies and extensive State control takes its place.

Systematic and Co-ordinated Effort. Planning has to be comprehensive and not isolated and piecemeal. Hence individualistic, isolated and independent action on the part of various sectors is naturally out of place. All economic efforts aiming at accelerated economic development must be properly co-ordinated. The plans of individual industries for instance must be dovetailed. This will secure the necessary balance between the various parts of the plan. Only an integrated and co-ordinated plan can bring a community nearer to the objectives it has set before itself. The economic endeavour must be regular, sustained and systematic and not haphazard, diffused, indiscriminate and fitful. Without co-ordination, a country will land itself into chaos and economic mess.

Growing Public Sector. Another important feature of a planned economy is the vital role played by the public sector and its growing importance. Private sector cannot be expected to sink capital in enterprises in which the return is long-delayed and is uncertain. It will avoid pioneering tasks which are naturally hazardous. Nor can the private sector be expected to build up a modern steel plant. In certain lines of industry, the market may not be sufficient to attract private capital. In under-developed countries, the entrepreneurs prefer to invest in commerce to investing in industry. Thus, many industries of vital national importance remain neglected. Heavy industries are beyond the means of private entrepreneurs but they are indispensable for building up a self-reliant and self-generating economy.

Planning in India has come to Stay.

The State as the custodian of national interests must step in where private enterprise is shy and is found wanting. The public sector really provides the essential framework for spreading out the planned economic activity. In India, quite a large number of important industries have been exclusively reserved for the public sector under the Industrial Policy Resolutions of 1948 and 1956. The public enterprises not only fill up the gaps in industrial structure but also provide the foundation and pave the way for further economic development. In all planned economies, the public sector is steadily expanding and assuming greater and greater importance.

Other Features. Better balance, more even distribution of economic power, greater economic stability, higher level of employment, fuller utilisation or resources, greater security for the workers, elimination of recurring business cycles are some other features of a planned economy.

Concept of Rolling Plan

The Indian Planning Commission decided in September 1977 to introduce the rolling plan concept with effective from April 1, 1978 with a view to ensuring greater flexibility and realism in planning. This decision constitutes a major departure from the past pattern of five-year plans.

It was felt that the past pattern proved to be vulnerable to changes in the domestic and international economies and did not adequately provide for the inevitable fluctuations in agricultural output.

Under the rolling plan concept, a five-year plan is formulated as before, but it is revised every year in the light of the performance of the various sectors of the economy and availability of resources. That is, there is an annual operational plan for each year with a fresh five-year perspective. Thus, there is a five-year plan in continuous existence, being reviewed and extended year by year.

Jawahar Lal Nehru (1889-1964) First Prime Minister and Architect of modern in India.

In essence, the new system provides a continuum of realistic annual plans each rolling on the other with a changing five-year perspective which would be readjusted in accordance with changing economic conditions.

For almost a quarter of a century, the Planning Commission in India has been formulating five-year plans in a bid to attain the nation's economic objectives more expeditiously and according to a scale of priorities. But each of its blueprints turned out to be bigger, more ambitious and yet less fruitful in its impact on the basic problems of poverty and unemployment. The common man's frustration mounted as each Plan failed to bring about noticeable improvement in his life. At many places there was gross accentuation of economic disparities despite all the grandiose planning exercises. These led to derisive comments and a widespread discontent. The practice of fixing a specific five-year period for each plan also posed other problems. The mounting price-spiral made nonsense of all estimates of costs and other projections. The tragedy of the Fifth Plan was particularly great on this account and much of the time spent on its formulation was a waste. The planners found it hard to finalise the schemes even after half the five-year period was over. Backlogs and overflows from one quinquennium to the next became a familiar feature of the planning process.

But it would be unfortunate if long-term perspectives are sacrificed on grounds of expediency and excessive reliance placed on short-term changes in programmes. The complexities of the situation and structural problems make a clear sense of direction imperative. It is equally true that ad hoc cuts in planned investment can disturb the basic plan balances.

In fact, the critics of the Rolling Plan complain that it may lead to no plan at all. They argue that a rolling perspective plan cannot take care of heavy industries with very long gestation periods. But it is not true that a rolling perspective plan cannot plan for heavy industries at all. Only, the attainment of the targets in their case will depend upon the prevailing circumstances in any one year.

Some people hold the view that it would usher in an era of "realistic and purposeful" planning in the country in the period to come. It is said that the rolling plan concept is eminently practical. It is considered that the rolling plan concept would make the government action-oriented, as accountability would increase when the yardstick for judging the results is short-term. It might help the administration cut bureaucratic red-tape, and corruption involved in clearing industrial licences, as the people are impatient for results.

Role of Government in Post Liberalisation Era

In Laissez-Faire economic system the government plays only a passive role. It is concerned with only the basic activities or a police state, Activities such as protection of citizens from external aggressions, maintainence of internal law and order, administration and provides certain basic infrastructures. In the welfare capitalism the government plays an active role so as to provide the economy stability and maintainence of full employment along with the basic function (as in the case of laissez-faire economy) through the use of monetary and fiscal policies. In Authoritarian Socialism the government takes complete control of the economy. Where only certain basic freedoms are allowed the rest of economic freedoms are not allowed and, all economic decisions are made by the government or the state. In Communism the government is in complete command of all economic activities to a greater extent complete equalities of income and wealth is achieved. The aim of a government in almost all the economic systems are to achieve maximum social and economic welfare. Economic welfare is at the root of social welfare. No government in the world can survive if they are unable to get the maximum economic and social welfare for the people.

In India soon after independence the government under Prime Minister Nehru followed a conciouse mixed economic policy, in which the government to a greater extent played some what direct role in achieving the desired economic and social welfare. The government introduced many industrial policies under which the industrial development was given priority as well as a dynamic role was assigned to public sector. In 1950 National Development Council was formed and the planning commission was established. Government opted for planned economic development on the lines of Russian experience, but our planning was that of decentralised planning as well as induced planning. This really helped us in achieving, rapid economic development in the later period specially during the 70's. Mrs. Gandhi further strengthened the philosophy of socialism and assigned further active role of government by nationalising banking system, abolishing the privy purses and announcement of starting three new steel plants in the south, *viz.*, Salem steel plant, Vijaynagara steel plant and Vishaka Patnam steel plant. Due to certain political turmoil, the economic system to a greater extent came to standstill. In the eightees, the government in India started looking at a different angle at the economy, with a privatisation vision. This was the need of the time as there were problems either created or existed in the economy.

On 14th February 1992, the first sign of privatisation started as the government announced the opening of airways industry to private sector. In 1991 as the government, took the step towards liberalisation and globalisation and the Indian economy was declared open as a part of the global economy. Disinvestment policy in public sector, more liberal monetary reforms under the chairmanship of Narsimhan a former governor of RBI, more liberal flow of foreign capital including NRI's deposits, and so on . . . . Many multinationals and transnationals were allowed to open their economic installations in the country. It is said, that in 1992-93, the total flow of foreign money is equal to that of the total amount borrowed from 1950's to 1992-93. Mc Donalds, Revolans, Wall's Enrons, Congentrix, Fords, General Motors, Kellogs *etc*, entered the economy. The main objectives of the government was :

(i) To obtain foreign capital/foreign investment.

(ii) To get the benefits of foreign capital in the form of quality products, technology *etc*.

(iii) To infuse competition.

(iv) To achieve certain pre-determined economic objective in the form of employment, income generation as well as infra-structure development. If we get these objectives, then the liberalisation and globalisation policy is the best, but this raises certain questions regarding the present role of government.

(i) Social responsibility of the government,

(ii) Profit as the only criteria of judging efficiency of an organisation,

(*iii*) Widening, inequalities of income and wealth and upper rich are getting very rich,

(*iv*) Domination of service sector,

(*v*) Threat to India's own culture, and

(*vi*) Dependence on developed countries as well as more foreign indebtedness.

Conclusion

Thus, the concept of Rolling Plans adopted by the Indian Planning Commission under the Janata Government is basically a rational one. Instead of a rigid framework, there has to be an annual operational plan with a fresh five-year perspective every year of a Rolling Five-Year Plan. This system, which marks a major departure from the past, calls for continuous adjustments in plan projections on the basis of resources availability, production trends and other economic developments. The Planning Commission is involved not only in updating the plan every year but also in keeping a continuous watch on the progress of plan projects, changes in price and production trends and other important developments which have a bearing on planning. However, the new system calls for more sophisticated techniques on the part of the Planning Commission to monitor not only the progress of plans but also other economic trends.

Key terms

Planning, Indicative planning, Physical planning, Financial planning, Structural planning, Core plan, Contigent plan, Planned and Unplanned economy.

QUESTIONS

1. Give the salient features of planned economy. Describe the advantages and disadvantages of economic planning.
2. What are the objectives of economic planning? What conditions are essential for success of planning?
3. Make out a case for economic planning for an under-developed country. Discuss the importance of economic planning in a developing economy.
4. Distinguish between (*a*) "Planning by Direction" and "Planning by Inducement". (*b*) Which of the two would you prefer and why? Totalitarian planning and democratic planning.
5. Do you agree with the view that economic planning is incompatible with economic freedom?

   Or

   "Planning under capitalism is a contradiction in terms". Discuss.
6. Distinguish between physical planning and financial planning. How can they be co-ordinated in the formulation of a development plan?

PART EIGHT

Economics of Welfare

Chapter

CHAPTER 82

WELFARE ECONOMICS

We studied the nature of Economics in the beginning of the book. Economics in a nutshell refers to the prudent management of scarce resources. The economists are generally agreed that the scarce re sources of the community should be so utilised as to maximise total satisfaction or welfare of the people. Economics has mainly concerned itself with welfare as some of the well-known definitions of Economics would incidate. For instance, according to Cannan, "The aim of Political Economy is the explanation of the general causes on which the material welfare of human being depends." According to Pigou, Economics studies "that part of social welfare that can be brought directly or indirectly into relation with the measuring rod of money." Thus, Economics in its origin, development and content has coincided, by and large, with welfare economics. But let us see what welfare economics means.

Definition of Welfare Economics

Welfare economics is a branch of Economics which is primarily concerned with the promotion of the welfare of a community as measured in the satisfaction derived from the economic goods at the disposal of the community. It is the function of welfare economics to help in the formulation of economic policies calculated to maximise social welfare. "The analysis of the efficiency of an economy with maximum total satisfaction as the yard-stick is known as welfare economics."[1] Quite a good definition would be : "Welfare economics is that branch of economic analysis which is concerned primarily with the establishment of criteria that can provide a positive basis for adopting policies which are likely to maximise social welfare."[2]

Maximizing social welfare.

According to the definitions given above, we can say that the principal function of welfare economics is to provide standards of judgment by which one can judge economic policies and events from the point of view of social welfare. As Scitovsky observes : "Welfare economics is that part of the general body of economic theory which is concerned primarily with policy."[3] In short, welfare economics has to define what an economic optimum may be. It has to lay down conditions for maximising welfare and prescribe policies with that end in view.

1. Bober, M.M.—*Intermediate Price and Income Theory* (First Edition), p. 483.
2. Syed Fakharul Hassan—*Introduction to Welfare Economics*, 1962, p. 1.
3. Scitovsky Tibor—*Papers on Welfare and Growth*, 1962, p. 174.

Economic and Non-Economic or General Welfare

A distinction may be drawn between economic welfare and general welfare. An individual's welfare may relate to his physical well-being, spiritual well-being or economic well-being. "The concept of welfare," according to Robbins, "embraces many states of mind, some of a merely 'sensual', some of more spiritual nature. . . . But the class 'economic' will not be one of them."[4] Obviously, economics is not concerned with physical or spiritual well-being. It is only concerned with that aspect of an individual's well-being which is derived from economic goods and services. In Pigou's words, "The range of our inquiry has become restricted to that part of social welfare that can be brought directly or indirectly into relation with the measuring rod of money. This part of welfare may be called economic welfare."[5]

Welfare refers to a state of mind or, as Pigou says, "The elements of welfare are states of consciousness." This is no doubt a subjective concept, but it can be imparted an element of objectivity by linking individual welfare to individual choice so that his welfare map is his preference map. For instance, if he chooses apples rather than oranges, he would increase his welfare by consuming apples rather than oranges. A person's choice is determined by a large number of variables some of which are economic and others not. Welfare economics ignores the non-economic variables. We might say that economic welfare refers to satisfaction derived from the consumption of economic goods, whereas general welfare refers to the satisfaction derived from both economic and non-economic goods.

But the two types of satisfactions are merged in a man's mind and cannot be clearly distinguished. Professor Little explains this by a metaphor thus : "The utilitarians imagined the mind to be like a well of known depth into which parcels of satisfaction, duly labelled economic or political or religious, were thrown. . . . On the later analysis it is imagined that the mind is like a well of unknown depth, partly filled with water, the level of which could be altered by turning on various taps labelled economic, political, *etc*. Once the water is in the well there is no way of saying which tap it came from and also it is impossible to say how much water there is in the well."[6] Hence, economic and non-economic welfare are not easily distinguishable.

As Professor Cannan says, ". . . there is no precise line between economic and non-economic satisfaction and, therefore, province of economics cannot be marked out by a row of posts or a fence, like a political territory or a landed property."[7]

It is possible that some economic causes affect economic welfare and total or general welfare differently. But there is a strong presumption that qualitative conclusions about effects on economic welfare hold good also of effects upon total welfare.

Positive Economics and Welfare Economics

We should now be in a position to lay down a clear line of demarcation between positive economics and welfare economics. We may refer once again to what we have discussed in the beginning of the book regarding the scope of economics. There we drew a distinction between positive economics and normative economics. That distinction practically holds good here.

Positive economics explains an economic phenomenon and normative economics comments on the desirability or otherwise of that phenomenon. For instance positive economics explains why wealth in the community is unequally distributed and normative economics would say whether the unequal distribution of wealth is desirable or not. The question of desirability falls in the purview of welfare economics.

Positive Economics — deals with facts of the economy

Normative Economics — deals with value judgements about the situation

Again, positive economics would explain why the price of wheat has risen so high welfare economics would suggest price control measures to promote the greatest good of the greatest number. In short, positive economics formulates economic generalisation or laws, whereas welfare economics is concerned with economic policies.

The idea underlying the essential difference between positive economics and welfare economics can be explained in another way. The principle of the economics can be falsified and rejected if they cannot be verified and established in the light of actual experience in the real world. The propositions of welfare economics are rather different. They are based on assumptions some of which may or may not be realistic. From the assumptions, we deduce conditions for maximising welfare. Even if the conditions are fulfilled, the welfare may not increase, because the assumptions may turn out to be inappropriate.

Also, it is difficult to say whether welfare has actually increased since welfare is not an observable

4. Robbins, L.—*Robertson on Utility and Scope, Economics*, May, 1953.
5. Pigou, A.C.—*The Economics of Welfare*, 1948, p. 111.
6. Little I.M.D.—*A Critique of Welfare Economics*, 1960, p. 51.
7. *Wealth*, pp. 17–18.

quantity like a market price or an item of personal consumption. Testing a welfare proposition is an exceedingly difficult affair for private estimation of welfare is likely to differ widely. "Whereas the normal way of testing a theory in positive economics is to test its conclusions, the normal way of testing a welfare proposition is to test its assumptions."[8]

Individual vs. society.

In positive economics assumptions are simplified and adopted as convenient to draw conclusions and one worries only when conclusions come to be applied in the real world. But the assumptions of welfare economics are a more serious affair. The have to be carefully scrutinised, since they are going to form a basis of actual policy. "It is clear that the interest attaching to a theory of welfare depend almost entirely upon the realism and relevance of its assumptions, factual and ethical in a particular historical contexts."[9]

Individual Welfare and Social Welfare

A student can say at once that individual welfare refers to the sum-total of satisfaction derived by a individual from the consumption of economic goods, whereas social welfare is the total satisfaction of the society as a whole. Social welfare has been defined as "an aggregate of the utilities or satisfaction of all the individuals in the society." But the matter is not so simple as that.

The individual welfare can be linked with his choice. We cannot say that social welfare depends on society's choice. The society consists of millions of individuals who choose differently. The society has no mind of its own apart from individuals. If in a society, an economic measure or policy makes some individuals better off and others worse off, we cannot say what has happened to social welfare: whether it has gone up or down.

Difficulty also arises from the immeasurability of utility or satisfaction. If the satisfaction derived by an individual could be measured cardinally (*i.e.*, by assigning definite numbers), as the Marshallian utility analysis made us believe, then it would have been possible to arrive at an exact measure of social welfare by adding the individual utilities. But utility is not an extensive magnitude like length and is not, therefore, measurable numerically. It is, on the other hand, an intensive magnitude and we can, therefore, speak of it as more or less. In other words, although cardinal measurement of utility is out of the question, ordinal measurement is possible as by indifference curve technique.

This, however, is sufficient for our purpose. We can assume rational behaviour on the part of consumers in the mass. It will be possible for us to see whether an economic event or policy will increase or decrease economic welfare. That is all what is needed for practical purposes.

In deriving social welfare from individual welfare, we are confronted with the problem of inter-personal comparisons which we shall discuss separately. In the meantime, let it suffice to say that the problem is not insoluble. All are agreed that a rich man enjoys a greater measure of economic welfare than a poor man. It is not really **inter-personal** comparison, *i.e.*, comparing the utility of a rich person with that of a poor person. It may, on the other hand, be considered an **intra-personal** comparison in which the same person compares the two situations. He can say if he became rich he would derive greater satisfaction. We shall see as we proceed that various theories of welfare economics have been put forward to facilitate the transition from individual to group or social welfare.

Divergence between Individual and Social Welfare

Broadly speaking, the welfare of the individuals is synonymous with the welfare of the society. But the cases of divergence are not uncommon. Pigou has mentioned several situations in which there is divergence between the value of marginal social and marginal private net product.[10] For Instance, when a tenant leaves the land in an improved condition at the end of the lease, the private net product will be less than the social net product. Such a divergence will be found to occur in all cases in which the contract between the two parties provides for the return of a durable producer's good in a better condition.

Again, there are cases when a person incidentally renders a service to some other persons, for which he gets no payment or no payment can be exacted. In such cases, again, private net product will be less than the social net product, *e.g.*, a light house benefiting ships on which no toll could be levied, investment made in private parks improving the air of the neighbourhood, lamps installed at the doors of private houses, investment on prevention of smoke from factory chimneys, etc. If the smoke is not

8. Graff J. De V.—*Theoretical Welfare Economics*, 1968, p. 3.
9. *Ibid.*, p. 3.
10. Pigou, A.C.—*Economics of Welfare*, 1948, Ch. IX.

prevented, the social net product will be less than the private net product, for the smoke inflicts a heavy uncharged loss on the community in the form of damage to buildings, vegetables increased expense on washing clothes, cleaning rooms, *etc*. Moreover, when investment is made on research leading to inventions which cannot be kept a secret or got patented, the investor passes on to the society a part of the benefit. Here also private net product is less than the social net product.

On the other hand, there are cases where social net product is less than the private net product. This will happen when there are technical difficulties of enforcing compensation for disservices incidentally rendered as in the case of a factory smoke inflicting loss or damage on the neighbourhood, as mentioned above. The other examples are the game preserving activities of some landlords resulting in damage to the neighbour's crops by rabbits and other wild animals, owner of a factory in the heart of the city, production and sale of intoxicants, evils arising out of foreign investments, a loan financing a foreign war, women working in factories immediately before and after confinement. In all such cases, private net product is greater than social net product. In other words, the individuals gain at the expense of the society. Individual welfare is promoted but social welfare is reduced.

Thus, divergence between individual welfare and social welfare arises from the existence of uncompensated services and uncharged disservices. They occur in all market forms, *viz.*, perfect competition, monopolistic competition, monopoly, *etc*. The state can reduce this divergence and bring about harmony between individual and social welfare through fiscal measures like bounties and taxes.

Light house - private net product is less than social net product.

Old Welfare Economics : Pigou's Analysis

Credit of systematising the study of welfare economics belongs to Professor Pigou. The basic postulate put forward by him relates to man's equal capacity for satisfaction when placed in similar circumstances. He says: "If we take random groups of people of the same race and brought up in the same country, we find that in any features that are comparable by objective tests, they are on the average pretty much alike." Again, "On the basis of analogy, observation and intercourse, inter-personal comparison can, I think, properly be made; and, moreover, unless we have a special reason to believe the contrary a given amount of stuff may be presumed to yield a similar amount of satisfaction, not indeed as between any one man and another but as between representative members of groups of individuals.[11]

Pigou, therefore, holds the view that inter-personal utility comparisons are possible. He observes, "Utilities though not measurable (strictly in cardinal sense) are comparable both intra-personally and inter-personally"[12]. He, therefore, accepts the ordinal measure of utility (*i.e.*, more or less and not measurable by assigning definite numbers).

Since, according to the postulate of equal capacity for satisfaction, different people derive the same satisfaction out of the same real income, it will increase social welfare if some real income is transferred from the rich to the poor. In keeping with the law of diminishing marginal utility, such a transfer will mean less of utility to the rich than the gain to the poor.

The relationship between the welfare of a society and the distribution of its income can be explained with the help of the following diagram (Fig. 80.1). Let us take the case of two individuals of identical capacity for experiencing utility but with extremely different incomes. Let us draw a curve to represent the marginal utility to each of these persons of added increments of money. They will, because of their different incomes, be able to consume different quantities of whatever gives them utility. The diagram shows the situation on a utility curve of two persons of extremely different money incomes. The rich man can easily settle at *D* beyond which there is no point in further outlay (because utility is negative beyond point *D*). The poor man may well be at *A* (because of his very much lower income). If the rich man's income is reduced, he may not have to contract his current consumption at all or, in any case, we may suppose him only to be forced to reduce from *D* to *C*. This transferred income to the poor man enables him to move from *A* to *B*. On these assumptions, redistribution of income from the very rich to the very poor cannot but help increase social welfare.

11. *Ibid.*, p. 292.
12. *Ibid.*, p. 293.

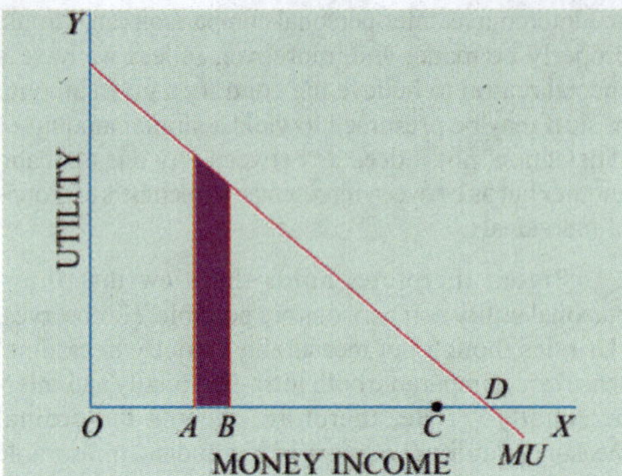

Fig. 80.1. Redistrubution of income from rich to poor

According to this view, a perfectly equal distribution of wealth will maximise social welfare. But it is objected that such a re-distribution of wealth will militate against capital formation and will reduce social welfare by damaging the productive capacity of the community. Pigou, however, takes care to say that such a transfer of real income should be accomplished so as not to affect adversely "production effect, enterprise and development of capital equipments."[13]

The principal objection put forward against this view is that the presumption of man's equal capacity for satisfaction is not scientifically tenable and cannot, therefore, form the basis of inter-personal comparisons of utility. In this connection, Robbins observes: "The postulate of equal capacity for satisfaction rests on ethical principle rather than upon scientific demonstration."[14] Since, according to this view, utility of different individuals is not comparable, economist is stultified as an adviser in policy matters.

Harrod, however, does not agree with this view. He says some postulate of this sort must be assumed if study of economics is not to lose its utility altogether. Even Robbins suggests "that such assumptions should be made and their implications explored with the aid of economist's technique." But under the weight of Robbins' criticism, welfare economics lost its scientific purity and ceased to be accepted as a guide to policy. It, however, was rescued from this situation by the new welfare economists like Kaldor and Hicks, which we shall study presently.

NEW WELFARE ECONOMICS

The New Welfare Economics represents a break with the utilitarian tradition in Economics. The new welfare economists claim to arrive at optimum conditions of production and exchange without adding the utilities of different persons or comparing the satisfactions of different individuals. The new welfare economics is claimed to be objective and scientific and not ethical. It is said that welfare economics furnishes as analysis of the causes governing the measure of welfare or an increase or decrease thereof. Pareto is said to be the founder of new Welfare Economics, although there have been introduced some subsequent refinements since then. About the welfare propositions laid down by Pareto even now there is general agreement. We shall, therefore, presently deal with them.

Pareto's Welfare Criterion

Italian economist Vilifredo Pareto has laid down the conditions for maximising social welfare or for achieving a social optimum. A Paretian optimum refers to a situation in which it is impossible to make any one better off without making some one worse off. For judging such a situation, Pareto has enunciated a very simple and straight forward criterion thus: "Any change which harms no one and which makes some people better off (in their own estimation) must be considered to be an improvement."

Graphical Representation. The Paretian criterion may be put in graphic terms as under:

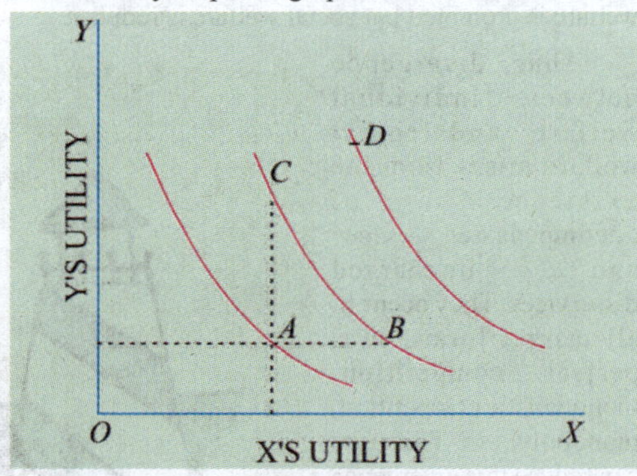

Fig. 80.2.

For simplicity, let us deal with a community in which there are only two persons *X* and *Y*. In Fig. 80.2 let us represent the utility of individual *X* along the horizontal axis and that of *Y* along the vertical axis.

The Pareto criterion state that if we start off from a situation which is represented by a point like *A*, then a policy change by the government is an improvement if it results in a move to any point like *B* or *C* which lies to the right of *A* or above. At *B*, *X* is better off than at *A* with *Y* as well off as before, whereas the move to *C* benefits *Y* without harming *X* and the move to *D*, benefits both the persons.

Conditions of Paretian Optimum

The conditions of Paretian optimum are given below:

13. *Ibid.*, p. 301.
14. Robbins, L.—*Interpersonal Comparisons of Utility*. E.J., December 1938, p. 637.

(i) Optimum Allocation of Products. Allocation of products to be optimal must be such as to make it impossible for any pair of individuals to exchange any quantity of any pair of consumer goods resulting in increase in one's satisfaction without decreasing that of another. That is, if any alternative allocation can increase some one's satisfaction without decreasing another's, it is not optimal. To put in terms of indifference curve technique, the marginal rate of substitution (*MRS*) between any two goods must be same for any pair of owners of the same two goods. We know that marginal rate of substitution (*MRS*) is the rate at which units of one good can be exchanged for the units of another without lowering the level of satisfaction.

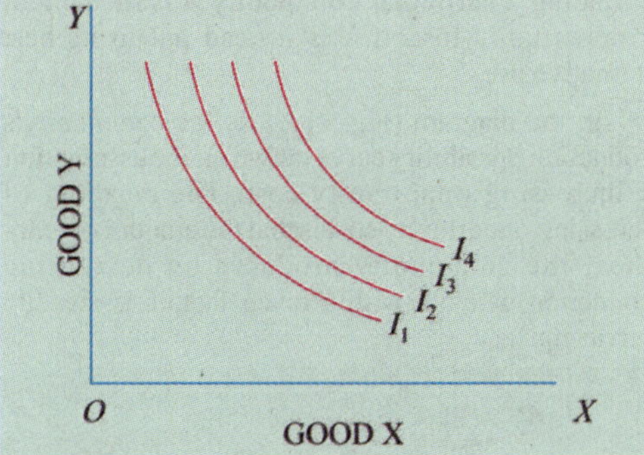

Fig. 80.3(*i*).

Fig. 80.3(*ii*). Indifference Curves.

This can be explained with the help of an Edgeworth Box diagram. The Edgeworth diagram for consumption shows the indifference curve preference maps of the two individuals and their derived levels of satisfaction from the various combinations of the goods. Fig. 80.3 (*i*) shows four ordinary indifference curves, *i.e.*, I_1, I_2, I_3 and I_4, showing the various combinations of the goods *X* and *Y* at different levels of income of *A*. Similarly, Fig. 3 (*ii*) shows four indifference curves, *i.e.*, I_5, I_6, I_7 and I_8, showing the various combinations of the two goods *X* and *Y* at different levels of income of *B*.

The indifference curve preference maps of both *A* and *B* have been combined and shown with the help of an Edgeworth Box in Fig. 80.3. (*iii*).

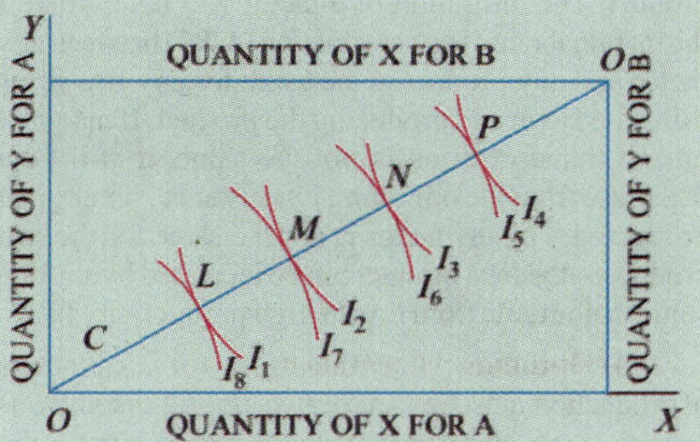

Fig. 80.3(*iii*) Centract Curve.

The indifference curve preference map of *A* starts from the origin, *O*, whereas the indifference curve preference of *B* starts from the origin *O'*. The slope of an indifference curve, as we know, at any point is the marginal rate of substitution between *X* and *Y* (*MRSxy*) at that point. We know that the *MRSxy* is the marginal amount of one good which is lost in order to get a marginal unit of the other, in order to maintain the same level of satisfaction. The point would be the optimal where the (*MRSxy*) of both the individuals is the same. If the marginal rate of substitution between any two goods is not the same for the two individuals, then with the help of exchange, it is possible to increase the level of satisfaction of one without diminishing that of the other. Now, if we join the points *L*, *M*, *N*, *P* where the different sets of indifference curve of the individuals *A* and *B* are tangent to each other, we get a curve known as **contract curve**, *i.e.*, *cc'*. The points *L*, *M*, *N* and *P*, lie on the contract curve *cc'* At each of these points, the *MRSxy* for *A* and *B* is the same. Therefore, each point along a contract curve *cc'* represents a Point of Pareto-optimality. In other words, any redistribution of the goods *X* and *Y* between *A* and *B* will yield a lower level of satisfaction.

(2) Optimum Degree of Specialisation. There is a necessary (through not a sufficient) condition for determining the optimum output of each product by each firm. The condition is that the marginal rate of transformation (*MRT*) between any two goods must be the same for any pair of firms producing both of them. The Marginal Rate of Transformation between two goods is the amount of one good which would have to be sacrificed to produce one unit of another good. This only means the ratio of marginal opportunity cost of the two goods. Obviously, if marginal rate of transformation is not the same for any pair of producers, it would be possible to increase the combined output of the two goods or increase the output of one without decreasing that of another. This will mean that the present degree of specialisation is not the optimum.

(3) Optimum Factor Utilization. This represents optimum relationship between the factor and the product. The utilisation of a factor will be optimal if the marginal rate of transformation (*MRT*) between any factor and any product is the same for any two firms using the factor and producing the product. If marginal rate of transformation is not the same, it will be a departure from the optimum. For instance, if marginal productivity of any factor is not the same for the two producers, the total product can be increased by shifting some factor units from low to high productivity firms.

(4) Optimum Allocation of Factors. All factors of production must be so allocated among the various uses that the marginal production in each use is the same. If it is not the same, it will pay to shift some units of a factor from one use to another. In terms of new economics, the marginal rate of technical substitution between any pair of factors must be the same for any two firms using both to produce the same product. Only then, the allocation will be optimal. If it is not, it will be possible to increase the total product by shifting a factor from one firm to another.

(5) Optimum Direction of Production. Another condition for maximizing welfare is that the marginal rate of substitution between any pair of products for any person consuming both must be the same as the marginal rate of transformation for the community between them. In terms of utility analysis, it means (*a*) that the ratios of marginal utilities of the two goods must be the same for all consumers, *i.e.*,

$$\frac{MU \text{ of } A}{\text{Price of } A} = \frac{MU \text{ of } B}{\text{Price of } B}$$

and so on. This will represent maximum satisfaction of the consumer. (*b*) The ratio of their marginal costs must be the same for all producers producing them, *i.e.*,

$$\frac{MC \text{ of } A}{\text{Price of } A} = \frac{MC \text{ of } B}{\text{Price of } B}, \text{ and so on.}$$

(*c*) These ratios must be equal. This condition relates to the maximum efficiency of the economic system. The goods must be produced in such combinations that they not only conform to consumers preferences but are also produced at the minimum average cost. If it is technically possible to substitute one good for another and make one better off without making another worse off, the production is not optimal.

This may be explained with the help of a diagram (Fig. 80.4). Let us take a community producing two goods. The quantity of each good it produces will depend on its factor endowments and on its existing technical knowledge. By factor endowments we mean the amounts of factors of production the community possesses. Let us assume that the community can produce either 100 bushels of wheat or 100 yards of cloth when all its factors are fully and most efficiently employed in the production of either wheat or cloth respectively. The various combinations of the goods, *i.e.*, wheat and cloth, that it can produce can then be shown by the production possibility curve or the transformation curve. If the community chooses to produce only wheat, it can produce 100 bushels. If it would also like to produce cloth, it must forgo the production of some of its wheat. The amount of wheat which the community foregoes in order to have an extra unit of cloth is known as the opportunity cost of wheat in terms of cloth. In other words, the opportunity cost of a particular service *X* in producing a particular commodity *A* is the benefit or opportunity lost, if *X* is instead put to its best alternative use.

In the diagram (Fig. 4) *AB* is the community's production possibility curve drawn on the assumption of increasing opportunity cost. The meaning of increasing opportunity cost is that the amount of extra wheat the community produces by decreasing production of cloth with a given factors is steadily increasing.

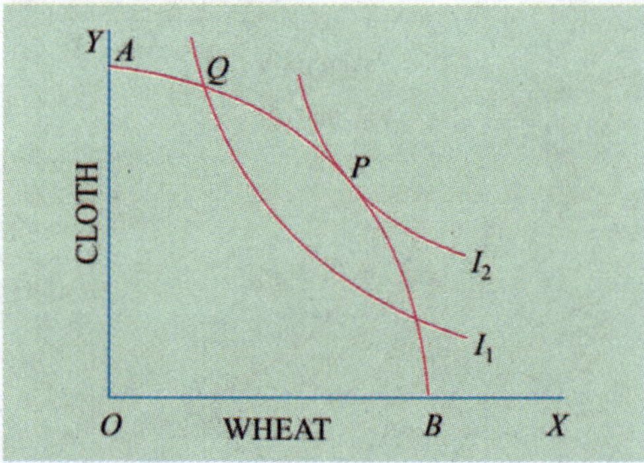

Fig. 80.4. Maximum efficiency of economic system.

Let us superimpose the indifference curve preference map, *i.e.*, I_1, and I_2 of an individual *A* on *AB*. Now the Pareto-optimal point would be where the slope of the production possibility curve *AB* and of the indifference curve of *A* is the same.

In this diagram, point P is the optimal point, as the slope of the indifference curve I_2 and *PB* on curve *AB* is the same. The point *Q* is not the point of optimum as here the slope of the production possibility curve *AB* and Indifference curve I_1 is not the same, and moreover the point *Q* lies on the indifference curve I_1, indicating that the consumer's satisfaction can be increased by moving from point *Q* to point *P* which lies on a higher indifference curve I_2.

(6) Optimum Allocation of a Factor-Unit's Time. The owner of a factor unit has the option of using the factor to render him a direct service or hiring it out to others for aiding in production. Hence, the problem for the owner of a factor is to allocate in an optimal manner the time of the factor unit between rendering direct services or working for a money reward. The condition for maximising welfare is that the marginal rate of substitution between the amount of product *X* received for aiding in its production and the time spent in rendering this aid must be the same (for each factor unit owner) as the marginal rate of transformation between the item of his factor unit spent in aiding production and the product *X*. This means that an individual's marginal valuation of his productive work must be equal to what his work adds to the community's total product. In other words, the money reward paid to the owner of a factor unit must be equal to the value of the marginal physical product of the factor unit. If it is not the same, the allocation will not be optimal, because it will then be possible to get more of *X* by transferring a moment of a factor unit's time from the production of direct service to production of *X* or *vice-versa*.

(7) Inter-temporal Allocation of Assets. Every firm (an individual) has to bring about an optimal allocation of factor inputs and product output over time. "A firm may produce a given output stream with various time patterns of factor inputs and, conversely, it may have various time patterns of outputs with a given input stream of factor services." This is only a special case of the more general problems of optimum allocation of products and factors, *i.e.*, cases where some of the products or factors may relate to different moments of time. In this case, the allocation will bring maximum welfare when the marginal rate of substitution between any pair of moments is the same for every pair of individuals or firms. One inter-temporal situation relates to borrowing and lending. The condition of maximum welfare in this case would mean that the rate of interest at which an individual is willing to lend a given amount of money (capital) must be equal to its marginal productivity to the borrowing producer.

Second Order Conditions. From the above, it is clear that the Pareto-optimum can be attained if the several marginal conditions as outlined above can be fulfilled. These are known as **first order conditions.** However, it is possible in some situations that the fulfilment of these first order conditions may not lead to welfare optimality. To achieve an optimum welfare position, it is very essential that the second order conditions along with the first order conditions should also be satisfied to achieve the maximum welfare. These second order conditions are no other than the stability conditions for equilibrium position. The fulfilment of second order conditions means that all the indifference curves and the production possibility curves should have the right curvature in the neighbourhood of any position where marginal conditions are satisfied. Prof. Reder puts it like this that in the neighbourhood of maximum welfare, all indifference curves must be convex to the origin and all transformation curves must be concave to it.

This is illustrated in the following diagram (Fig. 5). *AB* is the production possibility curve of the community. I_1 and I_2 are the indifference curves of an individual. The point *b* is a point of optimum welfare as the indifference curve I_2, is a tangent to the production possibility curve *AB*. At point *a*, the indifference curve I_1 is also a tangent to the production possibility curve *AB* but it is not a point of optimum welfare, as by moving from *a* to *b*, the community reaches on a higher indifference curve I_2.

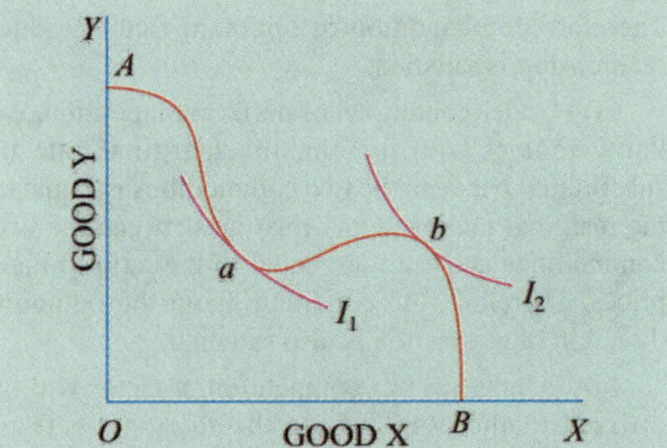

Fig. 80.5. Sufficient condition for optimality.

Conclusion. These are a few conditions of welfare maximisation. It may, however, be emphasised that these conditions are necessary but no sufficient for achieving optimum welfare. There may be other conditions in production and exchange which may have to be fulfilled in certain cases. Samuelson thus sums up: "Between any two variables, the marginal rates of substitution must be (subjectively) equal for all alternative processes with the common technical and subjective ratios being equivalent; otherwise there exists a physically attainable position that makes everyone better off."

Relation Between Paretian Optima and Perfect Competition

In what follows, we would discuss how far a perfectly competitive economy can be said to satisfy the optimal conditions given by Pareto.

(*i*) Under conditions of perfect competition, the consumer in order to maximize his satisfaction makes the marginal rate of substitution between any two goods equal to the ratio of their prices. At equilibrium, we know that the marginal rate of substitution between two goods is equal to the ratio of their prices for any consumer. Therefore, the first condition of optimum allocation of goods is satisfied under perfect competition.

(*ii*) Under conditions of perfect competition, the producer in order to have the minimum cost combination of the factors to produce a given output tries to equate the marginal rate of transformation between two factors to the ratio of their prices. At equilibrium we know, this condition is satisfied. Hence, the condition about the optimum allocation of factors is also satisfied.

(iii) The producer under perfect competition, in order to maximize his profits, tries to equate the marginal rate of transformation between the two commodities to the ratio of their prices and at equilibrium this condition is met. Thus, the condition about the optimum utilization of factor is satisfied.

(iv) The producer in order to maximize his profit tries to equate the marginal product of each factor to its price and, at equilibrium, this condition is satisfied. Therefore, the condition of optimum factor-product relationship is satisfied.

(v) Under conditions of perfect competition, we know that at equilibrium, the marginal rate of substitution between the two commodities is equal to the marginal rate of transformation between the two commodities and both are equal to the ratio of their prices. Therefore, the condition about the optimum direction of production is also satisfied.

(vi) Under perfect competition, a factor will be utilized to the point where the marginal rate of substitution between employment of the factor and its leisure equals the rate of payment made to it. Similarly, with a view to maximizing his profit, a producer equates the marginal rate of transformation between the factor and its product. Since the price of the product is the same for all the producers and the rate of payment is the same for all the factor units, the condition of optimum allocation of a factor unit's time is also satisfied.

(vii) An owner of an asset makes the marginal rate of substitution between present income and future income equal to his rate of time preference. In the same way, a borrower of the asset equates the cost of borrowing with the marginal rate of substitution between the present asset and future asset. Since under perfect competition, the rate of payment for all similar assets is the same, as also the cost to the borrowers, it is equal to the marginal productivity of the asset. In this way, the condition relating to the inter-temporal optimum allocation assets is also fulfilled under perfect competition.

From the above it is clear that under perfect competition all the marginal conditions of Paretian optimum are satisfied.

However, the fulfilment of these conditions subject to the following bold assumptions:

(i) There is perfect knowledge about both the future and the relevant activities of others in the present;

(ii) All the producers are genuine cost minimizers as well as profit maximizers;

(iii) There exist, perfect competition among the buyers and sellers;

(iv) There exists no external effects.

With the above-mentioned assumptions, if the economy comes to an equilibrium, so that demand and supplies are equal at some stable prices—then the resulting allocation of resources will be an optimal one.

However, in spite of all these bold assumptions, the resulting allocation of resources may not be an optimal one. Why?

(i) Under perfect competition, at equilibrium, there is an equality between price and marginal private cost of production and not between price and marginal social cost of production. Marginal private cost of production is calculated from the point of view of the producer, whereas the marginal social cost of production is calculated from the point of view of the society as a whole. And there may be a wide divergence between the marginal private cost and the marginal social cost. The following example will make this point clear. A producer may be responsible for polluting the air through the smoke emitted by his chimneys. He is not being charged for this disservice to the society. Now the price charged by the producer may be equal to the marginal private cost but not to the marginal social cost.

(ii) The conditions of optimum production and exchange, as dealt with by Pareto, do not take into account the optimum pattern of income distribution. The allocation which is brought about through the operation of the market forces under perfect competition can be said to be efficient only with respect to given distribution of income which may be far from the optimum distribution from the social point of view.

(iii) Finally, if there are external economies in an industry, under conditions of perfect competition, then the supply curve of the industry will be downward sloping and the equilibrium price then will be equal to the average cost of production and not to the marginal cost of production.

The above limitations have restricted very much the usefulness of the Paretian welfare analysis as a tool for policy recommendations.

Compensation Principle

A notable advance in welfare economies since Pareto has been the Compensation Principle, which is associated generally with the names of Kaldor, Hicks and Scitovsky.

Assumptions. The important assumptions on which this principle is based are as follows:

(i) There is constancy of individual's taste and the absence of external effects both in production and in consumption;

(*ii*) Inter-personal comparison of well-being are not possible;

(*iii*) Individuals are the best judges of their welfare.

This principle can be presented as follows: Let us consider the effects of any new economic policy introduced by the Government in a society. It is possible then to divide the society into three categories, *i.e.* those persons who would gain, those who would lose and those who would remain unaffected. In Hicksian terminology, or in terms of indifference curves, it means some would move to a higher indifference curve and others to a lower indifference curve and still others would remain on the same indifference curve. Here nothing is assumed about the quantities of satisfaction. It is argued that those who remain on the same indifference curve are quite indifferent about the change. We are therefore left with the gainers and the losers. Suppose the persons who have gained can compensate the losers, *i.e.*, can offer them something regarded by the loser as moving them back to their previous indifference curve. If the gainers are in a position to restore the losers to their original position and themselves move to an indifference curve lower than the one they were on after the initial change, but not so low as on the indifference curve they were on initiallly, *i.e.*, before the policy measure took place. Something has taken place in this situation that can be described as an increase in welfare on the part of the society. According to the advocates of this doctrine, this can be labelled as an increase in welfare.

To use Kaldor's words: "In all cases, where a certain policy lead to an increase in physical productivity, and thus of aggregate real income, the economist's case for the policy is quite unaffected by the question of the comparability of individual satisfactions; since in all such cases it is possible to make everybody better off than before, or at any rate to make some people better off without making anybody worse off. . . . In order to establish his (*i.e.*, economist's) case, it is quite sufficient for him to show that even if all those who suffer as a result are fully compensated for their loss, the rest of the community will be still better off than before."[15] In other words, no inter-personal comparisons of satisfactions are involved in judging a policy aimed at increasing aggregate wealth.

The compensation principle was endorsed by Prof. Hicks in these words: "A permitted reorganisation must be taken from now on to mean a reorganisation which will allow of compensation being paid and which will yet show a net advantage."[16] In other words, it is possible to increase welfare taxing the beneficiaries of an economic policy and out of the funds so raised to compensate fully the sufferers therefrom in the form of bounties and still develop a surplus. Thus, the gainers compensate the losers.

Kaldor-Hicks Compensation Principle

On *y*-axis *B*'s utility is measured and on *x*-axis *A*'s utility is measured. '*PQ*' is utility possibility curve. If the movement is from '*P*' towards '*Q*' then '*A*'s utility increases, and '*B*'s decreases if it is from '*Q*' to '*P*', then *A*'s utility decreases and *B*'s utility increases. If both consumers '*A*' and '*B*'s income distribution and output is at point '*R*', which is under the '*PQ*' utility possibility curve.

Now let us assume that due to some government policy measures the utility of '*B*' increases to point '*H*'. This shows that '*B*' is better-off and '*A*' is worse off. According to Pareto criterian. This is not welfare as one is better off by making other-one worse off. In the opinion of Kaldor and Hicks, movement from '*R*' to '*H*' does not mean '*A*' is worse off and '*B*'

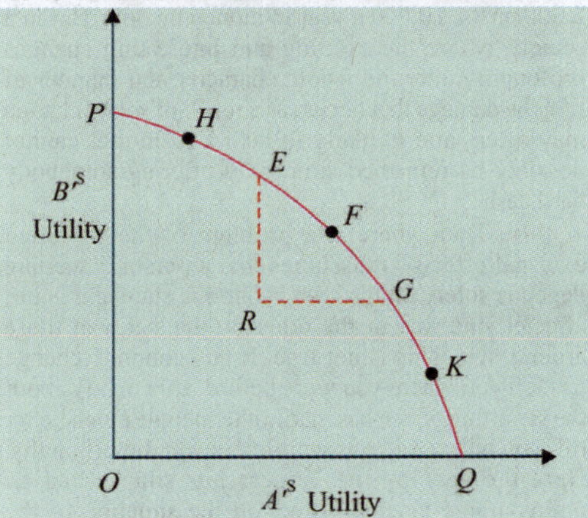

Kaldor - Hick's compensation principle.

is better off as it involves interpersonal comparison of utility, one cannot say whether or not social welfare increases according to Pareto criterion. Kaldor-Hicks says that even if '*B*' has moved from '*R*' to '*H*', even then, '*B*' can compensate '*A*' to the amount of '*EH*' as *A* is loser and '*B*' is the gainer. '*E*' is the point on '*PQ*' line which shows that '*A*' is not worse-off, but '*B*' is better-off which satisfies the Pareto-criterian.

Criticism. The compensation principle has been subjected to criticism by economists like Little, Baumol and Samuelson. The main points of criticism are:

(*i*) For the purpose of compensation, the theory assesses the loss and gain of individuals on the assumption of the equal marginal utility of money for the rich and the poor. This involves interpersonal comparisons which the new welfare economics wanted to avoid.

15. Kaldor, N.—*Welfare propositions of Economics and Inter-Personal Comparisons of Utility, E.J.* 1939, p. 550.
16. Hicks., J.R.—*The Foundation of Welfare Economics*, E.J., December 1939, p. 706.

(ii) This principle would work only if the compensation is actually paid by the gainers to the losers. If the compensation is not in fact made, some members of the society have in fact lost. Actually compensating the loser may prove quite a tall order. To begin with, we have to find out who they are, and this, in turn, raises the question as to what evidence bears on who is a gainer and who is a loser. Are we to take their word for it? And if not, how do we know whether someone is a gainer or a loser without making an interpersonal comparison?

(iii) The payment of compensation creates its own difficulties. Apart from estimating the exact magnitude of loss or gain without knowing everybody's utility scale, there are the administrative difficulties involved in the payment of actual compensation which make the principle impracticable.

(iv) The problem arises about the manner in which compensation is to be made. Typically, it was assumed that compensation would take the form of money payments. This may work, if someone has been damaged in a very obvious way, such as losing Rs. 5,000 or Rs. 10,000 a year in money income. But in a society, where the exciting and interesting changes profoundly alter the whole character and manner of life, the damage that occurs as a result of social change may often, and is likely to take a form that cannot possibly be remedied simply by offering somebody hard cash.

(v) Then, there is a problem of the so-called external effects.' It assumes that a person's welfare depends solely on his own economic state and is not affected one way or the other by the states of those around him. This is not true. If an economic change has left you where you were before, able to buy about the same things, but has made other people much better off, you will not feel as well-off as you did originally. Here the gain by the gainers has simply had an unfavourable external effect on the situation of the other group, without the other group's own actual economic situation having changed in any direct or observable way.

(vi) This theory isolates production and exchange from distribution and thus ignores distribution. It is impossible to ignore the nature of distribution while considering the problem of productive efficiency. The pattern of distribution depends on the composition of national output and it also affects marginal utilities of the mass of consumers. How can distribution, therefore, be ignored ?

(vii) Dr. Little and Prof. Scitovsky take exception to Prof. Hick's argument that it is possible that after the lapse of sufficient length of time all would be better off as a result of a certain reorganisation of economic activity. But good and bad effects of economic changes on real income distribution may not cancel out in the long run, especially major changes. Besides inter-personal comparisons at a certain time, it involves inter-temporal comparison which is even worse.

(viii) Kaldor's argument implies that the State is responsible for maintaining equitable distribution of income in the community. This can be the case only in a socialist state. In a free enterprise economy, it is, on the other hand, undesirable for the state to interfere in the distribution of income brought about by market mechanism.

Conclusion. Thus, we come to the conclusion that the compensation principle fails to put welfare economics on a sound footing so as to be beyond the criticism of positive economists.

Scitovsky's Double Criterion

In an article in 1941, Scitovsky has shown that the Kaldor-Hick's criterion may be contradictory in itself. According to Kaldor-Hick's criterion, let us assume that the position *B* is more efficient than the position *A*. Once the position *B* is chosen by the community, the same criterion can reveal that the return move from *B* back to *A* in which losers bribe the gainers to return to the original position *A* is an improvement as well. This inconsistency in the Kaldor-Hick's criterion is labelled as the 'Scitovsky Paradox' or the Reversal Test. In order to remove this inconsistency and to have a correct criterion of welfare, Scitovsky suggested that the non-fulfilment of the several test should be added to the Kaldor-Hick's criterion. The non-fulfilment of the reversal test means that the losers from an economic change may not be in a position adequately to bribe the gainers to oppose the change. In other words, the position *A* is socially better than the position *B* and also, the losers could not bribe the gainers into making the change.

Tribor Scitovsky (1910-2002)

Little's Criterion

According to Prof. I.M.D. Little, neither the Kaldor-Hick's test nor the Scitovsky's double test can be taken as a criterion of welfare. He develops a new welfare criterion which is based on two-value premises. First, that an individual becomes better-off if he is enable to reach a position higher up on his order of choice. Secondly, any social change that makes everybody better off is a good change. In the words of Little, this criterion can be stated as follows: "A change is economically desirable if it results in a good redistribution of welfare, and if a policy of redistributing money by lump-sum transfers could not make everyone as well-off as they would be if the change were made." In other words, this means that an economic change will constitute social improvement if (*i*) the resulting redistribution is no worse than the old one and (*ii*) it is impossible to make the community as well-off in the initial position as it would be after the change.

SOCIAL WELFARE FUNCTION

The social welfare function represents another new approach to welfare economics. This system of welfare economics was first worked out by Professor Bergson in his article, "A Reformation of Certain Aspects of Welfare Economics."[17] It has been endorsed and further developed by Professors Samuelson and Tintner. Since some sort of value judgment is essential for inter-personal comparisons, welfare economics, they say, is essentially a normative study, but it can be made a scientific study nevertheless. For this purpose, they have introduced into welfare analysis what has been called a 'Social Welfare Function.'

The Social Welfare Function consists of a set of value judgments in order to determine which of the alternative situations is socially most desirable. Bergson defines social welfare function "as a function either of the welfare of each member of the community, or of the quantities of products consumed and services rendered by each member of the community."[18]

The social welfare function is completely general in as much as it takes into account external economies and diseconomies as well as dependence of one person's satisfaction on other people's welfare. Professor Bergson says that the value of welfare function "is understood to depend on all variables that might be considered as affecting welfare: The amounts of each and every kind of good consumed by and services performed by each and every household, the amount of each and every king of a capital investment undertaken, and so on."[19] Thus, the social welfare function can be considered as a function of each individual's welfare, which in turn depends not only on his personal well-being, but on his assessment of the distribution of welfare among all the members of the community. It is a sort of collective utility function.

It can be seen how Bergson's theory differs from that of Kaldor and Hicks. Bergson emphasises inter-relations of the welfare of individuals whereas kaldor and Hicks assume them away and also ignore the problem of distribution. Bergson takes into account all possible determinants of individual welfare function and builds them into single social welfare function whose value is to be maximised.

But aggregating individual's preference into a single social preference presents serious problems: There is the problem of specifying the shape of the social welfare function and its exact dependence on the welfare of each individual. In order to determine the shape of the social welfare function, we have to decide about the relative weights to be attached to each individual's preferences. We have to decide whether everybody's preference is to be given equal weight or different weights are to be assigned and, if so, on what principle? It would then involve a value judgment which the new welfare economics wanted to eliminate.

Another difficulty has been pointed out by Professor Arrow in his **'Social Choice and Individual Values.'** He points out that a consistent and truly representative social welfare function cannot be constructed if choice is to be made from among more than two alternatives. A social ordering must be consistent (transitive) and non-contradictory. For instance, an ordering will be consistent (transitive) if *I* say *X* is better than *Y* and *Y* is better than *Z*, *I* also must say that *X* is better than *Z*. But professor Arrow shows that the majority rule will lead to contradictory social ordering. This, however, only shows its limitation and does not altogether rule out the use of the social welfare function.

Hence, social welfare function cannot be operationally defined and has little practical importance as a policy measure.

Welfare Criteria

From the above discussion, we can deduce some criteria for welfare judgments. These criteria enable the economists to make welfare pronouncements. That is to say, whether welfare has been increased or decreased or whether it has been maximised. The following criteria may be mentioned:

(*i*) Pareto Criterion. Italian economist Vilgredo Pareto enunciated a very simple and straightforward criterion thus: "Any change which harms no one and which makes some people better off (in their own estimation) must be considered to be an improvement." The optimum allocation of goods among consumers is based on this criterion. According to this criterion, points rationing which permits every consumer to benefit by adjusting his purchases in accordance with his own tastes and desires without harming anyone, is better than fixed rationing. Obviously, this criterion does not cover cases in which an economic change, while benefiting some, harms others. Such cases are simply brushed aside. Thus, the crucial issue of inter-personal comparisons is bypassed.

(*ii*) Kaldor-Hicks Criterion. According to this school of thought, economic welfare will be increased if those who benefit are made to compensate those who

17. *Quarterly Economic Journal* (1937-38), pp. 310-34.
18. Scitovsky, T.—*Papers on Welfare and Growth*, 1962, p. 184.
19. See Scitovsky, T.—*Papers on Welfare and Growth*, p. 186.

lose by an economic reorganisation and still retain a part of the gain for themselves. Thus, the change results in a net gain in welfare. Kaldor states the criterion thus: "A change is an improvement if those who gain evaluate their gains at a higher figure than the value which the losers set upon their losses."

Nicholas Kaldor.

***(iii)* Scitovsky Criterion.** It is a double criterion. It is possible that not only an economic change may be beneficial from the welfare point of view but reverting to the original position may also be an improvement. To avoid this paradoxical possibility, Scitovsky suggested double test, *i.e.*, (*a*) movement from the original position to a new position should be an improvement and (*b*) return movement should not be an improvement.

There is an implicit value judgment in both Kaldor and Scitovsky criteria, because the potential money compensation to the losers is a concealed value judgment through money. They have both thus ducked the basic problem of inter-personal comparison to evaluate policy change.

***(iv)* Bergson Criteria.** Bergson has suggested that the only way out of the problem is the formulation of a set of explicit value judgments, which assist in the evaluation of the situation. For instance, as to what is just or reasonable or desirable may be laid down by an outside authority, legislature or the highest executive. This involves the construction of social welfare function described in the previous section. By its help, one can judge whether one situation is an improvement on the other, because the social welfare function is an indifference map ranking different combinations of the satisfaction or utility which may accrue to the various individuals in the community. But how to get the welfare judgments is a task by itself.

Assumptions and Limitations of Welfare Concept

We give below a few assumptions on which the welfare concept rests:

***(i)* Measurability of Utility.** The early welfare economists assumed that utility was a quantifiable quantity and people's satisfaction could be measured. Man's economic welfare is said to be a sum of total of his satisfactions. Also, welfare of individuals could be added to arrive at total social welfare. But there is no objective measurement of a person's satisfaction since it is just a state of mind. Hence, according to some critics, welfare economics is hypothetical and lacks scientific character.

***(ii)* Inter-personal Comparisons.** We have said that social welfare can be increased by making some one more satisfied without making any one less satisfied. But we can assess the increase in welfare only if we compare satisfaction of one with that of another. Pigou implicitly assumed inter-personal comparison, but trenchent criticism by Professor Robbins made the economists sceptical. Later writers as we have seen, have attempted to formulate welfare theory independently of inter-personal comparison of satisfaction. This had led some economists to hold that inter-personal comparisons of satisfaction or happiness are illegitimate or unscientific. "I cannot believe," says Robbins, "that it is helpful to speak as if inter-personal comparison of utility rest on scientific foundations." Thus, assumption of inter-personal comparability of satisfactions imposes a serious limitation on welfare analysis.

***(iii)* Concept of Maximum.** Welfare analysis assumes that there is a determinate maximum. But actually, there may be several optima or points of maximum satisfaction. Economic theory has concerned itself with the movement from a lower to a higher optimum. Economic welfare concerns itself with a single optimum.

***(iv)* Consumer's Preferences.** It is assumed that consumer's preferences are independent of prices or other changes. This assumption is not realistic. The consumer's preferences are bound to be affected by changes in prices, or, say, changes in fashion. But the welfare economist says that if new indifference curves have to be drawn consequent on a change in price; "the diagrams of indifference maps melt into chaos."

***(v)* New Welfare Economics** has given up the assumption of measurability of utility and inter-personal comparability of satisfactions. This has rendered still more difficult to judge an economic policy or economic measure on welfare grounds alone, especially a measure resulting in redistribution of income. "Our refusal to attempt inter-personal comparisons of utility makes it impossible to judge, on welfare grounds, the propriety of measures involving (or aiming at) a redistribution of income or wealth."[20]

***(vi)* Normative.** Welfare economics necessarily involves value judgment and is thus essentially normative. "Welfare economics and ethics cannot be separated. They are inseparable because the welfare terminology is a value terminology. . . . Getting rid of value judgment would be throwing the baby away with the bath water."[21] This has made welfare economics

20. Reder, M.W.—*Studies in the Theory of Welfare Economics*, p. 20.
21. Little, I.M.D.—*A Critique of Welfare Economics*, 1960, pp. 79-80.

less scientific. But most welfare economists contend that welfare analysis is quite scientific and does not lean on any ethical assumptions. Pigou, for instance, says that economics is both light-giving and fruit-bearing.

Conclusion. In spite of the above limitations, welfare economics has assumed great importance in recent times. The governments are looking to the economists more and more for advice and suggestions in policy matters in order to promote welfare of the community.

APPLICATIONS OF WELFARE ECONOMICS

We know that welfare economic analysis is intended to enable the economist to make policy recommendations so that social welfare is maximised. Such recommendations may cover the diverse fields of the economy. Hence, policy implications of welfare economics can be numerous. We shall just pick up a few prominent ones.

Pricing Policy of Public Undertakings. The pricing policy of public undertakings occupies an important place in a mixed economy. The price and output policy of such undertakings must be such as to maximise welfare. The optimal pricing will be one which makes prices marginal cost ratio equal to the average prevailing elsewhere. When the marginal cost is zero, there is a prima facie case for rendering the service free. This is especially the case when there is some investment check and losses can be covered other than by marginal taxation and in an equitable manner. When average costs are considerably higher than the marginal cost, which is not small, the price charged should not be less than the average cost. But, where it is possible to finance losses, then there is a strong case for reducing prices below average cost. These undertakings should at least aim at covering total cost.

International Trade. There is no doubt that trade policies, free trade or protectionist, have welfare implications. If the post-trade position is actually better than the pre-trade position; and if the distribution of real income is not adversely affected, opening of international trade will increase welfare.

In a world of pure competition, imposition of a tariff results in mis-allocation of resources and in a reduction in net social welfare when all concerned nations are taken together. It is assumed that the pre-tariff allocation of resources was optimal. Imposition of tariff will affect prices and result in reallocation of resources which must be presumed to reduce welfare. The tariff levying country can gain but only at the cost of other nations. However, from the point of view of a backward country free trade is not ideal. Free trade maximising welfare presupposes optimum conditions of production and exchange within all countries which is unrealistic.

Rationing

From the point of view of maximising welfare, points rationing (which gives each consumer some fixed number of ration points) is better than fixed rationing which permits a consumer to buy only a fixed quantity of each commodity. This is so because the points rationing gives a consumer a wide choice in making his purchases even though his total consumption is restricted. The ration points will replace the money prices. Welfare will be maximised when each consumer purchases commodities in such proportions that the marginal rate of substitution any of one commodity for another will be equal to the ratio of their fixed point prices. The marginal rates of substitution for all consumers must be the same.

Taxation

When a Government has to resort to taxation to raise resources, welfare will be increased if the revenue is sought to be raised through direct taxation (*i.e.*, income tax) rather than indirect taxation (*e.g.*, sales tax or excise duty). If a person pays income tax (instead of the same amount as a sales tax on the purchase of a commodity), he can still purchase the combination of goods he prefers the most out of the combinations available to him. The sales tax tends to reduce his purchases. A sales tax or excise duty distorts prices from their optimum levels and forces the consumer to reallocate his expenditure among commodities in a less desirable fashion. On the other hand, the income tax only reduces his over-all purchasing power, but does not directly affect the relative prices. It does not, therefore, force him to readjust his expenditure.

There is no doubt that income tax also affects the tax payer's behaviour but it does not distort his consumption pattern; it only distorts his income earning plans. It may affect his will to work and save. However, excise duties have their own merits. They are anti-inflationary and fall on those who have a large propensity to spend.

Monopoly versus Competition. The welfare economist is opposed to monopoly since it stands in the way of optimum conditions of production and exchange. There is, therefore, strong support for perfect competition on welfare grounds. It is only under perfect competition that both by equalising utility to the price and by equalising marginal utilities of the various items, the consumers and producers can attain an equilibrium position. A consumer will be able to maximise his satisfaction by equating his marginal utilities of purchase. The producer is able to maximise his profit by producing that output at which marginal cost equals price. The marginal cost pricing, which brings about a social optimum, is possible only under conditions of perfect competition.

National Income

The welfare economist is able to demonstrate the intimate relation between national income and welfare. Increase in national income or favourable redistribution (*i.e.*, favourable to the poor) is bound to increase the measure of welfare in the community. This can be achieved through well-known fiscal devices of taxation, bounties or beneficent public expenditure. Thus, the egalitarian principle underlying public finance is provided by welfare economics.

Socialist Ideology

Welfare economics provides a strong support to socialist ideology. Only a socialist dictatorship can bring about conditions of production, exchange and distribution which may be conducive to welfare maximization. Free enterprise economy, where conditions of perfect competition do not exist, is helpless in the matter. A strong government action is called for to establish a social optimum.

Conclusions. Above are given a few illustrations (the lists are not exhaustive) which show that welfare economics has a strong say in shaping vital economic policies and in the introduction of far-reaching welfare-increasing economic measures.

OBSTACLES TO WELFARE MAXIMIZATION

If maximum welfare is to be attained, optimum allocation of factors of production is essential. This allocation must be in keeping with the consumer's preferences. For this purpose, there must prevail perfect competition. But, in the real world, perfect competition does not prevail; instead there is imperfect competition. This constitutes a big obstacle in the way of the attainment of maximum welfare. Imperfect competition may take the form of monopoly or monopolistic competition or oligopoly. We shall see how these market forms stand in the way of welfare maximization.

Monopoly. By pursuing restrictive price and output policies, the monopolists exploit the consumer's weakness by charging exorbitant prices and by restricting output. They reduce the national income. In all these ways, they reduce social welfare, especially because they cause mis-allocation of productive resources.

We have seen that a condition of welfare maximization is that the marginal rate of substitution between any two commodities (or, to use terms of utility analysis, the ratio of their marginal utilities) must be the same as the marginal rate of transformation between the same two commodities (or, the ratio of their marginal opportunity costs) for every producer in the economy. In this way (*i.e.*, by equating the ratio of marginal utilities of the goods with the ratio of their prices) the consumers get maximum satisfaction.

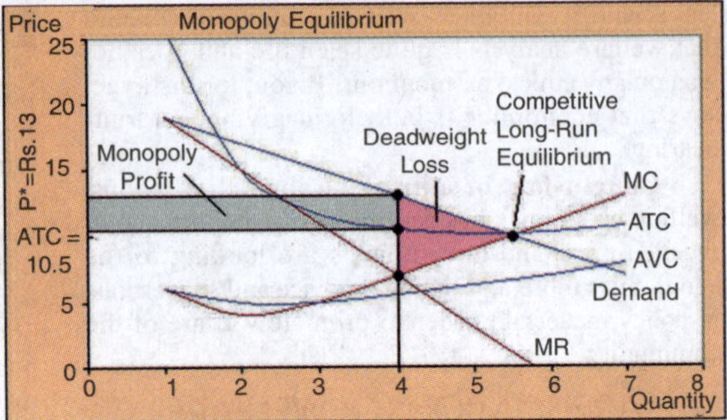

Monopoly vs. Competition – Competition ensures maximum welfare.

At the same time, the producers get maximum profits by equating the ratio of marginal costs with the ratio of prices. This is possible if there is perfect competition, because perfect competition ensures maximum efficiency of the economy and maximum satisfaction of the consumers. Under perfectly competitive conditions, private marginal utility or benefit tends to equal the social marginal utility or benefit on the one hand and private marginal cost and social marginal cost on the other, because the price is the same for all consumers.

The case is different in a monopoly. The monopolist faces a downward sloping demand curve (instead of horizontal straight line as under-perfect competition). Hence, marginal revenue is less than average revenue or price. In order to maximise profit, the producer will equate marginal cost and marginal revenue. But marginal revenue, we have seen, is less than price. Hence, his marginal cost is less than the price or price is kept higher than the marginal costs. Thus, the monopolist does not operate at the optimum output level. This means higher prices for the consumers and lower remuneration for the factor of production. By creating a divergence between factor price and the value of its marginal product, a monopoly distorts factor allocation. Too little resources are used in monopolised industries and too much in competitive industries producing too small quantities of certain good and too much of other goods; which is not in conformity with consumer's preferences.

Monopsony. It is a buyer's monopoly. It compels a firm to pay higher prices for factors in case of a buyer's monopoly in a factor market. Hence, the marginal cost of the factor will exceed its price per unit. For profit maximization, the factor will tend to be used up to a point where its marginal cost is equal to its marginal revenue product. But as said above, marginal cost exceeds price. Hence, the price paid to the factor is less than marginal product. Thus, the factor is not being paid its worth, which shows a faulty allocation of factors which in turn militates against welfare maximization.

Take the case of monopsony in a product market, *e.g.*, a consumer's co-operative being a single purchaser of some goods. In this case, the marginal cost of the product will be higher than the price paid

Monopsony – A single buyer.

by the monopsonist. The quantity purchased will be smaller and the price paid lower than under competition. This results in misallocation of resources in the economy.

Monopolistic Competition. In this case, there are too many firms in the industry operating at less than optimum scales of output having excess capacity which is socially wasteful. Product differentiation compels waste. Hence, a reduction in social welfare.

Oligopoly. In pure oligopoly (without product differentiation, *i.e.*, all firms producing identical goods), there is a misallocation of resource and hence a reduction of social welfare. In this case, a dominant firm determines the price and output policy. In order to maximise profit, the firm equates marginal cost with the marginal revenue. But the price will exceed marginal cost and distort resource allocation.

A FURTHER NOTE ON COMPENSATION PRINCIPLES

The Social Welfare Function and theory of Compensation Principles are sometimes treated as attempts to rehabilitate welfare economics and together are referred to as New Welfare Economics. This was necessary because of wide criticism of Pigovian and Paretian analyses. Pareto held that if any policy change benefited some people without harming others, it will be assumed that social welfare has increased. But in the real world, the economic situations are not so unambiguous that any policy change may benefit some people without harming others. Pareto appears to have deliberately confined his analysis to unambiguous changes in order to avoid value judgements and inter-personal utility comparisons. Kaldor, Hicks and Scitovsky, introduced the theory of Compensation Principles as a reformulated criterion on Paretian foundations. The theory of compensation principles states that whenever a policy change is effected it will benefit some and harm others. In case, those who gain compensate those who lose and still be gainers, then such a policy change may be considered desirable and shall be deemed to have increased social welfare.

The theory of compensation principles is based on the following assumptions:

(*a*) Individual, are supposed to be best judges of their welfare; (*b*) Changes in the level of production are assumed to affect social welfare; (*c*) There is no provision for interpersonal utility comparisons and cardinal measurement of utility is ruled out; and (*d*) Production and consumption are assumed to be unaffected by external factors and individual tastes are supposed to remain constant. Let us now examine the compensation principles as enunciated by Kaldor, Hicks and Scitovsky.

Kaldor's Compensation Principle

We start with situation *A*. Let us suppose that a policy change results in situation *B*. This change results in gain to some and loss to other. If gainers gain *X* and losers lose *Y*, then the gainers have to compensate the losers. Let the gainers pay X_1 of X ($X_1 > 0$) to losers so that $X_1 = Y$. If after compensating the losers, the gainers are still left with a positive net gains *i.e.*, $X–X_1 > 0$, the policy change is considered socially desirable and social welfare will be assumed to have increased. Thus $X–X_1$ is treated as an addition to the real income, hence to the economic welfare of society making policy change from an alternative *A* to alternative *B*.

This is a simple compensation principle. It advocates a change only when it produces net overall gain. The extent to what a section of society becomes' better off must be greater than the extent to which another section becomes worse off so that a marginal is left with the gainers which puts them in a better position than before.

Hick's Compensation Principle

Hicks's compensation principle is reverse of Kaldor's principle. As before, we take two alternative situations *A* and *B* and two categories-gainers and losers. If the losers bribe the gainers into not wanting a change, then the policy change may not be considered socially desirable, and as such not adding to the social welfare. If the losers cannot bribe the gainers then situation *B* is preferable to situation *A*.

The two compensation principles appear to be similar. In both the principles, gainers remain better off in the new situation. There is no marked departure from the Paretian analysis. It is an improvement over the earlier analysis by suggesting a few tests on the basis of which, after balancing positives and negatives of a policy change, we can form a judgement as to whether a policy change is socially preferable or not.

Scitovsky Compensation Principle

We may discuss this principle in two parts *viz.*, **the Scitovsky Paradox and Scitovsky Double Criterion.** Scitovsky pointed out a contradiction in Kaldor-Hicks Compensation Principle. Both Kaldor and Hicks considered a movement from situation *A* to situation *B* and the benefit resulting there from. Scitovsky pointed out that a backward movement from situation *B* to situation *A* may become socially gainful by the same criterion. There is thus a contradiction which is referred to as **Scitovsky Paradox.** To overcome this paradox, Scitovsky provided a **Double Criterion.** There can be a reverse movement from situation *B* to situation *A* if the gainers from such a move can profitably compensate the likely losers. Scitovsky therefore prescribes a double test for an economic change. One in the form of Kaldor-Hicks Principle *i.e.*, the gainers must be in a position to compensate profitably the losers and secondly there should be no possibility of returning to the original situation. In other words, while the gainers may be able to compensate the losers, the loser, should not be able to bribe the gainers to revert to the original position.

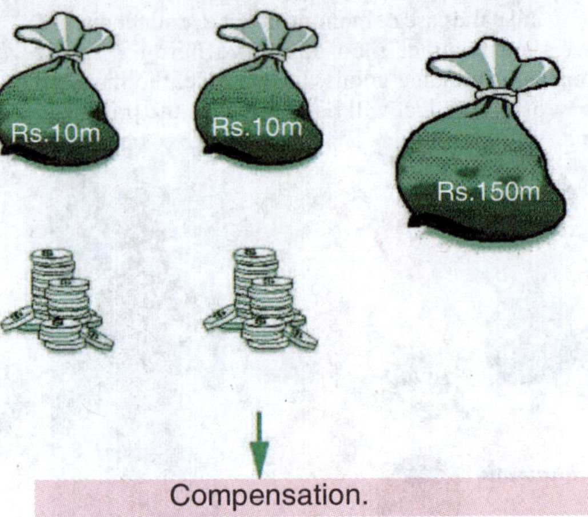

Compensation.

Criticism of the Compensation Principles

The compensation principles have been criticised on several grounds:

(i) These principles give an improved definition of welfare but do not provide any sound criterion to measure it. For assessing welfare, we cannot ignore income distribution. Compensation principles take a hypothetical income distribution which may be far from real.

(ii) Compensation principles are supposed to be value free, but actually value judgements are implicit in them. The principles work if the gainers overvalue their gain than the losers value their losses. This poses a serious problem of assessing the magnitude of gains and losses which cannot be tackled without value judgement. The gainers and losers constitute heterogeneous sections of people who measure their losses and compensations differently. This creates a difficulty about balancing the losses with gainer's compensation.

(iii) Compensations are only imaginary and hardly take a practical shape. It looks theoretically plausible but hardly practicable. In actual practice, it is impossible to identify the gainers and losers and determine the compensation payable by the former to the latter.

(iv) The theory of compensation principles suffers from the same limitations as the Paretian analysis in so far as the distribution analysis is separated from the problem of production. Viewed in relation to welfare, distribution is more important than the productive efficiency of the system. The ordinal utility analysis implied in the compensation principles does not facilitate the compensations by gainers to the losers. The difficulty of measuring the gains and losses makes the theory of compensation principles more rational than pragmatic.

Conclusion. We may thus conclude that the theory of compensation principles is not of much practical value in the matter of promoting social welfare.

MARKET STRUCTURE AND SOCIAL WELFARE

In the Paretian sense, if a policy change makes at least one individual better off without making any one worse off it is said to maximise social welfare. Let us see how this social optimum can be attained under different market structures. In this connection, we shall examine the possibility of attaining maximum social welfare under perfect competition, the monopoly, the monopolist competition and oligopoly.

Social Welfare Under Perfect Competition

To achieve maximum social welfare, the allocation of resources would be considered efficient if marginal rate of substitution between any two commodities for a consumer is equal to the marginal rate of transformation between these two commodities for every producer. This would lead to the equality of the ratio of marginal utilities and the ratio of commodity prices for the consumers and the equality between the ratio of marginal costs and the ratio of commodity prices for the producers because the former would result in maximum satisfaction and the latter in maximum profit. This results in equality of the ratio of marginal costs because both these ratios equal the ratio of prices under conditions of perfect competition.

The conditions of perfect competition also bring about the equality between the private marginal product and social marginal product. The basic condition for maximum social welfare is that social marginal utility be equal to social marginal cost. The equality between private marginal utility and social marginal utility will depend upon the distribution of money income in the community. The distribution must be such as would equalise its marginal utilities for all the consumers. The marginal cost of producing any alternative commodity would be the same as for the one that is being produced. This will lead to equality between private marginal cost with private marginal utility and hence the social marginal utility and social marginal cost. This is how conditions of perfect competition result in the attainment of maximum social welfare.

Monopoly

Since conditions of efficient allocation of resources as explained above do not exist in a monopoly, it does not lead to maximum social welfare. The monopoly equilibrium is based on the equality of marginal revenue and marginal cost. We know that under conditions of monopoly price is greater than marginal revenue of output. If follows therefore that price is higher than marginal cost too. The inequality between price and marginal cost represents the violation of the basic condition of efficient allocation of resources and hence of maximisation of social welfare. Under monopoly, the entrepreneur neither achieves optimum levels of output nor does he seek it. Also, a productive factor is not paid according to its marginal product because price exceeds the marginal cost of a commodity. Since productive factors do not get paid according to the principle of marginal productivity under monopoly, they are not attracted to this form of business enterprise to the fullest extent, whereas in the interest of maximum social welfare, factors must be employed where their marginal productivities are highest. It is thus clear that monopoly type of market structure is not consistent with the maximisation of social welfare.

There are some other obstacles too to the attainment of maximum social welfare under monopoly. Whatever the form of monopoly, whether in the commodity market or in factor market or buyer's monopoly (*i.e.*, monopsony), it works as a hindrance to the fuller utilisation of resources. For instance, trade unions pressure curtails employment opportunities and high labour costs stand in the way of expansion of industry to the optimum limit which means that other productive resources too are not fully utilised. Not only are these resources misallocated but it is also detrimental to social welfare. Thus monopoly market form is not conducive to the attainment of maximum social welfare.

Monopolistic Competition

Under monopolistic competition, efficient allocation of resources is not possible as under perfect competition. Under monopolistic competition, the demand curve is not tangential to the average cost curve

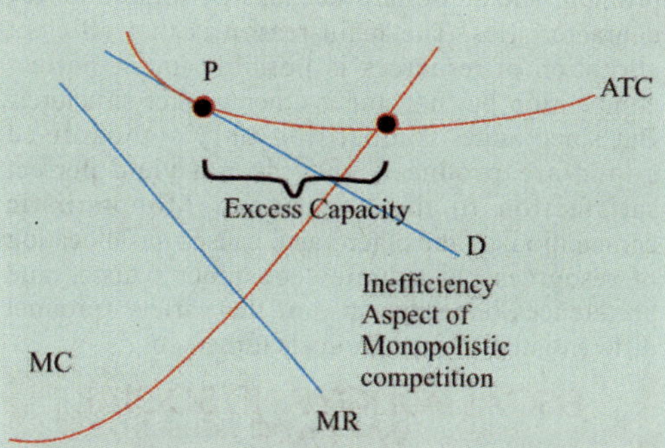

Monopolistic competition results in inefficiency.

at its lowest or optimum point. On the other hand demand curve is tangential to the average cost curve at a point higher than the optimum scale point. Since the levels of output produced are not optimum, the allocation of productive resources under monopolistic competition cannot be termed efficient. On the other hand, there is under-utilisation of capacity. If social welfare is to be maximised there must be fullest use of the installed capacity.

So far as there is product differentiation, monopolistic competition is better than perfect competition from the point of social welfare because variety in the products is calculated to give better satisfaction to the consumers of diverse tastes and temperaments. If the excess capacity under monopolistic competition is diverted to the production of a variety of goods, it will promote greater social welfare than it would be possible under perfect competition.

Oligopoly

Under oligopoly, there is misallocation of resources. That is why oligopoly is not considered consistent with the achievement of maximum social welfare. Misallocation of resources is due to the fact that a single firm determines the price of the commodity for the entire industry. The price is calculated to yield maximum profit *i.e.* where firm's marginal cost is equal to marginal revenue. Since price is higher than the marginal cost, it results in the misallocation of productive resources in the economy. When there are several competing firms, there is too much of product differentiation and unnecessary competition among the firms. This unwarranted competition causes considerable misallocation of resources and leads to considerable wasteful expenditure. Hence oligopolistic market structures do not promote social welfare.

Conclusion

We may thus conclude that perfectly competitive markets are consistent with the attainment of maximum social welfare. On the other hand, monopoly, monopolistic competition and oligopoly do not promote social welfare because of some inherent characteristics. The main reason is that efficient allocation of resources is possible under perfect competition but not under other market structures. But since under competition only standardised goods are produced, they do not yield perfect satisfaction to the consumers. Monopolistic competition, on the other hand, causes misallocation of resources but satisfies consumer's tastes and preferences better because of the variety (product differentiation) of the products turned out.

FISCAL POLICY AND SOCIAL WELFARE

In considering the impact of fiscal policy on social welfare we shall take income and tax structure. Let us first see the impact of income distribution.

Impact of Income Distribution on Social Welfare

It is generally believed that more even distribution of income promotes social welfare. We assume that monetary income is an index of real income, although price variations cannot be ignored altogether. Price variable may be kept constant assuming that the State assures an optimum distribution of goods through a public distribution system or other policy measures. Subject to these assumptions, we may say that optimum distribution of money income is conducive to maximisation of social welfare.

Take a situation A with a given income distribution and levels of satisfaction. Any change in this situation would be undesirable if (*a*) it makes some people more worse off than those whom it makes better off, and (*b*) if the losses of the losers and the gains of the gainers balance with each other leaving the society at a level, which in totality is not better off than the situation A. On the other hand, if a change in money income distribution makes at least some people better off without making any one worse off, it may be considered a desirable change on welfare grounds.

We can make use of the law of diminishing marginal utility of income in determining the effect of a shift in income distribution on social welfare. From the point of view of social welfare, we have to see that in any redistribution of money income the marginal utility of gainers is higher than the marginal utility of the losers. Until that happens income redistribution would be desirable for promoting social welfare.

However, it is not certain that equalisation of marginal utilities of all the individuals would tend to maximise the total satisfaction and hence welfare of society. We may have to be content with the maximisation of the probable total satisfaction with an egalitarian distribution of income. In other words, for the purpose of maximisation of social welfare it is

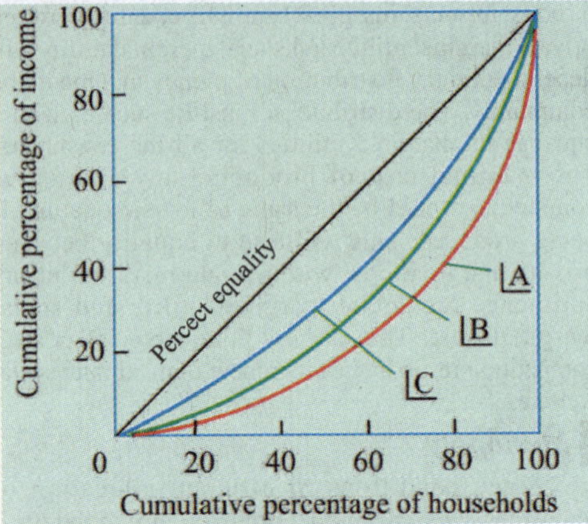

Income redistribution reduces inequality and increases welfare.

desirable that there should be income redistribution from the rich to the poor *i.e.*, from those with less marginal utility to those with higher marginal utility.

Impact of Tax Structure on Social Welfare

It goes without saying that social welfare is vitally affected by the tax structure of a country. There is no doubt that individual welfare is adversely affected by taxation. In the absence of a tax, an individual would have derived much greater satisfaction from his money income. But we cannot be sure whether society as a whole would benefit from the abolition or reduction of taxes. If taxes are reduced money incomes would increase. But if output and employment levels remain unchanged prices will rise. Rise in prices will harm the low income groups. Their standard of living will fall and social welfare will decrease.

When taxes are aimed at providing funds for economic development and public utility projects or for promoting efficient utilisation of resources, they are welfare promoting. Welfare is affected by the type of commodities taxed. If a tax is levied on commodity *A* and not commodity *B* those who consume more of *A* and less of *B* will suffer and those who use less of it and more of *B* will benefit. That is why compensation principle is advocated to increase social welfare. The losers should be compensated by subsidies and other concessions so that they are not worse off than before the tax is levied. If after this, some people still enjoy better levels of satisfaction than before, the tax may be regarded as welfare increasing rather than welfare decreasing. We usually find that public utility projects benefit the society at large though taxes are not levied on all sections of society. But the fact that taxes may enable the reorganisation of resources in such a way that those who pay taxes are not worse off than before and at the same time promote welfare of others makes the tax ideal for welfare.

All taxes, direct and indirect, sales tax and excise duties are levied in the interests of public good but there are some gainers and some other losers from the tax which necessitates compensating practices so that total welfare is not reduced. A careful study has to be made of the incidence of various taxes in other to find out which are conducive to social welfare. Pros and cons of each tax have to be weighed. In this way, fiscal policy should be designed so as to maximise social welfare either by increasing the satisfaction levels of all people or at least of some of them without reducing that of others.

Arrow's Impossibility Theorem

Arrow's Impossibility Theorem has dominated the discussions on welfare economies in recent years. It is well recognised that welfare as a concept is broad based and depends both on economic and non-economic variables. Measurement in welfare economics is not easy. We cannot quantify all that falls within the scope of welfare economics inspite of increasing use of mathematics in economics.

Kenneth Arrow, 1921 – Nobel Laureate in economics in 1972.

In the new welfare economics, stress is laid on social welfare and not on individual welfare. But social welfare function is much more complex than individual welfare function. The individual's welfare, though subjective can be made objective through his choice. But the choice criteria cannot be applied to social welfare, as we cannot think of a social choice. The society consists of individuals whose choice are seldom uniform. The problem therefore is how to make social decisions consistent with individual preferences. Kenneth Arrow has provided lucid analysis of this problem. He has demonstrated that it is impossible to make social decisions consistent with individual preferences on the basis of a majority vote as in a democratic set up. This is his Impossibility Theorem.

If, however, we make certain reasonable assumptions about human behaviour, it would be possible to construct a social welfare function that may satisfy some reasonable conditions. According to Arrow an effective social welfare function must satisfy the following conditions:–

(i) One condition is that social choices must be consistent. For instance, if choice *A* is preferred to choice *B* and Choice *B* is preferred to *C* then choice *C* must not be preferred to *A*. In other words, if an equal proportion of people prefer *A* to *B*, *B* to *C* and also *C* to *A*, then social choices are not consistent or transitive, and in such a case no social welfare function can be constructed.

(ii) Another condition is that a social welfare function should be non-responsive to perverse changes in individual preferences. If, for instance, in an initial ordering of the choices, an alternative is selected to reflect the social choice, this must not be altered because some individuals have changed their preferences or ranking of other alternatives. Even when a social welfare function is revised an alternative may be given a higher rank but in no case rank lower than one given to it initially.

(iii) A social welfare function must include only those choices or preferences which are capable or being realised. It should not be dependent on irrelevant or impossible individual choices.

(iv) The individuals should have full freedom to express their choices or ranking of alternatives. That is, a social welfare functional should not be dictatorial. No one individual's choice should be permitted to determine the social welfare function.

(v) Social welfare function must not be imposed on a community either by custom or by constitution. The individuals should be free to express their choices.

Arrow was guided by two conventional axioms in formulating these conditions *viz*., *(a)* Individual preference can be ranked and *(b)* every individual ranks his preferences in a consistent fashion. This Arrow developed the conditions of consistency and non-perversiveness of individual choices in a social welfare function. Arrow's Impossibility Theorem states that it is impossible to formulate a social welfare function which does not violate at least one of the above mentioned conditions.

Alternative Social Choice Theories

'*DD*' is grand utility frontier. On *y*-axis, utility of '*B*' and on *x*-axis utility of '*A*' is measured. *OG* line is 45° line drawn through the origin which passes through the point '*K*'. Point '*K*' is on '*DD*' curve and shows that $UB = UA$.

1. Equality Criterion : At point '*K*', distribution of goods and optimal allocation of resources between goods, between individuals is determined under this equality criterion. The equality of utilities of both the individual is required rather than equality of goods between the individuals.

2. Classical Utilitarian Welfare Criterion : Social welfare increases when the sum total of welfare of individuals increases.

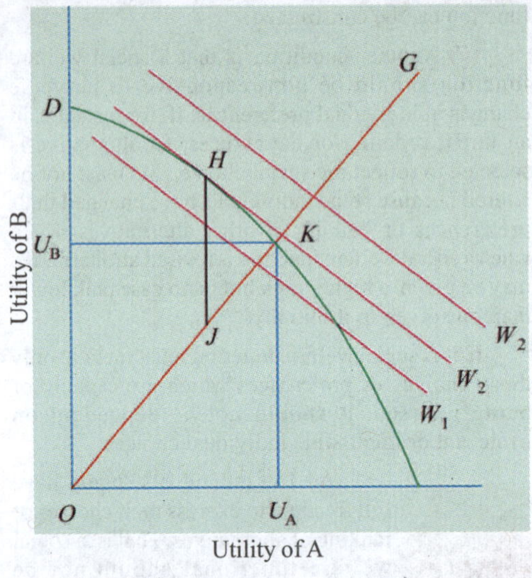

$W = \Sigma\, W (u_1 + u_2 + u_3 \ldots\ldots\ldots u_n)$

In the above diagram W_1, W_2 W_3 are social welfare indifference curves. At point '*H*' W_2 is tangent, which shows that U_A and U_B is maximum. According to classical welfare function point '*H*' on '*DD*' grand utility possibility frontier is socially optimum choice.

3. Rawl's (maximin) Welfare Criterion : According to Rawl's welfare criterion when the welfare of the worst-off individual increases that is the point when social choice is optimum. Point lying between '*JK*' an equal distribution line '*OG*' is socially preferable point to efficient position point '*H*'.

In Rawl's opinion, for the promotion of welfare among the down-trodden, poor or under previleged section of the society, certain amount of efficiency in resource allocation should be sacrificed.

Conclusion

We may conclude by saying that Arrow's Impossibility Theorem is an outstanding contribution to welfare economics. But it has its own limitations which mainly arise from the conditions he has laid down. If some of these conditions are relaxed a bit, it may be possible to construct a social welfare function.

Key terms

Economic and noneconomic welfare, Positive and normative economics, individual and social welfare, Pareto optimality, Contract curve, Compensation principle, Social welfare function, Arrow's impossibility theorem.

QUESTIONS

1. What is economic welfare? To what extent can the study of economics help in the achievement of economic welfare?
2. What is meant by economic theory? Point out the relation between economic theory and economic policy.
3. "Economics is neutral between ends as such". Discuss the validity of this statement in a welfare state.
4. Clearly bring out the relation between positive economics and welfare economics.
5. Account for divergence between individual welfare and social welfare and offer suggestions for bringing about harmony between the two.
6. Lay down a few criteria relating to economic welfare.
7. Clearly define the welfare concept and mention the various assumptions on which it is based.
8. What are the obstacles in the way of welfare maximisation?
9. Briefly mention the conditions necessary to achieve maximum welfare.
10. Write notes on– (*a*) Compensation Principle. (*b*) Social Welfare Function.
11. Explain the concept of Economic Welfare. How is it affected by (*a*) size and (*b*) distribution of national income?
12. State and explain the necessary conditions of Paretian maximum of economic welfare. Are they sufficient conditions also?
13. Show that much of welfare economics remains valid even if it is assumed that individual behaviour lines are kinked.
14. How can criteria of economic welfare be framed in the absence of inter-personal comparability of utility?
15. Examine the use of the Principle of Compensation as a means of ascertaining changes in community's welfare.
16. Write short notes on: (*a*) The Hicks-Kaldor criteria in New Welfare Economics. (*b*) Social Welfare Function. (*c*) Social Transformation Function.

INDEX

F

G

H

I

J

K